MW01026224

# THE BIBLICAL ILLUSTRATOR

## I THESSALONIANS

THE

# BIBLICAL ILLUSTRATOR

BY
JOSEPH S. EXELL

I THESSALONIANS

BAKER BOOK HOUSE
GRAND RAPIDS, MICHIGAN 49506

Library of Congress Catalog Card Number: 54-11086
ISBN: 0-8010-3280-6

Twenty-three Volume Edition

Printed in the United States of America

# INTRODUCTION TO THE FIRST EPISTLE TO THE THESSALONIANS.

I. THESSALONICA. 1 The city. When St. Paul first landed in Europe (Acts xvi. 11), and had preached at Philippi, he passed through Amphipolis and Apollonia to Thessalonica, immediately to the south of which lie the snow-clad slopes of Mount Olympus. This city, situated on the Thermean Gulf, and once the capital of Macedonia, had formerly the name of Thermæ, a name nearly similar to our *Bath*, or Hotwells. Under that name we read of it as one of the camping places of Xerxes. Cassander enlarged it, and bestowed upon it a new name in honour of his wife Thessalonica, daughter of Philip of Macedon. "As a commercial port," says a recent traveller, "Salonica must always hold a high place, and under a different gôvernment must become one of the most important centres of trade in the East, whether one regards its natural advantages as a harbour, or the richness and fertility of the back country, to which it forms the outlet." It was the largest and most populous city in Macedonia, and enjoyed considerable commercial relations. Under the Romans it was placed in the division called Macedonia Secunda, and became the residence of a Prætor. The city appears at a later period in unhappy connection with the Emperor Theodosius. It was the scene of a defeat of Constantius by the Saracens, and was afterwards sold to the Venetians by Andronicus, but captured by the Turks. Salonica is now looked upon as the third city of the Turkish Empire, Smyrna being the second. The population is estimated at 85,000, of whom about half are Jews. (*Bp. Alexander.*)    2. St. Paul's ministry here. The Acts contain little or no account of the apostle's labours among the Gentiles. We only read of three weeks' preaching in the synagogue, followed by the conversion of many Jews, "devout Greeks," and "chief women." Upon this the unbelieving Jews, enlisting the "roughs" of Thessalonica, created a riot which led to the departure of Paul and Silas by night. It is evident, however, from the Epistle, that the apostle's work here was both more extensive and of longer duration than the history would seem to intimate. For—(1) The bulk of the Church consisted of converts from idolatry (chap. i. 9). (2) There was already an organized Christian community when the Epistle was written (chap. v. 12). It was the custom for the apostles to appoint presidents or rulers on a second visit (Acts xiv. 21). If the ordination was affected during the first visit, as the narrative would seem to show, Paul's stay must have been much longer than three weeks. (3) The apostle gives a detailed description of his life in the city, which can scarcely be supposed to apply to so brief a sojourn (chap. ii. 5–12). (4) The same conclusion is corroborated by Phil. iv. 15, 16, Philippi being eighty miles away. Then we must remember— (*a*) That St. Luke has necessarily omitted many things in the apostle's history. (*b*) That nothing in the narrative forbids the interposition of a considerable space between the three weeks' ministry in the synagogue, and the assault upon the house of Jason. (*c*) That "turning to the Gentiles" was so habitual with the apostle, that the history of his work in any city would be incomplete without it. (*S. G. Green, D.D.*)    We can draw from the Epistles in connection with the Acts a clear picture of the apostle's manner of life. They lodged in the house of a be-lieving Jew of the name of Joshua (Gr. Jason) (Acts xvii. 5; Rom. xvi. 21), but accepted nothing from him but their lodging. To none of the Thessalonians would they be indebted (1 Thess. ii. 9; 2 Thess. iii. 8), but maintained themselves partly by the contributions twice forwarded to them from Philippi (Phil. iv. 16), but chiefly by hard manual labour, which occupied not the day only, but extended far into the night to make up for daylight hours devoted to preaching. They were determined to be model operatives (2 Thess. iii. 9), and not merely eloquent preachers: and besides the work of public teaching, the apostles followed their usual method of dealing with the converts' souls (chap. ii. 11). (*A. J. Mason, M.A.*) 3. The Thessalonian Church. By means of maps and descriptions we can form a picture to our mind of the Bay of Thessalonica, and see the semicircle of houses rising towards the hills with something of the air of an inferior Genoa. But it is much more difficult for us to see the earliest Christians exactly as they were. We instinctively think of something like churches. In modern Salonica three of these are still found which have been turned into mosques. One of these (St. Sophia) has a very ancient pulpit of beautiful marble, from which tradition reports that Paul preached. Yet, of course, they could have had no separate build-ings, and must have been content to meet in the houses of Jason (Acts xvii. 5), Aristarchus, Secundus (Acts xx. 21), or some other believer. But there are certain lines of church life which we can fairly trace. (1) There was an organized body addressed as a Church: which implies the sacrament, at least of baptism, without which a Church could not be. (2) This Church had a stated ministry (chap. v. 12–13). (3) The Church was gathered together at convenient opportunities. (*a*) The "holy kiss" (chap. v. 26), according to Justin Martyr, was given in connection with the Holy Communion. (*b*) The Christians met to be instructed by reading (chap. v. 27) of St. Paul's Epistles as the Law and the Prophets were in the syna-gogue. (*Bp. Alexander.*) It is hardly possible to realize the position of this infant community. Conflicting habits of thought and life, conflicting interests and aims, must everywhere have been prevailing. Amid the grosser forms of licentious-ness there was the difficulty ever felt by these Christians of keeping themselves unspotted from the world. Amid the ever-shifting subtleties of a vain philosophy there was the difficulty of holding fast the form of sound words. Amid the undis-guised contempt of the Gentiles, and the ceaseless, restless enmity of the Jews, there was the difficulty of "standing fast in the Lord." Amid the errors and dis-orders within their own bounds there was the difficulty of keeping "the unity of the Spirit in the bond of peace." In a word, the world was against them, and they were against the world. Perhaps the most vivid portrayal of the city life of the ancient world in its contact with Christianity is to be found in Kingsley's *Hypatia*. What is there depicted of Alexandria holds to a large extent true of Thessalonica. (*J. Hutchison, D.D.*)

II. THE EPISTLE TO THE THESSALONIANS. 1. The date and place of writing. It could not have been written after St. Paul's abode at Corinth, for Silvanus was with him, who after that, and 2 Thess. ii. 1, disappears from the apostle's com-pany. It could not have been written before; for those who had to bring St. Paul news from Macedonia found him not at Athens, but were allowed to join him at Corinth (Acts xvii. 15–xviii. 5; 1 Thess. iii. 1). It was not, then, written at Athens, according to the subscription of many MSS., misled by chap. iii. 1, but at Corinth. Nor was it written at the beginning of St. Paul's stay in that city. Chap. i. 7–8 proves that St. Paul must have remained at Corinth some time for the reputation of the Thessalonian Church to have acquired such currency, and for believers to have fallen asleep in Christ. (*Bp. Alexander.*) The contents of the Epistle bear every sign of an early date.   None of the great Pauline doctrines are touched upon in it, such as "faith," in its special sense, or "justification."   There is no Judaic legalism to oppose as in Galatians; St. Paul "can still point to them"—the Churches of Judæa—"as examples to his converts at Thessalonica" (chap. ii. 14). There is no Gnosticism to confront as in Colossians and Timothy.   Again the great prominence given to the doctrine of the Advent seems an indication of what St. Paul calls "the beginning of the gospel" (Phil. iv. 15).   The earliest gospel must needs consist in teaching that Christ was alive from the dead, and giving each Christian a vital interest in His present life, and this cannot be effected without much preaching of the Advent. (*A. J. Mason, M.A.*)   This Epistle was penned at the close of A.D. 52, or some time in 53, or at all events not later than 54.   If this last date be accepted, it is interesting to notice that it was the closing year of the Emperor Claudius' reign—a year specially memorable throughout the Roman Empire for alarming portents which attracted universal attention, and disturbed the popular mind with gloomy forebodings.   The prevalent mood produced by these portents, especially in such a city as Thessalonica, may have had its influence even on Christians, and may help to account for the excitement in the Church of which this Epistle takes so much notice.   Catching the general contagion—the current belief that something very wonderful, some awful crisis was about to happen, and giving it at the same time the colouring of their own Christian faith, connecting it more particularly with part of the apostle's teaching which they had misunderstood— they were straining their eyes to catch, as it were, the first glimpse of their risen and glorified Saviour returning with the clouds as the dust of His feet.   Hence the duties which pertain to Christian fellowship and daily toil were neglected. (*J. Hutchison, D.D.*)   2. The occasion.   Though St. Paul had quitted Thessalonica he had not forgotten his infant Church, and had not intended to be absent from it so long.   Twice at least (chap. ii. 18) he had seriously endeavoured to make his way back, "but Satan hindered."   Persecution had by no means abated, as he had hoped, by the expulsion of the missionaries; and he dreaded lest the temptation should have been too fiery for the Christians so imperfectly taught and organized (chap. iii. 10).   In his extreme agony of mind, unable himself to reach them, he determined at the cost of utter loneliness in a strange and unsympathetic town (Acts xvii. 16; 1 Thess. iii. 1), to send Timothy to see how they fared and to help them. To St. Paul's great relief, his friend brought back, on the whole, an excellent report. True there were several most grave faults, but the practical apostle had evidently not expected so much progress, and was overjoyed (chap. iii. 8).   And this Epistle, its author's earliest, and perhaps the earliest book of the New Testament, contains St. Paul's comments on Timothy's report. (*A. J. Mason, M.A.*)   3. Analysis. A. HISTORICAL.   (1) Brief greeting (chap. i. 1).   (2) Thanksgiving for their conversion and holiness (chap. i. 2–10).   (3) Appeal to them as to the character of his ministry (chap. ii. 1–12).   (4) Renewed expression of thankfulness for their constancy under persecutions, and bitter complaint of the Jews (chap. ii. 13–16).   (5) His personal feelings towards them and the visit of Timothy (chaps. ii. 17–iii. 10). (6) His prayer for them (chap. iii. 11–13).   B. HORTATORY.   (1) Warning against impurity (chap. iv. 1–8).   (2) Exhortation to brotherly love (chap. iv. 9, 10), and honourable diligence.   (3) The only doctrinal portion of the Epistle (chap. iv. 13– v. 11).   (*a*) Consolation about the dead (chap. iv. 13–18).   (*b*) Duty of watchfulness since the Lord's advent is uncertain, but will be sudden (chap. v. 1–11).   (4) Their duties to one another (chap. v. 12–15).   (5) Spiritual exhortation (vers. 16–22).   (6) Prayer for them (vers. 23–24).   (7) Last words and blessing. (*Archdeacon Farrar.*) 4. Its characteristics and contents.   (1) In general.   Simplicity of style, and absence of controversy and developed doctrine.   Its keynote is hope, as that of the Philippians is joy. (*Ibid.*)   These Epistles are full of practical precepts, and in this respect they remind us of the Epistle of James; other portions approach more nearly than any other part of the New Testament to Revelation, the first vision of the Church descending out of heaven, the image of the hope and faith of the earliest believers. They breathe the spirit of the earlier chapters of the Acts where the apostles are waiting for their Lord, and watching the signs of those things that were coming to pass upon the earth. They say nothing of justification by faith, or of mystical union with Christ, or of the Church which is His body but no more does the earliest narrative of the Church, or James, or Revelation. They exhibit the revelation of Christ in one external form by such figures as recall the prophecies of Daniel. Lastly they set before us the likeness of a gospel simple, real, practical—looking to Christ as its Author and Finisher, but not yet entering into the deepest recesses of the human soul. (*Prof. Jowett.*)        (2) Its social revolutionary teaching. These Epistles mark an era in the formation of Scripture. The letter claims its place beside the prophecy and the history, and the first specimen of the new form of Scripture directly meets one of the deepest wants of the old society.    Much might be said of the new virtue of purity—of the new and awful line drawn round the citadel of the human soul by the gift of the Holy Spirit (chap. iv. 8). But there is another vein pregnant with momentous social consequences. Just before that glorious passage, which St. Paul's unrivalled tenderness and majesty never exceeded—in which he tells of the descent of the Lord from heaven and the gathering of the redeemed—he speaks with peculiar emphasis of a class of duties, in his mind evidently connected with "brotherly love" (chap. iv. 9–12). Their ambition should be to be quiet, &c. The result of this will be twofold—a peculiar dignity of aspect in the eyes of outsiders, and the honourable independence which can enable them to dispense with the contemptuous pity of any man's alms. In the Second Epistle he assumes a severer and more sarcastic tone against those who are only busy with that which is no business of theirs; and commands them, with impassioned earnestness, to eat their *own* bread, not that of other people. Few have remarked how significant this style of exhortation is of a new world and a new order of ideas. For, in spite of ultra-democratic appearances, there was in Greek society an ultra-aristocratic spirit in its most evil form—that of culture as well as position. As regards the former, tradesmen and mechanics were held to be incapable of true philosophy, or spiritual religion or refined thought. As regards the latter, one of the worst influences of slavery was the discredit it threw on free labour and all the smaller forms of commerce. Aristotle treats with cold cynicism everything of the sort. The tradesman or mechanic is but a higher kind of slave—differing from him in kind, not in degree—bearing the same relation to the public as the slave bears to the individual. To do anything which marks or curves the body; to live on daily pay; to be connected with the detail of fabrics or with bales in markets—this was to degrade a freeman, and to plebeianize his spirit as well as his body. Such were the ideas of Aristotle, who knew Macedonia so well, and had lived in it so long—such were the ideas which were in the very air of Thessalonica when Paul wrote. It is full of significance that the First Epistle speaks out so boldly and earnestly upon the dignity and becomingness of industry—the nobility of working with our own hands, though they may be blackened by the work; the duty of preferring our own coarse bread won of the sweat of our brow, to the precarious food of the beggar or the ignominious luxury of the parasite. This was one great social and moral result of the message which came from a carpenter's shop, and was published by a company of fishermen, among whom a tent-maker of Tarsus had obtained admission. (*Bp. Alexander.*)        (3) Its teaching concerning our Lord. A. Christ is Divine. 1. Titles. The Lord Jesus (chap. ii. 15); our Lord Jesus Christ (chap. ii. 19; v. 23); the Lord Himself (chap. iv. 16); the Lord.    2. Divinely conjoined with the Father (chap. i. 1). 3. Prayed to with the Father

(1 Thess. iii. 11). B. Christ is in heaven (chap. i. 10; iv. 16). C. Christ coming again, the Resurrection and the Life (chap. iv. 14–18). D. Christ the Redeemer. 1. Ever delivering us from wrath (chap. i. 11). 2. The medium of salvation (chap. v. 9). 3. Giving us life through His death (chap. v. 10). No Christology or Soteriology in the New Testament can go beyond this. (*Ibid.*) (4) Its eschatology. There are three principles by which to interpret the eschatological element in the New Testament generally and in these Epistles in particular. First, many of the passages are to be interpreted according to the analogy of all prophecy. Except in a few specified passages, time is not defined by the prophets. The future is projected, like a timeless picture, before the soul of the seer. Objects which are near seem to touch those which are remote. This may be illustrated by the beautiful optical illusion which causes the broad disc of the setting sun to seem as if it crushed down upon the western hills, or the moon to appear as if its white fire were actually interwoven through the sombre mass of a grove. The prophets were not historians by anticipation. They saw in juxtaposition, not in succession. A lyrical ode is sometimes connected by threads more delicate, though not less real, than those which bind together the parts of a closely-written essay. There are various kinds of method—logical, sermonic, poetical, historical; but method in the true sense is the apt disposition of a number of topics which may be referred to a common centre. Let us allow the prophets to follow a deeper order of their own. Swiftly and noiselessly from the luminous centre of some Divine principle, the prophetic spirit radiates to the furthest circumference of human events with an order which is generally real, not chronological. Then, secondly, all history is viewed as it is viewed by God, as even we can view it when we see it in plan rather than in section. That is, it is a cycle of typical judgments completed in the Last Judgment, of which each successive crisis possesses some of the general characteristics. In the history of the Jews we have an unveiling of the principles of God's judgment. "Wheresoever the carcase is, there will the eagles be gathered together." Wherever there is a body of spiritual death—a dead church, a dead state—there the carcase is. Such to a believer is the aspect of history. Still the eagles are gathering together. Still He comes with clouds. Still the saints cry, "The great day of the Lord is near." So has it been through many cycles of history—the destruction of Jerusalem, the fall of Rome, the Reformation, the French Revolution, our own time. So shall it be until, passing through all typical judgments, the Last Judgment shall darken over the human race. Thirdly, it was the evident intention, for great moral ends, of our Lord and His apostles to use language which should place their own and each successive generation in the position of those who *might* be alive at His coming, at the same time adjusting the perspective of teaching that those who lived far away should be able to apprehend the precise point of view better than contemporaries. This certainly is the meaning of Matt. xxiv. 48, xxv. 5, 19. We need not dwell upon the commission "to go into all lands," upon the institution of a Church and of a morality adapted to a world which was destined to last. Consider, then, 2 Thess. i., &c. The view of the immediate coming of Christ does arise. How is it treated? As a fanaticism, a falsehood, and a delusion. But further, admit not merely that the primitive Christians looked for and expected Christ (which they did, with an excessive tension), but that they considered that "experience would belie Him cruelly if the world were obstinate enough to last on after that generation"—what would have been the result? Why this: that when the last survivor of Christ's immediate followers died, Christianity would have died with him. Perhaps as the storm darkened the sky of Palestine, or as by the shores of the Ægean the sun went down in a dark cloud or in the burning sky, a knot of poor fanatics might have looked for the sign of the Son of Man. But if the gospel had been committed to

that false hope, it must have been carried from its cradle to its grave. The gospel has survived the persecutions, the syllogism, the epigram, the scaffold, caricatures of its doctrines and abuses of its holiness; but there is one thing which it will never survive—a refutation before the face of honest reason. But just at the time when, according to M. Renan's interpretation of the great teacher's words, their falsity was manifested, martyrs were preparing to bleed for them, and missionaries were starting, with a lie in their right hand, to announce it to the ends of the earth. The gospel did not die, as it must have done if committed to this doctrine; therefore it was not committed to it. Then, further, St. Paul did not expect the close of the present dispensation without a great ingathering of the Jews. Could he, who knew their obstinacy so well, suppose that this would be the work of the few years which yet remained to him? (Rom. xi. 25, 26.) And, again, there are passages in which he speaks clearly of his own death and resurrection (1 Cor. vi. 14; 2 Cor. iv. 14, v. 2; Philip. i. 23; 2 Tim. iv. 6). These expressions are inconsistent with a formulated belief on the part of St. Paul that Christ would come before he died. The practical point to be perceived in regard to the eschatological element in these Epistles is this: One vision fills the souls of the Thessalonian converts—that of the Great Coming. At first it is in danger of assuming fanatical proportions, and shaking their lives to the very centre. A few calm words (2 Thess. ii. 1) plead for the honour of the great Advent, and of the majestic gathering to the Redeemer. Then the perspective, for a while disturbed, was permanently readjusted, and remains at the same point even now, securing the perfect practical coincidence of the natural order of things with the supernatural expectation. When men seek to state the exact day, and that a near day, St. Paul, speaking through the ages, blames such fanaticism, and points us back to our Lord's words (1 Thess. v. 1). He puts down the childish fingers that count the number of the days. "Of that day and hour knoweth no one" (Matt. xxiv. 36). (*Ibid.*)

5. Its relation to, and difference from, the other Epistles. There is an absence of those higher but more controverted doctrines which occupy so much space in Paul's later Epistles. But it must be remembered that the Thessalonians had not long turned from idols to the living God. He would be an unwise missionary who should try and instil the more advanced doctrines of a matured Christianity into the minds of children in the faith. But we do find it impressed upon them that the part of the Christian life lies in the work of faith, &c. (chap. i. 3), and in entire sanctification (ver. 23); and the great articles of our faith are strongly emphasized; the death and resurrection of Christ, the general resurrection, the second advent to judgment, and the eternity of future rewards and punishments (chap. iv. 13–18, v. 1–10, 23, 24)—the substance of all Paul's after-teaching. (*F. A. Malleson, M.A.*) Reading the Epistles in chronological order, many will be tempted to trace in them a development of doctrine. Others, again, will seek to impress upon them the same fixed type of truth held from the beginning. Neither of these views is justified by an examination of the Epistles. There is a growth, it is true; but it is a growth of Christian life, not of intellectual progress—the growth, not of reflection, but of spiritual experience, enlarging as the world widens before the apostle's eyes, passing from life to death, or from strife to peace, with the changes in the apostle's own life, or the circumstances of his converts. There is a rest also in them, discernible not in forms of thought or in types of doctrine, but in the person of Christ Himself, who is his centre in every Epistle, however various may be his modes of expression or his treatment of controversial questions. (*Prof. Jowett.*) The theology of this Epistle is very simple and, as we should say, elementary, the contents being mainly practical. With wonderful perversity this fact has been employed as indicating a change of view in St. Paul himself, as though his creed were of a simpler kind than when he addressed the Church in Rome.

Rightly estimated, this very abstinence from the profounder topics of the Christian faith establishes, indirectly, the genuineness of the Epistle. The Church was young. The controversies which would hereafter lead to the scientific statement and argumentative unfolding of Christian doctrine had not as yet troubled the Churches. They needed milk rather than strong meat. To the Thessalonians the gospel was mainly a call to turn from idols, to serve the Father, to trust the Redeemer, and to honour both by faith, hope, and love. Such, to them, was the teaching which came in word, power, and the Holy Ghost. And "the present truth," the means of uplifting from the world, and of bringing invisible realities near, was the prophecy of Christ's second appearing, the call to await "the Son from heaven." These primary truths, in their breadth and fulness of ethical application, are the staple of this Epistle, as they were the strength of the earlier Churches. The contents of the letter thus precisely accord with its place in the series. It is interesting, also, to trace secret links of correspondence between hints and phrases of this Epistle and the more detailed teaching of the apostle's later productions. In the letters to Corinth especially, St. Paul follows out in a more extended form many a suggestion in those written *at* Corinth. In the association of faith, hope, love (chap. i. 3, v. 8), the apostle had evidently in his mind the thoughts so nobly wrought out in 1 Cor. xiii. Compare, again, chap. i. 5 with 1 Cor. ii. 4; chap. i. 6 with 1 Cor. xi. 1; chap. ii. 4 with 1 Cor. iv. 3, 4. The anxiety to revisit the Thessalonians has its counterpart in the apostle's desire to see the Corinthians again (chap. ii. 17; 2 Cor. i. 15; 1 Cor. v. 3); and the arrival of Timothy with good news from Thessalonica (chap. iii. 6) is paralleled by the "coming of Titus" (2 Cor. vii. 6). On the whole, it is the same man who writes to Corinth and from Corinth, in no sense repeating himself, but revealing the character of his mind and heart by his very turns of phrase, while his soul is ever filled with the most earnest, tender, and jealous affection for those whom he has been the means of leading to Christ. (*S. G. Green, D.D.*)     6. Its genuineness. The external evidence is chiefly negative; but this is important enough. There is no trace that it was ever disputed at any age or in any section of the Church, or even by any individual, till the present century. The allusions to it in writers before the close of the second century are confessedly faint and uncertain—a circumstance easily explained when we remember the character of the Epistle itself, its comparatively simple diction, its silence on the most important doctrinal questions, and, generally speaking, the absence of any salient points to arrest the attention and provoke reference. It is more important to observe that the Epistle was included in the old Latin and Syriac versions, in the Muralorian Canon, and in Marcion. Towards the close of the second century—from Irenæus of Lyons downwards, we find this Epistle directly quoted and ascribed to Paul. The evidence derived from the character of the Epistle itself is so strong that it may fairly be called irresistible. The fineness and delicacy of touch with which the apostle's relations towards the Thessalonians are drawn—his yearning to see them, his anxiety in the absence of Timothy, and his heartfelt rejoicing at the good news— are quite beyond the reach of the clumsy forgeries of the early Church. And then the writer uses language which, however it may be explained, is evidently coloured by the anticipation of the speedy advent of the Lord—language natural enough on the apostle's lips, but quite inconceivable in a forgery written after his death, when time had disappointed these anticipations, and when the revival or mention of them would serve no purpose, and might seem to discredit the apostle. Such a position would be an anachronism in a writer of the second century. (*Bp. Lightfoot.*)

# THE BIBLICAL ILLUSTRATOR.

## I. THESSALONIANS.

### CHAPTER I.

VER. 1. **Paul, and Silvanus and Timotheus to the Church of the Thessalonians.**
After the usual superscription in which St. Paul associates with himself his two
missionary companions, we have—I. THE APOSTOLIC GREETING. 1. "Grace and
peace" blends the Greek and Hebrew modes of salutation, "that union of Asiatic
repose and European alacrity." But these formulæ had become like some precious
antique vases, prized for their beauty more than their use, and empty of significance
or at least of blessing. But now they are lifted into a higher sphere and attain a
holier meaning, grace representing gospel blessing as coming from the heart of God;
peace, gospel blessing as abiding in the heart of man; embracing together the fulness of salvation. The right reception of them brings the peace of inward conscience,
of brotherly love, of eternal glory. 2. This grace and peace—(1) come from God
the Father as the source of all good. No designation brings God nearer the heart
than that favourite one of Paul's, "the God of peace." It can never come through
ourselves or others. (2) It comes through Him who is "our Peace," who reconciles
things on earth and things in heaven (Rom. v. 1). (3) When we receive the
adoption we have "the peace which passed all understanding." II. THE APOSTOLIC
PRAYERFULNESS. 1. Paul's life was one of unexampled activity. The care of all
the churches rested on him. But he was not too busy to pray. The busier a
servant of God is, the more prayerful he needs to be. Devotion and labour are two
sides of the one renewed life. With the Word the preacher influences the world;
with prayer he influences heaven. But the intimation here is that Paul had his
stated seasons for prayer. It was said of him at his conversion, "Behold he
prayeth," and ever after the words held good. 2. But in Paul's prayers the element
of thanksgiving was always present. (1) No prayer can be complete without it.
It is peculiarly characteristic of Christian prayer. There are prayers in Homer's
poems, but how few thanksgivings. The Gentile world "glorified Him not, neither
were thankful." (2) This thanksgiving was for others. It sprang from his loving
contemplation of the Thessalonians' excellences. While prayer for others is
common, gratitude for others is rare. It is a duty, notwithstanding, arising from a
community of interest in each other's welfare. III. THE APOSTOLIC CONGRATULATION.
He has much to say in reproof, so he will begin with praise. This was Christ's
method towards the Seven Churches. Let the same mind be in us. 1. The ground
of his commendation, the three graces of the renewed life—not in themselves however, but as they manifest themselves in the life. (1) "Your work of faith," *i.e.* the
work which faith produces. Wherever faith is it works onwards to this. This is
the Christain's duty towards self. (2) "Labour of love" is his duty towards his
neighbour. Love is infused by God and effused in good works. (3) "Patience of
hope" is duty in reference to the future and towards God. Manly endurance under
trial and stedfast expectation of a happy issue when the just and gentle monarch
shall come to terminate the evil and diadem the right. 2. These graces exist and
prove their existence—(1) "In our Lord Jesus Christ." All three proceed from
Him as their origin and terminate in Him as their end. (2) "In the sight of God
the Father." This issue of evil works as well as good, but the thought brings
no peace to the evil worker, whereas it is the joy and life of the Christian.
(*J. Hutchison, D.D.*)    *In God the Father :*—A man cannot be as a house with

doors and windows closed against the light, yet standing in the midst of light. A ship may take refuge in a harbour without receiving any one on board or sending any one ashore; but a man cannot so deal with God; he cannot take refuge in God without letting God in. The diver goes down into the water to find treasure, but carefully excludes the water; a man cannot so deal with God and the treasures hid in God. In the very act of finding safety and rest in God he must open his soul to God. (*J. Leckie, D.D.*)  *The introduction to the Epistle:*—I. A SPECIFICATION OF THE PERSONS FROM WHOM THE LETTER WENT. 1. The name of Paul stands first because —(1) He only possessed full apostolic authority. (2) He alone wrote or dictated the Epistle (chap. ii. 8, iii. 5, v. 27). 2. The connection of Silvanus and Timotheus with Paul and with the Thessalonians is illustrated in the Acts. When Paul set out from Antioch on his second tour, he chose Silas to attend him (Acts xv. 34, 40). In the course of their journey they met with Timothy (Acts xv. 1–3). The three proceeded to Troas (Acts xvi. 8, 9), where they crossed the sea and conveyed the gospel to several Macedonian towns. On leaving Philippi, Paul and Silas, if not Timothy, proceeded to Thessalonica (Acts xvii. 1–9). Silas and Timothy remain behind at Berea (Acts xvii. 13, 14). Paul proceeded to Athens and Corinth. (Acts xvii. 15; xviii. 1). Here Silas and Timothy, the latter of whom had been sent from Athens to encourage and confirm the Thessalonians, at length rejoined him, and here Paul wrote the Epistle. 3. These details account for three things in this specification. (1) How natural it was for Paul to address a letter so paternal to a Church he was instrumental in founding. (2) How appropriate that he should associate with himself men who had been active in ministering to the Thessalonians. (3) How fitting that Silas the elder should take precedence of Timothy (2 Cor. i. 19). II. THE PERSONS TO WHOM THE EPISTLE WAS SENT. 1. Thessalonica was a town of Macedonia. Anciently it bore the names, successively, of Eurathia and Therma. It was restored and enlarged by Cassander, and was called Thessalonica after his spouse, the daughter of King Philip, or, according to another opinion, from a victory which Philip himself achieved. It was a rich commercial city, distinguished for profligacy. It is now called Salonichi, and retains considerable traces of its ancient splendour. 2. There Paul preached on successive occasions in the Jewish synagogue. His doctrine is specified in Acts xvii. 2, 3, and his success in ver. 4. But idolaters were also converted (chap. i. 9). 3. The combined converts formed a Church. (1) The word means " called out," and is used to denote an assembly of persons. The Thessalonian Christians had been set apart by a Divine call in respect of faith, character and profession, and were associated as a religious brotherhood, a commonwealth of saints. (2) This Church was " in God the Father," signifying intimacy of relation. They were protected by His power, guided by His counsel, and cherished by His grace. (3) " In the Lord Jesus Christ " denotes the union between Christ and believers, elsewhere likened to that subsisting between the vine and the branches, the members and the head, &c. III. THE BLESSINGS INVOKED. 1. Grace: the favour of God. 2. Peace. (1) Quiet and tranquillity. (2) Prosperity (Psa. cxxii. 6, 7; 3 John 2). (*A. S. Patterson, D.D.*)  *Phases of apostolic greeting:*—I. IT IS HARMONIOUS IN ITS OUTFLOW. 1. Paul, though the only apostle of the three, did not assume the title or display any superiority. The others had been owned of God equally with himself in Thessalonica and were held in high esteem by the converts. Timothy was only a young man, and it is a significant testimony to his character that he should be associated with men so distinguished. Each had his distinctive individuality, talent, and mode of working; but there was an emphatic unity of purpose in bringing about results. 2. The association also indicated perfect accord in the Divine character of Paul's doctrines. Not that it gave additional value to them. Truth is vaster than the individual, whatever gifts he possesses or lacks. 3. What a suggestive lesson of confidence and unity was taught the Thessalonians by the harmonious example of their teachers. II. RECOGNIZES THE CHURCH'S SUBLIME ORIGIN. 1. The Church is divinely founded. "In" denotes intimate union with God, and is equivalent to John xvii. 21. 2. The Church is divinely sustained. Founded in God, it is upheld by Him. Thus the Church survives opposition, and the fret and wear of change. But this is withdrawn from apostate churches. III. SUPPLICATES THE HIGHEST BLESSINGS. 1. Grace includes all temporal good and all spiritual benefits. The generosity of God knows no stint. A monarch once threw open his gardens to the public during the summer months. The gardener, finding it troublesome, complained that the visitors plucked the flowers. " What," said the king, " are my people fond of flowers? Then plant some more! " So our

Heavenly King scatters on our daily path the flowers of blessing, and as fast as we can gather them, in spite of the grudging world. 2. Peace includes all the happiness resulting from a participation in the Divine favour. (1) Peace with God, with whom sin has placed us in antagonism. (2) Peace of conscience. (3) Peace one with another. 3. The source and medium of all the blessings desired. "From God our Father, and the Lord Jesus Christ." The Jew could only say, "God be gracious unto you, and remember His covenant;" but the Christian "honours the Son, even as he honours the Father." The Father's love and the Son's work are the sole source and cause of every Christian blessing. Learn—1. The freeness and fulness of the gospel. 2. The spirit we should cultivate towards others: that of genuine Christian benevolence and sympathy. We can supplicate for others no higher good than grace and peace. (*G. Barlow.*)     *The pastor's prayer:*—I. THE BLESSINGS DESIRED. 1. Their nature. (1) Grace. (2) Peace. 2. Their connection. (1) Grace may exist without peace, but not peace without grace. (2) Yet peace flows from grace. II. Their SOURCE. 1. God the Father is the Fountain of all grace. 2. Christ is the Medium of communication. III. Their SUPPLY. 1. Free. 2. Sufficient for all. 3. Constant. 4. Inexhaustible. (*J. Lyth, D.D.*)     *Timotheus* was a Lyconian born in Derbe or Lystra, where he was religiously trained. He was probably converted by St. Paul during his first visit to Lycaonia (A.D. 45, Acts xiv. 6, 7). He was taken on a second visit to be Paul's companion, and circumcised (A.D. 51, Acts xvi. 1, &c.). He was sent from Berea to Thessalonica (Acts xvii. 14; 1 Thess. iii. 2); with Silas he rejoins Paul at Corinth (A.D. 52, Acts xviii. 5; 1 Thess. iii. 6) and remains with Paul (1 Thess. i. 1; 2 Thess. ii. 1). He was with Paul at Ephesus (A.D. 57, Acts xix. 22; and was sent thence to Corinth (Acts xix. 22; 1 Cor. iv. 17; xvi. 10). He is again with Paul (A.D. 58, 2 Cor. i. 1; Rom. xvi. 21). He journeys with Paul from Corinth to Asia (Acts xx. 4); and is with Paul in Rome (A.D. 62 or 63, Phil. i. 1; Col. i. 1; Philemon 1). Henceforth his movements are uncertain (A.D. 63–66). He is probably left by Paul in charge of the Church at Ephesus (A.D. 66 or 67; 1 Tim.); received the second Epistle, and sets out to join Paul at Rome (A.D. 67 or 68). Ecclesiastical tradition makes him first bishop of Ephesus and to suffer martyrdom under Domitian or Nerva. (*Bleek.*) *Silvanus* or Silas was an eminent member of the early Christian Church. The first, which in his full name, is given him in the Epistles, the latter contraction by the Acts. He appears as one of the leaders of the Church at Jerusalem (Acts xv. 22), holding the office of inspired teacher. His name, derived from the Latin *silva* "wood," betokens him a Hellenistic Jew, and he appears to have been a Roman citizen (Acts xvi. 37). He appointed a delegate to accompany Paul and Barnabas on their return from Antioch with the decree of the council of Jerusalem (Acts xv. 22, 32). Having accomplished this mission, he returned to Jerusalem (Acts xv. 33). He must however have immediately revisited Antioch, for we find him selected by St. Paul as the companion of his second missionary journey (Acts xv. 40, xvii. 40). At Berœa he was left behind with Timothy while Paul proceeded to Athens (Acts xvii 14), and we hear nothing more of his movements until he rejoined the apostle at Corinth (Acts xviii. 5). Whether he had followed Paul to Athens in obedience to the injunction to do so (Acts xvii. 15), and had been sent thence with Timothy to Thessalonica (1 Thess. iii. 2), or whether his movements were wholly independent of Timothy's, is uncertain. His presence at Corinth is several times noticed (2 Cor. i. 19; 1 Thess. i. 1; 2 Thess. ii. 1). He probably returned to Jerusalem with Paul, and from that time the connection between them seems to have terminated. Whether he was the Silvanus who conveyed I. Peter to Asia Minor (v. 2) is doubtful. The probabilities are in favour of the identity. A tradition of slight authority represents Silas as Bishop of Corinth. (*W. L. Bevan, M.A.*)     To the Church in Galatians, Corinthians and Thessalonians, but to the Saints in Romans, Ephesians, Philippians and Colossians. It is remarkable that this change of form should take place in all the later Epistles; perhaps because the apostle, more or less in his later years, invested the Church on earth with the attributes of the Church in heaven. The word *ecclesia* is used in the LXX. for the congregation, indifferently with synagogue. It is found also in Matthew, in the Epistles of John and James as well as in Hebrews and Revelation. It could not, therefore, have belonged to any one party or division of the Church. In the time of St. Paul, it was the general term, and was gradually appropriated to the Christian Church. All the sacred associations with which that was invested as the body of Christ were transferred to it, and the words synagogue and ecclesia soon became as distinct as the things to which they were applied. The very rapidity with which "ecclesia" acquired its new meaning, is a proof of the life and force which from the first the thought of communion with one another must have exerted on the minds of the earliest believers. Some indication of the transition is traceable in Heb. ii. 12, where the words of Psa. xxii. 23 are adopted in a Christian sense; also in Heb. xii. 23, where the Old and New Testament meanings of ecclesia are similarly blended. (*Prof. Jowett.*)    *The note of a true Church:*— There were heathen assemblies in Thessalonica, numerous and powerful; but these were for the worship of false gods. The only true Church was this recent, despised, persecuted one, which rejoiced in the knowledge of the Creator of heaven and earth as their heavenly Father through Christ. There was also a congregation of Jews. A synagogue stood there for the worship of the God of Abraham, Isaac and Jacob, the only living and true God. But its people, by rejection of the Messiah and persecution of His saints, had transformed it into "a synagogue of Satan." But the Church, which Paul had planted, was "in the Lord Jesus Christ." It was a Christian community. It was "in God the Father," having been originated by Him, being His possession, receiving the tokens of His favour, and being governed by His laws. It was "in the Lord Jesus Christ," its members having been gathered in His name, being knit together in His love, existing for His service, and preserved for His glory. (*J. Hutchison, D.D.*)    Grace be unto you and peace.—Let us look at the blessings. I. APART. 1. Grace—favour shown to one who has no claim upon it; and so either the kindness existing in God's heart towards us, or as some operation of that kindness. In the one case, we cannot see it—it is a boundless ocean hidden in God's infinite mind; in the other case, if we cannot see it we can enjoy it—it is a stream flowing out of that unseen ocean into our hearts. This grace—(1) Quickens. (2) Enlightens. (3) Upholds and strengthens. (4) Transforms. (5) Elevates. (6) Comforts. We are lost till grace finds us, undone till it saves us, naked till it clothes us, miserable till it comforts us. Grace finds us poor and makes us rich; sunk, and never leaves us till it has raised us to heaven. 2. Peace, *i.e.*, of mind through reconciliation with God. Naturally we are all strangers to this. We accordingly find men everywhere flying from thought and feeling to pleasure, business, science, and even cares. But quiet is not thus obtained. The soul slumbers but is not at peace. The peace of the text is not absence of thought and feeling, it is tranquillity and comfort while thinking and feeling. It spreads itself over the whole mind. (1) The understanding no longer harassed in its search for truth feels that in the gospel it has found truth to repose upon. (2) The conscience is quieted. Its tormenting fears go when the blood of Jesus cleanseth it from sin. (3) The affections which no natural man can indulge without disquiet, have such objects as satisfy while they exercise them, as regulate while they excite them. (4) The will before quarrelling with God's dealings now acquiesces in them and enters into perfect peace. II. CONJOINED. 1. The connection is very close. Paul mentions them together in all his Epistles except Hebrews, and so does St. Peter. Nearly twenty times are they coupled together and prayed for in the New Testament. So the connection cannot be accidental. 2. They are always mentioned in the same order—nowhere "peace and grace." 3. They are united as cause and effect. Grace is the root of peace, peace the flower of grace. They are not found together like two trees that grow side by side, their roots and branches intertwined. Where grace is, peace is or will be. 4. We may apply this to rectify the errors of— (1) The worldling. He cuts them in two. He wants peace without grace, happiness without holiness. But he might as well go round the world and search for a day without a sun. (2) The penitent who looks for grace but despairs of peace. III. THEIR TWOFOLD SOURCE. 1. From the Father, because His free everlasting love is the fountain of them. The work of Christ did not make God love, it was the way God's love was manifested. 2. From the Lord Jesus Christ, as the great Medium through which our prayers for grace and peace ascend, and through whom these blessings flow from God. Man in union with Christ—man's poor, empty, disquieted heart is the cistern into which the streams of grace and peace run. 3. In every instance in which Paul uses this benediction the two names are conjoined—an emphatic witness to the co-equality of Christ with God. IV. THE LIGHT IN WHICH THIS PRAYER PLACES THEM. It represents them as—1. Exceedingly valuable. If we have but these we need nothing more. 2. Needed by all. (1) By sinners. (2) By the comfortless. (3) By saints of all kinds, as here. They are not given once for all, but moment by moment. 3. Copious—sufficient for all times, &c. (*C. Bradley, M.A.*)    *Peace of Christ:*—A friend once asked Professor Francke, who built the Orphan-house at Halle, how it came to pass that he maintained so constant a peace of mind. The benevolent and godly man replied, "By stirring up my mind a hundred times a day. Wherever I am, whatever I do, I say, Blessed Jesus, have I truly a share in thy redemption? Are my sins forgiven? Am I guided by thy Spirit? Thine I am. Wash me again and again. By this constant converse with Jesus, I have enjoyed serenity of mind, and a settled peace in my soul." (*Scottish Christian Herald.*)   *Peace :—*The ordinary salutation of the East was one of peace, and is so still. Seated on his fiery steed and armed to the teeth, the Bedouin careers along the desert. Catching, away to the haze of the burning sands, a form similarly mounted and armed approaching him, he is instantly on the alert; for life is a precarious possession among these wild sons of freedom. His long spear drops to the level; and grasping it in his sinewy hand he presses forward, till the black eyes that glance out from the folds of his shawl recognize in the stranger one of a friendly tribe, between whom and him there is no quarrel, no question of blood to settle. So, for the sun is hot, and it is far to their tents, like two ships in mid-ocean, they pass; they pull no rein, but sweep on, with a "Salem Aleikum"—"Peace be unto you." Like their flowing attire, the black tents of Kedar, the torch proces-sion at their marriages, this salutation is one of the many stereotyped habits of the East. The modern traveller hears it fresh and unchanged, as if it were but yester-day that David sent it to Nabal. Beautiful as the custom is, like the fragrant wall-flower that springs from the mouldering ruin it adorns, it sprung from an unhappy condition of society. Why peace? Because frequent wars made the people of these lands sigh for peace. War does not take us unawares. We see the black storm-cloud gathering before it bursts; and by prudent policy may avert it, or, if it be inevitable, prepare bravely to meet it. But this curse of humanity fell on those countries with the suddenness of a sea-squall that strikes a ship, and, ere time is found to reef a sail or lower a boat, throws her on her beam ends, and sends her, crew and cargo, foundering into the deep. Look at the case of Job, at Abraham's rescue of Lot, at the spoiling of Ziklag (1 Sam. xxx.), and it is easy to understand how the most kind and cordial greeting in such countries was "Peace be unto you." With these words our Lord on returning from the grave accosted His disciples. How well did they suit the occasion! The battle of salvation has been fought out, and a great victory won; and in that salutation Jesus, His own herald, announces the news to the anxious Church. He has fulfilled the anthem with which angels sang His advent to this distracted, guilty world. Though He had to recall her from heaven, where she had fled in alarm at the Fall, or rather, had to seek her in the gloomy retreats of death, He brings back sweet, holy peace to the earth. Suppose that instead of descending in those silent and unseen influences of the Spirit, our Lord were to come in person, how would He address us? It would be in these very words. (*T. Guthrie, D.D.*)

**Vers. 2-4. We give thanks to God always for you all, making mention of you in our prayers.**—*Ministerial thanksgiving :*—I. Is EXPANSIVE IN ITS CHARACTER. It is our duty to be grateful for personal benefits, but it displays a nobler generosity to be thankful for the good of others. Paul thanked God—1. Because of their work of faith. (1) Faith itself is a work; it is the laying hold of Christ for salvation. In its exercise man meets with opposition, and it becomes a fight. (2) It is the cause of work—the propelling and sustaining motive in all Christian toil. "Faith without works is dead." 2. Because of their labour of love. Labour tests the strength of love. We show our love to Christ by what we do for Him. Love makes even drudgery an enjoyment. It leads us to attempt what we would once have shrunk from in dismay. 3. Because of their patient hope. It was severely tried, but not quenched. It is hard to hope in the midst of discouragement. It was so with Joseph in prison, with David in the mountains of Judah, with the Jews in Babylon. But the grace of patience gives constancy to hope. 4. Because of their election, not as individuals, this could not be, but as a people. St. Paul here means that from what he saw of the operations of Christian grace in them he knew they were God's elect. As Bengel says, "Election is the judgment of Divine grace, exempting in Christ, from the common destruction of men, those who accept their calling by faith. Every one who is called, is elected from the first moment of his faith; and so long as he continues in his calling and faith, he continues to be elected; if at any time he loses calling and faith, he ceases to be elected." Observe the constancy of this thanksgiving-spirit—"We give thanks always for you all." As they remembered without ceasing the genuine evidences of conversion so did they assiduously thank God. II. EVOKES A SPIRIT OF PRACTICAL DEVOTION. "Making mention of you in our prayers." The interest of the successful worker in his converts is keenly aroused; he is especially anxious the work should be permanent, and resorts to prayer as the effectual means. Prayer for others benefits the suppliant. When the Church prayed, not only was Peter liberated from prison, but the faith of the members was emboldened. III. Is RENDERED TO THE GREAT GIVER OF ALL GOOD. "We give thanks to God." God is the author of true success. In vain we labour where His blessing is withheld. (*G. Barlow.*) *Intercessory prayer :* A praying engineer used to run from Boston on the morning express train. A very faithful man he was in his business; and he was a man of ardour and enthusiasm for souls. He used to make me ride with him, and he would give me an account of his hunting and fishing for souls. I suppose he was the means of rescuing fifty men from the devil's grasp, clothing them and getting them into business. Even while he was running his engine he was thinking of his work—for his real work was among souls. The moment he got to the terminus off went his engineer's clothes and on went his ordinary dress, and he started around town to look after some of his cases to inquire about them, and to speak with them. He drew out his praying list one day! I found that he had a strip of paper on which were written ten or fifteen names; and he said that each day he prayed for every single one of them. Sometimes he was more particularly moved in behalf of this one, and sometimes in behalf of that one. Said he, "As soon as one of these is converted I put another on the list. There are ever so many waiting to get on the list; but I cannot put more than fifteen on." He was always praying somebody on or somebody off from that list of his. He gave me some of the most affecting accounts that I ever heard in my life. (*H. W. Beecher.*) *Prayer for individuals :*—There is nothing better than to always have before your mind some one at whose conversion you are aiming. There may be a withering plant in your garden, but it will respond to the touch of the water with which you sprinkle it, and there will be an awakening to new strength and beauty. And who will say that less effective will be the power of the Holy Ghost; that the Christian may not pray down an influence like the waters of life to any soul wasted away by sin? It is so hopeful, this personal work in behalf of souls. It is most effective when its aim is single, and one by one you separate men and make them special, individual objects of your attention. Such work, if persisted in, will tell wonderfully by and by. The results will grow into mountains. They may not aggregate as rapidly as did Dr. Hopkins, the old Newport parson, and the famous author of Hopkinsonism. He made a list of the members of his congregation, and for each one made separate supplication. There were thirty-one conversions after those separate prayers. You may not have such a success, but enough stars will shine in your crown to make a constellated glory there for ever!

Vers. 3, 4. **Remembering without ceasing your work of faith.**—*The three graces at work :*—I. THE WORK OF FAITH. Faith is an active principle, and St. James has dealt with it as such, and told Antinomians of every age that "faith without works is dead." Some assert that he was antagonistic to St. Paul on this subject. But this is refuted by St. Paul's example, and by the text, which accords with all that James has written. 1. Faith is the awakening of the soul to the realities of life. To apprehend the truth is to feel its power, without the consciousness of that power life is a dream. To grasp the truths of the gospel with the hand of faith is to stir up the powers of human nature and load them with responsibilities. 2. Faith is the inspiration to discharge the duties of life. The mere sense of obligation is not enough. It is a man's duty to pay his debts whether he has the means or not. Honesty of purpose and hope of success will encourage the debtor to labour until he is able to discharge his liabilities. The work of faith, although not without its reward, is a present effort to secure future fruits. The good seed is cast into the ground in expectation of a harvest. Work follows belief. II. LABOUR OF LOVE distinguishes between the ordinary work of the Church, and the supreme efforts necessary to maintain the Christian name. The cross was often very heavy. Fiery trials came to overcome faith, but love stood in the breach, and drove back the enemy. Where trust may fail, love never will. 1. It is a labour of love when everything seems to go against us. Peter and his fellow-disciples, although they had toiled in vain all night, yet cast the net once more out of love for the Saviour. It does not appear that they believed success would attend the second effort, but they did it in loving obedience to Christ. Apostolic labours were often carried on in the same spirit. Ministers, Sunday-school teachers, and Christian workers, when faith falters, should do as the second officer does when immediate danger is apprehended—send for the captain. In heavy seas let love take the command of the vessel. "Charity never faileth." 2. It is a labour of love when we are persecuted by those whom we seek to save. It is a trying ordeal to benefit others while they are injuring us. We have a severe lesson to learn when we must love those who hate us. In this the believer approaches nearer the Saviour. 3. It is a labour of love when we leave all the fruit for others to gather and enjoy. Disinterested love labours not for itself, but for those who follow. This is a grand movement in the Church. III. PATIENCE OF HOPE. This is the climax. Work must bear fruit. The glory of God in what we do may be beyond the ken of faith. The storm may rage furiously, threatening to outdo the wisdom and the courage of love. Hope sees beyond all this to the desired haven. 1. Abide God's time. With the Lord a thousand years are as but one day. Faith may become dispirited because there is a seeming slackness on the part of God to fulfil His promise. Love may be beaten by the storm for a longer time than was expected. Hope brings forward the visions of the future to cheer the one and to strengthen the other. 2. Lay hold on God's arm. Hope feels for the strength of the Lord, and leans upon it. (*Weekly Pulpit.*) *A favourite triology :*—These were St. Paul's "favourite triology of Christian principles." And they were fundamental also. An eminent theologian puts it thus :—"As the three principal colours of the rainbow—red, yellow, and blue, representing heat, light, and purifying power—supply in their combination all the other colours, so, by a sort of moral analysis, faith, hope, and love lie at the foundation, or enter into the composition, of all other Christian excellences." They are, in a word, inseparable graces. Faith always works by love, and these two virtues can wait patiently and hopefully for ultimate results. They are the crown of Christian believers, and the forces of the whole Church. And they must succeed. Faith says—"I labour in the full confidence that I shall finally accomplish all I would;" Love says—"I delight in my work, and therefore will not slacken in my efforts until I have secured all I desire;" and Hope says—"I can wait patiently for all I joyfully anticipate." These three divine graces are a created trinity, and have some glimmering resemblance of the Trinity uncreate; for as there the Son is begotten of the Father, and the Holy Ghost proceeds from them both; so here a true faith begets a constant hope, and from them proceeds charity. In the godly these three are united, and cannot be sundered. We believe in God's mercy, we hope for His mercy, and we love Him for His mercy. (*T. Adams.*) *The vital graces :*—The leading graces of Christianity are "faith, hope, and charity." On these all other graces essentially depend; so that where these are, there will all others most assuredly be found. But of all these graces there are counterfeits: there is "a faith that is dead;" there is "a love which is dissimulation;" and there is "a hope of the hypocrite that perisheth." Such, however, were not the graces which had been exercised among the Thessalonians: in them the apostle had seen— I. AN ACTIVE FAITH. True faith is active: it brings to the Christian's view the Lord Jesus Christ, as having in Him a fulness of all imaginable blessings treasured up for the use of the Church; just as the vine has in its root and trunk that sap of which all the branches partake, and by which they are nourished. Faith, moreover, brings the Christian to Christ for daily supplies of those blessings which his various necessities require. And having received communications of grace according to his necessities, he is stirred up by it to improve them to the glory of his Redeemer's name. In a word, whatever the Christian has to do for God, he does it through the operation of this principle, by which, and by which alone, he overcomes the world, and purifies his heart. This faith St. Paul had seen in his Thessalonian converts; yea, so eminently had it shone forth in them, that they were celebrated for it in almost every Church throughout the Roman empire, and were held forth as patterns and ensamples of it to all the Christian world. II. A LABORIOUS LOVE. Love is that fruit by which, above all, the truth and reality of faith will be discerned. It is by this, above all, that we can assure ourselves, or be known to others, as faithful followers of Christ. If we have it not, all else that we can have is of no value. But love is a laborious grace: it is always seeking for something which it may *do* either for God or man. It cannot endure to be idle. Whether it can do little or much, it delights to be doing what it can. Nor is it diverted from its pursuit by slight obstacles; no—like the water obstructed by the dam, it will overcome them, and will evince its strength and ardour in proportion to the difficulties that impede its exercise. Love is a self-denying grace; and where it exists in due measure, it will prompt a man not only to sacrifice ease and interest, but even to lay down his life itself for the brethren. This grace was so conspicuous in the Thessalonian converts, that St. Paul judged it quite unnecessary to write to them on the subject: they were so taught by God Himself respecting all its duties and offices, that he could add nothing to them, but only to exhort them to abound more and more in the conduct which they had already pursued. III. A PATIENT HOPE. Hope is the offspring of faith and love, or at least of that faith which worketh by love. St. Paul calls it "hope in our Lord Jesus Christ," because "in Him all the promises of God are yea and amen." It is a patient grace, leading us to expect all that God has promised, however long we may have to wait for it; and to fulfil all that God has required, to the utmost possible extent; and to suffer all that God has ordained us to suffer, in hope of a final recompense; and, finally, to continue in a constant course of well-doing, even to the end. Such was the hope which the Thessalonians had manifested, and in which they had greatly rejoiced even in the midst of all their afflictions. (*C. Simeon, M.A.*) *The character of Thessalonian Christianity*:—I. ACTIVE FAITH shown in—1. A full persuasion of the truth of the gospel. 2. Steadfast adherence to it in the midst of trial. 3. The great change which it had already wrought in their life and character. 4. The efforts in which they had engaged to extend the gospel. II. LABORIOUS LOVE implying—1. Great anxiety for the temporal and spiritual well-being of others. 2. Self-denying exertions to promote that well-being. III. PATIENT HOPE. 1. A conviction that Christ will come. 2. A preparedness for His coming. 3. An expectation of it. 4. An earnest desire for it. (*T. Hughes.*) *Faith, hope, and love*:—Faith hangs on the word of promise, love on that God who gives, hope on the promised inheritance. Faith receives and has, love gives, hope waits. Faith makes the heart firm, love makes it soft, hope expands it. Faith holds fast to what it has received, love gives up what it has received, hope triumphs over what is wanting. Faith capacitates us for dominion over this world, love for ministering to this world, hope for renunciation of this world. Faith is the confidence in what one hopes for; love, the proof of this, that one has faith; hope, the taking possession, before we have reached the goal, of that which we have learned by faith and love to yearn after. Faith is what it ceases to be in sight; hope is what it ceases to be in full possession; love is that which it never ceases to be, for God is love. (*Prof. Harless.*) Faith is childlike, hope is saintlike, but love is Godlike. (*Prof. Eadie.*) *The work of faith*:—I. As it regards GOD. 1. To depend on His guidance—(1) In His word. (2) In the opening up of providential opportunities. 2. To trust in His help. Without Him we can do nothing. (1) The mind is dark as to duty—He must enlighten it. (2) The will is irresolute or rebellious—He must subdue and strengthen it. (3) The energies are enfeebled—He must invigorate them. 3. To use His power. (1) It is offered freely. (2) It must be employed faithfully and energetically. 4. To bide His time. As in nature, so in grace, there is seed-time and harvest: how often the Christian husbandman confounds the two. 5. To aim at His glory. (1) This is His due inasmuch as He is the great Agent, we the implements. (2) This will lift our efforts on to a higher platform and endue them with an irresistible motive power. II. As it regards SELF. 1. To believe that God has qualified us for a certain work in a certain way. (1) God has qualified some mentally. It is for such to believe that God has fitted them for literature, teaching, organization, &c. (2) God has qualified some physically. It is for such to believe that although not gifted intellectually, they can still work for God in visiting the sick, &c. (3) God has qualified some financially: they should believe that their work is beneficence. (4) God has qualified some with only a quiet influence: such should not believe that they can do nothing. God sometimes qualifies by disqualifications. How can the sick work? In many ways. By prayer, the example of Christian resignation, &c. "They also work who only stand and wait." 2. To believe that God intends and will help us each to work in his own way. Do not, then, ape any one else. That is unbelief in our God-given individuality. Yet it largely obtains. The born preacher thinks he should organize: the visitor that he should teach: but it is misplaced faith and therefore unbelief. Be yourself, and rely on yourself as called and qualified by God. 3. To believe that through God's strength we are sufficient for anything that He calls us to. Unbelief here is the paralysis of Christian effort and the nurse of much sinful indolence. 4. To believe that God will accept and consecrate us as we grapple with our tasks. Faith is the spring of devotion to God. III. As regards our WORK. 1. To believe in the Divine sanction. Unbelief here is ruinous. Any doubt about our Divine call will not be compensated by the most transparent sincerity and the most prodigious effort. All work must fall to pieces without faith in its Divinity. 2. To believe that it is worthy of the best energies that we can devote to it, the best time that we can spend in its preparation and execution, the best appliances we can use in it. We must regard it as the noblest work in which a human spirit can engage: which it really is. 3. To believe in its ultimate success. Who would stand long hours behind a counter unless he believed that his work was going to pay? And who can preach and teach with any power unless he believes that God's word shall not return to Him void. IV. As regards OTHERS, viz., those for whose benefit we work. 1. To believe that they want our service: that the sinful need cleansing, that the degraded need elevating, &c. 2. To believe that our service will meet this need. If we have any lingering doubt that the gospel is not quite effective, and must be abandoned for, *e.g.*, some methods of social reform—farewell to all power and prospect of success. Learn—1. That Christ is the Author and Finisher of our faith. "It is the gift of God." 2. That faith having secured personal salvation, it henceforth becomes practical. 3. That faith grows and strengthens by exercise, and nowhere so effectually as in Christian work. (*J. W. Burn.*)   **And labour of love.**— *The labour of love:*—I. THE LABOUR WHICH LOVE INSPIRES. Love is the mightiest motive: the one which never fails. This is needed in all work that is worth doing: much more Christian work. Love regards either the work itself, as in the case of an artist, or the object for which the work is done, *i.e.*, to please a friend or to feed a family. Christian work is animated by the threefold motive: the work is worth doing, God is worth serving, souls are worth saving.   II. THE LABOUR WHICH LOVE DOES. 1. It undergoes any sacrifices. Mark the self-denial of the student, *e.g.*, in his pursuit of learning. Shall the Christian then avoid any discipline that will perfect his character, or is necessary for his equipment for war or service? 2. It succumbs to no fatigue. Of mere task-service we soon tire. 3. It spares no energies. When a man begins to pick and choose, it is easy to see that he has no heart in it. Christian love asks not how little can I do and escape condemnation, but how much can I do of this glorious work for this dear Master.   III. THE LABOUR WHICH LOVE PERFECTS. Its work must be worthy of itself. So—1. It is ingenious in contriving to do the best thing in the best way. What pains are taken about mother's birthday present; and shall we be less solicitous for Christ. 2. It adds beauty to ability so that the gratification may be complete. There is a holy extravagance about love which excites the query, "To what purpose is this waste?"   IV. THE LABOUR WHICH LOVE REWARDS. 1. The labour of love is its own reward: to have produced a book which has edified thousands is a reward to which the most handsome remuneration is out of all proportion. To have brought a soul to Christ is worth more than the wealth of a Rothschild. 2. The smile of the beloved one recompenses the labour of love. Your work is worth so much— which will you have—twice its value or the warm word of appreciation? The Master's glad "well done" is heaven. Lessons: 1. Learn to love what you do either for its own sake or for the sake of some one. This will make "drudgery divine." 2. Let your love grow with your work and your work under your love. (*Ibid.*)   *Products of love:*—Fear produceth unwilling, servile performances, as those fruits that grow in winter or in cold countries are sour, unsavoury, and un- concocted; but those which grow in summer or in hotter countries, by the warmth and influence of the sun, are sweet and wholesome. Such is the difference between those fruits of obedience which fear and love produceth. (*Bishop Reynolds.*)   *Love wrought this:*—A century ago, in the north of Europe, stood an old cathedral, upon one of the arches of which was a sculptured face of wondrous beauty. It was long hidden, until one day the sun's light striking through a slanted window, revealed its matchless features. And ever after, year by year, upon the days when for a brief hour it was thus illuminated, crowds came and waited eager to catch a glimpse of that face. It had a strange history. When the cathedral was being built, an old man, broken with the weight of years and care, came and besought the architect to let him work upon it. Out of pity for his age, but fearful lest his failing sight and trembling touch might mar some fair design, the master set him to work in the shadows of the vaulted roof. One day they found the old man asleep in death, the tools of his craft laid in order beside him, the cunning of his right hand gone, the face upturned to this marvellous face which he had wrought—the face of one whom he had loved and lost in early manhood. And when the artists and sculptors and workmen from all parts of the cathedral came and looked upon that face they said, "This is the grandest work of all; love wrought this." (*Christian Advocate.*)

**Patience of hope.**—*Patience of hope* is the point of this verse that we shall insist upon. But what is hope? It is an emotion; but it is more nearly allied to an intellectual state, perhaps, than a good many others. It is cheerfulness; it is happiness in expectancy; or, it is a bright view of the future. Memory takes care of the past; realization considers the present; anticipation works in the future, but it is a purely intellectual state of fore-looking: it may run along the line of cause and effect; it is a kind of prophecy from the known side of the relation of causes to effects. Hope acts in the future; it distils joy in the present by reason of that which it sees in the future. Anticipation does not: anticipated joys do not make one necessarily joyful now; anticipated success does not bring the remuneration of success in the present; it may bring courage, but not joy. Hope does bring joy, it irradiates the present; trials, struggles, temptations, defeats, are all made radiant by hopefulness. Not only is it an active state, but under certain circumstances it is a state that beds itself in, or is upheld by, the condition of patience, as if patience were a candlestick, and hope were the candle. It is looking at things in the future in a bright and cheerful light—the light of happiness. In this regard there are those that have no hope, or, rather, that have a hope that is torpid. I recollect having to deal with a saintly and notable woman, who, at the breaking out of a revival of religion, was in the very depths of despair, and felt that her hopes were blasted, and that she was foredoomed to eternal destruction. She had been so excessively active in all the preliminary stages of the religious excitement that she had simply exhausted herself; and, being of a bilious temperament, she had gone into a condition of absolute paralysis, if I might so say, of hopefulness. I did not address one single consideration of hopefulness to her. When her confidence was secured, so that she could follow implicitly my directions, I forbade her to go to church, to read one word in the Bible, or to utter a syllable of prayer until I gave her permission. She was filled with amazement; but resting absolutely, and freeing herself from that which had already been an over-anxiety in her case, at last nature rebounded, and she sent me word that if I did not free her from her promise she would have to break it, for her heart was overflowing with joy, and she could not help it though she tried ever so hard. If I had gone on describing the sin of her forgetting Christ and so forth, it would have been adding to her overstraining, and there would have been no chance for nature to rebound and come to her help. So, while there is this state of a probably diseased condition of mind, there must be other than mere moral treatment. There be many persons that have been injured by a too intense application, to their cases, of religious stimuli. We should have care not to plunge men into despondency; but, on the other hand, we ought all of us to be taught, in the very beginning, that of ourselves we are scarcely to attain anything that is very high—that the light which is in us, tending toward good, is the atmosphere of God Himself. Have hope—not despair; and above all things, do not get caught in the devil's puzzle as between that which is in you by reason of God's stimulus, and that which is dependent on your own exertion and your own will. (*H. W. Beecher.*) *The patience of hope:*—I. THE RELATION OF HOPE TO PATIENCE. 1. It begets patience. Where there is no hope there is no patience, but either apathy or recklessness. The man who feels there is no hope of retrieving his ruined fortunes simply folds his hands or drowns his despair in self-indulgence. 2. It fosters patience. While there is a hope of anything, we feel that it is worth while waiting for it. But just in proportion as hope fades does patience relax its hold. 3. It justifies patience. If there is nothing to wait for, why wait? A friend's promise, *e.g.*, is sure to be redeemed. The hope of that warrants the patience of years. Apply these principles—(1) To God's salvation. To despair of this as some have done is to grow careless and indifferent—but what weary days and months have been spent in the hope of the smile of God's countenance. This hope encourages us to wait for salvation in God's time and way, and the object is so great as to justify any amount of patience. (2) To Christian work. The prospect of winning souls calls forth the patient use of means. When we despond, the means are abandoned or only feebly employed. But hope lures the labourer to plod on. The seed is sown in tears; but it is sown; and the harvest will repay patient continuance in well-doing. (3) To family duties. The mother's lot is brightened by hope. Alas! what would it be without it? That troublesome boy may grow up to be a great man. In the hope of this plod on, mother! II. THE RELATION OF PATIENCE TO HOPE. 1. It keeps hope alive. The impatient are most subject to fits of despondency. The patient are often disappointed, but what do they do? Turn their energies into another channel. Bruce and the spider, "Try, try, try again." The man

who quietly plods on in spite of discouragement augments his hope. 2. It brings hope nearer its fruition. Every step brings the traveller nearer home. Apply these principles—(1) To the Christian conflict. The more strenuous your efforts to subdue the flesh and to resist temptation, the easier becomes the warfare and the brighter the hope of victory. (2) To the prospects of the Church. Our Lord delayeth His coming! What shall we do? Abandon Missions? No. "Hold the fort, for He *is* coming," and every day's service brings Him nearer. (*J. W. Burn.*) *The patience of hope :*—In the year 1683, Vienna, the capital of Austria, was besieged ; a great army of Turks, who were then making war with the nations of Europe, lay before it. When it was known that they were near Vienna, the Emperor of Austria fled from the city, and the poor people in it were left in sad fear and distress. The only person they thought likely to save them was the King of Poland, John Sobieski, and they sent entreating him to come to their help. They knew that he could only come to them over the northern mountains, and day after day they rose early, and watched for the first morning light, in the hope of seeing the Polish army on the mountains. It was anxious waiting, but hope sustained them. The siege began in July ; on the 11th of September some weary watchers were looking out from the ramparts to the mountain of the Kalimburg, when—oh, delightful sight !—they saw something bright on the mountain-side, and discerned the lances and armour of the brave Poles marching to the rescue. That very day Sobieski fought a bloody battle, defeated the Turks, and set Vienna free. (*Family Treasury.*)  *The effects produced by the vital graces in St. Paul's mind :*—
I. A LIVELY INTEREST IN THEIR WELFARE. A person less connected with them than he could not but have admired such excellences ; but he was their father ; he had begotten them in the gospel, and therefore might well boast of them as his "glory and joy." Accordingly we find that whenever he came into the presence of his God and Father, he both gave thanks for them, and prayed for their still greater advancement in everything that was good. Most exalted was the joy which he felt on their account. When he saw the transcendent eminence of their attainments, he quite forgot all his own afflictions ; the sight inspired new life and vigour into him ; and he felt in himself a recompense which richly repaid all that he had done and suffered for their sake. This shows what are the feelings and views of every faithful minister when he sees his people thus adorning the gospel of Christ. That so great an honour should be conferred on themselves—that such advantages should be imparted to their perishing fellow-creatures, and that such glory should be brought to God by their means, is to them a subject of almost stupefying amazement and overwhelming gratitude. And, while they render thanks to God for these things, they pour out their heart before Him in prayers and supplications on their behalf. In a word, these things form a bond of union between a minister and his people, such as does not exist in the whole world beside.
II. AN ASSURED CONFIDENCE IN THEIR STATE. When the apostle beheld these fruits produced by his Thessalonian converts, he had no doubt of their "election of God ;" the graces they exercised were manifestly wrought in them by the power of God, who had wrought thus upon them in consequence of His own purpose, which from all eternity He had purposed in Himself. The same blessed assurance may now be entertained wherever the same ground for it exists. Assurance, so founded, can never be productive of any bad effect. When such fruits as those which the Thessalonian converts produced are visible in any, then may we indulge the pleasing thought respecting them, as they also may respecting themselves, that "God loved them with an everlasting love," and therefore with loving-kindness hath He drawn them. Only we may observe—that this assurance is no farther justifiable than it is warranted by the graces which exist in the soul ; with the increase of those graces it may justly rise, and with their diminution it must proportionably fall. Any other assurance than this is unscriptural and vain ; but this not only *may* be entertained, but is the privilege and comfort of all who believe in Christ. (*C. Simeon, M.A.*)
**In the sight of God and our Father.**—*The habitual recognition of God :*—
I. WHAT IT IS TO ACT AS EVER IN THE SIGHT OF GOD. To maintain a supreme and habitual regard for God in the relations He sustains towards us. 1. Some act with a perpetual self-consciousness. They care for no one's esteem or condemnation. Their one object is to please self—a poor master when best pleased. 2. To act with a perpetual consciousness of others : ever fearful to offend, and offending from very fearfulness ; ever over-anxious to please, and failing through very over-anxiousness. 3. The Christian is ever conscious of, "Thou God seest me." (1) As a Being of infinite perfection. (2) As Lawgiver and Sovereign. (3) As Creator,

Preserver, Benefactor. (4) As Redeemer and Sanctifier. (5) As Judge and Rewarder. (6) As Father. II. THE ADVANTAGE OF ACTING AS EVER IN THE SIGHT OF GOD. 1. It would make the whole of life a continued act of religion. Apply this to business, politics, domestic duties. 2. It would give us the comfort of knowing that some one whose appreciation is worth having is cognizant of little acts upon which men set no value. Who regards the widow's mite or the cup of cold water? God is also observant of those little trials in the warehouse or home, the aggregate of which constitute a great trial. He is looking down with sympathy— be brave; He is looking down with justice—beware. 3. It would strengthen against temptation. There is enough in that omniscient Being to gratify every longing. Why, then, try to fill your belly with the husks that the swine do eat? 4. It would make us stedfast in all holy obedience. We should be prepared for all the duties of devotion. The sense of God with us amid all the cares and bustle of the world would help to maintain all the graces in lively exercise. 5. It would prepare for death and eternity. (*N. W. Taylor, D.D.*) *Realization of God's presence:*—The realization of the Divine presence is the central thought of the Christian's whole life. All the graces of his character spring from that one root. Just as all life, animal or vegetable, forms round a nucleus, a centre, a mere point or speck at first, but containing the germ of the animal or plant that is developed from it; so the spiritual life of the believer all forms itself from this one centre, the realization of the presence of God. (*Dean Goulburn.*) *An eye fixed on man:*—What would you say if, wherever you turned, whatever you were doing, whatever thinking in public or private, with a confidential friend, telling your secrets, or alone planning them, if, I say, you saw an eye constantly fixed upon you, from whose watching though you strove ever so much you could never escape; and even if you closed your own eye to avoid, you still fancied that to get rid of it was impossible—that it could perceive your every thought? The supposition is awful enough. There is such an Eye, though the business and struggles of the world would often enough prevent us from considering this awful truth. In crowds we are too interrupted, in the pursuit of self-interest we are too much perverted, in camps we are struggling for life and death, in courts we see none but the eye of a human sovereign; nevertheless, the Divine eye is always upon us, and, when we least think of it, is noting all, and, whatever we may think of it, will remember all. (*De Vere.*) *Man in the sight of God:*—Let us ask ourselves seriously and honestly, "What sort of a show would I make after all, if the people around me knew my heart and all my secret thoughts?" What sort of a show then do I already make in the sight of Almighty God, who sees every man exactly as he is? But take comfort also, and recollect however little you and I may know, God knows; He knows Himself and you and me and all things; and His mercy is over all His works. (*C. Kingsley, M.A.*)

Vers. 4-6. **Knowing, brethren beloved, your election of God.**—*Election:*—I. THE ELECTION "of God" is not connected with "knowing" nor "election." The meaning is that the Church was "beloved" of God, not merely of the missionaries. And the proof of their being the subject of the Divine love is their election. This election was their historical selection out of the Western World to be the earliest European recipients of the gospel. The narrative in Acts xvi. 6-10 is expository of it. The missionaries' course was narrowed off from this and that place until the vision of the man of Macedonia. Thessalonica being the chief city of Macedonia, the vision was a declaration of the election of its inhabitants. The term "election" is a rare one in Scripture, and is absent, except in this case, from all Paul's earlier Epistles. It had been used of Paul to Ananias in reference to his own similar selection: "He is a vessel of election unto Me." In both cases it means selection for privilege, and therefore for service. The same election is ceaselessly seen—one nation, city, family, individual, called before another. Many perplexities gather round the subject, and its ultimate solution is to be found in the Divine sovereignty alone. Often, however, the thing is clear. Here, *e.g.*, there was a fitness in the choice of Thessalonica as a centre for Christian influence (ver. 8). Thessalonica was a great emporium of commerce by sea. It lay also on the line of one of the great Roman roads. Cicero describes it as "placed in the bosom of the Roman Empire." II. THE GROUNDS OF THE APOSTLE'S KNOWLEDGE OF THIS ELECTION were—1. Subjective—on his part. (1) "Our gospel," a phrase implying—(*a*) Heart possession of it. "I believed, therefore have I spoken." This is the first prerequisite of a faithful ministry. As Melanchthon used to say to his students, "It is the heart that makes the theologian." (b) Apostolic commission—a gospel committed to him for declaration to others. (2) This gospel came not in word only; although it did come, of course, in word. Cornelius was told about "words whereby thou and all thy house shall be saved." These words were proclaimed by the apostle's lips. Human instrumentality is employed in what is in the strictest sense God's work. But often it is in "word only." Even from the lips of Christ the message fell ineffectual, and Paul has his share in this. But it was far different here. (3) This gospel came "in power"—not miraculously, but persuasively. It was no cold, formal performance of duty, but in a very exceptional degree heart work. (4) It was therefore "in the Holy Ghost." The presence and energy of the Divine Spirit were recognized by Him. His utterances were more than the struggles of an earnest human spirit; they were the winged words of the Spirit of Truth. (5) Hence it came "in much assurance," i.e., in the firm conviction that his message was from heaven, and that it was not in vain (1 Cor. ii. 1–5). So he knew from within himself that they were "appointed unto salvation." From this we may gather—(a) Every minister feels sometimes powerless, unaided by the Spirit, and oppressed with doubt. In such a case he is bound to search for causes in his own heart. But he is also entitled to look without; to trace the cause of his own feebleness in the apathy of the people. He may even, after the example of Paul, conclude in some cases from this ineffective preaching that they are not the chosen people of God. Pulpit and pew react on each other. "Like people, like priest." (b) The apostle appeals to their knowledge of his bearing and conduct as well as his words. Personal influence is far more direct and effective than official. Truth must be taught by example as well as precept. An infidel once said to Fenelon, with whom he had been residing: "If I stay here any longer I shall become a Christian in spite of myself." (c) This bearing was not self-interested, but for their sakes, as every minister's should be. 2. Objective—the eager joyfulness with which the Thessalonians received Paul's preaching. The two grounds cannot be separated. The first could be no safe evidence without the second. Their having been chosen of God is shown by their having chosen God's gospel (chap. ii. 13). It became theirs as well as Paul's. They became followers, i.e., imitators, of Paul and Christ. How? Not in their reception of the truth. In this they might be imitators of Paul, but not of Christ, who was the Truth. The point of imitation is the joyful endurance of suffering. Paul preached the gospel "in much affliction with joy of the Holy Ghost," as Christ had wrought it out: "Who for the joy that was set before Him endured the cross." In this sphere of trial, and of spiritual joy in the midst of it, Christ and His apostles and people are at one. Embracing Christ entailed suffering; but sorrow from without could not destroy inward joy. Afflictions come from men, but joy from the Holy Ghost. The gospel cannot be received without joy. Paul, then, would encourage them to greater endurance still, by his grateful recognition of this evidence of their election. (*J. Hutchison, D.D.*) *Evidences of election :*—I. THE WORD OF GOD COMING HOME WITH POWER. The power of the gospel—1. Does not lie—(1) In the preacher, otherwise men would be the converters of souls. (2) Nor in the preacher's learning, or it would consist in the wisdom of men. (3) Nor in the preacher's adaptation to his work; that is a secondary agency, not the cause. (4) Nor in the pathos the preacher may employ. People may weep at a theatre. No, there is something more wanted. A half-drunken man said to Rowland Hill, "I am one of your converts." "Yes," said he, "I dare say you are one of mine; but if you were one of God's, you would not be in that state." 2. It does lie in the power of the Holy Ghost. (1) Did you ever—never mind where—in listening to the Word, feel a Divine power coming with it? Not an impression—that may be wiped out—but a power convincing of sin, making you tremble under it, and then wooing you to Christ, in whom you believed and then became a changed man? (2) And since that has the Word rebuked you, filled you with God's love and light and joy, and desire after holiness? If not, you lack a proof of your election. Not that it will be so every time, for the preacher is not always in a fit frame. II. RECEIVING THE WORD WITH MUCH ASSURANCE—not full assurance; that comes afterwards. There are some people who play fast and loose with principles; put a hymn-book in their pockets when they are going to meeting and a song-book when they are going somewhere else. They can hold with the hare and run with the hounds. Such people have never much confidence in their religion: and it is very proper that they should not, for their religion is not worth the time they spend in making a profession of it. But the true Christian, when he gets hold of principles, keeps them. His religion is part of himself. He believes the truth, not because he has been taught it, but because it is true to him; like the servant-girl who, when she could not answer her infidel master, said, "Sir, I cannot answer you, but I have a something in here that would, if it could speak." Now, if you have received the gospel with much assurance, you can say, "Christ is mine. I know that Christ is precious, not by 'Paley's Evidences' or 'Butler's Analogy,' but by my heart's inward evidence, the analogy of my soul's experience." If you can say that, whether you believe the doctrine of election or not, you are one of the elect. III. BECOMING FOLLOWERS OF US AND OF THE LORD; by which the apostle does not mean that they said, "I am of Paul, I of Silas, I of Timothy." No, they imitated them so far as they imitated Christ. Are you Christ-like, or do you want to be? Can you forgive your enemy, love him, and do him good? Are you prayerful as Jesus was? If a man follow not Christ, whatever he may say about election he is not the Lord's. IV. ENDURANCE OF AFFLICTION WITH JOY. (C. H. Spurgeon.)    Conditional election :— A man of colour who had received the gospel became a preacher among his black brethren. He was addressed on one occasion by his master in these words : "And so I hear that you have become a preacher, Sam, and that you believe in the doctrine of election." "Well, yas, sah, I believe dat truth is clearly revealed in the Word of God." "And I suppose, Sam, that you think that you are one of the elect." "Well, sah, I'se prepared to say dat I gib all diligence to make my calling and election sure, dat is true." "But I suppose you don't think that I am one of the elect," said Sam's master. The sable preacher gave an answer that is worth quoting. Sam knew his master was given to the pursuit of pleasures, money, and the service of sin. Very quietly he replied, "Well, massa, I am not sure about that; dis I know—I nebber knew of an election wher' dar was no candidate." (H. Varley.)    Knowledge of election :— An Arminian being about to pay a Calvinist a sum of money, asked, "Is it decreed that I shall pay thee this money?" "Put it in my hand, and I will tell thee," was the reply. Is it not to be wished that many professors of religion would infer their "election of grace" by their actual possession of grace? (New Testament Anec-dotes.)    God's electing providence :—Henry IV., King of France, was in every point of view a great man. It is said that on an anniversary of his birthday he made the following reflection : "I was born on this day, and, no doubt, taking the world through, thousands were born on the same day with me; yet, out of all those thousands, I am probably the only one whom God hath made a king. How pecu-liarly am I favoured by the bounty of His providence!" But a Christian, reflecting on his second birth, may, with greater reason, adore the free and sovereign grace of God.    Proofs of election :—The way by which the apostle knew the election of the Thessalonians must be the method by which we are to know ours. We have known some men who pretended to know their election by their impudence. They had got into their head the presumption that they were elected, and though they lived on in sin, and still did as they liked, they imagined they were God's chosen. This is what I call presuming upon election by sheer impudence. We know others who have imagined themselves to be elect, because of the visions that they have seen when they have been asleep or when they have been awake—for men have waking dreams— and they have brought these as evidences of their election. They are of as much value as cobwebs would be for a garment, and they will be of as much service to you at the day of judgment as a thief's convictions would be to him if he were in need of a character to commend him to mercy. You may dream long enough before you dream yourself into heaven, and you may have as many stupid notions in your head as there are romances in your circulating libraries, but because they are in your head they are not therefore in God's book. We want a more sure word of testimony than this, and if we have it not, God forbid that we should indulge our vain conceits with the dainty thought that we are chosen of God. I have heard of one who said in an ale-house that he could say more than the rest, namely, that he was one of God's children; meanwhile he drank deeper into intoxication than the rest. Surely he might have said he was one of the devil's children with an emphasis, and he would have been correct. When immoral men, and men who live constantly in sin, prate about being God's children, we discern them at once. Just as we know a crab-tree when we see the fruit hanging upon it, so we understand what spirit they are of when we see their walk and conversation. "Without holiness no man shall see the Lord." If we are God's elect, we shall have some substantial evidence to attest it. (C. H. Spurgeon.)

Vers. 5–10. **For our gospel came not unto you in word only.**—*The coming of the* *gospel and its effects :*—I. THE MANNER IN WHICH THE GOSPEL SHOULD COME TO A PEOPLE. 1. In word. (1) In the word written. It is of no use without this. The preacher's voice cannot reach where it can go. (2) In the word preached— stated in naked and clear propositions. Religion is no dark, unintelligible impulse of the mind. A trumpet must give a certain sound, or who will prepare himself for the battle. A herald's business is to make himself understood. (3) In the word apprehended. For the want of effort in this direction many are living in the grossest presumption, supposing themselves to be saints whereas they are in the utmost danger; on the other, there are many embarrassed with doubts and fears who ought to be enjoying the gospel. 2. In power. (1) Doubtless in miraculous power, but this is subordinate. The importance of a document lies in its contents, not in the seal. (2) Certainly in moral power—the intrinsic energy and efficacy of the truth. "Is not my word a hammer," &c. "The word of God is quick and powerful." This was seen in the case of Felix and Agrippa. When the truth is emphatically announced, there is a majesty, authority and force in it which are not found in moral, philosophical, or scientific disquisitions and harangues. Let me testify that you are a sinful man, a dying creature, that eternity is about to open, &c., and there is a power in those truths to strike upon the conscience and cause alarm, and if rejected it is in defiance of the dictates of the understanding and heart. 3. In the Holy Ghost, who—(1) Convinces of sin, righteousness and judgment, creating a sense of the need of the Saviour and preparing for the reception of the message of mercy. (2) Applies the gospel salvation to the heart and sheds abroad the love of God in it, and renovates the whole nature. 4. In much assurance. The image is that of a vessel richly freighted with all its sails spread, and wind and tide directly in its favour, going gallantly into port hailed by the acclamations of the people on the beach. (1) The gospel came on our part with full knowledge, invariable conviction, and certainty. (2) It was received by you like a vessel richly freighted, commissioned by Providence, sent of God, and the treasure, by appropriation, at once fully became your own. This implies, of course, that they saw the evidence, and felt the power of the word, so that no room was left for doubt. The primitive believers were not entangled as we are by metaphysical subtleties and difficulties respecting faith. They knew at once, with the simplicity of children, that a cordial reception of Christ was salvation. (3) It is the privilege of every believer to rejoice in the fulness and felicity of his justification. This full assurance is nothing else than a simple and perfect belief. (4) With joy of the Holy Ghost amidst much affliction. The design of the gospel is to produce joy where nothing else can produce it. Animal spirits, the delights of science or of sense, where are they in affliction? But Christian joy flourishes and sings in trials, "Though the fig tree shall not blossom," &c. II. THE EFFECTS WHICH THE GOSPEL IS TO PRODUCE WHEN IT HAS SO COME. 1. They turned from idols. Is there no idolatry amongst us which the gospel ought to dethrone? What about the worship of mammon, of the world, of self? 2. They turned to serve the living and true God. (1) Who has the right to our service which no one else has. (2) Who will reward us for our service as no one else will. 3. To wait for Jesus. (1) He delivered us from the wrath to come—hence there is nothing in the future to fear. (2) Jesus comes at the Judgment; at death. 4. They became imitators of Christ. He is our supreme example. His followers are to be imitated only as they truly follow Him. "Take My yoke upon you," &c. 5. They became examples to others. There was light upon the candlesticks at Philippi, Berea, &c., but none so brilliant as here. A Christian is not required to set an example of learning, wealth, &c., but of goodness. III. THE REPORT WHICH MAY GO ABROAD. It was just the same as when a modern people renounces idols and wickedness. The rumour gets abroad and is substantiated by changed lives. It is the same when a revival of true religion breaks out anywhere. (*J. Stratten.*) *Power through the Spirit :*—" The best way I can explain how the Christian worker, in complete contact with Christ, is a power to save souls, is by the following example. Take a common bar of iron, and first bending it into the shape of a horseshoe, apply it to a battery. The stream of magnetism flows through it, and by this power it is enabled to hold, even though there be suspended from it extremely heavy weights. As long as the iron is in contact with the battery, so long does the power endure; but the moment the connection is broken the power ceases, the weights fall, and the magnet becomes only a piece of iron. Similarly the Christian worker, in immediate contact with Christ, has His Spirit flowing through him, and this Spirit is the power, and by it we are enabled to do great works for Christ: but the moment we lose touch of Christ, that moment is our power gone, and we become, for God's purpose, a mere worthless piece of clay. (*C. White.*) *The gospel the only power unto salvation:*—Bishop Lavington, when addressing his clergy in a pastoral charge in the last century, said, "We have long been attempting to reform the nation by moral preaching. With what effect? None. On the contrary, we have dexterously preached the people into downright infidelity. We must change our voice; we must preach Christ and Him crucified; nothing but the gospel is the power of God unto salvation." *How the gospel came to the Thessalonians :*—I. A FACT ASSERTED. "Our gospel came unto you." 1. Our gospel, not by way of revelation, but dispensation. They had it in trust for the advantage of others. And so sure were they that it came from God that they said, "If we or an angel from heaven preach any other," &c. 2. What is this gospel? Good tidings; but the goodness of the news must regard the state of the receiver. The proclamation of deliverance will be acceptable only to captives. To offer pardon to the innocent or alms to the wealthy would be an insult. The gospel finds every man a sinner, and the relief it gives is adapted to his condition. Is he lost? Here is a Saviour. Is he unholy? Here is renewing grace. 3. This gospel came to them; they did not go to it or send for it. Nor did our heathen forefathers; nor did we. "I am found of them that sought me not." II. THE MANNER OF IT EXPLAINED. It came—1. In word—by the translated scriptures and the preached word to you. Thus it must come to be received at all. But a mere theoretic knowledge—(1) Cannot answer the design of the gospel. God has not inspired men to write His word and then magnified it to amuse your minds or furnish you with materials for controversy. "All scripture . . . is profitable," &c. (2) Will aggravate your sin and increase your condemnation. It is a medicine which will either kill or cure: it will prove either the savour of life or death. "See that ye refuse not Him that speaketh." 2. In power. When this is the case—(1) It produces conviction of sin. The word at Pentecost was quick and powerful. It pricked men to the heart, &c. It is the same now. But it works conviction only for saving purposes. Believe on the Lord Jesus Christ, and the word will come with power. (2) It gives comfort—and the comfort increases with the tribulation. "Ah," said Bolingbroke, "I find my philosophy fail me now in this affliction." Does the gospel fail? "Although the fig tree shall not blossom," &c. (3) It sanctifies. It calls us to be and makes us saints. Plato often complained that he could not bring the inhabitants of a single village to live according to his rules. But did the fishermen of Galilee complain in a similar way? We have seen the profligate become moral, the covetous liberal, the implacable ready to forgive. 3. In the Holy Ghost. This marks the nature and source of the power. The apostle does not refer to miraculous power—for that ceased with the early age, and miracles failed over and over again when they were worked to secure belief. This power is common to every age, and when exerted never fails. "Not by might nor by power." Melanchthon, in his zeal for God, hoped that all he addressed on the love of Christ would embrace Him as a Saviour; but he soon found that old Adam was too strong for young Melanchthon. 4. In much assurance—(1) of understanding, (2) of faith, (3) of hope. (*W. Jay.*) *The power, spirit, and assurance of the gospel:*—I. THE WORD OF THE GOSPEL. 1. Not man's gospel (Gal. i. 6; 2 Cor. xi. 4). 2. But God's gospel (Acts xx. 24). 3. To some a hidden gospel (2 Cor. iv. 3, 4). 4. But to others a revealed one (Matt. xi. 25). II. THE POWER OF THE GOSPEL. 1. It reveals the Saviour (1 Cor. i. 24). 2. It quickens the dead (1 Cor. iv. 15). 3. It enlightens the mind (1 Pet. ii. 9). 4. It reveals wrath (Mark xvi. 16). III. THE SPIRIT OF THE GOSPEL. 1. It expounds the nature of truth (1 Cor. ii. 10). 2. It gives the knowledge of freedom (Rom. viii. 2). 3. Helps the soul against its infirmities (Rom. viii. 26). 4. And gives us the seal of glory (Eph. i. 13). IV. THE ASSURANCE OF THE GOSPEL. 1. The assurance of pardon (Psa. ciii. 12, 13). 2. Assurance of righteousness (Isa. xxxii. 17). 3. Assurance of hope (Heb. vi. 18–20). 4. Assurance of love (Col. ii. 2). (*T. B. Baker.*) *A gospel of power:*—I. The gospel is not simply a system of morals; it is A DIVINE POWER WORKING IN HUMAN LIFE, the power of the Holy Ghost. It comes not in mere word or theory or philosophy, but as a supernatural power direct from God. In this respect we distinguish religion from simple morality. Morality does not profess to go any higher than good motives. But the religious man looks to God for Divine strength and help to supplement his own feebleness. II. The gospel is not the mere word of a creed or ritual, but THE POWER OF A LIFE. What Christ most of all desires for us is that every true affection should be strengthened within us; that every noble aspiration should rise up to attainment; that every generous impulse should lead you to help and bless your fellows; that you should abhor the evil and love the good. III. CHRISTIAN ASSURANCE WILL COME TO HIM WHO LIVES BY THE POWER OF THE HOLY GHOST. Prove Christ's words by personal experiment, venture all on His sayings, surrender yourself to Him wholly, follow His counsel; and there will grow up within you such invincible conviction of His truth that neither death nor life shall shake His power over you. (*Prof. James Legge.*)    *The gospel in word:*—I heard two persons on the Wengern Alp talking by the hour together of the names of ferns; not a word about their characteristics, uses, or habits, but a medley of crack-jaw titles, and nothing more. They evidently felt that they were ventilating their botany, and kept each other in countenance by alternate volleys of nonsense. Well, they were about as sensible as those doctrinalists who for ever talk over the technicalities of religion, but know nothing by experience of its spirit and power. Are we not all too apt to amuse ourselves after the same fashion? He who knows mere Linnæan names, but has never seen a flower, is as reliable in botany, as he is in theology who can descant upon supralapsarianism, but has never known the love of Christ in his heart. "True religion's more than doctrine, Something must be known and felt." (*C. H. Spurgeon.*)    *Word and power:*—The gospel in two aspects. I. HUMAN. "Our." It is human—1. In its instrumentality. It was revealed to man, its blessings are enjoyed by man; it is preached and propagated by man (Rom. x. 14, 15). 2. When not crowned with success. "In word only." Apart from the unction from above, the gospel is a dead letter, a savour of death unto death—the good seed falls by the wayside, among thorns, on stony places. The impressions are superficial and defective. II. DIVINE. "In the Holy Ghost." It is Divine—1. In its origin. It is God's plan of salvation. It could not have been originated by man, because the idea is beyond the limit of his thoughts. Man can never give existence to what is Divine. "That which is born of the flesh is flesh." The gospel bears the image of the heavenly. It is God's scheme. 2. In its revelation. None could disclose God's secrets but Himself. Salvation is one of God's deep things. That which was not originated with man could not be revealed by Him. The gospel salvation was revealed early, unexpectedly, gradually, completely. 3. In its efficacy. The three clauses show the blessed and saving influence of the gospel. (1) In the emancipation of sinners from the slavery of sin and Satan. The gospel is truth, and the truth makes free and destroys the stronghold of Satan. (2) In establishing the kingdom of God in the heart. The gospel produces faith, hope, love; it enlightens the understanding, spiritualizes the affections, and purifies the heart. (*J. Jenkins.*)    *The gospel in word:*—You have passed through a bleak, barren moorland, where the soil seemed sown with stones, and disfigured with stumps of trees, and the only signs of vegetative life were scattered patches of heather and flowerless lichen. After a while you have again traversed the same region, and observed fields of grain ripening for the harvest, and budding saplings giving promise of the future forest. Whence this transformation? The cultivator has been at work. Not less apparent was the change effected in Thessalonica by the diligent toil and faithful preaching of the apostles. We have here two prominent features in the successful declaration of the gospel. I. THE GOSPEL IN WORD. "Our gospel came unto you in word." In the history (Acts xvii.) we learn the leading themes of apostolic preaching. It is worthy of note that the inspired apostle grounded his discourse on the Scriptures. Even he did not feel himself free from their sacred bonds. He taught—1. That the promised Messiah was to be a suffering Messiah. The Jewish mind was so dazzled with the prophecies of the regal magnificence and dominion of Jesus, that they overlooked the painful steps by which He was to climb to this imperial greatness. Out of their own scriptures he proved that the only Messiah announced was to be "a man of sorrows." 2. That the Messiah who was thus to suffer and die, was to rise again. This declared the Divine dignity of His person and was the pledge of the success and stability of His work. 3. That the Jesus who thus suffered and died and rose was the very Messiah promised in their scriptures. The grand topic of apostolic preaching must be the staple theme of the pulpit to-day. II. THE GOSPEL IN POWER. 1. In the exercise of miraculous power. The apostles were invested with this, and used it in substantiating the facts of the gospel. 2. In the Holy Ghost— not only in His miraculous manifestations, which were necessary in that age; but in the ordinary exercise of His power, as continued down to the present day— enlightening, convincing, renewing. 3. With much assurance. Literally, "with full assurance, and much of it." "Plerophoria" is from a word that means to fill up, and is used to denote the hurrying a ship on her career, with all her sails spread and filled with the wind. So the soul, filled with the full conviction of truth, is urged to a course of conduct in harmony with that conviction. 4. An assurance enforced by high integrity of character. "As ye know what manner," &c. Their earnest labours and upright lives showed they were men moved by profound conviction—a blending of evidence that is not less potent in these days. (*G. Barlow.*) *The powerful gospel :*—I. THE WORLD NEEDS A POWERFUL GOSPEL. The great want of men in all ages is an impulse to carry them out of spiritual lethargy. The first requisite is not light. Those who sit in darkness may see a great light, but not have the disposition or energy to seek it. The blight of society is not virulent hatred to good, but indifference, spiritual paralysis. The knowledge of truth is far ahead, not only of the practice but of the ability to pursue it. Theories of the universe have been formulated by the cartload, and the world is little the better for them. There is no hope of salvation in one more theory. No gospel that is not inspired with energy, however fertile in thought or beautiful in sentiment, will meet the world's need. But beware of mistaking sensation for energy. Sensational preaching may excite interest and stir emotion : yet it may be impotent as the thunder which only comes when the lightning has gone. We want a real energy though it be as silent as sunlight. II. THE GOSPEL OF CHRIST IS FULL OF POWER. Christianity is not merely a specific religious system ranking with the Egyptian, Indian, Grecian, &c. Nor is it only a better system in dignity, purity, &c. It is more than the noblest solution of the riddle of the universe. Its striking peculiarity is that it is alive, while other systems are dead. There is much truth in the Vedastic ideas of God, in the Zoroastrian teaching about sin, in the Egyptian eschatology, in the Greek dramatists' views of moral government, in the Greek philosophers' thoughts concerning the chief good. But all these lack power to change the heart. Christianity does this. Christ struck the keynote when He wrought miracles—" mighty signs " of His spiritual work. The " might " of them was an indication of His power. He was " moved with compassion " ; but His sympathy showed itself in energetic deeds of charity. He promised that His exaltation on the cross should draw all men unto Him. Thus Paul writes of the Cross as " the power of God " (1 Cor. i. 18). When the apostles were " endued with power from on high " their preaching was effectual. The power of the gospel is seen by its effects in the great apostolic missions, in the regeneration of the Roman world and the creation of Christendom, in Christian law, literature, society, home life, and individual character, in missionary victories of modern times. III. CHRIST IS THE SOURCE OF THE POWER OF THE GOSPEL. 1. He is the Truth (John xiv. 6). Errors are never lastingly powerful. When a false religion wins its way it is because of the truth mixed up with its errors. Mohammedanism, *e.g.*, was a grand protest of Monotheism against idolatry. If Christianity were false it must ultimately have failed. The truth of Christ is the first secret of His power ; and the power of the gospel is a proof of its truth. Mere external success may not go for much, but success in spiritual regeneration cannot be begotten of a lie. Christianity is not merely powerful : it is powerful for good, and therefore cannot have been cradled in a delusion. 2. Christ is seen in self-sacrificing love. He wins by the attractions of His Person and character. The great secret of His power is His Cross. A Christless gospel must ever be a futile one, and Christ without His Cross will be shorn of His strength. Without this, Christian ethics and theology are weak. 3. Christ sends His Spirit with His gospel. Conclusion : The power of the gospel may be frustrated—1. If the gospel is untruly, unfaithfully, unspiritually preached. 2. If the help of the Divine Spirit is rejected or neglected. 3. If the hearer wilfully rejects its influence. (*W. F. Adeney, M.A.*) *Power of the gospel :*—I wish I could take you to a scene in the kingdom of Hyderabad. The people had risen in a mob to drive us out, because we tried to speak of another God than theirs. The throng was filling the streets. They told me if I tried to say another word I should be killed ! I must leave at once, or never leave that city alive ! I succeeded in getting their permission to tell a story before they stoned me. They were standing around ready to throw the stones, when I told them the story of all stories—the love of the Divine Father that had made us of one blood. I told them that story of the birth in the manger at Bethlehem ; of that marvellous life ; of the gracious words that He spake. I told them the story of the Cross, and pictured, in the graphic words the Master gave me that day, the story of our Saviour nailed to the cross for them. When I told them that, I saw the men go and throw their stones into the gutter, and down the cheeks of the very men that had been clamouring the loudest for my blood I saw the tears running. And when I told them how He had been laid in the grave, and how after three days He came forth triumphant and then ascended into heaven, where He ever lives to make intercession for them, and that through Him every one of them might obtain remission of sins and eternal life, I told them I had finished my story, and they might stone me now. But no! they did not want to stone me now. They came forward and bought Scriptures, Gospels, and tracts, for they wanted to know more of the wonderful Saviour. (*D. Chamberlain.*)     *The quiet power of the gospel :—* A celebrated divine, who was remarkable in the first period of his ministry for a boisterous mode of preaching, suddenly changed his whole manner in the pulpit, and adopted a mild and dispassionate mode of delivery. One of his brethren then inquired of him what had induced him to make the change. He replied : " When I was young I thought it was the thunder that killed the people ; but when I grew older and wiser I discovered that it was the lightning. So I determined to thunder less and lighten more." (*W. Antliff, D.D.*)     *The penetrating power of the gospel :—* Down by Mitcham, when the lavender is growing, if you take a house there you will discern a smell of lavender ; you may shut the windows and close the doors, but when any persons enter a whiff of lavender enters with them—you cannot help it ; and if you live where the gospel is preached at all, you will be sure to hear it and made to know of it. It is God's intention that you should. It is a voice that comes unasked and undesired, but come it does. (*C. H. Spurgeon.*)     *The subduing power of the gospel :—*Amongst the very first comers at an open-air service was a well-dressed, respectable young man. He took a position close to where we were standing. He evidently did not come prepossessed in our favour. He looked severely on us, and there were hard lines about his mouth, as though he were contending with internal passion. I saw this and said to him, " Do you know why we have come here to-day ? " His reply was a prolonged stare at me. I took no notice of this, but said, " We have come to tell you and these gathered here about a Father in heaven who loves you." The effect upon the man was instantaneous. A whole battery of arguments could not have produced a more sudden effect than these few unpremeditated words. His face at once softened down ; the stern, severe lines about his mouth melted away, and though he made no reply, I could see he was touched. He remained rooted to the spot, an earnest listener all the time we remained there. (*J. Macgowan of Amoy.*)     *Degrees of power attending the gospel :—* Paul claimed two things as necessary to success in the ministry. 1. He could call the gospel " our gospel." We must be saved before we can preach salvation. Ezekiel had to eat the roll of his prophecy. As well think of steering the *Great Eastern* across the ocean without knowing the first principles of navigation ; as well think of setting up as ambassador without your country's authority, as of preaching before the gospel is your own. No amount of education will suffice if you lack a personal interest in salvation by Christ. 2. He was able to point to " his manner of life." And so must we. We must show in our lives what we preach with our lips. Woe to the minister when he is compelled to say, " Do as I say, not as I do." We shall use the text—I. For DISCRIMINATION. The gospel comes to all who hear it ; to the unregenerate as to the regenerate. But some preachers give one gospel to one class and another to another. Unlike the old sowers who sowed indiscriminately, they want to find the good ground before they sow. Instead of going out into the highways and hedges they want to know who are appointed to come, and then they will give the unnecessary invitation. But the apostles delivered the same gospel to non-elect and elect. The point of distinction is not in the gospel, but in its being applied by the Spirit or left to be rejected of men. 1. To some the gospel comes only in word. Even here there are gradations. (1) Some scarcely know what it is all about. They go to a place of worship and sit out an hour and a half of penance, and when done think they have done the proper thing, but are stolid, unthinking worshippers of an unknown God. (2) Others understand it in theory, and are pleased with it if preached in a manner to suit their tastes ; but the gospel remains in them as drugs in an apothecary's drawer : they are there, but produce no effect. It is an unloaded canon or barrel of gunpowder ; it has no force because the fire of God's Spirit is absent. (3) Others are really affected by it. They weep, resolve to amend, are alarmed, but the morning cloud is not more fleeting than their emotions. But these are produced by words, not by the Spirit. But men weep at a theatre. I am afraid that much of the holy water which is spilt from eyes in our places of worship is of no more value than the holy water at Catholic chapels. It is not heart sorrow. At this point let me ask, " Do you know the gospel only in word ? "

There is a class who are professional sermon-hearers. They go one Sunday to hear Mr. A., another to hear Mr. B., and appraise, criticise, &c. They are no better than spiritual vagabonds, neither getting nor doing good. 2. There are those to whom the gospel comes with three accompaniments. (1) There is sometimes an effect produced by the gospel which may be called "power," but it is not the power that saves. (a) It comes with power on the understanding. You have heard, weighed, judged, and received it as being Divine—you assent to its propositions. (b) To the conscience. It has convinced you of sin. Like Felix, you tremble. (c) On the feelings. Your desires have been awakened. You have said, "Oh, that I were saved!" and even advanced as far as Balaam, "Let me die the death of the righteous." (d) On the life. The gospel has done you much good, although it has not saved you ; though, alas! there are others to whom it has only for a time been as bit and bridle. (2) We come now to a nobler elevation, and speak to those to whom the Word has come "in the Holy Ghost." This is a great secret and cannot be expounded, but many of you know it experimentally. The Spirit has come— (a) As a quickening power. You have now different feelings, joys, sorrows, to what you had before, because while you listened to the letter which killeth, the Spirit came with it and made you live. (b) As an illuminating power. He showed you your sins and your Saviour. (c) As a comforting power. Your burdens were removed as He opened up to you the promises. (d) An inflaming power. He has rested on you when you have heard the Word as a Spirit of burning. (e) A rejoicing power. (3) The highest point in the text is "much assurance." (a) They were fully persuaded of the truth of the gospel, and had no staggering or blinding doubts. (b) They had the fullest conviction of their interest in that truth. They were saved, and they knew it. II. For INSTRUCTION. It is not enough to preach the gospel ; something more is wanted for conversion than even that. We must have the energy of the Holy Ghost. Then—1. It becomes more and more imperatively necessary that we should be much in prayer to God for that blessing. Luther said, "I have so much business to-day that I cannot get through it with less than three hours' prayer." Most people say, "I have so much business that I must only have three minutes' prayer." 2. Let us learn our own indebtedness to distinguishing grace, and bless God that the Word has come to us with power. 3. Inasmuch as there are degrees of attainment, let us seek for the highest degree. The "rest-and-be-thankful" policy is not much approved in politics, and in religion it will never answer. 4. A privilege may become a curse. If you have received the gospel in word only, it will aggravate the condemnation of those who might have received it with the Holy Ghost but would not. (C. H. Spurgeon.) The gospel in power :—On hearing these words of the apostle, who is not immediately disposed to say, "Happy man, who could thus address the objects of his ministry and the fruits of his evangelical labours"? But who is not also disposed to say, "Happy minister, with whomsoever associated in religious life, in whatever age or country he may exercise his ministry, who, when addressing those among whom he has been preaching, can employ similar language—'For our gospel came not unto you in word only, but also in power, and in the Holy Ghost, and in much assurance.'"? Now, how came this gospel to the Thessalonians? I. NOT IN WORD ONLY. Words are symbols of thought, and idea, and sentiment ; and it has pleased God the Holy Spirit to honour words, and He has been pleased to sanctify and dignify words through the medium of which to make known His thoughts and sentiments, His designs and dealings in reference to us men and our salvation. He, therefore, inspired holy prophets, and they announced the great things which belong to the salvation of the soul ; and then they were directed to record this ; and we read the words which God the Holy Ghost taught—the word of this salvation—how "that Christ died for our sins, and rose again the third day, according to the Scriptures"; and they state the doctrines founded on these facts, the privileges connected with them, the practical tendency of the whole, and the ordinances and institutions of the gospel : and thus in language they announced the good news, the glad tidings to the people. And still whenever the gospel comes, it must come "in word"; words must be employed, and the minister of the sanctuary must still employ "the words of this life." But then the great danger is lest it come in word only : then the great design of the gospel is defeated; all the high and important particulars relating to our salvation are not realized wherever the gospel comes only in word. We can suppose the case of a minister of Christ, possessing talents—talents of no common order, with a highly cultivated intellect, a very fertile imagination, and a genius which leads him to employ figures of poetry, and to suggest thoughts that captivate the attention and strike the minds of those who listen to his discourses from time to time; there are multitudes who throng to hear him wherever he goes; and, to use the words of the prophet, he is to them "as a very lovely song of one that hath a pleasant voice, and can play well on an instrument." And oh, how well attended are his ministrations! But where, amidst all this, is the instance of the poor sinner pierced to the heart by the two-edged sword of the Spirit and feeling the pungent smart of conviction? Where is the instance of the man smiting on his breast, and crying, "God be merciful to me a sinner"? But thus came not the gospel to the Thessalonians. II. ALSO IN POWER. What power? 1. Not the civil power; because in the days to which the apostle refers Christianity was not even protected by the civil government, but opposed by it. It was not with them as it is happily with us, where Christianity forms part and parcel of the very constitution and laws of the country, and where the broad shield of legal protection is thrown over us, and where we "sit under our own vine and fig tree, none daring to make us afraid." 2. Neither could the apostle refer to the power of eloquence or human talent. St. Paul himself tells us that his "speech and his preaching was not with enticing words of man's wisdom, but in demonstration of the Spirit and of power." This was "the power"; it was a Divine power; and it was Divine in two points of view: first, there was miraculous power to mark the propagation of the gospel; secondly, there was a secret energy accompanying the administration of the Word, bringing it home to the conscience and heart of those who heard. There is an awakening power, a convicting power; and there is a regenerating power, and a sanctifying power, and a consoling and satisfying power. Oh, what an energy there is in the gospel of the Lord Jesus Christ! III. AND IN THE HOLY GHOST. As surely as there was miraculous power in the first age of Christianity, so surely was the Holy Ghost there; for the miracles then wrought were the miracles of the Holy Ghost—"God also bearing them witness, both by signs and wonders, and with divers miracles and gifts of the Holy Ghost, according to His own will." And as surely as there must always be an efficacious power to give efficacy to the gospel wherever it is administered, the Holy Ghost must be there. The gospel is the dispensation of the Spirit; and where the gospel is preached, the Spirit of God is present to bear testimony to the truth. Who and what is the genuine Christian? Why, he was once in the dark, but now he is "light in the Lord." How came he to be so? "Ah," says one, "the preacher told us the gospel is light." True; and the gospel is the great light of the system, and the gospel is shining in the zenith of its splendour and glory. But what avails to me the noon-day sun, with all the blaze of day, if I have not the organs of vision. It is not only necessary that the light be there, but we must have the organs to discern it. And how comes this change to pass on us? By the mighty energy of the Spirit. He removes the scales from our mental eyes; it is He that gives the organ of spiritual vision and of perception; it is the Spirit that giveth light, IV. AND IN MUCH ASSURANCE—a plenitude of assurance. This phrase is significant of the manner in which the gospel was received by the people. 1. The assurance of the truth of the message. I do not know that the first believers in Christianity waited on the outside of the great temple of truth, to examine the two external pillars on which the temple reposes and by which it is supported. You know what those two pillars are: unmoved they stand where they ever stood, and all the shafts of infidelity have been unable to make any impression on them. (1) Prophecy; and the argument is this: Where there is genuine prophecy there is God, because God alone sees the end from the beginning: now in this Book is genuine prophecy; then here is God. (2) Miracles: where there are genuine miracles there must be God, for He alone can control nature, and act in opposition to its laws. But here are such interpositions recorded; therefore here is God. Now I do not know, I say, that these primitive believers waited outside the temple to examine then its two grand pillars in the first place; I rather believe they went in at once. The temple of truth, and wisdom, and grace—"Like the cerulean arch we see, Majestic in its own simplicity." 2. They saw the sanctity of those who officiated there. "You know," says the apostle, "what manner of men we were amongst you." Their simplicity, their self-denial, their purity, their benevolence, their zeal; are these characters that belong to infidelity? Then there was the Architect—the Architect of the temple of truth spoke in the temple of truth; and the people heard, and the truth came home to their hearts and consciences, and examined the inmost recesses of their hearts: they were judged of all, and condemned of all, and approved of all; and they were assured that it was the great Architect of truth Himself who thus spoke. (*Robert Newton, D.D.*) *The practical application of the gospel :*—The important question is—has the gospel really come to you; and has it come to you " in power, and in the Holy Ghost, and in much assurance"? If so, you must have experienced—I. A CON-VICTION OF SIN. The man who is a real Christian must have been taught the plague of his old nature, and what an evil thing it is to sin against God. II. AN ACQUAINTANCE WITH THE CHARACTER OF GOD'S HOLY LAW. This is a very necessary piece of knowledge. A mere professor, who has never known what real conviction of sin is, may be capable of amendment of life to a certain extent, but can have no just conception of the enormity of transgression against a holy and just God. When a man is made experimentally acquainted with the operations of the Holy Ghost, he feels that he has transgressed against God, and against the reasonable law of a mighty and righteous God, in every particular. " He who hath broken the law in one point, hath broken it in all." III. A BELIEF IN THE LORD JESUS CHRIST. When a man is in this condition there is no difficulty at all in persuading him that all his hopes upon his own efforts and his own righteousness must be dispensed with, and that he must rest on the imputed righteousness of Jesus Christ, the perfect work of the Son of God, the salvation of the Divine Saviour. Every man who is saved is saved by himself. God comes to a man personally; the Holy Ghost comes to a man personally; the merits of Jesus come to a man personally. This is real religion. (*H. Allon, D.D.*) *The power of a felt gospel :*—Once on a time an obscure man rose up to address the French Convention. At the close of his oration Mirabeau, the genius of the French Revolution, turned round to his neigh-bour and eagerly asked, "Who is that?" The other, who had been in no way interested in the address, wondered at Mirabeau's curiosity; whereupon the latter said," That man will yet act a great part ; " and added, on being asked for an explana-tion, "He speaks as one who believes every word he says." Much of the pulpit power under God depends on that—admits of that explanation, or of one allied to it. They make others feel who feel themselves. (*T. Guthrie, D.D.*) *The might of the gospel :*— There is power of the highest created order where there is mind. We need not quote an adage but two centuries old—" Knowledge is power "—when we can find the sentiment far more nobly and anciently expressed in our Bible—" A wise man is strong; yea, a man of knowledge increaseth strength." How mind acts upon mind! What vibrations bound from a single thought! But the gospel awakens a man dead in trespasses and sins. Through its precepts he gets understanding. It reminds him of the image in which he was created, and which he has lost. It fills him with shame and confusion that he has sunk so low. It informs him of the infinite gentleness which can once more make him great. It brings out the stamina of his mental and moral sensibilities by the same objects, alone touches him at all joints, stirs every inmost depth, and unbinds each latent energy of the spirit. The power of Christ rests indeed upon him. There is thus a mightiness in the gospel. I. IT IS THE POWER OF TRUTH. The gospel founds itself upon facts —upon what was done and upon what was taught. This is substantial truth ; and it justifies unfeigned faith. II. IT IS THE POWER OF AUTHORITY. It is Divine obligation ; the binding power and sanction is precisely this—" He that believeth shall be saved, and he that believeth not shall be condemned." III. IT IS THE POWER OF REALIZATION. Sooner or later, it is more or less surrounded by something like itself. It provokes inquiry, and compels to take a part. It tells of the death of Christ: it realizes futurity. In us is found every doctrine and blessing of the gospel in actual form and rudiment. Ours is a present salvation. The work of grace bears its fruits. Faith groweth exceedingly; love aboundeth more and more; peace passeth all understanding; and patience hath its perfect work. This is surely power—the kindling of a living light over the written Word, and the inward interpretation—the witness of the soul closing with it. (*R. W. Hamilton, LL.D.*) *The power and assurance of the gospel :*—It came and comes—I. WITH POWER. Who shall declare this mystery of power ? All ages and sciences have worked at the problem. 1. Power in its lowest conceptions belongs to the material. It is in the storm, the wave, the flashing lightning. Latent or active it belongs to every atom in the universe. 2. Higher up is the power of thought which gives man empire over the world ; temples, machines, pictures, &c., are embodied thoughts. Fling your mind back on the infinite past, and you find a period when every force existed as a thought in the Eternal Mind. 3. Highest of all is the power of the gospel. What is this? The power that slumbers in the great, Divine, essential seed thoughts of Christianity. The gospel is a gospel of—(1) Incarnation. The historic conceptions of God are all true and grand, but how cold and distant! But turn to the gospel, and you see the mighty God in the cradle of Bethlehem, in the streets of Nazareth, on the cross of Calvary, that He might take my nature up into Himself. (2) Unbounded benevolence. No truth of history is better authenticated than this, that outside the influence of Christianity there is but little sympathy. Into this world God flashed a new thought, that of atonement and self-sacrifice for the good of others. This is the power of the Cross. "I, if I be lifted up, will draw all men unto Me." From that hour the world entered on a new era. There was a fountain opened for guilt and also for sorrow by the Cross. From the moment of Pentecost there was a disposition to save others. Clothes were made for the poor, and asylums began to be founded. (3) Resurrection and immortality. Who shall tell the shadows which fall upon the land and home where Christianity has not come? II. IN THE HOLY GHOST. 1. In all the faiths there is the doctrine of the Divine influence coming to the spirit of man. The Pantheism of the old Brahmin involved this. The Theosophites of Egypt clung to this. The inner light of Platonism meant this. From Montanism downwards this was the prime doctrine of mysticism. This finds its culmination in the gospel. It is seen in creation educing beauty out of chaos; in civilization; in the achievements of the gospel. The world is rich in literature, but imagine the greatest Genius saying, "Weary one, believe My word and be saved!" But let the Spirit take the word of the gospel, and it is spirit and life to every one that accepts it. 2. A Holy Ghost must have a Holy Ghost ministry. Take a man, however gifted, but not anointed with the Spirit, and his word will be like the summer lightning which hits nothing. But give the Holy Ghost to but a rough fisherman, and he will smite the consciences of three thousand. III. IN MUCH ASSURANCE. 1. There is the assurance which comes from demonstration to others. There are tens of thousands who are better men to-day by this power; and its effects are seen in the walks of commerce and the sanctities of home. 2. That of an inner experience. He that believeth hath the witness in himself. 3. That of ultimate triumph. "Oh!" said a great savant, as he trembled upon the verge of the sepulchre, "my philosophy fails me here." Yonder, in a darksome dungeon and manacles about his limbs, is an old man. What sayest thou, Paul? "I am now ready to be offered," &c. (G. Douglass, D.D.) **Much assurance.**—I. MUCH CERTAINTY. II. MUCH FULNESS OF SPIRITUAL GIFTS. III. MUCH EFFECT OR FULFILMENT. (*Prof. Jowett.*) *Luther's assurance:*—Look at him when he stood up for the glory of his God, was there ever such a dogmatist? "I believe it," he said, "and therefore I speak it." From that day when on Pilate's staircase he was trying to creep up and down the stairs to win heaven, when the sentence out of the musty folio came before him, "Justified by faith we have peace with God," that man was as sure that works could not save him as he was of his own existence. Now, if he had come out and said, "Gentleman, I have a theory to propound that may be correct; excuse my doing so," and so on, the Papacy had been dominant to this day. The man knew God had said it, and he felt that that was God's own way to his own soul, and he could not help dogmatizing with that glorious force of persuasion which soon laid his foes prostrate at his feet. (*C. H. Spurgeon.*)

**Vers. 6-8. And ye became followers of us and of the Lord.**—*Followers of the Apostles and of the Lord:*—This is a very interesting and beautiful account of the triumph of the truth and the progress of religion in Thessalonica. The eye rests with gladness and gratitude upon the bright spots and periods, in the history of our world, in which the religion of Jesus has subdued and overcome the vice, and infatuation, and ignorance, and stupidity of our race; and we are prepared to say devoutly—"Awake, O arm of the Lord; awake, as in the ancient time, in the generations of old! Let Thy work be repeated, and the lovely scenery be viewed again!" I. THE THESSALONIANS WERE CAREFUL TO FOLLOW THE EXAMPLE OF THE APOSTLES. And the apostles took every care to demean themselves well, not only for their own credit's sake, but for the benefit of others, by a conversation suitable to their doctrine, that they might not pull down with one hand what they built up with the other; so the Thessalonians, who observed what manner of men they were among them, how their preaching and living were all of a piece, showed a conscientious care to be followers of them; that is— to imitate their good example. And herein they became followers of the Lord also, who is the perfect example; and we should be followers of others no farther than they are followers of Christ (1 Cor. xi. 1). The Thessalonians acted thus notwithstanding the afflictions to which the apostles and themselves also were exposed. They were willing to share in the sufferings that attended the embracing and professing Christianity. Perhaps this made the Word more precious, being dearly bought; and the examples of the apostles shone very bright under these trying circumstances; so that the Thessalonians embraced the gospel cheerfully, and followed the example of the suffering apostles joyfully. Such spiritual, and solid, and lasting joy as the Holy Ghost is the Author of, when our afflictions do abound, maketh our consolation much more abound. II. THEIR ZEAL SO PREVAILED THAT THEY WERE THEMSELVES EXAMPLES TO ALL OTHERS. They were "stamps," or instruments to make impression. They made good impressions, and their conversation had a correspondent influence upon others. There is nothing which maketh the gospel sound louder, the sound of it to be heard better, and the offer embraced more readily, than when a sincere profession is beautified, and adorned, and seconded by a sober and conscientious practice; for it was such a profession, strengthened with such a practice, in the Thessalonians, which made the gospel sound from them in Macedonia and Achaia. The word signifies to sound shrill and far, as with the noise of a trumpet, or voice of lion-herald. So that the effects of the gospel in turning the Thessalonians from idols "to serve the living and true God," was so spread abroad that the apostles themselves "need not to speak anything." (*D. Mayo.*)    *The power of example :*—"Ye became followers"—imitators, or copiers—"of us." This is the first view Paul here takes of his Thessalonian converts. 1. They resembled himself and his fellow-labourers. But how? In their faith, their hope, their love, and their good works. Let us enter into this thought. Man is an imitative creature. The first voluntary efforts that are made by children, are always endeavours to mimic something which they have seen. But as man is a depraved creature, and as he is exposed to bad examples in this world, as well as good, and more to bad examples than to good, he naturally follows the multitude to do evil; and the question with him, therefore, concerning anything, is not—Is it true? or is this reasonable? or is it righteous? but—"What will people think or say of me? Shall I not be seen?" Why, all the Lord's people are "a peculiar people"; and it argues much more dignity of principle and purity of motive to advance alone than under the applause of thousands. This disposition was in the case of the Thessalonians sanctified, for it was turned another way; for the men they now followed were few, compared with the rest, and they had nothing of a worldly kind to recommend them. No; they were esteemed the very "filth and offscouring" of all. Yet, with Moses, these Thessalonians chose "rather to suffer affliction with the people of God, than to enjoy the pleasures of sin for a season." They "esteemed the reproach of Christ greater riches than the treasures of Egypt." Yes; with David they could say—"I am a companion of all them that fear Thee, of them that keep Thy statutes." So it always is when persons are made "wise unto salvation;" then they immediately see, that the righteous are more excellent than their neighbours, and that of them the world is "not worthy." Then they pray—"Look Thou upon me, and be merciful unto me, as Thou usedst to do unto them that love Thy name." Then they let go the sons and daughters of folly and vice, and run and take hold of the skirt of him that is a Jew, saying—"We will go with you, for we have heard that God is with you." 2. They resembled the Lord also; to show the apostles confidence that they were themselves conformed to Him, and those that followed them thus far would be followers of Him. Therefore, says the apostle to the Corinthians—"Be ye followers of me, even as I also am of Christ." Did he mean to place himself upon a level, then, with Christ? By no means; but to assert that he knew he was walking the same way, that he was influenced by the same principles, that he felt the same sentiments. And we must be conscious of this too. Yes; we must remember that "if any man have not the spirit of Christ, he is none of His." But it is added, to teach us that no men are to be our examples any further than they resemble Him; that we are not to give up ourselves absolutely to any leader, however distinguished by gifts or graces. We are not to pin our faith upon their sleeve, or to determine our action by their practice invariably. No; they are all fallible. The wisest of men have their follies; the best of men have their faults; the wisest and the best of men, therefore, may lead us astray. Abraham denied his wife at Gerah; Moses spake unadvisedly with his lips; Job cursed the day of his birth; Peter said with an oath, "I know not the Man." But here we have in the Lord Jesus an infallible pattern; and therefore we may give up ourselves entirely to His direction and influence, and, as it is said, "follow the Lamb whithersoever He goeth." 3. They who imitated others became ensamples to others:—"Ye became ensamples to all that believe in Macedonia and Achaia." It is very observable in nature that things in succession are alternately cause and effect, effect and cause. Thus, parents produce children, and children produce in time children ; thus, those now obey, who by and by command; thus, learners now become teachers ; and those who were followers become leaders themselves. This was the case here ; from following the apostles and the Lord Jesus, they "became ensamples to all that believed in Macedonia and Achaia." Indeed, what individual is there, who is not, more or less, an "ensample" to some? Which of you is entirely isolated? Who is not seen and heard of some? Who is not followed by some ? But how honourable was it for these converts! They were "ensamples," to whom ? "To them that believe." Oh ! it is easy for you to be "ensamples" to some. It is easy, to have goodness enough to censure and condemn the grossly wicked ; it is easy, to have goodness enough to be considered righteous, when compared with drunkards, and swearers, and thieves, and robbers. But these Thessalonians were ensamples to the good, to the godly, " to them that believed " ; yea, and what is more, "to all them that believed in Macedonia and Achaia"; though it is very probable that many of these had been in the Lord before them, and had believed before them. There are many cases in which " the first shall be last, and the last shall be first." (*W. Jay.*)  *The practical result of a true reception of the gospel:*—I. THE TRUE RECEPTION OF THE GOSPEL. 1. They received the Word in sorrow—" in much affliction " (Acts xvii. 5–9). Principally, sorrow on account of sin—their prolonged rejection of Christ, and obstinate disobedience. 2. In joy. " With joy of the Holy Ghost." They realized—(1) The joy of conscious forgiveness and acceptance with God. The sinless angels, placed beyond the necessity of pardon, are incapable of realizing this joy. It belongs exclusively to the believing penitent. (2) The joy of suffering for the truth. Cyprian, who suffered for Jesus, used to say, " It is not the pain but the cause that makes the martyr." That cause is the cause of truth. Suffering is limited to life, but truth is eternal. To suffer for the truth is a privilege and a joy. (3) The joy of triumph—over error, sin, Satan, persecution. This joy is the fruit of the Spirit. These twin feelings—sorrow and joy—are typical of the alternating experience of the believer throughout his earthly career. II. THE PRACTICAL RESULT. 1. They became imitators of the highest patterns of excellence —"us and the Lord." The example of Christ is the all-perfect standard. But this does not supersede the use of inferior models. The planets have their mission, as well as the sun, and we can better bear the moderated light of their borrowed splendour. The bravery of a common soldier, as well as the capacity and heroism of the most gifted officer, may stimulate a regiment to deeds of valour. So the apostles, in their patience, zeal, and integrity, became examples, while they pointed to the great Pattern. 2. They became examples to others. " So that ye were ensamples to all that believe." (1) In the reality and power of their faith. (2) In their zealous propagation of the truth. "For from you sounded out the word of the Lord." (3) The influence of their example was extensive in its range. Macedonia and Achaia were two Roman provinces that comprised the territory known as ancient Greece. Thessalonica, the metropolis of Macedonia, was the chief station on the great Roman road—the *Via Egnatia*—which connected Rome with the whole region north of the Ægean sea, and was an important centre, both for commerce and the spread of intelligence. Wherever the trade of the merchant city extended, there the fame of the newly-founded Church penetrated. Great was the renown of their own Alexander, the Macedonian monarch, and brilliant his victories : but the reputation of the Thessalonian Christians was of a higher order, and their achievements more enduring. Learn—1. The gospel that brings sorrow to the heart also brings the joy. 2. A genuine reception of the truth changes the man, and creates unquenchable aspirations after the highest good. 3. A living example is more potent than the most elaborate code of precepts, however eloquently explained or cogently enforced. (*G. Barlow.*)  *The divinity of a true man :*—I. He is a RECIPIENT of the Divine. The "word " here is the gospel. Their suffering in receiving it was more than counterbalanced by " the joy of the Holy Ghost." What matters bodily affliction if you have this joy. "We glory in tribulation," &c. A genuine Christian is a man who has received into him the Divine Word. God's great thoughts have come into his intellect, touched his heart, and given a new moral impulse to his being. He who has not received this Divine Word intelligently and with practical effect is no Christian. The Christian is a living Bible, the "word made flesh." II. He is an IMITATOR of the Divine. The apostles were Christians because they were "followers of the Lord"; and all who would be Christians must become the same. 1. Christ is the most perfect moral model. In Him we have all that commands the attention and admiration of the soul. 2. Christ is the most imitable moral model. Sublimely great as He is, no character has appeared in history so imitable as His. (1) Because none is so powerful to awaken our admiration. What we admire most, we imitate most. (2) Because none is so easily understood. He is perfectly transparent. One principle—love—explains all His moral features and activities. (3) Because none but His is permanently consistent. III. He is an EXAMPLE of the Divine. "So that ye were ensamples," &c. Macedonia and Achaia stand for all Greece, so that they became ensamples to the entire Greek race. Genuine Christian not only receives and imitates, but reflects and radiates the Divine. He is the brightest and fullest revelation of God on earth; there is more of the Divine seen in the Christly soul than there is in starry heavens and blooming landscapes. "Ye are My witnesses." IV. He is a PROCLAIMER of the Divine. "From you sounded out the word." This is an image from a trumpet filling with its clear sounding echo all the surrounding places. They sounded out the gospel, not only in enthusiastic utterances but in noble and generous deeds. Thessalonica was a large maritime and commercial city; and its Christian merchants would in all their transactions with foreign traders ring out the gospel. Conclusion: A genuine Christian, then, is a Divine man. There is in a moral as well as in a constitutional sense, a "divinity within him." He is the recipient, imitator, example, and herald of the Divine. (*D. Thomas, D.D.*) *Stimulating example :*—The leisure of Cæsar was spent in reading the history of Alexander the Great. Upon one occasion his friends found him bathing the book with tears. In deep concern they asked him the reason why he wept. The reply was, "Do you think I have not sufficient cause for concern, when Alexander at my age reigned over so many conquered countries, and I have not one glorious achievement to boast?" So the lives of the apostles and early saints may well be studied by us who are Christians, that we may be fired by their exploits to do greater deeds for God; and we should mourn bitterly when we compare our small achievements with His whom we call Master and Lord, and who, before He had attained the years of middle manhood, had performed deeds at which the stoutest frames might quake and the most faithful soul might blush. Comparisons such as these would first stir our gratitude that such an example has been left us, and then fire our valour, that at the end our lives might not be mere empty names, but such as men might gaze upon with admiration, and seek to copy. *Christ the only sufficient Exemplar:*— It is said, that, thinking to amuse him, his wife read to Dr. Judson some newspaper notices, in which he was compared to one or other of the apostles. He was exceedingly distressed: and then added, "Nor do I want to be like them; I do not want to be like Paul, nor Apollos, nor Cephas, nor any mere man. I want to be like Christ. We have only one perfectly safe Exemplar—only One, who, tempted like as we are in every point, is still without sin. I want to follow Him only, copy His teachings, drink in His Spirit, place my feet in His footprints, and measure their shortcomings by these, and these only. Oh, to be more like Christ!" *The noble army of martyrs :*—" Man can do without happiness, and instead thereof find blessedness," wrote Carlyle, and Paul preached it with his life. But that life was only a faint echo of a greater life. "The Man of sorrows" was "God over all, blessed for ever." If a man cannot understand how "many afflictions" may be consonant with "the joy of the Holy Ghost," he may be a Christian by courtesy, but he knows little of Christian experience. The calling of a son of God does not exempt from sorrow, but it opens beneath it a spring of joy. This was proved by Paul, and his life work was the noblest, and has left the deepest mark on the progress of the race. Where are the Cæsars? Much of their work abides, but their names are little more than shades. It is the man who brings regenerating work to bear upon his age who is shrined most lovingly in the reverence of mankind. And so Paul lives because Christ lived in him. Those who followed Christ live amongst us because Christ is amongst us. Three hundred years ago Paul shook Christendom as he shook heathenism and Judaism in his day. I. FOLLOWERS OF US AND OF THE LORD. 1. There is something startling in these words. A man of like passions with ourselves dares to propose himself for imitation to those who were seeking to follow the incarnate God. And the world is never without its Christlike ones. And there is nothing more wonderful than that men and women like ourselves may be and live like the Son of God. He does not shine in unapproachable isolation. As the elder among many brethren, a bright particular star amid a cluster of constellations, He leads the human host with which He has cast His lot and mixed up His life for ever. 2. Where are the points of likeness? (Gal. ii. 20; 2 Cor. xii. 10). In the power of self-sacrifice. It may seem strange to this self-loving age, but it is well worth noting, that these men whose lives have been so fruitful had no thought of any interest but Christ; no self-will, but were absolutely open to the will of God. Are we then to have no will of our own? God forbid! Paul had a mighty will of his own, and expressed it in defiance of the whole secular and religious world. But it was his own and yet·not his own; it was moulded and refined into harmony with a higher will; and just as the blood gets purified from its carbonic dross as the vital air breathes through it in the lungs, so the will of Paul was purged of the acrid leaven of self by prayer that God would use him, strengthen him to follow Christ, and teach him to spend himself for the service of mankind. 3. A man need not adopt the calling of an apostle to enter such a life as this. There have been soldiers, statesmen, merchants, whose deepest thought has been "I am not mine own." Hard as it may be, it is the beginning of peace to say it and try to live it. You may have your own way, and you will weary of it as soon as you have got it; while you may give up our own way, and make it your effort to care for others, and a glow of heavenly joy will enter and abide in your spirit. Likeness to Christ lies expressly in the power of self-sacrifice, and this is to grasp the difference between blessedness and happiness which the text expounds. II. THEY ENTERED INTO THIS FELLOWSHIP BY RECEIVING THE WORD WITH MUCH AFFLICTION AND JOY OF THE HOLY GHOST. 1. Confession or profession is in these days cheap work. Then it was dear work, and at any moment might cost dear life. It is not good to be out of fellowship with the heroisms of the past. How many a stout citizen has stained his hearthstone with his life's blood that you may sit with your loved ones without fears around yours? An age out of fellowship with the martyrs is neither noble nor blessed, however prosperous. 2. We learn from Acts xvii. and the Epistle something of these afflictions. Strain your imagination to realize them—(1) Feel the cords tightening, see the glaring eye of the lion, hear the hiss of the red-hot iron or the swing of the axe; and bethink you in the last dread moment of a gentle wife, or a dear boy, &c., whom you are leaving obnoxious to the same doom. Does it seem to you that you could utter the name of Christ with your last breath with passionate devotion? Then you can understand how none but as martyrs can taste the joy of the Holy Ghost. (2) Then there was the utter rupture of all the bonds of kindred and social relation, and the loss of means. It is evident, from the Second Epistle, that there was deep poverty in the Church. They received the Word as England did at the Reformation—as Hindoos, Chinese, and South Sea Islanders receive it to-day. (3) And this is independent of the sorrow which springs out of the stern struggle against the world and flesh and devil. 3. To understand this better, notice—(1) That the purest joys are independent of surroundings. What a man *has* is nothing in comparison with what he *is*. If two persons love each other, to be near, even in penury, is bliss; to be separate, even in wealth, is misery. (2) So the joy of the Holy Ghost is the joy of a man who has found the true Lover and Lord of His being, whom he can obey with supreme delight. It is the joy of the lonely soul that has found its kindred, of a sick man who feels within himself that the spring of his life is healed. Men can glory in tribulations if they but bring them fully into the sphere of Christ's fellowship and love. Suffering ceases to be pain if love consecrates it. 4. And let the careless understand that the choice in life is mainly between suffering with joy in the Holy Ghost, and suffering without it. Life is no holiday pastime for any of us; but the true agony of life must be with those who are without God and hope in the world. (*Baldwin Brown, B.A.*) **Followers of us and of the Lord.**—*Not disciples merely, but imitators:*—I. IN MEEK RECEPTION (Psa. xl. 6; Isa. l. 5). II. COST WHAT IT MIGHT. III. REJOICING ALL THE WHILE (Psa. xxii. 22; xlv. 7). (*Canon Mason.*) *Christ's example the universal rule:*—God never gave a man a thing to do concerning which it were irreverent to ponder how the Son of God would have done it. (*G. Macdonald, LL.D.*) *The possibility of following Christ:*—Christ's Divinity does not destroy the reality of His manhood by overshadowing or absorbing it. Certainly the Divine attributes of Jesus are beyond our imitation. We can but adore a boundless intelligence or resistless will. But the province of the imitable in the life of Jesus is not indistinctly traced; as the Friend of publicans and sinners, as the Consoler of those who suffer, and as the Helper of those who want, Jesus Christ is at home among us. We can copy Him, not merely in the outward activities of charity, but in its inward temper. We can copy the tenderness, the meekness, the patience, the courage, which shine forth from His perfect manhood. His human perfections constitute, indeed, a faultless ideal of beauty, which, as moral artists, we are bound to keep in view. What the true and highest model of a human life is, has been decided for us Christians by the appearance of Jesus Christ in the flesh. Others may endeavour to reopen the question; for us it is settled irrevocably. (*Canon Liddon.*) *The indispensableness of following Christ :—* Believing on Christ, learning of Christ, following Christ; this is what it is to be a Christian. You must believe on Him that you may learn of Him. You must learn of Him that you may follow Him. But believing is nothing, and learning is less than nothing, if they do not result in faithful following. (*W. Gladden, D.D.*) *The motive for following Christ :* — Francis I. of France had not reached his twentieth year when he was present at the celebrated battle of Marignan, which lasted two days. He performed prodigies of valour, and fought less as a king than as a soldier. Having perceived his standard-bearer surrounded by the enemy, he precipitated himself to his assistance in the midst of lances and halberts. He was presently surrounded, his horse pierced with several wounds, and his casque despoiled of its plumes. He must have been inevitably overwhelmed if a body of troops, detached from the allies, had not hastened to his succour. Francis hazarded this battle against the advice of his generals, and cut short all remonstrances by the expression, which afterwards became proverbial, "Let him that loves me, follow me!" (*Percy.*) **Much affliction, with joy of the Holy Ghost.—** *Affliction and joy :—*Plato makes Socrates say to his friends, after drinking the poison, "How singular is the thing called pleasure, and how curiously related to pain, which might be thought the opposite of it! For they never come to a man together; and yet he who possesses either is generally compelled to take the other! They are two, and yet they grow together out of one head or stem; and I cannot help thinking that, if Æsop had noticed them, he would have made a fable about God trying to reconcile their strife, and, when He could not, fastening their heads together; and this is the reason why, when one comes, the other follows." That is a heathen speculation on one of the great mysteries of human life. The mystery appears intensified in Christian life (2 Cor. vi. 10). Yet so far it is explained by that life's being an imitation of Christ. The believer, like his Master, being in a world of sin, is encompassed with tribulation; but, being a citizen of heaven, he is also "girded with gladness." He hears the voice of loving authority, and he yields to it loving obedience. "If any man will come after Me," &c. He knows that the *via dolorosa* which he thus has to tread is a path of true joy, for he recognizes his Saviour's steps in it. Hence he can "sing in the ways of the Lord," for fulness of consolation will be his at last. The stream of the renewed life is of two currents. As near Geneva, at the junction of the Rhone to the Arve, the two rivers, though joined, yet appear distinct—the blue stream of the one and the white stream of the other forming one volume of water, flowing within the same banks, at least for a time, towards the sea beyond—so it is with the Christian life. Its stream has two currents—distinct, yet united—of tribulation and joy, ever wending its course, troubled and calm, to the ocean of eternity beyond. (*J. Hutchison, D.D.*)

Vers. 7-10. **So that ye were ensamples to all that believe in Macedonia and Achaia.**—*Christian example and character :*—I. CHRISTIAN EXAMPLE. 1. Christians are first followers, then leaders; first imitators and then imitated (cf. ver. 6). They first look to Him who is the Light of the world; they then shine with reflected lustre, becoming lights of the world themselves. This is implied in the original, which means the impress of a seal. Believers are stamped with Christ's likeness, and thus become a die for others. (1) This is the law of the communication of the truth. Each Christian becomes a living Epistle, a new Bible. Example brings home more powerfully than precept the lessons of faith (Acts xii. 24). (2) In this the Thessalonians were most conspicuous. Other churches looked up to them as their model—(*a*) A noble dignity. (*b*) A sacred duty. (*c*) A constant danger. 2. This example is explained and defined by ver. 8. By this we are to understand —(1) Not the report of their conversion, or the influence of their example merely; but (2) Their missionary zeal. The figure of the trumpet, spreading as echo-like it repeated itself, is found nowhere else in Scripture, except in the silver trumpets of the Jews. It may suggest to us the watchman's voice or horn, which from some high watch-tower amid surrounding midnight darkness swells forth over town and village and plain, or the pealing forth, from some humble church crowning the brow of an Alpine hill, of the melody of bells, floating on the undulating air over valley and mountain and lake, summoning to prayer. 3. But it is possible to see here an allusion to a special missionary service. They had received a call to this (ver. 4); and because theirs was a centre of commanding influence. We must remember that these were Paul's first Epistles. Converts from heathenism needed such teaching. They needed also some historical record of our Lord's life and death and resurrection. It is not unlikely therefore that Luke wrote his Gospel for their use. That evangelist was Paul's companion in Macedonia, and Thessalonica was, from its position and commercial connections, peculiarly suitable for the work of circulating that Gospel. In this "labour of love" the Thessalonian Church became widely known and honoured. The praise which Paul gave to Luke (2 Cor. viii. 18) was theirs. As the Waldensian peasants wandered over the plains of Lombardy and Italy, carrying secretly many copies of the Word, and offering them along with their merchandise wherever "an open door presented itself," so possibly these early Christian traders carried copies of St. Luke's Gospel with them from Thessalonica, and thus from thence sounded out the Word of the Lord. II. CHRISTIAN CHARACTER. 1. Faith. This was conspicuous and widespread. It had extended over a broader area than even their direct exertions. Paul was now in Corinth, where varied streams of travellers met, and so had ample opportunity for knowing it. Aquila and Priscilla had just come from Rome (Acts xviii. 2), and to be known there was to be known everywhere, and they having heard it would naturally tell the apostle of it; so that any special mention of it was unnecessary. This is true fame, found when unsought, the natural reward of self-denying labour and abiding faith. These Christians in simply doing their duty "left their name, a light—a landmark on the cliffs of fame." 2. Conversion from idols. The heart of every man serves idols. Everything away from God in which he seeks his satisfaction is a phantom, an image, not reality. "Keep yourselves from idols" is what all need. 3. Serving God and waiting for Christ. One clause distinguishes the Thessalonians from the heathen, the other from the Jews; but more, they represent the universal Christian life in its two most prominent aspects, ceaseless action and patient waiting. The hope of Christ's coming gives strength for and perseverance in service, and faithful service justifies and consecrates hope. Service without its hope would merge into dry and formal routine; hope without its service would pass into indolent, sentimental, or restless excitement. (*J. Hutchison, D.D.*) *Example : its nature and value :*—Mathematicians demonstrate their theorems by schemes and diagrams, which, in effect, are but sensible instances; orators back their enthymemes (or rational argumentations) with inductions (or singular examples); philosophers allege the example of Socrates, Zeno, &c., to authorize their doctrine; politics and civil prudence is more easily and sweetly drawn out of history than out of books. Artificers describe models, and set patterns before their disciples, with greater success than if they should deliver accurate rules and precepts; for who would not more readily learn to build by viewing carefully the parts and framework of a well-contrived structure, than by a studious inquiry into the rules of architecture? or to draw, by setting a good picture before him, than by merely speculating upon the laws of perspective? or to write fairly and expeditely by imitating one good copy, than by hearkening to a thousand oral prescriptions, the understanding of which, or faculty of applying them to practice, may prove more difficult and tedious than the whole practice itself as directed by a copy? (*I. Barrow, D.D.*)      *Example : its superiority to mere precept :*—A system of precepts, though exquisitely compacted, is, in comparision, but a skeleton—a dry, meagre, lifeless bulk; exhibiting nothing of person, place, time, manner, degree, wherein chiefly the flesh and blood, the colour and graces, the life and soul of things consist, whereby they please, affect, and move us; but example imparts thereto a goodly corpulency, a life, a motion; renders it conspicuous and active, transforming its notional universality into the reality of singular subsistence. (*Ibid.*)      *Example : its influence instructive :*—There is no doubt but a good example doth far more effectually instruct than good precepts; because it not only expresses the same virtues that precepts enjoin, but with far more grace and emphasis. For whereas precepts and discourses of virtue are only the dead pictures and artificial landscapes and descriptions of it, a virtuous example is virtue itself, informed and animated, alive and in motion, exerting and exhibiting itself in all its charms and graces. And therefore as we know a man much better when we see him alive and in action than when we see him only in a picture; so we understand virtue better when we see it living and acting in a good example, than when we only behold it described and pictured in precepts and discourses. (*J. Scott.*)    The best teachers of humanity are the examples of great men. (*C. H. Fowler.*)    *Example: stimulating:*—No man or woman of the humblest sort can be strong, gentle, pure, and good, without the world being the better for it, without somebody being helped and comforted by the very existence of that goodness. (*Phillips Brooks, D.D.*)    *Example: converting:*—We can do more good by being good than in any other way. (*Rowland Hill.*)    A young infidel was one night in bed, contemplating the character of his mother. "I see," he said, within himself, "two unquestionable facts. First, my mother is greatly afflicted in circumstances, body and mind; and I see that she cheerfully bears up under all by the support she derives from constantly retiring to her closet and her Bible. Secondly, that she has a secret spring of comfort of which I know nothing; while I who give an unbounded loose to my appetites, and seek pleasure by every means, seldom or never find it. If, however, there is any such secret in religion, why may not I attain to it as well as my mother? I will immediately seek it of God." Thus the influence of Christianity, exhibited in its beauty by a living example before him, led Richard Cecil to know Christ Himself, and to glorify Him by a most successful and devoted life. (*F. Morse, M.A.*)    When native converts on the island of Madagascar used to present themselves for baptism, it was often asked of them, "What first led you to think of becoming Christians. Was it a particular sermon or address, or the reading of God's word?" The answer usually was, that the changed conduct of others who had become Christians was what first arrested their attention. "I knew this man to be a thief; that one was a drunkard; another was very cruel and unkind to his family. Now they are all changed. The thief is an honest man, the drunkard is sober and respectable, and the other is gentle and kind in his home. There must be something in a religion that can work such changes." (*S. S. Times.*)    *Example: self-propagating:*—Example is like the press: a thing done is the thought printed; it may be repeated if it cannot be recalled; it has gone forth with a self-propagating power, and may run to the ends of the earth, and descend from generation to generation. (*H. Melvill, B.D.*)    *Macedonia* is the first part of Europe which received the gospel directly from St. Paul, and an important scene of his subsequent labours. So closely is this region associated with apostolic journeys, sufferings, and epistles, that it has been truly called by Clarke, the traveller, a kind of Holy Land. Roughly speaking, it is the region bounded inland by the range of the Hæmus or the Balkan northwards, and the chain of the Pindus westwards, beyond which the streams flow respectively to the Danube and the Adriatic. It is separated from Thessaly on the south by the Cambunian Hills, and on the east from Thrace by a less definite mountain boundary. Of the space thus enclosed, two of the most remarkable physical features are two great plains; one watered by the Axius, which comes to the sea at the Thermaic Gulf, not far from Thessalonica; the other, by the Strymon, which, after passing near Philippi, flows out below Amphipolis. Between the mouths of these rivers is a peninsula on which Mount Athos rises nearly into the region of perpetual snow, and across the neck of which Paul travelled more than once. This was the territory over which Philip and Alexander ruled, and which the Romans conquered from Perseus. At first the conquered country was divided by Æmilius Paulus into four districts. Macedonia Prima was on the east of the Strymon, and had Amphipolis for its capital. Macedonia Secunda stretched between the Strymon and the Axius, with Thessalonia for its metropolis. The third and fourth districts lay to the south and west. This division was only temporary. The whole of Macedonia along with Thessaly and a large tract along the Adriatic was made one province and centralized under the jurisdiction of a pro-consul at Thessalonica. We have now reached the definition which corresponds to the usage of the term in the New Testament (Acts xvi. 9, 10, 12 and elsewhere, and in the Epistles). Nothing can exceed the interest and impressiveness of the occasion (Acts xvi. 9) when a new and religious meaning was given to the well-known man of Macedonia of Demosthenes, and when this part of Europe was designated as the first to be trodden by an apostle (Acts xvi., xvii.). The character of the churches then planted is set before us in a very favourable light. The candour of the Bereans is highly commended; the Thessalonians were objects of Paul's peculiar affection; and the Philippians, besides their general freedom from blame, were remarkable for their liberality and self-denial. It is worth noting, as a fact almost typical of the change produced by Christianity in the social life of Europe, that the female element is conspicuous in the records of its introduction into Macedonia (Acts xvi. 13, 14; Phil. iv. 2, 3). It should be observed that in

St. Paul's time, Macedonia was well intersected by Roman roads, especially by the great *Via Egnatia*, which connected Philippi and Thessalonica, and also led toward Illyricum. (*Dean Howson.*)   Achaia signifies a Roman province, which included the whole of the Peloponnesus and the greater part of Hellas proper, with the adjacent islands. This, with Macedonia, comprehended the whole of Greece. Hence both are frequently mentioned together. A narrow slip on the north coast was originally called Achaia, the cities of which were confederated in an ancient league, which was renewed, B.C. 280, for the purpose of resisting the Macedonians. This league subsequently included several of the other states, and became the most powerful political body in Greece; and hence it was natural for the Romans to apply the name of Achaia to the Peloponnesus, and the south where they took Corinth and destroyed the league, B.C. 146. In the division of the provinces by Augustus, between the Emperor and the Senate in B.C. 27, Achaia was one of the provinces assigned to the latter, and was governed by a pro-consul. Tiberius, in A.D. 16, took it away from the Senate and made it an imperial province, governed by a pro-curator. Claudius restored it to the Senate. This was its condition when Paul was brought before Gallio, the pro-consul (Acts xviii. 12). (*Sir G. Grove, LL.D.*) **For from you sounded out the Word of the Lord.**—*God's trumpet:*—The apostle employs a word never used anywhere else in the New Testament to describe the conspicuous and widespread nature of this testimony of theirs. He says, "The Word of the Lord sounded out" from them. That phrase is one most naturally employed to describe the blast of a trumpet. So clear and ringing, so loud, penetrating, melodious, rousing, and full was their proclamation, by the silent eloquence of their lives, of the gospel which impelled and enabled them to lead such lives. A grand ideal of a community of believers! I. This metaphor suggests THE GREAT PURPOSE OF THE CHURCH. It is God's trumpet. His means of making His voice heard through all the uproar of the world. As the captain upon the deck in the gale will use his speaking trumpet, so God's voice needs your voice. The gospel needs to be passed through human lips in order that it may reach deaf ears. The Church is worse than "sounding brass," it is as silent brass and an untinkling cymbal, unless the individuals that belong to it recognize God's meaning in making them His children, and do their best to fulfil it. "Ye are My witnesses," saith the Lord. You are put into the witness-box, see that you speak out when you are there. II. Another point that this figure may suggest is THE SORT OF SOUND THAT SHOULD COME FROM THE TRUMPET. 1. A trumpet-note is, first of all, clear. There should be no hesitation in our witness; nothing uncertain in the sound that we give. 2. The note should be penetrating. There is no instrument, I suppose, that carries further than the ringing clarion that is often heard on the field of battle, above all the strife. And so this little church at Thessalonica, a mere handful of people, just converted, in the very centre of a strong, compact, organized, self-confident, supercilious heathenism, insisted upon being heard, and got itself made audible, simply by the purity and the consistency of the lives of its members. A clear voice will fling words to a distance that a thick, mumbling one never can attain. One note will travel much farther than another. Do you see to it that your notes are of the penetrating sort. 3. And then, again, the note should be a musical one. There is nothing to be done for God by harshness; nothing to be done by discords and jangling; nothing to be done by scolding and rebuke. The ordered sequence of melodious sound will travel a great deal further than unmusical, plain speech. You can hear a song at a distance at which a saying would be inaudible. Which thing is an allegory, and this is its lesson. Music goes further than discord; and the witness that a Christian man bears will travel in direct proportion as it is harmonious and gracious and gentle and beautiful. 4. And then, again, the note should be rousing. You do not play on a trumpet when you want to send people to sleep; dulcimers and the like are the things for that purpose. The trumpet means strung-up intensity, means a call to arms, or to rejoicing; means, at any rate, vigour, and is intended to rouse. Let your witness have for its inmost signification, "Awake! thou that sleepest, and arise from the dead, and Christ shall give thee light." III. Then, still further, take another thought that may be suggested from this metaphor, THE SILENCE OF THE LOUDEST NOTE. If you look at the context, you will see that all the ways in which the Word of the Lord is represented as sounding out from the Thessalonian Church were deeds, not words. The context supplies a number of them. Such as the following are specified in it: their work; their toil, which is more than work; their patience; their assurance; their reception of the Word, in much affliction with joy in the

Holy Ghost; their faith to Godward; their turning to God from idols, to serve and to wait. That is all. So far as the context goes there might not have been a man amongst them that ever opened His mouth for Jesus Christ. We know not, of course, how far they were a congregation of silent witnesses, but this we know, that what Paul meant when he said, " The whole world is ringing with the voice of the Word of God sounding from you," was not their going up and down the world shouting about their Christianity, but their quiet living like Jesus Christ. That is a louder voice than any other. I do not mean to say that Christian men and women are at liberty to lock their lips from verbal proclamation of the Saviour they have found, but I do mean to say that if there was less talk and more living the witness of God's Church would be louder and not lower; " and men would take knowledge of us, that we had been with Jesus "; and of Jesus, that He had made us like Himself. IV. And so, lastly, let me draw one other thought from this metaphor, which I hope you will not think fanciful playing with a figure; and THAT IS THE BREATH THAT MAKES THE MUSIC. If the Church is the trumpet, who blows it? God! It is by His Divine Spirit dwelling within us and breathing through us that the harsh discords of our natural lives become changed into melody of praise and the music of witness for Him. Keep near Christ, live in communion with God, let Him breathe through you, and when His Spirit passes through your spirits their silence will become harmonious speech; and from you " will sound out the Word of the Lord." (*A. Maclaren, D.D.*) *The Word of the Lord sounding forth:*—I. IT WAS THE WORD OF THE LORD THAT WAS SPREAD (ver. 5). 1. Paul did not despise the power of words; he was a master of them; but he contrasted words with power. Words—the air is stirred by them, as it is by raindrops, but they pass away, perhaps not forgotten, the memory lives for ever, stinging like a serpent or ministering like an angel, blasting as the lightning or refreshing as the dew. " The words of the wise are as nails fastened." Paul did not despise the marvellous Greek language as a vehicle of thought and feeling, but he said there was something more. The word is the organism which contains the life, the body that holds the soul, the frame that surrounds the picture. Knowledge is power, and truth, and love. 2. We have the Word of God in power. Have we an infallible interpretation of it? Rome says she has, but we say that she has tampered with it, and reject her forgery. In order to the right understanding of the Word, we need—(1) A correct version. (2) The exercise of our own powers in its study. Christ demands not a blind credulity, but says, " Come and see." (3) The help of those who are able to throw light on it. (4) Prayer for the help of the Holy Spirit. II. THEY WHO RECEIVE THE WORD ARE TO SPREAD IT ABROAD. 1. Power always carries responsibility. The learned are to teach the ignorant, the strong to help the weak, the brave the timid. This may not be according to the law of " natural selection," by which the weak go to the wall, but it is according to the law of love, of Sinai, of Christ, which says, " Thou shalt love thy neighbour," &c. God's disapproval of selfishness is seen in this, that it is only by using His gifts that we can retain and improve them. Hoarded wealth is useless; stored grain is mildewed; the buried talent is forfeited. We get by giving and learn by teaching. God speaks to us that we may speak to others. 2. The gospel had been in this case conveyed through the land and other lands. The same joyful sound has been heard in this country. All that is happy in the condition and noble in the character of our people is owing to this. Let England be true to her vocation, and pass the blessing on. III. HOW ARE WE TO SPREAD IT ABROAD? 1. Negatively. (1) Not by force. When the knights of Germany offered their swords to Luther, he replied, " No, the Word shall do it." You cannot destroy error or propagate spiritual truth by swords or Acts of Parliament. You may make rules of music, but you cannot impose them on the songsters of the wood. You may guide the little brook that comes chattering through the fields, but who can cut channels for the dew? Men's thoughts are as free; they cannot be prevented by violence. (2) Not by ceremonies. An attempt is being made to undo the Reformation, and send back the dial on English civilization and freedom. All forms are mischievous which come between us and Christ. As some foolish people covered grand pictures and frescoes on church walls with plaster, superstition has covered over the faith which is " placarded before our eyes " with Roman cement. It was the work of Luther and others to chip off the crust and reveal the work of the Divine Artist; and it is our work to protest against all that would bind the Word or hide the Saviour. (3) Not by sensational worship or teaching. A truly earnest man will be ready to welcome almost anything that will arouse the indifferent and win attention to the truth.   Paul was ready to be all things to all men; but I do not think he included absurdities in the means he would employ.   There are two dangers attending religious excitement: one, that while the surface of the nature is affected men will be satisfied with that; the other, that when the excitement is over there will be a hurtful reaction.   The crowds that cried " Hosanna " also cried " Crucify." 2. *Positively.*   (1) With a spontaneity that will be of itself a presage of success. " From you sounded forth," &c., as a natural effect of reception.   (a) It is difficult to hide truth, for it naturally tends to show itself.   When a scientific discovery has been made it is unnatural for the discoverer to keep it to himself, the strong conviction being that truth is not the property of an individual, society, nation, but of the race.   It is as difficult to hide truth as to hide light; if there is a crevice anywhere it will dart forth.   It may be buried like seed, and the storms of a long winter may pass over it until it is almost forgotten; but the elements go in search of the seed; the dew asks, " Where is it ? "   The rain says, " I will find it "; and the sun stretches forth his long fingers of light to feel it, and the seed is vitalized, and comes forth; so truth rises again, perhaps in a new form, but with multiplied power.   (b) This is especially illustrated in the history of spiritual truth.   When the truth has free course in a man's nature it will sound forth spontaneously as fragrance from a June rose, as heat from the fire, as lustre from a diamond, as music from an Æolian harp.   (c) There are some who receive and never give.   They are like a blank object that absorbs the light and never reflects it.   They are not like that little spring upon the hill slope, that receives from the cloud, and then gives refreshment and beauty to moss and nodding fern, gives itself for the use of the world, singing as it gives.   But they are like the stagnant pool, that receives the showers, and remains in the same place, to poison the atmosphere, until at length the hot summer sun dries it up.   There are others who give, but never cheerfully, with a bad grace that spoils the gift.   There are others again who give so readily that it is like breathing the balmy air of May to ask them for a contribution.   (2) By a holy life.   " Ye were ensamples."   A holy life is the best transcript of the Word.   Gibbon attributes the early success of Christianity to " the pure and austere morals of the Christians."   And Christian life is the most powerful argument the Church can use to-day.   It may be that of a friendless young man in London who, in the midst of temptations, dares to live a pure life; or that of a domestic servant who " sweeps under the mats" because she acknowledges a Master in heaven.   To pray in the sanctuary and cheat on the Exchange is what the world regards with disgust.   (3) By active effort.   From the seaport of Thessalonica merchants and sailors would carry with them the good tidings.   The news of their faith was so widespread that the apostle had no need to speak of it.   What a commendation! There are some whose faith is so small that you are obliged to advertise it if you want it known.   Our *names* too frequently, not our faith, are spread abroad.   The message of the Church has often failed because there has been so little of living faith in it.   The earnestness of our piety is the best answer to the worldliness and scepticism of the day.   (*James Owen.*)   *The sounding forth of the Word :*—The Greek commentators in this picturesque word observe a metaphor derived from the trumpet's brilliant tone and power of distant resonance.   Thus Chrysostom : " The resonance of the trumpet fills the whole vicinity; but the fame of your excellence fills the world, and reaches all and everywhere with equal sound.   Great deeds are celebrated with the distinctest commemoration where they were performed.   They are indeed often celebrated far away, but not so much.   It is not so with you.   The glorious sound has gone through the earth."   It can scarcely be doubted that St. Paul was thinking of the geographical position of Thessalonica, which had been particularly noted by Cicero (" It is placed in the bosom of our Empire ").   It was indeed by land a chief station on the great Roman Military Road (*Via Egnatia*), as Cicero also observes; while by sea it had a principal share in the commerce of the Levant, and was in constant communication with almost every shore of the known world.   When we take into account St. Paul's subtle tact in dealing with men, there seems to be much reason for finding an allusion also to a history of which every Thessalonian must have been proud—an historical blended with a geographical reference.   The apostle may have lightly touched upon a new fame in the gospel, succeeding to and surpassing the ancient Macedonian glory.   In the verse generally, and more particularly in the vivid words, " Your faith is spoken as if of a living thing," Chrysostom seems to trace a reminiscence of the elastic and bounding symbol of Alexander's Macedonian Empire in Daniel viii. 5-8.   Rarely, indeed, could such words have afterwards been applied to the Church of Thessalonica.

Cyril and Methodius, however, belonging to the Sclavo-Bulgarian nationality, which extends from the Danube to Thessaly—Hellenized Sclaves—evangelized Moravia, Bohemia, and Pannonia. They were born in the ninth century at Thessalonica. (*Bp. Alexander.*)　　*Christian influence diffusive :*—If a man carry in his hand a lighted burning candle, it giveth not light to him only that carrieth it, but to all those which be in the house; and they also see it which are without. Even so, if any be the child of knowledge, and carry about him the light of God, he doth not only taste of the comfort thereof himself, and work comfort to those that appertain to the Church of God, but lighteneth also the hearts of pagans and infidels which are abroad. Such as are bathed or perfumed with precious ointments or powders have not only the pleasure to themselves, but the savour thereof casteth itself out, and is pleasant to all those which stand by. The gospel is the light of God; it shineth in the darkness of this world; it is the sweet incense and savour of God; wheresoever the breath thereof is received, it bringeth life. (*Bp. Jewell.*)　*The fame of Christian character better than worldly renown :*—As the lightning is seen from one part of the air to the other, and as the sound of great noise spreadeth itself far and wide, so doth the light of good conversation in the godly show itself forth. And therefore he telleth them they have filled all the country of Macedonia with knowledge and with wonder at their faith and stedfastness in the truth. As if he had said, Great is the renown of your king, Alexander, and your country is famous. He hath overrun the whole world, and subdued it. He hath conquered Greece, Asia, Arabia, Phrygia, Armenia, Scythia, and India. Kings and princes fell down before him: the whole world stood in awe of his name. Yet Alexander had but the power and force of men. He had great treasures of gold and silver; he had numbers of horses and camels and elephants; he had swords, bills, spears, and darts, and suchlike artillery and armour. These where the things wherewith he overcame his enemies; hereby both he and his people were renowned. What, then, may be said of the battle which you have fought? or of the victory which you have gotten? You have won that Alexander could never win. You have overcome yourselves; you have overcome the world. He conquered the bodies of many, and had them at commandment; but their souls stood out, and would not be conquered. You have subdued your souls, and brought them to the obedience of the gospel. You have overrun all the country, and triumphed among the people. And all this is brought to pass without force, without policy, without armour, without artillery, only by your patience and suffering for the gospel's sake. (*Ibid.*)　　*Pulpit reflectors :*— It was a very suggestive saying of Dr. Lyman Beecher, that the reason why he was so blessed to the conversion of men was that he had so many pulpit reflectors, who lived out and diffused everywhere the gospel.　　*Witnessing for Christ to the whole world :*—Never was there a land blessed with such peculiar facilities as Britain for acting as a witness for Christ to the world. Why is it that the gospel is at this time in trust with a people whose ships cover the sea, who are the merchants of the world? Has He who drew the boundaries of Judea with His own finger, who selected the precise spot for the temple, who did everything for the Jewish Church from design, abandoned the Christian Church to accident? And, if not, if He has placed the gospel here with design, what can the nature of that design be, but that it should be borne to the world on the wings of every wind that blows? Say, why is it that Britain, and her religious ally America, should divide the seas, should hold the keys of the world? Oh, were we but awake to the designs of God, and to our own responsibility, we should hear Him say, " I have put you in possession of the seas ; put the world in possession of My gospel." And every ship we sent out would be a Missionary Church, like the ark of the deluge, a floating testimony for God, and bearing in its bosom the seeds of a new creation. Christians, ours is, indeed, a post of responsibility and of honour! On us have accumulated all the advantages of the past; and on us lies the great stress of the present. The world is waiting breathless on our movements; the voice of all heaven is urging us on. Oh, for celestial wisdom, to act in harmony with the high appointments of Providence— to seize the crisis which has come for blessing the world. (*John Harris.*)　　**In every place your faith to Godward is spread abroad.**—*True fame :*—No true and permanent fame can be founded except in labours which promote the happiness of mankind. The highest greatness surviving time and stone is that which proceeds from the soul of man. Monarchs and cabinets, generals and admirals, with the pomp of courts and the circumstances of war, in the lapse of time disappear from sight; but the pioneers of truth, though poor and lowly, especially those whose example elevates human nature, and teaches the rights of man, so that "a government of the people, by the people, and for the people, may not perish from the earth"; such a harbinger can never be forgotten, and their renown spreads coextensive with the cause they served so well. (*Charles Sumner.*)    *The means of securing fame :*—Live for something! Do good and leave behind you a monument of virtue that the storm of time can never destroy. Write your name in kindness, love, and mercy on the hearts of the thousands you come in contact with year by year, and you will never be forgotten. Your name, your deeds, will be as legible on the hearts you leave behind as the stars on the brow of evening. Good deeds will shine as the stars of heaven. (*T. Chalmers, D.D.*)    **For they themselves show what manner of entering in we had unto you.**—*A summary of experience :*—I. THE ENTERING IN OF THE WORD. When we preach you listen, and so far the Word is received. But the preacher often feels that he is outside the door, because Christ has not entered the heart. In responding to a knock a man will sometimes open the door a little way to see and hear before admittance. The King's messenger has thus been treated, and has even got his foot in the doorway, but has received painful hurt when the door has been forced back with angry violence. But he has also heard the joyful cry, "Come in." The truth has many ways of entrance. 1. It affects the understanding. Men discover that the gospel is the very thing for which they have been waiting. 2. Then it works upon the conscience, that being the understanding exercised on moral truth. The man sees himself a sinner, and is thus made ready to receive Christ's pardoning grace. 3. Then the emotions are aroused —fear is awakened and hope excited. Repentance calls forth one after another of her sentinels. The proud man is broken down, the hard heart softened. 4. By and by the entrance is complete, for the truth carries the central castle of Mansoul, and captures the heart. He who once hated the gospel now loves it—at first he loves it hoping that it may be his, though fearing the reverse; then he ventures to grasp it, encouraged by the Word which bids him lay hold of eternal life. II. CONVERSION. "Ye turned." Conversion is the turning completely round of a man to hate what he loved and love what he hated. It is to turn to God distinctly by an act and deed of the mind and will. In some senses we are "turned," in others we "turn": not promise or resolve. Reformation is not enough, there must be a revolution: old thrones must fall, and a new king must reign. 1. They turned from idols. The streets of London are crammed with fetish worship. (1) Multitudes are worshipping, not calves of gold, but gold in a more portable shape. Small circular idols are much sought after. The epithet "almighty" is applied to an American form of these idols. (2) Many worship rank, name, pleasure, honour. (3) Most worship self, and there is no more degrading form of worship. No wooden image is more ugly. (4) Men worship Bacchus still. There is a temple to him at every street corner. Other trades are content with shops, this fiend must have a palace. (5) The gods of unchastity and vice are yet among us. If you love anything better than God you are idolaters. 2. Some turn from one idol to another. If a man turns from Bacchus and becomes a teetotaler, he may become covetous. When men quit covetousness they sometimes turn to profligacy. Nothing will serve but turning to the living and true God. III. SERVICE. 1. The object of this service is—(1) The living God. Many have a dead God still. They do not feel that He hears their prayers, nor take Him into their calculations. A living God demands a living service. (2) The true God, and therefore cannot be served with falsehood. Many evidently serve a false God, for they pray without their hearts. When men's lives are false and artificial, they are not fit service for the God of truth. A life is false when it is not the true outcome of the soul, when it is fashioned by custom, ruled by observation, restrained by selfish motives, and governed by a love of human esteem. 2. Notice the order. The entering in of the Word produces conversion, and conversion service. If you are converts without the Word you are unconverted; if professing to receive it you are not turned by it, you have not received it; if you claim to have been converted and are not serving God, you are not converted; and if you boast of serving God without being converted you are not serving Him. IV. WAITING. 1. Salvation is not a thing which only requires a few moments of faith and then all is over; it is the business of our lives. We receive salvation in an instant, but we work it out with fear and trembling all our days. 2. This waiting is also living in the future. The Christian looks for the second advent with calm hope; he does not know when it will be, but he keeps himself on the watch as a servant who waits for his Lord's return. He does not expect to be rewarded by men, or even by God in temporal things, but by Christ with heaven. (*C. H. Spurgeon.*)    *The character of*

*ministers involved in the conduct of professors:*—In this general talk (ver. 8) the converts and the preachers were greatly mixed up—" For they themselves show of us
what manner of entering in we had unto you." I do not know that it is possible
for the preacher to keep himself distinct from those who profess to be converted by
him. He is gladly one with them in love to their souls, but he would have it
remembered that he cannot be responsible for all their actions. Those who profess
to have been converted under any ministry have it in their power to damage that
ministry far more than any adversaries can do. " There ! " says the world, when
it detects a false professor, " this is what comes of such preaching." They judge
unfairly, I know ; but most men are in a great hurry, and will not examine the
logic of their opponents ; while many others are so eager to judge unfavourably,
that a very little truth, or only a bare report, suffices to condemn both the minister
and his doctrine. Every man that lives unto God with purity of life brings honour
to the gospel which converted him, to the community to which he belongs, and to
the preaching by which he was brought to a knowledge of the truth ; but the
reverse is equally true in the case of unworthy adherents. Members of Churches,
will you kindly think of this ? Your ministers share the blame of your ill conduct
if ever you disgrace yourselves. I feel sure that none of you wish to bring shame
and trouble upon your pastors, however careless you may be about your own
reputations. *(Ibid.)*          *Repudiating idols:*—A large Chinese heathen temple has
lately been turned into a Christian place of worship in the north of China. At a
place called Shih-Chia-Tang the missionaries, Stanley and Smith, looked at the
gulley where, at the dead of night, the gods were hustled in. The summer rains
had caused a bit of a large god to crumble off. The men call it " divine mud ! "
so the missionaries took up a handful of the moistened clay, and threw it down,
saying, " Dust to dust, mud to mud ! " The temple looks very pleasant in its
changed character. The two large bells now call the people to worship the living
God, instead of calling the idol, as they supposed, from his feast and slumbers. In
the front temple quaint pictures of flying spirits and genii, painted on the walls,
still remain. The larger temple makes a very neat mission chapel, with its
whitened walls and scarlet-painted posts and beams. The wooden incense table
has been cut down into a preaching table, and the benches are made from the platform which supported the larger idols. On the temple front hangs a large tablet,
with " Jesus' Chapel " in beautiful Chinese characters, replacing the old Taouist
sign. This temple now stands a distinct witness to the truth that God is a Spirit,
and His glorious gospel is proclaimed in it. *Absurdity of idol worship:*—A Cingalese boy living at Baddegamma, in Ceylon, went one day into a Buddhist temple to
offer his evening flower. When he had done so, he looked into the idol's face,
expecting to see a smile of approval ; but as the great eyes stared on without any
expression of pleasure in them, he thought that so great a god would not condescend to accept a child's offering. Soon after, a man came in, laid down his
flower, turned his back, and walked carelessly away. The boy again looked into
the idol's face, and thought he should see an angry frown at this disrespect ; but
the eyes stared as before. He then began to realize the fact that the image had no
life in it, and was alike powerless to punish or reward. As soon as a mission
school was opened in the neighbourhood he became one of the pupils and was converted to God, together with several of his family. He afterwards became a zealous
and devoted minister. His name was Abraham Gunasekara. He died, and his son
is now the minister of a congregation of Cingalese Christians in Kandy. *Idolatry
swept away :*—Not long ago a young man came from Raratonga to this metropolis,
and he was taken to see the British Museum. Among the rest of the wonders he
there saw was a row of idols, and amongst others there was a Raratonga god. He
looked with wondrous curiosity, and asked permission to take it in his hands. He
looked at it all round for a while with great interest, and passed it back to the
guide, and said, " Thank you ; that is the first idol I ever saw in my life." In the
time of the honoured John Williams there were more than 100,000 individual gods
in Raratonga ; and so clean a sweep has the gospel of Christ made of the whole
abomination, that a young lad of nineteen had never seen one of them from the
day of his birth. *(Jackson Wray.)*          *The notion entertained of the Christian
religion, and the principal doctrines of it, in the earliest days :*—The early account
of the Christian religion, so universally received, and so well approved by the
apostles, consists of two chief parts : I. THE SERVICE OWING TO THE LIVING GOD.
1. Religion, considered in this light, can be no other than natural religion. This
was the original religion of man, but had been so corrupted and abused that there

was hardly any sign of it when our Saviour appeared in the world. The preaching of the gospel revived the true ancient religion of nature, and prepared men for the reception of it; and has, by the additional supports of revelation, maintained it for many ages, and probably will maintain it to the end and consummation of all things. 2. These additional supports make the next great branch of Christian doctrine. These are revived upon the authority of revelation, and stand upon the evidence of external proofs : that we ought to turn from idols, and serve the living God; that we ought to serve Him in holiness and purity, in conforming ourselves to the example of His justice, equity, and goodness, are truths which every man may feel to be such who has any reason or natural feeling about him; but that we have been delivered from the wrath to come by Jesus the Son of God ; that God raised Him from the dead, and hath appointed Him to be judge both of the dead and of the living, are articles which no man's reason can suggest; which, when suggested, reason cannot receive upon any internal evidence, but must take them upon an authority sufficiently confirmed upon external evidence. II. OUR FAITH IN CHRIST, AND OUR HOPE AND EXPECTATION GROUNDED ON THAT FAITH. 1. The patience of faith. St. Paul teaches us to wait for God's Son from heaven. But this waiting implies not only the patience of faith, but well-doing, in expectation of the coming of our Saviour and Judge; which sense is completely expressed in the Epistle to the Philippians—"Be followers together of me, and mark them which walk so as ye have us for an example; for our conversation is in heaven; from whence also we look for the Saviour, the Lord Jesus Christ, who shall change our vile body, that it may be fashioned like unto His glorious body, according to the working whereby He is able even to subdue all things unto Himself." 2. The expectation of Christ coming to judge the world is peculiar to Christians; and it is supported by the belief of the resurrection of Christ—that great and main point of faith, which the Apostles were commissioned to teach and establish in the Church of God. This designation of Christ to be judge of the world is no impeachment of the authority of God. The Son acts by the Father's commission, who hath given all judgment to Him; but this makes no change in the nature of the judgment itself. Did the article of the resurrection make any alterations in our notions of God or religion; did it bring any new burden upon us of any sort, it would be no wonder to see men very careful how they admitted it; but now that it requires nothing at our hands but what reason and nature require, what pretence for being scrupulous concerning it. Admit the article, and our hopes are much improved, while our duty is the same; reject the article, and our duty is the same, while our hopes are much less. (*T. Sherlock, D.D.*)     *The Bible's exposure of idolatry :*—I was told by that distinguished missionary, John Williams, that he found the simple reading of Isa. xliv. more effectual in convincing the natives of the folly and sin of idolatry than any of his own teaching. Ver. 17, "And the residue thereof he maketh a god," were the words which at once laid hold of their understanding and their conscience. (*Earl of Chichester.*)     *Folly of idolatry :*—According to Jewish tradition, Terah was a maker and seller of idols, and being one day obliged to leave home, he charged his son Abram to attend to business in his absence. Presently an elderly man came in, and taking a fancy to an idol asked the price. In reply, Abram said, " Old man, what is thy age?" "Threescore years," replied the visitor. Whereupon Abram exclaimed, " Threescore years! And thou wouldest worship a thing that has been fashioned by the hands of my father's slaves within the last four and twenty hours! Strange that a man of sixty should be willing to bow down his grey head to a creature of a day!" At these words the man, overwhelmed with shame, went away.     *Vanity of idols :*—A missionary and his wife, some thirty years ago, went from Manchester to Samoa. Children were born to them there, and to one of these was sent, by an old servant of the family, a splendid doll, which opened and closed its eyes, and was richly clothed. Meantime, Roman Catholic priests had attempted to establish a mission in Samoa, and had gained a foothold. Among their wares was an image of the Virgin Mary, doubtless richly dressed ; but unfortunately its eyes were fixed. While the priests and this object of worship were still under discussion, it became known that the English people had received a box of gifts from their own country. The natives crowded to the sight, of which by far the most attractive part was the old servant's doll. After watching for a time the wonder of its opening and closing eyes, they began to say to one another, without any suggestion from the missionaries, " We have seen the God of the Roman Catholics; we have also seen the plaything of the English children; the plaything opens its eyes, but the eyes of the Catholic god are fixed : greater is the plaything of the Protestants than the idol of the Romanists. What must the God of the Protestants be ? " The priests were absolutely driven from the island by the doll, while the word preached by the missionaries had free course, and was well listened to. (*Family Treasury*.) **The living and true God.**—What a strange yet pregnant phrase ! Surely the Author of life must live ; yet here is an expression which hints that there are deities who are not alive. It was thus that the Hebrews distinguished between the true God and the false gods of the nations around them (Psa. xcvi. 5). The heathen deities were so much carving, sculpture, and colouring ; or they were so much human imagination or speculation ; they had no being independent of the toil, whether of the hands or the brains of men. It was true that evil spirits, by lurking beneath the idol forms, or draping themselves in debasing heathen fancies, might contrive to appropriate the homage which the human heart lavished on its own creations (Psa. cvi. 37). But the broad contrast, latent in the expression " the living God," is the contrast between an imagination and a fact ; between an existing Being and fancy personages ; between a solemn truth and a stupid and debasing unreality. Some truth, however, there certainly was in the most degrading forms of heathen worship ; since a religion which is undiluted falsehood could not continue to exist as a religion, and the false religions which do exist, only exist by virtue of the elements of truth which in varying proportions they severally contain. And this intermixture of truth yields the best starting-point for convincing heathens of the errors which they admit, and of the truths which they deny beyond. In this sense undoubtedly the science of comparative theology may be made really serviceable to Christian truth. It is a widely different thing to start with an assumption that all the positive religions in the world, Jewish and Christian included, are alike con-glomerate formations in very varying degrees, partly true, partly false ; and that the religion of the future—an etherealized abstraction, to be distilled by science from all the creeds and worships of mankind—will be something beyond and distinct from all of them. Certainly heathenism is not treated, either in the Old Testament or the New, with the tenderness which would befit such an anticipation as this. Practically speaking, and as contrasted with revealed truth, heathenism is represented as a lie. To live within its range is to live in the kingdom of dark-ness (Isa. lx. 2 ; 1 Pet. ii. 9) ; to practice its rites is to be an enemy of God by wicked works (Col. i. 21) ; to go after false gods is to have the earnest of great trouble, and to provoke the anger of the real Lord of the universe (Psa. lxxviii. 59, 60 ; cvi. 36–40). (*Canon Liddon.*)    **And to wait for His Son from heaven.**—*A body of Divinity :*—I. THE DEITY OF CHRIST. " His Son." II. HIS HUMANITY. " Whom He raised." Christ could not have been raised had He not died, and could not have died had He not been man. III. THE UNITY OF HIS PERSON. " Even Jesus." IV. HIS REDEMPTION. 1. Men are guilty, lost, or they could not have needed a deliverance by Jesus, the Saviour. 2. Christ died for men that He might deliver them. 3. His death was accepted by the Father, " Whom He raised." V. HIS RESURRECTION. We must not think of Christ as dead, or centre our faith wholly on the Cross. " He is not here ; He is risen." VI. HIS ASCENSION. " From heaven." Hence He must have gone thither. 1. He has gone first as our forerunner, and secured for us the Spirit. 2. He remains in heaven. (1) To prepare a place for us. (2) To intercede. (3) To watch His Church's conflicts, and to deliver it. 3. He is there with saving power—" Delivereth." He is at this moment delivering. VII. HIS SECOND COMING. 1. Certain and uncertain. He will come, but when we know not. 2. Sudden, as a thief in the night. 3. To deliver His people from the coming wrath. (*C. H. Spurgeon.*)    *The second advent of Christ :*—I. THE CERTAINTY OF THE ADVENT. Of this, according to the unbroken statements of the New Testament, there is not the shadow of a doubt ; but I would observe—1. The time of the coming is an uncertainty. If you examine a few of the statements with reference to that uncertainty, you will find a statement in the New Testa-ment as to that coming being a thing near. In the first Epistle to the Thes-salonians, the fourth chapter, and the fifteenth verse, you read—" For this we say unto you by the Word of the Lord, that we which are alive and remain unto the coming of the Lord, shall not prevent them which are asleep." Where-as, in the second Epistle, the second chapter, and the third verse, you find the statement which implies that that coming was not immediate : " Let no man deceive you by any means : for that day shall not come, except there come a falling away first." You will find in the Epistle to the Hebrews the same apparently con-tradictory statements. Then you find in the seventh verse of the fourth chapter of the first Epistle of Peter—" The end of all things is at hand." Again, in the third chapter, the ninth verse, of the second Epistle of Peter, you find the apostle speaking of the Lord being "longsuffering to us-ward, not willing that any should perish." You have the same apparent conflict of statement in our blessed Lord's own words. Thus in the twenty-fourth chapter of Matthew, and the thirty-fourth verse, He says —"This generation shall not pass, till all these things be fulfilled;" which seems to intimate a near approach of the second coming. Then you find in the nineteenth verse of the twenty-fifth chapter, in the parable of the talents—"After a long time the lord of those servants cometh, and reckoneth with them." Again there is another class of statements which expressly and distinctly aver that the time of the second coming is left in uncertainty. Thus, you find in the twenty-fourth chapter of Matthew, and the forty-second verse—"Watch therefore : for ye know not what hour your Lord doth come." And you find a still more remarkable statement in the Gospel of St. Mark—"But of that day and that hour knoweth no man, no, not the angels which are in heaven, neither the Son, but the Father ; " that is—the Lord Jesus in His human nature was not at that time acquainted with the day of His Second Advent. What, then, is the result which the Word of God seems intended to produce by this apparent conflict of statement? I believe the result which it intends to produce is this—that we should be always on the watch for the second coming of our blessed Lord. There is a tendency in some minds to anticipate that coming, to affirm and believe that that coming is immediately at hand. The Christians at Thesalonica were in danger of thus putting away temporal duties, and neglecting the present calls of life, in order that they might be ready for that which they immediately expected. There is a tendency in other minds to defer and put off that day, to think that it is sure not to take place soon ; and thus to live an indolent, a listless and a comparatively indifferent life, as regards that grand object of our hope. Now, if we read the New Testament aright, and if we receive the impression which these various passages are intended to leave upon our minds, with reference to the certainty of the fact and the uncertainty of the coming, I believe that the effect produced will be to make us feel that the Lord's coming, though uncertain at any moment, is possible at any moment. It will produce that state of expectancy, and that state of preparedness and desire with reference to it, in which our Lord sees to be the fittest condition for the spirits of His people to live and be. 2. The grand object presented. I can hardly read without emotion of the anticipation of the first Advent, on the part of the pious Jews, who preceded that advent. But how much grander and more sublime is that which is the object of our hope—the Second Advent ; the Lord Jesus coming, not in humiliation, but in glory ; not in weakness, but in power ; not to suffer, but to reign ! And when we think of all the attendant circumstances which are predicted—the rapture of the saints, the descent of the Lord from heaven, the Judgment, the binding of Satan, the renewal of this earth, and all those grand scenes to be produced by His glory—who can look at this great object of our hope without feeling his spirit awed and solemnized, without feeling that we have presented to us in the Bible one of the sublimest and most glorious objects which it is possible for the mind of man to conceive, as that upon which our hope is to rest, as that to which our expectations are to tend? II. THE INFLUENCE WHICH THIS HOPE IS DESIGNED TO EXERCISE. 1. Holiness. "Every man that hath this hope purifieth himself, even as he is pure." Now, it is impossible for a person who is living in daily anticipation of the second coming of Jesus, impossible for a believer in Christ whose mind is constantly turning towards that glorious appearing, to do otherwise than endeavour to have his moral image conformed, as highly as it can be, to the moral image of Him whom he is expecting ; and that it lies in the very essential nature of man, that if in love and hearty faith he is expecting the coming of the Lord, he must seek to purify himself even as his Lord is pure. 2. Gratitude and love. There is a very emphatic word at the close of our text, where the Apostle says that we are expecting Jesus "which delivered us from the wrath to come." Consider what that wrath is ! Who it is that has delivered us ! CONSIDER HOW He has delivered us—not by handing over some mercenary ransom, but by giving Himself to suffer and to die ; and that it is through this purchase Christ has paid that He has accomplished this mighty deliverance ; and then say whether the anticipation of meeting Him must not produce, in the mind of him who has this hope, an earnest feeling of gratitude and devoted love to Him, to whom he owes his salvation and his glory. 3. Unworldliness. If a man is living in anticipation of the advent of Christ, it is impossible for him to be so wholly immersed in the cares and pleasures and businesses of this world, as is the case with too many professing Christians. If we were certain that the coming of the Lord were nigh at hand, would any Christian be unduly engrossed with the things of the world? No. " Use the world, and not abuse it." (*E. Bayley, M.A.*)    *Waiting for the second coming of Christ :*—A minister once entered an ancient almshouse, of which an aged couple were the inmates.    Beside a little round table, opposite the fire, sat the husband, too paralyzed to move at his entrance, and with his hat on his head to keep off the gusts of wind which sifted through his chinky dwelling.    His wooden shoe pattered on the floor unceasingly, keeping time to the tremour of his shaking frame ; and, as he was very deaf, his visitor shouted in his ear—" Well, what are you doing? "    " Waiting, sir."    " For what ? "    " For the appearing of my Lord."    " And what makes you wish for His appearing ? "    " Because I expect great things then.    He has promised a crown of righteousness to all them that love His appearing."    Some further questions were asked as to the foundation of his hope, when he slowly put on his spectacles, and, turning over the leaves of the large Bible already open before him, he pointed to the text—" Therefore, being justified by faith, we have peace with God. (*E. P. Hood.*)    *The great Deliverer :*—I. OUR DANGER, " Wrath." 1. Deserved. 2. Destructive. 3. Dreadful. 4. Unavoidable.    5. " To come."    II. OUR DELIVERER, " Jesus."    He stepped into the awful breach, took our place, was " bruised for our iniquities."    His deliverance was therefore—1. Honourable.    2. Costly.    3. Vicariously effected.    4. Great : (1) It saves from unutterable gloom.    (2) It conducts to unutterable glory.    5. Complete in its nature.    6. Free in its bestowments.    7. Eternal in its duration.    8. Race-wide in its purposes. (*T. Kelly.*)    *The coming of the Redeemer :*—I. THE WRATH TO WHICH WE WERE EXPOSED BEFORE OUR DELIVERANCE.    II. OUR DELIVERANCE. Out of love to us Christ assumed our nature, placed Himself under our curse.    By this He rescues us.    III. THE PROOF THAT OUR FULL PURCHASE FROM WRATH IS PAID. His resurrection.    IV. CHRIST'S FUTURE COMING.    It is certain even if delayed— therefore we must not be impatient but wait for it.    Conclusion : 1. Be thankful for your redemption.    2. Do not fret because you are not released from present evils.    3. Patiently discharge every present duty, and so wait for the coming of the Lord from heaven. (*Dr. Belfrage.*)    *Different types of believers :*—It appears remarkable that St. Paul should make the essence of the gospel here consist, not in the belief in Christ or the taking up of His Cross, but in the hope of His coming again.    Such, however, was the faith of the Thessalonian Church, such is the tone and spirit of this epistle.    Neither, in the Apostolic times nor in our own, can we reduce all to the same type.    One aspect of the gospel is more outward, another more inward ; one seems to connect with the life of Christ, another with His death ; one with His birth, another with His coming again.    If we will not insist on determining the times and the seasons, or on knowing the manner how, all these different ways may lead us within the veil. The faith of modern times embraces many parts or truths ; yet we allow men, according to their individual character, to dwell on this truth, or that as more peculiarly appropriate to their nature.    The faith of the early Church was simpler and more progressive, pausing in the same way on a particular truth which the circumstances of the world or the Church brought before them. (*Prof. Jowett.*)    *Waiting :*—The figure is of a sentinel, who at night walks backwards and forwards, and is tired and faint, and longs for rest, and watches anxiously for the morning, when the guard will be relieved. Or it is of the watcher of the sick, who wearily passes the night in the sick room, where the tick of the clock and the groaning of the patient alternate and measure the long hours, and watches, as star after star rises above the horizon, for the morning star to appear. (*H. W. Beecher.*) *Believers kept waiting till death that men may witness their piety :*—Sometimes the sun seems to hang for a half-hour in the horizon, only just to show how glorious it can be.    The day is done ; the fervour of the shining is over, and the sun hangs golden—nay, redder than gold—in the west, making everything look unspeakably beautiful, with the rich effulgence which it sheds on every side.    So God seems to let some people, when their duty in this world is done, hang in the west, that men may look on them, and see how beautiful they are.    There are some hanging in the west now! (*Ibid.*)    *Joyfully awaiting Christ :*—It was an old woman who said—" Is He not a precious Saviour? so great and good, and willing to save all us poor sinners ! "    She was lying on a hard bed in the dreary infirmary-ward of a workhouse ; and the power of faith and love to create a happiness independent of circumstances came out with almost startling force in her answer to the inquiry, " You know Him then, and love Him ? "    " Yes ; I do know Him, and love Him : His presence makes a heaven of this room. If you heaped up my bed with gold and silver," she added ; " and if you could give me the queen's carriage and horses, and her palace and her garden, and all her beautiful flowers, and health and strength to enjoy it all, I would not take them, if they would hinder me from going home to my Saviour. They talk of the pains of dying : what will they be to me ? They will but hurry me to heaven and to Jesus." *Delivered from the wrath to come :*— I. THE AWFUL DESTRUCTION REFERRED TO. 1. The actual infliction of the Divine displeasure (Psa. xi. 6). Shut out—(1) From heaven. (2) From God. (3) Into miseries. (4) And torments. ·2. This wrath will respect body and soul (Matt. x. 28). 3. This intense fierceness of wrath is to come (Rom. ii. 5). 4. This punishment will be eternal (Mark ix. 44). II. A BLESSED LIBERATION DECLARED. 1. From the sentence of wrath (Rom. viii. 1). 2. From meetness to this wrath (Rom. vi. 14). 3. From the gloomy forebodings of wrath (1 John iv. 18). 4. From the possibility of wrath (Col. iii. 3). III. THE GLORIOUS DELIVERER ANNOUNCED, EVEN JESUS. 1. Meritoriously by Jesus Christ (Col. i. 14); 2. Instrumentally by His Word (John viii. 32); 3. Efficiently by His Spirit (Rom. viii. 14); 4. God will deliver us personally and eternally (2 Tim. iv. 8). (*T. B. Baker.*) *The wrath to come :*—Men in these times seem unwilling to hear of future punishment. Hell is no longer a word for ears polite. They talk as if "a certain class of preachers" invented hell and kept it burning to enforce their precepts. I was in Naples in 1884, the year that cholera was epidemic. The Neapolitans accused the physicians of bringing the cholera. The physicians predicted it ; they told the people that unless they cleaned up their city the scourge would come. They laid down rules and gave warning. So when the cholera came, the people thought the physicians brought it to intimidate them into washing themselves and keeping their backyards clean, so they threw stones at the physicians and drove them out of the city. These physicians had come to risk their lives for the ungrateful people who rejected them. Thus, when preachers begin to talk of the scourge which will follow sin, the people —that is, some of them—begin to think the preachers are in some way responsible for this scourge. The preachers are assailed as cruel, fanatical, behind the times, and all that. Our Lord is a Physician. He came and found the disease of sin and its fatal consequences here already. He did not bring them. He left His home to improve the sanitary condition of this world, to cleanse its filth. And in order to induce men to submit to His treatment, He warns them to flee from the wrath to come. (*R. S. Barrett.*) *The wrath to come :*—The most delightful and encouraging subject on which a sinner can fix his thoughts is the overflowing mercy of an offended God ; but he will also often be thinking of the awful justice of the Being from whom he has received it, and the fearfulness of that wrath from which it has rescued him. Thus a longing after the coming of the Saviour, and an expectation of heaven, will ever be connected with the recollection of danger escaped and wrath incurred. I. THE WRATH OF WHICH THE APOSTLE SPEAKS. 1. It is Divine wrath. Not the anger of a creature whose power is limited and whose duration is finite, but the displeasure of One who fills heaven and earth with His power, and eternity with His existence. 2. It is unmingled wrath ; that is—judgment without mercy, justice without the least mixture of goodness. "They shall drink of the wine of the wrath of God, which is poured out without mixture into the cup of His indignation." 3. It is provoked wrath. It was not the original inheritance of man. He who made us, loves us ; He visits us every hour with goodness, and sends us in His Gospel the freest and most gracious offers of reconciliation. But if we reject a salvation which cost Him the blood of His Son, we provoke Him to anger, and stir up His wrath. 4. It is accumulated wrath. Every repeated act of sin increases it, and will aggravate our misery in eternity. "After thy hardness and impenitent heart," says St. Paul, "thou treasurest up unto thyself wrath against the day of wrath and revelation of the righteous judgment of God." 5. It is future wrath. "Wrath to come," and when we have borne it millions of ages, it will still be "wrath to come," no nearer an end than it was at first, nor easier to be endured. It is eternal wrath, lasting as the holiness of Him who inflicts it, and the guilt of the sinner who bears it. II. THE WAY OF ESCAPE FROM THIS WRATH. The Apostle speaks of some who have actually escaped from it. 1. The deliverance from it is undeserved. It is true that they who have received it are a people who "have turned from idols to serve the living and true God ;" but what led them to choose His service ? No natural love. It was the power of the Word, accompanied by the Holy Ghost, which turned them. The deliverance, therefore, was not deserved by them, but was owing to the free and distinguishing grace of the very God whom they had long braved and hated. 2. Though undeserved, it is complete deliverance. "The wrath to come" can never touch those "whose iniquities are forgiven, and whose sins are covered." They are as perfectly delivered from wrath as though it had ceased to burn, or they had ceased to deserve it. 3. Hence the deliverance is an eternal deliverance. The salvation of all believers in Jesus is an eternal salvation, making a final separation between them and all possibility of condemnation. 4. The author of this deliverance. "Even Jesus." It is certain that man cannot be his own deliverer. "No man can redeem his brother, or give to God a ransom for him." Neither can the angels, though they "excel in strength," help him. The eternal Son, the sharer of the Father's own omnipotence, proposed Himself as the Mediator between heaven and earth, and arrested the sword of justice. "He bare our sins in His own body on the tree." And now, in consequence of His obedience unto death, "all that believe in Him are justified from all things;" their liability to punishment is done away, and done away for ever; they have "passed from death unto life." So that when "the Lord Jesus shall be revealed from heaven," they will lift up their heads with joy, and shout—"Lo! this is our God; we have waited for Him, and He will save us. This is the Lord; we have waited for Him; we will be glad and rejoice in His salvation!" (*C. Bradley, M.A.*) *The wrath—principle:*—Dr. Watts has left on record the fact that of all who have been led to a saving faith under his ministry, he could recall but one who had been first awakened by the amiable attributes of the Divine character. All the rest were first aroused by fear of the Divine anger. "The love of God," he said, "had been the suasive power, but the wrath of God had been the awakening power." The same succession of convictions in the order of time is confirmed by the history of conversions in the great revivals of the past. Before men discover in its saving power that "God is love," they discover in its condemning power that "God is a consuming fire." Dr. Bushnell has put this fact incisively. He says: "One of the things most needed in the recovery of men to God is this very thing—a more decisive manifestation of the wrath principle. Intimidation is the first means of grace. No bad mind is arrested by love and beauty till such time as it is balked in evil and put on ways of thoughtfulness. And nothing can be so effectual for this as a distinct apprehension of 'the wrath to come.'" There are of course exceptions to this rule. Wilberforce records that he never experienced a sense of the Divine anger till after he was persuaded to repentance by the love of Christ. But such cases are not relatively numerous in the histories of conversion.

---

## CHAPTER II.

VERS. 1, 2. **For yourselves, brethren, know our entrance in unto you, that it was not in vain.**—*Essential elements of success in preaching: Boldness:*—Outsiders testified of the success of the gospel; and the apostles could confidently appeal to the converts in confirmation of the report. "For yourselves," &c. Dr. Lillie observes: "Paul's entrance was no easy, random, careless matter—not at all an affair of rhetoric or ostentation—no holiday diversion or intellectual pastime; but a fact of the utmost gravity for him and for that renowned city—a crisis, an epoch in the history of both." We trace in their ministerial endeavours four essential elements that are ever found in all successful preaching—boldness, sincerity, gentleness, moral consistency. Consider, first. their boldness. I. THIS BOLDNESS MANIFESTED IN THE EARNEST DECLARATION OF THE TRUTH. "We are bold in our God," &c. 1. Bold in their conception of the Divine origin and vast scope of the gospel, and its adaptation to the wants of man, they were not less bold in its faithful proclamation. Their deep conviction of the supreme authority of the truth gave them unusual courage. We see the same spirit in Paul, when his fearless words roused the ire of Festus, shook the conscience of the thoughtless Felix, or swayed the heart of Agrippa. We see it in Elijah as he rebuked the sins of the wicked Ahab or threw the baffled priests of Baal into maddening hysteria—himself the while unmoved and confident. We see it conspicuously in Him whose burning words assailed every wrong, and who denounced the leaders of a corrupt Church as "serpents!" "generation of vipers!" 2. "With much contention"—amid much conflict and danger. This kind of preaching provoked opposition, and involved them in great inward struggles. The faithful messenger of God fears not the most violent assault from without: but the thought of the fatal issues to those who obstinately reject and fight against the gospel fills him with agonizing concern.

II. THIS BOLDNESS NO SUFFERING COULD DAUNT. "Even after that we had suffered before," &c. They had come fresh from a city where they had been cruelly outraged. But their sufferings only deepened their love for the gospel, and inflamed the passion to make it known. A German professor has lately made experiments with chalcedony, and other quartzose minerals, and he has demonstrated that when such stones are ground on large and rapidly revolving wheels, they exhibit a brilliant phosphorescent glow throughout their entire mass. So is it with the resolute worker. The more he is ground under the strong wheel of suffering and persecution, the more intensely will his character glow. III. THIS BOLDNESS WAS DIVINELY INSPIRED. "In our God." It was not presumption or bravado; but the calm, grand heroism of a profound faith in God. The prophet Jeremiah, in a moment of despondency, decided to "speak no more in the name of the Lord;" but when he could say, "The Lord is with me as a mighty terrible One," his courage returned, and he obeyed implicitly the Divine mandate—"Thou shalt go," &c. Similarly commissioned, Paul once exclaimed, "I can do all things through Christ which strengtheneth me." Endowed with the like spirit Luther uttered his noble protest at the Diet of Worms—"Here I stand; I cannot do otherwise; God help me!" Lessons: 1. Boldness is indispensable in attacking the evils of the age—not in the mass, but in detail. 2. Boldness acquired only by studious and prayerful familiarity with God and His message. (*G. Barlow.*)    *The true pulpit:*—I. ITS SUBLIME COURAGE. "We were bold in our God." True pulpit courage must not be confounded with that audacity, impudence, self-assurance, which, alas! is so prevalent. It is courage in God, and springs from—1. Love for God's character. Love is the soul of courage. Strong love absorbs all selfish fears and makes the soul heroic. Paul loved his God so strongly that he lost all selfish feelings in the passion. 2. Confidence in God's gospel. Paul knew that the gospel he had received and that he preached was not of men, but of God. No infidel argument could shake his faith in this. It was to him a subject beyond question and debate, settled amongst the immoveable facts of his own consciousness. Boldness in God is what the pulpit wants now. Some preachers speak as if they were bold in their theology, in their sect, in their own capacities; but Paul was "bold in God." He felt himself to be nothing. II. ITS TRANSCENDENT THEME. The glad tidings. 1. That God loves all men, although they are sinners. Nature shows that God loves all men as creatures; but the gospel alone reveals His love to sinners (John iii. 16). 2. That God's love for sinners is so great that He gave His only begotten Son. This is God's gospel; and what a transcendent theme for the preacher! This Paul preached: not theology, science, philosophy, metaphysical theories. (*D. Thomas, D.D.*)    *True courage* is cool and calm. The bravest of men have least of a brutal bullying insolence, and in the very time of danger are found the most serene and free. Rage, we know, can make a coward forget himself, and fight. But what is done in fury or anger can never be placed to the account of courage. (*Shaftesbury.*)    *Ministerial boldness:*—Archbishop Whately once said, when a friend asked him whether he did not feel nervous about preaching, that he dared not; for nervousness implied thoughts of oneself, when we ought only to be thinking of God's message. (*J. Hutchinson, D.D.*)    *A minister without boldness* is like a smooth file, a knife without an edge, a sentinel that is afraid to let off his gun. If men will be bold to sin, ministers must be bold to reprove. (*W. Gurnal.*)    *Influence of character:*— The daily influence of Christ-like ministers streams into the character of their people as the imponderable sunlight enters into the solid substance of vegetation. (*Boston Review.*)    *Christian devotion:*—Rev. Mr. Johnson, a Baptist missionary in China, relates this fact of a native convert who, when trying to persuade his countrymen to give up their idols and believe in Christ, was ridiculed and scorned, and at last pelted with mud and stones till his face was red with the blood that flowed from the cuts in his temples. Mr. Johnson meeting him said, "You have had bad treatment to-day." He smilingly replied, "They may kill me if they will love Jesus."    *A courageous preacher:*—Mr. Moody tells us that there was a celebrated preacher in one of the Southern States of America, who went to a place where they told him if he dared to speak they would rotten-egg him. But he went right on. He said he wanted to tell them a story. A man in Texas went to town and sold a drove of cattle; he put the money in his saddle-bags, got on his horse and started for home, his dog with him. He got tired after awhile, and laid down under a tree and went to sleep, laying the saddle-bags by him. After awhile he awoke, took up the bags, got on his horse and rode off. But his dog kept barking and running back, and would not go along with him and keep quiet. So he finally, in his anger, took out his revolver and shot the dog, and rode on. But the more he thought about what he had done, the more he was troubled. He turned his horse and rode back, and found that the dog had dragged himself along until he had reached the tree where he had slept. There he was, dying; but by his side was his master's bundle of money, which he had dropped and was going off without, and which his faithful dog had lost his life in trying to save. "Now," said the minister, "I am here like that dog, to tell you of the treasure you are losing. Rotten-egg me if you want to." But they didn't; they heard him gladly. *Not in vain :—* A young man was engaged in teaching a class of rather wild lads in a Sabbath school. He thought that he was not qualified to make any impression upon them, and got much discouraged. By the inducements of his fellow-teachers and super-intendent, he was prevailed upon to keep at the work for years, till at last he absolutely refused to continue it longer. Many years afterward an eminent missionary wrote home: "Is that gentleman who taught in the —— Sabbath school still living? If he is, please let him know that there is at least one living who dates his conversion to Christ from the lessons received in his class." So you see that, although the teacher gave up his work because he saw no fruit, yet the seed sown was not lost; one soul, if not more, was saved, and used as God's means for saving many others.

Vers. 3–6. **For our exhortation was not of deceit, nor of uncleanness, nor in guile.**—*Exhortation :*—The whole gospel preaching and message is so called, as permeated by, and living in, an atmosphere of gentle, soothing affection. Religion has been defined as "morality tinctured by emotion." Much more truly is the whole gospel a system "tinctured by emotion," *i.e.*, a *paraklesis*. Hence two different shades of meaning are blended in the word. As addressed to the careless, slothful, tempted, fallen, it is *exhortation ;* as addressed to the sad and seeking it is *solace* and comfort. It is the gospel exhortation, which is never without a certain soothing, sympathetic sweetness. The two senses of *paraklesis* exhortation and consolation, so easily passing into one another (ver. 11) are suggestive of the external state of the early Church, sorrowing amid the evils of the world, and needing as its first lesson to be comforted, and not less suggestive of the first lesson of the gospel to the individual soul of peace in believing. (*Prof. Jowett.*) *Essential elements of success in preaching : sincerity:*—This is no less essential than courage. As the mountain tarn reflects the clear light of the stars so the preacher reflects in his conduct the motives by which he is sustained. I. SINCERITY IN MOTIVE (ver. 3). The Apostle disclaims the harbouring of evil intentions. 1. In relation to God. "Not of deceit." Having received the truth from God and about God, he transmits it in all its integrity without error or imposture. 2. In relation to himself. "Not of uncleanness." Pure in his own affection and purpose, he preached a gospel that was pure in itself, in its tendency, and in its experienced results. 3. In relation to others. "Not in guile." He sought not to propagate the gospel by fraudulent wiles or false representations. He descended not to hypocrisy to catch men. "Hypocrites," says Bernard, "desire to seem, not to be good ; not to seem, but to be evil; they care not to follow or practice virtue, but to colour vice, by putting in it the painted complexion of virtue." The life of a man whose motives are sincere, will be transparent as the light. A certain king of Castile, who had only been too familiar with the duplicity of mankind, once arrogantly said, "When God made man, He left one capital defect : He ought to have set a window in his breast." The sincere man opens a window in his breast, by the whole tenor of his words and actions, so that his innermost thoughts are apparent. II. IN SPEECH. 1. They speak under a solemn sense of responsibility. "But as we were allowed," &c. (ver. 4). To their charge, as men tested and approved of God, was committed the precious treasure of the gospel; and conscious of its riches they were solicitous to distribute them in all faithfulness and sincerity. 2. They sought chiefly the Divine approval. "Not as pleasing men," &c. There is much in the gospel distasteful to the natural man—its humiliating exposure of our depravity and helplessness, its holiness, its mysteries, the unbending severity of its law, and the absolute character of its claims. The temptation is sometimes great to temper, and modify the truth to carnal prejudice, and sacrifice faithfulness to popularity. But the apostles risked everything, so that they secured the Divine approval. 3. They practised neither adulation nor deception. "For neither at any time used we flattering words," &c. (ver. 5). "Flattery," says Plutarch, "has been the ruin of most states." But alas! who can tell the souls it has for ever undone!

III. OF AIM (ver. 6). Seen—1. In the generous suppression of the authority with which they were armed. "When we might have been burdensome," &c. Whether in foregoing their legitimate claim of maintenance, or, as restraining the exhibition of the dignity and power of their apostleship as generally admitted—it was equally honourable to the pure and disinterested character of their highest aim. 2. In the absence of all selfish ambition. "Nor of men sought we glory." They could conscientiously aver—"we seek not yours but you." "I love a serious preacher," says Fénélon, "who speaks for my sake, and not for his own : who seeks my salvation and not his own glory." It is said of one of the ancient fathers that he would weep at the applause given to his discourses. "Would to God," said he, "they had rather gone away silent and thoughtful !" It is a sorry end to preach for mere ephemeral human praise. Such a man may sink into the grave with the touching lament of Grotius—"Alas ! I have lost my life in doing nothing with great labour !" Lessons—1. Sincerity in proclaiming the truth can be acquired only by a personal experience of its power. 2. Sincerity is deepened by a conscious Divine commission. 3. Sincerity is unmistakeably evidenced in word and deed. 4. Sincerity is satisfied only in aiming at the highest results in preaching. (*G. Barlow.*) *The gospel and its preachers :*—I. THE GOSPEL. 1. It belongs to God ; hence it is denominated, "the Gospel of God." He indeed was its author ; and because He is good, He bestows His gospel on men for their good. 2. It claims universal acceptance. If it is not received in the love of it, there is no other gospel for mankind ; it is the only star by which men can navigate the sea of life, and securely gain the shores of eternity. 3. It is benedictive in its influence. II. THE PREACHERS OF THE GOSPEL. 1. They were men and not angels. Angels know nothing experimentally of human failings and regrets—human difficulties and trials, therefore are incompetent to preach the gospel. It must be preached by such men as Paul and Silas—"men of like passions with ourselves." They are on the same footing with the Thessalonians and all of humankind. 2. They were holy men. In the Divine order of things the blessing of conversion precedes the call to the ministry as surely as the morning star precedes the orb of day. In other words—men are not preachers first and then true Christians, but true Christians and then preachers. 3. They were sincere and bold. They had suffered acutely for the gospel at Philippi, had been shamefully illtreated by its citizens ; but many waters could neither quench their love for the gospel nor for the souls the gospel could save. So they preached it at Thessalonica with the same burning zeal they had done at Philippi. (*J. Cumming, D.D.*) *St. Paul's ministry*—Described. I. NEGATIVELY. 1. Not of deceit. The word thus translated, as distinguished from "guile," denotes mental error without respect to any bad design (see Prov. xiv. 8). It was no false theory, wild vagary, empty speculation, that Paul preached. 2. Not of uncleanness. To understand by this fraud or imposture would not only introduce needless tautology, but would interfere with the acknowledged ethical sense of the word, which is bad morals, especially sensuality. The Apostle affirms that he and his associates did not preach a doctrine which warranted or connived at vice, and did not seek, by preaching, to gratify any sensual passions of their own. The contrary character is exemplified in Jezebel (Rev. ii. 20), and in the persons described in 2 Pet. ii. ; Jude iv. 10-13, 16-19. 3. Not in guile. They had not acted the part of imposters or hypocrites. II. POSITIVELY. 1. Paul and Silas were—(1) "Allowed of God"—a term denoting a much stronger idea than that of bare permission, viz., distinct choice or positive approbation. (2) "To be put in trust with the gospel," a phrase which not only represents their actual admission to the ministerial office, but sets forth their responsibility as ministers. 2. They spoke in a manner corresponding to the twofold fact of their vocation by God and their responsibility to Him, "Not as pleasing men," &c. (1) They neither acknowledged nor applied what was pleasing to men as a safe and satisfactory standard by which to regulate their ministerial conduct. (2) They recognized such a standard in what was pleasing to God. They saw cause for special vigilance, and for habitual reference to Him in the fact that "He searcheth the heart and trieth the reins," and was intimately acquainted with their secret thoughts and feelings. (3) Prompted by such considerations they asked of Him, "What wilt Thou have me to do." (*A. S. Patterson, D.D.*) *Deceit an unsafe element in moral building :*—It is difficult to maintain falsehood. When the materials of a building are solid blocks of stone, very rude architecture will suffice ; but a structure of rotten materials needs the most careful adjustment in order to make it stand. (*Archbishop Whately.*)

*Advantages sometimes acquired by guile :*—Advantages may sometimes be acquired by craft. A fox got into a hen-roost one night, and so gorged himself that he could not make his exit through the narrow hole by which he entered. So he lay down pretending to be dead when the hen-wife came to look for her fowls. Thinking reynard was really dead, in her vexation for the loss of her hens, she took him by his brush and threw him outside, when he scampered off. Sixtus, Pope of Rome, owed his election to his cleverly counterfeiting sickness and old age ; so he got most votes, as other cardinals, who probably hoped to be pope, thought he would soon die. (*H. K. Burton.*) **But as we were allowed of God to be put in trust with the gospel.** I. What does the word "allowed" mean? The Greek word means—1. To try. 2. To approve. 3. To see fit. As in Rom. i. 25, the heathen, it is said, did not like to retain God in their knowledge, *i.e.,* they did not see fit to do it. Allowed does not mean to judge fit, in the sense that Paul was made a minister on account of his own merits, nor on the ground of the foresight of what he would be, but it was an act of God's sovereign grace. So in the account of his conversion (1 Tim. ii. 13) he gives thanks to Christ. In 1 Cor. vii. 25, he says he had obtained mercy to be found faithful. He regarded his being put in the ministry as a great and undeserved mercy. II. What is the gospel? The glad news of salvation revealed in the Scriptures. It is not a code of morals, nor a cultus, nor a life ; it is the system of doctrines concerning God and man and Christ. It is called the wisdom of God, so contrasted with the wisdom of men, *i.e.,* what God has revealed as opposed to what reason teaches. Hence to be put in trust with the gospel means to be a steward of the mysteries, *i.e.,* the truths revealed by God. Two things are included in the gospel : the truth and its proclamation. The gospel is a report—something heard. III. In what sense is the gospel a trust. Two things are included in a trust or two duties of a trustee. 1. The safe custody of what is committed to his care. 2. Right administration. As to the first, it must be preserved in safety and preserved from deterioration. If gold is committed to a man, he must not deposit it in an insecure place ; he must defend and preserve it. He can't substitute worthless paper for it. The gospel is the most precious treasure, far more so than gold or power. The minister is bound to preserve it, and not substitute the worthless products of his own brain for it. He must use it, not keep it hid in a napkin. He must use it for the purpose for which it is designed, not for his own advantage. Paul says of himself, that he acted—(1) Not as pleasing men, but God. (2) Not using flattery. (3) Not covetously. (4) Not seeking glory of men. The guilt of an unfaithful trustee is great. His doom dreadful. The reward and blessedness of a faithful minister the greatest conceivable. (*C. Hodge, D.D.*) *The Christian ministry :*—I. Its privilege—" allowed of God." II. Its sublime responsibility—" put in trust." III. Its faithful administration—" even so we speak." IV. Its awful scrutiny—" God which trieth the hearts." (*W. Bengo Collyer, D.D.*) I. The Apostle's reasons for preaching the gospel. 1. He was a steward, "put in trust with the gospel." It was therefore not the Gospel of Paul, but the Gospel of God. All ministers of it have a great honour put upon them and trust committed to them. They must not dare to corrupt the pure Word of God, but diligently make use of what is intrusted with them, knowing they will be called to give an account of it. 2. His design was to please God and not man. God is a God of truth, and requireth truth in the inward parts. The gospel is not accommodated to the vain fancies and lusts of men ; but, on the contrary, it was designed for the mortifying their corrupt affections, and delivering them from the power of fancy, that they might be brought under the power of faith. 3. He acted under the consideration of God's omniscience. This is indeed the great motive to sincerity—to consider God not only seeth all that we do, but knoweth our thoughts afar off, and searcheth the heart ; and it is from God that we must receive our reward. II. The evidences of the Apostle's sincerity. 1. He avoided flattery. He and his fellow-labourers preached Christ and Him crucified, and did not aim to gain an interest in men's affections for themselves, by glorying, and fawning, and wheedling them : they were far from that. Nor did they flatter men in their sins, or tell them that if they would be of their party, they might live as they listed. They did not build them up with vain hopes, nor indulge them in any evil work or way, promising them life, and so daubing with untempered mortar. 2. He avoided covetousness. He did not make the ministry a cloak or covering for this carnal desire, as God was witness. He would not enrich himself by preaching the gospel ; so far from that, he did not burden them for bread. He did not out in anywise like the false apostles, who "through covetousness with vain words made merchandise " of the people. 3. He avoided ambition and vain-glory. He neither expected people's purses nor their caps, neither to be caressed or adored by them, and called rabbi. He might have used greater authority as an apostle, and expected greater esteem, and demanded maintenance; but some might perhaps have thought all this too great a burden for them to bear, and hence he avoided all mention of such things. He thought ever of his Divine Lord, and seldom of himself. (*R. Fergusson.*) *The minister's trust, faithfulness, and trials :*—I. The minister's trust. 1. Its basis. The Divine permission—" allowed of God." This is the minister's prerogative and authority. 2. Its subject—the gospel. (1) In its wonderful disclosures of the grace of God. (2) In its operative power upon the heart and life. (3) In its presentation of the Person and work of Christ. 3. Its object—the salvation, edification, comfort, and eternal blessedness of men. II. The minister's faithfulness. 1. The minister who is conscious of his responsibility speaks as one who will have to render an account of his stewardship, thoughtfully, cautiously, humbly, prayerfully, boldly. 2. This faithfulness is expressed in the singleness and sacredness of its object. "Not as pleasing men," &c. (1 Cor. ii. 1–5). 3. This singleness of purpose in pleasing God rather than man is also a test of our fidelity. The faithful minister is content to labour without human applause. III. The minister's trials. 1. He is subject not only to those trials which are common to all men, but to those which are peculiar to his office : discouragement, anxiety for souls, doubts as to past labours, a sense of his unworthiness in His sight who trieth the heart. 2. But God trieth the heart for wise and benevolent ends—(1) To make us purer. (2) More sympathetic. (3) More efficient. (*W. D. Horwood, M.A.*) *Trustees for God:*—I. The trustees. 1. Christian ministers are trustees for God. They have a charge to keep other than that which is common to Christians. It matters little by what channel the Great Head of the Church has communicated His will to the individual ; it is enough that he is " allowed of God." 2. A trustee is chosen as being a man of character, one who can be relied upon to administer his trust fairly. Generally he is a friend chosen because of his superior qualifications. And, whatever may be said about truth being independent of the preacher, yet as light is tinged and refracted by the window through which it passes, so it is impossible to separate a man from the system he advocates. It is difficult to believe that to be good which expresses the feelings of a bad man. " Take heed unto thyself and unto the doctrine." Self modifies doctrine. Men universally recognize this, and the first necessity of success is to give no occasion for slanderous lies. That which is culpable in an ordinary Christian is doubly so in a minister. 3. But while as trustees we do well to look to ourselves, yet that does not mean that we should be burdened with the sense of our own importance. It has been the reproach of priests in all ages that they have been more anxious to magnify than to use their office. Without falling back on the exploded fallacy of apostolical succession we may find a platform sufficiently strong and broad in the priceless value of what has been committed to our trust. The trustee of a prince, heir to an ancient throne, is necessarily charged with more responsibility than a homeless wanderer. II. Their trust. That one word " Gospel " suggests the nature of it. Not simply the proclamation of a sovereign to his subjects, though that would involve a heavy responsibility; but the revelation of the very nature of Deity, and how that nature has wrought his working for the salvation of men. 1. Even with the Bible in their hands, and the multiplied helps to its study, it is possible for ministers to under-rate its importance, and to allow the gospel to be only one among many agencies by which God is renewing the heart of mankind. There is a strong tendency among liberal thinkers to extol what is good in each of the religions of the world, and to conceal the defects which are everywhere visible. But we have a religion which has no defects, and is perfectly adapted to every man, and to make him wiser, nobler, and happier; and which God has designed as the one religion for man. To deal tenderly with false religions is to imperil our trust. 2. Without any intention of substituting another gospel for that of the New Testament, it is possible to so place the emphasis in teaching as to seriously weaken the force of our message ; possible so to present Divine love and truth as to add to the weight of the many burdens which almost crush humanity. Any presentation of this solemn trust which fails to strengthen faith, hope, and love, must necessarily be defective. If our gospel be one of perpetual condemnation, destroying the old and not building up the new, it is not in sympathy with Him who came not to condemn but to save, and will win no confidence, and stir no enthusiasm. III. The administration of this trust. 1. It is required of a steward that he be found faithful. (1) To be faithful costs something. Faithfulness to a congregation considered as a unit requires self-crucifixion, but faithfulness towards individuals, and to the convictions created by the study of Divine truth much more. (2) But faithfulness is not that ill-natured determination to assert oneself and one's own views simply because they are our own, and in the spirit of self-defence. It does not mean obstinate adherence to one mode of action, when that method has lost its adaptability, much less the candidating for a cheap martyrdom, by offensively pushing into the forefront unwelcome truths at any cost. We have to be faithful to love as well as to logic. 2. The danger of most is that they are called to administer a trust of which they have no adequate appreciation. Conceive of a man put in trust of an estate rich in gold and precious stones, and allowing an absolute lease of it for the value of the mere timber on it. What an outcry there would be against his intellectual and moral unfitness! Our peril is lest, overcome by the spirit of the age, we should take too great heed to all and everything that is said against the gospel, and fail to appreciate the force of the argument which comes from eighteen centuries of positive evidence. 3. Unwittingly we may be helping into popularity men and their theories whose influence but for us would be confined within a very narrow area. Nine out of every ten men in our congregations know nothing of these, and the tenth man who knows something is likely to be more advantaged by the preaching of positive truth than by mere controversy. When an epidemic is abroad, the men of robust health are least in danger of infection, and our aim should be to get and keep men in a state of robust moral health, by feeding them with the Bread of Life. 4. When men seem disposed to break away from our influence we ought to search our hearts and methods, and everything which concerns us and our ministry, and see if there be anything in the spirit of our action which accounts for such restlessness. We ought to ask ourselves whether our administration of our trust be right, or whether we are the mere teachers of a science of religion, which informs the mind, but leaves the heart unmoved; whether there be not some vital element in the gospel which we have largely left out, which would have roused men to defend a treasure so valuable. Ministers not seldom so present the truth as to convince without persuading. We have knocked men down by the force of argument, and despoiled them without giving them anything in return. 5. Instead of patiently and faithfully administering our trust, we are apt to fall into the error of supposing that men know all that is knowable of Scriptural truth, and thus work outside the facts and truths of the gospel. (*Reuen Thomas, D.D.*) *Gospel trustees:*—I. THE PRECIOUSNESS OF THE GOSPEL. It is precious because—1. It reveals God. (1) Who all men are more or less blindly groping after. (2) As a Father infinitely wise and good. 2. It offers salvation—(1) From the penalty of sin. (2) From the power of sin. 3. It breathes hope into every man. II. IT HAS BEEN ENTRUSTED TO US IN ORDER THAT BY ITS MEANS WE MIGHT SAVE OUR FELLOW-MEN. How great is our responsibility to let it speak in our words and deeds! (*W. Birch.*) **Not as pleasing men but God.**—This should be the supreme and controlling purpose of life. I. To PLEASE GOD IS POSSIBLE, because—1. He has revealed what will please Him: His will in His Word. 2. We know this or may learn it. 3. His Spirit will help us if we seek His aid. II. To PLEASE MAN IS IMPOSSIBLE. 1. As it is impossible to please all men, so it is almost as impossible to please one. The same man is different at different times. What may please him to-day may displease him to-morrow. 2. God has failed to please man even more signally than man himself. Chiefly see how He failed when He came in the likeness of man that He might purify him and fit him for heaven. 3. By seeking to please men instead of God, or more than God, men must doom the world to perpetual darkness and stationariness, or rather, as this is not possible, to sure retrogression and decay. How blessed, then, is the truth that it is easier to please God than man! (*E. Mellor, D.D.*) *The true missionary spirit:*—Brave Paul! He spoke the Word, whether sinners would hear or not, whether men were converted or not. If it pleased God he was content. Just like that grand man who kept working away in isolation in the heart of China, and for years saw no conversion. A lady said to him, "What good are you doing in China, Mr. Burns?" To which he replied, "Madam, I did not go to China to convert the Chinese, I went to glorify God." He went to serve and please his Master. I was asked to examine a young man who wanted to give up his business and go to Africa as a missionary. I asked him, "What is your motive in wanting to take this step? Suppose you go to the heart of Africa, and, seeing thousands bowing down before their idols and refusing to hear of Christ, what would you do?" He replied, "I'd just keep pegging away." That is the right spirit of service: to keep pegging away for the Master, not to please the society, not to have a large place on the statistics, not to have a great following, but to please God. If we go forth to any service according to the will of God, and only to please Him, He will bless us in our souls, and in the end give us to see His power in the salvation of sinners. (*G. C. Needham.*) *An unfaithful preacher :*—We were sitting under the shade of an oak-tree comparing notes and conferring with one another as to the best methods of service, especially in reference to effective preaching. "I always write my sermons," said my friend, "and then carefully revise them, so that, if anything is written calculated to offend any of my hearers, I may at once erase it." This was said by a young clergyman, who was evidently anxious to make his mark as a preacher. Desirous to know that I heard correctly, I replied, "Do you mean that forcible statements, either of your own writing or from Scripture, concerning sin and the terrors of the judgment to come, are either toned down or avoided?" "Yes," was the reply; "if I think they will offend any one I do so." I fear this candid testimony indicates the reason why so many ministers are powerless amongst their fellows. "The fear of man bringeth a snare indeed." (*Henry Varley.*) *The danger of popularity :*—To one who warned him (Whitefield) to beware of the evils of popularity he replied, "I thank you heartily. May God reward you for watching over my soul ; and as to what my enemies say against me, I know worse things of myself than they can say concerning me." "I bless God for my stripping seasons," he would say; "nothing sets a person so much out of the devil's reach as humility." (*J. R. Andrews.*) *Displeasing men :*—You know the anecdote of Louis and Massilon. After Massilon had preached rather an agitating sermon, I suppose, Louis sent for him. "Massilon," said he, "you have offended me." "That is what I wished to do, sire," said the preacher. And we would not give much for a minister who did not offend two-thirds of his congregation at times—arouse them up—smash against the conscience of the bigot, and baulk party prejudices, and touch the secret sin, which, if they do not confess, they still feel. *Tried by God :*—Some things, if they be tried once, they are tried for ever ; if we try gold, it will ever be as good as we found it, unless we alter it ; as we find it, so it will continue to be. But try the heart of man this day, and come again the next, and you may find it in a different condition; to-day believing, tomorrow unbelieving ; to-day humble, to-morrow proud ; to-day meek, to-morrow passionate ; to-day lively and enlarged, to-morrow dead and straightened;—pure gold to-day, to-morrow exceeding drossy. As it is with the pulse of a sick man, it varies every quarter of an hour, therefore the physician tries his pulse every time he comes, because his disease alters the state of his body : so it is with the distempered condition of man's spirit. God having tried our pulse, the state of our spirit, by crosses, or by mercies, this day, next day He tries us too, and the third day He tries us again, and so keep us in continual trials, because we are continually varying. Our comfort is, that there is a time coming, when God will establish our souls in such a spiritual and heavenly frame, so that He will need to try us no more. (*J. Caryl.*) *Disregarding the slanders of men :*—John Wesley once stood out very nobly in disregarding the eyes of men so long as he stood acquitted in the sight of God. Among his many persecutions are to be numbered the falling back of former friends, including his wife. These turned against him, and published many spiteful things, even defaming his character in a shocking manner. Brother Charles hastened off in alarm and indignation to inquire what defence Brother John would set up. There was no time to lose ! The eyes of the world were upon him, and God's enemies and his own would be glad to make capital out of so contemptible a business ! What was Charles's surprise to find that John was resolved on doing simply nothing ! The great preacher was calm and comfortable in mind, being entirely free from any concern for the future. Why should he be perplexed when he had entrusted God with his all—even with his reputation? None are so safe as those whose characters are in God's keeping. Such often consider that they dishonour God by setting up puny defences of their own against the cavils of the wicked. They think more of that one eye of God which is ever looking upon them, than of the eyes of men. **For neither at any time used we flattering words.**—*The mean between flattery and severity :*—Paul avoided the extremes alike of obsequiousness and churlishness. The man whose independence forbade him to use flattering words was yet gentle enough in persuading the Thessalonians to embrace and make progress in the truth. And he who would be truly useful must strike this golden

mean as we are warned by the following fable: A chameleon once met a porcupine, and complained that he had taken great pains to make friends with everybody; but, strange to say, he had entirely failed, and could not now be sure that
he had a friend in the world. "And by what means," said the porcupine, "have
you sought to make friends?" "By flattery," said the chameleon. "I have
adapted myself to all I have met; humoured the follies and foibles of every one. In
order to make people believe I liked them, I have imitated their manners, as if I
considered them models of perfection. So far have I gone in this that it has become a habit with me; and now my very skin takes the hue and complexion of the
thing that happens to be nearest. Yet all this has been in vain; for everybody
calls me a turncoat, and I am generally considered selfish, hypocritical, and base!"
"And no doubt you deserve all this," said the porcupine. "I have taken a different
course; but I must confess that I have as few friends as you. I adopted the rule
to resent every encroachment upon my dignity. I would allow no one even to
touch me, without sticking into him one of my sharp quills. I determined to take
care of number one; and the result has been that while I have vindicated my rights,
I have created a universal dislike. I am called 'Old Touch-me-not,' and if I am
not as much despised I am even more disliked than you, Sir Chameleon." *Flattery
discouraged:*—One of the first acts performed by George III., after his accession to
the throne, was to issue an order prohibiting any of the clergy who should be called
to preach before him from paying him any compliment in their discourses. His
Majesty was lead to this from the fulsome adulation which Dr. Thomas Wilson,
Prebendary of Westminster, thought proper to deliver in the Chapel Royal, and for
which, instead of thanks, he received from his royal auditor a pointed reprimand,
his Majesty observing, "that he came to the chapel to hear the praises of God, and
not his own." This circumstance operated wonderfully on the reverend orator, as
from that moment he became a flaming patriot. The Doctor took part with Wilkes,
was made liveryman of the Joiner's Company, and lavished large sums upon Mrs.
Macaulay, the Republican historian, in whose honour he caused a marble statue to
be erected in his church at Walbrook, though before he died he caused it to be removed, not indeed so much from a sense of the impropriety of the thing, as out of
resentment to the lady, who had displeased him by her marriage. *Flattering
words:*—"I resolve," said Bishop Beveridge, "never to speak of a man's virtues
before his face; nor of his faults behind his back;" a golden rule! the observation
of which would, at one stroke, banish flattery and defamation from the earth. (*Bp.
Horne.*) "*Flattery* is false money, which would not be current were it not for our
vanity." (*La Rochefoucauld.*) **Nor a cloke of covetousness.**—*Sin cloaked:*—
The word "cloke" here is very significant. In this fallen world of ours there
are some sins which men may even glory in—many the indulgence of which
entails little or no shame. But this sin of covetousness is one which no
man will ever dream of boasting of. Men, while they indulge it, always
try to hide it. As Bishop Sanderson says, "No man will *profess* himself covetous,
be he never so wretchedly sordid within; but he will for very shame cast as
handsome a cloak as he can over it—frugality, good husbandry, providence—
some cloak or other to hide the filthiness of it from the sight of others. But
filthy it is still, be it cloaked never so honestly. God abhorreth it as a filthy
thing (Psa. x. 3). It appears, then, that this covetousness, however often it
may evince its presence among men, must have its cloke or mask. Were it
at once and invariably to rythe in its real colours, even the children of the world
would not endure it. It would be loathsome. But the Apostle adds, "God is witness" (Rom. i. 9; 2 Cor. i. 23; Phil. i. 8). In reference to the language of flattery,
he says, "as ye know." Man can judge thereon. Hence he appeals to his
readers. They themselves were good enough judges as to whether he had ever
flattered them. But it is otherwise with covetousness and its mask. "Neither man
nor angel can discern hypocrisy, the only evil that walks invisible, except to God
alone. By His permissive will through heaven to earth." In regard to it—the
hypocrisy of covetousness—therefore, Paul lays bare his heart before the all-seeing
eye. (*J. Hutchison, D.D.*) *Unmercenary motives:*—"When I gave up my business
sixteen years ago, after three months of the severest struggle of my life, whether I
should go for dollars and cents or for souls, from that day to this I have no more
lived for money than I have lived for water. My friends have blamed me because
I have not laid aside something for my family. Some of them insisted upon my
wife having some money, and they bought her a home in the country, and the
rumour is that it cost 30,000 dols., and 30,000 dols. to furnish it. The home cost

3.500 dols., and there have been some improvements, and the furniture and every-thing cost 10,000 dols. It belongs to my wife and children. My father died at the early age of forty-one, and if I died to-morrow there will be a roof over the heads of my wife and children. I have been offered 500 dollars to lecture, when I might talk an hour, and then go to a comfortable hotel; but as it is now, I work at the Tabernacle all day, and talk till midnight with inquirers, and when I am done have hardly strength enough left to go to my room. The royalty on the hymn-books amounted last year to 68,000 dollars, but it all went to three trustees, and not one dollar came into the hands of Mr. Sankey or myself. It belongs to us as much as the income of your business belongs to you but we give it up. We do not want one dollar of your money in Boston. Give it to the Lord as long as you please. I would rather live on a crust of bread than have people think we came for your money. If any young man here wants to go into the work of the Lord for money, I advise him not to do it. Now, I do not want any one to go off and say that we preach for nothing, for we do not. We preach for souls, and the Lord takes care of us. I never have known what it is to want money in the sixteen years I have been at work for Him. The Lord has taken good care of me, and I have not known what it is to want." (*D. L. Moody.*) **Nor of men sought we glory.**—Why should the Apostle so repeatedly repudiate the im-putation that he sought glory of men? He was one of those who instinctively knew the impression produced by his character and conduct on the hearts of others. What was the motive of this " vain babbler " would be a common topic of conversation in the cities at which he preached. "To get money; to make himself somebody," would be the ordinary solution. Against this the Apostle protests. His whole life and conversation were a disproof of it. It may have been that he was aware also of something in his manner which might have suggested such a thought. It was not good for him to glory, and yet he sometimes spoke as a fool. Rightly understood, this glorying was but an elevation of the soul to God and Christ, or at worst the assertion of himself in moments of depression or ill-treatment, but to others he might have been conscious that it must have seemed a weakness, and may have been made a ground of the imputation of his adversaries. (*Prof. Jowett.*) *Glory claimed for God alone :*—Cromwell in announcing the victory at Naseby to the Speaker of the House of Commons, added, "Sir, this is none other but the hand of God, and to Him alone give the glory wherein none are to share with Him. (*C. E. Little.*) *Emptiness of worldly glory :*—When Henry Martyn went in for and obtained the high distinction of senior wrangler at Cambridge, his mind was kept, he tells us, in a state of calmness by the recollections of a sermon he had heard from the text, " Seekest thou great things for thyself, seek them not, saith the Lord." James Brainerd Taylor was announced as being Number One in the class of students at college. The emptiness of honours struck him as it had done Henry Martyn. " What are honours ? " he said. " What is fame ? These are not my God." In such a spirit, the soul, while using honours to God's glory, is freed from that vexation of spirit which chafes some men of the world in high life, because a few inches of riband have been bestowed upon a favoured rival. How touching, we may add, it is to see the vain pursuit of human ambition acknowledge its emptiness when gratified. Madame Maintenon, when elevated to the throne of France as wife of Louis XIV., wrote to her friend Madame de la Mainford: " Do you not see that I am dying with melancholy, in a height of fortune which my imagination could scarcely have con-ceived ? " When sick, too, of high society, the wife of Thomas Carlyle wrote to her gifted husband: " Ah! if we had been left in the sphere of life we belonged to, how much better it would have been for both of us ! " (*Sunday at Home.*) *All glory to God:*—Said a converted Hindoo, addressing a number of his countrymen, "I am by birth a man of low and despised caste—and yet God has called me not only to know His gospel, but to teach it to others. Do you know why He did so? I will tell you. If God had selected one of you learned Brahmins, and made you His preacher, and you were successful in winning converts, the bystanders would have said, 'It is the amazing learning of the Brahmin, the Brahmin's influence, the Brahmin's great weight of character that has done this;' but now, when hearers are convinced and brought to the truth by my instrumentality, nobody thinks of the preacher, and God gets all the glory." **When we might have been burdensome as the apostles of Christ.**—This has been referred in different senses either to what precedes or to what follows. In the first case the sense would be, although we might have been oppressive to you with our glorying and claims. But even though the words be thus humoured, the antithesis is not quite sound. Without wholly losing sight of what has preceded, it is better to connect them with what follows. The Apostle means to say that he might have oppressed them with apostolic claims and pretensions. He might have commanded where he entreated; he might have "come to them with a rod," and he came to them "in love and in the spirit of meekness" (1 Cor. iv. 21); he might have claimed the right of support from them as an apostle of Christ, and he waives it for their sake (comp. 1 Cor. ix.). It is true that this last point is not referred to until ver. 9. But nothing is more in the Apostle's manner than to drop a thought and then resume it. (*Prof. Jowett.*) *Labour of love :*—Sixteen years ago a godly man and his wife were sent out to evangelize these then heathen people (Sambaina, a remote place in Madagascar); and the people hated them, and for long they would not listen. They broke into their house at night again and again, and threatened to burn them out; but they would not go away, but quietly and lovingly waited and prayed and worked. By and by the contributions from Ambòhipòtsy, from the Society on which these good people depended, were completely dried up. And when the heathen people heard that they rejoiced, for "now at last they will go," they said. But they did not go, but held on to their work; and they are there yet, working "all for love and nothing for reward." And God has blessed their work and raised many helpers and spiritual children for them there. "The wilderness and solitary places are glad because of them;" and some of those who persecuted them at the first told me the story with tears standing on their faces. . . . On the Sunday a large congregation filled their new chapel. (*W. Montgomery.*)

Vers. 7, 8. **But were gentle among you, even as a nurse cherisheth her children.** —*The nurse--mother :*—Were the person here meant only the stranger to whom a feeble mother, or, when the mother is no more, the sad and stricken father, entrusts their little one, still the image would express the ideas of kindness and care. But the pronoun "her own" (ἑαυτῆς) clearly shows that the picture in the apostle's eye is that of the mother herself nursing her tender offspring. And oh! what a love is hers!—how deep, how mild, how strong, how practical! Who, from his observation of the world, and from his own experience—in other stages, haply, than that of infancy—does not associate with the name of mother the idea of a gentleness the gentlest that ever, in this low world, takes up its home in a human voice, a human hand, a human heart? And what "man of woman born" may not catch the meaning, and feel the force, of the prophet's words—"As one whom his mother comforteth"? (*A. S. Patterson, D.D.*) *Essential elements of success in preaching :* *Gentleness :*—There is a power in gentleness to subdue the mightiest opposition, and to triumph over the most gigantic difficulties. The gentle rays of the sun melt the ponderous iceberg more speedily than the rolling billows of an angry ocean; the silent action of the atmosphere wastes the rock which remains immovable under the strokes of the heaviest weapon. A look from Moses vanquished the calf-idolatry of the Israelites which the fluent eloquence of Aaron had been powerless to resist; a calm, quiet word from Jesus paralyzed with fear the band of soldiers who came to arrest Him in Gethsemane. True gentleness is never weak. It is the tough, indestructible material out of which is formed the hero and the martyr. This quality was conspicuous in the preachers at Thessalonica. I. It was the gentleness of patient endurance. 1. It enabled them to bear the insult and outrage of their enemies. Their preaching roused violent opposition. They retaliated by praying for their persecutors. Against physical force they fought with moral weapons; and this attitude had a powerful influence on their adversaries. The modern preacher can adopt no better method. The offence of the Cross still stirs the enmity of the carnal mind. "And the servant of the Lord must not strive," &c. The power of a man is seen, not so much in what he can do as in what he can endure. It is only the Christian spirit that unites the utmost gentleness with the utmost strength. 2. It enabled them to bear with the weakness and imperfections of their converts— "As a nursing mother cherisheth her own children." They watched over them with the tenderest assiduity, instructed them with the most disinterested solicitude, accommodated themselves to their infant standpoint, with parental devotion. In order to successful teaching, in spiritual as in secular subjects, we must study the child-nature. Take into account the influence of surroundings, early prejudices, capacity, temperament. See this illustrated in the Divine treatment of Israel under Moses, &c., and the intercourse of Jesus with the disciples. II. It was the gentleness of self-sacrificing love (ver. 8). 1. Their gentleness arose from a genuine love of souls. "Because ye were dear." Love is the power of the preacher. After this he toils with increasing earnestness as the years speed on ; and it is the grace that comes latest into the soul. No amount of scholarship, exposition, or eloquence can atone for the absence of love. The fables of the ancients tell us of Amphion, who, with the music of his lyre, drew after him the huge stones with which the walls of Thebes were built ; and of Orpheus, who, by his skill on the harp, could stay the course of rivers and tame the wildest animals. These are but exaggerated examples of the charm of love. " I have always been afraid," said a devoted young minister, " of driving my people away from the Saviour. I would rather err on the side of drawing them." John Fletcher once said, "Love, continual, universal, ardent love, is the soul of all the labour of a minister." 2. The intensity of their love awoke a spirit of voluntary self-sacrifice. "So being affectionately desirous of you, we were willing," &c. To accomplish the salvation of their hearers they were willing to surrender life itself. This was the temper of the Divine Preacher, who " came not to be ministered unto," &c. A similar spirit imbued the apostle when he met the weeping elders of Ephesus. The love of science nerves the voyager to brave the dangers of the Arctic ice, amid which many have found a crystal tomb ; but a nobler love inspires the breast of the humble worker who cheerfully sacrifices all this world holds dear, to rescue men from woe. Lessons : 1. That gentleness is a power, not only in patient endurance, but also in enterprising action. 2. That gentleness is indispensable to effectiveness, either in warning or reproof. It succeeds where a rigid austerity fails. 3. That gentleness is fostered and regulated by a deep, self-sacrificing love. (*G. Barlow.*) *Ministerial work and character* (text in conjunction with vers. 1–11) :—I. THE TRUST REPOSED IN THE MINISTER OF CHRIST (ver. 4). Other trusts are temporary and inconsiderable ; this unbounded in its consequences and spiritual in its effects. In stating the doctrines committed to him by this trust, the minister has—1. To prepare for the gospel by teaching men their guilt and condemnation as sinners, their accountability to God, and their impotency to save themselves. 2. To tell what is properly the gospel he must explain that salvation begins in the purpose and love of God the Father, is wrought out by the incarnation and obedience unto death of God the Son, and is communicated and applied by God the Holy Ghost. 3. To show the effect of the gospel (vers. 11, 12). II. THE MANNER IN WHICH THE MINISTRY OF THE GOSPEL IS TO BE DISCHARGED. Besides the announcement of doctrines, much depends on the spirit in which they are announced. 1. Fidelity (vers. 2–5) in the discharge of a trust is the primary quality, without which subsidiary qualities do not deserve the name of virtues. The minister must not aim at pleasing men, but God. Heathen priests and false apostles were notoriously guilty of guile, deceit, impurity. To gain their ends they flattered men and concealed what was displeasing. So, alas! some professed ministers of Christ hide some part of the truth, soften the declarations of God's anger against sin, weaken, if they do not deny, the doctrines of the gospel, pass slightly over repentance, regeneration, separation from the world, &c. 2. Disinterestedness (vers. 5, 6). "Filthy lucre" is the term Scripture employs for appetite for gain in the minister of Christ. He has a right to demand that, preaching the gospel, he should live of the gospel ; but the spirit of self-denial which willingly yields its strict rights, and is careful not to appear to drive a trade under the cloak of religion, and "seeks not yours, but you," is ever the distinguishing mark of the true minister. 3. Humility (ver. 6). The man that courts popularity, that frames his doctrines to the fashion of the day or the taste of his hearers, that cultivates the arts of human oratory, has his reward. But the faithful minister exhibits not himself, but Jesus Christ his Lord. 4. Mildness and gentleness of heart. What is there in nature so tender as a nursing mother ? Different ministers excel in different graces. Though possessing all in a measure, yet they commonly surpass in some one or more—some in boldness, some in judgment, some in zeal, but the most useful in love. III. THE CONDUCT OF A MINISTER OF CHRIST AS A RESULT OF THE DOCTRINES HE HAS IMBIBED AND THE SPIRIT WITH WHICH HE IS ANIMATED. 1. Laboriousness (ver. 9). The ministry is a "work." 2. Purity (ver. 10). 3. Godliness. 4. Inoffensiveness. 5. Usefulness. (*Bp. D. Wilson.*) *Ministerial affection and devotedness :*—The Apostle Paul had, in the former part of the chapter, reminded his Thessalonian brethren in what manner the gospel had been brought and preached to them, viz., "not of deceit, nor of uncleanness, nor in guile." After thus stating what was not the character of his ministrations among them, he proceeds to state what it was : "But we were gentle among you, even as a nurse cherisheth her children " (ver. 7, 8). What a beautiful description is this of the feelings and conduct of St. Paul to his Thessalonian converts ! It is proper that I should first inform you that the apostle was addressing real Christians, truly converted characters : "For yourselves, brethren, know our entrance in unto you, that it was not in vain" (ver. 1). So in the first chapter, vers. 2–7. He, indeed, bears them all in his heart, but not equally so : some are closer there than others. Think you not that although our Lord had a most tender and affectionate spirit towards all the Jews, He had yet a peculiar and stronger affection for those who faithfully and closely followed Him ? At the same time, of course, any unfair or undue partiality is to be carefully avoided. 1. "We were gentle among you, even as a nurse cherisheth her children." Gentleness, or kindness, and softness of manner, and of treatment, peculiarly characterizes a nursing mother. Her little infant is a tender, delicate plant, and will not bear rough usage. The outward frame of an infant is so very weak, that it is liable to sustain an injury even by improper handling, much more by any violent treatment; and its nerves are so very fine and tender, that any great shock would weaken them, perhaps ruin them entirely. 2. The very idea of a nursing mother is connected with the nourishment which she gives to her child. As a mother will not give her infant any strange food, so will not a faithful and judicious minister add anything to, nor take away from, what is written in the Bible. 3. Another characteristic of a nursing mother, by which she shows her gentleness towards her child, is being patient towards it—in not only waiting upon it in all the kind and affectionate offices of a parent, but waiting for it ; giving it time, not hurrying it, but bearing with its infirmities, it may be, even with its petulance, and fretfulness, and oppositions. So the "servant of the Lord must not strive ; but be gentle unto all men, apt to teach, patient, in meekness instructing those that oppose themselves" (2 Tim. ii. 24). We must not be disappointed if the tender plants of our spiritual nursery do not thrive as we could wish or hope. We must make allowances for their natural infirmities, as well as for their spiritual weakness. 4. The apostle goes on to say, "So, being affectionately desirous of you, we were willing to have imparted unto you, not the gospel of God only, but also our own souls." Here, again, the image of an affectionate mother strikingly represents the devotedness of affection which the apostle bore towards his spiritual children. Many a mother has sacrificed her life for the sake of preserving the life of her child ! And is not this precisely the spirit and the conduct of St. Paul ? What was his language to the Corinthians ? "I will very gladly spend and be spent for you" (2 Cor. xii. 15). Would that we could feel and manifest the same devotedness to our Master's cause, and the same love for souls ! There remains one point to be considered in connection with the declaration of the apostle in my text, and a very important point it is, viz., the motive or reason which he assigns for the affectionate interest which he took, and the devoted zeal which he manifested, on behalf of his Thessalonian brethren. It was this : "Because ye were dear unto us." And here, again, the image of a nursing mother will illustrate this feature in the apostle's character, and in the character of every faithful minister. What is it that impels the fond and anxious parent to cherish and nourish the child of her womb ? Does she do it from any interested motives ? Will she be repaid for all her care and all her labour ? Not always. She does it for this simple but strong reason, because her child is dear to her. That which is a natural feeling in the bosom of the mother, by Divine grace becomes a spiritual affection in the breast of every faithful minister of the gospel. Thus the spirit of a faithful minister of Christ is an affectionate, devoted, and enlarged spirit. And why ? Because it is the "Spirit of Christ." Of Him, indeed, it might be truly said, in the days of His flesh, "He was gentle among us," and was "affectionately desirous of us." Do you not remember the affecting and affectionate image under which He represented Himself as feeling for perverse Jerusalem ? (Matt. xxiii. 37). (R. Grant.) *Gentleness essential to nurses :*—After all, it is only the sympathetic person who is fit for the office of nurse. There are born nurses, as there are born artists or poets—gentle, soft-stepping creatures, who let in the sunshine with their very presence, just with their cheerful voices and beaming eyes, and all-embracing charity, which, Christ-like, places no blame on jangling nerves for the extorted word of impatience, when flesh and heart are fainting, and the silver cord is well-nigh loosed, but with softest touch and pitying eyes soothe in place of condemning, and help the poor sufferer just as a mother's warm breast lulls her babe to forget its pain. A cheerful inflection of the voice is often worth more than a whole apothecary's shop. Your dull, silent croake is a walking hearse in a sick-room. After all, in this, as in every other successful profession, intelligence must rule ; but, alas ! intelligence is the rarest of gifts. We may buy jellies and hothouse fruits, but who has intelligence to sell combined with kindness, though the mines of Golconda bid for it? (*Fanny Fern.*) *Ministers the nursing fathers of the Church:*—In a church in Verona stands, or rather sits, a wooden image of St. Zeno, an ancient bishop, with knees so ludicrously short that there is no lap on which a babe could be dandled. He was not the first nor the last ecclesiastic who has been utterly incapable of being a nursing father to the Church. It were well if all ministers had a heavenly instinct for the nourishing and bringing up of the Lord's little ones. Is there not much lack in this? At the Synod of Moscow, held by King Goutran, A.D. 585, bishops were forbidden to keep dogs in their houses or birds of prey, lest the poor should be bit by these animals instead of being fed. Should not all ministers be equally concerned to chase away all morose habits, angry tempers, and repulsive manners, which might encourage the approach of inquiring souls who desire to know of us the way of salvation? Sunday-school teachers may also take the hint. (*C. H. Spurgeon.*) *Ministers should be gentle:*—St. Anselm was a monk in the Abbey of Bec, in Normandy; and upon Lanfranc's removal became his successor as abbot. No teacher ever threw a greater spirit of love into his toil. "Force your scholars to improve!" he burst out to another teacher who relied on blows and compulsion. "Did you ever see a craftsman fashion a fair image out of a golden plate by blows alone? Does he not now gently press it and strike it with his tools; now with wise art, yet more gently raise and shape it? What do your scholars turn into under this ceaseless beating?" "They turn only brutal," was the reply. "You have bad luck," was the keen answer, "in a training that only turns men into beasts." The worst natures softened before this tenderness and patience. Even the Conqueror, so harsh and terrible to others, became another man, gracious and easy of speech, with Anselm. (*Dean Church.*) *Tenderness prepares for usefulness:*—Speaking of the temper requisite to the right discharge of ministerial duty, Payson said, "I never was fit to say a word to a sinner, except when I had a broken heart myself; when I was subdued and melted into penitency, and felt as though I had just received pardon to my own soul, and when my heart was full of tenderness and pity. No anger, no anger." (*C. H. Spurgeon.*) **So being affectionately desirous of you, we were willing to have imparted unto you, not the gospel of God only, but also our own souls.**—*The love of souls a necessary qualification for the ministerial office:*—History cannot furnish us with a more striking instance of the love of souls than we find in St. Paul. Here he may mean—1. That such was his affection for his converts, that he, as it were, breathed out his soul in every word. He spoke as though he would have died on the spot, through earnestness to affect them with what he said. 2. Or that so ardent was his love for them, that he was willing not only to preach to them, but to die for them. Some of the patriots of antiquity loved their country so well that they generously sacrificed their lives for it. And shall not love of souls be as heroic? (Phil. ii. 17; 1 John iii. 16). I. THE HAPPY EFFECT OF THE LOVE OF SOULS ON THE OFFICE OF THE MINISTRY. 1. It will contribute to ingratiate us with mankind, and so promote our usefulness. It is not to be expected that those should receive advantage by our labours to whom we are unacceptable. The ministry of a contemptible minister will always be contemptible, and consequently useless. But when a minister in his congregation appears in a circle of friends whose affections meet in him as their common centre, his labours are likely to be at once pleasing and profitable. When the heart is open to the speaker his words will gain admission. There will be no suspicion of imposition or sinister design. Even hard things will be received as wholesome severities. Love has a language of its own which mankind can hardly fail to understand, its own look, voice, air, and manner. When dissimulation mourns and puts on airs of sorrow and compassion it is but whining and grimaces, and when she smiles it is but fawning and affectation; so hard is it to put on the face of genuine love without being possessed of it; and so easy is it for a real friend to appear such. 2. It will enable us to affect our hearers and make deep impressions on their hearts. Love will render us sincere, and the sincerity of the speaker will have no small influence upon the hearers. 3. It will make us diligent and laborious. How indefatigable are we in pursuing a point we have at heart, and in serving those we love. Therefore, if the love of souls be our ruling passion, with what zeal shall we labour for their immortal interests! (2 Cor. xii. 15). There will then be no blanks in the page of life; all will be filled up with the offices of friendship. Ever-operating love will keep us busy (Acts x. 38; 2 Tim. iv. 2). As souls are equal in worth, this love is impartial. Love will inspire our prayers with an almighty importunity, and render idleness an intolerable burden. 4. It will enable us to bear hardships and difficulties with patience, and even cheerfulness. The love of fame, of riches, of honour, &c.—what obstructions has it surmounted, what dangers dared ! And shall not the nobler passion do vastly more? (Acts xx. 24). Labour is delight, difficulty inviting, and peril alluring in this benevolent enterprise. 5. It will restrain from everything unworthy the ministry. If the love of men be warm in our hearts—(1) We cannot address men in a manner that looks more like a scold than a Christian orator, and which tends to exasperate rather than to reform. (2) We shall be courteous without affectation, insinuating without artifice, engaging without flattery, and honest without huffishness. It will guard us against all airs of superiority, and a distant, imperious behaviour, and render us affable, sociable, and modest (Luke xiv. 11 ; xviii. 14). (3) It will render us patient under unkind treatment, and keep down unmanly and unministerial sallies of passion (1 Pet. ii. 23). (4) It will disable us from aiming at sordid ends and employing sordid measures (ver. 5 ; 1 Cor. xii. 14). II. WHAT MINISTERS ARE TO EXPECT FROM THEIR PEOPLE IN RETURN. 1. To be looked upon as the friends and lovers of their souls. 2. To be treated as such. To have their instructions, warnings, &c., regarded as those of friends, and to be obeyed as such. " We live, if ye stand fast in the Lord," but it kills us to see you destroy yourselves. 3. To be loved. Since your ministers love you, they deserve to be loved in return (chap. v. 13) ; and since they speak the truth in love, it should be received in love. 4. To be generously and cheerfully supported. (*S. Davies, A.M.*) *Loved into life :*—One of the most beautiful of the legends of classical mythology is that of Pygmalion the sculptor, who became so passionately enamoured of a statue of his own creation that he implored Heaven to bestow upon it life. As the story goes the prayer was granted, and the beautiful image that his genius had evoked from the rude block began to show signs of vitality. The cold marble grew warm as the life-blood began to course ; the hueless cheeks gradually glowed with a modest blush ; the dull, expressionless eye gave back an answering glance to the artist's ravished gaze ; the rigid tresses relaxed into a silky softness, and waved with a golden sheen ; the stony bosom heaved with deep-drawn breathing, and reciprocated the passion of that to which it was clasped ; until at last the fair creature stepped down from her pedestal to be the bride of him who had loved and prayed her into life. There is a lesson for us, as Christian workers, in this old-world fable. We must love the souls we would quicken. Love must be the inspiration of our prayers. It is so loving and so praying, with the arms of our affection and our faith around the objects of our solicitude, that we shall sooner or later witness the result on which our hearts are set, and behold them " alive unto God." (*J. Halsey.*) *Truth warmed by love :*—Humbolt, in his travels, observes : " It seems remarkable that in the hottest as well as the coldest climates people display the same predilection for heat. On the introduction of Christianity into Iceland, the inhabitants would be baptized only in the hot springs of Hecla ; and in the torrid zone, in the plains as well as on the Cordilleras, the natives flock from all parts to the thermal waters." The fact is not less noteworthy that men love spiritual warmth. Cold truth, even cold gospel truth, is never attractive. Ministers must be fervent, their spirit earnest, and their style energetic, or the many will not resort to them. Religion is a dish to be served hot ; when it once becomes luke-warm it is sickening. Our baptism must be with the Holy Ghost and with fire if we would win the masses to hear the gospel. (*C. H. Spurgeon.*)

Vers. 9–12. **For ye remember, brethren, our labour and travail.**—*Essential elements of success in preaching : Moral consistency :*—As time indicated on the dial answers to the perfect mechanism of the watch, so the personal example of the preacher must answer to the words he utters. The most accomplished elocution, the most captivating style, will be fruitless unless backed with the strength of a complete, beautiful, spiritual character. Their moral consistency seen—I. IN THE UNSELFISH PRINCIPLE THAT GOVERNED THEM IN THEIR WORK (ver. 2). The apostle invariably asserted the right of ministerial maintenance. In another place he affirms that, not merely naked equity and the spirit of the Mosaic law, but also a positive ordinance of Christ requires this. In this early stage of the work, the apostle waived this claim. It might be on account of the poverty of the converts, or on account of the calumnious charge of covetousness. To crush all suspicion of interested motives, these noble missionaries refused " to be chargeable unto any one of them," depending for their support upon the remittances of the Philippians, and on their own labour. Thus did they evidence their supreme desire to be, not gain, but the proclamation of the gospel ; an example which has its counterpart in the brave, devoted, self-denying labours of many a modern missionary. II. IN THE MAINTENANCE OF A BLAMELESS DEPORTMENT (ver. 10). A Roman prince of the celebrated house of Colonna, whose virtues had sustained him alike in prosperous and adverse times, was once driven into exile, and when reduced to extremity he was asked, " Where is now your fortress?" He laid his hand upon his heart, and answered, " Here !" A conscious sense of integrity threw a strength and majesty around him in his sufferings. An inward consciousness of purity prompted these workers to appeal to those who were best acquainted with them. They behaved holily toward God, justly toward men, and unblameably in every regard. " Among you that believe." Believers could best understand the secret of their whole life, its aims and motives, its tendencies and issues ; and on them it would have an irresistible impression. It is often the fate of the public teacher, while blameless, to be unmercifully blamed by those who are outside the circle of his work. The world retains all its historic enmity to the truth, and is as venomous as ever in its expression. III. IN THEIR ENDEAVOURS TO STIMULATE THEIR CONVERTS TO THE HIGHEST ATTAINMENTS (vers. 11, 12). Observe—1. The lofty standard set up. " That ye would walk worthy of God." How sublime and dignified the Christian character may become—to walk worthily of God ! in harmony with His nature, His law—with our profession of attachment to Him. To the production of this grand result all their efforts were bent. " As a father doth his children," so they " exhorted " with all earnestness, " comforted " with all loving sympathy, and " charged with all fidelity and authority." The preacher must be master of every art necessary to success. 2. The motive to reach the standard. " Who hath called you unto His kingdom and glory "—His own glorious kingdom. We are invited to enter this kingdom on earth, and participate in its blessings ; but the full splendours of that kingdom are reserved for the heavenly world. How brief and insignificant will the sufferings and sorrows of the present appear, contrasted with the ineffable bliss of the future state ! " Do you want anything?" eagerly asked the loved ones who surrounded the dying couch of Melancthon. " Nothing but heaven," was the gentle response, and he went smiling on his way. Lessons : 1. That in order to success in preaching, moral consistency of life must accompany and sustain the faithful declaration of the truth. 2. That the greatest success is achieved when the highest experience of the Christian life is constantly enforced by both precept and example. (*G. Barlow.*) *An unmercenary teacher :*—The *Evangelist* told the story of a young minister in whom the true spirit of his calling was evidently present. He went from a Congregational seminary to a Missouri town. His church was the feeblest one in the place, and soon men said, " No Congregational element in this town." He created one. Through many discouragements he remained at his post, never once complaining or " craning " his neck for a richer church, a larger field, or a more conspicuous position. At last he began to get influence, and to use it aright. He had a call to a stronger church at £1,500 salary. He quietly refused. Then a call came from a great church east of the Alleghanies, with a larger offer of salary and moving expenses. None of these things stirred him. He never even told of it in his parish. The call was repeated. He said, " No, my work is here till God shuts the door." And a goodly inheritance was his. *St. Paul's labours in Thessalonica :*—The narrative in the Acts, if very strictly pressed, might lead us to suppose that the apostle had only spent at Thessalonica twenty-seven days at the utmost—perhaps only twenty-one or twenty-two (Acts xvii. 1, 2, 10) ; but it does not absolutely demand such narrow limits of time, and two circumstances seem to require its extension—the conversion of many idolaters (1 Thess. i. 9), and Paul's own expressed statement that he remained long enough in Thessalonica to receive assistance " once and again " from Philippi (Phil. iv. 16). In any case, the spectacle of such an one as Paul so working, even for something less than a month, would be a memorable one—a thing to attract attention, and to be long remembered and discussed. This would especially be the case n the Church of Thessalonica. A shop-keeping and industrial community would instinctively know whether such an exhibition was a piece of charlatanism or a reality. Even if St. Paul's stay was cut short by a riot, they might be perfectly aware whether these few weeks were a fair representation of the frame and mould of his general life. It is certainly strange to think how far the idea which we instinctively form of the great apostle, as one utterly absorbed in theological thought or seraphic devotion, when not employed in preaching or missionary work, must be modified by such a passage as this. The language here used about " working night and day," would show that in Thessalonica, at least, *one* unbroken day in the week only could be undividedly given to directly apostolic labour. It is vain to conjecture how much time may have been at his disposal upon the other days of the week. It has been added to the list of St. Paul's difficulties that he thus worked manually "at an age when the bodily frame refuses to perform a new office." This is surely not so. Men of station and education among the Jews diligently learned trades. The same obligation has been imposed by custom upon persons even of royal birth in different nations and countries. Eginhard tells us that Charlemagne had his sons taught mechanic trades, and his daughters spinning and weaving. Each member of the Prussian royal family at the present time is apprenticed, and enters into a guild of tradesmen. St. Paul's motives in continuing to work were three—I. INDEPENDENCE, the being able to take what has been ingenuously called "a lay position." II. EXAMPLE (2 Thess. iii. 8, 9). III. CHARITY, having something to give in alms (Acts. xx. 34). (*Bp. Alexander.*)          **Ye are my witnesses, and God also, how nobly, and justly, and unblameably we behaved.** —*Apostolic behaviour and methods:*—The apostle had previously made an appeal to his readers, and an appeal also to God; he now blends the two into one. I. APOSTOLIC BEHAVIOUR (ver. 10). 1. "Holily," a word which looks specially towards God. A common Biblical phrase is "holy to the Lord." The Divine command is "Be ye holy towards your God," and the announcement is made, "The Lord will show who are His, and who is holy." The word is applied to—(1) God, the Father, Son, and Spirit, as infinitely holy above His creatures —"the Holy One," the source and end of all purity. (2) To angels. (3) To saints, as being sanctified, consecrated to a holy life, by the renewing of the Spirit of holiness. All believers in this sense live holily. With varying degrees of conformity to the will of God, they are all true men. Their devotion is sincere; their hearts turn towards God as the flower opens itself and turns toward the light of heaven. 2. "Justly" represents the side of the apostle's behaviour towards men. It means righteously, and defines the believer's conduct as upright in all its connections and dealings with others. He is just in God's sight, through the imputation of Christ's righteousness; and, standing in a new relation to God, he strives to live in obedience to God's law of love. We often use the word in a narrower sense, as when we say of a man that he is just but not generous. But that is an unwarrantable limitation. According to God's law, no man is just who is not generous, kind, forbearing, helpful. Love is a debt we owe to our neighbour, and we are not just if we neglect to pay it. "Owe no man anything, but to love one another." 3. "Unblameably" is a negative word, but on that account all the more comprehensive. As servants of Jesus Christ, they gave "no offence in anything, that the ministry be not blamed." In applying these three words to himself and his companions, Paul could speak not merely of a good heart and a good life, but also of a good name—"better than precious ointment." He who keeps his life free from sin does good to himself; he who keeps it clear of suspicion is merciful to others. The apostle is here a pattern to pastors and people; but we must ever rise from human examples to Divine. Christ is set before us as "the Holy One," "the Just One"; and as to blamelessness, He could say, "Which of you convinceth me of sin"; and the Roman governor could testify, "I find no fault in Him." It is when we stedfastly and lovingly look towards Him that we come at length to be "holy and without blame before Him in love." Note that this was the light that Paul and his associates appeared in the estimation of those that "believed." More than this could not be said, for by Jews and Gentiles their character and conduct were furiously assailed (Acts xvii.). Paul represents himself, therefore, as turning aside from the reproaches and enmity of the world to the judgment of his fellow-believers. In their hands his reputation was safe. II. APOSTOLIC METHODS (ver. 11). Already he had used the figure of a nursing mother in the tenderness of her self-sacrificing devotion to her children. He now shifts the figure, and is a father. Two points are to be noticed in the latter comparison —1. As a wise father suits his training and teaching to the case of each child, so he acted towards his converts—"every one of you." It was the apostle's invariable procedure to deal with individuals. He "ceased not to warn every one of" the Ephesian elders. To the Colossians he says, "Warning every man," &c. Christianity has brought out into clearest light, and assigned the greatest prominence to, the worth of the individual soul. The rulers and teachers of heathen society thought of men as a body, and used or influenced them in the mass, but seldom thought of the individual. But the religion of Christ takes account of each. Its foundation rests on individual conviction. Individualism, not multitudinism, is the law of its growth, until it comes to leaven the whose mass of humanity. 2. As a father is intensely earnest in giving his children right guidance and instruction, so was Paul in his yearning care of his converts. As he had described his behaviour in a threefold way, so he describes his ministry. (1) Exhortation is the more general term, and describes apostolic teaching as influencing the mind and will; in other words, instruction. (2) Comforting is friendly persuasion, touching the feelings, and so leading the heart to Christ and His truth—consoling and inspiriting those who, in the midst of tribulation, were doubting and desponding. (3) Charging or testifying is adjuring them with all solemnity, as in the sight of God. III. APOSTOLIC AIM (ver. 12). The method was necessarily diverse : some needing exhortation, others comfort, others charging ; but the end was one, because they all needed to walk worthy. 1. By "walking" we are to understand the whole character and conduct. (1) The figure implies energetic movement in the way of progress. (2) It is worthy walking only when the command has been heard and obeyed. " Walk before Me, and be thou perfect." " As ye have received the Lord Jesus, so walk in Him." (3) Such walking is "worthy of God," being " with God." 2. Calling means not merely God's invitation, but that invitation as accepted ; hence effectual calling. His Church is called out of bondage and corruption into the light and liberty of the gospel. We must, then, walk worthy of the dignity of God's freed men. This calling is unto—(1) His kingdom. We are, then, to walk worthy of the duties of this kingdom, to exhibit—(a) Faithful allegiance to its King. (b) Joyful obedience to its laws. (c) Affectionate interest in all its subjects. (d) Valiant fighting in its service. (e) Co-operation in all good work. (2) His glory—not simply to His glorious kingdom ; but while God calls His people to dignities and duties, He is also calling them to future rewards. Their destiny is glory. This glory is " the prize of our high calling " ; but even here we know something of it. It consists of—(a) Likeness to Christ (1 John iii. 2). Our glory will be " the beauty of holiness." (b) Sharing Christ's sovereignty. " To him that overcometh," &c. Believers walk worthy of this destiny when they share it as fully as may be here, and when they lovingly look forward to its perfection hereafter. (*J. Hutchison, D.D.*) *The faithful pastor :*—I. IN HIS PERSONAL CHARACTER, AS AN EXAMPLE TO THE FLOCK. Consider him as behaving 1. Holily before God. He was made a new creature in Christ Jesus. Throughout life he exhibited the evidences of, and made continual advancement in, the graces of the new creation. Notice some of the characteristics of Paul's holiness, which are always in some degree in every holy character. (1) Tenderness of conscience. (2) Deep humility. (3) Lively gratitude. (4) Prayerfulness. (5) Realization of the presence of God. (6) Living upon the promises of God. (7) Profitableness of conversation. 2. Justly before man—(1) In thought. (2) In word. (3) In deed. 3. Unblameable in general deportment. Free from minor (so-called) imprudences; abstaining from all appearance of evil. Blamed indeed he was, as all who live holily will be, but only " as concerning the law of His God " like Daniel. With regard to everything that involved duty and faithfulness he was firm as an oak, but in everything relating to personal convenience and benefit yielding in any way he could for the glory of God and the good of man. II. As THE INSTRUCTOR AND GUARDIAN OF THE FLOCK. 1. He "exhorted," setting forth the whole truth, not simply as a matter of theory but practically. There was no reserve in his doctrine, pandering to individual tastes or to the fashion of the day. Hence his preaching afforded tests—(1) To the unregenerate by means of which they might discover the absence of spiritual life and be led to repentance. (2) To the lukewarm, so that they should not be allowed to rest satisfied with mere profession. (3) To the believer, teaching him not to rest in present attainments, but to press forward. 2. He " comforted." His own heart was full of love to God and man, and rejoiced in the experience of Divine consolations, so that he was duly qualified to sympathize with others (2 Cor. i. 3–5). Cold is the comfort which arises from the mere theoretical statement of points calculated to give comfort; but when that consolation flows from a heart that can say, " I have tried it myself and know its power," then God works by means of the minister, and the heart receives comfort indeed. 3. With holy authority and deep solemnity. Paul " charged " the Thessalonians—(1) With discrimination, in language that was not vague and general, but such as enabled him to apply the different parts of his message to the conscience of " every one." (2) With tender affection " as a father." III. THE OBJECT HE HAD IN VIEW—" That ye would walk," &c. The arguments by which he enforced this charge were three-fold. 1. God had called them not only generally but effectually, and as He who had called them was holy so He urged them to be holy. 2. God had given them a place in His kingdom. That kingdom was one of—(1) Righteousness, peace and joy in the Holy Ghost; its members therefore must glorify the King by "righteousness and true holiness," and by "joy and peace through believing." (2) Liberty: its subjects are delivered from the thraldom of sin and Satan, and must live in loyalty to the royal law of liberty. (3) Light: its citizens must, therefore, walk as "children of the light." 3. God had prepared for them a state of glory. The heirs of that glory, therefore, must live— (1) In expectation of it. (2) In preparation for it. (*J. Hill, B.D.*) *The power of a Christian life :*—This does not sound like Christian modesty, but Paul frequently talked like this; yet he was one of the humblest of men, "less than the least of all saints." The fact is, that Paul felt it incumbent upon him to bear witness for Christ by his life as well as his lips, and there were circumstances which constrained him to vindicate the excellence of his life as well as the truth of his doctrine. I. The power of a Christian life AS IT SERVES TO VINDICATE AND RECOMMEND A CHRISTIAN'S DOCTRINE. 1. Men's principles have ever been tried by their practices. If we find Mohammedans or Mormons living good lives we feel sure that there must be some truth in what they believed. In this way men judge in relation to the gospel. When the life of a believer is bad it is taken as an evidence against the truth of the gospel; when good it is taken as a proof of its truth. And no wonder ; for it is easier to judge of a doctrine in a man's life than in abstract forms. And then the gospel comes not as a speculation that the intellect may be gratified, but that man's heart and life my be transformed, and professes that it can be brought to the test of experiment. It follows, then, that when the lives of Christians are bad they are the worst enemies of the gospel; when good its best friends. 2. Examples open on all hands. (1) What an argument for the truth of Christ's doctrine was Christ's own life! How often has it silenced those who assailed His teaching. That perfection could hardly have come from falsehood or delusion. How often has that same life strengthened the faith of the doubting. We have been oppressed by the mysteries of His doctrine, but when we have looked at His life we have felt that He must have uttered what was true, that He can be trusted, and may be followed in spite of difficulties. (2) The same thing appears in the examples of the early Christians. The apostles and the great master were anxious that the lives of converts should be in harmony with their belief, because the world was to believe the Christian doctrine because of what they saw of the Christian life. And that life in its purity, love, resignation, heroism struck both Jew and heathen. Nothing was harder to be answered than that, and it is that which contributed more than anything else to the triumphs of the Church. (3) The same thing is illustrated by the power of the biographies of good men. Have we not felt in reading them that there is no religion that could have produced such characters but that of Christ, and that the religion that could produce them must be of God. Nothing better can be placed in the hands of a sceptic than the record of a Christian life which has been in accord with Christian profession. (4) The same is illustrated by living examples. The life of many a father and mother has been a greater inspiration than all their instruction. So with friends, business acquaintances, &c. II. The power of a Christian life AS IT SERVES TO ENFORCE A CHRISTIAN SPEECH. There are some in every Christian man's sphere to whom he ought to speak on the subject of Christian faith and practice. To do this effectually it is necessary that there should be wisdom in the choice of time, circumstances, manner, subject &c., but more than all a life in harmony with what is spoken. The want of this is the real reason why professing Christians speak so little to others on these subjects. There are other reasons it is true—a humble estimate of self, delicacy and reserve, but the true reason is because they feel that they would be acting in a way that would bring condemnation on themselves. How can a man speak against bad tempers, if his children and servants see him indulging them? or speak about the Bible if he neglects it? Or about extravagance if he is expensive? Or about the value of the soul, if he cares little about his own? He cannot speak, because he is ashamed, and because he feels that it would be little use. But let the life speak as well as the words, and then the words will be effectual as witnessing to the sincerity and earnestness of the speaker. It is better not to talk at all about religion, if we do not live it; and if we live it religion will often speak when we are silent. III. The power of a Christian's life IN BLESSING HIS DEATH. 1. Inasmuch as because of the death, the power of the life is more forcibly brought before the mind. Often we do not know the value of our blessings until we lose them. When we do appreciate the worth of a Christian friend while living it is not as we do when he is dead. We were sufficiently alive to his imperfections, but now he is gone we think only of his excellence, and yield to the influence of that. 2. In its influence in drawing the Christian's affections upward. When our friends are with us shining in their consistent life this world satisfies us more than when they are gone. Their life is a force of attraction to this earth where they are: but their death attracts us to the heaven whither they have gone. If they had not lived Christian lives we should be thinking of them as somewhere we know not where, but recalling their lives as being Christian we are compelled to look upward for them in glory. Conclusion: Seeing that the power of a Christian life is thus great, it becomes us—1. To inquire very earnestly whether we have experienced it and yielded to it. We have all known some true Christians, and also some false professors. In regard to the latter many like well enough to see and condemn them, but with satisfaction as furnishing an excuse for irreligion. It is poor work to use Christian inconsistency for that end. If all Christians were inconsistent there might be something in it. But there are some who do lead Christian lives, and when near them we feel their power. What use are you making of them? Are you accepting their Saviour and imitating their example? And now if they are gone are you following them to heaven? You have to answer for the gift of every Christian man made unto you and not only for sermons, &c. 2. To inquire whether we are putting forth the power of a Christian life. Are we commending Christ's doctrine by our lives? When we are gone will men be remembering us to their advantage? 3. A Christian life is such a life that Christ requires and that Christ lived, and that Christ enables those who really follow Him to live. Without Him we cannot live it (Gal. ii. 20). (*D. Thomas, B.A., of Bristol.*) *Consistency at home:*—The son and biographer of Cæsar Malan, after describing the openness and impulsiveness of his father's nature, and the close intimacy in which he had always lived with him, remarks: " I never saw anything in him which did not renew the impression that he lived as seeing Him who is invisible. Never was I witness of a gesture, never did I hear a word, with respect to which I had to feel that it would become to him the subject of serious regret." *Holy instruments:*—How diligently the cavalry officer keeps his sabre clean and sharp! Every stain he rubs off with the greatest care. Remember you are God's sword, His instrument, I trust, a chosen vessel unto Him to bear His name. In great measure, according to the purity and perfectness of the instrument will be success. It is not great talents God blesses so much as likeness to Jesus. (*R. McCheyne.*) *The influence of a holy life:*—About the mere presence and person of good men there hangs a charm and a spell of good which makes them do good even when they are not consciously thinking of doing good at all. Their very presence does good as if there were an angel there, and from their mere silence there spreads an influence, a flowing in of higher motives and purer thoughts into the souls of men. It was said of the ancient Cato that when he entered the young Roman nobles blushed for their base amusements. It is said of one of old that even as a boy all bad words were hushed at once when he joined a crowd of his companions. (*F. W. Farrar.*) *A holy life recognized:*—It was said of McCheyne, of Scotland, that people felt him when he entered a meeting or private home. Although not a stern, sanctimonious man, but a very cheerful one, yet people recognized him as a man of God who carried the atmosphere of heaven with him, and lived out the gospel of Christ. The inward spirit shone out from him, in his language, and conduct, just as a blazing lamp always reports itself. *Sixty years of pure life:*—" Citizens," exclaimed Lamartine to a Parisian populace during the revolution of 1848, as he introduced an honest man to them—" Citizens! listen! for a sixty years of pure life is about to address you." The mob stood silent. And so the unconverted world will listen to a godly life in which the Divine Spirit dwells, when such a life comes in close contact with them. **That ye would walk worthy of God.**—It has often been charged upon Christianity that it is a narrow and belittling system, and that there is no scope in it for the highest development, and for the finest and most commanding type of character. If this be so it can only be because there is no fit conception of God, a thing which might have been affirmed with propriety at the foot of Olympus, but which it calls for a good deal of rashness to avow at the foot of that mountain on which the preacher said, "Be ye perfect as your Father which is in heaven is perfect." And here Paul adjures men to acquit themselves in a way to reflect and magnify the excellencies of Him in whom all excellencies meet and harmonize. There are two general thoughts involved in the idea of walking worthy of God. I. MEN ARE TO

KEEP ALWAYS IN MIND THAT THEY BEAR GOD'S IMAGE ON THEIR SOULS. 1. There are those who tell us that our creation in the Divine likeness is a myth; that mind is only a function of matter; that what we are pleased to call the soul is only the outcome of physical organs in a certain state of adjustment and action; and that we have simply struggled up through lower forms and survive because the fittest. There may be some truth in evolution. Subsequent to the great creative acts, and within the sweep of laws and orders established by God, something like the principle of evolution does come into play. But there is nothing in this to disturb our faith in a distinguishing creation of man in the image of the Maker. God's stamp is on the human heart and brain. Man is separated in his moral nature and boundless aspirations from all other orders because he has something of God in him. In virtue of this he is an evidence of God. His soul is a mirror which reflects God. Through this likeness our relation to Him is that of a child to a Father. 2. True this image is marred, but it is still on the soul. To be a man, no matter how low down or far away, is to have some trace of ancestry in God. It is the work of Christ to restore this image and bring men back to a filial acknowledgment of the Father. In every one who has accepted Him and is sincerely trying to do His will, this image is emerging into more and more of prominence, and by and by it will be complete. 3. To walk worthy of God this dignifying fact must be kept to the forefront. Princes are taught that they are sons of kings and must, therefore, conduct themselves in royal fashion. By every man it should be kept in perpetual remembrance that he is a child of the King of kings. What an uplifting power! What a help in the struggle to do the right! What a shield against evil assaults! Is there anything which gives us a larger notion of manliness, or supplies us with higher motive forces? II. THE NEW RELATIONS, PRIVILEGES, AND OUTLOOKS INTO WHICH ONE IS INTRODUCED BY FAITH IN CHRIST. 1. This is the central argument here. Men are to walk worthy because of the call into God's kingdom and glory. They have come into a new estate, and are expected not only to show gratitude for it, but to feel its inspiration and advance into a grander mood of life. It is a thing of immense import that a man should be taken out of the kingdom of sin and set down securely in the kingdom of God. Pardon is a great thing, conversion is greater, but heirship to all the wealth of the heavenly inheritance is greater still. 2. Being called by God " into His own kingdom and glory " means much more than a standing in the Church, and a hope of admission into heaven. It means a fellowship with God in His blessedness now and for ever. At present it is incomplete, but real. We see through a glass darkly; we know only in part; but we do see and know, and these experiences are prophetic of a seeing and knowing that shall one day be perfect. 3. No man can take this in without feeling that his walk ought to be very close with God and wholly in the line of His will. We are told that we are heirs of all the ages, that poets have sung, philosophers taught, legislators ruled, and martyrs suffered, &c., and that to us has fallen the precious fruitage of all this sacrifice and toil. But they who, through faith in Christ, have a standing in the kingdom and glory of God are heirs to something more than all this. Surely the thought that he is heir to the measureless riches of Divine favour is to put heart into a man and to stir him to the utmost stretch of endeavour. Within the sweep of these general thoughts there are some specific requirements. (1) The spirit and habit of loyalty to God. He is to be the first and final reference of all our actions. His will must be the rule and test of living. This loyalty was illustrated by Peter and John. " Whether it be right in the sight of God," &c. Front to front with prison doors they would be true to Him. Daniel is another example. Fidelity might cost him his life, but he would not swerve from it. So in the case of the heroes in Hebrews xi. The trouble with us is that God has not this regnant place in our lives. Secular codes are permitted to regulate our actions—political, social, professional, domestic — and which are allowed to determine what is right and wrong. (2) A very high degree of purity. The most careless reader must notice the stress laid upon this in the Bible; but we lay too little on it, and too much on sensationalism and æstheticism. Yet a higher measure of purity is one of the most pressing demands of our time. (3) A walk full of love —to God and man, for love is Godlike. (*F. A. Noble, D.D.*) *Walking worthy of God:*—I. THE KINGDOM AND GLORY TO WHICH GOD HAS CALLED US. He calls to possess—1. Himself—to take Him by the spirit, the heart, and the knowledge which is love. 2. Ourselves—we are lost if we lose God. 3. Our brethren. If we possess God we must possess as our brethren all who are His children. 4. All things— " All are ours for we are Christ's." II. GOD HAS CALLED US TO HIS KINGDOM AND

GLORY. 1. The ground of this call—His own character. 2. The methods. (1) The Gospel. (2) Christ. (3) The Sacraments. III. OUR DUTY WITH REFERENCE TO THIS CALL—to walk worthy of God, by contemplating the life and following the example of the only man who walked worthy of God—Jesus Christ, who gave Himself for us. (*N. Macleod, D.D.*)    *Not to disgrace religion :*—It was the custom among the old Greeks that every Athenian youth, as soon as he could carry weapons, should take this oath—"I will not disgrace the sacred arms entrusted to me by my country, and I will not desert the place committed to me to defend." (*W. Buxton.*)    *A walk worthy of God :*—1. Letters disclose the character of the writer. No two persons write exactly alike because no two persons have precisely the same character. In many cases we should know the writer even if the handwriting were concealed. There is a difference of tone and thought which either helps to form, or corresponds with our idea of the character of the writer. Some letters soothe, others irritate; some elevate us, others draw us down. 2. Letters disclose the character of the receivers. We write differently to different persons, and in the very act of revealing our own we indicate not obscurely our conception of another's character. 3. These remarks are appropriate to this epistle. Paul is writing to a Church about which he is particularly anxious and hopeful. He gives us a graphic picture of himself and of his mode of dealing with his congregations. It is a beautiful portrait of a Christian pastor. And how much does the letter tell us of the persons addressed. We seem to learn from the Acts that St. Paul had been but a short time at Thessalonica, and yet he is able to record "a work of faith," &c., and to speak to them throughout not only as persons interested in the gospel, but exemplifying its rules of life and acquainted with its deepest doctrines. We are taught—(1) That there is nothing to prevent any one from becoming, within a very short time, a Christian indeed. It only needs that we should receive Christ's message with prayer and watchfulness and try to act upon it. Then, the fruits of the spirit will speedily show themselves. God's work is not tied by rules of time and system. (2) The precariousness of Christian life. The more rapidly it grows the greater are its dangers; but whether it grows quickly or slowly, we have a watchful enemy, and if he succeeds in driving us back from our life of faith and labour of love, the labour bestowed upon us will have been in vain. Let us consider this worthy walk. **I. IN GENERAL.** The words are like, yet in one point different from, several other expressions elsewhere. The worthy walk in Ephesians is of the calling; in Philippians, of the Gospel; in Colossians, of the Lord; here, of God. 1. This, in all ages, must be the aim of all Christian teaching. Sometimes it may be done by giving details of duty; sometimes by laying down principles; sometimes, best of all, by touching the spring of motive, and dwelling upon that love of God which alone can make us love Him. But the object is ever the same. 2. "Walk" is a lively figure, and suggests—(1) That our life is a state of motion. There is no resting here. (2) It is motion within limits. The motion of to-day does not carry us out of the region of yesterday, and to-morrow will find us moving up and down the same area as to-day. And thus, as in our point of view, life is a journey; a journey of successive stages, no one of which is taken twice over; so, in another aspect, it is rather a walk, in which we start from our own door and return to it, traverse time after time the same space, and are still the same persons in the same region and home. (3) That region and home is not local, but personal. We may change our abode, but we carry our sameness with us wherever we go—the same habits, infirmities, affections, tastes and interests. We are the same, and so is the reality of life; its accidents vary, but the deep inner life changes not. 3. But though life be a walk rather than a journey, inasmuch as it traverses over and over the same ground, there is all the difference in the world in our mode of exercising it. We may live at random with no rule or guidance; we may live on a principle not the right one; we may live according to the direction or example of others which may lead us quite astray. Paul's is a very short rule—"Walk worthy of God." My conduct, then, in the little affairs of my daily life, so insignificant as they may appear, are in some way capable of high and glorious uses; capable of bringing honour upon, or detracting from the honour of God. We may help others to forget or to remember God. If we live in one way we show that we think God of importance; if we live in another, we show that we think He may be disregarded and no harm come of it. **II. IN PARTICULAR.** There are some ways in which we could not, if we would, walk worthily of God. We could never so live as to remind men of the creative power, eternal existence, absolute sovereignty of God : but in the following ways we may, and can, walk worthily of Him. 1. By the cultivation of reverence. No one walks worthily of God who takes His name on his lips lightly, or refers in a trifling spirit to the solemn realities of His word or judgment. These are the ways in which wicked or thoughtless persons put God out of sight amongst their companions. Let, then, those about you be aware that though you may be merry and amusing about other things, you are always grave and reverent when God is concerned, and that you are shocked at the slightest allusion to Him in any but a serious spirit. 2. The cultivation of thankfulness. The thankful spirit is that of one who gives God the glory for all he has, and looks not at what He withholds. 3. The cultivation of holiness. "As He which hath called you is holy," &c. He whose conversation is impure, whose heart cherishes impure thoughts, is doing the greatest dishonour to the God of holiness. On the other hand no one witnesses for God as one who is noticed for his perfect purity of speech and conduct. 4. The cultivation of kindness. When our Lord said, "Be ye perfect as your Father," &c., He said it with regard to kindness. This is what tells while a man lives, and is remembered when he is gone. (*Dean Vaughan.*) *Walking worthily :*—Here we have the whole law of Christian conduct in a nutshell. There may be many detailed commandments, but they can all be deduced from this one. We are lifted up above the region of petty prescriptions, and breathe a bracing mountain air. Instead of regulations, very many and very dry, we have a principle which needs thought and sympathy in order to apply it, and is to be carried out by the free action of our own judgments. We are told in our text to " walk worthy of God." Then again, we are enjoined, in other places, to " walk worthy of the Lord," who is Christ. Or again, " of the Gospel of Christ." Or again, " of the calling wherewith we were called." Or again, of the name of "saints." And if you put all these together, you will get many sides of one thought, the rule of Christian life as gathered into a single expression—correspondence with, and conformity to, a certain standard. I. We have this passage of my text, and the other one to which I have referred, "Walking worthy of the Lord," by whom we are to understand Christ. We may put these together and say that THE WHOLE SUM OF CHRISTIAN DUTY LIES IN CONFORMITY TO THE CHARACTER OF A DIVINE PERSON WITH WHOM WE HAVE LOVING RELATIONS. The Old Testament says, " Be ye holy, for I the Lord your God am holy." The New Testament says, "Be ye imitators of God, and walk in love." So then, whatever in that Divine nature of flashing brightness and infinite profundity is far beyond our apprehension and grasp, there are in that Divine nature elements —and those the best and divinest in it—which it is perfectly within the power of every man to copy. II. The next form of this all-embracing precept. The whole law of our Christian life may be gathered up in another correspondence, " Walk worthy of the gospel " (Phil. i. 27), IN A MANNER CONFORMED TO THAT GREAT MESSAGE OF GOD'S LOVE TO US. That covers substantially the same ground as we have already been going over, but it presents the same ideas in a different light. It presents the gospel as a rule of conduct. The Cross is your pattern, as well as the anchor of your hope and the ground of your salvation, if it is anything at all to you. And it is not the ground of your salvation and the anchor of your hope unless it is your pattern. It is the one in exactly the same degree in which it is the other. So all self-pleasing, all harsh insistence on your own claims, all neglect of suffering and sorrow and sin around you, comes under the lash of this condemnation. They are not "worthy of the gospel." And all unforgivingness of spirit and of temper in individuals and in nations, in public and in private matters, that, too, is in flagrant contradiction of the principles that are taught on the Cross to which you say you look for your salvation. III. Then again, there is another form of this same general prescription which suggests to us a kindred and yet somewhat different standard. We are also bidden to bring our lives into conformity to, and correspondence with, or, as the Bible has it, " TO WALK WORTHY OF THE CALLING WHEREWITH WE ARE CALLED " (Eph. iv. 1). God summons or invites us, and summons us to what ? The words which follow our text answer, " Who hath called us unto His kingdom and glory." Men that are called to high functions prepare themselves therefor. If you knew that you were going away to Australia in six months, would you not be beginning to get your outfit ready ? You Christian men profess to believe that you have been called to a condition in which you will absolutely obey God's will, and be the loyal subjects of His kingdom, and in which you will partake of God's glory. Well, then, obey His will here, and let some scattered sparklets of that uncreated light that is one day going to flood your soul lie upon your face to-day. Do not go and cut your lives into two halves, one of them all contradictory to that which you expect in the other, but bring a harmony between the present, in all its weakness and sinfulness, and that great hope and certain destiny that blazes on the horizon of your hope, as the joyful state to which you have been invited. "Walk worthy of the calling to which you are called." And again, that same thought of the destiny should feed our hope, and make us live under its continual inspiration. A walk worthy of such a calling and such a Caller should know no despondency, nor any weary, heartless lingering, as with tired feet on a hard road. Brave good cheer, undimmed energy, a noble contempt of obstacles, a confidence in our final attainment of that purity and glory which is not depressed by consciousness of present failure—these are plainly the characteristics which ought to mark the advance of the men in whose ears such a summons from such lips rings as their marching orders. And a walk worthy of our calling will turn away from earthly things. If you believe that God has summoned you to His kingdom and glory, surely, surely, that should deaden in your heart the love and the care for the trifles that lie by the wayside. IV. And the last of the phases of this prescription which I have to deal with is this. The whole Christian duty is further crystallized into the one command, TO WALK IN A MANNER CONFORMED TO, AND CORRESPONDING WITH, THE CHARACTER WHICH IS IMPRESSED UPON US. In Rom. xvi. 2 we read about a very small matter, that it is to be done " worthily of the saints." It is only about the receiving of a good woman that was travelling from Corinth to Rome, and extending hospitality to her in such a manner as became professing Christians; but the very minuteness of the details to which the great principle is applied points a lesson. The biggest principle is not too big to be brought down to the narrowest details, and that is the beauty of principles as distinguished from regulations. Like the fabled tent in the old legend that could contract so as to have room for but one man, or extend wide enough to hold an army; so this great principle of Christian conduct can be brought down to giving " Phœbe our sister, who is a servant of the Church at Cenchrea," good food and a comfortable lodging, and any other little kindnesses, when she comes to Rome. And the same principle may be widened out to embrace and direct us in the largest tasks and most difficult circumstances. " Worthily of saints"—the name is an omen, and carries in it rules of conduct. The root idea of " saint" is " one separated to God," and the secondary idea which flows from that is " one who is pure." All Christians are " saints." They are consecrated and set apart for God's service, and in the degree in which they are conscious of and live out that consecration, they are pure. So their name, or rather the great fact which their name implies, should be ever before them, a stimulus and a law. Walk " worthily of saints " is another way of saying, Be true to your own best selves. Work up to the highest ideal of your character. That is far more wholesome than to be always looking at our faults and failures, which depress and tempt us to think that the actual is the measure of the possible, and the past or present of the future. There is no fear of self-conceit or of a mistaken estimate of ourselves. The more clearly we keep our best and deepest self before our consciousness, the more shall we learn a rigid judgment of the miserable contradictions to it in our daily outward life, and even in our thoughts and desires. It is a wholesome exhortation, when it follows these others of which we have been speaking (and not else), which bids Christians remember that they are saints and live up to their name. (*A. Maclaren, D.D.*) *Walk worthy of God*:—I. BY CHEERFULNESS. Nothing is more Christlike and winsome. Every flower, even, tries to make itself as pleasant as possible. Let us copy the flowers. Our cheerfulness honours God, and shows that He is a good Master, and make him a blessing to his neighbours. When your loss comes do not dishonour God by fretting. Do not draw your joy from the world's broken cisterns, but from the inexhaustible fountain of happiness. II. BY NOT BEING AFRAID OF THE TRUTH. Many would be willing to follow the truth if it were fashionable; but if we would walk worthy of God we shall follow it not only at the risk of popularity but of life. Let the example of Christ and the martyrs and reformers nerve you to uphold and proclaim the truth. Show by your life that you dare rest your life on the word of Christ. This needs a new heart and a right spirit. III. BY EARNESTNESS IN ALL WE DO. Our Divine trusts will not bear trifling with, and there is but a short time in which to discharge them. How energetic all have been who have walked worthy of God—Christ, the Apostles, &c. We work hard for our worldly employers, shall we work less for our heavenly? IV. BY GENUINE DISCIPLESHIP. Our practice should, like a good sovereign, ring properly when it is sounded. God is foully dishonoured when we are inconsistent. Be Christlike—1. In word: truthful, clean, sympathetic. 2. In deed: pure, kind, helpful. (*W. Birch.*) *The dignity and duty of God's called ones :*—I. THIS VOCATION IS AN ACT OF GOD'S GRACE WHEREBY WE ARE INVITED TO FELLOWSHIP WITH CHRIST (1 Cor. i. 9; Luke xiv. 16). 1. It is therefore opposed to works (Rom. ix. 11; 2 Tim. i. 9). 2. This invitation may be regarded two ways: barely by the word, or as implying our consent. When a man is called to an office in Church or State, he is said to be called though he declines; but when election and acceptation meet together, then there is a call. This distinction is necessary in Divine things (Matt. xxii. 14; Rom. viii. 30). In a strict sense men are called only when they accept God's invitation. 3. This calling implies that men are afar off. We call men that are afar, we speak to those who are near (Acts ii. 14, 39). II. THE DUTY OF THOSE WHO ARE CALLED IS TO WALK WORTHY OF GOD. 1. There is a fourfold worthiness. (1) In regard of merit: so only Christ is worthy (Rev. v. 9). (2) In regard of acceptation: so the saints are worthy (Rev. iii. 4). (3) In regard of proportion (2 Cor. iv. 17). (4) In regard of meekness (Matt. iii. 8). This is the sense here. 2. We should walk worthy of God because—(1) Dignity calls for duty. What higher dignity than to be called to God's kingdom and glory? (2) The more dismal a man's condition is the more is he obliged to walk answerably to God who hath called him out of that condition (Eph. v. 14). (3) The more comfortable and glorious the condition a man is called unto, the more he is engaged to God who has called him to that condition. What is good or desirable but we are called to it in being called to God's kingdom and glory? Is light desirable? We are "called out of darkness into His marvellous light." Holiness? (chap. iv. 7). Peace? (1 Cor. vii. 5). Communion with Christ? (1 Cor. i. 9). III. WHEN MAY WE BE SAID TO BE CALLED, AND HOW MAY WE KNOW IT? 1. God ordinarily calls men by the preaching of the Word; but also by direct impressions made by the Holy Spirit on the heart, and by afflictions, &c. 2. A man may know that he is called when he is—(1) constrained by the love of Christ. (2) Begotten by the word of promise (Rom. ix. 7, 8). (3) Separated from the world (1 Pet. ii. 9). (4) Apt and willing to be ruled by the Word in all things (Acts ix. 6, x. 29). (5) When he can say, "all things work together for my good" (Rom. viii. 28). (6) When he celebrates God's praises (1 Pet. ii. 9). IV. WHAT SHALL WE DO TO WALK WORTHY OF GOD? 1. Observe the excellencies of God and let them shine forth. (1) God is a great God; do something great for Him. (2) He is a sovereign Lord, and absolutely free; do what He commands with a free spirit. (3) He is infinitely holy: "Be ye holy" (1 Pet. i. 15, 16). (4) He is God all sufficient (Gen. xvii.); trust Him fully. (5) He is faithful (1 Thess. v. 24; 1 Cor. i. 9); believe all His promises. (6) He is our chief good and last end; in all your affairs begin with Him, rest in Him, desire after Him. 2. Observe what the great design of God is, and labour all you can to advance the same. (1) "Your sanctification." (2) The world's salvation. (3) The glorifying of Christ (John xiv. 13). 3. Israel sacrificed to God the gods of other nations, and herein they honoured God; and so shall we if we surrender our idols to Him. 4. Take heed of sinning in secret, and be much in private duty because God sees you. Walking in the eye of an all-seeing God is most worthy walking. (*W. Bridge, M.A.*) *Christian magnanimity :*—I. THE PRINCIPLES OF MAGNANIMITY IN GENERAL AS A NATURAL QUALITY. As there is a difference between bodies as to size, so there is a real character of greatness or meanness applicable to the mind. It belongs to magnanimity—1. To attempt great and difficult things. Those who from love of ease neglect the improvement of their powers, or who apply them, however assiduously, to things of small consequence, are destitute of this quality, as are those also who fall below their rank in life. 2. To aspire after great and valuable possessions. A great mind has great capacities of enjoyment, and will not be satisfied with trifles. 3. To encounter danger with resolution. No weakness is more contemptible than cowardice. 4. To struggle against difficulties with steadiness and perseverance. Few things are more contrary to magnanimity than fickleness. We commonly identify weakness and changeableness. 5. To bear sufferings with fortitude and patience. This virtue has always had the greatest reputation. II. WHAT IS NECESSARY TO GIVE IT REAL VALUE AS A MORAL VIRTUE. 1. The object of our desires must be just as well as great. Some of the noblest powers of the human mind have been exerted in invading the rights, instead of promoting the benefit of mankind. Some of the ablest men have borne the most detestable of characters. 2. Our desires must be governed by wisdom and prudence, as well as justice. Exertion in feats, which have little value except their difficulties or rareness, is no more the operation of magnanimity than rope-dancing is the work of a hero. To spend a whole life in the accumulation of a vast fortune is of small merit. 3. The principle of action must be honourable, as well as the achievement illustrious. If a man does extraordinary things merely to make his name famous, it is mean; but the sacrifice of name and riches to duty and usefulness is glorious. 4. Every attempt must be possible and rational; otherwise it is only extravagant, not great. III. NOT ONLY IS THERE NOTHING IN REAL RELIGION CONTRARY TO IT, BUT THERE ONLY IT APPEARS IN ITS BEAUTY AND PERFECTION. 1. Religion calls us to the greatest and most noble attempts. (1) In a private view it bids us subdue every sinful passion, and to nurture every excellence. (2) In a public view, every good man is called to live for the glory of God and the good of others. What sphere of activity wider or nobler than this? 2. The truly pious man aspires after the greatest and most valuable possessions. He despises the unsatisfying enjoyments of time, and reaches out after God and heaven. 3. True piety encounters the greatest dangers with resolution. The fear of God is the only effectual antidote to the fear of man. 4. The Christian perseveres in opposition to continued trial. This is what distinguishes Christian warfare from every other. It lasts through life. 5. He endures suffering with patience and fortitude. Witness the martyrs. IV. PRACTICAL IMPROVEMENT. Learn from what has been said—1. That whenever honour differs from conscience, it is a treacherous guide. 2. That as Christian magnanimity is more excellent than that of the world, it is also more practicable and universal. It is open to all. (*J. Witherspoon, D.D.*) *Eagles and flies :*—Says Manton on this text: "Live as kings, commanding your spirits, judging your souls to be above ordinary pursuits. It is not for eagles to catch flies. As of old it was said, ' *Cogita te Cæsarem esse* '—' Remember that thou art Cæsar '—so say we to each believer, ' Remember that thou shalt one day be a king with God in glory, and therefore walk becomingly.'" This is important teaching, and much needed in these days. Many who declare themselves to be eagles spend the most of their lives in hawking for flies; we even hear of professing Christians frequenting the theatre. Instead of acting like kings, many who claim to be the sons of God act as meanly as if they were scullions in the kitchen of Mammon. They do not judge themselves to be Cæsars, but they demean themselves as if they were Cæsar's slaves, living upon his smile, and asking his leave to move. What separation from the world, what brave holiness, what self-denial, what heavenly walking with God ought to be seen in those who are chosen to be a peculiar people, the representatives of God on earth, and courtiers of the new Jerusalem above! As the world waxes worse and worse, it becomes men of God to become better and better. If sinners stoop lower, saints must rise higher, and show them that a regenerate life cannot share in the general corruption. O Lord, I know that in Christ Jesus thou hast made me a king, help me, then, to live a right royal life. Lay home to my conscience that question, What manner of persons ought we to be? and may I so answer it that I may live worthy of my high calling. (*C. H. Spurgeon.*)   *Preaching while walking :*—The good St. Francis of Assisi once stepped down into the cloisters of his monastery, and laying his hand on the shoulder of a young monk, said, "Brother, let us go down into the town and preach." So they went forth, the venerable father and the young man. And they walked along upon their way, conversing as they went. They wound their way down the principal streets, round the lowly alleys and lanes, and even to the outskirts of the town, and to the village beyond, till they found themselves back at the monastery again. Then said the young monk, "Father, when shall we begin to preach?" And the father looked kindly down upon his son, and said, "My child, we have been preaching; we were preaching while we were walking. We have been seen, looked at; our behaviour has been remarked; and so we have delivered a morning sermon. Ah! my son, it is of no use that we walk anywhere to preach unless we preach as we walk." (*Paxton Hood.*)

Ver. 13. **For this cause also thank we God.**—*A happy ministers' meeting* (text and ver. 14) :—Paul unbosoms his heart to the loving Church at Thessalonica. He knew what it was to be worried by others, but found rest when thinking of them. The most tried ministers have some bright spots. In setting forth his joyful memories of Thessalonica, the Apostle gives us a sight of three things. I. MINISTERS GIVING THANKS. "We also thank God." Ministers are not always weeping, though they often do so. They have their time of thanksgiving, as Paul had. 1. This followed upon sore travail (see ver. 9). As we sow in tears, we reap in joy. 2. This was backed by holy living (vers. 10, 11). Unholy ministers will have scant cause for joy. 3. It prevented all self-laudation. To thank God is the opposite of glorifying self. 4. It was of a social character. "We"—Paul, Silas, and Timothy—"we hold a fraternal meeting of joy when God blesses us among our beloved people." 5. It was of an abiding character. "Without ceasing." We can never cease praising the Lord for His goodness in saving souls. 6. It cheered them for further service. They wished (ver. 17) to visit the friends again, and further benefit them. What a mercy for us all when God's servants are glad about us! Their joy is in our salvation. II. HEARERS RECEIVING THE WORD. "Ye received." Not all receive it. How badly do some treat the gospel. Not all receive it as did the Thessalonians, for—1. They received the Word of God; they heard it calmly, attended to it candidly, considered it carefully. 2. They received the Word of God with a hearty welcome. They accepted it by faith, with personal confidence and joy. 3. They did not receive the word of man. It is well to keep the doors locked in that direction. We cannot receive everything; let us reject merely human teaching, and leave the more room in our minds for the Lord's word. 4. They did not receive the gospel as the word of men. Their faith was not based on the clever, eloquent, logical, dogmatical, or affectionate way in which it was preached. 5. They received it as God's revealed Word, and therefore received it with reverence of its Divine character, with assurance of its infallibility, with obedience to its authority, with experience of its sacred power. 6. They received it so that it effectually worked in them. It was practical, efficient, and manifestly operative upon their lives and characters. III. CONVERTS EXHIBITING THE FAMILY LIKENESS. 1. They were like Judæan Christians, the best of them—in faith, in experience, in afflictions. 2. Yet many of them as heathen began at a great disadvantage. 3. They had never seen the church of God in Judæa, and were no copyists, yet they came to be fac-similes of them. 4. This is a singular confirmation of the Divine character of the work. The same Lord works in all believers, and in the main the same experience occurs in all the saints, even though they may never have seen each other. This similarity of all regenerated men furnishes a valuable set of experimental evidences of the Divine origin of conversion. Let us not be daunted by opposition, for at Thessalonica Paul was persecuted and yet triumphant. Let us rejoice in the effects of the Word everywhere. (*C. H. Spurgeon.*)     *The correct estimate of Gospel truth :*—The population of Thessalonica consisted of two diverse classes—Greek and Jew—the one representing the philosophy of Paganism, the other being the custodian of the truths of revelation. Among the Hebrews, Moses was recognized as the head of their system, and his words were profoundly venerated; and the Gentiles were not less devout and ardent in their admiration of Plato. The gospel impinged on these ancient and revered institutions. The followers of Moses and Plato were compelled to admit the higher authority of the apostolic message. They formed a correct estimate of it when they "received it not as the word of men," &c. I. THE GOSPEL IS SUPERIOR TO ALL HUMAN WISDOM. Human wisdom is—1. Limited. The greatest mind is imperfect in its knowledge, and restricted in using what it knows. 2. Changeable. Aristotle said, "There is no difference between what men call knowledge and mere opinion; therefore, as all opinion is uncertain, there can be no certainty in human knowledge." 3. Unsatisfying. Another great thinker said, "Nothing can be known; nothing, therefore, can be learned; nothing can be certain; the senses are limited and delusive; intellect is weak; life is short." II. THE GOSPEL IS ESSENTIALLY DIVINE. 1. It is authoritative. When God speaks, unbelievers may well be filled with fear. His Word comes with the majesty of its own innate power. It bends the ear to attention, the mind to faith, the heart to reverence, the will and conscience to obedience. 2. It is immutable. It is "the Word of the Lord that liveth and abideth for ever." (1) Its promises are sure. (2) Its threatenings will certainly be executed. 3. It is complete. There is nothing to add, nothing to subtract. It contains the fullest revelation of God, of man, of eternal issues, such as can never be found elsewhere. 4. It is worthy of universal credence. "If we receive the witness of men, the witness of God is greater." It is to the everlasting commendation of the Thessalonians, and of millions since their day, that when they heard the Word of God, they "received it not as the word of men," &c. III. THE GOSPEL IS EFFICACIOUS IN TRANSFORMING CHARACTER. "Which effectually worketh also in you that believe." As the planet receiving the light of the sun is transformed into an imitation sun, so the believing soul, receiving the light of the Word, is changed into the image of that Word. Whatever the Divine Word prescribes, *that* it works in us. Does it prescribe repentance?—it works repentance; faith?—it works faith; obedience?—it works obedience; knowledge?—it enlightens to know. Its transforming power is continually demonstrated. It makes the niggardly generous, the profane holy, the drunkard sober, the profligate chaste. Faith is the vital force that connects the soul with this converting power. IV. THE COR-RECT APPRECIATION OF GOSPEL TRUTH IS MATTER OF CEASELESS THANKSGIVING TO THE PREACHER. "For this cause also thank we God without ceasing." No disappointment is keener than that of unproductive labour. Some of the choicest ministers of God have had to mourn over comparative failure. Think of the anguish of Jeremiah, when the Word of the Lord, which he declared, was turned into daily reproach and derision; and of Ezekiel, when he wept over rebellious Israel! But the joy of success is inexpressible; and the full heart pours out its thanks to God. "They joy before Thee according to the joy in harvest, and as men rejoice when they divide the spoil." Lessons: 1. The word of man, while it may charm the understanding, is powerless to change the heart. 2. The correct estimate of gospel truth is to regard it as the Word of God. 3. The Word of God is efficacious in the individual only as it is received believingly. (*G. Barlow.*)     *The gospel message: its instrument and reception* :—I. THE GOSPEL IS A MESSAGE FROM GOD TO MAN. A message is a special communication, directly sent by one person to another, affecting matters of immediate interest. It is in this light that the gospel was regarded by its first preachers. They were ambassadors for Christ to men. 1. The message is special. Creation and Providence declare the glory of God, His power, wisdom, goodness. They have spoken with a thousand tongues, but they have not told us all. Their speech could not convey to the heart of man the hidden thought of the gospel, "But the law of the Lord is perfect, converting the soul." 2. The message has been directly sent. At sundry times, and in divers manners, through dream and vision, by the prophets, the communication was made at first, but in these last days He has spoken to us by His Son. 3. It demands our immediate attention. The answer is to be made by return. We must not turn away from Him who speaketh from heaven. II. THAT MESSAGE IS CONVEYED BY HUMAN INSTRUMENTALITY. This is so obvious as to require no elucidation; but in the special light of the text it demands the closest attention. Touching this, St. Paul said to the Corinthians, "And my speech and my preaching was not with the enticing words of man's wisdom," &c. The preacher must be so impressed with the solemnity of his position as to make his own glorification impossible. This was a charge made by the Redeemer against the Pharisees, "Ye receive glory of men." The hearer must also rise above many of the peculiarities of the messenger to the message itself, "See how ye hear." III. THE MESSAGE, WHEN RECEIVED IN FAITH, EXERTS AN IMMEDIATE INFLUENCE. "Which also worketh in you that believe." The whole soul is moved to action. 1. There is a response to its call. "Lord, I believe; help Thou my unbelief." 2. There is a conformity to its demand. "Take up the Cross, and follow Me." 3. There is a realization of its peace. It is a message of mercy offering peace and joy to the believer. "Peace be unto you." (*Weekly Pulpit.*)     *The Preaching of the Word and its effects* :—I. WHEN MAY IT BE SAID THAT THE WORD, NOT OF MEN, BUT OF GOD, IS PREACHED—1. Negatively. Not— (1) When doctrine evidently false is preached, or such as is condemned in Scripture, as, *e.g.*, some branches of the Socinian, Antinomian, Pharisaic, and other doctrines. (2) When doctrine is preached which is not contained therein, and, therefore, at best, doubtful—speculation, mysticism, &c. (3) When trivial doctrine is preached, and such as Scripture lays little stress upon, such as kneeling or sitting at the sacrament. (4) When uninteresting doctrine is preached, and such as, however important at another time, and to another people, does not particularly concern those to whom it is delivered; as when Christian perfection is preached to a drunkard, or the promises of eternal life to the impenitent. (5) When the preacher is influenced by sinister motives—as by a view to wealth, or ease, or honour, or when his own practice contradicts his doctrine and gives the lie to it; for then, it appears, he does not believe it himself. 2. Positively. (1) When, like the first teachers of Christianity, the preacher has no worldly advantages to expect, but rather suffering; and when his conduct shows that he firmly believes his own doctrine, and that it has a powerful influence upon his heart and life. (2) When it is evidently scriptural, and therefore true, important, and of particular concern to those to whom it is declared. And, above all, when it is declared by the Scripture to be essential to salvation. It is not a sufficient objection to this that the doctrine is clothed in language neither elegant nor pure, without any proper arrangement of ideas, in a manner neither engaging nor affecting. II. WHAT IS IMPLIED IN THEIR RECEIVING IT, NOT AS THE WORD OF MEN, BUT THE WORD OF GOD? 1. Negatively. It is not received as "the Word of God, but as of man," if received with inattention, irreverence, unconcern, unbelief, or with after neglect and disobedience. **Not** that the word even of man may not be attended to and heard with much respect, belief, and obedience; but if what is really the Word of God be not attended to, believed, and obeyed, it is evident it is received only as the word of man. 2. Positively. It is received as the Word of God if received with fixed and serious attention. Shall not the creature attend when the Creator, Preserver, and Redeemer speaks, and we know that He speaks to us?—with deep reverence, self-abasing humility, lively concern on account of the interest we have in the things revealed; assured faith as to the truth, importance, and suitableness of what is spoken; fervent prayer, since we cannot understand the Word unless we are taught by God's Spirit (1 Cor. ii. 11); sincere gratitude. What a blessing to have God speak to us!—ardent love of the truth, though it may condemn and distress us, though it be "quick and powerful, sharper than a two-edged sword" (Heb. iv. 12); a meek and patient mind (James i. 19–21); a firm purpose of obeying the will of God (James i. 22). III. The effects produced by it when thus received. "It effectually worketh in you that believe." Amongst its happy effects, are repentance, viz., illumination, conviction, humiliation, hatred of sin, and change of life (Acts ii. 37; 1 Cor. xiv. 24, 25; 1 Thess. i. 5–10). Confidence, and peace with God (Rom. x. 17; v. 1); regeneration (James i. 18; 1 Pet. i. 23); a lively hope of immortality (2 Tim. i. 10, 12; Tit. i. 2, 3; 1 Pet. i. 3); a spiritual and heavenly mind (Col. iii. 1; Phil. i. 20); and deadness to the world (1 John v. 4); love to God and man (1 Thess. iii. 12); this love is humble, resigned, zealous, obedient (1 Cor. xiii. 4; John xiv. 15, 21, 23; 1 John v. 3); benevolence to all men; the Word of God, showing that all are the workmanship of one Creator, under the care of the same Divine providence, and the subjects of the same call in the gospel: a meek, gentle, and long-suffering mind towards all: a merciful, sympathizing, and liberal mind: a sober, temperate, and pure mind (Tit. ii. 11, 12): a watchful and serious mind (1 Thess. v. 4–9): the Word of God, revealing serious and awful things, should create a corresponding temper in us: a courageous and brave mind (2 Tim. i. 7, 8): a growing and progressive conformity to Christ (Eph. iv. 11–16; 2 Tim. iii. 10). (*J. Benson.*) *The authenticity of the Scriptures :*—They are the Word of God on several grounds. I. From the majesty and sublimity of the style in which they were written. II. From the great and holy design of their Divine Author, and the harmony of all their parts. III. From the character of the sacred writers. They lived at different times and in different parts of the world; their adversaries were many and mighty; they had no worldly advantages; they relate their own imperfections; they were either good or bad men. IV. From the testimony of God Himself. Miracles—prophecy, the evidences of which increases the farther it goes. V. From the satisfaction which believers obtain from the inward testimony of the Holy Spirit. The inspiration of the sacred writers was supernatural and extraordinary; that of believers is extraordinary, but not supernatural. (*A. Barber.*) *Receiving the Word :*—I. The description of the Gospel—the Word of God. 1. It was given by God to the World. 2. It reveals to us His will in the salvation of ruined man. 3. He has commissioned His ministers to publish it. II. The act of receiving it. 1. Hearing it as the Word of God, and not merely as the word of man. 2. Listening to it with attention. 3. Accepting it with the fullest credence. 4. Taking it wholly in all its parts. III. The effect it produces. 1. It works a complete conformity to the character of Christ. 2. It supports the mind under all the difficulties and trials of life. IV. The gratitude expressed for it. 1. Because it is all the gratuitous work of God's Spirit. 2. Because the safety and happiness it confers and ensures. Reflections: 1. Have we received the gospel? 2. Are we bringing forth its fruits? (*E. Brown.*) *The efficacy of the Word of God and the way of receiving it :*—Ministers and hearers are alike responsible, the one for preaching and the other for receiving. The Word of God is not to be trifled with. It is either a savour of life unto life, or the reverse. I. The description given of the Word. 1. As to its Author. (1) It is not the word of men. Men are employed as instruments for making it known, but it is not a "cunningly devised fable" of theirs. (2) It is the Word of God in truth. (a) Such was the gospel as preached by the apostles (chap. ii. 2; Gal. i. 11, 12; Matt. x. 20). (b) Such also is the Written Word—the Bible. Men wrote as they spoke, under the inspiration of the Holy Spirit (2 Tim. iii. 16; 2 Pet. i. 21). (c) The same may be said of the Word as preached by true ministers now. They claim no inspiration, but if their teaching be founded upon and drawn from the Bible it is "in truth the Word of God." 2. As to its effects. The Word is not only the channel of Divine revelation, it is the instrument of Divine quickening. The Spirit not only inspires it, but conveys Himself with it. Thus the Word is made effectual (1 Pet. i. 22, 23). Hence it is called "the rod of God's strength," a "fire," a "hammer" (Psa. cx. 2; Jer. xxiii. 29), and the converter of the soul (Psa. xix. 7). It works effectually in—(1) Producing conviction of sin. The Spirit does this with His sword (John xvi. 8; Eph. vi. 17; Heb. iv. 12). (2) Binding up the broken heart. It reveals the way in which the sin of which it convinces may be forgiven. II. THE MANNER IN WHICH IT OUGHT TO BE RECEIVED. 1. With attention, because of its importance. 2. With reverence, as coming from a holy God to sinful men. 3. With humility and teachableness, making the requisite effort to understand it, and when understanding it receiving it without question. 4. As God's appointed instrument for the conversion and edification of our souls. (*E. Cooper, M.A.*) *Hearing and receiving the Word :*—I. HEARING THE WORD. The temper of soul in the Thessalonians was so great a favour that Paul thought he could never praise the Author of it sufficiently. He knew his spiritual children could not but thrive when they received their meat in such a manner as the Word of God. It is the speech of Senaclæus concerning Diarius the martyr—"Methought when I heard him speak, I heard the Holy Ghost Himself preaching to me." Truly the want of this hearing is one main cause why the Word of God doth so little good. The devil is very diligent at duties: he is every Lord's day the first at church. The children of God never gather together but Satan is among them. His great design is to render this engine of the Word fruitless, whereby the strongholds of His kingdom have been battered and broken down. Therefore, as a jailer will sometimes let his prisoners have their hands and feet at liberty so long as the doors of the prison are barred that they cannot run away, so he will let men have their hands at liberty for some acts of charity, and their feet at liberty to walk in some paths of virtue, so long as he can have the doors of their ears and hearts locked fast that they cannot get from him. He knoweth that Christ waiteth at the outer door of the ear, that He might thereby come to the inward door of the heart, and deliver the poor captives out of his hands. For this cause, if it be possible, he will keep the street-door shut; he will hinder men from hearing as in God's presence; he will find them other work to do than to hear. It may be he will get them to play and toy, or to talk to their pew-fellows, or to be reading, or to have their hearts in their own houses, while their bodies are in God's house; or as a child, though they are at their book, he will make them look off, if but a butterfly come by; he will set them about some business or other, unless they are serious as in God's sight, that they shall never have so much leisure as to hear even when in church. Yet did they but believe the invaluable worth of their souls, the consequence and weight of their unchangeable estates, what a searching time the hour of death will be, and what dreadful things will be seen at the day of judgment! Good Lord, how would they hear! The minister need not then call them to attend to the Word of God; they would of themselves give it their ears, and minds, and hearts, and think all too little for it. II. RECEIVING THE WORD. The Word is a salve of sovereign virtue. Some talk of the weapon salve that it heals at a distance: but the Word will not; it must be applied to the sore, or it will never cure. The Word is seed; preaching is the sowing of this seed; application of it to the heart is the harrowing of this seed into the earth. If the seed be thrown on the ground and not harrowed in, it can effect no harvest. It must be received. A good hearer is said to eat the Word (Jer. xv. 16; Prov. ix. 5). It is not the bread in the cupboard of the Bible, or on the table of a sermon, which will nourish the soul, unless it be by application of it, eaten and taken into the stomach; the glass of wine in the hand will not make the heart glad; the precious promises in the ears will not rejoice the spirit; they must by application be drunk down, then they will refresh and comfort the conscience. Faith is both the mouth to receive in, and the stomach to digest, this spiritual food. It is worthy of observation how frequently the Holy Ghost attributeth the famous effects and heroic acts of the Word to this commander-in-chief, under whose courageous and wise conduct it warreth. The Word fighteth boldly, and worketh miraculously under the banner of faith (Rom. i. 16). If the threatenings and curses of the Law are preached, faith is to them as the powder is to the bullet, causing them to make great havoc upon the lusts of a man. Faith turns stones into bread, and helpeth the Christian, like Samson, to fetch meat out of the eater. If the precepts and commands of the Law are preached, faith is the eye to see the equity in them, and the excellency of them; and faith is the hand to put them into practice.

If the promises and comforts of the gospel are preached, faith is to them as induction to a minister; and gives him actual possession of them, making them his own. Faith in the threatenings causeth humiliation; faith in the precepts causeth subjection; and faith in the promises worketh consolation. If at any time thou goest from hearing both dead and undone, thou mayest say to faith as Martha did to Christ, "If thou hadst been here my soul had not died." The unbeliever, like a man in a swoon, shuts his mouth against those life-recalling cordials which are before him in the gospel. Other sins wound the soul, but unbelief, like Joab, strikes under the fifth rib, and kills outright. So it cometh to pass that the Word is preached to many, but not to their profit. They hear the minister as chickens hear the hen; the hen calls them to come to her; they lie scraping in the dust, and will not hear her, till the kite cometh and devoureth them. But when the Word cometh with power the soul heareth it, as Peter heard the cock; he goeth out and weepeth bitterly when he hears of the boundless mercy he hath deserted, the matchless misery he hath deserved, and the infinite love he hath abused. When we are hearing, like the Thessalonians, our souls must be changed into the similitude of the Word, that it may come to us with power. As the working of physic kindly and well commendeth both the physician and body of the patient, so the powerful operation of the Word doth highly applaud both the skill of the Saviour and the state of the soul. It is written of Philetus, a disciple of Hermogenes, that, going to dispute with St. James the elder, the apostle preached Christ to him so powerfully, that he returned to his master, and said to him, " *Majus abieram, Christianus redeo;* "—I went forth a conjurer, but am come back a Christian. Oh, how happy will it be for us, whatever our end in going to church, yet when we return, we may upon good ground say, " We went forth proud, but are come home humble! We went forth bond-slaves of Satan, but are returned free men of Christ! We went forth carnal, malicious, and obstinate sinners, but are come back spiritual, gracious, and heavenly saints! " (*G. Swinnock, M.A.*) *The Word and its works:*— I. THE RECEPTION OF THE GOSPEL. 1. There is something in the source of the Word which claims our reverential regard. It is not the word of man, but of God. Yet the word of man claims to be heard. The utterances of the wise and good cannot be disregarded without blame; how much more the revelations of the supreme intelligence and goodness. 2. There is something in the intrinsic importance and manifest adaptation of this word which gives it claim to our regard. It speaks to our deepest wants and longings, and unfolds the " unsearchable riches of Christ " for their satisfaction. 3. There is something in the truthfulness of God's Word which gives it certainty. Man yearns for certainty, and is unhappy till he find it. He cannot find it in philosophy and speculation, but he can in Him who is " the Truth," who reveals Himself and speaks in the Word. 4. There is that in the nature of this Word which gives it authority. Mere human teaching has always wanted this: but the Word like its Author "speaks with authority, not as the Scribes." II. THE OPERATION OF THE GOSPEL. To be effectual it must be received, but being received it works—1. The conviction of sin. To leave us in our spiritual slumber because of the unpleasant sensations of the awakening were false mercy; but the power which rouses conscience is beneficent. 2. It leads to reconciliation with God. There can be no happiness while the soul is estranged from God. The Word brings us back by revealing the fulness and sufficiency of redemption. 3. It sanctifies the heart (John xvii. 17). Pardon is not sufficient by itself. The Christian life is progressive holiness. The Word quickens holiness and promotes its growth. 4. It supplies consolation in time of trial. (*D. M. Jenkins.*) *God's Word intelligently received:*—The following strikingly interesting story was lately related to me by the Lord Bishop of Derry: During Lord Lyndhurst's last illness, he received a visit from Lord Harrowby. The latter's eyes happening to fall upon some books popular among infidels, Renan's " Life of Jesus " among others, which were lying upon a table by the side of the sick man's bed, and had evidently recently formed the subject of his reading, he expressed in his countenance no inconsiderable amount of distress and disappointment. Upon this Lord Lyndhurst, who observed this change come over him, assured him that he need not be in the least degree alarmed, for that he had studied with the utmost care both sides of the question (and never was there an abler and more expert judge of the nature and value of evidence, no matter how entangled and conflicting such evidence might be, than Lord Lyndhurst), and was accordingly perfectly acquainted with all that had been urged against as well as for Christianity, but that (observe, I pray, his beautiful conclusion), his belief in the mission and resurrection of Jesus Christ had never been even for one second shaken.

(*Maurice C. Hime, M.A.*)    *God's Word prayerfully received :*—Dr. Schauffler, the missionary at Constantinople, relates the following story : A Turk of Thessalonica bought a Bible and read it diligently. He was asked what he thought of the Bible— if it was a Bible like other books. " No," said he ; " this is a book which man could not have written. God must have written it Himself." " Have you not also found that Christ must have been the Son of God ? " He shook his head. On his next visit he returned again to the subject, and said, "When I visited you last I could not answer your question truthfully from my heart. That Christ was the Son of God was the only point I could not believe. I went away to my closet and prayed for light, that I might believe ; and in answer to my prayer that I might know Christ as the Saviour of the world, light broke on my spirit, and since then I have believed." (*Der Glaubensbote.*)    *God's Word soul-quickening :*—A lady who was present at the dispensation of the Lord's Supper, where the Rev. Ebenezer Erskine was assisting, was much impressed by his discourse. Having been informed who he was, she went next Sabbath to his own place of worship to hear him. But she felt none of those strong impressions she experienced on the former occasion. Wondering at this, she called on Mr. E., and stating the case, asked what might be the reason of such a difference in her feelings. He replied, Madam, the reason is this, last Sabbath, you went to hear Jesus Christ, but to-day you have come to hear Ebenezer Erskine.    *Life-giving energy of the Word of God :*—A native minister of Madagascar, who has since been an assistant in the revision of the book of Genesis, attributes his conversion entirely to his having accidentally met with a small scrap torn from a Malagasy Bible. While walking past the spot where the Memorial Church of Ambantan-kanga now stands, he saw upon the ground a small scrap of printed paper. Taking it up, he found that it was a mere fragment of the book of Psalms. He began to read, and was especially struck with one verse, which speaks of the power and majesty of God. He could not get rid of the impression it made on his mind, that the God revealed in the Bible was the true and living God. He accordingly sought out a Christian, and inquired about the faith they possessed. The result was that he accepted Christ as his Saviour, joined himself to the persecuted company of believers, and endured with them privation and loss for Christ's sake. He has now been for some years a native pastor, and is a most zealous and godly man. What other word is so full of life-giving energy as this ? What other book can so change men for time and for eternity ? Surely, this is God's book.    *A due reception of the gospel :*— I. The occasion of Paul's thankfulness. 1. The manner in which the Thessalonians received the Word of God. (1) As proceeding from God's love. (2) As sanctioned by His authority. (3) As assured to them by His truth and faithfulness. 2. The manner in which it operated in—(1) Their conversion. (2) Their subsequent support. (3) Their progressive sanctification. II. The ground which ministers have for thankfulness whose labours are so blest. 1. For the people's sake. 2. For the Church's sake. 3. For the world's sake. 4. For the Lord's sake. Learn—1. Whence it is that the Word preached is so generally ineffectual to any saving purpose. 2. How it may be made effectual to the good of souls. (*C. Simeon, M.A.*)    *The right reception of the gospel :*—I. The right reception of the gospel (chap. i. 5). 1. They listened to it not as the word of men, but as the Word of God. Paul refers to the danger of listening to the gospel as if it were the word of men. How many treat it as merely the preacher's message. (1) Man's word is mixed with error and should be sifted ; but in God's Word there is no error. (2) Man's message may not concern us, but God's Word is of momentous importance. When its infallibility and worth are realized, you will—(*a*) Listen to it with reverence. (*b*) Feel its authority. (*c*) Rejoice in its preciousness. (*d*) Be impressed with a due sense of responsibility. 2. They received it in faith, "Also in you that believe." This is the only way in which it can be received. Hearing is not receiving it, nor an intelligent comprehension of its nature and relationships. Not until a man accepts Christ as his Redeemer and Righteousness is the gospel received. It should be thus received because of—(1) Its inexpressible importance to us. (2) The infinite love of God in the Word of His grace. 3. It follows that in thus receiving the gospel as the Word of God—(1) They dismissed from their minds all prejudices and preoccupations (Acts xvii. 5). (2) They heard with personal application. II. The efficacy of the Word when rightly received. It will have an effect, but what each must choose. 1. The mighty power which the Word had on those who believed, " Which effectually worked." By means of it they were—(1) Convinced of sin. (2) Made new creatures in Christ Jesus (James i. 18). (3) Sanctified (John xvii. 17).

2. The explanation of this effectual working—because they believed (Heb. iv. 2). In proportion to our faith will be our profit from the Word. III. THE THANKFULNESS INSPIRED BY THIS RIGHT RECEPTION AND EFFECTUAL WORKING OF THE WORD. Paul felt. thankful because of—1. His sympathy with the Lord Jesus in His work and triumphs "He shall see of the travail of His soul," &c. 2. The blessings realized by those who received the Word. The liberator feels joy in freeing the slave ; the physician in making the diseased healthy. (*G. W. Humphreys, M.A.*) *The logic of life :*—I wish to point out the evidences of the faith of Christ in its effectual working ; that it is the Word of God is declared by its practical working ; its Divinity, its validity, its preciousness are alike evidenced by its action and consequences in the experience and life of all those who truly receive it. Its practical working shows that it is no cunningly devised fable, but the very truth and power of God. There are three grand tests. I. IN CIRCUMSTANCES THE TEST OF TRUTH IS UTILITY. A belief is not shown to be true because it works to the profit of one man or a few men, or because it works to the profit of many men during a limited period; but a belief is shown to be true if it works to the profit of vast masses of men, in all kinds of conditions, through one generation after another. That which uniformly tends to the enrichment of society is manifestly in harmony with the law of the world. Now, I am bold to affirm that the faith of Christ will bear this test. It vindicates itself by stimulating life, enriching it, adorning it. II. IN CHARACTER THE TEST OF TRUTH IS BEAUTY. What is false in doctrine and ideal will tell in deformity, weakness, incompleteness of character. What is true in doctrine and ideal will illustrate itself in nobility of character and life. Beauty is the splendour of truth. Here again Christianity finds attestation in the logical life. Proof that Christ brought the eternal doctrine was seen in His own personal perfection. He who was the Truth was the Beauty. And the same splendour of character has been revealed in all generations of Christ's saints. But it is objected that these characters are not what they are in beauty by virtue of Christianity. Some sceptic said of Sister Dora, "She's a noble woman, but she'd have been that without her Christianity." But we cannot accept that. Could we accept it if a man were to say of a great golden sheaf of wheat that had brought forth a hundred-fold, "Yes, it has grown on ploughed land, it has been manured, weeded, watched, but it would have grown just the same on a prairie"? III. IN CONSCIOUSNESS THE TEST OF TRUTH IS HAPPINESS. If a man's faith gives him joy of the very highest kind—a joy altogether pure and unselfish, a joy that is intelligent, a joy that promotes the growth of the moral nature, a joy that persists through change and sorrow—I say that in such gladness he finds one of the strongest proofs of the divinity of his creed. It is a matter of the first import that a faith makes myriads nobly happy. Now, the logic of life once more accredits the faith of Christ—it makes its disciples truly happy. (John xiv. 27). Those who rest in the great doctrines of Christ share the peace and joy of Christ. Just as the eye is delighted with the lustre of the sunshine, the ear with the concord of sweet sounds, the nostril with the fragrance of a flower, so the soul is delighted with the truths revealed in Jesus Christ (John xv. 11). (*W. L. Watkinson.*) *Inspiration of the spoken Word :*—The "Word" here is the spoken in contrast with the written Word (chap. i. 8), the Third Gospel which, it has been conjectured, had possibly been entrusted to the keeping of the Thessalonian Church. The bearing of the text on the doctrine of the inspiration of the spoken Word of the apostles is very evident. This effectual working, this energy which is ascribed to the Divine Word is seen in its revealing to men, both what they are by nature and may be by grace. It is, as it were, the mirror which, as legend has it, can alone stay the basilisk. That creature which neither fire nor sword can overcome, is destroyed at once so soon as, the mirror being set before it, it sees itself and its hideousness. The corruption of the natural man dies when it sees itself in the mirror of God's Word. Not only so, that Word is also like the fabled mirror, which, the longer it is gazed upon, transforms and beautifies the beholder, till at last it reflects to all who bend lovingly over it the perfected beauty of holiness. Such an all transforming energy pertains to God's Word in the experience of all who believe. (*J. Hutchison, D.D.*) *The unity of the Bible :*—"Word of God" is one of the most common, ancient, and accurate titles of the Bible. It is a name to be specially valued because it carries with it the doctrine that the Bible is one whole, has one Author, subject and object, and as the text states, works with like power in all who receive it. I. IN ANYTHING THAT HAS ORGANIC UNITY, ALL THE DIFFERENT PARTS, HOWEVER MANY AND ALIKE, ARE YET SO RELATED AS ORGANS THAT EVERY ONE OF THEM IS ESSENTIAL TO THE INTEGRITY AND COMPLETENESS OF THE WHOLE. 1. This needs illustration.

(1) In the human body there is a wonderful variety of parts as to substance, form, colour, size, &c.; but you cannot take away a bone or vein, &c., without effecting the unity of the body. The Mind that created it made every smallest part with reference to every other part. (2) In a heap of sand there is no such unity of parts or purpose. One particle has no necessary relation to others. Take away one or twenty of these separate grains, you make the heap smaller, that is all. (3) The same difference can be traced in the different states of a tree. The organic law of vegetable life makes every portion of a tree—bark, wood, sap, leaf—from the root to the topmost twig, one whole, in spite of the diversity of the parts. But cut the tree down, saw and split it, and then lay the pieces together, no matter how regularly—the unity is lost. But, again, take the same pieces of timber, shape them in a particular way so as to fit them for each other with other materials according to the design of our mind so as to make a building. Here we have unity again, though not of life. You look at the house or temple and say it is one thing. 2. These examples make it plain what organic unity is in any production of the mind whether of God or man. Remember, however, two qualifications—(1) While every portion is essential to the completeness it is not said that it is essential to the life of the thing. A tree will live with some of the branches or roots cut off. A body will live after amputation. (2) All the parts are not of equal importance. II. THE BIBLE HAS THIS UNITY. It came from one Spirit, as one whole, with one design. Every part has vital connection with every other and with that design. You cannot tear any portion out without vitally hurting the integrity and authority of it as one Book. Hence it is what it is declared to be, the indestructible "Word of God." If it has not this unity, then human reason may take it to pieces, like the useless links of a broken chain, and sit in judgment on each one, and throw any one away. This experiment has long ago been tried, but the Church has held the Bible fast, and kept it one. III. IN WHAT DOES THE UNITY OF THE BIBLE CONSIST. 1. Not in the absence of variety or diversity in the parts. No book ever written approaches it in the diversity of its contents. It is not like the unity of a Doric column, a blade of grass or a single portrait; but rather like the unity of nature in the variety of her manifestations and operations. 2. Look at this diversity as bringing out the unity by contrast in a striking and impressive light. (1) The division into two Testaments stamped with the characteristics of two unlike dispensations having centuries lying between. (2) There are more than threescore books with almost as many writers. (3) These volumes were produced in states of society utterly dissimilar and appeared at unequal intervals stretching over 1,500 years. (4) The history covers between three and four thousand years, is in three distinct languages, all dead. (5) Notice the diversities of style, chronicles, biographies, poems, statistics, songs, treatises, predictions, &c. Each author has a stamp of his own, clearly defined from the rest. 2. Yet after all it is one Word. This unity is—(1) a unity of doctrine. As to the being, personality and providence of God the Father; as to the history, character and offices of God the Son; as to the nature, gifts and works of God the Holy Ghost; as to man's origin, sin, recovery and destiny; as to his regeneration, redemption and retribution; as to the constitution and glory of the Church; as to holiness of life and the communion of saints, this book teaches by all its voices, substantially the same thing everywhere. (2) Of history, proceeding straight from the first man, by the chosen nation, expanding afterwards into the broader family all visited with "the Light" and all regathered before the throne, it is one perfect historic whole. (3) Of prophecy and its fulfilment. The predictions run on from that early one on the threshold of Eden, through different parts of the volume, including much special and minute foretelling, till the mysteries of another life are foreseen in Patmos. (4) Of types and their answering realities. One portion will tell us about men, places, acts or ceremonies of which we do not see half the significance till we read on to a distant part of the record. (5) Of one living Person who harmonizes these arguments in Himself. Central to all this wondrous universe of Scripture signs and symbols stands the Saviour's Cross, with unbroken tables of the broken law leaning against its feet. Jesus is its inward life—making it the Book of Life to us—as much as the blood in the veins is the life of the body. In conclusion notice two difficulties. 1. You say that you cannot see the connection of some parts of the Bible with its principal object. There are passages and even books so apparently detached from the main drift that you cannot trace the links which join them with the rest. This is just what might have been expected in a message sent by God to a short-lived and ignorant child, but meant also to be for all time, lands and conditions. If certain

pieces of mortar and timber from a building were brought to you, you would confess that you could not see what relation they bore to the structure. A young child sees no use in half the things that the grown-up world deems quite necessary to keep society safe and strong. Could you see as the inspiring Spirit sees you would confess that either to the narrative, or moral impression, or spiritual power, directly or indirectly, to some past, present or future, this very part was an essential contribution. 2. You say that some parts are unedifying. To you, perhaps, but not to differently constituted persons, nor even to yourself if you sought more prayerfully. (*Bp. Huntington.*) *Receiving the Scriptures as the Word of Man:*—I remember in Archbishop Magee's book on the Atonement, allusion to a commentary on a very difficult text, which seemed to the person who was handling it certainly to contain the doctrine of our Lord's pre-existence and divinity. The man who found this a hard nut to crack had no other way of solving it except by saying that probably the old apostle had dictated one thing, and his amanuensis had written down another. (*Archbishop Tait.*) *God's Word and man's; their relative value:*—There is gold in the rocks which fringe the pass of Splugen, gold even in the stones which mend the roads, but there is too little of it to be worth extracting. Alas, how like too many books and sermons! Not so the Scriptures; they are much fine gold; their very dust is precious. (*W. Baxendale.*) *God's Word and man's; their relative effect:*—A clergyman had prepared a certain sermon with great care, and had reason to hope that it would be attended with a great blessing, for which he had sought with earnest prayer. The sermon was preached with great effect, and he came down from the pulpit full of hope. A widow stopped him on his way to the vestry and begged a word. "Ah!" he said to himself "it is coming as I expected. I thought it would not be preached in vain." Then to the woman "What part of the sermon struck you most, the beginning or the ending?" "Well sir," she replied, "I do not know much about the beginning or the ending; but you said ' God so loved the world that He gave,' " &c. The doctor was struck to the heart. All his fine words forgotten, but one of God's words made effectual. (*Ibid.*) *The power of the Word:*—When I read Rom. ix-xi. to that fine old man, Mr. ——, at Ramsgate, he shed tears. Any Jew of sensibility must be deeply impressed by them. (*S. T. Coleridge.*) *Converted by the Word:*— It is well known that the Earl of Rochester was for many years an avowed infidel, and that a large portion of his time was spent in ridiculing the Bible. One of his biographers has described him as " a great wit, a great sinner, and a great penitent." Even this man was converted by the Holy Spirit in the use of His Word. Reading Isa. liii. he was convinced of the truth and inspiration of the Scriptures, and the Deity and Atonement of Christ. On that atonement he rested, and died in humble expectation of heavenly happiness. *Experimental evidence to the Word:*—In order to appreciate this come with me to some sequestered glen amid the hills of Scotland, to the patriarchal occupant of a lonely cabin, where you may behold the grey-headed man, amid intermingling smiles and tears, bending morning, noon and night, over one book, " the big ha' Bible." Let us ask him, "How do you know that that book is the Word of God? You never read the 'Evidences ' of Paley, the ' Analogy ' of Butler, the ' Credibility ' of Lardner, the eloquent ' Demonstrations ' of Chalmers; how came you to believe it?" "Come to believe it," would the peasant say, "I have felt it in my heart and conscience to be the Book of God; it has taught me the truths I never knew before; it has given me a peace the world could never give; it has calmed my beating heart; it has stanched my bleeding wounds; it has kindled within me the love of God, and the hope of glory. Not the Book of God! I am convinced of it as I am that I am here a living man." (*J. Cumming, D.D.*)

Ver. 14. **For ye, brethren, became followers of the Churches of God which are in Judæa.**—I. CHURCH FOLLOWERS. The Thessalonian believers, acquainted with the important fact that there were several holy brotherhoods in Judæa which were united to Jesus Christ by faith in His truth, strove to imitate them in their spiritual virtues, and thus show that they were one with them—were united to them in and through the same Lord. The union of Church members is not a mere outward adhesion, like the way in which the stones of a building are joined to one another, but it is a living organic union, like the members of one body, possessed of a common life, constituting together one living whole, so that all are parts of one and the same being; hence it is a union which cannot be severed without doing violence to that blessed Spirit by whose act it has been brought about. The Church of

Christ, which is His mystical body, cannot be otherwise than one, wherever it may be—in Judæa or Thessalonica, and its members, wherever living, cannot be otherwise than imitators of each other. II. CHURCH SUFFERERS. The Word preached to the Thessalonians had wrought so effectually in them that they became examples unto others not only in faith and good works, but in patience and suffering, also for the Word's sake. With unflinching courage and steady constancy they met the fierce opposition of their own fellow-tribe or clansmen, beside that of others—the Jews—all enemies of the Cross of Christ. Christ Himself never used anything like force or violence, except once, and that was to drive ungodly men not into the Temple, but out of it. To ill-treat, and stone, and crucify good men for their religion is not the gospel of Christ, but the direct instigation of the devil. He is the father of lies, and truth is almost invariably on the side of the persecuted. Yet, though believers suffer persecution for it, they are benefitted by persecution, just as the giant of the forest becomes all the stronger and more deeply rooted for the strong blasts which have shaken and tried it. (*M. F. Day, D.D.*) *Suffering the test of conversion*:—It often happens that suffering reveals new features of character and awakens powers before dormant. It is said that Agrippa had a dormouse that slumbered so profoundly that it would never wake till cast in a cauldron of boiling lead. So there are some natures which put forth their powers only when in extremity. The piety of God's people is often tested by affliction. The faith of thousands has sunk, while those who have borne the strain have gained an accession of moral nerve. The Thessalonians imitated the churches of God in facing the storm of persecution with unconquerable firmness. I. THEIR SUFFERING HAD A COMMON ORIGIN. "Ye of your own countrymen"—they "of the Jews." 1. It is the unkindest cut of all that comes from the sword of our own people—people with whom we have lived in amity, but from whom conscience compels us to differ (Psa. lv. 12), when natural love is turned into unnatural enmity. 2. What a revelation this of the devilish nature of persecution. Its insensate malice rudely sunders all bonds of fatherland, friendship, or kindred. The close affinity between Cain and Abel does not arrest the murderer's hand. The tender ties between Saul and David avail not to curb the mad cruelty of the king. 3. How deep and changeless is the truth—"All that will live godly in Christ Jesus shall suffer persecution." The suffering that tests is still from the same source— "A man's foes are they of his own household." II. THEIR SUFFERING WAS BORNE WITH EXEMPLARY CHRISTIAN FORTITUDE. The same thought is expressed in chap. i. 6. At the head of the long line is Jesus, the captain of salvation; and all whom He leads to glory walk in His steps, imitate His example, and so become followers one of another. 1. It is not suffering in itself that purifies, so much as the spirit in which it is borne. It was enough to cool the fiery ambition of the aspiring disciples when Jesus said, "Are ye able to drink of the cup that I shall drink of?" And yet the following of Christ in suffering is the true test of discipleship. "He that taketh not his cross and followeth after Me, is not worthy of Me." 2. It is a proof of the supernatural efficacy of the gospel that it inspires so intense a love of it as to make us willing to endure suffering for its sake. The love of truth becomes supreme. John Huss, lamenting the rupture of an old and valued friendship, said, "Paletz is my friend; truth is my friend; and both being my friends, it is my sacred duty to give the first honour to truth." 3. The soul, penetrated with this devotion, will pass unscathed the fiery test. On the destruction of the London Alexandra Palace by fire, it was found that, while many specimens of old English porcelain exhibited there were reduced to a black, shapeless mass, the true porcelain of Bristol, though broken into fragments, still retained its whiteness, and even its most delicate shades of colour uninjured by the fire. So the truly good, though wounded, shall survive the fiercest trial, and retain intact all that distinguishes the Christian character. Lessons:—1. Our love of the Gospel is tested by what we suffer for it. 2. The similarity of experience, in all times and places, is a strong evidence of the truth of the Christian religion. 3. Suffering does not destroy, but builds up and perfects. (*G. Barlow.*) *The secret of persecution*:—A wolf flies not upon a painted sheep, and men can look upon a painted toad with delight. It is not the soft pace, but the furious march of the soldier that sets men a-gazing and dogs a-barking. Let but a man glide along with the stream of the world, do as others do, he may sit down and take his ease; but if he once strive against the stream, stand up in the cause of God, and act for Christ, then he shall be sure to meet with as much malice as men and devils can possibly throw upon him. (*J. Spencer.*) *The honour of persecution*:—One who was persecuted in Queen Mary's time wrote thus, "A poor prisoner for Christ! What is this for a poor worm! Such honour have not all His saints. Both the degrees I took in the university have not set me so high as the honour of becoming a prisoner of the Lord." *Consolation in persecution:*—Do they cast us out of the city? They cannot cast us out of that which is in the heavens. If they who hate us could do this, they would be doing something real against us. So long, however, as they cannot do this, they are but pelting us with drops of water or striking us with the wind. (*Gregory Nazianzen.*) *Persecution elicits sympathy:*—A coloured man applied to a New York merchant for a subscription, who at once knocked him into the street. The coloured man started on telling the story of his abuse, won sympathy by it, and, before night, collected fifty dollars. The persecutor, hearing the story, desired to silence the man, sent for him, and gave him a liberal subscription. *Benefit of persecution:*—As frankincense, when it is put into the fire, giveth the greater perfume; as spice, if it be pounded and beaten, smelleth the sweeter; as the earth, when it is torn up by the plough, becometh more fruitful; the seed in the ground, after frost and snow and winter-storms, springeth the ranker; the nigher the vine is pruned to the stock, the greater grape it yieldeth; the grape, when it is most pressed and beaten, maketh the sweetest wine; linen, when it is bucked and washed, wrung and beaten, is so made fairer and whiter: even so the children of God receive great benefit by persecution; for by it God washeth and scoureth, schooleth and nurtureth them, that so, through many tribulations, they may enter into their rest. (*Cawdray.*) *Persecution a stimulus:*—A certain amount of persecution rouses a man's defiance, stirs his blood for magnificent battle, and makes him fifty times more a man than he would have been without the persecution. So it was with the great reformer when he said, "I will not be put down, I will be heard." And so it was with Millard, the preacher, in the time of Louis XI. When that sovereign sent word to him that unless he stopped preaching in that style he would throw him into the river, he replied, "Tell the king that I shall reach heaven sooner by water, than he will by fast horses." (*T. De Witt Talmage, D.D.*)

Vers. 15, 16. **Who both killed the Lord Jesus and their own prophets.**—*Paul's indictment of the Jews:*—The apostle "goes off" upon the word "Jews" to describe the evil deeds of his countrymen. I. THE EXPLANATION OF THE INDICTMENT. Various views have been offered. 1. That as the persecution of believers in Thessalonica, though from the heathen, was yet directly instigated by the Jews, it was natural that Paul should turn aside to speak of them and their wickedness. 2. That the apostle, at the very time of writing, was himself suffering at their hands (Acts xviii. 5, 6, 12). His mind, therefore, we can well conceive, was full of thoughts regarding these Jewish misdeeds, and hence he bursts forth into utterances of sorrowful indignation. 3. That the Thessalonians were converts from Polytheism to a monotheistic religion which was a growth out of Judaism. They could, consequently, hardly fail to stumble by seeing Jews everywhere its most violent opponents. Paul may have striven to meet this state of mind, by showing that the opposition of the Jews was in keeping with their whole character and conduct. II. ITS SUBJECT MATTER. 1. The culminating point in Jewish wickedness is the casting out and murder of their Messiah. In ignorance they did it, it is true. Yet that ignorance was no justification, for the prophets, whose testimony was to Christ, the Jews had also slain. This is the indictment of the Old Testament, and also of Christ (Matt. xxiii. 29-39). Paul's words are but an echo of his Master's. 2. Seeing, then, that such was their past conduct, Paul adds, as naturally following, "and have persecuted us." What had been meted out to God's servants in the past it was to be expected would be extended to the apostles and believers. Under new conditions the Jewish character would again assert itself. 3. Hence he declares "They please not God and are contrary to all men." The more he came in contact with Gentile life, the more he must have observed the intense dislike with which the Jews were everywhere regarded. Despising other nations, they were themselves only loathed by these nations in return; and now that Paul's feelings had broadened into the love of all mankind, he could not but recognize them as showing what Tacitus called "adversus omnes alios hostile odium." The mark of God's anger had been set upon them, and the Divine judgment had been ratified by men. "When God loathes aught, men presently loathe it too." 4. But here it is not the dislike felt by others towards the Jews as the animosity of the Jews towards all others. "Forbidding us to speak to the Gentiles," &c. Like their own Pharisees they would neither enter in themselves nor allow others to enter. 5. In thus standing in the way of the Gentiles' salvation they were acting so as "to fill up their own sins alway" with fearful perseverance; alike before Christ had come, when He came, and now that He had gone, they had been filling up the measure of their guilt. 6. And now retribution was approaching. Wrath had already fallen, and was falling upon them; but in a short fourteen years it came upon them to the utmost in the destruction of their city and the dispersion of their race. (*J. Hutchison, D.D.*) *The fury of the old religion against the new:*—The transition from the old to a new order of things in the progress of religion is not always accomplished without opposition. Age is naturally and increasingly tenacious: and the old religion looks upon the new with suspicion, jealousy, fear, anger. The Jews had resisted the attempts of their own Divinely-commissioned prophets to rouse them to a purer faith and life; but their fury reached its climax in their opposition to Christianity. Observe—I. THE FURY OF THE JEWS IN THEIR INHUMAN TREATMENT OF THE GREAT LEADERS OF RELIGIOUS THOUGHT. 1. They plotted against the life of the world's Redeemer; and, in spite of insufficient evidence to convict, and the endeavours of the Roman Procurator to release, they clamoured for His crucifixion, exclaiming, "His blood be on us and on our children"—a self-invoked imprecation that fell on them with terrible and desolating vengeance! 2. The sin of murder already darkly stained their race—the best and noblest of their prophets being the unoffending victims. Isaiah, Jeremiah, Amos, and Zechariah met with violent deaths. The charge of Stephen was unanswerable (Acts vii. 52). 3. The apostles were subjected to similar treatment—"Have chased and driven us out." They drove them out of Thessalonica, afterwards out of Berea, and were at that moment engaged in instigating an insurrection to drive the apostle out of Corinth. The spirit of persecution is unchanged. Wherever the attempt is made to raise the Church, it is met with a jealous, angry opposition. And yet what a wretched, short-sighted policy does persecution reveal! It is the idolized weapon of the tyrant and the coward, the sport of the brutal, the sanguinary carnival of devils. II. THE FURY OF THE JEWS WAS DISPLEASING TO GOD. They fondly imagined that they were the favourites of heaven, and that all others were excluded from the Divine complacency. They could quote the words of their law, such as Deut. xiv. 2, with the utmost facility, to support their assumption of superiority and exclusiveness, wilfully shutting their eyes to the difference between the holy intention of Jehovah, and their miserable failure to realize that intention. In all their opposition to Christianity they thought they were doing God service. How fatally blinding is sin—goading the soul to the commission of the most horrible crimes under the guise of virtue. III. THE FURY OF THE JEWS WAS HOSTILE TO MAN. 1. Their hostility was directed against the world of mankind. "Are contrary to all men." The Jews of that period were the adversaries and despisers of all. Tacitus brands them as "the enemies of all men:" and Apion, the Egyptian, calls them "Atheists and misanthropes, in fact, the most witless and dullest of barbarians." 2. Their hostility was embittered by a despicable religious jealousy. "Forbidding us to speak to the Gentiles," &c. Here the fury of the old religion against the new reached its climax. It is the perfection of bigotry and cruelty to deny to our fellow-men the only means of salvation! Into what monsters of barbarity will persecution convert men! Pharaoh persisted to such a degree of unreasonableness as to chastise the Hebrews for not accomplishing impossibilities! Julian the Apostate, carried his vengeful spirit to his deathbed. IV. THE FURY OF THE JEWS HURRIED THEM INTO IRRETRIEVABLE RUIN. 1. Their wickedness was wilfully persistent. "To fill up their sins alway"—at all times, now as much as ever. So much so, the time is now come when the cup of their iniquity is filled to the brim, and nothing can prevent the consequent punishment. The desire to sin grows with its commission. St. Gregory says, "Sinners would live for ever that they might sin for ever"—a powerful argument for the endlessness of future punishment—the desire to sin is endless! 2. Their punishment was inevitable and complete. "For the wrath is come upon them to the uttermost"—is even now upon them. The process has begun. Their fury to destroy others will accelerate their own destruction. Punishment descended upon the wicked, unbelieving, and resisting Jews; and utter destruction upon their national status and religious supremacy. Lessons:—1. There is a fearful possibility of sinking into a lifeless formality, and a blind, infatuate opposition to the good. 2. The rage of man against the truth defeats its own ends and recoils in vengeance on himself. (*G. Barlow.*) *Guilty of the death of Christ:*—Bridaine was one of the most celebrated of the French preachers. Marmontel relates that in his sermons he sometimes had recourse to the interesting method of parables, with a view the more forcibly to impress important truths on the minds of his hearers. Preaching on the passion of Jesus Christ, he expressed himself thus :—"A man, accused of a crime of which he was innocent, was condemned to death by the iniquity of his judges. He was led to punishment, but no gibbet was prepared, nor was there any executioner to perform the sentence. The people, moved with compassion, hoped that this sufferer would escape death. But one man raised his voice, and said, 'I am going to prepare a gibbet, and I will be the executioner.' You groan with indignation! Well, my brethren, in each of you I behold this cruel man. Here are no Jews to-day, to crucify Jesus Christ : but you dare to rise up, and say, 'I will crucify Him.'" Marmontel adds, that he heard these words pronounced by the preacher, though very young, with all the dignity of an apostle, and with the most powerful emotion; and that such was the effect, that nothing was heard but the sobs of the auditory.    **For the wrath is come upon them to the uttermost.**—*The Jews under the wrath of God :*—Bishop Patrick quotes the following affecting inquiry addressed by Rabbi Samuel Moraccanus to a friend in the eleventh century :—" I would fain learn from thee, out of the testimonies of the law, and the prophets, and other Scriptures, why the Jews are thus smitten in this captivity wherein we are, which may be properly termed the perpetual anger of God, because it hath no end. For it is now above a thousand years since we were carried captive by Titus; and yet our fathers, who worshipped idols, killed the prophets, and cast the law behind their back, were only punished with a seventy years' captivity, and then brought home again ; but now there is no end of our calamities, nor do the prophets promise any." "If," says Bishop Patrick, "this argument was hard to be answered then, in his days, it is much harder in ours, who still see them pursued by God's vengeance, which can be for nothing else but rejecting and crucifying the Messiah, the Saviour of the world." *Severity consistent with benevolence :*—Take the case of an earthly parent. Suppose him to be endowed with all the tenderest sensibilities of nature, conceive of him as delighting in the health and welfare of his children, and, in the exercise of every benevolent affection, lavishing on them all the riches of a father's kindness and a father's care. You say, on looking at his benignant countenance and his smiling family, this is an affectionate father. But a secret canker of ingratitude seizes one or more of his children, they shun his presence, or dislike his society, and at length venture on acts of positive disobedience; he warns them, he expostulates with them, but in vain, they revolt more and more ; and at length, in the exercise of deliberate thought, he lifts the rod and chastens them ; and he who once was the author of all their happiness has become also their calm but firm reprover. And who that knows the tenderness of a father's love will not acknowledge that, severe as may be the suffering inflicted, such a man doth not afflict willingly, nor grieve the children of his love? Again, conceive of a man of benevolent feelings invested with the office of magistrate or judge—conceive that Howard, the unwearied friend of his race, who visited the prisons of Europe to alleviate the miseries of the worst and most destitute of men—conceive of such a man sitting in judgment over the life or liberty of another, and can you not suppose, that while every feeling within him inclined him to the side of mercy, and his every sensibility would be gratified, were it possible to make the felon virtuous and happy, he might, notwithstanding, have such a deep moral persuasion of the importance of virtue and order to the well-being of the state, that he could consign the prisoner to a dungeon or the gallows, and that, too, with the perfect conviction that it was right and good to do so ; while, still, every sentiment of the heart within him, if it could be disclosed, would bear witness, that he afflicted not willingly, and that he had no pleasure in the death of the criminal? Such a father, and such a judge is God; and the sufferings which he inflicts, whether they be viewed as corrective or penal, are compatible with the loftiest benevolence in the Divine mind. (*Dr. J. Buchanan.*)

Ver. 17. **But we, brethren, being taken from you for a short time.**—*The power of Satan great but restricted :*—St. Paul had a very profound belief in the reality and activity of the evil one (Eph. ii. 2 ; 2 Cor. iv. 4 ; Acts xxvi. 18 ; 1 Tim. v. 15 ; Eph. iv. 27 ; 2 Cor. xii. 7). The powers of Satan—I. FORCING AN UNWILLING SEPARATION. 1. The separation was painful but temporary—"Being taken from you" literally, "being orphaned of you." Their grief was like that of a father bereaved of his children, or children of their parents. They hoped speedily to return, and after a lapse of five years, that hope was realized. Satan acted by means of wicked men (Acts xvii. 5-8, 13). 2. The separation did not lessen their spiritual attachment. "In presence, not in heart." Satan may deprive of the oppor-

tunity of social intercourse, but not of reciprocal Christian love. Augustine, referring to different kinds of friendship, shows the pre-eminence of the spiritual, when the link is grace and the Spirit of God. " Natural affections, want of presence diminisheth; mundane friendship, where profit makes the union, want of profit unlooseth; but spiritual amity nothing dissolves, no, not that which dissolves all others, lack of society." II. HINDERING AN EARNESTLY DESIRED VISIT. 1. Opposition intensified their desire to see their converts. "Endeavoured the more abundantly," &c. As lime is inflamed by water, as a stream grows more furious by the obstacles set against it, so genuine affection is increased by that which opposes it. 2. The opposition succeeded in baffling repeated attempts to carry out that desire. "Once and again, but Satan hindered us." The apostle halted at Berea on his way to Athens, and probably attempted then to return to Thessalonica, but was thwarted in his design. Though no express reference is made in the history to the agency of Satan, Paul had unmistakeable evidence of its operation in many ways. Satan hindered us—perhaps by sickness, imprisonment, tempests at sea, or by keeping him so fully occupied with incessant conflicts and ever new tribulations of his own, as to leave him no leisure for carrying out his plan. The verb signifies to cut a trench in the way of a pursuing enemy, so as to hinder his progress. III. UNABLE TO ROB THE CHRISTIAN WORKER OF THE JOY AND REWARD OF SUCCESS. Great as is the power of Satan, it is not omnipotent. The Christian warrior can successfully withstand it (Eph. vi. 11–13; Rom. xvi. 20). 1. Success in soul-saving is productive of joy. "For what is our hope," &c. The merchant rejoices over his gains, the warrior over his victories, the artist over the achievements of genius; but there is no joy so sweet as that of the successful winner of souls. 2. The joy of success in soul-saving will be among the highest rewards of the future. "In the presence of our Lord Jesus Christ at His coming?" &c. The return of Christ to heaven, after the judgment, is here compared to the solemnity of a triumph, in which the apostle is to appear crowned in token of victory over the false religions of the world, attended by his converts, and because they are the cause of his being thus crowned, they are, by a beautiful figure of speech, called his crown of rejoicing. Special honour is promised to the successful worker (Dan. xii. 3). (1) Joy enhanced by the recognitions in the future life. If Paul knows his converts in the heavenly world, shall not we know our loved ones who have gone before? (2) By the presence and approbation of the Lord Jesus for whom we have laboured. "In Thy presence is fulness of joy," &c. Lessons: 1. The power of Satan works through many agencies; therefore we have need of watchfulness. 2. The power of Satan is limited; therefore we need not be discouraged (*G. Barlow.*)    *Paul's absence from the Thessalonians:*—For this he apologizeth. I. HE WAS RUDELY FORCED AWAY FROM THEM, such was the rage of his persecutors, who, by certain lewd fellows of the baser sort, stirred all the city of Thessalonica into an uproar, and would have taken summary vengeance upon him and Silas; but their brethren interposed, and ere long they sent them away by night to Berea. The body of Paul was at Berea, but the heart of Paul was at Thessalonica. He could not forget the Thessalonians. Sooner might the stars forget their courses at night-time, or the sun forget to shine at noon-day. II. EVEN HIS BODILY ABSENCE WAS BUT FOR A BRIEF SPACE—the time of an hour, as it were. All time on earth is brief and uncertain, whether we are present with our friends or absent from them. This world is not a place where we are long together. It is in heaven holy souls shall meet and never part more. III. HE EARNESTLY ENDEAVOURED TO SEE THEM AGAIN. How strong and beautiful his words, " We endeavoured the more abundantly to see your face with great desire! " Who could doubt his affection for his converts after this? He knew they esteemed him very highly in love for his works' sake, and was therefore attracted to them by the force of the same holy passion. Love alway begets love, and hearts thereby influenced would never be separated. But even apostles are not masters of their own time. Paul did his best, and angels could do no more. IV. BUT SATAN HINDERED HIS RETURN TO THEM. The great enemy of mankind is especially opposed to those who would destroy his kingdom of lies by declaring the truth of another kingdom. The child of God can no sooner enterprise that which is really good, but he meets with some impediment; so, whoever be the means or instruments for impeding us in the way of duty, the devil himself, through God's permission, is the prime author of that woeful work, and all others do but fight under his banner; for, though other means were doubtless accessory to Paul's stay at Berea, yet Satan hindered him from returning at once to Thessalonica. (*D. Mayo.*)    *The discipline of absence:*
—A little party of friends had been making a fortnight's excursion among the Alps,

in high enjoyment and good fellowship. Among them were two lovers in the first happiness of their engagement. The company broke up by degrees, and on the shore of the Lake of Geneva the young man took leave for a while of his betrothed. As the little steamer carried her away, and the twilight fell upon the lake, she sat alone, and her face grew pensive with a loneliness which was new to her. Her friends were walking the deck—a husband and wife, who for many years had walked together, and to whom sweet alike were the deck or the shore, Switzerland or England, if they were side by side. Their glances fell on the girl, and they said to each other, " To-day she was happy, and now she is sad ; but she could not spare the sadness. She will be the fitter for a wife's joy if she learns to love through missing him as well as through having him." So, perhaps, may higher intelligences look upon us in our saddest hours, and say, " Now they are learning to love." (*Free Methodist.*)

Ver. 18. **Satan hindered us.**—*Satan the hinderer :*—It may be profitable to remind ourselves of two or three things bearing upon the non-fulfilment of our best purposes. We have schemes which come to nothing ; wishes which perish in disappointment ; vows which fall so far short of realization as to afflict our hearts with a sense of self-perjury and self-contempt. What is that malign power which hinders us when we start on any holy errand ? Why is there not a clear path to the soul's feet, so that we may run the way of the Lord ? The question is all-important. If we know the hinderer we may address ourselves to the speciality of his power ; but if we mis-conceive his individuality or resources we may exhaust our strength in profitless labour. I. THERE IS A HINDERER. Not only are there hindrances ; there is a per-sonal hinderer. He is not visible. He is not persuadable ; resist is the right word, not persuade. Is the tiger ever persuaded to spare the prey ? God can be entreated ; the devil must be resisted. One man says there is no devil. Who is that one man ? Where does he live ? What has he done for the race ? " Jesus I know, Paul I know, but who is this ? " The devil tempted Jesus, entered into Judas, desired to have Peter, hindered Paul. I prefer that my faith should run in the line of these statements, notwithstanding their mystery, than that it should espouse the suggestions of speculators who have not yet established their claim to the confi-dence of souls. II. THE HINDERER ASSAILS THE MOST EMINENT WORKERS IN THE CHURCH.—The Saviour even, and here Paul. We are apt to think that the greatest escape the temptations which fall to the lot of others. But the greater the man, the greater the temptation. It is so in other things. The more refined the taste, the more sensitive to vulgarities. Our temptations—1. Show our unity as members of a common race. 2. Should awaken our sympathy as partakers of a common suffering. III. THIS HINDERER SEEKS TO FOIL THE AGGRESSIVE INTENTIONS OF THE CHRISTIAN. 1. In being a hinderer the enemy has the decided advantage. (1) It is easy to hinder, *i.e.,* easy to do mischief, suggest difficulties, magnify obstacles. (2) It is easier to hinder than to counteract. Once let the seed be sown, &c. Once let a good impression be produced, &c. 2. Did Satan ever hinder a man from doing a bad action ? When we were about to give a pound to a good cause, did Satan ever say, " Give *two.*" 3. Remember the enemy deals with the purposes as well as the performances. He fights battles in the mind. What a wreck is the inner life of some of us ! Application—1. Satan comes to us sometimes through the medium of bad men. 2. Sometimes through the gratification of apparently harmless wishes (" There is no harm in it "). 3. Sometimes through friendly but incapable advisers —men who are so far below our level, as utterly to miscalculate us. But there is hope. There is a helper. The Holy Spirit alone can overcome the spirit of evil. (*J. Parker, D.D.*) *The hinderer :*—All agree about the hindrances, but some deny that there is a personal hinderer. They hoot at the idea that a God of infinite power and beneficence would permit so malignant a rebel to exist. But where have such people lived ? There are thousands of visible devils, why not one invisible ? The devil hinders—I. BY SUGGESTING DOUBTS. The terrible catastrophe of the fall was accomplished by a doubt. One of his greatest achievements is to create the doubt of his own existence. We live in an age in which nearly everything that is necessary to be believed is doubted. Depravity is seen in nothing more clearly than in the manner in which people act when in doubt religiously. Instead of wisely protecting our own interests, we often give Satan the benefit of our doubts. Nothing pleases Satan so well as to get people in doubt as to the Atonement, the Bible, Judgment, Hell, &c. If he can do this, he will soon have them acting in accor-dance with their doubts. II. BY MAGNIFYING DIFFICULTIES. By this means he hinders multitudes, young and old, from giving their hearts to God. He is not honest enough to tell people that this life is one of difficulty, whether they are good or bad; but insinuates that the most crushing difficulties are in the paths of righteousness. But he is a liar. We are not at home yet, only at school. Our work is to master the hard curriculum; but God's cheering promise is, "All things work together for good," &c. III. By DISTRACTIONS. He dislikes a fixed purpose for the right, and loves to disincline the mind to think on eternal realities. He does not mind men being piously inclined, and purposing to do better. If he can keep them from immediate surrender, he knows that all the rest will be of no avail in the final issue. Conclusion: 1. As a hinderer Satan is the cause of two things—(1) Much that we would do but cannot. Paul's visit to Thessalonica was frustrated. (2) Much that we could do if we would: as our sins of commission. 2. Our helper is greater than our hinderer. (*T. Kelly.*) *Satan as a hinderer:*—Satan bears a threefold character—tempter, accuser, hinderer. As a hinderer he is obstructive, while as a tempter and accuser, he is destructive. 1. He inspires indifferentism where there ought to be enthusiasm. 2. He influences men to oppose inertia to advancement. 3. He fosters extra-conservatism. They used to say of Lord Eldon, that "he *prevented* more good than any other man ever *did.*" Wilberforce breasted opposition for forty-six years, in fighting for abolition of the slave trade. William Carey for fifteen years faced the opposition of his own brethren in furthering missions. 4. He leads to criticism and ridicule of what is good. 5. He moves men to determined and open antagonism to what is good—under every pretext. (*Homiletic Review.*) *Satanic power:*—I. THAT THERE IS A PERSONAL HINDERER IN THE SPIRITUAL LIFE OF MEN. Both the tenor and history, and the assignment of personal attributes prove it. He is mighty, malignant, spiritual, invisible, and impersuadable. II. THIS HINDERER ASSAILS THE MOST EMINENT PERSONAGES AND WORKERS IN THE CHURCH. This shows the unity of the race, and suggests a common sympathy. III. THIS HINDERER SEEKS TO FOIL EVERY AGGRESSIVE CHRISTIAN INTENTION. Easier to "hinder" than counteract: to suggest difficulties and magnify obstacles. Satan hinders the cause of religion in the world by creating, and then pointing to the foibles and sins of professors. 1. Their inconsistencies—pride, worldliness, divisions, selfishness, covetousness, gloominess. 2. Their crimes—drunkenness, fraud, &c. 3. Lukewarmness. (*J. M. McNulty, D.D.*) *Satanic hindrances:*—Paul and his companions were unable to revisit Thessalonica. 1. Not from want of will. 2. Not through the interpositions of Providence. 3. But because Satan hindered them. The hindrance was perhaps—(1) the persecution which made it prudent for them to stay away. (2) Or the Athenian philosophers and Corinthian heretics, which made it necessary that they should stay and defend and strengthen the young Churches. (3) Or dissensions which Satan fomented in the Churches they were visiting, which rendered their prolonged stay imperative. Anyhow, Satan was the prime mover. But why should he take so much interest in these three poor missionaries? That he might weaken the young Church at Thessalonica and destroy it; that he might thwart a powerful ministry; that he might keep Christians apart, and thus weaken that unity which is the strength of God's people. Note—I. IT HAS BEEN SATAN'S PRACTICE OF OLD TO HINDER, WHEREVER HE COULD, THE WORK OF GOD. " Satan hindered us " is the testimony which every saint will bear against the arch enemy. He endeavours to hinder—1. The completeness of the personal character of individual saints. Take the case of Job. 2. The emancipation of God's redeemed ones. (1) Jannes and Jambres withstood Moses, imitating his wonders by their enchantments. Romanism is an ingenious imitation of, and a Satanic hindrance to the Gospel. (2) Korah and his company hindered Israel by their assumption of the priesthood. Satan hinders now by conspiring to deprive Christ of His sole right to the priesthood. (3) Achan hindered Israel seriously; so do Satan's traitors in the camp to-day. (4) When Ezra and Nehemiah were found to build the waste places, the devil was sure to stir up Sanballat and Tobiah to cast down. There never was a revival of religion without a revival of the old enmity. 3. The history of the New Testament Church no less than that of the Old is a history of Satan's hinderings. When Christ was on earth, Satan hindered Him personally, and through the Pharisees, &c. When the apostles began their ministry, Herod and the Jews sought to hinder them, and when persecution prevailed not, all sorts of heresies and schisms broke out. When the reformation dawned, if God raised up Luther, Satan brought out Loyala to hinder him. If God had His Wycliffes and Latimers, Satan had his Gardiners and Bonners. II. THE WAYS IN WHICH SATAN HAS HINDERED US. He is very busy in hindering—1. Coming to Christ: perplexing with the guilt of past sins, or with the doctrine of election. But you must surmount both, feeling that your great business is to believe in the Lord Jesus Christ. 2. Prayer. (1) Tempting to abstain from it. (2) To relax importunity in it. 3. Christian work. (1) When we are prompted to work, *e.g.*, to speak to one about his soul, to visit the sick and relieve them, to contribute to missions, to teach in the ragged school, then Satan hinders. (2) When we are embarked on the work, we never ought to expect success unless we have the devil making a noise. We are doing little good when the devil is quiet. 4. Christian union. 5. Communion with Christ: distracting us in our most sacred ordinance. III. THE RULES BY WHICH WE MAY DETECT SATANIC HINDRANCES. I do not believe that Satan generally hinders people from getting rich. He delights to see God's servants set upon the pinnacle of the temple, for he knows the position is dangerous. You may tell when Satan hinders. 1. By the object. Satan's object is to prevent our glorifying God. If anything has happened to prevent your growing holy, useful, humble, you may trace it to Satan. 2. By the method. God employs good motives, Satan bad ones. 3. By their nature. Whenever an impediment to usefulness is pleasing it comes from Satan. He never brushes the feathers of his birds the wrong way; he generally deals with us according to our tastes and likings. 4. By their season. They come in prayer and while engaged in God's work. But we ought carefully to watch that we do not put the saddle on the wrong horse. Do not blame the devil when it is yourself. On the other hand, when the Lord puts a bar in your way, do not say, "That is Satan," and so go against the providence of God. IV. Supposing that we have ascertained that our hindrance comes from Satan, WHAT THEN? Go on, hindrance or no hindrance. 1. If Satan hinders opposition should cheer you. It is your duty to show that Satan is your enemy; rejoice when a prospect of overcoming him transpires. 2 Stand out against him, because you have now an opportunity of making a greater gain than if he had been quiet. 3. Consider what you lose if you do not resist and overcome him. It will be eternal ruin; or at the very least the ruin of Christian usefulness. 4. Feed your courage with the recollection that Christ has overcome. 5. Remember the promise, "Resist the devil and he will flee from you." (*C. H. Spurgeon.*) *Satan hindering Paul:*—The word "hinder" is a metaphor taken from military operations—the breaking up of roads, the destroying of bridges, and the interposing of varied obstacles, to cut off the enemies' approach or retreat. Or the figure may be that of the racecourse, the upsetting of a chariot by being brought into violent contact with another. Either way we have a graphic description of the obstructions in the way of the apostle's advance. Just as an angel stood in the evil way of Balaam, the apostate prophet, to intercept him, so is Satan here represented as standing in the good way of Paul. It is worthy of note that the personal spirit of evil is mentioned by his Hebrew name in this, Paul's earliest epistle—an epistle, too, addressed to a Gentile Church, and containing no direct quotation of Scripture. How, then, had these Gentile believers come to know his name and nature? By Paul's oral teaching, and probably also by a written Gospel. Now, of all the Gospels there is none which speaks so clearly concerning the personality and operations of the tempter under the name of Satan than that written by St. Paul's fellow-traveller, Luke. Here we have, therefore, another incidental confirmation of the view that that Gospel may have been entrusted to the Church of Thessalonica to disseminate. However, such an allusion to the adversary of souls points very strongly to the doctrine of his personality. But to what form of hindrance does the apostle allude? It was not, we may be sure, to any pressure of labour; Paul would regard this as a burden of honour laid upon him by the Master. It may have been the danger to which he would be exposed, as he had been previously, if he repaired to Thessalonica; but this cannot have bulked very largely in his view at the time; he is so sympathetically alive to the same danger as besetting his much-loved friends. It is more likely that the restraint arose from trials befalling believers in the districts where Paul himself was; but this has no support from the context, for it would seem from that to have been one in which Paul pre-eminently was concerned—"Even I, Paul." He makes something like a severance of himself from his companion in regard to it, and the "once and again" seems to point not to habitual or prolonged hindrance such as arose from dangers besetting the Church, but rather to some sudden, unexpected, and powerful obstacle such as bodily sickness, which, after passing away, had come upon him once more. These considerations seem to point to the "thorn in the flesh, the messenger of Satan sent to buffet him." Like the mysterious agony which now and again seized King Alfred in the midst of intensest activity, this thorn in the flesh was an interruption for the time being to all apostolic plans. This hindrance, however, sent of Satan, as it was declared to be, was yet blessed of God to Paul himself, doubtless for the increase of his patience, the purifying of his desires, the quickening of his zeal, and his growth in grace. It was also blessed of God to others. To the apostle's enforced absence from Thessalonica we owe this Epistle, fraught with its words of warning, comfort, and direction for all time. (*J. Hutchison, D.D.*)    *Satan a hinderer :*—I remember standing in the front of the Cathedral of Notre Dame, in Paris, admiring its beautiful statuary. As I did so a Parisian approached me and said, "Do you not see something amusing up there?" "No!" I said, "it seems to be all religious." Inwardly I was asking myself, "Is this an Atheist, or is he making a fool of me?" "Do you see those figures?" he inquired, pointing to a group representing a soul being weighed to see if it should be found wanting. "You observe that there is an angel standing on the one side and Satan on the other. Satan seems as if he were just watching to see that there was fair play." "Yes," I answered, "but I fail to see anything amusing in that." "Just look under the scales!" he replied. I looked, and there underneath was a little imp pulling down the scale. That is the way Satan gives fair play. A man says, "I will reform. I'll mend my life. I'll give up drink." "All right," says Satan, and he seems to stand aside and give fair play. Do not trust him. He has some unseen imp hanging on against you. If it be not strong drink, it will be some other sin. The only way to get clear of all these is to get Christ beside you; His power and grace will outweigh all the evil influences of Satan. (*Christian Herald.*)

Vers. 19, 20. **What is our hope, or joy, or crown of rejoicing ?**—*Those we lead to Christ an element of our final reward :*—Paul wrote this letter from Corinth. He had, probably, just witnessed the Grecian games and the crowning of the victors. Then, says he, "What is our crown? Are not even ye?" They were also his glory. God desires and expects honour. We have a right to desire it. His prayer was that his pupils might be perfect in Christ at His coming. The "coming" is associated with the resurrection. Then the apostle's hope was to see his pupils complete in Christ at the resurrection. 1. PAUL WAS NOT CONCERNED ABOUT HIS OWN SALVATION. That was as far behind him as that spot on the way to Damascus. His hope, his joy, was in the salvation of others. II. HE EXPECTED TO KNOW THEM IN THE RESURRECTION. For this would be the source of his joy. They, for whom he laboured, would then be his crown. The indefinite thought that somewhere in the universe were a crowd of persons who had been saved through his labour would not have satisfied. There follows the inference that identity will not be destroyed. To destroy identity is to destroy the person. Nor is there continuity of existence save in memory. We go into the other world with the totality of our natures. There can be no reward save there is a consciousness of work done, and this consciousness will depend on the memory being intact. Otherwise, God may give joy, but that will not be reward; He may torture, but that will not be punishment. III. THEN IT WILL BE KNOWN TO THESE SAVED ONES WHAT PAUL HAD WROUGHT FOR THEM. Else, how could their salvation be his joy and his crown? He would need more than the unselfish thought of what he had done. God will have glory. Christ was never more unselfish than when on the cross, despising the shame, yet He thought of the "joy that was set before Him." An element in Paul's joy will be the honour and praise given him by those who will be conscious of the good he did them. IV. PAUL WAS NOT A MERE INSTRUMENT, BUT A CO-WORKER WITH GOD. He was a factor in the power that saved his pupils. He speaks of God and the Holy Spirit, and also of himself, and claims for himself a crown of rejoicing in the work wrought. Then God, Paul, and you are to work out the salvation of men. V. PAUL WILL TAKE HIS CROWN IN THE PRESENCE OF THE LORD. Christ will recognize him as his factor. Christ will not be jealous. The elder brother goes out to find the prodigal. Observe—1. Selfish motives are admissible in our Christian work. The Lord, perhaps, never had a more self-sacrificing servant than Paul. He cultivated such familiarity with the spiritual world as to make it present. He thought Christ might come any minute. His was a personal hope, a personal joy, a personal crown. Heaven to us is a pretty place, talked about in Revelation, or by Milton. It is not to us sufficiently real to dry our tears. 2. The selfish interests we aim at in this world are but trifles, compared with the crown, the joy, the hope, we may have. We take from this life nothing but our characters, and there await us cycles of eternities upon eternities, and yet what time we devote to our wardrobes, to trifles.

Think of our translation to that other world; think of meeting men, women, and children leaping for joy, harp in hand, singing praises to God, and, at the same time, acknowledging us, with grateful hearts, as factors in the power that secured their salvation. 3. What dignity this gives the work of the Church. We are living in a time when the dignity of Christianity seems endangered. (*T. T. Duryea, D.D.*) *The grand reward anticipated by the genuine gospel minister:*—It is natural for men to work for rewards, to have an eye in all their labours to compensation. There is a selfish and a disinterested aim after rewards. The selfish is not only seen in the mere worldling, whose rewards are confined to the present life, but also in the religious professor, who here works, sacrifices, and prays in order to get for himself a blessed heaven at last. The disinterested reference to rewards is peculiar to the genuinely Christian worker, and is exemplified in the text. Notice—I. THE NATURE OF THE GOOD WHICH HE REGARDED AS A REWARD FOR HIS LABOURS. It was not wealth or enjoyment on earth, nor his own heaven in the future, but the spiritual excellence of those for whom he laboured; their deliverance from moral evil; their restoration to the image of God. He sought nothing higher as a recompense. This was his highest hope—his joy. Nothing thrilled him with a keener delight than to see sin crushed and virtue triumphant. This was his crown of glorying. The pleasure which the victor in the Grecian games felt in the garland he had won was nothing compared to Paul's. II. THE PERIOD WHEN THIS GOOD WOULD BE MANIFESTED TO HIS ADMIRING EYES. "Are not ye," &c., which implies—1. His belief in the final advent of Christ. Paul never doubted this, nor did the early disciples. They were not inspired as to its specific time; hence the latter mistook and thought it just at hand. 2. His belief that at that period when he should meet and recognize all his converts, and they would be presented to the Great Head "without spot or wrinkle," filled him with joy. (*D. Thomas, D.D.*) *The minister's joy:*—1. Numerous causes of depression are connected with the lives of faithful ministers. Their office necessarily brings them into collision with the passions of others. Hostility to the truth frequently assumes the character of personal spite against the preacher, who is misrepresented, contemned, and persecuted. 2. During these seasons the apostles were able to state their possession of supports and consolations which had imparted to them animation and perseverance (2 Cor. iv. 8, 9, 16; vi. 9, 10). These are comforts permanently provided for the work of the ministry, and not the least is that of the text. I. THERE IS A STRONG RELIGIOUS AFFECTION CHERISHED BY MINISTERS OF THE GOSPEL TOWARDS THEIR BELIEVING HEARERS. This is well illustrated by previous expressions in this Epistle. 1. The relation of ministers to their people must of necessity always involve the exercise of kindly solicitude on their behalf. This is clear from Scriptural designations of their vocation. It is impossible to fulfil that vocation without feeling towards those whom they feed as shepherds, protect as watchmen, instruct as teachers, lead as guides, an affectionate interest. 2. This affection is also founded, as is all intelligent affection, on the possession of some common property. Both have been "called in one hope of their calling," received the same Divine grace in their hearts, brought from the same spiritual bondage, washed in the same fountain, justified by the same righteousness, &c. 3. This affection becomes still more powerful when pastors have reason to conclude that to their instrumentality believers have been indebted for their introduction to spiritual life. Thus it was here. This connection is more close than others. It is not the relation of a friend to a friend, but of a father to a son (3 John 2–4). II. THERE IS AN IMPORTANT EVENT WHICH IT BECOMES MINISTERS AND THEIR BELIEVING HEARERS TO ANTICIPATE. Those who are united in the bond of Christian attachment ought to hold in remembrance that their communion on earth must soon terminate. But we have not to stay our contemplation of the future with the point of death. We have to look beyond to a period of high restoration. Throughout the Epistle the thought of the Lord's coming is associated with the wellbeing of the saints. 1. Let the minister habitually anticipate this, and he cannot but be careful that he may answer the claims and fulfil the obligations of his office. 2. Let private Christians regard this, and they, too, will earnestly cultivate the graces appropriate to their station. III. THE EVENT ANTICIPATED WILL INVOLVE THE MUTUAL RECOGNITION OF THOSE WHO HAVE BEEN SPIRITUALLY RELATED ON EARTH. This involves the general principle that all pious friendships will be restored to be perpetuated for ever. 1. The ultimate recognition of the saints is a truth adapted to administer substantial consolation amidst the numerous and painful separations inflicted by death. What gratitude should arise towards that religion which affords such a hope! 2. This doctrine is applied to the recognition of preachers and believers.

That connection which on earth is the parent of so much pure enjoyment will then be restored. IV. THIS RECOGNITION WILL TO MINISTERS BE CONNECTED WITH ELEVATED JOY (2 Cor. i. 13, 14; Phil. ii. 15, 16, iv. 1). In contemplating the reasons for ministerial joy we may name—1. The consideration of the unspeakable misery which believers have avoided, and the happiness to which they are exalted. 2. Saved believers will be a public testimony to the universe of official faithfulness and success. What a transcendent honour to be acknowledged in the presence of the Father and the holy angels. Here we do not witness all the results of our ministry. 3. The salvation of others will add new and permanent value to ministerial reward. (*James Parsons.*)    *Culture of character the work of the Christian pastor :*—How thoroughly Paul's work is charged with personal feeling. There are times in which this personal feeling should be allowed its proper expression. I. THE AIM OF A TRUE MINISTRY. To get men ready to stand in the presence of Christ. The apostle lived in expectation of the appearance of the Saviour. That great hope was his own perpetual inspiration, and by the teaching of it he ever urges his disciples to live holier and more consecrated lives. II. THE JOY IT GIVES THE MINISTER TO WORK WITH THIS FOR HIS AIM. There is a passionate kind of joy known by the man who is the means of many conversions. There is surely a deeper, holier joy known by him who watches over the growth of holy character, and the settling of holy principle, and the arrangements of a holy life— those further stages of the work of conversion. There must have been a great thrill of joy in the heart of the old alchemist as he watched the metals simmering, and changing form; and as he fancied he caught, again and again, signs that the long-sought elixir was yielding to the fires. How intense must be the joy of the sculptor who works at the rough quarry-block, and sees under each chisel-stroke a new proof that the image of his soul is gaining form before him! The artist must know true joy in his work as the bare canvas gradually fills with the creations of his genius. The architect watches stone laid on stone, and fair proportions and graceful forms growing up before him with ever-new delight. We know there is no joy on earth like that of the mother who watches the babe unfold in strength and intelligence; and on up through the stages of childhood and youth that mother watches with a perpetual soul-thrill as intelligence and character are developed and perfected. I have sometimes tried to conceive the inconceivable, and imagine I stood beside Jehovah, and felt the thrill of His great joy as He watched creation unfold all its fitnesses and beauties before His Divine commands : as chaos broke up into movement, and rocks gathered round their centre, and water-floods separated themselves from the land. Who shall tell the joy of Him who watched the stages of that wondrous growth? It is but suggested in the words, "And God saw everything that He had made, and behold it was very good." But all these fail before the joy to God, and to the good, that is found in watching the new creation of a soul, the regeneration and sanctification of a soul. All these can be but images and suggestions of the far greater joy he knows who watches the growth of souls, and can say, "What is our joy? . . . are not even ye in the presence of the Lord Jesus at His coming?" God must have more joy in the sanctifying of a soul, for He gave His only Son to accomplish that end. III. THE HOPE THE MINISTER MAY CHERISH THAT IN SOME HIS AIM WILL BE REALIZED. When we stand in the presence of Christ we shall each have several persons to thank for helping us forward on the road to holiness and God. (*R. Tuck, B.A.*)    *The minister's joy :*—I. THE REASONS UPON WHICH CHRIST'S FAITHFUL MINISTERS ARE SO SERIOUSLY ENGAGED IN SAVING SOULS, making it the great object of their desire and hope, the scope of their prayers, and the business of their lives. 1. The Divine command and charge laid upon them (Acts xx. 28; Col. iv. 17; 2 Tim. iv. 1, 2; 1 Cor. ix. 16). 2. The Spirit and Grace of Christ. They preach no unknown Saviour, but one in whom and in whose work they have a special interest (Rom. x. 1; Gal. iv. 19; Acts xx. 31; 2 Cor. xii. 15). 3. The example of Christ, who came "to seek and save the lost"; and whose meat was to "do the will of His Father," &c. 4. The worth of souls. 5. The danger they are in from the world without and corruption within. 6. The price paid for souls (Acts xx. 28). 7. The strict account they will have to give of their ministry (Ezek. iii. 17, 18). 8. Future glory. II. THE JOY THEY WILL HAVE IN THE SOULS THEY WIN IN THE PRESENCE OF JESUS CHRIST. 1. Every recovered soul will be a jewel added to their crown. 2. Their converts will be eternally safe. 3. They will spend eternity in their company whom they have loved most below. 4. They will receive the special commendation of the Lord. Conclusion. 1. How important the work of labouring for souls. 2. The prospect should animate pastors and people in times of depression. 3. How heavy will be the doom of those who have despised the preached gospel. (*D. Wilcox.*)  *The pastor's joy and crown :*—(Farewell sermon). Let us consider—I. WHAT YOU ARE TO ME IN THE PRESENT. 1. Some of you are my hope. Joy comes of anticipations realized, but we hope for that we see not. Some of you are my hope because there are possibilities which have never been developed, aspirations which have never been fulfilled, blessings not yet experienced. At the same time you have not yet turned your backs upon them. You and I are hoping that the seed may yet bear fruit. (1) Some of you young men have not yet become corrupted by a life of sin; but you have not yet given your hearts to God. Turn my hope into joy by deciding for Christ. (2) Some of you maidens have not yet yielded to the fashions and frivolities of the world, and have indeed been drawn after Christ; but you have not yet embraced Him. Make my hope joy by doing so now. (3) Whether old or young you are my hope if you are convinced that what I say is and has been true. No longer halt, then, between two opinions. 2. Some of you are my joy. My hopes have been realized. You have tasted and seen that the Lord is good. Cleave to Him and work for Him so that you may continue to be my joy, and be something more by and by. II. WHAT YOU MAY BE TO ME IN THE FUTURE. We must all appear before the judgment seat of Christ: I as your pastor to render an account of my ministry. Whether I have done my work well or ill it cannot be altered now; but if you have been unprofitable hearers you may remember in days to come what you have heard, and by giving yourselves to Christ be my "crown of rejoicing." Then I shall be able to point to you and others and say, "Here am I and the children Thou hast given me." And if any shall say, "He did not feed the flock, comfort the sorrowful," &c., I shall be able to point to you in refutation. (*R. Davey.*)  *The pastor's crown of rejoicing :*—I. THE TEXT POINTS TO THE FUTURE. Instead of indulging in fond regrets, lamenting over the severance of old ties, and giving himself up to the fascination of sentimental reminiscences, Paul looks onward to the future—hopefully, cheerfully, anticipating renewed friendship, calculating on continued usefulness. But beyond the horizon of time, Paul's eager gaze penetrates eternity. He and his brother believers did not forget the first Advent, but they seem to have been more mightily moved by the hope of the second. When this hope will be consummated they could not tell, neither can we; but it will be some day. II. THE TEXT RECOGNIZES AN EVERLASTING BOND OF UNION BETWEEN A CHRISTIAN PASTOR AND HIS FLOCK. 1. Moral influences work for ever. Mind affects mind, and will affects will, and character character in everlasting consequences of action and reaction. People cannot live and work together without making one another different. All relationships may be said to be interminable, because the influence for good or evil is perpetually operative. 2. But the relation between pastor and people is noticed in Scripture in a way no other is. Nothing is said about the meeting of kings and subjects, brothers and sisters, &c. This relationship of ministerial labour and oversight is alone placed in the eternal light; because a preacher has to do a work which no others do. He toils for eternity; and the result of his employment will not appear till time shall end. Many kinds of efforts produce immediate results; but with our sacred occupation "the harvest is the end of the world." III. The text SUGGESTS THE CONDITIONS ON WHICH THE APOSTOLIC HOPE EXPRESSED MAY BE FULFILLED. This hope is sublimely disinterested. Paul here stands before us, a true philanthropist, who loses himself in the good of others, whose heaven is to lead others to heaven. The hope of the salvation of others is his own great hope; their joy his own joy; their crowns his own crown. The conditions upon which such a lofty hope can be fulfilled are these—1. The conversion of men to Christ through repentance and faith. The feelings with which one regards a pupil or adopted child may be very tender and grow into the semblance of paternal affection, but it is only a semblance at best. A father's love and joy no stranger intermeddleth with. And so there is pure ministerial satisfaction in being an instructor of Christianity; but to be really a father in God, to beget a soul for Christ through the gospel—that is a joy which no man knoweth save he who receiveth it. The thought of that fills an apostolic mind with ecstasy. 2. The edification, improvement, growth in holiness of those so converted, whether by the minister himself or his brethren. To educate one's child is a most precious task; to have under one's pastoral care a person who attributes to you his conversion is a similar and yet nobler employment. To carry on step by step the purifying and ennobling process; to help to polish pillars in the house of God that are to go out no more for ever; to add any touches to the likeness of Christ drawn in the lives of His people—that is to enter into the noblest kind of partnership, to share in the consummation of the grandest of purposes. And it all bears on the anticipated felicity at "the coming of the Lord Jesus." 3. *The consolation of the afflicted in this world of trial.* No man entered more deeply into the feelings of others than did Paul. Perhaps the strongest of all ministerial power is sympathy in affliction; and the prospect of spending eternity together with the sons and daughters of sorrow in that world where tears are wiped from all faces will form no small part of our crown of rejoicing. (*J. Stoughton, D.D.*) *The way to the crown:*—The crown of a man's life is that which he desires above all things. A crown of rejoicing is that which gives him the greatest joy. The apostle's life joy was bound up with the salvation of souls. If that failed his life was joyless. I. THE SWEETEST JOY THAT EARTH GIVES IS THE JOY OF DOING GOOD. 1. Here is a high hill, its sides rocky, its surface sterile, its contour uncomely. Nobody wants it or values it. Presently a wise man walks over it, purchases it, cuts away at its sides, and after long and expensive toil lays bare a wealth of precious minerals. So there is many a deed of kindness that waits to be done; yet no one does it. It seems an unpleasant, hard, costly thing; yet he who at last does it finds in it a treasure. In every kindness there is a joy locked up for your own soul, and the more difficult it is the sweeter the joy. It is sweet to take a loaf of bread to the starving, although it may leave you hungry; to deny yourself of some ornament to clothe the naked; to lose your own sleep to watch beside the suffering. Pearls are found in the unsightly oyster, so pearls of joy are found in tasks from which we shrink. 2. But the sweetest joy is that of saving souls. A man once saved a child's life by snatching it from under the feet of a galloping horse, and ever after that one deed illumined that man's life. He lay for years in prison cells, but the joys of that heroic hour shone ever in upon his gloom. If it is so blessed to save from physical, how much more to save from eternal death! When Dr. Lyman Beecher was dying some one asked him what was the greatest of all things. He answered, "It is not theology; it is not controversy; it is saving souls." As the Christian approaches the sunset of life he feels that this is the only work worth doing. A preacher may draw crowds, and be rewarded with academic titles, and achieve great fame; but if souls are not saved his ministry is a failure. II. THOSE WHOM WE LEAD TO CHRIST WILL BE OUR CROWN OF JOY IN HEAVEN. I. Reference is here made to the ancient games. At the end of the race the victor is crowned. So at the end of the apostle's course he should receive a crown jemmed with saved souls. He who gives a cup of cold water in the name of a disciple will be rewarded, and he who saves souls will receive the most glorious rewards. 2. There seems also to have been in the apostle's mind the thought that his spiritual children would be grouped round him as a glory, as children gather round a parent. Jesus is the Saviour around whom all the saved shall gather. But that one family will be broken up into countless groups gathered about those who have led them to Jesus. All whom we have helped to the Saviour will greet us as we pass inside heaven's gates. Every Christian pastor or worker will, in heaven, be like a tree with many or few branches on which all the fruits of his life will hang. Conclusion: Our joy in heaven will be measured by our deeds of kindness on earth. The gold and silver we have spent in benefitting our race, will be transmuted into crowns of glory. Those who are spending themselves for Christ are weaving fadeless garlands for their brows. They who are saving souls are gathering and polishing jewels for their heavenly crowns. (*J. R. Miller.*) *Believers the joy of ministers:*—I. INQUIRE WHEN CHRISTIAN PROFESSORS MAY BE STYLED THE HOPE, THE JOY, AND THE CROWN OF THEIR MINISTERS. 1. When they appear to be truly converted to God. 2. When they grow in grace and in the knowledge of Christ. 3. When they walk worthy of their heavenly calling, and bring forth the fruits of righteousness, such as closet duties, family religion, love for Divine ordinances, and Christian ministers, and consistent deportment in the world. II. THE SOLEMN TIME IN WHICH THEY SHALL BE THE HOPE, THE JOY, AND THE CROWN OF THEIR MINISTERS. 1. The second coming of Christ. 2. Ministers and hearers must then meet. 3. Their hope is to meet them at the right hand of God. 4. Their joy to see them partakers of Divine glory. 5. Their crown of rejoicing to behold them as the seals to their ministry. (*C. Evans, D.D.*) *Consistent Christians a minister's joy:*—I do not know when I ever felt more gratified than on one occasion, when sitting at a Church meeting, having to report the death of a young brother who was in the service of an eminent employer, a little note came from him to say, "My servant, Edward —— is dead. I send you word at once, that you may send me another young man; for if your members are such as he was, I never wish to have better servants around me." I read the letter at the Church meeting, and another was soon found. It is a cheering thing for the Christian minister to know that his converts are held in repute. Of another member of my Church an ungodly employer said, "I do not think anything of him; he is of no use to anybody; he cannot tell a lie!" (*C. H. Spurgeon.*) *Hope, joy, crown:*—There are some who are our hope, who are not our joy; and others who are our hope and joy too, for a time, who will never be our crown; who hold not out to the end, and therefore will never be our rejoicing in the presence of the Lord at His coming. Some are under serious impressions, and excite a hope and joy, like that felt at the sight of blossoms in the spring, and yet are afterwards blighted. There are some that have made even a public profession, and yet, like the thorny and stony ground hearers, produce no fruit. The object desired, therefore, is not only your setting out, but your holding on, walking in the truth, and holding fast your profession to the end. Then, indeed, you will not only be our hope and joy, but our crown of rejoicing. (*Andrew Fuller.*) *Paul's crown and glory:*—That one word "glory" gathers up all the rays of light which stream from the others into its focus. They are his halo of glory now and evermore. Believers, or at least those who are specially engaged in His service, are described in 2 Cor. viii. 23 as "the glory of Christ." They are also in a lower sense the glory of Christ's ministers. The pastor will find in his congregation either his glory or his shame. It was the boast of the Jews that to them had been given three crowns—the crown of the law, the crown of the priesthood, and the royal crown. These they highly prized, but they often added, better than these is the crown of a good name. Paul's crown of a good name in the presence of Christ Jesus was his converts. The same crown is offered to us all, and is in keeping for us all if we are found faithful. History tells us that when in Philip II's reign a rebel claimed and gained the crown of Granada, he bore at the ceremony of coronation in his right hand a banner bearing the inscription "More I could not desire, less would not have contented me." These words cease to be presumptuous and become the utterance of truest wisdom only, when they refer to the crown of heavenly rejoicing, and when they are the legend of the banner under which he fights in "the sacramental host of God's elect." In view of the truth that converts are the crown of boasting in store for all faithful witnesses for Christ, the words are invested with a solemn significance "*We* live if ye stand fast in the Lord." "Now, little children, abide ye in Him, that when He shall appear, we may have confidence, and not be ashamed before Him at His coming." (*J. Hutchison, D.D.*) *Heavenly recognition:*—It is natural for those who are travelling to an unknown land, in which they are soon to make their residence, to enquire frequently anent its manners, its customs, and its modes of intercourse; it is therefore not surprising that Christians, travellers to the kingdom of God, frequently endeavour to lift the veil which covers futurity, and to learn what are the holy delights of that heavenly world in which they hope to dwell for ever. To these inquiries, Paul's statement to the Thessalonians affords the most precious consolation: it teaches that the friendship founded on piety is imperishable—that those who were friends to the Redeemer, as well as to each other, shall have mutual knowledge and recollection in the future world, which shall result in intercourse with each other and the whole triumphant Church. I. THE DOCTRINE OF HEAVENLY RECOGNITION. 1. The enjoyments and occupations of heaven are uniformly represented as social; but where is the charm of society without mutual knowledge? 2. Heaven is uniformly represented as perfecting all our faculties. Is it then probable that it will diminish, nay, entirely abolish memory, one of the most important of them? 3. The chief grace that will be exercised in the regions of the blest, next to love to God, will be love to our companions in glory. But what kind of love is that which is felt for an object which we know not? 4. In the general judgment which is appointed to vindicate the ways of God to man, it is certain that every individual will be known to the vast assembly as distinct from all other persons. Is it probable that God, after thus making the blessed acquainted with each other, should immediately afterward obliterate this knowledge? 5. It is certain that we shall see and know the glorious manhood of our blessed Saviour, elevated above all the heavenly powers; and if we shall know one body, why not more? During His abode on earth, He afforded to three favoured disciples a glimpse of His Divine glory. He was transfigured, and Moses and Elias descended in celestial brilliancy: the disciples knew them distinct from the Saviour, and each as distinct from the other; and if they knew them on the solitary mount, why should they not know them in the New Jerusalem? 6. We find the apostle Paul very frequently consoling himself under the sufferings and persecutions which he had to endure, by the prospect of meeting in heaven those who had been converted by his ministry on earth. II. THE TEACHING OF THIS DOCTRINE. 1. What a delightful idea does it give of the felicity of the celestial world! Surely nothing, except the vision and enjoyment of God and the Lamb, can equal the joys of knowing and being known to all the Church triumphant above—of living in an eternal brotherhood—of forming an indissoluble connection with all the good men that ever have existed, or that ever shall exist, till the trump of the archangel shall shake the earth to its centre. Who can even conceive the raptures of such an intercourse? 2. The doctrine that in heaven we shall know each other, and all the pious who have preceded us, affords one of the sweetest consolations to the Christian against the natural fear of death. To a soul that has made its peace with God, death has nothing so terrible as those agonizing adieus which are to be given to those whom we love; but the anguish arising from this source is removed when the dying believer can strain his closing eyes upon those who surround his bed of death, and say to them, " Suffer me to go and join yon heavenly company with the bright hope that you will ere long come to me, and we shall be beyond the reach of death, in the presence of our Lord Jesus Christ." 3. The doctrine of future recognition teaches relatives and friends how they should act in order that the sentiments of affection which they entertain for each other may have their greatest force, and they be saved from the severest pains. Form your attachments for eternity; build them on the basis of religion; strive to cement the ties of relationship by the more indissoluble bonds of grace; and then your future will be ineffably blessed and glorious. (*H. Kollock, D.D.*)

---

### CHAPTER III.

VERS. 1, 2. **Wherefore, when we could no longer forbear, we thought it good to be left in Athens alone.**—There is a subtle play of feeling in the whole texture of these words. On the one hand sadness—"to be left alone in Athens"; on the other, a bright and tender pleasure beyond resignation, a consent that was not extorted—"we were well pleased." The former expression has about it a tinge of desertion and forlornness, as of leaving father and mother (Matt. xix. 5; Mark x. 7; Eph. v. 13 : from Gen. ii. 24, LXX.); the sheep in the wilderness (Luke xv. 4); the preaching of the Word (Acts vi. 2). In the Old Testament, of one leaving wife or children by death (Deut. xxviii. 54; Prov. xx. 7, in LXX.; *cf.* Mark xii. 19; Luke xx. 31). The word is suffused with a sadness which abides after a farewell. The word "alone" stands forcibly last. Upon the departure of Timothy, Paul and Silvanus felt themselves to be indeed alone. "Alone in London" has become a proverb. But there was something more to one like Paul in a place like Athens— the city which was so beautiful, but so far from God. (*Bp. Alexander.*) *A difficult and important mission :*—Paul had been compelled to leave Thessalonica in consequence of the malignant opposition of the Jews. But Timothy might venture where it would be perilous for the apostle to appear. Fearing that his absence might be misconstrued, and anxious to strengthen the faith of the infant Church in the midst of trial, the apostle determines to send a trusted messenger. It is a significant testimony to the sound judgment and prudence of Timothy, that he is selected for this difficult and important mission. I. THIS MISSION WAS THE SUGGESTION OF AN UNCONTROLLABLE ANXIETY. "Wherefore, when we could no longer forbear." This anxiety sprang from the intensity of the apostle's love. It is a striking feature of genuine Christian love, that while it bears external suffering with uncomplaining patience, it is impatient of delay in doing good. The mother can endure anything but restraint in her desire to promote the best welfare of her child. David was indifferent to exposure and danger, but his soul panted after God. II. THIS MISSION INVOLVED GREAT PERSONAL INCONVENIENCE. "At Athens alone." True love, in its unselfishness, ever prefers another's good to its own. Timothy had travelled so constantly with Paul, and had been so great a comfort, that his absence was a loss keenly felt. Specially was his sympathy and co-operation needed at Athens. What a sublime historical picture is pourtrayed in the words " at Athens alone." Christianity embodied in a single, lonely man, standing in the midst of the populous metropolis of pagan culture and idolatry. Yet the power enshrined in that solitary man broke up and scattered the huge fabric of heathenism. III. This mission was entrusted to a thoroughly qualified messenger. The high character of Timothy and his relations with Paul are brought out in the epithets—1. Brother. Elsewhere Paul calls him his " own son in the faith," his " dearly beloved son "; but in speaking of him to the Churches, he recognizes him on the equal footing of a brother. 2. Minister of God. Solemnly set apart by the voice of prophecy and by the hands of the presbytery, and of Paul himself. 3. Fellow-labourer in the gospel of Christ, not only as all God's ministers are—*i.e.*, working the work of the same Lord—but also on the ground of that special intimacy of personal intercourse and co-operation to which he was from the first admitted by the apostle. Thus Timothy was thoroughly qualified—(1) To carry out the apostle's wish concerning the Thessalonians : and (2) to sympathize with the Church's peculiar difficulties and trials. He was more than a mere courier. He was faithful to Paul's instructions, and valuable to the Church in himself. IV. This mission was charged with a work of high importance and necessity. 1. To establish, to confirm, or set fast their faith, by a fresh authoritative manifestation of the gospel truth and its Divine evidences ; and this would be done by private conversation and public ministration. 2. To comfort. The word means also—and especially here—to exhort, though, doubtless, comfort would be mingled with the exhortation. The Thessalonians were exposed to the storm of persecution that was everywhere raging against the gospel and its adherents, and they were exhorted to steadfastness, " that no man should be moved by these afflictions." Paul and Barnabas had a similar mission to the Churches in Lesser Asia (Acts xiv. 22). There are none so strong in faith but need confirmation ; none so courageous but need comfort. Lessons—1. The establishment of believers is ever a subject of anxiety to the true minister. 2. The desire to promote the highest welfare of the Church should ever be paramount. (*G. Barlow.*) *Paul and Timothy :*—I. The character Paul giveth of Timothy. Elsewhere he calls him " my son "; here he calls him " our brother." Timothy was Paul's junior in age, his inferior in gifts and graces, and of a lower rank in the ministry ; for Paul was an apostle, and Timothy but an evangelist ; yet Paul calls him " brother." This was an instance of the apostle's humility, and showed his desire to put honour upon Timothy, and to recommend him to the esteem of the Churches. He calls him also a "minister of God." Ministers of the gospel of Christ are ministers of God, to promote the kingdom of God among men. He calls him also " our fellow-labourer." Ministers of the gospel must look upon themselves as labourers in the Lord's vineyard ; they have an honourable office and hard work, yet a good work (1 Tim. iii. 1). And ministers should look upon one another as fellow-labourers, and should therefore love one another, and strengthen one another's hands ; not strive and contend one with another, which will hinder their work ; but strive together to carry on the great work they are engaged in—namely, to preach and publish the gospel of Christ, and to persuade people to embrace and entertain it, and live suitably thereto. II. The design Paul had in sending Timothy. This was to establish the Thessalonians, and comfort them concerning their faith. Paul had converted them to the Christian faith, and now he was desirous they might be confirmed and comforted—that they might be confirmed in the choice they had made of the Christian religion, and comforted in the profession and practice of it. The more we are comforted, the more we shall be confirmed ; because, when we find pleasure in the ways of God, we shall thereby be engaged to continue and persevere therein. The apostle's design, therefore, was a pre-eminently worthy one concerning his Thessalonian converts— their faith and the object of their faith, the truths of the gospel, and particularly that Jesus Christ was the Saviour of the world, and so wise and good, so powerful and faithful, that they might surely rely upon Him. He would also have them remember the recompense of faith, which was more than sufficient to balance all their losses and reward all their labours. III. The motive inducing Paul thus to act. He cherished a godly fear or jealousy lest the Thessalonians should be moved from the faith of Christ. He was exceedingly desirous that not one among them should waver or apostatize ; and yet he apprehended danger, and trembled for the consequence. They could not but perceive what afflictions the apostles met with ; and also those who made profession of the gospel were persecuted, as without doubt these Thessalonians themselves were, and these evils might possibly stumble them. But the danger did not end here ; there was the tempter's subtlety and malice. He had often prejudiced the minds of men against religion on account of the sufferings its professors are exposed to, and he would do his utmost to damage the faith of these converts. Naturally, therefore, the apostle feared lest his labour should be in vain. To prevent the consequence of the danger, he sent Timothy to them to put them in mind that, as concerning affliction, they were appointed thereunto. Troubles and persecutions do not come by chance, nor merely from the wrath and malice of the enemies of religion, but by the appointment or permission of God. (*R. Fergusson.*)    *Alone in Athens :—*1. St. Paul puts upon himself the sacrifice of solitude in a strange city simply because it comes in the line of his duty. To his tastes other appointments would be more agreeable. Some familiar place would suit better his longing for sympathy. He is a scholar, and would prefer retirement. He is the worn hero of many battles, and would like to rest in some peaceful household of faith. That he cannot do and be faithful; and this with any honest soul settles the question. At Athens, busy as he is, he remembers the affectionate little band left behind at Thessalonica. 2. In his person, on landing at the Piræus, the morning light of the new age rose on a second continent. Yet everything was bleak, every face unfriendly. Any courage less valiant than his must have quailed before the overpowering splendour and despotism of old heathenism in its stronghold. Paul had come to it as fearless of its sophistries and arrogance as he had been of the swords and dungeons of Syria. 3. Without some common interests, cities are wildernesses and society the saddest of solitudes. (1) From the moment that Paul's feet touched the pier, the monuments of the dominant mythology began to lift themselves forbiddingly before him, to make him feel himself " alone." His own heart burning with love to Christ, the first objects that greet him are the statue of Neptune, a sensual temple of the God of Wine, images of Mercury, Minerva, Apollo, and Jupiter. Reaching the market-place, his sense of separation deepens at every step. The buildings are memorials of a foreign history. Their walls are covered with paintings of barbarous exploits and alien manners. Processions of disgusting ceremonies meet him. (2) If he turns from the world of sight to the world of thought, he finds the schools of unbelieving speculation strong in great names, but distracted with debate between doubt and delusion, and full of eloquent error. What was all this to the man who could say, " It is no more I that live ; Christ liveth in me." Deeper and darker the solitude grew ; and yet he could banish himself into a completer exile for the sake of the little band of Christians at Thessalonica. I. IN GOD'S APPOINTMENTS THERE ARE TWO KINDS OF LONELINESS. 1. Outward and physical. (1) The providential conditions are so settled for many that they have much less than the average share of social communication. (*a*) Sometimes, by a shrinking turn of the constitution, or by natural reserve, or by lack of magnetic quality, or by a fatal propensity to say the wrong thing, or by necessities of occupation or residence, they are cut off from society. (*b*) There is the solitude of temperament, the earnest heart all the while yearning for companionship, and yet strangely held back. (*c*) There is a solitude of pride where social advantages are bitterly given up to escape making an appearance inferior to that of one's class. (*d*) There is the solitude of obligation, created by the necessities of toil or devotion, by poverty or pity, imprisoning body and mind alike. (*e*) There is the solitude of bodily infirmity. (2) Among the perils of such a situation we must set down—(*a*) A tendency to a belittling self-consideration. Finding nothing beyond self to fasten upon, affection stagnates or sours. Religion will have hard work to save such a life from contempt. It has been the snare of all monks. (*b*) In other cases we see censoriousness. Rigid standards are applied to others. Allowances are not made for unavoidable differences, and so the first commandment of love is broken. (*c*) Along with these bigoted ways of thinking, comes envy and cynicism. You have never had your fair chance. You are distanced by your contemporaries. Outside your sick chamber are the gay children of health and wealth. It needs a steady faith in God's impartiality to keep down your discontent. So Martha felt her solitude—" Carest thou not that my sister hath left me " ; and Peter—" What shall this man do ? "—contrasting John's brighter lot with his own martyrdom. (*d*) Add to these a certain unwholesome fastidiousness, which is apt to arise from constant pre-occupation with private tastes. The hand is withheld from many a useful office, and the tongue from many a cordial utterance. Opportunities for Christian benefaction are despairingly thrown away, and life miserably bereft of its true glory. 2. Involuntary and moral loneliness. While this, too, has its dangers, it may be made the occasion, as it was with Paul, of great spiritual gains. (1) It is indispensable that at some period souls who follow Christ should stand morally apart, without honour or sympathy. This is one of the crosses which brave men have to take up, a school where strong principles are planted, convictions nourished, and energies trained. Rules of action taken up out of deference to prevailing notions fluctuate; these, wrought into the conscience in solitude, are more apt to come at first hand from God. Here is the test for all real characters. Can you live, work, suffer, stand out, move forward alone? This settles it whether you are a mere piece of movable furniture, moulded by the hands of fashion, or a living independent soul, satisfied to walk with Him who had not where to lay His head while He was showing the world the truth and love of God, satisfied to live with the apostle who thought it good to be left in Athens alone. (2) In all the biographies of human greatness we find this proved by examples. I try in vain to think of one memorable saint who has not had the discipline of the desert or the mountain. It is there that great leaders have gathered gifts from on high, broken the bondage of ambition and vanity, and came so close to Christ that His sacrificial power has entered them. Out of the Bible, no less than in it, master men have been lonely men. (3) Hence the defect you are sure to find in people who have never accepted or made intervals of seclusion. They may be stirring characters, but thin; loud, but shallow, wanting in reverence and steady power, over-anxious about results and appearances, over-deferential to the popular cry; at home only in the multitude, but afraid of the mount. It is the earnest, hearty worker with God who knows how to be refreshed with fellowship at Thessalonica, and to be left at Athens alone. (4) In our fast and outward-living generation, and our noisy and showy age the Church needs most religious retirement and private prayer. The greater the tendency to secular arrogance and surface morality the more Christians ought to guard the sacred retreats. This nation would hardly have been what it is or done what it has if our ancestors had brought up their sons and daughters in the glaring parlours of a vast hotel. Strong character is a separate thing, and requires a separate, individual nurture. Promiscuous intermixtures never produce it. It might well be defined as the power of standing alone. How we see the want of it wherever men and woman meet together; wherever majorities browbeat an unpopular faith; whenever you are likely to be a loser in money, or to be laughed at. Righteousness never counts her companions. This is the heroic loneliness of all God's great ones from the beginning; of Jacob left alone through the long night wrestling with the Angel; of Moses receiving commission to emancipate a nation, alone in the mountains; of Elijah when he cried "I only am left"; of Daniel watched by an idolatrous monarch kneeling three times a day; of Peter answering the rulers "Whether it is right in the sight of God," &c., and higher yet, of Him who trod the winepress alone, and yet not alone, for the Father was with Him. II. THE GOD OF OUR LIVES PUTS INTO ALL OF THEM SOME SOLITUDE FOR A PURPOSE OF HIS OWN. 1. He arranges it for us that we cannot be always in anybody's company. Friend after friend departs. Misunderstandings arise. There is a night between every two days. Sickness is sent. Is it not plain that this is because the deepest and holiest exercises of the spirit are where no human presence is by? 2. Look back. If repentance ever took hold of you and bade you look up for mercy; if the great choice between God and self was ever made, was it not when you were alone with your Saviour. 3. Before the Spirit has done His deepest and best work in you, He will have you all to Himself. The question of everlasting love is a private question—"Wilt thou be Mine for ever?" Each succeeding struggle, when we make the tremendous sacrifice which carries us clear of some entangling alliance, is solitary work. Great griefs are solitary—the heart breaks alone. 4. Our communion with Christ only obeys the law of all lofty delicate friendships. Intervention is interruption; and even the best society on earth is not good enough to divide your intercourse with your Master. III. LONELINESS SOMETIMES BECOMES LONESOMENESS. The excessively secluded life is imbittered by a craving for sympathy. This would have been Paul's feelings at Athens, and he would not have thought it "good" to be left there, but for the one Divine Friend who stayed with him. It is in His felt presence that those hearts are to find their consolation which are separated from their kind. However thronged the streets or brilliant the season, these uncheered souls are all around us. By far the greater number of us have hours when we long for nothing so much as to hear some fellow soul say "I know how you suffer; one heart at least answers to yours." There are constitutions finely tempered which need continual protection, but have it only under coarse, sordid hands, lacerating wherever they touch. There are self distrustful, timid creatures, tortured with a despairing sense of failure who never get an encouraging look.

What is the comfort? Only one. For all these the Man of sorrows is the only companion, and His hidden love the only consolation. What would Athens have been to Paul without his Saviour? IV. CHRIST'S BLESSING RESTS AS GRACIOUSLY ON OUR MORE SECLUDED AND LEAST NOTICED SERVICES FOR HIM AS UPON THE MOST CONSPICUOUS OF HIS WORKMEN. Paul the despised missionary at Athens is as sure of his Saviour's presence and benediction as when the populace of Lystra are hailing him as a god. We are slow to learn that the spirit of the gospel is no more in the assembly of ten thousand than where one tired labourer watches by the sick orphan, or one daughter of fortune and culture cheerfully crucifies every taste to teach a group of unclean vagabonds how to pray. We hurry into publicity as if that were heaven, and are impatient to count converts and see results, as if that were salvation. The most glorious chronicles and monuments of Athens are not in her letters, temples, arms, but in that little record of the friendless traveller who thought it good to be left there alone. (*Bp. Huntington.*) *The solitude of a great city* (*cf* Acts xvii. 16, 17) :—I. AFFORDS A PAINFUL OPPORTUNITY TO REFLECT ON ITS MORAL CONDITION : "He saw the city wholly given to idolatry." II. AWAKENS PROFOUND CONCERN IN A GREAT SOUL : "His spirit was stirred in him." III. ROUSES TO IMMEDIATE ACTION IN PROMOTING THE WELFARE OF THE CITIZENS : "Therefore disputed he in the synagogue and in the market daily." (*G. Barlow.*) *Solitary saints* :—Think of God working in the solitary things, for the grass does not merely grow around our populous cities, but up there on the side of the bleak Alps, where no traveller has ever passed. Where only the eye of the wild bird has beheld their lovely verdure, the moss and the grass come to perfection, and display all their beauty, for God's works are fair to other eyes than those of mortals. And you solitary child of God, dwelling far away from any friend, unknown and obscure, in a remote hamlet; or you in the midst of London, hiding away in your little garret, unknown to fame and forsaken by friendship, you are not forgotten by the love of heaven. He maketh the grass to grow all alone, and shall He not make you flourish in loneliness? He can bring forth your graces, and educate you for the skies, in solitude and neglect. (*C. H. Spurgeon.*) *Loneliness with some is unfavourable to virtue* :—A monk who could fast seven days in the monastery tried to do the same thing alone in the desert. The effort was too much for him. He gave out the first day. "How came you to fail?" was the question put to him when he returned. "Ah," said the monk, "when I fast in the monastery I have the prior and the brethren to look on and encourage me." *Solitude* :—I. THERE ARE TWO CLASSES OF SOLITUDE. The first consisting of insulation in space, the other of isolation of the spirit. 1. The first is simply separation by distance. When we are seen, touched, and heard by none, we are said to be alone. And all hearts respond to the truth of that saying. This is not solitude, for sympathy can people our solitude with a crowd. The fisherman on the ocean alone at night is not alone when he remembers the earnest longings which are arising up to heaven for his safety. The traveller is not alone when the faces which will greet him on his arrival seem to beam upon him as he trudges on. The solitary student is not alone when he feels that human hearts will respond to the truths which he is preparing to address to them. 2. The other is loneliness of soul. There are times when hands touch ours, but only send an icy chill of indifference to the heart; when eyes gaze into ours, but with a glazed look that cannot read into the bottom of our souls; when words pass from our lips but only come back as an echo reverberated without reply through a dreary solitude; when the multitudes throng and press us, and we cannot say as Christ did, "Somebody hath touched Me"; for the contact has been not between soul and soul, but between form and form. II. THERE ARE TWO CLASSES OF MEN WHO FEEL THIS LAST SOLITUDE IN DIFFERENT WAYS. 1. The first are the men of self-reliance—self-dependent; who ask no counsel and crave no sympathy, who act and resolve alone, who can go sternly through duty, and scarcely shrink let what will be crushed in them. Such men command respect: for whoever respects himself constrains the reverence of others. They are invaluable in all those professions of life in which sensitive feeling would be a superfluity: they make iron commanders, surgeons who do not shrink, and statesmen who do not flinch from their purpose for dread of unpopularity. But mere self-dependence is weakness; and the conflict is terrible when a human sense of weakness is felt by such men. Jacob was alone when he slept in his way to Padan Aram, the first night that he was away from his father's roof, with the world before him, and all old associations broke up; and Elijah was alone in the wilderness when the court had deserted him, and he said, "I only am left." But the loneliness of the tender

Jacob was very different from that of the stern Elijah. To Jacob the sympathy he yearned for was realized in the form of a simple dream. A ladder raised from earth to heaven figured the possibility of communion between the spirit of man and the Spirit of God. In Elijah's case the storm and the earthquake and the fire did their convulsing work in the soul before a still, small voice told him that he was not alone. In such a spirit the sense of weakness comes with a burst of agony, and the dreadful conviction of being alone manifests itself with a rending of the heart of rock. It is only so that such souls can be touched that the Father is with them and that they are not alone. 2. There is another class of men who live in sympathy. These are affectionate minds which tremble at the thought of being alone; not from want of courage or weakness of intellect comes their dependence upon others, but from the intensity of their affections. It is the trembling spirit of humanity in them. They want not aid, nor even countenance, but only sympathy. (*F. W. Robertson, M.A.*) *The risks of solitude:*—The self-diabolizing spirit of man always reveals itself to the lonely contemplatist, either in moments of vacancy, or under the stress of spiritual crises. Eve was tempted when she was alone; the suicide succumbs when he is pushed into the last degree of loneliness; the darkest thoughts of the conspirator becloud the mind when he has most deeply cut the social bond: when man is alone, he loses the check of comparison with others; he miscalculates his force, and deems too little of the antagonisms which that force may excite. All these are among the risks of solitude. The solitary man either degenerates into a misanthrope and the tool of the diabolizing spirit, or he enriches and strengthens his life by reverent and subduing contemplation. (*J. Parker, D.D.*)

Vers. 2, 3. **And send Timotheus.**—*Timothy and his mission:*—This is the first of a long series of similar missions. As the context shows, the youthful evangelist gave full proof of his ministry from the first. I. THE QUALIFICATIONS OF THE MESSENGER. 1. Brotherhood. The man sent on an errand of mercy must have— (1) Brotherly relations with his fellow-messengers. There are extraordinary circumstances in which a man may legitimately break through all the trammels of ecclesiastical order and discipline in order to save souls. The prophets and apostles were examples of this; so were Luther and Wesley. But generally the messenger must sustain close relations of amity and colleagueship, if not of subordination, with those who hold a similar office. This gives—(*a*) Might to his utterances, when his solitary authority would be questioned or ignored. (*b*) Comfort in hours of despondency and loneliness, in the thought that he has sympathy and has brethren to fall back upon. (2) A brotherly feeling towards those to whom he goes: "*Our* brother"—mine and yours. The brotherly feeling in the Christian worker avoids the evils of—(*a*) Haughty superiority: "Lord over God's heritage." His office may be more dignified, but his spiritual nature is the same: "One is your Master," &c. (*b*) Feminine weakness—such as would pander to tastes and humours; fear to rebuke; suppress unpalatable truth. Brotherliness is the manly love of another's soul. (*c*) Selfish motives. The minister is to save men, not make money out of them: "I seek not yours, but you." As brothers our interests are common. 2. Divine ministry. A true minister is—(1) Called of God. No ecclesiastical sanction can compensate for the want of this. A man may be able to trace his "uninterrupted succession," and be instituted to an illustrious office, but unless he is inwardly moved by God he is an intruder and no minister of God. (2) Qualified by God. This does not, of course, dispense with human qualifications. Indeed, gifts of learning and eloquence carefully cultivated and employed are required as signs that qualifications essentially Divine are prized and made the most of. But the Divine qualification is distinct. It is the enduement of power for the conversion of souls. Without this a man may be a profound philosopher, a skilful dialectician; his mind may be stored with masses of erudition, and his tongue nimble with the most bewitching oratory. But without the Holy Ghost he is "a sounding brass and a tinkling cymbal," and no minister of God. (3) Supported by God. Hence—(*a*) Courage: "I have made thy face as a flint." (*b*) Expectation of success: "My word shall not return unto Me void." (4) Owned of God, in the conversion of souls. (5) Rewarded by God: "Well done, good and faithful servant." 3. Labour. The ministry is a "work" involving—(1) Mental preparation; (2) pecuniary sacrifice; (3) abnegation of comfort; (4) consuming zeal. II. THE PURPOSE OF HIS ERRAND. 1. Establishment. (1) To base moral life upon Christ: "Other foundation can no man lay," &c. Then men are basing their lives on no foundation at all. Morality, good intentions, hope in God's clemency, are castles in the air which the labourer for God must destroy, that he may induce men to build on the only foundation. This foundation is stable and everlasting (Matt. vii. 24, &c.). (2) To build up moral life in Christ by promoting the growth of the Christian graces. Is Christian life a building? Then "love, joy, peace, gentleness," &c., are stones and rafters. Is it a tree? Then these are the fruits. 2. Comfort. (1) Encouragement concerning the faith. Such is afforded when faith—(a) Is shown to be well grounded : " We have not followed cunningly-devised fables." (b) Is stimulated into vigorous exercise—(c) When its end, " the salvation of your souls," is kept steadily before the eye. (2) Consolation in trouble. " Tribulation " affects the body in times of persecution, as here ; the mind in times of scepticism and denial ; the soul in times of spiritual darkness. Comfort comes from the Divine promises, the Divine sympathy, and the Divine support. (*J. W. Burn.*) *Ministers of joy :*—Some men move through life as a band of music moves down the street, flinging out pleasure on every side through the air to every one, far and near, that can listen. Some men fill the air with their presence and sweetness, as orchards in October days fill the air with perfume of ripe fruit. Some women cling to their own houses, like the honeysuckle over the door, yet, like it, sweeten all the region with the subtle fragrance of their goodness. There are trees of righteousness which are ever dropping precious fruit around them. There are lives that shine like star-beams, or charm the heart like songs sung upon a holy day. How great a bounty and a blessing it is to hold the royal gifts of the soul so that they shall be music to some and fragrance to others, and life to all ! It would be no unworthy thing to live for, to make the power which we have within us the breath of other men's joy ; to scatter sunshine where only clouds and shadows reign ; to fill the atmosphere where earth's weary toilers must stand with a brightness which they cannot create for themselves, and which they long for, enjoy, and appreciate. (*H. W. Beecher.*) **To comfort you concerning your faith.**—*Comforted concerning the faith :*—1. These Epistles may pre-eminently be called letters of comfort. There are many streams of consolation which are shallow and apt to run dry. They are good as far as they go and as long as they last. God has filled life for us with consolations—the ministries of nature ; many little things that happen every day. The lesser consolations, however, do not supersede the necessity for the greater. After drinking of the former we " thirst again," but the latter " spring up into everlasting life." 2. Does the apostle refer to faith as objective truth, or the affection which embraces the truth ? Both. The faith that comforts must not only be true, but must be accepted and become a heart-possession. We are comforted concerning the faith—I. BY THE PERSUASION THAT THE FAITH IS TRUE ; that it is a real revelation of grace and salvation spoken by God to man. 1. Any doubt on this fundamental point will affect essentially all forms of comfort. Say that the gospel is false or fallacious, or, although historically true, that it is yet largely mythical, and it is bereft of all its consolation. The old words would remain, such as " God hath given us everlasting consolation," " Comfort one another," &c. ; but a dead tree, although still rooted, casts no shadow, yields no fruit ; a well may be deep, and have no water in it. With a sorrow deeper than that of Mary might the Church, and even the world, exclaim in that case, " They have taken away my Lord, and I know not where they have laid Him." 2. Are any of you in this sore trouble—intellectually at sea about the gospel? I shall make no attempt to meet your doubts intellectually. Doubts are solved by faith, prayer, Providence, time, love. But it may do no harm, but good, to speak out our own faith (Heb. i. 1 ; John i. 1, iii. 16 ; 1 John ii. 1, 2, &c.). You may question, but we *know* whom we have believed ; and He will take your souls in trust also, and keep them against that day. II. By the fact that TO THE HUMBLE AND SINCERE, DOUBT RUNS ITS COURSE, AND THEN SUBSIDES AND PASSES AWAY. The experiences of this changeful, troubled life explain the gospel wonderfully to some. The experiences of the heart explain it, reveal the need of it, make it welcome ; and then doubting Thomas is found among the rest, exclaiming, as He falls at His Master's feet, " My Lord and my God." III. Inasmuch as IT WILL BEAR THE STRAIN AND PRESSURE OF LIFE, howsoever heavy. The faith will bear it, although it is borne by persons. What we believe and know enables us to bear and pass through what would otherwise overwhelm us. Human nature, in itself, as the work of God, will do and bear a great deal. Heroic deeds are done and sufferings endured even without Divine help. If it were a matter of stern silent endurance, the old Stoics, Roman soldiers, and the Red Indians could set

us an example.  But such a state of mind is attained by almost uprooting the finer
sensibilities of our nature, by shutting out the future, by putting all our strength
into mere obstinate resolution.  But that is not moral greatness; for this we must
have our nature unabridged, nay, developed and enlarged, made responsive, sensitive, to spiritual things.  It is not a question of getting through this life, but of
getting through it worthily.  Christ comes to elevate and transform all.  The Man
of Sorrows reproduces Himself in His followers; but though "the sufferings of
Christ abound in us," our consolation also aboundeth by Christ.  IV. Because our
faith WILL BEAR ALL THE BURDEN AND STRAIN WHICH COME BY THE ENLARGEMENT AND
INTENSE ACTION OF THE POWERS OF OUR BEING.  The pain of life which is increased
by Christian sensibility will be assuaged by the Christian consolation and borne by
the Christian courage.  We have tried the plan of "no faith," and that has failed.
The new faith brings new pain, because it draws to us the pain of others; but it
brings the promise that "all things shall work together for good," &c.  We have
put that to the proof, and, resting upon it, have found it firm.  Pain has been
shown to have a Divine mission to bless and sanctify us.  By the sorrow of the
Saviour's soul all the Church is redeemed; and by the sorrows of individual souls,
when they are touched with grace, are those souls purified as they could be in no
other way.  Only "if we suffer with Him" in some way can we "be glorified
together."  Believing this, we are to go on the simple way of duty, whatever may
be the difficulty of it, trusting all the while to the sustaining power of faith in
Christ.  "My grace is sufficient for thee," &c.  V. In that our faith teaches us
THAT A TIME AND STATE ARE COMING WHEN THERE SHALL BE NO MORE PAIN.  "In His
presence is fulness of joy."  Conclusion: We must remember that however strong
and firm the objective truth may be, and whatever its power to carry us through the
straits of life and its adaptation to lift us towards a life to come, it will be and do
none of these things if we have not the subjective principle by which we embrace
what is true, trust what is strong, and rise to what is high and pure.  The gospel,
as a practical power and abiding consolation, is in our hearts, or it is nowhere for
us.  (*A. Raleigh, D.D.*)

Vers. 3–5. **That no man should be moved by these afflictions.**—*The perils of
suffering:*—God hath decreed the saints to distress.  As He fore-appointed them to
heaven, so He fore-appointed them to heaviness and hardships (ver. 3).  The
wilderness is the road to Canaan.  Christ went by Bethany—the house of grief, to
Jerusalem—the vision of peace.  What was said of Christ may be said of a Christian, "Ought not Christ to suffer these things, and to enter into His glory?"  None
ever yet went to heaven without conflicts.  I. THE MOTIVES TO QUICKEN THE CHRIS-
TIAN IN THIS CONDITION.  1. Affliction will search whether thou art sound or no.  Great
troubles are great trials; hence afflictions are called temptations (James i. 2).  Grace
is brought to the proof when it is brought to persecution, as gold when it is brought
to the touchstone.  The soldier's knowledge or ignorance, courage or cowardice, will
appear when the enemy, strong and subtle, meets him in the field.  So a saint
comes to the test when he comes to tribulation.  2. God intendeth to sanctify thee,
and to make thee better by affliction.  He sendeth prosperity to quicken thee to
praise, and He sendeth adversity to stir thee up to patience and prayer.  He forceth
thee, like the ark, to sail in deep waters, that thy soul may mount nearer to the
skies.  The husbandman throweth his seed into deep furrows, and is glad of a
sharp winter because it will thrive the better.  3. Many are the worse for affliction.
Though the fire heateth the water and makes it more serviceable, yet it wholly consumeth the wood.  The same flail that liberates the corn bruiseth the stalk.  Afflictions that better a saint harden a sinner.  Ahaz in his distress sinned more against
the Lord, and every plague in Egypt increased the plague of Pharaoh's heart.  4. If
godliness be thy business, under the cross thou mayest expect God's company.  The
worse the ways and the weather in which thou travellest, the more need of good
society.  Israel had the rarest manifestations of God when they were in the wilderness.  Whoever be neglected, the sick child shall be tended not by the maid, but by
the mother herself.  God may leave His prospering saints to the guardianship of
angels, but His afflicted ones may be sure of His presence and favour both in water
and fire (Isa. xliii. 3, 4).  II. THE POWER OF RELIGION MANIFESTS ITSELF IN AFFLIC-
TION.  1. It leads the Christian to avoid those sins which an afflicted estate is
prone to, such as despising God's hand, impatience under suffering and its continuance, and envying the condition of those who prosper.  2. It also helps him to
exercise those graces which are required and proper in adversity, such as faith, re-

joicing in the Lord, and contentedness with his condition. Whatsoever the rod be with which he is scourged, he kisses it. He blesses God taking from him as well as giving to him; and this turned his blows into blessings, the grievous cross on his back into a glorious crown on his head. III. THE DIVINE END IN THE CHRISTIAN'S AFFLICTION. 1. It is to discover the Christian to himself. Thieves, when endeavouring to break into a house, and are prevented, do this courtesy to the master of the house—they show him the weakest part of his dwelling. Satan, by the troubles he brings on the saints, doth them often this kindness—by his rough waters their leaks are made known to them. To try the truth of grace, God led Israel many years through the wilderness, when He could have carried them a nearer way in a few days to Canaan, but it was to prove them, and to know what was in their heart. 2. It is to purge out some sins from the Christian. A garment is stricken with a staff that the dust may be beaten out. Tribulation comes from *tribulus*—a flail, because it makes the husk fly off. Joseph spake roughly to his brethren to make them repent of their sin; and so doth God deal severely with His children to make them mournful for their sin; and when once He hath brought them to that, He smileth on them. 3. It is to increase the graces of the Christian. Wisps scour vessels and make them the brighter; the fire purifieth the vessels of gold, and maketh them more meet for the Master's use. True Christians, like the vine, bear the more fruit for bleeding. Speaking of great afflictions, the Seer of the Apocalypse saith, "Here is the faith and patience of the saints." Here they are exercised, and here they are increased; for frequent acts of grace strengthen the habits of grace. (*G. Swinnock, M.A.*)　　　*Necessary afflictions :*—Too long a period of fair weather in the Italian valleys creates such a superabundance of dust that the traveller sighs for a shower. He is smothered, his eyes smart, the grit even grates between his teeth. So prosperity, long continued, breeds a plague of dust even more injurious, for it almost blinds the spirit. A Christian making money fast is just a man in a cloud of dust—it will fill his eyes if he is not careful. A Christian full of worldly care is in the same condition. Afflictions might almost be prayed for if we never had them. (*C. H. Spurgeon.*)　　　*The object of afflictions :* —There is no more precious truth than that uttered by Archbishop Secker, "Afflictions are not a consuming but a refining fire to the godly." Fitly as Archbishop Trench said, "We sometimes wonder, with regard to some of God's dealings with His children, that He should cast them again and again into the crucible of trial. It seems to us as though they were already refined gold. But He sees that in them which we do not see, a further fineness which is possible; and He will not give over till that be obtained. It is just as in a portrait by some cunning artist, which is now drawing near to its completion. Men look at it and count it perfect, and are well-nigh impatient that the artist does not now withhold his hand and declare it finished, while he, knowing better, touches and retouches as he returns again and again to his work. And why? Because there floats before him an ideal of possible excellence at which he has not yet arrived, but which will not allow him to rest or be contented till he has embodied it in his work. It is thus with God and some of His dear children. A storm among the Highlands of Scotland often effects great and rapid changes. The huge mountain that slumbers harmlessly in the sunshine with such calm and sullen majesty, is transformed by the tempest into a monster of fury. Its sides are suddenly sheeted with waterfalls, and the ferocious torrents work devastation among the glens and straths that lie in their impetuous course. The trees and shrubs that are but slightly rooted are swept away, and only the firmly grounded survive. So it is when the storm of persecution breaks upon the gospel and its adherents. The new converts, the roots of whose faith have not penetrated so deeply into the soil of truth, are in danger of being disturbed and carried away. Their peril is matter of anxiety to the Christian worker. Hence the apostle sends Timothy and writes this Epistle to the Thessalonians to "confirm and establish them in the faith." He shows—I. THAT SUFFERING IS THE INEVITABLE LOT OF GOD'S PEOPLE. 1. Suffering is a Divine ordinance. "We are appointed thereunto." A strange way, one would think, of reconciling people to affliction to tell them they have nothing else to expect. Here lies the triumph of the gospel, that it prescribes such conditions and reconciles men to their acceptance. This it does by the grace it imparts, and the hope it affords. (1) The purity of the Church coming in contact with sin and misery produces suffering "Because ye are not of the world," &c. (2) Our trials do not happen without the knowledge, consent, and control of God. (3) The Divine appointment of suffering is for our highest culture; withdrawing our affections from the temporal, and fixing them on the eternal; cleansing our corruptions and strengthening us to the right. (4) The greatest suffering often brings us into the neighbourhood of the greatest blessing. 2. Suffering was the subject of frequent apostolic warning (ver. 4). Paul was an illustrious example of heroic fortitude (Acts xx. 23). It is both wise and kind to forewarn God's people of coming afflictions that they be not overtaken unprepared. The predictions of the apostle "came to pass." Their first acquaintance with the gospel was in the midst of persecution and trial. The violent opposition continued, but the warning and exhortations of the apostle were not in vain (2 Thess. i. 4). 3. The suffering of God's people is a cause of ministerial anxiety (ver. 5). It has been pithily said, "Calamity is man's true touchstone." The faithful minister, knowing the perils of suffering, and the awful consequences of apostacy, is anxiously con cerned about the faith of his converts. "There are three modes of bearing the ills of life: by indifference, which is the most common; by philosophy, which is the most ostentatious; and by religion, which is the most effectual" (Colton). II. THAT SUFFERING EXPOSES GOD'S PEOPLE TO THE DISTURBING FORCES OF SATANIC TEMP-TATIONS. "Lest by some means the tempter have tempted you." 1. A suggestive designation of Satan. "The Tempter"—what unspeakable vileness and ruin are suggested by that name! All human woe may be traced directly up to him. The greatest champions of Christendom, such as Paul and Luther, had the most vivid sense of the personality, nearness and unceasing counter-working of this great adversary of God and man. There is need of sleepless vigilance and prayer. 2. The versatility of Satanic temptations. "Lest by some means." He may descend suddenly, clothed with terror and burning with wrath, to surprise and terrify into sin. More frequently he appears in the seductive and more dangerous garb of an angel of light, the deceptive phantom of what he once was. Infinite are his methods, but his aim is one—to suggest doubts and impious inferences as to God's providential dealings of severity, and to produce apostacy from the faith. III. THAT THE TEMPTATIONS OF A SUFFERING STATE IMPERIL THE WORK OF GOD'S SERVANTS. "And our labour be in vain." In vain as regards the great end of their salvation; they would lapse into their former heathenish state, and lose their reward; and in vain as regards the joy which the apostle anticipated from their ultimate salvation. It is true, no work done for God is absolutely in vain; the worker shall receive his just reward, but it may be in vain with regard to the object. It is bitterly disappointing to see the work that has cost so much, frustrated by temptation. How different might have been the moral history of thousands if they had not yielded to the first fiery trial. IV. THAT GOD'S PEOPLE MAY TRIUMPH OVER THE GREATEST SUFFERING. "That no man should be moved." Drawn away by flattery, or shaken "by these afflictions." While piety is tried it is also strengthened by suffering. The watchful and faithful soul may use his troubles as aids to a richer experience and firmer consolidation of Christian character. Lessons—1. To live a godly life involves suffering. 2. A period of suffering is ever attended with powerful temptations. 3. The grace of God is sufficient to sustain and deliver. (*G. Barlow.*) *The Christian conditions of life* :—" Man was made for happiness " is the easy formulary concerning the nature and ends of life which seems generally accepted. But if that had been Paul's view, the text could hardly have been written, nor Christ borne the witness of Matt. xvi. 24, 25; nor the heroes of Heb. xi. been pourtrayed. That formula may sound the philosopher's roadsteads, but is lost in the great sea of life as we launch forth to the depths which have been fathomed only by the life of the Lord. We need only read casually the lives of the great ones pourtrayed in Scripture to see that happiness was just the last thing they were thinking of; for had that been their aim, life must have been to them a dreadful disappointment. Paul at any rate was not afraid to hold forth a widely different rule and end even to young converts. I. WHAT IS THE AIM OF MAN? What offers him the highest attraction, and puts him under the strongest restraint? To live a life after the image and mind of God, leaving the happiness question alone. 1. This may bring happiness or pain, but such a man has as his end something which transcends happiness and makes him oblivious of pain (Gal. ii. 20). Self-love has forgotten itself in the love of Him whose love is the intensest passion that can possess the spirit, and fills it with joy unspeakable and full of glory. But the joy springs out of the passion, the passion is not cherished as the way to the joy. 2. We shall never arrive at a true Christian philosophy of life until we purge out the leaven of the last century philosophy, and consider the aim of man's life as something more than a search for happiness. To be is greater than to be anything; to live is greater than to possess or enjoy. Being will include both happiness and unhappiness as long as the world and the

Spirit are at war, but it will not feel itself nearer its end in the one than in the other. To live God-like will alone satisfy it; and that is sharing the burdens and sufferings of Christ. 3. There is nothing to frighten a man in the vision of struggles and suffering for a worthy end. Nay, there is that which should attract him. All the nobler spirits will be more fired by the end than daunted by the suffering. A high end which God smiles upon and pursues, is what inspires men with indomitable courage, and exalted joy. You feel it in the smallest things. Your days of exultation are when you are toiling earnestly and bearing bravely for the sake of some noble end, on which you can ask God's blessing. Pain which you would feel keenly in lazier moods seems hardly to touch you. The most glorious moment of Jacob's life was that night of agonizing wrestling, though it left him a halting man and spoilt for much of happiness. It is life in its full beat and swing, not the satisfaction of desire which is bliss. II. THE APPOINTMENT OF AFFLICTION AS THE MEANS. 1. The ordinance of affliction, " I am not come to send peace but a sword." The first fruit of the advent of the Saviour to the world, to a soul, is to deepen the sorrow of life, and to increase the pressure of its burden. It was no part of Christ's plan to makes a fool's paradise of the world. He came to deepen its experience in every way : to make it a more solemn thing to live, by unveiling life's issues ; a more awful thing to sin, by unveiling God's holiness ; a more hopeful and, therefore, more blessed thing to suffer, by declaring " the sufferings of this present time are not worthy to be compared with the glory that shall be revealed in us." Easy had it been for Him to restore the beauty and joy of Eden ; but something larger He had set before Him to realize. The world's chief sufferers have been the world's chief blessed ones in time and in eternity. 2. The author of the ordinance, God Himself. There is something terrible in the idea of the Epicurean God, sitting calmly on high with no eye to pity, no hand to save. Even the Jew, with his sublime conception of the God of Sinai, shrank from this. Isaiah liii. tells a nobler tale. Dark as the ordinance of sorrow may seem, He ordained it to Himself, before He ordained it to you. If the law be " through much tribulation ye shall inherit the kingdom," if the symbol of the new life be the Cross, the God from whom the law issues Himself won the kingdom by tribulation, and consecrated the Cross as its emblem by His own death. No soldier murmurs if his captain but leads him through the deadly peril. We are not afraid or ashamed to suffer in the flesh, when the chief sufferer is incarnate God. 3. The reason of the ordinance. There are a thousand subsidiary reasons, but the supreme one is that we may have fellowship with God. Man made happy on easy terms might have held just such fellowship with God as a light-hearted, innocent child can hold with one who has borne the burden of life's battle. He feels a passing interest in the child's prattle but keeps *himself* for the friend who has fought or suffered at his side. And God wants the fellowship of friends, not the prattle of children in eternity ; friends whose powers have been exercised in the sternest of conflicts, and proved that they hate evil as He hates it, and love good as He loves it, by being willing to resist the one and to clasp the other even unto death. The suffering He ordains is precisely the fellowship of His suffering. Perfect through sufferings is the Divine perfectness whereby the perfected may converse with Him for ever. 4. The end of the ordinance : Supreme and perfect bliss. The hunters after happiness miss it utterly. Those who lift the Cross as their symbol of life, and bear it till they change it for a crown, find in bearing it a blessedness which is kindred with the blessedness of God. It is a deep truth that none but those who suffer keenly can enjoy keenly. " So you who are troubled rest with us " is Christ's promise to those who dare to look boldly into this mystery of pain. Rest where the warrior can recall the incidents of the battle and reap the fruit of the victory—where the purified spirit shall shine resplendent—where rest shall be untiring service without disappointment or pain. (*Baldwin Brown, B.A.*)    *The persecution of the early church :*—To what extent did the early Christians suffer persecution? Much has been said of the tolerant spirit of the Roman government, inclined to let all religions sleep peacefully under the shadow of its wings. But it is one thing to tolerate existing religions, another to sanction a new one, and that, too, not seeking to insinuate itself privately, but openly professing as its object the conversion of the world. Probably there has never been a civilized country in which such an attempt at proselytism would not have been at first met by persecution. Every page of the Acts is a picture of similar persecutions ; and more remarkable than any part of it is the narrative which St. Paul gives of his own sufferings (2 Cor. xi. 23–33), and which, amid many other reflections, suggests the thought, how small a part of his life has been preserved. From the state of Christianity in the time of Pliny or Tacitus, we can scarcely form an idea of its first difficulties. Everywhere it had to encounter the fierce spirit of fanaticism, wrought up in the Jew to its highest pitch, in the pagan just needing to be awakened. The Jews, the false brethren, the heretics, the heathen, were in league more or less openly at one time or other for its destruction. All ages which have witnessed a revival of religious feeling, have witnessed also the outbreak of religious passions; the pure light of the one becomes the spark by which the other is kindled. Reasons of state sometimes create a faint and distant suspicion of the new faith; the feelings of the mass rise to overwhelm it. The Roman government may be said to have observed in general the same line respecting the first preachers of the gospel, as would be observed in modern times: that is to say, of matters of faith and opinion, as such, they hardly took account, except in so far as they endangered the safety of the government, or led to breaches of the public peace. It seemed idle to them to dispute about questions of the Jewish law in Roman courts of justice; but they were not the less prepared to call to account those by whose supposed agency a whole city was in an uproar. Hence, when the really peaceful character of the gospel was seen, the persecutions gradually ceased and revived only at a later period, when Christianity became a political power. Allowing for the difference of times and seasons, the feelings of the Roman governors were not altogether unlike those with which the followers of John Wesley, in the last century, might have been regarded by the magistrates of an English town. And, making still greater allowance for the malignity and depth of the passions by which men were agitated as the old religions were breaking up, a parallel not less just might be drawn also between the feelings of the multitude. There was in both cases a kind of sympathy by which the lower class were attracted towards the new teachers. Natural feeling suggested that these men had come for their good: they were grateful for the love shown of them, and for the ministration to their temporal wants. There was a time (Acts ii. 47, iv. 21) when the first believers were in favour with all the people; but at the preaching of Stephen the scene changes and the deep irreconcilable hostility of the two principles is beginning to be felt; "it is not peace, but a sword"; not "I am come to fulfil the law," but "not one stone shall be left upon another." The moment this was clearly perceived, not only would the far-sighted jealousy of the chief priests and rulers be alarmed at the preaching of the apostles, but the very instincts of the multitude itself would rise at them. More than anything that we have witnessed in modern times of religious intolerance, would be the feeling against those who sought to relax the bond of circumcision as enemies to their country, religion and God. But another aspect of the new religion served to bring home these feelings even yet more nearly—the description of the family, as our Lord foretold, the father was against the son, &c. A new power had arisen in the world, which seemed to cut across and dissever natural affections. Consider what is implied in the words "of believing women not a few"; what animosities of parents and brethren, &c. An unknown tie, closer than that of kindred, drew away the individuals of a family, and joined them to an external society. It was not only that they were members of another church, or attendants on a separate worship. The difference went beyond. In the daily intercourse of life, at every meal, the unbelieving brother or sister was conscious of the presence of the unclean. It was an injury not readily to be forgotten, or forgiven in its authors, than which in this world none could be greater. The fanatic priest, led on by every personal and religious motive; the man of the world, caring for none of those things, but not the less resenting the intrusion on the peace of his home; the craftsman, fearing for his gains; the accursed multitude, knowing not the law, but irritated at the very notion of this mysterious society of such real though hidden strength—would all work together towards the overthrow of those who seemed to them to be turning upside down the political, religious and social order of the world. (*Prof. Jowett.*) *The need of the apostolic warning:*—An example of this was seen in the case of Demas, who was allured by the love of this world, and forsook Paul in his sufferings at Rome, and departed to Thessalonica (2 Tim. iv. 10). The devil is often more to be feared when he fawns than when he roars. The man of God at Judah overcame Satan at Bethel, but was ensnared by him under the oak tree (1 Kings xiii. 14). David vanquished Satan in the battle-field (1 Sam. xvii. 48), but was vanquished by him in the cool of the evening on the housetop (2 Sam. xi. 2). (*Bp. Wordsworth.*) *Appointed to affliction:*—Church history nowhere gives a more striking illustration of these words, and of the power which lies in them to strengthen and comfort, than in the story of the banishment of some five thousand bishops and presbyters,

with their adherents, into the desert, by Hunneric, during the African persecutions
of the sixth century.  They were torn from their homes, and shut up amid squalor
and hunger in a small prison, and afterwards driven, with every species of maltreatment, over the burning sands.  Yet the song of that suffering pilgrim band had
its constant refrain, " Such glory have all God's saints."   (J. Hutchison, D.D.)

Ver. 4. **When we were with you we told you.**—*The minister to warn his people of
future suffering* :—I. MINISTERS SHOULD WARN YOUNG CONVERTS OF THE DIFFICULTIES
OF THE CHRISTIAN.  They must be taught that a suffering hour will come, and they
must expect it.  Otherwise there will be inevitable disappointment, and unbelief
will be engendered in other matters and perhaps apostasy.  II. WHEN CHRISTIANS
HAVE RECEIVED THESE WARNINGS THEY SHOULD FOREARM THEMSELVES.  1. The greatest
calamities may be mitigated by forethought and prudence.  2. There are promises
of Divine grace of which the Christian should possess himself before they are
wanted.  3. Otherwise, in spite of the strongest caution and the most efficient provision, Christians will sink under their trials.  III. THE HEAVIER THE TRIAL THE
GREATER THE REWARD.  For our light affliction we shall have an eternal weight of
glory.  (W. Burditt, M.A.)      *Tribulation* :—We all know in a general way that
this word means affliction, sorrow, anguish; but it is quite worth our while to
know how it means this.  It is derived from the Latin *tribulum* which was the
threshing instrument or harrow, whereby the Roman husbandman separated the
corn from the husks; and *tribulatio* was the act of this separation.  But some
Latin writer of the Christian Church appropriated the word and image for setting
forth of a higher truth; and sorrow, distress, and adversity being the appointed
means for the separating in men of whatever in them was light, trivial, and poor,
for the solid and the true—their chaff from their wheat—he therefore called these
sorrows and trials " tribulations," threshings, that is, of the inner spiritual man,
without which there could be no fitting him for the heavenly garner.  (Abp.
Trench.)      *The benefit of tribulation* :—Thus God schooleth and nurtureth His
people, that so through many tribulations they may enter to their rest.  Frankincense, when it is put into the fire, giveth the greater perfume; spice, if it be pounded,
smelleth the sweeter; the earth, when it is torn up with the plough, becometh
more fruitful; the seed in the ground, after frost and snow and winter storms,
springeth the ranker; the nigher the vine is pruned to the stock, the greater grape
it yieldeth; the grape, when it is most pressed and beaten, maketh the sweetest
wine; fine gold is the better, when it is cast in the fire; rough stones with hewing
are squared and made fit for building; cloth is rent and cut, that it may be made a
garment; linen is bucketed, and washed, and wrung, and beaten, and is the fairer.
(Bp. Jewel.)      *How to deal with troubles* :—Wesley was one day walking along a
road with a Christian man who was relating his troubles, and at the same time
saying he did not know what he should do.  As his companion was expressing his
doubts they happened to pass a stone fence over which a cow was looking.  " Do
you know," asked Wesley, " why that cow looks *over* that wall ? "  " No," replied
the friend in trouble.  " I will tell you," answered Wesley, " because she cannot
look *through* it."  And that is what you must do with your troubles, look over and
above them. (W. Baxendale.)      *God's purpose in troubles* :—Troubles are often the
tools by which God fashions us for better things.  Far up the mountain sides lies a
block of granite, and says to itself " How happy am I in my serenity—above the
winds, above the trees, almost above the flight of birds!  Here I rest age after age,
and nothing disturbs me ! "  Yet, what is it ?  It is only a bare block of granite,
jutting out of the cliff, and its happiness is the happiness of death.  By and by
comes the miner, and with strong and repeated strokes he drills a hole in its top,
and the rock says, " What does this mean ? "  Then the black powder is poured in,
and with a blast that makes the mountain echo the block is blown asunder, and
goes crashing down the valley.  " Ah ! " it exclaims as it falls, "why this rending?"
Then some saws to fashion it; and humbled now and willing to be nothing, it is
borne away from the mountain and conveyed to the city.  Now it is chiselled and
polished till, at length, finished in beauty it is raised high in the air to be the
top stone on some monument of the country's glory.  (H. W. Beecher.)      *Unmoved by trial* :—I have seen a tree proudly crowning the summit of a naked
rock, and there, with its roots spread out over the bare stone, and sent down
into every cranny in search of food, it stood securely moored to the stormy
crag.  I have wondered how it could grow up there, starved on the bare,
naked rock, and how it had survived the rough nursing of many a winter

blast. Yet, like some neglected, ragged child, who from early childhood has been familiar with adversities, it has lived and grown and held itself erect on its weather-beaten crag when the pride of the valley has bent to the storm; like men who, scorning to yield, bravely nail their colours to the mast, there it maintains its defiant position, and keeps its green flag waving on nature's rugged battlements. (*T. Guthrie, D.D.*) *Christian tribulation:*—How is it, brother? I do not ask you whether you like the cup which you are now drinking; but look back twenty years. . . . What has made you so versatile? What has made you so patient? What has made you so broad, so deep, so rich? God put pickaxes into you, though you did not like it. He dug wells of salvation in you. He took you in His strong hand, and shook you by His north wind, and rolled you in His snows, and fed you with the coarsest food, and clothed you in the coarsest raiment, and beat you as a flail beats grain till the straw is gone, and the wheat is left. And you are what you are by the grace of God's providence, many of you. By fire, by anvil strokes, by the hammer that breaks the flinty rock, God played miner, and blasted you out of the rock, and then He played stamper and crushed you, and then He played smelter and melted you, and now you are gold free from the rock, by the grace of God's severity to you. (*H. W. Beecher.*) *Christian progress a cause of tribulation:*— Crossing the ocean, I used to hang over the side of the *Java* to watch the stroke of the wave against the ship's cut-water. I noticed, when it was foggy, and we were making only seven or eight knots an hour, there was but little stir in the water; but when, in fair weather, we went fourteen knots an hour, the ocean tossed in front of the prow and boiled on either side. So, just in proportion as a Christian makes headway in Christian enterprise, in that ratio will there be commotion and excited resistance in the waters. If nothing has been said against you, if you have never been assaulted, if everybody seems pleased with you, you are simply making little or no progress; you are water-logged, and, instead of mastering the wave, the wave masters you. (*T. De Witt Talmage, D.D.*)

Ver. 5. **For this cause, when I could no longer forbear, I sent to know your faith.** —*Christian solicitude:*—I. Its NATURE. "When I could no longer forbear." 1. As a moral quality and exercise it must be distinguished from personal anxiety. This is everywhere forbidden: "Take no thought," &c., "Be careful for nothing." And it is easy to see why it is prohibited. It is selfish, and is provocative of those vices which are detrimental to the Christian character—irritation, unbelief, fear, and general unfitness for duty. But Christian solicitude is for others, is unselfish, self-forgetful, benevolent, and inspires a good many of those virtues which are inseparable from an exemplary Christian life—sympathy, self-sacrifice, helpfulness. 2. In certain cases it warrantably assumes an intense form. When a relative or a friend is in perilous circumstances through travel, occupation, &c., it is legitimate to feel anxious about him. This we generally do. But how much keener should be our anxiety when his soul is in danger, either through being unawakened, or through being exposed like the Thessalonians to temptation? Yet how insensible most are to the latter duty. A father, terribly solicitous about his son's temporal advancement, never bestows a thought about his eternal interests. When a daughter is away in some sphere of fashion or frivolity the mother's care about her health, prospects of marriage, &c., will be carried to the point of distress; while the nature of the moral atmosphere which the daughter breathes will hardly enter the mother's mind. How different with Paul. As the context shows he had the deepest sympathy with them in their physical dangers, but his supreme concern is about their "faith." II. Its METHOD: "I sent." This was all he could do. And this is often all we can do. We cannot always be with our friends to give them the benefit of our counsel, sympathy, help and protection; but we can always send—1. Messages to them. How seldom are letters employed as means of usefulness! What an immense amount of correspondence many of us get through in a year, and yet how little of it is utilized for God. How trivial much of it is even with those who need that it should be serious and practical. Yet no means could be more effective for conveying admonition, encouragement, and advice. The spoken word passes to be often forgotten; the written word may remain to be pondered. And then there are those who are too diffident to speak, who have no difficulty in writing. 2. Prayers to God. We may be sure of the acceptableness of our solicitude when expressed to Him. He only can help in times of spiritual danger. Our anxiety as expressed to them is only helpful as it drives them to God; then equally helpful is that prayerful solicitude which brings God near to them. III. Its PURPOSE. 1. Deliverance from spiritual peril. 2. Maintenance of spiritual work. The temptations of one hour may undo all the efforts of parents, friends, pastors and teachers for years. How often has a timely word or message arrested a downward career and saved a soul. (*J. W. Burn.*)    **The Tempter.**—*Satan more prominent in the New Testament than in the Old:*—Very remarkable is the prominence which Satan assumes in the New Testament, compared with the manner in which he is kept in the background in the Old. There, after the first appearance of the adversary in paradise, he is withdrawn for a long while from the scene; nay, there is but a glimpse of him, a passing indication here and there of such a spiritual head of the kingdom of evil, through the whole earlier economy—as in Job i., ii.; Zech. iii. 1, 2; 1 Chron. xxi. 1; he is only referred to twice in the Apocrypha (Wisd. ii. 24; Ecclus. xxi. 27). This may partly be explained on the principle that where lights are brightest, shadows are darkest; it needed the highest revelation of good to show us the deepest depth of evil. But, no doubt in that childhood of the human race, men were not ripe for this knowledge. For as many as took it in earnest it would have been too dreadful thus to know of one who had been a prince of light. Those, therefore, who are under a Divine education are not allowed to understand anything very distinctly of Satan, till with the spiritual eye it is given to them to behold him as lightning fall from heaven; then the Scripture speaks of him without reserve. Notice the analogy in 1 John ii. 13 and 14. To some the doctrine of the tempter is a stumbling-block; but it is not by Scriptural arguments alone that it is supported. There is a dark, mysterious element in man's life and history, which nothing else can explain. All who shrink from looking down into the abysmal depths of man's fall, seem to count that much will have been gained thereby; although it may be pertinently asked, What is the profit of getting rid of the devil, so long as the devilish remains? of explaining away an evil *one*, so long as the evil ones who remain are so many? What profit, indeed? Assuredly this doctrine of an evil spirit, tempting, seducing, deceiving, prompting to rebellion, so far from casting a deeper gloom on the mysterious destinies of humanity, is full of consolation, and lights up with a gleam of hope spots which would seem utterly dark without it. One might well despair of oneself, having no choice but to believe that all the strange suggestions of evil which have risen up before one's own heart had been born there; one might well despair of one's kind, having no choice but to believe that all its hideous sins and monstrous crimes had been self-conceived and born in its own bosom. But there is hope, if "an enemy hath done this;" if, however, the soil *in* which all these wicked thoughts and works have sprung up has been the heart of man, yet the seed *from* which they sprung had been sown there by the hand of another. And who will venture to deny this devilish, as distinguished from the animal in man? None, certainly, who knows aught of the dread possibilities of sin lurking in his own bosom, who has studied with any true insight the moral history of the world. In what way else explain that men not merely depart from God, but that they defy Him? What else will account for delight in the contemplation or infliction of pain, for strange inventions of wickedness, above all, of cruelty and lust—"lust hard by hate"? What else will account for evil chosen for its own sake, and for the fierce joy men so often find in the violation of law, this violation being itself the attraction? The mystery is as inexplicable as it is dreadful, so long as man will know nothing of a spiritual world beneath him as well as above him; but it is only too easy to understand, so soon as we recognize man's evil as not altogether his own, but detect behind his transgression an earlier transgressor —one who fell, not as men fall, for man's fall was broken by the very flesh which invited it; but who fell as only spirits can fall, from the height of heaven to the depth of hell; fell, never to rise again; for *he* was not deceived, was not tempted as was Adam; but himself chose the evil with the clearest intuition that it was evil, forsook the good with the clearest intuition that it was good: whose sin, therefore, in its essence, was the sin against the Holy Ghost, and as such never to be forgiven. All is explicable when we recognize the existence of such a spirit; who being lost without hope of redemption himself, seeks to work the same loss in other of God's creatures, and counts it a small triumph to have made a man bestial, unless he can make him devilish as well. (*Abp. Trench.*)    *The subtlety of the Tempter:*—An enemy, before he besiegeth a city, surroundeth it at a distance to see where the wall is weakest, best to be battered, lowest, easiest to be scaled; ditch narrowest to be bridged, shallowest to be waded over; what place, if not regularly fortified, where he may approach with least danger, and assault with most advantage. So Satan walketh about surveying all the powers of our souls, where he may most probably lay his temptations,—as whether our understandings are easier corrupted with error, or our fancies with levity, or our wills with frowardness, or our affections with excess. (*J. Spencer.*) *Degrees in temptation :*—Satan seldom comes to Christians with great temptations, or with a temptation to commit a great sin. You bring a green log and a candle together, and they are very safe neighbours; but bring a few shavings, and set them alight, and then bring a few small sticks and let them take fire, and the log be in the midst of them, and you will soon get rid of your log. And so it is with little sins. You will be startled with the idea of committing a great sin; and so the devil brings you a little temptation, and leaves you to indulge yourself. " There is no great harm in this; no great peril in that; " and so by these little chips we are first easily lighted up, and at last the green log is burned. (*J. Newton.*) *Seduction of temptation :*—Of the Lurley-berg on the Rhine, with the whirlpool and deceitful eddies near it, where many a raft and fishing boat has gone down, many wild legends are related. Tradition makes the rock the dwelling place of a Syren, who, by her sweet songs, enchanted all who heard her. The mariners of the Rhine, heedless of the dangers which beset them at this point, when once they heard the seducing song of the water nymph, altogether abandoned their charge to the course of the current, and frequently perished in the whirlpool, or were wrecked against the rock. (*W. Denton, M.A.*) *Where temptation assails :*—There is a deep truth contained in the fabled story of old, where a mother, wishing to render her son invulnerable, plunged him into the Styx, but forgot to dip in his heel, by which she held him. We are baptized in the blood and fire of sorrow, that temptation may make us invulnerable; but let us remember that trials will assail our most vulnerable part, be it the head, or heart, or heel. (*F. W. Robertson, M.A.*) *Temptation comes unawares :*—Many horses fall at the bottom of a hill because the driver thinks the danger past and the need to hold the reins with a firm grip less pressing. So it is often with us when we are not specially tempted to overt sin, we are more in danger through slothful ease. "There is no devil," says Ralph Erskine, "so bad as no devil." (*C. H. Spurgeon.*) *Sinful hearts invite temptation :*—No one would make overtures to a bolted door or a dead wall. It is some face at the window that invites proffer. (*H. W. Beecher.*) *Resistance to temptation possible :*—It is the devil's part to suggest: ours not to consent. As oft as we resist him, so often we overcome him; as often as we overcome him, so often we bring joy to the angels and glory to God; who opposeth us that we may contend; and assisteth us that we may conquer. (*St. Bernard.*) *Trial endured :*— Constantius (father of Constantine the Great) once published an edict requiring all Christians in his dominions to abjure their religion on pain of losing all their civil honours and offices. Some thereupon, like Demas and Diotrephes, forsook Christ and embraced the present world, but others stood firm, being willing to count all things but loss for their faith and for the love of their Master. Constantius then, having discovered who the real Christians were, restored them to their places, and banished the hypocrites, saying: "They can never be true to their emperor who are false to their Maker." *Temptation without warning :*—One summer the earth heaved like a tumultuous sea, and Ischia and its capital were in ruins and death; and a few weeks later the ocean rolled its force over Eastern islands, and lands, and houses, and men disappeared beneath its waves. In this way, oftentimes without warning, does temptation sweep on the soul. And its assault comes when night is over, and our eyes are shut to duty, to God, and to good. Reason will not daunt the tempter, for he makes the reason his captive. Imagination and memory fly to his side; and even conscience assumes but a proud neutrality. Oh, that is the hour of humbling; we were, we are not! Heaven looks on in pity, and Satan exults over a sinner who had repented and has gone back. There is no influence, no possibility of escape for man unless in the interposed power of his God. The power that is in us, is it asleep often? Do we often fall? Oh! wake up that gift, stir it into energy; beat down the environing defences of your basest foe; and remember Him of whom you are to walk worthy, and that true and holy fellowship of the saints in which you are called to live. (*The Quiver.*)

**Ver. 6. But now when Timotheus came from you unto us.**—*News that gladdens :*— With what anxiety a father entrusts his son with a commission to visit an estate in a distant land and to investigate its affairs, which are threatened for the time being. He is in suspense until he receives intelligence of the safe arrival of his loved messenger, and of the prosperity of the estate. But when his son returns and assures him that everything is prosperous, the father's satisfaction is complete. "As cold water to a thirsty soul, so is good news from a far country." Such, in a higher sense, was the experience of Paul here. I. THE APOSTLE WAS GLADDENED WITH GOOD TIDINGS OF FAITH MAINTAINED. 1. Their faith in the great truths of the gospel was maintained. The revelation of Divine truth is the basis of all faith. This truth as it affected their salvation had been successfully declared to them. They comprehended its meaning, felt its force, embraced it, were transformed by it. Amid the shock of persecution, and the insidious whisperings of false teachers, they held fast to "the form of sound words." 2. Their faith as a principle of active spiritual life was maintained. True faith is not simply a belief, but a life: not merely an assent of the mind to truth, but the impartation of a spiritual force. It forms a new era in the experience and history of the soul. It unites us to the Living God, and expands to our view, however dimly, the vast outline of the life of God as the pattern of our own. II. THE APOSTLE WAS GLADDENED WITH GOOD TIDINGS OF LOVE MANIFESTED. "Brought us good tidings of your charity." Love is the fruit of faith, both in its inward experience and outward manifestation. Faith and love are indissolubly combined (1 John iii. 23). The first exercise of love is towards God; and then towards all whom God loves. Such love is impartial and universal—manifested towards all in whom we discern the image of God, whatever their country or condition. Where faith and love reign there is a living, healthy, and prosperous Church. III. THE APOSTLE WAS GLADDENED WITH GOOD TIDINGS OF CONTINUED PERSONAL REGARD. 1. The apostle was fondly remembered. "Ye have good remembrance of us always." There are some scenes of nature which, beheld but for a moment, never fade from the memory; there are some faces we can never forget; and there are some individuals whose influence remains with us through life. The Thessalonians had good reason to remember Paul. The minister who first led us to the Cross, will ever have the pre-eminence in our affection, and the choicest spot in our memory. A high appreciation of the Christian minister is one of the evidences of possessing genuine faith and love. 2. They were as solicitous as the apostle for a renewal of Christian fellowship. "Desiring greatly to see us, as we also to see you." There is no bond so tender, and strong, as that existing between the preacher and his converts. He must needs love the souls he has been instrumental in saving, and who are his glory and his joy. The intercourse between such is of the purest and highest kind. Never was there a more loving heart than that of the Apostle Paul. The Thessalonians warmly reciprocated that love; and longed to renew the fellowship by which they had so richly profited. Lessons: 1. That church has the best reputation where faith is maintained and love manifested. 2. The Christian minister is cheered by the affection and stability of his converts. (G. Barlow.) Faith and charity:—Your faith is the guide, but your love is the way that leads to God. (Ignatius.)

Vers. 7-10. Therefore, brethren, we were comforted over you in all our affliction. —The steadfastness of believers a source of ministerial satisfaction:—The scholar finds his happiness in intellectual exercises, and in accumulating knowledge; the politician in the excitement of debate, and the triumph of principles; the scientist in testing and harmonizing the laws of nature; the merchant in his gains; and the minister in the increase of converts to the truth, and in their consistency and perseverance. Observe: I. THEIR STEADFASTNESS WAS A SOURCE OF COMFORT. 1. The apostle was comforted in the midst of personal suffering (Acts xviii. 6). So great was his trouble that the Lord thought it needful to encourage him (ibid. 9, 10). The bitterness of his afflictions at this time was sweetened by hearing of the constancy of his Thessalonian converts, The faithlessness of the people is a grief to the true minister now: but at last the horror will be theirs. 2. The apostle was comforted concerning their faith. The Church is in danger, and cause of deep anxiety, when its faith wavers. II. THEIR STEADFASTNESS INTENSIFIED THE PLEASURE OF LIVING. The good news thrilled his soul with new life. For now, whatever else befall—now, in the face of Jewish fury and Gentile scorn—now, amid infirmities, reproaches, necessities, persecutions, distresses and deaths oft—now we live if ye stand fast in the Lord. The relation of the minister to his people is so close and vital that they have it in their power to make his life happy or miserable. There is a method of destroying life without its becoming utterly extinct. To lessen the cheerful flow of life, and depress the spirits of the man of God, is a species of murder: to starve him into submission by studied neglect and privation, is diabolical. The ministerial life and energy of even an apostle depended on the sympathy, faith, and steadfastness of the brethren (John iii. 4). III. THEIR STEADFASTNESS WAS PRODUCTIVE OF GRATEFUL JOY. 1. This joy was copious and sincere : "For the joy wherewith we joy before our God." The transitions of the emotions are rapid. From the midst of the apostle's grief a fountain of joy breaks forth. This joy filled his soul even in the presence of God. It was a pure, sincere, undissembled, overflowing joy, such as God could approve. 2. This joy arose from a disinterested love : "For your sakes." True love gives us an interest in the safety and happiness of others. He who possesses this never lacks joy : if it flows not on his own behalf, it does on behalf of others. Bernard has said, "Of all the motions and affections of the soul, love is the only one we may reciprocate with God : to re-love Him is our happiness : woe, if we answer Him not in some measure of re-loving affection." 3. This joy was expressed in fervent thanksgiving : "What thanks can we render," &c. His gratitude was so great that he could hardly give it expression. The grateful heart prizes blessings that seem to others of small value. IV. THEIR STEADFASTNESS EXCITED AN EARNEST LONGING TO IMPART ADDITIONAL GOOD. 1. The apostle assiduously prayed for the opportunity of a personal interview : "Night and day," &c. The longer the absence the more eager the desire. The good news of their constancy increased the desire. A love like his could be satisfied only with personal spiritual intercourse. It was not enough simply to write. Voice and manner have a charm of their own. Reading, praying, &c., will be unavailing if we despise prophesying—the oral declaration of the truth. 2. The apostle sought this interview to supply what was lacking in their faith. None are so perfect in faith as not to be susceptible of improvement. Faith is based on knowledge, and as knowledge is capable of indefinite extension, so faith may be continually increased. The less distinctly the great subjects of faith are understood, the more defective is faith. We all have to cry, "Lord, increase our faith." Lessons : 1. The true minister cannot be indifferent to the spiritual state of his people. 2. The fidelity and perseverance of believers is an inspiration and an unspeakable joy to the anxious worker. 3. Faith and practice powerfully react upon each other. (*G. Barlow.*) *The faith of the people the comfort of the minister :*—It is natural for labourers to look for wages : the minister's best wages is the faith of his people. The apostle's work was laborious and discouraging, but his comfort was the growing faith of the Churches. On this point he was more anxious than about his own safety (ver. 5). I. THE APOSTLE'S AFFLICTION. 1. The abuse of the world and the devil. This abuse is—(1) A sure sign of a valid ministry : "If I pleased men I should not be a servant of Christ." Christ sent His servants as sheep in the midst of wolves. (2) Natural. Satan claims the world as his kingdom. When havoc is wrought in it it is not to be expected that he will bear it quietly. The carnal mind which is enmity against God is opposed to the gospel, because it abates human pride, and calls for much humiliation and sacrifice. 2. Non-success in many Christian efforts. The apostles "essayed to go" hither and thither : but the Spirit forbade them. In other places they were rejected ; in others all their labour seemed to be in vain. There is no greater grief to a minister than to be hindered, rejected or fruitless. 3. The aboundings of heresy and wickedness. It is impossible to describe the anguish of Lot, who "vexed his righteous soul" on account of the iniquity of Sodom, and equally impossible to describe the pain of God's servants, to whom the honour of Jesus is dear, to hear His name degraded, His faith frittered away, and the work of His Spirit melted down into a little cold water. 4. Personal suffering, whether of a bodily or spiritual character. II. HIS SOLACE. "Your faith." The minister is comforted by the knowledge—1. That faith is wrought in his hearers ; that his preaching is owned of God to the working of faith in the soul. This faith is not an intellectual assent to his teaching—that would bring him a little glory, no doubt. What he wants is that faith which works not admiration but transformation. 2. That his hearers are living the life of faith ; when he witnesses the love which faith works and the purity that faith imparts. A faith that does not make a man love holiness and hate sin will never make the heart fit for Divine inhabitation. 3. That his hearers are growing in faith—in its possession and exercise—in the strength and stature of faith ; growing whether in the "child," "young man," or "father" ; whether in the "blade, ear, or full corn in the ear." 4. That his hearers have the full assurance of faith. 5. That the stability of their faith is evincing its reality : "not moved with afflictions." 6. That their faith strengthens his own. (*J. Irons.*) *Saved sinners a minister's joy :*—I do not know anything that can make a man forget his pain and weariness like grasping the hand of a sinner saved. I speak here from experience, for yesterday evening, when I was thinking of this subject, I was myself somewhat dull through pain and weakness, and as God would have it, I took up the last Report of the Baptist Missionary Society, and as I glanced over it I saw my own name. It seems that our missionary in San Domingo has had a discouraging year, but it was lighted up with one most pleasing incident. A man had come down from the interior of Hayti to ask for baptism on accepting Christ as his Saviour. The missionary asked how he came to know anything about it. In reply he told him that he had fallen in with a sermon translated into the French language, which was preached by Mr. Spurgeon. Oh, friends, I was dull no longer! I had meat to eat. Had an angel stood in the study, I could not have felt more delighted with his visit than I did when I read of a sinner saved. (*C. H. Spurgeon.*)    **For now we live if ye stand fast in the Lord.**—*The spiritual relation between the apostle and the Thessalonians :*—I. His WELLBEING DEPENDED ON THEM. 1. Paul's distress while he was at Corinth is represented as a species of death, as he says elsewhere, "I die daily." But from this, as it were, he revived. He felt himself raised again to the full enthusiasm and activity of life by learning of their faithful adherence to Christ. When Jacob had the good news brought to him that Joseph was alive, and governor of Egypt, "his spirit revived." His years of mourning had been a kind of death to him, and the tidings delivered him from it. In the same way was Paul quickened in the midst of all his sorrows. As Newman says, "He felt all his neighbours to be existing in himself." We may further say that he existed in them—his life was bound up in theirs. 2. This identity of interest and aim can only rightly manifest itself in those who are one in Christ. Human character in its nobler elements can be developed alone in sympathy with others, in the willingness to share in each others joys, sorrows, failures, triumphs. Isolation of spirit is spiritual death. It is with hearts as with the embers of the hearth—"Do you not see glimmering half-red embers, if laid together, get into the brightest white glow" (Carlyle.) 3. What a striking contrast to the apostle was such an one as Goethe, the apostle of mere worldly culture, the picture of a man living in "the miserable dream of keeping the course of his inward development free from all foreign interference," reluctant to devote himself and his inner life to anything, or any one outside of himself ; consumed with the desire, as he expressed it, "to raise the pyramid of my existence, the base of which is already laid, as high as possible in the air ; that absorbing every other desire, and scarcely ever quitting me." There is no more revolting picture to the Christian than that. We can never rise to God as long as we try to do so in the way of selfish isolation. We can only find ourselves when we first lose ourselves in others. It is thus that Christianity extends itself. "Till each man finds his own in all men's good, and all men work in noble brotherhood." II. THEIR STEAD-FASTNESS REVIVED THE APOSTLE. What is implied in it ? 1. That individually and collectively the members of the Church are "in the Lord," abiding in Him both in faith and practice. 2. That while in the Lord they are exposed to the danger of wavering. The language seems military (1 Cor. xvi. 13). Christ's Church, each section of it, is exposed to assault. The army of the living God is subject to having its ranks broken in upon. This is the aim of the tempter, of whom the apostle had just been speaking. Hence the exhortation to steadfast adherence to God and His truth, for "by faith ye stand" ; steadfast adherence, too, to one another, that so they may present the strength of a united phalanx to the enemy, and at last rejoice in a day of triumph. (*J. Hutchison, D.D.*)    *The steadfastness of the Church the life of the ministry :*—I. THE NATURE OF THIS STEADFASTNESS. It comprehends —1. Their steadfastness in the faith of the gospel. This faith is not merely the assent of the mind to its truth, but also the dependence of the heart on its salvation. The latter depends indeed on the former ; for if the word of the gospel be not received as true, the salvation of the gospel cannot be depended on as sure. Steadfastness, then, comprises a firm belief in the truth of revelation, and a firm reliance on the Saviour revealed ; believing with the heart unto righteousness, having the heart established with grace. 2. Their steadfastness in the profession of the gospel. The gospel not only reveals truths to be believed, and a Saviour to be depended on, but presents claims to be recognized. It not only invites the confidence of the heart, but the confession of the mouth. It requires an avowed separation from the world and sin, and a professed subjection to the authority of Christ. Two separate interests divide the world—the kingdoms of Satan and of Christ. Christ has fully declared His determination to allow of no compromise. Many at different times have gone over to the enemy again. To stand fast is to maintain our profession, and not to deny the Saviour's name and desert His cause. In the early Church there was much persecution and apostasy. Now there is not much persecution, but temptation; and probably more have been induced to desert by the smiles of the world than were ever driven by its frowns. 3. Their steadfastness in the practice of the gospel. The gospel not only requires belief and profession, but action. Christianity is a practical religion. If our faith is genuine and our confession sincere, they will lead to obedience. The practice of the gospel includes— (1) Self-government of the head, heart, hands; thoughts, words, and deeds must be brought into subjection to Christ. (2) Relative duty. The gospel finds man a social being, and is adopted to his circumstances as such. His relative duties are—(*a*) Natural; and the practice of the gospel consists in the discharge of duties owing to parents, children, &c. (*b*) Civil. Such as relate to governors, subjects, masters, &c. These are comprehended in the golden rule. (*c*) Religious—our duty to the Church. 4. Their steadfastness in the hope of the gospel. The religion of Christ is pre-eminently a religion of hope (Tit. ii. 12; Phil. i. 6; Heb. vi. 17). II. ITS EFFECT. That of the text is only one out of many. The most important benefit would arise to themselves, but it would not terminate in themselves. It had a happy effect on their connections, especially on their spiritual instructors. 1. It increased their joy—"Now we live," we are happy. Who that seriously reflects on the nature and design of the ministry can avoid the conclusion that the prosperity of the people is the happiness of the minister (chap. ii. 19, 20). 2. It promoted their diligence: "Now we live," are alive in our work, and can apply ourselves with energy. When his people's faith is firm, their profession uniform, their prayers fervent, their practice consistent, &c., the minister goes forth to his work like "a giant refreshed." 3. It contributed to their usefulness. The early history of the Church proves this (Acts ii. 41). The greatest obstacle to religion is the inconsistency of its professors, and their uniform consistency its most powerful auxiliary. Ministers preach to the Church; but the Church preaches to the world. III. THE OBLIGATION OF CHRISTIANS TO MAINTAIN IT. 1. The authority of God enjoins it: "If ye love Me keep My commandments." 2. Their own interest is involved in it: "It is a good thing that the heart be established with grace." 3. The good of others requires it: "Look not every man on his own things." 4. A due regard for ministers demands it: They are to be esteemed very highly in love for their works sake. 5. Experience of Divine mercy and hope of eternal life add strength to all other obligations. (*Essex Congregational Remembrancer.*) *We live, if ye stand fast in the Lord:*—Here the purest zeal for the honour of his Master, and the most generous love to the souls of men, are happily united, and expressed in the native language of a warm and upright heart: the *purest* zeal and the most *generous* love, for no tincture of selfishness appears in either; if Christ is glorified, if men are saved, Paul obtains his utmost wish; his happiness is independent of everything else; he enjoys all that in his own estimation is worthy to be accounted life, if his spiritual children stand fast in the Lord. (*R. Walker.*) *Zealous for the souls of others:*—So, in a later time, wrote Samuel Rutherford, to his parishioners at Anwoth: "I long exceedingly to know if the oft-spoken watch between you and Christ holdeth, and if ye follow on to know the Lord. My day thoughts and night thoughts are of you. While you sleep I am afraid for your souls that they be off the Rock." *Christian steadfastness:*—1. Are you standing fast, by the assurance of understanding, in the doctrines of the gospel? 2. There is danger of our not standing fast in regard to the adherence of our hearts to the doctrines of the gospel. That they be clearly apprehended by the mind is important, not in order to their becoming matters of idle talk or curious speculation, but in order to the sanctification of the heart, and the conduct of the life. 3. Endeavour to find out by another test whether you are standing fast in Christ. The test I mean is proposed by St. John, in his first epistle: "He that saith he abideth in Him (that is, in the Lord Jesus Christ), ought himself also so to walk even as He walked." I demand, then, whether you are taking Jesus Christ for an example, and following His steps? I proceed to point out some of the dangers which threaten your religious steadfastness. (1) Beware of false teachers, who may "come to you in sheep's clothing, but inwardly they are ravening wolves." "By their fruits ye shall know them." (2) Arm yourselves with the powerful hopes of the gospel against the hostility and terrors of the world. (3) If your steadfastness is endangered by the terrors of the world, it is yet in greater danger of yielding to worldly stratagems and fascinations. Many a stout soldier, after successfully contending against the world as an embattled foe, has fallen by its enchantments. (4) There is danger of losing our hold of Christ through disgust at the difficulties of a religious course. We find the road narrower, the enemies which infest it more numerous and troublesome, the seasons of refreshment less certain and frequent, than we had anticipated. And hence we grow faint and weary. 5. Moreover, spiritual pride is the stumbling-block of many a soul. Lastly: I charge you to bear constantly in mind, that it is by the help of the Holy Spirit, and by that alone, that any one stands fast in the Lord. (*J. N. Pearson.*) *The steadfastness of Christians the happiness of ministers :*—There is a most beautiful harmony and dependence in the works of God; so there must be in civil relations; so there should be between minister and people. 1. THE NATURE OF CHRISTIAN STEADFASTNESS. 1. It is distinct from an obstinate perverseness—the pursuit of a given course without reason, and against reasons when they favour a change. The Christian keeps his mind open to conviction even when strongly persuaded, and is ever ready to alter his conduct when truth commands. 2. It is consistent with advancement. Spiritual progress is the aim of every Christian. Having tasted the pleasures of Divine knowledge and grace he desires more. To stand still is not to stand fast (Phil. iii. 10). 3. It is identical with constancy; firmness and immovableness in spite of outward circumstances. Opposition we are warned to expect, but we are to be firm to the end. II. IN WHAT RESPECTS CHRISTIANS ARE TO BE STEADFAST. 1. In our attachments. (2) To Christ. (2) To Christians. (3) To truth. (4) To duty. 2. In our zeal. Earnestness is commendable in worldly things, much more in religion. Here coldness is criminal. Steadfastness demands uniformity — not hot to-day and cold to-morrow. 3. In our Christian profession. Some make no public avowal of Christ; others make it but contradict it in their lives. III. THE MOTIVES WHICH SHOULD LEAD TO STEADFASTNESS. " Now *we* live if *ye* stand fast." It—1. Confirms the truth and power of the gospel we preach. Every steadfast Christian is an evidence of it in circles which ministers cannot reach. 2. Indicates our call to the work. Usefulness is the best proof of Divine ordination. 3. Warrants of hope of meeting you in glory. (*Essex Remembrancer.*) *The pastor's life wrapped up with his people's steadfastness :*—Ministers who are really sent of God greatly rejoice in the spiritual prosperity of their people. If they see God's word prosper they prosper. On the other hand it is like death to them if God does not bless His word. They get depressed, and say, " Who hath believed our report." I. SOME ARE NOT IN THE LORD AT ALL. 1. A solid mass of infidelity and godlessness hems us in. Our heart is heavy because the city shuts its eyes to the light. 2. Our greater sorrow is that there are many who hear the gospel and are not in the Lord. Some of you contribute to God's work, and are in many points excellent, but you lack the one thing needful, and after having joined with God's people in outward acts of devotion are in danger of being driven from His presence for ever. 3. If there be a deadening influence about the thought that some amongst us are not converted, think of what the effect must be upon a minister's mind who has laboured long and seen no fruit. There may be instances in which a man has been faithful but not successful. Then the soil breaks the ploughshare, and the weary ox is ready to faint. Are you working for Jesus? Then you know what it is to feel the shadow of death when you do not win a soul. II. THERE ARE SOME WHO PROFESS TO BE IN CHRIST BUT ARE CERTAINLY NOT STANDING FAST. This is a Marah—a bitter well. 1. There are many over whom we rejoice who, nevertheless, apostatize. They run well, and begin in the Spirit, but by and by attempt to be made perfect in the flesh. Oh, foolish ones, who hath bewitched you? We can never be sufficiently grateful to our Lord for allowing a Judas to be among the twelve, for thus He bore Himself what has been to His servants the most crushing of griefs. 2. Many do not believe in such a way that we could remove their names from the Church-roll; but they decline in grace. Too many grow worldly, and it is especially the case when they grow wealthy. 3. Others whom we look upon as likely to become leaders and helpers are diverted from the work of God. We do not now expect to see them at a prayer meeting, &c., for they are careless about the salvation of souls. They were once full of zeal, but are now neither cold nor hot. 4. Some are always shifting their doctrinal positions. 5. Some are not steadfast in their service of Christ. 6. We stand fast in the Lord if the Lord keeps you true in the matter of holy conversation. I call that holiness which minds its work at home, which makes a kind father, an obedient child, an honest tradesman, &c. But when men turn round and fling in our teeth, " These are your Christians," then down goes our spirit, and we wish we could die. 7. Unless men are steadfast the Church is weakened. The strength of any Church must be the aggregate of the strength of all its members; therefore, if you have a set of weak brethren you multiply the weakness of each by the number of the membership. What a hospital is the result! 8. The minister is disappointed of his reasonable expectations when men do not stand fast. He is like a farmer who sees the seed grow, but just when it is about to yield him a crop he spies out black smut, and his wheat is blighted. He may well weep that it went so far and yet failed so utterly. Judge ye mothers what it is to nurse your children till they are near manhood, and then to see them sink into the grave. III. THERE ARE SOME WHO ARE IN THE LORD AND STAND FAST IN THE LORD, AND THESE ARE OUR LIFE. 1. Because their holy life fills us with living confidence. (1) In the reality of Christianity. (2) In the keeping power of God. 2. By stimulating us to greater exertion. We are able to speak many things which could never have been spoken, and to point to such and say, " See what God hath done." (*C. H. Spurgeon.*)     *The people's stability the minister's comfort:*—I. WHAT IS THAT STABILITY WHICH ALL CHRISTIANS MUST ATTAIN. When any persons first receive the gospel so as to yield themselves up to its influence, they are said to " be in Christ ; " when they make advances in grace they are said to " walk in Christ ; " and when they are established in a firm adherence of the truth, they are said, as in the text, " to stand fast in the Lord." This is that stability which is required of us. 1. In the faith of the gospel. 2. In the profession of it. 3. In the practice of it. That all may be stirred up to seek this stability, we observe : II. WHY THEIR ATTAINMENT OF IT LIES SO NEAR TO THE HEART OF EVERY FAITHFUL MINISTER. A minister stands related to his people as a pastor to his flock, over which he is to watch, and of which he must give a just account; and his solicitude about them, instead of terminating when they are brought into the fold, may be said then more properly to commence. He will be anxious about their attainment of stability in the Divine life. 1. Because the honour of God is deeply interested in it. 2. Because their salvation altogether depends upon it. 3. Because the great ends of the ministry are answered by it. We conclude with a few words—1. Of grateful acknowledgment. 2. Of affectionate warning. 3. Of joyful encouragement. (*C. Simeon, M.A.*) *Inspiring Christian steadfastness :*—An image of Cybele was carried round in one of her usual cars on one occasion, in the reign of the Roman Emperor, Marcus Aurelius, and accompanied by a great multitude of people. All fell on their knees ; but Symphorianus, a young man of high family, conceived that his conscience would not allow him to participate in this rite, and most probably, on being taken to task for it, took occasion to speak of the vanity of idolatry. He was instantly seized, and conducted before the governor, Heraclius, a man of consular dignity, as a disturber of the public worship, and a seditious citizen. The governor said to him, " You are a Christian, I suppose. As far as I can judge, you must have escaped our notice ; for there are but a few followers of this sect here." He answered, " I am a Christian ; I pray to the true God, who rules in heaven, but I cannot pray to idols ; nay, if I were permitted, I would dash them to atoms, on my own responsibility." The governor, on this avowal, declared him guilty of a double crime, one crime against the religion, and another against the laws of the state ; and, as neither threats nor promises could induce Symphorianus to abjure his faith, he was sentenced to be beheaded. As they led him to execution, his mother cried out to him, " My son, my son, keep the living God in thy heart ; we cannot fear death, which leads so certainly to life : up, my son ! let thy heart be up, and look to Him who rules on high. Thy life is not taken from thee to-day, but thou art conducted to a better. By a blessed exchange, my son, thou wilt pass this day to the life of heaven." (*Neander.*)     **For what thanks can we render to God again for you for all the joy.**—*The pastor's thankful joy :*—I. ITS NATURE. 1. It was a joy for their sakes. It implies a love towards them. We do not joy for the sake of those to whom we are indifferent. 2. It was a joy before God. Not a carnal joy, but a holy joy, which he could carry to the mercy seat in thanksgiving and praise. 3. An abundant, not a scanty joy—" all the joy." II. ITS CHARACTER AND CAUSES. It is to be traced to the fact—1. That God had owned His preaching among them (chap. i. 5, 9 ; ii. 1. 13). (1) This joy was not as over a triumph of his own wisdom and strength. The true minister does not say, " I have converted a soul," attributing that vast result to his own logic or rhetoric, but to sovereign grace. (2) He estimates this work by striving to follow it out in its eternal consequences. It is much, indeed, to trace the present effects of grace in reformation, comfort, peace, &c. ; but fully to estimate it the minister must look onward to the soul enjoying the eternal inheritance (chap. ii. 19, 20). (3) This joy, therefore, is not derived from the praise which may greet the minister in the vestry from a mere admirer, the drawing-room compliments of mere sermon hearers. These, if he be not watchful, are snares, and must puff up by ministering to vanity. But the artless acknowledgments of stricken hearts, the loving thanks of anxious ones who have been eased, of mourners who have been comforted, &c., do not puff up, but send him to his knees in thankfulness and tears. (4) It is hard to say whether the joy of conversion or the joy of edification is the greater. For the latter has to do with no secondary branch of the ministry. It is not only a ministry of reconciliation, but is also for the perfecting of the saints. 2. That the Thessalonians adorned the gospel by the practical exhibition of its power in their hearts and lives. They had received the word as the Word of God. They had not listened from the mere love of novelty, nor from being caught by the apostle's eloquence. They had not been as the men of Ezekiel's day (xxxiii. 30–32). No; in Thessalonica we read of a work of faith, &c. They were "ensamples to all that believe," &c., &c. Here was more than a name to live, more than the form of godliness—power, life, growth, fruitfulness. Here, then, is a distinct cause of ministerial joy; not only sinners added, but believers growing. This every faithful pastor covets. He would not have a congregation like any of those mentioned in Revelation. He desires that when the heavenly Bishop inspects the flock He may have nothing—not even "a few things" against them. No tampering with false doctrine, declension from the faith, barrenness in good works, &c.; but a spiritual people, a praying, loving, fruitful, unselfish people. Over such he can "joy." 3. The affection of the Thessalonians towards himself. Not that Paul's great object was to centre the affection of his converts on himself. "We preach not ourselves," &c. A minister preaches himself when he employs enticing words of man's wisdom to attract a congregation and to get a name; when he would attach his congregation as partizans to his own person and preaching; when he uses flattering words as a cloke of covetousness, when, to keep his seats full and his friends round him, he accommodates his preaching to their taste. But Paul preached not to make Paulines but Christians, not to enrich himself, but to enrich them with "the unsearchable riches of Christ." Yet he did not repel the affection of his people when called forth in lawful measure toward himself. Paul loved the pastoral tie. He loved his people, and rejoiced that his people loved him. (*Canon Miller.*)    *Ministerial gratitude and prayer:*—I. OBSERVE HOW THANKFUL THE APOSTLE WAS (ver. 9). When we are most cheerful we should be most thankful. What we rejoice in we should give thanks for. This is to joy before the Lord, to spiritualize our joy. Paul speaketh as if he could not tell how to express his thankfulness to God, or his delight and rejoicing for the sake of the believing Thessalonians; but he was careful God should not lose the glory of that comfort he received in the welfare of his converted friends. His heart was enlarged with love to them, and with thanksgiving to God; he was willing to express the one and the other as well as he could. As to thankfulness to God, this especially is very imperfect in the present state; but when we come to heaven we shall do this blessed work perfectly. II. OBSERVE HOW PRAYERFUL THE APOSTLE WAS (ver. 10). He prayed for the Thessalonians night and day; that is—evening and morning, or very frequently, in the midst of the business of the day, or between the slumbers of the night, lifting up his heart to God in supplication for them. Thus we should pray alway. And Paul's prayer was fervent prayer: he prayed exceedingly—was fervent in his utterances. When we are most thankful we should be most prayerful; for those we give thanks for have need to be prayed for. Those we most rejoice in, and that are our greatest comforts, must be our constant care in this world of temptation and imperfection. There was something still lacking in the faith of the Thessalonians Paul desired might be perfected, and to see their face in order thereunto. And is it not true that the best of men have something wanting in their faith, either in the matter of it, there being some mysteries or doctrines not sufficiently apprehended by them, or yet as to the clearness and certainty of their faith, there being some remaining darknesses or doubtings as to the effects and operations of it, these being not so conspicuous and perfect as they should be? The ministry of the Word and the ordinances of the Sanctuary are exceedingly helpful in such a truly important matter; they are, therefore, to be desired and used for "the perfecting of the saints." (*D. Mayo.*)    *Thankfulness for success:*— Telford stated to a friend, only a few months before his death, that for some time previous to the opening of the Menai Suspension Bridge his anxiety was so great that he could scarcely sleep, and that a continuance of that condition must have very soon completely undermined his health. We are not, therefore, surprised to learn that when his friends rushed to congratulate him on the result of the first day's experiment, which decisively proved the strength and solidity of the bridge, they should have found the engineer on his knees engaged in prayer. A vast load had been taken off his mind; the perilous enterprise of the day had been accomplished without loss of life; and his spontaneous act was thankfulness. (*S. Smiles, LL.D.*)    *Joy in the progress of the gospel:*—A pious Armenian, calling on Mr. Hamlin, the missionary at Constantinople, remarked that he was astonished to see how the people were waking up to the truth; how, even among the most uncultivated, some were seeking after it as for hid treasure. "Yes," said he, "it is going forward; it will triumph; but alas! I shall not live to see it. Alas, that I am born an age too soon!" "But," said Mr. Hamlin, "do you remember what our Saviour said, 'There is joy in heaven over one sinner that repenteth'? You may not live to see the truth triumphant in this empire, but should you reach the kingdom of heaven your joy over your whole nation redeemed will be infinitely greater than it could be on earth." He seemed surprised at this thought; but after examining the various passages to which I referred him, he seemed to be perfectly enraptured at the thought that our interest in the Church of Christ is something that death cannot touch, and which, instead of ceasing with this life, will only be increased and perfected in another. "Oh, fool, and slow of heart," said he, "to read the gospel so many times without perceiving this glorious truth." If this be so, no matter to what age a Christian is born, nor when he dies. (*W. Baxendale.*)

Ver. 10. **Night and day praying exceedingly.**—*Paul's prayer for the Thessalonians:* —I. Its CHARACTERISTICS. 1. It was incessant; his aspiration by day, the breathing of his heart in the stillness of the night. 2. Intensely earnest. Above ordinary measure. It was a wrestling with his covenant God that he might see their face again. Satan had hindered this; hence the importunity. 3. Prevalent. It *was* heard. II. Its OCCASION. He desired this boon not for the mere gratification of any feeling of friendship in him or them; but because there were what he calls "the lacking measures of your faith." 1. As to doctrine, their knowledge was defective. They were entertaining not only imperfect but erroneous views, *e.g.* about the coming of the Lord, about the state of those who had fallen asleep, and the shares these would have in the glories of the second advent. In matters of this kind the apostolic churches generally had less defined views than those to whom have come "the long results of time." 2. As to practice, there was much that called for correction. The apostolic churches, like the mission churches of our own day, were in the midst of a social corruption of which we can barely form even a conception. There were especially four classes of evils prevailing: (1) Licentiousness, in its most degrading forms, was the besetting sin of the heathen world. The Christian converts often became contaminated with it. It lingered in the flesh when the spirit had cast it off. Even within the pale of the Church it sometimes assumed the form of a mystic Christianity. There were those who imagined themselves to have found in licentiousness the true freedom of the gospel. Chap. iv. points in this direction. (2) In the Church itself there reigned the spirit of disorder—enhanced in the case of Thessalonica by the idleness engendered by belief in the nearness of the second coming. There are constantly recurring evidences of this in these two Epistles. (3) There were scruples of conscience as to the observance of days, and eating with the unclean and unbelievers. The contact of Jews and Gentiles in the privileges and work of the Church could hardly fail in those days to give rise to such questions. (4) Disputes about doctrines and teachers bred dissentions and marred the beauty of Christian life. In all these different ways "unreasonable and wicked men" (2 Thess. iii. 2) worked mischief which needed to be guarded against and withstood. III. Its PURPOSE—to "perfect that which is lacking." The word "perfect" means to re-adjust, to restore. It is used in surgical language, of the setting of a bone or joint, and of repairing nets, and also of refitting and strengthening of ships. 1. In each of these senses we have fitting illustrations of Paul's purpose. His aim and that of all ministers is that Christians may be—(1) "perfectly joined together" (1 Cor. i. 10; Eph. iv. 12). Whatever may be their graces they have still "lacking measures of faith." They need to be "fitly joined together" (Eph. iv. 16). (2) So perfected in knowledge and practice that there shall be no defects in the gospel net. (3) So ceaselessly to be repaired, built up, as the Ark of Safety, that they shall withstand all the rude billows of this world. 2. Thus filling up that which is lacking in faith on earth, Christ's Church will at last pass into heaven where there will be nothing lacking in glory. John Howe has said, "We read indeed of certain *afterings* of faith (as it may be significantly rendered) 'things lacking' we render it; but there will be no afterings of glory. What is perfect admits of no increase, it is already full; and why should not a full glory satisfy? It is fulness of joy." (*J. Hutchison, D.D.*)    *Ministerial solicitude :*—" Why," say you, " should a minister need encouraging? We have plenty of troubles all the week long, with our losses here, and crosses there, we want encouragements, but surely ministers do not." Ah! if you want to have a refutation of that idea you had better come into this pulpit, and occupy it a little time. If you would like to exchange, I would truly say that so far as the pleasure of my office is concerned, apart from the spiritual joy my Lord gives me, I would change places with a crossing-sweeper, or a man who breaks stones on the road. Let a man carry out the office of a Christian minister aright, and he will never have any rest. "God help," says Richard Baxter, "the man who thinks the minister's an easy life." Why, he works not only all day, but in his sleep you will find him weeping for his congregation, starting in his sleep with his eyes filled with tears, as if he had the weight of his congregation's sins resting on his heart, and could not bear the load. I would not be that man in the ministry who does not feel himself so fearfully responsible, that if he could escape from the ministry by going with Jonah into the depths of the sea, he would cheerfully do it; for if a minister is what he should be, there is such a weight of solemn concern, such a sound of trembling in his ears, that he would choose any profession or any work, however arduous, sooner than the preacher's post. "If the watchman warn them not they shall perish, but their blood will I require at the watchman's hands." To sit down and spell over the question—" Am I free of his blood?" is terrible. I have sometimes thought I must have a day or two of rest, but I frankly confess that rest is very little rest to me, for I think I hear the cries of perishing souls, the wailings of spirits going down to hell, who chide me thus: "Preacher, can you rest? Minister, can you be silent? Ambassador of Jesus can you cast aside the robes of your office? Up! and to your work again." (*C. H. Spurgeon.*)

Vers. 11–13. **Now God Himself and our Father, and our Lord Jesus Christ, direct our way unto you.**—*A comprehensive apostolic prayer :*—I. This prayer recognizes the essential Oneness of the Father and the Son. 1. Christ is invoked equally with the Father. The word " Himself " stands foremost in the sentence and refers to both persons, as if the writer said, " May our God and Father, and our Lord Jesus Christ, *Himself* direct our way unto you." It should be also noted that the verb " direct," belonging to both persons, is in the singular number. This fact was urged as an important point by Athanasius in the great Arian controversy. As the Son partakes equally with the Father in the honour of invocation, so also in excellency of nature. Divine properties are also ascribed to the Son in overruling by His providence the affairs of men. " What things soever the Father doeth, these also doeth the Son likewise." 2. It is the privilege of the believer to realize a personal interest in the Father and in the Son. By an act of appropriating faith we can say, God *our* Father and *our* Lord Jesus Christ. Similar phrases occur no less than twenty-six times in these two Epistles. Blessed confidence! What a wealth of tenderness, satisfying assurance, and joyous triumph is involved in *my* God! *my* Saviour! II. This is a prayer for providential guidance in securing a much desired interview. " Direct our way unto you." Hitherto the way had been blocked up. The brethren there were as eager to welcome Paul as he was to be present; but Satan had hindered. Nevertheless, let God give the signal and all impediments would vanish. God should be recognized in the simplest affairs of life. " It is not in man that walketh to direct his steps;" and only those journeys are prosperous wherein God is pilot. There are crises in life when everything depends on being guided in the right way—*e.g.*, in selecting a school or college, entering on the religious life, commencing business, contemplating marriage, or in change of residence. In these and all other matters acknowledge God, and He shall direct thy paths. Our prayer for guidance must ever be in submission to the Divine will. The apostle's prayer was not answered immediately; five years elapsed before he again visited Macedonia. That path is safest and best in which God's finger points. Let His call be our loadstar: His hand the cloud, to move or pause as He directs. III. This is a prayer for the bestowal of an increased measure of the highest Christian affection. 1. Christian love is progressive and mutual. " And the Lord make you to increase and abound in love one toward another." Love is the badge of the genuine Christian. He cannot have too much of it—the more the better. It grows with all other graces, and causes them to grow. There is no limit to its expansion but our finiteness. But love must be mutual " one toward another."

"For this is the message," says St. John, "that ye heard from the beginning, that ye should love one another;" and, "Seeing ye have purified your souls . . . . see that ye love one another," urges St. Peter.  2. Christian love is unselfish.  "And toward all men."  The old law declared "Thou shall love thy neighbour as thyself."  And the New Testament reiterates the truth, that charity out of a pure heart, and of a good conscience, and of faith unfeigned is the fulfilling of the royal law.  3. Here we have Christian love practically exemplified.  "Even as we do towards you."  Paul and his co-labourers had given unmistakable evidence of their love (chap. ii. 8, 9, 13; iii. 3-5).  Love is the soul of self-sacrifice. Ministers should exemplify in their own lives what they prescribe to others. IV. THIS IS A PRAYER FOR CONFIRMATION IN A STATE OF UNBLAMABLE PERSONAL PURITY. 1. There is no stability in Christian graces apart from love.  "To the end he may stablish your hearts."  If it were possible to possess every other grace but love, it would be like a varied summer landscape, beautiful but transient.  Above all other graces we are exhorted to "put on charity which is the bond of perfectness"—a girdle which adorns and binds together all the rest.  Love is the fulfilling of the law, the infallible test and evidence of stability.  2. An unblamable holiness is the legitimate and necessary outcome of love.  "To the end He may stablish," &c. Paul prays for an increase of love in order to the attainment of a higher personal purity.  All defects in obedience issue from a defect in love.  Our love of God makes us solicitous to know and obey Him, and fearful to offend Him.  Our love of man makes us careful to preserve his honour, life and possessions, and in no way to impair his happiness.  The whole law is love.  There is no duty to which it does not incline; no sin from which it does not restrain.  3. Holiness screens the soul from Divine censure at the second advent (ver. 10).  He who remains steadfast shall be blameless then.  That holiness alone is genuine which will bear the scrutiny of Omniscience.  Lessons: 1. Recognize God in every event of life.  2. To attain purity pray for love.  3. Act in all things so as to secure the Divine approval. (G. Barlow.)  Paul's ejaculatory prayer:—We have here an instance of a marked characteristic of Paul's Epistles—the tendency which the course of the argument ever has to break forth into prayer.  In this respect they bear a striking resemblance to David's Psalms.  I. To WHOM THIS PRAYER IS ADDRESSED.  1. It is quite evident that the apostle regarded Christ as standing in the same relation to prayer as God the Father.  The prayer is addressed to both, implying equality of power and unity of will, which imply a still higher unity—even unity of essence.  While, then, our Lord is distinguished from the Father in personality, He is one with Him in Godhead, and therefore is He rightly addressed in the language of prayer.  2. "Himself" is emphatic, suggesting a contrast.  Human agency had been frustrated.  Satan had (chap. ii. 18) so far prevailed.  But now Paul turns to God with the confidence of filial reverence and love, and prays that He may remove obstacles and prosper his desire.  His prayer was in the spirit of Jer. x. 23, and Rom. i. 9, 10.  II. WHAT HE PRAYED FOR.  1. That they might increase, and by so increasing abound in love.  To have this is to abound in true wealth which no outward reverses can lessen, which increases the more it is expended, which is always useful and can never be exhausted.  It has prominence assigned it here, for it is the essence of Christian life, the bond of perfectness, the soul of the graces.  As all beauty is cold and lifeless unless there be a soul speaking and breathing through it, so all the elements of moral beauty are worthless without love.  (1) This love is a Christian grace, for it turns first of all to Christ.  It lives only in fellowship with Him, and He makes His people to increase in it.  (2) This love in its inner circle is "one toward another."  It is far in advance of friendship, which was so admired by the ancient heathen.  The calumny that Christianity is inimical to friendship, and is a selfish care for the individual soul is refuted here. It broadened and transfigured friendship into "love of the brethren."  (3) This love was toward all men.  Christianity has broken down the barriers of race and creed, and struck "barbarian" out of the dictionary of mankind, substituting "brother." It tells them of a Divine philanthropy (Titus iii. 4), and bids them imitate it.  (4) This love was exemplified by Paul "as we do toward you."  2. Love may be regarded as the end of Christian striving, for it brings men nearest heaven; but it is represented here as a means (ver. 13).  (1) Christian love going out towards others in blessing comes back laden with new blessings to the soul.  The "hearts" of Christ's people become in this way established.  Where there is mutual and universal love there is of necessity a steady purpose and aim imparted to the whole life.  The heart in this way becomes united (Ps. lxxxvi. 11).  All its impulses go forth in the one direction of holiness unblamable before God, and is thus recompensed with the assurance of Divine love. (2) Even amidst the imperfections and limitations of earth and time the believer has something of this. But the more advanced he is in the Divine life the more does he mourn over his unholiness in the sight of God. Hence the apostle carries our thoughts forward to the second coming (1 Cor. i. 7, 8). This is the pivot on which the whole Epistle turns. Very naturally and tenderly does Paul refer to this in order to draw away the thoughts of his friends from the trials, sorrows, and sins of their present lot. He would have them think of the lot of their future inheritance that they may be faithful unto the end. (*J. Hutchison, D.D.*) *Prayer about a journey :—* In these profoundly interesting words we have one of the most unfeigned and earnest prayers of the apostle. He desired to be directly instrumental in the farther spiritual benefit of the Thessalonians; and the only way to do so while at a distance was by prayer for them, together with his writing or sending to them. I. THE HEARERS OF PRAYER. Prayer is made to God, even the Father and our Father, and also to Christ, even our Lord Jesus Christ; therefore Jesus Christ our Lord is God, even as God our Father is God. Prayer is to be offered to God as our Father (Matt. vi. 9): so Jesus taught His disciples, and so the Spirit prompts them to pray (Rom. viii. 15). And prayer is not only to be offered up to Christ as our Lord and Saviour, but in the name of Christ as the Lord our Righteousness. II. THE THINGS PRAYED FOR. He prays that he might have a prosperous journey to them, by the will of God. The taking of a journey to this or that place, one would think, is a matter depending so much upon a man's own will, and lies so much in his own power, that Paul needed not by prayer to go to God about it; but the apostle knew that we depend upon God in all our motions and actions as well as for the continuance of life and being— that Divine Providence orders all our affairs, and that it is owing thereto if we prosper therein—that God our Father doth direct and order His children whither they shall go, and what they shall do—that our Lord Jesus Christ in a particular manner directs the motions of His faithful ministers, "those stars which He holdeth in His right hand." He prayeth, too, for the prosperity of the Thessalonians, whether he should see them or not; and there are two things he desired for them, which we should desire for ourselves and our friends, namely—that they might "increase and abound in love one toward another, and toward all men;" and that they might be established unblamable in holiness. This last-mentioned spiritual benefit is the effect of increasing and abounding love. Our desire should therefore be—to have our hearts established in holiness; for then we shall be found blame-less at the last advent of our Lord Jesus Christ. He will surely come, and come in His glory; and when He cometh, His saints will come with Him. And then the excellency, as well as the necessity of pure and perfect holiness, will appear, because without such a state no hearts shall be established at that day, nor shall any one be unblamable, or avoid everlasting condemnation. (*R. Fergusson.*) *Prayer to Christ :—*At the very moment of his conversion Saul of Tarsus surrendered him-self by a prayer to Christ as the lawful Lord of his being. "Lord," he cried, "what wilt Thou have me to do?" And when afterwards in the Temple our Lord bade St. Paul "Make haste and get thee quickly out of Jerusalem," we find the apostle unfolding to Jesus his secret thoughts, fears, regrets, confessions; laying them out before Him, and waiting for an answer from Him (Acts xxii. 19, 20). Indeed, St. Paul constantly uses language which shows that he habitually thought of Jesus as of Divine Providence in a human form, watching over, befriending, con-soling, guiding with infinite foresight and power, but also with the tenderness of human sympathy. In this sense Jesus is placed on a level with the Father in these, St. Paul's two earliest Epistles (text and 2 Thess. ii. 16, 17), in one instance as directing the movements of the apostle's life, in the other as building up the inward life of Christians. In other devotional expressions the name of Jesus stands alone (Phil. ii. 19; 1 Tim. i. 12). Is not this the natural language of a soul which is constantly engaged in communion with Jesus, whether it be the communion of praise or the communion of prayer? Jesus is to Paul, not a deceased teacher or philanthropist, who has simply done his great work and then has left it as a legacy to the world; He is God, ever living and ever present, the Giver of temporal and spiritual blessings, the Guide and Friend of man in his outward and inward life. (*Canon Liddon.*) *Direction of the way and increase in love :—*I. PAUL'S GREAT PERSONAL DESIRE. 1. It was evidently more than a natural transcient longing such as would arise in any mind on the remembrance of dear friends who had been left, it was a fixed strong desire. " We are away from you for a time, in presence, not in heart. I endeavoured to see your face with great desire, but Satan hindered. I therefore sent Timothy—my dearest and best fellow labourer, and the tidings he has brought has comforted me. But this is not enough. May God direct my way unto you." The inferences from this are—(1) They must have been a very lovable people. For in this desire we can see more than apostolic function, or simple discharge of duty. Clearly here is that unpurchaseable thing—the whole heart's love on both sides. (2) This is one of the marvels and triumphs of Christianity that it can thus mutually unite, refine, endear people to each other in any circumstances. What were the circumstances? They had scarcely a day's peace in their connection. And yet how they hold on to each other. Is there any other department of life that can be likened to this? Say, that some merchant goes into a distant city, opens a large business, and supplies smaller traders. But unfortunate times comes on. Those who have bought cannot pay, and the merchant sees his capital sunk as in the sea. Would it be wonderful if he closed his stores and departed? Now see the contrast. Paul comes on his great business to Thessalonica —the city is in an uproar, and his friends are glad to get him away with life. And yet the strain " Taken from you in presence, not in heart, I shall be back again soon." The religion of Christ is a plant which storms cannot break, which will grow fresh and green above the very snows, and in the dark, damp air of prisons, and will bear some of its best fruits when all other trees are barren. 2. The religious rule he puts it under; the subordination of it to the will of God. He seems to say, " There is nothing more that I can do : Satan seems to hold the keys of the city, and he will not let me in if he can help it. People would advise me to give it up. But no, I hold a strange key, that has opened many a door for me, and perhaps it may fit the lock of that city gate. It is called the key of prayer, and it never rusts with me, for it never rests. I use it by night as well as day. Even while I thus write, I use it. Now God direct my way." The teaching is, have your human desire, hold it against all hostility and disappointment; but have it in subjection to the higher Will which knows all the circumstances of which we can only know a part. Says an old writer, " Let God be our Pilot if we mean to make a good voyage of it." Let our hand be on the stern, our eye on the star. Let our course as the mariners' be guided by the heavens. II. PAUL'S GREAT DESIRE FOR THE CHURCH. 1. This desire is not dependent on the fulfilment of the other. He was aware that unless he had an express Divine assurance that the former was not to be calculated upon with certainty. If he is permitted to see them he will supply, by God's help, what is lacking in their faith, and out of that will spring a fuller love. But if he is not allowed to see them, the Lord could do without his agency. 2. The love here mentioned is discriminated, but it is one thing. Love to God is one thing, with differentiations suited to the character of the individuals. Love in us—(1) Has its fullest expression when its object is God. (2) Next to that in excellence is love of God's own children—our brethren. Very beautiful is this affection when founded on mutual knowledge and esteem, when each sees in the other the Master's image, and are all kindly affectioned one to another. " Behold how good and pleasant," &c. (3) It has been said that this mutual love is apt to deteriorate in the very exercise of it, and to become exclusiveness. This is possible. Churches have so attended to the form of this great privilege and duty that they have allowed the spirit of it to evaporate. They have ceased to feel for the miseries about them. Well, we cannot say that the Scriptures have led us astray. For see how inseparably the two things are here joined. " And toward all men." There is only that word between them, and that unites and never disjoins. It is God's strong bridge over the river ; God's marriage service over the two affections, never to be severed more. " And what God hath joined together," &c. Let no one say he loves the brotherhood if he despises one human creature. But on the other hand let no man say that he loves the race while he sees nothing to love in his fellow Christians. (*A. Raleigh, D.D.*)     *The helplessness of man's self-guidance :*—A merchant, though he owns the ship, and hath stored it with goods, yet, because he hath no skill in the art of navigation, he suffereth the pilot to guide it. Certainly we shall shipwreck ourselves unless we give ourselves up to be guided by the Spirit of God according to His will. (*T. Manton, D.D.*)     Just as if a master, who had given his scholar charge to follow wheresoever he might lead, when he sees him forestalling, and desiring to learn all things of himself, should permit him to go utterly astray ; and when he had proved him incompetent to acquire the knowledge, should thereupon at length introduce to him what he himself has to teach : so God also commanded man in the beginning to trace Him by the idea which the creation gives; but since they would not, He, after showing by the experiment that they are not sufficient for themselves, conducts them again unto Him by another way. (*Chrysostom.*)    *The right and the wrong way of seeking God's guidance:*—The Israelites usually asked council of God by the Ephod, the Greeks by their Oracles, the Persians by their Magi, the Egyptians by the Hierophante, the Indians by their Gymnosophistæ, the ancient Gauls and Britains by their Druids, the Romans by their Augurs or Soothsayers.    It was not lawful to propose any matter of moment in the Senate before their wizards had made observations from the sky.    That which they did impiously and superstitiously, we ought to do in another sense—religiously, conscionably, *i.e.*, not to embark ourselves into any action of great importance before we have observed from heaven, not the flight of birds, not the houses of planets, or their aspects or conjunctions, but the countenance of God, whether it shineth on our enterprises or not, whether He approves of our designs or not. (*J. Spencer.*)    *Guidance honestly sought:*—I believe that wherever guidance is honestly and simply sought it is certainly given.    As to our discernment of it I believe it depends upon the measure in which we are walking in the light.    One indulged sin may so cloud the sky that it spreads a mist, so that to see what God is doing is impossible.    But neither the casting of lots, the opening of the Bible at a venture, nor the sudden impression of a text, nor freedom in prayer over a matter, nor a dream, furnishes any reliable direction.    The Lord rather opens and shuts, throws down the walls of difficulty, or hedges the way with thorns, for those who confidingly seek His guidance by prayer.    They know that their concerns are in His hands, and fear to run before He sends, or to delay when He directs an advance. (*J. Newton.*)    *God honoured by seeking His guidance:*— There is nothing so small but that we may honour God by asking His guidance of it, or insult Him by taking it into our own hands. (*J. Ruskin.*)    *God's guidance to be sought by prayer:*—As the sails of a ship carry it into the harbour, so prayer carries us to the throne and bosom of God.    But as the sails cannot of themselves speed the progress of the vessel, unless filled with the favourable breeze, so the Holy Spirit must breathe upon our hearts, or our prayers will be motionless and lifeless. (*A. Toplady, M.A.*)    *Divine guidance guaranteed:*—Do you feel that you have lost your way in life?    Then God Himself will show you your way.    Are you utterly helpless, worn out, body and soul?    Then God's eternal love is ready and willing to help and revive you.    Are you wearied with doubts and terrors? Then God's eternal light is ready to show you your way, and God's eternal peace to give you peace.    Do you feel yourself full of sins and faults?    Then take heart; for God's unchangeable will is to take away those sins and purge you from those faults. (*C. Kingsley, M.A.*)    *The mysteriousness and methods of God's guidance:*—In the daily events of our life we mistake the Divine for the human.    You may cross a street, and not know the reason why, and in that very crossing you may be unconsciously obeying a Divine suggestion.    You may hold over the letter-box a letter, and suddenly you may say, "I'll not send it by this post," and your not sending it may occasion you a blessing that you never thought of.    You cannot account for these things.    You say, "I thought just at the last moment I would not do so;" but that is a fool's explanation of life.    I rather believe that God's angels are overhead, or just by our side, and that we do things by Divine impulse without always knowing what we are really doing.    You say, "Yes, but don't let us be superstitious."    I answer, I am more afraid of people losing veneration than I am afraid of their becoming superstitious; and it is a poor life that does not begin in veneration and continue in worship to the end. (*J. Parker, D.D.*)

Vers. 12, 13. **And the Lord make you to increase and abound in love.**—*The effect of love on universal holiness:*—The grace which is most generally spoken of in the Holy Scriptures as establishing the souls of men is faith.    But there is a sense in which love also establishes the heart; hence the apostle prays that God would make the Thessalonian Christians to abound in love.    I. THE INFLUENCE OF LOVE ON UNIVERSAL HOLINESS.    Love is an extremely powerful principle in the heart of every one that is truly born of God: it is the great wheel which sets the whole machine in motion, and gives a vital energy to every part.    1. It rectifies all the powers of the soul.    2. It enters into every action of the life.    3. It prepares the soul for heavenly communications.    II. THE ATTENTION DUE TO IT UNDER THIS PARTICULAR CONSIDERATION.    Love, for its own sake, should be cultivated to the uttermost; but when we consider its vast influence both on our present and eternal welfare, we should strive for it with all our might. 1. Let us seek to abound in it. 2. Let us intreat God to work it in us. 3. Let us be stirred up to this especially from the consideration before us—the Lord Jesus is shortly coming with all His glorified saints to judge the world. Application: 1. How shall we know whether our love increases? By the difficulties it surmounts, the sacrifices it makes, the victories it gains. 2. What shall we do to get an increase in it? Nothing but love will beget love; nor will anything but a sense of God's love to us prevail to create in us any real love toward our fellow-creatures. (*C. Simeon, M.A.*) *Christian love:*—I. THE NATURE OF CHRISTIAN LOVE. 1. Heartfelt. 2. Holy. II. THE SOURCE OF CHRISTIAN LOVE. 1. God gives it susceptibility. 2. God maintains it in the heart. III. THE OBJECT OF CHRISTIAN LOVE. 1. The whole Christian Church. 2. The whole family of man. IV. THE DEGREE OF CHRISTIAN LOVE. 1. Abundant. 2. Increasing. V. THE EFFECTS OF CHRISTIAN LOVE. 1. They are blessed to each other. 2. They are blessed to the Church. 3. They are blessed at the coming of the Lord. Improvement: 1. The text leads to inquiry. (2) The text leads to humiliation. (3) The text leads to prayer. (*W. H. Cooper.*) *The abounding of charity:*—This is the first of St. Paul's formal prayers. Note: I. THE OBJECT TO WHOM IT IS PRESENTED. 1. Our Lord is expressly addressed: not as the Mediator only, by whom petitions are made acceptable, but as Himself, the Hearer and Answerer of prayer. Here the Saviour is asked first for a temporal and lower gift, for the prosperous direction of the apostle's course and therefore the highest blessing that man can receive. 2. Our Lord is invoked in the unity of the Father, for "God Himself our Father, and our Lord Jesus Christ," two persons, are yet one in the verb "direct." The very grammar expresses their unsearchable Oneness not only in counsel and act, but in nature and dignity. 3. Here at the outset there is more than a latent reference to the mediatorial Trinity. Who is that Lord who shall stablish the saints before God? It is the Holy Ghost, in the unity of the Father and the Son, but also in His own administrative function as having our holiness in charge. II. THE PRAYER ITSELF. 1. Paul's first invocation is for charity, that gift of God and grace in man which always has the pre-eminence. It is the ruling emotion of the regenerate which, assured by its very life of the love of God, goes back directly to Him in devotion, and indirectly in deeds of charity to man. In love, as in an element, the apostle prays that they may grow. (1) Here at the very threshold of His theology, Paul establishes the true character of love as it rests especially on the fellow elect and as it embraces all men. This distinction bears close analogy to the particular and catholic love of God. But the distinction, however important, belongs to a lower sphere, and has significance only for a season. The two are one in "the bond of perfectness"; and when the prayer asks for its largest aboundings it leaves all limitation behind: "and toward all men." (2) The specific increase will be seen if we consider the vehement language in which Paul describes it, and the standard he sets up in his own example. (*a*) "Increase and abound" might be interpreted as a compound expression including all that is possible to the heart's capacity. But more closely examined the former signifies the growth of the soul in the sphere of charity, and the latter its aboundings in outward manifestation. Elsewhere love is regarded as growing in us; here, we grow in love, which, like faith, is not only a grace within but an element around the soul. "Increase in love" means that we may become more and more enlarged in heart as our love is enlarged, growing with its growth. The other term makes the sentiment more intense, and asks that the evidence of our increase may day by day overflow. Not, however, to man only. In the next chapter (ver. 9), when the apostle speaks of love to our fellow Christians as "taught of God," he calls it "philadelphia," a branch of charity never separable from that other love that belongs to God; so here it is regarded as springing from the large effusion of the love of God. (*b*) Paul presents his own example as at once a standard, guide, and incentive. He felt himself to be expanding in the habit and exercise of that love which "puffeth not up," but "edifieth." This is the first instance of a practice of his with which we soon become familiar—the commendation of his own example. Nowhere is his love more vividly exhibited than here. The collective strength of the previous expressions present to us a perfect description of self-forgetting charity. It begins in ver. 5. There is more than human sympathy here. Having had "much forgiven," the apostle "loved much." But while we are pondering the exhibition, we hear his intercession diverting us from himself: "the Lord make you," &c. 2. The connection between this abounding love and unblamable holiness is one of the most important topics in experimental theology. (1) Love, whether regarded in its unity, or divided into devotion and charity, is the energy of all holiness. We are released from sin by love as the instrument of the Spirit in expelling every impure affection. The soul in which the Divine love is shed abroad in its fullness can give no place to evil desires. By it also we are strengthened into complete obedience: for "love is the fulfilling of the law." There is no limit to the increase of this love. St. Paul has chosen two terms that spurn restriction; which teaches us on the one hand that a love perfected in the sense of having reached an impassable limit there cannot be: the love of God can never be spent, nor can man's return of love to God. But it teaches also that there is nothing in the heart that shall resist it. Hence holiness is a state in which man's heart, *i.e.*, man himself, is already established by the power of God. (2) The idea of confirmation in unblamable holiness before God carries the view forward to that day which is the vanishing point of all the lines of the apostle's theology and hope. It is supposed to be brought under the more direct scrutiny of God; it is not created by His coming: neither does death destroy the body of sin, nor the appearing of Christ perfect the love of the saints; but then the eye of Supreme Justice will regard the perfect in love as unblamable in holiness. (3) The construction of the sentence suggests that at and by the coming of Christ we shall be confirmed in our unchangeable condition of holiness before God. This is not the establishment of an uncertain character; the abounding of love has accomplished that. It is not the establishment in brotherly love; that is a grace which may be supposed to end with time. But it is the establishment of the unblamable holiness of perfect love. (*a*) The holiness of perfect love is the permanent character of the saved. Love abideth; and without holiness no man shall see the Lord. Holiness is the consummation of all that religion has to accomplish, and love is the law of heaven as well as of earth. Faith will cease by finding its object; and hope will never be conscious of an object waited for. (*b*) This establishment implies the end of probation. Probation vanishes to the individual in death; but to the Church, and man's history generally, only at the coming of Christ. Not till then, but assuredly then, all that belongs to the warfare, suspense and growing victory of religion shall cease. Rest in God shall be the law of heaven; and that rest shall be movement in an orbit around the throne which shall never be purturbed. (*W. B. Pope, D.D.*) *Missionary love :*—There is a reflex influence attending acts of obedience to God which goes immediately to advance the doers still further in the ways of godliness. All holy and charitable works are replete with seeds of blessing for the Christian's own soul. In the text the grace which is exercised in the actings of obedience becomes a means of still further advancement. The reaction of Christian love is progression in holiness, whether to the individual or the Church. The history of missions furnishes no ordinary proofs of this. I. The nature of that love in which St. Paul desired his brethren to abound. 1. Its spirituality of intention. This is inferred from its declared origin, "The Lord." Carnal minds have their charity, which regards men as body and mind, and, therefore, when it has consulted their physical happiness and intellectual cultivation it has reached its limit. Devout but unenlightened minds have their charity, but it seeks only to win men from vice to forms of godliness. But the charity that is born of God will act in correspondence with the mind of God, who has not failed to provide for physical happiness, mental improvement, and moral amelioration, but only as a consequence of the restoration of the soul to union with Himself. His sacrifice of His Son—"the Just for the unjust"—was to this end, "to bring them to God." In harmony with this will be the intention of His people's love. It was so in Paul's day. Its care for man was a care for man's soul. And so now Christian missions, while they compensate the physical miseries, mental debasement, and moral perversion of men by humanizing influences, lifting the savage into civilization, it looks upon all this as subordinate to the conversion of the heart to God. 2. Its unrestrictedness of attachment. It suffers no limitation. It leads God's people to care not only for their brethren, but all mankind. The earliest disciples went everywhere preaching the Word. The Thessalonians were no less active; and besides doing mission work themselves, they succoured other missionaries. Would that this love had never grown cold! But first came dissention, then unhallowed speculation, and afterward superstition. And when superstition had been removed formality supervened. And so at this late era we are but beginning again the evangelization of the world which began in apostolic times. 3. Its progressiveness of operation. Let it live and be in healthy action, and that action will be one of advancing power. This the apostle intimates not only by his prayer, but by instancing his own example. St. Paul was a bright exemplification of the charity that never faileth. His personal intercourse with the Thessalonians had been brief—but how, notwithstanding his labours and trials, he loved them. So it was with his affection for other Churches, it deepened and widened at the same time. And may we not point to many of his followers struggling with discomforts, afflicted with the spectacle of myriads wholly given to idolatry, frequently standing alone as witnesses for the truth, growing only more devoted to the work and attached to their charge. Yea, and when compelled to return to a more congenial climate they labour in the interests of their distant converts, and long to return. And so, according to their ability, is the love of the Churches who support missions. II. THE SANCTIFYING RESULT WHICH ST. PAUL ANTICIPATED FROM THAT INCREASE OF LOVE WHICH HE INVOKED UPON HIS BRETHREN. Consider this as illustrated in the history of missions. 1. In relation to our individual piety. (1) It quickens within us the spirit of prayer. One glance at millions lying in their heathen state hastens every child of God to his Father's feet. "The harvest," Christ said, "is plenteous," &c. What, then, shall His followers do? Rush at once into the field? No. "Pray ye." Nor is this all. From every region we hear the cry, "Pray for us that the Word of God may have free course and be glorified." And our souls are stirred within us to respond; and thus it is that an interest in missions keeps us at the throne of grace. And experience soon proves that the spirit of supplication is the very life of the cause. (2) It brings us into conscious co-operation with God. "We are labourers together with God." If the evangelization of the world were a human adventure then our partnership would be with man only; but faith is sensible of God's presence, and association with God who is holy results in holiness. (3) It familiarizes our minds with the operations of the Divine Spirit on the souls of men, and promotes self-examination and conveys instruction and consolation. 2. In relation to the piety of the Church which is the aggregate of the holiness of its individual members. As they severally thrive the whole body is strengthened, and society around receives a corresponding complexion. A habit of caring for souls is established; attention is drawn to the spiritual condition of those who are near; home missions spring up, and the fountain which is pouring forth its streams to fertilize some distant wilderness, overflows with living water to bless its native soil. How strikingly this is illustrated in the religious history of our own country! Call to remembrance the condition of England when the great missionary societies were first established. From that day God has blessed us with a reformed country and a revived religion. (1) The various expedients devised for the support of missions have been the means of this. Missionary meetings, sermons, literature, have given an impetus to the cause of God. In how many of our children the first buddings of Christian emotion have burst under the impression of some missionary tale. (2) Consciences awakened, and hearts moved to care for the heathen abroad have been impressed with a responsibility towards those at home. In conclusion, consider the subject in relation to—1. Ourselves. Here is the antidote to the evils of secularity, luxury, priestcraft, and scepticism. 2. Our society. Our successes should stimulate this love; our failures make an imperative demand upon it. 3. Our Church. Here strength at home will be in proportion to her prosperity abroad. 4. Our country. Missionary extension is its best defence. (*J. Harding, M.A.*) *The holiness tone :*—One day when I was with Mr. Hicks, the painter, I saw on his table some high-coloured stones, and I asked him what they were for. He said they were to keep his eye up to tone. When he was working in pigments, insensibly his sense of colour was weakened, and by having a pure colour near him he brought it up again, just as the musician, by his test-fork, brings himself up to the right pitch. Now, every day men need to have a sense of the invisible God. A clear conception of the perfect One produces a moral impression; and it does not make any difference how you get it. If you are poetical you get it through the imagination. If you have large veneration you get it through that quality. If you are most easily affected through your emotions, you get it through these elements. If by the intellect, by the imagination, by the affections, or by the moral sentiments you are exalted into the conscious presence of God, then you have obtained that which renders prayer of transcendent value, and which gives tone to your whole nature. But no nature is of such magnitude that it does not need, every day, to be tuned, chorded, borne up to the ideal of a pure and lofty life. (*H. W. Beecher.*) *The savour of Christian holiness :*—Now give me a hundred men—not men that are glowing while they sing, and heavenly while they pray, though I would have them so; but men that are, morning, and noon, and night, born of God, and that so carry the savour of Christ that men coming into their presence say, "There is a Christian here," as men passing a vintage say, "There are grapes here"—give me a hundred such men, and I will make the world believe. I do not ask to be shown the grape-vine in the woods in June before I will believe it is there. I know that there are grapes near when the air is full of their odour; and the question under such circumstances always is, "Where is the vine?" and never, "What is it that I smell?" You are to be a savour of love, and peace, and gentleness, and gratitude, and thanksgiving, so that whenever you go, the essence of the truth that is in you shall go out to men. The most expressible thing in this world is the exquisite delicacy of a Christian grace. There are some excellent essences, like, for instance, the attar of roses, which you must not leave unstopped unless you would have it all exhaled; but the more a Christian grace exhales, the more there is in the bottle. (*Ibid.*)

---

## CHAPTER IV.

**Vers. 1–3. Furthermore then, we beseech you, brethren, and exhort you.**— *Earnest exhortations to a higher sanctity :*—Purity is the perfection of the Christian character. It is the brightest jewel in the cluster of saintly excellencies, and that which gives a lustre to the whole. It is not so much the addition of a separate and distinct grace as the harmonious development of all. As Flavel has said, "What the heart is to the body that the soul is to the man; and what health is to the heart holiness is to the soul." In the prayer just offered the apostle indicates that God will fill them with love to this end. He now urges the attainment. Human agency is not destroyed but stimulated by the Divine. Observe—I. THAT A HIGHER SANCTITY CONSISTS IN LIVING UNDER A SENSE OF THE DIVINE APPROVAL. 1. Religion is a life. A "walk" implies continual approach to a goal. Religion is not an ornament, a luxury, a ceremony, but a life, all penetrating, ever progressing, but sometimes concealed. 2. Religion is a life modelled after the worthiest examples. "As ye have received of us." The Thessalonians not only received the wisest counsels from their teachers but they witnessed their holy and consistent lives; and their attention was constantly directed to the all-perfect example—Christ Jesus. It is the tendency of all life to shape itself after the character of its strongest inward force. The love of God is the mightiest power in the life of the believer; and the outer manifestation of that life is moulded according to the pattern of the inner Divine ideal. 3. Religion is a life which finds its chief joy in the Divine approval. "And to please God." It is possible, then, so to live as to please God. What a powerful incentive to a holy life. Donne, on his death-bed, said, "I count all that part of my life lost which I spent not in communion with God, or in doing good." 4. Religion is a life capable of vast expansion. "So, ye would abound," &c. God has made every provision for our increase in holiness. There is no limit in our elevation but our faith. II. THAT THE NECESSITY OF A HIGHER SANCTITY IS ENFORCED BY DIVINE AUTHORITY. "For this is the will of God even your sanctification." 1. A higher sanctity involves a conformity to the Divine nature. God is holy, and the aim of the believer is to be like Him. There is to be not only an abstinence from impurity but a positive experience of purity. By faith we participate in the Divine nature, and possess qualities analogous to the Divine perfections—mercy, truth, justice, holiness. 2. A higher sanctity is in harmony with the Divine will. What God proscribes must be carefully avoided; what He prescribes must be done. His will is here emphatically expressed; it is supported by abundant promises of help; and it is declared that without holiness no man shall see the Lord. The will of God is at once the highest reason, the strongest motive, and the final authority. 3. The Divine will regarding a higher sanctity is enforced by duly authorized messengers, and well understood precepts (ver. 2). The apostle did not assume authority in any dictatorial spirit. He delivered unto others what he had received. These precepts were well known. Obedience should ever be in proportion to knowledge. Knowledge and practice are mutually helpful to each other. To know and not to do is to incur the heaviest condemnation. "Not My will, but Thine be done." III. THAT THE POSSESSION OF A HIGHER SANCTITY IS REPEATEDLY URGED BY EARNEST EXHORTATIONS. "We beseech you, brethren, and exhort you."

Doctrine without exhortation makes men all brain, no heart; exhortation without doctrine makes the heart full, leaves the brain empty. Both together make a man. The apostle laboured in both. Here we have a fine example of the combination of a tender, brotherly entreaty, with the solemn authority of a divinely commissioned ambassador. Some people, says a certain writer, are as thorns; handle them roughly and they pierce you; others as nettles; rough handling is best for your safety. A minister's task is an endless one. Has he planted knowledge?—practice must be urged. Is the practice satisfactory?—perseverance must be pressed. Do they continue in well-doing?—they must be stimulated to further progress. The end of one task is the beginning of another. Lessons: The believer is called to the attainment of a higher sanctity—1. By the voice of God. 2. By the voice of His faithful ministers. 3. And by the aspirations of the life divinely planted within him. (*G. Barlow.*) *A fuller consecration:*—A superstructure is nothing without a foundation; neither is a foundation anything without a super-structure. Each, indeed, has its appropriate place, but both are alike im-portant; for if, on the one hand, the superstructure will fall without a foundation, so, on the other hand, it is for the sake of the superstructure alone that the foundation is laid. St. Paul, "as a wise master-builder," was careful at all times to lay his foundation deep and strong; but, having done this, he was careful also to raise upon it a beauteous edifice, such as God Himself would delight to inhabit. This is evident in all his letters; and hence in this to the Thessalonians, having been the instrument of their conversion, he would excite them to the highest possible attainments in universal holiness. I. His APPEAL. He had not sought to amuse them by curious speculations; nor had he given them maxims whereby they might please and gratify their fellow creatures. His object had been to bring them to such a holy and consistent " walk " as would be pleasing and acceptable to their God. What kind of a walk that is it will be profitable for us to inquire. 1. Walk *in* Christ by a living faith. 2. Walk *after* Christ by a holy conversation. II. His ENTREATY. In this the apostle acknowledges that the Thessalonians had already done well; but he wishes them to redouble their exer-tions in their heavenly path. Let us notice here—1. The fact conceded. 2. The duty urged. He might well have enjoined these things in an authoritative manner, but " for love's sake he rather besought them." He calls them " brethren," and as brethren he entreats them—(1) By the consideration of all that Christ has done and suffered for them. (2) By the consideration of all the interest He yet took in their welfare. (3) By the consideration of the honour He would derive from them. (4) By the consideration of the glory that will accrue to Him in the day of judg-ment. (*C. Simeon, M.A.*) *A deepening consecration:*—I. THE IDEA OF A DEEPER CONSECRATION IS A FAMILIAR ONE. Moses was set apart for special work. Aaron and his brother priests were consecrated. Paul as an apostle, and others, were separated by the Holy Spirit. That is the Old Testament idea of consecration—" setting apart a person or thing for sacred uses." The person might not at first be holy in him-self; but because of his daily association with sacred things, holiness was required of him. In New Testament times holiness of person and holiness of service move along together. Conversion is the dedication of oneself for the first time to God. A revival of religion is a re-dedication to more faithful service. The discipline of sorrow, meditation, the work of faith and labour of love, &c., still further deepen its spiritual life, and strengthen its activities. II. THERE ARE OCCASIONS WHEN THE CALL FOR DEEPER CONSECRATION IS CLEAR AND LOUD. Such was the preaching of the Baptist, and of Peter and Paul, summoning to repentance. A great popular ex-citement that moves deeply a people is providential preparation. An exigency in life when one is hurled from his self-dependence down upon his dependence upon God; a responsibility that compels one to put up new bulwarks to faith and a new criticism upon life; a calamity that opens all the doors and windows of life—those things teach you of your exposure and of your need that some pavilion drop its curtains around you. These indeed are felt to be Divine exhortations to higher, closer walk with God. III. THIS DEEPER CONSECRATION IS NOT NECESSARILY THE DOING OF NEW THINGS, BUT DOING THE OLD THINGS BETTER. The advice of Paul to the Thessalonians was to abound more and more in the very things in which they had been active. We can fritter away strength in variety. We can make the moral nature nervous by seeking continually a new excitement. Perfection and finish are not gained in trying new things, but by repetition. We become perfect penmen by making the same letters over and over again. Skill in the mechanic arts, in sculpture and in painting, is gained by repetition of the fundamentals of each. Wear the channels of the old religious routine deeper then. Lean with more entire self-abandonment upon the tried methods of Church activity. The Christian teacher will find the occasion of deeper consecration in the deeper work along the old lines of fidelity, study, and prayer. The officers of the Church will find their open door into more satisfactory life along the tried ways of tender consideration, faithful regard to vows, bearing still better responsibilities. The Christian father and mother will find their life growing less troubled and worldly if they make the family altar a place of greater regard, and the religious oversight of the family a matter of more constant attention. "Which things also ye do, but I beseech you, abound more and more." Depth comes in running constantly in the old curriculum. IV. YOU ARE TO BE LED TO THIS DEEPER CONSECRATION BY AN OLD MOTIVE. "I beseech and exhort you by Jesus Christ." It was the love of God in Jesus Christ that first broke your heart from the ways of sin, and it is this same love that must lift the life to higher and finer activity. V. THE DANGER TO WHICH THIS CONSECRATION IS EXPOSED. The danger of routine, of system, of familiar acquaintance with Biblical truths, the very thing the worth of which we have been advocating. 1. Simply because consecration must run in the old channels and be drawn on by the same motive, there is danger that we miss the vital contact with the Lord Jesus, that the spirit dies out while the system goes on. Church and prayer-meeting attendance may degenerate into a profitless habit. Your soul may be satisfied with the form and die for want of sustenance. Class teaching may become as spiritless as school teaching—the mere teaching of the lesson. Great alarm about our own spiritual condition should smite us when we find ourselves doing Christian duties for the sake of getting rid of them and of appeasing the conscience. 2. Then, again, the performance of Christian duties leads us into expressions of faith and desire that they may become stereotyped. Biblical language is the fittest medium by which to express our prayer and our faith. And the quickened soul can find comfort and relief for itself in repeating the same form. But let the fire die out, and living contact with Jesus shrink, and the form of words will remain, and we will have the startling inconsistency of devout expression enveloping a shrivelled and dead heart. 3. There may be movement in Christian life but no progress. Like the water-wheel that turns round in the same place that it did ten years ago, may be the Christian life that runs the weekly round of Church services. Like the door that swings on the same hinge, but never moves from the door-post, may be the Christian life excessively busy, continually in and out, but never advancing into the interior truths of God's Word. Christian life is not a tread-mill round; Christianity is not meant to teach us how to talk, but to teach us how to walk, and walking is orderly, constant progress towards a terminus, a glory. The path of the just shineth more and more unto the perfect day. VI. THE PRACTICAL METHODS BY WHICH THE DEEPER CONSECRATION CAN BE MAINTAINED WITHOUT FALLING INTO SPIRITLESS FORM. 1. Let there be an act of consecration; a holy hour when we surrender ourselves anew to God. We know that specious argument of the evil one about "resolving and re-resolving, and doing the same." We know that timidity of the honest mind that shrinks from a new self-dedication where it has so often failed; and yet how is life to be lifted up to finer issues unless there is the strong desire and resolve of the spirit? We do not drift into consecration and holy life? 2. Assist the memory. We fail in our consecration because we forget. Business engrosses the mind. A multitude of cares drives out the one special thought of the heart. Time slips along, weaving into the web of life new things with bright or dark colours. The very success of the first efforts of consecrated days has a subtle danger. Against this flood of insidious attack we must rear a defence that shall remain with us. I have known a book, for instance, selected because its contents and aim were along the line of the consecrated purpose, to be to the memory a continual reminder. I have known a text of Scripture chosen for its appropriateness to some individual weakness or to fill up the gaps of failure, or to string the soul to its best music hung as a motto on the wall, that every time you looked you were reminded of the weakness, the failure, the hope of your life. I have known men who have sat down and drawn up for themselves rules of life, meeting their deficiencies and aspirations by specific regulations, making their daily activity run along these prescribed channels, and their biographies have proved how good, how conscientious, how holy they were. I need only mention the names of Jeremy Taylor and Jonathan Edwards. I have known a voluntary service given to some spiritual meeting whose regular recurrence was continual reminder, or to some charity whose blessed work was constant call for service, or to some personal visitation of the poor and the sick. 3. Assist the spiritual nature by renewed study of the character of Jesus. The sculptor who is to make a model of your face and head, the painter who is to paint your portrait, asks of you many sittings, and the more sittings you can give him the more perfect will be bust or portrait. The daily study of Jesus will fashion the life after the glorious model. (*S. B. Rossiter.*)      *The Christian's walk and its object :*—I. The Christian's walk. 1. You young Christians have just got a walking power. There was a time when you *thought* you could stand, and you tried, but fell helplessly by the way-side. But Jesus of Nazareth passed by and said, "Wilt thou be made whole." You responded in faith, and like the man at the Gate Beautiful you found a new energy and walked and leaped and praised God. 2. This new power was given you to enable you to realize that "they that wait upon the Lord shall . . . walk and not faint." The sun may be very hot, and you ready to give way, but remember this promise ; and remember it when the goal of the journey seems a great way off. Don't be discouraged. 3. Paul had given these Christians directions how to walk. He did not leave them to wander about in the darkness. We, too, have directions. Look up the word "walk" in your concordance. We are to—(1) "Walk by faith." We do not behold the form of Jesus leading us on to victory, nor is our reward visible, but we apprehend both by Faith. (2) "Walk in the Spirit," opposed to which is "walking after the flesh," by worldly considerations, and a desire for gratification. (3) "Walk in wisdom." Do not give unnecessary offence, or obtrude your religion in a disagreeable way. The perfect Christian is a perfect gentleman. (4) "Walk honestly," or rather honourably. There is a certain un-affected dignity that belongs to the friend of God, and commands the respect of men. The child of the heavenly royal household cannot stoop to social meannesses, or commercial sharp practices. (5) "Walk circumspectly," *i.e.,* accurately. Be particular about little things, little vanities, self-indulgences, worldlinesses, sins of tongue and temper. There are some who have only a vague, not an accurate notion of what a Christian's walk ought to be; others walk timorously always expecting to make mistakes. Some strike out wildly never thinking of where they are going; others go painfully as though they were walking on egg shells or glass bottles. Let us avoid these two mistakes—not to allow ourselves to be so bound and hampered as to lose our spiritual liberty; but not to disregard trifles which put together make such a great thing in the end. II. The motive. "To please God." We shall not walk rightly without a right motive. God looks at that as well as at the effect. 1. What are you going to live for ? To be happy ? To get to heaven ? You may get both, but these are not what you were sent into the world for. 2. If you want to find out what should be the object of your life, look at Jesus. From first to last He lived simply to please the Father. He came to do the Father's will, and He did it. (1) You may do a man's will because you are his servant paid to do it, and therefore your duty to do it, or because he is your friend and you delight to do it. Between these two classes of motives lies the difference between the law and the gospel. (2) There are two ways of seeking to please God. We often notice in earthly relationships that there is less of conscious anxiety to please where love and confidence are strongest, while on the other hand strenuous efforts to please are frequently the results of misgivings as to the disposition of the person they are designed to please. The same may be said of our relationship towards God. There are some who really wish to please Him, and yet say, " I wonder whether this or that has pleased Him." But the blessedness of the Christian position is this, that we are accepted in the Beloved so that He can regard us with complacency in order that we may go on to please Him. 3. Let the thought of pleasing God ever take precedence of the thought of pleasing ourselves and others. 4. You are pleasing God much if you are trusting Him much. To doubt Him is to cast a reflection on His changeless love. (*W. H. M. H. Aitken, M.A.*) *How to walk so as to please God :*—I. With faith. Without this "it is im-possible to please" Him. II. With humility. He abases the proud, show-ing His abhorrence of them, but exalts the humble because He delights in them. III. With obedience. 1. Active. "To obey is better than sacrifice." "Children, obey . . . for this is well pleasing unto the Lord." 2. Passive. When in sickness, trial, &c. Nothing is more acceptable than the spirit which says, "Thy will be done." "The servant that doeth not his Lord's will shall be beaten with many stripes." IV. In communion with His people. "They that feared the Lord spake often one to another ; and the Lord hearkened and heard." Would He have done so had He been indifferent or displeased ? "Where two or three are met together in My name, there am I in the midst of them." V. BENE-VOLENTLY. " With such sacrifices God is well pleased." (*G. Burder.*) *Walking so as to please God :*—I. WHAT IS IT TO PLEASE GOD? 1. Negatively. Not as if we could do anything in its own nature pleasing to God (2 Cor. iii. 5). 2. Positively. So that He may accept us in Christ (Matt. iii. 17). (1) Our persons (Eph. i. 6). (2) Our actions (1 Pet. ii. 5 ; Luke ii. 14). (*a*) So as not to be angry with us for them. (*b*) So as to be favourable to us (Prov. viii. 35 ; Zeph. iii. 17). (*c*) So as to give us a reward (Matt. vi. 4 ; x. 42). II. WHY SHOULD WE PLEASE GOD? Because—1. He is so great and mighty (Jer. v. 22). 2. So just. 3. So gracious (Psa. cxxx. 4). 4. His pleasure is the highest happiness (Psa. xxx. 5 ; lxiii. 3). 5. This is the end of Christ's incarnation and our profession (Acts iii. 26 ; 2 Tim. ii. 19). III. HOW MAY WE PLEASE HIM? 1. In general (Heb. xi. 5). (1) We must be renewed (Rom. viii. 8). (2) Do what He has commanded. (3) Therefore do it that we may please Him. (4) Do it with understanding and discretion (1 Cor. xiv. 15). (5) With cheerfulness (2 Cor. ix. 7 ; Psa. xl. 8). (6) In faith (Heb. xi. 6). (7) To His glory (1 Cor. x. 31). 2. Particularly, these things please Him—(1) Repentance (Ezek. xxxiii. 11 ; Psa. li. 17). (2) Humility (Isa. lvii. 15, lxvi. 2 ; 1 Pet. v. 8). (3) Trust in His promises (Psa. cxlvii. 11). (4) Submission to His providences (1 Sam. iii. 18 ; Psa. xxxix. 9). (5) Prayer (1 Kings iii. 10 ; 1 Tim. ii. 1–4). (6) Frequent meditations upon Him (Psa. xix. 14). (7) Justice (Micah. vi. 7, 8 ; Psa. li. 19). (8) Mercy and forgiveness (Psa. ciii. 9–11 ; Matt. vi. 14). (9) Charity to the poor (Phil. iv. 18). (10) Thankfulness (Psa. lxix. 30, 31). IV. USE : Endeavour to please God. Consider—1. Otherwise you cross His end in making you (Prov. xvi. 4). 2. So long as He is displeased you are in danger of hell. 3. If you please Him you need please none else (Prov. xvi. 7). 4. Nor take care of anything (Matt. vi. 33 ; 1 John iii. 22). 5. He will bless all His providences to you (Rom. viii. 28). 6. Pleasing God is the work of heaven (Psa. ciii. 20, 21). 7. Please Him here, and enjoy Him hereafter. (*Bp. Beveridge.*) *Pleasing God :*—There are in the world self-pleasers, men-pleasers, God-pleasers. The last only deserve our imitation. I. GOD CAN BE PLEASED. That being the case—1. He notices our conduct. 2. Observes the character of our actions. 3. Has a disposition with regard to men. II. HE CAN BE WELL PLEASED (Col. iii. 20). Those please Him best who are most like in character and action to Him in whom He was " well pleased." III. HE CAN BE EASILY PLEASED. He requires no impossible services. His approbation is not wrung from Him with difficulty. IV. HE CAN ALWAYS BE PLEASED. " He waiteth to be gracious." When the Christian walks in the way of His commandments, he walks with God. V. HE OUGHT TO BE PLEASED. This is required by— 1. Himself. His commands all amount to this. His glory is promoted by this. 2. Man. Pleasing God is the directest way of securing the welfare of the world. 3. Our own well being. To please God is to have a tranquil conscience, the approbation of the God, an endless reward. (*B. Pugh.*) *Pleasing God* is—I. POSSIBLE. He has been pleased with men—Enoch, Noah, Daniel, &c. This is wonderful—wonderful that the Infinite should condescend to notice any one individual so insignificant as man. Still more wonderful that He should be pleased with anything that man can do. God is a pleasable Being, and man can contribute something to His pleasure. II. INCUMBENT. " Ye ought." Why? 1. Because He is the absolute Proprietor of your existence. He has a right to everything you have. 2. He is the most righteous of sovereigns. He does not require you to do anything that is not right and just. 3. He is the most tender of fathers. The only way to please yourselves is to please Him. (*D. Thomas, D.D.*) **So ye would abound more and more.**—I. WHAT IS IT TO ABOUND? 1. Negatively. Not as if we could do more than is required. For—(1) We cannot do all that is required (Psa. cxix. 96). (2) We can do nothing as it is required (2 Cor. iii. 5). (3) Yet if we could it is no more than our duty (Luke xvii. 10). 2. Positively. (1) Endeavour to go beyond others (1 Cor. xii. 31). (2) Be more serious in pleasing God than in anything else (Eccles. ix. 10 ; Rom. xii. 11 ; Matt. vi. 33). (3) Every day excel ourselves and grow better (2 Pet. iii. 18). II. WHAT SHOULD WE ABOUND MORE AND MORE IN? 1. In works of piety towards God ; in—(1) Godly sorrow for sin (2 Cor. vii. 9–11)). (2) Turning from our present lusts (Rom. vi. 12). (3) Faith in Christ for pardon (Eph. i. 7) ; for grace (Acts iii. 26 ; John xv. 4, 5 ; Phil. iv. 13). (4) Dependence on God's mercy (Prov. iii. 5). (5) Making Him our only joy and love (Matt. xxii. 37). (6) Prayer (Rom. xii. 12). (7) Hearing His Word (Luke iv. 16), and receiving His sacrament. 2. In works of equity to our neighbour—(1) Wronging none (Matt. v. 44). (2) Endeavouring the good of all (Gal. vi. 10). (3) Being charitable to the poor (1 Tim. vi. 18; 2 Cor. ix. 6–8). III. WHY SHOULD WE ABOUND MORE AND MORE? 1. We are commanded (Heb. vi. 1; 2 Pet. i. 5, 6; Eph. vi. 10; 1 Cor. xv. 58). 2. Unless we grow better we shall surely grow worse. 3. We can never abound too much; nor indeed enough (Phil. iii. 11). 4. The more we abound the more glory we shall have (Luke xix. 16–19; 1 Cor. xv. 41, 42). IV. HOW SHALL WE ABOUND MORE AND MORE? 1. Often think of spiritual things—(1) Of God (Psa. lxiii. 6; cxxxix. 18). (2) Of Christ. (3) Of the world to come (Amos vi. 3). Conclusion: 1. Motives. (1) We have abounded in sin too long (1 Pet. iv. 3). (2) Our life is continued for that end. (3) The more we abound the more comfort we shall have. (4) Abounding is the best sign of the truth of grace (James ii. 26). (5) Heaven will make amends for all. 2. Uses. (1) Of reproof— (*a*) To those who never please God, but abound in sin. (*b*) To those who take more pains to abound in riches than in graces. (2) Of examination. Compare your present with your past. (3) Of exhortation. "Abound more and more." (*Bp. Beveridge.*) *Of abounding more and more:*—If any one wishes to see what it is to begin well in Christian faith and practice and at the same time what care should be taken not to depend too much on mere beginnings however praiseworthy, he cannot do better than examine carefully these two Epistles to the Thessalonians. The apostle seems hardly to know how to say enough of their faith and charity, or of the noble and self-denying way in which they had received the gospel (see chap. i. 5–8; iii. 7–10). There could not well be more promising converts; and yet the very next words show how anxious he was that they might not trust in their first promising conversion, "Praying exceedingly that we might see your face": to what purpose? not for his own pleasure, but "to perfect that which was lacking in their faith." The same feeling runs through the whole of the letter; his joy in what they had done is everywhere tempered by a real and serious anxiety lest they should stop short and begin to think that they had done enough. I. Now, with regard to the absolute necessity of continual improvement, it appears in the first place from this circumstance THAT IF WE RIGHTLY VALUE THE FIRST GOOD BEGINNING, WE MUST FROM THE VERY NATURE OF THE CASE GO ON FROM ONE DEGREE OF HOLINESS TO ANOTHER. Men may very well do something which looks like repentance upon poor imperfect worldly reasons, and may deceive themselves and others into a notion that they are true Christian penitents; as, for example, intemperance may be left off for health or character's sake, or a quarrel may be made up with a view to our worldly interest, or the fear of approaching death may drive men against their will to long-neglected ordinances of religion; and it is no wonder if such a repentance as this very soon begins to stand still: if, having reached such and such a point, the man imagines himself good enough, and takes no more pains to be better: but this is quite contrary to the nature of true repentance upon Christian principles. II. This is yet more absolutely necessary, because, IF MEN DO NOT IMPROVE THEY ARE IN PRACTICE SURE TO GO BACK. They cannot stay where they are; they must either grow worse or better. For it is the nature of all strong impressions to act vehemently on the mind at first, and after a little time to fade away as it were and gradually become weaker and weaker. Thus the fear of God and the dread of sin and punishment, in which repentance usually begins, if we do not resolutely and on purpose endeavour to keep them up, are sure to lose their force on our minds. III. IT MAY HELP US IN JUDGING MORE TRULY OF OUR DUTY IN THIS RESPECT IF WE PUT OURSELVES AS NEARLY AS WE CAN IN THE PLACE OF THESE THESSALONIANS, WHO HAD LEARNED CHRISTIANITY FROM THE LIPS OF ST. PAUL HIMSELF. For, indeed, we are very nearly in their place; we, like them, have received of the apostles how we ought to walk and to please God. The only difference is, that they received this knowledge by word of mouth, we by reading the apostolic letters and listening to the apostolic Church. Now what sort of a spirit and temper should we have judged these Thessalonians to be of, if we found that as soon as their teacher was gone away to Athens, they had become careless about his instructions, thought much of what they had done already, and took no pains whatever to improve? Whatever censure we pass on them we must acknowledge surely to be due to ourselves, in such measure as we neglect the duty of amending daily because our Teacher is out of sight. Yet this is what we are sure to do, if we be not constantly exhorted and reminded of it; nay, there is great reason to fear that all exhortation may prove in vain. 1. For, first of all, having been bred up from our cradle in the knowledge and understanding of our Christian duty, we are apt to fancy ourselves familiar with the practice of it too. We are convinced in our minds that we know it well enough; and this of itself inclines us to be too soon satisfied with our accustomed way of doing it. 2. Again, a sincere Christian will be on his guard that he make no dangerous comparisons between himself and his neighbours. It will never do to take it for granted that we keep our place in respect of piety and goodness—that we are no worse than we were, in fact— because we are no worse in comparison with them. It may be that all around you are gone astray from God, and in the way to everlasting ruin : if such turn out to be the case, you may excuse and flatter yourself now that you are no worse than they ; but it will be little comfort to you in the day of account, when you find that your condemnation is as bad as theirs. (*Plain Sermons by Contributors to " Tracts for the Times."*) *The necessity of progress :*—It is a sure law that, as Luther said, " He who *is* a Christian is no Christian." He who thinks that he has gained the fulness of the faith has lost it. Progress is a require- ment of spiritual vitality ; and the recompense of past progress is the assurance of progress to come. In the words of a famous Hebrew saying, " The reward of a precept is a precept." He, that is, who has fulfilled one commandment is allowed to receive another. He who has reached one height of truth catches a glimpse of a loftier height beyond. Each attainment in the Divine life becomes the occasion for the revelation of fresh duty. The crown of labour for a being such as man is not rest but longer and nobler toil. It is true, we know, that to him that hath more shall be given. And it is no less true that of him that hath done much shall more be required. Each achievement of the successful worker was indeed God's gift. And what we receive, what we realize, what we gain—however we call the process—is not for contemplation, or for hoarding, but for further service. What is reaped supplies the seed-corn for a richer harvest. The gifts of God answer to His requirements, and the requirements of God answer to His gifts. " Grace for grace "—grace to be used in return for grace already used—is the law which regulates God's blessing ; " from strength to strength " is the description of the Christian's course. " We must abound more and more." We must seek untiringly for signs of growing nearness to God, and show what we have found. The trained eye learns to see beauties which were once undistinguished. The trained ear learns to interpret voices which were once inarticulate. And is it so— do we confidently trust that it always will be so—spiritually with ourselves ? Are we able as the years go on to fix our eyes more steadily on God, shrinking with livelier sensibility from sin more than from suffering, realizing our fellowship one with another in Him with a more intense vividness, looking, and showing that we look, beyond the wild confusion of the hour to the one will of peace and righteous- ness which cannot at last want accomplishment ? Are we able to listen to the Divine wisdom conversing with us as with sons in the words of apostles and prophets, speaking to us in our own tongues, interpreting our own thoughts, answering the questions with which our hearts are full ? Are we able to rest with increasing peace in the contemplation of Him who is perfect light, and to bring before Him who is perfect compassion the unceasing prayer of sympathetic remem- brance for all with whom we are united as fellow-workers in the present and as fellow-heirs of the future ? Are we able to pause in the solemn stillness of thought till we are alone with God, and to offer ourselves to the fire of His love ; that so little by little all may be consumed in us—all passion and pride, all self-seeking and self-trust—which does not minister to His glory, which does not, that is, make clearer to men His infinite perfection ? Are we able to regard the world in its unspeakable vastness, life with its inevitable sorrows, nature with its contrasts (to our eyes) of beauty and terror, or grace and mocking grotesque- ness, as even now gathered up in Christ, and seek for ourselves the development of every faculty by which we may be taught to spell out better the One Name written in all that is finite ? We tremble perhaps as we put such questions to ourselves. But they stir us at least with a sense of what our faith is. They make plain to us to what we are called. They show an obligation to progress, a capacity for influences of which, it may be, we are habitually unmindful. They condemn us perhaps. But the sentence of condemnation is the message of hope. It is a revelation of God's love as well as of man's failure. The strength for service and the opportunities for service are still given to us through the gospel. (*Bp. Westcott.*) *Abounding more and more :*—An aged Christian man who had been much benefited through life by God's blessing, after thankfully referring to his more than fifty years of health, prosperity, and abounding mercies, remarked, " I am convinced that if I have to be any happier than I have been or am, I must get more religion." The Hindus have a legend that a very little man once got a promise from a great king that he should have as much territory as he could overstep in three strides. Then the little man began to grow till his head reached the sky, and at last, when he took his three strides, with the first he overstepped all the land, with the second he overstepped all the seas, and with the third he compassed all the heavens. If we grow in knowledge, in wisdom, in grace, and in everything that is good, as we ought, we may at length be able to compass much that will be most advantageous to ourselves and to others. (*H. K. Burton.*)

Ver. 2. **For ye know what commandments we gave you by the Lord Jesus.**—*The Lord Jesus and His commandments :*—I. JESUS IS LORD. 1. By Divine appointment "He shall reign." 2. By creative acts He has a right to rule over things and beings whom He has made. 3. By redemptive work : "Ye are not your own." 4. By the glad acknowledgment of His saints : "Unto Him that loved us." 5. By the ultimate recognition of the universe : "At the name of Jesus every knee shall bow," &c. II. As LORD JESUS HAS A RIGHT TO COMMAND. 1. This right is uniformly asserted. Christ never prefers a request, makes a suggestion, or expresses a wish ; it is always "Come," "Go," "Do this," "If I, your Lord and Master, . . . ye aught." 2. This right has been blasphemously usurped. They are impious usurpers who determine other means of salvation, or rules of moral conduct other than those He has laid down. "One is your Master." III. HIS COMMANDS HAVE BEEN PLAINLY REVEALED. "Ye know." 1. Directly by Himself. "Love one another," &c. 2. Instrumentally by His accredited ambassadors. "We gave you from the Lord Jesus." Their deliverances, however, are only applications of Christ's principles to particular persons and places. 3. Permanently in the Bible. (1) How clearly. (2) How accessibly. Ignorance is without excuse. IV. OBEDIENCE TO HIS COMMANDMENTS IS THE CRITERION OF DISCIPLESHIP. Commands are given —1. Not to be thought about. 2. Not to be the subjects of promise in regard to the doing of them. 3. But to be obeyed. "Ye are My disciples if ye *do*." This doing must be—(1) Universal. "Whatsoever I command you." (2) Prompt. There is no time to lose. (3) Cheerful. We are subjects of so good a King. Conclusion : 1. Christ as Lord is approachable. He is "the mighty God," but He is the Man Christ *Jesus*." Sovereigns are difficult of access, are surrounded by the pomp of circumstance, excite embarrassment and nervousness when they do not terrify. But we may "come boldly to the throne of grace." 2. His commandments are not grievous. They are reducible to a few plain principles which a child may learn by heart. If we grasp them we practically grasp all. And then they are simply the conditions upon which alone our wellbeing can be secured. 3. What He has bidden us do He has done Himself. It makes all the difference on a field of battle whether the commanding officer says "Go" or "Come." Christ says, "I must go . . . if any man will come after Me." "I have left you" not only commands but "an example," an embodied command. 4. In loving loyalty to Christ there is great reward. "Lo, I am with you," now ; "Well done," by and by. (*J. W. Burn.*)    *The authority of Christ :*—Christ does not appeal to men as the heathen philosophers did. They ask opinions, court criticism, and even the wily and garrulous Socrates gives men an opportunity of differing from him ; but Christ, with "the authoritative tone and earnestness" of the Son of God, says, "This is absolute ; believe it and be saved, or reject it and be damned." He says that He came from the Father, that He speaks the Word of the Father, and that He is returning to the Father. So there is nothing between Him and God ; immediately behind Him, though invisible, lies infinitude, and He sets Himself up as the medium on which the voice of the infinite is broken into human sounds. (*J. Parker, D.D.*)    *God's commandments a protection and a delight :*—Reconciliation to God is like entering the gate of a beautiful avenue which conducts to a splendid mansion. But that avenue is long, and in some places it skirts the edge of dangerous cliffs ; and therefore to save the traveller from falling over where he would be dashed to pieces, it is fenced all the way by a quick-set edge. That hedge is the Commandments. They are planted there that we may do no harm ; but like a fence of the fragrant briar, they regale the pilgrim who keeps the path, and they only hurt him when he tries to break through. Temperance, justice, truthfulness, purity of speech and behaviour, obedience to parents, mutual affection, Sabbath keeping, Divine worship—all these are righteous requirements ; and "in keeping of them there is great reward." Happy is he who only knows the precept in the perfume which it sheds, and who, never having "kicked against the pricks," has never proved the sharpness of the thorns. (*J.*

*Hamilton, D.D.*)  *God's commandments reasonable :*—There is mention made of one who willingly fetched water near two miles every day for a whole year to pour on a dead stick at the command of a superior, when no reason could be given for so doing. How ready then should every one be to do Christ service, whose commands are backed with reason, and whose precepts are attended with encouragements. (*J. Spencer.*)

Ver. 3–7. **For this is the will of God, even your sanctification.**—*Holiness :*—Holiness, like sin, is many-sided, and each separate side presents us with a different view of its requirements and perfections. In this chapter holiness stands for purity and chastity, and also for liberality in our dealings one with another. A man may be both pure and liberal, and yet, as being proud, wilful, and revengeful, may be very far from being holy. Purity and liberality, or just dealing, are two conditions of holiness—are essential to its presence—yet they by no means exhaust its qualifications. The highest form of holiness is love, a love which at once purifies the affections, exalts the heart, and conforms us to the likeness of Him in whom all holiness finds its example and perfection. I. THE SANCTIFIED IS ONE WHO IS LOVED BY GOD, AND WHO ASKS FOR HIS LOVE IN RETURN. All unholiness keeps us away from God. II. THE SANCTIFIED IS ALSO THE WISHED-FOR ONE. "This is the *wishing* of God," &c. The creation by God implied a dedication to God (Isa. xliii. 7 ; Col. i. 16). The wishing of God was made null and void by the fall ; yet in His infinite love for man He went on wishing for man still. The purpose of the Incarnation was to reconsecrate lost and fallen man. III. THE SANCTIFIED IS ALSO THE DEAR AND HONOURED ONE; he is precious in the sight of the Lord (Psa. xci. 15 ; John xii. 26). IV. HE WHO IS SANCTIFIED IS ALSO DUTIFUL AND REVEREND TOWARDS GOD ; not as being moved by threatenings or encouraged by promises, but as being brought within the sphere of the operations of God the Holy Ghost. I cannot be holy unless my holiness produce some kind of fruit and leads to some practical result. V. THE SANCTIFIED ONE IS ALSO ROOTED AND GROUNDED IN THE FAITH, since holiness is gained by faith passing into action. Every successive conquest over sin deepens his spiritual life, and becomes part of such office by which the soul is consecrated to God. VI. THE SANCTIFIED OR CONSECRATED ONE IS ALSO PURE. Sanctification involves regeneration, or a new birth. (*J. M. Ashley, M.A.*) *Of sanctification :*—The notion of the word sanctification signifies to consecrate and set apart to an holy use. Sanctification hath a privative and a positive part. 1. A privative part, mortification, which lies in the purging out of sin. Though it takes not away the life, yet it takes away the love of sin. 2. A positive part, vivification, which is the spiritual refining of the soul, which in Scripture is called a "renewing of your mind" and a "partaking of the Divine nature." The priests in the law not only were washed in the great laver, but adorned with glorious apparel ; so sanctification not only washes from sin, but adorns with purity. I. WHAT IS SANCTIFICATION ? 1. Sanctification is a supernatural thing : it is Divinely infused. Weeds grow of themselves. Flowers are planted. Sanctification is a flower of the Spirit's planting ; therefore it is called "the sanctification of the Spirit." 2. Sanctification is an intrinsical thing : "it lies chiefly in the heart." It is called the adorning "the hidden man of the heart." The dew wets the leaf, the sap is hid in the root. 3. Sanctification is an extensive thing : it spreads into the whole man. "The very God of peace sanctify you wholly." He is not a sanctified person who is good only in some part, but who is all over sanctified ; therefore in Scripture grace is called a "new man"; not a new eye or a new tongue, but a "new man." A good Christian, though he be sanctified but in part, yet in every part. 4. Sanctification is an intense ardent thing : "fervent in spirit." Sanctification is not a dead form, but it is inflamed into zeal. 5. Sanctification is a beautiful thing ; it makes God and angels fall in love with us, "the beauties of holiness." 6. Sanctification is an abiding thing : "His seed remaineth in him." 7. Sanctification is a progressive thing. II. WHAT ARE THE COUNTERFEITS OF SANCTIFICATION ? There is something looks like sanctification which is not. 1. The first counterfeit of sanctification is moral virtue. 2. The second counterfeit of sanctification is superstitious devotion. 3. The third counterfeit of sanctification is hypocrisy ; when men make a pretence of that holiness which they have not. A pretence of sanctification is not to be rested in. Many ships that have had the name of the Hope, the Safeguard, the Triumph, yet have been cast away upon the rocks; so many who have had the name of saintship have been cast into hell. 4. The fourth counterfeit of sanctification is restraining grace. When men forbear vice, though they do not hate it, this may be the sinner's motto, "Fain I would, but I dare not." Here is no change of heart. Sin is curbed, but not cured; a lion may be in chains, but is a lion still. 5. The fifth counterfeit of sanctification is common grace, which is a slight, transient work of the Spirit, but doth not amount to conversion. III. Wherein appears the necessity of sanctification? 1. God hath called us to it: "God hath not called us to uncleanness, but unto holiness." 2. The necessity appears in this: without sanctification there is no evidencing our justification; justification and sanctification go together: "but ye are sanctified, but ye are justified." 3. Without sanctification we have no title to the new covenant. If a man make a will, and settle his estate upon such persons as he names in the will, none else but they can lay claim to the will; so God makes a will and testament, but it is restrained and limited to such as are sanctified; and it is high presumption for any else to lay claim to the will. 4. There is no going to heaven without sanctification: "Without holiness no man shall see the Lord." 5. Without sanctification all our holy things are defiled: "Unto them that are defiled is nothing pure." IV. What are the signs of sanctification? 1. Such as are sanctified can remember a time when they were unsanctified. 2. The second sign of sanctification is the indwelling of the Spirit: "The Holy Ghost which dwelleth in us." 3. The third sign of sanctification is an antipathy against sin. 4. The fourth sign of sanctification is the spiritual performance of duties, viz., with the heart, and from a principle of love. The sanctified soul prays out of a love to prayer; he "calls the Sabbath a delight." 5. The fifth sign, a well-ordered life. "Be ye holy in all manner of conversation." Where the heart is sanctified, the life will be so too: the Temple had gold without as well as within. 6. The sixth sign, steadfast resolution. V. What are the chief inducements to sanctification? 1. It is the will of God that we should be holy. In the text, "This is the will of God, your sanctification." As God's Word must be the rule, so His will the reason of our actions: this is the will of God, our sanctification. Perhaps it is not the will of God we should be rich, but it is His will that we should be holy. God's will is our warrant. 2. Jesus Christ hath died for our sanctification. Christ shed His blood to wash off our impurity. 3. Sanctification makes us resemble God. 4. Sanctification is that which God bears a great love to. A king delights to see his image upon a piece of coin: where God sees His likeness, there He gives His love. 5. Sanctification is the only thing doth difference us from the wicked. 6. It is as great a shame to have the name of a Christian, yet want sanctity, as to have the name of steward, and yet want fidelity; the name of a virgin, yet want chastity. 7. Sanctification fits for heaven: "Who hath called us to glory and virtue." Glory is the throne, and sanctification is the step by which we ascend to it. VI. How may sanctification be attained to? 1. Be conversant in the Word of God: "Sanctify them through Thy truth." The Word is both a glass to show us the spots of our soul, and a laver to wash them away. 2. Get faith in Christ's blood; "purifying their hearts by faith." 3. Breathe after the Spirit; it is called "the sanctification of the Spirit." 4. Associate with sanctified persons. Association begets assimilation. 5. Pray for sanctification. (*T. Watson.*) *Distinctive features of a true sanctification:*—It is comparatively easy for some minds to grasp the outlines of a grand undertaking, but they fail in working out the details. They are more theoretical than practical. So it is possible to form a bold conception of some leading Christian virtue—beauty, dignity, and necessity; but all the while to ignore the little details which, in every-day life, constitute the essence of the virtue. Sanctification is the perfection of the Christian life, and is attained, not by some magical feat, but by patient plodding and stern conflicts. It is the sublime but little understood science of living aright, in the sight of God and man. Secretary Walsingham, in writing to Lord Burleigh, said: "We have lived long enough to our country, to our fortunes, and to our sovereign; it is high time that we began to live for ourselves and for our God." Observe: I. That a true sanctification consists in the maintenance of a personal chastity. 1. This involves an abstinence from gross and sensual indulgence. "Fornication" (ver. 3) designates not only the actual transgression, but all the sinful lusts of the flesh. This vice is the source of many others. It is like the fabled Hydra, of which it is said that when one head was cut off another grew in its place. It is the root of extravagance, drunkenness, disease, poverty, murder. It is bewitching, prevalent, most fatal in its tendencies; and against it terrible vengeance has been declared and executed. 2. Involves a rigid maintenance of bodily purity (ver. 4). The vessel of the body is the temple of the Holy Ghost, and whatever would defile that must be shunned.

The apostle implies that there is a kind of art in chastity which all should practice. " Know," *i.e.*, have skill, the power of self-control. Christianity is the science of sciences, the art of living well; and no small skill is necessary in regulating the exercise of the Christian virtues. To *possess*, to rule the body in purity, keep a diligent guard on the senses (Job xxxi. 1; Prov. xxiii. 33; Gen. xxxix. 6, 7); avoid the company and conversation of the sensual; be temperate, industrious, prayerful. 3. Involves a masterly restraint on the passionate outgoings of evil desire (ver. 5). Ignorance is the origin of unchastity; and the apostle shows to what an extent of wickedness a man may go who knows not God. An old writer says: " Ignorance is a master, a mother sin : pull it, thou pullest all sin." Evil must be restrained in its earliest manifestation; banished from the region of thought. The longer it is harboured, the more powerful it becomes. II. THAT A TRUE SANCTIFICATION CONSISTS IN THE UNIVERSAL EXERCISE OF STRICT JUSTICE (ver. 6). Note—1. That no violation of justice is allowable. The prohibition extends not only to acts of unchastity, but to all the transactions of life. The value of a commodity is governed by its relation to the immediate wants of man. In nature that which has life and sense is more excellent than an inanimate creature: in this view an insect is superior to a diamond. But with regard to use, a loaf of bread is of more value than a thousand insects. Justice requires there should be a fair proportion between a thing and its price. To exact a price which is beyond the worth of the commodity sold, or to give a sum which is below its due value, is to overreach on the part either of the seller or the buyer. The commercial world of the present day might ponder with advantage the wholesome lessons to be learnt from the practice of an ancient Christian simplicity. The man who begins a course of dishonesty by defrauding a stranger will soon reach the point of cheating his dearest brother and chuckle at his unjust success. 2. That every violation of justice will be certainly punished. The rogue will not always triumph; and his ill-gotten gains may be the instruments of his curse. An all-seeing Eye watches and an Unseen Hand rests on all his accumulations. The successful robber is apt to lull himself into a false security. But " the Lord is the avenger of all such " (Prov. xxii. 22, 23 ; xxiii. 10). Not that we are to act honestly from the fear of punishment; but while striving to act rightly from love to God and a sense of duty, it is also salutary to remember that vengeance belongeth unto the Lord, and He will recompense. Where human justice fails, the Divine vengeance will supply the deficiency. III. THAT A TRUE SANCTIFICATION RECOGNIZES THE SUPREME AUTHORITY OF THE DIVINE CALL (ver. 7). A holy life gives no license to sin. Everything is in favour of holiness; the caller is holy (1 Pet. i. 15), the instrument holy (John xvii. 17), and the Spirit, the immediate worker, is the fountain of all holiness. Religion is a holy calling, because it leads to holiness; and though it finds us not holy, yet it makes us so. They answer not their calling who commit any manner of sin. Unmercifulness, cruelty, fornication, fraud and uncleanness are not of God. In every temptation to evil remember the Divine calling. Lessons: A true sanctification—1. Provides for the chastity of the whole man. 2. Governs all the transactions of daily life. 3. Responds to the highest call of God. (*G. Barlow.*) *Sanctification of the Spirit :*—I. WHY THE SPIRIT WAS SENT. The first purpose which was to be answered by Christ's coming in the flesh was, as St. Paul tells us, that He might " redeem us from the curse of the law, being made a curse for us." Christ's death has answered that purpose fully ; for, as the same apostle declares, " Christ *hath* redeemed us from the curse of the law." But there are other things in Christianity beside the death of Christ; and they must have their purpose also. Why was the Holy Ghost sent to us ? and why does He vouchsafe to come ? He comes to sanctify us men. You remember that, in the account of the creation, God said, " Let us make man in our image, after our likeness. So God created man in His own image ; in the image of God created He him." This image of God in the soul of man—for that, of course, is the thing meant—did not descend from Adam to his children. He lost it at the fall, and so could not leave it to his posterity. Adam's first son was born in the likeness of sinful man. What was the consequence ? " All flesh corrupted his way upon the earth." At last it became quite clear that, so long as this evil root—this hereditary taint—remained within us uncorrected, so long men would go on sinning; nay, would grow worse and worse; just as a bowl with a bias, if you try to send it straight, the longer it rolls, the further it will swerve. Now, if this state of things could be allowed to go on, Christ would have died in vain ; therefore, that He might finish the work He had begun for us, He sent His Holy Spirit to correct the bias of our evil nature, and gradually renew the image of God in our souls. This includes the renewal "in the spirit of our minds," and the putting on "the new man, which after God is created in righteousness and true holiness." Here, then, is another great purpose which the plan of our redemption is meant to answer. The death of Christ was to redeem us; the coming of the Holy Ghost is to sanctify us. "For this is the will of God," &c. II. THE SPIRIT'S DIFFICULTY IN SANCTIFYING. That must needs be a great and difficult task which the Holy Ghost has taken upon Himself. Could a lesser arm have upheld us in our battle against sin, God would have sent us that lesser and weaker arm. But He sends us His own Spirit. The work, then, from its importance and difficulty, must be worthy of that eternal Spirit. It is a war against sin and Satan. Satan has lodged himself in the heart, and knowing the value of the heart, he will fight for it inch by inch. But the work of sanctification is something more than merely driving out Satan: it is binding the old man which has hitherto held a tyrannous sway within us, and replacing him by the new man, which after God is created in righteousness and true holiness. To sanctify or hallow a thing is to set it apart for God's service. Thus Christians are called in Scripture "holy" and "saints," because they are God's people and serve Him. So when we say that it is God's will we should be sanctified or hallowed, this is the same as saying that our hearts ought to be like a church. A church is a house of prayer; and our hearts should be full of prayer also. Again, a church is the place for reading and explaining the Word of God; and the Word of God must be the food of our minds and the delight and meditation of our hearts. Moreover, a church is the last place for doing any wicked thing; so should it be with the heart of a Christian. Above all, a church is devoted to God; and this is the chief mark of a Christian: he should be devoted—heart and mind, soul and body, wholly given up to God's service. Not always praying, not always reading the Bible; but he is to be always serving God. Strength, as well as liveliness, is necessary to a principle; and it is the principle of sanctification to give ourselves up to God, and to give up everything that offends Him. In fine, it is in a measure living the life of heaven upon earth. This is God's will, and this is our beatitude. (*A. W. Hare, A.M.*) *Our consecration the will of God :*—I. OUR SANCTIFICATION. 1. This word has been misunderstood and abused. (1) There are some who expect to become different beings, with different ideas and qualities from those they now have. Thus when they find old sins reappearing under new names, needing the revival of grace, they become disheartened, and doubt their Christianity. (2) Others take refuge in small improvements, and think the work of sanctification is going on because this lust has died out or that temper curbed. 2. Let us grasp its meaning. It is applied in Scripture—(1) To things: the Sabbath, Mount Horeb, the Tabernacle, Altar, Temple; and in each case means consecration, for no moral change can pass over these things. (2) To persons: priests, prophets, the Jewish nation; and still the idea is appropriation, the stamping with God's image and superscription. (3) We pass on to gospel times. (*a*) Sometimes it is the grand universal consecration which Christ made in redemption: "By the which will we are sanctified through the offering of the body of Jesus once for all." (*b*) Sometimes it is the first great individual consecration at conversion: "The blood of the covenant wherewith he was sanctified"; "But ye were washed, ye were sanctified." (*c*) Sometimes, as in the text, it is the progressive realization in spirit and conduct of the one all-embracing consecration; not a change of nature, but an increasing, brightening presence of the Holy Spirit in the soul, into transformation of character and life. (*d*) Sometimes the complete identification of the will of man and the will of God, which is consecration consummated. 3. It is impossible to exaggerate the importance of this view. This is the redeemed man living his redemption, the forgiven man living his absolution, the consecrated man living his consecration. (1) Here is the antidote to self-righteousness: "Nor I, but Christ liveth in me." (2) Here is the antidote to despondency: "In me" truly "there dwelleth no good thing"; but I am encouraged to look to God for help. (3) Here is the antidote to all that petty, piecemeal, retail righteousness which dwarfs the aspirations of many. There are many who are building their little separate towers for the chance of reaching heaven—one trying to build a treasure-house of charity, another to beautify taste into piety, another to construct a substitute for grace out of natural negative virtues, but all missing the very point of Christian perfection, the becoming in deed that which God has made us all in idea—His entirely. Consecration is the being absolutely, and of a glad heart, God's. 4. There are special foes of this consecration. (1) It is a ruinous error to dream of the ideal and to neglect the practical.

This is antinomianism. (2) There are sins which make havoc of this consecration, of which St. Paul speaks in the context—sins which divide allegiance, sully loyalty, and fill God's temple with foul and filthy idols. II. Our sanctification is THE WILL OF GOD. 1. God's will is the true law of our lives. This is expressed without reservation, and all amounts to this—our consecration. 2. What God wills He will help us to realize. If there is failure, it is attributable to want of prayer, faith, and co-operation with God. 3. There is no way of acceptance with God but in conformity to His will. God being what He is, must will our sanctification. "Without holiness no man shall see the Lord." (*Dean Vaughan.*) *Human holiness the great object of the Divine will:*—1. God has a will. Will implies reason; God is infinite reason. Will implies force; it is determination: God is infinite force. Will, free, uncontrolled, is the expression of the willer's nature. God's nature is holy, benevolent, unchangeable. 2. God has a will concerning man. Insignificant though man be as compared with the universe, and less than nothing as compared with his Maker, he, nevertheless, engages the mind and heart of God. Glorious truth this! 3. God's will concerning man is his holiness. "Sanctification" man's holiness, and holiness is moral excellence, assimilation to Himself. If this be the will of God concerning man, two conclusions deserve special notice. I. THAT MAN'S GRAND DUTY CHIMES IN WITH HIS MORAL INTUITIONS AND HIGHEST INTEREST. What is the grand duty of man? Obedience to the Divine will. Philosophy can return no other answer. 1. Our moral intuitions urge us to holiness. There is one ideal character which they are constantly intruding on our notice, urging us to cultivate. Moral souls everywhere on earth feel that they should be true, honest, generous, pure, and devout; in other words, that they should be holy. 2. Our highest interest urges us to holiness. The history of the world shows that men have been prosperous and happy in proportion to their virtues; and human consciousness attests that men are only inwardly happy as they feel that they have lived and done the thing that is right and true. So, then, the great demand of the Bible, instead of being in the slightest degree incongruous with human nature or its interests, blends in with the strictest accordance. II. THAT MAN HAS AN INFALLIBLE GUIDE TO DETERMINE THE SUCCESSFUL IN PRAYER AND EFFORT. He who goes with God's will goes with omnipotence, and if he goes rightly, must succeed. 1. Successful prayers are prayers for holiness. He who prays for health, long life, secular property, has no reason to expect an answer only so far as these are sought with the grand motive of promoting holiness. God has not promised to answer any prayer that has not the desire for holiness as its inspiration. 2. Successful efforts are efforts for holiness. Efforts after wealth, influence, power, fame, may, and frequently do, succeed; but what then? If the inspiring motive has not been holiness, the end, which is happiness, is not obtained. Since God's will is our holiness, no human effort for happiness not aiming at the grand end has ever been, or can ever be, successful. Whatever may be the appearance of things, all prayers and effort not aiming at holiness are failures. (*D. Thomas, D.D.*) *Sanctification the will of God:*—I. THE SANCTIFICATION OF MAN IS THE AVOWED OBJECT OF GOD IN ALL THE DISPENSATIONS OF HIS GRACE. 1. The patriarchal (Gen. xxx. 1). 2. The Mosaic (Exod. xix.; Lev. xi.). 3. The Christian (Eph. v. 25–27). II. GOD HAS SHOWN THIS TO BE HIS WILL IN THE CONSTRUCTION OF REVELATION, WHICH OFFERS A SYSTEM OF TRUTHS ADMIRABLY CALCULATED AS AN INSTRUMENT TO EFFECT IT. 1. Man's responsibility. 2. God's perfections. 3. The doctrine, exhibition, and temporal and eternal punishment of sin. 4. The provision and offer of redemption. 5. Holy precepts, to which are attached abundant rewards. III. THE SCRIPTURES REVEAL AND INSTRUCT US HOW TO RECEIVE THE AGENCY OF A DIVINE PERSON, WHOSE OPERATIONS ARE PARTICULARLY DIRECTED TO THIS OBJECT. 1. He is the Author of our regeneration, which is holiness began. 2. He is the Author of the truth, which is the means of holiness, and applies that truth to the heart. 3. He is the Fountain of continual supplies of that grace, growth in which is progressive sanctification. (*J. F. Denham.*) *Sanctification the will of God:*—It is God's will, the great purpose that He has at heart, that men should be holy. "Sanctify them through Thy truth," &c. Pardon and all other blessings are means to this end. The Great Sculptor plans and labours only for a torso in room of a statue without this; the Great Builder would never see the top stone in His chosen temple without this; the Great Husbandman would never taste of the fruit of His labour without this. Now, if our sanctification—our growing holiness here and our perfected holiness hereafter—is God's will, then—I. HOLINESS IS A GREAT AND BLESSED CON-

SUMMATION. "*Good* is the will of the Lord." There can be nothing so great and blessed for any creature as to have God's will perfected in it. Only in holiness are eternal life and blessedness possible. To have the thoughts pure, the life at every point and in all its interests set like music to the words of God's law, the soul moulded into the image of Christ, that is to have heaven begun. II. GOD WILL SPARE NO PAINS TO CREATE AND PERFECT HOLINESS IN A MAN'S SOUL. He *has* spared no sacrifice, in that He sent His Son; for it was the essence and heart of Christ's mission to "purify unto Himself a peculiar people," &c. And still towards and in us He will direct His working to this great end. He will prune this vine, that it may bear more fruit. He will cut, and chisel, and polish, till the fair image of Christ is seen. And as we smart, and weep, and wonder at our heavenly Father's severity, let us think of His great purpose. III. WE ARE BOUND TO CO-OPERATE WITH GOD IN THIS GREAT END. "God wills it," said the Crusaders, and buckled on their armour for the conquest of the Holy Land. "God wills it" that we should pray, and strive, and fight for a purer and higher conquest. And what a start God gives us in His forgiveness through Christ! He thereby gives us freedom, gratitude, momentum; and in our whole warfare with sin He gives His Holy Spirit to inspire, direct, and sustain. IV. WE ARE ASSURED OF SUCCESS. If it is His will, "who can be against us?" (*Family Churchman.*)    Sanctification:—I. DISTINGUISH IT FROM RELATED TERMS. From—1. Regeneration is once for all done, and is the beginning of holiness, whereas sanctification is its progressive advancement. One is the implantment of holy principles and affections; the other their issue in a holy character. 2. Justification, while it does not exclude the present, has special reference to the past, while sanctification is chiefly directed to the present and the future. The one is something done for us, the other something done in us. The one is a change of relation, the other a change of character. The one implies pardon, the other purity. 3. Morality. This may exist without sanctification, as is seen in the lives of many worldly men. But sanctification cannot exist without morality. Morality is not to be disparaged; but there is no perfection without Christ. II. WHAT DO WE MEAN BY SANCTIFICATION? Religion implanted in the heart and conspicuous in the life. 1. "The kingdom of God is within you." Christianity begins in the heart, and forms the life by forming the dispositions. It works from centre to circumference. It does not consist in having, but in being. 2. Its fruits will always be apparent. Grace in the germ is hidden, but it is always manifest in the life. It is a light that shines, a fire that burns. How grace grows is a mystery; but when grown it is read and known of all men. Your life as to its source and supply is "hid with Christ in God"; but as to its practical effect, it is "a city set on a hill." III. ITS CAUSE. 1. The ultimate cause is God the Holy Ghost. Men may fashion a block of stone into the figure of a man, so admirably that the sculpture seems to look, and breathe, and speak; but it is not a man. It is merely an image; it wants life, which no created power can give. So it is here. Spiritual life in all its stages is a direct inspiration from God, and impossible without such inspiration. And He who gives life alone can sustain it. 2. The instrumental cause is truth. "Of His own will begat He us," &c. "Sanctify them through Thy truth." Sanctification is the effect not of the separate, but conjoint influence of the Holy Spirit in the heart, and the Word on the understanding, the one removing prejudice, the other dispersing ignorance. IV. SANCTIFICATION IS A PROGRESSIVE AND HARMONIOUS WORK. 1. Where there is life there will be progress—in vegetation, physically, mentally, and spiritually, and in each case gradually. 2. This is a progress that affects the whole manhood, a harmonious development of an entire Christian character. Just as in the healthful growth of a tree there is growth, not only of the roots but the shoots, branches, foliage, and fruit; so in the Christian the development is not of one grace, but of all. There is much diversity. Grace does not produce uniformity in the human character; but still the finest specimen of a Christian is the man in whom all graces are in their proportion. 3. Its beginning is here, but its progress for ever. Heaven begins on earth, and earth merges into heaven. V. SANCTIFICATION IS THE WILL OF GOD. Not simply the command, but the good pleasure of God. 1. It is necessarily so. He who is Light cannot love darkness; He who is Life cannot love death. 2. It is wrought in harmony with the nature of the human will. God works in what we have to work out. 3. What an encouragement is this! In all our struggles after goodness we may be sure of Divine sympathy and help. 4. With what solemnity does this invest the subject, for it follows that without holiness no man shall see the Lord. (*J. Davies.*)    Sanctification:—I.

ITS NATURE. 1. It is the invariable result of union with Christ (John xv. 5). He whom the Blood cleanses walks in the light. He who has a lively hope in Christ purifies himself, as He is pure (1 John i. 7 ; iii. 3). 2. It is the outcome and in-variable consequence of regeneration. The new creature lives a new life (1 John ii. 29 ; iii. 9–14 ; v. 4–18). 3. It is the only certain evidence of the indwelling of the Holy Spirit, which is essential to salvation (Rom. viii. 9). The Spirit never lies idle in the soul, but makes His presence known by His fruits (Gal. v. 22). It is nonsense to suppose that we have the Spirit if we do not walk in the Spirit (Gal. v. 25 ; Rom. viii. 14). 4. It is the only sure mark of God's election. There is much that is mysterious about this subject ; but nothing is plainer than that the elect are known by their holy lives (chap. i. 3). 5. It is a thing that will always be seen. It cannot be hid. 6. It is a thing for which every believer is responsible. Every man has power to lose his own soul ; but believers are under special obliga-tion to live holy lives. 7. It is a thing which admits of growth and progress. 8 It depends largely on a diligent use of Scriptural means—Bible reading, private prayer, attendance on public worship, regular communion. There are no spiritual gains without pains. 9. It does not prevent a man having a great deal of inward spiritual conflict (Gal. v. 17 ; Rom. vii.). 10. It cannot justify a man, but it pleases God (Rom. iii. 20–28 ; Heb. xiii. 16 ; Col. iii. 20 ; 1 John iii. 22.). Just as a parent is pleased with the efforts of his little child to please him, though it be only by picking a daisy, so our heavenly Father is pleased with the poor perform-ances of His believing children. But they must first be believing—*i.e.*, justified children ; for " without faith it is impossible to please God." 11. It will be found absolutely necessary as a witness to our character in the day of judgment. It will then be utterly useless to plead our faith if it has not been evidenced by our works. 12. It is necessary to train us for heaven. Then hope to get there ; but the only way is " the way of holiness." We must be saints before we die if we are to be saints in glory. When an eagle is happy in an iron cage, a fish happy on dry land, then will an unsanctified man be happy in heaven. II. ITS VISIBLE EVIDENCE. 1. It does not consist in—(1) Talk about religion (1 John iii. 18). (2) Temporary religious feelings (Matt. xiii. 20). (3) Outward formalism and external devoutness. (4) Retirement from our place in life (John xvii. 15). (5) The occasional perform-ance of right actions (Mark vi. 20). 2. It will show itself in—(1) Habitual respect to God's law, and the habitual effort to live in obedience to it as the rule of life (1 Tim. i. 8 ; Rom. vii. 22). (2) An habitual endeavour to do Christ's will (John xv. 14). (3) An habitual desire to live up to the standard which Paul sets before the Churches in the closing chapters of nearly all his Epistles. (4) Habitual atten-tion to the active graces which our Lord exemplified, and especially the grace of charity (John xiii. 34, 35 ; Coll. iii. 10). (5) Habitual attention to the passive graces of Christianity, which are especially shown in submission to God and forbear-ance towards man (1 Pet. ii. 21–23 ; Gal. v. 22, 23). III. THE RELATION OF SANCTIFICA-TION TO JUSTIFICATION. 1. In what are they alike ? (1) Both proceed originally from the free grace of God. (2) Both are part of the great work of salvation which Christ has undertaken on behalf of His people. (3) Both are found in the same persons. (4) Both begin at the same time. (5) Both are alike necessary to salvation. 2. In what they differ. (1) Justification is the reckoning a man to be righteous for the sake of Christ ; sanctification is making a man righteous. (2) The righteousness we have by our justification is not our own, but Christ's ; that which we have by sanctification is our own, imparted by the Holy Ghost. (3) In justification our works have no place at all, simple faith in Christ being the one thing needful ; in sanctification our works are of vast importance, and are commanded by God. (4) Justification admits of no growth ; sanctification is essentially progressive. (5) Justification has special reference to our persons ; sanctification to our natures. (6) Justification gives us our title ; sanctification our meetness for heaven. (7) Justification is the act of God about us ; sanctification the work of God within us. IV. APPLICATION. 1. Let us awake to a sense of the perilous state of many professing Christians (Heb. xii. 14). 2. Let us make sure work of our own condition. 3. We must begin with Christ. We must first live and then work. 4. We must con-tinually go on as we began (Eph. iv. 16). 5. Let us not expect too much from our hearts here below. The more light we have the more we shall see our own imper-fection. Absolute perfection is yet to come. 6. Let us never be ashamed of making much of sanctification. (*Bp. Ryle.*)    *Our sanctification :*—I. THE IN-TRINSIC EVIDENCE OF THE FACT THAT GOD DESIRES OUR SANCTIFICATION. 1. Sancti-fication is the restoration of that which was ruined by the apostasy. If it were only to bring things back to the primitive order which He pronounced to be very good, it is in God's view most desirable that man should be made holy. We do not wish to see a ship dismasted, a man lame, or a machine out of order. It delights us to see them restored to their natural state. So God delights in a restoration to the primitive moral order. 2. Sanctification is the complete reconciliation of man to God. As a lover of order, He must be pleased to see man reconciled to the perfect order He has established. Sin is a quarrel with God's arrangements. Sanctification is a return to perfect harmony with God and His government. 3. It is the restoration of perfect loveliness to man. God abhors sin partly because of its moral repulsiveness, and loves holiness because of its moral beauty. II. THE ACTIONS OF GOD IN REFERENCE TO MAN'S SANCTIFICATION. 1. We see more than desire; we see great earnestness in these. This earnestness comes to us in the form of authority. We are made for law, and are susceptible to the requirements of authority. See, then, the eternal God coming down to Sinai to make a law requiring men to be holy, and throwing around that law all the sanctions of Divine approbation and displeasure. To this mighty influence He adds the potent discipline of His Providence pruning us that we may be fruitful. Then, further, there is the mission of Christ, and the ministry of the Spirit. 2. With our minds full of these facts, let us see their practical consequences. (1) We should rejoice in afflictions. God, in chastening us, is aiming at our perfection. Christ was made perfect through suffering. (2) We should be earnest in the use of religious ordinances. These are the appointed means. " Sanctify them through Thy truth." And we should be confident of success in the right employment of them. (3) We should labour for each other's sanctification. As we are bound to pray, " Thy will be done," &c., so we are bound to desire that every human being may carry out that will by being holy. Conclusion : If God wills the sanctification of all men, then—1. The condition of the irreligious is fearful. 2. Every one who knows what the will of God is, is bound at once to seek after holiness. (*E. N. Kirk, D.D.*)

**Vers. 4-7. That every one of you should know how to possess his vessel in sanctification and honour.**—*The vessel of the body :*—1. At best a vessel is only a frail thing; let it be of gold or silver, time and use make flaws in it, and its day is soon past. 2. It is a vile thing, being the creature and mere instrument of the hands. 3. To be of any use it must have an owner, and it must be always just what its maker chooses, and must ever do what its employer sets it to do. It may be employed for other purposes, but it does nothing suitably but that for which it was first intended. The putting of it to other work is generally the surest way of destroying it, as when a glass vessel is put on the fire. I. OUR BODIES ARE VESSELS. They are frail enough—made of dust and returning to dust. They can do nothing of themselves ; if there be not soul and spirit to put them to use, they are as lifeless and unserviceable as any other, and are put out of the way as useless. II. BUT THEY ARE HONOURABLE AND PRECIOUS VESSELS. Made by the hand of God to contain the immortal soul, and with it the treasure of the knowledge of God. They were made to promote His honour and glory, and when put to any other service they are put out of shape, broken, and destroyed. III. THEY HAVE BEEN DEGRADED AND INJURED BY VILE USES. Does not the commonest experience tell us this ? Does not the employment of them in the service of the world, the flesh, and the devil deteriorate them ? Do not anxiety, intemperance, impurity, passion, vanity, ambition, derange them with all manner of diseases? IV. IN CHRIST JESUS, WHO TOOK OUR BODY ON HIM, THESE VESSELS HAVE BEEN RESTORED TO THEIR FORMER HEAVENLY SERVICE. Christ is the Saviour of the body as well as of the soul. The Holy Spirit has been given to sanctify the body and keep it holy. V. THESE VESSELS ARE CHARACTERIZED BY ENDLESS VARIETY, according to our different posts and gifts. VI. BEING REDEEMED AND CONSECRATED VESSELS, THE BODIES OF BELIEVERS MUST BE USED FOR GOD ALONE. This involves—1. Carefulness. 2. Purity. 3. Temperance. 4. Holy employment. (*R. W. Evans, B.D.*) *A call unto holiness :*—I. THE CONTRAST. 1. Holiness is eternal and Divine—the everlasting God is the holy God. 2. Man was created in the image of the holy God. 3. By the first transgression holiness was lost; the flesh became prone to all uncleanness, inward and outward. 4. Abounding uncleanness was in the world before the flood, in Gentile nations, and in Israel. 5. Uncleanness, public and private, shameless and hypocritical, is in this professedly Christian land. 6. The world winks at uncleanness, and even tries to justify it. Not so God (Eph. v. 6 ; 1 Thess.

iv. 7). II. The call. 1. To Israel and the Church (Lev. xx. 7 ; 1 Peter i. 14–16). 2. Holiness was taught by outward purifications under the law (Exod. xxviii. 36). 3. The reason for the call : God's purpose is to make His children like Himself, to renew their lost holiness (Eph. i. 4 ; iv. 22–24). III. The grace. 1. The God of holiness is the God of grace. 2. Grace to cleanse from uncleanness, by the atoning blood of Christ (1 Cor. v. 11 ; 1 John i. 7 ; Rev. i. 5). 3. Grace to sanctify, by the indwelling of the Holy Spirit, which inspires holy desires and affections. 4. Grace to strengthen, by the Holy Spirit enabling us to keep under the body and to crucify the flesh. IV. Warnings and exhortations. 1. The Word written uses great plainness of speech on this subject ; so should the Word preached. 2. The judgment recorded in Holy Scripture on the unclean. In one day God gave twenty-three thousand proofs of His hatred of uncleanness and resolve to punish it (1 Cor. x. 8). 3. To despise the call is to despise God, and to bring down His wrath here and hereafter. 4. Secret sinner, your sin will find you out. He who exposed David's sin will expose yours. 5. The effects of despising the call and doing what the Holy One hates are defiling, debasing, deadening, destroying. 6. Your body is the temple of God. Guard it for Him against all profanation. 7. Strive by prayer to be like Jesus—like Him in holiness now, that you may be like Him in glory hereafter. (*F. Cook, D.D.*) *Purity of life :*—Having dealt with purity of heart in the first clause of ver. 3, the apostle now proceeds to deal with its correlative and manifestation. I. Chastity. He writes to converts who but a short time before had been heathens. It was necessary to speak plainly and solemnly, for they had been accustomed to regard impurity almost as a thing indifferent. But the will of God, our sanctification, involves purity. Without it we cannot see God. God is light ; in Him is no darkness at all. There is something awful in the stainless purity of the starry heavens. As we gaze into them we seem almost overwhelmed with a sense of our own uncleanness. It is a parable of the infinite purity of God. In His sight the heavens are not clean. He is of purer eyes than to behold evil ; therefore only the pure in heart can see Him. That inner purity covers the whole spiritual life. It implies freedom from all the lower motives—all that is selfish, earthly, false, hypocritical ; it is that transparency of character which flows from the consciousness of the perpetual presence of God. But that inner purity involves outward. Religion is not morality, but it cannot exist without it. The religion which the Thessalonians abandoned admitted immorality. Their very gods were immoral. They were served by rites often leading to impurity. Hence the urgency of Paul's appeal. Amid the evil surroundings and depraved public opinion of a heathen town the converts were exposed to constant danger. II. Honour. The unclean life of the heathen cities was full of degradation. The Christian life is truly honourable. The Christian's body is a holy thing. It has been dedicated to God (1 Cor. vi. 13). The Christian must acquire a mastery over it in honour by yielding its " members as instruments of righteousness unto God." The Christian husband must give honour to his wife. Marriage must be honourable, for it is a parable of the mystical union between Christ and His Church. Those who honour holiness honour God, the fountain of holiness. III. The knowledge of God (ver. 5). The heathen knew not God. They might have known Him. He had manifested in creation His eternal power and Godhead. But they did not like to retain God in their knowledge (Rom. i. 19–25). Men framed a conception of God from their own corrupt nature, and that conception reacted powerfully on their character. The Thessalonian Christians had learned a holier knowledge, and therefore their knowledge must act upon their life. They *must* be pure. IV. Impurity is a sin against man. " Satan is transformed into an angel of light." Impure desires assume the form of love ; uncleanness usurps and degrades that sacred name. The sensualist ruins in body and soul those whom he professes to love. He cares not for the holiest ties. He sins against the sanctity of matrimony. He brings misery on families. The Lord who calls us in sanctification will punish with that awful vengeance which belongeth to Him all who, for their wicked pleasure, sin against their brethren. V. It is a sin against God (ver. 8). The indwelling of the Holy Ghost makes the sin of uncleanness one of exceeding awfulness. Of what punishment shall that man be thought worthy who does such despite against the Spirit of Grace. He cannot abide in an impure heart, but must depart, as He departed from Saul. Lessons : 1. Long after holiness, pray for it, struggle for it with the deepest yearnings and most earnest efforts. 2. Flee from the slightest touch of impurity—the thought, look, word. It is deadly poison, a loathsome serpent. 3. Remember the indwelling of the Holy

Ghost. "Keep thyself pure." (*B. C. Caffin, M.A.*) *How personal purity is to be maintained :*—The "vessel" is not a wife, but a man's own body. If it meant a wife, it might be said that every one would be bound to marry. The wife is, no doubt, called the "weaker vessel," the evident meaning of the comparison being that the husband is also "a vessel." I. How THE BODY IS TO BE USED. 1. Negatively. (1) It is not to be regarded as outside the pale of moral obligation, as antinomian perverters say, basing their error on "It is not I that do it, but sin that dwelleth in me"; "in me . . . dwelleth no good thing." (2) It is not to be injured or mutilated by asceticism after Romish example. The apostle condemns "the neglecting of the body" (Col. ii. 23). (3) It is not to be made an instrument of unrighteousness through sensuality—"not in passion of lust." Sensuality is quite inconsistent with the very idea of sanctification. 2. Positively. (1) The body is to be kept under control; the Christian "must know how to possess himself of his own vessel." He must "keep under the body"; he must make it a servant, not a master, and not allow its natural liberty to run into licentiousness. (2) He must treat it with all due "honour." (*a*) Because it is God's workmanship, "fearfully and wonderfully made." (*b*) Because it is "the temple of the Holy Ghost" (1 Cor. vi. 19). (*c*) Because it is an heir of the resurrection. (*d*) Because it is, and ought to be, like the believer himself, "a vessel unto honour," sanctified and meet for the Master's use, for the body has much to do in the economy of grace. II. DISSUASIVES AGAINST PERSONAL IMPURITY. 1. The knowledge of God received by the Christian ought to guard us against it. Paul here attributes Gentile impurity to ignorance of God (ver. 5). The world by wisdom knew not God, was alienated from the life of God, and thus sunk into moral disorder (Rom. i.). 2. The regard we ought to have for a brother's family honour (ver. 6). A breach upon family honour is a far worse offence than any breach upon property. The stain is indelibly deeper. 3. The Divine vengeance (ver. 6). If vengeance does not reach men in this world it will in the next, when they will have their portion in the lake that burneth with fire and brimstone. They shall not inherit the kingdom of God (1 Cor. vi. 9). 4. The nature of the Divine call (ver. 7). They had received a "holy calling," a "high calling," and although "called unto liberty," they were "created unto good works." They were "called to be saints," for God says, "Be ye holy, for I am holy." 5. The sin involves a despisal of God, who hath given us His Spirit that we may attain sanctification (ver. 8). God has ordered all our family relations, and any dishonour done to them involves a contempt of His authority. Conclusion: We have in this passage God—Father, Son, and Holy Spirit—interested in man's salvation and holiness. (*Prof. Croskery.*) *A caution against impurity :*—Fornication is a sin directly contrary to sanctification, or that holy walking the apostle so earnestly exhorts the Thessalonians to observe. I. THE CAUTION IS DEFINITELY EXPRESSED. "That ye should abstain from fornication;" by which words we are to understand all uncleanness soever, either in a married or unmarried state: to be sure adultery is here included, though fornication is specially mentioned. Other sorts of uncleanness are also forbidden, of which it is "a shame even to speak," though such evils are perpetrated by too many in secret. Alas for those who do such things! They are an abomination to their species! All that is contrary to chastity in heart, in speech, and in behaviour, is alike contrary to the command of Jehovah in the decalogue, and the holiness the gospel requireth. II. THE ARGUMENTS TO STRENGTHEN THE CAUTION. 1. This branch of sanctification in particular "is the will of God." Not only is it the will of God in general that we should be holy, because "He that called us is holy," and because we are chosen unto salvation through the sanctification of the Spirit; and not only doth God require holiness in the heart, but also purity in our bodies, and that we should "cleanse ourselves from all defilement of flesh and spirit." Wherever the body is, as it ought to be, devoted to God, and set apart for Him, it should be kept pure for His service; and as chastity is one branch of sanctification, so this is one thing Jehovah commands in His law, and what His grace effects in all true believers. 2. This will be greatly for our honour; for this is "knowing how to possess our vessel in sanctification and honour;" whereas the contrary will be a great dishonour—"And his reproach shall not be wiped away." The body is the vessel of the soul that dwells therein, so 1 Sam. xxi. 5; and that must be kept pure from defiling lusts. What can be more dishonourable than for a rational soul to be enslaved by bodily affections and brutal appetites? 3. To indulge the lusts of concupiscence is to live and act like heathens; "Even as the Gentiles which knew not God." The Gentiles, especially the Grecians, were commonly guilty of some sins of uncleanness which were not so evidently forbidden by the Light of Nature. But they did not know God, nor His mind and will, so well as Christians do. It is not so much to be wondered at, therefore, if the Gentiles indulge their fleshly desires; but Christians should not walk as unconverted heathens, "in lasciviousness, excess of wine, revellings, banquetings, and other like evil ways," because they that are in Christ "have crucified the flesh with its affections and lusts." (*R. Fergusson.*) *Licentiousness* was the besetting sin of the Roman world. Except by miracle it was impossible that the new converts could be at once and wholly freed from it. It lingered in the flesh when the spirit had cast it off. It had interwoven itself in the pagan religions, and was ever reappearing on the confines of the Church in the earliest heresies. Even within the Church it might assume the form of a mystic Christianity. The very ecstasy of conversion would often lead to a reaction. Nothing is more natural than that in a licentious city, like Corinth or Ephesus, those who were impressed by St. Paul's teaching should have gone their way and returned to their former life. In this case it would seldom happen that they apostatized into the ranks of the heathen'; the same impulse which led them to the gospel would lead them also to bridge the gulf which separated them from its purer morality. Many may have sinned and repented again and again, unable to stand themselves in the general corruption, yet unable to cast aside utterly the image of innocence and goodness which the apostle had set before them. There were those, again, who consciously sought to lead the double life, and imagined themselves to have found in licentiousness the true freedom of the gospel. The tone which the apostle adopts respecting sins of the flesh differs in many ways from the manner of speaking of them among modern moralists. He says nothing of the poison which they infuse into society, or the consequences to the individual himself. Neither does he appeal to public opinion as condemning, or dwell on the ruin they inflict on one half of the race. True and forcible as these aspects of such sins are, they are the result of modern reflection, not the first instincts of reason and conscience. They strengthen the moral principles of mankind, but are not of a kind to touch the individual soul. They are a good defence for the existing order of society, but they will not purify the nature of man or extinguish the flames of lust. Moral evils in the New Testament are always spoken of as spiritual. They corrupt the soul, defile the temple of the Holy Ghost, and cut men off from the body of Christ. Of morality, as distinct from religion, there is hardly a trace in the Epistles of St. Paul. What he seeks to penetrate is the inward nature of sin, not its outward effects. Even in its consequences in another state of being are but slightly touched upon, in comparison with that living death which itself is. It is not merely a vice or crime, or even an offence against the law of God, to be punished here and hereafter. It is more than this. It is what men feel within, not what they observe without them; not what shall be, but what is; a terrible consciousness, a mystery of iniquity, a communion with unseen powers of evil. All sin is spoken of in St. Paul's Epistles as rooted in human nature, and quickened by the consciousness of law; but especially is this the case with the sin which is more than any other the type of sin in general—fornication. It is, in a peculiar sense, the sin of the flesh, with which the very idea of the corruption of the flesh is closely connected, just as in ver. 3 the idea of holiness is regarded as almost equivalent to abstinence from it. It is a sin against a man's own body, distinguished from all other sins by its personal and individual nature. No other is at the same time so gross and insidious; no other partakes so much of the slavery of sin. As marriage is the type of the communion of Christ and His Church, as the body is the member of Christ, so the sin of fornication is a strange and mysterious communion with evil. But although such is the tone of the apostle, there is no violence to human nature in his commands respecting it. He knew how easily extremes meet, how hard it is for asceticism to make clean that which is within, how quickly it might itself pass into its opposite. Nothing can be more different from the spirit of early ecclesiastical history on this subject than the moderation of St. Paul. The remedy for sin is not celibacy, but marriage. Even second marriages are, for the prevention of sin, to be encouraged. Even the incestuous person at Corinth was to be forgiven on repentance. Above all other things, the apostle insisted on purity as the first note of the Christian character; and yet the very earnestness and frequency of his warnings show that he is speaking, not of a sin hardly named among saints, but one the victory over which was the greatest and most difficult triumph of the Cross of Christ. (*Prof. Jowett.*)     **Let no man go beyond and defraud his brother in any matter.**—*Commercial morality :*—I. BE RIGHTEOUS IN BUYING. Take heed less thou layest out thy money to purchase endless misery. Some have bought places to bury their bodies in, but more have bought those commodities which have swallowed up their souls. Injustice in buying is a canker which will eat up the most durable wares. An unjust chapman, like Phocion, payeth for that poison which kills him, buyeth his own bane. A true Christian in buying will use a conscience. Augustine relates a story of a mountebank, who, to gain spectators, promised, if they would come the next day, he would tell them what every one's heart desired. When they all flocked about him at the time appointed he said "This is the desire of every one of your hearts, to sell dear and buy cheap." But the good man desires to buy as dear as he sells. His buying and selling are like scales that hang in equal poise. 1. In buying do not take advantage of the seller's ignorance. This would be as bad as to lead the blind out of the way, and, as the text saith, those who overreach men are within the reach of a sin-revenging God. Some will boast of their going beyond others in bargains, but they have more cause to bewail it, unless they could go beyond the line of God's power and anger. Augustine tells us a certain man was offered a book by an unskilful stationer at a price not half the worth of it. He took the book, but gave him the just price, according to its full value. Wares that are half bought through out-witting a silly tradesman are half stolen (Prov. xx. 14; *cf* 1 Chron. xxi. 22-24). Ahab never bought a dearer purchase than Naboth's vineyard, for which he paid not a penny. 2. Do not work upon the seller's poverty. This is to grind the faces of the poor, and great oppression. It is no mean sin in many rich citizens who take advantage of the necessity of poor tradesmen. The poor man must sell or his family starve: the rich man knoweth it, and will not buy but at such a rate as that the other shall not earn his bread. God made the rich to relieve, not to rob the poor. Some tell us there is no wrong herein; for if poor men will not take their money they may let it alone: they do not force them. But is this to love thy neighbour as thyself? Put thyself in his place, and read Neh. v. 2-4, 12, 13. II. Be righteous in thy payments. 1. Pay what thou contractest for. If thou buyest with an intention not to pay thou stealiest, and such ill-gotten goods will melt like wax before the sun. Mark how honest Jacob was in this particular (Gen. xliii. 12). How many would have concealed the money, stopped the mouths of their consciences with the first payment, and kept it now as lawful prize. 2. Let thy payments be in good money. It is treason against the king to make bad money and it is treason against the King of kings to pass it. He that makes light payments may expect heavy judgments. III. Be righteous in selling. Be careful whilst thou sellest thy wares to men thou sellest not thy soul to Satan. 1. Be righteous in regard of quality. Put not bad ware for good into any man's hand. God can see the rottenness of thy stuffs, and heart too, under thy false glosses. Thou sayest "Let the buyer beware"; but God saith "Let the seller be careful that he keep a good conscience." To sell men what is full of flaws will make a greater flaw in thy conscience than thou art aware of. If thou partest with thy goods and thy honesty, though for a great sum, thou wilt be but a poor gainer. But is a man bound to reveal the faults of what he sells? Yes, or else to take no more for it but what it is worth. Put thyself in the buyer's place. 2. Be righteous in regard of quantity. Weight and measure are heaven's treasure (Prov. xi. 1; Lev. xix. 35, 36; Deut. xxv. 13-15). 3. Be righteous in thy manner of selling. The seller may not exact on a buyer's necessity but sell by the rule of equity. It is wicked by keeping in commodities to raise the market (Prov. xi. 26). Conclusion: In all thy contracts, purchases and sales cast an eye on the golden rule (Matt. vii. 12; 1 Cor. x. 24; Gal. v. 24). (*G. Swinnock, M.A.*) *Conscientiousness:*—The late Mr. Labouchere had made an agreement previous to his decease, with the Eastern Counties Railway for a passage through his estate near Chelmsford, for which the company were to pay £35,000. When the money had been paid and the passage made, the son of Mr. Labouchere, finding that the property was much less deteriorated than had been expected, voluntarily returned £15,000 to the company. (*Quarterly Review.*) *The curse of fraud:*—Perhaps you may once or twice in your life have passed a person whose countenance struck you with a painful amazement. It was the face of a man with features as of flesh and blood, but all hue of flesh and blood was gone, and the whole visage was overspread with a dull silver grey, and a mysterious metallic gloss. You felt wonder, you felt curiosity; but a deep impression of the unnatural made pain the strongest feeling of all which the spectacle excited. You found it was a poor man who, in disease, had taken mercury till it transferred itself through his skin, and glistened in his face. Now, go where he will, he exhibits the proof of his disorder and of the large quantity of metal he has consumed. If you had an eye to see the souls that are about you, many would see—alas! too many—who are just like that; they have swallowed doses of metal—ill-gotten, cankered, rusted metal—till all purity and beauty are destroyed. The metal is in them, throughout them, turning their complexion, attesting their disorder, rendering them shocking to look upon for all eyes that can see souls. If you have unjust gains they do not disfigure the countenance on which we short-sighted creatures look; but they do make your soul a pitiful sight to the great open Eye that does see. Of all poisons and plagues, the deadliest you can admit to your heart is gain which fraud has won. The curse of the Judge is in it; the curse of the Judge will never leave it. It is woe, and withering, and death to you; it will eat you up as fire; it will witness against you—ay, were that poor soul of yours, at this precise moment, to pass into the presence of its Judge, the proof of its money worship would be as clear on its visage as the proof that the man we have described had taken mercury is plain upon his. (*W. Arthur, M.A.*) *Refusing to defraud:*—A young man stood behind the counter in New York selling silks to a lady, and he said before the sale was consummated: " I see there is a flaw in that silk." She recognized it and the sale was not consummated. The head of the firm saw the interview and he wrote home to the father of the young man, living in the country, saying: " Dear sir, Come and take your boy; he will never make a merchant." The father came down from his country home in great consternation, as any father would, wondering what his boy had done. He came into the store and the merchant said to him : " Why your son pointed out a flaw in some silk the other day and spoiled the sale, and we will never have that lady, probably, again for a customer, and your son never will make a merchant." " Is that all ? " said the father. " I am proud of him. I wouldn't for the world have him another day under your influence. John, get your hat and come—let us start." There are hundreds of young men under the pressure, under the fascinations thrown around about commercial iniquity. Thousands of young men have gone down under the pressure, other thousands have maintained their integrity. (*T. De Witt Talmage.*) **God hath not called us unto uncleanness, but unto holiness.**—*The Divine call :—* I. To WHAT DOES GOD CALL? 1. Negatively: " Not unto uncleanness." (1) Of mind. Let this warn us against impure imaginations, conceptions, reflections which will make the memory one day a sink of infamy. (2) Of heart. Let us beware of impure loves, desires. (3) Of tongue. Away the obscene anecdote or illusion. (4) Of life. Eschew the licentious associate, the unchaste deed. 2. Positively: " Unto holiness." (1) Let your thoughts be holy and be set on good subjects, such as are worth treasuring and will cause no pain in recollection. (2) Let your feelings be pure. Cherish worthy objects, and aspire after noble ends. (3) Let your words be clean, such as dignify the instrument and edify the hearer. (4) Let your life be spent in the society of the good and in compassing righteous ends by righteous deeds. II. WHOM DOES GOD CALL? " Us." Everybody in general—you in particular. God calls—1. The young. It is impossible to exaggerate the importance of the early cultivation of habits of purity. The Holy Being says : " My son, give me thy heart." All will follow if this be done. If the spring be pure so will the stream be. 2. Women. Christian women are the salt of the earth without whose influence the world had perished in its corruption. And a false delicacy should not seal the lips of those whose duty it is to remind them of their responsibility in this particular. And she whose very presence is sufficient to abash the profligate should be very tenacious and careful of her social power. 3. Men. (1) Public men are called by God to give effect to the commandment which is " holy and just and good" in the national and provincial parliaments, to make virtue easy and vice difficult. (2) Private men are called by God to purify society by precept and example. III. How DOES GOD CALL? 1. By His Word which reflects His holy nature and reveals His holy laws. All its legislation, narrative, biography, poetry, prophecy, doctrine, are summed up in this: " Be ye holy." 2. By His works. They were made very good. In an elaborate argument (Rom. i. 20–32) the apostle shows that the natural order of things is holiness, and that men guilty of impurity sin against nature as well as God. 3. By the course of His government. History affirms the existence and administration of " a Power above us, not ourselves, that makes for righteousness." Egypt, Babylon, Greece, Rome, perished by their own corruptions—a judgment in each case no less real than that which overtook the cities of the plain. It would be difficult to find a nation that was overthrown until all that was worth preserving was dead. " Righteousness exalteth a nation," &c. 4. By His economy of redemption. The Cross of Christ and the mission of the Spirit are loud protests against uncleanness and calls to holiness. " Ye are bought with a price." " Your bodies are temples of the Holy Ghost." 5. By the witness of conscience which is an echo of the voice of God. IV. WHERE IS THE CALL TO BE OBEYED ? 1. At home. Let that be guarded against desecration as sacredly as a church. Watch with scrupulous care the course of conversation, and the literature upon the table. 2. In the state. 3. In society. 4. In trade. (*J. W. Burn.*) *Purity :*—Have you ever reflected upon all that is meant by these words ? St. Paul was speaking to those who had but lately been heathens, who were young in the faith, natives of a heathen city, encompassed about with all the sights and sounds, the customs and habits, the fulness of the Pagan life. And what that life was, what those sights and sounds were, I suppose scarcely one of us, certainly none who have not made a special study of those times and of those customs, can even conceive. And we must remember, that it was not only an open external thing, a plague-spot in society which people could shun with horror and be left uncontaminated. For the deadliness of this sin is its depths of corruption, the way in which it lays hold of everything, and the external act a sight a sound becomes an inward principle, leaving nothing free. In the midst of this world of impurity, Christianity raised the standard of absolute undoubting purity ; and that standard the Church has never lowered. Other sins it may, with some colour of truth, perhaps, be said she has not always repressed ; religion may have tended to produce hatred and malice; the Church may have wavered at times from the strict duty of veracity ; she may have become corrupted by the cares of this world and the deceitfulness of riches ; but one sin she has never touched, one sin has obtained no foothold in the Christian character, one sin has only lifted its head to be detected and denounced and defied, and that is the sin of lust and impurity. We forget what Christianity has done for us because it has done so much ; we forget how natural impurity seemed to the heathen world, how they honoured it, and even deified it ; and we forget too, or we have not yet become fully aware, how, with all our Christian experience and civilization, irreligion, and even perverted religion, tend to drag men back into that corruption, from which we are preserved by the protection of the Church's faith and discipline. And this protection is given us above all by the ideal which Christianity holds up to us, the ideal of purity in the Person of Christ. Nor was the purity of Christ the purity of an anchorite ; but of One whose work lay among men, and with men, and for men. He who was Purity itself, by His Divine humility condescended to men, not only of low estate, but of sinfulness, impurity, corruption. In this we may see in Him the model for us, whose lives are in the world, who also have to deal with sin, and who also can only be saved by the protecting power of an instinctive purity. But there is a yet further meaning in this active purity. "Unto the pure all things are pure," not only because he cannot be touched and corrupted by what is impure, but because he himself makes them pure. The true Christian saint has been able to go forth into the world of sin and shame, and by the mere unconscious force of his instinctive purity, turn the corrupted and the impure from powers of evil into living manifestations of Christ's grace. Nor is it only our fellow-men that we have power to cleanse by means of our own purity and innocence : even the impure things of which the world is full are often, when brought into contact with a stainless mind, turned into means, if not of edification, at least of harmless and innocent pleasure. Remember the noble words of one of the purest of poets (Milton) who reading, as he says, the "lofty fables and romances" of knighthood, saw there "in the oath of every knight, that he should defend to the expense of his best blood, or of his life if it so befell him, the honour and chastity of virgin or matron; from whence even then I learnt what a noble virtue chastity must be, to the defence of which so many worthies, by such a dear adventure of themselves, had sworn. . . . Only this my mind gave me, that every free and gentle spirit, without that oath, ought to be born a knight, nor needed to expect the gilt spur or the laying of a sword upon his shoulder, to stir him up both by his counsel and his arm to secure and protect the weakness of any attempted chastity. So that even those books, which to many others have been the fuel of wantonness and loose living, I cannot think how, unless by Divine indulgence, proved to me so many incitements to the love and steadfast observation of virtue." Such is the reflection of the ideal purity which Christ has shown us, the ideal which we have to aim at. Not a selfish isolated habit of mind, a bare freedom from corrupt thoughts and foul deeds, which is only preserved by careful separation from the things of the world, but an energising spiritual motive, an impetuous, undoubting living principle of action, which can go with us into the sin-stained world, and by the strength of its own innocence, by the glad assumption of the purity of others can make even the sinner a holy penitent.   Every life should be a priestly life.   Whatever may be your profession, you will be brought into contact with the sins of impurity, and unless you will share in them or at least condone, you must by your personal example fight against them.   (*A. T. Lyttelton, M.A.*)     *Called to holiness:*—Remark the force of the apostle's expression, we are "called to holiness" : in modern language we should express the same idea by saying, that holiness was our profession.   It is thus we say that divinity is the profession of a clergyman, that medicine is the profession of a physician, and that arms are the profession of a soldier ; and it is readily understood and allowed, that whatever is a man's profession, to that he is bound to devote his time and attention, and in that it is expected he has made a proficiency.   And precisely in this sense does the Scripture represent holiness to be the profession of a Christian ; not merely that his profession is a holy profession, but that the very object and essence of the profession is holiness.   To this Christians are called, this is their business, this they are to cultivate continually, this is the mark to which all their endeavours should be directed.   (*Jones' Bampton Lectures.*)     *Desire for holiness:*—A group of little children were talking together.   Presently this question was started : " What is the thing you wish for most ? "   Some said one thing and some said another.   At last it came to the turn of a little boy, ten years old, to speak.   This was his answer : " I wish to live without sinning."   What an excellent answer that was !   King Solomon, in all his glory and with all his wisdom, could not have given a better.     *A holy atmosphere:*—The spider is said to weave about him a web which is invisible, yet strong, through which the water or air cannot pass.   This is filled with air, and surrounded and sustained by this tiny bubble, he descends beneath the surface of the water and lives where another creature would speedily perish.   So it is in the power of the Christian to surround himself with a holy atmosphere, and thus nourished, to live unharmed amid a world that is full of sin.   (*Dr. Williams.*)     *The importance of purity:*—By the ancients courage was regarded as practically the main part of virtue : by us, though I hope we are none the less brave, purity is so regarded now.   The former is evidently an animal excellence, a thing not to be left out when we are balancing the one against the other.   Still the following considerations weigh more with me.   Courage, when not an instinct, is the creation of society, depending for occasions of action on outward circumstances, and deriving much both of its character and motives from popular opinion and esteem.   But purity is inward, secret, self-suffering, harmless, and, to crown all, thoroughly and intimately personal.   It is, indeed, a nature rather than a virtue ; and, like other natures, when most perfect is least conscious of itself and its perfection.   In a word, courage, however kindled, is fanned by the breath of man ; purity lives and derives its life from the Spirit of God.   (*Guesses at Truth.*) *Holiness* is not abstinence from outward deeds of profligacy alone ; it is not a mere recoil from impurity in thought.   It is that quick and sensitive delicacy to which even the very conception of evil is offensive ; it is a virtue which has its residence within, which takes guardianship of the heart, as of a citadel or inviolated sanctuary, in which no wrong or worthless imagination is permitted to dwell.   It is not purity of action that we contend for : it is the exalted purity of the heart, the ethereal purity of the third heaven ; and if it is at once settled in the heart, it brings the peace, the triumph, and the untroubled serenity of heaven along with it ; I had almost said, the pride of a great moral victory over the infirmities of an earthly and accursed nature.   There is health and harmony in the soul ; a beauty, which, though it effloresces in the countenance and outward path, is itself so thoroughly internal as to make purity of heart the most distinctive evidence of a character that is ripening and expanding for the glories of eternity.   (*T. Chalmers, D.D.*)

**Ver. 8.   He therefore that despiseth, despiseth not man but God.**—*The sin of despising God :*—The things set at nought are not specified, because the apostle wanted to draw our particular attention to Him whom in them we despise. It is, however, easy to see that they are all religious duties, moral laws and precepts, the observance of which makes up the sum total of a religious life.   1. Instinctively our thoughts turn first to that low value which many persons entertain of life.   They live to waste, or, as they say, using an almost criminal expression, to " kill" time : they occupy themselves with worthless books or newspapers, and regard reading solely as the diversion of the hour; they take up some work which is good in itself, but having no perseverance, fling it aside unfinished the moment they are weary of it; they spend their days in one long course of pleasure, harmless or harmful they care not which, and at the end ask themselves the question, "Is life worth living?" They are earnest, if earnest at all, only about the things of time and sense, and treat all matters merely as pastimes, means by which serious thoughts of death and eternity may be diverted. 2. There is another more open, yet possibly not more perilous way of despising than the above. There are those who from their youth, if not from their childhood, have been steeped in the sins of the flesh, who not only commit such things, "but have pleasure in those that do them;" forgetful, it may be, of the apostle's words, that "the unrighteous shall not inherit the Kingdom of God." 3. Then there are those who are living in unbelief—open scoffers of things Divine—men who do not want to believe in a Lawgiver, because, if they did, they would feel obliged to keep His laws; men who ridicule religion in order to deny its claim on their lives; who think, or pretend to think, that religion is not true, because in their case the wish is father to the thought. To them this question should be brought home. Be honest with yourselves and say, what if, after all, the God whom you affect to deny be the Lord of the universe, the Sovereign to whom you owe allegiance? what if you find at the last that you have had light enough, and you are forced to admit then that you have had no excuse for your obstinate unbelief? How will it be with you then, when you shall see eye to eye, and the truth, no longer hidden beneath the veil of your own weaving, shall stare you in the face in all its tremendous reality? To refuse to see and hear Him is to despise Him to whom nature pays her willing homage; for when the voice of man is dumb, "the heavens declare the glory of God, and the firmament sheweth His handywork." (*C. W. H. Kenrick, M.A.*) *A word to the despiser:*—Notice: I. THAT THE CHRISTIAN MINISTER IS SPIRITUALLY COMMISSIONED TO EXHORT MEN TO HOLINESS. "Who hath also given unto us His Holy Spirit." The apostles were endowed for their special ministry by the extraordinary gifts of the Holy Ghost. Though miraculous gifts are no longer bestowed, Christian ministers are nevertheless called and qualified by the Divine Spirit (2 Cor. v. 20). II. THAT THE MOST FAITHFUL EXHORTATIONS OF THE CHRISTIAN MINISTER MAY BE DESPISED. This is done when men reject the word spoken, refuse to listen to it, neglect to meditate upon it, and decline to enter upon the course of holy living with its counsels. This conduct shows—1. The voluntary power of man. He can resist the truth, or accept it. He is responsible for the exercise of all his moral powers; and, therefore, incurs guilt by any abuse of those powers. 2. The blinding folly of sin. It darkens the understanding, perverts the will, petrifies the affections, and banishes the good that elevates and saves. To wilfully reject the overtures of righteousness is to relinquish eternal life, and to doom the soul to spiritual death. III. THAT TO DESPISE THE FAITHFUL EXHORTATIONS OF THE CHRISTIAN MINISTER IS TO DESPISE GOD. "He therefore that despiseth, despiseth not man but God." The contempt of the true minister does not terminate in his person but reaches the majesty of that Being by whom he is commissioned. To disregard the message of an ambassador is to despise the monarch he represents (Luke x. 16). As the edicts proclaimed by the public herald are not his own, but the Prince who gives them authority and force; so the commands published by the divinely-commissioned minister are not his own, but belong to Him whose will is the law of the universe. It belongs to God to reveal the law, it belongs to man to declare it. The exhortation, whether uttered by a Moses, or by a Simeon Niger, is equally the word of God, to which the most reverential obedience is due. To despise the meanest of God's ministers, is an insult to the majesty of heaven, and will incur His terrible displeasure. Lessons: 1. The Divine commands concern man's highest good. 2. Take heed how ye hear. 3. To despise the Divine message is to be self-consigned to endless woe. (*G. Barlow.*) *The causes which induce a despising of Divine revelation:*—I. The rejection of Christianity CANNOT ARISE FROM A SUPERIOR INTELLECT on the part of infidels. Infidelity is not an intellectual state. But if great names are cited as giving sanction to unbelief, we can quote greater names as allies of faith. II. Nor can it be traced TO THEIR SUPERIOR KNOWLEDGE. The same sources of learning are open to believer and sceptic, and it has yet to be shown that the former have been less assiduous in drawing from them than the latter. On the contrary, the infidel must be charged with ignorance of—1. The language of Holy Writ. 2. Philosophy. 3. Historical facts and monuments. III. Nor to THEIR SUPERIOR MORALITY. 1. Can the despisers point to superior moral examples? It is well known that many fall off to infidelity through immorality. 2. Can they produce a superior system? The world does not contain the equal of Christianity. 3. Can they present superior motives? Anti-Christian morality, whatever may be its achievements, and these are small indeed, is ever based upon the motive that is either weak or low. (*T. Archer, D.D.*) *The cause of despising:*—As they who are displeased with all things that profit them not; or as a blind man, who, groping by the walls of a fair house, doth find fault with the windows because they are not so smooth as the walls; even so, such are they that find fault with the Scriptures because they show the spots as well as the beauty, the vice as well as the virtue. (*W. Cawdray.*) *The impotence and folly of despising the truth:*—Rest thee well assured, O scorner! that thy laughs cannot alter the truth, thy jests cannot avert thine inevitable doom. Though in thy hardihood thou shouldst make a league with death, and sign a covenant with hell, yet swift justice shall overtake thee, and strong vengeance strike thee low. In vain dost thou jeer and mock, for eternal verities are mightier than thy sophistries; nor can thy smart sayings alter the Divine truth of a single word of the volume of Revelation. Oh, why dost thou quarrel with thy best friends and ill-treat thy only refuge? There yet remains hope even for the scorner—hope in a Saviour's blood, in the Father's mercy, in the Holy Spirit's omnipotent agency. (*C. H. Spurgeon.*) *The sinfulness of the despiser:*—Here is a man who says to his poor wife who is a Christian, who, because she sometimes has a slip in temper or does now and then what he does not approve, "Ah, that is your Christianity, is it? Well, if that be your church and chapel going, I will have none of it." Beast, fiend! There are such creatures to be found. They are to be found amongst men and amongst women. Oh, the unkindness, the cruelty, the heart-slaughter! It were nothing to kill a man—stab him right through the heart and let him die. But when he is struggling towards light, towards God, and has to fight with all these demoniacal passions and influences round about, over which he seems to have little or no control, when he just stumbles on the road and they point at him and say, "Ha, ha, that is your Christianity, is it?" that is thrice dying, that is intolerable pain! We know we are inconsistent, we know we are selfish, we cannot boast of ourselves. (*J. Parker, D.D.*)

Ver. 9-11. **As touching brotherly love ye need not that I write unto you.**— *Brotherly love Divinely taught:*—The love of the brethren is the test of our Christianity, and the badge of our Christian profession. It is even the essential of "the new man," and is Divinely taught by the fount of love. Without it, all religious profession is mere glitter, an empty show, a noisy cymbal. But what is this love? Let us examine and see. I. Its NATURE. It is admiration, estimation, and perfect complacency in the Lord's people. It recognizes them all as brethren in Christ, and fellow-heirs of the grace of life. It includes attachment, fellowship, communion, spiritual adhesion, and unselfish conduct and conversation. II. Its EXTENSIVENESS. It is not sectarian, denominational, local. It is not to be limited to persons of our order, creed, or mode of worship; but it embraces every true saint of the Most High God, every disciple and follower of the Lord Jesus, every real Christian adorning the doctrine of God in all things and walking in the ways of holiness and eternal life. III. Its SPECIAL TRAITS. 1. It is the love of the heart; therefore not tinsel and make-believe. 2. It is the love of a pure heart. Not the love of the person with fleshly attachment, but love transparent as the light, and purifying as the flame. 3. It is the love that is both fervent and lasting. It knows nothing of coldness, formality, pretentiousness. Its utterances are immediate and emphatic; and its altar-fire is ever clear and intense. Many waters cannot quench it. It will not be extinguished, nor will it expire, but burn and shine in loving words and loving deeds, always to the honour of religion, and the glory of God. (*J. Burns, D.D.*) *The great duties of the Christian life:*—I. THE MANIFESTATION OF BROTHERLY LOVE. This the apostle exhorts the Thessalonians to increase in yet more and more. The exhortation is introduced not with a compliment, but with a commendation, because they were remarkable in their exercise of brotherly love, which made it less needful he should write to them about it (ver. 9). Thus by his good opinion of them he insinuated himself into their affections, and so made way for his exhortation to them. We should follow his wise example; for it is well to take notice of that in others' conduct and spirit which redounds to their praise, that by so doing we may lay engagements upon them to abound therein while life itself shall last. I. Observe WHAT THE APOSTLE COMMENDETH in the

Thessalonians. It was not so much their own virtue as God's grace, yet he taketh notice of the evidence they showed of this grace in them. God Himself had taught them this good lesson; and whosoever do that which is excellent are instructed of God to do it, and hence God must have the glory of it. All that are savingly taught of God are taught to love one another. This is the livery of Christ's disciples and followers. Note also, that the teaching of the Spirit of God exceeds the teachings of men; and as no man should teach contrary to what God teacheth, so none can teach so effectually as He teacheth, and men's teaching is vain and useless unless God teach also. Nor is this all: those are easily taught whom God doth teach; and therefore, though eminent abilities are much to be wished for in ministers, yet we ought not to be so anxious about the feebleness or eminency of gifts in them, as fervently desirous to have God's teaching to come along with theirs; for Paul shows that God, by His teaching these Thessalonians, had made them stand less in need of being taught by him. So well indeed, had they been taught by their Divine Master that they not only loved the brethren of their own city and society, or such as were near them and just of their own sentiments, but "the brethren of all Macedonia." Such is genuine brotherly love: it embraces "all who love our Lord Jesus Christ in sincerity and truth." 2. But, like all other excellences, brotherly love is capable of increasement. Accordingly, their apostolic teacher exhorted the Thessalonians to pray for more and labour for more. There are none on this side heaven who love in perfection. All, therefore, who are distinguished in this or any other grace have every need of increase therein, and perseverance unto the end. II. THE MEET ACCOMPANIMENTS OF BROTHERLY LOVE. 1. Tranquillity of spirit. This passive virtue is to be studied (ver. 11). It is indeed a most desirable thing to have a temper calm and quiet as a lake unruffled by a zephyr, and to be of a peaceable behaviour to all men, especially to those of the household of faith. All this tends to our own as well as to others' happiness. We should be ambitious to possess our own souls in patience, to be meek and gentle, not given to strife or division. Satan is very busy to disquiet our minds, and we have that in our own hearts that disposeth us to be unquiet; therefore we, too, must "study to be quiet." 2. Diligence in business. And if this duty is rightly attended to, there will be little disquietude of spirit. Those who are busy-bodies, meddling in other men's matters, cannot have placid minds. They are restless like the sea, and do all they can to make their neighbours like themselves. If they were diligent in their own calling, they would neither have time nor inclination for intermeddling. 3. Creditable deportment. Those "that are without" are the unregenerate and unsaved, and when those who are professors of Christianity "walk honestly toward them," they adorn the doctrine of God their Saviour and commend the religion to others which they have embraced themselves. 4. Comfortable living. Such Christians "have lack of nothing." Others by their slothfulness or intermeddling frequently bring themselves into narrow circumstances, and reduce themselves to great straits. Not so the saints: they are burdensome to no friends. They labour with their own hands, and have bread enough and to spare. (*R. Fergusson.*) *Brotherly love the proof of a true sanctification:*—In the second century Lucian declared: "It is incredible to see the ardour with which the people of that religion help each other in their wants. They spare nothing. Their first legislator has put it into their heads that they are all brethren." The mutual exercise of love towards the brethren is an indisputable evidence of spiritual regeneration (1 John iii. 14); and in this chapter the apostle evidently alludes to it as the proof of a true sanctification. Observe—I. THAT BROTHERLY LOVE IS DIVINELY TAUGHT (ver. 9). 1. It is commanded by Christ (John xv. 17). This is a lesson the world never taught, and cannot teach. The natural heart is selfish and cruel, and delights in aggression and retaliation. Brotherly love is a fruit of Christianity, and is a powerful influence in harmonising the warring interests of humanity. If love prevail, other graces will not be absent. 2. It has the example of Christ. He reminds His disciples of what should be its scope and character. "As I have loved you." The same glorious example was also the constant burden of the apostle's teaching (John xiii. 34; xv. 12; Eph. v. 2). Brotherly love should be pure, humble, self-denying, fervent, unchangeable. 3. It is its own commendation. " Ye need not that I write unto you." Love is modest, ingenuous, and unobtrusive. We should not hesitate to commend whatever good we see in others. The Great Searcher of hearts does not pass over any good thing in a Church, though otherwise clouded with infirmities (Rev. ii. 2, 3). A word of prudent commendation will often stimulate the soul in its endeavours after holiness. 4. It is a grace Divinely wrought. "Ye yourselves are taught of God." The heart is inclined to this grace by the Holy Spirit, in conjunction with the outward ministry of the Word (Jer. xxxi. 33; Acts xvi. 14). Those are easily taught whom God teaches. II. THAT BROTHERLY LOVE MUST BE PRACTICALLY MANIFESTED (ver. 10). Love is not limited by locality or distance; it is displayed, not only towards those with whom we have communion, but towards others. Missions are a monument of modern Christian charity. Love should be practically manifested in supplying each other's need, in bearing one another's burdens, in forgiving one another, and, if necessary, in kindly reproving one another. III. THAT BROTHERLY LOVE IS SUSCEPTIBLE OF CONTINUOUS ENLARGEMENT. "Increase more and more." Notwithstanding the commendation of the apostle, he exhorts the Thessalonians to seek greater perfection. What is the sun without light? What is fire without heat? So what is life without love? The rich seek to increase their store, the wicked add to their iniquities; the saint should not be less diligent in increasing unto every good word and work. The growth of charity is extensive, and it adds to the number of the objects loved, and intensive as to its inward fervour and tenacity. The more we apprehend the love of God the more our hearts will enlarge in love. True brotherly love crushes all self-love, and is more anxious to hide than pry into the infirmities of others. Seldom is a charitable man curious, or a curious man charitable. Lessons: 1. That brotherly love is the practical manifestation of the love of God in man. 2. That brotherly love should be constantly cultivated. 3. That brotherly love is a crowning feature of the higher Christian life. (*G. Barlow.*) *Brotherly love :*—I. THE LESSON "brotherly love." This operates in a way of— 1. Esteem and affection. God esteems the saints highly, as "fine gold," His "portion," "inheritance," "jewels," "very precious and honourable." And so those who are born from above, as they love Him who begat, so they love the begotten. 2. Intercourse. If they are to be our associates in heaven we ought to know them on earth. Man was made for society, and grace sanctifies social dispositions. Thus as soon as Peter and John were let go, they went to their own company. "They that feared the Lord spake often one to another." When several Christians meet, they are like so many drops of water on the table: where they touch they run into one. This adjusts to some extent the inequalities of life, for the poor may be rich in faith, and qualified to teach the rich in goods. The intercourse of Christians encourages as Paul found at Appii forum. 3. Sympathy. "Rejoice with them that do rejoice," &c. Be like-minded with Him who is touched with a feeling of our infirmities. 4. Instruction. "That it may minister grace to the hearers." So much depends on a wrong course or a wrong step in a right one. 5. Reproof. Here is the trial of brotherly love. The way in which it is generally received makes it heroic to administer it. "Thou shalt not hate thy brother," says Moses, "but rebuke him." "Faithful are the wounds of a friend." "Let the righteous . . . reprove me, it shall be excellent oil." 6. Succour and relief. "Whoso hath this world's goods," &c. "Let us love not in word or in tongue, but in deed, and in truth." 7. Prayer. II. THE TEACHER—"God." He taught the Thessalonians, and He teaches us—1. By our constitution. The senses are inlets to the mind, and so we are affected by things without—the eye, *e.g.*, by the sight of distress. How many endeavour to elude occasions of this excitement as the priest and Levite. 2. By injunction. "The end of the commandment is charity," &c. "This is His commandment that we believe on the name of His Son, and love one another," &c. 3. By example. (1) Of those who live in our own neighbourhood. Kind, good men are to be found everywhere. (2) Of those who have gone before us. Apostles, martyrs, &c. (3) Of angels who are ministering spirits, &c. (4) Above all, of Christ. "If God so loved us, we ought to love one another." 4. By His Spirit. He can give not only the lesson, but the capacity. III. THE TRACTABLENESS OF THE PUPILS. "Ye need not that I write." 1. What a satisfaction it is to a minister to be able to appeal to his people for illustrations and proofs of his teaching, and what an advantage to the people not only to hear, but to see. And so our Saviour said, "Let your light so shine," &c. Such advantage and satisfaction had St. Paul. 2. Paul did not flatter them. All he admired in them was ascribed to the grace of God. Their love was as extensive as it was real. 3. We must learn to love all real Christians notwithstanding their failings. "If a man be overtaken in a fault," &c. Nor should our love be determined by a man's religious opinions, "Whosoever doeth the will of My Father, the same is My brother," &c. IV. THE PROFICIENCY THE APOSTLE WOULD HAVE THEM ATTAIN TO. "More and more." 1. Too much cannot be said in commendation or enforcement of it. 2. The Divine life is progressive, and admits of degrees. 3. Christians should never rest in present attainments. (*W. Jay.*) *The nature of brotherly love :*—When as a Christian Church, we cultivate a spirit of mutual trustfulness; when each esteems the other better than himself; when the strong delight to recover and support the weak; when the wise are patient and gentle towards those of fewer attainments; when we are careful of each other's reputation, and gentle to one another's infirmities; when we are pitiful, long suffering, condescending, unsuspicious, and self-sacrificing, then will men remember that it is written, "A new commandment I give unto you," &c. (*J. Parker, D.D.*) *Brotherly love, the sham and the real :*—When I was but a youth, the smallest boy almost that ever joined a Church, I thought that everybody believed what he said, and when I heard the minister say "brother," I thought I must really be his brother, for I was admitted into the Church. I once sat near a gentleman at the Lord's supper, and we received the bread and wine together; he thus practically called me " brother," and as I thought he meant it, I afterwards acted upon it. I had no friend in the town of Cambridge, where I was; and one day when walking out, I saw this same gentleman, and I said to myself, "Well now, he called me brother; I know he is a great deal better off than I am, but I don't care for that; I will go and speak to him." So I went and said, "How do you do, brother?" "I have not the pleasure of knowing you," was his reply. I said, "I saw you at the Lord's table last Sabbath day, sir, and we are therefore brethren." "There now," said he, "it is worth while seeing some one who acts with sincerity in these times; come in with me." And we have been the nearest and dearest bosom friends ever since, just because he saw I took him at his word, and believed that he meant what he said. But now-a-days profession has become a pretence and a sham; people sit down in the church together, as though they were brethren, the minister calls you brother, but he will not speak to you, or own you as such; his people are his brethren, no doubt, but then it is in such a mysterious sense, that you will have to read some German theologian in order to comprehend it. That person is " your very dear brother," or " your very dear sister," but if you are in distress, go to them and see if they will assist you. I do not believe in such a religion as this. (*C. H. Spurgeon.*) *Brotherly love the test of religion :*—The apostle says, " We know that we have passed from death unto life." Pause a moment, then, and let us try to find out the reason. Because we feel very comfortable in our hearts, because we like to sit very closely to the fire and read a favourite author, because we have occasional gushings of very tender feeling, is that how we know we have passed from death unto life? The apostle says, No. His argument is this:—We *know*—the same word that I have in the text, Jesus *knowing*—that we have passed from death unto life *because we love the brethren*. Alas, sirs! there is this danger about our religious life to-day : we think, when we get hold of a favourite book, and repeat certain familiar hymns, and look upon ourselves in relation to the social blessings with which God has gifted us, that we are doing everything that is needful to show our relationship, to prove our redemption by Christ. (*J. Parker, D.D.*) *The means of creating and promoting brotherly love :*—As the spokes of a carriage wheel approach their centre they approach each other, so also when men are brought to Christ, the centre of life and hope, they are drawn towards each other in brotherly relationship, and stand side by side journeying to their heavenly home. (*J. T. Serjeant.*) *The unifying power of brotherly love :*—We have here suggested to us the strong bond of union existing in the early Church between Christian communities which were yet geographically apart from one another. As having the same dangers to encounter, the same battle to fight, the same Captain to lead, and the same victory to win, they are seen taking an earnest and active interest in each other's welfare. As the ancient Greek colonists practised the rite of cherishing on the altars of their public halls the perpetual fire that had first been kindled at the parent hearth of home—the mother city of Athens; so we may say was it with these scattered sections of the early Church. Separate though they were, they yet felt that they were one in sympathy and interest. The triple flame of faith, hope, and love burned more or less brightly in them all. Thus they claimed the same origin, held the same truth, and sought the same ends. No religion but that of Christ could have produced such a commonwealth. (*J. Hutchinson, D.D.*) *Instances of brotherly love :*—During the retreat of Alfred the Great, at Athelney, in Somersetshire, after the defeat of his forces by the Danes, a beggar came to his little castle there, and requested alms. When his queen informed him they had only one small loaf remaining, which was insufficient for themselves and the friends who had gone abroad in request of food with little hope of success, the king replied, "Give the poor Christian one half of the loaf. He who could feed five thousand men with five loaves and two small fishes, can certainly make that half of the loaf suffice for more than our necessities." Accordingly, the poor man was relieved, and this noble act of charity was soon recompensed by a providential store of fresh provisions with which the foraging party returned. (*G. Barlow.*)  *Continuance in brotherly love:*—A gentleman of Marseilles, named Removsat, shortly before his death, desired that his numerous family might be assembled about his bed. He acknowledged the delight which his children had afforded him by their affection and attachment, and especially for the tender love which they bore to one another. "But," continued he, "I have a secret to disclose, which will remove one of you from this circle. So long as I had any hopes of living I kept it from you, but I dare not violate your rights in the division of the property which I leave you. One of you is only an adopted child— the child of the nurse at whose breast my own child died. Shall I name that child?" "No, no," said they with one accord; "let us all continue to be brothers and sisters." (*W. Baxendale.*)  *Practical brotherly love:*—Thomas Samson was a working miner, and working hard for his bread. The captain of the mine said to him, "Thomas, I've an easier berth for you where there is less to do and more to earn: will you accept it?" "Captain," said Thomas, "there's our poor brother Tregony. He has a sick body, and is not able to work so hard as I am. I fear his hard work will shorten his useful life. Will you let him have the berth?" The captain, pleased with the generosity, sent for Tregony, and gave him the berth, which he is now enjoying. Thomas was gratified, and added, "I can work a little longer yet." (*Sunday Magazine.*)  *Love one another:*—A little girl of three or four years old learned the Bible text, "Love one another." What does "love one another mean?" asked her next older sister, in honest doubt as to the meaning. "Why, I must love you, and you must love me; and I'm one, and you're another," was the answer. Who can improve on that exegesis? (*S. S. Times.*)  *Love in practice:*—The longer I live, the more I feel the importance of adhering to the rules I have laid down for myself in relation to the following subjects:—1. To hear as little as possible of what is to the prejudice of others. 2. To believe nothing of the kind till I am absolutely forced to it. 3. Always to moderate, as far as I can, the unkindness which is expressed towards others. 4. Never to drink in the spirit of one who circulates an ill report. 5. Always to believe that, if the other side were heard, a very different account would be given of the matter. I consider love as wealth; and as I should resist a man who came to rob my house, so would I resist a man who would weaken my regard for any human being. I consider, too, that persons are cast in different moulds, and that to ask myself what I should do in that person's situation, is not a just mode of judging. I must not expect a man who is naturally cold and reserved to act as one who is naturally warm and affec- tionate; and I think it a great evil that people do not make more allowance for each other in this particular. (*C. Simeon.*)  **That ye increase more and more.**—*Moral increase:*—I. WHAT IS THIS INCREASE? The law of growth stamped upon nature, and the human soul by the Creator. Nothing is stationary. Increase may be, and in most cases is imperceptible in its processes, but it is real. II. IN WHAT ARE WE TO INCREASE? In all the graces of the Spirit; in faith, knowledge, love, prayer, &c., and in all active duties. These particulars will vary in different men: some want growth in one grace, some in another. III. HOW ARE WE TO INCREASE? 1. By beginning to do what we have never done before. Pray. Keep holy the Sabbath, &c. 2. By doing more than we have done before: more frequently repeating acts of service, increasing the measure and number of them. 3. By doing what we have been wont to do in a better spirit, improving in the tone and temper with which we serve God. Increasing in fervour, life and love. IV. THE ADVANTAGES OF INCREASE. 1. It will bring us nearer to God. 2. It will secure more of God's blessing. 3. It will make heaven more secure. (*J. Armstrong, D.D.*)  *The Christian's growth:*—1. This world has been compared to a pyramid. Beginning with the mineral, passing upward into the vegetable, and rising into the animal kingdom, we find a man standing on its apex—the crowning work of God. In defining these kingdoms, Linnæus makes growth common to all; but, properly speaking, growth is a property that belongs only to life, and all living things, "increase more and more." 2. This is as true of spiritual as of natural life. According to the fable, Minerva sprung full grown and armed from the head of Jupiter. No man thus comes suddenly in perfect saintship from the hand of the

Holy Spirit. I. In what are we to increase. 1. There is a little or no advantage in the increase of some things. It but increases our danger and burdens and cares. (1) More riches will not make us happier, and with the augmented expenditure they entail, do not always make us richer. (2) Nor is the increase, even of wisdom, without its drawbacks. It is harder to work with the brain than with the hands, and knowledge is increased at the expense often of health, and with increase of "sorrow." 2. It is not the increase of these things that the text calls us to aim, but of such riches as makes it less difficult to get to heaven, of the wisdom that humbles rather than puffs up its possessor, of "love, joy, peace," &c., a tender conscience, a holier walk. II. How are we to increase? 1. Equally. (1) All our graces are to be cultivated to the neglect of none. If one side of a tree grows and the other does not, it is a misshapen thing. Nor are monsters among mankind made only by want of parts, but also by some one part growing in excess. Analogous to this is the unequal growth of Christian graces. Let godly fear, *e.g.*, grow out of due proportion to faith, and the result is despondency ; let zeal grow more than wisdom, and like a machine without director or balance wheel, generating steam faster than it can use it, zeal bursts into extravagance and fanaticism. (2) There are differences of character, which, springing from constitutional peculiarities or early education, grace will modify but never eradicate. There are also differences which imply no defect, just as there are countenances which are unlike yet all beautiful. The Church, like the meadows below and the heavens above, owes its beauty in part to that variety in unity which marks all the works of God and mars none. (3) Some saints are remarkable for having one grace in peculiar prominence, *e.g.*, faith, resignation, courage, zeal, or benevolence. Yet though this peculiarity may draw most eyes upon them and win them most praise, these are not perfect specimens of Christianity. As with trees so with men, the least symmetrical may be the most noticeable. (4) The finest-specimen of a Christian is he in whom all the graces, like the strings of an angel's harp, are in most perfect harmony. Therefore we are to beware of cultivating one grace or duty at the expense of others. In seeking to do good to others we may neglect the cultivation of our own hearts and the duties we owe to our families. On the other hand, like a lark that goes soaring up to heaven while the hawk below is rifling her nest, we may spend our hours in prayer when we should be down there fighting the devil, alleviating human misery, &c. The head, heart, hand : doctrine, devotion, work : should each have their share of our time and attention. 2. Constantly. (1) This idea is embodied in all those figures under which our spiritual life is set forth in the Word of God—the growth of the seed, the progress of the day, the development of human life. (2) This constant growth is silent, unseen, unfelt in its processes ; yet if not every day, every year at least our life should present a palpable difference, as a tree by the ring that every season adds to its circumference. (3) The nearer we reach the summit of a hill, the climb is harder ; and the higher the eagle soars, ever mounting into thinner air, its flight grows more arduous. In both there is a point where progress ceases. But the higher a believer climbs, his ascent becomes more easy, and he never reaches the final stage. Like the mathematical paradox of two bodies that are ever approaching, and yet though moving through infinite space and for eternal ages, never meet, and never can meet ; so though they shall never reach the infinite height and perfection of Divinity, the saints in glory shall be constantly approaching it. III. We are to make efforts to grow. 1. Some men believe that the peculiar adaptation of the bodies of certain animals to their habits, in which we see the wisdom of their Maker, has resulted from the efforts which they have made to adopt themselves to their circumstances. The theory is absurd ; but nevertheless in the spiritual kingdom the very wish and effort to do good has with God's blessing a tendency to improve us. In attempting to be better we grow better, even as the flapping of a nestling's wing, impotent though it be to raise the bird in the air, fits its pinions for future flight. It is to efforts, not idleness, that God promises His blessing. God works ; and we are fellow-workers with Him that we may "increase more and more." 2. Cast a sponge into water, and, the fluid filling its empty cells, it swells out before our eyes. There is no effort here ; but it is not so that God's people are replenished with grace. More is needed than just to bring ourselves in contact with ordinances. To such active, energetic, and self-denying labours Christ calls us, as " Search the Scriptures," " Pray without ceasing," " Fight the good fight," &c. (*T. Guthrie, D.D.*) *Christian advancement :—*A child that stayeth at one stature and never groweth bigger is a monster. The ground that prospereth not and is not fruitful is cursed. The tree that is barren and improveth not is cut down. So

must all increase in the way of godliness and go forward therein.  Unless we go
forward we slip back.  (*Bp. Jewell.*)     *Progress :*—Our life, in fact, is like a ship
working its way down a river, where the water grows deeper, and the banks grow
wider, and the view expands as we move on, till at death, as there, where the
waves roar upon the bar, we shall pass out on a great, broad, shoreless ocean, on
which, with no limits bounding our progress, we shall advance evermore ; growing
in the knowledge and love and likeness of Christ with the ages of eternity,
increasing yet "more and more."  (*T. Guthrie, D.D.*)     **And that ye study to
be quiet, and to do your own business.**—*The pacific spirit another proof of a true
sanctification :*—To pass from brotherly love to quiet industry is a natural transition.  Love, peace, work are related virtues.  Observe—I. THAT A PACIFIC SPIRIT
IS TO BE STUDIOUSLY CULTIVATED.  "And that ye study to be quiet."  The word
"study" signifies to seek after an object with ambition, as though it were the
highest honour to possess it.  There is nothing some people dread so much as
being quiet.  They delight in a row, and if one does not happen as frequently as
they wish, they make one for themselves.  The political agitator, the money-
getter, the advocate of war, all seek to attain their ends in the midst of tumult.
Nor is the sacred circle of the Church free from the violence of the irrepressible
disturber.  There are some people who never will be still : you cannot hold them
still.  They are full of suggestions for other people to carry out.  Their tongue is
a perpetual clatter.  They fly from one department of work to another, and create
distraction in each.  They try one's temper ; they harry one's nerves ; they break
one's peace.  To such people it would be the severest task to obey the apostolic
injunction—"That ye study to be quiet"—and yet no one in the wide world has
more need to do so than they.  A pacific spirit cannot be secured without much
self-denying effort ; but it is a jewel worth all the trouble and all the sacrifice
(Prov. xx. 3 ; Col. iii. 12–15).  II THAT A PACIFIC SPIRIT IS ATTAINED BY A PERSE-
VERING INDUSTRY IN PERSONAL DUTIES.  1. That personal duties have the first claim
upon our efforts.  "Do your own business."  Attend first to whatever comes within
your general or particular calling.  The man who is inattentive to his own duties
cannot with any reason dictate the duties of others.  To do one's own business is
the best safeguard against idleness and meddling curiosity.  All strifes—domestic,
social, ecclesiastical, and political, may be traced to meddlesomeness.  The meddling man is "a fool," because he gratifies his own idle curiosity at the expense of
his own well-being and the happiness of others.  See that the business you do is
your own business, and that you let that of your neighbours alone.  2. That
personal duties demand genuine hard work.  "And to work with your own hands."
The claims of religion do not release us from secular toil, but rather demand that
*all* the work of life should be done with consistency and diligence.  Manual
labour is not the only form of industry.  The mind has often the harder task.  The
industry of some of our public men is amazing.  There is no greater foe to piety
than idleness.  Many take more pains to go to hell than almost the holiest to go
to heaven.  Jerome used to say that a man who labours disheartens even the devil
himself.  3. That industry in personal duties is enforced by apostolic precept.
"As we commanded you."  The apostle frequently did so, and set an example
(2 Thess. iii. 7, 8).  Honest labour is not beneath the dignity of any, and he who
works the hardest has the greater influence in enforcing industry upon others.
III. THAT A PACIFIC SPIRIT, COMBINED WITH DILIGENCE, RECOMMENDS CHRISTIANITY
TO THOSE OUTSIDE THE CHURCH.  "That ye may walk honestly towards them that
are without" (ver. 11).  Industry is no small part of honesty.  A lazy man can
never be an honest one.  A restless, trifling busybody does unspeakable damage to
religion.  The unbelieving world, on the other hand, is impressed and attracted by
the peaceful and diligent behaviour of the faithful.  IV. THAT A PACIFIC SPIRIT,
COMBINED WITH DILIGENCE, ENSURES AN HONOURABLE INDEPENDENCE.  "And that ye
may have lack of nothing."  It is more honourable to work than to beg.  It is
more blessed to be able to give than to receive.  What a mercy it is not to know
those temptations which arise from pinching poverty, nor yet to be necessitated
to depend upon the cold-hearted charity of others.  The patient, quiet plodder in
the way of duty may not always be rewarded with affluence ; but he is
encouraged to expect enough.  And the very spirit he has striven to cultivate
has enriched him with an inheritance which few possibly attain—contentment
with his lot.  He, whose is the silver and the gold, will care for His loved and
faithful servants (Psa. xxxvii. 25).  LESSONS : 1. Quarrelsomeness and indolence
cannot co-exist with a high degree of sanctity.  2. To secure the blessings of

peace is worthy of the most industrious study. 3. The mightiest aggressions of
the gospel upon the world are made quietly. (*W. Barlow.*)      *The quiet spirit :*—
This is the exhortation of St. Paul in his first Epistle. His own life was anything
but quiet; but this made him rather value quietness. Paul the aged was as far
from tranquility as ever, for the care of disorderly Churches pressed upon him.
Yet in his last Epistles he gave direction for prayer that "we may lead a quiet and
peaceable life." I. THE DESCRIPTION OF THE QUIET TO BE AIMED AT. 1. What it
is not. (1) There are men of good character and abilities who are naturally quiet
in an extraordinary degree. They are interested in and could add to the conversation, but they prefer to keep silence. In this way they inflict a real loss on society
and leave room for those to say much who ought to say little. (2) Some are quiet
from melancholy, from the loss of a dear friend, distorted views of religious
dogmas, business or family cares. The quiet of the text is neither of these. (3)
Nor is it the cynical silence of those who wish to show how much they despise the
ordinary topics of conversation. (4) Nor is it the calm of mental or moral laziness and stagnation. 2. The quiet that is Divine—(1) Grows from faith in God.
It is trust in Him who guides us by His counsel and protects us by His providence.
(2) This quietness of trust must be connected with an honest faithfulness in the
discharge of the duties of life. It is a false peace if it does not mean conscientious labour for God and man. When we have done all we can, we may leave
results to God, and rest in Him. II. THE DIFFICULTIES IN THE WAY OF LEADING A
QUIET LIFE. 1. A defectively illuminated conscience. There are men whose conviction is that no one is right but themselves. Such are always getting themselves
into trouble. 2. Youthful impulsiveness and rashness that is putting everybody
right, and showing without adequate preparation and experience how the right thing
is to be done. Such are of course discouraged and disturbed by snubbing and
failure. 3. But are there not many evils that will involve us in their guilt if we are quiet
about them? Yes; but reform is better done quietly, slowly, thinkingly, than by
any fierce blaze of zeal that creates real cause of offence while striving to rectify
the evil. God has patience; let His imitators strive to be quiet. III. THE UN-
OBTRUSIVE LIFE OF CHRIST. The vision we have of Him in the midst of the storm
calmly sleeping or calmly hushing winds and hearts is a symbol of the quiet side of
a holy life. 1. During the early portion of His life Israel was full of tumult, but
He was quietly working in a carpenter's shop. During His active life while all was
excitement about Him nothing of the trouble disturbed Him. When vexed questions
were laid before Him He settled them by a story. 2. Was not this part of the
secret of His power. Words of rebuke could not but have a terrible significance
from the lips of One who was so calm. See how the money-changers fled from
Him. One of the mightiest sermons ever preached is that of His silence under
the indignities of the night before His death. (*A. Craig.*)      *Quiet work :*—The
text tells us that we must study to be quiet in doing the business of this life.
And that means that our work should be—I. STEADY work. The race is not
always to the swift or the battle to the strong. The feet that are to climb the
lofty mountain must first tread the lowly valley. We cannot enter heaven at a
bound. II. PATIENT work. If in the race of life you show me the brilliant, quick,
hasty runner, one who has no staying power, and if you show me the steady,
earnest plodder, I will tell you who will come in first at the end. III. CONTENTED
work. Without this it can be neither quiet nor successful. Those who murmur
simply neglect a great portion of their work. IV. MODEST work. A Spanish
fable tells us how, when a number of great men were boasting of their deeds,
how one had gained a great victory, and another had painted a great picture, and
another had made a great speech, a spider descended by his web into their midst
and claimed equal honour with them. Since all man's deeds are like a spider's
web, and when we hear of a man who has done something remarkable, we may
think of him as a spider who has spun his web a little better than other spiders.
V. OUR "OWN" work. Let the gossip and the busybody take this to heart.
The meddler in other folks' affairs, the tale-bearer, and the scandalmonger never
do their own business, and hinder honest people from doing theirs. Conclusion:
1. In religious work pre-eminently we are called upon to be quiet. There are some
Christians who make a great noise. Their religion seems to be formed on the
model of the earthquake, and the whirlwind, and the fire, and knows nothing of
the "still small voice." They have to learn that in "quietness and confidence" lies
their strength. In these hurrying excitable days this is more important than ever.
2. This quietness is not indifference or cowardice. You are Christ's builders and you

work for Him like the builders of the Temple, without the sound of a hammer; you are Christ's soldiers, and can fight His battles without a flourish of trumpets. 3. Every Christian worker has a model in Christ Jesus, who worked the salvation of men quietly. (*H. J. W. Buxton.*)    *The study of quietness and the practice of our own business* :—The sum of Christianity is to do the will of God (ver. 3 ; Eccles. xii. 13). This holiness stands as queen in the midst of all the graces, has patience to wait on her, compassion to reach out her hand, longanimity to sustain, and this placability of mind to keep her in an equal poise and temper. So that to holiness more is required than to believe, hope, and pray. What is my faith if my malice make me worse than an infidel? What are my prayers, if the spirit of unquietness scatter them? So St. Paul here commands us not only to "abstain from fornication," from those vices that the worst of men are ready to fling a stone at, but those popular vices, animosity and turbulent behaviour, and to be ambitious to be quiet. I. THE OBJECT IN WHICH OUR STUDY MUST BE SEEN. To be quiet is to be peaceable (1 Cor. xii. 25 ; 1 Tim. ii. 2 ; Col. iii. 15). 1. This is not—(1) Tyranny, although some think there is no peace unless every man subscribe to their unwarrantable demands. (2) Others call even disobedience peace, and are never quiet but when they are let loose to do as they please. (3) Others esteem themselves quiet who are rather asleep than settled, bound up with a frost until the next thaw. (4) There are those who are still by reason of a dull and heavy disposition, and who do no harm because they do nothing and are nothing. (5) Some there are who are so tender that they will not even bear witness to the truth for fear of disturbance, having so much of the woman and the coward that they count it a punishment to be just and honest. (6) There is a constrained quietness ; that of Esau, which would last but till his father's funeral, of an Ammonite under the harrow (2 Sam. xii. 31), of Goliath when his head was off, that of a dead man who is at rest because he cannot move. All turbulent spirits are quiet before opportunity or hope sets their spirits aworking. 2. To be quiet consists in a sweet composure of mind, a calm and contented conversation, a heart ever equal and like unto itself. To this our religion binds us. It is a plant that God only plants, which grows and raises itself above the love of the world, covetousness, malice, fraud, which disturb ourselves and others. (1) To this the vanity of philosophy and the weakness of the law could not reach. The philosophers cried down anger and gave way to revenge ; and under the law it was but a promise. (2) This it was the business of the Prince of Peace to effect (Matt. v. 38–45, xxii. 39). (3) By this the genuineness of our Christianity is to be determined. II. THE ACT. We must make it our study or ambition. There is nothing that deserves commendation but must be wrought out with study and difficulty ; and the love of peace and quiet is no obvious and easy virtue, that will grow up of itself. 1. We must make it our constant meditation and fill our minds with it. By our continual survey of its beauty, by fixing our thoughts upon it, and by an assiduous reviving and strengthening of those thoughts we make it more clear and applicable. 2. We must put our meditation into practice, which will fix it in the habit. This is no easy thing. We must unlearn many things before we can learn this. (1) We must cast out self-love which is the source of many troubles. (2) We must root out that "root of all evil," covetousness, which will never suffer us to be quiet (Isa. v. 8). (3) We must pull back our ambition, which is a busy and vexatious evil, carrying over our brother's necks to that pitch from whence we fall and break our own, never quiet till then. (4) Then we shall the more easily bind our malice which is ever lurking for the prey. (5) We must empty ourselves of all suspicion and discontent ; which never wants fuel to foment, but feeds on shadows, whispers, lies, empty reports. All this is our spiritual exercise. We must practice it over and over again, and be ambitious to excel in it. III. THE METHOD WE MUST USE. Our progress in studies and endeavours is answerable to the rules we observe. Every man would be quiet in his own place, and pretendeth he is so when he is busy abroad. The covetous man is in his own place when he "joineth house to house" ; the ambitious is in his place when he flieth out of it ; never at rest till he reach that height where he cannot rest. The parasite, tale bearer, &c., all desire peace when they move as a tempest, and are at last lost in the ruin which they make. 1. There cannot be a truer method in our study than "to abide in our calling" (1 Cor. vii. 20), as in our own sphere, castle, sanctuary, safe from those incursions and affronts which disturb us when we are out of it (2 Cor. xii. 20 ; x. 14 ; 1 Pet. iv. 15). (1) Christianity is the greatest peacemaker, and keeps every man to his own office (Rom. xii. 7, 8 ; Eph. vi. 7), which if every man would keep and make good there would be peace. When every part answers in its place, and raises itself no higher than that will bear; when the magistrate speaks by nothing but the laws, and the subject answers by nothing but his obedience; when the greater shadow the less, and the less help to fortify the greater; when every part does its part, and every member its office; then there is equality and harmony. (2) This is enjoined by nature, and is its method. Everything in its own place is at rest and nowhere else (Psa. civ. 19). (3) This duty is to be urged and pressed—(*a*) From the grace and beseemingness of it. What garment can fit us better than our own? What motion more graceful than our own? Apelles with an awl, or the cobbler with his pencil; Midas with an asses' ears, or an ass in purple; Nero with his fiddle, or a fiddler with a crown, are monstrosities. (*b*) From the advantage it brings. That which becomes us, commonly furthers and promotes us. When we venture out of our place, we venture as at a lottery, where we draw many blanks before we have one prize; and when that is drawn it does not amount to a fortieth part of our venture. When we do our own business we find no difficulty but in the business itself, and no enemy but negligence; but when we break our limits and leap into other men's affairs, we meet with greater opposition. We meet with those who will be as violent to defend their station as we are to trouble it. 2. Let us shake off sloth and "work with our hands," for idleness is the mother and nurse of pragmatical curiosity. He that will be idle will be evil; and he that will do nothing will do that which he should not. This is the primordial law, as old as Adam, that we must work with our hands (Gen. iii. 19). The food of our souls and bodies is God's gift, and He gives when He prescribes the means of procuring them (Psa. xxiv. 1; cxv. 16). Labour is the price of God's gifts, and when we pay it down He puts them in our hands. What more unworthy an active creature than to bury himself alive in sloth? What more unbeseeming than to have feet and not to go, hands and not to use them? (1) The sluggard is a thief (Prov. v. 15; 2 Thess. iii. 11; Eph. iv. 28; Prov. xii. 27). Besides robbing others, he robs his own soul of the service the body was made to render. (2) There are devout sluggards other than monks and as idle, but not cloistered up, who do not hesitate to leave their duty to gratify the itch and wantonness of the ear. The husbandman may pray and praise the Lord at the plough tail. He that hears but one sermon and acts it over in his life, labouring honestly in his calling, is more acceptable to God than he that neglects his calling and hears one hundred a week. These are worse than infidels (1 Tim. v. 8). (3) We must not pass by the idle gallant. We see too many who have no calling, who neither sow nor reap, the cankers of their country, pinned to the commonwealth as their feathers are to their caps, for show, not for use, or rather as warts upon a man's hand, which grow up with it and deface it, or as idols, which, though dressed up and painted and gilt, are "nothing in the world." They may reply that they were born rich, and what they possess is theirs by inheritance. This may be true, but they were not born fools, nor were luxury and idleness entailed upon them at the same time. They were born men, and not as beasts of the field to eat, drink, and straggle up and down, and then fall to the ground. (*A. Farindon, B.D.*) *Of quietness and doing our own business:*—I. SOME CASES IN WHICH IT IS ALLOWABLE TO MEDDLE WITH THE AFFAIRS OF OTHERS. 1. Superiors may meddle with the business of those who are subject to their charge: magistrates, fathers, pastors. 2. When the honour of God is concerned we may and must interpose in vindication, as Phineas, Elijah, John the Baptist, our Lord. 3. When the public weal and safety are manifestly concerned we may interfere to support or secure them. 4. We may meddle for the succour of right against palpable wrong and outrage. 5. We may interpose when our own just defence requires it. 6. When the life or welfare, spiritual or temporal, of our neighbour is concerned, we may yield our aid: for we are "our brother's keeper." 7. If any opportunity of doing our neighbour good, especially his soul, offers itself, we should in charity embrace it. In these cases we may intermeddle, and in doing so be quiet, and doing our own business. II. SOME GENERAL RULES ACCORDING TO WHICH SUCH MEDDLESOMENESS IS COMMONLY BLAMABLE. 1. We should never out of ambition, covetous desire, or self-conceit, so meddle as to invade any man's office, or to assume the exercise of it. 2. We should not without call or allowance, meddle with our superiors, so as to advise or blame them. 3. We should not meddle, indeed, with the affairs of our equals so as to control or cross them. 4. We should not without desire or leave intermeddle in the smaller temporal interests of others on pretence to further them, or with design to cross them. 5. We should not, indeed, in matters of an indifferent and innocent nature so far meddle, as, without considerable reason to infringe any man's liberty, cross his humour, obstruct his pleasure, however discordant with our judgment and taste.

6. We should never offer to put a force on any man's inclination, or strive to bend it in compliance with ours. 7. We should not in conversation meddle so as to impose our opinions and conceits on others. 8. We should not ordinarily in converse affect or undertake to teach, for this implies pretence to a kind of superiority. 9. We should be cautious of interrupting any man's discourse or taking the words out of his mouth; for this is a rude way of dispossessing men of that which, by the common law of society, they suppose themselves to enjoy. 10. We should be careful of entrenching on any man's modesty in any way, either of commendation or dispraise, so as to put him to the blush, or to expose him to scorn. 11. It is good to be cautious of talking about other men and their concernments in way of passing characters upon them (1 Tim. v. 13). 12. We should not be inquisitive into the designs of men, press into their retirements, or pry into their secrets. 13. We should not lie in wait to catch any man at an advantage. 14. We should not meddle with things we do not understand. III. Some directions concerning particular kinds of meddling. 1. As to meddling by advice we may do well to observe these directions. (1) Advise not (except on call) a superior or one more eminent than thyself in authority, dignity, or age. (2) Thrust not with violence or importunity advice on an equal, or any man not subject to thy charge who is unwilling to receive it. (3) Be not obstinate in pressing advice. (4) Affect not the office of a counsellor except through friendship or humanity. (5) Advise not otherwise than with reservation and diffidence. 2. As to meddling for reproof. (1) Reprove not a superior, which is to soar above our pitch, to confound ranks, and pervert the order of society. (2) Reprove not rashly, and without certain cognisance of the facts. (3) Neither rashly as to the point of right, or without being able to show that the affair is really culpable. (4) Reprove not for slight matters, or such faults as proceed from natural frailty or inadvertency. (5) Reprove not unseasonably, when a person is indisposed to bear rebuke. (6) But mildly and sweetly, in the calmest manner and gentlest terms. (7) Neither affect to be reprehensive, or willingly to undertake the office of censor. 3. As to interposing in the contentions of others. (1) We should never meddle so as to raise dissensions, or to do such things as breed them. (2) We should not foment dissensions already commenced, blowing up the coals that are kindled by abetting or aggravating strife. (3) Especially we should not make ourselves parties in any faction where both sides are eager and passionate. (4) Nor interpose ourselves, without invitation, to be arbitrators in points of difference; though we may perhaps cautiously meditate or devise agreement. (5) If we would at all meddle in these cases it should be only by endeavouring to renew peace by the most fair and prudent means. IV. Some considerations proposed, inducive to quietness and dissuasive from pragmatical temper. (1) Consider that quietness is just and equal, pragmaticalness is injurious to the rights and liberties of others. (2) Quietness signifies humility, modesty, and sobriety of mind. (3) It is beneficial to the world, preserving the general order of things, and disposing men to keep within their proper station, &c. (4) It preserves concord and amity. (5) Quietness to the person endued with it, or practising it, begets tranquillity and peace; since men are not apt to trouble him who comes in no one's way. (6) It is a decent and loving thing, indicating a good disposition, and producing good effects. (7) It adorns any profession, bringing credit, respect, and love to the same. (8) Quiet also is a safe practice, keeping men not only from the incumbrances of business, but from the hazards of it, and the charge of bad success; but pragmaticalness is dangerous from the opposite effects, &c. (9) It is consequently a great point of discretion to be quiet, and a manifest folly to be pragmatical. (10) We may also consider that every man has sufficient business of his own to employ him, to exercise his mind, and to exhaust his labour; but those who attend pragmatically to the affairs of others are apt to neglect their own : advice on this head from Scripture and philosophy. (11) But suppose that we have much spare time and want business, yet it is not advisable to meddle with that of other men; for there are many ways more innocent, pleasant, and advantageous to divert ourselves and satisfy curiosity. For instance, investigation of the works of nature; application to the study of the most noble sciences, to the history of past ages, and to the cultivation of literature in general. *(Isaac Barrow, D.D.)* *Considerations conducive to the quiet minding of our own business :*—Nature offereth herself and her inexhaustible store of appearances to our contemplation; we may, without any harm and with much delight, survey her rich varieties, examine her proceedings, pierce into her secrets. Every kind of animals, of plants, of minerals, of meteors, presenteth matter wherewith innocently, pleasantly, and profitably to entertain our minds.'

There are many noble sciences, by applying our minds to the study whereof we may not only divert them but improve and cultivate them. The histories of ages past, or relations concerning foreign countries, wherein the manners of men are described, and their actions reported, may afford us useful pleasure and pastime. Thereby we may learn as much, and understand the world as well, as by the most curious inquiry into the present actions of men. There we may observe, we may scan, we may tax the proceedings of whom we please, without any danger or offence. There are extant numberless books, wherein the wisest and most ingenious of men have laid open their hearts, and exposed their most secret cogitations unto us. In pursuing them we may sufficiently busy ourselves and let our idle hours pass gratefully. We may meddle with ourselves, studying our own dispositions, examining our principles and purposes, reflecting on our thoughts, words, and actions, striving thoroughly to understand ourselves. To do this we have an unquestionable right, and by it we shall obtain vast benefit, much greater than we can hope to get by puddering in the designs or doings of others. Pragmaticalness then, as it is very dangerous and troublesome, so it is perfectly needless. It is a kind of idleness, but of all idleness the most unreasonable. It is at least worse than idleness in St. Gregory Nazianzen's opinion. For " I had rather," said he, " be idle more than I should, than over-busy." Other considerations might be added ; but these, I hope, may be sufficient to restrain this practice so unprofitable and uneasy to ourselves, and for the most part, so injurious and troublesome to others. (*I. Barrow.*) *The business of life :*—Life is a business. Every man has a mission, a purpose to work out, for which he has been sent into the world. Man is organized for activity, and the circumstances in which he is placed necessitate work. The business of life is to be—I. PERSONAL : " Your own." By this is not meant that we are to be regardless of others in our labour, and aim only at self-gratification and aggrandisement; but that we have a sphere of labour entirely our own, which we are bound to fill. 1. That this is the case is clear from—(1) The peculiarity of each man's external circumstances. No man has exactly the same surroundings as another. He has relations all his own. (2) The peculiarity of each man's personal needs. Every man has some exigencies special to himself. (3) The peculiarity of each man's individual aptitudes. Every man has not only an opportunity but a power for doing something which no other man can do so well. (4) The peculiarity of each man's obligations. Man has duties to perform in relation to himself, his race, his God, which no one in the universe can discharge for him. His obligations are intransferable. Attending to his *own* business a man—(1) Will not be an officious meddler in the affairs of others. His hands will be so full of work in his own sphere that he will have neither the inclination nor the opportunity to interfere in the concerns of others. (2) He will most effectively serve the interests of others. By doing rightly the work of his own sphere, he will exert the most salutary influence around him. " No man liveth unto himself." II. QUIET. " Quiet and business " are often separated. There is a business in which there is no quiet— noisy, fussy, all rattle and din. There is a quiet to which there is no business— lazy inactivity. The two must go together in the true work of life. Quiet work is the true work. 1. It is the strongest work. In quiet labour there is the plan and purpose of soul. There is concentrated force. It is not mere limb force, but life force. 2. It is the happiest work. In the work of bustle, excitement, and hurry there is no happiness. But in quiet labour there is the harmonious play of all the faculties. 3. It is the divinest work. With what sublime quiet God works! His energy operates in the universe as noiseless as the sunbeam. He is the God of peace. How quietly Christ worked: " He shall not cry," &c. It is not the bustling tradesman, merchant, politician, preacher, that does the strongest, happiest, divinest work. It is the man of quiet, resolute, unostentatious energy. Quiet work is not slow work. Stars are silent, yet how swiftly they speed! III. INTELLIGENT. " That ye study." Quiet work requires study. Noisy work is the result of caprice. Quiet work is the result of study. The more mind thrown into any work the less noise. The most noisy preacher has the least mind. Study gives the worker—(1) A clear and definite object. This prevents the excitement contingent on doubt and uncertainty. (2) Adapts the means. It constructs a machinery of means adapted to reach the end. A machinery whose joints and wheels are so lubricated by thought that it moves on without creak or noise. Conclusion : Who amongst us is doing this quiet work? (*D. Thomas, D.D.*) *Work should be worship :*—I. WORK IS A PART OF OUR DUTY. It is needful not only for the comfort or advantage of men, but for the continual existence of the race. And God has so framed us that we are dependent, not merely each man on his own work, but each man on the working of others. As a race and as a Church, we are not a vast collection of separate and independent individuals, but are united together as members of a family, nay, as members of one body. And "the increase of the body" depends on the effectual working of every part. It grows "by that which every joint supplieth." II. If this be true, then OUR WORK, THE ORDINARY BUSINESS OF LIFE, SHOULD BE REGARDED BY US AS A RELIGIOUS DUTY, so done to God that it shall be a part of our worship, an act of homage to God, like our prayers or alms. When we do our ordinary and earthly work in such a spirit as this, it lightens our burden, ennobles our work, and elevates ourselves. It secures that the work shall be honestly done to the best of our power, and turns the most earthly employment into a holy act of religious worship. What can be more secular than painting, sculpture, or architecture? Yet many painters, sculptors, and architects have sanctified their brush, chisel, mallet, by employing them in the service of God. Some have sanctified their voices by singing the gospel as much as others in preaching it. And what is more secular or earthly than money? Yet many have sanctified it by employing it in the service of God, and for the good of souls. Ah! it is not merely the thing we do, but the end for which, and the spirit in which we do it, that makes it religious, or an act of worship. (*William Grant.*)    *Business :*—There is a word which has come to mean much in our daily speech; whose meaning as we use it cannot be expressed by any single word in any other language, and that word is "business." Like "home" and "neighbour" it enshrines a tradition and stands for a history. The old sneer that the English are a nation of shopkeepers has lost its point, though not its truth. More than all other secular agencies the business enterprise of the English-speaking race has blessed the human race. It has led the van in the triumphal progress of Christian civilization. It has opened up continents, peopled deserts, and whitened solitary seas with the sails of commerce. Therefore, the old English word "business" has come to have a definite and noble meaning. It stands for a mighty commonwealth, wherein men and nations are intimately related to each other. It has its own laws enacted by the Supreme Lawgiver, which senates and parliaments do not need to enact and cannot set aside. Business means the appropriation and subjection of the world by man to himself. Beginning with agriculture, which is its simplest form, and rising through all grades of industrial and commercial activity, whatsoever subdues the external world to man's will, and appropriates its power, its beauty, its usefulness, is business; and whoso worthily engages in it is helping to carry out God's design, and is so far engaged in His service. To conquer the earth and force the wild fen or stony field to bring forth bread to gladden the heart of man; to level useless hills, and say to obstructive mountains, "Be ye removed from the path of progress;" to summon the lightnings to be his messengers, and cause the viewless winds to be his servants; to bring all the earth into subjection to human will and human intelligence. This is man's earthly calling, and history is but the progressive accomplishment of it. Therefore it is that, rightly regarded, business is a department of Christian activity. The business of everyday life ought to be pursued with high aims and lofty motives, not only for what it enables man to do, but chiefly for what it enables man to be in the exercise of his kingly function, and in the development of his kingly character. (*Bp. S. S. Harris.*)    *The business of life is* I.—To BE. Not merely exist, to breathe as a blacksmith's bellows, to vegetate, or lead an animal life. This is not to be a man. What is meant is that we have been put here to live the higher life of man—to be a Christian. This is the most useful kind of work. Let no one complain that they have few opportunities of working for God; for we may all strive to do what He desires; and the best way of doing good to man is to be good. The noblest workers bequeath to us nothing so great as the image of themselves. II. To DO. It has been cynically remarked that no one is necessary, and that when we cease to exist we shall not be missed. But though God needs the help of none, He is good enough to allow us to be workers with Him in making the world better. The weakest and humblest in his daily course can, if he will, make a heaven round about him. Kind words, sympathizing attentions, watchfulness against wounding people's feelings, cost very little; but they are priceless in their value. We shall none of us pass this way again; and soon it will be too late to do anything. Religion is not thoughts about or addresses to God. They are the means to urge us to work for God in the natural outgoings of our life, which, blotting out the distinction between things sacred and things secular, should make both one, all work religion and all life worship. The business of the week is quite as religious as the devotions of Sunday, if done to God. III. To DO WITHOUT. A true Christian schools himself to sit loose to the things of this world. If he have them, well and good ; if not, he can do without them. He does not attempt to make this world his home. He is a stranger and pilgrim passing on to the house not made with hands. In these times of depression many persons are forced to learn the lesson of doing without. If these would learn of Christ He would teach them that the loss of these superfluities was a gain, and they, like Paul, would " know how to be abased and how to abound." A man is a slave until he has learned how to do without. It is fine discipline to give up for a week, a month, or year some harmless luxury which is becoming too much of a necessity. The better we have learned this lesson the easier will it be for us. IV. To DIE. " We brought nothing into this world," &c. Well for those who can say with Paul, "I die daily ; " *i.e.*, I am ready to die every day I live. " For more than forty years," said Havelock, "I have so ruled my life that when death came I might face it without fear." The way to prepare to die is to prepare to live. Nothing but a good life here can fit us to have a better one hereafter. " Turn to God one day before you die," said a Jewish teacher. " How can I know the day before my death ? " " You cannot, therefore, turn to Him now." John Wesley was once asked, "Suppose you knew that you were to die at twelve o'clock to-morrow night, how would you spend the intervening time ? " "Just as I intend to spend it now. I should preach this night at Gloucester, and again at five to-morrow morning. After that I should ride to Tewkesbury, preach in the afternoon, and meet the society in the evening. I should then repair to friend Martin's house, who expects to entertain me, converse and pray with the family as usual, retire to bed at ten o'clock, commend myself to my heavenly Father and wake up in glory." (*E. J. Hardy, M.A.*) *Peaceful, humble activity :*—I. THE IMPORTANCE OF THE CONDUCT ENJOINED. Very powerful and energetic is the language of the Holy Spirit in warning all who name the name of Christ to depart from iniquity, especially such kinds of iniquity as pride and self-confidence, and also from indolence and all self-indulgent tempers. As, for instance, how strong and vehement is this language of the zealous Peter to Christians—" Yea, all of you be subject one to another, and be clothed with humility ; " that is, be girded, tightly fastened, as it were, with your humility, so as never to put it off, or part with it ; adding the great sanctions, " For God resisteth the proud "—sets Himself against them—" but giveth grace to the humble." And so with regard to the other evil tendency, namely, that to indolence and want of energy the Divine warnings are very express, and in various forms repeated : " The fool foldeth his hands together, and eateth his own flesh." " He that is slothful in his work is brother to him that is a waster." " A slothful man hideth his hand in his bosom, and will not so much as bring it to his mouth again." " The slothful man saith, there is a lion without ; I shall be slain in the streets." How different the saying of Him who came from heaven to earth to leave us an example ! " I must work," said He, " the works of Him that sent Me while it is day ; for the night cometh when no man can work." His illustrious apostle imitated Him. " Yourselves know how ye ought to follow us : we behaved not ourselves disorderly among you, neither did we eat any man's bread for nought. And when we were with you, this we commanded you, that if any would not work, neither should he eat." " We beseech you, brethren, that ye increase more and more " in all Christian excellences, " and that ye study to be quiet, and to do your own business, and to work with your own hands, as we commanded you, that ye may walk honestly toward them that are without," that is—that ye may do nothing to bring disgrace on your holy profession, " and that ye may have lack of nothing," or of " no man," " that ye may not be obliged to depend on wicked heathen people for support." These, then, pride and indolence, are the two great evil principles or dispositions which hinder and entangle us in our daily path, while a humble, diligent course is that which is most sure of the Divine blessing. Only we must be careful not to separate these two heavenly graces. A diligent person may be vain and proud ; and a professedly humble person may be slothful and negligent. As a general rule, the graces of the gospel are so united that the want of any one may give us great reason to fear that we are deficient in all. II. THE WAY TO SHOW SUCH CONSISTENT CONDUCT. " Study to be quiet." The word " study " is, in the original, very expressive—that we take great pains to lead a quiet, peaceable life—that we make it the object of our ambition. But lest this quietness should be debased into idleness or cowardliness, the apostle immediately adds, " And to do your own business, and work with your own hands ; " implying, that as Christians must always be quiet and peaceful, so they must never be careless and idle, but ever be full of energy and spirit in the quiet accomplishment of their every-day duties. And all this must be done under a deep sense of Christian responsibility, as having great privileges in possession, and great promises in prospect, and as servants of the Lord Jesus Christ. (*J. H. Newman, D.D.*) *A precept on business :*—All have a work to do, and all are, more or less, indisposed to do their own work. If the gospel had entirely repealed the sentence—"In the sweat of thy brow shalt thou eat bread," many men would have liked it all the better. But this is not what the gospel does : it does not abolish labour; it gives it a new and nobler aspect : it sweetens the believer's work, and gives him fresh motives for performing it; it transforms it from the drudgery of the workhouse or the penitentiary to the loving offices and joyful services of the fire-side and the family circle. The gospel, then, has not superseded diligent activity; but it commands one and all—"Do your own business, and work with your own hands." I. THIS PRECEPT IS VIOLATED BY THOSE WHO HAVE NO BUSINESS AT ALL. Some are placed by the bounty of God's providence in such a situation that they do not need to toil for a subsistence; but such a life, though it certainly is the easiest, will neither be the happiest nor the most lawful. We must have some business in hand, some end in view. Those who are familiar with the seashore may have seen attached to the inundated reef a creature, whether plant or animal you could scarcely tell, rooted to the rock, and twirling its long tantacula as an animal would do. It's life is somewhat monotonous, for it has nothing to do but grow and twirl its feelers, float in the tide, or fold itself up on its foot-stalk when the tide has receded. Now, would it not be very dismal to be transformed into a zoophyte? Would it not be an awful punishment, with your human soul still in you, to be anchored to a rock, able to do nothing but spin about your arms or fold them up again, and knowing no variety except when the retiring ocean left you in the daylight, or the returning waters covered you in their green depths again? But what better is the life of one who has no business to do? One day floats over him after another, and leaves him vegetating still. He was of no real service yesterday, and can give no tangible account of occupation during the one hundred and sixty-eight hours of which last week consisted. He goes through certain mechanical routines; but the sea-anemone goes through nearly the same round of pursuits and enjoyments. Is this a life for an intelligent, immortal and responsible being to lead? II. THIS PRECEPT IS ALSO VIOLATED BY THOSE WHOSE ACTIVITY IS A BUSY IDLENESS. You may be very earnest in a pursuit which is utterly beneath your prerogative as a rational creature and your high destination as a deathless being. The swallow is abundantly busy, up in the early morning, for ever on the wing, as graceful and sprightly in his flight as tasteful in the haunts which he selects. Behold him zigzagging over the clover field, skimming the limpid lake, whisking round the steeple, or dancing gaily in the sky, or alighting elegantly on some housetop and twittering politely by turns to the swallow on either side of him, and after five minutes conversation off and away. And when winter comes, he goes to Rome, or Naples, or some other sunny clime; and after a while he returns. Now this is a very proper life for a swallow; but it is no life for a man. To flit about from house to house ; to pay futile visits ; to bestow all thought on graceful attitudes and polished attire ; to roam from land to land, and then return home—oh, this is not simply ridiculous, but really appalling! The life of a bird is a nobler one ; more worthy of its powers, and more equal to the end for which it was created. III. THIS PRECEPT IS VIOLATED, TOO, BY THOSE WHO ARE NOT ACTIVE IN THEIR LAWFUL CALLING. They are "slothful in business." They are of a dull and languid turn : they trail sluggishly through life, as if some adhesive slime were clogging every movement, and making their snail-path a waste of their very substance. Others there are who, if you find them at their post, are dozing at it. They are perpetual somnambulists, walking in their sleep; looking for their faculties, and forgetting what they are looking for. They are too late for everything—taking their passage when the ship has sailed, insuring their property when the house is burned, locking the door when the goods are stolen; and thus their work is a dream, and their life is worthless and in vain (Prov. ix. 10). Practical lessons : 1. Have a calling in which it is worth while to be busy. 2. Having made a wise choice, mind your own business, and go through with it. (*J. Hamilton, D.D.*) *Business life :*—I. THE CHIEF DANGERS OF A BUSINESS LIFE. What are they ? It is a misfortune in the path of a commercial trader to be kept in perpetual contact with the purely material value of all possible substances. The public sentiment of great business centres is apt to reckon a man's worth by his business profits. It is always tempted to erect an ignoble or defective ideal of success in life. And then there are the vulgar dangers to honesty and truthfulness which indeed beset men in all professions and classes. II. The safeguards of a business life. 1. Cherish to the utmost a thirst for truth and a sympathy with what is ideal, unselfish, grand in conduct. 2. Cultivate a sympathizing contact with men in other than mere business relationships. These are the safeguards of the secondary order. 3. The only primary and sufficient safeguard for any of us is the religion of Jesus Christ. Religion opens the widest, freest outlook for the mind into eternal truth, enlarging a man's range of spiritual sight, and enabling him to judge of all things in both worlds in their true proportion. Religion, moreover, supplies us for that reason with the only true and perfect standard by which to test the value of things, and so corrects the one-sided materialistic standard of business. Lastly, religion transforms business itself from an ignoble to a noble calling, inasmuch as it substitutes for the principle of mere profit the ideal of service. (*J. O. Dykes, D.D.*)          *Energy of quiet forces :*—Without storm or noise the winds in their usual course accomplish surprising feats. All expanses of shifting sand, whether maritime or inland, like the deserts of Africa and Asia, are yearly modified by the agency of wind-drift, the wind carrying the dry sand left by the tides forward and landward beyond the reach of the waters ; and where the aërial current blows steadily for some time in one direction, as the trade winds and monsoons of the tropics, it will carry forward the drifting material in that direction. Hence the gradual entombment of fields, forests, and villages that lie in the course of such progressive sand-waves as on the Biscay seaboard of France and on the western verge of Egypt. Results like these arise from merely the ordinary operations of wind ; its extraordinary operations are manifested in the destructive effects of the hurricane, the whirlwind, and tornado. Gentle as it may seem, the continuous drifting of sand over the surface of hard rocks has been known to wear and polish down their asperities, and even to grind out grooves and furrows like those produced by the motion of glacier ice or the flow of running water. Here, then, we may observe great effects produced without fuss, and we may easily observe, in the phenomena of social life, that there are plenty of illustrations there of the same principle. The whirlwind of revolutions and hurricane of insurrections have no doubt produced startling consequences. But the influence of noble ideas, spoken by undemonstrative men, or embalmed in unpretending volumes, and of pious lives lived in seclusion, has produced a far greater effect upon the civilization of the world than all the blustering storms of war raised by kings and factions and reverberating through history. (*Advanced Text-book of Geology.*)          *All things work :*—Dr. Franklin used pleasantly to repeat the words of his negro servant : " Everything, massa, work in this country ; water work, wind work, fire work, smoke work, dog work, man work, bullock work, horse work, ass work ; everything work here but the hog : he eat, he drink, he sleep, he do nothing all day—he walk about like a gentleman." We hope our young friends will try to be useful and active. They surely do not wish that the saying of the negro should be true of them. *The importance of attending to our own business :*—The Church of God is as the body of man. In a man's body every part hath its several office ; the arm, the leg, the hand, and foot, do that whereto they are appointed : and doing the same, they live together in peace. But if the arm would take in hand to do that is the duty of the leg, or the foot that is the part of the hand, it would breed great disorder in the whole body. So if every man in the Church of God seek to do that to them belongeth, the Church shall flourish and be in quiet. But when every man will be busy and take upon him to look into other ; when every private man will govern, and the subject take in hand to rule the prince ; all must needs come to wreck and decay. Busybodies ever find fault with their brethren and neighbours, with the state, the clergy, the commonwealth, the Church, the government, and with the prince. They are an unquiet kind of men, ever looking for that they may mislike, and never contented. From these men come privy whisperings, slander, backbiting, mutinies, conspiracies, treasons, deposing of princes, and utter decay of commonwealths. These are the fruits of curiosity. (*Bp. Jewell.*)          *A lesson for busybodies :*—A man who had become rich by his own exertions was asked by a friend the secret of his success. " I have accumulated," replied he, " about one half of my property by minding my own business, and the other half by letting other people's alone." (*Clerical Library.*) *Reproof of a busybody :*—A certain woman once called upon her minister to tell him how much her mind had been hurt. Her pastor received her with all tenderness, and inquired into the cause of her distress. She went on to say, " She could assure him that her mind was very much hurt indeed, but she did not know how to tell him." The minister judging it must be something serious, urged her to be explicit upon the subject of her distress. At last she said, "It is the length of your bands in the pulpit." "Oh," said the minister, "I will take care that that distresses you no more." So fetching his bands he said, "Here is a pair of scissors, cut them to your wish." After she had done this, she thanked him and professed to feel her mind relieved. "Well, my friend," said the minister, "I may tell you that my mind has also been very much hurt, perhaps even more than yours." "Oh, sir, I am sorry for that; what, sir, has hurt your mind so?" He replied, "It is the length of your tongue. And now, as one good turn deserves another, you will allow as much to be cut off as will reduce it to about its proper length." It need not be remarked that she was speechless, and it is hoped, learned an important lesson with respect to that unruly member. (*W. Denton.*)   A lady once made a complaint to Frederick the Great. "Your majesty," said she, "my husband treats me badly." "That is not *my* business," replied the king. "But he speaks ill of you." "That," rejoined he, "is none of *your* business. (*Clerical Library.*)   **To work with your own hands.** *The dignity of labour :*—Two men I honour and no third. First, the toilworn craftsman that with earthmade implement laboriously conquers the earth and makes her man's. Venerable to me is the hard hand; crooked courses; wherein notwithstanding lies a cunning virtu, indefeasably royal, as of the sceptre of this planet. Venerable, too, is the rugged face, all weather-tanned, besoiled with its rude intelligence; for it is the face of a man living manlike. Oh, but the more venerable for thy rudeness, and even because we must pity as well as love thee! Hardly entreated brother! For us was thy back so bent, for us were thy straight limbs and fingers so deformed; thou wert our conscript, on whom the lot fell, and fighting our battles wert so marred. For in thee, too, lay a God-created form, but it was not to be unfolded; encrusted must it stand with the thick adhesions and defacements of labour; and thy body like thy soul, was not to know freedom. Yet toil on, toil on; thou art in thy duty; be out of it who may; thou toilest for the altogether indispensable, for daily bread. A second man I honour and still more highly; him who is seen toiling for the spiritually indispensable: not daily bread but the Bread of Life. Is not he, too, in his duty; endeavouring towards inward harmony; revealing this, by act, or by word, through all his outward endeavours, be they high or low? Highest of all, when his outward and inward endeavours are one: when we can name him Artist; not earthly craftsman only, but inspired thinker, who with heaven-made implement conquers heaven for us! If the poor and humble toil that we may have food, must not the high and glorious toil for him in return, that he may have light, guidance, freedom, immortality? These two, in all their degrees, I honour: all else is chaff and dust, which let the wind blow wherever it listeth. Unspeakably touching is it, however, when I find both dignities united; and he that must toil outwardly for the lowest of man's wants, is also toiling inwardly for the highest. Sublimer in this world I know nothing than the peasant saint, could such now anywhere be met with. Such a one will take thee back to Nazareth itself; thou wilt see the splendour of heaven spring forth from the humblest depths of earth, like a light shining in great darkness. (*T. Carlyle.*)

Ver. 12. **That ye may walk honestly toward them that are without, and that ye may have lack of nothing.** *The disciplinary and educational function of business, and some of the dangers that assail those engaged in it :*—I. Whatever their motives may be, BUSINESS MEN ARE ACTUALLY PRACTISING DAILY AND HOURLY THE CHRISTIAN VIRTUES of faith or foresight, prudence, self-control, self-denial, temperance, uprightness. The characteristic virtues of the business world are Christian virtues every one, and in adopting them men have acknowledged the excellence of Christianity. Self-indulgence is recognized as folly, as the foe to all happiness and manliness. Self-denial, self-control, is known in the practical affairs of life to be the condition of all success. Thus far, then, men have learned the great lesson of the Cross, and have taken its principles to be the rules of business life. Therefore it is that, if rightly and wisely conducted, there is no better discipline for the formation of character than business. It teaches in its own way the peculiar value of regard for other's interests, of spotless integrity, of unimpeachable righteousness; and the busy activities of life, in themselves considered, are good and not evil. They are a part of God's great work, and are as much His appointment as the services of praise and prayer. II. Though beyond all question the business energies of the age have been reinforced and guided by the gospel, until discipline, temperance, and self-control have become their permanent characteristics, and though beyond all question the business pursuits of the age are recogn ẓed by Christian thinkers and economists as departments of human culture and as part of God's administration of the world, yet BUSINESS MEN, WITH ALL THEIR EARNESTNESS AND SAGACITY, ARE PECULIARLY LIABLE TO BE BLIND TO THESE HIGH CONSIDERATIONS AND IGNORANT OF THIS GREAT ECONOMY. There are two dangers by which they are continually liable to be betrayed : one is selfishness, and the other is worldliness. 1. Profit, of course, is the very essence of success in business. Yet the making of profit is apt to become an absorbing passion with the eager business man for its own sake. His ordinary relations with men are apt to be more or less controlled by it. He pretty soon begins to wish to make his association pay, and his friendships, and his politics, and everything that he is and has and does. And if he is successful, a certain selfish pride establishes itself in his heart. Then comes avarice, that amazing and monstrous passion of the soul which loves money for its own sake, which grows on what it feeds on, which never can be appeased, never has enough. Woe to the man who sinks into this slavery. 2. Men are simply absorbed and engrossed and satisfied with their business pursuits and interests, and so neglect and forget their religious and eternal interests. Man is more than a denizen of this world. There is a hunger of the heart which nothing but God can appease ; a thirst of the soul which nothing but God can satisfy. " That ye may walk honourably toward them that are without." What can give this, spite of poverty or wealth, but the Christian conscience which is void of offence toward man and God ? " That ye may have lack of nothing." What can assure this, but the Spirit of adoption, which bears witness with our spirit that we are children and heirs of God ? (*Bp. S. S. Harris.*)   *Motives to industry :*—I. IT IS RIGHT. " That ye may walk honestly." 1. Idleness exposes men to three forms of dishonesty—(1) Unlawful dependence on others. We have no right to ask or receive the produce of another's labour when we are perfectly able to have produce of our own. This belongs to him and we filch it when we take it without value returned. It is taking the bread out of his mouth. All beggars, loungers, and loafers of all classes come under this category—labourers, genteel placemen, ministerial sinecurists. (2) Thievery. The thief is not usually one who can't, but one who won't work. To rob requires abilities which if honestly employed would secure adequate remuneration. But the thief likes his calling because of the idle leisure it promises, and the love of display which its wicked gains may gratify. (3) Gambling—the vice of which consists in getting that for which nothing is given, involving the rightful owner in loss. That he *might* have been the gainer is no justification, but a condemnation of both parties. This, too, springs from love of ease, from love of excitement, and from the feverish desire to be rich without the legitimate pains. 2. Honest industry avoids these temptations and secures—(1) Independence, which is worth all that is requisite to secure it. The worker could not stoop to the base cringing necessary to reap the paltry gains of the parasite, and mercifully escapes the contempt to which the idle dependent is exposed. (2) Nobility of soul which would scorn to take an undue advantage of another. II. IT IS PROFITABLE. " That ye may have lack of nothing." This is perfectly legitimate as a subordinate motive, and is one of the mainstays of civilization and philanthropy. The idea involves—1. The economy of the results of labour. To gain a competence thrift, temperance, and forethought are necessary. How many men honest and industrious enough, and with every means of acquiring a competency from time to time " lack " everything from their thriftless ways. But while honest to others they are dishonest to themselves. Frugality must enter into any large meaning of honesty. 2. The use of the results of labour—(1) In domestic requirements. (2) For charitable purposes. (3) For the promotion of religion.   (*J. W. Burn.*)   *Honesty :*—When James II., sent his Jacobite emissary to seduce the commanders of the British navy, he reported that Sir Cloudesley Shovel was incorruptible ; " He is a man not to be spoken to," was the emissary's tribute. (*C. E. Little.*)   *Honesty rewarded :*—A farmer called on Earl Fitzwilliam to represent that his crop of wheat had been seriously injured in a field adjoining a certain wood where his lordship's hounds had, during the winter, frequently met. He stated that the young wheat had been so cut up and destroyed that in some parts he could not hope for any produce. " Well, my friend," said his lordship, " if you can procure an estimate of the loss you have sustained I will repay you." The farmer replied that he had requested a friend to assist him in estimating the damage, and they thought that, as the crop seemed entirely destroyed, £50 would not more than repay him. The Earl immediately gave him the money. As the harvest approached, however, the wheat grew, and in those parts of the field which were the most trampled the corn was strongest and most luxuriant. The farmer went again to his lordship, and said, " I am come, my lord, respecting the field of wheat adjoining such a wood. I find that I have sustained no loss at all; for where the horses had most cut up the land the crop is most promising, and therefore I brought the £50 back again." " Ah," exclaimed the venerable Earl, " this is what I like ! this is as it should be between man and man ! " His lordship then went into another room, and on returning, presented the farmer with a cheque for £100, saying, " Take care of this, and when your eldest son shall become of age present it to him, and tell him the occasion which produced it." *Honesty towards those without :*—Only a few weeks ago, a missionary in China took his gun to go up one of the rivers of the interior to shoot wild ducks; and, as he went along in the boat, he shot at some ducks, and down they fell ; unfortunately they did not happen to be wild fowl, but tame ducks belonging to some neighbours. The owner was miles away, but the boat was drawn up to the side of the river, and the missionary went about carefully endeavouring to find out the owner of the ducks, for he could not rest until he had paid for the damage he had ignorantly done. The owner was much surprised, he had been so accustomed to have people shoot his ducks and never say a word about it, that he could not understand the honesty of the man of God, and he told others, until crowds of Chinese gathered round and stared at the missionary as if he had dropped from the moon ; a man so extremely honest as not to be willing to take away ducks when he had killed them! They listened to the gospel with attention, and observed that the teaching must be good which made people so conscientious as the missionary had been. I should not wonder but what that little accident did more for the gospel than the preaching of twenty sermons might have done without it. So let it be with us ; let us so act in every position that we shall adorn the gospel which is committed to our trust. (*C. H. Spurgeon.*) *Exemplary honesty :*—When this church was built, the President of the Board of Trustees called together every contractor and every mechanic that had worked upon it to ask if any of them had lost money by a too close contract in its construction ; and the welcome reply came to us, on the part of every single man, " We are content : we have made a reasonable profit on the work." And I think the blessing of God has rested on this Church from that day to this, in that it was honest. Nor do I know that this Church has ever committed an act, even through carelessness or forgetfulness, of dishonesty in the matter of the management of its fiscal affairs. (*H. W. Beecher.*)

Ver. 13. **But I would not have you to be ignorant, brethren.**—*Sorrow for the dead :*—Observe—I. THAT SORROW IS A MERCIFUL RELIEF TO A SOUL BEREAVED. Sorrow is nowhere forbidden. It may be an infirmity; but it is at the same time a solace. The religion of the Bible does not destroy human passions. We do not part with our nature when we receive the grace of God. The mind that is capable of real sorrow is capable of good. A griefless nature can never be a joyous one. II. THAT SORROW FOR THE DEAD IS AGGRAVATED BY IGNORANCE OF THEIR FUTURE DESTINY. The radius of hope is contracted or expanded in proportion to the character and extent of intelligence possessed. The heathen who have no satisfactory knowledge of the future life, give way to an excessive and hopeless grief. It was the dictum of an old Greek poet—a man once dead there is no revival ; and these words indicated the dismal condition of unenlightened nature in all lands and ages. What an urgent argument for missions. III. THAT SORROW FOR THE DEAD IN CHRIST IS SOOTHED AND MODERATED BY CERTAIN GREAT TRUTHS CONCERNING THEIR BLESSEDNESS. 1. That death is a sleep: *i.e.*, to the body ; as to the soul, it is the birth into a progressive life ; a departure to be with Christ. (1) Sleep is expressive of rest. When the toil of life's long day is ended, the great and good Father draws the dark curtain of night and hushes His weary children to rest. " They enter into rest." (2) Sleep is expressive of refreshment. The body is laid in the grave, feeble, emaciated, worn out. Then a wonderful process goes on, perceptible only to the eye of God, by which the body acquires new strength and beauty, and becomes a fit instrument and suitable residence for the glorified soul. (3) Sleep implies the expectation of awaking. We commit the bodies of the departed to the earth in sure and certain hope of a glorious resurrection. 2. That the dead in Christ will be roused from their holy slumber and share in the glory of His second advent. "Will God bring with Him." The resurrection of the dead is a Divine work. "I will redeem them from the power of the grave." Christ will own His people in their persons, their services, and their sufferings. They shall receive His approval, be welcomed and crowned by Him. 3. That the resurrection of Christ from the dead is a pledge of the restoration and future blessedness of all who sleep in Him. " For if we believe," &c. Christ Himself is the Resurrection, not only as revealing and exemplifying it, but as effecting it (John v. 25; vi. 39). The Word of God sheds a light across the darkness of the grave, and opens a vista radiant with hope and immortal blessedness. A vital knowledge of Christ silences every murmur, and prepares for every emergency. Lessons: 1. An ignorant sorrow is a hopeless one. 2. To rise with Jesus we must live and die to Him. 3. Divine revelations regarding the future life greatly moderate the grief of the present. (*G. Barlow.*) *Ignorance concerning the dead :*—Having given his converts golden counsel respecting the treatment of the living, both Christian and heathen, St. Paul turns abruptly in thought to the holy dead, and informs the Thessalonians how they ought to think " concerning them which are asleep." His design was to comfort the bereaved. He does not say to them, as Jesus said to the widow of Nain, " Weep not "; but he will limit their grief, and have their tears to fall in the sunshine, like the raindrops which fall when the thunderstorm is over. Moderate grief is lawful; immoderate grief is sinful. But there are reasons for it, which we now examine. I. IT IS AS IF THE MOURNERS HAD NO HOPE CONCERNING THE HOLY DEAD. It is to act too much like the Gentiles, who have no hope of a better life after this; whereas we Christians, who have a most sure hope—the hope of eternal life after this, which God, who cannot lie, hath promised us—should moderate all our joys on account of any worldly thing. This hope is more than enough to balance all our griefs over any of the crosses of the present time. II. IT IS THE EFFECT OF IGNORANCE CONCERNING THE HOLY DEAD. There are some things which we cannot but be ignorant of concerning them that are asleep; for the land they are removed to is a land of darkness, which we know but little of, and have no correspondence with. To go among the dead is to go among we know not whom, and to live we know not how. Death is an unknown thing, and of the state of the dead, or the state after death, we are much in the dark; yet there are some things anent them especially that die in the Lord that we need not, and ought not, to be ignorant of; and if these things are rightly understood and duly considered, they will be sufficient to allay our sorrow concerning them; namely—1. The dead sleep in Jesus. They are " fallen asleep in Christ." Death, therefore, doth not annihilate them. It is their rest, undisturbed rest. They have retired from this troublesome world, and thereby put an end to their labours and sorrows. Being still in union with Jesus, they sleep in His arms, and are under His special care and protection. Their souls are in His presence, and their dust is guarded by His omnipotence; so that they cannot be lost; nor are they losers, but infinite gainers by death; and their removal out of this world is into a better, even a heavenly one. 2. They shall be awaked out of their sleep, and raised up from their grave, for God will bring them with Jesus. They, then, are now with God, and are ineffably better where they are than they could possibly be down here. Through virtue of that union betwixt believers and Christ, it cometh to pass that whatever hath befallen Christ, as He is the Head of all believers, shall in God's own time be verified in believers themselves, due proportion and distance being alway kept which is between Head and members; for He inferreth that we shall be raised because He arose, and this because of our union with Him. Hence the death and resurrection of Jesus Christ are fundamental articles of the Christian religion, and give us golden hope of a joyful resurrection; for " Christ, being risen from the dead, is become the first-fruits of them that sleep," and therefore, " they who are fallen asleep in Him are not perished " (1 Cor. xv. 18–20). His resurrection is a full confirmation of all that is said in the gospel by Him who hath brought life and immortality to light. (*D. Mayo.*) *The state of departed saints :*—I. COLLECT THE INFORMATION WHICH THE PASSAGE OFFERS OF THE STATE OF THE DEPARTED. 1. As to the body. " Sin entered into the world and death by sin." But what was originally intended for a punishment is transformed into a blessing. Death is now, through the mercy of God, only the unrobing of a Christian before he retires to rest, and the short repose he takes while the Redeemer is making ready the eternal mansions to receive him. The figure of our text involves the idea of—(1) Repose. The body in its present state of deterioration is incapable of enduring many years of active existence. It grows weary of its necessary exertions, and requires its exhaustion to be repaired by rest. To die is to terminate the conflict, finish the race, reach the goal, and then, as a successful competitor, having gained the prize, to retire from the scene of competition. (2) Security. It is to sleep *in Jesus*. His eye watches their bed, and His arm protects it. The bodies of the saints belong to Christ not less than their souls by redemption (John vi. 39). Death consequently is not annihilation. (3) Hope. Christ is risen and become the first-fruits of them that sleep. The sleep of death implies waking on the morning of the resurrection. 2. As to the soul. Reason asks many questions which revelation does not answer; but all that it is necessary or beneficial to know the Bible declares. "Sleep" does not apply to the soul, for the soul never sleeps, and there is not a text which lends a sanction to the doctrine that the soul shares the death of the body. When "the body returns into the dust, the spirit returns to God who gave it." Death is rather the arousing of the soul from her drowsiness into heavenly vitality. Dives and Lazarus were both conscious immediately after death; and Paul desired death because it was to be with Christ. In what part of the universe the departed dwell we know not; but it is sufficient to know that they are with Christ. 3. As to the ultimate glory awaiting both. "If we believe," &c. The period of Christ's coming is that to which all Scripture points, all Providence tends, and all time conducts. The saints will be brought to judgment, but, unlike the wicked—(1) For acceptance and reward. (2) To be the crown of the minister's rejoicing. (3) To swell and share the triumph of the Redeemer. II. ENFORCE THE TOPICS OF INSTRUCTION AND COMFORT THE TEXT SUGGESTS. 1. It ascertains what is the character in which we must die to be made partakers of this glory. Those only who fall asleep in Jesus, which implies being in Him before they fall asleep. Scripture carefully distinguishes between those who "die in the Lord" and the common dead. 2. It exhibits the death and resurrection of Christ as of infinite importance. All the hopes we entertain of a joyful resurrection are built upon them. 3. It suggests the only adequate source of consolation under bereavements (ver. 18). (*E. Steane, D.D.*) *Reasons for comfort concerning them that die in the Lord:*—OF WHOM DOES THE APOSTLE HERE SPEAK? Of them that "sleep in Jesus." 1. To term death sleep was usual with the inspired writers (Psa. lxxvi. 5; Dan. xii. 2; 1 Cor. xi. 30; xv. 51; 1 Thess. v. 10). The figure is appropriate, for in sleep the senses are locked up, the members are motionless, we rest on our beds (Isa. lvii. 2) from toil and pain, and awake (Dan. xii. 2); so in death. 2. It is not, however, of all who die that the apostle speaks (Rev. xiv. 13). Those who die in the Lord are first "in Him," not by being baptized and professing Christianity, not by merely attending ordinances, not by moral blamelessness, not by orthodox opinions, but by faith in Christ. This faith secures freedom from condemnation (Rom. viii. 1); a new creation (2 Cor. v. 17; Gal. vi. 15); obedience (John xiv. 21), in which obedience we must persevere if we would sleep in Jesus. II. WHAT ARE THE THINGS CONCERNING SUCH OF WHICH WE OUGHT NOT TO BE IGNORANT? 1. That being in Him, they belong to Him, and are precious in His sight. He is their God; their Shepherd who knows, acknowledges, and takes care of them (John x. 14, 15, 27–29): they are His disciples, His family, His spouse, His members. Hence not only in life but in death they are precious to Him (Psa. cxvi. 15). For this, like all other things, is under the direction of His providence, and shall promote their good. 2. That as He is not the God, the Shepherd, &c., of the dead, but of the living, they shall not die, but only sleep, and shall certainly awake (Dan. xii. 2; Isa. xxvi. 19; John v. 25–29; Rom. viii. 10), and be most gloriously changed (Phil. iii. 21). Of all this Christ's resurrection is an assurance. This sleep is not insensibility: for the soul does not sleep even here, much less when disunited from the body. 3. That death is gain, having many advantages over life —freedom from labour, care, temptation, sin, sickness, death, and presence with Christ and saints and angels. 4. That we shall meet our departed friends again, and know them, and be with them and the Lord for ever (vers. 14–18). III. THE END FOR WHICH WE OUGHT NOT TO BE IGNORANT OF THESE THINGS. 1. That we sorrow not as those who have no hope. Sorrow we may and must. Grace was not meant to destroy but to regulate our affections. Nay, not to mourn would be sinful and lamentable (Isa. lvii. 1; Jer. xxii. 18, 19). But we must not sorrow as heathen or unbelievers. 2. Moreover, sorrow is needless—(1) On their account, for theirs is not loss, except of things which it is desirable to lose, but gain. (2) On our own account, for the loss is but momentary (Heb. xi. 10). (*J. Benson.*) *Consolation for the bereaved:*—I. IT HAS PLEASED GOD TO SUBJECT THE RIGHTEOUS AS WELL AS THE WICKED TO THE DOMINION OF DEATH. In their death we see—1. The offensive character of sin in the sight of God. 2. The power and sufficiency of Divine grace. 3. Instruction for the righteous in the certainty of their death. They are admonished—(1) To be diligent in doing good. (2) To be patient in suffering. (3)

To improve their sacred privileges. II. SORROW FOR THE DEATH OF THE RIGHTEOUS IS NOT INCONSISTENT WITH PIETY. It is allowable—1. As an expression of nature and friendship. 2. As a tribute due to excellency of heart. 3. As an acknowledgment of the loss sustained by their removal—(1) To society; (2) to the Church; (3) to the world. (*W. Naylor.*) *The coming of the Lord :*—I. IN RELATION TO THE DEAD IN CHRIST (ver. 13). 1. Intelligence concerning this relation important. (1) Because of its bearing upon the resurrection of believers. (2) Because ignorance on this subject cast the Thessalonians into deep sorrow in respect to their departed friends. 2. Intelligence concerning this relation an all-sufficient consolation (ver. 14). (1) Because Christ's resurrection ensures the resurrection of His saints. (2) Because of the inseparable relation between Christ and all His followers in His glory (ver. 14; Col. iii. 4). II. IN RELATION TO THE LIVING SAINTS (vers. 15, 17). 1. The living saints will be glorified, together with the resurrected ones (ver. 17; 1. Cor. xv. 51, 52). 2. The change of the living saints into their glorified state shall not precede the resurrection of the dead in Christ (ver. 15). III. IN ITS ACCOMPANIMENTS (ver. 16; Acts i. 11). 1. Christ will come in person. 2. Christ will come in person and in great glory (Matt. xxiv. 30 ; 2 Thess. i. 7–16). IV. IN THE ENCOURAGEMENT IT SHOULD AFFORD BELIEVERS (ver. 18). 1. In the case of the Thessalonians this was peculiarly necessary. 2. Is not this exhortation now timely ? V. PRACTICAL LESSONS. 1. The importance and glory of the coming of the Lord demand more earnest study than is now generally given (Col. iii. 4). 2. Christians should so live that they may be ready at any time to enter into the presence of the Lord. (*Preachers' Monthly.*) *The second coming :*—I. THE COMING OF THE LORD (vers. 13–18). What was that coming ; when it would take place ; the attending circumstances ; why it was so earnestly looked for ; and the comfort they found in it. II. HOW WE SHOULD LIVE IN VIEW OF THIS COMING (vers. 1–8). Watch ; be sober ; be wakeful ; be armed ; be ready ; be hopeful. (*Christian Age.*) **Concerning them which are asleep.**—*The Christian view of death :*—I. THE TRANSFORMATION OF DEATH. 1. From all the ancient heathen, and even, in part, from the Jewish world, there was a loud wailing of the bodies of the departed as over an utter ruin of life. Christianity teaches us that the dead are only asleep, and therefore in Christian grief there is no excess or despair. There is in this a whole revolution of the faith and hope of the world. The ideas of destruction, loss, unconsciousness, King of Terrors, cruel mower, prison-keeper are gone. There is an evening of life as well as a morning. "Man goeth forth unto his labour until the evening," "and so He giveth His beloved sleep." 2. There has been much perplexity through forgetfulness of what sleep is. Men do not cease to live in sleep. It is only the suspension of direct relations with the sensible ; a temporary change from which much advantage is derived. Death is sleep—(1) as it is a cessation of conditions and escape from circumstances which waste power and wear and tire faculty. "The wicked cease from troubling," &c. "They rest from their labours." (2) As there is in it the gain of fresh power for future use. So far from suspending spiritual power, the change in our dependence upon the sensible and material increases and intensifies it. This is proved from dreams ; and so is it in the thing signified. (3) As its separations are to be followed by the resumption of holy fellowship—as its evening withdrawal is to be followed by a morning return. II. CONSEQUENT ON THIS TRANSFORMATION THERE IS A CHANGE IN THE FEELING OF THE BELIEVER REGARDING DEATH. "We sorrow not," &c. The wail of the heathen was a wail of despair ; and the wail of the Hebrew saints, under the light of their imperfect economy, was often heart-breaking. And there is much bitter grief in Christian homes arising partly from yielding to the susceptibilities, and partly from ignorance. But it is benumbing to faith, and dishonouring to the Lord of Life. But there is a natural human emotion tempered and directed by the light and grace of the Gospel. Sorrow is nature's tribute to her own weakness and dependence. When Jesus wept He sanctified our griefs. Christianity puts no undue strain on our nature. We may weep for ourselves, but it is not to be absorbing, and is not to be wasted upon those who are present with the Lord. III. THE GLAD ANTICIPATIONS WHICH CHRISTIANS ARE ENCOURAGED TO CHERISH. Mark—1. Its glorious and stable foundation of fact. What Jesus did and suffered is the ground of a new future for humanity. Despair died when He died, and hope was born when He rose. "Because I live ye shall live also." 2. Complete resurrection glory and escape from hell's power. It is impossible to fully explore the abundance of this revelation given by "the Word of the Lord." It was given to meet the actual need of those who mourned that through death their friends would be excluded from the triumph of Christ's second coming. The living will not take precedence, for the dead in Christ shall rise first. 3. The reunion of the dead and living with each other and the Lord (ver. 17). Conclusion : 1. What an attraction the glad and certain future should have for Christian hearts. 2. How glad and calm should our hearts be in anticipation of that future. (*W. H. Davison.*) *The sleep of the faithful departed :*—One great miracle in the new creation of God is that death is changed to sleep ; and therefore in the New Testament we do not read of the " death " of the saints (see John xi. 11 ; Matt. xxvii. 52 ; 1 Cor. xv. 51 ; Acts vii. 60, xiii. 36). Christians were wont to call their burial-grounds cemeteries, or sleeping-places, where they laid up their beloved ones to sleep on and take their rest. 1. We know that they shall wake up again. What sleep is to waking, death is to the resurrection—a prelude, a transitory state, ushering in a mightier power of life. 2. They whom men call dead do really live unto God. They were dead while they lived this dying life on earth, and dead when they were in the last avenues of death. But after they had once died death had no more dominion : they escaped as a bird out of the snare of the fowler ; the snare was broken and they were delivered. Once dead, once dissolved, the unclothed spirit is beyond the power of decay. There is no weakness, nor weariness, nor wasting away, nor wandering of the burdened spirit ; it is disenthralled, and lives its own life, unmingled and buoyant. 3. Those whom the world calls dead are sleeping, because they are taking their rest (Rev. xiv. 13). Not as the heretics of old vainly and coldly dreamed, as if they slept without thought or stir of consciousness from the hour of death to the morning of the resurrection. Their rest is not the rest of a stone, cold and lifeless ; but of wearied humanity. They rest from their labours ; they have no more persecution, nor stoning, nor scourging, nor crucifying ; no more martyrdoms by fire, or the wheel, or barbed shafts ; they have no more false witness nor cutting tongues ; no more bitterness of heart, nor iron entering into the soul ; no more burdens of wrong, nor amazement, nor perplexity. They rest, too, from the weight of " the body of our humiliation "—from its sufferings and pains. They rest also from their warfare against sin and Satan. Above all, they rest from the buffetings of evil in themselves. The sin that dwelt in them died when through death they began to live. The unimpeded soul puts forth its newborn life as a tree in a kindly soil invited by a gentle sky : all that checked it is passed away, all that draws it into ripeness bathes it with fostering power. The Refiner shall perfect His work upon them, cleansing them sevenfold, even as gold seven times tried ; and all the taint and bias of their spiritual being shall be detached and corrected. Theirs is a bliss only less perfect than the glory of His kingdom when the new creation shall be accomplished. Lessons : 1. We ought to mourn rather for the living than for the dead, for they have to die, and death is terrible. 2. It is life, rather than death, that we ought to fear. For life and all that it contains—thought, and speech, and deed, and will—is a deeper and more awful mystery. In life is the warfare of good and ill, the hour and power of darkness, the lures and assaults of the wicked one. Here is no rest, shelter, safety. Wherefore let us fear life, and we shall not be afraid to die. For in the new creation of God death walks harmless. (*Archdeacon Manning.*) *The sleep of the faithful departed :*—It seems a strange opinion, entertained by some, that the souls of the faithful during the interval between death and the resurrection are in a profound sleep and devoid of all power of perception. This opinion appears to be grounded upon such expressions as " to fall asleep in Jesus," a phrase which probably represents nothing more than the well-known resemblance between the appearances of death and of its cousin sleep—the eyelids closed in darkness, the face in calm repose, the voice hushed in silence. How could St. Paul (Phil. i. 23) think it better for him—yea, far better—to depart from the body than to remain in it, if on his departure from the body he should sink into the lethargy of an unconscious sleep ? Is it not better to have the use of our reasoning faculty than to be deprived of it ? Is it not better to praise God in the land of the living than to be in a state in which we can have no knowledge of God at all, nor any capacity of praising Him ? Besides, the apostle does not express a desire to die, merely that he may be at rest and freed from persecutions and the anxieties of his apostolic office, but chiefly or solely with this object—that he may be with Christ. Now, surely we are more with Christ while we abide in the flesh than when we depart from it, if, when we have departed this life, we have no perception of Christ at all. In 2 Cor. xii. 2-4 St. Paul speaks of visions and revelations of the Lord, which he had seen and heard in the third heaven and in Paradise ; whether he was then in the body or out of the body, he professes ignorance : he could not tell : God knew. But the inference is obvious, that of the two alternatives he thought one quite as likely as the other ; that neither of them was impossible or unreasonable, and therefore that the soul when it is out of the body is as capable of seeing and of hearing as when it is in the body. From what the same apostle says in 2 Cor. v. 8, we may argue that as absence implies separation, so presence implies conjunction. But surely there is no need of this argument ; the very phrase " to be present with the Lord " intimates a consciousness of that presence. In addition, is there not much weight in the consideration that in the state of separation from the body our souls have the same condition that the soul of Christ then had, because He took upon Him all our nature ; and it is certain that His soul, during its separation, neither slumbered nor slept, but visited the souls of the fathers and preached the gospel to the prisoners of hope (1 Pet. iii. 18-20). These several considerations all tend to one conclusion—that the death of the body is by no means the sleep of the soul. How, indeed, the spirits of departed saints are employed is not recorded. We are told that they " rest from their labours " ; but the rest here specified means a refreshment, a delightful repose from earthly trials and troubles ; it does not exclude a blissful activity in a new and heavenly sphere. St. Paul speaks of visions and revelations and angelic utterances transcending all human utterance. That departed saints in their new home are in the saving Presence seems certain ; that they are therefore blessed is equally certain. But in what their blessedness consists is known to God and it is known to themselves. (*Canon T. S. Evans, D.D.*) *Christ died that saints might sleep in death :*— In Scripture, the book of life, the death of the saints is called a " sleep." It is observable how the apostle varies the expression—Jesus *died*, and the saints *sleep* in Him ; He sustained death with all its terrors, that it might be a calm sleep to His people. They enjoy so perfect a rest in the beds of dust as even in the softest down. (*W. Bates, D.D.*) *Death a sleep :*—I. FOR WHOM DEATH IS SO MITIGATED AND SOFTENED AS TO BE REPRESENTED AS A STATE OF SLEEP ? Those who believe in and are thus spiritually united to Christ. To these death is softened because Christ has died, and thus deprived death of its sting by being pierced with it, and because Christ has risen, robbing death of its terrors by spoiling its principalities and powers. There is, therefore, nothing in it now to fear. II. WHAT ILLUSTRATION DOES THIS REPRESENTATION AFFORD AS TO THE CONDITION OF THE DEPARTED ? It is not designed to represent it as a state of unconsciousness, as some affirm. Apart from philosophical reflections this is refuted by the parable of the rich man and Lazarus, by the promise of Christ to the dying thief, and by Paul's confidence in and desire for the " gain " of dying and being with Christ. The figure illustrates—1. The repose of the saints. We know that " Tired nature's sweet restorer, balmy sleep," is a season of quiet repose, when faculties which have been wearied and worn by exertion are at ease and at rest. Death to the believer is as the beginning of repose after the labour of the day (John xi. 9-11). (1) Life is a day of toil. We walk, run, plant, sow, reap, watch, wrestle, fight, &c. Ours is a hard, toilsome course. The task of resisting indwelling sin, of enduring affliction, bearing the obloquy of the ungodly, contending against the powers of darkness, of acquiring the attainment of Christian character, and of extending Christ's kingdom—these constitute a work which we are to do with all our might. (2) When we have finished, as hirelings, our day, the body rests in the grave, the soul in the paradise of God. Are we labourers ? Then we leave the field and lay down our tools. Are we travellers ? Then we terminate our long and wearisome journey and cross the threshold of our Father's mansion. Are we soldiers ? Then we take off our armour. Are we mariners ? Then we heave over the last ocean billow and enter into the desired haven. The sleep of the labouring man is sweet, and how sweet is the slumber of those who rest in Jesus ! 2. Their security. The season of slumber is assumed to be the season of security ; and no man in ordinary cases would commit himself to the one unless he could calculate on the other. The Christian would not be at rest if he were not secure. (1) When the time has come for his spirit to enter into immortality it is safe for ever. They are with Christ, and you might as well talk about His insecurity as theirs. (2) The body also is safe, for it also has been redeemed. The dust of every Christian is sacred ; it may be scattered, but Christ watches it and protects it. 3. Their prospect of restoration. When men lie down to sleep it is with the prospect of waking again in recruited vigour. So the resurrection of the saints will—(1) Invest their bodies with ineffable dignity and splendour. (2) Communicate higher and more ecstatic pleasures to the soul. III. WHAT INFLUENCE SHOULD THESE REPRESENTATIONS PRODUCE ON THE LIVING ? 1.

We ought not to indulge excessive grief on account of those Christian friends whom it has been, or whom it may yet be, our lot to lose. 2. It becomes us as Christians not to dread the arrival of death for ourselves. Do you tremble when, at the hour of midnight, you go to the couch of repose? 3. It should impress upon us the propriety of desiring the same consolations for ourselves. (*J. Parsons.*)    *Death a sleep :*—The death of the Christian may be so called because of—I. ITS PEACEFUL NATURE. 1. He lies down to die calmly as the tired labourer to take his nightly rest: not like the man who dreads the hour of rest because of the recollection of sleepless nights. 2. The approach of death is often silent and soft as the approach of sleep. As the weary man sinks imperceptibly into a state of slumber, so the Christian sometimes without a struggle passes into God's presence. It is like the sinking of day into night, or more properly the rising of the night into day. II. ITS ATTRACTIVENESS. How the labourer, toiling beneath a burning sun, will sometimes long for the shades of evening when he may stretch his tired limbs! So does the Christian, only with an intenser longing, look for his sleep. Not that earth is without its attractions; but it is the place of his exile, strife, pilgrimage. Yonder is his home radiant with immortal glory, and thronged with bright multitudes, and death is attractive because it is the vestibule to that. III. IT IS TO BE FOLLOWED BY AN AWAKENING. The heathen might have no hope of a resurrection. Their poets might bewail the fleetingness of life and the unknown condition of the dead. Even the Jew might see but dimly the shadow of the resurrection. But to the Christian it is the object of sure and certain hope. We are apt to speak of the dead as "lost"; but that they cannot be, as they are under Christ's care. They sleep only till He bids them wake. IV. ITS REPOSE. It is that state of "rest which remaineth for the people of God." Life's fitful fever is over: they sleep well. Death is not a state of unconsciousness; the very figure of sleep forbids that. They rest from — 1. Their labours : all that makes work laborious will then be unknown. Work they will, but in congenial employment and with unweariable faculties. 2. From persecution, false witness, wrong, disappointment, &c. 3. From pain, mental and physical. 4. From warfare against sin. Satan and the world can tempt no more. 5. From the buffetings of evil in themselves. V. ITS REFRESHMENT. The difference between the labourer who rises in the morning refreshed by the night's repose but faintly shadows forth the difference between the wearied wasted body which sinks into the grave and the renovated body, blooming with immortal youth, exempt from infirmities, endowed with unknown strength which shall come forth on the morning of the resurrection. Conclusion: The subject should lead us—1. To moderate our grief over the loss of those friends who sleep in Jesus. When they so sleep we have no mourning as regards them. 2. To contemplate death with much less fear and aversion. 3. To devote ourselves with increased earnestness to our present labour. 4. But there are some to whom death is a very different kind of sleep. The poet says, "To die, to sleep. To sleep! perchance to dream! Ay, there's the rub." The sleep of the ungodly is disturbed by fearful dreams—nay, realities, from which there is no escape but by being "in Christ" now. (*W. Landells, D.D.*)    *Sleeping in Jesus :*— Unbelief in immortality existed generally before the Christian era. About that time implicit belief in the after life became a conviction with multitudes. We ask any unbeliever to account for that. What produced this result? There is no effect without a cause. Was there not some grand event that gave the truth that we are immortal such vital power that even the lowly, the poor, the humblest—not the learned, not the philosophers only—became thoroughly convinced of it? Walk through the Roman catacombs; mark the difference there is between the epitaphs of the Epicureans on the one side, and the Christians on the other. One of the Roman tombs has this inscription, "While I lived, I lived well—my play is now ended, soon yours will be;—farewell, and applaud me." Another says, "Baths, wine, and love ruin the constitution, but they make life what it is—farewell." Then comes the tender stroke of a mother's grief—"O relentless fortune, that delights in cruel death, why is Maximus so early snatched from me?" Then turn and see the epitaphs of the early Christians—"Zoticus laid here to sleep." "The sleeping place in Christ of Elipis." "Valeria sleeps in peace." Is not that an echo of those wonderful words that were uttered at the tomb of Lazarus: "He is not dead, but sleepeth," or, when He said of the ruler's daughter, "The maid is not dead, but sleepeth?" Is not that an echo of that wonderful teaching of Christ that death is sleep—that the cemetery is what the word literally means, "a sleeping place"? What can have brought about such a change in the world? Intuition failed utterly to do more than faintly discern that such a thing as immortality might be. Philosophical reasoning produced nothing but Epicurean carelessness and Stoical contempt for death. But here we see a poor mother lay down her daughter, slain it may be by the arrows of persecution, but she says, " She sleeps in Jesus." It is sleep that knows an awaking, a short night that breaks into a glorious morning. Immortality is not now a dubious opinion, it is positive conviction. Whence comes it? Only from Christ. His life, His death, and especially His resurrection unfold it with marvellous clearness. *Sleeping in Jesus :*—I. THOSE WHO SLEEP IN JESUS DIE CONFIDING IN HIS PROTECTION. We all know how pleasantly one goes to sleep when he enjoys the friendship, and can confide in the protection of those about him. In such circumstances the mind is unbent, the spirit soothed and tranquillized, and we give ourselves up to rest with peculiar confidence and satisfaction. We know that however profoundly we may slumber, however completely we may be wrapped in insensibility, our safety will be secured. As a familiar illustration, place a child in the arms of a stranger, and however inclined to sleep it may have been before, it becomes instantly aroused; discomposed and terrified, it cannot trust itself to sleep in such a situation. But transfer it to the arms of its mother; let it lay its head on the familiar bosom, and feel itself under the reassuring smile of maternal tenderness, and ere long its fears subside, and its eyes calmly close in the consciousness of safety. We are all children thus when we come to die. Every child of God has a long sleep to take. When the short wintry day of life is over, the night of death closes in and darkens around us. But the Christian knows with whom he is to take his rest: he falls " asleep in Jesus." He is not in the hands of strangers, whose dubious character and unknown intentions might fill him with alarm, but in the sweet custody of a fast and faithful friend. He has long trusted his soul to Jesus, and now, in the hour of death, he is not afraid to trust his body to Him. He may not depart singing a song of victory; but as he has lived by faith, and not by sense, so now he dies in faith. II. THOSE WHO SLEEP IN JESUS ENTER INTO A STATE OF PERFECT REPOSE. There is something revolting to nature in the associations of " the house appointed for all living "; but the grave wears no aspect of gloom or horror to the believer in Christ Jesus. To him it is simply the tabernacle for a night of that " flesh " in which, " at the latter day," he shall " see God "; a tabernacle, moreover, endeared and hallowed by the fact that his Redeemer occupied it before him. "There laid they Jesus "; and though the sepulchre did not permanently retain Him, He was yet long enough its tenant to strip it of every gloomy association—to season it, if we may so speak, and render it a sweet and grateful resting-place for the dust of his sleeping saints. When the Christian is laid in the grave he is consigned to consecrated ground; he occupies " the place where the Lord lay "; and the marshalled hosts of heaven are the guardians of his rest. But where is his soul while his body thus rests in sacred and dignified repose? " Absent from the body," it is " present with the Lord." III. THOSE WHO SLEEP IN JESUS REST IN HOPE OF A JOYFUL RESURRECTION. When a man of sound body and mind retires to rest with a good conscience, and with his heart full of a great event which on the morrow is to crown him with honour and happiness, how light and airy his slumbers are! how vivid and lifelike the pictures which his buoyant fancy paints for him of the joys which await his waking! Thus it is, so far as the illustration is apt and adequate, with the man who " sleeps in Jesus." He commits himself to the grave full of glorious anticipations; and exulting in the assurance, that as certainly as morning succeeds night in the natural world, so the morning of resurrection shall succeed the night of the grave; and then " this corruptible shall put on incorruption, and this mortal immortality." It is this glorious prospect, set before the saint in the act of dying, and contemplated by his living spirit after death, that lights up the darkness of the narrow house, and reconciles immortal man to his present mortal destiny. He fixes his eye upon this, till his soul realizes it in all its interest and grandeur, and with his heart swelling with triumph and overflowing with joy, he exclaims—" I know that my Redeemer liveth, and that He shall stand at the latter day upon the earth; and though after my skin worms destroy this body, yet in my flesh shall I see God!" (*J. Young, D.D.*) *The sleep of death :*—" Slept " in the New Testament is a word sacred to the dying of the righteous; hence that sweet inscription found upon hundreds of slabs in the Christian catacombs of Rome, " Dormit," he sleeps; while on Pagan monuments of the same age, spared as if on purpose to furnish a contrast, we read again and again the rebellious and plaintive inscription, " Abreptus," snatched away. In the one case a violent disruption of the tenderest ties, in the other a slumber falling as softly as the evening dew. (*R. D. Hitchcock, D.D.*)    *The soul does not sleep in death :*—When a person is asleep what is it that rests? It is simply the muscles and the nerves and the wearied limbs ; the heart goes on beating, the lungs respiring and expiring; and what is remarkable in sleep, the soul never sleeps at all. It seems that when one is asleep, the soul often travels to far-distant lands, or sails upon the bosom of the deep, amid the blue hills and green glens of other parts of the land; exploring, thinking, searching, studying. The soul is never literally dead (though it may sometimes forget) to every thought and object, to all that enters by the avenues of the senses. If sleep be the metaphor of death, it does not prove that the soul is insensible, but only that the body, the outward garment only, having been worn and wasted in the wear and toil of this present life, is folded up and laid aside in that wardrobe—the grave—a grave as truly in the keeping of the Son of God as are the angels of the skies and the cherubim in glory. (*J. Cumming, D.D.*)    *Pilgrims at rest :*—Our first thoughts have to do with the difference between the living and the dead. 1. In being. "There is a natural body and a spiritual body." We shall never be without a vehicle, a covering. Paul speaks about being "clothed upon." 2. In place. The place of the departed may not be far from us, if, as some have held, they are our guardian angels. The angel told John that he was his "fellow-servant." As to the size of the place, what circumscribed, narrow, cramped notions we have! Don't speak of it as if it were not larger than Rutland, and of our meeting with each other there as if we were neighbours in the same street. The region is measureless, and the inhabitants "no man can number." 3. Those who have gone thither were once among the living here. I. How DESCRIBED. "Them which are asleep." This means more than is usually supposed. It means much about this life. 1. Not conscious of sin and sorrow, but wholly freed from them—"asleep." There can be no sleep where there is great pain : "if he sleep he shall do well." What consolation this for the bereaved ! The last sigh breathed, groan uttered, pang felt. 2. Watched and protected by the heavenly Father as children "asleep." How easily and comfortably children go to sleep knowing that they will be cared for ! So with them that "sleep *in Jesus*." 3. Without recurrence of pain and anxiety. Continuous sleep, undisturbed by roar of battle or tremor of earthquake. 4. But we cannot say of the lost that they are asleep. "There is no peace to the wicked." II. WHAT OUR KNOWLEDGE IS ABOUT THEM. "Concerning." 1. In engagements. Not continual feasting and hymn-singing. Variety of work. Tastes and capabilities find suitable spheres here : and surely in the other world we shall be ourselves, and every want will be met. 2. In powers. Present powers improved, memory more accurate, judgment more sound, perception more vivid. And from altered conditions of being, new powers will be developed. 3. In intercourse. "Sit down with Abraham"; "know as we are known." Similarity of view, thought answering to thought, feeling to feeling. Many here never seem to meet with their *likes*. "Then face to face." The mentally great drawn together, and others grouping according to their kind. (*J. S. Withington.*)    *Different ideas of immortality :*—Each hopes to find that which for him is the best thing, eternized in the future. The Indian looks for a boundless war-path, with victories ever new over animals and men. The Mohammedan desires, as a good beyond all which earth can offer, the utmost reach of sensual pleasure ; where wines shall be quaffed from diamond cups, and the beauty of houris be enjoyed without stint ; where the soul shall be dissolved, yet for ever rejuvenated, in the utmost attainable physical luxury. The philosopher craves a vision of truth. And the artist looks for terraces of beauty and majestical structures; where the pillars shall be worlds, and the pediments milky-ways; where colours more brilliant, lines more light, and proportions more perfect than here have been imagined, shall for ever surround and instruct the fine spirit. Each people, and each person, according to the different attainments of each, and their several characteristics, delights to anticipate the possession in the future of that special good which to each is supreme. And in nothing is the progress of refinement and virtue more evidently shown than in the higher ideas which are entertained, in successive epochs and by different nations, of what may be thus aspired to and expected. Men differ in their estimate of the goods of the present life. But when they transfer that estimate to the future, as it becomes colossal and transcendent, so the differences between them, which are indicated and gauged by it, become most conspicuous. (*Dr. Storrs.*)    **That ye sorrow not, even as others which have no hope.** *Having no hope :*—We need hope to cheer us all along in life, and to sustain us at the end of it. A sustaining hope, in view of the inevitable, must look forward to a life, beyond the present, of permanent good and joy. It must be founded on sufficient reasons : such as (*a*) the promise of God, and (*b*) the earnest of the fulfilment of that promise in our experience. They can have no such hope who have—I. No GOD, whether they are atheists in belief, or are living atheistic lives in mere carelessness. II. No BIBLE ; who do not practically receive and rest on a revelation. III. No SAVIOUR ; do not rest on Christ. IV. No PREPARATION FOR THE FUTURE. Nothing but the gospel offers such a hope. Have you laid hold on this hope ? Are you giving diligence to the full assurance of it ? (*C. W. Camp.*) *Sorrow without hope :*—The mother of poor Tonda led me to the house where the body was laid. The narrow space of the room was crowded ; about two hundred women were sitting and standing around, singing mourning songs to doleful and monotonous airs. As I stood looking, filled with solemn thoughts, the mother of Tonda approached. She threw herself at the foot of her dead son, and begged him to speak to her once more. And then, when the corpse did not answer, she uttered a shriek, so long, so piercing, such a wail of love and grief, that tears came into my eyes. Poor African mother ! she was literally as one sorrowing without hope, for these poor people count on nothing beyond the present life. (*Du Chaillu.*) *Hopeless death :*—The dreary and cheerless aspect which the state of the dead presented to Homer's mind, even in the case of Achilles, his prime hero, and Agamemnon, king of men, and Ajax, whose peculiarly unhappy fate and brilliant services on earth would have entitled him to consolation, if there had been any to be found, hardly needs a comment. The first of these bitterly contrasts his shadowy primacy with the lot of the meanest hireling on earth. The dead have no prospect ; they only look back to the past, or seek to snatch a glimpse of the present. They dwell on the triumphs, or on the wrongs and sufferings, of this mortal life, and sympathize, after a forlorn and bereaved fashion, with those whom they have left behind. The picture is one of such blank desolation as came spontaneously to the poet's mind, on whom neither faith nor philosophy had yet dawned, but who yet could not so far renounce man's birthright of immortality as to conceive of the utter extinction of personality in what had once been a human soul. The dead of Homer have pride, they cherish grudges and curiosity, affection and resentment, but they have, in a later poet's phrase, " left hope behind." The casual exceptions of the few favoured heroes who were by birth or marriage connected with Zeus himself, only prove more pointedly the dismal universality of the rule by which the rest are bound. (*H. Hayman, D.D.*) *Without hope :*—Mr. Robert Owen, the sceptic, once visited a gentleman who was an earnest Christian. In walking out they came to the gentleman's family grave. Mr. Owen, addressing him, said : " There is one advantage I have over Christians—I am not afraid to die. Most Christians are afraid to die ; but if some of my business were settled, I should be perfectly willing to die at any moment." " Well," said his companion, " you say you have no fear in death ; have you any hope in death ? " After a solemn pause, he replied, " No ! " " Then," replied the gentleman, pointing to an ox standing near, " you are on a level with that brute ; he has fed till he is satisfied, and stands in the shade whisking off the flies, and has neither hope nor fear." *A suggestive contrast :*—Mirabeau, the infidel, who was the hero of the French nation, died as a Frenchman might be expected to die, with a great deal of show and talk about the grandeur of his own genius and the loss to his country, and his last words were, " Crown me with flowers ; I am about to sink into the last sleep ! " In the same month there died in London one upon whose lips thousands had hung, whose name was a household word in the towns and villages in this country ; he had lived till his white hairs were the joy and reverence of all classes of society, and as John Wesley fell asleep in Jesus, among his last words were :—

> " I'll praise my Maker while I've breath,
>   And when my voice is lost in death,
>     Praise shall employ my nobler powers."

Let any one trace the effects of those two lives ; mark the progress of revolutionary principles in France, and notice the influence of that great revival of religion, of which John Wesley was the means, in the subsequent history of the English nation, and you will be constrained to say that it was the influence of that revival that maintained the principles of freedom and constitutional government among us, besides extending true religion among the masses of the community. (*Handbook to Scripture Doctrines.*) *Hope in death :*—The old custom of using rosemary at funerals is thus explained by Wheatley, on the Common Prayer : " To express their hopes that their friend is not lost for ever, each person in the company usually bears in his hand a sprig of rosemary ; a custom which seems to have taken its rise from a practice among the heathens, of a quite different import. For they have no thought of a future resurrection, but believing that the bodies of those that were dead would for ever lie in the grave, made use of cypress at their funerals, which is a tree that being once cut never revives, but dies away. But Christians, on the other hand, having better hopes, and knowing that this very body of their friend, which they are now going solemnly to commit to the grave, shall one day rise again, and be reunited to his soul, instead of cypress, distribute rosemary to the company, which being always green, and flourishing the more for being crops (and of which a sprig only being set in the ground, will sprout up immediately and branch into a tree), is more proper to express their confidence and trust." *Hope in death :—* Helen Founleson, one of six Scottish martyrs executed at Perth in 1543, being denied the privilege of dying with her husband, kissed him at the foot of the gallows on which he was to suffer, and took leave of him with these words, "Husband, rejoice, for we have lived together many joyful days, but this day, in which we must die, ought to be the most joyful to us both, because we must have joy for ever. Therefore I will not bid you good-night, for we shall suddenly meet with joy in the kingdom of heaven." (*J. F. B. Tinling, B.A.*) *Gone before :—*The Rev. J. Newton once said to a gentleman who had lately lost his daughter, " Sir, if you were going to the East Indies I suppose you would like to send a remittance before you. This little girl is just like a remittance sent to heaven before you yourself. I suppose a merchant in charge is never heard expressing himself thus : ' Oh, my dear ship, I am sorry she has got into port so soon ! I am sorry she has escaped the storms that are coming ! ' Neither should we sorrow for children dying." (*Whitecross.*) *The victory of hope in sorrow :—*One of the lessons which our Master enforced was that there should be a marked contrast between His disciples and worldly men. If a Christian differs in no important respect from a man without Christian faith, wherein is he better ? Christians were not to be saved from the casualties of men, but there was expected to be in them, under the influence of God's Spirit, something that should enable them to endure the various experiences of life in a way that common men could not. They were to regard life and death with a marked difference from the world. It was in this spirit that Paul wrote these words. There is to be a difference between death in the Christian and death in the unchristian household. If you bow your head or are overborne as others, how are you any better ? If in anything one might be left to his own way we should suppose it would be in the sorrows of bereavement. But no : even here we are to be Christians. I. It is no part of Christian teaching that men should not sorrow ; but it is a part of Christian teaching that men should not sorrow as others who have no hope. Christ suffered and shed tears ; but both stood in the reflected light of the other world. The apostles suffered, but they gloried in the fact that if they suffered they would reign. Suffering is good if it arouses in men their divine rather than their lower human nature ; it is to be such as does not exclude joy and is in the light of joy. II. Neither is it the teaching of Christ that the affections and relationships of men are trivial and unworthy of regard. Indeed, we have no guides to go by except these. Who would know the love of God if we did not know the love of man? To say that human affections are nothing, and that to love one another is to love dust, is to destroy the potency and value and use of those very ordinances of the household and friendship by which God means to develop our spiritual nature. Some teach that we are to let all the relationships of life seem so little in comparison with Christ that it will make no difference to us whether they go or stay. I could not respect a religion which made love a mere currency for good in this world alone. The spirit of Christianity sanctifies the love of husband and wife, parent and child, &c. ; so that we may be sure if we love right here we shall love for ever. III. Least of all does Christ teach that pain is unworthy of manhood and is to be strangled. Any such violence is to destroy what He elaborately created. The teachings of the Bible, and the example of Christ and of His apostles and saints has inculcated anything but the stoical doctrine. The Christian idea is the great power of victory over suffering, the bush burning but unconsumed. IV. But Christ did require that we should look upon our sorrow as surrounded by considerations derivable from His life and truth. 1. A wanton and ungovernable sorrow is a violation of Christian duty. It acts as if there were no God or Christ. There is a great difference, of course, between the first burst of sorrows and a continuous state. When one has been worn out physically, the gracious God finds no fault with the uncontrollable sweep of anguish. Let the cloud burst, but do not let the waters become a deep flowing river. When the first rush of feeling is over there should be that in the believer which will bring him back to Christ. 2. It is not right sorrow that seeks every aggravation, employing memory as a drag-net to bring back refuse experiences, to create unhappiness, and recount miseries as if proud of them. Blessed are they who can shut the door on the past and not open it again unless to bring some fairer joy and better hope. 3. A true Christian bereavement ought not to narrow the disposition and take men away from active affairs. The same Christian instinct which seeks consecration to the Master's service should find in it an antidote to sorrow. If you suffer you will often find comfort in ministering to some one's affliction. Dr. Spurzheim used to say that no woman was fit to be wife and mother till she had been educated in suffering. I say that no man or woman is fit for the highest offices of friendship and life without it. 4. Every man that suffers bereavement ought to make it manifest that it is grace not nature that heals. It is true that grace employs nature, and that time is a good nurse; but a Christian ought to be ashamed if nothing can cure him but time. How many there are who wait until their griefs are worn out before they get over them. But the man who knows how to apply the promise and realize the presence at the right time, has not only comfort in himself, but is a living and powerful witness to the power of Christ such as refutes infidelity as nothing else can, and wins to the Gospel as no preaching can do. (*H. W. Beecher.*)    *Christian mourning:*—I. THE SORROW WHICH CHRISTIANS MAY LAWFULLY INDULGE FOR DEPARTED FRIENDS. Feel your griefs, bereaved and desolate believers; you are permitted to sorrow. Away with the sentiments of those who teach that we should evidence an utter insensibility, a stupid unconcern, under affliction! Such is not the command of that God, "who knoweth our frame, and remembereth that we are dust:" nor of that Redeemer who, "in all the afflictions of His people was afflicted." Look at the Scriptures, ye who cruelly chide those tears that relieve the wounded heart, and say if Abraham violated his duty when he came to Kirjarth-arba to mourn for Sarah, and weep there. The lustre of Joseph's character was not obscured when he grieved for his father at the threshing-floor of Atad "with great and sore lamentation." Jeremiah was not forgetful of his elevated office when his prophetical harp sounded such mournful tones over the corpse of the good Josiah. We do not feel less attached to the Christians of Asia because they wept sore on parting from Paul, "most of all, because they should see his face no more." We sympathize with the pious widows who stood by the body of Dorcas weeping, and "showing the coats and garments which she had made for the poor while she was yet with them." Those "devout men" were not less devout when "they carried Stephen to the grave, and made great lamentation." There is nothing inconsistent with the high character of that Mary who sat delightedly at the feet of Jesus, and yet poured out big bitter tears at the door of her brother's sepulchre. But why mention inferior cases? Behold Jesus—our law-giver and model, authorizing a submissive grief by His emotion and tears at the tomb of Lazarus. An unlamented death is divinely represented as a judgment and a curse (Jer. xvi. 5, 6; xii. 18). But we may mourn as Christians over our departed; and where can the soul that is bowed and overwhelmed better flee than to its Father? Where find more comfort than in the bosom of its God? Christianity does not destroy our nature; it only regulates it. In giving us a heart, God has permitted us to exercise its emotions, and sensibility, instead of being a weakness in the Christian, is one of his noblest prerogatives, since it is one great source of his virtues. No; it is not the soul of a Christian which can be callous and insensible while standing by the corpse or the grave of a departed friend. II. THE SORROW WHICH CHRISTIANS ARE FORBIDDEN TO EXERCISE. 1. When in their hearts, or by their lips, they murmur against the disposals of God, and blame Him for unkindness and cruelty to them. Jacob was faulty in this respect when, on the reported death of his favourite son, he exclaimed, "All these things are against me!" In our severest griefs we must be persuaded that God acts not only with infinite wisdom, but also with infinite goodness; and that not only are His general dispensations merciful, but the particular dispensation which has afflicted us is the fruit of covenant love. 2. When the grief of Christians unfits them for holy duties, and prevents the exercise of religious devotion. What, because one we loved is dead, shall our heart also become dead and lifeless in all spiritual employments, and as cold as is his inanimate body? What, shall our tears be ever flowing over a mouldering form, and our affections never be raised to a living God? 3. When sorrow does not lead Christians to inquire what was the design of God in afflicting them. As Christians, instead of being "swallowed up in overmuch sorrow," we should study by each bereavement to feel more deeply the vanity of earth, the importance of eternity, and the preciousness of Christ. 4. When Christians follow not their departed friends beyond the grave. They are not in the grave, their bodies only are there; they, as emancipated spirits, are with "the spirits of just men made perfect." Sorrow is criminal, therefore, if it relates only to the outer covering laid aside for a little while. 5. Sorrow is also criminal when Christians have no well-grounded hope of re-union and fellowship with their departed in heaven. Heaven is the glorious rendezvous of all saintly men (John xiv. 1–3). (*H. Kollock, D.D.*) *Consolations accompanying the death of saints:*—I. THERE ARE SOME WHO HAVE NO HOPE IN THEIR SORROW. 1. As far as we can, we should see that no relative passed away out of our home and left us in unmixed grief. 2. Are there any who would so treat a relative as to leave him in doubt as to their salvation? II. THERE ARE THOSE WHO HAVE GOOD HOPE MIXED WITH THEIR GRIEF. 1. Even when there is the strongest hope of salvation, there will be sorrow. 2. Sorrow mixed with hope is full of comfort. 3. This comfort depends upon acquiescence in the will of God disposing us as His own. 4. This hope draws its consolations amidst sorrow mainly because it is "full of immortality." III. THE GROUNDS OF THIS CONSOLATION AS HERE LAID DOWN. Death is compared to a sleep as indicating—1. The calm repose of a dying believer. 2. The security of the saints in Christ's hand. 3. The certainty of the resurrection. 4. The beauty and glory of the redeemed Church. 5. Recognition of the saints in heaven. (*J. Walker.*)

Ver. 14. **For if we believe that Jesus died and rose again, even so them also which sleep in Jesus will God bring with Him.**—*Christ's resurrection and ours:*—I. THE EVENT PREDICTED. "Will God bring with Him." 1. This is affirmed to meet the fear that God could not do so. The ground of their sorrow was that their departed friends would be deprived of the glories of Christ's advent, which was thought to be near. Paul now assures them that the dead will share it as powerfully as the living. 2. The Thessalonians thus believed in Christ's second coming. This was a subject often on our Lord's lips, and is a prominent feature in this Epistle. It is kept in the background by many Christians to their disadvantage. Frequent thought about it is requisite to spirituality of mind. Paul says, "Our conversation is in heaven," and his reason is "from whence also we look for the Saviour." Heavenly mindedness is the drawing of self to Christ. 3. If God brings departed saints with Him, they are with Him now, otherwise He could not bring them. They are "the general assembly of the first-born;" "Spirits of just men made perfect;" "Absent from the body, present with the Lord." The New Testament again and again asserts that the saints after death go direct into God's presence. 4. When departed spirits are brought by God they will know one another. It is amazing to suppose that we should know each other on earth and not in heaven; that we should have a less amount of perception as to each other's character and identity there than here. If this be admitted the passage which was intended to comfort is a mockery. How could the Thessalonians be comforted by the coming of their deceased friends if they were not to know them? Read chap. ii. 19, 20. How could Paul's converts be his crown of rejoicing if he was not to know them? The same doctrine is proved from the parable of the rich man and Lazarus and from the appearance of Moses and Elias at the Transfiguration. II. ITS CERTAINTY. 1. If we believe that Christ died and rose again it follows as a necessary consequence that those who sleep in Him He will bring with Him. Observe how everything is based on the death and resurrection of Christ; and in view of that it is no wonder that the first preachers were selected because they were witnesses of the resurrection. (1) The object of Christ's death was "to redeem unto Himself a peculiar people." When God speaks of the results of that death as to its primary purpose, He says, "He shall see His seed;" "He shall see of the travail of His soul and be satisfied." (2) The object of the resurrection was to be the guarantee that the work of redemption was accomplished, and to be the first-fruits of its accomplishment; to be followed by its proper results, a harvest. So that if we believe these two facts, *i.e.*, that Christ finished the whole work that the Father gave Him to do, we must believe that the Father will fulfil His covenant part of the transaction and give to Christ the seed, and that the seed shall be perfected and glorified.

To this it is necessary that He should bring the spirits of the saints to meet their bodies, which is the assertion of Paul here. 2. It follows, also, that the Church being thus perfected in herself must also be perfected in her circumstances. "Father I will also that those whom Thou gavest Me be with Me," &c. (ver. 17). III. ITS OBJECT AND PURPOSE. The re-union of the saints—1. With their bodies. 2. With their friends. 3. With Christ, body and soul. Conclusion : The passage is full of comfort, but there is a tremendous limitation in it. It refers exclusively to those who sleep in Christ and those who are living in Him when He comes. Are you " in Christ "? (*C. Molyneux, M.A.*) *Christ's resurrection the pledge of ours :*— At our birth our bodies became a battle-ground between life and death. During the first ten years death makes many conquests. At ten years death begins to fall back. At twenty, life is triumphant. At thirty, life foresees the future. At forty, the battle is hot. At fifty, death inflicts some wounds, and life begins an orderly retreat. At sixty, life feels her strength failing. At seventy, the retreat becomes a rout. At eighty, death waves the black flag and cries, "No quarter!" This is no fancy picture; it is no preacher's dream; it is a fact undeniable, inevitable, universal! Indifference cannot affect its certainty, and scepticism cannot refute its truth. There is only one other fact with which we can confront this fact of death, and that is the resurrection of Jesus. Here fact meets fact. That is what we demand. We want a fact, a case, an instance, one single instance of resurrection. Once a sea-captain found his crew on shore apparently dead. The surgeon took one of the men and applied remedies, and the poisoned man stood on his feet. The captain shouted with joy, for in that one risen man he saw the possibility to save them all. So Christ brings life and immortality to light. His resurrection is not metaphysics, but history. Not a speculation for the future, but a fact of the past. Not a problem to be solved, but the solution of all problems. (*R. S. Barrett.*) *The certainty and blessedness of the resurrection of true Christians :*—I. WHAT IS MEANT BY THOSE THAT SLEEP IN JESUS. 1. Sleep is a metaphor used by sacred and profane writers. The ancient Christians called their place of burial *Koimetrion* " sleeping place." The figure is applied to the death of the wicked, but more frequently to that of the righteous (Isa. lvii. 2). Fitly is death so called as signifying rest (Rev. xiv. 13), and as preparatory to waking. 2. Death is called a sleeping " in Jesus " in conformity with 1 Cor. xv. 18, 23 ; 1 Thess. iv. 16; Heb. xi. 13. To sleep in Christ, to be Christ's, to die in Christ, to die in the faith, all mean the same ; to die in the state of true Christians as to be " in Christ " (John xv. 4 ; Rom. xiii. 1), means to be a Christian. And it is observable that we share all Christ's acts—die, rise, ascend, &c. with Him. 3. Some think that this is the sleep of the soul, but, on the contrary, Scripture applies the figure invariably to the body (Dan. xii. 2 ; Matt. xxvii. 52 ; Acts xiii. 36) ; and it is inconsistent with those passages which clearly affirm the soul to be awake (Luke xvi. 22, 23 ; xxiii. 43 ; Phil. i. 23 ; 2 Cor. v. 6). II. WHAT IS MEANT BY GOD'S BRINGING WITH HIM THEM THAT SLEEP IN JESUS. 1. The death and resurrection of Christ are an argument and proof of ours. Christ's death is mentioned as part of the argument because the truth of the miracle of the resurrection depends upon it. If Christ did not die He could not have risen. The resurrection is shown in 1 Cor. xv. 20 to be the pledge and first-fruits of ours. And that Christ intended to lay great stress upon this argument, appears in that He foretold it so often as the great sign He would give to the Jews to confute their infidelity (John ii. 18, 19 ; Matt. xii. 39, 40). Christ's resurrection gives us satisfaction in general of immortality, and then of His power to raise us because He raised Himself. And then it assures us of His truth and fidelity that He will perform what He promised. He could not have promised anything more improbable than His own resurrection ; and, therefore, since He kept His word in this, there is no reason to distrust Him in anything else than He has promised (Rev. i. 18; iii. 14). 2. Wherein the blessedness of the just shall consist. (1) In the mighty change which shall be made in our bodies and the glorious qualities with which they shall be invested. (*a*) "Equal to the angels " in immortal duration, and " children of God " in the perfect possession of His happiness (Luke xx. 35, 36). (*b*) Fashioned like unto the glorious body of Christ (Phil. iv. 20). (*c*) (1 Cor. xv. 35, &c.). (2) In the consequent happiness of the whole man, the body purified from frailty and corruption, and the soul from sin, and both admitted to the sight and enjoyment of the ever-blessed God (Rev. xxi. 2-4, 27 ; xxii. 3, 4). (*Abp. Tillotson.*) *The dead Christ and sleeping Christians :*—I. JESUS DIED THAT WE MIGHT SLEEP. The thought is that He, though sinless, died like a sinner. He took the place of a sinner ; was treated as a sinner as far as possible without sinning. He became what we sinners are, that we, the sinners, as far as possible, might become what He, the Righteous, is. Jesus died, then; His disciples sleep. Jesus spake of Lazarus sleeping, but never referred to His own death as sleep: that was not sleep, but death in its utter awfulness. The sting of death, He felt it; the victory of death, He yielded to it; the curse of death, He bore it; the desolation of death, He endured it; the darkness of death, He dreaded it. "O death! where is thy sting? O grave! where is thy victory?" were not words of our blessed Saviour, though they may be of the blessed dead. II. IF WE BELIEVE THAT JESUS ROSE FROM THE DEAD, WE MAY ALSO BELIEVE THAT THOSE WHO SLEEP IN JESUS GOD WILL BRING WITH HIM. So far as we loved them, we may love them as ever, as we shall yet behold them perfect in Jesus, without a semblance of sin, pure as He is pure. When He died, His sorrows were over, His work was done. And observe a remarkable fact— the body of the Redeemer was preserved from every indignity after the spirit had departed. Up to the moment of His death, He was subjected to every outrage. He was like the sinner; He was acting for the sinner; He was suffering for the sinner; and, while He was a consenting party, every indignity was heaped upon Him. But from the moment His spirit left His body, every honour was done to Him. His body, after His resurrection, was very unlike His body previously—it was "a spiritual body," invisible, and passing when and where it would and doing what it would. That body will be the model of our bodies; and the prime thought of St. Paul is—He will bring our friends to us again, and we shall know them, and be with them for ever with the Lord. (*A. Lind, D.D.*) *Resting on God's Word:*—A pastor in visiting a member of his church found her very sick, apparently dying. He said to her: "Mrs. M., you seem to be very sick." "Yes," said she, "I am dying." "And are you ready to die?" She lifted her eyes upon him with a solemn and fixed gaze, and, speaking with great difficulty, she replied: "Sir, God knows—I have taken Him—at His word—and—I am not afraid to die." It was a new definition of faith. "I have taken Him at His word," What a triumph of faith! What else could she have said that would have expressed so much in so few words?

Ver. 15. **This we say unto you by the Word of the Lord, that we which are alive and remain.**—*The waiting congregation of the redeemed:*—It is important here to observe that the apostle's language is not to be pedantically restricted as if "we" were necessarily to be taken literally. It is the broad, emotional, imaginative, not the restricted and historical "we"—the *we* not of him who associates himself with some accidental and arbitrary class, but of him who believes in the "Holy Catholic Church, the communion of saints"—the *we* of a true member of the supernatural community. He writes as a living man to living men, from the point of view of intimate communion with them; with that prophetic sympathy with the Church of the future which makes his pulses throb in unison with the waiting congregation of the redeemed. He puts himself in the same attitude with those who shall be alive at the Great Advent, "All who are alive on earth as we now are." Speaking as the mouthpiece of a generation which, like each of its successors, represents those who shall be alive at the Lord's coming, he says, "*We*"—*we*, the *living*, the "left over"—a word which is not without a tinge of sadness, in subtle harmony with the purpose Paul had in view. The fear which the Thessalonians had for their beloved ones was lest they might have suffered loss. They pitied them because they were taken. By this twice-repeated word, the pathetic refrain of this wonderful dirge (vers. 15, 17), the apostle seems to say—not that they are to be pitied; rather we who are left over, left without them in the world. If there is any leaving out in the case, it is we who are left out, not they. (*Bp. Alexander.*) *The Second Advent of Christ:*—Among the words of consolation in the valedictory discourse of Christ is the promise that He would come again and receive His people unto Himself. Time has sped noiselessly along. For nearly nineteen hundred years the Church's eyes have been strained with intense expectancy; but it has not lost confidence in the promise. Faith in the Second Advent of Christ is more widely spread and firmly held than ever. Long waiting has sharpened the longing, brightened the hope, and clarified the vision. Observe—I. THAT THE SECOND ADVENT OF CHRIST IS THE SUBJECT OF DIVINE REVELATION. "By the Word of the Lord." In a subject of such vast moment Paul was anxious to show that he spoke on the most incontrovertible authority. He had a special revelation, and spoke under the immediate inspiration of the Divine Spirit. The Second Advent is emphatically taught in the Scriptures. II. THAT THE SECOND ADVENT OF CHRIST WILL BE DISTINGUISHED BY SIGNAL TOKENS OF TERRIBLE MAJESTY. 1. There will be the triumphant shout of the Divine Redeemer (ver. 16).   Just before Jesus expired on the cross He cried with a loud voice, and, though there was the ring of victory in that cry, it sounded more like a conscious relief from unutterable suffering. But the shout of Jesus on His second coming will be like the battle-shout of a Great Conqueror.   It will break the silence of the ages, startle the universe into attention, raise the dead, and summon all people to the presence of the victorious Messiah. Formerly He did not cry (Isa. xlii. 2).   But now is the revelation of His power (Psa. l. 3, 4).   2. There will be the voice of the archangel (ver. 16), the chief of the heavenly multitude.   In response to the majestic shout of the descending Lord, he lifts up his voice, like the loud cry of a herald, announcing the glorious advent, and the sound is caught up and prolonged by the vast hosts of celestial attendants.   3. There will be the trumpet blast.   " With the trump of God " (Matt. xxiv. 31; 1 Cor. xv. 52).   Among the Hebrews, Greeks, and Latins it was the custom to summon the people with the trumpet.   In this way God is said to gather His people together (Isa. xxvii. 13; Jer. iv. 5; vi. 1).   The whole passage is designed to show that the Second Advent of King Messiah will be attended by the most imposing evidences of pomp and regal splendour.   III. THAT THE SECOND ADVENT OF CHRIST WILL BE FOLLOWED BY IMPORTANT CONSEQUENCES TO THE PEOPLE OF GOD—LIVING AND DEAD.   1. The pious dead shall be raised (vers. 15, 16).   The living at that day shall have no advantage over the dead.   Before any change takes place in the living, to fit them for the new condition of things, " the dead in Christ shall rise first," and be clothed with immortality and incorruptible splendour.   Whatever disadvantages may be the lot of some of God's people over others, they are ever recompensed by some special privilege.   The best state for us is that in which God places us.   And yet every man thinks another's condition happier than his own.   Rare, indeed, is the man who thinks his own state and condition in every respect best for him.   2. The living and the raised shall unite in a simultaneous greeting of their descending Lord (ver. 17). The living, after passing through the wondrous change, shall not anticipate the newly-raised bodies of the pious dead, but together with them—in one reunited, loving, inseparable company—shall be caught away in the chariot of clouds, to meet the Lord in the air, and greet Him in the descent.   He comes to fulfil His promise (John xiv. 3).   3. All believers in Christ shall be assured of eternal felicity with Him.   " And so shall we ever be with the Lord " (ver. 17)—in familiar companionship, in rapturous communion, in impending glory, in ever-enchanting revelations.   With Him, not occasionally, or for an age, or a millennium, but uninterruptedly, for ever.   How great the contrast with the brightest experiences of this changeful life!   There are three things which eminently distinguish the heavenly life of the soul—perfection, perpetuity, immutability.   The exact locality is not mentioned.   It is enough to be assured that we are to abide with Jesus in some place where parting is unknown.   IV. THAT THE CONTEMPLATION OF THE SECOND ADVENT OF CHRIST IS CALCULATED TO MINISTER CONSOLATION TO THE SORROWING (ver. 18).   The best consolation is that which is drawn from God's Word.   The bereaved were sorrowing for their loved ones, and were full of uncertainty about the future.   The teaching of inspiration assures them that their departed relatives shall be rescued from the power of death, that they shall meet again in glory to be for ever with each other and with the Lord.   The wants and distresses of certain individuals may be the occasion for the revelation of given truths, and the truths once revealed remain in the Church for ever.   Lessons: 1. The Church is justified in looking for the Second Advent.   2. That Advent will bring an everlasting recompense for the sorrow of the present life.   3. The record which reveals that Advent should be prized and pondered.   (*G. Barlow.*)

Vers. 16–18. **For the Lord shall descend from heaven with a shout.**—*The second coming of Christ:*—I. THE LORD'S DESCENT.   " He " and no other, in His august personal presence, in that same human body, too, with which He ascended into heaven (Acts i. 11).   And yet, while Himself unchanged, how changed the surroundings!   He will descend, not in humiliation to tabernacle with men, but to take His people to Himself, in heaven ; not emptied of His glory, but with the symbols of majesty and Divine power.   1. With a shout, one which indicates command.   The word is used of a charioteer's call to his steed, a huntsman's call to his dogs, the call, by voice or sign, of the boatswain giving time to the rowers, the music played to set an army or fleet in motion.   The angelic host and company of the spirits of the just are compared to a vast army, and Christ, the Captain of salvation, by His word of command, sets it in motion, and it, in the alacrity of joyful obedience, accompanies Him to judgment (Jude, ver. 14). The shout will possibly be, " Behold the Bridegroom cometh ; go ye out to meet Him." 2. The voice of the archangel. " The Lord Himself" and " the archangel " cannot be identified. Here and in Jude, ver. 9, the word designates the leader of the angelic hosts. Angels have been, and will yet be, Christ's ministering spirits. They served Him when on earth ; they ascend and descend upon Him in the advancement of His cause ; they will be His ministers of judgment hereafter. The shout may be that of command caught up by the archangel from the lips of the Lord, and repeated to the gathering hosts. 3. The trump of God, belonging to God, used in His service ; that probably of Rev. xi. 15. Under the old dispensation there is special prominence assigned to the trumpet. By it assemblies were summoned, journeys started, feasts proclaimed. It is employed by our Lord, as in the text. Paul calls this " the last " (1 Cor. xv. 52) ; and as such it will gather up all previous meanings. It will call together the rejoicing saints to the heavenly Zion ; like Joshua's trumpet, it will be to some the signal of dismay ; it will mean weal or woe according to the character of those who hear. II. THE RESURRECTION AND CHANGE OF CHRIST'S PEOPLE AT HIS COMING. 1. " The dead in Christ shall rise first." The emphasis rests on " first," and is designed to bring comfort to the Thessalonian mourners. Their departed friends, so far from being placed at a disadvantage, were to occupy a position of privilege. Those who are living will be " caught up." " We shall not all sleep, but we shall all be changed," not unclothed of their bodies, but clothed upon with immortality, a kind of death and resurrection in one. Thus changed, these shall be caught up " together " with the others in one united and rejoicing company ; " caught up " with a quick and resistless rapture, as the word implies, rising from the troubled and imperfect earth—changed and sublimated, as the blossom of the fabled Indian tree, transformed into a bird, flies upward into heaven. " In the clouds " ; not *into*, nor in multitudes (Heb. xii. 1), but as if in a triumphal chariot. Nor do clouds represent a veiling of the awful transaction, but simply supply an imagery which lends grandeur and awe to that event which is awful beyond all human language and thought. 2. The meeting-place : " In the air." We naturally place alongside this the ascension of Elijah, or that of our Lord. In this, as in all else, He has gone before His people and pointed out for them the way. " The air " is not the atmosphere, but infinite space as opposed to earth. The ancients fancied that the milky way is the path trod by the immortals to the palace of the King. The fable is but a distorted reflection of the truth. What it fancied the apostle declared—a pathway in the skies on which the saints are yet to pass to meet their Lord, that He may conduct them home. 3. " And so shall we ever be with the Lord." Less than this can never satisfy Christ's saints ; more than this they cannot desire or conceive — perfect security, sinlessness, happiness, glory. (*J. Hutchison, D.D.*) Of all the solemn associations connected with this verse few can surpass the following : " At the earthquake of Manilla (1863), the cathedral fell on the clergy and congregation. The mass of ruin overhead and around the doomed assemblage was kept for a time from crushing down upon them by some peculiarity of construction. Those outside were able to hear what was going on in the church, without the slightest possibility of clearing away the ruins, or of aiding those within upon whom the building must evidently fall before long. A low, deep, bass voice, doubtless that of the priest officiating, was heard uttering the words, " Blessed are the dead which die in the Lord." As this sentence came forth, the multitude burst in a passion of tears, which was soon choked. For some deep groans issued from within, apparently wrung from the speaker by intense pain, and then the same voice spoke in a calm and even tone, as if addressing a congregation, and all heard the words : "The Lord Himself shall descend," &c. (*Bp. Alexander.*) *Christ's coming :*—One coming —once, for one act—the simultaneous gathering of all before the judgment-seat. All this is a far-off view—the regarding the Second Advent in a kind of prophetical foreshortening. Seen near, this one event is manifold, having chronological order, and falling into many acts. I. THE ACTUAL COMING OF JESUS CHRIST AND ITS GLORY. 1. In the glory of His Father (Matt. xvi. 27). 2. In His own glory (Luke ix. 26). 3. With His angels (Matt. xvi. 27 ; Mark viii. 38 ; 2 Thess. i. 7). 4. Coming in the clouds of heaven (Matt. xxvi. 64 ; Acts i. 11). 5. Bringing His saints with Him (1 Thess. iii. 13 ; Col. iii. 4 ; 1 Thess. iv. 14). II. THE EVENTS WHICH WILL FOLLOW THE COMING OF CHRIST IN THE AIR. 1. The resurrection of the bodies of the sleeping saints. " The dead in Christ shall rise first." 2. The change into a glorified condition of all the living saints (1 Cor. xv. 51). All shall meet the Lord in the air.

All this august series of events precedes judgment. This is the very dawn of the day of the Lord. Later on will be the judgment on the nations, judgment on Israel, judgment on apostate Christendom, judgment on Satan; but from all that the saints are safe; they are already and for ever with the Lord. III. THIS COMING OF THE LORD IS FOR SAINTS—raised saints, living saints, both quick or dead, quickened or changed saints, and saints only. 1. Will His coming be for me? Shall I certainly have part in that glorious first resurrection? If I remain till He come, shall I certainly be changed in that moment of wondrous rapture? 2. Consider who are saints (1 Cor. i. 2; 2 Cor. v. 17; Eph. i. 1; 2 Tim. ii. 22; 1 Pet. ii. 9). Such only are looking for that blessed hope; and such only will see Christ with joy. (*J. Gritton, D.D.*) *The doctrine of the resurrection:*—I. THE CERTAINTY OF THE RESURRECTION. The heathen quite derided the idea of the resurrection (Acts xvii. 18, 32), deeming it incredible (Acts xxvi. 8); and some who professed Christianity explained away the doctrine relating to it, and represented the resurrection as a merely spiritual change which had passed already (2 Tim. ii. 18). Even some of the Thessalonian Church did not appear to be well-grounded in it; and hence St. Paul affirmed that it was a doctrine on which they might fully rely. 1. They did believe in the death and resurrection of Jesus Christ. On these two facts all Christianity was founded. If Jesus had not risen, all their faith in Him, and all their hope from Him, was altogether in vain (1 Cor. xv. 13–18). These two facts admitted, the resurrection of man would follow, of course. The resurrection of Jesus Christ was both an evidence that God can raise the dead, and a pledge that He will. The same omnipotence that raised Him can raise us. He is "the first-fruits of them that sleep." II. THE ORDER IN WHICH THE RESURRECTION WILL BE EFFECTED. This, perhaps, is a matter of curiosity, rather than of any great practical importance; but Paul would not that the Thessalonian Christians should be ignorant of it, and therefore it is worthy of our attention. 1. The dead will all be raised from their graves. All that have ever departed out of the world will be restored to life, each clothed in his own proper body. 2. Those who remain alive upon the earth will be changed. They will remain unchanged until all the dead are raised. Their change will be instantaneous. Without dissolution as preparatory to it, the mortal will put on immortality, the material will assume the spiritual. All will then be in that form which they will bear through the everlasting ages. What an amazing difference will then appear in them! The godly—how beautiful! the ungodly—how deformed! and both having either heaven or hell depicted in their very countenance! 3. Then will they be caught up to meet the Lord. Yes, into the presence of their Judge they must go; and as the earth would not be a theatre sufficient for such an occasion, they must meet the Lord in the air. Blessed summons to the godly! awful indeed to the ungodly! III. THE ISSUE OF THE RESURRECTION TO THE SAINTS. 1. They will receive a sentence of acquittal, or, rather, of unqualified approbation—"Well done, good and faithful servants." 2. They will ascend with Christ and His bright attendants to the heaven of heavens. 3. They will then behold His glory which He had with His Father before the world was. Oh, how bright their vision of His glory! how unbounded their fruition of His love! Nothing now could add to their felicity; nor could anything detract from it. That, too, which constitutes its chief ingredient is—that it will be "for ever." Were this supreme happiness to be only of limited duration, it would be incomplete; the idea of its ultimate termination would rob it of half its value. But it will be pure and endless as the Deity Himself. (*C. Simeon, M.A.*) *The dead in Christ:*—I. THOSE WHO ARE IN CHRIST DIE. They are not exempted from the common fate. 1. To walk by faith, not sight, is their rule of life; hence there is this barrier between themselves and the unseen universe. 2. Subjection to death is an essential part of moral discipline to the righteous. Christ Himself became obedient unto death, and was made perfect through suffering. 3. The dying scene affords occasion for the greatest triumphs of grace and displays of God's mercy and love. How many, by such a spectacle, are moved to repentance and faith in Christ! 4. The death of Christians is needful to render the resurrection of them at all possible. A true and complete conquest over death demands that his victims should be recovered from his dominion. 5. Saints die to express God's irreconcilable hatred to sin. They just taste one drop of the bitter cup which Christ has drunk for them, and feel one lash of the chastisement which He has endured. This gives them a keener sense of the value of salvation. II. BELIEVERS AFTER DEATH ARE STILL IN CHRIST. They retain their innocence before God, their purity, their enjoyment of the Divine favour, their hope of final and perfect happiness. Nay, in all these respects their position is incomparably superior to what it was on earth. They are with Christ in paradise. Hence death is no real evil to them. It is an immense boon to them. It cuts them off from some enjoyments, but it enriches them with enjoyments of a far surpassing order, while also it snatches them away from all care, pain and fear, for evermore. Applications : 1. To believers in anticipating death. Look forward to it calmly, acquiesce in its infliction resignedly, and triumph over its terrors in the full assurance of faith. 2. Here is comfort for the bereaved. If your deceased friends are among the dead in Christ, you may be assured of their perfect happiness, and may hope soon to be reunited with them. 3. Address the unconverted. You are not in Christ—yet you will die ! And think of the dead out of Christ—how horrible their eternal doom ! Oh ! then, now seek an interest in Him, that for you to live may be Christ, and to die, gain. (*T. G. Horton.*)     *The resurrection of the dead :*— Just as the ripe ears of corn which grew on the plains and the mountain sides of Palestine were immediately brought into the Temple, and waved before the Lord, as a pledge that every ear of corn standing on and growing in Palestine should be safely reaped and gathered in, so the resurrection of Christ is a demonstration that we, His people, shall be raised again. If we sleep in Jesus, God will raise us with Him ; because He lives, we shall live also. Dry up your tears, then. Sometimes you go to the churchyard ; sometimes you attend the remains of your relatives to their long homes, you go to " The house appointed for all living " ; and sometimes you see the bones lying round the grave, and you are tempted to take them up, and ask, " Can these bones live ? Can these dishonoured, dishevelled, and denuded bones live ? Can the dead live again ? "  " Come, see the place where the Lord lay." As surely as the sepulchre of Christ became an empty sepulchre, so surely the sepulchres of His people shall become empty sepulchres ; as surely as He got up, and sang a jubilee of life and immortality, so surely shall His people come out of the grave. How beautifully has the Prophet Isaiah expressed it : " Thy dead men shall live, together with my dead body shall they arise. Awake and sing, ye that dwell in dust ; for thy dew is as the dew of herbs, and the earth shall cast out the dead." (*Dr. Beaumont.*)     **And so shall we ever be with the Lord.**—*Ever with the Lord :*—The phrase implies—I. New, living, direct social relationships with the Redeemer. There is more intended than being associated together in one glorious scene. It is not only to see Him and live in His house, one of His family, always in His presence ; it is the getting rid for ever of what is un-Christlike in character, the gaining of the real perfect sympathy with the Christ life. We are with our Friend, not only when we are in His society, but when we blend our thought, our love, our life with His ; when we become His other self. There is here the intimacy and closeness of spiritual fellowship and spiritual resemblance : " We shall be like Him, for we shall see Him as He is." We shall be like Him in faith, in spiritual emotions, in purpose, in tendency, in character. We shall then reach our lost ideals of manhood. The spotless radiance of the perfect Christ shall then be associated with a perfect Church, which He has loved and redeemed, every member of which shall be " without spot, and blameless." " Perfect in Jesus Christ." We shall be with the Lord in perfect holiness, " unblamed and unblamable," and " unreprovable" ; in untemptable purity, in power not to sin. The spirit shall with Him be possessed of indestructible good. II. We shall be with the Lord also in the unfolding light of His new revelations. We shall see light in His light. Truth shall no longer be seen in broken parts and through media which distort and mislead. Now the glass is flawed, and much we see is out of harmony and proportion. There are faults in ourselves which hinder the perception of Truth's harmony and beauty. There are also Divine withholdings of Truth which now we cannot bear or receive. But when we live our life with the Lord, all will be changed. We shall know Him, who is the Infinite Truth, and " that which is in part shall be done away." III. We shall be with Him in the blessedness of His own perfect life, and reign and joy. Fulness of joy and pleasures for evermore are with Him. Holy desires shall only be cherished, to be satisfied out of the Infinite fulness. The life will surpass all we have known or can imagine. We call it, therefore, from its plentitude, and perfection, and blessedness, Eternal. It is the adjective of quality, not of duration. It exceeds exceedingly ; is " a joy unspeakable and full of glory," " an eternal weight of glory." The joy is the joy of marriage. We sit down " at the marriage supper of the Lamb." The life is ever new, the joy is ever fresh, the fulness exhaustless. " Thou shalt make them drink of the river of Thy pleasure." IV. And the crown of all is SECURITY, CHANGELESSNESS, CONTINUANCE. "Ever with the Lord." They go no more out for ever. No possibility of fall is here. There is no change here. "Change and decay in all around we see." The familiar faces are missed. Every Sabbath is an anniversary of our losses. Every act of our life has in it the memory of a past joy, which was and is not. The social life of heaven will complete its blessedness. The thought throws a halo of tenderness and affection over that world. The relational emotions are not cut off and sundered by death. The new life will be ordered by them. What the most hallowed sacramental experience foreshadows and typifies will be then enjoyed in full sweetness and elevating power. The sacred signs will not be needed, because we shall have the reality in its unspeakable grace. ((*W. H. Davison.*) For ever with the Lord:—I. THE LOFTIEST IDEA OF THE GLORIFIED LIFE. To be with the Lord. Our conceptions of the future are coloured by our human tastes and prejudices. 1. To some it is a state. It is all within. Perfect freedom from sin, and the joy of spiritual fellowship with Christ. 2. To others it is a place. There must be trees, rivers, golden pavements, &c. 3. Probably a combination of both will give us the true idea. State and place combine to make complete happiness. 4. But more is required—social enjoyments. The idea of those who have been bereaved is reunion. But the saint exclaims, "Whom have I in heaven but THEE!" "The altogether lovely." The Saviour reciprocates this desire. "I go to prepare a place for you." "Father, I will that they whom Thou hast given Me be with Me," &c. 5. The duration augments the joy of this fellowship. Here it is intermittent; there it will be "for ever." II. WHAT THIS IDEA OF A GLORIFIED LIFE ENSURES. 1. Continual contemplation of Christ. Here that meditation, which is the sweetest of our spiritual enjoyments, is broken; yonder it shall be uninterrupted. 2. Continual assimilation to Christ. Here it is a slow progress, and incomplete at best; but in heaven there will be no obstacles, but every help, in growing into the likeness of our Lord. 3. Unceasing reflection of Christ. As long as the sun shines upon it, the water pours forth its gladness; but often a cloud intervenes, and night shuts out the glory. But when we stand before the throne, we shall eternally catch the light of Christ's countenance on the polished surface of our holiness, and He shall be admired of all them that believe. III. FROM THIS IDEA OF HEAVEN LET US LEARN—1. That heaven is the one meeting-place of the redeemed. Here they are, and must be, separated. 2. That our sorrow for the departed should be restrained. (*G. D. Evans.*) For ever with the Lord:—We have here—I. A CONTINUANCE. Nothing shall prevent our continuing to be for ever with Him. Death shall not separate us, nor the terrors of judgment. As we have received Him, so shall we walk in Him, whether in life or death. 1. We are with Christ in this life. "Your life is hid with Christ in God." If we are not with Him, we are not Christians. Separated from Him, we are dead. We are constantly with Him—(1) In the sense of abiding union; for we are joined unto the Lord, and are one Spirit. In consequence we feel an intense joy, even Christ's own joy fulfilled in us. For the same reason we are bowed in sorrow, having fellowship in Christ's sufferings. This companionship should be manifest to others by its fruits. Men should take knowledge of us that we have been with Jesus. (2) In the sense that His unchanging love is always set upon us, and our love never dies out, "Who shall separate us," &c. (3) By the continual indwelling of the Holy Spirit. (4) Whenever we are engaged in His work. "Lo! I am with you alway." 2. We shall be with Christ in death. "Yea, though I walk," &c. 3. After death, in the disembodied state, we shall be "absent from the body," but "present with the Lord," as was the dying thief. And the body shall sleep *in* Jesus, and awake and say, "When I awake, I am still with Thee." 4. In due time the last trump shall sound, and Christ shall come; but the saints shall be with Him (ver. 14). Whatever the glory of the Second Advent, we shall be with Jesus in it. 5. There is to be a reign of Christ, and whatever that reign is to be, we shall reign also. 6. And when cometh the end and the mediatorial kingdom shall cease, we shall ever be with the Lord. II. AN ADVANCEMENT. 1. It is an advancement on this present state for—(1) However spiritually-minded, and therefore near Christ, we may be, being present in the body we are absent from the Lord. To "be with Christ," we must "depart." (2) Though our souls are with the Lord, yet our bodies are subject to corruption, and after death the separation will continue; but the time will come when this corruptible will put on incorruption, and the whole manhood be perfectly with the Lord. 2. What this glorious state is to which we shall be advanced. We shall be with the Lord in the strongest sense of the term; so with Him, that there will be no business to take us away from Him, no sin to becloud our view of Him ; we shall see Him as a familiar Friend, know His love and return it, and this " for ever." 3. We shall be with the Redeemer, not as Jesus only, but as the Lord.   Here we have seen Him on the Cross, and lived thereby ; but we shall there see Him on the throne, and obey Him as our King.   III. A COHERENCE.   " With " signifies not merely being in the same place, but a union and identity.   Even here our lives run parallel in a sense.   We live to Him, die with Him, so shall we rise and ascend, and then we are to be for ever with the Lord.   1. By sharing His beauty.   2. By being made partakers of all the blessedness and glory He now enjoys.   Conclusion : 1. This " for ever " must begin now.   2. What must it be to be without the Lord?   (*C. H. Spurgeon.*)   *Ever with the Lord :*—This will be the fruition of the brightest hopes, the fulfilment of the precious promises, the accomplishment of the purpose of Christ's Advent, departure, and coming again.   I. IN WHAT SENSE with the Lord ?   1. Referring to the present state of things, Jesus said, " Where two or three are met together." And we may not overlook that presence now.   He is now with us—(1) By God's testimony in the Scripture.   (2) By personal ministrations of His Spirit. (3) By His work within us.   (4) By His providence over us.   (5) By His government of us.   And we with Him.   (*a*) By our faith in His testimony and use of it. (*b*) By frequent thoughts of Him, and much love for Him, and close intercourse with Him.   (*c*) By our work for Him.   2. But the text points to being with Him personally, so as to see His glorified, but now hidden, humanity, hear His voice, and speak to Him as a man speaketh to His friend.   II. WHERE ?   In the place prepared by Himself, designed by the genius of His love ; built up by the energy of His power, enriched by the resources of His wealth, adapted to us by the depth of His knowledge and wisdom.   You have looked into the home prepared for the bride ; you have looked into the cot prepared for the first-born.   Why so beautiful? To receive an object of love.   III. HOW LONG ?   Only a little time were His first disciples with Him ; not long enough to know Him.   None of us are long enough with each other to know each other perfectly.   It is only when some loved one is taken away, and you put the different passages of His life together, and read them as one continuous story, that you can know what that life has been.   While living in the bustle of life we cannot know each other.   But hereafter we shall be with Christ uninterruptedly for ever.   IV. WITH WHAT RESULT ?   Occasional absence is desirable between man and man.   The wife prefers that the husband should be away for a few hours a day at least following his occupation, while she follows hers. Children are all the better for leaving home.   But this has no application here. To be always with the Lord is to be always blessed by the Lord.   We shall see Him as He is, be like Him, have the advantage of His ceaseless ministrations.   Then all that is involved in being with Him will be for ever.   1. Life for ever.   2. Light for ever.   3. Love for ever.   4. Rest for ever.   5. Joy for ever.   (*S. Martin.*) *Being ever with the Lord :*—These words imply—I. PERSONAL NEARNESS TO CHRIST. At present the saints may be said to be at a distance from Him.   " While we are at home in the body," &c.   Spiritually, of course, Christ is with "two or three who meet together in His name."   But after the resurrection we shall be brought near Him, body and soul, and in His presence find fulness of joy and pleasures for evermore.   II. IMMEDIATE VISION OF CHRIST.   He prayed for His disciples to be with Him, that they might behold His glory.   This was seen once at the Transfiguration ; but Christians are not now fitted to enjoy such glory ; it would overpower our sight as it did Saul's, and prostrate us as it did John.   We can only see it by the eye of faith, and this partial sight is sufficient to make Christ the object of our supreme affection and esteem.   But the time will come when we shall see Him with the eye of our glorified body, and be able to bear the stupendous sight.   There we shall see that face, which on earth was marred more than any man's, smiling with more than the brightness of a thousand suns ; that head, which was pierced with thorns, crowned with glory and honour ; that body, which was arrayed in mock majesty, shining with a beauty of which we can form no conception.   III. PERFECT RESEMBLANCE TO CHRIST.   We are predestinated to be conformed to the image of God's Son.   This resemblance commences at regeneration ; but the features are faint at first ; but by constant contemplation of the glory of Christ, they become more marked.   This now is the case with the spirit ; at the resurrection our bodies will be fashioned like unto Christ's glorious body.   And then the progress of both in likeness to Christ shall be eternal.   IV. A CONSTANT SENSE OF THE PRESENCE, LOVE AND FRIENDSHIP OF CHRIST.   We have these here, but not constantly.   Clouds of doubt and sinfulness on our side, and of displeasure on His, intervene. But in the heavenly world there shall be nothing to bar intercourse and manifestation for a single moment. V. Social enjoyment. Where Christ is all His people are, and none but His people. Here society is mixed, the bad blended with the good. The good are removed, and leave us to mourn their departure. But in heaven no one departs, and all are good. It is an inspiring thought that we shall for ever be with all the good. VI. Felicity satisfactory in its nature and eternal in its duration. Our best earthly enjoyments are unsatisfactory—they do not fill the soul; transient—they do not last. Even our highest enjoyments of Christ are not all that we should like them to be. But "we shall be satisfied when we awake in His likeness." (*J. McKinlay, D.D.*) "For ever with the Lord! for ever! for ever!" were the last words of Robert Haldane. *Ever:*—Oh, how sweet is that word—"ever"! Ever to be happy, and ever happy; to enjoy Christ fully, immediately, and everlastingly! Certainly, as the word "ever" is the hell of hell, so it is the heaven of heaven. Frailty is a flaw in the best diamond of nature, and abateth its price; but eternity is one of the most precious jewels in the crown of glory, which increaseth its value exceedingly. (*G. Swinnock, M.A.*) **Wherefore comfort one another with these words.** There is comfort—I. For the bereaved. Our friends are only asleep. They are with Christ, and we shall one day join them. II. In the suggestion that perhaps we shall not have to die after all. Who knows when Christ shall come? III. In knowing that when Christ comes it will not be as the crucified Nazarene, but as the Son of God. Our daily prayer will then be answered, and His will done. IV. In holding communion even here with a Redeemer out of sight; for our highest joys are only a foretaste of the fulness of joy to be revealed when we shall see Him as He is. V. In the recollection that time hurries on to the great consummation. Every hour brings the time of the Church's marriage and glorification nearer. VI. In the thought that every grace we attain will give our Lord pleasure when He comes. Wealth and social pleasure will then go for nothing. In relation to the future these can give us no comfort. VII. In knowing that fidelity is all that Christ requires till He comes. (*C. S. Robinson, D.D.*) *Christian comfort:*—I. Christians are often in circumstances to need comfort. 1. In time of persecution (2 Tim. iii. 12). 2. In the season of affliction (Job v. 7). 3. In the prospect of death. II. The words of Scripture are peculiarly calculated to give comfort (vers. 13–17). Here is promised—1. A resurrection. 2. A triumph with Christ. 3. Rest in eternity. III. This comfort should be mutually administered. (*T. Massey, B.A.*) *Words of comfort:*—Comfort means help as well as consolation. When the Saviour was anointed to comfort all that mourn, it was not to speak words of kindness only, but to reach forth the hand of beneficence so that sorrow might not only be soothed but turned into joy. This also is the office of the Paraclete; and Christianity calls us to be fulfillers of the law of Christ by bearing one another's burdens. Whilst we mourn the departure of Christian friends, let us remember—I. That death is no strange thing. "It is appointed unto men once to die." Were death of rare occurrence, if some only were singled out by the arrows of the last enemy, then our sorrow might admit of no mitigation, but it is not so; Flesh and blood *cannot* enter the kingdom of God. II. That death is the Lord's messenger summoning the saints to His presence. "Precious in the sight of the Lord is the death of His saints." It may be difficult to see the hand of God in the departure of those we love. Our selfish hearts would have prolonged their stay, forgetting that death is gain to them. III. That death terminates the toil and warfare of this life. Whilst they were in this tabernacle they groaned, being burdened; now the burden is lifted and they have entered into rest. Here they fought the good fight of faith; there they are crowned as conquerors. Here they suffered; there they enter into the joy of their Lord. IV. That death is the beginning of perfection. The best and happiest of saints were here imperfect; now they are "the spirits of just men made perfect" in holiness and happiness; for they are like Christ, because they see Him as He is. V. That death is a revival of sacred friendships, and an introduction to the general assembly and Church of the first-born. Most of us as we look into the heavenly world can recognize a sacred kindred there. When you pass away it will be to meet with old associates, and the whole company of the redeemed. Compared with such fellowship as this, what can earth offer? VI. That death will be a season of reunion for us. They have only gone before, a little in advance. The great gulf will be crossed at the Master's call, and our communion recommence, never to be disturbed again. VII. That every death is part of that process which will

ISSUE IN THE DISPENSATION OF THE FULNESS OF TIMES. Heaven is enriched by the departure of every saint. (*R. W. Betts.*) *The duty of comforting one another :*—I. THE PERSONS—" One another." 1. One man is the image of another, because the image of God is upon all. One man interprets another. We are as glasses, and one sees in another what he is and what he himself may also be. He may see himself in another's fear, grief, complaints. In another's sickness, he may see the disease which may sieze on himself; in another's poverty, his own riches with wings; in another's death, his own mortality. They are also a silent but powerful appeals to his compassion to do as he would be done by in like case. 2. " One another " takes in the whole world. One is diverse from another, yet we can hardly distinguish them, they are so like. (1) From the same rock are hewn out the feeble and the strong. Of the same extraction are the poor and rich. He that made the idiot made the scribe. Who then shall separate? (2) Besides this, the God of nature has also imprinted our natural inclination which carries us to love and comfort one another. One man is as another, by himself weak and indigent, needing the help and supply of others (1 Cor. xii. 4, 5), and so provided. One man excels in wisdom, another in wealth, another in strength, that they may serve one another in love (Gal. v. 13). 3. A nearer relation binds men together—their relation in Christ. In Him they are called to the same faith, filled with the same grace, ransomed with the same price, and shall be crowned with the same glory. And being one in these, they must join hand in hand to uphold one another, and so advance one another to the common glory (Matt. xxii. 38, 39; 1 Cor. xii. 12). As each man, so each Christian is as a glass to another. I see my sorrow in my brother's eyes; I cast a beam of comfort upon him, and he reflects a blessing upon me. And in our daily prayer, " Our Father " takes in " one another," even the whole Church. II. THE ACT. 1. Comfort is of large signification. It may be to be eyes to the blind and feet to the lame, to clothe the naked and feed the hungry. Speak and do something that may heal a wounded heart, and rouse a drooping spirit. 2. To comfort is a work of charity which is inward and outward. What a poor thing is a thought or word without a hand; and what an uncharitable thing is comfort without compassion. Then I truly comfort my brother when my actions correspond with my heart. And if they be true they will never be severed; for if the bowels yearn, the hand will stretch itself forth. 3. We must look to the motive. Our comfort may proceed from a hollow heart; then it is Pharisaical; it may be ministered through a trumpet, and then it is lost in the noise; it may be the product of fear. All these are false principles, and charity issues through them as water through mud—defiled. Christ is our motive and pattern (Mark ix. 41). 4. Let us be ambitious to comfort, for we have great occasions. Every day presents some object. Here is an empty mouth; why do we not fill it? Here is a naked body; why do we not part with our superfluities to cover it? Here God speaks, man speaks, misery speaks; and are our hearts so hard that they will not open, and so open mouth and hands (Phil. ii. 5). III. THE MANNER OR METHODS—" with these words." 1. In every action we must have a right method. He that begins amiss is yet to begin, as the further he goes the further he is from the end. As James speaks of prayer (chap. iv. 3), so we seek comfort and find not because we seek amiss. Our fancy is our physician. We ask ourselves counsel, and are fools that give it; we ask of others and they are miserable comforters. In poverty we seek for wealth; and that makes us poorer than we were. Wealth is no cure for poverty, nor enlargement for restraint, nor honour for discontent. Thus it is also in spiritual evils. When conscience holds up the whip we fly from it; when it is angry we flatter it. We are as willing to forget sin as to commit it. We comfort ourselves by ourselves and by others, by our own weakness and others' weakness, and by sin itself. But the antidote is poison, or, at best, a broken cistern. 2. The apostle's method is—(1) In general, the Word of God. For the Scripture is a common shop of comfort, where you may buy it without money and without price. The comforts of Scripture are—(*a*) Abiding (1 Peter i. 23)—its hope (1 Peter i. 3); its joy (John xvi. 22); its peace (Psa. lxxii. 7); so all its comforts (2 Cor. i. 20). All else is perishing. (*b*) Universal. Nothing, no one is hid from the light of them. But we must be careful how we apply them and prepare ourselves to receive them. God's mercy is over all His works, but it will not cover the impenitent. Nevertheless, the covetous comforts himself by the ant in Proverbs (chap. vi. 6); the ambitious by that good ointment in Ecclesiastes (chap. vii. 1); the contentious man by the quarrel of Paul and Barnabas; the lethargic in God's forbearance; and thus turn wholesome medicine into poison by misapplication. (2) In particular, the doctrine of the resurrection and the coming of Christ. These are the sum of all comforts, the destruction of all ills. (*A. Farindon, B.D.*) *A child's faith :*—A gentleman walking in one of the metropolitan cemeteries observed kneeling beside a tombstone a little girl about ten years of age. In her hand she held a wreath, which she placed upon the grave. Going up to her, he asked if any one very dear to her lay there. "Yes," she replied, "my mother is buried here." "Have you a father, or sisters, or brothers, little one?" inquired the stranger. "No, they are all dead, and I am the only one left. Every Saturday afternoon I come here, and bring flowers to lay on mother's grave. Then I talk to her, and she talks to me." "But, dear child, if she be in heaven, how can she talk to you?" "I don't know," was the artless reply, "but she does, and tells me to be truthful, and do what is right, so that one day Jesus will take me to live with her in heaven." *The gospel telescope :*—What the telescope does for science, the gospel does for those who believe it. It converts hazy conjecture into immovable certainty, and interprets the feeble hopes and dreams which glimmer in the eye of reason into demonstrated and well-defined truths. "Oh, that all my brethren," said Rutherford, when dying, "may know what a Master I have served, and what peace I have this day. This night shall close the door and put my anchor within the veil." *An exulting prospect :*—Rowland Hill, when very aged, preached for the Rev. George Clayton, of Walworth. The services exhausted him, and while going feebly down the aisle, after all the congregation had gone, Mr. Clayton heard him repeating softly to himself the hymn he most delighted in during his last years :—

> " And when I'm to die, receive me I'll cry,
> For Jesus has loved me, I cannot tell why;
> But this I can find, we two are so joined,
> That He'll not be in glory and leave me behind."

" To my heart," said Mr. Clayton, "this was a scene of unequalled solemnity; nor can I ever recur to it without a revival of that tender and hallowed sympathy which it originally awakened." *Preparing for heaven :*—Some years ago a traveller, who had recently returned from Jerusalem, discovered, in conversation with Humboldt, that he was as thoroughly conversant with the streets and houses of Jerusalem as he himself was; whereupon, he asked the aged philosopher how long it was since he visited Jerusalem. He replied, "I have never been there, but I expected to go sixty years since, and I prepared myself." Should not the heavenly home be as familiar to those who expect to dwell there eternally? *Heavenly comfort :*—It is rarely we read anything more touchingly beautiful than the way in which Catherine Tait, wife of the late Archbishop of Canterbury, tried to comfort her own heart and the heart of her husband after they were suddenly deprived by death of "five blessed little daughters." Other parents, who mourn because of empty cradles and desolate places by the fireside, may be strengthened by their example. Mrs. Tait writes :—" Now, constantly, with our daily prayers, we say the thanksgiving and commemoration for them : 'Lord, Thou hast let Thy little ones depart in peace. Lord Jesus, Thou hast received their spirits, and hast opened unto them the gate of everlasting glory. Thy loving Spirit leads them forth in the land of righteousness, into Thy holy hill, into Thy heavenly kingdom. Thou didst send Thy angels to meet them and to carry them into Abraham's bosom. Thou hast placed them in the habitation of light and peace—of joy and gladness. Thou hast received them into the arms of Thy mercy, and given them an inheritance with the saints in light. There they reign with Thy elect angels and Thy blessed saints departed, Thy holy prophets and glorious apostles, in all joy, glory, felicity, and blessedness, for ever and ever. Amen.' "

## CHAPTER V.

VERS. 1–11. **But of the times and seasons, brethren, ye have no need that I write unto you.**—Perhaps because the apostle had told them, or because the sudden coming of Christ was a universal belief. So in modern times a preacher might say, "There is no need for me to speak to you of the uncertainty of life." (*Prof. Jowett.*) *The attitude of the Church towards the Second Advent of Christ :*—As when we ascend a winding river some well-known landmark appears to alter its position seeming now distant, now near, so at different points on the circuitous stream of life the coming of Christ reveals itself as a near or remote event. " It is plain," says Archer Butler, " that that period which is distant in one scheme of things may be near in another, where events are on a vaster scale, and move in a mightier orbit. That which is a whole life to the ephemera, is but a day to a man ; that which in the brief succession of human history is counted as remote, is but a single page in the volume of the heavenly records. The coming of Christ may be distant as measured on the scale of human life, but may be near when the interval of the two advents is compared, not merely with the four thousand years which were but its preparation, but with the line of infinite ages which it is itself preparing." The uncertainty;of the time of the Second Advent and its stupendous issues define the attitude of the Church. I. IT IS AN ATTITUDE OF EXPECTANCY. 1. The time of the Second Coming is uncertain (ver. 1)—a gentle hint that all questions on that subject were unnecessary, as there was nothing more to be revealed. The curiosity and daring of man tempt him to pry into secrets with which he has nothing to do, and to dogmatize on subjects of which he knows the least. Many have been fanatical enough to fix the day of the Lord's coming (Mark xiii. 32). This uncertainty is a perpetual stimulant to the people of God to exercise the ennobling virtues of hope, watchfulness, fidelity, humility, inquiry, and reverence. 2. The Second Coming will be sudden (vers. 2, 3). The thief not only gives no notice of his approach, but takes every possible care to conceal his designs : the discovery of the mischief takes place when it is too late. The prudent will take every precaution to avoid surprise, and to baffle the marauder. 3. The Second Coming will be terrible to the wicked. " They shall not escape " (ver. 3). Wicked men are never more secure than when destruction is nearest. The swearer may be seized with the oath on his tongue : the drunkard while the cup is trembling on his lips. The destruction of the wicked and all they prized most in life will be sudden, painful, inevitable. Now there is place for mercy, but not then (Rom. ii. 8, 9). II. IT IS AN ATTITUDE OF VIGILANCE. 1. This vigilance is enforced on the ground of a moral transformation (vers. 4, 5). Believers are translated out of the kingdom of darkness into the kingdom of light. They are " children of the day," when the sun shines the brightest, when privileges are more abundant, when opportunities multiply and responsibility is therefore increased. 2. This vigilance must be constant (vers. 6, 7). Let us not, like the drunkard steeped in sottish slumber, be immersed in the sleep of sin and unconcern, neglecting duty, and never thinking of judgment ; but let us watch, and, to do so effectually, be sober. We are day-people, not night-people ; therefore our work ought to be day-work ; our conduct such as will bear the eye of day, the veil of night. A strict sobriety is essential to a sleepless vigilance. III. IT IS AN ATTITUDE OF MILITANT COURAGE (ver. 8). The Christian has to fight the enemy, as well as to watch against him. He is a soldier on sentry. The Christian life is not one of luxurious ease. The graces of faith, love, and hope constitute the most complete armour of the soul. The breastplate and helmet protect the two most vital parts—the head and the heart. Let us keep the head from error, and the heart from sin, and we are safe. The best guards against both are—faith, hope, and charity ; these are the virtues that inspire the most enterprising bravery. IV. IT IS AN ATTITUDE OF CONFIDENCE AS TO THE FUTURE BLESSEDNESS OF THE CHURCH. 1. This blessedness is divinely provided. 2. This blessedness consists in a constant fellowship with Christ. " That whether we wake or sleep, we should live together with Him " (ver. 10). The happiest moments on earth are those spent in the company of the good ; so will it be in heaven. 3. The confidence of inheriting this blessedness encourages edification (ver. 11). Lessons : 1. The great event of the future will be the Second Coming of Christ. 2. That event should be looked for in a spirit of sobriety and vigilance. 3. That event will bring unspeakable felicity to the good, and dismay and misery to the wicked. (*G. Barlow.*) *Times and seasons* are often found together, but always in the plural in the New Testament (Acts i. 7), and not unfrequently in the LXX., and the Apocrypha (Wisd. vii. 18 ; viii. 8), both instructive passages, and Dan. ii. 21) : and in the singular (Eccles. iii. 1 ; Dan. vii. 12). Grotius conceives the difference between them to consist merely in the greater length of the former. But this is insufficient, and fails to reach the heart of the matter. *Chronos* is time simply as such ; the succession of moments (Matt. xxv. 19 ; Rev. x. 6 ; Heb. iv. 7). *Keiros* is time as it brings forth its several births ; thus " time of harvest " (Matt. xiii. 30) ; " time of figs " (Mark. xi. 13) ; " due time " (Rom. v. 6) ; and, above all, compare, as constituting a miniature essay on the word (Eccles. iii. 1-8). Time, it will thus appear, embraces all possible seasons, and being the larger, more inclusive word, may be often used where season would have been equally suitable, though not the converse; thus "full time" (Luke i. 57), "fulness of time" (Gal. iv. 4), where we should rather have expected "season," which phrase does actually occur in Eph. i. 10. So we may confidently say that the "times of restitution" (Acts iii. 21) are identical with the "seasons of refreshing" (Acts iii. 19). Here, then, and in Acts i. 6, 7, "times" are spaces of time, and these contemplated under the aspect of their duration, over which the Church's history should extend; but the "seasons" are the joints and articulations in this time, the critical epoch-making periods fore-ordained of God (Acts. xvii. 26); when all that has been slowly and without observation ripening through long ages is mature and comes to birth in grand decisive events, which constitute at once the close of one period and the commencement of another. Such, *e.g.*, was the passing away with a great noise of the old Jewish dispensation; such again the recognition of Christianity as the religion of the Roman Empire; such the conversion of the Germanic tribes settled within the limits of the Empire; such the great revival which went along with the first institution of the mendicant orders; such, by better right, the Reformation; such, above all others, the Second Coming of the Lord in glory (Dan. vii. 22). (*Abp. Trench.*)　　*The uncertainty of the time of the Second Advent*:—Of this true advent season of eternity, though much is known, much too is hidden. There are secrets the Divine Bridegroom whispers not; that the "Spirit and the Bride" may still "say, Come." Between the Church and the Church's Head there still subsists, even in this intimate union, a mysterious separation; and on the period of that separation is a holy reserve. It has already lasted for ages, and we cannot dare to predict at what epoch it is to close. The veil that hangs before the celestial sanctuary is still undrawn; and it is vain for us to "marvel" as of old the expectants of Zacharias, that the High Priest of our profession "tarrieth so long in the temple." He has willed it that, certain of His eventual arrival, we should remain in uncertainty as to its destined moment. This mingling of ignorance and knowledge on the part of Christ's people is best suited to keep alive in their breasts the hope whose breathed utterance is "Even so, come, Lord Jesus." The Thessalonians knew that the time could not be known, hence there was no need for Paul to write about it. (*J. Hutchison, D.D.*)　　*The Second Advent and its issues*:—I. THE APOSTLE TELLS THE THESSALONIANS IT WAS USELESS TO INQUIRE ABOUT THE PARTICULAR TIME OF CHRIST'S COMING (ver. 1). The event is certain—Christ *will* come, and there is a certain time divinely appointed for Christ's coming; but there was no need that St. Paul should write about that specially, and he had no revelation from heaven concerning it. Nor should we inquire into this secret "which the Father hath reserved in His own power." Christ Himself did not reveal "that day and hour" while on earth; for it was not included in His commission as the great Prophet of the Church; nor is it in that of His apostles. A vain curiosity desireth to know many things which there is no need soever of our knowing, and which if we knew them thoroughly would do us no good, but perhaps harm. II. THE APOSTLE TELLS THEM THE COMING OF CHRIST WOULD BE A GREAT SURPRISE TO MOST MEN (ver. 2). And this is what they knew perfectly, or might know, because the Lord Himself had so said (Matt. xxiv. 44). As the thief usually cometh in the dead time of the night, when he is least expected, such a surprise will the day of the Lord be—so sudden and surprising His appearance. And the knowledge of this fact will prove more useful than to know the exact time, because this will lead us to watch, that we may be ready whenever He cometh. III. THE APOSTLE TELLS THEM HOW TERRIBLE WILL BE THE COMING OF CHRIST TO THE UNGODLY (ver. 3). It will be to their destruction. It will overtake and fall upon them in the midst of their carnal security and jollity; when they dream of felicity, and please themselves with vain amusements of their fancies or their senses, and think not of it. And it will be unavoidable destruction too. "They shall not escape:" there will be no means possible for them to avoid the terror or the punishment of that day; no shelter from the storm, nor shadow from the burning heat that shall consume the wicked. IV. THE APOSTLE TELLS THEM HOW COMFORTABLE THE COMING OF CHRIST WILL BE TO THE GODLY (vers. 4, 5). And here he sketches their character and privilege. They are "children of light." They were "sometime darkness, but were made light in the Lord." They were "the children of the day," for "the Sun of Righteousness had risen upon them with healing in His beams." They were not under the dark shadows of the law, but under the bright sunshine of the gospel, which brings life and immortality to light. But this, great as it is, is not all: the day of Christ will not overtake them as a thief, but will be "a time of refreshing from the presence of the Lord." They " look for Him, and His appearance to them will be their full salvation." (*R. Fergusson.*)    *The profanity of attempting to determine the time :*— Mark what Paul saith, " Ye have no need that I write unto you of times and seasons " ; and that our Saviour saith, "It is not for you to know the times or the seasons." What may we think then of them that write books and almanacks, and say, "Such a year, and at such a time, Christ shall come " ; and with these speeches frighten and mock the world ? Paul was the apostle of Christ, an elect vessel of the Holy Ghost : he said, I have no need to write of it ; you cannot know it. What need is there now that such books and pamphlets should be written? Why should the world be troubled with such vanities ? Spare me your patience, and give me leave a little to deal with these wizards. Tell me, thou that dost measure and behold the compass of heaven, and markest the conjunctions, and oppositions, and aspects of the stars ; and by that wisdom canst foretell the things that shall be done hereafter : where learnest thou this skill? how comest thou by this deep knowledge ? Paul was taken up into the third heaven, and heard words which cannot be spoken, which are not lawful for man to utter : yet he knew not this secret, nor might not know it. What art thou then ? art thou greater than the apostle of Christ ? hast thou been taken up into some place higher than the third heaven ? has thou heard such words, as are not lawful to utter ? If this be so, why dost thou utter them ? Wilt thou take that upon thee, which the holy apostle dareth not ? Art thou of God's privy council ? The angels and archangels know not hereof : and shall we think that thou knowest it ? art thou wiser than an angel ? Consider thyself : thou art a miserable man ; thy breath fadeth as the smoke ; thou art nothing but dust and ashes : thou canst not attain to the knowledge hereof. (*Bp. Jewell.*)    *Under sealed orders :*—A Government vessel was about to leave the dock, to sail away for some port. No one knew her destination, whether it was to be near by or far away. Those who had loved ones on board felt sad and anxious ; were they to be within reach of cheering words, of letters full of love and encouragement, or were they to be sent afar to some foreign port from which no word could come in weary weeks and months ? They could ask the question many and many a time, but there was no echo to the words, no answer to be had. The ship was to sail under sealed orders ; orders from the Navy Department that were sealed by Government zeal, which could not be opened until the ship was far out at sea, and away from all possible communication with land. The Captain of our salvation sends us away on sealed instructions. Whither ? You do not need to know. You might not like your destination ; you might object to the buffeting waves, the billows of trouble might threaten to wreck your soul ; the harbour might be hard to reach and the rocks of danger might lie between you and it. Do you care? Does it matter to you if the passage is a stormy one when you know that safety is at the end ? that there is a harbour that leads to the Eternal City ? and (most comforting thought) when the Father is at the helm, and that He neither slumbers nor sleeps ? Let go your moorings, spread the canvas, and in storm or sunshine, by day or by night, go forth with " sealed orders.'

Ver. 2. **For ye yourselves know perfectly that the day of the Lord so cometh as a thief in the night.**— *Christ coming as a thief in the night :*—Here we have a striking comparison—one which, to all appearance, had passed into a recognized formula, yet one which no Christian would have dared to use had it not been hallowed by our Lord's own lips. And so we find it first of all in His own parable (Matt. xxiv. 43 ; Luke xii. 39, 40). Next we find it caught up by His disciple Peter (2 Pet. iii. 10). Then we find it adopted by Paul ; and last of all we hear it again from our Lord (Rev. iii. 3 ; xvi. 15). The formula means—I. That as the thief comes UNEXPECTEDLY, so His coming will be stealthy, under cover, as it were, of darkness ; when the children of night and darkness, the dreamers (Jude ver. 8), do not in the slumber of carnal security, even momentarily think of His approach. But if this were all, the idea would lack much of aptness and dignity. Therefore—II. As the thief comes TO STEAL, so the day of the Lord comes to take away by force the so-called goods—the possessions of the worldling. The children of the night have their most valued substance snatched from them. They are robbed of their soul (see Rev. xvi. 15). Vigilance is needed that the garment may be kept—not torn from him—that he may not be found robbed of the robe of the Redeemer's righteousness, but clothed therewith, and accepted at last. (*J. Hutchison, D.D.*)    *The suddenness of the Second Advent :*—This present state of things is ever close upon the next world, and resolves itself into it. As when a man is given over, he may die any moment, yet lingers; as an instrument of war may any moment explode, and must at some time; as we listen for a clock to strike, and at length it surprises us; as a crumbling arch hangs, we know not how, and is not safe to pass under, so creeps on this feeble, weary world, and one day, before we know where we are, it will end. (*J. H. Newman, D.D.*) *A reminder of mortality :*—One of Gotthold's friends had a little scent-box, made in the shape of a death's head, with a screw at the skull for opening and taking it asunder. It then showed various cells filled with fragrant balm. Being asked why he had made the box in this particular shape, he replied, "In order to have something continually reminding me of my mortality." On this, Gotthold rejoined, "You have done well if such was indeed your object, and not, rather, to possess a curiosity for people to gaze and wonder at. The thought of the mortality to which, like all your race, you are subjected, may be infinitely more profitable to you than all kinds of balm. If seized with the delirium of pride, reflect that death will one day reduce you to dust and ashes, and wither your pomp like a flower. If overcome by angry passion, take to heart that death stands behind you with his axe, and only waits the signal from God to reduce you in an instant to the impotency of a dead gnat. If your heart ache, and your head be distracted with cares, recollect that all your trouble and anxiety will one day come to a blessed end." *Preparedness :*—When war was declared between France and Prussia, Von Molkte was fully prepared. The news was brought to him late one night: he had already gone to bed. "Very well," he said to the messenger, "the third portfolio on the left," and went to sleep again until morning. (*H. D. Mackay.*) *The day of the Lord :*—The day of the Lord, yet future, is the day on which, most assuredly, all thoughts will turn to Him, whether willingly or by constraint, whether in terror or in joy; the day in which His truth will silence into nothingness all human errors and guesses at truth, in which His justice will take the place of all that is named justice, rightly or wrongly, among the sons of men; the day in which everything else but He will be lost sight of, and will be as though it were not, in which the eternal reality of His relation to the world and to man will also be the acknowledged reality. As surely as we have seen this morning's sunlight, we shall hereafter behold the eternal Judge upon His throne, the countless multitudes before Him, the division between His creatures deep and irreversible, the disciplined activities of His angels, the issues on this side and on that, as all gradually settles down into the last unchangeable award. (*Canon Liddon.*)

Ver. 3. **When they shall say, Peace and Safety.**—*The day of days :*—If Scripture did not warrant the figure in which the future coming of the Lord is compared to the act of a felon breaking into a house at night to plunder, we should not have ventured on it. The comparison is suggested by the Lord Himself : "Watch, therefore, for ye know not what hour your Lord doth come. If the good man of the house had known in what hour the thief would come, he would have watched." I. THE DAY STATED. By the expression, "the day of the Lord," must be meant a day in some unique sense *His* day; for all days are really days of the Lord of time. 1. By the day of the Lord is signified that day on which He will take the first place in the thoughts of His responsible creatures. 2. It is the day on which He will bring the vast moral account between Himself and His responsible creatures to an end. II. THE FIGURE EMPLOYED. What are the ideas suggested by the words, "As a thief in the night"? 1. They are suggestive of fear. The old prophets spoke of the coming day of universal doom as "the great and terrible day of the Lord"; and we cannot but echo their language. But if we will, the Judge may be our Friend and Saviour. It is during the years of time that men decide how they will meet Him. 2. They are suggestive of suddenness. There is the contrast which it will present to many of God's judgments in the present life. They approach with measured steps. Neither war, nor famine, nor pestilence, come generally like a thief in the night. But not so will be the Second Advent of Christ. A Christian's first practical anxiety should be expressed in his Master's words, "Lest coming suddenly He find me sleeping." 3. They are suggestive of that which cannot be prevented by our own efforts. We cannot prevent the coming of Christ in the clouds of heaven : all that we can do is to prepare to meet Him by judging ourselves in self-examination. We may erect in our own heart a tribunal, and bid all our life pass before it ; and then we may hear, if we will, the echoes of the voice of Christ, in mercy or condemnation, as that voice will sound to us hereafter from the judgment-throne. Thus we may make a business-like preparation for death ; for death, like judgment, comes as a thief. Death is the ante-chamber of the judgment-hall of

Christ. To prepare, therefore, for death, is a man's true and most serious business during his life. "Ye are not in darkness that that day should overtake you as a thief." (*Canon Liddon.*) *The sinner's doom :*—I. IN THE MIDST OF IMAGINED SECURITY. When enjoying riches, and contemplating, as the rich fool, their further augmentation; and when, perhaps, trusting in the infinitude of the Divine mercy, and thinking "the day" afar off. II. SUDDEN. Without notice : nothing in the course of nature, or the affairs of men, to indicate the catastrophe. III. UNAVOID-ABLE : reputation, good works, &c., will be as cobwebs. IV. TERRIBLE. "Destruction." (*Sir E. Bayley, D.D.*) *Delusions :*—Manton says well, "As the madman at Athens challenged all the ships that came into the harbour for his own, so carnal men claim an interest in heavenly things which are none of theirs. Deceived hearts believe they are running to heaven when they are posting to hell; like rowers in a boat, they look one way, and go contrary." Religious delusions may be very comfortable while they last, but what will be the misery of their breaking up! To have all your fancied godliness vanish like the mists before the sun will be grievous indeed. In proportion to the confidence inspired will be the despair involved. The poor madman in Bedlam in the olden time placed a straw crown upon his head, and issued orders like a Cæsar; it was his madness which made such a farce a comfort to him. In the next world the sinner's madness will be over, he will be sobered by his despair : what then will he think of his former fancies and fond self-flatteries? What an awaking, from the dreams of bliss to the realities of hell! O my soul, see thou to it that all thy hopes are well grounded! Call not Christ thine, and heaven thine, if they are not so. Do not play the fool with eternal things, but get a sure title to everlasting blessedness. (*C. H. Spurgeon.*) *False over-confidence :*—You may have a strong faith in everything else but Christ, and yet perish. There was an architect who had a plan for building a lighthouse on the Eddystone Rock. It quite satisfied his mind, and as he sat by the fire looking at the plan, he was quite sure that no storm that ever came could shake the building. He applied for the contract to build the lighthouse, and he did build it, and a very singular-looking place it was. There were a great many flags about it and ornaments, and it looked very promising. Some shook their heads a little, but he was very, very firm, and said he should like to be in it himself in the worst wind that ever blew. He was in it at the time he wanted to be, and he was never heard of again, nor was anything more ever seen of his lighthouse. The whole thing was swept away. He was a man of great faith, only it happened to be founded on mistaken principles. (*J. L. Nye.*) *False peace :*—Your peace, sinner, is that terribly prophetic calm which the traveller occasionally perceives upon the higher Alps. Everything is still. The birds suspend their notes, fly low, and cower down with fear. The hum of bees among the flowers is hushed. A horrible stillness rules the hour, as if death had silenced all things by stretching over them his awful sceptre. Perceive ye not what is surely at hand? The tempest is preparing; the lightning will soon cast abroad its flames of fire. Earth will rock with thunder-blasts; granite peaks will be dissolved; all nature will tremble beneath the fury of the storm. Yours is that solemn calm to-day, sinner. Rejoice not in it, for the hurricane of wrath is coming, the whirlwind and the tribulation which shall sweep you away and utterly destroy you. (*C. H. Spurgeon.*) *Secure in sin :*—"A Swiss traveller," says the *Edinburgh Review*, "describes a village situated on the slope of a great mountain, of which the strata shelve in the direction of the place. Huge crags directly overhanging the village, and massy enough to sweep the whole of it into the torrent below, have become separated from the main body of the mountain in the course of ages by great fissures, and now scarce adhere to it. When they give way, the village must perish; it is only a question of time, and the catastrophe may happen any day. For years past engineers have been sent to measure the fissures, and report them constantly increasing. The villagers, for more than one generation, have been aware of their danger; subscriptions have been once or twice opened to enable them to remove; yet they live on in their doomed dwellings, from year to year, fortified against the ultimate certainty and daily probability of destruction by the common sentiment 'Things may last their time and longer.'" Like the dwellers in this doomed village, the world's inhabitants have grown careless and secure in sin. The scoffers of the last days are around us, saying, "Where is the promise of His coming? For since the fathers have fallen asleep, all things continue as they were from the beginning of the creation." But in saying this, they are too confident. Nothing is permanent that has sin about it, nothing secure that has wrath above it, and flames of fire beneath it. Sin has once deluged the world with water, it shall deluge it again with waves of fire. Sodom and Gomorrah are the types that foreshadow the doom of those that live ungodly in these latter times, and he who can walk this reeling world unmoved by all the tokens of its fiery doom, must either have a rock of refuge where his soul may rest secure, or else must have fallen into a strange carelessness, and a sad forgetfulness of God. (*Ibid.*) *Procrastination leads to sudden destruction :*—Do any of you remember the loss of the vessel called the *Central America ?* She was in a bad state, had sprung a leak and was going down, and she therefore hoisted a signal of distress. A ship came close to her, the captain of which asked, through the trumpet, "What is amiss ? " "We are in bad repair, and are going down : lie by till morning," was the answer. But the captain on board the rescue-ship said, " Let me take your passengers on board now." " Lie by till morning," was the message which came back. Once again the captian cried, " You had better let me take your passengers on board now." " Lie by till morning," was the reply which sounded through the trumpet. About an hour-and-a-half after, the lights were missing, and though no sound was heard, she and all on board had gone down to the fathomless abyss. Oh, unconverted friends, for God's sake, do not say, " Lie by till morning." To-day, even to-day, hear ye the voice of God. (*Ibid.*) *A deadly peace :*—The old fable described the vampire bat, in tropical countries, as hovering above its victims, and drinking their life-blood, while it soothes them to sleep on by fanning them with its wings all the while. So the devil soothes souls into deadly sleep. (*J. W. Hardman.*) *Danger near and man unconscious of it :*— Many years ago there was a terrible murder in one of our rural counties. A desperate man determined to kill the squire of the village. No danger was thought of, no such peril was dreaded. With unclosed shutters the doomed man sat in his house, his family moving in and out, his books, his papers around him in perfect security, as he thought. But meanwhile, creeping behind the shrubs of the lawn, in the gathering twilight, with his loaded gun, crept the armed assailant, till the bringing in of the evening lamp cast its glow through the comfortable chamber within, and enabled a sure and deadly aim to be taken by the murderer outside. Even so does the devil plot our ruin. (*Ibid.*) *Unconsciousness of the approach of death :*—Even when death is not absolutely sudden, how often have I seen persons, who were ill, wholly refuse to believe or realize that their sickness was unto death. Almost till the day of their departure they have talked quite confidently of what they intended to do when they rose from the bed of sickness; have perhaps even seemed to themselves to be much better just before they sank into the long swoon which can only end in the last fluttering sigh. "O God, they have deceived me then; and this is death ! " was the startling exclamation of a sinful English king, and with those words he sank back and died. And very commonly for hours, and even days, before death, men and women lie quite unconscious ; the pulse still beats, the breath still labours, possibly the tongue still murmurs, as the imagination floats amid the confused reminiscences of the past, and babbles of green fields far away. But no voice of exhortation can reach them then ; they can gather no thought into consecutive meaning ; they can breathe no prayer unto Him into whose awful presence they are about to enter. (*Canon Farrar.*) *Men lured to destruction :*—The other day I was going down the street and I saw a drove of pigs following a man. This excited my curiosity, so that I determined to follow. I did so, and to my great surprise I saw them follow him to the slaughter-house. I was very anxious to know how this was, and I said to the man, "My friend, how did you manage to induce those pigs to follow you here ? " " Oh, did you not see ? " said the man ; " I had a basket of beans under my arms, and I dropped a few as I came along, and so they followed me." Yes, and I thought, so it is ; the devil has a basket of beans under his arm, and he drops them as he goes along, and what multitudes he induces to follow him to an everlasting slaughter-house ! Yes, friends, and all your broad and crowded thoroughfares are strewn with the beans of the devil. (*Rowland Hill.*)

Ver. 4. **But ye, brethren, are not in darkness.**—*Responsibility for religious privileges :*—It is universally admitted that the extent of our responsibility is to be measured by the amount of our privilege. Hence our Lord said, " To whom men have committed much, of him will they ask more." It is in harmony with this that the apostle makes the appeal in our text. I. OUR PRIVILEGES AS A CHRISTIAN CHURCH. " Not in darkness," but in light as regards—1. A knowledge of the true God. This lies at the foundation of religion. It is only by knowing God that we come to know ourselves. Had we no perfect standard of what is pure and lovely, were we allowed to frame some model of perfection, each would select that character for imitation, which reflected least discredit on his own.  But tell us what God is, and you tell us what God loves; and what He loves man should love also.  But the Thessalonians not only enjoyed through the gospel light a correct doctrine of God: they, as are all true Christians, were brought into an experimental knowledge through peace with Him.  2. The Word and ordinances of God (ii. 13; v. 12).  (1) By the use of these we foil the craftiness, which would " carry us about with every wind of doctrine"; we set at nought the schoolmen who would " teach for doctrine the commandments of men"; whilst we bind and fetter the discursive genius of infidelity, by allowing no objection to be valid unless founded on the Word.  (2) Nor is it of use to vindicate our faith to others only; it serves much to confirm and strengthen it in ourselves.  The humblest Christian who loves his Bible because he has felt its power, finds in it many things hard to be understood; but he can repose with child-like confidence in the thought—"Hard as these things may seem, the Lord hath spoken them;" and He would never have left a mystery where plainness would have made me happy.  He has told me all that concerns my comfort here, and will reveal hereafter what I know not now.  3. We can understand now the propriety of this appeal.  "Once ye had no knowledge of God and Divine things.  This darkness has passed.  Yours must be the fault, therefore, if the day should overtake you as a thief."  II. THE MOTIVES WHICH SHOULD URGE US TO THE RIGHT IMPROVEMENT OF CHRISTIAN PRIVILEGES.  1. Their tendency to promote personal religion.  (1) We are so much the slaves of habit, the mind so easily slides into the ordinary occupations of life, that without some periodical admonition that it has higher objects to seek, its power would be expended in considering " What shall we eat."  We might know that " We have no continuing city" and that it is our duty to " Seek one to come," but if we were not occasionally reminded, every week would find us less punctual, and at last we should neglect it altogether.  But how the hour of prayer, the Sabbath, &c., rouse us to the call of duty.  (2) A disposition to slight these outward means is a concealed aversion to the religion which enjoins them.  It is an index of that self-sufficiency which will only accept a blessing if obtained in a way of our own choosing.  (3) Men ask " Why cannot I be religious without going to church?  I can go forth into the fields and look through nature up to nature's God."  Possibly you can, but *will* you?  2. The danger that we may suddenly lose them.  The " day" here is the day of judgment, but practically for us that is the day of death.  When that will come we know not; but lest it should find us slumbering, let us be on our guard always, and not flatter ourselves with a false peace.  (*D. Moore, M.A.*)     *Two views of death:*—" I am taking a fearful leap in the dark," said the dying infidel, Hobbes.  " This is heaven begun, I have done with darkness for ever, nothing remains but light and joy," said the dying believer, Thomas Scott.  (*Sunday at Home.*)     *Ready to die:*—When Gordon Pasha was taken prisoner by the Abyssinians he completely checkmated King John.  The King received his prisoner sitting on his throne, or whatever piece of furniture did duty for that exalted seat, a chair being placed for the prisoner considerably lower than the seat on which the King sat.  The first thing the Pasha did was to seize this chair, place it alongside of his Majesty, and sit down on it: the next to inform him that he met him as an equal and would only treat him as such.  This somewhat disconcerted his sable majesty, but on recovering himself he said, " Do you know, Gordon Pasha, that I could kill you on the spot if I liked?"  " I am perfectly well aware of it, your Majesty," said the Pasha.  " Do so at once if it is your Royal pleasure.  I am ready."  This disconcerted the King still more, and he exclaimed, " What! ready to be killed?"  " Certainly," replied the Pasha, " I am always ready to die, and so far from fearing your putting me to death, you would confer a favour on me by so doing, for you would be doing for me that which I am precluded by my religious scruples from doing for myself—you would relieve me from all the troubles and misfortunes which the future may have in store for me."  This completely staggered King John, who gasped out in despair, " Then my power has no terrors for you?"  " None whatever," was the Pasha's laconic reply.  His Majesty, it is needless to add, instantly collapsed.

Ver. 5. **Ye are all children of the light.**—I. What it is to be of THE NIGHT AND DARKNESS.  This is a fitting symbol of a soul away from God, blind in understanding and heart and will.  There is implied in it—1. Ignorance of God.  2. Wickedness.  " Men love darkness rather than light," &c.  3. Misery.  Days of sorrow are days of darkness.  II. What it is to be CHILDREN OF LIGHT AND OF THE DAY.  Theirs is a state of—1. Knowledge. They are "enlightened," having turned the eye of their heart to Him who is the Light of the world. 2. Holiness. As God is clothed with light as with a garment, so are His people clothed even now with the white robe. 3. Happiness. "Joy cometh in the morning." 4. Future glory. In God's light they shall see light. Conclusion: This being the state of Christ's people, it cannot be that the day should overtake them as a thief; that day loved and longed for can never come upon them as something unwelcome. (*J. Hutchison, D.D.*) *Children of the night and darkness :*—A colonial governor who was about to return to England offered to use his influence with the home government and procure any favour the colonists might desire. The unanimous reply was as startling as the demand for the head of John the Baptist. "Tell them to tear down the lighthouses, they are ruining the colony." The people were wreckers. (*W. C. Church.*) *The children of the day :*—I. It is evident that ALL THOSE ON WHOM THE TRUE LIGHT SHINES ARE, IN A VERY IMPORTANT SENSE, THE "CHILDREN OF THE DAY." Christendom is the domain of light as contrasted with the early world or the regions beyond. Its very dimmest parts are luminous in comparison with any portion of the world to which the rays of the gospel have not penetrated. None can dwell where the gospel is known without deriving from it great accessions of knowledge on most important and essential questions. What elsewhere is conjecture, surmise, hope, there is certainty. What heathen sages, by the reflection and research of a life, laboured to make probable, the Christian child learns at its mother's knee, and grows up to know and believe with an implicit and unwavering confidence, yea, and many things besides, which the efforts of natural reason were never able so much as to excogitate even into the rudest sketch or outline. II. But there is a higher sense in which WE ARE THE CHILDREN OF THE DAY, AS WE ARE BAPTIZED INTO THE BODY OF CHRIST, AND MADE TO PARTAKE OF THE PRIVILEGES OF THE CHURCH. And this also is happily true of most of us; sad to think, that in a land that calls itself Christian, it should be untrue of any. The ancient fathers often called baptism "illumination"; because it introduced and pledged to its recipients the enlightening influences of the Holy Spirit. III. There is still another form and grade of illumination, by virtue of which the partakers of it are made in a still higher and more glorious sense the children of the light and of the day. This is THAT ILLUMINATION WHICH REACHES THE HEART AND THE LIFE, AND BRINGS THEM UNDER THE PRACTICAL CONTROL OF THE TRUTH WHICH IT COMMUNICATES. This is the end and design of all inferior illumination. A spiritual illumination, one that takes hold upon the moral and active powers of our nature, quickens the conscience, controls the will, hallows the affections, gives truth supremacy and dominion, and stamps the visible impress of every revelation it makes upon the character and practice, is the illumination that makes us children of the day in the only sufficient sense, and thereupon heirs of salvation. (*R. A. Hallam, D.D.*) *Children of life and light :*—I looked from my window this morning across the fields. I noticed a dwelling-house whose roof was exposed to the early and cheerful sun. There had been a storm in the night, and snow covered the roof. In an hour the warmth of the sun had melted it, save where the shadow of the chimney fell. That long, dark shade kept firm grasp of the iciness. It gave me a morning lesson, like a text from Scripture. The ice of our lives lingers only where the shadow is. If we have no Christly warmth, it is because we live in the dark. If our love is chilled and our nature sluggish, there is something between us and the light. What then? We must go forth from shadows. The sun shines and its beams are full of life. If we walk in this life the ice will melt, and instead of deathly conditions, we shall become rivers of living water. An army officer was called to the French and Indian war a century and a half ago. He left a wife and five children at home. A fearful throat ailment carried every child in a few weeks to the grave. The wife sat alone and desolate at home. What did she say? "I must not stay indoors and weep; I will go into the sunshine." And her neighbours daily said, "Madame Ringe is in the sunlight again." And this legend of her is told till this day. Christ is the Sun. Shadows do not belong to us. They savour of death. The one aim of God is to make us children of life and light; then follows holy fellowship and hallowed communion. (*A. Caldwell.*) *Judged by the light we give :*—In Connecticut recently, the parents of a young lady in a school at Bridgeport sent to her a collection of beetles from Cuba. Among them were two or three specimens known as *Elater Noctilucus*, or fire beetle of the West Indies. They measure about an inch in length. On each side of the thorax is a large, oval, velvety black spot, like an eye, and some of them have in place of the oval spot two translucent, opal-like spots on the sides of the thorax, and from these at night the insect throws at will a strong light, resembling two tiny electric lamps in full glow. The light from one insect is sufficiently strong to enable one to read fine print with ease. When agitated the insect also gives out a similar light from the tissue between the segments on the under side of the body. The beetles were taken to a photographic artist in the city, who found that the light emitted from them, though of a greenish hue, contained abundant actinic rays by which, with a sensitive plate, he could obtain negatives. After a few experiments he succeeded in taking a picture of one of the beetles by no light but that emitted by the beetle itself. It is too often forgotten that pictures of human character are taken in the same way; every man is judged by the light he gives. *Children of light:*—We may learn a lesson on this subject from an article in common use—our coals. Long, long ages ago our earth was filled with immense forests of fern trees. It was sunlight that made them grow. Sunlight was bottled up in those ferns. After a while those ferns became our coal-beds, and coals are really bottled-up sunlight. We put the coals inside the grate, we apply a match, we release the bottled-up sunlight, and the light and heat previously latent in the coals warm and cheer us during the dark, cold days of winter. These coals may be described as "children of light." The light so played upon them thousand of ages ago that it got into their very nature, so that they only require a little stimulus to pour forth floods of radiance and warmth. And if we believe and walk in God's light when it visits us, we shall become "children of light;" the light will get into our inmost natures, so "that we shall become fountains of light." (*Free Methodist Magazine.*) *Light and liberty:*—Going to Helena I saw piles of boxes and goods on the landing, and I said to the superintendent, "Do the slaves buy as much as their masters used to do for them?" "A great deal more." "And what things do they buy?" "Looking-glasses and candles." "Looking-glasses, of course; candles, however!" said I. "What do they want with candles?" "In the old slave times, a slave was never allowed a light in his cabin unless it were a fire, and the candles became in their sight the signal of liberty, and the moment they were free they said, 'Give us light.'" (*H. W. Beecher.*) *Light within diffuses radiance without:*—1. In reducing chaos to the order of a well-constituted world the first work of God was the creation of light. "And God saw the light that it was good," &c. (1) Light is indeed an admirable production of the Creator. It imparts beauty to all that delights the eye of man; since, in the absence of light, beauty could have no existence. It brings to the eye all the knowledge and pleasure we derive from a survey of the Divine workmanship, the works of art and the face of man. Its properties are astonishing. It requires only a few minutes to come from the sun, whence, falling in parallel rays, it illumines the face of the earth in the twinkling of an eye. And how admirable its influence in conveying warmth and activity to all things. (2) It is no wonder that it should be used as an emblem of all that is excellent in the spiritual world. (*a*) As revealing the figure, position, and qualities of things light is an emblem of truth, which assigns to everything its real attributes. (*b*) Of knowledge, which apprehends and forms a just estimate of things. (*c*) Of moral purity, as preserving its own essence without being contaminated with the objects it approaches. (*d*) Of true piety, as conveying life and health. (*e*) Of the happiness attendant on true goodness, as imparting gladness. (*f*) Of God Himself, who is "the Father of lights," in whom is "no darkness at all." 2. Darkness is the absence of light, and in an ordinary sense its opposite. Here it had precedence of light, and still retains a periodical influence, contributing to the well-being of the universe. But though useful in the physical world, morally darkness is emblematical of all that is evil. (1) As concealing objects around us, and precluding the right apprehension of them, it is the emblem of ignorance and error. (2) As favouring the machinations of the wicked and shrouding them from detection it is a metaphor for sin which hates the light. (3) As associated with danger and terror it intimates the peril and punishment of guilt. (4) The grand enemy of all goodness, as the deceiver, defiler and destroyer of men is the prince of darkness and his kingdom the kingdom of darkness. The children of light are distinguished —I. BY THE KNOWLEDGE OF THE TRUTH. 1. As in the material world darkness preceded light and was only banished by Divine command, so ignorance precedes the light of saving knowledge. This was exemplified in the case of the Thessalonians and other Gentiles "Having their understanding darkened" as to God, duty, destiny. The Jews were better off; but their's was only "a light shining in a dark place." But when the Sun of Righteousness arose it scattered the gross darkness of heathenism and the shadowy emblems of Judaism. 2. But in order to enjoy the light we must have an eye to see, since if that organ be covered with a scale or be injured light will fail of its purpose. Pride and prejudice are a film to quench the intellectual eye in reference to Divine things. For the things of this world man retains the light of intelligence, but " the natural man receiveth not the things of the Spirit of God." 3. The eyes of the children of light have been opened. That which was formerly rejected as fantastical or unimportant has become the " one thing needful." Instructed by the Word and Spirit of God light shines within and around ; they see the glory of God in the person and work of Christ. The path of life lies open, and perceiving both its difficulties and encouragements they walk on in safety. The love of the truth characterizes them as children of the light. " He that doeth the truth cometh to the light," &c. II. BY HOLINESS, in opposition to what is offensive to God. 1. Sins of the life are called works of darkness, and sins of the affection are similarly characterized (1 John ii. 9–11). The darkness of ignorance is naturally associated with vice, and the blindness of the understanding with that of the heart. "If the eye be single," &c. If the guide be blind the other faculties placed under his direction will stumble continually; and the guide himself partaker in pravity is led astray by the perverseness of those whom it is his duty to govern. If the mind through prejudice, passion, the allurements of the world, embraces error for truth, good for evil, what can be expected but that, betrayed by its counsellors, it should advance on the road to ruin. And men manifestly walk in darkness. How else can they barter immortality for the shadows of time. 2. The children of the light, however, have the eyes of their understanding enlightened. God's Word is a " light to their feet," &c. The planets, irradiated by the sun, may be called " children of light "; so should the believer, irradiated by Christ, let his light shine. III. BY USEFULNESS in opposition to the influence of the workers of iniquity. 1. Error serves only to deceive—sin only to beguile and destroy ; and every one who promotes the one or the other injures his fellows. Their influence is as the lengthened night of the Polar regions spreading sterility over the earth, and destroying life. 2. But the children of light diffuse a salutary influence. Not only are they "blameless and harmless," they "shine as lights in the world, holding forth the Word of life." Such come to be esteemed sure guides. They are as a pilot skilled in the perilous passes of his own rocky course, whose vessel breaks the way, leaving a luminous track, by which the fleet may steer its course in safety. IV. BY A BLESSEDNESS peculiar to themselves. We all appreciate the advantages of light, and pity those who are deprived of them. But if to one born blind it were an inexpressible happiness to obtain sight should not a purer joy pervade him who is made to behold the imperishable beauties of the spiritual world. (*H. Grey, D.D.*) *Vigilance and sobriety :*—The text is for the Lord's people ; and as they have great privileges to enjoy, so they have great duties to perform, and that, too, distinct from others. I. Two CLASSES ARE SPOKEN OF IN CONTRAST. 1. The children of the night and of darkness. Of ignorance, unbelief, and wrath. They are in the regions of moral rebellion and imminent danger. 2. The children of day and of light. Illumed by the Word and the Spirit of God. Transformed ; brought out of spiritual Egypt, and translated into the Divine kingdom. They are now of God's family—sons and heirs. Hence they have heavenly light within them—knowledge, love, and holiness. Their path is light itself, and it leads to " the inheritance of the saints in light." So that while they are on earth, they are " the lights of the world." II. THE COURSE OF THE CHILDREN OF THE DAY. " Therefore, let us not sleep as do others." 1. That which they are to avoid. Moral sleep, soul lethargy, conscience slumbering, spiritual drowsiness. This is a state of helplessness, vague and illusory dreams, wasted opportunities, real perils. 2. That which they are to attend to. Watchfulness against the snares of the world, the stratagems of Satan, and the deceitfulness of the heart. As the sentinel at his post ; as the mariner on stormy ocean looking for day ; as the wise virgins waiting with their lamps burning, so all Christians are exhorted to do. 3. That which they are to be, " sober." Physical sobriety—avoiding revelling, banquetting, intemperance, and all tendencies to them, avoiding the very appearance of evil. Mental sobriety—walking in humility and self-abasement, not intoxicated with vanity, nor the praises of men. Social sobriety—avoiding foolish excitements and a vapid and silly conversation. Moral sobriety—seeking even lawful things with moderation, such as the increase of riches and innocent pleasures. Such sobriety includes a well-balanced mind, a serious spirit, and a becoming walk before God and men, and is real, entire, and constant. III. THE MOTIVES BY WHICH THIS COURSE IS URGED. 1. The enemies and

perils which surround us.  An evil world ; a malignant devil ; a weak nature, liable
to err, and leaning to sin.  2. The sad results which may ensue.  Spiritual declension ; open apostacy ; personal degradation ; unutterable misery.  Application :
The text to be prayerfully considered and solemnly pondered—(1) In the light of
our Christian profession ; (2) In connection with our peace and happiness ; (3)
With our usefulness and honour ; (4) With our final acceptance and salvation. (*J.
Burns, D.D.*)    *The relation of Christianity to intellectual culture :*—The text is a
declaration of the relation of Christianity to all enlightening agencies.  Christians
are born of light and day.  They walk in the light and are in kinship with all
illuminating agencies.  I. THE NATURE AND METHODS OF RELIGION NECESSITATE
MENTAL CULTURE.  It does not and cannot rely upon force or fashion or gain or
favour for its propagation in the world.  The instances where a Church, secularized
by an alliance with temporal power, has endeavoured to use these agencies, illustrate the apostacy of that Church rather than the character of Christianity.  1.
Christianity is a spiritual light and force.  It is a revelation.  Like a newly-dis-
covered truth in science or a new invention, it must be tested.  And so it appeals to
the thought of the world.  It is the light of the world.  It ignores blind force.
Jesus says, " My kingdom is not of this world," &c.  2. It does battle in the domain
of thought, conscience and the affections.  In no other way can it secure the conquest of the human will.  It recognizes the integrity and dignity of each individual.
3. It believes in one God, the author both of nature and revelation.  To its faith
every truth of science, every fact of nature is a revelation.  If they seem to disagree
with the Bible it is stimulated to further research.  It is, therefore, the friend of all
science and all scientific investigation.  Most great scientists have been Christians.
II. THE PRESENCE OF THE GOSPEL A STIMULUS TO MENTAL ACTIVITY.  It is no accident,
but in the nature of things that progress, discovery, civilization, wealth and power
go hand in hand with a pure Christianity.  1. The great ideas of religion stimulate
mental activity.  The law of mental development is this : thrust a fact or great
idea before a mind, and as the mind contemplates it, in many lights, new ideas are
born and the mind expands, enlarges, strengthens.  So you teach children in the
schools.  You give them a fact of physics or history, and as their minds contemplate it they grow.  Given the thought, " steam possesses an expansive force," and
engines are constructed.  Show Columbus a carved stick that drifted in from the
Western ocean, and a new continent is discovered.  A falling apple observed, leads
to the discovery of gravitation.  Now, by the same law, project upon the mind
thought of God, immortality, sin, redemption, judgment, &c., and that mind will
wake up to an activity of thought that will make it wiser.  It will study conscience,
law, evidences, life, responsibility, till it becomes educated.  2. Christianity lifts
man into a position that justifies him in trying to become a thinker.  If a man lives
on the borders of a desert thought to be worthless, he will never explore it.  But
let him know its mineral wealth and he will soon know it.  So with the future.
Let the soul have no knowledge of God and righteousness, and it will not awake ;
but let it contemplate itself as an heir of glory, and how it will wake up.  Ask a
slave to study kingcraft, and he tells you he has no use for it ; but you ask an heir-
apparent with different result.  So the Christian studies God's ways and Word.
III. FACTS CONFIRM THESE PROPOSITIONS.  Christianity has ever been the friend of
liberal thought and learning.  It originated our educational institutions, and maintains a good many of them.  What phenomena are presented in Sunday schools,
the Christian press and pulpit !  (*C. N. Sims, D.D.*)

Ver. 6. **Therefore let us not sleep as do others, but let us watch and be
sober.**—*Sleep :*—I. THE SLEEP OF SIN.—Scripture teaches us, with the utmost
explicitness, that a state of sin is a state of slumber.  Sleep is a figure
which is commonly employed to illustrate man's natural and unrenewed state.
Sin is the sleep of the soul—the spirit.  1. Both natural and spiritual
sleep are characterized by forgetfulness.  We speak, and not without reason,
of the oblivion of sleep.  A man falls into a sound sleep, and immediately he
forgets the past, "forgets himself," to use a very common and not inappropriate
expression.  Look at men in a state of sin, in an unrenewed, unawakened state—
are they not the subjects, the victims of forgetfulness, to an almost incredible
extent ?  Do they not forget what manner of men they are ?  Do they not forget
all the great lessons of God's Word and God's providence, which have been so
repeatedly addressed to them ?  Do they not forget what they owe unto their Lord ?
Are they not oblivious to those immense accumulations of guilt which are invoking

the long-delayed vengeance of Heaven? 2. Both spiritual and natural sleep are characterized by insensibility to the present. In bodily slumber a man is insensible to all that transpires around him: he is shut off from all surrounding influences; a mysterious, and, for the time, impenetrable veil separates him from the external and material world. Is not this, again, illustrative of the moral, the spiritual condition of the unrenewed, the unawakened sinner? He is in the midst of a spiritual world, full of realities the most stupendous, the most amazing. He has no spiritual discernment. There are the truths of Scripture, there is this wide-spreading spiritual universe, with all that it contains of beauty and terror, with its sweet whispers of invitation and its thunder-tones of warning, all of which things are not the less real because he is asleep: but to him they are as though they were not, while he is asleep; for him they have practically no existence; on him they exert no appreciable influence. 3. In both spiritual and natural sleep we see not only forgetfulness as to the past and insensibility as to the present, we see, also, the entire absence of apprehension as to the future. In the case of natural slumber, though some great peril be actually threatening the sleeper, there is no uneasiness, no dread, no desire or effort either to avert the danger or to escape from it. That I am not overstating the case will appear, if you will take the trouble to compare your feelings in reference to some object of earthly interest, with your feelings in reference to some object of spiritual interest. But with spiritual danger it is otherwise. You see it not—it is intangible —it is mysterious—it is future. 4. Both natural and spiritual sleep are often disturbed by dreams. But there is the widest difference between the dreams which disturb the natural and spiritual sleeper. In natural sleep the objects of our dreams are unrealities, fantastic and improbable assemblages of familiar things, grouped upon we know not what principle of association. The man wrapped in spiritual slumber dreams, but of what is actual and real. 5. In the case both of natural and spiritual slumber we see that persons who are soundly asleep are very unwilling to be awakened. And in all deep sleep, if the awakening be not a very thorough and complete one, there is an almost irresistible tendency to fall asleep again. God often, in His providence, disturbs the sleep of men. But, whatever may be the cause, there is in such cases only a partial awakening, and we see plainly enough that the sleeper does not like to be thus disturbed. II. Let us now notice THIS SLEEP OF DEATH which is so often referred to in God's Word. The same natural state is, as you know, employed to symbolize two things, sin and death; and if we are but truly emancipated from the slumber of sin, we shall be able to look forward without foreboding to the sleep of death. As we compare sleep and death, we distinguish several points of correspondence, which are not only very obvious, but which are also very interesting. 1. We see sleep exercising its dominion over the entire world. In all ages, and in all countries, we see men yielding to its influence. And just so the power of death is universally exercised and submitted to. "Death has passed upon all men, inasmuch as all have sinned." 2. Though men have been sleeping and dying for six thousand years, there is an infinite mystery still attaching both to sleep and death. There is no one wise enough to say precisely what the one or the other is. 3. Sleep and death agree in this also, that their dominion extends no further than the body. While the body lies fettered in sleep, the soul enjoys an unbounded and unwonted liberty, which it scarcely knows how to use. 4. In sleep and in death there is the apparent enjoyment of rest and quiet. In reference to the grave we say, "There the wicked cease from troubling; there the weary are at rest." 5. In sleep and in death men lie down with the hope and the expectation of rising again. 6. You know, in the case of natural slumber, that they who would sleep well at night must not sleep much in the day. And I would remind you, that if you spend the day of your life sleeping the sleep of sin, the sleep of death will be a troubled sleep, and your awakening, on the resurrection day, one full of terror. If you will sleep when you ought to be awake, you will not be able to sleep when the time for sleep cometh. (*T. M. Morris.*) *Let us not sleep :*—Many thoughtless and irreligious men think that they live in a manner that is the furthest off from sleep. And, indeed, they may be in a perpetual fever; and yet spiritually they are like men who sleep. I. When a man is asleep he is in a state of INACTIVITY. You no more expect activity from the sleeping than you do from the dead. Whatever may be the fervid life of a godless man, yet with respect to God, prayer, preparation for eternity, religious duties, he does nothing; and Scripture says that he is not only asleep, but dead—and this, notwithstanding his pursuit of knowledge and pleasure.

II. A man asleep is UNCONSCIOUS of all around him. He may be asleep in the sunshine, on a bank of beauty and fragrance, surrounded by the most gorgeous scenery on earth, but he is insensible to it all. Such is the condition, spiritually, of the sinner. A man that has religious faith in him sees that God has surrounded him by another creation; but this is for ever shut from the sight of the godless. What is the scenery of earth to that of the universe of truth, to which the worldly have their whole soul closed? III. They that sleep DREAM, and are therefore liable to be affected by the unsubstantial and the untrue. A sluggard perhaps dreams that he is rich and prosperous; a hungry beggar, that he is a king. The most absurd and grotesque visions may flit over the dreamer and be to him as affecting as the realities of life, or he may be disturbed by dreams of terror equally unsubstantial. And worldly men will often be agitated by superstitious fears; their very ignorance of religion will be a positive and operating evil. But principally they dream that they are " rich and increased in goods," &c.; while they are in reality "poor and miserable," &c. The worldly man goes on fearing nothing because unconscious of the actual condition of his nature, and there is nothing so absurd as the dreams of irreligious dreamers; aye, and of religious dreamers too, thinking that they have enough of religion, and resting satisfied with repeating their creeds. IV. Sleep is SOMETIMES PRODUCED BY INDULGENCES that make sleep heavy (ver. 7). When men sleep through grossness and sensuality it is very difficult to awake them. Loud voices and violent shaking will scarcely do it; and if you should succeed, they are irritated and want to sleep again. So when men's souls are drugged. Startling providences, such as a death next door, or an arousing sermon, which makes the deepest impression on others, have none on them. If some kind friend takes them by the arm, and will make them hear, they are vexed and feel insulted. Their conscience may be probed for the moment, but it is soon over, and they go to sleep again. So men go on crying "Peace and safety," and by the constant neglect of their spiritual nature closing the heart against the gospel, they get into a state of complete hardihood, and then " sudden destruction cometh." " Let us not sleep like " these, " but watch and be sober." (*T. Binney.*) *Spiritual sleep:*—I. SLEEP IS A TIME WHEN THE REASON HAS NO CONTROL OVER A MAN. This is the state of the sinner. Boast as he may, his reason cannot exercise its full powers till God gives light to the understanding. How manifest it is that men are in a state in which they are not acting with a proper view to their well-being. Though hastening to eternity, they are making no provision for it. II. SLEEP IS THE TIME WHEN THE POWERS OF BODY AND MIND ARE WITHDRAWN FROM ACTIVE AND USEFUL LABOUR. True a sinner's mind is active, but not about the chief good, the glory and honour of God. The body is active, but what are its powers wasted upon? Are they not frequently "instruments of righteousness unto sin." And though men may not have sunk into licentiousness, yet, unless consecrated to God, their highest powers are thrown away. III. SLEEP IS A TIME WHEN DANGER MAY BE VERY NEAR WITHOUT BEING PERCEIVED. The sinner is like a man whose house is in flames, or into which robbers have gained entrance. He may have upbraidings of conscience, and make resolutions, and see that a course of sin is a course of misery. But all pass away unless there be the quickening power of heaven upon them. Take heed then, sinner, and awake. (*J. Morison, D.D.*) *The soul asleep:*—I. THE EVIL. There are three kinds of sleep in Scripture. The sleep of the body; of the grave; of the soul. It is of the last that Paul speaks. There is—1. The sleep of indolence, indifference, thoughtlessness. We use a like term in the affairs of life. Of a man who lets all his opportunities pass, and makes no provision against evil, obvious to all but himself, we say, "He must be asleep." Such a sleep, spiritually, is described in Isaiah xxix. The Bible is a sealed book, and eternal things a matter of little consequence. The Bible is not opposed; but all we can extort is a vacant assent, and then sleep. 2. The sleep of security and false peace. Attention has been awakened; "things belonging to peace " have been apprehended; but after having been thus enlightened there has ensued a delusive tranquillity of soul, trading in past conversion, little thinking of the use their sleepless adversary is making of their guilty slumber. 3. The sleep of sloth and inactivity. All the emblems of the Christian life support the necessity of earnestness and diligence—the racer, &c. Hence the idea of an unadvancing Christian is a practical contradiction. Imagine the case of a babe remaining always a babe, a warrior without victory. All stationary conditions in religion are slumbering conditions. II. THE DANGER. Spiritual sleep, like natural, is a thing of degrees. There is a deep sleep from which a man can with difficulty be aroused, and yet there is a lighter sleep in which though every noise be sufficient to disturb, yet it may not be sufficient to arouse. These two states are types of the unawakened sinner, and the unwatchful Christian. 1. With regard to a man in the confirmed slumber. (1) There is the awful danger that none of the warnings and providential rebukes by which other souls are stirred up should reach him; he cannot hear them. Sickness stretches him on his bed; death bereaves him of friends; decaying faculties predict his latter end; but he sleeps only to waken in the prison of the invisible world. (2) But deep as his slumbers are, they allow of his being amused with dreams. He can hear the whispers of Satan, when he cannot hear the thunders of vengeance. The word is represented as paradise; religion is an affair of observances; repentance is a dying man's employment; and death, perhaps, an eternal sleep. In that sleep of the soul "What dreams do come!" What contradictions to truth, what impiety against God! What frauds upon a rational intelligence! 2. In the sleep of a lighter character, unwatchfulness and supineness of soul, the danger is lest it should deepen into the heaviest. Men thus asleep are like those under the influence of an opiate; their only safety lies in keeping their eyes open; once close them, they die. But at best such can expect to have no evidence of their acceptance in a dying hour: they have none now. (*D. Moore, M.A.*) *Sleep not:*—We do not usually sleep towards the things of this world. In this age of competition most men are wide awake enough for their temporal interests; but we are all very apt to sleep concerning the interests of our souls. The text applies—I. To THE PEOPLE OF GOD. 1. Let us not sleep as did the disciples who went with their Lord to the garden, and fell a slumbering while He was agonizing. Think of what Christ has done, is doing, and wants you to do. Where is our zeal for God, and compassion for men in view of all this? 2. Let us not sleep as Samson, who, while he slept, lost his locks, strength, liberty, eyes, and at last his life. Carnal security is a Delilah always. It gives us many a dainty kiss, and lulls us into tranquil slumber, which we imagine to be God's own peace, whereas the peace of Satanic enchantment is upon us. Here there are perils of the deadliest sort. The Philistines do not sleep. Our Samsonian lock, the secret of our strength, is faith. Take away that and we are weak as other men. 3. Sleep not as those did when the enemy came and sowed tares. When false doctrines and unholy practices creep into a Church, it is when the watchers are asleep. An unwatchful Church will soon become an unholy Church. 4. Sleep not as the ten virgins whom the coming of the Bridegroom surprised. Suppose the Lord were to come to night; are you ready, with your loins girt and your lamps trimmed? II. To THE UNCONVERTED. 1. Do not sleep as did Jonah. When all the rest were praying in the tempest he was insensible to it all. Every man called upon his God, except the man who had caused the storm. He was most in danger, but he was the most careless. Do not some of you live in houses where they all pray but you? Yours is the only soul unblest, and yet yours is the only one unanxious. 2. Do not sleep like Solomon's sluggard. He slept hour after hour. He only meant to slumber a few minutes; but minutes fly rapidly to men who dream. Had he known he would have been shocked at his own laziness. Now there are men who say that they will attend to religion soon, but must first enjoy a little pleasure. They will not risk their soul another twelve months, they will but stay till next Sunday. But so it has been year after year. 3. Do not sleep like Eutychus. It is true that he was restored to life; but many a Eutychus has fallen dead under the Word and has never revived. If preaching does not wake you it rocks your cradle and makes you more and more insensible. 4. Do not sleep like Saul and his guards. Abishai said "Let me strike him: it shall be but this once." That is what Satan says and what he will some day do. 5. Do not sleep as Sisera. Those who profess to be your friends will prove your assassins. (*C. H. Spurgeon.*) *Why Christians should not sleep :*—I. God has done more for them than for others. II. They have made promises to Him which others have not made. III. God has made to them exceeding great and precious promises which He has not made to others. IV. So much is expected of them, and such a great work is laid upon them, if "they sleep as do others," it will not be done. V. While Christians sleep the enemy is busy—sinners perish—the world rushes madly to ruin! (*Preacher's Monthly.*) *On guard :*—"Let us watch." I. THE IMPORTANCE OF WATCHFULNESS. It is the mainstay of the soul, which, if once called off, we lie open to the shot of every enemy. This, like one of the Nethinims, must stand constantly porter at the door of our hearts—God's temple, to keep out whatever is unclean. Watchfulness is a diligent observation of ourselves in all things, and at all times, that we may please God always. He that watcheth hath his eyes in his head, according to the wise man's phrase, and seeth, as the Chinese say of themselves, with both eyes. David expresseth it fitly: " I said, I will take heed to my ways; " that is, I will ponder my paths, and consider where I set my feet, lest I should tread awry. Without this wariness there is no safe walking. Like Laish was, the secure soul is made a prey to its enemies. Soul lethargies are most dangerous, most deadly. He who watcheth not is led about like one in his natural sleep, by any temptation, he knoweth not how nor whither When the wolves in the fable once prevailed with the sheep to part with the dogs they soon devoured them. If Satan can but get Christians to forego this means of their safety, he will soon make them his prey. It is reported of the dragon that, while he sleepeth, a jewel is taken out of his head. Noah lost the jewel of temperance, David the jewel of chastity, during their sleep. If the eye of watchfulness be once shut, the soul is open to all wickedness. II. THE OBJECTS OF WATCHFULNESS. 1. Watch against sin, against all sin. The gardener doth not only watch over his flowers to water and cherish them, but over all weeds to pluck and root them up. 2. Watch against thine own sin. A wise governor will have a special eye upon that particular person in his garrison whom he knoweth to be a traitor. 3. Watch for the doing of good. The countryman watcheth for the bell ringing on the market-day, when he will open his sacks, that he may sell corn to the needy. 4. Watch in duties. The child must be watched at school, or he will play and toy, instead of learning his lesson thoroughly. 5. Watch after duties. When the garden is dressed and the seed sown in it, it must be watched, lest hogs get into it, and root all up. It was a wise speech of Marcus Aurelius after he had won a great battle, " I tell thee of a truth that I stand in greater fear of fortune at this moment than I did before the battle, for she careth not so much to overtake the conquered as to overcome the conqueror." Satan is like Fortune. 6. Watch thy senses. These are the Cinque Ports, as one calls them, of the Isle of Man, which, if not well garrisoned, will let in strangers and disturbers of the peace. Shut up the five windows—guard the five senses, that the whole house may be full of light, according to the Arabian proverb. " Blessed is that servant whom his Lord when He cometh shall find watching." Surely blessedness is worth our waking; bliss is worth keeping our eyes open. Apollonius, coming early in the morning to Vespasian's gate, and finding him, then a prisoner, up and at study, said to his companion, " This man is worthy to reign and command an empire ; " which afterward came to pass. He that watcheth for the Advent of Christ the short hour of his life, shall be counted worthy to reign with Christ in His kingdom for ever. (G. Swinnock, M.A.)    Watch!—Temptation comes—I. As A WHIPPED FOE, and begins to say, " Oh, I am worsted; there is no danger in me." Watch it ! Firemen watch the smouldering coals that the wind may again inflame. Men watch closely that place in an embankment which has once given way. II. WITH A NEW FACE, and says, " I am not your weakness." Take heed ! Faithful Abraham lost his faith, meek Moses was impatient, David became sensual, and lion-hearted Peter trembled. III. As A CHILD, and says, " Oh, I am so little, I cannot do anything." Watch it ! Little temptations are seeds of the upas-tree, eggs of the serpent, sleeping dynamite. The devil puts the little Oliver Twist through the window to open the door for him, the big robber. Hell is first lit with shavings. IV. As A SMILING FRIEND, and says, " You know me and love me ; fear not." Watch it ! The beloved Delilah betrayed the strong Samson to death. Watch and pray. The sentinel's power lies in his communication with the power that supports him, and then watchfulness. If he watch only, he can do nothing when the enemy comes He is one, the enemy is an army. But if he too can summon an army, then is his watching effective. So is prayer the Christian watchman's communication with the powers above him. If he watch only, he can do nothing, for he contends with principalities and powers and spiritual wickedness in high places. But if he watch and pray, he, too, can summon powers omnipotent to his rescue. And prayer is communication with the power. (R. S. Barrett.)    The danger of spiritual slumber :—There was, a paragraph in a local newspaper tells us, a foreign sailor at Cork, who, having been late for his train, lay down to sleep during the short summer night on the first broad flat wall he came to. After a time, in his sleep, he rolled over the edge, for it was—though he had not noticed the fact—the boundary wall which separated the road from a precipice fifty feet in depth. He would have been instantly killed, had he not, as he fell, instinctively grasped at the ivy which clothed the wall. Here for three-quarters of an hour he hung, clinging with all his strength, and shouting as loud as he could for aid. At last he was rescued, but so soon as he was in safety the strong man fainted, so terrible had been his position. Thus is it with many a soul. Men sleep thoughtlessly on the brink of eternity. They dream of earthly joys; but suddenly, by some unexpected crisis, by some dangerous illness, they are awakened, and made to feel their danger. They perceive that they must expect to meet that God whom they have forgotten. The great fault of modern preaching is its soothing and sugary character. There is a tendency always to be putting forward the mercy and pardoning character of God, whilst His justice and His needful severity as a moral Ruler is kept out of sight. The difficulties of repentance, the awful doom of sin when persisted in, are matters unnoticed. Away with this twaddle and prattle about the simplicity of faith; the easiness of " being saved"; the empiric remedies of the " only believe " school; the supply of comfortable pillows to induce spiritual slumber. Away with the sweet but fatal syrup which suggests that men may at any time with the greatest facility become eminent Christians! How much more vigorous and robust was the piety of olden days. For instance, St. Hugh of Lincoln, refusing to hurry over a poor man's funeral, though he received a message that the king was waiting dinner for his arrival. " In God's Name," said the enthusiastic prelate, "let the king go to dinner. Better that he dine without my company, than that I leave my Master's work undone." (*J. W. Hardman, LL.D.*) *Awake thou that sleepest :*—I. THE NATURE OF THIS SLEEP. 1. If a Christian man is said to sleep it must be in reference to inactivity. In sleep the whole body is at rest, but the mind is not. Never have we more graphic pictures of scenes and persons, nor more curious uprisings of buried pleasures and pains. But while the worker sleeps the loom is still. Now, while Christians sleep all aggressive energy is suspended; the minister sleeps in the pulpit, and the hearer in the pew, neither do nor get good. 2. While men are asleep they have no interest in their work-a-day life. So to a sleepy Christian, souls may perish at his threshold, but he cares as little for them as they for him. Besides, he is immovable to all appeals. What is the use of spending argument or wasting speech on a sleeping man? This slumbering spirit spreads itself over everything else. If he comes to a prayer meeting he goes away without wrestling with the angel of mercy. 3. There is such an experience as walking in the sleep, aye, and in dangerous places where men awake would hardly go. By some strange influence somnambulists can go safely past the dangers. So, professors have a carnal security, and go terribly near the fire of sin. 4. When a man is asleep he is unprotected. Were we not unconscious of danger we could not sleep: but it is very real. Samson slept till Delilah cut his hair, and Sisera till Jael drove the nail into his temples. When a Christian is asleep he lays himself open to the devil, "who as a roaring lion," &c. He lies down in the enchanted ground till Giant Despair hauls him away to Doubting Castle. 5. In sleep there is no waste and decay. It is by sleep we are refreshed, but we do not eat or drink when we are asleep. So, when professors are asleep they raise no cry for the living Bread, and have no sense of hunger; feel no need of a Bible or a Saviour; conscious of no want they offer no prayer, and if they sleep long enough, they will sleep on to death. 6. Mark the insidious character of this sleep. (1) A Christian may be asleep and not know it. He may imagine himself rich while in reality he is poor and miserable. (2) He may have taken precautions against being disturbed. There is a way of bolting and barring your heart against anybody. Beware of antinomianism: a draught of that may send you into a sleep that will know no awaking. (3) You may be doing much to make people imagine you were anything but asleep. People can talk and walk in their sleep, and so may you; and you may have fine dreams and grand projects. II. THE CAUSES OF THIS SLEEP. 1. It is the evil of our nature. While we are asleep about Divine things we are wide awake about worldly things. 2. It is easy to send a man to sleep with the chloroform of bad doctrine. If he believes that God is too merciful to punish he goes to sleep and cares nothing for his soul. Or if holding true doctrine he perverts them that will send him asleep. 3. Another cause is absorption in the things of the world, even when lawful. Every one knows that there is something he likes exceedingly, and that if he were to give full swing to it it would become an everlasting passion. 4. The sultry sun of prosperity. Those are generally the most spiritually minded who have drunk deep of the cup of suffering. 5. Spiritual pride. III. THE APOSTLE'S ADMONITION. 1. The first thing to do is to open the eyes and let in the light. Open them to God in His Word, works and conscience. Just as the sun in the heavens shining in the eyes of a sleeper drives away sleep, so let the beams of the Sun of

Righteousness shine into your hearts and wake you from your slumber. 2. Sleep not, for it is love that would have you awake. A mother's love will lull a child to sleep; but if there is a house on fire that love will take another turn. The wisdom of Christ would have you awake. The thief pilfers, and tares are sown while you are asleep, and therefore it is the highest wisdom to respond. You are commanded to awake, and by One who redeems you with His blood. IV. INDUCEMENTS TO THIS AWAKENING. 1. Christ will give thee light—the light of truth and joy and glory. 2. It is high time to awake for the old, the middle aged, the young. (*Prof. Croskerry.*)    *Awake! Awake!*—I. AN EVIL TO BE AVOIDED.    " Others " may be translated " refuse," the common herd who have no mind above earth. The refuse of mankind are in a state of—1. Deplorable ignorance. The sleeper knows nothing. So, talk to the sinner of Divine doctrines and they are a riddle; of sublime experiences, and they seem to be enthusiastic fancies. They know nothing of joys and are oblivious of evils to come. 2. Insensibility. Rob or destroy his property, and yet he sleeps as though guarded by the angel of the Lord. How few there are that feel spiritually; although they feel acutely any injury to their person or estate. 3. Defencelessness. How helpless was sleeping Sisera. So the refuse of mankind have no power to resist temptation. 4. Inactivity. The sleeping farmer cannot plough, the sailor direct his ship, the tradesman attend to his shop. And how many there are who rise up early to toil for themselves do nothing for the glory of God or the good of men. Some say they have no time, others frankly that they have no will. 5. Unwatchfulness. II. REASONS FOR AVOIDING THIS SLEEP. 1. We are the children of the light and of the day, *therefore* let us not sleep. It is no marvel that men sleep at night; but were a whole city to be wrapped in slumber at noon-day, what room there would be for astonishment or alarm. Sleep in the daytime is incong'uous. So, for a Christian to slumber in ease now that the Sun of Righteousness has arisen is untimely and unseemly. 2. It is war time (ver. 8). What have warriors to do with sleep when the citadel is attacked or when the foe is in the field? So spiritual sleep is madness. 3. It is service time. Shall men sleep at the plough, and God's servant sleep over his work. (*C. H. Spurgeon.*) *A slumbering church:*—You have all read the fairy tale: A great Eastern city, beleaguered by fierce foemen, was arming in resistless strength to issue from her gates and sweep away the invader. But from the camp of the foe came forth a mighty magician, and with a breath of his sorcery changed the whole city into stone. Everything where life had been became a cold, dead statue. There stood the pawing war horse, with nostril distended, caparisoned for the battle. There stood the mailed champion, ready to spring to his seat and lay lance in rest for the onset. But, alas! the strong arm was cold stone on the neck of the petrified charger. There stood the serried infantry, with armour and plumes, and upfloating banners, but each man cold, breathless, lifeless. The eye had a stony glare. Hand, brow, lips, were frozen to marble. All still, silent, deathstruck! Alas! picture sadly truthful of Christ's slumbering Church to-day. (*C. Wadsworth, D.D.*)    *The deadening effects of the gospel when it does not arouse:*—You know the great boiler factories over here in Southwark. I am told that when a man goes inside the boiler to hold the hammer, when they are fixing rivets, the sound of the copper deafens him so that he cannot bear it, it is so horrible; but, after he has been a certain number of months in that employment, he hardly notices the hammering: he does not care about it. It is just so under the Word. People go to sleep under that which once was like a thunderbolt to them. As the blacksmith's dog will lie under the anvil, where the sparks fly into his face, and yet go to sleep, so will many sinners sleep while the sparks of damnation fly into their faces. If I must be lost, let it be as a Zulu Kaffir, or as a Red Indian, who has never listened to the truth; but it is dreadful to go down to the pit with this as an aggravation: " You knew your duty, but you did it not! " may this never be said of any of us! May we never sleep under the Word as others lest we die in our sins. (*C. H. Spurgeon.*)    *The insensibility of the sinner:*—When a man is asleep he is insensible. The world goes on, and he knows nought about it. The watchman calls beneath his window, and he sleeps on still. A fire is in a neighbouring street, his neighbour's house is burned to ashes, but he is asleep and knows it not. Persons are sick in the house, but he is not awakened; they may die, and he weeps not for them. A revolution may be raging in the streets of his city; a king may be losing his crown; but he that is asleep shares not in the turmoil of politics. A volcano may burst somewhere near him, and he may be in imminent peril; but he escapeth not; he is sound asleep, he is insensible. The winds are howling, the thunders are rolling across the sky, and the lightnings flash at his window; but he that can sleep on careth not for these, and is insensible to them all. The sweetest music is passing through the street; but he sleeps, and only in dreams doth he hear the sweetness. The most terrific wailings may assail his ears; but sleep has sealed them with the wax of slumber, and he hears not. Let the world break in sunder, and the elements go to ruin, keep him asleep, and he will not perceive it. Christian, behold your condition. Have you not sometimes been brought into a condition of insensibility? You wished you could feel; but all you felt was pain because you could not feel. You wished you could pray. It was not that you felt prayerless, but it was because you did not feel at all. You sighed once; you would give a world if you could sigh now. You used to groan once; a groan now would be worth a golden star if you could buy it. As for songs, you can sing them, but then your heart does not go with them. You go to the house of God; but when "the multitude that keep holy day" in the full tide of song send their music up to heaven, you hear it, but your heart does not leap at the sound. Prayer goeth solemnly like the evening sacrifice up to God's throne; once you could pray too; but now, while your body is in the house of God, your heart is not there. You feel you have brought the chrysalis of your being; but the fly is gone away from it: it is a dead, lifeless case. You have become like a formalist. (*Ibid.*)　　*The enchanted ground :*—There is a portion of the road which leads from the city of Destruction to the Celestial City which is more dangerous than any other. It does not abound in lions, dark woods, deep pitfalls, yet more pilgrims have been destroyed here than anywhere. The great geographer, John Bunyan, well pictured it when he said "I then saw in my dream, that they went on till they came into a certain country, whose air naturally tended to make one drowsy, if he came a stranger into it. And here Hopeful began to be very dull and heavy of sleep wherefore he said unto Christian, 'I do now begin to grow so drowsy, that I can scarcely hold up mine eyes; let us lie down here and take one nap.' Christian: 'By no means, lest sleeping we never wake more.' Hopeful: 'Why my brother? sleep is sweet to the labouring man; we may be refreshed if we take a nap.' Christian: 'Do you not remember that one of the shepherds bid us beware of the Enchanted Ground? He meant by that, that we should beware of sleeping; wherefore let us not sleep as do others, but let us watch and be sober.'" There are no doubt many of us who are passing over this plain. I. WHAT IS THAT STATE OF SLEEP WITH WHICH CHRISTIANS SOMETIMES FALL? It is not death but—1. A state of insensibility. 2. A state in which they are subject to divers delusions. 3. A state of inaction. 4. A state of insecurity. II. SOME CONSIDERATIONS TO WAKE UP SLEEPY CHRISTIANS. 1. The Lord is coming (ver. 2). Would you wish to be sleeping when the Lord comes? Would you like Him to find you at a ball? 2. Souls are perishing. Sailor, wilt thou sleep when the wreck is out at sea, and the life-boat is waiting for hands to man it? III. WHEN IS THE CHRISTIAN MOST LIABLE TO SLEEP? 1. When his temporal circumstances are all right. See the parable of the rich fool. 2. When all goes well in spiritual matters. The disciples went to sleep after they had seen Christ transfigured. 3. When we get near our journey's end. The enchanted ground is nigh to Beulah, and Bunyan gives the reason why. IV. GOOD ADVICE TO SLEEPING CHRISTIANS. 1. One of the best plans is to keep good company and talk about the ways of the Lord. 2. If you look at interesting things you will not sleep. A Christian never slept at the foot of the Cross. 3. Let the wind blow on thee. Seek to live daily under the influence of the Holy Spirit. 4. Impress thyself with a deep sense of the value of the place to which thou art going. (*Ibid.*)　　*The pilgrims on the enchanted ground :*— Pursuing their journey, they come to the enchanted ground. I. HOPEFUL KEPT AWAKE BY GOODLY COUNSEL AND DISCOURSE. 1. He gives an account of his life before conversion. 2. He gives four reasons why he resisted the light. 3. Eight circumstances that revived his conviction. 4. He vainly tried to ease himself by a moral reformation. 5. The way of salvation. 6. He persisted in prayer until the answer came, and Christ was revealed to him. 7. Believing and coming to Christ explained. II. IGNORANCE COMES UP AGAIN. 1. Ignorance explains the ground of his hope. 2. Christian explains what good thoughts are. 3. Christian gives answer to Ignorance's confession of faith. 4. Ignorance speaks reproachfully about things he knows not. 5. He again falls behind. III. CHRISTIAN AND HOPEFUL RENEW THEIR CONVERSATION. 1. Reflections over the conduct of Ignorance. 2. The proper use of fear. 3. Why ignorant persons stifle conviction. 4. Talk about one called Temporary. 5. Four reasons why some backslide. 6. How they backslide. IV. SOME LESSONS ON THIS STAGE. 1. In times of danger it is wise to recall former experiences. 2. Human philosophy may seem very wise, but the Bible is an unfailing touchstone. (*L. O. Thompson.*) *Life the time for work :*—The apostle sounds a note of warning. Men should attend. I. THERE IS A DIVINE PURPOSE IN EVERY MAN'S LIFE. We do not come into this world by accident, necessity, nor our own choice. We are sent, and, therefore, we have some distinct mission to fulfil. It is the duty of every man to love God, to watch the interests and good of His universe. This is what He sent us for. II. THERE IS A DIVINE LIMIT TO EVERY MAN'S LIFE. It is but "a day." Sleep is the time for dreams. It is the season of darkness. He who sleeps knows nothing as it really is, and is, for the most part, insensible to pleasure or pain. Our time is unsuitable for sleep. It is too short. It is too full of duties. It is the only time wherein they can be discharged. Spiritual sleep is sin, death—and God calls us to awake. There is a business to be done in our mortal life which cannot be done hereafter. (*Preacher's Monthly.*) **Watch.**—I. WHAT ARE WE TO WATCH AGAINST? 1. Sin. 2. The temptations of the enemy. 3. Ourselves. 4. The lust of the flesh and of the eye and the pride of life. II. WHAT ARE WE TO WATCH FOR? 1. Opportunities—(1) To instruct the ignorant. (2) To confirm the weak. (3) To comfort the afflicted. (4) To glorify Christ. 2. The promises. 3. Answers to prayer. 4. The Second Coming of Christ. (*C. H. Spurgeon.*) *Taking observations :*—They who in a crazy vessel navigate a sea wherein are shoals and currents innumerable, if they would keep their course, or reach their port in safety, must carefully repair the smallest injuries, and often throw out their line, and take their observations. In the voyage of life, also, he who would not make shipwreck of his faith, while he is habitually watchful and provident, must make it his express business to look into his state and ascertain his progress. (*W. Wilberforce.*) *Salutary watchfulness :*—A king had an unwise and reckless son, so reckless that when all entreaty and rebuke proved in vain, he condemned him to death. Still he was allowed three months' respite, in which he was to prepare himself for death. After this had flown, the father called him again into his presence. But what a change in the appearance of the son! His figure was abject, and his countenance bore the traces of an entire inward transformation. "How comes it now," says the king to him, "that thou, my son, appearest before me in so different a character?" "Ah, my father and king," replied he, "how should I not be changed, having death for three months constantly before my eyes?" "Well," responded the father, "since thou hast so earnestly considered the matter and become of a different mind, thy punishment is remitted; yet see that thou keep within thee for ever this new feeling!" "That is too hard for me; how could I, amid the manifold enticements of my newly-granted life, possibly be able to stand?" Then the king ordered a shell to be handed to his son, which was filled up to the brim with oil, and said to him, "Take this and carry it through all the streets of the city. But two men with drawn swords are to follow immediately behind thee on foot. If thou spillest only one drop of the oil, in the same moment thy head is to roll off into the street." The son obeyed. With slow, but sure, steps he traversed the streets of the great capital, ever holding the full shell in his hands, followed by the two armed servants, who were ready at any moment to decapitate him. But, happily, without having spilled even a drop of the oil, the young man returned to his father's palace. "Tell me, my son," said he, "what hast thou seen in thy wandering through the city?" "Nothing, my father, nothing at all have I seen." "And why not, since, too, this is our yearly market-day? Tell me what kind of shops, wares, people, animals, &c., fell under thy notice?" "Indeed, sire, I have seen nothing whatever on the entire route, for my eyes were ceaselessly directed toward the oil in the shell that it might remain in the right position and not run over. And how should I not have been thus watchful, when the executioners were close behind, and my life hung upon the point of their sword?" Then said the king, "Now keep well in mind what thou hast been forced to learn in this hour. As the shell of oil, so bear thy soul always in thy hands; direct thy thoughts away from the distractions of sense and the things of earth in which they are so easily lost, towards the eternal which alone has worth, and ever reflect that death's executioners follow at thy heels, and so thou wilt not so easily forget what is needful for thy soul, and so needful to keep thee from the old disorderly life that must necessarily lead to perdition." And the son hearkened, and lived happily. (*A Tamil Parable.*) *Duty of watchfulness :*—A believer's watchfulness is like that of the soldier. A sentinel posted on the walls, when he discovers a hostile party advancing, does not attempt to make head against them himself, but informs his commanding officer of the enemies' approach, and leaves him to take the proper measures against the foe. So the Christian does not attempt to fight temptation in his own strength; his duty is to observe its approach and tell God of it by prayer. (*W. Mason.*) *Watchfulness must be constant :*—When the station of Moriah was planted among the Basutos, the missionaries (Mr. Casalie and two companions) were greatly disturbed by hyenas. Each missionary had to mount guard in his turn for one-third of the night. The hyenas' plan was evidently to wear out the dogs, which they seemed to fear more than the man with the gun, by incessant prowling and howling round the enclosure. For hours together the dogs maintained a corresponding watchfulness and activity, hurrying from one point of apparent attack to another, until even canine nature was on the point of exhaustion. Relief seemed to come shortly before dawn, for the howling became rarer and more distant, until it ceased altogether. Of course the dogs were soon asleep, but their slumber was almost immediately broken by a tremendous uproar. The hyenas had broken in silently, had seized their prey, and were off with it before the missionary had time to fire a shot. Like a greater enemy of man, the hyenas, failing to intimidate, had trusted to a surprise, and by a pretended peace had worn out the watchfulness of the defenders of the flock. (*J. F. B. Tinling, B.A.*) *Watchfulness overcome :*—Argus is fabled to have had a hundred eyes in his head, only two of which ever slept at once. Jupiter sent Mercury to slay him. Mercury put on his winged slippers, took his sleep-producing wand, and hastened to the side of Argus. He presented himself in the guise of a shepherd with his flock. Argus listened, delighted with the new kind of music, and invited the young shepherd to sit beside him. Mercury sat down, told stories, and played the most soothing strains upon his pipes, till it grew late, hoping to lock in sleep the watchful eyes of Argus. At length, as Mercury played and told a long story of the discovery of his wonderful instrument, he saw the hundred eyes all closed. The head of Argus leaned upon his breast, and Mercury cut it off with a stroke, and tumbled it down the rocks. The hundred eyes availed not while the watcher slept. Juno took them, and set them in the feathers of the tail of her peacock, where they remain to this day. (*J. L. Nye.*) **Be sober.**—I. PHYSICALLY. Abstain altogether from intoxicating liquors, or, at least, from their excessive use. II. MENTALLY. By avoiding vanity, ambition, and other extravagant and unreasonable passions. III. SPIRITUALLY. By keeping free from wild and unregulated enthusiasm in religion. IV. CIRCUMSTANTIALLY. Don't make haste to be rich; and "when riches increase set not thy heart upon them." V. SOCIALLY. Don't make too many friends, and don't impose on the kindness of those whose friendship you make. (*A. S. Patterson, D.D.*)

Ver. 7. **They that sleep sleep in the night, and they that be drunken are drunken in the night.**—*A manifold drunkenness :*—The drunkenness here spoken of is not that from wine only, but that also which comes of all vices. For riches and the desire of wealth is a drunkenness of the soul, and so carnal lust; and every sin you can name is a drunkenness of the soul. On what account, then, has he called vice sleep? Because, in the first place, the vicious man is inactive with respect to virtue; again, because he sees everything as a vision; he views nothing in its true light, but is full of dreams and oftentimes of unreasonable actions; and if he sees anything good he has no firmness. Such is the present life. It is full of dreams and fantasy. Riches are a dream, and glory, and everything of that sort. He who sleeps sees not things that are and have a real subsistence, but things that are not he fancies as things that are. Such is vice and the life that is passed in vice. It sees not things that are, but things that are fleeting and fly away, and that soon. (*Chrysostom.*) *The Christian view of drunkenness :*—In Thessalonica Paul had his first experience of an European rabble. The Jews employed the tactics by which every sinking cause has fought for life. "Lewd fellows of the baser sort" who were not unaccustomed to the sight of "the world turned upside down," loungers confused oftener than not with drink, and could be bought for any shameful purpose, children of the darkness and the night, "set the city in an uproar." There is no need to further describe these birds of evil omen; the scum and the froth are the same everywhere and all time through. But these miserable creatures were not always so. The wildest of that mob was once a happy, innocent child. Some of them eventually came to be children of the light. And such may every drunkard become through Christ. I. THE ASSERTION WHICH PAUL MAKES. "Drunken in the night." 1. The words were probably meant to be taken literally. "Man goeth forth to his work and to his labour *until the evening.*" There is little drunkenness till then. Between this and midnight the work is done (Rom. xiii. 13). 2. But they were also meant to bear a figurative application. "The night" was the whole life of the world, of the nation, of the man, until Christ rose like a glorious sun (1 Pet. iv. 3). (1) Explain the mystery that a habit so degrading should from the earliest time have obtained so firm a hold. What originates drunkenness? Night, says Paul, in the intellectual and moral nature. Paul's method, and that of the gospel, differs from that of many temperance advocates in going deeper. Get rid of drunkenness, urges the reformer, and you will get rid of most of your crimes. Get rid of the night, says Paul, and you will get rid of drunkenness. (2) What night? The night of ignorance, says one—let the man be taught; the night of discomfort—give the man a happy home; of solitude—find the man companions; of dullness—furnish wholesome excitement; of idleness—keep the man employed. Well, these are shadows of the night, but not night itself. Paul's "night" is that of Christlessness. "Without God and hope in the world." Jesus said, "I am the Light of the world," &c. (John viii. 12). (3) There is one thing which the prince of darkness cannot do when attacked in his citadel of drunkenness. If you say that education will cure this evil, he will take the intellectual powers and stimulate them into fascinating play by the wine cup. He can furnish the public-house with comfort, provide companionships, give excitement, and keep the hands busy. Try every weapon, but remember that the public-house will catch the cue and point them at your own heart. But there is one power to which the devil will not appeal, and that is Christ (1 John iii. 8). II. THE APPEAL WHICH PAUL URGES. "Let us who are of the day be sober." 1. Paul was addressing Christians. A line was then drawn, clear cut, between the believer and the unbeliever. Now things have got somewhat mixed. The sad truth that we have to face is that it is an easier thing for thousands around us to grow up in drunken than in sober habits. Your free library may not be open on Sunday, but by command of government your public-houses must. Whatever weight your legislation has over the first day of the week is in favour of drunkenness rather than intelligence. Moreover, you cannot choose your neighbours or keep your children from contamination. Count and contrast the public-houses and sanctuaries; which has the need of bell, ritual, sensational element to attract to its services "lewd fellows of the baser sort"? In one large town in England 10 per cent. go to a place of worship once a week, and 25 per cent. go every day to the public-house. 2. Under the deep conviction that this vice must be grappled with, barriers are built behind which- the young and tempted may find shelter. The pledge, guild, league, and society are all to be honoured. But they are nothing to the Christian for his own sake. He has higher ground to occupy. He dreads not so much breaking his bond as sinning against God. Christ outweighs every other consideration. 3. High ground this. Yes, and we dare not lower it. Prove that drunkenness is profitable to the National Exchequer, that it is a characteristic of the best workman, that it is the fashion, which are all dead against the evidence; but I am not careful to answer in this matter. The end of life is not an overflowing exchequer, a ready hand, an entrance into society. "What shall it profit a man?" &c. The drunkard is degraded, unsafe; therefore bind him with pledges and securities. But I look beyond the present, beyond the beggared home, the loathsome death, to something worse—damnation. In that city where there is no night there is no drunkard. Conclusion: Here is a message for all mankind (vers. 9, 10). (*T. H. Pattison.*) *Prayer against drunkenness:*—Dr. M'Cosh tells the story of a negro who prayed earnestly that he and his coloured brethren might be preserved from what he called their "upsettin' sins." "Brudder," said one of his friends at the close of the meeting, "you ain't got de hang of dat ar word. It's 'besetting,' not 'upsetting.'" "Brudder," replied the other, "if dat's so, it's so. But I was prayin' de Lord to save us from the sin of intoxification, and if dat ain't a upsettin' sin, I dunno what am."

Ver. 8. **But let us, who are of the day, be sober.**—*Good counsel:*—I. THE CONDITION TO BE SHUNNED. Christians must keep their natural desires and appetites after the things of this world within due bounds. "Let your moderation be known to all men" is a Divine injunction. St. Paul enjoins sobriety. Now, sobriety is usually opposed to excess in meats and drinks, and here he particularly opposes it to drunkenness. But it also extends to other temporal things. Hence the Great Teacher warned His disciples to "take heed lest their *hearts* were overcharged with surfeiting and drunkenness, and cares of this life, and so that day come upon them unawares." It was a most reproachful state for men to sleep away the daytime, which is specially for work, but, after all, it was not so strange that those who had the benefit of Divine revelation suffered themselves to be lulled by Satan into carnal security, and laid the reins on the neck of their appetites, and indulged themselves in all manner of riot and excess. It was night with them. They were not sensible of their danger, therefore they slept; they were not sensible of their duty, therefore they were drunk. But it ill becomes Christians to do thus. What! shall Christians, who have the light of the glorious gospel shining in their faces, be careless about their deathless souls, and mindless of the world to come? They that have so many eyes upon them should carry themselves not only decently, but holily. II. THE EQUIPMENT TO BE WORN. The whole armour of God. And this is indispensable to be put on and worn, in order to such sobriety as becomes us, and will be a preparation for the day of the Lord, because our spiritual enemies are many, and mighty, and malicious. They draw hosts to their interest, and keeping them in it, by making them careless, and secure, and presumptuous; by making them intoxicated with pride, intoxicated with passion, intoxicated with self-conceit, intoxicated with sinful gratifications; so that we have every need to arm ourselves against their attempts, by putting on the spiritual breastplate to keep the heart, and the spiritual helmet to protect the head. We must live by faith, and that will keep us watchful and sober, and be our best defence against all the assaults of our enemies. We must get a heart inflamed with love; and this also will be our defence. We must make salvation our hope; and this will hinder our being intoxicated with "the pleasures of sin, which are but for a season." Having "the hope of salvation," we must do nothing to shake our hope or render ourselves unfit for the great salvation we hope for. (*D. Mayo.*) *Aspects of Christian life* :—I. THE CHRISTIAN IDEA OF THE PRESENT LIFE AND OF THE BEST PREPARATION FOR GETTING THROUGH IT. 1. Life is a battle. There is peril of some sort. Men do not want a breastplate and helmet sitting under their own vine and fig-tree in unbroken repose. 2. Life is a great and noble thing, but a wise man, observing the spiritual faculty in man, gets the idea that it is not an ultimate state. It is full of beginnings. Things do not seem completed. Wonderful as the universe is, it does not fill the soul, but leaves a continual yearning for something more. Man is capable of forming an idea of what mind might become, and then he looks abroad and sees himself a little man among little men, being pulled down by the worser part of his nature, and tempted to rest satisfied with the present condition of things. 3. See, says the apostle, that you are not engrossed by the lesser to the neglect of the greater. Guard those sublimer parts of your nature, that head and heart, those thoughts and affections that wander through eternity. (1) Put on the breastplate of faith and love. Have within you the principle of faith which shall penetrate the material and visible and realize the spiritual, substantial, and eternal, and in the midst of all that greatness and splendour remember that faith will bring before you God, infinitely holy; and along with faith there will be a love which shall bring your moral being into contact with all good; the love of infinite excellence will raise you above the present and bring you into harmony with itself. (2) But more: You must have a personal interest in the infinite future "for a helmet," &c. You must not be satisfied with looking about this universe and thinking that it has been from and will be through eternity, and that you are just come to appear for a little moment, and then pass away, as some philosophers allege; you are yourself to be eternal. A hope of this sort will preserve you from those temptations to grosser forms of folly and sin. You will not be satisfied to associate with them that are drunken, and who enjoy the pleasures of sin, which are but for a season. Combine these, and you have an element of strength which will preserve you amidst all spiritual danger. II. WHENCE MAN IS TO GET THIS EQUIPMENT FOR THE BATTLE OF LIFE. By the actual revelation and interposition of God. In this dislocated world I want a Divine hand to put it right. If I am to have faith to realize the infinite, love to bring me in harmony with the good, and hope to secure a personal interest in eternity, then I want God to speak, to help. Christianity comes and delivers such a message as we want: "God hath not appointed us unto wrath," &c. (ver. 9). 1. I could take that the world over, and call to guilty men, "Forsake your sins, for God hath not," &c. God hath spoken to you and acted for you. While you belong to the natural system it goes on, and you with it. The law takes its course, and there is nothing but destruction for you, for you have broken it. But God has interfered and enforced a remedy by which you may be saved. If you accept that, then you may escape the result which must otherwise ensue ; for God's design is your salvation. 2. But this is true in a more emphatic sense of those who have received the gospel. In a higher and profounder sense " God hath not appointed you," &c.—the very object for which it was offered and by you believed. You have come in contact with this Divine element, and by it you are preparing, while here, for the ever-lasting blessedness which is the future adornment of saved humanity. Christianity, then, is not merely a system ; Christ is more than a perfect Teacher and Example : He has died for us and wrought out for us a redemption. Men may take their stand on the abstract improbability of the thing ; but let them reject the Bible also, for if there is one thing clearer in that than another it is that Christ has made an atone-ment for sin. Christ's death is the point upon which the salvation of humanity turns ; we may not be able to say how, but the thing is uncontestable. III. THE SORT OF WORLD TO WHICH WE ARE PASSING AND THE KIND OF THING OUR LIFE IS TO BE (ver. 10). 1. "Awake or sleep " means alive or dead. The great object of the gospel is that as long as you live you should live with Christ, have a Divine life from Him, and walk in harmony with Him, and that when you are dead you shall be with Him also. 2. But Paul meant more than this. He had in his mind chap. iv. 15–17, and his object was to show how the great end of the gospel was to be answered, and that the death of the disciples would not frustrate its accomplish-ment. When Christ is manifested, whether they are alive or dead the result will be the same : they will all be alive together with Christ. 3. Here, then, is—(1) Immortal life for man. Though I may die and see corruption, I shall rise up like Christ into a glorious and eternal life. That is something like a consummation. There is something ultimate about that, with which I can be satisfied ; so different from this world of beginnings, temptations, warfare and dislocations, where the spiritual is dragged down to the flesh. (2) Life of the noblest and Divinest sort ; life with Christ. You cannot make a man more miserable than to take him out of his own sphere in society and put him in one opposite ; but to place a Christian in the immediate presence of Christ is to bestow upon him the highest happiness. His sanctified and glorified nature will find itself at home by the side of Christ. (3) Life of the highest character in respect to general society. We shall not only live with Him, but " together." It will not be a solitary blessedness. A multitude which no man can number made like each other, by Christ having made them like Himself, will live together in harmony, love, and mutual confidence, and their happiness will be complete. IV. CHRISTIAN MEN HAVING THIS FAITH, LOVE, AND PROSPECT, SHOULD—1. Edify one another, which implies that there is a foundation laid, upon which the edifice is to be built. Christians should help each other to become temples for the Holy Ghost. Now, a glorious thing like that could never have sprung up in a world like this : it must have come from God. 2. Comfort one another with the testimony we have received—under trial, under loss of friends, in the family, and in Christian intercourse. Conclusion : 1. The perfect beauty and harmony of the Christian system as a theory. If one could not believe it true, it would be relinquished with regret. What a glorious thing, then, to feel no such pity, but to be certain of its truth. 2. The strong feelings of gratitude, hope, and determination which ought to inspire us with respect to life. (*T. Binney.*) *Christian sobriety, or seriousness :*—The two great elements indispensable for the existence of a really grand character are elasticity and steadfastness— elasticity, without which a man gets crushed by every slight failure ; and steadfastness, without which he will be turned aside from his purposes by unworthy motives, and be tempted to forget the end of his efforts in the contem-plation of the means whereby they are to be attained. For keeping alive this elasticity, a man must know how to be wisely gay ; for keeping up this stead-fastness, he must know how to be sober. And so Christian sobriety must be based upon a reasonable estimate of the importance of life and the seriousness of all things here below. The trifler who has no higher ambition than to amuse himself, mistakes the meaning of all things on earth. He sees no further than the outside of things, and treats them as a savage does a toy, which, when it does not frighten him, affords him endless mirth. The man or the boy who has got to feel that God's eye is on him morning, noon, and night, and who is learning to realize that the smallest incident of every hour has and must have an influence upon all his future prospects for good or evil—the man or the boy who is impressed with the momentous truth that every day as it passes carries with it an imperishable record of his deeds and words and thoughts, and that the time *must* come when he will stand before the judgment-seat of Christ and give an account of the deeds done in the body—he cannot fail to be serious, and will become more and more so in proportion as he realizes these things, and in proportion as he lives in remembrance of them every hour. But as he lays hold of the fact that God loves him and all men, and that, with all his weakness and inconstancy, he is yet not left unsupported by the Spirit's grace—though he may be serious, he will not be sad. (*A. Jessop, D.D.*) *The sober-minded children of the day :*—I. THE PERSONS. 1. Their character. (1) They are in God and Christ (chap. i. 1). (2) They know their election of God—not in theory, but in fact, in the heart, by virtue of their union to Christ. 2. Their privilege. "Of the day." (1) The day itself is the gospel day (Zech. xiii.), the day of the fountain opened for sin: the Lord's day, well called *Sunday* because of its brightness; but that brightness shines inward through the indwelling Spirit. "I was in the spirit on the Lord's day." (2) Its manifestation (Eph. v. 8) revealing sin, salvation (Mal. iv. 2), progress, Divine supplies, future glory. II. THE DUTY: "Be sober." 1. Towards God. (1) Humble, and not intoxicated with pride. (2) Believing, and not intoxicated with false doctrine. (3) Truthful, and not intoxicated with anxiety and fear. 2. In respect of our enemies. (1) Patient, and not hasty. (2) Courageous, and not fearful. (3) Forbearing, and not wrathful. 3. As regards ourselves. (*A. Triggs.*) *The work and armour of the children of the day :*—I. THE CENTRAL INJUNCTION, into which all the moral teaching drawn from the Second Coming is gathered: "BE SOBER." 1. The context shows that we are not to omit a literal reference (ver. 7). Temperance is moderation in regard to the swinish sins of drunkenness and gluttony. None need the precept more than we. Any doctor will tell you that the average Englishman eats and drinks a great deal more than is good for him. It is melancholy to think how many professors have the intellectual and spiritual life blunted by senseless table indulgence. 2. The higher meaning. (1) It is not an unemotional absence of fervour in Christian character. Some are always preaching down enthusiasm, and preaching up "a sober standard of feeling," which is nothing more than Laodicean lukewarmness. But the last thing the Church of this century needs is a refrigerator; a poker and pair of bellows are far more needful. The truths we profess are so tremendous that nothing but a continuous glow of enthusiasm will correspond to their majesty and importance. Paul was the very type of an enthusiast. Festus called him mad; so did some at Corinth (2 Cor. v. 13). Oh for more of that insanity which rouses the Pentecostal charge, "These men are full of new wine"! (2) It means the prime Christian duty of self-restraint in the use and love of all earthly treasures and pleasures. (*a*) It is clear from the make of a man's soul that without self-control he will go all to pieces. Human nature was made not for democracy, but for monarchy. Here are within us many passions, tastes, desires, which ask nothing but "Give me my appropriate gratification, though all the laws of God and man be broken to get it." So there has to be an eye given to these blind beasts and a hand laid on these instinctive impulses. The true temple of the spirit has the broad base laid on these instincts; above them and controlling them the will; above it understanding which enlightens it and them; and supreme over all conscience, with nothing between it and heaven. Where that is not the order you will get wild work. The man who lets passion and inclination guide is like a steamboat with all the furnaces banked up, the engines going at full speed, and nobody at the wheel. (*b*) That self-control is to be exercised mainly in regard of our use and estimate of the pleasures of life. It is not only man's make that makes it necessary. All about us are hands reaching out drugged cups; and whoever takes Circe's cup turns into a swine, and sits there imprisoned at the feet of the sorceress for ever. Only one thing can deliver us: "Be sober" in regard to the world and all it offers. Ye cannot serve God and mammon. II. A MOTIVE WHICH BUTTRESSES THIS EXHORTATION. "Let us, since we are of the day, be sober." 1. What day? Not exactly the Day of Judgment, although there may be some allusion to that; but the apostle has passed from that to day in general. Christians are the children of that which expresses knowledge, joy, and activity; they should, therefore, be brave, not afraid of light, cheerful, buoyant, hopeful, transparent, and walk in this darkened world, bearing their radiance with them, and making things, else unseen, visible. 2. But while these emblems are gathered into that name there is one direction in which the consideration ought to tell—that of self-restraint. "*Noblesse oblige*"; the aristocracy are bound to do nothing dishonourable. Children of the light are not to stain themselves with anything foul. Indulgence may be fitting for the night, but incongruous with the day. III. THE METHOD BY WHICH THIS GREAT PRECEPT MAY BE FULFILLED. 1. Faith, love, hope, form the defensive armour of the soul, and make self-control possible. Like a diver in his dress, who is let down into the ocean, a man whose heart is girt with faith and charity, and whose head is covered with hope, may be dropped down into the wildest sea of temptation and worldliness, and yet will walk dry and unharmed. 2. The cultivation of these three is the best means for securing self-control. It is an easy thing to say, "Govern yourself." The powers that should control are largely gone over to the enemy. Who shall keep the keepers? You can no more "erect yourself above yourself" than you can lift yourself by your coat collar. But you can cultivate faith, hope, and charity, and these will do the governing. Faith will bring you into communication with all the power of God. Love will lead you into a region where temptations will show their own foulness. Hope will turn away your eyes from looking at the tempting splendour around, and fix them on the glories above. (*A. Maclaren, D.D.*) **The breastplate of faith and love.** I. FAITH GUARDS AGAINST INTELLECTUAL TEMPTATIONS. 1. We are surrounded by an all pervasive, subtle, penetrating atmosphere of scepticism. We meet with it in our educational agencies, and drink it in with our learning; in society, and imbibe it with our interchange of thought and conversation; in our ephemeral literature, and take it in in our recreation; in our pulpits, alas! and receive it along with our religious instruction. In these and other ways doubts are insinuated into the heart on the all-important subjects of God, Christ, salvation, duty, destiny. Escape it we cannot. To fight it seems only like combatting the air, so agile is the adversary. Our only safety lies in wearing an insulator. A mariner wrapped in oilskin can defy the elements though he cannot allay them. Such an insulator is faith; not firmly held theological opinions, but practical and realizing trust in God and truth. Faith *knows* whom and what it has believed, and passes unscathed through the trial. 2. We are surrounded by circumstances which tend to agitate the mind and excite our fears. Our duties, responsibilities, dangers, in business, home, travel, Churches, are calculated to engender anxiety, and when once anxiety gets into the heart it is difficult to dislodge, and, if allowed sway, the citadel is gone and despair enthroned. The only course is to keep anxiety out by the breastplate of faith. Trust in God and in His promise is the sure antidote. "No weapon that is formed against them shall prosper," &c. "All things work together for good," &c. II. LOVE GUARDS AGAINST MORAL TEMPTATIONS. These, too, abound, and to escape them we must needs go out of the world. Some, of course, we must fight, but against each and all we need protection. 1. Love to God is the supreme motive for resistance. No other is sufficiently strong and durable. Prudence, self-respect, consideration for friends, &c., are well as subordinate motives, engravings on the breastplate, but are unavailing by themselves. The true, abiding, invincible motive is "How can I do this wickedness and sin against God?" What God has done for and to me, and what He is to me and I to Him, are sufficient inspirations when strongly held to resist the most powerful advance. 2. Love to God creates moral habits and tastes which render temptations innocuous. "What fellowship has light with darkness?" While this Sun rules the children of the day, the night of sin can have no place. (*J. W. Burn.*) **For an helmet, the hope of salvation.** I. HOPE. 1. Subjectively considered hope is the expectation and desire of future good. Christian hope contemplates—(1) The highest exaltation and perfection of our nature. We shall be like God, conformed to the image of His Son in soul and body. (2) This exaltation arises from the enlargement of all our powers to do and all our capacity to receive. (3) Dominion or exaltation in dignity as well as in excellence and power. (4) The presence and vision of God in Christ. 2. Its foundation is—(1) The promise of God. (2) The infinite merit of Christ. (3) The love of God. From what we know of that love we infer that there is no benefit which it is not ready to confer. (4) The witness of the Spirit that we are the children of God. II. HOPE AS A HELMET. 1. Protects the believer's most vital part. In the old hand to hand conflicts the head was the worst exposed, and its protection of the first importance. Hence the helmet was as necessary as the shield. With the Christians the hope of salvation gives security, and, therefore, confidence, courage, and endurance. (1) From the assaults of Satan against our faith and confidence in God; and from our proneness to neglect eternal things. (2) From the attractions and allurements of the world. (3) From the corruptions of our own hearts. 2. Adorns the believer. The helmet is the most attractive part of the warrior's equipment. So is hope to the Christian. It enables him to hold his head erect. (*C. Hodge, D.D.*) **The helmet:**—I. Its mention serves TO REMIND THE CHRISTIAN THAT HE IS A SOLDIER. 1. If you were not soldiers you would not need armour. This idea should govern the whole of life. Too many Christians try to be friends with God and with His enemies. Never take off your armour, or in some unguarded moment you may meet with serious wounds. 2. You are soldiers in the enemies' country. The sick are in the trenches, and the active are engaging the enemy. More or less all are exposed and always. 3. You are in the country of an enemy who never gives quarter. If you fall it is death. The world never forgives. What might be done without observation by any one else is noted and misrepresented in you. 4. You fight with an enemy who never made a truce. You may come to terms and parley; forces of evil never do. "Dread the Greeks, even when they bring you gifts"; and let the Christian dread the world most when it puts on its softest speeches. 5. You have to do with an enemy who cannot make peace with you nor you with him. If you become at peace with sin, it has conquered you. II. Being a soldier LOOK TO YOUR HEAD. 1. A wound in the head is a serious matter. Being a vital part it needs to be well protected. A good many Christians never think of defending the head at all. If they get their hearts warmed by religion, they think that quite enough. But it is not: a hot head and a hot heart may do a good deal of mischief, but a hot heart and cool head will do a world of service for Christ. Have right doctrine in the head, and then set the soul on fire. 2. A helmet is of no use to any part but the head. (1) The head is peculiarly liable to temptation. It is not easy to stand on a high pinnacle without the brain beginning to reel: and if God puts a man on a high elevation of usefulness he had need to have his head well taken care of. So with wealth, popularity, &c. (2) The head is liable to attacks from scepticism. He who has a hope of salvation is not afraid of its quibbles. He may hear them all, and be for a moment staggered, as a soldier under a sudden shock, but he recovers himself. A man is not often a very thorough democrat after he gets a little money in the savings bank, and when a man gets a stake in Christianity he gets to be very conservative of old-fashioned truth. (3) The head is in danger from the attacks of personal unbelief. Who of us has not doubted his interest in Christ at times? but the man who has a good hope may be of good cheer. These doubts and fears will pass away. (4) Some are attacked by threatenings from the world. The world brings down his double-handed sword with a tremendous blow, but it only blunts itself on the helmet. III. Consider THE HELMET WITH WHICH GOD WOULD HAVE YOUR HEAD PROTECTED. 1. Its Giver. The soldier gets his regimentals from Her Majesty, and from the Monarch Himself we must get our helmets. Those of your own construction are of no use in the battle, and the hope of salvation is not purchasable. 2. Its Maker. Weapons are valued according to the maker; the name of the Holy Ghost is on our helmets. The hope of salvation is His work in the soul. Rest satisfied with none that are made in the workshop of nature. 3. The metal of which it is made. Beware of getting a base hope, a helmet of paltry metal, through which the sword will cleave to your skull. 4. Its strength. It renders its wearer invulnerable in all assaults. Recollect David, when pressed with troubles on every side. "Why art thou cast down? . . . Hope thou in God." 5. It will not come off. It is of main importance to have a headgear that cannot be knocked off in the first scrimmage. So ours must not be a commonplace hope that will fail us in extremity. 6. The old helmets were oiled to make them shine. When God anoints His peoples' hope, and gives them the oil of joy, it shines bright in the light of the Saviour's countenance. 7. The helmet was the place of honour. The plume was placed in it. The Christian's hope is his honour and glory: he must not be ashamed of it. IV. THERE ARE SOME WHO HAVE NOT THIS HELMET. Christ only provides for His own soldiers, but Satan also provides for his. His helmets are also potent ones. Nothing but the sword of the Spirit can cleave them. He has given some a thick headpiece of indifference. "What do I care!"—that is your helmet. (C. H. Spurgeon.) Hope of salvation:—Salvation is hoped for because it is already begun. This hope of salvation is a defence—1. Because that which we hope for is to be free from sin. 2. Because by this hope the heart is set on higher and nobler things. 3. Because, from the experience of salvation which provides our hope, we know the blessed rewards of salvation from sin. 4. Because heavenly life begun gives power to resist and overcome sin. 5. Because the blessings hoped for outdazzle the allurements of sin, and the delights it promises. 6. Because we know that all we hope for is lost if we yield to sin. (Christian Age.)

Vers. 9, 10. For God hath not appointed us unto wrath.—God's everlasting purpose:—I. GOD'S PURPOSE is—1. That we should not be lost. We all deserve wrath. All have sinned, and every sin the Divine indignation will avenge. The longer we live in sin, therefore, the greater the amount of wrath our iniquities are treasuring up. And yet, although we are daily provoking the Divine anger, God has not appointed us to wrath. He willeth not the death of a sinner. 2. That we should be saved. The kingdom He has prepared from the foundation of the world. (1) This should comfort us in trial. God's purpose none can frustrate. "Fear not, little flock," &c. (2) Don't distress yourselves about election. God has told you that His will is that "all men should be saved"; and, therefore, if any one perishes, it is not because of God's secret purpose, but His own want of inclination. "Ye will not come." II. ITS ACCOMPLISHMENT. 1. There is only one way in which God's purpose can be effected: "By our Lord Jesus Christ." "Neither is there salvation in any other." The grand subject of Christianity is Christ; and those who do not make Christ all in all are like those Jewish builders who refused "the headstone of the corner," or like the foolish man who built on the sand. 2. In what respect salvation is through Jesus Christ is plainly told us: "Who died for us." Christ's death rescues us from wrath. That which our sins provoked was borne by Christ. 3. How sad the mistake of those who think little or nothing of Christ's atonement, on which hinges our salvation. "He that believeth," and he only, "shall be saved." III. ITS EFFECTS. 1. Life with Christ on earth. "Whether we wake." "To me to live is Christ." To this end Christ was called Emmanuel. This life is in union with Christ. Wherever you go, Christ goes. He never leaves or forsakes you. 2. Life with Christ in heaven. Our bodies sleep, but not our souls. "Absent from the body," &c. "This day shalt thou be with Me in paradise." This association will be—(1) More intimate than that on earth. (2) More blessed. (3) More enduring. Conclusion: We hence perceive— 1. The nature of our present existence. If we are Christians, this life is only the porch to a better; if not, a porch to a worse. 2. The readiness of God to save. "He willeth not the death of a sinner." *(C. Clayton, M.A.)*      *Called to salvation:*—God is pleased to day to put up before your eyes the white flag of mercy, calling you to come to Jesus and live. But recollect, if you do not yield to it, He will put up the red flag of threatening, and then the black flag of execution will not be far off. Perhaps some of you have been suffering under bodily disease—take that as a warning. When our vessels of war would stop a suspicious vessel, they fire a shot athwart her bows as a warning. If she does not haul to, perhaps they give another; and if no notice is taken of this, the gunners go to their business in real earnest, and woe to the offender. Your affliction is the gospel's warning gun. Pause awhile, I beseech you; ask the Lord in mercy to look upon you, that you may be saved! As I think upon some of you here who are not saved, I feel something like the boy I read of yesterday in the newspapers: Last week there were two lads on the great rocks of Lundy Island, in the Bristol Channel, looking for sea-gulls' eggs; one of them went far down the cliff, and lost his footing, and when his brother, hearing a faint voice, looked down, he saw him clinging to a jutting crag, and striving in vain to find a place for his feet. There stood the anxious brother, alarmed and paralyzed with dread, quite unable to help the younger one in so much peril below, who soon relaxed his hold and was dashed to pieces far beneath. I feel somewhat like that alarmed brother, only there is this happy difference: I can hope for you, and bid you hope for yourselves. You are clinging now, perhaps, to some false hope, and striving to find a rest where rest is not to be found; but the strong-winged Angel of the everlasting gospel is just underneath you this morning, crying, "Drop now; simply drop into My arms; I will take you and bear you aloft in safety." That Angel is the Angel of the Covenant, the Lord Jesus Christ. You must be dashed to pieces for ever unless you rest in Him; but cast yourself upon Him, I pray you, and then, as you are carried in safety far off from every fear, you will magnify the grace of God and extol the glorious gospel. *(C. H. Spurgeon.)*     **Who died for us that whether we wake or sleep.** More exactly *watch.* So popular a motto of early Christian life—caught as it was from the lips of Christ (Mark xiii. 34–37)—that it took the form of a name—Gregory. It has been said that there are three sleeps for man—those of nature, sin, and death; and three corresponding awakenings—those of nature, righteousness, and life eternal. It is of the second that Paul speaks here. Salvation is through our Lord Jesus Christ, who died for us for this purpose, in order that, whether we keep life's long toilful watch, or fall asleep in what is called death, we should have our true life together with Him. *(Bp. Alexander.)*     *Salvation:*—I. It is LIFE. We shall live. This is the common Scripture designation of all we include in spiritual and eternal life. All that is opposed to death; the holy, happy, and immortal existence of the whole man, soul and body. II. LIFE WITH CHRIST. Association or communion. Companionship with Christ. 2. Participation of His life, its power, holiness, blessedness, glory. III. THE LIFE OF ALL. We shall all—all the redeemed, all those dear to us who belong to Christ, all in every age and nation who love Him, are to be made the subjects of this life. (*C. Hodge, D.D.*) *Assured salvation through Christ :*—The Thessalonians had groundless fears for their departed friends (chap. iv. 13). I. GOD'S PURPOSE. 1. We are not appointed to wrath. 2. We are appointed to salvation. 3. We are appointed to salvation obtainable by our Lord Jesus Christ. II. NOTHING CAN FRUSTRATE THIS PURPOSE. 1. Because Christ has died for us. A continent of truth is spread out in this one fact. III. OUR SALVATION IS ASSURED TO US. 1. In this present existence— "whether we wake." 2. In death—"or sleep." Salvation has two parts—that which is present, or the state of grace ; and that which is future, or the state of glory. IV. WE ARE UNITED TO CHRIST, and our life is joined to His life ; and thus, whether we live or die, we are the Lord's. It should be noticed, however, that "the glory and chief hope of the Church are not to be realized at death (of the individual), but at the Lord's coming : one is not to anticipate the other, but all are to be glorified together at Christ's coming (chap. iv. 14–17; Col. iii. 4; Heb. xi. 40). Death affects the mere individual, but the coming of Christ, the whole Church. At death our souls are invisibly and individually with the Lord ; at Christ's coming, the whole church, with all its members, in body and soul, shall be visibly and collectively with Him." V. HERE IS AN ENDURING BASIS FOR HOPE AND COMFORT. 1. Salvation is sure—as sure as Omnipotence can make it in view of Christ's death. 2. Salvation will be complete. The body shall be raised in immortal strength and beauty, and the soul shall be sinless and happy in the service of God. 3. Grief over the dead is natural (John xi. 31–35; Phil. ii. 27) ; but, with the hope of resurrection and recognition hereafter, it should be moderated. 4. In all this we perceive the immense benefits revelation and grace have conferred upon us. (1) In contrast with heathenism. The Greeks believed in the immortality of the soul, but knew nothing about the resurrection of the body. Their dead were called "shades." Even the Egyptians did not believe in the resurrection of the body, unless the return of the spirit, as it was believed, to inhabit the mummified body, can be called a resurrection. (2) As culminating in the Gospel. The Old Testament presented the two doctrines as counterparts to each other—the immortality of the soul and the resurrection of the body. But these two doctrines were not so clearly understood in the Old Testament times as in the New. That they were revealed is evident from such passages as relate to Enoch and Elijah, the raising of the dead, and from Psa. xvi. 9, 11, xvii. 15, lxxiii. 24; Prov. xiv. 32; Isa. xxxviii. 18, 19, &c. These doctrines were made illustrious by the death, resurrection, and ascension of the Lord Jesus Christ, and by explicit statements in the New Testament. Hence, in its clearer light, there is more of hope, joy, and comfort than was possible before the coming of Christ. He is the first-fruits of them that slept. (*L. O. Thompson.*) *Christ's desire for His people's company :*—How all-inclusive the passage is ! The whole of that grand purpose for which the Bible was written is contained in these few lines. What have you not in this verse ? You have Christ, His death, His substitutionary work, His resurrection, the fact of His present life, the assurance of His return, the saints' salvation, the saints' eternal glory. This text is also a window through which we look into the heart of Christ, and behold the Saviour's great desire that all His people should live together with Him. I. LOVE'S DESIRE. That we should live together with Him. 1. Viewed from one stand-point, this is only natural. Grant love, and you are necessarily compelled to grant something else—desire for the presence of the object beloved. I cannot imagine it possible for the two ever to be separated. Love is always restless until the object of affection is close by. In proportion as the love is pure and intense, so will the delight in the nearness of the object become intensified; and Christ finds His greatest happiness in having His people near Him. Have you joy in communion ? He joys more. As you look up to Him, do you feel constrained to sing ? He, too, when He looks down on you, feels that He must sing ; for "the Lord thy God in the midst of thee is mighty : He will joy over thee with singing." 2. And yet it is very marvellous. (1) Where did the love spring from ? Why did He love me at all ? Has any friend on earth treated any of us half so ill as we have treated Christ ? And yet His choicest desire is that we shall live together with Him. Is it not strange that, though there are some people who would not care to have you in their house, yet

Christ wants to have you in His home? (2) Mysterious? More so still when I call to mind the fact that I do not like to live with myself. Self is my plague. And yet how strange that, though I want to get away from self, Christ wants me to go and live with Him. 3. How all-inclusive the desire is. It is that we should not only live with Him, but *together* with Him. What is that? (1) Take it as including all His people, and then it teaches us that Christ is not content for one to be absent. He wants to see all the members of His family brought round the table. Is it not always so when there is love to all? What is the bliss of heaven? All His people together. Fathers united once more to the children who went before, husbands re-united with wives, friends with friends—all together; and then all together with Him. To Christ's eye that is the most beautiful picture that heaven itself can present—Christ and all His numerous family, without an absentee. (2) Or does "together" apply to Christ? And, if so, there is a beautiful thought in it. You may live in the same house with a person, and yet not live together. "Together" implies a certain amount of intimacy. When Christ brings His people together He brings them to a home. He does not merely collect a multitude of people. No; in heaven there will be holy familiarity. II. LOVE'S METHOD TO OBTAIN ITS DESIRE. Christ's was most costly. "Greater love hath no man than this," &c. If you would measure Christ's love, you can only do so by the Cross. Here is the explanation of Calvary. If you say that Christ died in order to satisfy Divine justice, to make an atonement for sin, to deliver from hell—all that is true. But now put it in a more beautiful way: that I might live together with Him "who died"—not on a soft bed, but hanging on hard timber; not with loving friends around, but a hooting crowd; not with death lit up by His Father's smile, but crying, "Eloi," &c., out on a felon's hill. And He died in my place. If He had not, I must. Now there is no room for doubt. If, when you were a sinner, Jesus loved you enough to die for you, do you not think that now you are one of His friends, He will love you enough to bring you home? III. THE ONLY CONDITIONS THAT CAN SATISFY CHRIST'S DESIRE. Christ is not going to be disappointed. Any way, whether we wake or sleep, He means that we shall be with Him. What is intended by these words? 1. Take them literally. Sleeping or waking, conscious or unconscious, the saint and the Saviour are never far apart. 2. "Awake or asleep" means living or dying. Christ will have our company living. Christ would not be satisfied merely to have our company in the glory. He wants it down here. His delight is to commune here with His ransomed ones. And suppose we fall asleep in death. Death is but the Lord's black chariot that He sends to bring His darlings home. The billow of death never washed a soul from the Saviour's arms. It washes the soul from a thousand other hands that try to retain it, but it only sweeps the spirit away to its eternal home. 3. The chief meaning is that, whether by resurrection or translation, we shall be with Him (chap. iv. 16). Then there are some who will fall asleep in death, and there are others who will be alive and awake at Christ's coming. Will He be satisfied only to have one of the companies with Him? No; He died for us that, whether we wake or sleep, we should live together with Him. We shall pass either through the portals of death, or over them as did Elijah; but, either way, the goal reached will be the same. (*A. G. Brown.*) *Oneness with Christ:*—A well-built stone gets to be one with the foundation. In the old Roman walls the mortar seems to be as hard as the stones, and the whole is like one piece; you must blow it to atoms before you can get the wall away. So is it with the true believer; he rests upon his Lord till he grows up into Him, till he is one with Jesus by a living union, so that you scarce know where the foundation ends and where the upbuilding begins; for the believer becometh all in Christ, even as Christ is all in all to him. (*C. H. Spurgeon.*)

Ver. 11. **Wherefore comfort and edify one another.**—*Comfort and edification :*—I. COMFORT implies—1. The presence of discomfort, and the duty of mutual support under trial. Men are troubled—(1) By sin. We must comfort by restoring such in the spirit of meekness, by pointing them to the Saviour. (2) By infirmities. Here we must comfort by bearing one another's burdens with sympathy and help. (3) Affliction. When we can do no more, we can console with a few simple words. "A word spoken in season," &c. 2. Owning our relationship with others. There is very deep comfort afforded to the solitary when we make them feel that they are not alone—*e.g.*, in Christian testimony before an ungodly world; in work for the Master. 3. Reminding people of what they must expect from the world on the one hand, and of

Christ's helpfulness on the other (John xv. 17). 4. Bringing before others the real grounds of comfort. (1) Present acceptance with God. (2) Future approval and reward. II. EDIFICATION. 1. Presupposes a foundation—Christ Jesus. 2. Consists in—(1) Christian conversation. "Forsake not the assembling of yourselves together" (Eph. iv. 29). (2) Mutual prayer. "If two of you shall agree," &c. (3) Unity of design. Conclusion: To fit yourselves for this work. 1. Search the Scriptures, which are full of words of comfort and edification. 2. Read Christian biographies. 3. Beware of Pharisaism. (*Bp. Villiers.*) *The power of comfort :* —So have I seen the sun kiss the frozen earth, which was bound up with the images of death and the colder breath of the north; and then the waters break forth from their enclosures, and melt with joy, and run in useful channels; and the flies do rise again from their little graves in walls, and dance awhile in the air, to tell that there is joy within, and that the great mother of creatures will open the stock of her new refreshment, become useful to mankind, and sing praises to her Redeemer. So is the heart of a sorrowful man under the discourses of a wise comforter. He breaks from the despairs of the grave, and the fetters of chains and sorrow; he blesses God, and he blesses thee, and he feels his life returning; for to be miserable is death, but nothing is life but to be comforted. And God is pleased with no music from below so much as in the thanksgiving song of relieved widows, of supported orphans, of rejoicing and comforted persons. (*Jeremy Taylor.*) *The power to comfort a test of religion :*—Shortly before his death, being visited by a clergyman whose features, as well as language, were more lugubrious than consoling, Hood looked up at him compassionately, and said, "My dear sir, I'm afraid that your religion doesn't agree with you." (*W. Davenport Adams.*) *Edification* is one of the metaphorical words which have passed into the language of Christianity from the lips of our Lord. The foundation and progress of the Christian life is likened by Him to the building of a house (Matt. vii. 24; *cf.* Luke vi. 1, 8; Col. i. 23; 1 Pet. v. 10), and the parable of the improvident builder (Luke xiv. 28). Christ said, "I will edify My Church" (Matt. xiv. 18). Thus the Christian Church and the Christian soul are alike compared to a building or temple. The building will not be finished out until Christ comes. Those who by sympathy, word, or deed, assist the growth of Christian wisdom, feeling, or life, are conceived of as builders, helping others or themselves to supply some part for the construction of the spiritual edifice, and are said to edify (1 Cor. vii. 1, xiv. 3, 4; Col. ii. 7). (*Bp. Alexander.*) *Edification the aim of Christian speech :*—When Handel's oratorio of the *Messiah* had won the admiration of many of the great, Lord Kinnoul took occasion to pay him some compliments on the noble entertainment he had given the town. "My lord," said the composer, "I should be sorry if I only entertained them: I wish to make them better." It is to be feared that many speechmakers at public meetings could not say as much; and yet how dare any of us waste the time of our fellow immortals in mere amusing talk! If we have nothing to speak to edification, how much better to hold our tongue. (*C. H. Spurgeon.*) *The Communion of saints :* —This forms an article of the Christian faith; but the profession of a truth and the experience or practice of it are widely different things. I. WHAT THIS COMMUNION IS. 1. Saints are those who have been convinced of sin and saved by Christ, and are now living under the sanctifying influence of the Holy Ghost. 2. Their communion is a union of heart with Christ and one another. This is confined to no Church, age, people, or place. If grace sanctify some poor heathen five thousand miles away, and any poor sinner amongst ourselves, let them meet, and there will be a communion of feeling and interests between them. This communion has its type in the walk to Emmaus. The topics are—(1) Themselves— their joys, griefs, failures, triumphs, fears, hopes. (2) Their Lord—His condescension, goodness, love, truth. (3) Christ's kingdom and doctrine—how most effectually they may further the one and adorn the other. (4) Their heritage—in its future and all glorious perfection. II. ITS ADVANTAGES. 1. Comfort. The followers of Christ, so far from being exempt from trial, are often most troubled; but by communion they comfort themselves together. When one member suffers, all suffer. 2. Edification. Sometimes it is humbling, sometimes encouraging or consoling; but it is always edifying to commune with believers. Such an interchange of thought, feeling, and affection, produces often a friendship as intimate and endearing as that which subsisted between Jonathan and David. In conclusion, I would recommend—1. Religious intercourse. (1) There is an intercourse which seems to be religious, but is far from being so. Many talk about religion without talking religion itself. (2) Many professors are wanting in Christian open-ness and candour. How freely worldlings communicate their ideas to each other. Should Christians be less communicative ? 2. Devout retirement. Without this the life and power of religion cannot be maintained, much less communion. (*W. Mudge, B.A.*) *Christian comfort :*—Luther, at Wittenberg, discerning a very melancholy man, whom formerly he well knew, said unto him, "Ah ! human creature, what doest thou ? Hast thou nothing else in hand but to think on thy sins, on death, and on damnation ? Turn thine eyes quickly away, and look hither to this man Christ, of whom it is written, ' He was conceived by the Holy Ghost, born of the Virgin Mary, suffered, died, buried, the third day arose from the dead, and ascended up into heaven.' Wherefore dost thou think all this was done? Verily, it was that thou shouldst comfort thyself against death and sin ; therefore, forbear, be not afraid, neither do thou faint, for truly thou hast no cause ; for Christ suffered death for thee, and prevailed for thy comfort and defence, and for that cause He sitteth at the right hand of His Father to deliver thee. Therefore, whosoever thou art that art possessed with such heavy thoughts, know for certain that the same is a work and devising of the devil ; for God hath sent His Son into the world, not to affright, but to comfort sinners. From hence these and the like sentences are often expressed in the Scriptures : ' Rejoice ; be joyful in the Lord.' ' Be not afraid.' ' Be not discouraged.' ' Be of good comfort : I have overcome the world.' " (*Luther's Table Talk.*)

Vers 12, 13. **We beseech you, brethren, to know them which labour** among you.—*Faithful ministers worthy of respect :*—I. THE PARTICULARS UPON WHICH THIS CLAIM FOR THE MINISTERS OF CHRIST IS FOUNDED. 1. The influence of the minis-terial office. They are " over you in the Lord " by a Divine appointment, by your own choice ; not as task-masters, nor by mere human patronage. Their influence is full of care, exertion, watchfulness, responsibility. 2. The employment of the ministerial office. They " admonish you." Ministers are builders, watchmen, teachers, soldiers. Their labours are—preparatory in studies, executive in duties, solitary in trials. II. STATE THE NATURE AND PRESS THE DUTY OF THAT RESPECT WHICH CHRISTIAN CHURCHES OWE TO THEIR MINISTERS. 1. The due proportion of that respect : esteem them in love. 2. The motive which should influence : " for their work's sake." A high valuation of the ministerial office. 3. The evidences which prove it is genuine. Attention to the comfortable support of a minister. A regular, devout, conscientious attendance on his ministry. A tender regard for his character. 4. The mode by which the text enforces the duty. " I beseech you, brethren." (*E. Payson.*) *Ministers and people :*—I. CHRISTIAN MINISTERS AS HERE DESCRIBED. Not by titles indicative of earthly honour or human power, not by any natural excellencies of temper or mind, nor by any acquired advantages of knowledge and skill, nor by any peculiar mea-sure of spiritual gifts ; but by their work and office. 1. " Them which labour among you." The original signifies to " labour with unremitting diligence, even to much weariness." This involves—(1) Due preparation for public ser-vices—the preparation of the man as well as of the sermon, &c. (2) The work—preaching, administering, visitation, &c. 2. They that " are over you." (1) Not by usurpation of the office or human commission (Mark x. 42–44). (2) But by Christ, the Head of the Church—(*a*) As examples. (*b*) Guides. (*c*) Governors and administrators of Christ's law. 3. Those who " admonish you." This is needed by the ignorant, the negligent, the inconsistent. II. THE DUTIES OF CHRISTIAN CHURCHES TOWARDS THEIR MINISTERS. 1. To know them. (1) As Christian friends. (2) Their character. (3) Their religious principles. (4) What belongs to their office and work, and their fitness for it. 2. To " esteem them very highly in love." The world may treat them with aversion ; hence the Church should treat them with affection and regard. And the text warrants the very highest. III. THE REASON FOR THESE DUTIES. 1. The plain command of God. 2. The work's sake. (*A. Wickens.*) *Pastoral claims :*—Your pastor claims from you—I. PROPER RESPECT FOR THE OFFICE HE SUSTAINS. It is a most sacred office, and because some men have disgraced it, and others made it the engine of priest-craft, or for other reasons, the minister is not to be stripped of official superiority and reduced to the rank of a mere speaking brother. Regard your pastor, then, not with feelings of superstitious dread, or slavish veneration, or frivolous famili-arity. Hold such in reputation as your friend, but also as an ambassador of God. II. DUE REGARD FOR HIS AUTHORITY. Office without authority is a solecism.

"Let the elders rule." "Obey them that have the rule over you." This is not independent, but derived from and resting on Christ. It is not legislatorial, but judicial and executive. "Thus saith the Lord." Should the minister advance anything unscriptural, they must try the minister by the Bible, not the Bible by the minister. Not that this confers the indiscriminate right of criticism, as if the end of hearing were to find fault. In performance of his duty it belongs to your pastor—1. To preside at the meetings of the Church. His opinion is to be treated with deference, even when it should not secure assent. 2. To be responsible to Christ for the peace and good order of the Church, which should secure for him freedom from obnoxious meddling. III. REGULAR, PUNCTUAL, AND SERIOUS ATTEND- ANCE UPON HIS MINISTRY. 1. Regular. There are persons upon whose attendance it is as impossible to depend as upon the blowing of the wind. How disheartening this is! What are the causes? (1) Distance, which reconciles them to one service on the Sabbath and none all the week besides. (2) The weather. (3) Home duties. (4) Sabbath visiting. (5) A roving spirit of unhallowed curiosity. 2. Punctual. Late attendance is a great annoyance to orderly worshippers, dis- respectful to the minister, and an insult to God. 3. Serious. Come from the closet to the sanctuary. The fire of devotion should be kindled at home. Remember where you are, whose Presence is with you, and what is your busi- ness in the house of God. IV. SINCERE AND FERVENT AFFECTION. This love should be—1. Apparent; for however strong, if confined to the heart, it will be of little value. A minister should no more be in doubt of the attachment of his people than of his wife and children. 2. Candid: for charity covers a multitude of faults. Not that you are to be indifferent to character. This candour is not asked for the manifestly inconsistent. The minister, like Cæsar's wife, must be above suspicion. The charity asked for is not for an unholy, but for an imperfect man: for those infirmities which attach to the best, the candour which thinks no evil, &c. It is surprising what insignificant circumstances will sometimes, quite unintentionally, give offence to some hearers. 3. Practical. It should lead you to avoid anything that would give him even uneasiness. His work is difficult at its easiest. Therefore you should be—(1) Holy and consistent. (2) Peaceful among yourselves. He cannot be happy with an inharmonious people. (3) Generous contributors to his support. 4. Minute and delicate in its attentions. 5. Constant. V. RESPECTFUL ATTENTION TO HIS COUNSELS, either public or private. VI. CO-OPERATION IN HIS SCHEMES OF USEFULNESS for—1. The Church, whose interests should be his and your first concern. Sunday schools, sick visiting, &c. 2. The town. The Church should not be behindhand in great public movements. 3. The world at large—missions, &c. VII. YOUR PRAYERS. The apostles needed this much more than uninspired men. Pray for your pastor at home, &c. (*J. A. James.*) *Pastors and people :*—I. THE PASTOR'S WORK. The Thessalonian elders—1. "Laboured among" the people committed to their charge. And the labour of a faithful Christian minister may be regarded as com- prehending—(1) The physical labour of preaching the gospel in public, and of visiting the people in private. (2) The intellectual labour of study. (3) The moral labour of keeping his own soul in order for the right discharge of his vocation. 2. They were "over" the people "in the Lord." The original denotes superintendence, and from the view given throughout the New Testament of the functions of Christian office-bearers, that it comprehends both pastoral vigilance and ecclesiastical rule. 3. They "admonished," *i.e.,* did not confine their instructions to general and abstract statements of Divine truth, but brought that truth closely to bear on particular circumstances and character. II. THE DUTIES OF PEOPLE TO MINISTER. 1. They were to "know" them, *i.e.,* own or acknowledge them "in the Lord," *i.e.,* in deference to the authority and accord- ing to the wise and salutary regulations of their Master. This acknowledgment, of course, was to be practical as well as verbal. The Thessalonians were to render it, not only by speaking of these office-bearers of their Church as their spiritual guides and overseers, but by attending to their ministry, asking their advice, submitting to their discipline, and providing for their maintenance. 2. They were to "esteem" them "very highly in love for their work's sake"; that is, regard them with mingled emotions of respect and affection, because of the nature of their office and because of their fidelity in fulfilling it. This twofold mode of treating ministers was calculated to promote the religious improvement of the people and to encourage pastors. 3. "And be at peace among yourselves." Social peace among true Christians is highly important, both for their own mutual improvement and personal comfort, and for the recommendation of religion to the world; and it is to be maintained by the cultivation both of unanimity of sentiment and of kindliness of feeling (Col. iii. 12–16; 1 Cor. i. 10–13; iii. 3–7). (*A. S. Patterson, D.D.*)      *Appreciation of a clergyman's work :*—The incumbent of Osborne had occasion to visit an aged parishioner.    Upon his arrival at the house, as he entered the door where the invalid was, he found sitting by the bedside, a lady in deep mourning reading the Word of God.    He was about to retire, when the lady remarked, " Pray remain.    I should not wish the invalid to lose the comfort which a clergyman might afford."    The lady retired, and the clergyman found lying on the bed a book with texts of Scripture adapted to the sick ; and he found that out of that book portions of Scripture had been read by the lady in black.    That lady was the Queen of England.    (*W. Baxendale.*)

Ver. 14. **Now we exhort you, brethren, warn them that are unruly.**—The verse contains four distinct, but co-ordinate and mutually connected exhortations. I. "WARN THEM THAT ARE UNRULY."    In pursuing peace, fidelity was not to be sacrificed ; and one of the methods in which Christian peace might be promoted was the faithful and tender rebuke of those whose quarrelsome temper or wayward conduct disturbed fraternal harmony.    The " unruly " were such as, either from lax principles with respect to ecclesiastical government, or from pride, ambition, or recklessness, refused submission to legitimate authority ; and such their fellow-Christians were to "warn."    In warning this class of persons, much, of course, depends on the manner in which the work is done.    But when it is performed by one true Christian to another with intelligence and tenderness, there is good reason to believe that it will prove successful ; nor can it be supposed that the spirit of the Psalmist's words (Psa. cxli. 5) is altogether alien from the followers of Christ. II. " COMFORT THE FEEBLE-MINDED," such as, from a natural want of energy and firmness, or from deficiency in Christian faith and confidence, were disquieted amidst the calamities of life. The worldling might despise them for their cowardice ; the religious censor might blame them for their culpable distrust. But Christianity took them under her protection, and here commands their firmer-hearted brethren to soothe and cheer them amidst the struggles of the faith and the adversities of time. III. " SUPPORT THE WEAK." Here, as in Rom. xiv. 1, 2 and 1 Cor. viii. 7–12, the word " weak " denotes a special deficiency in knowledge or faith, and liability to fall.    Such weakness might arise from the prejudices produced by a Jewish or Pagan education, from the recency of conversion, or from causes more obviously culpable.    But to whatever source the weakness might be traceable, one " whom Christ had received " was not to be despised by his older or stronger brethren.    The word rendered " support " denotes the act of taking another by the hand or arm.    IV. " BE PATIENT TOWARD ALL MEN."    By this command the apostle calls on the Thessalonian Christians to guard against being led, whether by the intellectual obtuseness and moral imperfection of members of the Church, or by the calumnious reproaches and persecuting rage of the enemies of the truth, to resort to bitter and upbraiding words, or to cease from efforts to do the individual good. " Love suffereth long and is kind " (1 Cor. xiii. 4).    (*A. S. Patterson, D.D.*) *Precepts :*—I. WARN THE UNRULY : those who, like disorderly soldiers, break the ranks, and become idle, dissolute and worthless.    This was a besetting sin in the primitive Churches.    Many entertaining false views about the nearness of Christ's Advent became indifferent to work, and sank into apathy or even worse.    The proverb says, "An idle mind is the devil's workshop " ; and when a man is not occupied he is apt to become an instrument of evil and a disturber of the Church. It is difficult to pin some people down to do a bit of fair honest work.    They are full of schemes for other people, and are for ever finding fault that other people do not carry them out.    These are the restless gipsies, the pests of every Christian community, the mischief-makers and busybodies in other people's matters.    Warn such. Admonish gently at first, putting them in mind of their duty. It is the fault of many to limit admonitions to gross and grievous sins, but in these cases warning often comes too late.    If admonition is not effectual, then proceed to sharper reproof.    If that is unavailing, separate yourselves from their society. II. COMFORT THE FEEBLE-MINDED.    More correctly—encourage the faint-hearted.    The reference is not to the intellectually weak, but to such as faint in the day of adversity or the prospect of it (chap. ii. 14), or who are disheartened in consequence of the loss of friends (chap. iv. 13).    It may also include those who are perplexed with doubt as to their spiritual condition, and who through fear are subject to bondage.    There are some people so weighed down with a sense of modesty as to incapacitate them from using their abilities. Others, again, are so oppressed with the inveteracy of sin that they despair of gaining the victory and give up all endeavours. These need encouraging with the promises of God, and with the lessons and examples furnished by experience. Heart-courage is what the faint-hearted require. III. SUPPORT THE WEAK. A man may be weak in judgment or in practice. There may be lack of information or lack of capacity to understand. Such was the condition of many who, not apprehending the abrogation of the Mosaic law, and thinking they were still bound to observe ordinances, were weak in faith. Some linger for years in the misty borderland between doubt and certainty, ever learning, but never coming to a knowledge of the truth. Defective faith implies defective practice. Support such with the moral influence of sympathy, prayer, counsel, example. IV. BE PATIENT TOWARDS ALL MEN, even the most wayward and persecuting. Consider the patience of God and imitate it. Lack of present success is no excuse. The triumphs of genius in art, science, and literature are triumphs of patience. (*G. Barlow.*) *The feeble-minded :*—Littleness is implied. The word occurs here only in the New Testament (see Isa. xxxv. 4; lxx.), and is almost unknown in classical Greek. The student of Aristotle will look upon it as implying the contradictory of the "great souled," with his high estimate of himself, "just contempt" for others, and freedom from excessive elation or depression. The whole passage here might well lead us to suppose that, as the Thessalonian Christians had a tender and almost feminine susceptibility about those they had loved and lost, so they would be likely also to have some of the rest of the characteristics which accompany that beautiful weakness. We may perhaps refer to "the chief *women* not a few" (Acts xvii. 4). The morbid conscientiousness, the form of self-torment known to spiritual writers as *scrupulousness,* would be well-expressed by the word "little-minded." (*Bp. Alexander.*) *Precept and practice :*—St. Paul gives an admirable precept to the Thessalonians, but precept must blossom into practice, and practice will prove the best commentary on precept. I. THE PRECEPT ILLUSTRATED BY PRACTICE. All the persons in God's great family are not of the same height and strength; though some are old men and fathers, and others are young and strong, yet many are little children, nay, babes in Christ: some can go alone, or with a little help, if you hold them but by their leading-strings; but others must be carried in arms, and will require much love and patience to overcome their childish forwardness. Christ winks at their weaknesses, who hath most reason to be moved with them. Though His disciples were raw, and dull, and slow to understand and believe, yet He bears with them; nay, though when He was watching for them, and in His bloody sweat, and they lay sleeping and snoring, and could not watch with Him one hour, He doth not fall fiercely upon them, and afterward excuseth them for their lack of service. Their spirit was willing, but their flesh was weak. It is no wonder that their pace was slow, when, like the snail, they have such a house—such a hindrance—on their backs. Who can think of this infinite grace of the blessed Redeemer in making such an apology for them when He had such cause to be full of fury against them, and not be incited to imitate so admirable a pattern? God's treatment of Jonah was very similar to Christ's treatment of His disciples. Jonah runs from His business: God sends him to Nineveh; he will go to Tarshish. Here was plain rebellion against his Sovereign, which was repeated. But lo! He cannot permit Jonah to perish; He will rather whip him to his work than let him wander to his ruin. But how gentle is the rod! God cannot forget the love of a father though Jonah forget the duty of a child, and will rather work a miracle and make a devourer his saviour than Jonah shall miscarry. Oh, the tenderness of God toward His weak and erring children! Now Christians are to be "imitators of God." If He, so glorious, holy, and infinite, beareth with His creatures thus, what cause have they to bear patiently with their fellows! "We that are strong ought to bear the infirmities of the weak." II. THIS PRACTICE IS GROUNDED UPON PRINCIPLE. It was love on the part of Christ and on the part of God that led these Divine Persons to act so graciously as They did; and the same love must ever prompt Christians to imitate Them—love to Jesus Himself and love to them for whom He died, but who need practical sympathy and help. There must be no bitterness, no envyings, no heart-burnings among the brethren, but they must love each other as each loves himself, and suffer together in all suffering. Oh, how sweet is the music when saints join saints in concert! but how harsh is the sound of jarring strings! A mutual yielding and forbearance is no small help to our own peace and safety. There is a story of two goats which may excellently illustrate this matter. They both met on a narrow bridge, under which a very deep and fierce stream did glide; there was no going blindly back, neither could they press forward for the narrowness of the bridge. Now, had they fought for their passage, they had both been certain to perish; this, therefore, they did—they agreed that one should lie down and the other go over him, and thus both their lives were preserved. While Christians are doing the reverse of this, they are like some small chickens, a prey to kites and other ravenous creatures. "In quietness shall be their strength." (*G. Swinnock, M.A.*) *Warnings :*—Warnings are given in love (1 Cor. iv. 14). Warnings are given in mercy. Warnings are given in duty (Ezek. iii. 20). I. THE WARNING OF EXAMPLE. Fallen angels (Jude 6). Ungodly men (Jude 7). Untrue professors (Jude 17–19). II. THE WARNINGS OF INSTRUCTION. God has given us warning in His Holy Word that life is uncertain (James iv. 13, 14); that it is an evil thing to offend God (Rom. ii. 8, 9); that it is a foolish thing to forsake Christ (Heb. ii. 3); that it must be foolish to run such risk (Acts iv. 12); that it must therefore be foolish to turn away from this only hope. III. THE WARNINGS OF EXPERIENCE. The experiences of sin are bitter (Rom. vii. 24). The enjoyments of salvation are sweet (2 Thess. ii. 16, 17). If warnings are to do us good they must be heard (2 Tim. iv. 3, 4), believed (Gen. xix. 14), obeyed (Matt. xxi. 28–31). This is our lesson—Prov. xxix. 1. (*J. Richardson, M.A.*) **Support the weak, be patient towards all men.**—Manton says: "Though we cannot love their weaknesses, yet we must love the weak, and bear with their infirmities, not breaking the bruised reed. Infants must not be turned out of the family because they cry, and are unquiet and troublesome; though they be peevish and froward, yet we must bear it with gentleness and patience, as we do the frowardness of the sick; if they revile we must not revile again, but must seek gently to restore them, notwithstanding all their censures." This patience is far too rare. We do not make allowances enough for our fellows, but sweepingly condemn those whom we ought to cheer with our sympathy. If we are out of temper ourselves, we plead the weather, or a headache, or our natural temperament, or aggravating circumstances; we are never at a loss for an excuse for ourselves, why should not the same ingenuity be used by our charity in inventing apologies and extenuations for others? It is a pity to carry on the trade of apology-making entirely for home consumption; let us supply others. True, they are very provoking, but if we suffered half as much as some of our irritable friends have to endure we should be even more aggravating. Think in many cases of their ignorance, their unfortunate bringing up, their poverty, their depression of spirit, and their home surroundings, and pity will come to the help of patience. We are tender to a man who has a gouty toe, cannot we extend the feeling to those who have an irritable soul? Our Lord will be angry with us if we are harsh to His little ones whom He loves; nor will He be pleased if we are unkind to His poor afflicted children with whom He would have us be doubly tender. We ourselves need from Him ten times more consideration than we show to our brethren. For His sake we ought to be vastly more forbearing than we are. Think how patient He has been to us, and let our hard-heartedness be confessed as no light sin. (*C. H. Spurgeon.*) *The contrast between heathenism and Christianity in the treatment of the weak :*—Heathen philosophy, even Plato's, was systematically hard on the weakly. It anticipated modern theories and practice in such matters as the struggle for existence, survival of the fittest, and happy dispatch. In the exercise of the art of medicine Plato held that it might serve to cure the occasional distempers of men whose constitutions are good; but as to those who have bad constitutions, let them die; and the sooner the better: such men are unfit for war, for magistracy, for domestic affairs, for severe study; and the best thing for such is to have done with life at once. In contrast with this Bacon vindicated the art of healing by appealing to the examp,eof Christ, and reminded men that the great Physician of the soul did not disdain to be the Physician of the body. Hawthorne asserts that most men have a natural indifference, if not hostility, towards those whom disease, or weakness, or calamity of any kind causes to falter and faint amid the rude jostle of our selfish existence. The education of Christianity, he owned, the sympathy of a like experience, and the example of women, may soften and possibly subvert this ugly characteristic; but it is originally there, and has its analogy in the practice of our brute brethren, who hunt the sick or disabled member of the herd from among them as an enemy. Faithful to which code of action, says Balzac, the world at large is lavish of hard words and harsh conduct to the wretched who dare spoil the gaiety of its fêtes and to cast a gloom over its pleasures: whoever is a sufferer in mind or body, or is destitute of money or power is a pariah. The weakly or deformed child of a Spartan was thrown, by order, into the cavern called apothetæ, in the belief that its life could be no advantage either to itself or to the state. The worst of charity is, complains Emerson, that the lives you are asked to preserve are not worth preserving. (*F. Jacox, B.A.*)    *The difficulty of the strong to sympathize with the weak :*—A disposition to despise weakness, observed Mr. Fonblanque, seems to be a law of nature which humanity prevails against with effort, by urging the sympathies and stimulating them by the imagination. Poor Boswell again and again makes piteous record of Johnson's unimaginative contempt for the sufferings of frailer constitutions; and he philosophizes on the fact that in full health men can scarcely believe that their ailing neighbours suffer much, " so faint is the image of pain upon our imagination." " At your age, sir, I had no headache," snapped the doctor at Sir William Scott once when the future Lord Stowell ventured to complain of one. When Fanny Burney fell ill at court, she wrote, " Illness here, till of late, has been so unknown that it is commonly supposed that it must be wilful, and therefore meets little notice till accompanied by danger. This is by no means from hardness, but from prejudice and want of personal experience." John Stuart Mill reckoned it as one of the disadvantages of Bentham that from his childhood he had never had a day's illness; his unbroken health helped to incapacitate him for sympathy with his fellows, and weakened his power of insight into other minds. (*Ibid.*)    *Helping the weak :*—A poor bee had fallen into the pond, and was struggling as well as her failing strength would allow. We seized a pole, and placed the end of it just under her. She took firm hold, and we lifted the pole and the bee. A little while was spent in drying herself and pluming her wings, and then our worker made a straight line for the hive, and doubtless was soon at her daily task rewarding us with honey. May not many a human worker be found in a sinking condition? A little sensible help might save him. Who will give it? He who does so shall receive the blessing of him that is ready to perish. Poor hearts are often in deep despondency, sinking for lack of a sympathetic word. Do not withhold it. Rescue the perishing. Be on the watch for despairing minds; if no other good comes of it, you will, at least, be more grateful for your own cheerfulness. But good will come of it in unexpected instances, and it will be heaven's music in your ears to hear sighs turned into songs. (*C. H. Spurgeon.*)    *Support the weak :*—In the town of Leeds I was waiting one wet wintry night outside the railway station, when a ragged, dirty boy, selling papers, came up to me and said: "Buy an evening paper, sir. Please do. Only seven left, and they's all my profit." The boy's eagerness to sell arrested my attention, and on looking down I saw a bright, intelligent face with a look of honesty in it. So I questioned him, and found his parents were, he supposed, "drinking at a public-house in Briggate." "Had he no cap to wear that rainy night?" "Yes," but he had lent it to his sister, who was waiting for him in an old doorway across the road till he "sold out." The cap wasn't on her head because she had "no boots and stockings, so I told her to put her feet inside my cap to keep 'em warm and prevent her ketchin' cold." Surely this was "a self-sacrificing chivalry worthy of the knights of old, for a boy who thus cared for his sister exhibited the true spirit of bravery." (*Told in Dr. Bernardo's "Night and Day."*)    *Patience* is a Divine attribute, and is repeatedly mentioned as a fruit of God's Spirit in the soul. In the text this grace is made a universal duty. It is not to be a tribute paid to the virtuous, but to all. And the man who enjoined it exercised it. I. THE NATURE AND SOURCES OF CHRISTIAN PATIENCE. 1. In respect to personal trial patience is exercised in its lower form. Patience in labour, fatigue, pain, &c., is not easy, but it is the easiest kind of patience. When, however, we are called to have patience with others, we enter a higher and more difficult sphere of duty. Men may endure their own trials from pride, hope, native firmness, duty, &c.; but when we are required to be patient towards bad dispositions, evil conduct, &c., this is a nobler achievement and proceeds from nobler motives. 1. Patience does not imply approval of men's conduct or character, nor indifference to them. On the contrary, we must see things as they are before God; and if we refrain from attacking it must not be construed into approbation. 2. This patience implies such benevolence and pity as shall make us tolerant, and which can only spring from that regenerated love that God works in the soul. II. THE CONDITIONS OF ITS EXERCISE AND ITS OBJECTS. It must be exercised towards all men. To be patient with those we ˡove is natural; but we must not stop there; nor with our own *set :* nor with the good even when they stumble; nor with those who hold our opinions; but also with—1. The dull and foolish, who are very trying, especially if you are nervous and they are not; if you are mercurial and they are phlegmatic. They are in your way, and make your tasks troublesome. Nevertheless, you must be patient with them. 2. The conceited; a very hard work indeed, to submit to haughty looks and arrogant conduct. 3. The selfish and cunning, patience with whom places you at a disadvantage. 4. The rude. 5. The passionate, &c. Wherever you find a man that has the brand of God's creation upon him, and immortality for his destiny, there you find the object of this command. Do you find this hard, impossible? Then consider—III. ITS MOTIVES. 1. It is only by having patience with men that you can retain any hold upon them. The man who is outside your pity is outside your diocese. You cannot do anything for a man you dislike, and one of the worst things that can befall a benevolent nature is to be incapacitated to do good. 2. Only in this way can we imitate Christ. "I say unto you, love your enemies," &c. 3. It is by this very patience on God's part that we ourselves are saved. (*H. W. Beecher.*)    *Patience and charity needed :—* "Lord, I can't make these sticks perfectly straight; I have lost all my strength. Send me to another field." But what is the answer of the Holy Spirit? "You were not sent to that field to take every crook out of those sticks; you can't perfect human nature; that is My work." Now there is something in every man —ministers included—that is a little gnarly. It is peculiar to the individual—a streak of the old Adam inwrought in his individuality. In one it is stubbornness, in another it is suspiciousness, in another reserve, in another a disposition to be critical, or fault-finding, or censorious. By whatever name it may be known, it is, in fact, a little twist of depravity, and no human influence, no preacher, can untwist it and straighten it out. It is a peculiar twist of self, inborn, inbred, inwrought. So when I discover what a man's peculiar twist is, I say, "The Lord only can take that out of him, and I won't touch it if I can help it." I tried my hand at this once on a good Scotch brother, and I will never try it again. He was a most uncompromising subject, and I am quite convinced that if I had had a little more charity for his peculiarities he would have been a very useful man. (*Dr. Spinning.*)

Ver. 15.  **See that none render evil for evil.**—*Negative and positive precepts:—* I. SEE THAT NONE RENDER EVIL FOR EVIL UNTO ANY MAN. Retaliation betrays a weak and cruel disposition. Pagan morality went so far as to forbid the unprovoked injuring of others; and it is not without noble examples of the exercise of a spirit of forgiveness. The Jews prostituted to purposes of private revenge the laws which were intended to administer equitable retributions. It is Christianity alone that teaches man to bear personal injuries without retaliation. "Hath any wronged thee," says Quarles, "be bravely revenged; slight it, and the work is begun; forgive it, and it is finished. He is below himself that is not above an injury." Public wrongs the public law will avenge; and the final recompense for all wrong must be left to the Infallible Judge (Rom. xii. 19, 20). II. BUT EVER FOLLOW THAT WHICH IS GOOD, BOTH AMONG YOURSELVES AND TO ALL MEN. The noblest retaliation is that of good for evil. In the worst character there is some element of goodness. Our beneficence should be as large as an enemy's malice (Matt. v. 44, 45). That which is good is not always that which is pleasing. Goodness should be sought for its own sake. It is the great aim and business of life. Goodness is essentially diffusive; it delights in multiplying itself in others. It is undeterred by provocation; it conquers the opposition. Lessons: 1. The perceptive morality of Christianity is a signal evidence of its transcendent glory. 2. Practice is more potent than precept. 3. The Christian spirit is the root of genuine goodness. (*G. Barlow.*) It is not strictly true to say that Christianity alone at first forbade to return evil for evil. Plato knew that it was not the true definition of justice to do harm to one's enemies. The Stoics, who taught the extirpation of the passions, were far enough from admitting of revenge to be the only one that should be allowed to remain. It is a higher as well as a truer claim to make for the gospel, that it kindled that spirit of kindness and good-will in the breast of man (which could not be wholly extinguished even towards an enemy), until it became a practical principle; and that it preached as a rule of life for all, what had previously been the supreme virtue, or the mere theory of philosophers. (*Prof. Jowett.*)    *Following the good :*—**Ever follow that which is good among yourselves and** to all.—1. In political effort men can unite, and so they ought in religious; for religion means the link which binds men for good work. Is it more important to put one's political friends in Parliament than to win one's neighbours for heaven? 2. Remember the unwearied diligence of political partizans. Ah, one cannot help regretting that Christians are less earnest. 3. In politics men will give up their dearly loved crotchets to promote the welfare of the general party. Why not, then, sink our individualism in following that which is good? We are to ever do so—I. IN BUILDING UP OUR OWN CHARACTER. 1. It is easier to do good than to be good. We are so apt to be discouraged by many failures. We have wished to grow in goodness like a tree, but we have more to contend with than a tree. We promise well in bud and leaf, and then the fruit does not ripen, and we get discouraged. Some of us have done worse. We have put forth the bud of innocence, but the blossom of virtue has been nipped by the frost of misfortune, or the blast of temptation, and we have given up. To all such let this exhortation come with power. Still set your face towards the good. Try again. Will you throw away your coat because it is soiled? Would you have your child despair of writing because he has upset the ink? 2. In following the good let us aim high. To copy from another may help us a little; but we shall make the surest progress if we follow only Christ. We teach children writing by setting the best copy before them. If we fall to-day, let us arise to-day and follow Him. II. IN THE CHURCH. Every Church should be a missionary society, and when a new member is received something should be found for him to do. It is true you cannot find a perfect Church; but this should not dishearten you. Go into an organ factory—what a horrible din! Yes; but what is the result? The Church is an organ factory. All our pipes have to be made and tuned. But if we are in earnest we shall not care for the discord; the instrument will one day play harmonious music. In battle, if a general see a brigade hardly pressed he orders out another to support it. So, if the Church's battalion in the slums is weak, the battalion in the suburbs should hasten to its help. Let us by our example make the Church vigorous and good. If the prayer-meeting is good, the Lord's supper, &c., follow them. Be as regular and earnest in Church duty as though you were paid for it. III. IN THE WORLD. Lift up your voices against war. Working men uphold arbitration against strikes. Do not blame statesmen for making war, when master and man fight and ruin one another. IV. IN YOUR OWN NEIGHBOURHOOD. There is much that you can do there. Conclusion: 1. Persevere in following the good. 2. Let your motive be the love of Christ. 3. If you keep following the good, your works will follow you. (*W. Birch.*) *Perseverance in following the good:*—When Columbus was sailing over the Atlantic, believing there was another continent in the west, his men were dispirited and almost in mutiny, he said, "Unless we have some sign of land within the next three days, we will turn back." Fortunately, they had some signs of land, and the ships steered on until they came to the American coast. Now, what you are doing is good, and you should tolerate no "if" about it. You have been preaching, and teaching, and doing good for a long time, and perhaps you are ready to say, "Unless I have some signs of good fruit from my labour, I will give up." Do not. If that which you are following be really for the benefit of mankind, be not weary in well-doing. The test of success is not in numbers. Remember that Jesus had no disciples with Him in His trial; at His crucifixion He had only one, and He ended His beautiful ministry by the cross. Therefore, do not despair. Keep on with your work and keep at it. Persevere. Follow that which is good continuously unto the end. (*Ibid.*) *Good for evil:*—Bacon said, "He that studieth revenge keepeth his own wounds green." Philip the Good, of Burgundy, had it in his power to punish one who had behaved ill to him; but he said, "It is a fine thing to have revenge in one's power, but it is a finer thing not to use it." Another king of France said of his foes, "I will weigh down the lead of their wickedness with the gold of my kindness." A minister remarked, "Some persons would have had no particular interest in my prayers, but for the injuries they did me." (*H. R. Burton.*)

**Vers. 16–18. Rejoice evermore.**—*A trinity of privileges:*—I. STUDY THESE ADVICES SEPARATELY. 1. "Rejoice evermore." Rejoice because of—(1) Your conversion. (2) Your privileges as children of God. (3) Your apprehension of Christ and His love. (4) Your hope of glory. These are always available, and if we sometimes rejoice in them, why not evermore? 2. "Pray without ceasing." (1) This implies a praying habit, and relates to our thoughts, affections, and feelings.

Oral praying is occasional, and is merely the outburst. (2) The reasons why we should pray at all always exist, and therefore we should "pray without ceasing." Prayer betokens—(a) danger, and our dangers surround us every moment. (b) A sense of personal weakness and destitution, which are permanent. (c) Is essential to dependence on God, which ought to be without intermission. All the reasons why we should pray at all urge us to pray unceasingly. 3. "In everything give thanks." (1) In everything; for however great the trial, it is invariably accompanied by many mercies. No case is so bad but that it might be much worse. (2) The "in" also means "for." "All things work together for good," &c. God's children cannot receive from God anything but mercies. Both for and in everything we should give thanks. Not afterwards merely, but in the midst. This is the real triumph of faith, and this is the will of God concerning us in Christ Jesus. II. VIEW THESE ADVICES IN THEIR CONNECTION WITH EACH OTHER. 1. How does a state of constant joy in the Holy Ghost lead to prayer? One would think it might lead to praise rather than prayer. Now, prayer is something more than a selfish craving, it is communion with God. But such is impossible without joy. When we rejoice in God, we are at once impelled to tell Him all our wants, lovingly and confidently; and thus the highest exercise of prayer results more from a sense of God's goodness than of our necessities. Supplies of blessing, then, provoke thanksgiving. 2. Why is not this our experience? We rejoice, &c., but not always. Our defectiveness is owing either—(1) To our shallowness or lack of thorough earnestness. (2) To our insincerity, or the mingling of selfish and worldly motives with our piety. (3) To our unbelief or want of hearty confidence in God's love and faithfulness. Or (4) To our sloth, which refuses to make the requisite effort for our growth in grace. Let these hindrances be removed. (*T. G. Horton.*) *A triple commandment:*—The apostle commendeth unto us three virtues, of greater price than the three presents the Magi brought unto Christ: the first is, "Rejoice evermore"; the second is, "Pray without ceasing"; the third, "In everything give thanks." All three are of one last, and are the things which one saith all men do, yet scarce one doeth them as he should; therefore the apostle, to show us how we should do them, doth put "continually" unto them, as though continuance were the perfection of all virtues. I. THE COMMAND TO REJOICE. It is not an indifferent thing to rejoice, but we are commanded to rejoice, to show that we break a commandment if we rejoice not. Oh, what a comfort is this—when the Comforter Himself commands us to rejoice! God was wont to say, "Repent," and not "rejoice," because some men rejoice too much; but here God commandeth to rejoice, as though some men did not rejoice enough; therefore you must understand to whom He speaketh. In the Psalms it is said, "Let the saints be glad"; not, Let the wicked be glad: and in Isaiah God saith, "Comfort ye My people"; not, Comfort Mine enemies. He who would have us holy as He is holy, would have us joyful as He is joyful; He who would have us do His will on earth as angels do it in heaven, would have us rejoice on earth as angels rejoice in heaven; He who hath ordained us to the kingdom of saints, would have us rejoice that we have such a kingdom to receive; therefore Christ saith to His disciples, "Rejoice that your names are written in heaven." II. THE COMMAND TO PRAY. As Elisha would not prophesy until the musician came, and while the musician played he prophesied, so when the heart rejoiceth in God, then it is fittest to call upon God. 1. It is such a pleasant thing that Paul joineth, "pray without ceasing" with "rejoice evermore," to show that no man hath such joy as he who is often talking with God by prayer; as if he should say, If thou have the skill to pray continually, it will make thee rejoice continually; for in God's company is nothing but joy and gladness of heart. 2. It is such a sweet thing, above other things that we do for God, that in Revelation the prayers of the saints are called "incense," because, when they ascend to heaven, God smelleth a sweet savour in them. Moreover, what a profitable thing unceasing prayer is! It doeth more good than alms; for with mine alms I help but three or four needy individuals, but with my prayers I aid thousands. 3. It is a powerful and victorious thing. As all Samson's strength lay in his hair, so all our strength lieth in ceaseless prayer. Many have learned more by praying than they could by reading, and done that by prayer they could not do by counsel; therefore one saith that he who can pray continually can do all things and always, because, like Jacob, he can overcome God, who helpeth him; and he who can overcome God can overcome Satan too, who trieth his uttermost to hinder all things. III. THE COMMAND TO PRAISE. What will we give to God if we will not afford Him thanks? What will we do for God if we will not praise Him? It is the least we can give and do, and it is all we can give and do. Shall the birds sing unto God, which is all they can do, and not they for whom God created birds? What a fool is he which will fight, and travel, and watch for himself, and will not speak for himself in psalms, and hymns, and spiritual songs, making melody in his heart unto God! God requires the sacrifice of praise from us as He did from the Jews. Therefore let us not say, God will not hear us. God Himself says, "Whoso offereth praise glorifieth Me ; and to him that ordereth his conversation aright will I show the salvation of God." (*H. Smith.*)    *Rejoice evermore:*—Some men are joyful by disposition. We like the jovial, merry men, the Mark Tapleys of the world, who are jolly even under adverse circumstances. Yet such joy in an irreligious man has something sad about it. It is like building a warm and comfortable house upon the winter's ice. There are also men who have learned cheerfulness because they know the wisdom and health of it. We admire this, too—the bravery of being joyful in this world. There is something almost tragic in the joyous shout of the crew that goes sailing to the polar sea. Of course they need all their hope and cheer. Soon the sunny air will chill, the cheerless ice will fleck the blue sea, the snow will hiss in the brine, and the black curtain of the Arctic night will fall over the scene. Wave your caps, boys, as your gallant ship slips out of the pier. Be merry if you can. But I do not understand how it is possible to be joyous if you look not beyond the grave into which all things that give you joy must so soon be swept. The joy, the merry laughter of sinful men— is it not reckless? It is like a lot of boys exhilarated by the motion of a maelstrom and shouting with delight as they are sucked into the fatal vortex. How different the Christian's joy. With God on his side, with his books balanced, with his peace sealed, with confidence in the eternal future, with the mighty conviction that all things work together for good to them that love God— why, such a man may indulge all of the exuberance of his soul. (*R. S. Barrett.*) *Rejoice evermore:*—I. THE POSITION OF THE TEXT. 1. It is set in the midst of many precepts. Note them. All these things are to be done as occasion requires, but rejoicing is to be done evermore ; and rejoice in each duty because you rejoice evermore. 2. It comes just after a flavouring of trouble and bitterness (ver. 15). The children of God are apt to have evil rendered to them ; but still they are bidden to rejoice. "Blessed are ye, when men shall revile you." Despondency is excluded, and yet among the curiosities of the Churches, I have known many deeply spiritual people who have been afraid to rejoice, regarding it as a sacred duty to be gloomy. But where is the command to be miserable? Then, is it not a sin not to rejoice, since it is so plainly commanded? II. THE QUALITY OF THIS REJOICING. 1. It is not a carnal rejoicing. If it were it would be impossible to keep it up evermore. There is a joy of harvest, but where shall we find it in winter? There is a joy of wealth, but where is it when riches are flown? So with health, friends, &c. If your joys spring from earthly fountains, those fountains may be dried up. You are forbidden to rejoice too much in these things, for they are as honey, of which a man may eat till he is sickened. But the joy which God commands is one in which it is impossible to go too far. 2. It is not presumptuous. Some ought not to rejoice : "Rejoice not, O Israel . . . for thou hast departed from thy God." It would be well for the joy of many to be turned to sorrow. They have never fled to Christ for refuge. Many have a joy that has accumulated through many years of false profession. If your joy will not bear looking at have done with it. 3. It is not fanatical. Some people of a restless turn never feel good until they are half out of their minds. I do not condemn their delirium, but want to know what goes with it. If our rejoicing does not come out of a clear understanding of the things of God, and has no truth at the bottom of it, what can it profit us? Those who rejoice without knowing why are driven to despair without knowing why, and are likely to be found in a lunatic asylum ere long. Christ's religion is sanctified common-sense. 4. It is not even that Divine exhilaration which Christians feel on special occasions. There are moments when Peter is no fool for saying, "Let us build three tabernacles." But you are not commanded always to be in that rapturous state, because you cannot be ; the strain would be too great. When we cannot mount as on wings, we may run without weariness, and walk without faintness. The ordinary joy of Christians is not the joy of jubilee, but of every year ; not of harvest but of all the months. 5. But it is the joy which is part of ourselves which God works in us by His Spirit, the cheerfulness of the new-born disposition, a delight in God and Christ, a sweet agreement with

Providence, a peace passing understanding. III. ITS OBJECT. 1. We can always rejoice in God. "God my exceeding joy." (1) God the Father, His electing love, unchanging grace, illimitable power, and transcending glory in being His child. (2) God the Son, Immanuel, His sympathizing humanity, His divinity and atonement. (3) God the Holy Ghost, dwelling in you, quickening, comforting, illuminating. 2. Every doctrine, promise, precept of the gospel will make us glad. 3. The graces of the Spirit : faith, hope, love, patience. 4. Holy exercises : prayer, singing, communion, Christian labour. 5. Bible study. IV. REASONS FOR REJOICING. 1. It wards off temptation. The armour of light is our effectual preservative. What can worldly mirth give to the man who is happy in God. 2. It encourages one's fellow-Christians. It is a half-holiday to look at the face of a rejoicing Christian. His words are ever cheering and strengthening. 3. It attracts sinners. (*C. H. Spurgeon.*)    *Rejoice evermore :*—I. IN YOUR PRESENT STATE. 1. You are pardoned sinners. 2. Have the testimony of a good conscience. 3. Have one who is able to bear your burdens. 4. Are related to God as children; to Christ as brethren. 5. Have free access to God and constant communion with Him. 6. Have a plentiful supply of grace. II. IN YOUR FUTURE PROSPECTS. 1. We are heirs of God and joint-heirs with Christ. 2. Every day brings us nearer our inheritance. Conclusion : 1. A sad Christian cheats himself all his journey. 2. We displease God if we are not joyful in His service. 3. By sadness we act like the spies who took an evil report of the good land. (*W. M. Hawkins.*)    *Rejoice evermore :*—1. This is a rule to which one would think all men should be forward to conform. Who would not embrace a duty the observance whereof is pleasure itself ? May it not be a plausible objection against it that it is superfluous since all men aim at nothing else but joy. Alas! When we consult experience we find the precept very ill obeyed. Who is not, at times, full of doleful complaints ? It is quite true that men are very eager in the pursuit of joy, and beat every bush of nature for it; but they find only transitory flashes of pleasure, which depend on contingent and mutable causes residing in a frail temper, and consist in slight touches on the organs of sense, their short enjoyment being tempered with regret ; so that men's usual delights are such that we should not if we could, and could not if we would, constantly entertain them : such "rejoicing evermore" being unreasonable and impossible. 2. It is a calumny on religion to say that it bars delight; on the contrary, it alone is the never failing source of true, steady joy, and not only doth allow us, but obliges us to be joyful. Such is the goodness of God that He makes our delight to be our duty, our sorrow to be our sin, adapting His holy will to our principle instinct; that He would have us resemble Him, as in all perfections, so in a constant state of happiness ; that as He hath provided heaven hereafter, He would have us enjoy paradise here. For what is the gospel but "good tidings,' &c.! and in what doth the kingdom consist but "righteousness, peace, and joy"? What is there belonging to a Christian whence grief can naturally spring ? From God, "our exceeding joy"; from heaven, the region of bliss ; from Divine truth, which rejoiceth the heart?" To exercise piety, and to rejoice are the same thing. We should evermore rejoice—I. IN THE EXERCISE OF FAITH. 1. In God's truth, there being no article of faith which doth not involve some great advantage, so that we cannot but "receive the word with joy." (1) The rich bounty of God in creation. (2) God's vigilant care in providence. (3) The great redemptive events and transactions of our Lord's earthly and heavenly life. 2. In the application of those verities wherein God opens His arms to embrace us, His invitations and soul remedies. Is it not, indeed, comfortable to believe that we have a physician at hand to cure our distempers, powerful succour to relieve our infirmities, an abundant supply of grace ? 3. In the real accomplishment of the "exceeding great and precious promises." How can the firm persuasion of heaven's glory be void of pleasure ? or confidence in God's fatherly care, on which we can cast our burdens, and from which we receive full supplies ? II. IN THE PRACTICE OF CHRISTIAN HOPE. "The hope of the righteous shall be gladness," "rejoice in hope." All hope, in proportion to the worth of its object and the solidity of its ground, is comfortable—much more when reposed in and on God. If it please men much to be heirs to a great inheritance, or to expect promotion or wealth, although death, and other accidents may interfere, how much more shall that "lively hope of our inheritance, incorruptible," &c., which can never be defeated, breed a most cheerful disposition. III. IN PERFORMING THE DUTY OF CHARITY. Love is the sweetest of all passions, and when conducted in a rational way towards a worthy object, it cannot but fill the heart with delight. 1. Such an object is God. He infinitely, beyond all else, deserves our affections, and may most easily be attained ; for whereas men are crossed in their affections, and their love is embittered, concerning God it is quite otherwise. (1) He is most ready to impart Himself, and loved us before we could love Him. (2) He encourages our love by sweetest influences and kindest expressions. Wherefore "they that love Thy name shall be joyful in Thee." 2. Who can enumerate or express the pleasures which wait on every kind and each act of charity towards men. (1) In giving. (2) In forgiving. (3) In sympathy and help. In these we gratify our best inclinations, oblige and endear ourselves to our brethren, most resemble the Divine goodness, and attract the Divine favour. (*I. Barrow, D.D.*)        *Rejoice evermore :—* I. WHAT IS IT TO REJOICE ? There is—1. A joy in outward things. (1) Natural. (2) Sinful (Eccles. xi. 9). (3) Lawful (Eccles. ii. 24 ; iii. 12, 13, 22). 2. A spiritual joy in God (Phil. iii. 1 ; iv. 4). II. WHAT IS IT TO REJOICE ALWAYS IN THE LORD ? To make Him the object of all our joy. 1. For what He is in Himself (Matt. xix. 17). 2. For what He is to us. (1) Our preserver (Psa. xlvi. 1, 2). (2) Our Saviour (Hab. iii. 18 ; Psa. xxvii. 1). (3) Our God (Heb. viii. 10). III. WHY OUGHT WE TO REJOICE EVERMORE ? 1. God commands it (Psa. xxxii. 11 ; Phil. iv. 4). 2. Christ prays for it (John xvii. 13). 3. The Holy Ghost works it (John xiv. 26 ; xvii. 7). 4 It is necessary and useful. (1) To lessen our esteem of the world and of sinful pleasures (Psa. iv. 7 ; lxxxiv. 10). (2) To enlarge our hearts and make them more capacious of heavenly things. (3) To facilitate our duties, and make us active in God's service (Deut. xxviii. 47 ; Neh. viii. 10). (4) To support us under our troubles (1 Pet. i. 7, 8). IV. HOW WE MAY ALWAYS REJOICE ? 1. Live above the world (2 Cor. iv. 18). 2. Live above the natural temper of your bodies. 3. Avoid such things as are wont to grieve and trouble you. (1) Sin (Psa. li. 8 ; Matt. xxvi. 75 ; 2 Cor. i. 12). (2) Needless questions—(*a*) about God's decrees. (*b*) The exact time of your conversion. (*c*) Judging yourselves according to your outward condition (Eccles. ix. 1). 4 Whatsoever happens still put your trust in God (Isa. xlix. 13, 14 ; l. 10 ; lv. 7 ; Heb. xiii. 6). 5. Act your faith constantly in Christ (John xiv. 1 ; Rom. viii. 33, 34). 6. Often meditate on the happiness of those who truly fear God. (1) In this world (Rom. viii. 28). (2) In the world to come (1 Cor. ii. 9). 7. Check thyself whensoever thou findest thy spirits begin to sink (Psa. xlii. 5, 11). (*Bp. Beveridge.*)        *Rejoice evermore :*—Real Christians are rare ; joyful ones more so. I. THE DUTY AND PRIVILEGE. 1. It must be carefully distinguished from levity or sinful mirth. " I said of laughter, it is mad," &c. Gravity, mixed with cheerfulness, becomes the man and the Christian. 2. We are not to drown our sorrow in gratification of the senses (Prov. xiv. 13), and thus obtain a temporary satisfaction. 3. This joy is not intended to render us insensible to affliction. There is a happy medium between impenitent indifference and overmuch sorrow. II. THE DISPOSITION TO BE CULTIVATED IN ORDER TO A HIGH STATE OF RELIGIOUS ENJOYMENT. 1. We must guard against whatever might incapacitate us for holy satisfaction : sin especially. The wine of heavenly consolation is poured into none but clean vessels. 2. Divine interpositions in our favour should be carefully noticed. If God keeps a book of remembrance of us, so should we of Him. As He treasures up our tears, we should treasure up His mercies. 3. We must watch and pray against a spirit of murmuring and unbelief. 4. We must guard against unreasonable doubts and fears as to our spiritual state, or our tears will drown our triumphs, and our lamentations silence our songs (Psa. xlvi. 1, 2). 5. The assistance of the Holy Spirit must be implored, who is the efficient cause of joy. III. THE REASONS WHICH SHOULD RENDER OUR JOY PERMANENT. Some duties are to be performed at particular times—this always. Godly sorrow, instead of being an impediment, is a preparative to joy. There are times which more especially call for joy—our conversion, the day of our espousals—the time of spiritual revival, &c. Yet there is no time in which it would be unsuitable. 1. Because its sources are unchangeable. The love, purpose, and promises of God are without variableness ; the blood of Christ never loses its virtue ; the efficacy of the Spirit is evermore the same. 2. Its benefits afford a powerful inducement for its continual preservation. " The joy of the Lord is our strength." It invigorates every grace, gives a fresh impulse to every duty, lightens our troubles, sweetens our mercies, and gives glory to God. 3. It will be the work of heaven, and should, therefore, be our employment on the way to it. (*B. Beddome, M.A.*) *Rejoice evermore :*—I. A CHRISTIAN PRIVILEGE. The Christian may rejoice evermore because—1. Nothing that befalls him can hurt him. 2. Everything must benefit him in proportion as it aims to injure him. II. A CHRISTIAN PRECEPT. The act

of rejoicing has a power—1. Remedial. 2. Acquiring. 3. Conquering. III. A
CHRISTIAN PROMISE. 1. As to the Christian's future. 2. That the cause for joy
should be inexhaustible. 3. That the duration of joy should be endless.
(*D. Thomas, D.D.*)  *Rejoice evermore* :—I. WHAT IS THIS REJOICING. There is a
carnal rejoicing (Luke xii. 19), and a spiritual rejoicing in God (Phil. iv. 4). 1. God
Himself, as God, is a lovely nature, and the object of our delight (Psa. cxix. 68 ;
cxlv. 2, 10 ; cxxx. 3). 2. We are to rejoice in God as revealed in Christ
(Luke i. 46, 47). 3. We rejoice in God in the fruits of our redemption (Rom.
v. 11 ; Psa. xxxii. 11). 4. We rejoice in God when we delight to do His will
and are fitted for His use and service (Psa. cxix. 14 ; 2 Cor. i. 12). 5. We
rejoice in God when we rejoice in the blessings of His providence, as they
come from Him and lead to Him (Joel ii. 23 ; Psa. v. 11 ; Deut. xxviii.
47, 48). II. HOW THIS MUST BE PERPETUAL. 1. In all estates and conditions.
(1) Affliction is not inconsistent with it (2 Cor. vi. 10 ; 1 Pet. i. 6 ; 2 Cor. vii. 4 ;
Acts xvi. 25). Whatever falleth out there are always these grounds for joy—
(*a*) God's all sufficiency (Hab. iii. 18). (*b*) The unshaken hope of heaven (Matt.
v. 12). (2) Affliction much promotes it (2 Cor. xii. 10 ; Rom. v. 3-5 ; Heb. xii. 11).
2. From first to last, because it is of use to us at all times. (1) Christianity is
begun with joy in the world, so in the soul (Luke ii. 10, 11 ; Acts viii. 8 ; xvi. 34 ;
Luke xix. 2 ; Acts ii. 41). (2) Our progress in the duties and hopes of the
gospel is carried on with joy (Phil. iii. 3). Rejoice evermore—(*a*) So as to
pray without ceasing (Job. xxvii. 10). (*b*) So as to give thanks in everything (Job i. 21). (3) The end comes with joy. (*a*) The joy of God
is the comfort of our declining years. (*b*) At death we enter into the joy of our
Lord. III. THE REASONS WHICH ENFORCE THIS DUTY. 1. God hath done so much
to raise it. (1) The Father gives Himself to us, and His favour as our
felicity and portion (Psa. iv. 6, 7). (2) The Son is our Saviour. Consider what
He has done to make our peace (Col. i. 20) ; to vanquish our enemies (Col. ii. 14,15) ;
to be the ransom of our souls (1 Tim. ii. 6) and the treasury of all comfort (John i.
16 ; Heb. vi. 18). Abraham rejoiced to see His day at a distance, shall not we now
it has come (Rom. xiv. 17). (3) The Holy Ghost as sanctifier lays the foundation
for comfort, pouring in the oil of grace, then the oil of gladness—whence " joy in
the Holy Ghost." 2. All the graces tend to this. (1) Faith (1 Pet. i. 8 ; Rom. xv.
13). (2) Hope (Rom. xii. 12 ; v. 2). (3) Love (Psa. xvi. 5, 6). 3. All the ordinances
and duties of religion are for the increase of joy. (1) Reading (1 John i. 4). (2)
Hearing (2 Cor. i. 24). (3) Prayer (John xvi. 24). (4) Meditation (Psa. cxl. 34).
IV. ARGUMENTS IN FAVOUR OF THIS DUTY. 1. Its necessity. (1) That you may own
God as your God; delighting in God is a duty of the first commandment (Psa.
xxxvii. 4). (2) That you may be thankful for the blessings God bestows in Christ.
(3) That you may follow the conduct of the Comforter (John xvi. 22). 2. Its
utility. (1) With respect to the temper and frame of our own hearts (Neh. viii. 10).
It quickeneth us to a life of holiness (Psa. xl. 8). (2) With respect to God's
acceptance. Rejoicing is—(*a*) More honourable to God (Micah vi. 3). (*b*) Most
pleasing to Him, since He so often calls for it. V. HOW TO PERFORM THIS DUTY. 1.
Be prepared for it. (1) Our state must be altered, for we are the children of wrath,
and under the curse. (2) Our hearts must be altered. (3) Our life. 2. Act it
continually. 3. Take heed you do not forfeit or damp it by sin (Psa. li. 8 ; Eph. iv.
30). 4. When lost renew your repentance and faith (1 John ii. 1). (*T. Manton, D.D.*)
*Rejoice evermore* :—How can man, constituted as He is, rejoice evermore? And if it be
the duty of the believer sometimes to think with sorrow of his sins, how can it be his
duty to be always glad ? Let two considerations serve for a reply. 1. The penitence required of the believer is not the unmitigated anguish of remorse, but a
feeling, painful, as from its very nature it must be, but soothed and sweetened by
the exercise of Christian faith and hope—a dark cloud, but gilded by the glorious
sunshine. 2. " Evermore " does not necessarily mean, without the slightest intermission, which is physically impossible, but without abandoning the practice—
habitually and onwards to the end. Even the calamities of life, and the sense of
his own unworthiness, must not make the believer permanently cease to be happy.
In order to the habitual experience of joy on the part of the child of God, his mind
must come into contact with what is fitted to make it glad ; and it is obvious from
the nature of the case, and from a multitude of texts (Isa. l. 10 ; Luke iii. 10, 11 ;
Acts viii. 39 ; Rom. v. 2, 11 ; xv. 13 ; 2 Cor. i. 12 ; 1 Thess. iii. 9, &c.), that spiritual
happiness may be derived from the following sources :—(1) The believing and
realizing apprehension of the gospel—the " glad tidings of great joy " ; (2) The

recognition, by faith and its fruits, of a personal interest in Christ; (3) Filial confidence in God; (4) The anticipation of the heavenly glory; (5) The promotion of religion in the world. (*A. S. Patterson, D.D.*) *Rejoicing according to individual capacity* :—Bless the Lord, I can sing, my heavenly Father likes to hear me sing. I can't sing as sweetly as some; but my Father likes to hear the crow as well as the nightingale, for He made them both. (*Billy Bray.*) *Christian rejoicing* :—Rejoice with a rejoicing universe. Rejoice with the morning stars, and let your adoring spirit march to the music of the hymning spheres. Rejoice with the jocund spring, in its gush of hope and its dancing glory, with its swinging insect clouds and its suffusion of multitudinous song; and rejoice with golden autumn, as he rustles his grateful sheaves, and clasps his purple hands, as he breathes his story of fruition, his anthem of promises fulfilled; as he breathes it softly in the morning stillness of ripened fields, or flings it in Æolian sweeps from lavish orchards and from branches tossing bounty into mellow winds. Rejoice with infancy, as it guesses its wondering way into more and more existence, and laughs and carols as the field of pleasant life enlarges on it, and new secrets of delight flow in through fresh and open senses. Rejoice with the second birth of your heaven-born soul, as the revelation of a second birth pour in upon it, and the glories of a new world amaze it. Rejoice with the joyful believer when he sings, " O Lord, I will praise Thee," &c. Rejoice with Him whose incredulous ecstasy has alighted on the great gospel secret; whose eye is beaming as none can beam save that which for the first time beholds the Lamb; whose awestruck countenance and uplifted hands are exclaiming, " This is my Beloved, and this is my Friend." Rejoice with saints and angels as they rejoice in a sight like this. Rejoice with Immanuel whose soul now sees of its travail. Rejoice with the ever blessed Three, and with a heaven whose work is joy. (*J. Hamilton, D.D.*) *The duty and the means of cheerfulness* :—If it be a part of Christian charity to alleviate the miseries of mankind, then the cultivation of a cheerful spirit is a Christian duty. Why should you lighten the sorrows of the poor by your alms, and make your own house miserable by your habitual gloom? And if you have learnt anything of human nature, you will know that among the pleasantest things that can find their way into a house where there is anxiety and want, are the music of a happy voice and the sunshine of a happy face. The best person to visit the aged and the poor—other things, of course, being equal—is the one whose step is the lightest, whose heart is the merriest, and who comes into a dull and solitary home like a fresh mountain breeze, or like a burst of sunlight on a cloudy day. No one can make a greater mistake than to suppose that he is too cheerful to be a good visitor of the sick and wretched. Cheerfulness is one of the most precious gifts for those who desire to lessen the sorrows of the world. It can do what wealth cannot do. Money may diminish external miseries; a merry heart will drive the interior grief away. It is possible to cherish and encourage this spirit of joyousness, even when it is not the result of natural temperament. Consider what it is that depresses you. If it is the consciousness of sin, often confessed, never heartily forsaken, appeal to Him who can pacify as well as pardon; master for a single week the temptation to which you habitually yield, and you will find yourself in a new world, breathing clearer air, and with a cloudless heaven above you. If it is incessant thought about your own personal affairs, escape from the contracted limits of your personal life by care for the wants of others. Determine, too, to think more of what is fair and generous and noble in human nature than of what is contemptible and selfish. Those who distrust the world and think meanly of it can never be happy. There is sin enough, no doubt; but there is more of goodness than some of us suppose. It makes my heart "merry" to think of the patience and courage with which many whom I know are bearing heavy troubles; the generosity with which some of the poor relieve the distresses of those more wretched than themselves; the firmness which some are showing in the presence of great temptations; the energetic devotion of others to the highest welfare of all whom their influence can reach. Christ has not come into the world for nothing. If sometimes it is necessary to dwell upon the moral evil which clings even to good men, and upon the terrible depravity of the outcasts from Christian society, I find in Him a refuge from the sore trouble which the vision of sin brings with it. He is ready to pardon the guiltiest, and to bring home to Himself those who have gone furthest astray. Why should those who have seen God's face be sad? " In His presence " both on earth and in heaven " there is fulness of joy." (*R. W. Dale, D.D.*) *Cheerfulness in God's service* :—This want of laughing, this fear of being joyful is a melancholy method of praise. It is ungrateful to God. I would rather dance like David than sit still like some Christians. I remember being in a church once in America. They certainly had a warm church, and that was pleasant; but in one sense it was a fine ice-house, for no one seemed to feel any joy. When we came out I was asked what I thought of the service. I said that if some negro had come in and howled out a " hallelujah," it would have been a joy; but nobody had shown anything but conceit—it was all intellectualism. (*G. Dawson, M.A.*)    *Happiness in all circumstances:*—When Richard Williams, of the Patagonian Mission, with his few companions were stranded on the beach by a high tide, and at the beginning of those terrible privations which terminated his life, he wrote in his diary: "I bless and praise God that this day has been, I think, the happiest of my life. The fire of Divine love has been burning on the mean altar of my breast, and the torchlight of faith has been in full trim, so that I have only had to wave it to the right or left in order to discern spiritual things in heavenly places." Later, when severe illness was added to circumstantial distress, he could say: "Not a moment sits wearily upon me. Sweet is the presence of Jesus; and oh, I am happy in His love." Again, though held fast by fatal disease, he wrote: "Ah, I am happy day and night, hour by hour. Asleep or awake, I am happy beyond the poor compass of language to tell. My joys are with Him whose delights have always been with the sons of men; and my heart and spirit are in heaven with the blessed." (*J. F. B. Tinling, B.A.*)    *Christian joy:*—If you have one joy now, and will become a Christian, you will have ten thousand joys then. The grace of God will not deplete you; it will not rob you of a single satisfaction. There is not one thing in all the round of enjoyments that will be denied you. God gives especial lease to the Christian for all sunlight, for all friendship, for all innocent beverages, for all exhilarations. I will tell you the difference. You go into a factory, and you see only three or four wheels turning, and you say to the manufacturer: "How is this? you have such a large factory, and yet three-fourths of the wheels are quiet." He says the water is low. A few weeks afterwards, you go in and find all the spindles flying, and all the bands working—fifty, or a hundred, or five hundred. "Why," you say: "there is a great change here." "Oh, yes," says the manufacturer, "the water has risen. We have more power now than before." I come into this man's soul, who has not surrendered himself to God, and I find there are faculties employed; but only a part of his nature is working. The water is low. After a while I come into that man's nature, and I find that all his capacities, all his energies are in full play. I say there is a great difference. The floods of Divine grace have poured their strength upon that soul, and whereas only a few faculties were employed then, now all the energies and capacities of the soul are in full work. In other words, he who becomes Christian is a thousand times more of a man than he was before he became a Christian. (*H. W. Beecher.*)    *The pleasantness of religion:*—Religion is often regarded as a morose and melancholy duty, a duty abridging delight rather than a delight irradiating duty. And much of the character both of the precept and conduct of the Christian Church has been well calculated to betray the world into this erroneous supposition. Extremes meet. And the extreme Puritan view of religion combines with the extreme Papal view in identifying religion with austerity. These opposite yet kindred asceticisms has done much to misinterpret to the world the true nature of religion. For surely it is obvious that God has not created His world to be a gloomy conventicle or intended the chambers of human life to be cheerless as a monastery. He has made the earth surpassingly beautiful and pleasant, rich in fragrance, song, and joy. And is it to be supposed that birds and trees and fields may laugh and sing, but that man, the top and crown of creation, is doomed to pass through life a sad and mirthless pilgrim? Does not the page of inspiration proclaim that (Prov. iii. 17). Angel voices all around us echo again the first Easter question, "Christian, why weepest thou?" "Rejoice," they say, "in the Lord always!" And again their message is, "Rejoice." No doubt the happiest religion has its yokes and crosses, its travails and its tears. Repentance and contrition are not things pleasant in themselves. The ascent up the hill of self-sacrifice is thorny, laborious, steep. But, like the brave mountaineer, the Christian enjoys the exhilaration of climbing, no less than he enjoys the serenity and largeness of the prospect from the summit. True pleasure is never the child of indolence. The intellectual giant, *e.g.*, who now sports with gladsomeness among the deep questions of the mind, found the first steps of his training wearisome and painful. It is only after years of mental effort that he has attained the elevation of pure and full intellectual delight. Similarly the pleasures of religion are not sweetest at the commencement. Ideals of pleasure also differ. The clearer and nobler the soul becomes, the deeper will be its delights in the pleasantness of religion. And what nourishment for the mind is comparable to the studies of religion? What contemplation so matchless as the contemplation of God? What ideals so beautiful as those of Christ? What aspiration so glorious as to copy Him? What manliness so robust, yet so refined, as the manliness of the Son of God? . . . The joys of meditation upon God, the delights of adoring the Author of the mysteries and the majesty of existence, the happiness of touching the hem of Christ's garment, and leaning on His breast, and shedding the tears of devotion at His feet, make the latest years of the religious life a continuous jubilee. (*J. W. Diggle, M.A.*)

Ver. 17. **Pray without ceasing.**—I. WHAT IS IT TO PRAY? 1. It is a desire. That is the nature of it. We may desire a thing—(1) With our mouths only (Isa. xxix. 13). (2) With our hearts only (1 Sam. i. 13). (3) Both with heart and mouth. This is prayer; and so prayer is both cordial and oral (John xvii. 1). 2. The subject: good things (1 Tim. iv. 8). (1) For our natural life. (a) For our being (James v. 14, 15). (2) For our well-being (Prov. xxx. 8). (3) For our spiritual life. (a) To understand the Scriptures (Psa. cxix. 18; James i. 5). (b) To repent of sin (Psa. li. 7, 10). (c) To believe in Christ (Luke xvii. 5). (d) To love God. (e) For pardon (Acts viii; Matt. vi. 13). (3) For our eternal life. (a) To hold out to the end (Psa. li. 12). (b) And then crown us with glory (2 Tim. iv. 7, 8). 3. The object: God, not saints. As appears—(1) From Scripture (Rom. x. 14; Luke xi. 2). (2) From reason. (a) Saints cannot hear us. (b) If they do they cannot help us (Isa. xlv. 20). (c) Prayer is a part of Divine worship. II. How DOTH IT APPEAR WE OUGHT TO PRAY. 1. God commands it (1 Tim. ii. 8). 2. It is part of His worship (Psa. xcv. 6, 7). 3. By this we give Him glory. (1) Of His sovereignty over us. (2) Of His immensity and omnipresence (Matt. vi. 6). (3) His all sufficiency. (4) His mercy. (5) His faithfulness to His promises. 4. This is the means appointed by God for our receipt of good things (Ezek. xxxvi. 37; Luke xi. 13). 5. He has promised good things to it (Matt. vii. 7). III. How SHOULD WE PRAY? 1. With outward reverence (Heb. xii. 28; Psa. xcv. 6; Isa. xlv. 23). The saints always did so: Daniel (iv. 10); Solomon (2 Chron. vi. 13); Peter (Acts ix. 40); Paul (Acts xx. 36; xxi. 5; Eph. iii. 14); Stephen (Acts vii. 60). Our Lord (Luke xxii. 41). 2. Inwardly. (1) With the understanding (1 Cor. xiv. 15). (2) The heart (Isa. xxix. 13; Ezek. xxxiii. 31; 1 Cor. xiv. 15). (3) In charity (1 Tim. ii. 8). (4) With respect to the promises (Gen. xxxii. 9-12). (5) In the name of Christ (John xiv. 13). (6) In faith (Heb. xi. 6). (7) To a right end (Matt. vi. 6; James iv. 3). (8) So as to expect the answer (Psa. xlv. 23). IV. WHEN SHOULD WE PRAY? Without ceasing. Not as if all our time was to be spent in prayer; but—1. So as always to have our hearts in a praying posture (Psa. lvii. 17). 2. So as to take all occasions of prayer (2 Sam. ix. 13; Luke ii. 37; xxiv. 53; Acts i. 14). 3. So as to pray in all conditions (Eph. vi. 18; James v. 13). 4. So as not to leave off praying for any mercy because God doth not at first hear us (Luke xviii. 1; 2 Cor. xii. 8, 9). 5. So as to pray every day (Luke i. 75; Matt. vi. 11). There is not a day we sin, nor a day but we want mercies. 6. So as to take all occasions to lift up our hearts to God in ejaculations (Luke xvii. 5; Neh. ii. 4; v. 19; xiii. 22; Mark ix. 24; 1 Sam. i. 13). (*Bp. Beveridge.*) *The nature, seasons, and obligations of prayer:*—I. THE NATURE OF PRAYER. It is an act of worship, consisting of four great parts. 1. Adoration. 2. Confession. 3. Petition. 4. Thanksgiving. II. THE PRINCIPAL SEASONS OF PRAYER. 1. The Sabbath. 2. Such occasional days as are warranted by the Word of God and appointed by the Church. 3. The morning and evening of every day. 4. The times at which we receive our food. 5. Besides these regular seasons of prayer, there are many others continually occurring which can be designated by no general name. The times at which all peculiar blessings are bestowed on us are times of prayer. In the same manner is prayer our especial duty at those seasons in which we are peculiarly distressed in body or in mind, are in peculiar danger, are exposed peculiarly to temptations, are sick, are bereaved of beloved friends, are threatened with alarming evils, or whenever we find ourselves the subjects of peculiar sloth, reluctance to our duty, or ready to repine at the dispensations of God's providence, or to distrust His faithfulness or His mercy. Nor are we less obviously called to the duties of prayer and thanksgiving by the peculiar prosperity or distresses, the dangers or deliverances, of our country. In the same manner the great concerns of the Church of God ought continually to be subjects of fervent supplications. III. OUR OBLIGATIONS TO PERFORM THIS DUTY. To pray—1. Is a dictate of conscience and common sense. 2. Is an injunction of Scripture. 3. Is after the example of Christ. 4. Promotes our own well-being. God has taught us that He will be "inquired of" by mankind for the good which He is pleased to bestow upon them. The only promise that He will give or that we shall receive blessings is made to such as ask. (*Timothy Dwight, D.D.*) *Habitual communion with God in prayer*:—There are two modes of praying mentioned in Scripture : the one is prayer at set times and places and in set forms; the other is what the text speaks of—continual or habitual prayer. The former of these is what is commonly called prayer, whether it be public or private. The other kind of praying may also be called holding communion with God, or living in God's sight, and this may be done all through the day, wherever we are, and is commanded us as the duty, or rather the characteristic, of those who are really servants and friends of Jesus Christ. These two kinds of praying are also natural duties. I mean we should in a way be bound to attend to them, even if we were born in a heathen country and had never heard of the Bible. For our conscience and reason would lead us to practice them, if we did but attend to these Divinely-given informants. Most men indeed, I fear, neither pray at fixed times, nor do they cultivate an habitual communion with Almighty God. Indeed, it is too plain how most men pray. They pray now and then, when they feel particular need of God's assistance; when they are in trouble or in apprehension of danger; or when their feelings are unusually excited. They do not know what it is either to be habitually religious or to devote a certain number of minutes at fixed times to the thought of God. Nay, the very best Christian, how lamentably deficient is he in the spirit of prayer! Let any man compare in his mind how many times he has prayed when in trouble with how seldom he has returned thanks when his prayers have been granted; or the earnestness with which he prays against expected sufferings with the languor and unconcern of his thanksgivings afterwards, and he will soon see how little he has of the real habit of prayer, and how much his religion depends on accidental excitement, which is no test of a religious heart. Or supposing he has to repeat the same prayer for a month or two, the cause of using it continuing, let him compare the earnestness with which he first said it, and tried to enter into it, with the coldness with which he at length uses it. Why is this, except that his perception of the unseen world is not the true view which faith gives (else it would last as that world itself lasts, but a mere dream, which endureth for a night, and is succeeded by a hard worldly joy in the morning? Is God habitually in our thoughts? Do we think of Him and of His Son our Saviour through the day? When we eat and drink, do we thank Him, not as a mere matter of form, but in spirit? When we do things in themselves right, do we lift up our minds to Him and desire to promote His glory? (*Plain Sermons by Contributors to "Tracts for the Times."*) *The spirit of prayer*:—Let us—I. EXPLAIN the injunction in our text. It is the practice of the Scripture writers to use broad and forcible terms to express the extent or the intensity of their ideas. Such a phrase demands—1. The frequent act of prayer. Thus, when St. Paul declares to the Romans (i. 9) that "without ceasing he made mention of them always in his prayers," he seems to refer to his intercessions for them at his stated approaches to the throne of grace; for when he tells the Ephesians (i. 16), in a similar phrase, that he "ceased not to give thanks for them," we find this to be his meaning, from the sentence that he immediately adds, "making mention of you in my prayers." Just as he writes to the Philippians (i. 3, 4). In all cases, habits are formed only by the repetition of acts; and therefore devotion is essential to devoutness. 2. The persevering habit of prayer—the patient waiting upon God in the face of difficulties and discouragement. For when the apostle says, "pray without ceasing," his object is, as may be gathered from the context, to animate them to persevere in supplication, notwithstanding their disappointment with respect to the immediate coming of the Lord, their sorrow for the loss of Christian friends, and their experience of unruly and unstable brethren. 3. The pervading spirit of prayer. For without this all stated acts and persevering diligence of outward supplication will be vain. Prayer consists not in those acts, but in the spirit and temper of devoutness, generated, exercised, kept up under difficulty by those acts. II. ENFORCE it. It might, indeed, appear at first sight strange that such a duty should need enforcement; that no very pressing argument would be necessary to persuade to such a privilege. Let me, then, press it upon you—1. As a remedy for perplexity. Man is ignorant and foolish; and he has daily proofs that it is not in himself to direct his steps. 2. As a consolation under trouble. 3. As your strength against temptation. No sin can be successfully resisted without fervent prayer. (*T. Griffith, M.A.*)　　*Pray without ceasing:*—The position of the text is suggestive. 1. It comes after " Rejoice evermore," and as if that had staggered, the reader, Paul now tells him how to do it: " Always pray." The more praying the more rejoicing. 2. In everything give thanks. When joy and prayer are married their firstborn is gratitude. I. WHAT DO THESE WORDS IMPLY? 1. That the voice is not an essential element in prayer. It would be unseemly and impossible to pray aloud unceasingly. There would be no opportunity for any other duty. We may speak a thousand words and never pray, and yet cry most effectually, like Moses, and never utter a word. The voice is helpful, but not necessary, to the reality or prevalence of prayer. 2. The posture is not of great importance. Kneeling is a beautiful token, but who could be always kneeling? and, besides, good men have stood, sat, &c. 3. The place is not essential; if it were, our churches should be large enough for us all to live in them; and if for the highest acceptance we need aisle, chancel, &c., then farewell green lanes, fields, &c., for we must without ceasing dwell where your fragrance can never reach us. But this is ridiculous. " God dwelleth not in temples made with hands." 4. The text overthrows the idea of particular times, for every second must be suitable for prayer. It is good to have seasons, but superstition to suppose that one hour or season is holier than another. Every day is a red letter day. 5. A Christian has no right to go into any place where he could not continue to pray. Hence many amusements stand condemned at once. Imagine a collect for the shooting match, the racecourse, the theatre. Anything that is right for you to do you may consecrate with prayer. II. WHAT DOES THIS ACTUALLY MEAN? 1. A privilege. Kings hold their levees at certain times, and then their courtiers are admitted; but the King of kings holds a constant levee. 2. A precept. It means—(1) Never abandon prayer for any cause. You must not pray until you are saved and then leave off ; nor after you are experienced in grace; nor because of Satan's temptation that it is all vain ; nor because the heavens are brass, or your heart cold ; nor because you cannot answer sceptical objections. No difficult problem about digestion prevents you eating. As we breathe without ceasing, so we must pray. (2) Never suspend the regular offering of prayer. Never give up the morning and evening prayer. The clock is to go all day, but there is a time for winding it up. 3. Between these hours of devotion be much in ejaculatory prayer. While your hands are busy with the world, let your hearts still talk with God. He who prays without ceasing uses little darts or hand-grenades of godly desire, which he casts forth at every available interval. 4. We must always be in the spirit of prayer. Our heart must be like the magnetic needle, which always has an inclination towards the pole. In an iron ship it exhibits serious deflections ; if you force it to the east, you have only to take the pressure away and immediately it returns to its beloved pole again. So let your hearts be magnetized with prayer, so that if the finger of duty turns it away from the immediate act, there may still be the longing desire, to be acted upon the first possible moment. As perfume lies in flowers even when they do not shed their fragrance, so let prayer lie in your hearts. 5. Let your actions be consistent with and a continuation of your prayers. The text cannot mean that I am always to be in direct devotion, for the mind needs variety of occupation, and could not without madness continue always in the exercise of one function. We must therefore change the manner of operation if we are to pray without ceasing. He who prays for his fellow-creatures and thus seeks their good is praying still. III. How CAN WE OBEY THESE WORDS? 1. Let us labour to prevent all sinful interruptions. 2. Let us avoid all unnecessary interruptions. If we know of anything that we can escape which is likely to disturb the spirit of prayer let us shun it. 3. Sometimes we are too busy to pray. This is a great mistake. Luther said, " I have so much to do to-day that I shall never get through it without three hours prayer." Sir H. Havelock rose two hours before the time to march that he might have time for Bible reading and communion with God. Payson, pressed by examinations, &c., abridged the time for private prayer, but when he corrected his mistake, he confessed that he did more in a single week than in twelve months before. God can multiply our ability to make use of them. 4. We must strive against indolence, lethargy, and indifference. We need waking up. Routine grows upon us. 5. Fight against despair of being heard. If we have not been heard after six times we must, like Elijah, go again seven times. Be importunate: heaven's gate does not open to every runaway knock. 6. Never cease through presumption. IV. WHY SHOULD WE OBEY THIS PRECEPT? Because—1. It is of Divine authority. 2. The Lord always deserves to be worshipped. 3. You want a blessing in all the work you are doing. 4. You are always in danger of being tempted. Carry your sword in your hand; never sheathe it. 5. You always want something. 6. Others always want your prayers. (*C. H. Spurgeon.*)    *Unceasing prayer :*—I. PRAYER MUST BE INCESSANT. 1. From the nature of the act. (1) Prayer is intercourse with God, the Being in whom the creature lives and moves. To stop praying, therefore, is to break the connection. A man must breathe without ceasing because thereby his whole physical system is kept in right relation with the atmosphere. It is as strictly true that religious being depend upon communication with God. (2) It may be objected that prayerless men suffer no distress. If a human body is removed from the air and shut up in the Black Hole of Calcutta, the report comes at once from the physical organization that the established relation of the fleshly nature and the world has been interfered with. (*a*) To this we reply that as man is composed of two natures, so he lives two lives, and for this reason he is able to gratify the desires of one nature and lead only one life here; it is possible for the flesh to live and the soul to be dead in sin. Like an amphibious animal, if man can absorb his lower nature in the objects of sense, he is able to dispense with intercourse between God and his higher nature without distress. If the amphibian can breathe on land, he need not gasp like a fish when taken from his native element. (*b*) But while this is so, the soul, the principal part of man, cannot permanently escape distress if out of communication with God. The half-way life is not possible in eternity. The amphibian cannot live year after year in one element. Each nature asserts its rights ultimately, and if its wants are not met suffocation is the consequence. And so man cannot live in only one of his natures for ever. (*c*) We appeal to the Christian and ask him whether complete cessation of prayer would not work as disastrously to his soul as the stoppage of breath would in his body. Suppose that that calming, sustaining intercourse were shut off, would not your soul gasp and struggle? What a sinking sensation would fill the heart of the afflicted or bereaved if it were found impossible to pray! Man has become so accustomed to this privilege that he does not know its full richness. Like other gifts, nothing but deprivation would enable him to apprehend its full value. 2. From the fact that God is continually the hearer of prayer. An incessant appeal supposes one incessant reply. God does not hear His people to-day and turn a deaf ear to-morrow. He promised to hear in His temple continually (2 Chron. viii. 12–16); nor does its destruction disprove the Divine faithfulness. If the worshipper ceases to go into the temple, God, of course, goes out of it. God, as Creator, has established such a relation between the body of man and the air that there must be a continual supply of air; and therefore He has surrounded him with the whole atmosphere. The instant he inhales with his lungs, he finds the element ready. And God, as Saviour, has established such a relation between the renewed soul and Himself that there must be unceasing communion, and therefore in the gospel proffers Himself, so that whenever the heart pants out its desire it finds one ever present supply. II. THE FEASABILITY OF UNCEASING PRAYER. The fact that prayer is the only mode by which the creature can hold intercourse with his Maker, goes to prove that such intercourse is practicable. It cannot be that God has called a dependent being into existence and cut off all access. If the intercourse is broken, it cannot be by God. To pray without ceasing :—1. Man must have an inclination to pray. (1) Volition is impotent without inclination. A man does not continuously follow an earthly calling unless his heart is in it. The two differ as stream from fountain. A man's resolutions spring out of his disposition, and in the long run do not go counter to it. Suppose an entire destitution of the inclination to draw near to God, and then by an effort of will lashing yourself up to the disagreeable work; even supposing such prayer acceptable, you could not make it unceasing by this method. You would soon grow weary. (2) But if the inclination do exist, prayer will be constant and uniform. A good tree cannot *but* bear good fruit, and year after year without ceasing; because there is a foundation laid for this at the root. So if the soul is inclined towards God, nothing can prevent it from approaching Him—not sorrows, imprisonment, death. 2. This inclination must be strengthened by cultivation. Because it is the product of the Holy Spirit, it does not follow that we may neglect the means of development. You cannot originate a flower; but you must supply it with means of nurture, or it will die. And so with the inclination to pray. The means are—(1) Regularity in the practice of prayer. Man is a creature of habit, and whatever he leaves to chance is likely to be neglected. He who has no particular time for winding his watch will often let it run down. There is a time for everything, and that Christian will be the most likely to pray without ceasing who at particular times enters his closet and shuts the door. (2) The practice of ejaculatory prayer. Prayer does not depend so much upon its length as its intensity. We are not compelled to go to some central point, as Jerusalem or Mecca. In any section of space or point of time, the ejaculation of the soul may reach the Eternal mind, and be rewarded by the Hearer of prayer. (*Prof. Shedd.*) *The spirit of prayer:*—The life of religion consists in dependence upon God; and prayer is the breathing forth of this life, the exercise and energizing of this life. I. THE EXPLANATION OF THE INJUNCTION OF THE TEXT. 1. The frequent act of prayer. 2. The persevering habit of prayer. 3. The pervading spirit of prayer. II. THE ENFORCEMENT OF THE TEXT. 1. As a remedy for perplexity. 2. As a consolation under trouble. 3. As strength against temptation. (*T. Griffith, A.M.*) *Unceasing prayer:*—I. THE DUTY. Two extreme errors are to be avoided—that of the ancient Euchites, who took these words literally, and that of those who fail in constant prayer. 1. For those who would never intermit this exercise. Let us explain the word. A thing is said to be done without ceasing which is done at constant times and seasons, as often as they occur (2 Sam. xix. 13; ix. 12; Rom. ix. 2; 1 Thess. ii. 13; 2 Tim. i. 3). The matter may bear a good sense if you interpret the apostle's direction either of—(1) The habit of prayer or praying temper (Psa. civ. 9). (2) Vital prayer. All duties may be resolved into prayer or praise (Psa. xxv. 5; Prov. xxiii. 27). (3) Continuance in prayer till we receive the answer (Luke xviii. 1; Matt. xv. 22–28; 2 Cor. xii. 8). (4) Frequency of return in the occasions of prayer. Praying—(*a*) At all times, never omitting the seasons of prayer, stated or occasional (Matt. vi. 11). (*b*) In all conditions, afflicted or prosperous (James v. 13; Jer. ii. 27; 1 Tim. iv. 5). (*c*) In every business, civil or sacred (Prov. iii. 6; Gen. xxiv. 12; 2 Thess. iii. 5). 2. To those who excuse unfrequent prayer on the pretence that they are not bound to pray always, and that the time of duty is not exactly stated in the New Testament. (1) Though there is no express rule, yet the duty is required in the strictest and most comprehensive terms (Eph. vi. 18; Col. iv. 2: Psa. lxii. 8; Luke xxi. 36). (2) The examples of the saints should move us. David (Psa. lv. 17); Daniel (Dan. vi. 10). (3) The ceasing of the daily sacrifice was accounted a great misery (Dan. ix. 27). (4) God trusts love, and would not particularly define the times of the duty; surely, then, we should be more open-hearted and liberal with Him. He expects much from a willing people (Psa. cx. 3). (5) God complains of His people's neglect (Jer. ii. 32). II. THE REASONS. 1. With respect to God—(1) We acknowledge His Being in prayer (Heb. xi. 6; Psa. lxv. 2). (2) We acknowledge His supreme providence (Matt. vi. 11). 2. With respect to the nature of prayer. It is the nearest familiarity which a soul can have with God. Now acts of friendship must not be rare, but constant (Job xxii. 21). Men that often visit one another are acquainted. Prayer is visiting God (Isa. xxvi. 16). This is necessary—(1) For present comfort; it gives boldness to come to God in your necessities if you daily wait upon Him (Eph. iii. 12). A child is not afraid to go to his father, nor a friend to a friend in trouble. (2) For future acceptance (Luke xxi. 36). 3. With respect to the new nature (Zech. xii. 10; Acts ix. 11). 4. With respect to the necessities of the saints (James i. 5; Eph. iii. 10; Heb. iv. 16). 5. With respect to its utility and profit. (1) The three radical graces—faith, hope, and love—are acted on and increased in prayer (Jude 20, 21; Psa. cxvi. 1, 2). (2) The three related duties—joy, prayer, thanksgiving—are promoted by frequent prayer (Phil. iv. 6, 7; Psa. cxvi. 2; 1 Sam. i. 27, 28). (*T. Manton, D.D.*) *Prayer all pervading:*—A man cannot really be religious one hour and not religious the next. We might as well say that he could be in a state of good health one hour and in bad health the next. A man who is religious is religious morning, noon, and night; his religion is a certain character, a mould in which his thoughts, words, and actions are cast, all forming parts of one and the same whole. He sees God in all things; every course of action he directs towards those spiritual objects which God has revealed to Him; every occurrence of the day, every event, every person met with, all news which he hears, he measures by the standard of God's will. And a person who does this may be said almost literally to pray without ceasing; for, knowing himself to be in God's presence, he is continually led to address Him reverently, whom he always sets before him, in the inward language of prayer and praise, of humble confession and joyful trust. (*J. H. Newman, D.D.*)        *The all pervasiveness of prayer :—* Prayer is to be regarded not only as a distinct exercise of religion, for which its own time must be set apart, but as a process woven into the texture of the Christian's mind, and extending through the length and breadth of his life. Like the golden thread in a tissue, it frequently disappears beneath the common threads; yet, nevertheless, it is substantially there, like a stream running underground for a certain period of its course. Suddenly the thread emerges into sight again on the upper surface of the tissue, and suddenly again disappears; and thus it penetrates the whole texture, although occasionally hidden. (*Dean Goulburn.*)        *Watching and prayer :—* Venice may well call upon us to note with reverence, that of all the towers which are still seen rising like a branchless forest from her islands, there is but one whose office was other than that of summoning to prayer, and that one was a watch tower only. (*J. Ruskin.*)        *Regularity in prayer :—* Sir Thomas Abney had for many years practised family prayer regularly; he was elected Lord Mayor of London, and on the night of his election he must be present at a banquet; but when the time came for him to call his family together in prayer, having no wish either to be a Pharisee or to give up his practice, he excused himself to the guests in this way : he said he had an important engagement with a very dear friend, and they must excuse him for a few minutes. It was most true; his dearest friend was the Lord Jesus, and family prayer was an important engagement; and so he withdrew for awhile to the family altar, and in that respect prayed without ceasing. (*C. H. Spurgeon.*) *Example of constant prayer :—* Fletcher's whole life was a life of prayer; and so intensely was his mind fixed upon God, that he sometimes said, "I would not move from my seat without lifting up my heart to God." "Whenever we met," says Mr. Vaughan, "if we were alone, his first salute was, 'Do I meet you praying?' And if we were talking on any point of Divinity, when we were in the depth of our discourse, he would often break off abruptly and ask, 'Where are our hearts now?' If ever the misconduct of an absent person was mentioned, his usual reply was, 'Let us pray for him.'" (*Life of Fletcher of Madeley.*)        *Necessity of constant prayer :* —"Some graces, like the lungs, are always in use." "Pray without ceasing"; "be thou in the fear of the Lord all the day long"; and such like exhortations appertain to continuous duties. Thus David says, "I have set the Lord always before me"—he was always living in the presence of God. Other parts of the human frame are exercised occasionally, but the lungs are always at work; and, even so, certain of the graces are in active motion in their appointed seasons; but faith never ceases to believe in the Lord Jesus, for it is essential to spiritual vitality. Hence we ought never to go where we shall be out of the atmosphere of heaven. Lungs must have air, and cannot endure a dense smoke or a poisonous gas; nor can faith bear error, false doctrine, and evil conversation. Since we always need the pure air of heaven, let us not go where it cannot be found. Who in his senses would desire to have been in the Black Hole of Calcutta? Who wishes to dwell where drunkenness and loose living abound? How can faith breathe in such a suffocating atmosphere? (*C. H. Spurgeon.*)        *Constant prayer in practice :—* At a monthly meeting of ministers in London, a question was proposed to be discussed at the next meeting, viz., "How can we pray always?" A woman at the bottom of the room, attending to the fire, turned round and said, "Why, gentlemen, I could answer that question now." Ah," said a minister, "Susan, do you know how to pray always?" "I hope so;" said Susan. "But," said the minister, "you have so much to attend to; how can you find time to pray always?" "Oh," said Susan, "the greater the variety I have to attend to, the more I am assisted to pray. In the morning, when I open my eyes, I pray, 'Lord, open the eyes of my understanding, that I may behold wondrous things out of Thy law.' Whilst I am dressing I pray, 'Lord, may I be clothed in the robe of righteousness, and adorned with the garment of salvation!' As I am washing myself I pray, 'O Lord, may I be washed in the fountain opened for sin and uncleanness!' When kindling the fire I pray, 'O Lord, kindle a fire of sacred love in this cold heart of mine!' And whilst sweeping the room I pray, 'Lord, may my heart be swept clean of all its abominations!' And so, gentlemen, I am praying all the day!" O happy woman! (*Clerical Library.*)        *Value of constant prayer :—* Can you stand on the beach a moment? You can scarcely see, but yet you may discern, by the lights of lanterns, sundry brave men launching the life-boat. It is out; they have taken their seats—helmsmen and rowers, all strong hearts, determined to save their fellows or to perish. They have gotten far away now into the midst of the billows, and we have lost sight of them; but in spirit we will take our stand in the midst of the boat. What a sea rolled in just then! If she were not built for such weather, she would surely have been overset. See that tremendous wave, and how the boat leaps like a sea-bird over its crest. See now again, it has plunged into a dreary furrow, and the wind, like some great plough, turns up the water on either side as though it were clods of mould. Surely the boat will find her grave, and be buried in the sheet of foam;—but no, she comes out of it, and the dripping men draw a long breath. But the mariners are discouraged; they have strained themselves bending to yonder oars, and they would turn back, for there is small hope of living in such a sea, and it is hardly possible that they will ever reach the wreck. But the brave captain cries out, "Now, my bold lads, for God's sake, send her on! A few more pulls of the oar, and we shall be alongside; the poor fellows will be able to hold on a minute or two longer—now pull as for dear life!" See how the boat leaps; see how she springs as though she were a living thing—a messenger of mercy intent to save. Again he says, "Once more, once again, and we will do it!" No, she has been dashed aside from the ship for a moment; that sea all but stove her in; but the helmsman turns her round, and the captain cries, "Now, my boys, once more!" And every man pulls with lusty sinews, and the poor shipwrecked ones are saved. Ay, it is just so with us now. Long have Christ's ministers, long have Christ's Church, pulled with the gospel life-boat. Let us pull again. Every prayer is a fresh stroke of the oar, and all of you are oarsmen. Yes, ye feeble women, ye confined to your beds, shut up in your chambers, who can do nothing else but pray, ye are all oarsmen in this great boat. Pull yet once more, and this week let us drive the boat ahead, and it may be it will be the last tremendous struggle that shall be required; for sinners shall be saved, and the multitude of the redeemed shall be accomplished. Not we, but grace shall do the work; yet is it ours to be workers for God. (*C. H. Spurgeon.*)    *Continuous and stated prayer :* —Prayer is the act of spiritual respiration; that true prayer can no more be limited to certain hours than respiration can. Yet even the image itself does not warrant us in thinking lightly of the virtue of stated prayer. It is true, indeed, that life can be supported even in the populous market, in the crowded street, nay, in the worst ventilated alleys, so long as respiration continues; but what a source of health and strength would the poor overwrought artizan find, if he could resort now and then to the transparent air of the open country, undefiled by smoke; to the purple-heathered down, where sweet gales fan the cheek; or to the margin of the ocean, over whose surface careers the invigorating wind! In spots like these we not only breathe, but breathe easily, freely, and spontaneously; the mere process of animal life is a delight to us, and with every breath we drink in health. Such is the effect of an hour of stated prayer after a day busily, yet devoutly spent. That hour wonderfully recruits the energies of the soul which human infirmity has caused to flag; and if we cannot say with truth that such an hour is absolutely necessary to spiritual existence, yet we can say that it is absolutely necessary to spiritual health and well-being. (*Dean Goulburn.*)    *Prayer independent of moods :*—The late Mrs. Prentiss, daughter of the saintly Edward Payson, was pre-eminently a woman of prayer. From her early years prayer was her delight. In describing the comforts of her chamber in the Richmond School, she valued as its crowning charm the daily presence of the Eternal King, who condescended to make it His dwelling-place. She was accustomed to speak of learning the mysterious art of prayer by an apprenticeship at the throne of grace. She saw that prayer is not to be made dependent on the various states of emotion in which one comes to God. "The question," she said, "is not one of mere delight." She illustrated in her own quaint way the truth that moods have nothing to do with the duty of prayer. "When one of your little brothers asks you to lend him your knife, do you inquire first what is the state of his mind? If you do, what reply can he make but this: 'The state of my mind is, I want your knife.'" (*J. L. Nye.*)    *Prayer a training for prayer :*—Manton says, "By running and breathing yourselves every day, you are the fitter to run in a race; so the oftener you come into God's presence, the greater confidence, and freedom, and enlargement it will bring." No doubt by praying we learn to pray; and the more we pray the oftener we can pray, and the better we can pray. He who prays by fits and starts is never likely to attain to that effectual, fervent prayer, which availeth much. Prayer is good, the habit of prayer is better, but the spirit of prayer is the best of all. It is in the spirit of prayer that we pray without ceasing, and this can never be acquired by the man who ceases to pray. It is wonderful what distances men can run who have long practised the art, and it is equally marvellous for what a length of time they can maintain a high speed after they have once acquired stamina and skill in using their muscles. Great power in prayer is within our reach, but we must go to work to obtain it. Let us never imagine that Abraham could have interceded so successfully for Sodom if he had not been all his lifetime in the practice of communion with God. Jacob's all-night at Peniel was not the first occasion upon which he had met his God. We may even look upon our Lord's most choice and wonderful prayer with His disciples before His Passion as the flower and fruit of His many nights of devotion, and of His often rising up a great while before day to pray. A man who becomes a great runner has to put himself in training, and to keep himself in it ; and that training consists very much of the exercise of running. Those who have distinguished themselves for speed have not suddenly leaped into eminence, but have long been runners. If a man dreams that he can become mighty in prayer just when he pleases, he labours under a great mistake. The prayer of Elias, which shut up heaven and afterwards opened its floodgates, was one of a long series of mighty prevailings with God. Oh, that Christian men would remember this ! Perseverance in prayer is necessary to prevalence in prayer. Those great intercessors, who are not so often mentioned as they ought to be in connection with confessors and martyrs, were nevertheless the grandest benefactors of the Church ; but it was only by abiding at the mercy-seat that they attained to be such channels of mercy to men. We must pray to pray, and continue in prayer that our prayers may continue. O Thou, by whom we come to God, seeing Thou hast Thyself trodden the way of prayer, and didst never turn from it, teach me to remain a suppliant as long as I remain a sinner, and to wrestle in prayer so long as I have to wrestle with the powers of evil. Whatever else I may outgrow, may I never dream that I may relax my supplications. (*C. H. Spurgeon.*)  *Ejaculatory prayer :*—Ejaculations take not up any room in the soul. They give liberty of callings, so that at the same instant one may follow his proper vocation. The husbandman may dart forth an ejaculation, and not make a balk the more ; the seaman, nevertheless, steer his ship right in the darkest night. Yea, the soldier at the same time may shoot out his prayer to God, and aim his pistol at his enemy, the one better hitting the mark for the other. The field wherein bees feed is no whit the barer for their biting ; when they have taken their full repast on flowers or grass, the ox may feed, the sheep fat on their reversions. The reason is, because those little chemists distil only the refined part of the flower, leaving only the grosser substance thereof. So ejaculations bind not men to any bodily observance, only busy the spiritual half, which maketh them consistent with the prosecution of any other employment. (*T. Fuller, D.D.*)  *Prayer without petition :*—Prayer is not always petition, thanksgiving, confession, adoration, &c. ; it is often an unuttered and unutterable communion. A nervous clergyman, who could only compose to advantage when absolutely alone and undisturbed, thoughtlessly left his study door unlocked, and his little three-year-old child softly opened the door and came in. He was disturbed, and, a little impatiently asked, " My child, what do you want ? " " Nothing, papa." " Then what did you come in here for ? " " Just because I wanted to be with you," was the reply. To come into God's presence and wait before Him, wanting nothing but to be with Him—how such an hour now and again would rest us ! We have a friend who leaves his business-place, especially when particularly burdened with care, and rides up to the great cathedral, where he sits down for an hour, and then goes back again to business. He says, " It is so quiet there, it rests and quiets me." How much more might we find a quiet resting-place for our weary souls and bodies, by just resting in the Lord, sitting without petition at His feet, or as John, leaning our heads upon His bosom. (*Independent.*)  *Prayer always seasonable :*—There is nothing which is right for us to do, but it is also right to ask that God would bless it ; and, indeed, there is nothing so little but the frown of God can convert it into the most sad calamity, or His smile exalt it into a most memorable mercy ; and there is nothing we can do but its complexion for weal or woe depends entirely on what the Lord will make it. It is said of Matthew Henry, that no journey was undertaken, or any subject or course of sermons entered upon, no book committed to the press, nor any trouble apprehended or felt, without a particular application to the mercy-seat for direction, assistance, and success. It is recorded of Cornelius Winter that he seldom opened a book, even on general subjects, without a moment's prayer. The late Bishop Heber, on each new incident of his history, or on the eve of any undertaking, used to compose a brief prayer, imploring special help and guidance. A physician, of great celebrity, used to ascribe much of his success to three maxims of his father's, the last and best of which was, "Always pray for your patients." *Continuous prayer :*—Dr. Raleigh used to say that he could not preach without communion with nature, and this meant, for him, communion with God. Those who knew him best knew that he lived in an inner world of prayer. He seldom spoke of such experiences; but he has said, " I cannot always pray when I would, but some days I seem to pray all day long." He used to think out his sermons during his solitary walks, and his freshest thoughts came to him under the open sky. (*Life of Dr. Raleigh.*) *Prayer a security :*—There is a curious fish found in some of the Indian rivers, which may be called the river Remora. Nature has provided it with a sucker beneath the jaws, which enables it to attach itself to a rock, and so resist the terrific current to which it is exposed in the rainy seasons. What that provision is to the fish, prayer is to you. By it you may cling to the rock, though all else threatens to sweep you away. *Given to prayer :*—" During his seclusion at Enderley," writes one of the biographers of Robert Hall, " almost entirely without society, he spent much of his time in private devotion, and not infrequently set apart whole days for prayer and fasting—a practice which he continued to the end of life, deeming it essential to the revival and preservation of personal religion. When able to walk, he wandered in the fields and sought the shady grove, which often echoed with the voice of prayer and witnessed the agony of his supplications. He was frequently so absorbed in these sacred exercises as to be unaware of the approach of persons passing by, many of whom recollected with deep emotion the fervour and importunity of his addresses at the mercy-seat, and the groanings which could not be uttered. His whole soul appears, indeed, to have been in a state of constant communion with God; his lonely walks amid the woodland scenery were rendered subservient to that end, and all his paths were bedewed with the tears of penitential prayer. Few men have spent more time in private devotion, or resorted to it with more relish, or had a deeper practical conviction of its benefits and its pleasures, as well as of its obligation as a duty binding upon all." (*Joseph Cook.*)

Ver. 18. **In everything give thanks, for this is the will of God in Christ Jesus concerning you.**—*Thanksgiving :*—The duty and privilege of praise are not appreciated. Worship—ascribing worth to God and describing His worth—is in His Word the leading feature, as in modern days it is the least feature of the assemblies of saints. Worship implies a thankful frame. Nothing left outside of the range of this injunction, because to a true believer all things work together for good. Compare Eph. v. 20; Col. iii. 17. I. It is THE FRUIT OF FAITH. Natural gratitude is the natural pleasure felt in prosperity ; gracious gratitude blesses God, like Job in adversity, because of faith in His wisdom and goodness. II. It is ONE OF THE FOREMOST OF BLESSINGS, and parent of all other graces. So says Cicero. It disposes to contentment in all conditions, and puts a bridle on desire. III. IT FINDS BLESSINGS as a magnet finds steel. IV. It FITS FOR GREATER BLESSINGS. God gives more abundantly where previous gifts are properly valued (Psa. l. 23). Chrysostom said " There is but one calamity—sin " ; and after many sorrows died, exclaiming, " God be praised for everything ! " (*A. T. Pierson, D.D.*) *Thankfulness :*—I. To WHOM MUST WE GIVE THANKS ? Only to God : because (Psa. c. 4) —1. It is only by Him we are preserved from evil (Psa. cxxi. 7). 2. It is only from Him that we have anything that is good (James i. 17). 3. He only is good in Himself (Psa. cvii. 1; cxxxvi. 1; Luke xviii. 19). II. How SHOULD WE GIVE THANKS TO HIM ? 1. By a humble confession of our own unworthiness (Gen. xxxii. 10 ; Eph. iii. 8), through sin (Psa. li. 5 ; 1 Cor. xv. 9), and our abuse of God's mercies (Jude 4). 2. By a humble acknowledgment of Him in all we have (Prov. iii. 6). His power (Psa. cxxxv. 1, 6) ; goodness (Psa. cxlv. 1, 2, 9); mercy (Psa. cxxxvi. 1-3). 3. By admiring Him in all we have, and praising (1 Chron. xxix. 12, 13). 4. By improving all for His glory (Prov. iii. 9). 5. By walking before Him in all well pleasing (2 Tim. i. 3). III. WHAT MUST WE THANK HIM FOR ? For all things (Eph. v. 20). 1. Our mercies. (1) Spiritual. (*a*) His sending Christ to die for us. (Luke ii. 14). (*b*) His quickening Spirit (2 Cor. ix. 15). (*c*) His gospel (Matt. xi. 25). (*d*) His restraining grace (1 Cor. xv. 57 ; Rom. vii. 25). (*e*) His renewing and sanctifying grace. (*f*) His comforts (Psa. cxlvii. 1-3). (*g*) His ordinances. (2) Temporal (*a*) Creation (Psa. xcv. 6; c. 1-3). (*b*) Preservation (Acts xvii. 28) (*c*) Provision (Psa. cxlvii. 7-9 1 Tim. vi. 17). (*d*) Health and strength (Psa. xviii. 32). (*e*) Gifts and parts (1 Cor. xiv. 18). (*f*) Life and liberty. (*g*) Protection. 2. Our afflictions

(Job i. 21). (1) Because they are not so great as we have deserved (Ezek. ix. 13). (*a*) Not spiritual (Psa. cxlvii. 20). (*b*) Not eternal (Lam. iii. 39). (2) Because they are still mixed with mercies. (3) Because they are really spiritual mercies (Rom. viii. 28 ; Heb. xii. 10). (*a*) For the deadening of our sins (Job xxxvi. 8-10). (*b*) For the quickening of our graces (Psa. cxix. 67). Uses—1. Reproof. (1) To such as never think of that God who gives them all things to enjoy (Psa. x. 4). (2) Who think upon Him, but are not thankful to Him. (3) Who thank Him with their mouths, but not their hearts (Col. iii. 16). (4) Who thank Him for some things but not for all (Eph. v. 20). 2. Exhortation. Be thankful. Consider—(1) This is all the requital God expects, or you can give (Psa. l. 10, 14 ; lxix. 30, 31). (2) You cannot expect a blessing on your mercies except you are thankful. (3) The more thankful you are for mercies received, the more ground you have to expect more. (*Bp. Beveridge.*)    *The duty of thankfulness :*—I. Some Christians are not eminent for thankfulness. 1. Some are very selfish. Unless the blessing alight on their actual self it matters not where it comes down. They cannot joy in the graces of their brethren. There are some so grievously selfish that they take as matters of right and of course every good and perfect gift, and regard the withholding of them as a personal injury. 2. Others are remarkable for peevishness. There is an ingenious fretfulness, dexterous in detecting flaws, industrious in embittering its own comfort, and wearisome by its pertinacious fault-finding. If the house be commodious, the situation is bad : if a friend be kind, he doesn't see you often enough ; if a book be otherwise good, there is a word or two you don't like. 3. Many are unthankful from inadvertency. They are surrounded with blessings, but from pure heedlessness they do not perceive from whom they have issued. Gratitude does not depend on the amount of mercies received, but on the amount known and prized. II. Materials for thankfulness. 1. Personal salvation. We have all felt the glow of returning health ; but what is this compared to the joy of salvation. 2. The Bible. How thankful the Psalmists were for the scanty portion of the Word of God possessed by them : how much more grateful should we be for a completed revelation. 3. Devout and congenial society. Who can estimate the blessings of friendship ; and if your friend has gone to God, few mercies call for more thankfulness than a friend in heaven. 4, Mercies in the disguise of affliction. These are topics which give scope for the holy ingenuity of loyal saints. " In everything," because " all things are working together for good." III. Appropriate expressions of Christian gratitude. 1. It should occupy a prominent place in devotion whether secret or social. 2. Recount God's mercies to others. In this way you will quicken your own soul to increasing fervour, and kindle the gratitude of others. 3. Sing praises. Few things are better fitted to dispel the evil spirit of censoriousness, selfishness, and sullenness than heart-sung hymns of thanksgiving. 4. Embody your gratitude in offerings of thankfulness. These are the only oblations for which room is left in our new economy. (*J. Hamilton, D.D.*)    *The habit of thankfulness :*—We hear a great deal of the power of habit. I know there is power in good habits. Is there any in evil habits ? Are good habits the greatest blessing in our life ? One-half of the best work performed by us is done largely through sheer force of habit. When a person is learning to play the piano, he or she goes over the keys awkwardly, and with difficulty, but soon becomes a good player through the force of habit. A man doing something that he is accustomed to will stand well the cares and anxieties which daily burden his mind. But put him at something which he knows nothing about, and they would kill him. Good habits enable one to resist temptation. The only way to conquer evil habits is to put good ones in their place. How often men discard their evil habits, but put nothing in place of them ! The bad habits soon return like the unclean spirits of the parable. I wish to speak of the habit of thankfulness. I. The value of such habit. It helps us to quell the repining over the ills of life. There is an old story of a young man who was walking along a road, full of life, but very poor, when, observing a carriage driven by containing an old man, he began to repine, saying ; "Oh, what a life I lead ! Just look at the genuine, quiet comfort enjoyed by that old man ; Oh, that I were in his place ! " The old man looked out of the window at the same time and sighed : " Oh, that I had the youth and strength of that man with all his splendid possibilities, I would give everything that I possess." Now the habit of thankfulness secures us against all this. A child will give thanks to any one who may make her a present of any kind, and shall we not return thanks to God for what He has given us ? Some of us may have sore troubles ; but when you remember the Lord's goodness and His consolations, you are able to bear them. Paul and Silas sang praises in prison. That's the way to do. Sing praises under all the ills of life. The Christian idea is to charge upon these ills. II. THE HABIT OF THANKFULNESS LEADS TO DEEPER PENITENCE. Repentance is the soundest, truest, and most acceptable thing in the eyes of God. All true penitence takes account of God's goodness, and incites cheerfulness and thankfulness to God. III. WE OUGHT TO BE THANKFUL FOR EVERYTHING PAINFUL AS WELL AS PLEASANT. "In all things." We can always be thankful that a thing is not worse. If it were worse it would be no more so than our sins make us deserve. When trouble comes over us, we learn to appreciate that as a blessing which is gone. A man does not know the blessing of good health until he loses it. (*J. A. Broadus, D.D.*)     *Thanksgiving to God:*—I. THE DUTY ENJOINED. Give thanks—1. With the soul (Psa. ciii. 1, 2). (1) With the understanding, which weights the value of the benefit conferred. (2) With the memory, which stores up the remembrance of benefits received. (3) With the affections, by which benefits are warmly embraced. 2. With the voice: otherwise thanks will be buried. How many aids and witnesses did David summon to assist him in this duty; the mountains to leap, the floods to make a noise, &c. Nature and art have found out many helps and signs—bells, musical instruments, feasting, &c. Yet these are but poor and senseless sacrifices performed by unreasoning deputies, if thanks have no more significant expression; and cheer of the countenance, bodily gestures, dancing, are dumb shows. But by speech one man's heart conveys to another the cheery conceptions and passions of the soul, and so multiplies praise and sets on others to bless God with him. 3. With obedience, which God prefers to all our sacrifices. He that in the way of thankfulness bows and performs the mortification of one sin, the addition of one duty, pleases God better than Solomon with all his beeves and sheep. The life of thankfulness consists in the lives of the thankful; otherwise it is but as one who should sing a good song with his voice and play a bad one with his instrument. II. THE EXTENT OF THE MATTER. 1. God will be praised in all His creatures whereof we have the sight or the use; for every one of us have no less benefit by the sun and air, than if we saw or breathed alone. 2. In all the works of His provident administration—public blessings—our country's good. 3. In all personal favours. Every man that sees another stricken and himself spared is to keep passover for himself. 4. In all crosses, counting it an honour to suffer for Christ's sake. 5. In all gifts: temporal or spiritual, and, above all, for Him who is all in all. 6. In all times and places. III. THE SUPREME MOTIVE. "This is the will of God." A sufficient answer to the foolish question "What addition shall I make to His honour who is self-sufficient?" God's will has binding authority enough, but the winning word is added, "In Christ." "I have so loved you as to give My Son; the return I expect and will is your thanks." An ingenuous child desires to know only what his father loves, and a grateful courtier only the pleasure of his sovereign. (*S. Ward.*)     *The perpetual thanksgiving of a Christian life:*— These words form the last of a series of apparently impossible precepts—perpetual joy, perpetual prayer, united in a life of perpetual thanksgiving. Of course these do not refer to acts, but to a state of heart. Yet even then the difficulty is not removed, for toil and rest, success and failure, events that cheer or overshadow, are all to be received not only submissively but thankfully, and so are the tremendous sorrows which shatter the human heart. How can this precept be obeyed? I. ITS DIFFICULTY. Why do we not trust God sufficiently to thank Him in every lot in life? 1. One source of the difficulty lies in the constant changes in the soul's life produced by temperament and circumstances. There are periods when it is comparatively easy to be thankful—days of sunshine when bare existence is a joy—times of sorrow, too, when we can trace the hand of love—hours of meditation when we get some deeper vision into the Divine meaning of life. But there are other periods when thanksgiving is the hardest task—days of dreariness, coldness of spirit, doubt. 2. But apart from this there are two sources of difficulty which are permanent. (1) Our fancied knowledge of life. We think we can tell what are great mercies, Whereas that which we pass by as a trifle or shudder as at a calamity may be heaven's greatest blessing in disguise. Constantly we are taught our ignorance, yet constantly we assume to know. Experience has revealed to us that what the child would have chosen the man passes by; and as we pass on in life we learn that the brightest rainbows of hope spring from the darkest clouds of trouble; and that in the deepest valleys of humiliation grow the fairest flowers of faith and love. Yet we forget the lesson, and fancy that we understand all. (2) Unbelieving distrust of God. (*a*) We are afraid to recognize His presence everywhere, acting through every little force in nature and through every trifling change in our careers.

(*b*) When we do discern the hand of God we are afraid to trust Him perfectly. In our submission we are tempted to bow to a kind of awful will that must have its way, rather than to believe that what God has chosen for us is most wise, just, and kind. II. THE MOTIVE. God's will is so revealed in Christ that, believing in it, we can give thanks in all things. Christ showed—1. That life was the perpetual providence of the Father. "Not a sparrow falleth." "Behold the lilies." His life was a ceaseless illustration of this. He went through the world whether men took up stones to stone him or shouted their hallelujahs, equally fearless as though He was sublimely safe, till His work was done. Realize that as true of your life, and if every moment and trifle of our history are under the Father's providence, for what shall we refuse to be thankful! 2. That that providence is a discipline of human character. Christ's teaching and life show us that not getting more, but being greater; not pleasure, but holiness; not success, but heaven is God's purpose in disciplining the life of men. The learning " obedience by the things which He suffered " was the end for which the Father's providence led the Divine man. And so with us. 3. That the discipline of life is explained by eternity alone. The life of Jesus, apart from the eternal glory which crowned it, seems only a failure and a mystery; and the Father, who ordained for Christ His strange dark way, is leading us by a way that must be dark till death lift the veil. We know not what we need for heaven's splendour, but know this that "the great multitude" have come out of great tribulation. III. THE METHOD OF ITS ATTAINMENT. 1. It is not to be reached by a single resolution, or in a day by an outburst of excited feeling. We may say sincerely, henceforth I resolve to trust God in everything. But little vexations soon shake our trust; greater troubles break down our resolution; the emotion has declined, and we say, " No man can be always thankful." 2. It is the gradual result of a life of earnest fellowship with God—a life that in daily meditation realizes the presence of the Father; that by prayer feels the reality of God's love—that comes at length to walk through all toils and temptations under a deep sense of the all-surrounding God. (*E. L. Hull, B.A.*)     *The faculty of thankfulness :*—If one should give me a dish of sand, and tell me there were particles of iron in it, I might look for them with my eyes, and search for them with my clumsy fingers, and be unable to detect them; but let me take a magnet and sweep through it, and how it would draw to itself the almost invisible particles by the mere power of attraction! The un-thankful heart, like my fingers in the sand, discovers no mercies; but let the thankful heart sweep through the day, and as the magnet finds the iron, so it will find in every hour some heavenly blessings; only the iron in God's sand is gold. (*H. W. Beecher.*)     *Thanksgiving with prayer :*—A child knelt at the accustomed time to thank God for the mercies of the day, and pray for His care during the coming night. Then, as usual, came the "God bless mother and—" But the prayer was stilled, the little hands unclasped, and a look of sadness and wonder met the mother's eye, as the words of helpless sorrow came from the lips of the kneeling child, "I cannot pray for father any more." Since her lips had been able to form the dear name, she had prayed for a blessing upon it. It had followed close after her mother's name. But now he was dead. I waited for some moments, and then urged her to go on. Her pleading eyes met mine, and with a voice that faltered, she said, "Oh, mother, I cannot leave him out all at once; let me say, 'Thank God that I had a dear father once,' so I can still go on and keep him in my prayers." And so she still continues to do, and my heart learned a lesson from the loving ingenuity of my child. Remember to thank God for mercies past as well as to ask blessings for the future. (*The Christian.*)     *Thankfulness and unthankfulness :*—At the dinner-table in the cabin of a steamboat there sat a conceited young man, who thought he displayed his own importance by abusing everything placed before him. A clergyman present, remonstrated with him, but in vain. Even on deck he continued his complaints of the ill-cooked, unsavoury fare, until the clergyman thoroughly disgusted, turned away, and, walking toward the steerage, noticed an old man, in his home-spun and well-worn shepherd's plaid, crouching behind the paddle box, where he thought himself unobserved. He took from his pocket a piece of dry bread and cheese, and laying them down before him, reverently took off his blue bonnet, his thin white hairs streaming in the wind, clasped his hands together and blessed God for his mercy. In the great Giver's hands lie gifts of many kinds, and to the scantiest dole of this world's fare we oftentimes see added that richer boon—a grateful heart. (*Christian Age.*) *Exemplary thanksgiving :*—Objects seem large or little according to the medium through which they are viewed. In the microscope, what a remarkable change they undergo! The humble moss rises into a graceful tree; the beetle, armed for battle, flashes in golden or silver mail; a grain of sand swells into a mass of rock; and, on the other hand, a mountain looked at through the wrong end of a telescope sinks into a mole-hill, and the broad lake contracts into a tiny pool. Even so, according as we look at them, with the eyes of self-condemning humility, or of self-righteous pride, God's mercies seem great or little. For example, a minister of the gospel, passing one day near a cottage, was attracted to its door by the sound of a loud and earnest voice. It was a bare and lonely dwelling; the home of a woman who was childless, old, and poor. Drawing near this mean and humble cabin, the stranger at length made out these words: "All this, and Jesus too! All this, and Jesus too!" as they were repeated over and over in tones of deep emotion, of wonder, gratitude, and praise. His curiosity was roused to see what that could be which called forth such fervent, overflowing thanks. Stealing near, he looked in at the patched and broken window; and there in the form of a gray, bent, worn-out daughter of toil, at a rude table, with hands raised to God, and her eyes fixed on some crusts of bread and water, sat piety, peace, humility, content-ment, exclaiming, "All this, and Jesus too!" *Grounds for thankfulness:*—I cannot enumerate all the sweet mercies for which you should be thankful—the personal mercies, a sound mind and a healthy body; restorations from sickness; preservations in imminent peril; a good education, abundance of books, and, perhaps, some leisure to read them; a competent share of the good things of this life, a home, food, raiment, occasional rest and recreation, the enlivening of a journey, and the enlightenment of travel. Family mercies: parents that were kind when you were helpless, and wise when you were foolish; the endearing associations of early days; the gentleness of kindred, who, if a little more remote, were scarce less tender than father or mother were; the amenities and joys of your present home; the household lamp and the household hearth, with all the fond familiar faces on which they shine; the voices which make blythe music in your dwelling; the lives which you have got back from the gates of the grave, and those glorified ones whom you would not wish to bring back; with all those numberless indoor delights, those visits of kindness, and advents of gladness, and solacements of sympathy which He, whose home was heaven, loved to witness or create in the homes of earth. Spiritual mercies: the Bible, the Sabbath, the house of prayer, the closet, the family altar, the great congregation, prayer-meetings, communion seasons, psalms and hymns and spiritual songs, Christian friends; perhaps a conscience void of offence towards man, and at peace with God through Jesus Christ; perhaps a victory over some temptation; perhaps progress in some grace; perhaps answers to prayer; along with what may either already be your own, or may as assuredly be made your own, as the Bible is already yours—the Comforter, peace in believing, hope in dying, a joyful resurrection, a home in heaven, a blood-bought harp, the inheritance of all things. These are a few of His mercies; but oh! how great is the sum of them! (*J. Hamilton, D.D.*) *Reasons for thankfulness:*—King George, at the close of the Revolutionary War, in which he had lost thirty colonies, proclaimed a day of thanksgiving because of the return of peace. His chaplain said to him, "For what would your majesty have us give thanks? for the fact that you have lost thirteen of the brightest jewels of your crown?" "No, not for that," said the king. "Because we have added millions to our national debt?" "No, not for that," said the king. "Because tens of thousands of people of the same race and religion have been destroyed?" "No, not for that," said the king. "Why, then," insisted the chaplain, "and for what shall we give thanks?" "Thank God," said the king, with great vehemence —"Thank God, because matters are no worse." (*J. L. Nye.*) *Unthankfulness:*— Like the Caspian Sea, which has some unseen way of disposing of its waters, so that whatever rains come down, and whatever rivers flow in, its great gulf never fills, and never a rill runs out from it again; so there is a greedy, all-devouring selfishness, which, whatever rivers of pleasure flow into it, and whatever mighty bursts of heaven-descended bounty exhaust their fulness over it, always contrives to dispose of the whole in the caverns and subterraneous passages of its capacious egotism—the vast *mare iternum* of self, without one drop of overflowing in kind-ness to man or gratitude to God. (*J. Hamilton, D.D.*)

Ver. 19. **Quench not the Spirit.**—*Positive duties:*—I. THE FIRST ADVICE—"Quench not the Spirit." The Spirit is quenched as a man doth quench his reason with

over-much wine; and therefore we say, "When the wine is in, the wit is out," because before he seems to have reason, and now he seems to have none; so our zeal, and our faith, and our love, are quenched with sin. Every vain thought, and every idle word, and every wicked deed, is like so many drops to quench the Spirit of God. Some quench it with the business of this world; some quench it with the lusts of the flesh; some quench it with the cares of the mind; some quench it with long delays, that is, not plying the motion when it cometh, but crossing the good thoughts with bad thoughts, and doing a thing when the Spirit adviseth not, as Ahab went to battle after he was forbidden. The Spirit is often grieved before it be quenched; and a man when he begins to grieve, and check, and persecute the Spirit, though never so lightly, never ceaseth until he have quenched it, that is, until he seem himself to have no spirit at all, but walketh like a lump of flesh. II. THE SECOND ADVICE. After "Quench not the Spirit" followeth "Despise not prophesyings." The second admonition teacheth how the first should be kept. "Despise not prophesying," and the Spirit will not quench, because prophesying doth kindle it. This you may see in the disciples that went to Emmaus. When Christ preached unto them from the law and the prophets, their hearts waxed hot within them. This is no marvel that the spirit of a man should be so kindled and revived with the Word; for the Word is the food of the soul. The apostle might have said, Love prophesying, or honour prophesying, but he saith, "Despise not prophesying," showing that some were ashamed of it. The greatest honour we give to prophets is not to despise them, and the greatest love we carry to the Word is not to loathe it. Prophesying here doth signify preaching, as it doth in Romans xii. 6. Will you know why preaching is called prophesying? To add more honour and renown to the preachers of the Word, and to make you receive them as prophets (Matt. x. 41). Hath not the despising of the preachers almost made the preachers despise preaching? III. THE THIRD ADVICE. After "Despise not prophesyings" followeth "Prove all things," &c., that is, try all things. This made John say, "Try the spirits." We read that the Bereans would not receive Paul's doctrine before they had tried it; and how did they try it? They searched the Scriptures. This is the way Paul would teach you to try others as he was tried himself; whereby we may see that if we read the Scriptures we shall be able to try all doctrines; for the Word of God is the touchstone of everything, like the light which God made to behold all His creatures (Gen. i. 2). A man trieth his horse which must bear him, and shall he not try his faith which must save him? And when we have tried by the Word which is truth and which is error, we should keep that which is best, that is, stay at the truth, as the Magi stayed when they came to Christ. We must keep and hold the truth as a man grippeth a thing with both his hands; that is, defend it with our tongue, maintain it with our purse, further it with our labour, and, if required, seal it with our blood. Well doth Paul put "prove" before "hold;" for he which proveth may hold the best, but he which holdeth before he proveth sometimes takes the worse sooner than the best. IV. THE FOURTH ADVICE. After "Prove all things, and hold that which is good," followeth "Abstain from all appearance of evil." As if the adviser should say, That is like to be best which is so far from evil that it hath not the appearance of evil; and that is like to be the truth which is so far from error that it hath not the show of error. Paul biddeth us abstain from all appearance of evil, because sin, and heresy, and superstition are hypocrites; that is, sin hath the appearance of virtue, error the appearance of truth, and superstition the appearance of religion. If the visor be taken away from them, they will appear exactly what they are, though at the first sight the visor doth make them seem no evil, because it covereth them, like a painted sepulchre the dead men's bones beneath. (*H. Smith.*)
*Words of warning:*—I. THE WORK OF THE HOLY SPIRIT. 1. The Holy Spirit is God, and so has all the strength of God. What He pleases to do He can do. None can stand against Him. This is of the greatest possible comfort to us, because we have enemies that are too strong for us; but no enemy is strong enough to hurt us if the Spirit of God is on our side. And again, as the Holy Spirit is God, so He has that wonderful power of working on the heart which belongs to God, and in purifying it, and making it holy like Himself. 2. The Holy Spirit dwells in the Church. His work is done upon those who belong to the Church. "He dwelleth with you, and shall be in you." What the soul of each one is to our body, so the Holy Spirit lives in the Church, and gives spiritual life to each member of the Church. He works through the ordinances of the Church, and what He gives, He is pleased to give through those ordinances. 3. The Holy

Spirit is like a fire in the heart of man. Fire gives warmth and light. Is not this exactly the character of the work of the Holy One. What is colder than the fallen heart of man toward God? Who warms it into real love to God but the Spirit by whom the love of God is shed abroad in the heart? Again, what is darker than the heart of man? Who pours light into it, and makes us to see that God is the true portion of the soul? It is the Holy Ghost. "We have an unction from the Holy One, and we know all things." II. THE QUENCHING OF THE HOLY SPIRIT. 1. The power we have to do this. We have already said that the presence of the Holy Spirit in the Church is like a fair shining light. Its rays fall on all hearts. It touches, it gilds, it beautifies all souls. It gives them a new fairness, like the golden rays which bathe the whole landscape, making each separate leaf to glisten as it dances on its branch, and hill and valley, wood and meadow, to wear a holiday aspect. Do not choose darkness rather than light by quenching the Spirit. We have power to do this. If we choose, we may say—I will not be changed, I will not give up my icy coldness of soul, I will go on in the hard-bound frost of my own selfishness, I will care for myself, live for myself; the fire may burn around me, but I will quench it. So we may put out the light which would lead us to God and heaven. 2. The way in which we may exercise this power. The Spirit of God may give us light in the Holy Scriptures, and we may refuse to read them at all, or read them without learning to know God and ourselves. The Spirit of God may give us light in the Church, which is the pillar and ground of the truth, and we may determine not to see what the Church would have us to believe and to do. The loving Spirit of God is longing to work among you, His heart is set upon you, He is opening out the treasures of His goodness before you. Oh! take care you do not check Him by your indifference. He will act to you as you act to Him. Just as fire cannot burn in a damp, unwholesome atmosphere—as there are places underground where the air is so foul that the brightest candle will go out at once, so if you choke the heavenly fire it will go out. The Holy Spirit will not work in the midst of cold, worldly, unbelieving hearts. By all that is dear and precious, "Quench not the Spirit!" (*R. W. Randall, M.A.*) *The working of the Divine Spirit:*—There are three active elements in nature—air, water, fire; and one passive—earth. The Holy Spirit is spoken of under the figure of each of the former, never of the latter. The Holy Spirit is always in action. St. Paul is writing with evident reference to the promise, "He shall baptize you with the Holy Ghost and with fire." Perhaps he may have had regard to some special manifestations of the Spirit (see ver. 20). A man might feel within him a fire burning, which was meant for expression, and which he was tempted to suppress, through feelings of modesty, false shame, indolence, or indifference, and he was anxious to caution against this. And there is now a bad economy of Divine gifts; men possessing talents of property, position, influence, persuasion, knowledge, grace, lock up that which was intended for the whole house of Christ. This is quenching the Spirit. Personally, as the Divine Spirit, no efforts or negligences of man could lessen His power or glory; but as the Divine Inhabitant of the soul it is otherwise. Note the manner of His working. He acts on—I. THE UNDERSTANDING. He spake to the understanding of prophets, psalmists, apostles, &c., and so we have in the Bible the truth brought home to our understandings. But the office of the Spirit is not bounded by the Bible. The Word of God is in the hand of every one, till it has become an ill-used book by its very plentifulness; and to him who has not the Spirit to shine with the light of His holy fire within the printed page all is darkness. The letter killeth, the Spirit alone quickeneth. So, then, a man quenches the Spirit who either neglects the Bible or is not taught by the Spirit out of it (Eph. i. 18). II. THE CONSCIENCE. The office of the Spirit is to bring sin to remembrance—a thankless office in one sense. Tell your best friend his faults, he must be one of a thousand if you have not lost him. Few can say, "Let the righteous smite me" (Psa. cxli. 5). But the Spirit knows how to reprove without irritating, and at the right time and in the right way. The still small voice takes conscience for its mouthpiece. When that voice is heard bringing to remembrance some half-excused sin, of the neglect of some half-denied duty, "Quench not the Spirit." III. THE WILL. The understanding may see the truth—the conscience may be alive to duty—is the work done? Answer all ye who know what it is to see the good, and yet to pursue the evil; to hate yourselves for your weakness, and yet do again the thing ye would not! The Holy Spirit, therefore, touches the will, the spring of being. He who says, "Stretch forth thy hand," will give the will and the power, and with the peace and reward. IV. THE HEART.

"Thou shalt love," &c. Who gives so much as a corner of his heart to God? The question is a self-contradiction, for the heart always gives itself whole or not at all. The Spirit enables us to cry Abba, Father. It is a dreadful thing to quench the Spirit in an intellectual scepticism; in a stubborn doggedness of conscience; in a settled obstinacy of will; but it is more dreadful to quench Him in a cold obduracy of heart; to say to Him when He says "Son, give Me thy heart"—"I will not—go Thy way—torment me not before the time" (Heb. x. 29). (*Dean Vaughan.*) *Quench not the Spirit:*—The word does not mean to resist, damp, or partially to smother, but to put out completely, as a spark when it falls into water. I. THE SPIRIT CAN BE QUENCHED. Else why the injunction? 1. The antediluvians quenched the Spirit. He strove with them to do them good, they strove against Him to their destruction, and the flood swept them away. 2. In Nehemiah ix. you will see how God strove with the Jews, and how they quenched the Spirit and were left to perish. 3. The same law is in operation still. God gives His Spirit to instruct men. They refuse to hear and God leaves them to their worst enemies—their sins. It is foolish to frame theories with which these facts will not harmonize. The striving does not, of course, refer to God's power; there could be no striving with that. But it is man's sins striving with God's love; and God tells us that He will not always strive with man's sins, but will relinquish the contest, leave the field, ~~Gen 6. 3~~ and allow him an eternity in which to learn the fearful misery of what it is to have quenched the Spirit. As unbelief tied the Saviour's hands so that He could not do any mighty work, so it can cripple the agency of the Spirit. II. HOW CAN HE BE QUENCHED. Fire may be extinguished—1. By pouring water upon it. The most direct way of quenching the Spirit is sin and resistance to His influence. He may act as a friend who, having been wantonly slighted, withdraws in grief and displeasure. 2. By smothering it. So the Spirit may be quenched by worldliness. The process may be a slow and partially unconscious one, but it is real and sure. 3. By neglect. Timothy was exhorted to "stir up" His gift. And as a fire will die out unless it receives attention, so will the Spirit if we indolently do nothing to improve the gift. 4. For want of fuel. And the Spirit will be quenched unless the Spiritual life is fed by the Word of God, "Sanctify them through Thy truth." 5. Through want of air. There may be abundance of fuel, but it will not burn. Not less essential to the flame kindled by the Spirit is the breath of prayer. (*E. Mellor, D.D.*)    *Quench not the Spirit:*—1. The Holy Spirit is represented as fire, the source of light and heat, because of His searching, illuminating, quickening, reviving, refining, assimilating influences. 2. It is implied that He may be quenched; not in Himself, but by the withdrawal of His influences, and so His graces, which are indicative of His presence, may be extinguished. 3. He may be quenched in others as well as in ourselves. (1) In ministers, by contempt of their ministrations. (2) Among Christians, by neglect of social prayer and religious conversation. Christians are like coals of fire which kindle into a blaze only when kept together. How disastrous to zeal are dissentions (Eph. iv. 30-32). I. THE INSTANCES, IN WHICH WE MAY QUENCH THE SPIRIT. 1. By slighting, neglecting and resisting His operations. When the Spirit stirs us up, and we neither stir up ourselves nor our gifts, we quench the Spirit. 2. By diverting the mind from spiritual concerns, and engaging in vain and unnecessary recreations. The love of pleasure will extinguish the love of God. Fulfilment of the lusts of the flesh renders walking in the Spirit impossible. 3. By inordinate affections towards any earthly object. The life and power of godliness are seldom found among those who are eager in the pursuit of worldly gain (Matt. xix, 16-22). 4. By robbing Him of His glory, by denying His Divinity, or the necessity and efficacy of His operations. 5. By sins of omission and commission. These are opposite to His nature. One will damp His sacred fire, a course of iniquity will extinguish it. II. THE REASONS WHICH SHOULD WARN US AGAINST THIS DANGER. If we quench the Spirit—1. He will be silent to us, and will cease to admonish and guide either directly or through His ministers (1 Sam. xxviii. 15). 2. He will suspend His influences and leave us in darkness. 3. We shall sin both against God and our own souls. (*B. Beddome, M.A.*)    *Quench not the Spirit:*—This is a little text, but it is full of large matters. I. WE HAVE A SPIRIT TO QUENCH. 1. The possession of the Spirit is the distinguishing prerogative of the gospel covenant; this it is which imparts a life, an energy, a fulness, a reality, to its every part and detail. 2. We are all the depositaries of this great treasure; the holders of a wonderful gift, for the abuse or improvement of which we shall one day have to answer. II. THE NATURE AND PROPERTIES OF THIS SPIRIT. 1. A consuming fire. (1) It destroys in us at once that curse which adheres to us as children of a fallen parent. (2) In those who yield themselves, gradually does one unholy habit of thought, one unsanctified desire, one impure affection after another, succumb beneath its power and influence. 2. A purifying fire; it does not wholly destroy the will, so as to make man a passive instrument; it only strips the will of that evil which makes it at enmity with God. Nor does the Spirit deaden and annihilate the affections, powers, faculties of our moral nature; it only withdraws them from low, base, unworthy objects, and fixes them on others whose fruits will be love, joy, peace. 3. A kindling fire. It raises in the mind of man the fervour of devotion and the heat of Divine love. 4. A defending fire. Like the sword of the cherubim, it turns every way to guard "the tree of life." 5. An enlightening fire. (1) The Christian, by the Spirit which is given him, is enabled to see what he is in himself. It shows him how degraded is his nature, how forlorn and hopeless are his prospects. (2) This reveals to him what he is in Christ—Child of God. Heir of glory. (3) This reveals to him the path of life. (4) This lays open to him the mysterious, hidden wisdom of the Word of God. III. WHAT IS MEANT BY "QUENCHING THE SPIRIT." 1. This is done by those who altogether fall away from Christ—by apostates. 2. It is not only, nor generally, by a sudden and violent wrenching and snapping asunder of the ties which bind him to Christ, that the obdurate sinner quenches the Spirit. The integrity and unity of his inner life is damaged and sapped little by little; he quenches the Spirit, more or less, in all the stages of his spiritual decay. IV. WHAT ARE THE MEANS, AND WHAT THE AGENCY, WHICH OPERATE IN BRINGING THIS ABOUT. 1. Floods of ungodliness swamp the soul. 2. Blasts of fierce and headstrong passions. 3. Want of fuel to nourish and preserve it. In many a soul the Spirit's fire is quenched because it is never replenished by prayer, meditation, self-examination, works of charity and mercy, attendance on Holy Communion, &c. V. THE AWFUL CONSEQUENCES. Let us quench the Spirit, and how shall the motions of sins which are in our members be rooted out? how shall we be able to purify ourselves from all filthiness of the flesh and spirit, and to perfect holiness in the fear of the Lord? (*Arthur G. Baxter.*) *On quenching the Spirit:*—"Quench not the Spirit." Put not out that heavenly fire which you did not kindle, but which you can extinguish. Put not out that holy fire which is the real heart of your life, and without which spiritual death is sure to follow. Put not out that fire by sensual pleasures and indulgence of fleshly appetites, as did Sodom and Gomorrah; by love of the world, as did Demas; by careless neglect, as did the lukewarm Church of Laodicea. I. THE FIRE CAN BE PUT OUT. 1. You may put it out by indulgence of the body. The brutalizing power of fleshly sins, of whatever sort, always blunts the conscience, and makes the spiritual eye unable to discern the true nature of God's requirements. A man who has given himself up to these becomes coarse. If the sins be such as men can see, he becomes visibly coarse and earthly. If the sins be of the far wickeder and yet more secret sort, he often retains much outward refinement and even softness of manner, but coarseness and earthliness of soul; with little sense of disgust at impurity, with a low and animal idea of the highest of all affections. 2. The fire can be put out by worldliness and a life devoted to self and selfish hopes. What can be more miserable than the condition of that man whose powers of mind have shown him the truth of God, whose understanding has been too highly cultivated to allow him to shut his eyes to the eternal laws of heaven, who can appreciate, perhaps, till his very heart thrills with admiration, the high examples of love, of self-sacrifice, of a pure and brave service, which history has recorded, and yet who cannot be, and who feels that he never can be, what he himself admires; who feels that while he admires the noble and the true, yet he is not attracted by it? The end of such a character generally is to lose even this much appreciation of what is good, and to retain admiration for nothing but refinement without a resolute will within; to despise all self-sacrifice, all generosity, all nobleness as romantic and weak; and, of course, either to give up religion altogether, or to make a superstition to suit the worldly temper. 3. Lastly, and most often of all, the fire of the Spirit can be put out by mere neglect. The Spirit holds before the sight, time after time, soul-stirring visions of what our lives and characters might be. As we read, as we live with our fellows, as we worship, as we listen, we are touched, enlightened, half roused to real resolution. But we hear not, or if we hear we make no effort; or if we make an effort, we soon give it up. The greatest thoughts, the noblest thoughts flit before the minds of men in whom their fellows suspect nothing of the kind; but they flit across the sky, and those who share in them, yet feel them to be as unreal as those clouds. There is no waste in nature equal to the waste of noble aspirations. What is the end of such coldness? The end is an incapacity to hear what they have so often heard in vain. In such men there comes at last an utter inability to understand that the message of God is a message to them at all. They hear and they understand, but they find no relation between their lives and what they learn. They will be selfish, and not know they are selfish; worldly, and not be able to see they are worldly; mean, and yet quite unconscious of their meanness. II. THE LAST, THE FINAL ISSUE of "quenching the Spirit," I cannot describe. A fearful condition is once or twice alluded to in the Bible, which a man reaches by long disobedience to the voice within him, and in which he can never be forgiven, because he can never repent, and he cannot repent because he has lost all, even the faintest tinge, of the beauty of holiness. What brings a man into such a state as this we cannot tell; but it is plain enough that the directest road to it is by "quenching the Spirit." (*Bp. Temple.*) *On the Holy Spirit*:—Some have thought that the words of our text are to be referred to the extraordinary gifts of the Spirit, which were enjoyed by the Church in the days of the apostle; such as the gift of healing, the gift of tongues, the gift of prophesying. All this may be very just, and very suitable to the Church of the Thessalonians; yet, if this were all, the words would have no application to us, since those miraculous gifts have ceased. Still, this admonition stands in the midst of precepts which are of lasting and universal obligation: "Rejoice evermore: Pray without ceasing: In everything give thanks;" and, a little onward, "Prove all things: hold fast that which is good." Who does not see that, both before and after the text, every precept belongs to all ages? I. Let us attentively consider THE SUBJECTS PRESENTED TO OUR NOTICE in this brief but comprehensive sentence. Here is a Divine person exhibited, the Spirit; a comparison implied, fire; a state of privilege supposed, viz., that this fire is already kindled; finally, a sin prohibited, "Quench not the Spirit." 1. The gifts and illuminations, which we must not quench, cannot be viewed apart; they are inseparable from an actual indwelling of the Holy Ghost. The Spirit, therefore, is a Divine person. Sins are committed against Him. He must be a Divine person. The work which He performs in our hearts requires infinite knowledge, infinite condescension, infinite wisdom, and infinite power. The admonition of our text acquires a peculiar force from this consideration. We live under the ministration of the Spirit. 2. Here is a comparison implied. But, without attempting to follow out this comparison in all its particulars, it shall suffice to observe, that these words, addressed to the Thessalonians, must refer either to the light kindled in them by His teaching, or to the affections inflamed by His influence. True religion is both; it is inward illumination, and a hidden and celestial fire, which purifies and warms the heart, originated and sustained by the Holy Spirit. Love to God, fervency in prayer, ardent zeal for His glory, joy, desire, hope, all mounting heavenward; to what else could they be compared, with equal propriety? They conquer, they possess, they fill, they purify the soul. This fire is communicated from above, like that which burned upon the altar of old. Like that, it must be kept burning continually. 3. My dear brethren, you are addressed in the text, as those in whom this Divine fire is already kindled. It supposes that you are true Christians, and that you have a concern to keep the grace you have received. But is it really so? Alas! you cannot quench what has no existence in the soul. 4. This leads us to inquire into the sin. What is it to quench the Spirit? How far is it possible for a true believer to be guilty of it? And, by what means? Now, there are two ways, as we all know, in which fire may be quenched. It may be quenched by not adding fuel, or by adding water, and, in general, anything of a nature adverse to it. Hence there are two ways in which the Spirit may be quenched, illustrated by this emblem, negligence and sin. II. We shall endeavour to ENFORCE THIS ADMONITION; for it is by far too important to be discussed only, without the addition of special motives, calculated to show the guilt and danger which would be involved in its neglect. 1. Therefore, consider that, if you quench the Spirit, you will provoke in an eminent degree the displeasure of God. No sins are reckoned so heinous as those which are committed against this Divine Agent. 2. Consider that this would be, in general, to destroy all your spiritual comfort; and, in particular, to silence the witness and obliterate the seal of your redemption, leaving you without any evidence of your interest in the great Salvation. 3. Consider, once more, that to be guilty of such an offence would open wide the floodgates of all sin, which it is the office of the Holy Ghost to subdue and destroy. It would leave you without strength and without defence against Satan and your own corruptions. Let me close by adding to this admoni-

tion a few words of exhortation.   1. Let me entreat you to conceive very affectionately of the Holy Spirit.   2. Let me exhort you to give honour to the Holy Spirit,
by a distinct and continual recognition of your dependence upon Him.   3. Finally,
if all this be true, then how miserably mistaken must be that ministry which casts
the name and office of the Holy Spirit into the shade!   (*D. Katterns.*)   *Quenching
the Spirit :*—The Holy Spirit is more than " Emmanuel, God with us." He is God
*in* us.   Until He so comes we are ruined; when He comes the ruin becomes a
living temple.   No man can explain this; and yet every striving, expanding soul
exults in the sacred belief.   How awful, then, the power given to a man to quench
the Spirit.   How? By any unfair dealing with the laws and principles of our
nature, by which He works.   He uses memory for conviction, conscience for condemnation or justification, understanding for enlightenment, will for invigoration,
affections for happiness; and if we refuse to allow these faculties to be so used, we
are quenching the Spirit.   The Spirit's work is—I. CONVICTION OF SIN.   He takes a
sinner, and makes memory a scourge to him : shows him the holiness of God and
the sinfulness of sin.   It is a most gracious opportunity; but, alas! he misses it,
stifles memory and silences conscience, and thus quenches the Spirit.   Christians,
too, when convinced of sin may quench the Spirit if they do not take heed.   II.
REVELATION.   " He shall receive of mine," &c.   In conducting this great work He
uses every kind of suitable instrumentality—the inspired writings, the spoken word,
thoughtful books, Christian conversation, &c.   It follows, then, that if we do not
search the Scriptures and take kindly the ministries of truth we are shutting out of
our hearts the waiting Spirit of God.   III. SEALING OR SETTING APART.   When men
are born by His regenerating power from above they are marked for their celestial
destination, and set apart for God.   He renews His sealing process again and
again, retouching His work and bringing out the Divine inscriptions.   Any one who
resists this process, who does not often think of the Father and the Father's house,
and who minds earthly things is quenching the Spirit.   Christian people, too, have
thoughts given to them purely as sealing thoughts; they are not needed for duty or
life here, but for higher service and the life to come.   One is earlier down some
morning than usual, and in the short moment of quietness looks far away into the
land of sunless light.   One is struck suddenly—at the high noon of city life—with
the utter vanity of all the fever and toil and strife.   Or at night there falls upon
the house a little visitation of silence.   Quench not the Spirit in any of these
His gracious comings.   (*A. Raleigh, D.D.*)   *Quenching the Spirit :*—I. SOME
DISTINCTIONS OF THIS SIN.   1. Total and partial.   (1) Total, when the Spirit's
impressions are quite erased so that no spark is left among the ashes.   "My Spirit
shall not always strive with man," and this Spirit departed from King Saul.   (2)
Partial, when the Spirit is weakened and brought to a very spark, as was the case
with David (Psa. li.).   2. Wilful and weak.   (1) Wilful, when men resolutely set
themselves to put out the holy fire, being resolved not to part with their lusts, they
go on in opposition to their light, strangle their uneasy consciences, murder their
convictions that they may sin without control (Acts vii. 51).   (2) Weak, which is
the result of carelessness rather than design (Eph. vi. 30; Solomon's Song v. 2–5).
II. HOW THE SPIRIT IS QUENCHED.   This holy fire is quenched—1. By doing violence
to it, as when one puts his foot on the fire or casts water on it, or blows it out.
Thus the Spirit is quenched by sins of commission.   As when one raises an offensive smoke in the room where his guest sits, he is grieved and departs; so the Spirit
is grieved by the offensive smell of our corruptions.   2. By neglecting it, as the lamp
will be extinguished if you feed it not with more oil, so the Spirit is quenched by
neglecting his motions, and not walking in the light while we have it.   III. WHY
WE SHOULD NOT QUENCH THE SPIRIT.   1. Because it is the holy fire; and, therefore,
it ought to be kept carefully, and it is dangerous to meddle with it (Lev. ix. 24).   2.
Because we can do nothing without it.   So far as the Spirit goes away, all true
light and heat go with Him, and then the soul is in death and darkness.   3. Because
when once quenched we cannot rekindle it.   We " cannot tell whence it cometh
or whither it goeth."   Were it the fire of our own hearths we might kindle it again;
but it is from heaven, and we have no command there.   4. Because the quenching
of this fire is the raising of another tending to the consuming of the soul.   This is
a fire of corruption within us.   When the Spirit departed from Saul he went to the
devil.   And some people never come to a height of wickedness till the Spirit has
been at work in them, and they have quenched Him.   Conclusion: 1. We may
quench the Spirit in others—(1) By mocking them.   (2) By speaking evil of the
way of God (Acts xix. 9).   (3) By diverting them from duty.   (4) By tempting them

to sin. 2. Quench it not in yourselves but cherish it. (1) By diligence in duties —Bible reading, Christian conversation, private prayer. (2) By keeping up a tender frame of spirit. (3) By strict obedience. (4) By making religion the one thing. (*T. Boston, D.D.*) *Quenching the Spirit :*—Light is the first necessity of life in this body ; without it we could not go about our business, and should lose health and die. Such also is knowledge to the soul, and the Holy Spirit is the means of it. This light we are to beware of quenching. A light may be quenched—I. BY NEGLECTING TO FEED AND TRIM IT. Coal, wood, oil, &c., serve as fuel for fire ; Christian practice serves to maintain Christian knowledge. Practice is necessary for the preservation of even earthly knowledge. The knowledge communicated by the Spirit is that of salvation. This may be extinguished by not caring for it. How few things we read in the newspaper we remember a week after, simply because we are not interested. Shut up a light in a close place where no ray can pass forth, and after a little flickering it will go out. So if the light of the knowledge of Christ does not shine in deeds of faithful service it becomes extinguished. II. BY CARE-LESSNESS. This engenders wilfulness, and then wickedness, and like the lamps of the virgins this light once quenched cannot be lighted again (Heb. vi. 4 ; Matt. vi. 23). *Quenching the Spirit :*—I. THE OBJECT TO WHICH THIS EXHORTATION RELATES. Not the essence of the Spirit, or His inherent attributes, but His agency. 1. This agency is symbolized by fire. " He shall baptize you," &c. (Acts ii. 1–3). (1) Fire imparts light, so it is the office of the Spirit to impart knowledge. " The eyes of your understanding being enlightened." (2) Fire is employed to purge metals from dross ; the Holy Spirit purifies men from sin and makes them holy. In the Old Testament He was " the Spirit of burning ; " in the New " the Spirit of holiness." (3) Fire imparts heat : it is the office of the Spirit to kindle in the soul emotions which animate and enliven—love, zeal, joy. 2. The value of that agency. Its preciousness is beyond all conception, transforming as it does the state and character and securing the blessings of eternity. 3. The responsibilities attached to it. It is not only a gift, it is a stewardship ; it is not only a privilege, it is a talent, to be cherished and improved. II. THE EVILS WHICH THE EXHORTATION DEPRECATES. The Spirit may be quenched—1. By the want of a due recognition of His agency. (1) A Christian may be tempted in his own case to ascribe that to himself which is really the result of Divine grace. (2) He may be tempted in the case of others to disbelieve in the existence of the Divine work in spite of evidence, either in individual characters, or masses affected by revivals of religion. Wherever there is this guilty incredulity there is a refusal to the Spirit of the attributes due to Him. 2. By a want of holy separation from the world. The great design of the Christian vocation is holiness, and this is the one purpose of the operations of the Divine Spirit (John xvii. 14–20 ; Eph. v. 7–15). If, then, a Christian permits himself to be so trammelled by earthly things as to conceal his character ; if he allows his affections to be earthly ; if he practices secular vocations which are forbidden, or pursues lawful ones inordinately ; if he mingles in scenes of worldly frivolity or worse, what becomes of the fire kindled in his heart ? Of course its light becomes faint, and its heat cools. 3. By a want of mutual forbearance and love. " The fruit of the Spirit is love," &c. The indulgence, therefore, of angry passions is incompatible with the influence of the Spirit (Eph. iv. 30–32). Here is the condemnation of the strife of sects, of unbrotherly conduct in a given Church, of family quarrels, of all unneighbourliness. 4. By neglect of the Word of God and prayer. The Word of God comprises the record and its proclamation, both of which are under the influence of the Spirit. To neglect to read the one or to hear the other is a sure method of quenching the Spirit, who convinces, converts, sanctifies, &c., by each. So with prayer, private, domestic, congregational. III. THE BLESSINGS WHICH COM-PLIANCE WITH THIS EXHORTATION WILL SECURE. If Christians do not quench the Spirit, if they rightly apprehend the nature of the Spirit's agency—illuminating, &c. ; if they do homage to it by nonconformity to the world ; if they cultivate love ; if they render a right regard to the Word of God and prayer they will secure—1. The eminent prosperity and happiness of their own souls. We shall become firm in faith, pure in life, glowing in love, burning in zeal. We shall not be dwarfish, stunted plants, but as trees planted by rivers of water ; others will take knowledge of us that we have been with Jesus, and " the very God of Peace will sanctify us wholly." And this prosperity will be our happiness. We shall thus walk in the light of God's countenance, enjoy His comforting, gladdening friendship here ; be animated by a sure hope, and finally enter into the joy of the Lord. 2. The true glory of the Church. This glory does not consist in high sounding ecclesiastical pretensions, in pompous ritual, but in humility, holiness, stedfastness to truth, &c. Let Christians cherish and honour the Spirit and they will secure the beauty, spirituality, and splendour of the Church. 3. The rapid diffusion of religion. As the Church becomes more holy and prayerful obstacles will disappear, revived energy will be given and exerted and nations will be born in a day. (*J. Parsons.*) *Quenching the Spirit :*—I. How DOES THE SPIRIT INFLUENCE THE MIND ? Not by physical agency but by means of the truth. He persuades men to act in view of truth as we influence our fellows by truth presented to their minds. Sometimes this truth is suggested by providence, sometimes by preaching; but whatever the mode the object always is to produce voluntary action in conformity to His law. II. WHAT IS IMPLIED IN THIS FACT AND WHAT MUST BE INFERRED FROM IT. 1. God is physically omnipotent, and yet His moral influences exerted by His Spirit may be resisted; but if the Spirit moved men by physical omnipotence there could be no resistance. The nature of moral agency implies the voluntary action of one who can yield to motive and follow light or not as he pleases. When this power does not exist moral agency cannot exist. Hence if our action is that of moral agents, our freedom to do or not do must remain. 2. If the Lord carries forward the work by means of revealed truth there must be most imminent danger lest some will neglect to study and understand it, or lest, knowing, they should refuse to obey it. III. WHAT IS IT TO QUENCH THE SPIRIT ? 1. The Spirit enlightens the mind into the meaning and self-application of the Bible. Now there is such a thing as refusing to receive this light. You can shut your eyes against it; you can refuse to follow it when seen; and in this case God ceases to hold up the truth before your mind. 2. There is a heat and vitality attending the truth when enforced by the Spirit. If one has the Spirit his soul is warm; if not his heart is cold. Let a man resist the Spirit and he will certainly quench this vital energy. IV. THE WAYS IN WHICH THE SPIRIT MAY BE QUENCHED. 1. By directly resisting the truth He presents to the mind. After a short struggle the conflict is over, and that particular truth ceases to affect the mind. The man felt greatly annoyed by that truth until he quenched the Spirit; now he is annoyed by it no longer. 2. By endeavouring to support error. Men are foolish enough to attempt by argument to support a position which they know to be false. They argue it till they get committed, and thus quench the Spirit, and are left to believe in the very lie they unwisely attempted to advocate. 3. By uncharitable judgments, which are so averse to that love which is the fruit of the Spirit. 4. By bad temper, harsh, and vituperative language, and intemperate excitement on any subject whether religious or otherwise. 5. By indulging prejudice. Whenever the mind is made up on any subject before it is thoroughly canvassed, that mind is shut against the truth and the Spirit is quenched. 6. By violating conscience. Persons have had a very tender conscience on some subject, but all at once they come to have no conscience at all on that point. Change of conscience, of course, often results from conscientious change of views. But sometimes the mind is awakened just on the eve of committing a sin. A strange presentiment warns the man to desist. If he goes on the whole mind receives a dreadful shock, and its very eyes seem to be almost put out. 7. By indulging appetites and passions. These not only injure the body but the soul: and God sometimes gives men up to them. 8. By dishonesty and sharp practices in business. 9. By casting off fear and restraining prayer. 10. By idle conversation, levity, and trifling. 11. By indolence and procrastination. 12. By resisting the doctrine and duty of sanctification. V. THE CONSEQUENCE OF QUENCHING THE SPIRIT. 1. Great darkness of mind. Abandoned by God, the mind sees truth so dimly that it makes no useful impression. 2. Great coldness and stupidity in regard to religion generally. It leaves to the mind no such interest in spiritual things as men take in worldly things. Get up a political meeting or a theatrical exhibition, and their souls are all on fire; but they are not at the prayer meeting. 3. Error. The heart wanders from God, loses its hold on truth, and perhaps the man insists that he takes now a much more liberal and enlightened view of the subject, and it may be gradually slides into infidelity. 4. Great hardness of heart. The mind becomes callous to all that class of truths which make it yielding and tender. 5. Deep delusion with regard to one's spiritual state. How often people justify themselves in manifest wrong because they put darkness for light and *vice versa*. (*C. G. Finney, D.D.*)     *Quenching the Spirit :*—Fire may be quenched—I. BY CASTING WATER ON IT. This is comparable to actual, wilful sin (Psa. li.). II. BY SPREADING EARTH UPON IT. This is applied to the minding of earthly things. 1. The cares of the world, and the deceitfulness of riches; excess of business which not only employs but entangles a man in the affairs of this life, by toil, scheming, speculation. The consequence is, the powers of the soul being limited, and when full, no matter of what, they can hold no more. As the water partakes of the quality of the soil over which it rolls, so our minds soon acquire a sameness with the object of our affection and pursuit. 2. Certain vanities and amusements erase the boundary line which should separate the Church from the world, and if they are not unlawful they have a tendency to destroy spirituality and a taste for devotion. 3. Worldly and political conversation which frets the mind, genders strife, and cools religious ardour. If we talk of that which we love best, where habitually are the thoughts and affections of many professed Christians ? Surely it becomes us to live so as to " declare plainly that we are strangers and pilgrims on the earth." III. BY THE SEPARATION OF THE PARTS. Apply this to our divisions. 1. With what earnestness does the apostle enforce unity and co-operation among Christians ! The enemy knows the importance of this ; he therefore loves to separate, and unhappily finds too much to favour his wishes in our ignorance, prejudice, and infirmities. 2. There are some families who are quarrelling all day, and then go to prayer in the evening. If prayer does not induce people to avoid passion, then evil tempers will make them leave off prayer or perform it in a manner that is worse than the neglect of it. 3. One truth aids another truth, and one duty another duty. Detach private devotion from public, or public from private, and both sustain injury. Separate practice from principle, works from faith, or promises from commands, and you destroy the effect of the whole. IV. BY WITHHOLDING FUEL. A real Christian will soon feel the disadvantage of disregarding the means of grace. You may keep in a painted fire without fuel, but not a real one. Conclusion : We cannot quench what we have not. The exhortation, therefore, supposes the possession of the Spirit. Yet there is a common work of the Spirit which accompanies the preaching of the Word, the effect of which may be entirely lost. Herod heard John gladly, but he cherished a criminal passion which destroyed all his fair beginnings. Felix heard Paul, but the trembler dismisses the preacher for a more convenient season which never came. He afterwards conversed with the apostle, but he never again experienced the feelings he had subdued. (*W. Jay.*) *Protecting the Spirit's light :—* A man has lost his way in a dark and dreary mine. By the light of one candle, which he carries in his hand, he is groping for the road to sunshine and to home. That light is essential to his safety. The mine has many winding passages in which he may be hopelessly bewildered. Here and there marks have been made on the rocks to point out the true path, but he cannot see them without that light. There are many deep pits into which, if unwary, he may suddenly fall, but he cannot avoid the danger without that. Should it go out he must soon stumble, fall, perish. Should it go out that mine will be his tomb. How carefully he carries it ! How anxiously he shields it from sudden gusts of air, from water dropping on it, from everything that might quench it ! The case described is our own. We are like that lonely wanderer in the mine. Does he diligently keep alight the candle on which his life depends ? Much more earnestly should we give heed to the warning, " Quench not the Spirit." Sin makes our road both dark and dangerous. If God gave us no light, we should never find the way to the soul's sunny home of holiness and heaven. We must despair of ever reaching our Father's house. We must perish in the darkness into which we have wandered. But He gives us His Spirit to enlighten, guide, and cheer us. (*Newman Hall, LL.B.*) *Instance of quenching the Spirit :—* Several years ago I was called to visit a young man who was said to be sick, and wished to see me. Approaching him as he was lying upon his bed, I remarked that he certainly did not look as though he was ill. He replied, " I am not sick in my body, but in my soul. I am in deep distress." Asking him the cause of his distress, he said, " During the revival in our Church, I have not only resisted its influence, but I have made sport of the young converts, I have ridiculed those who were seeking the salvation of their souls, and I feel that I have committed an unpardonable sin, and there is no hope for me." I said to him, " Your sins are indeed fearfully great ; but if you sincerely repent, and will now believe in the Lord Jesus Christ, He will pardon you." I referred to the Saviour's compassion to the thief on the cross, and to other cases that might awaken some hope in his mind. But everything that was said failed to reach his case. His reply to every argument, or appeal, or passage of Scripture that was quoted, was the same, " There is no hope for me." After an earnest prayer for his salvation, and commending him to the mercy of God, I left him. Calling the next day, I found he had passed a sleepless night, and the state of his mind was unchanged. Again, after pointing him to the promises of the Scriptures, and praying with him, he expressed the same feeling of utter despair. Not a ray of light crossed the dark cloud that hung over his soul. The third day on entering his room I found him in a raging fever. His mental agony had taken effect upon his body. Without any indications at first of physical disease he was now lying in a most critical condition. I pointed him once more to the bleeding Saviour on the cross, and pleaded with him at the throne of grace. But with him the harvest was passed, the summer of hope was ended. He had quenched the Spirit, not only by his personal resistance, but by hindering and laughing at others who were seeking to escape eternal death. The next day I found that his reason was dethroned. His fond mother was bathing his temples with ice-water. On my addressing him, he replied in an incoherent manner. He was beyond the reach of any gospel tidings. That night his soul passed into eternity. (*Rufus W. Clark, D.D.*) *The Spirit quenched:*—An old man came to a clergyman and said, " Sir, can a sinner of eighty years old be forgiven ? " The old man wept much while he spoke, and on the minister inquiring into his history, gave this account of himself:—" When I was twenty-one, I was awakened to know that I was a sinner, but I got with some young men who tried to persuade me to give it up. After a while I resolved I would put it off for ten years. I did. At the end of that time my promise came to my mind, but I felt no great concern, and I resolved to put it off ten years more. I did, and since then the resolution has become weaker and weaker, and now I am lost ! " After talking to him kindly, the minister prayed with him, but he said, " It will do no good. I have sinned away my day of grace ; " and in this state he soon after died. *Danger of deferring reformation:*—How dangerous to defer those momentous reformations which conscience is solemnly preaching to the heart ! If they are neglected, the difficulty and indisposition increase every day. The mind is receding, degree after degree, from the warm and hopeful zone, till at last it will enter the arctic circle and become fixed in relentless and eternal ice. (*J. Foster.*) *The Spirit quenched:*—A few months ago in New York a physician called upon a young man who was ill. He sat for a little by the bedside examining his patient, and then he honestly told him the sad intelligence that he had but a short time to live. The young man was astonished ; he did not expect it would come to that so soon. He forgot that death comes " in such an hour as ye think not." At length he looked up in the face of the doctor and, with a most despairing countenance, repeated the expression : " I have missed it—at last." " What have you missed ? " inquired the tender-hearted, sympathizing physician. " I have missed it—at last," again the young man replied. The doctor, not in the least comprehending what the poor young man meant, said : " My dear young man, will you be so good as to tell me what you——? " He instantly interrupted, saying : " Oh ! doctor, it is a sad story—a sad—sad story that I have to tell. But I have missed it." " Missed what ? " " Doctor, I have missed the salvation of my soul." " Oh ! say not so. It is not so. Do you remember the thief on the cross ? " " Yes, I remember the thief on the cross. And I remember that he never said to the Holy Spirit—Go Thy way. But I did. And now He is saying to me : Go your way." He lay gasping awhile, and looking up with a vacant, staring eye, he said : " I was awakened and was anxious about my soul a little time ago. But I did not want religion then. Something seemed to say to me, Don't postpone it. I knew I ought not to do it. I knew I was a great sinner, and needed a Saviour. I resolved, however, to dismiss the subject for the present ; yet I could not get my own consent to do it until I had promised that I would take it up again at a time not remote, and more favourable. I bargained away, insulted and grieved the Holy Spirit. I never thought of coming to this. I meant to have religion, and make my salvation sure ; and now I have missed it—at last." " You remember," said the doctor, " that there were some who came at the eleventh hour." " My eleventh hour," he rejoined, " was when I had that call of the Spirit ; I have had none since—shall not have. I am given over to be lost." " Not lost," said the doctor ; " you may yet be saved." " No, not saved—never ! He tells me I may go my way now ; I know it—I feel it here," laying his hand upon his heart. Then he burst out in despairing agony : " Oh, I have missed it ! I have sold my soul for nothing—a feather—a straw ; undone for ever ! " This was said with such unutterable, indescribable despondency, that no words were said in reply. After lying a few moments, he raised his head, and, looking all around the rooms as if for some desired object, turning his eyes in every direction, then burying his face in the pillow, he again exclaimed, in agony and horror: "Oh, I have missed it at last!" and he died. (*D. L. Moody.*) *The coated heart :*—I heard a few nights ago that if you take a bit of phosphorus, and put it upon a slip of wood, and ignite the phosphorus, bright as the blaze is, there drops from it a white ash that coats the wood and makes it almost impossible to kindle the wood. And so when the flaming conviction laid upon your hearts has burnt itself out, it has coated the heart and it will be very difficult to kindle the light there again. (*A. Maclaren, D.D.*) *Self-destroyed :*—When some poor distracted one in Paris determines to lift his hand against his own life, he begins by stopping up every nook and cranny in the room which lets in the sweet air of heaven. He closes the door, he closes the windows, he fills in every hole, one by one, before he kindles that fatal fire which by its fumes is to bring destruction. So it is when men deny the Spirit and quench the Spirit. They may not know it, for the madness of sin is upon them, but none the less is it true that one after another they close those avenues by which He might enter to save them, until God can do no more than stand apart in judgment, as over Ephraim of old, saying, "O Ephraim, thou hast destroyed thyself." (*W. Baxendale.*)

Ver. 20. **Despise not prophesyings.**—I. WHAT PROPHESYINGS ? 1. The Scriptures written (2 Pet. i. 20, 21 ; 2 Tim. iii. 16). (1) The truths asserted (Acts xxvi. 27). (2) Commands enjoined (Mark vii. 8, 9). (3) Promises made (Rom. iv. 20). (4) Threatenings denounced (Prov. i. 30 ; Amos iii. 8). 2. The Scriptures preached (1 Cor. xiv. 1–3), which they despise—(1) Who do not come to hear them (Luke iv. 16). (2) Who do not regard what they have heard (Luke iv. 20). (3) Who do not practice what they hear commanded (Lev. xxvi. 15 ; John xiii. 17). II. WHY NOT DESPISE THEM ? 1. They are the Word of God (chap. ii. 13). 2. They that despise them despise Him (Luke x. 16). 3. If we despise the Word we may be justly deprived of it. 4. If we despise His Word God will despise us (1 Sam. ii. 30 ; Prov. i. 25, 28). 5. By so doing we render it ineffectual to ourselves (Heb. iv. 2). (*Bp. Beveridge.*) *Despise not prophesyings :*—Prophesying in the ordinary sense means the foretelling of future events. Here the term denotes exposition of the Scriptures. 1. Because some who do not despise the office itself may be disposed to cast contempt on particular ministers, Paul forbids a contempt of prophesyings in general, lest by particular instances of neglect the office itself should be brought into disrepute. Ministers have peculiar gifts. One is learned, another eloquent, another argumentative, &c., but there is no faithful minister, whatever his gifts, from whom we may not reap some advantage. Those who hear with prejudice will never hear with profit, let the preacher be who he may. 2. But the apostle forbids us to despise prophesyings, intimating that an undervaluing of the one will lead to a contempt of the other. For our own sakes we are to receive the message, for His sake who sent him the messenger. Lydia's heart was open to the one, and her house to the other. I. THE CAUTION. Ministers are required to magnify their office, and to so discharge their duties as to preserve it from contempt (1 Cor. xiv. 39). The exhortation, however, applies more particularly to hearers. Whatever be our attainments there is always room for improvement. Those despise prophesyings who—1. Refuse attendance upon a preached gospel. Some are so openly profane as to make the Sabbath a day of worldly business or indulgence. Others pretend that they can profit more by prayer and meditation at home. Those who in former times forsook the assembling of themselves together, as the manner of some now is, did so from fear. But whatever the cause, such souls famish and are accessory to their own destruction. "Woe is me," says Paul, "if I preach not the gospel "; and woe is the man who refuses to hear it (Prov. xxviii. 9 ; 1 Cor. ix. 16). 2. Attend the gospel but with improper disposition. Part of their time is spent in drowsiness or trifling inattention, observing their neighbours instead of the preacher. Hence when they come home they can tell more of what passed in the seats than in the pulpit. Others are not contented with plain truths; wholesome truths must be garnished to their taste. Paul represents such as having "itching ears "; and though they "heap to themselves teachers " running from one church to another, they get but little good. 3. Are apparently serious in their attendance on the Word, but who neither receive it in love, mix it with faith, nor reduce it to practice (Ezek. xxxiii. 31, 32). The gospel is also despised when it is attended to for unworthy purposes : to hide some iniquity, to silence conscience, to raise our reputation, or promote our worldly interest (2 Pet. ii. 1, 2). II. THE REASONS. 1. The weakness or wickedness of those who dispense the Word of God. 2. Familiarity on the part of the hearer. Scarcity creates a longing, but plenty breeds contempt. The Word of God is "precious" when it is scarce. 3. Insensibility and unbelief. Sinners are at ease in their sins and love to be so. 4. Profaneness and desperate wickedness. The Word reproves such, and they cannot bear it. Knowledge aggravates sin and raises a tempest in the soul. III. THE SIN AND DANGER. None but fools despise wisdom, and to despise the wisdom that cometh from above is still more dangerous presumption (Prov. i. 7; Jer. xi. 10, 11). Those who despise prophesyings—1. Despise what God has honoured and will continue to honour (Isa. lv. 10, 11). 2. Are guilty of despising the Divine authority (chap. iv. 8). 3. Injure their own souls (Prov. viii. 34–36). 4. Will bring down contempt at length upon their own heads (Psa. l. 24; Heb. xii. 25). (*B. Beddome, M.A.*) *Careless listening:*—Father is ill and cannot go to church. Daughter, who has spent three years at a boarding-school and is a communicant and a teacher in the Sabbath-school, enters. "Well, Mary, did you have a good sermon this morning?" "Yes, splendid; I never heard Dr. X. preach better." "What was the text?" "Oh, I don't remember! I never could keep texts in mind, you know." "What was the subject? Don't you remember it or some of the ideas?" "No, papa, but I remember a beautiful figure about a bird soaring up into the air. Why, I could almost see it and hear its song!" "Well, what did he illustrate by the flight of the bird?" "Let me see. It was something about faith, or about going to heaven. I can't just recall now what it was, but the figure was splendid." And the father is satisfied. Why shouldn't he be? That was the kind of listening to sermons that he taught her by his own example. If he had heard it he could not have made a better report unless there had been something in it about politics or the news of the day. We are losing the habit of attention and the use of the memory in the house of God. The story of the Scotch woman and the wool has comforted a great many careless and forgetful hearers of the Word. When criticized for claiming to have enjoyed a sermon, and to have been edified by it, though she could not remember a single idea in it, or even the text, she held up the fleece she had just washed, wrung it dry, and said: "Don't you see the water is all gone, and yet the wool is clean. So the sermon is all gone, but in passing through my mind, as I listened, it did me good." We think that hers was an exceptional case. We don't believe in cleansing hearts as she cleansed wool. The Saviour said, "If ye abide in Me, and My words abide in you." And Paul wrote to the Corinthians, "By which also (the gospel he preached) ye are saved if ye keep in memory what I preached unto you." He evidently had no faith in the saving power of truth that merely rippled on the ear like water over a rock.

Ver. 21. **Prove all things: hold fast that which is good.**—The design of these precepts is to caution us against two pernicious extremes; one is taking opinions on trust without examination, the other is after a wise choice not being able to abide by it. Credulity and unsteadiness are alike dangerous, and the only way to prevent them is to examine every doctrine propounded to us in order to regulate our choice, and then, having made a wise choice, to hold it unalterably so as to reap the full benefit. We must be as cautious in the selection of our principles as of our friends, but once well chosen we must not lightly part with them. I. CARE AND DISCRETION IN CHOOSING. 1. The persons. Not pastors only, but the Church was thus addressed (see also 1 John iv. 1; 2 Cor. xiii. 5; 1 Pet. iii. 15; Acts xvii. 11). Vain, therefore, is the Romish contention that the laity are excluded from judging for themselves. It is also one of man's natural rights, resulting from his being a rational creature, to judge for himself, and to trust other men's eyes only when he cannot use his own; and even then only after he has tested their trustworthiness. 2. The rule of procedure—that of right reason. Whatever on the best inquiry appears most reasonable is to be received. It is assumed in all debates that reason is umpire. (1) Two classes seem to form an exception—those who advise the surrender of reason to the dictates of an infallible chair, and those who obtrude their dreams for Divine oracles. But they have to give reasons, and so suppose what they deny. They plead that reason is weak and fallible; but they can only know this by weak and fallible reason; and even taking that for granted we must either trust it or something blinder, such as fancy, passion or prejudice (2) To discard reason is to discard faith which is built upon it. We ought to have a reason for what we believe. We believe a doctrine because we find it in the Scriptures; we believe the Scriptures because they speak the mind and will of God; we believe that they do so because they have the marks of Divine authority. (3) Reason and faith are not opposite but assistant to each other. The glory of religion is that the best reasons go with it, and that it loves to be examined by the nicest reasons. 3. The use and application of this rule to the doctrines of Christianity. (1) In some points Scripture is plain and clear and the reason of the thing as well, as in its moral teaching. (2) Sometimes it is clear and express, but the reason of the thing dark, as in the mysteries of our faith. Here reason proceeds upon extrinsic evidence, the authority of the Revealer; and brings proofs to show that it has been revealed without pretending to say how or why it is. (3) In other points Scripture may be obscure and silent, but the reason of the thing clear as in infant baptism, and reason shows what by analogy or consequence though not directly Scripture allows or condemns. (4) Another case is where neither Scripture nor the reason of the thing are clear; both together affording only dark hints of what is or is not. Here, then, is ground only for a probable assent; it is, however, the business of reason to lay the things together, make the best of its materials, and lean to the most charitable side without being too positive in either. II. FIRMNESS AND STEADI-NESS IN RETAINING. To be always seeking without finding, ever learning and never able to come to a knowledge of the truth neither becomes a Christian or a man. Of course it is not implied that when we have once settled our opinions on good grounds, that we are never to alter them on better. The best judgment will some-times err, and men's judgments often ripen with their years. Yet as in civil matters wise men generally have some fixed leading principles, so the wise Chris-tians will have some fundamental articles of faith which once intelligently accepted he will not have canvassed a second time. The proofs, e.g., of the superiority of Christianity over Paganism and Mohammedanism, of the being of a God over the atheistical contentions are so full and clear that they need never be reargued. So with revelation and morality. And with regard to minor matters that we permit to be reopened, we must hold fast to this that reason and not caprice, vanity, ambition, fear is to be umpire; and then if its decisions are clear against us it is the truest constancy to change what is proved to be an error, for we are commanded to hold fast only what is good. (D. Waterland, D.D.)    Prove all things :—I. RELIGION ADDRESSES US AS SENSIBLE BEINGS. 1. Not every religion, nor even every section of Christianity. Some say, " Do not inquire ; submit implicitly to the teachings of your Church." Truth does not do this; it courts examination because it can afford it. (1) There are difficulties in our faith, but they yield before a clear mind, patient study and prayer, and a correct life. There are many things above reason, but reason proves that it is reasonable to believe them. (2) Surely this is what religion ought to be. Has God given us our mental faculties for nothing ? You are responsible for your beliefs, and while before God we shut our mouths ; yet before men we are bound to ask does God say it ? I must have faith, but it must be an intelligent and manly faith, else my religion will be unworthy a creature so highly endowed. 2. " Prove " refers to the process of testing coin whether genuine or counterfeit. " Lest by any means I should become a castaway," i.e., as a piece of money that could not bear the test, " Reprobate silver." So are you to prove whatever is presented to you, as carrying the mark of the King of kings, therefore asserting a Divine claim upon you, whether it be true or a forgery. II. WHAT IS THE TOUCHSTONE BY WHICH WE ARE TO GAUGE THE REAL AND THE FALSE? What is that spiritual alchemy which shall always make the base to precipitate to the bottom, and the right and holy to come up to the surface, separate and clear ? 1. The first criterion of religious truth is personal experience, " Come and see ; " have you come? (1) God will give everything He has promised to simple, earnest, persevering prayer. Have you proved this? (2) When a man turns to God in penitence and faith he is forgiven. Have you done this? (3) God speaks of " a peace which passeth understanding." Have you put yourself in the way to get an experimental proof whether there is such a peace or not. (4) So with happi-ness, wisdom, doctrine. Is it not sheer madness to refuse such gold and say " I will not test it." If it do not turn out what it professes to be, then is the time to reject it. 2. The grace of common sense and moral perception which God has given us. These, of course, are vitiated by wilful sin, and they will lead us wrong. But if a man will only be careful to have a good conscience, lay open his heart to the influences of the Spirit, and honour and obey them when they come, he will not make any great mistake. 3. God's Word is the measuring line of all moral truth. If we give up that ultimate appeal there is no resting place for the mind. This does not mean taking solitary verses which in the Bible as elsewhere may be made to prove anything you like. You must gather the general intention of the mind of God by study and prayer, dealing with the proportions of truth. 4. Above the Bible is Christ, the living Word. Everything is to be tested by Him. (1) Doctrine—where does it place Him? (2) Promise—does He seal it? (3) Duty—does He command it? (4) Pleasure—does He sanction it? (*J. Vaughan, M.A.*) *Prove all things :*—We see Paul's character here. He had been speaking with his wonted fervour ; but he sees nothing inconsistent in this with the soundest, calmest reasoning. I. THE FIRST DUTY HE URGES—" Prove all things." Be enthusiastic ; but test, try, examine well. Courses of sin need no testing. The apostle speaks of what seems good, wise, honourable. 1. At times indolence tempts to indifference. This is the greatest danger of our age ; but it is palsy to the mind, and death to the soul. 2. Some are afraid to think. But remember the greatest have stood firm ; and the doubts of our age are old and dry albeit they may seem new and fresh. III. THE SECOND DUTY THE APOSTLE URGES—" Hold fast that which is good." 1. Hold fast what we have proved for ourselves to be true and good. Immature convictions are generally abandoned, and wisely so. 2. But before we have had time and power to test, there is something good to grip. Even heathen know the great foundations of the fitting, the beautiful, and the true. We are not heathen born ; therefore we must not cast off all that we have learned at our mother's knee for the sneers of half-read women and the cavils of daring men, but the rather " be valiant for the truth." (*Bp. E. H. Bickersteth.*) *Prove all things :*—I. WHAT THINGS ? 1. Ourselves. The work of examination should begin at home—our state before God, our graces, our practice. 2. Others—friends (Prov. xxv. 19), candidates for Christian communion, ministers. 3. Doctrines—are they simply sanctioned by councils or by God ? Do they minister to pride of intellect, or humbleness of heart. 4. Actions. Do we walk after the Spirit or after the flesh ? Do we keep the ordinances of God or of men (Prov. xiv. 12)? II. BY WHAT RULES. Not by outward appearance : this was what Eve did, and what Samuel was in danger of doing. But—1. By fruits. This applies to both persons and doctrines, and is a test ordained by Christ. 2. The examples of good and wise men in so far as they follow Christ the supreme example. 3. The Divine Word : Search the Scriptures. 4. Our own experience corroborated by the word of truth. " He that believeth hath the witness in himself." (*B. Beddome, M.A.*) *Quinquagesima Sunday :*—The last clause of this verse is very commonly taken to mean, " Abstain from everything which looks like evil, from everything which a bystander would suspect to be evil." That St. Paul can never have meant his exhortation to bear the sense which we have forced upon it, a moment's thought will convince you. " Judge not," says our Lord, " according to the appearance, but judge righteous judgment." That passage cannot affect the construing of our text, for the word in St. John is ὄψις, not εἶδος. But it directly affects the question, whether we are to judge of evil by the mere look or semblance ; for remember the occasion which called forth the precept of Christ. He had healed a sick man on the Sabbath-day. This act had the appearance of evil. It appeared evil, not only to the accidental bystanders, but to the religious guides of the Jewish people. How carefully these parts of His conduct are recorded by the Evangelists ! How evidently they think that, if they were blotted out of His life, He would not have perfectly revealed His Father, or been a complete pattern to His disciples ! Do you suppose he would have taught his Thessalonian disciples that these conspicuous lines in the character of Christ were not to be copied, but to be treated as dangerous ? But did not St. Paul follow most strictly the steps of his Master, did he not depart altogether from the maxim which has been ascribed to himself, when he appeared in the eyes of the Jews, converted and unconverted, perhaps of apostles, to be violating sacred customs, and trampling upon the covenant of his fathers ? To which doctrine did he conform, when he ate openly with the Gentiles in the presence of Peter and Barnabas, who were striving to keep up what every Jew must have considered a graceful, if not necessary, recognition of the difference between the chosen people and all others ? How did he avoid the mere look of evil, when he left the impression upon the minds of his countrymen that he was overthrowing the righteousness of the Law, by preaching the righteousness of Faith ? The three clauses, " Prove all things ; hold fast that which is good ; abstain from all appearance of evil," are not associated by accident. Every person who has paid the least attention to St Paul's style will perceive how clearly the relation between them is indicated by the antithetical words κατέχετε, ἀπέχεσθε. " Hold on to the good, hold off from every form of evil." And it is clear that the thought which determines the force of both these clauses—the thought which is

uppermost in the writer's mind—is that which is expressed by the word "prove,"—
δοκιμάζετε. Now that word and its cognate substantive, whether it refers to things
or to persons, to the soundness of money, or to the qualifications for citizenship,
always denotes a process of testing. So, then, according to the popular interpretation of the text, St. Paul would say, in the first clause; "Be not content with
the mere semblance of anything you have to do with. Look into it; find out the
good of it, hold to that." And he would say in a second and corresponding clause,
"Be always afraid of semblances. The moment anything looks like evil, fly from
it. Throw away your tests and proofs; simply hold off from that which seems evil
to you or to the people about you." This is not an antithesis, but a contradiction.
I. He tells us first, to PROVE OR TEST all things. I do not know a more honourable
watchword to inscribe upon our banners than this of prove all things, if only we
know what it signifies, and how St. Paul used it. Assuredly he did not understand
it, as some of us do, "Bring all things to the standard of your private judgment;
see whether they accord with that; only hold fast that which does." If there is
not that which is true absolutely—true for all men—search and inquiry are very
fruitless; we had better lay them aside. If my judgment is to be the measure of
all things that I see and converse with, if I am at liberty to use it as such a measure, if there is no higher measure to which I can bring it, that it may be deepened
and expanded, it is certain to become narrower and feebler every day. Whereas, if
I continually acknowledge the presence of a Light which is greater than any organ
of mine can take in, but yet with which I am intented to hold communion, I shall
desire that that Light may enter more and more into me, to purify my vision and
enlarge its capacities. I shall desire to see all things in this Light. And it will so
distinguish between what is fantastic and what is real, between the shows of things
and their substance, that it will not be possible for me to accept one for the other,
either in obedience to my own natural taste and inclination, or at the bidding of
any earthly guides and authorities whatsoever, II. Next, St. Paul tells us to prove
ALL THINGS. He does not say, "Prove or test certain doctrines which are submitted
to you;" though those are of course not excluded. He assumes that everything
whatsoever with which we come into contact—the ordinary notions and maxims of
society, the habits and traditions of the literary, or philosophical, or professional, or
religious circle in which we are moving, the words we speak, the common every-day
experiences of life—all need sifting and testing, that we may know what there is of
good in them. Yes, believe that the good is in all things, in those that you have
made little account of, in those that you have been taught by others to hate, in those
which you have learnt to hate yourself. Do not shrink from confessing that there
is and must be a goodness, a beauty at the bottom of them all, else they would not
have continued to exist. Do not be afraid of inquiring for it lest you should fall in
love with the evil and ugliness which are also in them. III. St. Paul goes on,
"HOLD FAST THE GOOD." When you have perceived it, detected it, anywhere, then
cleave to it, hug it, swear that you will not let it go. Be sure that what you want
is the substantial good; the beauty in which is no flaw. Having that, you are sure
you have what God in His infinite love desires that you should have; you have what the
Son of God took your nature and died upon the cross that you might have; you have
what the Spirit of God is stirring you and all creatures to sigh and groan that you may
have. Not that it is yours, in any sense which can enable you to say to a neighbour,
"It is not thine." It is yours by faith; it is yours because it is God's, and He invites you to believe Him and trust Him, and so to inherit His own righteousness and
truth and blessedness. It is yours because it is not in your own keeping, because
you are lifted out of yourself that you may enjoy it. IV. And so we come at last to
the word with which I began, "ABSTAIN," or "KEEP YOURSELVES FROM EVERY FORM OR
APPEARANCE THAT IS EVIL." You have seen the good; you have grasped it; now have
nothing to do with whatever is not that, with whatever counterfeits it. There will
be every variety of evil shapes, forms, appearances; but if you have learnt to look
below, to try and test the heart of things, you will not be misled by this variety.
You will detect the evil, the lie, under each new disguise, and you will be able to
stand aloof from it; to shun the contact of it. Just so far as the truth has become
precious and familiar to you, this likeness, this double, this mockery, will be loathed
and kept at a distance. But I conceive, brethren, that the peril of our being vanquished by some of its manifold forms will be infinitely increased, if we adopt that
opinion which has gained such strength from the supposed authority of St. Paul.
To believe that we must fly from that which people think evil, from everything
which seems evil to ourselves at the first glance, is to become a prey of evil in its

worst sense. All reformation, in every age, has been retarded by this doctrine, all corruptions have been sanctified by it. And yet it has not restrained a single rash reformer; it has not preserved a single truth from outrage. The conscience of men cannot be bound by a rule, which must be transgressed before a single brave act can be done, a single right principle asserted. These are instances—your own experience may supply a hundred similar—where this maxim proves utterly ineffectual to accomplish its own ends. For every vulgar worldly argument which puts on a religious dress, and affects an authority that does not belong to it, must prove feeble and worthless. The only consequence of resorting to it is, that you benumb the moral sense, that you degrade the hearts of those whom you bring under its influence. They will plead it for deserting a friend, for refusing to maintain an unpopular cause; they will forget it the moment it interferes with any passion or propensity of their own. (*F. D. Maurice, M.A.*) *Prove—then hold fast:*—I. Two THINGS TO BE DONE. 1. Prove, *i.e.*, inquire into and decide upon after examination. Prove as gold and silver are tried, and as the strength of building materials are tested. Haste in reception or rejection are forbidden. The standards of proof are —(1) The Holy Scriptures. The Bereans were "more noble," &c.—there is something contemptible in a man refusing to look at statements put before him as though it were impossible for him to make a mistake; teachableness is noble. (2) Experience: "What fruit had ye," &c. "Unto you that believe He is precious." (3) Observation: "Ye shall know them by their fruits." (4) The spiritual and religious faculty sanctified by the Holy Ghost: "He that is spiritual judgeth all things." "Ye have an unction," &c. 2. Hold fast against indolence, prejudice, pride, perplexity, evil inclinations, influence of irreligious men, winds of doctrine, false teaching and the fallible teaching of Christ's best friends. II. THE SPHERE FOR THIS PARTICULAR ACTION. 1. Prove all things—opinions, doctrines, requirements, customs, professions, characters, modes of working. (1) All ancient things. Things are not better for being old. Sin is old. (2) New things. A thing is not wise or adapted to the times because new. It may be a new folly. (3) Common things. Things are not right because generally acceptable. (4) Singular things. (5) Attractive things which have too often misled our fallen nature—specious doctrines which have pandered to our pride. (6) Repulsive things—Christ, *e.g.*, may put in our path a cross, which it is better for me to bear than to wear a crown. 2. Hold fast the good. Not, of course, what is evil. If what is doubtful comes into your hand let it lie there, but do not close your fingers over it until you have proved it; then hold it fast, whether it be opinion and doctrine, custom and practise, communion and friendship, that which your mind, faith, love, hope embraces—anything that is good. 3. The giving heed to this requirement is of great importance. Here it is in the statute Book, and in vain do we call Christ Master unless we do what He bids us. (1) If we receive error we cumber our minds with what is profitless, deceive ourselves, impair our spiritual life, and reject the truth. (2) If we admit an evil custom, or have fellowship with evil-doers, we expose ourselves to corruption; and by rejecting Christian ordinances and fellowships, we deprive ourselves of means of grace. 4. These are times when the text is likely to be overlooked. In days of church-slumber, nothing is proved; in days of morbid wakefulness, nothing is held fast. And what is true of the Church is true of the individual. 5. In cherishing obedience to the text, we must—(1) In proving all things avoid—(*a*) seeking for a kind of evidence God does not give. (*b*) Encouraging a restless and captious spirit. (*c*) Entertaining foolish questions which gender strifes. (*d*) Misplacing the tests with which God has favoured us. The Bible is the supreme standard. (2) In holding fast the good, we must avoid prejudice, obstinacy, and pertinacity upon doubtful matters. Conclusion: Take this yoke of Christ on you. No one can bear it for you, neither Church nor individual, and for this you will be held responsible at the Judgment seat of Christ. (*S. Martin.*) *Hold fast that which is good:*—I. THE EXHORTATION. 1. What are those good things which we have to hold fast. (1) The Gospel and the way of salvation by Christ. (2) That truth, in particular, which relates to the person and work of Christ (Rev. iii. 8). (3) The good treasure lodged in our hearts or placed in our hands. (4) Our spiritual comforts and whatever contributes to the peace and purity of our minds. (5) A line of conduct consistent with the Word of God. (6) An open profession of religion. 2. How are we to hold them fast. It supposes—(1) That our judgment concerning them is fixed. (2) That we retain them in our memory (1 Cor. xv. 2; 2 Pet. i. 15). (3) A high esteem and warm affection. (4) Resistance to all opposition. II. THE MOTIVES. 1. The honour of God requires that we should hold fast what He has revealed. 2.

The things we are required to hold fast are good in themselves. 3. If we part with the good we shall retain the evil, and cannot easily recover what we have lost. 4. If we disobey, what account shall we give another day? Hence we learn—(1) That nothing but true religion will stand its ground. (2) That perseverance in the way of truth and holiness is necessary to eternal happiness (Heb. x. 38). (*B. Beddome, M.A.*)    *Holdfasts*:—There are many occasions when the soul feels that it has come to a crisis. It may be compared to the feeling of William Tell when he was taking aim at the apple. Everything depends on the action of the next moment. It is to decide for God or the devil, for heaven or hell. We all need a holdfast at such critical times. I will mention two. I. THERE IS A GOD. Unless we can hold on to that, life becomes hard and vexatious, and we are like people floundering on ice, but when our heavenly Father is a fact to us, life loses its bitterness and death cannot sting. God cannot be proved to any one. Every man must prove Him for himself. You cannot prove colour to a blind man, to know it he must see. If you seek God with the proper faculties, you will find and know Him. 1. One of the links in this holdfast is that God is perfect. You cannot trust men fully because of their imperfections, but you can fully trust God because He is all-wise, all-powerful. He does not learn by experience; what He does cannot be improved. 2. Another link is that God is loving. The sweetest and most self-sacrificing love this side of heaven is not in the least degree comparable to it. It was not exhausted on Calvary. It is treasured up for you. 3. It is possible for every man to find God. You are nearer to Him than you fancy. Open the door of your faith and He will enter in. II. THE TRUE MOTIVE OF RIGHT ACTION IS LOVE TO GOD AND MAN. When men act on this they cannot go wrong. Do true children need rules and regulations to tell them how to behave towards parents and brothers? If this law ruled all other laws would be needless. Hold then fast to this in—1. Business perplexities. 2. Conflicting duties. 3. Fierce temptations. 4. Death. (*W. Birch.*)    *Hold fast*:—Steadfastness is a prime virtue. "Be sure you are right, and then hold on though the heavens fall." "Prove all things," and adhere to the "good," and surrender it only with life. Hold fast—I. To YOUR FAITH. It is a lie of the devil that "it matters not what a man believes." As he believes so is he. Throw away or tamper with your faith in the inspiration and Divine authority of the Scriptures, and you are sure to go astray and perish in your unbelief. II. To YOUR INTEGRITY. To let go one particle of it—to compromise in the least with wrong—endangers your soul, and is sure to forfeit your peace of mind and your Christian standing and influence. III. To YOUR PROFESSION. Cleave to the Church which Christ purchased with His blood. Honour and magnify its mission. Sustain and advance its interests by all the means and influence which God has given you. IV. To CHRISTIAN EFFORT in behalf of souls. "Be not weary in well-doing." Guard against "an evil heart of unbelief." Do not doubt "the promises"—they are all "yea and amen in Christ Jesus." The night of fear and struggle and waiting may be long and dark, but the morning will come to gladden you, if, like Jacob, you hold on. V. To PRAYER. Be sure you get hold of the everlasting arm, and then not let go. Persevere in the face of a thousand obstacles. Let not God go till He bless. Be not denied. Turn rebuke and seeming denial into fresh pleas, as did the Syro-Phœnicia woman. The answer, the blessing, is sure, when God gives the grace of perseverance. To "hold fast" is to overcome. VI. "Hold fast" TO HEAVEN. Make it the pole-star of life. Never lose sight of it, no, not for an hour. Live daily "as seeing the invisible." (*L. O. Thompson.*)    *Holding fast the good*:—I would apply the text to the religion of Jesus Christ and assert that it is good, and because good that you are to hold it fast. By this is not meant theology, which is very good as science and art, but is not life. Nor do we mean imposing rites, splendid churches which are very beautiful and helpful to the weak, but are not the religion of Jesus Christ. This is—I. FAITH AS OPPOSED TO INFIDELITY—faith in God our Father, in the Lord Jesus who died for us, in the spiritual nature of man, in the spirit world. 1. This faith harmonizes with our natural instincts which lead us to feel that all that exists is not present to the bodily senses, that somewhere inside the temple of the universe is a holy of holies filled with a glory that the eye of flesh cannot behold, and our desire is to enter that inner temple, and behold what it is. A little bird in a London cellar knows instinctively that there is an outer world, although he has never been there, and he is brave enough in his gloomy place to make some attempts at singing and flying. 2. Infidelity says there is nothing to know—no God, &c. Matter is all. Well, a mole might say there is no sun, no bright worlds; yet these do exist, and if the mole would only come out of his hole he could catch some rays of glory. Let men cease then from burrowing in the earth. They will never find heaven there. Let them follow their deepest instincts and highest aspirations and they will reach the throne of God, and their first act will be to worship Him. 3. In this faith we can rest and find comfort, but the bed of infidelity is too short for my soul to stretch itself upon. II. HOLINESS AS OPPOSED TO SIN—all possible virtues and graces, all things true, good, beautiful. 1. The religion of Christ demands holiness, "Be ye holy." "Be ye perfect." In this demand we see the wonderful possibilities of the soul. It is said that we have descended from very humble ancestors. Then there must be in our nature some marvellous energy, for the development has been truly wonderful. I can turn my face upward, build steamers that can cross the ocean against the storm, &c., more, I can pass within the veil and lay my hand on that of the Father, and say, " Thy will be done." The artist takes the rough block of marble and transforms it into a majestic statue, and everybody speaks of his genius. Yes, but something must be said for the marble that has the power of being transformed. Very wonderful is the work of the Divine Artist upon the soul, but something must be said for the soul that is capable of being changed into His image, and it is nothing less than this that our religion demands of it. 2. But it not only demands, it gives the sure promise of attaining holiness—the Church is to be without spot, &c. The process may be sketched. God loved us—sent His Son to die for our sins—gave His Holy Spirit to transform our nature—by and by He will take us to Himself. Is not this religion good ? Ask not where it came from. Judge it on its own merits for once. III. GOODNESS AS OPPOSED TO SELFISHNESS. 1. Selfishness, as seen in the priest and Levite in the parable of the good Samaritan, passes by suffering, and avoids the inconvenience of sympathy: as seen in Lot's choice, it takes the best, indifferent to the claims of others. 2. Christianity says, "Bear ye one another's burdens," &c.—the burdens of ignorance, disappointment, anxiety, fear. Now selfishness is hateful, and self-denial admirable by common consent. We have examples in the three hundred at Thermopylæ and in the man who to save another's life imperils his own. But try and rise from these to the self-denial of Christ, "who loved us and gave Himself for us." Imitate that, and you are a Christian. IV. HOPE AND JOY AS OPPOSED TO DESPAIR. 1. The natural language of despair is, " Let us eat and drink for to-morrow we die," and that cry arises from materialism. There is no Father to care for us; the world formed itself; man is only organized matter; there is no heaven; we are dissolved when we die as prophets, apostles, reformers, martyrs, great statesmen, teachers, poets, and our own dear ones have been. But philosophers, poets, teachers of all the religions, believed that the dead lived. It is all a dream, says the materialist. Take what pleasure you can, don't sorrow for anything, laugh at distress. 2. The gospel brings joy to the distressed and sorrowful in the present. We look through our tears at the closed grave, but see standing there One saying, "I am the Resurrection and the Life." Is not our religion good? Then trust it, and don't be afraid that it is going to be overthrown. It may be captured like the ark, but it will give the Philistines more trouble than they bargain for. (*T. Jones, D.D.*)		*The Bible and free inquiry:*—"Despise not prophesyings," *i.e.*, preaching, the apostle has just said. Now comes the text. "Don't deify the preacher." Put what they say to the test (1 John iv. 1; Acts xvii. 11). Congregations should listen with a desire to profit, and then carry all the preacher says to the test of holy Scripture. I. THE END OUR INQUIRY SHOULD AIM AT—some real good. 1. There is such a thing as good. Philosophers have told us of a *summum bonum*, and common experience points in the same direction : "There be many that say, Who will show us any good ? " We have not only intellects that want to be satisfied, but hearts and wills that want to be cheered and guided. We want to be peaceful while we live and when we come to die, and nothing is really good that does not help us to this end (Isa. lv. 1–3). 2. This is the end our inquiry should aim at. Mere assault on error or ridicule of folly is poor and heartless work. Sometimes it is necessary, but if this is all you attempt you may break every idol and not increase man's happiness by one atom. Paul did something more than this at Athens. 3. Here is a model for the free inquirer. Let your object be to do all the good you can. All your skill as an iconoclast will do nothing to meet the cry, "Who will show us," &c. II. THE CHARACTER THE INQUIRY SHOULD ASSUME. Put everything to the proof. The inquiry should be—1. Careful. This is required in chemistry and astronomy, and the man who does not carefully examine the truths of religion will make the grossest blunders. 2. Comprehensive. You ought to examine the inquirer as well as the object, the instruments he uses, and the faculties he employs. A man once gazed through a telescope at the sun, and immediately turned away in alarm, exclaiming, " There is a monster in the sun." It proved, however, only to be an insect in the telescope. So with many who glance now and then at religion. Their instruments of inquiry are not clear, and they ascribe to the shining orb what really belongs to the foul tube. What would you think of a man who had no ear for music criticizing Handel's " Messiah "? Or a man colour-blind describing a garden in May? Or a prodigal judging the rules of his father's house? Do these illustrations apply? I am not saying that every free inquirer into religion is worse than other men, but that he is no better by nature. Ought he not, then, to take this into account? If I have unworthy passions I have a bias against a holy religion. 3. Free from pride, passion, sin, ambition. &c. III. The welcome which the Bible gives to such inquiry. It welcomes inquiry. 1. Of such a nature. Here is this Book of Truth, not hiding in darkness, but exposing itself. I tell you of—(1) A God, a great, intelligent Creator. Put it to the test. Is it not more reasonable than that there is no intelligent cause ? (2) A law ordaining perfect love to God and man. Put it to the test. What would the world have been had it kept it? What is it because it has broken it? (3) A Saviour. Prove Him. Does He not commend Himself to reason and conscience? (4) Mysteries. Prove this too. Is it not reasonable that the finite can never grasp the infinite? 2. To such an end. It is " good " we want. This the Bible brings. Its revelations were not given for our amusement, but for our advantage. It gives peace with God through Christ in obedience to the law, peace in our own souls and towards men, and leads to the world of perfect peace. And now it says, " Hold it fast ! " There is something rich and substantial about it. Hold it fast against the power and subtlety of the tempter. (*F. Tucker, B.A.*)      *The right of private judgment in matters of religion:*—I. Objections that are taken against the exercise of this right. It is said that if this be granted then every individual will have his own religion. 1. Our answer to this is, such would be a consequence not of the exercise of private judgment, but of human depravity. If imperfect men had all the privileges of angels consequences would follow very different from those characterizing the history of angels, but no one would say that they were the necessary effects of the enjoyment of angelic privileges. If, then, instead of assailing the depravity of man for abusing the right of private judgment we assail that right and forbid its exercise, we are mistaking the source of the evil and not taking the proper method to prevent it. 2. Then we may ask how interdicting the right can prevent the evil consequences ? Shall we issue a decree and enforce it by penalties? But that will only stop the expression, and will not interfere with the right of private judgment. The slave clad in iron fetters has still his private judgment, and with his mind, which is free, you cannot meddle. 3. But it may be affirmed that to suppress this expression is a good thing, and prevents evil. How so? This supposes an infallible instructor. How do we know that the public judgment of any body of men may not be as pernicious as the private judgment of an individual? Look at the past. Almost every heresy has at one time been protected and taught by public authority, and almost every orthodox sentiment has been put down by the same. II. Considerations in support of this right. 1. We find from Scripture that the right of private judgment in religious matters is the duty, not merely the privilege, of every individual to whom the Word of God should come. (1) This Epistle was addressed to the Church, not to any public functionary. Paul, Timothy, and Silas, inspired teachers of the mind of God, say, " Prove all things." If any say that the laity must defer to authority, the authority here says exercise your private judgment! Then what is the meaning of the general addresses to the Churches, as such, at the commencement of each Epistle, but that the minds of laymen as well as ministers should be exercised upon them? (2) When we come to Epistles addressed to individuals such as Timothy and Titus we find nothing investing them with the authority of interpreting against the private judgment of those they taught. Nay, they are commanded " in meekness to instruct those that oppose themselves," not to dictate to them on the ground of authority. (3) Then we have the doctrine that every one of us must give an account of himself to God, which implies the exercise of private judgment. How can we reconcile this with being compelled to follow the dictates of another? Shall we give an account of ourselves to God at the last whilst we are permitted to take no account of ourselves? Shall we carry mental slavery with us all the time we are in our state of probation, and in eternity only stand on our own foundation? Nay; if God tells us that every one of us must give an account then He means that we must prove all things against the day of that account. 2. The arguments derived from the powers and faculties that God has given us is no less conclusive. Why did God give us the power of judging at all? Is it possible that God would give men the exercise of public judgment for the things of time and forbid it in the affairs of eternity? III. DUTIES CONSEQUENT UPON THIS RIGHT. 1. Searching the Scriptures. We criminate ourselves deeply if we contend for the right of private judgment and neglect to search those oracles about which alone the faculty can be engaged. What should we think of a judge who insisted on his right to pronounce judgment while ignorant of the matter on which the judgment was to be pronounced. 2. Stimulating others by teaching them the great things of God. If it be our duty to search the Scriptures it is the duty of all. It is incumbent on us, then, not only to practice, but to encourage this exercise. 3. Duly appreciating the falsehood that revelation trammels the mind. On the contrary the text breaks every mental bond. (*J. Burnet.*) *Innovation and conservatism in matters of religion :*—This advice is always pertinent; yet there are periods in which it is specially relevant. While humanity on the whole is ever advancing, the stream at one time seems to stand still, and at another rushes on with noisy activity. When Paul wrote all was full of mental activity, religious conflict, political tumult, and the first century repeats itself in the nineteenth. Our age has three characteristics which bear on the interests of religion. 1. Intellect is all alive, more so perhaps than at any other period. This is the result—(1) Of those general laws by which the social progress of our race is governed. (2) Of our refined civilization, which by ever becoming more complicated is continually taxing the human mind. (3) Of the stimulus of advancing education, which begets emulation, and raises continually higher the standard of necessary acquirement. Hence—2. The age is one of mental freedom. The mind is goaded by internal cravings and external excitements. It goes forth to explore all regions, and will not be stopped by authority or opposition. The right of private judgment is conceded, and is exercised without scruple. Hence— 3. A clamorous war of opinion. The number of sects grows portentously. New opinions are started on almost every subject. All extremes of views on religion are zealously and ably advocated. If we be men and not children we cannot be unconcerned about these controversies, but don't be alarmed, "Prove all things,"&c. These words involve the doctrines of—(1) Individual responsibility for religious faith and practice. (2) Individual duty and right of private judgment. 1. THE LIBERAL ELEMENT in the text. 1. Candid inquiry. The disposition to know what others think is, when moderately possessed, an admirable trait of character. Some ensconce themselves within the limits of their hereditary creed, and listen with anger to opposing opinions deaf to all argument. These intellectual pigmies have in all ages proved a stumbling-block to educated men, and assumed a position unwarranted by Christianity as the text shows. The gospel as an innovation, courts the investigation that it has never scrupled to exercise, and aims at inspiring in its disciples the love of truth as truth. 2. Patient examination. Be not like the Athenians, who spent their whole time in hearkening to some new thing; but spend much of it in sifting the new things you hear. Neither novelty nor authority can supply the place of argument. 3. Wise and decisive selection. The text supposes that when all things are proved, some will be accepted, which are to be held fast. Some are ever learning, but never come to the knowledge of the truth, attempting an easy neutrality which speedily turns into treason against Christ. This discrimination between the good and the bad supposes the possession of a touchstone. Primarily man's reason is the touchstone. There are propositions which no man can accept. We can no more believe in the incredible than see the invisible. The Word of God is, of course, the final appeal, but not by superseding reason—only by assisting it. Reason has first to decide on the credentials of Revelation, and then to be consulted as to its contents. Reason, then, following the Word of God is to be the criterion by which we are to "prove all things." II. THE CONSERVATIVE ELEMENT: "Hold fast," &c. Which assumes—1. That truth is attainable. Some deny this. Let Christian men beware of this perilous frame of mind which leads inevitably to selfish misanthropy or unprincipled sensualism. A free thinker is frequently a man who does not think at all, but considers all things as not worth thinking about. Believe what all wise and good men have believed and proved, that there is such a thing as fixed truth, and having found it—2. Hold it fast, without fickleness or fear. Having made up your mind, after due deliberation, adhere to your decision, and make use of it for further acquisition; not refuse to hear anything more about it, but be not unsettled without fresh and weighty argument. Don't keep going over the old ground. This is the only means of attaining and retaining personal peace, and manliness of Spirit. (*T. G. Horton.*) *Man in relation to the vast and the specific:*—I. A VAST REALM FOR INQUIRY : " Prove all things." This implies—1. Freedom of thought. Go into all churches and systems, there is good everywhere : find it out. Confine not your mind to your own narrow creed or church. 2. A test of truth. This test is threefold—(1) Results : " By their fruits shall ye know them." (2) The Spirit of Christ. Whatever agrees not with His free, righteous and loving Spirit must be rejected. (3) Conscience : " Why even of yourselves judge ye not what is right ? " II. A SPECIFIC OBJECT TO ATTAIN : "Hold fast." It is the good you want. What is the good? The "truth as it is in Jesus," a living, beautiful, soul transporting reality. Get this and then hold it fast. There is a danger of losing it ; it is worth holding ; it is more precious than worlds, it is the pearl of great price—the heaven of souls. (*D. Thomas, D.D.*) *Testing the Bible:*—Let me caution you against putting off making up your mind about this Book. Ever since 1772 there has been great discussion as to who was the author of Junius's Letters, those letters so full of sarcasm, and vituperation, and power. The whole English nation was stirred up with them. More than a hundred volumes have been written to discuss that question, who was Junius ? who wrote Junius's Letters ? Well, it is an interesting question to discuss ; but still, after all, it makes but little practical difference to you and to me who Junius was, whether Sir Philip Francis, or Lord Chatham, or Horne Tooke, or Horace Walpole, or Henry Grattan, or any one of the forty-four men who were seriously charged with the authorship. But it is an absorbing question, it is a practical question, it is an overwhelming question to you and to me, the authorship of this Holy Bible, whether the Lord God of heaven and earth, or a pack of dupes, scoundrels, and impostors. We cannot afford to adjourn that question a week, or a day, or an hour, any more than a sea captain can afford to say, " Well, this is a very dark night ; I have really lost my bearings ; there's a light out there, I don't know whether it's a lighthouse or a false light on the shore. I don't know what it is ; but I'll just go to sleep, and in the morning I'll find out." In the morning the vessel might be on the rocks and the beach strewn with the white faces of the dead crew. The time for that sea captain to find out about the lighthouse is before he goes to sleep. Oh, my friends ! I want you to understand that in our deliberations about this Bible we are not at calm anchorage, but we are rapidly coming towards the coast, coming with all the furnaces ablaze, coming at the rate of seventy heart throbs a minute, and I must know whether it is going to be harbour or shipwreck. (*T. de Witt Talmage.*) *A life given to proving all things:*—I have really no history but a mental history. . . . I have seen no one, known none of the celebrities of my own time intimately or at all, and have only an inaccurate memory of what I hear. All my energy was directed upon one end—to improve myself to form my own mind, to sound things thoroughly, to free myself from the bondage of unreason and the traditional prejudices which when I began first to think constituted the whole of my intellectual fabric. (*Mark Pattison, B.D.*) *Proving the power of God's grace:*—It is related that Bishop Kavanagh was one day walking when he met a prominent physician, who offered him a seat in his carriage. The physician was an infidel, and the conversation turned upon religion. " I am surprised," said the doctor, " that such an intelligent man as you should believe such an old fable as that." The bishop said, " Doctor, suppose years ago some one had recommended to you a prescription for pulmonary consumption, and you had procured the prescription and taken it according to order, and had been cured of that terrible disease, what would you say of the man who would not try your prescription ? " " I should say he was a fool." " Twenty-five years ago," said Kavanagh, " I tried the power of God's grace. It made a different man of me. All these years I have preached salvation, and wherever accepted have never known it to fail." *Faith and reason:*—Faith and reason are, as it were, two keys which God has given us with which to unlock all spiritual mysteries. It is as if I had a drawer in which were stored away my valuable papers. The cabinet maker gives me two keys to my drawer, telling me that both keys will generally unlock the drawer, but always, if one will not, the other will—that therefore I must keep them securely, and keep them always tied together. But I untie and separate them, and, for safe keeping, place one key carefully away in the drawer itself and lock it up with the other key. With this other key I lock and unlock the drawer at pleasure. But the time comes at length when the key I have will not unlock the drawer, and now I need the other; but I have locked it up and cannot get it. Just so faith and reason are two keys that God, our Maker, has given us with which to unlock all spiritual mysteries. Generally, either will unlock and explain all difficulties in Revelation and Christian experience; but always, if the one fails, the other will unlock the mystery. But here is a man that goes and locks his faith up in his reason; and presently he encounters a spiritual truth which his reason will not explain or unlock—it transcends human reason. You tell him, for example, that he must believe in the Trinity, in regeneration, in the resurrection of the body. "But," says he, "I cannot—they are unreasonable." And why can he not believe these spiritual truths? Simply because he has gone and locked his faith up in his reason, and will not accept any truth which he cannot comprehend and which his reason will not fully explain of itself without the aid of faith. The rationalist is he who locks his faith up in his reason. Now it may be, and is, just as bad to lock your reason up in your faith. There, for instance, is the poor deluded Romanist, who believes implicitly anything that his Church teaches, whether reasonable or unreasonable. You remonstrate with him for believing in transubstantiation, in the virtue of relics, in the absurd traditions of his Church. You tell him these things are unreasonable. "So they may be," he replies, "but I believe them nevertheless, for the Church teaches them, and I believe whatever the Church teaches." And why does he believe such absurdities? Simply because he has locked his reason up in his faith and given the Pope the key—and whatever the Pope or the Church or his bishop teaches he believes implicitly, whether it be reasonable or unreasonable. It is impossible for one to be a true Roman Catholic without locking his reason up in his faith. But God demands that we shall use both our faith and our reason, and keep them both joined together. Doing this we shall be preserved from rationalism on the one hand, and from credulity and superstition on the other. Now God does not demand that we shall believe in anything that contradicts our reason; but He does demand that we shall believe in truths that transcend human reason. If the Bible should teach that black is white, that right is wrong, that a thing can be and not be at the same time, I would not and could not believe it, because it would plainly contradict my reason. But when it teaches that there is a God, a Trinity, a soul in this body, a heaven prepared for it, I may not and do not fully comprehend these spiritual truths; but I do not decline to believe them on that ground; for while they do transcend my reason, they do not contradict it. The Roman Catholic believes many truths that contradict human reason; the rationalist will believe no truth which transcends human reason; the true intelligent Christian believes nothing that will contradict, but many things that transcend, human reason. The first locks his reason up in his faith; the second locks his faith up in his reason; the third uses both his faith and his reason and keeps them ever joined together. (*Prof. Tillett.*)

Ver. 22. **Abstain from all appearance of evil.**—*Safe conduct:*—A man will never begin to be good till he begins to decline those occasions that have made him bad; therefore saith St. Paul to the Thessalonians, and through them to all others, "Abstain from all appearance of evil." I. THE WAY TO FULFIL THIS COUNSEL. You must shun and be shy of the very shows and shadows of sin. The word which is ordinarily rendered "appearance," signifies kind or sort; and so the meaning of the apostle seems to be this, Abstain from all sort, or the whole kind, of evil; from all that is truly evil, be it never so small. The least sin is dangerous. Cæsar was stabbed with bodkins, and many have been eaten up by mice. The least spark may consume the greatest house, the tinest leak may sink the noblest vessel, the smallest sin is enough to undo the soul, and, therefore, shun all the occasions that lead to it. Job made a covenant with his eyes (Job xxxi. 1), Joseph would not be in the room where his mistress was (Gen. xxxix. 10), and David, when himself, would not sit with vain persons (Psa. xxvi. 3–7). As long as there is fuel in our hearts for a temptation we cannot be secure: he that hath gunpowder about him had need keep far enough off from sparkles; he that would neither wound conscience nor credit, God nor Gospel, had need hate "the garment spotted with the flesh." In the law, God commanded His people not only that they should worship no idol, but that they should demolish all the monuments of them, and that they should make no covenant nor affinity with those who worshipped them, and all lest they should be drawn by those occasions to commit idolatry with them. He that would not taste of the forbidden fruit must not so much as gaze on it; he that would not be bitten by the serpent, must not so much as parley with him.

He that will not fly from the occasions and allurements of sin, though they may seem never so pleasant to the eye or sweet to the taste, shall find them in the end more sharp than vinegar, more bitter than wormwood, more deadly than poison. II. NOTED EXAMPLES TO INCITE US.  Scipio Africanus, warring in Spain, took New Carthage by storm, at which time a beautiful and noble virgin resolved to flee to him for succour to preserve her chastity.  Hearing of this, he would not suffer her to come into his presence for fear of temptation, but caused her to be restored in safety to her father.  Livia counselled her husband Augustus not only to do no wrong, but not to seem to do it.  Cæsar would not search Pompey's cabinet, lest he should find new matters for revenge.  Plato mounted upon his horse, and judging himself a little moved with pride, at once alighted, lest he should be overtaken with loftiness in riding.  Theseus is said to have cut off his golden locks, lest his enemies should take advantage by laying hold of them.  Oh, Christian people! shall the very heathen, who sit in darkness, shun and fly from the occasion of sin, and will not you, who sit under the sunshine of the gospel?  To prevent carnal carefulness, Christ sends His disciples to take lessons from the irrational creatures (Matt. vi. 26–32).  And to prevent your closing with the temptation to sin, let me send you to school to the like creatures, that you may learn by them to shun and avoid the occasions of sin.  A certain kind of fish, perceiving themselves in danger of taking, by an instinct which they have, do darken the water, and so many times escape the net which is laid for them.  And a certain kind of fowl, when they fly over Taurus, keep stones in their mouths, lest by shrieking and gabbling they discover themselves to the eagles, which are among the mountains, waiting for them.  Now, if all these considerations put together will not incite you to decline the occasions of sin, I know not what will. (*T. Brooks.*)      *Avoiding the appearance of evil:*—I. THE NATURE OF THOSE APPEARANCES OF EVIL WE ARE REQUIRED TO AVOID.  1. Whatever may be interpreted as evil by others, so as to become a stumbling-block or matter of reproach. Their consciences may be too scrupulous and their tempers censorious, yet we are not to offend or grieve the weak unnecessarily.  The omission of things indifferent, can neither be sinful nor injurious, their commission may be both (1 Cor. viii. 13).  This must, of course, be understood with some limitation, else there would be no end of conforming to men's humours and fancies; therefore good men must be left to act according to their own scruples and may disregard scruples which have no shadow of reason or Scripture to support them.  2. What may be an occasion of evil to ourselves.  Some things not evil may lead to evil. Peter's going into the palace of the high priest led to his denial of Christ. Achan's looking stirred up his covetousness; hence David prays to be turned away from beholding vanity, and our Lord taught us to say, "Lead us not into temptation, but," &c.  The fly that buzzes about the candle will at length singe its wings.  3. Whatever borders on evil or approaches towards it.  Instead of inquiring how far we may go in gratifying this or that appetite without offending God, let us keep as far away as we can.  If you would not swear do not use expletives : if you would be temperate do not load your table with superfluities.  4. The first risings of evil in the heart such as anger, covetousness, uncleanness.  " When lust hath conceived it bringing forth sin," &c.  " Keep thy heart with all diligence," therefore.  II. WHEN MAY WE BE SAID TO ABSTAIN FROM EVERY APPEARANCE OF EVIL ? When our whole conduct will bear the light ; when we are sincere in our intentions and circumspect in our actions ; when the Divine glory is our aim and the good of man our work.  To this end incessant watchfulness is required.  1. In the common concerns of life.  Everything like artifice or dishonesty is unworthy of the Christian character (chap. iv. 6).  2. In our amusements and recreations.  They must be innocent and lawful, few and inexpensive, healthful and select.  3. In our daily intercourse.  We must speak the words of truth and soberness (Eph. iv. 29; James v. 12).  4. In religious exercises, "Let not your good be evil spoken of." III. THE MOTIVES.  By abstaining from the appearance of evil.  1. Many of our falls will be prevented.  2. It will give credit to our profession, and tend to convince the world of the reality of our religion.  3. It will contribute much to the peace and satisfaction of our minds.  (*B. Beddome, M.A.*)      *Abstinence from the appearance of evil :*—The tendency is to place too high an estimate on appearances. Hence outward religion comes to be magnified at the expense of inward holiness. To guard against this great stress is laid in the Bible on piety in the heart : but this has lead people to say, "Appearances are nothing—it is with the heart God has to do."  The object of the text is to give appearances their real importance

It is therefore connected with several injunctions which relate to inward and practical Godliness and which issue in a prayer which shows that abstinence from the appearance of evil is an essential attribute of entire sanctification. I. THE IMPORT OF THE PRECEPT. There may be the appearance of evil where evil is not intended and where there is no evil in fact. 1. In our actions. (1) In our social intercourse we may aim to show a proper regard to men of the world for our improvement or for their own, but this association may appear to be the result of elective affinity. (2) In our pursuits we may seem to ourselves to be merely diligent in business, while we may appear to be contravening the prohibition of laying up treasures upon earth. (3) In our dress and furniture we may merely seek our own convenience, while to others we may appear conforming to the world. (4) In our contributions and other expenditure we may seem to be merely liberal, but to others prodigal. (5) In our intercourse with the other sex we may think ourselves only courteous, but appear to others amorous. Conversely—(1) We may shun society for the purpose of avoiding its contamination, but appear to others to forget our social relations and duties. (2) We may design to live above the world, but the world may think us negligent of business. (3) We may intend to be plain in dress, but appear to others to make religion consist in plainness. (4) We may be merely economical, but appear penurious. (5) We may think ourselves correct in our bearing to the other sex, but they may think us morose. It is difficult to determine on which side of the happy medium the greatest evil lies, but as the least appearance of evil is injurious we should always be on our guard. 2. In our words. (1) We may design to be free and pleasant and yet appear trifling. (2) We may be in earnest only, and yet appear to be in a passion. (3) We may be faithful in reproof and appear censorious. (4) We may only intend to use plain language but it appears course and indelicate. (5) We may be imparting instruction and be voted conceited. 3. In our spirit. (1) Zeal may have the appearance of fanaticism; (2) Elevation of mind, of haughtiness; (3) Promptness of obstinacy; (4) Calmness of stoicism; (5) Humility of mean-spiritedness; (6) Deliberation of infirmity of purpose. II. THE REASONS FOR THE PRECEPT. 1. Those which affect ourselves. Falling into evil appearances—(1) Results from the want of a correct taste, a well disciplined conscience, knowledge, watchfulness, evils which will ripen into bad habits if not checked. (2) Will mar our own enjoyment of religion when we find that it has done harm. (3) Will ruin our usefulness which depends on our influence, which acts through appearances, and is estimated by them. 2. Those which affect God's glory. We honour God in proportion as we exhibit a practical illustration of the purity of the Christian character before the world. The ungodly associate our blemishes with our religion. 3. Those which regard the well-being of others. All example consists in appearances, and "no one liveth to himself"; we are contributing by our appearances to the formation of the characters of those around us, and any one of those appearances may make all the difference between heaven and hell. III. INFERENCES. 1. That appearances are of high importance. 2. That appearances, and not what a man means, determine his influence as a member of the Church. 3. That the qualities which will enable us to avoid the appearance of evil should be sedulously cultivated—an accurate judgment, a tender conscience, perfect self-knowledge. 4. That the Scriptures which pourtray so minutely the appearances of evil should be diligently studied. (*G. Peck, D.D.*) *Avoiding sins of every appearance:*—1. The "appearance" of material things does not depend entirely upon their form, but largely upon the medium through which, the light in which, and the eye by which they are seen. Some men are colour-blind. Some men have the jaundice. Thoughts and feelings are still more liable to be misapprehended, because they must be addressed by one soul to another through the senses—the eye, the ear, the touch, by the pressure of the hand, by speech, by gesture, by writing. A thought or emotion, therefore, suffers a double refraction in passing from one mind to another. And thus it comes to pass that even in communities composed of most serene and wise intellects and loving hearts, the appearance does not always match and represent the ideal. 2. The difficulty of the rule as it stands in our version is this, that there is nothing so good but it may appear evil. To the evil all things seem evil, and you cannot help that. Was there ever a virtue that did not seem a vice to a man's enemy? Does not his liberality appear prodigality, his economy parsimony, his cheerfulness levity, his conscientiousness puritanism, his temperance asceticism, his courage foolhardiness, his devotion hypocrisy? How is it possible to avoid such judgments as these unless a man could have the whole world for his friends? Can the heavenly Father demand more of you than that you really be true and faithful and pure? Must you also fritter your strength away in striving to make your good life seem good in the eyes of perverse men? 3. The attempt to gain the favourable verdict of all men is not only impracticable, but it is demoralizing. It occupies a man with appearances, and not realities; with his reputation, and not with his character. There can be devised no shorter cut to hypocrisy than a constant effort to "abstain from all appearance of evil." 4. What, then, did the apostle mean? The difficulties of the text are removed by the translation "abstain from evil of every form." The lesson is total abstinence from what is really evil. The complementary thought is that evil can never be good by a mere change of appearance. Let us look at some of the ways in which we may follow what is really evil because its appearance is good, and show how Satan disguises himself as an angel of light. I. UNITY AND UNIFORMITY. The most important thing about any man is his faith. A thorough belief in a real truth is life: it will reproduce itself in the outward action. How easy it is here to find real evil that is apparently good. To strive to compel men to uniformity seems a good, whereas it is really an evil. One may even quote Scripture in justification. "One faith." A man may forget that the essential principle may be one, while the phenomenal presentation may be manifold. All compulsory uniformity is mischievous. The inquisition produced cruelties among good men, and hypocrisies among bad. In its essence truth has always unity, in its development seldom uniformity. Some think it would be delightful for all men to see truth at the same angle; but if there were but two men who should profess to do it, it would be either a mistake, or a falsehood. Give over the effort to secure ecclesiastical uniformity. Let grace be natural, and nature gracious. Give room for God in man, and in the Church as you do in nature. II. LIBERTY AND LICENTIOUSNESS. There is something very captivating in "liberty." The very word sounds open and breezy. Liberty has been made a queen and a goddess. More money has been spent for her, and more blood shed for her, than for any other. When one recollects the history of the race, one is not surprised that when Madame Roland was going to her doom, she should have saluted the statue of Liberty with the bitter exclamation, "O Liberty, what outrages are perpetrated in thy name!" It is exceedingly difficult to draw the line between licentiousness and liberty, and hence the danger is greater. True freedom of intellect and heart and life consists in voluntary and exact obedience to the law of God. A compulsory obedience is mere hypocrisy. An inexact obedience is a perpetual weakness. Every step taken in the statutes of the Lord with a free will is a step of freedom. David perceived this when he said, "I will walk at liberty, for I seek Thy precepts." But, the moment a man lifts his foot from the law of the Lord, and sets it down outside, he places it in the nets of evil, and is ensnared. But the modern and atheistic idea of liberty is the absence of all moral law, or the refusal to be controlled by law. In other words, it is licentiousness. Avoid it, no matter what its appearance. How vast are the hull and rigging of the largest vessel on the ocean, and how small is the helm; and yet that little helm turns that great bulk whithersoever the helmsman listeth. Suppose the great vessel should say, "I will not endure this impertinent interference, this incessant control," and should throw the helmsman overboard, and unship both helm and rudder. She would be free then, would she not? Yes, but a free prey to all winds and waves. Is that the freedom to be desired? And yet that is the idea of this age. The State, the Church, the family are to be overthrown, for men must be free! It is pitiful and painful to see human beings struggling to be free, to be hated, to starve, to die, to be damned. Avoid this evil. Remember that no splendour of dress can make a leper clean, and no brilliancy of appearance can make an evil good. III. JUSTICE AND INTOLERANCE. The dogma of infallibility is not a mere ecclesiastical development. Its seed is in every heart. If we are unconscious of it, who does not act upon it? We pronounce judgment as if there could be no appeal, and act upon such sentences as final. Nay, more. There is a disposition on the part of many to go beyond, and keep surveillance of society, making themselves general detectives. They are often heresy-hunters, self-constituted health boards, enforcing social sanitary regulations of their own. The plain fact is, they are censorious. The reason they did not "abstain from" this "evil" is, because it has the "appearance" of good. It seems to evince a high moral sense. It looks like loyalty to truth, and unselfish. The man is not seeking to be popular! He is a martyr to his sense of right? It is good and grand! He applauds himself. He feels that others ought to applaud him. He undertakes to execute his own sentences. The condemned is treated like a leper, like a lost man. All that is done that the purity of the judge shall be evinced. Men and women seem to think that kindness to a sinner is endorsement of, and participation in his sin. Hence the evil of social ostracism. A man that has fallen has so few helps to rise, and a woman who has fallen has no aids but what God gives. "Abstain from this evil" of censoriousness, whatever appearance it may have. It is very easy to get up the requisite amount of virtuous indignation, but it is difficult to keep indignation virtuous. While burning the sins I ought to hate, it will soon begin to burn the sinner whom I ought to love. IV. GENEROSITY AND PRODIGALITY. The latter is an evil under any name and in every guise. It leads men to be careless and lazy about their expenditures. Because there are so many easy givers, there are so many easy beggars. It is injurious to give to the undeserving as it is injurious to withhold from those who deserve. The man who walks through the streets talking or thinking, and pulls something out of his pocket for every beggar without looking the applicant in the face, or recollecting him ten minutes after, is not charitable. He is a thriftless prodigal. True charity, and true liberality, and true generosity know how much, and to whom, and why, they gave; not in remembrance of self-complaisance, but that they may see how much more they can do. Abstain from the evil of prodigality which has the appearance of liberality. V. ECONOMY AND STINGINESS. The grip of selfishness on money is the vice that makes a man feel that it is better ninety-nine worthy cases suffer than that one unworthy case be helped. It is a stone-blind vice. Men know when they are liars, thieves, murderers, but they do not know when they are covetous. Every sin committed by man against man has been admitted by some one who was guilty, except two; and one of them is covetousness. It puts on so good an "appearance!" It is called among men prudence, economy, thrift, any word which glosses over the inner viciousness. It was so in the time of David, who said, "Men will praise thee when thou doest well to thyself." But "abstain" from this "evil" of doing so well for yourself that you can do nothing for others, and remember that the Lord will praise thee when they doest well to another. VI. INDEPENDENCE AND CONTEMPT FOR APPEARANCES. We are not to do a thing that is wrong because it has the appearance of right in the eyes of many, and we are bound to do good, however it may seem to others; but we are also to see to it that our "good be not evil spoken of." There is in some men a swaggering boastfulness of independence of the opinion of others, of determination to do just what they think right, and of regardlessness of the feelings of others. They think it looks well. There is an appearance of stern virtue in all this; of character; of independence. Any voluntary hazarding of the appearance of evil is most foolish, if not criminal. No man has a right on any pretence to "give a just offence to the moral sentiments" of the community. (*C. F. Deems, D.D.*)     *Avoiding the appearance of evil:*—Venn was given to understand that a lady to whom his ministry had been singularly blessed, had been pleased to requite her obligations by making him heir to her property, which was very considerable. And we may not doubt that he gladly accepted the intended favour, and persuaded himself that it was a seasonable gift from God, for the relief of his mind, and for the comfort of his family. Perhaps he might have so reasoned and felt, in regard to it, but the following letter which he addressed to the lady, on hearing of her kind intention, will show in what a pure, lofty sphere his spirit moved: "My very dear friend, I understand, by my wife, your most kind and generous intention toward us in your will. The legacy would be exceedingly acceptable, and I can assure you the person from whom it would come would greatly enhance the benefit. I love my sweet children as much as is lawful, and as I know it would give you pleasure to minister to the comfort of me and mine, I should, with greater joy, accept of your liberality. But an insurmountable bar stands in the way—the love of Him to whom we are both indebted, not for a transient benefit, for silver or gold, but for an inheritance, incorruptible, undefiled, and that fadeth not away, reserved in heaven for us. His honour, His cause, is, and must be, dearer to His people than wife, children, or life itself. It is the firm resolve of His saints, yea, doubtless, I count all things but loss for the excellency of the knowledge of Christ Jesus my Lord. To be, therefore, a stumbling block in the way of any that are seeking Him—to give the least countenance to any that would be glad to bring His followers into contempt, and call in question their sincere and disinterested attachment to Him would grieve me while in health, darken my mind in sickness, and load me with self-condemnation on a bed of death. How would it also render all my exhortations feeble, and make them be accounted only as pulpit declamation, if, when I was pressing that solemn truth upon my people, 'Love not the world, neither the things in the world,' they could say, our minister, however, was careful to secure the favour of this rich proselyte, and, at length, to gain sufficiently by her! After the most mature deliberation, therefore, it is our request, which we cannot permit you to refuse us, that you will not leave us any other token of your regard than something of little value, but what it derives from the giver. If it should please God that our connection should be prolonged some years, we shall, in our hearts, still more abundantly enjoy your friendship when we are sure that we are not in danger of being influenced by a regard to our own interest. And if we must soon have the cutting affliction of losing you, you may depend on it, we shall not less affectionately make mention of your name, and your unfeigned love for us both in Christ Jesus, than if we had what the world esteems the only substantial proof of your regard. As for our children, whom many will think that we have not the love for that we owe them, by refusing your great favour, I would say only this, we both know of no inheritance equal to the blessing of God; and the certain way of securing it, as far as means can avail, is to be found ready to love or suffer any thing sooner than to incur the appearance of evil." (*Memoir of Venn.*)　　*The appearance of evil:*—A missionary magazine, in giving an account of the conversion to Christianity of a high-caste Brahmin in India, stated, as a good test of the new convert's sincerity, the following fact: A Christian friend, knowing that the Hindoo custom of wearing the hair long, and fastened with sacred flowers in a knot at the back of the head, was intimately connected with certain acts of idolatrous worship, advised the Brahmin to cut off this hair at once, and thus demonstrate to all men that he had really ceased to be an idolater. To this suggestion the convert promptly replied, "Yes, certainly, for it is the devil's flag." Accordingly, the hair was immediately cut off.　　*The appearance of evil:*—An old Chinese proverb says, "Do not stop in a cucumber field to tie the shoe." The meaning is very plain. Some one will be likely to fancy that you are stealing fruit. Always remember the injunction: "Abstain from all appearance of evil." Do not stop under the saloon porch to rest yourself, however shady the trees may be, or however inviting the chairs. Some one may fancy you are a common lounger there, and so your name is tarnished. Don't go to a liquor saloon to get a glass of lemonade, however refreshing it may seem to you. Rather buy your lemons and prepare the cooling beverage at home, where others may share it with you, probably at no greater expense than your single glass would cost you. Somebody seeing you drinking at the bar will be sure to tell the story, and will not be particular to state that you were drinking only lemonade. Then, too, if you are careless about the appearance of evil, you will soon grow equally careless about the evil itself. (*Great Thoughts.*)　　*Fear of sin:*—The old naturalist, Ulysses Androvaldus, tell us that a dove is so afraid of a hawk, that she will be frightened at the sight of one of its feathers. Whether it be so or not, I cannot tell; but this I know, that when a man has had a thorough shaking over the jaws of hell, he will be so afraid of sin, that even one of its feathers—any one sin—will alarm and send a thrill of fear through his soul. This is a part of the way by which the Lord turns us when we are turned indeed. (*C. H. Spurgeon.*)　　*The need of guarding against all evil:*—Manton says: "A man that would keep out the cold in winter shutteth all his doors and windows, yet the wind will creep in, though he doth not leave any open hole for it." We must leave no inlet for sin, but stop up every hole and cranny by which it can enter. There is need of great care in doing this, for when our very best is done sin will find an entrance. During the bitter cold weather we list the doors, put sand-bags on the windows, draw curtains, and arrange screens, and yet we are made to feel that we live in a northern climate: in the same way must we be diligent to shut out sin, and we shall find abundant need to guard every point, for after we have done all, we shall, in one way or another, be made to feel that we live in a sinful world. Well, what must we do? We must follow the measures which common prudence teaches us in earthly matters. We must drive out the cold by keeping up a good fire within. The presence of the Lord Jesus in the soul can so warm the heart that worldliness and sin will be expelled, and we shall be both holy and happy. The Lord grant, it for Jesus' sake. (*Ibid.*)

Ver. 23. **The very God of peace sanctify you wholly.**—*A short but comprehensive prayer:*—The apostle had told the Thessalonians in the beginning of his Epistle, that he always made mention of them in his prayers; and, now he is writing to them, and closing his Epistle, he lifteth up his whole heart for them. I. THE GOD TO WHOM THE APOSTLE PRAYS, namely, "the very God of Peace." He is sometimes denominated "the God of all grace," "the God of love," but here—"the very God of peace," not only because He is "the Author of peace," but also "the Lover of concord." There was a special reason for this: Paul felt that by the peaceableness and unity of the Thessalonians themselves they would best obtain those things for which he prays. God does not bestow His choice blessings on the members of a Church who are given to strife and disorder, but on those who are bound together in one by the golden cord of love. Such peace and fellowship are pleasant to behold both to men and angels; how much more to God Himself! (Psa. cxxxiii.). II. THE BURDEN OF THE APOSTLE'S PRAYER. 1. Sanctification. Not partial but entire— the whole man. Or, he prays that they may be more perfectly sanctified, for the best are sanctified but in part while in this world; and therefore we should pray for and press toward complete sanctification. 2. Preservation. Where the good work of grace is begun, it will be carried on, be protected and preserved; and all those who are sanctified in Christ Jesus shall be preserved to the coming of Christ Jesus. If God did not carry on His good work in the soul, it would miscarry; and therefore we should pray God to perfect it, and preserve us blameless, that is, free from sin and impurity, till at length we are presented faultless before the throne of His glory with exceeding great joy. III. THE APOSTLE'S ASSURANCE ANENT HIS PRAYER. "Faithful is He that calleth you," he writes to his converts, "who also will do it." The sovereign kindness and infinite love of God had already graciously appeared to them in calling them to the saving knowledge of His truth, and the sure faithfulness of God was their security that they would be Divinely helped to persevere to the end. Accordingly, the apostle assures them that God would do what he desired: He would effect what He had Himself promised: He would accomplish all the good pleasure of His goodness toward them. Verily, our fidelity to God depends upon God's faithfulness to us. (R. Fergusson.) Sanctification:—I. THE AGENT in our sanctification is the Spirit of God (2 Thess. ii. 13; 1 Pet. i. 2; 1 Cor. vi. 14; see also Rom. viii.). By the Father we are sanctified, as we are chosen by Him unto sanctification; as by His good pleasure and free grace the atonement of Christ and the sanctifying agency of the Spirit exist. By the Son we are sanctified, as His death is the only means by which we ever become holy, and by which the Spirit came into the world for the benevolent purpose of making us holy. By the Spirit we are sanctified as the immediate Agent in applying to us the blessings of Christ's redemption, particularly in renewing and purifying our hearts and lives. Thus, although this work is immediately performed by the Spirit as the proper Agent, yet we are truly, though more remotely, said to be sanctified by the Father, by the Son, and by the Godhead universally considered. II. THE INSTRUMENTS of our sanctification are generally the Word and Providence of God. 1. The Word of God is the means of our sanctification in all cases in which it contributes to render us better, whether it be read, heard, or remembered; whether it be pondered with love, reverence, wonder, or delight; or whether, with similar affections, it be faithfully obeyed; whether its instructions and impressions be communicated to us directly, or through the medium of Divine ordinances, or the conversation, or the communion, or the example of our fellow-Christians. The Providence of God becomes the means of our sanctification in all the ways in which it makes solemn and religious impressions on the mind. III. THE PROCESS of sanctification may be summarily exhibited in the following manner. 1. It is progressive through life. The first sanctifying act of the Spirit of God is employed in regenerating the soul. Succeeding acts of the same nature are employed in purifying it through all the successive periods of life. 2. This process is not uniform. By this I intend that it is not the same in manner or degree every day, month, or year. From whatever cause it arises, our views are at times brighter, our vigilance more active, our resolution stronger, our temper more serene, and our energy more vigorous than at other times. This is visible in all that we speak, or think, or do, whatever may be the objects of our attention. That a state of things in us, which so materially affects ourselves in our very nature, should have an important influence on our religious interests is to be expected of course. The changes are here wrought in ourselves; and we, the persons thus changed, are those whose religion is concerned. As we are changed, therefore the state of our religion must in a greater or less degree be changed also. 3. The process of sanctification is universal. By this I intend that it affects the whole man: his views, affections, purposes, and conduct, and those of every kind. It extends alike to his duties of every kind; toward himself, his fellow-creatures, and his Maker. It affects and improves indiscriminately all the virtues of the Christian character: love to God and to mankind, faith, repentance, justice, truth, kindness, humility, forgiveness, charity, generosity, public spirit, meekness, patience, fortitude, temperance, moderation, candour, and charitableness of judgment. It influences ruling passions and appetites, habits of thought and affection, of language and practice. It prompts to all the acts of piety: to prayer, praise, attendance upon the sanctuary and its ordinances, our sanctification of the Sabbath, Christian communion, and Christian discipline. 4. The progress of sanctification is conspicuous in the life. From the commencement of Christianity in the soul the Christian course is that of a general reformation. REMARKS: 1. The considerations suggested concerning this important religious subject furnish every professing Christian with an interesting rule for the examination of his own character. 2. The same considerations furnish abundant encouragement to the Christian. Think how much God has done to accomplish this work, and you can find no room for despondency. (*Timothy Dwight, D.D.*) *Entire sanctification:*—Short of being wholly surrendered to God, we are maimed and incomplete. Holiness is the science of making men whole and keeping them whole. Christ is not come to save bits of humanity, like spars of a floating wreck, men's souls only, but to restore the finished man which God fashioned at the first, entire and without blemish. And because this is our completed life, it is our only true life. Our true life can only be that in which all our faculties find room for their harmonious development. This differs greatly from some of the notions that have gathered about the doctrine which regard the body as an enemy and persecute it accordingly; or a weak effeminacy whose conscience is troubled as to the colour of a ribbon, the size of a feather, the metal of one's watch-chain; a life in which everything is suspected a ghostly mystery, a thing alike loveless and useless. Let us gladly welcome the word—entire sanctification; not the privilege of a few adventurous and favoured souls, but the every-day life of ordinary men and women in the every-day work. The word "sanctification" means everywhere that which is claimed by God, given to God, used for God. Take its first use, "God rested on the seventh day . . . and sanctified it." What the Sabbath was amongst days, that man is to be amongst creatures. I. THAT THIS IS OUR TRUE LIFE IS MANIFEST IN THE VERY NATURE OF MAN WHICH IS HERE REFERRED TO, BODY, SOUL, AND SPIRIT. 1. Man is a mystery, rent by two, we might say three, worlds. (1) In common with the animals he has a body taken from the same earth, dependent on the same conditions, returning to the earth in the same way. And yet the beasts in following their instincts fulfil the purpose of their being, whilst man is a true man only as these instincts are checked. The reason must come in to control the appetites, but what if the passion be stronger than reason? Reason may bid the man to do right, but it does not bring the power. And, worse still, what if the reason itself drag down the man, lower the animal, and he who was sensual becomes devilish, the subject of envy, malice, pride, covetousness, revenge? What then? (2) We turn to the other faculty—the spirit. That which looks out where reason cannot see, and listens where reason hears nothing, that which has the dread consciousness of a Presence at which reason may laugh, looking out into the dark to declare that there is nothing. But this faculty may contribute to the degradation of the man. To his other miseries this may add a thousand superstitions. Of all creatures man alone wants more than he needs, and in that one fact lies the source of man's misery. Of all animals man alone is the victim of excess. It is the infinite capacity of the spirit degraded and seeking its satisfaction through indulgence. 2. Such is this creature. In a world where all else fulfil their purpose and lie down in peace, he alone is distracted. He is too big for the world, with a mind that cannot fulfil its own ideal. Where can he find his true life, in which all that is within him can be made harmonious and balanced? Some have said, "Mutilate the body to save his nobler being." Others have said, "Blind the mind and mock the spirit, that the animal may be happy. Eat, drink, for tomorrow we die." But surely there is a power somewhere that can keep the creature whole. Think of a steamship, steam at full pressure, engines going, sails set, yet with no hand on the helm, no look-out, no eye on the compass, hurrying on in the darkness, none knows whither. Or think of such a ship manned, yet where the forces of steam are set to one end and the sails to another, where one part of the crew will make for the Southern Cross and another steer for the North Pole. What is the remedy? 3. Let the commander come on board with due authority, then shall all these antagonistic forces be brought into harmonious working. We, seeking for deliverance, turn instinctively to our Creator. He who made us at the first must understand these faculties and can restore them to their true ends and uses. In all gradations of life we find the need of the creature met with its supply. The higher capacities of man for friendship, service, brotherhood find room and satisfaction. And is it only in the highest that we are to be left deceived? Made conscious of the infinite, yet are we to be met with the finite? If that be so, then has all nature mocked us. Every instinct within us, everything about us, cries aloud that somewhere there is that which can set the man at rest. Instinctively we lift our hands upward, assured that help must come from God. The God of Peace, who made us for Himself, can adjust the wishes and aims to His will, and the man takes his true place in the world as one having dominion over it. Here is our only true life, a life of entire consecration. II. OUR KNOWLEDGE OF GOD MAKES THIS ENTIRE SANCTIFICATION OUR ONLY TRUE LIFE. In common with other creatures, we live and move and have our being in God. 1. But this wards us from all other creatures in the world, we can give to God. This it is which makes us capable of religion. According to our gift do we find our place in one of the three great classes which divide humanity. Only to give something that we have is the mark of the heathen. Only to give something that we do is the distinction of the Jew. To give that which we are is the privilege and glory of the Christian. "Take my goods and be no more angry with me," is the cry of the heathen. "Behold my righteousness and remember Thy promise," speaks the Jew. "I am not mine own, but Thine, live in me or I die," is the distinctive glory of the Christian. 2. But what we give to God is altogether the result of our knowledge of Him. If we know God only as Creator and Controller, who touches us only from without, we give that which is only from without. But if we know God as our Father, as Love—then is there but one offering which can satisfy Him or satisfy us, body, soul, and spirit wholly given up to Him. Before this demand of our complete surrender, there comes the revelation of God. The Epistle begins with, "Grace and peace from God our Father," &c. It is in this revelation of God's love to us that this claim finds its force. If He have given Himself to us there can be no other return than our whole being to Him. Amongst us the claims of love are such that true love is hurt and injured with less than love. If love be lacking, gifts, obedience, service do but affront and insult love. If the measure of God's love to us be nothing less than the shame and agony and death of the Son of God, then to give Him less than our body, soul, and spirit is to make religion itself only another bewilderment. III. CONSIDER THIS LIFE AS THE SUBJECT OF OUR PRAYER. "May the God of Peace Himself sanctify you wholly." This great work is to be done for us by God. What years of weary and wasted endeavour it would save us if we were willing to accept so obvious a truth! We linger about theories of sanctification. In seeking to make this life our own it will help us to dwell upon the three stages of sanctification as set forth in the Old Testament, the picture-book of the New. 1. Sanctification is the surrender of that which is claimed. "Sanctify unto me," or as it is in the original, "Cause to pass over unto us." That is where sanctification begins. The demand and command of God. We have thought so much about God's provision for our forgiveness that we have almost lost sight of the fact that forgiveness has this purpose, our perfect obedience to His will. Jesus Christ is come not to be Saviour only, but Lord. Holiness is obedience, and the beauty of Holiness is the beauty of a completed obedience. Religion may borrow the loftiest titles, and swell with the sublimest aspiration, and yet be a thing of flabby sentimentalism, without the strong pillars and girders of God's authority. Let this surrender to God be a definite act. Our fathers often made this surrender in writing, and it is a distinct gain to make the act visible and tangible. And the process of writing gives one leisure to see into the greatness of God's claim, and into the sincerity of our response. This is the first step we must bring into our life, the great, strong authority of God. There was an age in which the authority of God was so set forth that it concealed His love, and it produced men stern, perhaps, but grandly true, men all backbones and ribs. Let us beware lest by concealing the authority of God in His love we grow creatures without any backbones or ribs at all. 2. The second step in our sanctification is the cleansing blood. Nothing else could give such solemnity to the offering, nothing else so completely set it apart for God. This was the crimson seal upon the deed of gift. The Church of to-day has gone away from the Church of the first ages. The death of Christ is the ground of our salvation, that and nothing more. With them it was

the resistless claim.  Our answer is, " Go on your happy way to heaven"; theirs
was, " Glorify God in your body and your spirit, which are His."  The blood
meant ransom, redemption, but the deliverance found its purpose only in the
service of God.    That is the measure of the Cross of Christ—not safety only from
the destroying angel, but deliverance from the bondage of sin, our victory over the
world and the flesh.  And that not simply as the natural effect upon us of Christ's
love.  It is more than a passionate hatred of sin kindled by the sight of our crucified Lord ; more than an enthusiastic devotion fired and sustained by the memory
of Him who loved us and gave Himself for us.  As surely as the Cross of Christ
has put me into a new relationship to God, and made it possible for Him to be just
and the Justifier of him that believeth, so has that Cross put me into a new relation
to the world.    This is the great salvation which is provided for us.    Now, in the
name of Jesus Christ are we to rise to find the chains fall off, the bondage ended,
the doors of the prison open, the jealous foes powerless to hold us.  Redeemed
with the precious blood of Christ, now are we free indeed, that in everything we
may be His faithful soldiers and servants until our lives' end.    3. The last stage in
sanctification is the Divine indwelling.    Everything led up to that.    Everything
that was claimed was cleansed.    When Moses had done all that God commanded
him, then God came down and filled the place with His glorious Presence.    Earth
had no more to ask, and heaven no more to bestow.  Up to that point God is ever
seeking to lead us.    Just as earth led up to man, and found its use and completeness in his coming, so was it that man led up to God.    And when man came
God  rested  from  His  labours,  here  was  his  resting-place  and  home.    His
work  was  at  an  end,  and  with  that  indwelling  all  things  found  their  finish
and  completion.    And  up  to  this  all  the  great  provisions  of  grace  lead.    We
stand  and  look  down  through  the  ages  and  see  God  coming  nearer  to  earth,
until  at  last  there  cometh  One  who  standeth  and  knocketh,  saying,  " Open
unto Me."    Then, when He cometh in to dwell with us, paradise is restored.
Once more God hath found His rest, and we have found ours, and there comes
again the Sabbath calm, for that all is very good.  (*M. G. Pearse.*)     *Entire*
*sanctification:*—By regeneration the heart is renewed, by justification sins are
pardoned, in sanctification the life is made holy.  Romanists confound justification
and sanctification ; but while connected they must be distinguished.  The former
is what is done for us, changes our state, is perfect at once, and is through
the merits of Christ ; the latter is what is done in us, changes our nature, is
gradual, and is by the Spirit.  The one gives the title, the other the fitness for
glory.  I.  The nature of sanctification.  Separation from that which is common
to that which is holy.  So the furniture of the tabernacle (Exod. xxx. 29), and
priests  and  people  were  sanctified  (Exod.  xxviii.  46).    It  consists—1. In
mortifying the evils of our nature (Rom. viii. 12, 13).  If sin is not mortified,
it  will  prevent—(1)  Our  communion  with  God  (Ezek.  xiv.  7).    (2)  Growth
in grace. (3) Peace here and happiness hereafter.    That which makes clean
the  outside  merely  will  never  satisfy  a  holy  God,  make  a  holy  character
and  fit  for  a  holy  place.    2.  The  consecration  of  the  Christian  to  that  which
is  holy.  (1)  To  the  glory  of  God  of  all  that  he  is,  has,  and  does.  (2)  To  the
cause  of  Christ  which  is  the  good  of  man.    II.  The way of sanctification.
1. It is attributed to the redeeming, cleansing blood of Christ.  2. To the Holy
Spirit (2 Thess. ii. 13 : Rom. xv. 16).  His design is not simply to better our
nature, but to cure it entirely.  3. To the Word of God as the Spirit's instrument
(John xvii. 17), explaining the nature, applying the promises, and imparting the
hope of holiness.    4. To faith and prayer (2 Thess. ii. 13; Acts xv. 9; Matt. vii.
11).    Truth sanctifies only as it is received by faith, and by prayer obtains the
influence of the Spirit.  III.  The characteristics of sanctification.  1. Progressiveness.  We should aim at sinless perfection; and unless we increase in holiness
we are increasing in sin.  2. Visibility, not of course in its essence but in its effects.
We see that the tree grows, that its branches extend, that it bears fruit, although
we do not see it grow.  3. Entireness.  It must influence the whole man.  IV.
The importance of sanctification.  1. Without it the design of God's love to us is
in vain, " This is the will of God even your sanctification."  2. Without it we are
strangers to the Saviour's grace " who died for us that He might purify unto Himself," &c.  3. Without it we are a forsaken and desecrated temple of the Holy
Ghost.    4. Without it we are unfit for heaven.  None but " the pure in heart shall
see God."  Application : 1. Use the means of sanctification, prayer, Bible study.
2. Keep before you the perfect model of sanctification in the example of Christ.  3.

**Never be satisfied with your attainment in sanctification.** (*Dr. Jarbo.*)    *Entire sanctification :*—1. Note the position of this prayer. It forms a conclusion, and this gives it a specific character. (1) It is the natural close of the Epistle—an impressive course of precept and exhortation. Sanctification from all sins and also in its positive sense had been inculcated and prayed for, and now all previous petitions are gathered up into one. (2) It is the close of the strain immediately preceding. As far back as ver. 15, we perceive the signs of strong emotion. Paul's exhortations become very bold, and each bears the burden of perfection. The grandeur of this introduction prepares us for the grandeur of the prayer. Precisely at the point when man's ambition to be perfect has been stimulated to the utmost, the transition is made from what we can do for ourselves to what God can do for us. 2. The peculiarities of the prayer. It is marked off from the rest of Paul's prayers in that it has more of the temple spirit and phraseology. This suggests at once a comparison with our Lord's High Priestly consecration prayer (John xvii.). The Divine consecration separating believers from the world while keeping them blameless in it; having its end, on the one hand, in the unity of the mystical body in holiness, and on the other, the vision of Christ's glory at His coming; and brought to its perfection by the righteous or faithful God of the Christian vocation; these form a series of ideas common to Christ and Paul. 3. The expressions by which God is invoked in Paul's prayers are always great expository helps. (1) "The God of peace" is the author of reconciliation accomplished through the atoning mediation of Christ. Those only can be sanctified who have entered into the enjoyment of the Divine favour. Peace begins the state of grace, pervades it, and is its perfection (Rom. v. 1). (2) "He that calleth" (ver. 24). Sometimes the calling refers to the past—at conversion: sometimes to the final issue; here, however, it is the continuous call between the two extremes—always to holiness. This name is a remembrancer, every time we hear it, of an abiding obligation on our part, and a constant will on the part of God. (3) The third name is not mentioned but implied. God is the only sanctifier—the Father (John xvii. 17), the Son (Heb. ii. 11), the Holy Ghost (2 Thess. ii. 13). Only a lax religious phraseology speaks of a man's consecrating himself. We have words for duty and virtue in every form, but this must be sanctified or set apart from our common use. Only One could say "I sanctify myself." 4. Entering the prayer itself we mark its great central idea, the entireness of personal sanctification : but to clear the way we must consider what is not meant, that in which all accepted believers are entirely sanctified. (1) They are absolutely washed from the guilt of sin (Heb. x. 22). In this sense sanctification and justification are one. The soul that is justified in the forum or court mediatorial is in the temple and before the altar sanctified, and completely (Heb. x. 14). (2) They are presented to God upon an altar which makes everything holy, and they are thus set apart to the Divine service. Now that must be absolute or nothing. The offering must be either on the altar or not on it. But the oblation has yet to go up to heaven in the consuming fire as a whole burnt offering. (3) They are complete in Christ according to the foreknowledge of God (Rom. viii. 30; Heb. x. 14; 1 Cor. i. 30). (4) These several views unite in the element of imputation. But the apostle's prayer uses a word which takes us into an altogether different region, "Faithful," &c. (ver. 24). He does not ask that God may count, but that God may make them holy. The entireness of sanctification is here expressed in two ways. It is—I. A COMPLETE CONSECRATION OF THE WHOLE PERSON OR BEING OF THE CHRISTIAN. 1. Consider some objections arising out of the form and construction of the sentence. It has been said that the words are too rare and uncertain to admit of a doctrine so important being based upon them. But granted that they are unusual, they are chosen with extreme precision, and bear their sense in their very form. Passing by this, two other objections, based upon it, must be noticed. (1) One takes the form of an honourable but unsound explanation which assumes that "wholly" refers to the Thessalonian Church, and "blameless" to individual members. But there is no instance of any particular community being regarded as capable of entire sanctification. That blessedness is the prerogative of the Christian or the whole mystical body of Christ. (2) The other less-worthy subterfuge asserts that the plain meaning of the terms must not be unduly pressed; that Paul's theology ought not to be made responsible for his exuberant phrases. This loose theory of inspiration as here applied is condemned by the fact that the text begins and ends with the power of God. And with regard to "Faithful is He," it is remarkable that it is always used when the strength of the apostle's language might seem to demand the confirmation of a special Divine guarantee. 2. Entire sanctification as an end attained consists of—(1) A consecrating act of God put forth to the utmost necessary point. The work is one of Divine power which God begins, continues, and brings to perfection. " He will do it." This separates our sanctification from everything which man by his own effort may attain. It is not the result of a new direction or impetus given to our faculties; through no energy of the self-consecrated will; through no mighty outgoings of the regenerate feeling; through no contemplation of the regenerate reason. There is a power above and behind using them, but not leaving the recovery of holiness to them. It is not the moral agent retrieving himself by Divine aid, but a new and more abundant life infused, sustained and carried to perfection by God Himself. (2) This sanctifying power extends to all the elements of man's nature. (*a*) His spirit is that element of his nature which is his distinction. In it he is only a little lower than the angels for a season, and has no fellowship whatever with the lower creation. Here is the seat of the Divine image, marred but never lost, and whose perfect restoration must wait until sanctification is lost in glory. Meanwhile the reason is entirely dedicated to its original function of being the depository of the supreme first principles of goodness, rectitude, and truth; the conscience is sanctified unto perfect fidelity as an internal legislator true to the truth, as an incorruptible witness pacified, and as a fearless interpreter of the Divine judgment; the will is sanctified as the servant of its own supreme choice and intention, and as the master of its own acts, by release from every impediment of unholy motives and by the constant influence of the truth applied by the spirit; the impulse behind and the end before, and all its means between consecrated in the unity of one supreme principle—the glory of God. But we are apt to lose the noblest meaning of the term " spirit," by the use of these synonyms. It is the element in man's nature that is capable of God. Dead or asleep in the unregenerate, it is quickened into life by the Holy Spirit; and when it is entirely possessed by Him who quickens it—the spiritual man being " filled with the Spirit," and wholly spiritual—it is wholly sanctified to the vision of God. (*b*) The soul is consecrated as distinct from the spirit. This faculty, when mentioned apart from the spirit, comes between the higher and lower elements of our being. It is the sphere of the desires and passions, which are innocent in themselves, but transformed by the sinful will into worldly affections and lusts, which are restored, however, by being brought under the control of the Holy Spirit through the will, refusing them their unholy stimulants and nourishment in the world. (*c*) The body is also sanctified as the instrument of spirit and soul. As such it has abundant honour put upon it as the temple of the Holy Ghost. But like spirit and soul, its sanctification is limited till sanctification and glorification shall be one. (3) The entireness of the consecration. " Wholly " has reference to the person made up of these constituents. The three parts are not introduced to show that holiness becomes perfect by proceeding through these inwardly towards the centre. The sanctification is of the man in whom these unite. It begins with the self of the " new man," and the Holy Ghost dwelling therein, becomes a will within the will that rules the whole; and when He has confirmed that will in supreme devotion to God, sanctification is entire. II. THE PRESERVATION OF THE SAME INTEGRAL PERSON IN A STATE OF BLAMELESSNESS TILL THE COMING OF CHRIST. 1. The same power that sanctifies as an act preserves that sanctification as a state. Entire sanctification as distinguished from sanctification is the confirmed, habitual, no longer interrupted devotion of the whole being to God. As the power which created the world sustains it by an indwelling energy, so the power which can fix upon God the strength of the whole soul can keep it fixed upon Him. A strong influence of grace descending in answer to prayer may carry the whole soul to God for a season. When the prayer of faith which brings this blessing becomes unceasing this act becomes the tranquil state of the soul. " By faith we stand," and He who is faithful is " able to keep us from falling." 2. This consecration is the preservation of all that belongs to Spirit, &c., in the fellowship and service of God. The whole man becomes entirely the Lord's property and worshipper, His instrument and servant. Hence entire sanctification is the habitual communion with God as the supreme good of the soul; and the habitual reference of every act to the will and glory of God as the Lord of life. Love makes the whole being a whole burnt offering. 3. This state of entire consecration is preserved in blamelessness. (1) No blame is imputed to it; by virtue of the atoning blood it is in a constant state of acceptance. (2) It is a faultless sacrifice. The High Priest so entirely consecrates the offering to God that sin is no longer found in it. 4. The fidelity of

God is pledged to the accomplishment of this. (*W. B. Pope, D.D.*)    *The sanctification of the complete man:*—I. Its MEANING. 1. What does Paul mean by being sanctified wholly? (1) In man there is a trinity of powers linking him with three different worlds. (*a*) By the body, with its sensations, &c., we are connected with the earth. (*b*) By the soul, powers merely natural, faculties, passions, and affections, we are connected with the sorrowing, rejoicing, toiling world. (*c*) But there are deeper things linking us with a sublimer region, an emotion that pants for the eternal, prayers that cry out for the infinite—these are voices of the spirit. (2) These, Paul says, are to be sanctified, *i.e.*, consecrated. (*a*) The body, not by crushing and despising it, but using it as a gift of God for His glory. (*b*) The soul, not by despising its gifts as carnal, or shutting our ears to the appeals of affection, but by dedicating it to God; thus making hopes, ambitions, loves, holy. (*c*) The spirit must be sanctified, for when men have used the powers of their spirit as their own they have fallen into spiritual sins, intolerance, bigotry, pride. 2. Why does Paul lay such emphasis on the consecration of all our powers? Because they are gateways of temptation from three different worlds, and unless they are consecrated we are never safe. (1) Men have tried to purify their outward life alone, leaving soul and spirit unguarded, and then secret sins of pride and imagination break out. (2) Men have left the spirit unconsecrated. Guarding body and soul, subduing bodily fear, and ready to meet scorn and shame, Peter, relying on his own strength, fell at the first temptation. (3) Men have tried to hallow the spirit only, to keep their higher life apart, hence the dishonesties which have so often blemished men professing peculiar saintliness. We must be consecrated through the whole range of our powers or we shall not be consecrated at all. II. Its ATTAINMENT. 1. We cannot consecrate ourselves. We try it. (1) We subdue the body, but the soul, with its temptations, is too strong for us. (2) We strain all our energies to subdue sins of the intellect and affections; and then we are tempted with spiritual pride. Weary of the struggle, we say, "It is all vain." It is not. Admit your weakness, and cry to God the sanctifier. 2. God preserves the entire sanctification by imparting peace. The calmness He gives when we cease our own efforts is our truest might to maintain this complete consecration. III. Its MOTIVE. "Until the coming," &c. This coming is—1. A day of manifestation. Because that day is coming sanctify—(1) The body, that it may shine out a glorified body in that day; (2) The soul, that it may be able to receive the truth and light of that day; (3) The spirit, that it may be able to commune with the Eternal Love. 2. A day of everlasting gatherings. Sanctify, therefore, body, &c., "that you may be meetened for the Church of the firstborn." (*E. L. Hull, B.A.*)    *The prayer for entire consecration:*—The momentous warning of ver. 19 perhaps led to this prayer that the temple in which that holy flame was burning might be preserved in its integrity and blamelessness. "Whole" does not mean the three associated together, but that each may be preserved in its completeness. The prayer is threefold. I. THAT THEY MAY BE SANCTIFIED BY THE GOD OF PEACE. 1. Sanctification is the condition of outward and inward peace. 2. This sanctification is to be complete "wholly" in their collective powers and constituents. II. THAT EACH CONSTITUENT MAY BE PRESERVED TO OUR LORD'S COMING. Each part of the man and the whole man is immortal. III. THAT EACH SO PRESERVED MAY BE ENTIRE and complete, not mutilated or disintegrated by sin. 1. That the body may retain its yet uneffaced image of God, and its unimpaired aptitude to be a living sacrifice to its Maker. 2. The appetitive soul, its purer hopes and nobler aspirations. 3. The spirit, its everblessed associate the Holy Spirit of God. (*Bp. Ellicott.*)    **I pray God that your whole spirit, and soul, and body.**—The word rendered "whole," signifies literally, "whole inheritance or portion." It is applied metaphorically to a city, all whose buildings are standing, undamaged by fire or sword; to an empire, the provinces of which are entire; to an army, whose troops are yet undiminished by any casualty. St. Paul, therefore, may be considered to pray that the believer's whole inheritance may be kept inviolate. And what is this inheritance? It is threefold, a Body—a Soul—a Spirit. Man, that is, is delineated not as a simple, but as a compound being. He has three constituent parts, and the apostolic prayer is to the effect that every one of these parts may be kept without loss until the day of Christ's appearing. (*Bp. Woodford.*)    *The tripartite nature of man:*—I. BODY—sense-consciousness. II. SOUL—self-consciousness. III. SPIRIT—God-consciousness. (*J. B. Heard, M.A.*)    There are three things of which man in his entirety consists—flesh, soul, and spirit: the one, the spirit, giving form; the other, the flesh, receiving form. The soul is intermediate between these two: sometimes it follows the spirit and is elevated by it, and sometimes it consents to the flesh and falls into earthly concupiscences. (*Irenæus.*) *Body, soul, and spirit:*—An ancient philosopher once called the human frame "a harmony of bones," and a beautiful cathedral may be well called a harmony of stones. Following the same train of thought in a wider application, I might point out to you how man in his entire composite structure of body and soul and spirit was designed by his Creator to be, as it were, a living instrument of diverse chords attuned to one perfect harmony. How should I describe the relations to each other of these factors of our human fabric? Should I call the body the *sheath* of the soul, and the soul the *sheath* of the spirit? Or the body the *organ* of the soul, and the soul the *organ* of the spirit? Or the first the utterance of the second, and the second the expression of the third? What is the body for? Not for intemperance, incontinence, greed; "the body is for the Lord." He is its Builder and Redeemer: doubly Owner of it and twice Proprietor, first by creation and then by redemption. If, then, we would live to the Lord, let us keep our bodies in temperance, soberness, and chastity. But what did I say—let us keep the body in order? Why, the body is the organ of the soul; the soul rules it with a will, uses it with a will, bids it walk with feet, touch with hand, taste with tongue, speak with mouth, see with eyes. To keep the body in order, then, we must keep the soul in order—filling it with good desires, pure motives, wise counsels, noble aims and aspirations. Yes, but what is to keep the soul in order? Why, the soul itself is controlled by that of which it is the organ and the expression, even by the spirit. So, then, let each of us fill our highest nature, even the spirit, with good desires, pure motives, noble aspirations, lofty thoughts of God and heaven. But *can* we? Is a man's ego or self outside a man that he should pour into his own spirit good desires, as he would pour water into a cistern? A man's ego is *inside* the man, whether it be seated in the soul, or in the spirit, or in both. For behind the body is its ruler and director, the soul, behind the soul is its ruler the spirit: but behind the spirit of man is *what?* Is there no superior? Why, yes; some unseen power there is, that plays the part of King David to the harp, and makes the music of the instrument; that suggests, inspires, persuades, drawing to virtue or tempting to vice—an evil power drawing to evil, a good power to good. If God's Spirit penetrate, intensify, illuminate man's spirit and through that reach the soul, and bend the will submissive to good, until the man subdue his own flesh to his own spirit, that man, by faith in Christ, shall save his soul alive. But if, alas! the reverse of this—if the love of the world, the lust of the eye, the pride of life should smother, stifle, quench the nobler aspiration after holiness and happiness—such a man, if he resist to the end the strivings of the Holy Ghost in the domain of his own spirit, shall, in the words of our Lord, "lose his own soul—his own *self.*" We are fearfully and wonderfully made: our triple organism is a mystery, but our double destiny is a certainty. There is to life eternal a dread alternative. There is the one way to heaven before us, and Jesus Christ is this one Way; and there is another way leading to hell. Powers of evil and powers of good surround us: the angels of God attend upon us for our well-being, the angels of Satan hover about us, tempting us to our ruin. Environed by this conflict in the air between good and evil, we must be loyal to our Master, true to our only Saviour, stedfast in prayer and watching, doing our duty in our several stations, keeping our garments unspotted of the flesh: ever using the sacramental means of grace in the Holy Supper; and so, and only so, the Spirit of Christ, which flows through the mystical veins of His Divine humanity, shall fill with its goodness and gentleness, its purity and charity, our own spirits, through them controlling our souls and bodies. For in God's propriety of order, the body is the tabernacle of the soul, the soul is the temple of the human spirit, and the human spirit is the sanctuary of the Holy Ghost. (*Canon T. S. Evans, D.D.*) *Body, soul, and spirit:*—I. Every department of the universe of matter finds itself represented in the BODY of man. 1. Whenever he receives, digests, and is nourished by food, and experiences bodily pain, man lives the life of the animal. 2. The hair, which grows and is nourished, and yet which is endowed with no sensation, belongs to, and connects us with, the vegetable kingdom. 3. Mineral matter enters largely into the composition of the circulating lifeblood, whose current throbs in every extremity of our frame—and thus a link of sympathy, and community of nature, is established between man and a third great department of matter. II. The SOUL is that, which when held in combination with the body, connects us with the beasts of the field. For by the soul is probably to be understood the passions or affections—such as have no element of reason or the higher nature in them—perhaps natural instincts would be a more generally intelligible term. It will not be denied that brutes manifest fear, when they are threatened or punished; that there is a strong spirit of emulation and competition among horses; that anger and jealousy will lead stags to encounter one another; that all animals care for their young, and that in some the maternal instinct is developed with a power which almost surpasses that feeling as it exists in man. Now fear and emulation and anger and parental affection, and other such instincts—in their crude state, unmodified by reason, and the sense of right and wrong—constitute, I suppose, the ψυχή, or soul, of which the apostle is here speaking. III. The SPIRIT comprises all that higher part of human nature, by which man holds of God and blessed angels. The spirit gives him a sympathy with the world above, even as the soul gives him a sympathy with the animals, and as the body gives him a sympathy with the material universe. Angels are said to be "ministering spirits." And it is remarkable that when man is spoken of in the Scriptures as holding communion with God, the spirit and not the body is mentioned as the organ through which that communion is held (Rom. i. 9; John iv. 24). The beasts that perish cannot apprehend God, cannot understand the Divine Word and Will, or hold communion in any form with the Eternal. Why not? They have no natural capacity for doing so. Some link in their nature is wanting, which, if it were present, might make them competent to an exercise so sweet and yet so awful. That link is πνεῦμα —spirit. (*Dean Goulburn.*) *Body, soul and spirit sanctified*:—I. THE THREE- FOLD NATURE OF MAN. In ordinary language, which the Scripture itself does not hesitate commonly to adopt, a two-fold division of our nature is recognized—man is said to be made up of body and soul. By the word "soul" are understood both his moral and intellectual faculties—those points in his being which distinguish him from other animals, and to cultivate which is the proper business of his life. It is thus used to signify the highest part of his nature; and therefore in the language of those who know the true objects of his highest faculties, and the exalted state to which they might be raised hereafter, it expresses his immortal part in contradistinction to that which is to perish with this present life (Matt. x. 28). But as the notions generally entertained respecting the highest part of our nature were in many respects highly erroneous—as our relation to God as our Maker and Father was lost sight of, and further, as ceasing to regard Him as the great object and centre of our being, men naturally lost all clear and lively hopes of immortality, the word "soul" in its common acceptation among the Greeks was inadequate to express the loftier and more enlightened conceptions of a Christian, with respect to his best faculties and their most perfect state. We find, therefore, in several passages of the New Testament that a third term is employed in addition to those of body and soul, and intended to express something superior to the soul in its common sense, as the soul is superior to the body. The third term is "spirit," which, in the signification now alluded to, seems applicable to Christians only, and to denote that perfection of human nature which it was the object of the gospel to accomplish—an understanding that should know God, and affections that should love Him; or, in other words, a spiritual creature capable of enjoying communion with the Father of Spirits, and from that relation being naturally immortal. Thus, then, when this three-fold division of our nature is mentioned, the term "body" expresses those appetites we have in common with the brutes; the term "soul" denotes our moral and intellectual faculties, directed only toward objects of this world, and not exalted by the hope of immortality; and the term "spirit" takes these same faculties when directed toward God and heavenly things, and from the purity, the greatness, and the perfect goodness of Him who is their object, "transformed into the same image from glory to glory, even as by the Spirit of the Lord." II. THE PERFECTION OR BLAMELESSNESS OF THIS TRIPLE NATURE. With the government of the body all are engaged at some periods of their lives, and some through the whole of their lives. All more or less can understand the temptations to indolence and comfort, and to the indulgence of intemperance and sensuality. How many thousands there are who live like Esau! Their appetites are keen, and their enjoyments lively; the body is alive, while the soul and spirit are almost dead; and therefore the man lives what may be called an animal life; but as a man with a soul, and much more as a Christian with a spirit, he is in the lowest state of degradation, neither fit for the life that is to come, nor yet for the life of a reasonable being even in this present world. To keep down the body, therefore, and bring it into subjection, was the object of fasting and mortification; but what is specially wanted is to raise and strengthen the soul and spirit, that the body may be able and ready to aid them in their work, which it cannot do unless it be itself sound and vigorous. The soul is commonly strengthened by the growth and cultivation of the powers of the understanding, and by the various objects which attract the mind as we come forth into actual life. But the perfection of the soul must not be preferred to that of the spirit, any more than that of the body to that of the soul. The excellence of our spirit is to feel and hope as spiritual and deathless creatures. When this takes place, how beautiful is the sight to behold the spirit, and soul, and body, each healthy and strong, and each working in its proper order to perfect its own happiness, and thereby to advance the glory of the Triune-One! (*T. Arnold, D.D.*) *The spiritual nature:*—What Paul prayed for his friends we may well pray for both ourselves and our friends—a blameless spirit, a blameless soul, a blameless body. This is the whole man. 1. What we mean by the body we very well understand. Mystery even in the body there is, it is true; but still, on the whole, what is meant by a blameless body requires no great exposition. The man with a perfect physique, the man who is a picture of perfect health, verifies himself to our senses, with his broad shoulders, his brawny, muscular limbs, the glow of health upon the cheek, his unwearied vigour by day, his sweet, undisturbed sleep at night. 2. We look in the Greek, to find the same word indiscriminately rendered " life " and " soul." We look in the Latin, and find the word that stands for soul to be "*anima*," that which animates the body. The soul, then, is that which gives life to this physical organization, The brain is but ashes, without intellect behind it. The heart is a mere muscular valve, if there be no affection and love which make it beat quicker in the presence of the loved one. That which gives physical organism its use, that which makes it an instrument, that which links man to his fellow-man, that which deals with the transient and the visible, with that which is round about us, what philosopher's classify as " the intellect, the sensibilities, and the will"—we call this the soul. 3. But what is the spirit? It is by the spirit that we discern the truth. It is the spirit which is ever against the flesh, antagonizing, striving for full mastery of it. It is the spirit which links us to God. It is the spirit which is the Divine and immortal principle in man, undying. So that if there be no spirit, or if it be left to die, there is no immortal life. Let us look for a few moments, and see what are some of the characteristics of this spiritual nature, what some of the indications of the possession of this spiritual in man. But how shall you know what is the value, worth, character, of your spiritual nature? He that has a spiritual nature—I. WILL HAVE AT LEAST A HUNGERING AFTER THE SPIRITUAL. 1. This may be, indeed, the only evidence of spiritual nature in him. It certainly is the first. Before as yet the artist knows how to paint or draw, he has in him the desire for painting; and the little boy takes up his pencil and scrawls away, trying to make forms, so bearing witness to a seed-art within him that needs development. The bird has a wish for the air before its wings are fledged and it can soar out from the nest. Our hungers indicate what we are. 2. And as the Bible expresses and interprets the desire of spirituality, so it gives its promise to those desires. You may wish for wealth, and stay poor. But the soul that longs for a stronger conscience, a clearer faith, a more eager and joyous hope, a diviner reverence, shall not go unsatisfied. II. HAS IN HIM SOMETHING THAT PERCEIVES THE SPIRITUAL. III. WILL FIND EXPRESSION FOR THE SPIRITUAL. We are not all teachers, but we all live; and, after all, the true measure and final test of spiritual life is not what we think, nor what we say, but the way in which we live. I pray God that you present yourselves, spirit, soul, body, blameless before the throne of His grace. 1. Blameless in body, with no wart upon it of intemperance or sensual self-indulgence. 2. Blameless in soul, with no ignorant superstition degrading it, with no social coldness, no disfellowship of humanity, no idleness shackling the hands that should have been busy in service. 3. Blameless in spirit—what do I mean by that? I pray God that you may have—(1) A reverence that shall always show something higher and grander and nobler and diviner than the eye has ever shown you, and shall always make you bow before it and follow after it. (2) A hope that shall summon you to a nobler and diviner life than can be interpreted by anything the eye has ever seen or the ear has ever heard. (3) A conscience that shall hold you rigorously and undeviatingly in the path of rectitude, not turning to the right hand nor the left under beckoning enticement or under threatening pressure and menace. (4) A love so large, so catholic, and so inspired by Him that no wrong shall weary its patience, no iniquity shall blur or hinder its sympathy, no sorrow shall fail to touch its pity: for this makes manhood and womanhood. Not what we know: ignorance does not defile us. Not what we have done: doing does not make us. But what in the higher developments of our soul, what in our reverence, in our hope, in our faith, in our love, we are—that really makes us. (*Lyman Abbott.*)　　*The king's lodging :*—Manton says: "If an earthly king lie but a night in a house, what care is there taken that nothing be offensive to him, but that all things be neat, clean, and sweet? How much more ought you to be careful to get and keep your hearts clean, to perform service acceptably to Him; to be in the exercise of faith, love and other graces, that you may entertain, as you ought, your heavenly King, who comes to take up His continual abode and residence in your hearts!" We know a house in which an empress rested for a very short time, and the owner henceforth refused to admit other inmates. Such is his devotion to his royal guest that no one may now sit in her chair or dine at the table which she honoured. Our verdict is that he makes loyalty into absurdity by this conduct; but if we imitate him in this procedure in reference to the Lord Jesus we shall be wise. Let our whole being be set apart for Jesus, and for Jesus only. We shall not have to shut up the house; for our beloved Lord will inhabit every chamber of it, and make it a permanent palace. Let us see to it that all be holy, all pure, all devout. Help us, O Purifier of the temple, to drive out all intruders, and reserve our soul in all the beauty of holiness for the Blessed and Only Potentate. (*C. H. Spurgeon.*)

Ver. 24. **Faithful is He that calleth you.**—*The faith of man and the faithfulness of God:*—1. The highest object of man's existence is to hold communion with God. For this his nature was framed, and in this alone will it find repose. 2. But the vital tie that connected us with heaven is broken. We are as a limb of the body separated by paralysis, or any other internal cause, from the benefits of the general circulation. God is the heart: we have insulated ourselves from God, and deadened the nerve that conducted his influences. We have a name to live but are dead. 3. This is a state of things deeply to be lamented; but no one ever lamented that the brute creation was shut out from the converse of angels—because there are no faculties in brutes that point to a higher destiny; no traces of a fall, nothing about them which makes it a practical contradiction that they should be as they are and yet what they are. But even in the natural man there are faint gleams of a something over and beyond his present state, a perpetual unhappiness, proving his designation for a different state of things originally. 4. Now without some notion of the extent of the loss, you can never estimate the value or nature of the restoration. It is by the length of the dark shadow that you compute the height of the elevation beyond it. It is by summing up the long catalogue of woe that you will be able to conceive the importance of that manifestation of mercy, whose object is, by the descent of God, to bind once more the broken links of communion. 5. The nature of this restoration. Man is separated from God as a criminal, and as unholy; the communion is restored by free pardon on God's part for Christ's sake, and the acceptance of that pardon upon man's, and by the process of sanctification which makes a lost and ruined soul at length "meet for the inheritance of the saints." 6. Of this union with God the first great characteristic must be one which concerns both intellect and heart. It must behold God's holiness, justice, and mercy, and must love the holiness, dread the justice, desire the mercy. This complex act of knowledge and affection is faith. 7. But in every perfect union there must be mutual confidence, and a strict fulfilment of enjoyments on both sides. If man be trustful, God must be "faithful." This is the affirmation of the apostle. Thus faith in man and faithfulness in God are the two members of our spiritual harmony. I. The Divine faithfulness is gloriously characteristic of the spiritual system to which we belong. No words can go beyond the confidence of David in the faithfulness of God, and no doubt high and spiritual meanings belong to his expressions of such confidence. Holiness was to be the foundation of all, but yet a holiness triumphant in visible majesty and regal pomp. But the faithfulness of our text has exclusive reference to sanctification. It was no relief from temporal evils that Paul promised; the mercy of God might send them to the lions; it was still His mercy, if it but kept them unspotted from the world. How many are content with such faithfulness as this? Is this the tenor of your prayers? Is your heart busy in pleading with God His own eternal faithfulness in behalf of your sanctification and spiritual safety? II. The Divine faithfulness extends to the whole man. The entire, if feeble humanity, is sheltered under this canopy of Divine protection.

The body is subdued into its place as minister to the soul ; the soul is guarded from its own special corruptions; and the spirit is preserved undecayed amid an hostile world. Of a surety the sacred Trinity that occupies the throne of heaven will not forget this humble image of Their ineffable mystery. Surely the soul will be preserved by that creative Deity who first infused it into the frame; the body by that Eternal Son who was pleased to assume it; and the spirit, by that ever blessed Spirit who bestows it and may well guard His own inestimable gift. III. THIS FAITHFULNESS IS OF HIM " THAT CALLETH YOU." It is a fidelity to His own gracious engagement. He without destroying human freedom or responsibility, of His free grace commences, continues and ends the whole Christian work. Yet so faithful is His compassion that He represents Himself as bound and tied to the impulses of His own unconstrained mercy. There is no bond but His own love, yet that bond is stronger than iron; and He, whom the universe cannot compel, commands Himself. IV. WITH SUCH A GOD, SUCH PROMISES AND FAITHFULNESS, WHY IS THERE A DELAY IN APPROPRIATING SO GREAT SALVATION? If we believe that these things are true where is the earnest active faith, and where the life that answers to it? (W. Archer Butler, M.A.) God's faithfulness :—Grandly did the old Scottish believer, of whom Dr. Brown tells us in his " Horæ Subsecivæ," respond to the challenge of her pastor regarding the ground of her confidence. "Janet," said the minister, " what would you say, if after all He has done for you, God should let you drop into hell?" " E'en's (even as) He likes," answered Janet. " If He does, He'll lose mair than I'll do." At first sight Janet's reply looks irreverent, if not something worse. As we contemplate it, however, its sublimity grows upon us. Like the Psalmist she could say, "I on Thy Word rely" (Psa. cxix. 114, metrical version). If His Word were broken, if His faithfulness should fail, if that foundation could be destroyed, truly He would lose more than His trusting child. But that could never be. " For ever, O Lord, Thy word is settled in heaven. Thy faithfulness is unto all generations." Well then might Janet encourage herself in the Lord her God, and say, " God hath spoken in His holiness; I will rejoice." Assurance of victory :—I can never conceive that it dispirits the soldier, when he is fighting, to tell him that he must win the victory. This is what Cromwell's ironsides said when they saw the great general riding along the ranks, "'Tis he!" they said, "'tis he!" they felt the victory was sure where Cromwell was, and like thunderbolts they dashed upon their enemies, until as thin clouds before the tempest the foemen flew apace. The certainty of victory gives strength to the arm that wields the sword. To say to the Christian you shall persevere till you get to the journey's end—will that make him sit down on the next mile-stone? No; he will climb the mountain, wiping the sweat from his brow; and as he looks upon the plain, he will descend with surer and more cautious footsteps, because he knows he shall reach the journey's end. God will speed the ship over the waves into the desired haven; will the conviction of that on the part of the captain make him neglect the vessel? Yes, if he be a fool; but if he be a man in his wits, the very certainty that he shall cross the deep will only strengthen him in time of storm to do what he would not have dreamt of doing if he had been afraid the vessel would be cast away. Brethren, let this doctrine impel us to a holy ardency of watchfulness, and may the Lord bless us and enable us to persevere to the end. (C. H. Spurgeon.)

Ver. 25. **Brethren, pray for us.**—Prayer for missionaries :—I. THE GROUNDS OF THIS APPEAL. 1. The character of the men required. " Pray ye, therefore, the Lord of the harvest," &c. The work requires fully qualified workers. It must have apostolic, unselfish, unworldly, spiritual, sympathetic, brotherly men. Pray for such. Only God can send them. 2. The work they are called to accomplish.—(1) There are evils to be vanquished before the good can be created—apathy, a dead conscience, helpless dependence on others. On the other hand, the missionary has to create a spirit of hopefulness and of self-help, and the recognition of the Divine claim. He has to secure a quickened conscience to stand trembling in the presence of sin, and yet able to rest immovable in the recollection of free grace and dying love. (2) There are special difficulties he has to overcome. (a) He has no human constraints. At home if a man neglects his work his material interest suffers; the salary of the missionary is constant. At home the pastor has his equals; abroad he is supreme. At home we are under constant inspection; the missionary is thousands of miles away from criticism. These constraints are very helpful, however unpalatable; and lacking them the missionary needs our prayers. (b) He has no human helps of association and sympathy to which we owe so much, of these the missionary often knows nothing. What solitude of mind, heart and sorrow! far from country, kindred, home! All sights and sounds uncongenial. (c) He meets with frequent and bitter disappointment—rank hypocrisy where conversion seemed sound. (d) Then there is the climate and its effects. How much we are indebted to our much complained of and variable weather for the strength of our physique. In India the more regular climate seems to dry up all the energies. But this is nothing compared to the vitiating moral atmosphere. II. THE NATURE OF THIS APPEAL. 1. What it supposes. (1) Faith in prayer. Prayer is of the essence of religion, and if prayer be not availing then religion is an illusion and must die. But if it be availing then religion is a practical force and cannot die. (2) Faith in the gospel, for it is the universal law of God's service that no man shall take a share in His work without faith. Without it we cannot please Him, secure His Spirit, nor rouse and devote our energies to the conversion of souls. But given faith all things are possible. (3) Brotherly sympathy. Missionaries are " brethren " calling on the same Father, steeped in the same temper, going to the same reward. 2. What, if we comply with it, will it bring? (1) All will be occupied at the same time and in the same work. Some are strong, some weak; some are rich, some poor; some are learned, others ignorant—but all can pray, and this is the grandest privilege and mightiest power of all. (2) All will be benefitted by it. He who prays, he for whom prayer is offered. (3) It will be for the Divine honour, "Not by might nor by power," &c. (4) It will appropriate and apply God's benefits. (*J. Aldis.*) *The prayers of Christian people in relation to ministerial work :*—It is useless for any man to pray unless he has, even to every human being, this brotherly feeling. True prayer is the outflowing of a kind and loving heart. Ministers need specially the sympathies and prayers of their people on account of—1. The difficulties of their work. 2. The peculiar trials of their work; and 3. The twofold results of their work. I. THE DIFFICULTIES OF MINISTERIAL WORK. The first difficulty here is to be always in a proper mental mood for mental work. There is—1. A work of preparation for the pulpit, and—2. A work of communication in the pulpit. The result in either case depends upon the atmosphere which surrounds the preacher's soul—upon the current of his inmost feeling. It is the duty of every Christian minister, however great his mental culture and creative genius, to make special and careful preparation for the pulpit. To keep clear of all disturbing forces, so as, at the proper time to retain the power of fixing the mind upon the subject to be investigated, and to be just then in a state of spiritual repose " in the spirit," the state which is the condition of spiritual perception, as the truth is spiritually discerned, requires great grace. The second difficulty is the finding of a variety of subjects—subjects which shall—(1) Be taken hold of by the preacher's own mind. (2) Be relished by the people; and—(3) Prove permanently profitable to both. II. THE TRIALS OF MINISTERIAL WORK. The first of these trials arises from a deep consciousness of personal weakness and inadequacy for the work. These trials arise from want of success. III. THE TWO-FOLD EFFECT OF MINISTERIAL WORK. The final result of every human work is solemn. The day of final reckoning is solemn to every one, but yet the issues in that day, of ministerial work here, will be perhaps the most solemn of all solemn things. I have spoken of the minister's need of an interest in your prayers. I have spoken of the cheering influence which an assurance of this will have upon his own spirit, how it will actually give a richer tint to the glorious truths of God's Holy Book as they will be, from time to time, presented in his discourses. But, as all forces in nature are recriprocal in their action, so does prayer act upon him who prays as well as upon him for whom the prayer is offered. If you wish to be profited by the preaching, pray for the preacher. (*Evan Lewis, B.A.*) *The force of prayer :*—What is the prayer for which I ask? It is not the self-willed importunity of him who thinks he shall be heard for his much speaking. It is not the opening to God of thoughts which His love has not anticipated. It is not the pleading of our personal wishes as isolated objects of Divine favour ; say, rather, it is the humblest, tenderest, most unquestioning expression of our dependence, the confession of our wants and weaknesses, as we have felt them, the firmest resolution to rest in God's will, and to make His will our own ; the energy of a spiritual communion by which we realize our own well-being in the well-being of others ; the endeavour to quicken and chasten and hallow every prompting of duty by the light of heaven. In this sense, " brethren, pray for us." Such prayer corresponds—I. WITH OUR CHRISTIAN FELLOWSHIP. We are not, we cannot be, alone. In itself the fact is fitted to oppress us with the feeling of our powerlessness. But it can be transfigured.

And to pray one for another is to transfigure it. When St. Paul speaks of Christians being "in Christ," he has gathered up the gospel in two syllables; he has proclaimed the unfailing bond of fellowship, the adequate provision for effective ministry, the victorious sovereignty of redeeming love. II. WITH OUR PRESENT NEEDS. III. WITH OUR DIVINE ASSURANCE. Christianity deals with social problems, not accidentally, but in virtue of its existence. For us the Incarnation is the rule and the motive power. The Resurrection is the sign of God's purpose for all material and transitory things, the transfiguration of the completeness of human life. The Christian Church is, as we believe, the present organ of a living Spirit. We claim for it, in virtue of the assurance of the Lord, not simply the right of existence or the power of self-defence, but the certainty of conquest. (*Bp. Westcott.*)    *The ministers' plea for the peoples' prayers :*—I. DIRECTIONS. Pray for us. 1. That we may be furnished with all proper gifts and graces for our work. 2. That we may be preserved from the defections of the age. 3. That we may be helped to fulfil our ministry in the best manner. 4. That our ministry may be accepted of God in Christ, and of His people. 5. That we may be made successful in our work. 6. That the usefulness of our lives may be continued. 7. That we may be united with one another, and with the Churches of Christ, in carrying on the work of the Lord. 8. That our own souls may be saved, and that we may give up our accounts with joy in the day of the Lord Jesus. II. CONSIDERATIONS. 1. Our work is very important. 2. Our difficulties in managing it are many— arising from the work, ourselves, and our hearers. 3. Our strength is small. 4. The residue of the Spirit is with the Lord, and there is room for hope that, by the help of your fervent prayers, it may be brought down upon us. 5. Our prayers and labours for you call for a return of your prayers for us. 6. The answer of your prayers for us will turn to your own benefit, and to the advancement of Christ's kingdom and glory. (*J. Gouge, D.D.*)    *Prayer for ministers :*—Pray for us—I. AS TEACHERS, that we may be taught of the Holy Spirit, and have more of the mind of Jesus ; and that eschewing all false doctrine—the materialistic and the sensuous on the one side; and the rationalistic and the sceptical on the other—we may hold, and teach, and feel, the truth in all its proportions. II. AS PREACHERS AND EVANGELISTS, that we may never preach ourselves, but Christ only, in all His fulness, without limit: affectionately, earnestly, persuasively, lovingly, savingly: give true bread to our people: speaking as a dying man to dying men ; as a redeemed soul to souls for whom Jesus died. III. AS MINISTERS OF HOLY SACRAMENTS, THE WORD, AND SERVICES OF THE CHURCH. That her beauty and grace may never be injured by us, and that we may do all holy things with a holy mind; and that God will so honour His own ordinance, that, even at our lips, His Word may go with the greater power ; and when there shall be made a true confession, the assurance of absolving grace may reach comfortably even through us, to the yet unquiet conscience ; and true sacrifices arise at our hands, from fervent and united hearts; and the whole Church "grow up into Him in all things which is the Head." IV. AS MEN, "Brethren, pray for us." Acknowledging and claiming, by that word, a common brotherhood,—lest, perhaps, they might think of him only in his official capacity. "Pray for us" as men, subject as much—if not more—to the same infirmities that you are; poor, ignorant men, that know nothing as they ought to know it; wanting guidance at every step, and sympathy, and the blood of Jesus to wash both their bodies and their souls. (*J. Vaughan, M.A.*)    *The value of prayer for ministers :*—John Livingstone, of Scotland, once spent a whole night with a company of his brethren in prayer for God's blessing, all of them together besieging the throne ; and next day, under his sermon, eight hundred souls were converted. All the world has known how the audience of President Edwards was moved under his terrible sermon on "Sinners in the hands of an angry God." But the secret of that sermon is known to but few. Some Christians in the vicinity had become alarmed, lest while God was blessing other places He should in anger pass them by ; and so they met on the previous evening and spent the whole night in agonizing prayer. (*H. C. Fish, D.D.*)    *The minister's prayer-book :*—A worthy minister of the gospel, in North America, was pastor of a flourishing Church. He was a popular preacher, but gradually became less to his hearers, and his congregation very much decreased. This was solely attributed to the minister ; and matters continuing to get worse, some of his hearers resolved to speak to him on the subject. They did so ; and when the good man had heard their complaints, he replied, "I am quite sensible of all you say, for I feel it to be true ; and the reason of it is, that I have lost my prayer-book." They were astonished at hearing this, but he proceeded : " Once my preaching was acceptable, many were edified by it, and numbers were added to the Church, which was then in a prosperous state. But we were then a praying people. . . ." They took the hint. Social prayer was again renewed and punctually attended. Exertions were made to induce those who were without to attend the preaching of the Word. And the result was, that the minister became as popular as ever, and in a short time the Church was again as flourishing as ever. (*Clerical Library.*) *Prayer helps preaching :*—There was once in the old days a famous mission preacher ; whenever he preached he was accompanied by a little blind boy, his brother. As the great preacher stood on chancel step, or in pulpit, and people wept or trembled at his words, close by would be the blind child, with his sightless eyes turned upward, as though watching his brother. One night, the preacher saw a vision in church, he thought an angel touched him, and pointed to the blind boy. Then he saw a stream of light from heaven shining on the sightless eyes, and he understood now that it was not the eloquence of the preacher, but the prayers of the blind child which wrought such wonderful results. (*W. Buxton.*)

Ver. 26. **Greet all the brethren with an holy kiss.**—*The holy kiss :*—This exhortation in various forms is frequent (Rom. xvi. 16 ; 1 Cor. xvi. 20 ; 2 Cor. xiii. 12 ; 1 Pet. v. 14) ; and it must be borne in mind was addressed to men with respect to men, and to women with respect to women only. At this time worship would be conducted in accordance with the strict customs of the East, the men being separated from the women. It is still altogether contrary to " chastity " or " good fame " for a man and woman to greet one another in public, even though members of the same family. Hence the embarrassment of the disciples (John iv. 27). Had anything been intended so monstrous to the notions of the Greeks as the fact of all men indiscriminately kissing all women it must have been distinctly stated, and that with restrictions to guard against its abuse. Moreover, had such indiscriminate salutation been allowed it would have formed a damaging charge, sure to have been brought by Pagan and Jewish objectors ; but no such charge is discovered in the writings of the early centuries. The custom was practised for a long time. It was called " the kiss of greeting," " the kiss of peace," sometimes only " the peace." One special time when it was employed was during Divine service just before Communion. In the *Apostolic Constitutions*, a work of the third century, the author says, " On the other side let the men sit with all silence and good order ; and the women, let them also sit separately, keeping silence. . . . Then let the men salute one another, and the women one another with the kiss in the Lord." There are two distinct kinds of kissing—one is that of dependants or suppliant's kissing a supreme hand, feet, hem of garment, or dust on which he has trodden. The other is that which takes place between equals. When these are relatives or dear friends each in turn places his head face downwards upon the other's left shoulder, and afterwards salutes the right cheek, and then reverses the action (Gen. xxxiii. 4 ; xlv. 14, 15 ! Acts xx. 37). Between the first and last mentions of this custom stretches a period of more than eighteen hundred years ! What wonder, then, that after the lapse of another eighteen hundred years, we find it still the same in the changeless life of Bible Lands ! When a kindly, but somewhat more formal and respectful, salutation passes between those of the same rank, they will take hold of each other's beards and kiss them, and it is a great insult to take hold of a man's beard for any other purpose (2 Sam. xx. 9, 10). There is, however, another common occasion of kissing, viz., between a host and his guests, when one places the right hand upon the other's left shoulder and kisses the right cheek, and then the left hand on the right shoulder, kissing the left cheek (2 Sam. xv. 5). For the neglect of this Simon the Pharisee was rebuked (Luke vii. 45), by our Lord, committing, as he did, a gross breach of the laws of hospitality. Another formal mode of salutation between equals is to join the right hands ; then each kisses his own hand and puts it to his lips and forehead or over his heart. Most probably it was by laying the hand on the shoulder and kissing the cheek that the early Christians saluted one another. It was intended to teach believers of their common brotherhood in Christ, without distinction of caste or rank. It answers exactly to our hearty shaking of the hands. (*J. Neil, M.A.*) *Fraternal salutation :*—I. THE PRACTICE ITSELF. It was an ordinary mode of salutation, and had been practised at all times in eastern countries, sometimes even by men, and that, too, for opposite purposes. Hence Judas, when he wished to betray his Master, he did so with a kiss, testifying his apparent friendship on the one hand, and his abominable treachery on the other. A kiss was the sign of affection; and so by that slight artifice Judas thought to conceal his base purpose. Jesus, with severity, reproached him justly for it : " Betrayest thou," He said, " the Son of Man with a kiss ? " As if He had said, Dost thou violate all thy obligations of fidelity to thy Master, and thus deliver Him up to death ? The kiss is the outward token of inward affection, but thou dost employ it basely and wickedly, intending to add deceit, disguise, and the prostitution of a mark of esteem to the crime of treason. Every word of Christ's reproach must surely have gone to the heart of Judas. The same artifice, however, was frequently resorted to for a like purpose. Take, as proof, that between Joab and Abner (2 Sam. iii. 27). II. THE SANCTITY OF THIS PRACTICE. St. Paul speaks of " a holy kiss," to denote that he intended it to be an expression of Christian affection, and so to guard it against all improper familiarity and scandal. Thus he sends a friendly salutation from himself, and Silvanus, and Timotheus; and he would have them signify their mutual love and affection to one another by " the kiss of charity." So far this was well; but there are other ways of showing attachment to Christian brethren of a less suspicious and more certain character, such as rejoicing with them when they rejoice, and weeping with them when they weep, bearing their burdens and relieving their wants. This is indeed good and acceptable in the sight of God.     (*A. Barnes, D.D.*)    *Christian greeting :*— Shake hands with somebody as you go out of church. The more of it the better, if it is expressive of real interest and feeling. There may be a great deal of the spirit of the gospel put into a hearty shake of the hand. Think of St. Paul's four times repeated request, " Greet one another," after the custom then in common use, and one which is expressive of even warmer feeling than our common one of hand-shaking. Why not give your neighbours the benefit of the warm Christian feeling that fills you to your finger tips, and receive the like from them in return ? You will both be benefited by it; and the stranger will go away feeling that the church is not, after all, so cold as he had thought it to be. *A smiling greeting :*—A lady of position and property, anxious about her neighbours, provided religious services for them. She was very deaf—could scarcely hear at all. On one occasion, one of her preachers managed to make her understand him, and at the close of their conversation asked : " But what part do you take in the work ? " " Oh," she replied, " I smile them in and I smile them out! " Very soon the preacher saw the result of her generous, loving sympathy in a multitude of broad-shouldered, hard-fisted men, who entered the place of worship, delighted to get a smile from her as she used to stand in the doorway to receive them. Why do not the working classes attend the house of God ? They would, in greater numbers, if self-denying, Christ-loving Christians would smile them in and smile them out. (*The Christian.*)

Ver. 27. **I charge you by the Lord that this Epistle be read unto all the holy brethren.**—*The authority of St. Paul's Epistles :*—This is by implication a remarkable ecclesiastical sanction claimed for this Epistle. In the Jewish Church Moses and the Prophets were constantly read (Luke iv. 16; Acts xii. 27; xv. 21). The injunction here reminds us of the blessing in Rev. i. 3, and the impressive solemnity with which it is given is worthy of note. Surely it suggests the duty of reading passages of the New Testament in church, and even the guilt of neglecting it, or of keeping it from the people. This is one of the passages which give us an idea of the great authority attributed to the Epistles from the earliest times. They were carried by the apostle's delegates (like the *iggereth* of the synagogues); they were held to have equal dogmatic authority with the apostle himself ; they were read out and finally deposited among the archives of the church ; they were taken out on solemn days and read as sacred documents, with a perpetual teaching. Thus the epistolary form of literature was peculiarly the shape into which apostolic thought was thrown—a form well adapted to the wants of the time, and to the character and temperament of St. Paul. (*Bp. Alexander.*)    *Bible reading in the Church :*—The solemnity of this charge suggests —1. The co-ordinate authority of the Epistles with other portions of Holy Writ. The Old Testament lessons came as messages from God in the synagogue; the New Testament lessons come as the same in the church. 2. The prominent place they should occupy in public worship. Too many regard them as amongst the " preliminaries," and treat them accordingly. Singing, prayer, reading, preaching are each of the utmost importance. If any deserve prominence it is reading, for that is the declaration of the pure Word of God. I. How THE BIBLE SHOULD BE

READ IN CHURCH. 1. Distinctly. When mumbled the time is simply wasted, and the people deprived of edification and comfort. Those who protest against their being read in a dead language should beware of reading them in a dead voice. 2. Reverently. Carelessness is a grave fault; it begets careless hearing. The Word read is a savour of life unto life or of death unto death. What a responsibility, therefore, rests on the reader! 3. Impressively. The art of elocution is by no means to be despised. We take all possible pains to impress our own messages on the minds of those who listen. We are pathetic, earnest, persuasive, as the case may be; how much more then should we be with the message from God? 4. Without note or comment. This should be the rule, although there may be exceptions. Comment comes naturally in the sermon. The Bible should be allowed a fair chance to do its own work. "My Word"—not a comment on it— "shall not return unto Me void." "All Scripture . . . is profitable for doctrine," &c. II. WHY? 1. As a perpetual safeguard against heretical teaching. The preacher may err from the truth, but if the Bible be in the reading-desk, the antidote is always at hand. 2. As a continual supply of teaching, comfort, and edification. If the preacher be inefficient, the reading of the lessons will do much to supply the want. 3. As an ever-recurring reminder of the duty of searching the Scriptures. It is to be feared that the Scriptural knowledge of multitudes is just what they learn on Sunday. 4. As a constant witness of God's presence in His Church. The speaker is not far away from his speech. (*J. W. Burn.*) *A solemn mandate:*—This is not only an exhortation, but an adjuration by the Lord that must not be set aside for any consideration. What was the special reason for this serious order at Thessalonica is not stated; but it is possible that an opinion had begun to prevail even then and there that the Scriptures were designed to be kept in the hands of the ministers of religion, and that their common perusal was to be forbidden. At all events it is not unreasonable to suppose that the Holy Spirit, by whom this Epistle was dictated, foresaw that the time would come when this prohibition would be broached and upheld by certain ecclesiastics and councils, and that acted upon it would be one of the means by which a huge religious fabric would be established. Hence the mind of the apostle was supernaturally directed to give this solemn injunction, that the contents of this Epistle should be communicated without reserve to *all* the Christian brethren in Thessalonica. I. THE APOSTOLIC INJUNCTION IS AN EXPRESS DIVINE COMMAND. All the people must have access to the Word of God. So important was this considered that it was deemed necessary to enjoin those who should receive the Word of God, under the solemnities of an oath, and by all the force of apostolic authority to communicate what they had received to others. II. THE UNLIMITED CHARACTER OF THIS APOSTOLIC INJUNCTION. Not a single member of the Church at Thessalonica was omitted from it, whether high or low, rich or poor. The command is, indeed, that the Word of God be "read unto all the holy brethren," but by parity of reasoning it would follow that it was to be in their hands; that it was to be ever accessible to them; that it was in no manner to be withheld from them. Probably many of them could not read, but *in some way* the contents of revelation were to be made known to them; and not by preaching only, but by reading the words inspired by God. No part was to be kept back; nor were they to be denied such access that they could fully understand it. It was presumed that all the members of the Church would understand what had been written to them, and to profit by it. III. THE SIN OF VIOLATING THE INJUNCTION. If all be true we have stated, and true all is, it follows that there is great sin in all decisions and laws which are designed to keep the Scriptures from the people, and great sin in all opinions and dogmas which prevail anywhere, denying them the right of private judgment. The richest blessing of heaven to mankind is the Bible; and there is no book ever written so admirably adapted to the popular mind, and so eminently fitted to elevate the fallen, the ignorant, and the wicked; and there is no more decided enemy of the progress of the human race in intelligence and purity than he who prevents in anywise the free circulation of the Holy Volume, while there is no truer friend of his species than he who causes it to be read by all men, and who contributes to make it accessible to all the peoples of the world. (*A. Barnes, D.D.*) *Desire to know God's Word:*—The following is an extract from a petition which was signed by 416 Roman Catholics in the vicinity of Tralee, the parents and representatives of more than 1,300 children, and presented to the Roman Catholic Bishop of Kerry in 1826:—"May it please your reverence,—We, the undersigned, being members of the Roman Catholic Church in your bishopric, beg leave to approach you with all the respect and deference due to our spiritual father, and to implore your pastoral indulgence on a subject of much anxiety to us, and of great importance to the bodies and souls of our dear children. We approach your paternal feet, holy father, humbly imploring that you will instruct the clergy to relax that hostility which many of them direct against the Scripture schools, and to suspend those denunciations and penalties which are dealt to us merely because we love our children and wish to see them honest men, loyal subjects, good Christians, and faithful Catholics. In short, permit us to know something of the Word of God, so much spoken of in these days." (*Religious Tract Society Anecdotes*.)　*The authenticity of the Epistle*:—To produce a letter purporting to have been publicly read in the Church of Thessalonica, when no such letter in truth had been read or heard of in that Church, would be to produce an imposture destructive of itself. At least it seems unlikely that the author of an imposture would voluntarily and even officiously afford a handle to so plain an objection. Either the Epistle was publicly read among the Thessalonians during Paul's lifetime or it was not. If it was, no publication could be more authentic, no species of notoriety more unquestionable, no method of preserving the integrity of the copy more secure. If it was not, the clause would remain a standing condemnation of the forgery, and one would suppose, an invincible impediment to its success. (*Archdeacon Paley*.)　*The witness to Christ of the oldest Christian writing*:—This Epistle is of peculiar interest, as being the most venerable Christian document, and as being a witness to Christian truth quite independent of the Gospels. There are no such doctrinal statements in it as in the most of Paul's longer letters; it is simply an outburst of confidence and love and tenderness, and a series of practical instructions. But if it be so saturated as it is with the facts and principles of the Gospel, the stronger is the attestation which it gives to the importance of these. I have, therefore, thought it might be worth our while if we put this—the most ancient Christian writing—into the witness-box, and see what it has to say about the great truths and principles which we call the Gospel of Jesus Christ. Let us hear its witness—I. To THE DIVINE CHRIST. 1. Look how the letter begins (chap. i. 1). What is the meaning of putting these two names side by side, unless it means that Christ sits on the Father's throne, and is Divine. 2. More than twenty times in this short letter that great name is applied to Jesus, "the Lord"—the New Testament equivalent of the Old Testament Jehovah. 3. Direct prayer is offered to our Lord. Thus the very loftiest apex of revealed religion had been imparted to that handful of heathens in the few weeks of the apostle's stay amongst them. And the letter takes it for granted that so deeply was that truth embedded in their new consciousness that an allusion to it was all that was needed for their understanding and their faith. II. To THE DYING CHRIST. 1. As to the fact. "The Jews killed the Lord Jesus." And then, beyond the fact, there is set forth the meaning and the significance of that fact—"God hath not appointed us to wrath, but to obtain salvation by our Lord Jesus Christ, who died for us." I need but mention in this connection another verse which speaks of Jesus as "He that delivereth us from the wrath to come." It is a continuous deliverance, running all through the life of the Christian man, and not merely to be realized at the far end; because by the mighty providence of God, and by the automatic working of the consequences of every transgression and disobedience, that "wrath" is ever coming towards men and lighting on them, and a continual Deliverer, who delivers us by His death, is what the human heart needs. This witness is distinct that the death of Christ is a sacrifice, is man's deliverance from wrath, and is a present deliverance from the consequences of transgression. 2. And if you will take this letter, and only think that it was merely a few weeks' familiarity with these truths that had passed before it was written, and then mark how the early and imperfect glimpse of them had transformed the men, you will see where the power lies in the proclamation of the gospel. The men had been transformed. What transformed them? The message of a Divine and dying Christ, who had offered up Himself without spot unto God, and who was their peace and their righteousness and their power. III. To THE RISEN AND ASCENDED CHRIST. "Ye turned unto God . . . to wait for His Son from heaven whom He raised from the dead." And again, "The Lord Himself shall descend from heaven with a shout." The risen Christ, then, is in the heavens. 1. Remember we have nothing to do with the four Gospels here: we are dealing here with an entirely independent witness. And then tell us what importance is to be attached to this evidence of the resurrection of Jesus Christ. Twenty years after His death here is this man speaking about that resurrection as being the recognized and notorious fact which all the churches accepted, and which underlay all their faith. Then if, twenty years after the event, this witness was borne, it necessarily carries us back a great deal nearer to the event, for there is no mark of its being new testimony, but every mark of its being the habitual and continuous witness that had been borne from the instant of the alleged resurrection to that present time. The fact is, there is not a place where you can stick a pin in, between the resurrection and the date of this letter, wide enough to admit of the rise of the faith in a resurrection of the Church to the admission that the belief in the resurrection was contemporaneous with the alleged resurrection itself. 2. And so we are shut up to the old alternative, either Jesus Christ rose from the dead, or the noblest lives that the world has ever seen, and the loftiest system of morality that ever has been proclaimed, were built upon a lie. And we are called to believe that at the bidding of a mere unsupported, bare, dogmatic assertion that miracles are impossible. I would rather believe in the supernatural than the ridiculous. And to me it is unspeakably ridiculous to suppose that anything but the fact of the resurrection accounts for the existence of the Church and for the faith of this witness that we have before us. IV. To THE RETURNING CHRIST. That is the characteristic doctrinal subject of the letter. The coming of the Master does not appear here with emphasis on its judicial aspect. It is rather intended to bring hope to the mourners, and the certainty that bands broken here may be reknit in holier fashion hereafter. But the judicial aspect is not, as it could not be, left out. And the apostle further tells us that "that day cometh as a thief in the night." That is a quotation of the Master's own words, which we find in the Gospels; and so again a confirmation, from an independent witness, as far as it goes, of the Gospel story. And then he goes on, in terrible language, to speak of "sudden destruction, as of travail upon a woman with child; and they shall not escape." These, then, are the points of this witness's testimony as to the returning Lord—a personal coming, a reunion of all believers in Him, in order to eternal felicity and mutual gladness, and the destruction that shall fall by His coming upon those who turn away from Him. What a revelation that would be to men who had known what it was to grope in the darkness of heathendom and to have no light upon the future! I remember once walking in the long galleries of the Vatican, on the one side of which there are Christian inscriptions from the catacombs, and on the other heathen inscriptions from the tombs. One side is all dreary and hopeless, one long sigh echoing along the line of white marbles—"Vale! vale! in æternum vale!" ("Farewell, farewell, for ever farewell!")—on the other side, "In Christo, In pace, In spe" ("In hope, in Christ, in peace"). That is the witness that we have to lay to our hearts. And so death becomes a passage, and we let go the dear hands, believing that we shall clasp them again. (*A. Maclaren, D.D.*)

# THE BIBLICAL ILLUSTRATOR

## II THESSALONIANS

THE

# BIBLICAL ILLUSTRATOR

BY

JOSEPH S. EXELL

II THESSALONIANS

BAKER BOOK HOUSE
GRAND RAPIDS, MICHIGAN 49506

# INTRODUCTION TO THE SECOND EPISTLE TO THE THESSALONIANS.

I. THE OCCASION OF THE EPISTLE.—The apostle remained in Corinth for a year and six months (Acts xviii. 11), and it was undoubtedly during the latter part of this time that he wrote this Epistle. Silas and Timothy were still in his company (chap. i. 1); the former for the last time, as we may conclude from the silence of the history. Communications would naturally have passed meanwhile between himself and the Thessalonians. He would have heard, concerning his former Epistle, how far it had produced its effect, where it had been misconstrued and where it had failed. The effect of such tidings is very apparent in this letter. It was plainly written with a twofold intent: 1. The anticipation of the Lord's Second Advent, aroused by the teaching and former letter of the apostle, had been stimulated to an unhealthy activity by fanatical or designing teachers, who had even forged a letter in the name of St. Paul, and had filled the Church with anxiety and alarm. This state of feeling has indeed been supposed by many critics to have been occasioned simply by the misunderstanding of the former letter. Not to speak, however, of the unlikelihood that the calm prophetic words in which he had enjoined " the patience of hope " in reference to the great event should so have been perverted, his own language (chap. ii. 2) seems to show decisively that he referred to a supposititious letter. " Spirit " refers to a pretended prophecy; " word " to a pretended saying on inspired authority; " letter," therefore, would similarly mean a pretended epistle. Moreover the word *as*, in the phrase " as by us," would scarcely have been used by the writer, had he intended to indicate his own letter. We therefore conclude that an imposture had been practised on the Thessalonians, advantage, no doubt, having been taken of what the apostle had actually said and written. To prevent such imposition for the future, he now expressly states that his own signature and " salutation " would henceforth authenticate all his Epistles (chap. iii. 17). 2. The other circumstance was the disregard of one most important injunction of the former Epistle—there laid down briefly, almost with an apology, as though a hint in a matter so obvious would be sufficient (chap. iv. 11). But this gentle suggestion of Christian duty had proved inadequate. In the Church there were some who, influenced, perhaps, by the anticipation of an immediate catastrophe in the world's affairs, neglected the ordinary duties of life—" working at no business, but being busybodies." Thus early did religious fanaticism produce its natural fruit in selfish indolence; and the loftiest hopes of the Church were perverted into a plea for the most ignoble mendicancy. For such offences the fitting remedy, sharp and stern, was excommunication; while yet, as if to acknowledge the nobleness of the truth which had been so misread and degraded, the offender is to be dealt with tenderly, in the hope that he might learn to apprehend it aright. (*S. G. Green, D.D.*)

II. ITS GENUINENESS AND RELATION TO THE FIRST EPISTLE.—Like that of the First Epistle is practically uncontroverted. We seem to have very early testimony to its use—Polycarp appearing in two places to quote it, though anonymously, according to his custom; and Justin, speaking of the man of Sin, a manner which shows his acquaintance with this Epistle. The objections of a few modern scholars are chiefly drawn from the prophecy in chap. ii., from supposed contradictions between the two Epistles, especially in regard to the date of the advent; from fancied allusions to the persecution of Nero; from a mistaken notion that the doctrine of an Antichrist (which was in reality pre-christian) was only invented by the Montanists. Doubts have been entertained by a few critics, who acknowledged the genuineness of both, which of these two letters is the earlier. Ewald placed the second first. The arguments, however, are hardly worth considering in face of the fact that in 2 Thess. ii. 15, we have an allusion to a former Epistle. All the historical portion of the First Epistle (especially chap. ii. 17; iii. 11) bears evident tokens of being the earliest communication that had passed between St. Paul and his spiritual children since he had left them. (*Canon Mason.*) The Second Epistle may be regarded as continuing the first and as diverging from it, and in one respect, at least, forming a link of transition to the later Epistles. It defers the advent of Christ, and yet presents a more vivid and detailed account of the manner and circumstances of it. More fully in the apostle's mind, nevertheless, in its outward manifestation, it seems to remove further from him, the intervening objects overshadowing the distant vision. The very definiteness with which he conceives it, leads him, as it were, a step onward, to consider the stages of its revelation, to ask the question, not "when shall these things be, and the end of the world"? but what shall happen first. It was thought by Grotius that this Epistle must have preceded the first. Improbable as it is (comp. 2 Thess. ii. 15) that a previous Epistle could have interposed itself between the visit of the apostle and chapters two and three of the First Epistle; and inconsistent as 1 Thess. iv. 13–18 would then be with 2 Thess. ii., the opinion may serve to remind us that, in one sense it is true that the Second Epistle anticipates the First; that is to say, it is based on the lesson which the apostle had taught the Thessalonians while he was yet with them, and previously to either (chap. ii. 5). The subject of Antichrist was not new to them; they had been told what was meant, and what withheld that he should be revealed in his own time, whereas, in the former Epistle, he had led their minds exclusively to the heavenly vision. (*Prof. Jowett.*)

III. ANALYSIS.—I. THE SALUTATION (chap. i. 1, 2). II. THE RETROSPECTIVE PORTION (chap. i. 3–12). 1. Thanksgiving for progress made (vers. 3, 4). 2. Hopes thus afforded against the advent day (vers. 5–10). 3. Prayers for continuance in so happy a state (chap. i. 11, 12). III. THE INSTRUCTIVE AND HORTATORY PORTION. 1. On the date of the advent—(1) Caution against believing the advent close at hand (chap. ii. 1–3). (2) What must happen first (ver. 3–10). (3) Terrible fate of the apostates (vers. 11, 12). (4) Thanksgiving that their fate is so different (vers. 13, 14). (5) Thanksgiving and prayer (vers. 15–17). 2. On the necessity of work. (1) Request for prayers for himself, which skilfully serves to predispose the readers to obey the ensuing commands (chap. iii. 1–4). (2) Prayer for the same purpose (ver. 5). (3) Commands to make all work, and to excommunicate the refractory (vers. 6–15). (4) Prayer for tranquillity (ver. 16). (5) Final benediction, with attention drawn to the autograph (vers. 17, 18). (*Canon Mason.*)

IV. THE GOSPEL OF PAUL AT THESSALONICA.—What was the gospel brought to Thessalonica? Can we give to ourselves any precise account of the "good news" which "Paul and Silvanus and Timotheus" announced in this city, and which produced so powerful and enduring an effect? To these questions the indications of the two Epistles, compared with the story of the Acts, enable us to give a tolerable answer. 1. The foundation of St. Paul's teaching was laid in the proof of the Messiahship of Jesus, drawn from the prophecies of Scripture, compared with the facts of the life, death, and resurrection of the Saviour. The method of this proof, briefly indicated in Acts xvii. 3, is set forth at length in the report of his discourse at the Pisidian Antioch given by St. Luke in the thirteenth chapter of the Acts. 2. The purpose of Christ's death and its bearing on human salvation must have been abundantly explained by the apostles. So we infer not only from the central position of this subject in St. Paul's later Epistles, and from the prominence given to it in Acts xiii. 38, 39, where the announcement of forgiveness of sins and justification by faith forms the climax of St. Paul's whole sermon; but the language of 1 Eph. v. 8–10 leaves us in no doubt that the same "word of the cross" was proclaimed at Thessalonica which St. Paul preached everywhere. Here "salvation" comes "through our Lord Jesus Christ, who died for us"—a salvation from "the anger of God," a salvation in part received already, in part matter of "hope," and which belongs to those who "have put on the breastplate of faith and love." This salvation was the great need of the Gentile world, which "knew not God," and was enslaved to idolatry and shameful lusts (1 Eph. i. 9; iv. 5; 2 Eph. i. 8). Still it must be admitted, and it is remarkable, that very little is said in these two letters on the subject of the atonement and salvation by faith. Evidently on these fundamental doctrines there was no dispute at Thessalonica. They were so fully accepted and understood in this Church that it was unnecessary to dilate upon them; and the apostle has other matters just now to deal with. 3. The Church at Thessalonica being chiefly of heathen origin, St. Paul and St. Silas had said much to them of the falsity and wickedness of idolatry, completing the lessons which many of their disciples had already received in the synagogue. Their faith was emphatically a "faith toward God—the living and true God," to whom they had "turned from their idols" (this seems to imply that many Thessalonian Christians had been converted directly from paganism), and whom they knew in "His Son" (1 Eph. i. 9, 10). And this living and true God, the Father of the Lord Jesus, they had come to know and to approach as "our Father" (1 Eph. i. 3; iii. 11, 13; 2 Eph. ii. 16), who was to them "the God of peace" (1 Eph. i. 1; v. 23; 2 Eph. i. 2), who had "loved them and given them eternal comfort and good hope in grace," had "chosen" them and "called them to enter His kingdom and glory," who "would count them worthy of their calling and accomplish in them all the desire of goodness and the work of faith," who had "given them His Holy Spirit," whose "will" was their "sanctification," whose "word" was ever "working in" them, who would "comfort and strengthen their hearts" in every needful way and would reward them with "rest" from their afflictions in due time, whose care for His beloved was not limited by death, for He was pledged at Christ's coming to restore those whom death had snatched away (1 Eph. i. 4; ii. 12, 13; iv. 3, 7, 8, 14; v. 18: 2 Eph. i. 5, 7, 11; ii. 13, 16, 17). Such a God it must be their one aim to love and to please; St. Paul's one desire for them is that they may "walk worthily" of Him (1 Eph. ii. 12; iv. 1; 2 Eph. iii. 5). The good news the apostle had brought he speaks of repeatedly as "the gospel of God," while it is "the gospel of our Lord Jesus Christ" (2 Eph. i. 8), since He is its great subject and centre: cf. Rom. i. 1, 3, "the gospel of God—concerning His Son." It is important to note the prominence of God in these Epistles, and the manifold ways in which the Divine character and relationship to believing men had been set forth to the Thessalonian Church. For such teaching would be necessary, and helpful in the highest degree, to men who had just emerged from heathen darkness and superstition; and these letters afford the best example left to us of St. Paul's earliest instructions to Gentile converts. 4. So we come to that which was the most conspicuous and impressive topic of the Thessalonian gospel, so far as we can gather it from the echoes audible in the Epistles, viz., the coming of the Lord Jesus in His heavenly kingdom. 5. The moral issues of the gospel inculcated by St. Paul at Thessalonica, the new duties and affections belonging to the new life of believers in Christ, are touched upon at many different points; but not developed with the fulness and systematic method of subsequent Epistles. Most prominent here are the obligation to chastity, as belonging to the sanctity of the body and the indwelling of the Holy Spirit (1 Eph. iv. 1–8), and the claims of brotherly love, with the good order, the peace, and mutual helpfulness that flow from it (1 Eph. iv. 9, 10; v. 12–15; 2 Eph. iii. 14, 15). What is singular in these Epistles is the repeated and strong injunctions they contain on the subject of diligence in labour and attention to the ordinary duties of life (1 Eph. iv. 10–12; 2 Eph. iii. 6–15). A striking moral feature of the gospel proclaimed at Thessalonica is manifest in the conduct of the missionaries of Christ themselves—their incessant labour, their unbounded self-denial, the purity and devoutness of their spirit, and their fearless courage (1 Eph. i. 6, 7; ii. 1–12; 2 Eph. iii. 8, 9). (*G. G. Findlay, B.A.*)

V. The Style and Character of the Two Epistles.—They are the letters of a missionary, written to an infant Church but very recently brought from heathen darkness into the marvellous light of the gospel. They lie nearer, therefore, to the missionary preaching of the apostle of the Gentiles, as we find it, for instance, in Acts xiv. 15–17; xvii. 22–31, than do any of the later Epistles. This accounts for their simplicity, for the absence in them of controversy, and the elementary nature of their doctrine. They are addressed to a Macedonian Church, and they exhibit in common with the Epistle to the (Macedonian) Philippians a peculiar warmth of feeling and mutual confidence between writer and readers. They are singularly affectionate letters. From 2 Cor. viii. 1, 2; xi. 9, we gather that the generosity which endeared the Philippians to St. Paul (Phil. iv. 14–17) distinguished the Macedonian Churches generally. The apostle can scarcely find words tender enough or images sufficiently vivid to express his regard for the Thessalonians (1 Eph. ii. 7, 11, 17, 19, 20; iii. 9). He feels his life bound up with them (chap. iii. 8). He boasts of them everywhere (2 Eph. i. 4; 2 Cor. viii. 1, 2). If he exhorts them, his warnings are mingled with commendations, lest they should think he has some fault to find (1 Eph. iv. 1, 9, 10; v. 11; 2 Eph. iii. 4). Further, these two are especially cheering and consolatory letters. The apostle sent Timothy to "comfort" the Thessalonians "concerning their faith" (1 Eph. iii. 2), and in writing he pursues the same object. Persecution was the lot of this Church from the beginning (1 Eph. iii. 4; Acts xvii. 5–9), as it continued to be long afterwards (2 Cor. viii. 2; *cf.* what was written to Philippi ten years later, Phil. i. 28, 29). So the apostle bends all his efforts to encourage his distressed and suffering friends. He teaches them to glory in tribulation. He makes them smile through their tears. Lastly, these are eschatological Epistles: that is, in the language of theology, they set forth "the last things" in Christian doctrine—the second coming of Christ, the raising of the dead and transformation of the living saints, and the judgment of the world; they announce the advent of Antichrist as the forerunner and Satanic counterpart of the returning Christ (2 Eph. ii. 1–12). (*Ibid.*)

# II. THESSALONIANS.

## CHAPTER I.

**Vers. 1–3. Paul and Silvanus and Timotheus** (see 1 Thess. i. 1, 2).—The company which despatched the First Epistle had not yet broken up. This proves that the Second Epistle was written before the end of the second missionary journey, for after that time we do not read of Silvanus being in the company of St. Paul. The salutation is precisely the same as in the First Epistle, save for the last clause of ver. 2, which is wrongly added in that place, but stands rightly here. (*Canon Mason.*) **Unto the Church of Thessalonica.**—*The use of the Church:*—But what an astronomer he would be who should sit at his telescope, watching the instrument, praising its lenses, magnifying the honour of its maker, cleaning, fixing, and adjusting it, and never seeing anything through it ! It is what is beyond the telescope, it is what the telescope reveals and brings to you, that gives it its value. Without that, it is good for nothing. Now the Church is God's telescope ; and if it enables you to see through the visible to the invisible, if it brings you truth, if it brings your time-thoughts into the relations of eternity, if it brings God, as a veritable person—yea, as a Father—near to your heart and near to your moral sense, then it is the Church of God to you. Otherwise, it is the Church of man. If it be opaque ; if it stop your thought with itself ; if you have got only so far as that you are a Churchman, you have not started on the true Christian course. (*H. W. Beecher.*) *The value of the Church:*—What is summer worth in the desert of Sahara ? It found it sand, and leaves it sand. The sun and the summer are worthless to the desert. And what is the Church worth to you ? It is worth just what it develops in you, as an educating institution. Its whole design is to hold you up in weak hours ; to inspire you with higher thoughts and with sweeter dispositions ; and to give you power to lift yourself up to the invisible. The Church is neither to be worshipped nor to be rested upon. You are not safe because you are in it, any more than the child is learned because it has been at school. The school is of great value ; there knowledge is gained more readily than it can be gained elsewhere : but we do not undervalue it when we say that you should not worship it. And the Church—should I disparage that—I, a minister, that have received its blessings, and that have seen them imparted to others ? No ; but its value is in this : that it teaches you to neglect the lower, and to centre your affections on the higher. For nothing less than God can satisfy the human soul—no ordinance, no service, nothing but love, down-dropping from the everlasting Fountain of sympathy, of pity, and of compassion. The love of God can satisfy you; and the uniting with the Church is good to you just in proportion as you, through the Church, look up and see God. (*Ibid.*) **Peace.**—*The peace of the believer:*—Through the Middlesex Narrows, the Winooski River rushes with impetuous torrent. When nearly through the Narrows the waters dash with tremendous force against a great rock that rises majestically many feet into the air. On this rock, near the top, is a hollow place of considerable size into which the rain falling collects and so forms a beautiful pool. So tranquil this pool becomes that it lies there a mirror reflecting the blue sky, the fleecy clouds, and the glories of the setting sun. Below, at the foot of the rock, the waters are in wild commotion. So on the Rock of Ages, rising high above and withstanding the world's wild rushing flood, peacefully rests the believer reflecting the glories of the world above—kept in perfect peace. **We are bound to thank God always for you.**—*The duty of thanksgiving:*—I. Thanksgiving is a debt that we owe to God for His benefits. 1. Justice requires it, for our mercies were given on this condition (Psa. l. 15). We ourselves consent to this covenant. We seldom pray in distress without promising thankfulness (Hosea xiv. 2). Yet how backward are we to perform (Luke xvii. 18). It is a kind of theft if we crave help in our necessities, and then act as though it came from ourselves.

2. God expects it—not *de facto* actually; He expects no more than is given—but *de jure*, of right He might expect (Luke xiii. 7; Isa. v. 4; 2 Chron. xxxii. 25). Therefore a good man should make conscience of his returns (Psa. cxvi. 12). 3. It keeps up our intercourse with God. By the laws of Ezekiel's temple the worshippers were to go in at one door and out at another, that no back might be turned on the Mercy-seat (Ezek. xlvi. 9). God cannot bear to have men turn their backs upon Him when their turn is served. Prayer and praise should be our continual work (Heb. xiii. 15). 4. It provides for the succession of mercies. The more thankful we are the more we receive; as a husbandman trusts more of his precious seed to a fruitful soil. The ascent of vapours makes way for the descent of showers (Psa. lxvii. 5, 6; Col. ii. 7). 5. It exercises and promotes all spiritual graces. (1) Faith, when we see the invisible Hand that reaches out our supplies (1 Chron. xxix. 14; Hosea ii. 8). (2) Love (Psa. cxvi. 1, 2). Self-love puts us more on prayers, but the love of God on praises. (3) Hope, as Abraham built an altar in Canaan when he had not a foot of land in it (Gen. xiii. 18). (4) Humility. The humble are most delighted in the praises of God, the proud in their own (Heb. i. 16; Gen. xxxii. 10; 2 Sam. vii. 18). 6. It prevents many sins, as—(1) Insensibility to God's blessings. (2) Murmuring (Job. ii. 10; i. 21). (3) Distrust and carking cares (Phil. iv. 6; Psa. lxxvii. 10, 11). (4) Spiritual pride (1 Cor. iv. 7). II. In thanksgiving spiritual benefits are to be especially acknowledged, because—1. They are discriminating, and come from God's special love. Corn, wine, and oil are bestowed on the world, but faith and love on the saints (Psa. cvi. 4). Protection is the benefit of every common subject, but intimate love and near admission the privilege of favourites. Christ gave His purse to Judas, but His Spirit to the others. 2. They concern the better part, the inward man (2 Cor. iv. 16). It is a greater favour to heal a wound than to mend a garment. The soul is more than the body; and a soul furnished with grace than one furnished with gifts (1 Cor. xiii. 1–3). 3. They are secured at greater cost than temporal blessings. The latter are bestowed by God as Creator and Upholder; saving grace He bestows only as the God and Father of Christ (Eph. i. 3). 4. They are pledges and beginnings of eternal blessings (John v. 24; Rom. viii. 30; 2 Cor. iii. 18). 5. They incline and fit the heart for thankfulness. Outward benefits give us the occasion, these the disposition (Psa. lxiii. 5). 6. They are never given in anger, as temporal benefits sometimes are (Matt. xiii. 11; Phil. i. 19). 7. They render us acceptable with God. A man is more accountable for worldly blessings, but not of greater account (Luke xii. 48); but saving graces are acceptable (1 Pet. iii. 4). 8. They should be acknowledged, that God may have the sole glory of them (James i. 17; Rev. iv. 10, 11; Isa. xxvi. 12; 1 Chron. xxix. 14; 1 Cor. xv. 10; Luke xix. 16). III. Spiritual blessings vouchsafed to others must be acknowledged with thankfulness. 1. It suits with our relation as members in the same mystical body of Christ, and so is part of the communion of saints (1 Cor. xii. 26; Phil. i. 7; Rom. xii. 15; Col. i. 3, 4). 2. The glory of God is concerned in it. Wherever His goodness shines forth, especially with any eminency, it must be acknowledged (Rom. i. 8; Gal. i. 24). 3. Our profit is concerned in it, inasmuch as it conduces to a common good. The good of some is the gain of the whole; we are benefited by their example, confirmed in their companionship (1 Thess. i. 7, 8; 1 Cor. i. 4, 5; Rom. i. 2). 4. If the salvation of our brethren be dear to us, whatever is given in order thereto we must reckon among our benefits, and we should rejoice in one another's gifts and graces as our own. 5. We increase their faith and comfort by such thanksgiving (Phil. i. 3–6). IV. In thanksgiving for spiritual benefits, whether to ourselves or others, the increase of grace must be acknowledged as well as the beginning of it. The degree is from God. He that begins perfects (Phil. i. 6). 1. Not our own free will (John vi. 44). 2. Not the strength of our resolutions (Psa. lxxiii. 2). 3. Not the stability of gracious habits (Rev. iii. 2). 4. But God only (1 Pet. v. 10; Luke xvii. 5). (*T. Manton, D.D.*) *The prosperity of the Thessalonian Church:*—In some of the Epistles we have the Church presented in a declining state, and suitable admonitions are given to her; in other Epistles we see her prospering, and hear the counsels of infinite wisdom proclaimed unto her. The Thessalonian Church was of the latter character, and seems to have been eminently favoured of her God. She was high in the esteem of the apostle; and deservedly so, because conspicuous among all the Churches of that age for high attainments. I. The happy state of the Thessalonian Church. In her infant state she was highly commended for "her works of faith, and labours of love, and patience of hope"; but here we view her in her

adult state. 1. Her increasing faith. This "had grown exceedingly," being daily more vivid in its apprehensions, more vigorous in its actings, and more uniform in its effects. Their faith had evinced its growth in that it had enabled them to see, almost as with their bodily eyes, the Saviour they loved, enthroned above all powers, invested with a fulness of spiritual gifts, ordering all things in heaven and earth, and, by His prevailing intercession at the right hand of God, securing to His believing people all the blessings of grace and glory. A corresponding energy, too, was felt through all the powers of their souls, accompanied with a fixed determination to live for Him who lived and died for them. 2. Her abounding love. In almost every Church there are comparative alienations of heart, if not some actual disagreements; but here "the charity of every one of them all toward each other abounded." One spirit pervaded the whole body; and time, instead of giving occasion to the enemy to foment differences, had only cemented and confirmed their mutual affection, so that they were greatly assimilated to the very image of Him whose name and nature is Love. Happy people! 3. Her invincible patience. Great had been the trials of her members from the beginning (1 Thess. ii. 14, 15); but they were not intimidated: "they held fast the profession of their faith without wavering," "in nothing terrified by their adversaries "; "for they had respect unto the recompence of the reward." They even gloried in their sufferings; and so "possessed their souls in patience," and allowed "patience to have her perfect work." What an enviable state was this! II. The light in which the apostle viewed this state. 1. He regarded it as a fit subject of thanksgiving to God. "Of Him," and Him alone, "was their fruit found." To Him therefore St. Paul gave the glory, "as it was meet" he should, and as he felt himself "bound" to do. So should we acknowledge God in all that is good, and glorify Him for it. 2. He regarded their state also as a fit subject of commendation to other Churches. He gloried of them in those where he ministered, in order to stimulate them to greater exertions, and encourage them to expect greater measures of Divine grace, in order to their own more exalted proficiency. 3. He further regarded their state as a fit subject of congratulation to themselves. Their graces, exercised under very trying circumstances, sufficiently demonstrated that there must be a future state of retribution, where the present inequalities of the Divine procedure would be rectified, and when "they should be accounted worthy of that kingdom" for which they suffered so much. III. The lessons we should learn from this Church. 1. That opposition, how formidable soever it may be, is no excuse for our turning back from God. What are our persecutions in comparison of those which they endured? Yet they were "stedfast, immovable, always abounding in the work of the Lord." Should we then be intimidated? No; we should take up our cross cheerfully; and having counted the cost, should be content to pay it. 2. That whatever proficiency we have made in the Divine life, we should still press forward for higher attainments. The Thessalonians, through mercy, had attained a rare eminence in the Divine life: so should we, forgetting all that is behind, reach forward to all that is before. We should "grow up into Christ in all things." Application: (1) How different from the Thessalonian Church are the generality of those who call themselves Christians! (2) How diligently should the most exalted Christians press forward in their heavenly course! (C. Simeon, M.A.)    The matter of thankfulness:—Observe: I. It is a comfort that our inward man is in a good state whatever it be with our outward. The Thessalonians were poor and afflicted (1 Thess. i. 6). Yet their condition before God was prosperous, and matter of thanksgiving rather than lamentation (so 2 Cor. iv. 16). We should count this world's goods well exchanged if by the want of them our spiritual graces are increased. If God by an aching head will give us a better heart; by a sickly body a healthy soul (3 John 2); by lessening us in the world make us rich in faith (Jas. ii. 5), we should not barely submit, but be thankful (Psa. cxix. 71; 2 Cor. xii. 9, 10; Heb. xii. 11). II. It is not enough barely to be good, but we must grow from good to better and be best at last. 1. God's children wait on the Lord, and He is not wont to be sparing to those who attend upon Him (Isa. xl. 31). 2. They are planted in a fertile soil (Psa. xcii. 13, 14). 3. There are ordinances by which they receive a supply of the Spirit (Psa. lxxxiv. 7). 4. They find new encouragement in God's ways (Prov. x. 29). 5. Our reward should encourage us (Phil. iii. 14). 6. The way is so pleasant that we have no occasion to tire in it (2 Pet. iii. 18). 7. God expects it (Heb. v. 12; Luke xii. 48; John xv. 2). III. Their growth was considerable. Certainly they did not overgrow their duty, but it was a wonderful growth considering the difference between what they once were and what now, and between them and others, even their contemporaries in the faith. We should not only grow, but excel in grace. To this end we should be—1. More humble (James iv. 6). 2. Diligent in the use of gifts (Luke viii. 18). 3. Thankful (Col. ii. 7). 4. Obedient to the Word of God as our rule, and the sanctifying motions of the Spirit as our principle (Jer. viii. 9; Eph. iv. 30). IV. THEIR GROWTH WAS IN BOTH FAITH AND LOVE. 1. These are inseparable (Col. i. 4; 1 Tim. i. 13), the one concerning our personal, the other the Church's benefit. We are to edify ourselves in faith, others in love. 2. This connection is necessary, because all religion is exercised by these graces. The mysteries of religion are received and improved by faith, and its precepts and duties acted by love (1 Cor. xvi. 13, 14). 3. The qualification which entitles us to the privileges of the new covenant in faith working by love (Gal. v. 6). Faith without love is dead, and love without faith is but a little good nature. 4. Both graces are recommended by the same authority (1 John iii. 23). 5. The one refers to God, the other to man. The one keeps us from defection from God, the other from a schism with our fellow Christians. V. THIS GROWTH AND PROFICIENCY WAS FOUND IN ALL. Not only some were eminent for faith and charity but all. (*T. Manton, D.D.*) *Growing faith:*—I. IT IS THE DIVINE WILL THAT FAITH SHOULD GROW. Growth is one of the characteristics of God's work. The oak that breasts the storm, and fights in savage fury with the gale, is after all only the outgrowth of the acorn, once carried in a child's pocket, and thrown with childish glee down the ravine. The eagle, that looks with unblinking eye upon the sun, was once the tiny eaglet in the nest, who feared to spread the wing. The God of nature and the God of grace are one. Beloved, God's trees, the trees of His right hand planting, attain not their full proportion in a moment. Think not because you have not yet attained the faith and joy of So-and-so that there has been no work of genuine grace in your heart. He who has commenced the work will carry it on by successive stages, for growth is our Lord's method of working; perhaps some will ask the question " Why ? " May we not venture to suggest that the growth of a believer is part of God's joy ? There is a pleasure in watching growth. Is it not your greatest joy to mark the tender growth of the body, and the gradual development of the mind, of the little light of the home ? Shall He who implanted that joy lack it Himself ? Moreover, it is by this process of gradual growth that we best learn our Lord. Were we to attain maturity at once, we should lose many a sweet experience; we should have but little knowledge of His lovingkindness, and know but little of His long suffering tenderness. II. GROWTH IN FAITH IS GOD'S WORK. This we gather from the form of expression used in our text, "we are bound to thank God." Paul recognized the growth of faith in the Church at Thessalonica as God's doing. Man has never yet been able to place that secret thing into any of His works which will cause them to grow. The sculptor may chisel the marble block into a form of loveliness until it almost seems to breathe, but it has no inherent power of development, a century of time will find it, as his hand left it. The artist may fashion in wax, flowers that deceive the sight, but to impart that power which will cause the bud to open into a flower is beyond his skill. The prerogative to cause growth is God's alone, and that growth is as much His work as the first implanting of the principle of life. The tree grows not by violent efforts of its own, but simply by living in the sunshine, and God's children grow not by their own vows and resolves, but by dwelling in the light of His countenance, who is the " Sun of Righteousness." Do you ask, how He makes our faith to grow ? 1. By placing in faith itself, a principle that compels its growth. As in the infant so in faith there is that which naturally develops itself, a stillborn faith such as a devil may have can never grow, but a living faith, living because it's God-given, must grow. 2. But growth requires nourishment, and by nourishment God increases faith. The child grows by food, and the tree grows not unless it draws its nourishment from earth and air, and the author of our faith has provided for faith a continual banquet. I mean the promises. Now a child will not grow by nourishment alone, it wants exercise. Growth in bulk is not always growth in strength. It is not the sitting at the dinner table, but the running out of doors in healthy exercise that makes the child grow. The tree grows not alone through sunshine and soft summer breezes, but by the wintry gale. A week's campaign in the battle-field will make a better soldier than a year of parade. 3. God makes His children's faith grow strong by exercise. To Abraham's faith He gives a Mount Moriah; to Jacob's, the loss of a Benjamin. To Daniel's, a den of lions; and to Job's, a succession of messengers of evil; and think not believer that you

will be an exception.  III. GROWTH IN FAITH IS A CAUSE FOR REJOICING.  "We
are bound to thank God, brethren, because your faith groweth exceedingly."  1.
Because He knew that in proportion as their faith grew, so also would their
happiness.  Faith and happiness always walk hand in hand.  2.  I think also
Paul rejoiced because he knew that in proportion as their faith increased so
would their capacity for labour.  A great work is too much for the hands of weak
faith, and a heavy burden would break its back.  Weak faith walks in the rear, of
the army only, strong faith in the van.  Little faith can do a useful work in hoeing
and raking and watering the plants of the garden, but only strong faith is qualified
to go out as pioneer into the backwoods of sin, and with lusty blows make the first
clearing.  IV. FAITH SHOULD NOT ONLY GROW, BUT GROW EXCEEDINGLY.  I do not
think the apostle Paul so much thanks God in this text for the growth of faith in
the Church at Thessalonica, as for the fact that it grew exceedingly.  It was not a
small but a great increase of faith He saw in them.  Be not content with a mere
canoe faith, only meant for fine weather, and swamped through a capfull of wind;
but pray for a leviathan faith that sports itself in the deep when lashed in wildest
fury.  (*A. G. Brown.*)  *A lecture for little faith:*—I. THE INCONVENIENCES OF
LITTLE FAITH.  1. When faith begins it is like a grain of mustard seed, but as the
Spirit bedews it with His grace it germinates, begins to spread and becomes a great
tree.  When faith begins it is—(1) Simply looking unto Jesus, perhaps through a
cloud of doubts, with much dimness of eye.  (2) When faith grows it rises from
looking to coming to Christ.  (3) That done faith lays hold on Christ, sees Him in
His excellency, and appropriates Him.  (4) Then it leans on Christ, casting on Him
the burden of its sins and cares.  (5) Next, faith puts in a certain claim to all that
Christ is, and has wrought.  (6) Lastly, it mounts to full assurance, and out of
heaven there is no state more rapturous and blessed.  But there are some Christians
who never get out of little faith.  There are many such in the "Pilgrim's Progress."
There is Ready-to-halt, who went all the way to the celestial city on crutches, and
then left them when he entered Jordan; Feeble-mind, who only lost his weakness
when he came to the same place where he buried it; Mr. Fearing, who used to
stumble over a straw, and get frightened if he saw a drop of rain; Mr. Despondency
and Miss Much-Afraid, who were so long locked up in the dungeon of Giant Despair
that they were almost starved to death.  2. The inconveniences of this little faith.
(1) While it is always sure of heaven it seldom thinks so.  Little-faith is as sure of
heaven as Great-faith.  When Christ comes to count up His jewels, He will take to
Himself the little pearls as well as the great ones.  Little-faith cost as much as
Great-faith.  God loves Little-faith and will do so to the end.  Yet he is so afraid
—because he feels himself unworthy, doubts that he has been called aright, his
election, and that he will not hold out to the end.  But Great-faith is sure of all
these points.  (2) Although he has grace enough he never thinks so.  Great-heart
wont have more than sufficient to carry him to heaven, and this is what Little-faith
has.  But see the latter in trouble—he says he will never be able to keep his head
above water; in prosperity he is afraid that he will intoxicate himself with pride;
when he meets with the enemy he fears defeat.  How different with Great-faith!
(3) When tempted to sin he is apt to fall.  Strong-faith can well contest the enemy,
for his courage and strength are full and his weapons sharp.  II. RULES FOR
STRENGTHENING LITTLE-FAITH.  If you would have your little faith grow you must—
1. Feed it, by meditation on the Word.  He who deals largely with the promises
will soon find that there is room for believing them.  2. Prove the promise.  When
in distress take the promise and see whether it is true.  The older you are the
stronger your faith should become for you have so many facts to support it.  Every
instance of God's love should make us believe Him more.  3. Associate yourselves
with godly and much-tried people.  Young believers will get their faith much
refreshed by talking with well-advanced Christians.  4. Labour to get as much as
possible free from self.  Live above the praise and censure of self, and wholly on
Christ.  Self is like the sucker at the bottom of the tree which never bears fruit,
but only sucks away nourishment from the tree.  5. Many can only get faith
increased by great trouble.  How do the old oaks become so deeply rooted?  Ask
the March winds and they will tell you.  We don't make great soldiers in barracks.
So with Christians.  Great faith must have great trials.  6. Exercise what faith
you have.  The reason why the blacksmith does not tire is because he is used to it.
It is no wonder that lazy Christians have little faith.  It ought to be little; you do
but little, and why should God give you more strength than you mean to use.  If
you want to get warm, don't rub your hands in front of the fire, but run out and

work. True works won't save you, but without works faith is frozen to death. 7. Commune with Christ, then you cannot be unbelieving. When you cannot see Him, then you doubt Him. III. A CERTAIN HIGH ATTAINMENT TO WHICH FAITH MAY IF DILIGENTLY CULTIVATED, CERTAINLY ATTAIN. A man's faith can never grow so strong that he will never doubt. He who has the strongest faith will have sorrowful intervals of despondency; but he may so cultivate his faith that he may be so infallibly sure that he is a child of God, that all his doubts and fears will not get an advantage over him. A man may in this life be as sure of his acceptance in the beloved as he is of his own existence. " I know whom I have believed." (*C. H. Spurgeon.*) *A growing faith :—*St. John tells us that he had no greater joy than to hear that his children walked in the truth (3 John 4) ; and surely next to the joy of seeing the sinner receive the truth, the next that can fill the heart of a minister must be to see him walk in the truth, but especially in these days when a profession of the gospel is so easily taken up and laid down. But a man may abide in the truth and not walk in it, have faith and not increase in it, and look back on past happy days of progress with regret. I. There is such a thing as GROWTH IN THE DIVINE LIFE. It is so in human life. The babe becomes a boy, a youth, a man. It is so in vegetable life—the seed becomes a tree ; and so there are babes, children, men, and old men in Christ ; and the command is, " Grow in grace." Of this grace the central principle is faith, and in proportion as that grows all the rest will grow. There is weak faith, and it results in a weak Christianity ; but as it strengthens all the virtues strengthen and flourish with it. II. THE SYMPTOMS OF AN INCREASE OF FAITH. 1. When Christ becomes more exceedingly precious ; when we are taken more and more off self and reliance in the means to dependence on Christ. The question of questions is, " What think ye of Christ ? " Many, if they spake honestly, would have to answer, Only what we have been told or have read, but nothing in the way of personal value and real estimation. But a child of God regards Christ as his all, and as Christ gradually fills up the circumference of thought and action do we grow in faith. 2. When we become more and more conformed to Christ—in spirit, in word, in deed. For faith is the assimilating power. 3. When we distinguish more and more clearly between faith and feeling. Many Christians are occupied too much with feeling. Every feeling that is not based upon faith is worthless. Learn to depend on faith whether feeling results or no. III. THE MEANS BY WHICH FAITH IS INCREASED. Its source is the Holy Spirit, but He works through means. Amongst others we may note—1. Secret prayer. 2. A constant looking unto Jesus, the Author and Finisher of faith. (*J. H. Evans, M.A.*) *The necessity of a growing faith :—*To increase in faith is—I. A SUBJECT FOR DEVOUT THANKSGIVING. Paul gave thanks because—1. The blessing of increased faith is of unspeakable value. Little faith will save, but strong faith is that which builds up the Church, overcomes the world, and glorifies God. 2. The blessing came at a seasonable time—the time of persecution. Such a time tests the reality of faith. If sound it will grow in spite of obstacles, as Israel in Egypt. The present is a time of trade depression, abounding vice and grievous departure from the faith. What need to be rooted in the faith when the days are so evil. 3. If there be any growth in faith it is the work of God's spirit. Faith is all through the gift of God. In nature we ought to admire God's hand as much in growth as in creation. So progress in faith reveals the same power as its commencement. Let God have all the glory from its Alpha to its Omega. If thou be a strong man in Christ do not sacrifice to thine own net, glorify thine own experience as if thou madest thyself strong and rich in the things of God. II. AN OBJECT FOR DILIGENT ENDEAVOUR. If you have it not labour to attain it. 1. Why? Because—(1) The proof of faith lies in the growth of faith. A dead faith will not grow. If you have not more faith it is to be feared that you have none. (2) God's truth deserves it ; we, as children, ought to believe our Father by instinct even as the eyes see and the ears hear. (3) It will be so much for our own spiritual health and joy. As your being an Englishman does not depend on your health or wealth, so neither does your salvation turn upon the strength and joy of your faith, but much does depend on it. Why not have foretastes of heaven. These you cannot have without growing faith. 2. How ? By the Holy Spirit : but still He uses us for the increase of our faith. If we are to grow—(1) Negatively—(*a*) avoid continual change of doctrine. If you transplant a tree often it will yield scanty fruit. Those who are " everything by turns and nothing long," are " ever learning, but never able to come to a knowledge of the truth." (*b*) Do not give up the ground in which your souls should grow. If you dig away the earth from a tree you impoverish it. So doctrine after doctrine is given up until nothing is held to be important. The experiment of the Frenchman who had just brought his horse to live on a straw a day when he died is being repeated among us, faith being literally starved to death. (*c*) Do not overshadow your faith by worldliness, tolerated sin, love of riches, pride and care, and so prevent its growth. You cannot expect a sapling to grow under the shadow of an oak. (2) Positively. Faith grows by—(*a*) an increase of knowledge. Many persons doubt because they are not instructed—They doubt whether they shall hold on to the end : despair because they find evil in their hearts, &c. Study God's Word, and you will find how vain they are. (*b*) Experience. When a man has proved a thing his confidence is increased. When you have tested a promise again and again nobody will be able to shake you, for you will say, "I have tasted of this good word." (*c*) Meditation and walking with God. If you want to believe in a man you must know him. So with God : when your communion is close and stedfast your faith will grow exceedingly. (*d*) Prayer with faith and for faith. (*e*) Obedience. A man cannot trust in God while he lives in sin. (*f*) Exercise. The man who uses the little faith he has will get more faith. Brick by brick up rose the pyramids. III. THE SOURCE OF OTHER GROWTHS. Increasing faith promotes— 1. Increasing love. If we are not filled with brotherly love it is because we are not firmly believing that truth which worketh by love. 2. Unity. Who shall separate men who are one in Christ by the grip of a mighty faith? 3. Patience. Some Christians make large demands on our patience ; but faith in Christ and the possibilities of grace will work wonders. (*C. H. Spurgeon.*)　　*Constant growth :—* The growth of trees is no less complete than it is constant ; and, though it be little it is a little all over. An apt illustration of all growth, of all culture, which is real. It is not merely the growth of one faculty of the soul, but it is the cultivation of the whole soul itself ; and, though it be not much, it should be more and more. Even so, the foliage shall be fuller, the flowers more numerous, and the fruit more plentiful ; and, as in the case of the tree, every year shall leave its ringed record of expansion, and enlarged stem and lengthened branches shall tell of seemly and shapely growth. The trimly-cut pollard, on the one hand, and the stalk all awry, on the other, may tend to vary the view ; but they are miserable warnings, after all! You are not growing unless it is you that grows. (*J. Gordon.*)　　*Abounding charity :* —I. THE INTERNAL AFFECTION MUST INCREASE (Phil. **i.** 9) to God and our neighbours, especially to those who are God's. There are so many things to extinguish it, or make it grow cold, that we should always seek to increase this grace, that it may be more fervent and strong, and not grow cold and dead. II. THE EXTERNAL EXPRESSIONS SHOULD ABOUND. 1. As to acts. In duties of charity we should not be weary. Now we may be weary upon a double occasion—(1) because we meet not presently with our reward (Gal. vi. 9). Duties of charity have their promises annexed, which are not presently accomplished, but in their season ; they will be either in this life or in the next ; (2) or because of continual occasions, when there is no end (Heb. vi. 10, 11). As long as the occasion continueth, so long should the charity continue, that at length they might meet the reward, " Ye have ministered, and do minister." This is tedious to nature and to a niggardly heart, but love will be working and labouring still, and ever bringing forth more fruit. Where this heavenly fire is kindled in the soul, it will warm all those that are about them. But love is cold in most ; it will neither take pains, nor be a charge to do anything for the brethren ; but Christian love is an immortal fire, it will still burn and never die ; therefore we should continue the same diligence, zeal, and affection that formerly we had. 2. As to objects. Christ telleth us, " The poor ye have always with you " (Matt. xxvi. 11). As long as God findeth objects, we should find charity ; and the apostle saith (Gal. vi. 10), " As we have opportunity, let us do good to all men." Expensive duties are distasteful to a carnal heart. It may be they would part with something which the flesh can spare, and will snatch at anything to excuse their neglect ; they have done it to these and these ; but as long as God bringeth objects to our view and notice, and our ability and affection doth continue, we must give still. If our ability continueth not, providence puts a bar and excuseth ; but if our affection doth not continue, the fault is our own. (*T. Manton, D.D.*)　　*Christian progress :*—This is the will of God, that we wax and increase in all holiness. Hereby we know whether we be of God, or no. We may not stand at a stay, but must be renewed. " Whosoever mendeth not himself in the practice of virtue, he groweth worse." God hath placed us in a race to run : we must so run, that we may attain the prize. We are grafts of the Lord's planting : we must grow to the height and breadth of a tree, and bring forth fruit. We are pilgrims and strangers, and pass by the wilderness of this world into our heavenly resting-place ; we may not stay by the way, but must remove our tents, and continually march on forward, until that day come, when we shall enter into the land of promise. (*Bp. Jewell.*)

Ver. 4. **So that we ourselves glory in you in the churches of God for your patience and faith.**—*The apostolic commendation:*—I. THE MANNER. 1. The person commending—" We ourselves." In 1 Thess. i. 8 he speaks of their faith as praised by others : here he justifies common fame by His own testimony. (1) It is easy to deceive the credulous multitude, but to deserve esteem of those who are best able to judge is a comfort. (2) Where grace is eminent it may be praised without suspicion of flattery. (3) We should keep up the value of our testimony that it may be of weight to those who receive it. 2. The act of praising. Glorying imports exaltation or rejoicing of mind and the outward expression. The one comes from the apprehension of some excellency, the other from a desire that others may know how we are affected with it. This glorying became apostolic gravity for—(1) It was for the honour of God who had wrought these graces, and not himself. (2) For the encouragement of the Thessalonians. We ought to give a testimony to those who deserve it, not to curry favour with them, but to incite them to perseverance in the way of God. (3) For the example of others and the edification of the Church. (4) For his own comfort (1 Thess. ii. 20). 3. The persons before whom. Not in common meetings, but where God's people were met for worship and spiritual benefit. "Churches of God" are so called because :—(1) God instituted and founded them (Acts xx. 28). (2) There God is worshipped and acknowledged (Psa. xxii. 3). (3) There He manifests His power and presence (Eph. ii. 22). II. THE MATTER. 1. The graces wherein they excelled "faith and patience" ; before it was faith and love. These two are often joined (Heb. vi. 12 ; Phil. i. 29). Faith precedes suffering, for the sufferer must first be a believer ; but when God calls to it both must go together (Heb. x. 35, 36). 2. The grievousness of those temptations wherewith these graces were exercised. (1) They were many—"All." (2) They took effect : persecution worked tribulation (Rom. viii. 35). (3) But the Thessalonians continued firm, "endured." (*T. Manton, D.D.*) *The purpose of trouble:*—Tribulations and persecutions often befall God's dearest and choicest servants (2 Tim. iii. 12 ; Acts xiv. 22). It is—I. THAT WE MAY BE CONFORMED TO OUR LORD AND PLEDGE HIM IN HIS BITTER CUP (Col. i. 24). The sufferings of Christ personal are complete and meritorious ; they need not to be filled up ; but the sufferings of Christ mystical (1 Cor. xii. 12) are not complete until every member of His body have their own allotted portion and share. Christians should be animated to suffer patiently by the fact that the Captain of our Salvation was made perfect through suffering (Heb. ii. 10). Those who will partake with Christ in His kingdom must share with Him in sorrows. Paul counted all things but dross that he might know the fellowship of Christ's sufferings (Phil. iii. 10). II. FOR OUR TRIAL (1 Pet. i. 7). A man may be deceived at other times, and think that faith strong which a trial discovers to be weak : as Peter (Matt. xxvi. 35). A man may doubt, and think his faith weak, which a trial discovers to be strong (Heb. x. 32 ; xi. 34). III. THAT THE EXCELLENCY OF OUR SPIRITUAL STATE MAY APPEAR. What can be more excellent than that which affords joy under the saddest temporal condition (John xvi. 33 ; 2 Cor. i. 5). This will sweeten the bitter waters, like the wood in Marah. A drop of this honey will make our bitterest cup agreeable. IV. BECAUSE WE NEED THEM (1 Pet. i, 6). 1. To modify our pride. 2. To keep us close to God. 3. To tame our flesh. Great prosperity perverts the best. Conclusion : 1. With what thoughts we should take up the stricter profession of Christianity, viz., with expectations of the Cross. Many think they may be good Christians, yet all their days live a life of ease. This is just as if we should enlist as a soldier and never expect battle, or as if a mariner should go to sea and always expect a calm. 2. What fools they are that take up religion expecting honour, ease, and plenty. You may do so for a time, but the trials will come. The summer friends of the gospel, or those painted butterflies that flutter about in the sunshine of prosperity, must expect that a winter will come. (*Ibid.*) *Faith and patience :*— I. WHAT IS PATIENCE ? A contented endurance of painful evils. It is a moral virtue when by the argument of human prudence we harden ourselves to bear the evils that befall us. The spiritual grace is the fruit of the Spirit, and we bear these evils from Divine principles to Divine ends. The latter as it is wrought in us by God (Rom. xv. 5) so it fetcheth its strength from God's Word (Rom. xv. 4).

Now scriptural arguments are fetched either from the will of God who appoints us to this conflict (1 Thess. iii. 3), or from the glory of God, which is promoted thereby (Phil. i. 20), or else our final happiness (James i. 12) or from the example of Christ (1 Pet. ii. 21). This grace of patience may be considered— 1. Barely as tried. Some give up at the first assault (Matt. iii. 21). Others hold up against the first brunt, but begin to be tired and wax weary in their minds (Heb. xii. 3). 2. As tried with many and long afflictions (Heb. x. 32; Col. i. 4). Many cannot bear any evil; they have no faith. Some hold out in slighter temptations for a while; they have weak faith. But the constant and unconquered patience is the fruit of strong faith. II. WHAT OF FAITH IS MANIFESTED BY IT? 1. Assent, for we must believe the truth with a Divine faith before we can suffer for it. How can we endure afflictions for supernatural things, which merely depend on revelation, unless we are firmly persuaded of their truth? (Acts xiv. 22). 2. Consent, or fidelity to Christ in our covenanted duty (Matt. xvi. 24). In great afflictions we are tried whether we love anything above Christ (Matt. x. 37). The resolution of this consent is the thing tried, *i.e.*, whether we are prepared to endure anything for Christ's sake (Acts xxi. 13). It is easier to discourse of patience than to practice it, as it is easier to build a castle in time of peace than to defend it in time of war. 3. Confidence, or relying upon God's promises, which are our support. There are two sorts of promises. (1) That God will enable you to bear them (2 Tim. i. 12, iv. 18; 1 Cor. x. 13). (2) That He will graciously reward them (Rom. viii. 18; 2 Cor. iv. 17). III. THE REASONS. 1. Faith is the grace that is most struck at in our tribulations (James i. 3); therefore if a man know the strength of it in time of tribulation, then ordinarily he has a clearer proof of the truth and strength of that grace than at other times. 2. It is the grace that is of most use to us at such times (1 Pet. v. 9; Eph. vi. 16). Three benefits we have by it—(1) It keeps us so that we do not for these things question the love of God (Isa. xlix. 14; Psa. lxxvii. 9; Heb. xii. 5). (2) So that we take no sinful course for our escape (Psa. cxxv. 3, 5). It should not shake our constancy and persuade us to do as the wicked (Isa. xxviii. 16; Heb. xi. 35). (3) So that we may not faint and grow weary of duties, even of life itself, as Jonah (iv. 8; see Psa. xxvii. 13, xlii. 5). 3. In such times faith is manifested. The true and sensible discovery of faith is patience under manifold tribulations. (1) Because then we have nothing to stick unto but the comforts and supports of faith. (2) Its proper, genuine effect is then produced to the view of both conscience and the world. What courage our belief in God's promises has produced in us sensibly appears by enduring the greatest extremities rather than forsake the way of the Lord. (*Ibid.*)      *The power of patience :—* Among the regular and consistent worshippers at the Bohemian Church in Berlin during the ministry of Pastor Jänike was a colonel at the War Office. His brother officers mocked at his piety, and used every opportunity of turning religion into ridicule. Being unable by these means to provoke the good man to indiscretions, they determined to provoke him by a more definite act of rudeness and scorn. Accordingly one of his colleagues in the office sketched a caricature of the colonel kneeling in church and receiving the holy communion. It was plain, from the entire character of the work, that a deadly hatred against the holiness of the Lord had inspired the pen that drew it. The sketch was secretly placed on the desk of the colonel, and the perpetrators of the miserable jest watched his arrival, and counted on an outburst of wrath. However, when the good man came and saw the sketch, he gravely shook his head, folded the paper, put it in his pocket, and then went on with his work, conversing with his colleagues in the usual friendly manner. A few days after the man who had drawn the shameful sketch knocked at the colonel's door. The patience of the Christian was more than his conscience could bear. He came now, and with deep emotion, to apologise for his impertinence. The colonel gave him his hand, and assured him he had forgiven him everything. Not very long after this man knelt by the colonel's side to receive the Lord's supper, testifying with tears of gratitude that he had found Christ. From henceforth he became one of the warmest friends of the pious and long-suffering Christian. (*Sunday at Home.*)      *Patient endurance :*—I shall never forget as long as I live that day when, in the glow of the eventide, as the sun was sinking and as the mists were creeping over the land, I walked with one of our native brethren by the river-side, and saw a light in the dim distance, when he said to me, "Yonder is the only Christian in all that great town." Ten years ago he received Christ into his heart; his father and mother turned him out; his friends forsook him; his neighbours persecuted him; and all these years he stood his ground, scarcely getting food to eat. During all these ten years he maintained his Christian character unspotted in the midst of the heathen around him, and the native brother said to me, "Now his business is reviving, because people say he sells the best things and always means what he says." I entered his humble bamboo hut and sat down on the ground by his side, and as I discoursed about his loneliness and his sadness the tears sprang into his eyes, and he said, "No, I am never lonely; for as Christ was with the Hebrew children, and as He was with Daniel in the lions' den, so all these years He has been with me." (*A. H. Baynes.*)

Ver. 5. **Which is a manifest token of the righteous judgment of God.**—*Persecutions a demonstration of the Judgment:*—I. STATE THE POINT. 1. It concerns us to be fully persuaded of the truth of a future judgment for two reasons. (1) It establishes our comfort, for then our wrongs shall be righted (Phil. i. 28), and our labour of love recompensed. (2) It binds our duty upon us by the strictest tie (Eccles. xii. 14). 2. This judgment is a righteous judgment (Acts xvii. 31). The world is now tried in patience : all are not punished according to their deservings. 3. This judgment needs to be evidenced, not only by the light of Scripture, but of reason. Nature says, It may be ; faith, It shall be ; yet the former must not be rejected—(1) Because things seen in a double light work more strongly upon—(a) Our love and obedience (Philemon 16). (b) Upon our faith. When nature teaches us to expect such a retribution, all vain cavils are refuted. (2) Because all have not received the light of Scripture. To them, therefore, the light of nature is a preparative inducement either to believe or to believe more firmly. (3) Because in time of temptation we need all the succour which the nature of the thing can give. Then, besides the grounds of faith, we must study its helps. (4) Among other arguments of a future day of recompence persecution is a plain demonstration. (a) If God chastises so severely the relics of sin in His children, how much more the wicked (1 Pet. iv. 17 ; Luke xxiii. 31 ; Prov. xi. 31). (b) No righteous governor will suffer the disobedient to persecute the obedient, and therefore, though he permit it for a time, yet he will call them to account. II. HOW IT IS A DEMONSTRATION OF FUTURE JUDGMENT. 1. There is a God. This is the supreme primitive truth which lies at the bottom of all religion (Heb. xi. 6). It were to light a candle to the sun to prove this. 2. This God is just, for all perfections are in the First Being (Jer. xii. 1; Rom. iii. 5, 6). 3. This just God is the Governor of the world (Psa. xciv. 1, 2). 4. It is agreeable to the justice of His government that it should be well with them that do well, and ill with them that do evil. Conscience and natural reason own this truth (Rom. i. 32 ; Prov. xxvi. 1). 5. This reward and punishment are not fully administered in this world. The best often go to the wall, and many wicked prosper, and persecute the ungodly. Hence the complaints of the saints who have stumbled at this (Psa. lxxiii.; Jer. xii. ; Hab. i.). 6. Since God's justice does not make a sufficient difference here, there is another life where He will; for otherwise all these absurdities would follow : (1) God would seem indifferent to good and evil, yea, more partial to the evil ; but this were a blasphemy (Psa. lxxiii. 1 ; xi. 6, 7). (2) Man would seem left at liberty to break or keep God's laws at pleasure, and no harm come of it, but rather profit. But this would destroy all obedience (Deut. xxx. 19, 20; Zeph. i. 12). (3) Obedience would be man's loss and ruin, and so God would be the worst Master (1 Cor. xv. 19). (4) The most eminent virtue would be under perpetual infamy ; therefore things must be reviewed, and that which is good restored to its public honour (1 Pet. iv. 13, 14). (5) The children of wisdom would seem sons of folly in checking their lusts and renouncing all for their fidelity to Christ. (6) All the comfort of the saints in longing for this day is but a fanatical illusion, when yet this desire is quickened by God (Rom. viii. 23 ; 2 Cor. v. 5). 7. This justice will be administered at the last day. (*T. Manton, D.D.*) **That ye may be counted worthy of the kingdom of God, for which ye also suffer.**—*Worthiness of the kingdom of God:*—I. THE KINGDOM OF GOD is twofold. 1. The kingdom of grace is the gospel estate, and for this Christians may be said to suffer—(1) To promote it in the world. (2) Because they have entered it. 2. The text rather refers to the kingdom of glory (Matt. xxv. 34). Christians suffer for this that they may enter it. II. WORTHINESS OF THIS KINGDOM. There is a threefold worthiness. 1. Of exact proportion (Luke x. 7). This is justice proof both from the covenant and intrinsic worth of the action. But there is such a distance between God and the creature that none can make God his debtor (Rom. viii. 18 ; Rev. ii. 10). 2. Of fitness and congruity (Matt. iii. 8 ; Acts xxvi. 20; Phil. i. 27; Eph. iv. 1). There is—(1) A fitness in point of order. So they are worthy who are qualified according to God's order (Rom. viii. 17 ; 2 Tim. ii. 11, 12). It is agreeable to Christ's wisdom and love that He should own His faithful servants, and since they are willing to take His cross, that they should share His crown (Rev. iii. 4). (2) In point of preparation (Rom. ix. 23 ; Col. i. 12). It is the wisdom of God to put all things in their proper places, as fishes in the sea, beasts on earth. And persecutions are one means which fit the godly for heaven. As the hewing and squaring of stones fitted them to be set in the Temple at Jerusalem, so are we squared and meetened to be set in the heavenly temple. 3. Of acceptance, when God, for Christ's sake, is pleased to count us worthy in spite of failings (Luke xxi. 36). So here : III. THOSE SHALL BE COUNTED WORTHY TO ENTER THE KINGDOM WHO DILIGENTLY PURSUE IT. 1. What this is—(1) Diligence in doing good (Matt. vi. 33). It is not enough that we seek the kingdom ; we must seek it in the first place, and all must give way to it (Heb. iv. 11). (2) Evil must be suffered (Heb. x. 36 ; James i. 12). 2. The reasons for it. (1) These things are required as conditions of entering into life (Mark x. 38). (2) When this condition is fulfilled, then we have an evidence that God will count us worthy to enter into His kingdom (Phil. i. 28). Use. Let us seriously consider these things—1. The felicity here offered. What bustling is there in the world for a little greatness and advancement ? Yet all other crowns are but petty in comparison of the crown of life. 2. The certainty of conveyance (2 Tim. iv. 8). 3. You must submit to any terms (Phil. iii. 11). (*Ibid.*)  *Present suffering and future glory :*—What the woof is to the warp, crosses are to character. Without the latter the former is nothing but limp lines of threads without strength, without usefulness, without susceptibility of being made beautiful. But when crossed by the woof, it becomes cloth fit for various uses, and capable of receiving a finish and an ornamentation which transforms it into a thing of beauty. In like manner a man's character is limp, weak, unreliable, and unattractive, until it has been subjected to many tests and trials. These, like the woof, cross and recross one's natural tendencies until resistance to evil begets strength, endurance, growth, and moral beauty. Why, then, should one fret against one's crosses ? They are painful, vexatious, hard to be borne sometimes, but what are these ills, which are but for a moment, when compared with the exceeding and eternal weight of glory with which they are to be rewarded when the last one has been overcome ? The brilliants in one's eternal crown will be the crosses of one's present life crystalized in the love and light of heaven. (*Zion's Herald.*)

Vers. 6, 7. **Seeing it is a righteous thing with God to recompense tribulation to them that trouble you ; and to you who are troubled rest with us when the Lord Jesus shall be revealed.**—*The two troubles and the troublers :*—I. THE TERM APPLIED TO OUR LORD'S COMING " revealed." To reveal is to uncover what is hidden. This may be done in two ways—1. Spiritually, as Jesus is now evidently set forth in His gospel. 2. Outwardly. (1) In this way Christ has been already revealed, but only partially. Few saw Him, and those few very little. (2) By and by He will come without disguise and " every eye shall see Him." II. THE DIFFERENT PORTIONS WHICH WILL THEN BE GIVEN TO VARIOUS PERSONS. 1. The troublers and their portion. (1) Wherever God has a people there will sure to be troublers. (2) Sometimes God visits such with His displeasure here, just to show that He marks what they are doing, but generally He seems to let them alone. (3) Their position is—(*a*) Tribulation. Of this we all know something, but the deepest sorrow we have ever felt compared with this is as a summer cloud to winter midnight. (*b*) Recompense. It is to come upon them as a consequence of their unkindness to God's people. Wretched they would have been had they let these people alone, but because they would not they shall be still more wretched. (4) How seldom do some of us think of this. We regard " the hard speeches " of the ungodly as little more than the outbursts of prejudice, ill-humour, or harmless pleasantry ; but God regards them differently. (5) How this truth magnifies the love Christ bears to us, grounding His judicial proceedings on the conduct of men towards us as well as toward Himself. " He that toucheth you, toucheth the apple of My eye." 2. The portion of the troubled. (1) We must not think that we are in the number of these because the world ill-treats us. The world frequently torments its own followers. (2) The blessing pronounced is—(*a*) rest. The very thing for which most of us long. We are often grieved at this longing : but Christ in His compassion shows us that holy Paul had the same longings, and that they were lawful. This compassion is further shown in this revelation of heaven. Were we in that place where they " rest not day nor night " we should never call it by that name. That activity is quite in harmony with this rest ; but Christ does not dwell upon it because He is addressing weary men. (b) "Rest with us." It will be a rest of the same kind as that enjoyed by the highest saints. It may be enough to be with Christ; but if we love Him we shall love His people, and to meet with the latter also will augment our joy. Paul could enter into this. It gave him as much joy as them. III. THE RIGHTEOUSNESS OF THIS. 1. Christ came as a Saviour, and accordingly displayed love and mercy ; He will come as a Judge, and what we look for in a judge is equity. God's justice now is very much a matter of faith, but then it will be made fully manifest. 2. To bring this about there must be evident justice in the portions assigned to different men. Their destinies must be suited to their character and conduct. See standing before the Judge two separate companies. Here are those who bore willingly hatred and reproach for His name's sake—there are those who reproached and hated them because they loved His name. Without looking any farther we see the force of these words. (1) These latter have troubled God's people, and it is but their desert that they should be troubled in their turn. (2) The harassed people find rest. True they merit it not, and remembering what they are we should have expected the apostle to say, " It is a merciful thing with God to give you rest." This he does say elsewhere, but here he enters into his Master's feelings who thinks only of His people's services and forgets their sins. 3. What the grace of God leads Him to promise His justice will lead Him to perform. (*C. Bradley, M.A.*) *Divine retribution a manifestation of Divine justice :*—I. THE JUSTICE OF GOD. 1. Justice is God's attribute as Governor. It is twofold. (1) General—the perfection of the Divine nature. This is the same with His holiness. God loves righteousness and hates iniquity necessarily (Psa. v. 4 ; Zech. iii. 5). (2) Particular which respects His office as Judge of the world (Deut. xxxii. 4). 2. Of His government there are two acts. (1) Legislative justice, which determines man's duty, binds him to the performance and defines the rewards and punishments which shall be due upon man's obedience and disobedience (Deut. xxx. 15). (2) Judiciary or distributive justice, whereby He renders to all men according to their works (Rom. ii. 6 ; 1 Pet. i. 17). This is twofold. (a) Rewarding (Heb. vi. 10 ; 2 Tim. iv. 8). (b) Vindictive or punishing (Rom. ii. 7–9 ; John iii. 19 ; Heb. x. 29). 3. This distributive justice is exercised. (1) More darkly here : yet even here the wicked are punished and the righteous rewarded (Rom. i. 18 ; Psa. lviii. 11). (2) More plainly hereafter (Rom. ii. 5). The difference between the last time and this is—(a) That the righteous and the wicked have but the beginnings of their reward and punishment : the wicked inwardly (Heb. ii. 15 ; Eph. iv. 19 ; Psa. lxxxi. 12) and even outwardly, as witness the fall of nations, and the sudden and otherwise unaccountable destruction of individuals ; so the righteous have inwardly much of his love, peace, &c. ; and outwardly the wicked have it not all their own way (Mal. iii. 17, 18). (b) God's justice now appears more negatively than positively, *i.e.*, God does nothing contrary to justice. As to His rewards His servants have deserved nothing which they enjoy ; and as to His restraint of due punishment it is to bring the sinner to repentance. II. THIS JUSTICE AS APPLIED TO THE DIFFERENT RECOMPENSES. 1. " Tribulation to them that trouble you " for a double reason. (1) Their own disobedience to God's laws (Rom. ii. 8). (2) Their opposition to those that would obey God, so consenting with the devil in his apostasy (Matt. xxiii. 13 ; xxiv. 49). 2. " To you who are troubled rest." How is this just ? Things may be said to be righteous with God— (1) In respect of strict justice when what is done deserves reward by its intrinsic value. So no obedience of man or angel can bind God to reward it. (2) In respect of His bounty God is just. When He rewards man because he is in some way righteous. This capacity of reward respects either the righteousness of Christ (Rom. iii. 25, 26), or the difference between the person recompensed and others. General justice requires that He should put a difference between the godly and the wicked (Psa. xi. 7). (3) In respect of His promise (1 John i. 9). 3. Particularly discuss these two effects. (1) The troublers are to be troubled (Rom. ii. 9). The law of retaliation operates often in the course of providence (Judges i. 7 ; Obad 5). Ahab's blood was lapped up by dogs where Naboth was murdered. Haman was executed on the gallows he had erected for Mordecai. Henry III. of France was killed in the chamber where the massacre was contrived ; and Charles IX. died flowing in his blood in his bed. The rich glutton wanted a drop who gave not a crumb. (2) The troubled rest—and the rest in proportion to the trouble. (*T. Manton, D.D.*) *The thought of rest :*—While walking through the streets of the city we passed a man whose head was whitened and body bowed by the hardships of not less than sixty years. His limbs trembled under their heavy burden, and with much apparent effort he advanced but slowly. We overheard him talking in a low and subdued voice, evidently mourning over his weariness and poverty. Suddenly his tone changed and his step quickened, as he exclaimed, " I'll rest when I get home." Even the thought of rest filled him with new life, so that he pursued with energy his weary way. To us it was a lesson. If the thought of the refreshing rest of home encourages the careworn labourer so that, almost unmindful of fatigue and burdens, he quickens his step homeward, surely the Christian, journeying heavenward, in view of such a rest, should press onward with renewed vigour. This little incident often comes to mind amid the perplexing labours of the day, and stimulates to more constant and earnest effort. Each labourer toiling in his Master's vineyard, bearing the heat and burden of the day, can say, " I'll rest when I get home." *Rest after suffering :*—None of us who have not read deeply into history can understand how utterly the Russian and German peoples were threshed, as straw is threshed on the summer threshing-floor, by the iron flail of Bonaparte. So extreme was the suffering that it broke the heart of that most beautiful and noble woman, the wife of King William, the father of the late Kaiser. She died, as it were, struggling with the sorrows of her people. For her her husband erected a tomb in the environs of Berlin. I can hardly mention it without tears. It is peculiarly built, standing alone in a forest, with glass that throws a sombre light upon all the hither part of it, while on the far part the golden and natural light of the sun shines —as if this side, where you enter, represented the gloom of this world, and the other side, where she lies, carved in marble over her dust, represented the light and the glory of the more blessed land. When I first was there I had read about, but never had fairly conceived of, that which met my eyes. The queen, sculptured at full length, lies as one upon a bed at rest. There is the most exquisite expression of having at last come to full, perfect, and joyful rest. (*H. W. Beecher.*) *Rest for the troubled :*—I. WHAT IS THIS REST ? It is—1. A felicitating rest. In it there is—(1) Freedom from all troublesome evils. (*a*) Sin (Rom. vii. 24) is the most grievous, but in heaven there is no sin (Eph. v. 27). In paradise there was a tempter, but not in heaven. (*b*) Misery and affliction (Rev. xxii. 4). (2) An enjoyment of all good, even God. To our felicity three things are necessary. (*a*) A prepared faculty ; (*b*) a suitable object ; (*c*) the conjunction of these. In a state of glory these things concur. The faculty is more prepared than here as we are purged from sin and fleshly delusions—the object is more manifested (1 Cor. xiii. 12) ; the conjunction is more intimate ; for here it is by faith, there by vision, here by an imperfect, there by a perfect love. 2. A holy rest, a perpetual sabbatizing (Heb. iv. 9). The Sabbath is not a time of idleness ; on it the sacrifices were doubled (Numb. xxviii. 1). So our service is not ended with our lives ; holy work will be part of the blessedness of heaven (Rev. vii. 14, 15). 3. A rest for the whole person —body and soul. II. WHY OUR REWARD IS REPRESENTED AS REST. Because it suits —1. The aim of the saints. It is the end of motion. None have it but those that seek after it. We are all travelling to the other world. Some are posting to eternal torment on the broad road, others to life and rest by the narrow way (Matt. vii. 13, 14). Every day a Christian gets nearer the goal (Rom. xiii. 11). 2. The goodness of God, who delights to recompense His people for their pain and weariness. He has a care for His weary servants here and gives them rest (Isa. l. 4 ; Matt. xi. 28). III. " REST WITH US." 1. All Christians have the same felicity for substance though the degrees are different. Those who have been together in the labour, duty, and danger shall be together in the rest and recompense (Matt. xxv. 1). The grounds of essential happiness are the same to all. (1) The same Redeemer (Exod. xxx. 15 ; 1 Cor. i. 2 ; Rom. iii. 22). (2) The same covenant which is the common charter of the saints (Acts ii. 39). It is a covenant which— (*a*) Offers the same benefits, pardon, life (Rom. iv. 23, 24 ; 2 Tim. iv. 8). (*b*) Requires the same duties (Gal. vi. 16 ; Rom. i. 16). 2. Though the essential happiness of the saints is the same, yet there are degrees in glory. What relation holiness has to heaven, so more holiness here means more happiness there. 3. It is a comfortable adjunct to our felicity that we shall have such company there (Matt. viii. 11 ; Heb. xii. 22, 23 ; Eph. ii. 19, iii. 15). Let this promote church unity. (*T. Manton, D.D.*) *The craving for rest :*—No one will easily believe how anxiously, for a long time, I have wished to retire from these labours into a scene of tranquility, and, for the rest of my life (dwindled, it is true, to the shortest span) to converse only with Him who once cried, " Come unto Me all ye that labour," &c. In this turbulent and raging world, amid so many cares, which the state of the times heaps upon me in public, or which declining years and infirmity cause me in private, nothing do I find on which my mind can more comfortably repose than on secret communion with God. (*Erasmus.*)    *Rest not for the present :*—Epaminondas, before going into battle with the Lacedæmonians, sat down to rest for a few moments, when his seat fell under him. "That," quoth the soldiers, "bodes no good." "Nay," said their leader, with happy presence of mind; "it is an intimation to me that I have no business to be sitting here when I should be leading you against the enemy." (*Percy Anecdotes.*) *Rest not on earth :*—There is the tradition of an Indian chief who with his wife fled before the prairie-fires till he had crossed a broad river ; when he struck his tent-pole into the ground and cried, "*Alabama !* " ("here we may rest"). He was no prophet.  Hostile tribes overpowered them; and they found only their graves where they sought a home.  This is, may be, a parable of the soul ; for it earth has no *Alabama*. (*E. Foster.*)    *Rest at last :*—The pass of Glencoe in Scotland is reached by a long, steep, and winding path ; but at its top is a stone with the inscription "Rest and be thankful." Such is the pilgrim's path ; but at its end is heaven, on whose gates may be read a similar inscription. (*T. Guthrie, D.D.*)

Vers. 7–10. **When the Lord Jesus Christ shall be revealed from heaven.**—This passage both consolatory and doctrinal—consolation designed for a persecuted Church—instruction for the world.  Our subject : the general judgment.  We will regard—I. Its CERTAINTY.  May be argued from moral government.    1. Indicated by reason.  2. Attested by conscience.  3. Proved from Scripture.  II. Its SOLEMNITY.  Mark the attendant events.  1. The descent of the appointed Judge.  2. The glorious throne He will occupy.  3. The vast concourse of attendants.  4. The time and manner of advent.  5. The resurrection of the sleeping dead.  6. The transformation of the busy living.  7. The destruction of the universe.  III. Its REALITY.  Not fictitious or nominal, but sternly real.  1. Universal citation. 2. Impartial scrutiny.  3. Final separation.  4. Judicial sentence.  5. Eternal execution. (*J. Odell.*)    *Joy and terror in the coming of the Lord :*—The Lord will come the second time.  When, we cannot know.  Angels do not know.  But this does not detract from its certainty.  To us individually His coming is virtually near.  It is not long till we go hence, and time for us will be no more.  Eternity begins ; Christ, the Judge, deciding our state for happiness or misery.  Therefore we need not put His coming far away in the future.  We are graciously permitted to prepare for it, so that it may be to us an event of joy and not of terror.  I. To UNBELIEVERS THE LORD'S COMING WILL BE AN INDESCRIBABLE TERROR.  They rejected Him come to deliver them from sin.  Now they must behold Him as their righteous Judge to pronounce upon them the condemnation of their own choosing. This is their condemnation—that they believed not on Him.  Mercies slighted will make justice self-approved.  Not mercy, then, but the "wrath of the Lamb " will be upon them.    II. To BELIEVERS HIS COMING WILL BRING INCONCEIVABLE JOY. They have accepted Him in His mission of redeeming love in His first advent.  At His coming to judge the world He will receive His own to Himself.  Such a relation to Him carries with it a desire for His appearing, when they shall appear with Him in glory.  "They rest from their labours, and their works do follow them."    III. POINTS FOR REMARKS.  1. Great is the mercy of God in extending to us present salvation through the mediation of Christ.  Great is His mercy also in forewarning us of His coming again as the Judge.  2. Life appears short in view of the event of Christ's coming and the eternity awaiting us.  How important this life is, considered as a preparation. 3. Terrible as must be the coming of Christ to the wicked, to the Christian it is a joyous anticipation.  It has always been so.  Christ is the chiefest among ten thousand, and the One altogether lovely.  To see Him face to face and dwell with Him for ever is heaven to the soul.  This state may well awaken a desire to see Him. (*The Study.*)    *The coming of Christ with His angels :*—I. THERE IS A TIME COMING WHEN CHRIST SHALL BE FULLY REVEALED AND COME IN ALL HIS GLORY.  1. What is this revelation ?  The coming of Christ is set forth as an apocalypse and as an epiphany.  The former is in the text, and in 1 Pet. i. 13, 1 Cor. i. 7, and means an unveiling ; the latter is in 2 Tim. iv. 8, Titus ii. 13, and means a forth-flashing.  The former is used because—(1) Many have never seen Him (Acts iii. 21).  This does not hinder His spiritual virtue and influence although it does the enjoyment of His bodily presence (1 Pet. i. 8).    (2) His earthly state was obscure, His Godhead peeping through the veil in a miracle or so. (3) His spiritual glory is seen but in a glass darkly (1 Cor. xiii. 12). Vision is reserved for heaven (John xvii. 24). (4) His kingdom is not always clear to the world (Luke xvii. 20). (5) His subjects are under a veil (Col. iii. 3 ; 1 John iii. 2 ; Rom. viii. 19). 2. That this time is coming is evident from—(1) The promise of His coming. This ancient promise (Jude 14, 15) was ever kept afoot in the Church. The scoffers took notice of it (2 Pet. iii. 4). It has been revived by all the Lord's messengers. Moses, David, Samuel, Joel, Zechariah, Malachi, and more clearly by Christ (John xiv. 3). Christ would not flatter us into a fool's paradise. (2) His remembrancers in the Church (1 Cor. xi. 26 ; 2 Tim. iv. 1). (3) Our inward pledge of it. At parting there is a giving of tokens. Christ has gone to make ready for the day of His espousals. To prevent suspicion He left His Spirit to stir up in us expectation of that day (Rom. viii. 23 ; Rev. xxii. 17). (4) Our constant experience of His love and care. There are frequent messages of love passing between us and Christ, in His word, prayer, sacraments, to show that He does not forget us. (5) The interest of Christ which is concerned in it. (*a*) Partly that the glory of His Person may be seen and fully discovered. His first coming was obscure, in the form of a servant, with a poor retinue, &c. ; now He comes as the Lord of all in power and great glory. (*b*) That He may possess what He has purchased (1 Pet. i. 18, 19 ; John xiv. 3 ; Heb. iii. 13). (*c*) That He may overthrow the wicked (Isa. xlv. 23 ; Rom. xiv. 10, 11 ; Phil. ii. 10). (*d*) That He may require an account of things during His absence (Matt. xxv.). II. WHEN CHRIST COMES HE WILL BRING HIS MIGHTY ANGELS WITH HIM. 1. Those angels are mighty (Psa. ciii. 20). One slaughtered many thousands of Sennacherib's army in a single night. Their greatness is mentioned to show the excellency of our Redeemer who is greater than all. 2. He will bring them—(1) To show His glory and majesty. The most excellent creatures are at His command (1 Pet. iii. 22 ; Eph. i. 22 ; Heb. i. 4–7). (2) Because He has a service for them. (*a*) To gather the elect (Matt. xxiv. 31). This shall complete their many services on His behalf and ours (Luke ii. 13, 14 ; 1 Cor. xi. 10 ; 1 Tim. v. 21 ; Luke xv. 7, 10 ; Heb. i. 14 ; Psa. xxxiv. 7 ; Luke xvi. 22). (*b*) To execute His sentence on the wicked (Matt. xiii. 41, 42, 49). (*c*) To show that they are part of the army commanded by the Captain of our salvation. (Psa. lxviii. 17). (*T. Manton, D.D.*)

Ver. 8. **In flaming fire taking vengeance on them that know not God and obey not the gospel.**—*Christ's coming :*—I. THE TERRIBLE MANNER OF CHRIST'S COMING. "In flaming fire," which serves—1. To set forth the majesty of the Judge (Acts vii. 20 ; Deut. v. 22, 23 ; Psa. l. 3). 2. As the instrument of punishment on the wicked (Matt. xiii. 42 ; xxv. 41). 3. To burn up the world (2 Pet. iii. 10, 11). II. THE PERSONS BROUGHT TO JUDGMENT AND THE RULES OF PROCEDURE. 1. Some had no other discovery of God but from the course of nature and the instincts of conscience—these shall not be judged for not believing in Christ, but for not knowing God (Rom. ii. 12–15). Therefore among the Gentiles—(1) All Atheists who deny God's Being are obnoxious to judgment. (2) All idolaters who corrupt the worship of God. (3) All wicked men who when they know God glorify Him not as God, &c. (Rom. i. 21). (4) All who despise and resist God's authority (Exod. v. 2). What is all this to us ? To teach us—(1) That ignorance of God excuses no man from judgment. Whether foreign nations or His own people, God will punish them for wilful ignorance of necessary things. (2) That it is not enough to know God unless we know Him as we ought to know Him (Tit. i. 16). (3) That the more means there are of knowing God, the greater the crime if we do not know His will (Luke xii. 47). 2. Some having a discovery of Christ and His salvation are judged by the gospel. (1) All such obey not the gospel. (*a*) Who obstinately refuse to entertain the doctrine of Christ and His salvation (1 Pet. iv. 17). (*b*) Who profess to believe but practically deny (Eph. ii. 2 ; iii. 6). (*c*) Who apostatize (Heb. x. 39). (2) Who shall be judged by the terror of the gospel dispensation. (*a*) Those who have lived in the clear sunshine of the gospel (Mark xvi. 16). They are condemned because of their sins against God, and their refusal of the remedy (John iii. 18, 19). (*b*) Those to whom the object of faith was more obscurely propounded. (i) Those who lived before or after the Flood. Abel, Enoch, Noah, Abraham, Isaac, and Jacob are in the chronicle of faith (Heb. xi. ; 1 Pet. iii. 19, 20). (ii) Those who lived under the legal administration of the covenant of grace shall be judged according to that (Rom. ii. 12). The law was more manifest, but the way of salvation was clear enough (Psa. cxxx. 3, 4 ; cxliii. 2). (iii) Those who lived under the ministry of John and of our Lord

(John viii. 24). (iv) Those who, under the dispensation of the Spirit, know Christ more or less : Mohammedans and Jews. (v) Those Christians to whom Christ is offered more or less purely : Papists, Socinians, &c. However God may deal with the vulgar who err in the simplicity of their hearts, we know not ; but their leaders are terribly responsible. (*T. Manton, D.D.*) *Ignorance and disobedience :*—I. "Know not God." There is a twofold knowledge of God. 1. Speculative. (1) The bare sight of the truth ; empty and cold notions about God and religion. (*a*) Such as many of the heathen have (Rom. i. 21). (*b*) The Jews (Rom. ii. 19, 20). (*c*) Formal Christians (2 Tim. iii. 5). (2) There are different degrees of this knowledge. (*a*) Memorative, such as children have who are taught to speak of Divine mysteries by rote, but are not affected by them. (*b*) Opinionative, when not only the memory is charged but the judgment exercised, yet wisdom enters not upon the heart (Prov. ii. 10). This makes men disputers about, but not practicers of godliness (chap. ii. 10). (*c*) Sufficiently cordial to be reformative but not regenerating. 2. Practical and saving. We must know God—(1) So as to trust in Him (Psa. ix. 10). (2) So as to love Him (1 Cor. viii. 3). (3) So as to obey Him (1 John ii. 4 ; Jer. xxii. 16). Our practices must speak out our knowledge. So then all they that know not God so as to fear Him for His majesty and power, love Him for His goodness, trust Him for His wisdom, imitate Him for His holiness, obey Him for His authority, so as to seek Him and delight in Him, are obnoxious to Christ's judgment. He has no religion who has no god, and he has no god who prefers his lusts to obedience. II. "That obey not the gospel of our Lord Jesus Christ." It is not enough to profess the gospel, we must obey it. This obedience is necessary whether we consider—1. The gospel which is the sum of things to be believed and done. Its three commands are—(1) Repentance (Isa. i. 19, 20). (2) Faith in Christ (1 John iii. 23 ; Heb. ii. 3). (3) New obedience (Titus ii. 12). 2. Faith, which also implies obedience (Rom. x. 16, i. 5, xvi. 26 ; Acts vi. 7) : for it is a hearty consent to take the blessedness offered for our happiness, the duty required for our work, and so has an influence on our whole obedience. 3. Christ. (1) His example (Heb. v. 8, 9 ; Phil. ii. 8). (2) His authority and sovereignty (Acts v. 31). III. Uses. 1. If you would have the comfort and not the terror of the Day of Judgment, you must obey the gospel (Rom. vi. 16). 2. What we have to do is to study to know the Lord, that we may believe in Him and serve Him. (*Ibid.*) *Ignorance of God :*—We read of an ancient king who, desiring to ascertain what was the natural language of man, ordered two infants as soon as they were born, to be conveyed to a place prepared for them, where they were brought up without any instruction, and without ever hearing a human voice, and what was the event ! Why that when they were at length brought out of their confinement, they spake no language at all ; they uttered only inarticulate sounds like those of other animals. Were two infants in like manner to be brought up from the womb without being instructed in any religion, there is little room to doubt but (unless the grace of God interposed) the event would be just the same. They would have no religion at all : no more knowledge of God than the beasts of the field. Such is natural religion abstracted from traditional and from the influences of God's Spirit. (*J. Wesley.*) *Degrees of Divine knowledge :*—A young child who has hitherto fancied that the rim of the sky rests on the earth a few miles away, and that the whole world lies within that circle, sails down the Forth there, and sees the river banks gradually widening, and the river passing into a frith. When he comes back he tells his companions how large the ocean is. Poor boy ! he has not seen the ocean—only the widened river. Just so with all creature knowledge of God. Though all the archangels were to utter all they knew there would still remain an infirmity untold. (*J. Culross, D.D.*) *Loyalty and disloyalty to the Gospel :*—During the Civil War in America those who were loyal displayed the banner of the United States on every house almost throughout the country. Such was the case in Fredericksburg : but when the inhabitants found that Stonewall Jackson and a regiment of Confederates were approaching, they all, with one exception, were frightened and concealed their signs of loyalty. An elderly woman named Barbara Frike had the courage to display the banner outside her window. When the general saw it he ordered the soldiers to fire at it. In the midst of the fire and the smoke the old dame put her head out, and shouted, "Strike my grey head, but spare the banner of my country." Her courage overpowered the general, and he ordered his men to let her alone. (*Dr. Rees.*)

Ver. 9. **Who shall be punished with everlasting destruction from the presence**

**of the Lord.** *The punishment of the wicked :*—I. GENERALLY. We have here— 1. The estate " destruction " (1 Thess. v. 3 ; Matt. vii. 13 ; Rom. ix. 22 ; Phil. iii. 19), meaning thereby not an abolition of their being but of their well-being. Annihilation would be no loss. It is a destruction—(1) Of their carnal happiness, their glory, pleasure, gain, wherein they placed their contentment—(2) Of the true happiness which lies in the favour of God. 2. The duration " everlasting " (Matt. xxv. 41, 46). 3. The reasons—(1) The majesty of God against whom the sin is committed. (2) The nature of sin which is a preference of short sensitive good before that which is spiritual and eternal. (3) The will of the sinner. Their impenitence is endless, so is their punishment. (4) There is no change of state in the other world (Luke xiii. 25 ; xvi. 26). II. PARTICULARLY. 1. The punishment of loss " From the presence of the Lord." Concerning this note—(1) That all are equal in this. There may be degrees of pain, but all are equally excluded from the Divine presence. (2) That the punishment of the wicked is the opposite of the reward of the righteous. All our refreshment comes from the Divine presence (Acts iii. 19). (3) That it is fitting. They have forsaken God, and now God has forsaken them (Rom. i. 28 ; Job. xxi. 14). (4) That it is this greatest part of future punishment—(*a*) In itself, it is to be deprived of an infinite good (Psa. xvi. 11 ; Exod. xxxiii. 15). (*b*) In the deep sense of it. Here the wicked are insensible of it. (*c*) In its irreparableness. 2. The punishment of sense : " From the glory of His power " (Rev. vi. 15, 16). This is the greatness of His goodness, and to be deprived of that is to feel the might of His justice. III. THE LESSONS—1. To the unconverted. These considerations should—(1) Rouse them out of their security. (*a*) Many disbelieve. (*b*) Others think neither one way nor the other (Amos vi. 3). (*c*) Others do not closely apply what they believe and think. (2) Check their boldness in sinning against light and conscience. (3) Cause them to shake off all delays in the business of religion (Matt. iii. 7 ; Heb. xi. 18 ; Luke xiv. 32). 2. To the godly—(1) Bless God for your deliverance through Christ (1 Thess. i. 13 ; Rom. v. 9). (2) Let your love to Christ be quickened, and grow in His likeness (1 John iv. 17, 18). (3) Be courageous (Luke xii. 4, 5 ; Heb. xi. 35). (4) Warn your friends in time (Luke. xvi). *Banishment from God's presence :*—1. Of all the ways in which Scripture describes the future blessedness of the elect none has less attraction for the wicked than that which places it in the full enjoyment of God's presence. On all occasions direct reference to Him as near is painful. 2. Yet you would think it very strange and hard if whilst every day you were heaping marks of love on a child he regarded you simply as a mere machine operating beneficently because you could not help it. This is the treatment, however, to which men subject their Maker. 3. One main reason of this treatment is the constant flow of good gifts from God whether they make any return or not ; and so, having never discerned the invisible God in His works and gifts here, they see no reason why in another world it should not be the same. Where can the bliss be of seeing God's countenance shine full on the soul, no beam of which has been ever sought or wished for by them here. 4. But when it comes the punishment will be dreadful enough for—(1) All good things come from God. (2) But having rejected Him it is but equitable that we should be left to our own resources to find what happiness we may. Banishment from God means—I. EXCLUSION FROM THIS MATERIAL WORLD with all its natural sources of pleasure, every particle of which is God's. II. DEPRIVATION OF ALL THAT CAN SATISFY A SINNER'S LUSTS. Think of the misery of a never satisfied hunger and an always raging thirst. The good creatures of God which were once abused are now beyond the reach. III. THE WITHDRAWAL OF THE GODLY who are taken to God. No one knows how much the world owes to the intermixture of the righteous with sinners, leavening the corrupting mass and shaming evil into dark corners. But the angels will sever the two, and so precisely that no one true servant of God shall be left in the crowd. There is something unspeakably dreadful in the thought of a society which is one mass of sin. IV. LOVE WILL BE EXTINGUISHED. Very sweet is kindness which God has shed in our hearts as a solace for earthly ills, but there can be no love at all when God is withdrawn, for that means the withdrawal of love as effectually as light at sunset. V. THE HOLY SPIRIT WILL HAVE DEPARTED. Now, ever striving within, that Spirit does now and then give out a spark of goodness, and overrule here and there that utter wickedness which otherwise would prevail. And even in wicked men we see scattered up and down remainders of something better and higher, just as among the ruin of a great building you see here and there a beautiful fragment unbroken, to remind you of what the whole once was; or as you may sometimes see, when the sun is shining, beauty in things ugly, and when the

sun is withdrawn the beauty goes. So it will be with the soul in eternity. At
present strive as he will man cannot utterly unstamp his soul of the seal of God.
But when God removes His presence the spirit of man becomes wholly evil.
Conclusion: The sure Word of God teaches us much else about hell; but the
teaching of the text should be sufficient to warn us against it. (*J. Garbett,
M.A.*)    *Hell, a necessary truth:*—Assuming the general impression of
readers of the New Testament in relation to this doctrine to be correct; that
we are there taught that there is a hell, that a human being of certain
character may come and must come into a state of everlasting punishment; we are prepared to accept it as truth. The doctrine is as really required
as the immense vertebræ of some unknown animal require that the undiscovered ribs should be immense and of a certain character. An astronomer
observes in a planet a slower or quicker rate of motion at one point of its orbit: he
argues that there must be a world beyond it, not yet seen; and Neptune is
presently discovered. A hell is the full harvest of self-indulgence, evil, sin.
(*J. Christien, D.D.*)    *The reality of perdition:*—A dying man of large means
said: "I would give thirty thousand pounds to have it proved to me satisfactorily
that there is no hell." Such proof cannot be presented. But suppose you throw
overboard most of the testimony on this subject—is there not some slight possibility
that there may be such a place? If there should be, and you have no preparation
to escape it, what then? A young woman, dying, said to her father: "Father,
why did you not tell me there was such a place?" "What place?" "A hell!"
He said: "Jenny, there is no such place. God is merciful. There will be no future
suffering!" She said: "I know better! I feel it now! I know there is such a place!
My feet are slipping into it this moment! I am lost! Why did you not tell me there
was such a place?" It is the awful, stupendous, consuming, incontrovertible fact of
the universe. (*T. De Witt Talmage.*)    *Punishment irremediable:*—The law which
binds the earth in its orbital path finds expression in the being of a flower; the
being of a flower and the life of a human soul are governed by one and the same
law. Given, then, a flower with every capacity for strength, beauty, and sweetness;
put it beyond the range of the mighty sun's hand of blessing, put it in the "outer
darkness" of a cellar, whence the celestial sheen is excluded, into which no showers
can come, and through which no breeze can sweep: the flower will live for a time,
even will propagate life; but what life! Its stalk and branches will become poor,
weak, spongy, nerveless things; its leaves will grow more yellow and diminutive, its
flower less and less like the God-purposed thing it might have been, and its smell
will degenerate into a tainting impurity; why? Because by a mysterious chemical
communion with the sun, alone could the glory and goodness that were in it be
brought to blossom and fruitage. Light, not the mere need of light, quickens
strong life and paints the beautiful. The presence of the true, not its felt absence,
corrects the false. Communion with the grand, good, strong, and loving, alone can
recover and transform. If, therefore, the language of Christ and His apostles will
not admit of the interpretation that hell is the theatre of a more effective moral
discipline than earth, that future punishment is really disciplinary;—and will the
general mind admit the words "outer darkness—unquenchable fire—everlasting
punishment—place of torment—and depart, ye cursed," capable of the interpretation?—then the doctrine of an irremediable state of punishment in the life to come
is in harmony with the law which we recognize in the utter falling off from fruitage,
beauty, and trueness of uncultivated plants, and in the fearful degradation and mere
animalism into which isolated and neglected tribes of our race have fallen
"Destruction—death—perish—devour, for ever and ever":—do these Scripture
terms become more intelligible in the light of this law? (*J. Christien, D.D.*)
*The glory of His power:*—Not "from His power,"—this is impossible. Whither can
I go from His power? If I ascend up to heaven it is there: if I go down to hell, it
is there also. Nay, nay, it is only from the glory of His power. "I beseech thee,"
said Moses, "show me Thy glory." And He said, "I will make all my goodness
pass before thee." Well, then, the glory of God is the goodness of God. So the
glory of His power in that day will be the goodness of His power in the revelation
of the resources of His almighty will, as seen in the new heaven and the new earth,
in the righteousness that shall dwell therein, and in the blessedness of His saints
therein. To be banished from the glory of His power is to be given over to the fury
of His power. It is not only to forfeit the enjoyment of the resources of His power
administering goodness, but it is to come under the rigour of His power, administering justice. It is to feel Almightiness taking vengeance on body and soul without

limit to, or possible escape from it—vengeance, we are told by One who knew, which is as a worm that never dies, and a fire that never shall be quenched. Oh, one of old did indeed well say, " It is a fearful thing to fall into the hands of the living God ! "   (*C. J. P. Eyre, M.A.*)

Ver. 10. **When He shall come to be glorified in His saints, and admired in all them that believe.**—*Christ glorified in glorified men :*—There be the two halves—the aspect of that day to those to whom it is the revelation of a stranger, and the aspect of that day to those to whom it is the glorifying of Him who is their life. I. The remarkable words which I have taken for my text suggest to us, first of all, some thoughts about that striking expression that CHRIST IS GLORIFIED IN THE MEN WHO ARE GLORIFIED IN CHRIST. If you look on a couple of verses you will find that the apostle returns to this thought and expresses in the clearest fashion the reciprocal character of that " glorifying " of which he has been speaking. " The name of our Lord Jesus Christ," says he, " may be glorified in you, and ye in Him." So, then, glorifying has a double process involved. It means either " to make glorious," or " to manifest as being glorious." And men are glorified in the former sense in Christ, that Christ in them may, in the latter sense, be glorified. He makes them glorious by imparting to them of the lustrous light and flashing beauty of His own perfect character, in order that that light, received into their natures, and streaming out at last conspicuously manifest from their redeemed perfectness, may redound to the praise and the honour, before a whole universe, of Him who has thus endued their weakness with His own strength, and transmitted their corruptibility into His own immortality. 1. The artist is known by his work. You stand in front of some great picture, or you listen to some great symphony, or you read some great book, and you say, " This is the glory of Raffaelle, Beethoven, Shakespeare." Christ points to His saints, and He says, " Behold My handiwork ! Ye are My witnesses. This is what I can do." 2. But the relation between Christ and His saints is far deeper and more intimate than simply the relation between the artist and his work, for all the flashing light of moral beauty, of intellectual perfectness which Christian men can hope to receive in the future is but the light of the Christ that dwells in them, " and of whose fulness all they have received." Like some poor vapour, in itself white and colourless, which lies in the eastern sky there, and as the sun rises is flushed up into a miracle of rosy beauty, because it has caught the light amongst its flaming threads and vaporous substance, so we, in ourselves pale, ghostly, colourless as the mountains when the Alpine snow passes off them, being recipient of an indwelling Christ shall blush and flame in beauty. " Then shall the righteous blaze forth like the sun in My Father's Kingdom." Or, rather they are not suns shining by their own light, but moons reflecting the light of Christ, who is their light. II. And now notice, again, out of these full and pregnant words the other thought, THAT THIS TRANSFORMATION OF MEN IS THE GREAT MIRACLE AND MARVEL OF CHRIST'S POWER. " He shall come to be admired "—which word is employed in its old English signification, " to be wondered at "—" in all them that believe." So fair and lovely is He that He needs but to be recognized for what He is in order to be glorified. So great and stupendous are His operations in redeeming love that they need but to be beheld to be the object of wonder. " His name shall be called Wonderful." And wonderfully the energy of His redeeming and sanctifying grace shall then have wrought itself out to its legitimate end. Such results from such material ! Chemists tell us that the black bit of coal in your grate and the diamond on your finger are varying forms of the one substance. What about a power that shall take all the black coals in the world and transmute them into flashing diamonds, prismatic with the reflected light that comes from His face and made gems on His strong right hand ? The universe shall wonder at such results from such material. And it shall wonder, too, at the process by which they were accomplished, wondering at the depth of His pity revealed all the more pathetically now from the Great White Throne, which casts such a light on the Cross of Calvary ; wondering at the long, weary path which He who is now declared to be the Judge humbled Himself to travel in the quest of these poor sinful souls whom He has thus redeemed and glorified. III. And now a word about what is not expressed, but is necessarily implied in this verse, viz., THE SPECTATORS OF THIS GLORY. We need not speculate, it is better not to enter into details, but this, at least, is clear, that that solemn winding up of the long, mysterious, sad, blood and tear-stained history of man upon the earth is to be an object of interest and a higher revelation of God to other·

creatures than those that dwell upon the earth; and we may well believe that for that moment, at all events, the centre of the universe, which draws the thoughts of all thinking, and the eyes of all seeing creatures to it, shall be that valley of judgment wherein sits the Man Christ and judges men, and round Him the flashing reflectors of His glory in the person of His saints. IV. And lastly, look AT THE PATH TO THIS GLORIFYING. "He shall come to be glorified in His saints, and to be wondered at in all them that *believed*"; as that word ought to be rendered. That is to say, they who on earth were His, consecrated and devoted to Him, and in some humble measure partaking even here of His reflected beauty and imparted righteousness—these are they in whom He shall be glorified. They who "believed": poor, trembling, struggling, fainting souls, that here on earth, in the midst of many doubts and temptations, clasped His hand; and howsoever tremulously, yet truly put their trust in Him, these are they in whom He shall "be wondered at." (*A. Maclaren, D.D.*) *The final Advent*:—The context teaches two things concerning the final Advent of Christ. 1. The mode of His revelation to the world: "Revealed from heaven." He is now hidden within the veil; the veil will then be withdrawn and every eye shall see Him. But how will He be revealed "with the angels of His might." What are they, and how numerous? "In a fire of flame." Fire is often represented as the accompaniment of manifested Deity (Exod. iii. 2-18; xix. 18; Dan. ii. 9, 10; Mal. iv. 1; Rev. xix. 12). 2. The purpose of His revelation to the world. What is it? (1) To deal out retribution on the ungodly, "Taking vengeance," &c. What will be the retribution? "Everlasting destruction." What is that? Ah, what! Whence comes it? "From the presence of the Lord." His presence makes the heaven of the blest, constitutes the hell of the damned. (2) To confer immortal blessedness on His faithful disciples, "To be glorified in His saints." As the sun's glory is reflected in a mirror, so will Christ's glorious image be seen in the assembled universe in the perfection of His saints. How will Christ be glorified in this revelation of Himself? I. THE MAGNIFICENCE OF HIS MORAL TRIUMPHS will be universally recognized. When the millions of His disciples shall appear from all ages and lands, redeemed from all evil and resplendent with goodness, the glory of Christ's triumphs over the worst superstitions, over the strongest prejudices, over the mightiest depravities, over the wicked and most hardened of the race. The Hottentot, the Esquimaux, the Hindoo, the Chinese, the Japanese—men of all races, will appear as His. How will this strike every soul with admiration and praise. He who conquers the errors, bad passions, corrupt principles and habits of our soul, achieves a sublimer conquest than he who lays thousands of the mere bodies of men dead on the field of battle. But Christ's conquest of millions and millions of souls will appear on that day. II. THE PERFECTION OF HIS CHARACTER will be universally recognized. 1. Will not His love be seen in all these conquests, His disinterested, compassionate, persevering, all-conquering love? 2. Will not His faithfulness be seen in all these conquests? Will not every redeemed soul say He is true; all He has promised He has performed. 3. Will not His holiness be seen in all these conquests? He cleansed them from all their spiritual pollutions, and they appear before Him without spot or wrinkle or any such thing. 4. Will not His power be seen in all these conquests? Who will not be struck with His might in accomplishing this great work of gathering them all together into His everlasting kingdom. (*D. Thomas, D.D.*) *Christ glorified*:— What a difference between the first and second Advent of the Redeemer. One great reason for a judgment day was to manifest the glory of Jesus. I. CHRIST WILL BE GLORIFIED IN HIS SAINTS. In their—1. Countless number. Little as the flock of Jesus now appears, yet when all is collected what a mighty host will appear. 2. Diversity of character, nation, age, time. The persecutor Paul and the persecuted Stephen; the converted Greek and the believing Jew; patriarchs and modern missionaries. 3. Past experience of His grace, converting, consoling, providential. 4. Perfection and happiness of body and soul for ever. II. CHRIST WILL BE GLORIFIED IN HIS ENEMIES. In their punishment will be seen—1. His authority, now denied. 2. His faithfulness to fulfil His threatenings as well as His promises. 3. His holiness as the hater of iniquity. 4. His omniscience in detecting secret crimes. (*H. Kollock, D.D.*) *The Second Coming*:—I. CHRIST WILL ASSUREDLY COME AGAIN. This is no less certain than that He once dwelt on this earth. The time is still a secret to us, and perhaps to all orders of intelligent creatures; but the circumstance itself is indubitable. He will come again at the time appointed of the Father. At the ascension His disciples were expressly assured of it by two angels (Acts i. 11). Our blessed Lord also spoke frequently of it (John xiv. 2, 3); but He never states the time. "Watch," He says, "for ye know neither the day nor the hour when the Son of Man cometh." Though the exact time is not known, yet the Second Coming of Christ is a prominent object of faith. II. WHEN CHRIST COMES, HE WILL BE GLORIFIED IN THE HAPPY AND ADVANTAGEOUS CIRCUMSTANCES OF HIS PEOPLE. 1. In their perfection in holiness. This will then reflect honour upon Him. They will be presented "not having spot or wrinkle, or any such thing, being holy, and without blemish." 2. In their eternal glory. Soul and body being re-united, they will be freed from all the infirmities of sinful and mortal flesh; have enlarged capacities, fitted for the noblest services—celestial minds attached to celestial bodies (1 Cor. xv. 42–49; Phil. iii. 21; 1 John iii. 2). 3. In their number. Jesus spoke of His flock as a little one (Luke xii. 32); but in that day the number of His ransomed ones will be far greater than the stars of heaven; and they will be gathered from the east and the west, the north and the south (Rev. vii. 9, 10). III. WHEN CHRIST COMES, HE WILL ALSO BE ADMIRED IN THEM. 1. His wisdom (1 Cor. i. 30). 2. His power, demonstrated by His resurrection (John v. 20–29). 3. His faithfulness. His saints have believed and trusted in Him; now His truth is confirmed. It will thus be a glorious day to Christ, and a day of unspeakable joy to His people (Luke xii. 37, 38). (*N. Lardner, D.D.*) *The saints' estate of glory at the judgment :*—I. THE STATE ITSELF. It is one of glory. There is twofold glory put upon the saints. 1. Relative which consists of three things—(1) The free and full forgiveness of our sins by the Judge (Acts iii. 19). Which pardon is—(*a*) Constitutive by God's new covenant (Acts x. 43). (*b*) Declarative when God as a Judge determines our right. (*c*) Executively when He remits the deserved penalty, and gives glory and happiness. All this is done in part here, but more fully at the last day. (2) A participation of judicial power (1 Cor. vi. 2, 3; Luke xxii. 30). Here some of the saints judge the world by their doctrine; all by their conversation (Heb. xi. 7); there by vote and suffrage. (3) Christ's public owning them before God and His angels, by head and poll, man by man (Luke xii. 8; Col. i. 22; Jude 24; Eph. v. 27; Heb. ii. 13). 2. Inherent (Gal. i. 16 *cf.* Rom. viii. 18). This glory will be revealed—(1) In our bodies which shall be made—(*a*) Immortal and incorruptible (1 Cor. xv. 42). (*b*) Like Christ's glorious body (1 Cor. xv. 43; Matt. xvii. 2, xiii. 43). (*c*) A spiritual body (1 Cor. xv. 44). (2) In our souls which will be fully satisfied and filled up with God (1 John iii. 2). II. THE MEASURE OF THE GLORY CHRIST WILL IMPART. It is a thing so great that it is said—1. He shall come to be glorified in the saints. Paul does not say that the saints shall be glorified (Rom. viii. 17); that were less though much. Nor does he say Christ shall be glorified in Himself (1 Pet. iv. 13); but in the saints. He is glorified in the glory which results to Him from their glory. His experience shows—(1) The certainty of this effect of His coming. If His glory be concerned in our glorification, we may be the more confident of it. (2) The greatness; for how is Christ glorified in the saints? (*a*) Objectively. God is glorified by impression. So all His creatures glorify Him, *i.e.*, offer matter to set forth His glory (Psa. cxlv. 10; Eph. i. 12). Not speak but be. (*b*) Actively by expression (Psa. l. 23; 1 Pet. ii. 9). He will be admired in those that believe. We admire all those things which exceed knowledge and expectation. That glory shall exceed all hope; but who are the parties that shall wonder? (1) The good angels—the spectators, not the parties interested, but beings marvellously affected by the salvation of sinners (1 Pet. i. 12; Eph. iii. 10). (2) The wicked are amazed when they see those so much loved and advanced by Christ whose lives they counted madness and folly. (3) The saints themselves are filled with wonder, they finding their expectation so much exceeded; for admiration is the overplus of expectation. Even in what is revealed, the saints find many astonishing instances of God's love (1 Peter ii. 9). III. THE AUTHOR : Christ. How He is concerned in this; for it is not said the saints shall be glorified, but He. Our glory as it comes from Christ redounds to Him (Rom. xi. 36). 1. He is the procurer of this glorious estate for us by His death and sufferings (Eph. i. 14; Rom. viii. 13; Eph. v. 27). He gave Himself, not only to sanctify, but to glorify His people. 2. He has promised it in His gracious covenant (1 John ii. 25). 3. He dispenses it. As the husband rises in honour, so does the wife; when the head is crowned the members are clothed with honour; when the Captain enters glory it is with His followers (Heb. ii. 10). 4. He is the pattern of it (Rom. viii. 29; Phil. iii. 21; 1 John iii. 2). IV. THE SUBJECTS—"His saints," "All that believe." Mark—1. The connection between these two characters—saints and believers. It implies that those who by faith so separate themselves from the world and consecrate themselves to God shall be glorified (Acts xxvi. 18). 2. This glory is limited to saints and believers (John iii. 15 ; Col. iii. 12 ; Acts xx. 32 ; xxvi. 18). 3. Though it be limited to saints, yet there is a great difference between the saints. Some are eminent in grace; others weak and dark ; some will be raised, others changed; but they all agree in this that Christ will be glorified in all. The glory that will be put upon the humblest will be enough to raise the wonder of angels. V. The season: "In that day." For this public honour we must wait till the time fixed. It is not meet that the adopted children should have their glory till the Son of God by nature, be publicly manifested. There is no congruity between their present state and this blessedness. 1. The place is not fit it is so full of changes. 2. The persons are not fit. Our souls are not yet purified enough to see God (Matt. v. 8 ; 1 John iii. 3). When Christ presents us to God we shall be faultless (Jude 25). Old bottles cannot bear this new wine (Matt. xvii. 16). 3. The time is not fit. We must be some time upon our trial before we enter upon our final estate. It is fit that Christ should be admired now in the graces, but then in the glory of His people (1 Pet. iv. 4). Uses: 1. To wean us from the vain glory of this world. 2. To encourage us to seek after this glorious estate by continuance in well-doing. (*T. Manton, D.D.*) *The glory of Christ as exhibited in His people* :—I. In the excellence of their character. Whatever contributes to the honour of an individual must in some way reflect His worth. The productions of an author form the medium of His praise. Thus creation is the medium of the Creator's glory because it displays His wisdom, power, and goodness. So at the last day the vast assembly of the redeemed deriving all that they possess from the Saviour will be the medium through which the efficacy of His atonement, the power of His grace, and the extent of His love will be manifested in an admiring universe. 1. In estimating the improvement of an individual or the advancement of a community, it is necessary to bear in mind their original condition. So in forming a correct estimate of what the Saviour does for His people it is necessary to remember—(1) Their lowly origin. (2) Their ignorance of God, Christ, salvation, duty, destiny. (3) Their depravity. They were enemies of God, transgressors of the law, &c. 2. Who without grateful emotion can think of such as they shall finally appear in glory? (1) The mists of ignorance shall be dispelled. (2) All sin will be put away. (3) They as lesser luminaries will reflect the glory and the grace of the Sun of Righteousness. II. In the perfection and security of their bliss. 1. There was a time when they were strangers to joy— through the indulgence of evil passions, the gratification of evil propensities, distance from God. 2. At the judgment and onwards their bliss will be—(1) Perfect. After their conversion it was by no means contemptible, but it was incomplete, and so imperfectly reflected Christ's glory. (2) Secure. Here it is interrupted and not seldom destroyed; by and by no danger will alarm, enemy intrude, or temptation seduce. Conclusion : Hence we see—1. The dignity of the Christian character. 2. The Christian's glorious hope. (*J. Kay.*) *Christ glorified in His saints:* — "When He shall come." How many things are waiting that issue, how many mysteries to be solved, purposes to be unfolded, longing hopes to be at rest ! 1. Paul does not define the time—the word is one of studied indefiniteness—"Whenever He shall come." But the object is determined, viz., that Christ may be glorified and admired. Far and above everything else on this grand day this will be the end of ends. 2. In this, that day only puts its right climax on all that went before ; for this earth, from the beginning was made to be a platform to exhibit Christ— the Fall, sorrow, death, the material world. 3. This may be a comfort now. Who has not said, "I wish to glorify Christ—but do I, and can I?" And the poor divided, sin-stained Church—it is pleasant to be assured that it will fully glorify Christ then. 4. It does not say that Christ will be glorified, &c., *by* but *in* His saints —others will be the admirers, angels, the assembled universe—we shall be the reflectors. 5. "Saints" here are the perfectly holy. Now holiness is the final end of man. All else, election, redemption, grace, is only a means ; and for the reason that Holiness is the image of God. That there might be such an image was the end of the first creation and the second. Therefore when every grace is complete the whole Deity will be represented in its fulness—the Father's love in choosing, the Son's love in dying, the Spirit's love in moulding every man's life. That process which went on day by day and slowly here, will be finished. 6. To "believe" is to take God at His word. And those who believe look very strange here. Men cannot understand them. They seem to be giving up substances for shadows. But then the whole world will see with astonishment the triumphs of faith, and the faithfulness of Jesus to His own word. 7. You will do well to make much of the saints and to extol the virtues of the faithful, not for hero worship but to gather from them the features of Christ and to imitate them. (*J. Vaughan, M.A.*)  *Christ marvelled at :*—Many persons look upon Christians as common-place holders of a common-place creed.  Our Christianity is a story of marvels.  It begins in wonder; it will never end.  I. THE LORD JESUS WILL BE MARVELLED AT BY HIS SAINTS, WHO WILL SEE, FOR THE FIRST TIME, THE GREATNESS OF THE DELIVERANCE HE HAS WROUGHT OUT FOR THEM.  There are those who look upon sin as a slight thing to be delivered from; but all through the Bible we hear of Christ as the great Deliverer, because He comes to deliver us from sin.  He is great because He delivers from a great evil; and when we see how great Christ is He will be "marvelled at by all them that believed." At present we take our salvation very coolly, as if it were a small matter.  We only half understand it now; but it will be far better understood some day.  And when we see it as we ought, as it is, then Jesus, who has wrought it all, will indeed be "marvelled at" by us.  II. THE LORD JESUS WILL BE MARVELLED AT BY HIS SAINTS FOR THE COURSE OF PROVIDENCE BY WHICH HE HAS LED THEM HOME.  The Jewish people had a story of marvels.  Their rescue from Egypt was a wonder; their passage across the Red Sea was a wonder; the saving of their life when the destroying angel passed over the land was a wonder; the water for their thirst gushing from the rock was a wonder; the bread for their hunger falling from the heaven was a wonder; and, in fine, the whole history of the people was one chain of wonders.  So, in truth, is the whole history of all Christians, whether Jews or Gentiles.  Though there seems nothing particular in their lives, if they are looked at in a proper spirit, even those comparatively prosaic, are charged with the elements of mystery.  God has kept them in Jesus, has rescued them, has carried them over many an abyss.  They were not at all aware of it at the time; but they will be fully aware of it "in that day," and they will marvel at their marvellous Leader.  The history of His salvation is continued in the history of His providence.  So when they stand before Him as His accepted ones they will see that He verily is the great marvel of their past.  Many a marvel has He done; but He Himself is the marvel of marvels.  III. THE LORD JESUS WILL BE MARVELLED AT BY HIS SAINTS, FORASMUCH AS HE WILL BE SEEN AS HE IS.  Himself a wonder, He will awake a wondering sentiment in the hearts of those who, for the first time, see what He really is.  This is the one revelation waited for.  We have seen many things, but we have not seen Christ; we have seen many deliverances, but we have not seen the Deliverer; we have seen the temple, but we have not seen the Lord of the temple.  We talk to Christ every day, but we have not seen Him yet.  In our spirit we have seen Christ coming to our spirit—so seen Him that we have marvelled at His beauty, and understood somewhat why those who actually saw Him in the days of His flesh were so attracted to Him.  But Christ—"the chief among ten thousand, and the altogether lovely"—is sometimes darkness upon darkness to our sinning soul, and no light shines out of the gloom.  You remember the story of a child during an eclipse sobbing until the darkness became so intense that the sobs were hushed in terror; but when the darkness passed away, and the light came, the little one clapped her hands, and cried, "Beautiful!"  So with us; when He doth appear, and we see Him as He is, He will be marvelled at for all the forms of beauty in His one Person.  *Jesus admired in them that believe :*—1. What a difference between the first and second comings of our Lord.  When He shall come a second time it will be to be glorified and admired, but when He came the first time He was despised and rejected of men.  2. The design of Christ's return is to be glorified in His people.  Even now His saints glorify Him.  When they walk in holiness they reflect His light : their holy deeds are beams from the Sun of Righteousness.  When they believe in Him they also glorify Him, because no grace pays lowlier homage to the throne of Jesus.  3. We do not glorify Him as we could desire for too often we dishonour Him by our want of zeal and our many sins.  Happy day when this shall be no more possible.  I. THE SPECIAL GLORIFICATION HERE INTENDED.  1. The Time : "When He shall come."  For this He waits, and the Church waits with Him.  2. In whom this glorification is to be found.  He is glorified by what we do here, but at last He will be glorified in what we are.  (1) In His saints.  All will be holy ones; but inasmuch as they are believers the holiness with which they will honour Christ is a holiness based on faith in Him.  (2) "In all that believe." This is enlarged by the hint that they are believers in a certain testimony, according to the bracketed sentence.  The testimony of the apostles was concerning Christ—His incarnation, life, death, resurrection, and ascension.  All who believe this witness are saved.  But inasmuch as they are first said to be saints, this faith must be a living faith which renews the character and shapes the life after the model of Christ. 3. By whom will Christ be glorified? He shines in His people but who shall see the glory? (1) His own people. Every saint will admire Christ in Himself, and in his brother saints. (2) His holy angels. (3) Perhaps the inhabitants of other worlds. (4) Satan and his defeated legions. These shall glorify Christ in His people, in whom they have been completely overthrown. 4. In what degree? The very highest. Admiration means wonder; surpassing all conception. Every one will be astonished, none more so than the saint himself. 5. In what respects? (1) On account of the number of the saints. "A great multitude whom no man can number." Those who laughed will now see how the little one has become a thousand. (2) An account of their quality. They shall be "without spot or wrinkle or any such thing." Absolutely perfect. II. THE SPECIAL CONSIDERATIONS THIS TRUTH SUGGESTS. 1. That the principal subject for self-examination with us all should be—Am I a saint? 2. The small value of human opinion. When Christ was here the world reckoned Him a nobody, and while His people are here they must expect to be judged in the same way. Never mind the reproach which will then be silenced. 3. A great encouragement to seekers. If Christ is to be glorified in saved sinners will He not be glorified indeed if He saved you? 4. An exhortation to believers. If Christ is to be honoured in His people let us think well of and love them all. Some are uncomely, poor, ignorant; but do not, therefore, despise them. 5. An encouragement to all who love Jesus and bear testimony to His name. (*C. H. Spurgeon.*) *The beauty of God:*—When Charles Kingsley was dying he seemed to have a glimpse of the heavenly splendour into which he was going, and of God in His brightness and loveliness, and he exclaimed, "How beautiful God is!" Every revelation of God that is made to us is a revelation of beauty. Everywhere in nature, in flower that blooms, in bird that sings, in dewdrop that sparkles on leaf or plant, in star that shines, in sunset that burns with splendour, we see disclosures or reflections of God's beauty. In the Holy Scriptures, where the invisible God is manifested and interpreted, every revelation of His character presents God to us in surpassing loveliness. Christ was God manifest in the flesh, the brightness of the Father's glory, the express image of His person, and He was altogether lovely. Such enrapturing beauty the world has never seen incarnated, save in that one blessed Life. *Christ glorified:*—In historical paintings, the principal personages whose history is to be represented occupy the foreground, and stand out, as it were, from the other figures which occupy the background. In the painting of the death of General Wolfe, who fell at Quebec, the dying hero immediately arrests your attention; your eyes fasten upon him, and all your sympathies and feelings are united there. So with the believer, it is Christ who occupies the foreground of his vision. He is the glorious personage who continually fills his eye and secures his attention, and makes every surrounding object little in its dimensions beside Him. It is Christ who died for him at Calvary; this draws out his affections towards Him. All other objects are eclipsed in their beauty, and have no beauty in comparison with Christ. "Whom have I in heaven," &c. *Christ reflected in His people:*—You may have seen a room hung round with mirrors, and when you stood in the midst you were reflected from every point: you were seen here, and seen there, and there again, and there again, and so every part of you was reflected; just such is heaven, Jesus is the centre, and all his saints like mirrors reflect His glory. Is He human? So are they! Is He the Son of God? So are they sons of God! Is He perfect? So are they! Is He exalted? So are they! Is He a prophet? So are they, making known unto principalities and powers the manifold wisdom of God. Is He a priest? So are they! Is He a king? So are they, for He hath made us priests and kings unto God, and we shall reign for ever and ever. Look where you will along the ranks of the redeemed, this one thing shall be seen, the glory of Christ Jesus, even to surprise and wonder. (*C. H. Spurgeon.*) *Christ glorified in His people:*—As a king is glorious in his regalia, so will Christ put on His saints as His personal splendour in that day when He shall make up His jewels. It is with Christ as it was with that noble Roman matron, who when she called at her friends' houses and saw their trinkets, asked them to come next day to her house, and she would exhibit her jewels. They expected to see ruby, and pearl, and diamond, but she called in her two boys, and said, "These are my jewels." Even so will Jesus instead of emerald and amethyst, and onyx and topaz, exhibit His saints. "These are my choice treasures," saith He, "in whom I will be glorified." Solomon surely was never more full of glory than when he had finished the temple, when all the tribes came together to see the noble structure, and confesssd it to be " beautiful for situation, the joy of the whole earth." But what will be the glory of Christ when all the living stones shall be put into their places and His Church shall have her windows of agates and her gates of carbuncle, and all her borders of precious stones? Then, indeed, will He be glorified, when the twelve foundations of His new Jerusalem shall be courses of stones most precious, the like of which was never seen. (*Ibid.*) **That Day.**—Sometimes we read of " the last day," " the great day,"—here " *that* day "; because it is the day to which all other days point, in prospect of which all other days come with their duties, trials, responsibilities ; the day towards which the hopes of the Church, founded on the promise of God, and the course of the world governed by the providence of God, are both gradually tending, just as converging lines do to a point of contact. In heaven it is the day longed for, for it is the day of the revelation of the great King, and the completion of the brotherhood between angels and saints. On earth it is the day the Church sighs for, and over the grave of her departed children she says, "Accomplish the number of Thine elect. Hasten Thine appearing ! " In hell it is the day feared, because there the angels who left their first estate are reserved in everlasting chains, in darkness, unto the judgment of that great day. Of this day the conscience of every one of us warns. It is not the mere induction of logic from the prevalence of evil and the suffering and loss which attends goodness ; it is no mere depression of spirits through forfeiture of self-respect or fear of man, that punishes the poor victim of deep remorse, when he shrinks from the reckoning to come ; the evidence is in that man as surely as it may be seen without him in the government of God's world, as surely as it may be seen before him in the letter of God's Word ; it is a portion of the economy of his constitution, the economy of every rational mind, placed there by Him who made man. Scoffers in our day, as in St. Peter's, who keep their eyes on the apparent constancy of the present order of things, may say, " Where is the promise of His coming ? " but a coming of some kind to judgment their very fears will show, and the desire to shake the veracity of the promises of Scripture regarding that day is encouraged by these secret fears. The coming of that day is as sure a thing as the existence of the Person of God, the Judge of man. The revealed councils of the Trinity would be nugatory without it. If the Father is gathering to Himself a great family, of which the everlasting Son is not ashamed to be called the Brother, this is the day for the manifestation of that family. If He has promised to the Redeemer that He shall see of the travail of His soul and be satisfied, that there shall be a public acceptance of the children given Him and the possession of an earthly kingdom, this is the day for the fulfilment of the engagement. Of this day the Holy Ghost has written, and to prepare men for it He abides with the Church. And this day is called in Scripture, " the last day," " the day of our Lord and Saviour Jesus Christ." He humbled Himself to humanity in the prospect of this day ; He hung upon the cross to win this day ; the resurrection and ascension were only steps of preparation towards this day ; His heavenly life is an expectation of this day. Royalty not yet enjoyed, hope not yet satisfied, glory not yet perfected, all wait for their fulness on that day when " the Lord Jesus shall be revealed," &c. (*C. J. P. Eyre, M.A.*) *The day of Christ's glory and of the Church's joy :*—I. HE SHALL COME TO BE GLORIFIED IN HIS SAINTS. To glorify means to secure honour or renown for a person. This prerogative Christ claims for Himself (John xi.). He was glorified in Lazarus ; He shall be glorified in the saints : 1. In the number of His saints. Even now through a little flock, He receives honour through them. But so little are they in comparison with the world around that the glory Christ receives now is not worthy to be compared with that He will receive when " the multitude which no man can number " will be gathered round Him, the largest of the two which shall be there. Do we not read " All the earth shall be filled with the glory of the Lord," " All flesh shall see the salvation of God " ? We may fairly infer that previous to the judgment there will be a vast accession to the Church. One generation shall succeed to another each increasing, one and all combining to swell the number of those of whom Christ spoke when He said, " I, if I be lifted up," &c. 2. In the harmony of the saints. This harmony was regarded by our Lord as of great importance. It is true that this does not exist as it should to the shame of the Church. But there *is* unity, and that unity redounds to the glory of Christ. But how much more shall it do so when every difference is extinct, every error rectified, and every passion quelled. The great theological controversialists will then see eye to eye, and the Saviour will then see His desire accomplished. 3. The holiness of the saints. This was one of the objects of

Christ's death ; His honour is involved in it. How then will honour be secured, when body and soul, and the whole Church shall be perfect. II. HE WILL BE ADMIRED IN ALL WHO BELIEVE. You admire Him now even as seen in His ordinances, and in prayer, but the hour is coming when that admiration shall be past description. 1. His full possession of mediatorial glory shall lead you to admire Him. He will not come amidst poverty and shame, but in flaming fire, &c. If the Saviour appears now as the " altogether lovely," although we only see through a glass darkly, what will He appear to be when we see Him face to face. 2. The universal acknowledgment of His supremacy shall lead you to admire Him—devils, heathen, and all His enemies will bow before Him, and every tongue shall confess that He is Lord. 3. The knowledge of what He has done will lead you to admire Him. We can conceive now, in some measure, our obligation to Christ, but how little compared with what we shall know when the depth of the depravity from which we have been rescued, the dreadfulness of the danger from which we have been preserved, and the glory of the heaven to which we are introduced, are fully revealed. Application : 1. Let Christians, animated by such a prospect, and possessed of such an inheritance, cherish holy gratitude and practice grateful obedience. 2. Let the unconverted seriously consider the loss and peril of their position. (*W. Brock, D.D.*) **Because our testimony among you was believed.**—*The testimony believed :*—I. THE GREAT TEST OF CHRISTIANS IS BELIEVING. The promises run everywhere in this strain (Mark xvi. 16; John iii. 36). II. FAITH OF ANY SORT IS NOT ENOUGH, WE MUST TRULY AND SINCERELY BELIEVE (John viii. 31; 1 Thess. i. 5). We distinguish between the two when the truths believed have an effectual power to change our hearts and reform our lives (1 Thess. ii. 13; Titus. i. 16; Hosea viii. 2). III. THE MATTER WE ARE TO BELIEVE IS THE APOSTLE'S TESTIMONY CONCERNING GOD'S GOOD-WILL TO SINNERS IN CHRIST. 1. Christianity, or the doctrine of salvation by Christ, is a testimony. A testimony is the proof necessary in matters that cannot otherwise be decided by rational deduction : as in two cases—(1) In matters that depend upon the arbitrary will of another. If I want to know how a man stands affected towards me, I must know it by his testimony. So none can know God's good will, but those to whom He reveals it (Matt. xi. 27). (2) In matters of fact. Matters of law are argued by reason, matters of fact are only proved by credible witnesses ; and in this respect the gospel is a testimony. Its facts transpired necessarily in one place, but the knowledge of them concerns the whole world. 2. This testimony is given—(1) By Christ (John iii. 33; Rev. iii. 14). (2) By the apostles who were commissioned by Christ as His witnesses (Acts i. 8; ii. 32; x. 39–41). This testimony is valuable to produce a saving belief in Christianity. (*a*) They had the testimony of sense (2 Pet. i. 16, 17; 1 John i. 1–3). (*b*) They were men of holiness and integrity (1 Cor. xv. 15). (*c*) They were authorized by miracles (Heb. ii. 3, 4). (*d*) Their testimony they gave in word and writing (Acts iv. 33; 1 John iv. 12). (*e*) Christ prays for all who should believe through them (John xvii. 20). Use 1. Of information. (1) Of the nature of faith—belief of testimony. We can only believe on testimony; we know by sense and reason. (2) The ground of faith. Christ and the apostle's testimony as transmitted to us. 2. Of exhortation. Believe this testimony that you may make out your title to eternal life. If we receive it not it will be a testimony against us. Two sorts will never be allowed for true believers. (1) The careless (Matt. xiii. 19). (2) The unsanctified who deny the faith (1 Tim. v. 8). (*T. Manton, D.D.*) *Faith as a motive power :*—How could the question, Whether faith be a motive power, have ever been made the subject of controversy ? For many a year, every day and every hour has strengthened my conviction that what a man believes, and what he does not believe, is either the lever or the bar to all that he does. If I believe what, by his pale cheek, as well as by word of mouth, the messenger announces—that sentence of death has been pronounced against me, and that to-morrow's dawn will shine upon my scaffold ; if I believe the intelligent architect when he assures me that the beams which support the roof of my chamber must in a few hours give way ; if I believe the smooth tongue which whispers that my friend is a villain—is it possible that these things should not prove to me a spur and a goad ? Were faith, indeed, a mere imagination, and did it signify nothing but the presentation to the mind's eye, of so many possibilities and shadowy images of beauty, it might be otherwise. But faith is no such baseless picture drawn by the imagination. It is a piece of myself, and what we believe penetrates through secret and unexplored passages, into the deepest recesses of our being. It cannot be otherwise, therefore, than that a man's life is the reflex of his faith. If thou believest in the breath of another world, then that breath will become the soul of thy life. (*Prof. Tholuck.*)

Vers. 11, 12. **Wherefore also we pray always for you.**—*The good pleasure of goodness:*—At the point where the intercession rises out of the text we see St. Paul's manner of giving a devotional turn to every subject. He had been contemplating the glorification of God in the punishment of the wicked and the salvation of the saints. Whilst assuming that the Thessalonians were among the latter a change passes over his mind. The language of exultation becomes that of hope; and hope takes refuge in prayer —I. THAT GOD MAY COUNT THEM WORTHY OF SO HIGH A DIGNITY. Here he thinks only of the condescending grace that will confirm to the end a vocation resting only on an imputed worthiness. The call is one; but it may be viewed in a threefold gradation, and in each the honour is conferred on man as unworthy in himself but reckoned worthy through the grace of Christ. 1. The first call to salvation is altogether independent of our merit. The gospel invites all alike to an equal place in the Divine favour. The first summons to God's presence where mercy awaits the vilest is a distinction of which we are reckoned worthy for Christ's sake alone. 2. We are also called unto holiness, and those who are accepted and renewed are termed specifically "the called." But their name and place among the saints depend upon the gracious imputation of the Divine tolerance. The saint is always and only reckoned to be holy, not because his holiness is unreal, but because with all his sanctity he is only a sinner saved by grace. 3. We are called by God to His kingdom and glory; but that the consummate issue of the Divine purpose will be as much the conferring of an undeserved distinction as the first acceptance was. Their sanctity will be their garment of righteousness, unspotted from the world; but the judgment of God, which never forgets though it forgives the past, will bear witness that that garment was once stained. Their good deeds will follow them, but so will their forgiven sins. Hence we see the appropriateness of the term as introducing the prayer. It gives to God the glory of the full and complete salvation it supplicates. II. THAT HE MAY ALSO MAKE THEM WORTHY. 1. The combination of imputed and imparted worthiness. These always go together. The enemies of justification say that God never reckons a man to be what he is not, which is true. The Divine grace mercifully waits while the process is going on, and God is always making His justified ones worthy of their justification. Nor will He present them faultless and crown them until their sanctification is complete. The imputation of worthiness is complete at once, but the infusion is gradual. The reckoning awaits awhile for the reality, which will surely come; and then will the counting and the making be merged into one. 2. Hence we must regard the two phrases employed as embracing the entire compass of religion. "All the good pleasure of His goodness," &c., is one of those striking summaries in which the apostle delights to throw out his views of finished godliness. "All that goodness can delight in and desire " refers to the formation of a perfect character within; whilst the "work of faith " must include as the antithesis, all that the external duties of religion involve. 3. We must, however, mark more specifically the union of the Divine and human in the perfect holiness prayed for. Not that the Divine part is the pleasure of His goodness, and the human our work of faith. No such distinction is in the words. They speak of the complacency our own souls feel in goodness as a desire satisfied by God; and our work of faith as fulfilled in Divine power. Both and equally unite the two ever necessary elements. (1) Take the former. The apostle uses terms which make no distinction between the Divine energy in us and our own. The delight our regenerate souls feel in all kinds and degrees of goodness is no other than a fruit of the Spirit's renewing grace. It is the desire of God beating in our own hearts. The unregenerate may admire all excellencies, and yet sigh to think of them as an unattainable ideal; it is only the renewed soul that takes a tranquil delight in the thought of the attainment of these things. Abhorring that which is evil they cleave to that which is good; and thus delighting themselves in God, and aspiring after holiness, they have their heart's desire (Psa. xxi. 2). (2) Take the latter. The work of man's faith is his own work; but it is a work which God fulfils in us. Here again the prayer makes no distinction. Faith is man's acting in the strength of God. The Divine blessing does not simply assist and reward our efforts. When the dejected disciples said, "Lord, increase our faith," Christ told them that their faith, nourished by devotion, should be a principle of Divine power working within, and accomplishing wonders possible only to God (Matt. xvii. 20). 4. It remains to dwell upon the perfect attainment of worthiness during the present discipline of the Christian life. It is impossible to put too much strength into the words " fulfil with power," which belong both to the external and internal life of grace. And whether we think of the power of God or the fulfilment in us, there is obvious no limit to attainment. What can be impracticable to that Power? And as for "fulfil," that is a word always reserved for very high service. The prayer is that God may accomplish in our hearts all that we desire, all that goodness finds congenial, all that we have set our heart on. III. THAT HE MAY CROWN IMPUTED AND IMPARTED WORTHINESS WITH GLORY (ver. 12). These words are an echo of ver. 10. 1. The finished holiness of the saints, with every desire fulfilled and duty discharged, will redound to the glory of the name of Jesus. What they shall be He will have made them; and as the name of the Father is glorified in the Son, through the revelation of His redeeming Person and work, so the name of the Son is glorified in the saints in their full acceptance and sanctification through His atonement. 2. But we are also to be "glorified in Him." The "name" is not now mentioned; because it is only through our most intimate union with Himself that we attain our supreme glorification. Here the prayer of the servant is like the prayer of the Master, but supplementing what He left unexpressed (John xvii. 24). When we remember all that is meant by being "glorified in Him," we must needs feel persuaded that He whose name is thus spoken of is God. In God alone is the sphere of the creature's blessedness and glory. (*W. B. Pope, D.D.*) *Experimental Christianity :*—All the great principles of our common Christianity are stated in these verses by St. Paul, so far as the experience of believers is involved. I. CHRISTIANITY IN ITS NATURE. It renders Christians "worthy." While we guard against self-righteousness on the one hand, we should be careful against a mock humility on the other. There is a worthiness with which God is well pleased, and which is the blessed result of the working of Christianity in the soul (Col. i. 9, 10; Rev. iii. 4). Just as a tree is known by its fruits, so Christianity is known by the moral and spiritual effects it produces in those who profess it. II. CHRISTIANITY IN ITS SOURCE. "The good pleasure of His goodness." And this absolutely alone; for none could have merited it as a system of restoration. In fact, there is no merit either in unfallen angel or unfallen man, much less in fallen creatures such as we are. Christianity, then, originated in "the good pleasure of goodness," and that "goodness" was Divine. III. CHRISTIANITY IN ITS ACTIVITY. "The work of faith." Faith is its active grace. This produces all religious affections, and this sustains all religious affections. It is as coal to the fire, as oil to the lamp. IV. CHRISTIANITY IN ITS DESIGN. "That the name of our Lord Jesus Christ may be glorified in you and ye in Him." A double glorification—that of the Master, and that of His servant. What, has not Christ glory enough in heaven with His Father and the holy angels? If He has, can He receive glory from such creatures as His saints? Yes. The original signifies that He can be inglorified in His saints; that is, by something within them—by the gracious work he has wrought in them. V. CHRISTIANITY IN ITS MEASURE. "According to the grace of our God and the Lord Jesus Christ." The Father and the Son are the givers of grace, and by their names being linked together we are to understand that they will give grace in all its fulness. There is more grace in them than there can be sin in us, or in the whole world. Some sinners are allowed to run mightily on the Divine score, to manifest that, though they are beggared, Divine grace is not. Grace always rises higher in its tide than sin, and bears it down by its flow, just as the rolling tide of the sea rises higher than the streams of a river, and beats them back, with all they contain in them. Divine grace neither knows measure nor end. (*J. Burns, D.D.*)

Ver. 11. **That our God would count you worthy of this calling.**—*Salvation the result of the pleasure of God's goodness and His power :*—I. IT FLOWS FROM THE PLEASURE OF GOD'S GOODNESS. In the whole course of our salvation this is to be observed: 1. The coming of Christ (Luke ii. 14). 2. The covenant of grace (Col. i. 19, 20). 3. The ministry (1 Cor. i. 21). 4. The grace to embrace the covenant offered (Matt. xi. 26). 5. The blessings of the covenant. (1) By the way (Deut. xxxiii. 16), (2) at the end of the journey (Luke xii. 32). II. IT IS ACCOMPLISHED BY HIS ALMIGHTY POWER. The power of God is necessary—1. To bring us into a state of grace. Nothing but it can overcome man's obstinacy and change his heart (Job xiv. 4). The work is called a "new creation" (2 Cor. v. 17; Eph. ii. 10; iv. 24), and creation is a work of omnipotence, whether physical or spiritual. 2. To maintain us in a state of grace. Here consider—(1) The necessity of God's power (1 Pet. i. 5). None but this Almighty Guardian can keep and preserve us by the way, that we may come safe to our journey's end (Acts xvii. 28; Heb. xiii. 21). Remember the adversaries (Gal. v. 17; 1 Pet. v. 8); but remember the assurance (Matt. xix. 26). (2) The sufficiency of this power (Jude 24). (*a*) To enable for all duties (Phil. iv. 13; Eph. iii. 16). (*b*) To support in all trials (Deut. xxxii. 22). (*c*) To resist all temptations (1 John iv. 4; Eph. vi. 10). (*T. Manton, D.D.*)

*Worthiness of Divine calling :*—I. WHAT IS THIS CALLING? The Christian calling is holy (2 Tim. i. 9); heavenly (Heb. iii. 1). The one relates to the way, the other to the end; hence it is a calling to virtue and glory (2 Pet. i. 3). Both may be considered either as they are represented—1. In the offer of the Word. There God is often set forth as calling us—(1) From sin to holiness (1 Thess. iv. 7). (2) From misery to happiness (1 Pet. v. 10). 2. As impressed upon us by the operation of the Spirit (Rom. i. 7), by which we have a right to the heavenly blessedness (Heb. ix. 15). II. WHAT IS IT TO BE COUNTED OR MADE WORTHY OF THIS CALLING? There is a threefold worthiness—1. Of desert and proper merit (Rev. iv. 11). God deserves all that the creature can give Him, and infinitely more (Rev. v. 12). The workman is worthy in this sense of His meat (Matt. x. 10). When preachers are sustained by hearers, it is not our alms but a debt (1 Tim. v. 17). But it is not so between us and God (Gen. xxxii. 10). 2. Of meekness and suitableness (Col. i. 10: Eph. iv. 1). In this sense God makes us worthy when He makes us more holy and heavenly (1 Thess. ii. 12; Col. i. 12). This meetness consists in—(1) Holiness (1 Pet. i. 15). The calling—(*a*) Puts a holy nature into us. (*b*) Obliges us to live by a holy rule. (*c*) Offers us a holy reward. (*d*) And all to engage us to the service of a holy God, who will be sanctified to all who are near to Him. Therefore, to make His people such who were once sinners, He has appointed means (Gal. v. 26) and providences (Heb. xii. 10), and all accomplished with the operation of the Holy Spirit (chap. ii. 13). (2) Heavenliness; for God, by inviting men, draws them off this world to a better. The more they obey His will, the more heavenly they are. It is heaven —(*a*) They seek (Col. iii. 1, 2). (*b*) Hope for (1 Pet. i. 3). (*c*) Count their portion (Matt. vi. 20, 21). (*d*) Their home and happiness (Heb. xi. 13). (*e*) Their work and scope (Phil. iii. 14). (*f*) Their end, solace and support (2 Cor. iv. 18). Their course becomes their choice (Phil. iii. 20). 3. Acceptance (Acts v. 41), which notes liberality in the giver but no worth in the receiver (Luke xxi. 36; Rev. ii. 4). III. THIS IS AN EXCELLENT BENEFIT, AND THE MERE FRUIT OF GOD'S GRACE. 1. It is an excellent benefit. By this calling—(1) Our natures are ennobled (2 Pet. i. 4 ; 2 Cor. iii. 18). Holiness is the beauty of God. His image impressed on us. (2) We are brought into an estate wherein not only are we amenable to God, but He to us (1 John iii. 1; Rom. i. 6). (3) We are under the special protection of God, so that all things work together for good (Rom. viii. 28). (4) We are admitted to everlasting blessedness (Eph. i. 18; Phil. iii. 14; 1 Pet. iii. 9). 2. It is the fruit of God's grace (Rom. ix. 11; 2 Tim. i. 9). (1) For the beginning. He was pleased to call us at first. From what a state of sin and misery He called us (Col. i. 21). (2) For the progress. God that began the good work continues it (1 Pet. v. 10; 1 Thess. v. 24). (3) For the end. God must count us worthy to the last. Consider—(*a*) The infinite disproportion between our best services and greatest sufferings and the promised glory (Rom. viii. 18). (*b*) The imperfection of our best obedience (Isa. lxiv. 6). (*c*) Our unprofitableness to God, who is above our injuries and benefits (Job. xxii. 23 ; xxxv. 7, 8; Luke xvii. 10). (*d*) The interruptions of our obedience (James iii. 2; 1 John i. 10). Conclusion: Behave as a people called by God, because your calling is—1. A peculiar favour (Eph. v. 8). 2. A great honour (1 Thess. ii. 12). 3. A rich talent, faculty and power (2 Pet. i. 3). 4. A special trust (1 Pet. ii. 9). (*Ibid.*)     *Faith fulfilled :*—Let us conceive a chemist experimenting along a certain line, and presently beginning to suspect the existence of some great unknown law. He pursues his investigations. There are certain converging lines of evidence pointing to this conclusion. He stands on the verge of a great discovery. He multiplies experiments, and his suspicion becomes now a conviction—not a certainty. His mind has overleapt the interval and fastened upon the truth before the labouring processes of reason have verified it. This is faith. Nothing remains but to make the crowning experiment. All hangs on this, and we can conceive with what breathless interest he watches its development. It is successful, and a great tide of joy rushes in upon his soul that a new, great truth is born into the world, which shall for ever live, bearing his name imprinted upon it. We, then, are in the condition of that chemist in the interval between the conviction and the making of the last experiment. We see lines of evidence leading up to God. Faith overleaps the interval and fastens upon the truth. The crowning experiment shall be made in eternity, when sight shall set the seal to faith, and give us the last conclusive evidence which shall for ever silence question. We shall then leap all at once unto the full assurance of the things in which we believed. We shall have issued from the realm of faith into the serene everlasting certainty of heaven. (*W. Sparrow.*)

Ver. 12. That the name of our Lord Jesus Christ may be glorified in you.— *Christ glorified in His servants :*—I. WHEN THE WORK OF FAITH IS FULFILLED WITH POWER, CHRIST IS GLORIFIED IN HIS SERVANTS.    1. Christ is glorified— (1) Passively in all His creatures, as His glorious excellencies are visibly represented in them. Natural agents (Psa. xix. 1, 2; cxlv. 10). The new creature (Eph. i. 12). (2) Actively, as they conceive and declare His excellency. (*a*) In their hearts, by estimation and love (Luke i. 46; Psa. lxxiii. 25), and trust (Isa. xxvi. 3), and delight (Psa. iv. 6, 7; lxxiii. 3). (*b*) With their tongues (Psa. l. 23; James iii. 10). (*c*) In their lives, by fixing his glory as the end (1 Cor. x. 31), and by doing those things as may most suit the end (1 Pet. i. 15).    2. The work of faith fulfilled with power glorifies Christ. Christ is glorified by—(1) Our patience under troubles (John. xxi. 19; Phil. i. 21), which is a work of faith. (2) All holy conversation and godliness (Matt. v. 16; 1 Pet. ii. 12).    II. IN PROMOTING THE GLORY OF CHRIST WE PROMOTE THE SALVATION OF OUR SOULS.    1. God has appointed this order that we should first glorify Him before He glorifies us. It would redound to God's dishonour if he should glorify those that do not glorify Him, and make no difference between those who break His laws and those who keep them.    2. God has also appointed that we should glorify Him on earth before He glorifies us in heaven. In this we have Christ for an example (John xvii. 4, 5).    3. Christ takes special notice of those that glorify Him in the world (John xvii. 10). Christ is glorified—(1) In His Person, when He is owned as the Son of God (John xvii. 8, 27). (2) In His office (John xiv. 13). (3) In His doctrine, when it is believed and practised (Acts xiii. 48)    4. This glory is promised (1 Sam. ii. 30; John xii. 26; Rom. viii. 7).    5. The suitableness between His being glorified in us and our being glorified in Him. (1) Objectively, because this impression of honour upon us redounds to His glory (ver. 10). (2) Actively, because one part of our happiness is, that we love and praise Him. This is our glory, that we behold Christ's glory (John xvii. 24).    6. We may expect this glory—(*a*) With confidence (2 Tim. iv. 8; 2 Thess. ii. 13). (*b*) Without danger of presumption, because Christ is the Lord of glory (James ii. 1; 1 Cor. ii. 8), and because that grace whereby we glorify Him is given by Him (John xvii. 22).    III. OUR COMPLETE SALVATION, FROM FIRST TO LAST, FLOWS FROM THE GRACE OF GOD IN CHRIST. (*T. Manton, D.D.*) *Christ is glorious in the character of His followers* in that—I. THEY GIVE HIM THE THRONE, and cheerfully acknowledge His authority over them. II. WHATEVER IS EXCELLENT IN THEIR CHARACTER IS BUT THE REFLECTION OF HIS OWN. III. THEY ARE HIS WITNESSES IN THIS UNGODLY WORLD.    IV. THEY LOVE TO PROMOTE HIS GLORY and advance the interests of His kingdom. Application : 1. This is full of comfort to God's people, because they have the greatest security in His guardianship and love. 2. It is full of inducements to holy being. 3. It is full of rebuke to ungodly men, in that there are no indications of the Saviour's glory in their characters. (*G. Spring, D.D.*)    *A Christian is the reflex of Christ :*—It has often been said that the Christian virtues are only impressions of the image of Christ ; and that is true and good ; but these impressions must find expression in every-day life. We are called of God to make manifest the character of " Him that loved us." Once, in a large company of Christian men, the most lively regret was expressed that there is no authentic portrait of Jesus Christ as he lived and walked upon this earth. How gladly, it was said, would Christians often look on the features of that face ! But one of God's aged pilgrims stood up and said, " I cannot deplore that at all, because a true Christian is the true likeness of Christ." (*Pastor Funcke.*)

---

## CHAPTER II.

VER. 1. Now we beseech you, brethren, by the coming of our Lord Jesus Christ. *The coming of Christ :*—I. THE NATURE OF IT. Christ came. He comes. He

*II. THESSALONIANS.*

is to come. **1. He came in the flesh.** The long line of predictions from Adam to Malachi were accomplished at last, after long delay and anxious expectation. **2. He comes continually.** (1) In the extraordinary manifestation of His presence and power, whether for judgment or mercy. (2) In the special manifestation of Himself to His people. **3. He is to come.** (1) Personally and visibly. (2) With power and great glory. (3) The dead shall rise, the just and the unjust. (4) The judgment will then be held. (5) The world destroyed. (6) The kingdom of God consummated. The consequences to His people will be—(a) Their redemption, *i.e.*, their final deliverance from the power of death. (b) Their complete conformity to the likeness of Christ. (c) Their perfect enjoyment of that kingdom prepared for them from the foundation of the world. II. THE TIME. 1. It is unrevealed. 2. It is to be unexpected. 3. It will not be until the conversion of the Jews and the calling in of the Gentiles. Did the apostles expect Christ in their day? (1) They regarded His coming as they regarded the coming of death. (2) It was revealed to them that there should be a falling away first. We must distinguish between their personal expectations and their teaching. The latter alone is infallible. III. POINTS OF ANALOGY BETWEEN THE FIRST AND SECOND COMINGS. 1. Both predicted. 2. Anxiously and long expected. 3. The subjects of much speculation as to time and mode. 4. Disappointing in the one and the other. IV. THE STATE OF MIND WHICH THE DOCTRINE SHOULD INDUCE. 1. A firm belief in the revealed fact that He is to come. This faith should not be shaken by long delay. How long Abraham waited and died without the sight. 2. Earnest desire. The hopes of the ancient people were concentrated on the coming of the Messiah. This led them to bear patiently what they had to suffer. To set their hopes on the future and not on the present. The same effect should be produced on us. 3. Watchfulness and anxiety, lest that day should overtake us as a thief in the night. We should have our lamps trimmed and our lights burning. It would be a dreadful thing for Christ to come and find us immersed in the world. 4. Prayer and waiting. 5. Solicitous efforts to prepare others for His coming, and to prepare the way of the Lord. He will not come to the individual nor to the Church till His way is prepared. This includes—(1) Taking out of the way obstructions to His coming. (2) The accomplishment of the ingathering of His people. (*C. Hodge, D.D.*) *The coming of Christ:*—I. THE COMING OF CHRIST TO JUDGMENT IS A TRUTH—1. Well known by all the saints (Jude 14; Psa. xcvi. 13; xcviii. 9; Eccles. xii. 13, 14). 2. Firmly believed (2 Pet. iii. 3–5; Titus ii. 11–13). 3. Earnestly desired (Sol. Song viii. 14; Rev. xxii. 20). Why? (1) In respect of Him who is to come—that we may see Him who is our great Lord and Saviour. All who believed anything of Christ before He came desired to see Him (John viii. 56). And now Christians (1 Pet. i. 8; ii. 3). (2) In respect of the persons desiring—there is that in them which moves them to it. (a) The Spirit of Christ (Rev. xxii. 17). The Holy Ghost creates this desire: it is His great work to bring Christ and us together. (b) The graces planted in us—faith, which takes Christ at His word (John xiv. 2); hope, which is faith's handmaid (1 Pet. i. 3); love, which is an affection of union (Phil. i. 23). (c) Christian privileges; believers then find the fruit of their interest in Christ, and have their reward (Rev. xxii. 12; 2 Tim. iv. 8; 1 Pet. v. 4). II. WHEN CHRIST SHALL COME ALL THE SAINTS SHALL BE GATHERED WITH HIM. There shall be—1. A congregation (Matt. xxv. 32; 2 Cor. v. 10). Adam will then meet all his posterity at once. All distinctions of age, quality, wealth, nation, &c., will disappear. 2. A segregation (Matt. xxv. 32, 33). There may be some confusion now, but there shall be a complete separation then (Matt. xiii. 49). 3. An aggregation: believers are gathered together for several ends. (1) To make up the number of Christ's attendants (Jude 14; Zech. xiv. 5; 1 Thess. iv. 17). (2) To be presented to God by head and poll. We were given to Christ to be preserved for glory (John xvii. 6). Christ is to give an account (John vi. 40). The form of presentation (Heb. ii. 13). (3) To be brought in one troop to heaven (John xiv. 3). Conclusion: There is much comfort in this. 1. Real Christians seem few (Luke xii. 32): but when there assembled they shall be a multitude that no man can number (Rev. v. 9; vii. 9). 2. Christian friends are now separated—then they shall meet to part no more (Matt. xxiv. 31; 1 Thess. iv. 17). 3. The Church seems in a degenerate state—then it shall be without spot. (*T. Manton, D.D.*) *Reunion:*—1. The exact word occurs only again in Heb. x. 25, and that gathering is typical of this. When we meet in the House of God, for prayer, praise, instruction and communion, we are practising for that other gathering, which shall be perfect. The verb, however, occurs in two other places: one is where our Lord reminds Jerusalem how He would have gathered her children together. That idea of safe keeping, cherishing under the wing of the mother, is involved in the "gathering" of the Second Advent. The other text is Mark xiii. 27, the interpretation of the text before us. 2. The text is used not as a terror but as an attraction. "We beseech you by it," as those who would not part with it for their life. The Advent, as a regathering, is full of consolation. But it implies— I. DISPERSION. There are senses in which this is tolerable. The severance of nations by dividing seas and deserts, and by the Babel judgment of divided tongues, is no affliction. It is as a type that we must read it to enter into its significance for sorrow. 1. It tells of sons and mothers parted for a lifetime by calls of duty or self-made necessities; of friends closer than brothers bidding each other a long farewell at a noisy station or a sea-washed pier; of vows of lifelong friendship broken in sudden passion; of discords which a breath would have healed; hence severance. 2. There is a dispersion of divided tongues concerning Christ in God's behalf. Men made offenders for a word; men unable to read in identical phrase some microscopic doctrine; men, kneeling in the name of one Saviour, imputing wilful blindness to one another. 3. Then the uncharitableness of individual men must be made the watchwords and heirlooms of parties and Churches. Creeds and articles must adopt the quarrel, and anathematize the deviation as a crime. So Christ's house is divided. 4. Behind and beneath all these dispersions there lurks the giant disperser, Death. Those unaffected by the other dispersions are all doomed to suffer from this. 5. But the greatest is sin. Brothers and friends may part and not part; even in this life they may be divided, and yet know that they have one home and Father. But sin divides even in its joining. Where sin is there is selfishness, and selfishness is severance. II. THE REGATHERING. To Paul, and to all whose hearts are large and deep, there was a peculiar charm in the thought of this. "I beseech you," as though no motive could be more persuasive. 1. The scene thus opened is august even to oppressiveness. Expanded from one end of heaven to the other, enhanced by multiplication of generations, till it has embraced all the living and dead who have possessed the one Divine faith which makes the communion of saints, it overwhelms and baffles the soul's gaze. 2. But we must seek to refine and decarnalize our conceptions. "There is a spiritual body," doubtless like that of the risen Jesus which entered the room whose doors were shut. We must reassure ourselves by thoughts of the possibility of a communion in which mind shall touch mind, and spirit breathe into spirit, and soul kindle soul with no cumbersome machineries or limiting measurements. 3. Even now we feel within ourselves an instinct of the regathering. There are those who profess to have the key of death, and to hold commerce with the departed. We could better believe them if we found in their supposed communications profiting or solemnity. But the instinct of reunion is there; we read it even in its follies. 4. Still more do we long and yearn in ourselves for that kind of union which can come only to the immortal. Here we meet and part with a sense of unrest which leaves us to the end hungry and desolate. To the friend of our souls we cannot say one half of what we meant to say, and that was not fully understood. Our love he read not, and our passing humours he took as a changed affection. But then friend shall meet friend in absolute oneness, knowing as known, because loved as loving. 5. The condition is "unto Him." There are many human heavens for one Divine. We picture to ourselves a future bright with earth's joys, and cloudless of earth's troubles; but have we remembered that "the light thereof" is the Lamb. The promise of the text is vocal only to the Christian. Conclusion: Make now the great decision. If we will here trifle together, live for the world, neglect Christ, mock at sin, we must look abroad for some other hope: there is none for us in the gospel. The Advent regathering is for those only who in life "have loved the appearing." (*Dean Vaughan.*) *The Advent as a motive :*—"By" is not a formula of adjuration. There would be no point in saying, "I beseech you by the day of the Lord, not to suppose that the day of the Lord is at hand." It must be taken in the sense of "on behalf of," as though he were pleading in honour of that day, that the expectation of it might not be a source of disorder in the Church. (*Prof. Jowett.*) *Caution against error :*— I. THE ERROR WHICH THE APOSTLE DISPROVES—that the day of Christ was then at hand. II. THE EFFECT WHICH THIS ERROR MIGHT PRODUCE—trouble and unsettledness of mind. This implies—1. That errors breed this disquietude. 2. That Christians should be firmly established against them. III. A REMOVAL OF THE FOUNDATION OF THIS ERROR. The brethren were not to be shaken either by spirit, by word, or by letter. (*W. Burkitt, M.A.*)

**Ver. 2. That ye be not soon shaken in mind.**—*A firm anchorage :*—There lies a maritime figure in the word "shaken." Wordsworth well paraphrases it. "In order that you may not soon be shaken off from the anchorage of your firmly settled mind, and be drifted about by winds of false doctrine, as a ship in your harbour is shaken off from its moorings by the surge of the sea." They are warned against being driven out of their ordinary state of mental composure—shaken out of their sanctified common sense. "Thrown off their balance," is what we might say; "or be troubled:" the clause has a slightly climactic force—thrown into a state of unreasoning, and frenzied confusion (Matt. xxiv. 6). (*J. Hutchison, D.D.*) *Errors concerning the Second Advent :*—I. From THE ERROR DISPROVED, observe that the time of Christ's coming must be patiently expected. Not rashly defined or determined. But is this such an error (James v. 8; 1 Pet. iv. 7; 1 Cor. x. 11; Rom. xiii. 12)? Why then should the apostle speak so vehemently against the nearness of Christ? I shall show—1. That the apostle had reason to say that the day of the Lord was at hand. (1) With respect to faith : for faith gives a kind of presence to things which are afar off (Heb. xi. 1). Therein it agrees with the light of prophecy (Rev. xx. 12). The Second Coming is as certain to faith as if He were already come (Phil. iv. 5). (2) With respect to love. Love will not account it long to endure the hardships of this present world until Christ comes to set all things to rights (Gen. xxix. 20). Faith sees the certainty of it, and love makes us hold out till the time come about. (3) As comparing time with eternity (Psa. xc. 4; 2 Pet. iii. 8). The longest time to eternity is but as a drop in the ocean. All the tediousness of the present life is but like one rainy day to an everlasting sunshine (2 Cor. iv. 17). (4) Paul speaks to particular men, whose abode in the world is not very long. Eternity and judgment are at hand, though Christ tarry long till the Church be completed (2 Pet. iii. 9). Now what is long, and afar off to the whole Church, considered in several successions of ages is short to particular persons. Christ is ready to judge at all times, though the world is not ready to be judged. The Coming of Christ is uncertain, that men in all ages might be quickened to watchfulness, and make preparation (Luke xii. 40; Matt. xxiv. 42). 2. The seducers had little reason to pervert the apostle's speech, and the apostle had good reason to confute their supposition that Christ would come in that age. (1) To inquire after the time is curiosity (Acts. i. 7). It is a great evil to pry into our Master's secrets, when we have so many revealed truths to busy our minds about. It is ill manners to open a secret letter. The practice of known duties would prevent this curiosity which tends not to edification. (2) Much more was it a sin to fix the time (Matt. xxiv. 36). (3) The fixing of the time did harm—(*a*) It drew away their minds from necessary duties. (*b*) It pleased Satan who is the author of error. (*c*) It had a tendency to shake faith in other things when their credulity was disproved by the event. (*d*) It showed a diseased mind, that they were sick of questions when they had so much wholesome food to feed upon (1 Tim. vi. 4). (*e*) It engendered strife. II. THE EFFECT THIS ERROR WAS LIKELY TO PRODUCE. Trouble and unsettledness, in which is a two-fold metaphor, the one taken from a tempest, the other from the sudden alarm of a land fight. 1. Errors breed trouble in the mind : they do not only disturb the Church's peace (Gal. v. 12), but personal tranquility (Gal. 1. 7). How?—(1) They are on unsound foundation, and can never yield solid peace. We only find soul rest in true religion; others are left to uncertainties (Jer. vi. 16). (2) Because false peace ends in trouble. Every erroneous way is comfortless eventually. False doctrine breeds anxiety, and cannot quiet conscience; but truth breeds delight (Prov. xxiv. 13, 14; Matt. xi. 28–30). 2. Christians should be so established as not to be easily shaken. (1) Let us see how this is pressed. (*a*) From the encouragement of the great hope (1 Cor. xv. 58; Acts xx. 24). (*b*) From its absolute necessity (Col. i. 23). (2) Let us inquire what is necessary to this establishment. (*a*) A clear conviction of the truth, not some fluctuating opinion about it (James i. 8; 1 Thess. v. 21; 2 Pet. iii. 16, 17; Eph. iv. 14). (*b*) A resolution to adhere to the truth. The heart must be established by grace as well as the mind soundly convinced (Heb. xiii. 9; 1 Cor. vii. 37; Acts xxi. 13). This resolution of the heart is by faith and love (Heb. iii. 12; 2 Thess. ii. 10; Eph. 17). (3) The opposite to this is inconstancy (Gal. i. 6; Matt. xi. 7; Prov. xiv. 15), of which the causes are—(*a*) Want of solid rooting in the truth (Matt. xiii. 5, 20). (*b*) Want of mortification (2 Tim. iv. 10). (*c*) A readiness of mind which disposes men to conform to their company, as the looking-glass represents every face that looks into it (Jer. xxxviii. 5). (*d*) Want of a thorough inclination to God, so that they are right only for a while or in some things (1 Kings ii. 28; Hosea vii. 8). (*e*) Want of holiness and living up to the truths we know (1 Tim. iii. 9). (*f*) Libertinism. Men think they may run from one sect to another as the wind of interest blows. They would die rather than change their religion, but think nothing of the differences among Christians when their turn is to be served. (*T. Manton, D.D.*) *Calmness in view of the Second Advent :*—Two anecdotes of two very different men well illustrate that practical combination of energetic discharge of duty with Advent expectation which these Epistles have secured to the Church. When Francis of Sales was once, after intense labour, unbending himself at a game of chess, some morbid precisian who was near, asked him what he would do if he knew that the Lord's coming was even at hand, "Finish the game," said the bishop, boldly; "for His glory I began it." General Lee wrote a striking story to his son, "Last century, in New England, a day of sudden and unaccountable gloom, known yet by tradition as "the dark day," occurred while the senate of the State was sitting. The universal impression was that doomsday had indeed come. Suddenly a well-known member stood up, "President," said he, "I propose that lights be brought in, and that we pass to the order of the day. If the Judge comes He had best find us at our duty." (*Bp. Alexander.*) **Neither by Spirit, nor by word, nor by letter, as that the day of Christ is at hand.**—*Dangers of deception :*—These are the three ways in which the Thessalonians were in danger of being deceived and so troubled. A fanatical spirit had insinuated itself, and, as in all such cases, fraud was sure to follow closely on its footsteps. I. SPIRIT. Voices had been heard in their assemblies which professed to come from those who had the gift of prophecy. These had to be tried, for they might be full of error (1 Thess. v. 21). II. WORD. Not simply any rumour that might be gaining currency, or any reckoning as to the time which men might make; nor some unwritten saying of our Lord, or oral message from the apostle; but simply ordinary teaching in the Church. It would thus seem that unscrupulous or fanatical men, getting a footing in the Church, were busy in misleading and so troubling believers. III. LETTER. "As from us," is not to be connected with all three terms, for the spirit, as of the absent Paul, could not have been feigned. The manifestation must have been present in his own person. And so, if it cannot be attached to the first, it should not be to the second. Confining it to letter it refers not to some misconstruction of Paul's former Epistle, but to actual fictitious letters. Such are hinted at in chap. iii. 17. False or fanatical brethren had made such letters current in the Thessalonian community. Nor is this so very extraordinary. Literary forgeries, meant as pious frauds, were not uncommon, and the offence, daring as it was, is somewhat softened to our view when we reflect that Paul's letters, while they had the authority, were not yet invested with all the sanctity with which we now regard them. It is quite conceivable, then, that there were some who thought they were serving a good purpose, one that Paul had himself at heart, in circulating, perhaps anonymously, as a representation of Pauline teaching, letters which, as they thought, cleared up the obscurities of his instruction. (*J. Hutchison.*) *Dissuasives against error :*—I. WAYS AND MEANS GOD HAS APPOINTED TO SETTLE CHOICE AND OPINION IN RELIGION. 1. The light of nature antecedently to external revelation will sufficiently convince us of the being of God and our dependence upon Him (Rom. i. 19, 20). For I must know there is a God, or else I cannot believe in a revelation from Him. Nature will tell us that there is a First Cause of all things, of infinite power, wisdom, and goodness, that it is reasonable that He should be served by His creatures; that He will reward or punish men as they disobey or serve Him: but how He is to be served, and how after disobedience return is possible is revealed in the Word of God. 2. The written Word shows us the true way of worshipping and pleasing God, and being accepted with Him: therefore it is a sufficient direction to us. There is enough to satisfy conscience, though not to please wanton curiosity (2 Tim. iii. 15; Psa. xix. 105). There we have many things evident by the light of nature made more clear, and that revealed which no natural light has shown. 3. The natural truths of the Word of God are evident by their own light. The supernatural truths, though above natural light are not against it, and fairly accord with principles which are naturally known, and are confirmed—(1) By antecedent testimony (John v. 39; 2 Pet. i. 19). (2) By evidence in their own frame and texture (2 Cor. iv. 2–4). (3) Subsequent evidence, that of the apostles (Acts v. 32). 4. The Word being thus stated and put into a sure record is intelligible on all necessary matters (Psa. xxv. 8). To think otherwise were blasphemy or folly. 5. Besides, the illumination of the Spirit accompanies the Word and makes it effectual (2 Cor. iv. 6; Eph. i. 17, 18; 1 Cor. ii. 14). 6. There are promises of direction to humble and sincere minds (Psa. xxv. 9; Prov. ii. 4, 5; John vii. 17; James i. 5). II. THE CHRISTIAN WHO IS THUS ESTABLISHED IS FORTIFIED AGAINST—1. Pretended revelations, "Spirit"; because:—(1) Having his mind thus settled, he may boldly defy all revelations pretended to the contrary (Gal. i. 8). Any doctrine if different from, or besides the written Word, a Christian may reject. (2) A Christian is on better terms, having the written Word, than if God dealt with him by way of revelations (2 Pet. i. 19). (3) It is not rational to expect new revelation, now the canon of faith is closed up (Heb. ii. 1, 2; Matt. xxviii. 20; John xvii. 29). (4) If any such be pretended, it must be tried by the Word (Isa. viii. 20; 1 John iv. 1). (5) They that despise ordinary means, and pretend to vision or inspiration are usually such as are given over to error as a punishment (Micah ii. 11). 2. Unwritten tradition "Word." This should not shake the mind of a settled Christian, for it has no evidence of its certainty, and would lay us open to the deceits of men, blinded by their own interests and passions; and if such tradition be produced as has unquestionable authority it must be tried by the Scripture. 3. Epistle as from us—(1) Supposititious writings which the Church in all ages has exploded, having received only those which are theirs whose names they bare. (2) False expositions. These are confuted by inspection of the context, scope of the writer, comparing of obscure places with plain and clear. (*T. Manton, D.D.*) *Spirits to be tried :*—Genuine enthusiasm is the zeal of love for Christ and for human souls, guided by the Word of God. It is a very different thing from that blind zeal which is the fire and fervour of an overheated imagination, which exalts itself above the written Word, and is more properly named fanaticism, which is not a virtue but a vice. Wesley besought his followers to shun this rock in sober faith, saying, "Give no place to a heated imagination. Do not hastily ascribe things to God. Do not easily suppose dreams, voices, impressions, visions, or revelations to be from God. They may be from Him. They may be from nature. They may be from the devil. Therefore, 'Believe not every spirit, but try the spirits, whether they be of God.' Try all things by the written Word, and let all things bow down before it."

Ver. 3. **Let no man deceive you by any means; for that day shall not come except there come a falling away first.**—*Christ and Antichrist :*—The most marked features in this passage are—I. A CARICATURE OF CHRIST ; an exact counterpart and mockery of Christ in the man of sin. The latter has, like the former—1. An apocalypse (ver. 3. *cf.* 6–8). 2. A solemn coming on the stage of human history (ver. 3). 3. An advent (ver. 9). 4. Power, signs, wonders (ver. 9). 5. Designation (ver. 4). 6. A definitely appointed season of His own (ver. 6). II. A CARICATURE OF CHRISTIANITY. As some of the leading glories of Christ are studiously travestied in the "lawless one," and described in language which forces us to think of Christ; so several of the leading features of the Christian system are powerfully travestied by imitative anti-Christianity. This latter is—1. A mystery (ver. 7), imitative of the mystery of godliness. 2. Has an energy, an inworking (ver. 7, 11, *cf.* Eph. ii. 2), imitative of the energy and inworking of the Word of God (1 Thess. ii. 12; Heb. iv. 12), of God (Phil. ii. 13; Gal. ii. 8), of the indwelling Spirit (Col. 1. 29). "He shall work in them by such an energy as that of the Holy Ghost, who witnesseth in us concerning God ; not a mere apprehension, but an inworking of error, a regeneration into the faith of *the lie* " (E. Irving). 3. Has a faith—a solemn making of an act of faith—imitative of the faith of Christians (ver. 11). 4. The words eudokein, eudokia are used of God's good pleasure in His sinless Son, and of His good-will toward men (Matt. iii. 17; xii. 18; xvii. 5; Luke xii. 32; 1 Cor. i. 21; Gal. i. 15), or the good will of Christians in holiness and acts of love (1 Thess. ii. 8, &c.). The imitative good pleasure of anti-Christianity is in unrighteousness (ver. 12). (*Bp. Alexander.*) *Signs of the Second Advent :*—I. A CAUTION : "Let no man deceive you." A man may be deceived on this momentous subject. 1. All admit that Christ will come ; but few invest it with sufficient importance. Paul thought so much about it that he made it the main subject of these Epistles, and the New Testament is full of it. Little is said about death but much about the Second Advent. 2. There were false teachers who preached that the event was at hand, and many were abandoning the ordinary duties of life, and were troubled and shaken in mind. False expectations were calculated to produce such results. What awful disturbance there would be in the mind of every unconverted man were it now infallibly anounced that Christ would come to-morrow. But Paul was writing to the Church. How, then, could they be troubled who were encouraged to look for and hasten unto that event ? It is one thing to live in quiet expectation of

Christ, and another to feel that He will come to-morrow. We are forbidden to inquire into the day and hour. That is to keep the Church in a state of calm expectation. Think of the trouble many good people would be in were it known that Christ would come directly. Who would have any relish for work. And then there are many true believers whose evidence is not always clear; how it would trouble them. How agitated we should be about the condition of our friends. To prevent these evils, the hour is unrevealed. II. THE EVENTS WHICH MUST TRANS-PIRE BEFORE CHRIST COMES. 1. " The gospel must be first preached to all nations. as a witness," as our Lord said. His object was the formation of a Church as His witness. This Church, like a pilgrim, has gone from place to place. Churches have been formed, and then after a while the candlestick.has been removed, as in the case of those of Asia. The effect of this has been the gathering of a people, genera-tion after generation, to " the general assembly of the first-born." This, too, is the work of every preacher. He does not convert congregations, but individuals. The net is cast and fish are gathered of every kind forming what we call Christendom. With this body our Lord will deal when He comes, and then the final severance will take place. But before then there will be a great moral separation, viz.—2. " A great falling away." This will be of mere professors who, by withdrawing, will leave the whole body of believers sharply defined and intact (Rev. xiii. 8). This apostasy will not be of one or two, here and there; that began in Paul's time, and has been going on ever since; but one of a great and striking character. The cause of this will be the portentous development of the mystery of iniquity which began the work one thousand eight hundred years ago, ripening into all sorts of sin, Romanism, infidelity, religious indifference and worldliness, preparing the visible Church for the reception of a great pretender who is—3. " The man of sin." Some have identified this character with the Pope in his official character but this can hardly be the case inasmuch as the Pope has never exalted himself above God, &c., (ver. 4), and has not been worshipped by the world (Rev. xiii. 8). One of the marks of the beast is that all shall worship him but the elect; but surely every non-Papist is not a true believer. Whether a given Pope may yet appear as the man of sin is another matter, but it is quite certain that one has not yet been "revealed" as such. This individual will—(1) be a " man," (2) be qualified for his work by the energy of Satan—(3) be revealed by tribulation which shall sift and purify the elect, at the same time inviting to himself all the ungodly. III. THEN WILL COME THE END (chap. i. 7–10). (*Capel Molyneux, M.A.*) *The falling away* is either that of which he had spoken to them while he was yet with them, or that, which in his own mind was inseparable from the coming of Christ which was to follow. Of what nature was this falling away? What vision of apostasy rose before him as he wrote this? Was it within or without? permanent or passing? persecution of the heathen, or the disorganization of the body of Christ itself? Was it the transition of the Church from its first love to a more secular and earthly state, or the letting loose of a spiritual world of evil, such as the apostle describes in Eph. vi. 12? So ideal a picture cannot properly be limited to any person or institution. That it is an inward, not an outward evil, that is depicted, is implied in the very name apostasy. It is not the evil of the heathen world, sunk in grossness and unconsciousness, but evil rebelling against good, conflicting with good in the spiritual world itself. And the conflict is of the same nature, though in a wider sphere, as the strife of good and evil in the heart of the indi-vidual. It is that same strife, not as represented in Rom. vii., but at a later stage when evil is fast becoming good, and the remembrance of the past itself is carrying men away from the truth. (*Prof. Jowett.*) *An evil and presumptuous one :*—The apostle speaks in the eighth verse of the revelation of " that wicked," intimating the *discovery*, which should be made of his wickedness in order to his ruin : here he speaks of his *rise*, which should be occasioned by the general apostasy; and to intimate that all sorts of false doctrines and corruptions should centre in him. I. THE NAMES OF THIS PERSON. 1. He is called " that man of sin," to denote his egregious wickedness; not only is he addicted to and practises wickedness himself, but he also promotes, countenances, and commands sin and wickedness in others. 2. And he is " the son of perdition," because he himself is devoted to certain destruction, and is the instrument of destroying many others both in soul and body. II. THE PRESUMPTION OF THIS PERSON. 1. His towering ambition. He " opposeth and exalteth himself above all that is called God, or that is worshipped." Thus he has not only opposed God's authority, and that of the civil magistrates, who are called " gods," but exalted himself above God and earthly governors, in demanding greater regard to his commands than to the commands of God or the magistrate. 2. His dreadful usurpation. "He as God sitteth in the temple of God, showing himself that he is God!" As God was in the temple of old, and worshipped there, and is in and with His Church now, so Antichrist is the usurper of God's authority in the Christian Church, and the claimer of Divine honours, for, among the most blasphemous titles, this one has been given to him, "Another God on earth!" (*T. Scott, M.A.*)    *Apostasy and Antichrist :*—I. THE GENERAL APOSTASY WHICH MUST PRECEDE CHRIST'S COMING. 1. Apostasy is any defection from that lord to whom we owe fealty. In religious matters it is defection from our right and proper Lord. The devil was an apostate (Jude 6; John viii. 44); our first parents (Rom. v. 19); their posterity (Zeph. i. 6; Isa. lix. 13). 2. The apostasy of the text was not civil, the falling away of many kingdoms from the Roman empire; but of the visible Church from its Lord. This is proved—(1) From the fact that the Thessalonians did not intermingle with State affairs. (2) From the use of the word in Christian doctrine (Luke xiii. 13). (3) Because it was expressly foretold (1 Tim. iv. 1). (4) Because those who are most concerned to maintain the notion of civil apostasy are most notorious in this defection. 3. The proper Lord of the Christian Church is Christ (Rom. xiv. 9; Eph. v. 23). 4. Apostasy from Christ is determined by two things. (1) By undermining His authority. This is done when others usurp His place without His leave, *e.g.*, superinduce a universal head of the Church which Christ never appointed. (2) By corrupting and destroying the interests of His kingdom, which is the case wherever there is a degeneration from the purity and simplicity of the gospel (2 Cor. xi. 3), such as when the faith of the gospel is turned into dead opinions and curious questions; and its worship corrupted into giving Divine honour to saints and angels and turned into a theatrical pomp of empty ceremonies; and its discipline transformed into temporal domination and carried on by sides and interests. 5. This apostasy is notable and discernible, not of a few or many in divers Churches. There have always been backsliders (1 John ii. 18, 19; iv. 3, 5); but the great apostasy is in some visible Church where these corruptions are generally received and defended. Who then are they—(1) Who usurp Christ's authority by setting up a universal head over all Christians? (2) Who revive the worship of a middle sort of powers between God and man (1 Tim. iv. 1; Col. ii. 18), and invent so many lies to defend it, when Christians should keep themselves from idols (1 John v. 21), not contented with the only Mediator (1 Tim. ii. 5; 1 Cor. viii. 5)? (3) Who plead for indulgences and the supererogatory satisfaction of saints as profitable for the remission of sins? (4) Who keep believers from reading the Scriptures when expressly enjoined to do so (John v. 39; Psa. i. 2)? (5) Who deny one part of the Lord's Supper notwithstanding His institution to the contrary (1 Cor. xi. 25, 26)? II. THE REVELATION OF ANTICHRIST as—1. "The man of sin." (1) The Jews gave this name to Antiochus (1 Macc. ii. 48, 62), and it is given to Antichrist because he is a man given up to sin eminently, and giveth excitements to sin. Now how much open sin is allowed in the Papacy their own stories tell. Histories witness that the most abominable men have occupied the Papal chair; and no man can sin at so cheap a rate when, by dividing sins into mortal and venial, and these expiated by penance, faculties, licences, dispensations, indulgences until sin is distinguished out of conscience. (2) Because he is called "the man of sin" it does not follow that he is an individual. One is often put for a society and succession of men as kings (Dan. vii. 8; Isa. x. 5; xiv. 9); so the "man of God" is put for all faithful ministers (2 Tim. iii. 17); "high priest" (Heb. ix. 25); "the king" (1 Pet. ii. 17). So one person represents that succession of men that head the revolt against Christ. 2. "The son of perdition." Wherein he is likened to Judas (John xvii. 12). The term may be explained passively as one condemned to everlasting destruction (2 Sam. xii. 5; Eph. ii. 3), or actively as bringing destruction on himself and others (Rev. ix. 11, *cf.* Heb. v. 9). Note the parallel. (1) Judas was not a stranger, but a pretended friend and apostle (Acts i. 17). Turks and infidels are enemies to Christ, but Antichrist seeks to undermine Him under a pretence of friendship. There is no mystery in open enmity (ver. 7). (2) He sold Christ for a small matter; Antichrist makes a market of religion. (3) Judas betrayed Christ with a kiss, and where is there apparently such friends of Christ as at Rome? They are ready to worship the Cross, and yet they are its enemies, because they mind earthly things. (4) Judas was a guide to those who came to take Christ, and the main work of Antichrist is to be a ringleader in persecuting for religion. (5) Judas was covetous, and England to its bitter cost knows the exactions of the Papacy. (*T. Manton, D.D.*)    *The development of Antichrist :*—

I. It BEGINS IN A FALLING AWAY—1. From the power and practice of godliness, though the profession be not changed. (1) Because this disposes to the entertainment of error. When a people that are carried with great zeal for a while, lose their affections to good, and return to a worldly life, then the bias of their hearts easily prevails against the light of their understandings. And so unsanctified men may the sooner be drawn to apostasy; they never felt the quickening virtue of faith, and were never wrought by it to the true love of God or an holy life. (2) Because if a lively Christianity had been kept up, Antichrist had never risen, and it is the way to keep him out still (Matt. xiii.). A sleepy religion and corruption of manners made way for corruption of doctrine, worship, and order (Cant. v. 2). (3) Because there is such a compliance between the nature of Antichristianism and the temper of a carnal heart; for superstition and profaneness grow both upon the same root. To prevent this falling away from a lively godliness observe two things—(a) Coldness in duties, when the will and affections grow more remiss, and the worship of God, which keepeth up the remembrance of Him, is either omitted or performed in a careless and stupid manner (Jer. ii. 32; Job xxvii. 10; Isa. xliii. 22). When you seldom think or speak of God and do not keep up a delightful communion with Him, there is a falling away. (b) Boldness in sinning. When men lose their tenderness and strictness, and the awe of God is lessened in their hearts, and they do not only sin freely in thought, but in act, have not that hatred of sin and watchfulness they had formerly, but more abandon themselves to a carnal life, they are falling off from God apace (2 Pet. ii. 20). Consider the cause of it—(a) Want of faith in God (Heb. iii. 12). (b) Want of love to God (Rev. ii. 4, 5). (c) Want of a due sense of the world to come (Heb x. 39). (d) Love of the present world (2 Tim. iv. 10; vi. 10; iii. 4). 2. From a true religion to a false, which may be done two ways. (1) Out of weakness of mind as those do who were never well grounded in the truth (Eph. iv. 14; 2 Pet. iii. 16). Therefore we need to be established; but the forsaking of a truth we were bred in usually comes from some falseness of heart. Some errors are so contrary to the new nature, that they discern them by the unction (1 John ii. 20). (2) Out of vile affection, when they forsake the truth for the advantages of a fleshly, worldly life, some places to be gotten by it, &c., and as the whore of Babylon hath a golden cup, riches, and preferments, wherewith it inviteth its proselytes. Now these are worse than the former, for they sell the birthright (Heb. xii. 16). O Christians! take heed to yourselves. Apostasy brought Antichrist into the Church. Let it not bring him back again into the land, or into your hearts. II. The next step is THE MAN OF SIN. As the first apostasy of Adam and Eve brought sin into the world, so this great apostasy brought in a deluge of sin into the Church, and defiled the holy society which Christ had gathered out of the world. Idolatry is often called adultery or fornication; spiritual uncleanness disposeth to bodily, and bodily to spiritual. Usually a corrupt state of religion and corrupt manners go together; otherwise the dance and the fiddle would not suit. The world cannot lie quiet in a course of sin, if there be not some libertine, atheistical doctrine, and carnal worship to countenance it (Rev. xi. 10). III. The man of sin is also THE SON OF PERDITION. I. Actively. False religions strangely efferate the mind (Jude 11; Hosea v. 2). Men think no cruelty nor dishonesty unlawful which serveth to promote the interests of their sect, and lose all charity to those that are not of their way. 2. Passively, shall be destroyed. Sometimes grievous judgments come in this world for the corruptions of religion; but in the world to come, dreadful is the end of apostates (2 Pet. ii. 20, 21). (*Ibid.*) *The man of sin:*—Mark—I. THAT MORAL EVIL ON EARTH IS REPRESENTED IN HUMAN NATURE. Sin is connected with man in contradistinction to—1. Abstract systems. 2. Super-earthly sinners. II. THAT IT IS OFTEN FOUND USURPING THE PREROGATIVES of God, such as—1. Proprietorship in human life. 2. The taking away of human life. 3. Dominion over conscience. 4. The absolving from sin. 5. Infallibility of character. III. THAT IT IS SUBJECT TO RESTRAINT IN THIS WORLD, arising from—1. Civil law. 2. Social intelligence. 3. The monition of conscience. 4. Physical inability. IV. THAT IT IS ASSOCIATED WITH THE MYSTERIOUS (ver. 7). Evil is mysterious on account of—1. The darkness that enfolds its introduction. 2. The mask under which it works. 3. Its wonderful results. V. THAT IT IS SATANIC IN ITS OPERATIONS (ver. 9). These operations are—1. Sensuous. 2. Marvellous. 3. Deceptive. 4. Unrighteous. 5. Destructive. VI. THAT IT IS DESTINED TO BE DESTROYED BY THE AGENCY OF CHRIST. 1. By His Word. 2. By His manifestation. (*D. Thomas, D.D.*) *Judas a type of the Papacy:*—The term "son of perdition" occurs but once elsewhere, and that on our

Lord's lips in reference to Judas. The parallel between His character and conduct and the Papacy—not any individual Pope, but the whole system—is most close. We conceive the Papacy to be here intended, because the features of type and prophecy here delineated fit no other subject. I. JUDAS AND THE BISHOPS OF ROME ALIKE WERE MINISTERS—OFFICIAL MEN IN THE CHURCH. The antiquity of the Church of Rome, and the dignity, authority, and vast influence of its bishops is undisputed. II. BOTH BETRAYED THE TRUST REPOSED IN THEM. How fearfully Judas did this we all know ; and has not the Papacy? The trust committed to it was the "mystery of godliness," the maintenance of the gospel in its purity and simplicity, the care of Christ's flock, example not lordship. How was this trust fulfilled by successive bishops of Rome? They gradually began to seek for ascendancy, to accommodate the Scriptures to their own purpose, to vitiate the purity and simplicity of the gospel by tradition, ecclesiastical decisions, fables, and legends as of Divine authority, to set themselves more aloft, and to set the Saviour aside, usurping His pre-eminence by assuming the title of His vicars, as though He were not with His Church always. III. BOTH BETRAYED HIM INTO THE HANDS OF HIS ENEMIES TO DEATH. Judas literally, the Papacy in the persons of His persecuted representatives. Judas betrayed Christ into the hands of the civil power, and has not the wretched policy of Rome ever been to screen its own cowardice and heartlessness behind the pretended power of civil authority, to whom her victims after sham trials have been handed over for death? IV. BOTH BETRAYED THE LORD WITH A KISS. The Papacy makes a vain pretence of showing special homage to Christ. Witness its caricature of Christ's example when the Pope washes the feet of a few selected beggars, and the spurious honour given to Christ's dignity by the mediatorship of Mary and the Saints. V. BOTH BETRAYED THE LORD FOR MONEY. The covetousness of Judas gives point to the apostolic injunction to ministers not to be lovers of filthy lucre ; but history is witness that the Papacy from the first has been given to filthy lucre. The requirements and ordinances which Rome has substituted for the ordinances of the gospel have been so many channels for wealth to flow into her treasury. Almost as soon as the Papacy rose on the ruins of the Pagan Empire she imposed the impious tax known as Peter's pence. But this is not all. Merchandize is made of Christ. Rome professes that her priests, in the mass, transubstantiate the wafer into Christ, and the mass is offered for the sins of men, for money ; so that the priests must be paid as Judas for offering up the Lord Incarnate. And then she sells indulgences, deliverances from penance, prayers, &c., making salvation a matter of money. VI. BOTH BETRAY CHRIST AT THE INSTIGATION OF SATAN. We could not account for the structure of the Papacy except on this hypothesis. 1. If you trace back the policy of Satan to the beginning you find it to be threefold. (1) It was to blot out the idea of God. Hence we find no idolatry on the part of the ungodly before the flood. (2) Failing, then, to set aside religion altogether he corrupted it. No sooner was there knowledge of the true God than he introduced gods many ; side by side with prophets, miracles, the Word of God, he set up soothsayers, magic, lying oracles and legends. (3) When Christianity was set up, and his pagan throne in Rome overthrown, he set up his Papal throne, and repeopled the deserted pantheon with idols for Christians to worship. So exactly has this come to pass that there is scarcely a pagan ceremony that has not its shadow in Popery, and its mission abroad is to paganize Christianity rather than to Christianize paganism. 2. Note the satanic characteristics of the Papacy. (1) There is no doubt that Satan has much to do with the lying wonders of heathenism, and the strange appearances of power with which Rome caricatures the miracles of Christ. Did not the Pope know that the winking picture which he sent crowns to adorn, and which he endorsed as a miracle, was a most barefaced imposture? (2) Satan fell by pride, and we need scarcely to be reminded of the awful arrogance of the Papacy. Look at the servile homage the Pope receives when men kiss his feet ; and when on the day of his installation he is borne on the shoulders of bishops, and thrice adored ; and when on the pontifical throne he is placed on the high altar where the Divine wafer rests, thus "sitting in the temple of God, shewing himself as if he were God and is worshipped." VII. BOTH FULFIL SCRIPTURE AND ACCOMPLISH WHAT GOD IN HIS DETERMINATE COUNSEL AND FOREKNOWLEDGE DECLARED SHOULD BE DONE. How these and other instances in which the wrath of man praises God is a mystery ; but the existence of such a system of despotism, delusion, superstition, and cruelty, would be an intolerable burden on any other hypothesis. But when we see it all foretold in revelation, and that it shall at last serve to magnify Christ, and tend to the glorification of His Church, we bow submissive and tarry the Lord's time. VIII. BOTH ARE BRANDED "THE SON OF PERDITION," BECAUSE OF THEIR FEARFUL DOOM (ver. 8). (*Canon Stowell.*)

Ver. 4. **Who opposeth and exalteth Himself above all that is called God?—** *Antichrist :*—I. As OPPOSITE TO CHRIST. Christ is the true Head and Lord of the Church (Acts x. 36). That which is most remarkable in Christ, and should be in all His followers, is humility (Matt. xx. 28) ; 2 Cor. viii. 9). This is the grace recommended to His disciples (Matt. xi. 29) ; not especially to His ministers (Matt. xx. 25, 26 ; Luke xxii. 26). Dominion is allowed in the civil state, for there it is necessary ; but pre-eminence is the bane of the Church (1 John 9). The apostles everywhere disclaim lordship (2 Cor. i. 24 ; 1 Pet. v. 31) ; and if they would not assume lordship, who may ? Now in the Pope pride is conspicuous. See his progress : from the chief presbyter, a bishop over many presbyters in the same city ; then a metropolitan over many bishops in one province ; then a patriarch over many provinces ; then universal bishop ; then the only shepherd and bishop, and others but his substitutes. But yet exalting himself farther, he challengeth all power in heaven and earth. And the like is practised by his followers. From private priests they grow up into some prelature, as archdeacons, deans ; then a bishopric ; then a better and richer ; then archbishops, cardinals ; then pope. II. THE INSTANCES OF HIS PRIDE. 1. His exalting himself above all human powers. (1) "That which is called God," *i.e.*, magistrates, &c. (Psa. lxxvii. 1, 6 ; *cf.* John x. 34, 35). God hath clothed such with His honour, so far as He has put His name upon them, as being His vicegerents. Even this Antichrist exalts himself. (2) "Or is worshipped." The Greek is whatever is held in the highest degree of reverence, whatever is august or illustrious, as the Emperors of Rome were called Sebastoi (Acts xxv. 21). Antichrist exalts himself not only over magistrates but kings and emperors ; no less than twenty have been trampled upon by the Pope. 2. His usurpation of Divine honours. (1) The usurpation itself, "He sitteth as God," &c. (1 Cor. iii. 16, 17). The temple of God is the Church (2 Cor. vi. 16). But is the Church of Rome the Church of Christ? It was before it was perverted, and retains some relic of a Church, mangled as it is. In this temple of God the Pope *sits*, it is his *sedes*, cathedral, seat, whereas other princes are said to reign. And, again, he sits as God incarnate, for Christ is the true Lord of the Church ; his name is not Antitheos, but Antichristos ; not one who invades the properties of the Supreme, but those of the Mediator—(*a*) By usurping the titles of Christ, as Husband of the Church ; Head of the Church ; Chief Pastor (Pet. v. 4) ; *pontifex maximus*, greatest High Priest (Heb. iii. 1 ; iv. 14) ; so His vicar-general upon earth, whereas the ancient Church gave this to the Holy Ghost. (*b*) By usurping the thing implied in the titles—authority over the Church, which is due alone to God incarnate. Supreme authority may be considered as to, First, the claim and right pretended. By virtue of his office in the temple of God he claims the same power as Christ has, which is fourfold. (i.) An unlimited power over things in heaven and earth. This was given to Christ (Matt. xxviii. 18), and the Pope as his vicar challenges it ; but to set up himself as a vice-god without warrant is rebellion against Christ. (ii.) Universal headship and supremacy over all the Churches of Christ. This is Christ's right, and whoever challenges it sits as God in His temple. To exercise this power is impossible, and to claim it is sacrilegious, for none is fit for it but such as is God as well as man. (iii.) Absolute authority so as to be above control. Such a sovereignty belongs to none but God (Job ix. 12), yet the Pope is said to be above all law. (iv.) Infallibility and freedom from error, which is the sole property of God ; what blasphemy to attribute it to man ! Second, as to the exercise, there are two acts of supreme authority : Legislation, which is the peculiar and incommunicable property of Christ (Isa. xxxiii. 22 ; James iv. 12), they, therefore, who make laws to bind the conscience invade Christ's sovereignty. Judgment. The Pope exercises an authority no less than Divine when he absolves man from his duty to God, or the penalty which sin has made due, which he does by dispensation and by indulgence. Bellarmine says that Christ has given Peter and his successors a power to make sin to be no sin, and that "if the Pope should err in forbidding virtues and commanding vices, the Church were bound to believe vices to be good and virtues evil." And as to indulgences, to pardon sin before it is committed is to give licence to sin. (2) The degree of this usurpation, " showing himself that he is God" : that is meant not of what he professes in word, but what he doth in deed. He shows himself that he is God. (*a*) By accepting Antichrist's disciples, who call him our Lord God the Pope, and who say that he has the same tribunal with Christ, that from him no appeals are to be made even to God, that his words *ex cathedra* are equal to Scripture, and much more.   Now to accept these flatteries is to show himself that he is God. (*b*) By weilding Divine prerogatives, arrogating the right to be lord of conscience, to determine what is to be believed, and pardoning sins.   III. USES : 1. To give a clear discovery where to find Antichrist : every tittle of this is fulfilled in the bishop of Rome.   2. To show us how things should be carried in the true and reformed Christianity.   (1) With such meekness that our religion may be known to be that of the Crucified.   Pride and ambition have been the cause of all the disorders of the Church.   (2) With obedience to magistrates, which is the opposite of Antichristianity (Rom. xiii. 1 ; 1 Pet. ii. 13 ; 2 Pet. ii. 10).   (3) What a wickedness it is to usurp Divine honours (Acts iii. 12).   (*T. Manton, D.D.*)

Vers. 6, 7. **And now ye know what withholdeth.**—*The restraining power and its withdrawal :*—I. WHAT IS THIS RESTRAINING POWER?   1. The explanation, now so difficult, was no difficulty to the Thessalonians.   They knew what it was ; and the Church of the first three centuries said without hesitation that it was the Roman Empire.   2. History has taught us the literal incorrectness of this, for the Roman Empire has passed away, and it is to play with language to regard it as living on in the German or Austrian Empires.   This fact modified the interpretation of the later fathers, who regarded it as the restraining discipline of Divine order ; and Christian thinkers are now coming to regard it as the regulated social order, that spirit of obedience to law which is the direct antagonist to the spirit of lawlessness which was embodied in ancient Rome ; but this spirit is sustained by the working of the Spirit of God.   3. As a matter of fact the spirit of religion has been in all ages the restraining influence.   Man is naturally attracted to lawlessness. Within Christian nations there have been the elements of destruction, but they have been held in check in three ways.   (1) Christianity has created and sustained a public opinion which has supported law and is antagonistic to lawlessness.   (2) It has called the conscience in to the support of constituted order because it has taught men that that order has supernatural sanction.   (3) It has created and administered a healthy discipline and taught men that obedience to the law of righteousness is the true regulation of life.   For fifteen hundred years politicians have been ready to recognize this restraining influence.   4. By God's will there are two great co-ordinate authorities, the civil and the ecclesiastical ; He would have these work in their own sphere, the Church not invading the province of the State, and *vice versa*. And the Church has thus gone on in union with the State exercising its restraints. II. WHAT IS MEANT BY THIS POWER BEING TAKEN OUT OF THE WAY ?   I believe it to be that crisis in our race which in the Apocalypse is called the Fall of Babylon—the collapse of the ecclesiastical influence in politics.   1. Babylon is represented as a harlot, a term distinctly applied in the Old Testament, not to heathenism, but to a faithless Church.   And so in the New Testament it is only the professed Church that can fall into that depth of iniquity.   2. Turn to Rev. xvii. and Babylon is riding, controlling, guiding a scarlet-coloured beast.   Afterwards there is the bitterest antagonism, and the beast and ten kings rise up against the apostate Babylon and treat her shamefully.   3. Now go back to mediæval Europe, and the one arresting political feature is the Church.   The Pope is virtually king of kings and lord of lords.   In those days priests were judges, ecclesiastics, politicians, and the mystic woman is seen riding on the beast—the Church at least lending her authority to the maintenance of civil order.   But her position was full of danger.   It was the Master's temptation to world empire over again.   Christendom failed where the Master won, and sought to realize a true conception by false means.   She lost her spirituality and fell under the power of a mere secular ecclesiasticism.   Contrast the Church of the Middle Ages with that of the first.   4. You cannot be surprised at people identifying Babylon with the Papacy, for the description of the apostle almost necessarily leads us to think of Rome.   The spirit that rules the Roman see is of the earth earthy.   Its policy is ruled not so much by principle as by the intricacies of human politics, and it is ever swayed by the three sad spirits that are predicted of mystic Babylon—ambition, covetousness, and luxury.   The ideal of Ultramontanism, that the Church on earth is a perfect entity is true, but its sin is that it is the material realization of a conception that is emphatically spiritual.   5. What is the effect?   This, that as the claims of the ecclesiastical spirit have become more and more intense, the nations of the world have revolted against the power with which for centuries they have been in closest alliance.   Is not this the case in

France, Germany, Belgium, and even Spain? Where can we find a country whose Church gives obedience to the Papacy that is not in conflict with the Papacy? 6. But this is not only with the Churches that own obedience to Rome. What about the great Eastern churches who have delivered up so much of their power to the Czar? What about our own? Is truth never compromised for expediency? Nay, the spirit of corruption has permeated Christendom, and our position is one of humiliation before God. And now mark the movements that are going on. Society and civilization for fifteen hundred years have had a Christian basis, but both are being constructed on a secular basis (See Lecky's chapter on " the Advance of Secularizing Politics"). Conclusion: What then is our position? 1. We must recognize the withdrawal of this restraining influence of civilization, and in it a warning of the approaching Advent. Christ may see fit to delay—but " Be ye ready." 2. We should do all that in us lies to perpetuate the ministry and the restraining power that we may lengthen the days of opportunity for the race. (*Canon Body.*)    *Restraints removed :*—Since a body falls to the ground in consequence of the earth's attraction on each of its molecules, it follows that, everything else being the same, all bodies, great and small, light and heavy, ought to fall with equal rapidity, and a lump of sand without cohesion should, during its fall, retain its original form as perfectly as if it were compact stone. The fact that a stone falls more rapidly than a feather is due solely to the unequal resistances opposed by the air to the descent of these bodies. The resistance opposed by the air to falling bodies is especially remarkable in the case of falling liquids. The Staubbach in Switzerland is a good illustration. An immense mass of water is seen falling over a high precipice, but before reaching the bottom it is shattered by the air into the finest mist. In a vacuum, however, liquids fall, like solids, without separation of their molecules. The resistance opposed by the customs and ethics of society is the reason why many men are deterred in a rapid fall into ruin. Take away all the resistance which etiquette, conventional morality, philanthropy and religion, offer to the downfall of men, and, like things in a vacuum, how sadly fast the descent would become. Many men in respectable elevation owe their adventitious position to the happy accident of strong resistance offered to their fall by the circumstances and influences surrounding. (*Prof. Ganot.*)

Ver. 7. **For the mystery of iniquity doth already work.**—*Lawlessness and the lawless one :*—St. Paul has been telling the Thessalonians that there is much to be done in the world before things will be ripe for the Advent of our Lord Jesus Christ. This was the caution needed by the Church in those times; for, in the light of a new revelation—one of the foundation truths of which was the Second Advent of the Redeemer to judge both the dead and the living, and with the charge ever ringing in their ears to watch and pray, lest, coming suddenly, He should find them sleeping, it was natural that they should ask themselves, "Why should we take the trouble of living with any interest or earnestness the old life of time, when, at any moment, all may be interrupted and scattered to the winds by the sign of the Son of Man in heaven, to close, on the instant, the things that are seen and temporal, and to introduce, amid all kinds of fearful surprises, new heavens and a new earth?" Our danger is from quite a different quarter. Our difficulty lies not in not making enough of the life of time, but in preventing it from filling the whole field of our vision. On this very account there is something doubly striking in the scene here presented—of a Church restless and feverish in anticipation of the Advent. It shows us how far we have fallen from original Christianity if we are suffering in ourselves, under the influences of the infidel talk of the day, any doubt of the fact itself as we rehearse it day by day—"From thence He shall come again to judge the quick and the dead." I. LAWLESSNESS WILL PRECEDE IT. On this subject St. Paul leaves no room for doubt. He speaks of a certain particular growth and spirit of evil which must have full scope and play before the Advent. Nor does he leave us in any uncertainty as to the direction in which we must look for the rise of that state of things which will bring down upon itself God's latest, surest, and direst judgment. He selects for it a particular name, not one of the common names for sin in the Scripture, but a name which he only uses twice or thrice in all his writings, and which has always a very definite and precise meaning. Our English version renders this word in one verse as "iniquity," and in the next verse "the wicked one;" but in the original the word is substantially the same in both verses—in the one "the mystery of lawlessness doth already work;" and, in the other, "then shall the lawless one be revealed." St. Paul's statement is that already, when he was writing this letter eighteen hundred years ago, there was at work in the world, if not in some degree even in the Church, a spirit of lawlessness, which was, however, kept in check by some definite impediment, which he had evidently explained by word of mouth to the privileged Thessalonians.  He, perhaps, does not refer to the strength of civil and national government, as it was then exhibited in the great Roman Empire, as exercising a salutary, though rough, control over the tendencies of fallen nature toward insubordination and anarchy; but, he distinctly says, there will come a time when the controlling power will be weakened or withdrawn, and then lawlessness will come to the surface and front of the world; and will set up its own law, which shall be that of menace, intimidation, and violence ; or else these same things under more numerous and more subtle nomenclatures, and in full-blown insolence, shall bring matters to that pass, that nothing less than the intervention and interposition of the Divine Lord and Judge can restore tranquility and harmony to the dislocated and disorganized earth.  II. The lawless will then be revealed.  St. Paul seems to prepare us, in passing from lawlessness to the lawless one, for a sort of incarnation of lawlessness—principle, power, or person, sitting, as it were, in the very temple of God, "showing himself that he is God," and yet, in reality, deriving from Satan all "the powers and signs of lying wonders" by which he deludes the unhappy victims who are not fortified and pre-occupied by the devout love of the truth.  Why should it be a thing incredible with you that the Empire of Unrule shall at last have a personal head in whom the final discomfiture by the Advent of the great Lord shall manifest itself so that "he who runs may read"?  But the thought profitable to us all is this—"lawlessness" is the predicted characteristic of the last age.  May I not ask, Is it not now abroad on the Continent of Europe?  Is it not abroad in one integral portion of what we still fondly term "the United Kingdom"?  Is it not abroad in the family and the Church—in the workshop and the study—in the literature of a "science falsely so-called"—and in the lurking-places of political fanatics, who "count not their lives dear to them" if they can only but embitter an existence or topple down a throne?  It is working everywhere with ingenious industry among the time-honoured institutions of society itself.  Frightful outbreaks of lawlessness have startled us again and again, until they have almost ceased to startle.  Soon the newspaper will be flat and dull which records not one of them—assassinations and attempted assassinations of rulers crowned and uncrowned, despotic, constitutional, or democratic—it matters not.  "The foundations of the earth are indeed out of course."  The reign of lawlessness is begun, though a few years, or a few tens of years, may yet intervene before the actual unveiling of the lawless one.  (*Dean Vaughan.*)    *The mystery of iniquity :*—I. The "mystery of iniquity" is the power unseen, unknown except by its effects, which is ever working in the world for evil—working against the law and will of God, corrupting what has been well done and well begun by man, causing misery in the natural world in all that man has to do with, through the mischief which it works in the moral and spiritual world, in the heart and soul of men.  1. Try to trace evil back to its origin, and you soon see that your search is vain.  God did not create this to be the bane of His handiwork.  Are we then to conclude that evil is an independent being, self-subsisting, with a will and deadly energy of its own?  2. Here, then, is part of the "mystery of iniquity"; and another part is the mystery of its working.  See how we are born to evil, as surely as the sparks fly upward. Alongside the primeval blessing, "Increase and multiply," there has sprung up a countervailing curse on all our race in the increase and multiplication of sin.  The seeds of evil are propagated from parent to child, each little one bringing into the world as his spiritual inheritance a propensity to evil, which mingles with all his propensities to good—a fresh contribution to the already abundant growth of evil; a mere germ at first, but unfolding speedily, growing with the growth of the child as the worm in the bud, and strengthening beyond his strength.  3. So active, so subtle, so successful, is the "mystery of iniquity" in its working; and what is it in its consequences?  (Gen. iii. 17; Rom. v. 12).  How mysterious are the chastisements which fall upon us!  We may be sure our sin will find us out; though it be long, yet it will not tarry.  Still more mysterious is the working out of the consequences of the parent's sin upon the children, perhaps even unto the third and fourth generations.  The children suffer in body—they are a prey to the same virulent hereditary disease, they drag a blighted existence; or their minds are left untrained, unguarded, a seed-plot for every sinful thought that may alight upon them; they are left to drudge in indigence.  II. Great, therefore, without doubt, is the "mystery of iniquity"; but, thanks be to God, still greater, infinitely greater, is the "mystery of godliness" — the secret, unseen, unmeasured power which lies in the inspiration, guidance, comfort of His good Spirit, which is within us all, and is freely, abundantly poured out on all who truly seek it. Already it has bruised the serpent's head, it has shown us the way by which we may avoid the fascination of its basilisk eyes, and by which, even when it has fastened its fangs upon us, we may recover from its deadly sting. (*W. G. Humphrey, B.D.*) *The mystery of iniquity :*—In the former Epistle St. Paul wrote in such vigorous language about the approach of the Second Advent that the Christians had imbibed a stronger impression than he had intended. This he now corrects by the prophecy of the text. I. THE MYSTERY OF INIQUITY. 1. Its characteristics. (1) It is a mystery, something whose approaches are not open as those of a fair antagonist, but subtle and secret. The term is with two exceptions used in a good sense of some part of the hidden purposes of God's love, long concealed, but at length revealed. Thus we read of "the wisdom of God is a mystery "—the "mysteries of the kingdom "—" the mystery of godliness," &c. When, therefore, we find a word so consecrated to the deep things of God here applied to a principle of evil we are prepared for something extraordinarily dark and perplexing. This at once proves that the prophecy cannot apply to Mohammedanism, heathenism, or infidelity, or any avowed enemy of God's truth. (2) It is an iniquitous principle, and is expressly referred to Satan. It is not the contrivance of man (ver. 9). (3) It springs out of the bosom of the Church, and its workings are found within the precincts of that Church (ver. 4). 2. Trace the working of this fearful system. (1) In primitive times the Church was persecuted—who would have believed that in a brief lapse of time the Church herself should become a bloody persecutor? What could have effected such a frightful change but the working of Satan? (2) For what did the primitive Church endure affliction? It was because they abhorred idolatry. Who, then, would have believed it possible that the children of the martyrs would worship the Virgin Mary instead of Diana, and St. Catherine, St. Agnes, &c., instead of the Muses and the Graces? What but the "mystery of iniquity" could have accomplished this? (3) Take the stupendous miracles wrought by her first founders; miracles so unquestionable that none ventured to impugn them. How shall their credibility be assailed? By questioning or denying them? No; by base imitation and the multiplication of spurious miracles and lying wonders (ver. 9). As surely as pure Christianity is founded on true miracles, so surely is the whole superstructure of the mystery of iniquity raised upon false ones. 3. The deepest scheme of Satan's malignity is that he has worked the machinery of the Church against herself, and availed himself of Divine ordinances and spiritual institutions, as so many channels of destruction to souls. It is true that there are some parts of the Christian machinery that Satan never attempts to use if he can avoid it. (1) Take, *e.g.*, the Holy Scriptures. Wherever the mystery is fully developed the Word of God is withheld from the people. In Protestant countries, where the popular voice calls for the Bible, the priests are ashamed to withhold it, and there Satan draws weapons against the truth even from Scripture itself. (2) So with preaching; that is suppressed wherever the mystery fully works. But if men will preach, then even this shall be made a proclamation of error, and monks and friars shall publish the merits of saints, &c., instead of the merits of Christ, and their ministry shall arouse a dormant Church to deeds of blood. (3) But take the Christian ministry—how simple its origin and obvious its Scriptural duties. And what has Satan made of it? He has transformed the preaching, teaching, praying servant of the Church into an arrogant, sacrificing order with mysterious powers inventing the mystery of the confessional. Of all the transformation of the mystery that of priestcraft is the worst. (4) Nor have the sacraments escaped. To the simple element of water in Baptism superstition has added oil, and even spittle, and divers ceremonies and exorcisms, and has attached to the mere performance of the office necessary grace making it the instrument of regeneration, substituting the outward form for the inward power. But of how much further corruption has the other sacrament been the subject? What so simple and touching as its primitive institution? Could it have been believed possible to convert it into the Roman mass, with its denial of the cup and consequent destruction of communion, its consecrated wafer, said to contain the body, blood, &c., of Christ, its pompous ceremonial and idolatrous worship? What but Satanic working could have produced so deplorable a defection from truth? II. THE PERIOD OF ITS DEVELOPMENT. 1. The Evangelical prophet affirms that this mystery did already work; its ambitious purposes restrained by the dominance of the Imperial power. Yet it worked—it diffused itself through the Christian Churches as a baneful principle, corrupting the faith of some and the practice of others, at once introducing Judaizing teachers and heathen vices preparing the way for the successful corruption of the great apostasy " when he that now letteth shall be taken out of the way." The seeds of every corrupt principle and false doctrine, which has since disturbed and divided the Church, were sown by the great enemy under the very eyes of the apostles. 2. We must content ourselves with a birds-eye view of the rise and progress of this baneful power, observing its marvellous tenacity of life under the most adverse circumstances. (1) The conversion of Constantine closed the Pagan dynasty of Rome, and while this event seemed to favour the progress of the gospel it opened the door for the aggrandization of the priesthood, which ultimately led to the supremacy of the Bishop of Rome. (2) Scarcely had the man of sin been well seated on the eminence which marked him out as Antichrist than the Northern barbarians swept all before them in Europe, but amidst the general wreck the Popedom survives and converts the invaders to its creed. (3) Then arose Mohammedanism, which paralyzed the Eastern Church and leaves Rome without a rival worthy of the name. (4) The dark ages succeed, and the mystery reigns undisturbed during a period of spiritual and intellectual stagnation. (5) But soon a formidable enemy appears in Luther, and men fondly hoped that the reign of Antichrist was at an end. Sad delusion! Loyola appeared in the conflict, and luxurious Rome became ascetic and missionary, and won abroad what it had lost at home. (6) Time rolls on. Protestantism becomes lukewarm and worldly-minded; it makes no conquests, and the ancient mystery undermines its influence. Suddenly a new enemy appears in revolutionary and atheistic France, and Romanism seems to have received its death-blow. Not so; within half a century of her destruction the Archbishop of Paris announces the exhibition of a drop of the Saviour's blood and a drop of the Virgin's milk. (7) Never since the Reformation has this mystery pursued its war against light and liberty more rigorously than it has recently. III. How AND WHEN SHALL IT BE SUBDUED AND DESTROYED? Not until the Saviour's Advent (ver. 8). Some vainly hope that its overthrow will be accomplished by the cultivation of the human intellect and the diffusion of secular knowledge. Why then did not the talent and philosophy of atheistical France accomplish this? Have we forgotten that that dark Jesuit fraternity has embraced some of the most learned and intelligent of men. What then is to be done? 1. Let every man look to his own soul and pray to be preserved from the working of this mystery. 2. Let all true Protestants combine in spirit and effort to uphold the only one system which can effectually grapple with the system of iniquity. (*Dean Close.*)        *The mystery of iniquity :*—I. THE ACTUAL NATURE OF SIN : " Iniquity." The new revision will prove somewhat clearer than the old version upon this passage. 1. A crime which must be reckoned according to fixed law. The word is "lawlessness." So "iniquity" means inequality, or that which is not up to the standard. 2. A crime which is inherent in personal free-will. "That wicked" is the lawless one : a person, not a community. 3. A crime which is the vitiating force of our humanity : "already." It poisons and corrupts the age. II. THE INEXPLICABLE PECULIARITIES OF SIN. "Mystery of iniquity." This verse need not be wasted on the Pope; all sin is Antichrist (1 John iv. 3). 1. Its origin. We found it in the universe we entered : where did it come from? 2. Its power. It crushes barriers of the mightiest resistance. 3. Its omnipresence. It urges its way in at our purest moments. 4. Its gloom. It shadows every life and every age it touches. III. THE TREMENDOUS ACTIVITY OF SIN : "Doth work." The verb is the one which gives us our word "energy." 1. Perpetuating itself. No effort needed to keep it alive. 2. Propagating itself. Myriads of new shoots and species every year. 3. Intensifying itself. Malignity of spirit in old poisonous plants; greater responsibility comes from greater light in this age of ours. A proper consideration of this text will throw illumination upon several others in the Bible : 1. "This abominable thing that I hate" (Jer. xliv. 4). Sin is the one element of disturbance. 2. "The plowing of the wicked is sin" (Prov. xxi. 4). The warmth of even honest industry quickens poison in the blood. 3. "The ways of death" (Prov. xiv. 12). All sin in the system is absolutely fatal; it works. 4. "The latter end is worse" (2 Peter ii. 20). Relapses find men weaker to contend with corruption. 5. "There is no hope : no" (Jer. ii. 26). Sinners are positively helpless. 6. "A falling away first" (ver. 3). Things in the world are going to grow worse before they are better. 7. "Come, Lord Jesus." The whole cure is on the way (ver. 8; Rev. xxii. 20). (*C. S. Robinson, D.D.*)        *The mystery of godliness and the mystery of iniquity :*—I. THE MYSTERY OF GODLINESS is a mystery of—1. Light. (1) Its author is "the light that lighteth every man that cometh into the world." In the character, life, death, resurrection of

Christ you will find no shade of what is false or insincere. (2) So with His revelation. If it be dark it is with excess of splendour; but throughout there is an utter absence of unreality. (3) No man can understand it but he who has been made sincere and true by the Spirit of God. "The light shineth in darkness, but the darkness comprehendeth it not." But there is light within when the veil is removed from the heart, and the light that is "in the face of Jesus Christ" beams upon the soul. 2. Love. (1) It springs from a love that cannot be guaged, and exhibits a love that cannot be spanned. "Herein is love." The mystery of mysteries is that God "spared not His own Son," &c. (2) The love of Jesus is past finding out. "Greater love hath no man than this," &c. Therefore St. Paul prayed that the Ephesians might "know the love of Christ that passeth knowledge." (3) Christ's whole religion is a religion of love. "The love of Christ constraineth us." "Love one another." 3. Wisdom. (1) Christ is "the wisdom of God," and "in Him are hid all the treasures of wisdom and knowledge." (2) His religion is the most exquisite contrivance, and exhibits the most perfect adaptation to accomplish the purpose of its Author. How wondrous the wisdom that has brought the sinful creature back into fellowship and favour with the Holy Creator. 4. Holiness. Its grand end and aim is to accomplish holiness in the redeemed; hence it is emphatically the mystery of godliness. "Be ye holy for I am holy." II. THE MYSTERY OF INIQUITY is a mystery of—1. Darkness. Romanism is a perversion of the truth. It has a show and mask of retaining the truth, but only to make it subservient to its dark purposes; so that there is not a single Divine truth in the whole compass of Christianity which has not its parallel caricature. Thus if the wondrous transparency and purity of the "mystery of godliness" is an evidence of its Divine derivation, the wondrous "deceivableness of unrighteousness" in the "mystery of iniquity" is an evidence of its derivation from the prince of darkness. Truth must be from above, and error and falsehood from beneath. 2. Despotism and oppression. The object of the whole economy of Popery is the exaltation of the priesthood. The mysterious leaven which was working in the apostle's day, and ultimately produced this was—(1) On the part of the laity, that carnal mind which loves to indulge its pleasures and passions while it wants the conscience quiet. (2) On the part of the clergy the leaven was a love of power and aggrandisement, that mighty principle that cast down angels from heaven, and our first parents from paradise. So Rome has distorted the mystery of godliness so as largely to obscure its loving aspect. Jesus, instead of being the Mediator, requires to be propitiated. Man is enslaved by means of a sacerdotal system that makes him continually seeking a salvation but never finding it; continually working out a salvation he can never accomplish, hanging in the scales of doubt and vibrating between fear and hope. Thus man is kept submissive under his taskmasters; and inasmuch as Rome teaches that sins are never fully forgiven in this life, its devotees are kept in bondage to their latest breath. According to the principles of Rome a man should give himself up to his ghostly director as completely as a staff is wielded by a man's hand, or as wax is moulded by him who uses it. God only knows what are the fearful scenes of oppression and cruelty that are concealed beneath the mantle of Popery. 3. Subtlety. Of all the systems that ingenuity ever elaborated there is none that can compare with Romanism. Only the prince of darkness is equal to the task. There is more than human subtlety and art in it. Though the structure has been built in different ages, and the elements brought from many quarters, yet it so marvellously coheres, and is so wondrously propped by a thousand subsidiary principles that the only greater mystery in the universe is that "of godliness." It was Satan's last resource; he could not destroy Christianity, so he perverted it and made it subserve his own purposes. 4. Immorality. There are good Roman Catholics, and many have gone to heaven out of Rome; but that is because of the remnant of truth which defies perversion. The whole tenour of the system, however, is contrary to godliness. "The commandments of God are made of none effect through their traditions." Then they poison the springs of holiness by their system of casuistry which seems only intended to enable men to sin without being disturbed. The same effect is produced by their absolution, which stupifies the conscience without giving peace to the soul. Conclusion: 1. Let us adore and cherish the "mystery of godliness," share its power, and delight in its faith, and walk worthy of it. 2. Let us sympathize with, pray for, and endeavour to rescue the victims of the "mystery of iniquity." (*Canon Stowell.*) *Wickedness a mystery* in regard to—I. ITS ORIGIN. II. ITS CONNECTIONS AND THE MEANS IT EMPLOYS. III. ITS PROGRESS. IV. ITS TENDENCY. (*Heubner.*)

*The development of Antichrist:*—This mystery, saith St. Paul, doth already work. It shall increase, and go forward, and grow to a perfection. A thorn, when it is young, is soft and gentle; ye may thrust at it with your finger, it will not hurt you: but after it waxeth and groweth hard and stubborn, it will pierce the flesh, and draw blood. A bear, when he is young, is harmless and innocent; ye may dandle it, and dally with it, as with a whelp; it hath no chambers to gripe, no teeth to bite, nor paws to tear: but after, it will grow, and become fierce and cruel like the sire. A serpent, when it is young, is little and pretty; it hath no sting, nor poison; you may take it in your hand, and lay it in your lap, it will not hurt you: after, it will increase in venom, and grow in mischief, and be like itself; then it will shake the sting, and cast poison, and prove dangerous. Such a thorn, such a bear, such a serpent is Antichrist. At the first he shall seem soft, and gentle, and innocent. After, he shall grow fierce, and arm himself with sting and poison. But a thorn, though it be soft, is a thorn: a bear, though he be little, is a bear: a serpent, though he be pretty, is a serpent. Even so Antichrist, though he seem gentle, mild, and simple, yet is he Antichrist. He groweth by degrees, he will be like his sire; his paws will be dreadful, his mouth will be deadly. (*Bp. Jewell.*)

Ver. 8. **And then shall that wicked be revealed.**—*Antichrist:*—I. His TITLE. "That lawless one." It is the property of Antichrist to boast himself to be above all laws, in which he resembles Antiochus (Dan. xi. 36). It cannot, therefore, be hard to find him out, for—1. Who is that infallible judge that takes upon him to decide all controversies, who judges all things, is judged of none; who destroys with fire and sword those who question his authority, and who releases from their allegiance the subjects of those who dispute his supreme sovereignty? 2. Who is he that takes upon him, with faculties, licences, and pardons to dispense with the law of God, and to allow open and notorious sins? 3. Who is he that by his own writers is said to be freed from all human law, that has a paramount authority to all laws, that he cannot be bound by them? One expressly says that he is above law, against law, and without law; a plain description of the lawless one in the text; and another, not without a spice of blasphemy, "God and the Pope have their will for a law." 4. Who is he that has brought into the Church the worship of God by images, and the worship of saints and angels, which is the great lawlessness which is branded by the Christian law as such? If there be no such power extant, then we are yet to seek for Antichrist; but if there be, none so wilfully blind as they that cannot see wood for trees, and know not where to fix this character. II. His REVELATION. 1. His appearance in the world. He shall be in the world as soon as a certain hindrance is removed. (1) The most learned argue that this impediment was the Roman empire: that gone, Antichrist was to be revealed or the prediction proved false. (2) Things of great moment cannot be removed nor established in a minute. The removing of the Roman empire was not all at once, nor the rising of the pontificate, but by degrees. When Constantine began to remove the imperial throne to Byzantium, though the majesty of the empire continued at Rome, yet this was a step in removing the impediment; it lessened the Emperor's authority there and increased that of the Pope's. (3) The progress of Antichristian tyranny is, in short, this: About A.D. 600 their ecclesiastical power began to be raised when the majesty of the empire was weak in Italy. When John of Constantinople had usurped the title of universal bishop, Gregory the Great said, "The king of pride is near, and an army of priests is prepared to serve him as their general;" and in about six years Phocas conferred on Pope Boniface the same title. About 688 the Pope obtained the Pantheon, or temple of all devils, and consecrated it to Mary and all saints. The temporal monarchy was long in hatching, but began in that century. Pope Constantine would have his foot kissed like another Diocletian, and openly resisted the Emperor Philippius, and encouraged the treason of Justine and Anastasius. In the eighth century, Gregorys II. and III. continued the rebellion, and caused all Italy to withdraw their obedience from the Emperor Leo; and later Zachary assisted Pepin to depose Childeric. Afterward Adrian took upon him to translate the empire of the Greeks to the Latins, and ever since the Popes have made broils in kingdoms and assumed the right of deposing kings. 2. God's discovery of him to the world was also by degrees, in raising up witnesses against the tyranny and usurpation of Rome in every age. Five hundred years before Luther, Peter Bruis began, and Henry, his scholar, succeeded him, and to both succeeded the Waldenses and Albigenses; then Wicliffe, the Bohemians, Savonarola, and lastly Luther and the German and

English reformers. III. His RUIN. 1. The manner of his fall. (1) " Consumed."
Antichrist is not presently to be destroyed, but to waste away by a lingering consumption ; as his rising was by degrees so he will lose his authority. (*a*) The reason
for this is that God has a use for him as he has for the devil himself, and therefore
permits him some limited power to scourge his people for their sins, to try his
people's obedience, to cure their divisions, and to keep up a remembrance of His
mercies. (*b*) Observe how this consumption is accomplished. The pomp and
height was about 1,500 years after Christ, but what a decay has happened since by
the revival of religion and learning. (*c*) Caution. Antichrist is being consumed,
but he is not yet dead. What strength he may recover before his last destruction
God knows ; but it has re-entered many countries from which it was cast out, and
made havoc among the evangelical Churches. What, then, shall we do ? Watch
and pray (Matt. xiii. 25) ; reform and repent (Rev. ii. 5) ; be fortified and established
by knowledge (2 Pet. iii. 17), by grace (Heb. xiii. 9 ; 1 John ii. 20). (*d*) The author
and means of this consumption, " The Lord . . . with the breath of his mouth,"
which means either His providential Word (Isa. xi. 4 ; Psa. xxxiii. 6 ; Heb. i. 3 ;
John xviii. 6), or the efficacy of His Gospel (Eph. vi. 17 ; Heb. iv. 12 ; Rev. ii. 16).
Antichrist's destruction is to be by the victorious evidence of truth. It must needs
be so, for the tyranny is upheld by darkness which is dispelled by the light of truth ;
and therefore the Papists cannot endure the Scriptures. Again, his kingdom is
carried on by falsehood, and his impostures are discovered by the simplicity of the
gospel. (2) " Destroyed." The coming which is to accomplish this final annihilation is most likely the Second Advent (chap. i. 7, 8 ; ii. 1–3). Others conceive
some notable manifestation of his presence and power in his Church, but it is certain that at the judgment the beast and false prophet shall be cast into the lake of
fire (Rev. xix. 20). 2. The use to be made of this. Be not discouraged at the
survival of Antichrist : his doom is sealed. (*T. Manton, D.D.*) *The means of
the destruction of Antichrist :*—The gospel—" the breath of His mouth." And how
admirably adapted is the means to accomplish the end ! 1. The man of sin has
usurped the place of God in the throne of the Church. What is required to depose
the tyrant ? The proclamation and reception of the gospel. This shows that St. Peter
had no dominion over the consciences of his brethren or the faith of the Church to
which he ministered, and consequently that he never transferred such power to
others. The gospel shows that God is the only Lord of conscience : and as this is
known and appreciated will man fall from the position he has usurped, and God be
raised and worshipped. 2. The man of sin has dictated the creed of the Church :
and declared it to be the merit of human actions and sufferings. And what is
necessary to consume this fatal error, but the knowledge of the gospel which
declares that the just shall live by faith : that salvation is of grace, through faith,
and the gift of God. 3. The man of sin has vended and sold pardons and future
rewards. What is necessary to consume this power of the Pope, except the knowledge and belief that God only can forgive sins ; that He forgives freely through the
merits of Christ, and for His sake confers the kingdom of heaven on those that
believe. 4. The man of sin assumes a dominion over the invisible world, and professes to have power to deliver souls from the flames of purgatory. What is necessary to consume this error, but to circulate the Scriptures, which most clearly show
that God only has power to reach the inhabitants of the invisible world. 5. The
man of sin labours to keep men in ignorance. What is necessary to dispel the
darkness of the human mind, and thus to consume this his stronghold, but to send
men the light of life. (*C. Lee.*) *The Christian revelation of life :*—1. In " Modern
Painters " Ruskin reminds us of the delight we feel in view of a bright distance
over a dark horizon. At sunrise, beyond some line of purple hills, we have seen
the sky become a great space of light, and though the shadows of night were
lingering in the valley we have looked into the dawn. 2. In the Bible we are
always looking over a foreground in shadow into a bright distance. (1) In Old
Testament prophecy the waste and tumult of history were seen against the far
Messianic glory. (2) In the New Testament the apostles have learned to see all
the wickedness of the world horizoned by the manifestation of the Coming of
Christ. 3. In Christian vision, then, two aspects of Christian life and world history
should be viewed together. (1) If we have been compelled to observe the evil of
the world we need to look on until we see its darkness beneath the brightness of the
Lord's presence. (2) On the other hand, we must not shrink from any knowledge
of the evil of the world. The Good Shepherd will seek the lost sheep, and not wait
for the coming dawn. 4. Observe how Jesus always seemed to see both aspects.

Sin was an ever present fact to Him, but He saw it all set in the holy love of God; and because of this He could at once condemn sin and rejoice over it. 5. A similar juxtaposition characterizes this chapter. We do not know exactly of what Paul was thinking, but it is clear that he saw the darker foreground, and the bright distance, the mystery of iniquity still working, and the manifestation of the coming of Christ. I. THE TEXT DISCOVERS THE LAW BY WHICH THE MANIFESTATION OF THE PRESENCE OF CHRIST FOLLOWS THE REVELATION OF THE MAN OF SIN. The revelation of sin is necessary for its judgment. As soon as the man of sin becomes revealed, then follows his destruction. Things have to grow worse in order that they may become better. We can discover this principle when we survey great historic masses of sin. When Babylon's abominations were full, God's judgment brought all her pomp down to hell. So with pagan and mediæval Rome. The Goth and Vandals were let loose by Providence when the vices of a decayed civilization had filled the cup of wrath; and the Papal corruption was ripe for destruction when Luther sounded his appeal. What availed the voice of some New England divine to check the growing system of slavery in America? Both North and South were making money by letting it alone. But all the while it was growing up under the law of God's judgment. Providence lets wheat and tares grow till the harvest. And when at last that man of sin was fully revealed, the compromises which had restrained the full growth and revelation of slavery being taken away, then came the hour of its destruction. II. THERE IS ALWAYS, THEREFORE, REASON FOR HOPE WHEN WE SEE SOME EVIL THING COMING OUT OF ITS CONCEALMENT, and making its power felt with a more shameless impudence. Whether it be intemperance, the power of the saloon, or greed, or lust, or monopoly, or anarchy. This law is a reason for hope and courage in all Christian work. Something may have given you a moment's revelation of the mystery of iniquity in your neighbourhood, and discouraged, you are tempted to say What is the use of our feeble endeavour against such powers of evil? Or you may have run against some dead wall of indifference, or custom, or wrong method entrenched in some good institution, and because rebuffed where you expected sympathy you either drop the work or continue with heartlessness. But you have failed to look up until you saw some bit of God's sky at the end of your way. If we are sure we have seen the wrong and harm, we may be sure that it will be manifest in time, and that in time what hinders its revelation will be removed, and then it shall be consumed in the brightness of the Lord's Coming. This is the reason why the men who really have seen evil things, and fought mightily against them, as a rule have been not only the bravest men, the self sacrificing, the martyrs, but also the cheeriest and most hopeful men. It is the indifferent man, he who does not lift a finger to take any burden from men's shoulders, who fears that his country is going to destruction, as it might do for aught he does. III. THE SAME PRINCIPLE OBTAINS WITH REFERENCE TO OUR INDIVIDUAL SALVATION. Sins one after another come to revelation in our lives, and, as they are revealed will be consumed in some manifestation of Christ. A man goes on in a life that was not satisfactory to his conscience or heart. Something happens to bring that dissatisfaction to revelation. He sees a larger, diviner self rising before his present self, condemning it, and ready to consume it as by the presence of Christ. That is a crisis for any man. And if we disown the man of sin in us, and own the Christ self, we are converted. And every time any sin comes to revelation is God's opportunity of grace. When it reaches its full measure it may not prove to be a vehement passion, or devouring beast, but only some little meanness, selfishness, &c. But at last we see it as an evil thing, contrary to God. Then let it be consumed in the presence of Christ. "Behold now is the accepted time." And the progress upward is one of ever increasing quickness of perception of evil and power over sin. IV. SUCH is the benign law of growth and grace; BUT ITS ALTERNATIVE CANNOT BE ESCAPED. If the man of sin in us is revealed, and we will not let him go, what then? The sin must be punished. God cannot hold heaven safe in one hand, and let the sin of the world escape from the other. The man of sin must be destroyed, and if we cling to it how can God separate us from its fate? We must go where sin goes, if our hearts cleave to the sin. That is so in this world, why should it be different in any other? All dishonesties go straight and sure towards ruin, and eventually carry the defaulters with them. Hence the urgency of the gospel to us now. (*Newman Smyth, D.D.*)

Ver. 9. **Even he whose coming is after the working of Satan.**—*The agency of Satan:* —I. THE SCRIPTURE ACCOUNT OF SATAN. 1. He is represented as a spirit or immaterial being (1 Kings xxii.; Luke x. 17-20). 2. As an angel, preferable to man in understanding and might. 3. As a fallen angel (Jude 6). 4. As the prince or chief of infernal spirits (Matt. ix. 34; xii. 24; xxv. 41; Luke xii. 41). As lying under punishment, in reserve to be brought forth at the great day of retribution as a monument of God's hatred of sin. II. THE INSTANCES OF HIS AGENCY. 1. His introducing sin into the world (2 Cor. xi. 3-13). 2. The temptation of Christ (Matt. iv. 1-11). 3. Possession of bodies when Christ was in the world (1 John iii. 8; Acts x. 38). 4. The objects against which his force is directed are the dishonour of God and the ruin of men. 5. The subjects are good and bad men. 6. The ways in which he acts are two—force and fraud, fiery darts and subtle wiles (Eph. vi. 11-16). 7. He acts on persons and means with diligence, and constancy, and malice, as a roaring lion (1 Peter v. 8). 8. Be his activity ever so great, it is restrained and over-ruled by God, who has all evil spirits under His control. The practical improvement of the subject : 1. We should admire the wisdom and goodness of God in making a discovery of Satan. 2. We should watch against his manifold artifices. 3. We should pray for grace and power to resist him. (*J. Towle.*)    *Emissaries of Satan :*—Some years ago, when the cholera was raging in New Orleans, a steamer, near nightfall, put out from the city, laden with passengers escaping from the pestilence. The steamer had been but a little while out when the engineer fell at his post with cholera. The captain, in despair, went up and down among the passengers, asking if there were any one there who could act as engineer. A man stepped out, and said that he was an engineer, and could take the position. In the night the captain was awakened by a violent motion of the steamer, and he knew there was great peril ahead. He went up, and found that the engineer was a maniac ; that he had fastened down the safety-valves ; and he told the captain that he was the emissary of Satan, commissioned to drive that steamer to hell. By some strategy, the man was got down in time to save the steamer. There are men engineered by maniac passions, sworn to drive them to temporal and everlasting destruction. Every part of their nature trembles under the high pressure. Nothing but the grace of Almighty God can bring down those passions, and chain them. A little while longer in this course, and all is lost. (*T. De Witt Talmage.*)

Vers. 11, 12. **And for this cause God shall send them a strong delusion that they should believe a lie.**— *Judicial infatuation* follows upon wilful perversity and obstinate unbelief. God *sends*, not *shall send* (Authorised Version), still less "permits to be sent." It has the full force of the vivid prophetic present, "a working of error," *i.e.*, a working in them which issues in the increasing destructive power of error ; the hardening of Pharaoh's heart is the parallel which suggests itself. It lies in the nature of God's moral government and in the moral constitution of man, that sin, indulged, weakens the strength of resistance, and so invites and prepares the way for the more frequent and violent assaults of temptation. Thus yielding to sin receives at last its punishment in the slavery of sin. The working of error has its aim in this that they should believe *the* lie, as opposed to the truth just indicated. Man must believe something—if not the truth, with all the blessings which its reception brings, then the lie of the devil with the doom pronounced upon it. Unlike the Thessalonian believers who had "every desire of goodness," who had their pleasure in goodness, and their desires ever reaching forth towards its increase (chap. i. 11), these unbelievers have their pleasure in evil. They have said to it, "evil be thou my good." Hence with "the son of perdition," whose adherents they are, their end is destruction. (*J. Hutchison, D.D.*)    *Ill-disposed affections naturally and penally the cause of darkness and error :*—Of all the fatal effects of sin none is so dreadful as that every sin disposes for another and a worse. By gradations sin arrives at maturity; it is the only perpetual motion, and needs nothing but a beginning to keep it going. I. HOW THE MIND OF MAN CAN BELIEVE A LIE. There is such a suitableness between truth and the understanding that the latter of itself can no more believe a lie than a correct taste can pronounce bitter to sweet. If a lie is believed it can be only as it carries the appearance of truth. Before there can be an appearance there must be an object and a faculty, and from one of these must spring all falsehood. But the object cannot cause a false appearance of itself, and therefore the difference must rest in the perception. Objects are merely passive. Truth shows itself to be truth, and falsehood falsehood, whether men apprehend them so or no. What, then, are the causes on the believers part which make any object to appear what it is not. 1. An undue distance between the faculty and its object. Approximation is necessary to perception. Distance in space hinders corporeal perception; moral distance hinders spiritual perception of God and His worship. 2. The indisposition of the intellectual faculty which follows from sin. Where the soul has deviated from the eternal rules of right, reason, and morality, it is in darkness, and while in darkness it must necessarily pass false judgments upon most things that come before it. The understanding, like some bodily eyes, is disabled from exact discernment, both by natural weakness and supervening soreness. II. WHAT IS IT TO RECEIVE THE LOVE OF THE TRUTH. 1. To esteem and value it. Truth must first be enthroned in the judgment before it can reign in the desires. 2. To choose it as a thing transcendently good. To esteem is an act of the understanding; to choose of the will. This is the proper and finishing act of love. The great effect of love is to unite us to the thing we love, and the will is the uniting faculty, and choice the uniting act. Till we have made religion our fixed choice it only floats in the imagination; but it is the heart which must appropriate the great truths of Christianity. Then what was before only an opinion passes into reality and experience. 3. This will help us to understand what is rejecting the truth. Not because men think it false, but because it crosses their inclination. The thief hates the day; not but that he loves the light as well as other men, but he dreads that which he knows is the likeliest means of his discovery. The great condemnation that rests upon the world is that men see the light but love darkness, because their deeds are evil. III. How THE NOT RE-CEIVING THE TRUTH INTO THE WILL AND AFFECTIONS DISPOSES THE UNDERSTANDING TO DELUSION. 1. By drawing off the understanding from fixing its contemplation upon an offensive truth. For though it is not in the power of the will when the understanding apprehends a truth to countermand its assent, yet it is able to hinder it from taking that truth into full consideration. If a man has affections averse to the purity of the truth they will not suffer his thoughts to dwell upon it, but will divert them to some object that he is more enamoured with; and so the mind lies open to the treacherous inroads of imposture. 2. By prejudicing the understanding against the truth—the understanding in that case being like the eye which views a white thing through a red glass. This was how the Jews rejected the Saviour. They saw His miracles and heard His words through the medium of, "Is not this the carpenter?" "Can any good come out of Nazareth?" 3. By darkening the mind, which is the peculiar malignity of every vice. When wise men become vicious their wisdom leaves them. The ferment of a vicious inclination lodged in the affections is like an intoxicating liquor received into the stomach, from whence it will be continually sending thick clouds and noisome steams up to the brain. IV. How GOD CAN BE PROPERLY SAID TO SEND MEN DELUSIONS. "God is light, and in Him is no darkness at all"; and what is not in Him cannot proceed from Him. But God may be said to send delusions. 1. By withdrawing His enlightening influence from the understanding. The soul is not otherwise able to exert its intellectual acts than by a light flowing in upon it from the fountain of light. How reasonable, then, that God, provoked by gross sins, should deliver the soul to infatuation by a suspension of this light. 2. By commissioning the spirit of falsehood to seduce the sinner (1 Kings xxii. 22; 2 Cor. iv. 4). How dreadfully did God consign over the heathen world to a perpetual slavery to His deceits! And the truth is where men under the gospel will grow heathens in practice, it is but just with God to suffer them to grow heathens in their delusions. 3. By a providential disposing of men into such circumstances as have an efficacy to delude. He may place them under an heterodox ministry or in atheistical company, throw pestilent books in their way, all which, falling in with an ill-inclined judgment, and worse ordered morals, will recommend the worst of errors. And, therefore, as we find it expressed of him who kills a man unwittingly, that God delivers that man into his hands (Exod. xxi. 13), so when a man, by such ways as these, is drawn into false belief, it may be affirmed that God sends that man a delusion (2 Sam. xvii. 11, 12, 14; Ezek. xiv. 9). 4. By His permission of lying wonders. Thus when Pharoah hardened his heart against the will of God, God permitted him to be confirmed in his delusion by the enchantments of the magicians. And so with the lying wonders of the Church of Rome, which confirm the legends imposed for truth upon her deluded members. V. WHEREIN THE GREATNESS OF THIS JUDGMENT CONSISTS. 1. In itself. (1) That it is spiritual, and so directly affects the soul. The judgments affecting the body are insignificant in comparison. (2) It blasts the peculiar perfection of man's nature, his understanding; for ignorance and delusion are the disease of the mind, and the utmost dishonour of reason; there being no sort of reproach which a man resents with so just an indignation as the charge of folly. If slavery be that which all noble spirits abhor, and to lose the choicest of nature's freeholds, the reason, be the worst of slaveries, surely the most inglorious condition that can befall a rational creature is to be governed by a delusion (John viii. 32). And, besides this, it has a peculiar malignity to bind the shackles faster on it by a strange unaccountable love, for no man entertains an error but he is enamoured of it. 2. In its effects. (1) It renders the conscience useless. A blind watchman is a nuisance and an impertinence, and a deluded conscience is a counsellor who cannot advise, and a guide who cannot direct (Matt. vi. 23). (2) It ends in total destruction. Every error is in its tendency destructive. Hell is a deep place, and there are many steps of descent to it; but as surely as the first gloom of evening tends to and ends in the thickest darkness, so every delusion persisted in will lodge the sinner in the blackest regions of damnation. VI. What deductions may be made from the whole. 1. That since the belief of a lie is a sin it is not inconsistent with Divine holiness to punish one sin with another (Rom. i. 24, 26), and no punishment is comparable to this. 2. That the best way to confirm our faith in the truths of religion is to love and acknowledge them. 3. That hereby we may be able to find out the true cause of—(1) Atheism. (2) Fanaticism. (*R. South, D.D.*)          God and error :—Sceptics never tire in quoting this text, to prove, if they can, that God sends delusions to deceive mankind, and that men are doomed to everlasting perdition for what they could not avoid, simply because the Almighty so willed it. But the infidel's interpretation of the passage has been read into it by himself. Its real teaching is eternally true. There are four points in it to be considered by us. I. The class of men referred to. 1. They "believed not the truth." There is a rejection of the truth which arises from ignorance, and some excuse is to be made for it. But there is also a wilful rejection of the truth. Men close there eyes to the light, and grope in the darkness by their own free choice. Reason is made blind to give eyes to prejudice and passion, and excuses are invented, not so much to justify their conduct to others, as to salve their own consciences. In this way they smother the truth, until they come thoroughly to reject it. 2. They "had pleasure in unrighteousness ; " or, better rendered, "were well pleased in the unrighteousness." They not only practised unrighteous acts, but they took pleasure in doing them. Regardless of the law of God, which is the standard of righteousness and the basis of morality, they revelled in sinful delights. II. The delusion to which they were subject. The Greek term translated "delusion" is literally "the inworking of error." The expression is a very important one, and shows the source and mode of operation of the error. The whole thing is internal, and is opposed to the inworking of the Holy Spirit. Men pursue an evil course until they come to believe it to be right. Look at that fine boy who is just leaving his home for the workshop or the college. He has been brought up in a pure family, surrounded by all that is good and pious. But the first day in his new surroundings words fall on his ears which horrify him ; these, or similar, he will hear again and again, until they cease to affect him. Then, and at a later stage, he will himself indulge in coarseness and profanity with the rest, and perhaps become the very blackest of all that black company. The inworking of sin and error will destroy conscience, and that most fearful of all states be reached in which no remorse be experienced, but rather pride in sin. Man very largely moulds his own character, and with it his beliefs ; and very often, alas ! he comes to "believe a lie," and his doing so is entirely his own fault. III. This delusion, or inworking of error, is sent by God. Does error, then, come from God ? No ; but He abandons men to it when they have wilfully and persistently broken the law of righteousness, just as they fall into disease of body when a natural law has been violated. IV. The purpose of the inworking of error. "That they might be damned." This seems a most terrible doctrine, and hundreds have cavilled at it to the danger of their own souls. "Condemned" is certainly a milder word, but with very much the same meaning. "He that believeth not is condemned already." But the original word is better rendered in the Revised Version—"judged." The Judge of all the earth will do right; but that very right may involve most fearful consequences. If the inworking of error goes on till the judgment comes, it will be an awful calamity to that man in whom it occurs. When the Divine judgment is passed there can be no dissentient voice, no sympathizers with the condemned, and even the heart of the criminal himself will bear testimony to the righteousness of the sentence. (*G. Sexton, LL.D.*) God's logic of sin :—1. Every one who takes pleasure in unrighteousness is under a strong delusion. 2. Every one who is under a strong delusion believes a lie. 3. Every one who believes a lie has rejected the truth. 4. Every one who rejects the truth will be judged by God. 5. Every one who shall be judged by God shall be damned. 6. Therefore every one who receives the truth as it is in Jesus shall be saved (ver. 13). (*J. T. Wightman.*) *The infatuation of the followers of Antichrist* :—I. THE AUTHOR. God is not and cannot be the cause of evil. The avenger of sin cannot be the author of it. With sin as sin God has nothing to do, but with sin as a punishment of sin God has to do. 1. To understand this concurrence we must not say—(1) Too much, lest we leave a stain on the Divine glory. He infuses no sin, and conveys no deceit; these belong not to God but to man or Satan. (2) Nor too little as that God's judgments of blindness of mind (John xii. 39, 40), and hardness of heart (Exod. iv. 21), are simply said to be so because foreseen, or inevitable, or barely permitted. Besides all this there is a judicial sentence which is seconded by an active providence. 2. God's concurrence may be thus stated. (1) His withdrawal of the light and direction of His Spirit (Deut. xxix. 4). A greyhound held in by a slip runneth violently after the hare when it is in sight; as soon as the slip is taken away the restraint is gone, and his unbred disposition carries him. So men that are greedy of worldly things are powerfully drawn into errors countenanced by the world, when God takes off the restraint of His grace. In this God is not to be blamed. Voluntary blindness brings penal blindness; and because men will not see they shall not. (2) His delivering them up to the power of Satan (2 Cor. iv. 4) as the executioner of His curse (1 Chron. xxi. 1, *cf.* 2 Sam. xxiv. 1). Temptations come from the devil, but they are governed by God for holy ends (1 Kings xxii. 22). (3) His raising up such instruments and objects as meeting with a naughty heart do blind it. (*a*) Instruments (Job xii. 16; Ezek. xiv. 9). For man's ingratitude God raises up false prophets to seduce them that delight in lies rather than in the truths of God. (*b*) Objects (Jer. vi. 21). If we will find the sin, God will find the occasion. If Judas will sell his Master, he shall not want chapmen to bargain with him. II. THE DEGREE OR KIND OF PUNISHMENT. "Strong delusion," the prevalency of which is seen in—1. The absurdity of the errors. (1) Adoration of images (Psa. cxv. 8; Isa. xliv. 9–20). (2) The invocation of saints, a thing against reason, because they are out of the reach of our commerce, and against Scripture which always directs us to God by one Mediator, Christ. (3) Works of supererogation (Luke xvii. 10). 2. The obstinacy wherewith they cleave to them. In spite of Scripture, reason, and evidence of truth, they still cry the opinion of the Church and their forefathers; like the Jews, who denied the clearest matter of fact (John viii. 33: Jer. xliv. 16–19). 3. The efficacy of the causes. (1) The withholding of Scripture. (2) Gain and ambition (Acts xvi. 19–21, 25). (3) Pride and prejudice which will not disavow a welcome error or acknowledge an unwelcome truth. III. THE EFFECT. The belief of a lie. 1. The object: a lie, that is either—(1) False doctrines (1 Tim. iv. 2). (2) False miracles in their legends. (3) False calumnies against Protestants. 2. The act: given up to believe a lie. Some are doubtful, some almost persuaded, some espouse the common prevailing opinions, some adhere to them with much false zeal and superstition. IV. THE USES. 1. Information. (1) To show us the reason why so many learned men are captivated by Antichrist—the delusions of Satan. Four causes may be given. (*a*) Self-confidence. God will show the folly of those who depend on the strength of their own wit (Prov. iii. 5, 6; 1 Cor. i. 19). (*b*) Prejudice. The priests and scribes could readily tell that Christ was to be born in Bethlehem (Matt. ii. 4–6), yet who more obstinate against Him who was born there? (*c*) Pride. Many Jews believed on Christ, but would not profess Him, lest they should be put out of the synagogue (John xii. 42, 43). (*d*) The judgment of God. (Luke xix. 41, 42). (2) To show us that the prevalency of this wicked one is no blemish to providence; for permission of Him is one of God's dreadful dispensations. Hereby God would show us—(*a*) That there are deceits and errors as well as truth in the world, much of choice, not chance. (*b*) That although it is a great evil to be deceivers, it will not excuse us if we are deceived (Matt. xv. 14). (*c*) What need there is to pray not to be led into temptation. (*d*) To fear to slight the grace offered (Deut. xxviii. 28). 2. Of caution to take heed of spiritual infatuation that this judgment fall not on us. Take heed—(1) Of sinning against the light (James iv. 17). (2) Of hypocrisy in the profession of the truth (Prov. xxvi. 26). (3) Of pride and carnal self-sufficiency (2 Chron. xxxii. 31). (4) Of following the rabble (John iv. 20; Prov. xxiv. 13, 14). (*T. Manton. D.D.*) *Choice influences belief*:—This believing a lie does not necessarily denote intellectual, or what are called speculative errors, but perhaps refers more particularly to moral questions. And yet intellectual belief is not to be excluded. "The inworking of error" is potent here also. Much nonsense is talked in these days about irresponsibility for opinions. "A man always believes according to evidence," it is said. So he may, and yet it may be his own fault that more evidence was not obtained. In one of the numerous debates that I have held with leading sceptics, my opponent said that God could not be just if He punished him for his opinions, because he had used every means in his power to arrive at the truth. Then said I, "You are the first man in this world who ever did." I am sure no man can say before God that he has let no opportunity go by for learning the truth; that he has left no available evidence unexamined; that he has allowed no chance to escape him which might have been used to profit. Belief is largely influenced by the will. Don't let us forget that. Man very largely moulds his own character, and with it his beliefs. Every man has a free will, and by his voluntary choice he makes habits which become permanent. These constitute his character. In the end he comes to "believe a lie," and his doing so is entirely his own fault. (*G. Sexton.*) *Natural law in the spiritual world :*—"God shall send," or more correctly rendered, "God sendeth"—that is, He is ever sending. Spiritual laws are as certain in their operation as those which regulate material things. Indeed, material things and the laws of matter are but symbols of the deeper and more abiding spiritual realities. Does error come from God? No, but He abandons men to it when they have wilfully and persistently broken the law of righteousness, just as they fall into disease of body when a natural law has been violated. There is no help for this. It is in accordance with the eternal truth and righteousness of God. Why do our bodies suffer, if we commit acts of excess? Not because God wills that we should so suffer, but because the suffering is a necessary consequence of the violation of His laws. It is His means of directing us aright, and, if we fail to obey Him, the consequences must fall upon our own heads. The laws of nature are inexorable, and cannot be broken with impunity. Let a man ruin his constitution by dissipation, and, although God may forgive him for the sin, he will carry his diseased and enfeebled body to a premature grave. The pardon does not undo the consequences of the wrongdoing. "The inworking of error" necessarily carries with it its own penalty—a penalty stamped on it by God. Thus God does not directly send the delusion, but "the inworking of error" is as much one of His laws as gravitation. A man may close his eyes to the natural light, or live for years in darkness, and the result in the end will be blindness. Does God send the blindness? Directly, no. Indirectly, yes; for it is the violation of His law that caused it. So if we close our eyes to the spiritual light, we shall become spiritually blind, and live in darkness, mistaking the spiritual things that surround us; in other words, we shall be deluded. God sends this delusion, that is, it follows the evil course of doing what He has prohibited, and not doing what He has commanded. (*Ibid.*) *Punishment according to law :*—I have a clock, as very many have, which was made to meet certain exigencies of the future. It has a calendar which points out the day of the month, the hand moving one figure each day. If the month has 31 days, it moves from that to the 1 for the next month; but if the month has but 30 days, the hand jumps over the 31, and on February it moves from 28 over the 29, 30, and 31 to the 1 of March. But once in four years it stops at February 29, and then moves over two figures to the 1. Now, we do not have to run to the maker when these changes are needed, and ask him to come and move the hands. He knew the exigences would arise, and arranged for doing the work at the time he made the machinery. So the Lord has arranged His laws of the earth in such a way that they punish certain sins. The punishment is from the Lord, but He need work no miracle to bring it. Men defy the laws of health and cleanliness, and a pestilence breaks out, or contagious diseases rage. Men oppress their workmen, or kings rule with hard and selfish power, and rebellions and insurrections break out, and the oppressors lose far more than they seemed to gain. (*H. W. Beecher.*)

**Ver. 12. That they all might be damned who believed not the truth, but had pleasure in unrighteousness.**—*Progress in unrighteousness :*—This is a terrible judgment—filling up the measure of their obduration, that they may at length fall into condemnation. But it is equitable. They believed not the truth, received not the gospel in the simplicity of it, as revealed by Christ and His apostles, and recorded in the Scriptures, but wilfully and for their own interests' sake, gave themselves up to these corruptions. And more, they "had pleasure," &c. In ver. 10 it was, "they received not the love of the truth;" now they delight in its opposite. I. WHAT IS UNRIGHTEOUSNESS? Righteousness is giving every one his due—man and God (Matt. xxii. 21);

man (Titus ii. 12); God, in the way of worship and reverence (Psa. xxix. 2; xcvi. 8). This unrighteousness is principally meant in the latter sense. False worship is the greatest unrighteousness; for by this the glory of God is given to another (Rom. i. 18, 23, 25). II. THEY HAD PLEASURE IN IT; in those things they please themselves, not lapse into it out of simple ignorance and error of mind. And so the apostle parallels the two great apostasies from the light of nature and the light of the gospel (Rom. i. 32; Psa. xcvii. 7). III. THEIR CONDEMNATION. Observe—1. Errors of judgment as well as sins of practice may bring damnation on the souls of men. All sins do in their own nature tend to damnation (Rom. vi. 23), and errors of judgment are sins because contrary to the law of God (1 John iii. 4). There is nothing so wicked that a man blinded with error will not attempt against those that differ from him (John xvi. 2). A blind horse is full of mettle, but stumbles; therefore, if a man be not guided by sound judgment, his zealous affections will precipitate him into mischief (Rom. x. 2). How true this is of the papacy. 2. Though all errors may bring damnation, yet some are especially damning (2 Pet. ii. 1). This may be either from—(1) The matter held, if destructive of the way of salvation by Christ; or (2) The manner—(a) When men profess what they believe not and voluntarily choose error for worldly ends. (b) When they are vented by some Christian professor to the seducing of others (Acts xx. 30; Gal. v. 20). (c) When, though they should not err fundamentally, they so far debauch Christianity, as that God gives them up to believe a lie, and to defend and maintain corruptions of doctrine and worship. (d) When there is gross negligence, it is equivalent to standing out against the light (John iii. 20; 2 Pet. iii. 5). (*T. Manton, D.D.*) *God not the author of damnation :*—"God is too good to damn anybody," so we hear some say nowadays. They are quite right. God does not damn anybody; but many damn themselves. Damnation is sin and suffering producing and perpetuating each other. We see suffering producing sin in this world, and sin producing suffering. Look at the low dens, with their diseased, poisoned, putrescent inmates, their depravity, their profligacy, their brutality, their bodily torture, their mental anguish. Is not that damnation?—sin and suffering acting and reacting. God does not damn men; He tries to prevent it. He moves heaven and earth to prevent it. Was not the crucifixion moving heaven and earth? The crucifixion was God's supreme effort to keep men from hell. How unreasonable to charge God with your death! Suppose I went, sick and suffering, through the stormy night, to hold a light for you at some dizzy chasm; suppose you struck down the light which I had brought with so much pains; suppose you lost your foothold and fell into the abyss below, could I be charged with your death? Well, then, did not God bring you light? Did He not with scarred hand hold that light over your pathway? If you reject it and fall, can you charge Him with your death? No! oh, no! (John iii. 19). (*R. S. Barrett.*)

Vers. 13-17. **We are bound to give thanks.**—*Gratitude for salvation :*—The apostle is here contrasting the state of the Thessalonians with that of many who should, at a future period, arise in the Church, whose presumption should know no bounds, and who for their impiety would be given over by God to final impenitence. While those transgressors were doomed to everlasting misery, the Thessalonian converts were ordained to eternal life, having been from the beginning chosen by God to salvation, and having been in time called to the enjoyment of it through the ministry of the gospel which the apostle preached. For them, therefore, he gives thanks, as it was most meet for him to do, since it was the mercy that called for the devoutest praises from all. I. THEIR ELECTION OF GOD. 1. The end to which they were elected. It was "salvation," even "the salvation that was in Christ Jesus with eternal glory." It was not to the means of salvation merely; for many enjoyed the means of salvation on whose behalf he could not give thanks, yea, on whose account "he had continual heaviness and sorrow of heart;" but it was to salvation itself, with all its inconceivable and lasting blessings. 2. The means by which that end was attained. God has ordained the means as well as the end; and He has ordained the end no otherwise than by and through the appointed means. He had chosen the Thessalonians to salvation "through the sanctification of the Spirit." Further: He had chosen them to salvation through "belief of the truth." By faith we lay hold on the promises of God; by faith we become united to Christ; by faith we bring down from heaven all those supplies of grace which are necessary for us in this state of warfare. Thus faith and holiness are inseparably connected with salvation; and to them men are elected as much as to salvation itself. II. THEIR CALLING BY HIS MINISTRY. 1. The instrument is

His Word. As far as His Providence concurs in the salvation of men, it is only in subserviency to His Word. This is the rod of His might by which all the wonders of His grace are wrought. Miracles gave credibility to the testimony which Christ and His apostles bore ; but it was the testimony itself, as applied by the Holy Spirit to the soul, that wrought effectually upon the hearts of men. And in all ages it is the same Word, either read or preached, that is effectual to conversion. So the apostle reminds his converts at Thessalonica that, though they were from eternity chosen of God to salvation, they were called to the possession of it through the ministry of the gospel. 2. The same instrument, if received rightly, will operate effectually to the same end. It had turned the Thessalonians "from idols to serve the living God ; " and thus it will assuredly work on all who cordially embrace it. It " is quick and powerful, and sharper than any two-edged sword " : it " is mighty to the pulling down of the strongholds of Satan " : it " prospers in the thing whereunto God has sent it." When the time has come for the return home of His wandering sheep, He apprehends them by His Word, and brings them with His gracious energy to His fold, making them " willing in the day of His power." This is His invariable process—" Whom He did predestinate, them He also called," &c. Conclusion : 1. Those who have never yet obeyed the Gospel call must not say, "I am not of God's elect, and therefore I cannot help myself." They have been " called to a belief of the truth," such as should lead them to rely entirely upon the Lord Jesus Christ for salvation, and to the sanctification of the Spirit, even such a sanctification as should progressively transform them into the Divine image of righteousness and true holiness. They should therefore receive freely at His hands all the blessings offered thus to them. If, however, they will obey the Divine call, their blood will be on their own head. 2. Those who have obeyed the call should ever remember that God has chosen and ordained them to bring forth fruit to His honour and glory. He loved them, not from any good He saw or foresaw in them, but simply because He would love them. Hence they have every reason to give Him thanks ; nay, their every breath should be an effusion of praise. (*C. Simeon, M.A.*) *The nature, duty, and privilege of a Christian :*—I. WHAT IS IT TO BE A CHRISTIAN ? There are three characteristics in the text. 1. Belief of the truth. (1) There are various kinds of truth. All truth is not " the truth." There is natural and religious truth. Christian truth is distinguished from all other by being " the truth as it is in Jesus "—truth touching God, the soul, eternity. (2) So there are various kinds of belief. We believe things we see, results of reasoning, conclusions of argument, laws, things above reason, God and our own souls. The faith of our text, however, is (*a*) a faith of the heart—the verification of those truths which can be understood by the heart of man alone. This distinguishes it from mere intellectual effort. (*b*) A supernatural faith. Observe the company in which it is put—side by side with· the power of the Spirit of God. And everywhere in Scripture it is so. It is by the supernatural operation of the Holy Ghost, and is supernatural in its origin, operations, and results. 2. Sanctification of the Spirit. There is a question whether this refers immediately to the objective work of the Holy Ghost, or the subjective work in man's own spirit. But it is immaterial ; it amounts to the same in either case. Sanctification in its broadest, its Biblical as distinguished from its theological sense, is a triple work. (1) It is the purgation of the soul of him who believeth by the sprinkling of the blood of Christ. (2) It is the recreation of the moral nature by the Holy Spirit. (3) It is the dedication of the cleansed and renovated person to God. 3. Hope of everlasting life. Three things are connected with and result from sin : Disaster—" The soul that sinneth it shall die." Privation—of blessedness. Suffering—an accusing conscience and a dark outlook. Over against these in glorious and everlasting antithesis are— (1) Eternal life. (2) Positive blessing. (3) Present and eternal joy and glory. This is our hope. It is a good hope, a hope assured to us by warrant beyond dispute. II. WHAT IS THE DUTY OF A CHRISTIAN ? 1. Goodness (ver. 17). To be good. (1) Negatively, to put away that which is evil. This is a part of our duty of which we cannot afford to think lightly. Christ suffered for us that He might deliver us from the present evil world. Those who are born of God do not commit sin. (2) But there is no such thing as a merely negative goodness. It is always also positive and practical, and finds expression in speech and action. It is a recognition of God in the family and daily life in reverence and worship, in the government of self and in charity towards man. (3) This goodness must be as universal as it is practical. " Every good word and work." There is a goodness which is eclectic ; and it is right that we should devote attention especially to forms of goodness for which we are most fitted, but not to the neglect of those which are common to all : *e.g.*, Religious worship and carelessness about personal purity are often found together ; so are personal devoutness and neglect of missionary effort and *vice versâ*. Good words of every kind. (4) This goodness is to be robust and energetic, not infantile and feeble. We love the heathen, but how much do we give them. We love our brother, but how often does a fault reduce that love to microscopic proportions. 2. Steadfastness. This goodness is to be practised consistently, not by fits and starts; through life, and not for an hour ; not only when easy, but in the face of hardship and persecution. III. WHAT ARE THE PRIVILEGES OF A CHRISTIAN ? The characteristics and duties just mentioned. The three points are the same under different aspects. But specifically. 1. Consolation. This is needed at all times for the Church of God is now in its suffering state. (1) Christian life begins in self-sacrifice. The Christian passes from death into life through a strait gate, which excludes many a habit, &c., long cherished. (2) Christian life continues by sacrifice ; the bearing of the daily cross, the conflict with sin, the evangelistic effort which is the very life of the Church, all involve loss and pain which need consolation. This consolation is abundant and abiding, consisting as it does of the love and presence of " Our Lord Jesus Christ," &c. (ver. 16). 2. Sanctity. 3. Good hope through grace. 4. Glory. Conclusion : How great the prospects, responsibility, dignity of a Christian. (*J. D. Geden, D.D.*) *God's Salvation :—* I. CONSISTS in " obtaining the glory of our Lord Jesus Christ." This phrase is evidently an expansion and more exact specification of the term salvation in ver. 13. The believer is to share the glory which Christ possesses (John xvii.). Jesus has already given His glory of self-sacrificing love and union with the Father to His disciples in a measure, but hereafter it is to be given in fulness. What a great salvation ! II. Is OBTAINED—1. As a result of God's choice and call. Not that this lessens human responsibility, or should relax human watchfulness and diligence (ver. 15). 2. As a result of the Spirit's sanctification. 3. Through personal apprehension of the truth. III. Is A MATTER OF THANKFULNESS. (*Clerical World.*) *The favoured people :—*I. True Christians are OBJECTS OF A SPECIAL CHOICE. 1. The Author: God. The Scriptures unanimously declare that true Christians are chosen of God. Who dare question the right of the Most High to choose them. While He injures none, for this is impossible, surely He may, if He please, confer special benefits on some (Rom. ix. 20, 21). 2. The date—" from the beginning " (1 Pet. ii. 9; i. 2; Rom. viii. 29; Eph. i. 4). 3. The end—" to salvation." This determines its true nature and supreme excellency. The Israelites were chosen, but many fell, and we are admonished to take heed lest we " fall after the same example of unbelief." The twelve were chosen to apostleship, but Judas apostatised. This salvation is not only deliverance from sin in this life, but eternal glory in the world to come. II. True Christians are PERSONS OF A PECULIAR CHARACTER. God's chosen people are—1. Believers of the truth. (1) God's Word is emphatically " the truth." (2) Believing is giving hearty credit to the Bible as the record of God in such a way as to feel affected and influenced by it according to the nature of the things which it regards. Without this belief of the truth we have no evidence of our election, and only " deceive our own selves." 2. Partakers of the Spirit. " If any man have not the Spirit of Christ he is none of His." The Spirit in the heart is essential to the being of a Christian, for without Him there is no regeneration. Then His influence is necessary for every Christian enterprise. What reason there is for the admonitions " Quench not the Spirit," " Grieve not the Spirit." We must judge whether we are partakers of the Spirit by His fruit (Gal. v. 22-24). 3. The subjects of sanctification. The Spirit given to God's people produces and gradually promotes it. There is no way of attaining holiness but by the Spirit of Holiness. Faith bears a close connection with this state. Faith guards the Christian from sin and preserves him in the path of duty. Sanctification, therefore, is the best evidence of faith, and the best mark of election. We have proof that we are " of God " only as we are like God. III. True Christians FURNISH CAUSE OF LIVELY THANKSGIVING. Why? True Christians are— 1. A proof of the power of the gospel. 2. A credit to Christianity (Phil. i. 27). 3. Useful to others. (*T. Kidd.*) *Connection between faith and the sanctification of the Spirit :—*Religion has two factors, the Divine and the human. All the doctrines whose object and result are the salvation of lost souls, have an inseparable connection. They necessitate and include each other. In the text, sanctification of the Spirit is conjoined with belief of the truth. I. ELECTION IS PRESUPPOSED. 1. Its author is God. 2. It is from the beginning. 3. It is personal. 4. It

is comforting. Those that are chosen are beloved of the Lord. II. ITS DESIGN.
1. To produce holiness of thought, word and deed. 2. To secure salvation.
Holiness is salvation. 3. To obtain the glory of our Lord Jesus Christ. III. ITS
AGENCY. 1. It proceeds from the love and grace of God. 2. It is rendered possible
by the death of Christ. 3. It is carried into effect through the agency and influence
of the Holy Spirit. IV. ITS INSTRUMENT. This is the truth. 1. Men are called
by the truth. 2. Men are sanctified through the truth (John xvii. 17). V. ITS
EVIDENCE. 1. Illumination by the Spirit in order to understand things that are
spiritual (1 Cor. ii. 14). 2. Sanctification of the Spirit. 3. Belief of the truth.
Apart from these, no person has, or can have, any proof that he is chosen of God
to eternal life. VI. CONCLUSION. 1. Men are lost because they have pleasure in
unrighteousness, and believe not the truth. 2. No sanctification takes place in
any soul apart from the belief of the truth. 3. The end of faith is the salvation
of the soul. 4. Sanctification and faith have their roots in election. 5. Does any
one seek for evidence of his election, let him believe the gospel and live a holy life.
(*L. O. Thompson.*)     *Election :*—I. HOW IT IS HERE SET FORTH. 1. By the rise of it,
which is the mere love of God, for Paul calls these "brethren, beloved of the
Lord " (Deut. vii. 7, 8). There is no antecedent worthiness in those whom God
chooses (2 Tim. i. 9). 2. By the act itself "hath chosen you " making a distinction between them and others. Those whom God chooses He separates from
the world (1 John v. 19). Their names are kept in the records of heaven (Luke
x. 20; Phil. iv. 3), whereas others are not (Rev. xvii. 8; xx. 15). 3. By the
antiquity of it " from the beginning " (Eph. i. 4 ; Matt. xxv. 34). Love in God is
of old standing, even from eternity, and what is from everlasting is to everlasting (Psa. ciii. 17). 4. By the means of its accomplishment two are mentioned,
one on God's part and one on ours—Sanctification of the Spirit, and belief of the
truth. Where, note—(1) That God's decree is both of ends and means, for all His
purposes are accomplished by fit means. He who has chosen us to salvation has
chosen us to be holy, and to believe the truth. And without the means the end
cannot be attained ; for without faith and holiness no man shall see God or escape
condemnation (John iii. 36; Heb. xii. 14). What God has joined together let no
man separate. If we separate these things God does not change his counsel, but
we subvert His order to our own destruction. (2) That these are not causes but
fruits of election (Eph. i. 4; 1 Pet. i. 2 ; Acts ii. 47; xiii. 48). (3) That being the
necessary fruits they are also evidences of our election. All that are sanctified by
the Spirit and believe the truth belong to the election of God. (*a*) Sanctification
is not only an external dedication to God, but an inward and real change
(1 Cor. vi. 11). (*b*) Faith is not a cold assent to an opinion as to the Christian
religion, but such a lively trust as brings us under its power (vers. 10, 12).
The Thessalonians received the truth so as to obey it and suffer for it.
(4) The connection between the two—(*a*) There is a necessary connection
between them as of cause and effect, for none are powerfully drawn to believe
but such as are sanctified. To incline and bring us to God is a work wholly
reserved to the Spirit. (*b*) There is the connection of concomitancy between the
gospel and the Spirit. The Spirit only goes along with the gospel; and so both
external and internal grace are of God (John xvii. 17). (*c*) There is a subordination
of faith to this work of the Spirit by the truth; for the greatest things work not till
they are considered and believed (1 Thess. ii. 13). II. THIS IS THE GREAT MATTER
OF OUR THANKSGIVING TO GOD. Consider—1. That thanksgiving to God is a great
and necessary duty, expressly enjoined by Him, and expected from us (1 Thess. v.
18). 2. That we are to give thanks chiefly for spiritual and eternal mercies (Eph.
i. 3). 3. That the great expression of God's mercy is in election. (1) There we see
all our blessings in their rise, which is the love and grace of God. Waters are
sweetest and freshest in their fountain (John iii. 16). (2) It shows us God's distinguishing grace, and who it was that made us differ from others (John xiv. 22;
1 Cor. i. 26; Matt. xi. 25, 26). (3) Then we may see that grace takes off self-
boasting (Eph. ii. 8, 9; i. 6). (*T. Manton, D.D.*)     *Gratitude to God for salvation :*—I. THE PERSONS DESCRIBED AND THE DUTY ENJOINED. 1. Thanksgiving for
the salvation of others (Rom. vi. 17). 2. Thanksgiving is the constant duty of all
Christians (Eph. v. 20). 3. The cause is the revelation of God's love (Jer. xxxi. 3).
II. THE REASONS ASSIGNED FOR THIS GRATITUDE. 1. Election. (1) God's people are
a chosen people (Rom. viii. 29). (2) Chosen from the beginning, or eternity (Titus i.
2). (3) Without any regard to previous good works (Titus iii. 5). (4) Chosen in
Christ Jesus (Eph. i. 4). (5) To salvation here, and glory hereafter (Eph. ii. 10).

2. Sanctification. (1) The Spirit quickens the soul (Eph. ii. 1, 5). (2) The Spirit enlightens the mind (Eph. i. 18). (3) The Spirit leads the soul to glory (John xiv. 16, 17). 3. Faith. (1) Negative faith, or ceasing to trust in self (2 Cor. i. 9). (2) Faith in God's blessed Word (Psa. cxix. 41, 42). (3) Faith in Christ and His work (Acts xvi. 31). III. THE METHOD WHEREBY GOD DEVELOPS HIS PURPOSE OF LOVE TO HIS CHURCH, AND THE SUCCESS ATTENDING THE SAME. 1. They were called to believe these doctrines (Eph. iv. 4–6). 2. He always calls into Christian fellowship (1 Cor. i. 9). 3. He calls His people into liberty (Gal. v. 13). 4. The instrumentality employed. "Our gospel" (1 Cor. i. 23, 24). 5. The blessing obtained is eternal glory, called in the text, "the glory of our Lord Jesus Christ;" which denotes that the chosen, sanctified, and believing, and called people of God, shall never be separated from Him, or perish (Col. ii. 4). (*T. B. Baker.*)     *Effectual calling:*—A godly English minister of two hundred years ago, the Rev. Thomas Doolittle, used to "catechise" his congregation, more especially the young people, every Lord's Day. An incident that melted his hearers on one occasion is thus related. The question was on "effectual calling," and to bring it more closely home to them he suggested that they should recite the answer, changing the word *us* to *me*, and *our* to *my*. No one had the courage to begin, till a young man well known as one who had led a bad life arose, and with every sign of contrition repeated, amid the tears of the congregation: "Effectual calling is the work of God's Spirit, whereby convincing me of my sin and misery, enlightening my mind in the knowledge of Christ, and renewing my will, He did persuade and enable me to embrace Jesus Christ freely offered to me in the gospel." This young man had been convicted by being catechised—think of such a thing happening in these days of looser religious discipline! —and from being a wicked and ignorant youth he had become an intelligent Christian.     *Justification and sanctification:*—Manton says, "A malefactor that hath a leprosy on him needs not only a pardon, but a medicine; and in a broken leg, not only ease of the pain is desirable, but that the bone be set right. So we need both justification and sanctification." Justification saves the malefactor, and sanctification cures him of his spiritual disease: are they not equally desirable? Who would wish to miss the one or the other if in need of them? Pardon removes the pain of our broken bones, but spiritual renewal reduces the fracture. Let us not be content with half a gospel, but obtain a whole Christ for our broken hearts. Renewal of life is every way as desirable as forgiveness of sin. As well be full of guilt as full of guile. If a child has eaten unhealthy food it is well to cure the disease which is occasioned by it, but it is equally desirable to break him of the habit which led him to such foul feeding. (*C. H. Spurgeon.*)     *Holiness:*—When Dr. Livingstone asked one of the Bechuanas, What is holiness? the reply was, "When copious showers have descended during the night, and all the earth and leaves and cattle are washed clean, and the sun rising shows a drop of dew on every blade of grass, and the air breathes fresh, that is holiness."

**Ver. 14. Whereunto He called you by our gospel.**—*Effectual calling:*—I. ITS AUTHOR. "He," viz., God. 1. None else has authority to call—(1) To duties. Being our Creator, He is our owner; and being our owner, He is our sovereign and lawgiver, and may enact what laws He pleases (James iv. 12). (2) To privileges. His blessings are so great that none else can give us a right to them; and the soul can have no security that it does not intrude upon the possession of things till we have His warrant. None came to the wedding feast till bidden (Matt. xxii.), or went into the vineyard till hired (Matt. xx.). 2. None else can have the power; for to calling there is not only the invitations of the word, but the effectual operations of the Spirit. None else can change the heart (2 Pet. i. 3; Rom. iv. 17; 2 Cor. iv. 6; Eph. ii. 10). II. THE OUTWARD MEANS. 1. The means itself: the Gospel. This God uses—(1) Because, if God will invite the creature by his duty to His happiness, it is necessary that the call should be evident by some visible sign. The natural duty of man is much seen by the Creation (Rom. i. 19; Psa. xix. 1, 2). But this call made to fallen man as a remedy for his lapsed estate can only be known by revelation. (2) To convince and stop their mouths who refuse this calling, for the gospel brings grace home to us and leaves it to our choice (Acts xiii. 26; iii. 26). Great is the misery of those who refuse (Luke xiv. 24; Prov. i. 24–26). (3) Because He will preserve the liberty of His own workmanship, and therefore will not compel us, but will, at the same time teach and draw us (John vi. 44, 45; Acts xi. 21; xvi. 14; Rom. i. 16). 2. The interest the apostle challenges in it— "*our* gospel." Elsewhere it is called God's gospel (1 Tim. i. 11). He is the Author.

It is also called Christ's gospel (chap. i. 8), as the principal sub-revealer. And then the apostles' gospel, because they were the instruments chosen by Christ to declare it (1 Tim. i. 11). This expression is—(1) A word of fidelity (1 Cor. ix. 17). (2) A word of esteem and love; what we love we call ours (Rom. xvi. 25; Eph. i. 13). (3) A word importing diligence (Acts xx. 24). Paul was willing to suffer or do anything for the sake of it. (4) A word of mutual consent (2 Cor. iv. 3). III. THE ENDS. 1. Subordinate. "Whereunto"—(1) God calls us to the faith of the gospel (Rom. x. 14). (a) There must be a belief in it in general. (b) A particular affiance in Christ according to the terms of the New Covenant, i.e., the assent must be fiducial or accompanied with a trust in Christ (Eph. i. 15; 2 Tim. i. 12), and obediential, not a devout sloth or carelessness (Psa. cxix. 10; Jude 20, 21; Psa. xxxii. 2; Rom. viii. i.). (2) God calls us to holiness (1 Thess. iv. 7) on several grounds. (a) That there may be a likeness between the Person calling and the persons called (1 Pet. i. 15). (b) Because the nature of the calling enforces sanctification (Heb. iii. 1; 2 Tim. i. 9; Rom. i. 7). (c) Because the grace shown in our calling obliges us to be holy in point of gratitude (1 Thess. ii. 12). (d) Because the calling enables us to be holy, giving us all things necessary to holiness of heart and life (2 Pet. i. 3). 2. The ultimate end. "To obtain the glory," &c. (1 Pet. v. 10). (1) It is glory for body and soul (1 Pet. i. 9; 1 Cor. xv. 42, 43). (2) It is the glory of our Lord Jesus Christ. (a) It is purchased by Him (Eph. i. 7). (b) Promised by Him (John x. 28; 1 John ii. 25). (c) Prayed for by Him (John xvii. 14). (d) Bestowed by Him; at death (Acts vii. 59; Phil. i. 23; 2 Cor. v. 8); at judgment (John xiv. 3). (e) With Him (Rom. viii. 17; Rev. iii. 21). (*T. Manton, D.D.*) *Effectual calling and Divine glory :*—I. THE GOSPEL CALL. What is that? It is the invitation of Divine mercy to accept the blessings of salvation. 1. The call is one of sovereign mercy. Mercy for mercy's sake. God was under no obligation to show mercy. The act is of His rich grace, and of that only. 2. It is most free and open. Not clogged by difficulties. "Ho every one," &c. "Come unto Me," &c. "If any man thirst, let him come," &c. The message is to the world—to every creature. 3. It is most earnest and pressing. The ministers who bring it are to invite, persuade, beseech, compel men to be reconciled to God. There is not the shadow of a doubt respecting God's sincerity. II. THE WAY IN WHICH THE CALL IS TO BE MADE SURE. 1. It must be heard. "How can they believe in Him of whom they have not heard?" "O earth! earth! hear the Word of the Lord." "If any man hath ears, let him hear." "Hear, and your soul shall live." 2. It must be understood. The truth as it is in Jesus must be comprehended. 3. It must be believed. Truth only realizes the call. Matthew believed; Saul believed; the Samaritans believed. Thus the pardon of sin, the acceptance of the person, and every blessing for time is obtained. 4. It must be retained. The profession of faith must be held fast. "Abide in Me," says Christ. So we must continue Christ's disciples to the end. III. THE PROVISION MADE TO RENDER THE CALL SURE. 1. The Holy Spirit attends Divine truth. "My speech and my preaching," said St. Paul to the Corinthians, " was not with enticing words of man's wisdom, but in demonstration of the Spirit and of power; that your faith should not stand in the wisdom of men, but in the power of God." 2. The Holy Spirit is specially given when the call is accepted. So it came to pass on the Day of Pentecost. When the three thousand, pricked in their heart by the simple truth declared unto them by the burning earnestness of Peter, cried to him and the rest of the apostles, "What shall we do?" he said unto them, "Repent, and be baptized every one of you in the name of the Lord Jesus for the remission of sins, and ye shall receive the gift of the Holy Ghost." They did as they were told, and received the Divine gift of the Divine Spirit. And so it comes to pass now in the experience of all penitent believers. 3. All the blessings and privileges of the gospel follow its acceptance. Such, for example, as justification (Rom. v. i.); sonship (John i. 12); sanctification (1 Thess. v. 23); everlasting life (John iii. 16); heaven, or "the obtaining of the glory of our Lord Jesus Christ" (John xvii. 22, 24). Application: (1) To us the gracious call has come; (2) it may be accepted now; (3) All who receive it will be made happy and safe for ever; (4) and all who reject it by their unbelief and disobedience will be condemned by it for ever. (*J. Burns, D.D.*)

Ver. 15. **Therefore, brethren, stand fast, and hold the traditions.**—*Inspired traditions viewed in relation to the ministry and the Church* (Text, and vers. 13, 14):—I. THE DOCTRINES WHICH CONSTITUTE THESE TRADITIONS. 1. That human redemption had its rise in sovereign favour (ver. 13). 2. That we are indebted solely to the Scriptures for our knowledge of salvation. 3. That Christ is the central truth of the Bible. 4. That sanctification by the Spirit through belief of the truth is obligatory on all Christians. II. THE DUTIES OF THE CHURCH IN REGARD TO THESE TRADITIONS. 1. Stability. " Stand fast." 2. Fidelity. " Hold." (*J. Woodward.*) *The Scripture sufficient without unwritten traditions :*—I. OUR DUTY IS TO STAND FAST IN THE FAITH OF CHRIST AND PROFESSION OF GODLINESS WHATEVER TEMPTATIONS WE HAVE TO THE CONTRARY. "Stand fast," being a military word, alludes to a soldier's keeping his ground, and is opposed to two things—1. A cowardly flight, *i.e.,* our being overcome in the evil day. Wherefore we are exhorted to put on the armour of God (Eph. vi. 13), which helps us to withstand and to stand. The first is the act of a soldier, the second the posture of a conqueror. Here we make our way to heaven by conflict and conquest; hereafter we triumph. 2. A treacherous revolt, or yielding to the enemy, by complying with those things which are against the interest of Christ for advantage sake (2 Tim. iv. 10; Heb. xii. 15, 16). II. THE MEANS OF STANDING FAST IS TO HOLD THE TRADITIONS TAUGHT BY THE APOSTLES. 1. The doctrine of Christianity is a tradition. (1) Matters not evident by the light of nature or revelation must be either an invention or a tradition. (*a*) An invention is something in religion not evident by natural light, nor agreeable to sound reason, but is some cunningly devised fable, obtruded by various artifices upon the belief of the world (Eccles. vii. 29; Rom. i. 21, 22). (*b*) The gospel is none of this sort, but a tradition, or delivery of truth upon the testimony of One come from God to instruct the world and reduce it to Him (Heb. ii. 3, 4). Christ delivered it to the apostles, and the apostles to others (2 Tim. ii. 2), until it came to us. This testimony is as binding as if we had heard Christ or the apostles, for we have their word in writing. And that these are their writings appears by the constant tradition of the Church, the acknowledgment of enemies, the blessing of God upon them to the conversion of souls, their power to protect the Church and promote its conquests, and their survival in spite of persecution and debate. (2) The Christian religion must needs be a tradition. (*a*) Because it is built on matter of fact, viz., that the Son of God came from God to bring us to God, confirming the truth of His mission by such miracles as showed Him to be the Son of God and the Saviour of the world. Now a testimony or tradition is needful in matters of fact which must be confined to some time or place. Christ could not be always working, dying, rising, &c., everywhere. Those things were once to be done in one place before competent witnesses. But because the knowledge of them concerned all the world they were by them attested to others (Acts i. 8–22; ii. 32; iii. 15; x. 39–41.) (*b*) Because it is matter of faith, or doctrine, built upon matter of fact. We cannot properly believe a thing but upon testimony. If one asks, "Do you believe the sun shines?" you answer, "No, I see it." "Do you believe that twice two make four?" "No, I know it." But if he should ask "Do you believe that the sun is bigger than the earth?" you reply, "Yes," not because it appears so, but because competent judges tell you such is the case. Apply it now to the mysteries of the gospel. They cannot be seen by the eye, for they are invisible; nor comprehended by the reason, for they are above it; but we believe them because revealed to prophets and apostles. And this is more certain than sense. The eye may be deceived, and reason may err, but it is impossible for God to deceive or be deceived (1 John v. 9). 2. The holding this tradition is the great means of standing fast in the faith of Christ and the confession of His name. For in it there is sure direction to walk by, and sure promises to build upon (2 Pet. i. 16, 17; 1 John i. 2–4.). By this we have all that belongs— (1) To faith. There can be no faith till we have a sure testimony of God's revelation; for faith is a believing such things as God hath revealed, because He hath revealed them. (2) Nor obedience, for that is doing what God commands, because He commands (1 Thess. iv. 3; v. 18; 1 Pet. ii. 15). (3) Nor certain expectation of happiness. We are never safe till we know by what rule Christ will judge us (Rom. ii. 16; 1 Thess. i. 8). III. SINCE THE APOSTLES HAVE GONE TO GOD, AND WE CANNOT RECEIVE THEIR DOCTRINE BY WORD OF MOUTH, WE MUST STICK TO THE WRITTEN WORD. 1. Because we are taught to do so by Christ and the apostles (Matt. xv. 2; Luke xvi. 31; Acts xxvi. 22; 2 Pet. i. 19). 2. Because these things were written for our sakes (1 John i. 4). They knew the slipperiness of men's memory, and the danger of corrupting Christian doctrine, if there were not a sure authentic record left; therefore they wrote fully. 3. Because the Scriptures are perfect, and give us a knowledge of those things which concern—(1) Our faith. If there be enough written for that, we need not unwritten traditions to complete our rule (John xx. 30, 31).

What would men have more? (2) Our duty; that is sufficiently provided for (Titus ii. 12); therefore we need no other rule. (3) Our happiness: the doctrine that is able to make us wise unto salvation, is enough for us (2 Tim. iii. 15, 17). (*T. Manton, D.D.*) *Scripture and tradition*:—" There was a flute in the Temple," says the Talmud, "preserved from the days of Moses; it was smooth, thin, and formed of a reed. At the command of the king it was overlaid with gold, which ruined its sweetness of tone until the gold was taken away. There were also a cymbal and a mortar, which had become injured in the course of time, and were mended by workmen from Alexandria, summoned by the wise men, but their usefulness was so completely destroyed by this process that it was necessary to restore them to their former condition." Are not these things an allegory? Do they not imply that by overlaying the written Law with what they called gold, but what was in reality the dross and tinsel of tradition, the rabbis had destroyed or injured its beauty and usefulness. (*Archdeacon Farrar.*) *Stand fast*:—Let us stand fast as men who are appointed to keep their places until their guard is relieved by the coming of their Lord. If you have won the day, oh, do keep it! You must not suppose that the whole of religion is wrapped up in the day or two, or week or two which surround conversion. Godliness is a life-long business. 1. Stand fast doctrinally. In this age all the ships are pulling up their anchors. Now, put your anchors down. Learn no teaching but what Christ teaches you. If you see a truth in God's Word, grip it; and if it be unpopular, grip it the more. The one watchword now for the whole army of God is, " Stand fast." 2. Stand fast practically. All the barriers are broken down. People try to make the Church and world meet. Therefore, it becomes Christians to gather up their skirts, and be more precise than ever they were. 3. Mind that you stand fast experimentally. Pray that your inner experience may be a close adhesion to your Master. Stand fast without wandering into sin. Only so will you be preserved from the vortex of iniquity. Stand fast without wearying. Stand fast without dallying with any kind of error. The weather is very bad just now spiritually. Stand fast because of your citizenship. (*C. H. Spurgeon.*)

**Vers. 16, 17. Now our Lord Jesus Christ Himself, and God, even our Father.**— *Divine love and its gifts*:—It is an ill wind which blows no one any good. We owe this prayer to the needless alarms of the Thessalonians. I. THE BLESSED FACT of the Divine love. This is a fact not to be learned from a dictionary or uttered in speech, but to be felt. 1. God hath *loved* us. (1) The text does not say that God pitied us, although that would be true. You may pity a person whom you dislike. (2) Nor does it say that God has had mercy on us. A man is merciful to his beast, to his enemies, but it does not follow that he loves them. (3) Nor is the word benevolence. A mother is not benevolent to her child, a bridegroom to his bride. (4) Theologians talk of God's love of complacency, but that is too cold. (5) We must keep to the simple term, love. You know, mother, how you love the dear child in your arms. It seems part of yourself. Now, as God has united us to Himself by cords of love He thinks of us as He thinks of Himself. 2. He hath loved *us*, so insignificant, frail, foolish, sinful, and therefore so uncomely, ungrateful, provoking, deserving to be abhorred. We can understand His love to apostles, martyrs, &c., but that He should love us is wonderful. 3. This love is the great fountain of our Spiritual blessings. What is called the source of the Thames is a tiny rivulet; its real source is the whole watershed. But suppose the Thames a full-grown river from one fountain head, what a sight it would be. Now, the mercy of God to us in Christ leaps in all its fulness from the infinite depths of God's love. 4. The apostle joins the name of the Lord Jesus with that of God the Father, denoting not only equality of being, but holy concert in all that concerns our well-being. Christ is the gift of the Father's love, but Jesus loves His own. 5. Christ is here put first because He is first to us in our experience. We began our dealings with heaven not by going first to the Father, but to the Son. 6. Christ is "ours." Paul might have written, "*the* Lord," &c., but when he was testifying of this great love he must use a word of possession. Faith takes hold of Jesus and says, " He is all my salvation, and all my desire." 7. This love enables us, too, to say. "*Our* Father" (1 John iii. 1). 8. We are not told when that love began, only, "hath loved us." He loved us when we first came to Him repenting, when we were at the swine trough, ere we had a being, ere the world was formed, from everlasting. II. THE MANIFESTA- TION OF THIS LOVE. 1. Everlasting consolation. He found us wretched, when the arrows of conviction were sticking in our hearts; then He came to us with His consolations. Since then consolation has always followed on the heels of tribulation. What are our consolations? (1) That God has forgiven us. (2) That His promises are Yea and Amen in Christ. (3) That all things work together for our good. (4) That because Christ lives we shall live also, and live with Him. 2. Good hope. It is good because based on a good foundation. The fanatic's hopes will pass away with the vapours which produced them, but the believer's hope is founded in grace. Why is it, then, that some believers' hopes flicker? Because they get away from a hope in grace and look towards themselves. III. THE PRAYER FLOWING OUT OF THIS. 1. That God would comfort your hearts. This is of the utmost importance. Cheerfulness ought to be the atmosphere you breathe, and if you believe that God loves you, you cannot but be happy. 2. That he would stablish us in every good word and work. This establishment is derived from the consciousness of God's love. Don't be disheartened at the discouraging signs of the times. God loves you; work and bear witness for Him. Dark nights are but the prelude to bright days. (*C. H. Spurgeon.*)      *Free grace a motive for free giving :*—I. IT IS OF THE UTMOST IMPORTANCE THAT BELIEVERS SHOULD ENJOY CONSOLATION. Every commander knows that if he has not his soldiers in good heart, there may be a great many of them, and they may be well trained, but the battle is not likely to be won. This importance is seen—1. In the very existence of the text. It is the prayer of an inspired man. 2. In the fact that Christ is called upon "Himself," without any intermediate agency, and "God, even our Father" (chap. iii. 16). 3. In that it affects the Christian's heart. It is well to have a strong hand, how else shall we labour? to have a firm tread, how else shall we stand? Yet these are secondary matters compared with a healthy heart (John xiv. 1). 4. Because it is needful to prevent impatience and other evils. Perhaps it was the lack of comfort which led certain of the Thessalonians to preach the immediate coming of the Lord; their impatience excited the wish, and the wish the assertion. When men lose the present comfort of plain gospel doctrines, they are apt to begin speculating (chap. iii. 5). Laziness and despondency lead many to say, "Why are His chariots so long in coming?" 5. Because it promotes fruitfulness (ver. 17). When we are not happy in the Lord we do not give ourselves heartily to His service (chap. iii. 13). II. GOSPEL CONSOLATION IS FREELY BESTOWED. 1. It is described as a gift; and nothing can be freer than a gift. We have purchased nothing; what have we to purchase it with? 2. This freeness is seen in every part of it. (1) It covers the past, "Which hath loved us." Why? The sole reply is, "Even so father, for so it seemed good in Thy sight." Shall not the bridegroom elect his own bride. (2) As for the present, "He hath given us everlasting consolation." The pardon and perfect righteousness of Christ, lie in, union to, marriage with Him is ours, assuredly as a gift; how could it be otherwise? (3) As for the future, we have "good hope through grace," in which there is not a trace of legal claim. It comes not by way of reward, but of Divine favour. 3. This freeness is shown by the persons from whom the consolation comes. The comfort of the gospel must be free since it is brought to us by Christ, and God *our* Father. A father does not pay wages to his children, his gifts are freely bestowed out of the love of his fatherly heart. What father expects to be paid for what he does for his sons and daughters? 4. This freeness is shown by the source of consolation—the Divine love. What can there be in me for God to love? Love is unpurchaseable. Consolation is "through grace." III. SINCE THE CONSOLATIONS OF GOD'S LOVE HAVE BEEN SO FREELY BESTOWED, THEY SHOULD LEAD US TO A LIFE OF HOLY BENEVOLENCE. We ought to be free in our giving to others, since God has been so free in His giving to us. 1. In every benevolent enterprise Christian men should take a hearty interest (ver. 17). 2. This interest should be shown in actions as well as words. In the best MSS. "work" comes before "word." Some people think that word should be everything and work nothing. These professors speak a great deal about what they will do, talk much about what others ought to do, and more about what others fail to do. 3. This should be done without pressure. No one could lay constraint upon God to bless His people; no pressure was put upon Christ to redeem them. Even so should men give to God out of an overflowing heart. (*Ibid.*)      *Everlasting consolation:*—1. The prayer passes by a sudden transition from the human duty to the Divine grace. 2. The Lord Jesus is the Being addressed, but with a peculiar relation to the Father. In only one other instance are Father and Son united by a verb in the singular, and in no other instance is His name placed first. This should be noticed by those who hold that Paul's estimate of his Saviour only reached by degrees an exaggerated loyalty. 3. It is a rule that God should be addressed under an aspect appropriate to the specific supplication. The God of all grace turns a countenance infinitely varied towards His petitioners. Here the apostle is about to ask that the Thessalonians may be consoled, strengthened, and established, and accordingly, with exquisite precision, he calls upon Christ, and God as the everlasting Consoler and Strengthener through grace. I. THE INVOCA-TION. God in Christ is invoked as having loved us. 1. And more generally. (1) This is St. Paul's first allusion to the supreme and ultimate source of redemption. It is the first clear declaration that in the economy of human salvation love has the pre-eminence. The only saying that could surpass this was reserved for St. John in his first Epistle, the last document of revelation. (2) The link between the love that gave and the gift itself is grace. The love of God must by its very nature impart. There is something of grace in every Divine gift; but grace is the medium of the gifts of the love of God as they reach us through redemption. 2. More particularly in the gift of love. (1) The gift is twofold and comprises the whole sum of our benefit in Christ. The blessing is an " everlasting consolation " as it comes from God, and a "good hope " as we receive it. (2) "Everlasting consolation" is a phrase nowhere else used. It implies the healing of the great wound of sin, and the removal of its consequences; an eternal assuagement of a sorrow that would otherwise know no end. (*a*) Nothing is more certain than that of itself the misery of sin must last for ever; it has in its nature no resources of cure, no elements of change. (*b*) The consolation is eternal, unlike the beggarly and fleeting solaces of time, in which it is the joy that endureth for a night, while sorrow comes in the morning. It is an eternal consolation springing from an eternal redemption (Heb. ix. 12). (*c*) But it is treasured up only for those who flee to it for refuge. Hence the adjective of boundless meaning is elsewhere applied to the exact opposite " everlasting destruction." (3) The " good hope " describes that part of the gift which has reference to the future, and is another unparalleled expression, although it has near approximations. As the Epistle to the Hebrews supplies "eternal redemption," so it supplies "bringing in of a better hope." This hope embraces the whole Christian benediction, for such blessings as are received are only earnests of something better. It is a hope good in itself; "better" in relation to the promises given to the fathers; it is really the best inheritance that God can give, Christ merit, or we receive. II. THE PRAYER. 1. Generally we understand the purport of a prayer by its immediate occasion. Confidence within and stability without were the graces that the apostle aimed to strengthen (ver. 2). In the former Epistle the coming of death was the disturbing thought; in this it is the coming of the Lord of death foreshadowed by the " man of sin." Hence the abundance of hortatory language in both. But a higher comforter than Paul was necessary. Hence the sudden turn, " May the Lord Himself comfort your hearts." 2. The comfort prayed for is not what we call by the name. It is always in Scripture at once exhortation to the soul and invigoration as the result. The heart here is not the seat of the feelings, but the centre of the man; and the inner man is comforted when words are spoken to him by the Spirit which strengthens his own energies (John vi. 63). 3. The idea of establishment in Christian life is as familiar in this Epistle as that of consolation. By keeping the heart strong in His consolation, the Lord stablishes the life in His obedience. But all is dependent on firm faith in Christian doctrine (ver. 15). Whatever scruple may arise on this subject is obviated by the reflection that " word" and "work " are here linked into one idea. The Christian life is one of entire goodness, based upon and growing out of perfect truth. Conclusion: A touching comment on our prayer is given in chap. iii. 3. It is as if the Divine Spirit had without delay, " while he was yet speaking," ratified the request. (*W. B. Pope, D.D.*)

Ver. 16. **Everlasting consolation.**—*The comforts propounded to us in the gospel:* —I. ARE OF AN EVERLASTING TENDENCY AND BENEFIT—pardon and life, to free us from everlasting death, and bring us to everlasting happiness (1 John ii. 25 ; Heb. v. 9; Psa. cxix. 111; lxxiii. 26). When all other things fail, have spent their allowance, can afford us no more relief, then we begin to enjoy our proper portion. II. DEPEND ON EVERLASTING FOUNDATIONS. 1. The everlasting love of God (Psa. ciii. 17). 2. The everlasting merit of Christ (Heb. ix. 12). 3. The everlasting covenant (Heb. xiii. 20). III. ARE SUFFICIENT TO DO THEIR WORK. 1. To reduce us from temporal and flesh-pleasing vanities (Heb. xi. 25, 26; Psa. xvi. 11; 1 John ii. 17). 2. To make us steadfast in the truth, and cheerful under sufferings (Heb. x. 34 ; 2 Cor. iv. 17, 18). 3. To increase us in holiness and stablish us in every good work (1 Cor. xv. 58; John vi. 27). (*T. Manton, D.D.*) *False and true consolation:*—Trouble of some kind is universally diffused among men, and in the generality pretty equally distributed. Few of God's own children get through the world and into the heavenly home without trouble by the way. There is a sense in which Christians drink more deeply of the bitter cup than others, for in proportion as they are really Christians, they have refined and developed sensibilities. Trouble is to us what we ourselves are, and so is joy, and so is everything. Sympathy is a precious thing, but beyond a certain point every one has to bear his own burden; and since there is promised grace, let each one bear it like a man. But Christianity is not stoicism, and the Christian heart must have consolation. I. THERE ARE FALSE CONSOLATIONS. 1. The desperate consolation of complete thoughtlessness. 2. The presumptuous consolation of concluding that God is bound to make all turn out well in the end, and that therefore we need not trouble ourselves. 3. The superficial consolation which soothes the mind without going down to the roots of things. "If things are dark to-day—well, then, they will be brighter to-morrow." True enough; but what of the morrow beyond to-morrow? The darkness may be back again. We want the "everlasting consolation"; anything short of it is deplorably less than we need. II. THERE IS THE TRUE CONSOLATION. It is everlasting because it comes from an everlasting source—the unchangeable God. Never can we be consoled for the sorrow of the world, or our own share of it, until we meet with Him—the Father of our spirits, the God of our salvation, and receive what we need from Him. All consolation is in Him. He is everlasting; and He says that He has loved us from everlasting. Believe the gospel, accept its grace, hold its truth, do its duty, breathe its spirit, and you have the everlasting consolation of God. Observe, this is how it is to end for us here practically—in the comfort of our hearts, and stablishment in every good word and work; the everlasting comfort realized everywhere, amid the manifold cares of the household, in the honest trade of the city, in the pure speech and godly habits. God knows all, and that is enough; so I can go on with a quiet, yea, singing heart, seeking that steadfastness in every thing and place which the Father has promised. (*A. Raleigh, D.D.*) *The eternal comforters:* —The religion of Jesus Christ is one of consolation. It comes with sunshine, with help, with hopefulness. It is declared on many a page of Scripture, as in the letter of St. Paul, to be full of eternal consolations—consolations taken from that aspect of life which is afforded by looking at it from the immortal and spiritual side. Look then, at some of the elements of this eternal consolation which God our Father and the Lord Jesus Christ minister to us in our sorrow. I. OUR SORROW IS GREATLY ENHANCED BY THE MYSTERY OF LIFE. If we could only understand the reason of it, it would be easier to bear; but the tears seem to be so unnecessary, the wounding so needless, the pain and anguish so inexplicable! Life is a tangled skein, and we can get no clue. Whence we came, why we are here, what there is yet to come, we cannot comprehend. In this mystery and perplexity there comes One who says, "*Trust Me.*" He does not, indeed, throw scientific light on the mystery of life; He does not tell us what life means; but He says, "Trust Me." And we look up into that face, and that which looks down into ours inspires us with confidence; and we lay hold of that hand, and the grasp of that hand makes the thrill and throb of faith run through the very nerves of our being; and though we do not understand, and are still perplexed, yet we drink in confidence through the bright eyes that look into ours, and through the strong hand that grasps ours. It is not a philosopher who speaks to us, who has seen a little deeper into life than we have; nor is it a poet who speaks to us, who has gotten a little deeper insight into it than we have: it is the Witness-Bearer, who out of the eternal life has come, and into the eternal life is going. His is the witness; and in this is the root and ground of all that Christianity has offered us—faith, not in a philosopher, a poet, a theologian even, but *in a Witness-Bearer.* II. BUT THIS MYSTERY OF LIFE DOES NOT SO GREATLY ENHANCE THE PAIN OF LIFE AS THE FRAGMENTARINESS OF IT. It is not without semblance of reason, at least, that the broken column is put up in our graveyard—life seems to be such a series of separated fragments, so broken, so discordant! We look up the mountain-side, and we see not only the top enfolded in the cloud, but all above is thunder and lightning. And here Christ comes to us, and brings us this further message: "Life is not fragmentary: there is no break. You see the river flowing till it reaches the cleft in the mountain, but it goes on: you see your companion entering the dark cavern of the mountain-side; it is but a tunnel; presently he will emerge into a fairer, brighter land beyond." Life is like a song; and the singer goes from us, and the song grows dimmer and more indistinct, and then fades away; but the singer has not stopped his singing, though our eyes cannot follow him into the unknown whither he has gone. We get heart-broken, until we turn and find here this word brought to us—" That loved one has gone to the mountains, where there is neither pain, nor sorrow, nor temptation, but the everlasting sunlight and the undying song: follow thou on." Instead of the long, long wail of despair, this message of the ever-living Christ has put the throb of exhilaration and the song of triumph! III. BUT THE MYSTERY AND FRAGMENTARINESS OF LIFE ARE NOT SO HARD TO BEAR AS THE INJUSTICE OF IT. The best men suffer most, and the worst men suffer least. From the days of David down, men have looked thus at life, and felt the cruelty and seeming wickedness of it. So they have thought life ruled by a demoniac spirit—the god of this world; or life made up merely of the conflicting forces of human life, ruled by chance, with might makes right, and the strongest is the best, and a survival only of the fittest; or that it is ruled by cruel wrath and hate and jealousy—furies that pursue men, and are let loose upon them, because the gods are envious of their prosperity and their happiness; at all events, that life is a chaos over which there broods no Spirit of God bringing forth light, but only a spirit of darkness bringing forth darkness. But He who has shed on the mystery of life the light of trust, and He who has shed on the fragmentariness of life the light of hope, sheds on this awful unfaith in God —this awful sense of injustice and wrong against which we protest in vain endeavour, the light of love; for this is Christ's declaration everywhere and ever—the devil is not the master of this world, nor furies, nor a god of cruelty, but Infinite and Eternal Love is working out the web of human destiny. There is a higher and better life. The very thought of it is heaven. Blessed be God, even our Father, and the Lord Jesus Christ. (*L. Abbott, D.D.*)     *Everpresent comfort :—* More than a thousand years ago a company of refugees, escaping Attila's dreadful devastation of Northern Italy, settled on one of the muddy islands at the head of the Adriatic, and there founded the city of Torcello, and at a later time built up the magnificent commercial empire of Venice. The ruins of the old cathedral still stand in the ruined city, built by those stout-hearted men in a time of struggle and discouragement, as a symbol and stronghold of their religious faith; and in the cathedral the noticeable thing is the openness of the windows and the abundance of sunlight. None of the Gothic windows of the Northern churches or of the gloomy shadows clouding the high-arched ceiling; but all is luminous, bright, and fair, with not even dark colours in the frescoes. It was built by men of sorrows, but they were men who believed in God; and, therefore, while there was fear and depression enough around them, they made their house of worship joyous with all the beauty and cheer of Italian sunshine, and in this spirit they wrung from disaster the beginning of a grand success. The spirit that pervades a man's daily life is the measure of his real religion. He may be careless of sect and ceremony, but if he can carry heavy burdens with a light heart and meet calamities with serene courage, it must be that in the depth of his soul he has real faith, which, like a fountain in an oasis, keeps everything sweet and blooming. He may never put his faith into words, like a great theologian, or build it up into beautiful archi-tecture, like the brave people of Torcello; but, nevertheless, it is known and read of all men in the beauty and courage of his life, which may be more eloquent than any body of divinity and more impressive than cathedral or stately music. For courage and cheerfulness are, after all, the sincerest possible confession of man's real belief that all things are working together for good, and that Divine Providence is ever changing the darkness into light.     **Good hope through grace.**—I. HOPE. No man since the Fall can be satisfied with the present. Here is always either some evil pressing on us, some capacity of enjoyment unfilled, or some desire for the perpetuity of what we possess, which passes beyond the present into the future. This expectation and desire of future good is hope. Its object is the unseen. This hope is—1. The spring of all activity. 2. With regard to sinners under the sentence of the law, and in prospect of eternity, it is indispensable to any rational peace. II. GOOD HOPE, *i.e.*, well founded, and directed towards what is truly good. 1. Some men are insensible and indifferent with regard to their destiny. This state of mind is—(1) Irrational. (2) Unsatisfying. (3) Precarious. (4) Destruc-tive. 2. Others have a hope, but it is not good. It is founded on—(1) The general mercy of God. (2) Their relation to the Church. (3) The assumption that all are to be saved. (4) Spurious religious experience. (5)

The assumption of goodness. The general basis of a false hope is error either as to the purpose of God in reference to the punishment of sin, or as to the conditions on which exemption from sin is promised, or as to our having fulfilled or experienced those conditions. 3. A good hope is therefore—(1) A hope founded on the truth, on the promise of God and the work of Christ. (2) One which we have a right to entertain, *i.e.*, which is the genuine fruit of the Spirit; not an unauthorized anticipation on our part, but one which is inseparable from faith. (3) One which has for its object the infinite blessings of redemption, sometimes Christ's coming, sometimes the resurrection, sometimes the glory of God. Towards this the whole creation looks forward with earnest expectation. III. THROUGH GRACE, *i.e.*, a hope which God graciously gives, and gives in the exercise of His grace. God gives us this hope:—1. In that He promises to us the blessings which are the object of the hope. 2. Because He produces in our minds the exercise of our hope. IV. EVIDENCE THAT A HOPE IS GOOD. 1. That it has a Scriptural foundation; *i.e.*, that it rests on the promise of God clearly revealed in His Word. 2. That it has Scriptural blessings for its objects; not earthly good or millennial prosperity, but conformity to Christ, and the enjoyment of Him for ever. 3. That it sanctifies the soul, makes us pure even as He is pure (1 John iii. 3). 4. That it is the fruit of faith. V. THIS HOPE. 1. Is a helmet. 2. Is an anchor. 3. Is to the soul what wings are to the eagle. It elevates it above the world, raises it to heaven, fells us with its spirit. (*C. Hodge, D.D.*)     *Good hope through grace :—* Faith, hope, and love—the three master-principles of the true believer—are principles acted on in worldly things, by every man, every day. You need, then, no definition of the chief term in our text—" a good hope through grace." My theme is the best of hopes, a heavenly hope, a hope which cannot fail nor disappoint you—hope from God and in God, " good hope through grace." Such a hope was enjoyed by the Thessalonian saints. And this, in connection with their other gospel blessings, is here set forth in awful contrast with an opposite class of characters and destiny— the character and destiny of those who "received not the love of truth " to their soul's salvation, " but had pleasure in unrighteousness." The gospel-hope, then, is a " good hope." Why " good " ? It is good, I observe—I. In its OBJECTS. These are set forth to us in Scripture with much variety of phraseology. In ver. 14, just cited, they are designated in one comprehensive phrase, " the obtaining of the glory of our Lord Jesus Christ." In 1 Thess. v. 8, as in Eph. vi. 17, " The hope of salvation " ; Rom. v. 2, " And rejoice in hope of the glory of God " ; Col. i. 5, " The hope laid up for you in heaven" ; Titus i. 2, " Hope of eternal life " ; Heb. vi. 19, a hope " which entereth into that within the. vail " ; 1 Pet. i. 3, 4, the hope of " an inheritance, incorruptible and undefiled, and that fadeth not away, reserved in heaven for you " ; and ver. 13, " Hope to the end for the grace that is to be brought unto you at the revelation of Jesus Christ." In this last-cited passage, as in Titus ii. 13 and 1 John iii. 2, the realization of this hope is connected with the glorious advent of the returning Saviour : " Looking for that blessed hope, and the glorious appearing of the great God and our Saviour Jesus Christ " : " We know that when He shall appear, we shall be like Him ; for we shall see Him as He is." Other passages might be adduced to set forth the nature of the believer's hope, and to prove it " good," from the goodness of its objects. It were much indeed, it were a " good hope " for man—a sorrower in a sorrowing world—to have before him a heaven, where sorrow and sighing shall have fled away. It were much, it were a " good hope," for man, a sinner, with corruption within and conflict without, to have before him an inheritance undefiled ; the victor's palm and the victor's song. And these, all these, the believer's hope embraces. Yet, not these only. His eternity is to be spent not alone within reach of God, or near God ; but in God's very presence, with God. His glory is to come not only from God ; in a yet loftier and more wondrous sense, it is " the glory of God." II. But the hope which is engaging us is " good " by reason not only of its object, but, of its SECURITY. It shall assuredly be realized : it shall not confound nor make ashamed. Consider its foundation : " In hope of eternal life, which God, that cannot lie, promised before the world began " (Titus i. 2) ; which hope we have as an anchor of the soul, both sure and steadfast (Heb. vi. 17, &c.). If " hope deferred maketh the heart sick," hope confounded maketh it desolate. In the " good hope " of the Christian, uncertainty is no element. It is a deferred hope, a waiting hope, a tried hope ; but not an uncertain hope, not a speculative hope. It rests not upon probability. Its security is the word, the character, the nature of the unchanging and unchangeable Jehovah. III. The hope of which we speak is a " good hope "

IN ITS EFFECTS. Man's need is two-fold. He is a sinner, and, as a sinner, a sufferer. This hope meets alike his sin and his sorrow. 1. For, observe, it is a sanctifying hope. "Every man," writes St. John, "that hath this hope in him purifieth himself, even as He is pure." Thus, like the faith on which it rests, hope is a principle of no secondary influence in furthering the great work of holiness in the believer's soul, and in his growth in grace. The heir of glory must grow in grace. 2. But this hope is, further, a sustaining hope. It sustains under trial. It sustains, too, in the spiritual conflict. And this good hope sustains in death. IV. But it is further characterized as "a good hope THROUGH GRACE." It is "through grace" in a two-fold sense, as resting on grace, conveyed, that is, through a covenant of grace, even "the gospel of the grace of God"; and as imparted by grace to the individual believer. It is based on this: that for man, for me an undone sinner, powerless for my own recovery, with no ransom to atone, no escape from hell, God, in the richness of His unbought, unasked, undesired mercy, has provided a free and full salvation; that a propitiation has been made by Jesus the Lamb of God, which is of infinite efficacy for my pardon and reconciliation and peace. They are short and simple words—"good hope through grace." They bespeak the truth received, the gospel tasted in its power and sweetness, Christ known and won, Christ dwelling in the sinner, the sinner dwelling in Christ. The words of the same apostle to the Ephesians present the gloomy contrast: "having no hope." Such was the state of the Ephesians and Thessalonians in their heathen darkness. Why? They were "without Christ." (*J. C. Miller, M.A.*) *A superlative gift:*—I. THE SUBJECT—"a good hope." 1. Because it has a good Author—God. 2. Because it has a good object—the salvation of the soul by our Lord Jesus Christ. 3. Because it has a good foundation. 4. Because it has a good influence, for it tranquillizes the mind, purifies it, and establishes it. II. THE SOURCE—"through grace." 1. Grace is the spring from which it flows. 2. It is applied by the influence of grace, without human merit. 3. The objects on which it fixes are undeserving. (*R. Cope, LL.D.*) *A good hope:*—I. IT IS GOOD IN ITS NATURE. 1. As to its object. 2. As to its foundation. 3. As to its effects. II. IT IS GOOD IN ITS ORIGIN. 1. Derives existence from God. 2. Man by nature is destitute of hope. 3. God communicates the principle. 4. God maintains it. III. IT IS GOOD IN ITS IMPORTANCE. 1. In regard to man's comfort. 2. In regard to his duty. 3. In regard to his safety. (*E. Martin.*) *Good hope through grace:*—I. WHAT IT INCLUDES. 1. A serious, believing, habitual regard to a future state as represented in the Bible. No atheist denying God or deist rejecting the Scriptures can have it. 2. Preparatory to this hope there must be a humbling conviction of sin, and our danger and helplessness, for the good hope implies deliverance therefrom. Those can know nothing of hope who have known nothing of fear. 3. It implies an acquaintance with the gospel (Col. i. 23) for it is derived from gospel promises, and is connected with gospel faith. 4. The term "good" distinguishes it from every other kind of hope (Job viii. 13, 14; xxvii. 8; Prov. viii. 32). II. WHY IT IS CALLED A GOOD HOPE. 1. Its object is good—not worldly honour, filthy lucre, sensual delight, but the pure, spiritual, exalted felicities of the heavenly world. 2. Its foundation is good—not the stumbling stone of human merit, but the adamant rock of Divine love. 3. Its effect is good. The man who has it is the better as well as the happier for it (1 John iii. 3; Psa. cxix. 166). (*G. Burder.*) *Good hope through grace:*—I. THE GIFT. 1. What is this good hope? (1) Hope is sometimes put for the thing hoped for (Prov. xiii. 12; Col. i. 5) such as (*a*) The coming of Christ to our comfort (Titus ii. 13; 1 Pet. i. 13). (*b*) The resurrection (Acts ii. 26; xxiv. 15; xxvi. 6-8). (*c*) The vision of God (1 John iii. 2). (*d*) Our heavenly inheritance (1 Pet. i. 4; Titus i. 2; Rom. v. 2). (2) Sometimes hope is put for the reasons and causes of hoping; and so he who gives me solid reasons for hoping gives me good hope (Heb. vii. 19; Rom. xv. 4). (3) The act or grace of hope is good in respect of itself (Lam. iii. 26) or the measure of it. That is good hope which is most able to do its office (1 Pet. i. 3; Heb. vi. 11). Briefly the grace of hope is twofold. (*a*) There is a hope which is the immediate fruit of regeneration, and is a constitutive part of the new creature (1 Pet. i. 3). (*b*) There is a hope which is the fruit of experience, and belongs to the seasoned Christian, who has approved his fidelity to God, and made trial of God's fidelity to him (Rom. v. 4). 2. The effects of this hope. (1) Support in troubles. When we are persuaded of a happy issue, we are the better kept from fainting (Phil. i. 19, 20). (2) Encouragement in working. It is hope that sets the whole world a-work (1 Cor. ix. 10) and the Christian (Acts xxvi. 7). 3. This hope is the free gift of God. (1) It is His gift. He not only gives us objective grace—the mercy of the gospel, or its warrant in the promises, but subjective grace by His Holy Spirit whose work is necessary. (*a*) By way of illumination that we may see what is the hope of His calling (Eph. i. 18 ; 2 Pet. i. 9). A short-sighted man cannot see things at a distance ; not from any defect in the object, but through the fault in his eyes. (*b*) By way of inclination that one may seek after these things as our portion and happiness (Acts xvi. 14 ; Gal. v. 5). (*c*) By way of excitation (Rom. xv. 13). (2) It is free gift. (*a*) The matter of hope is God's free, undeserved mercy (Psa. cxxx. 7). Without this there were no hope, and therefore the saints make this their anchor hold (Psa. xiii. 5 ; Jude 21). (*b*) The grace of hope is the fruit of the Lord's mercy ; such are our ill deservings that nothing else could incline Him to give it us (1 Pet. i. 3). II. WHAT ENCOURAGEMENT IT IS TO PRAYER THAT GOD HAS GIVEN US A GOOD HOPE THROUGH GRACE. 1. God would not invite and raise a hope to disappoint it (Psa. cxix. 49). 2. He who gives us the hope will give us all things necessary to the thing hoped for (1 Pet. v. 10). 3. Those who have received good hope through grace have these to rest upon. (1) God's nature as He is merciful and gracious (Judg. xiii. 23). (2) His promise, so that we may trust His faithfulness (Rom. viii. 28 ; Jer. xxxii. 40). (*T. Manton, D.D.*) *The inspiration of hope :*—Hope is an active grace. It is like the spring in the watch : it sets all the wheels of the soul in motion. Hope of a crop makes the husbandman sow his seed ; hope of victory makes the soldier fight ; and a true hope of glory makes a Christian vigorously pursue glory. (*T. Watson.*) *The inspiration of hope:*—The hope of Christ is a staff in the hands of the weary before the arm of Christ is stretched out on which he may be privileged to lean. Hope is a marvellous inspiration which every heart confesses in some season of extremest peril. It can put nerve into the languid, and fleetness into the feet of exhaustion. Let the slim and feathery palm-grove be dimly descried, though ever so remotely, and the caravan will on, spite of the fatigue of the traveller and the simoom's blinding, to where, by the fringy rootlets, the desert waters flow. Let there glimmer one star through the murky waste of night, and though the spars be shattered, and the sails be riven, and the hurricane howls for its prey, the brave sailor will be lashed to the helm, and see already, through the tempests breaking, calm waters and a spotless sky. Oh ! who is there, however hapless his lot or forlorn his surroundings, who is beyond the influence of this choicest of earth's comforters—this faithful friend which survives the flight of riches, and the wreck of reputation, and the break of health, and even the loss of dear and cherished friends. (*W. M. Punshon, LL.D.*) *Hope without grace :*—A " hope " is to some like a passport, which one keeps quietly in his pocket till the time for the journey, and then produces it. Or like life-preservers, which hang useless around the vessel until the hour of danger comes, when the captain calls on every passenger to save himself; and then they are taken down and blown up, and each man, with his hope under his arm, strikes out for the land : and so such men would keep their religious hope hanging until death comes ; and then take it down and inflate it, that it may buoy them up, and float them over the dark river to the heavenly shore. Or as the inhabitants of Block Island keep their boats hauled high upon the beach, and only use them now and then, when they would cross to the mainland ; so such men keep their hopes high and dry upon the shore of life, only to be used when they have to cross the flood that divides this island of time from the mainland of eternity. (*H. W. Beecher.*) *Hope and steadfastness :* —A good Methodist in a prayer meeting said that when, many years since, he crossed the ocean he was much in the habit of looking over the ship's side, particularly near the prow, and watching the vessel as she steadily ploughed her way through the waves. Just under the bowsprit was the image of a human face. The face to him came to be invested with wondrous interest. Whatever the hour or the weather that face seemed ever steadfastly looking to port. Sometimes in great tempests the waves would completely submerge the face of his friend. But as soon as the vessel recovered from its lurch, on looking again over the ship's side, the placid face was still seen faithfully looking out for the port. " And so," he exclaimed, " I humbly trust it is in my own case. Yea, whatever the trials of the past, the toils and disappointments of the present, by the grace of God I am still looking out for port, and not long hence I anticipate a triumphant and abundant entrance. (*W. Baxendale.*)

**Ver. 17. Comfort your hearts and stablish you in every good word and work.—** *Divine comfort :*—I. COMFORT. 1. What it is. (1) Our natural refreshment. We cannot enjoy our temporal mercies with any delight without God's blessing (Eccles.

ii. 24; iii. 13; Acts xiv. 17). (2) Our support in troubles (Psa. cxix. 50; 2 Cor. i. 4; Acts ix. 31). (*a*) God can give His people comfort in the greatest tribulation (Isa. li. 12). As long as we have God to stand by us and the promise of eternal life trouble will be counterbalanced (Rom. v. 2, 3; 2 Cor. iv. 17; Isa. xl. 1, 2; Matt. ix. 2). (*b*) There is special allowance of comfort for God's people in affliction (1 Pet. iv. 14). As the mother keeps most with the sick child, so God looks to the afflicted. This is the difference between God and the world; the world ever runs after those that are prosperous, as rivers into the sea, where there are waters enough. (*c*) Our comforts carry proportion with our sorrows (2 Cor. i. 5; 1 Cor. x. 13). 2. What it is to have our hearts comforted. The heart is the proper seat of spiritual comfort (Psa. iv. 7). God's comfort is like a soaking shower that goes to the root, whereas the dew only wets the surface. Other comforts refresh the outward man. The joy of the world makes a great noise but leaves the heart sorrowful. God in dealing with the heart uses means, but His Spirit works immediately by—(1) Opening the understanding to see the grounds of comfort (Rom. xv. 13). (2) By raising the heart to the lively act of joy (Acts xiii. 52). 3. In what sense it is of God. (1) When it is allowed by Him (Eccles. v. 18). (2) When the matter is provided by Him (John xiv. 1). (3) When by these means He worketh comfort (Rom. xiv. 17). II. Why this is of God. 1. Because God challenges as His own the right to comfort the heart (Job xxxiv. 29). 2. Though the grounds of comfort be never so clear, yet if God concur not, we find not the effect. 3. Because of the advantages springing from this source. Our comforts—(1) Come with more authority, and silence all our doubts and fears (Psa. xciv. 19). If comfort be made of our own fancy it will be like a spider's web that is weaved out of its own bowels, but is easily swept away. (2) Are full and strong. For God works like Himself, and therefore can and will support His people in the greatest difficulties. (*a*) They are full (Acts xiii. 52; 2 Cor. vii. 4; John xv. 11). (*b*) Strong (Heb. vi. 18). III. The uses. 1. To reprove Christians for over-much dejection and fainting in troubles. Why are we so much cast down? Is there no balm in Gilead or comfort in God? 2. If all comfort be of God, let us go to Him for it. (1) See that you are qualified for it. Comfort follows holiness, as heat fire. The Spirit is first a Sanctifier and then a Comforter (Eph. i. 13, 14). (2) Expect not a singular way of comfort besides the Word, prayer, Lord's supper, &c. 3. Consider the ends for which God gives comfort—to fortify us against the enemies of our salvation. (*T. Manton, D.D.*) *Divine comfort:*—When a man walketh in the sun, if his face be towards it, he hath nothing before him but bright shining light and comfortable heat; but let him once turn his back to the sun what hath he before him but a shadow? And what is a shadow but the privation of light and heat of the sun? Yea: it is but to behold his own shadow, defrauding himself of the other. Thus there is no true wisdom, happiness, comfort, but in beholding the countenance of God; look from that and we lose these blessings. And what shall we gain? A shadow, an empty image of ourselves instead of the reconciled face of God. (*J. Spencer.*) *Establishment:*—I. What it is. Confirmation in the grace we have received. It must be distinguished—1. With respect to the power wherewith we are assisted. There is—(1) Habitual confirmation, when habits of grace are more settled and increased. (*a*) Faith: for we stand by faith (Rom. xi. 20; 1 Pet. i. 5; Luke xxii. 32). (*b*) Love (Cant. viii. 6, 7). (*c*) Hope (Heb. vi. 19). (2) Actual establishment, when these habits are fortified and quickened by the actual influence of God; otherwise neither stability of resolutions (Psa. lxxiii. 2), nor of gracious habits (Rev. iii. 2) will support us. 2. With respect to the matter about which it is conversant—stability. (1) In the doctrine of faith (1 Thess. v. 21; Jer. vi. 16). We ought to be well settled lest our fluctuating opinions breed unbelief in others and shame to ourselves. Yet while we cry up constancy we must not cherish prejudice which shuts the door on the light. (2) In every good work, or holiness of life. Here the greatest establishment is needed. It is ill when the mind is tainted, but worse when the heart is alienated (1 Thess. iii. 13). This is difficult. (*a*) Because of the contrariety of the principles that are within us (Gal. v. 17). The garrison is not free from danger that has an enemy lodged within. (*b*) Because it is more hard to continue in conversion than to be converted. The latter is more passive, the former active. 3. With respect to the subject in which it is seated: the soul with its faculties. (1) The mind is established when we have a clear, certain, and full apprehension of the truth of the gospel (Col. ii. 2). (2) The will is established when it is firmly and thoroughly resolved for God against sin (Acts xi. 23; Psa. xxvii. 4; 1 Pet. iv. 1). (3) The affections are established when they stir us up to do what the mind is convinced of, and the will resolved upon as to the necessary duties in order to eternal happiness (Psa. cxix. 32). (*a*) Love fills us with delight (Psa. xl. 8 ; 1 John v. 3 ; Psa. cxii. 1). (*b*) Hope bears us up (Heb. iii. 6). 4. With respect to the uses which it serves. (1) Doing the will of God with delight, cheerfulness, and constancy (Eph. iii. 16). (2) Bearing afflictions with honour to God and safety to ourselves (Phil. iv. 13 ; Col. i. 11). (3) Withstanding temptations (Eph. vi. 10). 5. With respect to the degree, it is such a strengthening of the soul as prevents not only our fall but our shaking (1 Cor. xv. 58 ; Eph. iii. 17 ; Col. i. 23). II. How NEEDFUL IT IS. 1. Man at best is but a creature. As providence is a continual creation, so stablishing grace is the continuance of the new creation (2 Cor. i. 21). 2. The indisposition of our natures. (1) To every good word. The truths of the gospel are supernatural and must be settled and preserved by Divine power (Eph. ii. 8). (2) To every good work (Jer. xiv. 10 ; Psa. xcv. 10). 3. In regard of those oppositions that are made against us after conversion. Satan pursues us ever (Col. i. 13, *cf.* 1 John iv. 4) ; therefore there must be the same power to stablish us in grace that first brought us into a state of grace. 4. The saints miscarry when God withdraws His supporting grace, as Peter, David, &c. (Psa. li. ; 2 Chron. xxxii. 31). III. WHY IT IS TO BE SOUGHT OF GOD. 1. He only is able (Rom. xvi. 25 ; Jude 24 ; 2 Tim. i. 12). 2. He is willing (2 Cor. i. 10 ; 2 Tim. iv. 17, 18). 3. He has promised (Psa. lxxiii. 23). 4. This is the experience of saints (Psa. xciv. 18). Conclusion : Look up to God for establishment. 1. When you begin to decline and grow indifferent in the practice of godliness. If grace be weak, you must get it strengthened (Psa. xvii. 5 ; cxix. 133). 2. In unsettled times when we are full of fears, and think we shall never hold out (Psa. xvi. 8). (*T. Manton, D.D.*) *Sustained by Christ :*—There are men and women here who would have been dead twenty years ago but for Jesus. They have gone through trial enough to exhaust ten times their physical strength. Their property went, their health went, their families were scattered. God only knows what they suffered. They are an amazement to themselves that they have been able to stand it. They look at their once happy home, surrounded by all comfort. Gone! They think of the time when they used to rise strong in the morning and walk vigorously down the street, and had experienced a health they thought inexhaustible. Gone! Everything but Jesus. He has pitied them. His eye has watched them. His omnipotence has defended them. Yes, He has been with them. They have gone through disaster, and He was a pillar of fire by night. They have gone across stormy Galilee, but Christ had His foot on the neck of the storm. (*T. De Witt Talmage.*)

---

## CHAPTER III.

VER. 1. **Finally, brethren, pray for us.**—*The power of prayer :*—The Apostle Paul is now writing from Greece, either from Athens or from Corinth. The note at the foot of the epistle mentions Athens. The same ancient subscription testifies that the first epistle was written from Athens. There is, however, the strongest reason for believing that both the epistles were written from Corinth ; and without discussing the question we will assume that at least this second epistle was. Thus we see that Paul desired that the Word of the Lord might be as unimpededly spread and as illustrious in renown when he preached it in Corinth as when he had published it in Thessalonica. I. And first, AN APOSTLE ASKING HELP OF PRIVATE CHRISTIANS. God alone is really independent. Only God can say, " I am that I am." All the creatures of God within the range of our knowledge are mutually dependent, including man, the divinest of all terrestrial beings. The highest officers which the Church of Christ has known were apostles, and those were extraordinary functionaries ; yet one of these, and that the greatest, pens the words of our text, saying to the young men and to the little children in the Church of Thessalonica, " Brethren, pray for us." The eye cannot say unto the hand, I have no need of thee ; nor again the head to the feet, I have no need of you. Now, ye are the body of Christ and members in particular, and it is just this mutual dependence which is recognized in the request of Paul as embodied in the text. There are four things which are likely to make us forget our dependence upon others—gifts or endowments, office, position or standing, and past successful service. These four things—

gifts, office, position, successful service—are very likely to make us forget our dependence upon others unless we be on the watch against the mischievous influences which occasionally proceed from them. And there are four things in others which tend to make us overlook the assistance they can afford us—low temporal estate (especially in these days when wealth is becoming in our churches a false god), the possession of a single or but few talents, a retiring disposition, and the not holding any office in the Church of Christ. II. Let us look at PRAYER CO-OPERATING WITH PREACHING AND SECURING ITS SUCCESS. Who can tell what is being wrought, and what has been effected, by the ordinance represented by this little word "pray"? In asking his friends in Thessalonica for assistance the apostle said to them "Pray." Prayer is very different from preaching, and yet a moment's reflection will show how they work together. Prayer speaks to God for man; preaching speaks to man for God. Prayer seeks to bring God to man; preaching aims to bring man to God. Prayer moves God towards man; preaching persuades man to seek after God. Prayer makes known unto God man's request; preaching reveals to man God's mind and will. Preaching casts in the seed; prayer brings the rain and the sunshine. Preaching deposits the leaven; prayer secures the hand which adds its working. Preaching utters the good tidings; prayer carries the sound to the ear and makes that all sensitive. Preaching is doing the practical work which man can do; prayer asks for what God only can do, and for that which is necessary to the success of that which the man can do. But although prayer occupies this lofty position, we are all more or less in danger of being diverted from it. Those who reason much upon religious matters are diverted by a secret scepticism. Those who are carnal and walk as men are diverted by their fondness for a quick and visible return for all their efforts. Those who think of themselves more highly than they ought to think are diverted by self-sufficiency. Those whose estimate of human nature is too valuable are diverted by their too strong expectation of what may be done by the simple presentation of the truth; for there are men so excessively simple that even now, after eighteen centuries of trial, they will tell you that if you only put God's truth as well as you can before men they will take it in. III. Thirdly, at A CHURCH IN A MACEDONIAN CITY BEING REQUESTED TO SYMPATHIZE WITH A CHURCH IN A CITY OF ACHAIA. This request recognizes the common relations of man and the supreme relations of Christ. Thessalonica, as the schoolboy knows, was a chief city of Macedonia, a then northern and Roman division of Greece, as Corinth of Achaia was the southern division of the same country. The Macedonian city had become, under the Romans, great, populous, and wealthy, and contained a large number of Jews. It has been called, very justly I think, the Liverpool of Northern Greece, on account of its commerce, ships sailing from its harbours to all parts of the then commercial world. Corinth was also a magnificent mercantile city, extremely rich and densely populated; the population consisting of Jews, Greeks, and Romans, with a smaller proportion of Jews than were found in Thessalonica. Where Thessalonica has been compared to Liverpool, Corinth has been likened to modern Paris. Now considering that the two cities were but some four or five hundred miles apart—that they were chief cities in two provinces of the same country—and that they had several national and civic features in common, the existence of sympathy, it may be said, must be taken for granted, and as scarcely worthy of remark. But would such a saying be reasonable and true? Men in great cities are generally inclined to become isolated, and exclusive, and self-absorbed. Moreover great cities are proverbially envious, and jealous, and contemptuous of each other—compare, for instance, Glasgow and Edinburgh—so that it is no small thing to have the men of one city greatly concerned for the men of another. Now Paul would have the Gentile in Thessalonica lovingly interested in the Jew of Corinth, and the Jew of Thessalonica in the Gentile of Corinth. The disposition which looks upon all men now as a family, and all Christians as a household, is pre-eminently the spirit of Jesus Christ, and to this Paul appeals when he writes: "Brethren, pray for us that the Word of the Lord may have free course and be glorified, even as with you." IV. The latter part of the text expresses THE ONE THING TO BE DESIRED WHEREVER THE GOSPEL IS PREACHED. This is the fourth object at which we said we would look. The language here employed is evidently derived from the public races. The word here rendered "have free course" is elsewhere translated "run." Paul in passing from Athens to Corinth would go along the isthmus where the Grecian games were celebrated. He would see the stadia and theatre; he would look upon the busts and statues of successful competitors, and would see the very trees which yielded the corruptible crown. Accustomed, like the Great Teacher, to draw his illustrations from near sources, he would naturally use an institution which increased the fame of the renowned city. Hence he speaks of the Word of the Lord running as a racer without impediment, or as a chariot without a drag on the wheel, and being honoured and applauded at the end of the course. In plain language Paul requests the Thessalonians to pray that the Word of the Lord may speedily be communicated to man, may be cordially received, may appear to be not the word of man but the Word of God, and may produce all promised results, being universally acknowledged as worthy of all acceptation. Now these words imply that there were hindrances to the spread of the Gospel in Corinth. Some of these were peculiar to Corinth and others were common to all places. Our Lord Jesus Christ had forewarned his apostles of these obstacles when he spoke to them of the hatred and persecution which they would encounter for the Gospel's sake, also in some of the similitudes by which he represented the kingdom of heaven, especially in the parable of the sower. Therein Christ teaches that the counteracting work of sense, the want of comprehension and appreciation in the hearers, the lack of depth of feeling, the cares of the world, the deceitfulness of riches, the lust of other things, the wealth and pleasures of this life impede the Word. All this every hearer has more or less experienced, and every preacher more or less observed, ever since Christ spake the parable whose lessons we are quoting. Now from the commencement of his apostleship Paul saw this. Paul was not a man to look on the most pleasant side of an object. Invariably, as we all know, he turned a thing round and round, and looked at it on all sides. Heathenism and Judaism had opposed the spread of that Word in Thessalonica, especially Judaism. The Jews envied the apostles their miraculous powers and their influence over the Gentiles, and raising a fierce tumult against them, drove them from the city; but they could not banish the word of the Lord, and now in Corinth it found embodiment again. The luxury of the city, the vain show, the expensive habits of the people, the attractive immorality, the self-indulgent habits of the citizens, presented peculiar obstacles in Corinth, but the chief of them are common to all places, all races, and all ages of the world. Men do not care for any word of the Lord. They do not feel their need of this peculiar Word of the Lord that we call the Gospel. Men have their ears filled with the words of man. But, it here occurs to me that we have scarcely noticed recently WHAT IS MEANT BY THE WORD OF THE LORD. According to the text the Word of the Lord is something definite and positive. That of which Paul speaks, is not any or every word of the Lord, but some word which, on account of its importance and blessedness, he calls "The Word." It is the Gospel of our salvation, which is sufficiently definite to enable one to detect "another Gospel." Now some men seem to say that the Gospel of our salvation is not definite at all. As the God revealed in the Bible is a personal God, so the Word of the Lord is a peculiar and positive revelation that Paul here actually personifies, so distinct and well-defined does it appear to his eye. Then this Word of the Lord has a special mission to mankind. It needs to have free course. Its free course is like the going forth of the sun from horizon to meridian, spreading on its way light and heat, fruitfulness and life. Or, returning to the allusion of the text, its free course is like the successful running of a racer, or the driving of the charioteer, upon whose supremacy is staked, not the laurel, but liberty and life—not crowns, but the very existence of peoples and of kingdoms. Hence the prayer that the Word of the Lord may have free course, and be glorified. Brethren, you who know the Word of the Lord publish it. Keep it not as a sacred trust in the treasury of your spirit. As you, then, publish the Word of the Lord, lay your account to the existence and to the manifestation of impediments. Expect to see it proceeding, sometimes, slowly as a chariot whose wheels are locked—slowly as a racer encumbered by reason of long and heavy train. Yet imagine the reverse of this—the Word of the Lord having free course. Think of this; nay, more expect this. Remove impediments by your own hands if possible; but in every instance ask the Lord who spake the Word to give His Word free course. Give others who are publishing the Word of the Lord your interest. Pray for all mothers and fathers of the land. (*S. Martin.*) *Prayer for ministers:*—If Paul with all his supernatural endowments required the prayers of God's people, how much more ordinary ministers. The progress of the gospel is not to be attributed to the power of the minister, however great, but to the power of God in answer to prayer. I. THE NATURE OF PRAYER GENERALLY. 1. Sincere desire. 2. Believing expectation of the blessings supplicated. The prayer of the man who doubts, of the heart which wavers, refuses to give glory to God by confiding in the promises He has made. But there must be some ground on which the believing expectation rests, viz., the testimony of God concerning His Son, and not mere sincerity, good character, attendance or the ordinances of religion. 3. The influence of God's Spirit. Without the Spirit's regenerating power, we can have no spiritual vision or believing confidence. We cannot call God "Father" but by the Spirit of adoption, and therefore cannot offer the prayer of children. 4. Petitions in accordance with the revealed will of God. It is possible to seek what God has never promised, and even what He has forbidden. It is important, therefore, not to trust our own feelings, but to rely upon God's Word. II. THE DUTY OF PRAYER FOR MINISTERS IN PARTICULAR. Such prayer—1. Connects devotion with public instruction. Mere critical hearing or indifferent hearing destroys the chances of edification. We should remember that we are not only in the presence of the preacher, but of the preacher's God. When we link the pulpit to the throne, there will be a blessing in the feeblest ministrations. 2. Associates ministerial success with its true cause. There is a great danger of attributing this to the talent of the preacher, and giving the glory to man which is due to God alone. Prayer will help us to recognize the agency of God in the instrumentality of man. 3. Creates a right state of mind in regard to ministerial failure. The blame may be not his but yours. Success may be withheld not because of any failure in his powers, but in the failure of your prayers. III. THE INFLUENCE OF A PRAYING PEOPLE ON THE STATE OF THE WORLD AND THE CHURCH WITH REGARD TO THE DIFFUSION OF THE GOSPEL. Prayer exercises an important influence in this direction because it—1. Increases and maintains love to God. Prayer leads to acquaintance with God, and the more we are acquainted with God the more we shall love Him. 2. Love to man. Prayer for conversion is at once an evidence and a means of growth of that love. 3. Zeal. Without zeal there will be no success; but what promotes love to God and man will inflame zeal; and inflamed zeal gives energy to philanthropy. 4. Practical activity, which is inseparable from love and zeal. 5. Patience. Without prayer, difficulty assumes unreal proportions and begets despondency; but by prayer the believer knows that they are not unsurmountable, and works hopefully for their removal. 6. Devotedness. Prayer is the secret of entire consecration, without which there can be no success. (*J. Burnet.*) *The power of prayer :*—I once knew a minister who was constantly successful, who enjoyed a revival every year for twelve years, and could not account for it until one evening at a prayer meeting a brother confessed that for a number of years past he had been in the habit of spending every Saturday evening till midnight in prayer for his pastor the next day. That explained the secret, in part, at least. Such a man praying would make any ministry successful. (*C. G. Finney, D.D.*) *Prayer and success :*—No one can tell how much power may be imparted to a pastor's preaching if even one person be among his hearers whose thoughts are wrestling with God that the word may be made effective unto salvation. In a church it was noticed that for several years one young man after another became a communicant. This could not be referred to the preaching of the pastor, nor to any known agency. At last it was found that an old coloured woman who sat in the gallery had been doing this. She selected one young man whom she saw in the congregation, and made him the object of her prayers. She prayed for him in her home and when she was at church. After he united with the church she selected another. And thus for years she had been praying. This reminds us of the legend so sweetly put into verse by Adelaide Procter :

> " The monk was preaching : strong his earnest word,
>     From the abundance of his heart he spoke,
> And the flame spread,—in every soul that heard
>     Sorrow and love and good resolve awoke ;
> The poor lay brother, ignorant and old,
>     Thanked God that he had heard such words of gold.

> ' Still let the glory, Lord, be thine alone,'
>     So prayed the monk, his breast absorbed in praise ;
>         *       *       *       *       *       *
> ' O Lord, I thank Thee that my feeble strength
>     Has been so blessed ; that sinful hearts and cold
> Were melted at my pleading,—knew at length
>     How sweet Thy service and how safe Thy fold ;

> While souls that love Thee saw before them rise
> Still holier heights of loving sacrifice.'
>
> So prayed the monk, when suddenly he heard
> An angel speaking thus : ' Know, O my son,
> Thy words had all been vain, but hearts were stirred,
> And saints were edified, and sinners won
> By his, the poor lay brother's, humble aid
> Who sat upon the pulpit stair and prayed,"

God give us in all our churches the lay brother who prays.  He is the best prayer book.  (*George S. Mott, D.D.*)    *Confidence in prayer :*—Upon one occasion of great difficulty, Melancthon and Luther had met together to consult about the best means to be adopted.  After having spent some time in prayer, Melancthon was suddenly called out of the room, from which he retired under great distress of mind.  During his absence, he saw some of the elders of the reformed church, with their parishioners and families.   Several children were also brought hanging at the breast ; while others a little older were engaged in prayer.  This reminded him of that passage, " Out of the mouth°of babes and sucklings has thou ordained strength, because of thine enemies, that thou mightest still the enemy and avenger." Encouraged by this pleasing scene, he returned to his friends with a mind set at liberty, and a cheerful countenance.   Luther, astonished at this sudden change, said, " What now !  what has happened to you, Philip, that you are become so cheerful ? "   " O Sirs," replied Melancthon, " let us not be discouraged, for I have seen our noble protectors, and such as, I will venture to say, will prove invincible against every foe ! "   " And pray," returned Luther, filled with surprise and pleasure, " who, and.where are these powerful heroes ? "   " Oh ! "said Melancthon, " they are the wives of our parishioners, and their little children, whose prayers I have just witnessed—prayers which I am sure our God will hear : for as our heavenly Father, and the Father of our Lord Jesus Christ, has never despised nor rejected our supplications, we have reason to trust that He will not in the present alarming danger."  (*Scottish Christian Herald.*)    **That the Word of the Lord may have free course and be glorified.** —*The unfettered gospel :*—St. Paul had just prayed for the Thessalonians, he now asked them to pray for him.  But it is worthy of remark that the first point mentioned has no reference to himself, but to his work. His life was in danger, and in ver. 2 he begs them to pray that he may be delivered, &c. ; but this was not the thing nearest his heart.  I. THE WORD OF THE LORD.  What this was we may gather from the record of another missionary (Acts x. 36–43).   It included the heavenly mission, miracles, life, death, resurrection and future coming of Christ, and the certainty of pardon through trust in Him.   1. How inestimable this privilege. 2. How universal.   II. ITS FREE COURSE.  *Marg.* " run," indicating progress overcoming whatever obstructions.  The psalmist prayed that God's saving health might be " known among all nations: " how much more should we, the professed servants of Him who said " Go ye into all the world," &c.   We should pray that the gospel may have free course—1. In ourselves. 2. In our families, including servants. 3. In our neighbourhoods.   4. Among our countrymen in overgrown towns and neglected villages.   5. Among our emigrants, so many of whom go forth, no man caring for their souls, to found our colonies.  6. Among the heathen.  III. ITS GLORIFICATION, *i.e.*, its eminent success.  What kind of success the Apostle explains, " as it is with you."  How was that ?  The word of the Lord came to them—1. In power (1 Thess. 1–5), as a fire burning in the conscience ; as a hammer breaking their wills ; as a two-edged sword, discerning the thoughts and intents of the heart.   This glorious power was given to the Word by the Holy Ghost.  2. Bringing assured peace and joy.   They were not merely startled by it at first, but the more they heard the more they were edified.  3. Resulting in continued obedience.  4. Ministering to the increase of holiness.  IV. THE CONNECTION OF PRAYER WITH ALL THIS.  The gospel will not run and succeed as a mere matter of course.  But prayer lays hold of the power of God which alone can—1. Overcome difficulties.  " Is anything too hard for the Lord."  2. Make the gospel effectual in salvation.  (*D. Fenn.*)    *The glorification of the Gospel :*—I. THE GREAT OBJECT OF CHRISTIAN DEVOTION.  1. The free and unimpeded circulation of the gospel.   (1) There are impediments—the spirit of persecution, the prevalence of idolatry, superstition, and infidelity, the inconsistency and corruptions of the Church—all of which are resolved into the opposition of the human heart.  (2) The allusion is to the *stadium* or racecourse—in which it was necessary that every obstacle should be removed, crooked places made straight, &c. The Son of God is riding forth in the chariot of His gospel, and the prayer is that nothing may be allowed to stop His progress. 2. The removal of hindrances was only a means to the end of the glorification of the gospel. (1) It would not be enough if in every part the most unrestricted freedom were enjoyed, that all obstacles to evangelism were removed, that spacious churches were everywhere raised, and that all rank and authority were made subservient to the progress of truth. (2) The word of God is glorified only when it is the medium of spiritual renovation, when its supreme authority is acknowledged by its professors, when its discoveries are cordially received, its injunctions practised, its holy influences exemplified. II. THE DUTY OF FERVENT PRAYER IN ORDER TO ITS ACCOMPLISHMENT. The connection between prayer and the success of the gospel involves many important principles. 1. Prayer honours the agency of God. If we have the ear of God we are sure of His hand. If the spirit of supplication be poured out upon us, that itself is a pledge of success. And God honours prayer because prayer acknowledges that "it is not by might, nor by power," &c. 2. Prayer is expressly enjoined. "Ask, and it shall be given you." "For all these things I will be inquired of," &c. 3. All history demonstrates that the spirit of prayer is invariably connected with success. No one ever prayed for himself that did not succeed. Let this encourage the anxious inquirer. Can you refer to any praying church that was not a successful church? 4. Those engaged in promoting this object have especial claims on you. "Pray for us." It is the prayer of the Christian minister. Like Moses of old, he is upheld in the hands of prayer. 5. In proportion to the spirit of prayer shall we cherish the spirit of activity, liberality, and zeal. III. KNOWN INSTANCES OF SUCCESS ARE GROUNDS OF ENCOURAGEMENT. "As it is with you." Not that we are to be satisfied with success; on the contrary, notwithstanding it, we have much cause for humiliation. Still humiliation is not incompatible with thanksgiving for what has been done in and by us. The apostle quotes the case of the Thessalonians as an illustration of what God can do and a pledge of what He will do. Look upon the history of your own conversion. What God can do for you He can do for every one. Conclusion: The subject—1. Demands inquiry. 2. Encourages hope. 3. Enjoins activity. (*J. Fletcher, D.D.*) *The success of the gospel:*—I. THE OBJECT PROPOSED. That the Word of the Lord may have free course, &c. 1. By the Word of the Lord we understand that revelation of God's will contained in the Holy Book, a revelation of every doctrine necessary to be believed, and of every duty to be practised. This is the Word of the Lord—(1) For it bears the stamp of Divinity upon it, being authenticated by miracle and fulfilled prophecy. (2) Because the subject matter is what God alone could reveal. Creation, man's nature, the way of salvation through redemption by Christ, and regeneration by the Spirit. 2. This gospel is the great instrument which is intended for human salvation. It is God's instrument for enlightening the mind; His tender of pardon; His directory of the way to heaven. The age prior to the gospel abounded with great men; but the world by wisdom knew not God. The gospel, however, is the power of God unto salvation. 3. The object proposed is that this Word of God may have free course. Some see here a reference to the Greek races. Here is a course to be run, and the glory relates to the crown and the plaudits of the spectators. But the more natural view is that of a river. The gospel is the river of the water of life. Wherever it comes the wilderness and solitary place are made glad. Trees of righteousness laden with fruits of peace overhang its margin. (1) The gospel in its course has met with opposition from high and low, rich and poor, &c. Heathens and infidels have entered the lists against it. Its progress has been impeded by subtle errors. But the greatest obstacle has been the inconsistencies of its professors. (2) The text contemplates this gospel as rising and bearing down every opposing barrier, and rolling the majestic tide of truth to the utmost regions. 4. "And be glorified." It is glorious in itself, but it is the manifestation of this glory that the text has in view. The Word of the Lord is glorified—(1) In its rapid and extensive progress. This was the case when three thousand were converted under the ministry of Peter, when Luther arose, and Wesley, and in modern missions. (2) In its effects on the character of its converts, *e.g.*, Saul of Tarsus. (3) In the happy deaths of Christians. II. THE MEANS INDICATED. Pray for your ministers because—1. They are instruments of God for the dissemination of the gospel. The gospel is an offer of peace and they are ambassadors of God; it is good news and they are the messengers; it is a mystery for man's benefit and they are the stewards; the world is a field and they are the cultivators; the Church is an edifice and they are the builders. Other powers are auxiliary, *e.g.*, Sunday schools, tract and Bible societies; but preaching leads the way and has the special sanction of Christ. In view of all this, "pray for us." 2. They meet with many discouragements, arising from their weakness, their responsibility, and their failures. 3. The efficacy of their preaching depends upon the unction of the Spirit, and this can be secured only by prayer. 4. It is your duty. It is enjoined by God. They pray, study, preach for you; the least that can be asked is that you should pray for them. 5. It will be beneficial to yourselves. Without prayer you cannot expect to profit by their ministrations. Conclusion: 1. Great is the efficacy of prayer. 2. You cannot be neutral in this work. You are either for the gospel or against it, and prayer or the neglect of it will determine which. (*J. Brown.*)    *The gospel's conquests:*—A captain once rushed into the presence of the general in hot haste, and said: "General, we can never fight them, they are so numerous." "Captain," said the general, coolly, "we are not here to count them, but to conquer them, and conquer them we must." And conquer them they did. (*J. Ossian Davies.*)    *The diffusion of the gospel:*—It begins in the individual's heart; and secretly, silently, but powerfully, it spreads till the whole nature is penetrated by its influence, and animated to a new character. It is silent as the dew of heaven, but as saturating also. Like a sweet stream, it runs along many a mile in silent beauty. You may trace its course, not by roaring cataracts, and rolling boulders, and rent rocks, but by the belt of verdure and fertility that extends along its margin. The fact is all great forces are silent; strength is quiet; all great things are still. It is the vulgar idea that thunder and lightning are the mightiest forces. Gravitation, which is unseen, binds stars and suns in harmony. The light which comes so silently that it does not injure an infant's eye, makes the whole earth burst into flowers, and yet it is not heard. Thus love and truth, the compound elements of the gospel leaven, are quiet but mighty in their action; mightier far than hate, persecution, bribes, falsehood, and swords. Souls are won, not by might, or by power, but by the Spirit of the Lord of Hosts; and this Spirit is secured by the quiet efficacy of prayer. (*J. Cumming, D.D.*)    *Spreading the gospel:*—At the close of the war with Great Britain I was in new York. One Saturday afternoon a ship was discovered in the offing, which was supposed to be a cartel, bringing home our commissioners at Ghent from their unsuccessful mission. The sun had set before any intelligence from the vessel had reached the city. Expectation became painfully intense as the hours of darkness drew on. At length a boat reached the wharf, announcing the fact that a treaty of peace had been signed, and was waiting for nothing but the action of our government to become law. The men on whose ears these words first fell, ran in breathless haste to repeat them to their friends, shouting as they rushed through the streets, "Peace, peace, peace!" Every one who heard the sound repeated it. From house to house, from street to street, the news spread with electric rapidity. The whole city was in commotion. Men bearing lighted torches were flying to and fro, shouting like madmen, "Peace, peace, peace!" When the rapture had partially subsided, one idea occupied every mind. But few men slept that night. In groups they were gathered in the streets and by the fireside, beguiling the hours of midnight by reminding each other that the agony of war was over. Thus every one becoming a herald, the news soon reached every man, woman and child in the city; and in this sense the whole city was evangelized. All this, you see, was reasonable and proper; but when Jehovah has offered to our world a treaty of peace, why is not a similar zeal displayed in proclaiming the good news? Why are men perishing all around us, and no one has ever personally offered them salvation through a crucified Redeemer? (*Dr. Wayland.*)    *The progress of Christianity:*—In the first 1,500 years of its history Christianity gained 100,000,000 of adherents; in the next 300 years 100,000,000 more; but in the last 100 years 210,000,000 more. Make these facts vivid. Here is a staff. Let it represent the course of Christian history. Let my hand represent 500 years. I measure off 500, 1,000, 1,500 years. In that length of time how many adherents did Christianity gain? 100,000,000. I add three finger breadths more. In that length of time how many adherents did Christianity gain? 100,000,000. In the 300 years succeeding the Reformation Christianity gained as many adherents as in the 1,500 years preceding. But I now add a single finger's breadth to represent one century. How many adherents has Christianity gained in that length of time? 210,000,000 more. Such has been the marvellous growth of the Christian nations in our century, that in the last eighty-three years Christianity has gained more adherents than in the previous eighteen centuries. These are facts of colossal significance, and they cannot be dwelt on too graphically and too often. By adherents of Christianity I mean nominal Christians, *i.e.*, all who are not Pagans, Mohammedans, or Jews. At the present rate of progress, it is supposed that there will be 1,200,000,000 of nominal Christians in the world in the year 2,000. (*Joseph Cook.*)

Ver. 2. **That we may be delivered from unreasonable and wicked men.**—The curious word rendered "unreasonable" is rendered "amiss" in Luke xxiii. 41, "wickedness" in Acts xxv. 5, "harm" in Acts xxviii. 6, occurring nowhere else in the New Testament. It properly means something "misplaced," hence "extravagant," "monstrous." Thus the dying robber says that our Lord has done "nothing so monstrous" as to deserve crucifixon; Festus ironically invites the priests to a serious journey to St. Paul's trial, "if there be something so monstrous in him"; the Maltese "say that nothing so monstrous happened to him after all." So St. Paul wishes the Thessalonians to pray for his deliverance "from those monstrous and depraved people." He is evidently meaning some particular foes whom he fears, for the original has the definite article. Who, then are those monstrous persons? If we turn to Acts xviii. 6, 9, 12, and observe the circumstances under which the letter was written, we can hardly doubt that they are the unbelieving Jews of Corinth. From these Jews he was narrowly delivered. It was perhaps in direct answer to the prayers for which St. Paul here asks that he received the vision and assurances of our Lord, and that Gallio was moved to quash so abruptly the proceedings of the Jews. (*Canon Mason.*)   *A marvellous deliverance:*—A worthy servant of God, pastor in one of the cantons of Switzerland, took a lively interest in a prisoner condemned to death. On the evening before the execution the pastor could not account for a strange repugnance to perform a duty that he had hitherto discharged without hesitation. A voice within him seemed to say, "Do not go." Fearing to neglect a duty, he ran to the prison. Arrived at the gate, the same irresistible voice seemed to say to him, "Do not enter." The pastor returned to his study, assured that he was obeying the will of Him whom he desired to serve. He afterwards learned that the prisoner had resolved to make a desperate effort to escape, and as soon as the pastor entered that day, to attack him, and then escape to some place of concealment. The unhappy prisoner, exasperated by disappointment, roared with anger. The gaoler, hearing an unaccountable noise, suddenly entered the cell. The condemned man, supposing this was his intended victim, threw himself, with the fury of despair, on the gaoler, and struck him on the head with his irons. The gaoler fell dead, while the prisoner ran towards the gate to escape, and was only secured after a terrible conflict. (*J. L. Nye.*)   *God a protector:* —Some years ago, a band of missionaries in the Fiji Islands found their home surrounded by a troop of savages armed for battle. Being both unable and unwilling to fight, they shut their door and began to pray. Presently the howling of the savages ceased. Then one of the missionaries went out, and found only one savage there. Said the missionary: "Where are your chiefs?" "They are gone. They heard you praying to your God; and they know yours is a strong God, and they are gone." The savages were right at last. God is a strong God; strong to help those who love Him—strong to punish His enemies. **All men have not faith.**—*Lacking the essential:*—I. WHAT FAITH IS. 1. It is taking God at His word. Noah did it about a thing unknown (Heb. xi. 7); Abraham did it about a thing untried (Heb. xi. 17–19); Moses did it about a thing untried (Heb. xi. 28). 2. It is trusting Jesus at His invitation. The Jews who had no faith, had no profit (Heb. iv. 2); Peter who had little faith, had little comfort (Matt. xiv. 28, 30, 31); the woman of Canaan, who had great faith, had a great blessing (Matt. xv. 28); the centurion, who had most faith, had most honour (Matt. viii. 10). Trust your souls to Christ's care (Acts vii. 59); trust your sins to Christ's cleansing (1 Peter i. 18, 19); trust your life to Christ's keeping (Col. iii. 3, 4). II. WHENCE FAITH COMES. 1. From God's grace (Eph. ii. 8; Rom. xii. 3). 2. From God's Word (Rom. x. 17; 2 Tim. iii. 15). 3. From God's working (1 John v. 1; Col. ii. 12). 4. From man's heart (Rom. x. 10; vi. 17). III. HOW FAITH WORKS. 1. It overcometh the world (1 John v. 4). 2. It purifieth the heart (Acts xv. 8, 9). 3. It worketh by love (Gal. v. 6). Two great benefits come from faith—(1) the preciousness of Christ (1 Peter ii. 7); (2) the blessedness of Christ (1 Peter i. 8). (*Archdeacon Richardson, M.A.*)

Ver. 3. **The Lord is faithful.**—*The faithfulness of God:*—No apostle insisted more strongly on the liberty of God than St. Paul. This is understood when we remember that he wrote to churches largely composed of Jews whose inveterate inclination was to believe that God had bound Himself to them by an inviolable and exclusive covenant. To uproot this he teaches that the covenant with Israel did not prevent God being the God of the Gentiles. But that teaching may raise a formidable objection. The freedom of God; is not that arbitrariness? No; Paul the great defender of Divine liberty is also the one who insists with most force on the Divine faithfulness, that attribute which affirms that God is without shadow of turning. The two truths thus balance each other. I. The Lord is faithful—HAS NOT GOD WRITTEN THAT THOUGHT IN ALL HIS WORKS? Do we not each spring read it in the renewed nature? 1. Alas! we can count on that faithfulness and not recognize its source. The peasant who, perhaps, has never bent his knee to God, turns up the ground, confides the grain to its furrows, and awaits the future with confidence. The atheist who denies the sovereign ordainer believes in universal order in nature. The scientist counts so on the exactitude of the laws of nature that a thousand years beforehand he announces the minute when two stars will meet in space. Everything in our plans for the future rests on the confidence that what God has done until now, He will do again. Yet the carnal man stays himself in this very fidelity in order to dispense with God, and because everything happens as it did in the time of his fathers, he infers the uselessness of prayer. The very faithfulness which ought to fill him with gratitude serves as an excuse for his unthankfulness. 2. What then is necessary that God's action may be manifested? That He interrupts the course of His benefits? This He does sometimes, and with what results? Man says "Chance alone governs us." Thus whatever God does, man succeeds in eluding Him. If order reigns, the sinner says "I can dispense with God"; if disorder occurs, "There is no God." II. GOD'S FAITHFULNESS APPEARS IN THE MORAL ORDER. 1. What are moral laws? Not variable commands which God is able to change when He likes, but expressions of His very nature, "Be ye holy for I am holy." 2. This being so, I can understand why God cannot contradict Himself, and that at all costs His law must be accomplished. You would regard him as a fool who would trifle with steam, but look without terror on the sinner who violates the Divine will. Yet which is the most certain. I can conceive of a world where the law of gravity does not exist, but not one where, by the will of God, evil would be good. I cannot believe, without tearing my conscience in two, that if the seed buried in the soil must appear, yet what a man sows he will not reap. 3. On what does the confidence of the greater part of men rest? On the idea that God's justice is never vigorous. Who told us so? Sinners interested in believing it. But is a criminal to witness in his own cause and pronounce his own verdict? Let us not abase God by such an idea under the pretext that He is good. God is faithful to Himself, cannot give the lie to His holiness, and according to His immutable laws sin must entail suffering. 4. Though all sinners should agree in denying God's judgment that will not hinder them from being carried each minute towards the judgment which awaits them. I can believe everything except that God ceases to be holy; and convicted of that, the only suitable prayer is "God be merciful to me a sinner." 5. There is the admission the gospel wishes to draw from us. And when repentant men by faith throw themselves on the Divine mercy, they find in God a reconciled Father, and the thought of His faithfulness becomes the source of the firmest assurance, and the sweetest consolation. 6. God's faithfulness, like the wilderness pillar, is at once dark and light: to the sinner it is justice, to the penitent mercy. 7. Not that God in pardoning sacrifices His righteousness; righteousness has received this sanction on-the Cross. 8. But will not such a doctrine countenance presumption. Yes, just as if you take one of the elements out of air you can make it poison. But the perversity of man must not prevent us from preaching God's mercy. For wherever that was believed it has produced obedience. Do you encounter the most lax lives among those who believe most in the love of a faithful God? The danger is in believing in it too little. At the time of the errors of your youth, did the pure and holy kiss of your mother make you indifferent and trifling? Inspire an army, weak and demoralized, with a steadfast confidence in its general, and they are already half-way to triumph; and the Christian's cry of victory is "The Lord is faithful." III. WHAT PART DOES THIS FAITHFULNESS PLAY IN OUR LIVES? 1. Have you understood it? Is there anything below more beautiful than a faithful attachment? Ah, perhaps you enjoyed it yesterday. That happiness was only lent you for a few days. Sooner or later the strongest and tenderest ties must be broken; but if you have known them only for a single day, you have caught a glimpse of the faithfulness of God. 2. The Lord is faithful. Lay hold of that word and oppose it—(1) to all the events of your life. It will help you to traverse the gloom. We must walk by faith, not by sight. When the sculptor attacks a block of marble, who could discern the noble image which one day will be disengaged? So let the Divine artist act, let all that ought to disappear fall under His faithful hand. (2) To all the failings and variations of your heart. If we are unbelieving, He abideth faithful. (3) To all the temptations which beset you. His faithfulness will provide a way out of it. (4) To all the discouragements which would paralyze your activity. (*E. Bersier, D.D.*) *Divine faithfulness and Christian obedience :*—I. ENCOURAGE-MENT TO DEPEND UPON GOD. 1. The Divine Promiser. "The Lord is faithful" to His promises, and is the Lord who cannot lie (Num. xxiii. 19), who will not alter the thing that is gone out of His mouth. He is faithful to His relation to us, to His own truth, to His own character. Men may be faithless and false, but God never. They may refuse to embrace the gospel, and set themselves against it, but God will not abandon His great purpose on which He has set His heart, and on which He has pledged His word. Even many who are members of the Church may forget their sacred and solemn vows, and may show no fidelity to the cause of their Redeemer, but God Himself will never abandon that cause. To a pious mind it affords unspeakably more consolation to reflect that a faithful God is the friend of the cause which we love, than it would were all men, in and out of the Church, its friends. 2. The Divine Performer. When once the promise has been made, performance is sure and certain. There may be indifference in man on the one hand, and opposition on the other, but "the Lord will work, and who shall let it?" and the result will correspond both with the work and the Worker. II. A FURTHER GROUND OF ENCOURAGEMENT. 1. Their obedience in the past. The Apostle had, in the Lord's stead, commanded them to do certain things, and for the Lord's sake they had done all they were commanded to do. They were not like Saul, the first king of Israel, who, tempted by Satan, preferred rather to do as he wished than as he was divinely directed, not knowing then that obedience was better than all the sacrifices ever offered to the Lord, and hearkening to Him than the fat of countless rams (1 Sam. xv. 16-23). 2. Their obedience in the future. The experience the Apostle had of their obedience in the time past was firm ground for his confidence that they would do the things commanded them for the time to come, and it was also firm ground to hope that whatever they asked of God they should receive from Him, beause they kept His commandments, and did those things that were pleasing in His sight (1 John iii. 22; v. 14, 15). 3. But chiefly the Apostle's confidence in them was founded upon his confidence in God. Though they had done well in the past, they might, some time or other, weary in well-doing; but the Lord would remain faithful; and though heaven and earth might pass away, not one jot or tittle of His word would fail. "The foundation of the Lord is sure." (*D. Mayo.*) *The certainty of final salvation :*—I. THE FAITHFULNESS OF GOD. 1. God is faithful to His covenant engagements (Heb. x. 23). 2. Faithful to His Son Jesus Christ (Heb. vii. 21, 22; viii. 6). 3. Faithful to His redeemed people (Isa. xlix. 15). 4. Christ is faithful as a Mediator (Heb. ii. 17). 5. The Spirit is faithful in His administration (1 Cor. i. 9). II. THE ESTABLISHMENT OF THE CHURCH. 1. To fix and settle our faith in Christ (Col. ii. 7). 2. To confirm the understandings of His people in His truth (Col. ii. 2). 3. Establishing them in the fulfilment of His promises (2 Cor. i. 20). 4. To bring to a good issue all that concerns us (Psa. lxxiii. 24). 5. To give fixation to our love in Him (2 Cor. i. 21). This establishment is— 1. By the written Word. 2. By the preached Word. 3. By the sacraments. 4. By Divine ordinances. 5. But always by His Holy Spirit. III. THE DIVINE PRESERVATION OF HIS PEOPLE. 1. From the torments of the damned (Job xxxiii. 24). 2. From the condemnation of the law (Rom. viii. 1). 3. From the anger of God (Isa. xii. 1). 4. From the injury done by persecutions (Mic. iv. 10). 5. From sin and overcoming temptations (2 Peter ii. 9). He will keep them—1. In sickness (Psa. xli. 3). 2. In health (1 Cor. iii. 21, 22). 3. In fear (1 Cor. ii. 3). 4. In peace (Isa. xxvi. 12). 5. In war (Rom. viii. 37). 6. In their bodies (Rom. viii. 13). 7. In their souls (1 Cor. iii. 16). 8. In ordinances (Ex. xx. 24). 9. In providences (Rom. viii. 28). 10. In life and death (1 Cor. xv. 57). 11. And for ever (John vi. 51). (*T. B. Baker.*) **Who shall stablish you.**—*The established Christian character :*—I. THE CHRISTIAN IS TO BE ESTABLISHED. Consider what this means—1. Progress. The foundation is laid; now the superstructure must be built upon it. 2. Fixity. The progress is not that of a flowing river, but that of a building in the course of erection. We are to hold fast what we have attained. A periodic unsettlement, pulling down to day what we built up yesterday, will have a poor result. 3. Strength. The building is to be no mere bower of branches, no tent of the wilderness, for temporary occupation, but a permanent, solid house in the eternal city of God. It will have to stand the stress of wind and weather. 4. Order. That which is established is not heaped together in a rude formation, like the cyclopean walls seen in granite mountains. The true building follows the designer's plan. The Christian life must be built on the pattern of its great Architect. 5. Elevation. The house is built up. We raise the structure tier after tier. So in Christian life we should rise nearer heaven. Like the soaring pinnacles of a Gothic cathedral, the latest aspirations of the Christian experience should rise far above the earth and point to the sky. 6. Room for contents. The house has its inhabitants and furniture. The established Christian should have room for Divine stores of truth and holy thought, and for thief and fire proof safes which can keep his treasures in security. The complete building is not to be a solid pyramid for the sole purpose of hiding the mummy of its owner, but a glorious temple in which God may dwell. II. THE CHRISTIAN IS TO BE ESTABLISHED BY GOD. Men tried to raise the tower of Babel up to heaven, but failed in their pride and self-will. We cannot build up our own characters. God is the great Builder, and He is raising the structure of the Christian life by all the discipline of daily experience. 1. Truth. Solid character must be built of solid materials—realities, facts, truths. By His revelations in nature, the Bible, Christ, God brings the stones of truth with which to establish our characters. 2. Work. The human building, unlike the material, is not inactive. Character is built up by means of service. God sets us this, and raises us from childish pettishness to manly largeness of soul by the discipline of duty. 3. Trial. Trouble and temptation help to wedge the character into place, as the arch is strengthened by the very weight laid upon it, driving its stones more closely together. 4. Spiritual grace. We are built up from precious stones hewn in the quarries of the everlasting hills of God, not from the clay bricks of earth. The great Builder brings His own heavenly materials. III. THE ESTABLISHMENT OF THE CHRISTIAN IS ASSURED BY THE FAITHFULNESS OF GOD. 1. It is not yet accomplished. It took forty years to build Herod's temple. It takes well nigh twice forty years to establish the characters of some of God's children. Nay, who shall say that the process is completed when brief life is done? Christian people die in all stages of imperfection and partial progress. Are they to be fixed for ever in these initial conditions, half a column here, a wall commenced there, arches not yet locked with their key-stones? There must be a continued establishing in the future life, till the last golden spire gleams aloft in the cloudless blue of heaven. 2. How do we know that this will ever be realized? We are often tempted to despair at our own slow progress. Now it is much to be assured that it is all assured by the faithfulness of God. Of course, this implies our continued faithfulness. The whole tenor of God's Word implies that He will not abandon the good work He has commenced. (*W. F. Adeney, M.A.*) *The soul's establishment and safety secured by the faithfulness of God :*—I. THE PROMISE. 1. Establishment. (1) The Bible lays great stress on this (Rom. i. 11; 2 Cor. i. 21; Col. ii. 6; 1 Thess. iii. 12; Heb. xiii. 9; 1 Pet. v. 9; Jude 24). (2) Unsettledness is the attribute of the unregenerate man. He is compared to—(*a*) A wave of the sea. (*b*) A house built on the sand. (*c*) A plant that has no root. (3) Establishment is needful to the true Christian. He has root, he is in Christ, but He needs to be daily established in grace. This applies to some especially, but to all more or less, and especially at some times, and in some particular graces, *i.e.* in faith, hope, and love. 2. Preservation. (1) This is needed moment by moment, because of the multiplicity of our snares, and the power and vigilance of our great adversary. (2) But a man who is established in the life of faith and a holy walk—where is there room in him for Satan's access? (3) The establisher and defender is God. "Except the Lord build the house," &c. II. THE FOUNDATION OF THE PROMISE. 1. There are several ways of denying God—grossly by atheism, practically by ungodliness, mentally by want of trust in His faithfulness. 2. Faithfulness is the glory of Deity. (1) It is the effect of God's veracity. He has pledged His word and will faithfully execute it, because He is a true God. (2) It stands connected with His omniscience; for if God knows all things, what inducement can there be to deny His word. (3) It stands intimately bound up with His holiness; to break His word would be a breach of His holiness. (4) It stands involved in His immutability: it would show that He was of various minds. (5) It would be a breach upon His perfect love; for how could that be perfect love which promises good and fails to perform (Psa. lxxxix. 1, 5, 8, 14, 35). 3. This perfection makes all His threatenings certain as to their accomplishment. Look at the flood, Sodom, Babylon, Jerusalem! Was He not faithful to His threatenings in these instances? 4. But it is the foundation of all His promises. "He cannot deny Himself." Conclusion: 1. What a sweetness there is in this truth! We may be weak and in danger, but here is the promise. And remember who gives it; Jehovah Himself. In God's dealings there is always something that exhibits His own grandeur. He establishes and defends just like Himself. 2. Seek these blessings, and remember the means of securing them. God gives them, but we must pray and watch. 3. These blessings come in God's way, not yours. The unlikeliest ways may be the best. (*J. H. Evans.*) **And keep you from evil.**—*An effectual guard:*—The expression imports an effectual guard. We know what the garrison of a city is; to keep watch by night and by day, summer and winter, in the brightest sunshine and the thickest midnight, foul weather and fair, from the beginning of the year to the end. The protection of the city is its guard. We know the comfort, peace and well-being of the inhabitants of that city stand most intimately connected with their indoor arrangements; but if you ask what is the security of the city, it is not their domestic arrangements—it is the guard of the city. Thus is it with the people of God. How much there stands connected with the watchfulness of God's saints, as to their peace and well-being and holy walking, no language of mine can ever describe. "Keep thy heart with all diligence," says the wise man. "What I say unto you I say unto all," says our blessed Lord; "watch." And by His apostle—"Watching thereunto with all perseverance and supplication." But if you ask who is the Guardian of the city, he gives but a blind answer who will say anything short of a covenant God. Let me just refer you to the hundred and twenty-seventh Psalm. "Except the Lord build the house, they labour in vain that build it; except the Lord keep the city, the watchman waketh but in vain." I would pray that yours might be that state of watchfulness, that the outgoings of thought might be watched over, the first elements of evil and the first mark of spiritual declension: but I would have you live upon this as a cardinal truth never to be lost sight of—that the Guard of the city is Jehovah Himself—Father, Son, and Holy Ghost—the covenant God of Israel. The expression is most blessedly extensive: "The Lord is faithful, who shall stablish you and keep you from evil." Is it evil men? He "will keep you." Is it Satan, the evil one? Is it sin, the evil thing? He "will keep you." From its condemning power He "will keep you;" 'for there is no condemnation to them that are in Christ Jesus. From its reigning power He "will keep you;" and that, by the power of His love "shed abroad in your heart through the Holy Ghost." And He "will keep you" from its inbeing, in that happy world, where you shall have to sing the praises of this triune God throughout an endless eternity. (*Ibid.*)

Ver. 5. **The Lord direct your hearts into the love of God, and into the patient waiting for Christ.**—*Soul elevation:*—There are many kinds of elevation that man aspires to. 1. Mercantile elevation: men struggle to become the leading merchants of the age. 2. Civic: men strive hard for the posts of magistrate, mayor, statesman, premier. 3. Ecclesiastical: men labour to attain the posts of canon, dean, bishop. But all these involve not the true elevation of man. What, then, is true elevation? I. A CERTAIN STATE OF HEART IN RELATION TO THE DIVINE. 1. "The love of God"—the love of gratitude for the kindest Being, the love of reverence for the greatest Being, the love of adoration for the holiest and best Being. And all this is supreme. Thus centreing the soul on God we dwell in love, and therefore dwell in Him. 2. "Waiting for Christ." Looking forward and anticipating His advent to release us from all the sorrows and sins of this mortal state. This waiting requires patience: the wheels of His chariot seem to tarry. II. A CERTAIN STATE OF HEART PRODUCED BY THE DIVINE. "The Lord direct your hearts." The hearts of men in their unregenerate state are everywhere but in this direction, they are as sheep that have gone astray, prodigals that have left their Father's house, stars that have wandered from their orbits. Who shall bring them back? None can but the Almighty. Ministers may argue and entreat, but unless the Lord come to work their labour is all in vain. (*D. Thomas, D.D.*) *Love and patience:*—1. This prayer bears that peculiar triune stamp which we often meet, and which cannot be satisfactorily accounted for save on the theory of a Trinity in all Christian supplication. The Holy Ghost is always to be regarded as referred to when a Third Person joins the Father and the Son. 2. The prayer is one of those terse sentences which exhibit all religion in a symmetrical pair of counterparts, the precise relation of which is shown by the context. (1) The promise (ver. 3) pledges the faithfulness of the Lord, *i.e.*, Christ, to their confirmation in grace and the restraint of the evil one, the two kinds of guardianship being alike necessary and mutually supplementary. By confirming our inward stability, the Lord often keeps the tempter from us, and when he comes, the blessing of the Lord on our resistance tends to confirm our steadfastness. But—(2) The apostle does not leave all to the Lord's fidelity. He rejoices in the confidence that the Lord's protected ones will protect themselves (ver. 4) by fortifying their own minds with truth and their lives by obedience. The Divine and human are balanced in our protection. "The Lord is faithful if you may be trusted." (3) But as God must have, in all things, the pre-eminence, the prayer follows which gives to the Spirit the prerogative of directing the soul into the love of God which confirms the soul, and into the patience of Christ which will endure and survive the enemy's attacks. I. THE LOVE OF GOD is exhibited under two aspects in the New Testament. 1. Our love to God; but that is not here meant. When the Apostle makes that the object of prayer, he asks it as a benediction of God. 2. It means here God's love to us. (1) That love beams through Christ upon all the world; but those only rejoice in it who are brought into a state of mind from which every impediment is removed. (2) It is not the heart as the sphere of the affections that is here meant, but the whole man. In the strength of the love of God there is no duty past performance, and no difficulty that may not be overcome. (3) No higher prayer can be offered than this, that by the influence of the Spirit we may be drawn from every lower affection and have an entire being open to the unhindered operation of the love of God. II. THE PATIENCE OF CHRIST. 1. The Apostle prays literally for the steadfastness of patience of which Christ is at once the source, example, and reward. "Patient waiting for" or "patience for the sake of" Christ would have required different words, although both meanings are included and are appropriate. The Divine Spirit does direct the souls of believers into tranquil and earnest expectation of Christ's coming, and into the patient endurance of trials for His sake. But the specific meaning here is, that it may please the Lord to remove every hindrance to our perfect union with Christ in His example of obedience unto death. 2. Our way is directed into this patience when we are led into self-renouncing submission, when all things that minister to earthly mindedness are put away, and when we are brought into fellowship with His mind, who "endured the cross" for the joy that was set before Him. 3. We can offer no more important prayer than that we may have our self-will bound, and be girded and led by Another into the way of our Saviour's self-sacrifice. III. THE FULL FORCE OF THE PRAYER IS NOT FELT UNLESS WE UNITE ITS TWO BRANCHES. Love and patience are here for the first and last time joined. 1. In our salvation their union has its most impressive exhibition. The mercy of the Father reaches us only through the endurance of the Son: at the Cross the love of God and the patience of Christ are blended in the mystery of their redeeming unity; and only that union saved the world. 2. The mercy of God waits on the free-will of man with a patience that owes its long-suffering to the intercession of Christ. 3. The economy of grace provides the full power of the love of God for the progressive salvation of the saints, waiting for their full conformity to holy law with a patience that is the most precious fruit of the Redeemer's passion. 4. Eternal glory will be the last demonstration of the love of God and the crowning victory of the patience of Christ. IV. WE MUST REGARD THIS COMBINATION AS THE OBJECT OF OUR PRAYER. With St. Paul, all that the Christian needs for the struggle and victory of life is the love of God in the heart as an active principle, and the patience of Christ as a passive grace. But the form of the prayer shows that he did not separate the two as much as we do. All duty and resistance find their strength in the love of God, and must be perfected in the patience of Christ In due time the patience of Christ shall be lost in the "partaking of Christ," and the great surviving grace, the love of God in us, will abide for ever. *(W. B. Pope, D.D.)*    *The love of God and the patience of Christ ;—*I. THE LOVE OF GOD is employed in three senses—God's love to us; our love to Him; and Divine love in us, *i.e.*, a love like God's. The latter is probably the meaning here. What then is God's love? And may the Divine Spirit direct us into the enjoyment of it. God's love is—1. The very Being of God; and when love is the supreme and dominating motive and energy in us, swaying all the powers and manifesting itself to the utmost, we are directed into the love of God. 2. Comprehensive: it knows no limit. So our love, if Divine, will not be fettered by circumstances or the character of the objects. Like God's, it will be discriminating, and discern differences in moral character, but it will seek the good of all. 3. Unstinting. God gave His only-begotten Son—this is the characteristic of true love everywhere. It never calculates the cost, and when the best is done there is the willingness to do more. 4. Constant in its manifestation : it never wearies or ceases:

And Divine love in man knows no discouragement, is baffled by no obstacles, succumbs to no injury. II. THE PATIENCE OF CHRIST—a patience like Christ's. How much this is needed is shown by the fact that Christ our example was and is patient, and taught patience by word and life. 1. To understand this we must travel beyond the millenniums to the foundation of the world when, the Lamb to be slain was foreordained for sacrifice. Then over the long centuries during which sin held sway when the Son was waiting for the fulness of time. And then during that earthly life in which he endured unimaginable suffering waiting for the accomplishment of His baptism. Then waiting for Pentecost; and now waiting with unwearied patience until those in Christian countries who are resisting the Spirit shall yield, and those in heathen lands shall own His sway, and those who profess to be His people shall consecrate themselves wholly to His work. 2. It is a patience something like that we want. And if Christ can afford to work and wait, surely we can. What are you? A Sunday-school teacher? A preacher? A church officer? Working, praying, your heart discouraged, and sometimes ready to question whether the glad day will ever dawn? He can be patient; be patient with Him and like Him. The counsel of the Lord, it shall stand. (G. W. Olver, B.A.)    The love of God:—I. THE NATURAL FEELINGS OF THE HEART TOWARDS GOD. Originally man delighted in God; but the moment he sinned, fear and distrust entered his mind, and he became a "child of wrath." Notice—1. Man's enmity against God, "the carnal mind," &c. We think it would be a happy thing were there no God to trouble us. It is this feeling that makes prayer burdensome instead of delightful, and duty irksome instead of a means of happiness. And so men converse with God, and do for Him as little as possible. 2. The consequent misery of man. Cut off from the fountain of happiness, he hews broken cisterns, and places his delight in the disappointing creature instead of the unchangeable Creator. II. THE MIND OF GOD TOWARD MEN IN THIS CONDITION. Consider—1. The love of God to sinners. This is the true source of His dealings with men, and His love is not like ours, but disinterested, free, costly, pure. How we wrong it when we try to merit it! "God commendeth His love," &c. 2. The effects of this love. (1) Forgiveness. (2) The provision of His Spirit. (3) Divine likeness. (4) Eternal life. III. THE HEART DIRECTED INTO THIS LOVE. 1. The means. Ample provision is made for its enjoyment. No man can direct his own heart, nor his parent or minister. But Christ has given His Spirit who can change the heart by directing it into the love of God. This Spirit is secured by prayer. 2. The consequence. Love begotten in our hearts to God and men. (E. Bickersteth.)    The love of God:—It is sometimes difficult when we meet the expression, "the love of God," to discriminate whether it means God's love to us, or our love to God. But the truth is, they are one and the same thing. We cannot love God, but as He loves us; it is the consciousness of His love to us which makes our to Him. Just as any object I see is only an image of the object formed on the retina of my eye, so whatever love I feel is only the reflection of the love of God laid upon my heart; and the ray which lays the image is the Spirit of God. The love of the saints in heaven is the brightest and truest because the Original is nearest and dearest. (J. Vaughan, M.A.)    Waiting for the second Advent:—The first epistle was written to correct certain enthusiastic views concerning that advent; but the second tells us that the effort had failed. For meanwhile a forged epistle (chap. ii. 2), asserting that the day was near, opened the floodgates of fanaticism. Consequently men forsook their employments, and, being idle, indulged in useless discussions and in prying curiously into the affairs of others. Hence the injunctions (1 Thess. iv. 11; 2 Thess. iii 6–8). Moreover two opposite lines of conduct were adopted by persons of different temperament. Some greedily received every wild tale about the advent; others perceiving that there was so much imposture, concluded that it was safest to believe nothing. To the first Paul says, "Prove all things," &c.; to the second, "Quench not the Spirit," &c. These opposite tendencies of scepticism and credulity will be found near together in all ages; some refusing to believe that God speaks in the signs of the times; others running after every book on prophecy, and believing anything providing it be marvellous. To meet this feverish state Paul takes two grounds. He first points out the signs which will precede the advent; self-idolatry, excluding the worship of God—sinful humanity, "the man of sin." These signs worked then and now. Next Paul called the Church to a real preparation for that event in the text. The preparation is twofold. I. THE LOVE OF GOD. 1. The love of God is the love of goodness. God is the Good One—personified goodness. To love God is to love what He is. (1) No other love is real; none else lasts. Love based on personal favours, e.g., will not endure. You may believe that God has made you happy. While that happiness lasts, you will love God. But a time comes when happiness goes as it did with Job. The natural feeling would be "Curse God and die." Job said, "Though He slay me," &c. Plainly he had some other reason for His love than personal favours. (2) The love of goodness only becomes real by doing good—otherwise it is a sickly sentiment, "If any man love Me, he will keep My commandments." 2. The love of God is the love of man expanded and purified. We begin with loving men. Our affections wrap themselves round beings created in God's image—then they widen in their range. "No man hath seen God at any time. If we love one another . . . His love is perfected in us." "He that loveth not his brother whom he hath seen," &c. An awful day is coming. How shall we prepare for it? Not by unnatural forced efforts at loving God, but by persistence in the appointed path of our common attachments. "Inasmuch as ye did it unto the least of these," &c. 3. It is not merely love of goodness, but love of goodness concentrated on the Good One. Nor merely love of man, but love of man expanded into love of Him in whom all that is excellent in men is perfect. II. PATIENT WAITING. 1. What is waited for? There are many comings of Christ, in the incarnation, at the destruction of Jerusalem, as a spiritual presence when the Holy Ghost was given in every signal manifestation of redeeming power, in any great reformation of morals and religion, in revolutions which sweep the evil away to make way for good, at the end of the world, when the spirit of all these comings will be concentrated. Thus we may see in what way Christ is ever coming and ever near, and how the early Church was not deceived in expecting Christ. He *did* come, though not in the way they expected. 2. What is meant by waiting? Throughout St. Paul's writings, the Christian attitude is that of expectation—salvation in hope. Not a perfection attained, but one that is to be. The golden age lies onward. We are longing for, not the Church of the past, but that of the future. Ours is not a yearning for the imaginary perfection of ages gone by, nor a conservative content with things as they are, but hope. It is this spirit which is the preparation for the advent. 3. It is patient waiting. Every one who has longed for any spiritual blessing knows the temptation to impatience, "Where is the promise of His coming?" The true preparation is not having correct ideas of how and when He shall come, but being like Him (1 John iii. 3). III. THE LORD WILL DIRECT US INTO THIS. Not an infallible human teacher, but God. (*F. W. Robertson, M.A.*) *Love begets love :*—Love begets love. It is a process of production. You put a piece of iron in the mere presence of an electrified body, and that piece for a time becomes electrified. It becomes a temporary magnet in the presence of a permanent magnet, and as long as you leave the two side by side, they are both magnets. Remain side by side with Him who loved us, and gave Himself for us, and you too will become a permanent magnet—a permanent attractive force; and like Him you will draw all men—be they white men or black men—unto you. That is the inevitable effect of love. Any man who fulfils that cause must have that effect produced in him. Gentlemen, give up the idea that religion comes to us by chance, or by mystery, or by caprice. It comes to us by natural law; or by supernatural law, for all law is Divine. Edward Irving went to see a dying boy once, and when he entered the room, he just put his hand on the sufferer's head, and said, "My boy, God loves you," and went away. And the boy started from his bed, and he called out to the people in the house, "God loves me! God loves me!" One word; one word! It changed that boy. The sense that God loved him had overpowered him, melted him down and begun the making of a new heart. And that is how the love of God melts down the unlovely heart in us, and begets in us this new creature, who is patient and humble and unselfish. And there is no other way to get it. There is no trick about it. Oh, truth lies in that!—we love others, we love everybody, we love our enemies, because He first loved us. (*Prof. Drummond.*) *A brief prayer for great things :*—Two blessings only are here prayed for, but they are of transcendent moment. I. THAT THE HEARTS OF THE THESSALONIANS MIGHT BE BROUGHT INTO THE LOVE OF GOD. To be in love with God as the most excellent and suitable Being—the best of all beings, is not only most reasonable and necessary in order to happiness, but is happiness itself. It is the chief part of the beatitude of heaven where this love will be made perfect. But none can ever attain to this unless the Lord, by His grace and Spirit, direct the heart aright; for the love of the best creature is apt to go astray after other things. Great damage is sustained by misplacing the affections upon wrong objects; but if He who is infinitely above and before all things, control and fix the love of the heart on Himself, the rest of the affections will thereby be rectified. II. THAT ALL PATIENT WAITING FOR CHRIST MIGHT BE JOINED WITH THIS LOVE OF GOD.

There is no true love of God without faith in Christ. To wait for Christ, supposeth faith in Him—that He came to our world once in flesh, and will come again in glory. This second coming must be expected, and careful preparation must be made for it. There must be a patient waiting, enduring with courage and constancy all that may be met with in the interval. We not only have great need of patience, but of great need of Divine grace to exercise it—" the patience of Christ," as some interpret the words, that is—patience for Christ's sake and after Christ's example. (*R. Fergusson.*)　*St. Paul's kindness :*—The Apostle meant only to express a benevolent wish on behalf of the Church at Thessalonica : but he expressed it in such terms as a person habituated to the doctrine of the Trinity would naturally use : he prayed that the Lord the Spirit would direct their hearts into the love of God the Father, and into the patient waiting for Christ.　I. THE OBJECTS OF THE APOSTLE'S WISH.　A very little observation of the world is sufficient to convince us that the love of God is not the supreme passion of mankind, nor a due preparation for a final advent of Christ. Nevertheless, to possess this state of heart and mind is essential to the Christian character. Of ourselves we never shall, or can, attain to this. In full persuasion of this fact, St. Paul poured out the benevolent aspiration that the Christians to whom he wrote might experience more deeply the truths they possessed.　II. THE REASONS OF THAT WISH.　Among the most important of these were doubtless two.　1. The attainment of such a state would prove highly conducive to their present happiness. This the Apostle knew : he knew it from the universal tenor of the Holy Scripture (Psa. lxiii. 5 ; Matt. v. 3–12) ; and he knew it from his own experience (2 Tim. iv. 7, 8).　2. It was also indispensably necessary to their eternal welfare. What is a Christian without the love of God ? He cannot call himself a disciple of Christ who has no delight in following the steps of Christ, or in looking forward to His future advent.　Application—(1) We express the same benevolent wish respecting you ; (2) and we also request that you will adopt the same wish for yourselves. (*C. Simeon, M.A.*)

Ver. 6. **Now we command you, brethren, in the name of our Lord Jesus Christ, that ye withdraw yourselves from every brother that walketh disorderly.**—*Apostolic authority :*—I. THE NEEDS-BE FOR THIS COMMAND. Rather abruptly, the Apostle turns from a very important and pleasant subject to one of a totally different character—the proper method of treating those who were idle and disorderly in the Church. He had adverted to this subject in his previous epistle, but in the mild language of exhortation. When he wrote to the Thessalonians, he was aware that there were some among them who were disposed to be idle, and he had tenderly exhorted them "to be quiet, and to mind their own business, and to work with their own hands." But it seems that the exhortation, and the example of Paul himself when at Thessalonica, had not been effectual in inducing them to be industrious. It, therefore, became necessary to use the strong language of command, and to require that if any members would not work, the Church should take due action concerning them. What was the original cause of their idleness is not known. There seems no reason, however, to doubt that it was much increased by their expectation that the Saviour would soon appear, and that the world would soon come to an end. If this was to be so, of what use would it be to labour ? Why strive to accumulate property with reference to the wants of a family, or to a day of sickness, or to the requirements of old age? Why should a man build a house that was soon to be burnt up ? Or why buy a farm which he was soon to leave ? The effect of the expectation of the speedy coming of the Lord Jesus has alway been to induce men to neglect their worldly affairs, and lead idle lives. Man, naturally disposed to be idle, wants the stimulus of hope that he is labouring for the future weal of himself, his family, or society ; nor will he labour if he believes that the Lord is just about to appear.　II. THE AUTHORITY FOR THE COMMAND. " In the name of our Lord Jesus Christ," says the Apostle, using all the appellations of his Divine Master to stamp his mandate with full authority. By thus using " the name," he means that he was acting on the behalf of Christ, or by His commission or power (Acts iii. 6 ; 2 Cor. ii. 10). A judge occupies the seat of justice on behalf of the monarch who rules the kingdom, and pronounces judgment in his stead on the guilty. But St. Paul's authority was higher than that from the kings of the earth ; it was authority derived from the Divine Head of the Church, and his command therefore was paramount.　III. THE MATTER OF THE COMMAND. " That ye withdraw yourselves from every brother that walketh disorderly, and not after the tradition which he received of us." This is the true notion of Christian discipline toward an erring member. Cease to have fellowship with him: do not regard him any longer as a Christian brother. No effort to affect him in any other respect must be made : neither name nor standing must be injured ; nor must he be held up to reprobation, or followed with a spirit of revenge. When he shows that he is no longer worthy to be recognized as a Christian brother, leave him to himself and his God. Peradventure God may bring him to repentance. (*A. Barnes, D.D.*) *Withdrawal from the disorderly :*—The striking word " withdraw " is, in its simple form, found only besides in 2 Cor. viii. 20. In a still more striking compound it occurs in Acts xx. 20-27; Gal. ii. 12; Heb. x. 38. It is a metaphor from the language of strategy; a cautious general shrinking from an engagement and timidly drawing off under cover. Perhaps we might illustrate it by the familiar " fight shy." A social excommunication rather than ecclesiastical seems chiefly meant, though the latter might be involved. The word " disorderly " is rendered " unruly " in 1 Thess. v. 14. The kind of irregularity is made clear in vers. 10, 11. Bengel quaintly makes this an opportunity for denouncing the Mendicant Orders. " An order of mendicants is not an order ; if the Thessalonians had bound themselves to it by a vow, what would Paul have said ? " (*Canon Mason.*) *Withdrawal from such as walk disorderly :*—1. The matter of the text is separation from those that walk out of line, and keep not their ranks : a word borrowed from military discipline, which requires every soldier to march in his file. But because there can be no irregularity without a rule, and no disorder where no orders have been given, the Apostle explains that he means those who walk not after the tradition, &c., *i.e.*, the doctrine of the apostle. The following therefore are branded—(1) All who commit gross wickedness (1 Tim. vi. 3). (2) All who are erroneous and heretical. Others transgress, these destroy the rule. (3) Turbulent and factious persons : such as rend the Church, and despise government because not of their own devising. (4) Idle and impertinent tattlers and tale-bearers (ver. 11). 2. To this we are bound by an express and urgent command, on authority the most absolute and sovereign ; but we are reminded that the sinner is still a brother. I. STATE THE DUTY. 1. Cases wherein we are not bound to withdraw from them that walk disorderly. (1) In the management of civil affairs, and whatever is necessary for subsistence. This was allowed to Christians among heathens, and cannot be denied to us among ungodly professors. (2) So as to violate the bonds of nature, or the respects which are due to them. A godly son must not withdraw himself from the authority of a wicked father ; those unequally yoked must not therefore relinquish their relation or neglect its duties ; nor servants reject the commands of profane masters. Dominion is not founded in grace, and it would be a wild world if inferiors should acknowledge no superiors but such as are cordially subject to God. No : we ought to converse with all persons according to the relations in which we stand to them. (3) When we have great hopes and strong probabilities of reforming them. This is to act the physician, and to follow the example of Christ (Matt. xi. 19 ; ix. 12). Yet two cautions must be observed. (*a*) Watchfulness over the heart and actions when in wicked company even with a design of doing good, else we may get the infection instead of curing it. (*b*) That we venture not unless we have good grounds for the hope that we shall do them good. This we may expect if we have prudence enough to divert them, authority enough to affright them, or reverence enough to overawe and shame them. Otherwise it is hazardous whether we shall keep our conscience safe or maintain our zeal. (4) In the service of God. We may join them in prayer and ordinances, and be glad that they give religion any, though only a complimental, respect. The great scruple is concerning the Lord's Supper. But—(*a*) Christ ate with Judas (Luke xxii. 20, 21 ; Mark xiv. 23). (*b*) Admitting the contention, your duty is not to withdraw yourselves but to remove them. If you have followed out Matt. xviii. 15, 16, the offender will be removed by the proper authority, or if not you do not partake of his sin by partaking of the same ordinance. 2. Cases in which we are bound to withdraw. (1) From all unnecessary converse. We are not to make them our bosom friends. (2) We are to withdraw from them our inward respect and esteem (Psa. xv. 4). How can we value the companionship of the Devil's slaves, however bedecked, and esteem these whom God condemns ? (3) This inward dislike should be manifested, at least so far as to show that we have very different feelings for true Christians. But here let us beware of running into extremes, and mistake a proud disdain for a holy dislike and by the sourness of our converse fright them from our converse and our religion too. (*a*) We ought to distinguish between our brother's person and his vices, and neither hate nor love the one for the other. He who loves his person for his vices is a devil ; he who loves his vices for his person is a flatterer; he who hates his vices for his person is a murderer; and he who hates his person for his vices is unchristian (Lev. xix. 17). This duty is difficult, and can only be done by using the utmost efforts to reclaim our brother, for thereby we express our hatred of his sins by seeking to destroy them, and our love for his person by seeking to save him. (*b*) We must not withdraw the civility which is due to his station, nor refuse the offices of humanity. The one is not religion but rudeness, and the other unnatural. Religion teaches not churlishness but obligingness. II. REASONS TO ENFORCE THIS DUTY. 1. It is an act of the greatest love to their persons. We are not to separate out of spite or peevishness, but out of goodwill, it being the last and probably the most effectual means of reclaiming them (ver. 14). 2. It is an act of self-protection. There is no plague so catching as sin, for—(1) Our hearts are naturally corrupt. (2) It is the glory of wicked men to rub their vices on as many as they can. They would make all like themselves. (3) Our society with them may involve us not only in their guilt but in their punishment (Prov. xiii. 20; Numb. xvi. 26; Rev. xviii. 4). (4) If no other punishment overtake you, yet their very society must be a burden to the conscientious Christian (Psa. lvii. 4; cxx. 5). (5) Our converse with them must be a great hindrance from doing our duty. (6) We have other company to keep, and need not be beholden to the wicked for society—the good, our own consciences, God. III. APPLICATION. Ought we to withdraw from those that walk disorderly? Then—1. Let not wicked men condemn conscientious Christians as though they were proud or unsociable. 2. Let this serve to break all combinations of wicked men. God has prescribed this rule, and converse not regulated by it is conspiracy against heaven. Flee then from wicked companions. 3. See the misery of the wicked. They are deemed unfit for Christian society on earth, much more for that society in heaven. 4. Christians! be exhorted to withdraw. (1) Get your hearts off those things in which the wicked abound. (2) Be as little beholden to them as possible. (3) Let them see your courage and resolution. 4. Christians! so demean yourselves that the wicked shall see that your company is the more desirable. (1) Let your practice be agreeable to your profession. This brings great credit to religion. (2) Labour to outstrip the wicked in those things in which they gain the affections of others. (*a*) Some pretend to be very exact in giving every one his due—and triumph over those professors who do not. (*b*) Others brag of their courtesy and affability. (*c*) Others of their love and agreement among themselves. (*d*) Others of their charity and good works. (*E. Hopkins, D.D.*)　　*Withdrawal from the disorderly :*—A military metaphor lies in the latter word (1 Thess. v. 14). It describes the unruly as men who are not in their places in the ranks of the Christian army, men who are setting aside the strict rules of discipline, thereby causing disorder and courting disaster. In every such case of insubordination the offender is to be first warned (1 Thess. v. 14); but continued contumacy is to be punished by withdrawal. In this word some see a nautical figure, suitable to a maritime and commercial community like the Thessalonians, and we have such a figure in chap. ii. 2. It would thus mean, "As you take in your sails to steer clear of a rock or reef, so give a wide berth to every disorderly brother. He and all like him are hidden rocks of danger" (Jude 12, R.V.). But it is better to take the metaphor as military, and a natural continuation of the previous one. Thus understood it suggests a strategic movement—the withdrawing, prudent and cautious, but not necessarily timid, on the part of a general with his soldiers from the enemy. It is wise to withdraw from such stragglers out of the ranks; they give the Christian army a bad name, they exert a bad influence, lower the general feeling, and retard progress. They have, therefore, to be avoided even more than if they were openly ranged on the opposite side. They are the most dangerous of foes who belong to the ranks and yet are out of them. It is the disorderly *brother* and not the heathen who is to be shunned; yet although thus severely treated, he is to be looked upon as a brother after all (ver. 15). (*J. Hutchison, D.D.*)　　*Coming clear out :*—Ko-san-lone, a converted Chinese, when in America on a visit, was deeply impressed with the little difference he saw between the style of living of many professing Christians and the people of the world. Adverting to the matter on one occasion, he said, making at the same time a large sweep with his arm, "When the disciples in my country come out from the world, they come clear out."

Vers. 7-9. **For yourselves know how ye ought to follow us.**—*Apostolic example and precept concerning industry :*—1. Paul found it expedient on many accounts to commend industry. (1) The early Christians felt a most lively sense of the evidence and importance of Christianity, were greatly affected by its promises, and looked with indifference on a world from which they had little to expect but persecution. The zeal engendered by all this, however, had its dangers. A contempt for the world may be carried too far, and Paul was afraid it might be here, and lead to a widespread negligence of work and consequent ruin to many families. (2) The apostles had assurances of support from Christ, and there was a danger lest Christians should apply them generally. (3) The opinion of the nearness of the Second Advent led some to regard work as superfluous. (4) The eminent liberality of the first believers was a temptation to dishonest and lazy men. Thus there was a danger lest the Church, instead of being a society of honest, busy men, should become a nest of drones. 2. St. Paul, therefore, recommended industry by precept and example. He had a strong claim to maintenance as an apostle of Christ, and especially to the Gentiles, and a very small sum would have been sufficient for a man who only required food and raiment. Yet he chose to waive this right, and laboured night and day rather than eat any man's bread for nought. Such a person, therefore, might well lay the stress he does here on labour; elsewhere he condemns what we should regard as carelessness or indolence, denial of the faith and infidelity. Consider this example as a precept of industry in—I. OUR WORLDLY CALLINGS. This is necessary, because—1. We came naked and destitute, both physically and mentally, into the world. But both body and soul are designed by God, the one to improve in understanding and the other to increase in strength. Thus, by the voice of nature, God teaches us to be improvable and industrious beings. 2. The Scriptures echo the voice of reason, and command and commend industry throughout. 3. God has made us dependent on others, and teaches us, by the voice of reason, that we ought in return to promote the welfare of others. 4. The Gospel commands us to do good—*i.e.*, what an idle person has not the power or inclination to perform. He who is negligent of his own interests will hardly be serviceable to others. 5. Whosoever is slothful in business will be a slothful Christian, for the same temper disposes to both. 6. Idleness is the parent of vice. He who has some good end to pursue is too busy for temptation; but the idle, having nothing else to do, is tempted to yield. A vacant mind is a proper habitation for the devil. An idle person loathes his own company, and thus gets into worse, and, unless favoured by an extraordinary concurrence of circumstances, falls into want and thence into wickedness. 7. Of all bad dispositions, laziness is the most vexatious. The love of ease and pleasure produces idleness; yet such is the nature of things, idleness produces neither ease nor pleasure, but the reverse. 8. By industry we obtain credit and reputation. 9. By industry we shut out many fretting desires, sorrowful reflections, and turbulent passions. 10. By industry we become beneficial to others, and thereby secure many blessings for ourselves. II. OUR RELIGIOUS AFFAIRS. 1. The shortness and uncertainty of life warn us not to neglect it, since upon our present behaviour depends our future state. 2. The reward before us excites us to it. 3. Gratitude to Him who has done so much for us moves us to do something for Him. 4. The punishment allotted to the idle and wicked servant calls us to it. 5. Our present interest invites us to it, bringing as it does peace of mind and the blessing of God upon our worldly affairs. (*J. Jortin, D.D.*)

Ver. 9. **Not because we have not the power, but to make ourselves an ensample unto you to follow us.**—*Example :*—Paul relinquished his right to support, that he might set a much needed example of industry- Let us consider—I. EXAMPLE IN RESPECT OF OTHER THINGS WHICH HAVE GREAT INFLUENCE ON CONDUCT. 1. Advice is persuasive, but example more so. Let a man advise his friend contrary to his own conduct, and his friend will imitate his conduct and reject his advice. 2. Authority is great, but example is greater. A parent's habits have more force than his precepts. 3. The law of the land is not equal to the law of example. Written law must yield to common law, and common law is only immemorial example. II. THE FORCE OF EXAMPLE ON THE VARIOUS STAGES OF LIFE. 1. Children are wholly subject to it. 2. Youths, thrown into the society of men, immediately assume the airs and manners of men, have their own leaders, and follow them. 3. Men aim at distinguishing themselves, but can only do so by imitating the distinguished in every department of active or studious life. 4. Old men both set and follow examples. III. THE INFLUENCE OF EXAMPLE ON HUMAN SOCIETIES. 1. A family is a small but important society; and here it is not so much what parents command or others advise as what everybody does, that forms the characters and manners of children. Take a child from one family (although a foreign one), and place him in another, and he will more resemble that in which he was brought up than that in which he was born. 2. If you go into a little neighbourhood, parish, or town, you will find a similarity in their manners and customs which can be due to nothing but the force of example. 3. If we consider the peculiarities in national characters, we must ascribe them to the same. A nation takes its character from the stock from which it originates. IV. EXAMPLE GOVERNS ALL THE MODES OF HUMAN CONDUCT. 1. The modes of speaking, reading, writing, vary according to the practice of the best instructors. 2. The higher branches are subject to the same sovereign authority. Sometimes mathematics, sometimes metaphysics, sometimes fine arts are in fashion; and each of these is principally cultivated according to the example of those who reign in the republic of letters. 3. Example governs the various modes of building. Different nations, states, towns, and even villages, commonly construct their houses in a different manner. 4. Example fixes the various degrees of reputation which belong to various stations and employments. Among the Jews it was reputable to labour in any of the mechanic arts. To cultivate the soil was honourable among the Romans. Elsewhere manual labour is thought a degradation. 5. The same law applies to the affairs of government. A single nation follows some great general or politician, and one nation treads in the steps of another. 6. So even in religion. The peculiarities and ceremonies of each took their origin from the opinion and practice of one or a few; and when a sect is formed, example preserves its existence and its peculiarities. Take the Friends, for examples. 7. Modes of mourning and rejoicing take their rise from the same cause. Savage nations mourn and rejoice according to nature; polished nations according to art. 8. In dress, modes of living, and diversion, example reigns alone and supreme. Example commands the French always to change, and forbids the Spaniards ever to alter. V. THE IMPROVEMENT. We learn from the great influence of example—1. Why parents are so unsuccessful in the education of their children. They defeat their instructions and corrections by their examples. 2. Why it is so difficult for any not to deviate from the path of virtue. It was through example that so many of the good men of the Bible went astray. 3. The importance of avoiding bad company. 4. That no man can live in the world without doing good or hurt to others. 5. The account which great and influential men will have to give for their use of example. 6. How easy it is to effect a reformation. A few can do it anywhere by a good example. (*W. Emmons, D.D.*)          *Example better than precept:*—Felix Neff, pastor of the High Alps, finding his people miserably poor, through ignorance of the proper methods of agriculture, endeavoured in vain to persuade them to a change. At length, having himself a garden at Queyros, he determined to plant it with potatoes. They watched him planting in the way he had recommended to them, and ridiculed what they were sure was a waste of labour. But when the gathering time came, and they saw him turning up plants with sixty tubercles, they begged that he would teach them next season to do the same. (*J. F. B. Tinling, B.A.*)          *Commands to be enforced by example:*—During the siege of Sebastopol, Gordon was one day going the round of the trenches when he heard an angry altercation between a corporal and a sapper. On examining the cause, he learned that the men were instructed to place some gabions on the battery, and that the corporal had ordered the sapper to stand on the parapet, where he would be exposed to the enemy's fire, and to place the gabions, while he, perfectly sheltered, handed them up from below. Gordon at once jumped on the parapet, ordering the corporal to join him, while the sapper handed them the gabions. When the work was done, and done under the fire of watchful Russian gunners, Gordon turned to the corporal and said, " Never order a man to do what you are afraid to do yourself." (*Life of General Gordon.*)

Ver. 10. **We commanded you that if any man would not work, neither should he eat.**—*The law of labour:*—It is a curious circumstance that the first subject that disturbed the apostolic church was not of a profound character. It was the question of temporal relief—the early budding of a poor law. From that time forth the mode and measure of the administration of charity has been a vexed question in church and state. Here St. Paul lays down the grand principle which is applicable to all relief. We have here a common law to guide all our alms, national and individual. It is a law against wilful idleness. This is plain from the context. But we are not to withhold the hand from the necessitous (ver. 13). Let us apply this law that labour is life and life is labour to—I. THE IRRATIONAL CREATION. 1. The inanimate creation is God's great chemical laboratory. 2. His animated creation is one enormous fáctory where the law of labour is rigidly enforced, from the royal eagle to the meanest reptile. The swallows skimming round us seem to be only sporting in the air. In reality they are working for their food, opening their beaks as they fly, and carrying home insects to their young. How many miles daily does a sheep walk to get its living? Look into the insect world (Prov. vi. 6; xxx. 24) at the ant hills, spider's webs, coral reefs, marvels of scientific, artistic, and laborious industry. The law everywhere is—no work, no life. II. THE SPIRITUAL LIFE OF MAN. 1. Here we might imagine that another great law meets us in opposition—the law of grace. Scripture teaches us that we are saved not by our own endeavours but by God's free and unmerited mercy. May we then lie down in antinomian security? That moment we cease to live. Antinomianism is spiritual suicide. Hear the word of God: "Agonize to enter into the strait gate." "Labour for the meat which endureth," &c. How is a Christian described? As a soldier, husband-man, pilgrim, and by other figures, every one of which implies exertion of the most strenuous character. Every promise is held out to the energetic; and not only so, but the result is proportionate. "The diligent soul shall be made fat." The more we pray and toil, the richer will be our present harvest in peace of conscience, the sense of pardoning love, and in the world to come eternal glory. 2. And if this be true individually in what we have to do in working out our own salvation, how much more in our labours of love. Here nothing is done without toil. You need but look at all the benevolent institutions of the country to see that no real good is done without trouble. III. MAN IN HIS NATURAL STATE. Work was the law of Para-dise; it only became a painful one after the fall. From the moment of its utter-ance, "By the sweat of thy brow," this law has ruled all human life. There is not a man who has attained to eminence save in obedience to it. In our country, whose distinction is that the paths of fame and wealth are open to the meanest, it is a fact that the vast majority of our greatest men in Parliament, the army, science, the law, the Church, have sprung from the lower or middle classes. It is not the poor mechanic only, but all must work or die. But what about the born wealthy? Well, that is the result of their ancestor's labour. It did not originally come by chance or fortune. And even those who are under no obligation to toil for their daily bread are obliged to have recourse either to it or to artificial labour in travel or sport to maintain their health and save their life. (*Dean Close.*)     *Idlers :*—In writing to his step-brother Johnston, who had requested a loan of money, Abraham Lincoln says: "The great defect in your conduct is, not that you are lazy, but that you are an idler. This habit of uselessly wasting time is the whole difficulty, and it is vastly important to you and to your children that you should break the habit. Go to work for the best money wages you can get, and for every dollar that you will get for your own labour I will give you another one. If you will do this you will soon be out of debt, and what is better you will have gained a habit that will keep you from getting in debt again." (*H. O. Mackey.*)     *No work, no pay :*—Here is a large vineyard. Many men and maidens are busy on the hillside. They are coming and going, and singing the vintage songs. Here is the master. He sees that the rules are kept. There must be no disorder, no profanity. Each must keep his place. The baskets must be clean. The master is counting the baskets that are brought to the vats. After each name he writes the number of baskets brought. At last the week is ended, and the men and maidens come to receive their pay. Here among them is a man whom the master has been watching day by day. He kept his basket clean; he kept his place; he used no profane language; he enjoyed the companionship of the others; he joined merrily in the vintage songs. But in all this time he gathered no grapes. "What is your name?" says the master. "Menalque," says the man. "I find your name upon the book," replies the master, "but I do not find that you gathered a single cluster; there is therefore no pay for you." "No pay?" says the man. "What have I done wrong? I have kept my place, used no improper language, kept my basket clean, and joined heartily in the songs." "You did no wrong," says the master, "but you did no work. There is nothing for you." "No pay for me!" exclaimed the man. "Why, that is the one thing I came in the vine-yard for. The pay constituted my chief interest in it." Is not this the history of thousands in the Lord's vineyard? They come, their names are upon the book. They do no special wrong; they do not swear, or steal, or commit adultery. They break no rule. They sing the vintage songs. They hear sermons, if they are entertaining. They attend church, if it is quite convenient. But are they in any true sense labourers in God's vineyard? Have they done any honest work for Christ and His Church? Have they performed one hard task, done one unpleasant duty, spoken one brave word, lifted one fallen sinner, lightened one heavy burden, crucified one loved comfort, or done any one thing or series of things that would justly entitle them to the name of labourer, or the hope of reward when the great day of reckoning comes? (*R. S. Barrett.*) *Work necessary for man :*—John the Dwarf wanted to be " without care like the angels, doing nothing but praise God." So he threw away his cloak, left his brothers and the Abbot, and went into the desert. But after seven days he came back and knocked at the door. " Who is there ? " asked the Abbot. " John." " John is turned into an angel, and is no more among men." So he left him outside all night, and in the morning gave him to understand that if he˙was a man he must work, but that if he was an angel he had no need to live in a cell. *The danger of idleness :*—Notice the invention used by country people to catch wasps. They will put a little sweet liquor into a long and narrow-necked phial. The do-nothing wasp comes by, smells the sweet liquor, plunges in and is drowned. But the bee comes by, and if she does stop for a moment to smell, yet she enters not, because she has honey of her own to make ; she is too busy in the work of the commonwealth to indulge herself with the tempting sweets. Master Greenham, a Puritan divine, was once waited upon by a woman who was greatly tempted. Upon making inquiries into her way of life, he found she had little to do, and Greenham said, " That is the secret of your being so much tempted. Sister, if you are very busy, Satan may tempt you, but he will not easily prevail, and he will soon give up the attempt." Idle Christians are not tempted of the devil so much as they tempt the devil to tempt them. (*C. H. Spurgeon.*) *The cure for idleness :*—The wife of a certain chieftain who had fallen on idle habits, one day lifted the dish-cover at dinner, and revealed a pair of spurs ; a sign that he must ride and hunt for his next meal. (*H. O. Mackey.*) *How to deal with beggars :*—Oberlin was distinguished by his benevolence and charity ; hence he was beset with beggars. " Why do you not work ? " said he to a man one day. " Because no one will employ me." " Well, then, I will employ you ; there, carry those planks ; break these stones ; fill that bucket with water, and I will repay you for your trouble." Such was his usual mode, and idle beggars were taught to come there no more. (*J. L, Nye.*)

Vers. 11, 12. **For we hear that there are some which walk among you disorderly, working not at all, but are busybodies.**—*A busybody :*—Apelles, who flourished in the time of Alexander the Great, never permitted a day to pass without practice in his art. He was accustomed, when he had completed any one of his pieces, to expose it in some public place to the view of the passers-by, and seating himself behind it to hear the remarks which were made. On one of these occasions a shoemaker censured the painter for having given to the slippers a less number of ties than it ought to have. Apelles, knowing the man must be correct, at once rectified the mistake. The next day the shoemaker, emboldened, criticised one of the legs, when Apelles indignantly put forth his head and bid him keep to that line of criticism which he justly understood. Here we have the disorderliness of vers. 6–7 defined. There is a scornful play of words here in the Greek which is lost sight of in the English : the word for busybodies being merely a compound form of the word " working." Quite literally, the compound means " working enough and to spare," " being over busy," " overdoing "; then, as a man cannot possibly overdo what it is his own duty to do, it comes to signify—I. Doing useless things, things which concern no one, and might as well be left alone : as, *e.g.*, magic, which is described by this word (Acts xix. 19) ; or natural science, which is so described in the Athenians' accusation of Socrates ! II. Meddling with matters which do not concern the doer, but do concern other people (1 Tim. v. 13). Bishop Lightfoot suggests that the play can be kept up through the words " business " and " busy ; " we might perhaps say, " not being business men, but busy bodies." But which of the two notions mentioned above is to be considered most prominent here, we cannot tell for certain. 1. The Thessalonians do not seem to have been much carried away by the first class of dangers—idle speculations such as those of the Ephesian and Colossian churches. Yet we cannot altogether exclude this meaning here. St. Paul's readers had been overbusy in theorizing about the position of the departed at Christ's coming (1 Thess. iv. 15), and had been so eager over their idle doctrines of the Advent as to falsify, if not actually to forge, communications from St. Paul (2 Thess. ii. 2). Such false inquisitiveness and gossiping discussions might well be described by the Greek word we are now considering. 2. Everything, however, points to a more practical form of the same disposition to mask idleness under cloak of work; feverish excitement, which leads men to meddle and interfere with others, perhaps to spend time in " religious " work which ought not to have been spared from everyday duties (1 Thess. iv. 11, 12). There is nothing to show definitely how this busy idleness arose, but it may very probably be the troubled and shaken condition of mind spoken of in chap. ii. 2. (*Canon Mason.*) **That with quietness they work.**—*The blessedness of work :*—1. There is probably no means of grace more strengthening against temptation, more healthful for the spirit, more uplifting towards God, than honest, earnest work. When God placed man in the Garden of Eden, He placed him there not for the sole purpose of contemplation, but to dress the garden and keep it. The Saviour is reputed to have worked at His foster-father's bench, and thus to have consecrated all human toil. Even His Sabbaths were spent in worship and in doing good. The most religious life is often thus a life of unremitting toil. 2. Upon the scroll of Nature is written the gospel of work. For Nature seldom supplies our necessities or meets our conveniences by provisions ready made for use. Nature furnishes the raw material : the clay to be fashioned into bricks, the iron to be converted into machinery, the fertility of the soil to be husbanded by cultivation, the produce of distant lands to be first transferred by the seaman's endurance and the merchant's enterprise to the place of manufacture, and then to be spun and woven by the diligence of the artizan into cloth suitable for wear. Even Nature declines to satisfy our wants unless we work in her laboratories, and recognize the Divine obligation of earning our bread by the sweat of the brow. Nature thus exalts every labourer into a disciple of God, learning in the Book of Nature the dignity and value of toil. 3. History harmonizes with Nature in the pronouncement of this verdict upon the blessedness of work. The most forward nations of the world are those which have been compelled by the necessities of climate and geographical position to labour most diligently for their daily sustenance. The most backward races are those which dwell in sunny lands, where fruits grow without strenuous husbandry, and where the glow and inspiration of effort are only partial and weak. 4. The experience of the Church may be added in favour of the elevating influence of work. Where does infidelity most abound ? Not among the busy and industrious classes, but among the luxurious, the leisurely, the indolent. Doubters may not be always drones, but drones are commonly doubters. The pests of the commonwealth and the poisons of society are its loungers, its idlers, its non-working element; those who simply " eat the fruits of the earth and do no good and die " ; who neither work for their own private advantage, nor devote themselves to the public weal. The idle man is in the full glare of temptation, and upon the high road to iniquity. 5. Work is a great preservative for the soul. It drains off the evil humours of the flesh ; it parries the thrusts of temptation ; it yields the fruits of a peaceable heart ; it delights with the reflection of useful service to others ; it gives to man the exalted sense of being a co-operator with God in Nature, in the world, and in the Church. (*J. W. Diggle, M.A.*)

Ver. 13. **But ye, brethren, be not weary in well-doing.**—*St. Paul's tact :*—The last verse was addressed to all those whose consciences would prick them on hearing it read at the Eucharist. Now the writer turns to the orderly brethren, as quite a distinct class. The rhetorical effect of this quick apostrophe would be the same as in the well-known story of Napoleon addressing the rioters, and requesting the gentlemen to separate themselves from the *canaille.* The distinction is so invidious that every one would hasten to join the ranks of the respectable. (*Canon Mason.*) *Weariness in well doing :*—Read the two previous verses, and mark the apostle's censure of those who are busybodies, "working not at all." 1. A church should be like a hive of working bees. 2. There should be order, and there will be order where all are at work. The apostle condemns disorder in verse 11. 3. There should be quietness ; and work promotes it (ver. 12). 4. There should be honesty ; and work fosters it. 5. The danger is, lest we first tire of work, and then fancy that we have done enough, or are discharged from service by our superior importance, or by our subscribing to pay a substitute. While any strength remains we may not cease from personal work for Jesus. 6. Moreover, some will come in who are not busy bees, but busy-bodies : they do not work for their own bread, but are surprisingly eager to eat that of others ; these soon cause disturbance and desolation, but they know nothing of "well-doing." The apostle endeavours to cure this disease, and therefore gives—I. A SUMMARY OF CHRISTIAN LIFE. He calls it "well-doing." 1. Religious work is well-doing. Preaching, teaching, writing books and letters, temperance meetings, Bible-classes, tract-distributing, personal conversation, private prayer, praise, &c.   2. Charitable work is "well-doing."   The poor, the widow and the fatherless, the ignorant, the sick, the fallen, and the desponding, are to be looked after with tender care,   3. Common labour is "well-doing."   This will be seen to be the point in the text, if we read the previous verses.   Well-doing takes many forms : among the rest—Support of family by the husband.   Management of house by the wife.   Assistance in house-work by daughters.   Diligence in his trade by the young man.   Study of his books by the child at school.   Faithful service by domestics in the home.   Honest toil by the day-labourer.   4. Certain labour is "well-doing" in all these senses, since it is common labour used for charitable and religious ends.   Support of aged people by those who work for them. Watching over infirm or sick relatives.   Bringing up children in the fear of the Lord.   Work done in connection with the Church to enable others to preach the gospel in comfort.   5. Everything is "well-doing" which is done from a sense of duty, with dependence upon God, and faith in His Word ; out of love to Christ, in good-will to other workers, with prayer for direction, acceptance, and blessing. Common actions become holy, and drudgery grows divine when the motive is pure and high.   We now think it will be wise to gather from the epistle—II. A WARNING AS TO CAUSES OF WEARINESS IN WELL-DOING.   1. Unworthy receivers of charity weary generous workers (ver. 10).   2. Idle examples tempt the industrious to idleness (ver. 11).   3. Busybodies, and disorderly persons in the church, hinder many from their diligent service (vers. 11, 12).   4. Troublers, such as "unreasonable and wicked men," dispirit those who would serve the Lord (ver. 2).   5. Our own flesh is apt to crave ease, and shun difficulties.   We can make too much of works, and it is equally easy to have too few of them.   Let us watch against weariness.   Let us now conclude with—III. AN ARGUMENT AGAINST WEARINESS IN WELL-DOING.   "But ye, brethren, be not weary in well-doing."   1. Lose not what you have already wrought.   2. Consider what self-denials others practise for inferior things : soldiers, wrestlers, rowers in boat-race, &c.   3. Remember that the eye of God is upon you, His hand with you, His smile on you, His command over you.   4. Reflect upon the grandeur of the service in itself as done unto the Lord, and to His glorious cause. 5. Think upon the sublime lives of those who have preceded you in this heavenly service.   6. Fix your eye on Jesus, and what He endured.   7. Behold the recompense of reward : the crown, the palm.   If others tire and faint, be not ye weary. If others meanly loaf upon their fellows, be it yours rather to give than to receive. If others break the peace of the church, be it yours to maintain it by diligent service, and so to enjoy the blessing of verse 16.   (C. H. Spurgeon.)   Perseverance : —If I mistake not, there is one of our noble families which has for its motto the single word "Persevera."   It is a very grand motto, and I can well believe that a man whose forefathers had that single word inscribed upon their banners, and who himself had lived with that word ever speaking to him from the escutcheon of his house, would be a braver and more steadfast man by reason of the influence which such an eloquent motto would exercise upon his character.   And yet there is a very great inclination in certain stages of society, and certain periods of our lives, to feel a kind of contempt for this same perseverance.   Mere patient labour is thought but meanly of for the most part ; we give it all sorts of bad names.   We sneer at a "plodder."   We half suspect a "painstaking" boy of being a stupid one.   We become considerably amazed where unpresuming "carefulness" carries the day over more dashing "style."   It seems dull to us to go on from year to year, practising at the same thing, toiling at the same kind of work, and so very slowly rising towards perfection in anything.   We are inclined to fancy when we start in life that great talents—that indefinable power which we call genius—will be sure to bear all before it, and must carry the world by storm.   By and by we get to find that the world is very much larger than we fancied, and that there is a great deal of talent—nay, a great many geniuses in it, and that eminence is not to be obtained at a bound, but only by long and patient climbing.   But this is a hard lesson to learn, and we dislike the learning it too.   When we begin to see that it *must* be learnt, many of us revolt from the necessity ; some are discouraged, and fairly give in at once; some few bow before the law, and these succeed.   This is true of all things.   What makes the savages in the Pacific able to swim for miles, so that they are almost as much at home in the water as on the land?   What makes the Australian native able to follow and track by such slight indications as you and I could not even understand?   What makes the tea-taster in London able to tell whether this chest of tea was packed in Shanghai or that in Canton ?   What makes the clerk at the Bank of England able to detect in an instant the single forged note out of a heap of a thousand genuine ones which he handles too rapidly for our eyes to follow? It is persevering carefulness, without which all the natural gifts in the world would not avail for the doing of any one of these things. But is all this true of the *highest* things? Is it true that in religion, in godliness, it is perseverance that best serves to produce the true Christian temper and the truly Christian life? God forbid that we should lose sight for an instant of the co-operating grace of the Holy Spirit, or put anything into the place which His grace can alone occupy; but with that reservation it *is* undoubtedly true that even in religion, and the building up of a Christian character, it is perseverance that is of the most vital and essential importance, and that, indeed, without a persevering continuance in the painful practice of what our conscience sanctions and commands, there can be no real godliness, no true religion. If there be one thing more than another which marks the man of genius, it is his courageous steadfastness. They say that the tiger once balked in its first spring, will not again renew the charge, but skulks back into the jungle cowed and ashamed. We know that it is ever so with the craven spirits in the world; the first check and discouragement crushes them, they have no heart to recover from a fall. Such men do not bargain for work; they only bargain for success. But God's Word says, bargain for work only, and leave success to follow or not as it may. Working *is* success, for after doing, something—something I say—must be done; and after well-doing, something *good* is done. (*A. Jessop, D.D.*)   *Weariness in well-doing :*—I. THE CAUSES TENDING TO FAILURE IN WELL-DOING. 1. Love of ease. 2. Necessity of self-denial. 3. False humility. 4. Deficient co-operation. 5. The fact that in God's cause the object and effect of well-doing are much less palpable than in some other provinces of action. 6. Distrust in God. II. SOME MOTIVES AGAINST BEING WEARY. 1. The consciousness and the pleasure of pleasing God. 2. This is the fittest introduction and discipline for the other world. 3. No relief is gained by yielding to weariness. (*John Foster.*) *The tendency to weariness in well-doing illustrated and opposed :*—Among the Thessalonians some were acting inconsistently. But while the apostle reproved such, and directed the Church to withdraw from them, they were not to be given up in despair. The Church was not to weary in their reclamation. I. THE CAUSES OF WEARINESS IN WELL-DOING. 1. Love of novelty. This works in us when our own interests are concerned, and much more when the interests of others only are at stake. To go on in a steady course of kind exertion requires great strength of principle and perseverance. On first hearing of a distressing tale our feelings are strongly agitated, but by degrees ardour naturally cools. Familiarity with suffering blunts the edge of the feelings towards it. Some new object presents itself which engenders remissness towards the former one. 2. Want of success. Having been disappointed we are apt to become tired, discouraged, despairing. The sinner we have tried to reclaim seems inveterate, the enemy we have endeavoured to conciliate is implacable, and the temptation is to abandon an apparently impossible task. 3. Injurious treatment. We may have met with ingratitude, or been deceived by designing persons; our attempts at conciliation have only inflamed resentment; reproach and calumny seems the only fruit of our labour. In these and other cases the temptation to desist from our labour of love is strong. II. SOME CONSIDERATIONS WHICH MAY HELP TO OPPOSE THIS TENDENCY. 1. The example of Christ. This is binding on all His followers. Was He weary in well-doing? Remember the ingratitude, reproach, and persecution He endured. 2. The conduct of Christ toward yourself. While He has been forward to do you good, have you not abused His kindness? He might justly have been wearied of you, and shall you then be wearied of well-doing to your fellow-creatures? "Freely ye have received, freely give." 3. There is an express promise given to perseverance in well-doing. "In due time we shall reap if we faint not." (*E. Cooper.*)   *The cure of weariness :*— The well-doing of the text refers to the duties of life generally. The Apostle was informed that there were in the Church at Thessalonia persons who walked disorderly, working not at all, but were busybodies. The hospitality of the members enabled them to go from house to house, and the less spiritual would welcome them for the sake of gossip. They were commanded to work, and eat their own bread. Then the text follows as a general exhortation. I. THE DUTIES OF LIFE ARE ONEROUS. Every man who lives an earnest life knows the pinch of the shoe. 1. The initiatory stages of life involve labour. There are hundreds in the world this moment whose entire failure, through an undisciplined youth, will end in idleness and misery. You can bend the twig, but not the sturdy branch. Parents should teach their children that life is a matter of paramount importance. " Train up a child," &c. 2. The discharge of life's duties demands energy and perseverance. God has ordained labour more for the development of man's powers than for its own sake. Every branch of human work has its difficulties. It is the case with some that they think other avocations or professions easier than their own. It is a mistake. Do not run from one thing to another in search of ease; you must work hard in whatever department, or fall a victim to fancy. 3. There are special circumstances of a crucial nature to overcome. So far we have only touched on the general, but men do not go through life without an occasional tension that taxes all their strength. The mariner encounters storms. In the lives of great men trials are great, but in the lives of ordinary men trials are as great as they can bear. The Book of Proverbs is a great monitor. II. LIFE'S DUTIES CAN BE DISCHARGED—faint not "in well-doing." God has measured your task by your strength. He will not lay upon us more than we can bear. 1. Faint not, because well-doing is divinely ordered. Men fail because they look on labour as a human imposition. The first man, who was lord of all he could survey, was a gardener. All nature is at work. 2. Be not weary, because there is a sweetness in well-doing. Work is its own rewarder. The indolent speak of drudgery, but the industrious think of satisfaction in labour. It has a harvest to follow. 3. Faint not, because industry and perseverance form character. "Not slothful in business; fervent in spirit, serving the Lord." Some think that they are Christians because they sing hymns, while business is going to the dogs. Life is the occasion to develop principle. 4. Faint not, because God will continue your strength. (*Weekly Pulpit.*) *Christian activity :*—Dr. Adam Clarke said that "the old proverb about having too many irons in the fire was an abominable old lie. Have all in it—shovel, tongs, and poker." Wesley said, "I am always in haste, but never in a hurry: leisure and I have long taken leave of each other." Coke crossed the Atlantic eighteen times, preached, wrote, travelled, established missions, and at nearly seventy years of age started to Christianize India. (*J. L. Nye.*) *Motive and work :*—All indolence is infectious. It may be contracted by contagion; but it may be a malaria with which the atmosphere is charged. However the evil is communicated, it captures men just in the measure of their predisposition to it. Not even an apostolic Church was free from the spell which paralyzes Christian energy in these later days. But Paul's greatest concern was for those who had not entirely given up godly effort, but were in danger of yielding to self-indulgent idleness. Surrounded as they are by cavillers, grumblers, and obstructionists, Christians at work run a great risk. I. WEARINESS IMPLIES WORK. 1. There is a vast difference between weariness *in* and weariness *of* work. There is good hope for the first, but very little for the last. Like Gideon's three hundred, these Thessalonians were "faint, yet pursuing." Their enthusiasm was not as great as it had been, their schemes of aggression not so far-reaching, their blows not so vigorous; but they had not thought of becoming like Ephraim, who, "being armed and carrying bows, turned back in the day of battle." Yet they were somewhat infected by the indolence that was about them. Like the stupor of the Arctic frost-sleep, it is only to be cast off by renewed exertion. 2. What would all the promises of the heavenly rest be worth if Christians did not experience the fatigue, discouragement, and reaction of active effort. The comfort of home is just in proportion to the sense of weariness which business has wrought. 3. With every day's work for Jesus it becomes a more joyous thing to dare and do. Easier becomes His yoke and lighter His burden, till we in heaven with winged obedience follow the Lamb whithersoever He goeth. 4. Be not cast down with the consciousness of flagging zeal. It is a plain proof that you have not always been a sluggard. The slothful man is weary only of idleness. Defraud Satan of his purpose by renewed consecration. II. WORK EXPRESSES MOTIVE. 1. Force is never lost either in physics or morals. It changes its form and applications, but is never annihilated. The heat from the sun is not buried in sod or sea. It appears again in the exhalations which in time descend to give freshness, fulness, beauty to vegetation. The revolving wheels, ascending piston-rod are all the story of the heat which is the motive force. It may propel a gigantic steamer through a boisterous sea, turn the spinning-jenny or the corn-mill; but however grand or commonplace the application, the motive is the same. And then the intensity of the cause appears in the effect. Precisely the amount of heat employed in machinery is distributed in the friction of its many parts. 2. The same holds good in the mental and moral forces. (1) Work expresses and discriminates the measure and character of motive. Duty and love are two diametrically opposed incentives, and have a way of showing themselves in their achievements. There is a difference between prison labour and that outside the walls. Love for his last can make even a shoemaker an artist. (2) Christian work follows the same rule. "If ye love Me, ye shall keep My commandments." What a difference between primitive Christianity with its constraining love of Christ, and mediæval Christianity with its legalism and penances. (3) But every Christian workman in the measure of his energy determines to what degree he is controlled by the love of Christ. Duty may do for a day, but love alone can govern a life. If you have been labouring as galley-slaves it is no wonder that you are weary. If you have been counting your charities as so many compensations for your sins, your life must indeed be joyless. III. FAILING MOTIVE MAKES FAINTING WORK. Love is always lavish. It does not stop to compute values. It breaks its alabaster and fills the house, the church, and the world with its fragrance before legalism has finished its calculation. If you are conscious of weariness, is it not because your estimate of the preciousness of Jesus has been dwarfed? And if you would be awakened to energy again you must contemplate first the fulness of His propitiatory work and the loveliness of His character, so that gratitude and love may twine together on the lattice of His promise, and bring forth much fruit that shall remain. Go measure the love of Calvary. Tell your soul again the gospel story. Be found "looking unto Jesus." Then shall your Christian work be an ever-growing delight. (*S. R. Tyng, jun.*) *The base life and the beautiful :*—These words are spoken to a young Church whose growth in grace had been marvellously rapid. St. Paul was able to call to mind a "work of faith," &c., such as we associate rather with mature Christian life. They were on the one hand so young that weariness might seem to be the least of their perils, and yet on the other so strong that the cloud was scarcely visible in their horizon. I. WELL-DOING is not found elsewhere in the compound. It is not beneficence or "doing good," but the moral beauty of the new man in Christ. St. Paul had a keen eye for the beautiful in grace, if not in nature. He loved to contemplate the grander attributes of humanity as developed under the "healthful spirit of God's grace" and the "continual dew of God's blessing." This thought has a powerful persuasion for the heart of a young man, who would bitterly resent the idea of having parted with his manliness or taste by becoming a Christian. II. BE NOT WEARY. The collision of the two opposites, the "beautiful" and the "base," is striking. "Wax not base in your beautiful life." This baseness is that faint heart which makes cowards of us; that sinking of spirit in the face of trial or peril, which in one case breeds sluggards and in the other deserters. Be not faint-hearted in that glorious work which is yours as Christians, for if you suffer that ugly influence to steal over you, there is an end at once of all nobleness and greatness. You will be mere cumberers of the ground in common times, and in some crisis may be seen as runaways first, and then castaways. III. HOW NATURAL THIS WEARINESS IS TO US. The daily resumption of the common duties of praying and reading, the daily recurrence of the same troublesome attacks from indwelling, soliciting, besetting sin, the finding myself always beginning, never advancing in the work of duty and the fight of faith—how wearisome is all this. To look forward to a long life of this perpetual to and fro, how many have intermitted the struggle and gone back into the world. IV. THERE IS AN ALTERNATIVE. This last stage of weariness is not reached unconsciously. There are beginnings which may be watched, and by earnest prayer counteracted. God is on our side. Deal truly with yourself, and He will deal bountifully with you. Concentrate yourselves on your duties till they become all to you. Place yourself in thought each day before the great white throne. Above all, live much in His presence who quickened the dead. (*Dean Vaughan.*)

Vers. 14–15. **If any man obey not our word by this epistle, note that man.**— *How to deal with the erring :*—No Christian duty more delicate and difficult than that we owe to the unbelieving, the disobedient, the erring, even for the haters and despisers of Christ and His Church. 1. "Note this man." There should be a full realization of his error; no ignoring of it, or acquiescence in it; no belittling of it. 2. We are to note all such, separate ourselves from them, have no fellowship with them. And this implies—(1) A defence of the truth, a vindication of the right. (2) A bearing open, faithful witness for Christ, for the Church, &c. 3. But we are not to cast them off—abandon them as hopeless reprobates—withdraw sympathy, anxiety, prayer, effort in their behalf. "Count him not as an enemy, but admonish him as a brother." Kindness, gentle entreaty, Christian endeavour, persisted in, may finally make him "ashamed," and win him over. Oh, had heretics, schismatics, apostates, erring brethren of every kind, been always dealt with in this Christian way, how different had been the result! It is not too late to begin. (*Homiletic Monthly.*)　　*Church discipline:*—The Revised Version well brings out the meaning—"Note that man, that ye have no company with him." It is no mark that is to be set upon him—no stigma, though this as a matter of fact would follow. It is to be a mental marking, and the purpose of it no formal excommunication but an avoidance (ver. 6), which would in the nature of things carry with it a kind of ecclesiastical censure and suspension. Thus it appears that such a one sets a mark upon himself. The disorder of his life is the mark of spiritual disease—the beginning of what may end in death. Like the spots on the body, indicating the first stages of the plague, which the Armenians call the *pilotti*, the pilots or harbingers of death, so upon the character of such "unruly" ones there are spots, which are pilots of the ruin of the soul. It is therefore dangerous for those who are whole to have company with these; but it is especially needful for the good of the erring brother himself. He may be led in this way to a wholesome shame, which Carlyle has called "the soul of all virtues, of all good manners, and good morals." Yet he is still one of them, "a brother," notwithstanding the severity of the treatment to which he is to be subjected. He is to be won back in the right way by brotherly admonition. "Too harsh chiding," says Gregory Nazianzen, "is like an axe which flieth from the handle. It may kill thy brother, when it should only cut down the briars of sin."　　*A faithful admonisher:*—Do you know nine-tenths of the trouble in this world is the manifestation of a wrong spirit? There was a man down in Georgia, one of the leading members of the Methodist Church in his place. He paid liberally, was wealthy and respected. There was a renter on his farm who belonged to the same church. They had a quarrel, came to harsh words, almost to blows. On Friday the preacher heard of this difficulty. On Saturday he came to his appointment. He first went to the renter and said, "I hear that you and Brother So-and-So have had a difficulty. That won't do for brethren. I want you to agree with me, your pastor, that you will settle it and bury the whole question." "I am perfectly willing to do anything that is right about it. I am ashamed of the way I did and talked. I am perfectly willing to do anything that you and the congregation say is right to do." He drove over to the rich man's and said, "I understand you had a quarrel or difficulty with another brother of our church. I want you to promise me that you will drop the whole matter, and let us all go along as if nothing had happened." This brother said, "That man has treated me badly. I will quit myself if you don't turn him out of the church." The pastor soon saw that he was possessed of a bad spirit. They walked out in the grove together, and the pastor said, "Let us pray," and said he, finally, "My brother, for the cause of Christ, for the sake of souls and harmony in the church, will you not give me your promise?" "If you don't turn him out I will never pay another cent." The preacher looked at him and said, "I have done my best on you, and unless you become reconciled to your brother I will turn you out, if you paid 1,000,000 dols. a year!" That man left the church and became a common drunkard, and has gone to ruin. What was the matter with him? Just a bad spirit. O Lord, create in us a right spirit. If you have a right spirit you will do right. (*S. Jones.*)

Ver. 16. **Now the Lord of Peace Himself give you peace always by all means.**— *Peace from the Lord of peace:*—There is another reading of this passage, which modern editors have preferred, and I think with good reason; for τρόπῳ they substitute τόπῳ—"in every place" for "by all means." The expression in our version may, no doubt, have a good and important sense; but it sounds like a tame addition to the words which have preceded. The other suggests a new thought, which enlarges and completes the prayer. "May the Lord of Peace give you peace at all times and in all places." Such a petition must needs have a deep and solid ground to rest upon. "The Lord of Peace," he says, "give you peace." This he assumes as the very name of God. A god of war they had all heard of. He was said to have watched over the infancy of the greatest city in the world, to have been the father of its first king. Whithersoever the Roman Eagle had been borne, there were the tokens of his presence. The name Thessalonica testified that he had been on that soil. He knew that the heathens had never been satisfied with the idea of a god of war, however much it might have possessed them. They felt that the olive was a sacred emblem as well as the laurel. There must be some One from whom it came—of whom it testified.  The quiet homestead, the growth of trees and flowers, the power and art of tillage, must have an origin, as well as the skill and feats of armies.  Surely tempests did not witness of unseen power more than a still lake or an evening of clear starlight.  All sweet notes and their intricate combinations told of some secret source of harmony.  The heart which responded to these sights and sounds demanded a Lord of Peace nigh, and not afar off.  Was He a different Being from the other?  It was the misery of Polytheism to believe that He must be different.  How could such opposite effects proceed from the same Cause?  It was the blessed privilege of the Jew to be taught in direct words, and by the whole course of his history, that the Lord his God was one Lord, that the God of armies was the same as the Lord of Peace.  The acts of His power were the manifestations of His righteous will.  He was the Lord God, merciful and gracious, slow to anger, and plenteous in mercy; therefore would He not clear the guilty; therefore was all evil, everything unmerciful and oppressive, hateful in His eyes; therefore was He pledged to destroy it.  There was no actual or implicit contradiction in His nature.  I. The words are very EMPHATIC.  May He HIMSELF give you peace.  As if he had said, "I know and am persuaded that no one else can give it you; not I, not all the preachers and doctors in the universe.  Properly speaking, you do not even receive it at second-hand through us.  He gives you the thing itself; we present you with the seals and sacraments of it.  He opens a direct communication with your hearts; he conveys into them that which we only stand offering to them from without.  "May He," says the apostle, "Himself give it you!  Be not content to take it from any other."  II. And be sure also that He GIVES it.  You do not purchase it by prayers or faith or good deeds.  He receives the gift of a higher life, or he sinks into death.  In other words, God gives him peace, or he continues in a state of perpetual war.  III. THIS PEACE the apostle desires for the Thessalonians.  Not some image or shadow of peace, but peace itself, in its full meaning.  Not a peace which depends upon pacts and bargains among men, but which belongs to the very nature and character and being of God.  Not a peace which is produced by the stifling and suppression of activities and energies, but the peace in which all activities and energies are perfected and harmonized.  Not a peace which comes from the toleration of what is base or false, but which demands its destruction.  Not a peace which begins from without, but a peace which is first wrought in the inner man, and thence comes forth to subdue the world.  Not a peace which a man gets for himself by standing aloof from the sorrows and confusions of the world into which he is born, of the men whose nature he shares, choosing a calm retreat and quiet scenery and a regulated atmosphere; but a peace which has never thriven except in those who have suffered with their suffering kind, who have been ready to give up selfish enjoyments, sensual or spiritual, for their sakes, who have abjured all devices to escape from ordained toils and temptations; the peace which was His who bore the sorrows and infirmities and sins of man, who gave up Himself that He might become actually one with them, who thus won for them a participation in the Divine nature, an inheritance in that peace of God which passeth understanding.  IV. St. Paul could then say boldly, "The Lord give you peace IN ALL TIMES."  He was living in a time of exceeding restlessness.  All about him were wars and rumours of wars.  The Jewish commonwealth was breaking to pieces, from the hatreds of its sects, from its mad desire to measure its strength with its Roman masters.  St. Paul was the object of the fiercest spite of those fighting sects.  They did not abhor each other so much as they abhorred him.  And he knew that the end was coming —that God Himself had pronounced the doom of the city of David; that if he did not witness the fall of that nation, to save which he was willing to be accursed, it would be only because some violent death would take him sooner than it out of the world.  In this time, which affected all his disciples as well as himself, which had caused great sufferings to the Thessalonian Church, both from present Jewish persecutions and from the dim feverish apprehension of some day of the Lord which was near at hand; in this time, he could ask the Lord of Peace to give himself and them peace.  He could ask it confidently, nothing doubting that the petition would be heard and answered, nay, that the very tumults in the world and in themselves were intended to awaken it and to accomplish it.  He knew that easy and comfortable circumstances do not impart the peace which men want.  He knew that the most disastrous may drive them to that centre where it dwells and where they may possess it.  V. He prayed also, if the reading I have spoken of is the true one, that they might have peace IN EVERY PLACE.  He had some experience of different places, of Greek cities and Jewish, if he had not yet seen Rome, as he purposed to do ; and all his experience hitherto had been of strifes, tumults, persecutions. He had come to Thessalonica because he had been thrown into prison at Philippi. He escaped from Thessalonica to Beræa, thence to Athens. In Corinth the continued Jewish opposition was trifling compared with the struggle in his own spirit, which made him despair even of life. At Ephesus he was destined to fight with men who assailed him as the beasts assailed those who were exposed in the Amphitheatre. At Jerusalem voices cried, "Away with such a fellow from the earth! it is not fit that he should live." Bonds and imprisonments awaited him in the capital of the world. And yet he could say, "The Lord of Peace give you peace in all places." In the prison he had found it; in that infinite tumult and despair of his own spirit he had found it. And this, he was certain, was not because he was an apostle—because he had Divine revelations—because he had singular gifts. It was because he was a man, sharing the temptations of men, experiencing in himself the redemption which had been wrought out for men. VI. Do WE NOT NEED TO HEAR AT THIS TIME, IN THIS PLACE, THE SAME MESSAGE ? VII. But is not THE WEEK THAT WITNESSES OF THE SACRIFICE OF THE VICTIM ONE THAT BRINGS PEACE, IF IT FINDS BUT LITTLE ? Is not the week that commemorates the completion of the sacrifice one that carries peace even into the midst of war ? Yes! this, and nothing less, is what these days signify. "The Lord of Peace Himself give you peace in all places." You want a Lord of Peace, One in whom Peace dwells always, under all conditions, amidst all turmoils. Here, in the agony of the garden, on the cross of Calvary, behold Him ! (*F. D. Maurice, M.A.*) *Peace from the Lord of Peace:*— I. THE LORD OF PEACE is Jesus. St. Paul habitually calls Him Lord, and brings His name into special relation with peace. This is an apt compendium of His other titles and gives in one perfect phrase the whole sum of His mediatorial work. 1. The appellation is only another form of the title by which His coming was fore-announced. It was declared that He should vanquish Satan, turn aside the Divine displeasure, and establish a government of peace. Isaiah makes all His glorious names merge into " The Prince of Peace." His mediatorial obedience is bearing " the chastisement of our peace." The increase of His kingdom would be the "abundance of peace " (Isa. ix. 6, liii. 5, ix. 7 ; Psa. lxxii. 7). 2. The manner of His coming was a token of peace. "God with us." " Peace on earth." These announcements declared that the world's Peace was born, and that the alliance of God with our nature was the reconciliation which had been preached. This was the " everlasting sign that should not be cut off " (Isa. vii. 14 ; lv. 13). 3. But He who brought that sign was Himself cut off that it might be everlasting. Though the reconciliation was virtually effected from the beginning, for the " Lamb was slain from the foundation of the world," yet it required the atonement of " the blood of the Cross " (Col. i. 20–22). 4. The title, however, is a glorious one, and directs our thought to Christ's exaltation. Our Melchizedek became King of Salem, *i.e.* peace, by virtue of the sacrifice which He first offered as Priest of the Most High God. But the Royal title tells us that He has achieved our peace with the power of an endless life. Yet, like His ancient type, He was never other than a King. 5. Whilst this is true, it must not be forgotten that the term " Lord " is for the most part applied to Christ in respect of the jurisdiction He obtained in death (Rom. xiv. 9 ; Matt. xxviii. 18 ; Acts x. 36). Everything became Dominical from that time : the Lord's "house," " supper," " day," and so " peace." 6. Christ is Himself the Publisher of His own peace. The terms on which the sinner may make his peace with God are prescribed by the Lord Himself; nor does He permit any human authority to interfere with them. (1) Repentance ; no peace that was ever pronounced upon those who are careless of this condition was ever ratified by Him. (2) But when this condition is complied with He demands only a supreme reliance upon Himself; and those who encumber the sinner's approach by any human inventions have no sanction from Him. II. THE BESTOWMENT OF PEACE. 1. Our Saviour Himself administers His own government by His Spirit, and imparts with His own hands the blessings of His peace. As He presents His atonement in heaven He imparts it on earth (Rom. v. 11). He dispenses the forgiveness of sins, permitting none to interpose between Himself and the penitent save as the simple ambassadors of His will. He commanded His apostles to preach and to utter the salutation of peace, but the assurance of remission He reserved for His own lips. But in proportion to the restraint upon them was the freedom with which He dispensed it to the penitent. And still "the Lord of Peace" speaks the word that tranquillizes the conscience and gives the heart rest. 2. "Give you peace always." This means— (1) At the outset, that the humble petitioner may expect a permanent assurance of acceptance. The prayer for forgiveness which ascends "without ceasing" is heard and answered "always." (2) But the peace of Christ is larger and deeper than reconciliation; it includes all spiritual prosperity (John xiv. 27; xv. 11). 3. "By all means." We must expect it to come through strange and seemingly discordant methods. He who is "Lord of Peace" shows His supremacy in this, that He can make all things contribute to His servants' prosperity. We pray not merely that the Redeemer may shed peace through His Word and ordinances, but in tribulation, and make that minister to the profound communion of the soul with God; that He may preserve to the spirit interior peace, whilst the surface is harassed by temptation; that the very turbulence of the world may be made not only to heighten our peace by contrast, but to confirm it by driving us to more perfect fellowship with Him (John xvi. 33). III. THE GUARANTEE OF THIS PEACE. "The Lord be with you all." Where He dwells there must be peace, but this indwelling is only secured by prayer. He commanded His disciples to pronounce their peace in every house they entered. Much more does He observe His own law. Entering our hearts, He speaks His "peace"; abiding in us, He gives us peace "always"; and by the secret energy of His grace He turns all events to our good "by all means." (*W. B. Pope, D.D.*) *Benediction and invocation:*—Before closing his letter to the Thessalonians, St. Paul desires three Divine things for them. I. THAT THE LORD OF PEACE WOULD GIVE THEM PEACE. By peace some understand all manner of prosperity; but the apostle meant, in particular, peace with God—peace in their own conscience— peace among themselves—peace among others. And this peace he desired for them always, and in everything, and by all means. As they enjoyed the means of grace, he would have them successful in the use of all the means and methods of grace; for peace is often difficult, as it is always desirable. The gift of peace is God's, who is "the Author of peace and Lover of concord." And of this we may be firmly assured—that we shall neither have peaceable dispositions ourselves, nor find men disposed to be at peace with us, unless the Lord of Peace Himself give us both. II. THAT THE PRESENCE OF THE LORD MIGHT BE WITH THEM. How intensely the great leader of Israel desired the Divine Presence to go with him and the people to the land of promise may be gathered from his own words to Jehovah Himself: "If Thy Presence go not with me, carry us not up hence." He knew full well not only the absolute need of His presence to guide them, but also that His presence really included every other good. Paul felt as did Moses. He was sure that if the Lord was with the Thessalonians, all would be well with them. And we need nothing more to make us safe and happy, nor can we desire anything better for ourselves and our friends than to have the Lord's gracious presence with us and them. This will be a guide and guard in every path we may go, and a real comfort in every condition in which we may be placed. It is the presence of God that maketh heaven to be heaven, and the presence of God will make this earth, albeit cursed with sin and sorrow, like unto heaven. No matter where we are if God be with us; no matter who is absent from us if God be present with us. III. THAT THE GRACE OF THE LORD JESUS CHRIST MIGHT ALSO BE WITH THEM. Whatever the eminence of the Thessalonians for their inherent virtues and gracious qualifications, yet the apostle knew that it was only God's sovereign grace, and not their own merit, which must be relied upon for obtaining any temporal or spiritual mercy from the hands of God; for though he commended them for their faith, and love, and patience, and other excellences, yet he closeth and crowneth all by wishing God's free grace and favour to them as the fountain-cause of all they stood in need of or could expect. This grace or favour flows to us through Jesus. And it is this that is "all in all" to make us pure and happy. The apostle admired and magnified this grace on all occasions: he delighted and trusted in it: it had made him the saint, and the preacher, and the hero that he was; and no marvel that, as he loved his Thessalonian converts with a deep and holy passion, he took his leave of them with words so meet and precious. (*D. Mayo.*)     *The jewel of peace:*—I. THE MANY-SIDED BLESSING. The peace of the text is a gem with many facets, but—1. Its main bearing is towards God. (1) The Atonement has wrought perfect reconciliation and established everlasting peace. Into the enjoyment of this all believers enter. (2) Our hearts should be at peace by being fully in accord with God's will. Some of God's children complain of His dealings with them and so have not perfect peace. (3) There is also the peace of conscious complacency, the sense of Divine love which is lost when God hides His face through our sin. Peace because sin is forgiven is the fruit of justification (Rom. v. 1). Peace because the heart is made to agree with the will of God is the result of sanctification. "To be spiritually minded is . . . peace." Peace through consciousness of Divine love is attendant on the spirit of adoption. 2. This peace spreads itself abroad, and covers all things with its soft light. He who is at peace with God is at peace with all things that are God's, and all things work together for his good. 3. This practically shows itself in the Christian's inward peace with regard to his present circumstances. He sees God's hand in everything, and is content. Is he poor? The Lord makes him rich in faith. Is he sick? The Lord endows him with patience. 4. This peace is mainly to be found in the soul itself as to its thoughts, believings, hopings, and desires: "the good man is satisfied from himself." Some minds are strangers to peace. (1) How can they have peace where they have no faith. (2) When they are much afraid. II. THE SPECIAL DESIRABLE-NESS OF THIS PEACE. 1. It is essential to the joy, comfort, and blessedness of the Christian life. 2. Without peace you cannot grow. A shepherd may find good pasture for his flock, but if they are hunted about by dogs they will soon become skin and bone. 3. Without peace you cannot bear much fruit. If a tree is frequently transplanted, you cannot reasonably look for many golden apples. 4. Stability is dependent on peace. The doctrine can soon be driven out of a man's head which affords no light and comfort to his heart. 5. You must have peace for your soul's wealth. As war spends and peace gathers the riches of nations, so does inward strife devour us, while spiritual peace makes the soul fat. III. THE SOLE PERSON FROM WHOM THIS PEACE MUST COME—the Lord Jesus, the Prince of Peace. Who else can it be but He whom the angels announced with "Peace on earth"; who made peace by the blood of His Cross; who is "our Peace," having broken down the middle wall of partition; who said, "My peace I leave with you," &c.? 1. The apostle does not say, "May the Lord of Peace send His angel or His minister to give you peace," or "May you have it at the communion table, or in reading the Word, or in prayer." In all these we might be refreshed—but "Himself" give you peace. (1) We do not obtain peace except from the Lord Himself. His Person is a source of peace. (2) He "gives" this peace; not merely offers it to you, or argues with you that you ought to have it, or shows you the grounds. 2. "The Lord be with you all"—as much as to say, "That is what I mean; if He is present, you must enjoy peace." Let the sea rage, yet when Jesus arises there will be a great calm. IV. THE SWEEP OF THE PRAYER. 1. "Always." On week-days as well as Sundays; in the prayer-meeting and in the workshop; with the Bible and with the ledger; at all times, under all circumstances, and everywhere. Why are we troubled, when we may have this peace always? 2. "By all means." Some agencies evidently make for peace, but He can give us peace by opposing forces; by the bitter as well as the sweet; the storm as well as the peace; loss as well as gain; death as well as life. There are two grand ways of giving us peace. (1) By taking away all that disquiets us. Here is one who frets because he does not make much money, or has lost some. Suppose the Lord takes away his covetousness; he is at peace, not because he has more money, but less of grasping desire. Another is ambitious. Suppose the grace of God humbles him so that he only wishes to be and to do what the Lord wills; how readily he rests. Another has an angry temper; the Lord does not alter the character of the people round about him, but makes him gentle. What peace he now feels! (2) By discoveries of Himself and His grace. Conclusion: "There is no peace, saith my God, to the wicked." (*C. H. Spurgeon.*) *Peace of conscience and heart the element of holiness* :—1. "Always"—*i.e.*, absolutely permanent. The same word is used of the angels, who always behold the face of God; and of Christ, who "foresaw the Lord always before Him." The constancy of the Christian's peace is to be the same as that wherewith angels wait on the behests of God and Jesus realizes God's presence. 2. "In every manner." There are different modes and circumstances of its manifestation, according as the heart is burdened with anxiety, or depressed with a sense of sin, or feverish with excitement, or distracted by business. We may taste it in every form, according to the special need of the moment. 3. The Lord of Peace, its Author and Source, is called upon to bestow it (John xiv. 27; Phil. iv. 4-7). 4. This peace is a main essential to holiness; it is not only the root out of which it grows, but the strength in which alone it can be successfully pursued, and the element in which it moves. Its spheres are—I. THE CONSCIENCE. 1. It must be admitted by faith in Christ—such an act as shall shed abroad in the heart a sense of God's pardoning love. This act is simply a cordial acceptance of God's gift of Christ. Having performed this, we place ourselves in the condition described in Rom. v. 1. 2. But it must be detained. It is a sensitive guest, apt to take flight at the slightest affront, The conscience, once cleared by faith, must be kept clear by effort, the use of appropriate means, and repeated acts of faith. "Herein do I exercise myself to have always a conscience void of offence." But as faults will accrue, we need for the maintenance of peace periodical examinations of the conscience. II. THE HEART. Peace under the vexations and frettings of life. 1. This fretting may arise from anxieties, the right method of dealing with which is in Phil. iv. 4–7. Whatever may be your wishes on the subject which makes you anxious, refer them to God in prayer; and having done so, leave them with Him, assured that He will order the matter for the best. Drop them altogether. They are off your hands now, and are in better hands. They are no longer your business; they need not be your care. Thinking is utterly fruitless, and fruitless thinking is waste of the energy needed for progress, and is also a positive breach of God's precept—"Be careful for nothing." The spiritual life of the present moment is the one thing needful. As for future evil, it may never come; and if it does, it will prove less in reality than in anticipation. The women going to the sepulchre troubled themselves unnecessarily about the stone, for it was rolled away. 2. This discomposure may arise from things going cross in daily life, rubs of temper, annoyance, &c. The rule for the maintenance of peace is here the same. Never let your thoughts dwell on a matter in which another has made you sore. If you do, a hundred aggravations will spring up. With a brief prayer for him who has offended you, keep your thoughts away from what he has done. Try to realize God's presence. "My presence shall go with thee, and I will give thee rest." But the great point is to let the mind settle. Turbid liquids will clear themselves, and precipitate their sediment simply by standing. Be still, then. Conclusion: 1. Those who indulge fretful feelings, either of anxiety or irritation, give an opening to the devil in their hearts. "Fret not thyself, else thou shalt be moved to do evil." "Let not the sun go down upon your wrath, neither give place to the devil." Peace is the sentinel of the soul; only so long as this sentinel is on guard the castle is kept secure. 2. Be careful to maintain peace, if thou wouldst not only resist the devil, but receive the guidance of God's Spirit. That Spirit cannot make communications to a soul in a turbulent state. The Lord is not in the wind, or the earthquake, or the fire. Not until these have passed, can His still small voice be heard. (*Dean Goulburn.*)  *Peace versus war* :—I. First, then, we have A PEACEFUL DESIGNATION. 1. He who is the eternal and omnipotent Jehovah—"The man of war," "The lion of the tribe of Judah," is here described as "The Lord of Peace." He is so in His disposition. Peace, like silver sheen, is woven in His nature. His life manifested it, His words breathed it, His looks beamed with it, His prayers pleaded for it, His chastisement was to procure it, and His death was to seal it. 2. This fact may be yet more clearly seen if we remember how longsuffering He is with His enemies. What trifles prove sufficient to light the torch of war, if there be the desire first. Contrast with this what our Lord bears from His avowed foes, and His longsuffering towards them, and you will then be enabled in some measure to grasp the peaceableness of His disposition. Oh, what affronts does He receive, and yet forbears to smite! What indignities are heaped upon Him! How is His name profaned, His Sabbath desecrated, His laws broken, His Book derided, His worship neglected! What monarch on earth has ever been so openly defied, and that by creatures who are at His mercy for their very breath and bread? 3. This peace-loving disposition of our Lord can also be demonstrated by His forbearance with His friends. A slight from an open enemy is insignificant in its power to wound, compared with one that comes from a professed friend. What weakness, what base ingratitude, what falseness of affection are shown to Him, by the very ones whose names are engraven on His heart. And yet He bears with us and loves us still. Surely God's grace is not more marvellous in its first love than in that love's continuation. 4. The Lord is also the "Lord of Peace" in His actions. This is seen in the fact that He purchased it at a tremendous cost. Peace could only be procured by His own humiliation, agony, and death. At His baptism the peaceful nature of His mission was again made known, by the descent of the Holy Spirit. In what form was it that the Spirit alighted upon Him? He is His people's Ambassador above; and whilst He remains our representative there, our peace is secured, and glorious truth, "He ever liveth to make intercession for us." 5. The peace that was purchased by His blood is now secured by His life, and He only waits to place the crown upon the whole by perfecting our peace. Peace without the alarm of battle; peace beyond the noise or even rumour of strife; peace, deep and calm as mountain lake unruffled by a breeze, yet glittering in the sunlight, is the sweet consummation of the dealings of the Lord of Peace with us. II. We have, in the second place, A PEACEFUL SUPPLICATION. "The Lord of Peace, give you peace." 1. A conscience peace. This is one of the greatest gifts the Lord can bestow. What is a man without it? He may be surrounded by every luxury; but if he lacks this, he lives in a perpetual hell. That this happy experience might be theirs was prayed for by the apostle. 2. But as these words were addressed unto the Church at Thessalonica, they may also be understood as praying for their Church peace. A Church without peace is in just as wretched a condition as a heart without it. No country has ever suffered half so much through the ravages of war as has God's Church from its internal strifes. And, alas! as in other wars, what trifles kindle the flame. Some little grievance between two members, which a word of explanation on either side would heal at once, is allowed to grow and rankle, whilst partisans flock to the rival standards, and the few neutrals left find themselves powerless to avert the calamity. 3. Notice, further that the peace desired was a perpetual one. "Peace always" was the apostle's prayer. Very different this to the peace which has been Europe's of late. A peace so long, that war shall be forgotten; a peace so complete, that the probability of war shall cease. 4. It was also to be a peace that came by all means. May every privilege (Paul seems to say) which, as Christians, you possess, be so many golden pipes conveying to your hearts the oil of joy and peace! When you pray, may you lose your burdens and your cares, and find in it sweet peace. When you gather for the holy purposes of public worship, may a heavenly calm be yours, and may you find the sanctuary a means of peace. When alone, you meditate upon the promises, may they be to you as songs of consolation. III. A PEACEFUL BENEDICTION. "The Lord be with you all." 1. His presence be with you to comfort. May you never miss His smile or mourn His absence. 2. His power be with you to keep. In the seasons of temptation, may He hold above thy head His shield. 3. His Spirit be with you to guide. In the daytime may a cloudy pillar go before thee, and in the night season may one of fire direct thee. IV. AN INTERROGATION. "Have you this peace?" Is there within your breast a pacified conscience and a soul that has found its rest? (*A. G. Brown.*)

Ver. 17. **The salutation of Paul with Mine own hand, which is the token in every epistle.**—*Paul's token* was the mark by which to tell an authentic epistle of his from those forged letters with which false brethren had troubled the Church (chap. ii. 2). At first sight it seems to us too audacious for any one to have conceived the thought of writing a letter under the name of Paul; but, on the other hand, we must recollect several points. 1. St. Paul's genuine first epistle, in spite of its claim to inspiration (chap. iv. 15), could not yet have acquired in the eyes of the Thessalonians the sanctity it wears for us. They had no notion of such a thing as Holy Scripture; and even if they had, St. Paul was a familiar figure, a mechanic, who had just left them, not yet invested with the heroic halo. 2. Such literary forgeries were not uncommon in that age, and scarcely considered reprehensible, unless they were framed to inculcate with authority some heretical teaching. Apocryphal gospels soon after abounded, under false titles, and works fathered on Clement and other great Church teachers. 3. There need not always have been a direct intention to deceive the readers as to the authorship; but the renowned name acted as a tempting advertisement for the work, and the theories thus shot forth hit their mark; whether the real authorship were discovered or not mattered little in comparison. Such points must be borne in mind before we accept as genuine any of the early Christian writings. (*Canon Mason.*) There is the suggestion here that other letters may have passed between the apostle and the Thessalonian believers. If there were such a correspondence, we may regard it as having no doctrinal interest, and so was allowed to disappear. The amanuensis —probably Timothy—has now finished his work, and the apostle authenticates it. He gives his sign manual as a guarantee of the genuineness of the letter. He calls attention to it. Though his readers were doubtless acquainted with it, he asks them to mark it well—its large and, it may be, uncouth characters (Gal. vi. 11) were to be "the token" in every epistle he might in future send to them or to others, where attestation was needful. "So I write." (*J. Hutchison, D.D.*)

**Ver. 18. The grace of our Lord Jesus Christ be with you all. Amen.**—*The benediction :*—I. Its CONTENTS. Grace. II. Its COMPREHENSIVENESS. It embraces all. III. Its POWER. It is yea, and amen. (*J. Lyth, D.D.*)    What Paul calls his "salutation" is the prayer, showing that the whole business they were then about was spiritual; and even when he must give a salutation there must go some benefit along with it, and it must be a prayer, not a mere symbol of friendship. It was with this he would begin, and with this he would end, fencing round that which he said with mighty walls on either side; and safe were the foundations he laid, and safe the conclusion that he laid thereon. "Grace to you," he cries, "and peace"; and, once more, "Peace always," and "The grace," &c. (*Chrysostom.*) The benediction is the same as in the First Epistle, with the significant addition of "all." It serves a loving purpose here. Caught up, as it may be, from verse 16, where it is so prominent, it is meant to include the disorderly brethren, regarding whom he had painfully dictated words of severity. He would, indeed, have the censure written; but he would, before he closes, take away its sting. All, without exception, are enfolded in his loving embrace. Upon all he asks the Divine grace to descend. (*J. Hutchison, D.D.*)    *Grace :*—I. Its SOURCE. II. Its FULNESS. III. Its FLOW. IV. Its POWER. (*J. Lyth, D.D.*)    *Without the grace of Christ :*— The late Rev. Mr. Brown, of Haddington, towards the close of life, when his constitution was sinking under his multiplied and unintermitted labours, preached on the Monday after the dispensation of the Lord's Supper, at Tranent, a serious and animated sermon from these words : "The grace of our Lord Jesus Christ be with you all. Amen." After the service was concluded by prayer and praise, and he was just about to dismiss the congregation, it occurred to him that he had made no direct address to those who were destitute of the grace of the Lord Jesus ; and, though worn out by his former exertions, he at considerable length, and with the most intense earnestness, represented the horrors of their situation, and urged them to have recourse, ere the season of forbearance was past, to the rich and sovereign grace of the long-despised Saviour. This unlooked-for exhortation apparently made a deep impression, and was long remembered by the more serious part of the hearers. (*J. Whitecross.*)

# THE BIBLICAL ILLUSTRATOR

## I TIMOTHY

THE

# BIBLICAL ILLUSTRATOR

BY
JOSEPH S. EXELL

I TIMOTHY

BAKER BOOK HOUSE
GRAND RAPIDS, MICHIGAN 49506

Library of Congress Catalog Card Number: 54-11086
ISBN: 0-8010-3280-6

Printed in the United States of America

# INTRODUCTION TO THE PASTORAL EPISTLES.

THE GENUINENESS OF THESE EPISTLES.—As we read the Epistle to the Philippians, we feel that the apostle in his Roman prison was looking for speedy martyrdom. In many respects he regarded his work as finished. At the same time he felt that his "abiding in the flesh" was a help to the Churches which he had founded, and would fain visit once again (Phil. i. 24). In this aspect there seemed still a work for him to do. We are not told in the Acts which of the two possibilities was realized. In its closing verses it refers to the two years of Paul's captivity in Rome, but does not tell us to what issue they led. We are inclined to accept as the more probable, the idea that the apostle was set free, and was thus enabled to renew his labours for the good of the Church either in the East or West. We know that his plan, when in the year 59 he left Corinth to repair to Jerusalem and thence to Rome, was not to take up his abode in Rome, but simply to pass through it on his way into Spain, that he might fulfil the ministry which he had received of the Lord, to carry to the very end of the earth the testimony of the gospel of His grace. Was it given him to fulfil this purpose? Thirty years after the death of St. Paul, Clement, bishop of Rome, writing to the Corinthians, says that "Paul, after preaching the gospel from the rising to the setting sun, and teaching righteousness throughout the whole world, arrived at the extremity of the West; and after suffering martyrdom in the presence of the rulers, he was set free from this earth and reached the holy place prepared for him." Now it does not seem to me possible to suppose, as so many critics do, that by this expression, "the *extremity* of the West," Rome is meant: especially after the words going before, "from the rising to the setting sun," and "throughout the whole world." Rome, so far from being the "extremity" of the world, was rather regarded as its centre. We are confirmed in the idea that this is not Clement's true meaning by another passage also written at Rome, and bearing testimony to the tradition then current in that Church. It occurs in the Fragment of Muratori, where the writer refers to the "passion of Peter and the departure of Paul from Rome for Spain." We are not so much concerned at present with the question whether Paul went into Spain, as whether, in the event of his liberation, he again visited the Churches of Macedonia, the Church at Philippi, and the Churches in Asia, according to the hope expressed by him in the Epistle to Philemon. This question is inseparable from that of the authenticity of the Pastoral Epistles. It is impossible to find, during Paul's active ministry in Greece and in Asia Minor, or during the two years of his first captivity in Rome, circumstances corresponding to the biographical details contained in them. Either the Pastoral Epistles are genuine, and in that case, they date from the time between the liberation of the apostle and his martyrdom, and are the latest monument we have of his apostolic work; or they are spurious productions. On the latter supposition, criticism must find some explanation of the purpose of such a forgery. The majority of the critics at the present day incline to the view last given, though the evidence of tradition is as strong in favour of the authenticity of the Pastoral as of any of the other Epistles. There is a correspondence scarcely to be mistaken between certain expressions in the Epistle to Titus and the First Epistle to Timothy, and the Epistle of Clement of Rome; while it is impossible to deny the allusions to the Pastoral Epistles in the letters of Ignatius and Polycarp. The ancient Syriac Bible, as well as the Latin, in the second half of the second century, contained the Pastoral Epistles with all the others, and the Fragment of Muratori expressly records their admission into the canon, notwithstanding their originally private character. The Fathers at the close of the second century quote them as unanimously accepted. The two Gnostics, Basilides and Marcion, seem indeed to have rejected them, but this is not to be wondered at. If then in modern times the majority of critics coincide in denying the authenticity of all three, or of one or other of them, it must be on account of their contents. One thing is clear : these Epistles do differ from all the rest in certain very marked particulars. The apostle seems in them to be more occupied than was his wont with the future of the Church, and attaches greater importance to the various ecclesiastical offices on which that future might largely depend. He has before him dangerous teaching, which is spreading among the Churches, and which, if it became prevalent, would gravely undermine true piety. This teaching is of an altogether different character from the Pharisaic, Judaizing doctrine, against which he had protested in his earlier Epistles. Lastly, there is an evident want of cohesion in the ideas expressed and in the subjects treated, and a frequent repetition of certain forms of speech, which do not occur in the earlier Epistles. What conclusion must we draw from these various indications ? Is it true that there never was a period in the life of the apostle when new considerations, of which there is no trace in his earlier Epistles, may have come to occupy his mind ? Is it true that there is no reason to suppose that towards the close of his life, his teaching may have taken a new direction, and may have found expression in new modes of speech appropriate to the changed conditions ? Is it true that the unsound teaching against which he charges his colleagues to contend earnestly, can be no other than the Gnostic heresies of the second century, which would necessarily imply that these Epistles are the work of some forger assuming the name of St. Paul ? Is it true, lastly, that the ecclesiastical organization, to which the writer distinctly refers, belongs to a time long subsequent to the life of St. Paul ? 1. *The teaching of the apostle*, both as to form and substance. It is asserted that the conception of the gospel presented in these letters differs notably from the well-known teaching of Paul. The great fundamental doctrines of the apostle of the Gentiles, justification by faith and regeneration by the Holy Spirit, are scarcely touched upon. The great theme in these Epistles is the application of the gospel to outward conduct. For the most part the practical side of the Christian virtues is alone brought into prominence. We shall see presently what particular reasons the apostle may have had for insisting on this aspect of Christian truth. But independently of such considerations, it is easy to understand that the gospel teaching having been once clearly formulated, and thoroughly established by the earlier labours of the apostle in the Churches founded by him, as well as in the minds of his colleagues, he might now feel it opportune to insist rather on the practical application of the truths learned to daily life. The present writer has personally known preachers, who, after being foremost among their brethren in re-discovering, so to speak, the foundation-truths of the gospel, took a no less prominent part when the preaching again assumed a decidedly practical character. If such a change as this has been traceable in our own day, why may we not suppose a similar modification in the apostolic teaching of St. Paul, especially if the circumstances of the time seemed to demand it ? Criticism exacts, however, that the mode of speech at any rate should not change, and that the style of the apostle in these Epistles should not differ markedly from that of his other Epistles recognized as genuine. But we are told that such a strongly marked difference does exist. It is shown that a number of words are used in these three Epistles which do not occur in any of the earlier letters. Several expressions also occur repeatedly, which are not found in any of the earlier writings, and some entirely new terms descriptive of the unsound teaching leavening the Church at this time. To this we reply that diversity of verbiage is a marked feature throughout the literary career of the apostle. It results partly no doubt from the wealth and creative fulness of his genius, partly from the ever varying experiences through which he passed in his intercourse with the Churches. Other indirect influences may be added ; as for instance, the natural wealth of the Greek language and the fruitfulness of Christian thought. We conclude then that the teaching of these letters furnishes no proof, either in form or in substance, that they are not from the pen of St. Paul. It only shows that they belong to a particular period—the closing period of his apostolic labours. This conclusion is confirmed by the analysis we are about to make of the teaching against which he contends, and which presented itself to his two fellow-labourers in the Churches where they were at work. 2. *The teaching protested against in the Pastoral Epistles.* It has been said that this heretical teaching cannot be of an earlier date than the second century ; that the different Gnostic systems of that advanced period are clearly described, particularly those of Valentinus and Marcion. Other critics dispute this, and suppose the heresies referred to to be those of Cerinthus and the Ophites, at the beginning of the second or the close of the first century. This theory is equally opposed to the authorship of St. Paul. But two features of the heresies indicated by the apostle are incompatible with either of these suppositions. The first is that they do not appear to contain elements directly opposed to the gospel, as do the systems of Marcion and Valentinus. Had the writer been a Christian of the second century trying, under the name of Paul, to stigmatize the Gnostic systems, he would certainly have used much stronger expressions to describe their character and influence. He would have found in the first chapter of the Epistle to the Galatians a model of the Pauline polemics with regard to teachings subversive of the gospel. The second characteristic of the heresies referred to in the Pastoral Epistles is their Jewish origin. The doctors who propagate them are called "teachers of the law, though they understand neither what they say nor whereof they confidently affirm." They are Judaizing Christians ("they of the circumcision," Tit. i. 10), raising foolish contentions about the law (chap. iii. 9), and teaching "Jewish fables" (chap. i. 14), to which they add "endless genealogies," evidently also Jewish, for they are classed by the writer with "fightings about the law" (Tit. iii. 9; 1 Tim. i. 4), and form part of the teaching of those who call themselves "teachers of the law" (ver. 7). The natural solution presents itself, if we accept the Pastoral Epistles as closely connected with the Epistle to the Colossians. There we read of teachers who were trying to bring the Church into legal bondage, advocating the law as a higher means of sanctification and illumination; making distinctions between days and meats, like the weak Christians spoken of in Romans xiv., and taking up the worship of angels, in order to obtain from them revelations as to the celestial world (Col. ii. 16–18). One step further in the same direction will put us in touch with the false teachers of the Pastoral Epistles, who only represent a further stage of degeneracy in the direction of Judaism. They are the precursors of the Cabbala, which is a natural outgrowth of their doctrine. 3. *Church organization.* Several modern critics, following Baur, have assumed that the ecclesiastical offices referred to in the Pastoral Epistles indicate a much later date than the apostolic age. The functions of presbyter and deacon seem much more strictly defined than is likely to have been the case in the first century. The position of Titus and of Timothy in relation to the elders or presbyters, seems suggestive rather of the monarchical episcopate of the second century. The ministry of widows, as described (1 Tim. v.), can hardly be anything else than the office of deaconess-sisters, spoken of in ecclesiastical writings of a later date; as, for instance, when Ignatius says to the Christians at Smyrna, "I salute the virgins, called widows." But there are two insuperable difficulties in the way of this theory: (1) the plurality of presbyters in each Church (Tit. i. 5; 1 Tim. iv. 14), and (2) their complete equality of position. These are the distinctive marks of the presbytery or episcopate of apostolic times, in opposition to that of a later period, when the bishopric was entrusted to one man, who was set over the college of presbyters. Undoubtedly reference is made in 1 Timothy iv. 14 to a council of presbyters as an organized body, which had concurred with Paul in setting Timothy apart for his office, by the laying on of hands. But, in the first place, that which was thus conferred on Timothy was not the office of bishop, but simply a call to evangelistic work (2 Tim. iv. 5). And this rite of the laying on of hands to set apart to some work of ministry was practised in the Church from the earliest times, as for example, at Antioch, where the prophets and teachers laid hands on Barnabus and Saul to designate them for their missionary journey among the Gentiles. Even earlier than this the same practice is referred to in the Church at Jerusalem, when the apostles laid hands on the "seven men of good report" chosen to administer the alms of the Church to the poor. It is, indeed, an Old Testament usage, for Moses laid his hands on Joshua to transmit to him his office; and the same practice was observed when the heads of an Israelite household transferred to the Levites the duty properly devolving on their eldest sons, to serve in the sanctuary. It is then perfectly natural, that when Timothy departed from Lycaonia with Paul and Silas for a new mission among the Gentiles, the elders of the Church should have united with Paul in imploring for him the unction of the Holy One to qualify him for his evangelistic work, to which he was thus set apart. It is no matter of surprise then if, in 1 Timothy iii., Paul speaks of the diaconate as a recognized office, especially in a large Church like that of Ephesus. The opening words of the Epistle to the Philippians show that in another and probably much smaller Church, this office was already existing side by side with that of the bishop. If the Epistles before us had been written in the second century, by some one assuming the name of Paul, why should he have omitted the deacons in the Epistle to Titus ? On the other hand, it is quite natural that if the Church of Crete had been only recently founded, this second office should not yet have been required. In the passage referring to widows in 1 Timothy v., careful attention should be paid to 'he transition in ver. 9 from those who are widows in the ordinary sense to those who may be enrolled as such for the service of the Church, in the care of orphans and strangers and the poor. Whatever Weizsäcker may say on this point, it seems to us perfectly clear that it is in this sense of a recognized servant of the Church, that the title of deaconess is given to Phœbe, in Romans xii. 1, 2. All the references then in the Pastoral Epistles to offices in the Church seem to be closely connected with the elements of Church organization which we find mentioned in the earlier Epistles. The apostle is indeed more occupied than formerly with the duties and responsibilities of these servants of the Church. This arises no doubt partly from the ever-increasing gravity of the danger to the Churches from these unsound doctrines, and from the yet more deadly errors which he forecasts in the future. Then the apostle has a prevision of his own approaching end ; and to these two causes of anxiety on the Church's account, a third is to be added, of which we must now speak more at length. In the early days of the Church at Jerusalem, reference is made to presbyters or elders, in whose hands Barnabas and Paul placed the moneys collected at Antioch for the poor of the flock at Jerusalem (Acts xi. 30). These same elders are spoken of again as taking part in the assembly which decided the conditions of the admission of the Gentiles into the Church (Acts xv. 2, 6, 22). But it does not appear that these elders, as such, were preachers. Their office seems rather to have been administrative. Paul and Barnabas, in their first mission into Asia Minor, before leaving the Churches which they had founded there, appointed elders whom they set apart with fasting and prayer. It is probable that the ministry of these elders was of a spiritual as well as administrative character. For the apostles, not being themselves present in the Churches, the oversight and spiritual guidance of them would naturally devolve on these elders. This could not be the case to the same degree in Jerusalem, where the apostles themselves still resided. Somewhat later, at Thessalonica, there were in the Church leaders or overseers, who carried on the work among the faithful. The reference here is clearly to a ministry of a spiritual nature, but only under the form of the cure of souls (chap. v. 12–14), not under that of preaching. This is spoken of as the gift of prophecy, and was doubtless bestowed on those who filled the post of teachers in the Church (chap. v. 19, 20). At Corinth, the spontaneous manifestation of the Spirit under the three forms of prophecy, the gift of tongues, and teaching, seems exceptionally abundant. Yet the regular officers could not be dispensed with. Why should not Paul have instituted them here as well as in Lycaonia and at Thessalonica ? They are indeed mentioned in the long enumeration of the various gifts, under the name of " helps " and " governments," ἀντιλήψεις, κυβερνήσεις (1 Cor. xii. 28). Both are spoken of in the plural, because these two functions had their various spheres of duty ; but both offices were certainly recognized. For if they had no existence, why does the apostle say at the commencement of this passage, " Now there are diversities of gifts, but the same Spirit ; and there are diversities of ministrations, but the same Lord " (xii. 4, 5) ? Certain gifts then were to be freely exercised : those, namely, which the apostle describes by the special name of " gifts " (χαρίσματα). But there were others which were to be exercised by regular functionaries appointed by the Church itself, as in the case of the gifts of " helps and governments," which belonged to the presbyters and deacons. In the Epistle to the Romans, instead of the twelve gifts which flourished at Corinth, we find only seven (Rom. xii. 8) ; prophecy, ministry (διακονία)—which includes no doubt the two offices of which we have just spoken—teaching, and a series of other gifts appertaining to the individual life. We feel that the extraordinary outpouring of gifts at Corinth was a local and temporary fact. The tongues disappeared, and teaching took their place ; the gift of prophecy was directly perpetuated in the offices of the Church. Everything tends to settle down into a calmer and more settled state. Strong confirmation is given to this view by the Epistle to the Ephesians. Here Paul embraces the ministry in all its breadth, as concerning not only the particular Church, but the Church universal. He sees the gifts bestowed by the risen and glorified Lord, and the functions arising out of them taking three forms. First, there is the foundation ministry, represented by the apostles and prophets. Secondly, a ministry of extension carried on by the evangelists or missionaries. Thirdly, a ministry of edification entrusted to the pastors and teachers (iv. 11). And this is all. The rich abundance of gifts enumerated in the

Epistle to the Corinthians, seems to have vanished; or at any rate their place in the Church is a subordinate one. Of all the gifts and offices belonging to the Corinthian Church, there remain only two—those of pastors and teachers—the pastorate as an office, the teaching as a free gift. The first of these terms clearly includes presbyters and deacons; the second refers to public teaching. But it must be observed that the way in which the apostle expresses himself (using a singular article for the two names) implies a very close connection between the functions of pastor and teacher. Very much the same state of things is suggested by the superscription of the Epistle to the Philippians, "To all the saints which are at Philippi, with the bishops and deacons." Doubtless it is natural, that in addressing a letter, only the offices should be mentioned, the gifts being too uncertain an element to be enumerated. But the absence of any allusion to these gifts in the course of the Epistle, shows how far we are receding from the early Corinthian phase of Church life. If now we turn again to the Pastoral Epistles, we shall naturally expect to find a continuance of the same tendency to blend the gift of teaching with the office of elder. And so it is. According to Titus i. 9, the choice of a presbyter or bishop must only fall on a man who "is able both to exhort in the sound doctrine and to convict the gainsayers." According to 1 Timothy iii. 2, the bishop must be a man "apt to teach" (see also 2 Tim. ii. 24). Lastly, according to 1 Timothy v. 17, there are two classes of elders—those who confine themselves to administering the affairs of the Church, and those who in addition to this "labour in word and in teaching." The latter are to be "counted worthy of double honour." We see that in proportion as the extraordinary gifts of primitive times cease, the offices in the Church increase in importance and in influence, and that the principal gift—that of teaching—which survived all the rest, came to be more and more closely identified with the office of the regular ministry. (*Prof. F. Godet.*) 1. The first of the difficulties, around which the others revolve, is the chronological puzzle. If Luke had told us that Paul was beheaded at the close of the imprisonment of which he records the commencement, and if he had thus forced us to intercalate the narrative of the "Acts" with otherwise unrecorded biographical detail, even then, we should feel convinced that a forger would have been more careful in his mention of names, persons, places, and seasons, and would not have courted immediate detection by the fabrication of a series of journeys and missionary labours which clashed with universally-accredited documents. But Luke is silent about the conclusion of Paul's life; and the possibility thus granted of the hypothesis of a second imprisonment becomes the salvation of the Epistles from this irreverent handling. Baur is fully aware of this, and endeavours to show that the statement made by Clement of Rome throws no weight into the balance of probability in favour of a second imprisonment. Granting, however, that the Epistles to the Philippians and Colossians give no hint of any continued expectation of a visit to Spain, and that Luke's narrative leaves no space for Paul's intended journey from Rome to Spain (Rom. xv. 24), yet the hint given by Clement lends high probability to such a visit having been paid; and so, from the time of Eusebius to our own day, this solution of the difficulties has been thought by a long catena of competent scholars to be satisfactory. 2. A second class of difficulties arises from the use of a number of words and phrases which are peculiar to one or more of these Epistles, and are not found in other portions of the Pauline writings. This argument appears very convincing to some writers, but investigation into the circumstances under which these letters were written, the persons to whom they were addressed, and the purposes for which they were composed, is more than sufficient to account for the occurrence of these peculiarities. If a group of Bishop Berkeley's letters about his intended college at Bermuda were compared with several chapters of his "New Theory of Vision," very similar phenomena would appear. Each class of composition would have, to some extent, its own vocabulary. To say that certain expressions, like "doctrines of devils," are not apostolic because not found in the earlier Epistles, is reasoning in a vicious circle. We cannot know that this and other terms and phrases are not Pauline until, on other grounds and by irrefragable evidence, it is shown that these Epistles were not written by the apostle. Many of these expressions, such as "healthy," or "sound doctrine," which in some form occurs six times in the Pastoral Epistles, are perfectly comprehensible if we reflect on the growth of dogmatic ideas and ecclesiastical discipline, on the diffusion of poisonous doctrine, and the prevalence of diseased forms of thought during the course of the four to six years which must have elapsed between writing the Epistle to the Philippians and the Epistles before us. Take, again, a fresh and beautiful form of expression which repeatedly occurs : "This is a faithful saying." It reveals a new but indubitable characteristic of the early Church. Holy, trust-worthy, Divine words had begun to pass from lip to lip and from land to land. They were sacred coins stamped in the mint of religious experience, and passing current as pledges and symbols of new and supernatural fellowship. Who can wonder if such watchwords as, "Christ Jesus came into the world to save sinners," or as "If we die with Him we shall also live with Him"—words expressive of the very centre and scope of the whole gospel—had already become the recognized bonds of mutual understanding; that the rise of a custom, which developed ultimately into creeds and liturgical forms, should have received Paul's imprimatur? Psalms, hymns, spiritual and responsive songs, had, as we may judge from 1 Cor. xiv. 16, Col. iii. 16, been growing into customary use in the early Church. These Divine "proverbs," created we know not by whom, polished by deep emotion, tested in the furnace of sorrow, proved in the hour of conflict, were among the sacred pos-sessions of the martyr Church, and we need not suppose that a reference to the habit is post-apostolic. There are many approximations to the same conception in the undoubted Epistles of Paul. Again, why should Paul not use the word *epiphaneia*, instead of *parousia*, to denote the coming of our Lord? Had not earlier Epistles shown that the feverish expectation of a visible *parousia* was requiring modification, and that the apostle himself anticipated a "manifestation," which was even more than the old notion of a "coming," and might prove to be the final revelation and unveiling of the fact that He had already come? It is true that the verb (*arnoumai*) "deny" is frequently used in these Epistles of those who repudiated the Lord Jesus, and it is also used in Jude, 2 Peter, and 1 John—a circumstance vindicated by the subversive character of the later developments of heretical feeling which came under Paul's observation after his deliverance from his first imprisonment. One of the most striking peculiarities to which adverse critics call attention is the use, thirteen times, of either *eusebeia, eusebein, eusebôs*, for godliness or piety towards God in Christ. Some equivalent form occurs five times in the Acts, but hardly anywhere else in the New Testament. This may have arisen from Paul having contrasted the great Christian "mystery of godliness" with the heathen conception of relation to the gods. Paul, by his long residence in Rome, came upon this grand definition, and then, having once used it, he found the various derivatives of the word embrace for him the whole circumference of Christian experience and conduct. Another phrase is used in both Epistles to Timothy characteristic of the position and duties of the evangelist, but borrowed from the style of the Old Testament, and never elsewhere adopted in the New. I refer to the expression, "O man of God" (1 Tim. vi. 11), and "The man of God" (2 Tim. iii. 17). This peculiarity is in harmony with the apostolic idea of the Christian ministry, and it corresponded with the prophetic rather than with the priestly order of the old covenant. If it were necessary to follow these terms and phrases in detail, it would be far more just to the materials before us to imagine a more or less sufficient reason why the apostle should have adopted them, than, on account of their presence, to perform the rough and sweeping process of handing these Epistles over to a *falsarius*. Surely a writer who was anxious to make his compositions pass for those of the apostle Paul, could easily have kept scrupulously within the vocabulary of his undoubted Epistles. 3. A third class of difficulties has arisen from the numerous digressions of the author of these Epistles. It is stated that, without warning, he departs from the matter in hand to introduce broad statements of Christian principle or compendiums of truth ; and 1 Tim. i. 15; ii. 4–6; iii. 16, are cited in illustration. This peculiarity is sufficiently marked, but not more so than it is in the Epistles to the Galatians, Ephesians, and Corinthians. Thus in Gal. i. and ii., Paul digresses to recount portions of his own life ; and in stating what he said to "Peter before them all," he unfolds the whole doctrine of justification by faith. In the Epistles to the Corinthians, the digressions run into whole chapters, and it becomes difficult in consequence to follow the argument. Compare also Eph. iii. 1, and iv. 1, for a similar idiosyncrasy of style. 4. De Wette has urged the author's exaggeration of the moral and doc-trinal elements in the Epistles in a manner said to be un-Pauline. But though we may admit a more concise and clearly-cut phrase for certain theological concep-tions, and discover the use of the word "hairetikos" in Titus iii. 10 in a sense which savours of a later signification of the word "hairesis," yet it is clear that "hairesis" in Paul's undoubted Epistles did mean a faction or sect, and that "heretick" might mean a person who fomented and agitated for sects and with a party spirit. But since such a spirit always arose from some strongly-held idea, some truth, or half-truth, or untruth pertinaciously maintained, the word probably had always carried with it an antithetic reference to the faith of Christ; and now, when opposition had crystallized itself into definite shape, "heresy" was an appropriate term for Paul, at the end of his life, to use when writing to a Church officer concerning the root principle of dissension and schism. 5. The most formidable agreement among the impugners of the authenticity of the Epistles turns upon the indications afforded by them of an ecclesiastical constitution which was not developed until after the supposed date of Paul's death. In our opinion, there is nothing more than may be safely gathered from the Epistle to the Philippians i. 1, 2, where the only Church officers referred to are "the bishops and deacons." "The elders" to be appointed in every city in Crete are clearly identical in person with the bishops, whose qualifications are immediately recorded (Titus i. 5, 6, 7; Comp. Acts xx. 17 and 28). Even in the Epistle to the Romans (xii. 8) there is special advice given to the ruler in the Church, and the same word is used that describes the ruling functions of the elder in the Pastoral Epistles. See 1 Tim. iii. 4; comp. also 1 Thess. v. 12 and 1 Cor. xii. 28, where the *charism* of government is reckoned as one among the many gifts of the Spirit. (*H. R. Reynolds, D.D.*) 1. The external evidence of their reception by the universal Church is conclusive. They are distinctly quoted by Irenæus, and some of their peculiar expressions are employed in the same sense by Clement, Paul's disciple. They are included in the Canon of Muratori and in the Peschito, and are reckoned by Eusebius among the canonical Scriptures universally acknowledged. Their authenticity was never disputed in the early Church, except by Marcion; and that single exception counts for nothing, because it is well known that he rejected other portions of Scripture, not on grounds of critical evidence, but because he was dissatisfied with their contents. 2. The opponents of the genuineness of these Epistles have never been able to suggest any sufficient motive for their forgery. Had they been forged with a view to refute the later form of the Gnostic heresy, this design would have been more clearly apparent. As it is, the Epistles to the Colossians and Corinthians might have been quoted against Marcion or Valentinus with as much effect as the Pastoral Epistles. 3. Their very early date is proved by the synonymous use of the words πρεσβύτερος and ἐπίσκοπος. 4. Their early date also appears by the expectation of our Lord's immediate coming (1 Tim. vi. 14), which was not entertained beyond the close of the apostolic age. (See 2 Pet. iii. 4.) 5. Their genuineness seems proved by the manner in which Timotheus is addressed. How can we imagine a forger of a subsequent age speaking in so disparaging a tone of so eminent a saint? 6. In the Epistle to Titus, four persons are mentioned (Artemas, Tychicus, Zenas, Apollos); in 1 Timothy two are mentioned (Hymenæus and Alexander); in 2 Timothy sixteen are mentioned (Erastus, Trophimus, Demas, Crescens, Titus, Mark, Tychicus, Carpus, Onesiphorus, Prisca, Aquila, Luke, Eubulus, Claudia, Pudens, Linus). Now, supposing these Epistles forged at the time De Wette supposes—viz., about A.D. 90—is it not certain that some of these numerous persons must have been still alive? Or, at any rate, many of their friends must have been living. How, then, could the forgery by possibility escape detection? If it be said that some of the names occur only in the Pastoral Epistles, and may have been imaginary, that does not diminish the difficulty; for would it not have much surprised the Church to find a number of persons mentioned in an Epistle of Paul from Rome whose very names had never been heard of? 7. De Wette himself discards Baur's hypothesis that they were written in the middle of the second century, and acknowledges that they cannot have been written later than about the close of the first century—*i.e.*, about A.D. 80 or 90. Now, surely, it must be acknowledged that if they could not have been *later* than A.D. 80 or 90, they may well have been *as early* as A.D. 70 or 68. And this is all which is required to establish their genuineness. (*Conybeare and Howson.*) "It is an established fact," as Bernhard Weiss rightly points out, "that the essential fundamental features of the Pauline doctrine of salvation are, even in their specific expression, reproduced in our Epistles with a clearness such as we do not find in any Pauline disciples, excepting, perhaps, Luke, or the Roman Clement. Whoever composed them had at his command, not only St. Paul's forms of doctrine and expression, but large funds of apostolic zeal and discretion, such as have proved capable of warming the hearts and guiding the judgments of a long line of successors. Those who are conscious of these effects upon themselves will probably find it easier to believe that they have derived these benefits from the great apostle himself, rather than from one who, with however good intentions, assumed his name and disguised himself in his mantle.  (*Alfred Plummer, D.D.*)

TIME AND PLACE OF WRITING.—The design with which these Epistles were written—their subject-matter—their very phraseology—all bespeak a date of composition distinct from and later than that of any other Epistle of St. Paul. The apostle's declining years, the death of so many of his apostolic brethren, the breaking out of the persecution of the Christians under Nero in A.D. 64, the foresight of his own martyrdom not far distant, the anticipation also perhaps of the death of the Apostle of the Circumcision, St. Peter, for which that apostle was looking, as our Lord had showed him (2 Pet. i. 14 ; John xxi. 18), the foreboding of evil days at hand for the Church (Acts xx. 29 ; 2 Tim. iii. 1)—these and other considerations would impress themselves on the apostle's mind with great force and solemnity, after his release from his two years' detention at Rome, and would inspire him with earnest solicitude, and with a vehement desire to provide for the future spiritual welfare of the Churches, which would soon be bereft of his personal presence and fatherly care.  He would, therefore, now bequeath to the Church an apostolic directory for her future guidance in spiritual regimen and polity.  This he did by constituting the Churches of Ephesus and of Crete, and by setting Timothy and Titus over them respectively as chief pastors of those Churches, which were thus presented to the eye of Christendom as specimens and models of apostolic Churches ; and by addressing to the chief pastors of those Churches these Epistles, which were designed to be to them, and to all bishops and pastors, like a sacred manual and a heavenly oracle for their guidance (1 Tim. iii. 15).   It may also be remarked, that the form of religious error, against which St. Paul provides an antidote in these Epistles, is of a peculiar character, such as belonged to the last age of the Jewish polity and to the decay of the Jewish ritual at Jerusalem.  It is not the rigid Pharisaism and strict legal self-righteousness which had been condemned by St. Paul in the Epistles to the Galatians and Romans. But it was a speculative Gnosticism, a theorizing profession of faith, a spurious religion of words, vaunting, in boastful hypocrisy, its own spiritual illumination, but hollow, barren, heartless, profitless, and dead ; not "maintaining good works," but rather disparaging them : explaining away the doctrine of the resurrection of the body (2 Tim. ii. 17, 18) by an allegorical process of interpretation, afterwards fraught with so much moral mischief to the world ; and deluding its votaries with a specious show and empty shadow of godliness ; and puffing them up with presumptuous notions of superior holiness, and tempting them to cauterize their consciences with a hot iron (1 Tim. iv. 2) ; and inveigling them to make compromise between God and mammon, and enticing them with earthly allurements to make religion a trade, and to wear away their days in hypocritical unfruitfulness, and to live as liars to themselves, and indulging them in antinomian licentiousness, worldly lusts, carnal concupiscence, and sensual voluptuousness. It was, in fact, that hypocritical form of religion which had incurred the stern censure of St. James, foreboding the coming woes of Jerusalem (James i. 22-27 ; ii. 14-26) ; and which is also denounced in the Epistles of St. Peter and St. Jude (2 Pet. ii. 1-3, 13, 19 ; Jude 4, 10-12, 16, 19) ; and which afterwards developed itself in the full amplitude of its hideous deformity in the organized systems of the Gnostics, and particularly in the mystical allegories of Valentinus, and the moral oppositions of Marcion, subverting the foundations of faith and practice, and bringing disgrace on the Christian name by its moral profligacy and dissolute enormities.   This is the form of Judaizing Gnosticism that is presented to the eye by St. Paul in these Epistles, and evoked from him those solemn denunciations which characterize these Epistles concerning the moral guilt of heresy, and on the necessity of shunning all profitless and barren speculations, and of teaching wholesome and sound doctrine, fruitful in good works. The peculiar phraseology of these Epistles also deserves notice.  It has indeed been arbitrarily represented in recent times as an argument against their genuineness.  But it may rather be adduced in confirmation of the statement that they belong to a distinct period of their own (and this a late one) in the apostle's career.  Some of the most remarkable features of this phraseology are—1. πιστὸς ὁ λόγος used to introduce a memorable saying, a formula peculiar to these Epistles (1 Tim. i. 15 ; iii. 1 ; iv. 9 ; 2 Tim. ii. 11 ; Tit. iii. 8), and very appropriate to a time when the apostle would leave certain memorable sentences as "faithful sayings," to be like "nails fastened by the masters of assemblies, which are given by one Shepherd "—even Christ Himself, the Chief Shepherd.   2. ὑγιαίνουσα διδασκαλία, λόγοι ὑγιαίνοντες, λόγος ὑγιὴς, ὑγιαίνειν τῇ πίστει (1 Tim. i. 10; vi. 3; Tit. i. 9, 13; ii. 1, 2, 8; 2 Tim. i. 13; iv. 3)—words equally proper to be sounded in the ears at a time when the Church was suffering from such spiritual diseases as the apostle describes under such names of a *canker, fables, profitless questions, idle talk.*   3. The same observation may be applied to the perpetual inculcation of the terms *sound, sober, holiness,* and such like.   They are like protests against that empty profession of religion, which was like a foul and deadly gangrene preying on the vitals of the Church.   (*Bp. Chris. Wordsworth.*)      Set free from his captivity in the spring of the year 64, Paul departed for the East, as he had said to Philemon and to the Philippian Church.   Embarking at Brindisi, the most frequented port of Italy on the eastern side, he arrived at Crete.   There he found Titus, who had already preached the gospel there and founded Churches.   Here Paul remained some time with Titus.   Then, desiring to fulfil his promise to the Philippians, he left there his faithful servant, who was still to carry on the work, and departed into Macedonia.   Trophimus, who accompanied him, fell sick as the ship coasted along the shores of Asia Minor, and was left at Miletus.   Paul had only a glimpse in passing of Timothy, who was at this time stationed at Ephesus.   Paul exhorted him to remain at his difficult post, instead of becoming his companion, as Timothy would doubtless have preferred.   As it was Paul's intention in any case to visit Asia Minor before leaving for the West, he promised Timothy to come back shortly, and continued his voyage.   He disembarked at Troas, where he left his cloak and books with Carpus, meaning to take them up again on his return.   Arrived in Macedonia, his mind full of anxious thoughts about the grave duties devolving on his two young companions in labour, he wrote to them both—to Timothy with a view to encourage him, to give him fresh counsel, and assure him again of his speedy return; and to Titus to tell him that some one was being sent to take his place, and to beg him to come without delay to join Paul at Nicopolis, probably the town in Thrace, where he proposed to pass the winter, before starting again in the spring for Asia Minor.   As far as we can gather, St. Paul seems to have been prevented by some unforeseen circumstance from carrying out this plan.   He was not able either to go back to Troas to fetch the things he had left there, or to rejoin Timothy at Ephesus, or to avail himself of Philemon's hospitality at Colosse.   He was compelled suddenly to return west.   Either he was carried there as a prisoner, having been arrested in Macedonia, or he went of his own accord into Italy in response to some urgent demand upon him.   This sudden call may have been the dispersion and comparative destruction of the Church of Rome under the persecution by Nero.   It needed a hand like Paul's to raise again the building from its ruins.   It is possible that after performing this duty, he may, at length, in the course of the year 65, have left for Spain, as says the Fragment of Muratori (perfectionem Pauli ab urbe ad Spaniam proficiscentis).   There he must soon have been again taken prisoner and brought back to Rome.   From his prison he wrote the Second Epistle to Timothy, in which he describes his almost utter loneliness, and begs him to come to him before the winter of 65–66.   Notwithstanding the favourable issue of his first appearance at the imperial tribunal, when he was enabled to bear his full testimony before the heads of the State, he was soon condemned and executed (probably beheaded) on the Appian Way, near which his tomb was still shown in the second century.   We do not see what valid objection there can be to this hypothetical explanation, which bears out all the allusions contained in the three Epistles before us.   Even the prophetic words spoken to the Ephesian elders at Miletus (Acts xx. 25) thus find their fulfilment: "Behold, I know that ye also, among whom I went about preaching the kingdom, shall see my face no more"; for he was never able to carry out his purpose of again visiting Asia Minor.   His presentiment of his coming end (to which, as we see from his words to Philemon, he did not attach the certainty of prophecy) proved truer than at one time he himself supposed.   (*Prof. F. Godet.*)

DISTINGUISHING CHARACTERISTICS.—The two Epistles of St. Paul to Timothy with the Epistle to Titus form a clearly distinct group in the apostolic writings.   They have been designated *The Pastoral Epistles;* and though the expression, like that of *The Synoptic Gospels,* has the disadvantage of attributing to them in too great a degree a general design, and of thus diverting attention from their individual peculiarities, it marks with correctness the most important element which they have in common. The First Epistle to Timothy and the Epistle to Titus are, indeed, mainly concerned with instructions and exhortations to those disciples of the apostle respecting their duties as overseers of the two Churches committed to their charge, and with advice and warning in view of the special dangers they would have to meet. But the Second Epistle to Timothy starts from more personal considerations, and is in a far greater degree occupied by them. The apostle writes it while under imprisonment at Rome, and in expectation of imminent martyrdom (2 Tim. iv. 6, 7). In a tone of deep emotion, natural to such circumstances, St. Paul writes to Timothy, entreating him, if possible, to come to him soon; and occasion is taken to address to him some earnest exhortations that he should be stedfast in the faith, and fulfil his course like the apostle himself. But the duties which Timothy has to discharge in this course are those of a chief pastor; the apostle is thus led to direct his advice in great measure to these special duties; and so far the Epistle resembles the other two. It should, indeed, be borne in mind, since the fact has considerable weight in estimating some of the peculiarities of these Epistles, that they are personal as well as pastoral, differing in this respect from all the other Epistles of St. Paul, except the brief one addressed to Philemon on a special occasion. But so far as they are concerned with the general interests of the Church, it is with the duties of pastors that they deal; and it is impossible to overrate their importance in this respect. The other Epistles afford us all needful instruction respecting the great dogmatic truths of Christianity, and the chief points of Christian morals. But respecting the practical organization and government of the Church, they furnish only incidental hints. The deficiency is supplied by these three Epistles. They were written near the close of the apostle's career, when it was becoming necessary for him to provide for the due government, after he should have passed away, of the Churches he had founded. Brief as they are, they afford a clear insight into the principles by which he was guided, and they give advice which in all ages of the Church has been accepted as the apostolic standard of pastoral duty. (*H. Wace, D.D., in Speaker's Commentary.*) These Epistles are marked by peculiarities of their own, which distinguish them from each of the other groups. They were not addressed to Churches, but to individuals—to two younger men, friends and companions of Paul's travels, who were in perfect sympathy with him—to men who had submitted themselves to his personal influence and were familiar with his methods of thought. To them there was no need to expound the philosophy, whether of law, or of sin, or of redemption. It was unnecessary for him, in these Epistles, to vindicate his apostolic office or to recount either his afflictions or his services. Timothy and Titus had suffered with him. They had difficult duties to discharge, and needed both advice and stimulus. The principles and details of Church discipline, the motives and law of Christian service, were the themes on which he dilated. It is in harmony with these obvious peculiarities of the Epistles that they should abound in phrases suitable to confidential intercourse, and that they should refer to matters which were not included in other and earlier correspondence. (*H. R. Reynolds, D.D.*) (1) The ever-deepening sense in St. Paul's heart of the Divine mercy, of which he was the object, as shown in the insertion of ἔλεος in the salutations of both Epistles to Timothy, and in the ἠλεήθην of 1 Tim. i. 13. (2) The greater abruptness of 2 Tim. From first to last there is no plan, no treatment of subjects carefully thought out. All speaks of strong overflowing emotion, memories of the past, anxieties about the future. (3) The absence, as compared with St. Paul's other Epistles, of Old Testament references. This may connect itself with the fact that these Epistles are not argumentative, possibly also with the request for the " books and parchments " which had been left behind (2 Tim. iv. 13). He may have been separated for a time from the ἱερὰ γράμματα, which were commonly his companions. (4) The conspicuous position of the " faithful sayings " as taking the place occupied in other Epistles by the Old Testament Scriptures. The way in which these are cited as authoritative, the variety of subjects which they cover, suggest the thought that in them we have specimens of the prophecies of the apostolic Church which had most impressed themselves on the mind of the apostles and of the disciples generally. 1 Cor. xiv. shows how deep a reverence he was likely to feel for such spiritual utterances. In 1 Tim. iv. 1, we have a distinct reference to them. (5) The tendency of the apostle's mind to dwell more on the universality of the redemptive work of Christ (1 Tim. ii. 3–6; iv. 10), his strong desire that all the teaching of his disciples should be " sound," commending itself to minds in a healthy state, his fear of the corruption of that teaching by morbid subleties. (6) The importance attached by him to the practical details of administration. The gathered experience of a long life had taught him that the life and well-being of the Church required these for its safeguards. (7) The recurrence of doxologies (1 Tim. i. 17 ; vi. 15, 16 ; 2 Tim. iv. 18) as from one living perpetually in the presence of God, to whom the language of adoration was as his natural speech. (*Dean Plumptre in Dict. of Bible.*)

WITNESS OF THESE EPISTLES TO THE APOSTOLIC MINISTRY. The Pastoral Epistles are the *locus classicus* in the New Testament on the subject of the Christian ministry. Elsewhere St. Paul writes to Churches or to a private Christian like Philemon, but here he writes to his own representatives, evangelists, and ministers of Christ like himself, on the duties of their office. And these Epistles themselves supply the answer to the question, what may have prompted the change of method. It was because the circumstances of St. Paul's last days led him to emphasize the necessity for government in the Church. In the department of doctrine he saw an unpractical profane spirit of speculation springing up on a Jewish basis, but already displaying that sort of false spiritualism, that horror of what is material and actual, which has constantly characterized Oriental thought, and which found such a conspicuous development, in a direction most opposed to Judaism, in the Gnostic movements of the second century (1 Tim. i. 4–7 ; iv. 1–5 ; vi. 20, 21 ; 2 Tim. ii. 16–18 ; Tit. ii. 10-16 ; iii. 8, 9). This speculative tendency was frequently joined to a self-seeking proselytism and a thinly-veiled covetousness (Tit. i. 10, 11 ; 2 Tim. iii. 6, 7 ; 1 Tim. vi. 4, 5) ; and it allied itself with a terrible tendency to lawlessness, which clouded the whole moral atmosphere of the Christian Church, whether in the department of civil authority and secular occupations, or in the relations of master and servant, or in the inner sphere of Church life (1 Tim. vi. 1, 2 ; Tit. ii. 9 ; iii. 1–3 ; 2 Tim. iii. 1–8). There was a special need of government, then, in the circumstances of his last years, and this not only in face of the needs of the moment, but even more in view of the future (2 Tim. iv. 6–8, *cf.* iii. 1–6, iv. 1–5 ; 1 Tim. iv. 1–5, *cf.* Acts xx. 17-35). St. Paul in these Epistles is emphasizing no new thing. Just as in the Epistle to the Colossians he develops a doctrine of the person of Christ which had been implied in the expressions of his earlier Epistles, and in the Epistle to the Ephesians works out the doctrine of the Church which had been more briefly suggested in his Epistles to the Corinthians, so now he emphasizes that idea of governmental and doctrinal authority in the Church which had been an element in his earlier teaching, especially in his Epistles to the Thessalonians and Corinthians, and consequently lets that gift of government, which in the Corinthian Church had been associated with other more exciting but less permanent and necessary endowments, emerge into greater isolation and distinctness. 1. As to the local ministries of bishop and deacon, if we do not gain much new information, on the other hand we have a greater clearness and definiteness given to the picture we can form of their office. Thus the "episcopus" is also called "presbyter," and, though the latter title would naturally suggest a dignity associated with the reverence due to age, and indicate rather a position than (like the first title) a definite office, yet this will not bear being pressed. A word is used for old men (Tit. ii. 2) distinct from the title of presbyter, and the latter is markedly identified in Tit. i. 5–7 with the title of bishop. These " bishops " constituted a college or group of " presidents " in each Church (1 Tim. iv. 14, *cf.* Tit. i. 5), and are spoken of as being really entrusted with the care of the Church (1 Tim. v. 17 ; iii. 5). They share the apostolic stewardship, and that not only in the sense of administration, but also in the sense of being entrusted, really, though subordinately with the function of teaching (Tit. i. 7, 9 ; 1 Tim. ii. 2 ; v. 17 ; 2 Tim. ii. 2). The proper discharge of their office is secured by their being carefully chosen, after due probation, in view not only of their moral fitness, but also of their capacities as rulers and teachers (1 Tim. ii. 1–7 ; Tit. i. 6–9). The lower ministry of the deacons is provided for in the older and more developed Church of Ephesus, not in the newer Churches of Crete, and it too is to be entrusted only after a due scrutiny of the moral fitness of the man who is to hold it (1 Tim. ii. 8–13). We gain no light upon the functions of the diaconate, except so far as that the deacons would not be required, by contrast with the presbyters, to teach or to rule. 2. We gain important information as to the extension of the apostolic office. In Timothy and Titus we are presented with apostolic delegates, exercising the apostolic supervision over the Church of Ephesus and the Churches of Crete respectively. They are not, indeed, what St. Paul and the other apostles were, the original proclaimers of a revelation; they stand in this respect in the second rank, as entrusted on'y with the task of maintaining a tradition, of upholding a pattern of sound words (2 Tim. i. 13, *cf.* 1 Tim. i. 3; iv. 11, 13; vi. 3). But in this task they exercise the supreme apostolic authority, and not in this respect only. To them belongs the function, in Titus' case of founding, in both cases of governing, the Churches committed to them. They ordain men to the Church orders, after being duly satisfied of their fitness, and exercise discipline even over the presbyters (Tit. i. 5; 1 Tim. v. 22). Again, as it is their function to maintain the truth, so in defence of it they are to oppose false teachers, and when these exhibit the temper of separatists and heretics, and will not "hear the Church," they are to act in the spirit of Christ's directions and leave them to their wilful courses, having nothing further to say to them (Tit. iii. 10, 11). We do not, however, gather that they possessed the miraculous power to inflict physical penalties, which St. Paul describes in his phrase "delivering unto Satan for the destruction of the flesh." As apostolic delegates, then, Timothy and Titus exercise what is essentially the later episcopal office, but it would not appear that their authority, though essentially *permanent*, is definitely localized like that of the diocesan bishop. Nor do we gather from these Epistles any clear intimation that Timothy and Titus, though they were to provide for a succession of sound teachers (2 Tim. ii. 2), were to ordain men to succeed them in their apostolic office in the local Churches. All then we can fairly conclude is that St. Paul, after ordaining, or with a view to ordaining, the local ministers, bishops, and deacons, appointed delegates to exercise the apostolic office of supervision in his place, both before and after his death; and it must be added that the needs which required this extension of the apostolic ministry were not transitory ones. No definite title is assigned to Timothy and Titus, though their function is spoken of as a "ministry," and as "the work of an evangelist," and in Timothy's case at least is distinguished from that of the presbyters by the attribute of comparative youthfulness (1 Tim. iv. 6; 2 Tim. iv. 5). No doubt the necessity for fixed titles grew greater with lapse of time and increase of controversy. 3. The Pastoral Epistles give us a clearer view of St. Paul's conception of the ministerial office. Over and above what constitutes the gift of the Christian life, the apostolic "minister" is qualified for his work by a special ministerial gift or "charisma"—"a spirit of power, and love, and discipline"—imparted to him after his fitness has been indicated by a prophetic intimation, in a definite and formal manner, by means of the laying-on of the hands of the apostle, by means also of a prophetic utterance, accompanied with the laying-on of the hands of the presbytery (2 Tim. i. 6, 7; 1 Tim. iv. 14; i. 18). In this process there were features which were not destined to be permanent. Thus the prophetic indication of the person to be ordained ceased; and the prophecy, which St. Paul speaks of as the medium through which with the laying-on of his hands the spiritual gift was communicated, passed from being an inspired utterance into an ordinary prayer or formula of ordination. But it is only a very arbitrary criticism which can fail to see here, with slight miraculous and transitory modifications, the permanent process of ordination with which we are familiar in later Church history, and that conception of the bestowal of ordination of a special "charisma," which at once carries with it the idea of "permanent character," and that distinction of clergy and laity which is involved in the possession of a definite spiritual grace and power by those who have been ordained. It is also arbitrary to deny that St. Paul, when he appointed Timothy and Titus to ordain other ministers, as we gather, by a similar process (1 Tim. v. 22), would have hesitated to use the same language about the subsequent ordinations made by them or to attach to them the same ideas. (*Chas. Gore, M.A.*)

# INTRODUCTION TO THE FIRST EPISTLE TO TIMOTHY.

TIMOTHY.—Timothy was the son of one of those mixed marriages which, though condemned by stricter Jewish opinion, and placing their offspring on all but the lowest step in the Jewish scale of precedence, were yet not uncommon in the later periods of Jewish history. The father's name is unknown; he was a Greek, *i.e.*, a Gentile by descent. If in any sense a proselyte, the fact that the issue of the marriage did not receive the sign of the covenant would render it probable that he belonged to the class of half-converts, the so-called Proselytes of the Gate, not those of Righteousness. The absence of any personal allusion to the father in the Acts or Epistles suggests the inference that he must have died or disappeared during his son's infancy. The care of the boy thus devolved upon his mother, Eunice, and her mother, Lois. . . . It would be natural that a character thus fashioned should retain throughout something of a feminine piety. A constitution far from robust (1 Tim. v. 23), a morbid shrinking from opposition and responsibility (1 Tim. iv. 12–16; v. 20, 21; vi. 11–14; 2 Tim. ii. 1–7), a sensitiveness even to tears (2 Tim. i. 4), a tendency to an ascetic rigour which he had not strength to bear (1 Tim. v. 23), united, as it often is, with a temperament exposed to some risk from "youthful lusts" (2 Tim. ii. 22), and the softer emotions (1 Tim. v. 2)—these we may well think of as characterizing the youth, as afterwards the man. (*Dean Plumptre in Dict. of Bible.*)     When Paul, on his second missionary journey, came into closer connection with him, he was already a disciple, and possessed a good reputation among the believers in Lystra and Iconium. Paul calls him his τέκνον (1 Tim. i. 2, 18; 2 Tim. i. 2; 1 Cor. iv. 17), from which it would appear that he had been converted by the preaching of the apostle, probably during the apostle's first stay in Lystra (Acts xiv. 6, 7); and according to the reading, παρὰ τίνων, in 2 Tim. iii. 14, by means of his mother and grandmother. Paul, after circumcising him, because his father was known in the district to be a Gentile, adopted him as his assistant in the apostleship. From that time forward Timothy was one of those who served the apostle (Acts xix. 22), his συνεργός. The service consisted in helping the apostle in the duties of his office, and was therefore not identical with the office of those called evangelists. Timothy accompanied the apostle through Asia Minor to Philippi; but when Paul and Silas left that city (Acts xvi. 40), he seems to have remained behind there for some time, along with some other companions of the apostle. At Berea they were again together. When Paul afterwards travelled to Athens, Timothy remained behind (with Silas) at Berea; but Paul sent a message for him to come soon (Acts xvii. 14, 15). From Athens Paul sent him to Thessalonica, to inquire into the condition of the Church there and to strengthen it (1 Thess. iii. 1–5). After completing this task, Timothy joined Paul again in Corinth (Acts xviii. 5; 1 Thess. iii. 6). The two Epistles which Paul wrote from that place to the Thessalonians were written in Timothy's name also (1 Thess. i. 1; 2 Thess. i. 1). When Paul, on his third missionary journey, remained for some considerable time in Ephesus, Timothy was with him; where he was in the interval is unknown. Before the tumult occasioned by Demetrius, Paul sent him from Ephesus to Macedonia (Acts xix. 22). Immediately afterwards the apostle wrote the First Epistle to the Corinthians, from which it would appear that Timothy had been commissioned to go to Corinth, but that the apostle expected him to arrive there after the Epistle (1 Cor. iv. 17; xvi. 10, 11). When Paul wrote from Macedonia the Second Epistle to the Corinthians, Timothy was again with him; for Paul composed that Epistle also in Timothy's name—a very natural act if Timothy had shortly before been in Corinth. He next travelled with the apostle to Corinth; his presence there is proved by the greeting which Paul sent from him to the Church in Rome (Rom. xvi. 21). When Paul, after three months, left Greece, Timothy, besides others of the apostle's assistants, was in his company. He travelled with him as far as Philippi, from which the passage across to Asia Minor was usually made. From there Timothy and some others went before the apostle to Troas, where they remained till the apostle also arrived (Acts xx. 3-6). At this point there is a considerable blank in Timothy's history, since he is not mentioned again until the apostle's imprisonment in Rome. He was with the apostle at that time, because Paul put his name also to the Epistles to the Colossians, Philemon, and the Philippians. This fact is at the same time a proof that no other of his assistants in the apostleship stood in such close relations with him as Timothy. When Paul wrote the last Epistle, he intended to send him as soon as possible to Philippi, in order to obtain by him exact intelligence regarding the circumstances of the Churches there (Phil. ii. 19, &c.). From the two Epistles to Timothy we learn also the following facts regarding the circumstances of his life :—According to 1 Tim. i. 3, Paul, on a journey to Macedonia, left him behind in Ephesus, that he might counteract the false doctrine which was spreading there more and more. Perhaps on this occasion—if not even earlier—Timothy was solemnly ordained to his office by the laying on of hands on the part of the apostle and the presbytery. At this ordination the fairest hopes of him were expressed in prophetic language (*cf.* 1 Tim. i. 18; iv. 14 ; 2 Tim. i. 6), and he made a good confession (1 Tim. vi. 12). Paul at that time, however, hoped soon to come to him again. Later on, Paul was a prisoner in Rome. When he was expecting his death as near at hand, he wrote to Timothy to come to him soon, before the approach of winter, and to bring him Mark, together with certain belongings left behind in Troas (2 Tim. iv. 9, 11, 13, 21). Timothy is only once mentioned elsewhere in the New Testament (Heb. xiii. 23). It is very improbable that the Timothy there mentioned is another person; and from it we learn that when the Epistle was written he was again freed from an imprisonment, and that its author, as soon as he came, wished, along with him, to visit those to whom the Epistle was directed. According to the tradition of the Church, Timothy was the first Bishop of Ephesus. (*Joh. Ed. Huther, Th.D., in Meyer's Critical and Exegetical Handbook.*)    If he continued, according to the received tradition, to be Bishop of Ephesus, then he, and no other, must have been the " angel " of that Church to whom the message of Rev. ii. 1–7 was addressed. It may be urged, as in some degree confirming this view, that both the praise and the blame of that message are such as harmonize with the impressions as to the character of Timotheus derived from the Acts and the Epistles. The refusal to acknowledge the self-styled apostles, the abhorrence of the deeds of the Nicolaitans, the unwearied labour—all this belongs to the " man of God " of the Pastoral Epistles. And the fault is no less characteristic. The strong language of St. Paul's entreaty would lead us to expect that the temptation of such a man would be to fall away from the glow of his " first love," the zeal of his first faith. The promise of the Lord of the Churches is in substance the same as that implied in 2 Tim. ii. 4–6. (*Dean Plumptre in Dict. of Bible.*)

CONTENTS.—The Epistle consists of two parts. 1. In the first the apostle treats of three subjects—(1) The true gospel teaching, which must be preserved from any admixture, and especially from any legal element. It was with a view to this that when Paul was departing into Macedonia he desired Timothy to remain at Ephesus· There he would have to contend with persons who, while calling themselves doctors of the law, have no true comprehension of it, and apply it to the faithful, while it is really only given for evil-doers. The gospel which Paul teaches, and which he has himself been taught by deep experience, excludes any such admixture. It was to be Timothy's task to uphold in its purity this gospel which others were thrusting from them (chap. i.). (2) Worship. It is the duty of the Church to pray for the pagan rulers of the land, and for all men without distinction. In the assemblies of the Church the women are to wear modest attire, and to keep silence. Their sphere is home (chap. ii.). (3) The ministry. Reference is made to the bishopric and the diaconate—two offices indispensable to the life of the Church, and in regard to which Timothy is enjoined to use special vigilance. The apostle describes the moral qualifications required in bishops and deacons, without which they could not command the respect of the Church (chap. iii. 1–13). 2. In the second part of the Epistle (beginning chap. iii. 14) instructions are given to Timothy as to the way in which he ought to conduct himself towards the Church in general, and to its various classes in particular. And first towards the Church as a whole. He must keep before him its high destiny. It is the pillar on which the mystery of salvation is inscribed that all the world may read. Timothy is charged to use the more watch-fulness over it, because the spirit of prophecy foretells a time coming when there shall be a great falling away from the faith, when a spirit of false asceticism will creep into the Church under the guise of superior sanctity, but based in truth upon the impious idea that the whole material part of the works of God is to be ascribed to the spirit of evil. Timothy is to put the Church specially on its guard against such teaching, and is himself sedulously to avoid any approach to this error. He is to command the respect of the Church in spite of his youth, and is not to allow anything to quench the gift which is in him, and which has been imparted " by prophecy with the laying on of the hands of the presbytery " (chap. iii. 14–iv. 16). Then follow counsels as to his behaviour towards the older members of both sexes, and towards the younger sisters and widows. The apostle here adds some injunc-tions with regard to widows who may be called to a ministry of practical benevolence in the Church. He then gives rules as to the treatment of presbyters, or elders, who are evidently the same as the bishops spoken of in chap. iii. They were there designated bishops or overseers, with reference to their function in the Church ; here they are spoken of as presbyters or elders, in recognition of their dignity. Paul adds on this subject a word of counsel to Timothy himself (chap. v.) ; and con-cludes with some further admonitions to slaves who have become " believers and beloved " (chap. vi. 1, 2) ; to those who have already been led away from the truth by false teachers ; and to the rich in this world's goods (chap. vi. 17–19). A brief salutation, and one final word of warning (chap. vi. 20–22), bring the Epistle to a close. (*Prof. F. Godet.*)

# THE BIBLICAL ILLUSTRATOR.

## I. TIMOTHY.

### CHAPTER I.

Ver. 1. **Paul, an apostle of Jesus Christ.**—*The apostle's claim to authority :*—The beginning of this Epistle is so formal and solemn that it is evidently intended to give a tone of authority to all that follows. I. His office as being that of "an apostle of Jesus Christ." He often laid stress upon his apostleship, and not without good reason, for if it had not been recognized he would have been powerless to mould the Churches, which by God's blessing he had been enabled to form. Apostles are still wanted by the world, and Christians ought not to speak either with faltering voice or with apologetic tone. The confidence of the Church must be strengthened before the world will submit to its teaching. II. St. Paul refers here not only to his office as "an apostle of Jesus Christ," but also to the basis on which his appointment rested—namely, "the commandment of God our Saviour." Nothing could give a man more courage than belief in such a Divine call. It sustained that noble hero, General Gordon, amidst difficulties and perils which made his life an epic poem; indeed, in all ages the men who have had that belief have dared and done the mightiest deeds. Turn over the pages of history, and you will see that the invincible Ironsides—the dauntless pilgrim founders of the new world —the noblest evangelists and fathers of the early Churches, were all victorious because each said to himself, "I am here by the commandment of God our Saviour, and Lord Jesus Christ, which is our hope." And going back farther still in Church history, we see Jeremiah standing amidst his persecutors like a brazen wall and a defenced city; Daniel defying the wrath of the king, without a sign of braggadocio, or of any seeming consciousness of his nobility; and Elijah opposing the court, the hierarchy, and the fanatical people—without a tremor, because he looked beyond them all, and spoke of "the Lord God of Israel, before whom I stand." III. Here we may encourage ourselves, as Paul did, by remembering the giver of this office and work. The expression "God, our Saviour" is frequent in the pastoral epistles, but is only met with elsewhere in Jude's doxology, and in Mary's Magnificat. Probably Paul used it here with a special view to certain false teaching which was springing up in the Christian Church at this period. (*A. Rowland, LL.B.*) *God commanding human life :*—Many men wreck their lives by determinedly carrying out their own plans without reference to the plans of God. In an army every part, every brigade and regiment, must wait the commander's orders. If any battalion moves independently, though ever so heroically, it not only confuses the whole plan of battle, but brings disaster to itself as well in the end. So each individual must always wait for God's command to move. Keep your eye on the pillar of cloud and fire that leads. Never lag behind, but be sure you never run ahead. You can make the clock strike before the hour by putting your own hands to it, but it will strike wrong. You can hurry the unfolding of God's providence, but you will only mar the Divine plan unless you wait for Him. You can tear the rosebud open before the time when it would naturally open, but you destroy the beauty of the rose. So we spoil many a gift or blessing which God is preparing for us by our own eager haste. He would weave all our lives into patterns of loveliness. He has a perfect plan for each. It is only when we refuse to work according to His plan that we mar the web. Stop meddling with threads of your life as they come from the Lord's hands. Every time you interfere you make a flaw. Keep your hands off, and let God weave as He pleases. Do you think you know better than He does what your life ought to be? (*The Presbyterian.*) *The minister's authority should be as much regarded as his sufficiency :*—Two things are considerable in a minister : his sufficiency and his authority. The people listen much to his sufficiency, but take little heed to his authority; and therefore come they to church rather to judge than to be judged, forgetting that many may be as skilful but none can be so powerful in binding and loosing as is the minister. A judge or a justice of peace may have less law in him than a private man, but he hath much more power, and they that appear before him regard his acts according to his power : so should it be in the Church. But men fear the magistrates that are under earthly kings, because the pains which they inflict are corporal; our hands, our feet, feel their manacles and fetters. And did but our souls as truly feel, as indeed they should, the pastor's binding and loosing of them, we would make more account of those offices than we do. And it were good we did so, for they so bind as that they can loose again; but if we neglect them, when our Lord and Master cometh He will command all contemners so to be bound hand and foot that they shall never be loosed again. (*J. Spencer.*)    **Our hope.**—*Our hope :*—In the Word of God we find many brief but precious sentences, the introduction of which appears to be incidental. I do not say accidental, but incidental. They stand upon these sacred pages, beautiful as the dew-drops on the flowers, and as the rain-drop on the leaf; while they are as useful for the purposes of our spiritual life, as are essences to the chemist, and to the medical practitioner, and to others, in cases where bulk involves inconvenience and difficulty. Such a sentence you find in the words we have read, which are the inscription of Paul's first letter to Timothy. I refer to the words, " LORD JESUS CHRIST OUR HOPE." These words are not necessary to the inscription ; they are no part of the general course of remark. Three names are here given to one being, and they express three things—rank, service, and qualification. The Lord, the Lord Jesus, the Lord Jesus Christ—the " Lord Jesus Christ our hope." Hope, as you know, is a complex emotion, constitutional, universal, and most powerful, and a compound emotion which is most fully brought forth in Christian experience. We desire you to look at the Lord Jesus Christ as the Author of hope, that by thus looking to Him, your own hope may be strengthened. But why is hope within you so weak ? Is the Lord Jesus Christ your hope ? Then your hope should answer to His character, and to His attributes, and to His resources, and to His throne. If you are in a tiny boat upon a stormy sea, you rock with the billows ; but if you stand upon the firm rock which guards the sea-shore, although tempests may be raging, you stand firmly with that rock. Now, if you base your hope upon self ; if you rest it upon any creature ; if you are trying to root it and ground it in circumstances ; you will find that your hope will be feeble and mutable. If, on the other hand, it be grounded in Christ, it ought to be strong enough to answer the purpose of an anchor to your soul in any storm, however long or fierce the storms and tempests may be which play around you. I. THE LORD JESUS CHRIST GIVES HIS DISCIPLES NEW OBJECTS OF HOPE. You all know well what hope is—that it consists of desire and expectation. Jesus Christ puts good things before His followers, things that awaken desire, and that call forth expectation. His followers look for these things, and they long for them ; and in looking and longing for them, they hope. The Saviour puts new objects of hope before His followers. These are such as the following: the consummation of their salvation. And, passing from things great to things comparatively small, we may mention another new object of hope: the supply of the disciple's temporal need by his Father in heaven. Some men are reckless about the future—I mean this low, earthly, temporal future. Now, to the reckless and to the fearful ; to the self-dependent, and to the sinfully dependent upon others ; our Lord Jesus Christ saith, " Your heavenly Father knoweth that ye have need of all these things " ; so that the expectation of supply—supply of daily bread to life's last hour, is built upon the loving and watchful care of our Father in heaven. Here again is a new object of hope. Connected with these new objects are others, such as everlasting life in heaven—life eternal in our Father's house, holy, happy, godly, celestial life. And besides this, the establishment of Christ's own kingdom on this earth, and the setting up of His kingdom in the new earth, which, by-and-by, He will create. You, therefore, see that these new objects of hope are numerous and great and benevolent and godly. II. JESUS CHRIST ALSO LAYS NEW FOUNDATIONS FOR OLD HOPES. Before our discipleship to Jesus Christ, if our hope was for temporal good, then the hope was built upon money, skill, energy, prudence, wisdom, the treasures of our own information, the confidence of our fellow-men in us, our ability to commend ourselves to the good feelings and to the judgment of our fellow-men. But in the case of the Christian, as we have already shown you, the hope, even of temporal good, is built upon the Father's care of us

and love for us. Before our discipleship, we were wont to say, " I am rich, I shall
have need of nothing," but Christ hath taught us to sing, "Jehovah is our Shepherd, we shall not want." Now, here is a new foundation for an old hope ; and
what say you about the foundations as they appear contrasted? Do you not agree
with me, that the one is miserably loose and shifting sand, and that the other is the
rock of ages that can never, never be moved? Or if, before discipleship to Christ,
we hoped for salvation, for the forgiveness of our sins, and for eternal life, then
the basis of that hope has been changed likewise. We used to boast, " I have never
done any harm to anybody " ; or we said, " I have always attended a place of
worship " ; or we said, " God is merciful, and I have never done much harm to
anybody, and I am quite sure He will forgive." Now, the disciple of the Lord Jesus
Christ, as we have shown you, hopes first and supremely for the consummation of
his salvation ; but what about the foundation? Hear the disciple now, " What
things were gain to me, those I count but loss for Christ, I count all things loss for
the excellency of the knowledge of Christ Jesus my Lord." The Lord Jesus Christ
our hope ; He gives us new objects of hope, and He lays new foundations for our
old hopes. And yet more—III. OUR LORD JESUS CHRIST CONSTITUTES HIMSELF THE
SECURE FOUNDATION OF ALL LAWFUL HOPES, WHETHER THEY BE OLD, OR WHETHER THEY
BE NEW. The Lord Jesus Christ is the foundation. His sacrifices and His mediation open the windows of heaven for us, and the door of heaven to us. Look at
this sacrifice and mediation of our Lord Jesus Christ as the basis of hope. Further,
the government of our Lord Jesus Christ secures our possession of all that He
ordains for us. The " government is upon His shoulder." All power is given unto
Him both in heaven and on earth. All that He means to work out for you will be
thoroughly and perfectly wrought out; and it is one of our great mercies, that
Christ will not work out our foolish and sometimes wicked schemes and plans,
which, if they were wrought out, would ruin us. His government secures our
possession of all that He ordains for us. Jesus Christ's love keeps Him ever awake
toward our welfare. We often talk of the love of a mother as watchful. Her love
is her eye ; she sees by her heart ; affection is her power of observation. Nobody
can see, with respect to her children, what she sees, just because her power of love
is a second sight. IV. THE LORD JESUS CHRIST IS HIMSELF AN OBJECT OF HOPE.
He has promised to come again ; and those who love Him look for Him. Now,
think for one moment ; what is the master hope in your soul? What do you long
for most eagerly? I have read in my Bible, in this glorious New Testament, of men
" having no hope," that is—no good hope, no hope worth having, no hope worth
retaining, no hope that will not make ashamed. Is that your case? There are
hopes in your soul ; for objects of hope are ever appealing to, and calling out,
desire and expectation, and these hopes are the sources, or the occasions, of joy.
Well, do tell me a little about them. Are these hopes worth cherishing?
(*S. Martin.*)　　*Christ our hope :*—Of all the ingredients that sweeten the cup of
human life, there is none more rich or powerful than hope. Its absence embitters
the sweetest lot ; its presence alleviates the deepest woe. Surround me with all the
joys which memory can awaken or possession bestow—without hope it is not
enough. But though you strip me of all the joys the past or the present can confer,
if the morrow shineth bright with hope, I am glad amid my woe. Of all the busy
motives that stir this teeming earth, hope is the busiest. Is it so in regard to the
pleasures and possessions of time?—how much more should it be in regard to
eternity? How should, how can that man be happy amid the brightest joys of
time, who sees his little span of life shelving down precipitously into the dark,
dreary, desolate abyss of nothingness or into a more dreadful eternity of woe? and
how should, how can that man be greatly saddened by the ills of time, who sees a
blissful eternity fast drawing nigh? Thus then we realize the value of hope as a
source of happiness. It gladdens the pilgrimage of earth, it irradiates the dark
horizon of death, and provides for the eternity beyond. I. WHAT IS THE FOUNDA-
TION OF OUR HOPE? Most men live in hope of happiness beyond the grave. Few
men, I suppose, are altogether destitute of it. But when we ask for a reason for
the hope that is in them, how often do we find it a dream and a delusion and a lie!
Some, acknowledging their sins, trust that by their prayers and penitence and
performances they can atone for bygone sin ; and others who, confessing the
worthlessness of all they can do, throw themselves on the general mercy of God.
In none of these do we recognize the foundation on which our hope is resting. And
what then have we seen in the work or person of Christ to awaken hope? We
reply—1. Looking back on the past work of Christ we find a sufficient remedy for

the guilt of sin. 2. Looking at His present work, we find a remedy for our pollution. He purifies His people as well as pardons them. He regenerates and renews them by His Spirit, as well as redeems them by His blood. He reconciles them to the holiness as well as to the justice of God. 3. How is the strength of this foundation proved when, turning from the work to the Workman, we contemplate the surpassing excellencies of His Person! Who is this that undertaketh to provide pardon for the guiltiest, and purifying for the most polluted? It is " the Lord "—the Lord of Glory—the only-begotten of the Father—the eternal Son of God. What virtue, then, in His atoning death! what prevalence in His prayer! what power in His hand to purify! It is " Jesus," the Son of Mary, an Elder Brother, partaker of flesh and blood, made in all things like unto His brethren, a Man of sorrows and acquainted with our griefs. How true and real, then, were the sufferings which He endured when He died for men, and how tender are His sympathies as now He pleads for or with us—" a High Priest, touched with the feeling of our infirmities "! Once again, this is the " Christ "—anointed by God, commissioned for this very work. He does not stand alone; the Father sent Him. II. But now, in the second place, some may ask, WHERE IS THIS WARRANT OF OUR HOPE? Who are you, or what have you done more than others, that you should thus confidingly draw near to Jesus? The warrant of His holy Word—yes; with unfaltering voice we proclaim aloud that Christ speaking to us in the Word was, and is, the sure and only warrant of our hope. III. But again, in the third place, we have learned to say, The Lord Jesus Christ accepted, appropriated, built upon by us, is THE SUBSTANCE OF OUR HOPE. Received and rested on He became our Saviour. IV. But then, in the fourth place, we learned to say THAT CHRIST IN US, CHRIST FOUND AND DWELLING IN US IS THE EVIDENCE, THE ASSURANCE, OF OUR HOPE. " I live," said Paul—" I live ": there was no uncertainty here, no dim or doubtful hope, but all the certainty of conscious life—" I live, yet not I, but Christ liveth in me." " The Lord Jesus Christ is my hope," the principle of life in me. As the sap of the root dwells in every branch and leaflet, imparting life and verdure; as the volition of the head lives in every member, guiding all its actions; as a master dwells in his own house, controlling all its arrangements, so Christ dwelleth in His people by His Holy Spirit, quickening, controlling, guiding them, conforming them to His own likeness. Well then may the Christian say, " Christ in me is the hope of glory." This is indeed a step in advance in the Christian's life! It is more than salvation provided, however fully; it is more than salvation offered, however freely; it is more than salvation accepted, however surely. It is salvation in possession. V. But now, when thus we have considered THE SECURITY OF THE CHRISTIAN'S HOPE AS CONTRASTED WITH THE FALSE HOPES OF THE WORLD, let us consider THE BRIGHTNESS OF THIS HOPE. It is not only sure, but glorious, transcending all else that men have ever pictured for themselves. For what does the Christian hope? I know not what I shall be, but when He shall appear, I shall be like Him. I am called to " the obtaining of the glory of the Lord Jesus Christ." This is our destiny. We are " predestinated to be conformed to His image." Say, then, how dazzling is the glory of the Christian's hope! Jesus stands revealed not only as our Saviour, but as Himself the pattern of our salvation. Where He is, there we hope to be. What He is, that we hope to be. What He has, we hope to have. VI. But now, in the last place, it may be asked, WHEN SHALL THIS HOPE PASS INTO POSSESSION? Bright as the salvation of which I have spoken may be, it is not yet fulfilled, it is only hoped for. Hope deferred maketh the heart sick. Till fulfilled, it is fragmentary and incomplete. What, then, it may be asked, is the period when hope shall pass into full possession? An earnest and foretaste we have in this life, yea, unspeakable joy when our sins are forgiven and our hearts are purified. An amazing increase we shall have at the hour of death, when our disencumbered spirits shall break away and be with Jesus. To those, then, who now ask us, as we live on earth, Is your joy complete? is your hope fulfilled? we answer, Not yet; not even when our sins are pardoned and our hearts are purified; not even when at a communion table we hold fellowship with our present Lord. The Lord Jesus Christ is Himself the climax of our hope. When He appears in glory, but not till then, shall we appear with Him, our joy completed and all our hope fulfilled. (*W. Grant.*)

Ver. 2. **Unto Timothy, my own son in the faith.** *Spiritual paternity :*—A friend talked solid doctrine to a man who said, " I am a father in Israel. I have been a child of God now, so many years; I have had such a deep experience that I am a father in Israel." My friend said to him, "How many children have you?" "Well," he answered, "I do not know." "How many have you brought to Christ? How many have been converted by you?" "Well, I do not know that any have." "Then don't you call yourself a father until you have got some children." (*C. H. Spurgeon.*)    *The relations of Paul and Timothy* :—To understand this relationship think first of—I. TIMOTHY'S CONVERSION. He had been prayerfully taught in the Jewish faith by his mother and grandmother, and was therefore, with them, prepared to receive the gospel.    II. TIMOTHY'S SETTING APART FOR SPECIAL WORK did not take place until seven years after this. God does not call us to high service until we have proved our fidelity in what is lower.    III. Now and then we get a glimpse at TIMOTHY'S HAPPY COMPANIONSHIP with Paul, which was never afterwards broken for any length of time, and which was the more remarkable because of the difference between the ages of the two men. But it is good for the aged to keep the heart young by their association with youth ; and it is even better for those who are in the spring-time of their life to yield reverence and love, and considerate kindness, to those who are older and more experienced than themselves ; indeed it is an ill sign when there is resentment of home authority, repudiation of responsibility to the aged, and a wish to have only the companionship of those who live for the pleasures of this life.    Conclusion : Those of us who, like Timothy, are teachers of others, may learn from the reception of this letter that we need continuous instruction in order to accomplish our ministry.    It is not enough that we should begin our work with memories stored with truths, and with hearts consecrated to the Master's service. (*A. Rowland, LL.B.*)    *The relation between older and younger workers* :—Few relations between men are more interesting than that of a man, who has for years been doing a work, with some younger man, to whom the work is to be given over to finish or to carry on.    That work is to pass through new developments, and new circumstances which the man who is passing away may not be able to comprehend.    But if there is true generosity in the mind of the older man, he always rejoices that the work is to go on after he has passed away.    The older gives to the younger promises and opportunities.    All that the older man has done is not going to perish with him.    His work projects itself into the future.    It is not stopped short by the wall of his own death.    The younger man, looking back on the experience of the older teacher, which seems to have lasted longer than it really has lasted, gets some sort of background for his own work.    That work is not something which he has started, thought out for himself.    The older man gives to the younger a sense of a long-continued past ; the younger gives to the older a sense of a long-continued future. (*Phillips Brooks, D.D.*)    *Friendship complemental* :—In the relation of St. Paul to Timothy we have one of those beautiful friendships between an older and a younger man which are commonly so helpful to both.    It is in such cases, rather than where the friends are equals in age, that each can be the real complement of the other.    Each by his abundance can supply the other's want, whereas men of equal age would have common wants and common supplies.    In this respect the friendship between St. Paul and Timothy reminds us of that between St. Peter and St. John.    In each case the friend who took the lead was much older than the other ; and (what is less in harmony with ordinary experience) in each case it was the older friend who had the impulse and the enthusiasm, the younger who had the reflectiveness and the reserve. These latter qualities are perhaps less marked in St. Timothy than in St. John, but nevertheless they are there, and they are among the leading traits of his character. St. Paul leans on him while he guides him, and relies upon his thoughtfulness and circumspection in cases requiring firmness, delicacy and tact.    Of the affection with which he regarded Timothy we have evidence in the whole tone of the two letters to him.    In the sphere of faith Timothy is his " own true child " (not merely adopted, still less supposititious), and his "beloved child." (*A. Plummer, D.D.*)    **Grace, mercy, and peace.**—*Grace, mercy, and peace* :—There is always some interest in the first or the last of anything—an interest in proportion to the importance of that which is begun or ended.    A birth or a death, each creates a sensation peculiar to itself, distinct from any other event ; they are the beginning and the ending of that most solemn mystery, life.    Viewed in the light of eternity, there is something peculiarly affecting in the first or the last act of a Christian ministry.    This text presents in summary the leading doctrines of the gospel—" Grace, mercy, and peace "—grace as the origin, mercy as the development, and peace as the result of man's salvation.    I. There is, then, first of all, THE GRACE THAT ORIGINATES.    Grace is the Alpha of all salvation.    It is grace in the eternal counsel, grace in the Divine election, grace in the heavenly calling, grace in the individual conversion, grace in every gift of the Holy Ghost, grace in the conviction of sin that realizes its danger, in the godly repentance that mourns over it. It is grace that transplants the flower from the wilderness into the garden of the Lord, waters it with the dews of heaven, and makes it bud and bloom, and so shed its sweetness all around, that even in decay and death its scent survives imperishable. It is grace that gives the lowly man his humility, the loving man his kindly affections, the benevolent man his charity, the zealous man his ardour, the young Christian his spiritual strength, the old Christian his experience, the suffering Christian his patience, and the dying Christian his support. Thus the first practical inquiry, that enables us to ascertain our own state before God, is, Have we realized the truth, not as a mere point in theology, but as a point in personal feeling, that " in me, that is, in my flesh," in my natural character or capacity, " dwelleth no good thing " that without Christ we are nothing, can do nothing? II. There is, secondly, THE MERCY THAT DEVELOPES THE COUNSEL OF REDEMPTION. As grace is something that is given as a gratuity, that is neither merited, nor purchased, nor obtainable by other means, nor deserved, nor even desired, so mercy involves an absolute demerit—not merely a negation, but a disqualifying clause. Grace might be applicable to an order of beings to which mercy was not applicable. I say, mercy involves an absolute demerit. A judgment incurred, but respited—a forbearing stroke, where the blow was not only merited but provoked and challenged! Hence it is described by the terms, " the longsuffering of God," " the forbearance of God." And yet the word mercy still implies a victim. If no penalty of an earthly law, for instance, were ever inflicted upon any man, as was the case with some of our own laws till of late years, the suspension of such a law would be no mercy to any man, it would be practically disannulled, and the idea of mercy under such a statute would merge into repeal. It is when some men actually suffer the penalty from which others are exempted by the interposition of the sovereign, that the mercy is said to be shown to those who are exempted. When a criminal sees another man suffering the death to which his guilt had condemned himself, he understands then the royal prerogative of mercy. It is so with the sinner. Mercy is the great development of the love of God. It is not the exercise of a Divine attribute, which, like His power or wisdom, cost the Father nothing. " God so loved the world, that He gave His only begotten Son, that all who believe in Him should not perish." This was the Father's sacrifice, of which Abraham's was the figure, just as Isaac's self-submission was a type of the Son's. An act of mercy costs earthly princes nothing beyond the word pardon; it cost the King of kings the immolation of His Son, " whom He had appointed Heir of all things." Who is to wonder, then, at the magnificent things which are said in Scripture about the mercy of God? Mercy gave birth to the " Man of sorrows "; mercy clothed the Heir of heaven in coarse Galilean raiment, as a poor man among the poor; mercy made Him toil, and hunger, and thirst, and travail, and suffer, and die; mercy rose with Him from the grave; mercy speaks by Him from the seat of intercession, and promises to come again in glory, to gather His elect, and to establish His kingdom. Mercy is the main element, the uniform ingredient, in every act of grace. It was mercy that fixed our own native lot in a land of light, and Christian ordinances, and social privileges, instead of among howling savages, with minds as dark and bare as their disfigured bodies; it was mercy that provided some of us with the goodly heritage of pious parents, however little we may have profited by their example and prayers; it was mercy, if our hearts were reached at last, if we turned to " flee from the wrath to come, and to lay hold upon eternal life." It is mercy still, O Lord, that we are living this day to praise Thee, that health, reason, strength, apprehension, and multiplied opportunities, and means of grace, and channels of good works by which we shall glorify Thee, and benefit ourselves and others, are yet spared to us. It is mercy, in short, that meets us in the hour of sorrow, and whispers consolation. Hence the next practical test of our condition in the sight of God is—Have we felt our need of mercy? Have we realized our lost, wretched, forlorn condition without a Mediator? III. Thus mercy, joining hands with grace, like the outstretched wings of the cherubim that met over the ark, crown and complete God's covenant with His people; and finally THEY PUBLISH " PEACE "—PEACE BETWEEN THEM. This was our closing proposition. The seal and consummation of the plan of redemption is peace. Have you remarked, that the angels singing from heaven called it " peace on earth "? that is, peace here, peace now; not simply that poetical peace in the grave, of which some men sing, or the peace in heaven to which the believer aspires, but something that he has in his heart at once ; and that is called by the angels " peace on earth "—peace at once, peace with all men, peace with ourselves. " Mark the perfect man, and behold the upright ; the end of that man is peace." The external incidents of life no longer break the calm of the full assurance of faith, or hope, or understanding, in the life of the believer; but " when a man's ways please the Lord, He maketh his enemies to be at peace with him." " The God of peace beats down Satan under your feet shortly." The Son of peace is an abiding and delightful guest in your dwellings ; your vision of peace is not like Jerusalem's, hidden from your eyes, but fixes a distinct, lofty, lovely impression upon your minds—like an horizon that seems to fence in and shield us with the clouds of heaven, yet opens heaven itself to the far-seeing gaze of faith. The world in its own way is seeking for this peace ; amid all its pleasures and cunning variations of pleasure and amusement it is seek- ing, over the wreck of every present enjoyment, the peace which it hopes to find in the future. It is seeking it where the poor disconsolate Elisha sought his master —in the wilderness, instead of looking up to heaven where he was gone. And hence the search is vain ; men do not find it. (*J. B. Owen, M.A.*) *A Christian salutation :*—The salutation which Paul gives to his own son in the faith is an exquisite example of what a Christian greeting should be. It is no idle compliment, but an earnest prayer. I. THE MANIFESTATION OF DIVINE LOVE desired on Timothy's behalf is threefold, consisting of " grace, mercy, and peace," for the sympathetic mind of Paul analyzed and displayed it, much as a prism will catch a ray of sun- shine, and reveal more clearly the wonderful beauty that is latent in it. 1. Grace is the free favour of God, pouring itself forth upon the soul which is yearning for it, and filling it with gladness and praise. So that a prayer for God's " grace " to be with us is really a prayer that our sins and doubts may be dispersed ; for as with nature's sunlight, it is not any alteration in the sun, but a change in the earth's atmosphere, or in the earth's attitude towards the sun, that brings brightness in the place of gloom, daylight in the stead of darkness. 2. The association of the idea of mercy with grace is striking, and is peculiar to these Epistles to Timothy and to the Second Epistle of John. But it was characteristic of Paul, who was profoundly conscious of his own need of " mercy," to pray for it on behalf of his comrade, who was engaged in similar work. It is not to the erring Galatians nor to the backsliding Corinthians, but to this honoured servant of the Christian Church, that he prays for God's " mercy " to be evermore extended ; for from his own experience he knew how much that mercy is needed by those who are sensible that their character comes far short of their ideal, and that their work for Christ is marred by their faults and follies. We may occupy the highest position in the Church, yet instead of being thereby exalted above the need of mercy, we must the more humbly cast ourselves upon it. Nothing but the realization of the Divine forbearance will embolden us to continue in spiritual service, which is awful in its responsibilities, and likely to be ill done by us through our sinfulness and ignorance. The noblest saint falls back in life and death on Divine mercy as his one and only hope. 3. Peace flows from the " grace " and " mercy " of God. It is a sense of reconciliation with Him—of rest in Him, which will give calmness in hours of trouble and peril, and will spread a sacred and happy influence over those around us. As good Bishop Patrick says, " Peace is the proper result of the Christian temper. It is the great kindness which our religion doth us, that it brings us to a settledness of mind and a consistency within ourselves." II. THE SOURCE OF THESE BLESSINGS is pointed out in the assurance that they flow from " God our Father and Jesus Christ our Lord." 1. If God is our Father we may surely expect such blessings, for they are just what in our lower sphere we fathers (whose fatherhood is but a broken reflection of His) would gladly give our children. We are not happy unless they are living in our " favour "; we are eager to show them " mercy " directly and whenever they come to us in penitential grief ; and if there is one blessing we desire for them above others, it is that their minds may be at " peace." 2. But grace, mercy, and peace, can only come to us through Jesus Christ our Lord, because we are undeserving and sinful. (*A. Rowland, LL.B.*) *The price of peace :*— The other day I was preaching in my own church upon this subject. I said that if a man wanted to have peace with God, he must be prepared to put away his sin. After the sermon a wealthy gentleman, a member of my own congregation, came up to me and said, " You have broken me down to-day. For the last two or three months I have not been able to sleep. You know I have retired from business, but the fact of the matter is, I have beem gambling on the Stock Exchange, though people did not know it. Whenever the funds go down I begin to tremble. Although

I believe I gave my heart to God some years ago, I have been trying to serve two masters—gambling for money, and at the same time pretending to serve God. Now, I have made up my mind that I must destroy this sin. It will cost me £4,000, but I am determined to make a clean sweep of it altogether." The gentleman added, " I think peace of mind is cheap at £4,000 " ; and I think so too. (*A. E. Stuart.*)

Vers. 3, 4. **As I besought thee to abide still at Ephesus.**—*Timothy's charge :*—Our translators have supplied two words at the close of the fourth verse, in order to complete the sentence which the apostle left unfinished ; but it would have been better had they inserted them earlier, for the meaning is more clear if we read, " As I besought thee to abide still at Ephesus when I went into Macedonia, so I beseech thee now to remain there." It is an example of the way in which Paul's living thoughts leaped ahead of the words which might have clothed them.    I. THE PERIOD to which he refers in the phrase, " when I went into Macedonia," cannot be certainly fixed.    There was, indeed, one occasion mentioned in Acts xx. 1, when, in consequence of the peril in which he was placed through the uproar raised by Demetrius, he did leave Ephesus for Macedonia ; but in the chapter preceding that narrative we read that he had already sent Timothy and Erastus thither; and we know that he joined them there, because in the First Epistle to the Corinthians, written thence, he mentions Timothy as being then with him.    II. THE MODE OF ADDRESS to Timothy demands a word or two.    " I besought thee "—not I commanded thee. No doubt this is expressive of the gentleness and affection with which Timothy was regarded, but it is also an indication of the kind of authority which was exercised by the apostles over their fellow-workers.    There was nothing dictatorial about it, nothing of the military discipline which is so popular and effective in an aggressive section of the Church in our day.    Influence then was that of character; authority was the outcome of inspiration ; and even the chosen twelve were better pleased to rule by love than fear.    It must be admitted this may give rise to abuses and perils. III. THE PURPORT of Paul's entreaty was that Timothy should check the progress of false doctrine in the Ephesian Church.    There was a ferment going on in the minds of men at that time, such as usually accompanies or follows a great religious movement.    False notions of God, and of His law, arising from an imperfectly understood Judaism, combined with a speculative heathen philosophy, were threatening to destroy the simplicity of the gospel.    A sort of cabalistic system was being constituted in the Church, by an incongruous mixture of Jewish fancies with heathen speculations, and this threatened disaster—just as the ivy, climbing slowly but surely, thrusts in a root here and a tendril there, till the once strong wall has every stone loosened, and in the storm it falls.    IV. THE REASON given for opposing such teaching is, that it " ministered questions rather than godly edifying." The Revised Version adopts another reading, and rightly so.    The meaning is, that these questionings did not subserve God's " dispensation "—His specific plan for admission to His kingdom, His method of salvation unfolded in the Gospel ; for that dispensation consists " in faith."    And as a matter of experience we know that questions which merely excite the fancy, or even the intellect, tend to make the objects of faith distasteful.    For example, a course of sensational novel reading, which peoples the mind with unrealities, does extrude earnest thoughts on spiritual realities.    And this which is true of the rites of the Church is equally true of its organizations, and we have constantly to be on our guard lest the occupation of the mind with the details of Church work should divert us from the cultivation of personal Christian life.    But the apostle here condemns chiefly the unhealthy practice of giving prominence to unimportant questions, whether it be in the sphere of philosophy or of religion.    When a settler has to grow his own corn to provide himself with daily bread, he will let speculation on the strata beneath the surface wait till he has found time to sow and to reap. (*A. Rowland, LL.B.*)    *The doctrine condemned in the Pastoral Epistles a Jewish form of Gnosticism : the Gnostic's problem :*— It is of more importance to inquire what was the nature of the " different doctrine " which Timothy was to endeavour to counteract.    And on this point we are not left in serious doubt.    There are various expressions used respecting it in these two letters to Timothy which seem to point to two factors in the heterodoxy about which St. Paul is anxious.    1. The heresy is Jewish in character. Its promoters " desire to be teachers of the Law " (ver. 7).    Some of them are " they of the circumcision " (Tit. i. 10).    It consists in " Jewish fables " (Tit. i. 14). The questions which it raises are " fightings about the Law " (Tit. iii. 9).    2. Its Gnostic character is also indicated.    We are told both in the text and in the Epistle to Titus (i. 14; iii. 9) that it deals in "fables and genealogies." It is "empty talking" (ver. 6), "disputes of words" (vi. 4), and "profane babblings" (vi. 20). It teaches an unscriptural and unnatural asceticism (iv. 3, 8). It is "Gnosis falsely so called" (vi. 20). A heresy containing these two elements, Judaism and Gnosticism, meets us both before and after the period covered by the Pastoral Epistles: before in the Epistle to the Colossians; afterwards in the Epistles of Ignatius. The evidence gathered from these three sources is entirely in harmony with what we learn elsewhere—that the earliest forms of Christian Gnosticism were Jewish in character. It will be observed that this is indirect confirmation of the genuineness of the Pastoral Epistles. The Gnosticism condemned in them is Jewish; and any form of Gnosticism that was in existence in St. Paul's time would almost certainly be Jewish. Professor Godet has pointed out how entirely the relation of Judaism to Christianity which is implied in these Epistles, fits in with their being the last group of epistles written by St. Paul. At first, Judaism was entirely outside the Church, opposing and blaspheming. Then it entered the Church and tried to make the Church Jewish, by foisting the Mosaic Law upon it. Lastly, it becomes a fantastic heresy inside the Church, and sinks into profane frivolity. "Pretended revelations are given as to the names and genealogies of angels; absurd ascetic rules are laid down as counsels of perfection, while daring immorality defaces the actual life." This is the phase which is confronted in the Pastoral Epistles: and St. Paul meets it with a simple appeal to faith and morality. It is quite possible that the "fables," or "myths," and "genealogies" ought to be transferred from the Gnostic to the Jewish side of the account. And thus Chrysostom interprets the passage. "By fables he does not mean the Law; far from it; but inventions and forgeries, and counterfeit doctrines. For, it seems, the Jews wasted their whole discourse on these unprofitable points. They numbered up their fathers and grandfathers, that they might have the reputation of historical knowledge and research." The "fables" then, may be understood to be those numerous legends which the Jews added to the Old Testament, specimens of which abound in the Talmud. But similar myths abound in Gnostic systems, and therefore "fables" may represent both elements of the heterodox teaching. So also with the "endless genealogies." These cannot well refer to the genealogies in Genesis, for they are not endless, each of them being arranged in tens. But it is quite possible that Jewish speculations about the genealogies of angels may be meant. Such things, being purely imaginary, would be endless. Or the Gnostic doctrine of emanations, in its earlier and cruder forms, may be intended. By genealogies in this sense early thinkers, especially in the East, tried to bridge the chasm between the infinite and the finite, between God and creation. In various systems it is assumed that matter is inherently evil. The material universe has been from the beginning not "very good" but very bad. How then can it be believed that the Supreme Being, infinite in goodness, would create such a thing? This is incredible: the world must be the creature of some inferior and perhaps evil being. But when this was conceded, the distance between this inferior power and the supreme God still remained to be bridged. This, it was supposed, might be done by an indefinite number of generations, each lower in dignity than the preceding one, until at last a being capable of creating the universe was found. From the Supreme God emanated an inferior deity, and from this lower power a third still more inferior; and so on until the Creator of the world was reached. These ideas are found in the Jewish philosopher Philo; and it is to these that St. Paul probably alludes in the "endless genealogies which minister questionings rather than a dispensation of God." (*A. Plummer, D.D.*) *Speculations condemned:*—St. Paul condemns such speculations on four grounds. 1. They are fables, myths, mere imaginings of the human intellect in its attempt to account for the origin of the world and the origin of evil. 2. They are endless and interminable. From the nature of things there is no limit to mere guesswork of this kind. Every new speculator may invent a fresh genealogy of emanations in his theory of creation and may make it any length that he pleases. If hypotheses need never be verified—need not even be capable of verification—one may go on constructing them *ad infinitum.* 3. As a natural consequence of this (αἵτινες) they minister questionings and nothing better. It is all barren speculation and fruitless controversy. Where any one may assert without proof, any one else may contradict without proof; and nothing comes of this see-saw of affirmation and negation. 4. Lastly, these vain imaginings are a different doctrine. They are not only empty but untrue, and are a hindrance to the truth, they occupy the ground which ought to be filled with the dispensation of God which is in faith. Human minds are limited in their capacity, and, even if these empty hypotheses were innocent, minds that were filled with them would have little room left for the truth. But they are not innocent : and those who are attracted by them become disaffected towards the truth. The history of the next hundred and fifty years amply justifies the anxiety and severity of St. Paul. The germs of Gnostic error, which were in the air when Christianity was first preached, fructified with amazing rapidity. It would be hard to find a parallel in the history of philosophy to the speed with which Gnostic views spread in and around Christendom between A.D. 70 and 220. Throughout the Christian world, and especially in intellectual centres such as Ephesus, Alexandria, and Rome, there was perhaps not a single educated congregation which did not contain persons who were infected with some form of Gnosticism. Jerome's famous hyperbole respecting Arianism might be transferred to this earlier form of error, perhaps the most perilous that the Church has ever known : " The whole world groaned and was amazed to find itself Gnostic." However severely we may condemn these speculations, we cannot but sympathize with the perplexities which produced them. The origin of the universe, and still more the origin of evil, to this day remain unsolved problems. No one in this life is ever likely to reach a complete solution of either. (*Ibid.*)

Ver. 4. **Neither give heed to fables.**—*Old doctrines enduring :*—At Cudham, in Kent, is an old church. Walking round it on one occasion, I observed a portion of the roof falling to decay and needing to be propped up with a timber stay. On closer investigation, however, I discovered that the decaying portion was none of the old structure, but a modern addition. We need not fear for the ancient fabric of Christian truth. The new-fangled doctrines will fall to the ground, while the old gospel " endureth for ever." (*J. Halsey.*) *Modern gospels false :*—The very commendations which some people give of the so-called gospel they preach arouse our suspicion. When we hear of its recent and human origin, we at once begin to doubt its validity. We are reminded of the boy who went into a shop to change a sovereign. " Are you sure it is a good one ? " asked the man behind the counter. " Oh, yes, quite sure, sir ; for I seed father make it this morning." We do not believe in a gospel which was coined but this morning. We preach a gospel which was minted in heaven, which bears the image and superscription of Christ, which has the ring of true metal, and which will pass current in all the dominions of the King. (*C. W. Townsend.*) *Self-made gospels useless :*—When some men come to die, the religion which they have themselves thought out and invented will yield them no more confidence than the religion of the Roman Catholic sculptor who, on his death-bed, was visited by his priest. The priest said, " You are now departing out of this life ! " and, holding up a beautiful crucifix, he cried, " Behold your God, who died for you." " Alas ! " said the sculptor, " I made it." There was no comfort for him in the work of his own hands ; and there will be no comfort in a religion of one's own devising. That which was created in the brain cannot yield comfort to the heart. The man will sorrowfully say, " Yes, it is my own idea ; but what does God say ? " (*C. H. Spurgeon.*) *Unprofitable speculations :*—In reviewing some of the questions which occupied my attention at an early period, I have seen reason to bless God for preserving me at a time when my judgment was very immature. When I have seen the zeal which has been expended in maintaining some such peculiarities, I have thought it a pity. Bunyan would have called them " nuts which spoil the children's teeth." They have appeared to me as a sort of spiritual narcotics, which, when a man once gets a taste for them, he will prefer to the most wholesome food. A man who chews opium, or tobacco, may prefer it to the most wholesome food, and may derive from it pleasure, and even vigour for a time; but his pale countenance and debilitated constitution will soon bear witness to the folly of " spending his money for that which is not bread." (*A. Fuller.*) *Unprofitable disputes to be avoided :*—Avoid disputes about lesser truths, and a religion that lies only in opinions. They are usually least acquainted with a heavenly life, who are violent disputers about the circumstantials of religion. He whose religion is all in his opinions, will be most frequently and zealously speaking his opinions ; and he whose religion lies in his knowledge and love of God and Christ, will be most delightfully speaking of that happy time when he shall enjoy them. He is a rare and precious Christian who is skilful to improve well-known truths. Therefore let me advise you, who aspire after a heavenly life, not to spend too much of your thoughts, your time, your zeal, or your speech upon disputes that less concern your souls ; but when hypocrites are feeding on husks and shells, do you feed on the joys above. I would have the chief truths to be chiefly studied, and none to cast out your thoughts of eternity. (*Richard Baxter.*)   *The groundwork of Christianity :*—In his confidential letter to Timothy, he struck very hard blows, and more nearly in language of contempt than I remember his using in any other of his writings.   He made a distinction in this way : he warned against that method of teaching which led to discussions, questions, janglings, disputes, envyings, and urged Timothy to pursue that line of teaching which had in it the power of building men up, of edifying them—this being the architectural word for building.   Those doctrines which tended to educate men in a noble manhood he told him to preach ; but those other doctrines which resulted not in the change of men's dispositions, but in debates and questionings, he counselled him to avoid.   That which tends to develop right sentiments he declares to be gospel teaching and preaching, whereas that which tends to develop nice distinctions, nice arguments, nice points of orthodoxy, and to make men think that they know ever so much, so that they are proud of their knowledge, though they are fools all the time, is false teaching and preaching.   And here we have the foundation on which men should be united.   Unity is not to exist in governments, ordinances, and doctrines, but in things that pertain to godliness of life.   It is said, "If a man is sincere his convictions do not make any difference."   Don't they ?   A man says to you, "I saw you break into a bank." "Oh, no," you say, "That is only a joke."   "Yes I did.   And not only that, I saw you pick a man's pocket."   He sticks to it that he saw you do these things ; and the more sincere he is the worse it is for you.   Do not you think it makes any difference what a man's convictions are when he is talking about you ?   You demand that a man shall think right when he talks about you, and your wife, and your daughter, and your credit, and your interests.   Everybody holds. in regard to certain technical speculative ideas which lie outside of positive knowledge, that men should believe right.   In the great realm of which we are speaking, and in reference to things which relate to manhood and character, everybody holds that right believing is essential.   We hold every man responsible for his beliefs so far as his conduct is affected by them : not for his speculative beliefs, but for those of his beliefs which pertain to human life in the family, in business, and in government.   Of the great laws to which men are accountable, spiritual laws are the highest, civil laws are next, social laws are next, and physical laws are next ; and belief in the existence of these laws is important. A belief that men are accountable to them, and that obedience to them brings happiness, while disobedience to them brings unhappiness, is also important.   You may leave out men's beliefs in regard to certain philosophical views of responsibility, and that which is woven in the loom of apprehension may be scattered, and no harm may result ; but the great fact remains that men are accountable to those laws ; and every man stands on that.   Men are accountable ; and if they do right they are rewardable ; but if they do wrong they are punishable ; and the greatest danger would result from teaching that it made no difference what men thought and did.   It would be a fatal blow at morality.   It would reduce man to the level of the animal, that acts according to instinct and not according to reason.   There could be no greater mistake than that.   While there may exist differences of opinion in regard to minor points connected with this fact, it is all-important that men should recognize the fact itself, that under the Divine government, and under the laws that belong to that government, men are held accountable for their conduct, for their feelings, and for their thoughts in life.   Men are also in agreement with regard to the ideal of character—that is, in regard to the architectural plan, which is laid down in the New Testament for godliness, or true Christian manhood.   They believe that the New Testament requires that the whole man shall be shaped and educated into a perfect obedience to all the laws of his condition here and hereafter. They believe that the body must be wholesome in a perfect Christian man.   They believe that where there is a perfect Christian manhood, the intellect must be healthy and regulated.   They believe that a man's disposition must be perfectly developed and harmonized before he can be a ripe Christian man.   We hear a great deal about the way being obscure, so that one cannot tell what the truth is.   Men complain that if you go to one church they tell you one thing, if you go to another church they tell you another thing, and if you go to another church they tell you still another thing.   It is true that churches differ on various minor points ; but they agree on great essential points.   In those things in which they are at agreement, they are like the body of a shawl ; and in those things in which they differ they are like the fringe of that shawl.   The body of the shawl is solid ; and there is division only in the fringe. It is the outer edge of truth about which men quarrel more than about anything else. In regard to the great central truths there is substantial unity. A man might better go into a desert in a sand-storm, or he might better put his glass into a blinding mist, in the hope of getting a view of the stars, than attempt to come to an understanding of the interior nature of the Divine life and government, by means of philosophical thought or discussion. That is a subject about which there is no controversy. It is here that the Christian world agree. About the ineffable love of God, about His inconceivable excellence, about His wondrous goodness and mercy, men are all agreed. Secondly, what is called "orthodoxy" in each sect falls, for the most part, into that category about which men differ, and may differ; as also do what are called "fundamental doctrines." Fundamental to what? That is the question. The doctrines which are fundamental to right living, to reverence and love toward God, and to love and self-sacrifice toward man; the doctrines, in other words, which are necessary to build up godliness in each particular man—about those doctrines there is no variation of belief. They are fundamental to conduct, fundamental to character, fundamental to duty; and about them men do not squabble. But what is fundamental to Calvinism in another thing. "Fore-ordination" is necessary to Calvinism; but it is not necessary to higher piety. Being "irresistibly called by efficacious grace" is essential to the Calvinistic scheme; but it is not necessary to true Christianity. Though such things as these may be fundamental to the forms, and ceremonies, and rituals, and usages, and governments of Churches, they are not fundamental to piety in its highest sense. I do not say that these outward elements have no value: that is not the point; I say that whatever their value may be, no man has any right, in the face of Christendom, to call them fundamental to Christianity when they are only fundamental to a side-issue—to something on either side of which a man may stand in his belief, and yet be a Christian and go to heaven. (*H. W. Beecher.*)

Vers. 5-7: **Now the end of the commandment is charity.**—*The end of the commandment :*—These verses are occupied with a description of what God's dispensation was meant to produce, and indicate how it came to pass that many failed of it. "The commandment" or charge which Timothy had received had this as its end or purpose—the promotion of "love out of a pure heart, and of a good conscience, and of faith unfeigned." By love is meant the right relation of the whole nature both to God and to man; for love to man is in the highest sense a consequent of love to God. I. THREE CONDITIONS of this love are specified. 1. A pure heart. This is essential to any vision of God. Unless we are purified our affections will naturally fasten upon selfish objects, or even upon those which are evil. 2. A good conscience is often insisted upon in Scripture as one of the inestimable blessings enjoyed by God's children. Conscience is the activity of consciousness towards the ethical aspect of things. But conscience is "good" if it is healed and purged by the Saviour's touch; if, instead of condemning us, it gives us confidence towards God; if it is reliable and unbiassed in its decision on all questions brought before its tribunal; and if it not only directs the will, but spurs it into instant activity. 3. Faith unfeigned is the third condition of God-accepted love. Though mentioned last, "faith" is the germ grace—the seed principle. To us fallen men there is no way to a "good conscience" and a "pure heart" but that of "faith" in Jesus Christ—that faculty which, laying hold of Him the Mediator, brings us into fellowship with God and all unseen realities. The apostle now turns from the conditions of love to—II. ITS COUNTERFEITS, exhibited in those who, professing to aim at it, miss their mark and swerve aside to "vain janglings"—that is, to empty talking and disputation. Too often the Church has had members who have been destitute of moral and spiritual perceptivity, but have made themselves at home in speculations and controversies. And the worst tempers are to be found among the members of the more talkative and disputatious sects. Paul heartily abhorred "vain babbling"—talk on religious subjects which was sometimes made a substitute for holy living; and in the Epistle to Titus, as well as here, some sharp stern words are uttered against it. False teaching is not to be lightly regarded or easily welcomed, as if it could have no evil effect on moral and spiritual life. For example, the philosophy of materialism, which represents our thoughts and affections as nothing but the emanations of movements in our physical bodies and brains, is ultimately destructive of moral responsibility and of belief in a coming immortality. "Continue thou in the things wherein thou hast been taught." Do not foolishly give up the faith which was associated with all that was sacred in your childhood. Remember that there is a sphere of existence outside the range of your senses, beyond the proof of your reason, of which you know nothing unless you accept the glimpses given of it in this Divine revelation. Beware lest, like these Ephesian heretics, you swerve from the faith, having turned aside unto vain jangling. (*A. Rowland, LL.B.*)  *The use and the abuse of the gospel:*—I. The USE of it. What is the use of it? First: The production of love in the soul. "The end of the commandment is charity." Secondly: The production of purity in the soul. "A pure heart." Thirdly: The production of a sound moral sense in the soul. "A good conscience." Fourthly: The production of a genuine confidence in the soul. "Faith unfeigned." II. The ABUSE of it. "Some," says the apostle, "having swerved have turned aside," *i.e.*, have missed the mark. The apostle mentions some out of the many great abuses of the gospel. Their talk was "jangling." Miserable discussions about forms, ceremonies, traditions, &c., &c. How much in all ages has there been of this in connection with the gospel. What miserable jargon, what *jejeune* gabbling. Their talk was—(1) Vain—vain, in the sense of emptiness and unsatisfactoriness. It had no substance of truth in it, and therefore nothing in it to satisfy either the intellect or the heart. (2) Ambitious. "Desiring to be teachers of the law." In how many thousands in Christendom does the gospel awaken little more than the ambition to be teachers? All it does for them is to strike into their hearts a desire to talk about it, mainly for the purpose of self-parade. Perhaps there is no greater abuse of the gospel than a certain kind of pulpiteering. (3) Ignorant. "Understanding neither what they say nor whereof they affirm." As a rule, the men who are most anxious to preach are the most ignorant. (*The Homilist.*)    **Charity.**—*The importance of heart love:*—John Wesley wrote to a student, "Beware that you are not swallowed up in books. An ounce of love to God is worth a pound of transient knowledge. What is the real value of a thing, but the price it will bear in eternity? Let no study swallow up or entrench upon the hours of private prayer. Nothing is of so much importance as this, for it is not the possession of gifts, but of grace, nor of sound knowledge and orthodox faith, so much as the principle of holy love and the practice of Christian precepts, which distinguish the heir of glory from the child of perdition." *Charity and almsgiving:*—The word "charity" is confined, in common acceptation, to two meanings, neither of which gives a just idea to a general reader of its original and scriptural meaning. It is, first, applied to modes of thinking or speaking respecting things and persons; and in this sense is often grievously misemployed by the insincere and the worldly; and, secondly, charity to the poor is used as another term for almsgiving. Either of these methods of employing the term is a corruption of this large and noble word, and an instance how the depravity of our nature has a tendency to spoil every thing it touches. Indifferent to the rules and practices of a holy life, some call that charity which glosses over gross vice and ruinous error; and others, under a total indifference to the meaning of the text—"Charity covereth (or hideth) many sins," hope to compound for a sinful life by contributing, as they think, largely of their own substance to the poor of their neighbourhood or to some charitable institution. That neither of these apparent results is really the fruit of Christian charity is too often evident, from the change induced by some slight provocation, which immediately quickens us into a vivid perception of wrong; what appeared charity is then seen to have been indifference either to truth or to holiness. But charity, in its real and scriptural sense, has a far more enlarged signification. It is a love to God, which is thence reflected upon all the creatures of God. It embraces cheerful devotedness and submissiveness to His will, founded on a faith in His declarations, a trust in His righteousness, an awful estimate of His character and counsels; and thence issues forth in sentiments of kindness, compassion, and good will, to all with whom we have a direct or distant intercourse. Patient under wrong, candid in its constructions in the world, slow to wrath, easy to forgive; it cheerfully sacrifices self, whenever such sacrifice can promote the Saviour's glory, or the temporal and moral welfare of mankind. It is evident, therefore, that whatever goes by the name of charity, is unworthy of that name, unless it be the fruit of that devotion of the affections, to which that name is confined in Scripture. Hence, almsgiving is no charity, unless it proceed from love. And since "the end of the commandment is charity"; since He who was rich and for our sakes became poor, has left us His example as well as His command; since in that world of rest, which lies all but exposed before the Christian's gaze, the heavenly Canaan—there will be no sorrows, no ignorance, no distress, no dangers, no toils, no death—let us esteem it no mean privilege, that now living in a world of varied grief and suffering, we have at once the means and the opportunity to imitate Christ—and while we have the time, " let us do good to all men." (*C. Lane, M.A.*)   **A good conscience.**—*A good conscience :*—Every man has a conscience. As without the physical senses I could never feel my connection with this material system—the green earth beneath my feet and the blue heavens that encircle me would be nothing without them ; so, without this conscience, this moral sense, I could have no idea either of moral government or God. Had you no conscience, I might as well endeavour to give to one that is born blind and deaf the idea of beauty and sweet sounds, as to give to you the idea of duty and God. What is a good conscience? Three things are necessary to it.  I. IT MUST LIVE. There are two classes of dead consciences. First : Those that have never been quickened. Conscience is in the breast of all in the first stages of childhood : but it is there as a germ unquickened by the sunbeam of intelligence, it is there as the optic nerve on which no light has fallen, it is dead. Secondly : Those which have been quickened but are now dead. II. IT MUST RULE. There are consciences with some vitality in them, but no royalty ; they are enslaved. They are found some-times in subjection to—(1) Animalism. They are " carnally sold under sin." (2) Worldliness. Worldly interests govern them. (3) Superstition. No conscience is good in this state. Conscience is the imperial faculty in the human soul ; it is not only self-inspecting, self-judging, but should be self-ruling. III. IT MUST RULE BY THE WILL OF GOD. If it rule—and it often does—by a worldly expediency,'a con-ventional morality, or a corrupt religion, it is a bad conscience. It must rule by the will of God, it must have no other standard. A good conscience is essential to every man's spiritual growth, power, peace, and usefulness. Without a good con-science what is he ? A moral wreck tossed on the billows of passion and circum-stances. (*The Homilist.*)   *A good conscience :*—Oh, for a good conscience, to meet the terrors of that day without apprehension ! But to have it then, we must possess it now. What is a good conscience? Its importance and necessity.  I. THREE THINGS ARE ESSENTIAL TO A GOOD CONSCIENCE. 1. Illumination. 2. Pacifica-tion. 3. Sanctification. (1) I say, first, the conscience must be enlightened. In itself it is not an infallible guide. Its province is not to teach men truth, not to correct erroneous principles, but simply to show a man when his conduct is, or is not, at variance with his knowledge and convictions of what is right. That know-ledge must be obtained elsewhere ; and then conscience will dictate the course of rectitude and consistency. If the judgment be under the influence of false principles, the conclusions of conscience will also be false. Some of the vilest things that have ever been done in this world have been done in its name and under its authority. It is evident, therefore, that a conscience, to be rightly directed, must have light ; so far as it is instructed it invariably conducts a man in the right way. Therefore, seek illumination. Be concerned to have correct principles, and labour after proper views of Divine truth ; for if the clouds of ignorance and error hang over the mind, not the greatest firmness of character, not the utmost integrity of purpose, no, not even the most decided sincerity of conviction, can preserve the vessel of the soul from pursuing a false track till, finally driven upon the quick-sands or dashing against the rocks, it makes shipwreck of faith and of good conscience, and thus through ignorance is for ever cast away. From this cause arise the calmness and complacency of the unconverted sinner. He is in darkness : he is the victim of false judgments, false views of the character of God, false views of the claims of His most holy law, false views of the true nature and enormity of sin, false hopes and schemes of salvation. (2) A conscience, when it has been thus enlightened, requires to be appeased. A conscience that is only enlightened is a torment, an accuser ; the greatest enemy of the soul's peace ; a fire in the veins, the bones, the marrow ; a worm that gnaws with insatiable cruelty. Such was the state of Cain when he had lifted up his arm against his brother Abel. " His innocent and injured shade seemed to pursue him." Such, too, was the case of Herod, who had been betrayed in an unguarded moment into the murder of John the Baptist. Such was the state of Belshazzar, at a time when he was surrounded with all his pomp and power, and everything yielded to his authority. Are any of you in this condition? Behold here, in the gospel, your remedy ; here, in the sacrifice of God's dear Son, the spotless victim, "the Lamb slain from the foundation of the world." Carry your broken spirit, then, to the feet of Jesus. If His precious blood distil upon it, every gaping wound will heal. (3) But conscience may be appeased on false grounds. Various devices are employed to pacify it when awakened, but it is " a good conscience " only when appeased in a way of sanctification. There remains, however, one question which deserves our serious consideration before we quit this branch of the subject. May not a worldly man possess a good conscience without vital religion, and to what extent? Here we must distinguish between the duties of the first and those of the second table. In so doing we shall distinguish between a conscience void of offence toward God and a conscience void of offence toward men. He who has been thus just to man has not satisfied the claims of God. Before the All-seeing Eye he stands convicted of imperfection and transgression in every thought, word, and deed. A conscience void of offence toward men has crowned him with moral glory while he lived; a conscience not void of offence toward God will cover him with eternal confusion when he stands before the great tribunal! Thus we reach a momentous and an inevitable conclusion. Every man is a sinner against God by the decision of Scripture, and in most cases by his own confession. Therefore, first let every man seek to comprehend and feel the extent of his guilt and the magnitude of his transgressions. II. We shall point out THE IMPORTANCE AND NECESSITY OF A GOOD CONSCIENCE. 1. And here let me remind you that this judge is enthroned in you by God Himself and cannot be cast down. It may be kept in ignorance, it may be bribed, it may be lulled to sleep, but there it is, not to be dispossessed of its rightful authority. It cannot be extinguished either by fraud or by force. Since, then, you cannot help entertaining this inmate because God has erected its tribunal, there remains but one remedy, to bow to its decisions. To fight against it will be but to beat the air. If we have true wisdom we shall be concerned to make a friend of a companion that we cannot shake off, and whose decisions, for or against us, will be confirmed at the last day. 2. Consider, again, how great and how solid is the peace which a good conscience is capable of conveying to the soul. It is an inestimable treasure, a constant and an unchangeable witness to our sincerity. There may be disquietudes without, there may be pains of body, there may be assaults and temptations, there may be losses, afflictions, and persecutions, but, amidst the wildest storms, it maintains inward serenity. Let self-convicted sinners tremble in proportion as they draw near to the throne of an offended God: the accepted Christian can defy death, and enter eternity with unextinguished joy. 3. Consider what strength and spirit a good conscience imparts through all the journey of life. Without it the hands become weak in duty, the feet weary in travel, and the heart is languid and depressed in religious engagements. You cannot approach the mercy-seat with confidence, for, while you do not approve yourselves, what hope can you have of acceptance with God? He can find no comfort or satisfaction in the world, and yet he is shut out from the comfort of religion. Present things have no relish, and yet he dares not appropriate the future. Give me an unclouded conscience; let it bear me witness in the Holy Ghost: then I shall stand upright in the presence of the enemy. My arm will be strong to wield the sword of the Spirit. There will be an inward vigour and elasticity that shall rise in proportion to opposition. 4. Consider that subjection to the dictates and decisions of conscience anticipates and prevents an adverse verdict in the great day. "If we would judge ourselves," says the apostle, "we should not be judged of God"; that is, not so judged as to be condemned. We shall close this important subject with a few words of practical application. 1. In the first place, to the true Christian who is deeply concerned to keep a good conscience, we would offer the following directions. Be anxiously vigilant against all evil, and watchful as to all opportunities of good. The conscience of a saint is like the eye of the body, extremely sensitive, requiring to be guarded with most jealous care. The least mote that enters into it makes it smart and agonize. Remember, believer, that your sins are, in some points of view, worse than those of all other men. They are committed against greater light and knowledge. Let it be your constant concern to live and act as under the eye of your great Master, to whom all things are naked and open, before whom the heart is anatomized as it were, and all its secrets are perfectly known. Realize the presence of Christ with you, and carry it into all the engagements of life, striving to do nothing which you would not be willing that He should behold. Be diligent and habitual in the work of self-examination, without which it is certain that no one can be satisfied as to the reality of his condition. What a shame it is to some men, that they know everything but their own hearts and characters! (*D. Katterns.*) *Importance of a good conscience :*—A good minister, whom we will not name, while sitting at the dinner table with his family, had these words said to him by his son, a lad of eleven years; "Father, I have been thinking, if I could have one single wish of mine, what I would choose." "To give you a better chance," said the father, "suppose the allowance be increased to three wishes; what would they be? Be careful, Charley!" He made his choice, thoughtfully; first, of a good character; second, of good health; and third, of a good education. His father suggested to him that fame, power, riches, and various other things, are held in general esteem among mankind. "I have thought of all that," said he, "but if I have a good conscience, and good health, and a good education, I shall be able to earn all the money that will be of any use to me, and everything else will come along in its right place." A wise decision, indeed, for a lad of that age. (*S. S. Chronicle.*) **And of faith unfeigned.**—*Unfeigned faith:*—An agnostic (or infidel), being present one day in a circle of refined people, was surprised when told that a certain lady, noted for her intelligence and her boldness and originality of thought, was a firm believer in the sacred Scriptures. He ventured to ask her at the first possible opportunity, "Do you believe the Bible?" "Most certainly I do," was her instant and unhesitating reply. "Why do you believe in it?" he queried again. "Because," she confidently added, "I am acquainted with the Author." Poor souls, that know not God in Christ as their Saviour, think, like the leaders of our nineteenth century philosophical infidelity, that He is "unknowable," and so reject His Word. But true believers have a blessed acquaintance with both.

Vers. 8–10. **The law is good, if a man use it lawfully.**—*The purpose of the law:*— The value of God's gifts largely depends upon the use we make of them. There are powers within our reach which may with equal ease destroy our welfare or increase it. Every reader of the Epistles, every student of Pharisaic teaching, and every one who understands the work of the Judaisers, is aware that even the Mosaic law was grossly abused. The law is good if a man use it lawfully. The apostle next endeavoured to explain more fully the purpose of the law, and his explanation may be summed up under three heads:—I. THE LAW WAS NOT MEANT AS AN INSPIRATION. "The law is not made for a righteous man." The statement is true, whether you think of a man "righteous" by nature or by grace. Those edicts and prohibitions were not intended for one who was eagerly inclined to obey their spirit. Such a revelation of God's will would not have been needed if Adam had continued in his righteousness, for things forbidden with pains and penalties after his fall were not at first attractive to him. If you walk through a private garden with the children of its owner, as one of themselves, you do not see anywhere the unsightly notice-boards, which are necessary in a place open to the public, asking you to move in this direction or in that, and to avoid trespassing hither or thither. Amongst the children, and as one of them, you are consciously above the need of such laws as those. Restrictions and warnings are always meant for those inclined to break them. Another example might be drawn from society. The laws on our statute books, the police who tramp through our streets, the vast organization represented by prisons and courts, by judges and magistrates, would no longer be necessary, and would never have been called into existence, if every man loved his neighbour even as himself. It is those who are disobedient in nature who make law a necessary institution. Similarly in the home. When your first child comes as a gleam of sunshine into your home, you parents do not begin to make a theoretical code of restrictions; but when the children grow older, and there are conflicts of will between them, and the household is likely to be disorderly by their thoughtlessness and faults, you begin to say, "You must not do this or that; it is to be from this time forward forbidden." But as the years roll on and good habits are formed by the young people, and from the love they bear you they instinctively know what you wish and readily do it, even these wise rules practically fall into desuetude. Because they are ruled by a right spirit they are set free from law. This leads to our second assertion, namely, that the law which was not meant for an inspiration was—II. INTENDED FOR THE RESTRAINT OF THE DISOBEDIENT. A lawless man is everywhere the least free. Carried hither and thither by his ungoverned passions; swayed now this way, now that, by his inexcusable carelessness and neglect, he nevertheless finds himself perpetually clashing against a will mightier than his own. Sometimes it is the law of his country which seizes him by the throat and holds him in restraint. Sometimes it is disease, the direct result of his own sin, which falls like a curse upon himself, and even upon his children. Sometimes it is conscience which protests and rebukes, until his whole life is made miserable. And these are but premonitions of what is coming when the Judge of all the earth will appear to give every man according to his works, and the thunders of outraged law will supersede the gentle voice of Christ's gospel. Terrible is the list of offences against human relationships which follows; though the first of the phrases in our version is at once too strong and too narrow. "Murderers of fathers" should be "smiters of fathers and smiters of mothers." The allusion may be to such crimes in the literal sense of the word, of which now and again we are horrified to hear, and which are commonest with those who are under the influence of drink—the cause of innumerable crimes! Or it may refer with equal force to those who smite their parents with the tongue, loading them with scorn and reproach, instead of encircling them with considerate love. "Cursed be he that setteth light by his father or his mother, and let all the people say Amen." "Man-slayers"—those who, by their exactions and oppressions, indirectly destroy the lives of men—as well as murderers, who are regarded as the pariahs of society. "Whoremongers and they that defile themselves with mankind," are terms which are meant to include all transgressors of the seventh commandment, a law which our Lord Jesus so broadened out in its application as even to include indulgence in lustful thought. "Liars and perjured persons" are forms of that false witness against one's neighbour which the ninth commandment so strongly condemns; and nothing is clearer as an evidence of the rule of Christ's spirit than the transparent truthfulness of character, which wins the admiration of the world, and suns itself in the favour of God. This list is formidable enough, and the fact that the apostle does not confine himself to the phraseology of the Mosaic decalogue, is a sign that we do not evade the penalties of the law by keeping its letter. III. THE APOSTLE ASSERTS THAT THE PURPOSE OF THE LAW IS AMONGST THE THINGS REVEALED IN THE GOSPEL OF THE BLESSED GOD. The "sound doctrine" he mentions is the teaching of our Lord and His apostles; which, as the phrase denotes, was thoroughly "sound" or wholesome, especially as opposed to the weak and distempered doctrines propounded by the false teachers whom Timothy had to oppose. (*A. Rowland, LL.B.*) *The use of the law:*—It would appear from this text that there is a way in which the law may be used lawfully, or rightly, from which we infer that there is also a way in which it may be used unlawfully, or unrightly—it may be put to a right use or to a wrong one. And there is a real distinction between this right and this wrong use of the law, which, if steadily kept in view, would be a perfect safeguard, both against the error of legality and the equally pernicious one of Antinomianism. First, then, we use the law unlawfully when we try to make out a legal right to the kingdom of heaven. There are two ways in which one may proceed who purposes to make out his right by his obedience to the law. If he have a sufficiently high conception of the standard, then he is paralyzed, and sinks into despair because of the discoveries that he is making of his exceeding distance and deficiency from that standard; and thus he is haunted at all times by a sense of his great insufficiency, and he never can attain to anything like solid peace. But there is another way—he may bring down the law to the standard of his own obedience, and may bring his conscience and conduct into terms of very comfortable equality with one another. But this is what the Bible calls a peace which is no peace. The ruin of the soul comes out in either way of the enterprise. 2. Having said this much on the wrong use of the law, I have only time in this discourse to instance one right use of it. When we compare our conduct with its command-ments, we cannot fail, in our deficiency and in our distance, to be convinced of sin. (*T. Chalmers, D.D.*) *The use of the law:*—Observe, then, of the law of God, that it has another and distinct object from that of holding out a method by which men acquire a right to its promised rewards, even that of holding out a method by which they acquire a rightness of character for the exercise of its fruits. The legal right is one thing; the moral rightness which obedience confers is another. For the former object the law must now become useless, and having fallen short of perfect obedience in ourselves, we must now found our whole right only in the righteousness of Christ. For the latter object, the law still contains all the use and all the impor-tance which it ever had. It is that tablet on which are inscribed the virtues of the Godhead; and we, by copying these into the tablet of our own character, are re-stored to the likeness of God. We utterly mistake the design and economy of that gospel, if we think that while the first function of the law has been superseded under the New Testament dispensation, the second has been superseded also. Obedience for a legal right is everywhere denounced as a presumptuous enterprise; obedience for a personal righteousness is everywhere said to be an enterprise, the prosecution of which forms the main business of every disciple, and the full achieve-ment of which is the prize of his high calling. For the one end the law has alto-gether lost its efficacy; and we, in order to substantiate its claim, must seek to be justified only by the righteousness of Christ. Let me now, then, expound more particularly the uses to which our observance of the law may be turned, in giving us not a right to heaven, but the indispensable character without which heaven never will be entered by us. If, after having laid hold of the righteousness of Christ, as your alone meritorious plea for the kingdom of heaven, you look to the law as in fact a transcript of the image of the Godhead, and by your assiduous keeping of this law, endeavour more and more to become like to God in Christ, this is the legitimate and proper use of the law, and by making this use you use it lawfully. You must not discard the law as being a thing that has no place in the system of the gospel. The great end of the gospel is to work in you a life and law of God, and by impressing the traits of that law on your character, to make you more and more like the Lawgiver, and fit you for His companionship. Therefore, although you discard the law in one capacity, that is not to say that you are to discard it altogether; for there remains this other capacity—the law is that to which you must conform yourselves in order to render you meet for the inheritance of the saints. We see, then, that though this obedience of ours to the law of God never can make out for us a judicial right for heaven, yet that this obedience, and this alone makes out our personal meetness for heaven. We can separate, in idea, the judicial from the personal meetness for heaven, and while we lay an entire stress on the former we also count the latter indispensable. Now, what helps us to do this is the arbitrary connexion which obtains between a punishment and a crime in civil society. I trust you see the relation of this to our present subject. One part of the law of God is that we should be forbearing and forgiving one with another. The circumstance which leads us to transgress that law is just the natural heat and violence of our temper. Suppose a man set out on the enterprise of seeking to establish a right to heaven by his obedience to the law, then it is his duty to restrain all the outbreakings of a furious temper, but he sees he never can succeed in making out the right by his obedience to the law, and, transgressing in one particular, he has failed in all. Now, some thinking that they have discarded the law, in as far as its power to obtain for them a right to heaven is concerned, and that in discarding it they have gone to Christ, are apt to think they are quit of the law altogether. But we say they are not because there still remains another end—another important capacity in which they are still to use the law even after they have united themselves to Christ. What is this capacity? and of what use is the law after this step has been taken? Here is the use of the law. All that you have gotten by your faith in Christ is a right to the kingdom of heaven. But the kingdom of heaven is peace and righteousness and joy. The kingdom of heaven is within you, and the essential joy of heaven is that joy which springs from the exercise of good, and kind, and virtuous affections. You have obtained a right of entering heaven and a release from the punishment of hell. But if the temper which prompted you to those transgressions of the law still remains within you, then the essential misery of hell remains within you. You are still exposed to all the misery that is incurred by the exercise of furious and malignant passions. You must have a rightness of character—you must get quit of all those immoral, vile, and wretched things which by nature adhere to you, and your salvation is begun here by a gradual process of deliverance from the wickedness of your hearts and lives, and which, perfected, renders you meet for the inheritance of the saints; so that this use of the law is an indispensable thing, although the law has failed, or rather you have failed, in making out your right to heaven by your obedience to its precepts. If a believer could be delivered from the fear of hell and were to remain in character and effect just what he was, a portion of the misery of hell would still adhere to him. His mind, in respect of all these painful sensations, may be as unrelenting as ever. The man that has this unsanctified feeling in his heart carries hell about with him. In respect of the material ingredients of torture, it is conceivable that he may be saved by being justified, but in respect of the moral ingredients to be saved he must be sanctified. Therefore we see that though the law is of no use, it is just by obeying this law that you make out your sanctification, and the one is just as indispensable as the other. The thing I want is that you will not put asunder what God has joined. It is not enough, then, to obtain a mere translation from what is locally hell to what is locally heaven. There must be an act of transformation from one character to another. Or, if faith is to save them, they must be sanctified by faith; and if it is not by the law that they are to obtain their right of entering into heaven, most assuredly it is by their obedience to the law that they have obtained that heaven shall be to them a place of enjoyment, for without it heaven itself would be turned into a hell. And without going for illustration to the outcasts of exile and imprisonment, the very same thing may be exemplified in the bosom of families. It is not necessary that pain be inflicted on bodies by acts of violence in order to make it a wretched family. It is enough that pain be made to rankle within every heart; from the elements of suspicion, hatred, and disgust, an abode of enjoyment may be turned into an abode of the intensest misery. Having thus endeavoured to make palpable to you that the hell of the New Testament consists mainly in the wretchedness which attaches naturally and necessarily to character, let me touch on the opposite and more pleasing side of the picture—the heaven of the New Testament, as consisting mainly in the happiness which attaches naturally and necessarily to character. I have no idea of a man carrying in life with him the security that he is a justified person, and at the same time a bad member of society, making his whole family miserable. If he perseveringly and presumptuously go on with his disobedience to the law, that man is not in the way of salvation at all. Were it real, the first doing of faith in Christ would be to work love in his heart. It would show itself in all sorts of ways in the walk and conversation. But the main happiness of heaven is just the happiness that springs from righteousness, peace, and joy in the Holy Ghost. And though you have the right of entering there if you have not these things you have no heaven at all. If your life has in it the character of hell, taking you out of one place and putting you into another will not make you happy. The kingdom of God is not in you. To enjoy a brilliant and picturesque heaven a man must be endowed with a seeing eye; to enjoy a musical heaven he must be endowed with a hearing ear; to enjoy an intellectual heaven he must be endowed with a clear and able understanding; and to enjoy the actual heaven of the New Testament into which all who are meet on earth are soon to be transported, he must be endowed with a moral heart. So that the very essence of salvation shall consist in the personal salvation by which man is rendered capable of being a happy and congenial inmate of heaven. This might be made obvious to you in the lessons of your own experience with man—the connection between the character and the happiness of man. (*Ibid.*) *The lawful and unlawful use of law :*— He does not, like a vehement polemic, say Jewish ceremonies and rules are all worthless, nor some ceremonies are worthless, and others essential; but he says the root of the whole matter is charity. If you turn aside from this all is lost, here at once the controversy closes. So far as any rule fosters the spirit of love, that is, is used lawfully, it is wise, and has a use. So far as it does not, it is chaff. So far as it hinders it, it is poison. I. THE UNLAWFUL USE. Define law. By law, Paul almost always means not the Mosaic law, but law in its essence and principle, that is, constraint. This chiefly in two forms expresses itself—first, a custom; second, a maxim. As examples of custom we might give circumcision, or the Sabbath, or sacrifice, or fasting. Law said, thou shalt *do* these things; and law, as mere law, constrained them. Or again, law may express itself in maxims and rules. Principle is one thing, and maxim is another. A principle requires liberality, a maxim says one-tenth. A principle says, "A merciful man is merciful to his beast," leaves mercy to the heart, and does not define how; a maxim says, thou shalt not muzzle the ox that treadeth out thy corn. A principle says, forgive; a maxim defines "seven times"; and thus the whole law falls into two divisions. The ceremonial law, which constrains life by customs. The moral law, which guides life by rules and maxims. Now it is an illegitimate use of law: 1. To expect by obedience to it to make out a title to salvation. By the deeds of the law shall no man living be justified. Salvation is by faith: a state of heart right with God; faith is the spring of holiness—a well of life. Salvation is not the having committed a certain number of good acts. Salvation is God's Spirit in us, leading to good. Destruction is the selfish spirit in us, leading to wrong. For a plain reason then, obedience to law cannot save because it is merely the performance of a certain number of acts which may be done by habit, from fear, from compulsion. Obedience remains still imperfect. A man may have obeyed the rule, and kept the maxim, and yet not be perfect. "All these commandments have I kept from my youth up." "Yet lackest thou one thing." The law he had kept. The spirit of obedience in its high form of sacrifice he had not. 2. To use it superstitiously. It is plain that this was the use made of it by the Ephesian teachers (ver. 4). It seemed to them that law was pleasing to God as restraint. Then unnatural restraints came to be imposed—on the appetites, fasting; on the affections, celibacy. This is what Paul condemns (chap. iv. 8). "Bodily exercise profiteth little." And again, this superstition showed itself in a false reverence—wondrous stories respecting angels—respecting the eternal genealogy of Christ—awful thoughts about spirits. The apostle calls all these, very unceremoniously, "endless genealogies" (ver. 4), and "old wives' fables" (chap. iv. 7). The question at issue is, wherein true reverence consists: according to them, in the multiplicity of the objects of reverence; according to St. Paul, in the character of the object revered. 3. To use it as if the letter of it were sacred. The law commanded none to eat the shewbread except the priests. David ate it in hunger. If Abimelech had scrupled to give it, he would have used the law unlawfully. The law commanded no manner of work. The apostles in hunger rubbed the ears of corn. The Pharisees used the law unlawfully in forbidding that. II. THE LAWFUL USE OF LAW. 1. As a restraint to keep outward evil in check. . . . "The law was made for sinners and profane." . . . Illustrate this by reference to capital punishment. No sane man believes that punishment by death will make a nation's heart right, or that the sight of an execution can soften or ameliorate. Punishment does not work in that way. The law commanding a blasphemer to be stoned could not teach one Israelite love to God, but it could save the streets of Israel from scandalous ribaldry. And therefore clearly understand, law is a mere check to bad men: it does not improve them; it often makes them worse; it cannot sanctify them. God never intended that it should. Hence we see for what reason the apostle insisted on the use of the law for Christians. Law never can be abrogated. Strict rules are needed exactly in proportion as we want the power or the will to rule ourselves. It is not because the gospel has come that we are free from the law, but because, and only so far as, we are in a gospel state. "It is for a righteous man" that the law is not made, and thus we see the true nature of Christian liberty. 2. As a primer is used by a child to acquire by degrees, principles and a spirit. This is the use attributed to it in verse 5. "The end of the commandment is charity." Compare with this two other passages—"Christ is the end of the law for righteousness," and "love is the fulfilling of the law." "Perfect love casteth out fear." In every law there is a spirit, in every maxim a principle; and the law and the maxim are laid down for the sake of conserving the spirit and the principle which they enshrine. Distinguish, however. In point of time, law is first —in point of importance, the Spirit. In point of time charity is the "end" of the commandment—in point of importance, first and foremost. The first thing a boy has to do is to learn implicit obedience to rules. The first thing in importance for a man to learn is to sever himself from maxims, rules, laws. Why? That he may become an Antinomian, or Latitudinarian? No. He is severed from submission to the maxim because he has got allegiance to the principle. He is free from the rule and the law because he has got the Spirit written in his heart. (*F. W. Robertson, M.A.*) *The moral teaching of the Gnostics: its modern counterpart:*—The speculations of the Gnostics in their attempts to explain the origin of the universe and the origin of evil, were wild and unprofitable enough; and in some respects involved a fundamental contradiction of the plain statements of Scripture. But it was not so much their metaphysical as their moral teaching which seemed so perilous to St. Paul. Their "endless genealogies" might have been left to fall with their own dead weight, so dull and uninteresting were they. But it is impossible to keep one's philosophy in one compartment in one's mind, and one's religion and morality quite separate from it in another. However unpractical metaphysical speculations may appear, it is beyond question that the views which we hold respecting such things may have momentous influence upon our life. It was so with the early Gnostics, whom St. Paul urges Timothy to keep in check. "The sound doctrine" has its fruit in a healthy, moral life, as surely as the "different doctrine" leads to spiritual pride and lawless sensuality. The belief that Matter and everything material is inherently evil, involved necessarily a contempt for the human body. This body was a vile thing; and it was a dire calamity to the human mind to be joined to such a mass of evil. From this premise various conclusions, some doctrinal and some ethical, were drawn. On the doctrinal side it was urged that the resurrection of the body was incredible. Equally incredible was the doctrine of the Incarnation. How could the Divine Word consent to be united with so evil a thing as a material frame? On the ethical side the tenet that the human body is utterly evil produced two opposite errors—Asceticism and Antinomian sensuality. And both of these are aimed at in these Epistles. If the enlightenment of the soul is everything, and the body is utterly worthless, then this vile clog to the movement of the soul must be beaten under and crushed, in order that the higher nature may rise to higher things. The body must be denied all indulgence, in order that it may be starved into submission (chap. iv. 3). On the other hand, if enlightenment is everything and the body is worthless, then every kind of experience, no matter how shameless, is of value, in order to enlarge knowledge. Nothing that a man can do can make his body more vile than it is by nature, and the soul of the enlightened is incapable of pollution. Gold still remains gold, however often it is plunged in the mire. The words of the three verses taken as a text, look as if St. Paul was aiming at an evil of this kind. These Judaizing Gnostics " desired to be teachers of the Law." They wished to enforce the Mosaic Law, or rather their fantastic interpretations of it, upon Christians. They insisted upon its excellence, and would not allow that it has been in many respects superseded. "We know quite well," says the apostle, "and readily admit, that the Mosaic Law is an excellent thing; provided that those who undertake to expound it make a legitimate use of it. They must remember that, just as law in general is not made for those whose own good principles keep them in the right, so also the restrictions of the Mosaic Law are not meant for Christians who obey the Divine will in the free spirit of the gospel." Legal restrictions are intended to control those who will not control themselves; in short, for the very men who by their strangest doctrines are endeavouring to curtail the liberties of others. In a word, the very persons who in their teaching were endeavouring to burden men with the ceremonial ordinances, which had been done away in Christ, were in their own lives violating the moral laws to which Christ had given a new sanction. They tried to keep alive, in new and strange forms, what had been provisional and was now obsolete, while they trampled under foot what was eternal and Divine. "If there be any other thing contrary to the sound doctrine." In these words St. Paul sums up all the forms of transgression not specified in his catalogue. The sound, healthy teaching of the gospel is opposed to the morbid and corrupt teaching of the Gnostics, who are sickly in their speculations (chap. vi. 4), and whose word is like an eating sore (2 Tim. ii. 17). Of course healthy teaching is also health-giving, and corrupt teaching is corrupting ; but it is the primary and not the derived quality that is stated here. It is the healthiness of the doctrine in itself, and its freedom from what is diseased or distorted, that is insisted upon. Its wholesome character is a consequence of this. The extravagant theories of the Gnostics to account for the origin of the universe and the origin of evil are gone and are past recall. It would be impossible to induce people to believe them, and only a comparatively small number of students ever even read them. But the heresy that knowledge is more important than conduct, that brilliant intellectual gifts render a man superior to the moral law, and that much of the moral law itself is the tyrannical bondage of an obsolete tradition, is as dangerous as ever it was. It is openly preached and frequently acted upon. The great Florentine artist, Benvenuto Cellini, tells us in his autobiography that when Pope Paul III. expressed his willingness to forgive him an outrageous murder committed in the streets of Rome, one of the gentlemen at the Papal Court ventured to remonstrate with the Pope for condoning so heinous a crime. "You do not understand the matter as well as I do," replied Paul III. : "I would have you to know that men like Benvenuto, unique in their profession, are not bound by the laws." Cellini is a braggart, and it is possible that in this particular he is romancing. But, even if the story is his invention, he merely attributes to the Pope the sentiments which he cherished himself, and upon which (as experience taught him) other people acted. Over and over again his murderous violence was overlooked by those in authority, because they admired and wished to make use of his genius as an artist. "Ability before honesty" was a common creed in the sixteenth century, and it is abundantly prevalent in our own. The most notorious scandals in a man's private life are condoned if only he is recognized as having talent. It is the old Gnostic error in a modern and sometimes agnostic form. (A. Plummer, D.D.) The right use of the Divine law :—When we look around us, we see that God governs all by established rules. His government enters into all the minutiæ of providence. But when we leave this government, where we ought to leave it, in the hands of almighty wisdom and power, and ascend to the spiritual world, there we find the great difference there is between created and uncreated, between the imperfection of man and the perfection of God. Let us consider—I. THE INFINITE PERFECTION OF THE LAW OF GOD. "The law," says the apostle, "is holy ; and the commandment holy, just, and good "; and why? because God Himself "is holy, just, and good." 1. To understand the perfection of this law we must consider also the relation subsisting between the Governor and the governed. They are all dependent for everything, both now and for ever, upon Him. No man upon earth has a right to legislate, but as the representative of God Himself. Why is a father a legislator in his own family? because he is a father? No; but because God has invested him with that right. Moreover, legislation is not a something arbitrary in the Deity; His legislation flows from His own essential perfection. It must be what it is, it cannot be otherwise. 2. Consider the law of God as to its commandments. It requires, in the first place, supreme love to God; involving the exercise of all the affections of the heart. The commands of this law require, also, fraternal love. 3. Consider the law of God as to its curse. In this respect, also, it will appear to be " just and good." Does it seem unkind? No; for it throws the sinner no farther from God than he throws himself. 4. The law of God, then, is immutable and eternal. The law of God must necessarily relate to every inhabitant of heaven, of earth, of hell. 5. Consider the law of God under the Adamic covenant. It connected life with obedience, death with disobedience. 6. Consider the law of God under the Mosaic dispensation. II. THE USES OF THE LAW OF GOD. " The law is good, if a man use it lawfully." 1. The law is abused and insulted by transgression. What is said of wisdom may be said of this law; " he that sinneth against Me wrongeth his own soul." 2. The law is insulted and abused when men endeavour to justify themselves by it. This must arise, first, from ignorance of themselves; and, secondly, from ignorance of the law of God. Paul says of the Jews, " they have a zeal of God, but not according to knowledge. For they, being ignorant of God's righteousness, and going about to establish their own righteousness, have not submitted themselves unto the righteousness of God." The whole ceremonial law taught men that they were to be justified by another—that sin was to be atoned for. 3. And the law is insulted and abused whenever men endeavour to justify themselves, in the least degree, by it. 4. And not only is the law insulted and abused when men reject the law, but also when they reject the remedy for their disobedience. The rejection of the gospel is the greatest and most dreadful act of disobedience to the law. It is an insult offered to the government of God, and a wanton rejection of His goodness. But what are the uses of the law? 1. We should view it as fulfilled by Jesus Christ. But Christ died also for His brethren, that He might bring them to a state of perfect conformity to the law, and preserve them in that state for ever. The apostle speaks of being " under the law to Christ"; this is the state of the believer on earth, and this will be his state for ever. 2. To use the law aright, is to study it perfectly, and to see its beauty as it was exemplified in Christ. 3. To use the law aright is to connect it intimately with faith. There is a more intimate connection between faith and the law of God than we can possibly describe. By believing in Christ we honour the law as a covenant, in its commands, and its curse; and when we take it as a rule of life we honour it altogether. 4. The law is used and honoured as it should be, when we make it the guide of our daily conduct, when we aim to bring all our actions as near to the law of God as possible. (*W. Howels.*) *The right use of the law :—* The apostle speaks like one possessed of the full assurance of understanding, in the mystery of God and of Christ. " We know," says he, " that the law is good : " we know it by Divine inspiration, by rational deduction, and also by experience. This may be applied to the ceremonial law, by which the Jews were distinguished from all other nations as God's peculiar people. They were hereby directed how to worship God, and how they were to be saved. It was a shadow of good things to come, and afforded a typical representation of the blessings of the gospel. But it is the moral law which the apostle principally intends : and this is truly good in itself, whether we use it lawfully or not. It is a copy of the Divine will, a transcript of the Divine perfections. If we do not approve of this law, it is because we are ignorant of its nature and are at enmity against God. " The law is holy, and the commandment holy, just and good : " and " I delight in the law of God after the inward man " (Psa. cxix. 28 ; Rom. vii. 12, 22). I. NOTICE SOME INSTANCES IN WHICH THE DIVINE LAW IS USED UNLAWFULLY. 1. In thinking that Christ's obedience to it renders our obedience unnecessary. 2. When, instead of judging ourselves by the law, we take occasion from it to judge uncharitably of others, we use it unlawfully. Thus did the Pharisees: " This people who know not the law are cursed," said they. 3. In depending upon the works of the law for justification before God, we make an improper use of the law; and that which is good in itself ceases to be good to us. II. CONSIDER WHAT ARE THE PROPER USES OF THE DIVINE LAW. " The law is good, if a man use it lawfully." 1. It serves as a glass or mirror, in which we may behold the majesty and purity of God, and the guilty and wretched state of man. 2. It acts as a restraint upon our lusts and corruptions. If it be asked, " Wherefore serveth the law?" The answer is, "It was added because of transgressions"; that is, to prevent them by curbing the unruly passions and appetites of men. 3. The law is properly used as a means of conviction. "By the law is the knowledge of sin," and without it sin could not be fully known. "When the commandment came," says Paul, "sin revived, and I died." 4. It is a complete directory, or rule of conduct. One great end of the law ever was, and ever will be, to instruct us in our duty towards God, ourselves, and our neighbour. Like the pillar of fire which guided the Israelites through the wilderness, it is a light to our feet, and a lamp to our paths. 5. It serves as a criterion by which to judge of our experience, and whether we be the subjects of real grace. (*B. Beddome, M.A.*)  *On the law :*—I. In the first place, then, we beg your attention to THE CHARACTER AND REQUIREMENTS OF GOD'S LAW. 1. This law, in the first place, is holy. It is the offspring of the mind of Deity, which is perfectly pure. It is the spotless transcript of God's holiness. It is the faithful representation of His moral excellence and perfection. 2. It is not only holy, but it is just. It is the standard of right, and the infallible standard of right. In all that it claims, in all that it forbids, in all that it inculcates, it is perfectly just to God the Lawgiver, and perfectly just to man the subject of His laws. 3. Moreover, the law is good. It is a kind and merciful law. The motive which prompted the promulgation of it was a motive of benevolence. 4. I beg to remind you that it is a supreme law; universal in its obligations, and binding on the consciences of every rational, intelligent, and accountable being. 5. I must beg you to remark, in the fifth place, that the law is unchangeable; and for this plain reason, because it is perfectly holy, perfectly just, perfectly good. Whatever change there is wrought in the law, it must be either for the better, or for the worse. If the law be already perfect, it cannot be changed for the better; and that God should change His law for the worse, is an idea not for a moment to be admitted into any rational understanding. 6. Let me further observe that this law is also eternal; for the very reasons to which I have already adverted. It requires not only a personal obedience but a perfect obedience. We must not only obey in some things but in all things—"all things which are written in the book of the law to do them." This obedience, also, must be perpetual. It is not a man's obeying the law to-day and violating it to-morrow, which will constitute the obedience which it requires: for "Cursed is every one that continueth not in all things written in the book of the law to do them." II. "WHEREFORE THEN SERVETH THE LAW?" If such are its characters, and such are its requirements, and every living man must feel that he is utterly incapable of rendering that personal, perfect, and perpetual obedience which the law requires, "wherefore then serveth it?" 1. The law of God serves for instruction. It holds up to our view the standard of right and of wrong. 2. The law serves for conviction—conviction of sin: and this it does in three ways. First, it demonstrates to us the evil of sin in its direct contrariety to God's nature and will. "I had not known sin"—I had not been acquainted with sin—"except the law had said, Thou shalt not covet." But the law of God not only demonstrates what sin is, but it brings home a sense and a conviction of it, to the conscience of the sinner. Once more, the law serves for conviction, inasmuch as it utterly silences and stops the mouth of every transgressor, by showing him that he stands without excuse in the presence of the Lawgiver, on the ground of his manifold delinquencies and his innumerable breaches of this law. The law serves, in the third place, for condemnation. It will be the rule by which every sinner who perishes will be condemned at the last great day : for "the wages of sin is death." Fourthly, the law serves to magnify the all-sufficiency and perfection of that justifying righteousness, which Christ, as the surety of His people, has supplied. In the fifth place, this law serves as a rule of life and a directory of conduct to all who are the subjects of God's moral govern- ment. Some persons have adopted that most pernicious sentiment, that the law of God is not a rule of life to the believer. But I ask, why not? Cannot you easily conceive that the law of God may be annulled and abrogated in one view of it, and remain altogether in full force in another view of it? As a covenant, it is utterly taken out of the way; because it has been gloriously fulfilled in the person of the Surety. And therefore, now, "by the deeds of the law no flesh living shall be justified." But it would be indeed a strange and most anomalous thing, if God, in removing His law as a covenant, should have disannulled that law as the rule of life. I speak it with all reverence, this is a thing which God Himself could not do; and for this plain reason, that the law is just a transcript of His own pure and perfect mind ; the law is just the revelation of His holy and unchangeable will; and unless He could destroy His own perfect mind, and unless He could alter His own immutable will, then His law must ever remain the rule of life and manners, not only to all His redeemed children, but to all intelligences in heaven and in earth. III. THEN, WHAT IS NECESSARY IN ORDER THAT WE MAY USE THE LAW LAWFULLY? 1. We should daily appeal to it, as the standard of action, the rule of self-examination, and the instrument of penitential conviction. 2. In the next place, be it remarked, that when we habitually divorce ourselves from the law as a covenant, as a means of justification, and as a ground of hope, we use it lawfully. 3. We use this law lawfully, in the third place, when Christ becomes inexpressibly dear to our hearts, as having honoured and fulfilled the law, placed it in the position of its just authority and importance, and at the same time redeemed us from its curse and from its punishment. 4. We use the law lawfully when, conscious of our own weakness and incapacity to fulfil its requirements, we are earnest in prayer for the Spirit of grace to renew and sanctify our nature, and to strengthen us to a compliance with all the known will of God. 5. Again, the law is used lawfully when we make it our constant study, and aim, to exemplify its holy requirements—to show the law of God in our habitual walk, in our life, our spirit, our behaviour. " Ye are a chosen generation, a royal priesthood, an holy nation, a peculiar people; that ye should show forth the praises of Him who hath called you out of darkness into His marvellous light. (*G. Clayton, M.A.*) *The proper uses of the law :*—" The law is good," says the apostle, "if a man use it lawfully." Consequently there is an unlawful use of the law. What, then, is the lawful use of the law ? I. TO SHOW US OUR NEED OF A SAVIOUR. "By the law is the knowledge of sin." And again, " The law was our schoolmaster to bring us to Christ." Let us take but a cursory view of the various commandments, and we shall find that we have individually violated them all, and thus are verily guilty before God. II. Observe, then, that in this case the law serves AS A RULE TO REGULATE OUR BEHAVIOUR. Like so many poles or beacons placed along a difficult navigation, or so many finger-posts erected along a road, the several commandments serve to indicate our course heavenward. If we wish to secure in the most effectual manner the fidelity of a son or a servant, we shall not proceed by a system of terror, but rather by one of authority, tempered by gentleness and kindness. Precisely such is the system adopted by the Father of mercies in the gospel. Seeking not the compulsory " eye-service " of the convict, but the cheerful and cordial obedience of an attached child, He employs a plan exquisitely suited to this desired end. He deals with us as creatures of reason and feeling. He knows that affection must be won, not forced; that men are not to be driven, but drawn into love. Accordingly the Christian, now that he is " justified by faith," obeys the law immeasurably better than he ever did, or could do before. 1. For now he obeys it not merely in the letter, but in the spirit ; not as of necessity, but willingly ; not partially, but universally. He esteems God's commandments concerning all things to be right. 2. And then he has now what he had not before, namely, the aid of the Holy Spirit working in him both to will and to do, and causing him, like water at the roots of a tree, to bring forth the fruits of righteousness to the Divine praise and glory. And now behold the necessary, the indissoluble connection between justification and sanctification. A person is justified through faith, which, uniting him to Christ, gives him an interest in His righteousness. Then this faith produces obedience by producing love. "Faith worketh by love." It becomes a living principle in the heart, urging to the performance of all such good actions as God has prescribed ; and therefore this is termed " the obedience of faith." (*J. E. Hull, B.A.*) *The use of the law :*—I. We consider THE INSTITUTION, EXTENT AND APPLICATION OF THE LAW. When God formed man upright in His own image, the moral law, which inculcates eternal, unchangeable truth and perfect goodness, was written in his heart. By the fall, the fair image of God's purity was defaced, some faint lines of distinction only of right and wrong being left upon the natural conscience. When God was about to separate to Himself the people of Israel, with a view to preserve and perpetuate in the earth the knowledge of His character and will, He gave them the law from Sinai, not now inscribed on their hearts as before, but engraven on two tables of stone. Such was the institution of the law. We proceed to its extent and application. The moral law of the ten commandments is a complete summary of all human duty to God, to each other, and to themselves. We are not to limit the commandments to their literal meaning ; otherwise a great part of our thoughts, and words, and even of our actions would be exempt from the notice and control of the law of God. It has the whole Word of God for its expositor, the regulation of the whole sphere of human principle and action for its object. "The law is spiritual." It does not merely regard the outward action, it goes down into the heart and motives, and tries every thought, intention, and principle of the soul. II. To consider HOW IT IS LAWFULLY USED. 1. We use it lawfully when we receive and respect it in its full extent, and in every part of it. There is hardly any man, however wicked, who does not feel something like reverence for some parts of God's commands. A man will coolly break and profane the Sabbath who dares not curse and swear. 2. We use the law lawfully when we bring every part of our character, the inward as well as the outward man, to the test of its requirements. An action, though apparently agreeable to the law of God, if it originate in some base, selfish, unholy motive, is in His sight an act of disobedience, a positive sin. Jehu did an action which the law required, when he rooted idolatry out of the land; but it soon appeared that his object was not the glory of God, but his own distinction and advancement. Neither was Amaziah's conduct better than splendid sin, "who did that which was right in the sight of the Lord, but not with a perfect heart." 3. We use the law lawfully when we seriously believe, and fully admit that it contains eternal and unalterable truth, that our holy God could not have given a law less holy, less extensive; that every being, in proportion as he is holy and fit for heaven, loves the law; that every transgression of it must expose us to Divine justice as guilty offenders; that the penalty of every sin is death eternal; and that till we seek mercy and forgiveness in His appointed way for each sin of our lives, the curse of the law, and the wrath of God abide upon us. All this must be true in the very nature of things. III. THIS LAWFUL USE OF THE LAW ANSWERS GOOD ENDS, PRODUCES HAPPY EFFECTS UPON US, WHATEVER OUR STATE AND CHARACTER MAY BE. 1. This lawful use of the law is good for the unconverted, whether a wicked or a self-righteous man. When, under a serious and spiritual understanding of the law, he not only surveys his actions but enters with its light into the secret chambers of his heart, he discovers his true character in all its horrid deformities. He perceives that his heart has never felt the love of God, the principle of all true obedience. His best actions are now seen in their proper light, as needing the mercy, not claiming the reward of his holy God. He cannot be saved by works under the law, except he keep it perfectly. But if he could forget all his past sins, he finds that the law is so pure and extensive that he cannot keep it for a day. The more he tries the more he is condemned. In this awful state the gospel points his despairing eye to the Cross. "Behold the Lamb of God which taketh away the sins of the world." Thus "the law is our schoolmaster to bring us to Christ." It drives us from Sinai to Calvary. It pulls down every false foundation of hope, that we may build on Christ alone, the rock of ages. 2. After the law has brought a penitent sinner to Christ for pardon, peace, and life, it is, if lawfully used, good and useful to him as a justified believer. He is called to be holy; and the practical part of the Word of God, which is a comment upon the law, shows him at large what is sinful and what is holy. It therefore becomes a light to his feet and a lamp to his paths. To be conformed to the law is to be conformed to the image of God, and to be capable of heavenly happiness with Him. (1) Let me entreat you, if you regard your immortal souls, diligently to read, hear, and meditate upon the Word of God at large, which explains the law and will of God by precept, and illustrates them by example. (2) Let your hearing and study of the Word of Life be ever accompanied with earnest humble prayer to God, for the powerful aid of His grace to give you a spiritual taste and judgment to dispel your ignorance, to guide you into all truth, and to fasten it with power on your hearts. (3) In considering the several parts of the law of God your object should be to comprehend its full bearing, extent, and meaning. In order to succeed you cannot take a better model than our Saviour's view and explanation of a part of the law in His sermon on the mount. (*J. Graham.*) *Using the law :*—A Chinese correspondent of the New York "Christian Weekly" sends some instances of how Chinese preachers meet questions and preach, of which the following is one :—"Bishop Russell, of Ningpo, recently told us of a helper of his who was preaching on the Ten Commandments, when a man suddenly entered and walked rapidly forward to the desk. 'What have you got there?' he asked in a loud voice. The helper immediately replied, 'I have a foot-rule of ten inches' (the Chinese foot has ten inches, as the foot everywhere ought to have), 'and if you will sit down I will measure your heart.' And he proceeded with his ten-inch rule to show how 'short' his hearers were according to God's measure." *The law good :*—No doubt the law restrains us ; but chains are not fetters, nor are all walls the gloomy precincts of a jail. It is a blessed chain by which the ship, now buried in the trough, and now rising on the top sea, rides at anchor, and outlives the storm. The condemned would give worlds to break his chain ; but the sailor trembles lest his should snap ; and when the gray morning breaks on the wild lee-shore, all strewn with wrecks and corpses, he blesses God for the good iron that stood the strain. The pale captive eyes his high prison-wall to curse the man who built it, and envies the little bird that perches upon its summit ; but were you travelling some Alpine pass, where the narrow road, cut out of the face of the rock, hung over a frightful gorge, it is with other eyes you would look on the wall that restrains your restive steed from backing into the gulf below. Such are the restraints God's law imposes. (*T. Guthrie, D.D.*) *Applying the law :*—The Bishop of Moosonee, whose diocese is in the region of the Hudson's Bay territory, and inhabited chiefly by Ojibbeway Indians and Esquimaux, said, "Let me take you in thought to a place a hundred miles distant from my own home in that country—a place called Rupert's House. One morning I had before me a large congregation of Indians. I knew that among them there were four men who only a month or two before had murdered their fathers and mothers, and I intentionally placed those men directly in front of me. I called attention to the Ten Commandments. I read the Fourth Commandment and explained it, and I also read the sixth and explained it, and when I had done I put questions to the four men to whom I have just alluded. I said to the first, ' Who killed his father ? ' I said to the second, ' Who killed his mother ? ' I said to the third, ' Who killed his mother-in-law ? ' I said to the fourth, ' Who killed his father ? ' And each of those men replied without blushing, ' It was I who did it.' Of what crime were those poor murdered people guilty ? They were guilty of a crime of which we may any of us be guilty, and of which some of us here already begin to be guilty—the crime of growing old. Accordingly the old father and mother were told that they had lived long enough and that it was time for them to die, and the bow-string was speedily placed round their necks, and with one son pulling at one end, and another son or perhaps a daughter at the other, the poor old people were deprived of life, and then hastily flung into a grave. Happily this state of things has now passed away." *Design of the law :*—An American gentleman said to a friend, "I wish you would come down to my garden and taste my apples." He asked him about a dozen times, but the friend did not come, and at last the fruit-grower said, " I suppose you think my apples are good for nothing, so you won't come and try them." " Well, to tell the truth," said the friend, "I have tasted them. As I went along the road I picked up one that fell over the wall, and I never tasted anything so sour in all my life ; and I do not particularly wish to have any more of your fruit." " Oh," said the owner of the garden, " I thought it must be so ! Those apples around the outside are for the special benefit of the boys. I went fifty miles to select the sourest sorts to plant all around the orchard, so the boys might give them up as not worth stealing ; but if you will come inside you will find that we grow a very different quality there, sweet as honey." Now you will find that on the outskirts of religion there are a number of " Thou shalt nots," and " Thou shalts," and convictions and alarms ; but these are only the bitter fruits with which this wondrous Eden is guarded from thievish hypocrites. If you can pass by the exterior bitters, and give yourself up to Christ and live for Him, your peace shall be like the waves of the sea. (*C. H. Spurgeon.*)   **Sound doctrine.**—*Sound doctrine* is not a thing separate from its purpose. It is not spoken from heaven merely for the sake of informing men's minds. Is not this the heresy pervading Christian teaching ; that Christian teachers have thought of doctrine as something given them that they might exercise their minds upon it, rather than as something which came to them in order that what God supremely loves—a holy life—might be built up ? The one great thing which has perverted man's study of the Christian gospels is, that men have dared to forget that the gospel came to a world of sinners that they might be reclaimed from the paths of sin and brought to righteousness again. Wonderfully few are the mistakes which men make when they read the Bible as the law of life. Wonderfully few are the men able to read the Bible rightly when they fasten their eyes on it for speculation. The soul which goes to the Bible to get the thing for which it was given, gets the thing it goes for. The soul laying hold on the heart of the New Testament finds what was in the heart of God. It is expressed by St. Paul in the phrase, " the will of God, even your sanctification." It is certainly easy to find in the New Testament the truth of Jesus Christ. A man comes to the Bible and says, " Is not this strange and mysterious ? " And he points to some marvellous proof he seems to have extorted from the plain text of the New Testament. He is using the Bible for that for which it was not given. He is sure to go wrong, and gather from it some strange doctrine, a fantasy which never was in the simple teaching of the Holy Spirit. Another man goes to the Bible hungering for a better life, desiring to escape from sin; weary of the barren sinfulness of this world he goes to the Bible for a picture of the kingdom of heaven; goes to the Bible to learn how this world can be made the habitation of the Holy God. That man can understand, not perhaps every truth there, for there are truths yet to be developed by certain exigencies of the world; but he will come away full of the learning which he at present needs. The New Testament will become to him a book of life. When St. Paul writes back from Europe to Asia, he bids Timothy teach the disciples that the law is to be used lawfully. He tells him and them the same lesson which we need. Let us go to our Bible for our Bible's purpose, inspiration, and a law of life, and the idea of what God would have man to be, and the power to become what it is the purpose of our Father that we should become. This is the teaching of the First Epistle to Timothy. The fundamental thing which Paul said to Timothy was that he should send the Ephesians to the Bible for the Bible's purpose. Always, spirituality is to go back to morality. The idea that man is to be wise with the wisdom of God is to refresh itself with the idea that man is to be good with the holiness of God. (*Phillips Brooks, D.D.*)

Ver. 11. **According to the glorious gospel of the blessed God.**—*The glorious gospel :*—The gospel is here characterized as glorious. It depends not for its glory on any incidental circumstances. In its essential elements it is the same for all lands and nations, conveying " glad tidings of great joy to all people." The language of the text, with all other gloriousness, implies the glory of perpetuity. Indeed, what is here called "the glorious gospel" is elsewhere called " the everlasting gospel " (Rev. xiv. 6). Bringing these phrases together, we have " glory everlasting " ; changeless amid changeful seasons. But having fully stated this evangelical commonness, let us now remark that the manner in which persons are brought into connection with the gospel varies. One is persuaded by the terror of the Lord, another is drawn by His mercy and constrained by His love. And every one who has tasted of the joys of salvation will find his estimate of them affected, not only by their intrinsic excellence, but by their particular adaptation and application to his individual exigencies and personal experience. Let us, then, in these words, transplant ourselves to Paul's position. Let us contemplate what he speaks of from his own point of view. I. The apostle may thus have spoken in RELATION TO THE MESSIAH. As a Jew, Paul had longed for Christ. This was the grand promise made to the fathers; the seed of the woman was to bruise the serpent's head ; in Abraham and his seed should all families of the earth be blessed; Shiloh should come, and to him should the gathering of the people be. Other nations glory in their founders, and look back. The Jews expected a Deliverer, and looked forward. And hence Christ, when He came and was recognized, gratified a peculiar, earnest, and ever-growing anticipation. The Lord whom they looked for came to His temple, even the messenger of the covenant whom they delighted in. It is true that Paul, in the first instance, was disappointed in Jesus—bitterly disappointed. But that disappointment enhanced, by contrast, his delight, when he came after all to perceive that this was indeed the Hope of Israel. He had abhorred the Christians for neglecting the Aaronic ritual. And what an exposition of their conduct was now before him!—that the rites had been exchanged by them for the reality; that the sacrifices were but shadows, and found their substance in Christ; and that the Mosaic ordinances received the utmost honour in being so fulfilled—in being done away by the accomplishment and verification of all their foreshadowings. In one aspect the revelation was appalling. The stupendousness of the remedy gave Paul impressions which he had never had before of the dreadfulness of the evil, compelling him to reason that " if one died for all, then were all dead." Ruined must that state have been which called for such redemption. Paul stood aghast—sank aghast —at these thoughts. He had supposed himself, as touching the righteousness which is of the law, to be blameless. But under the teaching of the Cross, sin— that is the sense of sin—revived and expanded into such gigantic dimensions, that, at the thought of it, he died : all life of self expired within him ; all personal merit paled and perished in a sense of penal desert. And what was now his relief ? What was now his refuge? That very Cross which had previously so shocked him. Thus the grandeur of the remedy exposed to him the evil of sin; and the evil of sin commended reactively the gloriousness of the gospel. Surely when redemption exposes the evil of rebellion—when the bitterness of the curse is evolved by contrast with curative blessing—when blackness of darkness is discerned only afar off, and as rendered visible by light streaming from heaven and guiding us to its portals, we may well hear such instruction, and hail in it the "Glorious gospel of the blessed God!" II. Paul might characterize the gospel as glorious, viewing it in relation to THE GIFT OF THE SPIRIT. Palestine had had its prophets; and wondrous characters had these teachers been. These prophets might be persecuted while they lived, but monuments were soon erected to them when they died. Hence the disappearance of prophets was more deprecated than their severest reprimands, and lamentation found its climax in saying, "We see not our signs, there is no more any prophet, neither is there among us any that knoweth how long" (Psa. lxxiv. 9). The ancient seers were never numerous. Two or three distinguished a period. But now there is a whole company of apostles, and inspiration is not limited to them. God pours His spirit on all flesh, and sons and daughters prophesy in multitudes. Nor does the privilege terminate with preternatural qualifications. These accompany and promote transforming influences far more precious. "According to His mercy He saved us by the washing of regeneration and the renewing of the Holy Ghost, which He shed on us abundantly through Jesus Christ our Saviour." Now was the fulfilment of the promise: "Behold, the days come, saith the Lord, that I will make a new covenant with the house of Israel, and with the house of Judah. . . . I will put My law in their inward parts and write it in their hearts, and will be their God and they shall be My people." "The law of the Spirit of life in Christ Jesus," Paul says, "hath made me free from the law of sin and death." The apostles exemplified such renewing power. They manifested a spiritual-mindedness before which all grovelling sordidness might well be confounded, and, as ashamed, hide its head. Quit a partial and suspicious discipleship! rise to the heights of a high calling! and still multiply achievements, and still heighten attainments, till your religious profession bear its own proof, and all your aims, and aspirations, and efforts, beam with the glory of the gospel of the blessed God. III. Paul may be supposed to have used the language of the text in relation to A FAVOURED PEOPLE AND A PROMISED LAND. Paul had an enthusiastic patriotism. Even self-love seemed feeble when vying with love to his people (Rom. ix. 1–3). With such fervency of affection for his countrymen, Paul beheld and deplored their imperilled condition. The Roman tyranny was becoming every year more intolerable, and defeated insurrections only riveted and aggravated its domination. To what would these things grow? The question was inevitable and ominous; and, whatever desire might answer, probability, verging on certainty, pointed to the extinction of the Jewish name and nation. What was his joy, then, when an occasion of dismay became a source of solace, when spiritual illumination pointed beyond impending ruin to eventual recovery, and foretold the time when all Israel should be saved. Yet another and more cheering aspect of the case now burst upon his contemplation. The promise, that in Abraham and his seed should all families of the earth be blessed, was apprehended by him in its vastness. His survey, restricted before to the literal Israel, suddenly compassed the world, and embraced in all nations the true Israel of God. (*D. King, LL.D.*) *The beatific God: the gospel a transcript of the character of God:*—The only security at any time either for sound doctrine or earnest moral practice is the gospel. The fallacy with which the apostle contended is found operating in every time. Many would apparently make a divorce in their own minds between the moralities of every day life and the gospel—between works and faith. Because man is an intelligent being and must have a clear notion of what he is doing, if he is to act worthy of his nature, his conduct must be regulated by principle, and especially his moral conduct by a clear understanding of God's will. What, then, is the will of God? It is the system of truth revealed in the Scriptures; in other words, it is orthodoxy. Of course there must be an orthodoxy, or system of right doctrine. I. GOD IS BLESSED IN HIMSELF, AND THEREFORE HE HAS GIVEN A GOSPEL TO MAN. The epithet blessed, as applied to God, is one of singular grandeur and felicity. In the highest and richest sense of the word, God is the happy or beatific God. God is blessed in Himself, blessed in the manifestation of Himself, and blessed in the communication to others of His own blessedness. 1. God is blessed in Himself. This is a necessity of His being. To be God is to be infinitely happy; for God is just, good; and to be good is to be blessed. To say that a being is good is to say that he is happy. The purity or holiness of God is one of the fountain-heads of His blessedness. Jesus says, "Blessed are the pure in heart." A pure heart is a well-spring of blessedness; it is a bower of fragrance, and an abode of spiritual beauty. It is a bright sky in which the thoughts sing to each other as birds in the sunny air; it is a home of the Holy Ghost. What, then, must be the blessedness of God! He is the holy heart of the universe; the light of light. God is happy because He is perfect. We have never known what it is to be perfect. From first to last in this life we are imperfect, and it is a painful thing to be imperfect. Not only to be so, but to know it—to have the clear consciousness that we carry imperfection within us ; to feel that there is a discord at the very centre of our life—that surely is a sharp thorn in the heart. To have come to the vision of an ideal life, which we recognize to be our true and proper life, and love as such, while at the same time we are in bondage to a variety of mean restrictions; this is the cause of unhappiness and unrest. But God is the all-perfect One— harmonious, complete, self-sufficient, and therefore He is the blessed God. God is happy because He is almighty. Our weakness is to us a constant source of pain. We think we should be happy if only we had strength for every emergency, and if the arm could always fully second the will. But we live and die with the sorrowful conviction that, however splendid our projects, our performances are mean. With God, however, there is nothing of this. Above all, God is happy because He is the God of Love. The living essence of the Godhead has a name, and that name is Love. This is the one supreme joy of the universe; that great affinity, that beautiful spiritual attraction, which draws all souls together in peace and concord, by drawing them unto God. God is love, and therefore He is happy. This is the reason why God might not, and did not keep His blessedness to Himself. Although He was infinitely blessed in Himself in eternity, before angel, or world, or man appeared, He did not remain the sole possessor of this immense, this uncreated felicity. He decreed to unfold the hidden wealth of eternity ; to manifest Himself, and to bring forth an image of Himself, in the form of an intelligent and moral being, who should be able to reflect His glory and to share His blessedness. Hence creation ; hence the manifested wonders of providence in time ; and hence eternal redemption. And so, having looked for a little at the self-possessed, inherent blessedness of God, let us now glance at—2. God is blessed in the manifestation of Himself. All true work is a pleasure. It is a joy to produce anything. The exercise of power, the facility to act, the creation of a thought, the production of a work of art—each of these manifestations gives pleasure to the person who puts its forth. A child has pleasure in the gradual awakening of its nature, and the first exercise of its faculties. It delights in the discovery and manifestation of its powers, one by one. It delights to be able to walk and to speak. A school-boy, who is a true student, has pleasure first in mastering a problem, and, after that, in exhibiting his mastery over one domain of knowledge after another. A young artizan has pride in the performance of his first piece of independent work, and in earning his first wage. He feels that he is of some worth to the world. In the higher walks of human effort—in the productions of art and literature, the true artist has a pure joy. As the poem, or the picture, or the statue is slowly elaborated, the artist is bringing forth into palpability the fair image that has hitherto dwelt in the ideal world of the soul. There is a blessedness in the manifestation of one's true self. Let these faint analogies remind us of the blessedness of God in the forth-putting of His power. He is the Creator, the Supreme Worker, the one Original Producer. He has brought forth the universe. The universe is God's work. And what a work is that! So vast, so beautiful, so profound! Because God is God it must be a joy to Him to bring forth angels, and worlds, and men; and the proof that God rejoiced in His own creation is to be found in the fact that He Himself blessed it, and called it very good. 3. God is blessed in the communication to others of His own blessedness. He who works a work merely that he may delight himself therewith, even although that work is beautiful and good, has not reached the highest blessedness. This consists in making others blessed. He who lives for himself alone can never know what the highest blessedness is. To seek to shut up happiness in one's own heart is to embitter and destroy it altogether ; for selfishness and blessedness can never keep company. Men are unhappy just in proportion as they are selfish; and consequently God is blessed because He is absolutely unselfish. Even in eternity God was not alone in His blessedness ; for there are three persons in the adorable Godhead, and from eternity there was fellowship in God, and the high interchange of love. The Gospel was an eternal purpose of God. Yea, how marvellous it is that sin has become the very occasion in connection with which

God has revealed the wonders of His grace, and given the highest manifestation of His own happiness and glory. The highest joy of God is the joy of saving souls. It is a blessed thing to communicate happiness to the unfallen, and preserve them in their felicity; but it is more blessed to give joy to the miserable, and open up a way by which the wretched and the impure may return to the very bosom of God. And since these are the tidings; since this is the message of gladness that the gospel brings to every man, how fitly may it be styled the glorious gospel of the blessed God! II. GOD HAS GIVEN A GLORIOUS GOSPEL TO MAN, AND THEREFORE MAN SHOULD BLESS GOD. In the verse from which the text is taken the apostle speaks of the gospel as something committed to his trust. Notice here some of the particulars in respect of which the epithet "glorious" may be applied to the gospel. The gospel is glorious in its own character; in its authorship; in its unfoldings; and in its everlasting issues. 1. It is glorious in its own character. It is the Almighty God proclaiming an amnesty to sinful men. Surely that is a great fact in the history of this universe. What can exceed in glory such a proclamation? 2. The gospel is glorious in its authorship. Everything God has made is glorious in having Him as its author. Throughout the whole of God's workings, everything speaks of His glory. 3. The gospel is glorious in its unfolding. All the other manifestations of God in creation and providence are but introductory and preparatory to this. Creation is but the scaffolding, and providence but the great stairway leading to the gospel. 4. The gospel is glorious in its eternal issues. It is through it alone that we come into the possession of eternal life. What, then, is our response? It is for us to reflect in some measure this glory. It is for us, in turn, to bless the blessed God. We do so, first of all, by believing the gospel—by listening to this message, and accepting it as the truth of God. Can there be anything more awful than for a human being to reject such a gospel? And yet this can be done—this is done every day. What is worthy of the entire and unreserved homage of our being, if the glorious gospel of the blessed God is not worthy of it? In conclusion, there are four warnings that come sounding out to us from this text, to which we would do well to take heed. 1. Beware of ignoring the gospel. This is what many are doing at the present time. They quietly and complacently set it aside. 2. Beware of caricaturing the gospel. It is a caricature of the gospel to represent God as sitting merely on a throne of justice, manifesting only the sternness and severity of the law, and insisting on the law being satisfied at whatever price, and with whatever results. But the gospel has been so caricatured. Its enemies have said that it is a wrathful and vindictive system. 3. Beware of undervaluing the gospel. There are some who regard Christianity as a form of natural religion. 4. Beware of finally rejecting the gospel. (*F. Ferguson.*) *The glorious gospel :*—The gospel!—"the glorious gospel!" whence did it come? Its birth-place was the bosom of God. What its end and aim? To save a world of souls. Whence does it rescue? From the fellowship and destinies of hell. Whither does it lead? Back to its birth-place—to heaven—to God. The single inquiry into the reason and propriety of the epithet here bestowed upon the gospel —"the glorious gospel." Let this then be our point, to prove that the gospel is a "glorious" scheme—a "glorious gospel." "The glorious gospel!" What is it to be "glorious"? Need I define this to you?—need I tell you what it is to be physically, what it is to be morally "glorious"? Who can need that I define to him the term "glorious," as applied to natural things, that has seen the bright orb of heaven shedding abroad his noon-day splendour? Who that has gazed upon the mighty sea, as it careered along, so bold, so free, so wild, gilded but untamed by that bright orb's beams? Or who so lost, I say, not to religion, but to all sense of moral beauty and grandeur, as to see no glory, no dignity, no greatness, in virtue? And the "gospel" is "glorious!" Why? It is "glorious," I observe—I. IN ITS AUTHOR. Think you that even the most presumptuous hope would have whispered, that perhaps the very Being whom he had offended would Himself bear the penalty, that his Judge would perhaps be his Saviour, that grace should flow to him and his race through the blood-shedding of the only begotten Son of God, the Son in the bosom of the Father—God Himself? No, the brain of man devised not the "glorious gospel"—the heart of man conceived it not! II. The gospel was "glorious" IN ITS MEDIATOR. Now this notion that such a free pardon, such a remission of the penalty of guilt, would have been a "glorious" act on God's part, is derived from human analogy, but so far from being a "glorious" act, it would have sullied the brightness of God's glory for ever, for He would have denied Himself, would have appeared before His creation as a Being uttering threatenings which He had no final and real intention of executing. Mercy might have been magnified, but to a woful disparagement of justice and holiness and truth. But "Jesus" is "the Mediator of the new Covenant"—He who is "so much better than the angels"— the Creator and "heir of all things"—the "Beloved Son"—the "very and eternal God!" How "glorious" a gospel flowing through such a mediation! how great the price of its salvation! III. The gospel is "glorious" IN ITS OBJECTS AND RE-SULTS. It is the gospel of salvation, a "gospel of peace." It finds God and man at variance—God offended, man lost. How "glorious" then the object of the gospel—to reconcile God and man—to offer salvation, not to the Jew only, but to all the world—to utter a cry free as the air we breathe: "Ho, every one that thirsteth!" But how "glorious" its results! And these, in all their eternal fulness, who shall tell? But how "glorious" now!—how "glorious" Christ Jesus in the heart, "the hope of glory!"—how "glorious" to see "the Ethiopian change his skin, and the leopard his spots!"—to see the "blasphemer," the "persecutor, and injurious," preach "the faith which once he destroyed!"—how glorious to hear the savage gaoler cry: "What must I do to be saved?" But time shall one day be no longer, and shall the gospel glory be entombed in the grave of time? Rather shall its glorious results then truly begin. IV. The gospel is "glorious" AS CONTRASTED WITH THE LAW. See, then, the glory of the gospel as a scheme of salvation for man, when contrasted with the law. See the law demanding (and that justly) what man cannot render—hear it, as the penalty of non-fulfilment and disobedience, proceed to call for vengeance, the death of the transgressor. See the gospel not only not refusing to recognize man's need, and frailty, as a lost sinner, but taking man up at this very point, the pinching point of his need, that he is a lost sinner. The very object, then, of the gospel is to vindicate God's law, and yet save the transgressor of that law, to exhibit a God all-just as a God all-merciful. But the gospel is more "glorious" yet! for as its only source was the grace of God, as God only "gave His only begotten Son" up to the death, because "He so loved the world," so from first to last is the gospel one of grace, and grace alone. But the gospel is more "glorious" yet! The law, we saw, had no pardon to bestow, no righteousness to give, still less could it restore the fallen nature, renew the alienated heart, or rectify the perverted and biassed will. It could not purify the springs of action. No law does this. But the Spirit of Christ to sanctify, no less than the righteousness of Christ, and the blood-shedding of Christ to justify, is the gift of the gospel. Such is the gospel—so "glorious" to God, so "glorious" to man. (*J. C. Miller, M.A.*)    *The glory of the gospel:*—I. It is "the glorious gospel" BECAUSE IT IS A SYSTEM OF ETERNAL TRUTH, IN WHICH THE MORAL PERFECTIONS OF THE GODHEAD ARE MOST TRANSCENDENTLY DISPLAYED. 1. Now, in reference to this "glorious gospel," we say, that in it all the perfections of the Divine nature are strikingly displayed. 2. But in this "glorious gospel" there is, besides the exhibition of all the perfections of the Godhead, the most striking development of them. For though all the attributes of the Godhead are infinite, yet their manifestation may be varied in an endless diversity of degrees and forms: but in this "glorious gospel" there is the most striking display of the whole. Is love an attribute of the Divine nature? Is justice an attribute of Divine nature? Where do we see it displayed so effectually as in "the glorious gospel of the blessed God"? Is wisdom an attribute of the Divine nature? Where have we such a display of it as in "the glorious gospel of the blessed God"? 3. We must, however, advance a step further: here is the most harmonious exhibition of the perfections of the Godhead. II. It is "the glorious Gospel of the blessed God," BECAUSE IT IS ADMIRABLY ADAPTED TO THE MORAL AND SPIRITUAL NECESSITIES OF MAN. Those necessities are vast and varied; but there is no want that it cannot supply, no guilt that it cannot pardon, no depth of misery that it cannot explore. 1. But when we say that this gospel is adapted to man as an ignorant being, I would remind you that it is so, not merely as adapted to convey to him the truth he should understand, but, by a light directed to the understanding and to the heart, first to instruct the judgment, and then to renovate the soul. There is all the difference in the world between mere intellectual and spiritual light; between that knowledge that may be obtained by the unaided efforts of the human mind, and that which is to be acquired by the teaching of the Spirit of God. The one is as different from the other as the mere picture of a country as it is painted on a map is from the country itself, where, with its hills and dales, and rivers, it stretches itself before your view. 2. It is adapted likewise to man as a guilty being. 3. This gospel is still further adapted to man as a polluted being. 4. It is "the glorious gospel" because it is adapted to man, as a miserable being. Misery and guilt are linked to each other in an unbroken chain; and no man can be the voluntary slave of sin, without, in a proportionate degree, being the victim of wretchedness. 5. This gospel is adapted to man as an immortal being. 6. It is so, in the last place, because it is adapted to man as an impotent being. III. It is "the glorious gospel of the blessed God," because IT IS DESIGNED TO ACHIEVE ULTIMATELY THE MOST IMPORTANT BLESSINGS TO THE WORLD AT LARGE. IV. I must now come to the concluding part of the subject, TO DEDUCE SUCH REMARKS AS ITS NATURE WILL SUGGEST. First, I remind you both of the privileges and the obligations with which you are invested who possess this gospel. Secondly, we infer from this subject how pitiable must be the condition of those inhabitants of the earth to whom this gospel has never been sent! (*T. Adkins*.) *The glorious gospel:*—It seems, as a revelation, so to eclipse every other, that earth with all its wonders grows dim by its side, and the firmament with all its hosts is no longer effulgent with Deity. And this is, we think, what St. Paul in our text designs to assert of the gospel. He speaks as though the carrying that gospel to a land were the furnishing such a revelation of God as must necessarily, even if it did not overcome the unbelief in man, redound immeasurably to the glory of its Author. He will not allow that it could at all depend on the reception which the gospel might meet, whether or not God would be glorified by its publication. Why should it? Suppose that it were to please the Almighty to give some new and striking exhibition of His existence and His majesty to a people that had been indifferent to those previously and uniformly furnished; suppose that on a sudden the vault of heaven were to be spangled with fresh characters, the handwriting of the everliving God, and far outshining in their burning beauty the already magnificent tracery of a thousand constellations; would not God have splendidly shown forth His being and His power—would He not have given such demonstrations of His greatness as must vastly contribute to His own glory, even if the people for whose sake the overspread canopy had been thus gorgeously decked, were to close their eyes against the glittering evidence, or to hearken to infidel philosophers, who should resolve into natural causes, or explain by their boastful astronomy, the mighty phenomenon which announced the immediate agency of the Creator? God is sublimely independent of man; and if He have made a discovery of Himself—His nature—His perfections—He can contemplate that discovery with ineffable complacency, however it may be regarded by His creatures. He does not wait their admiration in order to be assured of its beauty; He does not require their approval, to be confirmed in His delight. We read, that when God rested from the work of this creation, He "saw everything that He had made, and behold, it was very good." He surveyed His own work with unspeakable pleasure; He saw and He knew it to be glorious; and if no anthem of lofty gratulation had ascended to His throne from intelligent creatures, He would have reposed, in majestic contentment, on those vast performances, and have felt Himself so praised in His deeds, that neither angels nor men could break the chorus. And why should not we hold the same in regard of the gospel? Why, if this gospel be an incomparably more brilliant and comprehensible revelation of Himself than could have been made by His coming forth from His inaccessible solitude with a fresh retinue of suns and systems—why should not God regard its publication with ineffable complacency, whether men hear, or whether they forbear? Are we to hold it to be in the power of such creatures as ourselves to prevent, by our infidelity, the accruing of any glory to God, from that into which He may be said to have gathered Himself—which is nothing less than a focus, in which all the Divine attributes meet, or from which they diverge, to irradiate the universe? Oh! we are not thus mighty in evil. We may shut our eyes to a manifestation of God, but this is the utmost that we have in our power. We cannot obscure that manifestation; we cannot despoil it of one atom of its beauty; we cannot make it a jot less worthy or expressive of Godhead. And therefore may it well be supposed, that God would regard the ambassadors of His Son—those who with the cross in their hand hastened to publish to the ignorant the tidings of redemption—as more really and more emphatically the revealers of Himself than all those worlds, gorgeously apparelled, with which His creative skill had peopled infinite space. We may well understand, that as these apostles went from shore to shore, making proclamation, wherever they stood, of the mystery of "God made manifest in the flesh," they would be viewed by Him whose commission they bore as finer witnesses to the stupendous, and the awful, and the majestic, and the beautiful properties of His nature, than stars as they marched in their brightness, or angels as they moved in their purity.   Who, then, can be surprised at the lofty tone which has been assumed by St. Paul, when speaking of the gospel committed to his trust?   But now let us go on to speak of the two separate cases, in order to show you, with greater precision, how this character of the gospel holds good in regard equally with those who are saved and of those who are lost.   Is the gospel, indeed, ever detrimental to the hearer?  and if detrimental, can it still be styled "glorious"?   Yes, the gospel may prove injurious to the hearer, but it cannot prove otherwise than glorious to its Author.   You are not to think that the gospel can be a neutral thing, operating neither for good nor for evil.   There is a self-propagating power in all kinds of evil; and every resistance to God's Spirit, operating through the instrumentality of the Word, makes resistance easier, and facilitates for the future the hearing without obeying.   So that preaching, where it produces no salutary effect, unavoidably hardens the hearer.   But if it be admitted that in various ways men may be actually injured by the gospel, making it the occasion of their own aggravated condemnation, what have we to say to such a result being in any sense or degree glorious to God?   But we are to blame in confining our thoughts to the ends in which man has an immediate concern, in place of extending them to those in which God Himself may be personally interested.   We forget that God has to make provision for the thorough vindication of all His attributes, when He shall bring the human race into judgment, and allot to the several individuals a portion for eternity.   We forget that in all His dealings it must be His own honour to which He has the closest respect, and that this honour may require the appointment and continuance of means of grace, even where those means, in place of effecting conversion, are sure to do nothing but increase condemnation.   For the great point, so far as we can judge, which will have to be made out in respect of every man who perishes hereafter, is the inexcusableness of that man—his being nothing less than his own wilful destroyer; and the making out this, in regard of those condemned for neglecting the salvation provided by Christ, will require that it be abundantly proved that this salvation was offered, yea, pressed on their acceptance.   Think ye that the minister of Christ has nothing to do but to confirm the righteous in their faith, and rouse the careless to repentance?   Indeed it is at these that he is avowedly labouring, but in acting upon man he is acting for God.   He may seem to you to labour in vain, just because those to whom he speaks forsake not their iniquities; but it is not in vain.   He preaches for the day of judgment; he preaches as an evidence of God's forbearance, as a witness against the impenitent—an evidence and a witness which shall be called forth and displayed when the trumpet hath sounded, and the Judge is on His throne.   And St. Paul knew, and felt this.   He knew, and he felt, that when He preached Christ to a people, he was making that people without excuse if they persisted in iniquity, and therefore providing that God should be "glorious" in dealing with them in vengeance.   (*H. Melvill, B.D.*)   *The gospel of the glory of the happy God:*—Two remarks of an expository character will prepare the way for our consideration of this text.   The first is that the proper rendering is that which is given in the Revised Version—"the gospel of the glory," not the "glorious gospel."   The apostle is not telling us what kind of thing the gospel is, but what it is about.   He is dealing not with its quality but with its contents.   It is a gospel which reveals, has to do with, is the manifestation of, the glory of God.   Then the other remark is with reference to the meaning of the word "blessed."   There are two Greek words which are both translated "blessed" in the New Testament.   One of them, the more common, literally means "well spoken of," and points to the action of praise or benediction; describes what a man is when men speak well of him, or what God is when men praise and magnify His name.   But the other word, which is used here, and is only applied to God once more in Scripture, has no reference to the human attribution of blessing and praise to Him, but describes Him altogether apart from what men say of Him, as what He is in Himself, the "blessed," or, as we might almost say, the "happy" God.   I. THE REVELATION OF GOD IN JESUS CHRIST IS THE GLORY OF GOD.   The theme, or contents, or the purpose of the whole gospel, is to set forth and make manifest to men the glory of God.   Now what do we mean by "the glory"?  I think, perhaps, that question may be most simply answered by remembering the definite meaning of the word in the Old Testament.   There it designates, usually, that supernatural and lustrous light which dwelt between the cherubim, the symbol of the presence and of the self-manifestation of God.   So that we may say, in brief, that the glory of God is the sum-total of the light that streams from His self-revelation, considered as being the object of adoration and praise by a world that gazes upon Him. And if this be the notion of the glory of God, is it not a startling contrast which is suggested between the apparent contents and the real substance of that gospel? Suppose a man, for instance, who had no previous knowledge of Christianity, being told that in it he would find the highest revelation of the glory of God. He comes to the Book, and finds that the very heart of it is not about God, but about man; that this revelation of the glory of God is the biography of a man: and more than that, that the larger portion of that biography is the story of the humiliations, and the sufferings, and the death of the man. Would it not strike him as a strange paradox that the history of a man's life was the shining apex of all revelations of the glory of God? And that involves two or three considerations on which I dwell briefly. One of them is this: Christ, then, is the self-revelation of God. If, when we deal with the story of His life and death, we are dealing simply with the biography of a man, however pure, lofty, inspired he may be, then I ask what sort of connection there is between that biography which the four Gospels give us, and what my text says is the substance of the gospel? Brethren! to deliver my text and a hundred other passages of Scripture from the charge of being extravagant nonsense and clear, illogical *non sequiturs*, you must believe that in the Man Christ Jesus " we behold His glory—the glory of the only begotten of the Father." And then, still further, my text suggests that this self-revelation of God in Jesus Christ is the very climax and highest point of all God's revelations to men. I believe that the law of humanity, for ever, in heaven as on earth, is this, the Son is the Revealer of God; and that no loftier—yea, at bottom, no other communication of the Divine nature can be made to man than is made in Jesus Christ. But be that as it may, let me urge upon you this thought, that in that wondrous story of the life and death of our Lord Jesus Christ the very high-water mark of Divine self-communication has been touched and reached. All the energies of the Divine nature are embodied there. The " riches, both of the wisdom and of the knowledge of God," are in the Cross and Passion of our Saviour. Or, to put it into other words, and avail oneself of an illustration, we know the old story of the queen who, for the love of an unworthy human heart, dissolved pearls in the cup and gave them to him to drink. We may say that God comes to us, and for the love of us, reprobate and unworthy, has melted all the jewels of His nature into that cup of blessing which He offers, to us, saying: " Drink ye all of it." And my text implies, still further, that the true living, flashing centre of the glory of God is the love of God. Christendom is more than half heathen yet, and it betrays its heathenism not least in its vulgar conceptions of the Divine nature and its glory. The majestic attributes which separate God from man, and make Him unlike His creatures, are the ones which people too often fancy belong to the glorious side of His character. Of power that weak Man hanging on the cross is a strange embodiment; but if we learn that there is something more godlike in God than power, then we can say, as we look upon Jesus Christ: " Lo! this is our God. We have waited for Him, and He will save us." Not in the wisdom that knows no growth, not in the knowledge which has no border-land of ignorance ringing it round about, not in the unwearied might of His arm, not in the exhaustless energy of His being, not in the unslumbering watchfulness of His all-seeing eye, not in that awful Presence wheresoever creatures are, not in any or in all of these lies the glory of God, but in His love. These are the fringes of the brightness; this is the central blaze. The gospel is the gospel of the glory of God, because it is all summed up in the one word—" God so loved the world that He gave his only begotten Son." II. THE REVELATION OF GOD IN CHRIST IS THE BLESSEDNESS OF GOD. And so I would say, the philosopher's God may be all-sufficient and unemotional, the Bible's God " delighteth in mercy," rejoiceth in His gifts, and is glad when men accept them. But there is a great deal more than that here, if not in the word itself, at least in its connection, which connection seems to suggest that howsoever the Divine nature must be supposed to be blessed in its own absolute and boundless perfectness, an element in the blessedness of God Himself arises from His self-communication through the gospel to the world. All love delights in imparting. Why should not God's? He created a universe because He delights in His works and in having creatures on whom He can lavish Himself. The blessed God is blessed because He is God. But He is blessed too because He [is the loving and therefore the giving God. III. THE REVELATION OF GOD IN CHRIST IS GOOD NEWS FOR US ALL. It means this: here are we like men shut up in a beleaguered city, hopeless, helpless, with no power to break out or to raise the siege; provisions failing, death certain. Some of you older men and women remember how that was the case in that awful siege of Paris, in the Franco-German War, and what expedients were adopted in order to get some communication from without. And here to us, prisoned, comes, as it did to them, a despatch borne under a Dove's wing, and the message is this: God is love; and that you may know that He is, He has sent you His Son who died on the cross, the sacrifice for a world's sin. Believe it and trust it, and all your transgressions will pass away. Is not that good news? Is it not the good news that you need—the news of a Father, of pardon, of hope, of love, of strength, of heaven? (*A. Maclaren, D.D.*)    *The gospel, glad tidings:*—Show what the gospel of Christ is, by illustrating the description given of it in our text. 1. The gospel of Christ is "tidings." This is the most simple and proper conception we can form of it. It is not an abstract truth, it is not a merely speculative proposition, it is not an abstruse system of philosophy or ethics, which reason might have discovered or formed; but it is simply tidings, a message, a report, as the prophet styles it, announcing to us important intelligence, intelligence of a connected succession of facts; of facts which reason could never have discovered; intelligence of what was devised in the counsels of eternity for the redemption of our ruined race, of what has since been done in time to effect it, and of what will be done hereafter for its full completion when time shall be no more. It is true, that, in addition to these tidings, the gospel of Christ contains a system of doctrines, of precepts and of motives; but it is no less true, that all these doctrines, precepts and motives are founded upon the facts, communicated by those tidings in which the gospel essentially consists; and that to their connection with these facts, they owe all their influence and importance. Perfectly agreeable to this representation, is the account given us of the primitive preachers, and their mode of preaching the gospel. They acted like men who felt that they were sent, not so much to dispute and argue, as to proclaim tidings, to bear testimony to facts. 2. The tidings which constitute the gospel of Christ are glad tidings; tidings which are designed and perfectly adapted to excite joy and gladness in all who receive them. That they are so, is abundantly evident from the nature of the intelligence which they communicate. They are tidings of an all-sufficient Saviour for the self-destroyed. And must I prove that these are glad tidings? Does the sun shine? are circles round? is happiness desirable? is pain disagreeable? And is it not equally evident, that the tidings we are describing are glad tidings of great joy. But it may in some cases be necessary to prove even self-evident truths. To the blind it may be necessary to prove that the sun shines. And in a spiritual sense we are blind. We need arguments to convince us, that the Sun of righteousness is a bright and glorious luminary; that the tidings of His rising upon a dark world are joyful tidings. Such arguments it is easy to adduce, arguments sufficient to produce conviction even in the blind. If you wish for such arguments, go and seek them among the heathen, who never heard of the gospel of Christ. See those dark places of the earth, filled not only with the habitations, but with the temples of lust and cruelty. Enter into conversation with the inhabitants of these gloomy regions. Ask them who made the world; they cannot tell. Who created themselves? they know not. Ask them where happiness is to be found, they scarcely know its name. Ask for what purpose they were created, they are at a loss for a reply. They know neither whence they came, nor whither they are to go. View them in the night of affliction. No star of Bethlehem, with mild lustre, cheers or softens its gloom. If this be not sufficient, if you still doubt, go and contemplate the effect which these tidings have produced wherever they have been believed. We judge of the nature of a cause by the effects which it produces, and, therefore, if the reception of the gospel has always occasioned joy and gladness, we may justly infer that it is glad tidings. And has it not done this? What supported our trembling first parents, when sinking under the weight of their Maker's curse, and contemplating with shuddering horrors the bottomless abyss into which they had plunged themselves and their wretched offspring? What enabled Enoch to walk with God? Here the well-spring of salvation was first opened to the view of mortals; here the waters of life, which now flow broad and deep as a river, first bubbled up in the sandy desert; and thousands now in heaven stooped and drank and live for ever, tasting the joys of heaven on earth. Then pause and say, whether the tidings which excite all this joy are not glad tidings? Have patriarchs and prophets been deceived? Were the apostles and primitive Christians mad? Are the angels of light infatuated or blind? Is the all-wise God in an error?

Does He call upon all His creatures to rejoice, when no cause of joy exists? You must either assert this, or acknowledge that the gospel of Christ is glad tidings of great joy. 3. The gospel is not only glad tidings, but glorious glad tidings. That it is so, is asserted in other passages, as well as in our text. St. Paul, contrasting the gospel and the law, with a view to show the superiority of the former, observes that if the ministration of death was glorious, the ministration of the Spirit must be still more glorious; for if the ministration of condemnation be glory, much more doth the ministration of righteousness exceed in glory. Glory is the display of excellence, or perfection. That the gospel contains a grand display of the moral excellences and perfections of Jehovah, will be denied by none but the spiritually blind, who are ignorant of its nature. If any doubt respecting the character of the gospel still exists in your minds, it must surely vanish when you recollect that it is—4. The gospel of God, of the blessed God. What that is not glorious can proceed from the God of glory? What that is not calculated to give joy to all holy beings, can proceed from the God of happiness and peace? II. CONSIDER ITS HUMAN ADMINISTRATION. It was committed, says the apostle, to my trust. But why? I answer, the gospel was no more designed to remain locked up in the breast of its author, than the rays of light were intended to remain in the body of the sun. In condescension to our weakness, therefore, God has been pleased to commit the gospel to individuals selected from our ruined race; individuals, who, having experienced its life-giving and beatifying power, are prepared to recommend it to their perishing fellow sinners. Of these individuals, the first to whom it was committed were the apostles; it was committed to them as a proclamation is committed by earthly princes to their heralds, not to be retained, but communicated. (*E. Payson.*) *The glorious gospel:*—I. THE MANIFESTATION WHICH THE GOSPEL GIVES OF THE GLORY OF GOD. There are many sources whence we may derive some faint glimpses of the Divine glory. We may see it in the world around us, wherever we cast our eyes. This, then, we take it, is the glory of God; the revelation of His mercy and grace to sinful man. And this revelation is only to be found fully developed in "the glorious gospel of the blessed God." Here we see the attributes of Deity brought out with surpassing and undimmed lustre. Do we speak of Deity as the only wise God? We see this attribute also strikingly brought out in "the glorious gospel of the blessed God." Wisdom consists in the employment of the best means for the best ends; and although evident traces of this attribute are scattered all around us in the fitness of things to the manifest design contemplated, it is in the gospel alone that we discover the mightiest effort of Divine wisdom. II. THE COMPREHENSIVENESS OF ITS BLESSINGS. In this point of view, also, we shall see significantly brought out the truth of the text, that it is "the glorious gospel of the blessed God." The blessings of the gospel are calculated to meet all the wants and longings of man as a pilgrim destined for eternity. Here knowledge is offered, which, while it is worthy of the highest intellect to expend its gifted powers in boundless research, is also adapted to the meanest capacity; here is knowledge far superior to any that the philosophers of Greece ever taught, or the proud sons of Rome ever knew; here is knowledge which can penetrate with its illuminating influences the innermost darkness of the understanding, refine the affections, purify the heart, and regulate the life of man in his upward aspirations for heaven. Do you feel yourselves guilty before God? In the gospel you may learn the way to obtain redemption through the blood of Christ, even the forgiveness of sins. But more than this: the gospel offers the cleansing and renewing influences of the sanctifying spirit. It belongs to the glorious gospel alone to afford substantial and enduring joy. III. THE MAGNITUDE OF ITS TRIUMPHS. The triumphs of the gospel were soon made manifest, even in the earliest days of Christianity. IV. THE SIMPLICITY OF ITS REQUIREMENTS. Now the grand scheme of the gospel presents us with many things inscrutable to our understandings, which things, like the angels, we "desire to look into" (1 Pet. i. 12); but what affects us much more than all is, the simplicity of the means by which the most mighty and blessed results are accomplished. In this simplicity of arrangement, so available by all, the glory of the gospel shines conspicuously and pre-eminently forth. Herein we discover the master-wisdom of the great Contriver, and are led to ascribe "glory to God in the highest." (*W. J. Brock, B.A.*) *The happiness of God:*—I. I will consider WHAT WE ARE TO UNDERSTAND BY THE BLESSEDNESS OR HAPPINESS OF GOD, AND WHAT ARE THE ESSENTIAL INGREDIENTS OF IT. 1. Perfect knowledge, to understand what it is that constitutes happiness, and to know when one is really possessed of it. For as he is not happy, who is so only in imagination or a dream, without any real foundation in the thing ; for he may be pleased with his condition, and yet be far enough from being truly happy : so, on the other hand, he that has all other necessary ingredients of happiness, and only wants this, that he doth not think himself so, cannot be happy. 2. To perfect happiness is likewise required a full power to do whatever conduceth to happiness, and likewise to check and control whatever would be a hindrance and disturbance to it ; and therefore no being is as happy as it can be, that is not all-sufficient, and hath not within its power and reach whatever is necessary to a happy condition, and necessary to secure and continue that happiness against all attempts and accidents whatsoever. 3. There is wisdom also required to direct this power, and manage it in such a manner, as it may effectually conduce to this end ; and this is very different from mere power abstractedly considered ; for one may have all the materials of happiness, and yet want the wisdom and skill to put them so together, as to frame a happy condition out of them ; and he is not happy, who doth not thoroughly understand the proper method and means of compassing and securing his own happiness. 4. Another most considerable and essential ingredient of happiness is goodness ; without which, as there can be no true majesty and greatness, so neither can there be any felicity or happiness. 5. Perfect happiness doth imply the exercise of all other virtues, which are suitable to so perfect a Being, upon all proper and fitting occasions ; that is, that so perfect a Being do nothing that is contrary to or unbecoming His holiness and righteousness, His truth and faithfulness, which are essential to a perfect Being. 6. Perfect happiness implies in it the settled and secure possession of all those excellences and perfections ; for if any of these were liable to fail, or be diminished, so much would be taken off from perfect and complete happiness. 7. In the last place, infinite contentment and satisfaction, pleasure and delight, which is the very essence of happiness. II. I propose, to show, THAT THIS ATTRIBUTE OF PERFECTION DOTH BELONG TO GOD, AND THAT THE DIVINE NATURE IS PERFECTLY BLESSED AND HAPPY ; and this is so universal an acknowledgment of natural light, that it would be a very superfluous and impertinent work to trouble you with particular citations of heathen authors to this purpose ; nothing being more frequent in them than to call the Deity, " the most happy and most perfect Being," and therefore happy, because felicity doth naturally result from perfection. It shall suffice to take notice of these two things out of heathen writers, to my present purpose. 1. That they accounted happiness so essential to the notion of a God, that this was one of the ways which they took to find out what properties were fit to attribute to God, and what not ; to consider, what things are consistent with happiness, or inconsistent with it. 2. Whatever differences there were among the philosophers concerning the perfections of the Divine nature, they all agreed in the perfect felicity of it ; even Epicurus himself, who so boldly attempted to strip the Divine nature of most of its perfections, by denying that God either made or governed the world ; whereby he took away at once His being the first cause and original of all things, and His goodness likewise, and wisdom, and power, and justice, or, at least, made all these useless, by taking away all occasion and opportunity for the exercise of them ; yet this man does frequently own, and profess to believe, the happiness of the Divine nature. For thus Lucretius, the great disciple of Epicurus, describes his opinion of the Divine nature :—"It is necessary that the Divine nature should be happy, and therefore altogether unconcerned in our affairs ; free from all grief and danger, sufficient for itself, and standing in need of nobody, neither pleased with our good actions, nor provoked by our faults." This was a very false notion both of God and happiness, to imagine that the care of the world should be a pain and disturbance to infinite knowledge, and power, and goodness. III. HOW FAR CREATURES ARE CAPABLE OF HAPPINESS, AND BY WHAT WAYS AND MEANS THEY MAY BE MADE PARTAKERS OF IT. As we are creatures of a finite power, and limited understandings, and a mutable nature, we do necessarily want many of those perfections, which are the cause and ingredients of a perfect happiness. We are far from being sufficient for our own happiness ; we are neither so of ourselves, nor can we make ourselves so by our own power ; for neither are we wise enough for our own satisfaction. All the happiness that we are capable of is, by communication from Him, who is the original and fountain of it. So that, though our happiness depend upon another, yet if we be careful to qualify ourselves for it (and God is always ready to assist us by His grace to this purpose), it is really and in effect in our own power ; and we are every whit as safe and happy in God's care and protection of us, as if we were sufficient for ourselves. But to what purpose, may some say, is this long description and discourse of happiness? How are we the wiser and the better for it? I answer, very much, in several respects. 1. This plainly shews us that atheism is a very melancholy and mischievous thing; it would take away the fountain of happiness, and the only perfect pattern of it. 2. If the Divine nature be so infinitely and completely happy, this is a very great confirmation of our faith and hope concerning the happiness of another life, which the Scripture describes to us, by the sight and enjoyment of God. So that the goodness of God is the great foundation of all our hopes, and the firmest ground of our assurance of a blessed immortality. 3. From what hath been said concerning the happiness of the Divine nature, we may learn wherein our happiness must consist; namely, in the image and in the favour of God: in the favour of God, as the cause of our happiness; and in the image of God, as a necessary inward disposition and qualification for it. All men naturally desire happiness, and seek after it, and are, as they think, travelling towards it, but generally they mistake their way. In a word, if ever we would be happy we must be like " the blessed God," we must be holy, and merciful, and good, and just, as He is, and then we are secure of His favour; "the righteous Lord loveth righteousness, and His countenance will behold the upright." (*Archbishop Tillotson.*) *The happiness of the eternal mind :*—The word here translated *blessed* is the same that occurs in the beautitudes, signifying *happy*, and is to be distinguished from another word, also translated blessed, but signifying to be blessed or adored. This phrase " the happy God " stands out in bright contrast with the dark dream of Asia, that there were two gods—one good, one evil—Ormuzd and Ahriman, against which Jewish religion had witnessed from the beginning. The Jewish faith was distinguished from all other ancient beliefs by maintaining the unity and blessedness of the King Eternal, and by asserting the recent origin, the reptile quality, and the final destiny of evil. I. Let us, then, observe THAT OUR OWN SOULS, IN THEIR PROFOUNDEST INSTINCTS, COMPEL THE BELIEF IN THE HAPPINESS OF THE ETERNAL MIND. Our minds revolt at once at the idea of a miserable everlasting cause. We cannot steadily conceive of an everlasting and boundless power otherwise than as resting on its own ocean depths in unfathomable bliss. We cannot even imagine it as suffering eternally, whether from weakness, or weariness, or pain, disappointment, or malignity, or through sympathy with everlasting misery of created beings. The necessity of indestructible being, which supports the eternal life, necessitates its blessed life. The very heathen, as in Homer, always speak and sing of "the happy gods." If we are to follow in our thoughts the instincts of our own nature (and we have no other means of thinking of the boundless life), then it is blessed for ever. For life here—its product—in all its orderly states is identical with enjoyment. It is disorder alone which produces misery. Think of the life on this planet, from its lowest to its highest ranges, from the dance of animalculæ seen in the magnified drop of water up to the pleasures of the highest races that frequent the atmosphere, the land, the ocean. To breathe the pure air, to drink in the pleasant sunlight, to seek for and enjoy each its proper food, is the law of life, for if their life is short they have no sense of its shortness, and while it lasts it supplies the pleasures of motion, of rest, of vision, of action, and of love. For mankind there opens a new world of delights. Words fail us to describe the heights and depths of human enjoyment. What must that blessed existence be as a life of thought! To us thought is one of the chief and steadiest sources of enjoyment even amidst all our darkness, and deficiency of light, and baffled inquiries, and unsatisfied longings for intelligence. But what must be the delights of that infinite intellect, the energy, the reach, and the force of that Spirit, whence have sprung all the worlds, all the sciences, and all the minds in the universe. What must be that life of inexhaustible power in design, radiant within all the archetypes of beauty in form and colour, the mind in which have dwelt for eternity the patterns of all loveliness in earth and heaven; in which have bloomed the floral splendours of all the worlds; all the lovelinesses of figure, and form, and face, and scenery in earth, and sky, and air, and in the heaven of heavens? What, again, must be that life of creative energy from whose eternal love of life-giving have sprung all the delights of parental and life-giving love through the creation? What ideas can man form of the intrinsic and eternal blessedness of God before and apart from the creation? In that past creationless eternity, the Son, we are told, "was in the bosom of the Father"; He " had a glory with the Father or ever the world was." And in Him were gathered up all the thoughts and purposes of God as to creation, moral government, and redemption (John xvii. 5-24). This gives a ledge of solid ground for one further step upward in our thought. In the past eternity the self-existing wisdom and power revolved the whole infinite future of His manifestation to an everlasting universe, including the redemption of man, the incarnation of the Word; and this eternal counsel of love was the outcome of the holy and loving blessedness of the Sun of spirits. For God is love. He was never alone in eternity. II. LET THIS SAME TEMPER APPEAR IN OUR WORSHIP. Let us "sing unto the Lord." (*E. White.*) *The glorious gospel:*—I. THE IMPORT OF THE GOSPEL AS HERE CONVEYED. You are all doubtless aware that the true meaning of the word gospel is glad tidings, or good news. The gospel tells us of the grace and love of the Father, of the condescension and sacrifice of the Son, and of the mission and influence of the Holy Ghost. "God so loved the world that He gave His only begotten Son," &c. This is good news for all men, and this is the gospel. We all like to hear glad tidings. The intelligence of the relief of Lucknow and the salvation of our countrywomen and children sent a thrill of joy and gratitude throughout the country—it was good news. But no tidings ever proclaimed to men can equal in sublimity, and joyousness, and importance, the good news of the gospel. 1. The gospel is good tidings to man as a rational and intelligent being. The possession of a thinking soul is the distinction and glory of man, and knowledge is necessary for the welfare of his soul. The desire for knowledge under various modifications is one of the natural desires of the human heart. Nowhere is there such a treasury of the highest knowledge for man as in the gospel of Jesus Christ. On the loftiest and most important themes it yields the surest information—the only information which can fill and satisfy the human soul; throwing the purest light on the pilgrimage of man; unfolding his dignity, his duty, and his danger; dispelling doubts, dissipating darkness, and offering certainty on questions about which men have perplexed themselves in vain. 2. Further, the gospel is good news to man as a moral and sinful being. Man is a moral being, and everywhere gives evidence of the possession of a moral nature. In all countries, amongst all peoples there are moral judgments, distinctions between right and wrong, or between what it believed to be right and wrong. The presence of conscience is universal. It is a sad and solemn truth that man is a sinner, and that he is guilty. But the gospel brings good news to him. It tells him of a Divine provision by which he may be pardoned and saved. It tells him of a sacrifice which has been offered for sin—a sacrifice of boundless value, which has met all the requirements of righteousness, and laid the foundation for mercy. How glorious the news for a guilty soul! And this is not all. Man, as a sinner, is not only guilty, but polluted, more or less, under the power of sin. How shall he be purified from this pollution, rescued from this dominion? The same gospel that tells him of pardon, tells him also of purity. "The blood of Jesus Christ cleanseth from all sin." And further—3. It is good news to man as a social and a suffering being. Man's life here is, more or less, in company with others, a pilgrimage of sorrow. He is born to trouble. And perhaps sometimes you are perplexed, and strange thoughts come into your mind, so that you call the proud happy, and the wealthy blessed, and wonder what kind of a Being it is that governs the world with such apparent inequality. Is this world left to chance, or left to the sport of fiends? The gospel comes to our relief, and tells us that an Almighty Father governs all; that He numbers the very hairs of our heads, and that not even a sparrow can fall to the ground without His permission. It tell us that now we are in a state of probation and discipline, and provides the richest consolation, with the assurance that God is too wise to err, and too good to be unkind. 4. The gospel is glad tidings to man as a dying and immortal being—dying, and yet immortal. Yes, both. It is the gospel only,—not philosophy, not reason, not infidelity, not atheism,—but the gospel of Christ alone that can teach us to say and sing, "O Death, where is thy sting? O Grave, where is thy victory?" II. THE CHARACTER OF THE GOSPEL AS HERE GIVEN. It is glorious—"the glorious gospel." Few descriptive terms are more commonly used, and yet, perhaps, none more difficult of exact definition than "glorious." There are many kinds of glory recognized and spoken of in the world, and many things called glorious. There is regal glory, military glory, political glory, intellectual glory. We speak of a glorious day, a glorious scene, a glorious achievement, a glorious victory. It is expressive of lustre, excellence, and beauty. Glory belongs to God; and that which belongs to Him or comes from Him is alone truly glorious. Nowhere has the word so fitting and true an application as in reference to the gospel of God. It is the expression to us of the supremacy, greatness, and moral excellence and perfection of the Almighty Father, and is especially glorious in two respects: as a revelation, and as a remedy.

1. The gospel is glorious as a revelation. It makes known to us, what we nowhere else can learn, the loftiest truths connected with the character of God, and with our relationship to Him. It is the highest revelation of God, and of His law, of His government, and grace. Nature speaks of Him, and providence speaks of Him, but it is the gospel only that fully unfolds His moral character—reveals His grace. There, too, we see— as nowhere else can be seen—the value of man's soul, the terrible act of sin, the majesty of moral law, and the glory that may yet be ours. By the revelation of such momentous truths, the gospel may well be designated " glorious." But it is not only in the truths revealed, but in the manner and mode of the revelation that the gospel is especially glorious. "God, who at sundry times, and in divers manners, spake in times past unto the fathers by the prophets, hath in these last days spoken unto us by His Son." It is not a mere proclamation from heaven, nor a Divine theory, nor a set of holy doctrines, but a revelation of facts—facts the most wonderful and glorious in the world's history. It is this especially that constitutes the distinction and grandeur of the gospel. " Great is the mystery of godliness, God was manifested in the flesh." The full and final revelation is in Jesus Christ, in what He was, and what He did. To rest on His love, to trust His righteousness, to look up into His radiant countenance, is to see the glory of the gospel. 2. The gospel is glorious as a remedy. It is a remedy, perfect and sufficient for human care and crime, for sin, and wretchedness, and death. We have seen that something is wrong with humanity ; for there is everywhere the consciousness of evil and guilt. The gospel of God meets that which is wrong and sets it right. It is a perfect remedy, never-failing if fairly tried. In its universality, its adaptation and its efficacy, we see its glory. That gospel is, indeed, a glorious remedy for all, good news to the thoughtless, the outcast, the prodigal, the penitent. It contains within itself the test of its truth, its adaptation, and its power. Try it. III. THE DESIGN OF THE GOSPEL IS HERE INFERRED. It is " the glorious gospel of the blessed God." The word that is rendered blessed, might perhaps be more familiarly rendered happy, for that is its meaning. The good news about Jesus as the Saviour, and the Friend of sinners, is from the blessed, the happy God. God is infinitely happy ; nothing can disturb His serenity, or interfere with His enjoyment, or hinder His pleasure. But happiness is eminently diffusive. A cheerful, happy man will soon make his presence felt in any company; if we may so say, he cannot help it; his influence will be from the outgoing of his own nature. Thus the gospel is to us the expression of God's blessedness, and His provision for the happiness of His sinful creatures. We learn, then, that its design in reference to men is to make them happy—truly, eternally happy. Oh ! that they would believe this and turn to the gospel of God as to the fountain and means of solid, durable enjoyment. Happiness, true, abiding happiness, can only be found in the glorious gospel of the blessed God. Would you then be happy, happy in your souls, and in your homes, in your daily toil, and duty, happy even when you have to pass through scenes of sorrow, and when the shades of death fall upon you? Accept the good news of the gospel. No intelligence can affect you, except it is believed. The best earthly tidings will neither sadden nor elevate if you do not credit them. So every man must receive God's message, and believe the gospel for himself if he would feel its preciousness, and realize its power. (*J. Spence, D.D.*) *The pre-eminent glory of the gospel*:—I had a great affection for Algernon Wells, and I now distinctly call to mind that blended pathos and humour which gave an exquisite charm to his unaffected manly character. He had, like Thomas Aquinas, " the gift of tears," and was apt to weep on public occasions when his heart was touched, or his carefully finished plans were interrupted; but he had a fund of humour in conversation, and could pour forth sunny smiles and hearty, healthy laughs, such as I do not think often irradiated and warmed the countenance of the angelic doctor. His death was like his life, full of faith and love and joy; and when his end was drawing nearer than he apprehended, he said to Dr. Burder: "My dear friend, if it please God, I hope to be able to preach as I have never yet done. Not that I reproach myself with having concealed or forgotten it. No, but more than ever I would fain speak of it as I have thought and felt here. I would make it the first thing, the pre-eminent. All gathered knowledge, all history, all poetry, all pleasant thoughts and happy things—all that I have, and am, and know, and think, shall range round and illustrate, but be subordinate to this the glorious gospel ! The more I think of it in my long and quiet ponderings, the more precious and needful it becomes to me !" (*J. Stoughton, D.D.*)

Ver. 12. **Putting me into the ministry.**—*The summons to service:*—I. IT WAS A
SIGN OF DIVINE GRACE. In God's abounding grace he found himself not only
forgiven, but summoned to service ; "made a chosen vessel" to bear God's treasure
unto the Gentiles. He never ceased to be filled with wonder, that the Lord had
"counted him faithful," or esteemed him to be worthy of trust ; and his highest
ambition was to respond to this gracious confidence. For that is one of the best
results of being trusted—it develops a sense of responsibility, and appeals to all
that is noblest in the nature. Trust your child with some important message, or
duty, and he will be more careful over it than over what is trivial. The apostle was
put in trust of the gospel ; in other words, he was commissioned to make known
God's way of salvation through Christ, and upon him largely rested the responsibility of winning men to God, and then combining them in Christian communities.
A higher work could not be sought for than this, and no ambition is more sacred
and divine than that which prompts one to pray for it. He speaks expressly of
" the ministry "—" the service," as the Revised Version has it—which might vary
in form, but had as its essence the doing of something for Jesus Christ. And those
who have any experience of this service feel that they need the superabounding
grace of God to guide and sustain them in the work to which they have been
Divinely called. The oil from the olive tree must flow to the golden candlestick, or
the light will die out. The well must be fed from heaven, indirectly through many
a hidden channel, or it will soon be exhausted. And of Christ Jesus we may say,
"All my springs are in Thee." In the law we find restraint, in the Christ we find
inspiration. II. But lest it should be thought that there was any natural innate
worthiness of such a trust on Paul's part, he goes on to show that THIS SUMMONS TO
SERVICE CAME TO ONE WHO WAS UTTERLY UNDESERVING. 1. It was like Paul, and
therefore another indication of the authenticity of this Epistle, to call prominent
attention to what he had been before his conversion. Like David he could say,
" My sin is ever before me." The remembrance of past sin with Paul was not a
source of sorrow only, but it was a source of thanksgiving. It was something like
one of those wonderful clouds we see at sunset. At first it looms ominously on the
horizon, as if the blackness of darkness were resting on the distant hill, but at last
the sunlight streams forth, the edges of the cloud become dazzlingly bright, and
soon the whole is suffused with purple, and crimson, and gold ; the dark cloud is
glorified, and we feel the evening would have lost half its beauty if the cloud had
not been there. Paul's description of his previous career is painted in colours black
enough. Let the thought of that infinite love lead you to repentance, lest you be
found at last not only to have disobeyed Divine law, but to have rejected Divine
mercy. 2. It was not with a desire to lessen the enormity of his guilt that
he adds, " I obtained mercy, because I did it ignorantly in unbelief." Paul was a
persecutor, not because he was indifferent to the claims of God, but because in his
ignorance he thought he ought to do many things contrary to the name of Jesus.
III. Finally, it is evident that DIVINE GRACE WHICH GAVE THE CALL AND FORGAVE
THE SINNER, HAD AS ITS SIGNS IN THE HEART OF THE CONVERT—"FAITH AND LOVE."
" The grace of our Lord was exceeding abundant, with faith and love which is in
Christ Jesus "—that is, they found their sphere of action in Christ. It was not
merely that the former persecutor was led to see the transcendent excellence
of Jesus, but such faith in Him, such love towards Him were aroused in his
heart, that the persecutor became the apostle, who said, " The love of Christ
constraineth us." (*A. Rowland, LL.B.*) *Ministers thankful for their office :*—
I. CHRIST FURNISHES MEN FOR THE MINISTRY. This Paul more than intimates in the words of the text. And everywhere in the New Testament,
ministers are represented as the servants and ambassadors of Christ, and as
his peculiar, ascension gifts to the Church. Hence we may justly consider
Christ as forming and qualifying, as well as authorizing, all His own ministers,
in every age of the Church. Thus a good capacity, a good education, and a
good heart, are the noble qualifications which Christ bestows upon those whom
He raises up, and employs in the sacred work of the gospel ministry. II.
REASONS WHY THE MINISTERS OF CHRIST ARE THANKFUL FOR THEIR OFFICE. 1.
The ministerial office bears a favourable aspect upon a life of religion and vital
piety. His duty carries him among lively Christians, among mourning saints and
distressed sinners ; where the beauties of religion, the worth of souls, and the
presence of God, serve to solemnize his mind and to warm his heart with devout
and heavenly affections. Besides all this, the peculiar difficulties which attend his
office yield him a fair opportunity of improving his mind in some of the most

amiable of the Christian graces. 2. The ministers of Christ are thankful for their office because it gives them peculiar advantages to enrich their minds with useful and Divine knowledge. A man might be as great a metaphysician as Locke, as great a philosopher as Newton, as great a naturalist as Solomon, and yet, in point of the noblest knowledge, fall far below the apostle Paul, who understood the deep things of Divine revelation, which alone can explain all the works and ways of the Supreme Being. His business therefore requires him to extend his researches to matters of a higher nature, and of more importance, than those which employ the attention of the sons of science; and so affords him a happy opportunity of feeding his mind with the same glorious truths which angels now desire to look into, and which all holy beings will for ever contemplate, with growing ardour and delight. And this is a good reason why he should be thankful for his office. 3. A greater reason is, that it opens before him the largest sphere of usefulness. It belongs to his office to strengthen the cords of civil society, by condemning vice, by inculcating virtue, and by enforcing the righteous laws of man from the Word of God and the motives of eternity. And it is a part of his duty to attend to the rising hopes of his flock, and instil into their young and tender minds the first principles of virtue and wisdom; which lay the broadest foundation for peace and harmony among families, among societies and larger communities. But his widest sphere of usefulness lies in that Divine authority with which he is invested, to bear the messages of God to men, and teach them those great and important truths by which they may become wise to salvation. By virtue of this authority Paul become so extensively useful in the first age of Christianity. 4. Their work is of such a nature as to carry its own present and future reward with it. The ministers of Christ receive no inconsiderable reward as they go along, before their labours and their lives are ended. REFLECTIONS: 1. The office of the ministry is the most desirable office in the world. " This is a true saying, if a man desire the office of a bishop, he desireth a good work." 2. The ministerial office needs no foreign aid to recommend itself to those who are qualified for it. Some are ready to apprehend that the ministry would soon become vacant if it should once unhappily lose the protection and support of the civil power. 3. The ministerial office is no burden to the people. One, who calls himself a moral philosopher, undertakes to prove in the face of stubborn fact, that the people of Israel were utterly unable to support their expensive priesthood. And many, at this day, seem to have the same opinion concerning the ministers of Christ. 4. The ministers of the gospel ought to give themselves wholly to the duties of their office. 5. The ministers of the gospel should cheerfully submit to that state of self denial, in which the nature of their office requires them to live. 6. Christ has laid His ministers under the most endearing obligations to be faithful in their office. 7. It is a privilege to hear, as well as to preach the gospel. It is a privilege of the Gentiles to hear Paul, as well as a privilege of Paul to preach to the Gentiles. (*N. Emmons, D.D.*) *The attractions of the Christian ministry :*—It was a wise proverb that the king of Israel quoted to a boastful Syrian invader, when he said, "Let not him that girdeth on his harness boast himself as he that putteth it off." Our text is not the boastful exultation of an untried soldier, but rather the calm, joyful expression of the gratitude of a veteran. He had faced the angry eyes of those who at Damascus regarded him as a heretic, because he had seen more light than they. The estimate which a man of such experiences puts upon his vocation, after a trial covering about thirty years, is worthy of careful consideration. Paul was thankful for the privilege of these thirty years in the ministry of God's dear Son. Let us consider some of the attractions of the Christian ministry. It is not forgotten that earnest, scholarly and religious men are needed in all the ministries of human life. We may, perhaps, best set forth our theme by an examination of the grounds of our satisfaction and joy in the ministry of Jesus Christ. I. THE CHARACTERISTICS OF THE GOSPEL. Paul had zeal and joy in his work because he knew he was presenting a religion which is the outcome of—1. A Divine revelation. God has spoken. Paul went forth, not with a Bible, but with the Word of God. 2. A system of Divine power: not a philosophy, a guess, a theory to be entertained ; but a life, a present working of a Divine energy in the soul. 3. The remedial character of the gospel gives zeal and joy to those who preach it. 4. The historic connections of Christianity have given and now give impulse to zeal and joy to those who are set for its defence. This thing was not done in a corner. Christianity is no beggar in the world of thought, asking for recognition, but a system rooted firmly in the soil of human history, and bearing fruits of which its adherents need never speak with hesitation. 5. Its power to satisfy the wants of the human soul. II. THE ATTRACTIONS OF THE WORK ITSELF. 1. Our contact with good men. In religious and charitable work, much of our time is spent in contact and converse with the excellent of the earth. 2. The affectionate regard in which we are held by our people. 3. The opportunity afforded for the growth of character. 4. The opportunities afforded in the ministry for the cultivation of scholarship. III. THE CROWN SET BEFORE US. The work of the Christian ministry is not completed on earth. Allow me to conclude with a few words of fraternal exhortation as to the claims of this work and the kind of men that are required in it. And need I say that, first of all, men are wanted of an unworldly spirit. The spirit that was in Agassiz when he said, "I have no time to make money," is that needed in the ministry of reconciliation. Again, the ministry needed calls for men of good common sense, and a good stock of it. Finally, the times demand in the Christian ministry men of solid learning. (*T. F. Burnham.*)

Ver. 13. **Who was before a blasphemer.**—*I was before:*—Note here, before we come to the special purpose we have in view, that godly men never think or speak lightly of their sins. When they know that they are forgiven, they repent of their iniquities even more heartily than before. You have probably read biographies of John Bunyan, in which the biographer says that Bunyan laboured under a morbid conscientiousness, and accused himself of a degree of sin of which he was not guilty. Exactly so, in the view of the biographer, but not so in the view of John Bunyan, who, startled into sensitiveness of conscience, could not find words strong enough to express all his reprobation of himself. Job said once, "I abhor myself." I. IF WE THINK OF WHAT WE WERE, IT WILL EXCITE IN US ADORING GRATITUDE. Paul was full of gratitude, for he thanked Christ Jesus that He counted him faithful, putting him into the ministry. II. A SENSE OF WHAT WE WERE SHOULD SUSTAIN IN US VERY DEEP HUMILITY. 1 Cor. xv. 9. I have heard of a good man in Germany who used to rescue poor, destitute boys from the streets, and he always had them photographed in their rags and filth, just as he found them; and then, in years afterwards, when they were clothed and washed and educated, and their characters began to develop, if they grew proud he would show them what they were, and try to teach them what they would have been likely to be if it had not been for his charity. If you are inclined to lift up your head, and boast what a great man you are now, just look at the likeness of what you were before the Lord made you a new creature in Christ Jesus. Oh! who can tell what that likeness would have been but for the interpositions of Divine grace? III. THE REMEMBRANCE OF OUR FORMER CONDITION SHOULD RENEW IN US GENUINE REPENTANCE. When you leave off repenting, you have left off living. IV. THE RETROSPECT OF OUR PAST LIVES SHOULD KINDLE IN US FERVENT LOVE to the Lord who has redeemed us. I think there is nothing better than to retain a vivid sense of conversion in order to retain a vivid sense of love. Do not be afraid of loving Christ too much. Oh for more love arising out of a deep, intense sense of what we once were, and of the change which Christ has wrought in us! V. REMEMBERING WHAT WE WERE, ARDENT ZEAL SHOULD BE AROUSED IN US. Look at Paul. He says, "I was before a blasphemer, and a persecutor, and injurious." What then? Why, now that he has become a follower of Christ, he cannot do too much. He put many saints in prison; now he goes into many prisons himself. I remember one who lived four or five miles away from a place of worship, who used to say, "You old legs, it is no use being tired; for you have got to carry me. You used to take me to the place of amusement when I served the devil, and you shall carry me now to the house of God, that I may worship and serve Him." When sometimes he had an uneasy seat, he used to say, "It is no use grumbling, old bones, you will have to sit here, or else you will have to stand. Years ago you put up with all kinds of inconveniences when I went to the theatre, or some other evil place, when I served Satan; and you must be content to do the same now for a better Master and a nobler service." I think some of us might take a lesson from that old man, and say to ourselves, "Come, covetousness, you are not going to hinder me from serving the Lord. I used to be liberal to the devil, and I do not intend now to be stingy to God." VI. If we remember what we were, and how grace has changed us, IT OUGHT TO MAKE US VERY HOPEFUL ABOUT OTHER PEOPLE. VII. WHAT GOD HAS DONE FOR US SHOULD CONFIRM OUR CONFIDENCE FOR OURSELVES—our confidence, not in ourselves, but

in God, who will perfect that which He has begun in us. (*C. H. Spurgeon.*)
*The memory of forgiven sins :*—God's forgiveness is full, free, and thorough.
Yet, forgiving, He does not forget.  God remembers forgiven sins, but He
does not, will not, remember them against us.  We should remember them.
I. The memory of forgiven sins is favourable to humility.  Spiritual pride
is a sin to which the eminently holy, gifted, and useful Christian is peculiarly
liable.    Let the first remember how he formerly defiled himself ; the second,
to what unworthy objects he directed his noble faculties ; the third,
that his pardoned sins may be—probably are—working fatal mischief in
the world ; and where is there room for pride?  How much reason for
self-abasement?  Why did Paul describe himself as "less than the least of all
saints"?  II. The memory of forgiven sins is conducive to watchfulness.
Forgiveness has not destroyed our liability to sin.  Forgiven sins have left weak
places in our souls.  He who keeps in view those remitted sins which had the
strongest hold on his nature, will vigilantly watch against the return of "the
unclean spirit."  III. The memory of forgiven sins is productive of compassion.
We pity sinners.   The unforgiven are the unforgiving, the unmerciful and stony-
hearted.   IV. The memory of forgiven sins awakens gratitude.   We are in
danger of forgetting "all" the Lord's "benefits," but we cannot if we remember
our sins. (*The Homilist.*)         *Transformation of the vilest :*—Mr. Ruskin, in his
"Modern Painters," tells that the black mud or slime from a footpath in the outskirts of a manufacturing town—the absolute type of impurity—is composed of four
elements—clay, mixed with soot, a little sand, and water.  These four may be
separated each from the other.  The clay particles, left to follow their own instinct
of unity, become a clear, hard substance, so set that it can deal with light in a
wonderful way, and gather out of it the loveliest blue rays only, refusing the rest.
We call it then a "sapphire."  The sand arranges itself in mysterious, infinitely
fine parallel lines, which reflect the blue, green, purple, and red rays in the greatest
beauty.  We call it then an "opal."  The soot becomes the hardest thing in the
world, and for the blackness it had obtains the power of reflecting all the rays of
the sun at once in the vividest blaze that any solid thing can shoot.  We call it
then a "diamond."  Last of all, the water becomes a dew-drop, and a crystalline
star of snow.  Thus God can and does transform the vilest sinners into pure and
shining jewels, fit for His home in heaven.      *A wonderful change :*—The following is one of many well-authenticated cases of converted infidels given in the *Anti-
Infidel :*—Walking along a street in the "second city of the empire" a few days
ago, I saluted a middle-aged man dressed in the semi-clerical garb of a mission
preacher, and I rather surprised a friend who was with me by telling him that he
who had just passed us was a converted infidel.  The story of his being "brought
back," as I heard it from his own lips, may not be uninteresting.  Mr. B——, then,
was at one time an avowed atheist, a professed and prominent infidel.  He possesses
a fine intellect ; but, alas! he devoted his talent to the wicked purpose of "proving"
the non-existence of the Divine Giver thereof.  One evening a mock debate was
held among his athiest associates, in which Mr. B—— assumed the part of a
Christian, and towards the close of the discussion said to his opponent, in solemn
tones, "Now, my young friend, when you go home, take and read your Bible for
the truth of what I have stated, and pray for help and guidance!"  This was considered to be a rich bit of sarcasm, and made a "great hit."  Some time after,
Mr. B—— was accosted by the same young man, who, to his surprise, asked him
in real earnestness, "My friend, how about your soul?"  "Oh, don't bother me
with such stuff," replied Mr. B——, impatiently.  "Do you remember that debate
we had?" said the young man.  "Well, I took the advice you gave me then ; I
studied the Scripture, I prayed over it, and I have found peace ; and, oh! my
friend, you cannot do better than take your own advice.  You gave it then to
ridicule the cause you were supposed to be upholding.  Now, I beg of you to think
of it seriously, and it will really do you good."  Mr. B—— did take his own
advice, with the result that he saw the error of his ways, embraced Christianity,
and has been for years zealously preaching that doctrine which he formerly
reviled.

Ver. 14. **And the grace of our Lord.**—*The Saviour's grace in its freeness and
effects :*—I. Consider the grace of our Lord Jesus Christ.  It was this that led
Him to remember you in your low estate ; to interpose on your behalf ; to assume
your nature, and to give His life a ransom for many.  "Surely He hath borne our

grief and carried our sorrow." "Behold, how He loved him!" said the spectators around the grave of Lazarus, when they saw only His tears. Behold, how He loved them! was surely the exclamation of angels, when, at His cross, they beheld His blood. For was He compelled to submit to this undertaking? No. Did we deserve it? "When we were yet without strength, in due time Christ died for the ungodly." In the application, as well as the procuring of our salvation, the grace of the Lord Jesus appears. Means were used; but they derived all their efficacy, and their very being, from Him. But whence sprang this desire? From conviction. What produced this conviction? Reflection. And what produced this reflection? A train of events. And what are events? Providence. And what is Providence? God in action; and God, acting for the welfare of the unworthy, is grace. The progress is equally from the same source. He who quickens us, when dead in trespasses and sins, renews us day by day; and enables us to hold on our way, and wax stronger and stronger. As this laid the foundation, so it will raise the superstructure; and He shall bring forth the top-stone thereof, with shoutings, crying, "Grace, grace unto it!" But, though all are saved by this grace, some individuals seem to be, in a peculiar manner, the trophies of it; and, were it necessary, we could make, even from the records of Scripture, a marvellous selection of instances. Manasseh; the dying thief; the murderers of the Son of God; the Corinthian converts. II. THIS GRACE IS EMINENTLY DISPLAYED IN THE CONVERSION OF PAUL: "And the grace of our Lord," says he, "was exceeding abundant." Never did His heart pity a more undeserving wretch, or His hand undertake a more desperate case. Perhaps, you say, this made the apostle so humble. It did. But humility is not ignorance and folly. Christians are often ridiculed for speaking of themselves in depreciating terms: especially when they call themselves the vilest of the vile, or the chief of sinners. It is admitted and lamented that such language may be insufferable affectation, and is sometimes used by persons who give ample evidence of their not believing it. When show is a substitute for reality, it is generally excessive. III. THIS GRACE IS ALWAYS PRODUCTIVE OF SUITABLE INFLUENCES AND EFFECTS. "In faith and love," says the apostle, "which are in Christ Jesus." 1. Divine grace produces faith. Faith is the belief of the gospel; a firm and lively persuasion of the truth of the record that God has given of His Son, accompanied with acquiescence, dependence, and application. It will lead me to have recourse to Him for all I want. 2. Divine grace will equally produce love. To whom? To the Saviour Himself; His name, His word, His day, His service, His ways. 3. Divine grace will produce both these in the same subjects. Faith, according to the apostle's order of statement, goes before love; for faith precedes everything in religion—it is an original principle; it is the spring from which flow all the streams of pious temper and practice; it is the root from which grow all the fruits of Christian obedience and affection. But love follows after faith. We are told that "faith worketh by love." And how should it be otherwise? Is it possible for me to believe the compassions of the Saviour, and to realize as my own the blessings of His death, and not feel my heart affected? and my gratitude constraining me to embrace Him, and my fellow-Christians, and my fellow-creatures, for His sake? By the latter of these, therefore, you are to evince the reality and genuineness of the former. The subject admonishes Christians. It calls upon you, like Paul, to review the grace of our Lord Jesus Christ. Remember where you were, and what you were, when He said unto you, "Live!" Look unto the rock whence ye are hewn, and to the hole of the pit whence ye are digged. This will prove the destruction of pride and ingratitude. (*W. Jay.*) *The exceeding abundant grace of God:*—It is the most difficult thing in the world for a man to speak in a becoming and consistent manner concerning himself. He speaks of himself very humbly and penitently: "Who was before a blasphemer, and a persecutor, and injurious; but I obtained mercy because I did it ignorantly in unbelief." He speaks also most encouragingly to others : "Howbeit for this cause I obtained mercy, that in me first," or in me principally, "Jesus Christ might show forth all long suffering for a pattern to them which should hereafter believe on Him to life everlasting." I. THE GRACE OF GOD AS THE ONLY SOURCE OF HOPE AND SALVATION TO GUILTY AND APOSTATE MAN. 1. The very terms of this proposition suppose that man is in a guilty and apostate state. The effectuation of that great scheme into which the angels desired to look, the contrivance of infinite mercy, is of grace : "Ye know the grace of our Lord Jesus Christ, who, though He was rich, yet for our sakes became poor, that we through His poverty might become rich." The application of the Divine contrivance for man's recovery is of grace. The Holy Spirit, the third person in the glorious Trinity, stands engaged in the economy and covenant of mercy, to "take of the things of Christ, and show them unto us." The completion of this great and glorious work is of grace. Were we to trace the whole process from the commencement to the perfection of it, it would be seen that in every step the grace of God is manifested to be "exceeding abundant." Now, do consider that this is the only source of hope and salvation for guilty man. Tell me of any other if you are able. Will you talk to me of penances, and pilgrimages, and bodily austerities? II. IN THE CIRCUMSTANCES ATTENDANT UPON THE CONVERSION AND SALVATION OF THE APOSTLE PAUL, THIS GRACE WAS " EXCEEDING ABUNDANT." 1. This will appear, in the first place, if you consider his previous character. He was, before, an impious blasphemer, a treacherous persecutor, an injurious reviler. What does this prove? That where a man is not chargeable with gross immoralities, yet the sins of the mind, the intellect, the temper and disposition of the heart, may stand out in the sight of God in the most odious, the most culpable, and in the most guilty form. 2. In the second place, the grace of God was exceeding abundant towards this apostle, if you consider the period of time at which he thus became the subject of renewing and converting mercy. It was at the very moment when, with impetuous fury, he was proceeding to Damascus under the authority of the high priest to make havoc of the Church of God. 3. In the third place, the exceeding abundant grace of God was conspicuously manifest in the completeness of the change which was produced on his condition and character. It was a very remarkable change, because Paul the disciple presents a contrast so direct, so strong, and so striking, to Saul of Tarsus. Once more, the grace of God was exceeding abundant toward him if you consider the subsequent employment to which he was appointed, the eminent qualifications with which he was endowed, and the great success which attended him in his apostolic career. III. THE CHARACTER TO WHICH THE GRACE OF GOD WILL ALWAYS FORM THOSE WHO ARE THE SUBJECTS OF IT. "With faith and love which is in Christ Jesus." The two grand characteristics of the apostle antecedently to his conversion, were his unbelief and his malignity. Now the character to which he was wrought by the operation of Divine grace on his heart, exhibits an entire contrast to these two characteristic qualities; for you find in him faith taking the place of unbelief, and love taking the place of malevolence; he becomes an entirely changed man, the principles of his whole conduct are completely altered. In closing this subject— 1. It offers hope to the most hopeless; I say hope to the most hopeless, because we have discovered that the grace of God is the spring and the source of man's salvation. 2. Let us examine, pointedly and seriously, whether we know anything of the grace of God which we have seen exemplified in so remarkable and transcendent a degree in the conversion of the apostle Paul. Has this grace reached your heart? 3. What gratitude do we owe for the manifestation of this grace, for the revelation of it to our sinful world? If the sun could be extinguished and blotted out from yonder heavens, it would be a less calamity inflicted on the natural world than if the doctrines of grace were banished from the Christian system. Let us close, therefore, by considering the animating and exhilarating prospect which the grace of God opens beyond the grave. (G. Clayton.) Abundant grace:—Grace and its fruits are, you perceive, the two themes of the apostle's thankfulness, as they should be the two great themes of our thankfulness. I. CONSIDER, IN THE FIRST PLACE, THE GRACE OF OUR LORD, WHICH WAS "EXCEEDING ABUNDANT." If there was one theme on which Paul dwelt oftener, and lingered longer than others, it was this theme of Divine grace. He took pleasure in giving it prominence, and securing for it attention. It was with him a great central truth, from which other truths radiated, and towards which they again converged. It was a seminal truth, a seed out of which other truths sprang and grew. It was a foundation truth, on which he continued to build a structure of strength and holiness and beauty. In this respect, all saints are very much alike. " By grace are ye saved." Grace is one form of Divine love. I say one form, because there are others. God loves Himself. He loves His perfect works—the high intelligencies that surround His throne. But this is a love of complacency. Grace is pity—it is love unconstrained by any governmental necessities—unmerited by any moral qualifications. It is worthy of notice that Paul characterizes the grace of God to himself as " exceeding abundant." He adds one term to another for the purpose of expressing his sense of its freeness and fulness. This is a proper way of speaking. Nothing but grace, nothing but "exceeding abundant " grace, could have moved God to give His only begotten Son for the forgiveness of sins; nothing less than grace, "exceeding abundant" grace, could have converted and saved Isaac the son of faithful Abraham, and Samuel, for whom the devout Hannah prayed, and Solomon, brought up in the house of the man after God's own heart, and Timothy, who had known the Scriptures from a child. However great our religious advantages, or excellent our character, or refined and elevated our tastes, the heart by nature is corrupt, and the life is bad, and nothing short of "exceeding abundant" grace can purify the former and rectify the latter. After all it comes to this, that every Christian finds in his own conversion the most illustrious manifestation of the grace of God. There is another peculiarity in Paul's language which we must not overlook. He speaks of the grace shown in his salvation as "the grace of our Lord." By our Lord he evidently means the Lord Jesus Christ. Elsewhere he attributes his salvation to the Father; he recognizes, also, the sovereign agency of the Holy Spirit; here he refers, in an especial manner, as in other places, to our Lord Jesus Christ. He calls himself "Paul, a servant of Jesus Christ;" he says, "I am crucified with Christ: nevertheless I live; yet not I, but Christ liveth in me: and the life which I now live in the flesh I live by the faith of the Son of God, who loved me, and gave Himself for me." It was Christ who sent him to preach the gospel; and when in prison he was "the prisoner of Jesus Christ"; he could do all things through Christ, who strengthened him; he could say, with truth, "I count all things but loss, for the excellency of the knowledge of Christ Jesus my Lord, for whom I have suffered the loss of all things, and do count them but dung, that I may win Christ." "For me to live is Christ." What a comment all this is on his saying to the Corinthians, "For I am determined not to know anything among you, save Jesus Christ, and Him crucified." The grace of our Lord, towards us and in us, has been "exceeding abundant." II. Now, let us consider THE FRUITS OF GRACE, of which Paul speaks—"Faith and love which is in Christ Jesus." These two elements of Christian character are put, if you will look at the chapter, in opposition to the apostle's previous character. Speaking of himself, in the preceding verse, he says, "I, who was before a blasphemer, a persecutor, and injurious, did it ignorantly in unbelief," but now, instead of unbelief and blasphemy there is simple, yet strong faith, and instead of persecution and injury, there is ardent, self-denying love. Look at the reality and strength of the faith! It overturned all the prejudices of the mind fortified by parental example and early education. It made him bold as a lion in the advocacy of the Redeemer's cause, before the philosophers and monarchs of the age. How ardent and consuming was this man's love. His love to Christ led him to renounce friends and fame; it burned out the old enmity of his heart against Jesus, and filled him with a consuming zeal. It prompted him to undertake the most arduous labours, it enabled him to endure hardships by sea and land, and to brave persecution by his countrymen. It was the great secret of his life and labours. "What mean ye to weep and to break my heart? for I am ready not to be bound only, but also to die at Jerusalem for the name of the Lord Jesus." And to this supreme love to Jesus Christ, there was united a warm affection for His followers, a tender compassion for all mankind. He loved and enkindled love. Such were the fruits of a Divine grace in the apostle Paul, and just in proportion as that grace is in our hearts, will these fruits appear in us. Like causes produce like effects. Let us try ourselves to see whether or not we are partakers of the grace of God in truth. Observe, for a moment, the order in which the apostle places these Christian virtues—faith and love. Faith first, love second. We find this order in other parts of his writings; they are not by chance here—"Faith which worketh by love." "Let us who are of the day be sober, putting on the breastplate of faith and love." You see how natural this order is. The sinner has, first, a believing apprehension of Christ. There can be no real love to Christ, or love to men for His sake, without faith in Him. You may admire His character, but you cannot feel that personal obligation and attachment which He demands. Burke could appreciate to some extent the philanthropic career of Howard; Pollock and Cowper could sing his praises; but how vastly different from their emotions towards the great philanthropist, was the love cherished by the prisoners whose lot he alleviated, and the distressed whose sorrows he removed. Remember this also—If you profess faith, you will show it by love. "Faith which worketh by love." If you desire to know whether you believe in Christ, ascertain this by asking whether you love Christ. Paul mentions only faith and love as the fruits of Divine grace in Him. Not that these were the only fruits produced, but because these are the chief, and where these are found all the others will surely be found with them. The Christian virtues hang together like grapes in clusters. Where you find faith and love you will find also obedience, patience, purity, meekness, and everything that is excellent and of good report. (*W. Walters.*)

Ver. 15. **This is a faithful saying.**—*The gospel in a sentence :*—I. THE MISSION OF THE SON OF GOD is here set forth—He " came into the world." This expression would be an extravagance if it referred only to ordinary human parentage. The pre-existence of our Lord in a higher state was unquestionably an accepted axiom among the early Christians, a commonplace of primitive Christian belief ; and we, believing in His deity, offer Him our lowly adoration as well as our thanks and love. II. THE PURPOSE OF HIS MISSION could not be set forth more clearly and concisely than in the words, He came " to save sinners." His object was not to become the temporal king of the Jewish people, nor yet to give the light of scientific, or philosophical, or even ethical knowledge to the Gentiles ; but to redeem men from the condemnation of the law, and to deliver them from their sins. To reverence Him as a kingly man, or to honour Him as a great teacher only, is but an imperfect acknowledgment of His claims. III. THE EXEMPLIFICATION OF THIS PURPOSE, given by Paul, is drawn from his own experience. He says, respecting himself, of sinners, "I am chief." The word "sinners" is the same as occurs in the ninth verse, where it denotes those for whom the law was a necessity, for rebuke and restraint. Whom the law came to condemn, Jesus came to save. When, under the influence of chloroform, some critical operation is performed, and the patient wakes up to find that it is over, a great feeling of thankfulness rises up in his breast at the whisper, " thank God it has been successful," for he knows that life is saved ; but he would feel still more thankful if he knew what the skilful surgeon does, that there was only a fractional part of an inch in this direction or in that between him and death. Paul knew better than we do what he had been saved from here and hereafter, and his intensity of feeling about sin was an element in his spiritual greatness. May God give us also humbling views of ourselves and adoring thoughts of Him who has saved us ! Conclusion : The truth that Jesus Christ came into the world to save sinners, is " worthy of all acceptation." " It is a faithful saying," worthy of implicit credence, of absolute reliance, for it will not give way though you lean the whole weight of your soul's salvation on it. It is worthy of acceptance by all men. And it is worthy of every kind of acceptation ; worthy of being embraced by every faculty of mind, and heart, and will. You may understand it as a theological doctrine, but that is not enough ; you may love it as a familiar pleasant-sounding phrase, but that is not enough. It deserves the homage of your entire nature. (*A. Rowland, LL.B.*) *The object of Christ's coming into the world :*—The person of the Saviour is to be considered ; and " what think ye of Christ ? " In the text, it is true, He is described by terms especially significant of His mediatorial character and work—He is called " Christ,"—a title of office, significant of the proper designation of the world's Redeemer by the Father, to the distinct and essential offices of Prophet, Priest, and King—the Anointed, the Great Teacher ; and who teacheth like Him ? the anointed High Priest and the great High Priest who hath offered Himself a sacrifice, once for all, in His own body on the tree—and the anointed King in Zion who sits upon His throne, who rules in the midst of the earth—rules for the subjugation of His enemies, and for the protection of His friends ! His advent into our world is here announced. " He came "—but the very language supposes His pre-existence—He necessarily was before He " came " into the world—yes, pre-existing with the Divine Father from everlasting ; for " In the beginning was the Word, and the Word was with God, and the Word was God." He came into our world after He had been promised, in the earlier periods of time, to the patriarchs—and this promise they saw, and this promise they believed, and this promise they embraced, and they died in the faith of the Redeemer that should come. He came into the world after He had been shadowed forth by the various types and symbols which marked the Mosaic Institute ; and at last, " when the fulness of the time was come, God sent forth His Son, made of a woman, made under the law," to redeem them that were under the law. " Christ Jesus came into the world." And what a world, my friends ! Not a world prepared to greet and hail Him as its Lord—not a world prepared to receive and welcome Him, no ! a world of rebels, a world of sinners—a fallen world, a guilty, perishing world, a world that was going down to ruin ; and to ruin it inevitably would have gone, had it not been for the intervention of this high, this almighty Deliverer ! What, then, was His errand in coming into our world ?

When God becomes incarnate there must be some mighty object to achieve—there must be some great end to accomplish to justify such an interposition. To this inquiry the text furnishes the answer, "Christ Jesus came into the world to save sinners." This was the great object. He came to procure salvation for us—He came that He might bestow salvation upon us—the former in order to the latter. Still, however, though our sin is atoned and salvation procured, an unapplied remedy, you know, is of no service. It is not enough that the ransom has been paid; we must be liberated and share the blessings of freedom. If it be true that Christ has come to procure salvation for us, by His meritorious obedience unto death, then is it equally necessary that He should be exalted to bestow it. He saves from the power of sin by the power of grace richly communicated to the heart of the believer—a power that overturns the power of sin! Yes; and "sin shall not have dominion over you," says the apostle; "for ye are not under the law but under grace." He saves from all the condemnation and defilement of sin, by the cleansing virtues of His blood, by the healing power of His grace. Still, however, the salvation of Jesus Christ is not merely a negative thing—it consists not merely in deliverance from the guilt and positive evils to which, by sin, we are exposed. He walks in the light of God's countenance, he derives comfort from the great Fountain of all Consolation; now it is that the Word of God is the rule, now it is that the love of God is the principle, now it is that the glory of God is the grand end of all his actions! But then, we have to leave this world—this is not our home; here we have no continuing place of abode; and we want not only saving while we live, but when we die. The salvation of Jesus is commensurate with all our necessities, it is adequate to all our demands, it contains all that our circumstances require; and He who saves us in life will not abandon us in death! Well do I remember—never, while memory holds her seat, shall I forget—what was spoken to me by the late Mr. Robert Spence, of York. Passing through that city, I had once an opportunity of calling upon that excellent man, who had himself been a preacher of righteousness for more than half a century; and said he, "I thought, ere now, that I would have been at the end of my journey—that ere now I should have arrived at my Father's house; but it has pleased the Heavenly Grace to spare me a little longer, and I feel considerably stronger than I was. But when I came into this room and happened to pass that glass, I caught a sight of myself—I was struck," said the venerable man; "I thought what a little, old, infirm creature I had become—a mere remnant of myself; but instantly," continued he, "I lifted up my heart to the Lord, and I was favoured with such a manifestaton of His grace and love that, though alone"—but he was not alone, for God was with him—"I said, 'Well, welcome, old man! welcome, infirmity! welcome, death! and welcome, heaven!'" Yes; and the religion of Jesus can make him rejoice in the midst of affliction, and welcome infirmity, welcome old age, and welcome death; because death, to the Christian, is but the gate of life. Then, though the body go down to mingle with the clods of the valley, the ransomed spirit wings its etherial flight to the regions of eternal day! The body, too, is to be saved! One said to me lately, "Oh, never mind the body!" but Jesus Christ remembers the body. He is the Saviour of the body as well as of the soul; and we look for Him in this way; we look for Him that He may "change our vile bodies and fashion them like to His own glorious body, according to the working of that mighty power whereby He is able to subdue all things unto Himself." II. WHAT IS THE LIGHT IN WHICH MANKIND OUGHT TO REGARD THIS SAYING? First, as "a true saying"; and then, as "worthy of all acceptation." Let it be remarked, then, that those whom it pleased God to employ in order to propagate this saying, in the first instance, always affirmed that it was true. Besides, the God of essential and eternal truth has been pleased to affix His broad seal to this saying. He could not give His seal to a lie. How is this? Why, He enabled those men to perform miracles in order to attest it. How do you prove, inquired another, that what you declare is true? Bring hither yon leper, excluded from all intercourse with his fellow beings, standing afar off, bring him hither to me, and in the name of this Jesus, and to prove that He "came into the world to save sinners," I pronounce the word, and his leprosy shall immediately depart from him! And it was so! The saying again is pronounced and the question is repeated. Bring hither the dead body, says an apostle, you are about to cast it forth into the tomb; but no, bring it hither; I pronounce the word, and that dead body shall start into life! And it was so! There is another way, however, in which the truth of this saying is to be ascertained, and it is, of all others, the most satisfactory and consoling. It is in the way of experiment, bringing this truth to trial, to the test. How is this? Why, here is a man, and I have now present in my mind's eye a case which, I suppose, twenty years ago actually occurred—here is a man who in early youth begins to think it would be to his credit to begin to evince independency of mind, to throw off all the fetters of education and early impressions, and to think for himself. He associates with those who speak with great disrespect of this Divine volume, who begin to sneer, or have been in the habit of sneering, at all serious religion and serious Christians: by and by he begins to imbibe their spirit, and to acquaint himself with all the objections urged against revealed religion; by and by he begins also to sneer and laugh at the Bible, he casts off fear and plunges headlong into infidelity; he is then, perhaps, admired as a man of liberal mind, of genius, and of intelligence; and the individual I refer to was a man of fine understanding and cultivated mind; but by and by disease marked him out as its victim, he saw some of his companions in infidelity die; not one of them died comfortably—some of them died most awfully; he began to consider with himself, Whither, after all, am I going? I never disbelieved the Being of a God; but then, although I have always regarded Him as a good and benevolent Being, have I acted as I should, as a creature—as a dependent being, sustained by His power and bounty? Have I always revered and loved and served Him as I ought? This I have not done! What have I done? I go to my natural religion, as it is sometimes called; I study moral virtue, I endeavour to do good, and thus endeavour to recommend myself to this benevolent Being. But in natural religion he finds no relief for a troubled mind, no balm for a guilty conscience. What, thought he, shall I do? I will have recourse once more to the Bible, I shall begin to read it seriously. He did read it, the more he read it the deeper was the impression on his mind, that this is no human fabrication, in this book surely God has spoken: he read, and on every page he saw something of this Saviour and about this salvation. The thought flashed upon his mind, and he exclaimed, Oh, that this were but true! Oh, that I could believe this! I should find relief immediately: here is a system adapted to my condition. Oh, if it were but true, that "Jesus Christ came into the world to save sinners," make an atonement for sin, and procure salvation for me! Here is a system that suits my case and provides for my necessities! Oh, that it were true! At last he resolved to make the experiment: he read this book, and sincerely prayed to God to teach him what is truth. I believe he read this very text, "This is a faithful saying, and worthy of all acceptation, that Christ Jesus came into the world to save sinners." Is this the saying, and is this Jesus the Saviour of sinners? Oh, help me, he prayed, to believe this, teach me to believe this, I desire to believe this, I would believe this! Lord, I believe this—help Thou my unbelief! I venture my soul on this Saviour—I cast myself on this atoning sacrifice. What happened? "His chains fell off—his heart was free!" His load of guilt was removed, his misery was banished; joy and peace and love unspeakable sprang up in his heart, and his soul began to exult, disburthened of its load. Not many days had elapsed before he met one of his old companions, who had grown gray in infidelity. What is this, he inquired, that I hear of you? I hear you have become a Christian! How do you know that there is a word of truth in the whole affair? How do you know that such a being as Jesus ever existed? Know! was the reply, know! I know it by an argument of which you never were the master,' I know it by a process to which you are a total stranger, I know it is true that "Christ Jesus came into the world to save sinners," for Jesus Christ has saved me! Well, then, but it is not only "a true saying" and worthy merely of all attention, examination, and observation, commending itself to the approbation of every well-regulated mind, but it is also "worthy of all acceptation." It is worthy of acceptance because of its truth; if not true, it could have no just claim upon—it would be unworthy our acceptation. It is worthy of acceptance, again, because it is so vitally interesting. A thing may be true and yet not interesting to me; but here is a saying which is proved to be true, and which is surpassingly interesting to all the children of men. What so worthy the acceptance of the diseased man, as some sovereign specific which shall not only remove the malady but restore to health and vigour his emaciated frame? The saying has been accepted by the great, the wise, and the good, in different countries and ages of the Church; yes, and some of the greatest and wisest of men that ever lived, of learning, too, various and profound, have received this saying—have stedfastly believed its truth and realized its power. And who art thou who art giving thyself credit for having superior lights and superior intellects? But not only is this saying worthy of acceptance, but "of all acceptation "—of the acceptance of all. If, in the next place, any portion of our race in any part of our world, could be found, who were absolutely and irrevocably excluded from all interest and benefit in this saying, I honestly confess to you, that I see not how such a portion of our race could regard this saying as worthy their acceptation. That is not, that cannot be worthy my acceptance, in which I cannot, by any possibility, have any interest. And not only is this worthy the acceptation of all, but of the highest acceptation of all. As though the apostle had said, This is no ordinary saying; it is a message from the throne—a message of mercy from the throne; oh, hail it, welcome it, receive it as coming from the throne, "Christ Jesus came into the world to save sinners!" And having thus realized the truth and power of this saying ourselves, let us do all that we can to circulate it—let us always speak well of this Jesus, and endeavour to recommend the Saviour to all our fellow creatures.     (*R. Newton, D.D.*) *The faithful saying* :—I. CHRIST JESUS CAME INTO THE WORLD TO SAVE SINNERS. 1. Jesus Christ was somewhere in existence before He was seen here. He "came into the world." Think of a new planet or star just created in our system and shining forth. We should never say, it is come here; we should say this of a planet or star that had travelled into our system from some distant region. And it was from a region distant indeed that Christ came here, from a heavenly one; and the place He held in that region, was the most distant and the highest. He was not an angel in heaven; He was the everlasting God. He came from the very summit, the lofty throne, of heaven to save us. 2. There are lost sinners in our world, whom it was needful for Christ to come into our world to save. Every man that breathes in our world is a sinner. And every sinner everywhere is necessarily a lost sinner. This is the nature of sin, it ruins whomsoever it touches; ruins him fatally and irrecoverably; in Scripture language, it destroys him. And on this property of sin, the ruinous nature of it, is grounded partly the necessity of Christ's interposition in our behalf. We say that His coming from His throne to save us, shows the greatness of His love to us, and so it does; but it shows as plainly the greatness of our misery. 3. And when Christ came into the world to save sinners, He came determined to save them. He knew He could do so, otherwise He would not have come. We do not go to the frozen regions of the north to gather there the flowers and fruits of sunny climes. We never think of going into vaults and charnel houses to raise the dead. Nor would our blessed Lord have come into the world for our salvation, had He not felt as He came, that He could work out salvation for us. II. THE DESCRIPTION ST. PAUL GIVES US HERE OF THE TRUTH HE STATES. He calls it a "saying," "a faithful saying," and one "worthy of all acceptation." 1. It is a saying. And who says it? God Himself, Christ Himself. He might have come into our world, and never have told us that He had come here, or why He had come. And it is not God or Christ only, who says this. The prophets declared it before it took place : the glorious company of the apostles said it afterwards; the noble army of martyrs died rather than not say it; the holy Church throughout all the world has in every age acknowledged it; and as for the Church above, it says this oftener, perhaps, than it says anything else, and loves to say it better. Heaven often resounds with this saying and other sayings like it. 2. And this is a faithful saying, a true one. It is not only said, but it ought to be said, for it is true as truth itself. He had what St. John calls a testimony or witness of this truth within himself. He knew it, just as we know at this moment that our hearts are beating, and our pulses going, and that we are living and breathing men. He had experience of the fact. And valuable as are the many outward testimonies we have to the truth of the gospel, and convincing as they are to a sound, unbiassed judgment, they are all nothing in comparison with this 3. This saying too, we are told, is worthy of all acceptation. The words will admit of two interpretations. It is, first, as our communion service renders the passage, "Worthy to be received of all men." Few sayings are so. Many things which we hear are worth no man's attention. They are either false or trifling; they are better not listened to. And others have only a limited interest. They may be worthy of one man's notice, but not another man's, for they do not concern him. This saying, however, concerns every man, and concerns him deeply. O how eagerly will some of us listen to some things! the news of the day perhaps, the scandal of our neighbourhood, and the trifling occurrences that fill up the trifling lives of our fellow-men!—things, it may be, in which we have little more interest than the inhabitants of some distant planet; but this saying, to which sometimes we have scarcely an ear to give, involves in it the highest interests of us all. This saying is worthy also of the utmost reception we can give it, the most entire and cordial acceptance. Some things that we hear are worth putting into our memories but not into our hearts; they are dry matters of fact. But here is something worthy of our memories and hearts also; worthy of being attended to, worthy of being remembered, worthy of being thought on and studied, worthy of being delighted in, worthy of being laid hold of by our whole heart and mind—in this sense, "worthy of all acceptation." A feeble or cold reception of this saying is no reception at all of it. Where the gospel saves the soul, the heart first opens itself to receive it, and when it is in the heart, the heart feels it to be its treasure and its joy. III. THE VIEW WHICH THE APOSTLE TAKES OF HIM-SELF WHILE CONTEMPLATING THIS TRUTH. Of the sinners, he says, whom Christ Jesus came into the world to save, "I am chief." (C. Bradley, M.A.) Worthy of all acceptation:—I. It is worthy of all acceptation BECAUSE IT IS THE FULL DEVELOPMENT OF THE THEME WITH WHICH REVELATION IS CHARGED; it lies not only in the track, but it is the full outcome of all that God has been aiming at in all His providential guidance and government of men, from the first days of the creation to the hour when the "Child was born, the Son was given," whom He had from of old promised to the world. From the first chapter of Genesis to the last chapter of the Apocalypse, the main thread in the Scripture is this work, the saving of sinners. And if we study it we shall find that it is the vital core of all the great movements of human society. The Bible opens with the statement that the great burden of man's existence here is sin, and that the great need of man's being is salvation. The inner meaning of it is true for all time, and is the key, I believe the Divine key, to human history. The theme there is sin, wilful, conscious, guilty transgression, revealed as the root of all man's infirmity, degradation, and misery. II. It is worthy of all acceptation, FOR IT ALONE EXPLAINS AND JUSTIFIES THE WHOLE COURSE OF HUMAN HISTORY. This life of ours is altogether too sad, too burdensome, too dark a thing to be suffered to live on, if there be no great hope for the future to lighten it. The world is very beautiful and glorious, you may say; it is a happy thing to be born with faculties finely touched like ours into a world like this. Yes, unspeakably beautiful and glorious is this earth of ours, and our life here might well be a paradise of pure delights. But sin poisons all. Despite of all the beauty, all the joy, the great masterpieces of human thought and utterance are in the minor key. Sadness is the dominant tone in all our literature, sorrow is the staple experience of mankind. I say frankly, that if I were compelled to look at life and the world, cut off from all the comfort and hope which streams down upon us through the Christian faith, I should be sorely tempted to the conclusions of the pessimist philosophy, that there has been some terrible blundering in the constitution of the world. But set in the heart of it all Christ's mission to save, and the darkness lights up in a moment. This dread experience of sin becomes through grace a stage in an unending progress. This school of our discipline, this house of our bondage, this field of our conflict, is but a stage of development, a step of progress, and all its deepest experiences have relation to blessed and glorious issues in eternity. III. It is worthy of all acceptation, FOR IT IS ESSENTIAL TO THE DIGNITY AND THE WORTH OF LIFE. Is life worth the living? Yes, a thousand times yes, if it is the life of a forgiven man in a redeemed world. What man needs is not to forget sin, to make light of it, to shut out the world of spiritual terrors which it unveils. It will not be shut out. What man needs is free loving and righteous forgiveness—forgiveness which is not a weak winking at trans-gression, or an idle peace, peace where there is no peace, but a forgiveness resting on an atonement which reveals righteousness, magnifies law, and satisfies the deepest convictions of man's righteous conscience on the one hand, and the holy heart of God on the other. This horrible doctrine of the absolute indelibility of transgression has been the cause of untold anguish through all the ages of human history. Sin must fruit in sorrow, and forgiveness cannot annul the act of sin, or obliterate its issues. But there is an infinite difference between the experience of the man who is working out the penalty of sin, with the sense that behind the sorrow there is the vindictive hand of the law-giver, who will exact the uttermost farthing of retribution, and that of the Christian, who knows that behind all that he endures, and is entirely reconciled to enduring, is the eye and the hand of the Almighty Father of his spirit; an eye which watches his struggles and sorrows with the tenderest compassion, a hand which is guiding and ruling all the discipline to blessed and glorious issues in eternity. This is a faithful saying, and worthy of all acceptation; for through it, "where sin abounded grace doth much more abound; that, as sin hath reigned unto death, even so might grace reign, through righteousness, unto eternal life, by Jesus Christ our Lord." IV. It is worthy of all acceptation, because, while it lends dignity and worth to life, IT ALONE LENDS HOPE TO IMMORTALITY. An essential part of the benign work of love is the reconciliation of man with law. Forgiveness is a blessed fact, unspeakably blessed, but chiefly as the means of realizing a still more blessed fact—purification. On that absolutely the well-being and the bliss of the soul rests in eternity. And what is the cry of all the nobler heathen faiths? Deliverance from self. This is a faithful saying, and worthy of all acceptation, because it is charged for man with the promise of eternal life; not eternal existence under these dread and soul-crushing conditions, but eternal life, free, pure, noble, blessed life, finding its spring of perennial joy and fruitfulness in the sunlight of the face of God. The salvation which is by Christ Jesus offers to man not only pardon and peace, but renewing, restoration; a new heart, a new life, a new power, a new supreme attraction, drawing man ever by its sweet but resistless constraints into closest and holiest fellowship with the life of God through eternity. And this is Christianity. (*J. B. Brown, B.A.*) *The world small for so great a transaction as redemption:*—It seems a little place, this world of ours, to be the scene of such transcendent transactions. But size, as we measure it, counts for nothing on high; as far as we can see, it is the method of God everywhere to work from what man calls insignificant centres over vast areas of life. It is emphatically thus in history. England is but a little country, Greece was less, Judea least of all; and yet from these intense radiating centres influences have streamed forth which will be fruitful of high results throughout eternity. The cultivated homes of men are but little oases in the midst of desert and ocean spaces, of vast extent and dreary monotony; fruitless and useless in our weak judgment; though we are now beginning to see that they are essential to the high development of the limited regions which can nourish the noblest forms of life. Who shall tell what is to grow out of the transactions of which this little, but most highly developed and glorious, earth has been the theatre, to the great universe and the kingdom of heaven in eternity? (*Ibid.*) *The gospel and its recommendation:*— I. THE GOSPEL. It means good news. Here is a man ill; the word that tells him how he may be cured of his disease is gospel—good news. It claims to be the best news. Such is our text, and that because it tells about three things—1. It tells of a divinely-appointed Saviour. It tells of "Christ Jesus," and there is gospel in the very name. I thank God for that name. I have sometimes ventured to compare it to what we are all familiar with—the sign-board above a shop-door, telling what is to be got there; or the name on the door of a lawyer or physician, telling what men may expect there. A sick man sees the doctor's name on his door, and applies to him without hesitation. He says, "The man is a physician, a doctor; that is his profession; he is there for the very purpose of receiving and curing the sick and dying, and I have a claim on his services which he cannot, dare not, refuse." And so here is One who has His name, as it were, on His door; His profession, His business described in His very name—"Jesus." It tells His occupation—the Saviour. But He is also spoken of as the "Christ," that is, the Anointed One. Let us go back to the olden times again. There is one who has been guilty of some sin, which lies heavy on his conscience and heart. He takes the prescribed offering, a lamb, and goes with it to the priest, that that lamb may suffer and die for him, as his sacrifice, his substitute; and when its blood is shed, his sin is atoned for and put away. But the question comes up, "Is He a right priest? Has He a Divine commission?" Yes; because He is "anointed," the holy oil was poured on Him, setting Him apart to the holy office; and as He is an anointed priest, there is no cause to fear. Or take another case: a crime has been committed, and the offender is sent to the king, who alone can give pardon for such an offence. The pardon is given; the man hears it from the king's own lips. But here, too, the doubt arises, "Has He a right to give it? Is He commissioned to grant a pardon? Is He the real king? Will the pardon stand?" Yes; because the holy anointing oil was poured on Him, which marks Him out as the God-anointed king. And like other great official persons, He carries His credentials with Him. 2. It tells of the mission and work of Christ. By His "mission," I mean His being "sent," His coming on His great errand of mercy and love. "Christ Jesus came into the world." What a word of wonder is this! I have been in one of our Highland cottages, and have had the place pointed out where our Queen has sat. There is a sacredness about the spot that can hardly be told, so that you scarcely wonder that some of our humble Scottish peasants have said, "None shall ever sit on that seat again!" You can fancy the mingled pride and enthusiasm with which they tell of the condescension of the greatest sovereign in the world visiting their lowly dwellings. "She came into this humble cottage of mine!" And yet what was that to this— "Christ Jesus came into the world"? There is a lazar-house for the reception of lepers in all the stages of their dreadful disease. No man who enters comes out but for burial. One of these good, devoted men, the Moravian Brethren, has his heart filled with compassion for the sufferers, and with the desire to point them to Christ and to heaven; and knowing that he bids a life-long farewell to all outside, he cheerfully enters, and the door closes, shutting him up in a kind of living grave. You say, What a marvel of love and pity! And yet, what are all these as compared with this—"Christ Jesus came into the world"? And then, in regard to the work which He came into the world to do, notice the words—"to save sinners!" Most wonderful of all! Strangers, enemies, rebels—these are some of the descriptions that you have in the Word of God of those whom He came to save. 3. It tells of the objects of His care and love. I have spoken of these, in the general, as "sinners." We now get a step further forward—"sinners of whom I am chief," or "first." II. Having spoken of THE GOSPEL itself, I ask your attention now to its RECOMMENDATION: "This is a faithful saying, and worthy of all acceptation." 1. It is true. The great drawback about many things that are very attractive is that they are not true. You have met with some entertaining volume. It interests you deeply, and lays thorough hold of your heart. You would rather lose a meal, or an afternoon's play, or an hour's sleep, than lay aside your book. And as you finish the reading of it, with the tear in your eye, and your young heart beating quick, you say, "That is a fine story, a wonderful story. I have seldom read anything like it." Ay, but do you know it is not true; it is just "made up"; it is all unreal. Sometimes you have pleasant dreams; you are happy as can be; you have gained some object on which your hearts have long been set; but you suddenly wake up, and it is but an empty dream. Friends who have come home from India have told us, that when passing through the desert, they have seen the "mirage," with its grassy slopes and graceful trees casting their shadow on the lake beside which they seem to be growing, most beautiful to the eye; but it is only a vision, and in a moment vanishes out of sight. But I have this to say in favour of the wondrous gospel story, that it is true. I wonder if you ever got the length of doubting it? There is an old man who is often to be found in his humble cottage, with his large family Bible spread out before him, always open at the 14th chapter of John. A youth, who is a frequent visitor, coming in to ask for him, says, "I wonder why you are so often reading these words, when you know them all by heart; I should be for reading what I did not know." "Well, master," is the old man's reply, "you are right enough, I dare say; but it seems to do me good to get a look at the real words; it helps an old man's faith, for when I see them, I say, There they be, and I cannot doubt them. You see the thought of a mansion in heaven for an old sinner like me, and my Lord going before to prepare it, and coming back to take me to it—why, it is all so wonderful, that if I could not get a look at the words sometimes, I am afraid I should be just doubting again." 2. It is trustworthy. Paul tells here that he has tried it, he has made the experiment, and can now recommend it from personal experience. I fear to trust myself on such a slender support, and gaze with dismay upon the abyss below. I look for another way, but there is none. At length I hear a voice from the other side saying, "The plank bears; I have tried it; I have crossed it; it will bear you; plant your foot firmly on it, and you will get safely across." I look across, and see a man larger and heavier than myself; and when I see him, I pluck up heart, plant my foot on the plank, and cross in safety; and once I am over, I too can testify, The plank bears; I can say, It is trustworthy; I can give others the benefit of my experience: "It has saved me, and now I can recommend it to you." 3. It is all-important. It is worthy of all acceptation, and therefore of all attention. It is no trifling matter. 4. It is welcome-worthy. It is spoken of here as being "worthy of all acceptation." "Oh, that dreary gospel," I think I hear some one saying, "I suppose we must needs have to do with it, or we cannot be saved. It is very much like a medicine. I am ill, I must take it, or I shall not recover, but it is bitter and repulsive." Not so, says Paul; this gospel is "worthy of all welcome." I might compare it to those letters from beloved friends, which the arrival of the mail from some distant country brings to us. (*J. H. Wilson, M.A.*) *For whom is the gospel meant?*—I. EVEN A SUPERFICIAL GLANCE AT OUR LORD'S MISSION SUFFICES TO SHOW THAT HIS WORK WAS FOR THE SINFUL. 1. For the descent of the Son of God into this world as a Saviour implied that men needed to be delivered from a great evil by a Divine hand. You would never have seen a Saviour if there had not been a fall. Eden's withering was a necessary preface to Gethsemane's groaning. 2. If we give a glance at the covenant under which our Lord came, we soon perceive that its bearing is towards guilty men. If there had been no sins and iniquities, and no unrighteousness, then there had been no need of the covenant of grace, of which Christ is the messenger and the ambassador. 3. Whenever we hear the mission of Christ spoken of it is described as one of mercy and of grace. In the redemption which is in Christ Jesus it is always the mercy of God that is extolled—according to His mercy He saved us. 4. The fact is, when we begin to study the gospel of the grace of God we see that it turns its face always towards sin, even as a physician looks towards disease, or as charity looks towards distress. 5. The gospel representations of itself usually look sinnerward. The great king who makes a feast finds not a guest to sit at the table among those who were naturally expected to come, but from the highways and hedges men are compelled to come in. 6. And ye know that the gospel has always found its greatest trophies amongst the most sinful: it enlists its best soldiers not only from amongst the guilty, but from amongst the most guilty. II. THE MORE CLOSELY WE LOOK THE MORE CLEAR THIS FACT BECOMES, for the work of salvation was certainly not performed for any one of us who are saved on account of any goodness in us. 1. All the gifts which Jesus Christ came to give, or at least most of them, imply that there is sin. What is His first gift but pardon? How can He pardon a man who has not transgressed? 2. Our Lord Jesus Christ came girded also with Divine power. He says, "The Spirit of the Lord is upon Me." To what end was He girded with Divine power unless it be because sin had taken all power and strength from man? 3. I will not omit to say that the great deeds of our Lord, if you look at them carefully, all bear upon sinners. Jesus lives; it is that He may seek and save that which is lost. Jesus dies; it is that He may make a propitiation for the sins of guilty men. Jesus rises; He rises again for our justification, and, as I have shown, we should not want justification unless we had been naturally guilty. Jesus ascends on high, and He receives gifts for men; but note that special word, "Yea, for the rebellious also, that the Lord God may dwell among them." 4. And all the gifts and blessings that Jesus Christ has brought to us derive much of their radiance from their bearing upon sinners. It is in Christ Jesus that we are elect, and to my mind the glory of electing love lies in this, that it pitched upon such undeserving objects. III. Now it is evident that IT IS OUR WISDOM TO ACCEPT THE SITUATION. IV. THIS DOCTRINE HAS A GREAT SANCTIFYING INFLUENCE. 1. Its first operation in that direction is this: when the Holy Spirit brings the truth of free pardon home to a man it completely changes his thoughts concerning God. "What," says he, "has God freely forgiven me all my offences for Christ's sake? And does He love me notwithstanding all my sin?" 2. Moreover, this grand truth does more than turn a man, it inspires, melts, enlivens, and inflames him. This is a truth which stirs the deeps of the heart, and fills the man with lively emotions. 3. Besides, this truth when it enters the heart deals a deadly blow at the man's self-conceit. 4. Moreover, where this truth is received there is sure to spring up in the soul a sense of gratitude. 5. And I think you will all see that free forgiveness to sinners is very conducive towards one part of a true character, namely, readiness to forgive others. (*C. H. Spurgeon.*) *A faithful saying*:—I. Here is a WONDERFUL saying. It was but thirty years since the gospel of the Lord Jesus Christ had been preached, yet these words had become a saying, a blessed proverb. It summed up briefly and yet fully the source and purpose of the gospel—its height and depth, its length and breadth. "Christ Jesus came into the world to save sinners." Look into it. No such wonderful saying was ever heard in the world before or since. The Jew was willing to believe that the God of Israel could admit into His high presence the holy men to whom He had entrusted some great enterprise, and who had proved themselves worthy of such an exceeding honour. Abraham, Moses, Elijah—for such men God might come in all the majesty of His splendour and commune with them. The Greeks believed that for the gifted and the great, for splendid heroes who had wrought prodigies of valour on the battle-fields or in the games, the gods might stoop to give some token of their favour and protection. That was familiar enough. But that God should care so much for men who had slighted Him, and forgotten Him, and insulted Him, and rebelled against Him! That God should care for coarse, low, ignorant people, whom it was a disgrace to notice, and who were incapable of any goodness! This was ridiculous, worse than merely incredible. To the Greeks such an idea was a folly, to the Jews it was an offence. Yet still more wonderful was the saying—that God, the God of Glory, should come down as a man, should become one of us and one with us, taking upon Himself not only our nature, but our curse—the awful load of the world's sin; and that He should bear for us all shame and agony! II. Experience has proved it a FAITHFUL saying. The early disciples passed from one to another, setting their seal to its truth, until it came to be supported by a host of witnesses. And since St. Paul wrote that, the great cloud of witnesses has ever been growing. There is nothing in the world to-day that has such testimonies to commend it as this gospel of our salvation. I call up the memory of saintly men and women in my own little native town, dear old souls, many of them poor, but with such purity in their faces, such love in their hearts, such peace in their lives. With others life was a hot and fevered unrest, but about these there was an atmosphere of holy calm. What was it that made them so bright, so happy, so hopeful, that kings might well have envied them? They are ready with the reason—"It is a faithful saying, and worthy of all acceptation, that Christ Jesus came into the world to save sinners." Go to-day whither you will, north or south, east or west, and find the homes that are happiest, the lives that are sweetest, the souls that are sunniest, the hearts and hands that are most eager and most earnest in helping others—you shall find it amongst those who set their seal to this as true—"It is a faithful saying, and worthy of all acceptation, that Christ Jesus came into the world to save sinners." Come yet again and stand by the deathbed; that rends the veil from all pretences. I see the face pinched and pale with sickness, yet is it lit up with a brightness as if the eyes did look within the veil. Fear is gone, and all is peace. Bend and listen as the lips are parted for their last utterance. "It is a faithful saying, and worthy of all acceptation, that Christ Jesus came into the world to save sinners." My brother, this gospel is no fancy of fanatics; no delusion of the dark ages. Nothing in this world comes to us so hallowed and so commended. Can I find another Christ Jesus? Can I find another salvation which comes with such evidence of its faithfulness as this? Surely it is worth my accepting. I will take for my own that Saviour who has come into the world to save sinners. If this is a faithful saying, then are there three things that do greatly concern us every one. 1. If Jesus Christ has come into the world to save us, then we must be in great danger. Whatever is the use of trying to save a man if he is not in any peril! 2. If this be a faithful saying that Christ Jesus came into the world to save sinners, then surely none but Jesus Christ can save me. My struggles and resolutions cannot avail, or Christ need not have come. 3. If this be a faithful saying that Jesus Christ came into the world to save sinners, then He has come to save me. If He has come to save sinners He means people who have sinned—real sinners—not good people who call themselves sinners because it sounds humble. The desperate cases are those which my Lord ever seeks first of all. Luther tells us, once upon a time the devil said to him, "Master Luther, thou art a great sinner, and thou wilt be damned." "Stop, stop," I said, "one thing at a time. I am a great sinner, it is true—though *thou* hast no right to say so. I confess it. What next?" "Therefore thou shalt be damned," quoth he. "That is not good reasoning," said I. "It is true that I am a great sinner—but it is written, 'Christ Jesus came to save sinners': therefore I shall be saved! Now go thy way. So did I cut off the devil with his own sword, and he went away sorrowing, because he could not cast me down by calling me a sinner." (*M. G. Pearse.*) *Christ's power to save:*—I seem to see Saul rising on that road to Damascus, brushing the dust from his cloak, and wiping the perspiration from his excited brow, and then swinging out his hands towards all ages as he cries, "This is a faithful saying, and worthy of all acceptation, that Christ Jesus came into the world to save sinners, of whom I am chief." In my church in Brooklyn, at the close of the service one day, a man came from the back part of the house and sat down near the pulpit. I saw him waiting, so I came down at the close of the service, and asked him if he would not go in amongst those making inquiry for their souls. He said, "No, sir; you cannot do me any good. I came from the Far West, but you cannot do me any good. The gospel is not for *me*—I am a victim of strong drink." He said, "I won't tell you my name; you know it. I rose to be one of the first men of my State. I have a beautiful wife and beautiful children, but am bringing them all to ruin. I thought if I came here I *could* be saved; but find I can't. Yesterday I was coming down on the Hudson River train. There was a man sitting beside me with a flask of strong drink. He asked me if I would have some of it. I said 'No'; but, oh, how I wanted it! The arid tongue of the liquor seemed thrusting itself from the side of the cork, and I felt I must fly from that presence. I went to the platform of the train and thought I would jump off; but we were going at the rate of forty miles an hour, and I came back. That thirst is on me, and you cannot do *me* any good." I said, "You do not know the grace of God. Come in here, and we will pray for you." We prayed for him, and I then went to the drug store, and said to the doctor, "Can you give this man anything to help him to destroy that thirst?" Well, the physician put up a bottle to help him. I said, "Give him a little more," and he put up another bottle. I then said to the man, "Put your trust in God, and when this paroxysm comes on take your medicine." He passed away from me into Boston, and was gone from me some weeks, when I got a letter enclosing the small amount of money I had paid for the medicine, and saying, "Thank God, Mr. Talmage, I have got cured, and the fear of the thirst is put off, and I have not taken any of the medicine. I am preaching every night on righteousness, temperance, and judgment to come, in one of our large halls, and I send you two papers to show how the Lord is blessing me." I have heard from him since, and the Lord has seen him through, and will see him through. Oh, the grace of God! Try! Try it! (*T. De Witt Talmage.*) *The mission of Christ to the worst :*—All the great hereditary and historical religions of mankind, both of the East and the West, are religions designed for morally respectable people, for men who, in their own opinion, are good and deserving persons, or are earning merit and future bliss by trying to become so. That was and is the essence of Bhuddism, of Brahminism, of Laoutsaism, of Islam, and of the natural, philosophical religions of Europe and America. They are the religions of men who "are going about," like the Jews of the first century—the Jews of corrupted Judaism, "to establish their own righteousness" and title to immortal life, or to Nirvana. The genuine Christianity, taught by the Lord Jesus, the Christ of God, the one genuine message of the Eternal Creator to the human race, is the one and only religion proposed to, and pressed upon, the wicked. It is sent forth over all the world, as salvation for the lost, as complete and immediate salvation. (*E. White.*) *The sinner's door :*—When I began my ministry in Dundee, I had the privilege of meeting many of those who were blessed under the preaching of the sainted Murray M'Cheyne. I was told of one case of conversion which is rather peculiar. The person was much troubled, his mind was filled with gloomy darkness, and he had no peace nor rest. One day, as M'Cheyne was preaching to Christians, not to those outside of Christ's fold, the man got peace. After the service he went round to the vestry to see the minister, who did not need to inquire if the visitor had got peace, it shone in his face ; so he simply asked, "How did you get it?" He answered, "All the time I've been trying to enter in at the saints' door, but while you were speaking I saw my mistake, and entered in at the sinners' door." It is the only way; you need not come to God as a saint, or a pretty good sort of a person, but simply as a sinner, wanting and needing salvation. (*W. Riddell.*) *A gospel text :*—Mr. William White, one of the London City Missionaries, relates the following interesting fact: "Some years ago, through the kindness of the late Joseph Sturge, Esq., of Birmingham, a large grant of copies of *The British Workman* was made to the London City Mission, a portion of which was allotted for my district. Some time after distributing my share of that grant in my district, I visited a man who was very ill. After some conversation, I said, 'Well, my friend, the best news that any one can ever bring you is contained in this text from the Bible, "This is a faithful saying, and worthy of all acceptation, that Christ Jesus came into the world to save sinners."' His face was immediately lit up with a smile, and raising himself in the bed, he pointed to the patched window and said, "Oh, sir, I know that already. Look there: that's a piece of the paper you once gave me. My wife tore it up, and mended the window with just that piece of it that has that text on it. And since I've laid here, day after day, I've read it over and over till I've got it off by heart."'" The City Missionary adds: "I believe the Holy Spirit made that text on the patched window a blessing to the man's soul." **Of whom I am chief.**—*The chief sinners objects of the choicest mercy :*—I. The salvation of sinners was the main design of Christ's coming into the world. II. God often makes the chiefest sinners objects of His choicest mercy. For the last, that God doth so, observe—1. God hath formerly made invitations to such. See what a black generation they were (Isa. i.) by the scroll of their sins. They were rebels, and rebels against Him that had nursed them : " I have nourished and brought up children, and they have rebelled against Me " (ver. 2). He comes to charge them "laden with iniquity" (ver. 4). They had been incorrigible under judgments. "Why should ye be stricken any more? Ye will revolt more and more" (ver. 5). 2. God hath given examples of it in Scripture. Manasseh is an eminent example of this doctrine. His story (2 Chron. xxiii.) represents him as a black devil, if all the aggravations of his sins be considered. (1) It was against knowledge. He had a pious education under a religious father. An education usually leaves some tinctures and impressions of religion. (2) His place and station: a king. Sins of kings are like their robes, more scarlet and crimson than the sins of a peasant. Their example usually infects their subjects. (3) Restoration of idolatry. (4) Affronting God to His very face. He sets up his idols, as it were, to nose God, and built altars in the house of the Lord, and in the two courts of His temple, whereof God had said He would have His name there for ever (vers. 4, 5, 7). (5) Murder. Perhaps of his children, which he caused to pass through the fire as an offering to his idol (ver. 6); it may be it was only for purification. "Moreover, Manasseh shed innocent blood very much, till he filled Jerusalem with blood from one end to the other" (2 Kings xxi. 16). (6) Covenant with the devil. He used enchantments and witchcraft, and dealt with a familiar spirit (ver. 6). (7) His other men's sins. He did not only lead the people by his example, but compelled them by his commands: "So Manasseh made Judah and the inhabitants of Jerusalem to err, and to do worse than the heathen God had rooted out" (2 Chron. xxiii. 9), to make room for them. Hereby he contracted the guilt of the whole nation upon himself. (8) Obstinacy against admonitions: "God spake to him and his people, but they would not hearken, or alter their course" (2 Kings xxi. 10). (9) Continuance in it. He ascended the throne young, at twelve years old (ver. 1). It is uncertain how long he continued in this sin. 3. It was Christ's employment in the world to court and gain such kind of creatures. The first thing He did, while in the manger, was to snatch some of the devil's prophets out of his service, and take them into His own (Matt. ii. 1), some of the Magi, who were astrologers and idolaters. To call sinners to repentance, was the errand of His coming. And He usually delighted to choose such that had not the least pretence to merit (Mark ii. 17): Matthew, a publican; Zaccheus, an extortioner, store of that generation of men and harlots, and very little company besides. He chose His attendants out of the devil's rabble; and He was more Jesus, a Saviour, among this sort of trash, than among all other sorts of people, for all His design was to get clients out of hell itself. What was that woman that He must needs go out of His way to convert? A harlot (John iv. 18), an idolater; for the Samaritans had a mixed worship, a linsey-woolsey religion, and, upon that account, were hateful to the Jews. What was that Canaanitish woman who had so powerful a faith infused? One sprung of a cursed stock, hateful to God, rooted out of the pleasant land, a dog, not a child; she comes a dog, but returns a child. 4. The commission Christ gave to His apostles was to this purpose. He bids them proclaim the promise free to all: "Go ye into all the world, and preach the gospel to every creature" (Mark xvi. 15). All the world; every creature. He put no difference between men in this respect, though you meet with them in the likeness of beasts and devils, never so wicked, never so abominable. This commission is set out by the parable of a king commanding his servants to fetch the maimed, halt, and blind, with their wounds, sores, and infirmities about them (Luke xiv. 21, 23). 5. The practice of the Spirit after Christ's ascension to lay hold of such persons. (1) Some out of the worst families in the world; one out of Herod's (Acts xiii. 1), "Now there were in the Church that was at Antioch certain prophets and teachers, as Barnabas, and Simeon that was called Niger, and Lucius of Cyrene, and Manaen, which had been brought up with Herod the tetrarch, and Saul." It is likely to this intent the Holy Ghost takes particular notice of the place of Manaen's education, when the families where the rest named with him were bred up are not mentioned. Some rude and rough stones were taken out of Nero's palace. Yet some of this monster's servants became saints (Phil. iv. 22): "All the saints salute you, chiefly they that are of Cæsar's household." To hear of saints in Nero's family is as great a prodigy as to hear of saints in hell. (2) Some of the worst vices. The Ephesians were as bad as any, such that Paul calls darkness itself (Eph. v. 8). Great idolaters. The temple of Diana, adored and resorted to by all Asia and the whole world, was in that city (Acts xix. 27). Take a view of another corporation, of Corinth, of as filthy persons as ever you heard of, "such were some of you" (1 Cor. vi. 11). Well, then, how many flinty rocks has God dissolved into a stream of tears! Great sins are made preparations by God to some men's conversion; not in their own nature (that is impossible), but by the wise disposal of God, which Mr. Burgess illustrates thus : as a child whose coat is but a little dirty has it not presently washed ; but when he comes to fall over head and ears in the mire, it is taken off, and washed immediately. So when a wicked man falls into some grievous sin, which his conscience frowns upon him and lashes him for, he looks out for a shelter, which in all his peaceable wickedness he never did. III. Why God chooses the greatest sinners, and lets His elect run on so far in sin before He turns them. 1. There is a passive disposition in the greatest sinners, more than in moral or superstitious men, to see their need; because they have not any self-righteousness to boast of. This self-righteous temper is like an external heat got into a body, which produceth an hectic fever, and is not easily perceived till it be incurable ; and naturally it is a harder matter to part with self-righteousness than to part with gross sins, for that is more deeply rooted upon the stock of self-love, a principle which departs not from us without our very nature ; it hath more arguments to plead for it, it hath a natural conscience, a patron of it ; whereas a great sinner stands speechless at reproofs, and a faithful monitor has a good second and correspondent of natural conscience within a man's own breast. Just as travellers that have loitered away their time in an alehouse, being sensible how the darkness of the night creeps upon them, spur on, and outstrip those that were many miles on their way, and get to their stage before them ; so these publicans and harlots, which were at a great distance from heaven, arrived there before those, who like the young man, were not far off from it. As metals of the noblest substance are hardest to be polished, so men of the most generous, natural, and moral endowments are with more difficulty argued into a state of Christianity than those of more drossy conversations. 2. To show the insufficiency of nature to such a work as conversion is, that men may not fall down and idolize their own wit and power. Two things are certain in nature : (1) Natural inclinations never change, but by some superior virtue. A loadstone will not cease to draw iron while that attractive quality remains in it. The wolf can never love the lamb, nor the lamb the wolf ; nothing but must act suitably to its nature ; water cannot but moisten, fire cannot but burn ; so likewise the corrupt nature of man, being possessed with an invincible contrariety and enmity to God, will never suffer him to comply with God. And the inclinations of a sinner to sin being more strengthened by the frequency of sinful acts, have as great a power over him, and as natural to him, as any qualities are to natural agents ; and being stronger than any sympathies in the world, cannot by a man's own power, or the power of any other nature equal to it, be turned into a contrary channel. (2) Nothing can act beyond its own principle and nature. Nothing in the world can raise itself to a higher rank of being than that which nature hath placed it in. A spark cannot make itself a star, though it mount a little up to heaven ; nor a plant endue itself with sense, nor a beast adorn itself with reason, nor a man make himself an angel. It is Christ's conclusion, "How can you, being evil, speak good things?" (Matt. xii. 33, 34). Not so much as the buds and blossoms of words, much less the fruit of actions. They can no more change their natures than a viper can cashier his poison. Now, though this I have said be true, yet there is nothing man does more affect in the world than a self-sufficiency and an independency upon any other power but his own. This temper is as much riveted in his nature as any other false principle whatsoever ; for man does derive it from his first parents, as the prime legacy bequeathed to his nature. If a putrefied rotten carcase should be brought to life, it could never be thought that it inspired itself with that active principle. God lets men run on so far in sin, that they do unman themselves, that he may proclaim to all the world that we are unable to do anything of ourselves at first towards our recovery without a superior principle. The evidence of which will appear if we consider—1. Man's subjection under sin. He is " sold under sin " (Rom. vii. 14), and brought into captivity to " the law of sin " (ver. 23) ; law of sin, that sin seems to have a legal authority over him ; and man is not only a slave to one sin, but divers (Titus i. 3), "serving divers lusts." 2. Man's affection to them. He doth not only serve them, but he serves them, and every one of them, with delight and pleasure (Titus iii. 3). They were all pleasures as well as lusts, friends as well as lords. Will any man leave his voluptuousness, and such sins that please and flatter his flesh ? No piece of dirty muddy clay can form itself into a neat and handsome vessel ; no plain piece of timber can fit itself for the building, much less a crooked one ; nor a man that is born blind give himself eyes. IV. God's regard for His own glory. 1. The glory of His patience. We wonder, when we see a notorious sinner, how God can let His thunders still lie by Him, and His sword rust in His sheath. "I will not execute the fierceness of mine anger, I will not return to destroy Ephraim; for I am God, and not man" (Hosea xi. 9). If a man did inherit all the meekness of all the angels and all the men that ever were in the world, he could not be able to bear with patience the extravagances and injuries done in the world the space of one day; for none but a God, *i.e.*, one infinitely longsuffering, can bear with them. Not a sin passed in the world before the coming of Christ in the flesh but was a commendatory letter of God's forbearance, "To declare His righteousness for the remission of sins that are past, through the forbearance of God" (Rom. iii. 25). And not a sin passed before the coming of Christ into the soul but gives the same testimony, and bears the same record. "Howbeit, for this cause I obtained mercy, that in me first Jesus Christ might shew forth all long-suffering, for a pattern to them which should hereafter believe on Him" (ver. 16). This was Christ's end in letting him run so far, that He might show forth not a few mites, grains, or ounces of patience, but all longsuffering, longsuffering without measure, or weight, by wholesale; and this as a pattern to all ages of the world; ὑποτύ-πωσιν, for a type: a type is but a shadow in respect of the substance. To show that all the ages of the world should not waste that patience, whereof He had then mani-fested but a pattern. A pattern, we know, is less than the whole piece of cloth from whence it is cut; and as an essay is but a short taste of a man's skill, and doth not discover all his art, as the first miracle Christ wrought, of turning water into wine, as a sample of what power He had, was less than those miracles which succeeded; and the first miracle God wrought in Egypt, in turning Aaron's rod into a serpent, was but a sample of His power which would produce greater wonders; so this patience to Paul was but a little essay of His meekness, a little patience cut off from the whole piece, which should always be dealing out to some sinners or other, and would never be cut wholly out till the world had left being. This sample or pattern was but of the extent of a few years; for Paul was but young, the Scripture terms him a young man (Acts vii. 58), about thirty-six years of age, yet he calls it all longsuffering. Ah, Paul! some since have experienced more of this patience; in some it has reached not only to thirty, but forty, fifty, or sixty years. 2. Grace. It is partly for the admiration of this grace that God intends the day of judgment. It is a strange place: "When He shall come to be glorified in His saints, and to be admired in all them that believe in that day" (2 Thess. i. 10). It is the glory of a man to pass by an offence (Prov. xix. 11), *i.e.* it is a manifestation of a property which is an honour to him to be known to have. If it be thus an honour to pass by an offence simply, then the greater the offence is, and the more the offences are which he passeth by, the greater must the glory needs be, because it is a manifesta-tion of such a quality in greater strength and vigour. So it must argue a more exceeding grace in God to remit many and great sins in man, than to forgive only some few and lesser offences. (1) Fulness of His grace. He shews hereby that there is more grace in Him than there can be sin in us or the whole world. That grace should rise in its tide higher than sin, and bear it down before it, just as the rolling tide of the sea riseth higher than the streams of the river, and beats them back with all their mud and filth. It was mercy in God to create us; it is abundant mercy to make any new creatures, after they had forfeited their happiness (1 Peter i. 3). (2) Freeness of grace. None can entertain an imagination that Christ should be a debtor to sin, unless in vengeance, much less a debtor to the worst of sinners. But if Christ should only take persons of moral and natural excellencies, men might suspect that Christ were some way or other engaged to them, and that the gift of salvation were limited to the endowments of nature, and the good exercise and use of a man's own will. Therefore it is frequently God's method in Scripture, just before the offer of pardon, to sum up the sinner's debts, with their aggrava-tions; to convince them of their insolvency to satisfy so large a score, and also to manifest the freeness and vastness of His grace (Isa. xliii. 22–24). It is so free, that the mercy we abuse, the Name we have profaned, the Name of which we have deserved wrath, opens its mouth with pleas for us (Ezek. xxxvi. 21). Not for their sakes. It should be wholly free; for He repeats their profaning of His name four times. This name He would sanctify, *i.e.*, glorify. How? In cleansing them from their filthiness (ver. 25). His name, while it pleads for them, mentions their demerits, that grace might appear to be grace indeed, and triumph in its own freeness. (3) Extent of His grace. The mercy of God is called His riches, and exceeding riches of grace. He pardons iniquities for His name's sake; and who can spell all the letters of His name, and turn over all the leaves in the book of mercy? Who shall say to His grace, as He does to the sea, Hitherto shalt thou go, and no further? His exchequer is never empty; "Keeps mercy for thousands" (Exod. xxxiv. 7), in a readiness to deal it upon thousand millions of sins as well as millions of persons. He hath a cleansing virtue and a pardoning grace for all iniquities and transgressions (Jer. xxxiii. 8). (4) Compassion of His grace. The formal nature of mercy is tenderness, and the natural effect of it is relief. The more miserable the object, the more compassionate human mercy is, and the more forward to assist. Now that mercy which in man is a quality in God is a nature. How would the infinite tenderness of His nature be discovered, if there were no objects to draw it forth? Now the greater the disease, the greater is that compassion discovered to be wherewith God is so fully stored. (5) Sincerity and pleasure of His grace. Ordinary pardon proceeds from His delight in mercy; "Who is a God like unto Thee, that pardoneth iniquity, and passeth by the transgression of the remnant of His heritage. He retaineth not His anger for ever, because He delighteth in mercy" (Micah vii. 18). If He were not sincere, He would never change the heart of an enemy, and shew kindness to him in the very act of enmity; for the first act of grace upon us is quite against our wills. It is so much His delight, that it is called by the very name of His glory: "The glory of the Lord shall follow thee" (Isa. lviii. 8): *i.e.* the mercy of the Lord shall follow them at the very heels. Christ does not care for staying where He has not opportunities to do great cures, suitable to the vastness of His power (Mark vi. 5). 3. Power. The Scriptures make conversion a most wonderful work, and resemble it to creation, and the resurrection of Christ from the dead, &c. What vast power must that be that can change a black cloud into a glorious sun? This and more doth God do in conversion. He doth not only take smooth pieces of the softest matter, but the ruggedest timber full of knots, to plane and show both His strength and art upon. 4. Wisdom. A new creature is a curious piece of Divine art, fashioned by God's wisdom to set for the praise of the framer, as a poem is, by a man's reason and fancy, to publish the wit and parts of the composer. It is a great skill of an artificer, with a mixture of a few sands and ashes, by his breath to blow up such a clear and diaphanous body as glass, and frame several vessels of it for several uses. It is not barely his breath that does it, for other men have breath as well as he; but it is breath managed by art. And is it not a marvellous skill in God to make a miry soul so pure and crystalline on a sudden, to endue an irrational creature with a Divine nature, and by a powerful word to frame so beautiful a model as a new creature is! The more intricate and knotty any business is, the more eminent is a man's ability in effecting it. This wisdom appears—(1) In the subjects He chooseth. We will go no further than the example in our text. Our apostle seems to be a man full of heat and zeal. I say, to turn these affections and excellencies to run in a heavenly channel, and to guide this natural passion and heat for the service and advancement of that interest which before he endeavoured to destroy, and for the propagation of that gospel which before he persecuted, is an effect of a wonderful wisdom; as it is a rider's skill to order the mettle of a headstrong horse for his own use to carry him on his journey. (2) This wisdom appears in the time. As man's wisdom consists as well in timing his actions as contriving the models of them, so doth God's. He lays hold of the fittest opportunities to bring His wonderful providences upon the stage. His timing of His grace was excellent in the conversion of Paul. (*a*) In respect of Himself. There could not be a fitter time to glorify His grace than when Paul was almost got to the length of his chain; almost to the sin against the Holy Ghost. Christ suffered him to run to the brink of hell before He laid hold upon him. (*b*) In respect of others. Behold the nature of this lion changed, just as he was going to fasten upon his prey. And was it not a fit time, when the devil hoped to rout the Christians by him, when the high priests assured themselves success from this man's passionate zeal, when the Church travailed with throws of fear of him? (3) This wisdom appears to keep up the credit of Christ's death. The great excellence of Christ's sacrifice, wherein it transcends the sacrifices under the law, is because it perfectly makes an atonement for all sins; it first satisfies God, and then calms the conscience, which they could not do (Heb. x. 1, 2), for there was a conscience of sin after their sacrifices. Not a light, but a great transgression. Now, if Christ's death be not satisfactory for great debts, Christ must be too weak to perform what God intended by Him, and so infinite wisdom was frustrate of its intention, which cannot, nor ought not, to be imagined. Now, therefore, God takes the greatest sinners, to show—(*a*) First, the value of this sacrifice. If God should only entertain men of a lighter guilt, Christ's death would be suspected to be too low a ransom for monstrous enormities. (*b*) The virtue of this sacrifice. He is a " priest for ever " (Heb. vii. 17) ; and therefore the virtue as well as the value of His sacrifice remains for ever : He hath " obtained an eternal redemption " (Heb. ix. 12), *i.e.*, a redemption of an eternal efficacy. And those who were stung all over, as well as those who are bitten but in one part, may, by a believing look upon Him, draw virtue from Him as diffusive as their sin. Now the new conversion of men of extraordinary guilt proclaims to the world, that the fountain of His blood is inexhaustible ; that the virtue of it is not spent and drained, though so much hath been drawn out of it for these five thousand years and upwards, for the cleansing of sins past before His coming, and sins since His death. (4) For the fruitfulness of this grace in the converts themselves. The most rugged souls prove most eminent in grace upon their conversion, as the most orient diamonds in India, which are naturally more rough, are most sparkling when cut and smoothed. V. The fruits of converting grace, &c. 1. A sense of the sovereignty of grace in conversion, will first increase thankfulness. Converts only are fit to shew forth the praises of Christ (1 Peter ii. 9). But suppose a man had been all his lifetime like a mole under ground, and had never seen so much as the light of a candle, and had a view of that weak light at a distance, how would he admire it, when he compares it with his former darkness ? But if he should be brought further, to behold the moon with her train of stars, his amazement would increase with the light. But let this person behold the sun, be touched with its warm beams, and enjoy the pleasure of seeing those rarities which the sun discovers, he will bless himself, adore it, and embrace that person who led him to enjoy such a benefit. And the blackness of that darkness he sat in before, will endear the present splendour to him, swell up such a spring-tide of astonishment, as that there shall be no more spirit in him. God lets men sit long in the shadow of death, and run to the utmost of sin, before He stops them, that their danger may enhance their deliverance. 2. Love and affection. The fire of grace cannot be stifled, but will break out in glory to God. God permits a man's sin to abound, that His love after pardon may abound too (Luke vii. 47). 3. Service and obedience. Such will endeavour to redeem the time, because their former days have been so evil, and recover those advantages of service which they lost by a course of sin. They will labour that the largeness of their sin may be answered by an extension of their zeal. 4. Humility and self-emptiness. As no apostle was so God-magnifying, so none was so self-vilifying as Paul. Though he was the greatest apostle, yet he accounts himself less than the least of all saints (Eph. iii. 8). 5. Bewailing of sin, and self-abhorrence for it. 6. Faith and dependence. (1) At present, in the instant of the first act of faith. Great sins make us appear in the court of jurisdiction, with a naked faith, when we have nothing to merit it, but much to deserve the contrary (Rom. iv. 5). The more ungodly, the more elevated is that faith which lays hold on God. (2) In following occasions. Pardoning such great sins, and converting such great sinners, is the best credential letter Christ brings with Him from heaven. Men naturally would scarce believe for His own sake, but for His work's sake they would, because they are more led by sense than faith. For every great conversion is as a sea-mark to guide others into a safe harbour. As when a physician comes into a house where many are sick, and cures one that is desperate, it is an encouragement to the rest to rely upon his skill. If men believe not in Christ after the sight of such standing miracles, it is an aggravation of their impenitence, as much as any miracle Christ wrought upon the earth was of the Jew's obstinacy, and does put as black a dye upon it : " Ye, when you had seen it, repented not afterward, that you might believe Him " (Matt. xxi. 32). Further, such conversions evidence that God's commands are practicable, that His yoke is not burdensome. 1. First, the doctrine manifests the power of the gospel. God gains a reputation to the gospel and the power of Christianity, that can in a moment change persons from beasts to men, from serpents to saints. 2. Groundlessness of despair. Despair not of others, when thou dost reflect upon thy own crimes, and considerest that God never dealt with a baser heart in the world than thine was. Comfort of this subject : If God has made thee of a great sinner the object of His mercy, thou mayest be assured of—(1) Continuance of His love. He pardoned thee when thou wert an enemy, will He leave thee now thou art His friend ? (2) Supplies of His grace. Thou hadst a rich present of His grace sent thee when thou couldst not pray for it, and will He not much more give thee whatsoever is needful when thou callest upon Him? A wise builder does not begin a work when he is not able to finish it. God considered, before He began with thee, what charge thou wouldst stand him in, both of merit in Christ and grace in thee; so that the grace He hath given thee is not only a mercy to thee, but an obligation on Himself since His credit is engaged to complete it. (3) Strength against corruptions. Can molehills stand against him who has levelled mountains? Can a few clouds withstand the melting force of the sun, which has dissolved those black mists that overspread the face of the heavens? No more can the remainders of thy corruption bear head against His power, which has thrown down the great hills of the sins of thy natural condition, and has dissolved the thick fogs of thy unregeneracy. 1. To those that God hath dealt so with. (1) Glorify God for His grace. (2) Admiration is all the glory you can give to God for His grace, seeing you can add nothing to His essential glory. 2. Often call to mind thy former sin. It hath been the custom of the saints of God formerly. When Matthew reckons up the twelve apostles (Matt. x. 3) whereof he was one, he remembers his former state, "Matthew the publican"; but none of the other evangelists call him so in that enumeration. (1) It makes us more humble. Thoughts of pride cannot lodge in us, when the remembrance of our rags, bolts, and fetters is frequently renewed. (2) It will make us thankful. Sense of misery heightens our obligation to mercy. Men at sea are most thankful for deliverance when they consider the danger of the foregoing storm. A long night makes a clear morning more welcome. (3) It will make thee more active in the exercise of that grace which is contrary to thy former sin. (4) It will be a preservative against falling into the same sin again. The second branch of exhortation is to those that are in a doubting condition. The main objection such make is the greatness of sin. Oh, there was never such a great sinner in the world as I am! But—1. Art thou indeed the greatest sinner? I can hardly believe it. Didst thou ever sin after the rate that Paul did? or wert thou ever possessed with such a fury? 2. Suppose thou art the greatest, is thy staying from Christ the way to make all thy sins less? Art thou so rich as to pay this great debt out of thy own revenue? or hast thou any hopes of another surety? 3. Are thy sins the greatest? Is not the staying from Christ a making them greater? Does not God command thee to come to Christ? and is not thy delay a greater act of disobedience than the complaint of thy sinfulness can be of humility? 4. Were thy sins less than they are, thou mightest not so easily believe in Christ, as now thou mayest. Great sins and a bad heart felt and bewailed, is rather an advantage; as hunger is an incentive to a man to seek for meat. If men had clean hearts, it is like they would dispose of them otherwise, and rather think Christ should come to them. Men's poverty should rather make them more importunate than more modest. If, therefore, thou art afraid of drowning under these mighty floods which roll upon thee, methinks thou shouldst do as men ready to perish in the waters, catch hold of that which is next them, though it be the dearest friend they have; and there is none nearer to thee than Christ, nor any such a friend; catch hold therefore of Him. 5. The greatness of thy sin is a ground for a plea. Turn thy sins into arguments, as David doth, "for it is great" (Psa. xxv. 11). If thy disease were not so great, Christ's glory would not be so illustrious. Pardon of such sins enhanceth the mercy and skill of thy Saviour. Plead therefore—1. The infiniteness of God's mercy. It is strange if thy debts should be so great, that the exchequer of the King of kings cannot discharge them. Hast Thou not said that Thou art He "that blots out transgressions for Thy own sake"? (Isa. xliii. 25); that Thou dost "blot out iniquities like a thick cloud"? (Isa. xliv. 22). Is there any cloud so thick as to master the melting power of the sun; and shall ever a cloud of sin be so thick as to master the power of Thy mercy? Has not Thy mercy as much strength and eloquence to plead for me, as Thy justice has to declaim against me? Is Thy justice better armed with reason than Thy kindness with compassions? Have Thy compassions no eloquence? Oh, who can resist their pleasing rhetoric! 2. Christ's, and God's intent in His coming, was to discharge great sins. He was called Jesus, a Saviour, because He was to save His people from their sins. And do you think some of His people's sins were not as great as any men's sins in the world? 3. Christ's death was a satisfaction for the greatest sins, for God could not accept any satisfaction, but what was infinite. "One sacrifice for sins for ever," &c. (Heb. x. 12); not one sin, but sins; not little sins, but sins without exception. Let thy objections be what they will, Christ shall be my advocate to answer for me. 4. Christ is able to take away great sins. Did He ever let any one that came to Him with a great infirmity, go back without a cure, and dishonour Himself so much, as that it should be said, it was a distemper too great for the power of Jesus to remedy? And why should there be any sin that He cannot pardon? But, may the soul say, I do not question His power, but His will. Therefore —5. Christ's nature leads Him to show mercy to the greatest sinners. 6. Christ was exalted by God upon this very account (Heb. vii. 25). 7. Christ is entrusted by God to give out His grace to great sinners. Christ is God's Lord-almoner, for the dispensing redemption, and the riches of His grace. Fourthly, the caution which this subject suggests. 1. Think not thy sins are pardoned because they are not so great as those God has pardoned in others. A few small sands may sink a ship as well as a great rock. Thy sins may be pardoned though as great as others, but then you must have equal qualifications with them. They had great sins, so hast thou; but have you as great a hatred and loathing of sin as they had? 2. Let not this doctrine encourage any person to go on in sin. God never intended mercy as a sanctuary to protect sin. 1. It is disingenuous to do so. Great love requires great duties, not great sins. Freeness of grace should make us increase holiness in a more cheerful manner. 2. It is foolish so to do. Would any man be so simple as to set his house on fire because he has a great river running by his door, from whence he may have water to quench it; or wound himself, because there is an excellent plaster which has cured several? 3. It is dangerous to do so. If thou losest the present time, thou art in danger to lose eternity. There are many in hell never sinned at such a presumptuous rate. He is merciful to the penitent, but He will not be unfaithful to His threatenings. (*S. Charnock.*) *The pattern convert; or, the chief sinner saved:*—I. THIS PATTERN CONVERT HAD BEEN THE CHIEF OF SINNERS. 1. He had displayed invincible zeal in opposing the gospel. He believed in the Jewish religion, and he hated and persecuted the cause of Christ. He executed his mission in right earnest. He ever felt that no arm but the Almighty arm could have reached and delivered him from this terrible depth of ruin. 2. He had been an excessively proud man. Saul of Tarsus possessed a haughty spirit. His unconquerable love to the law arose from the pride and arrogance of his unregenerate heart. 3. His mental power, too, aided him in his work. He was a scholar of no ordinary character, blended with natural energy and grasp of intellect. II. THE SALVATION OF THIS PATTERN CONVERT ILLUSTRATES THE MEDIATORIAL STRENGTH OF CHRIST. The chief of sinners has been saved. 1. The salvation of Paul is an evidence of the sufficiency of the atonement. 2. The salvation of Paul is a proof of the efficacy of victorious grace. 3. The salvation of Paul proves the worth of intercession. Who first arrested the man on his way to Damascus? Christ—He pleaded with the persecutor and conquered him by love. 4. The salvation of Paul exhibits Divine patience. "That in me first Jesus Christ might show forth all long-suffering"—patience. III. THIS PATTERN CONVERT PROCLAIMS THE SAVIOUR IN THE GOSPEL AS WORTHY OF ALL ACCEPTATION. Why? 1. Because He is the revelation of the highest intelligence to man's reason. He is the manifold wisdom of God—"God manifest in the flesh." Reason could trace out the handiwork of God in every star that glitters in the heavens, but in Christ it sees God in human form. No such revelation of God was ever made before the incarnation as the one which we possess. Sir Isaac Newton revealed the great law that binds atom to atom, and all to its mighty centre; and angels have made glorious revelations; but in Christ we see God interested in, and saving His enemies. 2. He is the only antidote for sin. 3. He alone reveals the hope of immortality. Christ meets the highest aspirations of our nature by His resurrection and ascension; He has drawn aside the veil of futurity and "opened the kingdom of heaven to all believers." 4. This revelation is based in truth. Other books contain pretended revelations, but they have no foundation in truth. The Koran, to wit: the gospel however is "a faithful," a true "saying." Prophecy, miracle and history, as well as its own almighty efficacy, prove that it is true. (*J. H. Hill.*) *The chief of sinners:*—It was a characteristic of the religion of Paul, that it was eminently personal and practical. The idea, therefore, to which we direct your attention is this: That true religion, and great experience in it, cause the believer to regard himself peculiarly a sinner. We have several considerations to prove this. I. THE VIEW WHICH A BELIEVER HAS OF HIS OWN HEART IS MORE MINUTE, AND MORE EXTENSIVE ALSO, THAN ANY VIEW HE CAN TAKE OF ANOTHER'S. He cannot draw upon another's memory as he can upon his own. His quickened recollections furnish him with many a dark chapter, as his mind roves back upon forgotten years; and there is a vividness and freshness in the recollection of what a sinner he has been, which throws over his own experience an aspect of peculiarity. He can number his own sins as he cannot another's. He can recollect the smallness of temptation, and the tender, and touching, and terrible motives which would have restrained him from his sins if he would only have felt them. Conscience, with an eye of fire, will look into his soul, and the aggravations of sin, which arose from a thousand circumstances of his condition and God's forbearance toward him, will seem to invest his sinfulness with a criminality and an abomination beyond anything that he will dare to attribute to other people. II. VERY MUCH IN PROPORTION TO THE EXTENT OF A BELIEVER'S GRACIOUS ATTAINMENTS IS PURE CONSCIENCE BROUGHT INTO EXERCISE. We mean by this pure conscience an exercise of that faculty as such, in its own nature and for its own ends, not mingled with other affections. And one great difference betwixt the convictions of a believer and the convictions of an unbeliever consists simply in this; the different impressions they have of the mere wrong of sin. A believer sees that wrong as an unbeliever does not. In sin itself he sees an evil which an unbeliever does not. III. THE RULE OF CONSCIENCE IS NOT A THING WELL UNDERSTOOD BY AN UNCON-VERTED SINNER IN HIS ORDINARY FRAME OF MIND. The deceptions of sin have been flung over it. But when the Holy Spirit justly convicted him, he saw sin in himself that he never saw before, and hope died within him. He discovered what God's law meant and where it applied. Law reigns; and now, better and better understood, sharper than any two-edged sword, a discerner of the thoughts and intents of the heart; it is no wonder that every just conception of God's law should tend to make the grace-enlightened believer conceive of himself as the chief of sinners. He sees that that code of spiritual purity has strange applications to his erring soul. His very spirit cannot hide from it for a single moment. It pursues the soul everywhere. IV. THE RELIGIOUS ATTEMPTS OF A BELIEVER CONSTITUTE ANOTHER CONSIDERATION. They have been many, and he is fully conscious that they have sometimes been sincere and earnest; but oh! how often have they been baffled! What vain purposes! How little his strength! How many sinful desires! He utters the deep-toned cry, Chief of sinners! Chief of sinners! V. THROUGHOUT ALL THE SUC-CESSFUL ATTAINMENTS OF GRACE, A BELIEVER IS INVARIABLY BECOMING BETTER ACQUAINTED WITH GOD. The knowledge he has of the Divine character constitutes one of the most efficacious aids and impressive influences. The better he knows God the better he knows himself; and while his knowledge of God increases both his reverence and his attachment, his knowledge of himself fills him with humiliation and shame. Sin appears worse and worse to him as he knows God better. VI. A CHRISTIAN, ESPECIALLY AMID HIS ATTAINMENTS IN GRACE, IS A CREATURE OF NO LITTLE REFLECTION. His knowledge increases, especially his knowledge of himself; and amid reflections and increasing knowledge in Divine things, again and again he is surprised and disappointed in a most painful and humiliating manner. Sometimes he is astounded, and disheartened, and driven to prayer by a wave of despondency that rolls over his soul. His reflection discovers sin as he did not expect, discovers it wherein he had little suspicion of its existence. He finds the imperfection of his repentance, that his very repentance (according to the graphic description of the apostle) needs to be repented of. VII. THAT PROCESS OF SANCTIFICATION CARRIED ON IN A BELIEVER'S HEART BY THE OMNIPOTENT POWER OF THE HOLY SPIRIT IS VERY MUCH CARRIED ON THROUGH THE INFLUENCE OF TWO SPIRITUAL OPERATIONS: first, the discovery of sin, and second, faith in the Redeemer of sinners to procure pardon and justification unto life eternal. There is the combined influence of compulsion and attraction; of violence and persuasion. The believer is driven off from himself at the same moment he is drawn toward God. But this process and these affections are sometimes interrupted. His soul wanders from God. And that it should ever wander seems to him one of the strangest anomalies in the universe! The conclusions from this subject are worthy of remembrance. 1. Never despair. There is mercy for the chief of sinners. 2. Never seek hope, consolation, or any comfort or encouragement to your soul by diminished ideas of sin. 3. Never judge of your Christian condition by the smallness of your humiliating convictions. Rather judge of it by the magnitude of them. 4. Never allow pride to have any place in your religion. Self-complacency all rests on ignorance and deception. 5. Never imagine that a deep sense of sin and all the humiliating ideas that grow out of it, are things of unhappiness and gloom. Quite the contrary. They are matters of peace and joy to a believer. (*J. S. Spencer, D.D.*) *The chief of sinners:*—I. I have TO TRY AND HUNT OUT THE CHIEF OF SINNERS. Now who are they? They come under various characters, and may be classified in different lists. 1. We will begin with those who directly oppose themselves to God and to His Christ. These are chief among sinners. Paul did join their ranks. 2. And here I ought to put down those who hold views derogatory of the Deity and the person of Christ. 3. Another group of princes and peers in the realm of evil may be described as those who attack Christ's people, and who seek to pervert them from the right way. 4. There is another group whom you will all allow to be of the chief of sinners—those who have sinned foully in the world's esteem; violating the instincts of nature, and outraging the common sense of morality and decency. 5. And surely I may find another class of the chief of sinners among those who have become not only adepts themselves, but the tutors to others in the school of evil. 6. In this section we include those who have had much light, and yet have sinned against it; who have been taught better, who have had a knowledge of the way of truth, and yet have turned aside to crooked paths. 7. There are those, too, who sit under an earnest ministry, and yet go on in sin—they surely belong to the class of chief sinners. 8. Drawing the bow at a venture, there is another class I would single out, those who are gifted from their childhood with a tender conscience. 9. Yet again ; if you have had warning in sickness, and especially if on your sick bed you have vowed unto the Lord that you would turn to Him, then you that are covenant-breakers, you that violate vows made to the Most High, you must also be put among the first and foremost of transgressors. II. Why those who are proverbially the chief of sinners are very frequently saved. 1. One reason is to illustrate Divine sovereignty. 2. Another reason is, that He may show His great power. Oh ! how hell is made angry when some great champion falls ! When their Goliaths are brought down, how the Philistines take to their heels ! How heaven rings with songs when some chief of sinners becomes a trophy of the Divine power ! 3. And next, how it shows His grace ! 4. Again ; great sinners are very frequently called by God for the purpose of attracting others. 5. And then, the saving of the chief of sinners is useful, because, when they are saved they generally make the most fiery zealots against sin. Have we not a proverb that " The burnt child dreads the fire " ? I noticed my host, on one preaching excursion, particularly anxious about my candle. Now, as everybody ought to know how careful I am, I was a little surprised, and I put the question to him why he should be so wonderfully particular. " I had my house burnt down once, sir," said he. That explained it all. No man so much afraid of fire as he, and they who have been in sin, and know the mischief of it, protest against it the most loudly. They can speak experimentally. Oh! what revenge there seems to be in the apostle's heart against his sin! 6. And then, again, they always make the most zealous saints. (*C. H. Spurgeon.*) *The chief of sinners :*—I. Why, then, did St. Paul call himself the chief of sinners ? It is a startling designation, and the more you think of it the more startling you will feel it to be. It is a mere truism to say that the success of a religion depends to a large extent upon the personal veracity and goodness of its founders. Now, St. Paul was practically the founder of Christianity over a large area of the heathen world. It was he who had told them almost everything they knew of Christ. It was his version of Christ's teaching, his view of the meaning and scope of His work, with which they were most, if not exclusively familiar. And he frequently declared that he himself was the style of man a Christian ought to be. " Be ye followers of me," he said, " as I also am of Christ." How, then, were they to understand him when he asserted himself to be the chief of sinners ? It can hardly be denied that had such a confession escaped from the lips of any but a Christian apostle it would have produced a very perplexing, if not a thoroughly suspicious impression. Would any of the great heathen philosophers, or any one who aspired to found a religion, have ventured to terminate his career by an assertion of his own incomparable sinfulness? And if he had, would it not have discredited his mission or been considered too absurd to be serious? But it was not so with St. Paul's confession. It gave no uneasiness to his most sensitive converts, no occasion for reproach to his most implacable foes. Does not this prove that Christianity had a way of dealing with sin peculiar to itself, and produced a type of character absolutely unique ? But assuming that St. Paul used the words seriously, *i.e.*, without any intentional exaggeration, what did he really mean ? We are very apt to entertain defective and partial conceptions of sin. Many virtually restrict it to those modes of its expression which they themselves have experienced. They are troubled by some particular evil which natural inclination, or continued indulgence, has invested with special power. It may be the lust of avarice, or an envious and angry passion, or an unholy and impure desire. But whatever it may be, it is the sin which engages the attention and alarms the conscience of the man whom it attacks ; and if he be a Christian it is the sin which he struggles against, and whose very touch fills him with a self-reproach almost too heavy to be borne. It is very natural that any one in this condition should come to conceive of sin as almost identified with his peculiar temptation. It is the sin he thinks about when any reference is made to the subject. And it is entire deliverance from its defilement that constitutes his highest idea of happiness. Was it, then, because St. Paul was pressed by some special thorn of this kind that he called himself the chief of sinners? We can hardly think so, if we remember the language and style of his Epistles. There is scarcely a sin which he does not mention and tell us something about. He points out wherein the enormity of certain transgressions consists. He shows us the disposition and temper out of which others are likely to spring, and how to resist or baffle their attacks. He draws up exhaustive catalogues of offences, for the purpose of reminding us that not one of them, however much it might be tolerated in heathen society, is consistent with citizenship in the kingdom of God. But if the apostle was not likely to exaggerate in this particular way, was it not possible he might do so in another? There are not a few who know the many shapes which evil may assume, but who know them theoretically, rather than practically. The world they know is a world of respectability, and perhaps of high moral principle. But they do not know the outer circles of our social life, the broad zone of lawlessness that surrounds the region of decency. And you feel accordingly that the conceptions of evil which such people have are necessarily defective. They may be filled with an intense conviction of the guilt of the sins they know, but their knowledge does not go far. And their self-accusations, when they are expressed, strike you, for this reason, as being unreal. They have an air of extravagance, unperceived by those who utter them, but quite discernible by anybody else. Was St. Paul, then, a person of this sort? Was it ignorance of life, or of human nature, that made him place himself first in the catalogue of sinners? It can hardly have been this, either, for he lived at a time when the world was at its worst, and very few men of his day had seen so much of it as he. He had known the chief priests and rabbis of Jerusalem, and the philosophers of the Grecian schools. He had traversed the rougher districts of heathendom, where passion gave itself vent in coarse and brutal fashion. He had beat about the slums of the largest cities, and lain in the common prisons with the scum and offscouring of the earth. You may depend upon it that the man who had written the first chapter of the Epistle to the Romans, and had lived in Rome two years during the reign of Nero, a reign when all kinds of devilry literally ran riot—knew perfectly well what he was about when he declared himself the chief of sinners. The truth is that St. Paul had a very rare and exceptional insight into his own heart, and also into the nature of sin. There was no part of him allowed to be at rest, no reserve of energy which lay idle, and which might have developed, had it roused itself up, an unsuspected weakness or liability to excess. The whole force of the man went into his work. He was always on the stretch, always expending every particle of strength in following after the one aim of his efforts. Hence he felt himself all through. Every weak place betrayed its weakness. Every temptation to swerve from his path pierced him like an arrow. Every sluggish or selfish impulse acted like a drag upon his eager limbs. The very ardour of his devotion, the keenness of his pursuit, made the least hindrance an unspeakable pain. But not only so, he saw it with an eye that penetrated farther into its depths than that of any other has done. He detected the fearful possibilities of ruin that lie wrapped in its every germ. He knew the pervasive power that enables it to infect the whole nature of a man, if it once be suffered· to escape from restraint. He knew how terrible were the passions that once strove in his own heart, and still slumbered there. And above all his bright vision of the holiness of God, his sublime conception of Christ's purity threw a white light that beat upon his sin and exposed its every line, and feature, and movement. He saw it so distinctly and plainly that other men's sins were hazy and vague, and dwelt in the region of comparative shadow. II. WHY ST. PAUL APPENDED THIS REMARK ABOUT HIMSELF TO THE STATEMENT IN THE VERSE. The drift of the passage leads us to believe that he meant it to confirm the faithfulness of the saying. It was equivalent to putting his subscription at the foot of it, as one who endorsed it or attested its truth. In proof of the assertion that Christ Jesus had come into the world to save sinners, he appealed to his own case as specially to the point. There was no room for despair when he had found mercy. It would not do much to recommend the skill of a physician that you declared he had healed you of a most virulent disease, if it turned out, after all, that your ailment had existed chiefly in your own imagination, and been little more than a touch of hypochondria. I should say that the most desperate man is he who is neither careless, nor a profligate, nor a formalist, but one who, earnest and correct in conduct, is conscientiously attached to a false or defective creed, and bent enthusiastically on pushing its claims. Such a one, sustained by the proud consciousness of always having done what he considered his duty, and therefore troubled by no compunctions of conscience, free from every impure or unseemly indulgence, convinced that he is right in his opinions, and so far enamoured of their excellence, or filled with contempt for their rivals, that he finds the greatest satisfaction in urging them upon the world, is not likely to be easily turned from the course he pursues. The fact is he cannot conceive any reason for a change. So there is no opening by which you can approach him. Was not St. Paul very much such a character as this? Christ proved able to accomplish what, humanly speaking, seemed impossible. He saved the man who of all men in the world seemed the least likely, and the most difficult, to be saved. And St. Paul never could look back to his conversion but with feelings of the most reverent awe and adoring thankfulness. III. THE STATE-MENT ITSELF—THAT CHRIST JESUS CAME INTO THE WORLD TO SAVE SINNERS. Sinners were the object of His mission, and sinners without any distinction. Now, what He has promised is not merely to rescue us from some future danger, indeed has nothing to do with the future directly at all. " Christ saves us from sin," he says, " here and now, and my case substantiates the statement." And if you should ask how this can be, since he has just told us, not simply that he was the chief of sinners before his conversion, but is so still, the answer is, that Christ does not save us by any magical or mechanical process. He does not entirely sever us from the past and its transgressions, though He does secure that they shall not involve us in the destruction which is their natural result. He leaves us to fight a hard battle with the root of sin that still survives in our nature. Having robbed it of its power of irreparable mischief, He enlists us in completing its extinction. He spoils it of its old fascination. He exposes its emptiness and folly. He counteracts its force by revealing attractions that lift us above the sphere of its influence. And our present actual superiority to its rule is won through the gradual emancipation and strengthening of our character. Surely it is a much more crushing defeat to what has brought such misery upon us that it should be despised and baffled by its former victims. St. Paul, then, could say that he was the chief of sinners, and yet appeal to himself as an illustration of Christ's power to save. Indeed, his very confession was itself an evidence of his redemption. It revealed a humility that implied the overthrow of pride and self-complacency, the very qualities in which the strength of sin resides. You are saved from its final triumph. Only see that you keep hold of the promise of mercy and of grace to help us in Jesus Christ. Let no onset of sin drive you from Him, no fresh development of its resources tempt you to distrust Him. You can only fight and overcome as you fall back on His word, and grasp the hope which it reveals. (*C. Moinet, M.A.*)    *Fourth Sunday after Trinity* :—I. HOW ARE WE TO UNDERSTAND THIS LANGUAGE OF THE APOSTLE RESPECTING HIMSELF? You will, I hope, at once dismiss from your minds any thought that the apostle was exhibiting to his son Timothy what some would call a graceful humility. We ought to assure ourselves that no humility can be graceful, because none can be gracious, which has not its foundation in truth. Of all qualities, this is the one which it is most monstrous to counterfeit. He would speak of himself as he would of another man, honestly and simply. If it was the fact that he had laboured more abundantly than all the apostles, he did not shrink from announcing it. Neither must we say that St. Paul was led to give himself this title because he had a sudden and keen remembrance of his life when he was a persecutor of the faith. But he could not think himself —we know from the words which he uses when describing his previous history that he did not think himself—worse than other persecutors merely because he was more zealous than they were. He was certainly not the chief of sinners because he acted out a wrong conviction more vigorously than others did. Nor must we forget that the words, literally taken, do not warrant us in supposing that St. Paul referred wholly or chiefly to the past. If he says, " I am first, or chief," Timothy must have understood that he was not charging himself with the crimes of other days, but was expressing what was in his mind at the time he wrote. The law proved its justice by affixing to each palpable outrage and overt act its meet recompense of reward. St. Paul had been a zealot in enforcing the law; he had never brought himself within the range of one, even the mildest, of its formal censures. " But by the law," he says elsewhere, " comes the knowledge of sin." It prohibits offences; it awakens a man to perceive that there is in him a disposition to commit these offences. Here then St. Paul found himself "first." Yes, in a most awful sense, alone. He had no means of ascertaining how far other men had separated themselves from the righteous, loving mind of God. The law said, " Thou hast done it." And by degrees he found that the law was only echoing without what a Living Voice was saying to him within. The Spirit of God convinced him of sin. And since the more he knew of the attraction of the Divine magnet, the more he knew the strength of the inclination there was in him to wander from it, the more he attributed any right direction of his spirit to its influence—he could say, with no affectation, with the inmost sincerity, " Of sinners I am first. More of this love has been shown to me than to any I know; my resistance therefore has been greater than that of others. If the light has overpowered me, there has been a struggle with it, there is a struggle with it, which I dare not say is equally mighty and desperate in them." If this was the warrant for this mode of speech, you will not wonder that he should have used it with even more emphasis in the later days of his earthly pilgrimage, than in the earlier. You will think, perhaps, that St. Paul's large and intimate acquaintance with the moral abuses and corruptions that sprang up in the members of the different Churches which he had planted, may have diverted his mind from this contemplation, and may have proved that there was a wickedness about him which had never penetrated within him. But you must not fancy that he thought more gently of himself as he became acquainted with the party-spirit and sensuality of the Corinthians, or when he found the Galatians regarding him whom they had once loved with such a violent affection, as their enemy because he told them the truth. I rather suppose that he detected in himself all the evils which caused him such bitter pain in them, that he understood their heresies and carnality and suspicions by the seeds of the like which he found in his own heart; that he never condemned them without passing sentence upon tendencies which might at any moment start to life in him. I apprehend that in this way the more he did this—the more he understood his relation to his flock as their minister and priest—the more he perceived that he was the first among sinners. By such processes, he was, I conceive, trained to a real, not a mock humility.

II. THE WORDS, " CHRIST JESUS CAME INTO THE WORLD TO SAVE SINNERS," SOUND TO US LIKE A COMMONPLACE WHICH WE HEARD IN THE NURSERY. There was some strange hostility between his mind and the mind of a righteous Being, his Creator. Could they be reconciled? There was some bondage upon his will. Could it be set free? This experience, this demand, is met by the broad announcement: " One is come from that righteous Being with whom thou art at war, expressly to make peace. One is come to save sinners out of their sins." He might doubt long and ask earnestly whether news so good could be true. He must have a real emancipation, real peace with God. The claim of every one calling himself a Deliverer and Reconciler must endure the severest of all tests. Was He able to do that which none else had been able to do? Could He accomplish what the law and sacrifices, that he held to be most Divine, had not accomplished? No one could settle them for him. An archangel could not force him to accept the gospel merely on his authority. The poorest man might bring it with such evidence to his conscience that he could not but say, "It is true." And when he had said this, the repetition of the truth to which he had given his adhesion could never become a flat or a stale one. Was this all? Was there no brighter light coming to him every moment from that heaven into which he believed the Son of God had ascended? no clearer and deeper insight into the effects of His coming to our world than had been vouchsafed here at first? Surely there was. It is contained in the plural, " sinners." His experience had been personal. He had known sin in himself. He had known deliverance in himself. But that sin consisted in separation from his fellows as well as from God. That deliverance consisted in reunion to his fellows as well as to God. Jesus Christ had saved him; but He had not come into the world to save him. There was not a man who had not the same needs as he had; there was not a man who had not the same Helper as he had. (*F. D. Maurice, M.A.*)

*Sin:*—Let us begin by thinking what St. Paul could possibly mean by calling himself " the chief of sinners." We know very well that he did not mean, that, either before his conversion or since, his life had been anything but most decorous and respectable. " Men and brethren, I have lived in all good conscience before God unto this day." And, in writing to friends, he could describe himself in those early years before his conversion, as " touching the righteousness which is in the law blameless." It is equally certain that he did not mean that his life had ever been careless, and thoughtless, and worldly. He speaks of himself in one of his Epistles as "profiting," that is, making progress, "in the Jews' religion above many my equals," that is, my cotemporaries. He had also been a very religious man; religious after a wrong pattern of religion, it is true, but still thoroughly and ardently religious after the common type and pattern of the day. And yet this man of blameless life and strict religion, writing quietly in advancing years to a favourite friend and pupil, can speak of himself as the "chief of sinners." What can he mean by such language? One thing is already quite clear. St. Paul must have thought of sin in a way very different from that in which most of us are in the habit of thinking of it. To us, the "chief of sinners" would be a man of utterly profligate and vicious life, who had broken the commandments of God in the most reckless and high-handed way. And so little does our notion of "the chief of sinners" agree with what we know about St. Paul, that, when he calls himself so, while we admire his humility, we barely give him credit for sincerity. He can scarcely have meant it, we think. But I am sure we shall make a great mistake, if we resolve that "I am chief" of our text into a passing pang of pain, shot into his mind by the sudden recollection of those old days, when, as the historian says, "he made havoc of the Church," and "breathed out threatenings and slaughter against the disciples of the Lord." None of us would dream of denying the fact of our sinfulness. That we are sinners we all confess. But the confession is often a very hollow one; means very little; means often only this—that we know we are not perfect, but we believe we are not worse than most people, and are a good deal better than some, and may reasonably expect to do well enough at the last. That St. Paul should speak of himself as the "chief of sinners," seems to persons, who are thinking thus of sin and meaning no more than this by their confession of sinfulness, only an outrageous extravagance of language—a temporary fit of morbid self-reproach. We may be quite sure of this, that so long as we go on comparing ourselves with other people, and judging other people, we shall never come to any real sense of sin, or to any true penitence for it, or to any heartfelt desire for its forgiveness. Such comparison of ourselves with others is utterly false and misleading. Neither must we rest satisfied with judging ourselves by any external standard or rule of life, whether it be the law of God, or the law and custom and fashion of the society of which we are members. We may be models of propriety; exemplary in every department of conduct and life. And yet that may be true of us, which Jesus said was true of the religious world of His own day: "This people honoureth Me with their lips; but their heart is far from Me." For indeed, this terrible matter of sin goes far deeper than outward conduct. Outward conduct may reveal the depths of sin within, may reveal them to the man himself, as well as to the world around. But no outward conduct is a measure of sin. Judged by outward conduct one would have said of St. Paul, that he was as near perfection as a man could be. At this point of our inquiry we must try to get nearer, if we can, to St. Paul's experience. The recollection of those old persecuting days was lying very heavily on his conscience, when he wrote the words of our text; not heavily in the sense of making his forgiveness doubtful, but heavily in the sense of revealing the possibilities of sin within. When he came to himself in the moment of his conversion, the fact that he had been a persecutor of the disciples of Christ, fancying all the while that he was doing God's service, must have made the first rude breach in the self-righteousness of Saul the Pharisee. Time and thought would only enlarge that breach and make it more practicable. If he had deceived himself so grossly once, fancying that to be right and virtuous which was so manifestly wrong and wicked, why not again? It is often such a rude shock as this to vanity and self-confidence that marks an epoch in a man's spiritual life, awakening, and ultimately transforming him. In this way it is that "men may," and often do, "rise by stepping-stones of their dead selves to higher things." We must learn humility. We must learn the bitter lesson of self-distrust. No true progress is possible until this lesson has been learned. Along with this experience —perhaps as part of it—there went another. It was part of the sorrow and humiliation of Saul's conversion, that it revealed to him the painful fact, that his life and work had been set hitherto in a wrong direction; that he must break with his past, and begin all over again; that he had not only missed the mark, but had been aiming at a wrong one. Steadily did he set himself, nobly and courageously, to retrieve the past; to undo what he had done, and to do the very opposite. And again and again that old past rose up against him, to make the new course more

difficult.  In this way, I fancy—or in some such way as this (for who are we, that
we should dare to gauge the experience of a Paul ?)—he seems to have come to those
deeper views of sin, with which his letters are pervaded.  Our English word " sin "
suggests little or nothing of itself to us ; but the Greek equivalent, certainly, and,
I think, the Hebrew also, have their meaning printed broadly and legibly upon
them.  To "sin" in those languages, is to miss the mark ; to fall short of the
mark ; to go wide of the mark ; to fail ; to come short of the true standard.  Now
the moment we lay hold of this, as the deepest meaning and real essence of sin,
that moment self-righteousness becomes impossible to us.  There may be those
here, who cannot bring the sense of sin home to their consciences with any keenness,
so long as sin is regarded merely as "transgression of law" ; so innocent and
blameless have their lives been.  But let them think of "sin" in this deeper, truer
aspect, as missing the mark, failing to be that, which it is in us to be, and which God
by His Spirit and His Providence is calling us to be, and who can hold out against the
conviction, that he is in very truth a sinner, and a very grievous sinner, if not the very
chief of sinners ?  And this sense of sin will become deeper, and this confession of sin
will become more penitent and genuine, in proportion as we pass out of our natural
darkness into the light of God, and begin to discern more clearly what our true
standard is, and what our gifts and capacities are : what it is in us to be, and what
God is seeking to make of us.  The greater the gifts and capacities and endowments,
the more keen will be the sense of failure and shortcoming.  Such reflections as
these, honestly pursued, cannot fail, to use St. Paul's expressive phrase, to "conclude
us all under sin " ; to bring the weight and pressure of a genuine sense of sin to
bear upon us all.  Now, however painful this may be, it is unquestionably the first
step in the right direction.  We cannot become what God would make us until we
are made deeply and sincerely conscious of sin and infirmity, of unworthiness and
unprofitableness.  But we must not leave the subject so.  St. Paul could never leave
it so.  His own personal confession of sin, deep and contrite as it is, is set in the
midst of a burst of triumphant hope.  " This is a faithful saying, and worthy of
all acceptation, that Christ Jesus came into the world to save sinners ; of whom I
am chief."  Yes—"sinners of whom I am chief " ; but then " Christ Jesus came
into the world to save sinners," and, therefore, to save me.  (*D. J. Vaughan, M.A.*)

Ver. 16. **Howbeit for this cause I obtained mercy.**—*Praise for salvation :*—The
narration of personal experience may be very helpful to those who are wanting
instruction or sympathy.  Men are better able to grasp truth in the concrete than
in the abstract.  To see a sinner saved from sin is more helpful than to read of
salvation.  No one recognized this more clearly, or acted on it more wisely, than
Paul ; and some of the most instructive parts of his Epistles are those in which he
recounts his own religious experience.  We may similarly help others, especially
our own children, and those who are within the sacred circle of friendship ; but
the narration of experience may be as harmful as beneficial, if it becomes frequent
or formal.  There is danger of egotism, till our own personality covers the whole
horizon of our thought.  There is risk of affected singularity, as if we wished to be
distinguished from others and considered superior to them.  Referring to himself
he says—I. THAT SALVATION CAME TO ONE MOST UNDESERVING.  "Chief of sinners
though I am," he exclaims, " I obtained mercy," " that in me," in the very depths
of my nature, in my whole future destiny, Jesus Christ might "show forth all long-
suffering."  II. THAT HIS CONVERSION WAS A PATTERN FOR ALL THE FUTURE.  III.
THAT SUCH CONVERSION SHOULD EXPRESS ITSELF IN PRAISE TO GOD is evident from
the noble doxology which follows—" Now unto the King eternal, immortal, incorruptible, invisible, the only (wise) God, be honour and glory for ever and ever.
Amen."  Paul was always ready for a song of praise, and could sing as heartily in
prison at Philippi as at the prayer-meeting beside its river.  It is not often that
God is spoken of as " King," and the expression rendered by our translators " the
King eternal," but more correctly in the margin of the Revised Version  " King of
the Ages," is quite peculiar to this verse.  What a helpful assurance this is that
our God, our Saviour, the Father of our Lord Jesus Christ, is the supreme Lord of
all the successive ages which stretch from the forgotten past into the infinite future ;
that He controls all stages of development in the natural realm, in the creation and
dissolution of worlds, and in the kingdom of grace !  (*A. Rowland, LL.B.*)    *Saul
of Tarsus obtaining mercy :*—I. LET US CONSIDER THIS MERCY IN REFERENCE TO HIM-
SELF.  1. In the first place, the mercy which he obtained pardoned all his sins.
His sins, numerous and aggravated as they were, instead of being visited with

deserved punishment, were all forgiven. The hand of mercy blotted out his iniquities as a cloud, and his transgressions as a thick cloud, so that in his own condition the promise of God to the penitent was fulfilled, "I will be merciful to their unrighteousness, and their sins and iniquities will I remember no more." How complete and efficacious is the pardon which the penitent transgressor never fails to receive when he confesses his iniquities and cries, "Lord, save me, or I perish"! 2. The mercy which he obtained renewed and sanctified his heart and character. By this Divine and sanctifying illumination an entire change was effected in his sentiments, and feelings, and character; and though no new faculties were imparted to his mind, yet the original faculties of his mind received a new impulse and direction. His mind acquired new associations of ideas; new trains of thought and feeling; new views of himself, and of Christ, and of religion in general; so that he began to love what he once hated, and to hate what he once loved, and to declare, as the result of his own experience, "If any man be in Christ he is a new creature; old things are passed away; behold all things are become new." How warm and constant was his love to Christ, whose mercy he had obtained! "Many waters could not quench it, neither could the floods drown it." With what tender and earnest compassion did his spirit yearn over those who wilfully rejected the mercy which he had obtained, and which, in his estimation, was infinitely valuable! "Of whom," says he, "I have told you often, and I now tell you, even weeping, that they are the enemies of the cross of Christ, whose end is destruction." How entirely was he devoted to the work in which he was engaged! What steady and unflinching fortitude and magnanimity he manifested, in the midst of all the afflictions and persecutions he endured! "None of these things move me," said he. And yet what deep humility was associated with all his holy excellencies, and his abundant usefulness! He was "not a whit behind the very chiefest apostles." II. CONSIDER THIS SAME MERCY IN REFERENCE TO JESUS CHRIST. For He was its source and giver, and by Him was this apostle constituted a "vessel of mercy, and a vessel unto honour, sanctified and meet for the Master's use." And if such a character as Paul's was formed by Christ, what, think you, must be His own character? If Paul was the workmanship of Christ, what, think you, must be the skill, and purity, and power of the heavenly Architect? There was much in the character of Paul that was great, and much in it that was glorious; but every attribute of his greatness and every beam of his glory was derived from Christ. 1. In the first place, the mercy which Jesus Christ exercised towards him was long-suffering mercy. "In me," says he, "Jesus Christ hath showed forth all long-suffering." And in him it was indeed shown most evidently and extensively. Why did not flames from heaven descend, and consume him to ashes? Why?—for the same reason that they have not yet fallen upon you. "Because He is long-suffering to us-ward, not willing that any should perish, but that all should come to repentance." 2. The mercy which Jesus Christ exercised towards him was sovereign mercy. And so far was he from even expecting it, that his thoughts and affections were fully occupied in anticipating the havoc which he intended to make in the church at Damascus. Such was his character up to the very moment when the persecuted Saviour met him in the way. And yet, though he neither deserved this mercy nor desired it, nor expected it, he most abundantly obtained it, with faith and love which is in Christ Jesus. No reason, I apprehend, can be assigned, by us at least, why he should be converted at all, or why his conversion should take place at that time, and under those circumstances, except "the good pleasure" of the Saviour's will. "Even so, Father, for so it seemeth good in Thy sight." 3. The mercy which Jesus Christ exercised towards him was efficacious mercy; for it came to him, "not in word only, but in power." If ever any case of depravity and crime appeared to be invincible and desperate, this was the case. III. CONSIDER THIS MERCY IN REFERENCE TO OURSELVES AND TO SINNERS IN GENERAL. The apostle further says in our text, that the mercy which he obtained at his conversion was intended to render him "a pattern to them which should hereafter believe on Christ to life everlasting." 1. In the first place, this pattern shows us that the conversion and salvation of a sinner's soul is effected by Divine mercy. Yes, throughout the whole work of man's redemption by the incarnation and sufferings of Christ, and throughout the pardon, and sanctification and spiritual progress of every saved sinner, mercy, sweet mercy reigns. Mercy determined on our salvation in the ages of eternity, and provided a Saviour for us in the fulness of time. Mercy arrests the sinner in his course, and enlightens his mind, and softens his heart and teaches him to pray, and enables him to be faithful even unto death.

And mercy opens for him the gates of the celestial city, and conducts him to the throne, and places on his head the crown of everlasting life. 2. In the second place, this pattern shows us the ability and willingness of Christ to show mercy to the greatest sinners, who repent and believe His gospel. 3. This pattern shows what a believer may become through the Saviour's mercy. (*J. Alexander.*) *The character and conversion of Saul of Tarsus:*—Judgment and mercy are to be our songs in the house of our pilgrimage; and judgment and mercy are the chief subjects of God's Word. In one page of that Word we read of God's destroying the world with a deluge—in the other, of saving Noah and eight persons in the ark. In one page we read of His giving up the nations of the earth to the basest idolatry—in the other, of His calling Abraham from Ur of the Chaldees, and bidding him separate himself in mercy from them. In one page we read of His destroying the cities of the plain, and the inhabitants with them—in the other, of His rescuing Lot and his family lest he should be devoured in the coming devastation. God's wisdom and love are surprisingly manifest in these portions of Holy Writ, and in thus setting before us judgment and mercy. Some are monuments of His wrath, to alarm, arouse, and convict the impenitent, hardened, and profligate sinner; while others are monuments of His grace, His free mercy, and His sovereign love, to show how boundless it is in its extent, and to animate penitent sinners to come to the same source from whence these individuals obtained so large a share. The apostle tells us that his conversion was "a pattern to them who should hereafter believe on Christ to life everlasting." Is there any one supposing that his sins are too peculiar and too aggravated to find mercy? I call upon him now to look at the peculiar case presented, at the specimen of the divine workmanship here brought to his view. It is to be held up as "a pattern," to show the vast and boundless extent of the grace of God in the conversion of the sinner, and the plenitude of the mercy of Christ in its extending to the utmost bounds of a sinner's guilt. Those of us who have believed through grace, ought to find our minds refreshed by looking at these patterns which God has set up in His Word. I. THE SIN-FULNESS OF SAUL'S LIFE BEFORE HIS CONVERSION. 1. He was a horrid blas-phemer. "I verily thought," he says, "that I ought to do many things contrary to the name of Jesus of Nazareth; which things I also did in Jerusalem." His name was like poison to his very soul; he never spoke of Him but with the most daring impiety; he would never examine the evidences of His mission, never look to the prophecies of olden time, never examine the types which the prophets represent and set forth of the great Messiah who was hereafter to come: but he took it for granted that He was an impostor, and he treated Him as such. He was a man of great learning, and he turned all his learning to despise his Saviour. He insulted Him and His disciples, and as far as lay in him he was determined that the name of Christ should never be known in the world, but as a name of execration fit only for the mouths of swearers and blas-phemers. This was his determination. 2. He was a furious persecutor as well as a blasphemer. Whoever professed the name of Jesus Christ was the object of his inveterate rage. But let us trace the gross features in his cha-racter as a persecutor, in order to discover the strength of his enmity to Jesus Christ and His disciples. (1) He tells us that he was "exceedingly mad against them." And in Acts ix. 1, there is a peculiar phrase used: "Saul yet breathing out threatenings and slaughter." You have seen a man in a great passion; the passion affects his breathing, so that he breathes out his words; he cannot utter them with that coolness, and conciseness, and readiness, which he does when he is quite free from passion; but he breathes them out; it seems to affect all his powers. This is the exact metaphor used in the words of the passage: "breathing out." He was "exceedingly mad against them": not only angry, but mad; and not only mad, but exceedingly mad. (2) He threatened them with "slaughter." His tongue was a servant which he employed in the devil's service to a vast extent; he used the most desperate threats to these poor individuals, these lamb-like persons, of confiscation, of imprisonment, and even of slaughter. (3) He "compelled them to blaspheme." And methinks this is the cream of his defilement, that he was not content to be an infidel himself, that he was not content to degrade Christ himself, but he made this the price of being let loose from his grasp, that they should deny Christ, that they should forswear Christ, that they should give up Christ, and that they should sever themselves for ever from Christ. (4) He "haled men and women to prison": not only men but women. Their sex might have excused them and pleaded for pity; but that was nothing to him; women were no more regarded than men: his bowels were shut against the mother with the child at her bosom; she might plead them—it was of no use. (5) Look at another point of his character: "many of the saints did he shut up in prison"; not one family, but many, numbers; all within his own reach or power—he not only took them before the magistrates, but "shut them up in prison." And mark what he also tells us in Acts xxvi; he was not content with his rage exerting itself in Jerusalem, but he persecuted them "even unto strange cities." He extended this madness of persecution not only to Jerusalem and its suburbs, but to strange cities, cities that he had no connection with, and among whose inhabitants he had no need to go; only if there was a saint there, if there was one who named the name of Jesus there, that would bring him to that city. (6) He "caused them to be put to death," and triumphed over them in their sufferings. Acts xxvi. 10. This was the character of Saul previous to his conversion. I do not know whether there is a persecutor present; of course I could not suppose that there is such a persecutor as Saul was. God be thanked that in happy Britain the government of the country would not allow it, or else the spirit, in numbers, is the same. But I refer to that man whose wife has just begun to be serious; he does not take a razor and cut her throat; he does not shoot her with a pistol; he does not drag her before a magistrate; but everything that can embitter her life, everything that can cross and aggravate her temper—this he does; and in this manner he persecutes her because she prays for him, because she loves Christ, and serves Him, and delights in His service. Art thou here, O man? Look at the spirit of the individual whom I present before you this evening, and see yourself, and hate yourself while you look at it. 3. He was not only a furious persecutor, but he was an injurious neighbour. He himself tells us this: "Who was before a blasphemer, and a persecutor, and injurious": that is, he never did any real good; that is, he never sought God's glory, or his fellow creatures' true happiness: he would not only not enter in himself, but he would not let others enter in. How many widows did this man make! How many orphans did he make! How many hearts did he break! How much poverty did he occasion! 4. There was another point in his character: he was a proud Pharisee. This may appear light to some, but this was the crown of his character, this is the greatness of his guilt; this is (if I may use the expression) his scarlet and his crimson sin—that he went about to set up and establish his own righteousness, not submitting himself to the righteousness of God. "Publicans and harlots," says our Saviour, "enter into the kingdom of heaven before them." Now there are many individuals who are similar to Saul. We hear numbers say, "I am not a liar; I am not a drunkard; I pay my way; I live respectably in the world, and endeavour to train up my children respectably; and if I don't go to heaven, who ought to go?" And where is Christ, and where is the Saviour of sinners? "Yes, but then," you say, "I know I have done wrong in many things; we are all guilty in some respects: but then I have never been a great sinner, and I do hope that if I do as well as I can, the Lord Jesus Christ will help me, and give me some of His merit that I may die in peace." Now this, though not uttered in such plain and direct language, is often implied, and is the meaning of thousands of sinners. II. THE FREE GRACE OF CHRIST EXHIBITED IN HIS CONVERSION. Perceive how his conversion was effected by Christ. Imagine yourselves in Jerusalem a few minutes, and see Saul just as he is setting out on his journey to Damascus, for the sake of persecuting the poor saints in that city. See him mount his horse; see the numbers around him—what a splendid guard the man has. Look at the Sanhedrim, the chief priests and the great men of his nation coming to him, shaking hands with him, and saying, "God speed your way, and give you the success of your mission": look how the people are congratulating him all around. See the poor saints trembling. "Now," they say, "I fear for the safety of my sister, who has gone to Damascus. Now is my dear friend who lives in that city about to be butchered by this furious tyrant." See the people all running to John Mark's house, to engage in prayer, and bring down the blessing of heaven, that this man be stopped in his persecution; and going home to write letters, to prevent, if possible, the danger to which some of their friends and relations will be subject by this man's arrival. Never man thought himself more secure; never man thought he was going on a more virtuous embassy; and he had pretty nearly reached Damascus, he was within sight of the gates; and just as he was going forward, and some of the saints perhaps looking out of the windows, seeing him advancing, and trembling for fear of his entry—just as he approached the gate, the Lord Jesus Christ opened a window in heaven, and let one single ray of His glory fall down from heaven upon him. This was the manner of his conversion; now let us see what effect did his conversion produce? What effect did it produce on the spot? It turned proud Saul into humble Paul: he that was raging with madness against the disciples, was now trembling and astonished for himself. See what it did for him the three days afterwards. The light that came from heaven had taken away his natural sight, but how it had illuminated his mind. How great his anguish now he saw his past life! Oh, the grace that could soften such a heart, melt such a mind! But see what his conversion did for him in after days. And here mark, there was not only grace to make him a Christian, but there was grace to make him a minister: he was not only taken from the world as the Church are, but he was taken from the Church as Aaron was, and made a minister of the Lord Jesus Christ. And now let us see him in his ministry. What was the subject of it? "I determined not to know anything among you, save Jesus Christ, and Him crucified." And he went and preached boldly before kings, and rulers, and magistrates, and assemblies of different classes, the glories of his Saviour, and the triumphs of His grace. Oh, the labours of this man! Oh, the prayers of this man! Oh, the zeal of this man! Oh, the melting pity of this man over lost souls! Oh, the subjugating power of Divine grace, and the influence of Divine love! III. THE DESIGN OF CHRIST IN HIS CONVERSION. I know not which to admire most, the sovereignty and grace of Christ in converting him, or the sovereignty and grace of Christ in exhibiting his conversion as a pattern to others, as an example from which they might take encouragement as long as time should last. 1. Here is the pattern of the infinite merit of Christ's death. The atonement of Christ reaches back to the first sin, and extends itself to the last: "He was made sin for us who knew no sin, that we might be made the righteousness of God in Him." "He is able to save to the uttermost all that come unto God by Him." 2. The unquestionable willingness of Christ's heart. 3. You here see the great design of Christ's gospel. Why is the gospel published? This is the pattern. To show you the great design of Christ's gospel—that is to encourage the souls of sinners to come to Him and be saved. 4. Again: look here and see the pattern of the renovating power of Christ's grace. Oh, how it changes the hearts and lives of sinners! In one of my village stations, a little time ago, I looked in at a cottage, and inquired of a poor woman there how things were going with herself and family. She said, "Oh, sir, I have more reason to bless God for the gospel than I can tell you. When we first came to this cottage, both my husband and myself were drunkards, our children were but barely clothed, and everything we had in the world was marked by the extremest poverty and misery; but now, instead of that, the Lord laid hold of my husband's heart first, then He was pleased to convert me by the preaching at the place of worship; and now the children are blessed, and I am blessed, and we are all happy together." And now you will see her one of the most respectable women in the village, with a little money in the savings' bank: on the Sunday all the children are catechised, and the husband delights to read and pray with his wife and children. Is not this an exhibition of the renovating power of Christ's grace? And this is not a solitary instance: you yourselves know instances like this in the neighbourhoods wherein you reside, where Christ's renovating power has been manifested. You are to look at this for a pattern if you are ever downcast for any individual. Here see what the power of Christ's grace can do. In the first place, corruption has a power over the individual, and makes him a blasphemer, a persecutor, injurious, and a Pharisee: and now the grace that has renovated his heart makes him a humble seeker of the Saviour, a zealous disciple of Christ, an anxious neighbour, desirous of the good of others, and pondering the way to heaven, and walking in it. (*J. Sherman.*) *Salvation for the chief of sinners :*—I. THE FACT WHICH IS HERE ASSERTED BY ST. PAUL. "I obtained mercy." II. THE USE WHICH ST. PAUL MAKES OF THIS GREAT FACT IN HIS HISTORY. St. Paul speaks here of his conversion, not only in its reference to himself, but also in its reference to others. Perhaps more than any person that ever lived St. Paul lived for others; perhaps more than any person that ever lived St. Paul was the most useful to others. It was a great fact for himself; it brought salvation to his soul, and he rejoiced in God for it. But it was a great fact for the world. Two things are especially, I think, to be noted in St. Paul's conversion. The one is its distinctness—it was a very marked conversion. His life was very decided before it and very decided after it. He was a prominent character, a well-known man, and it was a very distinct and a very decided conversion; but it is not upon that which he dwells in our text. There was another thing to be noted about the conversion of St. Paul, that it afforded a very wonderful exhibition and illustration of the long-suffering of Jesus Christ. The other apostles had been called by the Lord Jesus Christ to serve and follow Him from a life of innocence, comparatively speaking, at all events from a life that was void of any opposition to Him. (*E. Bayley, M.A.*) *Paul an example of mercy :*—I. The IMPROBABILITY of Paul's obtaining mercy. "Howbeit, I obtained mercy." II. The MERCY which, notwithstanding the improbability of the case, Paul did receive. 1. It was sovereign in its source. Whence did it spring ? Through what medium did it flow ? Human merit could have nothing to do in the gift of mercy to the chief of sinners. Mercy always excludes merit, and most evidently so in the instance before us. 2. It was great in its degree. We estimate the greatness of mercy by the guilt of the offender, and by the effects it produces. 3. It was boundless in its blessings. Hear the elevated sentiment of this apostle, writing to the Ephesians : "Blessed be the God and Father of our Lord Jesus Christ, who hath blessed us with all spiritual blessings in heavenly places in Christ " ; blessings of the best kind ; blessings adapted to the nature and necessities of the soul ; blessings that are from heaven, that lead to heaven, that bring us into intimate connection with heavenly realities, and that are durable as their eternal enjoyment. It is the observation of a late author, Though God is sovereign in the bestowment of mercy, He is not niggardly. He goes beyond the humbled sinner's highest expectation. Where he looked for a single drop, there descends the copious shower. Where he hoped to receive the alms of one mite, he finds the collected treasures of a thousand ages, the great mountain of solid gold. III. The DESIGN of its bestowment. 1. It was to illustrate Divine long-suffering. 2. It was to promote human encouragement. We here behold its majesty, its energy, and its triumph. (*T. Kidd.*) *On patterns in religion :*—Some men speak only of a salvation which they have heard of from others. Some teach others a salvation which they have experienced themselves. Paul was the chief of these. This personal element runs through all his writings. The stream of his teaching sprang at first, and still springs, from the fountain depths of his own soul, and it was, therefore, a living stream, like the river in Ezekiel's prophecy, which deepened as it flowed and healed wherever its waters descended. God had fulfilled to him the words, " The water that I shall give him shall be within him a fountain of water springing up to everlasting life." The point which comes before us to-day is this—his salvation ended not in himself, it was a pattern to encourage all other sinners to trust in the like forgiving mercy. We are very dependent on fashions and patterns in all parts of our life, to assist our labours, to stimulate our energies, to encourage our hopes. Examples act upon us more powerfully than arguments. Happy the Church which can say to all around, not only " Believe the Gospel," but " See what it has done for us !—that it has given us peace with God, a new and nobler life within, of thought, of design, of love, of hope, of action. Come with us, and we will do you good." The best recommendation of a remedy, and of a teaching, is its visible effect on ourselves. Let us see, by looking more closely into the history of St. Paul, how remarkably he was a typical pattern of salvation by Christ in all its stages and developments from first to last. I. IN HIS CALL. This was a supernatural and gracious work of God, brought about by an act above and beyond all ordinary moral laws. The act of placing saving truth before us as a heavenly vision is always the act of God alone, in His providence and grace. It is the result of a purpose of God, a call. Men do not discover truth savingly by mere study or experiment, as they find out the secrets of nature. Flesh and blood hath not revealed this unto thee, but My Father which is in heaven. It is the Spirit who says to Philip on behalf of the Treasurer, " Draw nigh to this chariot," and opens to him the book of Esaias the prophet. If you have been visited with a view of the reality of Jesus Christ as your Saviour, this has been the act of God. "Of Him are all things." So it was with Saul of Tarsus. II. Paul's life is A PATTERN OF ARBITRARY AND SOVEREIGN SELECTION TO SPECIAL SPIRITUAL ADVANTAGES AND SPECIAL APPOINTMENTS—the result of an everlasting purpose of God. He is a chosen vessel to Me to bear My name before kings and peoples—a splendidly embossed golden vase in which sweet odours of truth shall be burned before all nations. The world is full of such special and individual destinations that can be traced to no other source than the special will of God. Thus, too, some nations, as Israel of old, and now the Saxon race. Yet this Divine predestination is quite consistent with man's ultimate freedom. The predestinations of God do not enslave, but liberate and energize the will of man. " He worketh in us—to will." The will is ours, the inspiration is God's. "I was not disobedient to the heavenly vision." But the special vocations of God's servants are not for their own private and personal behoof. They look toward the profit of many, that they may be saved. If Paul is a chosen vessel, it is that he may " preach the Gospel to every creature." " To make all men see the fellowship of the mystery." III. St. Paul was A PATTERN IN HIS PARDON. "In him first Jesus Christ showed forth all long-suffering," to encourage others, though vile as he, to wash in the same life-giving fountain. We need other and nearer patterns. And they abound around us. Would that some whose experience is large and exact, and who have seen into the secret of the salvation of many different kinds of souls, would write for us a variety of biographies to serve as encouraging patterns, suited to modern contemporary society. It seems useless to tell the modern young man, whose form of alienation from God, his heavenly Father, is not that of a cruel persecutor, that he may take courage to trust in the mercy of God from the example of St. Paul. It does not touch him. A pattern of modern spiritual life that sprang out of a modern callousness and love of trifling amusements, just like his own, is what he requires. Tell them of such " patterns " as these, and they prove very helpful. God reveals Himself in many ways in nature, and Christ reveals Himself in many ways in the spiritual providence —not by books only, much less by sermons only—but by lives, somewhat akin to our own, and likely to move and touch and animate us by their example in kindred spheres of action. And so with women, and young women. The " patterns " which are likely to affect them, in a way to draw them to Christ, in closer love, are not those set before us in " Foxe's Book of Martyrs," where men had to burn at Smithfield for denying transubstantiation, at the behests of Mary Tudor and her bishops. They must be drawn from nearer home and from our own day. And such " patterns " of loving and noble lives, inspired with tender compassion, and industrious obedience, and diligent zeal in home duties are so numerous nowadays that a girl must live in a very heathenish circle if she knows of none which can help her to serve her Saviour. Let us not be so blind as to see no transfigurations of character except in the dead. There are around us not a few who shine already in the garments of immortality; who can be depended on for truth, for gentleness, for industry, for serious tenderness, and for active sympathy; and whose uplifted faces already gleam with the reflected light of that city of the living God to which they are moving upwards. But when all is said of the helpfulness of patterns of salvation in aiding us to believe and love the Lord, it remains true that earthly lives are but patterns of things in the heavens, and not " the very image of the things." They serve but as the shadows of the heavenly realities. They are but prophecies of a more glorious dawn. For the end is not yet, and when that which is perfect is come, that which is imperfect shall be done away. " Then shall I be satisfied when I wake up in Thy likeness." (*E. White.*) *Paul's conversion a pattern:*—I. IN THE CONVERSION OF PAUL THE LORD HAD AN EYE TO OTHERS. The fact of his conversion and the mode of it—1. Would tend to interest and convince other Pharisees and Jews. 2. Would be used by himself in his preaching as an argument to convert and encourage others. 3. Would encourage Paul as a preacher to hope for others. 4. Would become a powerful argument with him for seeking others. 5. Would, long after Paul's death, remain on record to be the means of bringing many to Jesus. II. IN HIS ENTIRE LIFE PAUL SPEAKS TO OTHERS. 1. In sin. His conversion proves that Jesus receives great sinners. 2. In grace. He proved the power of God to sanctify and preserve. III. IN HIS WHOLE CASE HE PRESENTS A CARTOON OF OTHERS. 1. As to God's longsuffering to him. In his case longsuffering was carried to its highest pitch. Longsuffering so great that all the patience of God seemed to be revealed in his one instance. Longsuffering which displayed itself in many ways, so as to let him live when persecuting saints; to allow him the possibility of pardon; to call him effectually by grace; to give him fulness of personal blessing; to put him into the ministry and send him to the Gentiles; to keep and support him even unto the end. 2. As to the mode of his conversion. He was saved remarkably, but others will be seen to be saved in like manner if we look below the surface of things. Saved without previous preparation on his own part; saved at once out of darkness and death; saved by Divine power alone; saved by faith wrought in him by God's own Spirit; saved distinctly, and beyond all doubt. Are we not also saved in precisely the same way? (*C. H. Spurgeon.*) *The Divine mercy unlimited:*—John Newton, speaking of the sudden death of Robinson, of Cambridge, in the house of Dr. Priestly, said: " I think Dr. Priestly is out of the reach of human conviction; but the Lord can convince him. And who can tell but this unexpected stroke may make some salutary impression upon his mind? I can set no limits to the mercy or the power of our Lord, and therefore I continue to pray for him. I am persuaded he is not farther from the truth now than I was once." (*S. Charnock.*)    *Encouragement from the case of St. Paul:*—I have heard it said of the elephant, that sometimes before he crosses a bridge he puts his trunk, and perhaps one foot, upon it; he wants to know if it is quite safe, for he is not going to trust his bulky body to things that were built only for horses and men. Well, after he has tried it, if he finds it strong enough, away he goes, and his great carcase is carried right across the stream. Now, suppose you and I sat on the other side, and said we were afraid the bridge would not bear us! Why, how absurd our unbelief would be. So when you see a great elephantine sinner, like the apostle Paul, go lumbering over the bridge of mercy, and not a timber creaks, and the bridge does not even strain under the load, why, then methinks, you may come rushing in a crowd, and say, "It will bear us if it will bear him; it will carry us across, if it can take the chief of sinners to heaven!" (*C. H. Spurgeon.*)    *John Newton's conversion:*—I have never doubted the power of God to convert the heathen world since He converted me. (*J. Newton.*) *An encouraging reflection:*—It is no small encouragement to a sick man, to hear of some that have been cured of the same disease as his own, and that in a higher degree of prevalence. (*J. Flavel.*)

Ver. 17. **Now unto the King eternal.**—*The King of the Ages:*—"The King eternal," or, literally, as in the margin of the Revised Version, "The King of the Ages," words which do not simply tell us something about the King, but also give us some account of His rule; and put into the hands of Faith a key to the highest positions of modern thought and science. For in all their realms—of matter, mind, and spirit—there is one common element, viz., Law. Whether we look around us, or within, order and rule are being ever more clearly and universally demonstrated. But the Christian attitude is becoming more candid; and now accepts, or is learning to accept the truth of a widespread reign of law with less of fear than of gratitude. For is not this state of order and harmony just what we should expect in His working whose Being is the perfect harmony? For while we know this as an age of Law, and are sometimes perplexed by its inexorableness, the thoughtful mind asks: "Have all the ages been as ordered? In the world of spirit and of matter have there not been whole epochs of distraction and ravage by undisciplined forces? For example, does not the earth on which we tread, bear in her very structure the record of ages of confusion and chaos, darkness and death? when lawlessness, not law, seemed to rule? when, so far as we can judge, there was no guiding thought, no ruling hand? In fact, does not the same defiance of law meet us to-day in the earthquake? Is law universal or only widespread?" But the deeper readings of science assure us that it is not only the quiet processes which gladden the eye and heart that have their ordered course. The silent and regular development through blade and ear to the full corn, is not more determined and invariable than is the dread convulsion that entombs its thousands; and it was through the exercise of unyielding law that that strife was wrought which has made the structure of our earth what we find it. This decided every event and ordered all the disorder of those ages of seeming unrule. And shall we not take the comfort the spiritual reading of this truth can give? For it is not only in the world of matter such a record of strife and confusion is written. In the brief history of our race there is the same tale in human characters. What is the meaning of such scenes as the French Revolution, for example? Are they the rough sport of unruled passion? Is there nothing determining their methods or moulding their results? What if that struggle and ruin, decay and destruction were the working and manifestation of a Divine health and order, casting away that which it could not assimilate and arrange? the removing of those things which could be shaken that those things which could not be shaken might remain? And these words, which speak of a "King" of the Ages, tell us why. They point to its source—to One who makes and administers that law, who is in and yet above it. But the faith of a Divine rule of each separate age is not enough. The heart of man craves something more than even such a confidence. There is inwrought into our very being a longing for Unity; and the words we are now considering justify this instinct, and pledge its fulfilment. For we are assured that, if He is "King of the Ages" in any adequate sense, they are bound together by the strong band of His will, which gives to them its own oneness and intimacy. They are no longer isolated units, but parts of a whole; and it is as a whole and not simply as units they are subjected. As the successive points of a circle stand in harmonious relation, not only to their common centre, but through this to each other; so the ages, which make one mighty cycle, having but one Lord and one law, stand related amongst themselves with an inner harmony as deep and true as their hearts. And not only so. There is more than this close relation and perfect agreement between the ages. If this were all it would leave unfulfilled another instinctive craving of the heart—that of Progress and Consummation. But these words which speak of the " King of the Ages " tell us there is one supreme will and word which they obey—one harmonious thought, which being the King's thought, must be a growing and deepening one. There is but little appearance of all this at times. Judging only of the part we see—that displayed on the earth and amidst ourselves—is not the show of things rather that of age at war with age? A backward movement, in which much that has been hardly won through centuries is easily lost in a moment? But it is only as the flow of the tide rolling inland, which surely advances, though seeming to recede; receding but to rally its forces and sweep onward to larger conquests. One perfect plan is being achieved, in many times and many ways indeed; yet in all, and through all, God is ever fulfilling Himself. Let us not, then, be troubled as though the issue is or could be uncertain, or the plan be marred. Trust—not only for the ages gone and the ages to come; but what is harder, for the age that now is. The " King of the Ages " is Himself invisible; He is not, therefore, less King. Nor is His kingdom less real because its presence is silent and unsuspected. For there are latent glories in this rule of the "King of the Ages"; a glorious mystery which was hidden from the ages and generations until the " fulness of the time," when the " Word became flesh and tabernacled amongst men," whose humanity He thus united with Deity, that He might reconcile man, and in man, all creation unto God. (*A. A. Dauncey.*)     *King immortal:*—Queen Elizabeth was once seized with a violent illness, accompanied with high fever. The Privy Council was hastily summoned from London, and in the ante-chamber of the room where she was believed to be dying, they sat with blank faces, discussing who was to be her successor. In the morning the worst symptoms abated, and in a few days she was convalescent. Our Monarch can have no successor. He is " alive for evermore," and of His kingdom there can be no end. (*H. O. Mackey.*)

Ver. 18. **This charge I commit unto thee.**—*Timothy's charge and warning:*—The " charge " to which Paul alludes does not refer to what he said in the third and fifth verses, but points on to what follows—to that good warfare which Timothy was summoned to undertake against evil. I. THE CHARGE, of which Timothy was reminded—1. Had been indicated by inspired prophets in the Church. Very significantly Paul says these prophecies " went before on thee " ; that is, they were not only uttered upon, or over him, but they went forth " before " him in his future course, revealing it and inspiring him to follow it—just as the consciousness of having a courier in front would direct and encourage the traveller. Hence Paul adds that " by them," or in them, Timothy might wage a " good warfare "; he was to feel like one clothed and armed in those prophetic hopes, in those believing prayers. And do not we know something of this? No man has ever done great work in the world unless he has a deep moral conviction that he is predestined to do it; and this was never exemplified better than in General Gordon, who, in more than one campaign, felt that he was invincible and resistless till his work was done. And in our lowlier spheres we should be the more watchful, earnest, and hopeful, because others have had great hopes about us, and because we have been set apart to be God's servants by many an act of dedication. It is a great thing to have prophecies going before us, and the prayers of dear ones encircling us so that in them we may war a good warfare. 2. For this charge involved conflict. 3. And for success in this warfare " faith and a good conscience " are essential. " Faith," without a " good conscience," is like a garrison summoned to defend one gate of the fortress, while a traitor is opening the other gate to relentless foes. This leads the apostle to give Timothy—II. THE WARNING which is contained in the last two verses. 1. He speaks of some who had put away a good conscience, stifling its voice and thrusting it from them, with this result, that they had made shipwreck of faith. And this experience has often repeated itself in the history of the Church. Balaam put away a " good conscience " when he paltered with his convictions to his soul's undoing. Saul, the king, did so when he disobeyed the distinct command of God, until he was no longer able to hear the Divine voice and resorted to the witch of Endor. Judas Iscariot did so when he resisted the promptings of the Holy Spirit and betrayed his Lord and Master; and in each case the sacrifice of conscience brought about " the shipwreck of faith." May God keep us undefiled, that we may never make shipwreck of faith! 2. Examples of this are pointed out to Timothy: "Hymenæus and Alexander." The latter was a very common name, so that we cannot confidently identify this man with "Alexander, the coppersmith," who, Paul declares, in the Second Epistle, did him much evil; but Hymenæus was so uncommon a name that we may be sure it was he of whom the apostle says, in the Second Epistle, that he and Philetus were in grievous error, denying the doctrine of the resurrection, and declaring that it was past already. A blunted conscience evidently accompanied a darkened mind. 3. Paul did what he could to save and warn them, saying of them, " Whom I have delivered unto Satan, that they may learn not to blaspheme." A difficult passage, chiefly because we know so little of apostolic modes of Church discipline. It certainly did not mean that they were given over to perdition, for the object of the punishment was their salvation, "that they might learn not to blaspheme," that is, not to misrepresent and calumniate the truth of God. Here, as well as elsewhere, Satan is spoken of not as an independent hostile power, but as one who is allowed to work evil for a given purpose, which is often beyond the range of men to discover. Thus Job was left in the power of the adversary for a season; and similarly, the Lord Jesus said to Peter, "Simon, Simon, Satan hath desired to have you, that he might sift you as wheat; but I have prayed for thee that thy faith fail not." Paul himself speaks of the " thorn in the flesh " as being " the messenger of Satan to buffet " him. And when in the light of these passages we read this solemn declaration and couple it with 1 Cor. v. 5, where Paul says of the incestuous offender, " With the power of the Lord Jesus Christ to deliver such an one unto Satan for the destruction of the flesh, that the Spirit may be saved in the day of the Lord Jesus," we come to the conclusion that the apostles were gifted with, and sometimes used, the solemn power of inflicting disease on the body, in order to awaken in the offender, or in others, convictions of sin and longings for salvation. In the terrible cases of Ananias and Elymas, we see evidences of a power to punish given to those who could heal diseases and cast out devils, a power which no doubt was demanded by the exigencies of the Church, and certainly died with the apostles, who could not transmit it. But underlying its exercise was a principle of Divine discipline, which is applicable in every age; for there is no loss we sustain, no affliction we suffer, but may work for our spiritual welfare, warning us against evil, and stimulating us to holier endeavour and more earnest prayer. (*A. Rowland, LL.B.*) **War a good warfare.**—*A good warfare:*—I. WAR, THEREFORE, IS INEVITABLE. You must fight or fly; be the victor or the vanquished. Nay, if you mean to make sure your own salvation, and please Him who hath called you to be a soldier, there is not even that alternative. You are surrounded with foes you cannot shun. Flight would be ruin. The conflict cannot be avoided. Every step will be contested. Yet be not discouraged. The more strenuous the struggle, the more glorious the achievement. Your aid is omnipotent, your resources are infinite, and you "war a good warfare." Few, indeed, of the warfares waged by the powers of this world are worthy of the means employed and the men sacrificed to win them. But the Christian soldier " wars a good warfare "; emphatically, pre-eminently and peculiarly good; good in all its agencies, its aspects, and its issues. II. Have we not A GOOD CAUSE? Did the Israelites glory in a good cause, contending for the Land of Promise? the Crusaders, marching to the rescue of the Holy Sepulchre? your forefathers, asserting with the sword their independence of Great Britain? But the Christian cause is the purest and noblest that ever kindled the enthusiasm of a people or won the admiration of the world. It is identified with all that is important in truth, beautiful in virtue, sublime in charity, or glorious in hope. It is the cause that marshals the cherubim, and stirs the deep vengeance of hell; that brought Jehovah from the throne of the universe to the manger. We fight, not to desolate provinces and degrade princes, but to convert earth into a paradise and enthrone humanity with its Redeemer. No wrongs have we to avenge, no malice to gratify, nor cruel thirst for blood. III. And have we an unworthy CAPTAIN? What Hebrew warrior did not glory in his Joshua or his David? What mediæval crusader did not proudly follow his Richard, his Philip, or his Bertrand? What Frenchman did not rejoice in the name of Napoleon, what Englishman in the name of Wellington, what American in the name of Washington? Who of all the myriads that took part in your late civil conflict, was not ready to cheer for Grant or Lee, for Sherman or Jackson? But "who is this that cometh from Edom, with dyed garments from Bozrah? this that is glorious in His apparel, travelling in the greatness of His strength?" "I that speak in righteousness, mighty to save." It is the Captain of the Lord's host, the champion of our redemption. He comes to avenge us of our enemies, and lead our captivity captive. What are the qualities most desirable in a military leader? In the highest perfection, they are all found in Christ. Is it wisdom? He is the embodied wisdom of God. Experience? Ever since the original revolt in heaven He has been battling with the hosts of hell. Valour? Single-handed and alone He went forth to meet the Prince of darkness with all his dire array. Success? He foiled the cunning foe in the wilderness of Judæa, and triumphed over his embattled myriads upon the cross. Kindness? Once He died to save His enemies, and now He wears the name of every follower punctured with a spear upon His heart. Ability to reward? The thrones of heaven are His, and a kingdom such as earth never knew He promises hereafter to every conqueror. Such a Captain, who would not joyfully follow? IV. And what say you of our ARMOUR? Our panoply is ample and impenetrable, and our weapons are effective because they are Divine. V. And what think you of our SUPPLIES? "Who goeth a warfare at his own charges?" "My God shall supply all your need according to His riches in glory by Christ Jesus." What a measure is that, and what a medium of communication! "He is able to do exceeding abundantly above all we can ask or think." "They who trust in the Lord shall not want any good thing." Our Divine commissariat is furnished with all that we can possibly require in any emergency of the campaign. VI. And how like you our DEFENCES? "God is our refuge and strength, a very present help in trouble. Therefore will we not fear, though the earth be removed, and the mountains be carried into the midst of the sea; though the waters thereof roar and be troubled, though the mountains shake at the swelling thereof." VII. And have you not seen the array of OUR ALLIES? "The angel of the Lord encampeth round about them that fear Him, and delivereth them." "The chariots of God are twenty thousand, even many thousands of angels; the Lord is in the midst of them, as in Sinai, in the holy place." "Are they not all ministering spirits, sent forth to minister for them who shall be heirs of salvation?" See them leading righteous Lot and his family forth from Sodom, before the fire-tempest descends upon the doomed city. See them deploying from the host of God to meet Jacob, returning from Padan Aram, about to encounter the formidable bands of his offended brother. See them, with their flashing cavalry and flaming artillery, covering all the moun tain round about Elisha, and delivering a whole army into the hands of a single man. If heaven could spare so splendid an escort for the patriarch, so glorious a body-guard for the prophet, what millions on millions incalculable must be engaged on behalf of the whole Church militant in the wilderness! And if one angel could slay all the first-born of Egypt in a night, or destroy seventy thousand men of Israel at a stroke, or stiffen in death a hundred and eighty-five thousand Assyrian soldiers with a blast of his breath, what have we to fear, around whom encamp myriads of celestial warriors? What power of hell shall scatter the cohorts of heaven? VIII. And WHO EVER HAD BETTER COMRADES? They are called, and chosen, and faithful. Like Saul and Jonathan, they are stronger than lions and swifter than eagles. Like the intrepid son of Jesse, they can run through a troop and leap over a wall. One can chase a thousand, and two can put ten thousand to flight. The saints of all ages form but "one army of the living God," and the militant rear hold fellowship with the victorious van. IX. AND WHO EVER FOUGHT WITH GREATER SUCCESS? What power has prevailed against the Lord's redeemed? Their interest is His; and to defeat them were to defeat Omnipotence. X. AND WHO EVER WON SO RICH A REWARD? Where centres the ambition of earthly heroism? In the victor's palm, the monarch's crown, the empty plaudits of the multitude, "a fancied life in others' breath," a name on the scroll of history, a niche in the temple of fame, a monumental column in the Capitol, a memory embalmed in the nation's heart, a tuneful immortality in the songs of ages. But your reward is "a far more exceeding and eternal weight of glory." (*J. Cross, D.D.*)

Ver. 19. **Holding faith, and a good conscience.**—*Faith and a good conscience :*—I. WHAT THEY ARE:—1. Faith. The term is in the Scriptures applied both to the revealed truth which a disciple believes, and to his act in believing it. Faith is objective, or subjective. It is at one time the truth which you grasp, and at another time your grasp of the truth. Both in the Scriptures and in their own nature these two are closely interwoven together. It is impossible everywhere to preserve and mark the distinction between the light that I look on, and my looking on that light. True, my looking on it does not create the light, but it makes the light mine. Unless I look on it, the light is nothing to me. If I am blind, it is the same to me as if there had not been light. In some such way are faith and the faith connected and combined. It is quite true that the gospel remains, although I should reject it: my unbelief cannot make God's promise of none effect. Yet my unbelief makes the gospel nothing to me—the same to me as if it had not been. The faith stands in heaven, although faith be wanting on earth; but if faith is wanting, the faith does not save the lost: as the sun continues his course through the sky although I were blind; but my blindness blots out the sun for me. 2. A good conscience. It is not necessary to explain what conscience is: my readers know what it is better than I can tell. Here the principal question is, Whether does the epithet "good" refer to the conscience that gives the testimony, or to the testimony that the conscience gives. The term "good" here belongs not to the testifier, but to the testimony. In one sense that might be called a good conscience, that tells the truth even though the truth torment you. When the conscience, like an ambassador from God in a man's breast, refuses to be silent in the presence of sin, and disturbs the pleasure of the guilty by uttering warnings of doom, that conscience is good, in the sense of being watchful and useful; but it is not the good conscience of this text, and of ordinary language. Both here, and in common conversation, a good conscience is a conscience that does not accuse and disturb. It is the same as peace of conscience. It is no doubt true that in an evil world, and through the deceitfulness of an evil heart, the conscience may sometimes be so drugged or seared that it may leave the soul undisturbed, although the soul is steeped in sin. It sometimes says "Peace, peace," when there is no peace. "There is no peace, saith my God, to the wicked"; but the conscience sometimes contradicts God, and says that there is peace to the wicked. This is, however, an abnormal state of things; as when an ambassador at a foreign court turns traitor to the king who commissioned him, and refuses to deliver his lord's commands to the court where he has been accredited. The conscience in man is intended to be God's witness, and to speak to the man all the truth. Taking conscience, not as twisted and seared by sin, but as constituted by God in the conception and creation of humanity, then a good conscience is peace of conscience. You have and hold a good conscience when that present representative of God in your bosom does not charge you with sin. By the light of Scripture we know that, as matters go among the fallen, a good conscience, if real and lawfully attained, implies these two things:—(1) The application of the blood of sprinkling for the pardon of sin; and (2) Actual abstinence from known sin in the life through the ministry of the Holy Spirit. A good conscience—if it is not a cheat—implies a righteousness on you and a righteousness in you. Pardon and renewing combine to constitute, under the gospel, a good conscience. What God hath joined, let not man put asunder. The conscience is good when it truly testifies that God is at peace with you, and you are at peace with God. II. Their relations:—The text consists of two parts. The first is a command, the second is an example. The example, as is usual both in human teaching and Divine, is adduced for the purpose of enforcing the precept. Doubtless, Paul could have called up from his own experience many examples to show how good it is to hold both faith and a good conscience; but it suited his purpose better, in this instance, to adduce an example which shows the dread consequence of attempting to separate them. In point of fact, an example of these two rent asunder is more effective in proving the necessity of their union than a hundred examples in which the union remains intact. Thus, if proof were necessary, to divide a living child in two with Solomon's sword would constitute more vivid evidence that in a human being the left side is necessary to the life of the right, and the right to the life of the left, than the sight of a hundred unharmed children. When one side is wrenched off, the other side also dies: this is shorter and surer proof that the two are mutually necessary to each other's existence than a hundred examples of positive, perfect life. Besides, it is easier to find a foundation for a negative than for a positive example. In buoying a channel, they cannot well set up a mark where the ship ought to go; they set up a beacon on the sunken rock which the ship ought to avoid. Here a question of the deepest interest crosses our path and claims our regard. Granted that faith and a good conscience are linked so intimately together that the one cannot live without its consort, what is the specific character of the relation? Whether of these two is first in nature as cause, and whether follows as effect? Looking to the form of expression in the text, which is exact and definite, we find that in the case adduced it was not the dissolution of faith that destroyed the good conscience, but the failing of the good conscience that destroyed faith. These men put away the good conscience; then and therefore, they lost the faith. What then? As the continued possession of the faith depended on maintaining the good conscience, is it through prior possession of a good conscience that one may attain faith? No. The converse is the truth, fully and clearly taught in the Scriptures. You do not reach faith through a good conscience, but a good conscience through faith. A good conscience grows on faith, like fruit on a tree, not faith on a good conscience. A good conscience in both its aspects, as already explained, is the fruit of faith. Without faith it is impossible to please God, either by the righteousness of Christ in justifying, or the new obedience in sanctifying. Now this specific relation is not reciprocal. The good conscience does not produce faith, as faith produces a good conscience. What then? If faith goes first as the cause, and a good conscience follows as the fruit, the good conscience obviously cannot subsist without faith; but may faith subsist without a good conscience? No. As to production at first, the relation is not reciprocal; but as to maintenance it is. We cannot say, as a good conscience springs from faith, faith also springs from a good conscience; but we can say, as the want of faith makes a good conscience impossible, so, also, the loss of a good conscience is fatal to faith. Some species of trees retain life in the roots although the head and stem are cut away. A young tree may spring from the old stump, and grow to maturity. But other species, such as the pine, will not thus spring a second time. When the mature tree is cut off, although the root, with a portion of the stem, is left, the tree does not revive. The root dies when the head is severed. There is an interesting analogy between a pine-tree and the pair which are joined in the text. It is not the tree's towering head that produces the root; the root produces the towering head. We can, therefore, safely say, If the root is killed, the head cannot live; but we may also say, If the head is severed, the root will die. Precisely such is the relation between faith and a good conscience. Faith is the producing, sustaining root, and a good conscience the stem that it sustains. Consequently, cut off faith, and a good conscience falls to the ground. Yes, this is the truth; but it is not the whole truth. We can also say, Destroy the good conscience, and faith cannot stand. Thus in one way only may the good conscience be obtained; but in either of two ways both may be lost. Let faith fail, and the good conscience goes with it; let the good conscience be polluted, and the faith itself gives way. In the first place, then, speculative error undermines practical righteousness. As belief of the truth purifies the heart and rectifies the conduct, so a false belief leads the life astray. The backsliding begins more frequently on the side of conduct than on the side of opinion: the good conscience is lost in most cases, not by adopting a heretical creed, but by indulging in the pleasures of sin. The conscience is more exposed in the battle of life than the intellect. And it is on the weak point that a skilful adversary will concentrate his attack. While the calamity is substantially in all cases the same, the faith may be shipwrecked in any of three distinct forms,—a dead faith, an erroneous faith, and no faith. In the first a form of sound words remains, but they are a dead letter; in the second, false views of Christ and His work are entertained; and in the third, the backslider sits down in the chair of the scorner, and says, No God, with his lips as well as in his heart. Among ourselves, perhaps a dead faith is the most common form of soul shipwreck. Faith and covetousness, faith and any impurity, cannot dwell together in the same breast. These cannot be in the same room with living faith. As well might you expect fire and water to agree. I knew a young man once who became what was called a Socialist. He attained a great degree of boldness in the profession of ungodliness. No God, or no God that cares for me, was his short, cold creed. But I knew him and his communications before he had made shipwreck concerning faith. The second table of the law had, by indulgence of sinful pleasure, been rusted out of his heart before the first table was discarded from his creed. He had cruelly dishonoured his father and his mother before he learned to blaspheme God. It cannot be comfortable to a young man in his strength to come day by day to open his heart to God, if day by day he is deliberately disowning and dishonouring his parents in the weakness of their age. The dishonourer of his parents finds it necessary to his own comfort to cast off God. This man put away his good conscience, and therefore his faith was wrecked. I knew another, who had in youth made higher attainments, and who, on that account, made a more terrible fall. He had experienced religious impressions, and taken a side with the disciples of Christ. I lost sight of him for some years. When I met him again, I was surprised to find that he had neither modesty before men nor reverence before God. He was free and easy. He announced plainly that he did not now believe in the terrors spiritual that had frightened him in his youth. I made another discovery at the same time regarding him. He had deceived, ruined, and deserted one whom he falsely pretended to love. Through vile and cruel affections he had put his good conscience away; and, to pacify an evil conscience, he had denied the faith. The belief of the truth and the practice of wickedness could not dwell together in the same breast. The torment caused by their conflict could not be endured. He must be rid of one of the two. Unwilling to part with his sin at the command of his faith, he parted with his faith at the command of his sin. But though the shipwreck of faith is often, it is not always, the issue of the struggle. When the conscience of one who tried to be Christ's disciple is defiled by admitted, indulged sin, the struggle inevitably, immediately begins. The Spirit striveth against the flesh, and the flesh against the Spirit. The sin often casts out the faith; but the faith also often casts out the sin. The outcome is often, through grace, the discomfiture of the adversary. "Thanks be to God, who giveth us the victory." "The steps of a good man are ordered by the Lord. Though he fall, he shall not be utterly cast down; for the Lord upholdeth him with His hand." (*W. Arnot.*) *A good conscience :*—I. A GOOD CONSCIENCE. This expression may be used in more ways than one. 1. A clean or pure conscience is a "good conscience." Keep your conscience pure. Do not sully it. Every wrong thing you say or do leaves a stain on your conscience—just like a black mark on a white piece of cloth or a sheet of paper, and your great concern should be, not to have your conscience thus made black and foul. This applies alike to those who are Christians, and to those who are not. The best conscience has stains enough, and, as we shall see, needs to be cleansed. But in so far as your decision as to any action or course of conduct is concerned, it is of the last importance to keep your conscience clean. I need not say that this is not easy. It requires a constant effort—ay, a constant fight. Paul knew what this was. Good man as he was, he required to be ever on the watch to keep his conscience pure. 2. A cleansed and pacified conscience is a "good conscience." Perhaps some of you say, "Alas, what you have said about the pure conscience is of little concern to me. At least, it can only be a thing of the future to me. What about the past? My conscience troubles me. It is defiled." Now it is here that the gospel comes in, with the good news of cleansing for the conscience. It not only tells of provision of grace and strength in the Lord Jesus, to enable us to keep the conscience clean, and do what it bids. It does more. It tells of pardon for sin, through the blood of Christ, who, by taking the guilt of sin upon Himself, and dying in the sinner's stead, removes the guilt, washes out the stains, and so brings back peace to the conscience. There is no conscience that does not need this cleansing, that does not need it again and again, whether the conscience is troubled about the sin or not. I have heard of an Indian having a dollar which did not belong to him. Pointing to his breast, he said, "I got a good man and a bad man here, and the good man say, the dollar is not mine; I must return it to the owner"; and so he did. He could not have got the "good conscience" otherwise. 3. A tender conscience is a "good conscience." This comes pretty near my first gremark, instead of second, because it seems to come in most suitably after speakin of the cleansed and pacified conscience. If I can get peace for my conscience by going to the blood of Christ, does it matter very much my sinning again? Ah, yes. I heard the other day of a man having a "strong conscience." That is to say, he could go a great length and do very questionable things without his conscience being troubled. Perhaps in order to create a laugh, or to be thought clever, and make himself "good company," as it is called, he might exaggerate or go beyond the exact and literal truth without it disturbing his conscience much. Now, that is not a tender conscience. "Old Humphrey," speaking of such a one, says that he "puts too much red in the brush!" All such things should be avoided. It is very important to cultivate tenderness of conscience. Even if a thing is not altogether wrong or bad, if it has a doubtful look about it, it should not be done. There are some pieces of machinery which the smallest pin would damage or stop. Take a watch and let a grain of sand get into it, and all would go wrong. Let a grain of sand get into your eye, and you know what comes of it. Now, your conscience should, in this respect, just be like the watch—should just be like your eye —the least thing of wrong should be feared, and felt, and avoided; and if it does get in, there should be no rest till it is out. II. WHAT IT LEADS TO. What is the

effect of having a good or evil conscience ? 1. A good conscience leads to happiness and peace; an evil conscience to misery and despair. 2. A good conscience inspires with courage, independence, and fearlessness; an evil conscience fills with cowardice and shame. (*J. H. Wilson, M.A.*)    *Wrecked through losing a good conscience :*—I had a friend who started in commercial life, and as a book merchant, with a high resolve. He said, "In my store there shall be no books that I would not have my family read." Time passed on, and one day I went into his store and found some iniquitous books on the shelf, and I said to him, "How is it possible that you can consent to sell such books as these?" "Oh," he replied, "I have got over those puritanical notions. A man cannot do business in this day unless he does it in the way other people do it." To make a long story short, he lost his hope of heaven, and in a little while he lost his morality, and then he went into a mad-house. In other words, when a man casts off God, God casts him off. (*T. De Witt Talmage.*) *Faith the cabinet of conscience :*—If faith be a precious pearl, a good conscience is the cabinet that contains it. This heavenly manna must be laid up in a heavenly pot. (*T. Secker.*)    *A good conscience :*—We have compared conscience to the eye of the soul. We may also compare it to the window of the soul. A window is of use for letting light into a room; and also for looking through that you may see what is outside of the window. But if you want a good, correct view of the things that you are looking at through a window, what sort of glass is it necessary to have in the window? Clear glass. Suppose that the glass in the window, instead of being clear glass, is stained glass; one pane red, another blue, another yellow, and another green. When you look through the red glass, what colour will the things be that you are looking at? Red. And so when you look through the blue glass, all things will be blue. They will be yellow when you look through yellow glass, and green when you look through the pane of that colour. But suppose you have thick heavy shutters to the window, and keep them closed, can you see anything through the window then? No. And can you see anything in the room when the shutters are closed? No. It will be all dark. And conscience is just like a window in this respect. You must keep the shutters open, and the windows clean, so that plenty of pure light can get in, if you want to see things properly. God's blessed Word, the Bible, gives just the kind of light we need to have a good conscience. (*J. H. Wilson, M.A.*)    *Good conscience a man's longest friend :*—It is a witty parable which one of the fathers hath of a man who had three friends, two whereof he loved entirely, the third but indifferently. This man, being called in question for his life, sought help of his friends. The first would bear him company some part of his way; the second would lend him some money for his journey; and that was all they would or could do for him; but the third, whom he least respected, and from whom he least expected, would go all the way, and abide all the while with him—yea, he would appear with him, and plead for him. This man is every one of us, and our three friends are the flesh and the world and our own conscience. Now, when death shall summon us to judgment, what can our friends after the flesh do for us? They will bring us some part of the way, to the grave, and further they cannot. And of all the worldly goods which we possess, what shall we have? What will they afford us? Only a shroud and a coffin, or a tomb at the most. But maintain a good conscience, that will live and die with us, or rather, live when we are dead; and when we rise again, it will appear with us at God's tribunal; and when neither friends nor a full purse can do us any good, then a good conscience will stick close to us. (*J. Spencer.*)
**Have made shipwreck.**—*Shipwrecks :*—I. THE NATURE OF SUCH SHIPWRECKS. We shall confine our meditations to the special aspects of this subject as they are here presented; "concerning faith have made shipwreck." But when has a man made shipwreck concerning faith? 1. When he has lost his hold of spiritual truth. We know but little of these men, Hymenæus and Alexander, but what we do know shows us that they had lost their grasp of Divine and apostolic teaching. Hence we read respecting Hymenæus in the second chapter of the Second Epistle to Timothy, "And their word will eat as doth a canker; of whom is Hymenæus and Philetus ; who concerning the truth have erred, saying that the resurrection is past already, and overthrow the faith of some." Here we see then departure from "the truth"; also that such departure, in Paul's conception, was shipwreck. We read of Alexander in the fourth chapter of the Second Epistle. "Alexander, the copper-smith, did me much evil; of whom be thou aware also ; for he hath greatly withstood our words," or the gospel which Paul preached. These men then had made "shipwreck concern-

ing faith." They had lost their faith in the truth as embodied in Christ: and in the resurrection as taught by Him and His apostles. But such "shipwrecks concerning faith" occur in the quieter and less keenly intellectual spheres of human life. The freshness of spiritual life is lost amidst life's cares, temptations, and prosperity, and with the freshness of the spiritual life there goes the beautiful and childlike grasp of faith. Let me ask you, what scepticism has to give you better than the truth, which you have already received from the lips of Christ. 2. Shipwreck is made concerning faith when men and women lose their faith in the nobleness of human destiny, and in the importance and possibility of attaining it. 3. A man has made shipwreck concerning faith when he loses those elements of character which are the results of faith. "They that will be rich fall into temptation and snares; for the love of money is the root of all evil." II. THE CAUSES OF SUCH MORAL SHIPWRECKS. 1. Trifling with conscience, or the severing of a good conscience from faith. This is clearly the thought of the apostle in these words. "Holding faith, and a good conscience; which, some having put away concerning faith, have made shipwreck." "A good conscience," says Dr. Fairbairn, "is here faith's necessary handmaid," and is as essential as a living faith; indeed, is its necessary fruit. But there are men who sever the two. They imagine that a mere intellectual holding of the truth is enough; that it is not essential that it should influence the life. Such were the views of Hymenæus and Alexander. They made shipwreck by trifling at first with the instincts and enforcements of conscience. It was this trifling with sin which led to the overthrow of faith. Sometimes faith goes first, and the obligation to morality is subsequently relaxed. But the converse of this is also true. 2. Another cause of moral shipwrecks is, according to the apostle, "hurtful lusts." There is, for instance, the lust after money. There is special reference to this here. "They that will be rich," rich at any cost, social, mental, or spiritual. "Which some coveted after." There is the lust after sinful pleasure. Pure pleasure is right enough: but any pleasure indulged at the expense of conscience, any pleasure which soils the spiritual nature is altogether wrong. The pleasures of sinful gratification, of reading and amusements which appeal to the lowest passions, the bewitchment of drinking, are daily drowning men in destruction; leading to shipwrecks. III. THE CONSEQUENCES OF THESE MORAL SHIPWRECKS. 1. There is the shipwreck of happiness. "Pierced themselves through with many sorrows"—with pangs of remorse. And what hell can be worse than that? 2. This is consummated in final retribution and overthrow. "Drown men in destruction and perdition." What these terrible words mean I cannot say. (*R. A. Davies.*) *Making shipwreck of the soul:*—I do not wonder that such an illustration should readily occur to the mind of Paul. He had not forgotten his terrible experience in the autumn of 62, just three years before. For fourteen weary days—the fierce Euroclydon blowing, and neither sun nor stars appearing—he had been tossed up and down on the angry sea of Adria, the vessel a mere plaything to the gale. Nor was this by any means his sole experience of the dangers of the deep. In writing two years earlier to the church at Corinth, he made mention of "perils of the sea" he had already encountered, and stated that "thrice he had suffered shipwreck." As the first Christian missionary, he had made repeated voyages from Cæsarea to Tarsus, and Antioch, and Cyprus, and various parts of Asia Minor, and had probably been eyewitness of many a sad maritime disaster. The records of Trinity House may inform us how many ships have been wrecked in one year, but, ah! where is the record that shall tell us how many souls have been lost? How many young men, for example, who left their peaceful, pious homes, perhaps a few years ago, and have been launched upon the open sea of city life with all its dangers and temptations, have, within the past few months, been caught by some fierce blast of vice or error, and hurled to moral and spiritual ruin? I. A FAIR START. This thought is suggested by St. Paul's reference to the early promise which Timothy gave of a pious and useful life. When he speaks of "the prophecies that went before on him," I understand him to allude not to inspired predictions, in the usual sense of the term, but to the hopes which had been cherished, and the anticipations which had been expressed, regarding him, even from his childhood. People who knew the lad, his character, his training, his environments, augured for him a bright and honourable career. They said, "That boy will turn out well. He will be a good man. He will make a mark on society. He will live to purpose." And those "prophecies" were justified. 1. By the fact that he came of a good stock. What language can express the blessing that comes of a wise and godly upbringing! Many of us owe more than ever we can tell to the holy influences that gathered around us in our early days. Oh, with what tender and delightful associations is that paternal dwelling linked! Ay, and old grannie Lois, too, we remember how she would take down her spectacles from the chimney corner, and show us Bible-pictures that delighted our young minds, and then would urge us to give our lives to God. You came out of an admirable nest. The ship was launched from a first-rate building yard. 2. Those "prophecies" were justified in the case of young Timothy, by his thorough acquaintance with Holy Scripture. What is that we read in Paul's Epistle to him (iii. 15, Revised Version)? From a babe. It is the same Greek word which Luke uses when he says, "And they brought unto Jesus infants, that He would touch them." As soon as he was capable of learning anything he was taught the Word of God. The first impressions his mind received were of religious truth. His mother, as a pious Hebrewess, regarded it as her main duty to her child, to make him acquainted with Holy Scripture. Such instruction may be expected to have a salutary influence on the whole future life. A boy who knows his Bible, and is well up in Scripture studies, starts life with great advantage. He gives promise of keeping on the right rails. 3. There was yet another thing that justified those early "prophecies" of a good career for Timothy. And this was the personal character of the lad. He was a well-disposed, quiet, thoughtful, serious youth. He never gave his mother any trouble. We read as much in the Acts of the Apostles, for it is there stated that "he was well reported of by the brethren that were at Lystra and Iconium." It is a good sign of a young fellow, when, in the town or village where he was born and bred, every one is ready to speak well of him. Thus we have seen what is meant by a fair start in life. It is like a vessel gliding down the slip on the launching day, when, all the hammering ended, and gay bunting flying everywhere, and loud huzzas rending the air, she softly glides out on to the open main! Who, on such a day, would augur her lying a pitiful wreck on some foreign reef? II. Now for THE GOOD EQUIPMENT. It is thus described: "Holding faith and a good conscience." Two very excellent and necessary things. Shall we call conscience the compass to direct the ship's course, and faith the sails that are to impel her on her way? Well, no vessel that wants either of these things is fit to go to sea. Without the one, her path through the deep will be uncertain, and therefore dangerous; without the other, she will have no force to carry her forward. A man has a poor chance of a happy and successful voyage over the sea of life, if, in entering upon it, he lacks either a good conscience or a sound faith. 1. "A good conscience." I take them in this order, because, generally, the whisper of conscience is heard even prior to the adoption of a definite faith. In matters of spiritual navigation, the compass is fixed before the canvas is set. Yours, sir, is a bad conscience, when, without upbraiding and making you miserable, it allows you to go into bad company, to frequent the haunts of dissipation, to profane the Lord's day, to neglect His ordinances, to read unclean literature, and to satisfy yourself with all sorts of vain excuses. Yours is a drugged and evil conscience, William, when you can lie down to rest at night and sleep soundly, though you have offered no prayer to God, and have no reason to know that He is at peace with you. "A good conscience" is one that is tender, sensitive, and pure; like a sound compass, whose magnetism has not been injured, it will guide you aright. To be altogether safe and good, it must be under the direction of God's truth; for the mere moralist may be scrupulously conscientious, and yet far from the standard which the gospel requires. But—2. You want something more. If you are to be fully equipped, you must also have a sound and living faith. You will not come to much good without this. A compass is an admirable thing, but you will not secure much speed if that is all the ship is provided with; there must also be the unfurled canvas, which, filled with the breath of heaven, will give it energy and motion. A living faith must be based on a definite creed. You cannot be a believer unless there is something that you believe. There is an affectation very popular at the present day, to believe nothing. No, no. Take away a young man's religion, and he is the easy prey of all manner of evil. If you want to destroy a man's morals, rob him of his Bible. A brig fifteen hundred miles out from land, without one square yard of canvas, is better off than a young man who has no religion and no faith. A man's very accomplishments have proved his ruin. Who will deny that decided genius has shipwrecked many a promising life? I have not a doubt that Burns, and Byron, and Shelley, and Goethe, and Paine, and Voltaire, that each of them, in the absence of a sustaining faith, suffered moral disaster just in proportion to his genius. If a ship is heavily freighted with costly treasures, all the more does it need to have its sails well spread to the wind. Thus furnished with a good conscience and a true faith, you will sail the voyage of life in safety, and at last reach the everlasting haven. But stay, our text tells us—III. Of A FATAL DISASTER—a spiritual shipwreck. The apostle says that some persons—and he goes on to mention two instances, "Hymeneus and Alexander"—having put away a good conscience, and lost their faith, had become morally shipwrecked. Paul does not for a moment hint that Timothy would do so. Nay, as he indicates in his Second Epistle, he was sure he would not do so. He who had begun the good work in him, would carry it forward to perfection. The compass is thrown overboard; the sails are carried away; the vessel is shattered on the rocks. Nearly every man who goes wrong begins by tampering with conscience. So long as a young Christian keeps a good conscience, I am not much afraid of his lapsing into scepticism. Foolish men! they hoisted their mutinous flags, and thought to draw away after them the whole Christian fleet: and, lo! there they are, lying two pitiful wrecks, over which the wind moans its eternal dirge. This has been the history of hundreds and thousands since. (*J. T. Davidson, D.D.*) *The great shipwreck :*—I. THE SUM OF THE CHRISTIAN LIFE. That is the whole, the union of all the parts. It has two chief parts: "faith and a good conscience." Faith is an outgoing, grasping, clinging, leaning mood of the soul. The Christian is always "holding faith and a good conscience." The word conscience means a fellow-knowledge—from *con* together, and *science* knowledge. And who is your fellow in this knowledge? The answer is—God. Conscience is the knowledge I have along with God. It makes me perfectly sure that its voice is the voice of God. God is thus in the conscience, judging all my actions. The heathen has his household god: yours is conscience. Conscience is very strong in the young. We knew perfectly what it was to hold a good conscience. And so did an Irish boy, whose master wished to lengthen a web that was short measure. He gave the boy the one end and took hold of the other himself. He then said, "Pull, Adam, pull!" But the boy stood still. "Pull, Adam!" he shouted again; but the boy said, "I can't, sir." "Why not?" the master asked. "My conscience will not allow me." "You will never do for a linen manufacturer," the master replied. That boy became the famous Rev. Dr. Adam Clarke, and persuaded many to hold faith and a good conscience. You must not think that it is easy to keep a good conscience. You do yourself the greatest injury when in youth you disobey conscience. When men put away a good conscience, oh what tortures they often endure, day and night, in after years! I wish now to show you how faith and a good conscience always go together. They are like the right and left sides of a living man; there can be no health or power when either is palsied. Or they are like the sisters Martha and Mary in the home Christ condescends to visit, only they unite their gifts without blaming each other. The Christian is thus kept right towards God and man, and does equal justice to both worlds. The old fathers used to say that the Book and the Breast agree, and that conscience is naturally Christian. Perhaps you would be pleased with an illustration of this truth from the old world. About five hundred years before Christ, a Greek poet showed the workings of an evil conscience. Agamemnon, prince of men, just returned from the wars of Troy, was murdered by his own wife. His son, Orestes, must avenge his death, and so slew his own mother. After that deed of blood all joy forsook the lighthearted, dashing prince. Guilt lay heavy upon his soul, and he felt that he was hated of the immortals. The Furies, with their snaky hair and cruel scourges, were upon him, and chased him night and day. But who are the Furies? You know them well: they are self-accusing thoughts, which the poet describes as heaven-sent avengers of sin. Byron knew them well, for he says—

> " My solitude is solitude no more,
> But peopled with the Furies."

Orestes fled to the temple of Apollo, god of light, and kneeled at his altar, seeking guidance. While he knelt, the Furies slept on the altar steps. Is not that a beautiful idea? It is a sort of sermon teaching that the accusing conscience finds rest only in prayer to God. Apollo bid him go and give himself up to Divine justice, as represented by the sacred judges at Mars Hill in Athens. He did so, the Furies following him all the way. He owned his guilt before the judges, and declared himself ready to do whatever they recommended. In wellnigh such words as a Christian uses, they told him that he must have an atonement, and be cleansed by water and blood. Even they believed, in their own dim way, that "without shedding of blood is no remission." He was so cleansed, and then even the Furies were satisfied, and ceased from troubling. And the smile of heaven again came to Orestes, and he walked in the land of the living, a forgiven and joyous man. Oh, how perfectly Christ meets all the felt needs of such an awakened conscience! Thus the Christian is a man of faith and of a good conscience; not of faith without conscience, nor of conscience without faith. He is no spiritual paralytic, powerless on the one side: he is no miserable, limping cripple, whose doing is shamefully shorter than his believing; but his soul moves like the successful runner, on equal feet. Our text likens the soul to a ship. Now, a ship sails best when it is kept even by not being overloaded on one side. And thus balanced between faith and a good conscience—between a deep sense of sin and a thorough trust in the Saviour—the good ship of heaven, with swelling sails, catches the favouring breeze, and heads for the "Fair Havens" above. II. THE RUIN OF THE SOUL. The history of this ruin has three stages; for it begins with the conscience, then reaches faith, and ends in shipwreck—"which (good conscience) some having put away, concerning faith have made shipwreck." Now your soul is an immortal ship in a dangerous sea. Conscience is the captain, reason the steersman, the Bible your chart, and your natural appetites are the sturdy crew—good servants they, but the worst of masters. Only conscience can guide the vessel safely through the rocks and quicksands of temptation. But the crew sometimes mutiny and put conscience overboard, and then passion becomes the master and owner of the ship, and seizes the helm. "Conscience," our text says, "which some having put away"—that is a phrase of violence. Only after a fierce struggle can conscience be put away. Unless the command be given again to the rightful captain, the ship drifts among the rocks, and the sea rushes in through the yawning bows, and ruin claims the whole for its own. The ruin of the soul begins with conscience, and usually with littles. Conscience is like the outer dyke in Holland, which the flood first assails. Little lies, hid under the cloak of outward decency, are like the little fox the Spartan boy hid under his dress till it gnawed into his very heart. Oppose the little beginnings of evil. When the conscience is wounded, faith decays and dies. A bad life is a marsh from which poisonous mists arise to becloud the mind. A bad heart forges notions to suit itself. Evidently Paul believes that our faith is shaken not so much by wrong arguing as by wrong living—Hymeneus and Alexander. Perhaps they grew too fond of wine, and fell upon mean tricks for hiding it; or they were very fond of money, and told lies to get it. And so they put overboard the troublesome captain, good conscience. Then they began to find fault with Paul's preaching; this sermon was not plain, and that did them no good; he was too hard on people, and pushed matters too far. Very likely they gave some fine name to their doubting, and protested that they could not endure bigotry, and that they wished more sweetness and light. But their falling away went from bad to worse, till they became stark blasphemers, and had publicly to be cut off from the Church. When Paul was shipwrecked, the crew lightened the ship by casting overboard the tackle and the cargo. Should you be caught in any hurricane of temptation, part with everything rather than lose a good conscience. All the money in the world, all the honours and pleasures on earth, cannot make up for the loss of that. Pray that to the Christian faith you may add Christian honour. The putting away of a good conscience, unless repented of, ends in shipwreck. A shipwrecked soul—what a thought! But this dark passage is not so dark as it seems. Hymeneus and Alexander had been cut off from the Church that they might "learn not to blaspheme" (ver. 20). The apostle would not despair even of these two blaspheming backsliders. He had a great hope that they would lay this warning to heart, and come again as penitents to the feet of Christ. Ours is a religion of hope, which teaches us not to despair of the greatest sinner, but to pray that even shipwrecked souls may be saved. (*J. Wells.*)

---

## CHAPTER II.

VERS. 1, 2. I exhort, therefore, that, first of all, supplications.—*Prayer for others*:—The true Christian, however, recognizes in human history the moral government of God. He believes, because God has declared it, that a mysterious but all-wise Providence governs the nations upon the earth; and that Jehovah continually regards the moral qualities of human agencies. He believes that the decay and calamities of successive empires have ever had a close and direct connection with their contempt of virtue and religion. I. THE DUTY OF PRAYER FOR OTHERS, AND MORE ESPECIALLY FOR PERSONS IN AUTHORITY. Intercessory prayer is here stated to be a duty; for when the apostle says "I exhort," he speaks by Divine command. If we recognize the authority of revelation, we must admit the act of intercession for others to be an act in precise conformity with the revealed will of God. But there are two results of the most beneficial kind which necessarily arise from intercessory prayer. 1. In every case in which we implore God on behalf of others, we recognize Him as the source of power, authority, mercy and grace. The address we make to Him implies our conviction that He is the Preserver and the Benefactor from whom all succour is derived. 2. But prayer for others is, besides this, an act of charity. We cannot voluntarily exercise this duty but in the spirit of charity. Prayer for others implies, by its very act, our participation in their wants, our sympathy in their sorrows, our general interest in their welfare. II. But the nature and importance of this duty will be rendered more evident as we consider THE DESIGN FOR WHICH PRAYER FOR OTHERS IS TO BE OFFERED—" that we may lead a quiet and peaceable life in all godliness and honesty." There are two ways in which public prayer may be supposed to be the direct channel of benefit to the community. 1. In the first place, there is nothing which so tends to allay irritation, to excite compassion, to restrain envy and revenge, to calm the turbulent passions of every kind, as social prayer. Were large bodies of men honestly and frequently united in prayer to God for a blessing upon the community; were they to connect earthly government with God's kind purposes to the world of social order and of mutual good will, these united prayers would be found to be the strongest cement of the various parts of the social fabric, by bringing out before the minds of all the highest and the noblest motives by which intelligent beings, and at the same time capable of affection, can be influenced. Imagine the rich unfeignedly imploring God's blessing upon the poor—and where could be found room for the exercise of injustice and oppression? Imagine the poor praying for the rich—and where would be found room for the exercise of envy, of violence, of revenge, and of robbery? Imagine the rich praying for the rich—and where would be room for the display of rivalry, contention, and selfish ambition? Imagine the poor praying for the poor—how much kindness and mutual affection would be immediately drawn out into active operation! Imagine those in authority imploring God for a blessing on every measure they undertake, and upon all their national policy—and where would be any scope for individual and selfish aggrandizement? where would be any disunion of the interests of the ruler and the ruled? Or imagine the minds of the community united in prayer for those whom God has set over them—and where would be the wish for riot, for outrage, for insubordination, or violence? 2. But a second method in which prayer will powerfully act upon a nation is through the direct blessings which God, the righteous and the Almighty Governor, will certainly bestow. It is evident that God designs to bestow these blessings through this very channel. How easily can He send healthful seasons and external peace! How easily can He enlighten the minds, and prompt the measures of those by whom the affairs of the State are administered! (*G. Noel.*) *Prayer for those in authority:*—I. THE DUTY ENJOINED in the words of our text—namely, "that supplications, prayers, intercessions, and giving of thanks be made for all men; for kings, and all that are in authority." 1. The constituent parts of this important duty. The several parts of public worship are comprehended in the text, in what the apostle denominates "supplications, prayers, intercessions, and giving of thanks." By supplications we understand the deprecation of those calamities to which we are exposed in common with all men. The apostle next speaks of "prayers"—by which we understand petitions—which it is our privilege to present to the throne of the heavenly grace, through Jesus Christ, for the supply of our various wants. The apostle, in connection with prayer, speaks of "intercessions"—that is, prayer—for others; those petitions which we are called to offer for all sorts and conditions of men, according to their several necessities. To supplications, prayers, and intercessions, the apostle adds "giving of thanks," as an expression of our gratitude for all the benefits vouchsafed to us by the great Author of our being. 2. The extent of our Christian obligations in regard to this duty. The apostle teaches us that in our acts of public devotion we are "to pray for all men." Here is nothing partial, exclusive, or sectarian. But we are not only taught to pray for all men in general, but for our rulers in particular, whether supreme or subordinate. And as it is the Lord "that giveth salvation unto kings," to Him we ought to pray on their behalf, that He may bless them in their royal persons, families, and government. The honour, welfare, and happiness of nations depend much on the wisdom, piety, and government of those who reign. But in praying for all that are in authority, we should not only pray for kings and for ministers, but also for magistrates, who may either be a great blessing or a great curse. It becomes us to pray, from a consideration of the importance of their office. 3. The order in which this is presented by the holy apostle. "I exhort, therefore, that, first of all, supplications and prayers be made for all men." This is not a secondary duty, a thing merely optional; no; it is a duty of paramount importance, which ought to take the precedence of every other in the public assemblies of the Church of God. The prayers of the people of God are more to be depended on than all the strength of our fleets or armies. II. THE ARGUMENTS BY WHICH THIS IMPORTANT DUTY IS ENFORCED. 1. That as professing Christians we may give no just cause of offence to the government under which we live; "that we may lead a quiet and peaceable life in all godliness and honesty"; that we may be preserved "from all sedition, privy conspiracy, and rebellion"; so live as the gospel may not be blamed; but that we who, by the principles of our Divine religion, are taught to abhor everything that would be injurious to others, conduct ourselves so as to prove that we are the friends of all and the enemies of none. If the State be not in safety, the subjects cannot be secure; self-preservation, therefore, ought to lead men to pray for the government under which they live. The psalmist, a true patriot, inspired with the love of his country, a holy zeal for the glory of God, and an ardent desire for the prosperity of both Church and State, says, when speaking of the people of God, "I was glad when they said unto me, Let us go into the house of the Lord. Our feet shall stand within thy gates, O Jerusalem. For my brethren and companions' sakes, I will now say, Peace be within thee. Because of the house of the Lord our God, I will seek thy good." Let us, then, cultivate the spirit of true loyalty, patriotism, and religion, as that which is best calculated to promote our individual interest, the Church's good, and the commonwealth of the nation. 2. That we may secure the Divine approbation of our conduct, which is done by sincerely, faithfully, and affectionately praying for all men; "for this is good and acceptable in the sight of God and our Saviour," and therefore has the highest possible sanction. It is not said that it is good and acceptable in the sight of God to speak evil of dignitaries, by railing against those who are higher in rank, power, or authority than ourselves, whether in Church or State. The evil is prohibited; "it is written, thou shalt not speak evil of the ruler of thy people"; and, therefore, to indulge in it were a crime in the sight of God, as well as contrary to the rules of that society by which many of us profess to be governed, which says, that "We shall neither speak evil of magistrates nor of ministers." It is not said that it is good and acceptable in the sight of God our Saviour to treat the office of rightful governors with contempt. 3. That the will of God, in reference to the salvation of our guilty race, may be accomplished. If we ask, what is the will of God our Saviour concerning the human race? we are taught to believe that it is gracious and merciful. He "would have all men to be saved and come to the knowledge of the truth." Many have been saved in answer to prayer; and we have good reason to believe that more would if we had prayed more. III. THE INFERENCES which may be deduced from the subject. 1. That we are not good subjects unless we pray for all our constituted authorities. In early times, the members of the Jewish Church were called to pray for heathen princes, even for those who carried them away captive into Babylon, "unto the God of heaven, for the life of the king and of his sons," and in obedience to the command of God Himself, by the prophet Jeremiah, as a means of securing their own interests—"that ye may be increased therein and not diminished; seek the peace of the city whither I have caused you to be carried away captives, and pray unto the Lord for it; for in the peace thereof shall ye have peace." 2. If we are not praying subjects, we are not good Christians; for all good Christians are men of prayer, and no Christian can be satisfied with merely praying for himself, his family, or the Church of God. 3. We conclude, from the nature of this duty, that if we are not good Christians we shall never yield a conscientious obedience to the apostolic exhortation recorded in our text. (*A. Bell.*) *The duty of prayer for all who are in eminent place:*—1. ON THE OBJECT OF GOVERNMENT. I leave it to men of another taste and profession to enter minutely into the inferior objects of government, as well as into the means by which those objects may be obtained; and, keeping within the boundary of the text, shall observe that government is intended to promote security, happiness, piety, and religious influence. It has often been stated that a large portion of all codes of law, as of all history, is a proof of human depravity. Men have fallen from God; and, corrupted in their social propensities, they envy, injure, and destroy each other. All communities, therefore, have found it necessary to agree to some restraint, and to lodge in some hands a controlling power; the individual is to be blended with the general good, that the general may return individual advantage. Security, then, is one great object of government. And it is the glory of government to hold the shield over all—to defend the poor, the fatherless, and the widow, as well as the men of might, and the great, and the noble. Now, though under God, men's personal and social happiness greatly depends on their own industry and carefulness, yet has it some connection with the government under which we live. There are numerous ways in which religion and piety may be aided by the men who are in authority, and especially by kings becoming nursing fathers, and their queens nursing mothers. The word we render honesty is of rather questionable meaning; some translate it "gravity"; its general import is to behave decorously and worthily. As connected with godliness, it implies a desire that Christians may be allowed to conduct religious worship, and the whole of their profession, in a way suitable to religion itself; and that, being delivered from the evils of persecution, they may be exempt from temptation to act inconsistently with their high vocation. The gravity and dignity here mentioned convey, however, to me the idea of Christian influence—influence of character, of benevolent exertion. II. THE BEST WAY OF SECURING THIS OBJECT. There are numerous ways in which some good may be done, and in which, therefore, it is our duty to act. Home, and its immediate vicinity, and the nearest relations, are the great sphere of our influence; and here the Christian must act in promoting the morals, the intelligence, and the spirituality of all around him. The Christian, too, has political privileges; and in votes, and in petitions, and in every peaceful and constitutional way, it is his duty to act for the public good in the fear of the Lord. The laws, too, must be supported in their majesty by all— even by the humblest in society; as, without the countenance of the many, the few who have to enforce them, however elevated their rank and unbroken their integrity, will be too feeble, and the object of government will not be obtained. Nor must it be forgotten that well-directed charity is a most efficient way of promoting the security and happiness, as well as the godliness, of the community. The way, however, of securing this object marked out in the text is prayer. I attach importance to prayer, for the following reasons:—1. God generally deals with nations according to their moral character and piety. From the times in which the Assyrian, the Persian, the Grecian, the Roman Powers were punished, to the days of revolutionary and sanguinary France, Providence has preached this awful doctrine. Hear Isaiah: "If ye be willing and obedient, ye shall eat the good of the land." 2. That a nation's morals and piety will be in the degree of its prayerfulness. 3. I urge prayer, because the hearts of kings, and of nobles, and of senators —of all in authority—are at the disposal of Him who hears His people when they call. He can turn the counsel of Ahithophel into foolishness; He bringeth to nothing the devices of the wise; He inspired Solomon with wisdom; by Him kings reign and princes decree righteousness. III. OUR PRESENT INDUCEMENT TO SEEK THIS OBJECT IN THIS WAY ESPECIALLY. 1. You will see the necessity of prayer for the nation when I remind you of the hazard which always attends measures which have not been tried. 2. You will see the necessity of prayer for the nation when I remind you of the important business which its parliament has to transact. 3. The delicate position of the nations, and our connection with them, will further show the need of grace to enlighten all who take a lead in our public affairs. 4. There is another reason why, at this time, we should be earnest in prayer of a more religious kind—viz., the near approach of the latter-day glory in the Church. (*J. K. Foster.*)    *On intercession for others:*—I am led by these words to consider the great Christian duty of praying for others. Perhaps there is none more neglected, with so little consciousness of sin in the omission of it. It is enforced by the example of the most eminent saints. Thus Abraham interceded with God for Sodom; and He said, in answer to his prayer, "I will not destroy it for ten's sake." Moses, the illustrious type of the great Intercessor, prayed for the people; and we learn that

God would have destroyed the Israelites had not Moses His chosen stood in the gap : " I prayed," saith he, " unto the Lord, and said, O Lord God, destroy not Thy people and Thine inheritance, which Thou hast redeemed through Thy greatness." " God forbid," said Samuel, " that I should sin against the Lord in ceasing to pray for you." The Psalmist exhorts to pray for the peace of Jerusalem, " They shall prosper that love thee. . . . Peace be within thy walls, and prosperity within thy palaces." Isaiah expresses his determination not to hold his peace for Zion's sake, and for Jerusalem not to rest " until the righteousness thereof go forth as brightness, and the salvation thereof as a lamp that burneth." Daniel humbled himself before God day and night, and fasted and prayed for the sins of the Jews. I would not, however, enforce this duty merely, or chiefly, because it is enjoined to us by the precepts and recommended to us by the practice of patriarchs, judges, psalmists, prophets, and apostles, and of Him who is in all respects our great Example : it is rather because this duty is included within the general obligation of Christian love, of which it forms an essential part. Leaving, therefore, the question of the duty of intercession, I proceed to consider its advantages. I. INTERCESSION FOR OTHERS MAY BE CONSIDERED AS THE MEANS OF EXCITING BENEVOLENT AFFECTIONS IN OURSELVES. Ask me, What is the glory of an angel above a devil ? I answer, It is the spirit of love which animates the one, of which the other is destitute. It is not the absence of external splendour, it is not the suffering and misery, it is the want of benevolence, by which a fallen spirit is degraded, and which makes him odious. Ask me, What is the peculiar glory of the gospel above every other religion ? I reply, It is the spirit of love which breathes in it. The providence of God seems purposely to have placed the Christian in a scene where the exercise of love is needed, and his benevolent affections continually called forth ; where wants and miseries present themselves on every side amongst his fellow-creatures and his friends. What can he do for them ? His own means are insufficient to relieve them ; but he can pray ; he can implore God to supply what he cannot do. Have you a dear relation sick or afflicted ? Are you indebted to a generous benefactor to whom you cannot repay the debt of gratitude ? O what a just and noble return may you render him by your prayers ! II. INTERCESSION FOR OTHERS WILL ALSO PRODUCE THE SPIRIT OF LOVE IN THOSE FOR WHOM WE PRAY. Love creates love. You cannot meet your friend, after your heart has been engaged in fervent supplication for him, without expressing that genuine tenderness which will produce a reciprocal regard in him. Intercession enlarges the exercise of friendship : it opens a new source of love. Let not a Christian say, I am forsaken—I meet with no acts of kindness. Has he then no Christian friends ? Let him think of them as interceding for him. Intercession for our friends refines our friendship and redeems it from those debasing feelings by which the attachments of worldly men are so often degraded. III. THE THIRD ADVANTAGE OF INTERCESSION FOR OUR FRIENDS CONSISTS IN ITS EXCITING OUR LOVE TOWARDS GOD. This is its direct influence. Can you go to the Father of Mercies day by day imploring blessings upon all you love? can you diversify these petitions, adapting them to the various necessities, sorrows, and circumstances of your friends? and do you not exclaim, How infinite the riches, how boundless the power, how vast the bounty of the Being I address ? He is the Giver of all good things to my children, to my friend, to my neighbour, to my country, to the whole world, to the universe ! IV. THE LAST ADVANTAGE WHICH I SHALL MENTION IN INTERCESSION FOR OUR FRIENDS IS THAT IT IS THE DIRECT MEANS OF PROMOTING THEIR WELFARE. Why, when He intends to bless, may He not do so through the medium of prayer and intercession? Can anything be more consonant to the general analogy and constitution of the world? Even the great benefits of redemption are conveyed to us through the intercession of the Redeemer. What an example did He exhibit of the performance of this duty ! V. LET US LEARN WHO HAS BEEN OUR TRUEST FRIEND, TO WHOM WE HAVE BEEN MOST INDEBTED. Think often of Him who has laboured the most for your welfare, who has most watched over your soul, and prayed the most effectually for you. Think of Him who now liveth to make intercession for you. That Friend is Christ. (*J. Venn.*)    *Gordon and intercessory prayer :*—Canon Wilberforce told the following characteristic incident about General Gordon :—" Just before General Gordon started, as he believed for the Congo, he sent to a prayer-meeting over which the Canon was presiding, asking for the prayers of those assembled. He said in his letter, ' I would rather have the prayers of that little company gathered in your house to-day than I would have the wealth of the Soudan placed at my disposal. Pray for me that I may have humility and the guidance of God, and that all spirit of murmuring may be rebuked in me.' When he reached London on his return from Brussels, and his destination was changed, the General sent the Canon another message, ' Offer thanks at your next prayer-meeting. When I was upborne on the hearts of those Christians I received from God the spiritual blessing that I wanted, and I am now calmly resting in the current of His will.' " *Pray for those in authority :*—When Abraham Lincoln was going from Springfield to Washington he stood upon the platform of the car, and his old friends and neighbours were gathered round him to wish him an affectionate God-speed in the course upon which he was entering. He had come to rule and reign in times of difficulty and trouble, and he said, " Well, friends and neighbours, there is one thing you can do for me that I ask you to do, and that is—pray for me," and the train went off, bearing him to Washington. That is the spirit that one would desire to see amongst those who are in authority and influence, and it is the spirit that we well may cultivate towards those in authority over us. *Prayer for those in authority :*—Methodism in Ireland was, at the time of its union with England, looked upon with suspicion, and this was especially the case during the time of the rebellion. Lord Cornwallis happened to spend a few days with Speaker Foster. At that time Mr. Barber was stationed in that circuit as the minister. He and Mr. Foster's gardener, who was also a Methodist, were walking in Speaker Foster's grounds one day, when Barber, who was instant in season and out of season, asked the gardener to engage in prayer. They both knelt down, and Barber was praying aloud, when Lord Cornwallis and Speaker Foster, who were out walking, heard voices, drew near, and listened. Among the requests made to God were appeals for assistance to the Government, who were placed in such trying circumstances, and that God would bless and direct the counsels of the Lord-Lieutenant—Lord Cornwallis. Barber in his prayer breathed the deepest loyal devotion, and concluded by imploring a blessing upon the Methodists, and that they should be saved from the devil and Squire Ruxton of Ardee. " Who is this squire ? " asked Lord Cornwallis, and Mr. Foster replied that he was a neighbouring squire, who persecuted the Methodists. " And what does this praying mean ? " asked Lord Cornwallis. " Oh," replied Mr. Foster, " this gardener of mine is one of those Methodist fellows, and I must dismiss him." " You will do no such thing," said the other. " Did you hear how he prayed for me, for the Council, for the King, and for the Government? Indeed, these Methodists must be a loyal people; and as for Squire Ruxton, just take my compliments to him, and tell him that I think these Methodists are very good people, and that he must leave them alone." That prayer of poor Barber's put a stop to the worst persecution ever endured in that neighbourhood, and, while passes were required of others, free permission was given to the Methodist preacher to go where he liked and do what he liked. *Prayer for rulers :*—I. WE OUGHT TO PRAY FOR THOSE WHO ARE IN AUTHORITY MORE FREQUENTLY AND EARNESTLY THAN FOR OTHER MEN, BECAUSE THEY MORE THAN OTHER MEN NEED OUR PRAYERS. In other words, they need a more than ordinary share of that wisdom and grace which God alone can bestow; and which He seldom or never bestows, except in answer to prayer. 1. This is evident from the fact that they have a more than ordinary share of duties to perform. All the duties which God requires of other men, considered as sinful, immortal, and accountable creatures, He requires of rulers. It is incumbent on them, as it is on other men, to possess personal religion; to exercise repentance toward God and faith in the Lord Jesus Christ ; to love and fear and serve their Creator ; and to prepare for death and judgment. In addition to the various personal duties of a moral and religious nature which are required of them as men, they have many official duties which are peculiar to themselves— duties which it is by no means easy to perform in a manner acceptable to God and approved of men. 2. They are appointed and they are required to be ministers of God for good to those over whom they are placed. There is no power but of God ; the powers that be are ordained of God. Since, then, legislators, rulers, and magistrates are the ministers and vicegerents of God for good, they are sacredly bound to imitate Him whom they represent ; to be such on earth as He is in heaven ; to take care of His rights and see that they are not trampled upon with impunity ; to be a terror to evil-doers and a praise and encouragement to such as do well. 3. As the influence of their example must be great, it is their indispensable duty to take care that this influence be ever exerted in favour of truth and goodness ; and to remember that they are like a city set upon a hill which cannot be hid. Now consider a moment how exceedingly difficult it must be for a weak, short-sighted, imperfect creature like man to perform these various duties in a proper manner, and how large a share of prudence and wisdom and firmness and goodness is necessary to enable him to do it. Surely, then, they who are called to perform such duties in a peculiar manner need our prayers. II. THOSE WHO ARE INVESTED WITH AUTHORITY NEED MORE THAN OTHER MEN OUR PRAYERS, BECAUSE THEY ARE EXPOSED MORE THAN OTHER MEN TO TEMPTATION AND DANGER. While they have a more than ordinary share of duties to perform, they are urged by temptations more than ordinarily numerous and powerful to neglect their duty. They have, for instance, peculiarly strong temptations to neglect those personal, private duties which God requires of them as men, as immortal and accountable creatures; and a performance of which is indispensably necessary to their salvation. They are exposed to the innumerable temptations and dangers which ever attend prosperity. How powerfully, then, must they be tempted to irreligion, to pride, to ambition, to every form of what the Scriptures call worldly-mindedness? It can scarcely be necessary to add that persons who are exposed to temptations so numerous and powerful need our prayers. III. This will appear still more evident if we consider THAT, SHOULD THOSE WHO ARE CLOTHED WITH AUTHORITY YIELD TO THESE TEMPTATIONS AND NEGLECT EITHER THEIR PERSONAL OR OFFICIAL DUTIES, THE CONSEQUENCES WILL TO THEM BE PECULIARLY DREADFUL. They will, like Jeroboam, make their people to sin. We are informed by an inspired writer that one sinner destroyeth much good. This remark is true of every sinner, but it is most emphatically true of sinners who are placed in authority. IV. We ought to pray with peculiar earnestness for all who are in authority, BECAUSE OUR OWN INTEREST AND THE GREAT INTERESTS OF THE COMMUNITY REQUIRE IT. This motive the apostle urges in our text. Pray, says he, for all in authority, that we may lead quiet and peaceable lives in all godliness and honesty. These expressions plainly intimate that if we wish to enjoy peace and quiet—if we wish godliness and honesty, or, in other words, religion and morality, to prevail among us, we must pray for our rulers. Farther, the peace and prosperity of a nation evidently depend much upon the measures which its rulers adopt in their intercourse with other nations. Once more, the peace and prosperity of a nation depends entirely on securing the favour of God. (*E. Payson.*) *Christians exhorted to pray for the Queen and Parliament :*—I. In the first place, with respect to THE DUTY ITSELF. 1. The nature of it stands very distinctly expressed and announced in the text. Observe, however, that you are not to suppose from this, that kings, princes and senators, and "all that are in authority," are always to be considered as ungodly, unconverted men; not, it may be, a part of God's Church themselves. 2. As to the external circumstances, in which the duty is contemplated as being discharged, I would just remark that the apostle is giving direction to Timothy for regulating the actings and order of the Church as a society; and is, therefore, in the text, more especially contemplating the Church as such. 3. The internal feeling and state of mind with which the duty is to be discharged. There is emphatically demanded from us, in this duty, earnestness and warmth, sincerity and faith. Try to call into exercise a calm, resolute, honest sentiment of hearty faith in this agency which you exercise. 4. And consider, again, that in relation to this duty, every heart and every lip has its importance. It is the sum and amount of faith in the mass of the people, which is represented in the Scripture as prevailing with God. II. TO MENTION SOME CONSIDERATIONS, WHICH SHOULD BE FELT TO ENFORCE AND URGE UPON US ITS DISCHARGE. 1. In the first place, to go to the highest at once, we have the Divine command as it stands in the text, and as that text is corroborated and sustained by other passages of the Divine Word. The will of God is the supreme source of moral obligation. 2. A consideration enforcing the discharge of this duty on Christians arises from the fact, that the possession of any power whatever involves an obligation to its proper and efficient employment. If, therefore, it be true that Christian men are contemplated as having the privilege of offering intercession for others, if they are possessed of this amazing power of presenting supplications which shall actually exercise a real agency with God and a beneficial influence upon man, the very possession of that power, that spiritual function, involves an obligation to its conscientious exercise. 3. But we go on to observe that there are these special considerations. You may put them to yourselves in some such way as this. The important position and aspect which these parties sustain in relation to God's government of the world. For kings and rulers, and men in authority, are represented as God's ministers. Because of this, we are called upon, both for their sake and our own, to commend them to God, that they may indeed be His ministers, by intelligently falling in with His will, and seeking voluntarily to accomplish His purposes. 4. Another consideration is the influence which the character, conduct, and determinations of those in authority must have upon the rest of mankind for evil or for good. 5. Another consideration which specially commends persons in authority to the intercessions of God's Church, is the view which Christians may perhaps feel themselves compelled to take of their condition and character. It may be, that Christians may be compelled to feel that a king is necessarily surrounded by circumstances dangerous to his religion, perilous to his soul. It may be, that Christians may think that the circumstances connected with distinguished rank are unfavourable to the proper exercise and culture of those principles and sentiments, which it becomes man as a sinner to entertain, and therefore to that state of mind which is a necessary preparation for the reception of the Gospel of God. It may be, that Christians may sometimes be compelled to think that persons in these high stations are not surrounded by the best, the most enlightened and scriptural, spiritual guides. III. CONCLUDING OBSERVATIONS. I think this subject should be felt to present to us the primitive Church in an interesting aspect, and in various ways to illustrate the greatness of our religion. This little society of Christian men—despised, persecuted, contemned—they had prayers for their persecutors; they had love for them. Let me observe, that the important Christian duty which I have been enforcing upon you to-night, must not be made a substitute for all other duties, which as Christian Englishmen you are called to perform. By being Christians, you ceased not to be citizens; as citizens, all your political duties remain the same; the only thing is, that you are to discharge them under religious motives, and with a conscientious desire in them to be "accepted of God," whether or not you are approved of men. (*T. Binney.*) *Prayer for kings :*—I. THE APOSTLE EXHORTETH CHRISTIANS TO "PRAY FOR KINGS" WITH ALL SORTS OF PRAYER; with δεήσεις, or "deprecations," for averting evils from them; with προσευχαὶ, or "petitions," for obtaining good things to them; with ἐντεύξεις, or "occasional intercessions," for needful gifts and graces to be collated on them. 1. Common charity should dispose us to pray for kings. 2. To impress which consideration, we may reflect that commonly we have only this way granted us of exercising our charity toward princes; they being situated aloft above the reach of private beneficence. 3. We are bound to pray for kings out of charity to the public; because their good is a general good, and the communities of men (both Church and State) are greatly concerned in the blessings by prayer derived on them. The prosperity of a prince is inseparable from the prosperity of his people; they ever partaking of his fortunes, and thriving or suffering with him. For as when the sun shineth brightly, there is a clear day, and fair weather over the world; so when a prince is not overclouded with adversity or disastrous occurrences, the public state must be serene, and a pleasant state of things will appear. Then is the ship in a good condition when, the pilot in open sea, with full sails and a brisk gale, cheerfully steereth on toward his designed port. Especially the piety and goodness of a prince is of vast consequence, and yieldeth infinite benefit to his country. So, for instance, how did piety flourish in the times of David, who loved, favoured, and practised it! and what abundance of prosperity did attend it! What showers of blessings (what peace, what wealth, what credit and glory) did God then pour down on Israel! How did the goodness of that prince transmit favours and mercies on his country till a long time after his decease! How often did God profess "for His servant David's sake" to preserve Judah from destruction; so that even in the days of Hezekiah, when the king of Assyria did invade that country, God by the mouth of Isaiah declared, "I will defend this city to save it for Mine own sake, and for My servant David's sake." We may indeed observe that, according to the representation of things in Holy Scripture, there is a kind of moral connection, or a communication of merit and guilt, between prince and people; so that mutually each of them is rewarded for the virtues, each is punished for the vices of the other. 4. Wherefore consequently our own interest and charity to ourselves should dispose us to pray for our prince. We being nearly concerned in his welfare, as parts of the public, and as enjoying many private advantages thereby; we cannot but partake of His good, we cannot but suffer with him. We cannot live quietly if our prince is disturbed; we cannot live happily if he be unfortunate; we can hardly live virtuously if Divine grace do not incline him to favour us therein, or at least restrain him from hindering us. 5. Let us consider that subjects are obliged in gratitude and ingenuity, yea in equity and justice, to pray for their princes. They are most nearly related to us, and allied by the most sacred bands; being constituted by God, in his own room, the parents and guardians of their country. To their industry and vigilancy under

God we owe the fair administration of justice, the protection of right and innocence, the preservation of order and peace, the encouragement of goodness, and
correction of wickedness.  6. Whereas we are by Divine command frequently enjoined to fear and reverence, to honour, to obey kings ; we should look on prayer
for them as a principal branch, and the neglect thereof as a notable breach of those
duties.  7. The praying for princes is a service peculiarly honourable, and very acceptable to God; which He will interpret as a great respect done to Himself ; for
that thereby we honour His image and character in them, yielding in His presence
this special respect to them as His representatives.  8. Let us consider that whereas wisdom, guiding our piety and charity, will especially incline us to place our devotion there where it will be most needful and useful ; we therefore chiefly must
pray for kings because they do most need our prayers.  II. THE OTHER (THANKS-
GIVING) I SHALL BUT TOUCH, AND NEED NOT PERHAPS TO DO MORE.  For—1. As to
general inducements, they are the same, or very like to those which are for prayer ;
it being plain that whatever we are concerned to pray for, when we want it, that we
are bound to thank God for, when He vouchsafeth to bestow it.  2. As for particular
motives, suiting the present occasion, you cannot be ignorant or insensible of the grand
benefits by the Divine goodness bestowed on our king, and on ourselves, which this
day we are bound with all grateful acknowledgment to commemorate.  (I. Barrow.)
*The duty of public intercession and thanksgiving for princes :*—I. It recommends a
great duty to us, the duty of MAKING SUPPLICATIONS, PRAYERS, AND INTERCESSIONS,
AND OF GIVING THANKS FOR KINGS, AND ALL THAT ARE IN AUTHORITY.  II. FOR THIS IS
GOOD AND ACCEPTABLE IN THE SIGHT OF GOD OUR SAVIOUR.  1. Our applications to
God in behalf of the princes and rulers of this world are highly reasonable, as they
are proper expressions of our good-will to mankind, whose fate is in their hands,
and whose welfare in great measure depends upon their actions and conduct.  2.
As the virtues and vices of those who govern, operate on all inferior ranks of men
in the way of natural causes, so have they another and a more extraordinary effect ;
inasmuch as God doth often take occasion to reward or punish a people, not only
by the means of good or ill princes, but even for the sake of them.  3. The cares
of empire are great, and the burthen which lies upon the shoulders of princes very
weighty ; and on this account, therefore, they challenge, because they particularly
want our prayers, that they may " have an understanding heart to discern between
good and bad, and to go out and in before a great people."  With what difficulties
is their administration often clogged by the perverseness, folly, or wickedness of
those they govern !  How hard a thing do they find it to inform themselves truly
of the state of affairs ; where fraud and flattery surround and take such pains to
mislead them !  4. That the providence of God doth, in a very particular manner,
interpose towards swaying the will and affections, directing, or overruling the
intentions of those who sit at the helm ; for the king's heart is in the hand of God,
as the rivers of waters ; He turneth it whithersoever He listeth (Prov. xxi. 1).  He
gives a bent to it this way or that, which it takes as certainly and easily as a stream
is derived into the channels, which the hand of the workman prepares for it.
These prayers are never so becomingly and forcibly addressed to God as in the
great congregation.  Blessings of a public nature and influence require as public
and solemn acknowledgments ; and the proper way of obtaining mercies, which
affect many, is by pouring out the joint requests of many in behalf of them ; for in
the spiritual, as well as the carnal warfare, numbers are most likely to prevail.  III.
I proceed to consider THE SPECIAL MOTIVE THERE PROPOSED, TO QUICKEN US INTO THE
EXERCISE OF IT, that so we may lead a quiet and peaceable life in all godliness and
honesty.  I shall briefly show in what respects the devotions recommended by the
apostle contribute to this end ; and how far, therefore, our own ease, advantage,
and happiness are concerned in paying them.  And—1. They have a plain
tendency this way, as they are a prevailing argument with God so to dispose and
incline the minds of princes that they may study to promote the quiet, good, and
prosperity of their kingdoms.  2. Such prayers facilitate our leading a quiet and
peaceable life in all godliness and honesty ; inasmuch as they express, in the most
significant manner, our love, and zeal, and reverence towards the persons of
princes ; and by such instances of duty invite them to make us suitable returns.
They effectually prevent those jealousies, which men clothed with sovereign power
are too apt to entertain of their inferiors, and promote that good understanding
between them, which is the common interest, and should be the common aim of
both, and wherein the security and happiness of all well-ordered states chiefly
consist.  3. A quiet and peaceable life is the fruit of these public devotions, as we

ourselves derive from thence a spirit of meekness, submission, and respect to our
superiors, and are led into an habitual love and practice of those mild graces and
virtues which we, at such times, solemnly exercise and pray God to inspire us with;
and which, when generally practised, make crowns sit easy on the heads of princes,
and render them and their subjects equally a blessing to each other. IV. PRESS
ON CHRISTIANS THIS DUTY. 1. The princes for whom the apostle pleads were
infidels, without Christ, aliens from His commonwealth and strangers from the
covenants of His promise (Eph. ii. 12); and such also they were, by the permission
of God, to continue for three hundred years after the coming of our Saviour, that
so His gospel might not owe its first establishment, in any degree, to the secular
powers, but might spread and fix itself everywhere without their help and against
their will, and manifest to all the world its Divine original by the miraculous
manner in which it should be propagated. If then the tribute of supplications and
thanksgivings was due to those heathen princes, is it not much more due to those
who are Christians, who are ingrafted as principal members into that mystical body,
of which Jesus Christ is the head? 2. That the Roman emperors, for whom the
apostle here directs that prayers should be made, were usurpers and tyrants, who
acquired dominion by invading the liberties of a free people, and were arbitrary and
lawless in the exercise of it. Their will and pleasure was the sole standard of
justice; fear was the foundation of their government, and their throne was upheld
only by the legions which surrounded it. Even for such rulers the first Christians
were exhorted to supplicate and give thanks. How much more reasonably and
cheerfully do we, who are met here this day, now offer up that sacrifice for a Queen,
who wears the crown of her forefathers, to which she is entitled by blood, and
which was placed on her royal head, not only with the free consent but with the
universal joy and acclamations of her subjects. 3. Those who governed the world
at or near the time of St. Paul's writing this epistle, had no personal merits or
virtues to recommend them to the prayers of the faithful. Tiberius, Caligula,
Claudius, and Nero, under whom the Christian faith was disseminated, and for all
whom, we may presume, the faithful equally made their supplications were not
only bad princes but bad men, infamous for their lust, cruelty, and other vices; but
they were in authority, and that gave them a right to be mentioned in the sacred
offices of the Church. How different from their case is ours, whose eyes behold on
the throne a Queen who deserves to sit there, as well by her virtue as by her birth.
4. The emperors of Rome, for whom the primitive Christians were obliged to
pray and to give thanks, were their avowed enemies and persecutors, who did what
they could to hinder the establishment of the Church of Christ, and to suppress
those very assemblies wherein these devotions were offered up to God in their
behalf. Whereas she, for whom we now adore and bless the good providence
of God, is, by her office and by her inclination the defender and friend, the patroness
and nursing-mother of His Church established among us. (F. Atterbury, D.D.)
Prayer for others:—This stands out in the history of Paul more eminently than in
that of any of the other apostles. He ceases not to make mention of others in his
prayers. We may well suppose that that which was manifest in the example
of the Lord, and that which the disciples, doubtless, took from His example,
was eminently acceptable before God. 1. A habit of praying for others, keeps
our minds on a higher plane than does always thinking about our own
selves. Praying for others increases in you those compassions and kindnesses
toward men which society needs in every part. There is yet much rude and
savage nature left among men. There is much of the forest and the wilderness
left in society. We speak of them as "the mass," "the rabble," or "the common
people." We think of them as we do of flocks of birds, without individualizing
them; without specializing their wants, and temptations, and trials; without
bringing ourselves into personal relations with them. They are mere animated
facts before us. It is a bad thing for men to live, and grow up, and call themselves
Christians, and form the habit of looking at the great mass of men and seeing
nothing in them but their physical constitution and external relations. And the
habit of praying for men brings back the manhood to your thought, and sympathy,
and heart in such a way as to lead you to imagine their history, and to feel for
them with a true-hearted interest. As we look at men without individualizing
them, we are apt to think of them as so many forces without attributes. We see
them working, delving, earning, achieving. They are to us very much like rains,
like winds, like laws of nature. And the sight is a bad one because it hardens the
heart. It is dangerous to look upon the weak side of men. Anything is danger-

ous to your manhood which takes your sympathy away from your fellow-men, and makes your heart hard toward them. What we need is to have such sympathy with men that every day we shall carry their cases before God, and look at their vulgarities in the light of God's pity, and not in the light of our own contempt and cynical criticism. 2. The habit of praying for men tends, also, to increase our patience and our tender helpfulness towards them, and prepares us for just thoughts concerning them. There is many a man who would not smite his neighbour with his fist, but who smites him unmercifully with his thoughts. There is many a man who would not pierce a fellow man with an instrument in his hand for all the world, but who does not hesitate to pierce him and wound him to the very quick with his thoughts. In the court-room of our own secret souls, we condemn men unheard. We argue their case, and they have no chance to make plea in return. And if we are Christian men, we shall see to it that that inside, silent hall of judgment, the soul, is regulated according to the most scrupulous honour, and conscience, and manhood, and sympathy. Nor do I know of any other way in which this can be so well done as by the habit of praying for others. Having, then, considered the duty, more particularly, of praying for all men, let us specialize. 1. We naturally pray for our children first. We remember them in our family prayer. And how much better it is, in praying for them, to follow out the line of their disposition, and, as it were, to bathe our affection for them in the heavenly atmosphere! How much more beautiful they will be to us! 2. Then I think we ought to pray for our associates and our friends, not in the general way alone. General good wishes are not without their use; but special prayers are needful. I do not think that we sufficiently search out and know our friends. We are to pray for all that are despised. It is wholesome that from day to day we should send our mercies out, as it were. It is wholesome that we should have something to compare our lot with. As sweet is better to our taste when we have taken something sour, so joy is better for having the touch of sorrow near to it. 3. We are to pray for all those who are in peril and distress; for all those who are shut up in various ways. Prayer for such people keeps alive pity. It deepens humanity. 4. Then we are to pray for our enemies. That duty is made special. It is made one of the fundamental evidences of the relationship of God Himself. Once more. 5. We cannot fulfil the spirit nor the letter of this command if we pray only for our own sect. (*H. W. Beecher.*) *Praying for others :*—The ties which bind Christians to one another are at once so subtle and so real, that it is impossible for one Christian to remain unaffected by the progress or retrogression of any other. Therefore, not only does the law of Christian charity require us to aid all our fellow-Christians by praying for them, but the law of self-interest leads us to do so also; for their advance will assuredly help us forward, and their relapse will assuredly keep us back. (*A. Plummer, D.D.*) *Aspects of the times; or, what the Church has to say of earthly governments :*—I. GOVERNMENT IS OF GOD. It has its germ and root in the fatherly relationship. The early patriarch was monarch of his own house, lord of his own castle and flocks, and of the keeper thereof. II. GOVERNMENT AS OF GOD IS TO BE OBEYED. Conscience, which binds us by direct ties to the throne of God, must, of course, always be obeyed. III. GOVERNMENT AS OF GOD IS TO OCCUPY A FOREMOST PLACE IN OUR PETITIONS. First of all—too often, indeed, it is last of all, and sometimes seldom at all. IV. GOVERNMENT BLESSED BY GOD WILL THUS ENSURE THE WEAL OF MAN. (*W. M. Statham.*) *Intercessory prayer :*—Prayer is a first necessity of the Christian life. Without it we are like soldiers in the arid desert, who grow more and more weary as they think of distant wells separated from them by relentless foes, and we are ready to exclaim, " My soul thirsteth for God, for the living God. As the hart panteth after the waterbrooks, so panteth my soul after Thee, O God." When we pray we become conscious of the reality of unseen things until they completely outweigh in importance worldly affairs, and then it becomes possible to us, and even natural to us, to live as " strangers and pilgrims." The connection with what precedes is tolerably clear. Timothy had been exhorted to wage a good warfare on behalf of the truth, but prayer for himself and others was essential to victory, because it alone would bring into the field of conflict the unseen powers of heaven. Even the Pagan Greeks were said to be inspired in their fight against the Trojans by the thought that the gods were with them; but theirs was only dim and superstitious remembrance of the truth that heaven fights for those who pray—as Elisha found when the Syrians encircled the city. Prayer offered by the church in Ephesus in Rome, in Jerusalem, received answers in the spiritual victories of believers, and in the effects produced through their witness-bearing upon the hearts of the people. I. THE VARIETY OF PRAYER is indicated by the use of these differing phrases, "supplications, prayers, intercessions, and giving of thanks." We may think of these phrases separately in order to get a clearer notion of the meaning of each; but one shades off into another; and you can no more exactly define each than you can say of the colours of a sea at sunset, "the blue begins just here, and the glow of crimson and the sheen of the gold just there." The more you pray the more you will discover the variety of soul-utterances to God; the calm contemplation; the agonizing supplication; the childlike talk with the heavenly Father; and the seraphic praisefulness. These are only known through experience. When the untaught, unmusical lad takes up a violin, it is as much as he can do to produce one steady tone, but in the trained hands of the accomplished musician that same instrument wails, and pleads, and sings. Much more varied are the utterances of the human soul, when a full answer is given to the prayer of the disciples, "Lord, teach us to pray." II. THE SUBJECTS OF PRAYER specially referred to in this passage are not the necessities of the saints themselves, but the wants of other men, and especially of all those who had authority and who exercised influence over society. Listen to what Tertullian says in his apology respecting the practice of these early Christians. "We Christians, looking up to heaven with outspread hands, because they are free from stain; with uncovered heads, because there is nothing to make us blush; without a prompter, because we pray from our hearts; do intercede for all emperors, that their lives may be prolonged, their government be secured to them, that their families may be preserved in safety, their senates faithful to them, their armies brave, the people honest, and the whole empire at peace, and tor whatever other things are desired by the people or the Cæsar." If that was the custom under heathen rule, how much more is it our duty under a Christian government! Therefore let us pray that our national affairs may be guided with wisdom; that amidst the tortuous channels of foreign policy, where so many cross currents and hidden rocks abound, the ship of state may be firmly and safely steered; that questions likely to provoke anger and suspicion may be settled on fair principles of justice; and that in all home legislation inequalities and injustices of every kind may be swept away, the needs of a chronic pauperism met, temptations to drunkenness and profligacy lessened where they cannot be removed; and thus "God, even our own God, will bless us, and all the ends of the earth shall fear Him." We may fairly widen the application of these words still further. Some of our truest "kings" are uncrowned. A man who directs and rules the thought of a nation has more power than one who gives expression to it; and we have seen instances in which a man has lost far more than he has gained by exchanging the position of an editor for that of a legislator. III. THE ISSUE OF SUCH PRAYERS is thus described—"That we may lead a quiet and peaceable life, in all godliness and honesty," or rather "in all godliness and gravity," as those who are not perturbed by earthly strifes, but see in the state of society around them the germs of the righteousness and peace which are of heaven. IV. THE ACCEPTABILITY OF SUCH PRAYERS in the sight of God is expressly asserted. (*A. Rowland, LL.B.*) *Kings over-ruled by God :*—And how many instances do we find in Scripture history, and in ancient and modern history, in which God has over-ruled the counsels of kings for the welfare of his Church! See how the heart of one Pharaoh was turned towards Joseph; how the madness and stoutheartedness of another issued in his own ruin and in the glory of God; how Nebuchadnezzar and Darius, and even the wicked Belshazzar, all advanced the holy Daniel in the kingdom; how Cyrus and other Persian monarchs assisted in rearing the temple of the God of Israel; how Constantine was brought to acknowledge the true God; and how, in the days of our own glorious Reformation, a wicked and ungodly king was yet made an instrument in God's hand of conferring the most unspeakable blessings on our land and on the world. (*H. W. Sheppard.*)

Vers. 3, 4. **In the sight of God our Saviour.**—*The Saviour God :*—Prayer is not everything, but it is "good." Effort is not everything, but it is "good." Fervent prayer and earnest work, blended in a good man's experience, become means of grace in no small degree. I. Let us think, by way of preparing our minds for this broad truth, of THE TITLE CHOSEN BY OUR APOSTLE—"God our Saviour," or "our Saviour God." It is the good pleasure of God as the Saviour, that is uppermost in his mind. The intercessions of the Church as well as the intercessions of the Christ, are but the outgrowth of a Divine purpose, a saving purpose. Surely here is abundant proof, that whatever may be said of mediation, it cannot be an intervention by a third party between a guilty world and a holy Creator. Surely, also, we ought to look upon redemption as having its spring and source in an unsolicited love of the Divine heart. It would have been well had there been more use made of this beautiful phrase, "God our Saviour," and less of "God the Sovereign," which is not a Scriptural one. When the lost are found, they are found through the mercy of God our Saviour. II. Then let us observe, that if there be any meaning in words, HERE IS ALSO A DIVINE PREFERENCE DISCLOSED TO US; yes, and more than a preference, an energy going forth in order to attain the object of that preference— "who willeth that all men should be saved." It is not that, of the two, He would rather men should be saved than that they should be lost. This would be a poor and pitiful rendering of the teaching here conveyed to us. Nor is it that there is a sentimental preference; this again might be very unpractical in its results. Many people are conscious of decided preferences, but the preferences are not thrown into their wills. "God willeth." Oh that is a strong will of God. He willeth, and lo, the creation became a fact. Are you afraid to allow that there is a strong will—the will of God our Saviour, behind all the acts and processes of Redemption? You say that a purpose may be thwarted and a preference crossed. Yes, yes, but don't let this beguile you into any loss of comfort which these words ought to bring you. Especially let them not rob you of any conviction about the absolute and irreversible favourableness of God to your personal, your present, and your future salvation. III. THE BREADTH AND GRANDEUR OF THIS STATEMENT MAY STARTLE US. But what will familiarity with it do for us? "Oh," says one, "it will not do to speak it out too boldly. Men will grow daring in their sins; and they will come to believe that if love be indeed almighty and all-embracing, they may do just as they like, and all will be right at last." Do you not see, however, that, though our apostle entertained this conviction, he saw that all men needed to be prayed for and laboured for? He who is our Saviour God wills that all should be saved; therefore it is good and acceptable in His sight that we should pray for all without distinction. A true prayer becomes a purpose. He who prays for what God loves and wishes, must come to love what God loves; else his prayer is not a true prayer. Why was the Cross planted? Not that the good might be strengthened in their goodness, but that the bad might be assured there was a means whereby they might be recovered. The salvation of Christ is not simply a protection of virtuous men, but a recovery of the vicious; not simply an incentive to continuance in well-doing, but a restoration from evil-doing. What that salvation is, at which our apostle glances, you must look elsewhere to find. If he says, "knowledge of the truth," do not think that this requires a vast deal of learning to reach. Do not suppose that mere opinion, or Scripture knowledge even, is what he means. He means, that associated with salvation is a true knowledge, a true recognition of God as the Saviour. The false lie gives place to the true knowledge: there is nothing more than this in the phrase. You have believed Satan's lie, now believe God's truth. Salvation, again—do you ask what it is? It is a renewed moral energy—the power to do right, the strength to overcome evil. It is safety when the enemy may tempt or taunt. It is eternal life in Christ. It is to have God dwelling with, in us—the assurance of victory. (*G. J. Proctor.*) *The Saviour—God:*—The first name by which the great infinite Being was known to His creatures was that of the Maker of the world; but unless sin had entered into the creation, He could not have been known by the name of God the Saviour. The text says, it is His will, even our salvation. The good, the wise, the gracious will of our God and Maker is our salvation, and His will is the motive of all His actions. I. The apostle remarks, that THERE IS ONE GOD. It has been said that the idea of eternity and the idea of a God are too much for us to meddle with. It is not too much to meddle with, but too much fully to understand. One God, one eternal Jehovah, who is above all, and over all, and in all, the only One depending upon none, and derived nor proceeding from none. II. The second thing in the text is, that THERE IS ONE MEDIATOR. Here an interesting scene presents itself to our view. Three parties, God on the one hand, man on the other, and a Mediator, coming, mediating and acting between these two parties at difference, to bring them into union. Now, in order to be qualified to act between both, he must be acquainted with the nature, sentiments, and feelings of both. Agreeably to this, Jesus is revealed as truly and properly God, and therefore He has the same names given to Him, the same attributes ascribed to Him. Nor are we to confine His mediation to the days after His appearance in the flesh; He was the one Mediator from the beginning of the Creation. It was through faith in the seed of the woman who was to appear in the fulness of time to take away sin by the sacrifice of Himself that Adam and Enoch, Noah, Abraham, and all the fathers, entered into glory. He, as the alone Mediator, does and will continue to mediate until the whole scheme of mercy be completed. There is one God and one Mediator, the man Christ Jesus. " Who will have all men to be saved, and come to the knowledge of the truth." This implies, that the truth must be revealed, or made known. But how is the truth to be made known for its acknowledgment and belief ? God does not, as it is asserted in the Apocrypha, take a prophet by the hair of the head, and place him where his work awaits him ; the truth is made known by the use of ordinary means. Now, let us consider the present state of human means. The progress of science and the perfection of navigation have opened up the possibility of sending the truth to every land to be acknowledged and received. Many motives might be urged. What Christ has done for you calls upon you to do something for promoting His interest in the world. The value that you yourselves put upon the salvation of your souls should induce you to send the truth to others. (*A. Clarke, D.D.*)     *Our Saviour :*—God is our Saviour. 1. He is a seeking Saviour. Were a king to enter a city he would expect and receive honour and applause. But the world would be astonished if instead of asking to be shown the principal buildings of the city, the king were to say to the mayor, " Now let me go to your poor men and women who need my kingly help and sympathy : it gives me no pleasure to look on your splendour while I know your back slums are crowded with the miserable and degraded." Ah, no king ever did this except the One who was crowned with thorns, and whose throne was a cross. 2. God is a gracious Saviour. He not only loves His friends, but He dies to save His enemies. 3. God is a truthful Saviour. His word may be relied on. No man yet, so far as I have been able to learn, ever trusted God and was lost. 4. He is a loving Saviour. A mother who has a crippled child, from whom all other people draw away and shudder because of its distorted face, will hug her babe to her breast and rejoice because she has love for it. Now, like a mother, God is our loving Saviour, not because there is anything good in us, but because His heart contains love for us. 5. The Lord is a powerful Saviour. 6. God is our present Saviour. He saves now. 7. God is our everlasting Saviour. If He were not able to " keep us " I should doubt, and you would fear ; but we rejoice to know that God is our everlasting Saviour. (*W. Birch.*)     **Who will have all men to be saved.**—*God would have all men to be saved :*—Benevolence is a distinguishing feature of the gospel, which bears an aspect of mildness and compassion to every man. And it transfuses its spirit into the hearts of all who understand it, and submit to its influence. This disposition is founded upon two great principles which are recognized by Christianity—that we are all the children of an equal, creating love; and all redeemed by the same Divine sacrifice. I. To THE APPELLATION GIVEN BY THE APOSTLE TO THE GOSPEL—it is " the truth." The unhesitating manner in which the founders of Christianity apply this epithet to the religious system they were charged to unfold to the world is a circumstance not to be passed over in silence. Had they been conscious of the absence of inspiration, and that the Christian code of doctrine had been an invention of their own, it would have been insufferable arrogance in them to have dignified it with the appellation of " the truth." They knew that this system was " the truth," because they knew that it came from God. The heathen sages had reason which was dark and beclouded, because it was only the reason of fallen creatures. The apostles had revelation, the mind of the Spirit, who searches the deep things of God. The gospel which they preached had the evidence of the old revelation of the law ; for its principles were seen pictured in the hieroglyphics of the tabernacle. It had the evidence of the prophets; for they had jointly testified of Christ, His sufferings, His glory, His doctrines, in language of easy interpretation. They had the evidence of miracles wrought by Jesus Himself, in confirmation of His mission, and which they themselves had seen. But by designating the gospel " the truth," the apostle not only proclaims its divinity, and consequent infallibility, but also calls the attention of men to it as a system of the utmost importance to them, and bound up with their best interests. It is represented in the text as truth which relates to salvation. God willeth all men to be saved by coming to the knowledge of the truth. It is this circumstance which strikes so deep an interest into our religion, and distinguishes it as " the truth," by way of eminence. All truth is not interesting to man ; or, at least, every other truth is but partially so. It shows us the true propitiation—the blood of a Divine sacrifice. It exhibits the terms of man's acceptance—his deep humiliation of soul, and his faith in the merits and intercession of the appointed Redeemer. It has promises for man's encouragement, warnings for his caution, precepts for his direction. It proclaims him immortal ; teaches him that he is on his trial ; sets before him the solemnities of the general judgment ; and carries his hopes and fears into their highest exercise, and renders them of the best possible service to him, by opening to him the penalties of eternal destruction, and the glories of endless felicity.  II. We observe in the text, THAT THE KNOWLEDGE OF THIS TRUTH IS CONNECTED WITH SALVATION, AS A MEANS TO AN END ; and connected, too, by no less an authority than the will of God. He that willeth "all men to be saved " willeth them also "to come to the knowledge of the truth "; and from this the inference is irresistible, that the knowledge of the truth is essential to salvation.  This subject deserves our serious attention ; and there are two questions which arise out of it—What degree of that truth is necessary to be known in order to salvation; and how it must be known.  The first question presents a point of necessary discussion ; because if it were meant that, before a person could be saved, he should have a complete and accurate knowledge of all the truths of the gospel, every one would be excluded from the benefit.  The truths revealed are the revelations of an infinite mind, and partake of its infinity. They relate to spiritual operations, of which we know little; and to a future state, of which we practically know nothing.  For this reason the gospel must ever present something more to be known, as well as to be experienced ; and it is to be the subject of development for ever.  This is its perfection.  But there are considerations which prove that a perfect knowledge of every part of the truth is not essential to mere salvation.  Hence it is that divines have divided the truths of the gospel into two classes—those which are essential, and those which are non-essential. The distinction is just.  There are truths which it is necessary we should know in order that we may be saved.  The best way of determining what is essential for us to know, is to consider what is essential to faith.  It is said, "He that believeth and is baptized shall be saved."  Whatever, therefore, is essential for us to know, in order that we may believe, must be essential for us to know, in order that we may be saved.  In order to faith we must know the purity of the Divine law in such a degree as shall convince us that we have violated it, and incurred the penalty of its maledictory sanction.  We must know our inability to make atonement; for without this the undertaking of Christ is vain in respect to us. We must know so much of the evidence of Christ's mission as to receive Him as the divinely-appointed Redeemer.  We must know His meritorious death to be so satisfactory to the offended Deity, that for the sake of that He will impute our faith for justification. We must know the provisions made in the promises for supplying us with the help of the Holy Spirit for the renewing of our nature, and the support and comfort of our minds; and we must know the precepts of the gospel law, by which our minds and lives may be regulated according to the will of God.  This knowledge is necessary for mere salvation : but we are far from saying that a higher degree of knowledge is useless.  A higher degree of knowledge is, indeed, necessary in order to a confirmed faith ; to enable us to meet and answer the objections by which we may be assailed; to qualify us to instruct the ignorant; to be a means of carrying us up to high attainments in religion ; and to prepare us for extensive usefulness in the Church. The second question, how the truth must be known, in order that we may be saved, seems to be answered in the phrase, "come to the knowledge of the truth."  This knowledge supposes curiosity to know the truth.  It is lamentable that there is so little of this amongst men.  In many instances truth is never thought of.  This knowledge supposes the admission of truth into the understanding, and its influence upon the practice.  Some men shrink back from this knowledge.  They will not come to the light lest their deeds should be reproved. Whatever it cost us, we must know the truth, that we may walk by it, and be saved by its instrumentality.  III.  The text presents us with an interesting view of THE CONNECTION OF THE DIVINE WILL WITH THE SALVATION OF MAN.  "Who will have all men to be saved."  1.  The object of this will is the salvation of man.  This has already been alluded to, but deserves a more distinct consideration.  It is this which so gloriously displays the benevolence of God by the gospel.  2.  That in the same sense He willeth all men to be saved.  That this is Scripture doctrine, and that the word "all " is to be taken in its most extensive sense, scarcely any other argument is necessary to prove than that of the apostle in the context.  It is a feeble criticism to say that the apostle meant by the expression, "all men," all ranks of men; for that is the same thing.  "All ranks of men " are "all men " (2 Cor. v. 14, 15). Here the remedy is declared to be as extensive as the disease.  3. The mode in which the Divine will is connected with human salvation remains to be considered.

It is a natural question, "If God willeth all men to be saved, why is it that any perish?" The answer is, If God willeth to save men by overcoming their wills by His omnipotent influence, all men must be saved; but He wills to save them according to the nature which He has given them; and we have the evidence of His Word, and of our own consciousness, that His will is a resistible will, and that His willing us to be saved does not effect our salvation without a corresponding determination of our own will. The principal opinions on this subject are these. Some persons have considered man, when under the gracious influence of God exerted upon him in order to his salvation, as wholly passive, and carried by irresistible force into a new condition. But if this be the case, then man is a machine. Another opinion therefore is, that the will is necessarily influenced in its determinations by motives of good and evil discovered to the understanding; and that in the case of those who are saved, such motives as must command the assent of the will are impressed by God upon the mind; and thus it is supposed that the person so operated upon is infallibly brought into a state of salvation without any violence to his free agency. If, however, God willeth all men to be saved, and proceeded in this way to the execution of His purpose, their salvation would be as certain as if they were machines. The doctrine is the same, though cloaked with a metaphysical garb. The opposite extreme to these opinions is, that man has a natural power to discern the right, and to choose it, independent of a Divine agency exerted upon his mind. Had man been left without any supernatural aids, he must have been as blind to discern what is good as he was unable to choose it. The plain facts before us, then, are, God willeth our salvation; He has appointed effectual means to this end; He has given us all the power to use these means; and to the use of them He has promised His blessing. Whether we will actually "come to the knowledge of the truth," or not, is left ultimately with ourselves; but whether we will hear the voice of God, or whether we will forbear, we have motives, exhortations, promises; all that can move upon our fear, our love, our interest. To apply these motives is a part of our ministry. We are made ambassadors for Christ to persuade you to be reconciled to God. (*R. Watson.*) *All men to be saved :—*This large thought comes in primarily as an argument and a measure of intercessory prayer. It is one of the reasons that St. Paul gives why, "first of all, supplications, prayers, intercessions, giving of thanks, should be made for all men." The first reason is his own individual case—he himself was the monument of the power of intercession, when, with his dying lips, St. Stephen prayed for him as one of his murderers. The text is the second reason—Pray for all, for God loves all. Pray for persecuting kings—pray for Nero—for God wills the salvation of all. We are never so safe as when we are taking great views of God. Most of our sins and troubles are from having narrow previsions, which limit the Holy One of Israel. It is not a merely future tense, but it is the expression of the Divine wish and intention, which are to be the same for ever, whatever man may do to frustrate it—"who wills that all men should be saved." But the great point to which I wish to draw your consideration is, the Catholicity of the salvation which God wills and presents to man. That magnificent "all"—who can reduce it?—"all" to be saved. Has not God plainly shown you that He wishes you to be saved? Has not He so drawn, chastened, so converted, so held, so protected, so borne with you, so blessed you, that He has given the most unmistakable evidence that He would have you to be saved? And did you ever meet with the man who could tell you the contrary, of his own experience? It is remarkable, in the Old Testament, how often God is called, "the God of the whole earth." And David, probably in prophecy, loves the expression, "The King of all the earth." But if you ask me, more logically, Why it is that I believe that God wills the salvation of all His creatures? I answer—I find it in the congruity of all things. I find it in the law which must regulate the mind of a great Creator. I find it in the Fatherly character of God, and the "tender mercies that are over all His works." I find it in the immensity of the gift of His own Son, that blood is an equivalent, and much more to the sins of the whole world. I find it in the imagery of the Bible, which suits every land, and in those provisions of His grace, which are accommodated to the minds of the inhabitants of every clime. I find it in the free flowings of that Spirit, like the four winds of heaven, "I will pour it upon all flesh." "If God wills the salvation of all men, why are not all saved? For who can resist His will?" If God willed the salvation of all His creatures, He willed also that the world which He had made should be a world of discipline and probation. Therefore He willed that the will of every living man should be free—for this is an essential condition of probation. But what shall we say respecting the heathen? They have not even "the knowledge." But why? God willed them to have it, and made the most express provision that they might have it; for He laid it upon every soul that should ever know Him, and made it almost a condition of His presence in that soul, that it should impart again that knowledge to another. And this commission He gave to His whole Church. Am I to say then that, because, through my neglect, and selfishness, all men are not saved, and brought to the knowledge of the truth, therefore God did not will it? (*J. Vaughan, M.A.*)    *Redemption universal:*—Let us go simply into these two investigations, what is pre-supposed of all men when we are bidden, as we are, in our text to pray for all men? and, secondly, when we are bidden, as we equally are, in our text to give thanks for all men. I. Now it can scarcely have escaped your attention that there is in our text AN ACCUMULATION OF PHRASE WHICH MUST PREVENT OUR THINKING THAT ANY PRAYER, EXCEPT THE LARGEST AND MOST URGENT, WILL COME UP TO THE SCOPE OF THE APOSTLE'S EXHORTATION. These words forbid our thinking that St. Paul simply requires that we should be, in general terms, the well-wishers of mankind. Had his discourse referred exclusively to the household of faith, he could not have used more unrestricted language, nor sent us to our knees with a broader view of the blessings to be sought for in our wrestlings with God. We just wish by these means to show at the outset the wrongness of the opinion that we are only bidden to solicit for the mass of our fellow-men the common mercies of existence, that we may reserve petitions which have to do with God's nobler gifts for our pleadings on behalf of a select company of mankind. If you consider prayer attentively, whether it be for ourselves or for others, you must regard it as the most wonderful act which can ever be attempted by a fallen creature. We shall not hesitate to say that so long as the scheme of our redemption is kept out of sight, prayer is nothing but a great proof of human ignorance. There is a great deal taken for granted in prayer. When I pray, I assume that an access has been opened for me to the Father; I assume, that in spite of my apostasy, born though I have been in sin and cradled in corruption, God's compassions towards me may not be shut up nor alienated. I assume that some amazing corrective, as it were, must have been applied to human guiltiness, so that the pollution which naturally and necessarily clings to the fallen, is no hindrance to free admission to an audience of Him who is of purer eyes than to look unmoved upon iniquity. And how can I assume all this, unless I bring within my contemplations the mysteries of redemption, and, making my appeal to the wondrous achievement which Christ hath effected on my behalf, fetch from that an assurance that there lies no barrier between myself and the Lord? The whole work of human reconciliation is gathered into God's permitting prayer. The globe was convulsed and shaken to its very centre before it could become a platform on which man might kneel. It is a truth sufficiently simple to commend itself to every capacity, that if prayer is literally based upon redemption, then all who can be rightly the subjects of prayer must be strictly the subjects of redemption. I cannot pray for a man whom I know to have never been redeemed—a man for whom Christ Jesus did not die. Can I ask God to have mercy on that man's soul? Such is the use that we would make of the exhortation of our text. We infer from it the grand doctrine of Christianity, even that of Christ's having died for the whole world; and lest it should be thought that this inference is in any degree far fetched, we will just show you how St. Paul supports or authorizes his exhortation. You observe that the announced reason that all should be prayed for is that God is willing that all should be saved; and if God wills that all should be saved, assuredly all must have been put into a salvable state; in other words, all must have been redeemed by the precious blood of Christ. It does not fall within the scope of our argument to examine into the mystery of God's willing the salvation of all, when it is certain that nothing more than a remnant shall be saved. The character given to the living God—and who doubts that at the root of true religion lies the character of God?—the character given by St. Paul of the living God is that He is the Saviour of all men, especially of those who believe. In this same sense—for He is not spoken of as a different kind of Saviour, in the different senses, but as the same in kind though different in degree—in the same sense that God is especially the Saviour of believers, He is generally the Saviour of all men. This is St. Paul's statement; and if the living God is the Saviour generally of all in that very sense in which He is especially the Saviour of believers, then beyond question all must have been redeemed by Him; for redemption is that incipient form of salvation which may be common to all, and yet applied effectually only to some. O blessed

Saviour, Thou didst take upon Thyself our nature, and didst ransom that nature, and therefore didst place within the reach of all who are born of this nature the choice things of forgiveness and acceptance ; therefore is it that our prayers may, and must, go up to the mercy-seat on behalf of all ; all shall be the subjects of our petition, for all are the objects of redemption; and we may now acknowledge and appreciate the justice of the ample terms in which the text is expressed : " I exhort therefore, that, first of all, supplications, prayers, intercessions, and giving of thanks, be made for all men." II. We turn now to the second question—WHAT IS PRE-SUPPOSED IN REGARD OF ALL MEN, WHEN WE ARE BIDDEN, AS WE FURTHER ARE, TO GIVE THANKS FOR ALL MEN ? You will observe at once that thanksgiving must assume the existence of benefit. If I am to give thanks for all men, it is clear that I must be acquainted with some manifestation of kindness towards all, which may justly summon forth my praise on their account. But if we were guilty of an exaggeration in designating prayer as a giant act, we fall into no over-wrought statement if we apply such an epithet to the thanking God for our creation. Conscious to myself of the struggles within me of a principle which can never be extinguished, never be mastered by any process of decay, knowing that the present scene, whatever its cares or its joys, is but the first stage of an unlimited career along which I am appointed to pass—shall I praise God for having endowed me with existence, unless I have assurance that it is not impossible for me to secure myself happiness throughout the infinity of my being ? Shall I thank God for the capacity of being miserable, unspeakably miserable, throughout unnumbered ages ? I cannot do this. I cannot praise God for the bright sunshine that must light me to the dungeon; I cannot praise God for the breeze that must waft me to the whirlpool ; I cannot praise God for the food that must nourish me for the rack ! Life, the present life, that single throb, that lonely beat—can I praise God for this, if it must unavoidably usher me into a sphere of wretchedness whose circumference cannot be reached, or turn me adrift on an ocean of fire without a shore, or consign me to that mysterious death which consists in the being for ever dying, that wondrous immortality of being restored as fast as consumed and consumed as fast as restored ? Better, oh ! infinitely better for me if I had never been born, I cannot praise God for this. Creation can be no more a blessing than annihilation if I am not a redeemed man ; it is this, and this alone, for which you require me to praise God. If I am a redeemed man it is possible that I may be saved ; if I am not a redeemed man, then, so far as is revealed, it is impossible. As far as we know from the Bible it is impossible that any man shall be saved for whom Christ did not die. And how then can I give God thanks for all men, unless I believe that Christ died for all men ? Shall I praise Him for the creation of others though I cannot praise Him for my own ? Shall I sweep the harp strings, and bring out the melodies of gratitude, because God has so dealt with tens of thousands of my fellow-men ; that if He had dealt in like manner with myself, I should have worn sackcloth and gone all my days in inconsolable mourning ? No ! I cannot thank God for all men except on the noble principle that Christ has redeemed all men. Creation is a blessing if connected with redemption, but not dissociated from it. Thus, as we trust, we have sufficiently shown you that the universal redemption of mankind is pre-supposed when we are bidden to pray for all, and when we are bidden to give thanks for all. Our two topics may, therefore, be considered as sufficiently discussed, and it only remains to bid you strive to obey in your practice the exhortation of which we have shown you the propriety. (*H. Melvill, B.D.*) **Knowledge of the truth.**—*Salvation by knowing the truth :*—I. IT IS BY A KNOWLEDGE OF THE TRUTH THAT MEN ARE SAVED. Observe that stress is laid upon the article: it is *the* truth and not every truth. Though it is a good thing to know the truth about anything, and we ought not to be satisfied to take up with a falsehood upon any point, yet it is not every truth that will save us. We are not saved by knowing any one theological truth we may choose to think of, for there are some theological truths which are comparatively of inferior value. They are not vital or essential, and a man may know them and yet may not be saved. It is *the* truth which saves. Jesus Christ is *the* Truth: the whole testimony of God about Christ is *the* truth. This knowledge of the grand facts which are here called the truth saves men, and we will notice its mode of operation. 1. Very often it begins its work in a man by arousing him, and thus it saves him from carelessness. Perhaps he heard a sermon, or read a tract, or had a practical word addressed to him by some Christian friend, and he found out enough to know that " he that believeth not is condemned already, because he hath not believed on the Son of God." That startled him. "God is angry with the wicked every day"—that amazed him. He had not thought of it, perhaps had not known it, but when he did know it, he could rest no longer. 2. The truth is useful to a man in another way : it saves him from prejudice. Often when men are awakened to know something about the wrath of God, they begin to plunge about to discover divers methods by which they may escape from that wrath. Consulting, first of all, with themselves, they think that if they reform—give up their grosser sins, and if they can join with religious people, they will make it all right. They have done all that they judged right and attended to all that they were told. Suddenly, by God's grace, they come to a knowledge of another truth, and that is that by the deeds of the law there shall no flesh be justified in the sight of God. They discover that salvation is not by works of the law or by ceremonies, and that if any man be under the law he is also under the curse. 3. Moreover, it often happens that a knowledge of the truth stands a man in good stead for another purpose : it saves him from despair. 4. A knowledge of the truth shows a man his personal need of being saved. 5. A knowledge of the truth reveals the atonement by which we are saved : a knowledge of the truth shows us what that faith is by which the atonement becomes available for us : a knowledge of the truth teaches us that faith is the simple act of trusting, that it is not an action of which man may boast. II. A MERE NOTIONAL KNOWLEDGE OR A DRY DOCTRINAL KNOWLEDGE IS OF NO AVAIL. We must know the truth in a very different way from that. How are we to know it, then ? 1. Well, we are to know it by a believing knowledge. You do not know a thing unless you believe it to be really so. 2. In addition to this, your knowledge, if it becomes believing knowledge, must be a personal knowledge—a persuasion that it is true in reference to yourself. 3. But this must be a powerful knowledge, by which I mean that it must operate in and upon your mind. A man is told that his house is on fire. I will suppose that standing here I held up a telegram, and said, " My friend, is your name so-and-so ? " " Yes." " Well, your house is on fire." He knows the fact, does he not? Yes, but he sits quite still. Now, my impression is about that good brother, that he does not know, for he does not believe it. 4. This knowledge when it comes really to save the soul is what we call experimental knowledge —knowledge acquired according to the exhortation of the Psalmist, " Oh, taste and see that the Lord is good "—acquired by tasting. I am now going to draw two inferences which are to be practical. The first one is this : in regard to you that are seeking salvation. Does not the text show you that it is very possible that the reason why you have not found salvation is because you do not know the truth ? Hence, I do most earnestly entreat the many of you young people who cannot get rest to be very diligent searchers of your Bibles. The last inference is for you who desire to save sinners. You must bring the truth before them when you want to bring them to Jesus Christ. (*C. H. Spurgeon.*)

Ver. 5. **One Mediator between God and man.**—*The mediation of Christ :*—That there has been a Mediator in this world is conceded by all except Jews and heathens. But respecting the precise nature of the work which He has undertaken and accomplished, there has not been even in those to whom the knowledge of this salvation has come, clear conceptions, nor correspondent emotions of gratitude and thanksgiving. With what distress would you gaze on the Divine power and infinity, and say, " He is not a Man as I am, that I should answer Him, and we should come together in judgment; neither is there any days-man betwixt us, that might lay his hand on us both " ? With what anguish would you look around and inquire for some being able and ready to rescue you from perdition ? But what, in such circumstances, you would look for in vain is now declared unto you. You are now taught on the authority of inspiration that there is one God and one Mediator between God and man. I. WHAT IS IMPLIED IN THE IDEA OF A MEDIATOR BETWEEN GOD AND MAN ? The fact of a mediation between one man and another implies a difficulty which it is not easy to reconcile. This is equally implied in the employment of a government to mediate between two other nations. Such measures are never adopted in the times of peace and of mutual friendship. So of our attitude to God. The fact that there is a Mediator between God and man unquestionably proves that there is an alienation which it is exceedingly difficult to reconcile. II. ALIENATION DOES NOT IMPLY CRIMINALITY IN BOTH THE PARTIES WHICH ARE THUS BROUGHT INTO CONFLICT. On this subject a proverb seems to have obtained among men, that in cases of alienation there is transgression in both the conflicting parties. "Both are to blame" is a maxim which has prevailed. It may perhaps be important to show the fallacy of the principle itself against which I am here contending. We are often asked, with a confidence amounting almost to the authority of inspiration, "Do you not believe that in all cases of alienation there is blame on both sides?" To this we reply, "We do not, we cannot believe it." If the question still be pressed, we ask our inquirer, "Do you not know that there is an eternal alienation between sheep and wolves; and have the sheep ever committed any aggression on the wolves?" You have all heard of the warfare which goes forward between the angels which kept their first estate and those spirits which have revolted from God. And is it not to be assumed that in this controversy the angels, who have always been spotless in the eyes of Jehovah, were free from the imputation of guilt? Pre-eminently is this principle applicable to Jehovah. Of what wrong, respecting us, has He ever been guilty? Who amongst those that have in former times charged Him with injury or injustice has ever been able to sustain it? "Let no man say, when he is tempted, I am tempted of God," &c. The objects around us were never created and never designed to be the cause of our transgressions. Our sins are not the result either of the example of those individuals or circumstances which God has placed around us. They are the fruit of our own hearts. There is an alienation from Him in the sons of men, and the causes of this alienation are not mutual: the criminality is altogether with us. III. BUT WHO IS THERE THAT IS ADEQUATE TO UNDERTAKE THE MEDIATORIAL WORK? In human affairs there are many individuals who are equally competent to settle a difficulty and remove the causes of alienation which exist between a man and his neighbour. And in a great share of the instances which occur, any individual of a multitude that can be mentioned is equally as well qualified to undertake the work as any other individual that can be selected. Not so in the work of human redemption. Here there is but one Being in the universe who is competent to be a Days-man, a Mediator between Jehovah and His offending subjects (Isa. lxiii. 5). IV. TO INQUIRE WHY NO OTHER BEING BUT CHRIST IS QUALIFIED FOR THIS WORK. And here I must frankly confess that of my own unaided reason I am incompetent to tell. And I apprehend that had the family of man been left to ascertain by their own intellectual powers what Mediator is suited to their circumstances, no one of them would have been able to discover the truth. His agony for reconciliation burst forth in the affecting question, "Wherewith shall I come before the Lord and bow myself before the high God? Shall I come before Him with burnt-offerings and calves of a year old? Will the Lord be pleased with thousands of rams, or with ten thousands of rivers of oil? Shall I give my first-born for my transgression; the fruit of my body for the sin of my soul?" Let us go to the Scriptures to ascertain what Christ is; and having thence derived a knowledge of His character, let us draw the only safe conclusion, that on account of the respects in which He differs from every other being in existence, He is chosen to be the Mediator between God and man. V. WHAT, THEN, ARE THE RESPECTS IN WHICH HE DIFFERS FROM EVERY OTHER BEING? It must here be remembered that in certain respects He is God. I here refer to His original nature. Of Him, John in his Gospel says, "In the beginning was the Word, and the Word was with God, and the Word was God." Nor was He God only. In some respects He differed in His mediatorial office from the Father. He assumed into immediate connection with Himself a human body and a rational soul. This was done in accordance with the prophets. Isaiah in prophetic vision declared, "Unto us a Child is born," &c. These expressions show the union of divinity with humanity in our Lord Jesus Christ, and indicate His wonderful adaptedness to the work of redeeming men from their sins and reconciling them to God. Are we, then, asked in what respects Christ differs from every other being? Is it demanded in what respect He differs from the Father? We reply, by the addition unto His own glorious nature of all the powers and faculties of man. He is at once Divine and human. Is it again demanded in what respects He differs from men? I reply, He is human and Divine. In these respects He is altogether diverse from any other being in the universe. And viewed in this attitude, we may wonder, and say in the language of the prophet, "There is none like unto Thee, O God!" Having now learned from the Scriptures the qualifications of Him who undertook to be the Mediator for us, we can see His wonderful adaptations to the work which He has undertaken. Human salvation requires a thorough acquaintance with all the wants, perplexities, and temptations of man. In this respect, such a Mediator as He who has become flesh is wonderfully suited to our condition. He did not undertake to help the angels. The work of human salvation also requires a thorough knowledge of all the causes and a complete control of all the beings who have power either to advance or retard it. And what eyes but those which run to and fro through the universe are competent to see all the wants, and all the exposures, and all the means of relief which pertain to the condition of ruined man? What hands but those which formed the universe are competent so to direct all the influences of the material and the spiritual worlds in such a manner as to subserve the welfare of His people and cause them to conspire together for the promotion of their salvation? What other Presence, except that which pervades the universe, can be co-extensive with all the wants of His people who dwell in every part of the earth, who call upon Him for aid at every hour of the day and of the night? What other knowledge but that which transcends all limitation, and is strictly infinite, can be adequate to an acquaintance with the condition, the thoughts, the emotions, the feelings, and the actions of all the immortal beings who inhabit the vast regions of His Mediatorship? And what memory short of that to which all past, present, and future things are equally known is competent to bring together all the particulars of thought, of feeling, and of action, which constitute the life of a human being; and accurately to weigh in the balances the gold and the dross of his character; and not only this, but to extend the process to all the sons of men, all the apostate, and all the holy angels? Yet all this knowledge must be possessed by the Son of Man; and all the powers to which we have referred must be held by Him who undertakes the work of a Mediator between God and man. This work has commonly been regarded and taught under three separate heads. The first is His office as a Prophet. This portion of His work was referred to by Moses when he said, " A Prophet shall the Lord your God raise up unto you of your brethren, like unto me. Him shall ye hear in all things, whatsoever He shall say unto you." In this office it pertained to Him to reveal the character, the law, and the gospel of God to the children of men, and cause it to be written and preached unto them. It also pertained to His work to open the understandings of His people, that they might know the excellency of the Father and of His Son Jesus Christ. The next particular in the work of a Mediator is that of a Priest. He was a Priest, not indeed according to the order of Aaron, but of Melchizedek. As in the Mosaic history no priest is named as the predecessor of Melchizedek, so in human redemption there is no other priest but Jesus Christ. And in this Priesthood His work differed widely from that of other priests. They first offered sacrifices for their own sins, and afterwards for those of the people; but He had no occasion to offer sacrifices for Himself. " He was holy, harmless, undefiled, and separate from sinners." He is able to save to the uttermost those that come unto God through Him, seeing He ever liveth to make intercession for them. A third particular in this work is His office as the Ruler and Defender of the people of God. This is called His kingly office. In this respect the apostle declares that God "hath put all things under His feet, and given Him to be Head over all things to the Church" (Eph. i. 22). Such is the Mediator between a ruined world and the Holy One of Israel. A Mediator in some respects Divine, in other respects human. A Mediator who in the Scriptures is sometimes denominated God, at other times He is called Man. A Mediator who is set apart by Jehovah Himself to be the Prophet, the Priest, and the King of your souls; a Mediator whom, if you accept, on whom, if you rely, to whom, if you commit your immortal interests, you shall yet stand on Mount Zion with songs and eternal joy. This subject calls loudly on us to admire the wisdom and goodness of God. What could He have seen in us or any of our depraved race that induced Him to confer on us such an immense favour as this? Ah, He saw nothing but evil in our hearts, nothing but vice in our deeds. It was not owing to any righteousness in us, but of His mercy, that saved us. The subject calls on us to consider what our condition would have been had not Jesus undertaken to be Mediator between God and man. (*J. Foot, D.D.*) *The one Mediator:*—" It is good for me," said the Psalmist, " to draw near to God." It is the idea of all true religion that it can be nothing but good to get near to God—the nearer the better; that he who gets near Him finds peace, blessing, satisfaction of all wants; that away from Him is darkness and unrest. But why have a Mediator at all? Why have any one standing between you and God, instead of going direct to Him, and dealing with Him, without any Mediator? Just because our nature needs the Mediator. We cannot understand the mysteries of God, which pass our understanding. Out of the limits of our capacity, and out of the infinitude of God, springs that need of One who shall stand between Him and us, revealing the Infinite to the finite, the Divine to the human. And He who does this is called here emphatically " the man Christ Jesus " ; " for what man knoweth the things of a man, save the spirit of man which is in him ? " And thus, in order that the life and character of God should be understood by us, they must be revealed to us by a man ; by one in human form, and living under human conditions. It is only thus you can come to a real knowledge of any person. You must learn his character. Is it hard or tender ; generous or narrow ; wise or foolish ? And so your only true knowledge of the living God must be a knowledge of His character, of His life, of His ways. And as these, the life, the character, the ways of the infinite and eternal God are far above, out of human sight, they must be brought near enough for us to see, revealed to us by a Mediator who is Himself a man, the man Christ Jesus. A God thus revealed we can know, can understand. This is the idea of the mediation of Christ; the revealing of what otherwise would be unknown and unknowable in God; so that we, seeing His face and understanding His character, may lose the ignorance that is full of darkness, and the fear that is full of torment, and may draw nigh to Him with true hearts, and in the full assurance of faith. The end was spiritual perfectness; the Church was but the means, and only useful as it served the end, and subject to such changes as might make it serve the end better. But the belief, in which many people seem to find the essential nutriment of their spiritual life, is altogether different from this. To them the Church is all in all, while Christ recedes into the distance; and where the Church is not He is not and cannot be. They do not deny that He is the original source of Christian life and all its blessings; but to this truth they add the error, that these blessings can reach the individual soul only through one channel of sacraments and ministries. They thus interpose between God and man a certain mediation of the Church's, apart from which they do not recognize any reality of Christian life at all, thus drawing across the Holy of Holies a veil as thick as that which was rent in twain on the day of the crucifixion. Be on your guard lest you should ever learn to regard any system, or creature, as possessing a right to come between you and your own Lord and master; or as having the power to add to or to take from what He has done, and is doing, for you as the one Mediator between you and God. Now, you may see another example of the tendency I speak of — to substitute a lower mediation for the mediation of Christ, in the idea which many have (especially persons in whom feeling is stronger than reason) as to the relations which should exist between them and those who occupy the position of their spiritual guides and instructors, and whose duty it is, as such, to guide and instruct them. There is a strong desire in all minds, and particularly in minds of that class, for sympathy where feeling is deeply stirred, for counsel where the highest interests are involved; and there is, too, a strong inclination to depend on and defer to those, with whom that sympathy and that counsel are found. Sympathy is good; but it is dangerous, when in order to evoke or to secure it, you unbare the secrets of the soul, and have to relate, even to the friendliest and justest ear, the trials and difficulties which you find besetting your inner life. A human director or guide or counsellor is safe, not because he fills a certain office and is ordained to a certain ministry ; but when his character is such, that you know by the instinct of the spirit that there is in him the mind of Christ, and that communion with him is communion with one who is near the Master, and who will help to bring you near. Unless he is this, he can do nothing for you; he cannot bring you nearer to Christ, he can only stand between Christ and you. Now, in these instances (and more might be mentioned) we see the one tendency, to push Christ away, and set something of our own, a church, a system, a sacrament, a priest, a teacher, in the Mediator's place; so that the truth becomes obscured to us that the life of every human soul is wrapped up in its direct communion with its God, through faith in God as Christ revealed Him, and service of God after the pattern of the Divine life of Christ. (*R. H. Storey, D.D.*)    *Christ Jesus the Mediator* :—I. THE NECESSITY OF A MEDIATOR. But there are difficulties existing—a mighty gulf separating God and man. He cannot cross to us ; we cannot cross to Him. His holiness is one obstacle. "He is of purer eyes than to behold evil." Guilty and polluted as we are, we cannot approach that Holy Being without being at once consumed as were Korah and his companions. We at once see the necessity of a mediator. His justice is another obstacle. "Justice and judgment are the habitation of His throne." Maintaining the honour and dignity of His government was another obstacle. The great Legislator of heaven has enacted a law that sin must be punished, that death must be the penalty of disobedience. That peace on earth and glory to God may harmonize, there must be a mediator. Thus we have noticed the need of a mediator on the part of Jehovah. The mediator is equally necessary on the part of man. Man needed One who would descend into the depths of ruin, place underneath him the arms of omnipotent love, and raise him up—One who could enter into his dungeon, strike off his fetters, and throw open the prison door for his release—One who can reveal the Most High as a God of mercy, compassion, and love, yearning over the wandering prodigal, and anxiously watching for the first sight of a trembling penitent returning home. II. CHRIST JESUS THROUGH THE COMBINATION OF THE TWO NATURES IS ADAPTED TO ACT AS MEDIATOR. 1. He is equal with God; He is "the mighty God." 2. He is acquainted with the mind of God. Christ being human possesses three qualifications to act as mediator:—1. An affinity to our nature. 2. A sympathy with our infirmities. 3. An interest in our cause. From this subject we learn—1. To admire the wisdom of God in providing such a mediator. 2. The love of Christ in occupying such a position. 3. The folly of sinners in rejecting this mediator. (*I. Watkins.*) *The mediator of the covenant, described in His person, natures, and offices :*—Communion with God is our only happiness ; it is the very heaven of heaven, and it is the beginning of heaven here on earth. The only foundation of this communion is the covenant of grace ; and it is the great excellency of this covenant of grace, that it is established in such a mediator, even Jesus Christ. I. THE ONLY WAY OF FRIENDLY INTERCOURSE BETWEEN GOD AND MAN. It is through a mediator; that is implied. Whether man in the state of innocency needed a mediator, is disputed among persons learned and sober ; but in his lapsed state, this need is acknowledged by all. God cannot now look upon men out of a mediator but as rebels, traitor, as fit objects for His vindictive wrath ; nor can men now look up to God but as a provoked Majesty, an angry Judge, a consuming fire. II. THE ONLY MEDIATOR BETWEEN GOD AND MEN. "One mediator," that is, but one. Some acknowledge one mediator of reconciliation, but contend for many of intercession. So is Christ said here to be "one mediator," that is, but one. This mediator is here described partly by His nature—"the Man"; and partly by His names—"Christ Jesus." 1. His nature—"the man"; that is, "That eminent man," so some; "He that was made man," so others. "But why is this mediator mentioned in this nature only?" (1) Negatively : not by way of diminution, as if He were not God as well as man, as the Arians argue from this Scripture; nor as if the execution of his mediatorship were either only, or chiefly, in His human nature, as some affirm. (2) Positively : to prove that Jesus Christ was the true Messiah whom the prophets foretold, the fathers expected, and who had in that nature been so frequently promised: as in the first gospel that ever was preached (Gen. iii. 15), He is promised as the Seed of the woman. 2. His names—"Christ Jesus." Jesus, this was His proper name ; Christ, this was His appellative name. Jesus: that denotes the work and business for which He came into the world. Christ: that denotes the several offices, in the exercise whereof He executes this work of salvation. III. THAT THERE IS NOW NO OTHER WAY OF FRIENDLY COMMUNION BETWEEN GOD AND MAN, BUT THROUGH A MEDIATOR. And, indeed, considering what God is, and withal what man is; how vastly disproportionable, how unspeakably unsuitable our very natures are to His ; how is it possible there should be any sweet communion betwixt them, who are not only so infinitely distant, but so extremely contrary? God is holy, but we are sinful. In a word: He an infinitely and incomprehensibly glorious majesty, and we poor sinful dust and ashes, who have sunk and debased ourselves by sin below the meanest rank of creatures, and made ourselves the burden of the whole creation. If ever God be reconciled to us, it must be through a mediator ; because of that indispensible necessity of satisfaction, and our inability to make it (Rom. viii. 7). If ever we be reconciled to God, it must be through a mediator ; because of that radicated enmity that is in our natures to everything of God, and our impotency to it. IV. THAT THERE IS NO OTHER MEDIATOR BETWEEN GOD AND MAN, BUT JESUS CHRIST. "And one mediator" ; that is, but one. And indeed there is none else fit for so high a work as this but only He. 1. The singular suitableness of His person to this eminent employment. To interpose as a mediator betwixt God and men, was an employment above the capacity of men, angels, or any other creature ; but Jesus Christ, in respect of the dignity of His person, was every way suited for this work. Which you may take in these four particulars. (1) That He was truly God, equal with the Father, of the same nature and substance. For the further confirmation, take these arguments—(a) He whom Scripture honours with all those names which are peculiar unto God, must needs be God. That Christ hath these names ascribed to Him appears from these instances: He is not only styled God—"the Word was God" (John i. 1). (b) He in whom are those high and eminent perfections, those glorious attributes, of which no creature is capable, must needs be more than a creature, and consequently God. (2) As He is truly God, so is He complete and perfect man; having not only a human body, but a rational soul; and in all things was like to us, sin only excepted. That He had a real, not an imaginary, body, appears from the whole story of the gospel. (3) He is God and man in one person. V. THE SINGULAR FITNESS OF CHRIST FOR THIS WORK OF MEDIATION ARISES FROM HIS BEING GOD-MAN IN TWO NATURES, UNITED IN ONE PERSON WITHOUT CONFUSION OR TRANSMUTATION. 1. Had He not been truly God, He had been too mean a person for so high an employment. It was God that had been offended, an infinite Majesty that had been despised; the person therefore interposing must have some equality with him to whom he interposes. Had the whole society of persevering angels interposed on man's behalf, it had been to little purpose; one Christ was infinitely more than all, and that because He was truly God. 2. Had He not been completely man, He had been no way capable of performing that indispensably-necessary condition, upon which God was willing to be reconciled; namely, the satisfying of that righteous sentence which God had pronounced: "In the day that thou eatest thereof, thou shalt surely die" (Gen. ii. 17). 3. Had He not been God and man in one person, the sufferings of His human nature could not have derived that infinite value from the Divine nature. We could not have called His blood " the blood of God," as it is called (Acts xx. 28): it would have been no more than the blood of a creature, and consequently as unavailable as the blood of bulls, &c. (Heb. ix. 12; x. 4). 4. Had He not been God-man without confusion of natures, His Deity might either have advanced His humanity above the capacity of suffering; or His humanity might have debased His Deity below the capability of meriting, which is no less than blasphemy to imagine. And this is the first reason, the singular fitness of Christ for this work, because of the dignity of His person. The singular fitness of Christ for this employment in respect of the suitableness of His offices. There is a threefold misery upon all men, or a threefold bar to communion with God. (1) The guilt of their sins, which themselves are never able to expiate, or satisfy for. (2) The blindness of their minds, the cure whereof is too difficult for any creature-physician. (3) Their bondage and captivity to sin and Satan, which are enemies too strong for man to deal with. Suitably to these three great necessities, Jesus Christ is anointed of God to a threefold office, of a Priest, a Prophet, a King: the former of which offices he exercises on our behalf to God, and the last two from God to us. (a) The priestly office of Christ is the great, the only relief we have against the guilt of sin. The work of the priesthood consisted, under the law, chiefly of these two parts. (i) Satisfaction for the sins of the people (Lev. iv. 15–19, &c.). (ii) Intercession unto God on their behalf (Lev. xvi. 15–17). Both which were verified in Christ our "great High Priest" (Heb. iv. 14). His satisfaction, in discharging those debts which His people had run into with Divine Justice to the utmost farthing. (iii) His intercession; this is the other part of His priestly office. His satisfaction—that was performed on earth; His intercession is performed chiefly in heaven. By the former He purchased pardon and reconciliation (2 Cor. v. 19, compared with verse 21), by the latter He applies the benefits He hath purchased. (b) The prophetical office of Christ is the great, the only relief we have against the blindness and ignorance of our minds. He is that great Prophet of His Church whom Moses foretold, the Jews expected, and all men needed (Deut. xviii. 15; John i. 24, 25, 45; vi. 14); that Sun of Righteousness, who by His glorious beams dispels those mists of ignorance and error which darken the minds of men; and is therefore styled, by way of eminency, "that Light" (John i. 8), and "the true Light" (John i. 9). The execution of this prophetical office is partly by revealing so much of the will of God as was necessary to our salvation; partly by making those revelations powerful and effectual. (i) In revealing the will of God. (ii) In enlightening effectually the souls of His people. In causing the blind to see, and making them who were once darkness to be "light in the Lord" (Eph. v. 8). Thus He instructs by His word and by His Spirit (1 Peter i. 12). (c) The kingly office of Christ is the great, the only relief we have against our bondage to sin and Satan. He to whom "all power is given in heaven, and in earth" (Matt. xxviii. 18). (*W. Whitaker, M.A.*)

*Christ Jesus the only Mediator between God and men:*—I. THAT GOD HATH APPOINTED BUT ONE MEDIATOR, OR ADVOCATE, OR INTERCESSOR IN HEAVEN FOR US, in whose name, and by whose intercession, we are to offer up all our prayers and services to God. Besides that it is expressly said here in the text, "there is but one mediator between God and men, the man Christ Jesus," and that the Scripture nowhere mentions any other: I say, besides this, we are constantly directed to offer up our prayers and thanksgivings, and to perform all acts of worship in His name, and no other; and with a promise, that the prayers and services which we offer up in His name will be graciously answered and accepted (John xiv. 13, 14; xvi. 23, 24). St. Paul likewise commands Christians to perform all acts of religious worship in the name of Christ (Col. iii. 16, 17). And indeed, considering how frequently the Scripture speaks of Christ as "our only way to God, and by whom alone we have access to the throne of grace," we cannot doubt but that God hath constituted Him our only mediator and intercessor, by whom we are to address all our requests to God (John xiv. 6; Eph. ii. 18). And we have no need of any other, as the apostle to the Hebrews reasons (Heb. vii. 24, 25). "But this person (speaking of Christ) because He continueth for ever, hath an unchangeable priesthood," "since He abides for ever, is able to save to the uttermost all those that come to God by Him, seeing He ever liveth to make intercession for us." II. I proceed to show THAT THIS DOCTRINE OR PRINCIPLE OF ONE MEDIATOR BETWEEN GOD AND MAN, IS MOST AGREEABLE TO ONE MAIN END AND DESIGN OF THE CHRISTIAN RELIGION, AND OF OUR SAVIOUR'S COMING INTO THE WORLD, which was to destroy idolatry out of the world; which St. John calls "the works of the devil" (1 John iii. 8). III. IT IS LIKEWISE EVIDENT FROM THE NATURE AND REASON OF THE THING ITSELF, THAT THERE IS BUT ONE MEDIATOR AND INTERCESSOR IN HEAVEN, WHO OFFERS UP OUR PRAYERS TO GOD, AND THAT THERE CAN BE NO MORE. Because under the gospel there being but one high priest, and but one sacrifice once offered for sin; and intercession for sinners being founded in the merit and virtue of the sacrifice, by which expiation for sin is made, there can be no other mediator of intercession, but He who hath made expiation of sin, by a sacrifice offered to God for that purpose; and this Jesus Christ only hath done. He is both our high priest and our sacrifice; and therefore He only, in the merit and virtue of that sacrifice, which He offered upon earth, can intercede in heaven for us, and offer up our prayers to God. (*J. Tillotson, D.D.*) *Only one Mediator:*—Dora Greenwell's seemed to be a kind of dual nature religiously. On one side, as it were, she was High Church to the verge of Romanism; on the other, an earnest and simple evangelical Protestant. "However much," she said, "I may appreciate the value of great Catholic ideas. . . . When I kneel down to pray I am a Protestant; with Christ only between me and God, and between me and Christ—faith." (*Sunday at Home.*) *The atonement:*—I. THE NECESSITY FOR A MEDIATOR is distinctly implied. Christ is a true mediator, because He blends two natures in His own, the Divine and the human. When a man is down in a horrible pit, a rope dangling above him would be a mockery if it were far out of his reach ; and a ladder set in the miry clay beside him would be equally useless, if the ground above were at an unreachable distance from its highest rung. The only means of communication, which can bring him salvation, must reach the sunlit plain above him, and yet be within his grasp. So is it with the "one Mediator." As the God-man He reigns in the highest, yet reaches the lowest, and as the Son of man rather than the Son of David or the Son of Abraham, He touches every man, whatever his race or condition. II. THE ESSENCE OF THE ATONEMENT appears in the statement that He, the mediator, Christ Jesus, "gave Himself a ransom for all." The idea of substitution, however little it commends itself to the judgment of some who have often very imperfectly considered it, is unquestionably involved in this. The Greek word translated here "ransom," means the redemption price paid for the deliverance of a slave or captive, and when Jesus "gave Himself" (not money or power) a ransom for all, He was like one who takes the place of a prisoner that the prisoner may go free. If the captive refuses freedom he perishes, but the love of his would-be deliverer is none the less. Most of those who have rejected this great doctrine have done so because they have had pressed home upon them only one phase of it—as if that were in itself a complete and satisfactory account of a profound mystery. The atonement has sometimes been spoken of as a sort of legal transaction, having no essential bearing upon moral character, which will procure acquittal for the sinner at the bar of judgment without setting him free from the usurpation of sin. 1. The God-ward side of the atonement is as important as it is mysterious, but it is not to be insisted upon as if it were all. The Scripture asserts again and again in types and in texts that it is in virtue of the death of Christ that God can justly forgive; that except for His sacrifice the Divine love could not reach us; that by Him satisfaction was made to the law of God, and that pardon was not, and could not be, a bare act of grace. These statements are beyond proof. They concern a sphere of existence about which we know absolutely nothing except what is revealed in Scripture. They have to do with the relations between the Eternal Father and the Only Begotten Son, about which the wisest of us are profoundly ignorant. We do not understand how the law of the Father required the sacrifice of the Son, nor how the death of the God-man affected the purpose of the Father; but are we to say, therefore, that there is no connection between them? Is that the only mystery in life? Why, what do you know of your own existence in its deeper relations? Yet it has been a frequent and grievous mistake of popular theology to dwell upon this aspect of the atonement only as if it contained the whole truth. But we must also remember that Christ's giving of Himself as a ransom for all was meant to have its influence on human hearts. This leads us to contemplate—2. The man-ward side of the atonement. The Cross of Calvary assured the world that the Divine love, even for sinners, was capable of the utmost self-sacrifice, which taught many to say, "We love Him because He first loved us." But there is yet another phase of Christ's atoning work which must not be lost sight of. We have seen that it vindicated Divine law, and revealed Divine love so as to touch the hearts of those who saw it, but it was meant also to exert an ethical influence over men. 3. The moral power of the atonement. Many sneer at professing Christians as men who persuade themselves that they are relieved from the punishment of sin, but who show no signs whatever of being redeemed from its power. But love such as God calls for, and the sacrifice of Calvary demands, is really a strong and active affection; indeed, we are told that "love is the fulfilling of the law." III. THE PROPAGATION OF THIS FUNDAMENTAL TRUTH through the world is to depend upon testimony. Paul says that he himself was a living witness of it. This is our duty too. It may be that we have not any remarkable gifts like Paul's, but we may reveal to others the power of Christ to save from sin, if only we ourselves experience that power. (A. Rowland, LL.B.) Jesus Christ the one Mediator between God and man:—Before entering upon the discussion of our text, we would offer a few remarks on the precise meaning of the term "mediator," in this passage. Now, by the word "mediator," in its general meaning, we understand one who interposes between two parties, either to obtain some favour from one to the other, or to adjust and make up some difference between them. But such a mediation may be either voluntary or authorized, assumed or commissioned. Moses was a mediator in the former sense, when he showed himself to his brethren "as they strove, and would have set them at one again" (Acts vii. 26). His interference was rejected, when "he that did his neighbour wrong thrust him away, saying, Who made thee a ruler or judge over us?" It is not such a mediator that the text speaks of. It is not presumption, not unauthorized good intention in Christ when He mediates. But, again: the meaning of the term is modified by the relative condition of the parties to be brought together. These may be equal; and then each is privileged to commit his own part in the matter in hand to the care of the common arbitrator. A mediator, under such circumstances, becomes an umpire, a judge, a referee, to whom the interest of each party is committed, and by whose decision each party is bound. But this does not come up to the idea of Christ's mediation. A further notion of a mediator is that of one interposing between unequals: one that has been appointed by a superior, who has a right to make his own terms with an offending inferior, and to depute to whomsoever he may see fit the regulation of the manner in which intercourse is to be carried on between him and those with whom he may be willing to communicate. Moses, when called of God to the direction of Israel, is an instance of this authorized mediation between unequals; and, as such, was representative of the one great Mediator of whom our text speaks. By the term "mediator," then, we are here to understand one duly commissioned by God, with whom the power rests, to negotiate between Himself and man, in order, as God's vicegerent, to receive man's submission and obedience; and, as man's representative and advocate, to propitiate God's justice, and to procure and communicate God's blessing. I. THE PARTIES TO BE RECONCILED ARE "God and man"; the Creator and the creature; the rightful Sovereign and the rebellious subject; the kind Father and the ungrateful child. Strange, it may be said, that there should be variance between such: was it always thus? No: once all was harmony and peace and love. Whence, then, did the estrangement arise? From

God? No: the profusion and magnificence and beauty of Eden forbid the entertainment of such a thought. It was in man that the alienation began. But how is the estrangement perpetuated? "The carnal mind is enmity against God": here is the sinner's having learned to hate what he feels he has abused, and manifesting the identity of interest and feeling between himself and that evil one whose cause he now maintains. The very purity of the Being he has injured makes his hatred but the more malignant: the very lack of palliation for his disobedience confirms him in his settled purpose still to sin with a high hand. Thus, what folly and pride began, folly and pride perpetuate. II. THE PERSON MEDIATING—"the man Christ Jesus." 1. As to His nature, we may remark, that the expression, "the man Christ Jesus," must not be considered as declarative of His humanity to the denial of His divinity. He is "Wonderful, Counsellor, the Mighty God"; "God over all, blessed for evermore." But the Mediator is still the "man Christ Jesus." Our high notions of His Divinity must not cause us to overlook or deny His humanity. As His Divinity fits Him to act with God for man, so His humanity fits Him to act with man for God. But He must be sinless man. The slightest flaw in His moral character would make Him a criminal, and not an Advocate—would make His mediation offensive. The circumstance of having a tendency to sin would imply partiality: He would be prone to palliate rather than to condemn, and have a tendency to lower the standard of the Creator's requirements, in order to make easier terms for the creature. 2. Again, as to His commission. He is authorized and empowered by Him with whom alone the power rests. 3. His work is threefold: His atonement, intercession, and mission of the Spirit. III. THE DESIGN OR END OF THIS MEDIATION. Now, we must bear in mind that a mediator is required to consider the interests of both parties in behalf of whom he acts, and to make terms by which the honour of the superior, and the restoration to favour of the inferior, may be most effectually secured. With regard to the Almighty Ruler, His honour and sovereignty must be maintained, and His glory acknowledged and admired. Man's position is naturally now one of rebellion; but he must be brought to lay down his arms. Christ, in the person and place of man, has tendered and paid the penalty incurred, met the demands of offended justice, and now He tenders the submission of each individual child of man that receives Him as his Mediator by faith. The construction of man in his original form was a wonder of Divine skill: the formation of his spirit in knowledge, holiness, and happiness, bespoke a master hand; but, when all the beauty of this wondrous production had been marred by the fall, to re-construct, re-adorn, re-glorify the whole, was the act only of Him whose thoughts are not as our thoughts. Yet such is the effect of Christ's mediation. Intelligence continually enlarging and expanding in the unclouded presence of the very Source of truth; holiness everlastingly increasing in those regions where nothing entereth that defileth; love for ever glowing with increasing intensity before Him who is its very essence; happiness continually accumulating in the presence of Him who supplies it in inexhaustible abundance—these are the prospects of the redeemed soul: this is the high perfection to which the wisdom and power and love of Jehovah will bring the frail fragile thing that Satan shivered, and sin defiled. The glory of the perfections of Jehovah, then, are acknowledged and illustrated. But another end of this mediation was the good of man. Christ came to procure the outpouring of the blessing which sin had checked and intercepted. God now can visit those who had loved Him in Christ Jesus. We would now proceed to offer a few general observations which seem to be suggested by the whole subject. 1. And, first, how great is the unfairness of those who affirm, and the folly of those who can be persuaded, that the tendency of the doctrine of justification by faith only, is to engender a careless and an antinomian spirit. 2. But another observation is this: How great are the injury and injustice done to Christ by the addition of other mediators! To endeavour to make out a necessity for the interposition of the virgin, of saints, or of any priestly mediator on earth, in order to our availing ourselves of the mediation of the Redeemer, is grounded on no warranty of Scripture, and reflects injuriously on the character of the blessed Jesus. *(John Richardson, B.A.)* **The Man Christ Jesus.**— *Christ's—a true and proper humanity:*—In whatever way God is pleased to manifest Himself, the medium of manifestation must be limited and finite. His union with our humanity, as an organ of revelation, is no more inconceivable than with any other nature which is restricted and confined. He was pleased to assume our humanity as the form through which to reveal the Divinity, and had He not been conscious of a complete participation in human nature, He never would have adopted or employed the designation—Son of Man. Having taken our nature, the man Christ Jesus followed the laws of purely human development both in body and in mind. He not only represented but passed through every successive period or stage of life. In every sense He was a child—in every sense a youth—in every sense a man. The social affections enter immediately and inseparably into the very idea of our humanity. With these social feelings our Creator has endowed us, and has fixed our abode in a world in which they are ever being called into joyous play, and in which there exists the most beautiful provision for their gratification. Nor does Christianity interfere with these social ties and relationships. We are formed to love. Nor can we conceive of any principle, human or Divine, stronger or more impressive. It is the conservative principle of families and of society at large. A world without love would be a world in which every social bond would soon be loosened and broken, and the human passions become the play of so many lawless forces, which would ultimately involve society in eternal enmity and opposition. One of the most touching scenes in the social life and history of Christ is connected with His death. Not far from His cross, and just as He was in the act of giving up His spirit into the hands of His Father, He beheld His mother standing at a distance, burdened with sorrow and bathed in tears. While His development was from first to last without sin—while He was a living and pure model of that conduct which is pleasing to God—yet His fellowship with humanity was emphatically a fellowship of suffering. In suffering He surpassed all men. In proportion to the perfection, refinement, and sensibility of His nature, was the depth and keenness of His affliction. Never was sorrow like unto His sorrow. We wonder not, therefore, that Christ should have a deep and unmistakeable sympathy with suffering and with sorrow. Not that His sympathies could flow out only amid scenes of grief and distress. The subject of the purest social affections, He could freely mingle in the intercourse of men, and share in all their human joys. In Him we behold that Spirit of liberty with which the Divine life takes hold of, and appropriates to itself the relations of the world and of society. Christianity is eminently social in its character. True piety is cheerful as the day, and sheds its radiance over every scene. That school of spiritual life in which the Saviour taught His disciples differed from every other. Instead of a sour, austere, unyielding asceticism, He trained them to a comparatively unrestrained mode of life. Nor was it with poverty only that the Saviour sympathized. Nor must we lose sight of the truth, that the sympathy of Christ sprang from the purest and most intense love—that love, which, in seeking and in blessing its objects, asks not how, or when, or where. It is true that this loving, compassionate, sympathizing Saviour, has left this lower sphere of being, and hath passed into those higher heavens, in which room is found for nothing but the most refined and the most sublime enjoyment; and yet even there is " He touched with the feeling of our infirmities." His sympathies are still with us, whether we be in joy or in sorrow, and He can so communicate with our spirit, as to give us the consciousness of Divine succour and support. We are conscious of the fellowship of mind with mind. And what shall we say of those kindred virtues which clustered and shone like the most brilliant constellation in the life and character of the Man ? Humility is the queen of graces. It is one of the rarest and the truest virtues. It is far removed from everything approaching to meanness of spirit. Having come into the world to offer himself a sacrifice for man, there was no act of hazard or of self-denial to which the Saviour was not prepared and willing to descend. Allied to this humility is meekness. Self-denial is nothing if clamorous and noisy. It does not lift up and cause its voice to be heard in the street. It is silent, unobtrusive, and retiring. If humility be not servility, neither is meekness to be looked upon as softness. Hence it is that we read of the gentleness of Christ. Not only was He harmless in life, but in death He was led as a lamb to the slaughter, and as a sheep before her shearers is dumb, so He opened not His mouth. Not that He can be charged with timidity and weakness. His soul was full of manly energy. A spirit so humble, and meek, and gentle, could not be wanting in forbearance ; but forbearance must not be understood as involving any thing of timidity or cowardice. It is the highest manifestation of self-control. It follows that this forbearance carries with it the corresponding idea of patience. In forbearance there must be the power of enduring. But patience is not to be resolved into insensibility, any more than forbearance is to be resolved into cowardice. The Saviour of man could not only face opposition and danger, but He could with calm assurance bear every species of wrong and suffering which could be inflicted on His deeply sensitive and susceptible nature. It now only remains to add, that this patience was allied to the most child-like submission—the most perfect resignation. To give up our own individual will for the will of another in circumstances of deep suffering, is the perfection of Christian virtue. Nor were these virtues embodied and exemplified in the life of Christ otherwise than as a model and example to man. Our character and life should be the mirror in which His virtues are reflected; or rather, our life should be the counterpart of His. We must copy after our great pattern. It is not forbidden us in the arrangements of infinite wisdom and love to cultivate and cherish the social affections to the highest possible point, so long as they do not withdraw the heart from God, and the sublime objects of immortality. Nor can our Christianity have its full development but amid the scenes, and friendships, and enjoyments of our present being. Whatsoever things are true, whatsoever things are honest, whatsoever things are just, whatsoever things are pure, whatsoever things are lovely, whatsoever things are of good report—if there be any force, and if there be any praise in them, think on these things, and these things do, and the God of peace shall be with you. (*R. Ferguson.*) *The man Christ Jesus:*—To pray for all, even for those that are most hostile or most alien (ver. 3), is good and acceptable in the sight of God our Saviour. It may well be so, it must be so. For it is in accordance with His mind and will as Saviour. He is our Saviour, it is true; but not ours only (ver. 4). He will have all men— His greatest enemies, the most outcast prodigals, not excepted—He will have all men to be saved, and to come to the knowledge of the truth. If there are any for whom we cannot pray directly out of sympathy with them, we can pray for them out of sympathy with the Lord, who is our Saviour, and who is willing also to be theirs. All the rather will we pray for them all, when we bear in mind that they and we are all one. Yes! all are one, they and we are one; inasmuch (ver. 5) as there is one God for all, one Mediator for all, one Saviour for all. There are not many Gods, so that one might belong to one God and some to another. There are not many Mediators, many Captains of salvation, under whose separate banners men might rank themselves at pleasure. There are not many ransoms, with blood of various hues to meet varieties of taste among the sprinkled worshippers. There is but one God, to whom all belong. One God for all. One Mediator for all. One ransom for all. And the ransom, the Mediator, Christ Jesus, is "the man." Not a man of a particular colour, whether fair, or dark, or of Ethiopian dye. Not a man of particular race, Jew or Gentile; of Shem, of Japhet, or of Ham. Not a man of a particular class or rank, whether of royal ancestry or of lineage proper to His birth in the stable of an inn. Not a man of a particular temperament, whether sanguine or morose, grave or gay. Not a man of a particular history, walking in a path apart. He is "the man Christ Jesus"; everywhere, always, to every one, the same; the man. Therefore they who love Him, the man Christ Jesus, may well be exhorted to pray for all men. I. He is the man all through; OUT AND OUT THE MAN. In soul, body, spirit; in look, voice, carriage, walk; in mind, heart, feeling, affection. In Him—in all about Him, all He is, and all He does, you see the man; not the man of honour, the man of piety, the man of patience, the man of patriotism, the man of philanthropy; but the man. The manhood in Christ Jesus is very noble, but it is very simple. And it is because it is so simple that it is so noble. None have ever succeeded in drawing His character since. Do you ever think of Him but just as the man? Other men you think of as distinguished by their features. You remember other men by their peculiarities of manner. But by what peculiarity do you remember the man Christ Jesus? Oh! it is a blessed thing to know that Jesus Christ is the man. The man for you, brother, whoever you are—and the man also, I thank God, for me! The man for the strong—the man for the weak! The man for heroes, for who so heroic as the man Christ Jesus? The man for you who toil in the carpenter's shop; in the like of which once He toiled, like you—the man Christ Jesus! II. He is simply man throughout; IN EVERY EXIGENCY, in every trial, simply man—the man Christ Jesus! In all His earthly and human experience, you never find Him other than man; you never find Him less than man; and you never find Him more than man. He is the Son of God, you know; the Father's fellow. But you never think of His being the Son of God as making His manhood at all different from yours. No! For you never find Him taking shelter from the ills to which flesh is heir in any power, or privilege, or prerogative of His Divine nature and heavenly rank. Thus, as the man Christ Jesus, He lies in His mother's bosom, and works at her husband's trade, He is subject, all His youth, to His parents, He is weary, hungry, thirsty, He is vexed, grieved, pained, provoked, His soul is exceedingly sorrowful, and at times His anger is stirred, He cries, and groans, and weeps, He bleeds, and quivers, and dies. Man's capacity of attainment, man's power of endurance—what man is fit for, what man can stand, with the help of God, you learn from the human history of the man Christ Jesus! III. He is the man exclusively, pre-eminently, PAR EXCELLENCE, to the absolute exclusion of all others, He is the man, the only man, complete and perfect. He stands alone as man. Manhood, in its integrity, belongs to Him alone. Not otherwise, Oh, my brother sinner, could He be the man for you; the man for me. Let one gather up in himself all the fragments of the manhood which you and I share together. Let him collect in one heap, as it were, every particle of glory and beauty to be found anywhere among the ruins of humanity. Let him take every great man's quality of greatness, every good man's element of goodness. Take all the good, of all sorts, you can possibly discover in the records of good men of all the ages. Mix, compound, combine as you may please, you cannot get the man! For the man to meet my case, and satisfy the craving of my soul—must be no thing of shreds and patches; but complete, perfect, an unbroken round, in himself one whole. No composite will do. He must be a single and simple unity; one, like the seamless coat, woven from the top throughout. But humanity, manhood, has never been thus one, inwardly and intensely one, since the fall. Men there have been, good and great. But they have been fragmentary; a bit of manhood in each; often a very beautiful bit of manhood; but set, alas! and often well-nigh lost, in a confused, chaotic jumble of inconsistencies and incoherences! And here is the man; the man Christ Jesus. All manhood is His; manhood such as yours and mine; but untainted, incorrupt, one and indivisible, which yours and mine is not. He is holy, harmless, undefiled; and separate from sinners. Nay, even if we could fancy a man more complete still, more completely uniting in himself the excellences of all other men, and more completely excluding their infirmities and faults; we cannot reach the idea of one who would not be more to some than he might be to others; who might be everything to you, and little, if anything at all, to me. No! If we would find one who is to be the man for me, for you, for all; we must ascend the stream of time, and fetch his manhood from beyond the flood, from beyond the fall! Then, in the unbroken image of God, manhood, human nature, the very self of man, was truly and indeed one. Since then the manhood among men has been manifold and broken and fragmentary. The man who is to gather up the fragments must himself be whole. The only one who can be the head of all, because He can be the same to all, is He who takes our human nature—not as it is now, rent and torn by sin—but as it once was; one in unbroken, pure, and holy innocence, one in immaculate likeness to the Holy One. And who is this but the man Christ Jesus? IV. HE IS THE MAN TO MEDIATE BETWEEN GOD AND MAN. To be the one Mediator, He must be pre-eminently and distinctively the man; the representative man; the one man. If mediation is a reality; if it is a real transaction outside of us; not an internal process, but the adjustment of an external relation, as all Scripture teaches us that it is; the mediator must be a third party, distinct from both the parties between whom He mediates. He may and must represent both. But He is to be confounded with neither, He is to be merged in neither. A man cannot have a mediator within himself; nor can he mentally create a mediator out of himself. He cannot be his own mediator. Every man is not a mediator, nor is it any man indiscriminately who can be a mediator. Nor will an ideal man, springing, as it were, fully grown, from the thoughtful head or fond heart, the living ideal outcome and expression of those human instincts that are opposed to evil, and yearn for good, suffice. No. Not though we give it a local habitation and a name, and call it the man Christ Jesus of Nazareth. If there is to be real and actual mediation in the fair and honest sense of the term, the man who is to be mediator must be found for me, not found by me, least of all found by me in myself. He must be born, not from among us, but from above. He must be the man, not by assent or consent on the part of earth merely, but by the decree of heaven, or rather by the creative act of heaven's Lord, doing a new thing on the earth, bringing in anew the man, the second Adam! Thus three conditions come together and coalesce as identifying the man who is to be the mediator. First, He must be the man, not as manhood exists and appears, marred and broken, among the children of the fall, but as it was in its original oneness and perfection, when man really bore the image of his Maker. Secondly, He must be the man, not as suggested by men's own instincts, and impulses, and cravings, but as directly chosen, appointed, introduced by God Himself. And, thirdly, He must be the man, as being, in His wondrous person, one with God in the same true and real sense in which He is one with men. All these three conditions meet in the man Christ Jesus. And they meet in Him as the man who sounded the utmost depths of human experience, and in the strength of His pure and simple manhood, aided only by prayer and by the Spirit, withstood evil, mastered pain, and by suffering overcame the wicked one. Truly there is and can be but one Mediator between God and men, the man Christ Jesus. The man—(1) Made, as to His human nature, by special miracle, in the unbroken image and likeness of God. The man (2) Who comes forth from God, bearing His commission to negotiate peace. The man (3) Who in respect of His Divine nature, unchanged, unchangeable, is one with God— the Son dwelling evermore in the Father's bosom. V. HE IS THE MAN TO GIVE HIMSELF A RANSOM FOR ALL. He who would do this—must be one who is willing to take your place, and be your substitute ; and fulfil all your obligations, and meet all your responsibilities. But more than that, He must be Himself free, under no obligations, under no responsibilities of His own. He must be one who owes nothing to God on His own account ; no service, or righteousness, or obedience ; and one also who lies under no penalty on His own account ; against whom no charge can be brought. In whom are these qualifications found combined but in the man Christ Jesus ? For His willingness who can doubt it ? "Lo, I come," He says (Psa. xl. 7). But willingness alone will not suffice. He who is to be your surety, your ransom, must be no common man. If He is one who, as a mere creature, is made under the law, as all intelligent creatures are made under the law, He cannot answer for others ; He can but answer for Himself. Not even if He were the highest of the angelic host could He do more. Brother, thou needest a ransom, an infinite ransom, a perfect ransom, a ransom sufficient for the cancelling of all thy guilt and the perfecting of thy peace with God. No such ransom canst thou find in thyself, in me, in any angel. But God has found it. VI. HE IS THE MAN TO BE TESTIFIED IN DUE TIME. A testimony for fitting seasons, a great truth to be attested as a fact at the right crisis of the world's history, to be ever afterwards preached and taught as the source of life to men doomed to die—is this marvellous constitution of the manhood of Christ Jesus ; fitting Him for being the one Mediator, the one Ransom. It is the testimony for which I am ordained a preacher, an ambassador for Christ. 1. It is my ordained and appointed testimony, or rather the Lord's by me, to thee, O sleeper—to thee, O doubter—to thee, whosoever thou art, who art living a godless, unholy life, unrenewed, unreconciled, unsanctified. It is a testimony in due time to thee. 2. It is the testimony with which I am charged to thee also, O downcast soul, who art afflicted, tossed with tempest and not comforted, sin-laden, sorrow-laden, unable to see thy warrant for having peace and life with thy God. I testify to thee, the Lord testifies by me to thee, that all thou needest is in the man Christ Jesus, the Mediator, the Ransom, and in Him for thee. 3. It is a timely, seasonable testimony to thee also, O man of God, my son Timothy, O child of God, who hast quiet peace in believing, and art walking at liberty, having respect to all God's commandments. The testimony to thee this day is of the man Christ Jesus, the Mediator, the Ransom. And it is for every due time, every fitting season. For thyself, I urge thy recognition always of Him of whom I testify, the man Christ Jesus. For, whatever the time, whatever the season, it is a due time, a fitting season, for His being testified to thee, by the Spirit, as being present with thee. As thou walkest the streets, or journeyest along the road, He talks with thee by the way, and opens to thee the Scriptures concerning Himself ; the man Christ Jesus, who taught thus of old in Galilee and Jewry, speaking as never man spoke. As thou sittest at meat, He breaks bread with thee, the man Christ Jesus, in whose living, personal, human, and Divine fellowship, the first disciples at Jerusalem did eat their meat with gladness and singleness of heart. As thou visitest the fatherless and widows in their affliction, He goes with thee, the man Christ Jesus, who in all their affliction is Himself afflicted. As thou art wearied among the workers of iniquity whom thou art seeking to turn to righteousness, ready to complain, "Who hath believed our report ?" see, ever near thee, at thy side, the man Christ Jesus, who endured such contradiction of sinners against Himself, and whose prayer on the cross was, "Father, forgive them, for they know not what they do !" (*R. S. Candlish, D.D.*) *Christ, the mediating man :*—Jesus Christ as standing for mediatorial purposes between God and man, is doing a work necessary to be done before satisfactory relations can be established between the sinner and the holy God. Our sins have separated us from God, and Christ lives to intercede, to mediate for us. Now, this fact has been so stated at times as to produce false impressions concerning God and His feelings towards men. It has been spoken of as though Jesus Christ had to stand for us in the presence of God, to offer Himself as a sacrifice, to persuade the Supreme to have pity, to take us back into His favour. God is thus represented as One who sustains a stern anger against the entire race, and who is determined to hold out in His terrible wrath against them. Now, I venture to assert that any teaching which leaves that idea of God upon the hearts of men is a gross libel of the Divine nature, utterly contrary to Scripture, and solemnly untrue. We could not feel any conscious gratitude for such compulsory pardon as that. If we realized any love or gratitude, it would not go forth to Him, but to the Mediator who had interposed to save us from the impending wrath. We should regard God as One to dread, and Christ only as One to love. If there is one clear testimony of Scripture that we are invited to receive, it is that God's mercy is the fountain and source of the grace we receive. Christ is the expression of God's mercy. Christ is God's gift. Yet, it may be asked, could not God have saved and reconciled the world without the intervention of the man Christ Jesus? He is a very bold dogmatist who would say that God could not have redeemed without the aid of the appointed Mediator. That would be to shut Him up to necessity, to surround Him with limitations, to restrict Him within the sphere of a single method, forgetting that with God all things are possible. That God has arranged that this shall be, warrants us, not in saying that the end could not have been accomplished in some other way, but that this was in the Infinite Wisdom the best, and that it met a necessity which could not have been otherwise so well and adequately met. If you ask what was that necessity which resulted in the life and death of Christ, then Scripture is silent. There it stands, a sublime history, an accomplished fact, in some way unexplained to us. Our salvation depends upon that mediatorial work; the Christ has come between us and God, and so achieved our ransom; and He now appears in the presence of God for us. Yes, there it is; though, I repeat, so far as the Divine side of the work of Christ is concerned, we know nothing more than this, that it has satisfied the Divine Father, and made salvation possible to all. So we rest assured that it was the best way. When, however, we turn to the human side, we perceive how wonderfully gracious is the arrangement that the Mediator should have been what He was—a man, the man Christ Jesus. This is what we are asked to fix our attention upon as of supreme and vital importance to us. He who undertakes our case and pleads our cause is not an angel, is not to be regarded as standing in any degree aloof from us; for though He had a supernatural birth, that in no sense was meant to separate Him from the race: He is still essentially one with it. It is just what we want to realize. He is distinctively the man—the man belonging alike to all. His nationality is not prominent in our minds, and in no way estranges our sympathy from Him, or affects our feeling towards Him. The fact is, as you read the exquisite record of His life, you feel that no nation has any special claim upon Him. He lives, and acts, and speaks, and dies as One who belongs to all humanity. Then, carry the thought further. Your study of the character and conduct of Jesus Christ will have revealed to you this great truth— that He does not impress you as manifesting any particular temperament. We mark off men according to certain peculiarities of disposition which they possess: their individuality puts them into classes. We speak of the reserved and the frank, the serious and the gay. Now you find nothing of all this in Christ. He shows no one quality of mind or heart predominant over any other. There is a rounded completeness of nature in Him altogether unique. What is the consequence of this? That He repels none, and is attractive to all. Men of varying temperaments, like those who formed the first group of disciples, cluster around Him, accept Him as their guide and teacher. He is the Christ for all—the Mediator in whom all can trust. He can draw all temperaments and natures to Himself. See in this again another proof of His fitness for the office He holds, and the work He undertakes— the man Christ Jesus, the One Mediator. The world wants no other, no multiplied agency. Take notice again that He has none of the faults and flaws and imperfections of common manhood. Here indeed is His peculiarity. Yes, but even then you have proof that He is the Man. In Him you have manhood in its integrity. You have manhood in its grandest possibilities. But how does that complete manhood of our Lord help us to rejoice that He is the right One to become our Mediator? I reply that you could not conceive the idea of an imperfect one representing the case of sinners; you could not be content to trust it in his hands; you could not be sure of the result. His infirmities might interfere with and mar his grand work. It would not be to such a one that we could look hopefully to be the means of redeeming us, for he would need himself to be redeemed. He is a man, knowing us altogether, yet free from our defects and evil, and so fitted to achieve the work of reconciling us and leading us back to God. Thus the very integrity of His manhood is the reason why He should be the Mediator for all other men. You are linked to God through Him, and through Him will come every blessing that God has to give to His children. Let none fear to come to God, since the way is opened for reconciliation through the Mediator—the man Christ Jesus—and all that Christ is and all that He has accomplished are for you. (*W. Braden.*)

Ver. 8. **Pray everywhere.**—*Prayer :*—I. Let us consider THE SUBJECT OF ATTENTION. This is prayer. And what is prayer? Prayer is the breathing of desire towards God. Words are not essential to it. As words may be used without the heart, so the heart may be engaged where words are wanting. Words are not always necessary to inform a fellow-creature, and they are never necessary to inform God, who "searcheth the heart," and knoweth what is in the mind. What interesting looks will the hunger of the beggar at the door display! How is it in the family? You have several children : the first can come and ask for what he wants in proper language, and the second can only ask in broken terms, but here is a third who cannot speak at all : but he can point, he can look, and stretch out his little hand ; he can cry, and shall he plead in vain? "No! no!" says the mother, refuse him? his dimpled cheeks, his speaking eye, his big round tears, plead for him. Refuse him? Further, we notice the kinds of prayer. Prayer may be considered as public. There is also domestic prayer, by which we mean the prayer that is offered every morning and every evening at the family altar. Mr. Henry observes, "A house without this has no roof." Prayer may be considered as private. "When thou prayest, enter into thy closet, and shut thy door, and pray to thy Father which seeth in secret, and thy Father which seeth in secret shall reward thee openly." Prayer may be considered as ejaculatory, a darting up of the mind to God, as the word signifies. This may be done at any time, and under any circumstance. Nehemiah was the king's cup-bearer, and while he was in the room attending upon his office, he prayed to the God of heaven. II. Observe THE INJUNCTION. "I will that men pray everywhere, lifting up holy hands, without wrath and doubting." III. WHERE IT IS TO BE OFFERED. "Everywhere." Now, this is opposed to restriction or respect. Let us see what we can make of it in either of these views. You remember the Assyrians thought that the God of Israel was the God of the hills, and not of the valleys. And when Balaam was baffled in one of his endeavours to curse Israel, he went to another place to see if he could be more prosperous, and to try if he could curse them from thence. You see how the devotions of the heathens always depended upon times, and places, or pilgrimages. Among the Jews, who were for a time under a Theocracy, God chose a place where He might reside, and where were the symbols of His presence, and there all the males resorted thrice in the year ; but even then God said to Moses, "In all places where I record My name, I will come unto thee and bless thee." What think you of those sons and daughters of superstition and bigotry who would confine God to particular places and stations? Where was Jacob when he said, "This is none other than the house of God and the gate of heaven"? Where did Paul take leave of his friends? "He kneeled down on the seashore." Where did the Saviour pray? "He went out into a private place," "He went into a desert place," "He went up into a mountain to pray." When Jones, a famous Welsh preacher, was commanded to appear before the Bishop of St. David's, the bishop said to him, "I must insist upon it that you never preach upon unconsecrated ground." "My lord," said he, "I never do ; I never did ; for 'the earth is the Lord's and the fulness thereof' ; and when Immanuel came down to set His foot upon our earth, the whole was sanctified by it." God is no more a respecter of places than of persons. This should also encourage you when you are under disadvantageous circumstances. For instance, if you are called to assemble in a very poor place, or in a very small place, He Himself hath said, "Where two or three are gathered together in My name "— let it be where it will—"there am I in the midst of them." But now, further, as men may pray everywhere, so they ought to pray everywhere. The injunction not only allows, but enjoins, universal prayer. The duty is more opposed to neglect than even restriction. Men should pray everywhere, because they may die everywhere. They have died in all places : they have died in a bath, they have died in a tavern, they have died upon the road, they have died in the temple of God. You are therefore to pray everywhere. But what are we to say of those who, instead of praying "everywhere," pray nowhere? IV. Let us notice HOW THIS DUTY IS TO BE

DISCHARGED. It is to be offered up under three attributes. 1. The first implies purity, "lifting up holy hands." Solomon says, "The prayer of the wicked is an abomination to the Lord." David says, "If I regard iniquity in my heart, the Lord will not hear me." You have heard the Dutch proverb, "Sinning will make a man leave off praying, or praying will make a man leave off sinning." These will not do well together, therefore they must be separated. It would be better for a man to neglect his benefactor than to call at his house to spit in his face, or to smite him on the cheek. James says, "Can a fountain bring forth at the same place sweet water and bitter?" 2. The second attribute is kindness. This is expressed by the opposite extreme. "Without wrath." There are those whose lives may be far from egregious vices, but whose tempers do not partake of the meekness and gentleness of Christ; they bring their rancorous spirit into their worship, and think to appease the anger of God for their uncharitableness by offering it up on the altar of devotion. "He that dwelleth in love, dwelleth in God, and God in him." 3. The third attribute is confidence. This is expressed negatively: "I will that men pray everywhere," not only "without wrath," but "without doubting." Our Lord says in the Gospel by St. Matthew, "Whatsoever ye shall ask in prayer believing, ye shall receive." This confidence includes a persuasion in the lawfulness of the things we pray for. Then it takes in confidence in the power of God. "Believe ye that I am able to do this"? This confidence takes in the disposition of God towards you; you are not only to "believe that He is," but that "He is a rewarder of them that diligently seek Him." Especially you must have confidence in the mediation of Christ. (*W. Jay.*) *A Scripture description of prayer :*—I. THE EMPLOYMENT WHICH IS HERE COMMENDED. 1. That prayer must be addressed exclusively to God. This grand truth is introduced, and ought to be solemnly and uniformly affirmed, in direct contradiction to those mistaken propensities and systems by which men have addressed invocations to idols—mere imaginary beings, or beings really existing but created and inferior. 2. Prayer must be offered to God through the Lord Jesus Christ. It is an established and a cardinal principle in all revealed religion that man as a guilty sinner can have no access to God but through a Mediator—One whose merits, as having offered a sacrifice for sin, must be alleged as constituting a satisfactory ground for favour and acceptance. 3. Prayer offered to God through the Lord Jesus Christ must be presented by all mankind. The statement of our text is, that men are to "pray everywhere"; wherever men exist, men are to pray. The universal call to prayer arises from the fact that men are universally in precisely the same relationship to God. They are everywhere characterized by the same guilt, the same wants, the same responsibility. II. THE SPIRIT WITH WHICH THIS EMPLOY-MENT IS TO BE INSEPARABLY ASSOCIATED. "I will therefore that men pray everywhere, lifting up holy hands, without wrath and doubting." 1. First the apostle recommends importunity. Importunity is symbolized by the figure of the "lifting up of hands"—an attitude which was practised in prayer in ancient times, as externally indicating the place from whence man expected blessing, even heaven the dwelling-place of God, and the spirit with which they desired to receive blessing, laying hold (as it were) by eagerness and by strength of what they desired to receive from Him. Who, for example, can pray for pardon, for sanctification, for knowledge, for love, for protection, for comfort, for victory over death and hell, and for the final enjoyment of a happy immortality in heaven—without importunity? It is palpable that coldness to a rightly regulated mind must be utterly and finally impracticable. 2. But again ; the expressions of the apostle, when they recommend importunity, also recommend purity. "Lifting up holy hands"—these expressions, or the epithets with which the expressions we have noticed already are connected, referring to a custom, frequent or universal among the Jews as well as other Oriental nations, of carefully washing the hands before they engaged in the performance of any act of devotion, this being intended to be the sign and symbol of moral rectitude and of the preparation of the heart. Hence it is that in the Old Testament Scriptures you find a connection established between the cleanness of the hands and the purification or holiness of the heart. For instance, in the Book of Job we have this statement —"The righteous shall hold on his way, and he that hath clean hands shall be stronger and stronger"—there being of course an identification between the two expressions. In the twenty-fourth Psalm David inquires thus—"Who shall ascend into the hill of the Lord? or who shall stand in His holy place? He that hath clean hands and a pure heart." This being the import of the expression, we might refer it to the state, which must be rendered judicially pure or holy by the imputation of Christ's righteousness, dependence on whom we have already advocated and required; but we must especially regard it as referring to the heart, which must undergo the sanctifying influence of the Holy Spirit, so as to be morally conformed to the character and the law of God. In all ages, God demands to be worshipped in " the beauties of holiness." 3. The apostle also recommends benevolence. "I will that men pray everywhere, lifting up holy hands, without wrath." The expression " wrath " of course must be regarded as having respect to other men; we are to be careful against indulging towards them resentment or dislike, arising from whatever source, and we are to cultivate towards them the spirit of benevolence and of good-will, these prompting on their behalf intercession for their interests before the throne and in the presence of God. The apostle well knew that there is a great disposition to the indulgence of selfishness in prayer; and hence it was that he bore in the present instance his solemn protest against it. 4. The apostle at the same time recommends faith. "I will that men pray everywhere, lifting up holy hands, without wrath and doubting"; the term "doubting" is placed as the converse of faith. Faith in regard to the exercise of prayer, must not merely have respect to the Lord Jesus Christ, as the Mediator through whom prayer is to be presented, but must have respect to the entire testimony of God regarding prayer—in its mode, matter, and results. There may perhaps be stated certain limitations to the exercise of faith, as connected with the employment of prayer. Those limitations may justly have respect to the desires we are accustomed to present before the Divine footstool, for the impartation of what we deem temporal blessings. III. THE REASONS BY WHICH THIS EMPLOYMENT IN THIS SPIRIT MAY ESPECIALLY BE ENFORCED. 1. First, this employment in this spirit is directly commanded by God. 2. Again; this employment in this spirit is connected with numerous and invaluable blessings. Is it not associated with blessing to ourselves, and have we not been distinctly informed that the great instrument of the continuance of spiritual blessings to us, when converted by Divine grace, has been the agency of prayer? 3. And then it must be observed that the neglect of this employment in this spirit is attended and succeeded by numerous and by fatal evils. No man is a converted man who does not pray. No man can be a happy man who does not pray. No man can possess the slightest indication of the spiritual favour of God who does not pray. (*J. Parsons.*) *Prayer without anger:*—"Anger," says he, "is a short madness, and an eternal enemy to discourse and a fair conversation: it is a fever in the heart, and a calenture in the head, and a sword in the hand, and a fury all over: and therefore can never suffer a man to be in a disposition to pray. For prayer is the peace of our spirits, the stillness of our thoughts, the evenness of recollection, the rest of our cares, and the calm of our temper; prayer is the issue of a quiet mind, of untroubled thoughts: it is the daughter of charity and the sister of meekness: and he that prays to God with an angry, that is, with a troubled and discomposed spirit, is like him that retires into a battle to meditate, and sets up his closet in the out-quarters of an army, and chooses a frontier garrison to be wise in. For so have I seen a lark rising from his bed of grass, and soaring upwards, and singing as he rises, and hopes to get to heaven, and rise above the clouds; but the poor bird was beaten back with the loud sighings of an eastern wind, till the little creature was forced to sit down and pant, and stay till the storm was over: and then it made a prosperous flight, and did rise and sing, as if it had learned music and motion from an angel." (*Jeremy Taylor.*) *Praying everywhere:*—Forty years ago, Audubon, the distinguished American naturalist, was pursuing his vocation in a wild, remote, and, as he believed, perfectly uninhabited district of Labrador. Rising up from the bare ground after a cold night's rest he beheld, on one of the granite rocks which strew that desolate plain, the form of a man accurately outlined against the dawn, his head raised to heaven, his hands clasped and beseeching. Before this rapt and imploring figure stood a small monument of unhewn stones supporting a wooden cross. The only dweller on that inhospitable shore had come out from his hut to the open air, that without barrier or hindrance his solitary supplication might go up directly unto Him who does not dwell in the temples that are made with hands. *Wrath and prayer:*—Prayer is represented in the gospel as a holy and solemn act, which we cannot surround with too many safeguards, in order to prevent anything of a profane and worldly nature from interfering with the reverential freedom of this converse between the creature and its Creator. Prayer prepares for acts of self-denial, courage, and charity, and these in their turn prepare for prayer. No one should be surprised at this double relation between prayer and life. Is it not natural that we should retire to be with God, that we may renew our sense of His presence, draw on the treasures of light and strength which He opens to every heart that implores Him, and afterwards return to active life, better provided with love and wisdom? On the other hand, is it not natural that we should prepare by purity of conduct to lift up pure hands to God, and carefully keep aloof from everything that might render this important and necessary act either difficult, or formidable, or useless? The words introduced at the end of the verse so unexpectedly, and which we believe, for a moment, excite surprise in every reader—these words, "without wrath and doubting," contain a very marked and impressive allusion to the circumstances in which Christians were then placed. The question is anew brought before you at every new attack of your enemies; in other words, every new attack will necessarily tempt you to wrath and disputation as you are men, if it do not urge you to prayer as you are Christians. You cannot escape from wrath except by prayer, nor from hatred except by love; and not to be a murderer, since hatred is murder, you must as much as in you lies give life to him to whom you wished to give death. At least it is necessary to ask it for him, it is necessary by your prayers to beget him to a new existence; it is necessary in all cases, while praying for him, to exert yourselves in loving him. It is necessary that wrath and disputation be extinguished and die away in prayer. Two classes of men may excite in us wrath and disputation. The former are the enemies of our persons, those who, from interest, envy, or revenge, are opposed to our happiness, and more generally all those who have done us wrong, or against whom we have ground of complaint. The latter are those who become our enemies from the opposition of their views and opinions to ours, or the opposition of their conduct to our wishes. Both are to us occasions of wrath and disputation. The gospel requires that they be to us occasions of prayer. In regard to the former, I mean our personal enemies, I might simply observe that God does not know them as our enemies. God does not enter into our passions, or espouse our resentments. He sanctions and approves all the relations which He has Himself created, those of parent and child, husband and wife, sovereign and subject. But the impious relation of enemy to enemy is entirely our work, or rather the work of the devil. God knows it only to denounce it. Besides, in His eye the whole body of mankind are only men, and some in the relation which they stand to each other, only brethren. You would wish to pray for your friends alone; but this very prayer is forbidden, and remains impossible, if you do not extend it to your enemies. And if you persist in excluding them from your prayers, be assured that God will not even accept those which you offer to Him in behalf of the persons whom you love. Your supplications will be rejected; the smoke of your offering will fall back upon your offering; your desires will not reach that paternal heart which is ever open. Not only ought we to pray for our enemies, although they be our enemies; but we ought to pray for them because they are our enemies. As soon as they again become to us like the rest of mankind another distinction takes place, and a new right arises in their favour. They are confounded for a moment with all our other fellows, in order afterwards to stand forth from the general mass as privileged beings, with a special title to our prayers. When we meet with an opposition which frets and irritates us, Christian prudence counsels us to pray that the temptation may be removed; and, in particular, that our self-love and injured feelings may not weaken our love for our neighbour. But this prudence, if it counsels nothing further, is not prudent enough. If the same feeling which disposes us to pray does not dispose us to pray for our enemies or opponents, it is difficult to believe that it is a movement of charity. Charity cannot be thus arrested. Its nature is to overcome evil with good, and this means not merely that it does not render evil for evil, but that in return for evil it renders good. It would not be charity if it did less. Its first step overleaps the imaginary limit which it does not even see or know. It does not restrict itself to not hating; it loves. It would not do enough if it did not do more than enough. Can we renew our hatred for one for whom we have prayed? Does not every desire, every request which we send up to God for him endear him to us the more? Does not each prayer set him more beyond the reach of our passions? No; not till then is the work of mercy accomplished. We have no evidence of having pardoned an enemy until we have prayed for him. For to allege the gravity, the extent of the offence which we have received, has no plausibility. If we have brought ourselves to pardon him who has committed it, we might surely bring ourselves to pray for him; and if we cannot pray for him we have not pardoned him. An offence! But think well of it; can we really be offended? The term is too lofty, too grand for us. The offence may have grated very painfully on our feelings, or thwarted our interests, but it has gone no farther. Whatever injustice may have been done us, whatever cause we may have to complain, that is not the real evil. What evil absolutely is there in having our faith tried and our patience exercised? Because our fortune has been curtailed, our reputation compromised, our affections thwarted, does the world go on less regularly than it did? Not at all. The evil, the only real evil is the sin of that soul, the infraction of the eternal law, the violence offered to Divine order; and if any other evil is to be added to this, it will be by our murmurings, since the effect of them will be to make two sinners in place of one. Do you then seek a reason for refusing your intercession, and consequently your pardon to your adversaries? I have found one, and it is a fit ground for resentment: God your Father was insulted in the insult which you experienced. But show me, pray, the extraordinary man who, quite ready to pardon on his own account, cannot resolve to pardon on God's account! It may belong to God to be angry with them; us it becomes only to pity them, and pity them the more, the more grievously God has been offended. But alas! instead of seeing in the injury which we have received only an injury done to God, we insolently appropriate to ourselves the offence of which He alone is the object. In what hurts Him we feel ourselves offended, and consequently become angry, instead of being grieved. It will be well if, instead of praying, we have not cursed! Contrast the ordinary fruits of wrath and debate with these results of prayer. In yielding to the former, not only do you place yourself in opposition to the holy law of God, but you destroy the peace of your life and the peace of your soul; you aggravate the evils of a situation already deplorable; you kindle up hatred in the heart of your enemy; you render reconciliation on his part, as well as on yours, always more difficult; you run from sin to sin in order to lull your pride, and this pride gives you only a bitter, poisoned, and criminal enjoyment. How much better, then, is prayer than wrath and strife! But personal enemies are not the only ones who are to us the occasion of wrath and strife. The class of enemies, as we have already said, includes all those whose opinions, views, and conduct are in opposition to our interests or our principles. How little does the impatience which they excite differ from hatred! With regard to such enemies, our usual method is to hate in silence if we feel ourselves weak, or to dispute obstinately if we believe ourselves strong. The gospel proposes another method. It approves neither of hatred nor strife. Zeal, courage, perseverance, indignation itself, must all be pervaded with charity, or rather, proceed from charity. Indignation and prayer must spring from a common source; the former from love to God, the latter from love to men, and consequently both from love. How widely different is this conduct from that which is commonly pursued in the world! Let Government commit an error, it is greedily laid hold of and bitterly commented on; and this is all that is done. Let a religious teacher profess a system which is judged dangerous; his minutest expressions are laid hold of, and isolated so as to distort their meaning; his life is boldly explained by his opinions, or his opinions by his life, and there the matter rests. To pray, to entreat the Lord to shed His enlightening Spirit on this government, on that teacher, on that individual; to wrestle for them in presence of the Divine mercy, ah! this is what is seldom thought of. Ah! the Divine Intercessor must have fully established His abode in the soul before the spirit of intercession can dwell there! How difficult is it for the old leaven to lose its sourness! What seeds of hatred, what homicidal germs are in the heart which has received Jesus Christ! How much of Cain still remains in this pretended Abel! And what avails it to believe much if we love little, or to believe if we do not love? And truly, what have we believed, in whom have we believed, if we do not love? (*A. Vinet, D.D.*)

**Vers. 9, 14. That women adorn themselves in modest apparel.**—*Woman's true dignity*:—If we lived in Turkey or in India, we should be better able to appreciate the wisdom of Paul's counsel in respect to the women of his day: and I am not prepared to mitigate or to apologise for his brave and wise words. Remember it was due to him more than to any other apostle that women had been so far emancipated as they were when this Epistle was written, for it was he who had taught that in Christ Jesus there was neither male nor female. But he grieved over some of the evils which at first arose from the great changes effected in their social position. Seclusion had been rigorously maintained by the customs of those Eastern cities. The picture in the Royal Academy, which represents a young girl, with slippers in her hand, drawing aside the curtain of the seraglio, and stepping across the body of a black slave, who is sleeping with naked sword in his hand, fairly represents the slave-like treatment of women in Ephesus in Paul's days. Indeed, even among the Jews the women who came to the synagogue were (and still are) kept out of sight in a carefully screened gallery. It was therefore not to be wondered at that the Christian women emancipated from such treatment felt themselves not only at liberty to assert their new-born rights but bound to do so, and that they claimed a prominence and a freedom which were good neither for themselves nor for the Church. And we must not forget that, so far as women had greater publicity in the heathen cities, it was at the risk of the virtuous reputation which Christians would be the most anxious to preserve. The priestesses of the temples, for example, were notoriously immoral, and the Hetairae were not only a recognized, but even a respectable class in Pagan society. I. He speaks of it first NEGATIVELY, declaring that her dignity does not depend upon outward adornment; and this is always and everywhere true. It is probable that the women who came to the Christian assemblies in Ephesus arrayed themselves in costly attire, and sometimes made unbecoming display of their personal charms till the custom was becoming the sensation, if not the scandal, of the city. No one professing godliness ought to spend time, and taste, and money to the extent many do on mere personal adornment, as if the body was everything and the mind nothing, or as if the chief end of a woman's life was to win admiration not respect, to please man and not God. Even from a lower standpoint it is a mistake, and I venture to think that many a marriage has been prevented, and many a possibly happy home is fraught with anxiety, because of an expenditure on dress, which cannot be reasonably or rightly met. There are lives which might have been unspeakably happier if only they had been united, if the two young people had been content to face the world together with plain fare and simple habits. Listen to John Ruskin, "I say further, that as long as there are cold and nakedness in the land around you, so long can there be no question at all but that splendour of dress is a crime." II. WOMAN'S DIGNITY IS NEXT SET FORTH POSITIVELY. "I will," says Paul, "that women adorn themselves in—1. Modest apparel, with shamefastness and sobriety." Society owes its tone more to women than to men. What they frown upon will be tabooed; what they thoughtlessly tolerate will grow in evil influence. 2. But in addition to this influence, which may be almost unconsciously exercised, the Christian woman is to adorn herself with "good works." She often does this behind the veil which is drawn over every home. There are those whose "good works" are noble in their self-sacrifice and far-reaching in their issues of whom the Church hears little. Many a man can sympathize with that soldier who said, "I can stand before the enemy, but I cannot stand before my sister's prayers." And who does not know of more public work done by Christian women—such as that of our visitors and Sunday-school teachers; of saintly pleaders with the drunkards and the profligate;—of noble women whose writings have purged the atmosphere of moral corruption; of heroines like Florence Nightingale and Sister Dora, who have trodden closely in the footsteps of the Lord. These have been clothed with "good works." (*A. Rowland, LL.B.*) *The position of woman :*—This was—I. A BOLD DECLARATION on the part of the apostle. "Let the woman learn in silence (or rather in quietness) with all subjection, for I suffer not a woman to teach, nor to usurp authority over the man, but to be in quietness"; but the course he followed in this matter was wise, in the condition of life then prevailing. In our days there is no doubt a change of those conditions, which would make the rigorous application of such a rule unwise and unjust. Women, in larger numbers now than then, are of necessity independent, and are compelled to earn their own livelihood, and make their own homes; and being, in some respects, the weaker, they should have no artificial barriers put in the way of their doing so. There are disabilities, the relics of feudal times, which slowly, yet surely, are being swept away, though much still remains to be done. Under our English laws, for example, a woman may be compelled to pay taxes, though she has no right to influence the election of those who impose them—as her gardener or coachman may do. But the general law laid down by Paul still holds good. The public work of life, whether in the world or in the Church, is, broadly speaking, not woman's but man's. His is the life of turmoil, hers of quietude. She is receptive; he is aggressive: and it is not so much in her conspicuous activity as in her yielding affectionateness that her true strength is found. II. BY A SCRIPTURAL ARGUMENT. He goes back to Eden for a justification of his teaching—for he was accustomed to regard the facts of the Old

Testament as symbolical and parabolical sources of perpetual instruction. "Adam was first formed," says he, "then Eve." Man's priority in creation, standing as he did alone and in immediate relation to God, was an indication of his place and power, as having the headship over her whom God made to be his helpmeet. But if the helpmeet becomes the head, and the head weakly yields, there comes an overthrow of the Divine order, as there did come in Paradise. Practical shrewdness and discernment; the firm and regulative judgment which should characterize the ruler, are less hers than man's. Her very excellencies, connected as they are with the finer sensibilities and the stronger impulses of a noble and loving nature, disqualify her for the headship, whereas the balance in man's nature is the other way; in the direction of the intellectual and the governing. But it is here asserted that "Adam was not deceived," and was therefore more guilty, because with his eyes open to the wrong he yielded to conjugal love. In other words, the will and the judgment were sacrificed to the affections—the essence of moral fall. Paul closes his remarks on woman by alluding to—III. A BLESSED ASSURANCE. "Notwithstanding she shall be saved in childbearing"; or, as the R.V. has it, "through the childbearing." Perhaps there was some hint here of the blessing that comes through pain and travail, of whatsoever kind it be; and also of the great and noble work possible only to motherhood. But the more correct translation gives us rather the thought of what may be called pre-eminently "*the* childbearing"—when Jesus Christ, the world's Saviour, was born of a woman, and appeared in the likeness of sinful flesh—for it was thus that the great promise was fulfilled which brought a gleam of hope into the darkness of Eve's despair, "the seed of the woman shall bruise the serpent's head." (*Ibid.*) *Advice against jewellery:*—As to jewels, let me advise you not to buy any—even though you have the purse of Fortunatus, or may hereafter become wealthy. Some may be given you, but still I would say, do not wear them—unless, perhaps, now and then, with the pure desire of affording pleasure to the donors. A fancy for the possession and display of jewellery soon generates into a craze, ever growing, or unsatisfied unless in the ownership of gems superior to those of others around you. It is an unhealthy and vulgar feeling, which has not seldom led to the ruin of women in all classes. Other reasons may be advanced against the indulgence of this false taste. Valuable jewels cannot but become, at times, a source of trouble and anxiety; and if lost or stolen, a bitter feeling of annoyance is retained. Opportunities for display are few; and often then, through disadvantageous comparison with others, are apt to give rise to heart-burning and envy—feelings which would never be experienced in such a way were the face resolutely set against such vanities. (*Lady Bellairs.*) *A passion for extravagant dress:*—The Empress Josephine had twenty-four thousand pounds for her personal expenses, but this sum was not sufficient, and her debts increased to an appalling degree. She rose at nine o'clock. Her toilet consumed much time, and she lavished unwearied efforts on the preservation and embellishment of her person. Huge baskets were brought to her containing different dresses, shawls, and hats. From these she selected her costume for the day. She possessed between three or four hundred shawls, and always wore one in the morning, which she draped about her shoulders with unequalled grace. The evening toilet was as careful as that of the morning—then she appeared with flowers of pearls, or precious stones in her hair. Bonaparte was irritated by these expenditures; he would fly into a passion, and his wife would weep and promise to be more prudent; after which she would go on in the same way. It is almost incredible that this passion for dress should never have exhausted itself. After her divorce she arrayed herself with the same care even when she was no one. She died covered with ribbons and pale rose-coloured satin. As long as the heart is unrenewed by Divine grace, regard for the outward is even greater than regard for the inward. True religion reverses all this, and gives "the things unseen and eternal" their rightful place. The most humbly dressed believer in Christ has a better garment than the empress, even the wedding garment of Christ's righteousness. *A good use for ornaments:*—Some of you might do great good with articles which you might very readily spare. You have ornaments which Christian men and women are better without, which, if broken up or sold, would aid the good cause. I wish many would follow the example of Oliver Cromwell, when he went into Exeter Cathedral, and saw twelve massive images of the apostles in silver. "Oh, oh," said he, "what do these gentlemen here?" "They are the twelve apostles," was the reply. "Very well," said he, "melt them down, and send them about doing good." I wish Christians would do that with some of their gold and silver jewellery. Anyhow, for our own sakes, lest the canker get into our gold, and the rust into our silver, use it for doing good. (*C. H. Spurgeon.*)     *A becoming adornment:* — Goethe was in company with a mother and daughter, when the latter, being reproved for something, blushed and burst into tears. He said to the mother : " How beautiful your reproach has made your daughter ! The crimson hue and those silvery tears become her much better than any ornament of gold or pearls ; those may be hung on the neck of any woman ; these are never seen unconnected with moral purity." A full-blown flower, sprinkled with purest hue, is not so beautiful as this child, blushing beneath her parent's displeasure, and shedding tears of sorrow for her fault. A blush is the sign which nature hangs out, to show where chastity and honour dwell.     *The charity purse:* — Howard, soon after his marriage, " sold some jewels his wife had no longer any inclination to wear, and put the money into a purse called by herself and her husband the charity purse." (*J. Stoughton, D.D.*)     *Woman's sphere of influence:* — For so far as a woman is sincere to the nature God has given her, her aspiration is not so much that the world should ring with her fame, or Society quote her as a leader of fashion, but that she should bless and be blessed in blessing. It is not that she should wish for power, but that she should wish for a noble, not an ignoble power. It is not that she should not wish to queen it in this world, but that she should wish to queen it, not by ostentation of dress or life, nor by eclipsing others, but by manifestation of love, by nobility of gentle service, by unconscious revelation in her life, and conscious maintenance in others by her influence, of all things true and pure, of stainless honour in life, of chivalrous aspirations in the soul. (*Stopford A. Brooke, M.A.*) *Silence of women:* — " Why, Doctor," exclaimed a shallow, talkative lady, who was in the room with Dr. Johnson, but of whom he took little notice, " I believe you prefer the company of men to that of ladies." " Madam," he replied, " I am fond of the company of ladies ; I like their beauty, I like their delicacy, and I like their silence."     **Professing godliness.**—*The profession of godliness:* — Such is the description and character of Christians in early days, such of all true Christians in every day. In no one point of view is the inconsistency of the Christian world more strikingly apparent: they would be thought to embrace the gospel of godliness without an idea of becoming godly. What should we think of a physician who had no interest in the science or practice of medicine? What of a husbandman who disliked and avoided the employments of the field? What of a soldier who declined all discipline and all obedience? But, to say the truth, and to do men justice, such instances in the natural world are extremely rare ; it is only in the spiritual world, only where God, and the soul, and eternity are concerned, that we find men lost in apathy, and acting in contradiction to their pretended faith ; and casting off the consideration of those liabilities and duties upon which they have openly entered. There are men, indeed, who, when charged with such palpable inconsistency, and feeling uneasy under the shame of it, at once deny that they do set up any profession at all ; and make a sort of merit of saying that they do not pretend to any of the distinguished excellencies of the Christian character. But this flimsy pretext of honesty can avail them but little. If they pretend not to what the gospel requires, why pretend to the gospel at all? Nay, it is a melancholy fact that the generality of heathen in our Indian and other foreign possessions manifest a far more abiding sense of their various deities and idols than the generality of Christians do of the true and holy God. They fear the object of their worship, they respect it, they daily remember it. The wicked enemy, who drove man from paradise with a corrupted flesh into a corrupted world, still uses that flesh and that world as instruments of keeping up and increasing our estrangement from God. I have a message to deliver to-day to every soul that is in earnest in the great work of salvation ; not to teach, but to remind you of what the truth really is : be it then understood, be it taken to heart, that godliness is the great good, in the present life, to which Christ came to bring us, as the means of our final recovery and blessedness. (*J. Slade. M.A.*)

**Ver. 13. For Adam was first formed.**—*Man and woman: their relative work :*— As to the question, " Which is the most important, man or woman ? " if I may be allowed to speak in editorial style, I should say, " the discussion must now stop." Let those who like it " sit apart upon a hill retired " and discuss the kindred questions, " which is the most important, convex or concave, night or morning, east or west, green land or glancing water?" For ourselves we are, I hope, content to take Florence Nightingale's advice—"Keep clear of all jargons about man's work and woman's work, and go your way straight to God's work in simplicity and singleness of heart," each one to do what each one can do best. Now, we know that, as a rule, some things that women can do right nobly at a crisis, are not best for them to do when men are to be had. As a rule, I think it is not best for women to man a lifeboat; but one black night at Teignmouth last year, when the men were all out of the way, or else were not sharp enough, the women got the lifeboat out. With shrill, quivering cheers they carried it through the battling breakers, dragged a vessel off the sand-bar, and saved precious life. When we hear that they did all this without any help from the unfair sex, who can help saying, "Well done!" I go farther and say that, as a rule, in my private opinion, it is not best for women to preach in public, but where, in exceptional cases and with extraordinary gifts, women like Mary Fletcher and Priscilla Gurney go out of their way, and all by themselves publicly launch the lifeboat of the gospel to snatch souls from the sea of sin and from the rocks of death, again I say to the praise of grace, "Well done!" They remind me of the Roman who said, "I have broken the law, but I have saved the State!" They are under a higher law than the law they violate, and I am no more able to doubt the validity of their orders than I can doubt the sanity of the New Testament. (*C. Stanford, D.D.*)     *Punishment no hindrance to salvation:*—1. The punishment of the woman—"in child-bearing." 2. The comfort of the woman—"she shall be saved." 3. The condition of the salvation—"if they continue." Wherein is implied an exhortation to continue in faith, &c. Many observations might be raised. 1. The pain in child-bearing is a punishment inflicted upon the woman for the first sin. 2. The continuance of this punishment after redemption by Christ, doth not hinder the salvation of the woman, if there be the gospel-conditions requisite. 3. The exercise of faith, with other Christian graces, is a peculiar means for the preservation of believers under God's afflicting hand. I shall sum them up into this one. The continuance of the punishment inflicted upon the woman for the first sin doth not prejudice her eternal salvation, nor her preservation in child-bearing, where there are the conditions of faith and other graces. I. CONCERNING THE PUNISHMENT. Child-bearing itself is not the punishment, but the pain in it. For the blessing, Increase and multiply, was given in innocency. And because this punishment is the greater, it is disputed in the schools whether Adam's or Eve's sin were the greater. We may, I think, safely make these conclusions. 1. In regard of the kind of sin, it was equal in both. They both had an equal pride, an equal aspiring to be like God. 2. In regard of the first motion to this sin, Eve's sin was the greater. She was the seducer of Adam, which the apostle expresseth in the verse before the text. 3. In regard of the woman's condition, the sin was greater on Adam's part. (1) Because he, being the man, had more power to resist, more strength to argue the case. (2) Eve had a stronger and craftier adversary to deal with, the subtlest of all the beasts of the field (Gen. iii. 1), animated and inspired by a craftier devil. The stronger the tempter, the more excusable the sin. (3) Eve had the command of not eating immediately from her husband, which laid not altogether so strong a tie upon her as it did upon him, who had it immediately from the mouth of God, and therefore was more certain of the verity of the precept. II. OF WHAT NATURE IS THIS PUNISHMENT? 1. It is not a punishment in a rigid sense, nor continued as such. (1) Because it is not commensurate to the nature of the sin, neither is it that penalty which the law required. Death was due, and death immediately upon the offence; but death was kept off by the interposition of the Mediator, and this which is less than death inflicted at present. Where death is deserved, and a lighter punishment inflicted, it is rather an act of clemency than strict justice, and may be called by the name of a partial pardon or reprieve, as well as a punishment. (2) It is not a reparation of the injury done to God. One reason of the institution of punishment is to repair the damage the person offended sustains by the malefactor, as far as he is capable. (3) It is not continued as a part of satisfaction to the justice of God; as though Christ needed the sufferings of the creature to make up the sum which He was to pay for us, and which He hath already paid. These punishments are to awaken men to a sight of their first sin. (4) The proper impulsive cause of punishment is wrath. In inflicting it He preserves the authority of a Judge; in preserving under it, and pardoning the sin for which it was inflicted, He evidenceth the affection of a Father. 2. Yet it is in some sort a punishment, and something more than an affliction. (1) In respect of the meritorious cause, sin. This is not inflicted as an act of absolute sovereignty, but a judicial legal act upon the demerit of sin. (2 Because if man had stood in innocency, neither this grief, nor indeed any other, had been. III. THIS PUNISHMENT DOTH NOT HINDER SALVATION THOUGH IT BE CONTINUED. 1. God intended not in the acceptance of Christ's mediation to remove in this life all the punishments denounced after the Fall. God takes away the eternal, but not the temporal. Some parts of Christ's purchase are only payable in another life, and some fruits of redemption God intends for growth only in another soil; such are freedom from pain, diseases, death, and sin. But the full value of Christ's satisfaction will appear when there shall be a new heaven and a new earth, when the day of redemption shall dawn, and all tears be wiped from believers' eyes. But God never promised the total removal of them in this life to any saint; no, though he should have all the faith and holiness of all the catalogue of saints in the Book of Life centred in him. 2. Christ never intended, in the payment of the price of our redemption, the present removal of them. He sent, after His ascension, the Spirit to be our Comforter, which supposeth a state wherein we should need comfort; and when are we under a greater necessity of comfort than when the punishment of sin is actually inflicted on us? 3. Christ intended, and did actually take away the curse of those punishments from every believer. 4. Hence it will follow that to a believer the very nature of these punishments is altered. In the one the sting remains; in the other it is pulled out. The cord that binds a malefactor and a patient may be made of the same hemp, and a knife only go between; but it binds the malefactor to execution, the other to a cure. 5. Therefore all temporal punishments of original sin, though they remain, do not prejudice a believer's present interest. (1) They cut not off his relation to God. (2) They debar not from the presence of God. God may be and is as near to us in supporting as He is in punishing. (3) They break not the covenant. His rod and His stripes, though they seem to break our backs, make no breaches in His covenant (Psa. lxxxix. 32-34). 6. Add to all this, that the first promise secures a believer under the sufferings of those punishments. God's affection in the promise of bruising the serpent's head was more illustrious in His wrath than the threatening. There are the bowels of a father in the promise before there was the voice of a judge in the sentence. But it may be asked, What is the reason these punishments are continued since the redemption wrought by Christ? There are reasons—(1) On God's part. (a) It is congruous to the wisdom of God to leave them upon us while we are in the world. (b) It is congruous to the holiness of God. God keeps up those punishments as the Rector and Governor of the world, to show His detestation of that sin which brought a disorder and deformity upon the creation, and was the first act of dishonour to God, and the first pollution of the creature. (c) It is a declaration of His justice. (d) It is useful to magnify His love. We should not be sensible of what our Saviour suffered, nor how transcendently He loved us if the punishment of sin had been presently removed upon the first promise. (2) On our parts. It is useful to us— (a) To make us abhor our first defection and sin. (b) To make us fear to sin and to purge it out. Sin hath riveted itself so deep that easy medicines will not displace it. It hath so much of our affections that gentle means will not divorce us from it. We shall hate it most when we reap the punishment of it. (c) To exercise grace. 1. Faith and trust—" She that is desolate trusts in God " (chap. v. 5). The lower the state, the greater necessity and greater obligation to trust; such exercises manifest that the condition we are in is sanctified to us. 2. Obedience in a believer hath a greater lustre by them. It was the glory of Job that he preserved his integrity under the smartest troubles. 3. Humility. These punishments are left upon us to allay our pride, and be our remembrancers of our deplorable miscarriage. 4. Patience. Were there no punishments there would be but little occasion for patience. (*S. Charnock.*)

## CHAPTER III.

VERS. 1-7. **The office of a bishop.**—*The office of a bishop a good work :*—If a man desire the office of a bishop from right principles, he desireth—not a secular

dignity—not a good benefice—not a post of honour or profit—not an easy idle life
—but he desireth a work; a good work indeed it is: but still it is a work. I. It may
properly be called a WORK, if we consider the duties of the office, which require the
utmost assiduity, and some of which are peculiarly painful and laborious. II. It is a
GOOD WORK, whether you consider, for whom, with whom, or for what you work.
The ministers of the gospel work for God, who is carrying on the grand scheme of
salvation in our world. His immediate service is the peculiar business of their
lives. Ministers also work for Jesus Christ. It was He that originally gave them
their commission; it was He that assigned them their work; it is He that is
interested in their success. Again, the ministers of the gospel work for the souls
of men. To do good to mankind is the great purpose of their office. Let us next
consider with whom the ministers of the gospel work; and we shall see how good
their employment is. " They are workers together with God." (2 Cor. vi. 1).
They are also co-workers with Jesus Christ, promoting the same cause for which
He became man; for which He lived the life of a servant, and died the death of a
malefactor and a slave. They may also be called fellow-workers with the Holy
Spirit, whose great office it is to sanctify depraved creatures, and prepare them for
the refined happiness of heaven. They also act in concert with angels; for what
are these glorious creatures but " ministering spirits sent forth to minister to them
that shall be heirs of salvation "? (Heb. i. 14). An angel once condescended to
call a minister of the gospel his fellow-servant (Rev. xix. 10). Ministers also
are engaged in that work in which the apostles went before them. The office
of a bishop will farther appear a good work, if it be considered for what it
is that ministers work. They do not indeed work for a reward upon the
footing of personal merit; but they hope for it on the plan of the gospel, through
Jesus Christ. In this view, like Moses, they have " a respect to the recompense of reward" (Heb. ii. 26). And thus it appears, their laborious and painful
work is good—good in itself, good for the world, and good for themselves.
(*S. Davies, M.A.*)        *The ideal minister:*—The apostle who most boldly maintained
the brotherhood of believers clearly recognized the necessity for order and office in
Christian communities. I. The MORAL CHARACTERISTICS of the ideal pastor are strongly
insisted upon. Strangely enough, nothing is said about his piety, his love to God, his
communion with Him, his delight in Him, his devotion to Him; but this is naturally
presupposed as the basis of the rest. It is not alluded to here, partly because
Timothy did not require to be reminded that personal religion is the first essential
in all spiritual work, and partly because he was less able to judge of inward piety
in others than of the qualities mentioned here. 1. Self-rule is one of the principal of these, and it is to display itself in all directions. The bishop is to be sober,
exercising habitual self-restraint, not only in respect of intoxicating drinks, but also
in respect of indulgence in pleasures of all kinds, setting an example of dominion
over the carnal and sensuous. But temper is to be as much under control as other
passions, for the Christian teacher must be no " brawler," no striker, " but
patient." 2. Again, sound judgment is a qualification much needed by every
pastor and teacher. This is no doubt one reason of Paul's for urging on Timothy,
as he does in the sixth verse, that a pastor in the Church should not be a " novice,"
*i.e.*, a recent convert. If the young life of a plant be exposed to the glare of the
sunshine, death will supervene. And in the life of every creature—insect, and
bird, and beast, and most of all in the life of man—the period of development
must precede the period of manifestation. 3. Another characteristic of the ideal
minister should be open-heartedness and open-handedness. The phrase " given
to hospitality " in Authorized Version, or more correctly "a lover of strangers,"
denotes what was relatively more important then than now. II. THE RELATIONS
OF THE MINISTER TO THOSE AROUND HIM, his right relation with God being
pre-supposed. 1. He is to be the husband of one wife. 2. Then allusion is
made to the pastor's own house as distinguished from God's house. So it
is urged that any leader in the Church should rule well his own house, having
his children in subjection with all gravity. On which Dr. Reynolds has
beautifully said, " The child-life of the pastor's home should suggest the sacredness of a temple and the order of a palace." And is not this true for us all? Is
it not in the home that we are the most tested, and is it not there we can best glorify
God? 3. The relation the pastor should hold towards the world. Much stress is
laid in this passage on being " blameless," and having " a good report of them that
are without "—those, namely, who are outside the kingdom of Christ. We cannot
afford, as Christ's representatives, to defy the world's opinion about us so far as

moral reputation is concerned. The world is a poor judge of doctrine, of motive, and of religious hopes and thoughts; but it is a keen and on the whole an accurate judge of character; and when the members and leaders of the Church are recognized by the world as honest, sincere, trusty, pure men and women, Christ will win the day against His foes. (*A. Rowland, LL.B.*)        *Preference for the ministry :*— A remarkable avowal of the late Senator John A. Logan is reported by a clergyman in a letter to us. He says that in talking with the senator not long before his death, Logan said: "I have often thought that I would like to be in the ministry." I replied: "To have done that, general, you must have surrendered many ambitions." "That," was his noble reply—"that would be nothing. The end will soon come, and these things will then be seen to be worthless." I was convinced of his transparent honesty when he uttered these words, and am of opinion that he simply spoke as he believed and felt. (*Philadelphia Press.*)        *The dignity of the Christian ministry :*—Moreover, if we weigh all things in the balances of justice, we shall see that there is no king, whatever may be the pomp that surrounds him, who as a king is not in dignity below, I will not say a bishop only, but even a simple village pastor, regarded as a pastor. We have only, in order to realize the fact, to cast our eyes on the functions of the pastor and of the king respectively. What do the labours of princes regard? Is it not that evil-doers may be kept down by the vigilance of the law, and that the good may not be disturbed? That is to say, so to act that the persons and property of the citizens of the state shall be in safety? But how much more excellent is the aim of the minister of the gospel, who desires to establish in each individual soul the serenest tranquility by quieting and subduing the lusts of the world! The king's labours are intended to secure that the state shall live at peace with its neighbours; the priest's aim is that every one may be at peace with God, that each may possess peace within, and that no one may have it in his heart to injure another. The prince designs to protect the house, lands, and cattle of particular persons from the violence of depredators. But what does the priest design? To defend the property of the souls entrusted to him, their faith, their charity, their temperance, their purity against the assaults of the devil; property which confers happiness on those who possess it, and the loss of which plunges them into the direst misfortune. . . In one word, all that comes under the management of the prince is earthly and transient; but that which occupies the pastor is divine, celestial, eternal. And, therefore, as much difference as there is between the heaven and the earth, between the body and the soul, between temporal goods and eternal possessions, so much difference is there between the functions committed to the king and the trust devolved on the priest. (*Erasmus.*)        *A well-governed family :*—When there is to be a real order and law in the house, it will come of no hard and boisterous or fretful and termagant way of command. Gentleness will speak the word of firmness, and firmness will be clothed in the airs of true gentleness. How many do we see who fairly rave in authority, and keep the tempest up from morning till night, who never stop to see whether anything they forbid or command is in fact observed! Indeed, they really forget what they have commanded. Their mandates follow so thickly as to crowd one another, and even to successively thrust one another out of remembrance. The result is, that by this cannonading of pop-guns, the successive pellets of commandment are in turn all blown away. If anything is fit to be forbidden or commanded, it is fit to be watched and held in faithful account. On this it is that the real emphasis of authority depends, not on the windstress of the utterance. Let there be only such and so many things commanded as can be faithfully attended to; these in a gentle and firm voice, as if their title to obedience lay in their own merit; and then let the child be held to a perfectly inevitable and faithful account; and by that time it will be seen that order and law have a stress of their own, and a power to rule in their own divine right. The beauty of a well-governed family will be seen in this manner to be a kind of silent, natural-looking power, as if it were a matter only of growth, and could never have been otherwise. (*Horace Bushnell.*)        *Luther and his children :*—Luther used to teach his children to read the Bible in the following way. First, to read through one book carefully, then to study chapter by chapter, and then verse by verse, and lastly word by word, for, he said, "It is like a person shaking a fruit tree. First shaking the tree and gathering up the fruit which falls to the ground, and then shaking each branch and afterwards each twig of the branch, and last of all looking carefully under each leaf to see that no fruit remains. In this way, and in no other, shall we also find the hidden treasures that are in the Bible."

(*J. Stewart.*) *A minister above the love of money :*--A little while ago, in Calcutta, a native, a Christian merchant, was deeply interested in a community of "outcasts," and he made an offer of £60 a-year to any native Christian who would go and live among these people, and teach them the Word of Life. The offer had no sooner been made than a candidate for the office appeared. Who was he? As humble and devoted and consistent a Christian as you ever met. He was a professor in a missionary college, M.A. and LL.B. of the Calcutta University, and drawing a salary of £200 a year. Such was the candidate for this office of £60 a-year! (*Christian Herald.*) *A liberal bishop :*—Bishop Baring's generosity and munificence were unbounded. One instance may be given out of many. He was spending the Sunday with a vicar blessed with very moderate means and a large family. His lordship noticed the pale faces of the children, and said to their mother, "You must take these little ones to the seaside, and their father, too, must have a complete rest. I will provide his duty for six weeks." The good lady wondered where she was to find the wherewithal to carry out this excellent scheme. As the bishop, however, shook hands with her on leaving he put a £50 note into her hand in the kindest way, and solved the difficulty. It is not, however, every one who has such hereditary wealth as the late Bishop of Durham. (*Ibid.*) *Ministers not contentious* (Revised Version) :—How a soft answer can turn away wrath, as well as dissatisfaction, is illustrated in the following anecdote of the late President Wayland. Deacon Moses Pond went to Dr. Wayland once with the complaint that the preaching did not edify him. " I'm sorry," said the pastor; " I know they are poor sermons. I wish I could make them better. Come, let us pray that I may be able to do so." The deacon, telling the story, used to say, " Dr. Wayland prayed and I prayed; he cried and I cried. But I have thought a hundred times that it was strange that he did not turn me out of the house. I tell you there never was a better man nor a greater preacher than Dr. Wayland." (*W. Baxendale.*) **Apt to teach.**—*The pulpit a light and power :*—These three words are but one in the Greek. Ignorance is the inheritance of our fall in Eden. The grand work of the ministry of Christ is to illuminate the darkened mind. There is a fire that does not give light, and a cold phosphorescent flame that yields no heat. Our teaching, while it dispels the darkness of sin, must shed its beams to warm the frozen virtues into life. 1. To meet the claims of a good teacher one must be willing to learn. The apostles, dropping their nets and other worldly craft, went to a school of the prophets, such as never before or since existed on earth. Its sole instructor was the Great Teacher, the Creator of all things. They learned wisdom without a book from the source of all knowledge. 2. If we would be apt to teach, we must have a lesson to impart. 3. To be apt to teach, one must be master of the lesson he would impart. 4. To be apt to teach, a sacred enthusiasm is indispensable. 5. To be apt to teach under the wings of the Eternal Spirit, Holy Dove, we must gather strength and success by prayer. 6. Apt to teach, finally, has the element of faith. (*W. H. Van Doren.*) **Take care of the Church of God.**—*Pastoral care :*—Observe the sacred charge committed to God's appointed bishops, or shepherds, or pastors. I should, first of all, insist that Christ's pastors, who take care of the Church committed to their charge are to take care of their food—that they shall have nothing to eat but what is pure and wholesome. That in the care which God's servants have to take of the Church committed to their charge, they have to nourish three descriptions of character, or three classes of the family specified in Scripture—as babes, young men, and fathers. This care taken of the Church must be with all tenderness, but with all firmness, and under the consciousness of responsibility. It must be with all tenderness. We must be gentle, as the apostle says, " even as a nurse cherisheth her children; and because we were desirous of your welfare, we were ready to impart unto you our own souls, because ye were dear to our souls." But we are not only to use tenderness—" in meekness instructing those that oppose themselves "—towards the lambs, the weaklings, the little ones; but we must use all firmness. Moreover, if we would take care of the Church of God, it must be by keeping our hearts and thoughts fixed on our responsibility. (*J. Irons.*) **Not a novice.**—*Vanity in preachers :*—I. YOUNG PREACHERS ARE ESPECIALLY SUBJECT TO SUCH VANITY. It is the novice that is liable to be " lifted up with pride." 1. The young are naturally disposed to over-rate their abilities. 2. They are peculiarly susceptible to adulation. The more unenlightened and unreflective men are, the more they are given to flattery. II. THE DEVIL'S DESTINY MUST FOLLOW SUCH VANITY. " Fall into the condemnation of the devil." (*The Homilist.*)      *Ministerial pride rebuked :*—An aged Scotch divine had occasionally to avail himself of the assistance of probationers. One day, a young man, very vain of his accomplishments as a preacher, officiated, and on descending from the desk, was met by the old gentleman with extended hands, and expecting high praise, he said, "No compliments, I pray." "Na, na, na, my young friend," said the parson, "nowadays I'm glad o' onybody." *Rowland Hill on ministerial work :*—No man ever had stronger views than Mr. Rowland Hill of the true nature of the ministerial work, and of the necessity of a humble dependence on the Lord's assistance for a blessing in it. One of his remarks was, "If favoured at any time with what is called a good opportunity, I am too apt to find myself saying, 'Well done I,' when I should lie in the dust, and give God all the glory." Another was, "Lord, make me distrustful of myself, that I may confide in Thee alone; self-dependence is the Pharisee's high road to destruction." He was accustomed strongly to urge on all who entered the sacred office the necessity of maintaining Christian and heavenly tempers among their people. "Some folks," he would say, "appear as if they had been bathed in crab verjuice in their infancy, which penetrated through their skins, and has made them sour-blooded ever since; but this will not do for a messenger of the gospel; as he bears a message, so he must manifest a spirit of love." He used to like Dr. Ryland's advice to his young academicians —" Mind, no sermon is of any value, or likely to be useful, which has not the three R's in it—Ruin by the Fall, Redemption by Christ, Regeneration by the Holy Spirit." Of himself he remarked, "My aim in every sermon is a stout and lusty call to sinners, to quicken the saints, and to be made a universal blessing to all." It was a favourite saying with him, "The nearer we live to God, the better we are enabled to serve Him. Oh how I hate my own noise, when I have nothing to make a noise about! Heavenly wisdom creates heavenly utterance." In a letter to Mr. Jones, he observes, "There is something in preaching the gospel, with the Holy Ghost sent down from heaven, I long to get at. At times I think I feel somewhat like it, and then I bawl almost as bad as the Welshman. If we deal with Divine realities, we ought to feel them such, and the people will in general feel with us, and acknowledge the power that does wonders on the earth; while dry, formal, discussional preaching leaves the hearers just where it found them. Still, they who are thus favoured had need to be favoured with a deal of humility. We are too apt to be proud of that which is not our own. Oh humility, humility, humility!" It is no wonder, with such impressions as to the nature of his work, and the state of his mind, that Mr. Rowland Hill's preaching was so honoured and blessed of God. "Lord, help!" was his constant and earnest prayer, and it was heard. (*Scottish Christian Herald.*)      *Humility in ministers :*—The Rev. George Gilfillan, who died in 1877, was not only an author of some distinction, but a wit. A congregation to whom he had been preaching presented him, when a probationer, with a suit of clothes; and after he had put them on, the old ones were tied up in a bundle. "Where shall I send them?" said the tailor. "I will take them myself," said Mr. Gilfillan; "I have carried them too long upon my back to be ashamed of carrying them under my arm." There was no false pride about him. He gave due honour to old friends. (*Christian Herald.*)      *Ministerial pride rebuked :*—The American religious journal, the *Independent*, relates the following story of rebuked vanity, which was told recently in a gathering of ministers, by the Rev. Dr. Gould, of Worcester. "A certain Rev. Samuel Smith had been discoursing very learnedly and loftily, and was now walking home with his brother, eagerly waiting for some word of commendation. Not finding it forthcoming, he dropped a slender oblique hint, to see what could be drawn out. He was somewhat startled and shocked by the outburst: "I tell you, Sam, what it is. Instead of preaching "Jesus Christ and Him crucified," you seem to have been preaching Samuel Smith and him dignified." How necessary it is for preachers of the gospel to hide themselves in the shadow of Christ's Cross, and to forget themselves in the majesty of the message which they deliver! *A minister of good report :*—About thirty years ago the present Bishop of Minnesota went to Chicago, and built a church near the business centre of the city. In those days there were no street cars, and it happened that the reverend gentleman took up his residence in West Chicago, convenient to an omnibus line. It frequently occurred that the omnibus would be crowded, and many obliged to take "deck passage." The writer was riding on the seat with the driver one Saturday night, when the conversation turned upon Sunday labour and the consistency of professed Christians, the driver thinking it rather hard that he should be obliged to labour on Sunday, while others should take their rest. It appeared from his conversation that his faith in Christianity was rather weak; but turning to me he said, with considerable emphasis, "There is one clergyman whom I respect and believe to be a consistent Christian." Being a little curious to know who the clergyman was, and upon what evidence he had based his opinion, I asked him for an explanation. "Well," said he, "there is the Rev. Mr. Whipple, who built that church down town; he has a free pass over this line, but walks down and back on Sundays rather than compromise his Christianity; that proves to me that he is a consistent Christian." It sometimes occurs that a clergyman's most eloquent sermon is being preached when he least expects it; and any private Christian may preach the same kind of sermon. (*Christian Age.*)    *The causes and remedies of pride:*—You can hardly fail to perceive that this reasoning of St. Paul's proceeds on the supposition that they who know but little are most in danger of pride. It is just because man is a novice that he is likely to be lifted up. Is it not a confessed and well-known fact that the arrogant and conceited person is ordinarily the superficial and the ignorant? You will hardly ever find the man of real power and great acquirement other than a simple and unaffected man. It would scarcely ever lead you to a false estimate of persons, were you to take it as a rule, that where there is the manifestation of conceit, there is shallowness of intellect. And why is this, but because he who knows most is most conscious how little he knows? Can he be vain of his mental power who, having applied it to the investigation of truth, has discovered little more than that truth would exhaust power a thousand-fold greater? Can he be proud of his scientific progress who, having laboured long and hard, finds himself only a beginner, so vast are the spreadings which lie dimly beyond? Oh! it is not, and it never will be, the man of experience who shows himself haughty and conceited. We have thus taken the case generally of a novice in knowledge, as it helps to place under a clearer point of view the gist of St. Paul's argument—namely, that ignorance is the great parent of pride. But we will now confine ourselves to such particular branches of life as must have been referred to by the apostle, when he penned the direction for the exclusion of a novice; and forasmuch as it is the novice in Christian doctrine of which he speaks, we shall perhaps thoroughly compass his argument if we give our attention to knowledge of ourselves, in the two grand respects of our state by nature and our state by grace. Of all knowledge there is confessedly none which is either more valuable in itself, or more difficult of attainment, than self-knowledge; none more valuable, for a man has an immeasurably greater interest or deeper stake in himself than in the whole surrounding universe; none more difficult of attainment, for we have it on the authority of the Bible itself, that none but a Divine Being can search the human heart. And if we were not able to show of all knowledge whatsoever that it is a corrective of pride, or at least reads such lessons to each, as to his incompetence and insignificance, as leaves him inexcusable if he be not humble, we should have no difficulty in doing this in regard to self-knowledge. Let it be, if you will, that the study of stars in their courses might tend to give a man high thoughts of himself; for, indeed, till you look closely into the matter, there is something ennobling—something that seems to excuse, if not to form, a lofty estimate of power—when, with daring tread, the astronomer pursues the heavenly bodies into untravelled regions, tracking their wanderings and counting their revolutions; but in regard, at all events, of self-knowledge, there can be no difficulty in showing to any one who will hearken that pride can subsist only where this knowledge is deficient. If we consider man in his natural condition, how could any one be proud who thoroughly knew that condition? Self-knowledge—knowledge of the body—as appointed to all the disorders of the grave, would be the most effectual corrective to the self-complacency, of which beauty is the food. Who, again, could be proud of rank, puffed up because of some petty elevation above his fellow-men, who was deeply aware of his own position as an accountable creature? Who, once more, could be proud of his intellectual strength, of his wit, his wisdom, his elocution, who knew the height from which he had fallen—and saw in himself but the fragments—we had almost said the rubbish—of what God designed and created him to be? Indeed, you have here in the general the grand corrective to pride. Men have but to know themselves as fallen and depraved creatures, and we might almost venture to say that they could not be proud. But we have spoken of self-knowledge as though it were knowledge of man in regard only of his natural condition. We must, however, consider him as a redeemed being, and not merely as a fallen; for possibly, though knowledge of him in his ruined state be the corrective of pride, it may not be the same with knowledge of him in his restored state. Yes, a slight knowledge of the gospel, so far from generating humility, may even tend to the fostering pride. There is such an opposition between man ruined and man redeemed, if in the one state he may be exhibited as loathsome and worthless, in the other he may be thought of some such importance as ransomed by Christ whilst angels were left to perish, that it is hard to avoid on first hearing of the gospel, feeling that, after all, our degradation must have been exaggerated and our insignificance overdrawn. Thus the novice is once more in danger of being lifted up with pride. As the novice in that knowledge which has to do with man fallen, so the novice in that knowledge which has to do with man redeemed, is liable, through his knowing but little, to the thinking more highly of himself than he ought. And will not the danger diminish as the gospel is more thoroughly studied and understood? Yes, indeed; for what were it but the worst libel on the system of Christianity to suppose it not adapted to the producing humility? And if to this argument for humility, which is interwoven with the whole texture of the gospel, you add the constant denunciations of that gospel against pride—its solemn demands of lowliness of mind as essential to all who would inherit the kingdom of God—you will readily see that the further a man goes in acquaintance with the gospel, the more motives will he have to the abasing himself before God. Redemption as a scheme of wonders into which the very angels desire to look, may kindle in him a dream of his importance; but redemption as emanating from free grace, will convict him of his nothingness; and redemption as requiring from him the mind which was also in Christ, will cover him with confusion. And thus we reach the same conclusion, when we examine self-knowledge in regard to our condition as redeemed, as we reach when we examine it in regard of our condition as fallen. It is the novice who is in most danger of pride; it is his being a novice which exposes him to danger. (*H. Melvill, B.D.*)

Vers. 8–13. **Likewise must the deacons be grave.** — *The ideal deacon:*—I. Deacons should be of noble character (ver. 8). 1. They were to be grave— *i.e.*, of serious deportment—not sharing in the follies and gaieties of pleasure-loving cities like Ephesus, but revered as men living in a higher and purer atmosphere. 2. Not double-tongued, saying one thing to this man and another to that, and thus giving rise to misunderstandings and differences. Gossip is sometimes as harmful as slander. 3. Not given to much wine. Such temperance should be a characteristic of any true Christian, and is absolutely essential to one who would lead and represent the Church. 4. Not greedy of filthy lucre, or "base gain." II. Deacons should be strong in the faith (ver. 9). "Holding the mystery of the faith in a pure conscience." III. Deacons should be trusted by the Church (ver. 10). "Let these also first be proved," for their qualifications ought to be evidenced and recognized, in order that they may have the confidence of their brethren. IV. Deacons may look for the recompense of reward (ver. 13). The phrase "purchase to themselves a good degree," or, as in Revised Version, "gain to themselves a good standing," includes the idea of obtaining high reputation amongst the brethren; and that is not without its value. But it implies, also, advance in faith, in courage, and in wisdom, as the result of active and faithful service. And this is the preparation for, and the pledge of the honour which will be given in, the last great day—honour which will vary among the saints according to the measure of their capacity and fidelity. (*A. Rowland, LL.B.*) *Double tongued:*—During the civil war in America, three Northern officers were appointed on a commission with three Southern officers, after the battle of Prairie Grove, to negotiate an exchange of prisoners. While the commission was sitting, an aged farmer strayed into the room, thinking it was the provost's office. His eyes were dim, but he quickly noticed the uniforms, and supposing himself in the presence of the Northern staff, began protesting his loyalty to the Union. One of the officers facetiously advised him to be cautious, and, pointing to the Southern officers, told him to look at them. The old man put on his spectacles, and recognizing the uniform, explained that his heart was with the South in the great struggle, and that his only son was a soldier in the Southern army. Gazing around the room, he recognized the Northern uniforms also, and was bewildered. At last he leaned both hands on the table, and surveying the entire party, he said, "Well, gentlemen, this is a little mixed; but you just go on and fight it out among yourselves. I can live under any government." (*Christian Herald.*) *An equivocal life to be avoided:*—Some time ago two travellers went to Africa. Coming to a lake, one sought to find whither the current tended by throwing a float on its surface; and slowly, but surely, it floated eastward. "The current is eastward," said the traveller, satisfied with his discovery. Some time afterwards another traveller stood by the same lake, asking himself the same question, "Whither does the current tend?" He, too, cast a float upon the surface of the water, which at once floated westward. "The current is towards the west," he said; and, following out his discovery, he gained its out-let, and so traced it to where it emptied itself into the Atlantic Ocean. Let us see to it that our life is not uncertain, like this lake, at one time seeming to be going heavenward, and at another seeming to be going with the world. But rather may we, who bear the name of Jesus, let our lives run like a quiet and steady stream, and, as we go, leave a bright record of our lives behind us. (*Ibid.*) **Holding the mystery of the faith.**—*Accepting mysteries of the faith :*—I can drink of the clear cold spring, and be refreshed, though I may not hope to pierce the awful foundation of granite from whence it comes rushing up. I can take of the grain of the tawny sheaves, or of the laden vine, though I cannot tell how the unconscious root and fibres select, elect—never mistaking—out of a common soil that which shall produce their specific fruit. I can rejoice in the shining sun, and fan my cheek with the breathing wind, though I am ignorant as an infant of the great palace of light, and "know not when the wind cometh, nor whither it goeth." Even so ; I stoop my parched lips to the "living water," and I rise revived; and I know not man nor woman who ever sought to do so and was hindered. I am content with that. (*A. B. Grosart.*) *The mystery of the faith :*—I. Now there is a prevailing error to which we are exposed in the present day, of NOT SUFFICIENTLY RECOGNIZING IN REVEALED TRUTH MYSTERIES WHICH LIE BEYOND THE REACH OF HUMAN COMPREHENSION. By far the greater portion of the doctrines which compose the scheme of Christianity are mysteries which pass man's understanding. Such, for example, is the doctrine of the Trinity in Unity. Here, however, let me observe that although a mystery, it is a mystery of faith. It is not a revelation of which the mystery affords any excuse for unbelief. It is a mystery, I confess, upon God's part, of incomprehensible wisdom, power, and love; but yet it is a mystery upon which we may rely with the fullest assurance. It is the more important to observe this, because there are many minds before which the mysteries of Divine truth present themselves as an apology for unbelief. The facts of Christianity, and the doctrines which flow out of them, are amply attested. There is a marvellous self-evidencing property in the Gospel. Crowded though it be with mysteries, it is so constructed as to bespeak its suitableness to the moral necessities of the fallen. We appeal, then, not only to the evidence upon which the truth of the gospel rests, as contained in God's Word, but also to the results which have attended its proclamation, in corroboration of its claim, mystery though it be, to implicit faith. It is this mystery which has conferred upon mankind ten thousand blessings for time, the pledges and foretokens of yet richer blessings in eternity. II. But here the practical question arises, WHAT IS IT TO "HOLD THE MYSTERY OF THE FAITH IN A PURE CONSCIENCE" ; or, in other words, to what course of action are we summoned by the direction which the apostle here gives? Now, a pure conscience is "a conscience void of offence towards God and towards man." It is a conscience enlightened by the Holy Ghost, and free from accusation, whether on the ground of duty omitted or of precept infringed. To hold the mystery of the faith in a pure conscience, is therefore to be so under the influence of revealed truth as to be thereby impelled to practise all that God has enjoined, and to avoid whatsoever God has forbidden. Now, for nothing is the Bible more remarkable than for the practical nature of all its disclosures. There is not a doctrine of revealed truth which is not both designed and adapted to influence the daily life and conversation ; and never can the truth be held in a pure conscience but where the creed which is professed is exemplified in the conduct. Take, for example, any of the elementary truths of revelation, and you may discern at once their practical character. There is the revealed truth of the omnipresence of God, a truth which no man can hold the mystery of the faith and yet deny. According to this doctrine, we believe that God is everywhere and at all times present. Never can we escape from His observation—never elude His watchful inspection. This is a part of the mystery of the faith. And so with regard to every component part of the mystery of the faith. To hold it in a pure conscience is to allow every Christian doctrine to have its legitimate influence over the entire walk and conversation. This, then, it is to "hold the mystery of the faith in a pure conscience." It is to make every revealed doctrine a fresh motive for striving after moral perfection. Alas! there may be a "holding the mystery of the faith," but not "in a pure conscience." There may be familiarity with Christian truth, ortho-doxy of creed, clearness in the enunciation of the Gospel mysteries, zeal in the maintenance of the truth, and skill in contending against error, where, nevertheless, we look in vain for a correspondence between the profession of the lip and the language of the daily life. The mystery of the faith is held; it is expounded, professed, defended, and yet it is not held in a pure conscience. Its influence is counteracted by a life not regulated by the principles confessed. (*Bp. Bickersteth.*)

Ver. 11. **Even so must their wives be grave.**—*The pastor's wife :*—A good example is the pastor's first ministry, and Paul associates the wife in this ministry, when he wishes the wives to be " grave, not slanderers, sober, faithful in all things." This has been felt to be so important that in certain churches, those of Hungary, the minister has been made positively responsible for the conduct of his wife. He is everywhere so morally, and the responsibility is a grave one, the ministry may suffer considerably if it is not regarded. How much may the humours and vices of the wife (slander, avarice, negligence, display, &c.), compromise the respectability of the pastor? And conversely : Julian the apostate, observing that one cause of the success of the gospel was the purity in the manners of its followers, and especially its ministers, and wishing to enable paganism to compete with Christianity, ordered the pagan priests to maintain their wives, children, and domestics in the same sanctity of manners. (*Vinet.*)     *Talebearing discouraged :*—Hannah More had a good way of managing tale-bearers. It is said that whenever she was told anything derogatory of another, her invariable reply was, " Come, we will go and ask if this is true." The effect was sometimes ludicrously painful. The tale-bearer was taken aback, stammered out a qualification, or begged that no notice might be taken of the statement. But the good lady was inexorable ; off she took the scandalmonger to the scandalised, to make inquiry and compare accounts. It is not very likely that anybody ever a second time ventured to repeat a gossipy story to Hannah More. Milton being asked if he intended to teach his daughters languages, replied, " No, one tongue is enough for a woman ! " (*E. J. Hardy, M.A.*)

Ver. 12. **Husband of one wife.**—*A negligent father :*—I was once the guest, says Mr. Moody, of a Christian man, whose children were turning out badly. One night a conversation took place about them; and with tears trickling down his cheek he said, " My four eldest sons turned out badly, and I am afraid that the others are following their example." I said : " Let us look into this thing. Tell me about your family. How many nights do you go to church? " " On Sunday night. I am an officer in the church, and I am there on Sunday night." " What about Monday ? " " Oh, I am a deacon, and I am at the church on Monday night." " What about Tuesday night? " " I am connected with the city goverment, and I have to attend committee-meetings of the council." " Wednesday night is prayer-meeting, and you go to church? " " Yes." " That is how you are occupied four nights. What do you do the other three? " " I belong to the Masons. I hold a high office in the lodge, and have to be there." " That accounts for five nights. Of course, as you hold a high social position, you are often out at dinner-parties and committees. You go out perhaps one night each week to dinners and committees." " It will average all that." " Then," I said, " there is one more night, that is, Saturday night; what do you do then? " " Oh, I am superintendent of the Sabbath school, and I lock myself in my room and prepare the lesson for my Bible-class on the following day." " You don't let your children into your room then, do you ? " " No ; certainly not." " Then your children have to get off early in the morning, and they are away from family prayer? " " Yes ; some get off early, and others rise late, and they are not present at morning worship." " And you have to get away as early as possible to your business." " Yes ; as soon as I get through worship I am off." " What time do you take dinner? " " At six o'clock." " You see your children at six. But you are not always prompt. I suppose half-past six, is it not? " " Yes, that is about the average." " And your meetings begin about half-past seven ; so that you have but little time with your children. What have you done for them? " And at that very time he was trying to be made mayor of the city. He dropped his head, and said that he had never thought of it in that light before. There are many just like that. They are giving their time to public affairs, to the utter neglect of their children and their homes.     *Evils of polygamy :*— Titus, brother of Africaner, was the only individual on the station who had two wives, and fearing the influence of example, I have occasionally made a delicate reference to the subject and by degrees could make more direct remarks on the point which was one of the barriers to his happiness; but he remained firm, admitting, at the same time, that a man with two wives was not to be envied, and added, " He is often in an uproar, and when they quarrel he does not know whose part to take." He said, he often resolved when there was a great disturbance, he would pay one off. One morning I thought the anticipated day had come. He approached my door leading an ox upon which one of his wives was seated. " What is the matter ? " I inquired. Giving me a shake of his hand, and laughing, he replied, " Just the old thing over again. Mynheer must not laugh too much at me, for I am now in for it." The two wives had quarrelled at the outpost, and the one in a rage had thrown a dry rotten stick at the other, which had entered the palm of her hand, and had left a piece about an inch long, and the thickness of a finger. The hand had swollen to nearly four times its usual size. " Why " I asked, " did you not bring her sooner ? " " She was afraid to see you, and would not come till I assured her that you were a *maak mensche* " (a tame man). Having made an incision and extracted the piece of wood, she was melted into tears with gratitude, while I earnestly exhorted her to a better way of life. (*Dr. Moffatt.*) **Purchase to themselves a good degree.**—*The good degree :* — The words refer, in the first place, to a faithful discharge of the duties attached to the office of the deacon. They that have " used the office of a deacon well " are they who have laboured in the diaconate with honour to themselves and glory to their Master; for " well " is the same word used in the latter part of the verse, and translated good—a good degree. It is the specific term for the beautiful in human action, in contrast to the grudging discharge of mere obligation. It implies in the labourer not only diligence and zeal, but also carefulness and purity of motive; and the best use of every power and opportunity that God has entrusted to us—the frank, loving, self-abandoning, self-forgetting discharge of a holy obligation. Such an idea cannot be confined to any special office, and it is not, therefore, the particular work done which is thrown into the front, but the grace shown in the mode of doing it—the beautiful discharge of duty for God, in whatever sphere of the Church it may be, and whatever the exact nature of the duty which is done. But, further, the words furnish a stimulating motive to this earnest discharge of duty, by setting before the soul's desire a certain advantage that is to be secured by it. Here we must carefully put away the idea of buying—that is, of meriting in any way, as if we bargained with God. It has been thought that the word " degree " refers to ecclesiastical position and church office ; but such a meaning would be an appeal to professional selfishness, and would be utterly out of harmony both with the spirit of St. Paul, and with the meaning of his language. We must look much deeper to find the mind of God. A good degree is a degree full of honour, praise, and joy, and such as the soul may covet with all the force of a renewed and sanctified affection. In what consists the good degree, which results from the honourable discharge of duty ? I. IT CONSISTS IN A HIGHER STATE OF SPIRITUAL LIFE, A STRONGER FAITH, A BRIGHTER HOPE, A MORE ENTRANCING AND CAPTIVATING LOVE ; IN SHORT, A LARGER POSSESSION OF GOD, as if the Deity within flung His own grace and glory over the soul in which He dwells. Grace is but the soul's health, the restoration of a sin-stricken creature into the full enjoyment for which it was intended. A large measure of grace is, therefore, a high measure of health—and is not health delightful ? Is there pleasure in the aching head, in the weary limb, in the scorching fever, or the racking pain, or the feebleness and languor and strange incapacities of sickness and disease ? But must not the same thing be true of the soul ? Doubts, fears, alarms, conflicts, strange searchings of heart, dim gropings of spirit, and occasional agonies of conscience, and the gnawing aching pain of a self-upbraiding memory, are all the symptoms of spiritual sickness. That the honourable discharge of every duty promotes the health of the soul is clear enough. The more constantly duty is done, the more constantly faith and hope and love are present ; and then they grow by exercise till they become the soul's habit, its very life, the breath of its being, a part of the living self in the all-pervading presence and power of God. That this high measure of spiritual life is the good degree of the text, is shown by the last words, " great boldness in the faith." The literal meaning of the word translated " boldness " is freedom, frankness, and confidence of speech. It has two relations. One looks toward man when the soul, rich in its own love for Christ, and actually overflowing with joy in the Holy Ghost, pours out to others the fulness of its own affection—not with an effort, but freshly, naturally, spontaneously, as the living spring within the soul itself, the power of the Holy Spirit of God flows forth into utterance. Such a boldness of speech to others about their souls implies a glow and warmth of emotion, a strength of experience, and a power of love such as might fill the soul of an angel. Then there is another meaning of the word. It is used elsewhere for boldness of access to God. II. But a good degree includes a further idea, and THAT IS A HIGHER STATE IN GLORY, a place nearer God in the world to come, a more perfect knowledge of Him, and a more entrancing enjoyment of Him for ever and ever. This, we must bear in mind, springs from the other, and is but its completion. God is infinite. His gifts will be boundless as Himself; His gifts of knowledge, of holiness, of strength, of joy and rapture, will be infinite. There is in God no limit whatever. If for all eternity we shall enjoy more and more of God, it will be because the power to enjoy grows by enjoyment as the soul becomes larger and larger with the God who fills it. Grace here increases the capacity for glory hereafter. The more grace, the more glory. (*E. Garbett, M.A.*) *Faithfulness in an inferior position leads to a higher :*—Dr. Morrison wrote to his friends in England and asked them to send him out another missionary. A young man from the country came and offered himself. He came to the office of the Missionary Society and was introduced to the gentlemen of the board and had a long talk with them. They then asked him to call again in an hour or two, and they would give him an answer. In talking the matter over after he was gone, they came to the conclusion that this young man would not do to go as the colleague of Dr. Morrison. Finally, they said to Dr. Phillips, one of their members : " Doctor, you see the young man and tell him that we do not think him fit to be a missionary; but that if he would like to go out as servant to the missionary we will send him." The doctor did not like much to do this; but he did it. He told the young man just what the board said. Now, many a young man would have been angry on hearing this, and would have said : " No, I shall do no such thing. If I can't go out as a missionary, I won't go at all." But this young man did not feel or act so. After hearing what the doctor said, his answer was : " Well, sir, if the gentlemen don't think me fit to be a missionary I will go as a servant. I am willing to be a hewer of wood, or a drawer of water, or do anything to help on the cause of my heavenly Master." He was sent out as a servant, but he soon got to be a missionary, and turned out to be the Rev. Dr. Milne, one of the best and greatest missionaries that ever went to any country. (*R. Newton, D.D.*)

Ver. 15. **That thou mightest know how thou oughtest to behave thyself in the house of God.**—*What the Church should be :*—I. THE GLORIOUS NAME OF THE CHURCH— "The Church of the living God." 1. It is called the Church. What is a church? It is an assembly; and a Christian Church is an assembly of faithful men ; of men who know the truth, believe it, avow it, and adhere to it. The Greek word signifies an assembly summoned out of the whole population to exercise the right of citizenship. An ecclesia, or Church, is not a mob, nor a disorderly gathering rushing together without end or purpose, but a regular assembly of persons called out by grace, and gathered together by the Holy Spirit. Those persons make up the assembly of the living God. 2. But the title grows upon us when we read it as " the Church of God." There is a synagogue of Satan, and there is a Church of God. There are churches so-called which are not of God, though they take upon themselves His name ; but what an honour it is to be one of the assembly of God, to be one of those whom God has chosen, whom God has called, whom God has quickened, whom God has sanctified, whom God loves and calls His own ! How honoured is that assembly in which He resides ! The title is enhanced in its excellency by the word which it is applied to God. 3. It is " the Church of the living God," not thy congregation, O Diana, though they said of thee that thou didst fall from heaven, for thou art a lifeless image ! What was Diana of the Ephesians ? What life or power was in that senseless block ? Timothy knew that the assembly which gathered in the name of Diana was not called out by a living god. It is a glorious fact that our God, the God of the Church, liveth and reigneth, and that He shows His life all around us. We see Him sustaining nature, ruling providence, and reigning in the midst of His Church ; and while we see Him we adore Him. If you have never been quickened by the Spirit of God, if you are dead in trespasses and sins, what have you to do with the Church of the living God? Oh ye dead and corrupt, how can ye have communion with the living in Zion. II. HER DESIGN IN REFERENCE TO GOD. The apostle speaks of the Church of the living God as the house of God. 1. I suppose we are to understand by the Church being God's house, that it is the place of His worship. As of old the Temple was the holy place to which the children of Israel went up in pilgrimage, the point towards which they opened their windows when they prayed, and the place of the one altar and the one sacrifice; so now the Church of God is the sole place of God's true worship. He is spiritually worshipped nowhere else. Do not dream, ye ungodly, that ye can worship the living God. The first essential to your acceptance is that ye accept His salvation. 2. But I like better still to get away from the somewhat ceremonious idea of a temple to the more familiar thought of a house or home. The Lord makes the Church the place of His indwelling. The thought itself is charming. It is that old prophecy fulfilled, "I will dwell in them and walk in them." God calls His Church a house in the sense of His residing there. Of the Church we read, "God is in the midst of her, she shall not be moved." 3. In his own house a man not only dwells, for he might do that in any inn; but there he feels himself to be at home, and therefore it is the place of his manifestation. You do not see the man on the bench, for there you see the judge; nor on business, for there you see the trader; but at home, with the children, as one of them, you see the man, the father, the husband; you see his heart and soul. And God is not seen in all the universe with anything like the degree of clearness that He is beheld in the midst of His people. The Lord God is more gloriously manifested in His people than in all the works of creation. 4. A man's house is also the place of his paternal rule. In the Church we are under the present rule of our heavenly Father. In the Church of God you will sometimes see this very remarkably. 5. Once again, it is for his own house that a man works and spends his strength; it is the object of his choicest purposes. If a man shall compass sea and land to gain gold, it is for his house. If he rise up early and sit up late and eat the bread of carefulness, it is still for his house. And so the great Householder ruleth all things for His chosen family, and the end and the design of all providence, if we were to trace it to its ultimate object, is the good of them that love God, and are the called according to His purpose. We will not leave this point without observing how holy, then, should all members of Christian Churches be! "Holiness becometh thine house." How obedient also should we be; for if we are a part of the house of God, let it be our joy to submit ourselves to the Master. How struck with awe ought every church member to be to think that he is built into God's house. "How dreadful is this place! It is none other than the house of God." At the same time, how full of love ought we to be, for God is love! A house is no home if love be absent, and a Church is unchurchly if there be division among the brethren. III. THE DESIGN OF THE CHURCH IN REFERENCE TO THE TRUTH. Paul compares it to a pillar and its pedestal or basement; for that, I think, would be a fair translation. The temple of Diana, at Ephesus, was adorned with more than a hundred columns of stupendous size. They were mostly of Parian marble, and were either furnished by the various cities of Asia as offerings to the goddess, or were contributed by wealthy men and princes. These pillars are said to have been immense monoliths: single stones of sixty feet in height, and they were set upon a basement which was elevated ten steps above the surrounding area. Diana had her pillar and her basement, but she had no pillar or basement of truth, hers was all imposture throughout. Now, Paul calls the Church of God the basement and pillar of the truth. What does he mean? Notice, that she is not the creator of the truth, nor the inventor and fashioner of doctrine. Let it be remembered also, that the figure must not be pushed beyond what it was meant to teach. In a certain sense the Church cannot be the pillar and ground of the truth. Truth is true of itself, and owes its origin to God Himself and the nature of things. The Church is not here described as the deepest foundation of the truth, for the basement of the pillar of truth rests on a rock, and the Church rests on God, the Rock of ages. But truth in itself is one thing, as truth as existing in the world is another thing. I daresay the proverb is true, but truth never prevails till some living mind believes it, vindicates it, and proclaims it abroad. The person who thus takes up a grand truth, declares it, fights for it, and makes it known, may be very properly called the pillar and the basis of the cause; for the spread of the principle depends upon him. We may say of the Reformation, Luther was its pillar and basement; or of Methodism the same might be said of Wesley. Note how in another place Paul says that James and Cephas and John seemed to be pillars; that is to say, they were upholders of the good cause. Notice that the text speaks of "the Church of God," meaning all the people of God, and not the clergy alone. What does the expression mean—the pillar and basement? 1. I think it means, that in the Church the truth should abide. In the Church of the living God it always does abide, even as a pillar stirs not from its place. In the confession of the Church made by each one of her members, in the teaching of her ministers, and in the witness of the whole body, truth will be found at all times. The Church of God is not the quicksand of the truth, but the pillar and pedestal of it : she is not the floating island of the truth, but the eternal column of it. 2. It means that in the true Church the truth is uplifted as upon a pillar. Truth not only rests there as a pedestal, but it stands upright as a pillar. It is the duty and the privilege of the Church of God to exalt the truth into the open view of all mankind. Possibly you may have seen the column of Trajan, or the column in the Place Vendôme in Paris ; these may serve as illustrations. Around these shafts you see the victories of the conqueror pictured in relief, and lifted into the air, that all may see them. Now, the Church of God is a pillar which lifts up and publishes, far and wide, the achievements of our conquering Lord. 3. Again, a Church is intended by God to set forth the truth with beauty ; for in a temple pillars and columns are meant for ornaments as well as for service. God's service should be formed in the beauty of holiness. 4. Once more, it is the Church's business to maintain the truth with all her might. She is set as a brazen wall and an iron pillar against all error. The truths which may be derived from the text are of one order. 1. The whole Church is to maintain the truth. 2. Next, remember that a Church is unchurched which is not faithful to the truth. 3. Next, recollect that any Church fails in her design as being the pillar and pedestal of the truth in proportion as she departs from the truth. (*C. H. Spurgeon.*) *Proper behaviour in God's house :*—It was no vain superstition which prompted old Dr. Johnson to uncover his head, while standing within the deserted walls of a ruined chapel, in the Orkneys, saying to his less devout companion, "I look with reverence upon every place that has been set apart for religion." The crying sin of our own day is the sin of irreverence. The only occasion when our blessed Lord is said to have been angry, was when He saw His Father's house profaned. Many years ago, a worthy minister of the Scottish Kirk, attended a missionary meeting in London, and spent a Sunday there. A journey from Scotland to the great city was then not so common an occurrence as to pass without notice, and, on appearing in his own pulpit again, he wished to "improve" the occasion for the spiritual benefit of his flock. He accordingly remarked, in the course of his morning sermon, "I have three wonders to tell you of to-day, which I saw when in London," and then went on in his usual vein of preaching, without the slightest reference to his promise. On leaving the place of worship, many inquiring looks were cast at the worthy man, as much as to say, "You have forgotten to tell us the three wonders!" At the afternoon service the building was crowded to overflowing, curiosity (as usual) bringing out more people than a sense of duty. After concluding the accustomed worship, the venerable preacher remarked, "Well, my friends, I have now to tell you of the three wonders I saw in London." Amidst breathless silence, he thus went on : "The first wonder I have to tell which I saw in London is, when I took my place in the pulpit, the folks were all waiting for me, and I had no occasion to wait for them ; and I never saw the like of that here. The second wonder which I saw in London is, that as the prayer was drawing to a close, there was no jostling and making a noise ; and I never saw the like of that here. The third wonder is, that there was no reaching for hats, and bundling up of Bibles, when the last psalm was a-singing, and no going out while the blessing was being pronounced ; and I never saw that here, till this afternoon." Church manners have certainly improved very much, everywhere, since then, but the day has not yet dawned when most congregations would not be the better for hearing this simple story. We have come to this place to worship God, and we may properly ask ourselves whether we have really been doing what we came for? Have we borne our part in the solemn service with heart and voice ? The responsive part of our beautiful worship is one of its most striking and important features. There is something so animating in the hearty acclaim of a multitude of voices, that every tongue should be unloosed, and every heart give utterance to its gratitude and joy. "What would be thought if but a single bird should celebrate the dawn with his feeble note ? It is when the air is filled with melodious voices, and, when from every bush and tree-top, and through all the fields and groves, there is the cheerful commingling of tuneful praise, that the responses of the birds are worthy of the morning. And, surely, the service of the temple calls for a spontaneous utterance from all the worshippers. Who that has listened to the waves, as they come breaking upon the shore in distant, strong and stately rhythm, has not felt their power ? And there is nothing like this massing of sound to be moving and inspiring. There are times when the still small voice shall suffice; but, for the ends of public worship, even the inanimate world bespeaks something more " (John Cotton Smith). We are learning to behave ourselves properly in God's holy temple, here, that we may enjoy the worship of the heavenly sanctuary hereafter. The things which we now behold are but shadows of the true and the enduring. (*J. H. Norton.*) *The Church the house of God:*—I. Here is THE CHURCH OF GOD. In common discourse, we generally mean by this word a building set apart by Christian people for public worship; but it is doubtful whether the Greek term which we translate " church," is ever used in Scripture in this sense. The original word signifies an assembly, an assembly of any kind; and it is frequently so translated in our English Testament. But we must follow the word yet farther. It is often used to signify all the churches that are in existence at the same time on the earth. And even yet we have not done. There is one meaning more which the expression bears, and the highest of all. It has nothing to do now, however, with the merely nominal Christian; it takes now a purely spiritual though a wide sense. By the Church, then, as we are using the word to-day, we mean all the people of God of every age and nation viewed as one assembly. This we are now to look on in a particular light. II. It is A HOUSE. 1. It has a foundation. And it is one part of vital godliness, and the main part, to understand this. It is not self-evident. Men do not see the foundation of a building. The child that comes into this house of prayer never thinks of the buried work which bears up its walls. Set him to build a mimic church in imitation of it; he lays no foundation whatever. But the architect, the practical workman, begins with the foundation. He cannot overlook it, for he understands its importance. So the mere pretender to godliness thinks that the Church has little to do with the Lord Jesus, but to bear His name. He imagines that he himself can do without Him. 2. The materials, too, of this house are found mentioned in Scripture. They are, however, the very last we should have thought likely to build it. We come, then, to this conclusion—no meanness, no guilt, will cause God to reject any one of us. But though all alike earthly and all vile, yet these materials, in some points, differ very much from each other. We see among them men of all countries, all classes, all characters, all ages; here a poor man, there a rich and noble one; here a man of the loftiest intellect. One thing more, however, must be said of these materials—in all this diversified mass there is nothing to be found which is not prepared for the heavenly building before it goes to it. True, God does choose in His wonderful mercy earthly and base materials wherewith to build His house; there could not be baser; but He does not leave them base, no, nor yet earthly. He works on them. Though He does not find them fit for heaven, he makes them so. 3. But materials, however selected and prepared, will not of themselves form a building, no, not even if cast on a good foundation. There must be, further, a putting of them together. They must be sorted and arranged and united; each one must go into its proper place; otherwise they will be a confused heap, not a house. Now, there is a great overlooking of this fact amongst us, as applied to the Church. We almost forget that God has a Church. We feel as though we stood alone before Him, and were to be saved alone. III. We have now looked at the Church as a house, but the text goes farther; it calls it THE HOUSE OF GOD. 1. He is the Builder of this house. The plan of it is His, and so is the progress and completion. 2. He is also the Owner of this house. He is building it for Himself. " This people," He says, " have I formed for Myself." 3. And He, too, is the great Inhabitant of this house. It is built for this very purpose, to be " a habitation of God through the Spirit." " Behold," says St. John, when speaking of it as the new Jerusalem, " Behold, the tabernacle of God is with men." (*C. Bradley, M.A.*) *In the house of God:*—1. Thou oughtest to behave thyself quietly. 2. Thou oughtest to behave thyself attentively. 3. Thou oughtest to behave thyself seriously. (*P. Carter.*) *The house of God:*—I. THE HOUSE OF GOD IS THE DWELLING-PLACE OF GOD. II. THE HOUSE OF GOD SHOULD BE THE ABODE OF LOVE. The Church is not only the place where the Father dwells, but where His sons and daughters live in mutual confidence under the sway of supreme love to Him. It is this loving confidence which is the essence of a home. A splendid house with luxurious appointments is not a real home if love is not in it. III. THE HOUSE OF GOD SHOULD BE THE SPHERE OF SERVICE. The Church is our Lord's instrument of working. IV. THE HOUSE OF GOD IS TO BE THE MAINTAINER OF GOD'S TRUTH. There seems to be little doubt that Paul meant what the grammatical structure of the sentence states—that the Church, which is the house of God, is also " the pillar and ground (or basement) of the truth." The Church, then, is to be what Christ was, the Witness of the Truth. It is through human experience that the world will know it. God's truth cannot become influential and living if it is left in texts and creeds, in symbols and in formulas. It must enter into men's consciousness; it must become a living experience; it must find expression in character and action, and reveal itself in love, worship, and obedience. (*A. Rowland, LL.B.*) **Which is the Church of the living God.**—*The Church and soul-life.* I am to treat of the Church as the promoter of soul-life among men who are already really regenerate. Let us proceed, then, to inquire whether or not the Church sustains a developing and perfecting relation to the soul-life of its own numbers. I take the ground that it does sustain such a relation, and I argue this—I. From the general drift of Divine revelation as to the influential position which the Church sustains in the great redemptive economy. One of the grandest facts in the history of man is, that God has never taken one discoverable step, nor put forth one visible act, for his redemption, but through the Church. This is true both of the primary and completed history of redemption. Not a priest was consecrated, not an altar was built, not a victim was appointed, not a bard touched his lyre, not a prophet raised his voice, and not a hope was cherished in the primary dispensation under the law, but through the Church. When the elaborated principles and purposes of redemption were fully enunciated in the finished acts of the gospel, still God spoke and acted by the Church. His disciples were living scions of the same goodly fellowship. Not a miracle did Christ work, not a truth did He utter, not a pang did He endure, but for His Church. And His servants were as their Master in this matter. Every journey which they made, every insult which they received, every book which they penned, and every martyrdom which they welcomed, was for the Church. From all this, it is clear that the Church is not a matter of trivial import in the world, but is one of the great moral forces in the universe. She is no less than the subservient apparatus of redeeming love, the scaffolding which men and angels mount to pry into the secret architecture, and steal a thought from this stupendous temple. So that the Church is not the arbitrary mandate of the servant, but is the authoritative institution of the Lord. She was to form a sort of centre in Jehovah's boundless empire, the palace of the great King, from which He should sway the sceptre of moral administration in mercy and in peace. II. From the intimate relations which exist between her and "Christ our life." One of the most difficult points in this discussion will be to define, with anything like clearness and comprehensiveness, the specific union which binds Christ and His Church together. Happily our text introduces us into the central idea of this unity by the use of the one word "living"—"The Church of the living God." This fearful appellation of the Deity is used very seldom in the Scriptures, and never but upon occasions and subjects of very great importance. For instance, we find it in the deep soul-struggle of David when he cries, "My soul thirsteth for God, the living God," indicating the most intense longings of an immortal soul after its original life-sources. Again, it is used in the supernatural revelation of Christ's Divinity, made to Peter: "Thou art the Christ, the Son of the living God." She is called the "Church of the living God." Now, we never read of the Church as the "Church of the most high God," although we read of the "servants of the most high God." We never read of the Church of the everlasting God, although we read of the "commandment of the everlasting God." We never read of the Church of the holy God, although we read that the "Lord our God is holy": nor of the Church of the mighty God, although we read of Christ, that "His name shall be called the Mighty God." But when the inspired pen comes to give us the intricacies of His relations to the Church this mystical language is invoked. She is coupled with Him either as the Church of the living God, the pillar and ground of the truth, or as Mount Zion, the city of the living God. Herein we discover the nice distinction which the Holy Spirit uses in gospel definition. The Church is united to Christ, not as a dead bride, "for He is not the God of the dead, but of the living." She is allied to Him, not as to a God of the imagination, but as to the Fountain of all vitality. She possesses Him, not as the personated ideal life of God, but as the God of life—"the living God." Here, then, life throbs after life. To be sure, God is the cause of all causes, the life of all lives, the prolific original of every existence. He is not only the Universal Life, but the "living God" universal. In Him all lives "live and move and have their being," from leviathan that lashes the ocean into fury, to the insect that imperceptibly wheels in the eddies of the air. But in the Church there is an embodiment of every attribute and perfection of "the living God," which forms an inherent indwelling, and not a mere relation of influence. The life of His inferior creatures gives expression to His government, but the Church gives expression to His personality, to all His moral nature, and you can see it nowhere else as you find it there. God dwells in the midst of His Church in tangible reality. The Church can say, as no other body of men can say, "We are made partakers of the Divine nature." The life of the Church has been her most glorious characteristic; for it is a remarkable fact that, outside of the Church, no great moral forces have yet been discovered in the elevation and salvation of the race. III. FROM THE GENERAL TENOR OF SCRIPTURAL THOUGHT AND EXPRESSION, WHICH TREATS OF THE CHURCH AS THE CHURCH. IV. FROM THE HISTORICAL LIFE-DEVELOPMENTS OF THE CHURCH ITSELF. Real soul-life has always been found in the Church, and it has not been found out of it. God has always largely wrought out the life of the Church by the Church. Men never look elsewhere for light but to the sun. Men never look for soul-life but to the Church. Sometimes that life has been extremely feeble in the Church. The reason is, that, like all other sorts of life, it has always dissolved itself in a succession of classified manifestations. You always find it in the same place and under the same conditions. You always find flower-life in the rosebud, and forest-life in the forests. You always find sympathetic life in the heart, and intellectual life in the brain. Where, then, will you look for soul-life but in the Church? Where will you look for this overmastering impulse but where the living God has planted it? Life of His planting is deep seated in that palpitating soul-nature which is so nearly allied to His own essence. You can only see it in its developments. But where it exists there will inevitably be "first the blade, then the ear, then the full corn in the ear." The Divine life will develop itself in its fecundity of blessings. A living Deity must have a living temple. Yet no device of man can fabricate this life; every spark of the fire and every form of the flame is from "the living God." Man's appendages may enfeeble it, mystic observances may out-dazzle it, but it burns divinest in its own radiance. These are my arguments in support of the proposition that the Church sustains a developing and perfecting relation to the soul-life of its own members. Soul-life in the Church is capable of enkindling the same life in others. The newly-awakened power of this fellowship outweighs all other feelings, and subordinates them to itself. It betokens a coincidence of motive, sentiment, and principle, which enhances the life of the whole body, and blends the common force of the community into the tenderest relationships. Their organic life is a sacred trust, and "the living God" claims its use. They are the leaven, and in a silent, secret process of fermentation they are, by the forces of their continued operations, to diffuse the moisture through every particle of the mass. And yet no one must lose himself in the aggregate—no one must invite insignificance. The most self-depreciating member can stamp the impress of his moral life on every other living soul of the fellowship. (*T. Armitage, D.D.*) *The Christian Church, the House of God:*—Sacred tropology, by which I understand the various figures and similitudes whereby persons, characters, and events are brought under our notice, and made familiar to our minds, in the Bible, opens to the student of Holy Scripture, a field of thought and inquiry at once most beautiful and instructive. God the Father, for instance, is represented as a King, a Governor, a Householder, a Parent, a Master. God the Son is brought before us as the Word, a Shepherd, a Kinsman, a Redeemer, Rock, Light, Vine, Door, Bridegroom, Prince of Peace; God the Holy Ghost, as Fire, Water, Comforter, Witness, Spirit of Adoption, Fountain. Faithful Christians are called saints, disciples, children, servants, friends, priests, and kings unto God. Ministers are designated by suitable titles—watchmen, shepherds, ambassadors, stewards. I. THE HOUSE itself, called pre-eminently "the house of God." There is fitness, design, beauty, and force in comparing the Church of the living God, wherewith we have membership, and to which we owe allegiance, unto His house. 1. Its Builder is God Himself. A system at once so simple and stupendous, as that exhibited in the origin and end of the Church, could no more have been the result of human device, than the creation of the universe, with all the harmonies of its movements, and all the beauty of its parts. Unfathomable love designed, unsearchable wisdom contrived, and Power Almighty executed that device of goodness to a lost and ruined world embodied in the gospel. When the command of the Most High came to Moses in the wilderness, whither he had lead the chosen host, saying, "Make Me a tabernacle that I may dwell among them," every portion of that mysterious tent, even to the very meanest, was to be made according to a pattern shown him by God

Himself. And wherefore? Because it was to be a type of His Church, in which, as to its spiritual form, character, use, appointments, end, nothing was to be of human device. 2. Its chief corner-stone is Christ Jesus. The voice of prophecy attests this glorious element of the Church's stability. 3. The apostles and prophets are the foundations on which the Church is built. II. THE INHABITANTS OF THE HOUSE. 1. He hath given Jesus Christ to be the Head over all things to His body the Church, the fulness of Him that filleth all in all. He, then, is the High Priest over the house of God. He is the Master of that great family, both in heaven and earth, which is called by His name. 2. The indwellers of this house of God are all they who enter the Church by baptism, in the name of the Father, and of the Son, and of the Holy Ghost. III. THE BLESSINGS OF GOD'S HOUSE, THE CHURCH. 1. The Church affords shelter and sanctuary to its faithful indwellers. "The sparrow," saith the inspired Psalmist, "hath found a house, and the swallow a nest for herself where she may lay her young; even Thine altars, O Lord of Hosts, my King and my God." Without the Church's pale, the sinner is houseless, naked, miserable. 2. The Church, God's house, is a state of discipline and government. Order is heaven's first law, and without it the whole frame and fabric of Society would fall into cureless ruin. 3. But food is also necessary to the family of heaven, and the Church of God affords it. 4. The great Head of the spiritual family administers His house by stewards. 5. One of the chief blessings in the Church, considered as the house of God, here or in heaven, is gracious intercourse and communion. IV. THE END FOR WHICH THAT HOUSE WAS FOUNDED, AND THAT FAMILY ORGANIZED. (*R. P. Buddicom, M.A.*)     *The Church of the living God:*—I. In the first place, then, I observe that THE CHURCH BEARS TESTIMONY TO A TRUTH—to a special truth—and in this relation it may be termed "the pillar of the truth." It is a pillar of testimony. That truth is the revelation of God in Jesus Christ. Of that revelation the Church holds the record, maintains the verity, and illustrates the power. The Church itself is a witness that such a revelation has been given. We trace this body of Christian believers through past ages, until we reach a period when it did not exist. It bears witness to the New Testament account of its own origin. It is itself an abiding evidence to the authenticity of that account. We may try this evidence by negative and positive tests. In the first place, if the New Testament does not furnish a satisfactory account of the origin of the Christian Church, nothing else does. Or, if we assume that there never was an actual personality such as that to which the Church bears witness, and upon which it is founded—that this is only an ideal life, which, by a process of mythical evolution, has been developed from a slender reality into that which stands on the pages of the Gospel—we may well ask, how has this accretion crystallized into such harmony, and produced an ideal that satisfies the loftiest conceptions of all ages and all men? If such a person could not have been fabricated, or mythically evolved within the time when we must admit the existence of our written records, we are driven upon the positive test that such a Being did live and teach and act, and the Church stands firm as a pillar of testimony to that Divine manifestation in Jesus Christ. Moreover, while the Church preserves the record and maintains the verity of this revelation, it also illustrates its power. Again, taking the Church as it stands to-day—an undeniable, existing institution—and tracing back we come once more upon the fact to which it ascribes its origin. I need not say what a remarkable period that was in the history of mankind. An exhausted world, a troubled world, a world lying in the sad twilight of an eclipse. And then, suddenly, a new era emerging from the old—a sharp, distinct furrow breaking up the surface of history, new ideas, a new faith, a new life. An evident transformation—in its rapidity, depth, and thoroughness, really a miracle of transformation. There is no effect without a cause. And for such a stupendous effect as this there must have been a special cause. Where can we find such a cause? In the conditions of the old world, just alluded to? That Church stands yet, an unimpeachable witness to the revelation of God in Christ, and the operation of that truth in the earth. Divine in its origin like the creative act in the material world, like the procedure of the material world since the creation it now works by ordinary laws and in human conditions. It is advanced by human instrumentalities. It is distorted by human errors. It is hindered by human sins. And yet it manifestly triumphs, as an intrinsic power, through these instrumentalities. It dissipates these errors. It melts away these sins. It evidently acts as a special truth, a Divine force, in the world. It changes customs. It moulds manners. It works into laws. It springs up into beneficent institutions.

It transfigures the lives of men. It survives the wreck of dynasties. It abases the proud. It exalts the humble. It reveals the worth of humanity. It gives to the lowliest a faith that is more glorious than a crown, a dignity grander than coronation robes. Even when evoked for evil, it serves the good. II. I have been speaking of the Church as the witness, the pillar of testimony to a special truth. In the next place, let me refer to it as in a certain sense the GROUND OF ALL TRUTH. And, as I have suggested, there is a sense in which the Church is not only the " ground of the special truth" which characterizes the New Testament, but, as it rests upon, so, in turn, it enshrines—or, I might say, incarnates—the ultimate verity which exists behind all forms of truth, behind the visible facts which science explores and the invisible things which faith apprehends. Thus it affirms an "eternal and immutable morality," enthroned above the fluctuations of expediency and the caprice of self-will—a reality of Spiritual Being from which all life springs forth—and so authenticates conscience, vindicates prayer, explains the order of the physical world, and interprets the aspirations of the human soul. And this also is certain: the facts of science cannot be cancelled. Therefore, in relation to the great interests of religion, they must be adjusted. The Church, as assuming to be the " ground of truth," must try them by the simple truth. And, in this computation, what are facts? The naturalist verifies the objects of his senses and his reason, and calls them "facts." But the Christian believer, in his own consciousness, has the same evidence of " facts." The geologist is not more confident as to the trilobrite in the rock, or the astronomers as to Sirius in the sky, than is the devout soul as to communion with its Saviour and its God. The philosopher points his telescope, or arranges his microscope, and tells what God has done in the world without—in the glittering armies of heaven, or the infusorial myriad fold throbbing with the universal life. But the mourner takes the lens of faith, and gazing through the broken tomb of Jesus, commands the horizon of the immortal world. Through the clear-shining of his tears the penitent looks into his own heart, and in the illumination of Divine love beholds new hopes, new purposes, new possibilities, quickened in the transfiguration of a regenerated life. He knows in whom he has believed. He knows what Christ has done for his soul. He knows into what an atmosphere he mounts by prayer. And here let me make a practical suggestion based upon this unity of truth. No exhortation to the young minister is more common than that he should " study the Bible." But this does not imply mere textual study. We are studying the Bible when we study any truth. That live Scripture is to be read, and learned, and applied in the presence of all nature and all history. We must carry its light into the world around us, and come back with our knowledge and experience to find in it fresher reality and profounder depths of meaning. III. But I proceed to observe that this is " the Church of the LIVING God." Not only does it bear witness to a special truth—not only does it affirm all truth—it is also the vehicle of Divine life. (*E. H. Chapin.*) *The Church of the Living God:*—But what does it mean when it is said so expressly, " the Church of the Living God"? Is it in contrast to the temples of the heathen, whose gods are dead, and cannot hear, or speak, or see. Or does it mean more expressly that it is " the Church of God " who is " living" to keep, guide, bless, and give life to His people ; and, therefore, because it is " the Church of the Living God," it can never die. It may be changed, but it cannot die. Christ lives, and we are all members of Christ. Living members of a Living Head ; and from that Head life is ever flowing down into the body. Therefore, " the Church " in Him cannot help being " a living Church." And we are " the temple of the Holy Ghost who liveth in us." But this is only a part of what it means. It must, like its great Author, if it is a Living Church, show signs of life. Now, what are the evidences of life? Let us take the analogy of the human life. 1. To make human life there must be the breath. Every one who lives must, of necessity, breathe. So it is with " the Church," and with every member of the Church. There is a breath. The Holy Spirit is the breath. We must breathe that breath of the Spirit; and thus breathe warm thoughts, loving thoughts, happy thoughts, holy thoughts. 2. But the breath requires feeding with words which look and express this inward feeling. Words o fpraise, words of prayer, words of glory, words of power. Can there be life without expression? If it be not in speech, will it not be by some other way? 3. And can it go on without growth? If the man be a man of God, and if the Church be " the Church of the Living God," there must be growth. The man's soul must grow. All the fruits of the Spirit must grow in him. It is equally the consequence and sign of life. A Church which does not grow may doubt whether it is a Church at all! 4. And with the growth and the breathing will come action! Action in accordance with the principle which is working within us. 5. There must be expansion. It is the principle of all true religion, and of every Church. (*J. Vaughan, M.A.*)     *The Church: its nature and functions* :—Laying aside the notion of infallibility, let us proceed to consider how properly, without any such futile and arrogant claim, the Church is called the pillar and ground of the truth. 1. In the first place, and chiefly, the Church is so called, because, to use the language of our Twentieth Article, she is a "witness and keeper of Holy Writ." Christianity is found in the Bible, and originally and purely nowhere else. Who should keep the book but those that use it? Who be anxious for its preservation but those who value it, make it the rule of their life? This is at once natural and necessary. Who keep the records of literature and science but men of learning; and who the divine record of religious knowledge but men of religion? They ever have kept it and ever will keep it, as long as religion exists in the world. 2. But further, the Church does not barely keep the volume, attesting its authenticity and watching over its integrity, and so acting as a pillar and ground of the truth; but she seeks to promote the truth by a system of instruction, the basis of which is the contents of that volume. She does not act simply as a publisher of the book, but as a lecturer upon it. Her thoughts are not her own. She makes no such arrogant pretension. She has light, but it is borrowed light. She shines, but it is by reflection from the Holy Book. It is further worthy of remark, that the Church in the discharge of this function, is not doing a merely optional thing; she is necessitated to do it. The office is inseparable from her being. 3. It would be a further illustration and enforcement of this point to show in what manner the Church is required to discharge this duty. She is required to circulate the Scriptures. (*William Sparrow.*)     **The pillar and ground of the truth.—** *The pillar and ground of truth* :—I. THAT THE CHURCH IS THE PILLAR AND GROUND OF TRUTH.—1. That by the Church in this text he does not mean only the ministers. 2. It is far from concluding that one Church is the pillar of truth to another. 3. It is plain from all reason as well as Scripture, that truth is the pillar and growth of the Church, and not the Church of truth (Eph. xi. 20, 21; 1 Cor. iii. 9, 10, 11). Here we may inquire what that truth is which the apostle speaks of. There is a truth of history that we take delight in; to know what is doing in distant countries, or has been done in former ages, but this is rather our entertainment than our concern. There is a truth of argument. This is still more engaging, as it is the proper food of our reason. There is also a truth of conversation; which is what we call integrity. Besides these, there are truths of philosophy, that have no concern with the doctrine of Christ Jesus. But the truth that our apostle means is of another kind. 1. It is about the greatest concerns. 2. It comes with the fullest evidence. 3. It is always the same. 4. It is followed with the best effects. (*T. Bradbury.*)     *The pillar and ground of the truth* :—I. LET US CONSIDER THE APPROPRIATE ATTRIBUTE HERE ASCRIBED TO GOD. He is called the "living God"; and He is thus designated not in this place only, but also in numerous other places. He is self-existent and independent. There never was a time when He began to exist, and there never will be a time when He will cease to exist. He has "neither beginning of days nor end of life." He is also "the Fountain of Life" to all other beings throughout the whole creation. There is also a higher life, which, if we are Christians indeed, we have received from Him. II. LET US CONSIDER THE SIGNIFICANT NAME HERE GIVEN TO THE CHURCH OF GOD. It is called the house of God. "The house of God, which is the Church of the living God." He dwells in them individually, taking up His abode in their heart, and making it a holy temple unto Himself. "Know ye not," asks our apostle in writing to the Corinthians, "that your body is the temple of the Holy Ghost which is in you, which ye have of God?" He dwells also among His people collectively, being present in all their assemblies, as it is written, "In all places where I record My name, I will come unto thee, and I will bless thee." But there is another sense in which the word house is used in Scripture, and in which it may with propriety be understood here. It sometimes stands for the inhabitants of the house, the household, or the family. Thus it is said of Cornelius, the Roman centurion, that he was "a devout man, and one that feared God with all his house"; meaning all his family. The Church is the family of God. How great, then, is the privilege of those who belong to the house and family of God! III. LET US CONSIDER THE IMPORTANT OFFICE SUSTAINED BY THE CHURCH IN THE WORLD. It is present in the text as "the pillar and ground," that is, the stay and support "of the truth." In furtherance of this object, its ministers are to preach the truth, the whole truth, and nothing but the truth. The members of the Church also are to co-operate with its ministers in giving support and currency to the truth. IV. To CALL YOUR ATTENTION TO THE MANIFEST DUTY THAT RESTS UPON US AS MEMBERS OF THE VISIBLE CHURCH OF CHRIST, and particularly as members of that apostolical branch of it established in these kingdoms. "That thou mayest know how thou oughtest to behave thyself in the house of God, which is the Church of the living God, the pillar and ground of the truth." There is also another duty that rests upon us as members of the Church—we must live the truth. In other words, we must exemplify its holy effects in our life and conversation. But there is a third duty which we are called upon to discharge as members of the Church, namely, to make known the truth, as far as we can, to those who are ignorant of it. (D. Rees, M.A.)    Security of the Church :—Speaking of that enormous mountain peak known as the Matterhorn, which is the universal admiration of Alpine travellers, a writer says that the materials of which it is composed are remarkable, and he goes on to gives the following description : "Few architects would like to build with them. The slope of the rocks to the north-west is covered two feet deep with their ruins, a mass of loose and slaty shale, of a dull red brick colour, which yields beneath the feet like ashes, so that, in running down, you step one yard and slide three. The rock is indeed hard beneath, but still disposed in thin courses of these cloven shales, so finely laid that they look in places more like a heap of crushed autumn leaves than a rock, and the first sensation is one of unmitigated surprise, as if the mountain were upheld by miracle ; but surprise becomes more intelligent reverence for the Great Builder when we find, in the middle of the mass of these dead leaves, a course of living rock, of quartz as white as the snow that encircles it, and harder than a bed of steel. It is only one of a thousand iron bands that knit the strength of the mighty mountain. Through the buttress and the wall alike the courses of its varied masonry are seen in their successive order, smooth and true as if laid by line and plummet, but of thickness and strength continually varying, and with silver cornices glittering along the edge of each, led by the snowy winds and carved by the sunshine." Now, all this suggests a parable. The Church of God, that glorious mountain of His habitation, is apparently built of very frail materials. The saints are, to all appearance, more like "a heap of crushed autumn leaves than a rock," and beneath the feet of tyrants and persecutors they seem to yield like ashes ; and yet the Church defies the storm and towers aloft, the obelisk of the truth, the eternal pillar of almighty grace. Faith, with eagle gaze, perceives the thousand iron bands which prevent the disintegration of the mass, and the central foundation harder than a bed of steel upon which the colossal fabric rests. The Church abideth for ever : infinite love, faithfulness, and power sustain her, and the gates of hell shall not prevail against her. (C. H. Spurgeon.)

Ver. 16. And without doubt great is the mystery of godliness.—*Mystery* :—I shall deliver the nature of the thing itself in this definition, viz., that a mystery is a truth revealed by God above the power of natural reason to find out or comprehend. 1. That it is a truth. By which we exclude everything from being a mystery that is absurd and contradictious, since a truth can by no means be so. 2. That it be revealed by God, viz., as to its existence, that there is such a thing. For otherwise, as to the nature of the thing itself, and several other respects in which it may be known, the revelation of it is not supposed to extend so far. 3. That it surpasses all the power of natural reason to discover or find it out. 4. That it be such a thing as bare natural reason (even after it is discovered) cannot comprehend. I say comprehend, that is, know it perfectly, and as far as it is capable of being known (1 Cor. xiii. 12). That the mysteriousness of those matters of faith is most subservient to the great important ends of Religion, and that upon these following accounts. I. Because religion, in the prime institution of it, WAS DESIGNED TO MAKE IMPRESSIONS OF AWE AND REVERENTIAL FEAR UPON MEN'S MINDS. Distance preserves respect, and we still imagine some transcendent worth in things above our reach. Moses was never more reverenced than when he wore his veil. Nay, the very *sanctum sanctorum* would not have had such veneration from the Jews had they been permitted to enter into it, and to gaze and stare upon it as often as they did upon the other parts of the Temple. The high priest himself, who alone was suffered to enter into it, yet was to do so but once a year, lest the frequency of the sight might insensibly lessen that adoration which so sacred a thing was still to maintain upon his thoughts. In all great respect, or honour shown, there is something of wonder; but a thing often seen (we know), be it never so excellent, yet ceasing thereby to be new, it ceases also to be wondered at. Forasmuch as it is not the worth or excellency, but the strangeness of the thing, which draws the eyes and admiration of men after it. For can anything in nature be imagined more glorious and beautiful than the sun shining in his full might? and yet how many more spectators and wonderers does the same sun find under an eclipse? But to pursue this notion and observation yet farther, I conceive it will not be amiss to consider how it has been the custom of all sober and wise nations of the world still to reserve the great rites of their religion *in occulto.* Thus how studiously did the Egyptians, those great masters of all learning, lock up their sacred things from all access and knowledge of the vulgar! II. A second ground of the mysteriousness of religion (as it is delivered by God to mankind) IS HIS MOST WISE PURPOSE THEREBY TO HUMBLE THE PRIDE AND HAUGHTINESS OF MAN'S REASON. In short, man would be like God in knowledge, and so he fell; and now, if he will be like Him in happiness too, God will effect it in such a way as shall convince him to his face that he knows nothing. The whole course of his salvation shall be all riddle and mystery to him; he shall (as I may so express it) be carried up to heaven in a cloud. Instead of evidence springing from things themselves, and clear knowledge growing from such an evidence, his understanding must now be contented with the poor, dim light of faith, which guides only in the strength and light of another's knowledge, and is properly a seeing with another's eyes, as being otherwise wholly unable to inform us about the great things of our peace, by any immediate inspection of those things themselves. For as the primitive effect of knowledge was first to put up and then to throw down, so the contrary method of grace and faith is first to depress and then to advance. The difficulty and strangeness of some of the chief articles of our religion are notable instruments in the hand of God to keep the soul low and humble, and to check those self-complacencies which it is apt to grow into by an over-weening conceit of its own opinions more than by any other thing whatsoever. For man naturally is scarce so fond of the offspring of his body as of that of his soul. His notions are his darlings; so that neither children nor self are half so dear to him as the only begotten of his mind. And therefore in the dispensations of religion God will have this only begotten, this best beloved, this Isaac of our souls (above all other offerings that a man can bring Him) to be sacrificed and given up to Him. III. God has been pleased to put a mysteriousness into the greatest articles of our religion, THEREBY TO ENGAGE US IN A CLOSER AND MORE DILIGENT SEARCH INTO THEM. He would have them the objects of our study, and for that purpose has rendered them hard and difficult. For no man studies things plain and evident, and such as by their native clearness do even prevent our search, and of their own accord offer themselves to our understandings. The foundation of all inquiry is the obscurity as well as worth of the thing inquired after. And God has thought good to make the constitution and complexion of our religion such as may fit it to be our business and our task; to require and take up all our intellectual strength, and, in a word, to try the force of our best, our noblest, and most active faculties. For no man can outlive the reasons of inquiry so long as he carries any thing of ignorance about him. And that every man must, and shall do, while he is in this state of mortality. For he, who himself is but a part of nature, shall never compass or comprehend it all. Truth (we are told) dwells low, an I in a bottom; and the most valued things of the creation are concealed and hidden by the great Creator of them, from the common view of the world. God and diamonds, with the most precious stones and metals, are couched and covered in the bowels of the earth; the very condition of their being giving them their burial too. So that violence must be done to nature before she will produce and bring them forth. And then, as to what concerns the mind of man, God has in His wise Providence cast things so as to make the business of men in this world improvement; that so the very work of their condition may still remind them of the imperfection of it. (*R. South.*) *The mystery of godliness :—*I. THAT THE SCHEME OF GODLINESS IS GREATLY MYSTERIOUS WITH REGARD TO ITS CONTRIVANCE. Thus, how the case of man's fall was to be met, and how his salvation was to be wrought out in perfect harmony with all the Divine attributes, remained a profound secret, until God Himself was pleased to announce it to the world. Even angelic intelligence was inadequate to its contrivance. II. THAT THE SCHEME OF GODLINESS IS GREATLY MYSTERIOUS WITH REGARD TO ITS MODE OF DEVELOPMENT. That, in fact, its main and most important truths should have been so long concealed from the world, or only be darkly shadowed forth by types and figures; that their revelation should have been so gradual, and so late in reaching its consummation may well be reckoned a mystery. Why did He suffer so many millions of the race for whose benefit it was designed, and for whose salvation a knowledge of it seems necessary, to die without even having heard of it? III. THAT THE SCHEME OF GODLINESS IS GREATLY MYSTERIOUS WITH REGARD TO THE NATURE AND MODE OF ITS OPERATIONS. We gather from the words of our Lord, that the operations by which the Holy Spirit regenerates men through the system of evangelical truth would be inscrutable. "The wind bloweth where it listeth," &c. How, for instance, does this system of truth illuminate the mind, convey conviction to the judgment, awaken and alarm the conscience, gain the assent of the understanding, fill the sinner with penitence and godly sorrow, win his affections, subdue his whole soul to God, and transform him, a guilty and polluted spirit, into a new creature in Christ Jesus? What is the nature of those unseen, impalpable operations by which man is enlightened, pardoned, and born again? How is celestial light produced in the sin-darkened mind? IV. THAT THE SCHEME OF GODLINESS IS GREATLY MYSTERIOUS WITH REGARD TO ITS TRIUMPHS. The external means and agency by which these triumphs are secured may be plain and obvious enough as facts; but then they seem altogether inadequate to achieve them. V. THAT THE SCHEME OF GODLINESS IS GREATLY MYSTERIOUS WITH REGARD TO ITS CONSUMMATION. Its character is thus uniform from the beginning to the end. This grand drama of truth and mercy was opened by the most mysterious resolutions and stupendous acts; it is sustained and carried on by the sublimest evolutions and agency; and it will close amid the most transcendent and ineffable scenes of grandeur and bliss. All the dead are to be raised. Men and devils are all to be arraigned before the judgment-seat of Christ. The old heavens and earth are to pass away. A new heaven and earth of surpassing beauty and holiness are to be created for the reception of the redeemed. 1. This subject teaches us the necessity of implicit faith in all the truths and doctrines which God has revealed in His Word. This, indeed, we shall often find to be necessary. Mysterious facts which baffle our reason, demand our faith. In His darkest utterances, God must be implicitly credited. 2. This subject teaches us the necessity of cherishing the spirit of patience and humility. This, too, we shall find to be all-important. We cannot anticipate the end, nor rush to its disclosures before the time appointed by the Father. 3. This subject teaches us that we ought most gratefully to receive the unspeakable and eternal benefits which this grand and mysterious scheme of godliness was designed to confer on redeemed men. To refuse them, or even to be unconcerned about them, is surely the blackest and most hateful ingratitude, and must form the very climax of rebellion and guilt! (*S. Lucas.*)      *The mystery of godliness :*—I. A MYSTERY is something kept secret, locked up from the view of men. This sense of it agrees to the doctrines of Christianity upon a threefold account. 1. As they were concealed from former ages. 2. As they are yet so from the greatest part of the world. 3. As they continue so in some degree to God's own people. The temple of God is not to be opened till we get to heaven, and there we shall see the ark of His covenant. Upon these accounts it may be said our gospel is hid; it was so to the Jews, it is so to those that are lost; and, in part, it is so to the believer himself; and therefore it may be called a mystery. 1. It is called a mystery from its importance. 2. It is called a mystery because it never could have been known but by revelation. 3. A mystery is something above the comprehension of our reason. The things of God knows no man, but the Spirit of God. And this leads me to—II. SHOW THAT THE MYSTERY OF ANY DOCTRINE DOES NOT HINDER IT FROM BEING TRUE. 1. The difficulty or easiness of a doctrine does not make it the matter of our faith, but we go entirely upon the sufficiency of the evidence. 2. This obtains in every part of life, and it is strange we should exclude it from religion. 3. It is no way unaccountable that the nature and the designs of God should be incomprehensible to us. 4. It is necessary that our understanding should honour the revelation of God by a subjection, as well as our wills by a compliance. 5. These are not mysteries of man's forging, but we have them in the Book of God. 6. They are not concealed by any party or tribe among us, but lie open to be seen and read of all men. Therefore—7. The design of preaching them is not to set up the tyranny of priests, but to lead people to a veneration for their God, a dependence upon Him, and an application to Him. III. WHAT IS THE BENEFIT OF HAVING MYSTERIES IN THE CHRISTIAN RELIGION? Why could not our lawgiver have done as others did, only laid before us a set of rules, and distributed them under the several heads of practice, without ever engaging our faith in any speculations at all? When the law is established by faith, it gets a firmness and an influence that it could never have had any other way. 1. By the mysteries of the gospel we are led to an esteem for the salvation itself that God has given us, because thus we see that it was the contrivance of infinite wisdom. 2. We have the best arguments for our duty from the incarnation, satisfaction, and resurrection of Jesus Christ. 3. We have the noblest example of all practical holiness from God's being manifest in the flesh. 4. We are in particular inclined and encouraged to the duty of prayer, by this new and living way that is consecrated for us through the veil, that is to say, His flesh. (Heb. x. 20). 5. We have the best hope of succeeding in the whole work of our duty, from the redemption that is now established. 6. By these mysteries the principles of all practical religion are enlarged and encouraged. It is in a meditation upon these that we stir up the grace of God that is in us. 7. We are by this means kept low in our own eyes; as we find there are things above the reach of nature, and beyond the comprehension of faith. 8. This shows us the necessity of depending upon the Spirit for illumination, as well as upon Christ for acceptance. 9. This teaches a greater value for the revelation God has made of Himself. 10. This draws out our desires towards heaven, without which there can be neither the purity nor the comfort of religion. We long to be where the veil is taken off from the object, and the fetters from the faculty. IV. When the apostle calls this A GREAT MYSTERY, I SUPPOSE HE DOES IT IN A WAY OF PRE-EMINENCE to what is contained in other religions, more especially these two. 1. The mysteries of the heathen. 2. There were mysteries in the Jewish religion. (Psa. cxi. 4; xlviii. 9), in the midst of His temple, and He was terrible out of His holy places. (1) The mystery of godliness is in this respect greater than any among the heathen in that we learn it at once. Here are no years thrown away in a tedious preparation. There is no keeping of people in a preparatory dulness. (2) This mystery is about matters of more importance to our final happiness. This is life eternal, to know the only true God, and Jesus Christ whom He has sent. (John xvii. 3). (3) These mysteries were given us by God Himself. (4) These mysteries are to be diffused and made known. 2. There were undeniable mysteries among the Jews. (1) Our mysteries are distinguished from those that God gave to the Jews by their continuance. (2) Our mysteries refer us to themselves. The Jews had a respect to something else. (3) Our mysteries come in a nobler way, in a method more agreeable to the lofty nature of a rational soul. (4) This mystery is attended with a greater influence, both as to purity and peace. It is further said that this mystery is great without controversy. 1. It does not mean there should be no dispute about it. The natural man never did, and never will receive the things of the Spirit of God; they are foolishness to him. 2. This mystery is without controversy to all the ages of God's people. 3. This mystery is without controversy to those whom the grace of God has brought from the darkness of infidelity. 4. This is a mystery without controversy, because it still continues to be a mystery after all the ways that men have taken to explain it. A few practical directions about the use that should be made of mysteries in religion. 1. If you would treat Christianity or any particular article as a mystery, be careful to separate the doctrine from all the mixtures that curiosity or superstition have brought into it. 2. Read the Scriptures diligently, comparing spiritual things with spiritual. 3. Attend the ordinances of the gospel. He that walks with wise men shall be wise. 4. Pray for the Spirit. 5. Take care of quarrelling about these mysteries, and becoming vain in your imaginations. 6. Be more concerned about the improving of a mystery than the explaining it. (*T. Bradbury.*) *The mystery of godliness :—* I. Let us inquire WHAT ARE THE FEATURES OF MYSTERY WHICH BELONG TO THE SCHEME OF REDEMPTION. 1. It is a mystery if we consider the subjects of that redemption. 2. There is mystery in the mode of this redemption. 3. There is mystery in the magnitude of the accruing consequence of this redemption. The feud between heaven and earth has been adjusted by it. 4. It is a mystery, because no human wisdom could ever have devised it. It is a gem of grace dug from the deepest mine of the Divine intelligence, and lifted from the profoundest recess of the Divine compassion. 5. It was a mystery which baffled the malignant wit of devils to explain. 6. And if it passed the understandings of the dark confederacy of hell, it equally exceeded the capacity of angels to unravel its intent. 7. It is a mystery which will need eternity to explore it. II. Observe THE APPROPRIATENESS OF THE PHRASE—" the mystery of godliness." 1. It is so, because it reveals the only basis of godliness. 2. By a belief in this we become entitled to all the blessings of godliness. 3. By its influence on heart and life it leads to the practice of godliness. 4. Because the whole redounds to the honour and glory of God. From this mystery we may learn to raise our appreciation of the greatness and sublimity of the Christian revelation. (*A. Mursell.*) *The mystery of godliness :*—I. THE MYSTERY OF GODLINESS ITSELF. 1. The fact that God was manifest in the flesh. (1) The manifestation affirmed is the manifestation of God. It is the manifestation of Jehovah — of the Creator, Preserver, and Lord of all—of Him to whom all worship is due, and all dominion and glory belong. This much lies upon the very surface of the text. Is there nothing more to tell? There is more. God is One. But the Persons of the Godhead are three. And this is not the manifestation of the First, or of the Third, Person of the Godhead, but of the Second. It is the manifestation of God the Son. (2) As to the other question—the nature of this manifestation—we remark that it was personal. There are many manifestations of God—manifestations of Him in the world and in the Church, in His works, and in His Word. But these are manifestations of character and perfections. A manifestation of the Divine wisdom, and power, and holiness, and love, is a manifestation of God; but it is not a personal manifestation. It is a manifestation of the attributes and glory of God, and of the attributes and glory of the Persons in the Godhead ; but it is not a manifestation of the Persons themselves. There is a manifestation of the Father in those who are His children ; there is a manifestation of the Son in those whom He is not ashamed to call His brethren ; and there is a manifestation of the Spirit in all whom He regenerates and sanctifies. Yea, doubtless, the Divine Persons are thus manifested. But, though the manifestation be a manifestation of Persons, it is not a personal manifestation of them. They are manifested mediately, not immediately—as the worker is manifested by his work. There is no immediate personal manifestation of God, which has been afforded to man, except that manifestation of Him which constitutes the mystery of godliness. We do not overlook the manifestations of God that were enjoyed by the patriarchs —such as that which Abraham had in the plains of Mamre, and that which Jacob had at Peniel. These were foreshadowings of that mystery of godliness which the fulness of time disclosed. The personal manifestation of God is highly to be prized. We may judge of it by the desire which is felt to see the sage or philosopher who has enriched the stores of our knowledge by his speculations and discoveries. We may have read the great man's history again and again ; we may be familiar with what he has achieved ; we may have seen the fruits of his genius, his toil, his valour ; we may possess his portrait too ; but the effect of it all will be, not to diminish, but to increase, the desire to behold his person, and to see himself. Just so it is in the case before us. The knowledge of God's ways and doings, the light cast upon His character and glorious perfections by the teachings of Scripture and the experience of the Church, will never quench the desire for the vision of God Himself. We must further remark, with respect to the nature of this manifestation of God, that it was a manifestation "in the flesh." " God was manifest in the flesh." We read of the Holy Ghost coming down in a bodily form, like a dove. But the Holy Ghost was not a dove. He took, for the occasion, the visible form of a dove ; but there was no real dove in the case, any more than there is in the image or likeness of a dove which the pencil of the artist may create. God the Son, however, was man. He was Man as truly and really as He was God. Had He come with no more than the figure or likeness of a man—that likeness being temporarily assumed—it could not so well be said that God was manifested. It may serve to open up still farther this manifestation of God in the flesh, if we explain a little, as we can, and as Scripture enables us, how the manifestation was brought about. This much we are in a condition to say—that God was manifested in the flesh by the assumption into His Person, on the part of the Son, of the human nature, as consisting of a true body and a reasonable soul. The Son assumed human nature into His Person. He assumed it into His Person so that God the Son and the man Christ Jesus were not two Persons, but one. It was not that a new Person was constituted out of two Persons previously existing. His human nature never existed by itself, or as a person ; and the Person of the Son was eternal. Into that Person the human nature was taken, or assumed, as has been said—the identity of the Person remaining unchanged. There was no conversion of the Divine into the human nature. Had that been the case, He must have ceased to be God by becoming man. Nor was there any mixture of the natures. The two natures did not become one nature, combining their attributes. There was a union, however, between the two natures. But this union was not like other unions with which we may be acquainted. It was unlike the union between the soul and body of man. It was unlike it in this—that body and soul make but one nature between them. It was unlike the union between Christ and believers; for that is a union where distinct personality is preserved. And it was unlike the union among the Persons in the Godhead. The cases, indeed, are completely in contrast. There, we find distinct Persons, and one nature. Here, we find one Person, and distinct natures. 2. Passing now from the fact declared, that God was manifest in the flesh, we come to the reason of it. The reason was no other than the salvation of sinful man. A created nature was necessary, because a created nature alone could suffer, and on a created nature alone the stroke of wrath could fall. He took not, however, the nature of angels. The human nature was necessary, to connect Him more closely with our broken covenant, on the one hand, and with us who broke it, on the other. It was flesh that He took, because He was to be the second man, the last Adam; and, in that capacity, to magnify the law and make it honourable, and bruise the serpent's head. But a finite nature must have failed by itself. It need not have failed in purpose, or for want of will; but it must have failed in sufficiency, and for want of strength. II. THE CIRCUMSTANCES THAT COMMEND THE MYSTERY OF GODLINESS TO OUR FAITH AND ADMIRATION. (*A. Gray.*) **God was manifest in the flesh.**—*The important mystery of the Incarnation :*—I. I AM TO ILLUSTRATE THE DOCTRINE OF GOD MANIFEST IN THE FLESH. It is an undoubted truth, that the perfections and glory of God the Father were manifested in the Incarnation, life and death of His only begotten Son. If these, in one respect, veiled the Divine glory, they gave, in another, a new and fuller view of its brightness. The Scripture conceals not the reasons why God was thus manifest in the flesh. Perhaps, some may inquire, how can it be said that God was manifest in the flesh? Did not the nature He assumed, and the purposes of humiliation and suffering for which He assumed it, obscure, rather than manifest, His Deity? If, however, some circumstances of Christ's incarnation indicated meanness and abasement; in others, Divine majesty and greatness were manifested. Heaven and earth, angels and devils, kings and subjects, friends and enemies, unite to do honour to His birth. Let me now direct your attention to the practical improvement of this subject. Judge not the opinions or character of any man, or society of men, by their outward circumstances. Despise not, for His birth, His poverty, or mean appearance, the man who teaches an excellent doctrine, or who exhibits an eminently virtuous example. Just ideas, and a correspondent behaviour, not wealth or indigence, are the true tests of worth. Think how wretched and forlorn thy circumstances, which required so great and astonishing means of deliverance. Admire and improve this amazing condescension. Let the warmest gratitude inflame every breast while contemplating the love which gave rise to this condescension. Labour that He who was manifested in your nature may also be manifested in your persons: or, as Paul expresses it, " That the life of Jesus may be made manifest in your body " (2 Cor. iv. 10). Reflect how highly human nature is dignified and ennobled by the incarnation of the Son of God. Improve and exult in the foundation laid, by God manifest in the flesh, for the encouragement of faith. Sink not under thy doubts and fears; for to rescue sinners from destruction He, who was in the bosom of the Father, pledged His heart as their ransom that, as their Advocate, He might approach to God and successfully plead their cause. II. Paul describes this doctrine as a MYSTERY. The word "mystery" is borrowed from the secret religious rites and exercises among the heathen, to which only a few, after trial of their secrecy, were admitted by the Hierophant or Mystagogue. Hence, it is transferred to the incarnation of Christ, and its important causes and consequences, which could be discovered only by the Spirit, not by our senses, imagination, or intellectual powers. To men, who have no other guide than nature's light, the wonders of redeeming love were wholly unknown : and unknown they must have for ever remained, had not the first stewards of the mysteries of God learned them by inspiration, and been authorized to teach them. Under the Old Testament the Jews had only dark types and obscure prophecies of those good things to come. The wisdom of God in a mystery was a hidden wisdom, which none of the princes of this world knew; for, had they known it, they would not have crucified the Lord of Glory. Again, the gospel is a mystery; for to few who enjoy the external dispensation of the gospel is its native beauty and Divine energy inwardly revealed. Saints alone are divinely enlightened to perceive its certainty and glory. III. THE DOCTRINE OF OUR LORD'S INCARNATION, AND OF ITS CAUSES AND CONSEQUENCES, IS, WITHOUT CONTROVERSY, A GREAT MYSTERY. It has not only been confirmed by the fullest evidence; but it is without controversy to all to whom Jesus hath manifested the Father's name. Well, too, may this doctrine be termed great. It exhibits truths in their own nature transcendently excellent. All this, however, will not excuse our stumbling at this wisdom of God in a mystery, or these deep things of God. IV. THE DOCTRINE OF OUR LORD'S INCARNATION IS A MYSTERY OF GODLINESS. It is allowed that truths altogether unknown, and doctrines perfectly unintelligible, can be no motives to piety. But, notwithstanding this, motives to piety may be derived from that, in a mystery, which is known and understood. Though I cannot comprehend the doctrine of the Trinity, or the Divinity and Sonship of Christ, I may understand enough of the love of the Father, in sending His Son to be the Saviour of the world, and of redemption being purchased by His blood, to influence my temper and conduct. Articles of natural religion deeply affect us which yet are obscurely and imperfectly known. Now, all this was revealed that we might be sanctified through the truth. The view which it exhibits, both of the justice and goodness of God, affords the strongest motives to reverence of God's authority, value for His favour, trust in His mercy and obedience to His laws. V. THE DOCTRINE OF THE INCARNATION IS THE PILLAR AND GROUND OF THE TRUTH: NOT OF TRUTH, OR EVEN RELIGIOUS TRUTH IN GENERAL, BUT OF THE WORD OF TRUTH, THE GOSPEL OF OUR SALVATION, IN WHICH THAT PLAN OF REDEMPTION IS PUBLISHED, WHICH REASON COULD NEVER HAVE DISCOVERED. The original word, rendered *ground*, occurs nowhere else in the sacred writings. But it evidently signifies that upon which anything firmly rests. Here, therefore, where it relates to a building, and is joined to the word "pillar," it means foundation. A pillar only supports part of a fabric. A foundation bears the weight of the whole building. The metaphor intimates that the doctrine of the Person and Incarnation of Jesus is necessary to the support of the whole doctrine of redemption; and that, if the doctrine of the Incarnation were taken away, the whole doctrine of redemption would fall to the ground. Every other article of faith rests upon, and derives stability from, its connection with this. If the Son of God did not assume a true body and a reasonable soul, He was not the "Lamb of God which taketh away the sins of the world." The first thing in a building is the laying the foundation; and the first thing peculiar to Christianity which the apostles taught was the incarnation of Jesus, and His redeeming us to God through His blood: though to pave the way for this truth being received, they also inculcated the principles and obligations of natural religion, and the evidences of Christianity, from prophecy and miracles (1 Cor. xv. 1–3). And now, what is the conclusion of the whole matter? Think it not strange that the gospel often meets with bad entertainment, that some pronounce the mysteries of its foolishness, and others account the godliness these mysteries tend to produce an insupportable yoke. Learn from this subject to distinguish true religion and genuine piety from counterfeit appearances. Heathenism and popery have their mysteries; but they are mysteries of iniquity. Entertain this doctrine in a manner suitable to its nature. It is a mystery. Affect not to be wise above what is written. Admire and adore what thou canst not fully comprehend. It is a mystery of godliness. By indulging ease and security, while profligate and immoral, act not as if it were a mystery of iniquity. Remember that mere speculative knowledge will condemn, not save thee. It is the pillar and ground of truth. Prize that gospel which has published to thee a doctrine so transcendently glorious and important. (*J. Erskine, D.D.*) *The mystery of godliness:*—The greatness and importance of the truth which the Church was to maintain is given as a motive to fidelity on the part of Christians. I. THE CONTRAST BETWEEN FLESH AND SPIRIT. "He was manifested in the flesh, justified in the spirit." For it is not what appeals to our natural observation, to our sensuous nature, or to our purely intellectual faculties, which awakens the conviction that He is our Lord, but it is His Divine touch, felt upon heart and conscience, which leads us, like Thomas, to fall at His feet and say, "My Lord and my God." II. THE SECOND SUGGESTED CONTRAST IS BETWEEN THE ANGELS AND THE NATIONS. "He was seen of angels and preached unto the Gentiles." These are again natural opposites. Angels are the blessed inhabitants of a higher sphere; Gentiles are the most corrupt and debased inhabitants of this lower world. And it is His glory that His claims have been admitted by opposing and divergent nationalities, by the most varied types of men, as rightful King of all the world. III. THE LAST CONTRAST DRAWN HERE IS BETWEEN THE EARTHLY AND THE HEAVENLY. "He was believed on in the world, received up into glory." What a contrast between the celestial brightness and purity in which He is enshrined, and the disease, the death, and the sin prevailing in the world.   I know not how we Christians could still work hopefully if it were not that Jesus, the Almighty purifier, the one Saviour, can be believed on, and is believed on by us in the world—as One able and willing to bring salvation to the lost and degraded.   (*A. Rowland, LL.B.*) *The fountain opened; or, the mystery of godliness revealed :*—1.  Godliness is either the principles of Christian religion, or the inward disposition of the soul towards them, the inward holy affection of the soul.   The word implieth both: for godliness is not only the naked principles of religion, but likewise the Christian affection, the inward bent of the soul, suitable to Divine principles.   There must be a godly disposition, carrying us to godly truths.   These blessed truths of the gospel, they require and breed a godly disposition ; the end of them is godliness ; they frame the soul to godliness.   Thus we see the truths themselves are godliness, carrying us to God and holiness.   Hence follows these other truths briefly.  1. First of all, that no truth breeds godliness and piety of life but Divine truths; for that is called "godliness," because it breeds godliness.   All the devices of men in the world cannot breed godliness.  2. Again, hence, in that Divine truth is called godliness, it shows us, if we would be godly we must be so from reasons of Christianity ; not, as I said, by framing devices of our own, as graceless foolish men do.   But if we will be godly, it must be by reasons and motives from Divine truth.   That breeds godliness.  3. Again, hence we may fetch a rule of discerning when we are godly. What makes a true Christian ?   When he nakedly believes the grounds of Divine truth, the articles of the faith, when he can patter them over—doth that make a true Christian ?   No.   But when these truths breed and work "godliness."   For religion is a truth "according to godliness," not according to speculation only, and notion.   Religious evangelical truth is "wisdom"; and wisdom is a knowledge of things directing to practice.   A man is a wise man when he knows so as to practise what he knows.   The gospel is a Divine wisdom, teaching practice as well as knowledge.   It works godliness, or else a man hath but a human knowledge of Divine things.   Therefore a Christian hath godly principles out of the gospel, and a godly carriage suitable to those principles.   Now this godliness is "a mystery." What is a mystery?   The word signifies a hidden thing.  1. A mystery is a secret, not only for the present, but that it was a secret, though it be now revealed ; for the gospel is now discovered.   It is called a mystery, not so much that it is secret, but that it was so before it was revealed.  2. In the second place, that is called a mystery in the Scripture which, howsoever it be clear for the manifestation of it, yet the reasons of it are hid.   As the conversion of the Gentiles, that there should be such a thing, why God should be so merciful to them, it is called a mystery.  3. In the third place, a mystery in Scripture is taken for that that is a truth hid, and is conveyed by some outward thing.   Marriage is a mystery, because it conveys the hidden spiritual marriage between Christ and His Church.   So, then, the whole evangelical truth is a mystery.   For these reasons :—1. First of all, because it was hid and concealed from all men, till God brought it out of His own bosom : first to Adam in paradise, after the Fall ; and still more clearly afterwards to the Jews ; and in Christ's time more fully to Jews and Gentiles.   It was hid in the breast of God. It was not a thing framed by angels or men.   Christ brought it out of the bosom of His Father.  2. Again, it is a mystery ; because when it was revealed, it was revealed but to few.   It was revealed at the first but to the Jews—" God is known in Jewry," &c. (Psa. xlviii. 3).   It was wrapped in ceremonies and types, and in general promises, to them.   It was quite hid from most part of the world.  3. Again, when Christ came, and was discovered to the Gentiles, yet it is a mystery even in the Church, to carnal men, that hear the gospel, and yet do not understand it, that have the veil over their hearts.   It is "hid to them that perish" (2 Cor. iv. 3).  4. In the fourth place, it is a mystery, because though we see some part and parcel of it yet we see not the whole gospel.   We see not all, nor wholly.   " We see but in part, and know but in part " (1 Cor. xiii. 9).  5. Yea, and it is a mystery in regard of what we do not know, but shall hereafter know.   But is the doctrine of the gospel itself only a mystery?   No.   All the graces are mysteries, every grace.   Let a man once know it, and he shall find that there is a mystery in faith ; that the earthly soul of man should be carried above itself, to believe supernatural truths, and to depend upon that he sees not, to sway the life by reasons spiritual ; that the heart of man should believe; that a man in trouble should carry himself quietly and patiently, from supernatural supports and grounds, it is a mystery.   That the carriage of the soul should be turned universally another way ; that the judgment and affections should be turned backward, as it were ; that he that was proud before should now be humble; that he that was ambitious before should now despise the vain world; that he that was given to his lusts and vanities before should now, on the contrary, be serious and heavenly minded: here is a mystery indeed when all is turned backward. In Christ all is mystery: two natures, God and man, in one Person; mortal and immortal; greatness and baseness; infiniteness and finiteness, in one Person. The Church itself is a mystical thing. For under baseness, under the scorn of the world, what is hid? A glorious people. 1. Is it so that religion is a mystery? Then, first of all, do not wonder that it is not known in the world: and that it is not only not known, but persecuted and hated. Alas! it is a hidden thing. Men know not the excellency of it. 2. Again, if it be a mystery, then it should teach us to carry ourselves suitable to it. Nature taught even the heathens to carry themselves reverently in their mysteries; *Procul este profani,* "Away begone all profane." Let us carry ourselves therefore reverently toward the truth of God, towards all truths, though they be never so contrary to our reason. 3. Again, are these things mysteries, great mysteries? Let us bless God, that hath revealed them to us, for the glorious gospel. Oh, how doth St. Paul, in every Epistle, stir up people to be thankful for revealing these mysteries! 4. Again, it is a mystery, Therefore it should teach us likewise not to set upon the knowledge of it with any wits or parts of our own, to think to search into it merely by strength of wit and study of books, and all human helps that can be. It is a mystery, and it must be unveiled by God Himself, by His Spirit. We must not struggle with the difficulties of religion with natural parts. It is a mystery. Now, therefore it must have a double veil took off: a veil from the thing, and the veil from our eyes. It is a mystery in regard of the things themselves, and in regard of us. It is not sufficient that the things be lightsome that are now revealed by the gospel, but there must be that taken from our hearts that hinders our sight. 5. Again, being a mystery, it cannot be raised out of the principles of nature, it cannot be raised from reasons. But hath reason no use, then, in the gospel? Yes. Sanctified reason hath to draw sanctified conclusions from sanctified principles. Thus far reason is of use in these mysteries, to show that they are not opposite to reason, They are above reason, but they are not contrary to it, even as the light of the sun it is above the light of a candle, but it is not contrary to it. Here it is the greatest reason to yield reason to faith. Faith is the reason of reasons in these things, and the greatest reason is to yield to God that hath revealed them. Is not here the greatest reason in the world, to believe Him that is truth itself? 6. Again, seeing it is a mystery, let no man despair. It is not the pregnancy of the scholar here that carries it away. It is the excellency of the teacher. If God's Spirit be the teacher, it is no matter how dull the scholar is. 7. It is a mystery, therefore take heed of slighting of Divine truths. The empty shallow heads of the world make great matters of trifles, and stand amazed at baubles and vanities, and think it a grace to slight Divine things. This great mystery of godliness they despise. How shall we come to know this mystery as we should, and to carry ourselves answerable? We must desire God to open our eyes, that as the light hath shined, as the apostle saith, "The grace of God hath shined" (Titus ii. 11); as there is a lightsomeness in the mysteries, so there may be in our eye. Now, the Spirit doth not only teach the truths of the gospel, but the application of those truths, that they are ours. 1. Again, if we would understand these mysteries, let us labour for humble spirits; for the Spirit works that disposition in the first place. 2. And bring withal a serious desire to know. with a purpose to be moulded to what we know; to be delivered to the obedience of what we know; for then God will discover it to us. Wisdom is easy to him that will. Together with prayer and humility, let us but bring a purpose and desire to be taught, and we shall find Divine wisdom easy to him that will. None ever miscarry in the Church but those that have false hearts. 3. And take heed of passion and prejudice, of carnal affections that stir up passion; for they will make the soul that it cannot see mysteries that are plain in themselves. As we are strong in any passion, so we judge; and the heart, when it is given up to passion, it transforms the truth to its own self, as it were. Even as where there is a suffusion of the eye, as in the jaundice, or the like, it apprehends colours like itself; so when the taste is vitiated, it tastes things, not as they are in themselves, but as itself is. So the corrupt heart transforms this sacred mystery to its own self, and oft-times forceth Scripture to defend its own sin, and the corrupt state it is in. It will believe what it list. Therefore it is of great consequence to come with clean hearts and minds to the mysteries of God. "Great mystery." 1. That is the adjunct.

It is a " great mystery." And here I might be endless; for it is not only great as a mystery—that is, there is much of it concealed—but it is a great and excellent mystery, if we regard whence it came, from the bosom of God, from the wisdom of God. 2. If we regard the end of it, to bring together God and man—man that was fallen, to bring him back again to God, to bring him from the depth of misery to the height of all happiness; a "great mystery" in this respect. 3. Again, it is " great," for the manifold wisdom that God discovered in the publishing of it, by certain degrees: first, in types, then after he came to truths; first, in promises, and then performances. 4. Again it is a great mystery, for that it works. For it is such a mystery as is not only a discovery of secrets, but it transforms those that know it and believe it. We are transformed by it to the likeness of Christ, of whom it is a mystery; to be as He is, full of grace. It hath a transforming, changing power. 5. If we consider any part of it—Christ, or His Church, or anything—it is a mystery, and "a great mystery." It must needs be great, that the very angels desire to pry into (1 Pet. i. 12). 6. If we regard those that could not pry into it; as it is 1 Cor. ii. 6, 8 that the wise men of the world understood nothing of it. 7. Again, it is a great mystery, because it makes us great. It makes times great, and the persons great that live in those times. What made John Baptist greater than all the prophets and others in those times? Because he saw Christ come in the flesh. Let us take heed, therefore, that we set a higher price on religion. It is a mystery, and a great mystery; therefore it must have great esteem. It brings great comfort and great privileges. 8. Again, it is a great mystery, if compared to all other mysteries. Creation was a great mystery for all things to be made out of nothing, order out of confusion; for God to make man a glorious creature of the dust of the earth, it was a great matter. But what is this in comparison for God to be made man? 1. First of all, learn hence from blessed St. Paul how to be affected when we speak and think of the glorious truth of God; that we should work upon our hearts, to have large thoughts and large expressions of it. St. Paul thought it not sufficient to call it a mystery, but a great mystery. He doth not only call it "riches," but unsearchable riches. Out of the riches and treasure of the heart the mouth will speak. (1) And that we may the better do this, let us labour to have as deep conceits in our understandings as we can of that mystery of sinfulness that is in us, and that mystery of misery. (2) Again, if we would have large and sensible thoughts and apprehensions of these things, such as the blessed apostle, let us set some time apart to meditate of these things, till the heart be warmed; let us labour to fasten our thoughts, as much as we can, on them every day; to consider the excellency of this mystery of religion in itself, and the fruit of it in this world and in the world to come. It is a good employment; for from thence we shall wonder at nothing in the world besides. What is the reason that men are taken up with admiration of petty mysteries, of poor things? Because their thoughts were never raised up to higher considerations. 2. Let us bring great endeavours to learn it, and great respect towards it, and great love to God for it. Let everything in us be answerable to this "great mystery," which is a " great mystery." "Without controversy." It is so under the broad seal of public confession, as the word in the general signifies; by the confession of all, it is " great." It is a confessed truth, that the "mystery of godliness is great." As if the apostle had said, I need not give you greater confirmation; it is, without question or controversy, a great mystery. (1) First, in itself, it is not to be doubted of. It is a great grounded truth, as lightsome and clear as if the gospel were written with a sunbeam, as one saith. There is nothing clearer and more out of controversy than sacred evangelical truths. (2) And as they are clear and light-some in themselves, so they are apprehended of all God's people. However it be controverted by others, yet they are not considerable. All that are the children of the Church, that have their eyes open, they confess it to be so, and wonder at it as " a great mystery." They without all doubt and controversy embrace it. Things are not so clear in the gospel that all that are sinful and rebellious may see whether they will or no. 1. I will only make that use of it that a great scholar in his time once did upon the point, a noble earl of Mirandula. If there be no calling these things into question, if they have been confirmed by so many miracles, as they have been in a strict sense, why then, how is it that men live as if they made no question of the falsehood of them? What kind of men are those that live as if it were "without controversy," that Christian truths had no truth at all in them? Men live so carelessly and profanely, and slight and scorn these great mysteries, as if they made no question but they are false. 2. Again, in that he saith, "without controversy," or confessedly, "great is the mystery of godliness": here we may know, then, what truths are to be entertained as catholic universal truths, those that without question are received. Now we come to the particulars of this great mystery. "God manifested in the flesh." This, and the other branches that follow, they are all spoken of Christ. Indeed, the "mystery of godliness" is nothing but Christ, and that which Christ did. Christ was "manifested in the flesh, justified in the Spirit, seen of angels, preached to the Gentiles, believed on in the world, received up in glory." So that from the general we may observe this, that "Christ is the scope of the Scripture." Christ is the pearl of that ring; Christ is the main, the centre wherein all those lines end. He begins here with this, "God manifested in the flesh"; not God taken essentially, but taken personally. God in the Second Person, was manifested. All actions are of persons. The Second Person was incarnate. The Three Persons are all God; yet they were not all incarnate, because it was a personal action of the Second Person. And why in that Person? 1. Because He was the image of God. And none but the image of God could restore us to that image. He was the Son of God, and none but the natural Son could make us sons. By "flesh," here, is meant human nature; the property of human nature, both body and soul. And by "flesh" also is usually understood the infirmities and weakness of man, the miserable condition of man. In that God, the Second Person, appeared in our nature, in our weak and tainted disgraced nature after the Fall; from hence comes—1. First of all, the enriching of our nature with all graces in Christ, as it is in Col. ii. 3. 2. The ennobling of our nature. In that God appeared in our nature it is much ennobled. 3. In the third place, hence comes the enabling of our nature to the work of salvation that was wrought in our nature. It came from hence, "God was in the flesh." 4. And hence comes this likewise, that whatsoever Christ did in our nature, God did it, for God appeared in our nature. He took not upon Him the person of any man, but the nature. 5. Hence comes also the union between Christ and us. Whence is it that we are "sons of God"? Because He was the "Son of Man," "God in our flesh." There are three unions: the union of natures, God to become man; the union of grace, that we are one with Christ; and the union of glory. 6. Hence likewise comes the sympathy between Christ and us; for Christ is said to suffer with us. 7. Hence likewise comes the efficacy of what Christ did, that the dying of one man should be sufficient for the whole world. It was, that "God was in the flesh." The apostle may well call this, "God manifest in the flesh," a "mystery," and place it in the first rank. 1. And shall we think that so great a mystery as this was for small purpose? that the great God should take upon Him a piece of earth? Oh what boldness have we now to go to "God in our flesh"! 2. Again, from this, that God was "manifest in our flesh," let us take heed that we defile not this flesh of ours, this nature of ours. What! Is this "flesh" of mine taken into unity with the Second Person? Is this "flesh" of mine now in heaven, "sitting at the right hand of God?" 3. Likewise, it should teach us to stoop to any service of Christ or our brethren. What! Did the love of God draw him into the womb of the virgin? Did it draw Him to take my nature and flesh on Him? Take heed of pride. God Himself emptied Himself, and wilt thou be full of pride? He became of "no reputation" (Philip ii. 7), and wilt thou stand upon terms of credit? 4. Lastly, let us labour that Christ may be manifested in our particular flesh, in our persons. As He was God manifest in the flesh in regard of that blessed mass He took upon Him, so we would every one labour to have God "manifest in our flesh." How is that? We must have Christ as it were born in us, "formed in us," as the apostle speaks (Col. i. 27). (*R. Sibbes.*)      *The mystery of the incarnate God:*—The Christian system is a great and holy mystery, presenting an important function for the maintenance of Divine truth. Mystery may only be a secret, and comprise nothing difficult in itself. When broken the secret may be the plainest thing. The calling of the Gentiles was such a concealment. But there are many who deride this view, who speak of mystery as incompatible with the purport of a revelation. Now this objection surely goes too far and urges too much. For it would then be inconsistent for any religion to pretend a Divine authority. Religion must, in addressing us, though its information be most scant, tell us of Deity, insisting on spiritual relations and eternal issues. The poorest pretext of any religion must be a theism. "Who can by searching find out God?" So vainly empty is the adage, Where mystery begins, religion ends! Nor less light is the remark, that ere a proposition be believed all its terms must be appreciated. There is something in every term of knowledge which defies this rigid perception. Others diversify the objection by taking for granted that revelation can only be an appeal to our reason, and that it will therefore contain no mystery; nothing but what is intelligible to reason. We cheerfully subscribe that reason must judge its evidence, that reason must ascertain its scope. The mystery is no object of our faith apart from the testimony which avouches it, and from the fact in which it consists. The proper notion for us to form of a revelation is that its essentials shall entirely exceed our powers of discovery. The light of reason has become so common a phrase that it may seem hazardous to call its correctness in question. But it is unmeaning. Reason can boast no light. It is only a capacity to judge upon any subject presented to it. It finds a general analogy of its function in the bodily eye. That does not impart the elemental light, but receives it, together with the impression of those images which it unveils. It is nothing more than an organ to be exercised upon things without. Reason is no more the source of knowledge than corporeal vision is that of day. A moral sun and a spiritual world are as much needed by the one as the physical sun and material world are for the other.   1. The ancient mysteries were only affectations of the wonderfulness ascribed to them. They surrounded themselves with a purposed reserve. They included nothing which might not readily be apprehended. If there was difficulty, they contrived it. If the course of revelation was slow, they made it slow. If the curtain was laboriously raised, they had hung it heavily that so it might be raised. All was intended to excite curiosity, to produce impression, to strike the aspirant with artistic effects. It was the scenery of a theatre. Unlike this wilful perplexity, this ample drapery to cover nothing, the mystery of godliness was really transcendent. It muffled itself in no fold, it was abhorrent from all disguise. It spoke in no swelling words of vanity. It encircled itself with no seeming of doubt and amazement. The cloud which was upon it was of its own glory.   2. The effect which initiation in the ancient mysteries wrought upon the mind of the candidate was generally that of disappointment and aversion. The man of intelligence, though he came to them a believer, could not go forth from them with any assurance. Indignation at the banded impostors was his first feeling. Contempt of the mummeries, however splendid, practised upon him would quickly follow. They had spoken " lies in hypocrisy." Their " deceit was falsehood." If any particle of the truth was in their possession, they had "held it in unrighteousness." But they who have " knowledge in the mystery of Christ " rise in every sentiment of gratitude and satisfaction with every step of that knowledge. Nothing has failed of their expectation. Nothing has sunk in their esteem. It is marvellous in our eyes !   3. Much delay attended the probation of those who sought enrolment among the enlightened in the ancient mysteries. Their trials were protracted. Before the profession was attained there was every harassing and tedious ceremonial. Lustration followed lustration, each power of endurance was tasked to the utmost, subterranean chambers reverberated to each other, there was a prison-house and escape from its horrors was not sure, panic congealed the stoutest frame, all extremes of sensation were combined, and the whole service was fenced round with every caution against eager impatience or inquisitive haste. But the mystery of godliness knows no such suspicious restrictions. " Learn of Me " is the language of its Founder. A docile temper is the exclusive condition. We haste and delay not.   4. The most awful vows of secrecy were exacted of those who received the supposed purgation of these mysteries. A universal execration fell on the betrayer. " We cannot but speak the things which we have seen and heard." " We having the same spirit of faith, according as it is written, I believed, and therefore have I spoken ; we also believe, and therefore speak." " To make all men see what is the fellowship of the mystery." They " used great plainness of speech." 5. The whole arrangement of this singular discipline was invidious. It looked unfavourably on the great mass of our race. Selfish in its aims, destitute of any noble philanthropy, it intended the perpetual thraldom of the multitude in ignorance and degradation. It was the most cruel and potent auxiliary of priestly device and political despotism. In contradistinction to this haughty insolence, this vile contempt, with which the Mystagogues spurned and branded the species, Christianity surveys our nature in its broadest features, its truest intimacies, its grandest generalities. If it be marked by a partiality, it is toward the poor. It says : " How hardly shall they that have riches enter into the kingdom of God ! " It says : " Let the brother of low degree rejoice in that he is exalted ! " Among its brightest evidences, crowning all its miracles, is this attestation : " To the poor is the gospel preached." Its mercies are unto all. We may suppose that the inspired writer of the text, in styling the mystery of God indubitably great, bore in mind the common separation of the less and the greater ceremonies through which the respective postulants were called to pass. These were deemed alone worthy of the epithet, and alone capable of justifying it. Now the greater mysteries of the Pagan world pretended to solve religious difficulty. They promised that a great portion of the popular credulity might be simplified. They construed facts into allegories. They stripped the fable of its accessories, and exposed the moral which was couched in it. But the mystery of godliness was a grand interpretation. It was a key to cyphers. It was the substance of shadows. It was the fulfilment of visions. It gave light and meaning to "the dark sayings of old." Those greater mysteries boasted of a predominant doctrine. We do not with certainty know what that was. Whether the unity of the Divine nature or the immortality of the soul has been questioned, we think that we may conclude, with perfect confidence, that it was neither the one nor the other. Now, the mystery of godliness has its cardinal truth. It is the Incarnate Word. All connected with this manifestation is like itself. It is sin-offering and propitiatory sacrifice. We receive the atonement. A form of doctrine is declared to us. It is the glorious gospel of Christ. Those greater mysteries commanded a powerful influence. The chambers of imagery would not be soon forgotten, even if its import was explained. Terror sometimes prevailed, or it yielded to joy and repose. Some felt an immitigable dread, others a calm relief. The mystery of godliness is power. Christ dwells in the heart by faith. All the springs of our being are moved. His love constraineth us. Those greater mysteries claimed to impart an inward life. The spirit was supposed to emerge from a mystic death, to acquire new powers, and to occupy new relations. The regimen of its noviciate was called its birth. The man who had passed through these exercises was publicly hailed as endued with an existence higher than intellectual. He was of a privileged class. This new birth is to holiness. It is regeneration, a making of us again. It is renewing, a making of us afresh. With a marked description is this mystery announced; it is the mystery of godliness. This mystery is characterised by its attributes of purity and pious excellence. They belong to it. It has a tendency to inspire them. They are its ever-present glories and its invariable emanations. But here rebuke is dealt. Those arcana to which the mystery of holiness is opposed, were the scandal of the ages through which they survived. They were "works of darkness." But the proposition of the text is not exhausted. It asserts a particular use which the mystery of godliness subserves in relation to the truth. How is the mystery of the Incarnation the pillar and ground of the gospel? Its importance to the whole scheme of redeeming mercy is thus declared, and that importance is easily vindicated. (*R. W. Hamilton, D.D.*) *The Incarnate God vindicated:*—I. THE FACT OF A DIVINE INCARNATION IN THE PERSON OF JESUS CHRIST. The proposition is complex, and we will, in the first instance, reduce it to its parts. 1. The manhood of Messiah. 2. That Messiah always possessed the Divine nature while He has assumed our own. Though there may be none who argue from His Godhead against the reality of His Manhood, however it is to be feared that too many extenuate it, it is most common to argue from His Manhood against His Godhead. (1) Titles of Divinity and Manhood are given to Him. He is the Son of God and the Son of Man. (2) Attributes of infinity and limitation are ascribed to Him. (3) Representations of self-sufficience and dependence are assigned to Him. II. This great mystery of godliness, God the Son taking our nature, is entitled A MANIFESTATION. The light of the knowledge of the glory of God is in the face of Jesus Christ. To know the only true God is to know Jesus Christ, whom He hath sent. As we cannot understand God, who is a Spirit, God is manifest in the flesh. It is the sensible copy, the transparent mirror, by which He will be known. A manifestation is a making clear of that which is difficult and obscure. It is of frequent occurrence when the later Scriptures speak of Christ. "The life was manifested, and we have seen it, and show unto you that eternal life which was with the Father and was manifested unto us." Now there were works which He was to do as well as revelations to unfold. Nor let us suppose that this manifestation was always unperceived and unappreciated. He was actually recognized. "In the beginning of miracles He manifested forth His glory, and His disciples believed on Him." (*Ibid.*)    *The mystery of Godliness :*—1. It agrees to the main design of godliness. 2. It has a tendency to promote it. 3. It has the best influence upon it. 1. There is nothing in the mysteries of religion inconsistent with holiness to God, and beneficence to men. 2. The doctrines of Christianity have a tendency to promote all godliness. 3. The mysteries of religion have not only a tendency to promote godliness, but they give the best influence to it. I. WHAT IS THE GODLINESS HERE MENTIONED? Looking into this will give us an argument for those doctrines that promote it. 1. One article of godliness, and indeed the chief of them is, that we should bow down, and worship, before the Lord our Maker. 2. Our likeness to God. Godliness is God's likeness. 3. Godliness consists in a communion with God, which is the exchange of love between Him and us. 4. This same godliness takes into it our expectation from God. 5. Godliness takes into it our regard to the Divine institutions. 6. Godliness takes into it our love to godly people. 7. Our usefulness to those who are yet without, is no small part of religion. II. WE SHALL NOW INQUIRE HOW THIS GODLINESS, AS IT COMPREHENDS OUR DUTY TO GOD AND OUR BENEFICENCE TO MAN, IS PROMOTED BY THE MYSTERIES OF RELIGION. 1. Were it not for these mysteries we could not have had an open way to the throne of grace. 2. Another principle of godliness which the mysteries of religion do improve, is a reverence of the Divine Majesty. 3. It is in the belief of these doctrines that we feel the principles of our love to God, which are but the rebound of His to us. 4. We find by experience that this makes the worship of God our delight and plea- sure. 5. In this revelation we have the greatest and best examples of our duty. 6. By this they were inspired with hope. 7. This has given good people a prin- ciple of charity to those that differ from them, and the truest value for those for whom they are agreed. I will close what you have heard with a short application. 1. If these are mysteries of godliness, then you see the true spring of the opposition that is made to them, not because they are above reason, but because they are against corruption, and hide pride from man. 2. Let us improve the doctrines of religion to this purpose, to make us better as well as wiser. (T. Bradbury.) The mystery of godliness :—I. JESUS CHRIST WAS FLESH—A REAL MAN. This has been denied. Some have said that Jesus was a mere phantasm or phantom —that men felt they saw a body like our own, but it was a spectre, a vision—- the eyes with which they beheld were the eyes of imagination. Others have said He was more than an airy appearance, but not flesh; that the nature of Christ was a special material manifestation, say, a cloud acted upon by Divine power and made to appear a human body. Some have said that the flesh was heavenly substance, and not of the earth earthy; something ethereal which ultimately became absorbed in the sun. Others, again, have held that in the body of Jesus there was no common principle of life and no human soul. Jesus Christ was flesh—real man— flesh—and bones and blood spirit and soul and body. II. JESUS CHRIST WAS GOD MANIFEST IN FLESH. In this one Being we may see real Man and true God. He is not a godly Man, but God-man. A double life—higher and lower is indicated by many circumstances. He is born of a woman and conceived by the Holy Ghost. From Bethlehem to Olivet, and from Olivet to the great white throne, God is manifest in Jesus Christ's flesh. III. THAT JESUS CHRIST IS GOD MANIFEST IN FLESH IS A PROFOUND MYSTERY. The fact is declared, but the explanation is with- held. The manifestation of God in Jesus is proclaimed—the mode is hidden. Christian philosophers have, through centuries, tried to penetrate this manifestation ; it is mystery still. IV. THIS MYSTERY IS GREAT. Not a sham and a trick, not puerile and ridiculous, not useless and injurious as the mysteries of the ancient heathen and of corrupt churches, but real and magnificent, momentous, solemn, and blessed in intent. The incarnation does not exist for the mystery, but mystery necessarily enshrines the fact. And the fact, although great in wonderfulness, is equally great in wisdom and in power, in goodness and in love. V. BUT THIS GREAT MYSTERY IS THE MYSTERY OF GODLINESS. The mysterious fact, not the mysteriousness of the fact, is God's means of working godliness in us, and our means of working godliness to ourselves. Knowledge of God is essential to godliness; and this mystery is God manifest. The reality of God, His positive existence, His independence, His truth, His might, His wisdom, His knowledge, all the attributes that constitute Him the true God, are shown forth by Christ. The grace of God, His affection for His children, His graciousness to the penitent, these are revealed by Christ. A true and merciful God is manifested by the God-man. Faith in God is essential to godliness. Submission to God is essential to godliness ; and this the mysteriousness of the incarnation secures. Love to God is essential to godliness. And to this the great mystery especially appeals. So that Jesus Christ as God manifest in flesh is a means of our knowing God, of our believing in God, and submitting to God, and loving God. This leads to devotion, entire consecration to God. This produces piety, the performance of every duty to God. The foundation of true religion is hereby laid bare, the object of religion is hereby disclosed, the nature of pure religion is hereby taught, the blessedness of godliness is hereby revealed, and godliness is hereby actually produced. VI. GREAT IS THE MYSTERY OF GODLINESS WITHOUT CONTROVERSY. That is, by the consent of all, God manifest in flesh is a great mystery. How many use the light of day without holding any theory as to its nature, or even knowing that theories have been formed ! How many breathe the air in ignorance of its component parts and unable to comprehend the explanation which science can give ! A knowledge of the chemistry of food and of the physiology of digestion is not essential to nutriment ; and a man may live by his labour without having an idea of the philosophy of toil. Now here is spiritual light in which, mystery although it be, we may walk. And here is a moral atmosphere which, mystery though it be, we may breathe. And here is a sphere of godly life in which, mystery though it be, we may move and act. God manifest in flesh is the great mystery of godliness. The lessons hereby taught are these :—1. To be godly we must respond to God-manifest. God cannot be correctly and adequately known except through Christ ; and knowledge of God is essential to real religion. 2. To receive God-manifest we must bow to mystery. 3. If we have received this mystery let us do our duty by it. (*S. Martin.*) *God manifest in the flesh :*—I. THE PERSON THAT HE SPEAKS OF IS GOD. II. The great mystery of godliness tells us that this God was MANIFESTED. The revelation he has made of Himself is the ground of all our religion. 1. One manifestation that God has made of Himself is in a character that gives us our most early concern with Him, that He is the former of all things. 2. He is manifested as the object of universal worship. This flows from the former as a practical inference. 3. Another manifestation that we have of God, and in which the gospel exceeds all that went before, is that He is a lawgiver. 4. The gospel gives us a manifestation of the great God under the character of a judge. 5. God is manifested to us as one whom we have dishonoured ; the offended party. 6. When God manifests Himself, it is as the author of our reconciliation. 7. God is manifested to us as the author or contriver of that righteousness in which we are justified. 8. God is manifest as the author and fountain of those graces by which we are wrought into his image. 9. God has manifested Himself as the great example and pattern of all our holiness. 10. Another manifestation that we have of God is, as He is the author and giver of those joys that are laid up for us in another world. III. We are now to consider that particular MANIFESTATION of God which the text has led us to, and this is said to be IN THE FLESH. 1. He has manifested Himself in voices : He used to speak out to the world. 2. He manifested Himself by dreams and visions of the night (Job xxxiii. 15, 16). 3. He used to manifest Himself by raising up eminent persons, either as prophets to teach His people, or as saviours to defend them. 4. He manifested Himself in miracles. 5. He manifested Himself in a written law. 6. He manifested Himself by several ordinances. 7. He also manifested Himself by appearing frequently to them. The angel of His presence saved them (Isa. lxiii. 9). 8. The last and greatest manifestation that we have of God is in the flesh. (1) His being manifest in the flesh exceeds all the other manifestations that He gave of Himself, as it is more familiar. (2) This manifestation of God is most certain and convincing. Many times they could not tell whether it was God who spake to them or no. (3) This manifestation in the flesh is most expressive of our union to Him (Psa. lxviii. 20). (4) This manifestation in the flesh was for the working out of a great atonement (Heb. ii. 17). (5) By this manifestation in the flesh He gave the best instructions in the matter of our duty. (6) This gives us the greatest assurance of our happiness, because He has carried His body up with Him to heaven : Thither Jesus our forerunner is for us entered (Heb. vi. 20). (7) This shows the goodness of God our Saviour towards men (John iii. 16). IV. THE NOBLE CHARACTER THAT IS HERE GIVEN OF IT, AS A MYSTERY OF GODLINESS. Under this head there are two parts. 1. That it is a mystery. (1) Is it not a mystery that He who dwells in that light to which none can approach became visible to us ? (2) Another thing mysterious in this doctrine is, that He who has prepared His throne in the heavens should dwell among men. (3) Another part of the mystery is, that He who has derived no being from a man should be born of a woman. (4) He who was Lord of all takes upon Him the form of a servant. This carries the wonder a little deeper. (5) He who was eternally holy came in the likeness of sinful flesh. (6) He whose kingdom rules over all is a man of sorrows and acquainted with grief. (7) It is another mystery, that He who is blessed for ever should become a curse for His people. (8) It is another part of this mystery that the Prince of Life should be obedient to the death of the cross. V. THIS IS A MYSTERY OF GODLINESS, AND HAS A HAPPY INFLUENCE UPON ALL PRACTICAL RELIGION. People are the better for believing it. 1. This doctrine is a great argument of our duty to God. 2. The belief of God's being manifest in the flesh is raised upon our value for the revelation He has given us; and denying it carries the most dangerous conclusion against the best dispensation that ever a people were under. 3. This doctrine is the chief ground of our hope, and without that I am sure there can be no religion. 4. This doctrine is apparently the concern of good men, such as work out their own salvation with fear and trembling. 5. There is no practical inconvenience in believing that God was manifest in the flesh; it does no harm to our seriousness in any one article of piety or comfort. 6. It is certainly a thing very desirable, and to be wished for, that He who was manifest in the flesh should be God. (1) It will be easily owned that for a God to be manifest in the flesh is infinitely more kind and condescending than for the highest creature that ever was formed. (2) In this we have a greater proof of the satisfaction that He has made. (3) In this doctrine we have a better ground for our dependence upon Him. Application: 1. Hence we see it is quite wrong to pretend any explication of this doctrine, because that is the way to destroy all the mystery. There are two glories in the article: First, that it is true; and secondly, that it is too great for the comprehension of human reason; and I am sure it is no service to the former if we are striving to lay aside the latter. 2. If it is a mystery there is no knowing it without the help of the Holy Spirit (1 Cor. ii. 10). (*T. Bradbury.*) *Christ, the manifestation of God:*—We have no faculty by which to obtain an immediate perception of the Great Supreme. The King eternal, immortal, invisible, is by all unseen; and in His existence, His perfections, His purposes, He is to all beings a profound secret, except as He voluntarily discloses Himself to them. With what angels may know of God, or with what devils may know of God, we are not now particularly concerned. The text speaks of a manifestation of God to man. Man was not created to eat, and drink, and die; to pass his earthly existence absorbed in carnal pursuits, and earthly cares, and transitory pleasures. He was made to have communion with God, to serve Him, to contribute to His glory. But a God unknown and unrevealed cannot be worshipped nor obeyed. "God was manifest in the flesh." I do not feel it necessary to prove to you now that this actually took place at the incarnation of Jesus Christ. It is as plain as it can be upon the face of the passage, that this is the event to which the sacred writer refers. We wish to consider the Incarnation as a manifestation of God. It does appear as though God, whose it is to bring good out of evil, and to make the wrath of man to praise Him, had made the guilty trespass of man which needed the Incarnation in order to its atonement, the occasion of bringing Himself nearer to His creatures, and laying Himself more open to their astonished and admiring gaze, than He could have done, had not that which He abhors presented the occasion. We mean not to imply, of course, that God was wholly unknown in the world before the Incarnation, and that no other way existed or was possible than this, of arriving at a knowledge of His existence and attributes. There is a light in nature which reveals God, and there are lessons respecting Him spread out before the eyes of all men. But revelation has surpassed nature. We speak not now of its meeting those new necessities which the apostasy has introduced, and for which nature has not the semblance of a remedy; but of this one particular, which is now before us—the making known of God. Prophet and priest fulfilled each their course to teach the people knowledge; psalmists added their heaven-born strains; the Spirit of God, Himself the Author of these various lessons, taught them to the heart illumined by His grace. And here, again, if we knew not, from the actual fact, what was yet in reserve, we might be ready to ask what farther could be added to these teachings, so abundant, so comprehensive and so explicit of the Word of God, to make Jehovah better known? And yet, though the language of inspired communication may leave nothing untold which words can convey, and nothing farther to be desired, nothing even possible, in the way of description of the nature and perfections of the Most High; still it would introduce us to a nearer acquaintance with this dread Being if, instead of merely distantly hearing about Him, we should be made witnesses of His acts, and be permitted to gaze direct upon positive exhibitions of those attributes of power, and justice, and grace, of which we had been told. Here is another advance in the presentation of the knowledge of God. Thus, the fearful overthrow of Sodom, the plagues sent on hardened Pharaoh, the judgments on murmuring Israel, speak more impressively than any language, the holiness, the justice, and the dreadful vengeance of our God. So the various interpositions of God on behalf of His people, for their deliverance from danger and for their rescue from their foes, the magnificence of His descent on Sinai, the food He vouchsafed them in the desert, the guidance of the pillar of cloud and of fire, give a more vivid conception of God, and let us more into the beatings of His gracious heart, and show us more of the glory of His nature than any words can express. And now one might, with strong appearance of reason, conclude that the various modes of revealing God must be complete, and that nothing more can be imagined to be added to those already recited. And still the wisdom of God has shown us that it was not yet exhausted, that there was something yet possible, superior to them all. We would have pronounced it incredible had it not actually occurred. It is for the invisible God to make Himself visible, and assume a habitation among men, to be born, and live, and die. This, which was in appearance forbidden by His spirituality, His omni-presence, and His eternity, was nevertheless accomplished by God being manifested in the flesh. The unseen, eternal, omnipotent God dressed Himself in a human form, and gave Himself a local, temporal, tangible existence, so as to bring Himself within reach of our corporeal senses; He came down to dwell among us, not by a mere symbol of His presence, but really, personally, visibly. And thus He disclosed Himself to man, not at second hand, through the ministry of His servants, nor by occasional and momentary displays of His own dread power and magnificence, but by a life of intimate, uninterrupted converse in their midst. And now we ought, for the proper presentation of our subject, to go in some detail regarding the various perfections of the Divine nature, and show how, in respect to them all, our knowledge receives new confirmation and additional clearness by this manifestation of God in the flesh; and how, in the case of many, it receives large accessions above all that was previously known, or could, apart from the Incarnation, be known regarding them. And here be it observed, that we are not now speaking of Jesus as a teacher. The very existence of God receives new confirmation here. Indeed, some have referred to the miracles of Jesus as affording to their minds the only argument which was absolutely irrefragable, that there is an intelligible Being, the Author and the Lord of Nature. The unity of God is also freshly demonstrated both against the thousand deities of an idolatrous Paganism, and the two independent principles of good and evil of the Persian superstition, by the unlimited authority which Jesus freely exercised, commanding obedience in the kingdom of darkness as well as that of light. But we cannot delay on these and similar points. We pass to the holiness of God. This was set in a light by the Incarnation in which it never appeared before, and in which (without designing to limit the wisdom or power of God) we may say that, as far as we can judge, it could not have appeared without it. Our proof of this is drawn not from the fact, melancholy as it is, that the idea of holiness is entirely lost among the heathen, to whom God has not made Himself known. And thus it is with all the attributes of God. They all gather fresh lustre from the mystery of the Incarnation; and when they are viewed in the face of Jesus Christ, they appear with an impressive-ness which they never before assumed. Where was the long-suffering of God ever so exhibited as we see it in Jesus? If He had given proofs before of His regard for the human race, what a nearness does this induce beyond anything else that is conceivable, that He should come and live among us and wear a human nature, become bone of our bone and flesh of our flesh, partake of our infirmities and weaknesses, that He might deliver us from them, and take our nature with Him to glory. We would like to have pointed out to you how the feelings of man's natural heart toward God were exhibited here likewise, in their treatment of God manifest in the flesh; how perfect goodness and celestial excellence raised against Him the malice which betrayed, condemned, and crucified Him; and how it is the same enmity of the natural heart still which leads so many to side with His persecutors, and if they do not madly cry, " Away with Him! " nevertheless to show by their lives as well as by their professions, that they will not have this Man to reign over them. (*W. H. Green.*)    *The mystery of the incarnate God :*—I. IN IT WE HAVE DISTINCTLY ANNOUNCED THE REDEEMER'S SUPREME AND ESSENTIAL DIVINITY. "God was mani-fested in the flesh." This is affirmed of Christ, of the Son. II. THESE WORDS ANNOUNCE THE REDEEMER'S PERFECT MANHOOD. Flesh here means our common humanity. You need not be told that it does not mean corrupt human nature; nor yet does it mean the body as distinct from the spirit; but human nature in its entireness as distinct from the Divine nature. "For both He that sanctifieth and they who are sanctified are all of one: for which cause He is not ashamed to call them brethren." He did not merely seem man, nor merely assume the human shape, as He did when He appeared to the patriarchs and prophets previous to His Incarnation; but He was really and truly man, having flesh and blood, and body and spirit, and every element and characteristic of our common humanity. III. The third important doctrine announced in the text is, THE UNION OF TWO DISTINCT AND WIDELY DISSIMILAR NATURES IN ONE PERSON. "God was manifest in the flesh." The doctrine of Scripture plainly is, that He is perfect God and perfect Man in one Person. The two natures were united, not blended: the human nature could not absorb the Divine, nor did the Divine absorb the human. IV. The text affirms, THAT THIS MYSTERIOUS PROCEDURE RESULTED IN A SPECIAL AND PECULIAR DISPLAY OF THE GODHEAD. "God was manifested in the flesh." It does not merely mean that Deity became incarnate in our nature; but that through this mysterious event and others which were consequent upon it, the will, nature, attributes, and character of Jehovah were especially unfolded to the world, and made palpable to human observation and intelligence. "No man hath seen God at any time; the only begotten Son, which is in the bosom of the Father, He hath declared Him." He is "the brightness of the Father's glory, and the express image of His person." "God was in Christ"; and Christ is manifested God. The representation is accurate, full, perfect, and, in most condescending and attractive form, supplies the identical vision of paternal Deity. "I and My Father are one." Nor is the manifestation confined to earth. In the person and work of the God-man, Jehovah stands forth revealed to angels as well as to men. The manifestation is made on a higher stage, on a wider theatre, and before intelligence more penetrating and lofty. What a wonderful and condescending method to teach us how to look on God! V. THE GREAT OBJECTS WHICH THIS MYSTERIOUS EVENT WAS DESIGNED TO ACCOMPLISH. They were doubtless such as call for these wonderful means, and as required and justified their adoption. The vast and mysterious display of condescension and love furnished by God manifest in the flesh would not be made to secure trifling ends, nor for purposes which might have been accomplished by means lest costly and extraordinary. The objects contemplated, in short, are infinitely important. "God was manifested in the flesh" to teach us the Divine will and character,—to furnish a perfect Example for our imitation; that He might die to make a full atonement for our sins; that He might make an ample provision for our pardon and sanctification; that He might become our faithful and merciful High Priest, our sympathizing Friend, and powerful Advocate with God: that He might destroy the works and power of the devil. 1. We learn from this subject, that the Saviour provided for us is pre-eminently suited to His office. 2. We learn from this subject how confidently we may commit ourselves to this Saviour, and trust in Him for acceptance and life. (*S. Lucas.*) *Why did God become incarnate?*—I. GOD INTENDED THEREBY TO REVEAL HIMSELF MORE CLEARLY AND LOVINGLY TO MAN. II. THAT HE MIGHT UNITE CREATED BEINGS TO HIMSELF BY THE CLOSEST TIE, AND GIVE THE MOST AFFECTING PROOF OF HIS REGARD TO CREATED INTELLIGENCES LIKE OURSELVES. III. THAT HE MIGHT IN OUR NATURE, AND AS ONE OF OURSELVES, GIVE THE MOST DISINTERESTED AND DECISIVE TESTIMONIES THAT HE WAS IN THE RIGHT. IV. THAT HE MIGHT THEREBY GIVE THE STRONGEST EVIDENCE THAT THE DIGNITY AND HAPPINESS OF CREATURES WAS NOT ONLY COMPATIBLE WITH A STATE OF SUBJECTION, BUT THAT IT REALLY CONSISTED IN AN ENTIRE CONFORMITY TO THE DIVINE WILL. V. THAT GOD MIGHT SHOW MORE HATRED TO SIN BY PARDONING THE TRANSGRESSOR THAN BY PUNISHING HIM. VI. THAT HE MIGHT AFFORD THE FULLEST SECURITY OF HIS PEOPLE'S SALVATION. (*John Hall.*) *The divinity of Christ:*—Like a coronation crown robbed of its jewels, so is the gospel divested of the divinity of Christ. It is true there is pure gold left in the moral teaching and the matchless precept, but gaping cavities show where once the chief glory shone. Nor is the gospel alone mutilated by denying the divinity of Jesus. The character of Jesus as a man is brought down from a calm, consistent teacher to a sincere, insane enthusiast. From divinity to insanity—that is an awful descent! But there is no alternative. Not only is the gospel and the character of Jesus mutilated by a denial of His divinity, but my relation to Him is desolated. I find that I cannot touch the divinity of Jesus without touching my respect for His person. I might respect Him if He were a prophet like Moses or Elijah, or if He were a hero like Charlemagne or Luther. But as one who made the claims that He made, as one who demands my whole heart and my adoration, I must give Him that or nothing—or at most a tear. Without Christ's divinity my life's light dims, my love chills, my hope fades, the sunlight dies out of the spiritual landscape, and all things lose their clearness in the universal shadow. (*R. S. Barrett.*) *The incarnation of God :*—Paganism is misplaced incarnation. Some of these fancied incarnations are very revolting, and some of them are really sublime. The Egyptian's cat and crocodile are gross forms for God to take. The horrid fetiches of the Dark Continent are even worse. The Greek mythologies are classic and beautiful: There is something imposing in the fire-worship of the Parsees, and the Indian's river-god moving in majesty. But when God did really come to dwell among us, He came as a human child, an infant in its mother's arms. This is at once the most mysterious, the most beautiful, and the most universal form God could take, as far as we can think. The most mysterious, because Darwin and Huxley acknowledge no more baffling mystery than that of mother and child. The most beautiful, because Raphael and Murillo attempted to paint nothing more beautiful than a child in its mother's arms. The most universal, because the traveller who encircles the earth hears no voice which declares the brotherhood of man like the voice of an infant. It is a universal language, always the same, whether the plaintive cry come from the Indian papoose hanging from the bending bow, or from the Italian bambino among the sunny hills of Tuscany. The same one touch of nature, whether coming from Laplander's furs, or Hottentot's booth, or Hindoo's bungalow, or Turk's kiosk, or Arab's tent, or the silken curtains of a palace, or the squalid poverty of a garret. Mysterious ! Beautiful ! Universal ! (*Ibid.*) *Of Christ's humiliation in His Incarnation :*—Why was Jesus Christ made flesh ? 1. The especial and impulsive cause was free grace ; it was love in God the Father to send Christ, and love in Christ that He came to be incarnate. Love was the intrinsical motive. 2. Christ took our flesh upon Him that He might take our sins upon Him. He took our flesh that He might take our sins, and so appease God's wrath. 3. Christ took our flesh that He might make the human nature appear lovely to God, and the Divine nature appear lovely to man. As when the sun shines on the glass it casts a bright lustre, so Christ, being clad with our flesh, makes the human nature shine and appear amiable in God's eyes. As Christ, being clothed with our flesh, makes the human nature appear lovely to God, so He makes the Divine nature appear lovely to man. Now we need not be afraid to look upon God, seeing Him through Christ's human nature. It was a custom of old among the shepherds, they were wont to clothe themselves with sheep-skins to be more pleasing to the sheep ; so Christ clothed himself with our flesh that the Divine nature may be more pleasing to us. 4. Jesus Christ united Himself to man " that man might be drawn nearer to God." God before was an enemy to us by reason of sin ; but Christ taking our flesh doth mediate for us, and bring us into favour with God. If Solomon did so wonder that God should dwell in the temple, which was enriched and hung with gold, how may we wonder that God should dwell in man's weak and frail nature ? Behold here a secret riddle or paradox, " God manifest in the flesh." The text calls it a mystery. That man should be made in God's image was a wonder ; but that God should be made in man's image is a greater wonder. From hence, " God manifest in the flesh, Christ born of a virgin," a thing not only strange in nature, but impossible, learn that there are no impossibilities with God. He would not be our God if He could not do more than we can think. He can reconcile contraries. How apt are we to be discouraged with seeming impossibilities ! How do our hearts die within us when things go cross to our sense and reason ! What will it profit us, that Christ was born into the world, unless He be born into our hearts : that He was united to our nature, unless He be united to our persons ? Be like Christ in grace. He was like us in having our flesh, let us be like Him in having His grace. (*T. Watson.*) **Justified in the spirit.**—*The Incarnate God vindicated :*—Flesh and spirit are opposed to each other as terms. The spirit is not made to stand for the human soul, for that is included in the word flesh ; signifying all the constituents of humanity. Nor does the spirit intend the Third Person of the Trinity, for there is antithesis, and the contrast must be found in the same person respecting whom it is affirmed. God was manifest in the flesh, in His flesh : was justified in the spirit, in His spirit. Now, then, we proceed to inquire, Is the assurance of our Lord's Divinity, its perfect evidence, the justification of all His acts and undertakings during His manifestation in flesh amongst us ? 1. A manner of very original dignity and pre-eminent authority was assumed by

Jesus Christ. 2. Jesus Christ was punished with death under the accusation of blasphemy. 3. Imposture was laid to the charge of Jesus Christ. 4. Jesus Christ undertook mediatorial suretyship and representation. 5. Jesus Christ bore the Imputation, and was subjected to the stigma, of human guilt. 6. The methods which the Saviour pursued for the accomplishment of His ends seemed unlikely and ineffective. 7. Certain promises were made by the Son of God to His people, which must always have tested His power to fulfil them. 8. The dispositions and exercises of mind which the Redeemer inculcated on His disciples in respect of Himself, may create a strange suspense. (*R. W. Hamilton, D.D.*) *Justified in the spirit :*—These words are added to answer an objection that may rise from the former. He was "God manifest in the flesh." He veiled Himself. He could not have suffered else. He appeared to be nothing but a poor man, a debased, dejected man : a per-secuted, slandered, disgraced man in the world. He was thought to be a trespasser. It is no matter what He appeared, when He was veiled with our flesh ; He was "justified in the spirit," to be the true Messiah ; to be God as well as man. "Justified." It implies two things in the phrase of Scripture: a freedom and clearing from false conceits and imputations, and declared to be truly what He was ; to be otherwise than He was thought to be of the wicked world. "In the spirit." That is, in His Godhead : that did show itself in His life and death, in His resurrection and ascension. He was "justified" in a double regard. 1. In regard of God, He was justified and cleared from our sins that He took upon Him. He "bore our sins upon the tree," and bore them away, that they should never appear again to our discomfort. Now, the Spirit raising Him from the dead, showed that the debt was fully discharged, because our Surety was out of prison. All things are first in Christ and then in us. He was acquitted and justified from our sins, and then we. 2. And then He was justified by the Spirit from all imputa-tions of men, from the misconceits that the world had of Him. They thought Him to be a mere man, or a sinful man. No. He was more than a mere man; nay, more than a holy man ; He was God-man. The reason why He justified Himself to be so. 1. It was the more to strengthen our faith. All His miracles were but so many sparkles of His Divine nature, so many expressions of His Divine power ; and—2. To stop the mouths of all impudent rebellious persons. "Justified in the spirit." Then first of all—1. Christ will at length justify Himself. This is a ground of faith. However He be now as a sign set up that many speak against and contradict, yet the time will come when He will gloriously justify Himself to all the world. That is our comfort. Now, as it were, His offices are darkened : His kingly office is darkened and His prophetical office is darkened ; but at length it will appear that He is King of the Church, and all kingdoms will be Christ's. There are glorious times coming, especially the glorious day of the resurrection. Christ at length will be cleared, He will be justified. The sun at length will scatter all the clouds. Again, as Christ will justify Himself, so He will justify His Church and children, first or last, by His Spirit. His children are now accounted the offscouring of the world. Therefore in our eclipses and disgraces let us all comfort ourselves in this. How do we justify Christ? (1) We justify Christ when, from an inward work of the Spirit, we feel and acknowledge Him to be such an one as He is : Christ is God. (2) Those that have Christ illuminating their understandings, to conceive the mysteries of religion, they justify Christ to be the Prophet of His Church ; because they feel Him enlightening their understandings. (3) Those that find their consciences pacified, by the obedience and sacrifice of Christ, they justify Him to be their Priest ; for they can oppose the blood of Christ sprinkled on their hearts, to all the temptations of Satan, and to the risings of their own doubting conscience. (4) In a word, we justify and declare and make good that He is our King, and put a kingly crown upon His head, when we suffer Him to rule us and to subdue our spirits and our rebellions ; when we cherish no contrary motions to His Spirit ; when we rest in His word and not traditions, but stoop to the sceptre of Christ's Word. In particular, we justify Him, that "He rose from the dead," when we believe that we are freed from our sins, our Surety being out of prison. In the next place, for our direction ; as Christ justified Himself by His Spirit, by His Divine power, so let us know that it is our duty to justify ourselves, to justify our profession, justify all Divine truth. Let us make it good that we are the sons of God, that we are Christians indeed ; not only to have the name, but the anointing of Christ ; that we may clear our religion from false imputations ; or else, instead of justifying our profession, we justify the slanders that are against it. How shall this be ? The text saith, "by the Spirit." For as Christ "justified" Himself, that is, declared Himself to be as He was " by His Spirit," so every Christian hath the " Spirit of Christ, or else He is none of His " (Rom. viii. 9). (*R. Sibbes.*) *Justified in the spirit :*—There is in the words a twofold antithesis, or distinction from what went before. 1. The first is in the nature or kind of the revelation ; in the flesh He was manifest, in the spirit He is justified. The former does not carry the discovery far enough for His whole glory ; many saw that who were strangers to the latter. 2. The other distinction here is about the manner of the discovery. He was manifest in the flesh, He is justified in the spirit ; which may be understood these three ways. (1) He was justified in the spirit, *i.e.*, the seat of this justification, the place where it is fixed, is the soul of man. That He was manifest in the flesh we could see with our eyes ; but when He is justified, that lies all within ; there the mind, the conscience, the affections, take in the argument. And this is the great work of the Holy Spirit ; the thing that He has in charge. (2) The nature of this justification is all spiritual. As it is delivered to the mind and conscience, so it impresses these in a way suitable to the spirit of man. His manifestation was in the flesh, by miracles, signs, and wonders, to show His power ; by meekness, humility, and patience, to show his purity ; by trouble, shame, and death, to declare His merit. These were external, the facts upon which He sustained His character were seen abroad, the thing was not done in a corner ; but the manner of conveying this to the soul is different. The things of the Spirit of God are spiritually discerned (1 Cor. ii. 14). (3) That the Spirit is the Author of this justification ; it is He that works upon our souls in the manner that I have been describing. I. We shall inquire into the sense of the words, that Christ Jesus was JUSTIFIED. 1. He had a Divine approbation, both to His character and to His actions. That He was the Messiah, the anointed of the Lord ; and that what He did was right and good (John viii. 29). 2. He was also praised and admired as another part of His justification (Rom. iii. 4). II. ON WHAT HEADS IS CHRIST THUS JUSTIFIED ? 1. As to His mission, that He was sent of God. 2. As to His personal glory. 3. As to His fitness for the undertaking. 4. As to the propriety of those methods that He used. 5. As to His claim of the great reward above. 6. As to His actual possession of it. III. THE SCRIPTURE HAS FURNISHED US WITH SEVERAL PARTICULARS. CHRIST WAS JUSTIFIED IN THE SPIRIT. 1. By the prophetical warnings that were given of Him. 2. By His personal furniture. 3. At the hour of His death and suffering. 4. More especially at His resurrection. 5. At the day of Pentecost. 6. In the conviction of sinners. 7. In the consolation of believers. IV. HE WHO IS THUS JUSTIFIED IN THE SPIRIT IS NO OTHER THAN THE MOST HIGH GOD. V. THAT IT IS A MYSTERY OF GODLINESS. 1. It is a thing mysterious in its own nature, that He who was manifest in the flesh should be justified in the spirit. (1) One testimony given to our blessed Lord was concerning His death ; and you may look upon it as a mystery that He should take such a way to carry on His design, as all mankind imagined would be fatal to it (1 Cor. i. 25). (2) It is a mystery that He should be owned by the Father at the same time that He thought Himself forsaken. (3) Another mystery is this, that the very thing which seemed to hinder the faith of men should afterwards encourage it. I mean the death of our blessed Lord. (4) It is still further a mystery that He who appeared at His death, as if He was entirely in the enemies hands, should soon after declare His own power at the resurrection. (5) The manner of the Spirit's justifying Christ in a soul that was filled with prejudice against Him is very mysterious. Application : 1. If the justification of Christ in the Spirit is such a mystery, it is no wonder that the honour of our Lord is so much struck at. 2. This shows us how vain all the ways of promoting the knowledge of Christ will be that are not agreeable to the Spirit. VI. You will see that it is a mystery of GODLINESS, by considering the influ-ence it has upon the following principles. 1. By this we learn to approach with reverence to Him with whom we have to do. 2. If God is justified in our spirits it will fill us with a care to please Him. 3. This gives us humble thoughts of our-selves. 4. This inspires us with charity to others. 5. Another principle that the testimony of the Spirit has an influence upon is, that peace and hope that runs through the lives of believers. 6. It prepares him for a dying hour ; he dare trust his soul to the care of a Redeemer at last. Lord Jesus receive my spirit. (*T. Bradbury.*)　　*Jesus justified in the spirit :*—I. JUSTIFYING IS THE ABSOLVING FROM A CHARGE AND PRONOUNCING INNOCENT. Thus, wisdom is justified of her children. They clear her from the accusations of her enemies, and declare their sentiments of her as excellent and lovely. But from what charge was He justified ? It is an important truth that, by His glorious resurrection, and the consequent effusion of the Spirit, He was declared absolved from the sins which were laid upon Him as our Surety and Substitute. 1. He was justified by His Divine nature, or by those beams of Divinity which often broke forth, and brightly shone, in His darkest nights of humiliation and suffering. He did not display His royalty by a splendid equipage, by sumptuous entertainments, or by advancing His followers to worldly honours. But He displayed it more gloriously by giving, what no earthly prince could give, health to the diseased, life to the dead, virtue to the profligate, and pardon to the guilty. When He discovered the signs of human infirmity He also discovered the attributes of Divine glory and power. 2. Jesus was justified; and the charges of enthusiasm or imposture, which ignorance or malice brought against Him, were confuted by the Holy Ghost. The character of the Messiah, which inspired prophets had delineated, fully proved that Jesus was indeed the Christ. His Spirit that was in them testified, long before His appearance, the time, place, and manner of His birth; the circumstances of His life and death, His deep humiliation and abasement; and the glory which should follow. John, who was filled with the Holy Ghost from his mother's womb, pointed Him out as the Lamb of God which taketh away the sin of the world. In the meantime, let your temper and conduct justify those claims of Jesus, which others reject and condemn. Justify His claim of divinity. Did Jesus, by the Spirit, justify His claims? Under the influence of the Spirit, justify your pretensions to the character of Christians, and display the excellency of that character. (*J. Erskine, D.D.*) *The vindicated Saviour:*—I. THE SPIRIT VINDICATED THE SAVIOUR BY DEMONSTRATING THE GODHEAD WHICH HE PROFESSED. The evidence is spread over a wide field, but it is clear and decisive. The Spirit testified of Him in the prophets, foretelling His Divine character, as well as sufferings and subsequent glory. Amid His lowest forms of abasement and reproach the prophet seers recognise in Him the full majesty of the Godhead, and all the prerogatives of the Infinite. Not less clear and decisive are the inspired statements of the New Testament. His Godhead is announced without faltering or hesitation. And that nothing might be wanting to the demonstration, the Spirit raised Him from the dead. II. THE SPIRIT VINDICATED THE SAVIOUR BY ATTESTING HIS RIGHT TO THE CLAIMS WHICH HE PUT FORTH. These claims were of the most lofty character, embracing, in fact, the office of the Messiah, and all the prerogatives and perfections of the Most High God. He claimed to be the Light and Life of the world, the authorized Teacher of the will of God, the Head and Sovereign of the Church, and the Creator, Ruler, and Judge of all men. He challenged as His right the government and homage of the universe. These lofty claims the Spirit solemnly attested and justified. III. THE SPIRIT VINDICATED THE SAVIOUR BY CLEARING HIM FROM ALL THE ASPERSIONS WITH WHICH HIS ENEMIES CALUMNIATED HIS PERSON AND CHARACTER. IV. THE SPIRIT VINDICATED THE SAVIOUR BY COMPLETING THE REVELATION WHICH HE HIMSELF COMMENCED. By new or fuller revelations He finished the Divine system of truth which had already been largely unfolded by the personal teaching and history of Christ. V. THE SPIRIT HAS VINDICATED THE SAVIOUR BY BESTOWING THE BLESSINGS WHICH HE PROFESSED TO HAVE PURCHASED. He not only revealed the truth which Christ left partially or wholly unrevealed: but also communicated the blessings which He claimed to have procured for man by His sufferings and death. VI. THE SPIRIT VINDICATED THE SAVIOUR BY DISPLAYING HIS GLORY. He has lifted and removed the veil which shrouded him, and shown us the awful splendour of the August One who tabernacled in the likeness of sinful flesh in the person of Jesus of Nazareth. To unfold the Redeemer's mantled glory was one great object of the revelation which the Spirit inspired. It illuminated the deepest depths of His humiliation and reproach, and shone through the darkest eclipse of His Divinity. The prophets saw the Redeemer as Jehovah of hosts, with His train of ineffable glory filling the temple, and shining through heaven and earth. The Spirit, in short, led them to a height of vision whence they saw eternity and immensity filled with the majesty of His infinite Being, and flaming with the brightness of His immeasurable perfections. Then again, how did the Spirit display the Redeemer's glory through the stupendous miracles which He wrought! (*S. Lucas.*) **Seen of angels.**—*Jesus seen of angels:*—I. FOR EXPLAINING THIS SUBJECT, I OBSERVE —1. Angels were witnesses of the most important events which concerned the Redeemer. 2. The angels, who beheld this amazing scene, were honoured to minister to Jesus in these His sufferings. Thus, after our Lord's temptation in the wilderness, we read, "Then the devil leaveth Him, and behold angels come and minister unto Him" (Matt. iv. 11). 3. Angels behold and pry into the grand designs, for which Infinite Wisdom ordained all this scene of condescension and suffering. They not only saw God manifest in the flesh, but they saw the purposes for which He was thus manifest, for which He lived, for which He died. 4. While beholding the love which prompted the Son of God thus to condescend and thus to suffer, angels learn to love, and willingly to attend upon, and minister to the meanest of those whom the Lord of angels loved, and for whose salvation He stooped so low. 5. Angels, who saw God manifest in the flesh, were the first publishers to man of some of the most important events which they witnessed. An angel acquainted Daniel that the Messiah should be cut off, though not for Himself. An angel was the first publisher of the Saviour's birth. II. AND NOW TO CONCLUDE WITH A FEW PRACTICAL REFLECTIONS. (1) How shocking the folly and ingratitude of many! Angels desire to look into the mysteries of grace : and men, more nearly concerned in them, esteem it a disparagement to bestow upon them one serious thought. They shut their eyes, despise and scoff, while angels gaze, and wonder, and adore. (2) Imitate angels. The sufferings and glory of the Redeemer are their favourite meditation. Let them also be yours. Count all things loss and dung for the excellency of the knowledge of Christ. (3) Rejoice that He who was seen of angels was manifest in the flesh. Triumph, oh Christian, in that name Immanuel, God with us. In creation man was made a little lower than the angels. In redemption, the Son of God, by assuming our nature, has done infinitely greater honour to us than to them. (4) Ask your hearts, Have we ever seen the Lord? You have heard of Him with the hearing of the ear. Have you, by the eye of faith, so seen Him as to abhor yourselves, and repent in dust and ashes? Doth beholding His glory remove prejudice against Him, captivate your hearts, and transform you to His image? (*J. Erskine, D.D.*) *Seen of angels :*—The word is not altogether so fitly translated, for it is more pregnant than it is here rendered, "He was seen." It is true. But He was seen with admiration and wonderment of angels. 1. They saw Him with wonderment. For was it not a wonder that God should stoop so low as to be shut up in the straits of a virgins' womb? It was matter of admiration to the angels to see the great God stoop so low, to be clothed in such a poor nature as man's, that is meaner than their own. 2. And because He was their Head, as the Second Person, and they were creatures to attend upon Christ, their sight and wonderment must tend to some practice suitable to their condition. Therefore they so see and wondered at Him, as that they attended upon Christ in all the passages of His humiliation and exultation—in His life, in His death, in His resurrection and ascension. 3. They saw Him so as they were witnesses of Him to men. They gave testimony and witness of Him. (1) Shall angels see and wonder at these things? at the love and mercy and wisdom of God in governing His Church, in joining together things irreconcilable to man's comprehension, infinite justice with infinite mercy in Christ, that God's wrath and justice should be satisfied in Christ, and thereby infinite mercy showed to us? Shall they wonder at it, and joy and delight in it, and shall we slight those things that are the wonderment of angels? There are a company of profane spirits—I would there were not too many among us—that will scarce vouchsafe to look into these things, that have scarcely the book of God in their houses. They can wonder at a story, or a poem, or some frothy device ; at base things not worthy to be reckoned of. (2) Again, from hence, that Christ was seen and attended on and admired by angels, there is a great deal of comfort issueth to us. So we have a derivative comfort from the attendance of angels upon Christ. But surely, whatsoever they did to Him they do to us, because there is the same respect to Head and members. And hence we have the ground of the perpetuity of it, that they will for ever be attendants to us ; because their love and respect to us is founded upon their love and respect to Christ. Likewise, it may comfort us in all our extremities whatsoever, in all our desertions. The time may come, beloved, that we may be deserted of the world, and deserted of our friends ; we may be in such straits as we may have nobody in the world near us. Oh! but if a man be a true Christian, he hath God and angels about him alway. A Christian is a king ; he is never without his guard, that invisible guard of angels. (*R. Sibbes.*) *God manifested to angels by the scheme of human redemption :*—I. IN THE DEPTH OF HIS CONDESCENSION. It is probable that even angels cannot directly see God in the Person of the Father, and in His infinite essence. They see Him only in the displays of His glory. His condescension reaches to the lowest depth. They see Him reigning with the Father amid the ineffable glories of heaven, " making Himself of no reputation, and taking upon Him the form of a servant, and humbling Himself to become obedient unto death, even the death of the Cross." II. In the scheme of godliness, GOD WAS SEEN OF ANGELS IN THE MYSTERY OF HIS INCARNATION. This event, so strange and unparalleled in its character, would awaken their deepest interest, and largely engage their attention. They would learn something of it from the first promise, although it doubtless involved much more than they at first perceived. We are not to suppose, however, that the whole mystery of His incarnation was then made known to angels. III. In the scheme of godliness GOD WAS SEEN OF ANGELS IN THE SUPREME WISDOM OF HIS COUNCILS. In its contrivance and execution, they saw a display of intelligence which had never before impressed them. IV. In the scheme of godliness, GOD WAS SEEN OF ANGELS IN THE SOLEMN MAJESTY OF HIS JUSTICE. Never had they seen this attribute stand out in such tremendous manifestation, as when they saw Christ made " a propitiation to declare the righteousness of God for the remission of sins that are past." V. In the scheme of godliness, GOD WAS SEEN OF ANGELS IN THE IMMENSE ACHIEVEMENTS OF HIS POWER. They saw all power in heaven and in earth committed to the incarnate Son, and omnipotently wielded for the rescue of man, and for the overthrow of his enemies. VI. In the scheme of godliness, GOD WAS SEEN OF ANGELS IN THE INFINITE TENDERNESS OF HIS LOVE. Here they saw the fullest manifestation of this attribute, and gathered their loftiest conceptions of its depth and height. Here they first saw its peculiar mode, mercy. They had seen it developed as goodness, as infinite benignity before, but not its peculiar form, mercy. They required no sacrifice. VII. In the mystery of godliness, GOD WAS SEEN OF ANGELS IN THE PERFECT HARMONY OF HIS ATTRIBUTES. VIII. In the scheme of godliness, GOD WAS SEEN OF ANGELS IN THE GRANDEUR OF HIS ULTIMATE PURPOSES. What a host of unparalleled events rush on their brightening view! Earth redeemed!—devils vanquished!—death destroyed!—angels established!—the universe conserved!—sin and ruin all confined to hell!—man saved!—Messiah enthroned, and crowned with all power and glory!—the whole Godhead illustrated! —the Father glorified!—and all the faithful host of God united into one great and rejoicing family for ever! What purposes are unfolded here! We thus learn that the scheme of our redemption deeply interests the whole universe. (S. Lucas.) Seen of angels:—I. WHAT IS IT FOR THAT GOD WHO WAS MANIFEST IN THE FLESH AND JUSTIFIED IN THE SPIRIT TO BE SEEN OF ANGELS? 1. We may hence collect the esteem they had for the person of our Lord. 2. The esteem the angels had for our blessed Lord appears from their care to promote the design that He came about. Christ is seen and admired of the angels in His design as well as His person because it is their care to spread the gospel. II. The next general head is to consider it as a MYSTERY that our God should be seen of angels. Now this part of the story, that He was seen of angels, is wonderful. 1. This was a Saviour of whom they had no need, for they never sinned. 2. It farther enhances this wonder that they should pay so much regard to one who came down into a nature beneath their own. III. I have no more to do upon this branch of the Christian religion than to show you how it is a mystery of GODLINESS. 1. The belief of this gives life and soul to our duty. 2. Another act of our duty is a courageous profession of His name. 3. From His being seen of angels, in the way that I have described, we are encouraged in our dependence upon His grace, as that which is sufficient for us. 4. Here is an argument for your care and love to the people of a Redeemer. **Preached unto the Gentiles.**—*Preached to the Gentiles:*—First of all, there must be a dispensation of Christ. See the equity of this even from things among men. It is not sufficient that physic be provided; but there must be an application of it. It is not sufficient that there is a treasure; but there must be a digging of it out. It is not sufficient that there be a candle or light; but there must be a holding out of the light for the good and use of others. It was not sufficient that there was a " brazen serpent," but the brazen serpent must be " lifted up " that the people might see it. It is not sufficient that there be tapestry and glorious hangings, but there must be an unfolding of them. What it is to preach. 1. To preach is to open the mystery of Christ, to open whatsoever is in Christ; to break open the box that the savour may be perceived of all. To open Christ's natures and person what it is; to open the offices of Christ. And likewise the states wherein He executed His office. First, the state of humiliation. But it is not sufficient to preach Christ, to lay open all this in the view of others; but in the opening of them there must be application of them to the use of God's people, that they may see their interest in them; and there must be an alluring of them, for to preach is to woo. And because people are in a contrary state to Christ, " to preach Christ " is even to begin with the law, to discover to people their estate by nature. A man can never preach the gospel that makes not way for the gospel by showing and convincing people what they are out of Christ. This preaching is that whereby God dispenseth salvation and grace ordinarily. And God in wisdom sees it the fittest way to dispense His grace to men by men. Why? (1) To try our obedience to the truth itself. He would have men regard the things spoken, not for the person that speaks them, but for the excellency of the things. (2) And then God would knit man to man by bonds of love. Now there is a relation between pastor and people by this ordinance of God. (3) And then it is more suitable to our condition. We could not hear God speak, or any more excellent creatures. (4) And it is more proportionable to our weakness to have men that speak out of experience from themselves that preach the gospel, that they have felt the comfort of themselves. It works the more upon us. Let us therefore set a price upon God's ordinance. There must be this dispensation. Christ must be "preached." Preaching is the chariot that carries Christ up and down the world. But then, in the next place, this preaching it must be of Christ; Christ must be "preached." But must nothing be preached but Christ? I answer, Nothing but Christ, or that that tends to Christ. The foundation of all these duties must be from Christ. The graces for these duties must be fetched from Christ; and the reasons and motives of a Christian's conversation must be from Christ, and from the state that Christ hath advanced us unto. The prevailing reasons of a holy life are fetched from Christ. Now Christ must be preached wholly and only. We must not take anything from Christ, nor join anything to Christ. Christ must be preached; but to whom? "To the Gentiles." Here lies the mystery, that Christ, who was "manifest in the flesh, justified in the spirit," &c., should be "preached to the Gentiles." But why did God suffer the Gentiles to "walk in their own ways"? (Acts xiv. 16). Why did He neglect and over-look the Gentiles, and suffer them to go on "in their own ways," so many thousand years before Christ came? Were they not God's creatures as well as the Jews? I answer, This is a mystery, that God should suffer those witty people, that were of excellent parts, to go on "in their own ways." But there was matter enough in themselves. We need not call God to our bar to answer for Himself. They were malicious against the light they knew. They imprisoned the light of nature that they had, as it is Rom. i. 21. They were unfaithful in that they had. It is God's sovereignty. We must let God do what He will. Therefore we cannot be too much thankful for that wondrous favour which we have enjoyed so long time together under the glorious sunshine of the gospel. Hence we have a ground likewise of enlarging the gospel to all people, because the Gentiles now have interest in Christ; that merchants and those that give themselves to navigation, they may with good success carry the gospel to all people. There are none shut out now since Christ in this last age of the world; and certainly there is great hope of those western people. (*R. Sibbes.*) *Jesus preached unto the Gentiles :*—I. I AM TO REPRESENT IN WHAT MANNER CHRIST WAS PREACHED TO THE GENTILES. 1. The great truths which relate to Christ were declared and explained to them. Christ, therefore, was the chief, though not the only subject of the apostle's sermons; and everything else was preached in reference to Him. What we are told of Paul's sermons at Corinth and Rome is equally true of the sermons of the rest of the apostles. What were the things concerning Christ which they taught it is impossible to say in one sermon. The undertaking of Christ in the covenant of redemption and the promises then made Him by the Father; His personal glory, both as the Equal and Fellow of the Almighty, and as anointed in His human nature with the Holy Ghost and with power; His fitness as God-man for redeeming lost mankind. 2. The apostles laid before their hearers sufficient evidence of the truths concerning Christ in which they were instructed. Thus Paul confounded the Jews which dwelt at Damascus, proving that Jesus is very Christ. At a synagogue in Thessalonica, as his manner was, he went in unto them, and three Sabbath days reasoned with them out of the Scriptures, opening and alleging that Christ must needs have suffered and risen again from the dead, and that Jesus is the Christ. 3. The apostles invited and commanded their hearers to believe on Christ, to receive Him, and to rest on Him alone for salvation. Christ and the blessings of His purchase were freely offered to all, and all were invited and enjoined to accept them. II. I am next to show IN WHAT RESPECT CHRIST PREACHED TO THE GENTILES IS A MYSTERY. It was mysterious that, for a long period, God suffered them to walk in their own ways, giving His statutes unto Jacob and His testimonies unto Israel, while He dealt not so with other nations. This, however, was a mystery of wisdom. Still, however, it remains a mystery that to the Gentiles

Christ was preached when they were at the very worst. Search the inspired Epistles and tell me was Rome, Corinth, Ephesus, or Crete celebrated for sobriety, charity, justice, benevolence, and other humane and social virtues, when the apostles were sent to publish in their ears the religion of Jesus? Did they generally resemble a Socrates, an Aristides, a Fabricius, a Camillus? Alas! wisdom and goodness were far from them. What can we say to these things? How unsearchable are God's judgments, and His ways past finding out! When offers of salvation were made in the amplest manner to a generation so enlightened and yet so profligate, does not this manifest that all, however vile and unworthy, are welcome ot the Saviour? The confirmation of Christianity might be another end of this mysterious dispensation. The gospel was intended to subdue sinners to Christ. God, therefore, first sends it on that design, in an age where it was to meet with the greatest opposition, that its amazing conquests might manifest its Divine original. And this leads me to observe that the effects of the preaching of Christ to the Gentiles were mysterious and amazing. When the men of Cyprus and Cyrene spoke to the Grecians, preaching the Lord Jesus, the hand of the Lord was with them; and a great number believed and turned to the Lord. (*J. Erskine, D.D.*) *The proclaimed Saviour:*—I. HE WAS PREACHED UNTO THE GENTILES AS THE DIVINE SON OF GOD. II. THE INCARNATE GOD WAS PREACHED UNTO THE GENTILES AS HAVING BY HIS DEATH ON THE CROSS PRESENTED AN ATONING SACRIFICE FOR THE SINS OF THE WORLD. III. CHRIST WAS PREACHED UNTO THE GENTILES AS THE HIGH PRIEST AND DAYS-MAN APPÓINTED TO MEDIATE BETWEEN GOD AND MAN, AND TO RECONCILE MAN TO HIS OFFENDED CREATOR. IV. THE INCARNATE GOD WAS PREACHED UNTO THE GENTILES AS THE GRAND CENTRE AND MEANS OF UNION TO THE WHOLE CHURCH OF GOD. V. CHRIST WAS PREACHED TO THE GENTILES AS THE SUPREME AND UNIVERSAL JUDGE. (*S. Lucas.*) *Preached unto the Gentiles:*—I. I am to explain the thing itself that is here said of Christ Jesus, that the God who was manifested in the flesh, justified in the Spirit, and seen of angels, is now PREACHED UNTO THE GENTILES. What is the import of the expression that He was preached? The word signifies the office of a herald, or, as some think, of an ambassador. 1. To preach Christ is to declare that He is the only Mediator between God and man; and when this is preached among the Gentiles, it is to turn them from the error of their way, and the vile abominations they were got into. 2. When we preach Christ, we represent Him as sufficient to answer all the danger that our souls are in. 3. Preaching Christ is telling these things in the plainest and most open way we can. 4. We preach Christ as One who is willing to seek and save that which is lost. 5. Our preaching of Christ signifies the pains we are at in persuading people to come to Him. 6. We assert His authority over the whole creation, and especially over the Churches; that He has the government upon His shoulder; that all power is given to Him in heaven and in earth. 7. In this preaching of Christ we have an eye to that state where His glory shall be seen and ours complete. II. The other part of the truth contained in this text is, that He was preached unto the Gentiles; by whom we are to understand all the rest of the world, who had been, by the providence of God, a long while distinguished from one particular people. 1. You will see, by going over some historical accounts, that until the gospel came to be preached in this last and best edition, religion confined and drew in itself by every new dispensation. As, for example—(1) When God had revealed that promise, which was the blooming gospel, that the seed of the woman should break the serpent's head, as it was delivered to our first parents, so it equally concerned all their posterity. (2) After the flood, when our whole nature consisted of no more than what came out of the ark, Noah had three sons—Shem, Ham, and Japhet—and it is only the first of these among whom the true worship was maintained. (3) Here is still a farther narrowing of the Divine interest; for though Abraham's whole family were taken into an external covenant during his own days, yet one-half of them are cut off afterwards. (4) Here is a farther limitation; for though Isaac had the promise renewed to him—that in his seed should all the families of the earth be blessed—yet that is only to be understood of one-half. (5) Jacob's whole family, indeed, remain possessed of the true religion, and all the twelve tribes are brought out of Egypt; but in Jeroboam's time ten of them fall off both from their king and their God. (6) Whether the ten tribes returned with the two or not—as to me it seems probable they did—yet you find in a little time they revive the old prejudice. The Samaritans were supposed by the Jews not to be of the stock of Israel; but it is plain they always claimed it. (7) There seems to be a yet narrower distinction; for the people who lived at some distance from the temple, though there was no dispute of their lineal descent, are accounted afar off. 2. From that period the Divine mercy entered into other measures. You may then see how religion widened in pursuance of ancient prophecies. (1) Our Saviour was a Minister of the circumcision, and only sent to the lost sheep of the house of Israel : but yet even then He gave a dawn of His being preached among the Gentiles. (2) Accordingly, at His death, He took away all that which had kept up the distinction between Jew and Gentile, and so laid the foundation for their having the gospel. (3) He gave orders to His disciples, soon after the resurrection, that they might be witnesses for Him in Jerusalem, Judæa, Samaria, and to the uttermost ends of the earth. (4) For this He gives them qualifications. They are endued with power from on high ; the Holy Ghost came upon them. (5) He did it in accomplishment of His ancient prophecies. The Book of God is full to this purpose. Promises are made to those people who seemed the farthest off from mercy. II. He who thus distinguished Himself by an honour that had not been known for many ages could be no other than the Most High God. Jehovah is to be King over all the earth ; and in that day there shall be one Lord, and His name one. 1. We can preach no person to the Gentiles as the only Mediator between God and man, but one that is God as well as man. 2. In preaching Christ Jesus, we represent Him to the world as sufficient to answer all the necessities of their souls, both by way of atonement for them and of conquest over them ; that He paid a full price, and that He is possessed of a complete fund. We durst not say of a creature, let him be never so glorious, that by one offering he has for ever perfected them that are sanctified. 3. I told you that in preaching Christ Jesus we are to make a public discovery of Him. We must not conceal His righteousness and His truth from the great congregation, and in that are to run all hazards ; but this is more than we owe to a creature. 4. In preaching Christ Jesus we declare His willingness to save them that are lost. 5. Our preaching is persuading sinners to come to Him, that they may have life. 6. We proclaim Him as the great Head over all things unto His Church. III. We are to consider this branch of our religion as a MYSTERY. 1. It is mysterious that the Gentiles, who were neglected for so many ages, should have Christ Jesus preached among them. 2. These Gentiles were no way prepared to receive the news of a Saviour when He came to be preached among them (Acts xiv. 16). 3. It is still more mysterious that the Jews should reject a Saviour who was to be preached among the Gentiles. 4. After His disgrace from the Jews, He is made the subject of our ministry. 5. That Christ should be preached to the Gentiles is what He Himself put a bar in the way of. He acted all along as a Jew, as a minister of the circumcision. 6. This was a thing never to be conceived of by the Jews. 7. It is what the apostles themselves came into very unwillingly ; their thoughts were of a national cast as well as others ; and this stuck by them a long time. 8. It is some part of the wonder that the preaching among the Gentiles should be put into such hands. "Are not these men that speak Galileans ? and how is it that we hear among them in our own tongues the wonderful works of God"? 9. The persons He employed were no way prepared by education for that life of public service into which He called them (1 Cor. i. 27–29). 10. It is still farther a mystery in the way that God took to spread this gospel among the Gentiles ; that He should raise up these men to run all manner of dangers, who might have lived secure and protected (1 Cor. iv. 9–13). 11. The great wonder of all is, that they should be qualified with the gift of tongues. 12. He called most of them to seal this truth with their blood, which was the highest testimony that nature could give to what grace had taught. IV. I am now to show you that this branch of Christianity enjoys the same beautiful character that is given of all the rest; that it is a mystery of godliness, and promotes a pure and undefiled religion before God and our Father. 1. That minister who preaches up the Divinity of Christ, and tells the world plainly that He is no other than the Most High God, is likely to promote religion among men, because he speaks out. We see, we know what he means. 2. They who preach up Christ as the Most High God do insist upon such an object of their ministry as deserves to be so. 3. When we preach Christ as God, it answers the demand of your duty to Him. 4. This agrees to the nature of your dependence upon Him. Our gospel tells us there is salvation in no other. 5. This provides for all the comfort that we can stand in need of. The application of this is what I have but little room for; I will therefore confine myself to these three particulars. (1) If it is God whom we preach to the Gentiles—a God manifest in the flesh—then you may be very sure we have no reason to be ashamed of the testimony of our Lord. (2) Let us, upon this account, recommend ourselves to your friendship and hearty prayers. (*T. Bradbury.*) **Believed on in the world.**—*Believed on in the world :*—After " preached to the Gentiles," he joins "believed on in the world," to show that faith "comes by hearing." Indeed, "preaching" is the ordinance of God, sanctified for the begetting of faith, for the opening of the understanding, for the drawing of the will and affections to Christ. Therefore the gospel unfolded is called " the Word of faith," because it begets faith. God by it works faith; and it is called the " ministry of reconciliation " (2 Cor. v. 18), because God by it publisheth reconciliation. As preaching goes before believing, so it is the blessed instrument, by reason of the Spirit accompanying of it, to work faith. We see the excellency and necessary use of this grace of faith. How is Christ to be believed on ? 1. We must rest upon no other thing, either in ourselves or out of ourselves, but Christ only. 2. And whole Christ must be received. We see here Christ " believed on in the world "—the world that was opposite, that were enemies, that were under Satan. Who shall despair, then ? Now, I shall show how this is a mystery. 1. First, if we consider what the world was, an opposite and enemy to Christ ; and under His enemy, being slaves to Satan, being idolaters, in love with their own inventions, which men naturally doat on ; here was the wonder of God's love and mercy, that he should vouchsafe it to such wretches. It was a mystery that the world should believe. If we consider, besides their greatness and wisdom, the inward malicious disposition of the world, being in the strong man's possession, for these men to believe the gospel, surely it must needs be a great mystery. 2. Again, if we consider the parties that carried the gospel, whereby the world was subdued—a company of weak men, unlearned men, none of the deepest for knowledge, only they had the Holy Ghost to teach and instruct, to strengthen and fortify them—which the world took no notice of—men of mean condition, of mean esteem, and few in number: and these men they came not with weapons, or outward defence, but merely with the Word, and with sufferings. 3. Again, if we consider the truth that they taught, being contrary to the nature of man, contrary to his affections ; to enforce self-denial to men that naturally are full of self-love. 4. Again, if we consider another circumstance, it adds to the mystery ; that is, the suddenness of the conquest. 5. Again, it is a wonder in respect of Christ, whom the world " believed on." What was Christ ? Indeed, He was the Son of God, but He appeared in abased flesh, in the form of a " servant." He was crucified. And for the proud world to believe in a crucified Saviour, it was a mystery. 6. Lastly, it is a great mystery, especially in respect of faith itself, faith being so contrary to the nature of man. (*R. Sibbes.*) *Jesus believed on in the world :*—I. The import of Christ being believed on in the world. Doubtless Paul here speaks of saving faith. What that is we are told : " Whosoever believeth that Jesus is the Christ, is born of God." Yet faith, though it views Jesus in all His mediatorial characters, in its first acts chiefly beholds Him as purchasing for us salvation by His meritorious sufferings. And hence, in many scriptures the death and sacrifice of Christ is represented as the peculiar object of faith. II. The mysteriousness of Christ being believed on in the world. 1. It is a mystery that even under the most encouraging external circumstances, men savingly believe. Many are so immersed in business, or intoxicated with pleasure, that their attention is in vain courted to objects which strike not their senses. A humbled, self-condemning sinner, coming boldly to the throne of grace, for mercy to pardon, and grace to help, is indeed a wonderful spectacle. Faith is the gift of God ; and no common inconsiderable gift. 2. In the apostolic age the multitude brought to believe was mysterious. (*J. Erskine, D.D.*) *The accepted Saviour :*—I. The success of the first preachers of the gospel will appear mysterious when we consider the themes which they proclaimed. II. The success of the first preachers of the gospel appears greatly mysterious when we consider the human agency by which it was secured : an agency, humanly speaking, the most inadequate to such success, and the most unlikely to realize it. III. The success of the first preachers of the gospel appears mysterious when we consider the numerous and formidable obstacles arrayed against them, and which they had to surmount. IV. The success of the first preachers of the gospel appears greatly mysterious when we consider the mode in which it was achieved. V. The success of the first preachers of the gospel appears greatly mysterious when we consider its rapidity and extent. 1. We thus learn by whom all the past success of the gospel has been achieved. That success most clearly and distinctly announces the exertion of the power of God. 2. Hence we also learn from whom we are to expect all success in future. "God giveth the increase." "Our sufficiency is of God." "It is the Spirit that quickeneth." God must be entirely depended upon, and must have all the glory. 3. We further learn, that no matter how weak the instruments are, if they are only called of God, and humbly depend upon Him, and plainly declare the truth as it is in Jesus, success will crown their efforts. But, we must ask, Have you believed in Christ? (*S. Lucas.*) *Believed on in the world :—*I. WHAT IT IS FOR ANY PEOPLE TO BELIEVE ON CHRIST. 1. I begin with that which seems to be the lowest act of faith : and that is receiving the testimony He has given of Himself ; believing that His doctrine is of God, that it came from above. 2. They that believe on Christ look upon Him as the only Saviour of a lost world. 3. Believing in Christ is relying upon the righteousness, that He has brought in for our acceptance with God. 4. Believing in Christ is deriving from His fulness the principles of a new life. The satisfaction that He has made was with a view to this. 5. Believing in Christ is growing in the spiritual life. 6. When we believe in Christ, we regard Him as our great Comforter in every time of need. 7. They that believe in Christ are obedient to Him in all manner of conversation. 8. In particular, they that believe in Christ, live in the acts of religious worship to Him. 9. Believing in Christ is trusting Him for protection to the end of life. 10. Believing in Christ is looking to Him as the finisher of our faith ; as one that is to give the completing stroke to His own work. II. I am now to open this account that is given of Him, as an argument of His DIVINITY ; that He in whom the world are to believe, can be no other than the Most High God. In believing we look upon Him as the only Saviour of the world ; and this cannot be affirmed of one that is not God. III. As it is a MYSTERY. The nature of the work. 1. Believing itself is a mystery ; as it is acting without the direction of sense and reason, and very often against them, and therefore in opposition to the example and practice of others. So that it must proceed from something that we feel only in ourselves. (1) Believing is acting without the direction of sense and reason; it is depending upon what we do not see, and admiring what we cannot understand. (2) Believing is oftentimes acting against these two principles, by which we are to be conducted in other things. (3) Believing is acting in opposition to the practice and example of others ; and it is no easy matter to get thus high, (4) This proceeds from something within ourselves. IV. To what is said of believing in general, we may add the circumstance of place where men are to look for it, which leads us farther into the mystery. 1. You will observe the mystery of believing in Christ, if you regard it as a thing to be met with in this world, and not in heaven. Had it been said of Him now, that He is received up with glory, we could easily come into the report, because there He is revealed with a brightness unconfined : there is no veil upon His face, no limitation to their eyes. 2. It is mysterious that He is believed on in a world where He had been refused. 3. To this you may add another consideration, which heightens the wonder, that He is believed on in a world where the greatest evidence has already proved in vain (John iii. 32). 4. He is thus believed on in a world where He appears no longer. 5. He is thus believed on in a world possessed of the greatest prejudice against Him (John xv. 18). 6. It is farther strange that He is believed on in a world that is under the power of His most obstinate enemy. 7. It is strange that people should believe on Christ in a world when nothing is to be got by it. I do not affirm this in the strict sense of the words, for you know godliness has the promise of all things ; but my meaning is, that the soul, in the recumbence of his faith upon Christ Jesus, looks above all riches, honours, and every endearment of life. V. I am now to show, that for the world to believe in Christ Jesus as GOD who was manifest in the flesh, is a means of promoting that religion that ever was and ever will be the ornament of any profession. It is a mystery of GODLINESS. This will appear if you do but consider what the great business of religion is, and to what purposes it is both recommended as a practice, and promised as a blessing. I take it to consist in these four things—1. A subjection to Christ's authority, and a conformity to His image ; this may be called inward religion, and thus I shall consider it in the principle. 2. There arises from this a duty both to God and man, which is commanded in the two tables of the moral law. 3. It is a branch of this religion to make a profession of Christ, to own Him in the world, and show forth His praises. 4. The joys and satisfaction that Christ gives to His people who thus wait upon Him may come into the general notion that we have of godliness. Now all these are begun, advanced, and extended by the belief of those mysteries that we meet with in the faith, and in particular that He is a God who was manifest in the flesh.

Application : If it is part of the mystery of godliness that Christ is believed on in the world, then—1. You see how both ministers and people do best fall in with the design of Christianity ; the one by preaching up this faith, and the other by receiving it. 2. If that is one branch of religion, that Christ is believed on in the world, no wonder that Satan sets himself in opposition to it (2 Cor. iv. 4, 5). 3. How great a wickedness must theirs be who would hinder the faith of Jesus in the world ! 4. What need have we to be very earnest for that faith which is of the operation of God ? 5. See that this end is answered upon your souls (Col. i. 28). 6. Be sure that in believing on Him you regard all His perfections. (*T. Bradbury.*) **Received up to glory.**—*Received up to glory :—* Glory implies three things. It is an exemption from that which is opposite, and a conquering over the contrary base condition. But where these three are—an exemption and freedom from all baseness, and all that may diminish reckoning and estimation, and when there is a foundation of true excellency, and likewise a shining, a declaring and breaking forth of that excellency—there is glory. It will not be altogether unuseful to speak of the circumstances of Christ's being " taken up to glory." 1. Whence was He taken ? He was taken " up to glory," from Mount Olivet, where He used to pray, and where He sweat water and blood, where He was humbled. 2. And when was He taken " up to glory " ? Not before He had finished His work, as He saith, " I have finished the work Thou gavest Me to do " (John xvii. 4). 3. The witnesses of this were the angels. They proclaimed His incarnation with joy ; and without doubt they were much more joyful at His ascending up to glory. Now this nature of ours in Christ, it is next to the nature of God in dignity ; here is a mystery. Among many other respects it is a mystery for the greatness of it. We see after His ascension, when He appeared to Paul in glory, a glimpse of it struck Paul down ; he could not endure it. In this glorious condition that Christ is received into, He fulfils all His offices in a most comfortable manner. He is a glorious Prophet, to send His Spirit now to teach and open the heart. He is a glorious Priest, to appear before God in the holy of holies, in heaven for us, for ever ; and He is a King there for ever. To come to some application. 1. First of all we must lay this for a ground and foundation of what follows, that Christ ascended as a public person. He must not be considered as a particular person, alone by Himself, but as the " Second Adam." 2. In the second place, we must know that there is a wondrous nearness between Christ and us now ; for before we can think of any comfort by the " glory of Christ," we must be one with Him by faith, for He is the Saviour of His body. 3. Again, there is a causality, the force of a cause in this ; because Christ, therefore we. Here is not only a priority of order, but a cause likewise ; and there is great reason. 4. And then we must consider Christ not only as an efficient cause, but as a pattern and example how we shall be " glorified." It is a comfort, in the hour of death, that we yield up our souls to Christ, who is gone before to provide a place for us. Likewise, in our sins and infirmities. When we have to deal with God the Father, whom we have offended with our sins, let us fetch comfort from hence. Christ is ascended into heaven, to appear before His Father as a Mediator for us ; and, therefore, God turns away His wrath from us. Consider the wonderful love of Christ, that would suspend His glory so long. Hence, likewise, we have a ground of patience in all our sufferings from another reason, not from the order but from the certainty of glory. Shall we not patiently suffer, considering the glory that we shall certainly have ? " If we suffer with Him we shall be glorified with Him." (Rom. viii. 17). Again, the mystery of Christ's glory tends to godliness in this respect, to stir us up to heavenly-mindedness. (Col. iii. 1). (*R. Sibbes.*)     *Jesus received up into glory :—*Consider the glory into which Jesus is received as Mediator. 1. He is invested with the glorious office of interceding for lost sinners, and thus procuring their reconciliation and acceptance with God. Never was there a priest or advocate so truly glorious. 2. Jesus is invested with the high and honourable office of imparting saving light and life to the world by the influences of His Spirit and grace. 3. Jesus is advanced to the glory of universal dominion. To Him whom men despised ; to Him whom the nation abhorred ; to a Servant of rulers dominion and glory and a kingdom are given, that all people, nations and languages should serve Him. 4. Christ is received into glory as the Forerunner of His people, and the Pattern of their approaching bliss. Conclusion : 1. Let our conversation and hearts be where our Lord is. 2. Let, O Christian, the majesty and greatness of thy Lord excite thee to a bold undisguised profession of thy regards to Him. 3. Debase not that nature which God hath thus exalted in the person of Christ. Our nature, in Him, is advanced above the angels, and is next in dignity to the nature of God. 4. How great the happiness of those who are admitted to heaven, and who there behold the glory of the Redeemer! (*J. Erskine, D.D.*) *Received up into glory :*—I. HIS GLORY MAY BE CONSIDERED—1. As He is man, He has— (1) The imperfection of our nature. (2) Complete rest from all His labours. (3) A glory and reputation in His person. (4) His soul is satisfied with joys. (5) His body is independent on all supplies. Because it is a glorious body, it is received into an immortal life, and an eternal settlement. 2. He has the office of judge; but the greatest glory is—(1) The union of the human nature to the Divine. 3. As He is mediator, His glory appears in—(1) The stupendous union of the two natures. (2) His separation to the work of a Saviour. (3) His discharge of the trust. (4) His acquittance from the Father. (5) The union between the two natures is confirmed. (6) In this union He receives the praises of heaven. (7) He continues the mediation between God and man. 4. As He is God, He has the glories of the Deity. II. BEING RECEIVED INTO THIS GLORY MAY BE CONSIDERED WITH REFERENCE TO—1. His human nature : A cloud received Him; angels attended Him; He abides in heaven; He has received the reward. 2. His mediatorial office in the union of natures: He is owned by the Father; recognized by saints and angels; declares His resolution to continue so ; proceeds in this character through all His works, of nature, of grace, of providence ; He rules the Church ; He will judge the world. 3. His Divine nature ; the glory of this appears in throwing off the veil that was upon it, and laying that aside for ever; a fresh exposing Himself to the worship of angels ; speaking the language of a God in heaven, and thus revealing Himself on earth. 4. Therefore He will keep His glory, in His authority over the Church, in His full and proper Deity, and expects we should keep it. III. GREAT IS THE MYSTERY—God received into glory. 1. An account of mysteries in general, of this in particular. He who was destitute below has all fulness above. The object of God's wrath lives in His favour. He was deserted of men and angels, and is now their head. A suffering nature is united with an eternal. 2. A vindication of this mystery. IV. THIS IS A DOCTRINE OF GODLINESS. It promotes—1. Faith, by which we rest on the bare word of God, we make an honest profession of Him, we live with duty to Him. 2. Hope, by owning His Deity, we rest upon His righteousness, we trust Him for protection, we resign to Him at death. 3. Charity, the several senses of the word. A belief of Christ's divinity teaches forbearance of one another. Union in the faith the foundation of charity. (*T. Bradbury.*) *The exalted Saviour :*—I. THE EXALTATION OF CHRIST SUPPLIES DEMONSTRATIVE PROOF THAT HE HAS FINISHED THE GREAT WORK OF EXPIATION. II. THE EXALTATION OF CHRIST SUPPLIES THE FULLEST PROOF OF THE COMPLACENT ACCEPTANCE OF HIS SACRIFICE. III. THE TEXT EXPRESSES THE ACTUAL INVESTITURE OF THE REDEEMER WITH MEDIATORIAL POWER AND GLORY. This it is both important and necessary to observe. Distinctions must be made. The "glory" up into which the Redeemer was received, was not, of course, the essential glory of His Godhead. This He always possessed, and could not indeed do otherwise without ceasing to be God, it being inseparable from His nature as a Divine person. We need not again remind you that, as God, the Redeemer was incapable of exaltation, or of an accession of glory. To suppose Him thus capable is to suppose Him not God, and thus implies a contradiction. But as Mediator He was, economically at least, inferior to the Father, and acted as His servant, finishing the work which He had given Him to do, and was thus capable of being honoured and glorified by Him. IV. The statement includes THE INSTALMENT OF CHRIST IN HIS INTERCESSORY OFFICE. V. THE EXALTATION OF CHRIST SUPPLIES THE SUREST PLEDGE FOR THE FULL ACCOMPLISHMENT OF ALL JEHOVAH'S REDEEMING PURPOSES. VI. THE EXALTATION OF CHRIST SUPPLIES THE HIGHEST GUARANTEE FOR THE UNIVERSAL SPREAD OF HIS KINGDOM. (*S. Lucas.*)

---

## CHAPTER IV.

VERS. 1-3.—Now the Spirit speaketh expressly that in the latter times.—*A great heresy :*—"The Spirit" referred to is unquestionably the Holy Spirit of

God, who had been promised to the Church as its abiding teacher and comforter. In all their agencies and appointments the apostles sought His direction. It sometimes came in outward events, sometimes in strong impulses, and sometimes in the distinct utterances of men who were recognized by their brethren as inspired prophets. The trained ear of a musician can discover meanings and suggestions in a harmony which to an ordinary listener is nothing but a pleasant sound. And the conscience of one who habitually lives near God and listens for Him is sensitive to His whispers, and finds the meaning and the value of the promise "I will guide thee with Mine eye." Among the functions of the Holy Spirit was the occasional revelation of coming events; for there were in this sense "prophets" in the Christian Church, as truly as there had been under the Jewish dispensation. Nor were these always prominent and well-known men. Ananias and Agabus. Glimpses of the future came to some whose one qualification was that they stood on heights of spiritual communion—just as from the summits of the Rigi we have seen flashes of distant scenes through the broken clouds, which would be utterly hidden from one standing on a lower level. It was probably through one of the unknown prophets of the early Church that the distinct prophecy had been given to which Paul here alludes, which pointed out the speedy coming of a great heresy, the main outlines of which were definitely foreshadowed. Let us look at this great heresy, which has often and in various forms repeated itself even down to our own day. I. As to THE SOURCE OF THE HERESY Paul speaks in no wavering tones. 1. He traces it through the human agents to demon power. The Scriptures affirm that this world is the scene of conflict between evil and good, and that outside the range of our senses is, on the one side, the Holy Spirit of the living God, and on the other side are principalities and powers, the rulers of the darkness of the world. The alternations of night and day, of storm and calm, are not more real than are the vicissitudes of this great contest going on in the hearts of men. Allusion is made here to "seducing spirits"; but mysterious and mighty as may be their power, they are not omnipotent, nor are they resistless, but have control over those only who (to use Paul's phrase) "give heed" to them. Whether we are tempted to false thoughts, or to impure acts, or to anything else that is evil, it is not in vain that the summons is heard, "Resist the devil and he will flee from you." 2. But while we must guard against the evil thoughts which sometimes, as we are conscious, do not arise from ourselves, we have to give heed to this warning against the human agents of wickedness, of whom the apostle says, "They speak lies in hypocrisy, having their conscience seared with a hot iron." If there was one iniquity which more than another aroused the anger of our Lord, it was hypocrisy. A man who is false and unreal has no part in the kingdom of light, but is silently, if not openly, fighting against it. And the evil man here described has his "conscience seared with a hot iron"—a phrase which blazes with the apostle's holy indignation, but expresses a tremendous fact. Just as seared flesh has lost its sensibility, the once delicate nerves in it being destroyed, so there are consciences which nothing can affect. Appeals to honour and to shame are alike useless. The fatal influence exercised by such men was seen in the early Church, and is felt around us still, for no one can fail to be a power either for good or evil. Dr. Chalmers admirably puts it in these words: "Every man is a missionary now and for ever, for good or for evil, whether he intends or designs it or not. He may be a blot radiating his dark influence outward to the very circumference of society; or he may be a blessing, spreading benediction over the length and breadth of the world; but a blank he cannot be. There are no moral blanks; there are no neutral characters. We are either the sower that sows and corrupts, or the light that splendidly illuminates and the salt that silently operates; but, being dead or alive, every man speaks." II. THE NATURE OF THE HERESY thus originated, and propagated, next demands notice. The danger in our day is not towards unwholesome asceticism but towards unwholesome indulgence. Not fasting, but feasting, is the peril of the modern Church. Why then did Paul speak so strongly as he does here against asceticism? That error, which appeared and reappeared like the fabled Phœnix, was this: that there was an evil creator as well as a good creator, and that while the flesh with all the matter belonged to the evil one, only the spirit belonged to the latter. That was the philosophical reason given for neglecting the body, for eschewing all fleshly relations, and for abstaining from the material satisfaction of appetite; and against it the apostles protested with all their might, and no wonder. For if this were true, God was not the good creator of all things. If this were true, God had not come really in the flesh, seeing that flesh was the product of an alien and hostile power.  Hence many came to deny the true humanity of our Lord; they said His body was only a phantasm, not a reality, which implied that His temptations, His sufferings, His death and resurrection took place in appearance only.  Paul was not " striving about words to no profit " when he struck out vigorously against this pernicious doctrine; and before you dismiss such language in the New Testament as exaggerated, try to see what really lay behind it.  Even Satan may appear as an angel of light, especially when seen down the vista of eighteen centuries.  (*A. Rowland, LL.B.*) **Forbidding to marry.**—*The doctrine, which forbiddeth to marry is a wicked doctrine:*—I. HOW FAR THE POPISH DOCTRINE FORBIDDETH TO MARRY.  II. That THE POPISH DOCTRINE WHICH FORBIDDETH THE MARRIAGE OF THE CLERGY, AND OF ALL UNDER THE CELIBATE VOW, IS A WICKED DOCTRINE.  1. That doctrine which is a false doctrine, and contrary unto the Word of God, is a wicked doctrine: but the popish doctrine which forbiddeth the marriage of the clergy, and of all under the celibate vow, is a false doctrine, and contrary unto the Word of God: therefore it is wicked.  (1) The popish doctrine which forbiddeth the marriage of the clergy, and of all under the celibate vow, forbiddeth that which the Word of God alloweth.  (*a*) The Word of God alloweth marriage, and maketh no exception of the clergy, or any under the celibate vow.  That which God did at first institute and appoint, surely the Word of God doth allow (Heb. xiii. 4).  (*b*) The Word of God is so far from excepting the marriage of the clergy, that it doth plainly allow the marriage of such persons.  (i.) In the Old Testament times the prophets, priests, Levites, and all those who attended more immediately the service of God, and at the altar under the law, were allowed to marry.  Abraham, who was a prophet and priest in his own house, did not take Sarah to be his wife without God's allowance; otherwise, surely, God would not have so signally owned his marriage, as to make promise of the Blessed Seed unto him hereby.  Rebekah was a wife of God's choosing for Isaac.  God never blamed Moses, that great prophet, for marrying Zipporah; neither was Aaron faulty because he had his wife and children.  Isaiah, that evangelical prophet, was married, and had children too, in the time of his prophecy; which the Scripture, in the recording of it, doth not impute to him for any iniquity.  The priests and Levites generally did marry; and, however some of them are reproved in Scripture for divers sins, yet matrimony is never in the least charged upon them for any crime.  (ii.) In the New Testament times ministers have a plain and express allowance to marry, as will appear by two or three places of Scripture (1. Cor. ix. 5; Titus i. 6; 1 Tim. iii. 2, 4, 5, 11, 12).  (2) The popish doctrine, which forbiddeth the marriage of the clergy, and all under the celibate vow, forbiddeth that which the Word of God in some case doth command (1 Cor. vii. 1, 2).  2. That doctrine which, under the show of piety, doth lead unto much lewdness and villainy, is a wicked doctrine: but the popish doctrine, which forbiddeth the marriage of the clergy, and of all under the celibate vow, under the show of piety, doth lead unto much lewdness and villainy: therefore this doctrine is a wicked doctrine.  Whatever it be that leadeth unto lewdness and villainy, is devilish and wicked.  " He that committeth sin is of the devil " (1 John iii. 8).  3. That doctrine which forbiddeth the marriage of any, that hereby they may merit the kingdom of heaven is a wicked doctrine: but the popish doctrine which forbiddeth the marriage of the clergy, and of all under the celibate vow, forbiddeth the marriage of such, that thereby they may merit the kingdom of heaven.  4. That doctrine which is a badge or character of antichrist is a wicked doctrine: but the popish doctrine which forbiddeth the marriage of the clergy, and of all under the celibate vow, is a badge or character of antichrist: therefore this popish doctrine is wicked.  III. ANSWER THE POPISH ARGUMENTS WHICH THEY BRING TO PROVE THE UNLAWFULNESS OF THE MARRIAGE OF THE CLERGY, AND SUCH WHO ARE UNDER THE CELIBATE VOW.  1. Their first argument is drawn from the uncleanness which they affirm to be contracted by marriage; such as the clergy, and all who are more immediately devoted unto God, must abstain from.  This they endeavour to prove—(1) By the Levitical uncleanness (Lev. xv.); and the speech of Abimelech unto David (1 Sam. xxi. 4).  (2) Such as are married, they say, " are in the flesh," therefore unclean, and so " cannot please God" (Rom. viii. 8).  Answer 1. There is no uncleanness or unholiness in marriage itself, or in any use thereof; which is evident, because marriage was instituted in Paradise, in the state of man's innocency; and marriage, being God's ordinance, must needs be holy, because all God's ordinances are so.  Moreover, the Scripture calleth marriage " honourable in all," where " the bed is undefiled " by adultery (Heb. xiii. 4).  2. The papists will find it difficult to prove that there was ever any Levitical uncleanness by the use of marriage ; that Scripture in Lev. xv. speaking of something else, as will appear unto such as read and seriously weigh the place.   3. It is a gross misinterpretation of Rom. viii. 8, to apply it unto married persons, as if they were the persons spoken of by the apostle " that are in the flesh," and " cannot please God."   4. As to their inference from 1 Cor. vii. 5,—because such as would " give themselves to fasting and prayer," must abstain for a while, therefore ministers must abstain from marriage altogether, is such a *non sequitur*, as the schools will hiss at.   2. The second popish argument is drawn from 1 Cor. vii. 1, " It is good for a man not to touch a woman "; and, verse 8, " I say therefore unto the unmarried and widows, It is good for them if they abide even as I."   If it be good for the unmarried and widows to abide in a single estate like unto the apostle, then, say they, it is evil for such to marry; and therefore the clergy should abstain from this evil.   That may be good for some, which is evil for others.   A single estate may be good and best for such as have the gift of continency, and are persuaded in their heart that in this estate they may most glorify God ; whereas this estate may be evil for such as are without this gift, or in likelihood may most glorify God in a married estate.   It may be good at some time not to marry ; namely, in the time of the Church's persecution ; and all that have the gift at such a time, should choose the celibate estate, that they might be the more ready both to do and suffer for Christ, and be the more free from temptations to apostasy.   The apostle is so far from asserting it to be an evil for any in the worst of times to marry, that he asserteth the quite contrary when there is a necessity for it : " If need so require, let him do what he will, he sinneth not : let them marry "; (vers. 36, 38). 3. The third popish argument is drawn from 1 Cor. vii. 32-34 : Answer 1. It is not universally true, that all who are " unmarried do care for the things which belong to the Lord, how they may please the Lord," and that hereby they are taken off from minding and caring for the things of the world.   As to the latter, who intermeddle more with secular affairs than many of the popish unmarried clergy? 2. Neither is it universally true, that such as " are married do care for the things of the world " chiefly, so as to neglect the things of God ; as instance may be given in the holiness of many married persons, which the Scripture doth take notice of.   It is said that " Enoch walked with God after he begat Methuselah three hundred years, and begat sons and daughters " (Gen. v. 22).   Abraham, who is called "the friend of God"; Moses, unto whom the Lord "spake face to face "; Samuel, who was so highly in favour with God ; David, who was " a man after God's own heart "; Isaiah, Ezekiel, and almost all the prophets, were married persons : and we hardly read of any in the Old Testament that were famous for integrity and zeal for God, but they were such as were married.   3. Men may " care for the things that belong unto the world " moderately, and labour to please their wives in the Lord subordinately, and not transgress the bounds of their duty.   (*T. Vincent, M. A.*)     *Celibacy, its advantages and disadvantages :*—This state is as honourable, useful, and blessed as that of marriage.   John was the unmarried disciple whom Jesus loved.   The family at Bethany of two sisters and a brother was the family that Jesus loved.   They had all loveworthy characters even by Him.   The advantages of celibacy are threefold—1. It is a state of larger liberty.   2. It allows more money to give away.   3. It affords more time for direct work for God.   The dangers are twofold—1. For the women ; they are liable to become shallow and frivolous, mere butterflies or wasps.   2. For the men ; they are liable to become selfish and sensual, mere octopi, grasping all for their own self-indulgence.   The one safeguard is to live close to Christ.   (*R. A. Norris.*)

VERS. 4, 5.—**For every creature of God is good.**—*Our charter of freedom :*—In meeting the heresy which he foresaw, the apostle asserted one of the noblest principles in our heritage as Christians : " Every creature of God is good, and nothing to be refused if it be received with thanksgiving; for it is sanctified by the Word of God and prayer."   In other words, a common meal may become a sacrament to us if it be rightly received : and to a true follower of Christ no relationship will prove more saintly than that between husband and wife ; nothing more pure than fatherly and motherly love ; nothing more promotive of spiritual life than the duties and responsibilities of sons and daughters to their parents.   All things and all relationships may become holy to us.   This was the teaching of Paul, and of his Lord and ours.   You see, then, that Paul wisely meets the error by stating the truth, which must conquer it.    I. THE EXPLANATION OF THIS PRINCIPLE.    The apostle maintained a truth, which being received will always save the Church from the old error, in whatever form it comes.    He declared that everything was made by God, and that everything God made was good, and only became bad when used in a wrong spirit.    Our heavenly Father would have us take His gifts as constituting a holy eucharist, bringing blessing to us and evoking praise and thanks to Him.    A truth which condemns alike the ascetic in the Romish Church, and the Plymouth Brother, who thinks that business is worldly, social joys pernicious, and newspapers fatal to one's spiritual welfare.    Be brave and be trustful in the use of all that God has given you.    It was characteristic of the religious faith of the Hebrews that it maintained the doctrine, that all things were of God ; that there was one Creator, all-wise and all-good.    II. THE APPLICATION OF THIS PRINCIPLE.    1. In its application to the natural world it is doubtless generally believed amongst us.    Flowers and fruits, and golden corn and waving trees, all originated in God's thought, and are the products of His laws.    But do not these words of Paul warrant us in going further ?    Is not the ever-living, ever-present God, who makes the flowers and rules the world, the ordainer of our lot, the appointer of our circumstances ?    And if this be so, does not belief in it give sacredness to earthly duties, and dignity to those which are most trivial?    2. Make application of this truth to the occupation of life. There are times when we feel as if we could do better work than falls to our share. In the depressed condition of commerce especially, well-educated men are forced to take up employment which leaves their best and most cultivated powers unused. But we believe that what God has ordained, as well as what He has created, will prove to be good and best in the long run: that drudgery is as Divine as dignity ; and that training for the hereafter is more valuable than triumph here.    Everything depends on how you receive and do your work.    You may go to your office as a grumbling slave, or you may go as Christ's happy servant.    No occupation (unless there be sin in it) is to be spurned, no creature of God is to be rejected, but we are to say with the apostle, "I know, and am persuaded of the Lord Jesus, 'that there is nothing unclean of itself.'"    Evil is not in the thing, but in the spirit which wrongly receives, or uses, the thing.    III. THE TESTING POWER OF THIS PRINCIPLE. Nothing is to be rejected if it be received with thanksgiving.    But that implies that you ought to reject what you cannot receive with thanksgiving to God.    Prayer and thanksgiving to God may be to you what the legendary Eastern king found his formula to be, for when a cup of poison was put within his reach, and he took it into his hand, he named the name of God and made the sign of the cross over it, according to his constant custom, and the poisoned chalice was suddenly shattered in his hand and all the poison was spilled.    Name God's name over everything doubtful, and no poison of sin shall hurt you.    IV. THE TWOFOLD REASON GIVEN FOR THIS PRINCIPLE.    In the fifth verse the apostle explains more fully how common things are made sacred.    I say advisedly *made* sacred, for the word he uses means just that.    It does not signify that the things are declared to be holy, but that they are actually made holy by the Word of God and prayer.  1. Now the " Word of God " is not the utterance of His name over food as a sort of talisman.    The allusion is to " the Word," or command of God, which expressly gave permission and authority to man to use whatever was suitable for him in the vegetable and in the animal kingdom—"Every moving thing that liveth shall be meat for you ; even as the green herb have I given you all things."    That Divine ordinance makes all things sacred for the use of man ; but man's loyal and grateful acceptance of it must be combined with the ordinance, in order to make his use of things a right and not a usurpation.    Hence the apostle says, everything is made sacred by the Word of God.    2. And prayer, and these which God has joined let no man put asunder.    In the former phrase you see the top of the ladder which reaches heaven, in the latter you see the foot of it resting on the earth—and to a prayerless man it is only a vision of glory beyond his reach.    God's Word to you bestows the gift, but your word to God must appropriate the gift, or else it is not sacred and Divine.    (*A. Rowland, LL.B.*)    *Water the good creature of God :*—A minister who had lately occupied the pulpit of a brother was dining with the family of the absent minister, when the conversation turned upon the subject of teetotalism.    The lady who presided at the table said, "Ah! I do not like your doctrines ; you go too far in refusing the good creatures of God."    No notice was taken of the remark for some time ; the minister kept on with his dinner, but at last he said, " Pray, madam, can you tell me who made this ?" pointing to a glass of water that stood before him.    The lady replied, "Why, God, I suppose."    "Then," said the minister, "Madam, I think you do us an injustice when you accuse us of refusing the good creatures of God." Silence again reigned. By and by he said, "Madam, can you tell me who made yours?" pointing to the glass of beer that the lady preferred. "I can't exactly say I can." "Then, madam," replied he, "allow me to say there is some apparent inconsistency in your first remark. You prefer taking a thing man has made to that which God has bountifully provided, and yet you accuse me of rejecting God's creatures, because I prefer water to beer. Madam, I leave the matter to your more serious consideration." The lady has since seen her error, and joined the ranks of the total abstainers. **If it be received with thanksgiving.**—*Grace at meals :*—I. WHAT THE SCRIPTURES TEACH. 1. That it consecrates food to a holy use (1 Sam. ix. 13 ; Matt. xv. 36 ; 1 Cor. x. 30, 31 ; 1 Tim. iv. 4, 5). 2. That danger or the need of utmost haste should not interrupt it. Acts xxvii. 35. 3. That it is a religious duty (Rom. xiv. 6 ; Col. iii. 17 ; 1 Tim. iv. 3). 4. That we do not live by bread alone (Matt. iv. 4). II. REASONS FOR SAYING GRACE. 1. Because we have health. 2. Because we have appetite. 3. Because we have food. 4. Because we depend upon God's bounty for the providential supply of daily food (Psa. cxlv. 15, 16). 5. Because analogy confirms its practice. When we receive presents from friends, it is a pleasure to express our thankfulness ; how much more to acknowledge our gratitude to God for food to nourish us and for temporal comforts. III. WHAT ITS OMISSION SHOWS. 1. That we are unrenewed in heart. 2. Or, that we are thoughtless and ungrateful. How base a thing is ingratitude. How inconsistent in a professor of religion. IV. BENEFITS. 1. It sets a good example and lets others know that we are the Lord's. 2. It promotes gratitude. 3. It promotes morality and religion in the family. (*L. O. Thompson.*) *A lesson in thanksgiving :*—King Alphonso X., surnamed "The Wise," succeeded to the throne of Leon and Castile in 1252. On learning that his pages neglected to ask the Divine blessing before partaking of their daily meals, he was deeply grieved and sought diligently to point out to them the evil of this omission. At length he succeeded in finding a plan. He invited the pages of his court to dine with him. A bountiful repast was spread, and when they were all assembled around the table the king gave a signal that all was in readiness for them to begin. They all enjoyed the rich feast, but not one remembered to ask God's blessing on his food. Just then, unexpectedly to the thoughtless guests, entered a poor, ragged beggar, who unceremoniously seated himself at the royal table, and ate and drank undisturbed, to his heart's content. Surprise and astonishment were depicted on every countenance. The pages looked first at the king, then gazed upon the audacious intruder, expecting momentarily that his majesty would give orders to have him removed from the table. Alphonso, however, kept silence ; while the beggar unabased by the presence of royalty ate all he desired. When his hunger and thirst were appeased he rose, and without a word of thanks departed from the palace. "What a despicable, mean fellow!" cried the boys. Calmly the good king rose, and with much earnestness said : "Boys, bolder and more audacious than this beggar have you all been. Every day you sit down to a table supplied by the bounty of your heavenly Father, yet you ask not His blessing, and leave it without expressing to Him your gratitude. Yes, each and all of you should be heartily ashamed of your conduct, which was far worse than was the poor beggar's."

Vers. 6–10.—**If thou put the brethren in remembrance of these things.**— *Counsels to God's servants :*—The wise counsels given here to Timothy have their value in every age, and in every land, for those who are called upon to teach and warn their fellows. I. MAKE KNOWN THE TRUTH, AND THE TRUTH WILL STRENGTHEN YOU.—"If thou put the brethren in remembrance of these things, thou shalt be . . . nourished." The verb used by Paul does not signify, as our translation of it does, the reminding people of what they knew already but had forgotten; it simply means that the doctrine unfolded in the previous verses was to be presented in a suitable way to the minds of others. 1. It is to be noted that neither here nor elsewhere was Timothy called upon to be a dictator, but a teacher, he was to give counsels rather than commands. Religious truth demands the willing assent of mind and of conscience, and is valueless if it is imposed as a creed by force or fraud. Like the germ of life in a seed of corn it must be received into a kindly soil ; for only when soil and seed work together is a harvest possible. You may build a wall or a house on any soil—clay, or rock, or chalk—delving away till a smooth surface is prepared to receive the bricks and mortar superimposed upon it, and the stability of your building will not be much affected by the nature of the ground. But it is not thus you can get a harvest. A harvest cannot be had on every soil, because it is the product of life, and life needs to be in contact with certain forces before it can multiply itself. So in the higher sphere. You can make a child learn a creed and repeat it without fault, but that mental structure is only like the dead work of the builder. Truth needs to be welcomed by love, and thought, and will, as the seed must be received into good soil, and then the increase comes. 2. Observe also the reflex action of such teaching. If you put others in mind of these things you will yourself be "nourished." This is but throwing into another form the familiar truths, "There is that scattereth, and yet increaseth"; "Give and it shall be given you." How true this is, especially in mental and spiritual experience. We give our sympathy, without stint, to some one in trouble, and our tenderness of feeling is thereby intensified. We use what little knowledge we have of God's Word, or of Christian experience, and our knowledge grows. II. REJECT THE FALSE AND TRIVIAL FOR THE TRUE AND REAL. 1. Timothy is warned against "profane and old wives' fables," or in modern parlance, against stories which are the veriest chatter of old women. Probably Paul alludes to the fables and endless genealogies of which he elsewhere speaks. Foolish and trivial discussions and fanciful theories have often been allowed to overlay the truth of God, to its complete hiding, or at least to its sad enfeeblement. They are like a heap of decaying refuse covering the verdant grass, whose pale and enfeebled shoots show what its effect has been even after it has been cleared away. Let the truth about sin, and about Christ the Saviour from sin, be kept in the light; and beware lest it be covered over and forgotten under oratorical prettinesses, or philosophical speculations. 2. The man of God has something better to do than amuse his imagination or the imagination of others, and must "exercise himself rather unto godliness." God does not ask us to give up pleasures or even follies for the mere sake of cultivating an ascetic temper, but in order that we may be the more free for higher pursuits and a nobler service, knowing that those who would attain unto godliness must "exercise" themselves thereunto. To spend the week in thoughtlessness and triviality, and then to sit with inert mind under the preaching of the truth on Sunday, with an occasional spasm of repentance, or a feeble attempt at the repetition of a prayer, is only to mock God with unreality. III. KEEP THE BODY IN ITS TRUE PLACE AS SUBORDINATE TO THE SPIRITUAL LIFE. The Revised Version is to be preferred to the Authorized in its rendering of the eighth verse, "bodily exercise is profitable for a little, but godliness is profitable for all things." The apostle's reference is not to the asceticism which by flagellations and vigils kept the body under, but to the gymnastic exercises of the athlete, of which he had been reminded by the verb used in the preceding verse. IV. LET HOPE IN THE LIVING GOD BE YOUR INSPIRATION IN LABOUR AND SUFFERING. "For therefore we both labour and suffer reproach, because we trust in the living God, who is the Saviour of all men, especially of those that believe." This verse explains what Paul meant by living a life of godliness. "Life" is not mere existence, however prolonged, nor mere enjoyment of existence; but existence used for others, in the strength and under the blessing of God. The true saint "labours and suffers reproach"—or rather, "toils and strives"—in the service of his God; and he is not troubled when ill-requited, nor disheartened by seeming failure, because he trusts in the living God, in whom he has an endless heritage of peaceful and most blessed life. (*A. Rowland, LL.B.*) *A good minister of Jesus Christ :*—I. A man's goodness as a minister of Christ IS DISCLOSED IN THE FAITHFULNESS OF HIS SUBORDINATION TO THE AUTHORITY OF CHRIST. II. A man's goodness as a minister of Christ is disclosed IN THE PERSISTENCY OF HIS ADHERENCE TO THE DOCTRINE OF CHRIST. III. A man's goodness as a minister of Christ is disclosed IN THE STEADFASTNESS OF HIS IMITATION OF THE EXAMPLE OF CHRIST. IV. Lastly, a man's goodness as a minister of Christ is disclosed IN THE DEVOUTNESS OF HIS DEPENDENCE ON THE GRACE OF CHRIST. (*J. Brock, D.D.*) *Nourished in the words of faith :*—M'Cheyne seems invariably to have applied for his personal benefit what he gave out to his people. To do so was a fundamental rule with him; and all pastors will feel that, if they are to prosper in their own souls, they must so use the Word— sternly refusing to admit the idea of feeding others until satiated themselves. And for similar ends, it is needful that we let the truth we hear preached sink down into our own souls. We, as well as our people, must drink in the falling showers. Mr. M'Cheyne did so. It is common to find him speaking thus, "July 31, Sabbath Afternoon,—on Judas betraying Christ: much more tenderness than ever I felt before. Oh, that I might abide in the bosom of Him who washed Judas' feet, and dipped His hand in the same dish with him, and warned him, and grieved over him —that I might catch the infection of His love, of His tenderness, so wonderful, so unfathomable!" (*Memoir of M'Cheyne.*)          *Soul food :*—A great man had a camel that was wasting away, until it seemed at the point of death. "See," cried he, to the simple son of the desert, "here is my camel : I have tried cordials and elixir, balsams and lotions. Alas! all are in vain." The plain man looked at the hollow sides, the staring bones, the projecting ribs. "Oh, most learned philosopher," said he, "thy camel needeth but one thing!" "What is it, my son?" asked the old, wise man, eagerly. "Food, sir—good food, and plenty of it." "Dear me," cried the philosopher, "I never thought of that!" Friend, are you in low spirits? There's your cure. You don't want pity, don't deserve it. Give your starved soul more prayer, more communion with God, more meditation on the Word. Then go and try to do good to somebody about you. That's the sure cure for your misery.

Ver. 7. **And exercise thyself rather unto godliness.**—*The believer exercising himself unto godliness :*—I. The NATURE OF THE DUTY WHICH THE TEXT RECOMMENDS. 1. This duty includes a strict and impartial inquiry into our own hearts, as to what may be therein likely to prevent our advancement in godliness. 2. This duty requires an habitual attention to the duties of the closet. 3. This duty involves the exercise of much holy watchfulness and care in the ordinary pursuits of business, so that they may not be permitted to take away the heart. 4. This duty will call for occasional communion with our Christian friends. 5. This duty requires an earnest solicitude for the right improvement of our respective trials. 6. This duty demands of us a careful avoidance of such companions, conversation, and pursuits, as we have found in time past to be injurious to the advancement of personal piety. II. The MOTIVES WHICH SHOULD INDUCE US TO THE PERFORMANCE OF THIS DUTY. 1. We shall do well to remember that no great advancement will be made in godliness without this exercise. 2. Let us seriously consider that our progress in true godliness will make ample amends for whatever difficulties we may have to encounter in its attainment. 3. There is much reason to believe that this exercise unto godliness will never be sincerely made in vain. 4. It is of importance to consider that unless we exercise ourselves unto godliness, so far from making further advances in the Divine life, we shall go backward, not forward. 5. It is worthy of our serious regard, that so far as we feel an unwillingness to exercise ourselves unto godliness, we give affecting proof of the want of a principle of godliness in our hearts. (*Essex Congregational Remembrancer.*)          *The law of spiritual growth :*— The man who is content to pass along with an aimless existence; or, only seeking daily supplies for daily needs, never looking hopefully into the future, and never seeking to excel; does injustice to his higher nature, and grovels on a plane but little elevated above the demands of animal existence. No aim can so call out all the powers of the human mind, and soul, as the aim after God-likeness. For what is godliness? Is it not God-likeness? a seeking to be like God? Yet the question at once arises, How can man be like God? God is infinite, man is finite. Yet with all this disparity, the Bible exhorts us to set the Lord always before us, and to grow up into His likeness. What may be termed the physical attributes of God, those which pertain to Him as Maker of all things, Ruler over suns and systems, the Upholder of the universe; these man can neither comprehend nor copy, they are beyond his reach. It is God's moral qualities that we are to copy and emulate. All of God's moral attributes are comprised in His holiness. For holiness is moral perfection. As applied to God, it means that wholeness and completeness of the Divine nature, from which nothing can be taken, to which nothing can be added. It includes, therefore, truth, love, mercy, goodness, and the like; because the absence of either would mar the wholeness and completeness of the Divine character. The presence of every virtue is needed to make complete the full circle of holiness, and they are all found in perfect fulness in God. The man, then, who sets before himself the aim to be God-like, places above him the grandest aim that a created mind can reach after. Godliness, then, as spoken of in the text, is only another name for holiness in action, *i.e.*, practical piety. But you may say this holiness or godliness is not attainable. It is not to the full extent of the original which you are told to copy, because there are two elements in God's holiness which can never exist in man so long as he tabernacles in the flesh—the complete absence of sin, and the presence in full perfection of every virtue. The result of this godliness will show itself in a variety of ways. It will give a man the victory over himself. The cultivation of this holiness will enable a man to overcome the world. This godliness, so grand in itself, and in its results, can be secured only by exercising ourselves to attain it. It does not come of itself, nor by retired meditation, nor by earnest prayer, nor by diligent reading of God's Word. All these things are aids and adjuncts, but none of them, nor all combined, will give us godliness. It is the result of moral principles put into active exercise ; and demands the full bent, and strenuous exertion of the mind. There is much meaning in the original word which the apostle here uses, and which is translated "exercise." The literal rendering is—Be gymnasts in godliness. The idea, then, of the apostle is, that in order to attain unto godliness, we must be moral gymnasts, willing to use as severe discipline ; to undergo as painful privations ; to bear as torturing an exercise of flesh and blood ; as the gymnast did, who trained himself to win the wreath of ivy at the Isthmian festival, or the garland of wild olives which crowned the conqueror at Olympia. And why should we not ? The aims are infinitely higher, and the rewards are infinitely greater. The arena in which we are to perform this exercise is in the Church of God. Thus true religion is a very personal and practical thing. Personal ; because it is thyself that is to do the exercise ; it is an individual act, and no amount of exercise done by those around you in the same family, the same Church, can avail to your benefit. It is thyself that must be the moral gymnast in this spiritual conflict. And it is practical ; because the things in which we are to exercise ourselves unto godliness are all around our daily life. And to this repressive work, which demands constant exercise, there is to be added an aggressive work ; a watching of opportunities for good, a going out into the field of active Christian exertion. Moral powers, like the muscles of the body, are developed by exercise. The unused arm shrivels up ; the unused hand loses its cunning ; the unused brain loses its force. Our moral character is a thing of growth, and of slow growth ; first the blade, then the ear, after that the full corn in the ear. Character is principle put into practice and developed under trial. (*Bishop Stevens.*)    *Exercise unto godliness :*—Religion is not a dead, inoperative thing ; but vital, active, energetic, self-diffusive. There is an exercise unto health. This is necessary for students and persons of sedentary occupations, and the neglect of it has ruined many a fine constitution. But what is the health of the body to that of the soul ? What is the discipline of the muscular system to that of the moral affections ? There is an exercise unto gain. This is one of man's chief pursuits ; and what efforts have we all witnessed, what strenuous and unresting toil, what sleepless vigilance and incessant study, to lay up treasures here below ! But what are earthly goods to heavenly ? There is an exercise unto pleasure. There is an exercise unto knowledge. This is nobler, but not the noblest. Wisdom is better than knowledge, and the fear of the Lord is the beginning of wisdom. There is an exercise unto glory. This was the all-controlling and all-absorbing pursuit of the great military nations of antiquity, and some of them made all virtue to consist in this single aim. There is an exercise unto patriotism. This is a worthy competition, by all admired and praised. How many of you who hear me have begun this exercise ? Be not ashamed of it, nor weary in well-doing. It is a holy service, and fraught with perfect freedom. How many of you have hitherto neglected this exercise ? Enter upon it at once. It must be done, or all is lost. (*J. Cross, D.D.*)    *A heart exercised unto godliness necessary to make a good minister :*—I. I am to show WHAT THIS HEART EXERCISE UNTO GODLINESS IS. 1. It pre-supposeth a man to be truly godly. That professor or minister that is not godly can never exercise himself to godliness. It is impossible to act without a principle of acting, and exercise doth naturally require a power of it. He can never exercise himself to running, that wants feet to run with ; or to wrestling, who wants arms ; nor the ungodly exercise themselves to godliness ; on the contrary, "an heart they have exercised with covetous practices." 2. Making religion our business. In this the apostle gave himself a pattern to us. "Herein," says he, "do I exercise myself to have always a conscience void of offence, toward God and toward men." Godliness should be our great work, how to advance it in ourselves and others. Now we will make religion our business, if we take it not only by fits and starts, but make it our daily work, as men exercise themselves in their callings. 3. It imports a vigorous following of it, as wrestlers and runners ply their work vigorously. To be a little more particular, I will touch at four things. (1) We should exercise ourselves to the knowledge of these things pertaining to godliness, that we may be full of eyes, and "by reason of use, have our senses exercised to discern both good and evil." (2) We should be exercised in combating the lusts of our hearts, beginning the war against the devil at home. Like Paul, " we should keep our bodies under, and bring them into subjection; lest that by any means, when we have preached to others, we ourselves should be castaways." (3) We should be exercised to the performing of our duties, and that in a spiritual manner. (4) We should be exercised in the life of faith, without which, in vain will we attempt the other parts of the exercise of godliness. II. To show THE NECESSITY OF THE EXERCISE OF THE HEART UNTO GODLINESS, TO MAKE A GOOD MINISTER. 1. It is necessary to make a man faithful in his work, and to cause him to take God for his party, with whom he hath to do. 2. It is necessary to give a man a sense of the weight of the work, and the worth of souls, without which he cannot be a good minister (2 Cor. v. 9, 10). It is a weighty work. 3. It is very necessary to fit a man to suffer for truth. 4. It is most necessary to fit us for the performance of the several duties of our calling, whether in preaching, administering the sacraments, visiting families, or the sick. (*T. Boston, D.D.*) *A heart exercised unto godliness necessary to make a good Christian :*—The apostle gives us here a short, but substantial description of the Christian life. It is an exercise, it is not a name. Again, Christianity is not an easy exercise, but such as wrestlers or runners used, exerting all their might and skill to gain the victory. The true Christian life is heart exercise to godliness. For illustrating this I shall—I. SHOW SOME WEIGHTY TRUTHS IMPORTED IN THIS. 1. Habitual godliness is absolutely necessary to salvation. 2. No person goes to heaven sleeping. The Christian life is an exercise. 3. They must have true courage that shall come to heaven. They have to wrestle also with the world. No man can go through it to heaven, but he will find it a place filled with snares, and that will require courage to face the difficulties in it. 4. People must either give up the name of Christians, or else abandon their old exercise to sin and ungodliness. II. SHOW SOME THINGS IN WHICH THE EXERCISE TO GODLINESS CONSISTS. 1. In carrying on a constant trade with heaven, through our Lord Jesus Christ. Again, the exercised soul is employed in exporting his weakness, poverty, and wants, and importing strength and fulness from God. " They that wait upon the Lord shall renew their strength." 2. In a spiritual performance of duties. (1) In getting the soul fixed in that point, what is sin and what is duty in particular cases, before we put hand to it. (2) In doing the duty because it is the will of God, which must be not only the rule but also the reason of your duties, otherwise they are but bodily exercise. (3) In doing our duty to the glory of God. (4) In doing our duties in the strength of Christ. (*Ibid.*)

Ver. 8. **For bodily exercise profiteth little; but godliness is profitable unto all things.**—*The profit of godliness :*—Not only is this the testimony of a great man, but the testimony of a good man, the testimony of a Christian man ; a man, therefore, who had experience as to the utility of that concerning which he makes affirmation. He did not speak on the report of others, but he had brought the matter to the test of personal experiment ; and from what he had realized in himself he could say, " Godliness is profitable unto all things." I. WHAT IS GODLINESS ? It is real, vital, experimental, practical religion—genuine Christianity—a religion concerning God, the great, the wise, the blessed God. 1. Godliness comprehends a genuine fear. For where there is no fear of God there is no genuine piety—there is no religion. 2. Godliness means the saving knowledge of God, " whom to know is life eternal." 3. And then, where there is knowledge of God, saving knowledge, there must be love to God ; and no man can love an unknown object. 4. Then just in proportion as we love God (and this is essential to godliness) we shall be concerned to entertain intercourse with God. 5. Then perceive that this will lead to conformity to God—likeness to God. Such, indeed, is the very nature, such the constitution of the human mind, that it contracts a resemblance to those objects with which from inclination it is the most conversant. Apply the remark where you will, it will hold. Look at the man of this world ; where are his thoughts ? Why, the world is his object, and he becomes more and more worldly : and so of every other class. Now look at the man of God : his thoughts rise to God, his affections are spiritually placed on God : there is his object, there is his all ; and, beholding the glory of God in the face of Jesus, he catches the impress of it. 6. Let me say, too, that all Scriptural piety is practical. All that godliness which is genuine must lead to holiness of life and conversation. II. WHAT, THEN, ARE THE ADVANTAGES OF GODLINESS ? " Godliness is profitable." As though the apostle had said, " It is not merely a very harmless and innocent thing, and therefore no person should be afraid of it." This would have been very low praise, if it had been praise at all. It is not merely said " that it is profitable for some things "; nor is it affirmed concerning it that it is profitable for many things ; but the affirmation is without qualification, " Godliness is profitable for all things." " The life that now is." You cannot hear this without at once in your minds adverting to the beneficial influence of godliness on a man's external circumstances. Then consistent godliness gives a man character. Besides, godliness saves a man from intemperance : and what a vast benefit is this ! When a man becomes truly godly, he becomes industrious. You never saw an idle Christian. And then the Lord will bless the man that fears Him. Besides, godliness is beneficial considered in its influence in preserving and prolonging the life that now is. Then is it not true'that ungodliness tends to impair and destroy life ? Godliness is profitable in its beneficial influence on all the relations of life—on all the grades in society. Let me just add here that godliness is profitable at all the periods of life. It is profitable in the morning of life. Oh ! how it brightens the morning : and is not morning the best part of the day ? And if it be bright in the morning, oh ! may it not bless the noon ? Then if it brighten the morn and bless the noon, how will it cheer the evening of life ! Learn the inconsistency and folly of those who, while they admit the profit of godliness, make no effort to avail themselves of its advantages. Let me recommend this religion to you on the principle of self-interest. (R. Newton.)    The advantage of godliness :—Among the other advantages which it secures on this side eternity, one is the improvement of the human mind—I mean of his intellectual qualities : the improvement of his judgment, his discrimination, his mental faculties. I shall draw your attention to four reasons why the religion of Christ, when received into the heart, improves the human mind. I. ITS TENDENCY IS TO SUBJUGATE THE PASSIONS. It is more than its tendency ; it is its direct effect. Not that man is wholly without restraint ; there are three things which may operate to check the evil passions of the heart. 1. Conscience has some power. 2. Reason. 3. Self-interest. Self-interest can do something to check the passions, because it will say, " This will do you an injury." But they are unable to do this perfectly, and that for two reasons. 1. That passion is greatly assisted by powerful allies. Satan sits at the right hand of the human heart, blowing up the coals of evil which are in the heart into a flame of sin, which marks the demon's power over fallen man. But religion comes to counteract this ; the grace of God, by applying to the mind Divine truth and disposing the mind to love and embrace it, improves the mind--(1) By strengthening it. It gives such views, and principles, and motives, as direct the conduct. (2) By enlightening it. The tendency of religion on the mind is to make it see more accurately, reason more correctly, and feel more properly. II. IT PRESENTS RIGHT PRINCIPLES OF ACTION. 1. It presents a principle extremely weighty to regulate the mind aright and make it decide right on such things as it is called to judge respecting it. It enables the mind to realize eternity ; to be influenced by it at such times and in such places as an individual living in preparation for it should be influenced and guided in relation to an appearance before the great tribunal. 2. Religion produces the realization of another object which tends to guide the mind aright. What is that which will decide the rectitude of the whole life ? The apostle has stated it—" Whatsoever ye do, do all to the glory of God " ; because all that is not done according to this motive is not done according to the will of God. 3. Religion influences the mind and will aright, and therefore elevates the mind, because it furnishes a directory—the Scriptures. Religion has this influence, because—III. IT PRESENTS TO THE MIND THE HIGHEST SUBJECTS OF CONTEMPLATION. 1. It brings to the mind the things of God. It takes the mind, by contemplation, up into the mount, as Moses was taken up to converse with God ; or as the disciples were taken up into the Mount of Transfiguration to behold the glory of Christ and to hear Him talk with Moses and Elias. It has an elevating effect. 2. It makes the mind serious ; and seriousness improves the mind. Trifling is the mark of a light mind, and does not improve it. Religion, as it induces habits of seriousness, cannot fail to improve the mind. 3. The study of God's Word tends to strengthen the mind ; and that which strengthens the mind improves it. 4. Religion gives acquiescence to the will of God ; and this improves the mind. The mind that is opposed to the will of God is always battling ; but the mind that yields to the will of God is always going right. IV. BY THE INTERNAL PEACE, the peace of soul which religion is calculated to produce, and which it actually does produce; it raises the human mind. When the mind is at peace, it can operate calmly, and is therefore more likely to regulate the judgment and guide it aright. It has often been remarked what effect religion produces in seasons of great danger. This was strikingly observed in the case of the loss of the *Kent* East Indiaman. There were some persons on board under the influence of religion; and some of these, even females, became objects of admiration, because of their remarkable presence of mind. And this power of religion has often been remarked in our pious soldiers and sailors: their minds have been composed in the hour of danger and of battle; and they have been distinguished by their energy and calmness. In fact, almost all that distinguishes the rational from the irrational is seen in the Christian. The Christian in this world is always in danger. We cannot but observe, then—1. How superior is the state of the human mind in those who have religion to the state of the mind in those who have it not. 2. In attentively reading the history of the world, we may state, without fear of contradiction, that the minds of men have been improved in proportion to the degree of religion they have possessed. (*R. Sibthorp.*)  *The advantages of practical religion :*—1. " Godliness is profitable," as it tends greatly to alleviate the sorrows of life. 2. Godliness is profitable because it imparts sweetness to the enjoyments and an additional relish to the pleasures of life. It is a libel on piety, to represent it as something gloomy and morose. 3. " Godliness," because it confers upon its possessors pleasures peculiarly its own, " is profitable." 4. Godliness is profitable, as it disarms death of its terrors and the grave of its gloom. 5. " Godliness is profitable," for it prepares its possessor for eternal glory. From this subject we learn the importance— the value of religion. But, in fine, if religion is so profitable, I need scarcely, except for the purpose of excitement, remind you that it is personal religion that alone can be beneficial to any of you. (*Dr. Beattie.*)  *Godliness :*—I. THE NATURE OF GODLINESS. 1. Knowledge of the perfections of God—of the person and work of Christ as the Mediator—of man's state as a fallen creature—of his duty and privileges as redeemed by Christ. (1) As to the perfections of God. This knowledge is to be found nowhere but in the Book of God. (2) Here alone we obtain a knowledge of the Lord Jesus Christ. (3) Here we are made acquainted with man's state as a fallen creature. (4) As to his duty and privileges. Now, the knowledge of all this is essential to true religion in any soul. 2. Obedience to the commands of God. 3. The transformation of the soul into the image of God. II. THE FRUITS, OR TENDENCIES AND EFFECTS, OF GODLINESS. 1. For the increase of worldly comfort. 2. For the establishment of respectability of character in the world. 3. For the improvement of the human mind. (*P. M'Owan.*)  *The gain of godliness :*—I. And, first, WHAT IS GODLINESS? It is a real belief in God, the Father, the Son, and the Holy Ghost; our Maker, our Redeemer, and our Sanctifier. It is believing in Him, as He is made known to us in the Bible, in the gospel of Jesus Christ. Let us see, whether, even in this world, godliness is not great gain. In the first place, the Scripture gives a general promise that the godly man shall have good things in this world. 1. For godliness fits a man for every station. It is that character on which favour, honour, and esteem surely follow. 2. The godly man alone really enjoys the things which God gives him here. 3. But further, the godly man alone has the privilege of knowing that all things shall work together for his good. 4. But after all, if you would know the great gain of godliness, even in this life, you must try it. II. And this word BRINGS US TO THE FULL GAIN OF GODLINESS. If in this life only the believer had hope in Christ, he might still be deemed of all men most miserable. (*E. Blencowe, M.A.*)  *That godliness generally makes men happy in this life :*—I. It is to be observed that under the Jewish dispensation temporal promises were most expressly made to obedience, and most particularly with regard to the national success of the righteous against their public enemies (Deut. xxxii. 29). II. Therefore it is to be observed in the next place, and the observation holds more universally true, that religion and virtue, whenever they obtain generally so as to prevail in a nation, do bring along with them very great temporal blessings. III. As to the case of particular and private persons, about whom is much the greatest difficulty, there are several considerations necessary to be taken in in order to determine with any exactness how far godliness having the promise of the present life can be applied to them in this mixed and disorderly state of things. And—1. Religion and piety does not generally alter the natural circumstances or the relative states and conditions of men. If a man be poor or be a servant or slave, his being pious and religious will not certainly make him rich or gain him his freedom. 2. Godliness and true holiness does not exempt men from the unavoidable casualties of nature, such as sickness, death, and the like. 3. Righteousness and piety do not exempt men from such afflictions as God sees necessary either to make trial of their virtue or to make an example of it. 4. Religion and virtue do not always secure men from all the consequences of their own former sins. 5. Righteousness and true holiness do not secure men from the consequences of other men's sins also: from oppression and unrighteous judgment. (*S. Clarke, D.D.*)

*The profitableness of godliness:*—How generally men, with most unanimous consent, are devoted to profit, as to the immediate scope of their designs and aim of their doings, if with the slightest attention we view what is acted on this theatre of human affairs, we cannot but discern. Profit is therefore so much affected and pursued, because it is, or doth seem, apt to procure or promote some good desirable to us. It hath been ever a main obstruction to the practice of piety, that it hath been taken for no friend, or rather for an enemy to profit; as both unprofitable and prejudicial to its followers: and many semblances there are countenancing that opinion. For religion seemeth to smother or to slacken the industry and alacrity of men in following profit many ways: by charging them to be content with a little, and careful for nothing; by diverting their affections and cares from worldly affairs to matters of another nature, place, and time, prescribing in the first place to seek things spiritual, heavenly. It favoureth this conceit to observe that often bad men by impious courses do appear to thrive and prosper; while good men seem for their goodness to suffer, or to be nowise visibly better for it, enduring much hardship and distress. 1. We may consider that piety is exceeding useful for all sorts of men, in all capacities, all states, all relations; fitting and disposing them to manage all their respective concernments, to discharge all their peculiar duties, in a proper, just, and decent manner. If then it be a gross absurdity to desire the fruits, and not to take care of the root, not to cultivate the stock, whence they sprout; if every prince gladly would have his subjects loyal and obedient, every master would have his servants honest, diligent, and observant, every parent would have his children officious and grateful, every man would have his friend faithful and kind, every one would have those just and sincere, with whom he doth negotiate or converse; if any one would choose to be related to such, and would esteem their relation a happiness; then consequently should every man in reason strive to further piety, from whence alone those good dispositions and practices do proceed. 2. Piety doth fit a man for all conditions, qualifying him to pass through them all with the best advantage, wisely, cheerfully, and safely; so as to incur no considerable harm or detriment by them. Is a man prosperous, high, or wealthy in condition? Piety guardeth him from all the mischiefs incident to that state, and disposeth him to enjoy the best advantages thereof. It keepeth him from being swelled and puffed up with vain conceit. It preserveth him from being perverted or corrupted with the temptations to which that condition is most liable; from luxury, from sloth, from stupidity, from forgetfulness of God, and of himself; maintaining among the floods of plenty a sober and steady mind. Such a wondrous virtue hath piety to change all things into matter of consolation and joy. No condition in effect can be evil or sad to a pious man: his very sorrows are pleasant, his infirmities are wholesome, his wants enrich him, his disgraces adorn him, his burdens ease him; his duties are privileges, his falls are the grounds of advancement, his very sins (as breeding contrition, humility, circumspection, and vigilance), do better and profit him: whereas impiety doth spoil every condition, doth corrupt and embase all good things, doth embitter all the conveniences and comforts of life. 3. Piety doth virtually comprise within it all other profits, serving all the designs of them all: whatever kind or desirable good we can hope to find from any other profit, we may be assured to enjoy from it. He that hath it is *ipso facto* vastly rich, is entitled to immense treasures of most precious wealth; in comparison whereto all the gold and all the jewels in the world are mere baubles. He hath interest in God, and can call Him his, who is the all, and in regard to whom all things existent are "less than nothing." The pious man is in truth most honourable. The pious man is also the most potent man: he hath a kind of omnipotency, because he can do whatever he will, that is, what he ought to do; and because the Divine power is ever ready to assist him in his pious enterprises, so that "he can do all things by Christ that strengtheneth him." The pious man also doth enjoy the only true pleasures; hearty, pure, solid, durable pleasures. As for liberty, the pious man most entirely and truly doth enjoy that; he alone is free from captivity to that cruel tyrant Satan, from the miserable slavery to sin, from the grievous dominion of lust and passion. As for all other profits, secluding it, they are but imaginary and counterfeit, mere shadows and illusions, yielding only painted shows instead of substantial fruit. 4. That commendation is not to be omitted which is nearest at hand, and suggested by St. Paul himself to back this assertion concerning the universal profitableness of piety; "For," saith he, "it hath the promise of the life that now is, and of that which is to come." As for the blessings of this life, although God hath not promised to load the godly man with affluence of worldly things, yet hath He promised to furnish him with whatever is needful or convenient for him, in due measure and season, the which he doth best understand. Particularly there are promised to the pious man, A supply of all wants.—"The Lord will not suffer the soul of the righteous to famish." A protection in all dangers.—"The eye of the Lord is on them that fear Him, on them that hope in His mercy; to deliver their soul from death, and to keep them alive in famine." Guidance in all his undertakings and proceedings.—"The steps of a good man are ordered by the Lord." Success and prosperity in his designs.—"Commit thy way unto the Lord; trust also in Him, and He shall bring it to pass." Comfortable enjoying the fruits of his industry.— "Thou shalt eat the labour of thine hands." Satisfaction of all reasonable desires.— "The desire of the righteous shall be granted." Firm peace and quiet.—"Great peace have they which love Thy law." "The fruit of righteousness is sowed in peace." Joy and alacrity.—"Light is sown for the righteous, and gladness for the upright in heart." Support and comfort in afflictions.—"He healeth the broken in heart, and bindeth up their wounds." Deliverance from trouble.—"Many are the afflictions of the righteous, but the Lord delivereth him out of them all." Preservation and recovery from mishaps, or miscarriages.—"Though he fall, he shall not be utterly cast down: for the Lord upholdeth him with His hand." Preferment of all sorts, to honour and dignity, to wealth and prosperity.—"Wait on the Lord, and keep His way; and He shall exalt thee to inherit the land." Long life.—"The fear of the Lord prolongeth days." A good name endureth after death.—"The memory of the just is blessed." Blessings entailed on posterity.—"His seed shall be mighty on earth: the generation of the upright shall be blessed." "The root of the righteous shall not be moved." It is indeed more frequently, abundantly, and explicitly promised unto God's ancient people, as being a conditional ingredient of the covenant made with them, exhibited in that as a recompense of their external performance of religious works prescribed in their law. The gospel doth not so clearly propound it, or so much insist on it as not principally belonging to the evangelical covenant, the which, in reward to the performance of its conditions by us, peculiarly doth offer blessings spiritual, and relating to the future state; as also scarce deserving to be mentioned in comparison to those superior blessings. But infinitely more profitable it is, as "having the promises of the future life," or as procuring a title to those incomparably more excellent blessings of the other world; those "indefectible treasures," that "incorruptible, undefiled, and never-fading inheritance, reserved in heaven for us." (*I. Barrow.*) *The profitableness of godliness:*—1. We may consider that religion doth prescribe the truest and best rules of action; thence enlightening our mind, and rectifying our practice in all matters, and on all occasions, so that whatever is performed according to it, is done well and wisely, with a comely grace in regard to others, with a cheerful satisfaction in our own mind, with the best assurance that things are here capable of, to find happy success and beneficial fruit. Of all things in the world there is nothing more generally profitable than light: by it we converse with the world, and have all things set before us; by it we truly and easily discern things in their right magnitude, shape, and colour; by it we guide our steps safely in prosecution of what is good, and shunning what is noxious; by it our spirits are comfortably warmed and cheered, our life consequently, our health, our vigour, and activity, are preserved. The like benefits doth religion, which is the light of our soul, yield to it. Pious men are "children of the light"; pious works are works of light "shining before men." What therefore law and government are to the public, things necessary to preserve the world in order, peace, and safety (that men may know what to do, and distinguish what is their own), that is piety to each man's private state and to ordinary conversation: it freeth a man's own life from disorder and distraction; it prompteth men how to behave themselves toward one another with security and confidence. 2. We may consider more particularly, that piety yieldeth to the practiser all kind of interior content, peace, and joy; freeth him from all kinds of dissatisfaction, regret, and disquiet; which is an inestimably great advantage: for certainly the happiness and misery of men are wholly or chiefly seated and founded in the mind. If that is in a good state of health, rest, and cheerfulness, whatever the person's outward condition or circumstances be, he cannot be wretched : if that be distempered or disturbed, he cannot be happy. 3. Seeing we have mentioned happiness, or the *summum bonum*, the utmost scope of human desire, we do add, that piety doth surely confer it. Happiness, whatever it be, hath certainly an essential coherence with piety. These are reciprocal propositions, both of them infallibly true, he that is pious is happy ; and, he that is happy is pious. All pious dispositions are fountains of pleasant streams, which by their confluence do make up a full sea of felicity. 4. It is a peculiar advantage of piety, that it furnisheth employment fit for us, worthy of us, hugely grateful and highly beneficial to us. Man is a very busy and active creature, which cannot live and do nothing, whose thoughts are in restless motion, whose desires are ever stretching at somewhat, who perpetually will be working either good or evil to himself; wherefore greatly profitable must that thing be which determineth him to act well, to spend his care and pain on that which is truly advantageous to him; and that is religion only. It alone fasteneth our thoughts, affections, and endeavours, on occupations worthy the dignity of our nature. 5. It is a considerable benefit of piety, that it affordeth the best friendships and sweetest society. (*Ibid.*)    *Temporal blessings, support under trouble, and sanctified afflictions:*—I. GODLINESS IS PROFITABLE FOR THE OBTAINING OF ALL TEMPORAL GOOD THINGS THAT WE STAND IN NEED OF. In that catalogue of the Christian's possessions and treasures, which St. Paul has drawn up (1 Cor. iii. 22). 1. As to riches. " The blessing of the Lord it maketh rich " (Prov. x. 22). To all this we may still add, that religion brings contentment to the mind, and " godliness with contentment is great gain " (chap. vi. 6). If it does not bring the estate to the mind, it brings the mind to the estate; and that is much the same thing, it is altogether as well. Thus it is that " a little that a righteous man hath, is better than the riches of many wicked " (Psa. xxxvii. 16). And he is truly richer with a little, than the others are with a great deal. 2. To honour and good reputation. A blessing which the wise man rates at a higher price than gold and silver, or any of the riches of this world (Prov. xxii. 1). 3. Pleasure. " Her ways are ways of pleasantness, and all her paths are peace " (Prov. iii. 17). (1) As to bodily health, without which we can neither enjoy ourselves, nor anything. (2) A peaceable mind. If the mind be not in tune, the sweetest harmony will make no music in our ears. I must not here pass by an objection or two which may possibly be made against the pleasantness of religion. One is, that it requires some difficult and distasteful duties, as repentance, self-denial and mortification. But as well may one object against the pleasantness of health, because it may be sometimes necessary to take distasteful medicines, either to recover or to preserve it. Another objection against the pleasure of godliness is taken from the uncomfortable lives of some godly persons. II. GODLINESS IS PROFITABLE FOR THE LIFE THAT NOW IS, TO SUPPORT US UNDER TROUBLES AND AFFLICTIONS WHENEVER THEY BEFALL US. Here let us inquire what those peculiar supports under afflictions are, which are the proper fruits of godliness. They are chiefly these—1. The testimony of a good conscience. This, St. Paul tells us was his rejoicing in all his tribulations, and at last in the near views of death (2 Cor. i. 12). 2. A sense of pardon and reconciliation with God is a further support under worldly troubles. Pardon takes away the curse from affliction, and a sense of pardon is a sovereign balm to ease the anguish of the mind. 3. The comfortable hope of heaven, where these present afflictions shall be felt no more, and where they shall be abundantly compensated with fulness of joy for ever. 4. There are the supporting influences of the good spirit of God, which are promised in the gospel to all believers. III. THAT IT SECURES A SANCTIFIED USE OF AFFLICTIONS, AS WELL AS A HAPPY ISSUE OF THEM ; which is therefore a present, as well as a future benefit. (*D. Jennings.*) *The present life:*—1. It is a mysterious life. 2. It is a trying life. 3. It is a preparatory life. 4. It is a short life. 5. It is a precarious life. (*The Homilist.*) *Godliness :*—I. THE PRINCIPLE. II. THE PRACTICE. Godliness must be exercised ; religion is a personal matter. He must exercise himself vigorously. III. THE PROFIT. (*D. Thomas.*)    *The profit of godliness :*—I. " BODILY EXERCISE " IS OF CONSIDERABLE PROFIT. St. Paul is speaking of the training in the gymnasium. He allows it profits a little. Yet it is not all. No man is necessarily better in heart and life for having the muscles of his arm increased in girth half an inch or an inch. A sound constitution does not necessarily involve goodness in character. If so the Kaffir or Zulu would be the best man upon earth, which he is not. "Bodily exercise profiteth little : but godliness is profitable unto all things, having the promise of the life that now is, and of that which is to come." The discipline of godliness does make a man better inwardly. And the goodness passes from the centre outwards. It includes even that measure of advantage which may be derived from the culture of the body. II. There is another view of this phrase, "bodily exercise," which we ought to notice before passing on. A large class of writers understand by it not so much athleticism as ASCETICISM. The soul should bear empire over the body; but it should also reverence and care for the body. The laws of the body, of health, of sustenance are equally laws of God, with those of the soul. The perfection of manhood is attained when the laws of both, according to their kind and function, are duly observed. Asceticism is immoral, because it violates wantonly the law of God in one of the fairest provinces of His creation—viz., the delicate, sensitive, serviceable body of man. Yet even asceticism, in certain forms, profiteth a little. "Allow not nature more than nature needs," says Shakespeare. Self-denial in bodily indulgence might put some of us into more robust mental health, and impart to us a finer spiritual tone. I am not sure but that "bodily discipline" might (as St. Paul says) "profit a little." If any bodily appetite or habit rises into mastery over the mind or soul, it must be put in check with a firm hand, and with patient self-denial. So far "bodily exercise," discipline, is not only profitable, but imperative. III. THE HIGHER PRINCIPLE IN-CLUDING ALL THAT IS SERVICEABLE IN BOTH ATHLETICISM AND ASCETICISM, AND IMMEASUR-ABLY MORE BESIDE, IS GODLINESS. It grows also by use. "Exercise thyself unto godliness." We grow patient by being patient. We become industrious by refusing to be indolent and by working hard. We learn to love best by loving. We become religious by praying and communion with God. Begin to make God's law a ruling influence and power in your life. Think out what His will is about, say, that temptation which is coming to you to-morrow; then keep to His will, and pass the temptation by. That is the discipline of godliness. IV. THIS IS PROFITABLE FOR ALL THINGS—unlike athleticism, which profits only for soundness of health and tough-ness of muscle. 1. For the body itself godliness is profitable. Disease, weakness, morbidness are far more the devil's work than God's. 2. For the mind. He who ordered the planets in their orbits, and the seasons in their unvarying round, has not left the human mind without its law. Godliness brings man into harmony with the Author of his being. 3. For faith. But godliness advances faith. The more godlike we grow, the simpler, clearer, stronger is our faith in God. Live holier lives, live less selfish lives, and you will believe more in God and His Son. 4. The affections. This great reverence for the God who is great and good and loving enlarges our heart and our affections. Godliness is instinctive chivalry. If by your evil passion and harshness, your self-indulgence, your weakness and wanton folly, you blight the lives of others, I tell you, you are ungodly men. Godliness is profitable to the home. 5. Business. Be a godly man. Fear God rather than turns of fortune or than opinion. Be like God—true, reliable in your word and deeds. (*A. J. Griffith.*) *The profitableness of godliness* :—I. A MAN QUICKLY LEARNS IF HE WISHES TO LIVE PROFITABLY HE MUST HAVE REGARD TO LAW. We cannot violate law without suffering for it. Disobedience entails destruction, obedience informs with life. II. Let us carry this examination into greater detail. THE MOST PROFITABLE HUMAN EXISTENCE IS THAT EXISTENCE WHICH SECURES THE GREATEST BENEFIT TO THE GREATEST NUMBER OF FACULTIES. If we resolve a human being into its elements, we shall find it divisible into body, mind, and soul, or, as some would put it, moral instincts. The true philosophy of living consists in the development of this tripartite. We pass, then, to consider the influence of rigidly religious life upon these sides of our nature. 1. If we practise the precepts of the gospel we will eschew those evil acts which occasion uneasiness and remorse; our temperament will maintain an even tran-quility, our happiness will be full and satisfying. It has been truly said that an atheistic age is a barren age. We may safely say, then, that for the growth of the mind a godly life is best. 2. But the mind sends down its roots deep into the encompassing body upon which it acts and is acted upon. Physiologists tell us that a healthy mind conduces to a healthy body. If a Christian life produces vigour and clearness of intellect, then it must have a similar effect on the body. A religious life, then, we assert to be physically beneficial. 3. Passing to the region of the spiritual we are relieved from all necessity for discussion. Spirituality can only exist amid holy influences. The man who sins deadens his moral instincts, makes them useless here, and entails the penalty which such misuse is visited with hereafter. 4. But we cannot have obtained anything like a reliable knowledge of the relative value of two courses of life if we have excluded from our calculations all thought of suffering and sorrow. As we cannot by human device stave off sorrow, it behoves us to consider how it can be most successfully met. Mr. Spurgeon has said that if we take our troubles to God He will carry them for us; but if we take them anywhere else they will roll back again. III. Passing from the individual man to his business interests, we proceed to CONSIDER WHETHER GODLINESS IS INIMICAL TO WORLDLY SUCCESS. Now, all that Christianity enforces is the necessity of strict honesty. Religion will not transform the dunce into a genius, but sinfulness will transform the genius into a dunce. And if all things are considered, I feel confident that the just man gains in more than mere clear-headedness. Deceit is a most deceitful helper. Henry Ward Beecher tells a story of a man in the Canadian backwoods who, during the summer months, had procured a stock of fuel sufficient to serve the winter's consumption. This man had a neighbour who was very indolent, but not very honest, and who, having neglected to provide against the winter storms, was mean enough to avail himself of his neighbour's supplies without the latter's permission or knowledge. Mr. Beecher states that it was found, on computation, that the thief had actually spent more time in watching for opportunities to steal, and laboured more arduously to remove the wood (to say nothing of the risk and penalty of detection), than had the man who in open daylight and by honest means had gathered it. And this is oftener the case than we are disposed to allow. What appear to be short cuts to wealth are never safe ones, and very generally they prove to be extremely circuitous. Relaxation, too, is necessary for all men. Consider, then, whether the frivolous and enervating gaiety so frequently indulged in, or the innocent and energizing merriment of the godly, will best enable a man to recuperate the waste occasioned by business life. IV. WE CANNOT ISOLATE OURSELVES FROM OTHERS; WE ARE BOUND BY INNUMERABLE BONDS TO THE SYSTEM OF HUMAN INTERESTS. Our welfare is knit up with the welfare of the world. The man, then, who strives to suppress swindling, and who by the nobility of his own character rebukes all cheatery, is doing a grand service for mankind. He is making property more secure, and society more stable. If irreligion was crushed prosperity would visit this country with her brightest blessings and most permanent happiness. The gospel is also the more potent than all the antidotes which economists prescribe for the diminution of crime. V. IT IS TRUE GODLINESS, NOT SHAM OR SELFISH GODLINESS, THAT PROVES PROFITABLE. VI. Having thus glanced at the profitableness of religion in this life, LET US BESTOW A MOMENT'S THOUGHT UPON THAT OTHER LIFE WHICH IS ETERNAL. If we lose this, what profit is it that we have been successful in business! We have gained the lesser by losing the greater. The course which in the end will prove profitable cannot be a selfish one. Love to God is indissolubly intertwined with love to man, and the glory of God must issue in man's exaltation in the best and truest sense. (*J. G. Henderson.*) *What is the profit of godliness?*—That men, by godliness, should reap a fruition and harvest hereafter is not surprising to those who have at all been instructed in religious things; but there are many who have supposed that godliness was in a man's way here. What is godliness? So that godliness means something more than merely religion, in the narrow and technical sense of the term. It means having a wise view of all the laws of our being and condition, and living in conformity to them. Moreover, when it is said that it has in it "the promise of the life that now is," we are not to narrowly interpret it. A man with a clumsy hand, without skill and without inventive thought, is not justified in attempting to be an inventor simply on the general ground of godliness. We are not to suppose that a man who has no commercial training is to plunge into business and make this plea: "I live in conformity to the laws of my being, and shall be prospered in my pursuits." We are to have a larger idea of prosperity than is seen in any of these special things. That which, on the whole, promotes their greatest happiness must be considered. Their prosperity now means their welfare. It does not consist in the development of any one part of their nature, but the whole of it. Godliness has an immediate relation to that which is the foundation of all enjoyment—a good, sound bodily condition. The condition of enjoyment in this life is that one is in a sound state of bodily health. Godliness, or a conformity to the great laws of our condition, includes physical health—works toward it. Moderation of appetite; restraint of undue desires; that quietness of spirit which comes from the belief in an overruling Providence; that undisturbed equilibrium which comes from faith in God—all these are, looking at them in their very lowest relations, elements of health—of a sound physical condition. Next consider how much a man's happiness in this life depends upon his disposition—both with reference to himself and with reference to his social surrounding. It is not what you have about you, but what you are, that determines how happy you shall be. Excessive pride takes away from the power of enjoyment. Godliness, by its very nature, reduces a man to a certain conformity with the laws of his condition, and makes him content therein, and so works upon his disposition that it becomes amenable to the law of happiness. It is made to be more childlike and simple. It is brought into conditions in which happiness may distil upon it from ten thousand little things. A man who wishes to see beauty in nature must not watch for it in gorgeous sunsets always—though they will come once in a while. Let him watch for it in ten million little facets which glisten in the light of the sun, by the roadside as well as in the rich man's adorned grounds. We must see it in the motes and bugs, in the minutest insects, everywhere. So, then, we are to reap happiness and satisfaction, not so much from great cataclysms and paroxysms as in little things, that have the power to make us supremely happy. Another thing. Men's happiness depends more upon their relations to society than we are apt to think. Where men have the art of fitting themselves to their circumstances and their companions there is great satisfaction in these also. There is a true sympathy, a true benevolence, which is godly. If you go among men with a mean, selfish spirit, how little happiness will you find in your social intercourse! But if in the child and in its sports you see something to make you smile; if toward the labouring man you have a kindly good will, and if you find companionship with all who are virtuous in the various walks of life—with those who are high for certain reasons, and those who are low for certain other reasons; if you feel a generous brotherhood and sympathy of men, then there is a vast deal of enjoyment for you in this life, which comes simply from your aptitudes for fellowship and friendship. Now it is the peculiar office of a true godliness to subdue the heart to this universal amnesty and sympathy, so that they who are godly, who live in conformity to the will of God, in all their circumstances, shall reap more or less enjoyment. Godliness, by changing men's condition, prepares them to be happy; and by giving them affinities for things about them produces conditions of happiness. There are also other ways in which godliness works towards happiness. It gives to men a motive in this life without concentrating on their worldly endeavours the utmost of their powers. The outgoing of a man's own self, legitimately and industriously, with the constant expectation of success—there is great enjoyment in this. At the same time, let this enjoyment be coupled with the moderating, restraining feeling that if earthly enterprises fail and come short, this world is not the only refuge, and worldly affairs are not the only things of value—that though the house perish, and the garments be wasted, and the gold and silver take wings and fly away, and all things perish, yet there is a God, there is a providence, there is hope, there is a home, and there is immortality; then the happiness is greatly increased. Then there is the consideration of those qualities which go to make success in business. Men do not believe you are as honest or as faithful and prompt as you believe yourself to be. But where all the parts of a man are morally sound; where he is free from vices of every sort; where he has fidelity, conscientiousness, industry, good judgment, and intelligence; where he is so trustworthy that you can bring the screw to bear upon him, and, though you turn it never so many times, not be able to break him until you crush him to death—he is invaluable. And I say that just in proportion as men approach to that, they are more and more important in a commercial age, and in a great commercial community. Now, it is the tendency of the ethics of Christianity to produce just such men. If religion does not produce them, it is so far spuriously or imperfectly administered. There is a difference between ethical religion and ecclesiastical and doctrinal religion. But where a man has Christian ethics; where a man is truth-speaking and reliable; where a man is founded upon the rock Christ Jesus, and cannot be moved from it, I say that godliness tends to success in commercial affairs. If you take the different classes of religionists, where shall you find more Christian ethics than among the Quakers? Where shall you find more carefulness in daily life? And among what class will you find more worldly prosperity, and more enjoyment in it, than among them? When I lived in the West, a merchant told me that during twenty years he never suffered the loss of a quarter of a dollar from a whole Quaker neighbourhood. You might take whole settlements, and say that they were exemplifications of the fact that "godliness is profitable unto all things, having the promise of the life that now is, and of that which is to come." Many a poor man goes along the street whose name would not be worth a snap on a note. He could not get a bank in New York to lend him a hundred dollars for a month. He is of no market value whatever. But if your dear child was dying, and you did not know how to pray, he is the very man that you would send for. You would say to him when you were in distress, "Come to our house." Ah! a man may not have outward prosperity, and yet prosper. He may have that which money cannot buy—peace, happiness, joy. The power of making joy he has; and is he not prospered? Is he not well off? Finally, taking society at large, those who get the furthest from the rules of morality; those who have the most doubt and distrust in regard to the overruling providence of God; those who have a leaning to their own wisdom; those who are proud and selfish, and do what they have a mind to regardless of the welfare of others—they are not pre-eminently prosperous, even in material and commercial things. (*H. W. Beecher.*)　　*The profit of godliness in this life :*—With regard to this life, let it be remarked that the religion of our Lord Jesus Christ neither undervalues nor overvalues this present life. It does not sneer at this life as though it were nothing; on the contrary, it ennobles it, and shows the relation which it has to the higher and eternal life. There are many who undervalue this life; let me mention some of them to you. Those undervalue it who sacrifice it to indulge their passions or to gratify their appetites. Too many for the sake of momentary gratifications have shortened their lives, and rendered their latter end bitterly painful to themselves. Some evidently undervalue their lives, because they make them wretched through envy. Others are richer than they are, and they think it a miserable thing to be alive at all while others possess more of this world's goods than they. Oh poison not life by envy of others, for if you do so you miserably undervalue it! The slaves of avarice undervalue their lives, for they do not care to make life happy, but pinch themselves in order to accumulate wealth. The miser who starves himself in order that he may fill his bags may well be reasoned with in this way: "Is not the life more than the meat, and the body than raiment? So also do they undervalue it who in foolhardiness are ready to throw it away on the slightest pretext. He that for his country's sake, or for the love of his fellow-creatures, risks life and loses it, truly deserves to be called a hero; but he who, to provoke laughter and to win the applause of fools, will venture limb and life without need is but a fool himself, and deserves no praise whatever. Yet there can be such a thing as overvaluing this life, and multitudes have fallen into that error. Those overvalue it who prefer it to eternal life. Why, it is but as a drop compared with the ocean, if you measure time with eternity. They overvalue this life who consider it to be a better thing than Divine love, for the love of God is better than life. Some would give anything for their lives, but they would give nothing for God's love. It appears from the text that godliness influences this present life, puts it in its true position, and becomes profitable to it. I. First, let me observe that GODLINESS CHANGES THE TENURE OF THE LIFE THAT NOW IS. It hath "the promise of the life that now is." I want you to mark the word —"it hath *the promise* of the life that now is." An ungodly man lives, but how? He lives in a very different respect from a godly man. Sit down in the cell of Newgate with a man condemned to die. That man lives, but he is reckoned dead in law. He has been condemned. If he is now enjoying a reprieve, yet he holds his life at another's pleasure, and soon he must surrender it to the demands of justice. I, sitting by the side of him, breathing the same air, and enjoying what in many respects is only the selfsame life, yet live in a totally different sense. I have not forfeited my life to the law, I enjoy it, as far as the law is concerned, as my own proper right: the law protects *my* life, though it destroys *his* life. The ungodly man is condemned already, condemned to die, for the wages of sin is death; and his whole life here is nothing but a reprieve granted by the longsuffering of God. But a Christian man is pardoned and absolved; he owes not his life now to penal justice; when death comes to him it will not be at all in the sense of an infliction of a punishment; it will not be death, it will be the transfer of his spirit to a better state, the slumbering of his body for a little while in its proper couch to be awakened in a nobler likeness by the trump of the archangel. Now, is not life itself changed when held on so different a tenure? "Godliness hath the promise of the life that now is." That word changes the tenure of our present life in this respect, that it removes in a sense the uncertainty of it. God hath given to none of you unconverted ones any promise of the life that now is. You are like squatters on a common, who pitch their tents, and by the sufferance of the lord of the manor may remain there for awhile, but at a moment's notice you must up tents and away. But the Christian hath the promise of the life that now is ; that is to say, he has the freehold of it ; it is life given to him of God, and he really enjoys it, and has an absolute certainty about it ; in fact, the life that now is has become to the Christian a foretaste of the life to come. The tenure is very different between the uncertainty of the ungodly who has no rights and no legal titles, and the blessed certainty of the child of God who lives by promise. Let me add that this word seems to me to sweeten the whole of human life to the man that hath it. Godliness hath the promise of life that now is ; that is to say, everything that comes to a godly man comes to him by promise, whereas if the ungodly man hath any blessing apparent, it does not come by promise, it comes overshadowed by a terrible guilt which curses his very blessings, and makes the responsibilities of his wealth and of his health and position redound to his own destruction, working as a savour of death unto death through his wilful disobedience. There is a vast difference between having the life that now is and having the promise of the life that now is—having God's promise about it to make it all gracious, to make it all certain, and to make it all blessed as a token of love from God. II. THE BENEFIT WHICH GODLINESS BESTOWS IN THIS LIFE. Perhaps the fulness of the text is the fact that the highest blessedness of life, is secured to us by godliness. Under ordinary circumstances it is true that godliness wears a propitious face both towards health and wealth and name, and he who has respect to these things shall not find himself, as a rule, injured in the pursuit of them by his godliness ; but still I disdain altogether the idea that all these three things together, are or even make up a part of the promise of the life that now is. I believe some persons have the life that now is in its fulness, and the promise of it in its richest fulfilment, who have neither wealth, health, nor fame ; for being blessed with the suffering Master's smile and presence, they are happier far than those who roll in wealth, who luxuriate in fame, and have all the rich blessings which health includes. Let me now show you what I think is the promise of the life that now is. I believe it to be an inward happiness, which is altogether independent of outward circumstances, which is something richer than wealth, fairer than health, and more substantial than fame. This secret of the Lord, this deep delight, this calm repose, godliness always brings in proportion as it reigns in the heart. Let us try and show that this is even so. A godly man, is one who is at one with his Maker. 1. It must always be right with the creature when it is at one with the Creator. But when godliness puts our will into conformity with the Divine will, the more fully it does so, the more certainly it secures to us happiness even in the life that now is. I am not happy necessarily because I am in health, but I am happy if I am content to be out of health when God wills it. I am not happy because I am wealthy, but I am happy if it pleases me to be poor because it pleases God I should be. 2. The Christian man starting in life as such is best accoutred for this life. He is like a vessel fittingly stored for all the storms and contrary currents that may await it. The Christian is like a soldier, who must fain go to battle, but he is protected by the best armour that can be procured. 3. With a Christian all things that happen to him work for good. Is not this a rich part of the promise of the life that now is ? What if the waves roar against him, they speed his bark towards the haven ? 4. The Christian enjoys his God under all circumstances. That, again, is the promise of the life that now is. 5. I am sure you will agree with me that the genuine possessor of godliness has the promise of the life that now is in his freedom from many of those cares and fears which rob life of all its lustre. The man without godliness is weighted with the care of every day, and of all the days that are to come, the dread remembrance of the past, and the terror of the future as well. 6. And as he is thus free from care, so is he free from the fear of men. 7. Moreover, the fear of death has gone from the Christian. This with many deprives the life that now is of everything that is happy and consoling. Another application of the text is this. There is a bearing of it upon the sinner. It is quite certain, O ungodly man, that the promise of the life that now is belongs only to those who are godly. Are you content to miss the cream of this life ? I pray you, if you will not think of the life to come, at least think of this. (*C. H. Spurgeon.*)    *Happiness of godliness :*—Christianity a gloomy system ! The world and devils may say so ; but a thousand eyes that sparkle with a hope that maketh not ashamed, and a thousand hearts that beat happily with the full pulse of spiritual life, can tell thee thou liest. Christianity a gloomy system ! Why, it is the Christian only that can thoroughly enjoy the world. To him, to his grateful vision, earth is garlanded with fairer beauty, heaven sparkles with serener smiles; to him the landscape is the more lovely, because it reminds him of the paradise of his hope in prospect which his father once lost, but which his Saviour has brought back again, as a family inheritance for ever; to him the ocean rolls the more grandly, because it figures out the duration of his promised life; to him the birds in their forest minstrelsy warble the more sweetly, because their woodland music takes him upwards to the harpers harping with their harps in heaven; to him the mountains tower the more sublimely, because their heaven-pointing summits are the emblems of his own majestic hopes. (*W. M. Punshon.*)    *Secret of happiness:*—A thoroughly loyal subject of God's kingdom is qualified to dwell happily in any world to which God may call him. Because he is what he is, it matters less where he chances to be. The star which shines by its own light may traverse the infinite space of the heavens, but it can never know eclipse. On the other hand, a peevish, uneasy, and wilful spirit is not much helped by outward condition. King Ahab, in his palace, turns his face to the wall and will eat no bread, because he cannot have Naboth's vineyard. How many a proud man is so unweaned and pulpy that he cannot bear a cloudy day, an east wind, the loss of a dinner, the creaking of a shutter by night, or a plain word! You will meet travellers who take their care with them as they do their luggage, and grasp it tightly wherever they go, or check it forward from place to place, although, unlike their luggage, it never gets lost. You may carry an instrument out of tune all over the world, and every breath of heaven and every hand of man that sweeps over its strings shall produce only discord. Such a man's trouble is in his temper, not in his place. You can hardly call it "borrowed" trouble either, for it is mostly made, and so is his own by the clearest of all titles. (*Wm. Crawford.*)    *The blessedness of religion:*—Religion makes a man happier all the way through. You may have to work hard for your daily bread, but you hear reports of a land where they neither hunger nor thirst. You may have a great many physical distresses and pangs of pain, but you hear of the land where the head never aches, and where the respiration is not painful, and where the pulse throbs with the life of God! You may have to weep among the graves of the dead, but against the tombstone leans the Risen One pointing you up to that sphere where God shall wipe away all tears from your eyes. Ask those who are before the throne, ask those who have plucked the fruit of the tree of life, ask those who are waving the palms in glory whether this is the happy side or not. I knew a minister in Philadelphia (he was not poetic, he was not romantic—they called him a very plain man), who, in his last moment, as he passed out of life, looked up and said, "I move into the light." Oh! it is the happy side—happy here—it is happy for ever. (*T. De Witt Talmage.*) *Happiness is attainable in this life:*—Is happiness attainable? First, there is something in our condition as sinners against God, that militates against our happiness. God "made man upright, but he hath sought out many inventions." I. In order to show that happiness is attainable, I shall first appeal to the INFALLIBLE ASSURANCES OF GOD'S INSPIRED WORD (2 Chronicles xx. 20; xxvi. 5; Job xxxvi. 11). In the first Psalm there is an encomium upon the happiness of the godly (Matt. vi. 33). II. The MANIFEST AND UNQUESTIONABLE TENDENCY OF TRUE GODLINESS TO IMPART AND INSURE HAPPINESS. Health is by universal consent considered an essential ingredient to happiness. Cheerfulness is a part of happiness. And who can pretend to cheerfulness on such just grounds as the real Christian, the man of genuine godliness? His principles make him happy. Look at the influence of those principles on friendship; which is essential to happiness. Mark how the principles of godliness bear upon a man's usefulness. How can I be happy unless I am useful? III. The EXPERIENCE OF THE POWER OF THE GOD WHOM WE SERVE. If I can show you that happiness has been actually attained, it will be quite clear that it is attainable. Look, therefore, at the history and experience of the servants of God. I will grant the straitness of their circumstances, for they are often a poor and an afflicted people. Let me call your attention to the case of the prophet Habbakuk. "Although the fig tree shall not blossom neither shall fruit be in the vines, the labour of the olive shall fail and the field shall yield no meat, the flocks shall be cut off from the fold and there shall be no herd in the stalls, yet I will rejoice in the Lord, I will joy in the God of my salvation." Look at Paul and Silas—their backs lacerated with the Roman scourge, their feet made fast in the stocks, condemned to spend the night in a prison; "at midnight they prayed and sang praises to God; and the prisoners heard them." Now either these persons must be grossly deceived, or happiness is

attainable.   IV. In the fourth place, I must make an appeal to the fact of the EX-
ISTENCE OF HYPOCRITES IN THE CHURCH.   The counterfeit itself proves the value and
the existence of the genuine coin.   V. Finally, I make my appeal to the CONFES-
SIONS AND LAMENTATIONS OF THE UNGODLY THEMSELVES; who, having discarded
religion, both in principle and in practice, have been left to rue their own folly,
and to admit that their happiness was indeed illusory and vain, ending in bitter
disappointment.   Some have been honest enough to confess this; that they
have "forsaken the fountain of living waters," and they have heaped to themselves immeasurable bitterness and sorrow of heart.   1. In conclusion, then,
let this subject, in the first place, rectify our judgments.   2. In the next place,
let this subject decide our choice.   The consideration of it will do us good, if the
decisions of the will should follow the enlightenment of the understanding.   3. Let
this subject, thirdly, awaken our gratitude.   4. Finally, let this subject serve to
stimulate our desire for a more full and complete and final happiness beyond the
grave. (*G. Clayton.*)   *The profit of godliness in the life to come :*—There is another
life beyond this fleeting existence.   This fact was dimly guessed by heathens.
What was thus surmised by the great thinkers of antiquity, has been brought to
light in the gospel of Jesus Christ.   I. GODLINESS CONCERNING THE LIFE TO COME
POSSESSES A PROMISE UNIQUE AND UNRIVALLED.   1. I say a unique promise, for, observe,
infidelity makes no promise of a life to come. It is the express business of infidelity
to deny that there is such a life, and to blot out all the comfort which can be
promised concerning it.   Man is like a prisoner shut up in his cell, a cell all dark
and cheerless save that there is a window through which he can gaze upon a glorious
landscape.   2. No system based upon human merit ever gives its votaries a promise
of the life to come, which they can really grasp and be assured of.   No self-righteous man will venture to speak of the assurance of faith; in fact, he denounces it
as presumption.   Godliness hath a monopoly of heavenly promise as to the blessed
future.   There is nothing else beneath high heaven to which any such promise has
ever been given by God, or of which any such promise can be supposed.   Look at
vice, for instance, with its pretended pleasures—what does it offer you?   And it is
equally certain that no promise of the life that is to come is given to wealth.   Nay,
ye may grasp the Indies if ye will; ye may seek to compass within your estates all
the lands that ye can see far and wide, but ye shall be none the nearer to heaven
when ye have reached the climax of your avarice.   There is no promise of the life
that is to come in the pursuits of usury and covetousness.   Nor is there any such
promise to personal accomplishments and beauty.   How many live for that poor
bodily form of theirs which so soon must moulder back to the dust!   Nor even to
higher accomplishments than these is there given any promise of the life to come.
For instance, the attainment of learning, or the possession of that which often
stands men in as good stead as learning, namely, cleverness, brings therewith no
promise of future bliss.   "Godliness hath the promise of the life that now is, and
of that which is to come," but to nothing else anywhere, search for it high or low,
on earth or sea, to nothing else is the promise given save to godliness alone.   II. I
pass on to notice, in the second place, that THE PROMISE GIVEN TO GODLINESS IS AS
COMPREHENSIVE AS IT IS UNIQUE.   In the moment of death the Christian will begin
to enjoy this eternal life in the form of wonderful felicity in the company of Christ,
in the presence of God, in the society of disembodied spirits and holy angels.   III.
I have shown you that the promise appended to godliness is unique and comprehensive, and now observe that IT IS SURE.   "Godliness hath promise"; that
is to say, it hath God's promise.   Now, God's promise is firmer than the hills.
He is God, and cannot lie.   He will never retract the promise, nor will He leave it
unfulfilled.   He was too wise to give a rash promise: he is too powerful to be
unable to fulfil it.   IV. This promise is A PRESENT PROMISE.   You should notice
the participle, "having promise."   It does not say that godliness after awhile
will get the promise, but godliness has promise now at this very moment.
When we get a man's promise in whom we trust, we feel quite easy about the
matter under concern.   A note of hand from many a firm in the city of London
would pass current for gold any day in the week; and surely when God gives
the promise, it is safe and right for us to accept it as if it were the fulfilment
itself, for it is quite as sure.   You cannot enjoy heaven, for you are not there, but
you can enjoy the promise of it.   Many a dear child, if it has a promise of a treat
in a week's time, will go skipping among its little companions as merry as a lark
about it.   When the crusaders first came in sight of Jerusalem, though they had a
hard battle before them ere they could win it, yet they fell down in ecstacy at the

sight of the holy city. When the brave soldiers, of whom Xenophon tells us, came at last in sight of the sea, from which they had been so long separated, they cried out, "Thallasse! Thallasse!"—"The sea! the sea!" and we, though death appears between us and the better land, can yet look beyond it. V. This promise which is appended to godliness is A VERY NEEDFUL ONE. It is a very needful one, for ah! if I have no promise of the life that is to come, where am I? and where shall I be? Oh! how much I want the promise of the life to come, for if I have not that I have a curse for the life to come. (*C. H. Spurgeon.*)    *The life to come :*—It is a singular and lamentable fact, that while men are so sensitive and eager in pursuing temporal interests, they are so obstinately careless with regard to those spiritual interests, which are far more expanded and enduring. The correction of the evil now adverted to, must of course be considered as a matter of transcendant importance. I. First, notice SOME OF THE PROOFS THAT A "LIFE TO COME" DOES REALLY EXIST. There are evidences upon the subject of a future life, apart from any direct connection with revelation, to which nevertheless no insignificant weight must be assigned. I refer you especially to the masterly work of Dr. Butler, whence I imagine no candid mind can arise, without being satisfied that there is a strong probability, arising from analogy, of the continuance of conscious being after the death of the body, and entirely and absolutely uninjured by it. We may notice, again, the common consent of mankind, who, in all nations and in all ages, have admitted a futurity, although frequently with acknowledged and grievous defects : a fact, I conceive, which can only be properly accounted for by receiving the substantial and final truth of the thing which is believed. We may notice, again, the aspirations after something far beyond this transitory and mortal sphere —"longings of immortality." We may notice, again, the operations of the momentous faculty of conscience, in the judgment which it forms as to the moral qualities and deserts of actions and thoughts, and the feelings which it inspires in the bosom (by reason of its decisions) of pleasure or pain, hope or fear, satisfaction or remorse ; and all these, which are entirely independent of the opinions of other men, are to be regarded as prophetic indications of a subjection to other principles of decision, and to a great system of moral government, the sanctions of which are to be found in the yet impervious and impalpable future. But we must direct our regard to revelation itself : by which, of course, we mean the Scriptures of the Old and New Testament, "given by inspiration of God," and unfolding all the truths relating to the condition and to the destinies of man. II. THE CHARACTERISTICS BY WHICH "THE LIFE TO COME" IS DISTINGUISHED. It will appear to you important, besides the contemplation of the general fact, to notice the particular attributes, which the fact involves. It is very possible, to admit the general fact, and yet to indulge great and perhaps fatal mistakes as to the detail. The heathen admits the general fact, but grievously errs as to the detail. 1. And we observe, in the first place, that "the life to come" will comprehend the whole nature of man. 2. We are to observe, that "the life to come" is purely and entirely retributive. God has arranged it as the scene, where He will apply to His intelligent creation the sanctions of that great system of moral government, under which they have existed. 3. Again, "the life to come," which thus will comprehend the whole nature of man, and which is purely retributive, will be unchangeable and eternal. We can conceive nothing of what is indestructible in "the life that now is "; all around us breathes with decay and dissolution. The attributes which now are noticed do not merely apply to abstract existence, but to the condition of existence. In other words, the rewards and the punishments, which have been adverted to, will be unchanging and will be everlasting too. III. THE POWER, WHICH THE PROSPECT OF "THE LIFE WHICH IS TO COME" SHOULD POSSESS OVER THE MINDS AND HABITS OF MEN. 1. First, "the life which is to come" ought to be habitually contemplated. It has surely been revealed that it might be pondered ; and admitting the fact that there is a life to come, a mere sciolist, a child, would be able to arrive at the conclusion, how it ought to be made the object of thought and of pondering. Think how noble and how solemn is your existence. 2. Again "the life to come" ought to be diligently prepared for. Your contemplations are for the purpose of leading you to preparation. And how are we to prepare, so as to escape the world of punishment and to receive the world of reward ? The merit of penitence is nothing ; the merit of what you regard good works is nothing. There is only one method of preparation ; and that is, according to the announcements of the system of grace, in the volume which is before us. For the "life to come" many of you are prepared. Are there not some, who have never offered these aspirations, who themselves are not yet prepared? (*J. Parsons.*)

Ver. 10. **We both labour and suffer reproach.**—*Trust in God the support of Christians in their labours and sufferings* :—I. THE COURSE PURSUED BY THE APOSTLE AND HIS BRETHREN WAS ONE OF LABOURS AND SUFFERINGS. If we must be reproached, let us not be reproached for evil-doing, but for well-doing : let us not have conscience against us, exasperating our sufferings ; but secure in our conscious integrity and adamantine guard. II. WHAT IT WAS THAT SUSTAINED THE APOSTLE AND HIS BRETHREN IN THE COURSE WHICH THEY PURSUED : IT WAS THE PRINCIPLE OF CONFIDENCE IN GOD. " We trust in the living God, who is the Saviour of all men, especially of them that believe." 1. God is here regarded as " the living God " ; that is, the true God, as distinguished from dumb and lifeless idols, described by the Psalmist as " having eyes that see not, ears that hear not, mouths that speak not, feet that walk not." God appeals to this distinction, when He says, " As I live." This suggests the idea of the infinite perfection of the Deity, and consequently His ability to protect His servants. 2. As " the Saviour of all men, especially of those that believe." (1) " The Saviour of all men." His mercies are over all His creatures. (2) But in a far higher sense He is " the Saviour of those that believe." He saves them from consequences far more awful than any temporal calamities. Now, from the first of these views we infer that the power of God is pledged to assist His servants to do His will, and execute His commission : and, in whatever we do in obedience to God's will, we have reason to depend on the support of Him who has ordered it to be done. And, in the next place, this may be especially applied to that part of God's will, in which His glory is most concerned. In the gospel the honour of God is most of all concerned : men are to be saved by believing the gospel : therefore we may be confident that God will help them in all that relates to the success of the gospel : " He is the Saviour especially of them that believe." III. AS IMPROVEMENTS OF THIS SUBJECT, observe—1. How highly we should value that gospel, which the apostles preached amidst so much labour and suffering! 2. Imitate the apostles in their course of labours and sufferings. Be " fervent in spirit, serving the Lord." 3. And, lastly, as the apostles were supported by trusting in the living God ; so shall we also be, if we follow their example. If we trust in God, His favour will be our joy ; if not, His comforts will fail us. (*R. Hall, M.A.*) **We trust in the living God.**—*Trust in the living God :—* Trust—confidence—is an essential element of human nature. We begin life in a spirit of trust, and cling with confidence to our parents and the guardians of our infancy. As we advance in years, though deceived and betrayed, we still must anchor our trust somewhere. We cannot live without some being to lean on as a friend. Universal distrust would turn social existence into torture. We were born for confidence in other beings ; and woe to him that cannot trust! Still confidence brings with it suffering ; for all are imperfect and too many are false. Observe what a harmony there is between our nature and God. The principle of trust, as we have seen, enters into the very essence of the human soul. Trust seeks perfect goodness. Its natural tendency is toward an infinite and immutable being. In Him alone can it find rest. Our nature was made for God, as truly as the eye was made for the light of God's glorious image, the sun. I. WHAT IS THE PRINCIPLE OF RELIGIOUS TRUST ? I would observe, that religious confidence rests on God's parental interest in in individual persons. To apprehend and believe this truth is to plant the germ of trust in God. This truth is not easily brought home to the heart as a reality. The first impression given to a superficial observer of the world is, that the individual is of no great worth in the sight of the Creator. The race of man is upheld, and seems to be destined to perpetual existence. But the individuals, of whom it is composed, appear to have nothing enduring in their nature. They pass over the earth like shadows cast by a flying cloud, leaving for the most part as slight a trace behind. They break like meteors from the abyss, and are then swallowed up in darkness. According to this view, God is the Author of fugitive, mutable existences, from love of variety, multiplicity and development, however transitory these several existences may be. If we rest in such views of God, our confidence must be faint. Can we believe that human nature was framed by such a Being for no higher spiritual development than we now witness on this planet? Is there not, in the very incompleteness and mysteriousness of man's present existence, a proof that we do not as yet behold the end for which he is destined ; that the infinite Father has revealed but a minute portion of His scheme of boundless mercy ; that we may trust for infinitely richer manifestations than we have experienced of His exhaustless grace? But there is another reply to the sceptic, and to this I invite your particular attention. Our trust, you say, must be measured by what we see. Be it so. But take heed to see truly, and to understand what you do see. How rare is such exact and comprehensive perception. And yet without it, what presumption it is for us to undertake to judge the purpose of an infinite and ever-living God. Whatever creature we regard has actually infinite connections with the universe. It represents the everlasting past of which it is the effect. He then, who does not discern in the present the past and the future, who does not detect behind the seen the unseen, does not rightly understand it, and cannot pass judgment upon it. The surface of things, upon which your eye may fall, covers an infinite abyss. Are you sure, then, that you comprehend the human being, when you speak of him as subjected to the same law of change and dissolution, which all other earthly existences obey? Is there nothing profounder in his nature than that which you catch sight of by a casual glance? Are there within him no elements which betoken a permanent and enduring existence? Consider one fact only. Among all outward changes, is not every man conscious of his own identity, of his continuing to be the same, single, individual person? Is there not a unity in the soul, that distinguishes it from the dissoluble compounds of material nature? And further, is this person made up of mutable and transitory elements? On the contrary, who does not know that he has faculties to seize upon everlasting truth, and affections which aspire to reach an everlasting good? Have we not all of us the idea of right, of a Divine law older than time, and which can never be repealed? Has such a being as man then no signs in his nature of permanent existence? Is he to be commingled with the fugitive forms of the material world? Seeing, you see not. What is most worth seeing in man is hidden from your view. You know nothing of man truly, till you discern in him traces of an immutable and immortal nature, till you recognize somewhat allied to God in his reason, conscience, love and will. Talk not of your knowledge of men, picked up from the transient aspects of social life! It is not then to be inferred, from what we see, that God does not take an interest in the individual, and that He may not be trusted as designing great good for each particular person. In every human mind He sees powers kindred to His own—the elements of angelic glory and happiness. These bind the heavenly Father's love indissolubly to every single soul. And these Divine elements authorize a trust utterly unlike that which springs from superficial views of man's transitory existence. II. WHAT IS THE GOOD FOR WHICH, AS INDIVIDUAL PERSONS, WE MAY TRUST IN GOD? One reply immediately offers itself. We may not, must not trust in Him for whatever good we may arbitrarily choose. Experience gives us no warrant to plan such a future for ourselves, as mere natural affections and passions may crave, and to confide in God's parental love as pledged to indulge such desires. Human life is made up of blighted hopes and disappointed efforts, caused by such delusive confidence. We cannot look to God even for escape from severest suffering. The laws of the universe, though in general so beneficent in their operation, still bring fearful evil to the individual. For what then may we trust in God? I reply, that we may trust unhesitatingly, and without a moment's wavering, that God desires the perfection of our nature, and that He will always afford such ways and means to this great end, as to His omniscience seem most in harmony with man's moral freedom. There is but one true good for a spiritual being, and this is found in its perfection. Men are slow to see this truth; and yet it is the key to God's providence, and to the mysteries of life. Now how can man be happy but according to the same law of growth in all his characteristic powers? Thus the enjoyment of the body is found to be dependent on and involved with the free, healthy and harmonious development—that is the perfection—of its organization. Impair, or derange any organ, and existence becomes agony. Much more does the happiness of the soul depend upon the free, healthy and harmonious unfolding of all its faculties. Now for this good we may trust in God with utter confidence. We may be assured that He is ready, willing, and anxious to confer it upon us; that He is always inviting and leading us towards it by His Providence, and by His Spirit, through all trials and vicissitudes, through all triumphs and blessings; and that unless our own will is utterly perverse, no power in the universe can deprive us of it. Such I say is the good for which we may confide in God, the only good for which we are authorized to trust in Him. The perfection of our nature—God promises nothing else or less. We cannot confide in Him for prosperity, do what we will for success; for often He disappoints the most strenuous labours, and suddenly prostrates the proudest power. We cannot confide in Him for health, friends, honour, outward repose. Not a single worldly blessing is pledged to us. And this is well. God's outward gifts—mere shadows as they are of happiness—soon pass away; and their transitoriness reveals, by contrast, the only true good. Reason and conscience, if we will but hear their voice, assure us that all outward elevation, separate from inward nobleness, is a vain show; that the most prosperous career, without growing health of soul, is but a prolonged disease, a fitful fever of desire and passion, and rather death than life; that there is no stability of power, no steadfast peace, but in immovable principles of right; that there is no true royalty but in the rule of our own spirits; no real freedom but in unbounded disinterested love; and no fulness of joy but in being alive to that infinite presence, majesty, goodness, in which we live and move and have our being. This good of perfection, if we will seek it, is as sure as God's own being, Here I fix my confidence. When I look round me, I see nothing to trust in. On all sides are the surges of a restless ocean, and everywhere the traces of decay. But amidst this world of fugitive existences, abides one immortal nature. Let not the sceptic point me to the present low development of human nature, and ask me what promise I see there of that higher condition of the soul, for which I trust. Even were there no sufficient answer to this question, I should still trust. I must still believe that surely as there is a perfect God, perfection must be His end; and that, sooner or later, it must be impressed upon His highest work, the spirit of man. Then I must believe, that where He has given truly Divine powers, He must have given them for development. Human nature is indeed at present in a very imperfect stage of its development. But I do not, therefore, distrust that perfection is its end. We cannot begin with the end. We cannot argue that a being is not destined for a good, because he does not instantly reach it. The philosopher, whose discoveries now dazzle us, could not once discern between his right hand and his left. To him who has entered an interminable path, with impulses which are carrying him onward to perfection, of what importance is it where he first plants his step? The future is all his own. But you will point me to those who seem to be wanting in this spirit of progress, this impulse towards perfection, and who are sunk in sloth or guilt. And you will ask whether God's purposes towards these are yet loving. I answer: Yes! They fail through no want of the kind designs of God. From the very nature of goodness, it cannot be forced upon any creature by the Creator; nor can it be passively received. What a sublime doctrine it is, that goodness cherished now is eternal life already entered on! Thus have I spoken of religious trust, in its principle and its end. I have time to suggest but one motive for holding fast this confidence as a fountain of spiritual strength. We talk of our weakness. We lack energy, we say, to be in life what in hope we desire. But this very weakness comes from want of trust. What invigorates you to seek other forms of good? You believe them to be really within your reach. What is the soul of all great enterprises? It is the confidence that they may be achieved. To confide in a high power is to partake of that power. It has often been observed, that the strength of an army is more than doubled by confidence in its chief. Confide, only confide, and you will be strong. (*W. E. Channing.*) *Christly trust:*—First: Man is a trusting being. Trusting is at once the grand necessity and leading tendency of his existence. Secondly: His trust determines the character and destiny of his being. Trusting wrong objects or right objects for wrong purposes, is at once sinful and ruinous. On the other hand, trusting rightly in the living God is at once a holy and a happy state of being. Two remarks are suggested in relation to this Christly trust. I. IT FORMS A DISTINCT COMMUNITY AMONGST MEN. The apostle speaks here as "those that believe." All men believe. Men are naturally credulous. 1. There are some who believe in a dead God—an idol, a substance, a force, an abstraction. Most men have a dead God—a God whose presence, whose inspection, whose claims they do not recognize or feel. 2. There are others who believe in a "living God." To them He is the life of all lives, the force of all forces, the spirit of all beauty, the fountain of all joy. With these the apostle includes himself, and to these he refers when he says, "Those that believe." II. It secures the special SALVATION OF THE GOOD. The living God is the Saviour, or Preserver of all. He saves all from diseases, trials, death, damnation, up to a certain time in their history. All that they have on earth which go to make their existence tolerable and pleasant He has saved for them. But of those that believe He is specially a Saviour, He saves them—1. From the dominion of moral evil 2. From the torments of sinful passions—remorse, malice, jealousy, envy, fear. 3. From the curse of a wicked life. What a salvation is this! Christly trust gives to the human race a community of morally saved men. (*D. Thomas, D.D.*) **Who is the Saviour of all men.**—*The first Sunday after Epiphany:*—Whether, then, we take the words " the living God " in our text to apply to Christ Himself, or to the Father acting by Christ, it is equally asserted that Christ is the Saviour of all men : that the salvation which He wrought is, in and of itself, co-extensive with the race of man. What He did, He did for, and in the stead of, all men. If we wish to corroborate this by further Scripture proof, we have it in abundance. I will take but three of the plainest passages. St. John in his first Epistle, ii. 1, 2. St. Paul, 2 Cor. v. 14. In Rom. v. 10 he goes further into the same truth. See also 1 Cor. xv. 22. Adam, when he came fresh from the hands of God, was the head and root of man-kind. He was mankind. She who was to be a helpmeet for him was not created a separate being, but was taken out of him. The words spoken of him apply to the whole human race. The responsibility of the whole race rested upon him. When he became disobedient, all fell. Figure to yourselves—and it is very easy to do so, from the many analogies which nature furnishes—this constitution of all mankind in Adam : for it is the very best of all exponents of the nature of Christ's standing in our flesh, and Christ's work in our flesh : with this great difference indeed, inherent in the very nature of the case, that the one work in its process and result is purely physical, the other spiritual as well. The race, in its natural constitution in Adam, *i.e.*, as each member of it is born into the world and lives in the world naturally, is alien from and guilty before God : has lost the power of pleasing God : cannot work out its own salvation in or by any one of its members; all being in-volved in the same universal ruin. " In Adam all die." Now that rescue must not, cannot in God's arrangements, come from without. It must come upon mankind from within. God's law respecting us is, that all amendment, all purifying, all renewal, should spring from among, and take into itself and penetrate by its influ-ence, the inner faculties and powers wherewith He has endowed our nature. We know that our redemption was effected by the eternal Son of God becoming incar-nate in our flesh. Now suppose for a moment that He, the Son of God, had become an individual personal man, bounded by His own responsibilities, His own capacities, His own past, and present, and future. If He had thus become a personal man, not one of His acts would have had any more reference to you or me than the acts of Abraham, or David, or St. Paul, or St. Peter have. He might have set us an example ever so bright ; might have undergone sufferings ever so bitter ; might have won a triumph ever so glorious ; and we should merely have stood and looked on from without. No redemption, no renovation of our nature could by any possi-bility have been made. And He, thus being the Divine Son of God, and having become the Son of man, was no longer an individual man, bounded by the narrow lines and limits of His own personality, but was and is God manifest in the flesh ; a sound and righteous Head of our whole nature, just as Adam was its first and sinful head. Hence it is, that whatever He does, has so large a significance. Hence, that when He fulfils the law, His righteousness is accepted as ours. He did nothing, if He did not the whole. He redeemed none, if He redeemed not all. If there existed on earth one son or daughter of Adam not redeemed by Christ, then He, who had taken it upon Him to put away sin by the sacrifice of Himself, had not accomplished His work, and had died in vain. And let us see what this uni-versality of redemption implies, as regards the sons of men themselves. It enables the preacher of good tidings to come to every son and daughter of Adam, every out-cast and degraded one of our race, and at once to lay before them Christ as theirs, if they will believe on Him. It is the key, and the only key, to the fact of justifi-cation by faith. " Believe, and thou shalt be saved." Why? Believe in a Man who died and rose again, and thou shalt be saved ? Now this at once brings us to the second part of our text. In the broad sense on which we have hitherto been insisting, Christ is the Saviour of all men : of the whole of mankind. All have an equal part and right in Christ. And on this foundation fact, the whole mission work of the gospel is founded. We are to go into all the world, and we are to pro-claim the glad tidings to every creature. That redemption by Christ, which is as wide as the earth, as free as the air, as universal as humanity, is no mere physical amendment which has passed on our whole race unconsciously : but it is a glorious provision for spiritual amendment, able to take up and to bless and to change and to renovate man's spiritual part, his highest thoughts, his noblest aspirings, his best affections. And these are not taken up, are not blest, are not renovated, except by the power of persuasion, and the bending of the human will, and the soft promptings of love, and the living drawings of desire. (*Dean Alford.*) *The Christ-likeness of God :*—In several texts God is called our Saviour. God, then, is to us what Christ is. God Himself, then, is essentially Christlike. He must have in Himself some Christ-likeness, for He is, as Christ, our Saviour. Let the energy of these two truths once enter into a man's heart—the truth that in everything we have to do with the living God, and the truth that our God is the Christlike One, and they are enough to revolutionize a man's life. I. OUR HOPE IS SET ON THE LIVING GOD. This is a familiar Biblical phrase. This word, the living God, had not become an echo of a vanishing faith to the Psalmist, longing for the communion of the temple, who uttered Israel's national consciousness in this prayer: "My soul longeth, yea, even fainteth for the courts of the Lord: my heart and my flesh crieth out for the living God." It was a word intense with faith. A professor of chemistry, with whom sometime since I was talking about nature, and what it really is, said to me, thoughtfully: "The order of nature is God's personal conduct of His universe." It is not with a dead nature, or an impersonal order of laws, but with the living God in His personal and most Christian conduct of the universe, that we living souls have to do here and hereafter. I. OUR HOPE IS SET ON THE LIVING GOD, OUR SAVIOUR. It is a principle of far-reaching sweep and reconstructive power in theology, to think of our God above all as most Christlike in His inmost being and nature. I once saw in the city of Nürnberg, I think it was, a religious picture, in which God the Father was represented in heaven as shooting down arrows upon the ungodly, and midway between heaven and earth Christ, the Mediator, was depicted as reaching forth and catching those arrows, and breaking them as they fell. The painting was true to methods of conceiving Christ's work of atonement into which faith had fallen from the simplicity of the Bible; but it should not be called a Christian picture. "God, our Saviour," said apostles who had seen God revealed in Christ; and Jesus Himself once said: "He that hath seen Me, hath seen the Father." It is one thing to obtain from the Scriptures some adequate doctrine of the divinity of Christ. But it is another thing to have God through Christ brought as a living and inspiring presence into direct contact with all our plans and work and happiness in life. In sincere acceptance of Jesus' word that He knew the Father, and came from God, let us read the gospels for the purpose of learning what God Himself is towards us in our daily lives; how our world appears in the pure eye of God; how He thinks of us, and is interested in what we may be doing, suffering, or achieving. And He who opens His mouth, and teaches the multitude, utters God's heart to us upon that mountain-side. This is God's own blessedness showing itself to the world. Such is God, blessing with His own blessedness the virtue which is like His own goodness. Yes, but as Jesus, in His own speech and person, realizes God before us, how can we help becoming conscious of our distance of soul from perfection so Divine? He speaks for God. So God is towards man; this word is from the bosom of the Father; there is on earth Divine forgiveness of sin. But the fear of death is here in this world of sepulchres. We might love to love were it not for death. The worst thing about our life here is, that the more we fit our hearts for the highest happiness of friendships, the more we fit ourselves, also, for sorrow: love is itself the short prelude so often to a long mourning. What does God think of this? What can God in heaven think of us in our bitter mortality? Follow again this Jesus who says He knows—what will He show God's heart to be towards human suffering and death? Lord, show us in this respect the Father, and it sufficeth us. There, coming slowly out of the gate of the city, is a procession of much people. We do not need to be told their errand; often we have followed with those who go to the grave. The Christ who says He knows what God our Father is and thinks, meets them who are carrying to his burial the only son of a widow. It is all there, the whole story of man and woman's grief. The Christ sees it all; and more than all which disciples see;—He looks on through the years, and beholds death's broad harvests, and the generations of men passing each from earth in pain and tears; the whole history of death through the ages He bears upon the knowledge of His heart. What will God do with death? "And when the Lord saw her, He had compassion on her, and said unto her, Weep not. And He came nigh and touched the bier: and the bearers stood still. And He said, Young man, I say unto thee, Arise." It was not a miracle, but only an illustration beforehand of the larger law of life. While the widow wept, while the sisters of His friend Lazarus could not be comforted, Jesus knew that life is the rule in God's great universe, and death the exception. Yes, this is a glad gospel from the bosom of the Eternal. This earth is full of human cruelty and oppressions. Let us go, then, once more with this Jesus into the city, and see what He will do with the Scribes and Pharisees, hypocrites. In the world from which He says He came, and into which He declares He is going soon—for a little while to be unseen by His own friends

—in that world will He suffer these men to be? "Woe unto you, Scribes and Pharisees, hypocrites;—How shall ye escape the judgment of Gehenna?" It is the same Christ who is speaking—He whom we heard saying, Blessed, and in words which seemed to be a song from the heart of His own life—He who went weeping with the sisters at Bethany—who once sent that procession of mourners back in triumph and joy to the city. It is He who now stands before those extortioners and hypocrites, and says in God's name: "Woe unto you!" It is enough. The face of God is set against them that do evil. No lie shall enter the gates of that city of the many homes. Yes—but again our human thoughts turn this bright hope into anxiety. These men may not have known. We would go into the city and save all. We would let none go until we had done all that love could do; we would not suffer any man to be lost if love could ever find him? How, then, does Jesus show us what God is towards these lost ones? Listen; He sees a shepherd going forth in the storm over the bleak mountain-side, seeking for the one lost sheep; and this Wonder of divinity with man—He who came from God and knows—says, Such is God; "Even so it is not the will of your Father in heaven, that one of these little ones should perish." This is the picture of the heart of God drawn by Christ's own hand—the shepherd seeking the one lost sheep. Two consequences of these truths remain to be urged. God Himself is to be seen through Christ, and Christ is to be studied through all that is best and worthiest in the disciples' lives. Therefore through human hearts also which reflect in any wise Christ's spirit, we may seek to realize what God is. God is what they would be, only infinitely better; His perfection is like man's, only infinitely transcending it. Let us be very bold in this living way of access to God. (*Newman Smyth, D.D.*) *Jesus the Saviour of all men:*—St. Paul calls Him "the Saviour of all men"! Are all men, then, His people? Are not multitudes His enemies? Which witness shall I believe—the apostle, or the angel? Both of them! They do not gainsay each other. When you tell me that Dr. D. is the physician of this Poor-law District, you do not mean that he heals all the poor residing within his district, but only that he is appointed to heal them. His commission includes them all. Some may neglect to come to him, and others may prefer another doctor; but, if they will, they all may come to him, and have the benefit of his skill. In the same sense "Jesus is the Saviour of all men." He is appointed to save all men—"Neither is there salvation in any other"! (*J. J. Wray.*) *Trusting in God:*—During the burning of a mill in our town there was a strong threatening of a large conflagration. People even two blocks off began to pack their household treasures. From many blocks around the coals from the flaming building were scattered over the white snow. From my window the scene was truly magnificent. The wild, hot flames soaring aloft, the burning elevator looking as if suspended in the heavens, the countless millions of sparks ascending, the sway and surge of this terrible power of fire. It seemed to me that a row of cottages within my sight must soon be swallowed up too, and as I thought of an elderly friend—helpless in her bed—I wrapped myself up warmly, and went out in the night to her. She was white and trembling with excitement, for the fire was only two buildings distant, and her room was light as day, illumined by the flames. "I was just wondering whether it was best to get her up upon her chair," said the girl to me. "No, don't," I said, "I do not believe there is any danger, and if there is, she shall not suffer." "Don't you believe there is any danger?" asked the invalid as I reached her bedside. "No, I do not, unless the wind should change. Just lie still and don't worry. If the next house should catch fire we will come for you the first thing." She accepted our word and kept her bed, thus escaping a cold; and morning found her all right. I wonder, then, why we could not accept our loving, helpful Father's word as unquestioningly as she did the word of a mortal. Why will we persist in borrowing trouble, when He has promised "As thy day so shall thy strength be"? Why do we always assert proudly, yet humbly, "I will say of the Lord, He is my refuge and my fortress; my God; in Him will I trust"? (*E. Gilmore.*)

Vers. 11–16. **These things command and teach.**—*Characteristics of the Christian teacher:*—With true affection, and with heavenly wisdom, Paul exhorts his son in the faith to be mindful of his conduct and character. Here, as well as elsewhere, the apostle exhorts to—I. THE MAINTENANCE OF MORAL DIGNITY. 1. The tendency of Timothy was to yield rather than to command, to sacrifice truth for the sake of peace, and to lessen his own authority by morbid self-depreciation. Probably this is not so common amongst us as self-confidence; but it is a serious fault, and may be a grievous hindrance to usefulness. Unless you believe yourself to be capable of doing something better than you are now doing you will hesitate to attempt it. If you cannot trust God to help you through an onerous duty, you will be in danger of evading it. Much noble service has been lost to the Church and to the world by a foolish self-depreciation. I remember one who became a very successful man telling me that his early youth was blighted by this morbid tendency, and that he owed all his prosperity to a wise-hearted, loving, motherly woman, who took pity on the sensitive, shrinking lad, and made him believe in himself as one gifted by God to do something in the world. "Let no man despise thy youth." Be manly, and brave, and firm, lest you sacrifice interests which God has entrusted to your charge. 2. But the way to overcome the disadvantage of youth in the opinion of others, and to gain influence over them, is clearly suggested here. It is not to be done by noisy self-assertion, by the evident desire to be prominent, but by becoming, through Divine grace, an exemplar of real Christian worth. "Be thou an example of the believer, in word, in conversation (or behaviour), in charity, in faith, in purity." (The phrase "in spirit" is properly omitted from the Revised Version). (1) It is through our "word" that we chiefly manifest to others the nature of our inner life, and the tone and temper thus exhibited either weakens or strengthens our influence for good. (2) But words must be in harmony with conduct, and he would be a poor maintainer of Christ's cause whose words were admirable while his general behaviour was frivolous or faulty. (3) Nor is it enough to watch over our words and behaviour, but we must pay regard to motive and impulse, because we have to do with and to bear witness for the great Searcher of hearts, and should see that love and faith are the twin motive powers of our life—love which really cares for the interests of others, faith which lays hold upon the strength and wisdom of an unseen yet ever-present God. (4) And added to all these must be unquestioned purity, which will make us so scrupulous about moral improprieties that the breath of slander will fade away instantly from the polished shield of our reputation, and will keep the inner life clear and chaste, while it gives us the fulfilment of the Lord's words, "Blessed are the pure in heart, for they shall see God." II. Again, PREPARATION FOR CHRISTIAN WORK is inculcated here as well as maintenance of moral dignity. The apostle appears to have expected an early return to Ephesus, and hence writes— 1. "Till I come give attention to the reading, to the exhortation, to the teaching." The reference is primarily to the public duties of the Christian teacher. The "reading" of Holy Scripture in religious assemblies, which had been transferred from the synagogue, formed no inconsiderable part of the public worship of those days, as any one can imagine who reflects on the cost and rarity of manuscripts. "Exhortation" was often heard—appeals to affection and to enthusiasm, which led many a believer to give himself up entirely to the service of the Lord. And coincident with this was steady consecutive "teaching," by means of which God's Word was expounded, applied, and illustrated. 2. But the work to which Timothy was called required in the first place "a gift," which the apostle says was given him instrumentally—"by prophecy, with the laying on of the hands of the presbytery." The word used for "gift" denotes that it came from the Holy Spirit, with whom it is always associated in Paul's writings. These two—the gift of God and the recognition of it by the Church—should ever be combined in the pastor who is working for Christ. 3. But he is foolish and sinful who relies on the possession of a gift or the recognition of it by others. Neglected, the gift will perish, and the life of promise will end in miserable failure. The phrase rendered "give thyself wholly to them" might be more literally translated "be in them"—have your life in such thoughts and truths; let them constitute the atmosphere you breathe, and then your religious work will not be a something artificial and foreign to your nature, but the necessary outcome of your inward life. 4. Give heed, then, unto thyself and unto the doctrine. Cultivate such gifts as you have, and use them without stint in your Master's service; and see to it that the teaching you give is not the chance utterance of a thoughtless mind, but the product of earnest thinking and of believing prayer. III. Finally, Paul looked to see in Timothy (and God looks to see in us) READINESS FOR THE PROMISED REWARD. 1. It is no small blessing which is promised in the 15th verse, "that thy profiting" (or rather thy progress) "may appear unto all." You should be a living epistle, known and read of all men. 2. Nay, more than this, "Thou shalt both save thyself and them that hear thee." A traveller who was sinking from exhaustion in a snowstorm on the mountain saw his companion suddenly drop helpless at his side; straightway his own peril was forgotten, and, flinging himself beside him, he chafed his hands and rubbed his chest; and by the effort which brought life back to the dying he kept himself alive—he saved both himself and the friend beside him. For your own sake, and for the sake of others, spend and be spent in this glorious service, and not only will your own life be the fuller here, but heaven itself will be made incomparably more full of joy. (*A. Rowland, LL.B.*)    **Let no man despise thy youth.**—*On the duties of youth* :—1. Among the good qualities of the young which first discover themselves, and which we regard as the sure indications of everything excellent in morals, is a nice sense of what is good and what is evil, what is truly praiseworthy and what is not, with an early and earnest attention to the forming of their principles.    When embarked on the ocean of life innumerable dangers will surround them, and various temptations, under the specious forms of pleasure, will assail their hearts. To rush blindly on in a course so perilous, without either the benefits of experience or the guidance of wisdom, must quickly lead to inextricable difficulties perhaps, if not to misery and ruin.    But, to descend from general reflections to the discussion of a few particular subjects, permit me to observe that too great confidence in our own strength is always dangerous, and sometimes fatal.    But modesty in youth should be a natural virtue; it should be derived from other, more abundant sources than mere reflection, a feeling of comparative ignorance, or a sense of common propriety; it should spring spontaneously from sensibility—from a heart alive to every sentiment of shame, before it has been hackneyed in the ways of men or rendered callous by a long intercourse with the world.    Among the more innocent excesses of youthful passions and the less dangerous delusions of the mind may be ranked the extravagancies of hope and expectation.    But the loss of some distant good, however heightened by the powers of imagination or overrated by the blind partiality of our hearts, is by no means the only, or most important evil, that springs from this vain exaltation of the mind.    From being so long conversant with imaginary happiness we lose our relish for that which is real.    The mind also, soured with disappointments and irritated by frequent vexations, becomes, at a more advanced period, incapable of sharing in the social intercourses of life.    At the same time that they should take particular care to avoid the many false and artificial notions of life, which we are but too eager to embrace with blind credulity (and which, for that reason, indeed, the fanciful writers of romance are but too apt to communicate), they ought to acquire those enlarged ideas of men and things which have their foundation in truth, and, in some measure, supply the want of experience by habits of thought and reflection.    Above all, they should have recourse to the blessed gospel of our Lord and Saviour Christ, and deeply impress their hearts with those Divine truths which illumine the natural mind of man, as the rays of the sun enlighten the globe.    What I would next warn young persons against is an inordinate love of pleasure.    Suffer me to conclude by observing that every age and condition brings with it, beside the ordinary obligations of virtue and religion, certain peculiar and appropriate duties—duties to which young persons must diligently attend if they wish that "no man should despise their youth," and which the aged must duly cultivate and regularly practise if they would have "the hoary head found in the way of righteousness" and reverenced as "a crown of glory."    There are also a thousand secondary graces of character, which must be studied, and a thousand indirect modes of temptation to be guarded against, if we wish to make any considerable advances towards perfection and to lead "a godly, righteous, and sober life." (*J. Hewlett, M.A.*)    *The least man in the ministry not to be contemned* :—As in a building, some bring stones, some timber, others mortar, and some perhaps bring only nails—yet these are useful; these serve to fasten the work in the building: thus the Church of God is a spiritual building.    Some ministers bring stones—are more eminent and useful; others, timber; others, less—they have but a nail in the work; yet all serve for the good of the building.    The least star gives light, the least drop moistens, the least minister is no less than an angel, the least nail in the ministry serves for the fastening of souls unto Christ.    There is some use to be made even of the lowest parts of men ; the weakest minister may help to strengthen one's faith.    Though all are not apostles, all are not evangelists, all have not the same dexterous abilities in the work, yet all edify ; and oftentimes so it cometh to pass that God crowns his labours, and sends most fish into his net, who, though he may be less skilful, is more faithful, and though he have less of the brain, yet he may have more of the heart, and therefore not to be contemned. (*J. Spencer.*)    *Achievements of youth* :—It is often late ere genius shows itself; just as often, however, does distinction come early.    Thus at twenty-two Gladstone was a member of Parliament, and at twenty-four Lord of the Treasury.

Bright never went to school after he was fifteen. Sir Robert Peel entered Parliament at twenty-one, and was Lord of the Admiralty at twenty-three. Charles James Fox became a legislator at nineteen—an age when young men are given to breaking rather than to making laws. Bacon graduated at Cambridge when he was sixteen, and was called to the bar at twenty-four. Washington was a distinguished colonel at twenty-two. Napoleon commanded the army of Italy at twenty-five. Before he was seventeen Shelley was already an author—had translated the half of Pliny's " Natural History," and had written a number of wild romances. (*Palace Journal.*)     *Youth not to be despised :*—Mr. Spurgeon began his remarkable career early enough to preach with a juvenile face many astonishingly effective sermons. His fiftieth anniversary, just celebrated, recalls an anecdote worth repetition. Mr. Spurgeon was asked, in what to most preachers would have been salad days, to deliver a discourse in a near village. Accordingly he went. On meeting the pastor, whose name was Brown, that good old gentleman was sadly disconcerted at his supply's youthful appearance. " Well, well," said he to Mr. Spurgeon, " I really did not dream that you were only a boy. I would not have asked you to preach for me if I had thought so." " Oh! well," said Mr. Spurgeon, laughing, " I can go back." But Mr. Brown would not permit this, and into the pulpit his boyish guest ascended. How he comported himself is thus narrated: " Mr. Brown planted himself on the pulpit stairs. Mr. Spurgeon read a lesson from the Proverbs, and upon coming to the passage, ' Grey hairs are a crown of glory to a man,' he said he doubted that, for he knew a man with a grey head who could hardly be civil. But the passage went on to say: ' If it be found in the way of righteousness,' and that, he said, was a different thing. When he came down from the pulpit Mr. Brown said to him : ' Bless your heart, I have been thirty years a minister, and I was never better pleased with a sermon; but you are the sauciest dog that ever barked in a pulpit '; and they were always good friends afterwards."

Ver. 13. **Give attendance to reading.**—*Lecture on reading :*—I. First, THE CHOICE OF BOOKS. In this there is a great need of caution ; particularly in the spring season of life, while the mental and moral habits are yet in a process of formation. A person may be ruined by reading a single volume. It is a maxim, then, ever to be borne in mind, take heed what you read. To acquire useful information ; to improve the mind in knowledge, and the heart in goodness; to become qualified to perform with honour and usefulness the duties of life, and prepared for a happy immortality beyond the grave—these are the great objects which ought ever to be kept in view in reading. And all books are to be accounted good or bad in their effects just as they tend to promote or hinder the attainment of these objects. Taking this as the criterion by which to regulate your choice of books, you will, I think, be led to give an important place to historical reading, especially to that which relates to our own country. History is the mirror of the world. In addition to a knowledge of our own history, some acquaintance with the government and laws of the society in which we live would seem an almost indispensable qualification of a good citizen. Nearly related to history, and not less important, is biography. This is a kind of reading most happily adapted to minds of every capacity and degree of improvement. Few authors can be read with more profit than those that illustrate the natural sciences, and show their application to the practical arts of life. Authors of this character teach us to read and understand the sublime volume of creation. Not less valuable are those writers that make us acquainted with our own minds and hearts ; that analyse and lay open the secret springs of action ; unfold the principles of political and moral science ; illustrate the duties which we owe to our fellow-men, to society, and to God; and by teaching us the nature, dignity, and end of our existence, aim to elevate our views and hopes, and lead us to aspire after the true glory and happiness of rational and immortal beings. Especially must this be said of the Bible. One of the greatest and best of men, I refer to Sir William Jones, a judge of the supreme court of judicature, in Bengal, has said of the Bible, " I have carefully and regularly perused the Scriptures, and am of opinion that this volume, independent of its Divine origin, contains more sublimity, purer morality, more important history, and finer strains of eloquence, than can be collected from all other books, in whatever language they may have been written." Were I now to give you one rule for all, for regulating your choice of books, it should be this—" Books are good or bad in their tendency as they make you relish the Word of God the more or the less after you have read them." Having made these remarks to assist you in a proper choice of books, I

will—II. SUGGEST A FEW RULES IN REGARD TO THE BEST MANNER OF READING THEM. " There are many who read a great deal, and yet derive very little advantage from what they read. They make an injudicious choice of books ; they read without method and without object, and often without attention and reflection. As a man may be eating all day, and for want of digestion receive no nourishment ; so these endless readers may cram themselves with intellectual food, and without real improvement of their minds, for want of digesting it by reflection." It is of great importance, then, not only that we take heed what we read, but how we read. 1. In the first place, then, read with discrimination. The world is full of books ; no small portion of which are either worthless or decidedly hurtful in their tendency. 2. Read with attention. Never take up a book merely for amusement, or for the sake of whiling away time. Time thus spent is worse than lost. 3. Read with reflection. 4. Read with confidence. It is often said man does not know his weakness. It is quite as true, he does not know his strength. Multitudes fail to accomplish what they might because they have not due confidence in their powers, and do not know what they are capable of accomplishing. Hence they yield their understandings to the dictation of others, and never think or act for themselves. The only use they make of reading is to remember and repeat the sentiments of their author. This is an error. When you sit down to the reading of a book believe that you are able to understand the subject on which it treats, and resolve that you will understand it. If it calls you to a severe effort, so much the better. Call no man master. Yield not your minds to the passive impressions which others may please to make upon them. 5. At the same time, read with humility and candour. We know so little, in comparison with what is to be known, that we have always much more reason to be humbled by our ignorance than puffed up by our knowledge. Real science is ever humble and docile ; but pedantry is proud and self-conceited. 6. It is a happy method to improve by reading, when several persons unite in reading the same book, or on the same subject, and meet occasionally to interchange their thoughts and compare their opinions respecting the authors they have been studying. 7. Read for improvement, and not for show. Recollect that the great object of reading is not to be able to tell what others have thought and said ; but to improve your minds in useful knowledge, establish your hearts in virtue, and prepare yourselves for a right performance of the duties of life, and for a joyful acceptance with God on the great day of account. III. In conclusion, let me call your attention TO THE IMPORTANCE OF MAKING A DILIGENT USE OF THIS MEANS OF INTELLECTUAL AND MORAL IMPROVEMENT. 1. In the first place, then, reading is a most interesting and pleasant method of occupying your leisure hours. 2. It is a consideration of no small weight that reading furnishes materials for interesting and useful conversation. Those who are ignorant of books must of course have their thoughts confined to very narrow limits. (*Joel Hawes, D.D.*)
*Good literature—its pleasure and profit :*—And here we come to the first reason why we should give attention to reading. Because—1. There is so much to be had for so little. This too is true, that truth is cheaper than error, as found in the types to-day. The father of lies knows the appetite for a certain kind of reading which is upon the age. But, ministering to the lower tastes, he makes us pay his printers. He is up to every device, but always with an open eye to profit. 2. Reading is made more and more readable, and especially reading of the best kind. Those who had a taste for philosophy in the days of Plato, for poetry in the days of Chaucer, for history in the days of Gibbon, for natural science in the days of Richelieu, for metaphysics in the time of Locke, for sacred learning in the ages when monasteries had all the books and students—at what trouble every learner of old time was put to obtain intelligence. But, by contrast, how accessible is every sort of knowledge now. (1) One should read no more than he takes time to reflect upon. A paragraph or a page mentally masticated and digested is of more service than a whole volume swallowed whole. To get a single truth so at one's service as to handle it as skilfully as David did his sling and stone is more effective than the apparel of Saul's armour. Many a great case at law, involving precious life and costly property, has been lost or won through the happy knowledge of a single fact. (2) Read chiefly on the side of ascertained truths. Let us plant ourselves upon the rock, that some things have been settled. There are some facts of religion which can no more be made flux by the slow or the fierce fires of the crucible of criticism, than gold can be melted by the flicker of a fire-fly. It seems no less than an unpardonable concession to admit that everything in this world is uncertain and unstable, and that the least stability and certainty are found in the realm of religion and requirements of faith. (3) Read

for the sake of final character as well as, or even more than, for present culture or professional calling. Is family government becoming feeble? Is the French disease of domestic corruption sickening our most sacred fane, the family? Then it will do it still more unless there shall come on us a holy purpose to purify our homes by raising the quality of the reading there allowed above the merely professional, above the evanescently fashionable, above the utterly ephemeral, up to that high order in which what is read shall sweetly allure to brighter worlds, by making sin of every gilded and grosser sort abominable in this. (*J. L. Withrow, D.D.*) *Reading: a talk with young folk:*—I. And, first, remember what a great and good book is, and especially what the Holy Book is. I want you to read the best books. Never waste your time and money over a poor, worthless, bad book. A bad book is a poison; a good book, the product of a wise soul, is health and strength and joy to mind and heart. II. Then, consider what a great and good book may do for you, especially what the Bible may do for you. A bad book may pollute your moral life with foul and hideous stains; a weak and worthless book will waste your time, and destroy the force of your mind, but a wise strong book will ennoble and enrich you for ever. III. Then, consider how a great and good book may help you, especially how the Bible will help you. We need the sympathy and strength of greater men than ourselves. No mind should feed upon itself. It should commune with other minds, with the golden words of men whose hearts God hath touched. IV. Then, do not let us forget how a great and good book may teach you, especially how the Bible can teach you. It can teach you secular wisdom. The best business precepts are to be found in the Bible. (*G. W. McCree.*) *Reading:*—The art of writing is an old as well as an invaluable art, though printing is a comparatively modern invention. Paul was a reader (Acts xvii. 28; Titus i. 12), and he exhorts Timothy, his son, to read. Right attendance to reading means—I. Read the BEST books. The world abounds with books, most of which are rubbish, many of which are pestilent, few only are good. A good book should be—1. Enlightening. It should brighten the firmament and widen the horizon of the soul. 2. Truthful. Whether in the form of fiction, history, or discussion, it should be true to the great realities of existence. 3. Suggestive. Every page of a good book should involve much more than it expresses, and charm the reader into fresh fields of inquiry. 4. Disciplinary. A good book is a book that aims at disciplining both the intellect and the heart. To aid the intellect to think with freedom, force, and precision, and the heart to flow with pure loves and high aspirations. II. Read the best books in a RIGHT WAY. 1. Thoughtfully. 2. Earnestly. 3. Practically. If men would "give attendance to such reading" a glorious change would come over the world, a new order of things would spring up in every department of social life. (*D. Thomas.*) *Experimental knowledge must be added to book knowledge:*—It is well known that the great doctors of the world, by much reading and speculation, attain unto a great height of knowledge, but seldom to sound wisdom; which hath given way to that common proverb, "The greatest clerks are not always the wisest men." It is not studying of politics that will make a man a wise councillor of state till his knowledge is joined with experience, which teacheth where the rules of state hold and where they fail. It is not book knowledge that will make a good general, a skilful pilot—no, not so much as a cunning artizan—till that knowledge is perfected by practice and experience. And so, surely, though a man abound never so much in literal knowledge, it will be far from making him a good Christian, unless he bring precepts into practice, and, by feeling experience, apply that he knows to his own use and spiritual advantage. (*J. Spencer.*) *How to read with profit:*—As it is not the best way for any that intendeth to make himself a good statesman to ramble and run over in his travels many countries, seeing much and making use of little for the improving of his knowledge and experience in state policy, but rather stay so long in each place till he have noted those things which are best worthy his observation: so is it also in the travels and studies of the mind, by which, if we would be bettered in our judgments and affections, it is not our best course to run over many things slightly, taking only such a general view of them as somewhat increaseth our speculative knowledge, but to rest upon the points we read, that we may imprint them in our memories, and work them into our hearts and affections, for the increasing of saving knowledge; then shall we find that one good book, often read and thoroughly pondered, will more profit than by running over a hundred in a superficial manner. (*Ibid.*) *The taste for reading:*—If I were to pray for a taste which should stand by me in stead under every variety of circumstances, and be a source of happiness and cheerfulness to me through life, and a shield against its ills, however things might go amiss, and the world frown upon me, it would be a taste for reading. I speak of it, of course, only as a worldly advantage, and not in the slightest degree derogating from the higher office and sure and stronger panoply of religious principles—but as a taste, an instrument, and a mode of pleasurable gratification. Give a man this taste, and the means of gratifying it, and you can hardly fail of making him a happy man, unless, indeed, you put into his hands a most perverse selection of books. You place him in contact with the best society in every period of history; with the wisest, the wittiest, with the tenderest, the bravest, and the purest characters who have adorned humanity. You make him a denizen of all nations—a contemporary of all ages. The world has been created for him. It is hardly possible but the character should take a higher and better tone from the constant habit of associating in thought with a class of thinkers, to say the least of it, above the average of humanity. It is morally impossible but that the manners should take a tinge of good breeding and civilization from having constantly before our eyes the way in which the best-bred and best-informed men have talked and conducted themselves in their intercourse with each other. There is a gentle, but perfectly irresistible coercion in a habit of reading, well directed, over the whole tenour of a man's character and conduct, which is not the less effectual because it works insensibly, and because it is really the last thing he dreams of. It cannot be better summed up than in the words of the Latin poet, "*Emollit mores, nec sinit esse feros.*" It civilizes the conduct of men, and suffers them not to remain barbarous. (*Sir J. Herschel.*)

Ver. 14. **Neglect not the gift that is in thee.**—*An ordination charge :*—If the supernatural gifts with which Timothy was endowed were in danger of suffering injury from the neglect of the zealous, ardent, devoted evangelist, how much greater is your danger of neglecting the gift that is in you, and of suffering injury from its neglect? I have seen the desolation of a negligent ministry, if you have not. By neglect his gift seems to have decayed and died out of him. He preaches, but not as he once preached. Let me not be misunderstood. I do not say that every unsuccessful minister has neglected the gift that is in him. I am very far from saying so. Some have small ministerial gifts, little preaching power. Paul, in his younger days, made full proof of his ministry. He neglected not the gift that was in him. What gift have you? What qualification for the ministry which all true ministers have? You have the one great gift of the Holy Ghost, a renewed heart. Is this your gift? Do not neglect it. Strive to attain more of this blessed, living experience of the great truths you have to preach. I once heard a good man and a good preacher well known and greatly honoured in this town, say, in the retrospect of a long and prosperous ministry, " I have nothing to boast of, for my voice has done more for my success than my intellectual power." I admired the modesty of the preacher, who, though favoured by a musical voice, had no reason to speak disparagingly of his intellectual powers. But he was wise enough to form a right estimate of the adventitious gifts of which, without being vain, he knew how to make a good use. To be vain of such things would be indeed a little, pitiable vanity. Yet, like John Angell James, " Neglect not the gift that is in thee." "Neglect not the gift that is in thee." The words seem to say, Cultivate your own gifts; those which are natural to you. Do not be solicitous about gifts which God has not given you. (*R. Halley, D.D.*) *Benefit of using personal gifts :*—Think, too, of the benefits to be derived in our own souls by personal service. God will never let a man be a loser by serving Him. The dense vapours that rise from earth to heaven return in pure water ; so he who gives to God such as he has, shall receive from Him a good return. The spear that is used contracts no rust ; the sword that is continually wielded remains untarnished ; the arm in constant use becomes occasionally weary, but increasingly strong ; so the child of God who labours for his master, though often wearied, gains great strength through that which he expends. The placid lake is sealed up in winter's frost from shore to shore, but the running rivulet escapes its power. The bewildered traveller on the Alps, half benumbed with cold, gets fresh circulation and warmth by his exertions to restore animation to the body of another. The reason why we have so many benumbed and frozen Christians in the present day is, that there are few personally employed in the work. We long for the time when every believer like the little waterfall and the alpine traveller shall be too active to freeze. Personal service brings its own reward ; watering others, we are watered ourselves ; warming others, we are ourselves warmed ; blessing others, we ourselves are blessed. Do you say, what can God do by one? I reply, very much! By one He brought forth His chosen people from Egypt's thraldom; by one (and that a youth) Goliath was slain while the whole army of Israel trembled before him; by one the assembled Israelites were convinced that "The Lord He is God," and the prophets of Baal were slain; by one sermon, and that a simple one, three thousand hearts were opened. Time would fail to tell of what God has done by such men as Wickliffe, Luther, Calvin, Huss, Whitfield, Wesley, Pounds, Harlan Page, and why not you? (*G. Brown.*)

Ver. 15. **Give thyself wholly to them.**—*Ministers wholly given to their work:* —I. THAT MINISTERS MUST GIVE THEMSELVES WHOLLY TO THEIR WORK BY GIVING THEIR HEARTS TO IT. No man ever gives himself wholly to any business to which his heart is opposed. Paul gave his heart so much to the ministry, as to esteem it a great and distinguishing privilege. "I thank Christ Jesus our Lord," says he, "who hath enabled me, for that He counted me faithful, putting me into the ministry." His life was bound up in his work. Their hearts are so absorbed in their work that it becomes the source of their highest joys and deepest sorrows. II. Ministers must give themselves wholly to their work, by giving their THOUGHTS to it. Men always meditate upon their supreme object of pursuit. III. Ministers must give themselves wholly to their work, by giving their STUDIES to it. The apostle exhorts Timothy to "give attendance to reading." This includes study and thinking, and every mode of intellectual improvement. IV. Ministers must give themselves wholly to their work, by devoting all their TIME to it. They may employ their whole time in their work; because it is a work which may be done, not only on the first and the last, but on every day of the week. Ministers, indeed, should be frugal of time. They should divide it properly, and devote each part to some particular part of their duty. They should live by rule. V. Ministers must give themselves wholly to their work, by giving all their INTERESTS to it. The apostles were obliged to do this literally. They would not have been the ministers of Christ, without literally following his injunction, to forsake all that they had. Not to insist, however, on such extraordinary cases, I would go on to observe that every minister is called, at least, to make all his worldly interests subservient to his holy and Divine employment. VI. Ministers must give themselves wholly to their work, by making their SECRET DEVOTIONS subservient to it. They should give themselves to reading, meditation, prayer and self examination; and in all these secret devotions have a particular reference to their public office. VII. That ministers must give themselves wholly to their work, by LIVING AGREEABLY to it. Their lives should resemble their sacred character, and be worthy of the imitation of the best of Christians. Having shown, in various respects, how ministers must give themselves wholly to their work, I now proceed to suggest several reasons why they must give themselves wholly to it. I. And here the first reason that occurs is, that by giving themselves wholly to the ministry they will make the duties of it more EASY AND PLEASANT. Their work is truly great and laborious, which needs to be made as light and easy as possible. And though by giving themselves wholly to it, they will neither omit nor curtail any of its duties and labours, yet they will render these very duties and labours more pleasant and delightful. II. Ministers should devote themselves wholly to the service of their people, because this is THE WISEST AND BEST WAY TO SECURE THEIR LOVE AND RESPECT. We love to see a person heartily and zealously engaged for our good. This is human nature. The sick man esteems and values the physician who devotes himself to his service, and stands by him day and night, to watch his every motion, and to extend his healing hand at every call. III. Ministers must give themselves wholly to their work, because this will be THE BEST SECURITY AGAINST THE SNARES AND TEMPTATIONS TO WHICH THEY ARE EXPOSED. IV. Ministers must give themselves wholly to their work, because this is THE BEST WAY TO BECOME EXTENSIVELY USEFUL. Every industrious man, in every lawful calling, is a useful man. Industry makes the useful farmer, the useful mechanic, the useful physician, and the useful magistrate. V. Ministers must give themselves wholly to their work, because THEY ACTUALLY ENGAGE TO DO IT. VI. That the IMPORTANCE of the ministry requires those who undertake it to give themselves wholly to their office. I have now finished what I have to say upon the nature and obligation of ministers giving themselves wholly to their work, and proceed to improve the subject. 1. We learn, that if ministers do give themselves wholly to their work, they will make it appear. 2. We learn, that if ministers do not give themselves wholly to their work, they will also make it appear. 3. We learn, why the vineyard of Christ bears, at this day, such a disagreeable and melancholy appearance. 4. We learn, the great criminality of those who sustain the sacred office, but do not give themselves wholly to their work. (*N. Emmons, D.D.*)    *Meditation :*—Meditation chews the cud, and gets the sweetness and nutritive virtue of the Word into the heart and life : this is the way the godly bring forth much fruit. (*Ashworth.*)    The naturalists observe that to uphold and accommodate bodily life, there are divers sorts of faculties communicated, and these among the rest—1. An attractive faculty, to assume and draw in the food.  2. A retentive faculty, to retain it when taken in.  3. An assimilating faculty, to concoct the nourishment.  4. An augmenting faculty, for drawing to perfection.  Meditation is all these.  It helps judgment, wisdom and faith to ponder, discern, and credit the things which reading and hearing supply and furnish.  It assists the memory to lock up the jewels of Divine truth in her sure treasury.  It has a digesting power, and turns spiritual truth into spiritual nourishment; and lastly, it helps the renewed heart to grow upward and increase its power to know the things which are freely given to us of God.  (*J. Ranew.*)    *The secret of success :*—A man who commenced life as an errand boy rose rapidly, through his untiring industry and earnestness, to the head of an extensive business, which he conducted very successfully.  Meeting an old friend one day, he spared a few moments to describe to him briefly the extent of his prosperity and of his prospects.  His friend inquired the secret of his success.  "I put my soul into it," replied the prosperous shopkeeper.  "It is only by throwing my soul into my business, that I made it succeed."  So must the teacher do.    **That thy profiting may appear to all.**—*Growth in grace :*—Nothing but an evident progress in knowledge and holiness should satisfy the Christian.  God expects from him a constant ripening towards perfection.  But the duty is plain enough.  And the subject of inquiry to which I would rather direct attention is, whether in our long continued enjoyment of religious privileges, there has been any apparent profiting.  I. And the first test by which we may judge that we have grown in grace will be found IN AN INCREASING CONVICTION OF OUR SINFULNESS AND WEAKNESS BY NATURE.  The young convert's views of sin may be more startling, because new ; but that which flashes before his eyes works its way down into the very heart of the more mature Christian, and assumes there the shape of an abiding, humbling assurance of utter sinfulness and helplessness in himself.  Here, then, Christians, is a mark by which to measure whether we have grown in grace.  Have years of acquaintance with ourselves made us feel our depravity more deeply ?  When we hear any boasting of the goodness of human nature, do we listen as a sick man does, who knows death is at his vitals, to one complimenting him upon his good looks ?  If we realize our sinfulness more and more the longer we live, then we may be sure that there " our profiting appears."  II. Another point of contrast between our present and our former state, our early and our mature experience, will be found IN OUR VIEWS OF CHRIST, AND DEPENDENCE UPON HIM.  A young Christian rests indeed upon Christ, but it is as the newly laid wall rests upon the foundation, while the cement is fresh, and when a little blow will cause it to totter ; but the mature Christian is like that wall when it settles down, and the uniting medium hardens, so that wall and foundation seem but one solid structure.  In our early experience we said much of our dependence on the Saviour, now we feel it.  III. If there be any profiting to appear, it will seem again IN OUR INCREASED CHARITY.  A young Christian is often a young bigot, filled with self-conceit and pride, and disposed to severity of censure and condemnation.  Like a young watch-dog, he means well for his master's interests, but will often snarl at his master's friends, and upon such as an older guardian would recognize and welcome.  An advanced Christian will grieve more over the dissensions of Christians, and pray earnestly for the time when all shall be one.  IV. AND THERE ARE VARIOUS OTHER POINTS IN WHICH " OUR PROFITING WILL APPEAR," IF WE HAVE GROWN IN GRACE.  A young Christian is much troubled by the remembrance of particular acts of sin.  A young Christian, again, sets a very high value on religious sensibility, on excited feeling, on gifts, and estimates his own religious character by his fervours in devotion, his tears for sin.  The piety of the young believer, again, depends very much on external aid.  It must be fed by constant converse with fellow-Christians, and its warmth must be sustained by frequent attendance on religious meetings.  But our " profiting will appear," if we have learned to delight more in our own private meditations on God's Word, and in communion with Him, and to be less dependent on our Christian ministers and our Christian brethren.  "The mature Christian, like the sack well filled, can stand alone, while the young convert must be held up in his emptiness."  The young Christian lives much upon the opinion of others.  To the young Christian, one or two doctrines of God's Word seem exclusively important, and he would be glad if every sermon were upon conversion and faith in Christ, and is apt to regard a preacher as not evangelical who dwells upon the moral duties of life; but our "profiting will appear," if we have learned to magnify all God's Word, to feel that all should be unfolded, and to love it as a whole. And there will be, if our profiting is apparent, an increased dependence on prayer and all the means of grace. But of all other points an increasing heavenly-mindedness will appear as the most striking evidence of a growing Christian. So small is our improvement, however, that most of us are obliged to say, we hardly know at times whether we are any better than we were years ago. When a ship is moving slowly into port, so that we can scarcely perceive that she advances at all, it is pleasant to fix our eye upon some landmark, and watch it till we can exclaim, Oh, yes, I do see now that we move a little; and these marks which I have given may help us to know whether we are progressing at all towards the haven of peace. Happy are they who can thus perceive an advance in the Divine life. It is a comfort in itself, because every degree of progress in holiness is like every step in recovery from sickness, attended with positive and present pleasure. (*W. H. Lewis, D.D.*)

Ver. 16. **Take heed unto thyself, and unto the doctrine.**—*The comparative influence of character and doctrine:*—In counselling his friend and follower as to the best method of doing good in the sphere of duty allotted to him, the apostle seems here to lay the chief stress, not on doctrine or teaching, but on life or conduct. "Take heed," is his admonition, not first to what you teach, and then to what you are; not primarily to your verbal instructions, and then to the spirit of your own character and life, but first "to thyself" and then "to the doctrine." For it is nothing less than the broad principle that, in order to do good, the first and great effort must be to be good,—that extent and accuracy of religious knowledge, however important, are secondary, as a means of influence, to the moral discipline and culture of our own heart and life. Both reason and experience are against the notion that it needs great personal piety to be an accurate expositor of the theory of Divine truth, or that none but men of very holy lives can be profound theologians or able preachers. To be versant in a science does not of necessity imply that we must be skilled in the correlative art. Theory and practice, science and art, the knowledge of principles and the power to apply them, are attainments which depend on totally different faculties, and which may be, and in actual experience very commonly are, dissociated from each other. The able or eloquent writer on the principles of government would not always make the best practical statesman, or the acute expounder of theories in political economy the most sagacious financier. It is possible to know scientifically the principles of music without being able to sing a note,—to discuss and enforce the principles of grammar and rhetoric, and yet be a feeble speaker or inelegant writer. And the same remark is borne out in the sphere of man's spiritual life. The facts and data being given, a man may play with the terms of theology as with the terms of algebra. The experience of mankind in all ages has shown how possible it is for a man to draw fine fancy-pictures of the beauty of virtue amidst a life that is sadly unfamiliar with her presence, to utter pathetic harangues on charity with a heart of utter selfishness, and to declaim on purity and self-denial, whilst living in sloth and luxurious self-indulgence. The truth of God may thus be studied as a mere intellectual exercise, and preached as a feat of rhetorical address, whilst yet the premises of the preacher's high argument are utterly foreign to his own godless experience. Like a sick physician, the preacher may prescribe, perhaps successfully, to others for the disease of which himself is dying. We fall back with not less confidence on the assertion, that an experimental acquaintance with Divine truth—deep religious earnestness, is the first and grand qualification in the teacher, incomparably the most powerful means of usefulness, and the surest pledge of success. To be duly effective, truth must not merely fall from the lip, but breathe forth from the life; it must come, not like incense from the censer that only holds it, but like fragrance, from a flower, exhaling from a nature suffused with it throughout. In one word—and this is the principle which I wish now to illustrate—the first qualification of the religious instructor is, not knowledge, but piety. I. That life is in some respects of prior importance to doctrine may be perceived by reflecting THAT LIFE TENDS VERY GREATLY TO MODIFY A MAN'S OWN VIEWS OF DOCTRINE; in other words, that personal character tinges a man's perceptions of truth. Whether it be things material or moral, objects of sense or objects of thought, in most cases we perceive according as we are. The same objects may be externally present to a hundred spectators, and yet be practically different to each of them. Every one knows, for example, that the varied colours wherewith the face of the visible earth seems to be clothed, exist not literally in the objects themselves, but owe their splendour to the eye that surveys them. It is only the unknown or occult causes of colour that exist in nature; colour itself is in the organism and mind of the observer; and through physical disease or organic defect our perceptions of colour may be marred or destroyed. The jaundiced eye blanches nature. Or if we pass from the mere organism through which man's spirit converses with the outward world to that spirit itself, still more obvious illustration have we of the principle before us. It is the state of the inner eye, the condition of that spirit within us which looks out on nature through the loopholes of sense, that makes the world's aspect to be to us what it is. It is the same world which is beheld by the man of deep thoughtfulness and sensibility, and by the dull observer in whom the sense of beauty has never been evoked, and yet how different that world to each! Now the same law attains in that higher province to which the text relates. As our perceptions of beauty, so our perceptions of moral and spiritual truth are modified by the inner spirit and character of the percipient. Self conditions doctrine. A man's own moral state is very much the measure of his moral convictions. The highest spiritual truths lie beyond the range of a soul that is not in harmony with them, and the glimmerings of truth which a defective nature gains, take their complexion from its moral tone and spirit. The glorious discoveries of Divine things on the page of inspiration are lost to the soul in which the moral sense, the vision and faculty divine, is dull or dormant. God is but a name to the mind in which no Divine instinct, no godly sympathies and aspirations, have begun to stir. Moreover, consider how notoriously our opinions in secular matters are affected by our prejudices and passions. Who of us, where personal interest is at stake, can trust with unerring certainty to the conclusions of his own judgment? Experience proves that agreeable falsehoods are at least as likely to be believed as disagreeable truths. Endeavour to introduce new opinions, uncongenial to educational or class convictions, and often all the force of truth will in vain be exerted to obtain for them a place in the rugged and reluctant mind. Thus even on the lower ground of secular truth it needs, in the formation of opinion, the rarest candour and self-watchfulness to conduct the process aright. But this discipline is still more indispensable to the religious inquirer. For there are no interests so tremendous as those which are involved in our religious beliefs. In no other province of inquiry are deeper passions stirred, or prejudices, associations, habits, more numerous and inveterate, called into play. As the chemist seeks to render his balances exquisitely sensitive, and carefully eliminates from his results all variations of temperature or other disturbing elements; so should the student of Divine things strive by God's grace to attain the acuteness and delicacy of a judgment freed from all deflecting influences, and poised with an exquisite nicety of discrimination on which not the slightest grain of truth is lost. He should cultivate, in one word, by the discipline of a holy life, a truer and philosophic calmness and candour —the calmness of a spirit that dwells in habitual communion with God, the candour of a mind that has nothing to lose, and everything to gain, by truth. II. In further illustration of the principle that life or character comes, in order of importance, before " doctrine," it is to be considered that LIFE OR CHARACTER AFFECTS not only a man's own views of truth, but also HIS POWER OF EXPRESSING OR COMMUNICATING TRUTH TO OTHERS. For if, from any cause, the organ of spiritual perception be impaired or undeveloped in a man's mind, of course he can communicate to others no clearer views than he himself has received. The stream can rise no higher than its source. The medium lends its own defects to the light which passes through it. To exert real power over men's minds and hearts, what you speak must be not only true, but true to you. For the conveyance of thought and feeling from mind to mind is not a process which depends on mere verbal accuracy. Language is not the only medium through which moral convictions and impressions are transmitted from speaker to hearer. There is another and more subtle mode of communication, a mysterious moral contagion, by means of which, irrespective of the mere intellectual apparatus employed, the instructor's beliefs and emotions are passed over into the minds of his auditory. Strong conviction has a force of persuasion irrespective of the mere oral instrument by which it works. The magnetic force must saturate his own spirit ere it flow out to others in contact with him. No stereotyped orthodoxy, no simulated fervours, however close or clever the imitation, will achieve the magic effects of reality. Bring your own spirit to the fount of inspiration, live in habitual communion with the infinite truth and life, and the words you speak to men, whether rude or refined, will possess a charm, a force, a power to touch their hearts and mould their secret souls, which no words of eloquent conventionality can ever attain. There will be an intuitive recognition of the Divine fire which has touched your lips. III. The only other consideration I shall adduce in support of the principle involved in the text is—THAT LIFE OR CHARACTER HAS IN MANY RESPECTS AN INFLUENCE WHICH DIRECT TEACHING OR DOCTRINE CANNOT EXERT. Actions, in many ways, te··h better than words, and even the most persuasive oral instruction is greatly vivified when supplemented by the silent teaching of the life. 1. Consider, for one thing, that actions are more intelligible than words. Ideas, reflections, deductions, distinctions, when presented in words, are liable to misapprehension; their power is often modified or lost by the obscurity of the medium through which they are conveyed, and the impression produced by them is apt very speedily to vanish from the mind. But whatever the difficulty of understanding words, deeds are almost always intelligible. Let a man not merely speak but act the truth; let him reveal his soul in the articulate speech of an earnest, pure, and truthful life, and this will be a language which the profoundest must admire, while the simplest can appreciate. The most elaborate discourse on sanctification will prove tame and ineffective in comparison with the eloquence of a humble, holy walk with God. In the spectacle of a penitent soul pouring forth the broken utterance of its contrition at the Saviour's feet, there is a nobler sermon on repentance than eloquent lips ever spoke. The living epistle needs no translation to be understood in every country and clime; a noble act of heroism or self-sacrifice speaks to the common heart of humanity; a humble, gentle, holy, Christlike life preaches to the common ear all the world over. 2. Consider, again, that the language of the life is more convincing than the language of the lip. It is not ideal or theoretical, it is real and practical; and whilst theories and doctrines may be disputed, and only involve the learner in inextricable confusion, a single unmistakable fact, if you can appeal to it, cuts the knot, and sets discussion at rest. The theory is a fine one, they admit, but constituted as poor human nature is, there is this inseparable objection to it, that it will not work. But in this, as in many other cases, experiment will be the test of truth. Men may dispute your theory of agriculture, and explanation or discussion might only serve to confirm them in their error; but show them, rugged though be the soil and ungenial the climate, your fair and abundant crops, and objection is silenced. 3. Consider, finally, that the teaching of the life is available in many cases in which the teaching of the lip cannot, or ought not, to be attempted. But in all cases in which formal instruction or advice is precluded, how invaluable that other mode of access to the minds of men on which we are now insisting—the silent, unobtrusive, inoffensive, yet most potent and persuasive teaching of the life. The counsel you may not speak you may yet embody in action. To the faults and sins you cannot notice in words, you may hold up the mirror of a life bright with purity and goodness and grace. The mind which no force of rebuke could drive from sin, may yet be insensibly drawn from it by the attractive power of holiness ever acting in its presence. Let your daily life be an unuttered yet perpetual pleading with man for God. Let men feel, in contact with you, the grandeur of that religion to whose claims they will not listen, and the glory of that Saviour whose name you may not name. Let the sacredness of God's slighted law be proclaimed by your uniform sacrifice of inclination to duty, by your repression of every unkind word, your scorn of every undue or base advantage, your stern and uncompromising resistance to the temptations of appetite and sense. Preach the preciousness of time by your husbanding of its rapid hours, and your crowding of its days with duties. And, be assured, the moral influence of such a life cannot be lost. Like the seed which the wind wafts into hidden glades and forest depths, where no sower's hand could reach to scatter it, the subtle germ of Christ's truth will be borne on the secret atmosphere of a holy life, into hearts which no preacher's voice could penetrate. Where the tongue of men and of angels would fail, there is an eloquence of living goodness which will often prove persuasive. (*J. Caird, D.D.*) *The teacher and the taught:*—1. Let your teaching be Scriptural. You are students of God's revealed Word. Let me, then, earnestly entreat you to lay the basis of all that you have to say upon the clearly ascertained revelations of Holy Scripture. Do not suppose that you can find within yourself better moral illustrations, or more comprehensive principles of action, than you will find within the sacred volume. 2. Take heed to your doctrine, that it be not only Scriptural, but comprehensive. Do not rest satisfied with a truth because it is found in Holy Scripture, but discover for yourself whether there be not other truths, closely-related truths, in God's revelation, without which the truth in question cannot be understood. Do not be satisfied with the truth that merely meets your own views and fancy. Believe me, nearly all the errors which have desolated the Church of God have arisen from this want of comprehensiveness, this exaggeration of some truths, this conference upon them of unwonted importance. There are those who have so exclusively dwelt on the Divine sovereignty and counsels, that they have lost sight of the responsibility and defiled the conscience of man. There are those who are so overpowered by His divinity, that they have lost the practical force of His brotherhood, and conferred His humanity on His mother, His sisters, and brethren. 3. Take heed to the manner of the doctrine, that it be connected and ordered upon some plan, some prayerfully-considered purpose. Do not treat the Scriptures as a conjuring-book, nor open it at random, nor read it with carelessness ; but endeavour to get at a meaning of a period, of a stage, of an epoch, of a division of God's revelations ; or, if you will, pursue the Scriptural teaching, on some great thrilling themes, from the beginning of the Bible to its close. 4. Take heed to your doctrine, that it is appropriate to the class of minds with which you have to deal. Paul spoke in Hebrew to the Jews, and in Greek to the philosophers of Athens. He adopted one style when addressing the Orientalists of Ephesus, and another when reasoning with the prejudices of Roman Jews. "Take heed," said the venerable apostle to his son in the faith, "take heed unto THYSELF." We who are workers for God, students of truth, servants of the Church, teachers and pastors, watchers for souls, have a great work to do with ourselves : we have great temptations to resist, yet we are to be "patterns even to believers, in word, in conversation, in charity, in spirit, in faith, in purity." Take heed to thyself, O man of God ! Thou mayest deal with heavenly realities and Divine truths until they are mere chess-men that thou art shifting over the board and fighting imaginary battles with. Thou mayest substitute the intellectual appreciation of the truth which thou hast discovered, for the spiritual reception of it into thy own heart. The inducements by which the apostle urges this stirring appeal are comprehensive and inspiring : "in so doing thou shalt both save thyself and those that hear thee." My fellow-workers, there is one salvation for our hearers and for ourselves. The most powerful preacher, the most devoted teacher, the most distinguished apostle, the holiest martyr, must be saved by the same means as the most ignorant and guilty sinner to whom he speaks. There are no special passports to heaven, no short cuts, no sideways, no reserved seats, no privileged admissions there ; a spiritual reputation on earth is no watchword at the gates of heaven. However, patient perseverance in such godlike work is a way not only of securing the salvation of others, but our own salvation too. Our own salvation, without the salvation of those that hear us, is a thought we can scarcely endure. (*H. R. Reynolds, B.A.*)

*Self-improvement :*—"Genius," says a modern writer, "is the passion for self-improvement." It has been assumed that if a man has genius he does not need to be careful of himself, he does not need to aim at self-improvement. The very opposite is the true state of the case. It is the blood horse that needs the most careful training. "Take heed to thyself" is a word necessary for us all, but it is especially necessary for those of full vitality : for those in whose veins the hot blood seems to course rapidly ; for those of highly-strung nervous organization ; for those whose impulses are fiery ; whose temperament is ardent ; whose souls have in them a craving that seems insatiable. If these do not take heed to themselves, there will be disaster. A well-balanced nature, in which the physical, mental, and moral seem to be in happy equilibrium, is not always found, perhaps seldom. Some one department of our organism seems to predominate. The tendency is to cultivate that which it is most easy to cultivate, to the neglect of the other. Consequently, the whole nature is thrown out of balance and a condition of chronic unhappiness is the result. I would ask you to remark upon the advice which the great apostle gives to Timothy, one of the earliest presbyters of the Christian Church. Though this man must have had special qualifications for his work, yet these special qualifications did not preclude the necessity for diligent improvement of his mental powers. He is urged to do everything he can towards self-improvement. On that must depend his usefulness. There is no recognition here of any supernatural grace which would relieve him from the use of those means whereby ordinary men bring their minds into an ability of perceiving what is truth and what error. He must take heed to himself first, or his teaching will not be as full of light and of force as it ought to be. " Take heed unto thyself." Every man of us is a trinity in unity, body, soul, spirit. We have physical, mental and spiritual needs ; physical, mental and spiritual abilities—these constitutionally. They are included in the word " manhood." The physical is the pediment on which the mental and spiritual stand. It is that which confines them to this earth. It limits and modifies their use. There is something that we have to learn within these present limitations, which will be useful to us always. We soon come to the end of our physical growth ; and strange though it seems, very many seem soon to come to the end of their mental growth, although it must be only in seeming. But no one ever comes to the limit of spiritual growth so long as he is on this earth. Now, we have to recognize distinctly and clearly that the lower is for the sake of the higher. It is in service to it. The physical is for the sake of the mental, the mental for the sake of the emotional, and all for the sake of the spiritual. Nor is there any possibility of improvement until that which is uppermost in man constitutionally becomes uppermost in thought. Inadequate views of human nature are at the root of personal miseries and social perplexities. Man's view of himself as to what he is and what destined for must affect him beneficially or otherwise in all relations of life and in all that he does. Supposing a man has this view of life, " I am here to be as happy as I can make myself, here to enjoy myself, here simply to have a good time." That is the dominating idea. You see at a glance its limitations. No heroism can ever come out of it ; nothing really good or great or sublime. No man moving under the influence of that idea has ever done anything of worth or value. Take another view of life, that in which a man sees something to be done out of which comes a material reward. The idea of duty dawns upon him, eventually takes possession of him, masters him, and under its influence he denies himself much to which other men are inclined, and becomes the world's successful man in that region concerning which we cannot use any other words than those which convey respect—the commercial. This man becomes stoical. He uses one department of his nature only. We might bring other types of men forward in illustration, but these two will suffice. In both cases the nature is depreciated below that for which it was predestinated. Neither man will ever be good or noble. There is no possibility of it. The idea which these men have of manhood and its meaning and purpose is very much lower than God's idea written in the constitution of man. The first man never could be happy and the second man never can be satisfied. Why? Because, in both cases, the nature is larger than the idea which controls and dominates it. The spiritual part of man is clamorous. It wants its dues, or its wine turns to vinegar ; its milk of human kindness to gall. The physical is not here for itself, but for the sake of the mental, the mental is not here for itself, but for the sake of the emotional and the affectional ; and the emotional and the affectional are here for the sake of that which is permanent and indestructible in man's nature—the spiritual. As a child cries for its mother so the spiritual in man cries out for its Father, God. We see, then, that there is a limit soon reached to physical self-improvement, and a limit also soon reached to improvement arising out of any type or style of life which is dominated by the idea of pleasing oneself simply, or of doing duty which has relation only to that which is seen and temporal. Every man, even the smallest and meanest, is larger constitutionally than his business and larger than his pleasures—using that word as it is ordinarily used. Man's self, what the philosophers would call " the ego," is that which needs to be continuously improved. And with its improvement everything else belonging to the man will be raised, will be expanded, will be developed into a higher power. If a man be an artist, he is a better artist when his spiritual nature is awakened. The costliest pictures in all Europe are those in which the artists have aimed at bodying forth spiritual themes. No man is really himself until the Spirit within him is awake. The New Testament calls him " dead " till then. It is all but literally true that a man is never alive until that which is characteristic of him, as man, is alive. A type of religious life has been prevalent, we might say dominant, in the past which has almost lost sight of three-fourths of the Pauline theology, anyway of the Pauline ethics. To get a man converted according to the Calvinistic idea of conversion, and then pretty much to leave him as necessarily in a condition of safety, this has been dominant. Conversion means turning the life Christwards instead of turning the back upon Christ and His salvation. But to turn round and stand still is not the apostolic idea of being a Christian. Any new truth entering the mind brings light, and light means life, and life means activity. We are at school—learning how to be men and women according to God's idea of men and women. How is our spiritual nature to be developed into more and yet more until it becomes the undisputed sovereign of our constitution? It is impossible to compel any man to be a Christian because it is impossible to compel love. The heart of man must feel drawn to the object set before it. And so we fail to do any justice to the Christian religion unless its relation to the heart of man be presented so as to wake that heart into response. Along this line all self-improvement must proceed. We must take heed to ourselves. I venture to add that there is no spiritual self-improvement that is worth anything apart from plan and purpose. A spasmodic religiousness will do little. If a young man at college should study only when he feels in the humour he would be disgraced. If a man of business should go to his store or office only when the fit takes him he would be bankrupt. (*R. Thomas, D.D.*) *The principles of the ministerial character :*—We shall note some of those features of character, which were probably intended when the apostle urged Timothy—and in him all who should come after him—to "take heed unto himself." I. We may suppose him, in the first instance, to mean, Take heed that thou art FAITHFUL. No qualification is more commonly associated with the gospel ministry than this. "Moreover," says this apostle to the Corinthians, "it is required in stewards, that a man be found faithful"; "I have obtained mercy of the Lord to be faithful": whilst to Epaphras and Tychicus he assigns the distinction of "faithful ministers of Christ and his fellow-servants in the Lord." II. But again: in warning Timothy to "take heed to himself," the apostle would have him be FEARLESS. He says to him in another epistle, "God hath not given us the spirit of fear, but of power and of love and of a sound mind." It is remarkable to observe how prophets, evangelists and apostles concur in warning us against the fear of man. III. Another ministerial quality, which we may well consider as included in the apostle's caution, "Take heed unto thyself," IS THAT OF A PRUDENT REGARD TO EXTERNAL CIRCUMSTANCES. A Christian, a real Christian, we ought to remember, is a public man—an instrument in the world's renovation— taken up into a system of agencies, which are to issue in the regeneration of a new and righteous universe : so that "whether he lives, he lives unto the Lord; or whether he dies, he dies unto the Lord." Neither is it less a part of this ministerial prudence, to take heed to the intellectual signs of the times in which we live. (*D. Moore, M.A.*) *The principles of ministerial doctrine :*—I. We inquire, then, WHAT AUTHORITY IS TO BE CONSULTED IN DECIDING UPON THE TRUTH OF DOCTRINE. One pervading fault of all the religious systems of antiquity was the absence of any universal and accredited standard, either of faith or of practice. Men did not know what they were to believe. Their mysteries were locked up among human deposits ; their precepts proceeded from human oracles ; and as there were no means of securing uniformity among the teachers' thoughts, that which was set down as truth to-day, might cease to be truth to-morrow. Why, his security is, that all essential and saving truth is lodged, confined, inseparably bound up in a volume, whose pages were penned by the finger of the living God ; so that a curse would light on him, be he seraph from the throne of light or ambassador from the realms of darkness, who should knowingly preach as an essential doctrine of the gospel, that which could neither be found therein, nor yet be proved thereby. Now, it must be owned, that even if there be nothing else to recommend the recognition of this principle, it has at least the advantage of great simplicity ; that it would preserve us from all those fluctuations of doctrine and of practice, which would be sure to result, so long as men's cameleon views were permitted to determine what should be truth and what should not. But here it may be asked, does the fact of this system being locked up in a single book secure this much-desired uniformity? The Almighty has made the way of holiness plain as a sunbeam to him that on his knees will seek for it; but He certainly has made no provision for the blindness that will not see. II. We come now to THE CLAIMS OF HUMAN REASON IN REFERENCE TO THE MODE OF INCULCATING DOCTRINE. Born as man is, in common with myriads of other creatures, subject to appetite, passion, disease and death, he has one faculty which distinguishes him from the whole intelligent universe—the faculty of reason; that power by which he thinks and forms his conclusions. In this respect, man stands alone. It is plain, therefore, that no system of instruction would be complete, which disregarded the claims of this noble faculty. And yet it has been, from ill-advised endeavours to satisfy these claims, that the unity of the Church has suffered some of its severest shocks, and the cause of truth its deepest injuries. Teachers and taught have too often lacked the courage to acknowledge that the line of their puny intellect could never fathom "the deep things of God"—that there were doctrines in their system, which could never be comprehended by finite beings. Now, we have no hesitation in telling you, that we have no desire to see these lofty subjects pared down and refined to the presumed level of human reason. "Without controversy," such a doctrine as that of " God manifest in the flesh," is a mystery. Neither, as we shall hope to show you, whenever any of these sublime doctrines are brought under your notice, are any demands made upon your faith, which it is not the duty of an intelligent creature to concede. III. We proceed now to THE USE AND EFFICACY OF EXTERNAL ORDINANCES TOWARDS STRENGTHENING OUR FAITH. IV. THE LEADING TRUTHS TO BE INSISTED UPON AS ESSENTIAL POINTS OF DOCTRINE. (*Ibid.*) *Improvement of religious anniversaries:*—I. I shall EXPLAIN THE ADMONITION, " Take heed to thyself." 1. The object of your solicitude, this will be yourself. It is your soul—a man's soul is himself. What is the garment to the body which it clothes? What is the body to the soul which inhabits it? 2. The manner in which this solicitude for the soul is expressed—" Take heed." How often is that admonition repeated in Scripture; and generally to some subject connected with man's spiritual and eternal interests! Man is heedful enough in reference to his worldly concerns, but he is the most heedless being in reference to his spiritual interests. Salvation is not a trifling work; religion is not an insignificant matter;—it requires that we " take heed." II. I am TO ENFORCE THIS ADMONITION. And here the motives are so numerous that selection is more difficult than enumeration. 1. But, in the first place, 1 would remind you of the inconceivable value and infinite importance of that for which your solicitude is demanded. 2. Take heed to the soul, for the soul's salvation is the most rational, the most befitting exercise of that self-love which our Creator has implanted in our nature as our impetus to happiness. There is a great difference between selfishness and self-love. It cannot be vicious for a man to desire to be happy, nor is there any virtue in it. It is only an instinct of nature, but then it is a most important one; and the man that is not taking heed to his soul is acting in opposition to this self-love—this instinct of his nature after happiness. 3. But I observe there is another motive to take heed to thyself—it is the command of God. If it were only advice on the part of the Creator—since He knows the whole of the case, since His eye looks onward to eternity, since He comprehends the whole range of being, since He knows what is destined for the righteous and the wicked in another world —the creature must be under the influence of a total disregard to his own happiness, who refuses the counsel of the Almighty. 4. I remark, that if we do not take heed to ourselves, all the solicitudes which others may have cherished, or may still feel for us, will be all in vain. 5. I urge this admonition to take heed to yourselves by the consideration that it is indispensably necessary—you cannot be saved without it. There are difficulties connected with salvation. If you are saved, there must be striving, watching, and praying. Can all this be done without taking heed to your souls? 6. I admonish you to take heed to yourselves, by showing you that all the solicitude you may feel, or profess to feel for others, cannot be accepted in you for solicitude for yourselves. 7. I urge this on you from the consideration, that so far from interfering with or injuring your doings for the benefit of others, the more heed you take to yourselves, the better qualified will you be to take heed to others. There is nothing in a strict attention to your own personal salvation, incompatible with the salvation of others. And now permit me, in conclusion, to take up the subject—1. By way of examination. 2. Let me take up the subject by way of expostulation, what have you taken heed to if you have not taken heed to yourselves? How has your time been occupied? How have your faculties been employed? What have you found more valuable than your soul, more important than salvation, more endurable than eternity, more desirable than heaven? (*J . A. James.*) *Thyself and thy teaching:*—The text consists of three parts. It presents—1. An object of watchful care. 2. An admonition to persistency in watchfulness. 3. A reason for this care in its happy results. I. THE OBJECT OF WATCHFULNESS and caution is apparently twofold. Take heed to thyself and to thy teaching; but as we shall examine the admonition a little more carefully, we shall discover that the two parts are of one piece and made up of one thought. For the present, however, let us consider them separately. Take heed then, first, to thyself; or literally, hold thy attention fixed upon thyself. The gospel gives us two classes of admonition which, while apparently pointing in different ways, are nevertheless quite consistent. On the one hand, it is constantly directing our thoughts away from self; its very key-note is deny self; treat it as if it were not. On the other hand, it is most intensely personal. While it tells us that no man liveth unto himself, it also tells us that every man shall give account of himself to God. In one and the same breath we hear "Bear ye one another's burdens," and "Every man shall bear his own burden." In one place we find Paul insisting on the independent right of the individual conscience, asserting that every man stands or falls to his own master; and in another saying, "If meat make my brother to stumble, I will eat no meat while the world standeth." In our text we find the same thing. Timothy is exhorted to take heed to himself; but the last clause of the verse shows that not only himself but all his hearers are to be in his mind; that his very heedfulness of himself is to be for their sake quite as much as for his own. Hence our text, carefully studied, may show us how these two classes of admonition may be reconciled. "Bend thine attention on thyself." The fair inference is that self needs careful watching; that a man who undertakes to look after himself has a great piece of work upon his hands, and one which admits of no negligence. In a worldly sense most men find taking care of themselves a very serious business; it is an infinitely more serious business in a moral sense; it is transcendently serious in a Christian sense; at least our Lord seemed to think so when He asked, "What is a man profited, if he gain the whole world, and lose or forfeit his own self." The difference between taking care of self in the ordinary sense and in the Christian sense, is very radical and lies in this; that the ordinary sense implies taking care of the natural self; gratifying its desires, encouraging its tendencies, assisting its proclivities, trying to make it by culture, on a larger scale, essentially what it is by nature; while the Christian sense implies making self something which it is not by nature; the development of a renewed, Christ-like self, the ideal self of the Gospel; the training of a new creature in Christ Jesus. We often hear people exhorted to be true to themselves, as if all virtue were summed up in that. There are not a few men who, if they were true to themselves would be false to every man. Certain people talk as though if a man only acts out that which he really is at heart, he is thereby shown to be virtuous. On the contrary, he may be shown to be essentially vicious. A serpent is true to himself when he stings you; a tiger when he rends you; a traitor when he betrays you. The burglar, the pickpocket, the assassin, the more false they are to themselves the better for us. The gospel, therefore, challenges this fine moral sentiment, and admits it only under conditions. Be true to yourself, yes; but to what self? There is something before being true to yourself, and that is, "Take heed to yourself." Look well what that is to which you propose to be true. Christian training has not only to bring us to a certain point of attainment, it has also to detach us from very much; and it is to the work of detachment as well as to that of attainment that our taking heed to ourselves is directed. When a boy goes to West Point and is enrolled as a cadet, perhaps the most exasperating thing about his new life is that he is constantly being checked in doing the things which it is natural for him to do. The soldier self he finds out is something quite different from the schoolboy self, and the transition from one to the other is neither easy nor pleasant. "Look out for yourself. That is no way for a soldier to stand." His head or feet fall into their natural positions. "Take care! Eyes right!" And so at every point where the natural habits assert themselves, the boy is corrected and reproved. His natural self is the very thing he has to take heed to and guard against while he is cultivating the new soldierly self until it becomes a second nature. Just so, when a man sets out to become a good soldier of Christ, a great part of the hardness he has to endure grows out of the struggle with himself in the effort to develop the new and better self. Hence the emphasis is laid by the apostle justly upon this point. The first thing is that you yourself be right; that you yourself be under Christ's new law, pervaded by Christ's new life, guided by Christ's new unselfish principle of action; that you be such a self as Paul describes in the words, "Not I live but Christ liveth in me." Therefore, take heed unto thyself. Take heed too unto thy teaching. Christianity, such is our Lord's general principle, wherever it informs a life and a character, carries a power of instruction. Ye are the light of the world. The very quality of Christian life is that something should go out from it to enlighten and purify. Here, therefore, is the point of connection with the former charge. Take heed to thyself, because that self teaches; because no man liveth unto himself; because you cannot be a Christian and not give men some impression about Christ and Christianity. You must teach. You cannot help it. Men will learn something from you whether you will or not. Thus, then, all that has been said thus far is easily summed up. Clergy and people alike are admonished simply on the ground of their discipleship. Discipleship in every case carries with it a power of teaching. That power resides first of all in the disciple's Christian personality; in what he himself is as a Christian. I repeat it—you all teach. Every one of you who professes faith in Christ is a teacher in virtue of that fact. You teach by your spirit. This is a thing hard to define or explain. If one should ask you to explain the odour which fills your room from that beautiful climbing honeysuckle, you could not do it; but you are conscious of the fragrance none the less. II. We come now to the second element of the text—PERSISTENCY. Continue in these things; that is, in care for yourself and for your teaching. Christian self-culture requires continuous care. The old self is like the treacherous ocean lapping at the dykes and assailing the smallest break, and must be constantly watched. The new self is a growth, not a complete creation, and like all growths must be tended. And this persistency is related also to the teaching power of the Christian self. It is behind all the good and lasting impressions which holy character makes. When a man strikes a blow which stuns his adversary the effect is sudden; but behind that lightning-like stroke are years of slow muscular compacting and gymnastic training. When intellectual power goes out of another man to you, and you instinctively recognize, in your first contact with him, an intellectual king, behind that impression are years of mental discipline and laborious study. Just so spiritual character often makes itself felt at once. It takes no time nor reasoning to convince you that you are talking with one who has walked with God: but crude character, shallow character, half-way character does not and cannot affect you thus. Such impression is made by the man who has long taken heed to himself, who has been scarred in many a fight with the old self, and has watched and tended with prayer and tears the growth of the new man in him. Then again, even when character is not ripened there is a lesson in steady, persistent growth. A double-minded man, unstable in all his ways, ceases to be a lesson except of warning. When a man's whole life is seen to be concentrated upon the service of God and the attainment of a heavenly recompense, that life is a lesson. Many a time, as you have been walking the street, you have seen a man stop at a corner, and look fixedly upward at something or other. Your first impulse is to look up too. There is always a peculiar interest in anything that is above this earth, though it may be only a little way above. Then you stop, and still look up. Perhaps you ask, " What is it?" The next man that comes along and sees you two looking up, stops also, and the next, until a crowd is gathered, for no other reason than that one man in the hurrying throng stood steadfastly looking upward. And this familiar incident is a type of something better. When a man is seen living for heaven; when every day's life says to men, " One thing have I desired of the Lord: that will I seek after," there is a power and a lesson in that fact. Men ask, " What is it he sees which we do not see? What is he after which thus concentrates his energy, and makes him live in this world as if his home were elsewhere?" III. And now the third element of the text—THE RESULT OF THIS CAREFUL AND PERSISTENT SELF-CULTURE. "Thou shalt both save thyself and them that hear thee." In the economy of this world for a man to take heed to himself means to let other people go; not to save them, but to let them be lost if they will. In the Christian economy, to take heed to oneself is to save not only the self, but others. Thou shalt save thyself. It is very clearly implied that salvation is not an easy matter. Salvation is not a thing which God works out for us while we take our ease. But this promise, " thou shalt save thyself," is bound up with our influence upon others. You know very well that in teaching another any branch of knowledge, you broaden your own knowledge. You know how the labourer who toils for the sake of wife and little ones, strengthens his own arm; and in like manner, the exertion of spiritual energy for the sake of others, reacts to make the man who puts it forth spiritually stronger. The man who feels that he must take heed to himself because his life affects other lives, and who watches and disciplines himself, not only for his own salvation, but to save others—himself grows apace in spiritual power. So, too, you shall save them that hear you. There is a saving power in a life which is watchful over itself as in God's sight. Here we strike, I think, the true idea of the Church of Christ. The Church is ordained of Christ to save. Men talk of revival. For one I want a revival on a larger scale than is popularly conceived. A means of saving men—a mightier means than any temporary or spasmodic efforts. I long to see whole Churches, as bodies of Christ, glowing with the radiance of concentrated character. (*M. R. Vincent, D. D.*) *Conduct and doctrine :*—Let us look first at that member of the pair which is least popular—DOCTRINE. What does the word mean? It means simply "teaching," or "what is taught." St. Paul, writing to Timothy, who was by office a teacher, says "take heed unto the doctrine, to what you teach"; and of course writing to the people he would have said "take heed unto the doctrine, unto what you are taught." We are all being taught constantly; persons and things and events are constantly giving us lessons; the process of doctrine-making is for ever going on within us, and we cannot help it, as long as we are receptive and reasoning beings. And very often we hear some man give expression to a doctrine under the influence of a sudden event, which only puts in shape and brings to light what has been forming in his life for years. Since then the warning is about teaching, it must mean that we are to be careful of our subject and our teacher; for those are the important things in all teaching, and it is just those that give the characteristics to Christian doctrine. The subject is God and the teacher is Christ. It exalts God to His place as the very centre of all our life; it says that under Christ alone can we really learn about God worthily, although there will be many subordinate teachers, to whose word He will give the right place and due importance. This is the essence of Christian doctrine. Look at it thus as regulating, systematizing, correcting all the teaching that is for ever poured into our minds, and there is nothing so terrible in its aspect. It is not dry or unimportant; it is a matter of vital interest; it does not consist of things that cannot be understood, but has its beginnings in the simplest facts that all can comprehend. II. And so doctrine is put before us as a necessity of all life. And now we can turn to the other side which men appreciate so much more readily—to CONDUCT, which is contained in those words, "take heed to thyself." Care of our conduct, which we all willingly grant to be three-fourths of man's evident life, everybody feels the need of in this world. 1. In the first place we can see how conduct serves doctrine. This process of learning is not an easy one; the best side of a lesson is easily passed over, because some other side appeals to us more. We have been accustomed to think only of ourselves; sin has turned us away from God and He is a hard, dry subject to us; we are not what God made us to be, and so we are not able to appreciate what our God's word is to us. But diligent care of oneself tones up the mind. The man is used to being rigid with himself, to looking away from his own immediate comfort to higher and better. Doctrine is the learning in God's school: and just as it makes a great difference from what kind of a home a child goes to the school, as to how much he learns when he arrives there, so to learn in God's school we need to go there with lives that have appreciated the vileness of all sin and the value of all struggle against it. 2. This is the value of conduct, then, as a preparative for doctrine: look at it next as the interpreter of doctrine. God's teaching must be very great, and often beyond us; and we never shall know it, until we have tried it at point after point and found how powerful it is. Human conduct creates strange emergencies; and we, in our cowardice, are often afraid that we shall not be able to meet them, and so we are almost afraid to take heed unto ourselves. We think that we had better close our eyes to many things in our lives for fear that we shall not know how to deal with them. We do not know what we shall find in ourselves if we look too closely. But put conduct and the study of God's teaching together, and we find that all the emergencies of one answer to the possibilities of the other. The care of our conduct becomes like an experimental lecture on God's teaching; it supplies the illustrations for God's book of doctrine, which can help all poor ignorant scholars who say that they cannot understand God's teaching here. God's doctrine of mechanics is to be found in no text-book; it is written in the formation of our bodies, in the movements of the heavenly bodies, in the connection of all substances of this earth here. Men, like children, are led by these illustrations; they read page after page, they learn the doctrine, they go on and spread it in inventions of their own embodying those same principles, and so the world is furnished with what it needs. God's laws of morals and doctrine of salvation ask the same illustration; they are not all plain; they have obscure points as all God's thoughts must have to us. How shall the world get at them and use them? Only by their being embodied, so that men can study them in human lives and then use the principles in forming those new lives which the world so sadly wants. Take heed unto thyself and unto the doctrine. Find out your own wants and infirmities and go to the doctrine for their supply; take the doctrine and write it in your own life. And there is something more that conduct gives to doctrine besides illustration: it is life and warmth. No wonder that doctrine is often declared to be dry and hard. It is teaching about God coming to many men who know nothing about God Himself; He is a mere name to them; they do not appreciate His existence or His being at all. What shall give this same strange living power to doctrine? The man hears of God, but He is far away. But his own life he does appreciate; let him value that: it is a precious thing; it can live on nothing that the world furnishes; it calls out for the living God: take heed unto thyself, says the apostle. In thee is a voice which does tell of the nearness of another world, which demands the knowledge of a higher being. Living men make living doctrines. By those the world is saved. The doctrine received into men's lives is the power of God. And so when God would save the world He sent Christ to it. There was the complete union of doctrine and life. All the teaching of God was there; He was the Son of God direct from the Father. And in the last place, look how great the work is that such care of the doctrine and of conduct accomplishes. "Thou shalt both save thyself and those that hear thee." We do not save ourselves by our conduct and our neighbour by our doctrine. The two together save both of us. The two paths are one, the two goals are one. (*A. Brooks.*) *Man's highest work, and the way to achieve it:*—These words of Paul to Timothy should not be confined to ministers. They have an application to all men. I. MAN'S HIGHEST WORK. 1. The moral salvation of self. "Save thyself." What is salvation? Not mere deliverance from an outward hell, or introduction to an outward heaven, but it is restoration to the soul itself of what it has lost through depravity—the restoration of lost love, lost purity, lost harmony, lost usefulness. 2. The salvation of others. "And them that hear thee." All men, besides ministers, have hearers; and it is the duty of all men to preach, to speak that which will tend to the moral salvation of men, to raise them from ignorance to knowledge, from selfishness to benevolence, from materialism to spirituality, from Satan to God. II. MAN'S QUALIFICATIONS for the highest work. 1. Self-heedfulness. "Take heed unto thyself." See that self is all right, rectify thy own mistakes, train thy own faculties, purify thy own affections, discipline thy own character. This is the first step. You must be good, in order to do good. 2. Genuine teaching. "Unto the doctrine." The word doctrine here includes the whole matter of teaching. See that the teaching is true—true in its doctrine, in its spirit, in its aim. There is no teaching work where there is not a teaching life. He alone knows the Divine doctrine that does the Divine will. 3. Perseverance in goodness. "Continue in them." Continue in the work of self-culture and in genuine teaching. Do not let your efforts be capricious, but systematic; not occasional, but persistent. "Be instant, in season and out of season." (*D. Thomas, D.D.*) *Heed to life and doctrine:*—Two outstanding things are to be noted in the text; first of all, the connection between our doctrine and ourself: "Take heed unto thyself and unto thy doctrine"; and, secondly, the connection between two great results: "So shalt thou save thyself and them that hear thee." Take heed to save yourself. That is the best way to save them. "Take heed to thy doctrine." Yes, take heed to thyself, and thy doctrine will take heed of itself. Now, let me just run over that chain of thought. I am going to take the things the reverse way. "Take heed unto thy doctrine." There is a deal of talk about doctrine at the present day, with some wisdom in it and a great deal of folly. Downright good people are going about saying, "Doctrine does not matter; life is everything." Now, if that merely means that doctrines unpractised and which are hypocrisy are worthless, it does not say enough; they are accursed. But that is not just what is meant. I think that it is often taken to mean this—that it does not matter at all what a man believes; it does not matter at all what a man teaches about God, about the human soul, about salvation, about faith and duty, if only the man's heart be right, and if he means well. Now, to a certain extent, that is true. There are doctrines and there are doctrines; and I wish we had two very distinct names to indicate those utterly diverse classes of beliefs. If a man eats bread and meat every day, as much as he wants, it really matters very little if that man's doctrines about the chemistry of meat and bread are nonsense. He may be under utter delusions as to the way the meat and bread feed his body. If the man eats wholesome meat and wholesome bread, that is everything. If another man holds the most orthodox theories of chemistry and of physiology and of nutrition, and is not eating the actual meat and bread, then he dies. The other man lives in spite of his false doctrine. Now, that is true to a certain extent of theological beliefs. There are elaborate and subtle and noble theories about the inner, mysterious nature of God, the construction of Christ's person, the ultimate decrees of God, the precise explanation of how the dying love and obedience of Jesus Christ cleanses us actually from sin—theories and explanations of how these things are and are done; and I am bound to own frankly that it does not matter very much what a man thinks about this. If that man with his whole full heart lives on the Lord Jesus Christ, and takes Him to be his real Saviour from real sin, and has His Holy Spirit dwelling in him—ah, he is feeding on the bread of life; and even if his theories of how that bread of life is life to us are not quite correct it is a small matter; at least, it is a small matter by comparison with a man who is for ever teaching and working and battling about the theories and the explanations, while his heart is a desolate howling wilderness, with no love of God, no love of man, in it. But now let me say this. It is a pity that such questions should be raised. You cannot answer them quite rightly. You must give replies that may be misused and misinterpreted. There ought to be no such antagonism. Still, if the question comes up let us speak the truth. But now there is another class of doctrines—beliefs which are things not of the mere intellect, not of speculation, but which are convictions of the heart, which throw a man into a certain attitude towards God, and towards duty, and towards sin, and towards holiness. And it matters a great deal to a man what he believes about these. It counts for everything. But mark you, now, I mean what he believes not with his head, but with his heart, with his very being; and the only faith that the Bible deals with and speaks of as saving faith, is not the faith of the correctest theological intellect, but it is a faith which is the outgoing of a man's soul, of his whole being. The poor dying thief on the cross believes with the despairing outgoing of his heart to Christ to make him a good man. Yes, and it saves him. If a man believes that fire will not burn him, he will pay for that heresy. If a man has a mistaken notion how it is that fire has got heat in it, and how it warms and serves man, that does not so much matter, so long as he makes a rightful use of the fire; but if he has delusions about the relations of fire to himself, he pays for it. Now, I want to say something about doctrines. I want to say it with a little personal feeling, because if doctrines are so trivial (doctrines meaning teaching), then preaching is hardly worth doing. But I believe in preaching, not as we ignorant, half-hearted men do it, but as the great saints and heroes of Christendom have done it. It will be done by teaching—the teaching that comes with the very power of God in it. Doctrines? Why, the greatest thing within these last centuries this world has seen—the reformation in Europe—all grew out of one new thought about God, or, rather, the recovering of a lost thought about God—a new grand conviction that God is the living, loving, warm-hearted God, a Spirit whom men worship in spirit and in truth; not the horrible, mechanical, materialized God of priestcraft and superstition. And it all grew out of a doctrine; but, mark you, not a theory of the intellect spun out of things we knew nothing about and should not try to understand, but a great heart-belief about the living God. Therefore, " Take heed unto thy doctrine," surely is addressed to men that are not orthodox? No, Paul addressed it to the orthodox Timothy, " Take heed to thy teaching." But if a man has once learnt a form of sound words, surely he does not need to be guarding, and watching, and studying, and examining his preaching and his teaching? Does he not? Do you think that, having once seen the truth, having once learnt it, will guard a man from perverting it? No, try that with any secular accomplishment. Learn a language, and then give over practising it. Give over pains to keep up your accuracy and your fluency; and how long will you retain it? How soon will errors creep in? Ah! I tell you that a great many men think that they are preaching the orthodox doctrines which they were taught, and through indulgence or slothfulness, or through the unconscious pressure of one-sidedness and error, which the mis-shapen make of every common, frail, erring man's soul and intellect imposes upon his thinking and teaching, they have gone far astray. I do not mean, perchance, that the man actually says things that are false; but, mark you, you may make utter distortion of God's portrait if you are always working at the bits you like best, dwelling on a one-sided conception of Him. Now I must go on to the rest of my text very rapidly, but I can do it much more briefly. What I have to try to show you is that, while our doctrine is that by which we influence others, the best way to keep our doctrine true and right is to look after our heart. Ah, doctrines are one thing when they come from a man, simply repeated by hearsay at second hand, and preached just as things of the intellect, but they are another thing when they come out of a man's heart. Oh! I think it almost has an unhallowed effect to hear the story of the atonement argued out in a controversial fashion. (*Professor Elmslie.*)

**Both save thyself and them that hear thee.**—*By what means may ministers best win souls?*—I. MINISTERS' DUTY IS IN THREE THINGS HERE—1. Take heed unto thyself.

Thou art set in a high office, in a dangerous place; take good and narrow heed, look well to thyself, thy heart and way. 2. Take heed unto thy doctrine. Though thou be never so well-gifted and approved both of God and men; though thou be an extraordinary officer, as Timothy was; yet "take heed unto thy doctrine." 3. Continue in them. This hath relation, it appears, unto verses 12 and 15, as well as unto the preceding part of this verse. (1) Continue in thy work. Thou who art a minister, it is a work for thy life-time, and not to be taken up and laid down again, according as it may best suit a man's carnal inclinations and outward conveniences. (2) Continue in endeavours after greater fitness for thy work. No attainments in fitness and qualifications for this work can free a man of the obligation that lies on him to increase and grow therein more and more. (3) Continue in thy vigour and painfulness and diligence. II. THE DOUBLE ADVANTAGE PROPOSED TO ENCOURAGE MINISTERS TO THIS HARD DUTY. 1. Thou shalt save thyself. Thy own salvation shall be promoted and secured thereby. But how doth faithfulness in the ministry of the gospel further the minister's salvation? (1) Faithfulness in man's generation-work is of great use and advantage to salvation. "Well done, good and faithful servant." (2) Thou shalt save thyself from the guilt of other men's sins and ruin, if thou be faithful in the ministry. "Thou hast delivered," or "saved," "thy soul," (Ezek. xxxiii. 9). (3) Faithfulness and painfulness in the ministry of the gospel promote a man's own salvation, in so far as the work of Christianity is woven in with the right discharge of the office of the ministry. Many ministers can say, that if they had not been ministers, they had in all appearance lost their souls. 2. Thou shalt save them that hear thee. There is little hope of that man's being useful to save others, that minds not his own salvation: and therefore the apostle puts them in this order, "thyself," and then, "them that hear thee." Thou shalt save them. The great end of both preaching and hearing is salvation; and if salvation were more designed by preachers and hearers, it would be more frequently the effect of the action. Thou shalt save them. Not that ministers are of themselves able by all their endeavours to carry on this great end; they are only God's tools and instruments (1 Cor. iii. 6, 7). Concerning this—(1) We find that the Lord hath appointed this great ordinance of the gospel-ministry for this end—the saving of men (Eph. iv. 11-13). (2) He hath also given many promises of His presence, blessing, and success, to follow and attend them whom He sends on this great errand. (3) He hath also revealed much of His mind about ministers' duty in order to this end of saving men. This also makes the end more hopeful. (4) We find that the Lord doth qualify and fit them whom He makes successful. He makes men "able ministers of the New Testament," the word of life (2 Cor. iii. 5, 6). Now we return to the question to be resolved, by what means may ministers best win souls? I. What this text speaks about this matter. It looks two ways upon this question. 1. Take heed unto thyself. (1) Take heed that thou be a sound and sincere believer. (2) Take heed to thyself, that thou be a called and sent minister. This is of great importance as to success. He that can say, "Lord, Thou hast sent me," may boldly add, "Lord, go with me, and bless me." (3) Take heed unto thyself, that thou be a lively, thriving Christian. See that all thy religion run not in the channel of thy employment. It is found by experience, that as it fares with a minister in the frame of his heart and thriving of the work of God in his soul, so doth it fare with his ministry both in its vigour and effects. A carnal frame, a dead heart, and a loose walk, make cold and unprofitable preaching. (4) Take heed unto thyself in reference to all the trials and temptations [which] thou mayest meet with. Be on your guard; "watch in all things" (2 Tim. iv. 5). No men are shot at more by Satan than ministers; and he triumphs not more over the foils of any than theirs: and Christ is liberal in His warnings of dangers, and in His promises of help in them. 2. Take heed unto thy doctrine. Art thou a minister? thou must be a preacher; an unpreaching minister is a sort of contradiction. (1) Take heed unto thy doctrine, that it be a Divine truth. "Let a man speak as the oracles of God" (1 Peter iv. 11). And therefore it is needful that ministers be well acquainted with the Holy Scriptures. [It is] a bad token of the temper of that man that relishes any book more than the Word of God. (2) Take heed unto thy doctrine, that it be plain, and suited to the capacity of the hearers. "Learned preaching," as it is called, is a vanity, pleasing principally to such as neither design nor desire edification. Two things would help to plain preaching—(a) Clearness of knowledge. The alleged depth of our doctrine often proceeds from our own darkness. (b) Humility and self-denial. (3) Take heed unto thy doctrine, that it be grave and solid and weighty. "Sound speech, that cannot be condemned" (Titus ii. 8). II. But now we come to the second thing proposed,—to give some answer to this question from other things in the Word. And I shall—(I) Show some things that must be laid to heart about the end,—the saving of souls. (II) And then shall give some advice about the means. (I) About the end—the winning of souls. This is, to bring them to God. It is not, to win them to us, or to engage them into a party or to the espousal of some opinions and practices, supposing them to be never so right and consonant to the Word of God; but the winning of them is, to bring them out of nature into a state of grace, that they may be fitted for, and in due time admitted into, everlasting glory. Concerning which great end, these few things should be laid deeply to heart by all that would serve the Lord in being instrumental in reaching it—1. The exceeding height and excellency of this end is to be laid to heart. It is a wonder of condescendence, that the Lord will make use of men in promoting it: to be workers together with God in so great a business is no small honour. 2. The great difficulty of saving souls must be laid to heart. The difficulty is undoubted: to attempt it is to offer violence to men's corrupt natures, and a storming of hell itself, whose captives all sinners are. Unless this difficulty be laid to heart, ministers will be confident of their own strength, and so miscarry and be unfruitful. 3. The duty of winning souls must be laid to heart by ministers. That it is their principal work, and they are under many commands to endeavour it. 4. The great advantage there is to the labourer by his success is to be pondered. Great is the gain by one soul: "He that winneth souls is" happy as well as "wise" (Prov. xi. 30; Dan. xii. 3). Won souls are a minister's "crown and glory and joy" (Phil. iv. 1; 1 Thess. ii. 20). (II) For advice about the means, I shall add these few, besides what hath been said—1. Let ministers, if they would win souls, procure and retain amongst the people a persuasion of their being sent of God. That they are "Christ's ministers" (1 Cor. iv. 1). 2. Let ministers, if they would win souls, purchase and maintain the people's love to their persons. 3. It would further the winning of souls, to deal particularly and personally with them. Not always nor altogether in public (Col. i. 28; Acts xx. 20, 21). 4. Ministers must pray much, if they would be successful. The apostles spent their time this way (Acts vi. 4). Many good sermons are lost for lack of much prayer in study. But because the ministry of the Word is the main instrument for winning souls, I shall therefore add somewhat more particularly concerning this; and that both as to the matter and manner of preaching. (1) For the subject-matter of gospel-preaching, it is determined by the apostle expressly to be "Christ crucified" (1 Cor. ii. 2). (2) As for the manner of successful preaching, I shall give it in a negative and positive from these two places—1 Cor. i. 17; and ii. 1–4. I shall only instance in things that this Scriptural negative doth check and reprove in the way of preaching. (a) The establishing and advancing of Divine truth upon the foundation of human reason. (b) It is to preach "with excellency of speech" and "words of man's wisdom," when men think to reach the gospel-end on sinners by force of even spiritual reason and persuasion. (c) This also is checked in the apostle's words—the setting forth the beauty of the gospel by human art. The truth of the gospel shines best in its bare proposal, and its beauty in its simple and naked discovery. (3) The positive is—"In demonstration of the Spirit and of power" (1 Cor. ii. 4). (a) Paul preached so, as gave a demonstration that the Holy Ghost was in him, sanctifying him. (b) Paul preached so, as gave a demonstration that the Spirit of God was with him, assisting and helping him in his work. (c) Paul preached so, as [that] a demonstration of the power of the Holy Ghost was given to the hearts of the hearers. III. To conclude: you that are ministers, suffer a word of exhortation. Men, brethren, and fathers, you are called to a high and holy calling: your work is full of danger, full of duty, and full of mercy. And, lastly, for people. It is not unfit that you should hear of ministers' work and duty and difficulties: you see that all is of your concernment; "all things are" for your sakes, as the apostle in another case. Then only I entreat you—1. Pity us. We are not angels, but men of like passions with yourselves. 2. Help us in our work. If you can do anything, help us in the work of winning souls. 3. Pray for us. How often and how earnestly doth Paul beg the prayers of the churches! (*R. Trail, M.A.*) *Soul saving to be aimed at:*—I do not believe that a devout minister ever yet went to his pulpit with a single-eyed desire to do good and to glorify his Saviour, without some measure of Divine blessing upon his efforts. The most valuable hint I ever received came to me from a baker in Saratoga. I had been preaching there during my ministerial boyhood. The baker met me the next day, at the railway station, and said: "I believe you are the young man who spoke in our meeting-house yesterday." "Yes ; I am." "Well," said he, "I felt sorry for you ; because I thought you did not know what cultivated and critical people there are here in summer. But I have noticed that if a minister can convince the people in the first five minutes that he only aims to save their souls, he will kill all the critics in the house." That was one of the wisest things ever uttered. It ought to be written on the walls of every theological seminary and every pastor's study. (*T. Cuyler.*)

---

## CHAPTER V.

VERS. 1, 2. **Rebuke not an elder.**—*Christian reproofs :*—I. THE NECESSITY AND THE NATURE OF CHRISTIAN REPROOF are both suggested. Though age was always to be reverenced, even those in advanced life were to be rebuked when their conduct was inconsistent with their Christian profession. This requires not only a sincere regard for our brother's welfare, but also at times considerable moral courage. Some find it by no means easy to point out faults even to their own children ; but they fairly tremble at the idea of being faithful to those who are in a better social position than themselves, or to those whose age, experience, or learning give them in other departments of life influence and authority. All who have sought to do this are conscious of its difficulty. Speak as you may, you will not improbably offend ; for your brother needs as much grace to listen as you need to speak. II. THE MODE AND SPIRIT IN WHICH CHRISTIAN REPROOF SHOULD BE GIVEN in specified cases is suggested by the apostle here: "Rebuke not an elder, but entreat him as a father; and the younger men as brethren ; the elder women as mothers ; the younger as sisters ; with all purity." The word translated "rebuke" means to reprimand sharply, to chide in a rough or arrogant manner, or in a domineering temper; and this is condemned by all the teaching of our Lord about humility and charity. In pointing out faults, we are to be reverent and cautious, as well as earnest and manly ; and in discharging this duty of the Christian life we are called upon in the first place to be—1. Reverent towards age. "Rebuke not an elder" should be, "Rebuke not an elderly person." The apostle makes no reference here to official standing, but to age. This is obvious from the fact that he speaks first of older and younger men, and then of older and younger women. Ours should be the spirit of Samuel, who, even when he had to convey a message from God, modestly hesitated, waiting for a good opportunity to deliver it, and then spoke with the reverence due to Eli's age. 2. Love towards the brethren should be conspicuous in every word of reproof. Not anger, nor hatred, nor suspicion, but love—for they are our brothers in Christ. 3. Purity towards women, in thought, as well as in word and act. Nowhere was the exhortation more necessary than in Ephesus, and no one needed it more than Timothy, whose interviews with them were of necessity frequent. (*A. Rowland, LL.B.*) *Brotherly rebuke :*—Mr. Rothwell, surnamed by the godly of his day the Rough Hewer, from the solemn and powerful manner in which he opened up the corruptions of the human heart, and delivered the judgments of God against all iniquity, was, in his early days, a clergyman without any true sense of religion : he was brought to know the power of Divine things through an admonition given to him by a godly Puritan. Clarke, in his "Lives," says, "He was playing at bowls among some Papists and vain gentlemen, upon a Saturday, somewhere about Rochdale, in Lancashire. There came into the green to him one Mr. Midgley, a grave and godly minister of Rochdale, whose praise is great in the gospel, though far inferior to Rothwell in points and learning, He took him aside, and fell into a large commendation of him ; at length told him what a pity it was that such a man as he should be companion to Papists, and that upon a Saturday, when he should be preparing for the Sabbath. Mr. Rothwell slighted his words, and checked him for his meddling. The good old man left him, went home, and prayed privately for him. Mr. Rothwell, when he was retired from that company, could not rest, Mr. Midgley's words stuck so deep in his thoughts. The next day he went to Rochdale Church to hear Mr. Midgley, where it pleased God so to bless the Word that he was, by that sermon, brought home to Christ." The earnest man who was sent by his Master upon this errand of rebuke, must have felt that he was well rewarded for his holy courage in the after usefulness of Mr. Rothwell; but even had the message failed to bless the person to whom it was delivered, it would not have lacked a recompense from the Great Taskmaster. (*C. H. Spurgeon.*)

Vers. 4, 8, 16. **But if any widow have children or nephews.**—*Home responsibilities :*—We are reminded here—I. THAT HOME RESPONSIBILITIES ARE TO BE ACCEPTED AS THE APPOINTMENT OF GOD. The sacredness of family relationship is constantly insisted upon both in the Old Testament and the New. All transgressions against it were severely punished under the Mosaic economy, and were condemned still more solemnly by our Lord. A word of exposition on the first clause in the fourth verse is desirable, "If any widows have children or nephews, let them (*i.e.*, not the widows, but the children or nephews) learn first to show piety (filial love) at home." The word "nephews" is used by our translators in its old English sense, and is rendered in the Revised Version by its nearest modern equivalent, "grand-children," for in the writings of Chaucer, Sir Thomas More, and John Locke, "nephews" is used to denote grandchildren. And similarly, when it is said they are to requite their "parents," more is included than fathers or mothers, for the apostle's word is equivalent to the Scotch "forbears," for which the English language has no exact synonym. The idea is that we owe a debt of gratitude to those from whom we have derived existence, and to whom we owe the support, care, and education we have received. We are bound to see that to the utmost of our ability their wants in old age are met. II. THAT AMONG OUR GOD-GIVEN RESPONSI-BILITIES IS THE DUTY OF LABOURING FOR THE SUPPORT OF THE WEAK. Among the blessings of our human relationships is this : that honest work is necessitated. We have seen instances in which a young fellow who has spent all his salary on cigars, dress, and amusements, has after his marriage buckled to work, and dis-played an energy and ability for which none had given him credit before. Many a brave young wife and self-sacrificing mother has been ennobled through her home duties, having completely abandoned the foolish and trivial pursuits to which she was once addicted. And what numberless instances there are of men, whose dili-gence and self-abnegation are beyond praise, who have become what they are by first feeling the responsibility of caring and working for a widowed mother! III. Paul emphatically declares that THOSE WHO FAIL IN THESE RESPONSIBILITIES HAVE DENIED THE FAITH AND ARE WORSE THAN INFIDELS. Stern as the words are, they are true! Even the heathen, certainly the better class of them, were wont to acknowledge filial duties, and would have condemned cynical disregard of parents and refusal to fulfil natural duties towards them. This is an offence against humanity, and therefore, in the deepest sense, an offence against Christ. But a Christian professes to have higher motives in duty than others. Let us never for-get that the test of character is to be found in family relationships rather than in those which are ecclesiastical ; and that it is in the home first and chiefest of all that Christ's disciples are to adorn the doctrine of God their Saviour. (*A. Row-land, LL.B.*) **Piety at home.**—*Life at home :*—A church within a church, a republic within a republic, a world within a world, is spelled by four letters —Home! If things go right there, they go right everywhere ; if things go wrong there, they go wrong everywhere. The door-sill of the dwelling-house is the foundation of Church and State. A man never gets higher than his own garret or lower than his own cellar. In other words, domestic life over-arches and underguides all other life. George Washington commanded the forces of the United States, but Mary Washington commanded George. Chry-sostom's mother made his pen for him. As individuals, we are fragments. God makes the races in parts, and then He gradually puts us together. What I lack, you make up ; what you lack, I make up ; our deficits and surpluses of character being the wheels in the great social mechanism. One person has the patience, another has the courage, another has the placidity, another has the enthusiasm ; that which is lacking in one is made up by another, or made up by all. Buffaloes in herds; grouse in broods; quails in flocks; the human race in circles. Our usefulness, and the welfare of society, depend upon our staying in just the place that God has put us, or intended we should occupy. For more compactness, and that we may be more useful, we are gathered in still smaller circles in the home group. And there you have the same varieties again ; brothers, sisters, husband, and wife ; all different in temperaments and tastes. It is fortunate that it should be so. If the husband be all impulse, the wife must be all prudence.

If one sister be sanguine in her temperament, the other must be lymphatic. Mary and Martha are necessities. Then there are those who will, after awhile, set up for themselves a home, and it is right that I should speak out upon these themes. 1. My first counsel to you is, have Jesus in your new home, if it is a new home; and let Him who was a guest at Bethany be in your new household; let the Divine blessing drop upon your every hope, and plan, and expectation. Those young people who begin with God end with heaven. 2. My second advice to you in your home is, to exercise to the very last possibility of your nature the law of for-bearance. Prayers in the household will not make up for everything. Some of the best people in the world are the hardest to get along with. Sometimes it will be the duty of the husband and sometimes of the wife to yield; but both stand punc-tiliously on your rights, and you will have a Waterloo with no Blucher coming up at nightfall to decide the conflict. The best thing I ever heard of my grandfather, whom I never saw, was this: that once, having unrighteously rebuked one of his children, he himself—having lost his patience, and, perhaps, having been misin-formed of the child's doings—found out his mistake, and in the evening of the same day gathered all his family together, and said: " Now, I have one explanation to make, and one thing to say. Thomas, this morning I rebuked you very unfairly. I am very sorry for it. I rebuked you in the presence of the whole family, and now I ask your forgiveness in their presence." It must have taken some courage to do that. 3. I advise, also, that you make your chief pleasure circle around about that home. It is unfortunate when it is otherwise. If the husband spend the most of his nights away from home, of choice and not of necessity, he is not the head of the household; he is only the cashier. If the wife throw the cares of the household into the servant's lap, and then spend five nights of the week at the opera or theatre, she may clothe her children with satins, and laces, and ribbons that would confound a French milliner, but they are orphans. 4. I advise you also to cultivate sympathy of occupation. Sir James McIntosh, one of the most eminent and elegant men that ever lived, while standing at the very height of his eminence, said to a great company of scholars: " My wife made me." The wife ought to be the advising partner in every firm. She ought to be interested in all the losses and gains of shop and store. She ought to have a right—she has a right—to know everything. Your gains are one, your interests are one, your losses are one; lay hold of the work of life with both hands. Four hands to fight the battles. Four eyes to watch for the danger. Four shoulders on which to carry the trials. It is a very sad thing when the painter has a wife who does not like pictures. It is a very sad thing for a pianist when she has a husband who does not like music. 5. I have one more word of advice to give to those who would have a happy home, and that is: let love preside in it. (*T. De Witt Talmage.*)      *Home, sweet home :*—How many are longing for grand spheres in which to serve God. They admire Luther at the Diet of Worms, and wish they had some such daring opportunity in which to exhibit Christian character. Now, the apostle comes to such persons, in my text, and says: " I will show you a place where you can exhibit all that is grand, and beautiful, and glorious in the Christian character, and that place is the domestic circle." " Let them learn first to show piety at home." Indeed, if a man does not serve God on a small scale, he never will serve Him on a large scale. I propose to speak to you of home as a test, of home as a refuge, of home as a political safeguard, of home as a school, of home as a type of heaven. I. The home, in the first place, is the most POWERFUL TEST OF ONE'S CHARACTER. A man's disposition in public may be in gay costume, while in private it is in *déshabille.* The play actor does differently on the platform from the way he does behind the scenes; and public life is often a very different thing from private life. A man will receive you in his parlour with so much gracefulness that he seems to be the distillation of smiles, while in his heart there is a swamp of nettles. Private life is often public life turned wrong side out. The lips that drop with myrrh and cassia—the disposition that seems to be warm and bright as a sheaf of sunbeams, may only be a magnificent show-window to a wretched stock of goods. The harp that all day sang like an angel, may at night grate like a saw. There are those who are philanthropists in public life, who in home life are the Nero with respect to their slippers and their gown. The great Newton, after he had spent half of his life on one manuscript, came into his study one day and found that his dog had torn the manuscript to pieces. All he said was: " Little Diamond, you know not how much trouble you have given your master." Audubon, the great ornithologist, with gun and pencil, went all through the forests of this country for the purpose of bringing down and sketching the birds of the land; then went home, put the valuable documents in a trunk, and, after an absence, found that the rats had completely devoured the manuscripts, so that again he took gun and pencil, and again went through the forests of the land, reproducing that which was destroyed; while there are many in private life who, at the loss of a pencil or an article of clothing, will act as though they had met with a severe and irreparable loss, and will blow sharp, and loud, and long as a north-east storm. Let us learn to show piety at home. II. Again: I remark that HOME IS A REFUGE. The home is the tent we pitch to rest in, our bayonets stacked, our war caps hung up, our heads resting on the knapsack until the morning bugle sounds, warning us to strike tent and prepare for marching and action. Oh, what a pleasant place it is to talk over the day's victories, and surprises, and attacks, seated by the still camp-fires of the domestic circle. Life is a stormy sea. With shivered mast, and torn sail, and hulk aleak, we put into the harbour of home. Into this dry-dock we come for repair. Blessed harbour! The candle in the window is to the labouring man the lighthouse guiding him into port. May God pity the poor miserable wretch who has not any home. III. Again: I remark that the home is a POLITICAL SAFEGUARD. The safety of the State depends upon the character of the home. The Christian hearthstone is the only foundation for a Republic. In the family virtues are cultured which are a necessity for the State; and if there be not enough moral principle to make the family adhere, there cannot be enough political principle to make the State adhere. No home, no free institution. No home makes a nation of Goths and Vandals; makes the Nomads of Central Asia; makes the Numidians of Africa, changing from month to month, and from place to place, as the pasture happens to change. IV. I go further, and speak of HOME AS A SCHOOL. Old ground must be upturned by a subsoil plough, and harrowed and re-harrowed, and then it will not yield as good a crop as new ground with less culture. Now, infancy and childhood are new ground, and all that is scattered over that ground will yield luxuriantly. Make your home the brightest place on earth if you would charm your children into the high path of rectitude and religion. Do not always have the blinds turned the wrong way. Let God's light, that puts gold on the gentian and spots the pansy, stream into your windows. Do not expect your children to keep step to a dead march. A dark home makes bad boys and bad girls to be bad men and bad women. Above all, take into your homes thorough Christian principle. (*Ibid.*) *Home piety* :—I. OUR FIRST ENDEAVOUR WILL BE TO SHOW WHAT PIETY IS. This is all the more needful, as mistakes, numerous and fatal, exist on this vital subject, not only in the world, but also in the Church. It is "the mind that was in Christ, leading us to walk as He also walked." 1. Piety has its principles. It is not like a tree without a root; or a stream without a spring. It is originated, sustained, and cherished by an experimental acquaintance with God in Christ; for "this is life eternal, to know Thee, the true God, and Jesus Christ whom Thou has sent." Here, then, we have the principles of piety—knowledge, faith, love, submission, and holy fear. A cluster of good things; the soul and spirit of true religion; the gift of the Divine hand; the fruit of the Spirit; the purchase of Messiah's blood; and the earnest of everlasting life. 2. Piety has its enjoyments. "Her ways are ways of pleasantness, and all her paths are peace. She is a tree of life to them that lay hold upon her." The forgiveness of sins, access to God as a Father, the communion of Saints, the hope of everlasting life, the possession of a new nature, constitute a well-spring of blessedness to the humble, believing, obedient soul. 3. Piety has its duties. "If ye love Me, said the Saviour, keep My commandments; not every one that saith unto Me, Lord, Lord, shall enter into the kingdom of heaven, but he that doeth the will of My Father which is in heaven." With what frequency and earnestness has practical piety been enforced in the law and the prophets, as also by our Lord and His apostles! II. WE PROCEED TO SHOW WHERE PIETY IS TO BE MADE MANIFEST. If the principles and rootlets of piety be out of sight, their existence and power may easily be made apparent. Vegetable life in this sweet jessamine, or in yonder blushing rose, is far beyond our ken; but the effects of life are plain enough to be seen—the rind, the bud, the leaf, the flower, tell us that life is there. As to animal life—the sparkling eye, the ruddy countenance, the cheerful voice, the active limb, show us that life is there; but it is as much a mystery as ever; as far out of sight as ever. Steam, as it lies in the bosom of the boiler, is invisible; but the stroke of the piston, the sweep of the wheel, and the speed of the train, as well as the condensing power of the atmosphere, tell us that it is there. So of piety: much of it is hidden from the public gaze—its depths are not seen.

Christian life is hid with Christ in God. Yet if spiritual life exists, it will give proof of its existence and power. Hence at Antioch, when Barnabas "had seen the grace of God, he was glad." And exhorted them all that with purpose of heart they would cleave unto the Lord. Fire must burn, a fountain must flow, a good tree cannot bring forth bad fruit—Therefore show piety. 1. In general, wherever the providence of God may place you. The shop, the ship, the market, the farm, the factory, the counting-house, will afford you opportunities for confessing your Lord. 2. In particular, let your piety appear at home. Show to those around you, that the fear and love of God control your desires, purposes, words, and deeds; whatever your relation to the family circle—in whatever department your duty lies, act your part with cheerfulness, fidelity, and to the extent of your ability. See, that your piety is such as never can be reasonably questioned. (1) Shows its reality; let "the root of the matter" spring up and bring forth good fruit. (2) Maintain its spirit, humble, gentle, kind, forgiving: "Let this mind be in you, which was also in Christ Jesus." (3) Manifest its power, to restrain you from evil, to sustain and comfort and bless you, amid the ills of life; and to enable you by a patient continuance in well-doing, to seek for glory, honour, immortality, and eternal life. Mind that your piety be uniform; let no child be forgotten, no aged parent neglected, no poor widowed relative forsaken, no duty omitted. One word more: let your home religion be steady and growing; and as a general rule, rather seen, and felt, than heard. 3. The considerations by which this important duty may be enforced are numerous and weighty. Would to God we could rightly see and feel them. God, our Saviour, has made Christian believers "a chosen generation, a royal priesthood, a holy nation, a peculiar people, to show forth the praises of Him who has called them out of darkness into His marvellous light." And shall they not do His pleasure? Shall not Christian people acknowledge their Owner—and the claims of Him who hath made, redeemed, and saved them—by giving up themselves to His service, by glorifying Him, both at home and abroad, in their body and spirit, which are His? Besides, as members of the family circle, are we not bound to promote its comfort, safety, and welfare to the extent of our ability? If you feel any interest in the prosperity of the Church, the conversion of poor sinners, the general good of society, show piety at home. Be followers of them who through faith and patience inherit the promises. Tread in the steps of faithful Abraham, the pattern of believers, and the friend of God, who commanded his children and household after him to keep the way of the Lord. Drink into the spirit of Joshua, who served the Lord himself, and put forth all his strength to lead his family to do likewise. (*J. J. Topham.*) *The Christian at home :*—Some characteristics of home piety. 1. A careful respect for the rights of each member of the family. It is our first duty to be just towards each other, and a duty which is obligatory all round, as between husband and wife, parents and children, brothers and sisters, families and their relatives, employers and servants. It is not always easy to be just. It requires thoughtful consideration and some power of imaginative sympathy even on the part of those who desire to do as they would be done by. A great deal of the wrong that is suffered in the world arises out of unwitting injustice. Some persons are grossly and habitually unjust to those about them, misrepresenting their opinions, and imposing upon them sacrifices of feeling and trouble, while in other respects they are singularly generous. Another frequent cause of unhappiness in families is the partiality shown to a favourite child. This also justice forbids. 2. Next to careful respect for the rights of others I may mention great forbearance in asserting our own. A small thing in family life, but most significant as an index to character, is the self-pleasing with which some persons secure their own preferences at table. Even if they make a show of giving up what others like, they do it so ostentatiously that their generosity is generally declined. But real self-denial, that can find pleasure in the gratification of others, will conceal its preferences so that they may enjoy what they like without knowing that it is at the expense of any one else. 3. A third characteristic of home piety is the endeavour to please those about us for their good. A cheerful manner, a flow of wise and genial conversation, sparkling here and there with some bright corruscation of wit, flavoured always with the salt of cultured taste, and sometimes suggestive of serious thoughts, is a fine means of pleasing and benefiting others. Show piety at home by learning to talk well and wisely. 4. Lastly, piety should be shown at home in a devout regard for the honour of God. At the principal meals of the day, and morning or evening, if not both morning and evening, reverence should find suitable expression in acts of worship. You must be guided by your own sense of fitness as to what arrangements you shall make for this purpose. Let us systematically choose the good part, seek first the kingdom of God and His righteousness, endeavour to catch the spirit of our Master, and let its influence be diffused throughout our whole life. (*E. W. Shalders, B.A.*) *Piety at home:*—The radiance of a Christian character is to shine around the family hearth. In most minds the word home awakens emotions both sweet and solemn. Our tenderest relations, our strongest affections, our highest joys, our deepest sorrows, all are touched by the thought of home. The great duty which our text enjoins is the cultivation of piety at home. I. HOME IS THE PLACE WHERE CHARACTER IS MOST TESTED; AND IF PIETY BE NOT SHOWN THERE, IT CANNOT BE SHOWN ANYWHERE. Our real character is not so much shown in what we do intentionally and with a purpose, as in what we do impulsively and without reflection. Abroad in the world men may wear a cloak—they may deceive others, they may deceive themselves as to their true character; but at home the cloak generally slips aside, the true character comes out, and those who see them in their unguarded hours know them as they really are. Often a word, a look, or even a gesture in the family will give more insight into a man's heart than years of observation of his public life. The close intercourse of home life tries as well as reveals the real character. That which tries character also helps to form it. Home not only shows what we are, it helps to make us what we shall be for ever. The education which is deepest and most enduring is that of the home school. II. HOME IS SOMETIMES THE SCENE OF OUR DEEPEST SORROWS: AND PIETY IS THE BEST HELP TO ENABLE US TO BEAR THESE. The causes which disturb the happiness of home are manifold. Unwise marriage unions are the cause of much family misery. Bad habits are a frequent occasion of home sorrow. Evil tempers sometimes ruin the happiness of home. A practical carrying out of our text would speedily correct the evils to which we have referred, and change the character of the home-life where they have been endured. Were all the members of a family to "learn to show piety at home," what a scene of blessedness that would be! But there are other trials which sometimes convert the home into a "house of mourning," and which piety alone can enable us to meet. There are homes in which the pinching of poverty has to be endured. There are homes where disease presses with his heavy hand; and homes over which death spreads his black and chilly wing. But if there be only one pious member of the family, how the others will look to him and lean upon him in their hour of bereavement and sorrow! The influence acquired by consistency of character now operates for the good of his afflicted friends. III. HOME OUGHT TO BE THE SCENE OF OUR HIGHEST JOY; AND PIETY IS THE ONLY MEANS TO MAKE IT SO. The mutual love and confidence so essential to family happiness, can be produced and secured by nothing so certainly as by a common affection for the Saviour. How blessed are the ties of nature when they are sanctified and strengthened by grace! (*G. D. Macgregor.*) *Selfish children:*—An old Virginia minister said lately, "Men of my profession see much of the tragic side of life. I have seen men die in battle, have seen children die, but no death ever seemed so pathetic to me as the death of an aged mother in my church. I knew her first as a young girl, beautiful, gay, full of joy and hope. She married and had four children. Her husband died and left her penniless. She sewed, she made drawings, she taught, she gave herself scarcely time to eat or sleep. Every thought was for her children, to educate them, to give them the advantages their father would have given them had he lived. She succeeded. She sent her boys to college and her girls to school. When all came home they gave themselves up to their own selfish pursuits. She lingered among them some three years, and then was stricken with mortal illness brought on by overwork. The children gathered around her bedside. The oldest son took her in his arms. He said, 'You have been a good mother to us.' That was not much to say, was it? It was much to her, who had never heard anything like it. A flush came over her pallid face, and with faint voice she whispered, 'My son, you never said so before!'" (*Dr. Hoge.*) *John Gough and his mother:*—I remember, when my father was away in the Peninsular war, my mother, who used to work lace very nicely (and she grew very nearly blind by it), went one day from Sandgate to Dover, eight and a half miles, to sell it. I went out to play, having the whole day to myself till she came back. I was a famous reader when I was a little bit of a thing, and I never remember the time when I learned to read, and I can't remember when I could not read with the book the wrong side up. As I was playing, a boy came up to me and said, "Johnny Gough, Mr. Purday wants you in the library." Well, I ran into the library, and I remember being taken into a little room, and a girl dipped her hands in water and rubbed my face, and brushed my hair back, to make me look decent, and then took me into the reading-room, where there was a venerable looking gentleman, whom I distinctly remember they called "my lord." Mr. Purday said, "This is the boy I was speaking of"; and he then put a newspaper into my hands, and asked me to read a certain column to him, which I did. He gave me a five-shilling piece; another gentleman gave me sixpence; and the proprietor of the library gave me two pennies. Oh! how rich I was! I went out to play with the boys; I put my hands in my pockets now and then, and jingled my money, and then went on playing again. After a while a boy came to me and said, "Johnny, your mother has got home." I ran into the house, and there sat my poor mother upon a stool, faint and weary, with her basket of lace at her side. Her face was buried in her hands; I heard her sob, and I never could bear to hear my mother cry. "Mother, mother," said I, "what is the matter?" "My poor child," she said, "I have not sold a farthings-worth to-day, and what we shall do God only knows!" Said I, "Mother, just look at this!" and she did look at it; and she said, "Why John, where did you get that?" "I have been into the library; one gentleman gave me that, another gave me that, and Mr. Purday gave me these two pennies." My mother went upon her knees, clasped me around the neck, lifted up her eyes, thanked God, and then gave me a halfpenny all to myself! And what do you suppose I did with it? I went out and changed it into two farthings, and I never enjoyed money as much as that all the days of my life. (*J. B. Gough.*) *A widow's trust in God:*—M. Poinsot, the devoted Protestant Scripture-reader at Charleroi, has been much blessed in his arduous and heroic work for Christ. He says in his journal—"I visited a poor woman of seventy-six years of age, alone, poor, and ill. I said to her, 'The nights must seem very long to you, being always alone?' 'If I were alone,' she replied, 'I should have been dead long ago, but I have a Friend who never leaves me day nor night; I commune always with Him, and His Word comforts me.' 'But,' I said, 'if you became worse in the night?' 'He would take care of me,' was the reply; 'He is the best Doctor in Belgium.'"

Ver. 6. **But she that liveth in pleasure.**—*A life of pleasure a life of death:*—If this be true—and, being part of the Word of God, it must be true—then the world of pleasure is a region of death, and a life of pleasure is a living death. These are strange tidings for those who live only for pleasure, and who boast that they alone, of all mankind, enjoy life. I. WHO IS MEANT BY THE PERSON THAT LIVETH IN PLEASURE? And this point does require explanation; for the word "pleasure," is one strangely abused; it has quite a different meaning in different companies, and among different men. There are pleasures in science, pleasures in sin; pleasures in holiness here, and in heaven, we know, there are pleasures for evermore. "Now, she that is a widow indeed, and desolate, trusteth in God, and continueth in supplications and prayers night and day. But she that liveth in pleasure is dead while she liveth." Now this is evidently a character just the reverse; that of one who trusteth not in God, who neglects supplication and prayers. The same character is further described more at length in the eleventh and the thirteenth verses: wantonness, idleness, wandering about from house to house, tattling, the spirit of busy-bodies, speaking things which they ought not—are given as characteristics of her that liveth in pleasure. The original word, "liveth in pleasure," is very peculiar, and is used in only one other place in the New Testament, namely, in James, v. 5. Now, in that passage of St. James, he is addressing the wealthy, and the luxurious: "Go to now, ye rich men, weep and howl for your miseries that shall come upon you. Your riches are corrupted, and your garments are moth-eaten." Then, in the fifth verse, "Ye have lived in pleasure on the earth, and been wanton; ye have nourished your hearts as in a day of slaughter": where the word that is translated "ye have been wanton," is the very same word with that which, in our text, is rendered "liveth in pleasure": and the whole passage strikingly describes what kind of character is intended. Thus it is plain already, that to live in pleasure, is to live without trust or faith in God, without constant prayer; in wantonness, idleness, trifling, the pride of wealth; in luxury, sensuality, and self-indulgence. This is the life of worldly pleasure. But there are yet many other Scriptures which describe the life of pleasure; and I am anxious you should feel the Scriptural force of the subject. Thus, in the prophet Amos, in the sixth chapter: "Woe to them that are at ease in Zion, and trust in the mountain of Samaria, which are named chief of nations, to whom the house of Israel came," &c.

Again you see the spirit of the child of pleasure, he makes himself "at ease," he "puts far away the evil day" : he is self-indulgent, luxurious, gay, and jovial ; he feels not for the affliction of God's afflicted people.　In the book of Job, we have another description of men living in worldly pleasure—in his twenty-first chapter : "Wherefore do the wicked live, become old, yea, are mighty in power ?　Their seed is established in their sight with them, and their offspring before their eyes.　Their houses are safe from fear, neither is the rod of God upon them."　Here, again, you see the life of pleasure to be a life of unsanctified prosperity, festivity, mirth, wealth ; with the spirit of infidelity mocking at religion, asking, what good in prayer—what end to serve God ?　Oh, ye that have lived in pleasure, does not your conscience feel, "My life is detected ; my character has been described " ?　So in our Lord's parable ; the rich man, who fared sumptuously every day, and was clothed in purple and fine linen, was evidently a man of pleasure—luxurious, self-indulgent, fond of dress.　The city of Sodom was a city of pleasure.　Then think of Babylon, once filled with the gayest of the gay ; see that city of pleasure described in the prophet Isaiah : "Come down and sit in the dust, O virgin daughter of Babylon, sit on the ground : there is no throne, O daughter of the Chaldeans : for thou shalt no more be called tender and delicate.　Take the mill-stones, and grind meal : uncover thy locks, make bare the leg, uncover the thigh, pass over the rivers," &c.　And let none think that the Scriptural description of one that liveth in pleasure applies only to the rich and the great of this world.　But the temptation is common to all ranks, persons in middle life, and persons in the lowest walks of life, may be found to live continually in pleasure.　This do all the intemperate.　Oh, what sums the poor and labouring classes spend in the present day on needless, noxious, inflammatory drink !　II. Then this is God's judgment of the state of such "SHE THAT LIVETH IN PLEASURE "— WHOEVER LIVETH IN PLEASURE —"IS DEAD WHILE ALIVE."　Now that is the sentiment, or rather the sentence, of God Himself. "What does it mean ?　'She that liveth in pleasure is dead while she liveth ' :— how can one be dead while alive? "　Think of that serious, pious Christian, once in the circle of your acquaintance, once a friend, and even a brother ; but now he seems as one dead to all your pleasures, dead to the world, dead indeed unto sin. You say in scorn, that you might as well ask a dead man as ask him to join your worldly pleasure, he has become what you term a poor lifeless creature ; he is buried alive.　How true, how just, how striking that description !　The dead neither move, nor see, nor hear, nor smell, nor feel.　Your heart moves not in love to God ; your mind's eye sees no suitableness in the Saviour ; you hear not His voice, you perceive no fragrance in His name, like that of ointment poured forth ; you feel not the constraining force of His dying love.　Then death is, further, a state of insensibility and helplessness.　But further still, "She that liveth in pleasure, is dead while she liveth," because under sentence of death.　If a criminal were convicted of murder, or some capital crime, and sentenced to death, in the interval between his sentence and his execution he is considered as dead in the eye of the law.　But are you afraid that you shall now lose all pleasure ?　You will lose the phantom, and gain the substance ; you will throw away the counterfeit, and receive genuine gold ; you will drop worldly pleasure, which is connected with death, which has death inseparably tied to it, and enjoy spiritual pleasure, which is connected with eternal life.　But I had not meant to say much more which might seem harsh to those who will still be of the world ; I was endeavouring to lead those who are desirous of coming out of the world to come into new life.　" Her ways are ways of pleasantness, and all her paths are peace."　Then how noble, sublime, and glorious, are the objects with which religion is conversant.　I add but another thought. Religious pleasures are the best, for they have the approving smile of God on them now, and they can be carried with the soul into another world, and there be ripened into perfection. (*J. Hambleton, M.A.*)　*The woman of pleasure :*—It is a strong way of putting the truth, that a woman who seeks in worldly advantage her chief enjoyment, will come to disappointment and death.　My friends, you all want to be happy. You have had a great many recipes by which it is proposed to give you satisfaction —solid satisfaction.　1. And, in the first place, I advise you not to build your happiness upon mere social position.　2. I go further, and advise you not to depend for enjoyment upon mere personal attractions.　3. Again, I advise you not to depend for happiness upon the flatteries of men.　4. Again, I charge you not to depend for happiness upon the discipleship of fashion. (*T. De Witt Talmage.*) *True living :*—A Persian monarch asked an aged man, "How many of the sun's revolutions hast thou counted ? "　"Sire," said the old man, "I am but four years of age." "What!" interrupted the king, "fearest thou not to answer me falsely, or dost thou jest on the very brink of the tomb?" "I speak not falsely," replied the aged man; "eighty long years have I wasted in folly and sinful pleasures and in amassing wealth, none of which I can take with me when I leave this world. Four only have I spent in doing good to my fellow-men, and shall I count those years which have been utterly wasted?"      *A living death:*—Alas! many a man is dead while he liveth; yea, all are dead who live in impenitence and presumptuous sins. God is the soul of our soul, and the life of our life; and Christ must dwell in our heart by faith, and be the heart of our heart, to enable us to say with St. Paul, "I live, yet not I, but Christ liveth in me." Just as the heart is the workshop of the soul, from which it distributes natural heat and vital energy into all the veins and members, even so must the Lord Jesus generate in us spiritual life, and diffuse His spirit into all our powers, senses, desires, thoughts, and motions. The ungodly man is a living corpse; the worm of sinful desire consumes his conscience; he is an abomination in the eyes of the Saviour, and offensive to God and the holy angels. (*J. Gotthold.*)

Ver. 8. **But if any provide not for his own.**—*The necessity and excellence of family religion:*—I. I SHALL PROVE THAT FAMILY RELIGION IS A DUTY, FROM THE LIGHT OF NATURE AND OF SCRIPTURE. 1. If family religion be a just debt to the supreme Being, upon account of His perfections and the relation He sustains to us as families, then it must be our duty to maintain it according to the law of nature. Now this is the case in fact. God is the most excellent of beings, and therefore worthy of homage in every capacity, from His reasonable creatures. Again, God is the author of our sociable natures, and as such claims social worship from us. Again, God is the proprietor, supporter, and benefactor of our families, as well as of our persons, and therefore our families as such should pay Him homage. He is the owner of your families, and where is the man that dares deny it? 2. If family religion was the principal design of the institution of families, then is family religion our indispensable duty. And that family religion was the principal end of the institution is evident; for can you think that God would unite a member of immortals, heirs of the eternal world, together in the most intimate bonds, in this state of trial, without any reference to their future state? Were your families made for this world only, or for the next? 3. If family religion tends to the greatest advantage of our families, then it is our duty; and to neglect it is wickedly to rob ourselves and ours of the greatest advantage. 4. You are to consider family religion not merely as a duty imposed by authority, but as your greatest privilege granted by Divine grace. I now proceed to some arguments more purely Scriptural, which prove the necessity of family religion in general, or of some particular branch of it. (1) We may argue from the examples of the saints, recorded and commended in Scripture (Gen. xviii. 16, 18; xxvi. 25; xxv. 1, 3; xxxiii. 20). (2) We may argue from several Scripture precepts, which either directly or consequentially refer to the whole, or to some branch of family religion. The apostle Paul, having given various directions about relative duties in families, subjoins, "Continue in prayer, and watch in the same with thanksgiving" (Col. iv. 2). Peter exhorts "husbands to dwell with their wives according to knowledge, &c., that their prayers might not be hindered" (1 Peter iii. 7), which certainly implies that they should pray together. I proceed—II. TO SHOW IN WHAT SEASONS, OR HOW FREQUENTLY, FAMILY RELIGION SHOULD BE STATEDLY PERFORMED. Now it is more than intimated in Scripture, that it should be performed every day, and particularly morning and evening. Thus the sacrifices under the law, which were attended with prayer, were offered daily, morning and evening. To this the Psalmist alludes: "Let my prayer be set before Thee as incense," which was offered in the morning, "and the lifting up of my hands as the evening sacrifice" (Psa. cxli. 2). He elsewhere resolves, "Every day will I bless Thee" (Psa. cxlv. 2). Yea, his devotion was so extraordinary, that he resolves, "Evening, and morning, and at noon, will I pray and cry aloud" (Psa. lv. 17). So Daniel performed family worship thrice a day. III. I shall consider, WHAT PARTICULAR OBLIGATION THE HEADS OF FAMILIES LIE UNDER, and what authority they are invested with to maintain religion in their houses. In all societies there must be a subordination, and particularly in families, and it is the place of the head of such societies to rule and direct. Particularly it belongs to the head of a family, when there is no fitter person present, to perform worship in it, to use proper means to cause all his domestics to attend upon it. IV. And lastly, I COME

TO ANSWER THE USUAL OBJECTIONS AGAINST THIS IMPORTANT DUTY OF FAMILY RELIGION. 1. " I have no time, and my secular business would suffer by family religion." 2. " I have no ability to pray; I am too ignorant." 3. " I am ashamed." 4. " But, alas! I know not how to begin it." 5. " But my family will not join with me." 6. " But I shall be ridiculed and laughed at." (*S. Davies, M.A.*) *Home claims :*—If any one provide not for his own kindred, and for those of his own house, as parents or children, he lives in a manner so contrary to the Christian faith, that he, in fact, denies it, and is worse than an infidel. "Indeed," says Archbishop Secker, " Nature as well as Christianity enjoins this domestic duty so strongly, that the whole world cries out shame where it is neglected." That man, therefore, deserves censure, who, intent on the interests of others, disregards his own. The astrologer who was looking at the stars, and telling the fortunes of his neighbours, did not see the pit which lay at his feet, and into which he fell. It is well to do a good turn to a stranger, or even to an enemy, but " not to bulge our own vessel in attempting to raise that of our neighbour," as the following story from Æsop may show. " A wolf that lay licking his wounds, and extremely faint and ill from the bite of a dog, called out to a sheep passing by, ' Hark'ye, friend, if you would but help me to a sup of water out of yonder brook, I would manage myself to get something to eat.' ' Yes,' said the sheep, ' I make no doubt of it ; but when I bring you drink, my carcase shall serve you for meat.' "

Ver. 14. **The younger women marry, bear children, guide the house.**—*A wife's sphere :*—Every mother should occupy in the family the position of commander-in-chief. Her spirit should rule through the whole establishment, for in proportion as " she looks well to the ways of the household," with intelligence and discretion, the servants and other members of the family will follow in her path. There is nothing which ought to occupy a more prominent position than this power to rule the house diligently and well. Nor are we alone in this opinion. Goldsmith, in his " Vicar of Wakefield," says, " The modest virgin, the prudent wife, the careful matron, are much more serviceable in life than petticoated philosophers, blustering heroines, or virago queens. She who makes her husband and her children happy, who reclaims the one from vice, and trains the other to virtue, is a much greater character than the ladies described in romances, whose whole occupation is to murder mankind with shafts from their quiver or their eyes." Every wife, therefore, should seek, then, to be worthy of the position she occupies and in this way to become " a crown to her husband." (*John W. Kirton.*) *True womanly service :* —Most heartily do we go with Mrs. Fawcett's remarks upon the industrial and professional employment of women, in connection with which she said that a woman with a family, which she brought up well, was doing as great a work, economically and socially, as any person was capable of performing. Scores of mothers, whose sphere of activity is bounded by the walls of their home, and who sometimes deplore their inability to engage in outside work, may take heart on being reminded of this most certain truth. To train a family of children in the fear of God, and the best habits of feeling and conduct, is as precious a work as any that is done under the sun, exercises the very highest qualities of love, patience, and self-denial, and will be recognized on high as the truest service of Christ. (*S. S. Chronicle.*) *Homely duties :*—The Princess Alice, the beloved daughter of Queen Victoria, after an ancient custom of royalty, chose the lark as her emblem, because, as she said, while it lived on the ground and obscurely, it taught that in the discharge of homely duties we find the strength, the knowledge, and the inspiration to fill the air with joyous and soul-stirring music. If this woman of noble birth, the Lady Bountiful in the little state over which her husband ruled, the founder of orphanages and schools, could choose such an emblem, it may well be appropriated by those who move in the ordinary circles of influence and experience. It is in everyday life that opportunity comes to do the best things and gains its sweetest reward of happiness. (*Christian Age.*) *A Christian mother :*—Nearly forty years ago in the South of England there was an earnest minister of Christ, whose duties often called him from home. He had a large family, and he feared sometimes he was paying them but little attention because of his many obligations outside. One day he was about to start on a journey, and he stood at the door half-way downstairs, and he heard a voice in prayer. It was the voice of his wife. He listened, and she was praying for the children by name, and when she came to one name, Charles, she said, " Lord, he has a daring spirit ; whether for good or for evil, make it Thine own."

And the minister, as he wiped away a tear said, "It is all right; I can go and serve the Lord; it is right with the children"; and that Charles for whom prayer was offered is the beloved brother whom we listened to in St. Andrew's Hall yesterday —Charles Spurgeon. Who will say that that mother is not a Christian worker? She toiled in her own home, and laboured for her own children; and if there are mothers here I would say, "Go, and do likewise."

Ver. 16. **May relieve them that are widows indeed.** —*Charity ruled by wisdom:*— The first of these main principles of Church charity is—I. THAT THOSE RECEIVED TO PERMANENT SUPPORT SHOULD BE ONLY SUCH AS ARE AGED OR WEAK. In the ninth verse we read, "Let not a widow be taken into the number under threescore years old"; or (as the R. V. more correctly has it) "Let none be enrolled as a widow under threescore years old." A woman over sixty in Asia Minor (though it would be otherwise in our healthier, cooler climate) could no longer work, nor do much for the Church either, except by her prayers and supplications (another proof that officials are not referred to). Widows thus infirm and aged were to receive constant and generous support. But nothing was to be done, even under the sacred name of charity, which would paralyse personal exertion or weaken the sense of responsibility in relatives and friends. Paul's second principle is this—II. THAT THOSE WHOSE CHARACTER IS CHRISTIAN HAVE SPECIAL CLAIMS ON THE SUPPORT OF THE CHURCH. He is not referring here to the relief of distress which is the duty of every Christian, but to the use of the charitable funds given by the Church for distribution among her members. How beautiful is the picture of the true Christian matron, as depicted by the few touches of this masterhand in verses 5 and 10. Think of her motherliness, one who has brought up her children aright. Very beautiful, too, are the thoughts suggested of her lowly, loving ministry. Entertaining strangers, for the Lord's sake; not necessarily because she was rich, but because she was kind. III. The last principle which should guide us in the selection of those who may live on the charity of the Church is this, THAT THEY SHOULD BE REJECTED WHO WOULD BE MORALLY INJURED BY DEPENDING ON IT. At first sight the apostle seems rather hard upon the younger women; although it is evident from the 15th verse that he was not speaking from theory, but from actual and painful experience, and that some in the Church at Ephesus had already fallen into the evils to which he refers, having lost their first simple faith in Jesus Christ, and their former consecration to Him. He implies that ecclesiastical arrangements had aggravated their temptations, and he strongly urges that younger widows who might properly receive special help and solace for a time, ought not to be put on the roll of the Church for perpetual relief. His reason is given plainly enough. "They learn to be idle," says he, "wandering about from house to house; and not only idle, but tattlers also, and busybodies, speaking things which they ought not." Right as it was to support the aged and infirm, it would be morally injurious to support by charity these younger women. Idleness is always a fruitful parent of sins, of which gossip, meddlesomeness, and unprofitable talk are not the greatest; and the best preventive of this would be to throw Christian women as far as possible on their own resources, to let them take a good opportunity for settling in life, to exert themselves for their own maintenance, or to care for another household, as the brave and patient servants of Jesus Christ. Any one who knows the pernicious effects produced by ill-regulated charity, any one who reflects on the vices common to the idle classes of society, any one who has noticed the moral deterioration of young people who have nothing to do but to while away their time, will thank God for these wise counsels. (*A. Rowland, LL.B.*)

Vers. 17, 22. **Let the elders that rule well.** —*Duties towards the ministry:*— I. ITS FAITHFULNESS SHOULD BE HONOURED. "Let the elders that rule well be counted worthy of double honour." II. ITS REPUTATION SHOULD BE CHERISHED. 1. We ought to be slow to believe evil. "Against an elder" (here used in the official sense and not with reference to age) "receive not an accusation, but before two or three witnesses," or (as the Revised Version has it), "except at the mouth of two or three witnesses." The reference is obviously to a well-known Mosaic law. Timothy was not to be credulous of evil reports, he was to pay no attention to mere gossip, and still less was he to show any encouragement to slanderers. He was not appointed specially as a judge; but in contentions, such as unhappily arose in the

Church, his authority would often be appealed to. Again and again noble reputations have been ruined by slander, and the injustice and wickedness of the charges have only been demonstrated when it was too late to repair the wrong. But while we are to be slow to believe evil—2. We ought to be brave in the rebuke of evil. No fear of man, no mincing words to please fastidious ears, no wish to smother up iniquity, should be ours. "Them that sin rebuke before all, that others also may fear." III. ITS ASPIRANTS SHOULD BE APPROVED. "Lay hands suddenly (or hastily) on no man." The custom of the laying on of hands dates back to patriarchal times. Jacob laid his hands on Ephraim and Manasseh when he blessed them. It was an appropriate indication of the subject of prayer, a solemn act of designation and of dedication; and in the apostolic days it was used to sanction and ratify the elective act of the Church. In such work we are not to be ruled by caprice, excluding one we dislike; nor by partiality, appointing our personal friends, or those having some claims upon us. "I charge thee" (says Paul) "before God, and the Lord Jesus Christ, and the elect angels, that thou observe these things without prejudice, doing nothing by partiality." What could be a stronger inducement to the keeping of these commands than the realization of the fact that an unseen God and holy angels are near us, and that all our works, and even our purposes, are open and naked before Him with whom we have to do! And there is yet another word here for every Christian, especially for those who work for the Master, namely this— "Be not partaker of other men's sins; keep *thyself* pure," for the emphasis in the original is to be laid just there. It is easy enough to see other people's faults, and even to rebuke them; but beware lest any have occasion to turn on you and say, "Physician, heal thyself." Purity in the sense of chastity is, no doubt, included here, for an impure life is fatal to a Christian and ruinous to his influence for good —nay, even if such evil is only harboured within, it will prove the paralysis of spiritual life. (*Ibid.*) *Gifts to ministers :*—I became an usher in a school at Cambridge, and at the same time, when only sixteen years of age, accepted the pastorate at a Baptist chapel in the neighbourhood. After a while I gave up my post at the school, and was thrown on the generosity of the people, and they gave me a salary of £45 a year; but as I had to pay twelve shillings a week for two rooms which I occupied, the salary was not enough. But the people, though they had not money, had produce, and there was not a pig killed by any one of the congregation that I had not some portion of, and one or other of them would bring me bread, so that I had enough bread and meat to pay my rent with. An old man in that place who was a great miser, one afternoon gave me three half-crowns, and as I was wanting a new hat at the time I got it with the money. The following Sunday the old man came to me again, and asked me to pray for him that he might be saved from the sin of covetousness, and said, "The Lord told me to give you half-a-sovereign, and I kept half-a-crown back, and I can't rest of a night for thinking of it." (*C. H. Spurgeon.*) *Providing for the minister :*—Claude, the Indian preacher, after his conversion a few years ago in Russian America, began to sing hymns and tell gospel truths to his idol-worshipping fellow-countrymen. The old medicine men there wept, cowed by the felt presence of God's Holy Spirit. "Claude," said his companions, "it is too bad for you to chop wood. You ought to tell the people these things all the time." "I should not have anything to eat if I did not chop wood," he replied. "We will chop harder and later and get enough for you to live on too," said they. So Claude began to preach and teach. His support was salmon. Salmon for his breakfast, dinner, and supper, every day all the year. This was the salary of the first Protestant missionary to Alaska. Soon he had sixty scholars and an audience of from four to five hundred. God's Spirit was poured out. There were sixty converted, and hundreds gave up their devil worship. *Payment of ministers :*—In one of his conferences with working men Dr. Parker said: Some people sneered at preachers because they accepted pay. He contended that the question of payment ought never to arise in estimating the value of a true ministry. He could order a table to be made and delivered at any time, but where could he order a character to be made and delivered on such a day? The man who gave them a thought gave them inestimable riches. The man who gave them an inspiration lifted them up above fog and cloud and depression and difficulty and gave them a new start in life. If he were asked to go and speak to the humblest outcasts of London, then the question of payment ought not to arise: they were his brethren and sisters and friends and were in darkness, and he had the light. They should have the light for nothing. But when men came to him and said, "The well-to-do people of Bath, and Newcastle-on-Tyne, and Bristol want to hear you," he asked, Were they to escape without remunerating the man who instructed them and ministered to their enjoyment? He was prepared to preach for nothing if the landlord, the butcher, the baker, the candlestick-maker were agreeable, but these showed a brutal disregard for his feelings at quarter-day. *A question of payment :*—When addressing a body of working men, Bishop Wilberforce speaking of the nobility of true work, said, "Though I am addressing an audience of working men, I may claim to be a working man myself, for I work as hard as any man here present." A voice called out from the middle of the room, "But how about the pay?" A burst of general laughter followed, which was, with some little difficulty, hushed down by those who thought that the bishop would be offended. But not a cloud passed across his face. His eye twinkled as he joined himself in the general merriment, and then, when silence was restored, without a moment's hesitation, and the smile still playing upon his face, he said, "My friend asks, how about the pay? I will tell him at once. You see I am paid the same whether I work or whether I don't." His audience saw at once the significance of his words : Work done for its own sake, not for greed or necessity. And the rafters of the roof above us rang again and again with their cheers. (*Memoirs of Bp. S. Wilberforce.*)  *Ministers need encouragement:*—I know of a parsonage to which the death-angel came, and took to heaven a faithful and beloved under-shepherd. The kind members of his flock went to that desolate home, and could not say enough in praise of him whom they did truly love. A volume of his sermons was published, and widely circulated. Then the broken-hearted wife said : " Oh, if they had only said one-half to him which they now say to me, how it would have lightened his labour and rejoiced his heart ! " I know of another parsonage to which a pastor returned, after a Sabbath of extreme mental fatigue, and of intensely loving work for his people. The almost agonizing tone with which he said : " Not one kind word to-day, and I've done my very best," would have met a kind response from every parishioner's heart, could all have heard it. " Not one kind word to-day." I know of a pastor to whom a parishioner said one Sunday evening : " I have been benefited by both sermons to-day." When his pastor replied : " It always helps me to hear that," this warm-hearted man said : " If I always told you when I feel benefited by your sermons, it would be very often." I wish you could have heard the prayer of humble thankfulness which went up to heaven from the family altar in that pastor's study that night. (*Dr. Hoge.*)  **Doing nothing by partiality.** —*Partiality to be avoided :*—A suggestive anecdote comes to us just now from New York. One of the good clergymen of that city lately travelling, was engaged in pleasant conversation with a friend. He presently found himself greatly annoyed by a drunken fellow-passenger on the seat in front, who recognized him, and persisted in trying to take his share in the conversation. At last, losing all patience, our clerical friend arose, and, pushing his annoyer aside rather roughly, exclaimed : " You are drunk, and I don't want to have anything to do with you." At this his unfortunate interlocutor was for a moment silent, and then, turning and gazing reproachfully at the irritated clergyman, replied, in a tone so loud as to be heard nearly through the entire car : " Mr. ——, 'pears to me you don't care very much about my soul." It is one thing, truly, to care about the souls of the intelligent, and the cultivated, and the agreeable and the clean, to say nothing of the temperate, and quite another thing to care about the souls of the ignorant and the ill-mannered and the unclean. And yet it must not be forgotten that the claims of this latter class are just as strong upon the Christian Church and the Christian worker, as the former, and that in our efforts to bring men to God we are not to select those who present themselves agreeably to us, but are to take them as they come.

Ver. 22. **Neither be partaker of other men's sins.**—*How must we reprove, that we may not partake of other men's sins ?*—I. How A MAN MAY BE SAID TO PARTAKE OF OTHER MEN'S SINS. 1. By contrivance. Thus Jonadab was guilty of Amnon's incest, by his subtle contrivance of that wickedness, by being a pander to that villainy (2 Sam. xiii. 5). When a man shall wittingly and willingly spread a snare in his brother's way, and either drive him in by provocation, or decoy him in by allurement, he makes himself a partaker of his sin. For example : to provoke a man to passion, to tempt a person to drunkenness and uncleanness, to put a man upon murder and bloodshed, to draw souls into error, heresy, blasphemy, &c.,—this is to espouse and adopt the sin, and to make it a man's own. You know the story there,

2 Sam. xi. : Uriah was slain with the edge of the sword ; David was many miles off when Uriah was slain : "Thou hast killed Uriah the Hittite with the sword, and hast slain him with the sword of the children of Ammon" (2 Sam. xii. 9). The Ammonites slew him, but David murdered him. St. Paul tells us he was a "blasphemer, and a persecutor, and injurious." 2. By compliance. By consenting and complying with sin and sinners: so a man makes himself partaker. Though he has no hand in it, yet, if he has a heart in it ; though he does not act it, yet if he likes it, and loves it, and approves it. Saul—He had no hand in St. Stephen's death, he did not cast one stone at him ; but because he looked on with approbation, and stood by with consent—"Saul was consenting unto his death" (Acts viii. 1). You may murder a man with a thought, as they say the basilisk will with a look. 3. By connivance. By a sinful dissembling, flattering, and winking at others in their wickedness and sins, so men become guilty of others' sins : "The leaders of this people cause them to err" (Isa. ix. 16) : it is in the Hebrew, "The blessers of this people cause them to err." Beloved, the blessers of men in wickedness are the leaders of men in wickedness. 4. By sufferance. By permitting the sins of others, so we become guilty, by suffering others to sin, whom we are bound in duty, and may be able by authority, to hinder. 5. By influence of bad example. By setting loose and bad examples for others to imitate. So men are guilty of other's sins ; as, namely, when children sin by the examples of their parents, those very parents are guilty of their children's sins. So it is here : he that sets an evil example sins not alone ; he draws hundreds, it may be, into sin after him. He is like a man that sets his own house on fire ; it burns many of his neighbours', and he is to be answerable for all the ruins. 6. By inference from a bad example, or by imitation. So a man is guilty of another man's sin, not only by pattern, in setting bad examples, but also by practice, in following bad examples ; and thus that man that will be drunk because another was drunk, or that breaks the Sabbath because others do the like—he is not only guilty of his own particular sin, but he is guilty also of their sins whom he imitates and follows ; and the reason is, because bad examples are not land-marks for us to go by, but they are sea-marks for us to avoid. And this is the woful, intricate, perplexed labyrinth into which sin doth precipitate careless and ungodly sinners. If thou committest that sin which none before committed but thee, thou art guilty of all the sins of future generations by thy example—as Adam was in the world, and Jeroboam in Israel. And if thou committest any sin because others have committed it before thee, thou art guilty of all the sins of former generations by thy imitation : and so sin never goes alone ; a single sin is as great a solecism in divinity as a single "thank" is in grammar and morality. 7. By countenance. By delightful society and company with wicked men to countenance them, so we become partakers of their sins. 8. By maintenance. By upholding and encouraging men in their sins, though thou never committest them thyself, yet thou art guilty. "He that biddeth him God-speed is partaker of his evil deeds" (2 John 11). II. WHY A CHRISTIAN MUST BE CAREFUL TO AVOID, AND NOT TO PARTAKE OF, OTHER MEN'S SINS. 1. Out of a principle of charity to our brethren. 2. Out of a principle of pity to ourselves. 3. Out of a principle of piety to God. III. APPLICATION : 1. Is there such a thing as "partaking of other men's sins" after this manner ? (1) Hence you may be informed of the equity and justice of God's proceeding in punishment. (2) Hence be informed what piety, and strictness, and watchfulness are more especially required of those that have the care of others. (3) Hence take an account why the wicked of the world do so hate the godly, and reproach and revile them. It is this : They will not be partakers of their sins : they will not commit them, neither will they connive at them ; and this is the reason why the world hates them. (4) Here is matter of reproof and humiliation this day for our want of watchfulness in this kind. 2. The second use is of exhortation and caution together. Is it so, that it ought to be every man's care not to partake of any man's sin? 1. To lay down the arguments. (1) Consider : You have sins enough of your own, you have no reason to partake of other men's. It is cruel to "add affliction to your bonds." (2) Consider : It is a most monstrous sin, it is a most dreadful sin, to partake of other men's sins. The apostle speaks of committing iniquity "with greediness" (Eph. iv. 19). (3) Consider : If you partake of other men's sins, you shall certainly partake of other men's plagues. "Come out of her, My people," says God, namely, from Babylon, "that you be not partakers of her sins, and that ye receive not of her plagues" (Rev. xviii. 4). See Prov. xiii. 20. 2. What sins we must especially take heed of partaking of. Of all sin whatsoever ; "Abstain from all appear-

ance of evil" (1 Thess. v. 22); but especially of three sorts of sin, which may be called epidemical plagues. (1) Church sins. (2) National sins. (3) Family sins. 3. Now, and in the last place, we come to the antidotes: How we must so carry it. and order the business, as not to partake of other men's sins. (1) Exercise an holy jealousy over others. Job, sacrificing for his children, said, "It may be that my sons have sinned" (Job i. 5). (2) Watch against the sins of others. Have your eyes about you: take heed of contriving, complying, winking at them. (3) Pray against them. (4) Mourn for them. (5) Reprove them (Ezek. iii. 17-19). If we would not partake of the sins of others, we must reprove the sins of others (Lev. xix.; Ezek. xxxiii. 7-9). So the apostle saith expressly (Eph. v. 11). (*J. Kitchin, M.A.*) *Partaking of other men's sins:*—It was a frequent petition of the illustrious St. Augustine, "Lord, forgive other men's sins!" It is a petition which we all should constantly present to God; for we, all of us, in a greater or less degree, have been instrumental in producing that iniquity which deluges the world. I. We are to show you BY WHAT MEANS WE MAY PARTAKE OF OTHER MEN'S SINS. We partake of other men's sins by uttering those sentiments which tend to subvert morality, or diminish our horror for guilt. If we propagate loose doctrines, if we scoff at serious piety, if we persuade men that an holy and heavenly life is not necessary, "if we call evil good and good evil," we are murdering souls. II. That we may in future be more guarded, LET US ATTEND TO SOME OF THOSE MOTIVES WHICH ENFORCE THE IN-JUNCTION OF THE APOSTLE. III. SOME DIRECTIONS, TO ENABLE YOU TO COMPLY WITH THE INJUNCTIONS OF THE APOSTLE. 1. Be careful that your own heart and life are holy. Sin is infectious; and as long as you are polluted with it, you must communicate its poison to those with whom you asso-ciate. Besides, if your own life is unholy, your conscience will prevent you from faithfully reproving sin in others, or your ill example will render your reproofs inefficacious. 2. Cultivate a high value and love for the souls of men. That which we love we shall not readily injure; and if we have a proper regard for immortal souls we shall rather forego many pleasures than give a wound to them. 3. Mourn before God for the sins of your brethren. When God passed through Jerusalem to smite it, He spared none but those who cried and sighed for the abominations that were done within it (Ezek. ix. 4). 4. If we would not partake of the sins of others, we must reprove them. (*H. Kollock.*) *Participation in other men's sins:*—I. WHEN DO WE MAKE OURSELVES PARTAKERS OF OTHER MEN'S SINS? 1. Ministers make themselves partakers in the sins of their people, when those sins are occa-sioned by their own negligence, by their example, or by unfaithfulness in the dis-charge of their official duties. 2. Parents participate in the sins of their children, when they occasion, and when they might have prevented them. But further, parents partake in the guilt of their children's sins when they might and do not prevent them. 3. The remarks, which have been made respecting parents, will apply, though perhaps somewhat less forcibly, to masters and guardians, and all who are concerned in the government and education of youth. 4. Churches become partakers of the sins of an individual member, when these sins are occa-sioned by a general neglect of brotherly watchfulness and reproof, and when they are tolerated by the Church in consequence of a neglect of Church discipline. 5. We all make ourselves partakers in other men's sins, when we either imitate or in any other way countenance and encourage them. 6. Members of civil communities partake of all the sins which they might, but do not prevent. 7. If private citizens partake of all the sins which they might have prevented, much more do rulers and magistrates. Subjects who have the privilege of choosing their own rulers and magistrates, make themselves partakers of all their sins, when they give their votes for vicious or irreligious characters. II. To STATE SOME OF THE REASONS WHICH SHOULD INDUCE US TO GUARD AGAINST PARTAKING OF OTHER MEN'S SINS. 1. If we partake of their sins, we shall share in their punishment. 2. It is impossible not to perceive how completely our subject justifies the con-duct of those much insulted individuals, who have voluntarily associated for the purpose of assisting in executing the laws, and suppressing vice and im-morality among us. (*E. Payson, D.D.*) *Participation in the sins of others:*— I. TO SPECIFY SOME OF THE WAYS IN WHICH WE MAY BECOME PARTAKERS IN OTHER MEN'S SINS. 1. When, through the influence of custom, we fall in with habits which Scripture and conscience condemn. 2. When we fail to exert the power or influ-ence we may possess, for the prevention or discountenance of sin. 3. When we connive at them, or lend our sanction to their improper concealment. 4. When we fail to manifest our abhorrence, on either witnessing or hearing of their commission. 5. By inconsiderately introducing them to stations, the duties or dangers of which they are utterly incompetent to meet. II. How HARDENING AND INJURIOUS WILL PROBABLY BE THE INFLUENCE OF SUCH CONDUCT ON THE MINDS OF SINNERS. III. How ADAPTED SUCH CONDUCT TOO TO WEAKEN IN THE BELIEVER'S OWN MIND IMPRESSIONS OF THE EVIL OF SIN IN HIMSELF. (*Essex Congregational Remembrancer.*) *Other men's sins:*—However hideous and hateful our own sins may be, still, from long familiarity with them, or from the pleasure they afford us, we excuse, or palliate, or forget them. But you look with unaffected and unmitigated horror and disgust on the sins of other men. The rich look with horror on the sins of the poor, and the poor with equal indignation loathe the sins of the rich. Now it is this which gives its horror to the thought expressed in our text. It speaks in a language which all can understand. It says to each man, "Be not partaker in other men's sins." Let us consider, then, how, or in what way, we may partake in the sins of other men. I. We may become partakers in other men's sins BY LEARNING TO PRACTISE THEM. However alien to our own natural disposition, we are in danger of catching the infection of other men's sins—in danger of being corrupted and contaminated, and led to commit them, of learning to do and to delight in doing them. This world is like a hospital crowded with patients afflicted with various diseases. And here in our text the physician warns us to take heed lest in addition to our own disease we catch the infection of other diseases from our fellow-men, and aggravate and complicate our own by introducing their poison into our system. Each man has a sin which more easily besets him—a sin to which he is predisposed, which seems born in his nature. But there is no sin, however alien to our disposition at first, which may not be superinduced on our character, and become a second nature. Perhaps of all sins, acquired sins are the most inveterate. Though we escape the infection of other men's diseases, we may be responsible for their diseases and their death—diseases which we loathe and abominate. This is emphatically the lesson of the text. II. We become partakers in other men's sins WHEN WE WILFULLY AND KNOWINGLY ENTICE OR ENCOURAGE THEM TO SIN—ay, even though we should scrupulously keep our hands from doing or our own hearts from desiring to do it. This is an acknowledged principle of eternal justice. It is acknowledged and acted on in our courts of law. He who instigates, or encourages, or countenances a theft is held as guilty as the actual thief. He who loosens the stone from the mountain's brow is responsible not only for the blade of grass which it crushes in its first tardy movement, but for all the evil that it does in its downward career till it loses the momentum which he gave it, and lies motionless in the plain below. He is responsible for all the ruin it effects though he stands calmly at the top. Even so do we become partakers in all the deepening sins to which our first enticement gave birth. The schoolboy who has whispered in his companion's ear a filthy word, or taught him an evil thought; the merchant who has shown his apprentice the tricks and fraudulent dishonesties of trade; the master who has enticed his servant to despise the Sabbath; the giddy youth who has defiled the mind of maiden purity or seduced from the paths of innocence—all these are partakers, not only in the first sin to which they were tempted, but in the long, black, ever-deepening catalogue of sins to which that first sin gave birth. True, indeed, the responsibility of their victims is not lessened by their participation in it. III. We involve ourselves in other men's sins WHEN WE, THROUGH HEEDLESSNESS AND INATTENTION, COUNTENANCE OR GIVE THEM OCCASION TO COMMIT SIN. Observe, I do not now speak of those who allow themselves to be corrupted by other men's sins, as under the first head, nor yet of those who intentionally corrupt others, as under the second head, but only of those who, through heedlessness and inattention, are the unwitting and unwilling occasions of countenancing others in sin. The guilt in this case is less than in the former instances, and the consequences are not so fearful to ourselves. This no less than the last is an acknowledged principle of justice. It is acknowledged and acted on in our courts of law. Has any one through heedlessness or want of attention caused the death of a fellow-man, he is acquitted of the crime of murder, but he is brought in as guilty of culpable manslaughter. His guilt is less, but is as clear. His punishment is less, but it is as sure. Does the traveller mèet some accident, to the loss of property or the injury of his person, through the heedlessness or inattention of those who conveyed his property or himself, they are held responsible as persons guilty of culpable negligence, and if still persisted in to the frequent injury of others would be liable to severer punishment. But so it is in sober truth, and this for the first time is the point at which I take up the precise lesson of our text. I do not suppose that Paul thought it needful to warn Timothy against being corrupted by other men's sins. Nor can I imagine that he thought it necessary to forbid him from intentionally corrupting others. What, then, did he mean, unless it was to warn him that with the best intentions he might inadvertently, through inattention, involve himself in the guilt of other men's sins, sins which he hated himself, and which he mourned over in others? And so it was. "Lay hands suddenly on no man," said Paul, and as an argument or motive to care and consideration, he added, "Be not partaker in other men's sins." Having thus endeavoured to illustrate the general principles suggested by or embodied in our text, I might now allude to the encouragement and countenance that is given to drunkenness by the multiplied and unnecessary drinking customs which even good men maintain, but by which they become partakers in the sin of those who are thereby led away to excess. (W. Grant.) Partaking of other men's sins:—There is something which is very striking and very awful in the thought which is suggested to our minds in the words which have just been read. We have often heard it said that it is quite enough for any man in this world to answer for his own doings or misdoings; it is not fair to lay upon him any burden of guilt beyond that which is properly his own; or to attach to him any discredit because he comes, perhaps, of an ill-doing family; or because some one closely related to him has fallen into gross sin and shame. And if, in the nature of things, it is possible for us to help feeling as though a reflected disgrace were cast upon that person whose near kinsman has broken the laws of his country, for instance, and died a felon's death, still we are ready at once to confess, when the thing is fairly put to us, that it is not fit or just to hold any human being responsible for that which has been done by another; and that it is quite enough to answer for the wrong which he has done himself. We tremble to think of the heavy load of responsibility and guilt which we have accumulated for ourselves. But can it be that this is not all; can it be that we have all of us more to answer for than we have ourselves done. There is a sense in which it is not possible for any man to be partaker in the sin of another. You cannot transfer responsibility. No man can justly be held responsible for that which he did not do; but then a man may do many things besides those which he does directly. A man may do many things at second-hand, so to speak; and in that case he is quite as responsible for them as if he had done them with his own hand. For instance, you can all understand that if any person hires another to commit a murder for him, both parties in that transaction are equally guilty of the crime of murder. And, indeed, in many cases the accomplice is worse than the actual sinner, for in the case of the accomplice there is all the original guilt, with cowardice and meanness added. But may you not likewise be partaker in sins of which at their commission you did not know, and at whose commission you would shudder? May you not, in the moral world, sometimes set the great stone rolling down the hill, with little thought of the ruin it may deal below? As, for instance, you, a parent, neglect the training of your child, that child grows up into guilt which appals you—guilt which terrifies you; but are you not still partaker in that guilt—answerable for that guilt at the bar of God? Ah, you know you are; you know full well that if that neglected child should end at the gallows, the fault, the sin, the shame will still be in a great measure your own! Ah! you may live after you are dead to do mischief—live in the evil thoughts you instilled, the false doctrines you taught, the perverse character you helped to form. When you stand before the judgment throne, you may find yourself called to answer for myriads of sins besides those which you directly committed; and you will feel that your condemnation for these sins is just and right. Let us, then, look somewhat more closely into this great principle which I have been endeavouring to set before you. Let us look more particularly at some of the ways in which we may become "partakers of other men's sins." And in thinking, first, of how we may make others to sin by suggesting evil thoughts and feelings, let us take an extreme case by way of example: an extreme case, indeed, but unhappily not an unprecedented one. Let us think of a great genius: of a man to whom God has been pleased to give that rare and wonderful power of excogitating beautiful thoughts which shall come home to the heart and brain of other men, and clothing these beautiful thoughts in words which shall fall like music on the ear. Let us think of such a man applying the noble powers which God gave him for high and pure designs to surround vice with all the fascinations of poetry and romance, to strip it of all its grossness, while leaving all its guilt; let us think of him writing tales and poems, all of the most corrupting tendency; going to undermine the very foundations of all morality and all religion; and wrapping up infidelity and profligacy in thoughts that breathe and words that burn. And in every such case, is not that perverted genius justly chargeable with a share of that sin to which his writings have tempted? You may have done in a lower degree what the bad great man did on a grander scale. Even then, when you allow vice to pass without reproof, for fear of giving offence, are you not thus tacitly encouraging it? Even then, when you soften down the stern requirements of religion, for fear of making some one uncomfortable whom the truth would make uncomfortable, are you not thus practically encouraging him to remain worldly as he is? So far, then, for certain fashions in which by the lip, by speech or by silence, you may become accessory and abetting to other men's sins; and next we remark that by your life and example you may do so even more effectually. Example, whether good or bad, is always more efficient than precept; and you know quite well that many a man has taken heart to do a sinful deed because he saw another do it, who but for that would never have done so. The higher a man's profession of religion, the more closely will his practice be watched, both by such as have little religion and by such as have none at all; and who does not know how any inconsistency, any lapse, on the part of a professing Christian is laid hold of by ungodly men to countenance their ungodly lives, and to show that all religion is a pretence and a delusion! The evil principle we instilled, the evil example we set, may ripen into bitter fruit in the murderous blow which shall be dealt a century hence upon Australian plains. How strange, yet how inevitable, the tie which may link our uneventful life with the stormy passions of numbers far away! It is but as yesterday that we heard of the success of that marvellous achievement of science which has set the old world in momently communication with the new; and the most sluggish imagination must have been awakened somewhat in the thought of that slender cable which, far beneath the waves of the great Atlantic, lying still in stirless ocean valleys, and scaling trackless ocean cliffs, maintains the subtle current through those thousands of miles; but more wonderful still, surely, is that unseen fibre along which, from other men's sins, responsibility may thrill even to our departed souls—a chain whose links are formed, perhaps, of idle words, of forgotten looks, of phrases of double meaning, of bad advice, of cynical sentiment hardly seriously meant; yet carried on through life after life, through soul after soul, till the little seed of evil sown by you has developed into some deed of guilt at which you would shudder, but from some participation in responsibility for which you cannot clear yourself. Yea, the thought widens out beyond anything which I have hitherto suggested; for surely it is nothing more than a legitimate extension of the great principle of the text to say that in some measure we are responsible for the sin which we failed to do our utmost to prevent; and so that even heathen cruelty and heathen idolatry may be in so far chargeable on us, because, though we never bowed to the senseless image, though we never imbrued our hands in a fellow-creature's blood, we yet failed to give of our means, our efforts, our prayers, to send to those dark lands that gospel light, which might have bidden these things die out for ever. In truth, the only way in which it is possible for us to cease to sin in the person of others, is by ceasing to sin in our own; for every sin may waken its echo, every sin is repudiated and reiterated, in other souls and lives. (A. H. K. Boyd.) Refusing to be a partaker in other men's sins:—Joseph Sturge, the Christian philanthropist, remonstrating one day with a drunken man whom he met, was startled by his reply that he had got drunk at a public-house, adding, "The beer was made from your barley." His mind was at once made up, and the next Mark Lane Express announced that under no circumstances would the Messrs. Sturge supply barley for malting purposes. This conscientious decision struck off £8,000 a year from their income. **Keep thyself pure.**—A caution to young men:—In the abstract, the text, brief as it is, contains a precept impossible to be fulfilled. For who does not know that in His judgment "God looks upon the heart"? and yet, who can say, "I have made my heart clean, I am pure from my sin"? The solution of the apparent difficulty lies upon the surface: we can do relatively what we cannot do absolutely; we can do in association with the grace of God what we cannot do without it. We then, accordingly, as ambassadors for Christ, say to each young man whom we address, as the apostle said to Timothy, "Keep thyself pure." Keep thyself, as one from the beginning separated and set apart for Christ, from everything which is inconsistent with the allegiance which thou must owe to Him; with the attachment which thou oughtest to feel for Him; with the attainment of those blessings which are the purchase of His blood, and which God will bestow on thee through Him alone. "Keep thy heart with all diligence; for out of it are the issues of life." Watch against the beginnings of evil. 1. "Keep thyself pure," then, young man, as to "doctrine" (for doctrine is the foundation of duty). 2. And not only let Holy Scripture stand first, but let it stand alone. Let it be received, not as "the word of man," but, as to doctrine, the teacher of truth alone. 3. Again, we say to the young man, "keep thyself pure" from error, by taking Scripture, in all that seems to require "reproof" or refutation, as a test. Whatever is repugnant to thy inherent and instinctive sense of right, whether to be denied as a principle, or to be deprecated as a practice, try it by its agreement or disagreement with God's Word. 4. Next, "keep thyself pure" in act, by taking the Word of God "for correction," or setting upright that which hath fallen down, restoring what hath been damaged or decayed through sin. And here the Word is a supreme, unerring standard of right and wrong; and "correction" is but another name for bringing into harmony or accordance with the Word. 5. "Keep thyself pure," by looking to the Word "for instruction in righteousness"; for instruction, which must extend itself throughout the whole of life, though life were protracted, as of old time, far beyond the narrow limits of threescore years and ten. 6. "Keep thyself pure," then, young man, but only by the grace of God in Christ. Once throw aside that buckler, and thou wilt become vulnerable by every weapon of the foe. Wilt thou "keep thyself pure," or shall that impurity, which is now thy shame, become thy companion and thy curse throughout eternity? Wilt thou be refined as the pure gold, or cast away as the "reprobate silver"? "Keep thyself pure," then, young man! because "thy breath is in thy nostrils"; because thy sun of life may go down ere it is yet high noon; and that purity of life is essential to the peace of death. But once more we add, "keep thyself pure" for the improvement—yes, and even for the true enjoyment of life. But by the observance of this salutary caution everything is gained, and nothing can be lost; time is rightly occupied, and talent profitably improved. Diligence in the practice of business, coupled with uprightness in its principles, rarely fails to prosper, even in a worldly view. (*T. Dale, M.A.*) *Purity in a minister:*—I admire Mr. Whitefield's reasons for always having his linen scrupulously clean. "No, no," he would say, "these are not trifles; a minister must be without spot, even in his garments, if he can." Purity cannot be carried too far in a minister. (*C. H. Spurgeon.*) *A clean record:*—The last words of a man are of comparatively little importance, but surely Mr. Gough could have uttered no sentence which would have pleased him better if he had known he would never speak again than the last words which he ejaculated as he sank unconscious in the Presbyterian church in which he was lecturing, "Young man, make your record clean!"

Ver. 23. **Drink no longer water.**—*Timothy charged to take care of his health.*— I. The first thought presented is, THAT A LIVING AND DEEP PIETY, A CHRISTIAN ACTIVITY, EXTENDED AS FAR AS CAN BE IMAGINED, SHOULD NEITHER EXTINGUISH IN US A CERTAIN INTEREST IN THE THINGS OF THE EARTH, NOR ABATE THE FORCE OF THE NATURAL AND LEGITIMATE TIES WHICH UNITE US TO PARENTS AND FRIENDS. St. Paul is certainly a proof of it. What faith was firmer and more ardent than his! A man who said (and what he said he felt): "It is no longer I who live, but Christ that liveth in me, and the life which I now live in the flesh, I live by the faith of the Son of God, who loved me and gave Himself for me" (Gal. ii. 20). A man who affirmed that he had "a desire to depart, and be with Christ; which was far better" (Phil. i. 23). Well! it is that apostle who, in the midst of a life so filled up, in spite of so many engagements and perplexities of every kind, preserves that freedom of mind necessary to remember the physical infirmities of one of his disciples; it is he who, in a letter of such grave contents and of so serious a tone, in which he discourses on the duties of the evangelical ministry, and where he imparts to him his own personal experiences, finds time, place, and means of reminding him to take care of his health, which, perhaps, he neglected. Does not that attention, so fraternal and so delicate on the part of the apostle, serve to put in the clearest light this truth, which, nevertheless, issues with sufficient clearness from the general contents of the gospel, that a purely contemplative religious life is rather an abuse than the fruit of true Christianity; that faith has by no means the effect of filling our heads with frothy and mystic ideas which are not applicable to every-day life, and that if it elevates us above the world, it is in order to help us over its troubles and free us from its miseries, but not to make us strangers to the various relations which we have to sustain, nor to the duties which we have to practise here? And to speak only of the ties of blood and of friendship, or of those still sweeter and more powerful ones, of Christian brotherhood, does not St. Paul, when exhorting his disciple not to enslave himself to a plan of abstinence which might have become fatal to him, teach us that if we are sincere disciples of the Saviour, His love, which lives in our hearts, should perfect us in that respect and render us capable of sympathizing more and more with the necessities of our suffering and afflicted friends, of understanding their position, of giving us just ideas of their perplexities, of taking part in their burdens. There are Christians who are pre-occupied with the concerns of heaven, to the extent of forgetting a part of the duties which they have to fulfil on this earth, as parents, as friends, as citizens. In their religious rigour the human element is blotted out, rather than freed from the impure alloy of evil. II. If St. Paul, exhorting his disciple Timothy NOT TO IMPOSE UNNECESSARY ABSTINENCE UPON HIMSELF, AND TO TAKE CARE OF HIS HEALTH, PRESENTS TO US THE MODEL OF THAT TENDER, VIGILANT, AND DELICATE CHARACTER WHICH IS FULLY ALLIED WITH THE HIGHEST DEGREE OF THE RELIGIOUS LIFE. Timothy, who on his part seems to have placed himself in the position of needing that lesson—teaches us, by his example, that a lively concern for the interests of our souls ought not to make us neglect the care of our bodies. This would prove, so to speak, by the way that the most pious and sincere men are subject to fall by excess of zeal into exaggerations, which the Word of God is far from approving of; and it ought to make us feel the necessity of enlightening ourselves more and more on the will of God as regards us, by always joining intelligence with piety, the understanding of Divine things with fervour, or, to speak with the apostle St. Peter, by "adding to faith, knowledge" (2 Pet. i. 5), lest we should give way to whims and take peculiar paths from which it would be difficult later on to return. No doubt it is better, in the act, to go astray after the manner of Timothy, than to sin after the example of men of the world; and it is beyond all dispute that he who impairs his health through the effect of long and persevering labours, undertaken with the view of advancing the Saviour's kingdom, and on account of having listened to nothing but the inspirations of a zeal which knew no limit, and which yielded to no obstacle, is, without comparison, infinitely less culpable before God than the carnal man who, on account of having altogether given way to his senses and slackened the bridle of his passions, has ruined his strength and destroyed his body. But, viewed in connection with God, the body is the work of the Creator, and, although degraded by sin, it still bears certain marks of Divine origin. Estimated with relation to our soul, it serves as its organ; it is intended to be the instrument of its desires, the executor of its volitions. Considered in connection with our fellow-men, it has been given us to be a means of communication with them, and in general with the objects and beings which compose the visible world in which we are placed. "Nevertheless to abide in the flesh is more needful, in order to your furtherance and joy of faith" (Phil. i. 24, 25). And it was that conviction which led him to save himself for the work of God and for the salvation of the Church. Let us live for heaven, but let us never forget the task which we have to fulfil on earth. III. Yet, you will have observed, that whilst putting Timothy on his guard against the dangers of an overstrained abstinence, and recommending him not to deprive himself of a natural drink which God has created for the benefit of man, the apostle gives us in passing a lesson of temperance; for instead of simply recommending his disciple to have recourse to the use of wine as a cordial and as a remedy, HE TAKES THE PRECAUTION OF SAYING TO HIM, "USE A LITTLE WINE." Unquestionably that restriction was scarcely necessary as regards Timothy, since there is no appearance of his having ever abused the liberty which his teacher gave him; but can we doubt that if St. Paul had expressed himself in a manner more general and without employing that moderation of language, libertines would have hastened to seize upon his words, to confirm themselves in their irregularities? Sobriety, indeed, is, however, at all times obedience to a law established by God Himself in creation, and for the benefit and interest of the man who accepts it and who submits to it. God has so ordered things in the world where He has placed us, that the moderate use of the good things which He dispenses to us brings with it blessing; whilst the abuse of the same enjoyments has for its consequence a curse. It is the same with all the gifts of the Creator— intemperance turns them into poisons, the want of sobriety transforms them into means of destruction. Too much sleep, for example, weakens the body; too much pleasure enervates it; too much rest benumbs it; too much food thickens the humours; too much drink agitates and consumes it. "Therefore let us not sleep, as do others; but let us watch and be sober" (1 Thess. v. 6). Sober in our sufferings as well as in our joys ; in our sadness as well as in our pleasures ; sober in rest, sober in activity ; sober when watching, sober in sleep ; sober in body, sober in mind.    IV.  In fine, the advice addressed by Paul to Timothy to drink no longer only water, but to use a little wine on account of his frequent indispositions, gives occasion to a last question which might appear idle at first sight, but which is certainly not so when viewed in its practical consequences ; and that question is this :  "How is it that St. Paul, who had received from Christ the gift of working miracles, does not apply that gift in order to heal his disciple ? "  Would it have cost him much, who, in the town of Lystra, restored to an impotent man the free use of his limbs, formerly paralyzed—him who chased from a poor young woman at Philippi the lying spirit with which she had been possessed for a long time—him who at Troas had only to bend over the body of a young man fallen from the third story of a house into the street, in order to call him back into life ; would it have cost him, I say, much to deliver Timothy from a malady slight in itself, although serious enough to have brought him into a state of weakness ?  To these various questions we believe that we can answer, that it does not appear that the apostles could work miracles every time that they wished ; that they were in that respect directed from on high, and that in this particular case it is probable that Paul, after having consulted the Lord by prayer, was turned aside from the idea of freeing Timothy from his physical infirmities by means of a miraculous cure, or, at least, that he did not feel free to do it.    Miracles are for those who do not believe, to predispose them to faith ; but for those who already believe, of what necessity could they be ?  Timothy, converted to Jesus Christ and a minister of the gospel, had then no need of the manifestation of the power of Jesus Christ in his body, because he felt that same power work in the regeneration of his soul.  But what was more necessary than a miracle for him, more profitable than a supernatural cure, was affliction ; and that is, without doubt, the reason why the apostle, taught in that respect by his own experience, did not wish to heal him suddenly, although he employed all the counsels of a wise friendship to bring him over gradually and by natural ways to a state of health which he could wish for him, but which he did not believe himself authorized to procure for him instantaneously.  Is there any school so good as that of trial ?  We have seen that we should not voluntarily and by our own fault create trials for ourselves ; we should be satisfied with those which the Lord sends us.  But if, on the one hand, it would be culpable to plunge into, or to complain in, afflictions of which we ourselves are the manufacturers, we must not, on the other hand, harden ourselves under the hand of the Saviour when it lies heavy upon us. *(J. Grandpierre, D.D.)*      *Paul's advice to Timothy :—*  I.  The speaker, who is undoubtedly the apostle Paul.  We have not only to notice his friendship and regard for his son Timothy, but we may learn that it is the duty, and should be the practice, of the ministers of Jesus Christ, to attend to the state of the health of their people.  It may be observed, that the apostle recommended the ordinary means ; we never find a miracle wrought where common and usual means would answer the purpose.    The apostle John could not heal his friend Gaius, and therefore prays heartily for him.  Nor could Paul heal Trophimus, and therefore left him sick at Miletus. This proves that the apostles' power of working miracles, or performing cures, was confined and limited ; and it was wise and kind in Providence in confining the prerogative in His own hand, as some, no doubt, would have neglected the use of ordinary means ; and in some instances the apostles might have employed their power on improper occasions.    II.  The person addressed.  Timothy, the pious descendant of a pious mother Eunice, and grandmother Lois.  But Timothy, with all his piety, has imperfections ; and this furnishes us with the idea, that good men are liable to indispositions.  It has been often observed, that the last step of a virtue and the first of a vice are nearly contiguous.  Frugality is commendable, but how likely is it to lead to covetousness, which is a vice.  This should teach us to avoid extremes, as extremes in all cases are dangerous.  From Timothy, the person spoken to, we learn that good and useful men are subject to many infirmities. Besides the many instances left us on record in the Scriptures, we may notice those of more modern ones.  That great advocate for reformation, Dr. Owen, the pious and heavenly-minded Richard Baxter, the seraphic James Hervey, and the sweet singer in British Israel, Dr. Watts, not forgetting that laborious preacher George Whitfield, are all instances of the truth of this observation, and could all say many years before their death, "The graves are ready for us."    III.  The import of the advice given.  "Take a little wine for thy stomach's sake," &c., which furnishes two observations, namely—1. That it is the duty of Christians to use means, and to take care to restore and preserve the state of their health. Instances may be referred to where this advice, if it had been observed, would have prevented many a fatal sickness. The benefit and blessing of health may be considered in the humble walks of life; in the poor labourer, the support of whose family depends on his labour, and whose labour depends on his health. It may be considered among the higher ranks of life. What is the benefit or enjoyment of a well-spread table, of a well-furnished mansion, of extensive possessions without health? But health is of importance in a religious view. 2. We may observe, that the Christian is not forbid the use and enjoyment of any created good. (*W. Jay.*) *Bodily infirmities :*—I. We believe that the sacred Scriptures would be found far more edifying and consoling than they are at present by many experienced to be, if we were to endeavour to realize to ourselves the personal habits and circumstances of the saints and martyrs whose acts form the groundwork of the inspired volume. Nay, inasmuch as the life of most men is private and domestic, we may think that it would be most advantageous if we possessed a narrative of the secret life of Christ. In the contemplation of St. Timothy harassed with a sick body, and of St. Paul plying his trade of tent-making, in order to obtain daily bread, and probably to provide the funds for future apostolic journeys, we have a lesson of infinite value. We are all, more or less, accustomed to find excuses for our religious deficiencies in the accidents of our state and condition. But every individual has his own excuse : the trade of one occupies his time; the ill health of another prevents his going about doing good; the poverty of a third incapacitates him. As with the laity so with the clergy, we have each our own plea for not doing all that we might, for labouring less than we know in our hearts it is our bounden duty to do. And a very marked rebuke to all such is the contemplation of the old saints and apostles, as we now present them. They had their own private lets and hindrances, drawbacks to their utility, impediments to their efficiency ; yet what a work was theirs ! To be the reformers and restorers of the world, the regenerators of the universe ; to bring about the overthrow of idolatry, and the recognition of the one true God. Timothy was overwhelmed with "often infirmities." And yet these were the men who changed the religion of the world! Oh, noble triumph of the spirit over matter! Oh, glorious victory of Divine grace! What excuse have we for our carelessness and remissness, our sluggishness and indolence? What hindrances have we, which they had not tenfold? Are we poor, and therefore seemingly unable to help others? St. Paul worked at tent-making. Are we delicately nurtured and weak in health? Timothy was a man of many infirmities. Are we slow of speech, and unused to address our brethren? St. Paul's utterance was indistinct. II. What we have hitherto endeavoured to set before you has been simply this, that the first disciples of Christ had to contend not only with extraordinary but ordinary difficulties. Sickness and infirmity was their portion, even as it is ours, yet they did their work ; they did not make their personal weaknesses or their poverty any excuse for spiritual idleness. The lesson is easy. If they, in the face not merely of a hostile world, but in spite of all sorts of personal drawbacks, fought so long and well the fight of faith, how utterly inexcusable are we in making our private engagements, or want of means or health, pleas for remaining idle. Yea, this is the account we have to give you of Timothy, as implied in the text. Wonderfully met in him, health and disease, strength and infirmity. Called to severe labour in the vineyard of his Lord, with the charge of an entire Church upon him, how needful we think must it have been that his frame should be strong, and his health firm. Nevertheless, when God sent him sickness, he desired not to be rid of it. (*Bp. Woodford.*)      *Wine and health :*—Dr. B. N. Richardson, of London, the noted physician, says he was recently able to convey a considerable amount of conviction to an intelligent scholar by a simple experiment. The scholar was singing the praises of the "ruddy bumper," and saying he could not get through the day without it, when Dr. Richardson said to him, "Will you be good enough to feel my pulse as I stand here?" He did so. I said, "Count it carefully. What does it say?" "Your pulse says seventy-four." I then sat down in a chair, and asked him to count it again. He did so, and said, "Your pulse has gone down to seventy." I then lay down on the lounge, and said, "Will you take it again?" He replied, "Why, it is only sixty-four! What an extraordinary thing!" I then said, "When you lie down at night, that is the way nature gives your heart rest. You know nothing about it, but that beating organ is resting to that extent ; and if you reckon it up it is a great deal of rest, because in lying down the heart is doing ten strokes less a minute. Multiply that by sixty, it is six hundred; multiply it by eight hours, ..nd within a fraction it is five thousand strokes different, and as the heart is throwing six ounces of blood at every stroke, it makes a difference of thirty thousand ounces of lifting during the night. When I lie down at night without any alcohol that is the rest my heart gets. But when you take your wine or grog you do not allow that rest, for the influence of alcohol is to increase the number of strokes, and instead of getting this rest you put on something like fifteen thousand extra strokes, and the result is that you rise up very seedy, and unfit for the next day's work till you have taken a little more of the 'ruddy bumper,' which you say is the soul of man below." (*Naval Brigade News.*) *Health a duty :*—Health underlies all there is of a man. I think a man ill-bodied cannot think healthily. It would surprise people to see how many things which have shaken the world with controversy, and burdened it with error, had their origin in indigestion. Health is a duty. If a man would carry his mind aright, and have it work with power, let him seek to be healthy. (*H. W. Beecher.*) *Christians should not encourage wine drinking :*—Some say, "You must not force your principles on other people. I am a teetotaler myself; I would not touch alcohol, but then I will put it on my table for other people." They say you must not take the liberty of people away. A man that preached the gospel told me that some time ago. He said that some men had to drink it as a medicine, and that was the reason he placed it on his table. I said to him, "Then why don't you put a dish of pills on the table as well?" We have heard enough about it as a medicine, and it will be a grand day for England when you just sweep the stuff out of the island—the whole of it right out from your tables. Dare to be singular! (*D. L. Moody.*)          *Asceticism :*—I. A CHRISTIAN IS CALLED UPON TO CARE FOR HIS PHYSICAL HEALTH. The body is not to be despised or neglected. It is the temple of the Holy Ghost, to be thought of, and dealt with, reverently. Disordered nerves and deranged functions have much to do with gloomy views of God and hopeless views of men. For the sake, therefore, of one's moral and religious life, all that can be done to keep the body and brain in healthy condition and exercise, should be done religiously. II. A CHRISTIAN IS BOUND TO CONTROL ANIMAL APPETITE. (*A. Rowland, LL.B.*)

Vers. 24, 25.—**Some men's sins are open beforehand.**—*The law of moral recompenses :*—Let us proceed to a consideration of this law of recompenses, whether in relation to the bad actions of the sinner, or to the good works of the righteous, I. And first, let us see how the text brings out the principle we have spoken of, AS APPLIED TO THE CASE OF BAD MEN,—that is of hardened and incorrigible offenders : "[Some men's sins are open beforehand, going before to judgment." 1. Of this one illustration is to be found in the consequences which, even in the present state, follow upon the commission of sin. That principle of our religious philosophy, laid down by Bishop Butler, that the general constitution of this world's government is, upon the whole, favourable to virtues and adverse to wrong-doing, is in nothing more manifest, than in the unalterable connection which subsists between sin and misery. Dissipation leads to want, sensuality to enfeebled health, dishonesty drives sleep from the eyelids through the fear of being found out, and it is often literally true that "bloody and deceitful men scarce live out half their days." Thus, to the end of their days, sinners are constantly finding out that "they who plough iniquity and sow wickedness reap the same." In the spirit of the Psalmist, though often without his hope, they are left to cry out daily, "My sin is ever before me." For their first sin haunts them with its consequences to the close of their career. They never escape from its revenges. It tracks their path like a bloodhound. In its initial forebodings the plague of retribution begins here : "Their sins are gone beforehand to judgment." 2. Again, it is a part of the penalty of the transgressor in this life, and that which sends his sins before him, as it were a herald, to get his place and portion ready, that the longer he continues in a course of evil, the more violently and inevitably is he urged in the same direction. The thought is not sufficiently realized by us, that, in moral things, like produces like ; that each separate act of transgression which a man commits leaves its own seminal deposit of evil in the soul, which, unless eradicated by a higher power than his own, must fructify and gather strength till the time of harvest, —till the end of life, or till the end of the world. The process of moral deterioration may be subtle und unobserved, like the stealthy cre ping of a pestilence, but, in the majority of cases, it is sure and uniform. The youth determines what the man shall be. And the man determines what the grey hairs shall be. It is a righteous thing with God to let the wicked be the forger of his own fetters, and to leave him with his own hands to bind them on. Such is a law of our moral nature. Thus, while a man is continuing in sin everything is preparing for the end, and hastening the advent of the end. Each repeated act of disobedience exerts an influence upon character; tends to its consolidation and settlement in evil; helps to bring about that which, as far as can be seen, will be its final and everlasting form,—that of hatred of God, and resistance to all good. Except the final consummation of their misery, they have nothing more to wait for. "Their sins are gone beforehand to judgment." 3. But further, in relation to this great law of retribution, attaching itself to sinful actions, it is added, "some men their sins follow after." The thought here suggested would seem to be this, that in estimating the penalties due to transgressions we must take into the reckoning the unquestioned fact that the consequences of some men's sins follow after them, live to produce their mighty havoc and harvest of evil when the men themselves are gone. This is a law of social influences which altereth not. A bad man cannot restrict the consequences of his misdoing to himself. For the evil follows after, even unto many generations. Jeroboam, the son of Nebat, set up two calves, and the consequence was that within a few years two nations fell into the practice of idolatry. Indeed, in its consequences, and, as far as the present economy is concerned, every kind of sin may be regarded as having immortality. Infidelity and falsehood are immortal. The exposed sophistry and the ribald jest will be propagated from mouth to mouth, and from book to book, to the end of time. Thankful should we be to know that there may be an arrest laid upon the mischief, in some cases, or that the grace of God may, and often does, raise up a counteracting influence for good. But too commonly the seed of evil is left to bring forth fruit after its kind: "With some men their sins follow after." II. But I proceed to notice, in the second place, the application of this law of recompenses to the GOOD ACTIONS OF THE RIGHTEOUS. "Likewise also the good works of some are manifest beforehand, and they that are otherwise cannot be hid." 1. First, it is said that the good works of some are manifest even in the present life. "Ye are the light of the world," said our Lord; "a city that is set on a hill cannot be hid." "Thy Father, which seeth in secret, Himself shall reward thee openly." 2. Again, his good works are manifest beforehand, because they will be sure to take the form of active benevolence, and of endeavours to promote the moral and spiritual happiness of mankind. 3. "And they that are otherwise cannot be hid." What further lesson may we draw from this? why, that no good works of a righteous man can ever be altogether thrown away; can ever fail of producing fruit; can ever, whether in this world or in that which is to come, miss of its fitting and merciful reward. We know that, of vessels chosen for the Master's use, some are for greater honour, and some for less. "Cannot be hid," first, because of the effect which a course of good works has upon a man's own character, and the lasting peace they leave behind. "The path of the just is as the shining light, which shineth more and more unto the perfect day." Faith makes larger discoveries of God, and of the fitness and fulness of the provided atonement. Hid from the world, but not from himself, is his tranquil joy in prayer, his nearness to God in sacraments, his derived strength from Christ, his interchange of thoughts with heaven, as he meditates on the written Word. Hid from the world, but not from himself, are his peace in conflict, his supports in temptation, his thankfulness after a gained victory over the powers of evil, as to God, and to God alone, he gives the praise. Furthermore, a man's good works "cannot be hid," because, in all the parts and actions of our life, there are unknown eyes upon us. We, none of us, know the extent of our own influence, how many of those who are associated with us, in the common intercourse and work of life, may be, without acknowledging it, looking up to us as patterns, or at all events are taking observant note where our practice differs from theirs. "Cannot be hid," once more: because, like the bad man's sins, good works will follow after. Of every good man it may be said, as of Abel, "He being dead yet speaketh";— speaketh by the memory of his virtues. Such is the rule of the Almighty's procedure, whether in dealing with good men or bad. It is based on principles of everlasting rectitude. It is administered after methods of gentlest kindness. It commends itself to the conscience, as answering to the conditions of a reasonable service. It is in harmony with fact, with observation, and with the experience of our own hearts. (*D. Moore, M.A.*) *The method of penalty:*—I am certainly within the spirit of the text when I say that some sins anticipate judgment; they invoke it, and receive its sentence, and experience its penalty, apparently before the time; they run their course quickly, and incur their doom in this life. There are other sins that meet with little check; they are slow to overtake their consequences; they come upon little in this life that can be called penalty. Speaking from daily observation, we may say that the retribution of some sins begins in this world; while there are other sins that await their punishment in the next world. We shall best come to an understanding of this truth by looking a little into the method of retribution. It is, as its definition implies, a return of disobedience, or payment, when, in due time, it returns again. It is the natural and inevitable consequence of broken law. If we seek for an explanation of this law, we find none, except that it is so. We perceive its fitness and beneficence, but farther back we cannot go. The law is wrought into our moral nature, and also into our consciousness; certainly, it commands early and universal assent. We notice also that the penalty is akin to the sin; it is under the seed-law—like yielding like. We receive back the things we have done, changed only as mist is changed to water, and heat to flame. And the effect often bears so absolute resemblance to the cause as to arrest the imagination, and is called poetic justice; the murderer drinking the poison he had prepared for another. In human government it is not so, but only because of its imperfection. It is an increated principle, and cannot be superinduced to any great extent. When a man steals, all that human law has yet learned to do is to imprison, or otherwise injure him, inflicting an arbitrary, deterrent suffering. Society merely defends itself. It is seldom skilful enough to establish a natural relation between the crime and the penalty. But that part of human society which is not organized into government, the social relationship of men, is more skilful to connect evil with its natural punishment. If one sins against the conventional laws, or moral instincts, of society, he meets with exclusion or disgrace according to the nature of the offence. Cause and effect; natural order; congruity between the sin and its penalty; these are the unfailing marks that the great teacher put upon the subject. What wisdom, what truth, what justice, is the voice of universal reason and conscience. It is the weakness of human government that it does not employ this principle in the punishment of crime, so far as it might. It was a doubtful policy that abolished the whipping-post and pillory. If a brutal husband whips his wife at home, he can have no better punishment than a whipping in public; or, if this be corrupting to the people, then in private. If these suggestions be thought to imply a retrograding civilization, let me answer, they harmonize with the Divine order. There is but one sound, effective method of punishing wrong-doing, and that is to make the offender feel the evil he has inflicted. As we thus look at retribution in the mingled light of revelation and reason, we are prepared to understand why it is that some sins are punished in this world, while other sins await punishment in a future world. If we were to classify the sins that reap their painful consequences here, and those that do not, we would find that the former are offences that pertain to the body, and the order of this world; and that the latter pertain more directly to the spiritual nature. The classification is not sharp; the parts shade into one another; but it is as accurate as is the distinction between the two departments of our nature. In his physical and social nature man was made under the laws of this world. If he breaks these laws the penalty is inflicted here. It may continue hereafter, for the grave feature of penalty is that it does not tend to end, but continues to act, like force imparted to an object in a vacuum, until arrested by some outside power. But man is also under spiritual laws,—reverence, humility, love, self-denial, purity, and all that are commonly known as moral duties. If he offends against these, he may incur but little of painful consequence. There may be much of evil consequence, but the phase of suffering lies farther on. The soil and atmosphere of this world are not adapted to bring it to full fruitage. Stating our distinction again: punishment in this world follows the sins of the grosser part of our nature—that part which more especially belongs to this world—sins against the order of nature, against the body; sins of self-indulgence and sins against society. The punishment that awaits the next world is of sins pertaining to the higher nature, sins against the mind, the affections, and the spirit. The seed of evil sown in the soil of this world comes to judgment here. The seed of evil sown in the hidden places of the spirit, does not bear full fruit till the spiritual world is reached. Man is co-ordinated to two worlds. They overlap far into one another; the spiritual inter-penetrates the physical; and the physical sends unceasing influences into the spiritual. Still, each is a field whereon evil reaps its appropriate harvest. Illustrations of the first confront us on every side ; judgment pronounced and executed here ; sin punished here. Take the commonest but most instructive example—drunkenness. As soon as desire becomes stronger than the will, it begins to act retributively. Having sown to the flesh, he reaps to the flesh corruption. His sin works out its penalty on its own ground. I do not say that it ends here, because it is also linked with an order more enduring than this world. For, as one standing over against a mountain may fill the whole valley with the clamour of shouting, but hears at length an echo as if from another world, so these sins, having yielded their first fruits here, may stir up vaster penalties hereafter. The terrible feature of penalty, so far as any light is thrown upon it from its own nature, is that it cannot anticipate an end. The subject finds various illustration : indolence eating the scant bread of poverty ; wilful youthhood begetting a fretful and sour old age ; selfishness leading to isolation ; ambition overreaching itself and falling into contempt ; ignorance yielding endless mistake ; worldly content turning first into apathy, then into disgust ; these every-day facts show that if we sin against the order of this world, we are punished in this world. If we sin against the body we are punished in the body. We turn now to the other point, namely, that sins against the spiritual nature do not incur full punishment here, but await it in the spiritual world. We constantly see men going through life with little pain or misfortune, perhaps with less than the ordinary share of human suffering, yet we term them sinners. They do not love nor fear God ; they have no true love for man ; they reject the law of self-denial and the duty of ministration ; they stand off from any direct relations to God, they do not pray ; their motives are selfish ; their temper is worldly ; they are devoid of what are called graces except as mere germs or chance out-growths, and make no recognition of them as forming the substance of true character. Such men break the laws of God, and of their own nature, as really as does the drunkard, but they meet with little apparent punishment. There may be inward discomfort, pangs of conscience at times, a painful sense of wrong-ness, a dim sense of lack, but nothing that bears the stamp of penalty. These discomforts grow less, and at last leave the man quite at ease. These men seem to be sinning without punishment, and often infer that they do not deserve it. The reason of the difference is plain. They keep the laws that pertain to this world, and so do not come in the way of their penalties. They are temperate, and are blessed with health. They are shrewd and economical, and amass wealth. They are prudent and avoid calamities. They are worldly wise, and thus secure worldly advantages. But man covers two worlds, and he must settle with each before his destiny is decided : he may pass the judgment seat of one acquitted, but stand convicted before the other. It is as truly a law of our nature that we shall worship as that we shall eat. When, a half century ago, the famous Kaspar Hauser appeared in the streets of Nuremberg, having been released from a dungeon in which he had been confined from infancy, having never seen the face or heard the voice of man, nor gone without the walls of his prison, nor seen the full light of day, a distinguished lawyer in Germany wrote a legal history of the case which he entitled, " A Crime against the Life of the Soul." It was well named. There is something unspeakably horrible in that mysterious page of history. To exclude a child not only from the light, but from its kind ; to seal up the avenues of knowledge that are open to the most degraded savage ; to force back upon itself every outgoing of the nature till the poor victim becomes a mockery before its Creator, is an unmeasurable crime ; it is an attempt to undo God's work. But it is no worse than the treatment some men bestow upon their own souls. If reverence is repressed, and the eternal heavens are walled out from view ; if the sense of immortality is smothered ; if the spirit is not taught to clothe itself in spiritual garments, and to walk in spiritual ways : such conduct can hardly be classed except as a crime against the life of the soul. But one thing is certain. As the poor German youth was at length thrust out into the world for which he was so unfitted, with untrained senses in a world of sense, without speech in a world of language, with a dormant mind in a world of thought—so many go out of this world—with no preparation in that part of their nature that will most be called into use. There the soul will be in its own realm ; it will live unto itself, a spirit unto spiritual things. A spiritual air to breathe ; spiritual works to do ; a spiritual life to live, but the spirit impotent ! If there has been absolute perversion of the moral nature here, it must assert itself there in the sharpest forms, but the natural penalty of the greater part of human sin is darkness. This is the condemnation, that men have loved darkness. And the penalty of loving darkness, is darkness : a soul out of keeping with its condition, and therefore bewildered, dazzled by light it cannot endure, or blind from the disused sense, it matters not which ; it is equally in darkness. (*T. T. Munger.*)　　*Open and hidden sins :*—I. We are, first, to consider WHO THOSE PERSONS ARE WHOSE " SINS ARE OPEN BEFOREHAND, GOING BEFORE TO JUDGMENT." And, in making this inquiry, we must still keep in mind that all sin is condemning. The world makes strange distinctions between what it calls great and little sins ; but the word of God simply declares " the soul that sinneth, it shall die " (Ezek. xviii. 4). " The wages of sin," of all sin, " is death " (Rom. vi. 23). But though all sin is condemning, all sin is not equally open. Many sins which nevertheless subject the soul to eternal death, are kept hidden from man, while some are open and avowed. The unchanged nature may be restrained from exhibiting to the eye of man "sins open beforehand, going before to judgment "; but the evil prin- ciple of all sin is there, open to the eye of that God with whom we have to do. Causes there are which work upon the unchanged mind, from letting sin break out in the life ; though the real love of sin exists fully in the heart. Such a restraint is natural conscience ; such, the laws and expectations of civilized, much more of refined society. But where these restraints are broken through, then the whole body of sin and evil principles which were working in the inward soul before, now become manifest in all ungodliness. They have no fear of God before their eyes ; their hearts are hardened, through the deceitfulness of sin : they set the law of God always, and the law of man when they dare do so, at defiance ; and so spend their short day upon earth in " sins open beforehand, going before to judgment." II. Let us inquire, in the second place, WHO THOSE ARE WHOSE SINS " FOLLOW AFTER." In the judgment which is formed of sin by men of the world, their minds are manifestly under a great delusion from the father of lies. They do not judge of sin as " the transgression of the law of God," and therefore hateful in his sight ; but they measure it according to the effects which it produces against the safety or conveniences of society. They cannot see that all sin, whether it be " open beforehand," or whether it " follow after to judgment," is destructive to the soul, and dishonourable to almighty God ; and, consequently, that every child of Adam who dies in any unforgiven sin, is lost. But besides this kind of delusion, which comforts many in their unholy life, and so far prevents their sin from breaking out into open wickedness, there is another cause why sin is oftentimes kept from becoming " open beforehand." Moral virtue, and a certain external character of religion, have still a share of the world's permission, nay, in a measure, of the world's approbation ; provided that they do not make acknow- ledged reference to the power and obligations of the gospel of Jesus Christ. But all this only serves to make sin take deeper root. It is growing, though concealed from the world, in a soil congenial to it, and will increase unto all ungodliness. If, therefore, we retain sin in our heart by living in ignorance of the real state of our soul, while we succeed in establishing an outward character with men, we are passing through life deceiving and being deceived. Think, oh think, of the dreadful exposure in that day of all your secret bosom sins, hidden and unrepented of here, but then made manifest, to your "shame and everlasting contempt." III. It now remains that we consider the CASE OF THOSE WHO HAVE NEITHER SINS GOING BEFORE THEM TO JUDGMENT, NOR SINS FOLLOWING AFTER. And who are these ? where shall we find them ? Not among those who have never sinned : " For all have sinned, and come short of the glory of God " (Rom. iii. 23). Not among those who sin not now : " For their is not a just man on earth, that doeth good, and sinneth not," (Eccles. vii. 20). They will be found standing in their own peculiar lot : " washed, sanctified, justified in the name of the Lord Jesus, and by the Spirit of our God " (1 Cor. vi. 11) ; and none who are such have sins either going before to judgment, or following after. Think upon your privileges in your acceptance in the Beloved. " Ye are washed " from the guilt of past sins, because it is written, " the blood of Jesus Christ cleanseth us from all sin " (1 John, i. 7). It is the " fountain opened for sin and for uncleanness " (Zech. xiii. 1). (*H. Marriot, M.A.*)　　*The open and secret sinner :*—This is the condition of all open and notorious sinners. They are sold as slaves to sin ; everybody sees and knows them to be such ; they know it themselves, and are bitterly conscious of their bondage, however they may affect to think lightly of it, or even glory in it ; as there are those whose glory is in their shame, and who boast of being free from the restraints of religion, honour, and public decency. Who ever offended the general conscience of society by a great and public sin, and did not feel himself to be speedily judged, condemned, and degraded? and that not only in other men's judgment, which he would fain set aside or over-rule if he could, as partial, unreasonable, and unjust, but in the judgment of his own heart, which, in spite of himself, affirms and concurs in that of the world. For though the world itself is full of sin, yet, bad as it is, it does, in an imperfect and irregular way, respect virtue and rebuke vice. And hereby the judgment of the world becomes a token and intimation of God's judgment, and God makes the conscience and opinion even of wicked men testify against the wickedness of others, though perhaps less wicked than themselves. All open sin goes before to judgment. But how stands the case with regard to secret sins? There is in these, we may suppose, no manifest offence against the decencies and proprieties of society: the world knows nothing of the sin, character is not lost, the sinner's life may be in other respects unimpeachable. Cannot his sin be covered up? It is a vain hope; the covered sin corrupts the whole life. If open sin is like an overmastering fire, that blazes out at every window and flames up through the roof of the devoted house, secret sin is as the smouldering heat, that preys upon the main timbers, unobserved for a time, but stealthily eating its way from one to another, till at last the crash comes, and the building crumbles into dust and ashes. What calamity is so frightful and appalling as the sudden downfall of a man, long looked upon as of pure and honourable life, but found out at last to have been hiding wickedness under an outward show of virtue? And yet sad as this is, it is not so sad as if the cherished sin had passed undiscovered and unrepented of, till the sinner stood to answer for it before the great judgment-seat. I said that covered sin corrupts the whole life. And is it not so? Of course the secret sinner is ashamed of his sin; at least he is ashamed of it in reference to the effect it would produce against him, if it were known, in the minds of some people for whose opinion he cares. Then he must live in a constant disguise of false appearance. His daily life must be a lie, and he must be under a continual necessity of committing fresh sins to hide former ones. But besides the outward and visible consequence, what I may call the material penalty of sin, whether open or secret, there is an inward one of even greater severity; namely, the alienation of the mind from God, and consequent derangement of all the spiritual faculties and operations of the soul. Can a man who is consciously and designedly dishonest, or an extortioner, or a drunkard, or an adulterer, hold unreserved and refreshing communion with his Maker, who is of purer eyes than to behold iniquity? It is an old and most true remark, that nobody can go on both sinning and praying; for either praying will make him leave off sinning, or sinning will make him leave off praying. A wilful sinner might keep up the outward form, and be even all the worse for doing so, but he could not exercise the spirit of prayer. For though a person who is notoriously wicked in some particulars may, from mere worldly prudence, and a just appreciation of his own interest, be upright in others, this does not cleanse the blot of his character either to the world or to himself. The thief is not honoured by people of any discernment because he may happen to be sober, nor the adulterer because he may happen to be industrious. And much less can he, upon any reasonable estimate of his own spiritual state, appease his conscience, entertain a comfortable hope that he is in God's favour, or make it the serious business of his life to advance God's glory. He is, by his works, a manifest enemy to the kingdom of grace. And how stands, in this particular, the case of the secret sinner? We suppose his sin not to be known to the world; his example, therefore, creates no scandal, shocks nobody's feelings; it may not even be blemished by any apparent inconsistency; but the hidden sin defiles the sinner's conscience, and bars his approach to God, just as much as open wickedness does. And this is the way in which it operates. The man feels that there is a part of his habitual life that he cannot freely disclose and acknowledge to God; a condemning secret, which he would fain withdraw, if he could, even from the judgment of his own heart. The consequence is that the form of religion, which we are supposing the secret sinner to keep up, is but a deception, a hollow mask to hide the practical infidelity of his character. It is plain that the wilful sinner can have no comfort in the knowledge of God, or in approaching Him in prayer. He has chosen to set himself in opposition to God, and to be holden for an enemy by Him. It may be suggested that the law which forbids the darling sin is not God's law, the revelation which is supposed to declare it is misstated or misrepresented, or perhaps is no real revelation at all. Nobody wonders that the man who is profligate is also irreligious; and nobody thinks of taking his opinion or his practice into account in any matter in which religion is concerned. But the secret sinner may unsettle the faith of many souls besides his own. The secret sinner, again, will have to recollect, and, so far as he may, to repair any damage that he may have done to the cause of religion by the looseness of his conversation while he was supposed to be, though he really was not, a trustworthy companion for people of sincere and unpolluted minds. But whatever may be the proper outward manifestations of penitence for either open or secret sin, the work itself must be begun and wrought out within the sinner's heart. This season of Lent has been specially appointed by the Church for the work of self-examination and penitence: not but what we ought to be daily humbling ourselves for those faults which we daily commit, but because through our natural slowness and coldness to spiritual things we are apt to fall into a negligent way of performing these daily duties, and so require to be ever and anon awakened and warned to set ourselves more heartily to our painful task. Let us not, then, be withheld by false shame from owning to God and to ourselves, and, if it must be so, to man also, the heinousness of those sins which we may have openly and knowingly committed; nor let us attempt to take refuge in that ignorance of our own acts and of their quality, which, in whatever degree it is wilful, is in that degree an aggravation of sin, not an excuse for what is done amiss; but let us gladly accept the light which the Word and Providence of God afford to us, that we may come to know ourselves as we are known by Him. It may be a painful, but it will be a saving knowledge. (*Bp. S. Wilberforce.*)        *The sins that follow :*—I. Now there is no difficulty in fixing on the characters described under the former clause, "Some men's sins are open, going before unto judgment." From the day of Pentecost until now, the Church has had to contend with a body of men who have set themselves in direct and open hostility to holiness and God; who have mocked at His counsel and would none of His reproof. Their sins have been open; all the world has acknowledged their guilt, and anticipated their condemnation. Their offences go before them invoking God's judgment. Who are they, we will rather ask, described in the second clause of the text, whose wickednesses are not visible at the moment? In reply, we would remind you of the familiar division of all sin into ignorant and presumptuous. Indeed, indeed, it is quite possible for a man to be persuaded that he stands upright, when in God's sight he is grovelling in the dust. We will take the case of a man who rejects from his creed one of the articles of the Christian faith. These persons live on contented with their own condition; they are not sensible of any evil from the course they pursue. Now this licensed unbelief in which people, good and amiable in the main, indulge themselves upon particular points—this free thinking upon a few of the minor dogmas of the Church, which seemingly issue in nothing, leads to no harmful result, is just of the nature of those sins which follow after. The secret scepticism, Oh! it does not go before a man, calling down upon his head general reproach; it is not as the crime of dishonesty, or avariciousness, or cruelty, or impurity, which lift up their voices and imprecate judgment; but it hangs about an individual almost without his own knowledge. Noiselessly and stealthily it dogs his steps, never perhaps to be thoroughly developed in all its offensiveness, till the disembodied soul stands shivering in the eternal world. And they are not sins of faith alone which come under the category of the text. How many are they who permit themselves in some habitual breach of God's law, without ever realizing the fact that they are really guilty of actual sin. How many a tradesman suffers himself to take advantage of the ignorance of those with whom he deals, enlarging his profits by means not thoroughly justifiable, but which custom has sanctioned, and which, therefore, he never dreams of regarding as moral offences. So again a society, in its corporate capacity, will not hesitate to act in a manner in which its members would shrink from acting in their private capacity, as though the individual responsibility which God had stamped upon every unit of our species could be got rid of by associating together with our brethren. And what we have said with regard to things done or left undone, which men know not, and feel not, to be wrong, applies in its degree also to a variety of practices which people do know to be evil, but which yet appear too insignificant to be a cause of uneasiness. And this class of transgressions is one into which an age like the present is especially liable to fall. Men in a simple and uncivilized era are subject to gross vices, men of a refined and cultivated epoch sin small sins. Crimes of exceeding magnitude, as well as heroic virtue, belong to a nation in its infancy. Bloodshed, cruelty, incest, rapine, are the faults of a barbarous empire. Selfishness, coldness, covetousness, vanity, are the transgressions of modern times. II. We have hitherto considered the text as indicative of two descriptions of sin. The sins that follow after are the sins which men know not, or which they pass by as of little moment. But the words imply, we believe, more than that the sins in question are secret, or insignificant; they further indicate, that we have already indirectly insinuated, that although little recked of, they do in fact pursue a man to his hurt, and even to his condemnation. What is this? It is that these unknown or unregarded transgressions are not really without effect both here and hereafter. They may bear no fruit at the moment, but their fruit is not wanting. Again and again have we heard of individuals who, after a protracted career of uprightness and integrity, have been convicted of some fraud, and overwhelmed with sudden disgrace. The world marvels that one who stood so long should at last fall, that one so regular and steady and sober, and even religious should prove so false to his principles. But could we look deeper, and see as God sees, we should, perhaps, trace the final catastrophe to some single neglect, like that of abstaining from the Lord's Supper, which the mass never noticed, and if they had, would not have blamed; yea, which the unhappy one himself hardly knew. Yea, and we had almost said that it were well the result of the unknown sin should thus show itself now, even though its revelation be in the midst of dishonour and remorse. Better that the secret disease should be disclosed anyhow, whilst there is a possibility of cure, than that it should lie hid until the end. Death hath a strange power to banish delusions, and unravel self-deceit. When shaking itself free from the coil of flesh, the spirit often shakes off the former dulness of its mental sight, and begins to see things as they are. Then actions which once seemed right appear wrong, and practices once excused are perceived to be indefensible, and omissions which were thought pardonable look foul and terrible when the doors of eternity are unfolding. It is a very strong argument which we derive from the foregoing reasoning, for neglecting no means of grace, for undervaluing no transgression. The effects of such neglect are not wholly removed even by repentance. (*Bp. Woodford.*) *The seeming record of life, not always the actual one :*—The *Paper World* informs its readers that in using postal cards they may write so that only the initiated can read the message, and write a misleading message which will disappear. The true message, it says, should be written with a gold or quill pen dipped, not in ink, but in a mixture of one part sulphuric acid and seven parts water. When dry the card bears no trace of writing, but, as a blank card might excite suspicion, it may be covered with writing in tincture of iodine. When heat is applied to the card, the writing in iodine disappears, and the writing in diluted sulphuric acid becomes legible. There is reason to fear that the same process is going on in the record of some people's lives. In the day when all secrets are revealed and every one appears in the naked light of the great white throne, the records on the tombstones will disappear, and in their place will stand the hidden, true record of the actual life. *Fraudulent professors :*—A curious discovery of a diamond fraud has been made by a photographer in Boston, U.S. A diamond expert was offered a very large stone for £1,600. He applied to it all the tests used in the trade, and was satisfied that it was genuine. After he had purchased it, some circumstances occurred which led him to suspect that he had been cheated, notwithstanding the apparent genuineness of the diamond. He took the stone to a photographer, and asked him to send a ray of sunlight through it with his camera. Then it was discovered that there was an obstruction in the stone. A ray which passed through other diamonds clear and straight was stopped in the suspected stone. A powerful microscope was used upon it, and it was discovered that the obstruction was some cement which joined two small stones together, the two forming the magnificent gem the merchant had bought. The two stones were separated by chemicals, and were worth about £120 each. There are people who succeed in passing the tests of ministers and Churches who, when the light of God's throne falls upon them in the day of judgment, will be found fraudulent professors. (*Christian Herald.*) *Sin and judgment :*— Recent discoveries have revealed the carcases of prehistoric animals thrown out at the foot of a Siberian glacier. These animals were preserved unchanged, unseen, and unknown, for untold centuries, beneath the frozen mud and the solid ice of the never-hasting, never-resting, ever-moving glacier. And when, at last, these long-preserved carcases came out to the light and warmth and sun, they sent forth their horrid stench. Thus sin may be buried under the mud of materialism, and be frozen in indifference, and hidden in oblivion for years and centuries and cycles, but the on-moving glacier of time will at last reveal them to the light and glory of the judgment day, and then will they stink in the nostrils of God, and of angels, and of all the assembled multitudes. (*R. S. Barrett.*) **The good works of some.**—

*Good works which cannot be hid :*—I. Now it is clear THAT A WORK CANNOT DERIVE ITS
GOODNESS FROM ITS RELATION TO MAN. Water cannot derive its sweetness from a bitter
fountain. The limpid brook does not obtain its transparency from the muddy bed
over which it flows. A good work, we say, must derive all its goodness from God;
and, first of all, He must be its author; His Spirit must teach it; He must be its
originator. In other words, a man must be taught of God before he can do aught
which is pleasing in God's sight. But, again, in order to make a deed good, God
must be the doer as well as the author of it. We must be led by the Spirit, as well
as taught of the Spirit; God must work in us to do as well as to will. Not that our
own work is in any degree superseded—not that our diligence is rendered unnecessary—but we are fellow-workers with God. And yet the excellence of the work
is not derived from our share in the work, but from God's. And then for a work to
be good God must be the aim of that work. "Do all to the glory of God"—that is
our duty. "I have created him for My glory"—that is the Divine purpose. II.
Our text declares of such good works as we have described, THAT IT IS IMPOSSIBLE TO
HIDE THEM. "The good works of some are manifest beforehand, and they which
are otherwise"—that is, they which are not manifest beforehand—"cannot be hid."
It is therefore a mere question of time, and not of fact; all good works shall be
manifest, the only difference being that some are revealed beforehand in this life
whilst others are reserved till the life to come. But what is meant by this manifestation of works? Clearly not the display of a mere action whether of body or
mind. It would be no sort of consolation to the teacher, or visitor, or alms-giver if
you were to tell him that his lessons, or calls, or alms will all be published. That
might be a motive for the ostentatious and purse-proud pharisee, but it is no boon
to the self-denying and humble child of God. What then? Why, it follows that
our text declares, not that the bare works, but that the goodness of these works shall
be made manifest. And what is this goodness which shall be revealed? Precisely
that which attaches to the work as good in the sight of God, and which we have
already described. The origin and motive of the work will be manifested. Men
may misinterpret you now; they may call you a mad religious schemer; they may
say that the cross you have taken up is assumed to disguise some dishonesty of
heart; they may accuse you of a thousand motives rather than the true one; but
what matters it? It shall not always be thus. And then He will make manifest
the work's goodness of execution. He will demonstrate that it was "not by might
nor by power, but by the Spirit of the Lord of hosts." Men thought, and sometimes
even you thought, that the good work was done in a wrong way. And, finally, He
will make manifest the work's goodness of aim. But how will He reveal this fact?
Will He simply declare that His honour was your object, but unfortunately it failed?
No such thing. In every case He will reveal the full accomplishment of the end
whereto He sent the work; in every case He will display before you the most perfect success; in every case He will make manifest goodness consummated, a purpose
attained, and glory achieved. In His own way He will show it; but show it He
will; there will be no doubt about the fact; the end of the work will be proved good.
Sometimes God makes this aim manifest beforehand; He shows us even now that
His work is prospering in our hands; He proves to us that His glory is not only our
intention, but even the actual and present result of our labours. (*D. F. Jarman,
M.A.*) *Penetration of character :*—Years ago in Chicago crowded gatherings were
being held in the largest hall in the city, and Mr. Moody was "in command."
Suddenly his shrewd, quick eye fell on one of the ushers; he looked at him for a
minute, and then signalled to him to come to the vestry below. When they met
there Mr. Moody said: "Where do you come from—Does the senior usher know
you?" "No, sir." "What do you come here for?" "I wanted to be seen."
"Ah," said Mr. Moody, "you just drop that usher's rod and take a back seat, now
be smart." Mr. Moody had never seen the man before, but his wonderfully keen
penetration of character had detected something wrong in him. That man's name
was Guiteau, and within four years he murdered the noble Garfield, the President
of the United States. *Manifest beforehand :*—When the Sidonians were once going
to choose a king, they determined that their election should fall upon the man who
should first see the sun on the following morning. All the candidates, towards the
hour of sun-rise, eagerly looked towards the East, but one, who, to the astonishment
of his countrymen, fixed his eyes pertinaciously on the opposite side of the horizon,
where he saw the reflection of the sun's orb before the orb itself was seen by those
looking towards the east. The choice instantly fell upon him who had seen the
reflection of the sun; and by the same reasoning, the influence of religion on the

heart is frequently perceptible in the conduct, even before a person has made direct profession of the principle by which he is actuated. (*Saturday Magazine.*)

---

## CHAPTER VI.

**VERS. 1, 2. Servants as are under the yoke.**—*Under the yoke :*—The phrase "under the yoke" fitly expresses the pitiable condition of slaves, to whom Paul here addresses himself. Of all the hideous iniquities which have cried to heaven for redress, slavery, which places a man in such a position to his fellow, is one of the worst. It is as pernicious to the owner as it is to the slave. Dr. Thomson has well said, "It darkens and depraves the intellect; it paralyzes the hand of industry; it is the nourisher of agonizing fears and of sullen revenge; it crushes the spirit of the bold; it is the tempter, the murderer, and the tomb of virtue; and either blasts the felicity of those over whom it domineers, or forces them to seek for relief from their sorrows in the gratifications and the mirth and the madness of the passing hour." In the days of our Lord and of His apostles, slavery was a time-honoured and widely ramified institution. It was recognized in the laws as well as in the usages of the empire. So numerous were those "under the yoke," that Gibbon, taking the empire as a whole, considers it a moderate computation to set down the number of slaves as equal to the number of freemen. In Palestine the proportion would probably be less, but in Rome and other great cities the proportion would be far greater. Christianity, with its proclamation of equality and brotherhood, came face to face with this gigantic system of legalized property in human flesh, and we want to know how the gospel dealt with it. I. LET US FIRST SEE WHAT CHRISTIANITY DID NOT DO FOR THE SLAVES. That the followers of Him who cared most for the poor and needy, and who longed to break every yoke, pitied these slaves in their abject and humiliating condition, goes without saying. But they certainly did not urge the slaves to escape, or to rebel, nor did they make it an absolute necessity to church membership that a slave-owner should set all his slaves free. We may be quite sure that such a man as Paul would not be insensible to the evils of slavery, and further, that it was not from any deficiency in moral courage that he did not urge manumission; but told some slaves to remain in the condition in which they were, and, by God's help, to triumph over the difficulties and sorrows peculiar to their lot. Strange as this may seem at first sight, was it not wise? Did it not prove in the long-run by far the best thing for the slaves themselves, leading to a more complete extirpation of slavery than if more drastic methods had been tried at first? II. LET US SEE, THEN, WHAT CHRISTIANITY DID FOR THE SLAVES. 1. It taught masters their responsibilities. 2. It inculcated on the slaves a course of conduct which would often lead to their legal freedom. Under Roman law, liberty was held out as an encouragement to slaves to be honest, industrious, sober, and loyal; and, therefore, any Christian slave who obeyed the laws of Christ would be on the high road to emancipation. Liberty thus won by character was a better thing than liberty won by force or by fraud, and was more accordant with the genius of Christianity. 3. It gave dignity to those who had been despised and who had despised themselves. The work, which had once been a drudgery, became a sacred service; and this your toil and mine may surely be. 4. But, besides all this, Christianity laid down principles which necessitated the ultimate destruction of slavery. It taught that all men had a common origin; that God had made of one blood all nations; and that men of every class were to join together in the wonderful prayer, "Our Father which art in heaven." Learn, then, to trust to principles rather than to organization. Let life be more to you than law, and change of life more than change of law. Care for character first, believing that circumstance will care for itself. And, finally, in conflict with evils deep and wide-spread as ancient slavery, be patient, and have unwavering faith in the God of righteousness and love. (*A. Rowland, LL.B.*) *The slave winning his master for Christ :*—Many a heathen master was rebuked amid his career of profligacy by the saintly lives of Christian slaves, who had given themselves up to the Lord of purity; and probably the hearts of many were touched through the prayers of those they had despised. We have read of a negress in the Southern States who was caught praying by her master, and cruelly beaten for her pains. Stripped and tied fast to the post, as the blood-stained whip ceased for a moment to fall on the quivering flesh, she was asked if she would give over praying. "No, massa, never!" was the answer; "I will serve you, but I must serve God." Again the lashes rained down on her bleeding back; but when once more they ceased, the voice of the follower of Jesus was heard praying, "O Lord, forgive poor massa, and bless him." Suddenly the whip fell from his hand; stricken with the finger of God, he broke down in penitence. Then and there the prayer was answered—the godless master was saved through the faithfulness of the slave he had despised. (*Ibid.*)　　　*The power of custom to conceal sin:*—But we must not overlook the insidious and powerful influence of custom, which makes a sin so familiar that we do not trouble to investigate it. We deal with it as a sentinel does with one he has allowed to pass without challenge—he thinks it all right, and lets him pass again and again, until at last he is horrified to find he has been giving admission to a foe. John Newton, for example, after his conversion (which was as genuine as it was remarkable), carried on for years the inhuman traffic of slavery, and felt his conscience at rest so long as he did what he could for the bodily comfort of the slaves. He was quite insensible to the sinfulness of slavery until it pleased God to open his eyes, which had been blinded by custom. And, at the close of last century, an American gentleman left a plantation well stocked with slaves to the Society for the Propagation of the Gospel, and was evidently unconscious of any inconsistency. It is not to be wondered at that, in the early days of Christianity, disciples of Jesus were similarly deceived. Instead of condemning them, let us ask ourselves whether custom is not blinding us to other sins. (*Ibid.*)　　　**That the name of God and His doctrine be not blasphemed.**—*The imperfections of Christians exaggerated by the enemies of Christianity:*—It is objected to Christianity, which in my text may be considered as meant by "the name and doctrine of God," that many of those who profess to be regulated by its spirit and laws, instead of being better, are often much worse than other men; that, pretending to adhere to it as a system of truth and righteousness, they yet frequently neglect or violate the duties of those relations and conditions in which they are placed; that servants, for example, as here particularly alluded to by the apostle, bearing the name of Jesus, do, notwithstanding, act unfaithfully and disobediently; that the same remark is applicable to individuals of every other class and station in civil society; and that even some of the ministers of the gospel, who have studied it most, and should know it best, are themselves grievously addicted to the follies and vices of the world. 1. In the first place, then, the persons by whom the objection is adduced, seem, in many cases, to be influenced by a determination to censure, with or without reason, the conduct of Christ's professed followers. Whatever aspect we put on, and whatever deportment we maintain, they must discover, or imagine, something which they may use as a pretext for personal reproach, and which they may ultimately level against the doctrine or principles that we hold. If we are grave, they accuse us of being morose and gloomy. If we are cheerful, then we are light and joyous spirits, having as little seriousness and as much wantonness as themselves. 2. We remark, in the second place, that the fact which gives rise to the objection we are considering is not unfrequently exaggerated by the fault of an individual being transferred and imputed to the whole class to which he belongs. The ultimate aim is to bring Christianity into disrepute—to "blaspheme the name and the doctrine of God"; and in order to accomplish what is thus intended, the aberrations of every individual Christian are spoken of as descriptive of all who have embraced the religion of Jesus, and as a sort of universal and necessary accompaniment to the faith and character of His disciples. 3. It may be observed, in the third place, that the fact of which we are speaking is often exaggerated, by considering one part of the Christian's conduct as a test of his whole character. The splendour of their virtues is obscured by an individual spot, which malice or misconception has magnified far beyond its real size. And their character is appreciated, not by the tone of their principles, in connection with the habitual tenor of their conduct, but by a single vicious action, of which their mind is utterly abhorrent, which they bewail with unfeigned sorrow, and which a candid eye would trace to those imperfections of the heart, and those infelicities of condition, which adhere to humanity in its best estate. The unmanly equivocation of Abraham, the aggravated crime of David, and the unhappy strife between Paul and Barnabas, are held out as the characteristic features of these eminent persons; that faith, and piety, and humility, and zeal for the glory of God and the best interests of mankind, by which they were severally distinguished, go for nothing in the estimate that is formed. 4. In the fourth place, the fact by which unbelievers are furnished with the objection we refer to, is frequently amplified by a too rigid comparison of the Christian's conduct with the religion in which he professes to believe. Now, it would be fair enough to judge us by the standard to which we appeal, if they would take care at the same time to apply it under the direction of those rules, which the very nature and circumstances of the case require to be observed in such an important trial. They forget that the morality of the gospel must be perfect, because it is prescribed by a perfect Being, and that, had it been otherwise, they would very soon have discovered it to be unworthy of its alleged author. They forget that moral imperfection is an attribute of our fallen nature, and must therefore mingle in all our attempts to comply with the Divine will, and to imitate the Divine character. Conclusion: 1. And, in the first place, let it not be thought that we mean to plead for any undue or unlawful indulgence to the disciples of Jesus. 2. In the second place, let Christians beware of encouraging unbelieving and ungodly men in this mode of misjudging and misrepresenting character. 3. Lastly, let us scrupulously abstain in our own conduct from everything of which advantage may be taken, for that unhallowed purpose. (*A. Thomson, D.D.*) *The imperfections of Christians no argument against Christianity :*—Men may reject what is true, and disobey legal authority; that is what they do every day. But such rejection and disobedience neither alter the nature of that truth, nor destroy the legitimacy of that authority. In the same way the Christian religion, being established on grounds which have the sanction of God to support them, cannot be deprived of its claims to our submissive regard, because those who profess to believe in it do not act uniformly as it requires. "Let God be true, and every man a liar." The objection must suppose that the wickedness of professing Christians arises either from Christianity being directly immoral in its influence, or from its being deficient in power to make its votaries holy. Now, that its influence is far from being directly immoral will be granted, without hesitation, by every one who is at all acquainted with its spirit and its principles. It has a character so completely opposite to this, that it is commonly accused by its enemies of being severely and unnecessarily strict, inasmuch as it requires us to conform ourselves to a perfect law, and to imitate a perfect example. The objection, therefore, must owe its force to the other alternative that was stated. It must suppose that Christianity is deficient in power, or not properly calculated to make its votaries holy. Wherein, then, does its alleged deficiency consist? In what respect is it naturally inefficacious for making men virtuous and good? Is it defective in the plainness and energy of its precepts? Nothing can be plainer, or more forcible, than the manner in which it proposes its rules for the regulation of our conduct. Again, is Christianity defective in the extent of its morality? Its morality could not be more extensive than it actually is. There is no vice which it does not prohibit; there is no virtue which it does not enjoin. Is it defective in the principles on which its morality is founded? That might be affirmed, if it inculcated the principle of fictitious honour, which this moment stimulates to noble deeds, and the next gives its countenance to boundless dissipation and bloody revenge, or the principle of sentimental feeling. But the principles of Christian morality are of a quite different and infinitely more perfect kind, and fitted, by their natural and unfettered operation, to form a character of unblemished and superlative worth. Profound regard for the authority of Him who made us, whose subjects we now are, to whom we are finally accountable, and who possesses the most sacred and unquestionable title to our unreserved homage; firm and lively faith in the existence and perfections of God; supreme love and ardent gratitude to that Being who is infinitely amiable in Himself, and whose unbounded mercy in Christ Jesus has laid us under obligations to obedience the most cheerful and devoted; a heartfelt reliance upon that sacrifice of Himself by which the Son of God redeemed sinners from the guilt and the dominion of sin, and, by the influences of His Holy Spirit, extends as far as the habitations of men are found, elevates us above the sordid wish of living to ourselves, and consists in so loving each other as Christ has loved us. Is Christianity defective, then, in the sanctions with which its laws are enforced? These sanctions are fitted to awe the stoutest, and to animate the coldest heart. Is it defective in the encouragements which it gives to virtuous exertions? What encouragements greater than these: an assurance that "the eye of God is ever upon the righteous, and His ear open to their cry." Is it defective, I ask, in the last place, in the external means which it prescribes for promoting the spiritual improvement of the Christian? Here, also, it is wholly unexceptional. It puts into his hands a volume, which is " given by inspiration, and is profitable for doctrine, for reproof, for correction and instruction in righteousness, that as a man of God he may be perfect, thoroughly furnished unto all good works." It consecrates one day in seven to rest from ordinary labour, to give him a special opportunity of examining his heart, and of providing an additional store of knowledge and wisdom for his guidance in future. In all the views now taken of the moral influence of the gospel, it evidently appears that no defect whatever can be ascribed to it in that particular. On the contrary, it seems perfectly calculated, by the qualities we have found it to possess, to purify, in an extraordinary measure, the heart and the character of its adherents. (*Ibid.*) *The imperfections of Christians no argument against Christianity :*—The argument is not complete till we have considered the effects which Christianity has produced on the moral character of its adherents. 1. Let it be considered what a multitude of excellent characters have been formed by the influence of the gospel. From its first establishment down to the present day, every successive age has had a number of individuals and of families by whom its sanctifying power has been deeply felt and practically exhibited. On looking into the history of its progress and effects, we observe that it no sooner obtained a footing, than it began to change the moral aspect of society, wherever, at least, the profession of it prevailed. 2. But the holy tendency of the gospel is obvious, not only from its powerful effect on those who have truly believed its Divine origin, and given a candid reception to its doctrines ; the same thing may be seen in the improved moral condition of those also who have either given a mere speculative assent to it, or who are acquainted only with its tenets and precepts, or who live merely in countries where it is professed. The history of the gospel furnishes us with a detail of interesting and incontrovertible facts, which demonstrate that Christianity has neither been useless nor detrimental as a moral system : that it has maintained an influence peculiar to itself over the sentiments and manners of mankind ; and that this influence has been at once powerful, important, and extensive. 3. It is not enough, however, to state that there are many who show in their conduct the holy tendency and sanctifying power of Christianity ; that there are, and have been, multitudes of Christians who have adorned their religion by the exercise of every virtue ; it is proper to state, in addition to this, the contrast which their present conduct exhibits to their former conduct, and also to the deportment of others who have rejected the gospel, or who have never heard of its existence. It is right also to compare the moral character of the Christian with that of others who have not known or adopted the same religious faith. 4. It was formerly stated that the fact upon which the objection we are considering is founded, is frequently exaggerated by the fault of one Christian being transferred or imputed to the whole Church. But I have now to observe that the fact is also most unfairly and injuriously misapplied in another way. Our adversaries make no distinction between real and merely nominal Christians. 5. That the gospel has not been more generally efficacious in reforming mankind and in perfecting the character of its votaries, is to be accounted for in various ways. Without entering into any detail, however, I may merely mention one general principle which appears to solve the whole difficulty. The gospel is not a system of compulsion. (*Ibid.*) *The duty of Christians in reference to the objection founded upon their imperfections :* —We are called upon, by every motive of gratitude to the Saviour, of regard to the Divine honour, and of compassion to the souls of men, who must be saved by Christianity, or not be saved at all, to abstain from all those actions and indulgences by which "the name or the doctrine of God may be blasphemed." This is the exhortation of the apostle, which we shall now endeavour to illustrate, by pointing out the way in which it is to be complied with, so as most effectually to answer the end for which it is given. 1. And, in the first place, we exhort you never to forget that the gospel is a practical system. When you turn your mind to any one of its doctrinal truths, you will consider that it is not only to be believed, but that it is to make you free, in some respect or other, from the dominion of iniquity. When you meet with any precept, you will recollect that it is not merely a proof of the perfection of that morality which revelation inculcates, but a rule for your deportment in that branch of holiness to which it refers. When you cast your eye upon the delineation of a character, you will view it as not only held out to attract or to interest you, but as set before you to warn you against certain offences or to recommend the practice of certain virtues. 2. In the second place, with the same view we exhort you to a faithful and conscientious discharge of the duties which belong to the several relations in which you stand, and the various circumstances in which you are placed. Nor is this all. The circumstances, as well as the relations of life, come under the government of the rule we are considering. 3. In the third place, we exhort you to make a willing sacrifice even of certain privileges and comforts, when the exigences of the case require it, though, in ordinary circumstances, you would be warranted in refusing to make it, if it were demanded. "Let as many servants as are under the yoke," says the apostle, "count their own masters worthy of all honour, that the name of God and His doctrine be not blasphemed." While you recollect what is due to yourselves, you must recollect still more what is due to the gospel. (*Ibid.*) *The wicked lives of Christians no argument against the truth of Christianity :*—I. First I am to consider WHAT JUST GROUND OR COLOUR THERE MAY BE FOR A COMPLAINT OF THE EXCEEDING WICKEDNESS OF MEN NOW UNDER THE CHRISTIAN DISPENSATION. And here it may with truth be observed to the advantage of our holy religion, that, as bad as men are under it, they would have yet been worse without it. The rule by which Christians are obliged to walk is so excellent, and they are thereby so fully and clearly informed of the whole extent of their duty; the promised assistances are so mighty and the rewards so vast, by which they are animated to obedience; that their transgressions, as they are attended with a deeper guilt, so must needs appear to be of a more prodigious size than those of other men. And it is no wonder, therefore, if, on both these accounts, good and holy persons have spoken of them with a particular degree of detestation and horror. And as the vices of Christians are, for these reasons, open and glaring, so their virtues oftentimes disappear and lie hid. The profound humility and self-denial, which the Christian religion first enjoined, leads the true disciples of Christ, in the exercise of the chief gospel graces, to shun the applause and sight of men as much as is possible. On these, and such accounts as these, I say vice seems to have the odds of virtue among those who name the name of Christ, much more than it really hath. II. Secondly, THAT THEY ARE VERY UNREASONABLE IN SO DOING, I AM IN THE NEXT PLACE TO SHOW. For—1. The holiest and purest doctrine imaginable is but doctrine still; it can only instruct, admonish, or persuade; it cannot compel. The gospel means of grace, powerful as they are, yet are not, and ought not to be, irresistible. Let the gospel have never so little success in promoting holiness, yet all who have considered it must own that it is in itself as fit as anything that can be imagined for that purpose, and incomparably more fit than any other course that ever was taken. Did philosophy suffer in the opinion of wise men on account of the debaucheries that reigned in those ages, wherein it flourished most among the Grecians and Romans? Was it then thought a good inference that, because men were very dissolute when wisdom was at the height, and the light of reason shone brightest, therefore wisdom and reason were of little use towards making men virtuous? 2. The present wickedness of Christians cannot be owing to any defect in the doctrine of Christ, nor be urged as a proof of the real inefficacy of it towards rendering men holy; because there was a time when it had all the success of this kind that could be expected; the time, I mean, of its earliest appearance in the world; when the practice of the generality of Christians was a just comment on the precepts of Christ; and they could appeal from their doctrines to their lives, and challenge their worst enemies to show any remarkable difference between them. 1. There must needs be a great disparity between the first Christians and those of these latter ages; because Christianity was the religion of their choice. They took it up while it was persecuted. 2. Another account of the great degeneracy of Christians may be drawn from men's erecting new schemes of Christianity which interfere with the true and genuine account of it. 3. It is not to be expected but that, where Christians are wicked, they should be rather worse than other men; for this very reason, because they have more helps towards becoming better, and yet live in the contempt or neglect of them. III. SOME MORE PROPER AND NATURAL INFERENCES THAT MAY BE DRAWN FROM IT. They are many and weighty. And—1. This should be so far from shocking our faith, that it ought on the contrary to confirm and strengthen it; for the universal degeneracy of Christians in these latter days was plainly and punctually foretold by Christ and His apostles. 2. Consider the monstrous degree of pravity and perverseness that is hid in the heart of man, and to account for the rise of it. 3. Learn from thence not to measure doctrines by persons, or persons by doctrines : that is, not to make the one a complete rule and standard whereby to judge of the goodness or badness of the other. 4. To excite ourselves from thence to do what in us lies towards removing this scandal from the Christian faith at large, and from that particular church of Christ to which we belong; both by living ourselves as becomes our holy religion; and by influencing others, as we have ability and opportunity, to live as we do; that so both we and they may adorn the doctrine of God our Saviour in all things (Tit. ii. 10). (*Bp. Atterbury.*) *A faithful slave:* —Near the close of the civil war a gentleman residing in a Southern state deemed it prudent, the Northern army being within four miles of his residence, to conceal his State bonds, plate and other valuables. He decided on burying them in the woods; but as this concealment required assistance, it was necessary to take one of his slaves into his confidence. The man he selected was one whom he knew to be a consistent Christian. With this slave's aid he buried his treasure, and only he and his master knew the hiding-place. When the Northern troops came two days afterward, they were informed by the slaves, then emancipated, which of their number knew of the buried treasure. The man was ordered to disclose the spot where it was hidden, but he knew if he did so his former master would be ruined, and he refused. Six men with loaded pistols pointed at his head repeated the order, and gave him twenty minutes to decide whether he would obey or die. Life was very sweet, and the slave burst into tears, but told them he would rather die than break his word to his master. The rough soldiers were touched by the faithful fellow's heroism, and released him unharmed. It is often said that religion makes men weak and unmanly, but this Christian slave is an instance of the injustice of the charge. He was faithful even in peril of death. *Our social position:*—The position we have in society, when we come to think of it, ought never to make us unhappy. There is a kind of painting, or work, that they make in other countries, that they call mosaic. It is made by little pieces of marble, or pieces of glass of different colours. They are so small that each one represents merely a line. There are simply these little pieces of glass or marble, and, if one of the pieces falls or is trampled on, no matter; it is not worth anything at all of itself. And yet the artist takes that little piece, and places it by another, and hands out another, and proceeds until he makes a human face—the shape, the eyes, the mouth, the lips, the cheeks, the human form, part shaped to part—so that, standing off three or four feet, you could not tell it from an oil painting. Now, suppose that one of those little pieces should say, "I wish he would put me in the apple of the eye"; and another, "I wish he would put me on the lip"; and another the cheek—but the artist knows just where to put it, and to put it anywhere else would be to mar the picture. And if one should be lost, it would mar the picture. Each one has its place. I have thought it is so in society. God is making a great picture out of society. He is making it out of insignificant materials, out of dust and ashes; but He is making a picture for all eternity, and wherever God may be pleased to put me in that picture, if He puts me at all, it seems to me I should be glad to be there. We shall be glad of it, and the arch-angels shall contemplate God's picture. I cannot tell where I shall be; but God is putting us where we should be, and these plans are for our good and our glory and our triumph. And when we get to heaven, we shall not wish we had been much different from what we were, only that we had been better. But here we are so dissatisfied! (*Bp. Simpson.*) *The true motive in service:*—Let us invite servants to remember that they are working for God as well as for man. Their master's kitchen is a room in their Father's house. They may have bad employers who do not care for good work, or ignorant ones who do not appreciate it, or disheartened ones who have ceased to expect it. They must take for their guidance their heavenly Father's work in nature. His rain falls on the just and on the unjust, on the carefully tilled field which invites His blessing and on the stony ground which refuses it. Their ambition must be to make their work fit to be part of His. Their kitchen must be able to welcome His sunshine without being put to shame by it. There should be no vessel thrust away to the back of the cupboard too foul to receive the purity of His daisies or His primroses. When they find themselves hampered and defeated by thoughtlessness or selfishness, they must think how nature makes the best of everything, throwing ivy over ruins, and absorbing all decay into something new and good. (*Edward Garrett.*)

Vers. 3, 5. **Wholesome words.**—*Wholesome words:*—The opposite of wholesome in our common speech is that which tends to produce disease; but the opposite of the Greek word, of which this is a translation, is that which is already unsound or diseased. The thought of the apostle is, that there is nothing morbid or unhealthy about the words of Jesus. The words of the Lord are healthy, having nothing of the disproportion of monstrosity, or the colouring of disease about them ; and therefore they are wholesome, so that all who believe and obey them become thereby stronger, nobler, and sounder in all the qualities of moral manhood. Now let us see how this statement of Paul may be verified and illustrated. I. We may take first THE MATTER OF CREED, and we shall find, when we come to investigate, that in this department the words of the Lord Jesus were distinguished by two qualities which mark them as pre-eminently healthy. The first of these is their positive character. The Lord was no mere dealer in negations. Dr. Samuel Johnson complained of Priestley, as a philosopher, that he "unsettled everything and settled nothing"; but no one can read the four Gospels without feeling that in meeting Jesus he has come into contact with One who speaks in the most positive manner. On subjects regarding which the wisest minds of antiquity were completely uncertain, He has the fullest assurance. We may wade through volumes of metaphysics, from those of Aristotle to those of Kant, without getting any distinct notion of God, but "when we hear Jesus say, 'God is a Spirit, and they that worship Him must worship Him in spirit and in truth,' we feel that God is a personal reality; and though Christ does not define the nature of spirit, yet when He speaks of God as thinking, loving, willing— His Father and ours—we understand Him better than the philosophers, though He penetrates to the depth of a nature which they had vainly sought to define." He has settled our minds upon the subject, not by argument, but by awakening in us the God-consciousness which is one of the instincts of our being, and so bringing us to say, "It must be so, for I can rest in that." In like manner, when He enforces duty He evokes the conscience within us to a recognition of its responsibility. So, too, in reference to the future. He does not argue, He asserts with the speech of One who knows whereof He affirms, and forthwith the natural longing of the heart for immortality finds its craving satisfied, and settles in the certainty that "dust thou art, to dust returnest, was not spoken of the soul." Akin to this positive characteristic of the Saviour's words concerning creed is the discouragement which they give to all indulgence in speculations about things which are merely curious, and have no bearing upon our character or conduct. Thus, when one of His disciples asked, "Are there few that be saved?" He declined to answer the question, and fixed the attention of His hearers on the vital and urgent matter of individul duty, saying, "Strive ye to enter in at the strait gate." Everything that is profitless and without bearing on life and godliness He brands as unworthy of consideration or discussion, and all mere logomachies are unsparingly condemned by Him. Now in these two things you have the symptoms of mental and spiritual health. The man who accounts nothing certain never focuses his mind on anything; while he who runs after every sort of speculation, scatters his mind over everything. The one never gets ready to do anything; the other attempts so much that he really accomplishes nothing. Is it not, precisely, in these two respects that the unhealthiness of much of the thinking in our own age manifests itself? II. But now, passing from the domain of creed TO THAT OF CHARACTER, WE ARE EQUALLY STRUCK WITH THE HEALTHINESS OF THE SAVIOUR'S WORDS in reference to that. 1. For in dealing with that subject He is careful to put supreme emphasis, not on that which is without, but on that which is within. He distinguishes between the head and the heart, and never confounds intellectual ability with moral greatness. Now the healthiness of all this is apparent at a glance, for it goes to the root of the matter, and only One who was Himself whole-hearted could thus have prescribed for diseased humanity. 2. Again, in reference to character, the healthiness of the Saviour's words appears in that He insists, not on asceticism in any one particular, but on full-rounded holiness. He does not require the eradication of any one principle of our nature, but rather the consecration of them all. 3. But looking now, to the department of conduct, we have in that another equally striking exemplification of the healthiness of the words of the Lord Jesus. He was very far from giving any countenance to the idea that religion is a thing only of sentiment. He insisted, indeed, as we have seen, on the importance of faith in the great central doctrines; and He was equally emphatic in declaring the innerness of holiness. But He dwelt on both of these only that He might the more effectually reach that conduct which one has called "three-fourths of life." 4. But another illustration of the healthiness of Christ's words in regard to conduct may be seen in the absence of all minute and specific details. He lays down great principles, leaving it to the conscience of the individual to make the application of these to the incidents and occasions of life as they arise. The words of Christ are not like the directions on a finger-post at a crossing, or the indicators of the cardinal points upon a spire, which are of service only in the places where they are set up; but rather like a pocket compass, which, rightly used and understood, will give a man his bearings anywhere. Nothing so educates a man into weakness and helplessness as to be told in every emergency precisely what he must do. That makes for him a moral "go-cart," outside of which he is not able to stand, and the consequence is that he can never be depended upon. If the teacher shows the pupil how to work each individual sum, he will never make him proficient in arithmetic. The man who is continually asking himself, as to his food, what he shall eat and what he shall drink and what he shall avoid, is either a dyspeptic or a valetudinarian. He is not healthy. And in like manner, he who in the domain of morals is continually inquiring of somebody, may I do this? may I go thither? or must I refrain from that? has never rightly comprehended the healthiness of Christ's words, and is far from having attained the strength which they are calculated to foster. Here is the great law, "Watch and pray, lest ye enter into temptation." (*W. M. Taylor, D.D.*) *A contrast between true and false teaching :*—At the close of the second verse Paul urges Timothy not to be silent, but to "teach and exhort" the Christians in Ephesus on the subject in slavery. I. THE WHOLESOMENESS OF CHRIST'S TEACHING. The apostle speaks of "wholesome words," a translation which we prefer to that given in the Revised Version ("sound words"), because it conveys the idea of imparting health to men and to society. Christ's teaching is the ozone of the moral atmosphere. 1. It concerned itself with practical questions. The Sermon on the Mount (which is the chief specimen given us of His teaching) proves this to demonstration. As Jesus Himself put it : a candle was not lighted by Him in order to be looked at or talked about; but that it might give light to all that were in the house. In other words, the Christian religion is to be used rather than to be discussed, and is meant to throw light upon all the obscurities of life's pathway until it leads up to the light of heaven. 2. His teaching was embodied in His perfect life. This made it the more helpful. These slaves, for example, to whom the apostle had been speaking, wanted to know what they were to do under the provocations and hardships of their lot. And nothing could help them more than the knowledge of Him whose gentleness was never at fault; who, when He was reviled, reviled not again; when He suffered He threatened not, but committed Himself to Him that judgeth righteously. 3. His teaching tended to the increase of godliness. "The doctrine which is according to godliness," means the teaching which makes men more like God—in holiness and righteousness and love. But in sharp contrast with this is presented—II. THE UNWHOLESOMENESS OF FALSE TEACHING, the effects of which were visible in the character of those who accepted and taught it. 1. Self-sufficiency was written on the forehead of each of them. As Paul says, "He is proud," literally "carried away with conceit," "knowing nothing." A footman is generally more awe-inspiring than his master. And this was true of pretentious teachers in Paul's days, of whom he says they are "carried away with conceit." 2. Love of verbal disputes was another characteristic of theirs. The word translated "doting" indicates a distempered and sickly condition, which turns away from the "wholesome" food of the gospel; just as a child with a poor appetite refuses bread-and-butter, and can only daintily pick and choose among delicacies, and the more he has of them the worse his appetite becomes. It is a bad sign when society has unwholesome appetites, caring more for art than for truth—more for manner than for matter; for these are signs of decadence such as preceded the fall of the Roman empire. 3. A carnal appetite was displayed by these opponents of our Lord's wholesome words. Our translation, "supposing that gain is godliness," is incorrect and misleading. No one supposes, or ever supposed, that worldly gain is godliness, or leads to it; but many in all ages have been guilty of what Paul suggests, namely, of "using godliness as a way of gain." In other words, these men, corrupted as they were in mind, in the whole inner life, and "bereft of the truth," only professed the Christian faith so far as it was serviceable to their worldly interests. (*A. Rowland, LL.B.*) **Supposing that gain is godliness.**—*Gain not godliness :*—That men are greatly exposed to embrace the absurd doctrine that virtue exists in utility. I. I AM TO EXPLAIN THE MEANING OF THE DOCTRINE THAT VIRTUE CONSISTS IN UTILITY. This sentiment has been maintained by those who believe, as well as by those who disbelieve Divine revelation. The turning point is utility. Intention is of no farther value than as it leads to utility : it is the means, and not the end. "The result of this part of the subject is, that those persons have been grossly mistaken, who taught that virtue was to be pursued for its own sake. Virtue is upon no other account valuable, than as it is the instrument of the most exquisite pleasure." All who suppose that virtue consists in utility, agree in maintaining that virtue has no intrinsic excellence, as an end, but only a relative excellence, as a means to promote the only ultimate end in nature, that is, happiness. Since happiness is, in their view, the supreme good, and misery the supreme evil, they conclude that the whole duty of men consists in pursuing happiness, and avoiding misery. Upon this single principle, that virtue wholly consists in its tendency to promote natural good, in distinction from natural evil, Godwin has founded a scheme of sentiments which, carried into practice, would subvert all morality, religion and government. II. I proceed to demonstrate THE ABSURDITY OF SUPPOSING THAT "GAIN IS GODLINESS," OR THAT VIRTUE ESSENTIALLY CONSISTS IN UTILITY. This sentiment is not only false, but absurd, because it contradicts the plainest dictates of reason and conscience. 1. To suppose that virtue consists in utility, is to suppose that virtue may be predicated of inanimate objects. These have a natural tendency, in various ways, to promote human happiness. The mode in which a man is made subservient is by inducement and persuasion. But both are equally the affair of necessity. The man differs from the knife as the iron candlestick differs from the brass one; he has one more way of being acted upon. This additional way in man is motive, in the candlestick it is magnetism. Such is the natural and avowed consequence of the doctrine, that virtue consists in utility. It necessarily implies that mere material objects may be really virtuous; and some material objects may have more virtue than the most benevolent of the human race. 2. To suppose that virtue consists in utility, is to suppose that virtue may be predicated of the mere animal creation. It is no less absurd to ascribe virtue to the utility of animals than to ascribe virtue to a refreshing shower, or a fruitful field. 3. To suppose that virtue consists in utility, is to suppose that men may be virtuous, without any intention to do good. They certainly may be very useful, without having utility in view. Men are every day performing actions which have a tendency to promote that public good which lies beyond all their views and intentions. But the doctrine under consideration places all virtue in the tendency of an action, and not in the intention of the actor. Intention is of no farther value than as it leads to utility. This is stripping moral virtue of every moral quality, which is a gross absurdity. 4. To suppose that virtue consists in utility, is to suppose that men may be virtuous in acting, not only without any intention, but from a positively bad intention. If the virtue of an action consists altogether in its tendency, it may be as virtuous when it flows from a bad intention as when it flows from a good intention, or from no intention at all. The intention of an agent does not alter the tendency of his action. A man may do that from a good intention, which has a tendency to do evil; or he may do that from a bad intention, which has a tendency to do good. Some actions done from the worst intentions have been the most beneficial to mankind. Be it so, that no malevolent action has a natural or direct tendency to promote happiness; yet if virtue consists in utility the good effect of a malevolent action is just as virtuous as the good effect of a benevolent one. For the doctrine we are considering places all virtue in the tendency of an action, and not in the intention of the agent. 5. To suppose that virtue consists in utility, is to suppose that there is nothing right nor wrong in the nature of things, but that virtue and vice depend entirely upon mere accidental and mutable circumstances. There are certain relations which men bear to each other, and which they bear to our Creator, which create obligations that never can be violated without committing a moral crime. 6. To suppose that virtue consists in utility is to suppose that there is nothing in the universe intrinsically good or evil but happiness and misery. 7. To suppose that virtue consists in utility is to suppose that there is really no such thing as either virtue or vice in the world. If the actions of free agents are either good or evil, solely on account of their tendency to promote either pleasure or pain, then nothing can be predicated of them but advantage or disadvantage. Actions which promote happiness may be denominated advantageous, but not virtuous; and actions which produce misery may be denominated disadvantageous, but not vicious. III. MEN ARE GREATLY EXPOSED TO EMBRACE IT. This the apostle plainly intimates, by exhorting Timothy to withdraw himself from those who "supposed that gain is godliness." 1. From the resemblance which this error bears to the truth, though it be diametrically opposite to it. Those who maintain that virtue consists in utility, represent it under the alluring name of universal philanthropy, which is an imposing appellation. They pretend that happiness is the supreme good, and virtue solely consists in promoting it to the highest degree. They insinuate that this philanthropy directly tends to diffuse

universal happiness, and to raise human nature to a state of perfection in this life.
2. The danger will appear greater if we consider by whom this pleasing and plausible error is disseminated. It is taught by grave divines, in their moral and
religious treatises and public discourses. Law and Paley have been mentioned as
placing the whole of virtue in utility. Dr. Brown, in his remarks upon the Earl of
Shaftesbury's characteristics, maintains that virtue consists in its tendency to promote individual happiness. 3. There is a strong propensity in human nature to
believe any other scheme of moral and religious sentiments, than that which is
according to godliness. Men naturally love happiness, and as naturally hate holiness. (*N. Emmons, D.D.*)     *A mercenary motive :*—A Christian lady in America,
who has earnestly and prayerfully laboured to carry the gospel to the Mongolian
laundrymen around her, at length succeeded in getting one of them to attend
Sunday school and church regularly. The man was attentive and well-
behaved, and the lady had great hopes of him. She tried to interest others
in his welfare, too, and induced her friends to patronise his laundry. Visiting him
at his home a few days ago, she received a warm welcome. John gave her to understand that he enjoyed very much attending the Sunday school, information that
was exceedingly gratifying. Anxious, however, to receive more practical demonstration of the influence of the school upon him, she asked him if he did not think
it did him good. "Yi, yi!" came the convincing response, "washee fol le whole
conglogation." The Chinaman's idea of getting good is not an uncommon one ;
unhappily, it is the motive of many a church connection.

Vers. 6–8. **But godliness with contentment is great gain.**—*Contentment :*—I.
Seek the blessedness of godly contentment. 1. No doubt contentment apart
from godliness is a good thing. Seneca and Lucretius, and other pagan philosophers, were never tired of singing its praises ; and Socrates, when he walked
through the streets of Athens, and saw around him the evidences of wealth, art,
and culture, exclaimed, "How many things there are which I can do without."
(1) To some this feeling of contentment with their present condition seems constitutional. There are men and women who have an easy-going disposition, which
makes the best of everything. (2) Others again are content, not so much from
happy temperament, as from the fact that the lines have fallen unto them in
pleasant places, and they have a goodly heritage. Belonging to the rich and
leisured classes, they have no temptation to win a position, or to make money, by
unworthy means, for these are already theirs without effort. 2. It is not contentment, however, which is inculcated here so much as "godliness with contentment."
Many a man has been content without being godly, who might have been saved had
his content been disturbed and destroyed. II. Entertain a lowly estimate of
yourselves. "We brought nothing into this world." Of all God's creatures, the
human child is most helpless, most dependent upon kindly care ; and one of the
lessons taught by the coming of an infant into the home is the lesson of human
dependence. What have we, indeed, through life that we did not receive? The
very powers which enable us to win position or wealth are as much Divine gifts as
the wealth itself. No one here has reason for boasting or pride, but only for
reverent gratitude to Him who has crowned us with loving-kindness and with
tender mercy. III. Estimate justly the value of earthly things. However
precious worldly things may seem, it is certain "we can carry nothing out" of the
world when we leave it. It is a narrow bed which will form the last resting-place
even for the owner of a province or the ruler of a nation. (*A. Rowland, LL.B.*)
*Godliness :*—You know that all the waters in the world run towards the sea. The
little stream which you watch trickling through the green meadow runs on till it
joins another stream, and this again to a third, and so on, and it grows larger and
broader and deeper till it becomes a river, on which ships may ride, and down
which they may sail to the great ocean. The heart and mind of a godly person all
turn towards God as the waters flow towards the sea ; he loves Him above all other
things, admires Him above all other persons, trusts to Him above all other hopes,
and values Him above all other joys. (*E. Garbett, M.A.*)     *Godliness, the parent
of content :*—I. What is meant in Scripture by "godliness"? It frequently
means the gospel. As in this same first Epistle to Timothy (iii. 16),
"Without controversy, great is the mystery of godliness." In other
passages godliness means, as the word actually means in the old Saxon, God-
likeness, or a likeness to God ; because the object of the revelation of Christ
in the gospel is to show us the character of God in the person of a man, and

thereby set us a pattern for us to copy—and by offering grace to all, by which they may be able to copy that pattern, to make them Godlike by making them like Christ. II. Now THE EFFECT OF THIS GODLINESS IS IN THE TEXT STATED TO BE "CONTENTMENT"—"godliness with contentment"—that is, religion with the contentment which it always brings forth. Let us now, in examining this part of our subject, endeavour to learn how true religion produces contentment. 1. It teaches us to know God. The ideas which men are able to form of God's character, by observing His works, and without the help of revelation, are not such as to produce contentment. His works show the extent of His power; and the order and harmony of them, His own knowledge and perfection. But to know this will not produce contentment. We must know God's moral character for this. Now the Bible reveals God to us as a God whose name is "Love"; as a God whose goodness and mercy are as great as His power and wisdom. Thus the Bible reveals the Eternal God as the kindest friend of sinful man. And when this, which the Word of God thus discovers, is believed in the heart, then contentment must be produced, and will increase as the knowledge of God's character and the assurance of His love increase. For the Christian thus reasons: Is God all-wise? then surely He knows what is best for me. Is He as good as He is wise? then surely He will give what is best for me. 2. But, secondly, the Scripture teaches us to know ourselves, and thus leads us to contentment. Discontent always springs from pride and an overweening conceit of our own value and excellence. We are all by nature high-minded, and esteem ourselves at more than we are worth. Thus, true religion, by humbling a man, tends to produce contentment, for it shows him and makes him feel that he deserves nothing, so that every thing he has is more than he deserves; since he who values himself at nothing will count everything he receives to be above his value, and therefore a call on him for gratitude. And this contentment, the blessed fruit of godliness, were it spread through the world, were it growing in every heart, would set the foundations of the earth in course again, and bring into order what sin has thrown into confusion. It would teach men to keep to their place and to fulfil its duties. It would cut up all covetousness by the root, while it would give no check to honest industry and proper care to provide for our own household. It would put an end to that diseased love of change, and restless, excited spirit, which is continually agitating the mind of those who are in the world as the winds ruffle the unstable ocean. (*W. W. Champneys, M.A.*)      *The benefit of contentment :*—He was not content to call godliness gain, but he calleth it great gain; as if he would say, gain, and more than gain; riches, and better than riches; a kingdom, and greater than a kingdom. As when the prophets would distinguish between the idol-gods and the living God, they call Him the great God; so the gain of godliness is called great gain. The riches of the world are called earthly, transitory, snares, thorns, dung, as though they were not worthy to be counted riches; and therefore, to draw the earnest love of men from them, the Holy Ghost brings them in with these names of disdain, to disgrace them with their loves; but when He comes to godliness, which is the riches of the soul, He calleth it great riches, heavenly riches, unsearchable riches, everlasting riches, with all the names of honour, and all the names of pleasure, and all the names of happiness. As a woman trims and decks herself with an hundred ornaments, only to make her amiable, so the Holy Ghost setteth out godliness with names of honour, and names of pleasure, and names of happiness, as it were in her jewels, with letters of commendation to make her be beloved. Lest any riches should compare with godliness, He giveth it a name above others, and calleth it great riches, as if He would make a distinction between riches and riches, between the gain of covetousness and the gain of godliness, the peace of the world and the peace of conscience, the joy of riches and the joy of the Holy Ghost. The worldly men have a kind of peace and joy and riches. But I cannot call it great, because they have not enough, they are not contented as the godly are; therefore only godliness hath this honour, to be called great riches. The gain of covetousness is nothing but wealth; but the gain of godliness is wealth, and peace, and joy, and love of God, and the remission of sins, and everlasting life. Therefore only godliness hath this honour, to be called great gain. (*H. Smith.*)      *Enough :*—The godly man hath found that which all the world doth seek, that is, enough. Every word may be defined, and everthing may be measured, but enough cannot be measured or defined, it changeth every year; when we had nothing, we thought it enough, if we might obtain less than we have; when we came to more, we thought of another enough; now we have more, we dream of another enough; so enough is always to come, though too much be there already. For as oil kindleth the fire which it seems to quench, so riches come as though they would make a man contented, and make him more covetous. (*Ibid.*) *Contentment a commander*:—Such a commander is contentation that wheresoever she setteth foot an hundred blessings wait upon her; in every disease she is a physician, in every strife she is a lawyer, in every doubt she is a preacher, in every grief she is a comforter, like a sweet perfume, which taketh away the evil scent, and leaveth a pleasant scent for it. (*Ibid.*) *Poor capital for the next world*:—Once it was remarked to Lord Erskine that a certain man dying had left £200,000, whereupon he replied, "That's a poor capital to begin the next world with." Truly it was so, for if, on the other hand, the man had given it away in charity he would thus have really laid it up as treasure in heaven, where in a certain sense he would have possessed and enjoyed it, whereas in this case he left it all behind him on earth when he died, and thus really lost it. *Money of no use beyond the grave*:—At Andermatt, in Switzerland, recently, some workmen were repairing a wall that runs round the old churchyard when they suddenly came upon several skeletons, and on disturbing them there fell from the lower jaw of one, two gold coins of the reign of Charles VIII. of France, at the end of the fifteenth century. Further search revealed the presence in the bony hand of the skeleton of a piece of linen rag in excellent preservation, and on unfolding the rag the men brought to light ten silver coins of the sixteenth century, of the time of Francis I. of France. There is no means of knowing how the money came to be in so strange a place. It may have been placed there by superstitious friends of the dead, or death might have suddenly come upon a man who was carrying his money in that way. One thing, however, is certain, the money had not been used by him. When we see how men scheme, and labour, and hoard, it would seem that they have forgotten that it is of no use beyond the grave. *Folly of hoarding up wealth*:—We are told that when Alexander, the conqueror of the world, was dying, he gave orders that at his burial his hands should be exposed to public view that all men might see that the mightiest of men could take nothing with him when called away by death. The same lesson was taught us by Job when he said, "Naked came I out of my mother's womb, and naked shall I return thither." A mouthful of earth will one day stop the cravings of the most covetous. This makes the hoarding up of wealth so vain an occupation. He who died the other day worth three millions and a half, is now as poor as the beggar whom he passed in the street. "I would not mind dying," said a miserly farmer, "if I could take my money with me!" but when he ceased to breathe he left all behind him. What folly it is to spend all one's time in gathering a heap to leave it so soon. (*C. H. Spurgeon.*) *Leaving wealth*:—Mahmoud, the first Mohammedan conqueror who entered India, when a mortal disease was consuming him, ordered all his costly apparel, and his vessels of silver and gold, and his pearls and precious stones, to be displayed before him. In the royal residence at Ghuznee, which he called the Palace of Felicity, he drew from this display, wherewith he had formerly gratified the pride of his eye, a mournful lesson, and wept like a child. "What toils," said he, "what dangers, what fatigues, both of body and mind, have I endured for the sake of acquiring these treasures, and what cares in preserving them! and now I am about to die and leave them." (*Dictionary of Illustrations.*) *Exemplary contentment*:—A gentleman was once talking to Thomas Mann, a pious waterman on the river Thames, and having ascertained that he never laboured on the Sabbath, and was dependent on his labour for a living, he said, "Well, as your gains have been so small, you could not lay much up. Have you not been anxious, as you have proceeded in life, lest, from the very nature of your employment, exposed as it is to danger and to all weathers, you should be laid up by illness, and have nothing to support you?" "No, sir; I have always believed in God's Providence. I think I am just fitted for the situation which He has appointed to me, and that what He has fixed is best. I am, therefore, satisfied and thankful. I endeavour to do the duty which daily falls to me, and to be careful of my earnings: I have always had enough, and I have no fears about years to come." "Yet, my friend," said the gentleman, "if illness were to come, and you had not a provision made for the supply of your need in helpless old age, ought not this to give you some uneasiness?" "No, sir, that is not my business. Future years are not my business. That belongs to God, and I am sure that, doing my duty in His fear now, and being careful in what He intrusts to me, He will supply my need in future in that way which He shall think best." The gentleman then said, "We have heard that teaching the poor to read has a tendency to make them discontented with the station in which Providence has placed them. Do you think so ? " " No, sir; quite the contrary. All that I have read in the Bible teaches me to be content with the dispensations of Providence, to be industrious and careful. A Christian cannot be an idle or an ungrateful man." *Contentment :*—I. I am TO EXPLAIN GODLINESS. This consists in two things. 1. It consists in a godly heart. Godly signifies godlike. Those who have a heart after God's own heart are godly, and bear His moral image, in which man was at first created, and to which every renewed person is restored by the special influence of the Divine Spirit. The Spirit in regeneration enstamps the moral image of God upon the heart, which consists in righteousness and true holiness. There is nothing in which men so nearly resemble God as in a godly heart. 2. Godliness implies not only a godly heart, but a godly life. All men will live according to their hearts. (1) A sincere consecration of themselves to God. Those who mean to live a godly life, give themselves away to God in an everlasting covenant, never to be forgotten. (2) The godly not only devote themselves to God, but pay a sincere and habitual obedience to the intimations of His will. II. That THIS GODLINESS WILL PRODUCE CONTENTMENT. 1. Godliness leads those who possess it to realize that God always treats them as well as they deserve. They live under an habitual sense of their unworthiness in the sight of God. 2. The godly are sensible that God always treats them according to their prayers, which reconciles them to the Divine dispensations towards them. 3. That it leads men to live by faith in the perfect wisdom and rectitude of the Divine government. The godly believe that the hand and heart of God are concerned in all the events which actually take place. III. THAT GODLY CONTENTMENT WILL PRODUCE GREAT GAIN ; or rather, that godliness with contentment is great gain. 1. That godly contentment gains all the good in this world. Those who are contented after a godly sort, enjoy all the things that they possess, and they actually possess as much as they desire to possess ; which affords them complete contentment. The contented person is in just such a situation as He, all things considered, desires to be in. 2. That those who possess godly contentment, gain not only this world, but the world to come. Contentment here prepares them for contentment there. Godliness here prepares them to enjoy godliness there. Improvement : 1. If godliness produces contentment, then those have reason to doubt of the sincerity of their religion who do not derive contentment from it. 2. If godliness produces contentment, then none can be contented who are destitute of godliness. 3. If godliness be so gainful as we have heard, then none can be godly too soon. 4. If godliness be so gainful as we have heard, then there is no danger of being too godly. 5. If godliness be so gainful as has been represented, then the godly have good reason to pity the ungodly. 6. If godliness be so gainful as has been represented, then the godly ought to do all they can to lead others to be godly. Godliness is benevolence, and benevolence wishes well to all mankind. (*N. Emmons, D.D.*)      **We brought nothing into the world.**—*What we carry out of the world :*—There is a sense in which the text is true, and there is a sense in which it is not true. I. THERE IS A SENSE IN WHICH IT IS TRUE. It is true that we can carry nothing of our material possessions out of the world. We must leave behind our homes, our business, our property, our very bodies. This is—1. A fact the most obvious. 2. A fact the most practically disregarded. II. THERE IS A SENSE IN WHICH IT IS NOT TRUE. There are certain things which we did not bring with us, but which we shall carry away with us. 1. Our memories. We came without recollections, we shall carry thousands away. 2. Our responsibilities. We came without responsibilities, we shall carry loads away. 3. Our characters. We came without a character, we shall carry one away. 4. Our true friendships. We came without true friendships, we shall carry many away. 5. Our true sources of spiritual joy. Powers of holy meditation, hopes of approaching good, communion with the Infinite Father, &c., and all these we shall carry away with us. (*The Homilist.*)      *The responsibility of life :*—I. CONSIDER MAN'S DEPENDENCE AND MORTALITY. Everything that we possess and enjoy is not so much a gift as a loan. Strength to labour, and the reward of our labour, all worldly possessions and happiness, are merely for a time. They are only lent to us during our life, to be returned at our death. We often hear of a man having only a life interest in certain property. But who has more than a life interest in any worldly possessions ? But, as the text reminds us, we shall have to go out of this world. II. CONSIDER MAN'S MORAL AND SPIRITUAL NATURE, AND CONSEQUENT ACCOUNTABILITY. We brought much with us into this world, and we shall carry more out. 1. We brought a spiritual nature with us into this world, or, rather, we came into this world spiritual beings. Man is not a body, but a spirit. We have bodies, we are spirits. The universal consciousness of man testifies to the fact that he possesses a life higher than that of the brutes. Into the heavenly kingdom there cannot enter anything that defileth. "Be not deceived, God is not mocked ; for whatsoever a man soweth that shall he also reap. For he that soweth to the flesh shall of the flesh reap corruption, but he that soweth to the Spirit shall of the Spirit reap life everlasting." 2. We brought a moral nature with us into this world, or, to speak more correctly, we came into this world moral beings. Things affect us, not merely as pleasurable or painful, but as right or wrong. 3. We shall carry out of this world what we did not bring with us into the world. We must all carry with us the record of our life. 4. Besides the record of our life, which we must carry with us out of the world, we shall be blessed or condemned for what we leave behind us in the world. All of us will leave behind an influence which will live long after we are forgotten. (*A. F. Joscelyne, B.A.*)   **Having food and raiment.**—*Contentment with little :*—I. Let us consider THE NECESSITIES OF NATURE. These are few, and simple, and easily satisfied. For we should distinguish between real and artificial wants. In reference to happiness, a man only has what he can use. If he possesses a thousand pounds which he cannot use, it matters not, as to the benefit he derives from it, whether it be in his coffer or in the bowels of the earth. II. We should do well to consider THE INSUFFICIENCY OF THE CREATURE. When we see men dissatisfied with what they have, and all anxiety and exertion to amass an abundance of this "world's goods," we should imagine that there was a superlative excellency in these things, and that our happiness absolutely depended upon them. Happiness is an eternal thing. "A good man shall be satisfied from himself." III. To induce you to be satisfied with such things as you have, consider YOUR UNWORTHINESS. You murmur because you have not more—but should you not be thankful for what you have ? If a man owes you a debt, you ought to have your demand ; and if you do not receive the whole, you may justly complain. But it is otherwise with a beggar who asks alms. How much more therefore are we bound to say, with Jacob, "I am not worthy of the least of all Thy mercies"! Cease complaining, Christian. IV. Observe WHAT YOU HAVE ALREADY IN POSSESSION OR IN REVERSION. When I view the Christian—when I see him blessed with all spiritual blessings in heavenly places—when I see him a son of God, an heir of immortality—loved with an infinite love ; redeemed by the blood of the everlasting covenant ; called out of darkness into marvellous light. Oh why do not these blessings absorb us ! Once they did. When we were first induced to seek them— we thought of nothing else. We then said, If I succeed and obtain these—how willingly can I leave everything else ! V. Consider THE PROVIDENCE OF GOD. Suppose now a voice from heaven were to assure you that a little was best for you. You answer, I would try to acquiesce. And cannot God speak by actions as well as words ? VI. Consider HOW MUCH SAFER YOU ARE WITH LITTLE THAN WITH MUCH. Honey does not more powerfully attract bees than affluence generates temptations. Did you never see men ruined by prosperity ? Have you duly considered the duties as well as snares of a prosperous condition ? "Where much is given, much will be required." VII. Consider THE BREVITY OF YOUR CONTINUANCE UPON EARTH, WHERE ALONE YOU WILL NEED ANY OF THESE THINGS. "What is your life ? It is even a vapour that appeareth for a little time, and then vanisheth away !" And how much of this fleeting period is already consumed ! There may be but a step between you and death. Now if time be short, your trouble cannot be long. Were you ever so prosperous, it is only the sunshine of a day—the evening shades are beginning to spread, and will hide all your glories from your view. Read the verse before the text : "For we brought nothing into this world, and it is certain we can carry nothing out." (*W. Jay.*)

Vers. 9–11. **But they that will be rich.**—*Covetousness :*—I. THE DANGERS OF THIS TEMPER OF MIND ARE OBVIOUS. 1. It leads many to deception and dishonesty. 2. To get advantage to oneself is a false aim for any Christian life. If you know how insidious these and other perils are, you may well pray : "Lead us not into temptation, but deliver us from evil." II. DEFENCES AGAINST SUCH EVILS are within our knowledge, and many are finding moral security through using them. 1. Watch against the tendency to extravagant living. The absence of simplicity in some households leads to more evils than you think. Be brave enough to be simple in your habits. Seek to live without ostentation. 2. On the other hand, see to it that you do not bow down to worship the golden calf. No idolatry is more prevalent than this. 3. Cultivate love for higher things than the world offers. Good will conquer evil by its own inherent force. 4. Pray for the spirit of heroism in common life. (*A. Rowland, LL.B.*)     *Temptation :*—A careful examination of our text will show that it is in no sense exclusive. Those addressed in it are not such as have riches, but such as want riches, and are determined, whether or no, to obtain them. By further consideration of the chapter you will see that the reference to such as would be rich in our text, is only made as an illustration of the great truth for which the apostle is endeavouring to find impressive utterance. He selected the simplest and commonest illustration. He might with equal truth have said : They that will be wise ; they that will succeed; they that will get pleasure. I want to bring out into the light the general truth he illustrates, which appears to be this: There are certain kinds of character which are singularly exposed to the influence of temptation, and certain conditions of body and mind which seem to lay us open to the power of temptation. What Paul seems to say in our text, put into other words, is this: "Those with this moral disposition, the wish to be rich, are, in consequence of that disposition, exposed to the force of peculiar temptations " ; and so he leaves us to infer that what is true of that particular state will apply to many other similar conditions. The laws which regulate our mental and spiritual natures can often be understood by the help of analogous laws which we observe to rule our bodily frames. I. THERE ARE CERTAIN CLASSES OF CHARACTER SINGULARLY EXPOSED TO TEMPTATION. 1. Strong-willed and ambitious men. " These fall into temptation and a snare." From some points of view these strong-willed men may be regarded as the noble men of earth. They have a purpose in life, which holds in and guides, as with bit and bridle, all the forces of their being. They are the great men in our mills and warehouses ; the foremost as statesmen, and in carrying out great social and national enterprises. Yet this disposition lays men open to peculiar dangers. It comes too often to be opposed to that spirit of contentment which the apostle here intimates is peculiarly suitable to " godliness," and which is the result of a daily thankful dependence on that living God, who giveth us all things richly to enjoy. Especially do we find that this strong-will is liable to become self-will. And if you observe these strong-willed men carefully, you will find they are sadly often falling into sin in relation to their dependents and servants ; becoming imperious in their manners, forgetting the ordinary charities of social intercourse, and treating those who serve them as though they were an inferior kind of creature ; which is, in the sight of the one God who made us all, a sad and mournful sin against the common brotherhood. They that will be anything fall thereby " into temptation and a snare." If such is your disposition, remember, that is the side of your nature on which you are peculiarly exposed to danger. Do you then ask, May a Christian man be ambitious ? May he say, I will—I will be rich ; I will be great ; I will be successful ?—I reply, " Yes, he may ; but only when he can add, ' If God sees best.' " He may be ambitious if he can keep leaning on God all the while he pursues his ambitions. 2. Now, let us consider together two opposite classes of character—intense impulsive men, and inactive, sluggish men. These also " fall into temptation and a snare." They are very liable to sins of commission. So feebly swayed by prudential considerations, they often do things which they live very greatly to regret. In connection with Christian life and work, they are exposed to the sins of discouragement and failing perseverance. They, too, often live a butterfly life, emptying the nectar from no flower on which they settle, but flying hither and thither from flower to flower, and gathering no stores of honey. They are like those streams which are only fed by mountain rains, or melting snows ; they sometimes flow along in a very passion of excitement, but only for awhile ; they soon subside ; for weeks there is but a trickling rill, and often the stones lie bleaching in the sun for months together. There are few things which do more injury to a Church than the ebb and flow of its hopes and efforts through the influence of its impulsive members. There are many of the opposite disposition. It is exceedingly difficult to arouse them at all. They seem to have no personal wills. They are always requiring to be urged and pressed. Such persons have their peculiar liabilities to temptation ; mostly to sins of omission—the sins which come in connection with procrastination ; sins arising from neglect of duty. 3. Only one other phase of character I will mention. Men who must have company. These also " fall into temptation and a snare." God has set the solitary in families. " It is not good that man should be alone." But you must have observed that this spirit possesses some men very much more than others. There are some who feel as if they could not live without company. They feel restless in their very homes if no one beside their family is found there. I do not say that, on the very face of it, this is wrong; but need I point out to you how perilous such a disposition becomes? Need I remind you how many have, through it, been led astray into drinking habits, and so ruined in heart and in home, in body and in soul? II THERE ARE CERTAIN TIMES IN A MAN'S LIFE WHEN TEMPTATION HAS PECULIAR FORCE. One of the wonderful discoveries of this scientific age is that of the successive changes through which our bodies pass in the course of our lives. Now, these bodily changes are very remarkably associated with our moral conditions; especially are they connected with the varying force of bodily passions. In some conditions of our frame, no temptation to the indulgence of any bodily lust would exert an effective power on us. In other conditions of our frame, the least exposure seems to involve our fall, we feel to be actually "overtaken," "overwhelmed." There are three periods of life in which, for the most part, men fall under the power of evil. Most men that fall, fall either into young men's peril, full-grown men's sins, or old men's sins. The devil never appears so much like an angel of light as when he clothes himself to meet the rising passions of early manhood. A mournful proportion of our youth "fall into temptation and a snare," and are "drowned in destruction and perdition." Many a man has conquered the sins of youth, and then fallen before the sins of manhood. Sensual passion seems to acquire a new force then. The lust of gold. The thirst for position and fame urges men then. Men begin, for the most part, to be misers, or drunkards, or sensualists about this age. "A hoary head is a crown of glory if it be found in the way of righteousness." Yet old age has its special evils. Temptations to those sins which the Bible gathers up in the word "uncleanness." Often uncleanness of word and conversation; often, alas! of life and conduct also. It would appear that bodily lust and passion gathers itself in old age for one last struggle to gain the mastery. (*R. Tuck, B.A.*) *The love of money :*—You will notice, in the first place, the emphasis which is to be put upon the opening of this passage. "They"—not they that will be rich; because riches are ordained of God, and, rightly held and rightly used, are an instrument of most beneficent power, salutary to the possessor as well as the recipient of bounty—"They that *will* be rich" whether or not "fall into temptation," &c. They are willing to give the whole force and power of their being; for they will have it. They are men who, because they will be rich, cannot be conscientious; and who learn soon to say that most beggarly of all things, "A man cannot be a Christian and be in my business." How came you in it then? Yea, they have not time to cultivate refinement; they have not time for the amenities of life; they have not time for their household; they have not time for friendship; they have not time for love. And so, because they will be rich, they give up their heart also. And having given all these up, God blesses and blasts them: blesses, for they are rich, and that is what they call blessing; blasts, because it is not in the nature of God Himself, without an absolute change of the laws by which He works, to make a man happy who has, for the sake of gaining wealth, divested himself of those elements in which happiness consists. For what if the harp, in order to make itself blessed, should sell, first, its lowest base string, and then its next one, and then its next string, and then its next, and its next, until finally every string of the harp is sold? Then, when all the heaps of music are piled up before it, and it wants to play, it is mute. It has sold the very things out of which music must needs come. And men that will be rich give up sensibility, affection, faith, manhood, coining them all, emptying themselves: and when they get possession of their wealth, what is there left for them to enjoy it with? Their marrow is gone. There is no string in the harp on which joy can play. Not only will they who will be rich sacrifice everything, but they will not hesitate to do everything that is required—only, as men that will be rich require impunity, it must be safe. And so comes the long, detestable roll of mining, subterranean conduct, the secrecy of wickedness, collusions, plotting, unwhispered things, or things only whispered; that long train of webbing conduct which makes man insincere, pretentious hypocrites, whited sepulchres that are fair without, but that are inwardly full of death and dead men's bones. Men begin at first to make a little; they find how easy it is; they enlarge their ambition, and the conception dawns upon them, "Why am not I one of those who are appointed to be millionaires." In the beginning of life, a few thousands would have satisfied their ambition. Now, hundreds of thousands seem to them but a morsel. They grow more and more intense. Temptations begin to fall upon them. You can no more make money suddenly and largely, and be unharmed by it, than a man could suddenly grow from a child's stature to a man's stature without harm. There is not a gardener who does not know that a plant may grow faster than it can make wood; that the cellular tissue may grow faster than the ligneous consolidation; and that then it cannot hold itself up. And many men grow faster in riches than they can consolidate. Men who are tempted to make money suddenly, are almost invariably obliged to traverse the canons of morality. Avarice in its earliest stages is not hideous, though at the bottom it is the same serpent thing that it is at last. In the beginning it is an artist, and the man begins to think, "I will redeem my parents. Oh! I will repurchase the old homestead. Ah! will I not make my village to bud and blossom as a rose?" How many things do men paint in the sky which clouds cover and winds blow away, and which fade out with the morning that painted them. But where do you find a man who begins to make money fast, that does not begin to have narrower, baser, and avaricious feelings? Such men begin to be tempted to believe that success atones for faults. Men are tempted as soon as they get into this terrific fire of avarice, to regard morality as of little avail compared with money-making. They are dazzled. You will recollect our Saviour's words, "The deceitfulness of riches." Men are snared when they are given up to fiery avarice. They are snared because the very things by which they propose to gain success become in the long run the means of their own destruction. Cheating is another snare. No man cheats once without cheating twice. Like a gun that fires at the muzzle and kicks over at the breach, the cheat hurts the cheater as much as the man cheated. Cheating is a snare, and will always be a snare. The cheater falls into it. Conceit is another snare. Men lose wisdom just in proportion as they are conceited. It is astonishing to see how conceited men are in power. I have noticed how soon those that will be rich at any hazard, fall into drinking habits. They have come into a sphere in which they begin to fall not simply into "temptation and a snare," but into divers "lusts." Now comes extravagance. With extravagance come many more mischievous lusts. And when you see a man given to licentious indulgence, you may be sure that he will come to want a crust. Mark that man. Poverty is on his track; and he shall be surely overcome and destroyed by it. We are not to understand that money is the root of all evil; but the love of it—bestowing that which we have a right to bestow only on undying and immortal qualities upon God, and angels, and men—bestowing love, idolatrously, upon material gain. It is not said that all evil springs from this cause; but at one time and another this may become the cause of all evil. It has corrupted in its time every faculty and every relation in which a man stands connected with his fellows. It has divided families, it has parted friendships, it has corrupted purity. The love of money, often, is stronger than the love of kindred. I observe that as men come into this, one of two things takes place; they forsake the house of God, they forsake religious society, because either they have no taste for it, or because it irritates them, or annoys them, and they will not bear the restraint—or else, on the other hand, they betake themselves to religion because under certain circumstances, religion is an atonement for misconduct. It is a policy of life-insurance to men that are in iniquity. It is not, "What is true?" but, "What will make me feel good while I am a wicked man?" that they seek. They err from the faith. But now comes the solemn sentence, "They pierce themselves through with many sorrows." I wish you could see what I have seen. A sword is merciful compared with the sorrows that pierce men with pain through life. You do not dare to adopt economic courses, because men would rush in on you, and take possession of you. And so men go under false appearances. How they suffer! Ah! if a man is going to be ruined, and has the testimony of his conscience that he has been an honest man, there is some alleviation to his suffering; but frequently it is a ruin carrying with it blight. Is it not a terrible thing to see a man, in the middle of life, count death better than life? Thank God, a man does not need to be very rich to be very happy, only so that he has a treasure in himself. A loving heart; a genuine sympathy; a pure unadulterated taste; a life that is not scorched by dissipation or wasted by untimely hours; a good sound body, and a clear conscience—these things ought to make a man happy. A man may be useful and not be rich. A man may be powerful and not be rich; for ideas are more powerful than even dollars. If God calls you to a way of making wealth, make it; but remember do not love money. If God calls you to make wealth, do not make haste to be rich; be willing to wait. If God calls you into the way of wealth, do not undertake to make yourself rich by gambling. (*H. W. Beecher.*) *The love of money :*—The passion exists under various modifications. In some few of its subjects, it appears to be pure, unmixed, exclusive; terminates and is concentrated upon just the money itself—(that is, the property) the delight of being the owner of so much. "It is mine! so much!" But, in much the greater number of instances, the passion involves a regard to some relative objects. In some it is combined with vanity; a stimulating desire of the reputation of being rich; to be talked of, admired, envied. In some it has very much a reference to that authority, weight, prevailing influence, in society, which property confers; here it is ambition rather than avarice. In some the passion has its incitement in an exorbitant calculation for competence. So much, and so much, they shall want; so much more they may want, for themselves or their descendants. So much more they should like to secure as a provision against contingencies. Some are avaricious from a direct dread of poverty. Amidst their thousands, they are haunted by the idea of coming to want. And this idea of danger, from being undefined, can always hover about a man, and force its way into his thoughts. So described, this spirit, possessing and actuating such a number of our fellow mortals, bears an ill and a very foolish aspect. Let us now specify a few of its evil effects, with a note of admonition on each of them. One obvious effect is—that it tends to arrogate, and narrow, and impel the whole action and passion of the soul toward one exclusive object, and that an ignoble one. Almost every thought that starts is to go that way. Silver and gold have a magnetic power over his whole being. The natural magnet selects its subject of attraction, and will draw only that; but this magnetism draws all that is in the little world of the man's being. Or it is an effect like that of a strong, steady wind; every thing that is stirred and moveable, that rolls on the ground, or floats on water or air, is driven in that one direction. If it were a noble principle—if it were religion, that exerted over him this monopolizing and all-impelling power, what a glorious condition! The brief admonition upon this is, that if a man feel this to be mainly the state of his mind, it is a proof and warning to him that he is wrong. Observe, again, that this passion, when thus predominant, throws a mean character into the estimate of all things, as they are all estimated according to the standard of money-value, and in reference to gain. Thus another value which they may have, and, perhaps, the chief one, is overlooked, unseen, and lost. Again, this passion places a man in a very selfish relation to other men around him. He looks at them very much with the eyes of a slave-merchant. He cannot sell them, but the constant question is, "What, and how, can I gain by them? When this principle has the full ascendency, it creates a settled hardness of character. The man lives, as to the kinder affections, in the region of perpetual ice. He is little accessible to the touches and emotions of sympathy; cannot give himself out in any generous expansion of the affections. And here observe, again, that the disposition in question operates, with a slow but continual effect, to pervert the judgment and conscience. It is constantly pressing the line that divides right from wrong; it removes it, bends it away, by slight degrees. The distinction becomes less positive to the judgment. Self-interested casuistry is put in operation. But it comes nearer to the object of Christian admonition to observe the operation of this evil principle in ways not incompatible with what may be called integrity. It withholds from all the generous and beneficent exertions and co-operations, in which pecuniary liberality is indispensable; and excites against them a spirit of criticism, exception, cavil, and detraction. "They are sanguine, extravagant." "This is not the time." "They are unnecessary, impracticable." "There are many evil consequences." It causes to forego opportunities for gaining a beneficial influence over men's minds. It puts an equivocal and inconsistent character on Providence. "As to my own interests, Providence is not at all to be trusted—I must take the whole care on myself." We only add, it fatally counteracts and blasts internal piety, in all its vital sentiments. (*J. Foster.*) *The love of money :*—"The love of money," says the apostle, "is the root of all evil"; not that all evils have, but that all may have, their root therein. Take a rapid glance of a few of these, to which it certainly gives birth. And first, what root it is of idolatry; or rather it is not so much a root of this, as itself this idolatry—"Covetousness, which is idolatry" (Col. iii. 5). This sounds a hard saying, but it is one which can justify itself. For what is the essence of idolatry? Is it not a serving and loving of the creature more than the Creator; a giving to the lower what was due only to the higher, what was due only to Him who is the highest of all? And as this love of money disturbs the relations of men to God, drawing off to some meaner object affections due to Him, so it mingles continually an element of strife and division in the relations of men with one another. Again, what a root of unrighteousness, of untruthful dealing between man and man, of unfair advantage taken of the simple and the ignorant, of falsehood, fraud, and chicane, does the love of money continually show itself to be! And then—for time would fail me if I dwelt at large on all the mischiefs that spring from this, which even the heathen poet could style "the accursed hunger of gold"—what treading on the poor; what thrusting of them on unwholesome and dangerous occupations, with no due precautions taken for their health and safety; what shutting up of the bowels of compassion from the Lazarus lying at the gate; what wicked thoughts finding room in men's hearts, secret wishes for the death of those who stand between them and some coveted possession, have all their origin here. Consider, then, first, how powerless riches are against some of the worst calamities of our present life; how many of the sorrows which search men out the closest, which most drink up the spirit, these are utterly impotent to avert or to cure. Ask a man in a fit of the stone, or a victim of cancer, what his riches are worth to him; why, if he had the wealth of the Indies ten times told, he would exchange it all for ease of body, and a little remission of anguish. But why speak of bodily anguish? There is an anguish yet harder to bear, the anguish of the man whom the arrows of the Almighty, for they are His arrows, have pierced; who has learned what sin is, but has stopped short with the experience of the Psalmist, "Day and night Thy hand is heavy upon me; my moisture is like the drought in summer" (Psa. xxxii. 4), and never learned that there is also an atonement. What profits it such a one that all the world is for him, so long as he feels and knows that God is against him? Then, too, how often we see a man comparatively desolate in the midst of the largest worldly abundance. These considerations may do something; but take now another and a more effectual remedy against this sin. Let a greater love expel a less, a nobler affection supersede a meaner. Consider often the great things for which you were made, the unsearchable riches of which you have been made partakers in Christ; for coveteousness, the desire of having, and of having ever more and more, sin as it is, is yet the degeneration of something which is not a sin. Man was made for the infinite; with infinite longings, infinite cravings and desires. But finally, the habit of largely and liberally setting apart from our income to the service of God and the necessities of our poorer brethren is a great remedy against covetousness. (*R. C. Trench.*) *Fruit of covetousness*—(1) *oppression :*—The love of money is a root of every evil, and oppression is one of its many bitter fruits. The subject of this discourse is the multiform oppression of the poor, that results from a too eager pursuit of wealth. In ruder times, the rich often oppressed the poor in a very direct manner. When might took the place of right, they who had the power did not always take the trouble of covering their rapacity under legal forms. They kept back the labourer's hire, or seized his patrimonial field, or enslaved his person, according to the measure of impunity which their circumstances permitted them to enjoy. In this country, and in the present day, such vulgar robbery cannot be perpetrated. Love of money, a spring in the heart, when one channel of issue is blocked up, will force its way by another. Accordingly, this passion as certainly, and perhaps we should say as extensively, oppresses the poor now, as in ruder nations at earlier times. The same native evil is compelled to adopt more refined modes of action: but the oppression may be as galling to the poor and as displeasing to God although it keep strictly within the letter of human law. I have no doubt the law of Christ is violated amongst us—thoughtlessly, in ignorance, and in company with a multitude, it may be—but still sinfully violated, to a most alarming extent, in connection with the money-making efforts of this mercantile community. You have seen a street thronged from side to side with human beings, men, women, and children, all moving in one direction. The mass moves like a river. If every one keep his own place and glide along with the current, the motion will be gentle and harmless. But two or three strong men in the midst of that crowd conceive a desire to proceed at a much quicker rate than their neighbours. Yielding to that impulse, they bound forward with might and main. Observe the effect of their effort. They press on the persons that are next them. If these be strong men too, the only effect will be to push them faster forward, and the greater pressure may be only a pleasant excitement. But the pressure extends on either side, and is felt even to the outer edge of the crowd. Wherever there is a woman, a child, or a cripple, the feeble goes to the wall. The person originating the pressure may not be in contact with that sickly passenger—there may be many persons between them; but the pressure goes through all the intermediate links, not hurting any till it come to one who is unable to bear it, and hurting the helpless. In such a crowd you may sometimes see the selfishness of human nature in all is undisguised odiousness. The man seeks his own advantage, heedless of the injury that his effort may inflict on others. He is not guilty of a direct deed of injustice. He would not lift his hand to strike the feeble; he would not illegally wrest away his property. He endeavours to act justly: nay, he sometimes opens his hand in charity to the distressed. But really, though indirectly, he is an oppressor. He wriggles forward, although his movements necessarily hurt the poor. He looks to his own things; and disregards the things of others. He breaks the law of Christ. The oppressions which abound in our day, as the fruits of covetousness, are chiefly of this nature. They are by no means so gross as the tyranny which the feudal lords of the Middle Ages exercised on their serfs; but they spring from the same source, and are essentially of the same character in the estimation of the Judge. I shall now enumerate and briefly illustrate some of the forms which oppression assumes in modern society. 1. The reduction of wages below the point at which a labouring man can support his family, or a woman support herself. 2. The labour of children is another evil more or less remotely an effect of the haste to be rich. 3. Sabbath labour is one of the oppressions that the prevalence of the money-interest inflicts upon mankind. It is an evil that cries loud to the Lord of Hosts. 4. Yet another oppression let me name—the poor are in a great measure cooped up in crowded lanes, and miserable houses. This is one bitter fruit of a general selfishness. Conceive the force operating now within this city in the direction of money-making. If all the energies that are expended in that direction were added, how vast would the sum of them be! I know not a speculation more interesting than this. It would represent a power which, if collected and united, and turned upon the city's filth, and poverty, and ignorance, would sweep them away, as the stream of a mighty river rolling down our streets would carry off the mire that accumulated on their surface. (*W. Arnot.*) *Fruit of covetousness—* (2) *dishonesty :*—I. THE PATH BY WHICH COVETOUSNESS LEADS TO DISHONESTY is marked off step by step by the apostle in the text. 1. They "will be rich" (ver. 9). A class of persons are here characterized. They are described by the leading aim of their lives. It is not said what their religious profession was. Perhaps their belief was orthodox, and their zeal warm. All that we learn about them is, that in God's sight money was their "chief end." This is not a right—not a safe aim for an immortal being. 2. They "fall into temptation." The word conveys the idea of an unexpected fall—a stumble into a pit which you did not expect to be there. If the real movement of a man's life be toward money, while he diligently keeps his face turned round to maintain the appearance of being a Christian, he will certainly fall into every pit that lies in his way. The motion, too, is uneasy. Those who set out in pursuit of riches, making no other profession, get on more smoothly. 3. They fall into temptation. A man does not all at once go into vicious practices. He glides, before he is aware, into a position where he is exposed to the pressure of a strong temptation. Those who have rightly measured their own strength will avoid persons and places that put it to a severe test. He that trusteth to his own heart is a fool. 4. A snare marks another stage of this downward progress. The man who has thoughtlessly and in foolhardiness placed himself in the way of temptation, is soon surrounded—the meshes of a net compass him about. He got easily in, but he finds it impossible to get out again. He has recourse to a false entry, a forgery, or some other of the thousand tricks that the wit of hard-pressed men has invented, and the complicated forms of business has served to conceal. Behold the desperate, helpless fluttering of the bird in the snare of the fowler—dashing itself on the sides of an iron cage! 5. The next step is "into many foolish and hurtful lusts." These raging lusts are, as it were, watching, ready to fasten on their victim as soon as they see him in the toils of the net. You may have observed that a man whose pecuniary affairs are in a desperate position is peculiarly liable to fall into meaner vices. How frequently do the agonies and embarrassments that precede a shameful disclosure precipitate a man into the abyss of secret drunkenness! These lusts that covetousness leads to are "foolish and hurtful"; they pretend to cure, but they only deepen the wound. They apply a balsam that soothes the sore for a moment, but fixes disease more firmly in the flesh. I shall not trace this progress farther. II. THE DISHONESTY TO WHICH COVETOUSNESS LEADS. "Flee these things, but follow after righteousness." The vices that the love of money lands in are not named at length. In general, they are said to be foolish and hurtful. But the opposite graces are individually specified. The first on the list is righteousness. Of course, the opposite vice to which covetousness tends, and against which his warning is directed, is injustice. Righteousness is required in all our transactions—righteousness, not according to the conventional rules of society, which shift like the sand, but according to the immutable standard of the Divine law. The righteous Lord loveth righteousness.   How many are at this day put to shame for detected dishonesty, who once would have resented the supposition of it as keenly and sincerely as you ! I do not know your hearts : and what is more, you do not know them yourselves. One who does know them, however, testifies that they are deceitful above all things. Some forms of dishonesty, such as a false balance, that are prominently condemned in Scripture, we shall pass over without particular notice, because in modern society, though they still exist, they have been comparatively cast into the shade by other inventions.   Dishonesty is obliged to hide itself now under more elaborate devices. I mean the adulteration of goods offered for sale by the mixture of other ingredients. A false representation to a customer as to the original cost of your wares, or the rate of your profit, is manifestly dishonest.   Above all things, you who have others, especially young persons, employed in selling your goods, charge them to be true and honest.   I speak now not for the purchasers, but for the salesmen.   Breach of trust is a form of dishonesty alarmingly frequent in our day.   Righteousness is one and unchangeable.   It compasses about your mighty trafficking, and lays bonds on it, as completely and as easily as the smallest bargainings between a huckster and a peasant at the wayside : even as the same law with equal ease retains a little water in a cup, and the ocean's wave within the ocean's bed. (*Ibid.*)    *Haste to be rich :—* Now, why should " haste " be condemned ? for this is the voice of the Old Testament, not once or twice, but many times, either in direct terms or their equivalents. Why should haste to be rich be inveighed against, if riches are a great blessing ? In the first place, riches may either be produced or collected.   For the most part, the riches that bless men are the riches that are either produced, or are so improved by methods of ingenuity and industry that their service is much greater than it would be in the form of raw material.   The foundation of all prosperity is production.   The stone is good for nothing until it has been shaped.   Now, the man that produces wealth is the foundation man.   But that is a slow work.   It is impossible to hasten nature very much.   A man that could sow his wheat every night, and reap in the morning, would consider himself very fortunate and very happy. A man that, owning an iron mine, could draw metal as he did water from a fountain, and ship it abroad, would consider himself very fortunate.   But a man can do neither.   Man is the servant of the seasons.   He sows in the autumn or spring. With long patience he waits, as James says, like the husbandman for the harvest ; and little by little, and year by year, the man attains larger and larger means, greater competency, and, by and by, to riches ; and any man that undertakes to run ahead of processes of this kind in producing runs against natural law.   Natural, do we say ?   It is moral law, just as much as any other law.   It is the law of the production of wealth, that a man should render an equivalent for every stage of value. Sudden wealth is not hasty wealth, necessarily ;  I am speaking of the production and development of riches.   The production of wealth connects itself with benevolence, with sympathy.   A man that manufactures agricultural implements receives a certain reward for that ; but he is a benefactor ; he abbreviates labour everywhere. What is left at the end of every year, that which was not necessary to maintain the conditions of life, is what we may call the permanent wealth of a man.   It is a slow accumulation, taking the world at large.   Collectors of wealth that other men have produced may get rich speedily and safely; but producers of wealth, by the very Divine law, must go patiently, and continue through long times.   So he that makes haste to get rich is liable to fall into the violation of this fundamental law of equivalents—that is, into fraudulent ways.   But every man that is developing or producing riches is, at the same time, educating himself in morals, or should be ; for the fundamental conditions of increase lie in the man himself.   So, the development of wealth requires time, not only from the nature of production, but also because God designed it to be an education in all the minor moral qualities—as, for example, in moderation, in industry, in temperance, in loyalty, in fidelity, in respect for other's rights that co-operate with men ; for in the immense complication of riches men are in partnership with men they never saw.   Haste to be rich is also a great danger to men, because it tempts them to employ illegitimate means—sleights, crafts, disingenuous ways, greed, violations of honesty.   " Men have been fools to go through such long processes ; they have taken these circuitous routes, and have had a superstitious observance of moralities ; if they had the courage to go cross-lots they could come to the same results in less than half the time " ; and so they jump the boundary line, and run across the great roads that have been unfolded and developed by experience—and come to destruction.   They think they are weaving cordage ; but they are only running spider's webs up and down their ship ; and the first storm will break and destroy the whole of them.  A man, therefore, that is making haste to be rich is tempted to ostentation ; for riches quickly earned are like new wine, which is strong.  But ostentation is expensive, and there is many a man that is tempted to ostentation by the sudden increment of his riches, whether it be in houses, in lands, in equipage, in luxurious furnishings, in a sumptuous table, in yachts, in horses and hounds, in coaches, or what not.  Men having sudden wealth are apt to become cruel through indifference to other men's rights.  There is such a thing as a society-robber.  Then, too, anxiety, haste, is apt to change into idolatry ; and the very ends which men have in life are neglected, and the man's wealth becomes as an idol which he worships.  (*H. W. Beecher.*)     *Peril in handling wealth:*—In Washington, U.S., recently, it was found that some lady clerks engaged in sorting bank bills in the Treasury department found sores breaking out on their face and hands, and were obliged to leave.  This led to an inquiry, when it was found that the cause was the arsenic employed in the manufacture of the paper.  "I have known," says a journalist, "a half-dozen cases where ladies have been compelled to resign their positions.  There are three who were here six years before they were afflicted with sores.  About three months ago they were so visited by them that they had to quit work.  They have been away ever since, and the physician's certificate in each case says that their blood is poisoned with arsenic." This fact may be regarded as an illustration of the unnoticed peril sometimes lurking in handling wealth.     *Wealth a fatal weight:*—At Long Branch, some visitors, strolling on the beach, observed a large fish hawk swoop down into the waters of the bay and strike its talons into a huge plaice.  The bird rose with its prey, but its weight proved too great and dragged him down.  Several times the bird struggled to ascend, but failed, and, exhausted, it finally fell into the water still clinging to its captive.  Its talons were so embedded in the fish that it could not release them, and it was drowned.  The ·fish died of its wounds, and both were washed ashore, where with difficulty they were separated.  The death of the hawk in this effort to carry off its prize is typical of a disaster very common in life.  Covetousness and avarice only too often prompt men to struggle for a great financial prize, and in the struggle they sacrifice honour, integrity, and sometimes even life, natural and eternal.

Ver. 11. **But thou, O man of God.**—*The man of God:*—I. His RELATIONS TO GOD are suggested by the title itself, "man of God."  This had formerly been distinctive of a prophet, and especially of Elijah, the great reformer, who so realized the truth underlying it that he began many a message by the favourite formula, "The Lord God of Israel, before whom I stand."    In Ephesus, Timothy had to take up as decided a stand against prevailing evils as Elijah had maintained in the kingdom of Israel ; and he too was to find strength and wisdom in the presence of God, whence he might come forth to the people as God's representative and spokesman. Any devout man may be called a "man of God" if he is—1. Living near God and coming forth to his duties, as Moses came from the mount of communion, reflecting the light of heaven.  2. Representing God is the outcome of communion with Him. Reflection of light can only result from the incidence of light.  A mirror shut up in a pitch-dark cellar is not to be distinguished by the eye from a flagstone, but placed in the sunlight it may reflect a whole heaven of beauty.  If you would let your light shine before men, you must put yourself in true relation to the Sun of Righteousness.  And, again, no one would be called "a man of God" unless he was—3. Seeking God's ends.  It was because Timothy was by profession and in character "God's man" that the apostle assumes that his course would of necessity be different from that of the worldly—that he would flee the things they loved. Every one would discredit the assertion of one who said he represented a drapery establishment if, day after day, he was engaged in buying and selling timber or coal, and left all soft goods unregarded. II. His RELATIONS TO SIN are those of unconquerable repugnance.  1. The nature of these sins is exemplified in the words uttered just before by Paul against the love of money, the hurtful lusts of the human heart, and the foolish and evil practices to which these lead.  2. The means of escape from these are twofold.  Sometimes we may meet and conquer a temptation, and sometimes we may more wisely flee from it.  III. His RELATIONS TO VIRTUES.  Negative precepts distinguished the Old Dispensation, but the New Dispensation is not content with them.  The virtues mentioned here are arranged in pairs.  1. Righteousness and godliness include all conduct towards God :

obedience to His law, trust and reverence, devoutness and prayer. 2. Faith and love are the two essentials to such a life, for righteousness is the offspring of faith, and godliness is the offspring of love. 3. Patience and meekness have regard to our dealings with our fellow-men, especially with those who persecute or wrong us, and they are among the most difficult graces to exhibit. (*A. Rowland, LL.B.*) *Are you a man of God?*—I. The text speaks of a MAN. II. The text says that we are not only to be a man, but it tells us what sort of a man; it says—a "man OF GOD." There are two or three kinds of men. 1. There is the "man of the world." You hear such a person say, "Well, you know, I am a man of the world." A "man of the world" is supposed to know everything, but, as a rule, you find that what he knows is everything of indulgence and badness. But does he know how to bear trial when it comes? But the "man of God" feels that duty, principle, righteousness, are of first importance. The "man of the world" puts expediency before him; the "man of God" has principle for his guide. The "man of God" says, "It is not necessary for me to live, but it is necessary that the women and children should get out of danger before me." The "man of the world" always pushes himself first, because he is a "man of the world"; the "man of God" first lifts up others, because he is a "man of God." 2. Then there is the "man of business." All such a man is noted for is that he is a "man of business." His greatest characteristic is that his head is "screwed on the right way." The "man of God" seeks first the kingdom of God; the "things" of the world are of secondary importance. The "man of God" is, however, "diligent in business," but he is not a slave to it. 3. There are also other classes of persons called "men of wealth" and "men of learning." Being a "man of God" implies a man who has found God—God is in all his thoughts. Is God so hard to find as some of the Churches would have us believe? The "man of God" is one who has not only found God, but obeys His commandments. In the text the "man of God" is called upon to "follow righteousness"; that is, to train himself to act in a right or straight course of conduct. An old writer has pointed out that man has naturally a habit of walking askew. How difficult for a man to walk a hundred yards in a perfectly straight line! It is impossible for him to do so if he shut his eyes. I appeal to your recollection whether you ever saw a straight path across a field; it is always tortuous, in and out. Likewise, the path taken by a man's heart is not direct and straight by nature. The "man of God" is reliable; he can be trusted with uncounted gold, and his word is as good as his bond. The "man of God" should be godly; that is, like God, unselfish, not seeking exclusively his own good, but the good of all. The "man of God" will practise self-respect, self-control, and self-denial. (*W. Birch.*)     *Following righteousness :*—Ignorant though Stewart was of every technicality in trade, he was a man of undeviating truth and uprightness. He was aware that unjustifiable profits were made by shopkeepers, and that they had no conscience whatever about practising deception in order to place a fictitious value upon their goods. All such false ways he utterly abhorred, and he was determined to try his own plan. At all risks, he made up his mind that he would not look for more than ten per cent. profit, and that he would never deceive a buyer as to the prime cost of any article in his store. "Ten per cent. and no lies"—that was Mr. Stewart's motto for doing business. But it is a curious instance of the repugnance of the trade to carry on business on such terms that the salesman, who could not have suffered in any way by this arrangement, became irritated against his employer, and at the end of a month or so resigned his situation. He declared that he could no longer be a party to sell goods by such rules—that, in fact, Mr. Stewart was giving them away to the public; and, with very significant emphasis, he added, "Before another month is over you will be a bankrupt." Mr. Stewart's business, however, gradually enlarged, until, after being in business half a century, his property and stock was worth twenty million pounds, thus proving that "honesty is the best policy. (*Memoir of Stewart, the Millionaire.*)     **Patience.**—*Patience portrayed :* —Among all the graces that adorn the Christian soul, like so many jewels of various colours and lustres, against the day of her espousals to the Lamb of God, there is not one more brilliant than this of patience; not one which brings more glory to God, or contributes so much toward making and keeping peace on earth; not one which renders a man more happy within himself, more agreeable to all about him; insomuch that even they who themselves possess it not, yet are sure to commend it in others. I. In the first place, PATIENCE IS A VIRTUE COMMON TO US WITH GOD. Long-suffering is His darling attribute; and what is dear in His sight ought not to be less precious in ours. And how marvellous is His patience who daily pours His blessings on those men who as daily offend, affront, and dishonour Him! Yet God's blessings are abused to the purposes of luxury and lasciviousness; His truth is denied; His commandments are broken; His Church is persecuted; His ministers are insulted; His Son is crucified afresh; and His own long-suffering is made an argument against His existence—and He is still patient. What is man, then, that he should complain? II. The patience which we so much admire in God SHONE FORTH YET MORE AMAZINGLY IN THE PERSON OF HIS SON JESUS CHRIST. For was ever patience like that patience which, descending from a throne of glory, bore a long imprisonment in the womb to sanctify sinners, and lay in a stable to bring them to a kingdom. III. The patience thus practised by Christ IS ENJOINED BY HIS HOLY GOSPEL, being, indeed, the badge of that gospel and its professors. Is the mind tempted to impatience by the disappointment of its desires and the loss of worldly goods and enjoyments? The Scripture, to eradicate the temptation, is full of precepts enjoining us to contemn the world, and not to set our hearts upon things that pass away, and that cannot satisfy the soul when it is possessed of them. The worldly man is always impatient, because he prefers his body to his soul; the Christian prefers his soul to his body, and therefore knows how to give largely and to lose patiently. IV. WE FIND ALL THE SAINTS OF GOD who have been eminent for their faith in Christ TO HAVE BEEN AS EMINENT FOR THEIR PATIENCE, without which their faith must have failed in the day of trial; it being not through faith alone, but, as the apostle says, "through faith and patience," that they "inherited the promises." Faith begat patience, which, like a dutiful child, proved the support of its parent. Through patience Moses, so often abused and insulted, and only not stoned by a stiffnecked people, still entreated the Lord for them. V. THE PRESENT STATE OF MAN RENDERS THE PRACTICE OF THIS VIRTUE ABSOLUTELY NECESSARY FOR HIM if he would enjoy any happiness here or hereafter. Could we, indeed, live in the world without suffering, then were there no need of patience. "He that endureth to the end shall be saved. Be thou faithful unto death, and I will give thee a crown of life." VI. THE MANIFOLD INCONVENIENCES OF IMPATIENCE WILL SET THIS TRUTH OFF TO GREAT ADVANTAGE. As patience is the attribute of God, impatience had its beginning from Satan. "Through envy of the devil," saith the wise man, "came death into the world." And whence proceeds envy but from impatience of beholding the happiness of another? Impatience and malice, therefore, had one father, and they have grown together in his children ever since. (Bp. Horne.) Meekness:—It is recorded that after Thomas Aquinas had returned to Bologna a stranger came one day to the monastery, and, visiting the prior, asked that one of the brothers might carry a basket for him to the market to make some purchases. "Tell the first brother you see in the cloisters," said the prior. The brother happened to be Thomas Aquinas, who, at the curt command of the stranger, took up the basket and followed. But he was suffering from lameness, and the arrogant stranger turned round and scolded him for being so slow. The Bolognese, looking on with indignation at the treatment of the revered teacher of the Schools, said to the visitor, "Do you know who it is that you are treating in this way? It is Brother Thomas!" "Brother Thomas!" he exclaimed; and, falling on his knees, begged the saint's forgiveness. "Nay," said Thomas, "you must forgive me for being so slow!"

Ver. 12. **Fight the good fight of faith.**—*The good fight:*—War is a terribly earnest business which will not bear to be trifled with. Of all things under the sun, this work of fighting, if it is to be done at all, is one that must be done with all our heart and mind. It is no mere holiday affair of plumes and epaulettes, and drums and trumpets, and flags and fine parade. Only certain ruin will come to those who go into it in that spirit, with a light and careless heart. Well, now, it is to such a work that Paul likens the Christian life, and it is in the same earnest spirit that he would have us to deal with it. Of course, there are many points in which it differs altogether from the warfares of this world: they work sorrow and desolation and death, but this brings joy and fruitfulness and life. They doubtless call forth heroic qualities of courage and devotion, which, however, are often sullied by fierce and pitiless passion; but this conflict of ours, while it demands equal courage and devotion, is gentle also, and merciful, ready to suffer loss, but not to inflict loss. Oh, very true, in times like ours this conflict differs materially from that which Paul and Timothy had to wage in the early martyr ages of the Church's story. The wild beasts at Ephesus, the stonings in Jerusalem, the prison and the stake and the cross of those days, all have vanished from the warfare, which you may think, therefore, now hardly deserves so great a name. Yet a warfare it is still, not without its peril and its privation, and its enemy, and its conflict, partly within and partly without ; and it needs now, as ever, a brave and an earnest heart. Is our religion at all like a real, earnest battle? Were I speaking to you of your common everyday life, with its labour and weary wrestle to keep the wolf from the door, I might call it a hard battle for the poor man ; and some of you, I daresay, would be ready enough to reply, " Ay, that it is, and we know it well enough, too—a hard, weary, ceaseless struggle ; and sometimes we could almost wish we were well through it, and could be at rest." So, then, the words have clear meaning to many of us— I daresay to most of us. But could you say now as much about the affairs of your spiritual life? That is what Paul had in his eye. But have you ever maintained any such battle for integrity and truth, for the soul and for God, as you have often done for meat and drink, and raiment, and a respectable position? Assuredly, if we are true followers of Christ we shall find plenty of enemies to contend with—enemies who are ready to take advantage of every opportunity, and who are not to be overcome without long and resolute battle. You shall find these foes at the outset within yourselves. And the first part of every man's battle is to overcome and master these. I do not much value a warfare which is chiefly to get the better of other people. I do not believe that there is much good fighting in any one till he has first conquered himself. The battle begins, therefore, in our own heart and life. It is well to know that, for some are far more alive to their neighbour's danger than they are to their own ; and so long as they are of that mind they will never fight to any purpose the fight to which we are called. The nearest foes are those that are first to be dealt with, and there is no victory for us until these are overcome, and our nearest foes are those within ourselves. There are doubts, perhaps, perplexing your mind and chilling your faith, and you must fight your way into clearness, facing them like a thoughtful, earnest man ; for if you do not you may well chance to settle down in chill indifference to all that is at stake. Then there are lusts and appetites of the flesh which perhaps hotly assail you, and you must contend with them, and beat them into subjection, for otherwise they will grow just as they are gratified, and bind you in a bondage of shame. And there are still more malignant lusts of the mind, as envy, pride, malice, hatred, uncharitableness, revenge ; and we must do resolute battle with these and slay them, for if we let them live on they will soon leave no life in us. And there is the love of the world and the things of the world, and we must set ourselves to deny and resist that ; for oh, how many heartless souls there are that succumb to these allurements, and never strike one blow or win one victory in the good fight, because their hands have been weakened and their arms have been blunted by the world which they had folded to their hearts. But our warfare is not confined to these inward wrestles with deceitful lusts and hurtful snares ; it is not our own souls only that have to be saved. You might be religious after a fashion, and yet rather a selfish kind of man, if that were all that you were caring for. And the selfish man, no matter even though his self-seeking concerns his highest interests, the selfish man is not the true Christian man. Our battlefield is the world. We may not stand neutral in any righteous cause. Is there ignorance, breeding its poisonous crop of superstition, which we can in any wise help to remove? Is there injustice done which we can either arrest or redress? Then it will not do for you and me to stand by and say it is no concern of ours. This is called a "good fight," and surely with good reasons. Sometimes we are in the way of saying, "that was a good fight," when all we mean is that it was well and stoutly contested ; we praise the combatants simply because they did their part well. But here the phrase has a far deeper meaning than that. This is a good fight, whether we do our part in it well or ill. It is the cause that makes it good, as it is the cause alone that makes any warfare right. Alas ! how few of the world's wars can lay any claim to that name. And to do all this by persuasion, by pity, by tender sympathy, by bearing each other's burdens, by the truth spoken in love, by meek and patient suffering for righteousness' sake, by faithful example, by brotherly kindness and charity. So with good weapons the good fight is to be fought. Not with wrangling and bitterness, not by malice and cunning, not by persecution and hatred, but by the gentle drawing of all cords of love. Think not to gain the victory here by ways or by forces which Christ has never used. But it is also called a fight of faith. And for that, too, there is good reason. It is a fight for faith, but specially and still more it is a fight by faith. Only by faith can the victory be won. It is a fight for the faith. Always the Christian has to do battle for the faith once delivered to the saints, to retain it for himself, and to hand it down to his children, and to maintain it for the world. Sad it is to think that after so many centuries of Christian history, it would almost seem as if the enmity to the gospel only grew more intense and more bitter. The culture and highest education of this age has, alas! largely drifted away from it into atheism, agnosticism, esoteric Buddhism, and what not. What we have to contend for is faith in God, and for Christ as the revelation of God, and for faith in the immortal spirit and the life which is eternal; in short, for faith in its essential truth and in its purity, as Christ lived it and taught it, and as the apostles proclaimed it by inspiration of the Holy Ghost. And as our good fight is for the faith, so also it is by faith that it must be carried on. It will not be well if we take to other weapons. "This is the victory that overcometh the world, even our faith." He who said that was a master of clear and convincing reason. Very far was he from despising the intellect which God had given him for ordering all his thoughts aright. Always the soldier must have faith in his commander, faith in his skill, his courage, his loyalty, his capacity; and if he cannot trust these he is sure to be beaten. The rank and file, amid the smoke and dust of the conflict, perceive nothing but what lies close at their hand, and they may not be able to understand why they are ordered to keep this post or retire from that, why to rush on one peril, why to avoid another; but if they have faith in their leader they will say, "He knows best; it is our business to be where he would have us to be, and to do what he would have us to do, and if we fall what matter, so long as the fight only be won?" Without such a faith there would be no battle gained. There is nothing for us, then, but to fight on in faith: and if we do not, if we choose our own way and not Christ's, does not our past experience tell us that that way leads to sorrow and disaster? When was it that you fell before the tempter, and were brought, perhaps, to shame? When was it that your efforts to do good to others proved barren and fruitless? Was it not then, when you were full of self-confidence and had lost your faith in God? And when were your victories won, when did you make any progress in godliness? Was it not then, when you put your trust in Christ and did His will, and left Him to make it all clear in His own good time? (*W. C. Smith, D.D.*)     *The fight:*—It is a curious fact that there is no subject about which most people feel such deep interest as "fighting." This is a simple fact, whatever way we may try to explain it. We should call that Englishman a dull fellow who cared nothing about the story of Waterloo, or Inkermann, or Balaclava, or Lucknow. We should think that heart cold and stupid which was not moved and thrilled by the struggles at Sedan, and Strasburg, and Metz, and Paris, during the war between France and Germany. But there is another warfare of far greater importance than any war that was ever waged by man. This warfare, I am aware, is a thing of which many know nothing. Talk to them about it, and they are ready to set you down as a madman, an enthusiast, or a fool. And yet it is as real and true as any war the world has ever seen. It has its hand-to-hand conflicts and its wounds. It has its watchings and fatigues. It has its sieges and assaults. It has its victories and its defeats. Above all, it has consequences which are awful, tremendous, and most peculiar. I. TRUE CHRISTIANITY IS A FIGHT. True Christianity! Let us mind that word "true." There is a vast quantity of religion current in the world which is not true, genuine Christianity. The true Christian is called to be a soldier, and must behave as such from the day of his conversion to the day of his death. He is not meant to live a life of religious ease, indolence, and security. With whom is the Christian soldier meant to fight? Not with other Christians. Wretched indeed is that man's idea of religion who fancies that it consists in perpetual controversy! No, indeed! The principal fight of the Christian is with the world, the flesh, and the devil. These are his never-dying foes. Unless he gets the victory over these three, all other victories are useless and vain. He must fight the flesh. Even after conversion he carries within him a nature prone to evil, and a heart weak and unstable as water. He must fight the world. The subtle influence of that mighty enemy must be daily resisted, and without a daily battle can never be overcome. The love of the world's good things—the fear of the world's laughter or blame—the secret desire to keep in with the world—the secret wish to do as others in the world do, and not to run into extremes—all these are spiritual foes which beset the Christian continually on his way to heaven, and must be conquered. He must fight the devil. That old enemy of mankind is not dead. Remember the maxim of the wisest general that ever lived in England—" In time of war it is the worst mistake to underrate your enemy, and try to make a little war." This Christian warfare is no light matter. Saved souls will always be found to have fought a fight. Let us not think that in this war we can remain neutral and sit still. Such a line of action may be possible in the strife of nations, but it is utterly impossible in that conflict which concerns the soul. The boasted policy of non-interference—the "masterly inactivity" which pleases so many statesmen—the plan of keeping quiet and letting things alone—all this will never do in the Christian warfare. It is a fight of universal necessity. No rank, or class, or age, can plead exemption, or escape the battle. Ministers and people, preachers and hearers, old and young, high and low, rich and poor, gentle and simple, kings and subjects, landlords and tenants, learned and unlearned—all alike must carry arms and go to war. It is a fight of perpetual necessity. It admits of no breathing time, no armistice, no truce. On week-days as well as on Sundays—in private as well as in public—at home by the family fireside as well as abroad—in little things like management of tongue and temper, as well as in great ones like the government of kingdoms—the Christian's warfare must unceasingly go on. II. TRUE CHRISTIANITY IS THE FIGHT OF FAITH. Success depends entirely on believing. A general faith in the truth of God's written Word is the primary foundation of the Christian soldier's character. A religion without doctrine or dogma is a thing which many are fond of talking of in the present day. It sounds very fine at first. It looks very pretty at a distance. But the moment we sit down to examine and consider it, we shall find it a simple impossibility. We might as well talk of a body without bones and sinews. As for true Christians, faith is the very backbone of their spiritual existence. No one ever fights earnestly against the world, the flesh, and the devil, unless he has engraven on his heart certain great principles which he believes. A special faith in our Lord Jesus Christ's person, work, and office, is the life, heart, and mainspring of the Christian soldier's character. Habitual lively faith in Christ's presence and readiness to help is the secret of the Christian soldier fighting successfully. He that has most faith will always be the happiest and most comfortable soldier. Nothing makes the anxieties of warfare sit so lightly on a man as the assurance of Christ's love and continual protection. Let us turn to the pages of early Church history. Let us see how the primitive Christians held fast their religion even unto death, and were not shaken by the fiercest persecutions of heathen emperors. For centuries there were never wanting men like Polycarp and Ignatius, who were ready to die rather than deny Christ. Fines, and prisons, and torture, and fire, and sword, were unable to crush the spirit of the noble army of martyrs. The whole power of imperial Rome, the mistress of the world, proved unable to stamp out the religion which began with a few fishermen and publicans in Palestine! And then let us remember that believing in an unseen Jesus was the Church's strength. They won their victory by faith. Let us examine the story of the Reformation. Let us study the lives of its leading champions—Wycliffe, and Huss, and Luther, and Ridley, and Latimer, and Hooper. Let us mark how these gallant soldiers of Christ stood firm against a host of adversaries, and were ready to die for their principles. What battles they fought! What controversies they maintained! What contradiction they endured! What tenacity of purpose they exhibited against a world in arms! And then let us remember that believing in an unseen Jesus was the secret of their strength. They overcame by faith. III. TRUE CHRISTIANITY IS A GOOD FIGHT. "Good" is a curious word to apply to any warfare. All worldly war is more or less evil. The Scripture does not call the Christian fight " a good fight " without reason and cause. 1. The Christian's fight is good because fought under the best of generals. The Leader and Commander of all believers is our Divine Saviour, the Lord Jesus Christ—a Saviour of perfect wisdom, infinite love, and almighty power. The Captain of our salvation never fails to lead His soldiers to victory. 2. The Christian's fight is good, because fought with the best of helps. Weak as each believer is in himself, the Holy Spirit dwells in him, and his body is a temple of the Holy Ghost. 3. The Christian fight is a good fight, because fought with the best of promises. 4. The Christian's fight is a good fight, because fought with the best of issues and results. 5. The Christian's fight is good, because it does good to the soul of him that fights it. All other wars have a bad, lowering, and demoralizing tendency. They call forth the worst passions of the human mind. They harden the conscience, and sap the foundations of religion and morality. The

Christian warfare alone tends to call forth the best things that are left in man. It promotes humility and charity, it lessens selfishness and worldliness, it induces men to set their affections on things above. 6. The Christian's fight is a good fight, because it does good to the world. All other wars have a devastating, ravaging, and injurious effect. But go where you please, you will find that the presence of a few true Christians is a blessing. Surely this is good! 7. Finally, the Christian's fight is good, because it ends in a glorious reward for all who fight it. (1) It may be you are struggling hard for the rewards of this world. Perhaps you are straining every nerve to obtain money, or place, or power, or pleasure. (2) It may be you know something of the Christian warfare, and are a tried and proved soldier already. (*Bp. Ryle.*) *The Christian warfare; or, the good fight of faith :*—I. IN WHAT RESPECTS THE CHRISTIAN LIFE IS THE FIGHT OF FAITH. 1. There are enemies of our salvation, and there must be faith in the soul to set against them. Where there are not two parties, there can be no fight. There is no fighting in heaven, for there are no enemies there (Rev. xxi. 25). There is none of this fighting in the unbelieving world neither; for the enemies have all there alone, and there is no faith to set against them (Luke xi. 21). 2. Faith has the chief interest in this fight. In it there will be use for all the graces, the doing and suffering graces : yet the fight has its name from faith, as that which has the chief hand in it. It carries on the fight, and obtains the victory—"Whom resist, steadfast in the faith " (2 Pet. v. 9). 3. Lastly, the great design of a holy God, in that fight is the trial of faith. Hence says the apostle (1 Pet. i. 6, 7). II. IN WHAT RESPECTS IT IS A GOOD FIGHT? III. WHY IS THE CHRISTIAN LIFE, IN THE DISPOSAL OF HOLY PROVIDENCE, MADE A FIGHT? No doubt the Lord could have given His people a constant sunshine as well on this side as the other side of death, and cleared the way of those armed adversaries that are ready to attack them. 1. That the members may be conformed to their Head in their passage through the world. 2. That the nothingness, and utter unworthiness of the creature, which is to wear the crown of glory for ever, may convincingly appear; so as they themselves and all others may see it is owing purely to free grace, not to them (Deut. viii. 2). 3. For the greater confusion of the grand adversary, who, attacked Him in person in the world, and whom He causeth poor weak creatures to triumph over after they have maintained a fight with Him (Rom. xvi. 20). 4. For the greater glory of the Captain of their salvation, the more full display of the freedom of grace, and the efficacy of His blood and Spirit. 5. For that they may have a greater variety of experiences—"Patience worketh experience ; and experience, hope " (Rom. v. 4). 6. Lastly, that heaven may be the more sweet to them, when they come to it. IV. WHY THEIR FIGHT IS CALLED A FIGHT OF FAITH. The reason is, because by that means all the glory of the victories obtained redounds to free grace, not to the sinner himself, " It is of faith, that it might be by grace " (Rom. iv. 16). V. I WILL TOUCH AT SOME PARTICULAR FIGHTS OF FAITH THE CHRISTIAN MAY HAVE IN HIS COURSE HEAVENWARD, SUCH AS—1. In a call to some more than ordinary work or duty. 2. In desertion. 3. In temptations from Satan. 4. In afflictions. 5. With this present evil world. 6. With sin. 7. With death. Some have a fighting life with the world all their days: but, alas ! it is not the fight of faith with it, but a sinful faithless fighting with it, that carries on the ruin of their souls. Ye will know this faithless fight with it by these two things. 1. All their fight is to get something of the world, not to be kept from the spiritual evil of the world. 2. Their fight they have with the world takes away from them all favour of the Word of God and of religion. We must then stay our hearts by faith—1. Firmly believing the Scripture accounts of the unseen world (Heb. xi. 1). 2. Firmly believing the Scripture account of the way to heaven; that Christ is the way to it (John xiv. 6); and that by faith we walk in Him to it (Col. ii. 6). 3. Believing in the Lord Jesus Christ for your safe passage to the upper part of the unseen world (Psa. lxxiii. 24; xxxi. 5); committing your soul to Him, rolling the weight of your through-bearing on Him as the Captain of salvation appointed of God to bring many sons to glory. 4. Believing that your Lord Christ is Lord of the unseen world, and that the whole compass of it above and below is under His dominion (Rev. i. 18). (*T. Boston, D.D.*) *The problem of life :*—Human life is not a consummated and perfected thing ; it is a struggle, a conflict universally; and that not by accident, not by the intrusion of any unexpected obstacle, not by the re-establishment of the original and fundamental policy of creation, but by the very genius of creation. This conflict inheres in the very problem which the physical existence was set to work out. All acts of development from childhood to manhood are in the nature of aggression, of vigilance, of impulsion, of pressure onward, with more or less pain and penalty. The unfolding of every faculty is like a birth, and has its pain, its throe; and the organization of character comes by the drill of each separate organ. The making of a perfect man, according to the large ideal of Christ Jesus, obliges men to compel themselves in such a way that the whole process of education takes on the form of a conflict. Men recognize this outwardly. No man gains the aptitudes which are required for the maintenance of his physical existence without earnest study, without great patience, without much self-denial, without long drill, without hard work. You cannot acquire skill in your fingers without making them war against the tool, against matter, and against the laws by which matter is governed. Let us look at some points of the conflict which belongs to personal experience, which takes on different forms, and which all feel, more or less, in some form. There is, in the first place, the control of a man's own disposition, the control of his appetites and passions, which are indispensable servants, and strong-handed servants, but which are very dangerous masters, that slip easily into the seat of authority. Without appetites and passions, a man would languish as a plant without sap; there would be neither vigour nor success in his life; and yet, indispensable as they are as pioneers and engineers, they are dangerous. And multitudes of men, not knowing how to make suitable war upon domineering passions and appetites, are perpetually broken down. Then come the whole range of irritable and malign feelings. Irritableness is merely sensibility exercised in a certain direction. In general sensibility is a great blessing. Quickness to respond to fact, to truth, to that which is right, is a Divine blessing to any soul. At the same time, quickness is the peculiar difficulty of temper, which acts without thinking, without direction, and without discretion. A man who was without susceptibility to the impulse of anger would have no power of resistance or self-defence. Multitudes of evil which, if permitted to get control of us, would be most pernicious, and often fatal, are repelled by the sudden impulse of indignation. Thousands and thousands of temptations you must destroy at once, or they will destroy you. How many men, under such circumstances, know how to carry themselves evenly and justly, making anger turn to indignation, and making indignation turn to profit in moral results? How many are there who have no need to fight? Is your anger a patient steed so subdued to the saddle and bridle that you can ride it without watch and care? Is it an easy thing for you to maintain sweetness and equanimity? What man ever attempted to live a Christian life who has not had a painful consciousness of the need of conflict in regard to his temper and malign feelings? Then there is the more subtle danger of self-indulgence in every one of its forms. In this realm there is a perpetual seeking after immediate pleasure. There is, then, need that a man should rouse himself continually, and in every direction, that he should be up and around, that he should be vigilant and laborious as against this fatal spirit of quietude—this anchoring of the soul in still waters. But what shall I say of the conflict that every man has in life with pride, and with the love of praise, which leads one to violate others' rights, and to seek, in an undue measure, his own welfare? Let no one suppose that this conflict is necessarily one of dreariness, and that the Christian life, because it is a life of conflict, is therefore a life of morbid suffering or pain. It is a conflict that every man goes through who masters the mathematical science; but is it a painful conflict? When the awkward boy first goes to the school of manners, and is obliged to throw back his shoulders, and turn out the palms of his hand, and step with an appropriate instead of a clownish tread, it is a painful thing for him to do, and to do continually, and to form the habit of doing; but nobody says of children when they are sent to the dancing school, "Poor children! What a conflict they are going through!" And yet, it is a conflict that they are going through. And at every step of the education of his body or of his disposition, of his physical organs, or of his thought and feeling, a man is going through a conflict, and a conflict that sometimes is accompanied by bitter pain. There are sometimes exigences, though they are very rare, which bring men into an elevated condition without much struggle; but the ordinary experience of men in Christian life is one in which they press forward and overcome just as a man does who produces results by thought, by work, by patience in strife. The whole of Christian life is a conflict in that way. See how men are surrounded. See how the shopmate is obliged to repel the sagacious influences of him who stands near him. See how the moral tone of a man may be lowered by the vulgarity and impurity of the man who sits next to him, and thrusts

vile paragraphs under his eye, and narrates in his ear stories that are not fit for
him to hear or repeat. No thermometer in the open air was ever more subject to
the thermal influences of nature than men are to the influences that are exerted
upon them on every side; and we are constantly to wage a conflict of resistance
with every man we meet, and with all the circumstances in which we are placed,
that we may turn them to account, and that we may frustrate and thwart the
mischief that is in them. But these are comparatively small things. How is it
when you are father and mother, and a nest full of birds come down to you with
your faults exaggerated in them, and the faults of two or three of your ancestors
thrown in, and you are to bring up those children, strong-willed, and constantly
breaking out into this and that mischief? How many persons there are who have
been discouraged and almost heart-broken by the burden that God has laid upon
them to develop, to train, and to graduate successfully into life, a houseful of
children! It is a burden that you have to carry. It is a warfare that you have to
meet. Then there are social surroundings, infelicities, hardships, difficulties, tasks
of support, catastrophes, which overtake men in life. If you will be kind enough
to go down stream the water will not bubble around you a particle; it will make
your passage very easy; but now turn about and go up stream, and see how the
force of the current heaps the water about you. So long as a man is content to go
down stream in life, and does not attempt to go up stream, he goes easy; but let
him undertake to go up stream for the sake of a higher life, and see if on every
side he does not find difficulties to be overcome and trials to be borne. But, if he
perseveres, by and by so many of them will be mastered and he will have gained
such momentum that his career will be, comparatively speaking, joyous, though it
may not be easy. The rising from one plane or sphere to another plane or sphere
is always with difficulty. How, then, shall we maintain this conflict? Largely by
volition in respect to new things, and by reducing to habits, as far as possible,
things with which we are familiar. It is in the power of a man to make automatic
thousands of acts that at first he was obliged to force himself to perform. We
have not really learned a thing till we have learned it so that the learning ceases to
be conscious. We are also to fight this conflict as much as possible by adopting
the principle, or by recognising the fact and making it a principle of practical life,
that there is in every man an equipollent force over against each faculty that is in
him; that if there is selfishness there is generosity; that if there is hatred there is
love; that if there is avarice there is benevolence; that if there is fear there is
hope; and that in the discipline of a man's nature it is not so wise to directly
attack the evil as to excite the corresponding good, and let that take the control
of the evil. Is a man prone to think of things that he ought not to think of?
Let him think of things that he ought to think of. Let him give the mind another
direction and indulge in another class of thoughts. Does a child hurt itself? See
how the nurse or the mother catches up some mirror, some brilliant object, and
flashes it in the child's eye to divert its attention from its pain. It is not wise to
mourn over a child that is hurt or to look at its bruise; it is wise, rather, to direct
its thoughts to something else Then, aside from these things, fill your soul from
day to day with the great truths which are given to us in the gospel of Christ. (*H. W.
Beecher.*) *The good fight:—*I. IT IS SEVERE. Our enemies are many, strong, united.
II. IT IS PAINFUL. It is the house divided against itself. One desire in antagonism
to another. III. IT IS CONSTANT. Foes never tire, we must never rest. (*Homilist.*)
*The Christian warfare:—*I. SURVEY THE FIELD OF BATTLE. This world is a great battle-
field. Upon its bosom are two armies. They are disproportionate in numbers. The one
is large, united, armed, disciplined, and determined. The other is small, sometimes
trembling and irresolute, with here and there a bold and earnest hero, but for the
most part but indifferent soldiers. Their appearance and preparations are best
described in 1. Kings xx. 27; and it may be that this very passage was intended
as a type of them: "The children of Israel pitched before them like two little
flocks of kids; but the Syrians filled the country." In this position they are both
ready for the battle; but alas! the one is oftentimes more ready than the other.
The first is united, and it fills the country: the other is as two flocks of kids. The
first is armed with every conceivable weapon: the other has but one. The first is
disciplined and determined: the other is simple and feeble. And yet, withal, there
is no doubt of the issue. Every soldier in the little army is unconquerable. Many
and many an antagonist is conquered and subdued. To what, then, must we attribute
this remarkable success? Not to their numbers, certainly; for they are the fewest
of any people. Not to their wisdom; for they are the foolish of this world. Not

to their strength; for they are the weak things of it. It is to their Captain who commands them. He is the cause of this incessant victory against their overwhelming odds. The first army is commanded, indeed, by a mighty prince. No common general is he. Uniting every species of ability and strength save one, he is altogether invincible by any other might than that of our Commander; but before Him he has no success. II. We are now to investigate THE NATURE OF THEIR WARFARE. The apostle here calls it a "good fight," and a "fight of faith"; by which terms he shows us at once the object and method of warfare. 1. Take its object. It is the very opposite of the world. The object of the true soldier of Christ is to win souls to Him, to save men from hell, to make known the salvation purchased by Christ, and the promised freedom of the soul from sin. 2. Take, next, the principles of this warfare. Here again we see the difference between these two contending armies. In Satan's army every conceivable weapon is authorized. Lying, equivocation, misrepresentation, forging of books, corruptions of human writings, and the base and unholy trickery of false miracles, are resorted to as occasion may demand. Not such are the principles upon which Christians are called to fight. To them it is not permitted to act but according to the will and Word of God. 3. Let us regard, then, the methods by which the army of Christ are required to maintain their ground in the world. There are three modes of warfare by which they do this. They disarm their opponents, they silence the enemy, they bring them over to their side. These are the results of the Christian's mode of warfare. III. But I proceed to consider THE WEAPONS WHICH THE CHRISTIAN WARRIOR USES. Will all the tradition, or all the philosophy, or all the science of the world break any sinner's heart, or bring him into captivity, or destroy the power of his sins? They are not the Christian's sword, and with such shall no man prevail. But let us bring the gospel to bear upon these cases. Let us set before the young man, the infidel, or the selfish worldling the love of God in Christ, exhibiting as it does on the one hand the peril and necessary judgment of sin, and on the other the glorious remedy which is provided, and you bring the only weapon which will pierce their hearts. The Scripture, then, is our weapon. IV. THE DISCIPLINE WHICH IS NECESSARY FOR SO GREAT A CONFLICT. 1. Keep under the body. A habit of self-restraint is an essential element in Christian warfare. 2. Another direction is to endure hardness. Softness, and that temper which makes us shrink from opposition and the rough usage which we may meet with in our career, is often a sad hindrance to the Christian. 3. But the main thing is, that he should study the use of his weapon. 4. Last of all, pray. (*W. Harrison, M. A.*) **Lay hold on eternal life.** *Man's great duty:*—While there is eternal life in the gospel sufficient for all, none are specially excluded from its benefits. Those only are excluded who exclude themselves, and refuse to be saved on God's own terms. His proclamation of mercy to a lost, rebel world, is clogged with no exceptions. I. Consider OUR NEED OF ETERNAL LIFE. Greatest gift of God! eternal life is deliverance from eternal death, the curse of a broken law, and the doom of a burning hell. Eternal life is eternal blessedness—the pardon of sin's guilt, and freedom from its tyrannous power. II. Consider HOW WE OBTAIN ETERNAL LIFE. III. Consider more particularly WHAT WE HAVE TO DO, TO OBTAIN ETERNAL LIFE. Do! It is not to make ourselves worthy of it; nor to attempt to merit it; nor to wait till we are holy before we come to Christ. Salvation is not of works, but of faith. IV. Consider WHEN WE ARE TO LAY HOLD ON ETERNAL LIFE—When—but now? If the body is in great danger, and means of safety and escape are offered, there is no occasion to press them on men; to cry, lay hold on life, or say, do it now. *T. Guthrie, D.D.*) *Eternal life within present grasp:*—"Lay hold on eternal life." Observe that this precept is preceded by another "Fight the good fight of faith." Those who lay hold on eternal life will have to fight for it. As my text follows the command to "fight the good fight of faith," it teaches us that the best way of contending for the faith is, for ourselves personally to lay hold on eternal life. You cannot defend the faith by mere reasoning. There is a higher and a better life than that which is known to the most of men. There is an animal life which all possess; there is a mental life which lifts us up above the beasts; but there is another life as much above the mental life as the mental life is above the mere animal life. The bulk of men are not aware of this, and when they are told of it they do not believe the statement. Dream not that any of you will ever obtain eternal life hereafter unless you receive it in this life. Where death finds you eternity will leave you. I. "Lay hold on eternal life," that is, BELIEVE IN IT. You cannot lay hold on it unless you know it to be a reality. We do not lay hold on shadows, or fictions, or fancies. It is needful, therefore, to begin by a realizing faith. 1. That we may believe in this life, let me say that Holy Scripture constantly describes men unrenewed by Divine grace as being dead ; they are " dead in trespasses and sins." 2. The Scripture represents believers everywhere as possessing everlasting life. "He that believeth in Him hath everlasting life." 3. This life is produced by the operation of the Holy Spirit within the heart. 4. What a difference this quickening has made in those who have received it! What a marvellous life it is ! It brings with it new perceptions, new emotions, new desires. It has new senses : there are new eyes, with which we see the invisible ; new ears, with which we hear the voice of God, before inaudible. Then have we a new touch, with which we lay hold on Divine truth ; then have we a new taste, so that we " taste and see that the Lord is good." This new life ushers us into a new world, and gives us new relationships and new privileges. I want you all to get this idea into your heads—I mean all of you who have not learned this fact as yet : there is a life superior to that of common men—a life eternal, to be enjoyed now and here. I want this idea to become a practical force with you. Stephenson got the notion of a steam-engine into his brain, and the steam-engine soon became a natural fact with him. Palissy, the potter, had his mind full of his art, and for it he sacrificed everything till he gained his end ; so may you, by the teaching of the Holy Ghost, lay hold upon eternal life as being a blessed possibility ; and may you be moved to seek it ! There is an eternal life ; there is a life of God in the soul of man ; and I trust that you will each one resolve, "If it is to be had I will have it." Henceforth direct your thoughts and desires this way. II. But this is not enough : it is merely the door-step of the subject. "Lay hold on eternal life ": that is to say, POSSESS IT. Get it into your own soul : be yourself alive. How is eternal life grasped ? 1. It is laid hold of by faith in Jesus Christ. It is a very simple thing to trust the Lord Jesus Christ, and yet it is the only way of obtaining the eternal life. 2. This life once laid hold upon is exercised in holy acts. From day to day we lay hold on eternal life by exercising ourselves unto godliness in deeds of holiness and lovingkindness. Let your life be love, for love is life. Let your life be one of prayer and praise, for these are the breath of the new life. 3. In laying hold upon it, remember that it is increased by growth. Zealously grasp more and more of it. Do not be afraid of having too much spiritual life. Lay hold on it ; for Christ has come not only that we may have life, but that we may have it more abundantly. 4. Remember that spiritual life is enjoyed in the fullest sense in close communion with God. "This is life eternal, to know Thee the only true God, and Jesus Christ, whom Thou hast sent." III. "Lay hold on eternal life." That is, WATCH OVER IT, guard it, and protect it. Most men will preserve their lives at any cost. Unless they are drunk or mad, they will do anything for dear life : "Skin for skin, yea, all that a man hath will he give for his life." 1. Let every believer regard the life of God within him as being the most precious possession, more valuable by far than the natural life. It would be wise to lay down a thousand natural lives, if we had them, in order to preserve the spiritual life. 2. To that end the apostle bade Timothy flee from those things which are detrimental to that life. "Thou, O man of God, flee these things." A man that is very careful of his life will not remain in a house where fever has been rife. 3. Then the apostle tells Timothy to seek after everything that would promote his eternal life. He says, "Follow after righteousness, godliness, faith, love, patience, meekness " : seek after that which will exercise and develop your highest life. Frequent those hills of holiness where the atmosphere is bracing for your new-born spirit. 4. God help us to lay hold on eternal life, and to that end above all things lay hold on Christ ! We only live in Him : He is our life. To be divided from Christ is as surely death to us as it would be death to the body to be separated from the head. IV. "Lay hold on eternal life," that is, FULFIL IT. Labour that the time of your sojourning here shall be occupied, not with this poor, dying existence, but with the eternal life. 1. Fulfil the higher and the eternal life in every position of society. The chapter opens with advice to servants, who then were slaves. Their earthly life was wretched indeed, but the apostle bids them live, not for this present life, but for the eternal life. 2. Fulfil this better life, also, by leaving alone those questions which would swallow up the hour. See how Paul destroys these devourers —"Questions and strifes of words, whereof cometh envy, strife, railings, evil surmisings, perverse disputings of men of corrupt minds, and destitute of the truth, supposing that gain is godliness : from such withdraw thyself." 3. Further, the apostle bids us do this so as to surmount the temptations of selfishness. He warns us that "they that will be rich fall into temptation and a snare, and into many foolish and hurtful lusts, which drown men in destruction and perdition. V. Last of all, EXPECT ETERNAL LIFE. By the two hands of faith and hope lay hold on eternal life as the great reward of the righteous. 1. Let me suggest that we think much about the life to come. We shall soon be there in the endless home, let us send our thoughts thither like couriers in advance. 2. When you think of it, and your heart grows warm with the thought, then count it very near. Suppose you are to live a comparatively long life, yet no human life is really long. 3. Rehearse eternal life ! Rehearse the service and joy of heaven! They have rehearsals of fine pieces of music ; let us have a rehearsal of heaven's harmonies. The thing is practicable. (*C. H. Spurgeon.*)

Vers. 13-16. **I give thee charge in the sight of God.**—*Motives to steadfastness :*— When earnest Christians realize that they are about to leave the world, they are concerned that those who will fill their places should be loyal to the principles they have tried to maintain. The "commandment" which the young evangelist was to keep must be taken, in its broadest sense, as referring to the great principles of righteousness and truth which Christ Jesus had embodied and maintained. Although of celestial origin, this commandment would not appear to men " without spot," if its representatives were men of blemished reputation. Two motives to such steadfastness are suggested in the verses before us : the one being drawn from the example of Christ, the other from the greatness of God. I. THE EXAMPLE OF CHRIST is suggested in the allusion made to—1. His good confession before Pontius Pilate. It is well for us when we either suffer, or compel, all the incidents of life to lead our thoughts back to Christ. It was partly in order to make this possible that the details of His life and ministry are so fully given in the Gospels. Temptations, troubles, friendships, joys, conflicts, all that go to make up our experience, find counterparts in Him. He witnessed a good confession, though He knew the price of it would be agony, shame, and death ! There was a difference, however, between the Lord's confession and Timothy's or ours. Timothy " confessed " the good confession, Christ Jesus " witnessed " the good confession. Christ " witnessed " because He was identified with the truth He confessed, and was the source of every such confession after. Timothy " confessed," for his confession was responsive and secondary, and found its inspiration in that of his Lord. 2. Christ's achieved victory is another source of encouragement to His faithful followers. The Cross of Calvary was the immediate result of our Lord's good confession ; but that was not its final result. God, who quickeneth all things, has raised Him from the dead, and amongst the glorified and redeemed He already appears as Prince and Saviour. The victory of Christ is the encouragement and inspiration of all who are engaged in the conflicts of truth with error, of holiness with sin. Notice how this description of the expected appearing of Christ leads to the noble doxology which celebrates—II. THE GREATNESS AND GLORY OF GOD, " who is the blessed and only Potentate, the King of kings and Lord of lords; who only hath immortality, dwelling in the light which no man can approach unto ; whom no man hath seen, nor can see ; to whom be honour and power everlasting. Amen." If He be for us, who can be against us ? Timothy is fittingly reminded that—1. God is eternal. All time is at His disposal. 2. God is the blessed and only Potentate. If you substitute for " blessed " its synonym in modern English, you get the beautiful truth, that ours is a " happy " God—full of joy in Himself, the source of joy to all His creatures. 3. " God quickeneth all things." He can so quicken us that out of sadness and difficulties and torpor He can raise us to newness of life. 4. God is incomprehensible—as yet to us—in Himself and in His doings ; " dwelling in the light which no man can approach unto." It is a beautiful thought, that He is not hidden from us through absence of light, but through excess of light. Therefore, amid the gradual development of His purposes, we have only to witness a good confession, leaving all the results to Him. 5. God is Almighty, " the only Potentate, the King of kings and Lord of lords," the King of those who reign, the Lord of those who rule. All authority is in His hands. Let us not lose sight of Him to whom in this passage the great apostle ascribes honour and power everlasting. We too often regard ourselves as the rulers of the world, and forget our absolute dependence ; but, in relation to the blessed and only Potentate, we are far more insignificant than insects are in relation to us. (*A. Rowland, LL.B.*) **The blessed and only Potentate.**—*Christ's service :*

—One figure stands at the centre of man's history and dominates over it all—the figure of Christ. Now, there is no way to be securely and perfectly this except for him who takes Christ as his King, Would you resist temptation, would you be pure, kind, contented, truthful, honest? Well, then, enroll yourself with deliberate purpose as Christ's soldier, His scholar, His servant, His subject. Christ our King! What kind of a king is He? His kingdom is not of this world. To understand Him you must lay aside altogether your notions of earthly sovereignty. From the Cross He has reigned. The throne of Solomon had its golden lions and ivory steps, and gorgeous was the jewelled chair of Byzantium; but the throne of the King of kings was a cross of shame. And, strange to say, the world, in its penitence, in its satiety, in its remorse, has turned away from its own petty potentates, has dropped its weapons, has torn the garland from its brow, has fallen low upon its knees before the Son of Man on His instrument of torture. It has gazed on Him in the faded purple of mockery, and in His crown of thorns, and nations have said, in awe-struck whispers, "Behold your King!" Yes; and kings themselves have bowed down before that throne of sorrows. When Henry IV. of Germany cowered before the thin old Pope at Canossa; when Barbarossa received upon his neck the foot of the proud potentate; when our own Henry II. was scourged by monks before the shrine of Canterbury; when John received back his crown from Pandulf; when Godfrey refused to wear a crown of gold where his Saviour had a crown of thorns; when Rudolf of Hapsburg, not finding the sceptre in the temple of his coronation, seized upon the crucifix and swore that that should be his sceptre; when the most ancient crown of Europe was made, not of gold, but of iron, and that iron hammered, as men believed, out of a nail of the true cross—what was this but the homage of earthly kings to a Diviner royalty! Yes; and no power on earth has ever been able to resist Christ. Tell it out among the heathen that the Lord is King! Greece despised Him, and Greece glimmered into a dream; but the Cross remains. Rome hated Him, and Rome has crumbled into the dust; but the Cross remains. Philosophy rejected Him, and philosophy has sunk into impotence; but the Cross remains. Is He your King? Or will you choose in His place some vile and worth-less tyranny, some evil spirit, some despotic and besetting vice? Three centuries ago the Spaniards were besieging the little town of St. Quentin, on the frontiers of France. Its ramparts were in ruins, fever and famine were decimating its defenders, treason was gliding among its terrified population. One day the Spaniards shot over the walls a shower of arrows to which were attached little slips of parchment, promising the inhabitants that if they would surrender, their lives and property should be spared. Now, the governor of the town was the great leader of the Huguenots, Gaspard de Coligni. As his sole answer he took a piece of parchment, tied it to a javelin, wrote on it the two words, *Regem habemus*—" We have a king " —and hurled it back into the camp of the enemy. Now that was true loyalty— loyalty in imminent peril, loyalty ready to sacrifice all. But who was that king for whom, amidst sword and flame, amid fever and famine, Coligni was defending those breached and battered walls? It was the weak and miserable Henry II. of France, whose son, Charles IX., was afterwards guilty of the murder of Coligni and the infamies of St. Bartholomew. Have you a king? Is Christ your King? Ah, if He be, He is not a feeble, corrupt, false, treacherous man like Coligni's master, but a King who loves you, who died for you, who pleads with you even now on the right hand of the Majesty on High. Is Christ your King? If you are selfish and frivolous; if you are a better and a gambler; if you are a whisperer and one who delights in lies; if you are a fornicator or a "profane person, as was Esau"; if you worship Mammon; if your god is your ledger and you mind earthly things; if you are double-tongued, shifty, niggardly, worldly—say not that Christ is your King. Is Christ your King? If in sincerity and truth you will take Christ for your King and Captain I promise you two things. First, I promise you security. Principle is a noble thing; but in the fatal mirage of the passions principle is lost sight of, and amid the glamour of temptation principle not only loses something of its pristine splendour, but it becomes as if it were not. And the other blessing which Christ will give you is joy; for Christ says, " Peace I give you, My peace I leave with you; not as the world giveth give I unto you." " Not as the world giveth! " There has been a joy in dungeons and on scaffolds passing the joy of the harvest. Christ does not delude as Satan does with such promises as, " Serve me, and you shall be rich." (*Archdeacon Farrar.*) *The sovereignty of Christ:*—1. Jesus is a King in His own eternal and essential right. He is the Creator of all things; He is the Preserver of all things; He is the sovereign Lord and Proprietor of all things. But, then, He is a King in another sense, and it is to that, that allusion is here made. 2. He has a mediatorial kingdom which was given Him by the Father as a recompense for His great and glorious undertaking on behalf of our world: and thus He is a mediatorial King. Now, in this view of the subject as a mediatorial King, and having a mediatorial kingdom committed to His care, trust, management, and government, we may observe that this kingdom was small in its origin. At its first rising after His resurrection and ascension, the dimensions were small. 3. But, then, there is a third kingdom: if I may so speak, another kingdom within this kingdom—a kingdom in the hearts of His beloved people. "The kingdom of God," it is said, "is within you." It is in vain for men to pretend that they are the subjects of Christ merely because they are so outwardly. 4. I say He is a very bountiful Sovereign in whom you have trusted. He has promised to give everything which He possesses that He can give, and that His subjects can receive. He has made a covenant with them which is well ordered in all things and sure. "All things are yours." 5. Observe, again, He is a tender-hearted and sympathizing Sovereign. He feels for all His subjects; for every one of you, and for the meanest subject that He has; so that everything which concerns them concerns Him. There is no trial which presses sore on the mind which He does not feel, and in which He does not participate. 6. Then, observe, He is a condescending Sovereign. He entreats you to come to His bosom—to make known to Him your every concern. Solomon has this expression, "In the light of the king's countenance is life." There is doubtless here an allusion to the language of his royal Father: the father said, "Lord, lift Thou up the light of Thy countenance upon us." So he says again, "One thing have I desired of the Lord, that will I seek after; that I may dwell in the house of the Lord all the days of my life, to behold the beauty of the Lord, and to inquire in His temple." Then again it is said, "In Thy presence is fulness of joy; at Thy right hand there are pleasures for evermore." (*W. Wilkinson.*) **Whom no man hath seen.**—*God invisible:*—I. Consider WHAT THE EYE ITSELF IS, THE POOR IM- PLEMENT OF WHICH WE DEMAND SO MUCH. A ball of clay and mortality, it can act only on what is material and corruptible like itself. It is limited to a certain province even among these surrounding things. How delicate an organ it is, that is yet capable of taking in the broad scenes of the ocean and the land, and reaching as it were the stars at their immeasurable distances! At very short intervals of time it must be shut up within its fringes from the very light that it lives by; and when it is in its utmost vigour, the direct flash of a single sunbeam is more than it can bear. A tear dims it. A mote takes away from it every capacity but that of pain. A spark destroys it for ever. It cannot penetrate even the thin veils of outward nature. The true light may shine inward, though the body be dark. The soul sees otherwise and more nobly than through that narrow window. Is it through these lenses of flesh—so easily distempered, so often giving false pictures, so soon to perish—is it through these that we would gaze on the King Eternal? II. Think, further, WHO HE IS WHOM WE ASK TO BE THUS MANIFESTED TO US. The very idea of God absolutely excludes the possibility of His being an object of sight. He is a pure Intelligence, circumscribed by no form, bounded by no space, and to be communicated with only through the Spirit which Himself imparts. But the unconvinced may say: This is not what we seek, or have ever imagined. But we would lay our eyes upon some undeniable signs and represen- tatives of the Almighty Providence. Yet the Scriptures tell them, and their own religious reason tells them, that they are actually surrounded with just such signs and representatives in the natural creation. It is His spirit that gives it life. It is His wisdom that gives it law. It is not, however, with such as these, they may reply, that we are satisfied. We would have testimonies strictly miraculous, transcending all the powers of nature, and thus exhibiting an immediate connection with the Almighty One. The Scriptures and our religious reason then take up the word again and say: Foolish and slow of heart! unless ye see signs and wonders, ye will not believe. It does not seem, then, that there is the virtue you fancy in the spectacle that you ask. And why should there be? Why should transient visions and strange occurrences impart a steadier trust than the perpetual marvels of this glorious world, and the eternal chain of decrees and providences that can be held but in one sovereign hand? One thing more may be urged by those who withhold or utter faintly the ascription in the text, "To whom be honour and power ever- lasting," because "no man hath seen nor can see Him." They may say, It is not even such wonders as you have alluded to that we crave. They are for the individual only, or at most have their chief concern with but a tribe or a generation of men.

We would have a supernatural sign that should be permanent and universal. It should be for all eyes. To this suggestion we need not call on the Scriptures for a reply. It demands an open impossibility, and is inconsistent with itself. Whatever should be thus associated with the works of nature must necessarily be regarded as one of them, however marvellous and inexplicable it might appear. We can scarcely conceive of anything more wonderful than is somewhere or other already presented. From what has been said, I hope it has been made clear, that no one has cause for objection or mistrust because the Lord is invisible, for it is inconceivable how He should be otherwise. " To Him, whom no man hath seen or can see, be honour and power everlasting." " What we adore under the affection of our senses," says an old writer, " deserves not the honour of so pure a title. Nor is it strange that we should place affection on that which is invisible. All that we truly love is thus." The soul itself—is it not invisible, like its Source? To be born as we are, animal and moral beings, into two states at once—to dwell in a world like this we inhabit of pale reflections and shadows, where what is the most real is the least obvious— and at the same time to think the outward shape everything, and the secret intelligence and power that makes all to be what it is, nothing—this is to want the very sense that best becomes and exults us. The Scriptures, with a beautiful boldness of expression, speak of " seeing Him who is invisible." And when they thus speak, their meaning is twofold—to acquaint ourselves with him and to rejoice as in His presence. " He that doeth evil," says John, " hath not seen God." But " Blessed are the pure in heart," it is for them that the double privilege is reserved of knowing and enjoying Him. (*N. L. Frothingham.*) *The invisible God :—* The atheist never saw God, and therefore knows not how to believe such a being ; he cannot comprehend Him. He would not be a God, if He could fall within the narrow model of a human understanding. He would not be infinite if He were comprehensible, or to be terminated by our sight. How small a thing must that be which is seen by a bodily eye, or grasped by a weak mind ! If God were visible or comprehensible, He would be limited. Shall it be a sufficient demonstration from a blind man, that there is no fire in the room, because he sees it not, though he feel the warmth of it ? The knowledge of the effect if sufficient to conclude the existence of the cause. Who ever saw his own life ! Is it sufficient to deny a man lives, because he beholds not his life, and only knows it by his motion ? He never saw his own soul, but he knows he hath one by his thinking power. The air renders itself sensible to men in its operations, yet was never seen by the eye. If God should render Himself visible, they might still question as well as now, whether that which was visible were God, or some delusion. If He should appear glorious, we can as little behold Him in His majestic glory, as an owl can behold the sun in its brightness ; we should still but see Him in His effects, as we do the sun by its beams. If He should show a new miracle, we should still see Him but by His works ; so we see Him in His creatures, every one of which would be as great a miracle as any can be wrought, to one that had the first prospect of them. To require to see God is to require that which is impossible (1 Tim. vi. 16). (*S. Charnock.*)

Vers. 17, 19. Charge them that are rich in this world.—*The perils and possibilities of the rich :*—I. THE DANGERS OF THE RICH are manifold, but only two or three are suggested here. 1. The danger of self-conceit is hinted at in the words, " Charge them that are rich in this world that they be not high-minded." The vulgar boasting of wealth, and the ostentatious display of it, are indications of this. Again, the self-sufficiency that leads a successful man to attribute all his gains to his own shrewdness and diligence, and to speak contemptuously of those who never get on in the world, as if God had nothing to do with his physical energy and mental calibre, with the education and training of his youth, or with the unexpected opportunities of his manhood, is another sign of " high-mindedness." The pride which refuses to associate with those whose income is smaller, and which will hold aloof from intelligent and religious men and women, in order to cultivate acquaintance with those whose minds are shallow, but whose establishments are costly, and whose influence in the money market is great. 2. Another danger threatening rich men is that of trusting to uncertain riches. It is on this evanescence that Paul lays stress when he speaks of the folly of trusting to them. He hints at the conquest of this by exercising confidence in the living God, who giveth us all things richly to enjoy. The remembrance of the fact that God gave you money adds sacredness to it, a sense of responsibility in the use of it, and arouses the gratitude and praise which are His due. II. The opportunities of the rich are as noteworthy as their dangers. 1. They can "do good" to others, and many a noble institution has its source in the generous and wise gifts of those whom God has prospered. But besides this— 2. They can do noble things. The words used by Paul, which are both rendered "good" (in the R. V. as well as the A. V.), have not the same meaning in Greek. They would be better translated, "Charge them that they do good, and that they be rich in noble deeds." The latter word used by Paul signifies what is honourable and lovely in itself. It fell from the lips of our Lord when He described Mary's act of devotion. Rich men can afford to make wise and noble experiments in philanthropy and in Christian enterprise. III. The recompense of the rich who are thus faithful is not obscurely taught in the words which describe them as laying up in store for themselves "a good foundation against the time to come, that they may lay hold on eternal life." Of course, Paul does not mean that they gain eternal life by their good works. No one insists more strongly than he does on the fact that salvation is the gift of sovereign grace to the sinful and undeserving. But from its nature this grace becomes a talent, with which we are to do service for God. And since the nature of the future recompense is found in the development of life, all that makes that life more full of possibility and of result lays up in store a good foundation against the time to come. The fact is, that the connection between this life and that is far closer than many imagine it to be. (*A. Rowland, LL.B.*) *Trust in God, and not in riches* :—1. To trust in riches, is to trust in what we may never acquire; to trust in God, is to trust in Him whom we may always depend on finding. 2. To trust in riches, is to trust in what cannot avail us in the various calamities which occur in the course of human life; to trust in God, is to trust in One who will always be with us in all our straits and trials. 3. To trust in riches, is to trust in what cannot meet the wants of the heart, if it is found; to trust in God, is to trust in One who can fully supply all our need. 4. To trust in riches, is to trust in what we may be deprived of in a moment, or may gradually lose; to trust in God, is to trust in One whom we can never be deprived of, and never shall lose. 5. To trust in riches, is to trust in what we must all part with at last; to trust in God, is to trust in One who will be ours for ever. 6. Many and great are the blessings of every kind which this trust in God, rather than in riches, will secure to us. (1) It will teach us to moderate our desires after riches, and to be less eager than we often are in the pursuit of them. (2) It will show us how we may mingle the right pursuit of temporal things with that supreme regard to spiritual things which their paramount importance entitles them to. (3) It will enable us, when worldly losses come, to bear up patiently and hopefully under them, and to hear the voice of God speaking to us in them. (4) It will teach us the responsibility which is always connected with the possession of any portion of earthly things, and remind us of the account which we must give to God for the way we have used them. (*Alex. Reid.*) *Human affections raised, not destroyed, by the gospel:*—The apostle sets before us, in the text, two applications of the same human affection. He bids us not to "trust in uncertain riches," but to trust "in the living God." He assumes that this trusting impulse exists, and he would not destroy but reform it. He would exhibit the true and eternal object for a tendency in itself indestructible; and would intimate that there is prepared for the just desires of the soul a sphere of being, adequate to these desires, and from which the present detains us, only as the counterfeit and mockery of it! On the one hand "uncertain riches"; on the other the parallel announcement, that "God giveth us richly all things to enjoy." And thus the Spirit, that spoke in the exhortation of Paul, instructs in the great truth, that the faculties of men are themselves a mechanism for eternity; that it is not they—it is not Love, and Reliance, and Hope, and Desire—but their habitual objects, that man must toil to change. On this important matter, then, I shall first endeavour briefly to engage your attention, and I shall then attempt to illustrate the melancholy extent of the actual perversion of our nature, by showing how, even in their wanderings, these affections betray the higher purpose for which they were primarily intended, and how—more especially in the instance noted in the text, the "trust in riches"— man still unconsciously invests with the very attributes of perfect felicity, of heaven, and of God, the earthly idol to which he sacrifices both! There are those, then, who speak with solemn and prophetic truth of the change which comes over the aspect of the human soul, when, for the first time, "awaking to righteousness," it is introduced (while yet in the world of time) into the eternal world, and becomes cognizant of the glories, till then unseen, that surround "the throne of God and the

Lamb." But when, from the dignity and circumstances of the change, men pass to define its nature, there is often, it seems to me, much inaccuracy and some imprudence in their statements. We find it sometimes described as if no one element of human nature were to remain in the regenerate spirit. The declaration that a new heart is bestowed is taken in almost the fulness of a literal acceptation. All the old machinery of humanity is discarded; the "works" are, as it were, taken out of the case of the instrument, and a totally new organization of passions and affections provided. The spiritual renewal is thus falsely, I think, and dangerously, made to consist, not in "setting" our emancipated "affections upon things above"—not in the privilege of having "the whole body, and soul, and spirit preserved blameless until the coming of Christ," but in the acquisition of some indescribable affections (if such they may be called), which, though they be named love and desire, are no longer human love and human desire, but differing almost as much, it would seem, from these affections as they are in our hearts, as love and hate differ from each other! Hence that mystic and dangerous mode of representation too common among a large class of teachers, which would exalt the "love to God," for example, beyond all human conception, not merely in the dignity of its object (in which, I need not say, no language could overstate it), but even in the very nature of the feeling; as if the love of a devoted friend was one thing and intelligible, but the love to God quite another affection, and all but incomprehensible! The error of all such cases is the same—the notion that in the work of renewal new faculties are given us, instead of a new direction to the old ones; the notion that God annihilates human nature when He only perfects it; to destroy the channels themselves, instead of cleansing their polluted streams, and then replenishing them for ever with the waters of Paradise! As long as men conceived that the religious affections are in their essence wholly different from every other affection, they will inevitably conclude that the training and discipline for them must be itself equally different. So far for the general principle involved in the particular exhortation of the apostle, the principle that the same affections which cling to the lowly earth are those which must struggle, under celestial guidance, to find their rest in God. "Trust not in riches, but [trust] in the living God!" Blessed invitation! How it exalts, even while it reproves, our fettered nature! Trust, yes, trust with a devotedness such as the wildest frenzy of avarice has never exhibited! Trust, and fear not! It is among the noblest energies of your being —it was never given in vain. Trust, but "trust in the living God!" Preserve unbroken every element of your affections; they are all alike the property of heaven. Be ambitious, but ambitious of the eternal heritage. Labour after knowledge, but let it be "the light of the knowledge of the glory of God in the face of Jesus Christ!" Be it ours to find in the new world unveiled in the gospel the true materials of these holy desires, and so to train them while on earth for the society of heaven. I have but this moment glanced at a topic which might well demand deeper and fuller illustration. I mean the change which the fact of the incarnation of God most rightfully make in all that concerns the laws and regulation of the human affections. For, after all, these affections do, doubtless, strive, in the first instance, towards human objects; human themselves, they naturally cling to the human outside and beyond them. Ever since God became incarnate, this tendency precludes not their direct passage to heaven; nay, it quickens and guides it. It would have been little short of miracle, that even the most pious should maintain the state of perpetual contemplative affection towards the awful essence of the unmingled God. But when that God became man this difficulty was removed. The direct pathway to heaven was opened to the human heart. And the more you regard the passage, the more will you perceive that such views as those I have sketched were, in substance, the views which occupied the inspired teacher. His whole object is manifestly to contrast the two rivals for the human heart, the worlds visible and invisible; and hence it is that the text before us is the natural sequel to the preceding verse, where the glory of the eternal God is unveiled in all its majesty as the object which is to fix the affections of man. There is, proclaims St. Paul (ver. 15), a "blessed and only Potentate," who is hereafter to determine, "in His own time" (as it is emphatically called), the appearing of Christ Jesus in glory. This Being demands, as His inalienable right, all the energies of all the affections; for no inferior claimant can interfere with Him, who is "King of kings and Lord of lords." Then comes the exhortation. Seeing that such a privilege as this is ours (ver. 17), "charge them that are rich in this world," that they interpose not a veil between themselves and this Father of their spirits, or suffer the clouds and vapours of earth to sully or eclipse the beams of this eternal sun. " Charge them, that they be not high-minded, nor trust in uncertain riches, but in the living God, who giveth us richly all things to enjoy ! " Our earthly objects of pursuit are themselves clad by hope with colours that rightfully belong only to their celestial rivals ; our ordinary earthly longings themselves strain after a really heavenly happiness, while they miss so miserably the way to reach it ; that, in other words, in the treasuries of heaven are laid up all that you truly covet, even while, by a wretched illusion, you labour after their mockeries on earth ! Surely, if this can be proved, no conceivable argument can more powerfully demonstrate how we are made for religion, and can only find our true rest there ! Now the truth is, so wholly are we framed for the eternal world, that we must make a heaven of earth before we can fully enjoy it. God has so inwoven, in the innermost texture of our nature, the title and testimonies of the immortal state for which He made us, that, mingled with the perishable elements of earth, it is, even now, for ever around us ; it rises in all our dreams, it colours all our thoughts, it haunts us with longings we cannot repel; in our very vices it reveals itself, for they cannot charm us till they have more or less counterfeited it. There are aspirations turned astray, that, even in their distortion, attest their origin and purpose. There are warped, and crippled, and polluted hopes, that, even from their dungeon of flesh, still cry to heaven. In the spirit of these convictions, turn again to the text. To whom does the apostle enjoin the exhortation ? To " them that are rich in this world." What does he here assume ? He assumes the existence of wealth, and, involved in that existence, the desire to attain it, which is the necessary motive for its accumulation. He assumes that there resides in the heart of man the desire to build up around it the means of perpetual enjoyment, to secure to itself the materials of happiness—of happiness, for such is the specific essence of moneyed wealth, that may be independent of the moment, and which (as it were, condensed in its representative) may be preserved for a period indefinitely future. But what terms, save these, shall we employ, when we would depict the heaven of the Scripture revelation ? What characters are these but the very properties of God's eternal world ? And so far is it not manifest that the votary of earthly wealth does in fact, with all the energies of his nature, strain after that very security of unchangeable bliss which we preach ; but, mistaking the illusory phantom, weds his whole soul to the fictitious heaven, which the powers of evil have clothed in colours stolen from the skies ? The delusion produces its own delusive results. But these also are but the shadowy copies of a bright and holy reality. Every attribute of the eager candidate for earthly happiness and security is but the poor semblance of the very state the Christian already possesses or anticipates. The rich are first warned of the peril of what is here called " high-mindedness " ; a word whose happy ambiguity perfectly corresponds to my argument. But as there is a worldly and Satanic " high-mindedness," so is this, as before, but the counterfeit presentment of a high-mindedness God-given and celestial. Laying deep its foundations in self-abasement, the doctrine of faith alone bestows the blessed confidence, without which the Christian may be the inconsolable penitent, the mortified ascetic, the prostrate trembler before an offended God ; but without which he is, nevertheless, but half a Christian. The happy confidence of the children of God is an element which, though false teaching may exaggerate, no true teaching will ever discard. It is not for nothing that he is bid to rest upon the Rock of Ages, and to anticipate upon earth the repose of immortality. Here, then, is the " high-mindedness " of the Christian ; here is the truth to match that worldly falsehood, that high-mindedness base and debasing ; here is the bright, unchanging fire, which the votary of this world would rake among the dust and ashes of earth to enkindle ! Once more, the " rich in this world " is warned, not merely of the peril of self-exaltation, but also of that of unbounded "trust " in the fleeting riches he accumulates. The contrast I need not here insist on. We have already noticed it, and the apostle himself has expressly enforced it. The " living God " and His liberal graces arise to claim the homage of the " trusting " heart. The dependent on riches makes them his god, in making them the object of his dependence. Heaven is here again defrauded of its own, and all the charms of the Divine character, the charms that fix and fascinate the adoring believer in Christ—its abiding permanence, its just sovereignty, its fixed security, its unshaken faithfulness—all are torn from the throne of God to clothe the idol of the worshipper of wealth ! (*W. A. Butler.*) *The duties of the rich :*—Every condition of life hath its peculiar dangers to be avoided and duties to be done, but none hath dangers more threatening or duties more important than that of the rich and great : whose situation, notwithstanding, is seldom considered by those who are in it as having anything to be feared ; and is generally imagined by others to comprehend almost everything that is to be wished. To be thus environed with temptations, and probably sensible of none of them, is a most pitiable condition. Now the peculiar dangers of the rich and great arises either from the eminence of their station or the abundance of their wealth : and therefore the text points a caution against each. But I shall be able at present to treat only of the first: which is, THAT THEY BE NOT HIGH-MINDED. Every superiority of every sort, which men only imagine themselves possessed of, is too liable to be over-rated and improperly used. But superior fortune and condition are advantages so visible to all eyes, create such dependences, and give such influence, that it is no wonder if they tempt to uncommon haughtiness. Now undoubtedly distinguished rank is entitled to distinguished regard ; and the good order of society very much depends on keeping up that regard ; and therefore the great should in a proper manner be much more careful to keep it up than many of them are. But when they nurse up the consciousness of their own superiority into a contemptuous neglect of others and insolent expectations of unfit submissions from them, they have great need to be reminded that respect is paid to wealth and birth because the common good requires it, not because the persons who receive it are always worthy of it ; but their dishonourable behaviour will be the more conspicuous for their honourable station. And even supposing them guilty of nothing else to lessen the esteem they claim, yet claiming too much of it, or too openly, will frustrate their intention most effectually. For neither equals nor inferiors will suffer near so much to be extorted from them as they would have bestowed most freely on their own accord. But one sort of condescension to inferiors may be of peculiar advantage; I mean listening to useful information and advice from them, things which the great are very apt to think themselves above, when every one else sees they have much need of them. Neither affluence nor high rank by any means imply superiority of judgment. But if humility in the great could be no other way beneficial to them, yet avoiding the guilt of so injurious a behaviour as indulging a proud spirit prompts them to, is surely a motive important enough. Thus too many treat their tenants hardly, or permit them to be so treated. Another sort of persons, for whom superiors too commonly will not vouchsafe to have the consideration that they ought, are those who come to them upon business. Obliging such to an unreasonable attendance, making them wait long, and it may be return often, is a very provoking and a very injurious kind of stateliness. But there is another fault still worse frequently joined with this ; deeming it beneath their notice whether such of their inferiors as have just and reasonable demands upon them are paid when they ought. Another very blameable and very pernicious instance of high-mindedness in the great is imagining the management of their families an attention too low for them. Even that of their children they very commonly despise to an astonishing degree. Or if they have humility enough to inspect some part of their education, it is usually the outward and showy but less material part. Now proceed to the latter, TRUSTING IN UNCERTAIN RICHES: which phrase comprehends placing the happiness of life either in wealth itself or in those pleasures and amusements which it is commonly made the instrument of procuring. The prohibition therefore of doing this extends to regulate the acquisition, the possession, and use of a great fortune ; and to go through the subject fully, each of these points must be considered. 1. The acquisition. In speculation it seems hardly to be expected that any one who is once master of enough to answer his real and reasonable wants should feel any desire almost, on his own account, of having more : that he should take much pains about is very wonderful; and that he should do anything wrong for it quite unaccountable. No temptation is a warrant for doing wrong ; but to do wrong without anything that deserves the name of a temptation is exceedingly bad. And it cannot be nature, but merely an absurd habit wilfully indulged, that tempts men to accumulate what they have no need of. But though riches alone render eagerness for more very blameable and unbecoming, yet greatness added to them doubles the fault. For exalted rank absolutely calls for the exercise of honourable disinterestedness. 2. Concerning the possession of it. Now keeping a heap of wealth merely for the sake of keeping it is an apparent absurdity. Keeping it merely for the repute of having it is a very low inducement. And if laying up against future accidents be pretended, a moderate store will suffice for a reasonable security, and nothing can secure us absolutely. Indeed the larger the fortune, the more room for accidents in one part or another of it; and the loss of a small part will be as grievous to a heart set upon riches as that of a larger to another man. Besides, whoever lives only to the purpose of saving and accumulating will be tempted by this ruling passion to a sinful neglect of the poor and the worthy among his friends and dependants, perhaps among his relations and very children. But besides the sins which may be committed in the getting or keeping of wealth, there are—3. Others, committed too frequently in using it; which persons of superior fortune and rank must be charged to avoid, and which undoubtedly the text comprehends. For putting their trust in riches is just as much the description of those who place the happiness of life in the enjoyment of large estates as those who place it in the possession of them. Some trust in their riches so very inconsiderately that they trust there will never be an end of them, let them be squandered as extravagantly as they will. So they set out with gratifying themselves in everything. Others, if they do not dissipate their estates in so wild a manner, yet use them principally to minister to their sensuality and debauchery; vices which men of superior fortune somehow imagine they have a sort of right to be guilty of. Another very bad use of wealth, in which too many seem to place no small part of their happiness, is that of gaming. But supposing wealth be neither spent in this nor any of the gross vices mentioned before, yet if it be employed in ministering to a course of more decent and refined luxury, or in supporting such a pomp of life as nourishes vanity and pride, or in filling so much time with unprofitable entertainment, that little room is left in the mind for objects of importance: these things also the rich and great must be charged to amend. I proceed to THE DUTIES OF WHICH HE ENJOINS THEY SHALL BE PECULIARLY REMINDED. 1. The first is, to trust in the living God, who giveth us all things richly to enjoy. After warning them against placing their happiness in the pre-eminences, the possessions or pleasures of this world, it was very natural to direct them where they should place it: for somewhere we must. And his precept carries the proof of its own fitness along with it. For the living God must have the greatest power to reward our trust, and He who giveth us all things richly to enjoy hath shown Himself to have the greatest will also. Some persons, it may be, when they are pressed upon the subject, will plead that they are by no means without inward regard to God; though they cannot say they give much outward demonstration of it in acts of worship. But supposing them sincere, what reason can there be why respect to God should not be paid outwardly when respect to every superior besides is? But it is possible for us to keep up a sufficient possession of religion to secure both public order and domestic tranquility, yet by no means have a sufficient sense of it for obtaining eternal life; and what will the former avail us without the latter? We should all, therefore, learn to live more to our Maker; to imprint on our hearts and exert in our whole behaviour a stronger sense of His present providence and future rewards. It would be a direction, a security, an improvement, a comfort to us beyond expression. 2. The second duty prescribed in the text as peculiarly necessary for the rich and great is that they do good, that they be rich in good works. If men of rank and fortune observe duly the preceding part of the apostle's charge, they will easily be induced to observe the concluding one. If they are neither so high-minded as to neglect and despise their fellow-creatures, nor so selfish as to trust in uncertain riches, in the acquisition, the possession, or voluptuous enjoyment of them, for their happiness, but expect it only from their acceptance with the living God; they will naturally imitate Him whom they desire to please, particularly in His beneficence, the most amiable of all His perfections. And it is not by their wealth only that they are able and therefore called to do good, but by their whole behaviour. But still, though almsgiving is by no means the whole of beneficence, yet it is an essential part in those whom God hath qualified for it. And He hath given them all things richly and in plenty, not merely for themselves to enjoy in the vulgar sense, but that others may enjoy a due share of them and they the pleasure of imparting it; the worthiest and highest enjoyment of wealth that can be. But, in general, that both our charity and our generosity should bear some decent and liberal proportion to our abilities, and the rich in this world be rich in good works also. Nor is it sufficient for the rich to give plentifully, but they must do it on every fit occasion speedily; be ready to distribute and not stay till the circumstances of the poor are beyond recovery or their spirits broken under the weight of their misfortunes, but make haste to help them and, as far as possible, prevent distress. (*T. Secker.*) *God the giver of wealth :*—A good example of liberality was given by Mr. Thornton, of Clapham, a noble-hearted Christian merchant. One morning, when he had received news of a failure that involved him in a loss of no less than a hundred thousand pounds, a minister from the country called at his counting-house to ask a subscription for an important object. Hearing that Mr. Thornton had suffered that loss, he apologized for having called. But Mr. Thornton took him kindly by the hand : " My dear sir, the wealth I have is not mine, but the Lord's. It may be that He is going to take it out of my hands and give it to another; and if so, this is a good reason why I should make a good use of what is left." He then doubled the subscription he had formerly intended to give. **That they do good.**—*Live for some purpose :*—Live for some purpose in the world. Act your part well. Fill up the measure of duty to others. Conduct yourselves so that you shall be missed with sorrow when you are gone. Multitudes of our species are living in such a selfish manner that they are not likely to be remembered after their disappearance. They leave behind them scarcely any traces of their existence, but are forgotten almost as though they had never been. They are, while they live, like one pebble lying unobserved amongst a million on the shore; and when they die, they are like that same pebble thrown into the sea, which just ruffles the surface, sinks, and is forgotten, without being missed from the beach. They are neither regretted by the rich, wanted by the poor, nor celebrated by the learned. Who has been the better for their life ? Who has been the worse for their death ? Whose tears have they dried up ? whose wants supplied ? whose miseries have they healed ? Who would unbar the gate of life to re-admit them to existence? or what face would greet them back again to our world with a smile? Wretched, unproductive mode of existence ! Selfishness is its own curse ; it is a starving vice. The man who does no good gets none. He is like the heath in the desert, neither yielding fruit nor seeing when good cometh—a stunted, dwarfish, miserable shrub. (*J. A. James.*) *The opportunity of doing good :*—We shall then know better than we do now know that every soul on its way to eternity has its appointed times and seasons of good, which, if they be allowed to pass away shall never, never return again. Though the person be not lost, yet the innocence, the heroism, the saintliness, may be. We must, therefore, lose no opportunity of doing good to the souls and bodies of those whom God's good providence has put under our care, because if we miss it by our own fault, it may never again be allowed to us ; the persons whom God intended us to profit may be taken out of our reach, may be taken into another world before they come in our way again. (*John Keble.*) *Doing good :*—An eminent surgeon, who was also an eminent Christian, visited a lady who was a professed believer in Christ, but who, like some ladies I have heard of, was frequently troubled with imaginary diseases. The good doctor was frequently called in, until at last he said to her, " Madam, I will give you a prescription which I am certain will make a healthy woman of you, if you will follow it." " Sir," she said, " I shall be so glad to have good health that I will be sure to follow it." " Madam, I will send you the prescription this evening." When it arrived it consisted of these words, " Do good to somebody." She roused herself to relieve a poor neighbour, and then sought out others who needed her help, and the Christian woman, who had been so constantly desponding and nervous, became a healthy, cheerful woman, for she had an object to live for, and found joy in doing good to others. (*C. H. Spurgeon.*)

Vers. 20, 21. **O Timothy, keep that which is committed to thy trust.**—*Peril and preservation :*—I. THE PERIL against which the apostle warns Timothy was the intellectual pride and subtle speculation which, afterwards, in the second and third centuries, became formulated into a sort of philosophical system. It was then known as Gnosticism, because it exalted " gnosis "—knowledge—above faith, and was of a decidedly presumptuous and pragmatical tendency. The effect of such knowledge has ever been to cause men to err concerning the faith; to lose simplicity and devoutness; to wander into the pleasant meadows of Doubting Castle, till they are seized and imprisoned by Giant Despair ; and unless they there learn to pray, and bethink them of the key of promise, they are left at last to fumble and stumble among the tombs. " He who wandereth out of the way of understanding shall abide in the congregation of the dead." II. PRESERVATION from such peril is to be found in God's answer to the prayer which Paul breathed over Timothy—"Grace be with thee." We cannot by searching find out God. Intellectual acuteness has never yet succeeded in discovering Him.     (*A. Rowland, LL.B.*)     *The guarding of the deposit:*—What the deposit was, we may not doubt. It was the Christian faith, in its entirety and purity; and the contexts, in which the apostle's repeated warning occurs, present to us the occasions which even then rendered it necessary. "Profane and vain babblings, and oppositions of science falsely so called," were, even then, undermining the faith of their authors and of those who listened to them; and it was requisite that even one who had received from the lips of St. Paul himself "the form of sound words," should be exhorted to "hold it fast." But to us, at this far later stage of the Church's history, the admonition comes fraught with many a lesson, to be drawn from the experience of the past, and also from the peculiar circumstances in which we find ourselves placed, by the providence of God, as members of the Church of England. The deposit of the faith may be regarded under a more simple or a more complex form. Any Christian man who can recite the Apostles' Creed may be said to have the deposit of the faith stored in his memory; but how much more, "pertaining to life and godliness," does he not require, both for the enlightening of his understanding, and for the guidance of his life? Brethren, do we consider as we ought the precious form in which the Christian faith has been delivered to us in our Book of Common Prayer? It has been recently affirmed by a distinguished Presbyterian, that "the Church, if she would fulfil her mission, must avail herself of the riches which her children during all these ages have been gathering for her." Here is, indeed, the deposit of the faith, elucidated and interpreted in all its fulness. Learned and unlearned, the wayfaring man and little child, are here instructed, in respect of their manifold necessities and obligations, in respect of their diversified relations both to God and to man, what it is to believe the gospel of Christ. Again, there is a most important feature of our Church, in respect of which we must surely feel how urgent is the duty faithfully to guard the deposit which has been committed to our trust. We cannot but regard as a most signal instance of God's wondrous working for us, the circumstance that He accorded to us the power, which many others did not possess, of retaining in its integrity the constitution of the Church as it has existed from apostolic times. Surely a thoughtful man must ask, with all reverence, *why* God thus dealt with us; nor will he permit himself to hold the gift in less esteem, because it was not vouchsafed to others. If it be indeed our duty to regard our ecclesiastical polity as a blessing which has been secured to us by the grace and favour of God—if, in this regard, we have indeed cause to say, "The lines are fallen to us in pleasant places; yea, we have a goodly heritage"— then let us be very careful never ourselves to speak or to act, never to lead others to speak or to act, in the spirit of those of whom we read, that "they thought scorn of that pleasant land" which God had given them. Again, if our Book of Common Prayer be indeed a precious treasure house in which is stored for our use the deposit of the Christian faith, must we not be very careful to guard it from neglect, to secure to it its due honour? Are we, then, as careful as we should be here? We cannot be "guarding the deposit" if we give, or teach others to give, a non-natural sense to the language of the Baptismal Office, of the Catechism, of the Office for the Administration of the Holy Communion, or of the Ordinal: we are not handing on, as faithful stewards, that which has been committed to our trust, except we give their full significance to the teaching of the Prayer Book, as well as to that of the Articles. Suffer me to mention another point, which is essential to the "guarding of the deposit." A complaint is not unfrequently made of those who preach not Christ, but the Church. I do not deny that the want of a right understanding of Christian truth, and of a due feeling of its sacred character, may possibly lead to this monstrous result; but I would venture to remind you, that if we would "guard the deposit" faithfully, we must preach *both* Christ *and* His Church. It is, indeed, a fatal error not to "hold the Head, from which all the body by joints and bands, having nourishment ministered, and being knit together, increaseth with the increase of God"; but it is also a most grievous error, so to hold the Head as to ignore the divinely appointed organization, through which, as the apostle assures us, the nourishment of the body is dispensed, and its unity and strength secured. We cannot speak faithfully of Christ the Vine, of Christ the Head, of Christ the chief Corner-Stone, without speaking also of that wondrous, spiritual structure, His gracious relation to which is marked by the many names of love and power which are assigned to Him in Holy Scripture. Some persons may be tempted not to "guard the deposit" in certain points, by the hope of conciliating those who are unhappily separated from us. They may desire to withdraw what others regard as unauthorized pretensions, and so to occupy a common ground with them. What, then, must be the necessary effect of their doing so, while "the deposit," as enshrined in the formularies of our Church, remains what it is? They must deprive themselves of all excuse, before God and man, for using or assenting to those formularies. And, more than this, so far as their action is concerned, the Church becomes degraded into the most presumptuous and arrogant of sects, presuming, as she does from their point of view, to utter before God words of most awful and solemn import, to which her heart does not respond, and before men to make pretences and speak "great swelling words of vanity," while she yet repudiates her title to any real distinction from other Christian bodies which put forward no such claims. If we will not "guard the deposit" which has been committed to our trust as a Church, we have no alternative but to renounce it openly and honestly, having first put to ourselves with all seriousness the momentous inquiry, "Did that deposit come to us from the hand of God, or no?" But whither will men turn, if they should unhappily resolve to forsake the historic Church of the past, which we are taught to believe and to confess, as retaining to the end of the world her imperishable continuity, marvellously as she may be taught to adapt herself to the needs of successive generations, and to the various characteristics of "the nation of them that are saved, that shall walk in her light"? Once more, let me present to you that which appears to many a further and most cogent reason for unflinching steadfastness and faithfulness to our high trust. I refer to the remarkable position in which the Church of England has stood ever since the Reformation, in respect of all other Christian bodies throughout the world; and more than ever at this day stands, by virtue of her own wide extension and of her intercommunion with other branches of the Church Catholic, holding the same faith and observing the same order with herself. "If there be," says Bishop Lightfoot, "any guiding hand in the progress of history, if there be any Supreme Providence in the control of events, if there be any Divine Presence and any Divine call—then the position of England, as the mother of so many colonies and dependencies, the heart and centre of the world's commerce and manufacture, and the position of the English Church, standing midway between extremes in theological teaching and ecclesiastical order, point to the Church of this nation, with the very finger of God Himself, as called by Him to the lofty task of reconciling a distracted kingdom and healing the wounds of the nations." For the sake, then, of this inspiring hope, under the sense of this overwhelming responsibility, let us as members of that vast communion, whose worship ascends to God from well-nigh every portion of our globe, resolve by His help to "guard the deposit" which He has committed to our trust, and to stand still in the safe paths of duty and obedience, if haply our eyes or our children's eyes may be blessed by seeing this great "salvation of God." (*G. Whitaker, M.A.*) **Oppositions of science falsely so called.**—*Science and theology :*—There is no more vital and anxious thought in the religious life of to-day than the supposed conflict between science and religion. In certain quarters it has come to be taken for granted, that reason is necessarily opposed to faith; that nature and her teachings, so far as they can be understood and interpreted, are in conflict with the teachings of revelation; and that scientific men and theologians are therefore arranged in two hostile armies, having nothing in common, and engaged in a struggle which must ultimately end in the destruction of the one or the other. The result is, that scientific men and investigations are denounced as sceptical enemies of religious truth; and the compliment is abundantly returned by insinuations of bigotry and intolerance, as essential characteristics of religious teachers. And, in the popular mind, there is a vague and uncertain dread that the faith is to be overthrown, and the verities to which it clings, and upon which it is founded, are to be evaporated into myths and superstitions, which must take their place amid the exploded falsehoods of a too credulous past. A calmer and more comprehensive view of the contest will, however, justify us in saying, that the fear of the Christian is unfounded, and the sneer of the sceptic undeserved; that the apparent conflict is only an apparent one; and that the antagonism finds its field in the want of harmony, not so much between the verities of science and religion, as between scientific hypotheses and religious opinions; and that between nature and revelation, when properly understood, there must be a substantial harmony, since God is the author of them both. The misunderstanding is not between the things themselves, but between the guesses of men who seek to be their priests and interpreters. For science is simply our knowledge of nature, its facts, and its laws; and religion is simply our knowledge of God, and of our relations to Him. And, as the facts of nature reveal themselves slowly and almost reluctantly in response to patient research and careful study, it is but natural that the investigations and conclusions of one age should differ from those of another; that the latest deductions of science to-day should contradict the theories of a century ago, and that, in turn, they should expect to be contradicted by the theories of a century hence. Meanwhile, what is true remains; and this process of investigation and refutation carried on by scientific men from age to age, is but the method by which the truth concerning nature is separated from the fancies of men; and its result is, not the survival of the fittest, but the survival of the true. And yet the truthfulness of the true does not depend upon its having been discovered and known by men. No line or word on the vast page of the universe is altered by the most careful scrutiny; it is only that these mysterious words are spelled out, and read with fewer errors than other scholars made who had gone before. So, also, in religion there are certain facts which constitute its basis, and which are proposed to our faith, not as theories or opinions, but as facts. And along with these, there are systems of opinion, the deductions of human reason from the Divine premises, but which, as human deductions, are liable to be erroneous and false. And yet these human systems are but the honest efforts of men to understand the accepted facts of revelation, and to apply them to the circumstances and needs of human life. Devout men of science will never be wanting to refute the flippant sneer which, in the name of science, invades a domain beyond its proper grasp; and earnest men of theology will ever be ready to expose and correct the errors of other theological systems. And so, in science and in religion, each has, within its own adherents and disciples, its mutual check and safeguard, by which the truth is preserved, and the fancies of men, when inconsistent with it, are exploded. But the trouble begins when scientific men attempt to teach theology, or theologians assume to teach science. For as there is nothing in the study of science which necessarily makes a man a theologian, the theological views of the scientist may not be worth so much as those of an unlettered but earnest Christian; for that value is determined, not by intellectual acquisition, but by a devout habit of mind and heart. And there is nothing in the study of theology which necessarily acquaints a man with what is known as scientific truth; and therefore the scientific views of a theologian are of small value, since they are not in the line of study or thought to which he naturally devotes himself. And so long as scientists attempt to teach theology, and theologians insist upon refuting what they choose to dignify by the name of science, so long there will be a terrible warfare of words; but it will not touch nor jeopardize for a moment the indestructible harmony between true science and true religion, between a right reason and a devout faith, between the broad page of nature, written by His own finger through the long processes of His own law, and the page of inspiration, written by the human amanuensis of His own Spirit. There is one point, however, in the universe, in which nature and revelation meet; one point in which the visible creation comes in contact with the invisible and supernatural forces which pervade the universe. That solitary point is the incarnation of the Son of God. In it nature and revelation mysteriously meet and harmonize; as by it this human nature of ours—the very crown and glory of the visible creation—is taken into union with God. Here the ultimate mystery of science and religion meet and harmonize and are at one; as by the incarnation the nature of man is allied to the throne of God in a union which can never be divorced, and which waits for its final epiphany for the manifestation of the sons of God. (*W. A. Snively, D.D.*)

# THE BIBLICAL ILLUSTRATOR

## II TIMOTHY

THE

# BIBLICAL ILLUSTRATOR

BY
JOSEPH S. EXELL

II TIMOTHY

BAKER BOOK HOUSE
GRAND RAPIDS, MICHIGAN 49506

Library of Congress Catalog Card Number: 54-11086
ISBN: 0-8010-3280-6

Printed in the United States of America

# INTRODUCTION TO THE SECOND EPISTLE TO TIMOTHY.

THE AUTHORSHIP OF THE EPISTLE.—In several passages this Epistle bears the stamp of genuineness as a writing of St. Paul's, notably at chaps. i. 5–18 and iv. 9–22. In particular, the opening thanksgiving (chap. i. 3) is characteristic of Paul, eight of his ten other Epistles having a similar commencement. At the same time this is not such a prominent feature as to lead to imitation; and, as a matter of fact, it is not found in the two other Pastoral Epistles. A strong proof of genuineness is afforded by the proper names in the Epistle. They are twenty-three in number, including ten mentioned elsewhere. In connection with several of these ten, remarks are made which a forger would have been very unlikely to invent; e.g., "Demas forsook me, having loved this present world" (chap. iv. 10; cf. Col. iv. 14), is a record more like what we should have expected to find concerning Mark, in view of his former desertion of Paul (Acts xiii. 13); whereas we find favourable mention of him in this Epistle (chap. iv. 11). Dalmatia is also a strange place to have invented as a destination for Titus (chap. iv. 10), considering that he had been written to so recently at Crete. A striking argument has been derived from the occurrence of the name Linus in chap. iv. 21. The argument is based on the fact that Linus, Cletus, and Clement are the names of the first three bishops of the Church of Rome, preserved in her Eucharistic Service, dating from the second century. If the Epistle had been written in the post-Apostolic age, Linus, it is held, would have been sure to receive a more prominent place in the list of salutations, and his name would have been accompanied with that of Cletus, or at all events with that of Clement, as the latter was believed to have been an immediate disciple of Paul. (*J. A. McClymont, B.D.*)

OBJECT OF THE EPISTLE.—It was written from Rome shortly before the martyrdom of the apostle. It was written chiefly to urge Timothy to come to him, all his other companions in the service of Christ (excepting Luke) being away. One, Demas, had deserted him; others, as Tychicus, he had sent away. But, though apparently sent for the purpose of urging Timothy to come to him quickly, it contains the most precious exhortation to him, and through him to all ministers, "to make full proof of their ministry," and this it does in the words of a dying man, who is "ready to be offered, and the time of whose departure is at hand." Whatever special onslaughts of the evil one were yet in store for him, we have his expression of faith that God would carry him triumphantly through all (chap. iv. 18). (*M. F. Sadler, M.A.*)

CONTENTS.—This letter is of a more private, personal, and intimate character: hence in the superscription Paul omits the title apostle. In the body of the letter (chap. i. 6–iv. 8) three subjects are dealt with: 1. Timothy's own deportment. He is to stir up the gift which is in him, and not allow himself to be daunted by fear of the sufferings which the service of Christ may bring upon him.  Paul encourages him by four considerations : the grandeur of the gospel, his own example and that of the faithful Onesiphorus, and lastly by the sure hope of the Christian (chap. i. 6–ii. 13).  2. The Church.  This has been invaded by teaching to no profit, and tending only to barren disputations.  Nevertheless there still remains a nucleus of true believers, bearing the Divine seal of holiness.  Timothy must not be discouraged, therefore, but contend firmly and patiently for the truth.  There is even reason to expect that in the last times a moral corruption, like that of the heathen world, may find its way into the Church itself.  Already some Christians have become perverted.  In order to counteract their influence, the apostle gives Timothy three counsels.  He is to remember the example of constancy which he had witnessed in Paul himself (during his first sojourn in Lycaonia) ; he is to feed continually upon the Scriptures inspired of God ; and to redouble his vigilance and activity in evangelistic work (chap. ii. 14–iv. 5).  3. The apostle himself.  He speaks first of his approaching martyrdom, then he asks Timothy to come as soon as possible, because all his fellow-workers, except Luke, are absent.  He urges that Mark should come with him, and desires him to bring also the cloak and the books which he (Paul) had left in Asia Minor.  Lastly, he refers to his first appearance before the imperial judgment seat, which gave him an opportunity of fully proclaiming the gospel message, and yet did not lead to his condemnation.  In the concluding sentences he refers to, or explains incidentally, the absence of two of his fellow-workers (ver. 20).  Then come greetings to a few brethren, all of them bearing Roman names.  (*Prof. F. Godet.*)

# THE BIBLICAL ILLUSTRATOR.

## II. TIMOTHY.

### CHAPTER I.

Vers. 1, 2. **Paul, an apostle of Jesus Christ by the will of God.**—*The dignity of preachers :*—Preachers are to maintain the dignity of their persons. Because a good name is as precious ointment, above great riches, and more than the choicest silver and gold, to be regarded. It will rejoice the heart, whereas the contrary is a curse, and to be avoided. Otherwise, if ministers be ill reported of, their doctrine (be it never so sound or sovereign for the soul) will be despised, rejected. If the vessel be counted unsweet, who will with alacrity taste of the liquor? The Word will not speed if the preacher be despised. And for procuring a good report—1. Be diligent in the discharge of thy duty; avoid idleness in thy calling. 2. Take heed thou be not justly accused of that which thou hast severely censured in others. 3. Speak not evil of others, for with what measure we mete it shall be measured to us again. Could we cover others' infirmities, they would do the like for us. 4. Seek the glory of God in thy proceedings, for they who honour God shall be honoured of Him, whereas they who seek themselves shall be abased. The people also must take heed how they detract from the credit of their pastors. Nature, by a sacred instinct, will defend the head with the loss of the hand. Why, the preacher is the head of the people, and therefore to be respected; and it is an old axiom, "Do My prophets no harm" (Psa. cv. 15). (*J. Barlow, D.D.*) *Life shaped by the will of God :*—In 1798 a child was born at Rome, N.Y. His father was a mechanic. At school he showed good talents, and his father at length consented that he might attempt to get a liberal education. His heart was set on the law, but God made him a minister, turned his thoughts towards the Holy Scriptures as a field of study, and before he died (at the age of seventy-two years) a million volumes, of which he was the author, had been sold. This is a very brief sketch of the Rev. Albert Barnes. Now, did he do all these things of his own power and wisdom? Not at all. Hear his modest and truthful statement on the subject: "I have carried out none of the purposes of my early years. I have failed in those things which I had designed, and which I hoped to accomplish. I have done what I never purposed or expected to do. I have known what it was to weep at discouragements. I have been led along contrary to my early anticipations. I can now see, I think, that while I have been conscious of entire freedom in all that I have done, yet that my whole life has been under the absolute control of a Higher Power, and that there has been a will and a plan in regard to my life which was not my own. Even my most voluntary acts, I can see, have been subservient to that higher plan, and what I have done has been done as if I had no agency in the matter." (*J. Plumer, D.D.*) **According to the promise of life.**—*The promise of life :*—The specific form of the whole gospel is promise, which God gives in the Word and causes to be preached. The last period of the world is the reign of grace (Rom. v. 21). Grace reigns in the Word, only as promise. Grace has nothing to do with law and requisition of law, therefore the word of that grace can be no other than a word of promise. Hence χάρις and ἐπαγγελία form an indissoluble unity (Rom. iv. 16). For to this end Christ is the Mediator of the New Covenant, that we might receive the promise of the eternal inheritance (Heb. ix. 15). The promise of life in Christ-form is the word

1

of the New Covenant (chap. i. 1). The difference between the gospel of the Old Covenant and that of the New rests alone on the transcendently greater glory of its promise (Heb. viii. 6 ; xi. whole). That these great and precious promises are given to us (2 Pet. i. 4 ; 2 Cor. vii. 1) establishes the position of a Christian man ; if he calls himself a son and heir, he has no other title for this except that of promise alone, purely of grace (Gal. iv. 28, iii. 29 ; Rom. iv. 16). That, and how God for His own sake blots out our transgressions, and remembers our sin no more (Isa. xliii. 25), is the substance of the word of promise in the New Testament, and which confirms that of the Old. (*J. Harless.*)     *Promise and payment :*—Satan promises the best, but pays with the worst ; he promises honour and pays with disgrace ; he promises pleasure and pays with pain ; he promises profit and pays with loss ; he promises life and pays with death. But God pays as He promises ; all His payments are made in pure gold. (*T. Brooks.*)     *Through death to life :*—An unusual addition to the opening formula of St. Paul's letters, probably rising out of the sense that the promise was near its fulfilment, and that he was about to pass through death to life. (*E. H. Plumptre, D.D.*)     *The unwavering certainty of St. Paul in respect of his call to apostleship :*—1. Its foundation. 2. Its noble value. Ministry in the gospel is no function of death, but a proclamation of life in Christ Jesus. (*Dr. Van Oosterzee.*)     **Which is in Christ Jesus.**—*Ministerial relation with Christ :*—This must teach us who have any relation with Christ highly to esteem it and greatly to rejoice in it. Think it no small thing to be an officer in His house, a labourer in His vineyard, and a member of His body, for this is true nobility, unconceivable dignity, and the direct path to eternal felicity. Paul, a preacher of Jesus Christ, is a name of greater price and praise than all human titles and time's adjuncts (though in their nature good) in all the world. (*J. Barlow, D.D.*)     **To Timothy, my dearly beloved son.**— *Timothy, the pious youth :*—Timothy is one of the unblamed youths of the Bible. He ranks along with Abel, Joseph, Moses, Josiah, and Daniel. I. TIMOTHY'S BOOK. His father was a Greek and a heathen ; but his mother, Eunice, and his grandmother, Lois (who lived with them), were Jews and believers. They did their best for the godly upbringing of their boy ; and they would be left to do as they liked in the matter. For heathen fathers gave more attention to their young dogs and horses than to their young children. Books were then very scarce and dear, and probably the Old Testament was the only book in their house. They used it well, and found it to be a library in itself, and the best children's treasury. II. TIMOTHY'S HOME. The boy would be strongly tempted to follow his dashing heathen father, whose amusements would be such as boys most delight in ; yet he sided with and took after his devout mother and grandmother. That fact speaks volumes for him. I believe that he gladly gave himself up to all the best influences of his home. Thus his mother was his mother thrice over, for she gave life to his mind and to his soul as she had given life to his body. Obedience is only one of the outward signs of the true spirit of a child. A girl once heard a sermon upon this subject. On the way home, feeling uneasy, she said, " Mother, do I always obey you ? "   " You know best yourself, my dear," the mother replied. " Well, I never disobey you," the girl continued, " I always do what you bid me, but I sometimes go slow." The Bible shows concern chiefly about the kind and spirit of your obedience. " Children, obey your parents in the Lord." The right feeling to parents is so like the right feeling to God that people have used one word for both. The noblest characters are found among those men who in youth yielded most to a mother's influence. You will find many striking proofs of my view in such books as Smiles' " Self-help " and " Character." The reason is soon found. Boys like Timothy unite in their characters what is best in man and woman. They are rich in spirit beyond others, for Nature gives them manly strength, to which a mother's influence adds tenderness and sweetness. A well-known writer has said, " In my best moments I find again my mother in myself." Usually man is the son of woman in his best gifts. " A kiss from my mother," said West, " made me a painter." To love your mother well, then, is a liberal education of head and heart. III. TIMOTHY'S CONVERSION. Some, like Samuel, cannot remember a time when they did not trust God. Their love to the Saviour is not an after-love, but a first love. Others, like Timothy, have a well-marked and a well-remembered conversion. Paul calls him " my own son in the faith, . . . whom I have begotten in the gospel." Often the successful preacher but reaps what the mother had sowed, and watered with her prayers, and brought to the verge of harvest. Timothy must have been a mere boy at the time of his conversion. For he was quite young when he was ordained, and even when Paul wrote his Epistle to him, he was so boyish-looking that people might easily despise his youth. His early conversion was one chief reason why Timothy did so much good, and why he still remains such an inviting example of grace. It made him like Newton, of whom Bishop Burnet says, that he had the whitest soul he ever knew, and was as a very infant in purity of mind. Than youthful piety God has no better gift for you but heaven. (*James Wells, M.A.*) *The useful to be chiefly instructed :*—Such persons as are likely to prove good and excellent instruments in the Church are principally to be instructed and encouraged. We will water that plant most, hedge about it, and prune it, which is likeliest to bring forth much and good fruit; the beast of best hopes shall be put in the rankest pasture, the other turned to run in the common field and barrenest ground. (*J. Barlow, D.D.*)   **Grace, mercy, and peace from God the Father and Christ Jesus our Lord.**—*The universal need of mercy :*—The salutation in the three pastoral Epistles introduces between the customary "grace" and "peace" the additional idea of "mercy." It is a touching indication of the apostle's own humility, and reveals his deepening sense of the need of "mercy" as he drew near the glory of the unveiled Face. It records the fact that if in Ephesus, Rome, or England there are any children of God who fancy they can rise above an utterance of the cry, "God be merciful to me," apostles and ministers of Christ, even in view of the martyr's crown, cannot forget their profound need of Divine "mercy." The association of Christ Jesus with God the Father as the common source of "grace," "mercy," and "peace" shows what St. Paul thought of his Lord. As he commenced his Epistle with this blended petition, we are not surprised to find that his last recorded words were, "The grace of our Lord Jesus Christ be with you." This was the sum of all blessedness, and the exalted Lord, Christ, was Himself the source of it. (*H. R. Reynolds, D.D.*)   *Salutations :*—Salutations are not for compliment, but piety. (*J. Barlow, D.D.*)   *Conduits of grace :*—Hear the Word, search the Scriptures, read good books, receive the sacraments, pray, confer, for these be as so many conduits whereby the Creator conveyeth grace into the soul of the creature. (*Ibid.*) *Mercy and grace essential to true peace :*—Dream not, then, that all is peace that seems so; for what peace can a profane person have within him that wanteth faith and grace? Nay, how ever he carry the matter, he is at war within himself. The wounded deer runs and skips and leaps, yet the arrow or bullet stings, pains, torments at the very heart, and before long will cause a fall, a death. So, under a cheerful look, the soul may be sorrowful, and all that laugh in the face are not at peace within. Who, then, is he that would have true and sound peace? Let him strive for mercy and grace; for as the shadow the body, heat the fire, these follow the one the other. Many imagine they have it, yet are foully deluded, deceived. I deny not but the wicked may have a peace; but it is not worth the naming, for it runs not from a clear fountain, it springs not from a sweet root, and therefore one drop of this we have in hand is worth a thousand of that, as a little rose-water a whole glassful of mud. It is not constant neither, but often interrupted; every thunderclap will cause such to quake, to tremble, and at the last they shall certainly be consumed. Oh that men were wise to gather grace, so should they have peace at their latter end, and in the meanwhile be, like Mount Sion, unmovable! Grant that such may have outward troubles; yet they shall have inward peace that passeth all understanding. (*Ibid.*)

Ver. 3. **I thank God, whom I serve from my forefathers with pure conscience.**—*Serving God :*—Fifty years ago, when a poor black man of Jamaica wishing to go to Africa to tell the glad tidings of salvation, was told that, among other difficulties, he might be a slave again, he replied, "If I have been a slave for man, I can be a slave for God." (*Anon.*)   "*I serve*"*:*—At the battle of Crecy, in 1346, when King Edward III. of England defeated Philip, King of France, the Black Prince led a portion of the attack. Thinking himself very hotly pressed in the midst of the combat, he sent word to his father to send him some reinforcements at once, or he would be flanked by the enemy. The king, who had been watching the progress of the fight from a neighbouring hill-top, sent down word as follows: "Tell my son, the Black Prince, that I am too good a general not to know when he needs help, and too kind a father not to send it when I see the need of doing so." The historian tells us that, reassured by this promise, the Black Prince fought nobly, and put the motto *Ich Dien*, "I serve," upon his crest, which is on the Prince of Wales's escutcheon to this day. (*J. L. Nye.*)   *Disinterested service :*—After the completion of his great picture of "The Last Judgment" for the altar of the Sistine Chapel (which had occupied him eight years), Michael Angelo devoted himself to the perfection of St. Peter's, of which he planned and built the dome. He refused all remuneration for his labours, saying he regarded his services as being rendered to the glory of God. (*W. Baxendale.*) *The spirit of true service* :— My desire is that God may be pleased by me and glorified in me, not only by my praying and preaching and almsgiving, but even by my eating, drinking, and sleeping, and visits, and discourses ; that I may do all in the name of the Lord Jesus, giving glory to God by Him. Too often do I take a wrong aim and miss my mark ; but I will tell you what are the rules I set myself and strictly impose upon myself from day to day : Never to lie down but in the name of God, not barely for natural refreshment, but that a wearied servant of Christ may be recruited and fitted to serve Him better the next day ; never to rise up but with this resolution— well, I will go forth this day in the name of God, and will make my religion my business, and spend the day for eternity ; never to enter upon my calling but first thinking I will do these things as unto God, because He requireth these things at my hands, in the place and station to which He hath appointed me ; never to sit down to table but resolving I will not eat merely to please my appetite, but to strengthen myself for my Master's work ; never to make a visit but upon some holy design, resolving to leave something of God wherever I go. This is that which I have been for some time learning and hard pressing after, and if I strive not to walk by these rules, let this paper be a witness against me. (*J. Alleine.*) *True and false service :*—It is said of the Lacedœmonians, who were a poor and homely people, that they offered lean sacrifices to their gods ; and that the Athenians, who were a wise and wealthy people, offered fat and costly sacrifices ; and yet in their wars the former always had the mastery of the latter. Whereupon they went to the Oracle to know the reason why those should speed worst who gave most. The Oracle returned this answer to them : " That the Lacedœmonians were a people who gave their *hearts* to their gods, but that the Athenians only gave their *gifts* to their gods." Thus a heart without a gift is better than a gift without a heart. (*T. Secker.*) *Deceitful service :*—The observation of Augustine is founded on too much truth : " There is often a vast difference between the face of the work and the heart of the workman." (*Ibid.*) *Strength required for religious service :*— And to serve God, is it laborious ? We must then be of good courage, gather strength, and quit us like men. He that hath a hard task will proportion his power according to the toil. The longer the ground hath lain fallow, the stronger must be the team to tear it asunder ; and the farther we take a journey, the more pence must we put in our purse ; so the more difficult this duty is, the more must we look about us, arm ourselves, and be prepared for the well performance of it. And for the better discharge thereof we must labour for two things : the one is knowledge, the other strength. For these are absolutely necessary for the doing of any action, the one to direct us, the other to enable us in this duty. (*J. Barlow, D.D.*) **With pure conscience.**—*The Christian profession adorned by a pure conscience :*—And will not a pure conscience adorn our profession, give a comely gloss to our conversation ? Red, purple, and scarlet add no more gloss to a piece of fine cloth than this purity doth to the life of a Christian. *Conscience :*—Conscience is the judgment which we pronounce on our own conduct by putting ourselves in the place of a bystander. (*Adam Smith.*) *Conscience has a joint knowledge of life :*—Conscience imparts a double or joint knowledge : one of a Divine law or rule, and the other of a man's own action. (*J. South.*) *Conscience looking upon life :*—I am, I know, I can, I will, I ought—such are the successive steps by which we ascend to the lofty platform from which conscience looks out upon human life. (*W. T. Davison, M.A.*) *Conscience a delicate creature :*—Conscience is a dainty, delicate creature, a rare piece of workmanship of the Maker. Keep it whole without a crack, for if there be but one hole so that it break, it will with difficulty mend again. (*S. Rutherford.*) *Conscience in a Christian :*—The Christian can never find a "more faithful adviser, a more active accuser, a severer witness, a more impartial judge, a sweeter comforter, or a more inexorable enemy." (*Bp. Sanderson.*) *Conscience in everything :*—Trust that man in nothing who has not a conscience in everything. (*Sterne.*) *Conscience makes saints :*—Conscience makes cowards of us ; but conscience makes saints and heroes too. (*J. Lightfoot.*) *Conscience hurt by sin :*—Hurt not your conscience with any known sin. (*S. Rutherford.*) *A good conscience independent of outside opinion :*—In the famous trial of Warren Hastings it was recorded that when he was put on his trial in so magnificent a manner in Westminster Hall, after the counsel for the prosecution, Burke, Sheridan, and others had delivered their eloquent speeches, he began to think he must be the greatest criminal on the face of the earth; but he related that when he turned to his own conscience the effect of all those grand speeches was as nothing. "I felt," he said, "that I had done my duty, and that they may say what they please." (*J. C. Ryle, D.D.*)    *Integrity of conscience :*—Hugh Miller speaks of the mason with whom he served his apprenticeship as one who "put his conscience into every stone that he laid." (*S. Smiles.*)    *Obedience to conscience:*—Lord Erskine, when at the Bar, was remarkable for the fearlessness with which he contended against the Bench. In a contest he had with Lord Kenyon he explained the rule and conduct at the Bar in the following terms : " It was," said he, "the first command and counsel of my youth always to do what my conscience told me to be my duty, and leave the consequences to God. I have hitherto followed it, and have no reason to complain that any obedience to it has been even a temporal sacrifice; I have found it, on the contrary, the road to prosperity and wealth, and I shall point it out as such to my children." (*W. Baxendale.*) **Without ceasing I have remembrance of thee in my prayers night and day.**— *The inner life of St. Paul :*—These unstudied words tell us something of the inner life of such an one as St. Paul, how ceaselessly, unweariedly he prayed, night as well as day. (*H. D. M. Spence, M.A.*)    *St. Paul's delight in Timothy :*—I. THE SIGNS OF THE DELIGHT AND SATISFACTION WHICH THE APOSTLE TOOK IN TIMOTHY, AS RECORDED IN THE TEXT. St. Paul prays for Timothy with satisfaction, uniting thanks with his prayers (ver. 3). This proves what a well-grounded satisfaction the apostle felt in Timothy. The delight and satisfaction which the apostle took in Timothy are also evinced in his strong desire to see him (ver. 4). We cannot be surprised that the apostle craved the presence of Timothy. He was now a solitary old man, and a prisoner. Of his disciples and fellow-labourers, Titus was gone unto Dalmatia, Tychicus he had sent to Ephesus, Trophimus was sick at Miletus, Mark was absent, and only Luke remained with him. Besides, ingratitude and desertion had sorely tried his affectionate spirit: Alexander the coppersmith had done him much evil; Demas had forsaken him and the faith together ; and when first brought up for trial before the imperial tribunal, none of the disciples had stood by him to cheer and second him. To Timothy, therefore, and to the remembrance of his pious and unfailing affection, the apostle clung very closely ; and his presence he desired as his greatest earthly solace and support. The delight and satisfaction which the apostle took in Timothy he also testified by expressing his confidence in his Christian character, but especially in his faith, the root of all which is Christian in the character of any one (ver. 5). St. Paul knew him well. During fourteen or fifteen years had this friendship endured, and many were the trials to which it had been put—trials of the constancy of Timothy's affection, trials of the integrity of his principles. But Paul had found no decline in his affection, no instability in his Christian principles; he therefore trusted him unfeignedly. II. THE CAUSES OF THAT DELIGHT AND SATISFACTION. 1. As the great cause, the first cause, the mover and originator of all secondary and inferior causes, St. Paul thanks God for the gifts and graces with which He had enriched Timothy. 2. But God works by means. The means which He employed, the causes to which as to instruments we must look in creating in Timothy such a trustworthy and reliable Christian character, were these three—maternal piety, early biblical education, and the ministry of the apostle. (*H. J. Carter Smith, M.A.*)    *The Christian near heaven praying for others :*—I remember visiting a friend on his death-bed, who, besides being engaged in a life of business, had devoted a great amount of time and labour and thought to the benefit of his fellow-creatures. Visiting him on one occasion, he made to me this remark: " I pray but very little for myself now. It seems to me that the battle is fought and the prize is in view, and my devotions with regard to myself are not so much prayer as thanksgiving. I praise God many an hour during the wakeful night. But do not suppose I do not pray. I believe I pray more than ever I did in my life, because now I have more time to pray for my fellow-men and for the nations of the world." He went on to describe how each day, and certain parts of every day, were devoted by him as he lay there gradually sinking to his rest to prayer for those in whom he felt a special interest, and also for those whom he had never seen.    *A praying minister :*—The Rev. I. F. Oberlin reserved stated hours for private prayer, which became known to the people ; and it was usual for carters and labourers returning from the fields with talk and laughter to uncover their heads as they passed beneath the walls of his house. If the children ran by too noisily, these working people would check them with uplifted finger, and say, " Hush! he is praying for us." (*Sword and Trowel.*) *Remembrance :*—Remembrance hath in it four things—apprehension, reposition, retention, and production. A notion or thing is by the external or internal sense presented to the eye of reason ; she perceives it, that's apprehension; then it is committed unto memory as a place of conservation, that's reposition ; afterwards kept there in safety, that's retention ; and lastly, when occasion is given, it is called out again, and that's production. A man takes a shaft in his hand, puts it in his quiver, retains it there for a time, and, when he would recreate himself, pulls it forth again, this is a plain emblem of remembrance. (*J. Barlow, D.D.*)      *Friendly love outwardly manifested :*—This argueth that the love of many, as Lot said of Zoar, is but a little one. So weak a spring can have no deep fountain; so small branches no great virtue in the root; and so feeble a flame no abundance of fuel; for causes produce effects proportionable to their internal power, do they not? Try, then, as the truth, so the measure of thine own and thy friends' affection by the outward effects. He that loves much will declare it by many prayers and sundry actions. (*Ibid.*)

Ver. 4. **Greatly desiring to see thee.**—*Things of like nature desire union :*—Two flames will become one, and two rivers, if they meet, willingly make but one stream. And are not all the faithful baptized with fire, and of the like temperature and condition? A faithful man affecteth nothing above the Lord ; His image is the only object of his love ; and does not every good man in part resemble that, and carry it about with him? Do not the sparkles of grace and wisdom appear in their faces? Is there not a kind of Divine influence in their speeches? They in some measure resemble their father, as dear children ; and from the contrary ground the wicked are an abomination to the just. They will build up one another in their holy faith, consult for the good of the Church, and tell one another what the Lord hath done for their soul; yea, the very sight of a good man in the morning, a dream of him in the night, will make one walk with more cheerfulness all the day following. The face of the faithful is like the loadstone, it conveyeth strength to many, and yet is never the weaker, poorer ; and as the one is reputed a great wonder in nature, so is the other as great a wonder in grace. (*J. Barlow, D.D.*)      *The coming of an absent friend :*—The chilling cold of winter makes the summer's sun more pleasant; so doth long absence a friend's personal presence. (*Ibid.*)      *The faithful found in companies :*—And here may the profane learn a lesson or two, if they please, for this is the true cause why the faithful, like pigeons, flock to the house of God, and are to be found there in troops and companies. Is not that the congregation of the saints, and the royal exchange, where they all meet together? Again, they may see why some sigh in soul and desire to be loosed. For their best friends be gone to heaven before them, and Christ is absent from them (Phil. iii. 20). (*Ibid.*) **Mindful of thy tears.**—*Tears :*—He seems not merely to speak of the former tears of Timothy shed at bidding Paul farewell (for tears are usually elicited at parting, comp. Acts xx. 37), but of his habitual tears under the influence of pious feeling. In this respect also he had him like-minded (Phil. ii. 20) with himself. Tears, the flower of the heart, indicate either the greatest hypocrisy or the utmost sincerity. (*J. A. Bengel.*)      *The power of tears :*—There is no power that man can wield so mighty as that of genuine tears. The eloquence of words is powerful, but the eloquence of tears is far more so. What manly heart has not been often arrested by the genuine sobs of even some poor child in the streets. A child's tear in the crowded thoroughfare has often arrested the busy merchant in his hurried career Coriolanus, who defied " all the swords in Italy and her confederate states," fell prostrate before the tears of his mother : " Oh, my mother, thou hast saved Rome, but lost thy son." (*D. Thomas, D.D.*)      *Tears described :*—Tears have been described as the blood of the wounds of the soul, the leaves of the plant of sorrow, the hail and rain of life's winter, the safety-valves of the heart when too much pressure is laid on, the vent of anguish-showers blown up by the tempests of the soul.

Ver. 5. **When I call to remembrance [R.V., having been reminded of] the unfeigned faith that is in thee.**—*Unfeigned faith :*—Some recorded circumstance, some spoken words, some searching test, had convinced St. Paul that Timothy at the present time was shedding no womanish tears, that his faith had revealed its strength and reality. If put to a severe strain there was now no mistake about it.

His faith was not a mask of unbelief, not a mere species of personal affection for the apostle, nor was it an unpractical faith, or one dependent on circumstances. St. Paul may once have entertained some transient doubt about Timothy. His fears may have exaggerated to himself the significance of Timothy's excessive grief. The words of despair wrung from his lips at their parting may have distressed the apostle ; but now the ugly suspicion is suppressed and no longer haunts his nightly intercession. (*H. R. Reynolds, D.D.*)    *Unfeigned faith practical :*—A lady and gentleman were being shown over the Mint by the Master of the Mint, who took them from the gate where the rough gold came in until they saw it going out in the form of coins to the bank for distribution all over the country.    When they were in the melting-room, the Master said, " Do you see that pail of liquid ? "   " Yes." " If you dip your hand into it I will pour a ladleful of molten gold into your hand, and it will roll off it without hurting you."   " Oh ! " was the remark somewhat sceptically made.   " Do you not believe me ? " inquired the Master.   " Well ; yes, I do," replied the gentleman.   " Hold out your hand, then."   When he saw the boil-ing gold above his hand, ready to be poured out, the gentleman took a step back, and, in terror, put his hand behind his back.   The lady, however, stooped down, dipped her hand into the liquid, and holding it out, said,. " Pour it into my hand." She really believed, and could trust, but her friend had not the practical faith to enable him to trust.   (*J. Campbell White.*)    *Timothy's faith :*—I. THE PECULIAR EXCELLENCE FOR WHICH TIMOTHY IS HERE COMMENDED—" Unfeigned faith."   St. Paul goes to the root of all that was excellent in Timothy—namely, his faith.   Not but that he could at other times dwell with pleasure on the fruits of that faith ; especially when speaking of him to others.   A beautiful specimen we have in Phil. ii. 19–22.   But in writing to Timothy himself, he thinks it most profitable to insist upon the source of that excellent character—his faith.   II. THE INSTRU-MENTAL CAUSE TO WHICH THE FAITH OF TIMOTHY IS HERE ASCRIBED—namely, the previous faith of his pious mother, Eunice, and of his grandmother, Lois.   The only effectual cause to which unfeigned faith can be ascribed, is the grace of Christ and His Spirit.   Nevertheless, in conferring this precious gift, the Lord frequently works by instruments or means.   The case of these excellent women, then, may lead us to observe the special honour conferred on the weaker sex, in their being often made—1. Foremost in faith and piety.   Man fell by the woman's trans-gression ; but it is by the seed of the woman that he is redeemed.   The first convert in Europe was a woman—Lydia.   In every period of the history of the Church women have been more open to conviction, more simple believers in Christ, more devoted in their zeal for His cause, than others.   2. Foremost in spiritual usefulness. Such they were in the case before us.   Now this remarkable succession of piety, in three generations of the same family, was a blessing from God, in honour of female faith—" unfeigned faith."   " Them that honour Me," saith God, " I will honour." (*J. Jowett, M.A.*)    *The worth of faith :*—All other graces do still accompany it.   Where it is they all be.   Faith may be compared to a prince which, wheresoever he pitcheth his tents, hath many rich attendants (1 Cor. xiii. *ult.*), as love, hope, zeal, patience, &c. Faith expelleth infidelity out of the heart, as heat doth cold, wind, smoke, for they be contraries.   It cannot, nor will not, admit of so bad a neighbour ; it shoulders out all unprofitable guests (Acts xv. 9 ; Heb. iv. 2).   And besides this, faith makes our actions acceptable to God ; for without it it is impossible to please God : this is that true fire which cometh down from heaven and seasons all our sacrifices (Heb. ii. 6 ; Rom. xiv. *ult.*).   What, then, are they worthy of, that neither respect it in them-selves nor others ; many have no care to plant this flower in the garden of their hearts ; or, if they have it, to preserve it from perishing.   Jonah mourned that his gourd withered, yet we grieve not if faith be destroyed.   (*J. Barlow, D.D.*)    *Faith the chief thing :*—The world cries, What's a man without money ? but I say, What's a man without faith ?   For no faith, no soul quickened ; heart purified, sin pardoned ; bond cancelled, quittance received ; or any person justified, saved.   (*Ibid.*)    *Get faith :*—I say that to all, which I do to one, get faith, keep faith, and increase your faith.   A mite of this grain is worth a million of gold ; a stalk of this faith, a standing tree of earthly fruits ; a soul freighted and filled with this treasure, all the coffers of silver in the whole world.   What can I more say ?   The least true faith is of more value than large domains, stately buildings, and ten thousand rivers of oil.   If the mountains were pearl, the huge rocks precious stones, and the whole globe a shining chrysolite ; yet faith, as much as the least drop of water, grain of sand, or smallest mustard-seed, is more worth than all.   This will swim with his master ; hold up his drooping head, and land him safe at the shore, against all winds and weather, storms and tempests; strive then for this freight; for the time and tide thereof serveth but once, and not for ever. (*Ibid.*)    *Faith works like effects in divers subjects :*—The grandmother, the mother, and the mother's son, had the same faith; and the like fruits proceeded from them, else Paul would never have called it unfeigned, or said that it dwelt in them, or given them all three one and the same testimony. All three had faith, and unfeigned faith. For the likeness of actions were in them, and proceed from them, by the which it was called unfeigned, and equally appropriated to each particular person. And it is an undoubted position that faith produceth the like effects in all God's children; in truth, it must be understood, not in degree. For as faith increaseth, the effects are bettered. Many lanterns, with several candles, will all give light; but in proportion to their adverse degrees and quantities. Every piece hath his report, but according to the bigness, and each instrument will sound, but variously as they be in proportion, and that for these reasons. Because faith differs not in kind, but in degree, and like causes produce like effects. Every bell hath its sound, each tone its weight, and several plants, their diverse influences; yet not in the same measure, though they may vary in kind. Again, faith is diffused into subjects, though several, yet they are the same in nature and consist of like principles. Fire, put into straw, will either smoke or burn, let the bundles be a thousand; life in the body will have motion, though not in the same degree and measure; and reason in every man acteth, but not so exquisitely. The constitution may not be alike, therefore a difference may be in operation natural, and also from the same ground, in acts spiritual. A dark horn in the lantern dims the light somewhat. (*Ibid.*) *Unfeigned faith manifested :*—From this point we may learn how to judge of the faith in our times which so many boast of; they cry, Have not we faith? do not we believe as well as the best? But where be the fruits of faith unfeigned? hast thou an humble and purging heart? dost thou call upon God at all times, tarry His leisure, and rely upon His promise? art thou bold and resolute for good causes? canst thou resist Satan? cleave to God, and shun the appearances of evil? will neither poverty oppress thee by despair, or prosperity by presumption? Why, it is well, and we believe, that faith is to be found in thee, but if not, thou hast it not rooted in thee. For the tree is known by the fruit. Will not the flower smell? the candle give light? and the fire heat? and shall true faith be without her effects? Boast not too much, lest thou deceive thyself, taking the shadow for the body; and that which is not for that which should be. (*Ibid.*)    **Which dwelt first in thy grandmother Lois, and thy mother Eunice.**—*Lois and Eunice :*—Origen conjectured that Lois and Eunice were relatives of St. Paul. This is only conjecture. There is far more reason for believing that they were converts made by him on his first visit to Lystra. In the Jewish communities of these Asiatic towns there were elect souls who had begun to cherish larger hopes for humanity. If Lois had permitted her daughter to marry a Greek, and yet had retained her faith in the promises made to Israel, and if Eunice had so far yielded to her husband's views or habits as to have foregone for her only son the sacramental rite of admission to the Jewish nation, and yet, notwithstanding this, had diligently instructed him in the history and contents of Holy Scriptures (chap. iii. 15). We have a glimpse of light thrown upon the synagogues and homes of devout Israelites in Asia Minor. (*H. R. Reynolds, D.D.*)    Lois is the same with the more familiar Lais; Eunice is an equivalent of the Latin Victoria. (*H. D. M. Spence, M.A.*) *The day of Christian faith :*—Christian faith in its morning (Timothy), at noon (Eunice), and at the evening of life (Lois). (*Dr. Van Oosterzee.*)    *Celebrated mothers :*—Like the celebrated mothers of Augustine, of Chrysostom, of Basil, and of other illustrious saints of God, the life, sincerity and constancy of Lois and Eunice became vicariously a glorious heritage of the universal Church. (*H. R. Reynolds, D.D.*)    *Lessons :*—1. The infidelity of the father prevents not faith in the children. For if it had, Eunice and Timothy and many more should never have been found faithful (1 Kings xiv. 13; 1 Cor. vii. 14). 2. Succession of faith is the best succession. 3. Where we see signs of goodness, we are to judge the best. 4. When we give others instruction, we are first to possess them with the persuasion of our affection. For then they will take it in good part, and our words will have the deeper impression. (*J. Barlow, D.D.*)    *Memories of a mother :*—Among the reminiscences of a great statesman, Daniel Webster, it is related that on one occasion a public reception was given him in Boston. Thousands of his country's citizens crowded together and paid him homage. Bursts of applause had been sounding all day in his ears. Elegantly dressed ladies had thrown bouquets of the rarest flowers at his feet.   But as he ascended the steps leading to his mansion, crowned with the honours of the gala day, a little, timid girl stepped up and placed a bunch of old-fashioned garden pinks in his hand.   At sight of these old, familiar flowers, and their well-remembered fragrance filled the air, the old memories were stirred.   Just such pinks used to grow in his mother's garden when he was a child. Instantly that sweet face of the loved mother came to his vision; her tender, gentle voice sounded once more in his ears.   So overcome was he with the tide of old memories that crowded into his heart that he excused himself, and went to his apartments alone.   "Nothing," said he, "in all my life affected me like that little incident."   John Newton in his worst days could never forget his mother, at whose knees he had learned to pray, but who was taken to heaven when he was but eight years old.   "My mother's God, the God of mercy, have mercy upon me!" was often his agonising prayer in danger, and we all know how it was answered. (*Great Thoughts*.)     *Mother's influence*:—If we call him great who planned the Cathedral of St. Peter, with all its massiveness and beauty; if they call the old masters great whose paintings hang on monastery and chapel walls, is not she (the mother) great who is building up characters for the service of God, who is painting on the soul canvas the beauty and strength of Jesus the Christ?   (*A. E. Kittredge*.) *Christian mothers*:—Give me a generation of Christian mothers and I will undertake to change the whole face of society in twelve months.   (*Lord Shaftesbury*.) *Woman's influence*:—A missionary in Ceylon writes as a "noticeable fact" that where Christian women are married to heathen husbands, generally the influence in the household is Christian; whereas, when a Christian man takes a heathen woman he usually loses his Christian character, and the influences of the household are on the side of heathenism.     *Parental example*:—We may read in the fable what the mother crab said to the daughter: "Go forward, my daughter, go forward."   The daughter replied, "Good mother, do you show me the way!" Whereupon the mother, crawling backward and sidling, as she was wont, the daughter cried out, "So, mother!  I go just as you do."   (*Family Churchman*.) *Mother and child*:—Sir Walter Scott's mother was a superior woman, and a great lover of poetry and painting.   Byron's mother was proud, ill-tempered, and violent. The mother of Napoleon Buonaparte was noted for her beauty and energy.   Lord Bacon's mother was a woman of superior mind and deep piety.   The mother of Nero was a murderess.   The mother of Washington was pious, pure, and true.   The mother of Matthew Henry was marked by her superior conversational powers.   The mother of John Wesley was remarkable for her intelligence, piety, and executive ability, so that she has been called the "Mother of Methodism."   It will be observed that in each of these examples the child inherited the prominent traits of the mother. (*J. L. Nye*.)     *Mother's influence*:—"It was at my mother's knees," he says, "that I first learned to pray; that I learned to form a reverence for the Bible as the inspired word of God; that I learned the peculiarities of the Scottish religion; that I learned my regard to the principles of civil and religious liberty, which have made me hate oppression and—whether it be a pope, or a prelate, or an ecclesiastical demagogue—resist the oppressor."   (*T. Guthrie, D.D.*)     *Children to be taught young*:—First, for then they will remember it when they are old (Prov. xxiii. 13). Dye cloth in the wool, not in the web, and the colour will be the better, the more durable.   Secondly, to defer this duty is dangerous, for thou mayst be took from them.   Who then shall teach them after thy departure? (2 Kings ii. 24).   Thirdly, besides, what if they come to faith?   Will it not be with the more difficulty? Fallow ground must have the stronger team, great trees will not easily bend, and a bad habit is not easily left and better come by.   If their memories be stuffed with vanity as a table-book, the old must be washed out before new can be written in. Fourthly, what shall I more say?   God works strangely in children, and rare things have been found in them; and what a comfort will it be for parents in their life, to hear their children speak of good things, and at the last day, when they can say to Christ, Here am I, and the children Thou hast given me!   (*J. Barlow, D.D.*) *The secret of a good mother's influence*:—Some one asked a mother whose children had turned out very well, what was the secret by which she prepared them for usefulness and for the Christian life, and she said, "This was the secret.   When in the morning I washed my children, I prayed that they might be washed in the fountain of a Saviour's mercy.   When I put on their garments, I prayed that they might be arrayed in the robe of a Saviour's righteousness.   When I gave them food, I prayed that they might be fed with manna from heaven.   When I started them on the road to school I prayed that their faith might be as the shining light, brighter and brighter to the perfect day. When I put them to sleep, I prayed that they might be enfolded in the Saviour's arms." (*T. De Witt Talmage.*) *Training the young :*—Rightly to train a single youth is a greater exploit than the taking of Troy. (*Melancthon.*) *A good grandmother :*—" I owe a great deal to my grandmother," said a young man who was courageous and true above many in his Christian life. " Why, what did she do for you ? " " Oh, she just sat by the fire." " Did she knit ? " " A little." " Did she talk to you ? " " A little ; but grannie was not much of a talker ; she did not go in for all that, you know ; but she just sat and looked comfortable, and when we were good she smiled, and when we were wild in our talk she smiled too, but if ever we were mean she sighed. We all loved her, and nobody did as much for us, really, as grannie." (*Marianne Farningham.*) *A godly household :*—A household that fears God is another joy of my life. I would rather see it than the finest landscape. I can understand why Sir Walter Scott got his seat put down in his garden, within earshot of his bailiff's cottage, that he might always hear the sound of the psalms at morning and evening worship. There never was incense sweeter from morning or evening sacrifice ! A home, where the father and mother walk in the narrow way, is pretty sure to find their children accompanying them. Not that God's gifts are hereditary, but example goes a great way, and if the parent, who is the highest on earth to the child, live a Christian life, it is very seldom the child will not follow him. It depends on the parent. If the mother, or father, or both, be real Christians, gentle, kind, reverent, pure, the little ones grow accustomed to these graces and catch them almost unconsciously. *Suppressed lives :*—A few years ago a gentleman died in Germany whose name was almost unknown both in Great Britain and on the Continent. A physician by profession, and an inheritor of a title, he lived a life of comparative seclusion. He was never in the front at any pageant or ceremonial of any court. He was never known when treaties and alliances were made between reigning sovereigns. In diplomatic circles his name was never prominently mentioned. And yet no man of his time in all Europe had more influence in determining the destiny of nations than he. He was the power behind thrones. He was the intimate confidant of princes. He rendered the most important services to England and to Germany. His was one of those " suppressed lives " which are so often lives of commanding power. It was a suppressed life, expressed in kings, parliaments, and statesmen. Such lives are to be found in literary circles. It is often a matter of infinite surprise that such marvels of erudition and widest compass of reading in the domain of metaphysics, philosophy, theology, and ecclesiastical history, can be produced by a single man in the compass of so short a life as is given the world by many a German writer. But the secret is, that behind the life of the author, who may receive all the praise of the public, are scores of suppressed lives. These are the men of culture and training who are doing the toiling drudgery, wading through volumes, finding and verifying quotations. It is well known that in the business world these suppressed lives play a most important part. Many an employer is dependent upon the labours of faithful men, unknown to the world, who have mastered all the intricacies of a complex business, and upon whom they implicitly depend for advice in its management. St. Paul, after his somewhat depressing visit to Athens, found a home in the humble abode of Aquila and Priscilla, in the busy, sensual city of Corinth. In the house of this lowly artisan he found rest, refreshment, and strength. Working with him side by side, in the plebeian craft of tent-making, the great apostle to the Gentiles derived new zeal and energy for his great work from the life and conversation of this faithful disciple of Jesus Christ. In the same home the eloquent Alexandrian, Apollos, found shelter and instruction. In his life, full of eloquent thought and speech, and still more eloquent deeds, their suppressed lives found a brilliant and glorious expression. These two lives may justly stand for the lives of the great multitude of teachers in the Sunday Schools and other schools of our land. Suppressed lives mostly they are. Comparatively unrecognised is the influence these teachers are exerting upon the destinies of the millions of children intrusted to their care. In St. Paul's words to Timothy, as quoted in the text, we have the recognition of the power of suppressed lives in the charmed circle of the home. An ampler life has been opened to woman than heretofore in our day. The most thoroughgoing infidel cannot deny that Christianity above all other systems guards and glorifies the home ; that it has given to the wife and the mother the unique and the peerless position they hold in the countries where the highest civilisation is enjoyed. This Bible before me loves to honour the home. Who can estimate the influence of the suppressed lives in these homes ?　In that obscure country rectory at Epworth lived the mother of the Wesleys.　The husband was a dreamy, poetical, unpractical man. The household quiver was full and running over with children.　She was the teacher of them all.　John Wesley was taught by her the alphabet for the twentieth time, that. in her own language, '' the nineteenth might not be in vain.''　She kept up with the classical studies of her boys until they went away from home to school and college.　She managed her large family with the economy extolled by '' Poor Richard,'' with '' the discipline of West Point,'' and yet in the loving spirit of the home at Bethany.　She was the constant counsellor of her once seemingly stupid but now most gifted son John, and the earnest defender if not initiator of the greatest ecclesiastical movement of our day—the coming to the front in every Christian enterprise of the laymen of the Church.　She stood in her old age by the side of that son when, as the foremost religious leader of the centuries, he preached on Kensington common the memorable sermon to twenty thousand persons, and '' the slain of the Lord '' lay in windrows before him.　The grey-haired, bent, and silent mother was speaking in the burning words and ringing tones of the great reformer. The mother of Washington lived and triumphed in the matchless deeds of the father of his country.　(S. Fallows.)

Ver. 6. **Stir up the gift of God which is in thee by the putting on of my hands.**—*The graces of God's Spirit are of a fiery quality :*—And here we must all learn a double lesson.　First, to get this fire ; and next, to keep it from quenching. This is that one thing necessary ; and how should we rejoice if it be already kindled ! For without it we are blind, corrupt, cold, yea, stark dead.　We must make our hearts the hearth to uphold it, and our hands the tongs to build it ; it must lodge with us daily, send out flame from us, and our lamps must be continually burning ; then shall we glorify our God, give light to others, walk safely, as walled about with a defence of fire, in this pilgrimage ; and the Lord, at length, shall send us fiery chariots to carry us to heaven, where our lamps shall burn day and night, and shine as the sun in the clear firmament for ever and ever.　(J. Barlow, D.D.)　*The gifts of God are to be stirred up within us :*—For if they be not, will they not perish ?　Have you not heard that they are of a fiery quality, and therefore subject, without stirring, blowing, to decay and be extinguished ?　The things that put out the fire of the spirit in us, are—first, evil cogitations ; as smoke weakeneth the eye, cold frosts nip the tender bud, and stinking smells damp and dull the purest spirits, so do bad thoughts disturb, impoverish, and enfeeble the gifts of God that be in us. [Secondly, corrupt speech ; that troubleth the fountain, and stoppeth the spirit's spring ; it shakes the young plants of grace, as the boisterous winds do the late grafted scions : this will cause the new man to die before his time, and the best fruits he beareth to become blasted.　Thirdly, wicked works ; they raze the foundation, and, like the boar of the wood, root up all ; when these break forth into action, then falls grace suddenly into a consumption ; for they do not only wither the branches and change the complexion, but also kill the body, devour the juice of life, and destroy the constitution.　Fourthly, loud company ; this doth press down and keep under the gifts of God, that they cannot shoot up and spring ; as water to fire, green wood to dry, this quencheth all ; one grain of this leaven leaveneth the whole lump.　Let the Israelites live among the Egyptians, though they hate the men, yet they will learn their manners ; and Peter will grow cold if he warm his fingers at Caiaphas' fire.　Fifthly, the prosperity of the wicked ; that will buffet the soul, wound the very spirit, and make grace to look pale and wan.　How have the faithful fainted to see this, and the strongest foot of faith reeled, staggered ! This mud hath made the men of God almost to turn out of the way.　Sixthly, and finally, the pampering of the flesh.　It will impoverish the spirit, and make it look lank and lean.　If the one be cherished, the other will be starved.　When one of these buckets is ascending the other is descending.　Paul knew it well, therefore would beat down his body, and keep it in subjection.　These be the greatest impediments that hinder the gifts of grace from stirring, growing.　(*Ibid.*)　*Private helps to stir up grace :*—First, reading either the Scriptures or other holy writings.　This being done in a corner will refresh the spirit.　It is like food to the fainting passenger. Secondly, meditation.　He that sits long by the fire shall have his body to grow hot, and his cold spirits to become active, nimble.　Let this be done thoroughly, and it will make grace to stretch itself beyond its ordinary wont, and the Christian to be rapt out of himself.　Thirdly, prayer.　Who ever in his secret chamber went to God by earnest prayer but he was ravished in mind, and in the strength of that action spent all that day without weariness? God giveth the greatest gifts in secret; and, like man, revealeth Himself apart. Yea, private prayer doth both stir up and increase grace mightily; and as secret meals make a fat body, so doth that a well-liking mind. Fourth'y, observation, and that of the daily acts of God's providence. Fifthly, examples: not the worst, but the most excellent. Set before thine eyes the cloud of witnesses, that have far outstripped thee. Think what a shame it is for thee to come so far behind them. Will not a comely suite make some leap into the fashion? Sixthly, resolution; which must consist in propounding to ourselves a higher pitch of perfection. He that would shoot or leap further than before will cast his eye and aim beyond the mark. But if all these will not stir up this fire, then consider what a loss it is to be a dwarf and bankrupt in this grace. How God may forsake us, an evil spirit possess us, and Satan seek about to apprehend us, as the Philistines did Samson; so shall we pluck up our spirits, stir up our strength, rise out of this lethargy, and fly for our lives. (*Ibid.*) *The ordinances of God are not without profit, if rightly practised:*—It is not a trade, but the well using of it; not a farm, but the well husbandry of it, that will enrich the one and the other. Wherefore, be steadfast, immoveable, and abundant in the work of the Lord, knowing that your labour is not in vain in the Lord. (*Ibid.*) *Increase of grace:*—First, there may be an increase of grace in the best Christians. For Timotheus was an excellent man before this time; and were not his gifts now augmented? Secondly, that a minister hath need of more grace than a common Christian. This is the reason his gifts were increased. Thirdly, that the more worthy calling God sets us in, the greater portion of His spirit will He pour upon us. He did so by Timothy. Fourthly, that preachers may (above others) depend upon God for a blessing. For, are they not consecrated with great care and solemnity? enriched with extraordinary gifts and graces? Think on this, O ye men of God, and in contempt of the world let the honour of your calling, and hope of good success in the faithful execution, comfort your souls, and breed an undaunted resolution in you. (*Ibid.*) *St. Paul's concern about St. Timothy:*—The letter is a striking but thoroughly natural mixture of gloom and brightness. . . The thought which specially oppresses (the apostle) is "anxiety about all the Churches"—and about Timothy himself. Dark days are coming. False doctrine will be openly preached and will not lack hearers; and utterly un-Christian conduct and conversation will become grievously prevalent. And, while the godly are persecuted, evil men will wax worse and worse. This sad state of things has already begun; and the apostle seems to fear that his beloved disciple is not altogether unaffected by it. Separation from St. Paul or the difficulties of his position may have told on his over-sensitive temperament, and have caused him to be remiss in his work, through indulgence in futile despondency. The words of the text strike the dominant chord of the Epistle and reveal to us the motive that prompts it. The apostle puts Timothy in remembrance "that he stir up the gift of God which is in him." Again and again he insists on this and similar counsels (see vers. 8, 14, ii. 3, 15, iii. 14). And then, as the letter draws to a close, he speaks in still more solemn tones of warning (chap. iv. 1, 2, 5). Evidently the apostle is anxious lest even the rich gifts with which Timothy is endowed should be allowed to rust through want of use. Timidity and weakness may prove fatal to him and his work, in spite of the spiritual advantages which he has enjoyed. The apostle's anxiety about the future of the Churches is interwoven with anxiety about the present and future conduct of his beloved delegate and successor. (*A. Plummer, D.D.*) *Grounds of St. Paul's appeal to St. Timothy:*—In encouraging Timothy to stir up the gift that is in him, and not suffer himself to be ashamed of the ignominy, or afraid of the hardships, which the service of Christ entails, the apostle puts before him five considerations. There are the beautiful traditions of his family, which are now in his keeping. There is the sublime character of the gospel which has been entrusted to him. There is the teaching of St. Paul himself, who has so often given him a "pattern of sound words" and a pattern of steadfast endurance. There is the example of Onesiphorus with his courageous devotion. And there is the sure hope of "the salvation which is in Christ Jesus with eternal glory." Any one of these might suffice to influence him: Timothy cannot be proof against them all. (*Ibid.*) *Watching the heart flame:*—The Greek word rendered "stir up" literally means to kindle up, to fan into flame. We know that St. Paul frequently uses for his illustrations of Christian life scenes well known among the Greek heathen nations of the Old World, such as the Greek athletic games. Is it not possible (the suggestion is Wordsworth's) that the apostle while here charging Timothy to take care that the sacred fire of the Holy Ghost did not languish in his heart, while urging him to watch the flame, to keep it burning brightly, to fan the flame if burning dimly—is it not possible that St. Paul had in mind the solemn words of the Roman law, "Let them watch the eternal flame of the public hearth"? (Cicero, *De Legibus* xi. 8). The failure of the flame was regarded as an omen of dire misfortune, and the watchers, if they neglected the duty, were punished with the severest penalties. (*H. D. M. Spence, M.A.*)    *A neglected gift enkindled :*—Dr. Paley's great talents were first called into vigorous exercise under the following circumstances :—" I spent the first two years of my undergraduateship," said he, " happily, but unprofitably. I was constantly in society, where we were not immoral, but idle and rather expensive. At the commencement of my third year, however, after having left the usual party at rather a late hour in the evening, I was awakened at five in the morning by one of my companions, who stood at my bedside, and said, ' Paley, I have been thinking what a fool you are. I could do nothing, probably, were I to try, and can afford the life I lead ; you could do everything, and cannot afford it. I have had no sleep during the whole night on account of these reflections, and am now come solemnly to inform you, that if you persist in your indolence, I must renounce your society.' I was so struck," Dr. Paley continued, " with the visit and the visitor, that I lay in bed great part of the day and formed my plan. I ordered my bed-maker to prepare my fire every evening, in order that it might be lighted by myself. I arose at five ; read during the whole of the day, except during such hours as chapel and hall required, allotting to each portion of time its peculiar branch of study ; and just before the closing of gates (nine o'clock) I went to a neighbouring coffee-house, where I constantly regaled upon a mutton-chop and a dose of milk-punch. And thus on taking my bachelor's degree, I became senior wrangler." (*Life of Paley.*) *Individual gifts :*—What if God should command the flowers to appear before Him, and the sunflower should come bending low with shame because it was not a violet, and the violet should come striving to lift itself up to be like a sunflower, and the lily should seek to gain the bloom of the rose, and the rose the whiteness of the lily ; and so, each one disdaining itself. should seek to grow into the likeness of the other ? God would say, " Stop foolish flowers ! I gave you your own forms and hues, and odours, and I wish you to bring what you have received. O sunflower, come as a sunflower ; and you sweet violet, come as a violet ; let the rose bring the rose's bloom, and the lily the lily's whiteness." Perceiving their folly, and ceasing to long for what they had not, violet and rose, lily and geranium, mignonette and anemone, and all the floral train would come, each in its own loveliness, to send up its fragrance as incense, and all wreathe themselves in a garland of beauty about the throne of God. (*H. W. Beecher.*)    *Self-education :*— Every man has two educations—that which is given to him, and that which he gives himself. Of the two kinds, the latter is by far the most valuable. Indeed, all that is most worthy in a man, he must work out and conquer for himself. It is this that constitutes our real and best nourishment. What we are merely taught seldom nourishes the mind like that which we teach ourselves. (*A. Tynman.*)    *The stirred up will :*—I. It seems worth our while to remind ourselves that the source of all holy or vicious conduct is a virtuous or a depraved WILL. II. Next, in the review of our daily practice, it may be regarded as certain that we are wanting in our use of the most ordinary helps to a holy life, IF WE ARE INFREQUENT AND IRREGULAR IN PRAYER, AND IN OUR STUDY OF THE BIBLE. III. The present may further be a very fitting season for A STRICT EXAMINATION OF OURSELVES WITH REFERENCE TO ALL THOSE SEEMINGLY INDIFFERENT HABITS, ON WHICH (as a very little attention shows) THE VIGOUR OF OUR SPIRITUAL LIFE MAINLY DEPENDS. It is a point often overlooked by thoughtless persons, that a slow and undecided manner—habits of procrastination—sloth—want of punctuality and method— that these things, and the like of these, are fatal to the operations of the best-regulated will. (*J. W. Burgon, M.A.*)    *The Christian exhorted to stir up the gift of God that is in him :*—We must infer from this language that Timothy had become somewhat remiss since the departure of St. Paul, and needed a word of admonition and rebuke. But we must remember also, in justice to Timothy, that his position in Ephesus was an unusually trying one for a man of his age. He had been left in the city for the purpose of checking the outgrowth of heresy and licentiousness which had just begun to manifest itself. His ordinary duties were anxious and heavy : he had to rule presbyters, most of whom were older than himself; to assign to each a stipend in proportion to his work; to receive and decide on charges that might be brought against them; to regulate the almsgiving and the sisterhoods of the Church, and to ordain the presbyters and deacons. But, in addition to all this, there were leaders of rival sects in the city—Hymenæus, Philetus, and Alexander—men, probably, of considerable intellectual power, and certainly wielding great influence in the Christian community, who would exert themselves to oppose and to thwart the youthful bishop, and who would find in the absence of St. Paul their best opportunity of doing so with effect and success. Now Timothy, as it appears, was a man of a gentle and sensitive temperament. Lacking in the sterner fibre of character, he shrank from opposition and conflict. But although no mistake was made, as the sequel proved, the weaker nature of Timothy required on occasions the support and stimulus which the robust mind of the great apostle of the Gentiles was calculated to afford. One such occasion we have before us now. There came a visible slackening in the energy and vigour with which the youthful disciple held the reins of ecclesiastical government. St. Paul heard of this declension, and immediately spoke. The old man, ready to be offered, standing just on the confines of martyrdom, and just within reach of his crown, might well speak to his younger associate. And very touching are his words. The first thought on which we shall enlarge will be this—that there is a "gift of God" abiding in every one who names the name of Christ, and that this gift is "a spirit of power, and of love, and of a sound mind." The second thought will be this—that the gift in question may be permitted, through carelessness and neglect, to fall into decay; and that when this is the case, measures must immediately be taken to "stir up the gift"—to impart to it, by the use of suitable means, the vitality and vigour which it seems to have lost. I. Now, according to St. Paul, A CHRISTIAN IS ONE IN WHOM THE SPIRIT OF GOD—the personal Spirit, God the Holy Ghost—HAS TAKEN UP HIS ABODE, AND BECOME, AS IT WERE, A RESIDENT AND INMATE. What constitutes a temple is the inhabitation of Deity. It is just so with ourselves. Excellence of character and beauty of disposition are not things to be despised, but they only constitute the empty habitation; and the man is not a Christian unless the Spirit of God is dwelling within him. But, again, according to St. Paul, the Spirit of God does not supply to us the place of our spirit; but leaving the man in his completeness, pervades, animates, directs, that part of his nature by which he holds communion with the Divine. This gift of God "which is in us" is in the direction of "power, and of love, and of a sound mind." What does he mean? He means this. The office of God the Holy Ghost is to take of the things of the Lord Jesus Christ, and to "show" them to the true disciple. In other words, the Holy Ghost imparts to the soul a right understanding, a correct perception of Christian truth, and enables us to realise our own personal concern and interest in the things that are explained. II. The apostle tells us THAT THIS GIFT OF GOD WITHIN US MAY BE ALLOWED TO WANE—may require to be "stirred up." Yes; interest abates; novelty ceases to be novelty; variety is sought for; the first flush of early love passes away; the impulse which set us a-going is expended; duties become wearisome; regularity is monotonous. And are we always aware of the process that is going on within us? Not always. We attribute it to others—to causes that are outside ourselves. I have frequently visited consumptive patients. The poor fellow, with his wasted frame, and hectic flush, and racking cough, tells you that he is a little worse to-day—a little feebler; but then he knows how to account for it—he sat inadvertently in a draught yesterday. On the occasion of your next visit he is worse; but then—he took something at one of his meals which disagreed with him. The next time he is still worse; but he sat up too late—he overstayed his usual hour of retiring to rest. He has always a reason to assign that is not the real, the right, the true one. You, watching him pityingly, can give a better account of the matter. You know that the bodily frame is decaying,—that death is stretching on with rapid strides to claim his victim. So with the symptoms of spiritual declension. The man has one excuse or another to account for his decaying interest, for his waning spirituality, for his neglect of Bible study, for his less frequent attendance at the house of God or at the table of the Lord. "Business has increased"; "his health is not what it used to be"; "the preaching is not so interesting as it once was." Well, that is *his* account of the matter, as the poor consumptive patient has his account of the matter. You, looking on, know that the chill torpor of worldliness has seized upon the soul, and is threatening to bring it into the icy stillness of spiritual death. I fear we are all of us subject to the waning of the life within us. Let us be on our guard, then. The "gift of God" may be in us still; but it may need " stirring up." (G. Calthrop, M.A.) Our gifts, and how to use them :—I suppose that Timothy was a somewhat retiring youth, and that from the gentleness of his nature he needed to be exhorted to the exercise of the bolder virtues. His was a choice spirit, and therefore it was desirable to see it strong, brave and energetic. No one would wish to arouse a bad man, for, like a viper, he is all the worse for being awake; but in proportion to the excellence of the character is the desirability of its being full of force. There are many kinds of gifts. All Christians have some gift. Some have gifts without them rather than within them—gifts, for instance, of worldly position, estate, and substance. These ought to be well used. But we must go at once to the point in hand;—"the gift that is in you," we have now to speak of. I. First, then, WHAT GIFT IS THERE IN US? In some there are gifts of mind, which are accompanied with gifts of utterance. The stones in the street might surely cry out against some religious professors who make the Houses of Parliament, the council-chamber, the courts of justice, the Athenæum, or the Mechanics' hall ring with their voices, and yet preach not Jesus—who can argue points of politics and the like, but not speak a word for Christ—eloquent for the world, but dumb for Jesus. If you have the gift of the pen, are you using it for Christ as you ought? I want to stir up the gift that is in you. Letters have often been blessed to conversions; are you accustomed to write with that view? Another form of gift that belongs to us is influence. What an influence the parent has. Many of the elder members of the Church have another gift—namely, experience. Certainly, experience cannot be purchased, nor taught; it is given us of the Lord who teacheth us to profit. It is a peculiar treasure each man wins for himself as he is led through the wilderness. May you be of such a sort as a certain clergyman I heard of the other day. I asked a poor woman " What sort of man is he?" She said, " He is such a sort of man, sir, that if he comes to see you you know he has been there." I understood what she meant: he left behind him some godly saying, weighty advice, holy consolation, or devout reflection, which she could remember after he had left her cottage door. Another gift which many have is the gift of prayer—of prayer with power, in private for the Church and with sinners. There is another gift which is a very admirable one. It is the gift of conversation, not a readiness for chit-chat and gossip—(he who has that wretched propensity may bury it in the earth and never dig it up again)—but the gift of leading conversation, of being what George Herbert called the " master-gunner"; when we have that, we should most conscientiously use it for God. II. And this brings us, secondly to the consideration of—HOW WE ARE TO STIR UP OUR GIFTS. 1. First, we should do it by examination to see what gifts we really have. There should be an overhauling of all our stores to see what we have of capital entrusted to our stewardship. 2. The next mode of stirring up our gift is to consider to what use we could put the talents we possess. To what use could I put my talents in my family? 3. But, next, stir it up not merely by consideration and examination, but by actually using it. 4. And then, in addition to using our gift, every one of us should try to improve it. 5. And then pray over your gifts: that is a blessed way of stirring them up—to go before God, and spread out your responsibilities before Him. III. WHY IS IT THAT WE SHOULD STIR UP THE GIFT THAT IS IN US? 1. We should stir up the gift that is in us, because all we shall do when we have stirred ourselves to the utmost, and when the Spirit of God has strengthened us to the highest degree, will still fall far short of what our dear Lord and Master deserves at our hands. 2. Another reason is that these are stirring times. If we are not stirring everybody else is. 3. And then, again, we must stir up our gift because it needs stirring. The gifts and graces of Christian men are like a coal fire which frequently requires stirring as well as feeding with fuel. 4. If we will but stir ourselves, or rather, if God's Holy Spirit will but stir us, we, as a church, may expect very great things. (C. H. Spurgeon.) A missionary sermon:—Our gift, and the Divine claim on it:—What is in us or in our possession through the Divine benevolence? And what is the call made upon us in Divine providence and by the Divine Spirit, for the exercise of that gift, in order to the enlightenment and salvation of our fellow-men? I. THE ETHNIC OR RACE GIFT. No people can have enjoyed a larger gift in this regard than our own. " God hath not so dealt with any nation." See how this island-race is spreading over the earth! God has said to this nation, " Stir up the gift which is in thee—in thee by the slow deposit of My providence, by the sowings of centuries—stir up that gift, and use it for the world's good." II. THERE IS ALSO THE FAMILY GIFT.

All men receive from their ancestors something which goes into and becomes part of themselves, and this something has in it both help and hindrance. But to us, to most of this Christian assembly, the balance is largely on the side of help. It might have failed; for faith is not something mechanical, nor is it essentially and of necessity transmitted with the natural life. It might have failed, but it has not—"And I am persuaded that in thee also." "First in thy grandmother." Young men and maidens are apt to smile at the name of "grandmother." But the Scriptures glorify old age. So do the great poets. Seventy years ago some one lived, and loved, and was wedded, and listened to the music of her children's feet, from whom *you* have inheritance. Something lived in her which lives in you. "Stir up the gift which is in thee." Let the good thoughts of that far-off time live again. Let the tears then shed be a present tenderness in your breast. Let all the love of the old time have fulfilment and transmission, so that your children and your children's children may arise to call you blessed. In this life you are not atoms, units, severed personalities; but branches, links, conductors; receiving and giving, reaping and sowing, reaching back to the Eden behind you, and forward to the day of God that is coming. III. THERE IS TO EACH ONE A GIFT FROM GOD DISTINCTLY PERSONAL. There is something given to each, inhering in his own nature alone, not diffused, not shared by others, not flowing through his life from lives behind to lives before—something that begins and ends with himself. It is himself—the inner real self which presides over all outer relations of hereditary and historical kind. Stir up this gift of immortal life that is in thee by the creating Spirit, by the personal inbreathing of God. Be thyself. When a man is born, God gives him power to be something for his fellow-creatures and his God. That something may be like treasure "hid in a field," but never found. We know how certain great men have lived; how they became great by developing the inward energy. How then can a man truly and in the highest sense stir up his personal gift? Attila the Hun, "the scourge of God," had from God the gift which he developed, so that his life became like a stream of scorching fire. Napoleon had all that was masterly in his spirit from the God who made him; but the apostle would not have allowed that he stirred up his gift aright. And now, society is vibrating through and through with the action of various human gifts; statesmen striving against each other, and serving their country in the strife; prolific writers, working up to the full bent of their genius; merchants, making a very science of their commerce, and reaping ample harvest of the same. But beyond the stir and strife lies the question of spiritual motive, aim, tendency. From what fountain springs all this activity? To what goal is it tending? IV. THE CHRISTIAN GIFT. It is expressed in such a word as this: "For me to live is Christ, and to die is gain." Or this: "I am crucified with Christ: nevertheless I live; yet not I, but Christ liveth in me." Or this: "If any man be in Christ he is a new creature: old things are passed away, and all things are become new." And: "If any man have not the Spirit of Christ, he is none of His." Full religious development must take the form of Christian consecration. How much a man—any one of you young men—might do, would, I believe, be a discovery even to yourself. Now and again God gives us to see this, to see how much one can do, not by great original powers, not by the help of favouring circumstances, but just by consecration, by stirring up the gift—it may be a gift composed of many gifts, a general capacity of service. What in you is its measure? How far will it reach? How long will it last? How much will it achieve? I cannot tell; no more can you, until you try. Timothy the lad in Lystra knows nothing of Timothy the bishop of Ephesus. We all go on to meet, and as we go we make, our future selves. (*A. Raleigh, D.D.*) *Christian enthusiasm*:—What Timothy seems to have wanted most was fire. St. Paul could have no doubt as to his gifts, nor of the fidelity with which he would use them. But the work and the times demanded something more than talent and conscientiousness; they required enthusiasm. Hence the apostle urges his friend to "stir up the gift that was in him," or, as his words might be better rendered, "kindle the gift that is in thee into flame." For the want of this enthusiasm men of splendid parts prove splendid failures, and, although otherwise qualified to fill the highest places and to lead the grandest enterprises, are never heard of, from sheer inability to push their way. But our subject is not enthusiasm in general, but Christian enthusiasm in particular; and our text, with its context, supplies us with some useful hints respecting its subject, its nature, and its motive. I. ITS SUBJECT. To be enthusiastic it is obvious that we must have something to be enthusiastic about, and something worthy of our enthusiasm.  The enthusiasm of the Christian worker, like that of the poet, may be " fine frenzy," but, like the poet's, again, it is not aimless frenzy.  It gathers round a definite object, which has sufficient force of attraction to draw towards it the whole interest and strength of the man over whom it throws its spell.  In Timothy's case this subject was a gift for the office of bishop and evangelist.  Notice, then, that this capacity is—1. " The gift of God."  We take the greatest pride in the products of our independent genius and industry, or in the purchases of our wealth.  But here we have, as the bestowment of a generous benefactor, what all our money could not buy, and what all our skill could not fabricate.  We serve God just because God has given us the ability to serve Him.  In Christian work, therefore, boasting is shameful, and vanity ridiculous.  2. A constitutional gift.  God has invested us with two classes of gifts—gifts external and gifts internal—gifts which go to make up what a man has ; gifts which constitute him what he is.  Our capacity for Divine service is one of the latter class.  It is " in " us.  It is a soul faculty.  It entered into the original plan of our being.  Further, this capacity—3. Assumes different forms.  It is a common gift, but the idiosyncrasies of the individuals to whom it is given invest it, in each case, with a peculiar shape.  Thus painting and architecture, music and science, philosophy and poetry, statesmanship and wealth ; that subtle thing called influence, and that dreadful thing called war, that prosaic thing called trade, and that humble thing called home, have each and all been pressed into the service of illustrating our text.  And so Raffaelle in the Cartoons, Wren in St. Paul's, Handel in the " Messiah," Newton in the " Principia," Bacon in the " Novum Organum," Milton in the " Paradise Lost," Wilberforce in his Parliamentary achievements, Peabody in his munificent benefactions, Shaftesbury in the example he set before society, Gordon in the heroism with which he defended Khartoum, Moore in his work in the London warehouse, Susannah Wesley in hers in the Epworth rectory, and others in what they have done in the house, in the shop, or in the field, all seem to say, " There, that is what I mean by the gift that is in me."  And that we should ascertain what our special talent is, and in what our capacity should be employed, is of the utmost importance for many reasons.  How often do we hear the remark applied to some social failure—and true it is—" he has missed his calling."  A man who might have made something out in a walk in life for which he was suitably endowed, makes nothing out, because he has chosen one for which he is totally unqualified.  Once more, this capacity—4. Is intended for and must find employment in the service of the Church.  St. Paul's injunction carries with it the broad principle just laid down, but we must remember that the apostle had in view the interests of Christ's Church, and urged Timothy to promote those interests in the way for which he was Divinely qualified.  II. ITS NATURE.  We have the gift ; with what shall we kindle it ?  1. Like the capacity it has to kindle into flame, Christian enthusiasm is the gift of God.  No man ever purchased it ; no man ever created it.  It is not from beneath and human, it is from above and Divine ; " God hath given us the spirit . . . of power, of love, and of a sound mind."  And that a Divine person should provide the materials for the kindling of a Divine gift arises out of the necessities of the case.  Like produces like, and fire kindles fire.  You have in your grates blocks of a cold black mineral, the last things in the world, as far as appearances go, from which you would expect light and heat.  But you know that fire lies imprisoned and slumbering there.  And you know, also, that neither the most careful arrangement of the coals, nor the most vigorous use of the fire irons, will be of the least service in awakening the element and setting it free.  What you do, however, is to apply a light, and then the cold black mineral becomes fervent and radiant heat.  Eighteen hundred years ago a few weak and unlettered peasants formed all that there was of the Christian Church.  Who would have given them credit for a world-converting capacity ?  But within them lay dormant the Divine gift.  They formed no elaborate organisation ; they made no violent stir.  They simply waited and prayed ; and by and by fire from without met its counterpart within.  The Holy Ghost fell upon them, made them enthusiasts for Christ, and thus enabled them to kindle their gift into flame.  2. Christian enthusiasm is not " the spirit of fear."  This is obvious.  Until that spirit is laid there can be no enthusiasm.  It can only be conquered by the Divine Spirit, who, as He subdues the craven or the diffident temper, will make us instinct with that Christian enthusiasm which is—(1) The spirit of power.  And being this, it is distinguished from excitement, which is the spirit of weakness.  The two may, indeed, be confounded for a time, just as a meteor may, at first, be mistaken for a star.  No ; Christian enthusiasm is not a transient spasm of excitement; it is power, and that means stability, persistence, inexhaustible resources, unwearied and inextinguishable force. The spirit of power, however, although the first and basal element in Christian enthusiasm, is not the only one. For power, by itself, will make a man not an enthusiast, but a fanatic. Fanaticism is by no means weakness, it is force, often of the most vigorous kind, but force without regulation and control. Christian enthusiasm is, therefore—(2) The spirit of love. We all know the mighty part that love has sustained in the purest human enthusiasms. Love of children; for what heroisms has that not qualified the weakest of mothers? Love of country; what flames has that not kindled in the most phlegmatic of citizens? Love of man; for what endurance and what effort has that not nerved some of the feeblest of our race? Analyse any given case of noble enthusiasm, and you will find the very life of it to be love; either the love which manifests itself in devotion to a person, or the love which finds expression in consecration to a cause. In Christian enthusiasm both of these loves find play, for it is first devotion to a person. Christian love is love to God, and if I love God I must cling to Him. But Christian enthusiasm is also— (3) The spirit of a sound mind—a fact that is most frequently overlooked. Hence, by many, it is regarded as a symptom of goodness of heart, possibly, but certainly of weakness of head. In the world the enthusiast is not a mad speculator or simple dreamer; he is the man who, by the sagacity with which he lays his plans, the common sense lines on which he works them, the alertness with which he seizes every opportunity, and the tenacity with which he retains his hold on every advantage, builds up a colossal business and amasses a vast fortune. And we refuse to recognise as a Christian enthusiast the man who, by his wild vagaries neutralises the good of which he might have been otherwise capable, or the man whose sanguine temperament is imposed upon by impossible ideals. We claim for Christian enthusiasm rational as well as emotional qualities. It demands the consecration of the intellect at its freshest and its best, that it may help the body to render "a reasonable service." And what is this sound-mindedness? It is the self-control which conserves its energies, the patience which bides its time, the discernment which perceives that its time has come; it is the knowledge that understands its work, the judgment that determines where the work can be best done, the wisdom that suggests how to do it in the best way; it is the prudence which prepares for difficulties, the resolution which faces them, the tact which threads its way through them, or turns them to its own account. In one word, it is the mind in full health, in the health which consists of the wholeness, vigour, and harmonious activity of all the rational faculties; the intellect filled with the Holy Spirit of God. III. Its MOTIVES. We have the gift; by what considerations are we urged and encouraged to kindle it? 1. Timothy was reminded of his responsibility in the very terms of our text. 2. Timothy was reminded of his ancestral traditions. Men of noble lineage are supposed to have stronger motives to do nobly than those of meaner origin. They have a family as well as a personal reputation to sustain. 3. Timothy was reminded of his share in the great salvation. That we might kindle our gift, God, if I may so say, kindled His. 4. Lastly, Timothy was reminded that he had been honoured with a Divine call to stir up his gift. He was "called with a holy calling." There was nothing meritorious in him, as the apostle is careful to remind him, to occasion this call. It was of God's grace, and God, who had entrusted him with the gift, now laid formal claim to the use of His own. (*J. W. Burn.*) *An ordination sermon :—* They that think that every Christian may be a preacher, and that the ministry, considered as a distinct calling or employ, is nothing but usurpation, and some ambitious men's affecting a superiority over their brethren, like the cynic of old trampling upon Plato's cloak, make themselves guilty of greater pride than that which they pretend to condemn. The church is called a building, and we know that every flint or pebble is not fit to be a foundation or corner-stone, much less to be set into the ephod, and there to shine in oracles and responses. It is called a body too, and this hath various members, and these various offices, which cannot be all eyes and overseers; if they were, where would be the hearing? An ecclesiastical jurisdiction lodged in Timothy, an overseer constituted and appointed by St. Paul, even by the laying on of his hands, whereof he puts him in mind in the text, and of the gift that was bestowed upon him by that imposition of hands, and of his duty to exercise it. And here, before I enter upon the apostle's exhortation, or the duty contained in it, I cannot but take notice of the softness and gentleness of his address, "I put thee in remembrance." Practical discourses and salutary admonitions to men of learning and good education are a refreshing of their memories rather than teaching or illuminating their understandings. Discourses of this nature may put you in remembrance of a duty, which multiplicity of business would not suffer you to think of, or contemplations of other matters tempted you to overlook. I. WHAT THE GIFT IS WHICH WAS IN TIMOTHY, AND MAY STILL BE SUPPOSED TO BE IN ALL THOSE WHOM GOD CALLS TO THE SAME OFFICE. I shall particularise the gift communicated to Timothy; and if we take St. Paul for our guide, we shall find this gift was a Divine power vouchsafed to this man of God, which enabled and disposed him to teach, and live, and act, and do, answerable to the duties incumbent upon him, as a governor of the house of God. The apostle in the following verse calls it the spirit of power, of love, and of a sound mind; the spirit of Christian fortitude, of charity, and of sedateness and tranquillity of temper. 1. The spirit of fortitude, which consists in being undaunted at danger, fearless of the frowns of men while we do no more than our duty, and a steady freedom to vindicate the truth of the gospel and the honour of Christ Jesus, whatever may be the effect or consequence of it. 2. The spirit of love. It was not without very great reason that our Saviour asked St. Peter thrice, "Lovest thou Me?" and "Lovest thou Me more than these?" 3. The spirit of a sound mind. This seems to be a temper able to curb the passions, inordinate lusts, desires, and perturbations of the mind, an admirable spirit! To know when to be angry, and when to be calm; when to be severe, and when to be moderate and gentle. The mind is then sound when it keeps the lower faculties in good order, and it is an argument of wisdom to judge of things without heats, or prejudice, or prospect of self-interest, and to keep the wild desires of corrupted nature in awe, and to do things with prudence and moderation. II. HOW THIS GIFT WAS ANCIENTLY AND IS STILL BESTOWED AND COMMUNICATED. By the putting on of my hands, saith St. Paul; and in 1 Tim. iv. 14 he adds, by the laying on of the hands of the presbytery, *i.e.*, of the whole apostolical college, or the greater part of the apostles, who it is like were present upon the place. This rite or ceremony of imposition of hands on a person designed for Church offices and the service of the tabernacle, Isidore and others derive from Isaac's blessing his son Jacob, which they suppose was done by the Patriarch's laying his hands upon Jacob's head; from Jacob's laying his hands on his grandchildren and blessing them; from Moses's laying his hand on Joshua, and communicating part of his spirit to him. The ancient Romans used to lay their hands upon their slaves when they made them free; and Numa Pompilius had hands laid on him when he was made High Pontiff; but it is probable that even these fetched it from the Jews. The Christian Churches, who retained what was good and praiseworthy among the Jews, seeing nothing in this rite but what was grave, and decent, and solemn, and serious, adopted it into their service. In sacrificing beasts to the honour of God the priest laid his hands on the victim's head, to show he dedicated it to God, and from common, separated it to a holy use, and dismissed it from the service of men into that of the most high God; all which significations did wonderfully well agree with the end of the ministerial function under the gospel, and therefore the Christians had no reason to reject this useful and decent custom. This imposition of hands was no physical cause of conveying the Holy Ghost, but an external assurance, that as surely as the hands were laid on the head of the person ordained, so surely would the spirit of power, of love, and of a sound mind, light upon his soul if he did not obstruct it by wilful departing from the living God. That this rite hath lasted in the Church from the apostles' time unto this day is what the concurrent testimonies of all ages witness. III. HOW THIS GIFT IS TO BE STIRRED UP, AND WHAT IS THE BEST AND MOST PROPER WAY TO DO IT. In the original it is ἀναζωπυρεῖν, which is as much as stirring up the fire, or blowing the coals, and making the fire burn that lies mingled with the ashes. So that the Spirit of God conferred upon sacred persons by the imposition of hands is lodged in the soul, as the treasure in the gospel was hid in the field, which required digging and searching to make it useful. It is like gold in the ore, which requires melting, and cleansing, and purifying; like a stock of money which requires improvement by trading; like seed sown in the ground, which requires watering and other labour and industry to make it come forth, and grow, and spread, and yield fruit, and strengthen man's heart. This stirring up of the gift of God respects either the means that are to be used, or the duty itself. The means hinted in this and the preceding Epistle are chiefly three—prayer, reading, meditating. 1. Prayer. Who can live without it? Who can act or do anything of moment without the assistance of this spiritual engine? Nature teaches mankind to begin

their works of concernment with God ; grace therefore must be supposed to press
this duty infinitely more, on you particularly, the heirs of Timothy's office, in order
to this stirring up the gift of God that is in you, by the imposition of hands.
God that gives you talents intends not that you should bury them in the earth, or
lay them up in a napkin, but occupy and traffic with them, and be gainers by them ;
and to do this His help is necessary, who gives strength to the weak and power to
the feeble ; and this help is not to be had without importunate cries and solicitations.   These prayers must have fire ; it is their fervour that unlocks the secret
cabinet of the Almighty.   2.  Reading.   This the apostle expressly recommends to
Timothy (1 Tim. iv. 13) in order to his stirring up the gift of God.   Reading what?
No doubt the Holy Scripture, and therefore our Church proscribes, delivering a
Bible into the hands of the person upon whom episcopal hands are laid.   The great
examples you meet with here, the industry of Moses, the zeal of Elijah, the fervour of
St. Paul, the vigour of St. Stephen, the courage of St. Peter, the assiduity of Apollos,
the sincerity of Barnabas, what are these but so many motives to stir up the gift of God
that is in you ?   Add to all this the glorious, the precious, the large, the sweet, the
wonderful promises, promises of Christ's assistance, promises of comfort, of support, of
eternal life and glory, which will animate and enliven, and prompt you to blow up the
fire of the sanctuary and the coal of the altar, that it may consume the dross and tin,
not only that which cleaves to your own souls, but that also which sticks to others, that
see and hear you, and converse with you.   3.  Meditating.   This is also urged among
the means, not to neglect the gift of God.  " Meditate upon these things, give thyself
wholly to them " (1 Tim. iv. 15).   The bare reading will make no great impression.
Meditation digests and rouses the soul from her slumber.   This quickens the faculties, sets all the wheels a-going, incites to labour, prompts to industry, and moves and
even compels us to imitate the great examples set down in the Word of God, and to
follow their faith, and wisdom, and hope, and love, and charity.   But in what doth
the stirring up of the gift of God consist ?   Chiefly in these three particulars.   1.
Feeding the flock of God which is among you, taking the oversight thereof, not by
constraint, but willingly, not for filthy lucre, but of a ready mind, neither as being
lords over God's heritage, but being examples to the flock.   Ye are the captains,
the generals in Christ's army, while you bear the heat and burden of the day,
detract no labour, spare no pains, live like faithful stewards of the mystery of God,
vindicate your Master's honour, act like persons who have renounced the hidden
things of dishonesty, and by manifestation of the truth commend yourselves to every
man's conscience in the sight of God ; you make good the glorious titles and the
names which are given you, such as angels, and stars, and lights of the world,
and the salt of the earth, and a city set on a hill, &c.   2.  Labouring and making
it your business to reform abuses.   3.  Enduring hardness as good soldiers of
Jesus Christ, a duty very warmly recommended to Timothy (chap. ii. 3).   In
discharging your duty faithfully, you must expect obloquy, and slanders, and reproaches, and other inconveniences.  (A. Horneck, D.D.)          The latent spiritual
force in man :—I.  THAT THERE IS IN MAN SOME SPIRITUAL FORCE WHICH IS IN A
SPECIAL SENSE " THE GIFT OF GOD."   Indeed, our very existence, with all its
physical and mental attributes, is His gift.   But this spiritual force is something
special, and it may be said to comprehend at least three elements.   1.  The
sentiment of religious worship.   2.  The sentiment of moral obligation.   He has
an inbred feeling that there is an authority over him to which he owes
allegiance, that there are laws which he should recognise and obey.   3.  The
sentiment of social love.   The social love is something more than gregarious-
ness, than mere animal sympathy, which seem to belong to all sentient life.
It is benevolence, a well-wishing for the race.   Indeed, our life, with all its
attributes, is His gift, but this spiritual force is especially so.   It is bestowed upon
man only ; it is something greater than intellect, imagination, genius.   These it
works as its instruments.   It is in truth the substratum of his moral being, the
former of his character, the controller of his destiny.   II.  THAT THE URGENT DUTY
OF MAN IS TO ROUSE THIS SPIRITUAL FORCE INTO RIGHT ACTION.   To " stir up " into
right action this spiritual force is every man's paramount self-obligation.   He has
to rouse up into right action the spiritual power that lies within him and which is
God's greatest gift.   The command implies—1. That man has the power to do so.
Every righteous obligation implies the existence of adequate power of obedience.
But how can man do it ?  (1) How can he " stir up " the sentiment of worship into
healthy action ?   By devout meditations on the moral excellencies of the one true
and living God.  (2) How can he " stir up " the sentiment of obligation ?   By

contemplating the Divine will, which is the supreme law of life. (3) How can he " stir up " into right action the sentiment of holy love? By a devout study of the claims and needs of his fellow men. In this way every man can " stir up " this spiritual force, the gift of God that is within him. 2. On doing this depends his true dignity and bliss. Man can only become great by the right use of his great powers, by bringing out into right action all the great forces of his spiritual nature. The man who has not thus risen, has only risen as the stone has risen which has been hurled up into air, it must come down to the earth again. But he who rises by developing the spiritual forces of his nature, ascends heavenward, as the eagle that guides itself up from earth to heaven through clouds and sunshine. Conclusion: Man attend to thyself, not selfishly, and occasionally, but generously and constantly. There is an exhaustless field lying within thee fraught with countless germs of life and power. Throughout nature there are latent forces—fire mighty enough to burn up the universe sleeps in every atom of dust and drop of water. Powers sleep in the acorn sufficient to cover continents with majestic forests, and there is a spiritual force within us, rightly directed, that will build us into angels and lift us to the highest heavens of being. Let us, therefore, " stir up " this spiritual force, this " gift of God " within us. (*David Thomas, D.D.*) *Latent spiritual power :*—What is the course of the development of this spiritual gift, or, better, this gift of the Spirit? What is the manifestation and unfolding of this new energy of God in the highest branch of man's nature? It is quiet and gentle as all God's operations are in the hearts that yield to Him ; only an earthquake does it become when opposed by rocky natures, a desolating whirlwind among the stubborn oaks and cedars. It unfolds in willing hearts as seed in congenial soil, always with a promise of more and more ; the blade, the ear, the full corn in the ear ; the full corn in the ear multiplied thirty, sixty, an hundredfold, and each corn the promise and potency by a similar method of a hundred more. See how it increases. A young convert begins in an unobtrusive way to speak to a few wild boys whom he gathers together, one and another of whom become Christians ; the number grows, and with growth of responsibility the convert receives increase of power. The class becomes a congregation ; the few trembling, kind words he managed to speak at first become the powerful address ; the boys are joined by men and women ; the address becomes a sermon. That may be one way in which the gift of God may be developed and displayed. It is only one. For I hold the gift of the Spirit, which comes at conversion, to be also a gift for service. It is the same grace working through us to produce in other hearts precisely the fruits He has produced in us—repentance through our repentance, faith through our faith, love through our love, hope through our hope. The regenerated soul brings forth graces after their kind, just as the earth grass, and herb, and tree, yielding fruit whose seed is in itself, after its kind. But if all require His presence and help, none so manifestly require them as the minister who has to feed the flock of God. His nature ought to lie open to Divine influence at every point, and every call of his ministry should be a call to try and prove what the Spirit of Christ which is in him can accomplish for him and through him. He sometimes finds out the vastness of his supernatural resources through being made painfully conscious of the inadequacy of his natural powers for the work to be done. He sees the truth dimly, and therefore seeks for the light of the Spirit to be shed upon it and irradiate it. And here I would say that I am free to admit, as has been always held by those who intelligently believe that the God who created our natural powers is the same as He who sanctifies them and works through them, " that the greater the gifts by nature and cultivation, the greater the number of points at which the Holy Spirit may move us, and that Divine power is conditioned by human receptivity." The gift of the Spirit to Timothy was the same as to Paul ; and yet since Timothy's measure was not as capacious as Paul's, and, perhaps, because he did not so diligently stir up his gift as Paul, his life, beautiful and useful though it was, lacked the luxuriant fruitfulness of Paul's. The condition of our doing our best is that we allow God to do the best He can through us. And be our other gifts few or many, brilliant or humble, the reason for stirring up the flame of the great gift is just the same in all cases. For you would not have your poor gift without the fire that can make even it glow with fervour, as I have often seen the lips of poor, illiterate, feeble-minded men burn with rapture which gave beauty and charm to all they said. And you would not have your finer gifts, if you possess such, bereft of that energy which is a touch of omnipotence, nor left without that inspiration which is a pulse of the heart of infinite love. No one can tell the wealth of his gift in the possession of the Spirit of God. Let us put ourselves in remembrance that we may stir up the gift of God. Let us remember the day of our first submission, and how it ought to have implied a life-long submission, a continual yielding up of self and self-will. Let us remember the day of our consecration, the hopes which then gleamed in our heaven, the vows which then trembled on our lips. If the promise of these times has been blasted or dimmed, let us seek the renewing of our hearts by the Spirit which dwelleth in us. If the promise has been fulfilled, or even more than fulfilled, still let us honour the Spirit by whom we have been kept, sanctified, and used. (*J. P. Gledstone.*)     *Ordination :*—The poet Keble said on one occasion that he wished he could attend an ordination service every year of his life, that he might be reminded of first principles. *The Nemesis of neglected gifts :*—There is a terrible penalty attached to the neglect of the higher faculties, whether intellectual or moral ; a penalty which works surely and unerringly by a natural law. We all of us have imagination, intellect, will. These wonderful powers must have an object, must have employment. If we do not give them their true object, viz., the glory of God, they will find an object for themselves. Instead of soaring upwards on the wings supplied by the glories of creation and the mercies of redemption, they will sink downwards into the mire. They will fasten upon the flesh ; and in an atmosphere poisoned by debasing associations they will become debased also. Instead of raising the man who possesses them into that higher life, which is a foretaste of heaven, they will hurry him downwards with the accumulated pressure of an undisciplined intellect, a polluted imagination, and a lawless will. That which should have been for wealth becomes an occasion of falling. Angels of light become angels of darkness. And powers which ought to be as priests, consecrating the whole of our nature to God, become as demons, shameless and ruthless in devoting us to the evil one. . . . God's royal gifts of intellect and will cannot be flung away, cannot be left unused, cannot be extinguished. For good or for evil they are ours ; and they are deathless. But, though they cannot be destroyed, they can be neglected. They can be buried in the earth till they breed worms and stink. They can be allowed to run riot, until they become as wild beasts, and turn again and rend us. Or, in the spirit of power, of love and of discipline, they may be chastened by lofty exercise and sanctified to heavenly uses, till they become more and more fit to be the equipment of one, who is for ever to stand " before the throne of God, and praise Him day and night in His temple." (*A. Plummer, D.D.*)

Ver. 7. **For God hath not given us the spirit of fear, but of power, and of love, and of a sound mind.**—*Energy within right limits :*—The first characteristic stands opposed to faint-heartedness : the two other qualities are added, apparently, by the apostle, so that it may be distinctly manifest that he recommends no wild, rough exhibitions of force, but only such as were confined within legal limits. The ἀγάπη renders us capable for the offering of the greatest sacrifice for the cause of the Lord ; the σωφρονισμός is that Christian self-control which imparts power to a wise bearing in action, and in all things knows how to keep within true bounds. (*Dr. Van Oosterzee.*)     *Self-control :*—A sound mind, rather self-control, which keeps " a constant rein on all the passions and desires " (Trench), and would thus keep in check timidity and undue despondency. Some take " sound mind " to signify here " correction " of others, Church discipline, a meaning which the word will bear, but which is out of harmony with the other two elements of the special gift here enumerated, both of which are personal graces, not official powers. (*Speaker's Commentary.*)     *Self-mastery :*—The Spirit of God, by supplying us with power and love, launches within us forces which are capable, if they are not well adjusted, of producing either arrogance or laxity ; and which need, therefore, the central controlling energy of true self-mastery to harmonise them and save them from mutual destruction. We do not desiderate a neutral, colourless result, but a higher perfection, one in which both these forces have full play. (*H. R. Reynolds, D.D.*)     *The spirit of discipline :*—If it be asked whether the discipline be that which Timothy is to enforce in ruling others, or that which he is to practice in schooling himself, we may answer " Both." The termination of the word which is here used (σωφρονισμός) seems to require a transitive meaning ; and slackness in correcting others may easily have been one of the ways in which the despondency of Timothy showed itself. On the other hand the whole context here speaks of Timothy's treatment of himself. To take a more lively interest in the conduct of others would be discipline for himself and for them also. There may be as much pride as humility in indulging the thought that the lives of other people are so utterly bad that it is quite out of the power of such persons as ourselves to effect a reformation. This is a subtle way of shirking responsibility. Strong in the spirit of power, glowing with the spirit of love, we can turn the faults of others, together with all the troubles which may befall us in this life into instruments of discipline. (*A. Plummer, D.D.*)　　　*Christian courage:*—These words, though originally addressed to a bishop, and with reference to the ministerial office, yet need not be limited in their application. For of all who are duly baptized into the faith of the Lord Jesus, it is unquestionably required that they manfully fight under His banner against sin, the world, and the devil, and continue His faithful soldiers and servants unto their lives' end; wherein is implied, to say the least, that we strive earnestly and habitually to get rid of all mean cowardly fears, and go on in the path marked out for us by our Heavenly Guide, with all energy of conduct, and charity of heart, with such caution, too, and self-possession, as become persons who know what they are about. "First of all," says St. Paul, "God has not given us the spirit of cowardice"—for that is the proper meaning of the word, which in the original is not the same with that which is generally translated "fear," but quite different. It is used also, in a few other places, in the New Testament; as, *e.g.* (St. Mark iv. 40), when, after repeated demonstrations of the Almighty power and infinite compassion of the holy Jesus, His disciples were still weak and wavering, and alarmed at apparent danger, His gentle yet solemn rebuke was, "Why are ye so fearful [cowardly]? how is it that ye have no faith?" Whence we learn that this spirit of cowardice is so inconsistent with the character, as even to prove a want of faith, so far as it influences the heart. Again, on another occasion (John xiv. 27), when our blessed Lord was encouraging and cheering the fainting spirits of His disciples, perplexed and alarmed at the prospect of His leaving them: "Let not your heart be troubled," said He to them; "neither let it be afraid" (cowardly).—"Ye believe in God, believe also in Me." And again, in the description of those who shall be judged liable to the second death, the first-mentioned are (in our translation "fearful," but originally) the cowardly, and then next, the unbelieving (Rev. xxi. 8). These are all the places where the word is used in the New Testament. The spirit of cowardice, then, is opposed to the spirit of faith. But, says the inspired apostle, God hath not given us—us Christians—this spirit of cowardice—this base unworthy disposition is not from Him, nor among the fruits of His blessed Spirit. Rather we are taught to expect from that heavenly source a spirit most opposite to that of cowardice—a spirit of energy, charity, prudence; enabling us to proceed and go forward in our Christian course under every circumstance, to serve the Lord without distraction, to oppose men's errors without enmity to their persons, to walk warily as in days of danger and perplexity. That the word here translated "power" has this meaning, viz., of inspired energy and courage, we may know as from other passages in the New Testament, so from these two. In Acts vi. it is said of the holy martyr—"Stephen, full of faith and *power*"—as far as possible from any distrust or apprehension as to the holy cause of the gospel which he had undertaken. And in the Revelation of St. John, the Divine message to the Bishop of the Philadelphian Church, was, "Thou hast a little strength, and hast kept My word, and hast not denied My name;" a little strength, energy, or power—as not having like some others, altogether fallen away through indolence, or faint-hearted cowardly fear. Hence, we infer, that the spirit by which the faithful Christian is actuated is one of energy, resolution, and steady perseverance; and inferring this, we are bound to put it closely to our consciences, as follows:—Whether our life is one of diligence and activity, and this diligence and activity, not limited to this world, but actually in the cause and service of Almighty God. Whether we avoid, as much as possible, mixing in idle company, reading vain and trifling books, or other publications, indulging in useless, idle, unprofitable thoughts. Whether we try to know, and feel, the value of our precious, irreparable time. Whether we endeavour, from day to day, in that state of life to which it has pleased God to call us, to do our duty—*i.e.*, what in God's sight is expected of us; for very often much less will satisfy the world, and our own easy consciences. Whether we pray habitually, to be enabled to accomplish these our respective duties with resolution, steadiness, and perseverance; neither alarmed by danger, if it should happen, nor moved by scorn and contempt; but expecting such trials as part of God's discipline, to bring our hearts into a fit state for our admission into the everlasting habitations. We may further observe that the mean spirit of cowardice is always found in effect (in whatever way it is to be accounted for), a great hindrance to the growth of true charity, love for God and man. "The fear of man bringeth a snare"—even so great a snare as to with-draw the heart from loving and trusting Almighty God. Cowardice is a selfish feeling, makes men think only of themselves, their own present interests and com-forts—a state of mind quite repulsive of true charity and love. Hence (says St. Paul), "God gives not His servants the spirit of cowardice, but of power, and also of love," leads them both to be zealous and earnest in fulfilling their high duties, and at the same time tempers their zeal with meekness and love. If we would then know, whether we are such in heart and life as Christians ought to be, we must ask ourselves, not merely whether we are earnest in our religion, but also whether "all our things are done with charity," love to God and man. Again, you will observe that St. Paul intimates to us in the passage now considered, that it is not enough for the Christian to be zealous in his duty, even though his zeal be tempered and guided by love; unless also he be cautious and on his guard, so as in every emergency to retain his presence of mind, and always (as every person should who has any important matter in hand) to know what he is about. This, I say, is the spirit and disposition which as Christians we are still to labour and pray for, nor shall we seek it in vain—for to His faithful servants God gives, not only the spirit of power, and of love, but also of a sound mind; whilst by His grace He enables them to be harmless as doves, He would have them also wise as serpents, ever on their guard; on their guard, i.e., not so much against their earthly as their spiritual foes. (*Plain Sermons by Contributors to "Tracts for the Times."*) *The threefold gift:*—Our text presents to our view a striking contrast between that which constitutes the religion of a worldling, and that which constitutes the religion of a Christian. The religion of a worldling is a religion of slavish fear, but the religion of a Christian consists of a threefold gift, as specified in the language of my text. If you go to Pagan lands you will find all the Pagan tribes in possession of a religion of slavish fear; they fear their priests, and therefore they bow down to them as if they were a superior race of beings to themselves. They fear the devil, and, therefore, they worship him lest he should do them hurt, for theirs is a religion of slavish fear altogether. There are three words, or three features, of our subject, so distinctly marked that I want your attention to them separately. "God hath given us the spirit of power"—there is efficiency. "God hath given us the spirit of love"—there is attraction. "God hath given us the spirit of a sound mind"—that is a treasure in our vessels of infinite value. I. "God hath given us the spirit of POWER." I would have every person who is moved with the idea that God sends him to preach, "tarry at Jerusalem, until he has been endued with power from on high." II. Now a word or two about the attraction in the "SPIRIT OF LOVE." You will recollect reading that all the law is said by our blessed Lawgiver to be couched in this one word, "love"; and sure I am that all the gospel is couched in it, for "God is love." Hence it is the grand principle insisted on all through the New Testament. III. Now glance at the treasure in possession in earthen vessels, called A SOUND MIND. It is one of the rarest things in existence—a sound mind. I can meet with puerile minds, I can meet with frantic minds, I can meet with enthusiastic minds, I can meet with fickle and varying minds, not a few, and some of these bad and sad qualities even among Christians; I lament over them. A sound mind—what is it? There is not a child of Adam that possesses it until he gets it from above; it must be inspired. I grant that there are many men who have sound minds in temporal things; sound minds to judge rightly and consistently of worldly matters, so as seldom to make a mistake in matters of business; a sound mind to rule their house properly, to manage things with keenness and propriety, and with success; but, mark, I make a distinction between a sound mind, as the gift of God in a spiritual point of view, and a sound mind as existing in nature. A sound mind, as existing in nature, only regards natural things, and can rise no higher than its own level. I never knew a man of sound mind in spiritual things, until the Holy Ghost inspired it. (*Jos. Irons.*)    *Christianity: what it is not and what it is:*—I. WHAT GENUINE CHRISTIANITY IS NOT. It is not a "spirit of fear." The spirit of fear is that of a criminal and a slave. It haunts the minds of the guilty, and is only a prelude to those awful feelings which harrow up the soul that dies in a state of final impenitence. Such is not the spirit by which Christians are actuated. The great end for which our Saviour came into the world was to deliver men from their awful situation of exposure to the Divine wrath, and the fear consequent upon a knowledge of this state. But how are we to reconcile this passage with others, in which the spirit of fear is highly spoken of? Such as, "Blessed is the man that feareth always"; "I will put My fear in their hearts," &c. They are to be reconciled in this way. That spirit of fear which is not given to the people of God is a fear arising from a sense of guilt, a conviction that God is their enemy. But that fear which is implanted in the hearts of His people is a filial fear—a holy jealousy, lest by sin they should provoke the Lord to anger. II. WHAT IS THE NATURE OF GENUINE CHRISTIANITY? 1. Genuine Christianity is powerful and efficacious. "God hath given us the spirit of power." In 1 Cor. iv. 20 this apostle says, "The kingdom of God is not in word, but in power"—it is not in anything external, but in the experience of all the powerful effects of the gospel. The gospel is powerful to the salvation of all that believe. 2. Genuine Christianity is benevolent and kind. "God hath given us the spirit of love." This enters most essentially into the system of Divine truth, and also into the experience of every child of God. This spirit is not natural to man. Whatever obtains the name of love is only a selfish principle. But by grace it is overcome, and a contrary spirit is bestowed. "We love Him, because He first loved us." Where this love is felt in the heart, it is impossible but a reciprocal feeling of love to God must spring up within us. And not only love to God, but to all that bear His image—our brethren in Christ. But the love of the Christian is not confined to his brethren in the Lord; it extends to all mankind. 3. Genuine Christianity is in the highest degree rational, and peculiarly suited to the exigencies and circumstances of mankind. When a sinner is called out of darkness into light, he often becomes an object of derision; he is represented as an enthusiast, and beside himself. This was the case with Paul; but with respect and justice he repelled the charge; and this every child of God may do; for He has conferred upon him "the spirit of a sound mind." What is enthusiasm? It is the power given to the mind by some sublime conceptions which have broken in upon it. We praise this in many things—we praise it in the artist; and one once said, when fault was found with him for having employed so much of his time, "Art is a jealous thing, and requires the whole man." And is not eternity, is not religion a jealous thing? Does it not require the whole man? That the Christian is acting a most rational part is evident, if we consider what are the principles by which the prudent men of the world are guided; they are the same as those by which the Christian is guided, only changing the motives and the ends. These are indemnity for the past, enjoyment of the present, security and provision for the future. (*J. Henderson, D.D.*) *The spiritual endowment of the Christian Church:*—I. THE CHURCH OF CHRIST IS ENDOWED WITH THE SPIRIT OF COURAGE. 1. In being a disciple at all courage was demanded. 2. In proclaiming the gospel of God courage was manifested. 3. In enduring hardness courage was developed. II. THE CHURCH OF CHRIST IS ENDOWED WITH THE SPIRIT OF POWER. 1. The power of holy utterance is a spiritual gift. 2. The power of Christian legislation is a spiritual gift. 3. The power of righteous resolute volition is a spiritual gift. III. THE CHURCH OF CHRIST IS ENDOWED WITH THE SPIRIT OF LOVE. 1. Love of kindred is a spiritual gift of the Inspirer. 2. Love of country—patriotism—is a Divine spiritual gift. 3. The love of Christ and of God is an endowment of the Spirit of God. IV. THE CHURCH OF CHRIST IS ENDOWED WITH THE SPIRIT OF SOUNDNESS OF MIND OR OF HEALTH. 1. The capacity and consequent appetite for knowledge are spiritual endowments. 2. The energy of habitual holy action is a spiritual endowment. 3. The restoring power of a righteous life is a spiritual endowment. (*W. R. Percival.*) *The great purpose of Christianity:*—Why was Christianity given? Why did Christ seal it with His blood? Why is it to be preached? What is the great happiness it confers? I read the answer to them in the text. There I learn the great good which God confers through Jesus Christ. "He hath given us, not the spirit of fear, but of power and of love and of a sound mind." The glory of Christianity is, the pure and lofty action which it communicates to the human mind. It does not breathe a timid, abject spirit. If it did, it would deserve no praise. It gives power, energy, courage, constancy to the will; love, disinterestedness, enlarged affection to the heart; soundness, clearness, and vigour to the understanding. It rescues him who receives it from sin, from the sway of the passions; gives him the full and free use of his best powers; brings out and brightens the Divine image in which he was created; and in this way not only bestows the promise, but the beginning of heaven. This is the excellence of Christianity. In reading the New Testament I everywhere learn that Christ lived, taught, died, and rose again, to exert a purifying and ennobling influence on the human character; to make us victorious over sin, over ourselves, over peril and pain; to join us to God by filial love, and above all, by likeness of nature, by participation of His Spirit. This is plainly laid down in the New Testament as the supreme end of Christ. In the prophecies concerning Him in the Old Testament, no characteristic is so frequently named as that He should spread the knowledge of the true God. Now I ask, what constitutes the importance of such a revelation? Why has the Creator sent His Son to make Himself known? I answer, God is most worthy to be known, because He is the most quickening, purifying, and ennobling object for the mind; and His great purpose in revealing Himself is, that He may exalt and perfect human nature. God, as He is manifested by Christ, is another name for intellectual and moral excellence; and in the knowledge of Him our intellectual and moral powers find their element, nutriment, strength, expansion, and happiness. To know God is to attain to the sublimest conception in the universe. To love God is to bind oneself to a Being who is fitted, as no other being is, to penetrate and move our whole hearts; in loving whom we exalt ourselves; in loving whom we love the great, the good, the beautiful, and the infinite; and under whose influence the soul unfolds itself as a perennial plant under the cherishing sun. This constitutes the chief glory of religion. It ennobles the soul. In this its unrivalled dignity and happiness consist. I fear that the world at large think religion a very different thing from what has been now set forth. Too many think it a depressing, rather than an elevating service, that it breaks rather than ennobles the spirit, that it teaches us to cower before an almighty and irresistible being; and I must confess that religion, as it has been generally taught, is anything but an elevating principle. It has been used to scare the child and appal the adult. The main ground of the obligation of being religious, I fear, is not understood among the multitude of Christians. Ask them, why they must know and worship God? and, I fear, that were the heart to speak, the answer would be, because He can do with us what He will, and consequently our first concern is to secure His favour. Religion is a calculation of interest, a means of safety. God is worshipped too often on the same principle on which flattering and personal attentions are lavished on human superiors, and the worshipper cares not how abjectly he bows, if he may win to his side the power which he cannot resist. I look with deep sorrow on this common perversion of the highest principle of the soul. I have endeavoured to show the great purpose of the Christian doctrine respecting God, or in what its importance and glory consist. Had I time, I might show that every other doctrine of our religion has the same end. I might particularly show how wonderfully fitted are the character, example, life, death, resurrection, and all the offices of Christ to cleanse the mind from moral evil, to quicken, soften, elevate, and transform it into the Divine image; and I might show that these are the influences which true faith derives from Him and through which He works out our salvation. Let me only say that I see everywhere in Christianity this great design of liberating and raising the human mind. (*W. E. Channing, D.D.*) A *Whit-Sunday Sermon* :—Many readers of this passage, I doubt not, place the emphasis on the word *us.* They suppose St. Paul to say, "An ordinary man, who occupied the position which you occupy, the overseer of a society which is composed of various and contradictory elements, in which strange doctrines are appearing, which is exposed to all the influences of a commercial and corrupt city, would fear and tremble. It is your privilege to be as free from fightings and terrors as I, your spiritual father, am." What encouragement, then, could he give to Timothy? Precisely that which he had found necessary in his own case, precisely that to which he had been driven by the experience he has described to us. His spirit might be palsied with fear; but there was a Spirit near him and with him which was not a spirit of fear, to which he could turn as the Deliverer from fear, the Restorer of energy, the Quickener of hope. That Spirit had been given not to him (Paul), but to the Family of which he was a member;— if in any special sense to him, to him only because he was a servant of that Family, because he needed powers that were not his own, to make his ministries for it effectual. I. I suppose we have all felt tempted, at times, to use language which is just the reverse of the apostle's. We have read in records of the past—we have known on a larger or smaller scale among our contemporaries—such instances of strange panic and cowardice, of counsel and heart failing just when the need for them was the greatest, that we have been ready to exclaim, "Surely there is something Divine in this! We cannot attribute such a loss of nerve and energy to the pressure of outward circumstances; these often evoke the greatest courage when they are most appalling. We cannot attribute it merely to a natural want of courage; those same men, or bodies of men, at other crises, showed that they were capable of manly effort. Their fear is surely supernatural. God has given them this spirit of fear." Such a mode of speaking is not uncommon; it is not without strong excuse. But I think also that our consciences will tell us that we pervert such passages of Scripture if we set them in opposition to the doctrine of St. Paul in the one now before us. We need not study the records of the past, or the actions of our fellow-men, to learn what the spirit of fear or cowardice is. Each has, perhaps, known something of that cowardice which springs from self-distrust, from the apprehension of lions in his path, from doubtfulness, which of several paths he should choose, from the foretaste of coming evils. II. The Spirit of God is said to be a Spirit of POWER. Consider the different kinds of power before which men bow, and those which they covet most to exercise. There is none more familiar or more wonderful than that of the orator. There is another power mixed frequently with this, but yet different in its direction and its nature, which also can be limited to no country, or circumstances, or stage of cultivation. The physician, the healer, is welcomed in all lands by different titles, but always for this reason, that he can in some way act on the life of men, can oppose the powers that are threatening life. In some regions his functions are hardly distinguished from those of the priest, because he too is conversant about life and death, a life or death that may continue when the resources of the ordinary physician are exhausted. The most simple, naked exhibition of human power is in that royal Will, which obtains supremacy by claiming it—which compels individuals and nations, they know not how, to own that it is meant to rule them, and that they must needs obey. That such a force as this exists, it is as idle to deny as to deny the force of sea or wind. We are certain that the most settled, organised tyranny is still a rebellion, and must end as rebellions end. What is the warrant for this conviction? Whit-Sunday says it is this, that the highest power, the all-ruling Will, was manifested in One who took upon Him the form of a Servant. It says that His noblest gift to men is His own Spirit of Power. It says that to that Spirit all spirits must at last bow; that any will which is mere arbitrary will—which does not seek to deliver and to raise those whom it rules—must be broken in pieces; that the only effectual power will be proved at last to be that which can give up itself. III. If the world was to be instructed that all power of speech, of imparting life and wisdom to men, of governing societies, is of God, and is His gift to His creatures, certainly no teachers could be so suitable as those Galileans. And yet I know not whether there was not something even more wonderful in the selection of these men to show that all Love is of God; that His Spirit is the author of whatever love men are able to exhibit in acts or to feel within. For as Jews they had learnt to despise and hate all the uncircumcised; as Galileans they must often have been jealous of that more favoured part of their own race, which looked down upon them. They had been chosen, indeed, by a Teacher who bore all their narrowness and ignorance; who educated them by a careful and gracious discipline for the work to which He had destined them. Their affection had been drawn out towards Him; that affection had been a bond to each other, though interrupted by continual desires in each of them to be the chief in His kingdom. But their affection had been tried, and had broken down. It had failed towards the Master; what strength could there be in it towards any of their fellows? If love was their own, or had its springs in them, it must be utterly dried up. Then reflect how it burst forth, how it poured itself out first upon Jews, who scorned them; next upon Gentiles, whom it had been part of their religion to scorn; to see what it could endure. So they were trained to understand that there must be about them and with them a Spirit of ever-living, long-suffering love, the heights and depths of which they could never measure—of which they could only say, It is the Spirit of Him who died upon the Cross, and who in that death manifested the very nature of His eternal Father and His purposes to men. What is the original falsehood of all who speak of their love to God and man? This: they take credit to themselves for a love which is moving them to noble thoughts and good deeds, but which has another source than their hearts; which is Divine, not earthly; universal, not partial. IV. Finally, this Spirit is said to be the Spirit of a SOUND MIND. You cannot make any estimate or guess of the wildness and madness into which man may be led. And therefore you cannot provide the remedy for this wildness and madness, or any adequate protection against it. Do you think you know of some adequate remedy or protection? Perhaps you will say it lies in the Church. May not this be, after all, the one security against these excesses? May not the Spirit of God keep better watch over those minds which He has taken into His guardianship, than you can keep? A Spirit who knows how all are tempted—who knows what temptation is strongest for each—who is seeking to unite them in a common fellowship—who is guiding them to the same haven—who will suffer none who would act rightly to be without the necessary aids to action, none that would seek truth to be lost in falsehood; who will continually assist the desire to do right in those who are conscious of the inclination to wrong—who will for ever kindle afresh the zeal for truth in those who feel that they are beginning to acquiesce in plausible lies? To tell men that such a guiding Spirit of Power, of Love, of a Sound Mind, has been given them, and is with them—this is not dangerous, but safe. (*F. D. Maurice, M.A.*) *On soundness of mind in religion :*—The expression, sobriety, or soundness of mind, is used in the Scriptures in various senses. Sometimes it is opposed to madness; as where the demoniac was found sitting at the feet of Jesus, clothed and in his right mind. Madness disposes men to act irregularly, furiously, and extravagantly. Soundness of mind, therefore, implies recollection, calmness, and discretion, the guidance and control of reason. In other places, soundness of mind is opposed to levity and impropriety, as where women are required to adorn themselves in modest apparel, with sobriety; or to intemperance and sensuality, as where young men are exhorted to be sober minded, and, denying ungodliness and worldly lusts, to live soberly. Sometimes it is contrasted with pride and self-conceit: thus the apostle forbids the Romans to think extravagantly of themselves, instead of thinking soberly, as they ought to do. In my text the same expression is used in a more general and comprehensive sense. The general characteristic of all unsoundness of mind may be said to be false perceptions. He whose mind is in this state dares not see things as they really are; they appear to him extravagantly magnified or diminished, distorted, or confounded with different objects. A sound mind, on the contrary, forms a just view of the subjects presented to it; it estimates correctly the relative value and importance of different subjects, and is not governed by prejudice, caprice, or idle imaginations. I. Soundness of mind is opposed to CREDULITY. Credulity arises from a misapprehension of the nature and value of evidence. The credulous man believes on insufficient authority. He does not perceive the proportion which different kinds of evidence bear to each other. How many in the Church at this day receive the doctrines of Christianity, not on account of the evidence by which they are supported, nor because they are plainly delivered in Scripture, but because this or that particular man has held them! A man of sound mind will not indeed despise human authority, and, in the spirit of innovation, doubt a tenet because it has been generally maintained; but he will be very careful to found his faith upon the truth of Scripture rather than upon the opinions of men. II. Soundness of mind is opposed to SUPERSTITION. A person in the dark sees nothing distinctly, and is therefore very apt to form confused and erroneous ideas of every object around him, his imagination giving to them what form and colour it pleases. Such is the situation of a superstitious man with respect to all objects of a spiritual or religious kind—he sees nothing in its proper form and proportion. A frequent and dangerous superstition is that which lays an undue stress on mere external religious observances. A man, therefore, of a sound mind, while he attributes to forms and ceremonies their true value, will not substitute them for more substantial good. He will manifest the soundness of his mind by preferring the substance to the form, and by endeavouring to possess the spirit of religion rather than the mere shadow of it. III. Soundness of mind is opposed to ENTHUSIASM. Enthusiasm consists in unwarranted ideas of the nature of the relation between us and our Creator. A man of sound mind will cherish no extravagant notions of Divine communications. An enthusiast entertains lofty notions of himself, and degrading conceptions of the Deity; he conceives that the course of nature is to be regulated with a view to his interest. The ordinary rules, even of morality, must yield to his convenience. He and his immediate connections have a peculiar dispensation: they are the particular favourites of God, and all things are to minister to their exclusive good. IV. Soundness of mind is opposed to SCEPTICISM or INFIDELITY. I am well aware that infidels arrogate to themselves the distinction of being the only sound reasoners, and charge believers with credulity and superficial views. But the charge may justly be retorted on themselves: they do not possess a sound mind; for the body of evidence by which Christianity is established is incomparably superior to that by which any historical fact, or any other tenets whatever, have been supported. V. Soundness of mind is opposed to INSENSIBILITY, or INDIFFERENCE TO THE GREAT OBJECTS OF RELIGION. If you saw a man bartering his estate for a childish toy, or labouring to accomplish some object in its nature evidently

unattainable, or using the greatest exertions and the most powerful means to effect some frivolous or contemptible purpose; or, on the other hand, struggling to accomplish some end really important by means wholly inadequate, you would say, without hesitation, that such a man had not a sound mind. The great doctrines which religion teaches must be either false, or doubtful, or true. That they are false can never be positively proved. " Surely," says Pascal, " in a doubtful point of this most tremendous consequence, it is the duty of every rational person to endeavour, if possible, to obtain a solution of his doubts, and to remain no longer in suspense about a question of such immense consequence, in comparison of which all the sorrows or happiness of this life will not bear so much as a single moment's comparison. Yet we see persons, professing, too, to be wise, and raised above the vulgar herd, who not only doubt upon these points, but appear to be easy and composed, nay, declare their doubts with perfect indifference, and perhaps gratify their vanity in professing them. What words can be found to fix a name for such unaccountable folly? Yet you see the same persons quite other men in all other respects. They fear the smallest inconveniences: they see them if they approach, and feel them if they arrive. They pass whole days and nights in chagrin and despair for the loss of their property, or for some imaginary blemish in their honour; and yet these very same persons suppose they may lose all by death, and remain without disquiet or emotion. This wonderful insensibility with respect to things of the most fatal consequence, and that, too, in a heart so nicely sensible of the meanest trifles, is an astonishing prodigy, an unintelligible enchantment, a supernatural blindness and infatuation." You believe the Scriptures; you believe that there is a future life, in comparison of which this is a mere point; sit down and contemplate the duration of it. Yet, O strange absurdity! we see everything reversed: persons not at all interested about these fleeting moments, on account of their relation to eternity, but very anxious about them in themselves! The Bible informs us of our danger, and must be our only guide how to escape it. Here, then, is folly and unsoundness of mind in the highest degree, that men will not search the Scriptures and be guided by the Word of God. (*J. Venn, M.A.*)
*Power in the Christian:*—And here is condemned those, both preachers and people, who have it not themselves, neither can endure it in others. We commend the deep-mouthed hound, the shrill sound of the trumpet, the loud report of the piece; yet cannot away with, care not for the spirit of power and resolution in a Christian. Is not power appropriated to God? Did not Christ speak with authority and power, and not as the Scribes? For can a soldier be too strong? a traveller over-well limbed? then may a Christian be too well fenced, armed. Must he not wrestle with principalities and powers? combat with the sons of Anak? tread upon the lion and the ape? And who can tell what weight may be put on his shoulders for time to come? Will we not provander our beast for a long journey? rig our ships for a rough passage? build them strong for a long voyage? bend our staff before we leap? And shall we never fortify the inner man, repair the battered bark of our souls, nor try the truth of that stilt which must help us to heaven? Wherefore, gather spiritual greatness, strive for this strength, and purchase this power by all means possible, and that thou mayest do these things. (*J. Barlow, D.D.*)
*Sinful fear of God:*—One of our poets gives a grim picture of a traveller on a lonesome road, who has caught a glimpse of a frightful shape close behind him—

> " And having once turned round walks on,
> And turns no more his head."

The dreadful thing is there on his very heels, its breath hot on his check; he feels it though he does not see, but he dare not face round to it; he puts a strong compulsion on himself, and, with rigidly fixed face, strides on his way, a sickening horror busy with his heart. An awful image that, but a true one with regard to what many men do with their thoughts of God! They know that that thought is there, close behind them. They feel sometimes as if its hand were just coming out to be laid on their shoulders, and to stop them. And they will not turn their heads to see the Face that should be the love, the blessedness, the life of their spirits, but is—because they love it not—the terror and freezing dread of their souls. (*A. Maclaren, D.D.*)    *A sound mind:*—Dr. Arnold, of Rugby, gives, in one of his letters, an account of a saintly sister. For twenty years, through some disease, she was confined to a kind of crib; never once could she change her position for all that time. "And yet," said Dr. Arnold, and I think his words are very beautiful, "I never saw a more perfect instance of the power of love and of a sound mind. Intense love, almost to annihilation of selfishness; a daily martyrdom for twenty years, during which she adhered to her early-formed resolution of never talking about herself; thoughtful about the very pins and ribbons of my wife's dress, about the making of a doll's cap for a child, but of herself—save as regarded her improvement in all goodness—wholly thoughtless; enjoying everything lovely, graceful, beautiful, high-minded, whether in God's works or man's, with the keenest relish: inheriting the earth to the fulness of the promise; and preserved through the valley of the shadow of death from all fear of impatience, and from every cloud of impaired reason which might mar the beauty of Christ's glorious work. May God grant that I might come within one hundred degrees of her place in glory!" Such a life was true and beautiful. But the radiance of such a light never cheered this world by chance. A sunny patience, a bright-hearted self-forgetfulness, a sweet and winning interest in the little things of family intercourse, the Divine lustre of a Christian peace, are not fortuitous weeds carelessly flowering out of the life-garden. It is the internal which makes the external. It is the force residing in the atoms which shapes the pyramid. It is the beautiful soul which forms the crystal of the beautiful life without. *Latent power in churches :*—It is impossible to over estimate, or rather to estimate, the power that lies latent in our churches. We talk of the power that was latent in steam—latent till Watt evoked its spirit from the waters, and set the giant to turn the iron arms of machinery. We talk of the power that was latent in the skies till science climbed their heights, and, seizing the spirit of the thunder, chained it to our surface, abolishing distance, outstripping the wings of time, and flashing our thoughts across rolling seas to distant continents. Yet what are these to the moral power that lies asleep in the congregations of our country and of the Christian world? (*T. Guthrie, D.D.*) *True fearlessness :*—When young Nelson came home from a birds'-nesting expedition, his aunt chided him for being out so far into the night, and remarked, "I wonder fear did not make you come home." "Fear," said Nelson, "I don't know him." Fit speech for a believer when working for God. "Fear? I do not know it! What does it mean?" The Lord is on our side? Whom shall we fear? "If God be for us, who can be against us?" (*C. H. Spurgeon.*) *Unwarrantable fearlessness :*—When William Rufus heard of a rebellion at Le Mans, he flung himself, at the news of it, into the first boat, and crossed the channel in the teeth of a storm. When his followers remonstrated with him, he contemptuously replied, "Kings never drown." (*H. O. Mackey.*) *Christian courage :*—Some of the Indian chiefs having become the open enemies of the gospel, Mr. Elliot—sometimes called the Apostle of the American Indians—when in the wilderness, without the company of any other Englishman, was at various times treated in a threatening and barbarous manner by some of those men; yet his Almighty Protector inspired him with such resolution, that he said, "I am about the work of the great God, and my God is with me; so that I fear neither you nor all the sachims [or chiefs] in the country. I will go on, and do you touch me if you dare." They heard him and shrank away. (*W. Baxendale.*) *Intellectual virtues :*—1. Intelligence, which is that act of reason whereby we understand every particular concerning everything. 2. Science, which is that act of reason whereby we know all truth in all things. 3. Sapience, which is that act of reason whereby we understand and perceive what will follow from everything. 4. Prudence, which is that act of reason whereby we observe the fittest opportunities for the effecting of all things. 5. Art or skill, which is that act of reason whereby we know how to effect everything most skilfully. (*J. Barlow, D.D.*) *A sound mind not easily attained :*—We may perceive that sound minds are not easily come by, whatsoever the world may judge. Some think themselves wise with a little wit, as others do themselves rich with no great wealth. (*Ibid.*) *Power, love, and a sound mind are of absolute necessity for a resolute Christian, preacher, or private person :*—For power without love can work, but will not. Love without power would work, but cannot. And power and love can and will, but a sound mind is requisite to guide both. (*Ibid.*) *Contagion of fear :*—Speaking of his experiences in battle, a soldier-writer says, "How infectious fear is; how it grows when yielded to; and how, when once you begin to run, it soon seems impossible to run fast enough; whereas, if you can manage to stand your ground, the alarm lessens, and sometimes disappears." (*H. O. Mackey.*) *Needless fear :*— A lady was wakened up one morning by a strange noise of pecking at the window, and when she got up she saw a butterfly flying backwards and forwards inside the window in a great fright, because outside there was a sparrow pecking at the glass, wanting to reach the butterfly. The butterfly did not see the glass, but it saw the sparrow, and evidently expected every moment to be caught. Neither did the sparrow see the glass, though it saw the butterfly, and made sure of catching it. Yet all the while the butterfly, because of that thin, invisible sheet of glass, was actually as safe as if it had been miles away from the sparrow." It is when we forget our Protector that our hearts fail us. Elisha's servant was in great fear when he awoke in the morning and saw the city of Dothan encompassed with horses and chariots and a great host; but when his eyes were opened at the prayer of the prophet, his fears vanished, for he beheld the mountains full of horses and chariots of fire. "Thou wilt keep him in perfect peace whose mind is stayed on Thee, because he trusteth in Thee." "The Lord shall preserve thy going out and thy coming in from this time forth and for evermore." (*Jas. Inglis.*) *Love casting out fear :*—The love of God casts out all other fear! Every affection makes him who cherishes it in some degree braver than he would have been without it. It is not degrading to this subject to remind you of what we see away far down in the scale of living beings. Look at that strange maternal instinct that in the lowest animals out of weakness makes them strong, and causes them to forget all terror of the most terrible at the bidding of the mighty and conquering affection. Look at the same thing on the higher level of our own human life. It is not self-reliance that makes the hero. It is having the heart filled with passionate enthusiasm born of love for some person or for some thing. Love is gentle, but it is omnipotent, victor over all. It is the true hero, and martyr if need be, in the human heart! And when we rise to the highest form of it—namely, the love which is fixed upon God—oh! how that should, and if it be right, will, strengthen and brace, and make every man in whom it dwells frank, fearless, careless of personal consequences. (*A. Maclaren, D.D.*) *Power of love :*—Some time ago a poor fellow, who had been in penal servitude many years, came back to Manchester. He called on an old friend, a teacher of a ragged school, and in course of conversation said, "Can you tell me where Mr. Wright lives?" The teacher replied, "Did you know Mr. Wright?" The man answered "Yes; after I was sent to prison I was hardened; I cursed God, and the judge and jury; I cursed myself, and I cursed the prison; and in my rage I tried to commit suicide; but that day Mr. Wright came into my cell, and knelt down and prayed for me. I would not kneel at first; but when I saw the old gentleman kneel down, and saw his tears trickling down his cheeks, I could not help myself, and I also knelt down and prayed; and that day I gave God my heart. When I came out of prison, I made up my mind to seek him and thank him for his kindness to me." The teacher said, "Ah, my friend, Mr. Wright has been dead a long time." The converted thief exclaimed, "Dead! Mr. Wright dead!" The teacher said, "Yes, he is dead; but the same Spirit which prompted him to kneel down in your cell is in a Person whom I know, who can bless you in every time of need." He exclaimed, "Please tell me his name?" The teacher said, "His name is Jesus Christ." (*W. Birch.*)

**Ver. 8. Be not thou therefore ashamed of the testimony of our Lord, nor of me His prisoner.**—*Not ashamed of Christianity :*—It was natural and right that an old warrior whose armour was worn with use should charge the young soldier to bear himself bravely in the war. Cowardice is bad always, whether in the physical heroisms of the battle-field, or the moral heroisms of common duty. We are cautioned against being ashamed! And shame is the child of doubt as well as the child of fear! I. WE SHOULD NOT BE ASHAMED OF A TESTIMONY FOR CHRIST, BECAUSE CHRISTIANITY GIVES THE TRUE READING OF OUR MORAL NATURE. What are we? Apart from Christ, the world is just as much divided in its philosophical schools on this question as ever it was. The Utilitarian moralists enthrone the selfish instinct, and make the foundation of morals mere utility, or the greatest happiness principle; they test the morality of actions by their consequences, as if it were possible to trace them through all their sequences to their ultimate results, as if a man could thus judge, unless all the future ages were before him. But in setting up this standard, with one sharp and almost contemptuous sweep, they cut away the entire moral nature of man. Conscience has no place in their creed. "My own belief," says Mr. Mill, "is that the moral feelings are not innate, but acquired." Surely a fearful reading of human nature! "Let us make man in our image" becomes only a morbid dream of some early dramatist of creation! How this theory of human nature would, if adopted, ultimately affect society may perhaps best be understood by another sentence of Stuart Mill—" The proper limit to self-indulgence is that one shall neither hurt himself nor hurt others." Imagine this, a man is not to consult conscience, or the sense of right and wrong, he is neither to be cheered by conscience nor to be scourged by remorse, but is suffered to take his stand amongst his fellow-beings, as a mere conscience-less, calculating machine, weighing not the moral wrong, but the outward harmfulness of self-indulgence. If I turn from the school of Buckle and Mill to the modern scientific school, if captivated by the discoveries of modern science, I sit as a disciple at the feet of Huxley or Darwin, my power to realise any lofty conception even of this present life is gone! I feel like a man who has saved his purse and lost his gold, or who has kept safely the golden frame but lost the portrait it contained. Let us look at their position! We are declared to be the last and noblest form of a long series of developments; we trace these back to the elementary types of life. It may constitute a theory of physical nature, it cannot constitute a theory of human nature. It has no explanation whatever of the past of our race. Yes, the gospel makes us feel the grandeur of life as life; its rewards here are moral, its punishments the same. Instead of bidding us to think alone on consequences, it reminds us that God searcheth the heart. Its garland of victory is the well done of conscience, its scourge of woe is the agony of remorse. II. WE SHOULD NOT BE ASHAMED OF CHRISTIANITY, BECAUSE IT GIVES THE TRUE READING OF MAN'S RELIGIOUS NATURE. Man must worship. We all admit that. History proves it. A nation without its altars is as undiscoverable as a firmament without its stars! But what says Paul to Timothy?—" This is a faithful saying, and worthy of all acceptation, that Christ Jesus came into the world to save sinners," " This charge I commit unto thee, son Timothy." Yes! Yes! this was the message! Christ the Saviour of men! This it is that comes home to the heart and conscience of humanity everywhere. This is the great message we preach in the face of all modern endeavours to give the gospel only a place in the religions of the world. Yes! how that meets the soul-needs of man! Conscience is at rest beneath that cross where Christ the Lamb of God taketh away the sins of the world. Pardon, virtue, self-denial, sacrifice, peace, hope, joy, love, these are the growths of the Christian life—these blossom on no other tree but the Tree of Life. III. WE SHOULD NOT BE ASHAMED OF CHRISTIANITY, BECAUSE IT GIVES THE TRUE READING OF MAN'S HUMAN LIFE. Whatever the old theologies may have said, human life is divine. I mean by that, that the world into which we are born finds place and play for all our varied human faculties. It is manifest that man's nature is a mistake, and the world a mistake, if a man is to move on in a region of Asceticism, or a transcendental region of Mysticism. Take this life! I say this is a beautiful world to live in. It is a world of colour! It is a world of sound! It is a world of mystery! It is a world of enterprise! It is a world of motion! It is a world of taste! It is a world, in fact, full of manifestations of adaptation to the being to be placed upon it by God. Now, if it were worldliness to touch all these things, then we are tempted to worldliness every hour, every moment, and the world is a cruel enchantress, that meets us at every step. Surely you know well that this is not worldliness, that Christ did not teach us it was worldliness. Man's nature too would be a mistake. He has not only eyes to lift to heaven and knees to bend to earth, he has hands to toil with, a home to care for, a country to serve, and a whole round of earthly duties to discharge. Still it is a charge brought against Christianity that it is indifferent to human culture and affection. Now, I do admit this, that a man's personal relation to God is the first question which the gospel of Christ deals with: he is to be brought nigh by the blood of Christ, to be a temple of the Holy Ghost, to rejoice in a spiritual sonship. But it is also true that all other duties and relationships are lifted into higher spheres, and ruled by higher motives. Christianity is not responsible for the perversion of ascetics, nor is it responsible for the abuse of worldlings. The Christians of Apostolic times must keep themselves unspotted from the world, not by avoiding the very possibility of its stains, but by a life in God which preserves them from the power of evil. And so must we: the difficulties of the case are the difficulties of moral life. Christianity consecrates the life of the family, the life of the city, the life of the state. IV. WE SHOULD NOT BE ASHAMED OF A TESTIMONY FOR CHRIST, FOR CHRISTIANITY GIVES A TRUE READING OF LIFE, IN CHRIST HIMSELF. Christ is not only a Teacher; Christ is not only a Saviour; though He is both these. Christ is Christian life! He is His own religion alive and in action! When we study Christianity, we not only study the Evangels and the Epistles; we study Christ,

Christ's life is the ideal of all Christian life! As such I ask you to mark its practical side; its human side; its relation to all the interests, physical, social, and divine of the world Christ came to ransom and to save. Christ's hours of prayer occupied much of His earthly life, but He was not one-sided in His life. How active He was—"He went about doing good." How reasonable He was—He reasoned with the Jews out of their Scriptures. How home-loving He was—He abode at the house of Martha, and her sister Mary. How life's cheerful pleasures found Him a sharer in them—His first miracle was wrought at the marriage feast of Cana in Galilee. How social He was—He dined at the house of the Pharisee. How actively compassionate He was—"He healed all their sick." How wonderfully He carried the golden thread of the heavenly through the warp and woof of the earthly life. Oh! it is something beautiful indeed to possess that life. In all your experiences of emotion, awe, reverence, tenderness, it is not enough to feel the thrill of mere sensation. As Christ was consecrated to His Father, so must we be to Him! V. WE SHOULD NOT BE ASHAMED OF THE TESTIMONY OF CHRIST, FOR CHRISTIANITY NEGLECTED WRONGS OUR NATURE. All truth neglected wrongs our nature! I mean scientific truth, as well as religious truth. If I believe the world goes round, and if to propitiate priests, or to provide for some supposed protection of the Church's creed, I say the world does not go round, I wrong my mind. If I reject religious truth, I wrong my mind in the worst sense; I wrong my conscience and my heart. That man is to be pitied who bears about with him the murdered body of truth! There are such men, they know the gospel, they need no further commendations of it to the conscience and the heart. I say Divine demonstration has been made to the faculty of judgment, and to the faculty of feeling. And yet as the apostle says, "They know not the truth." They perpetuate that hideous immorality of bartering their souls for ease, pleasure, and sin! "Verily he that knew his Lord's will and did it not, shall be beaten with many stripes." VI. WE SHOULD NOT BE ASHAMED OF A TESTIMONY FOR CHRIST, BECAUSE CHRISTIANITY IN ALL THESE SCENES STANDS ALONE. Its position is unique! This one thing we know, that a Saviour such as I have been speaking of, is none other but Christ. If there is, and we are to be confronted with some new Saviour, it is time that the criticisms of the day gave us a new Christ. We exhaust other subjects, but we never exhaust Christ! With admiring and adoring homage we take our stand behind the Cross, and say to a world that wants a Saviour—"Behold the Lamb of God that taketh away the sins of the world." "Produce your cause," says the Most High to all who would now declare His Anointed One! "Beside Me, there is no Saviour!" (*W. M. Statham, M.A.*) *Power of personal testimony* :—Mr. Blackwood was the means of my conversion twenty-four years ago. And what was it that laid hold of me? I was then as worldly a young man as any in London, but I went to hear him speak at Streatham, having given a promise to do so to the young lady who was afterwards my wife, and is now in heaven. The sermon did not produce much impression upon me, but afterwards Mr. Blackwood walked up to me, and put his hand on my shoulder, and in his own loving way said: "Dear friend, I do not think that I have seen you at this meeting before. Are you a Christian? I know Christ; I have proved Him; do *you* know Him?" I had to say, "No, I do not." What the sermon did not do that testimony did, and I had no peace until I found the Saviour two days afterwards. Twenty-four years have passed since then; eighteen of them I have spent amongst the poor of the East of London, and I am more persuaded than ever that what the Church of Jesus Christ needs is not mere oratory, mere eloquence, mere wealth, but men who not only bear Christ's name, but come right out for Him, so that no one in their senses can doubt their being children of God. (*A. G. Brown.*) *Cowardice rebuked* :— Thirty years ago, more or less, there was a boy in Scotland who would go to sea. His name was James, and his father was a respected citizen of a good town six miles from the sea. On James's first voyage to Calcutta he kept up the habit of praying in the forecastle before turning in to his hammock, for he had been accustomed to do so regularly at home. Nobody said anything to him on the matter, but Bob Shearer, an able seamen, watched him. In Calcutta some of the seamen left the ship, and others were engaged in their place to work the ship home. One of these was a "rough," whose name was Robert. Hence he was called English Bob, and Shearer was called Scotch Bob. One night, soon after the homeward voyage began, James was on his knees, when the eye of English Bob happened to fall on him. "I declare," he cried, with an oath, "here's a younker praying. Did you ever?" And thereupon he flung a heavy shoe at his head with

3

excellent aim. Before James had time to rise Scotch Bob had the coward by the throat and told him to come upstairs and settle with him at once. The result was that English Bob got soundly and wholesomely thrashed. That night James went into his hammock without praying. But he had not time to fall asleep before Scotch Bob came and pitched him out. "What do you mean, you young coward? Say your prayers like a man! Do you think I'm going to fight for you and be disgraced in this way?" And so James never again failed to kneel before he slept, and feels to this day that his being ashamed of his Father in heaven and of the Saviour who died for him was well rebuked by the friendly courage of Bob Shearer. Long after, when his name had a title before it, and he was at the head of his profession, James had pleasure in finding Bob Shearer's mother, and bringing her to visit the mother who had taught him to pray. This story is related by James himself. *True friendship* :—Let me ask you a question. "What would you take for the greatest proof of downright friendship a man could show you?" "That is too hard a question to answer all at once." "Well, I may be wrong, but the deepest outcome of friendship seems to me, on the part of the superior at least, the permission, or better still, the call, to share in his sufferings." (*Geo. Mac-donald.*) *Definition of a friend* :—What is a friend but one whom I can trust; one who, in sorrow's hour, will mingle his tears with mine; one on whose support I can reckon when my back is at the wall! (*T. Guthrie, D.D.*) **According to the power of God.**—What power of God? has been asked. Not according to the power we get from God, but according to the power which God has displayed towards us in our calling and in our marvellous salvation. In other words, God with great power has succoured us; surely we may be confident that He will never leave us, never desert us; but in the hours of our sorest trouble incurred for Him will keep us and will bring us safely through it. (*H. D. M. Spence, M.A.*)

Ver. 9. **Who hath saved us, and called us with an holy calling.**—*The people of God effectually called in time* :—I. We may, in the first place, INQUIRE WHEREIN THIS HEAVENLY AND HOLY CALLING IS, OR WHAT SUCH ARE REPRESENTED IN SCRIPTURE AS CALLED TO. 1. They are called, in the first place, it is said, "out of darkness into marvellous light." 2. And then they are said, again, to be "called to the obtaining of the glory of the Lord Jesus Christ." But then they are called to the knowledge of Jesus as "the way" to eternal life, and to simple and humble faith in Him, and to see such glory in Him as shall lead them to find Him to be to them everything they can need, and possessed of everything they can receive and enjoy here and for ever. II. BUT THEN HOW IS THIS ACCOMPLISHED? We say, by the Spirit; it is the Spirit's work. But then He condescends to work by means, though He can work without means or by means, as He pleases. Generally speaking, the means is the Word of God, applied by His own almighty power and influence to the soul. III. BUT THEN HOW ARE WE TO TRACE THIS? The text teaches us to trace it, not to anything in the creature, or any thing that distinguishes those who partake of that heavenly calling from those who never partake of it, but to the sovereign and rich and distinguishing grace of the great Jehovah. "Not according to our works, but according to His own purpose and grace which was given us" long before we were born or had any existence, "given us in Christ Jesus" our spiritual Head, "given us in Him before the world began." You will find this great change described by emblems, which imply altogether the incapacity of man to accomplish it, and imply that he can have nothing in him to deserve it or merit it. It is called, you know, in one place, a resurrection—what none but God can possibly accomplish. (*W. Wilkinson, B.A.*) *Effectual calling, with its fruits* :—I. THE NATURE AND EXTENT OF THE GOSPEL-CALL. 1. We read in Scripture of an universal or general call, directed to all that live under the gospel. The invitation runs in the most comprehensive terms, that none may think themselves excluded. Salvation by faith in Christ was first proposed to the Jews, but upon their peremptory refusal it was offered without distinction to the Gentiles, who received it gladly; from which time the partition-wall has been broken down, and in every nation, they that fear God and work righteousness may be accepted of Him. But here, it must be carefully observed, the gospel-call is of a moral nature, and addressed to our reasonable powers. The blessed Jesus does not force men into His service by offering violence to their understanding and will; but convinces the former by setting the important truths of religion before it in a just and amiable light; and influences the latter by motives and arguments proper to dispose it to act agreeable to such conviction. If men complain their powers are broken, and that of themselves they cannot comply with the calls of God in His Word, He has directed them where to seek for necessary assistance, and has exalted His Son Jesus to give repentance, as well as remission of sins. So that if men finally refuse the gospel salvation, it will appear to have been owing more to a want of will than of power. 2. Besides this general call of the gospel, there is a more particular and personal call, when the Holy Spirit shines into the mind with such irresistible light as convinces the judgment, awakens the conscience, and engages the will to a compliance with every part of its duty. II. We are to inquire into THE AUTHOR OF EFFECTUAL CALLING, which my text says is GOD. If ministers had the tongues of angels, they could not of themselves prevail with sinners to believe and obey the gospel. By the representation the Scripture gives of the deplorable condition of fallen man, it is further evident that his effectual calling must be from God ; for it says, that his understanding is darkened, and "alienated from the life of God." That his will and affections are under invincible prejudices against virtue and goodness, and strongly biassed to sin and folly ; nay, that he is a slave to the devil, and carried captive by him at his pleasure. Is it not reasonable to conclude the necessity of a Divine agency, in order to accomplish the mighty change? Besides, effectual calling is compared in Scripture to those wonderful works that are peculiar to God Himself. It is called a New Creation, and a resurrection from the dead ; nay, 'tis compared to the mighty power of God, which was wrought in Christ when He was raised from the dead (Eph. i. 19). III. We are now to consider THE PROPERTIES BY WHICH THIS CALL OF THE SPIRIT IS DESCRIBED. 1. It is secret, God does not call sinners with an audible voice, but by secret and powerful impressions upon their souls. 2. It is a personal call ; ministers draw the bow at a venture, but the Spirit of God directs the arrow to the breast, where it is to enter. 3. Effectual calling is under the direction of the sovereign will and pleasure of God, as to the time, and manner, and means of it. Some are called into the vineyard at the third hour ; others at the sixth, and others not till the eleventh hour. The manner of God's calling men into the kingdom of grace is no less various. The like variety may be observed in the means of effectual calling. Some have been awakened by a sermon, others by a remarkable providence. Some by reading the Holy Scriptures, or books of devotion ; and others by religious conversation, meditation and prayers. 4. Effectual calling is without any regard to our works : so says the apostle in the text, "He has called us not according to our works." 5. The effectual calling of the Holy Spirit is always successful. IV. We are to consider THE FRUITS AND CONSEQUENCES OF EFFECTUAL CALLING. Before their conversion they were in a state of darkness, slavery, corruption and death ; now they are delivered from all this misery, and made partakers of the 'privileges of the children of God. But the more immediate consequences of effectual calling may be comprehended under these three particulars. 1. The first is, regeneration, or the new nature. 2. Sanctification by the Holy Spirit is another consequence of effectual calling. 3. A certain prophet of salvation. (*D. Neal.*)    *Effectual calling :*—I. I AM TO SHOW WHAT THE EFFECTUAL CALL IN THE GENERAL IS. An effectual call is opposed to an ineffectual one. An effectual call is the call that gains its real intent ; that is to say, when the party called comes when called. To apply this to our purpose, all that hear the gospel are called ; but, 1. To some of them it is ineffectual, and these are the most part of gospel-hearers, "For many be called, but few chosen" (Matt. xx. 16). They are called, invited ; but it is but the singing of a song to a deaf man that is not moved with it (Prov. i. 24). 2. To others it is effectual, and these are but few (Matt. xx. 16). II. I COME NOW TO SHOW WHO THEY ARE THAT ARE THUS EFFECTUALLY CALLED. The text tells us that this effectual call is according to God's purpose and free grace in Christ. 1. It is men, and not fallen angels, that are called. 2. It is some men, and not others, that are called effectually, and these naturally in as bad and sinful a condition as others (Eph. ii. 12). 3. It is for the most part those who have the least advantages as to their outward condition in the world (1 Cor. i. 26–28). III. I PROCEED TO SHOW WHENCE AND WHITHER THEY ARE CALLED WHO ARE EFFECTUALLY CALLED. 1. Called out of the world that lieth in wickedness (1 John v. 19). And hence the Church has its name in the prophetical and apostolical writings, Ekklesia ; *i.e.*, a company called out from among others, a gathered congregation. 2. Called unto Jesus Christ, and through Him to the blessed society of another world. IV. I PROCEED TO SHOW WHAT MAKES THE CALL EFFECTUAL TO SOME, WHEN IT IS NOT SO TO OTHERS. Negatively, 1. It is neither the piety, parts, nor seriousness of those who are employed to carry the gospel-call to sinners (1 Cor. iii. 7). 2. Neither is it one that uses his own free will better than another does (Rom. ix. 6). Positively. We may say in this case, "Not by might, nor by power, but by the Spirit of the Lord." V. IT MAY BE ASKED, WHAT NECESSITY IS THERE FOR THEIR BEING THUS CALLED? The necessity of it is manifest to all that know their natural case. 1. They are far off (Eph. ii. 13), far from God, and Christ, and all good (Eph. ii. 12). Hence the call is, "Draw nigh to God." 2. They are hard and fast asleep, and they need this call, "Awake, thou that sleepest, and arise from the dead, and Christ shall give thee light" (Eph. v. 14). 3. If they were awakened they know not where to go to (Acts ii. 37). 4. If they did not know where to go to, they are not willing to go thither (John v. 40). 5. If they are willing to go to Christ, yet being awakened, they dare not venture, guilt so stares them in the face, "Thou saidst, There is no hope" (Jer. ii. 25). 6. If they durst come, yet they cannot come, unless they be drawn (John vi. 44). VI. I SHALL MORE PARTICULARLY EXPLAIN THE NATURE OF EFFECTUAL CALLING. It is the work of the Lord's Spirit. 1. On the understanding. (1) An illumination of the soul from Mount Sinai. (2) An illumination of the soul from Mount Zion. 2. On the will of the sinner. This faculty of the soul needs also a saving work of the Spirit thereon, being fearfully depraved in the state of nature (Rom. viii. 7). Now, the Spirit's work on the will is, the renewing of it (Ezek. xxxvi. 26). (*T· Boston, D.D.*) *Salvation altogether by grace :*—It is somewhat remarkable—at least it may seem so to persons who are not accustomed to think upon the subject—that the apostle, in order to excite Timothy to boldness, to keep him constant in the faith, reminds him of the great doctrine that the grace of God reigns in the salvation of men. I. Very carefully let US CONSIDER THE DOCTRINE TAUGHT BY THE APOSTLE IN THIS TEXT. 1. The apostle in stating his doctrine in the following words, "Who hath saved us, and called us with an holy calling, not according to our works, but according to his own purpose and grace, which was given us in Christ Jesus before the world began," declares God to be the Author of salvation—"Who hath saved us and called us." The whole tenor of the verse is towards a strong affirmation of Jonah's doctrine, "that salvation is of the Lord." To say that we save ourselves is to utter a manifest absurdity. We are called in Scripture "a temple"—a holy temple in the Lord. But shall any one assert that the stones of the edifice were their own architect? No: we believe that God the Father was the architect, sketched the plan, supplied the materials, and will complete the work. Shall it also be said that those who are redeemed redeemed themselves? that slaves of Satan break their own fetters? Then why was a Redeemer needed at all? Do you believe that the sheep of God, whom He has taken from between the jaws of the lion, could have rescued themselves? Can the dead make themselves alive? 2. We next remark that grace is in this verse rendered conspicuous when we see that God pursues a singular method—"Who hath saved us and called us." The peculiarity of the manner lies in three things—first, in the completeness of it. The apostle uses the perfect tense and says, "who hath saved us." Believers in Christ Jesus are saved. This completeness is one peculiarity—we must mark another. I want you to notice the order as well as the completeness: "who hath saved us and called us. What! saved us before He called us? Yes, so the text says. But is a man saved before he is called by grace? Not in his own experience, not as far as the work of the Holy Spirit goes, but he is saved in God's purpose, in Christ's redemption, and in his relationship to his covenant Head; and he is saved, moreover, in this respect, that the work of his salvation is done, and he has only to receive it as a finished work. In the olden times of imprisonment for debt, it would have been quite correct for you to step into the cell of a debtor and say to him, I have freed you, if you had paid his debts and obtained an order for his discharge. Well, but he is still in prison. Yes; but you really liberated him as soon as you paid his debts. 3. When a speaker desires to strengthen his point and to make himself clear, he generally puts in a negative as to the other side. So the apostle adds a negative: "Not according to our works." The world's great preaching is, "Do as well as you can, live a moral life, and God will save you." The gospel preaching is this: "Thou art a lost sinner, and thou canst deserve nothing of God but His displeasure; if thou art to be saved, it must be by an act of sovereign grace." 4. My text is even more explicit yet, for the eternal purpose is mentioned. The next thing the apostle says is this: "Who hath saved us, and called us with an holy calling, not according to our works but according to His own purpose." Mark that word—"according to His own purpose." Do you not see how all the merit and the power of the creature are shut out here, when you are saved, not according to your purpose or merit, but "according to *His* own purpose"? 5. But then the text, lest we should make any mistake, adds, "according to His own purpose and grace." The purpose is not founded on foreseen merit, but upon grace alone. It is grace, all grace, nothing but grace from first to last. 6. Again, in order to shut out everything like boasting, the whole is spoken of as a gift. Do notice that, "purpose and grace which He gave us"—not "which He sold us," "offered us," but "which He gave us." 7. But the gift is bestowed through a medium which glorifies Christ. It is written, "which was given us in Christ Jesus." We ask to have mercy from the well-head of grace, but we ask not even to make the bucket in which it is to be brought to us; Christ is to be the sacred vessel in which the grace of God is to be presented to our thirsty lips. 8. Yet further, a period is mentioned and added—"before the world began." Those last words seem to me for ever to lay prostrate all idea of anything of our merits in saving ourselves, because it is here witnessed that God gave us grace "before the world began." Where were you then? What hand had you in it "before the world began"? II. SHOW THE USES OF THIS DOCTRINE. I would that free grace were more preached, because it gives men something to believe with confidence. (*C. H. Spurgeon.*)    *God's plan for man's salvation:*—I. THE ORIGIN OF OUR SALVATION. Three facts claim our notice. 1. It is with God. The last clause of the preceding verse shows to whom the pronoun "who" refers—"According to the power of God." It is God the Father to whom the apostle alludes. The Bible everywhere preserves the distinction between the origin and the means of our salvation. The last it invariably ascribes to God the Son: the first it as invariably ascribes to God the Father. In Ephesians ii. 4–7 we have a striking instance of this. In ver. 5, it is "with Christ"; ver. 6, "by Christ"; ver. 7, "through Christ." But all these expressions are introduced by the statement in ver. 4, "But God, who is rich in mercy, for His great love wherewith He loved us," &c. And so, in the text, the apostle says it is "in Christ Jesus"; but it originates so entirely with God the Father, that He is said to have "saved us." This Scripture distinction does away with the only apparently plausible objection that has been raised against the atonement of Christ—viz., that it represents the Father as unwilling to save sinners, or as needing to be appeased. The eternal Father, and the suffering Son, are united in one ascription of praise. In all our doctrinal statements, and in all our expressions of praise, let us give honour to both. 2. It is in His own purpose and grace. The idea of a purpose resulting from grace alone is prominent here. Our salvation not only originates with God, but in His gracious purpose alone. (1) It is not the result of necessity. Even acts of grace are sometimes necessary. The public voice demands them—the interests of the empire require them—the weakness of the government renders them expedient. Nay, the claims of justice itself may be satisfied, and grace steps forward. No voice in heaven—on earth—in hell—could have demanded salvation for guilty men. Believer, your damnation would not have tarnished His glory. Your salvation originated in His own purpose and grace. (2) It was not from the impulse of others. A generous heart is sometimes sluggish. It needs to be excited. One word from another has often stirred to benevolent action. Our merciful God needed no stimulus. It was not the offer of Jesus to die for us which roused Him to save us—it only met His own gracious desire. No pleading of angels or of men impelled Him. His loving heart did not wait for either. A few years ago a vessel was wrecked on the coast at Scarborough. It was in the night. The signals of distress aroused the crew of the lifeboat; the men were on the cliff, looking out and pitying; but the danger was so great that they stirred not. As soon as it was light crowds gathered on the spot. One voice was heard. It was the voice of a stranger. Pointing to the wreck, it appealed to the lifeboat's crew. It reached the hearts of the men. The boat was launched and manned. Soon it returned, bearing the saved ones to the shore. About the same time another wreck occurred on the same coast. It was the dead of night. A daughter and her father were sleeping in the lighthouse. The signal of distress awoke the young woman. She saw the peril. No voice was near to stir her to the deed of mercy. She aroused her father. Solitary and unstimulated they entered the boat—the wreck was reached—the wrecked ones were borne back in safety. Both deeds were noble; but you see the difference. The impulse from another stirred the crew of the lifeboat. No impulse was needed to stir the heart of Grace Darling. All illustrations must fail us; but we are speaking of Him who needed no impulse—waited for none—but acted at once from His own gracious purpose. (3) It was not by the counsel of others. The phrase "His own purpose" here is expressive. The generous heart is sometimes perplexed. It needs no stimulus, but it needs counsel. Difficulties stand in the way of following out its own promptings. Its language often is—"Oh! tell me what I can do to save him." How gratefully it welcomes the happy thought which removes all its perplexities. David's heart yearned towards Absalom, but his kingly office stood in the way of indulging a father's wishes. How welcome were the counsels of the woman of Tekoah, when she threw herself in his way to plead for the guilty one. But God was His own counsellor in man's salvation. He had no counsellor in creation—no architect— He was His own. He has no counsellor in providence. He needs no minister to advise, or privy council to deliberate—He is His own. It was yet more true as to man's salvation. It is " the mystery of His will, according to His good pleasure, which He hath pursued in Himself " (Eph. i. 9). He had no counsellor. No one can divide the honour with Him. 3. It is not according to our works. The apostle here intends to put good works in their right place; not to set them aside. By " good works" he invariably means not charities alone, however benevolent—nor prayers alone, however devout: he includes the whole works of a holy life. The daughter of Jairus was raised by Jesus. Think you not that, as the thrill of returning life passed through her veins, her first emotion would be that of love to Him who had rescued her from the grave, and that ever after she would be anxious to show it by every act which gratitude prompted? But Jesus raised her from His own gracious purpose. Her subsequent acts were the effect, not the cause. II. The MEANS OR METHOD OF OUR SALVATION. Three facts deserve attention. 1. It is in Christ. Paul teaches this: It is "according to His own purpose and grace"; but he adds, "which was given us in Christ Jesus." No views of God's purposes are right, then, which separate them from Christ Jesus. God has revealed no purpose except in Him. His very mercy, full as it is, knows no channel except through Him. Most men are ready to be saved—nay, wish it. The hard lesson for some to learn is, salvation by Christ. Strange that it should be so. The method which most honours God is the most suited to us. 2. It is by God's calling. 3. This calling is holy. The Apostle Paul has clearly explained his own meaning (2 Thess. ii. 13, 14). We pause not now to reason with those who would make it a salvation to sin, and not from sin. The text points higher than this. It is not enough to say that we are saved in the way of holiness: our very calling is holy—holy in its design, and holy in its spirit. It breathes spiritual purity, as well as life into the soul—a portion of the pure atmosphere of heaven itself. There is no calling by God which is not a holy calling. He stamps His own image as His own mark upon every soul He calls and saves. There are three classes to whom we wish especially to apply these statements. (1) To those inquiring after the way to salvation. Inquirer; we compared our text to a miniature map of the way of salvation. Take care that you follow it. John Bunyan's "Pilgrim" found his way out of the City of Destruction easily enough when alarmed. But his own mistakes, and the misleadings of others, led him into many perils. Nor was it until Evangelist met him the second time, and set him right, that he found the wicket gate, and the only way to the Celestial City. Take this verse with you at the beginning of your journey. Study it well. It will preserve you from serious perils to your salvation. (2) To those who object to God's plan of salvation. Our reference now is to those who object on the ground of its supposed tendency. It is thought by some that a salvation so arranged will check a holy life. If rightly viewed, it stimulates to it. If holiness be not always the result of the doctrine, the cause of failure is not in the truth, but in the heart on which it falls. When the soft fertilising shower has fallen on your garden, old flowers give fresh signs of life, and new flowers begin to open their buds. Nay, the seed hitherto buried, but invisible appears. And yet in one part of the garden you look, and although the same pure rain has fallen upon it, and the same seed lies buried beneath it, no flowers appears. The cause is not with the rain, but the soil. It was the doctrine of salvation by grace which transformed the frivolous dissipated young soldier of Corfu into the consistent, holy, religious hero of the Crimea—Captain Hedley Vicars. 3. To those who despise or neglect this salvation. Does its simple easy method offend you? How is this? The accomplishment of great ends by the simplest means is usually regarded as the greatest achievement of wisdom. This plan is the result of Divine wisdom alone. No other wisdom could have devised it. (*Samuel Luke.*)    *A holy calling:*— St. Peter (1 Pet. i. 15) gives the full force of this epithet: "As He which hath called you is holy, so be ye holy in all manner of conversation." (*Speaker's Commentary.*)    *God's call:*—The voice of Divine grace prevailing upon the will. This is the ruling meaning of " call," " calling," &c., in the Epistles; while in the Gospels it means no more, *necessarily*, than the audible invitations of the gospel (see, *e.g.*, Matt. xxii. 14). (*H. C. G. Moule, M.A.*)　　*A holy calling :*—1. For the causes of it are holy; God, Christ, the Spirit, and the Word are all said to be holy. And the ministers, for the most part, are holy, who be instruments in this action. 2. And in regard of the end too, and the subjects from which we are called, and to which we be called, it is a holy calling. For first, We are called from darkness to light. Secondly, From uncleanness to holiness. Thirdly, From wicked men and devils, to the communion of saints and angels. Fourthly, We are called from earth that is polluted, unto heaven the holy mountain of the Lord. 3. In the last place, this is to teach such as are called on this manner to walk worthy of their calling. Is it a holy calling? live thou holily. Shall a prince plod in the mire, defile his clothes, and pollute his person, by the base offices of poor subjects? How unseemly then is it for these holy brethren. (*J. Barlow, D.D.*)　　*Christianity a holy religion :*—To a young infidel who was scoffing at Christianity because of the misconduct of its professors, the late Dr. Mason said, "Did you ever know an uproar to be made because an infidel went astray from the paths of morality?" The infidel admitted that he had not. "Then don't you see," said Dr. Mason, "that, by expecting the professors of Christianity to be holy, you admit it to be a holy religion, and thus pay it the highest compliment in your power?" The young man was silent.　　*Grace does not lightly esteem :*—There is sometimes the thought that *grace* implies God's passing by sin. But no—quite the contrary; grace supposes sin to be so horribly bad a thing, that God cannot tolerate it. Were it in the power of man, after being unrighteous and evil, to patch up his ways, and mend himself so as to stand before God, there would then be no need of *grace*. The very fact of the Lord's being gracious shows sin to be so evil a thing, that man, being a sinner, his state is utterly ruined and hopeless, and nothing but free grace will do for him— can meet his need. (*Anon.*)　　*Salvation by grace :*—The late Rev. C. J. Latrobe visited a certain nobleman in Ireland who devoted considerable sums to charitable purposes; and, among other benevolent acts, had erected an elegant church at his own expense. The nobleman, with great pleasure, showed Mr. Latrobe his estate, pointed him to the church, and said, "Now, sir, do you not think that will merit heaven?" Mr. Latrobe paused for a moment, and said, "Pray, my lord, what may your estate be worth a year?" "I imagine," said the nobleman, "about thirteen or fourteen thousand pounds." "And do you think, my lord," answered the minister, "that God would sell heaven, even for thirteen or fourteen thousand pounds?"　　*Grace and free will :*—Mrs. Romaine was once in company with a clergyman at Tiverton, who spoke with no little zeal against what he called "irresistible grace," alleging that "such grace would be quite incompatible with free will." "Not at all so," answered Mrs. Romaine; "grace operates effectually, yet not coercively. The wills of God's people are drawn to Him and Divine things, just as your will would be drawn to a bishopric, if you had the offer of it." (*W. Baxendale.*)　　*The sovereign grace of God :*—Henry IV., King of France, was in every point of view a great man. It is said that on an anniversary of his birth-day he made the following reflection: "I was born on this day, and no doubt, taking the world through, thousands were born on the same day with me, yet out of all those thousands I am probably the only one whom God hath made a king. How peculiarly am I favoured by the bounty of His providence!" But a Christian, reflecting on his second birth, may, with greater reason, adore the free and sovereign grace of God.

Ver. 10. But is now made manifest by the appearing of our Saviour Jesus Christ, who hath abolished death.—*The appearing :*—Remarkable as the only passage in the New Testament in which the word ἐπιφάνεια (= manifestation) is applied to the incarnation of our Lord. (*E. H. Plumptre, D.D.*)　　The simple act of the Incarnation by no means covers the "appearing." The "appearing" (Epiphany) here includes not only the birth, but the whole manifestation of Christ on earth, including the Passion and the Resurrection. (*H. D. M. Spence, M.A.*)　　*Living in the days of Christ's appearing :*—Seeing that the days wherein we live are better than the days of old, we must thrive, and be better also. The more choice diet we feed on, the fatter and fairer should we be; the clearer light, the cleaner must we keep ourselves from pollution, contamination. When trees are removed to a more fertile soil, do we not expect that they should spread further, and be more fruitful than before? when cattle are put into a better pasture will we not look for better growth, more labour at their hands? Shall not we then grow strong, work mightily in the Lord's vineyard, and resolutely run the ways of His commands? Is not our light brighter, our spiritual food better, and our journey shorter? then why is there not some equal proportion? These things must be thought upon, made use of, or else our account one day will be the greater, the heavier; for unto whom much is given, shall much be required. They who have greater means for grace than others, must strive to be more gracious than others, or look for the more heavier reckoning. Our fathers were led in the night, the moon was their conductor; we are now in the day, when as the sun guideth us, shall we not then go faster, farther, with less fear, and more resolution, greater boldness? But alas! who taketh knowledge of these things maketh the true use thereof? We have the sun shining, yet sleep; or if awake, we cry, want we not light? I say no more, but with that our idleness cause not the Lord to remove our candlestick. (*J. Barlow, D.D.*) **Who hath abolished death.**—*Death abolished:*—The article is used here emphatically and designedly. The article is often used to express a thing in the abstract. *Death,* not merely in some particular instance, but in all its aspects and bearings, and in its very essence, being and idea is abolished. (*Jas. Bryce, LL.D.*) *Death of none effect:*—Christ Jesus is not only a living embodiment of the Eternal purpose and love of the Father, but He is also declared to be the Saviour who made death of none effect, abolished or rendered inoperative that death which is the universal curse of man, which "has passed through upon all men" (Rom. v. 12), and is grimly symbolised to us in the dissolution of the body. The Lord declared that those who lived and believed in Him should never die. St. John could never have recorded these words of the Master (John xi. 26) when a whole generation of Christians, including all the apostles, with the exception of himself, had passed away and come under the tyrannous sway of the last enemy, unless he had supposed the words to imply something far more and other than the death of the body. Wiesinger, Huther, Ellicott, and others are right in understanding by the word *thanatos,* "death," the entire antithesis to *zoe* or "life." Surely it is the entire principle of decay, corruption, and separation from God instituted by sin. It includes all the animosity that a living, self-conscious being feels against God for bringing him into a dying world, all the resistance to and departure from His supreme will. It is this otherwise irremediable curse, and painful looking for of condign punishment, this moral death and dissolution, which Christ has disarmed and rendered inoperative. (*H. R. Reynolds, D.D.*) *Death abolished:*—Everybody can feel the fitness of saying that sin and death are two of the greatest enemies of the human race. Expressive and appropriate is the habit we derive from Scripture of speaking of them as persons, hostile powers, who make war on us. Between the two there is a terrible alliance. They are in league against us; and though, if we are even victorious over them, we are told that death will be the last to be destroyed, yet sin was the first, and sin is the greatest. Not that, except for sin, these material bodies would be immortal. Eventual dissolution and decay into their elements belong to their constitution, as much as to that of vegetables in autumn. "We all do fade as a leaf." "All flesh is as grass." But though dissolution seems a characteristic of human bodies, the doubt and terror which accompany death are due to sin, which has estranged us from our Maker, whom, in consequence, we have ceased to think of as our Father. Thus the *sting* of death is sin. The voyage across the Atlantic is *one* thing to the slave, hurried by a captor, he knows not whither, and quite another to the traveller returning home. These, then, are the two greatest evils which afflict humanity; and, now, is there any remedy for them—any deliverer from them? Christianity professes to bring a remedy,—to announce a Deliverer both from sin and death. Hence, its message is called the gospel—the good news. "The Son of man was manifested, to destroy the works of the devil"; and "our Saviour Jesus Christ hath abolished death." I. DEATH MADE OF NONE EFFECT. Such is the meaning of "abolished." Not to do away with altogether, but to render imperfect, and in that sense to destroy. The entire destruction spoken of in the fifteenth chapter of the First of Corinthians will come later. Christianity has made no difference in regard to the dissolution and decay which befall all mortal bodies. It is still true that "all flesh is as grass." Its language, however, is not "Death shall never again strike down a human being, or make a happy home a house of mourning," but "O death, where is thy sting? O grave, where is thy victory?" "Blessed are the dead who die in the Lord." "To die is gain." So death is made of none effect. II. JESUS CHRIST, OUR SAVIOUR FROM DEATH. We may well ask, "By what rare enchantment can the king of terrors be transformed thus into an angel of light?" *Who* "can make a dying bed seem soft as downy pillows are?" Even He who said to a sister weeping at a brother's grave, "I am the Resurrection and the Life : whosoever liveth, and believeth in Me shall never die!" "To depart is to be with Christ, which is far better." But how so? Was He not the man Christ Jesus? And did He not Himself die in anguish? And was He not Himself laid in the tomb? Truly, if He was no more than man, our Christian hope of immortality is a baseless imposture. But the good news from God is that Jesus Christ was more ; that He is the Lord of life, the King immortal and eternal, who wrapped Himself awhile in perishable human clay, but whom it was not possible that death should hold. And the reason of His coming is thus expressed in Scripture : "Forasmuch as the children are partakers of flesh and blood, He also Himself likewise took part of the same, that through death He might destroy him that had the power of death." III. THROUGH DEATH HE ABOLISHED DEATH. By Himself passing down into the dark valley, into the silent tomb, He disarmed the grave of its terrors. And as we saw that death and sin are closely allied,—death the wages of sin, and sin the sting of death,— they are allied in regard to our deliverance from them. Our Saviour from the one, is our Saviour from the other. IV. LIFE AND INCORRUPTION BROUGHT TO LIGHT. A great shadow was spread over the world, and it lay the deepest over human life. Now, the great light, which the people who sat in darkness have seen in Christ, brings to view the novel and glorious fact of life associated with immortality, or incorruptibility. (*T. M. Herbert, M.A.*)      *Death abolished :* —He must have had strong faith who, writing amidst the signs of death ever near him in a populous city, could write, Jesus Christ hath abolished death. He felt within him the inspiration of an immortal life; and it gave a new character to all things around him. In his prison in Rome, heaven was his home. Adhering to a religion whose first preachers were martyrs, he saw no death in martyrdom. Having finished his course, and ready to be offered up, his time of *departure*—not of death—was at hand. Let us meditate upon this great subject, and see if we can understand the apostle. There is one doctrine of Christianity to which our hearts have not done justice, because our faith has not felt its power ; that doctrine is, that "Jesus Christ has abolished death." I. THE FACT—"Jesus Christ hath abolished death." 1. If you observe the connection, you will see this was the consequence of an everlasting purpose of grace. See the preceding verse. This glorious truth is not a thought of yesterday, not a thought that entered the mind of God on occasion of the fall of man, but a purpose made before man fell, before the world began. And this everlasting purpose is the firm and immutable rock on which rests the whole fabric of our salvation. I know some persons are afraid to think of an ever-lasting purpose, an immutable decree of God, as if it were an awful, an unapproach-able mystery. It is, indeed, awful, as is every attribute of Him who dwells in light inaccessible, but it need not be terrible. Observe the words : "according to His own purpose and grace." The purpose and the grace are intimately associated. The grace is as old as the purpose. Both are from everlasting. The purpose flows out of the grace, for the grace is the nature of the eternal God from which His purpose flows, and must be gracious like Himself. What is there to fear in a purpose of grace? Would you not be comforted in the trials of life, if you found in every emergency that your earthly father had made ample provision by a kind purpose before you were born? If for your infancy comforts were provided at his expense by a mother's care; and if you found a fund set apart to pay the expense of your good education, should any casuality deprive you of his immediate care ; and when you came of age you found a sum insured at your birth to enable you to commence business with respectability and good success ; and everywhere else, as parental forethought and love could foresee, a purpose appeared in a present supply of your wants ;—would not all this be an assurance and perpetual memorial of your father's good will? would it not endear him the more to your heart? and would you not cherish the memory of him who with so much forethought had provided for you with affectionate and loving regard? Just so with the gracious purpose of God. 2. But the fact of the abolition of death, connected with an everlasting purpose, was manifested in time by the appearing of our Saviour Jesus Christ. But how was it manifested? Wherein did Christ appear to abolish death? When did He accomplish this gracious purpose? We naturally look for the answer to His own death. Was that not really death? Was it a departure rather than a death? Did He ever say with regard to Himself that death was abolished? Did He meet death as if He had already destroyed him that had the power of death, that is, the devil? Go to Calvary and observe. What signs are there but true signs of death? Ho died, He tasted death. But, then, in dying He abolished death for all believers. It is as if He absorbed all the venom of the sting of death into His own soul and left none to distress the souls of His people; so that death, so dreadful to Him, is to them without a curse, without a sting, and but a shadow. Scripture has found for it a new name, a name of pleasant association, and calls it sleep (1 Thess. iv. 14). In saying Jesus really endured the pains of death, I refer not chiefly to the extreme bodily sufferings which He endured, but to the mental conflict and agony which to Him were the bitterness and curse of death. Christ hath abolished death, as every spirit in heaven feels with delight; and if we know it not now, we shall know it hereafter with rapturous delight. But must we wait till we reach the blissful life of heaven before we can say in the fulness of a joyful heart, "Our Saviour Jesus Christ hath abolished death"? Well, I fear we must—at least, many of us. Our faith seems as if it could not grasp and feel this great text. We are but sorry Christians if thus we pass our lives grovelling in clay, in bondage through fear of death. Worldling! you are right in fearing death, for it will strip you of all your beloved and prized possessions. Unpardoned sinner! you are right in fearing death, for to you it will be the dreadful doom and beginning of endless woe. Lover of pleasure! you are right in your fear, for it will turn your pleasure into pain, remorse, consternation, anguish. Worshipper of Mammon! you are right, for it will take away your gods, and what have you left? But Christians, are we not ashamed of ourselves? Christians, unworthy of the name, are you afraid of death? Do you not believe that Christ hath abolished it? Yes, you believe it as a fact; at least, you say so, and you think so. But do you know it as an experience —a truth of the heart as well as of the creed—a truth in which you rejoice as the conquest of the last enemy? II. THE EXPERIENCE THAT OUR SAVIOUR JESUS CHRIST HATH ABOLISHED DEATH. Paul rose out of these earthly shadows, awoke from these carnal dreams; saw the world, not as we see it, a substantial form, but as an evening cloud whose tints were fading, as a flickering flame whose glory was passing away. New light from the excellent glory came around him and gave new colour and character to all things about him. His prison was fading, and he scarcely saw it in the surrounding glory; his chain was melting off his hand and he scarcely felt it, for the day of his great deliverance was rising. Cæsar's tribunal, its attendants, pomp, lictors, sergeants, soldiers, executioners, what were they all in the full light of the great salvation all around him? They were virtually abolished too. Heaven was near, he could hear its sweet music. Eternal life was within him, he could feel its power. Immortality was brought to light, he could see it and rejoice in it. There was no more death, to obscure that light of unfading glory. They could not kill him, could not destroy that which he had learned to call himself, and which felt and knew everything in its relation not to time but to eternity. And there have been many others like him. (R. Halley, D.D.) Christ abolishing death:—" All men," says St. Paul, " are all their life-time, through fear of death, subject to bondage." And every one, who has at all watched his own mind, knows that this is true. The very heathen, as our mission-aries teach, tell us how death is known and feared, and looked forward to, with fearful expectation, as the great and universal enemy. Thus the fear of death is felt by all men, and is the fly in every pot of ointment, that, once found there, spoils and mars it: it is the sword hung overhead, whose keen point and sharp edge glitter ominously and threateningly in the light of every banquet; it is the hollow skull, with its eyeless sockets and its melancholy emptiness, that spoils every marble monument. I. MEN ALWAYS DID AND STILL DO ALL THEY CAN TO KEEP OFF THE UNWELCOME THOUGHT. The Greek and Roman, as they bound their heads with the wreath of roses, and stretched their limbs on the soft moss under the green arbutus, and drank off their goblets of wine, tried to forget that all this would soon be over, and that there would come one day the last disease. But it always was vain, and always will be, to attempt to quench the thought, though it may be staved off; the wine and flowers and song cannot last for ever. II. BUT WHAT IS IT THAT THUS MAKES DEATH AN OBJECT OF UNIVERSAL APPREHENSION AND DREAD? Is it always the act of death? is the mere dying always a dreadful thing? No! it is sin; it is the sense of accountability, and the solemn expectation of the account we have to render; it is " the fearful expectation and looking-for of judgment ": it is these which make death dreadful and dreaded, so that, " through fear of death men have been subject to bondage." III. Our text says THAT CHRIST " HATH ABOLISHED DEATH." Is, then, death dead? That cannot be. I see Christians die as well as other men. But the sting of death is drawn; for sin is taken away. Death, therefore, is not the summoner of God's court of trial, but the usher to call him into God's glorious presence-chamber. The Christian does not die when his body and his soul are for a time divided. He has in his spirit, that is, in himself, his truest self, a life which is eternal; from the moment he believes and trusts in Christ, from that moment " he hath eternal life." IV. BUT, IS IT ONLY THE CHRISTIAN TO WHOM DEATH IS THUS ABOLISHED ? "The fathers, where are they?" Did life and immortality begin with Christ? Were Christians the first to share and to enjoy them? Righteous Abel, when he fell by a brother's hand, and his fainting soul departed from his mangled body, took possession of the paradise of God. Noah and Abraham, Isaac and Jacob, David and Hezekiah, the glorious company of the prophets, the whole line of penitent believers—however unknown to men, yet known to God—inherited at death the same life that the Christian now inherits. But they did not know, as we know, the life and immortality which they received. Life and immortality existed as surely then, as now; but they then were "in the dark." The light had not risen : it was night with them ; and only the stars threw a trembling light on the things beyond the grave. The heathen had, indeed, their Elysian fields ; but that shadowy world was only a reproduction of the most pleasing portions of this present life, where, as the Indian hopes to use his bow and arrows to hunt the shadowy deer, as the Chinese hopes to employ the ghost of his loved paper money in that spectral world, so the heathens of Greece and Rome saw their heroes engrossed in the employments and amusements of this world—throwing the quoit, or driving the chariot, or reposing on beds of roses, in those fields of their own creation. And the views of the pious Jews and patriarchs were dim and obscure. "A land of darkness, as darkness itself, and of the shadow of death, without any order, and where the light is as darkness " (Job. x. 22 ; Isa. xxxviii. 10, 11 ; Psa. lxxxviii. 4, 5). (*W. W. Champneys, M.A.*)    *The death of death :*—I. THE EVIL IN QUESTION—It is death. We should suppose that this subject was very familiar to the thoughts of men, were we to judge from the importance and frequency of the event. But, alas! nothing is so little thought of. Let us examine what Nature teaches us concerning death ; and then go to the Scripture for additional information. 1. Suppose then there had been no revelation from God—what does Nature teach us concerning death ? (1) It sees plainly enough that it is a cessation of our being. The lungs no longer heave ; the pulse ceases to beat; the blood pauses and congeals; the eye closes ; the tongue is silent ; and the hand forgets her cunning. We are laid in the grave, where worms feed upon us. (2) It also teaches us the universality of death. (3) Nature teaches us that death is unavoidable. (4) Nature sees also that death is irreparable. It cannot produce a single specimen of posthumous life. (5) We may also learn from it that death is uncertain in its circumstances ; and that no man knows the place, the time, the manner, in which he shall expire. If it be objected that the generality of the heathen have had some other views of death than those which we have conceded, and had even notions of an existence beyond the grave—let it be observed, that the world always had a revelation from God ; and that when mankind dispersed from the family of Noah, they carried the discoveries along with them ; but as they were left to tradition, they became more and more obscure ; yet they yielded hints which led to reflections that otherwise would have never occurred. And if wise men, especially from these remains of an original revelation, were led into some speculations bordering upon truth, it should be remembered that in a case like this, as Paley observes, nothing more is known than is proved : opinion is not knowledge ; nor conjecture principle. 2. But how much more does the Scripture teach ! Here we learn—(1) Its true nature. To the eye of sense death appears annihilation ; but to the eye of faith it is dissolution. (2) Its true consequences. Very little of death falls under the observation of the senses; the most awful and interesting part is beyond their reach. It is the state of the soul ; it is the apprehension of it by devils or angels; it is the transmission of it to heaven or hell. (3) Its true cause. The Scripture shows us that man was not created mortal ; and that mortality is not the necessary consequence of our original constitution ; but is the penal effect of transgression. (4) The true remedy. What ! Is there a remedy for death ? Who said to His hearers, " If a man keep My sayings, he shall never see death " ? He hath abolished death. But let us— II. Consider this DESTRUCTION—for does not death continue his ravages? Does he not fall upon the people of God themselves ? Where then is the proof of this abolition ? It is undeniable that Christians themselves are subject to the stroke of death, as well as others. 1. He abolishes death, spiritually; that is, in the souls of His people. To all these, without exception, it may be said, in the words of

Paul to the Ephesians, " You hath He quickened who were dead in trespasses and sins." 2. He abolished death by His miracles while He was on earth. 3. He abolished death in His own person. His own rising from the dead is very distinguishable from all the former instances of resurrection. The ruler's daughter, the widow's son, Lazarus, and the saints in Jerusalem, were raised by the power of another ; but He rose by His own power. They rose as private individuals : but He as the head and representative of His people : and because He lives, they shall live also. 4. He abolished death penally. Thus He has destroyed death as to its sting. He has not abolished going home, and falling asleep, and departing ; but He has abolished death. This leads us to observe, that He has—5. Abolished death comparatively : I mean as to its terror. This is not the same with the foregoing particular. That regards all the people of God, and extends even to those who die under a cloud of darkness, and a load of depression ; it belongs to a Cowper, who died in despair, as well as to a Hervey, who said, " Lord, now lettest thou Thy servant depart in peace, according to Thy word ; for mine eyes have seen Thy salvation." All believers die safely ; there is no curse for them after death, or in death. In this sense, their end is peace ; peace in the result, if not in the passage. But their end is generally peace in experience as well as in result. There are, however, cases of constitutional infirmity that may not only exclude joy, but even hope. Sometimes the nature of the disorder is such as to hinder sensibility, or expression. Sometimes, too, God may allow the continuance of fear, even in those He loves, as a rebuke for loose or irregular walking ; and as a warning to others. 6. He will do this absolutely. He will abolish the very state : " He must reign till He hath put all enemies under His feet. The last enemy that shall be destroyed is death." (*W. Jay.*) *Death abolished :*—I. That we may feel the true impression of this Divine declaration, it will be necessary first to show WHAT IT IS NOT INTENDED TO TEACH. The state of fact, no less than the express averments of Holy Writ, forbid us to entertain the thought, that the appearing of our Saviour Jesus Christ has arrested the progress of that law of mortality which followed in the train of disobedience. Our present relations are formed but to be dissolved ; death, like a canker worm, preys at the root of all our comforts. We " have here no continuing city " ; and soon " the place that now knows us shall know us no more for ever." Philosophy may attempt to solve this mysterious problem ; may tell us that mortality is a law of our nature ; may point us to the analogies of creation around us. But withdraw from our view the inspired record which connects death with Adam's sin, and which exhibits it in the light of a penalty entailed upon transgression, and philosophy has no satisfactory reason to assign for a catastrophe so overwhelming and so universal. It may, indeed, affirm the state of fact, and argue from thence that it is the nature of man that he should die ; but how much more satisfactory is the philosophy of Scripture (which no sound philosophy ought to exclude), which tells us that man was made for life, that death is the forfeit of disobedience, and that but for sin the struggle of mortality would never have been beheld in our world ! II. In our text we are taught to look upon death as in some practical SENSE A VANQUISHED FOE ; and since it cannot be in the sense of staying its inexorable reign in our world, it becomes us to show the true and only sense in which it can be affirmed that " our Saviour Jesus Christ hath abolished death." The expression is very remarkable ; and the doctrine it contains is animating in the highest degree to all who embrace it with a realising faith. The idea conveyed by the original word is that of such an effectual counteraction of death, as involves a complete victory over it. 1. When the apostle asserts that " Christ hath abolished death," we must understand him, first of all, as proclaiming Christ's own personal victory over it. 2. But we must not forget that the victory which our Saviour Jesus Christ achieved in His own person over death was intimately connected with the nature and ends of that " decease which He accomplished at Jerusalem." Death, we must never forget, entered our world as the mark of apostasy, as the penalty of transgression ; if ever, then, it was to be " abolished," it must be by some dispensation which should effectually provide for the remission of sin, and for the restoration of apostate man to the favour and image of his God. In the hour of Messiah's deep agony, "the Lord laid on Him the iniquity of us all " ; and when with His last breath He exclaimed, " It is finished," the mighty work was then performed upon which depended the reconciliation to peace and life of untold millions of the human race. Having " finished the work which the Father gave Him to do," met every demand which devolved upon Him as the sinner's Surety, it was impossible, upon all the principles of the Divine government, upon all the arrangements of covenanted love, that He should be holden of the bands of death. 3. When the apostle asserts that "our Saviour Jesus Christ hath abolished death" we may assure ourselves that the real members of His body, all true Christians, will share His own triumph. Of this joyful fact there is a series of progressive evidence. The moment that any sinner is quickened to spiritual life, he is "quickened together with Christ," and is brought to feel in that conversion "the power of His resurrection and the fellowship of His sufferings," and is "made conformable unto His death." 4. The next stage of the proof that death shall be abolished will be supplied when believers are "absent from the body and present with the Lord." The fruition of the celestial paradise will divest them of every doubt or misgiving as to the resurrection of their mortal bodies. Every time they gaze on the glorified humanity of Him in whose presence they stand they will exult in the thought of that mighty exercise of power and love which shall quicken their tabernacles of clay, and unite them as spiritual bodies to their emancipated and happy spirits. They are waiting in glorious hope "for the adoption, to wit, the redemption of their bodies"; and, having received the first-fruits, they are looking forward to the harvest of the earth, when the number of God's elect shall be accomplished, and when all the objects of celestial hope shall be fully realised. At last the bright moment of perfected bliss shall arrive when death shall be literally "abolished"; when all the regions of mortality shall be divested of their spoils; when the whole redeemed Church shall stand complete in her glorified Head; when all shall be perfectly conformed in body and soul to the image of Him who is "the first-born among many brethren." 5. But there is one view of this subject which yet remains to be taken by us: it is the proof which is so often afforded of the truth of the apostle's declaration that death is "abolished," in the feelings with which departing saints are often enabled to look forward to their great change. Some there are, indeed, of God's servants who "through fear of death are all their lifetime subject to bondage"; their minds are perplexed with doubts and fears, and they cannot realise their title to the everlasting inheritance. But it is matter of great joy and thankfulness when faith is triumphant in the dying moment; when it can sing with an unfaltering tongue, "O death, where is thy sting," thy boasted sting? "O grave, where is thy victory? The sting of death is sin, and the strength of sin is the law; but thanks be to God, which giveth us the victory through our Lord Jesus Christ." (*J. Morison, D.D.*) *Death abolished:*—The question is, therefore, in what sense hath death been abolished by Christ. It means that He hath made death of none effect. In order to explain this we lay down three propositions. I. THAT THE FELT POWER OF DEATH OVER MAN IS ACCORDING TO THE STATE OF HIS SOUL. The power of death over man is not in the unconsciousness which he produces. So far as unconsciousness is concerned there is death in every sleep. Not in the dissolution it produces. For physical dissolution is going on every day in the body. Where then is the power of death? It is in the state of our souls in relation to it. Let us suppose that we had no capacity for forming any idea of death. What power would death have over us? None until it came; like the beast or the bird we should lie down on the green turf, and breathe out our last breath without one regretful or apprehensive thought. Or, let us suppose that we had ideas concerning death, all of which were of a pleasing character. What power would death have over us in this case? None. We should rejoice in it. II. THAT THE STATE OF A DEPRAVED MAN'S SOUL GIVES DEATH ITS FELT POWER. 1. All the affections of his soul are confined to earthly objects. All men whose natures are unchristianised love the world and the things of the world. All they love, all they plan and toil and hope for, are here. 2. He has terrible forebodings as to the consequence of death to him. III. THAT CHRIST HATH ABOLISHED THIS DEPRAVED STATE OF SOUL IN HIS DISCIPLES. How does He accomplish this? Not merely by the revelation of a future life, but by the impartation of a new spiritual life—a life of conscious pardon and of spiritual sympathy. This new life—1. Has a stronger sympathy with the spiritual than the material. The affections are set not on things below, but on things above. Hence, where is the dread of death to the true Christian? This new life—2. Has a stronger sympathy with the future than the present. Christ turns the hearts of His people to the future as their heaven. Who, therefore, would dread the dawn of the future into which the heart has gone? This new life—3. Has a stronger sympathy with the Infinite Father than with any other object. Christ sets the heart of His disciple upon the Infinite Father. Can death or any other event fill him with dread who loves the Infinite supremely? From this subject we learn—(1) The value of Christianity. (2) The test of godliness. (*D. Thomas, D.D.*) *The victor vanquished:*—We have here—1. An agent referred to by the word "Who," that is Jesus Christ. 2. We have a work which He has done—"abolished death." 3. A glorious disclosure which He has made, "brought life and immortality to light." 4. The means by which this revelation is made known—"the gospel." I. THE AGENT. When men have an important work to do, it is of great consequence to find a properly qualified person to do it. The Lord Jesus Christ possessed all the requisite qualifications for the great work of atoning for sins and reconciling man to God, since He was both God and man. Not merely that men might be pardoned and set free, but that they might be restored to the favour of God, and the long interrupted harmony and union between God and man re-established. II. Now let us glance at WHAT HE HAS DONE—"abolished death" (Rom. v. 12). But there is a threefold division of death: Temporal, or the death of the body; spiritual, or being dead to spiritual things; and eternal death, or the separation of soul and body from God for ever. Death is represented as a sovereign exercising dominion over the world, for it is said "death reigned from Adam to Moses, even over them that had not sinned after the similitude of Adam's transgressions." "Death reigned," says the apostle. The figure is a bold and striking one. It represents Death as a monarch exercising dominion or power. His reign is absolute. He strikes whom and where he pleases, there is no escape. All must bow beneath his sceptre. His reign is universal. Old and young, rich and poor, high and low, are alike the subjects of his gloomy empire, and but for the gospel, his reign would be eternal. The dominion of the gloomy tyrant has been shattered, and death itself has, as our text says, been abolished. Its terrors are abated and its sting removed. We come to consider how, and in what measure, this has been done. What is it to abolish anything? It is to cause it to cease, to put an end to it. Thus slavery was abolished in the British Empire and the United States. Its abolition cost Britain much, and cost the United States thousands of lives and millions of money. This whole accursed system of man-stealing, and all the horrors connected with it, is wiped out and destroyed. So has the Lord Jesus done with death. He has destroyed the stern tyrant by destroying that which is the cause of death—sin (Heb. ii. 9). Thus death was destroyed by dying; by His becoming obedient to the death of the Cross, He broke the empire and dominion of death for ever, and opened to man "the door of eternal life" and His resurrection was proof that God's justice was completely satisfied with the ransom offered. "Who hath abolished death." The apostle here seems to speak in some measure by anticipation. Sometimes the sacred writers represent things which are certain to be done as if they were done already. Sin, which is the cause of death, has been atoned for, and so death's empire has there received a fatal blow. Every evil habit, desire, and disposition overcome, every temptation to evil successfully resisted, every good word and work, all tend to lessen his power and wrest from Death his dominion. Thus life has prevailed over death so far as the gospel has made its way into the homes and hearts of men. So in various ways and on every side death has been losing his sway, and his empire is waning. Nowhere is the fact that death has been abolished seen in a clearer light than in the triumphant departure of God's children. Dr. Payson, a little before he breathed his last, said, "The battle's fought, the battle's fought, and the victory is won—won for ever. I am going to bathe in an ocean of purity and benevolence, and happiness to all eternity." "Why should I murmur," said John Howard, the noble Christian philanthropist, when ending his journey in a strange land, "Heaven is as near to Russia as it is to England." "My head is in heaven" (said the wife of Philip Henry, the Commentator); "my heart is in heaven, another step and I shall be there too." "Almost well, and nearly at home," said the saintly Richard Baxter, when asked by a friend how he did shortly before he died. And a lady, describing the last hours of that venerable patriarch of science, Sir David Brewster, says, "The sight was a cordial from heaven to me. I believed before, but now I have seen that Christ has truly abolished death." III. Now observe THE NEXT THING CHRIST HAS DONE FOR US. He has "brought life and immortality to light through the gospel." (*J. Reid.*)   *Of the immortality of the soul as discovered by nature and by revelation:*—In the handling of these words I shall—I. OPEN TO YOU THE MEANING OF THE SEVERAL EXPRESSIONS IN THE TEXT. 1. What is here meant by "the appearing of our Saviour Jesus Christ"? The Scripture useth several phrases to express this thing to us. As it was the voluntary undertaking of God the Son, so it is called His coming into the world. In relation to His incarnation, whereby He was made visible to us in His body, and likewise in reference to the obscure promises and prophecies and types of the Old Testament, it is called

His manifestation, or appearance. 2. What is meant by the abolishing of death. By this we are not to understand that Christ, by His appearance, hath rooted death out of the world, so that men are no longer subject to it. 3. What is here meant by bringing "life and immortality to light." Life and immortality is here by a frequent Hebraism put for immortal life; as also, immediately before the text, you find purpose and grace put for God's gracious purpose. The phrase of bringing to light is spoken of things which were before each either wholly or in a great measure hid, either were not at all discovered before, or not so clearly. I proceed—II. TO SHOW WHAT CHRIST'S COMING INTO THE WORLD HATH DONE TOWARDS THE ABOLISHING OF DEATH, AND THE BRINGING OF "LIFE AND IMMORTALITY TO LIGHT." I shall speak distinctly to these two: 1. What Christ's appearance and coming into the world hath done towards the abolishing of death, or how death is abolished by the appearance of Christ. (1) By taking our nature upon Him He became subject to the frailties and miseries of mortality, and liable to the suffering of death, by which expiation of sin was made. (2) As Christ, by taking our nature upon Him, became capable of suffering death, and thereby making expiation for sin, so by dying He became capable of rising again from the dead, whereby He hath gained a perfect victory and conquest over death and the powers of darkness. 2. What Christ hath done towards the bringing of "life and immortality to light." It will be requisite to inquire, What assurance men had or might have had of the immortality of the soul, and consequently of a future state, before the revelation of the gospel by Christ's coming into the world. And here are two things distinctly to be considered. What arguments natural reason doth furnish us withal to persuade us to this principle, that our souls are immortal, and consequently that another state remains for men after this life. But before I come to speak particularly to the arguments which natural reason affords us for the proof of this principle, I shall premise certain general considerations, which may give light and force to the following arguments: By the soul we mean a part of man distinct from his body, or a principle in him which is not matter. By the immortality of the soul I mean nothing else, but that it survives the body, that when the body dies and falls to the ground, yet this principle, which we call the soul, still remains and lives separate from it. That he that goes about to prove the soul's immortality supposeth the existence of a Deity, that there is a God. The existence of a God being supposed, this doth very much facilitate the other, of the soul's immortality. For this being an essential property of that Divine nature, that He is a Spirit, that is, something that is not matter; it being granted that God is, thus much is gained, that there is such a thing as a spirit, an immaterial substance, that is not liable to die or perish. It is highly reasonable that men should acquiesce and rest satisfied in such reasons and arguments for the proof of any thing, as the nature of the thing to be proved will bear; because there are several kinds and degrees of evidence, which all things are not equally capable of. Having premised these general considerations to clear my way, I now come to speak to the particular arguments whereby the immortality of the soul may be made out to our reason. And the best way to estimate the force of the arguments which I shall bring for it will be to consider beforehand with ourselves what evidence we can, in reason, expect for a thing of this nature. (1) That the thing be a natural notion and dictate of our minds. (2) That it doth not contradict any other principle that nature hath planted in us, but does very well accord and agree with all other the most natural notions of our minds. (3) That it be suitable to our natural fears and hopes. (4) That it tends to the happiness of man, and the good order and government of the world. (5) That it gives the most rational account of all those inward actions which we are conscious to ourselves of, as perception, understanding, memory, will, which we cannot, without great unreasonableness, ascribe to matter as the cause of them. If all these be thus, as I shall endeavour to make it appear they are, what greater satisfaction could we desire to have of the immortality of our souls than these arguments give us? 1. The immortality of the soul is very agreeable to the natural notion which we have of God, one part whereof is, that He is essentially good and just. (1) For His goodness. It is very agreeable to that to think that God would make some creatures for as long a duration as they are capable of. (2) It is very agreeable to the justice of God to think the souls of men remain after this life, that there may be a state of reward and recompense in another world. 2. Another notion which is deeply rooted in the nature of man is, that there is a difference between good and evil, which is not founded in the imagination of persons, or in the custom and usage of the world, but in the nature of things. To come then to my purpose, it is very agreeable to this natural notion of the difference between good and evil, to believe the soul's immortality. For nothing is more reasonable to imagine than that good and evil, as they are differenced in their nature, so they shall be in their rewards; that it shall one time or other be well to them that do well, and evil to the wicked man. III. This principle, of the soul's immortality, is suitable to the natural hopes and fears of men. To the natural hopes of men. Whence is it that men are so desirous to purchase a lasting fame, and to perpetuate their memory to posterity, but that they hope that there is something belonging to them which shall survive the fate of the body, and when that lies in the silent grave shall be sensible of the honour which is done to their memory, and shall enjoy the pleasure of the just and impartial fame, which shall speak of them to posterity without envy or flattery? IV. This doctrine of the immortality of the soul does evidently tend to the happiness and perfection of man, and to the good order and government of the world. This doctrine tends to the happiness of man considered in society, to the good order and government of the world. If this principle were banished out of the world, government would want its most firm basis and foundation; there would be infinitely more disorders in the world were men not restrained from injustice and violence by principles of conscience, and the awe of another world. And that this is so, is evident from hence, that all magistrates think themselves concerned to cherish religion, and to maintain in the minds of men the belief of a God, and of a future state. V. The fifth and last argument is, That this supposition of the soul's immortality gives the fairest account and easiest solution of the phenomena of human nature, of those several actions and operations which we are conscious to ourselves of, and which, without great violence to our reason, cannot be resolved into a bodily principle, and ascribed to mere matter; such are perception, memory, liberty, and the several acts of understanding and reason. These operations we find in ourselves, and we cannot imagine how they should be performed by mere matter; therefore we ought, in all reason, to resolve them into some principle of another nature from matter, that is, into something that is immaterial, and consequently immortal, that is incapable in its own nature of corruption and dissolution. I come now to the second thing I propounded, which is to show what assurance the world had, de facto, of this great principle of religion, the soul's immortality, before the revelation of the gospel. First, what assurance the heathens had of the soul's immortality. 1. It is evident that there was a general inclination in mankind, even after its greatest corruption and degeneracy, to the belief of this principle; which appears in that all people and nations of the world, after they were sunk into the greatest degeneracy, and all (except only the Jews) became idolaters, did universally agree in this apprehension, that their souls did remain after their bodies and pass into a state of happiness or misery, according as they had demeaned themselves in this life. 2. The unlearned and common people among the heathen seem to have had the truest and least wavering apprehensions in this matter; the reason of which seems to be plain, because their belief followed the bias and inclination of their nature, and they had not their natural notions embroiled and disordered by obscure and uncertain reasonings about it, as the philosophers had, whose understandings were prefixed with infinite niceties and objections, which never troubled the heads of the common people. 3. The learned among the heathen did not so generally agree in this principle, and those who did consent in it were many of them more wavering and unsettled than the common people. Epicurus and his followers were peremptory in the denial of it: but, by their own acknowledgment, they did herein offer great violence to their natures, and had much ado to divest themselves of the contrary apprehension and fears. The stoics were very inclinable to the belief of a future state; but yet they almost everywhere speak very doubtfully of it. Secondly, What assurance the Jews had of the soul's immortality and a future state. And of this I shall give you an account in these following particulars: 1. They had all the assurance which natural light, and the common reason of mankind, does ordinarily afford men concerning this matter; they had common to them with the heathens all the advantage that nature gives men to come to the knowledge of this truth. 2. They had by Divine revelation a fuller assurance of those truths which have a nearer connection with this principle, and which do very much tend to facilitate the belief of it; as, namely, concerning the providence of God, and His interesting Himself particularly in the affairs of the world. And then, besides this, the Jews had assurance of the existence of spirits by the more immediate ministry of angels among them. And this does directly make way for the belief of an immaterial principle, and consequently of the soul's immortality.

3. There were some remarkable instances of the Old Testament which did tend very much to persuade men to this truth: I mean the instances of Enoch and Elias, who did not die like other men, but were translated, and taken up into heaven in an extraordinary manner. 4. This was typified and shadowed forth to them by the legal administrations. The whole economy of their worship and temple, of their rites and ceremonies, and Sabbaths, did shadow out some farther thing to them, though in a very obscure manner: the land of Canaan, and their coming to the possession of it, after so many years' travail in the wilderness, did represent that heavenly inheritance which good men should be possessed of after the troubles of this life. But I shall chiefly insist on the general promises which we find in these books of Moses, of God's blessing good men, and declaring that He was their God, even after their death. 5. Toward the expiration of the legal dispensation there was yet a clearer revelation of a future state. The text in Daniel seems to be much plainer than any in the Old Testament: "And many of them that sleep in the dust of the earth shall awake; some to everlasting life, and some to shame and everlasting contempt" (Dan. xii. 2). 6. Notwithstanding this, I say that the immortality of the soul, and a future state, was not expressly and clearly revealed in the Old Testament, at least not in Moses' law. The special and particular promises of that dispensation were of temporal good things; and the great blessing of eternal life was but somewhat obscurely involved and signified in the types and general promises. And so I proceed to the second thing I propounded, which is to show what farther evidence and assurance the gospel gives us of it than the world had before: what clearer discoveries we have by Christ's coming, than the heathens or Jews had before. 1. The rewards of another life are more clearly revealed in the gospel. 2. The rewards of another life, as they are clearly and expressly revealed by the gospel, so that they may have the greater power and influence upon us, and we may have the greater assurance of them, they are revealed with very particular circumstances. 3. The gospel gives us yet farther assurance of these things by such an argument as is like to be the most convincing and satisfactory to common capacities; and that is, by a lively instance of the thing to be proved, in raising Christ from the dead (Acts xvii. 30, 31). 4. And lastly, the effects which the clear discovery of this truth had upon the world are such as the world never saw before, and are a farther inducement to persuade us of the truth and reality of it. After the gospel was entertained in the world, to show that those who embraced it did fully believe this principle, and were abundantly satisfied concerning the rewards and happiness of another life, they did, for the sake of their religion, despise this life and all the enjoyments of it, from a thorough persuasion of a far greater happiness than this world could afford remaining in the next life. (*J. Tillotson, D.D.*)
*Life and immortality brought to light by the gospel:*—But, supposing Moses or the law of nature to afford evidence for a future life and immortality, it remains to be considered in what sense the words of the text are to be understood, which do affirm that life and immortality were brought to light through the gospel. To bring any thing to light may signify, according to the idiom of the English tongue, to discover or reveal a thing which was perfectly unknown before: but the word in the original is so far from countenancing, that it will hardly admit of this sense, φωτίζειν signifies (not to bring to light, but) to enlighten, illustrate, or clear up anything. You may judge by the use of the word in other places: 'tis used in John i. 9—"That was the true light which lighteth [or enlighteneth] every man that cometh into the world." Jesus Christ did not by coming into the world bring men to light; but He did by the gospel enlighten men, and make those who were dark and ignorant before wise even to salvation. In like manner our Lord did enlighten the doctrine of life and immortality, not by giving the first or only notice of it, but by clearing up the doubts and difficulties under which it laboured, and giving a better evidence for the truth and certainty of it, than nature or any revelation before had done. If we consider how our Saviour has enlightened this doctrine, it will appear that He has removed the difficulty at which nature stumbled. As death was no part of the state of nature, so the difficulties arising from it were not provided for in the religion of nature. To remove these was the proper work of revelation. These our Lord has effectually cleared by His gospel, and shown us that the body may and shall be united to the spirit in the day of the Lord, so that the complete man shall stand before the great Tribunal to receive a just recompense of reward for the things done in the body. (*T. Sherlock, D.D.*) *Immortality brought to light:*—I. OUR LORD HATH GIVEN US A CLEARER KNOWLEDGE THAN WITHOUT HIM WE COULD EVER HAVE ACQUIRED OF OUR STATE AFTER DEATH. For, first, the best arguments which human reason suggests for the

immortality of the soul are founded upon right notions of God and of morality. But before the gospel was revealed the common people among the Gentiles had low and imperfect notions of these important truths, and consequently they were not persuaded upon good grounds of their future existence. The proofs of the soul's immortality, which are taken from its own nature, from its simplicity, spirituality, and inward activity, are by no means to be despised, they have much probability, and they never were or will be confuted. The moral arguments, as they are called, in behalf of the soul's immortality, as they are more familiar and intelligible, so are they more satisfactory. Now, it cannot be supposed that God, who is perfectly wise, would endue the soul of man with a capacity of well-doing, and of perpetual improvement, unless He intended it for other purposes than to live here for a very short space, and then perish for ever. He did not create the sun to shine for one day, and the moon to shine for one night, and then to be turned out of being. These sort of arguments, obvious and persuasive as they are, yet were usually overlooked in the Pagan world ; polytheism, vice, and ignorance had made men insensible of their force; these arguments shone forth along with Christianity, and were in a great measure owing to the gospel. They who argued justly enough to conclude from the nature of God and of man that it was reasonable to believe the immortality of the soul, and to hope that a future state of happiness should be the reward of a well-spent life, yet could not hence fairly draw any conclusions to their own full satisfaction. Many who believed the immortality of souls believed also a continual and successive removal of souls from one body to another, and no fixed state of permanent happiness. Our Lord hath opened to us a better prospect than this, promising us an incorruptible body, a life that shall not be taken from us, an unchangeable state, and a house eternal in the heavens. Some who in words acknowledged the immortality of the soul seem in reality to have taken it away, by imagining that the human soul was a part of the great soul of the world, of the Deity, and that upon its separation from the body it was reunited to it. 1. The gospel assures us that we shall rise again. 2. We are assured that the happiness of the good shall be complete, unchangeable, and endless. 3. We have also reason, from some places of Scripture, to suppose that the souls of the good are not deprived of thought, but are in a place of peace and contentment during their separation from the body. II. THE SECOND THING WHICH WE PROPOSED TO PROVE IS, THAT CHRIST, BY HIS RESURRECTION, HATH FULLY ASSURED US THAT HE CAN AND WILL RAISE UP HIS SERVANTS TO ETERNAL LIFE. If it be certain that Christ arose from the dead, the consequence is plain and unavoidable that the religion taught by Him is true. I have only a few inferences to lay before you. 1. Our Lord hath taught us that our souls are immortal. 2. Our Lord hath taught us that death is only the death or sleep of the body, that the souls of the good live to God, and that at the last day, when He shall appear, they shall be clothed with immortal and glorified bodies, and dwell for ever with Him. And to confirm these truths, He arose Himself in power and splendour, and became the first fruits of them that sleep. 3. The resurrection of Christ contains in it the strongest motives to cast off our sins, and to prepare ourselves for the glories which shall be revealed, and to take off our affections from this world, and to set them on things above. (*J. Jortin, D.D.*) *Life and immortality brought to light by the gospel :*—By the plain revelation of this state of immortality—1. Is most illustriously manifested to us the transcendent goodness and indulgence of our most merciful Creator, in that He will be pleased to reward such imperfect services, such mean performances as the best of ours are, with glory so immense, as that eye hath not seen, nor ear heard, nor can it enter into the heart of man to conceive the greatness of it. 2. By this revelation of immortal life is farther demonstrated the exceeding great love of our blessed Saviour, who, by His death and perfect obedience, not only purchased pardon for all our past rebellions and transgressions, not only redeemed us from hell and destruction, to which we had all rendered ourselves most justly liable, which alone had been an unspeakable favour, but also merited an everlasting kingdom of glory for us, if with true repentance we return to our duty. 3. This especially recommends our Christianity to us, which contains such glad tidings, which propounds such mighty arguments to engage us to our duty, such as no other religion ever did or could. I. TO THOSE WHO WOULD SEEM TO DOUBT OF THIS FUNDAMENTAL DOCTRINE OF A FUTURE LIFE. II. TO THOSE WHO PROFESS TO BELIEVE IT, BUT NOT FULLY AND HEARTILY. III. TO THOSE WHO DO REALLY AND CONSTANTLY BELIEVE IT. I. Let us for once be so kind to the sceptical disputers against religion as to suppose what they are never able to prove—that it is a very doubtful thing whether there will be another life after this. We ought to believe and live as if all these doctrines of religion were most certainly true ; for every wise man will run as little hazard as he can, especially in such things as are of the highest concernment to him, and wherein a mistake would be fatal and undoing. II. To those who profess to believe this immortal life, but yet do it not really and heartily. And this I fear is the case of the generality of Christians amongst us. Are any of those good things which men here court and seek after so desirable and considerable as the glories and joys of heaven ? Or are there any evils in this world that can vie terrors with hell ? III. To those who do heartily and constantly believe this great truth of another life after this ; who not only assent to this doctrine with their understandings, but have made this future happiness their ultimate choice and desire. This will fortify our minds against all the temptations we may meet with from this world, or any of its bewitching enjoyments. This faith will inspire us with strength and activity, and carry us out even beyond ourselves ; will animate us with such courage and resolution, as that we shall despise all dangers and difficulties, and think eternal happiness a good bargain, whatever pains or trouble it may cost us to purchase it. This conquers the love of life itself, which is most deeply implanted in our natures ; for what will not a man give or part with for the saving of his life ? Yet they who have been endued with this faith have not counted their lives dear to Him, so that they might finish their course with joy. This faith by degrees moulds and transforms the mind into a likeness to these heavenly objects ; it advances and raises our spirits, so that they become truly great and noble, and make us, as St. Peter tells us, partakers of a divine nature. It filleth the soul with constant peace and satisfaction, so that in all conditions of life a good man can feast himself with unseen joys and delights, which the worldly man neither knows nor can relish. Nay, this faith arms a man against the fear of death ; it strips that king of terrors of all his grim looks : for he considers it only as God's messenger to knock off his fetters, to free him from this fleshly prison, and to conduct him to that blessed place, where he shall be more happy than he can wish or desire to be, and that for ever. (*Dr. Callamy.*)     *Life and immortality revealed in the gospel :*—Life and immortality here seem to refer both to the soul and the body, the two constituents of our person. As applied to the body, life and immortality signify that though our bodies are dissolved at death, and return into their native elements, yet they shall be formed anew with vast improvements, and raised to an immortal existence : so that they shall be as though death never had had any power over them ; and thus death shall be abolished, annihilated, and all traces of the ruins it had made for ever disappear, as though they had never been. It is in this sense chiefly that the word "immortality," or "incorruptibility" is made use of in my text. But then the resurrection of the body supposes the perpetual existence of the soul, for whose sake it is raised ; therefore life and immortality, as referring to the soul, signify that it is immortal, in a strict and proper sense ; that is, that it cannot die at all, or be dissolved like the body. In this complex sense we may understand the immortality of which my text speaks. Now it is to the gospel that we owe the clear discovery of immortality in both these senses. As for the resurrection of the dead, which confers a kind of immortality upon our mortal bodies, it is altogether the discovery of Divine revelation. As for the immortality of the soul, Christian philosophers find it no difficulty to establish it upon the plain principles of reason. But it should be considered that those are not the arguments of the populace, the bulk of mankind, but of a few philosophic studious men. But as immortality is the prerogative of all mankind, of the ignorant and illiterate, as well as of the wise and learned, all mankind, of all ranks of understanding, are equally concerned in the doctrine of immortality ; and therefore a common revelation was necessary, which would teach the ploughman and mechanic, as well as the philosopher, that he was formed for an immortal existence, and, consequently, that it is his grand concern to fit himself for a happiness beyond the grave as lasting as his nature. Now, it is the gospel alone that makes this important discovery plain and obvious to all. It must also be considered that men may be able to demonstrate a truth, when the hint is but once given, which they would never have discovered, nor perhaps suspected, without that hint. Persons may be assisted in their searches by the light of revelation ; but, being accustomed to it, they may mistake it for the light of their own reason ; or they may not be so honest and humble as to acknowledge the assistance they have received. The surest way to know what mere unassisted reason can do is to inquire what it has actually done in those sages of the heathen world who had no other guide, and in whom it was carried to the highest degree of improvement. Now we find, in fact, that though some philosophers had plausibilities and presumptions that their souls should exist after the dissolution of their bodies, yet that they rather supposed, or wished, or thought it probable, than firmly believed it upon good evidence. What a vast inheritance is this, unalienably entailed upon every child of Adam! What importance, what value, does this consideration give to that neglected thing the soul! What an awful being is it! Immortality! The highest angel, if the creature of a day or of a thousand years, what would he be? A fading flower, a vanishing vapour, a flying shadow. When his day or his thousand years are past, he is as truly nothing as if he had never been. It is little matter what becomes of him: let him stand or fall, let him be happy or miserable, it is just the same in a little time; he is gone, and there is no more of him—no traces of him left. But an immortal! a creature that shall never, never, never cease to be! that shall expand his capacities of action, of pleasure, or pain, through an everlasting duration! what an awful, important being is this! And is my soul—this little spark of reason in my breast—is that such a being? I tremble at myself. I revere my own dignity, and am struck with a kind of pleasing horror to view what I must be. And is there anything so worthy of the care of such a being as the happiness, the everlasting happiness, of my immortal part? (*S. Davies, A.M.*) *Immortality brought to light by the gospel:*—Let us first advert to what may be called the physical state, and then to the moral state of the mind; and under each head let us endeavour to contrast the insufficiency of the light of nature with the sufficiency and fulness of the light of the gospel. I. An argument for its immortality has been drawn from the consideration of what we should term the physics of the mind—that is, from the consideration of its properties, when it is regarded as having a separate or substantive being of its own. For example, it has been said that spirit is not matter, and therefore must be imperishable. We confess that we see not the force of this reasoning. We are not sure by nature of the premises; and neither do we apprehend how the conclusion flows from it. Now, in the recorded fact of our Saviour's resurrection, we see what many would call a more popular, but what we should deem a far more substantial and satisfactory, argument for the soul's immortality than any that is furnished by the speculation which we have now alluded to. To us the one appears as much superior to the other, as history is more solid than hypothesis, or as experience is of a texture more firm than imagination, or as the philosophy of our modern Bacon is of a surer and sounder character than the philosophy of the old schoolmen. Let it be remarked that the word which we render "abolished" signifies also "made of no effect." The latter interpretation of the word is certainly more applicable to our first or our temporal death. He has not abolished temporal death. It still reigns with unmitigated violence, and sweeps off its successive generations with as great sureness and rapidity as ever. This part of the sentence is not abolished, but is rendered ineffectual. II. But another argument for the immortality of man has been drawn by philosophers from the moral state of his mind; and more especially from that progressive expansion which they affirm it to have undergone in respect of its virtues as well as of its powers. Still we fear that, in respect of this argument too, the flowery description of the moralists has no proof, and more particularly no experience to support it. Yes! we have heard them talk, and with eloquence too, of the good man and of his prospects; of his progress in life being a splendid career of virtue, and of his death being a gentle transition to another and a better world; of its being the goal where he reaps the honourable reward that is due to his accomplishments, or being little more than a step in his proud march to eternity. This is all very fine, but it is the fineness of poetry. Where is the evidence of its being any better than a deceitful imagination? Death gives the lie to all the speculations of all the moralists; but it only gives evidence and consistency to the statements of the gospel. The doctrines of the New Testament will bear to be confronted with the rough and vigorous lessons of experience. They attempt no ornament and no palliation. I cannot trust the physician who plays upon the surface of my disease, and throws over it the disguise of false colouring. I have more confidence to put in him who, like Christ the Physician of my soul, has looked the malady fairly in the face—has taken it up in all its extent, and in all its soreness—has resolved it into its original principles—has probed it to the very bottom, and has set himself forward to combat with the radical elements of the disease. This is what the Saviour has done with death. He has plucked it of its sting. He has taken a full survey of the corruption, and met it in every one quarter where its malignity operates. It was sin which constituted the virulence in the disease, and He hath extracted it. He hath expiated the sentence; and the believer, rejoicing in the assurance that all is clear with God, serves Him without fear in righteousness and in holiness all the days of his life. (*T. Chalmers, D.D.*) *Life and immortality brought to light by the gospel :*—I. FIRST LET US CONSIDER THE EVIDENCE WHICH THE WORLD HAD FOR THIS DOCTRINE PRIOR TO THE ADVENT OF CHRIST. The general and continued prevalence of this opinion, even admitting it to have originated in revelation, must be traced ultimately to the natural sentiments of the human heart. We are all naturally desirous of immortality. We naturally love our being, and of consequence naturally desire its continuance. The thought of being reduced into nothing is revolting to a rational soul. Numerous considerations tend to give it a rational support, and to some of these suffer me to direct your attention. 1. I observe that the very nature of the human soul itself, so far as we are capable of comprehending it, affords a strong presumption in favour of its immortality. It is perfectly distinct and essentially different from the earthly tabernacle in which it is enshrined; for we know that it thinks and acts independently of the body, and even when the body is at rest. 2. So far is this from being the case, that there is a strong probability, arising from the analogy of nature, of the continuance of our existence after the great change of death has passed upon us. All nature dies to live again. 3. This anticipation is still further confirmed by a consideration of man as a moral and accountable being. 4. If, from considering man, we turn our attention to God, whose creatures we are, and of whose government we are the subjects, the evidence in favour of immortality rises still further in its importance and strength. These evidences, however, are not to be represented, as has been done by some, as of so decisive and complete a character as to supersede the necessity of Divine revelation. To be convinced of this, we need only consider the case of those sages of the heathen world, who had no other light than that of unassisted reason to guide them. We find many of the best and greatest amongst them filled with doubts and perplexities on the subject. Brutus, a man of rigid and stoical virtue, was, by the principles of his sect, an assertor of a future state; but, finding his own cause and that of his friends unsuccessful, he sunk into despair, and, in the immediate prospect of his departure, made this extraordinary exclamation: "I have worshipped virtue as the supreme good, but have found it to be only an idol and a name." Socrates, who was confessedly the brightest character in the heathen world, seems to have possessed much clearer views of immortality than any other individual among the Greek philosophers. Yet even his opinions are not delivered without much hesitation and doubt, and are far from being either uniform or consistent. At one time we find him affirming it to have been his deliberate opinion, after the most dispassionate inquiry, that the good and wise had every reasonable hope of happiness in a future state of existence. And yet this conviction, though he distinctly avows it, was not so firmly settled in his own mind as to prevent him taking his last leave of his friends by these most impressive words: "It is time that I should go away to die, and that ye should return to the active business of life. Whether you or I have the better portion, is known only to the immortal gods, but I think cannot be known with certainty by any individual man." Cicero, though one of the most enlightened men of all antiquity, and one that wrote more on this subject than any other individual, yet seems to have no settled or deliberate opinion with regard to it; and, in one particular passage, in which he refers to the perplexing and contrary views entertained by philosophers, we find him declaring: "But of these doctrines which is to be received as true, some god must declare unto us; which is the more probable even, is extremely doubtful." II. Let us now examine THE SUPERIOR EVIDENCE WHICH THE GOSPEL GIVES US ON THIS SUBJECT. 1. In the gospel we have an express confirmation of the hope of nature, that the souls of men survive the dissolution of their bodies, and continue capable of exercising those powers and faculties which are essential to them. 2. Besides assuring us of the continued existence and consciousness of the spirit after death, the gospel informs us that the tabernacle of clay in which it was lodged, but which now lies mouldering in the dust of the earth, shall in due time be raised up in unfading life and activity, and re-united to its former spirit. 3. We are further assured in the gospel that the grand event of the resurrection will be the introduction to a state of retribution, which will admit of neither termination nor change. 4. While the gospel thus reveals to us a future state of inconceivable and endless bliss, it at the same time clearly points out the only certain way in which we can attain to the enjoyment of it. (*P. Grant.*)

*Death abolished, and life and immortality brought to light:*—In discoursing upon these words, it shall be my endeavour to show what Jesus Christ has effected—I. IN HIS OWN PERSON. Referring to the text, we find mention made of " Jesus Christ, who hath abolished death." It will, I doubt not, be readily admitted that, if the cause be removed, the resulting effects must necessarily cease. What, then, is the cause of death? It is a melancholy and humiliating reflection that man—the lord of this lower world, the vicegerent of the great Supreme on earth—should die, as do the brutes over whom he holds a delegated sway. Yet it is not more melancholy and humiliating than it is true—" His life is but as a vapour that appeareth for a little time, and then vanisheth away." Yet it was not always so. The mortality of man is the direful effect of sin. And when it is stated that Jesus Christ " hath abolished death," it cannot mean that we are consequently exempt from paying the debt of our fallen nature. By no means; " it is appointed unto all men once to die." The most merciless tyrants have, at some particular seasons, shown signs of a merciful and yielding disposition; and the tears of imploring loveliness have pierced even their hard and cruel hearts. But not all the fascinations of beauty can arouse one kindly feeling in the breast of the king of terrors, or make one single impression on his relentless nature. By the term " death " here, we are not to understand merely natural death, but the corruption and decomposition which take place in consequence of it; and, though we must allow it a short and momentary triumph, yet in the end it will be totally " abolished." And how has this been brought to pass? By Jesus Christ. By His righteousness and atoning sacrifice, satisfaction has been made for the sins of the whole world; by His resurrection and ascension, proof is given that the power and dominion of death must eventually terminate. Let us now proceed to consider what the same gracious Saviour has effected for us—II. BY MEANS OF THE GOSPEL. He has brought life and immortality to light." The literal translation of the original is: " He hath illustrated life and immortality by the gospel." This doctrine had never been illustrated and demonstrated before; it existed in promise, but had never been practically exhibited. But through what medium are we assured of this? It is the gospel alone which brings immortal life to light. It is this which rouses, extends, enlarges, and refines our limited views and sentiments. (*T. Massey, A.B.*)
*Immortal life:*—We will consider three things—first, the great subject " brought to light," " life and immortality"; secondly, the revelation—" He hath brought life and immortality to light "; and, thirdly, we will glance at the means by which this glorious subject is placed in the light of open day—it is " by the gospel." I. IMMORTALITY NATURALLY AND ESSENTIALLY BELONGS TO GOD ALONE, " who only hath immortality, dwelling in the light which no man approach unto; whom no man hath seen nor can see." By " life and immortality," in the language of the text, we simply understand immortal life, or existence incapable of decay. Human existence, or existence in the present world, is not, strictly speaking, immortality; it is liable to decay. The natural powers are liable to decay, and the natural members crumble into dust; and the intellectual powers are also liable to decay, in consequence of their being encased in, and connected with this crumbling and mouldering tabernacle. The gospel has brought to light this glorious fact: that there is an existence in another state for creatures such as we are, incapable of decay. By which we understand that it is an existence without sin; for in sin is involved and included all the elements of destruction, and nothing can remove the elements of destruction but the removal of sin. All the powers shall be cleansed, nicely balanced, rightly directed, and constantly employed; and they shall be raised beyond the reach of that which might tarnish, sully, deprave, or injure them for ever. As it is a state of existence without sin, so, consequently, it is a state of existence without sickness. And as there will be no sickness, as a matter of course there will be no pain. And that fear, which is such a source of torment, will be done away. And then as to gratification; there is nothing that can gratify a perfected intellect or a purified heart, but we shall possess it in all its fulness and purity, in order that we may enjoy it for evermore. " Life," with holiness; for as holiness is the principal perfection of God's nature, so holiness will be the principal characteristic of the Lord's people in a better state. " Life," with knowledge; for immortal life stands virtually in connection with spiritual knowledge. Hence Christ says: " This is life eternal, that they might know Thee the only true God, and Jesus Christ, whom Thou hast sent." It will be life, with peace in perfection, and life in the possession of joy; and all the future will be the anticipation of perfect satisfaction. It is, we may observe, life with God—we shall be " for ever

with the Lord "—life in the presence, life in the possession, and life in the enjoyment of God. We may remark that it is life of the most perfect kind, in the highest degree. Now we know not what life in perfection is. I conceive that the highest kind of life will, in all the experience of the Lord's holy ones, be wrought up to the highest degree of perfection, and, in that state, it will be spent to reflect His honour, to perpetuate the glory of His grace, and for the honour of His glorious perfections, for ever. For, in other words, we may say it is life in employment and in enjoyment. We associate these two together, for in our minds they always are associated: we can conceive of no suitable employment without enjoyment. II. THE REVELATION: "life and immortality are brought to light," intimating that immortal life was obscure before. The heathen had some idea of a state of immortal existence for the soul, but not for the body; although, according to the gospel, immortality is intended for the body equally with the soul. 1. He "brought to light," the purpose of God, which was to be wrought out through all the opposition of sin and Satan, and of man under their influence, that He would have a people possess an immortal existence incapable of decay—a life of the highest kind, in the most perfect degree. 2. He not only "brought to light" the purpose, but the promise. How frequently and how plainly does our Lord refer to this, particularly in the Gospel of St. John. We can refer but to one passage—the sixth chapter and the fortieth verse—"This is the will of Him that sent Me, that every one which seeth the Son, and believeth on Him, may have everlasting life; and I will raise him up at the last day." 3. He not only "brought to light" the promise, but He was Himself the example. You know He yielded to the death upon the cross. He came forth in the possession of immortal life, with an immortal body and an immortal soul. 4. He exhibited eternal life, as a blessing promised to the Church. "This," says the apostle John, with emphasis—"this is the record, that God hath given to us eternal life, and this life is in His Son." 5. He not only exhibited it to us as a blessing promised, but as a prize to be gained; for there is nothing in the gospel to sanction indolence. 6. It is represented as the end which grace has in view. Hence the apostle, drawing the parallel between the two heads, or public representatives, says (Rom. v. 20). It was "brought to light" as the great object of hope, upon which the eye of hope is to be fixed from time to time. And what made primitive Christians so cheerful, and dauntless, and bold, and courageous, was just this: they "were living," says St. Paul, "in hope of eternal life, which God, who cannot lie, promised before the world began." III. THE MEANS BY WHICH THIS BLESSING IS "BROUGHT TO LIGHT" IS "THE GOSPEL." 1. Now, in one view of it, the gospel is a kind of telescope, without which it is impossible to look so far into the distance as to see immortal life. There it is in the distance, but our faculties are so weakened by sin, and the mists of ignorance have so gathered between us and it that it is necessary there should be something to bring the mind's eye into contact with it. The gospel is that something. It brings the subject near, just in the same way as a telescope seems to bring the distant object near; so that we can look at it, gaze upon it, examine it, admire it, and enjoy it. 2. The gospel brings "life and immortality to light," because it shows us how we may get rid of sin, the cause of death. 3. The gospel not only tells how we may get rid of sin, the cause of death, but how we may obtain justification, the title to life. 4. As it tells us how to obtain justification, which is the title to life, so it informs us how we may surmount every obstacle that would keep us from the possession and enjoyment of it. It brings to our help the power of God, the wisdom of God, and the Spirit of God; in other words, it presents to us the Saviour, in all His fulness, and tells us how to every believer in Him He "is made wisdom, and righteousness, and sanctification, and redemption." *(Jas. Smith.)*
*Eternal life:*—By what means has Jesus Christ brought life and immortality to light? I bring a triple reply. By His teaching, by His redemption, by His resurrection. Let us touch upon each of these points. 1. By His teaching, I said; but I must explain my thought. Do I mean that Jesus Christ brought to men logical arguments in order to prove eternal life, that He made of them a learned, rigorous, invincible demonstration, that He gave to the proofs which the philosophers employed before Him an irrefutable value, that He Himself added new proofs which convinced the reason for ever? Never, brethren; I will not say that, because I do not think it. Jesus Christ never undertook to prove the future life, and you will seek in vain on His lips for a single scientific reasoning which had that aim: the gospel no more demonstrates the future life than it

demonstrates the existence of God. Brought it to light! How? What must be done in order to bring immortality to light? Ah! I understand you. The mysterious veil must be removed which hides the invisible world from us, that it may be penetrated and its secrets told to us. We ourselves are fatally arrested on the shores of the formidable ocean of death, and we do not know whether any new land shines there, beyond the flood, on the mysterious horizon. Darkness covers its waves; we try to throw light upon them, to direct the rays of our thought upon their depths; but that thought, which can follow the stars in their courses and calculate the laws of the world, is exhausted in the haze. We listen, and we hear only the monotonous noise of the billows in which the groanings of all past generations seem to be mingled, swallowed up in the common shipwreck which awaits us all. No one has come from that world, we say, to relate its secrets to us. But let some one appear, let him satisfy our ardent curiosity, let him tell us what heaven is, let him depict its beauties, let him recount the life which is the lot of the happy in glory, and our thirst will at least be appeased. Now, has Jesus Christ done that? Has He related to us what passes in heaven? Has He unveiled its mysteries to us? So little, as has been often remarked, that the gospel yields nothing here to our curiosity. If to bring immortality to light signifies to relate the secrets of the invisible world, it must resolutely be said, Jesus Christ has not done that. How striking does that moderation appear when we think that Jesus Christ could so easily have inflamed the souls of His disciples, and encouraged them to die, by depicting to them the splendours and the enjoyments of the world beyond! Recall the many founders of religion and false prophets who sent their disciples to death, intoxicating them with the promise of the delights which paradise reserved for them. In the teaching of Jesus Christ there is nothing like that. We see what Jesus Christ has not done, and what we might have expected from Him. I come back to my question: How has He, by His teaching, brought life and immortality to light? To solve it, to understand the novelty of His teaching as to this, let us see what ideas Jesus Christ found reigning around Him on this point. What did the book of the Jews, the Old Testament, teach on this matter? I hear it affirmed to-day that the idea of the future life is foreign to the Old Testament. In support of that idea the silence of the Old Testament is alleged as to the point. Let us examine it. I open the Old Testament, that book to which the idea of immortality has remained, so it is said to us, almost unknown, and in its first pages I see announced the startling fact that death was not in the first intention and will of God; that it is a disorder, an overthrow, fruit of that moral overthrow called sin. Whence this conclusion is imposed on us, that man, created in the image of God, is made by Him for immortality. And in the pages which follow, speaking of a patriarch who walked in the ways of God, the Bible tells us of Enoch, as further on it tells of Elijah, that he returned to God without passing through death. I come to the law of Moses. There is no mention made in it of eternity, I acknowledge this without hesitation; but I beg to remark that the question here is of a code addressed to a people, and that peoples do not live again as peoples. Legislation relates only to the present life; when even it should have to do with a religion like that of Moses, it would have to do with it only by its visible sides. The sole sanctions which it could promise are temporal sanctions; it has not to penetrate into the world beyond, for its mission expires there. After the law come the Psalms and the prophets. The Psalms—ah! I know they often express, with a bitter sadness, the idea that the activity of man ends at the tomb; but, to-day, could you not catch on the lips of a Christian similar expressions, when he thinks of the brevity of life, of the little time which is given him here below to serve his God? In addition to which, by the side of those longings, those presentiments of eternity, there are, I acknowledge, doubts, anxieties, uncertainties, in the presence of death among the believers of the Old Testament. It is still the age of twilight; shadows are everywhere mingled with the light. We can now imagine the state of beliefs in the centre where Jesus Christ appeared. What did Jesus Christ do? He sanctioned by His Divine authority belief in the Resurrection; He openly combated Sadduceeism; He returned unceasingly to the great thought of a last judgment; but is that all? If I wish to sum it up in one word, I do not hesitate to say that Jesus Christ has founded the faith in eternal life. And how? It was not always in simply supposing it, in illuminating all His teachings with that light, it was not only in speaking of heaven, as Fénélon has so admirably put it, as a son speaks of the house of his father; it is still, it is above all, in revealing to us an ideal of life to which our conscience is forced to subscribe, and which is a mockery if it should not continue and expand in eternity. What do all those words teach me ? Eternal life. Listen! " Blessed are they that mourn, for they shall be comforted ! Blessed are those who hunger and thirst after righteousness, for they shall be filled ! Blessed are the meek, for they shall inherit the earth ! Blessed are the merciful, for they shall obtain mercy ! " Say if each of those words does not open before your gaze like a splendid vista into eternity itself. Tell me if each of those words does not end by stretching into eternal life. This simple example shows, in a striking manner, how Jesus Christ has founded faith in the future life. He has founded it on the human soul itself, interrogated in its deepest and truest instincts. Taught by that reflection, let us now take His teaching in its central and ruling thought. Indeed, how shall we seek the kingdom of God, if eternity is a vain word ? How shall we pursue the ideal righteousness, if we ought to content ourselves with what the earth can give us ? How shall we follow after holiness, if we must negative our living some day freed from that law of sin which we carry in our members ? How shall we love, in short, how shall we give our heart to God and to all Divine things, if we should not some day find God, and in Him possess all in eternity ? Jesus Christ interrogates the human soul, and evokes in its depths those aspirations which eternity alone can satisfy. Hence, then, this is how the question shall be put : Faith in eternity will be faith even in the kingdom of God. The more we believe in the triumph of righteousness, of truth, of goodness, the more we shall believe in eternal life ; the more satisfied we are with the present life, the less we shall understand that eternity is necessary. Instead of saying then, as the mystics will do after Christ, " Let your imagination lose itself in ecstasy, and you will see heaven " ; instead of saying, as philosophers had said before Him, " Gather in your reason all the proofs which demonstrate immortality," Jesus Christ simply said, " Love, sanctify yourselves, thirst after righteousness ; the more you do that, the more will eternity be necessary to you, the more you will love it, the more you will believe in it ; for to live for holiness is to enter already, even here below, into eternal life." So, for Jesus Christ, eternal life begins, even here below, for every soul submissive to God ; that word is used forty times in the New Testament, and it always designates the state of a soul which has entered into communion with God. There alone is true life in reality. Eternity embraces the present and the past as well as the future. Eternity, we are in eternity. For him who has entered into the plan of God, the heavenly kingdom begins even here below ; only, while here below, everything is subjected to the blast of instability : in that other economy which we call heaven, life will be full and lasting, and joy will be there for ever. 2. That is how Jesus Christ, by His teaching, has founded faith in eternal life ; but even that teaching had never sufficed to found that belief, if the work of redemption had not followed and crowned it. Eternal life is communion with God. But is it sufficient to tell us so ? No, we have gone out from communion with God. Have we not all violated the law of the heavenly city, and can we enter it without a restorative act—without a holy pardon giving us access to it ? The road which leads us to God passes the foot of a cross, and if that cross had not been planted that road would never have been opened to a single person. Without redemption there is no eternal life. It is by His Cross as much as by His teaching that Jesus Christ has brought immortality to light. 3. But would the Cross itself have had that efficacy if the Resurrection had not followed it ? Listen to St. Paul. When he wrote to Timothy that Jesus Christ had conquered death and brought life and immortality to light through the gospel, on what, before all, did he place the accent if it was not on the resurrection of the Lord ? What would remain of the gospel without the Resurrection ? " The person of Jesus Christ and His teaching," you reply, " His life and His words, will always shine with the same lustre. What could a miracle add to the sublimity of His discourses, or of His character ? " The reply seems plausible ; and yet, I would ask your attention here to a fact. We have heard in our days many men holding the same language, who wanted a Christ without miracles and without a resurrection, who asked us what such prodigies added to His holiness. Years have passed, we have seen those men following the current of their thoughts ; little by little the perfect holiness of Christ is obscured in their eyes ; they have discovered blots in His life ; His Divine aureole has grown pale ; they see no more in Him to-day than the sage of Nazareth, sublime, but ignorant, and a sinner like all the children of men. In reflecting on this, I have found that the result of an irresistible logic was there. The person of Christ is one like His teaching. You cannot arbitrarily strike off such or such parts. All holds together in Him ; His life, His words tend to the Resurrection as to their natural fulfilment ; everything in Him supposes a victory over death; if that victory has not been obtained, His authority is shaken, His words lose something of their serene certitude, His ideal grandeur grows dim. As we have said, facts prove it every day. Let us suppose, however, that it is not so. Let us admit that Christ, conquered by death like all men, remains as grand, as holy. Have you reflected on the other side of the question? Have you asked yourself if faith in the future life would not for ever be shaken on the day when the fact of the resurrection of Jesus Christ should have disappeared from history? (*E. Bersier, D.D.*)

*The reasonableness of life:*—It may at first be thought that in the words of the text St. Paul has overstated the originality of his gospel in its doctrine of immortality. For, on the one hand, we find the tokens of firm belief in a life beyond the grave among the very lowest savages: it is shown in their legends, in their accounts of dreams, in their customs of burial. But St. Paul does not, could not, deny that the expectation of an eternal life and the suspicion of immortality were astir among men before Christ rose from the dead, the first-fruits of them that slept: what he does claim is that through the gospel of the Resurrection God has brought the truth to light, and substituted for the shifting glimpses, the twilight hope, the unfinished prophecy of the past, a fact as stable as his prison walls, a fact which brings immortality itself into the broad light of day, and sets it, for those who believe that Christ is risen, among the steadiest axioms of life. He is satisfied that his eyes have seen the form, his ears have heard the voice of One who liveth, and was dead, and is alive for evermore. The expectation of a future life had indeed long been in the world: but it had been a very different thing from this. In the infantile mind of the savage it had been little more than the mere inability to imagine how he could cease to be: it cost him less effort to think of the present as continuing than as stopping: he had not fancy or energy enough to conceive an end. It was impossible that a state of mind so purely negative should long take rank as an expectation among civilised men: in their higher and more active souls it must either become positive or pass away. It does become positive to the Greek and to the Jew: but at the same time it loses something of that unfaltering certainty with which it swayed the savage. Even David wonders "What profit is there in my blood, when I go down to the pit?" even Hezekiah cries to God, "The grave cannot praise Thee; death cannot celebrate Thee: they that go down into the pit cannot hope for Thy truth." Whatever Christianity has done, or failed to do, this at least we need not fear to claim for it: that it has availed to plant the belief of our immortality among the deepest and most general convictions of our race: that it has borne even into the least imaginative hearts the unfailing hope of a pure and glorious life beyond the death of the body: that it has shot through our language, our literature, our customs, and our moral ideas the searching light of a judgment to come and the quickening glory of a promised Heaven; that it has sustained and intensified this hope through countless changes of thought and feeling in centuries of quickest intellectual development: and that it is now impossible to conceive the force which could dislodge from so many million hearts the axiom which they have learned from the gospel of the Resurrection. But is there in this achievement any evidence that that gospel is true? Let us seek some answer to this question. And first, may not this be said with truth: that there are some conceptions of our life, of ourselves, and of this present world, which, as moral beings, we have no right to entertain? We have no right, for instance, to entertain, still less to impart, the theory that there is any sin which men cannot avoid, any vice which they had better practise: we have no right to say to ourselves or others that our humanity is naturally vile or brutal. Conscience can condemn a thought as distinctly and authoritatively as it can an act: and there are abstract views of ourselves and our life which can only be accepted by doing ruinous violence to the moral sense. Such, and so criminal, is or would be the belief that this present life is all unreal and meaningless, a thing to be mocked at or despised as silly and abortive: as though all its interests and issues, even when they seem most free and hopeful, were really in the relentless grip of a blind or cruel force, and its government or anarchy, with all that we call law and right and reason, a mere amusement for some scornful spectator of our manifold delusion. We have no right, even in thought, so to jeer at ourselves: no man, being rational and moral, may think so meanly of his manhood. We live then, we go on working, upon the belief that the main and dominant element in life is reasonable and righteous: it is a belief which morality inculcates as a duty; without which effort and progress are words drained of all meaning. But does this world, indeed, display the character which we are thus forced to impute to it, if all the issues of a human life are finished all its drama played, its accounts all balanced, and its story closed, when the frail body dies ; if life and immortality indeed have not been brought to light? But there are unnumbered souls for whom only the hope which Christianity has given them can justify the patient continuance of life, or arrest the quick growth of disappointment towards despair and madness. (*F. Paget, D.D.*) *The argument for immortality :*—It seems to me a very striking evidence of the pressure of the burden of life in our times that so many thoughtful and cultivated men and women outside the pale of our Churches are not only indifferent to, but contemptuous of, immortality. I trace the present terrible questionings, to use no stronger word, of the fundamental realities of our being, our relation to God as a living Being and our personal immortality, to no ignoble source. I believe that they are mainly due to the increased pressure of the burden of life under our present conditions of highly developed sympathies and lofty views of duty. Hence life seems full of sadness and confusion, and the doctrine is rather welcomed which finds many able, though sad, preachers in these days that at death we have done with it for ever. The doctrine of immortality is not so much formally asserted in Scripture as assumed throughout as the basis of its appeals, and of its treatment of the questions of conduct, of duty, with which it occupies itself. It is no new truth which the New Testament discovers and makes known ; an old truth, the oldest truth, old as the constitution of man's nature, is "brought to light by the gospel." The dim form of it is brought out into the daylight, and all men not only feel, but see, it to be a truth of God. Here, in the Bible, is the strong confirmation and assurance of the doctrine. No man can accept this revelation as containing God's counsel, and deny or question man's immortality. But while our faith rests securely on the revelation and the history which the ages have handed down, it is deeply important to consider how far the truth is supported or discredited by all that we can gather from other sources of the nature, the constitution, and the destiny of man. How far does the study of man's nature and history help or hinder our belief in immortality ? The argument is as follows : The belief that Christ, the risen Christ, was reigning with almighty power, and subduing all things to Himself, was a thought ever present with the men of all classes, orders, and callings, who wrought most mightily on the reconstitution upon a Christian basis of human society. I say, reconstitution on a Christian basis of human society. I wish I had time to go into the question ; I think it would not be difficult to show that human society within the civilised area was literally perishing of moral corruption, when the light and truth which Christianity brought into the world restored it at the very spring. Nothing is more marked in the apostolic age than the contrast between the despondent, despairing tone of the noblest pagan literature, which utters its deepest wail over the hopeless corruption of society, and the tone of vital animation, of buoyant, exultant hope which pervades the whole field of the intellectual and spiritual activity of the Christian Church. The one is manifestly the wail of a world settling into death, the other the joyful cry of a world new-born, and conscious of a vigorous, aspiring life. And behind the latter, its inspiring idea, its moving force, was the reign of the risen and living Lord. It was not the tale of Calvary simply, the history of the martyrdom of martyrdoms, mighty as was the influence which that could not but wield over men. It was distinctly belief in Christ as a reigning King: one who was a present and transcendent force in the government of all human affairs. I do not say that the result of this vision of the reigning Christ was such heavenly order on earth as reigns on high. Alas! no. Man's passion, selfishness, vanity, and lust are too strong. But I do affirm that this was the strongest principle, the conquering principle of resistance to all that had been wasting and destroying heathen society before Christ appeared. It was this which created the stern conflict against sin, vice, and wrong which has been fought out through all the Christian ages. So from the open tomb, whose bars the Saviour burst as He arose, a flood of glorious, kindling light streamed forth ; it spread as dawn spreads in the morning sky ; it touched all forms of things in man's dark and dreary world with its splendour, and called man forth from the tomb in which his higher life seemed buried to a new career of fruitful, sunlit activity, opening a wondrous depth of meaning in the Saviour's words, " The hour is coming, and now is, when the dead shall hear the voice of the Son of God, and they that hear shall live." The exceeding readiness and joyfulness with which a truth so transcendently wonderful, so far out of and above the visible order of things, was welcomed everywhere, penetrating men's hearts as though they were made for it, as sunlight penetrates the darkness of the world, would be utterly inexplicable, except on the theory that they were made for it; that there was that in their nature which was pining and longing for it; which was made to live and rejoice in the light of it, as flowers drink in the light and the dew. They received the truth as truly the most natural of all things, according to the order of the higher nature; and they lodged it at once as an unquestionable verity in the treasury of their beliefs and hopes. It is easy to say in answer to this that it was a fascinating doctrine, and won its way easily by the promise which it appeared to hold forth to mankind. No wonder, it is said, men naturally long for immortality, and catch easily at any doctrine, however delusive, which seems to respond to their longing and justify their hope. " Man naturally longs for immortality." Let us look at it a little, and ask ourselves why he longs; how the idea could rise and take such firm possession of the strongest and most progressive races of our world. If he longs, it is somehow because he was made to long. Out of something in his constitution the longing springs. Now nature through all her orders seems to have made all creatures contented with the conditions of their life. The brute seems to rest with full contentment on the resources of his world. His soul shows no sign of being tormented by dreams; his life withers under no blight of regret. All creatures rest in their orders, and are content and glad. Violate the order of their nature, rob them of their congenial surroundings, and they grow restless, sad, and poor. Rob a flower of light or moisture, and it struggles with something like agonising earnestness in quest of them. This well-known tendency in perverted things to revert to the primitive type seems to be set in nature as a wonderful sign that things are at rest in their natural conditions—content with their life and its sphere; and that only by ways of which they are quite unconscious, and which rob them of no enjoyment of or contentment with their present, they prepare for the farther and higher developments of life. This restless longing in man, then, for that which is beyond the range of his visible world, this haunting of the unseen by his thoughts and hopes, this " eager hope, this fond desire, this longing after immortality," what does it mean? Has Nature, which makes all things, in all orders, at rest in their sphere, wantonly and cruelly made man, her masterpiece, restless and sad? We are driven to believe by the very order of Nature that this insatiable longing, which somehow she generates and sustains in man, and which is the largest feature in his life, is not visionary and futile, but profoundly significant, pointing with the surest, firmest finger to the reality, the solid enduring reality, of that sphere of being to which she has taught him to lift his thoughts and aspirations, and in which he will find, according to the universal order of the creation, the harmonious completeness of his life. It spread, then, the belief in this truth, rapidly, joyfully, irresistibly, not by art, not by fraud, not by force, but because it was of the nature of light which inevitably conquers and scatters darkness. Men saw themselves and their life, their present, their future, in the light of it, and the revelation was convincing. We have here, not the longing only, but, to carry it no further, we have the life of Christendom for eighteen centuries built on it; we have it as the mainspring of human progress for incomparably the most civilised, developed, and progressive era of human history. How did it come there? Either—1. This result grew by natural development out of the precedent states and conditions of life, ascending under the guidance of what, for want of a better understanding of things, men call Nature—the vital force which is behind all the movement and progress of the world—through the successive stages of creature existence to the height of man. In that case, what men call Nature would be responsible for it—and then this would result. There is no freedom or intelligent choice in Nature, according to the materialists. Everything that is grows out of its antecedents by inexorable law. But what it is impossible to believe is that Nature, the vital force, call it what you will, has pressed on the development up to man, and endowed man with this propulsive movement of his whole being towards the sphere of the spiritual, the immortal, the eternal, and then confesses its failure to carry it further, leaving its noblest child a prey to aimless longings and barren hope. Is there everywhere glorious progress up to man, while for man the way onward and upward, which Nature has somehow taught him to look for and to struggle towards, is finally and for ever barred? Is a broken column the perfect emblem of this great universe? Is its highest achievement a sad, wistful, hopeless life? For that is what man's life inevitably becomes when he is cut off from God and immortality. Nature does nothing in vain in the creation. All works into a sublime procession of progress. Let no one tempt you to believe that the procession halts, and that the progress which stretches through the whole chord of being,

from a nebula to a constellation, from an atom to a world, from a cell-germ to a
man, is broken off in man and dies out for ever.  2. Still more impossible is it to
believe that this hope has no substance behind the veil to which it clings, and in
which as an anchor of the soul it holds, on the other hypothesis, that the
order of things is the work of a Divine hand, that the wisdom and power of God
are at work on all developments and progresses of life.  It seems blankly impossible
to believe that God could have created man to imagine, to frame to himself, a
picture of a whole universe of being behind the veil of sense, and beyond the river
of death ; could serenely watch him as he imagines it, and pleases himself with
forecasting it as the theatre of his immortal life ; could use it as an instrument to
stir and stimulate his sluggish nature, and keep his faculties on the strain of
effort by hope, when it is all a wretched illusion.  Can it be believed for a moment
that a wise Being can so have arranged His world that His loftiest creatures in
nature and endowment can only live the lower life by dreaming about a higher,
which is but a dream ?  If that is your scheme of the great creation, with man to
head it, what kind of demon do you make of your God ?  No !  Whether we look
at this aspect and attitude of man towards the eternal as the last outcome of the
vital pressure, be it what it may, which is working through creation, or as the fruit
of the design of an intelligent Creator, who saw this end from the beginning of the
processions of life—equally we are driven to the conviction which revelation makes
sure, that man on the topstone of the material creation plants his foot on the
threshold of a higher, a spiritual, an eternal world.  (*J. Baldwin Brown, B.A.*)
*Death abolished—life brought to light :*—If the railway runs to a particular station
and there stops, we call that station a terminus ; and the association of finality
springs up in our mind with regard to it, which has an influence upon our thoughts
and feelings during the whole of the journey, and especially towards its close.
" That is the station where we all stop and leave the carriages, having exhausted
the value of our tickets."  But if a new length of line be added, although the
station remains, it is a different fact ; its terminal character is abolished ; the
association of finality is dissolved from henceforth in our minds, and we think of
the station no longer as a place where we must all come to a standstill, but as a
point of brief tarrying on the way to other destinations.  Now Christ, by His
revelation of life and immortality, has added a line of indefinite length to the great
human journey ; it stretches away through prospects of vast extent and inconceivable grandeur ; in the thought of life the terminality of death is lost, and it becomes
only a fresh starting-point beyond which the noblest scenery begins to open.  Let
us, then, trace out some of those common experiences of our minds which lead us
up towards Christ's revelation, which predispose us beforehand to expect that such
a revelation would be given to us, and enable us the better to appreciate its evidences
and welcome its reality when it arrives.  1. Take first our natural reluctance at the
thought of death as a terminus.  It is easy to see that wherever men have thought
seriously, felt keenly, loved deeply, acted nobly, they have known this reluctance against
death which reason could not overcome.  Take as illustration those plaints which
break out again and again in the sad, sweet music of the Book of Job.  Listen again to
this strain of King Hezekiah on his recovery from a dangerous sickness : " I said in
the cutting off of my days, I shall go to the gates of the grave ; I am deprived of
the residue of my years.  I said, I shall not see the Lord, even the Lord in the
land of the living. . . . The grave cannot praise Thee, death cannot celebrate Thee ;
they that go down into the pit cannot hope for Thy truth. The living, the living,
he shall praise Thee, as I do this day."  We are struck, in these examples, with
the complete vacancy with regard to the future.  Apparently men had no power to
conceive of death in any other aspect than a terminus.  They could not get the
idea of continuation into their thoughts ; we cannot get it out of ours.  The explanation is that it has pleased God to reveal truth to the world by degrees ; and
the want of some one great truth leaves the mind helpless.  It cannot see what is
to be seen.  If we look at a Chinese picture we perceive that the artist does not
understand the truths of light and distance and gradation.  He sees nature as a
flat screen, and paints her so.  He cannot make the eye travel away into the background of limitless distance, as our great masters do.  He wants the knowledge of
a few truths which would at once alter his whole conceptions of nature and mode
of representing it.  I have stood in a gloomy chamber, where my vision was
bounded by its walls ; but suddenly a sliding door has been drawn, and there has
burst upon me a glorious view of rushing stream, and rock, and woodland, arched
by the blue sky, and suggesting enchanting distances.  If ever I enter that pavilion

again, I shall not look upon the dead wall with a blank and baffled gaze; I shall already seem to pierce it in imagination before the door is drawn, and be gazing out on the bright scene beyond. Men in those early days were groping for that sliding door unconsciously. The sadness and impatience at the bounding line of death impelled their thoughts to question whether it was really a bounding line. Their growing intelligent faith in the goodness of God worked in the same direction with the natural reluctance against death, till the first spark of the nobler truth was at last struck out; the first lines of gold appeared along the horizon, heralding the coming of the Divine Light-Bringer. 2. Next, we may note the great deterrent which the idea of immortality has proved to be in human life. When once an inkling of the great truth had entered men's minds it held them, and held them with increasing tenacity. It appears to be one of those truths which, once glimpsed, can never again be wholly lost sight of. There are, we know, to be found those who stoutly deny in words a future life; but it may be questioned whether they can shake off the yoke of the thought from their deliberations. No man can be certain there is not a future life, and this uncertainty is quite sufficient, as Shakespeare says in a well-known passage, to "puzzle the will," and make the man draw back from the verge of a crime. There are certain conditions of the human mind which appear to require the check supplied by the belief in immortality. It seems to be needed to ballast the temper under great sufferings and great temptations. Under the Roman Empire suicide was sadly common, because, there being no powerful belief of immortality, men thought themselves at liberty to dispose of their lives as they pleased. And we may justly argue that the full revelation of life and immortality by our Saviour Jesus Christ was called for by the saddened, wearied, dejected mental condition into which the world, with all its thought and civilisation, had fallen. The belief in a future life is doubtless an immense restraint upon wickedness, even although many do not know, or will not admit, what it is that restrains them. One of the keenest judges of human nature (Dr. Johnson) once said: "The belief in immortality is impressed upon all men, and all men act under an impression of it, however they may talk, and though, perhaps, they may be scarcely sensible of it." To this the reply was made that some people seemed to have not the least notion of immortality; and a distinguished man was mentioned as an example. "Sir," the great moralist replied, "if it were not for the notion of immortality, he would cut a throat to fill his pockets." History and human life in general show us that the nature of men requires repression; and that human laws and government are not sufficient for the purpose, although they act upon the same powerful principle of fear. Whenever and wherever the awful idea of a future has been pressed home upon men, there has been a speedy lessening of violence, ferocity, and crime. 3. Lastly, let us think of the belief of immortality as a needed incentive in human nature. We need stimulus, as well as repression. The one fact is as clear and constant as the other. We are naturally indolent except in the pursuit of our desires, tastes, interests. It is doubtful whether any man loves and pursues goodness purely for its own sake; at all events, to any considerable extent. The revelation of a future life comes in to meet this requirement; for all that goads and stirs up our spiritual energies draws its power from immortality, and from nowhere else. We are promised in an especial manner that we are to enjoy the sense of power and victory; and every pure and powerful instinct of our nature is offered its appropriate gratification in a state where God hath prepared for them that love Him things which eye hath not seen nor ear heard, neither hath it entered into the heart of man to conceive. (*E. Johnson, M.A.*)    *Continuity* :—The message of Easter, the gospel of the Resurrection, is the revelation of the Divine continuity of life, which shows us what life is already, with its mysterious connections and conflict; it shows us how we may conceive of life hereafter in its final consummation; it shows us how we may even now gain for the fulfilment of our appointed work the support of a Divine fellowship. The revelation of the risen Christ is the revelation of life present. Believers are undoubtedly to blame for allowing it to be supposed for a single instant that their faith deals only, or deals mainly, with the future. The clear voice of apostolic teaching is, "We have passed out of death into life." We have passed, and not we shall pass hereafter. "This is eternal life" in actual fruition, and not this will bring life as a later reward. "Our citizenship is in heaven." "We have come to Mount Zion, and unto the city of the living God, the heavenly Jerusalem." And, indeed, a gospel to be real must be present. No one can look upon the phenomena of life without feeling its oppressing riddles.

We need some light upon them. Earthly life is, and it must be, fragmentary, sorrow-laden, sinful. Who has not asked at some still moment, "How is my brief span of years crowded with little cares and little duties, relating to that past out of which it came, and to that future into which it will soon pass "? In the risen Christ we see the coherence, the unity of all action, and the real significance of simple work done in silence and obscurity. The manhood which Christ raised to heaven was enriched by the heritage of long ages, and matured in the fulfilment of the humblest offices of duty. A brief ministry only revealed what had been slowly shaped in unnoticed and forgotten ways. Looking to Him, living in Him here and now, we know that each human life is one in all its parts, and is essentially Divine; we know that it is one by the subtle influences which pass on from year to year, and from day to day; one by the continuous action of the will which shapes the fabrics of our character. We know that it is Divine; Divine in its present, if unseen, influence, Divine in the assurance of its future consummation. We know also that the unity of each single life is an image of the larger unity in which each single life is included. In the risen Christ we see the outcome of suffering; we cannot admit that in His life, closed to the eyes of men in betrayal, desertion, torture, there was one useless pang, one shadow of failure. All ministered to the same end. In the issue, even as we see it now, human judgments have been reversed. In the risen Christ we see the overthrow of sin. The end of sin is death, and Christ made death itself the way to life. The resurrection of Christ is thus a revelation of life present, disclosing the unity and the grandeur of the cause to which, with great services or small, we all minister, drawing joy, the joy of the Lord, out of our transitory sadnesses and disappointments, and pains, bringing the assurance that our last enemy shall be destroyed. It is also a revelation of life future. It is indeed a revelation of the future, because it is a revelation of the present. Future and present are essentially combined in the eternal. Under this second aspect the Resurrection conveys a two-fold lesson: it reveals the permanence of the present in the future; it reveals also in the future, as far as we can gain the thought, a form of life, fuller, better, more complete than this of our separated personalities. In Him, the representative of humanity, we see that the perfection of earthly life is undiminished by death; we see that what seems to be dissolution is only transfiguration; we see that all that belongs to the essence of manhood can exist under new conditions; we see that whatever be the unknown glories and the unimaginable endowments of the after life, nothing is cast off which rightly claims our affection and our reverence in this. This, however, is not all. Beyond this revelation of the ennobled permanence of the present in the life of the Résurrection, further depths of thought are open to us. Here on earth our lives are fragmentary and isolated; we are all separated one from another, and we are weakened by the separation. Our material frames are not, as we are tempted to think, the instruments of our union, but the barriers by which we are divided. The most active fellowship is at last irrevocably interrupted; the most intimate sympathy leaves regions of feeling ununited; but in the risen Christ we seem to have held out to us the image of a diviner life, in which each single believer shall be incorporated and yet not absorbed; the unity which is now foreshadowed in the unity of will with will is hereafter, as it seems, to be realised in a unity which shall embrace the whole being; each one will consciously share in the fulness of a life to which he has given himself, and will serve that by which he is maintained. To be in Christ is now the description of our vital energy; it will then be the sum of our existence; the body of Christ will then be no longer a figure, but a reality beyond all figures. And so it is given us to feel, even in the midst of our conflicts and estrangements, that the saddest differences of our mortal state are lost, as we are reminded by the most moving epitaph in our abbey: "Lost in the hope of the resurrection." (*B. F. Westcott, D.D.*)    *Life and immortality brought to light :*— If on a starlight night we undertake a journey on foot, and we know the general bearings of the country along which we pass and the general direction of the course we must take to reach the desired goal, we may with care and painstaking come to the end of our journey in safety. The moon is shining in the heavens, the constellations are glittering over our heads, and by the aid of the stars travellers can cross the trackless desert. But there are disadvantages in taking the journey by night which do not exist in the full light of day. With care we may keep the beaten path by night, yet sometimes there are difficulties in so doing. Mr. Forbes tells us that in his long night ride in South Africa he was obliged to alight from his horse to feel the ground, that he might be sure of the waggon-track. Then there are finger-posts here and there, but the light at night will not enable us to decipher the inscriptions. We pass by pleasant orchards and gardens, and in the daytime we see the fruits and flowers, but these are hidden in the night. There are avenues of trees whose boughs and branches interlace, which cast dark shadows in the night, but which in the day form cool resting-places. The beauty of the landscape is for the most part lost in the night, but in the day we look upon it with pleasure. The night journey is not so convenient and pleasant as the journey by day. Now, the journey by night represents to us the life of the saints of God before the advent of the Saviour into the world, and the gift of the Holy Spirit. The journey by day represents the life of God's children living in the broad daylight of the Christian revelation. Christ said of Himself, "I am the light of the world." Before His coming it was the night-time of Divine revelation. God's saints must walk by faith, as men walk in the night by the light of the moon and stars. When He came, the Sun of Righteousness arose to bless the world with His light. There were dark shadows for the ancient saints where we find quiet resting-places. There were mysteries which they could not decipher, which are clear to us in the light of Christs. I. CONSIDER CHRIST ABOLISHING DEATH. 1. Christ removed the uncertainty that hung over death. If we go down into the catacombs of Rome, the subterranean passages beneath the city, we may see the remains of heathen and Christian lying side by side. Over the heathen dead are inscribed words of hopeless sorrow. A Pagan mother writes words of bitter despair over her child, as if the handful of ashes were all that remained of the darling she once fondled and cherished. The ancient writings and funeral inscriptions of the heathen world, with few exceptions, corroborate the words of the Apostle Paul that they lived without hope, and that their sorrow for their departed friends was without hope. On the other hand, the words written over the Christian dead speak of the departed as being at rest with God. Over them we might write the words inscribed over the entrance to the catacombs of Paris, "Beyond these bounds they rest in peace, looking for the blessed hope." We must not attribute the same hopelessness to the Hebrew patriarchs, prophets, and righteous men of the elder dispensation. They seem to have had a persuasion of a life beyond the present. But a comparison of the words of the Old Testament saints with those of the apostles will present to us a contrast. "To die is gain." "Our home is in heaven, from whence we look for the Saviour." "I am now ready to be offered, and the time of my departure is at hand. There is laid up for me the crown of righteousness." Christ removed the uncertainty and obscurity which hung over death, and asserted the resurrection of all the dead, both of the just and the unjust. 2. Christ gives assurance of the full remission of sins and of the Divine favour to all who believe on Him. "The sting of death is sin." II. JESUS CHRIST HATH BROUGHT LIFE AND IMMORTALITY TO LIGHT. Mark the force of the words "life" and "immortality." Life, as will be seen by comparing the passages in which the word occurs in the New Testament, represents the highest blessedness to which we can attain. If we are in Christ, a new life has been implanted within us by the Holy Spirit, and that life will grow and expand until we reach the highest of which our nature is capable. This term includes all the blessedness to be found in communion with God, from the open vision of the Saviour and His glory, from the society of God's redeemed people, from the study of God's works in creation, providence, and redemption, from the fullest and most perfect service of God; in one word, all that we sum up in the word heaven. The word immortality completes the conception of the better life, showing that it is without decay or death. Whilst everything around us is suggestive of decay, the life of the Spirit is one of immortality. (*W. Bull, M.A.*) *Life and immortality brought to light by Jesus Christ:*—Death, as a physical fact, is inevitable and universal. The history of our race is a succession of generations; which march, with unceasing tramp, across life's narrow stage, each treading on the heels of its hurrying predecessor. Like the leaves of the forest in spring, they come; only to be soon swept away again, like the leaves of the forest in autumn. They chase one another to destruction, like snowstorms scudding across the insatiate ocean's breast. No man can hope that *he* will be one solitary leaf, which the autumn's blast will spare; or one solitary snowflake, which will not melt among the billows. Therefore are all men, "through fear of death, all their lifetime subject to bondage." But Jesus has "abolished death"—has robbed him of his terrors, and broken the horn of his power. He has illumed the dark recesses of the tomb; and by a most Divine camera, pictured on the disc of faith the distant future to our gaze. He has connected that future with our present life; and has thus restored to the latter its true dignity and significance, while He has for ever dissipated the notion that man's doom is annihilation. I. Before the appearance of Christ life and immortality were concealed in deepest darkness. The Egyptians, Phœnicians, Persians, and Chaldeans, seem to have had no idea of a future life whatever. Their wise men were merely students of nature. The materialism of the Chinese was, if possible, still more blank and absolute. In India the loftiest reach of speculation produced only the doctrine of Divine absorption. In Greece, philosophy, which means the study of religion, began about six centuries before Christ. Thales was born at Miletus, in Asia Minor. He ranked among the seven wise men. He lived to a good old age, and enjoyed a high reputation for virtue. He first uttered that magnificent aphorism "Know thyself." This reveals to us a man of solitary meditation. He was wont to wander along the pebbly beach of the muttering sea; and it seemed to him that water, by which all things are nourished and kept alive, was the prime source of creation. The gods were made of this element. So was every human being, and at death the soul is soaked up by the parent earth. How mournful the reflection, that our race had gone so far astray from wisdom and from God, as to invent only so poor and crude an hypothesis through the most intense thinking of its noblest sage! Next came one to say that the soul was air; another, that it was fire. Neither of these conjectures allowed a future life. Pythagoras, a mathematician, conceived that numbers were the beginning of creation. This mystical dogma was soon rendered more intelligible by one of his followers, an enthusiastic musician, who imagined that the human body was an instrument of music, and the soul but the symphony of its playing. When the chords of the lyre were snapped by death, then of course the melody departed, the soul became extinct. We now come to the prince of all Pagan religionists, Xenophanes. He was born in Ionia some five hundred years before Christ. He renounced all worldly grandeur, and applied himself, with most zealous devotion, to studies about God and man. He apprehended the Infinite One as a self-existent and eternal Spirit. But when he sought to know the truth about his own soul and its destiny, he was completely baffled. He bitterly complained that "error is spread over all things," and declared, in declining age, that he was yet, "hoary of years, exposed to doubt and distraction of all kinds." Time would utterly fail to tell of others, who sought with similar non-success to solve this great problem, "If a man die shall he live again?" None ever advanced one step beyond Xenophanes. He may fairly be taken as the type of man at his best state, with regard to religious knowledge, so far as the gospel is unknown. As to our own country, let me remind you of an anecdote about our druidical ancestors, which most beautifully and pathetically exhibits their utter ignorance of futurity. Their chieftains sat together in their council-hall, consulting about peace and war. It was the darkest hour of night. Resinous torches, rudely fastened against the walls, shed a few ghastly rays upon the grim countenances of the perplexed warriors. As they sat thus in deliberation, a poor bird, scared by some alarm and attracted by the light, suddenly fluttered into their midst through a small side window. More frightened than before, it hastily flew across to the opposite side, and escaped again, through another opening, into the darkness from which it had so transiently emerged. "Ah!" said the orator then speaking, "how like is our miserable life to that poor bird's passage! We come out of darkness, and know not why we are here: and then we are hurried into darkness again, not knowing whither we go." I have now established our position that, save for Christ and His gospel, men have ever been ignorant of life and immortality. It is so still. Without ranging over the heathen world, we may just state, that precisely the same questions are being agitated in Germany at this moment as were discussed in ancient Greece; and, apart from the Bible, with no better means of solving them, with no better hopes of success. "The united force of thousands of intellects, some of them among the greatest that have made the past illustrious, has been steadily concentrated on these problems without the least result. Centuries of labour have not produced any perceptible progress." But let us now turn to Christ and His gospel: and—II. Consider how He has brought life and immortality to light, thereby abolishing death. In explication of this delightful topic, we must declare, first, what Christ has taught, and, secondly, what He has done, in relation to our immortal life. 1. He has taught us the truth concerning the future. The Saviour's doctrine of immortality comprises four particulars: (1) That men are spiritual and immortal creatures. (2) That their future state will be one either of perfect happiness or of unmitigated woe. (3) That the decision of this alternative, in every case, will depend upon personal moral character; and (4) That the acquisition and formation of this character is confined to the term of our earthly life. 2. We are to state what He has done to secure for us individually an immortality of blessedness. It would not have been enough merely to inform us about the future. We need to be guided into it with safety. If others could have demonstrated to us a final world of blessedness, they could not have made it ours; but Jesus has procured for us a title to the felicities, whose existence He has proved. He has undertaken to be to us "the Way, the Truth, the Life." We were guilty—He takes away our sin, having "died, the just for the unjust, to bring us to God." We were polluted—He is our sanctification, purifying our souls "with the washing of regeneration and renewing of the Holy Ghost." We were undeserving, but He achieves for us a title to heaven. "The gift of God is eternal life through our Lord Jesus Christ." That He may actually lift us up to the mansions above, is the reason why He has enlightened us concerning them. (*T. G. Horton.*)    *The discoveries made in the gospel with respect to a future state* :—The vale of death is a road in which all men must travel; a path in which our fathers have gone before, and we ourselves must soon follow. It is therefore natural, and indeed of great importance, to inquire, whither it leads and where it will bring us. I. THE GOSPEL HAS CONFIRMED THE EVIDENCE AND ASSURED US OF THE CERTAINTY OF A FUTURE STATE. Our Saviour has done much more than merely confirmed the truth of a future state. II. As He has assured us of a life to come, so HE HAS REVEALED THE MANNER OF OUR DELIVERANCE FROM DEATH, BY A BLESSÈD AND A GLORIOUS RESURRECTION. This is the greatest and most important discovery that was ever made to the world. III. Our Saviour has revealed in the gospel not only the resurrection but also THE GLORIFICATION OF THE BODY. It is at present mortal, tending constantly to dissolution, and, at last, crumbling into dust; but it will be raised incorruptible, and capable of lasting through immortal ages, like the soul to which it is to be united. IV. Another important discovery made by the gospel IS THE GENERAL JUDGMENT BY JESUS CHRIST. This article of faith, as well as the two former, is matter of pure revelation. Whether God would sit in judgment Himself, or delegate that office to another; whether the judge would make a visible appearance, or remain invisible in judgment; and whether our fate should be decided by a particular trial of every person at death, or by a public and general judgment of the world, were unknown to mankind. To reveal these important circumstances was reserved for our Lord and Saviour Jesus Christ, who abolished death, and brought life and immortality to light by the gospel. Our Saviour's information extends beyond the future judgment. V. HE HAS INTIMATED TO US THE GENERAL NATURE OF THE HEAVENLY FELICITY, and the principal sources from which it will spring. The gospel plainly intimates that in the heavenly state good men shall be delivered from the natural evils of this life, which fall heavy on some, and from which none are entirely exempted; that they shall be delivered from the injuries of evil men; nay, that they shall be delivered from the sufferings which they frequently bring upon themselves here, by the irregularity of their passions, and the folly of their own conduct. In the future state, the gospel informs us, the understanding will be enlarged, and made capable of extensive acquisitions; the heart will be completely purified, and rendered susceptible of the finest feelings, especially of love; and, to give scope to these affections, we shall be admitted into the noblest society, and enjoy a delightful intercourse with angels and saints, with Christ and God, with all that is great and good in the universe. VI. To complete the discoveries of the gospel, OUR SAVIOUR HAS INFORMED US THAT THE FUTURE HAPPINESS IS ETERNAL. As the joys of heaven are complete and satisfactory, so they are permanent and perpetual; subject to no abatement, to no interruption or decay; not only large as our wishes, but lasting as our immortal souls. (*Andrew Donnan.*)    *Immortality is the glorious discovery of Christianity* :—I say discovery, not because a future life was wholly unknown before Christ, but because it was so revealed by Him as to become, to a considerable extent, a new doctrine. Before Christ, immortality was a conjecture or a vague hope. Jesus, by His teaching and resurrection has made it a certainty. Again, before Christ, a future life lent little aid to virtue. It was seized upon by the imagination and passions, and so perverted by them as often to minister to vice. In Christianity this doctrine is wholly turned to a moral use; and the future is revealed only to give motives, resolution, force to self-conflict and to a holy life. My aim, in this discourse, is to strengthen, if I may, your conviction of immortality; and I have thought that I may do this by showing that this great truth is also a dictate of nature; that reason, though unable to establish it, yet accords with and adopts it, that it is written alike in God's Word and in the soul. It is plainly rational to expect that, if man was made for immortality, the marks of this destination will be found in his very constitution, and that these marks will grow stronger in proportion to the unfolding of his faculties. I would show that this expectation proves just that the teaching of revelation, in regard to a future life, finds a strong response in our own nature. This topic is the more important, because to some men there seem to be appearances in nature unfavourable to immortality. To many, the constant operation of decay in all the works of creation, the dissolution of all the forms of animal and vegetable nature, gives a feeling, as if destruction were the law to which we and all beings are subjected. It has often been said by the sceptic, that the *races* or classes of being are alone perpetual, that all the *individuals* which compose them are doomed to perish. Now I affirm that the more we know of the mind the more we see reason to distinguish it from the animal and vegetable races which grow and decay around us ; and that in its very nature we see reason for exempting it from the universal law of destruction. When we look around us on the earth we do indeed see everything changing, decaying, passing away ; and so inclined are we to reason from analogy or resemblance, that it is not wonderful that the dissolution of all the organised forms of matter should seem to us to announce our own destruction. But we overlook the distinctions between matter and mind ; and these are so immense as to justify the directly opposite conclusion. Let me point out some of these distinctions. 1. When we look at the organised productions of nature we see that they require only a limited time, and most of them a very short time, to reach their perfection, and accomplish their end. Take, *e.g.*, that noble production, a tree. Having reached a certain height, and borne leaves, flowers, and fruit, it has nothing more to do. Its powers are fully developed ; it has no hidden capacities, of which its buds and fruit are only the beginnings and pledges. Its design is fulfilled ; the principle of life within it can effect no more. Not so the mind. We can never say of this, as of a full-grown tree in autumn, it has answered its end, it has done its work, its capacity is exhausted. The mind, by going forward, does not reach insurmountable prison-walls, but learns more and more the boundlessness of its powers, and of the range for which it was created. 2. I now add, that the system of nature to which the tree belongs requires that it should stop where it does. Were it to grow for ever it would be an infinite mischief. But the indefinite expansion of the mind, instead of warring with and counteracting the system of creation, harmonises with and perfects it. One tree, should it grow for ever, would exclude other forms of vegetable life. One mind, in proportion to its expansion, awakens and, in a sense, creates, other minds. It is an ever-enlarging source of thought and love. 3. Another distinction between material forms and the mind is, that to the former destruction is no loss. They exist for others wholly, in no degree for themselves ; and others only can sorrow for their fall. The mind, on the contrary, has a deep interest in its own existence. In this respect, indeed, it is distinguished from the animal as well as the vegetable. An improved mind understands the greatness of its own nature, and the worth of existence, as these cannot be understood by the unimproved. The thought of its own destruction suggests to it an extent of ruin which the latter cannot comprehend. The thought of such faculties as reason, conscience and moral will, being extinguished—of powers akin to the Divine energy, being annihilated by their Author—of truth and virtue, those images of God, being blotted out—of progress towards perfection, being broken off almost at its beginning—this is a thought fitted to overwhelm a mind in which the consciousness of its spiritual nature is in a good degree unfolded. In other words, the more the mind is true to itself and to God, the more it clings to existence, the more it shrinks from extinction as an infinite loss. Would not its destruction, then, be a very different thing from the destruction of material beings, and does the latter furnish an analogy or presumption in support of the former ? To me, the undoubted fact that the mind thirsts for continued being, just in proportion as it obeys the will of its Maker, is a proof, next to irresistible, of its being destined by Him for immortality. 4. Let me add one more distinction between the mind and material forms. I return to the tree. We speak of the tree as *destroyed*. We say that destruction is the order of nature, and some say that man must not hope to escape the universal law. Now we deceive ourselves in this use of words. There is in reality no destruction in the material world. True, the tree is resolved into its elements ; but its elements survive. and still more, they survive to fulfil the same end which they before accomplished. Not a power of nature is lost. The particles of the decayed tree are only left at liberty to form new, perhaps more beautiful and useful combinations. They may shoot up into more luxuriant foliage, or enter into the structure of the highest animals. But were mind to perish, there would be absolute, irretrievable destruction; for mind, from its nature, is something individual, an uncompounded essence, which cannot be broken into parts and enter into union with other minds. I am myself, and can become no other being. My experience, my history, cannot become my neighbour's. My consciousness, my memory, my interest in my past life, my affections, cannot be transferred. If in any instance I have withstood temptation, and through such resistance have acquired power over myself and a claim to the approbation of my fellow-beings, this resistance, this power, this claim, are my own; I cannot make them another's. I can give away my property, my limbs; but that which makes myself, in other words, my consciousness, my recollections, my feelings, my hopes, these can never become parts of another mind. In the extinction of a thinking, moral being, who has gained truth and virtue, there would be an absolute destruction. (*W. E. Channing, D.D.*)    *The Christian view of death:*—It is noticeable how small a space is given to death in the New Testament, as if our Lord Jesus made light of it! His idea of it is sleep. How full of peacefulness is this idea! There is nothing dreadful about it. "Lord, if he sleep he shall do well!" Beautiful and benign sleep! Our little children, when the time comes and the parent commands it, go to sleep. They laugh as they climb the stairs; there is a short silence as they kneel; then we hear them singing as the last evening sunbeams brighten the room, till sleep nestles down on their eyelids and they know nothing more till the morning's sun wakes the birds outside, and another day is here! Thus shall it be with God's children when they die. Their Father will, at the proper time, bid them put there work aside and go to rest. Not unwillingly, but with cheerful love they obey. Amid the evening glow of that Divine kindness which has brightened their working hours they will say "goodnight" to their friends and the world and peacefully "sleep in Jesus," "until the day break and the shadows flee away." (*I. E. Page.*)    *Life enlarged by death:*— A child that has been penned up in narrow quarters, with few playthings, and in constrained circumstances, has a grandfather and grandmother living in the country. There is the farmhouse full of rude abundance; there are the ample grounds; there is the brook, with fish in it; there is the big barn; and there are all manner of things in the barn-yard. The child has been out there once; and he had such liberty, and found his grandma such a dear old grandma, and his grandpa such a kind old grandpa, that the days were not long enough. He had so much sport, and was made so much of, and was never scolded, and never sent to school, and had nothing to do or to think of but to play, play, play all the time, that he would have liked to abide there. But he has been taken back to the city, and he lives in a narrow house, and has to go to school, and has to do this thing and that which are irksome to him, and is put through all the paces which are thought necessary for his education and development; and he longs for his country experience again. When spring comes round once more, the father and mother say to the little fellow, "Now, if you are a good boy, next June we are going to take you out to grandpa's." The idea of going out of the city to grandpa's! The child's mind is filled with all manner of delights. Ah, what perfect ecstacy he feels! He dreams about going, and rejoices in the thought. He does not analyse the intermediate steps, nor think much about them. His grandpa's is the place where, to his thought and affection, centres everything that is most heavenly—for a boy on earth, that is. I suppose that comes nearer to representing the feelings which the primitive disciples, the early Christians, had about dying, than any other illustration that you could well make. It was to go and be with the Lord. (*H. W. Beecher.*)    *A great may be:*—Rabelais, when dying, said, "I go to seek a great *may be.*" (*T. Carlyle.*)    *Immortality:*— Renan is unquestionably one of the most distinguished among those who deny the existence of a creative will and personal God. Yet Renan cannot make up his mind that he has lost for ever his beloved sister; that she has passed into the night of nothingness. He dedicates his "Life of Jesus" to her memory; . . . and invokes "the pure soul of his sister Henriette, who died at Byblos, September 24, 1861, to reveal to him, from the bosom of God in which she rests, those truths which are mightier than death, and take away the fear of death." (*J. H. Rigg, D.D.*)    *The lighted valley of death:*—In India a dreaded pass stretches between high rocks which frown from either side, as if ready to entomb the traveller who walks below. But when, towards evening, the sun in its westward journey reaches the head of the defile and pours its rays directly into it, the whole aspect of the valley is changed,

The sun, standing there, brightens the gloom into light and beauty. Who now would dread to pass that way? Thus shall it be with those who die in Christ. The living have always dreaded the gloom of the dark valley; but what if, as we pass, the Sun of Righteousness shall shine overhead? (*I. E. Page.*)     "*Now open your eyes*":—As one, taking his friend up a hillside in Scotland, that he might have a glorious view of Loch Lomond, bade him close his eyes, and led him by the hand till he could say, as the splendour of the landscape lay before him, "Now open your eyes," so Christ has a glory of heaven to show His people; but ere its full revelation they must close their eyes in death and clasp His hand for a few steps in darkness, to open them at His bidding amid the glories of heaven, and behold for themselves what "He hath prepared for them that love Him." (*Ibid.*)

Ver. 11. **A preacher, and an apostle, and a teacher of the Gentiles.**—I. A public PREACHER is one who may discharge his office ever in one and the same place. II. AN APOSTLE goes about everywhere; but he would have fully satisfied the requirements of his apostolic office if he had once for all declared his message. III. TEACHER. Here we have in addition diligence and perseverance in teaching: from which arose suffering. (*J. A. Bengel.*)     *The preacher a crier:*—It is an argument, that the preacher brings not stolen stuff nor bad commodity. He whose fruit is best, as we see in cities, crieth loudest. A low voice in the street argueth either an ill-commodity or a false way of obtaining it. (*J. Barlow, D.D.*)     *Not to cavil with the preacher:*—Again, this must teach the auditors not to cavil with the crier, but to hear the words of exhortation patiently. Some, like Festus, tell Paul, if he cry aloud, that he is beside himself; reputing the preacher rude, indiscreet, passionate. Why? Can a bell have too shrill a sound? a hound too deep or bass a mouth? a piece give too great a report? or a crier extend his voice too high? Shall not the shepherd shout when the sheep are wandering, or ready to be devoured by the wolf? Will ye not ring the bells awake, when the city is on fire? Discharge the greatest cannon, when the ship is in distress, and in danger to be lost in the haven? And shall not the preacher cry, roar, and, as John, bellow like an ox (for so the word is read), when men sleep and sink in sin, and be in hazard to be drowned and devoured by Satan, that cruel wolf, and pirate of the soul? (*Ibid.*)     *The servants of God take delight to dwell and discourse of good things* (Act xx. 7):—It's no burden or wearisomeness to the saints to enlarge their speech on heavenly subjects. A traveller when he hath taken a view of the situation of many towns and countries, beheld the rare monuments that he hath met withal, rejoiceth to make relation thereof unto his friends after his return; and so is it with a Christian, who is a spiritual traveller: when he hath seen into the mysteries of religion, found out the great secrets therein contained, by the painful travel of his mind, he maketh it the joy of his heart largely to discourse thereof unto his brethren. (*Ibid.*)     *Love makes teachers:*—But did they love the gospel they neither would or could be silent; for their word, like fire in straw, would burst forth. Will not the soldier speak of his wounds, the huntsman of his hounds, and the husbandman of his cattle and grounds? And shall we love the gospel and never make mention of it? No, no: this little speech of heavenly things argueth that the love of many is but cold. Love the word once, and say nothing of it, if thou canst. (*Ibid.*)     *A gospel preacher:*—Bramwell was a plain preacher in the States, and to some extent an uncultivated preacher; but he was full of faith and zeal, and his ministry was attended with marvellous power. He was preaching in a little village on one occasion, and the German minister, Trubner, was induced to go and hear him. Trubner was a very cultivated scholar, and a profound critic; and when some of Bramwell's friends saw him there they said, "Alas! alas! for poor Bramwell, how Trubner will criticise him!" Precious little did Bramwell care for him, or for all the philosophers under the sun. He preached, and set before his audience the everlasting gospel of Jesus Christ, and when Trubner went out of the church one of his friends said to him, "How did you like him? Don't you think he wanders a good deal in his preaching?" "Oh, yes," said the old Lutheran, "he do wander most delightfully from de subject to de heart." (*The Teacher's Cabinet.*)

Ver. 12. **I also suffer these things.**—*Pride in the profane causeth good men to suffer for welldoing:*—The Pharisees were zealous for the law and ceremonies, and Paul preached the gospel, called them beggarly and impotent rudiments; told that if they were circumcised Christ profited them nothing. Why, this so took down the pride of man, that he should not be justified by his own works, but by another's, that Paul was persecuted, and hardly intreated of his own countrymen. If a skilful tailor take measure of a crooked and misshapen person, and fit the garment proportionable to the pattern, a proud piece of flesh will pout, swell, and wrangle with the workmen; so let the ministers and men of God do good, divide the Word aright, high and lofty spirits will be muttering, for they cannot endure the light, or to be told of their deformities. Thus Paul was reputed an enemy for telling them the truth. A counterfeit and false glass is the fittest for old, withered, and wrinkled curtizans to view themselves in; for if it should show them their right shapes, all things to nothing, they split it against the walls. (*J. Barlow, D.D.*) **For I know whom I have believed.**—*The foundation of the Christian's hope:*—I. ONE GROUND OF THE APOSTLE'S ASSURANCE WAS A PERSUASION THAT CHRIST IS ABLE TO KEEP THE SOULS COMMITTED UNTO HIM. 1. It is implied that Christ is able to bring the soul into a state of salvation. 2. This persuasion of the apostle implied that Christ is able also to preserve the soul in a state of salvation. He added, as the other ground of his assurance—II. A CONSCIOUSNESS THAT HE HAD HIMSELF COMMITTED UNTO CHRIST HIS OWN SOUL. However firmly he might be persuaded of Christ's ability to save the souls committed to Him, he yet could not be assured that He would save his soul unless he felt conscious of the fact, that it was really committed unto Him. Let us now see what things this consciousness also implied. 1. It implied that he had knowingly given up all thoughts and hopes of saving himself by his own merits and doings. 2. It was further implied in it, that he now knowingly placed all his hopes and dependence on the sacrifice and mediation of Jesus Christ alone. 3. But it was also implied in it that, from the time in which he had thus renounced his own righteousness, and by faith had hoped in the righteousness of Christ, he had lived and acted consistently with such a faith and hope. (*E. Cooper.*) *The Christian's confidence in Christ:*—The faith of the Christian is here seen. I. In its OBJECT—" I know whom I have believed." II. In its CHARACTER. It is seen in many noble qualities and bearings, inseparably connected with each other in the triumphant profession made by the apostle. 1. Knowledge is here the foundation of faith—" I know whom I have believed." Yes, he knew by irresistible demonstration—such as extracted the venom of his heart against Jesus of Nazareth, and filled it with inextinguishable love and fervent devotedness to Him. 2. As knowledge is the foundation of faith, so faith is the reposing of an absolute trust—" I am persuaded that He is able to keep that which I have committed to Him." III. In its CONSUMMATION—" against that day." There is to be a consummation—when we shall receive "the end of our faith, even the salvation of our soul." The province of faith is but for a season, and it shall give place to the vision and fruition of God. (*W. B. Collyer, D.D.*) *The internal evidence of experience:*—The evidences for revelation have been commonly divided under two heads, external and internal. Under the head of external evidence, we may class all those proofs, which, though relating to what is found in the Scriptures, are nevertheless exterior to the Word of God; such, for instance, as the authenticity of the Books of Scripture, and the genuineness of their authorship, the miracles by which the truths that the apostles delivered were attested, and the sufferings and persecution which they underwent. But then the internal evidence is not less important. We might, first, take the internal evidence of Scripture which we gather from the Word of God itself—the harmony of one portion of it with another, and the circumstance that in our investigation of its bright and blessed pages, they seem at once to commend themselves, as what we might expect to come from the God of truth. And then there is the internal evidence, which may be gathered from the Christian's own experience—the attestation, so to speak, of a Christian's own experience to the truths which he finds revealed in the Scriptures of God. Now we believe that it is to evidence partaking of this character that the apostle alludes in our text. There was no confounding of his principles; there was no putting down of the truth which he maintained; nothing was able to terrify him out of what he had embraced as the truth of God. "For I know whom I have believed, and am persuaded that He is able to keep that which I have committed unto Him against that day." Now this class of evidence, we believe, will, more or less, be the evidence of every believer in the Lord Jesus. I. The first point which is presented for our consideration is THAT THE APOSTLE BELIEVED THE GOSPEL. This is the first act of the sinner with respect to Jesus. II. But the believer goes further. He does not rest with dependence upon the promise, that the Lord will be with him unto the end of the world; but he is assured of this, because he finds THAT SO FAR AS HE HAS TRUSTED THE PROMISE, GOD HAS ACTUALLY BEEN WITH HIM. He has found Him true to His word by positive experience. III. THE CONFIDENCE WHICH PAUL HAD IN THE FUTURE GATHERED FROM HIS EXPERIENCE OF THE PAST. (*H. W. McGrath, M.A.*) *The believer's confidence in the prospect of eternity :*—I. THE AWFUL PERIOD. It is not mentioned by name; but the apostle only calls it "that day." What day? The day of death, when "the dust returns to the earth as it was, and the spirit returns unto God who gave it"? Or the day of judgment? Doubtless the day of judgment. This is often in the Scripture called "that day," in order to show us that it is a very important, a very remarkable, a very distinguished day. II. WHAT THE APOSTLE DID in the prospect of this period. He deposited something in the Redeemer's hands; "that which I have committed unto Him against that day." What, now, was this deposit? You evidently see it was something personal, in which he acted as a believer. And it is not necessary, as far as I know, to exclude anything from the transaction; but principally we are to understand the eternal concerns of his soul. And if this required any confirmation, it may be derived from the example of poor Stephen, who, when he was dying, said, "Lord Jesus receive my spirit"—and from the experience of David, who in an hour of danger said, "Into Thy hand I commit my spirit; Thou hast redeemed me, O Lord God of truth!" It means, therefore, simply believing. The apostle's representation of faith here will remind us of several things. 1. The committing our eternal all into His hands implies conviction. The man before was deluded by error and blinded by ignorance; but now "the eyes of his understanding" are opened. (1) Now he is convinced of the value of his soul. (2) He is now convinced of the danger of the soul. (3) And now, too, he is convinced of his inability to save his soul. 2. And this act implies also a concern for its security and welfare. 3. The act of committing the soul to Christ also implies application to the Redeemer for the purpose of salvation. 4. It implies submission. III. THE SATISFACTION FELT in the review of the transaction. 1. You see what the satisfaction is derived from: and, generally considered, you observe that it takes in the apostle's acquaintance with the great Depository himself—"I know whom I have believed." 2. You have seen the satisfaction generally expressed; but here is a particular reference with regard to it. "And I am persuaded," says he, "that He is able to keep that which I have committed unto Him against that day." (*W. Jay.*) *Acquaintance with Christ the Christian's strength :*—Since the same source from whence Paul had all his high attainments is as open in all its fulness to each of us, as it was to him, let us consider the way in which that inexhaustible fountain was made available to him to draw supplies according to all his need, whether for support under the discouragement of his trials, or for direction under the perplexity of his difficulties. One word of the text will open the whole of this to us : "I know";—"I know whom I have believed," says he. Knowledge was the substance of his power. Nay, then, says the unlearned Christian, it is too difficult for me. Such knowledge is too wonderful and excellent. It is high, I cannot attain unto it. It is not for me. How discouraging! will the poor and busy man say. I have neither the leisure nor the means and opportunity of gaining it. How heartless the attempt, then, will the weak-minded and humble Christian say, conscious of his weakness. How can I ever hope to reach even a measure of that, when I feel my weakness and inability every step I take. But to the most unlearned, to the busiest, to the most feeble-minded, I say, that this knowledge and all the power it contains is for you. Mark the text. The apostle does not say, I know the support I shall receive, or the direction that will be given me, for I am wise and experienced, but, "I know whom I have believed." His knowledge was not of things, but of a person, and that but one. I. Here is mentioned HIS KNOWLEDGE OF THE TRUSTEE. Let us consider some particulars of the more obvious but important kind, wherein the apostle knew, and we should know Him. 1. He knew that He was faithful, therefore he believed Him. 2. He knew Him to be able. 3. He knew Him to be willing. 4. He knew Him to be all-wise, both to see his trouble, and the best way to get him out of it. 5. Nay, though clouds and darkness surrounded him, Paul staggered not at this, for he knew the ways of the Lord, that this is His method of dealing with His children. In a word he knew Him to be the sum of all happiness, the source of all strength, the pledge and faithfulness of all the promises, the depository of all power, the ruler of all events, the head over all things to His people, the Saviour both of soul and body. II. WHAT WAS IT THAT THE APOSTLE COMMITTED TO HIM? What was that deposit (as it is in the original), he was persuaded He was able to keep? I answer in one word, his treasure. But that would assume many forms under different circumstances. 1. When the guilt of sin would come upon his conscience, it would be the salvation of his soul. 2. When the power of temptation would come over him, it would be his integrity in serving God. 3, When personal dangers surrounded him, and left him no way of escape, it would be his self-preservation. 4. When assailed by the malicious insinuations of false apostles, and attacks upon his motives, as at Corinth, it would be his character. 5. When he heard of the entering in of grievous wolves into the flock he had fed so carefully, it would be the care of all the churches. Whatever it was, in short, that at the moment most occupied his thoughts and attention, that was what he had deposited for safe-keeping in the hands of Christ, and which he was persuaded He was able to keep against all assaults until that day, when the secrets of all hearts shall be revealed, and every man shall have his praise of God. (*G. Jeans, M.A.*)　　*Grounds of confidence in the Saviour's ability :*—We have here a strong expression of his confidence in the Saviour : let us consider, first, the nature, and then the ground of this confidence. I. Its NATURE. Some suppose the deposit, which the apostle mentions as committed to him, to denote the gospel trust in general : and this view is favoured by the similar expression in the context, " that good thing, which was committed to thee, keep—hold fast the form of sound words." But it seems more probable that he refers in the text to the interest of his salvation, the trust of his whole being, his body, soul, and spirit, which he had confidently committed to Christ, as Him who had " abolished death, and brought life and immortality to light." In the near view of martyrdom, dissolution, and eternity, his confidence remained unshaken. This is a trust unfit to be reposed in any created arm. No potentate can hold back his own spirit, much less another's, a moment from death : no angel could undertake such a trust ; he would abjure it. Some portion of our interests we commit to others, but never think of committing our whole spirit to a creature. Hence we infer that Jesus Christ is truly God : else it were highly improper, and indeed accursed, thus to trust Him. II. THE GROUNDS ON WHICH THE APOSTLE TRUSTS THE SAVIOUR. He saw that in His character which warranted such confidence, and he had a conviction of His ability. There was some peculiarity in Paul's case, to which we may advert, but which we need not anxiously separate from the general case of Christians. 1. The first ground, peculiar to Paul, is his vision of Christ at Damascus : this penetrated him with reverence and attachment for the glorious person then revealed : his heart was melted like wax, and he cried, " Lord, what wilt Thou have me to do ? " 2. He was confirmed in his trust by his subsequent experience of the favour and power of Christ. His eyes were opened by Ananias at Christ's command. Miraculous powers of great variety were conferred on himself ; so that he did perhaps even greater wonders than Christ had done. He was inspired to preach with power and boldness : " the power of Christ rested on him." In his soul such a renovation took place, as only Divine power could have effected : he was purified with humility and enlarged with love ; his prospects were extended far beyond time : and all this was the effect of Christ's ascension, and His gift of the Holy Spirit. 3. Jesus Christ had wrought the great salvation, and reconciled it with all the attributes of God. 4. The rank which Jesus Christ holds in heaven assures us that He " is able to keep that which is committed to Him." 5. As Jesus Christ is the appointed Judge of all, so eternal life is at His disposal in His judicial character. (*R. Hall, M.A.*)　　*A funeral sermon :*—I. THE SACRED DEPOSIT WHICH THE APOSTLE HAD MADE. All that concerned his soul, his hopes and his desires, his deliverance from guilt, and the enjoyment of the eternal favour of his God, comprised the whole amount of that deposit he had committed to the custody of his Redeemer. Now this transaction intimates—1. The perfect consciousness of a separate and immortal existence. 2. A deep sense of the supreme value of the soul. 3. A powerful conviction of the awful nature of death. II. THE HIGH SATISFACTION HE FELT WITH REGARD TO ITS SAFETY. 1. He knew Him in the power of His arm. 2. He knew Him in His sacred relation to the Church, as Prophet, Priest, and King. 3. He knew Him, in all the promises of His Word. 4. This persuasion was founded upon the certain return of the Saviour as the Judge of all. Hence he speaks of his soul being kept in safety against that day. (*J. E. Good.*)　　*The confidence of St. Paul :*—I. HIS KNOWLEDGE EXPRESSED —he knew whom he believed. It was not in himself he trusted, nor on his own foundation that he built ; he staked nothing on his own reason or imagination or self-begotten opinions ; nor had he any reliance on his own merits, or a high notion of the worth of his exertions, even for the cause of his fellow-creatures, or for the glory of God. It was not the world or the world's opinion that he trusted or followed, or any human judgment or conclusion that he rested upon, as apart from God's revelation. 1. He knew Him as the revealed Saviour spoken of and promised from age to age. 2. He knew Him as the Almighty Saviour, the eternal Son of the Father, fully sufficient for the wants of fallen man, and entirely adapted to the very work of redemption which He came from heaven to fulfil. 3. And he knew and believed this on the personal experience of that power in his own heart; the presence of the Spirit of Christ in his own soul, having already revived and quickened him from the death of his former corrupt and blinded state. II. THE TRUST he reposed in the object of his faith—"I am persuaded that He is able to keep that which I have committed to Him against that day." There was a persuasion, or, as the original describes it, a full reliance and settled repose in his mind on the object of his faith—the Saviour whom he believed. It is perhaps here a question, whether the apostle meant to say in these words, that Christ could and would keep that which he had committed to Christ; or, that which Christ had committed to him. Doubtless there is an interchange, as it were, an intercommunion between Christ and the soul of the believer; so that something is committed from Christ to the soul of His servant, and something also committed from the soul to Christ ; and both are kept by the power of Christ alone. Christ committed His truth, His word, His gospel to the apostle, to be received in the heart and proclaimed throughout the world; and the apostle committed himself, his all, to Christ. By His grace alone could the purity and perpetuity of Divine truth be upheld in the world; and by His Spirit alone could the apostle be himself upheld amidst the shocks of temptation and the inroads of time and the world, and conducted surely forward unto that day. It was in the former sense perhaps that, in a following verse, the apostle said to Timothy—"That good thing which was committed to thee, keep by the Holy Ghost which dwelleth in us." But take the text rather in the view given to us by our own translation, and we shall find that apostle had been persuaded, and not in vain, to entrust to Christ and His grace, his credit, his peace, his soul for ever. 1. His credit. He had to go forth truly, to Jew and Gentile, to preach what might seem a new religion—the one truth of God, hidden from ages and generations, and now made manifest by the gospel ; and he had to pledge himself that it was true, and worthy their acceptance. He was persuaded Christ could keep the word he had given, and fulfil the promises he had made. 2. He committed to Christ his peace. Peace, such as the world valued and sought after, the apostle was not very likely ever to ensure : he had to meet danger and want, to face enemies and bear insult. Happiness under such circumstances must have been very different from what the world calls happiness : but it was not the less so for that, nor could he the less confidently trust his inward peace and even outward circumstances to Him who judged and maintained his cause, and who had said— "Peace I leave with you; not as the world giveth give I unto you." 3. To Him, in fine, the apostle committed, doubtless, his soul, his all, for time and eternity. He acted here in the full spirit of his fellow-apostle St. Peter (1 Pet. iv. 19). (*C. J. Hoare, M.A.*) *Faith illustrated :*—I. THE GRANDEST ACTION OF THE CHRISTIAN'S LIFE. The apostle says, he committed himself into the hands of Christ. I saw the other day a remarkable picture, which I shall use as an illustration of the way of salvation by faith in Jesus. An offender had committed a crime for which he must die, but it was in the olden time when churches were considered to be sanctuaries in which criminals might hide themselves and so escape. See the transgressor—he rushes towards the church, the guards pursue him with their drawn swords, all athirst for his blood, they pursue him even to the church door. He rushes up the steps, and just as they are about to overtake him and hew him in pieces on the threshold of the church, out comes the bishop, and holding up the crucifix he cries, "Back, back! stain not the precincts of God's house with blood ! stand back !" and the guards at once respect the emblem and stand back, while the poor fugitive hides himself behind the robes of the priest. It is even so with Christ. The guilty sinner flies to the cross—flies straight away to Jesus, and though Justice pursues him, Christ lifts up His wounded hands and cries to Justice, "Stand back! stand back! I shelter this sinner; in the secret place of My tabernacle do I hide him ; I will not suffer him to perish, for he puts his trust in Me." The apostle meant that he did make a full and free surrender of himself to Christ, to be Christ's property, and Christ's servant for ever. I must add, however, that this act of faith must not be performed once only, but it must be

continued as long as you live. As long as you live you must have no other
confidence but " Jesus only." You may take Him now to-day, to have and to hold
through life and in death, in tempest and in sunshine, in poverty and in wealth,
never to part or sunder from Him. You must take Him to be your only prop,
your only pillar from this day forth and for ever. II. THE JUSTIFICATION OF
THIS GRAND ACT OF TRUST. Confidence is sometimes folly ; trusting in man is always
so. When I exhort you, then, to put your entire confidence in Christ, am I justified in so doing? " I have not trusted to an unknown and untried pretender. I
have not relied upon one whose character I could suspect. I have confidence
in one whose power, whose willingness, whose love, whose truthfulness I know.
I know whom I have believed." Paul not only knew these things by faith, but
he knew much of them by experience. Our knowledge of Christ is somewhat
like climbing one of our Welsh mountains. When you are at the base you see
but little ; the mountain itself appears to be but one half as high as it really is.
Confined in a little valley you discover scarcely anything but the rippling brooks
as they descend into the stream at the base of the mountain. Climb the first
rising knoll, and the valley lengthens and widens beneath your feet. Go up
higher, and higher still, till you stand upon the summit of one of the great
roots that start out as spurs from the sides of the mountain, you see the
country for some four or five miles round, and you are delighted with the widening
prospect. But go onward, and onward, and onward, and how the scene enlarges,
till at last, when you are on the summit, and look east, west, north, and south,
you see almost all England lying before you. Yonder is a forest in some distant
country, perhaps two hundred miles away, and yonder the sea, and there a
shining river and the smoking chimneys of a manufacturing town, or there the
masts of the ships in some well-known port. All these things please and
delight you, and you say, " I could not have imagined that so much could
be seen at this elevation." Now, the Christian life is of the same order. When
we first believe in Christ we see but little of Him. The higher we climb the more
we discover of His excellencies and His beauties. But who has ever gained the
summit? Paul now grown old, sitting, grey hair'd, shivering in a dungeon in
Rome— he could say, with greater power than we can, " I know whom I have
believed ! "—for each experience had been like the climbing of a hill, each trial
had been like the ascending to another summit, and his death seemed like the
gaining of the very top of the mountain from which he could see the whole of the
faithfulness and the love of Him to whom he had committed his soul. III.
THE APOSTLE'S CONFIDENCE. " I am persuaded that He is able to keep that which
I have committed to Him." See this man. He is sure he shall be saved. But
why? Paul! art thou sure that thou canst keep thyself? " No," says he, " I
have nothing to do with that " : and yet thou art sure of thy salvation ! " Yes,"
saith he, " I am ! " How is it, then? " Why, I am persuaded that He is able to
keep me. Christ, to whom I commit myself, I know hath power enough to hold
me to the end." Martin Luther was bold enough to exclaim, " Let Him that
died for my soul, see to the salvation of it." (*C. H. Spurgeon.*) *Assurance :*—I.
THE OBJECT OF FAITH—" I know whom I have believed." Well, now, whom
have you believed ? Have you believed Juggernaut ? Have you believed the
Hindoo Brahmins ? The glorious covenant Head of His Church—I have
believed Him. " He that believeth on the Son of God hath everlasting life ;
and he that believeth not hath not life." Where there is no believing of a saving
description upon the Person of the Lord Jesus Christ, there is no salvation. It is
in vain to tell me of all the excellencies of the creature, of all the attainments of
moral philosophy, and of all the pride of superstition, it only just makes a pious
road to hell for those who pretend to pursue it. There is no such thing as salvation,
no such thing as safety, for time or for eternity, but by believing on the Son of
God. " I know." I beseech you to mark the positive nature of the assertion. It is
not, " I hope, or trust " ; it is not, " I can, or shall, or may, believe in Him " ; but,
" I know whom I have believed." I do not like anything less than " I know," even
in things temporal. If I were to ask my servant whether such and such a matter
is safe, or right, or done properly, and I were to receive for an answer, " I think so,"
or "Probably it may be so " ; " Do not tell me that," I should say, perhaps somewhat angrily ; " Do you know it? is it really so ? " Surely, then, if I should
require this in temporal matters, what should I look for in things spiritual You
tell me God is merciful, and I shall do as well as others in the end. " I know whom
I have believed." The question might be put to the persons who make such an

assertion, "What do you know of Him?" "Well, I will tell you. I know very well that He is truly, properly, essentially, eternally God. I know enough of Him to be quite sure that He is truly, and properly, and sinlessly man. I know for certain of Him, that He is, in His complex character, as God and man, Mediator, Surety, Daysman for His Church, in official standing." Do you know all this? Do you know Him personally? Can you say, "I know that in His office He has accomplished all that is requisite for the salvation of His Church." Look at the word "believe" before we quit this part of our subject. "I know whom I have believed." What is believing? In the margin of our Bible we read "trusted." Well, believing is trusting, and trusting is believing. II. The nature of faith's actings—"that which I have committed to Him." There is something about this which enters at once into the daily experience of a child of God, and I think if it were more extensively practised in our experience, we should be happier Christians —the committing of everything to Him. I have committed to Him my soul's concerns; I have committed to Him the affairs of time; and I committed to Him His visible Church, which neither legislators nor monarchs care anything about, but to distract and to destroy. Look at these things for a few moments. I have committed to Him my soul's concerns. And these are of two descriptions; my soul's concerns for security, salvation, eternal life; and my soul's concerns in regard to spiritual existence, and spiritual prosperity, in my way to glory. I commit both to Him. Now the nature of faith's actings is to commit all to Jesus, in both these respects. If the filthy effluvia of human nature's risings annoy me, I shall cry, "Lord, subdue all my iniquity." I commit them all to Him; cannot do anything without Him, and I am sure it is no good talking about it. "Lord, conquer my depravity. Lord, fulfil Thy promises, that 'sin shall not have dominion.'" Then go on to mark, that it is faith's province to commit the affairs of this life to Him. They are not too little, they are not too mean for Him to notice, nor for Him to manage, and it may be viewed as the peculiar privilege of the Christian to carry to the throne of grace, and commit to Christ, every arrangement He may make, every bargain into which He may enter, every association He may form, and every companion He may choose. So with all His successes—to commit them all to Him, remembering that it is He who giveth power to get wealth. So, again, with regard to losses and crosses, painful events. III. The expectation of faith. "He is able to keep" it; and that is the point which fixes upon my attention. Blessings on His name, that He is as willing as He is able! He is interested in it. But this statement implies great danger or difficulty, or the Divine keeping would not be necessary. It implies that our beloved Zion is surrounded with every description of enemies and dangers, or it would not be said that it needs Divine keeping. Moreover, there seems in this expectation of faith enough to nourish assurance itself. "He is able to keep that which I have committed to Him." Well, then, assurance may lift up its head, and say, "If it be the soul's concerns, I have nothing to doubt—I trust it all in His hands. If it be the affairs of my family, or my business, I have nothing to harass me concerning them." One word more. "Against that day." We might mention the day of the termination of that trouble, the day of the accomplishment of that desire, the day of the consummation of a certain purpose or scheme in God's providence, relative to our spiritual or temporal affairs; but I must hasten to that day the apostle had immediately in view, "that day" when Christ shall claim His own; "that day" when all the election of grace shall appear before Him, and be presented to the Father "a perfect Church, without spot or wrinkle, or any such thing." (*J. Irons.*)

*The grounds of the believer's confidence:*—What a noble picture have we here! Elsewhere we are told that the apostle was "in presence weak, and in speech contemptible"; but he does not appear so now. We see in him a courage and calmness more than human. "What though my departure from this world be marked by infamy, and violence, and scorn—what though friends forsake, and the world revile, and foes pursue me with unresting hatred, I have one treasure of which they cannot rob me, one refuge to which I can always fly, one Friend who 'having loved me, will love me unto the end.'" I. The terms in which the apostle makes this noble declaration of his confidence. The apostle does not say, "what I have believed," as if his hope stood in his creed, which might be very exact—or in his Church, which might be very true—or in his labours, which were incessant and self-denying—or in his life, which was without reproach and blameless; but he says, "The proper object of my confidence is a Person; my religion consists in having found a Friend—a Friend with whom all my interests for time and for eternity may be entrusted. I cleave to a living, infallible, Divine Protector. 'I know whom I have believed.'" The expression, as you perceive, is in true keeping with the entire spirit of New Testament theology. When a sinner awakes to the first sight of his danger, the first words to be addressed to him are, "Believe on the Lord Jesus Christ, and thou shalt be saved." This is a principle of the Divine procedure which would commend itself were it only for its beautiful and pure simplicity. When pressed with the terrors of a guilty conscience, when despair and fear seem to be coming in upon me like a flood, I want something to fly to at once; I want to be directed immediately to an altar of safety. Tell me not of things to be believed, or learned, or sought for, or done, but tell me of one simple act which shall bring me within reach of mercy. Do not lose time in considering how "life and immortality are to be brought to light"—take Him as "the life." A convinced sinner cannot do better than embrace a theology of one article—"I know whom I have believed." Again, let us look at the word "believed." In the writings of St. Paul the expression stands for the highest form of moral persuasion. It implies the strength of an all-pervading practical conviction—the reposing of a loving, perfect, and confiding trust. The advance of this upon a mere intellectual faith you will perceive—for not only is it believed that Christ came for man's salvation, but that this salvation has become individually applied to ourselves. "I know whom I have believed." My faith rests upon my knowledge, just as my knowledge reacts upon my faith. I am not making a plunge into eternity in the dark. I have looked to the soundness of my Rock to see whether it will bear me; I have "tasted that the Lord is gracious," and therefore am "confident of this very thing, that He that hath begun a good work in me, will perform it unto the day of Christ." The word points out to us the danger of taking our religion on trust; the duty of subjecting our opinions to a diligent and inquiring search. An uninvestigated faith can never be a happy faith. Christ's work for us must be believed, but Christ's work in us must be proved. Let us take the next words, showing to us the nature of the Christian's deposit—"I know whom I have believed, and am persuaded that He is able to keep that which I have committed unto Him against that day." To the trust here spoken of we can place no limit. How great the privilege of having this treasure locked up in safe custody, feeling that whatever else is taken from us, our souls are enclosed in the sanctuary of heaven—that our Jesus puts His hand upon these and says, "These souls are Mine"—Mine to be kept, Mine to be watched over, Mine to be purged from all dross and defilement, and to be rendered back each to his own, "at that day!" And the apostle mentions this day, in preference to the day of his death, because although the earlier period would abundantly vindicate the Saviour's faithfulness, yet the other is the day when Christ shall formally give up His great trust—when, in the presence of all the intelligences of heaven, He shall show how carefully He has watched over souls, through the conflicts of life, through the terrors of death, through the long repose of the grave, now to hold them up as His jewels, and reward, and crown at "that day." II. THE GROUNDS ON WHICH THE APOSTLE RESTS HIS CONFIDENCE. These, as we should suppose, must consist in the personal qualifications of Him who was the subject of such trust, in the attributes of His holy nature, in the efficacy of His atoning work, in the virtue of His meritorious obedience, in the continued exertions of His resumed Divinity now that He is seated at the right hand of God. Thus, let us look at the attributes of His nature—at His power, for example; does He not say, "All things are delivered into My hand"; "all power is given unto Me in heaven and in earth"; "I open, and no man shutteth; I shut, and no man openeth!" Who, then, can harm us, if we have secured such a Friend as this? But, further, we know Paul would have a ground of persuasion in the work of Christ, in the sufficiency of His obedience, in the infinite reach of His atonement. The apostle was one who felt painfully the greatness of his own deficiencies. His language ever was "'In the Lord Jehovah have I righteousness and strength.' My only trust is 'that I may be found in Him.'" But once more, the apostle would find a comforting ground of persuasion in the thought that the Saviour in whom he believed, lived for ever. It is a sad reflection with regard to our earthly friends, that however cherished or however tried, death will soon take them away. (*D. Moore, M.A.*) *A safe deposit:*—We sometimes believe in men whom we do not know. We think we know them; but we are mistaken. We may inquire; we may observe; we may ask for testimony and receive it: we may even put men to severe test: still we are sometimes mistaken and deceived, and we have to confess, "I did not know the man whom I trusted." The case presented by the text is the opposite of that. In this instance we have trust leading to increased and enlarged knowledge—knowledge strengthening trust, and both producing the expression of full assurance. You observe that the language of the text is somewhat metaphorical. We have certain facts in the Christian life put before us here under the figure of a deposit—a depositor—a depositary, and the confidence of the depositor. I. WHAT IS THIS DEPOSIT? Was it the soul of the writer? Was it the well-being of Paul in his persecution, the getting good out of his sorrow (1 Pet. iv. 19). Was it the work of his salvation—that work to which he himself refers, when, addressing some of his converts, he says, " He which hath begun a good work in you will perform it "? Was it his future crown—the crown of righteousness? Was it his converts, for whom he was perpetually praying? Was it his apostolate? Was it the welfare of the Churches? Was it the truth, and the proclamation of the truth? The great care of a man on a dying bed is himself, and this should be our great care in life; yet to take charge of himself no man is capable. Whatever capacity a man may have had, or human nature may have had before the fall, the loss of capacity which sinfulness and transgression have occasioned is immense; and there is a fearful loss of position. The soul is guilty, and needs pardon, righteousness, and restoration. The spirit is polluted, and it is dark, dim, dull, and deathly, through its pollution—it wants light and life. A physician is needed to whom this soul, conscious of its guilt and of the disease of sin, may commit itself. A priest is needed, who can undertake the work of atonement; and an advocate, who can make intercession. Such an advocate, such a priest, such a physician, Paul had found in Jesus Christ; and to Him, who unites in His own person all that a sinner needs to find in a Saviour, Paul had given up himself. II. THE DEPOSITOR. This is Saul of Tarsus. Did Gamaliel teach him this? Some of Gamaliel's strongest and most prominent lessons were self-reliance. The tendency of his teaching was to lead the young Saul to depend upon himself, and he had, as we know, from the story of his life, an immense amount of self-confidence. There is nothing committed to God to keep—the man only talks of his own virtues and good deeds, comparing himself with another. This is not Saul the Pharisee, it is Saul the Christian. It is Saul, but it is Saul born again, it is Saul born from above, it is Saul a new creation, old things have passed away, behold all things have become new! New, this confidence in another; old, that self-confidence. " I can take care of myself," would have been his language a few years ago; " my prayers and almsgiving, and good works will save me," he would then have said; now, he is entirely changed, and he represents the state of his heart in writing, " I know whom I have believed, and am persuaded that He is able to keep that which I have committed unto Him against that day." Saul of Tarsus took charge of himself, but Saul the Christian committed himself to another. And who is that other? III. THE DEPOSITARY. Does Paul here refer to God, whose name he mentions in the eighth verse, or to our Saviour, Jesus Christ, whom he introduces to us in the tenth verse? We think he refers to our Saviour, Jesus Christ—not, of course, that we can separate God and our Saviour, Jesus Christ—because " God is in Christ, reconciling the world unto Himself." The depositary, mark, is Christ; the anointed Keeper of souls; one upon whom the unction of the Holy Ghost was poured out without measure, that He might take charge of souls; Christ—observe, Jesus Christ, the divine and devoted Keeper of souls. Now, to " Jesus Christ, our Saviour, who hath abolished death, and brought life and immortality to light "; to the " Word made flesh," " God manifest in flesh," " God over all blessed for evermore," to Him did Paul commit himself. It is in vain that you try to mingle these things—taking the responsibility of life upon your shoulders and committing yourself to another. You cannot do this; you must either madly and vainly try to bear the burden alone, or you must commit the whole to your Saviour, and all then that you are responsible for is, doing what He tells you, and not doing that which He forbids you. But, as to the charge, the charge is His; and as to the responsibility, the responsibility is His; and as to the care, all the care is His. Is there any danger of your abusing these truths? Is it possible that any of you can say, " Well, if this be the case, I have certainly asked Christ to take the charge of my soul, and I may be as careless as I please." When you put yourself into the hands of a physician, you feel that you are accountable for obedience to his instructions, and that his resources are made available to you just as you are submissive to his treatment. Just so with our Saviour Jesus Christ. IV. THE CONFIDENCE OF THE DEPOSITOR. " I know whom I have believed, and am persuaded that He is able to keep that which I have committed unto Him against that day." The confidence of Paul relates to four objects :—1. The general character of the depositary. "I know what He is, and what He can do ; I see and I appreciate all the attributes of His nature ; I know that He has an eye that never slumbers nor sleeps, an arm that is never weary, a working hand that is stretched out still, a heart of love—the extent and energy of which surpass knowledge. 2. Then it rests in the ability of the depositary with respect to this particular trust. "He is able to keep"—ABLE to keep. Few men had so seen the dangers of this world as Paul. God keeps some souls in a blissful, childish ignorance of their dangers, and they go through life with an amount of simplicity which is extraordinary, and which we cannot account for except upon the principle that God does literally hide them as in His pavilion. But there are others whose spiritual senses are so quickened, that they see almost every-thing relating to their religious life—at least the many of the spiritual and evil influences to which they are exposed. 3. This confidence relates to the continuous-ness of the present assurance. "He is able to keep that which I have committed to Him against that day." The fires of that day shall burn the wood, hay, stubble, and shall develop in grand contrast the gold, and the silver, and the precious stones. "Against that day 'He is able to keep that which I have committed to Him.' He knows what the test of that day will be, and against that day He is able to guard my trust, and nothing that I have committed to His hands, shall even in that day be lost." 4. Further, you observe, the apostle rests very much in the accuracy, and in the soundness of his own experience. "I know," he says, "whom I have believed." And how did he know? Did he know through having received the testimony of the prophets, who all bore witness to the Saviour? Did he know simply through having listened to Christian teaching, or to the teaching of such an one as Ananias? No; from these sources he did derive information, but he knew through following Christ, that He was able to keep that which he had committed to Him—he knew through taking advantage of Christ, that He was able—just as you know what a physician can do, by his attendance at your sick bed, or as you may know what a legal adviser is able to do, by the counsel he gives you in some time of temporal perplexity, or just as you may know a friend by his aid in the hour of adversity. He had, again and again, put Jesus Christ to the proof, and the proof had shown that not even God's words had fully described the Saviour. (*S. Martin.*) *Christian confidence :*—Let us look, first of all, at this persuasion, which I want you to be the subject of ; and then we will see the ground on which it rested ; and then the consequences of which it was productive. 1. "I am per-suaded that He is able to keep that which I have committed unto Him against that day." You see, it amounts to a perfect persuasion of security here ; here is absolute safety, and the experience of it. The word "persuaded" is as strong as possible. It was the deep inwrought conviction of his soul ; it was not liable to be disturbed ; it was a settled fact, as you dispose of a thing, and say, That is done, it is settled. It was the persuasion of his mind, that all was safe for eternity. Observe the remarkable use in this text of the word *that* by the apostle, which is very instruc-tive. He says, "I am persuaded that He is able to keep *that* which I have com-mitted unto Him against *that* day." He uses the word, you see, twice, with no antecedent in either case exactly, and no specific object mentioned to which it refers. There is something very striking about that. He takes for granted, that all will understand it ; that no mistake can possibly exist about it ; that no man will read the verse, and not at once interpret to what the word "that" refers in both instances. "Keep that!" Why, no child here doubts what he means. "My soul." "Against that day!" No child can doubt what day—the great day of His own coming. They are the two things in comparison with which everything else sinks into absolute, utter insignificance. The beauty of this passage, I think, is in that word "commit." As expressive and explanatory of the meaning of the word faith, I do not know any more beautiful term. People seem at a loss to understand what is meant at last by faith. The best interpretation, I think, is to be found in the idea which that word "commit" conveys. You commit your goods to a person you can trust ; you commit your body, your life, all you have got, exactly in proportion as you have grounds for trusting a man—your welfare, your character, your reputa-tion, your honour. You say, "I can leave my honour in your hands." That is exactly the meaning of the word here : "I have committed." There is something very beautiful in it, and it seems practically to be this : "I have put the matter out of my hands into His." Now, I wish you would quietly enter into that idea, and thoroughly understand it. I do not know anything that could positively give real comfort to a man, like the certainty that he has put his soul's interests out of his own hands into safe keeping. I think this word " commit " implies not only the apostle's sense of the value of the soul, but a man's practical inability to keep his own soul. Why do you commit your property to some one to keep ? Because you feel that you cannot keep it yourself, for some reason—never mind what. Why do you commit your health into the hands of a physician ? Because you feel that you cannot cure yourself. And so on with regard to anything else. You commit your child to an instructor, because you feel that you have more confidence in the instructor. So that the fact of committing anything to another supposes some inability on our part to do the thing. Just so with the soul. I dwell on that with unspeakable comfort. There is a relief to my soul in this idea, that with its tremendous responsibilities, with the awful destinies before it, I can hand it over into Jesus Christ's keeping, and that He will keep that which I commit unto Him. 2 But on what ground did the apostle arrive at this supposition—because there must be some ground for it ? For instance : if I were to say to you to-morrow, " Go and commit your property and your interests into the hands of some man," you would say, " Why that man ? On what grounds ? I know nothing about that man." But if I were to say, " That man that you know thoroughly well," and you were thoroughly alive to his capability and power, what would you say ? You would say, " Yes, I know whom you call upon me to believe ; I am persuaded that he is able to keep that, if I do commit it to him." You see, it would altogether depend upon the knowledge you have of the man. So Paul says here : " I know whom I believe ; therefore I am persuaded that He is able to keep that which I have committed unto Him against that day." Now, then, what do we know about Him ? What kind of knowledge is it that would warrant Paul, or that will warrant you and me, that we can commit all to Jesus Christ ? There might be, of course, endless particulars specified. This is the reason why I call upon you so much to study the whole work and character of Christ. It is, depend upon it, being thoroughly acquainted with the work of Jesus Christ, it is having an intelligent understanding of all that He has done, that gives this kind of unqualified assurance and happy confidence. Therefore we read, " This is eternal life, to *know* Thee." It is not just a sort of glimpse ; it is not merely saying, " I believed Christ died " ; but it is understanding and knowing these things. I often tell you, and I am persuaded of it, that throughout eternity our study will be the cross of Christ. " Against that day "—that is, right on from the present moment till that day comes. You will observe, that implies the state after death, as well as our present state. I have nothing to suffer in the intermediate state—no purgatory—no difficulties of any kind. He has kept me through life ; He will keep me afterwards, for He will keep that which I have committed unto Him to that day. It runs on from the moment a man commits his soul to Christ. The expression is very striking here. It seems to teach us, and to prove by implication, that after that day there is no danger. Then security will not be a matter merely of promise, but of circumstances. When I am perfected in body and soul, where will be my danger ? When I am in mansions where there is a gulf betwixt the mansions and hell where Satan is, and he cannot ferry it, all will be perfectly safe. Therefore we are to be as pillars in the temple of God, and to go no more out for ever. 3. Now, then, what was the consequence of it ? " I am not ashamed." Why was he not ashamed ? Because he was the subject of that glorious persuasion that all was safe. And I want you to believe, that there is the closest connection between boldness in a Christian's career and assurance in a Christian's heart ; that no man will take the walk of a Christian, and occupy the path as he ought to do, boldly and consistently and in a straightforward way, unless he feels that all is safe with regard to his everlasting state. He says, " For which cause I suffer." For what cause ? Because " I am appointed a preacher, and an apostle, and a teacher of the Gentiles ; for the which cause I suffer." When Paul was first brought to God, what did the Lord say about him ? He said, " I will show him how great things he must suffer for My name's sake." It is very remarkable, He did not say, " I will show him what great things he shall do," but " what great things he shall suffer." If we are consistent followers of God, we must be sufferers. Having alluded to his sufferings, he says, " I suffer " ; but he adds, " I am not ashamed." " I stand manfully forward and confess Him." Now, what is the ground ? I have already mentioned it. It is because of that persuasion. That is the antidote. (*C. Molyneux, B.A.*) *The use and abuse of dogma :*—A good man at the present day, writing a letter, with death staring him in the face, to an intimate friend, would be likely to write, not, " I know whom I have believed," but, " I know what I have believed." It comes more natural to us to express our religious convictions so—to think more of the " what " than of the " whom "—to cling rather to the creed, or doctrinal system, than to the Living Person, to whom system and creed bear witness. Of course, the doctrinal system implies the Living Person; but the system is nearer to our thoughts than the Person. With St. Paul it was otherwise. To him the Living Person—God our Father, Jesus Christ our Lord and Saviour— was everything, was all in all; the system was nothing—nay, we may say, had no existence. Therefore it is, that, in view of death and judgment, and all that is most trying to human faith and courage, he writes, " Nevertheless I am not ashamed "—I feel no fear—" for I know whom I have believed, and am persuaded that He is able to keep that which I have committed to Him against that day." Now this is a matter which both requires and deserves the most careful elucidation. It has a very important bearing upon present difficulties and pressing questions of the day. St. Paul was trained up, as a boy and a young man, in an elaborate religious system, of which the Scribes were the expositors, and the Pharisees the devoted adherents. He was at one time, as he tells us, an enthusiastic votary of this system himself. But the moment came at last when he found himself compelled to renounce this system utterly, to cast himself at the foot of the cross, and to consecrate his whole life to the love and the service of Jesus Christ. From that moment Christ was everything to him. Strictly speaking, he no longer had anything that could be called a religious system. All was Christ. Take one or two of his most expressive phrases, and you will feel how true this is : " To me to live is Christ." " I am crucified with Christ, and it is no longer I that live, but Christ liveth in me." We, too, have been trained up, more or less carefully, in an elaborate religious system. Must we break with this system, as St. Paul broke with the religious system in which he had been educated, in order to find, as he found Christ? Must we learn to say with him, in the sense in which he said it, " What things were gain to me, these I counted loss for Christ"? Or is it given to us to travel by a road which was denied to him—to preserve unbroken the continuity of religious thought. Here we are in fact touching what I have called one of the most pressing questions of the day, the use and abuse of dogma. And here we find ourselves in presence of two conflicting tendencies—two tendencies which run absolutely counter, the one to the other; one, an impatience, a fierce intolerance of dogma; the other, an equally fierce insistance upon dogma, as almost the one thing needful for these latter days, and the sole antidote for their disorders. You know the battle-cries of the two contending parties; one, demanding definite, distinctive, dogmatic, Church teaching; the other, demanding not dogma, but religion. Observe, then, first of all, that it is impossible for us to put ourselves exactly in St. Paul's position, or to get at his result precisely in his way. Eighteen centuries lie between us and him—eighteen centuries of controversy, of division, of development. Dogma is an inevitable growth of time, as every one may learn from his own experience. The opinions of any person who thinks at all, and in proportion as he thinks, pass with lapse of time out of a semi-fluid state into one that is fixed and solid. Such conclusions are to the individual thinker what dogmas are to the Christian Church. St. Paul had never formulated to himself the dogma of the Trinity in Unity : but in the lapse of centuries that dogma became a necessity of Christian thought. But then, this development of dogma—necessary as it is, beneficial as it may be—must never be confounded with the reality of spiritual worship —the worship of the Father in spirit and in truth. It moves along a lower level altogether—the level of the understanding, not of the spirit or of the soul. Herein lies the peril of that vehement insistance upon dogmatic teaching, which is so common in these days. Unless it be most carefully guarded, it leads straight to the conclusion that to hold the right dogmas is to be in the way of life. The light of life, the light which quickens, the light which is life, can be ours only on condition that we follow Christ. Dogmatic developments, then, are one thing; the religious or spiritual life of the soul is another thing. And the former may, certainly, be so handled and used, as to give no help to the latter. Yet there is, undoubtedly, a relation between the two; and the former may be made to minister to the latter, if we will. And the question is, What is this relation ? and, How may the dogmatic development be made subservient to the spiritual life? Christ says, " I am come that they might have life, and that they might have it more abundantly." Life, eternal life, salvation, redemption, righteousness : such words as these express the first and the last thought of the gospel of Christ, the aim of which is ever to touch and quicken and heal the souls of men. First in the historical order, and first in the order of thought, comes the spiritual reality, " the word of life " ; afterwards the dogmatic form and framework. The latter is, as it were, the body, of which the former is the soul. The words of Jesus are, as we should expect they would be, the purest conceivable expression of spiritual truth, with the slightest possible admixture of anything extraneous and unessential. For this very reason it is often exceedingly difficult to grasp their import—always quite impossible to exhaust their fulness. When we pass from the words of Jesus to the words of His apostles, we trace the first beginnings of that inevitable action of the human intellect upon spiritual truth, of which the growth of dogma is the result. It could not be otherwise. The disciple could not be altogether as the Master. But though we may thus trace in the Epistles of the New Testament the development of the first "organic filaments," out of which in time would be constructed the full-grown body of Christian dogma—the shooting of the little spikes of ice across the waters of life and salvation, which would eventually lead on to the fixity and rigidity of the whole;—yet are they so full of light, from proximity to the Fountain of all light, that the spiritual always predominates over the intellectual, and the spiritual elements of their teaching are visible on the surface, or scarcely below the surface, of the words in which it is couched. But, as time went on, the intellectual form began more and more to predominate over the spiritual substance; until, at last, it has come to be often no slight task to disentangle the one from the other, and so to get at that which is spiritual; and which, being spiritual, can be made food and refreshment and life to the soul. So far we have been dealing with the questions: "What is the relation of dogma to religion?" and "How may the dogmatic development be made to minister to the religious life?" And our answer to these questions may be summed up thus: Christ's own words, first and before all, go straight to the springs of the religious life, that is, the life of faith and hope and love, of aspiration and endeavour; and, after these, the words of His apostles. Christian dogma grows out of the unavoidable action of the human intellect upon these words, and upon the thoughts which they express. In order to minister to the soul's true life, such dogma must be translated back, by the aid of the Holy Scriptures, into the spiritual elements out of which it has sprung. When it becomes the question of the truth or falsehood of any particular dogmatic development, the testing process with reference to it will take two forms. We shall ascertain whether, or no, it can be resolved or translated back into any spiritual elements—into any rays of that light, of which it is said, "I am the light of the world." And, again, we shall ascertain, if possible, what are its direct effects upon human conduct and character. Does it tend, or not, to produce that new life, of which Jesus Christ is the pattern? If it does; then, unquestionably, there are in it rays of the true light, though mixed, it may be, with much error, and crossed by many bands of darkness. It must be our endeavour to disengage the rays of light from the darkness which accompanies them. Each generation of Christendom in turn has seen something of those riches, which was hidden from others. No one generation has yet seen the whole. Now, that this should be so, has many lessons for us; one or two of which we will set down, and so bring our subject to a conclusion. First of all, it devolves upon each generation in turn a grave responsibility; for each in turn may be put to the necessity of revising the work of its predecessors —such revision being rendered necessary by the peculiar circumstances of the generation in and for which the work is done. And whilst saying this, and claiming this our lawful liberty, we can also do full justice to the generations which have preceded us, and recognise the immense debt of gratitude which we owe to them. They have registered, for their own benefit and for ours, that aspect of the "unsearchable riches," which it was given to them to see. Every succeeding generation is bound to take full and reverent account of the labours of its predecessors, on pain of forfeiting something—some aspect of truth—which it would be most perilous and damaging to lose. And this, last of all, teaches us a much-needed lesson of humility, charity, and tolerance. (*D. J. Vaughan, M.A.*)     *Faith:*—In analysing those words I find three distinct ideas:—The faith of St. Paul expressed by the words, "I have believed"; the object of his faith which he recalls by saying whom he has believed; the certainty of his faith marked with so much strength and serenity by this expression, "I know whom I have believed." I. WHAT IS FAITH? Consult, on this subject the most widely spread opinion of this time and country. You will be told that faith is an act of intellectual submission by which man accepts as certain the teachings of religious authority. Faith would thus be to the intellectual sphere what obedience is to the practical. This idea early appears in the Church with the decline of Christian spirituality. Faith being thus understood, it resulted that the more numerous were the articles of faith which the believer admitted the stronger seemed his faith, and that the more difficult those articles were to admit it was the more meritorious. According to this way of seeing, he would be pre-eminently the man of faith who, refusing to know anything, to wish anything, to judge anything of himself, could say, " I believe what the Church believes," and he would have no other rule but absolute submission, without reserve, to the authority speaking by the voice of his spiritual director. I ask you if you there recognise the teaching of Scripture, if that is the idea which it gives us of faith? You have read those admirable pages in which the author of the Epistle to the Hebrews passes in review all the believers of the ancient covenant, all those men of whom the world was not worthy. Now, in all those examples, is faith ever presented to you as an abdication of the intelligence, as the passive acceptation of a certain number of truths? Never. I know, however, and God preserve me from forgetting, that there is an element of submission and of obedience in faith, but at the same time I affirm that all of faith is not included therein. Faith, according to Scripture, is the impulse of the soul grasping the invisible God, and, in its highest sense, the faith which saves is the impulse of the trusting soul apprehending in Jesus Christ the Saviour and the Son of God. Why talk to us of abdication? In the impulse of faith there is all the soul—the soul that loves and thinks, the soul with all its spiritual energies. It is said to us, one must be weak in order to believe. Are you quite sure? Take, if you will, one of the most elementary acts of faith, such as every honest man has performed in his life. Before you is easy enjoyment, but selfish and guilty; it is the pleasure which attracts you—go on, it is yours. But, just on the point of yielding, the cry of your conscience rouses you, you recover yourself and you assert your duty. . . . What are you doing then? An act of faith, for you assert the invisible; for duty neither is weighed nor is touched, for, to him who denies it, there is no demonstration that can prove it. Well! is that always an easy victory? Is it promised to the feeble? Is it necessary to abdicate to obtain it? In this example faith is not raised above moral evidence; but do you penetrate beyond, into the sphere of spiritual realities? Imagine a life entirely filled with the thoughts of God, entirely illuminated with His light, wholly inspired with His love, in one word, the life of St. Paul; when you contemplate it, are you not struck by the heroism it contains? Is there in the faith which is the moving spring of it only a passive submission, an intellectual belief in a certain number of truths? No; in this assertion of the invisible world there is a force and a greatness which lays hold on you; never, perhaps, does the human soul wrest from you a sincerer admiration than when you see it taking flight into the unknown, with no other support than its faith in the living God. In showing what it is we also answer those who say, " Of what good is faith?" II. WHOM SHALL I BELIEVE? To this question I reply with St. Paul, Jesus Christ. Jesus Christ? and why? To believe, I have said, is to trust. The question is to know to whom I shall trust the destinies of my soul. It is my whole future which I am to suspend on the word of a man; it is the inmost life of my heart, it is my eternal hopes. And if I am deceived, if it is found that I have built on the sand, if one day all this inward edifice of my life should fall to pieces! We must see clearly here. No illusion, no over-exciting of the imagination, no effervescence. Why? I will try and say it again in a few words. I will repeat what those millions of adorers, for eighteen centuries, have confessed, who have been able to say with St. Paul, " I know whom I have believed." Whom shall I believe? I have said it in the depth of my darkness, and have seen rising up before me the Son of Man. Alone amongst all He said, " I know whence I come, and I know whither I go." Alone, without hesitation, with sovereign authority, He showed the way which leads to God. He spoke of heaven as one who descended from it. Everywhere and always He gave Himself out to be the Sent of the Father, His only Son, the Master of souls. I have listened to His voice, it had a strange accent which recalled no other human voice; beautiful with a simplicity which nothing approaches, it exercised a power to which nothing can be compared. What gave it that power? It was not reasoning, nor human eloquence, but the radiance of truth penetrating the heart and conscience; in listening to it, I felt my heart taken possession of; I yielded to that authority so strong and sweet; in proportion as He spoke it seemed as if heaven opened and displayed itself to my eyes; I beheld God as He is, I saw man as he ought to be. An irresistible adhesion to that teaching rose from my heart to my lips, and with Simon Peter I cried " To whom shall we go? Thou hast the words of eternal life." Was it only my soul which vibrated at that speech? I looked, and, around me, hanging on the lips of Christ, I saw an ever-growing multitude assembled from all places, coming out from all conditions on the earth; there were poor and rich, ignorant and wise, children and old men, pure spirits and defiled spirits, and, like me, all were impressed with that word, all found, as I did, light, certainty, and peace. Can I let my whole destiny depend on a word of man, and have I not the right to ask Him who thus leads me on in His steps what entitles Him to my confidence, and how He can prove to me that He comes from God? " O Thou who callest Thyself the witness of God, Thou who speakest of heaven as if it had been Thy dwelling-place, Thou who enlightenest the mystery of death to our gaze, Thou who pardonest sin, show us that Thou art He who should come." Jesus Christ has replied to this demand of our soul. We ask Him if He comes from God, and He has done before us the works of God; I do not speak of His miracles, although they are still unexplained in their simple grandeur, in their sublime spirituality, in that indescribable truth which marks them with an inimitable seal. Jesus has done more than miracles, He has revealed God in His person; He has given the proof of His Divine mission in His life. It is holiness before which conscience perceives itself accused and judged. The more I contemplate it, the more I experience a feeling of adoration and of deep humiliation; and when at last men come and try to explain this life, and to show me in it an invention of mankind, I protest, I feel that the explanations are miserable, I feel that the reality breaks all that framework. Then, by an irresistible logic, I feel that if Christ is holy, He must have spoken truly, and ought to be believed. Is that all? Yes, if I only needed light and certainty; but there is a still deeper, more ardent, more irresistible instinct in my soul: I feel myself guilty, I thirst for pardon and for salvation. St. Paul felt himself a sinner, condemned by his conscience; he sought salvation in his works, he was exhausted in that sorrowful strife; he found salvation only on the cross. There he saw, according to his own words, the Just One offering Himself for the unjust; the Holy One bearing the curse of the sinner. In that redeeming sacrifice, St. Paul found assuagement for his conscience; the love of God as he recognised it in Jesus Christ penetrated his heart and life; is it not that which overflows in all his epistles, in all his apostolate? Is it not that which inspires, which inflames all his life? Is it not that which dictated to him these words, "I know whom I have believed"? It is also that which makes the foundation of Christian faith; it is that which millions of souls, led, like Paul, to the foot of the cross by their feeling of misery, have found in Jesus Christ; it is that which has transformed them, taken them out of themselves, conquered for ever by Jesus Christ. III. THE CERTAINTY OF FAITH! Do not these words rouse a painful sentiment in you? No one will contradict me if I affirm, that there is in our epoch a kind of instinctive neglect of all that is firm and exact in points of belief and Christian life. Let us examine it. We are passing through a time of grave crisis where all the elements of our religious faith are submitted to the most penetrating analysis, and whatever may be our degree of culture we cannot escape from it. So, something analogous to the artistic sentiment is made for the religious sentiment. In music, for example, no one, assuredly, preoccupies himself with truth. The most varied, the most opposed styles are allowed, provided that some inspiration and some genius are felt in them. One day, people will applaud a sombre and dreamy symphony; others will prefer a composition brilliant with force and brightness; others, again, the softened charm of a melody full of grace: as many various tastes as art can satisfy. Now, it is just so that to-day it is claimed religion should be treated. It is wished that man should be religious; it is said that he who is not so is destitute of one sense, as he to whom painting or music is a matter of indifference; but this religious sense should, it is said, seek its satisfaction there where it finds it. To some a stately worship is necessary, to others an austere worship; to some the gentleness of an indulgent God, to others the holiness of the God of the Bible; to some an entirely moral religion, to others dogmas and curious mysteries. Do I need to ask, what becomes with that manner of looking, of the certainty of faith and religious truth? Hence that sad sight of souls always seeking and never reaching to the possession of truth, always in quest of religious emotions, but incapable of affirming their faith, and, above all, of changing their life. Nothing is more contrary to St. Paul's certitude, to that firm assurance which makes him say, "I know whom I have believed." Can we be astonished that such a religion should be without real force and without real action? It could not be otherwise. It might be able, I acknowledge, to produce fleeting movements, vivid emotions, and sincere outbursts, but lasting effects never. I affirm, first, that it will convert nobody. And why? Because conversion is the most deep-seated change in the affections and life of man, and he will never exchange the known for the unknown, real life with its passions, its pleasures, however senseless they appear, for the pale and cold abstractions of a belief with no precise object and for the worship of a vague and problematic God. To fight against passions and lusts and refuse the compensation of satisfied pride, to bend the will, to conquer the flesh, and to submit life to the austere discipline of obedience, that is a work which a vague, indecisive religion will never accomplish. Without religious certainty there is no holiness and, I add also, no consolation. Let us also add that a religion without a certainty is a religion without action, without progressive force. How can it advance? Will it lay the foundations of lasting works, will it know how to conquer, will it send its missionaries afar? Missionaries, and why? Is it with vague reveries and floating opinions that they set out, like the apostles, to conquer the world? The life of St. Paul is the best explanation of his faith. Supported by his example, and by the experience of all Christians, I would say to you, " Do you wish to possess that strong immovable faith which alone can sustain and console? Fulfil the works of faith. Serve the truth, and the truth shall illuminate you; follow Jesus Christ, and you will believe in Christ." "There is no royal road to science," said an ancient philosopher to a prince who was irritated at finding study so difficult; so in my turn I would say, "There is no demonstration of Christianity, no apology which dispenses with obeying the truth, and with passing through humiliation and inward renunciation, without which faith is only a vain theory." The best proof of the truth of Christianity will always be a proof of experience; nothing will outvalue that irrefutable argument of St. Paul. (*E. Bersier, D.D.*) *Assured security in Christ:*—In the style of these apostolic words there is a positiveness most refreshing in this age of doubt. " I know," says he. And that is not enough—" I am persuaded." He speaks like one who cannot tolerate a doubt. There is no question about whether he has believed or not. "I know whom I have believed." There is no question as to whether he was right in so believing. " I am persuaded that he is able to keep that which I have committed to Him." There is no suspicion as to the future; he is as positive for years to come as he is for this present moment. " He is able to keep that which I have committed to Him against that day." Where positiveness is the result of knowledge and of meditation, it becomes sublime, as it was in the apostle's case; and being sublime it becomes influential; in this case, it certainly must have been influential over the heart of Timothy, and over the minds of the tens of thousands who have during these nineteen centuries perused this epistle. It encourages the timid when they see others preserved; it confirms the wavering when they see others steadfast. The apostle's confidence was that Christ was an able guardian. 1. So he meant that Jesus is able to keep the soul from falling into damning sin. 2. But the apostle did not merely trust Christ thus to keep him from sin, he relied upon the same arm to preserve him from despair. 3. Doubtless the apostle meant, too, that Christ was able to keep him from the power of death. 4. The apostle is also certain that Christ is able to preserve his soul in another world. 5. Paul believed, lastly, that Christ was able to preserve his body. " I cannot talk like that," saith one ; " I cannot say, ' I know and I am persuaded,' I am very thankful that I can say, I hope, I trust, I think." In order to help you to advance, we will notice how the apostle Paul attained to such assurance. 1. One main help to him was his habit, as seen in this text, of always making faith the most prominent point of consideration. Faith is twice mentioned in the few lines before us. " I know whom I have believed, and am persuaded that He is able to keep that which I have committed to Him." Paul knew what faith was, namely, a committal of his precious things into the custody of Christ. He does not say, "I have served Christ." No; he does not say, "I am growing like Christ, therefore I am persuaded I shall be kept." No; he makes most prominent in his thought the fact that he believed, and so had committed himself to Christ. 2. The next help to assurance, as I gather from the text, is this; the apostle maintained most clearly his view of a personal Christ. Observe how three times he mentioned his Lord. " I know *whom* I have believed, and am persuaded that *He* is able to keep that which I have committed to *Him*." He does not say, " I know the doctrines I believe." Surely he did, but this was not the main point. No mere doctrines can ever be the stay of the soul. What can a dogma do? These are like medicines, but you need a hand to give you them ; you want the physician to administer them to you ; otherwise you may die with all these precious medicines close at hand. We want a person to trust to. 3. The apostle attained this full assurance through growing knowledge. He did not say "I am persuaded that Christ will save me, apart from anything I know about Him"; but he begins by saying, "I know." Let no Christian among us neglect the means provided for obtaining a fuller knowledge of the gospel of Christ. I would that this age produced more thoughtful and studious Christians. 4. Once, again, the apostle, it appears from the text, gained his assurance from close consideration as well as from knowledge. "I know and am persuaded." As I have already said, persuasion is the result of argument. The apostle had turned this matter over in his mind; he had meditated on the pros and cons; he had carefully weighed each difficulty, and he felt the preponderating force of truth which swept each difficulty out of the way. How many Christians are like the miser who never feels sure about the safety of his money, even though he has locked up the iron safe, and secured the room in which he keeps it, and locked up the house, and bolted and barred every door! In the dead of night he thinks he hears a footstep, and tremblingly he goes down to inspect his strong-room. Having searched the room, and tested all the iron bars in the window, and discovered no thief, he fears that the robber may have come and gone, and stolen his precious charge. So he opens the door of his iron safe, he looks and pries, he finds his bag of gold all safe, and those deeds, those bonds, they are safe too. He puts them away, shuts the door, locks it, bolts and bars the room in which is the safe and all its contents; but even as he goes to bed, he fancies that a thief has just now broken in. So he scarcely ever enjoys sound, refreshing sleep. The safety of the Christian's treasure is of quite another sort. His soul, not under bolt and bar, or under lock and key of his own securing, but he has transferred his all to the King eternal, immortal, invisible, the only wise God, our Saviour—and such is his security that he enjoys the sleep of the beloved, calmly resting, for all is well. Now to close, what is the influence of this assurance when it penetrates the mind? It enables us to bear all the obloquy which we may incur in serving the Lord. They said Paul was a fool. "Well," replied the apostle, "I am not ashamed, for I know whom I have believed; I am willing to be thought a fool." (*C. H. Spurgeon.*)   *Assurance*:—It surely is evident that while justification is all that is necessary for safety, an assured knowledge of our justification on our own part must be necessary to give us the comfort and the joy of safety. Further, it is clear that the character of all our subsequent experiences must very largely depend upon such an assured knowledge; for I cannot feel, or speak, or act as a justified man unless I not only am justified, but know that I am justified. Nor can I claim my proper privileges, and enjoy the blessed results of my new relationship with God, unless I know certainly that this relationship exists. For our position is, that, though it be possible that you may be safe in God's sight, and yet not be safe in your own, you cannot lead the life that God intends you to lead unless you know of this your safety. First, you cannot draw near to Him with the filial confidence which should characterise all true Christian experience, and enter into the closest relations of true and trustful love. Next, you cannot learn from the happy results of this first act of faith the great life-lesson of faith. Then again you lose those mighty motives of grateful, joyous love which should be the incentives to a truly spiritual life, and instead of these there is certain to be an element of servile bondage even in your very devotion, and you must forfeit the glorious liberty of the child of God; and last, but not least, there can be no power in your testimony; for how can you induce others to accept a benefit of the personal effects of which you yourself know nothing? If your religion leaves you only in a state of uncertainty, how is it ever likely that you will have weight with others in inducing them to turn their backs upon those "pleasures of sin for a season" which, although they may be fleeting and unsatisfactory, are nevertheless a certainty while they do last. On the other side, let me point out that this knowledge of salvation is the effect and not the condition of justification. It would be absurd to teach that men are justified by knowing that they are justified. Of course they can only know it when it has happened, and to make such knowledge the condition of justification would involve a palpable contradiction. Indeed it would be equivalent to saying you must believe what is false in order to make it true. Look at these words of St. Paul; they sound bold and strong; yet just reflect for a moment. Would anything less than such a confidence as is indicated here have been sufficient to enable him to lead the life that he did? Would he ever have been fit for his life's work if his assurance of his own personal relations with God through Christ had been more dubious, and his standing more precarious? Would anything less than this settled conviction have enabled him fearlessly to face all the odds that were against him, and have borne him on through many a shock of battle towards the victor's crown? But now let us look more closely into this pregnant saying, and endeavour to analyse its meaning. On looking carefully at the words you will find that in stating one thing St. Paul really states three. FIRST, HE TELLS US THAT HE HAS ASSUMED A DISTINCT MORAL ATTITUDE, AN ATTITUDE OF TRUST TOWARDS A PARTICULAR PERSON. NEXT, THAT THE ASSUMPTION AND MAINTENANCE OF THIS ATTITUDE IS WITH HIM A MATTER OF PERSONAL CONSCIOUSNESS; AND NEXT, THAT HE IS ACQUAINTED WITH AND THOROUGHLY SATISFIED WITH THE CHARACTER OF THE PERSON THUS TRUSTED. Let us consider each of these statements severally; and turning to the first, we notice that St. Paul represents his confidence as being reposed not in a doctrine, or a fact, but a person. "I know whom I have believed." Many go wrong here. I have heard some speak as if we were to be justified by believing in the doctrine of justification by faith. Let me say to such what common-sense should have let them to conclude without its being necessary to say it, that we are no more justified by believing in the doctrine of justification by faith than we are carried from London to Edinburgh by believing in the expansive force of steam. Knowledge of the laws of the expansion of vapour may induce me to enter a railway train, and similarly, knowledge of the doctrine of justification may induce me to trust myself to Him who justifies; but I am no more justified by believing this doctrine than I am transported from place to place by believing in the laws of dynamics. Others seem to believe that our faith is to be reposed upon the doctrine of the Atonement, and not a few upon certain particular theories which are supposed to attach to that doctrine. But surely it is clear that our views of doctrine may be never so orthodox and correct, and yet our hearts may not have found rest in Him to whom the doctrine witnesses. Once again, some seem to regard our salvation as dependent upon belief in a fact; but surely it is possible to accept the fact, and yet come no nearer to Him who was the principal actor in that fact. Faith rests on a person, not a doctrine, or a fact; but when we believe in the person, this undoubtedly involves faith in the doctrine (so far as it is necessary for us to understand it) and in the fact. For if I believe in Jesus Christ, I believe in Him as God's express provision to meet the case of fallen humanity, and this involves the doctrine. Once again, if I believe in Christ, I believe in Him as having accomplished all that was necessary to meet the case of fallen humanity, and this involves the fact. The doctrine and the fact both meet in Him; but apart from Him neither is of any real spiritual value to me. Nay, I will go so far as to say that my apprehension of the doctrine, and even of the fact, may be very inadequate and incomplete, yet if with all my heart I rest upon the person, my confidence can never be disappointed. Now let us consider this statement that St. Paul makes as to his moral attitude towards Christ. He tells us that he knows whom he has believed. The phrase is especially deserving of attention, and yet, curiously enough, it is generally misquoted. How commonly do we hear it quoted as if the words were, "I know in whom I have believed." I fear that the frequency of the misquotation arises from the fact that men do not clearly discern the point to which the words of the apostle as they stand were specially designed to bear witness. The phrase, as St. Paul wrote it, points to a distinctly personal relation, and the words might, with strict accuracy, be rendered, "I know whom I have trusted." The words, as they are misquoted, may be destitute of this element of personal relation altogether. If I were to affirm of some distinguished commercial house in this city that I believed in it, that would not necessarily mean that I had left all my money in its hands. If I were to say that I believed in a well-known physician, that would not lead you to conclude that he had cured, or even that I had applied to him to cure, any disease from which I might be suffering. But if I stated that I had trusted that firm or that physician, then you would know that a certain actual personal relation was established between me and the man or the company of men of whom I thus spoke. How many there are who believe in Christ just as we believe in a bank where we have no account, or a physician whose skill we have never proved, and our belief does us as much good in the one case as in the other. But perhaps the true character of trust is, if possible, still more strikingly brought out by the word which St. Paul here employs in the original Greek. It is the word that would be used by any Greek to indicate the sum of money deposited, in trust, in the hands of a commercial agent, or, as we should say, a banker; in fact, the words used here simply mean "my deposit." If you carry about a large sum of money on your person, or if you keep it in your house, you run a certain risk of losing it. In order to ensure the safety of your property you make it over into the hands of a banker; and if you have perfect confidence in the firm to which you commit it, you no longer have an anxious thought about it. There it is safe in the bank. Even so there had come a time when St. Paul's eyes were opened to find that he was in danger of losing that beside which all worldly wealth is a mere trifle—his own soul; for what indeed "is a man profited, if he gain the whole world and lose his own soul?" Nay, it was not only that his soul was in danger amongst the robbers, it was actually forfeited to the destroyer, and then it was that, in his helpless despair, he made it over into another's hands—that other who had a right to preserve it and keep it alive, because He had ransomed it from the destroyer, and from that time forward there he had left it safe and secure, because He to whom he had entrusted it was trustworthy. Now have you done the same? Have you not only believed in Jesus, but have you trusted Him? Then this must lead us to the second of the three things that we saw St. Paul here affirms. Evidently St. Paul knew, and was perfectly sure, of his own moral attitude towards God; and here he explicitly asserts that his faith was a matter of distinct moral consciousness, for "I know whom I have believed" certainly contains within itself "I know that I have believed." Now turn this over in your mind. Surely it is reasonable enough when we come to think of it; for if we have something weighing on our minds that seems a thing of great importance, surely if we make it over into the hands of another, and leave it with him, we can hardly fail to be conscious of having done so. The question sometimes may be asked—and indeed it often is asked—"How am I to know that I have believed?" I confess that it is not easy to answer such an inquiry; but there are a good many similar questions which it would be equally hard to answer if people ever asked them, which, however, as a matter of fact, they never do. If I were to ask you to-night, "How do you know that you hear me speaking to you?" the only answer you could return would be—one that may sound very unphilosophical, but for all that one that is perfectly sufficient—"Because I do." If you answer, "Ah! but then that is a matter of sense," I reply, "Yes, but is it otherwise with matters that don't belong to the region of sense-perception at all?" If I were to ask you, "How do you know that you remember, or that you imagine, or that you think, or that you perform any mental process?" your answer must still be, "Because I do." You do not feel either able or desirous to give any further proof of these experiences; it is enough that they are experiences—matters of direct consciousness. But we need not in order to illustrate this point go beyond this question that we are at present considering. You ask, "How may I know that I believe?" This question sounds to you reasonable when you are speaking of Christ as the object of faith. Does it sound equally reasonable when you speak in the same terms of your fellow-man? How do you know, my dear child, that you believe in your own mother? How do you know, you, my brother, who are engaged in commerce, that you believe in your own banker? You can only answer in each case, "Because I do"; but surely that answer is sufficient, and you do not feel seriously exercised about the reality of your confidence, because you have no other proof of it excepting an appeal to your own personal consciousness. Let us now notice, further, that he knew well, and was perfectly satisfied with, the character of the person whom he did believe. Herein lay the secret of his calm, the full assurance of his faith. You may have your money invested in a concern which, on the whole, you regard as a safe and satisfactory one, yet when panics are prevailing in the city, and well-known houses are failing, you may be conscious of some little anxiety, some passing misgiving. You have faith in the firm, but perhaps not full assurance of faith. It is otherwise with the money that you have invested in the funds of the nation; that must be safe as long as Great Britain holds her place amongst the nations of the world. Clearly our sense of comfort in trusting, our full assurance of confidence lies in our knowledge of, and is developed by, our contemplation of the object upon which our trust is reposed—if indeed that object be worthy of it—and feelings of peace and calm will necessarily flow from this. (*W. Hay Aitken, M.A.*) *I know whom I have believed :*—"Whom—" Paul says. Quite another thing from "what." "I know what I have believed"; that is good. "I know whom I have believed"; that is better—best. Such believing has easily its advantages, several of them. When the thing we believe is a person, our believing, creed, becomes simple and coherent; the lines of our thinking all gather at a point, our creed is made one, like grapes growing in one cluster from one stem. I am interested on occasion to ask Christian people what their Christian belief is. It is instructive to note the wide divergence of answer. One believes one thing, another, another thing. "I know whom I have believed." To be a Christian is to believe in Christ. And what is it to believe in Christ? We reach too high for our answers; necessary truth grows on low branches. The boy says—" I believe in my father." All is told that needs to be told. Another thing about this creed with a person in it is, that it gives something for all our faculties to do. " I know what I believe." Such a creed is only intellectual ; it is an affair of thinking, reasoning, inference. Theological thought and discussion works so far only on the same lines as scientific. Mind only works; no heart, nothing volitional. A creed that gathers directly about person yields keen thinking, but yields much beside. It starts feeling, sets the affections in play, draws out the will and puts it to work. We each of us have one or more men that we believe in, with all our mind, heart and strength—men that are so far forth our creed; and they stir and stimulate us in every way, clearing our ideas, to be sure, but firing our hearts and making our resolutions sinewy and nervy. Christ made Paul a man of profound thinking, but a man of fervid passion and giant purpose—gave every faculty in him something to do. He was great all over. A third and consequent advantage in a personal creed is that it is the only kind that can produce effects, and work within us substantial alteration. I am not criticising creeds. It is an excellent thing to know what we believe, and to be able with conciseness and effect to state it. Paul does not say I know what I believe, but I know whom I believe, which goes wider and higher. Such a creed is not one that Paul holds, but one that holds Paul, and can do something with him therefore. No quantity of correct idea about the sun can take the place of standing and living where the sun shines; and standing and living where the sun shines will save from fatal results a vast amount of incorrect ideas about the sun. Belief in person works back upon me as an energy, alters me, builds me up or tears me down—at any rate never leaves me alone; it works as gravity does among the stars; keeps everything on the move. Such belief is not mental attitude, but moral appropriation ; it is the bee clinging to the clover-blossom and sucking out the sweet. It is regulative and constructive. We are determined by the person we believe in. Belief makes him my possession. Belief breaks down his walls and widens him out till he contains me. His thoughts reappear as my thoughts ; his ways, manners, feelings, hopes, impulses, motives, become mine. I know whom I have believed. We make our ordinary creeds, and revise and amend and repeal them. Personal creeds make us, and revise, amend and repeal us. No picture of a friend can be accurate enough to begin to take the friend's place or do the friend's work. No idea of a person can ever be enough like the person to serve as substitute. Knowing what God is to perfection would never become the equivalent of knowing God. If we bring this to the level of common life, its workings are simple and manifest. It is in the home. The mother is the child's first creed. He believes in her . before he believes what she says, and it is by his belief in her that he grows and ripens. If we cannot tell it all out in words what this believing in a mother or father means, we feel the meaning of it, and the deep sense is worth more than the wordy paragraph, any time. Education is an affair of person—person meeting person. Pupils do not become wise by being told things. Wisdom is not the accumulation of specific cognitions. It is men that educate. Person is the true schoolmaster. Even an encyclopædia does not become an educator by being dressed in gentlemen's clothes. What best helps a boy to become a man is to have somebody to look up to ; which is like our text—" I know whom I have believed." And out on the broader fields of social and national life we encounter the same principle over again. The present wealth of a people depends largely upon its commerce and productive industries. The stability of a people and its promise for the future, depends quite as much upon the quality of the men upon whom the masses allow their regards to fix and their loyalty to fasten. " I know whom I have believed." And believing in Christ in this way to begin with, issued in Paul's believing a host of particular facts in regard to Christ, and Paul's theology is his blossomed piety. No amount of faith in Christ's words will add up into faith in Him. You must have noticed how full all Christ's teachings are of the personal pronoun "I." Paul's Christianity began on the road to Damascus. The only man that can truly inform me is the man that can form himself in me ; that is what information means—immensely personal again, you see, as everything of much account is. And it is so everywhere. Religious matters, in this respect, step in the same ranks with other matters. The grandest convictions that we receive from other people are not constructed in us by their logic, but created in us by their personal inspiration. The gospel is not the

Divine book, but the Divine Man, and a great many miniature copies of that gospel are around us, working still effects along personal lines. We make Christianity hard by crumbling it up into impersonal propositions. It is no part of our genius to like a truth apart from its flesh and blood incarnation in some live man. It is a hard and awkward thing for me to believe in the doctrine of the immortality of the soul, for instance. I do not like the doctrine ; my intellect abhors it. No logic could persuade me of its truth, and I should never think of trying to syllogise anybody else into a possession of it. But my father is immortal and I know it. Your mother is immortal, and you cannot start in your mind a suspicion to the contrary. From all this we gather that a man who gets called an unbeliever, and even calls himself such, may believe a great deal more than he suspects. Unconscious orthodoxy is a factor of the times that needs to be taken into earnest account. There are quantities of unutilised and unsuspected faith. You do not believe in immortality. Did you ever see anybody that you had some little idea had about him something or other that death could not touch ? Let alone the abstract and come close to the concrete and personal, and let it work. You reject the doctrine of a change of heart; and it is a doctrine repugnant to our natures and a conundrum to our intelligence. Did you ever see anybody who stopped being what he had been and commenced being what he had not been ? If you find it hard work to square your opinions with the catechism, see whether you do not draw into a little closer coincidence with men and women whose lives transparently embody the gospel, and then draw your inference. To another class of uncertain hearers I want to add, Do not try to get your religious ideas all arranged and your doctrinal notions balanced. There is a great deal of that kind that is best taken care of when it is left to take care of itself. There is no advantage in borrowing some one's else opinion and no use in hurrying your own opinion. Begin with what is personal, as he did—"I know whom I have believed." Try to know the Lord. Draw nigh to God and He will draw nigh to you. " The fear of the Lord is the beginning of knowledge." There is no other way of beginning to be a Christian but the old way—"Come unto Me." And you and I, fellow Christians, owe it to these unsettled people among us and about us to help them to strong anchorage upon Christ ; and our qualifications for the work will be our own thorough rest in and establishment upon Christ and an ineffable commixture of love and tact, and tact considered not as a natural talent, but as a heavenly grace. In our relations to these people, there is another thing for us to remember of a more positive character, which is, as we have seen, that there is nothing that tells upon men and their convictions like life. Men believe in the personal. Truth pure and simple goes but a little way, except as it is lived. Abstractions are not current outside of the schools. The best preaching of a change of heart is a heart that is changed. These people are not going to be touched by anything that has not breath and a pulse. Living is the best teaching. So that if you and I are going to help these people to be conscious and pronounced Christians, we are not going to accomplish it by merely telling them about Christ and compounding before them feeble dilutions of Divine biography, but by being ourselves so personally charged with the personal Spirit of God in Christ that in our words they shall hear Him, in our love they shall feel Him, in our behaviour they shall be witnesses of Him, and in this way He become to them the Way, Truth and Life, all-invigorating power, all-comprehensive creed. (*C. H. Parkhurst.*) *Nothing to hold by :*—An infidel was dying, and his infidelity beginning to give way, was rallied by his friends, who surrounded his dying bed. " Hold out," they all cried, " don't give way." " Ah ! " said the dying man, " I would hold out if I had anything to hold by, but what have I ? " (*Anon.*) *Confidence in Christ :*—I. THE CHRISTIAN HAS IN HIS POSSESSION A TREASURE. 1. It is his greatest treasure. 2. At his own disposal. 3. Involves his whole welfare for ever. II. THE CHRISTIAN HAS ENTRUSTED HIS TREASURE TO THE PROTECTION OF CHRIST. 1. It is in danger of being lost. 2. Man cannot secure its safety himself. 3. Christ is the only Preserver. III. THE CHRISTIAN HAS ENTRUSTED HIS TREASURE TO CHRIST WITH UNBOUNDED CONFIDENCE. Because of his faith in Christ's—1. Power. 2. Promises. 3. Prestige. IV. THE CHRISTIAN'S CONSCIOUSNESS OF THE SAFETY OF HIS TREASURE IN CHRIST IS A SOURCE OF GREAT PEACE IN THE TROUBLES OF LIFE. 1. Because the greatest interest is secured. 2. Because trials will further this interest. 3. Because trials will soon end. (*B. D. Johns.*) *Knowledge conducive of assurance :*—This must move us all to get knowledge of God, if we would have faith in Him, yea, the best must grow herein ; for the better we know Him the more confidently shall we believe in Him. For it is so in all other things. When I know the firmness of the land I will the better rest my foot on it; the strength of my staff, the rather lean my whole body upon it, and the faithfulness of a friend, put and repose my confidence in him. And we must know God. First, in His power, how that He is able to do whatsoever He will. This confirmed Abraham's faith, and moved him to offer his son. Secondly, we must know Him in His truth and justice. Thirdly, we are to know God in His stability. How that time changeth not His nature, neither altereth His purpose. Fourthly, we are to understand that God is Sovereign Lord, that there is none higher than He; for if we should trust in an inferior we might be deceived. Fifthly, We must know God in Christ. (*J. Barlow, D.D.*) *It's all real :*—A Bible-class convert, who subsequently became a teacher, accidentally injured himself through lifting a heavy weight, and his sufferings in consequence were very severe. Yet, notwithstanding his pain and poverty, he was extremely happy, and clung to Christ with a triumphant faith. This poor fellow's dying testimony was very striking, and one of his last desires has never been forgotten. When just about crossing the river of death, he broke out into this expression, "Oh, Mr. Orsman, I would like to get well again, if only for one day, just to go round to my old companions, and tell them *it's all real.*" (*Sword and Trowel.*) *The love of Christ stronger than the terrors of death :*—At the conclusion of an evening service in a fishing village, a young man stood up, and with great earnestness began to address his fellows. He said, "You all remember Johnnie Greengrass?" There was a murmur of assent all over the gathering. "You know that he was drowned last year. I was his comrade on board our boat. As we were changing the vessel's course one night, off the Old Head of Kinsale, he was struck by the lower part of the mainsail and swept overboard. He was a good swimmer, but had been so disabled by the blow that he could only struggle in the water. We made all haste to try and save him. Before we got seated in the punt, we heard Johnnie's voice, over the waves beyond the stern, singing the last line of his favourite hymn, "If ever I loved Thee, my Jesus, 'tis now.' We made every effort to find him, but in vain. He was drowned; but the last words which we had heard from his lips assured us that the love of Christ had proved stronger than the terrors of death. He knew that neither death nor life could separate him from the love of Christ, and so he sank beneath the waves, singing, 'If ever I loved Thee, my Jesus, 'tis now.' " (*T. Brown, M.A.*) *Venturing on Christ :*—The Rev. Dr. Simpson was for many years tutor in the college at Hoxton, and while he stood very low in his own esteem, he ranked high in that of others. After a long life spent in the service of Christ, he approached his latter end with holy joy. Among other expressions which marked his love to the Redeemer, and his interest in the favour of God, he spoke with disapprobation of a phrase often used by some pious people, "Venturing on Christ." "When," said he, "I consider the infinite dignity and all-sufficiency of Christ, I am ashamed to talk of venturing on Him. Oh, had I ten thousand souls, I would, at this moment, cast them all into His hands with the utmost confidence." A few hours before his dissolution, he addressed himself to the last enemy, in a strain like that of the apostle, when he exclaimed, "O death, where is thy sting?" Displaying his characteristic fervour, as though he saw the tyrant approaching, he said, "What art thou? I am not afraid of thee. Thou art a vanquished enemy through the blood of the Cross." *Trusting Christ entirely :*—I have sometimes used the following experience as an illustration of salvation. For fifteen years I lived by the seaside, and was a frequent bather, and yet never learned to swim. I would persist in keeping one foot upon the bottom, for then I felt safe. But one day, in a rough sea, a great wave fairly picked me off my feet, and I struck out for dear life. I awoke to the fact that I could swim, that the waves would bear me up if I trusted them entirely, and I no longer clung to my own way of self-help. Even so does Christ save. How often the trying to help one's self keeps from peace and rest! and when the soul first abandons all to Christ, ventures wholly on Him, that soul finds, to its own astonishment, that Christ indeed bears up and saves him. (*H. W. Childs.*) *Jesus sufficient :*—An old lady who lately died in Melbourne said to her minister, "Do you think my faith will hold out?" "Well, I don't know much about that," replied the man of God, "but I am sure that Jesus Christ will hold out, and that is enough for you. 'Looking,' not to our faith, but 'unto Jesus.' " (*T. Spurgeon.*) *The safety of believers :*—I. The grounds upon which this comfortable persuasion is built. II. The manner in which this persuasion is produced and promoted in the souls of true believers. 1. The knowledge of Christ, which is necessary to produce and promote the comfortable persuasion expressed in the text, is partly derived from testimony. (1) God the Father has in all ages borne witness to the power and faithfulness of His own beloved Son, our blessed Saviour. This He did of old time by visions and voices, by prophecies and typical ordinances. (2) Christ Himself likewise thus testifies concerning His own power and readiness to save (Matt. xi. 28). (3) Nor must the testimony of the Holy Spirit be forgotten. "It is the Spirit that beareth witness, because the Spirit is truth." (4) All the saints who lived in former times, the whole company of the faithful, all the patriarchs and prophets, the apostles and martyrs, bear testimony to this interesting fact. They all died in the faith of its comforting truth. (5) Our fellow-Christians, likewise, in the present day, may be produced as witnesses to the power and faithfulness of the Redeemer. They live in different and distant places; their cases are various, and their attainments unequal; but they all will unite in declaring that ever since they were enabled to commit their souls to Christ, they have found a peace and joy to which they were strangers before, and that not one word of all that He hath spoken hath failed to be accomplished. 2. That this knowledge is likewise in part derived from the believer's own experience (see John iv. 42). Concluding reflections: 1. How much are they to be pitied, who have no interest in the Saviour, who have never been thoroughly convinced of their wretched condition as sinners, and who, consequently, have not committed the momentous concerns of their souls into the hands of Christ. 2. That we may abound more and more in this hope, through the power of the Holy Ghost, let us study to grow in grace, and in the knowledge of our Lord Jesus Christ. 3. Have we committed our immortal interests into the hands of Christ, and shall we not trust Him with all our lesser concerns? 4. Let us look forward with believing expectation to the day when it will appear with Divine evidence, how faithfully Jesus has kept all that has been committed unto Him. (*D. Black.*)     *Nothing between the soul and its Saviour*:—When Dr. Alexander, one of the professors of theology in Princeton University, was dying, he was visited by a former student. After briefly exchanging two or three questions as to health, the dying divine requested his old disciple to recite a verse of the Bible to be a comfort to him in his death struggles. After a moment's reflection the student repeated from memory that verse—"I know in whom I have believed, and that He is able to keep that which I have committed unto Him unto that day." "No, no," replied the dying saint, "that is not the verse: it is not ' I know *in* whom I have believed.' but ' I know whom I have believed.' I cannot allow the little word ' in ' to intervene between me and my Saviour to-day, I cannot allow the smallest word in the English language to go between me and my Saviour in the floods of Jordan." *The folly of not trusting Christ*:—I was busy at work during the deep, still hush of a hot July noon, when my attention was suddenly drawn to a fluttering sound in the room where I was sitting. A little bird from the neighbouring woods had entered by the open window, and was dashing wildly to and fro in its frantic efforts to escape again. I did not move at first, unwilling to increase its alarm, and hoping it would soon find its way out. But when after a little I again looked up, I saw that the little creature was circling round and round in desperate alarm; and, moreover, that the low, whitewashed ceiling was being streaked all over with blood from its poor head, which it grazed incessantly in its endeavours to get farther away from me. I thought it was time for me now to come to its help, but all my endeavours only made matters worse. The more I tried to aid its escape, the more blindly and swiftly did it dash itself against the walls and ceiling. I could but sit down and wait till it fell helpless and exhausted at my feet. The water stood in my eyes as I took it up and laid it in a safe place, from which, when recovered, it could fly safely away. "Poor foolish thing," I said, "how much alarm and suffering you would have been spared could you only have trusted me, and suffered me to set you at liberty long ago. But you have been to me a lively picture of the way in which we sinners of mankind treat a loving and compassionate Saviour."     *God a good Keeper*:—God hath all the properties of a good keeper. First, He is wise. Secondly, powerful. Thirdly, watchful. Fourthly, faithful. He hath given laws to be faithful, and then shall not He? *The certainty of salvation*:—When the soul is settled that person will be resolute in every good course. A faint-hearted soldier, were he resolved beforehand that he should escape death and danger, conquer his foes, and win the field, would he not put on his armour, gird his sword upon his thigh, and march furiously against his adversaries? And shall not then the Christian soldier, who is persuaded of victory, to have the spoil, and possess a crown of righteousness and glory, go on with an undaunted courage in the face of the devil, death, and hell? This doctrine reproveth those that for the most part never mind this duty. We see many who settle their houses on a good foundation, establish their trees that the wind shake them not, and by a staff to underprop their feeble bodies that they catch not a fall, the which we in its kind commend. But how few spend any time to have their souls settled in the certainty of salvation. (*J. Barlow, D.D.*)    *Faith and feeling:*—Dr. Archibald Alexander, eminent for learning and for consecration, when asked by one of his students at Princeton whether he always had full assurance of faith, replied, "Yes, except when the wind blows from the east." (*T. de Witt Talmage.*)    *Christian faith:*—Christian faith is the faith of a transaction; it is not the committing of one's thought in assent to a proposition, but it is the trusting of one's being to another Being, there to be rested, kept, guided, moulded, governed, and possessed for ever. (*H. Bushnell.*)    *Christian faith* is a grand cathedral with divinely-pictured windows. Standing without, you see no glory, nor can possibly imagine any. Nothing is visible but the merest outline of dusky shapes. Standing within, all is clear and defined, every ray of light reveals an array of unspeakable splendours. (*J. Ruskin.*)    *Faith a personal relation to Christ:*— If the object of faith were certain truths, the assent of the understanding would be enough. If the object of faith were unseen things, the confident persuasion of them would be sufficient. If the object of faith were promises of future good, the hope rising to certainty of the possession of these would be sufficient. But if the object be more than truths, more than unseen realities, more than promises; if the object be a living Person, then there follows inseparably this, that faith is not merely the assent of the understanding, that faith is not merely the persuasion of the reality of unseen things, that faith is not merely the confident expectation of future good; but that faith is the personal relation of him that believes to the living Person its object, the relation which is expressed not more clearly, but perhaps a little more forcibly to us by substituting another word, and saying, Faith is *trust.* (*A. Maclaren, D.D.*)    *Trust in Christ supported by cumulative evidence:*—I do not pretend to have a scientific knowledge of Divine things, or to rest my convictions upon a scientific demonstration; but I can venture to say that "I know whom I have believed." Such a belief will be supported by collateral evidence, acquiring from age to age a cumulative and converging force; but its essential virtue will in all ages be derived from the vital sources of personal love and trust. (*H. Wace, D.D.*)    *Character entrusted to God:*—When John Wesley was going over all the country proclaiming a crucified Saviour for sinners, the magazines and papers of the day slandered him as those of our day do God's servants still. In one paper there was an article so abusive and slanderous that a friend determined to contradict it. He laid the article and its reply before Wesley, who said, "When I gave my soul to Jesus, I gave Him my character to keep as well. I have to do my work and have no time to attend to it." Christians who are doing the Lord's work should go on with it, leaving themselves and their character in His hands.    *The soul entrusted to Christ:*—St. Paul says, "that which I have committed unto Him." This meant his soul. Suppose you have a precious jewel worth fifty or a hundred thousand dollars. It is so valuable that you are afraid you may lose it, or that some one may steal it from you. And suppose you have a friend who has a safe that is fire-proof and robber-proof. You take your jewel to this friend, and say to him: "Please take charge of this jewel, and keep it for me in your fire-proof." He takes it and locks it up there. And now you feel comfortable about that jewel. You know your friend is faithful, and your jewel is safe. You do not worry about it any more. You are ready to say about your jewel what St. Paul said about his soul, because you feel sure that it is safe. (*Richard Newton.*)    *Knowing Christ:*—There are two ways in which we are used to know persons. Sometimes it means to know them through some other person. Sometimes it means to know them ourselves. There is evidently a world-wide difference between the two. Let me illustrate it thus: We all know our Sovereign, her character, her state, her prerogative, her powers. But very few know the Queen. Yet it is very evident that those who have been admitted to her presence, and who have actually spoken and conversed in friendship with her, will have very different feelings towards her, and repose in her, and that their whole hearts will go out to her immensely more than those who know her only at a distance, and through the ordinary public channels. It is so with Christ. Some of you know Christ by the education of your childhood; some by the testimony of others; some by the reading of your Bible. Others have felt His presence. They have communed with Him. They have presented petitions, and they have had their answers from Himself. They have laid burdens at His feet, and He has taken them up. He has accepted their little gifts and smiled at their small services. *They* have proved Him. Isn't He another Being, isn't He another Christ to that man? They *know* Him. And what do they know of Thee, O blessed Jesus? They know Thee as the most loving and the loveliest of all—all grace, full of tenderness and sympathy, stooping to the meanest, and kind to the very worst. Our Brother, our Light, our Life, our Joy—who has taken away all our sins and carried all our load. That knowledge can never begin but in one way—by a certain inner life, by a walk of holiness, by the teaching of sorrow, in the school of discipline, from heavy leanings, by acts of self-abandonment, by goings down into the dust, by the grand influence of the Spirit, by Jesus revealing Himself. But once known—and from that moment it will be as hard not to trust as it is now difficult to do; as impossible for the heart to doubt as it is to that poor, prone heart now to question everything. If you really know, you cannot help believing. "If thou knewest the gift of God, and who it is that saith to thee, 'Give Me to drink,' thou wouldest have asked of Him, and He would have given thee living water." But there is a truth in St. Paul's words which I am very anxious to press upon you. See where the great apostle, the aged believer, the ripe saint, found all his argument and all his stand, as it were. Not—and if any man might he might—not in anything which had been worked by him; not in anything in him; not in his acts; not in his feelings; not in his faith; not in his conversion, however remarkable; not in his sanctification, however complete; but simply and absolutely and only in God. "I know"—as if he cared to know nothing else, all other knowledge being unsatisfactory or worse—"I know Him whom I have trusted." It may seem a strange thing to say, but it is really easier to know God than it is to know ourselves. It is remarkable that the Bible tells us a great deal more about God than it does about our own hearts. The great end of reading the Bible is to know God. (*J. Vaughan, M.A.*) *Confidence and concern:*—I. First, observe WHAT PAUL HAD DONE. 1. He had trusted a person—"I know whom I have believed." 2. Paul had gone further, and had practically carried out his confidence, for he had deposited everything with this person. A poor idiot, who had been instructed by an earnest Christian man, somewhat alarmed him by a strange remark, for he feared that all his teaching had been in vain. He said to this poor creature, "You know that you have a soul, John?" "No," said he, "I have no soul." "No soul!" thought the teacher, "this is dreadful ignorance." All his fears were rolled away when his half-witted pupil added, "I had a soul once, and I lost it, and Jesus found it; and so I have let Him keep it." II. The next thing is, WHAT DID PAUL KNOW? He tells us plainly, "I know whom I have believed." 1. We are to understand by this that Paul looked steadily at the object of his confidence, and knew that he relied upon God in Christ Jesus. He did not rest in a vague hope that he would be saved; nor in an indefinite reliance upon the Christian religion; nor in a sanguine expectation that all things would, somehow, turn out right at the end. He did not hold the theory of our modern divines, that our Lord Jesus Christ did something or other, which, in one way or another, is more or less remotely connected with the forgiveness of sin; but he knew the Lord Jesus Christ as a person, and he deliberately placed himself in His keeping, knowing Him to be the Saviour. 2. Paul also knew the character of Jesus whom he trusted. His perfect character abundantly justified the apostle's implicit trust. Paul could have said, "I know that I trust in One who is no mere man, but very God of very God. I have not put my soul into the keeping of a priest, like unto the sons of Aaron, who must die; but I have rested myself in One whose priesthood is according to the law of an endless life—a Priest for ever after the order of Melchizedek. He upon whom I confide is He without whom was not anything made that was made, who sustaineth all things by the Word of His power, and who at His coming shall shake both the heavens and the earth, for all fulness of Divine energy dwells in Him." 3. But how did Paul come to know Christ? Every page of Scripture, as the apostle perused it, revealed Jesus to him. This book is a royal pavilion, within which the Prince of peace is to be met with by believers who look for Him. In this celestial mirror Jesus is reflected. Paul also knew Jesus in another way than this. He had personal acquaintance with Him; he knew Him as "the Lord Jesus, who appeared unto him in the way." He knew the Lord also by practical experience and trial of Him. Paul had tested Jesus amidst furious mobs, when stones fell about him, and in prison, when the death-damp chilled him to the bone. He had known Christ far out at sea, when Euroclydon drove him up and down in the Adriatic; and he had known Christ when the rough blasts of unbrotherly suspicion had beaten upon him on the land. All that he knew increased his confidence. He knew the Lord Jesus because He had delivered him out of the mouth of the lion. III. Thirdly, let us inquire— WHAT WAS THE APOSTLE PERSUADED OF? 1. Implicitly Paul declares his faith in our Lord's willingness and faithfulness. 2. But the point which the apostle expressly mentions is the power of Christ—"I am persuaded that He is able." He that goes on board a great Atlantic liner does not say, "I venture the weight of my body upon this vessel. I trust it to bear my ponderous frame." Yet your body is more of a load to the vessel than your soul is to the Lord Jesus. Did you ever hear of the gnat on the horn of the ox which feared that it might be an inconveni- ence to the huge creature? Oh, friend! you are but a gnat in comparison with the Lord Jesus, nay, you are not so heavy to the ascended Saviour as the gnat to the ox. You were a weight to Him once, but having borne that load once for all, your salvation is no burden to Him now. Well may you say, "I am persuaded that He is able to keep that which I have committed unto Him." 3. What was this which Paul had committed to Christ? He committed to Him everything that he had for time and for eternity; his body, his soul, his spirit; all fears, cares, dangers, sins, doubts, hopes, joys: he just made a clean removal of his all from himself to his Lord. Those of you who are acquainted with the original will follow me while I forge a link between my third division and my fourth. If I were to read the text thus it would be quite correct—"I am persuaded that He is able to keep my deposit against that day." Here we have a glimpse of a second meaning. If you have the Revised Version, you will find in the margin "that which He has committed to me"; and the original allows us to read the verse whichever way we choose—"He is able to keep that which I have committed unto Him" —or "that which He has committed unto me." This last expression, though I could not endorse it as giving the full sense of the text, does seem to me to be a part of its meaning. It is noteworthy that, in the fourteenth verse, the original has the same phrase as in this verse. It runs thus—"That good deposit guard by the Holy Ghost which dwelleth in us." Inasmuch as the words are the same—the apostle speaking of "my deposit" in the twelfth verse, and in the fourteenth verse speaking of "that good deposit"—I cannot help thinking that one thought dominated his mind. His soul and the gospel were so united as to be in his thought but one deposit; and this he believed that Jesus was able to keep. He seemed to say, "I have preached the gospel which was committed to my trust; and now, for having preached it, I am put in prison, and am likely to die; but the gospel is safe in better hands than mine." The demon of distrust might have whispered to him, "Paul, you are now silenced, and your gospel will be silenced with you; the Church will die out; truth will become extinct." "No, no," saith Paul, "I am not ashamed; for I know that He is able to guard my deposit against that day." IV. This leads me on to this fourth point—WHAT THE APOSTLE WAS CONCERNED ABOUT. The matter about which he was concerned was this deposit of his—this everlasting gospel of the blessed God. He expresses his concern in the following words—"Hold fast the form of sound words, which thou hast heard of me, in faith and love which is in Christ Jesus. That good thing which was committed unto thee keep by the Holy Ghost which dwelleth in us." 1. He is concerned for the steadfastness of Timothy, and as I think for that of all young Christians, and especially of all young preachers. What does he say? "Hold fast the form of sound words." I hear an objector murmur, "There is not much in words, surely." Sometimes there is very much in words. Vital truth may hinge upon a single word. The whole Church of Christ once fought a tremendous battle over a syllable; but it was necessary to fight it for the conservation of the truth. When people rail at creeds as having no vitality, I suppose that I hear one say that there is no life in egg-shells. Just so; there is no life in egg-shells, they are just so much lime, void of sensation. "Pray, my dear sir, do not put yourself out to defend a mere shell." Truly, good friend, I am no trifler, nor so litigious as to fight for a mere shell. But hearken! I have dis- covered that when you break egg-shells you spoil eggs; and I have learned that eggs do not hatch and produce life when shells are cracked. 2. The apostle was anxious, not only that the men should stand, but that the everlasting gospel itself should be guarded. "That good thing which was committed unto thee keep by the Holy Ghost which dwelleth in us." It were better for us that the sun were quenched than that the gospel were gone. I believe that the moralities, the liberties, and peradventure the very existence of a nation depend upon the proclamation of the gospel in its midst. How are we to keep the faith? There is only one way. It is of little use trying to guard the gospel by writing it down in a trustdeed; it is of small service to ask men to subscribe to a creed: we must go to work in a more effectual way. How is the gospel to be guarded? "By the Holy Ghost which dwelleth in us." If the Holy Spirit dwells in you, and you obey His monitions, and are moulded by His influences, and exhibit the result of His work in the holiness of your lives, then the faith will be kept. A holy people are the true body-guard of the gospel. (*C. H. Spurgeon.*)

Ver. 13. **Hold fast the form of sound words.**—*Systematic knowledge of the gospel:*—While Paul was passing through Syria and Cilicia, confirming the Churches, he came to Lystra, where he found a certain disciple, named Timothy, who was highly esteemed by the Christian brethren in that city. This recommended him to the notice and acquaintance of the apostle; who being fully persuaded of his unfeigned piety and promising talents, determined to take him with him, and prepare him by proper instruction to preach the gospel. Timothy gratefully received and wisely improved this precious privilege, made great proficiency in theological knowledge, and soon became acquainted with the whole scheme of religious sentiments which the apostle embraced and taught. This form of sound words, or rather this system of sound doctrines, the apostle taught Timothy, and exhorted him to hold fast as a necessary and indispensable qualification for the gospel ministry. The opinion and practice of the apostle in this instance naturally leads us to conclude that a systematical knowledge of the gospel is still necessary to qualify other pious young men as well as Timothy for the same sacred office. 1. Young men who are preparing for the ministry should understand the harmony and connection which run through all the peculiar and essential doctrines of the gospel. These are so intimately connected that they cannot be clearly understood separately considered. 2. A systematical knowledge of the principal doctrines of the Bible is necessary in order to understand and explain the true meaning of the Scriptures in general. 3. Young men who are preparing for the ministry should have a systematical knowledge of the gospel, that they may be able to guard themselves against the religious errors to which they are peculiarly exposed. 4. It is necessary that those who are preparing for the ministry should have a systematical knowledge of the gospel in order to be able to refute as well as to avoid religious errors. 5. A systematical knowledge of the gospel is no less necessary in order to qualify pious young men to preach both the doctrines and duties of Christianity in the most plain, instructive, and profitable manner. It now remains to point out some things which seem naturally to flow from the subject. 1. The first thing suggested by the subject is that there can be no reasonable objection against all human systems of divinity. It is said that systems of divinity tend to promote religious controversies, which are highly prejudicial to practical religion. But it is very evident that they do not give rise to religious disputes, because religious disputes have always given rise to them. It is said that systems of divinity tend to prevent men from forming any real opinions of their own and to infringe upon their right of private judgment. No man can be said to have a real opinion upon any subject which is not derived from evidence; and if it be derived from evidence, it is totally immaterial whether he derives the evidence from his own investigation, or from conversation, or from reading, or from public or private instruction. It is said that systems of divinity are often the engines of designing men, and intended to propagate error instead of truth. It is not denied that theological systems may have been designed and employed to serve such an evil purpose. But it must be acknowledged, on the other hand, that they may have been designed and employed to counteract the baneful influence of error and to promote the cause of truth. 2. If the leading sentiment in this discourse has been sufficiently supported, we must conclude that it is generally improper for those to undertake to preach the gospel who have never acquired a systematical knowledge of it. In the next place, it appears from what has been said, that both an academical and theological education is highly necessary to qualify pious young men for the work of the ministry. 3. The whole train of the observations which have been made in this discourse now converge to a single point, and unitedly press the important duty of assisting pious and promising youths to furnish their minds with that literary and theological knowledge which is indispensably necessary to prepare them for the gospel ministry. (*N. Emmons, D.D.*)    *The form of sound words :*—The numerous and conflicting creeds, confessions of faith, and systems of divinity which are spread over the religious world are but of human authority. What volumes of needless controversy, what angry passions, what words of strife, and what deeds of violence had the world escaped by attention to this simple, obvious, all-important principle! But does it follow from this statement that we ought to have no system of religious opinions whatever; or that, having a system, it is a matter of indifference what that system is? By no means. We are not indeed to assume infallibility, either for ourselves or for the peculiarities of our creed; but it does not follow we should have no fixed creed at all. He who has no creed has nothing which he believes; and he who has nothing which he believes is an unbeliever, an infidel. The evil lies not in having a creed, but in having a wrong one; or in holding and propagating that which we have with tempers that are unkind and by measures that are unchristian. What we design at this time is a brief and plain summary of those religious principles avowed by the community of professing Christians with which we are more especially connected. If, on examination, the form of words we lay before you should be proved "sound," we may be allowed to admonish you in the words of the apostle to "hold it fast." 1. There exists an Infinite Being, the great first cause, whom we call God. There is but one God; but this one God subsists in three personalities or modes, commonly distinguished as Father, Son, and Holy Ghost. 2. The Holy Scriptures are the only sufficient and authorised rule of faith and practice. It is not intended to be affirmed that nothing is true but what is made known in the sacred writings; but that what is not there revealed cannot be required as an article of faith. 3. Man came out of the hands of his Creator in a state of perfect rectitude, holiness, and felicity. But man was at the same time constituted a moral agent; that is, he was put under a command or law which he had the power and liberty to obey or disobey. He disobeyed; and in consequence of that act of infidelity and rebellion fell from his primeval excellency; his nature became morally defiled; and that moral defilement he transmitted to all his posterity. 4. But mankind were not left to perish in this fallen, sinful, and wretched state: a great plan of redemption and salvation has been originated, and is now in actual existence and operation. This plan took its rise in the boundless benevolence of the eternal Jehovah; and the execution of it was laid on one that is mighty—on our Lord and Saviour Jesus Christ. 5. The Lord Jesus Christ, the Redeemer of mankind and the founder of our holy religion, is very God. But for us men and for our salvation the eternal Word became flesh and dwelt among us, so that the Saviour of the world is Man as well as God, or, in the style of the Scriptures, "God manifest in the flesh." 6. The sufferings and death of the man Christ Jesus are a proper and full satisfaction and atonement for the sins of mankind. 7. In that form of words which this Christian community has embraced, it is essential, not only that the blessed Jesus died for sin, but also that He died for the sins of all men; that in the design and appointment of Almighty God, the blood of the covenant extends its saving efficacy wide as the human race; and that, in consequence of the shedding of that blood, salvation is actually put within the grasp of every human soul. 8. We are justified before God and accepted into His favour, not by works of righteousness that we have done, but through faith in our Lord Jesus Christ, and through that alone. 9. It is the privilege of all who are thus accepted of God to have the assurance of it by the witness of the Spirit in their hearts. 10. As the nature of man is corrupt and sinful, before he can be admitted into the everlasting abodes of purity and bliss, he must undergo a great moral change—a change of disposition and desires—a change of heart and soul. This spiritual, happy revolution we are accustomed to express by such terms as "regeneration," "conversion," "the new birth," &c. 11. This regeneration and whatever else is necessary to the holiness and spiritual life of the soul is effected through the interposition and agency of the Holy Spirit. 12. The soul of man is immortal. 13. Perhaps no discovery of revelation is more stupendous or more consolatory than the doctrine of the resurrection of the dead. 14. "God hath appointed a day, in the which He will judge the world in righteousness by that Man whom He hath ordained; whereof He hath given assurance unto all men, in that He hath raised Him from the dead." 15. Finally, the solemnities of that great and final day of God will issue in the eternal blessedness and glory of the righteous, and in the endless punishment and misery of the wicked. Having thus submitted to you "the form," the plan, draught, or outline, as the word signifies, of what we consider "sound words," we solemnly request that it may be examined by that only proper test of religious truth, the Word of God. If it accord not with that standard, reject it; but if it do, then attend to the admonition in our text, and "hold fast the form of sound words." In the meantime, on this general admonition of the apostle, we may venture to establish the following exhortations. 1. Beware and do not exchange "the form of sound words" for the uncertainties and delusions of infidelity. 2. Beware of error in your religious doctrines. The mode of faith, the class of doctrines we espouse, cannot be a matter of indifference; for, as truth exerts an influence holy and happy, so the tendency of error is impure and destructive. 3. Finally, beware of holding "the truth in unrighteousness." Truth itself is of no value only as it influences to an upright, holy, and benevolent practice. (*J. Bromley.*) *The scope of the Scriptures :*—In these words there is—1. The character of Scripture-doctrine; it is sound words—sound and pure in itself, and sound in its effect, being of a soul-healing virtue (Ezek. xlvii. 9). 2. The sum of it, faith, showing what we are to believe; and love, what we are to do (1 John v. 3; John xiv. 15). This love has a particular relation to Christ, all our obedience being to be offered unto God through Him, as our faith fixes on God through Him. This was what the apostle preached. 3. Our duty with respect to it ; to hold fast the form of sound words. This signifies—(1) To have a pattern of the doctrine in our minds, to which all that ministers teach must be conformable. (2) To hold it fast; to cleave to, and keep hold of it, without flinching from it, whatever dangers or difficulties may attend the doing so. Both these senses are implied in the words. I. Let us consider THE NATURE OF THAT FAITH AND OBEDIENCE WHICH THE SCRIPTURE TEACHES, WITH THE CONNECTION BETWIXT THE TWO. 1. As to faith. Divine faith is a believing of what God has revealed, because God has said it, or revealed it. People may believe Scripture-truths, but not with a Divine faith, unless they believe it on that very ground, the authority of God speaking in His Word. And this Divine faith is the product of the Spirit of God in the heart of a sinner, implanting the habit or principle of faith there, and exciting it to a hearty reception and firm belief of whatever God reveals in His Word. Hence we may infer—(1) That there can be no right knowledge of God acquired in an ordinary way without the Scriptures (Matt. xxii. 29). (2) That where the Scriptures are not known, there can be no saving faith. (3) That there is nothing we are bound to believe as a part of faith but what the Scripture teaches, be who they will that propose it, and whatever they may pretend for their warrant. 2. As to obedience, it is that duty which God requires of man. It is that duty and obedience which man owes to God, to His will and laws, in respect of God's universal supremacy and sovereign authority over man ; and which he should render to Him out of love and gratitude. (1) That there can be no sufficient knowledge of the duty which we owe to God without the Scriptures. (2) That there can be no right obedience yielded to God without them. (3) That there is no point of duty that we are called to, but what the Scripture teaches (Isa. viii. 20). As to the connection of these two, faith and obedience are joined together, because there is no true faith but what is followed with obedience, and no true obedience but what flows from faith. Faith is the loadstone of obedience, and obedience the touchstone of faith, as appears from James ii. II. I proceed now to consider THE MANNER OF THE SCRIPTURE'S TEACHING. 1. The Scripture teaches some things expressly in so many words ; as, "Except a man be born again, he cannot enter into the kingdom of God," &c. 2. The Scriptures teach but externally. It is the Spirit that teaches internally. III. I come now to consider THE SENSE OF THE SCRIPTURE. The sense of the Scripture is but one, and not manifold. (*T. Boston, D.D.*) *The credenda of Christianity :*—I. LET US CONSIDER THE OBJECT OF TENACIOUS PRESERVATION : "the form of sound words which thou hast heard of me." What is this form of sound words? 1. I should answer explicitly, and without hesitation, in the first place, the whole of God's inspired truth, contained in the writing of the Old and the New Testament. In the Scriptures are contained all things necessary to be known and practised ; and, therefore, this Book must be held with a firm and a tenacious grasp. 2. By "the form of sound words," in the next place, it is not at all unreasonable to suppose that the apostle might intend a certain formulary, or system of Divine truth, which he might have given to Timothy, his "son in the faith," and a younger teacher in the Church. I say some formulary, or system of Divine truth, in which the great principles of the gospel might be condensed and epitomised. We have warrant in Scripture for such formularies, both in the Old Testament and in the New ; and though, indeed, as composed by mere human minds, they are not the object of a Divine faith, any farther than they are found in strict coincidence with the Holy Scriptures ; yet they are, nevertheless, profitable and desirable.  1. In the first place, it is of great advantage to have a concise, harmonious, connected view of the truth as it stands revealed in Holy Scripture.  2. In the next place, order is known to be a powerful assistant of the memory.  3. In the third place, it is well to have a summary of Christian truth, in order that our testimony among our fellow creatures may be clearly understood and explicitly declared.  4. And finally, that those who are enemies either to the truth or the practice of Christianity, may have that which can be lifted up as a standard against them, so that they cannot mutilate, corrupt, or destroy, "the truth as it is in Jesus." It cannot be doubted but that these systems and formularies of Divine truth, rightly exhibited, and sustained by Holy Scripture, have proved in every age a mighty bulwark to the faith of the Christian Church.  II. The duty which the Christian owes to the object which we have considered: to hold it fast with a firm and with a determinate grasp.  And this implies the following things—1. An accurate acquaintance with the truth which they embody and exhibit.  The understanding must be employed in ascertaining the sense and meaning of Holy Scripture, in comparing evidence, in deducing just conclusions from authentic premises, in tracing the harmony, the connection, and the bearing of one truth upon another, so that the various links of the chain may be held in their unbroken connection. 2. There must be a full persuasion of the truth.  3. Finally, there should be a conscientious determination to preserve the truth of the gospel at all hazards, and whatever consequences may possibly ensue with respect to ourselves, or our worldly interests.  III. The manner and the spirit in which the tenacity of the truth is to be attempted.  It is added, "in faith and love, which is in Christ Jesus." For there is always some danger lest human passion and infirmity should mix themselves even with our conscientious regard to the truth of God.  We have to guard against the wrath of the angry polemic; the bitterness of the prejudiced bigot; visionary and fanatic wildness of the enthusiast.  1. First, we are to hold fast the truth in faith, because faith is the only ground upon which we receive and retain the truth.  We do not receive it by tradition from our fellow-men; we do not receive it upon the authority or credit of any merely human teacher, however much that teacher may be valued by us; but we receive it on the ground of God's authority. He has revealed it.  We find it in His Book; a book of which the evidences fully substantiate the Divine original.  Then we have a witness which is more valuable, in point of fact, than ten thousand theories, or ten thousand merely speculative arguments.  This is the inward evidence which every real Christian derives from his own state of mind, his feeling, his character, his conduct; and by which he is able to demonstrate the truth of the blessed gospel.  Then we are to maintain the truth in love—"love which is in Christ Jesus."  I must show this determined and this courageous attachment to the truth, first, for the love of Jesus Christ, who came into the world both to reveal and to confirm it.  I must maintain it from love to my own soul.  Love to the souls of others should impel me to this courageous maintenance of the truth of the gospel.  Could we conceive of a readier method of destroying the entire population of a city than by poisoning the aqueduct, or the fountain, from which they were supplied with their daily drink?  What should we think of the guilt of that man who would knowingly drop poison into a living spring, that all who went to quench their thirst, instead of meeting with refreshment and health, should meet with their bane and their destruction?  And I never can suppose that man to be under the influence of a candid, generous, and benevolent spirit, who sacrifices the truth, and fails to maintain that which is of infinite importance to God's honour, to the salvation of the soul, and to the existence of Christ's kingdom amongst men, based, as they are, upon the everlasting and immutable truth of the gospel.  (*G. Clayton, M.A.*)       *The form of sound words :—* I do not suppose that by this it is intended that Paul ever wrote out for Timothy a list of doctrines; or that he gave him a small abstract of Divinity, to which he desired him to subscribe his name, as the articles of the Church over which he was made a pastor.  If so, doubtless that document would have been preserved and enrolled in the canons of Scripture as one of the writings of an inspired man.  I can scarce think such a creed would have been lost, whilst other creeds have been preserved and handed down to us.  I conceive that what the apostle meant was this:—" Timothy, when I have preached to you, you have heard certain grand outlines of truth; you have heard from me the great system of faith in Jesus Christ; in my writings and public speakings you have heard me continually insist upon a certain pattern or form of faith; now, I bid you, my dearly beloved son in the gospel, Hold fast the form of sound words, which thou hast heard of me, in faith and love which is in Christ Jesus." I. What is a "FORM OF SOUND WORDS"? Ten thousand persons will quarrel upon this. One will say, " my creed is a form of sound words "; another will declare that his creed also is sound, if not infallible. 1. We will not, therefore, enter into all the minutiæ which distinguish creeds from each other, but just simply say, that no system can be a form of sound words unless it is perfectly Scriptural. 2. But since it is said that texts may be found to prove almost everything, we must remark that a form of sound words must be one that exalts God and puts down man. 3. We think, also, that we may judge of the soundness of doctrine by its tendency. We can never think a doctrine sound, when we see plainly upon its very surface that it has a tendency to create sin in men. 4. We shall, perhaps, be asked, what we do regard as a form of sound words, and what those doctrines are which are Scriptural, which at the same time are healthful to the spirit and exalting to God. We answer, we believe that a form of sound words must embrace, first of all, the doctrine of God's being and nature, we must have the trinity in unity, and the unity in trinity. 5. Now, we hold, that a form of sound words must look upon man aright as well as upon God aright; it must teach that man is utterly fallen, that he is sinful, and for his sin condemned and in himself altogether hopeless of salvation. 6. And next, we think that a doctrine that is sound must have right views of salvation, as being of the Lord alone. II. Now let me show you THE NECESSITY OF HOLDING FAST THIS FORM OF SOUND WORDS, AND KEEPING IT FOR YOUR OWN SAKE, FOR THE CHURCH'S SAKE, FOR THE WORLD'S SAKE. 1. First, for your own sake, hold it fast, for thereby you will receive ten thousand blessings; you will receive the blessing of peace in your conscience. 2. "Hold fast the form of sound words," because it will tend very much to your growth. He who holds fast the truth will grow faster than he who is continually shifting from doctrine to doctrine. 3. I would beseech you to hold it fast for your own sakes, from a remembrance of the great evils which will follow the contrary course. If you do not "hold fast the form of sound words," listen to me while I tell you what you will do. In the first place, every deviation from truth is a sin. It is not simply a sin for me to do a wrong act, but it is a sin for me to believe a wrong doctrine. If it be a sin of ignorance, it is nevertheless a sin; but it is not so heinous as a sin of negligence, which I fear it is with many. 4. "Hold fast the form of sound words," because error in doctrine almost inevitably leads to error in practice. When a man believes wrongly, he will soon act wrongly. 5. And now, for the good of the Church itself, I want you all to "hold fast the form of sound words." Would you wish to see the Church prosperous? Would you wish to see it peaceful? Then "hold fast the form of sound words." What is the cause of divisions, schisms, quarrels, and bickerings amongst us? It is not the fault of the truth; it is the fault of the errors. There would have been peace in the Church, entire and perpetual peace, if there had been purity—entire and perpetual purity—in the Church. Going down to Sheerness on Friday, I was told by some one on board that during the late gale several of the ships there had their anchors rent up, and had gone dashing against the other ships, and had done considerable damage. Now, if their anchors had held fast and firm, no damage would have been done. Ask me the cause of the damage which has been done to our Churches by the different denominations, and I tell you, it is because all their anchors did not hold fast. 6. Keep to your faith, I say again, for the Church's sake, for so you will promote strength in the Church. I saw lying between Chatham and Sheerness a number of ships that I supposed to be old hulks; and I thought how stupid Government was to let them remain there, and not chop them up for firewood, or something else; but some one said to me, those ships can soon be fitted for service; they look old now, but they only want a little paint, and when the Admiralty requires them, they will be commissioned and made fit for use. So we have heard some people say, "There are those old doctrines— what good are they?" Wait; there is not a doctrine in God's Bible that has not its use. Those ships that you may think are not wanted, will be useful by-and-bye. So it is with the doctrines of the Bible. Do not say, "Break up those old doctrines, you can do without them." Nay, we want them, and we must have them. 7. "Well," says one, "I think we ought to hold the truth firmly; but I do not see the necessity for holding the form of it; I think we might cut and trim a little, and then our doctrines would be received better." 8. Again, I say, "hold fast the form of sound words," for the world's sake. Pardon me when I say that, speaking after the manner of men, I believe that the progress of the gospel has been awfully impeded by the errors of its preachers. I never wonder when I see a Jew an unbeliever in Christianity, for this reason, that the Jews very seldom see Christianity in its beauty. For hundreds of years what has the Jew thought Christianity to be? Why, pure idolatry. He has seen the Catholic bow down to blocks of wood and stone; he has seen him prostrating himself before the Virgin Mary and all saints; and the Jew has said, "Ah! this is my watchword—Hear, O Israel, the Lord thy God is one Lord; I could not be a Christian, for to worship one God is the essential part of my religion." So the heathen, I believe, have seen a false system of Christianity, and they have said, "What! is that your Christianity?" and they did not receive it. III. And now, LET ME WARN YOU OF TWO DANGERS. One is, that you will be very much tempted to give up the form of sound words that you hold, on account of the opposition you will meet with. But the greatest obstacle you will have is a sort of slight and cunning, trying to pervert you to the belief that your doctrine is the same with one which is just the very opposite. IV. I am to tell you of THE GREAT HOLDFASTS, WHEREBY YOU ARE TO HOLD FAST THE TRUTH OF THE GOSPEL. 1. If I might be allowed to mention one or two before coming to those in the text, I should say, in the first place, if you want to hold fast the truth, seek to get an understanding of it. A man cannot hold a thing fast unless he has a good understanding of it. I never want you to have the faith of the collier who was asked what he believed; he said he believed what the Church believed. "Well, but what does the Church believe?" He said the Church believed what he believed, and he believed what the Church believed; and so it went all the way round. Let me exhort you, parents, as much as lieth in you, to give your children sound instruction in the great doctrines of the gospel of Christ. I believe that what Irving once said is a great truth. He said, "In these modern times you boast and glory, and you think yourselves to be in a high and noble condition, because you have your Sabbath-schools and your British-schools, and all kinds of schools for teaching youth. I tell you," he said, "that philanthropic and great as these are, they are the ensigns of your disgrace; they show that your land is not a land where parents teach their children at home. They show you there is a want of parental instruction; and though they be blessed things, these Sabbath-schools, they are indications of something wrong, for if we all taught our children there would be no need of strangers to say to our children, 'Know the Lord.'" I trust you will never give up that excellent puritanical habit of catechising your children at home. Any father or mother who entirely gives up a child to the teaching of another has made a mistake. 2. But then, Christian men, above all things, if you hold fast the truth, pray yourselves right into it. An old divine says, "I have lost many things I learned in the house of God, but I never lost anything I ever learned in the closet." That which a man learns on his knees, with his Bible open, he will never forget. 3. But the two great holdfasts are here given—faith and love. If ye would hold the truth fast, put your faith in Jesus Christ, and have an ardent love towards Him. Believe the truth. Do not pretend to believe it, but believe it thoroughly. And then the second holdfast is love. Love Christ, and love Christ's truth because it is Christ's truth, for Christ's sake, and if you love the truth you will not let it go. It is very hard to turn a man away from the truth he loves. (*C. H. Spurgeon.*) *The Service of the Church of England.*—I. OF THE SYSTEM OF DIVINE TRUTH WHICH TIMOTHY WAS, and, consequently, all faithful ministers of the gospel are, to "hold fast," we remark, in the first place, that it is called a form. The great truths of revelation are scattered over the whole of the oracles of God; and in order to present those truths in a comprehensive manner to the bulk of mankind, who have neither time nor inclination to seek them out themselves, the Church has, in all ages, retained a summary of Christian doctrine like that which we call the Apostles' Creed. The apostles themselves knew well, that if they had left the doctrines of Christianity unguarded, or had depended on oral traditions to convey those doctrines uncorrupted to future generations, the Word of God would have been lost in an ungodly world, as was well-nigh the case with the Jews, who had made the Word of God void by their traditions. As it is, the truths of the gospel have had (if we may so speak) a narrow escape from the polluting hands of men. If our Reformers had not rescued the "form of sound words" from the errors of ten preceding centuries, we should not now be exhorting you, with St. Paul, to "hold fast the form of sound words which you have heard of us in faith and love." But whilst we see in the writings of St. Paul an authority for forms, we are far from attaching any importance to a form as such. To recommend itself to the heart and conscience of a believer, it must not be a mere form of words, but it must be a "form of *sound* words"—

" sound speech that cannot be condemned." In different places, and at different times, forms have been obtruded on the Church, framed according to man's device, and some peculiar interpretations of God's truth. But for a form to be worthy of being called " sound," it must be of sound words. We set up no standard of truth but the pure Word of God ; but we do think that a form of doctrine taken from that Word is the readiest mode of preserving the faith ; and the best and most precious legacy we can leave to our children is that sound form of words, in which we have been instructed—that sound form of worship, which, after all, is the glory of our land, and a powerful means of upholding Christianity amongst us. II. ON WHAT PRINCIPLE, AND IN WHAT SPIRIT OUR ADHERENCE TO OUR FORMS IS TO BE MAINTAINED. Timothy was to " hold fast the form of sound words " heard of Paul, on the principle of faith, and in the spirit of love, " that is in Christ Jesus." The strongest objection we have ever heard against forms, even admitting them to be of " sound words," is, that they are liable to impart a false security to the worshipper, and to become lifeless to the greater number of those who profess adherence to them. We cannot deny but that there is a danger here : we must admit, that the very best system which could ever be devised for maintaining God's truth will be sure to have something in it to object to. But this is not owing to the form : we are always too ready to find the blame that belongs to us in anything but our own hearts. A man who holds fast a form, merely because it is respectable, and that other persons may be assured of his orthodoxy, does not hold fast the form on a right principle. He should hold it in faith. It should be something that has life, and not a mere body without a form. Unless we get to that which is within the ark, it matters but little to look at the bending cherubim. Unless our faith is exercised upon the object of all our hope, namely, the Lord Jesus Christ, our forms will but serve to condemn us. But, lastly, we speak of the spirit in which we should adhere to our forms. They are not to be held fast in the spirit of bigotry and exclusion. This is not the spirit in which St. Paul taught Timothy to " hold fast the form of sound words " : he was to maintain his principles and his system of doctrine " in love " ; in love no doubt to his Saviour who had loved him to the death, but of charity towards all those who might differ from him on certain points. (*R. Burgess, B.D.*) *The Prayer-book a ready help in drawing near to God:*—The Book of Common Prayer, which has guided the devotions of so many millions, in all lands, to-day, and which has been the comfort of a great multitude which no man can number, in ages past, has been well described as " The Sanctuary of our Faith and our Language." Its words are familiar in every ear, and its ancient forms hallow our daily life. The Prayer-book speaks to us most tenderly of birth, baptism, marriage, and death. Forms of prayer and praise were used in the Jewish Church, by God's own appointment, and liturgies have given shape and permanence to the worship of the Christian Church since apostolic times. Our own Prayer-book is especially rich in its ancient treasures, from the fact that it embraces the choicest selections from those heirlooms of the past. It was not the work of a day, nor of a generation, but the legacy of saints and martyrs and confessors ; and the words now uttered by God's children in this distant age were once spoken by those who faced the rack and the devouring flames, and whose only abiding-places were the dens and caves of the earth. The Communion Service, by itself, is a compact and complete summary of the Christian's belief, and a powerful and persuasive sermon enforcing holiness of life. In our every-day, struggling, checkered existence, the Prayer-book bears an important part. When Archbishop Cranmer had resumed his manly courage, and was ready to seal with his blood his faithfulness to the truth of God, he reverently began his dying testimony by reciting the Apostles' Creed. John Rogers, as he was led in handcuffs through weeping crowds, to be burned at the stake, chanted, with loud and unfaltering voice, the thrilling words of the *Miserere.* The gentle and gifted Lady Jane Gray nerved herself to lay her head upon the fatal block by reciting the same sweet words, exchanging, in a moment, the earthly crown, with its thorns and trials, for an immortal diadem of glory. St. Augustine and St. Ambrose rise up before us when the grand *Te Deum* recalls the memorable baptism at Milan. Recent as are the historical records of the Church in this Western world, they are by no means lacking in interest and significance. On the sultry August day in 1583, when Sir Humphrey Gilbert landed on the craggy shores of Newfoundland, to take possession of the continent for England's queen, the Cross of Christ was set up, and the solemn offices of the Prayer-book were duly celebrated. Well may we rejoice that this Book of Common Prayer, so powerful for good, has been preserved, by God's kind providence, as the heritage of His people! The morning sun, as he rises successively on the nations of the earth, is ever followed by these prayers and praises of martyred saints, and he sinks, at close of day, behind no mountain nor plain nor ocean wave where these holy offices are not heard. After even so brief a summary of what might be said concerning this, the only meet companion volume for the Holy Bible, does not every one among us feel disposed to yield cheerful obedience to the apostle's direction concerning the preservation of the casket of sacred truth, " Hold fast the form of sound words "? The dying Hammond, amidst the most excruciating pains, stopped his friends, who were praying for him in irregular and unpremeditated words, saying, " Let us call on God in the voice of His Church ! " When the saintly George Herbert was asked what prayers should be offered in his death-chamber, he answered, with warmth, " The prayers of my mother, the Church of England ; there are no prayers like them ! " Hannah Moore records her testimony that " never, in the most rapturous moments of the saintliest minds, have they failed to find in the Prayer-book their most soaring and sustaining wings." The most devoted Churchman is not disposed to place the Prayer-book above the Bible, but, like the moon in the heavens, it is only a satellite of the Church, borrowing all its light from Christ, the Sun of Righteousness. (*J. N. Norton.*)    *The Thirty-Nine Articles of the Church of England :*—The words which I have chosen for the text intimate to us the great importance of the words by which our religious ideas are expressed. The Scriptures, indeed, as indited by the Spirit of God, contain words, of all others, the soundest and the best, by which to express such truths as are necessary for mankind to believe or know. The great God being the author, He has, without doubt, expressed everything there, in a manner of all others the most fit and proper. Nothing else would be consistent with infinite wisdom and goodness, and whatever words we employ, are either true or false, sound or corrupt, as they agree or disagree with the words of the Scriptures. But still there never has been any error, or heresy, or schism in the Church, but its authors have pretended to ground it on the Scriptures. In this all heretics, Greek and Latin, old and new, agree. They all plead Scripture for what they say, and each one pretends that his opinion, be it never so absurd and ridiculous, is in accordance with the words there used. This at first may seem strange, but on further reflection it is not to be so much wondered at ; it arises partly from the Scriptures being written in different languages to those with which most men are familiar ; so that, if in the translation (admirable as that translation on the whole is) there be any word that seems to favour an erroneous opinion to which men may be inclined, it is too readily concluded that the Scriptures favour it. This arises partly again from the circumstance, that though others are acquainted with the original languages in which the Scriptures are written, they yet are not so fully acquainted with them as to clearly understand the full meaning of every expression. Then again, the rites and customs of countries far distant, and ages far remote, were so different to our own, that they occasion difficulties and obscurities. A large part of the Bible is also written in the highest poetical language, and abounds with metaphors and figures. All classes of individuals have therefore been agreed on the desirableness of some form of sound words, based on the Scriptures. Every one of the foreign churches, I believe, possesses such a form of its own ; and those who in our own country left our own Church, also had such a form drawn up for themselves by the assembly of divines at Westminster, and still employ it as their catechism. There is, therefore, no difference of opinion as to the propriety of this —the necessities of the Church have established the approval of it. There are three especial excellencies in the articles, which deserve to be noticed, and which, perhaps, render them pre-eminent among all formularies of faith which have yet been drawn up. They are most eminently evangelical, moderate, and protestant. Evangelical in doctrine, moderate in discipline, and protestant in ceremonials. (*J. Garwood, M.A.*)    *The morning exercise methodised :*—" Hold fast "—Greek, Εχε. The word hath a double signification, namely, " to have," and " to hold," and both of these the apostle commends to Timothy, namely—1. To have such a form or collection of gospel-doctrines, as a type or exemplar to which he should conform in his ministry. 2. To hold it, that is, to " hold it fast," not to swerve from it in the course of his ministry, but pertinaciously to adhere to it, not to suffer it to be corrupted by men of erroneous principles, nor to part with it upon any terms in the world, but to stand by it, and own it, against all opposition and persecution whatsoever. Doctrine I. METHODICAL SYSTEMS OF THE MAIN AND SPECIAL POINTS OF THE CHRISTIAN RELIGION ARE VERY USEFUL AND PROFITABLE BOTH FOR

MINISTERS AND PEOPLE. In the managing of the doctrinal part of this observation, I shall only give you two demonstrations: 1. Scripture-pattern; 2. The usefulness of such modules. Demonstration 1. Scripture-pattern. The whole Scripture is a large module of saving truth. The Word of God is full of such maps and modules of Divine truths necessary to salvation. The whole gospel, in general, is nothing but the great platform or standard of saving doctrine. But now, more particularly, we may observe that, beside this great universal map or synopsis of Divine truth, there are to be found in Scripture more compendious abstracts containing certain of the main heads and points of saving doctrine, methodised into lesser bodies and tables, for the help of our faith and knowledge; and we find them accommodated, by the penmen of the Holy Ghost, to two special ends and purposes. 1. To inform the Church in the principles of religion. The Ten Commandments, a brief abstract of the whole law. Three modules delivered by Christ in His first sermon. The first module contains the beautitudes; a list of particulars wherein man's true and chiefest happiness doth consist (Matt. v. 3–11). The second module contains a list of duties; things to be done by every one that would be saved. This our Saviour doth by asserting and expounding the moral law (Matt. v. 17–48), confuting and reforming the false glosses which the scribes and Pharisees had put upon the Ten Commandments, thereby "making the law of God of none effect." (Matt. xv. 6). And these we may call the *facienda*, "things to be done." The third module contains a list of petitions, which (Matt. vi. 9–15) He commends to His disciples, and in them to all succeeding generations of the Church, as a form or directory of prayer. The holy apostles tread in our Saviour's steps. You may observe in all their epistles, that in the former part of them they generally lay down a module of gospel-principles, and in the latter part a module of gospel-duties. 2. A second sort of modules, or a second end and design of such modules, is to obviate errors, and to antidote Christians against the poison and infection of rotten, pernicious principles: for no sooner had the good husbandman sowed his field with good seed, but the envious man went out after him, and began to scatter tares (Matt. xiii. 25). In opposition whereunto, the apostles in their several epistles were careful to furnish the Churches with such modules and platforms of truth as might discover and confute those "damnable heresies" (2 Peter ii. 1). Demonstration 2. The advantages of such modules. Advantage 1. For the ornament of the truth. Whether it be delivered from the pulpit or from the press, in such systems and platforms the hearer or reader may, as in a map or table (sometimes of one sort, sometimes of another) behold Divine truths standing one by another in their method and connection, mutually casting light and lustre upon each other. 2. Such types and exemplars of Divine truths are of great help to the understanding. As the collection of many beams and luminaries makes the greater light, so it is in the judgment, a constellation of gospel-principles shining together into the understanding, fills it with distinct and excellent knowledge. 3. Such patterns and platforms, whether of larger or of lesser compass, are a great help to memory. In all arts and sciences, order and method is of singular advantage unto memory. We do easily retain things in our mind, when we have once digested them into order. 4. Such modules serve to quicken affection. Sympathy and harmony have a notable influence upon the affections. 5. It is a marvellous antidote against error and seduction. Gospel-truths in their series and dependence are a chain of gold to tie the truth and the soul close together. 6. Growth in grace is one blessed fruit of such systems and tables of Divine truths. When foundations are well laid, the superstructures are prosperously carried on. Uses. 1. In the first place, it serves to justify the practice of the Churches of Jesus Christ, which have their public forms and tables of the fundamental articles of the Christian faith drawn up by the joint labour and travail of their learned and godly divines, after much and solemn seeking of God by fasting and prayer; in the solemn profession whereof they all consent and agree. 2. It serves to show us the benefit and advantage of public catechisms. 3. Hence also I might commend to young students in divinity the reading of systems and compendious abstracts and abridgments. 4. It serves to commend methodical preaching. 5. It commends (not least) constant and fixed hearing. Especially when people sit under a judicious and methodical ministry. "Loose hearing may please, but the fixed will profit,"; skipping hearing, for the most part, makes but sceptical Christians. 6. From hence give me leave to commend to you the benefit and advantage of "the morning exercise." (*T. Case, M.A.*) *Keep:*—There is a fourfold keeping of this pattern, and all here meant. The first, in memory, not forgetting. Secondly, in faith, not doubting. Thirdly, in affection, not hating. Fourthly, in practice, not disobeying. And there can be none of the four without the first. Some read have; others, hold the pattern : all one in effect. (*J. Barlow, D.D.*) *The pattern :*—It is by some termed the true pattern, or perfect pattern, or form. It seems to be a word borrowed from a painter, who first draws but after a pattern, or from a carpenter that works by rule. (*Ibid.*) *Of sound words :*—A thing may be said to be wholesome or sound four ways. First, when it's sound in itself. Secondly, when it works soundness in another thing ; or thirdly, preserves it being wrought ; and fourthly, when it is a sign of soundness (John iii. 12). And all these be in the words of this pattern. (*Ibid.*) *Wholesome doctrine :*—For if the words be not sound, the pattern cannot but be unsound. When poison is mixed with good meats and wines it spoils all ; so when the words be not wholesome, the pattern and form of doctrine is defective. One rotten post maketh a weak building. We must be transformed into the doctrine ; and as the spirit in the meat we eat is turned into ours, so must the word we read or hear be converted into us (Rom. vi. 17). And if our spiritual food be not wholesome, our souls will grow sick and die. (*Ibid*). " *I pray you to fasten your grips* ":—This sentence I met with in one of those marvellous letters which Samuel Rutherford left as a priceless legacy to the Church of God in all ages. Truly he hath dust of gold. I thought it would make a capital text for a prayer-meeting address, and so I jotted it down. It gripped me, and so I gripped it, in the hope that it might grip you, and lead you " to fasten your grips." But do not imagine that I have taken a text from Rutherford because I could not find one in the Bible, for there are many passages of Scripture which teach the same lesson. As for instance, that exhortation, " Lay hold on eternal life," or that other, " Hold fast that thou hast," or that other, " Hold fast the form of sound words." The things of God are not to be trifled with, " lest at any time we let them slip." They are to be grasped, as Jacob seized the angel, with " I will not let thee go." Faith is first the eye of the soul wherewith it sees the invisible things of God, and then it becomes the hand of the soul, with which it gets a grip of the substance of " the things not seen as yet." A man has two hands, and I would urge you to take a double hold upon those things which Satan will try to steal from you. Take hold of them as the limpet takes hold upon the rock, or as the magnet takes hold of steel. Give a life grip—a death grip. " I pray you to fasten your grips." (*C. H. Spurgeon.*) *Faith in the minister :*—Whatever is held forth in the palsied hand of unbelief is itself made to quiver. Scepticism is a smoking lamp, which, while it gives no light, loads the atmosphere with a thick darkness, if not with a stench. (*Ibid.*) *Creed and life :*—I have heard people say that it cannot matter much what a man believes, so long as he lives up to right moral principles. They might as well remark that it does not matter if the beams of a house are rotten, so long as the door-plate is bright. Where will be the door-plate when the house falls ? A hazy creed means a mazy life. A man's faith is the mainspring of his actions. He who believes nothing will do nothing, till the devil finds him work. I record as my own experience that when the foundations of faith rocked the superstructure of practice reeled. (*Edwd. Garrett.*) *Men of unsettled creed :*—" I shape my creed every week," was the confession of one to me. Whereunto shall I liken such unsettled ones ? Are they not like those birds which frequent the Golden Horn, and are to be seen from Constantinople, of which it is to be said that they are always on the wing, and never rest? No one ever saw them alight on the water or on the land ; they are for ever poised in mid-air. The natives call them " lost souls," seeking rest and finding none. Assuredly men who have no personal rest in the truth, if they are not unsaved themselves, are, at least, very unlikely to save others. (*C. H. Spurgeon.*) *Faith and love :*—So that faith is necessary to keep the pattern ; for it purifieth the heart inwardly, and is the true ground of all outward and acceptable obedience. And for love, that's needful also. For love helpeth attention, strengtheneth the memory, setteth the will at work, uniteth to God and man, and therefore it is rightly said that by love we fulfil the law, for without this affection our best actions neither please the Creator, nor be profitable to the creature. Would we then practise the apostle's doctrine? then let us strive for faith and love. These two support the estate of a Christian, as the two pillars did the house of the Philistines. If these be removed, the foundation of our obedience and salvation fail and fall. He that would soar to heaven wanting either of these may as soon see a bird mount on high and take her stand who wanteth one wing. Faith, like the hand, takes hold on Christ, and love, like the feet, must carry

us to Him.   Thou wilt say, how may I know when an action is done in faith and love?
If it be done in faith: First, Thou must be in the faith, that is, in Christ, and Christ
in thee (2 Cor. xiii. 5).   Secondly, It must be guided by the rule of faith
(2 Pet. i. 19).   Thirdly, It must be done with faith, not doubtingly (Rom. xiv. 23).
Fourthly, It must be done to the object of our faith, viz., in obedience to God
in Christ, and for His glory (1 Cor. x. 31).   If an action be done in love: First,
It is done so freely that there is not the least expectation of any future recompense (Gen. xxiii. 15.)   Secondly, So secretly that (if possible) none might ever
come to the knowledge thereof.   Thirdly, So cheerfully, as there is equal (or rather
greater) joy in the doing, than receiving of the like favour.   Fourthly, so affectionately, that the more good we do to any, the more we find our hearts enflamed with
the love of that person.   Which is in Christ Jesus.   From the fourfold interpretation we may note so many doctrines.   I. THAT FAITH AND LOVE ARE GIVEN TO MAN OF
GOD THROUGH CHRIST JESUS.   II. THAT FAITH AND LOVE IN CHRIST SHOULD STIR US
UP TO KEEP THE PATTERN.   III. THAT THE OBJECT OF FAITH AND LOVE IS CHRIST
JESUS.   IV. THAT FAITH AND LOVE ARE COMPREHENDED IN CHRIST JESUS.   And
whereas our apostle hath now brought in this phrase five several times in this short
chapter, we may note divers things worthy our instruction.   I. THAT WE ARE HARDLY
BROUGHT TO BELIEVE THAT ALL GRACE AND MERCY COME THROUGH CHRIST JESUS.
DIVINE TRUTHS ARE NOT EASILY BELIEVED.   II. THAT THE BEST THINGS MAY OFTEN,
FOR GOOD ENDS, BE MENTIONED.   III. THAT WHEN WE SPEAK OF ANY GRACE OR FAVOUR
RECEIVED, WE SHOULD CONSIDER THROUGH WHOM IT IS CONVEYED TO US, VIZ., CHRIST
JESUS.   IV. THAT THE OFTEN REPETITION OF THE SAME THING IS PROFITABLE.   V.
THAT WHAT THE PEOPLE MOST NATURALLY ARE PRONE TO DOUBT OF, THAT IS PRINCIPALLY
AND OFTEN TO BE PREACHED.   VI. THAT A HOLY HEART IS NOT WEARY IN WRITING OR
SPEAKING THE SAME THINGS OFTEN.   (*J. Barlow, D.D.*)

   Ver. 14.   **That good thing which was committed unto thee.**—*The sacred trust :*—
I. THE CHARGE,—the truth, the Word of God, which—1. Unfolds the true God.
2. Proclaims life and salvation through the Redeemer.   3. Brings life and immortality to light.   II. THE DUTY.   We should have—1. A correct knowledge of the
Word.   2. A devoted attachment to it.   3. A desire to preserve it in its integrity.
4. A willingness to communicate it freely to others.   5. An abiding sense of its
responsibility.   III. THE ASSISTANCE.   1. Our necessities are connected with the
Holy Spirit's ability.   2. Rejoice in His readiness to help.   (*A. Reed, D.D.*)
*Good things :*—Here are those reprehended who never had any care to possess these
worthy things.   Nothing in man, or out of him, that is of greater worth, and
nothing less regarded.   We do count that person blessed that hath his house hung
with rich arras, his chests full of gold, and his barns stuffed with corn; and yet we
never have esteem of these excellent and rare things.   Truly, the least degree of
faith is more worth than all the gold of Ophir; a remnant of true love than all the
gay garments in the world.   Hope of heaven will more rejoice the heart of David
than his sceptre and kingdom.   But men do not think so, neither will they have it
so; yet the day of death, like an equal balance, shall declare it to be so.   Are they
worthy things?   Then put them to the best uses, and abuse them not.   And, in
the last place, seeing these be worthy things, let us all labour to possess them; for
of how much more value a thing is, by so much the more we should strive to obtain
it.   (*J. Barlow, D.D.*)      *Grace once gotten is to be preserved :*—Because, if grace
grow weak, the pattern will not be practised.   When all the parts of the natural
body be in a consumption, can we walk and work in the duties of our particular
callings?   And if the new man wax pale, and pine away, the paths of God's commands will not be run or trodden.   For, as all natural actions proceed from the
body's strength, and the purest spirit, so do all spiritual from the vigour of grace
and the new man.   When men have got some competency of wealth, they lie
long in bed, and will not up to work, and so their riches waste.   In like manner
it falleth out with God's children; for when they have attained to some competency
of gifts, they are highly conceited, grow idle, neglect the means, and so are overtaken with spiritual poverty, than the which what greater loss?   We must then
learn here, not only to get grace, but to keep it.   We will mourn if we lose our
money, grieve if we be deprived of our corn, natural strength and earthly commodities.   And shall the loss of grace never pinch us, pierce us?   Shall Jonah be
so dejected for his gourd, and we never be moved when grace is withered, ready to
perish?   Shall the earthworm sigh at the loss of goods, and we never shrink at
the shipwreck of heavenly gifts?   No greater damage than this, none less regarded,

more insensible. Let our plants begin to pine, our hair wax grey or fall, it will make some impression. But grace may decay, the spirit faint, and few be wounded in heart. Yet to such a time shall come of great mourning. Then get grace, keep grace ; so shall corruption be expelled, extenuated, and the pattern of sound words observed, practised. (*Ibid.*) *The Holy Spirit dwells in man :*—But He is infinite, therefore in all persons. True, yet He is in the faithful in a peculiar and special manner, both by His working and presence. Secondly, He is incomprehensible, not-withstanding, as we may say the sun is in the house, though a part of the beams be but there ; so the Spirit is said to be in man, although He be not wholly included in him. We account it a fearful thing to pull down or batter a prince's palace, it is death to wash or clip the king's coin, and shall we not tremble to wrong and injure this building, for such cannot escape the damna-tion of hell. This is for the comfort of the faithful. For what greater honour than this, to have the high God to dwell in our hearts ? Should our sovereign but come into a poor man's cottage, he would rejoice, and good reason, for that all his life long. And shall the King of Glory dwell with the sons of men; make His chamber of presence in their hearts, and they want hearts to solace themselves in the remembrance of that ? And here let man learn a lesson and wonder. Is it the spirit of God in Paul and others, where the spirit of all uncleanness not long before ruled ? Admire His humility that would descend so low as to dwell in so mean a habitation. He that dwells in that light that none can attain unto, now dwelleth where was a palpable darkness. Thirdly, where He takes up His lodging there is holiness. This fire purifieth the heart, cleanseth the inward man, though never so full of filthiness in former time (1 Cor. vi. 11 ; Ephes. v. 18). Thou wilt say, Sir, by what way may I come to this thing ? Why, thou must get a new heart, for He will never lodge in the old, for that's naught. (*Ibid.*) *The indwelling of the Holy Spirit :*—I. THE AUTHOR OF LIFE. 1. Before He dwells in us He quickens us (Eph. ii. 1 ; John iii. 5, 6 ; vi. 63). 2. Believers are temples of the Holy Ghost (1 Cor. iii. 16 ; vi. 19 ; 2 Cor. vi. 16). 3. True of all believers (Rom. viii. 9). 4. Christ's promise respecting it (John xiv. 16, 17). II. THE SOURCE OF UNITY. 1. His indwelling makes that unity a fact (Eph. iv. 4 ; 1 Cor. vi. 17 ; xii. 13–20). 2. That fact to be recognised and cherished (Eph. iv. 3). 3. One building inhabited by one Spirit (Eph. ii. 22.) III. THE PLEDGE OF GLORY. 1. The salvation bestowed and the salvation yet to be revealed. Grace and glory (2 Tim. i. 9 ; 1 Pet. i. 5 ; Psa. lxxxiv. 2). 2. The indwelling Spirit the earnest of our inheritance (2 Cor. i. 22 ; v. 5 ; Eph. i. 14). 3. Recognise His presence. 4. Honour and obey Him (Eph. iv. 30). (*E. H. Hopkins.*) *Real Christianity :*—The providence of God requires all Christians and all Churches to show what Christianity really is. Christianity is a larger and better thing than Christendom yet knows. Still the Holy Spirit dwells in the apostolic succession of the whole true Church of Christ, showing it what the things of Christ are, and helping it realise them in Christianity. How, then, are we to understand what the Christianity is, which we are still called to make real on earth ? I. THE CHRISTIANITY WHICH THE WORLD NEEDS PROBABLY TRANSCENDS ANY SINGLE DEFINITION OF IT WHICH WE SHALL BE LIKELY TO GIVE. Philosophers have tried many times to define the simple word " life," and at best they have had only clumsy success with their defini-tions of what every one knows by his own healthy pulse-beatings. The definition is not made easier when we prefix the adjective Christian to the word " life." If we labour to define in words so large and divine a reality as Christianity, we shall be sure to narrow it in our verbal enclosures, and we can hardly fail to leave whole realms of Christianity out when we have finished our fences of system and denomi-nation. II. CHRISTIANITY IS A LARGER THING THAN ANY ONE PARTICULAR ASPECT OR EXEMPLIFICATION OF IT WHICH MEN MAY BE TEMPTED TO PUT IN THE PLACE OF IT. Christianity, as a whole, is greater than the parts of it which men have hastily seized upon, and contended for as the faith of the saints. Christianity is that good thing which all the Churches hold in common, and it is greater than all. The Chris-tianity of Christ is that good thing committed unto us, which is large enough to comprehend all the ideals of Christian prophets, and prayers of devout hearts, as well as the works of faith which have been done on earth. It would be easy to illustrate from current life and literature the natural tendency of the human heart to substitute some favourite part of Christianity for the divine whole of it. And the unfortunate contentions and hindrances to the gospel which follow from this mistake are all around us. Thus one class of persons are called to benevolent works by the Divine charity of Christ, but in their zeal for man they may not realise sufficiently that the charity of God is the benevolence of universal law, and the Christ is the Life because He is also the Truth. Others, on the contrary, impressed by the order and grandeur of the truths of revelation, repeatedly fall into merely doctrinal definitions of Christianity; and, even while defending from supposed error the faith once delivered to the saints, they narrow that faith into a theological conception of Christianity which may have indeed much of the truth, but little of the Spirit of Christ. III. CHRISTIANITY IS THAT GOOD THING WHICH WE HAVE RECEIVED FROM CHRIST. In other words, Christianity is not a spirit merely, or idea, or influence, which we still call by the name of Christ, but which we may receive and even enhance without further reference to the historic Christ. Christianity is more than a spirit of the times, more than a memory of a life for men, more than a distillation in modern literature of the Sermon on the Mount, more than a fragrance of the purest of lives pervading history and grateful still to our refined moral sense. Jesus once said before the chief among the people, "I receive not honour from men"; and the patronage of culture cannot make for our wants and sins a Christ from the Father. Christianity is the direct continuation of the life and the work of Jesus of Nazareth in the world. Hence, it would be a vain expectation to imagine that the world can long retain the influence of Christ, the healing aroma of Christianity, and let the Jesus of the Gospels fade into a myth. Christianity, uprooted from its source in Divine facts of redemption, would be but as a cut flower, still pervading for a while our life with its charity, but another day even its perfume would have vanished. The Christianity of Christ is a living love. IV. CHRISTIANITY IS A CHANGED RELATIONSHIP OF HUMAN SOULS TO GOD THROUGH CHRIST. Go back to the beginning of Christianity to find out what it is. It began to exist on earth first upon the afternoon of a certain day when the last of the Hebrew prophets, looking upon Jesus as He walked, said, "Behold the Lamb of God." And two of his disciples heard him speak, and they followed Jesus. These men are now like new men in another world; in Christ's presence all Divine things seem possible to them; they are changed from the centre and core of their being; they are verily born again, for they live henceforth lives as different from their former lives before they came to Christ as though they had actually died out of this world, and come back to it again with the memory in their hearts of a better world. After a few years in Jesus' companionship, after all that they had witnessed of His death and resurrection, they are themselves as men belonging to another world, citizens of a better country, sojourning for a brief season here. "Old things are passed away," says the last-born of the apostles; "Behold, all things are become new." This, then, is Christianity—Peter, and John, and other men, living with Christ in a new relationship to God. It is a happy, hopeful, all-transfiguring relationship of human souls to God. Christ giving His Spirit to the disciples, disciples witnessing of the Christ—this, this is Christianity. What, then, is Christianity? It is, we say, the doctrine of Christ. What is the doctrine of Christ? Men sound in the faith; men made whole, men living according to Christ. The doctrine of Christ is not a word, or a system of words. It is not a book, or a collection of writings. He wrote His doctrine in the book of human life. He made *men* His Scriptures. His doctrine was the teaching of the living Spirit. The doctrine of Christ—lo! Peter, the tempestuous man, strong one moment and weak another, become now a man of steady hope, confessor, and martyr—he is the doctrine of Christ! The son of thunder become the apostle of love—he is the doctrine of Christ! The persecutor becomes one who dies daily for the salvation of the Gentiles—he is the doctrine of Christ! V. CHRISTIANITY IS THE COMPANY OF DISCIPLES IN NEW RELATIONSHIP WITH ONE ANOTHER, AND TOWARDS ALL MEN, THROUGH CHRIST. The new redeemed society is Christianity. A man cannot be a Christian, at least not a whole Christian, by himself alone. To seek to live a Christian life by one's self, in the secrecy of one's own heart, is an endeavour foreign to the original genius of Christianity. Christianity, when it is finished, will be the best society gathered from all the ages, the perfect society of the kingdom of heaven. How can a man expect to fit himself for that blessed society by neglecting here and now to enter into the fellowship of believers who seek to prepare themselves for that final society of the Lord by meeting and breaking bread together at His table? To be a Christian, therefore, is to be actually a follower of Christ with His disciples. And to make real and not merely nominal work of it we shall need often with deliberate resolution to give ourselves up to our own faiths, to throw ourselves manfully upon their current, and to let them catch us up and bear us whither they will. (*N. Smyth, D.D.*) *A sufficient endowment:*—"The influence of Mr. Moody is wonderful," said a lady to her minister; "he is not intellectual, nor eloquent, nor learned, and his appearance is not prepossessing." "Ah!" replied the minister, "but he has the Spirit of God in him." Yes," she responded, "and that is all." "All!" exclaimed the minister; "is not that everything?" *An essential provision of Christianity :*—Is not this power of God, through the Holy Ghost, an essential provision of Christianity? Could the Word of God be "a living Word" without it? We can no more conceive of Christianity as destitute of this Divine influence than as destitute of Christ. We look upon the face of nature and perceive that all its external forms are based upon one common principle of life; and were this withdrawn all things must die. So in like manner, looking upon external Christianity—its doctrines, its Sabbaths, its worship, its points of holiness, joy, and moral excellence, produced in perfect uniformity in all ages and amongst all classes—we perceive that there must exist beneath the surface some uniform power; and what can this be but the power of God through His Holy Spirit? And this belongs to the system, is inherent, permanent, certain. By the impulses of this power the "Word of God" effects its glorious triumphs; and, when it is withdrawn, Christianity sinks into the condition of an empty form. (*J. Dixon, D.D.*)

Ver. 15. **All they which are in Asia be turned away from me.**—*To revolt and turn from our former profession is a foul fault and great offence :*—For Paul doth complain against it, and sets it down as a sin to be abandoned of all men (John vi. 66; 1 Tim. i. 19, v. 11, 12). For in so doing we dishonour God; yea, no way more. For will not profane men judge that there is no profit or comfort in serving the Almighty when such forsake their profession? For thus they will reason: if that religion had been good, they and they would never have cast it off. Again, we weaken, as much as in us lies, the Church of Christ; for cut off a member, will not the body be the less powerful? And it gives the devil and his instruments the more encouragement. What? and may such cedars shake, totter, and fall? Then let the weak willows and poplar take heed of the wind. For blessed is he whom other men's harms do make to beware. And it shall not be amiss here to lay down some causes of falling away. And they be either, first, inward, or, secondly, outward. The inward be four especially. 1. Weakness. Thus many have fallen of infirmity. 2. Some affection not mortified. For one such a Jonah in the ship will unsettle all. 3. Infidelity. When men want faith, they are unstable in all their ways. 4. Want of experience of that secret comfort which the Lord enfuseth into the hearts of such as stand resolutely for His truth in an evil time. The outward causes are principally these: 1. Persecution. This hath turned millions backward, who in the days of peace had their faces to Sion-ward. 2. Some wrongs or injuries. 3. Scandal, or offences taken at some doctrine. "From that time many of His disciples went back, and walked no more with Him" (John vi. 66). 4. The example of great men. Doth any of the rulers or pharisees believe in Him? This is a cord that pulleth thousands from the true path and rule (John vii. 48). 5. When men have expected great promotion, but seeing their hopes frustrate, they turn aside. This is a great loadstone to draw an iron heart from the path to heaven. 6. Too much familiarity with men unsettled in the truth. Fearfully have some fallen by this stumbling-block. These be some of the main causes, both inward and outward, that have moved many to become backsliders. So that he that will go on constantly and with resolution must have an eye to all these things. (*J. Barlow, D.D.*) *Fickle friendship :*—What is sweeter than a well-tuned lute, and what more delightful than a faithful friend—one who can cheer us in sorrow with wise and affectionate discourse? Nothing, however, is sooner untuned than a lute, and nothing is more fickle than human friendship. The tone of the one changes with the weather, that of the other with fortune. With a clear sky, a bright sun, and a gentle breeze, you will have friends in plenty; but let fortune frown and the firmament be overcast, and then your friends will prove like the strings of the lute, of which you will tighten ten before you will find one that will bear the tension and keep the pitch. (*Christian Age.*) *Turncoats :* —The flounder is an ill-looking, dark-coloured, flat fish, which creeps close along the bottom, and frequents, for the most part, banks of mud, from which it is almost indistinguishable. Mr. Agassiz has experimented upon young flounders and their power of changing colour. Placing them upon blackish tiles, they quickly turned mud-colour; moved thence to the "sand" tiles, only a few minutes elapsed before their leaden skins had paled to dull, yellowish white; transferred to the mimic "sea-weeds," in less than five minutes a greenish hue overspread their skins, which would have served well in their native element to keep them unobserved against a mass of algæ. (*H. O. Mackey.*)          *Necessity of constancy :*—Without constancy there is neither love, friendship, nor virtue in the world. (*Addison.*) *Great wicked men fall by couples* (1 Tim. i. 20 ; 2 Tim. ii. 17) :—For the devil in all things seeks to imitate the Lord. If God have a Moses and an Aaron, he will have a Jannes and a Jambres. If Christ send out His true disciples by two and by two, Antichrist will do the like. We read of Joshua and Caleb, and of San- ballat and Tobiah : of Paul and Timothy, and of Philetus and Alexander. Because one will toil on and tempt another ; for sin uniteth sinners, as grace doth the godly; and by couples they seem to be the less faulty, the more able to defend their false cause. Learn we hence to rise by couples ; turn we and allure others to return. For woe to him that is alone when two strong men oppose him or a true cause. (*J. Barlow, D.D.*)

Ver. 16. **The Lord give mercy unto the house of Onesiphorus.**—*Onesiphorus of Ephesus:*—The man who now steps upon the scene does not reappear. One Epistle only mentions him, and in the Acts his very name is unrecorded. Let us mark, however, what letter it is which contains these references. It is the last of all the Epistles of Paul, written during his second imprison- ment, and not long before his death. He is again at Rome, but not, as on the former occasion, in his own hired house, with liberty to receive whom he will, and to speak all that is in his heart. Cold, and worn, and ill, Paul the aged lies in his prison cell ; and, of all his many companions, only Luke is with him now. So it happens that the very epistle which is full of the most heroic confidence in Divine protection, is marked by the tenderest yearnings after human sympathy ; and the heart of the apostle is swayed like the sea before the rough wind of unkind desertion, and again under the soft breeze of faithful solicitude and care. Onesi- phorus, it is clear, was an Ephesian ; for Timothy was at this time resident at Ephesus, and there this man's household dwelt. There, then, Paul and he had made acquaintance, during the long-continued campaign of the apostle in the city, now ten years ago. That earlier time is not forgotten. Every one knew, and Timothy had often heard, of what value his friendship had been. His house was one of the many which had opened to Paul and made him welcome. Children were there, now grown to manhood, who were taught to run to the door at his approach and to draw him joyfully in. Years passed, and they had not met. Business of some kind brings Onesiphorus at last to Rome. Paul is at Rome too, a prisoner, in close confinement, and it is not easy to get access to him. " No man stood by me, but all men forsook me : I pray God that it be not laid to their charge." This good Ephesian, however, is made of sterner stuff. He applied to the brethren, and, to his astonishment, they have nothing to tell about the apostle. He goes to the government offices and inquires there; there information is scornfully refused. He makes his way, nothing daunted, to the prisons, and gets referred from one jailer to another, till he is almost tired out ; but he perseveres, and at last here is a man who can tell him. But does he know the risk to his own liberty, perhaps to his own life? He knows ; he is prepared to face it, if only he may see Paul. " He sought me out very diligently, and found me "—found the solitary old man, with the chains on his hands, and the damp, dark prison walls round him. What a meeting must that have been ! Sunshine pouring into the mouth of a cave is a poor emblem of what the sight of that brave and cheerful countenance must have been to Paul. It was not, then, in vain, that Jesus had left the word on record for His disciples, " I was in prison, and ye came unto Me." Christian sympathy will find a way through every difficulty, and a key for every prison door. Paul has no silver or gold to give ; he is so poor that he cannot buy a cloak to keep off the cold; but he has something to be prized far more—a good man's prayers. Those prayers he offers both for Onesiphorus himself and his family. " The Lord give mercy unto the house of Onesiphorus." " The Lord grant it unto him." Nor is it Onesiphorus alone for whom Paul would pray. Let his household, too, be saved. Those sweet children, to whom he had so often spoken of the love of Jesus ; those faithful servants, who had their master's example to guide them ; the kinsfolk, who came to visit him ; may they all be bound in the bundle of life with the Lord their God ! See how great the blessing is of belonging to a godly home. Onesiphorus has been abundantly recompensed in time and in eternity for all that he had done and dared for Paul. Need we fear to be overlooked? We have the servants' prayers. We have the Master's promise. " Whosoever shall give to drink unto one of these little ones a cup of cold water only in the name of a disciple, verily I say unto you, he shall in no wise lose his reward." (*W. Brock.*)      *The brother born for adversity :—*A good man in these verses counts up what his friend had done for him, and then, to the best of his ability, he makes a payment. I. WHAT HAD ONESIPHORUS DONE FOR PAUL? 1. " When he was in Rome he sought me out very diligently." We cannot tell what it was that took Onesiphorus to Rome. Perhaps he was a merchant, and went there to buy and sell. Perhaps he was a scholar, and went there to listen to its poets and orators, and to acquaint himself with its works of art. But whatever he went for, he resolved to see his friend. It is possible that he was not at once successful. But he grudged no time, he spared no effort. And at length he succeeded. He found Paul. Some, perhaps, had they been in the place of Onesiphorus, would have been equally well pleased not to have found Paul. They would have reported to the Church, at their return home, that they had made various efforts, and had failed, and that probably the apostle was either dead or had been removed to another city. Their consciences would have been quieted, and perhaps their friends satisfied. But Onesiphorus was not anxious merely to quiet his conscience. What had Onesiphorus done for Paul? He had gone to see him not once, but many times. " He *oft* refreshed me." Perseverance in sympathy or in active kindness is more difficult than the being once sympathising, or once kind. Yet, though difficult, how valuable it is! 2. There is one characteristic of Onesiphorus' visits to Paul which is well worth noticing. The apostle was refreshed by them. " He oft refreshed me." Visits to the sick and the poor may be very depressing. We may go to tell them our own troubles instead of listening to theirs, or we may go to chide and scold—to tell how that, if we had been in their places, debts would not have been contracted, nor sicknesses taken, or we may go and " talk good," and that by the hour, while the weary or the bereaved one listens in submission. And the intention in all this may have been very kind. We went—for we felt it was our duty to go—and we did our best. But, alas! our visits healed no wound—they brought no sunshine. Yet how refreshing are the visits of some, and among them those of Onesiphorus. " He oft refreshed me." Do the words suggest to us any other visitant who comes in dark moments with " thoughts of peace and not of evil " ? Is there not One who says, " Come unto Me, all ye that travail, and are heavy laden, and I will refresh you." 3. Further, says the apostle, " he was not ashamed of my chain." If our friends are under reproach, our going to visit them, or in any manner permitting their names to be associated with our own, is a proof of our constancy. Most men are willing enough to worship the rising sun. If we hear of any one, with whom we have a casual acquaintance, becoming suddenly distinguished by a literary production, or a work of art, or an act of heroism, we are very swift to put forth our claims to recognition or companionship. But if a friend become poor, how prone we are to " cut " him, or, if he be dishonoured, to deny him. Onesiphorus despised the shame. 4. And be it observed that what was now done at Rome had been done elsewhere. For, says the apostle, " In how many things he ministered unto me at Ephesus, thou knowest very well." Perhaps at Ephesus the apostle had slept under his roof, had eaten, and that oft, at his table, had been helped by his purse, his time, his money. And now he shows that he had not become wearied in well-doing. And so he illustrated Solomon's proverb, " A friend loveth at all times, and a brother is born for adversity." II. And now we will look at THE PAYMENT THE APOSTLE RENDERED. " The Lord," says he, " give mercy unto the house of Onesiphorus." May children, and wife, and servants—all who dwell within the house or cluster round it—share the Divine bounty. May mercy engirdle its walls and canopy its roof. May it fall each night upon them that dwell therein as the soft dew. May it rise on them each morning as the blessed sun. In each breast may it settle like a gentle bird ; in each ear may it ring like the chime of church bells. May mercy take the hand of each and guide him, and watch over the plans of each and prosper him, and light up the prospects of each and cheer him. And, at last, may mercy make the pillow of each soft and easy, and enable each to close his eyes in the conviction that all beyond is well ; that the strange land to which he is going is still a land of mercy, and that in it there is a welcome waiting from Him who is the " Father of mercies and the God of all consolation." But a particular period is named to which the apostle's prayers pointed. " The Lord grant that he may find mercy of the Lord in that day." How blessed will it be to find mercy of the Lord in that day, and to find it as the kindly recompense for deeds done in days gone by. Who would have thought that there was any connection between those visits paid by Onesiphorus to a lonely man in irons in a gloomy prison, in a gloomy street, in the capital of the Cæsars, and the transactions of that period when the throne should be set and the books opened? What thread of connection is there between these? Only this: that seed bears its appropriate crop, that certain consequences follow certain antecedents to the end of time—yes, and after time! (*J. F. Serjeant, M.A.*)  *Onesiphorus :*—Onesiphorus comes into view as a ship appears upon the ocean when she crosses the pathway of the moon. Very little is known of his life before or after this brief contact with the life of Paul. The radiance which the apostle casts upon the page of history makes Onesiphorus visible. In this light the beauty of a noble character, whose gentle ministrations were the solace of one of God's servants, is evident. The moon discovers the model of a ship, and also her course; and an acquaintance is formed with a stranger of the ancient time because he stands near to, and sympathises with, a notable man. So true is it that life depends for its efficiency and its estimate upon the relations which it sustains, and that obscurity and fame are determined by the perspective. The apostle was a prisoner in a Roman dungeon. The comforts of " his own hired house " were no longer his. Nero was the Emperor. Christianity had been charged with political designs. The sword of the persecutor was red with blood. There was little hope of a favourable verdict at the bar of Cæsar. One companion after another had found it convenient to leave Paul. " Only Luke is with me," was the sad announcement which Timothy read when he opened the last letter of his honoured friend. It was not safe to visit such a prisoner. He was a marked man. The caprice of the Emperor was ready to seize upon any protest. His spies filled the city. A single word from his lips meant instant death. He had determined to hold Christianity responsible for a great disaster which befell Rome upon the 19th of July, in the year 64. For then a fire broke out in a valley between the Palatine and Cælian Hills, and marched steadily on its downward course for six days and seven nights. Some one must be punished, and Nero selected the Christians as the victims of his wrath. While Christianity was thus enduring persecution, Onesiphorus, an Ephesian, who had befriended Paul in his own city, reached Rome. He learned that the apostle, aged now and infirm, was in prison and in chains. He determined to go to his relief. His courage was equal to his sympathy. As we read these few sentences of Paul's letter to Timothy, we are impressed with the unfailing courtesy of the apostle. He appreciates the attentions of his friends, and he never fails to acknowledge them with great delicacy. His letters are models of correspondence, so dignified, so sincere, so frank, so affectionate! They are filled with personal allusions, which exhibit the social character of this eminent man. " The Lord grant unto him that he may find mercy of the Lord in that day!" How heart-felt! How genuine! How delicate! This sturdy soldier of the cross, whose valour has been displayed upon many a battlefield, commends the truth of the gospel by his courtesy. He does not repel men, but wins them. One of the wise sayings of Hillel, the distinguished Jewish Rabbin, was this: " Be thou of Aaron's disciples, loving peace and seeking for peace, loving the creatures and attracting them to the Law! " Hillel himself was a beautiful illustration of his own teaching. His gentleness of manner was associated with firmness of principle and strength of conviction. Paul, as a Pharisee, must have been familiar with the many traditions which were current among the Jews concerning the renowned teacher, and his own character must have been somewhat affected by his admiration for one whose virtues were praised in the schools of Jerusalem. " Let a man be always gentle like Hillel, and not hasty like Shammai," was an oft-repeated injunction. Gamaliel, the teacher of Saul of Tarsus, was the grandson of Hillel, and the school which the future apostle entered was pervaded with an atmosphere of courtesy. Then, when our Lord taught that zealous Pharisee, and led him to realise the sinfulness of his mistaken zeal which had made him a persecutor, and gave him a new appreciation of the excellence of humble service and gentle ministrations, he advanced to a new recognition of the duty and the opportunity of courtesy. I regard courtesy as one of the efficient graces of the Christian life. It is the polished mirror which reflects the most light. Bluntness, coarseness, rudeness, are not evidences of strength. The courtesy of Lord Chesterfield is not the courtesy of Paul. For Chesterfield, in his letters to his son, exhibits his lack of sincerity, his want of principle. His courtesy is only a thin veneer, which has received constant rubbing until it is worn out. Paul's courtesy is the real wood, which is solid down to the heart. The Christian heart is always ready to sustain the Christian manner ; and the Christian manner is Christ's manner. He commended truth by his address. Can you wonder that such courtesy as his secured him many friends among the poor and suffering? Does it seem strange that a similar courtesy has led mankind as with magnetic power? And yet we carry too little of it with us into the practical work of daily life. There is many a man whose business hours never hear a single kind word—a "thank you," an "if you please." Service becomes drudgery. The rich and the poor draw apart. Hostile camps are organised. Men who should be friends look angrily at one another. There is a better way for the home, the shop, and the counting-room. It is Christ's way, and Paul's way, and the way of all who manifest with them the true spirit of love. There is something very fine about this conduct of the large-hearted Ephesian. He was evidently a man of substance, for he had the means at his command which enabled him to help Paul in Ephesus and in Rome. Yet, when he visited the imperial city, where a money value was placed upon almost everything, he went about through the streets and among the prisons to find a despised Jew—one Saul of Tarsus—whose name had become a by-word and a reproach. Social life needs an illustration such as this. We are apt to forget—alas! we are apt to despise—the poor. Yet but for the poor—God's own poor—social life would perish in its corruption. It is well for us to appreciate the intimacy of this dependence which it obtains. Spiritual treasures are to be regarded as wealth. We must traffic more. Gold and silver must be exchanged for sympathy and prayer. The material blessings of this life are to be distributed just as the spiritual blessings are. The rich are to live for the poor, and the poor are to live for the rich. The man whose talents qualify him to command armies is to be the protector of the weak, and the man whose appreciation is sensitive is to be the teacher of the ignorant; the man who has this world's goods is to supply his brother's need, and the man who can prevail with God is to realise his responsibility in prayer. The ministrations of Onesiphorus exhibit the watchfulness of God, which is exercised through His servants. The poor saints understand this better than the rich saints can. Their poverty affords many occasions for the manifestation of special providences. And in their lives these special providences are very numerous. God feeds them, as He did Elijah by the brook Cherith. There is a wonderful adaptation of supply and demand. Nor should we fail to discover the dignity which is ours when we are selected by God as His messengers. Subjects always appreciate the preference of a sovereign. God honours us if He makes us His almoners. Let us appreciate the honour, and let us seek to discharge such duties with considerate love. "Blessed," says the Psalmist, "is he that considereth the poor." This is something more than giving; for it includes the manner of the giving. England has forgotten many of the leaders of fashion who were in favour thirty years ago, but she will never forget that cultured woman who went as nurse to the soldiers of the Crimea. Florence Nightingale once wrote that "the strong, the healthy wills in any life must determine to pursue the common good at any personal cost, at daily sacrifice. And we must not think that any fit of enthusiasm will carry us through such a life as this. Nothing but the feeling that it is God's work more than ours—that we are seeking His success, and not our success—and that we have trained and fitted ourselves by every means which He has granted us to carry out His work, will enable us to go on." Christianity waits for such service. When Onesiphorus came into helpful contact with the life of Paul, he secured an unconscious immortality. His is not a principal figure in the Scriptures. He is of secondary rank or importance. But he has secured a grand immortality, while other men, greater, wiser, more conspicuous then than he, are forgotten; and this immortality was secured by self-forgetfulness on the part of Onesiphorus. If we cannot work unless we are sure of a recognition, we shall have no part in the sweet charities which make life tolerable. We must learn of the coral insect, whose instinct teaches it to build until it dies, and which, by building, slowly lifts an island out of the seas, upon which flowers may bloom, and trees may wave, and man may find a home. This, my friends, is our immortality, sure and blessed. "We are labourers together with God." It may be that we can do but little. Never mind. We will do what we can. (*H. M. Booth, D.D.*)    *Was Onesiphorus dead?*—The only ground for the hypothesis of the death of Onesiphorus appears in the further reference to his household, rather than to himself, in the final salutations (chap. iv. 19). This might easily be explained on another supposition, as well as on that made by the advocates of the "prayer for the departed." If Onesiphorus of Ephesus had business in Rome, he may have had reasons for visiting Corinth, or Thessalonica, or Alexandria, or Spain, and may have been at too great a distance to receive personally the apostle's salutations. (*H. R. Reynolds, D.D.*) The balance of probability is decidedly in favour of the view that Onesiphorus was already dead when St. Paul wrote these words. There is not only the fact that he speaks here of "the house of Onesiphorus" in connection with the present and of Onesiphorus himself only in connection with the past; there is also the still more marked fact that in the final salutations, while greetings are sent to Prisca and Aquila, and from Eubulus, Pudens, Linus, and Claudia, yet it is once more "the house of Onesiphorus," and not Onesiphorus himself, who is saluted. This language is thoroughly intelligible if Onesiphorus was no longer alive but had a wife and children who were still living in Ephesus; but it is not easy to explain this reference in two places to the household of Onesiphorus, if he himself was still alive. In all the other cases the individual, and not the household, is mentioned. Nor is this twofold reference to his family, rather than to himself, the only fact which points in this direction. There is also the character of the apostle's prayer. Why does he confine his desires respecting the requital of Onesiphorus' kindness to the day of judgment? Why does he not also pray that he may be requited in this life? that he "may prosper and be in health, even as his soul prospereth," as St. John prays for Gaius (3 John 2)? This, again, is thoroughly intelligible if Onesiphorus is already dead. It is much less intelligible if he is still alive. It seems, therefore, to be scarcely too much to say that there is no serious reason for questioning the now widely accepted view that at the time when St. Paul wrote these words Onesiphorus was among the departed. (*A. Plummer, D.D.*) *Sympathy:* —Like the sea anemone, which feels the first returning wave upon the rock, and throws out all its tendrils, so the tender nature of some individuals will give forth all its sympathies at the slightest intimations of woe. (*J. Everett.*) *Sympathetic men:*—What a blessing are rest-giving men and women! People upon whose strong sense and deep and delicate sympathy we can fling ourselves as on to a welcome couch! People into whose presence the worries and irritabilities of life seem afraid to enter! Cathedral-like souls, full of softened lights and restful shadows! Oh, what a refreshment to meet with such! Large, deep natures which have found for themselves rest in God, and whose very presence brings over others what Christ's word brought over the Sea of Galilee—a great calm. Souls that are like a vast forest, rich and cool, filled with speaking silences and peopled solitudes, where one can recline for hours or wander for days a stranger to the heat that wearies and withers outside! Such, in some measure, we can all be, and the need for such service to humanity is not sufficiently insisted on. (*J. Dawson.*) *Prison fellowship:*—Who has not read the story of Picciola; how the prisoner knelt down and nursed the little flower which sprung up between the flagstones in his walk—how, in his loneliness, he talked to it as though it had a soul that could speak back to him—and how, at length, the strong heart was broken within him, when, with the heat of the sun, it at last withered and died? Or that stranger illustration of the prisoner of the Bastille who knit his affections to a spider, weaving his web in a corner of the cell, and then wept, as one weeps for his first-born, when it was killed through the wanton cruelty of the gaoler? Far beyond this is the joy we have in the fellowship of our own kind. *Religious friendship:*—Onesiphorus means "bringing profit." The man's life was true to his name. He brought profit to himself, others, God. A model minister's friend. I. RELIGIOUS FRIENDSHIP IS EMINENTLY PRACTICAL IN ITS SERVICE. 1. Invigorating. "Refreshed me." Like dew to shrivelled grass and drooping flower. 2. Painstaking. "Sought," &c. 3. Courageous. "In Rome." "Not ashamed of my chain." False friends are swayed by the signs of the times. Like a shadow, they leave us when we pass out of the sunshine. True friendship, based on character, not circumstances, hence unalterable. 4. Continuous. 5. Personal. 6. Proverbial. "Thou knowest very well." The true man loves to recount deeds of kindness. 7. Immortal. Kindness is undying. II. RELIGIOUS FRIENDSHIP IS HIGHLY DISTINGUISHED IN ITS REWARD. 1. It gained for him the influence of the mightiest Christian power. 2. It gained for him the influence of prayer for the best blessing. "Mercy." (1) The most needed blessing. (2) Involves every other. 3. It gained for him the influence of prayer for the best blessing on the most momentous occasion. "That day"—the judgment—the day of destiny— the final day of mercy. (*B. D. Johns.*) *Refreshing the poorest:*—And here the best may be taxed for omitting of the present occasion, or poor man's necessity. We are prone to commit sin instantly, and to put off good and charitable duties from time to time, and to do them lingeringly. But, beloved, this should not be so;

8

we gather fruit when it is the ripest; cut down corn when it is the hardest; let blood when it groweth rankest; and shall we not refresh our brethren being poorest? (*J. Barlow, D.D.*) *The needy not to be neglected :*—We may run from the poor, and his homely bed and cottage; but God and His swift curse will one day overtake us. (*Ibid.*)    *A welcome visitor :*—"I have read recently that in one of the English prisons there was at one time an underground cell, which was used as a place of punishment. Its remoteness, loneliness, and darkness made it a place greatly dreaded. Among the prisoners there was a man of refinement and nervous temperament, to whom the horror of this penalty was a fright that haunted him day and night. At length there was some alleged offence against the prison discipline, for which he was sentenced to four and twenty hours in this dungeon. He was led by the wardens to the place; the door was opened and he had to go down the stairs into its depths. The door was shut. The steps of the wardens died away in the distance; the outermost door was heard as its slamming echoed in the hollow places. Then all was still—a stillness that oppressed with terror amidst a darkness that could be felt. Nervous and full of imagination, the man sank down paralysed with fear. Strange and hideous shapes came out of the gloom, and pointed at him. His brain throbbed as with fever, and mocking voices seemed to come from all sides. He felt that before long the terror must drive him mad. Then suddenly there came the sound of steps overhead; and in a quiet tone the chaplain called him by name. Oh, never was any music so sweet! 'God bless you,' gasped the poor fellow. 'Are you there?' 'Yes,' said the chaplain, 'and I am not going to stir from here until you come out.' The poor man could not thank him enough. 'God bless you,' he cried. 'Why, I don't mind it a bit now, with you there like that.' The terror was gone; the very darkness was powerless to hurt while his friend was so near—unseen, but just above." And so beside us all ever is the unseen yet loving presence of our Master and Friend, and darkness and danger have no longer any power to frighten us. (*G. R. Dickenson.*)    **Was not ashamed of my chain.**—*Chains worth wearing :*—Here was Paul, in that large, grand company of men who, in all the ages, have been the victims of great ideals, of noble inspirations, of truth, of virtuous impulses, of high and generous purposes that reach out and beyond him; and there were a thousand men of all sorts coming against Paul's life, who appreciated his nobility, his gifts, his eloquence, his scholarship, his Judaism; and they saw nothing else in Paul or upon Paul but his chain, and then they walked away half ashamed and so sorry that so good a man as Paul had to wear a chain. There never was such jewellery in all the ages as that chain of Paul's. Never did any goldsmith melt together the rarest pieces from the mines and put them in such delicate and beauteous relationships with one another, as did the Providence of God, when, through countless years and by various circumstances, the prophecies worked out that chain for Paul. Here is a mother, and if she is really a mother she is far more certainly chained than the woman by her side who tosses her little head, for such heads are always small, and has no thought of responsibilities and cares; no thought about those relationships of life which ought to be the most sacred in the world. Here is a young man who has started out to make himself intelligent. He has only a few hours in which to do it. He takes those hours and by all the severe exactions of his noble spirit he is bound so to that ideal that he cannot do this, and he has not an evening for that, and he hurries to his work a chained man, but oh, how grand! Here is a girl who thinks, perhaps, that to-morrow she will begin to sew again, wearily but happily, chained to her work, because yonder in some lowly place in this city her mother is working and waiting, prayerfully doing what she can, for death to take her. But this brave girl is carrying that aged mother upon those weary arms as once the mother carried her, chained, but not with a chain bought at a jewellery store. She has not the kind of jewellery upon her that sparkles upon you at the great reception. No, her jewellery is made by Almighty God; it was mined in the vast secrets of goodness; it was brought out by the heat and fire of that eager life; and God has given her this chain as the mark that she belongs to that grand race of aristocrats. And I care not whether that girl lives in a garret, or lives in a mansion, she belongs to the aristocracy of heaven. In what contrast to these chains appear the chains that have rattled as you came here, my friend; for there are other chains of the most coarse and ignoble kind that bind us. Here is a man who comes and feels, when he sees the picture of that young man earnestly trying to become intelligent, that he is ignorant, and he never knows how much of a chain there is attaching itself to him. Other people do. His smartnesses are simply exhibits of his chain;

every time he tries to perpetrate a joke the chain rattles and people see how bound he is to utter ignorance. Here are men and women bound by chains of selfishness. To save your life you cannot conceive of a noble inspiration, The other day, when somebody told you of some one giving some money to a great cause, you sneeringly measured your own soul when you thought you were measuring his, and you said: "Well, he wanted to be advertised!" You know that is the way you would feel under the circumstances. Your chain rattled, and it rattled so awfully that those who were round about you saw the awful depths of selfishness into which you were about to fall. Here are men who are chained by habit. To save your life, you can't get home without feeling the pulling of a chain which you would rather break than to accomplish anything else in the world. But how different are these chains from the ones which Paul wore, as he stood there in the face of Israel and the whole world! That chain was rattling when he spoke, and he uttered that word with such eloquence that it has resounded through the centuries. "For the hope of Israel," he said, "I am bound with this chain. Other men have been bound to the past; I am bound to the future. Other men have been bound to iniquity; I am bound to righteousness. Other men have been bound to low ideals; I am bound to lofty ideals. Other men are in slavery, abject slavery, to those carnal purposes of life that debase; I am in slavery which is sublime, to the true and lofty ideals that exalt. For the hope of Israel, I am bound with that chain." (*F. W. Gunsaulus, D.D.*)

Ver. 18. **The Lord grant unto him that he may find mercy of the Lord in that day.**—*St. Paul's prayer for Onesiphorus :*—I. MERCY is a word we are often using, especially in our prayers. But there are some of us, perhaps, who have no very clear ideas of what mercy is. I must remind you again, that it is not mere kindness or goodness. To ask God to show us mercy is not simply to ask God to do us good. Such a petition includes in it a confession of our wretchedness and our guiltiness; for observe, misery is the proper object of mercy. Mercy, in the strict sense of the word, is kindness exercised towards the wretched; but then there is another use of the term and a more common one. Because our guilt is our greatest misery, mercy often signifies in Scripture pity shown to the guilty; in other words the forgiveness of our sins. In some respects mercy resembles goodness. It is indeed the very same thing, only its object is different. God is good to all, and always has been so; but He was never merciful, till misery appeared needing His compassion. He is good in heaven; every angel there feels and proclaims Him such: but there is no mercy in heaven, for there is no guilt there or wretchedness. And then again mercy is closely allied to grace. If it differs from it at all, it is in this—when we speak of grace, we have respect chiefly to the motive of the giver; when of mercy, to the condition or character of the receiver. Look at God, and then we call mercy grace; look at a man, poor, abject, guilty man, and then we call grace mercy. You see, then, that mercy is the perfection of the Divine goodness. It is that branch or exercise of it, which goes the farthest and does the most. It is goodness blessing us when we merit cursing, and saving us when we are well-nigh lost. Hence, God is said in the Scripture to "delight in mercy." His goodness can expand itself in it. He finds in it the freest scope, the largest indulgence, of His benevolence. It is not merely the work, it is the enjoyment, the feast and triumph, of His love. And you see also here another fact, that no man can ever deserve mercy. We often put these two words together, but we ought not to do so; there is a positive contradiction between them. Mercy is grace. It is kindness towards one who has no claim whatever to kindness and is totally undeserving of it. II. Let us pass on now to THE DAY THE APOSTLE SPEAKS OF. And observe—he does not describe this day; he does not even tell us what day he means: but there is no misunderstanding him: he means the last great day, the day when God will raise the dead and judge the world. 1. The apostle's thoughts were often dwelling on this day; it was a day very frequently in his contemplation. His mind had evidently become familiar with the prospect of it, and so familiar, that he could not help speaking of it as he would of any well-known and much thought of thing. And so it seems really to have been in the early ages of the Christian Church. We put the day of judgment far from us; we regard it as a day that will certainly come, but after so great an interval of time, that the thought of it need not press on us; but not so the first believers. Their minds were fastened on this day. They "looked for" it; that is, they were like men looking out anxiously in the east for the first dawn of some long wished for day, like men climbing the lofty mountain to get the first sight of the rising sun on some festal morning. They "hastened unto" it; that is again, they would have met it if they could. But there is something else implied in this expression. 2. It intimates also that this day is a most important one. There is the idea of pre-eminence contained in his language. We feel as soon as we begin to think, that we cannot estimate as we ought the importance of this day. It will affect every body and every thing on the face of the earth, and to the greatest possible extent. Other days are important to some, but this will be important to all. III. Turn now to HIS PRAYER. He brings together in it, you observe, the mercy and the day we have been considering. We cannot enter into the spirit of this prayer, unless we keep in mind throughout the character of this Onesiphorus. He was evidently a real Christian. And these kind offices, we may fairly presume, he rendered to the apostle for his Master's sake. This kind-ness under such trying circumstances, this steadfastness and boldness in the face of shame and danger, were the fruits of his faith in Jesus. They are evidences that he was not only a sincere believer in the gospel, but a man of extraordinary faith and love. The inference, then, that we draw from this prayer is this obvious one—our final salvation, the deliverance of even the best of men in the great day of the Lord, will be an act of mercy. It is sometimes spoken of as an act of justice, and such it really is, if we view it in reference to the Lord Jesus. Before he made His soul an offering for sin, it was promised Him that this stupendous sacrifice should not be made in vain. And the Scripture speaks of our salvation as a righteous thing in another sense—the Lord Jesus has led His people to expect it. But look to the text. The apostle implores in it mercy in that day for his godly friend; and what does he mean? If he means anything, he means this—that after all it must be mercy, free and abounding mercy, that must save that friend, if he is ever saved. He can talk of justice and of righteousness as he looks at his Master on His throne, and remembers what He has done and promised; but when he looks on a fellow-sinner, he loses sight of justice altogether, and can speak of mercy only. And observe, too, how this is said. It is not cold language. It is language coming warm from a most tender and deeply grateful heart. The good works of this man were all before Paul at this time—his boldness in Christ's cause, his steadfastness, his kindness; the apostle's mind was evidently filled with admiration of him, and his heart glowing with love towards him; yet what in this ardour of feeling does he say? The Lord recompense him after his works? No; he sees in this devoted Christian of Ephesus a miserable sinner like himself, one going soon to Christ's judgment-seat, and his only prayer for him is, that he may find mercy there. 1. We all still need mercy. There is a notion that a sinner once pardoned, has done with this blessed thing; that he may cease to seek it, and almost cease to think of it. It is error, and gross error. We can never have done with mercy as long as we are in the way to heaven; or rather, mercy will never have done with us. And notice also this remarkable fact—in all his other epistles, the salutation of this apostle to his friends is, "Grace unto you and peace"; but when he writes to Timothy and Titus, men like himself, faithful and beloved, eminent in Christ's Church, he alters this salutation. As though to force on our minds the point I am urging—a conviction that the holiest of men still need God's mercy—he adds this word "mercy" to the other two. In each of these epistles his salutation runs, "Grace, mercy, and peace." (*C. Bradley, M.A.*) *Paul's prayer for his friend:*—To the Christian mind the painful feelings occasioned by the recol-lection of violated friendship become unspeakably more poignant and intense, when we discover that the claims of friendship and the obligations of religion have been cast off together—that he whom we loved has made shipwreck at once of his faith and of his affection— of his duty to his God and to his friend. An affecting instance of this kind is recorded at the fifteenth verse of the chapter. Was it wonderful, therefore, that from the cold, cruel, and treacherous conduct of these men, he should turn with such a glow of kind and grateful emotion to the faithful and affectionate Onesiphorus? I. THERE IS A DAY COMING WHICH, FROM ITS TRANSCENDENT IMPORTANCE, MERITS THE EMPHATIC DESIGNATION OF "THAT DAY." And does not this day deserve the emphatic mention which is here made of it? Compared with every other period in the history of the universe, does it not stand out in unparalleled importance? There are days in the life of every one which, from the events that transpire in them, are invested with great and merited importance to the individual himself—such as the day of his birth, and of his death. But there is something in the day of final and universal retribution that sinks into obscurity any other eventful period in the history of man. The day of our birth introduces us into a scene empty and shadowy, both in its joys and sorrows, and proverbially brief and transitory in its duration ; *that day* ushers us into a state of being, in which we shall be conversant no more with the dreams only, but with the living realities of perfect felicity or woe, and conversant with them through a duration endless as the reign of the Eternal itself. The day of our death is chiefly interesting to ourselves, and to the little circle who have been connected with us by the ties of kindred or love ; the day of judgment is supremely interesting to any rational being who has lived and breathed on the face of our world—a day when the eternal destiny of the whole human race shall be determined with unparalleled publicity and solemnity. How important are those days, in the opinion of men, which have witnessed the fall or the rise of empires. How important was the day that dawned on the tribes of Israel marching from under the yoke of their Egyptian bondage—a day that ever afterwards was held sacred to commemorate their deliverance! How eventful that day that rose on the fall of the Assyrian monarchy, and beheld the empire of the East pass from Belshazzar and his impious race into the hands of the mild and virtuous Cyrus! How painfully memorable, at least to the nation immediately concerned, was the day that beheld the final destruction of Jerusalem, and the rejection and dispersion of its devoted race! How important to these lands of our nativity, and how worthy to be held in grateful remembrance, that day which witnessed the consummation of the glorious struggle that terminated in the vindication and establishment of our civil and religious liberties! But do you not feel that all these days, whether of transient or permanent importance, are so utterly insignificant, when viewed in relation to that day, that the comparison involves in it a kind of incongruity, and is truly a lowering of the awful dignity of the subject ? There are but two periods in the history of the world that can be consistently compared, in point of importance to men, with that day—the day that dawned on the creation of our race, which was hailed by the sweet acclaim of the angelic hosts and the day that shone on the birth of the Son of God. In every aspect in which we can view them, these were days big with consequence to the human family ; but they were only the introductory scenes to the consummation of the mightiest drama that ever was, or will be, performed on the theatre of the world. II. ON THAT DAY THE MERCY OF THE LORD WILL BE REGARDED BY ALL AS UNSPEAKABLY PRECIOUS. The mercy of the Lord is, in this world, regarded in a very different light by the various classes of men, if we may judge of their sentiments and opinions from their uniform practice. The great mass of mankind demonstrate by their conduct that, whatever may be their occasional fears and desires, the prevailing habit of their mind is an utter indifference either to the mercy or vengeance of God. But there are a few who are honourably distinguished by different sentiments, who avow it as their opinion, and evince their sincerity by a corresponding practice, that they esteem everything under heaven as utter vanity compared with the mercy of the Lord. And they who have practically esteemed the mercy of the Lord so highly in this world, will value it the more at that terrible day. With all their successful efforts, by the grace of God, to prepare their souls to meet the Lord in peace, and to be found without spot and blameless at His coming, they will impressively feel themselves still to be the objects of His mercy. Yes, and at that day Paul and his fellow-believers will not be singular in prizing the mercy of the Lord. Much as sinners have despised the mercy of the Lord here, they will then despise it no more. III. IN THE MIND OF A CHRISTIAN, THAT DAY POSSESSES TREMENDOUS CONSEQUENCE, AND TOWARDS IT HIS EYE IS HABITUALLY DIRECTED. Such consequence did this day possess in St. Paul's view, that the importance of everything on earth was estimated by its remote or immediate relation to it. Did he, from the hour of his conversion, despise all distinctions of wealth and honour when brought into competition with the knowledge of Christ ? It was, that by any means he might attain to a blessed resurrection on that day. Did he practise the most painful and persevering self-denial; or, to use his own words, did he keep under his body and bring it into subjection ? It was, that he might not be found disapproved on that day. Was he not ashamed of the sufferings he endured for the gospel ? It was because he knew in whom he had believed, and was persuaded that He was able to keep that which He had committed unto him against that day. Did he labour in season and out of season, warning every man, and teaching every man ? It was that he might present every man perfect in Christ on that day. Did he muse on the number and steadfastness of his converts ? He thought of them as his hope and joy and crown of rejoicing in the presence of our Lord Jesus Christ at His coming at that day. Did he engage in prayer for his converts ? It was that the Lord might make them to increase and abound in love, to the end that He might establish their hearts unblameable in holiness at the coming of our Lord Jesus Christ, with all His saints, on that day. IV. ENLIGHTENED CHRISTIAN AFFECTION IS ESPECIALLY SOLICITOUS ABOUT THE ETERNAL WELL BEING OF ITS OBJECTS. Deeply did the grateful and generous heart of Paul feel the kindness of Onesiphorus. There is no doubt he loved him before as a disciple, and very likely as a personal friend; but his conduct, when he visited Rome, awakened still deeper emotions of gratitude and affection towards him in the bosom of the apostle. And how did he express this sense of the kindness of Onesiphorus? Did he employ all his influence to improve the temporal fortune of his benefactor? Did he request his noble converts in the palace—for some such there were of the emperor's houshold —to exert their power to procure for Onesiphorus some post of honour and emolument in the civil or military establishment of Rome? Or did he write to the Ephesian Church, to which this person probably belonged, enjoining them to prepare some temporal reward, to be given to their deserving countryman for his kindness to himself? No; Paul attached too much importance to the solemnities of the last day and its immediate consequences; he was too much influenced by the scenes of the world to come, to ask for his beloved comforter so poor, so miserable a recompense. He loved him too well to solicit for him a fading, when he might ask for him an unfading crown. He knew too well the worth of his soul, the importance of an eternal well-being, to overlook these for the trifles for an hour, in his desire to reward him. V. GENUINE SAINTS HAVE IT EVER IN THEIR POWER TO REWARD THEIR BENEFACTORS. Looking at Paul as a poor despised prisoner in Rome, accused before the emperor of heresy and sedition, befriended by none but by a proscribed and despised sect, which was everywhere spoken against, with all the prejudice of the emperor, and the influence of the Jewish nation strenuously exerted against him— looking at Paul in this light one would speedily conclude, on the principles of the world, that he was a very unlikely person richly to reward his benefactors. But ten thousand times rather would I have laid this poor and apparently helpless captive under obligations to me by kindness to him, than have merited, by the most splendid civil or military services, the gratitude and reward of him who wore the imperial purple. What could Nero, even with a world at his nod, have conferred upon me? He might have lavished upon me all the favours of the imperial court. He might have made me the idol of fortune, and the envy of the proudest of the Roman nobility. He might have given me the conduct of the most honourable expeditions. He might have invested me with the command of the richest of the provinces. Paul had no imperial power or influence; he had even no imperial favour; but he was a favourite in a higher court, where he was every day, almost every hour, an acceptable visitant. He was one of those whose effectual fervent prayer reached the heavenly temple, and, through the channel of the atonement, drew down eternal blessings on his soul, and on the souls of those for whom he interceded. In conclusion, there is one inference very naturally suggested by the last remarks: If these statements are true, how wise it is, setting aside the pure love of benevolence altogether, to be kind to the people of God, especially to the pious poor! (*J. Mc Gilchrist.*)    *Mercy in that day* :—I. THAT THERE IS A DAY COMING, IN WHICH TO FIND MERCY OF THE LORD, WILL BE OUR ONLY CONSOLATION AND SECURITY. 1. The day here meant is the day so frequently mentioned in Scripture; and in which we are all most deeply concerned. It is described by many different names, as "the Day of Judgment," "the Day of the Lord," "the Last Day," "the Day of Wrath," "the Day in which God will judge the world." In that day, then, what will be our only consolation and security? The text reminds us, "To find mercy of the Lord." Mercy is another word for grace. It is an act of free and unmerited favour. Men sometimes say that such a person deserves to have mercy shown to him! But this is a very incorrect and careless way of speaking. A man can never deserve mercy. There may be some circumstances in his case, which may make him more particularly an object of compassion. When a criminal by his offence has forfeited his life, and is condemned to die; the king, from pity to the offender, or from some other consideration best known to himself, may grant a pardon and remit the sentence. Here is mercy, an act of free, unmerited grace to the undeserving and the guilty. But to say that there could be anything in the criminal which gave him a claim to mercy, would be to talk absurdly. The very idea, then, of mercy naturally shuts out all idea of merit. These two things are totally contrary to each other, and can never exist together. It is to be feared that many, when they talk of hoping to find mercy, mean in fact to say that they hope to find justice in that day; and that their hopes of being favourably received then are built not on God's free mercy, but on their own merits, and on their secret claims to reward. II. THAT THERE WILL BE SOME WHO IN THAT DAY WILL NOT FIND MERCY OF THE LORD. St. Paul, when he prays that Onesiphorus may find mercy in that day, clearly intimates it to be possible that he may not find it. And if it were not certain that Onesiphorus would find it, it is not certain that others will find it. Indeed, the Scriptures plainly tell us that all will not find it. We are expressly told that in that day some will say, "Lord, Lord, open to us"; to whom He will say, "Verily, I know you not." Let us see what the Scriptures teach us concerning those who will find mercy of the Lord in that day. 1. They are now seeking mercy, and seeking it in that one way, in which alone God has promised to bestow it. 2. They are duly affected and properly influenced by the views and hopes which they have of the rich mercy of God in Christ. There is a sad propensity in man to abuse the Divine mercy, and to take occasion, from this most glorious perfection of the Almighty, to run the farther and continue the longer in sin. How differently did a sense of God's mercy work on the pious David ! Hear what he says, " O Lord, there is forgiveness with Thee, that Thou mayest be feared." He felt that the goodness of God led him to repentance. The rich mercy of the Lord, far from hardening his heart, softened and overcame it. (*E. Cooper.*)  *Mercy in that day :*—Let us consider the language of the text as showing that the exercise of mercy towards us, especially in the proceedings of the final day, is an object of highest desire and hope. 1. The very nature of the occasion shows it to be so : the day of the end of the world. This will differ from all other days. On numbers of the days that are past, our eyes were never opened ; they appeared to our forefathers, but fled away ere we had our being ; while the days which we behold, they do not witness, for the darkness of death and the grave overshadows them. Thus different in their importance, ordinary days may be to different persons. The day of one man's prosperity may be the day of another man's adversity. For ancient days we are not responsible, and yet those days were concerned in the accountability of millions who have no concern with our own. But the day referred to in the text will be common to all the sons of Adam. If, then, we consider the period which it occupies, both as to what it follows and what it precedes, how manifest the need of mercy at that day. What recollections of time, what apprehensions of eternity will fill the mind ! 2. As it will be the period when God will display the effects of His probationary dispensations, the worth of mercy will then particularly appear. Such effects will be strictly discriminative of character and condition. Events will have reached their issues ; moral consequences will be brought together in vast accumulation, and will bear with all their weight upon the mind. Fruits will be reaped in kind and in degree, according to what we have sown. And while these effects will be so concentrated at that day, they will also be looked upon in their character of perpetuity. 3. As it will be the period when the Lord will reward His servants for all they have done in His name, the apostle could entreat mercy for his friend at that day. 4. It is also to be observed that the importance of an interest in Divine mercy at that day appears in the fact that if it be not then enjoyed the hope of it can be cherished no more. (*Essex Remembrancer.*) *Mercy in " that day" :*—I. WHENCE ARISES OUR NEED OF MERCY ? 1. Our need of mercy arises from our guilt, for mercy is kindness or favour shown to those who are undeserving of it. Our guilt arises from our personal disobedience to the Divine law. We inherit a depraved nature, but it is not for this that God holds us responsible. We are responsible not for what we have inherited, but for what we have done, and therefore it is not by our depraved nature but by our actions we shall be judged. 2. Guilt exposes to the retributive justice of God. There is always the feeling that sin deserves punishment at the hands of God. We know indeed from Scripture that it does so. Nothing could be plainer or more solemn than its statements, than the sinner is even now under the curse of the law which he has broken, and that hereafter he will come under a righteous retribution. But it is not to Scripture that I would now appeal. A man who has violated the laws of his country knows that he deserves to suffer their penalties. It is right, he says, I have sinned, and must bear the punishment. So the sinner against God feels that he deserves to be condemned, and that if God's justice were to deal with him he could not escape. From this indissoluble connection between sin and punishment arises our need of mercy. Therefore it is, that the prayer of the publican is the universal prayer of poor, sinful, and perishing humanity. Therefore it is, that in the presence of God's holiness, or confronted with His law, or in the near prospect of an eternal world, we shrink back appalled at the consciousness of our guilt. II.

WHETHER IT IS POSSIBLE TO OBTAIN MERCY? This is a question of grave importance; easily answered with the Bible in our hands, but, apart from it, filling us with strange perplexity. 1. Without a Divine revelation, we do not know that God is merciful at all. Granting that there is much to excite our hopes, there is as much to awaken our fears. We are ready to say, "God is good—His tender mercies are over all." But when the pestilence is abroad in the city, and the tempest in the field—when the rivers overflow their banks, and the mildew blights the precious fruits of the earth—when the crimson tide of war rolls through a land—when men's faces are black with famine—when the sea is strewn with wrecks—then we are filled with alarm, and say, "When I consider, I am afraid of Him." Think again: What are the conceptions which have been formed of God by those who are destitute of revelation? One of the best and wisest of the heathen doubted whether it was possible for "God to forgive sin." The sceptre of the Supreme God was a thunder-bolt—He was cruel, harsh and vindictive. Again: When we reflect on the nature of moral government, we perceive serious difficulties in the way of the exercise of mercy. Certainly this is not the end of government. The great object for which it exists is the administration of justice; that it may "render to every man according to his works." If mercy, not justice, be its ruling principle, it is not easy to understand why it should exist at all. The highest praise that can be given to an earthly ruler is, that he is "the terror of evil-doers and the praise of them that do well." Now apply this to the Divine government. Why does it exist?—whence its language and its laws? Is it not for the maintenance of order?—for the well-being of the creatures whom God has made? And, as far as we have an opportunity of observing, are not the laws of this government strictly carried out—in every case, sooner or later, exacting penalties from the disobedient? If you violate a physical law, there is no mercy for you. 2. But when we turn to the Scriptures, the subject is presented before us in a different light. (1) We learn, in the first place, that God is merciful in Himself. (2) We learn that this mercy is displayed to sinners through the atonement of Christ. III. WHY IS IT THAT AT THE DAY OF JUDG-MENT WE SHALL ESPECIALLY REQUIRE THE EXERCISE OF MERCY? It is the day that will terminate this world's history. Whenever it dawns, time will cease, the world will be burnt up, the heavens will pass away, there will be "no more sea." Wonderful was the day of creation, when God called things that were not as though they were, and His Spirit moved over the chaos, and light dawned, and the earth appeared. But more wonderful still will be that day when the purpose for which the world has been created shall have been accomplished, and, like a faded vesture, it shall be folded up. Then the world's history will end—its sad tragedies of sorrow, its scenes of suffering; and its works of nature, its wonders of art, the monuments of God's power, the trophies of man's skill, shall pass away. 1. Its absolute certainty. 2. Its scrutiny will be so strict. God will set our iniquities before Him—our secret sins in the light of His countenance. And that which we had forgotten shall be remembered; that which appeared to us but trivial shall assume a magnitude which will fill us with profound alarm; that which we supposed none had witnessed shall be proclaimed. 3. The award will be just and final. 4. It will come unexpectedly. All the representations given of the judgment-day describe it as a sudden and unlooked-for event. But what shall we say of the worldly, the ungodly, the profane? What sudden destruction will overtake them! When Pompeii was disinterred, there was discovered in the buried city the remains of those who still preserved the very attitude in which death had overtaken them. There was a skeleton before a mirror, another behind a counter; in the theatre, in the forum, in the temples, at a banquet, in every attitude and position they were found. It was the work of a moment, the burning lava fell, and they died. You are looking forward to many years of life, but the Judge may even now be standing at the door. Who then will find mercy? Those who have sought it and found it now—those who have confessed and forsaken sin—those who humbly rest on the merits of the Saviour's sacrifice. (*H. J. Gamble.*) *Paul's good wish on behalf of Onesiphorus:*—I. MEN ARE ALL ADVANCING TOWARDS A SOLEMN AND MOMENTOUS PERIOD. II. AT THAT PERIOD MEN WILL STAND IN NEED OF MERCY. When the apostle expresses a wish that his friend may receive mercy, it must be evident to every one that of course he needs it—that without its communication it is impossible that he can be happy. Another inference to be drawn from this principle is, that, in consequence of this transgression by which we are characterised, we are, of course, in danger of punishment by that great Almighty Being whom, in this manner, we have offended. But now, you must at once perceive the whole force of the statement from which these particulars have been deduced. For the purpose of escaping the condemnation of the last great day, there must be a communication of the mercy of the Lord. III. The mercy of God is diligently to be sought in the present world. 1. A portion in the provision of Divine grace ought to be sought by you as a matter of intense and impassioned desire. 2. A portion in the full provision of Divine grace should be sought in the spirit of fervent and importunate prayer. We must remark—IV. To receive mercy is to possess the enjoyment of a vast and incalculable blessing. I scarcely dare venture for a single moment to occupy your time by attempting to describe the blessed consequences of having the Judge for your friend on that day of eternal retribution, feeling, as I do, that the grandeur of the property may appear diminished by the feebleness of the description. V. Those who have the hope of mercy should desire its participation by others. It has already been observed, that the prayer of the apostle is that peculiar form of prayer which is known by the name of intercession. Here is a beautiful example of that spirit which we, as the possessors and heirs of mercy, should cultivate towards those in whom we feel an interest. (*James Parsons.*) *Mercy in the day of judgment:*—I. "That day." Its date is not given. It would but gratify curiosity. Its length is not specified. It will be long enough for the deliberate judgment of all men. Its coming will be solemnly proclaimed. Ushered in with pomp of angels, sound of trumpet, &c., none will be ignorant of it. Its glory, the revelation of Jesus from heaven upon the throne of judgment. This will make it most memorable. Its event, the assembly of quick and dead, and the last assize. Its character, excitement of joy or terror. Its personal interest to each one of us will be paramount. II. The mercy. To arouse us, let us think of those who will find no mercy of the Lord in that day:—Those who had no mercy on others. Those who lived and died impenitent. Those who neglected salvation. How shall they escape? Those who said they needed no mercy: the self-righteous. Those who sought no mercy: procrastinators, and the indifferent. Those who scoffed at Christ, and refused the gospel. Those who sold their Lord, and apostatised from Him. Those who made a false and hypocritical profession. III. To-day. Remember that now is the accepted time; for you are not yet standing at the judgment bar. You are yet where prayer is heard. You are where faith will save all who exercise it towards Christ. You are where the Spirit strives. You are where sin may be forgiven, at once, and for ever. You are where grace reigns, even though sin abounds. To-day is the day of grace; to-morrow may be a day of another sort, for you at least, and possibly for all mankind. The Judge is at the door. Seek mercy immediately, that mercy may be yours for ever. (*C. H. Spurgeon.*) *Going to receive mercy:*—When Thomas Hooker was dying, one said to him, "Brother, you are going to receive the reward of your labours." He humbly replied, "Brother, I am going to receive mercy." *The Christian manner of expressing gratitude:*—The enemies of Christianity, while stating its supposed defects, have asserted that it recognises neither patriotism nor friendship as virtues; that it discountenances, or at least does not encourage, the exercise of gratitude to human benefactors; and that its spirit is unfriendly to many of the finer feelings and sensibilities of our nature. But these assertions prove only that those who make them are unacquainted with the religion, which they blindly assail. Nothing more is necessary to show that they are groundless than a reference to the character of St. Paul. We readily admit, however, or rather we assert it as an important truth, that his religion, though it extinguished none of these feelings, modified them all. It infused into them its own spirit, regulated their exercises and expressions by its own views, and thus stamped upon them a new and distinctive character. It baptized them, if I may be allowed the expression, with the Holy Ghost, in the name of Jesus Christ. Hence, the apostle expressed neither his patriotism, nor his friendship, nor his gratitude, precisely as he would have done, before his conversion to christianity. These remarks, so far at least as they relate to gratitude, are illustrated and verified by the passage before us, in which he expresses his sense of obligation to a human benefactor. He did not idolise his benefactor; he did not load him with flattering applauses; but from the fulness of his heart he poured out a prayer for him to that God who alone could reward him as the apostle wished him to be rewarded. It is more than possible, that to some persons this mode of expressing gratitude will appear frigid, unmeaning, and unsatisfactory. They will regard it as a very cheap and easy method of requiting a benefactor; and were the case their own, they would probably prefer a small pecuniary recompense, or an honorary reward, to all the prayers which even an apostle could offer on their behalf. It is certain, however, that such persons estimate the value of objects very erroneously, and that their religious views and feelings differ very widely from those which were entertained by St. Paul. But what is the precise import of the petition—that he might then find mercy—and what did it imply? To pray that any one may find mercy of him at the judgment day, is to pray that he may then be pardoned, or saved from deserved punishment, and accepted and treated as if he were righteous. St. Paul, when he prayed that Onesiphorus might find mercy of his Judge at that day, must then have believed, that he would at that day need mercy or pardon. And if so, he must have believed that, in the sight of God, he was guilty; for by the guilty alone can pardoning mercy be needed. The innocent need nothing but justice. A distinguished modern philosopher, Adam Smith, well known by his celebrated treatise on the Wealth of Nations, has some remarks relative to this subject, which are so just and apposite, that you will readily excuse me for quoting them. "Man," says this writer, "when about to appear before a being of infinite perfection, can feel but little confidence in his own merit, or in the imperfect propriety of his own conduct. To such a being he can scarce imagine that his littleness and weakness should ever seem to be the proper object either of esteem or regard. But he can easily conceive how the numberless violations of duty of which he has been guilty should render him the object of aversion and punishment; nor can he see any reason why the Divine indignation should not be let loose without any restraint upon so vile an insect as he is sensible that he himself must appear to be. If he would still hope for happiness he is conscious that he cannot *demand* it from the *justice*, but that he must entreat it from the *mercy* of God. Repentance, sorrow, humiliation, contrition at the thought of his past conduct, are, upon this account, the sentiments which become him, and seem to be the only means which he has left of appeasing that wrath which he has justly provoked. He even distrusts the efficacy of all these, and naturally fears, lest the wisdom of God should not, like the weakness of man, be prevailed upon to spare the crime by the most importunate lamentations of the criminal. Some other intercession, some other sacrifice, some other atonement, he imagines, must be made for him, beyond what he himself is capable of making, before the purity of the Divine justice can be reconciled to his manifold offences." It may perhaps be said, if the apostle's views were such as have now been described, if he believed that justice must pronounce a sentence of condemnation on all without exception, on what could he found a hope that either himself, or his benefactor, or any other man, will find mercy of the Lord at that day? These questions are perfectly reasonable and proper, and it would be impossible to answer them in such a manner as to justify the apostle, were not a satisfactory answer furnished by the gospel of Jesus Christ. That gospel reveals to us a glorious plan, devised by infinite wisdom, in which the apparently conflicting claims of justice and mercy are perfectly reconciled. (*E. Payson, D.D.*) *Remember the reckoning day :*—What shall we think of such who never mind this day? Verily, they are much affected with earthly pleasures and profits, and have little regard of the greatest good. Many men in the inn of this world are like the swaggerers and prodigals in a tavern, who call freely, eat and drink, laugh and are fat, but never mind either the reckoning or the time of harvest; for they have sown no good seed, neither have wherewith to discharge the shot: therefore suffer these things willingly to slip and absent themselves out from their minds, because they have or can expect no commodity by either. But the faithful man is of a contrary mind; for he is sparing in expense, and hath scattered much good grain, the which will bring a goodly crop at his Master's appearing, the great day of reaping, both of which cause him often to look upward. (*J. Barlow, D.D.*) *Mercy on the judgment day :*—I. AN IMPORTANT SEASON. "That day." The day is that which is elsewhere called "the last day," because then the end of this world's history, as a place of trial at least, will be come; it is called also "the great day," because then scenes unparalleled before in grandeur will be unfolded, and affairs that have never been surpassed in magnitude will be transacted—such scenes and affairs as will throw into the shade the most splendid spectacles and momentous transactions of time. II. AN IMPORTANT BLESSING. For a man to find mercy even now, amid the trials and changes and imperfections of this present life, is to be truly blessed. It is to have guaranteed to him all that is included in eternal life—that gift of God—that munificent donation of infinite mercy. Nor will the largess be diminished, or the security invalidated, on the day of judgment. 1. There are many considerations besides which go to illustrate the high importance and exceeding desirableness of mercy on that day ; and one of these is, that it will then be felt to be peculiarly needful. 2. Another consideration, tending to enhance the value of the blessing, is that it will not be shared in by all. This is obviously implied in the apostle's intercessory petition. If the mariner who is saved from the wreck, when all his shipmates are lost, estimates his preservation more highly than he who has returned to the desired haven with them all in safety, must it not seem a glorious benefit to appear as " vessels of mercy prepared unto glory," when many fellow-sinners are found to be " vessels of wrath fitted to destruction"? 3. Another consideration still, which may well exalt the blessing in our eyes, is that if mercy be not found then, it will never be found. 4. And yet another circumstance which magnifies the value of the blessing is, that the condition of those by whom mercy shall not then be found will be pre-eminently wretched. Not to find mercy on that day is to be undone, altogether and eternally undone. Lessons : 1. If mercy is to be found at last, it must be sought now. 2. Again, if mercy is to be found at all, it must be sought through the mediation of Christ. 3. And, in fine, if mercy is to be found of the Lord, it must be sought in His service. (*D. Davidson.*)    *The requital of friendship :*— Paul was the friend of Onesiphorus, and how did he manifest his friendship ? Incarcerated and enchained, poor and destitute, he could not requite, in kind, his benefactor's generosity. But another mode of expressing friendship was left him, and as he was shut up to it by circumstances, so he turned to it with fondness. As the waters of a spring, when prevented from flowing forth in their natural channel, mount forcibly up towards heaven—as the portion that is prevented, by exhalation, from diffusing fertility along the course of the stream, descends afterwards in fertilising showers ; so the emotions of his overflowing heart, being pent up in one direction by the tyranny of man, ascended in devout aspiration to God, and though seeming to vanish in the vapour of fruitless wishes, entailed the communication of invaluable blessings. (*Ibid.*)    *The value of a good man's prayers :*—I would rather have the gift of a brother's faithful prayers than of his plentiful substance. And I feel that when I have given to a brother my faithful prayers I have given him my best and greatest gift. (*Edward Irving.*)    *Prayers for the dead :*—That Onesiphorus was dead is a gratuitous assumption. The fact that Paul *nowhere else* prays for the dead is fatal to the notion here. (*J. Bryce, LL.D.*)    In case even that Onesiphorus were really dead at the time of the writing of this Epistle, still the Roman Catholic interpreters are in error when they find in ver. 18 a proof of the lawfulness and obligation for intercessory prayers for the dead. The case here was altogether special, and cannot, without great wilfulness, be applied as the foundation of a general rule for all the dead. On the other side, it is often forgotten that the gospel nowhere lays down a positive prohibition to follow with our wishes and prayers, if our heart impel us thereto, our departed while in the condition of separation ; and hence, in any case, it is well to distinguish between the Christian idea which lies at the foundation of such inward needs, and the form of later Church rite and practice. (*Dr. Van Oosterzee.*)    *Beneficent wishes for the dead :*—On the assumption already mentioned as probable (that Onesiphorus was dead), this would, of course, be a prayer for the dead. The reference to the great day of judgment falls in with this hypothesis. Such prayers were, as we know from 2 Macc. xii. 41–45, common among the Jews a century or more before St. Paul's time, and there is good ground for thinking that they entered into the ritual of every synagogue and were to be seen in the epitaphs in every Jewish burial-place. From the controversial point of view this may appear to favour the doctrine and practice of the Church of Rome, but facts are facts apart from their controversial bearing. It is, at any rate, clear that such a simple utterance of hope in prayer, like the *Shalôm* (peace) of Jewish, and the *Requiescat* or *Refrigerium* of early Christian epitaphs, and the like prayers in early liturgies, though they sanction the natural outpouring of affectionate yearnings, are as far as possible from the full-blown Romish theory of purgatory. (*E. H. Plumptre, D.D.*)

## CHAPTER II.

VER. 1. **Thou therefore, my son, be strong in the grace that is in Christ Jesus.**—
*The connection :*—Οὖν points back to the defection of others, contrasting it with what
St. Paul is satisfied will prove the faithfulness of Timothy.   (*H. R. Reynolds, D.D.*)
*Imitate the loyal :*—It is as though he said, Imitate the one loyal follower (One-
siphorus), and make up to me for the faithless conduct of so many false friends.
(*H. D. M. Spence, M.A.*)     *Strength through partnership with Christ :*—Steven
Gerard once told a poor cartman to purchase a cargo of sugar, promising to
back him.   From that moment the cartman's wisdom and credit were equal to
Gerard's, for Gerard was his.   If the cartman had forgotten his wise, rich friend,
and acted on his own judgment and credit, he would have been weak again, and
as foolish as weak.   The cartman alone was nothing without wisdom or credit,
but the cartman and Gerard were strong.   Our strength is in partnership with
Christ.     *Christians strong in Christ Jesus :*—I. CONSIDER THE DUTY INCUMBENT
ON ALL WHO HAVE A MIND FOR HEAVEN, NAMELY, TO BE STRONG.   What is it to be
strong in the sense of the text ?   It presupposeth one thing, namely, they must be
spiritually alive.   To be strong imports three things.   1. To be ready for action,
according to the difficulties you may meet with in your way.   2. That you be
resolved.   Thus David exhorts Solomon, "Take heed now," said he, "for the Lord
hath chosen thee, to build an house for the sanctuary : be strong and do it."   That
is, be fully resolved and peremptory, so as not to be diverted by any emerging
difficulties.   3. That you be of good courage.   What need is there to be strong?
1. You have much work before you.   The work of your own salvation is upon your
hand (Phil. ii. 12).   You have also to serve your generation, by the will of God.
2. You will meet with much opposition in your work.   I now proceed—II. To
CONSIDER THE DIRECTION, NAMELY, THAT THOSE WHO WOULD BE STRONG, MUST BE STRONG
IN THE GRACE THAT IS IN CHRIST JESUS.   What is the grace that is in Christ Jesus?
1. Relative grace, that is the free favour of God to poor sinners, by which they are
embraced in the arms of His love unto salvation.   2. Real grace, that is the fulness
of the Spirit, and His graces, lodged in Jesus Christ, as the fountain and head of
influences, from which they are to be derived, into all His members.   "For it hath
pleased the Father, that in Him should all fulness dwell.   And out of His fulness
have all we received, and grace for grace."   What is it to be strong in the grace
that is in Christ Jesus?   1. It is to be animated to duty by the faith of that grace
that is in Christ Jesus for us, both relative and real.   2. It is to be strengthened to
duty by supplies of grace derived from Christ Jesus by faith.   Why must those that
would be strong be strong in the grace that is in Christ Jesus?   1. Because all
those that would be strong must be strong as members of Christ, as branches of the
vine.   2. Because the grace that is in Christ Jesus is only sufficient to bear us through.
(*T. Boston, D.D.*)     *Strength of grace :*—I. MULTIPLICITY OF ARGUMENTS SHOULD
PROVOKE TO OBEDIENCE.   "Thou, therefore."   II. MEN REGARD THOSE MOST WHO ARE
THE LIKEST MINDED TO THEMSELVES.   "My son."   III. STRENGTH OF GRACE IS NECESSARY
FOR A CHRISTIAN.   1. Comeliness pleads for it.   For is not Christ the root, we the
branches?   He the foundation, we the building?   Our head, and we His members?
And betwixt these ought there not to be an analogy, a just proportion, otherwise, would
it not be unseemly?   Should one finger stand still, would we not repute it a blemish?
and shall we not do the same in this mystical body?   2. Necessity requires it.   We
must fast, watch, and pray, fight with principalities, powers, and spiritual enemies,
which are in high places.   And will not crosses come, thick and threefold—temptations, desertions, sickness, and death, too?   What can or will do these, suffer these
things, anything but strength of grace, spiritual power?   What manner of men
ought ministers to be, thundering in preaching, fervent in prayer, shining in life,
burning in spirit?   And what is necessary for a preacher is required of every
Christian, strength of grace.   Strength is tried—(1) In prosperity : art thou humble
in thine own eyes?   Is thy heart, with the remembrance of the Lord's mercies,
made hot? and is it thy greatest care, how to promote his glory?   When the rain
falls, the waters swell : the sun shines, the sweetest flowers smell : the spring
approacheth, all creatures revive.   So when grace grows, our joy is full; our
mouths are trumpets sounding aloud, and every member of the body is an active
instrument, a never-wearied agent to fight the battles, and finish the great works
of our Lord and Master.   A willow bows with a small blast : an oak endures,
stands upright in a storm.   (2) In adversity : art thou patient? &c.   The horse

neighs at the trumpet; the leviathan laughs at the spear: so a strong man in grace, slights crosses, &c. Helps to grow strong in grace. 1. Hast thou, in thy apprehension some seed of sanctification? then seriously think of it, highly esteem of it, and bless thou the Lord for it. 2. Resolve with thyself the highest period of grace, whereof a created nature is capable. Scholars aim at the highest degree; citizens, at the most honourable office; and all tradesmen, at the increase of goods: so should weak Christians to be rich in the grace of God: strong in the Lord. 3. Add to these two, practice: exercise thy talent; put it forth, for thy own, and thy Master's advantage. Is it not written that many acts produce an habit, and to him that hath shall be given? 4. Neglect no means whereby grace is begun, or increased. IV. ALL GRACE IS FROM CHRIST JESUS. Whether we consider the beginning, kinds, or degrees; all grace is in Him, and by Him. Is it not written, that Christ ascended on high; gave gifts unto men? Of His fulness, are we not said to receive grace for grace? that is of all the kinds which are in the Head, the same be derived to His members. (*J. Barlow, D.D.*)    *Moral energy* :—I. MORAL ENERGY A DIVINE GIFT. This verse deals with the great motive power of the Christian religion, what imparts inward strength to frail humanity. Much besides is, so to speak, machinery, and this—the grace of Christ, is the steam, the driving force, without which the most perfect machinery is useless. Paul enjoins Timothy to obtain this force, this inward energy of the soul; and by calling it "grace" the apostle teaches that it is not like the unconscious forces of nature—the power of wind, or water, or fire, or gravity—which human skill can have at command and direct; but a power of a different, a spiritual order, and bestowed on other conditions. For it flows from the grace or kindness of God, and it is, therefore, called "grace," just as an act prompted by kindness is called a kindness, and the same with a favour. II. CHRIST THE SOURCE OF MORAL ENERGY. The Christian faith is that the Lord Jesus Christ is the fountain of all power, and the fire of all love, dwelling in the heart, as well as in heaven: "Who of God is made unto us wisdom, and righteousness, sanctification, and redemption." That is the faith of Christ; and it cannot be said of it that it is a weak, unsubstantial, and merely sentimental religion. It is based on the most sublime facts, for which it offers appropriate evidence; and the power of those facts to arrest, attract, rivet, and renew the hearts of weak and sinful men, and awaken in them an enthusiasm of trust, and gratitude, and devotion —the history of our religion for eighteen hundred years must declare, for no mere language can. III. THE COMMAND TO BE STRONG IN CHRIST. It is very characteristic of Scripture, and of its close conformity to human nature, even in its problems, that this great central thought, of the Divine source of moral energy, should be put into the form of a command to be obeyed—an injunction, for the observance of which man is responsible. It is not said to us, "Lie helpless till the Divine energy of Christ flows into your soul"; but, "*Be* inwardly strengthened in the grace that is in Christ Jesus." "I charge you to become empowered with that energy." Such is our strange life, our mysterious nature. Dependent on God yet responsible to Him! "It is God that worketh in you." "Work out your own salvation." "I, yet not I," says Paul. "By grace ye are saved" and healed; and this grace has its centre and fount in Christ. But it is your duty to have much of it. (*T. M. Herbert, M.A.*) *Our true strength* :—Luther relates concerning one Staupicius, a German divine, that he acknowledged that before he came to understand the free and powerful grace of Christ, he resolved and vowed a hundred times against a particular sin; yet could never get power over it, nor his heart purified from it, till he came to see that he trusted too much to his own resolutions, and too little to Jesus Christ; but when his faith had engaged against his sin, he obtained the victory. (*J. L. Nye.*) *Christ qualifies His servants* :—We are His "servants." A master does more than engage a servant: he also gives him the means whereby he may work. The tradesman does not put his servants into a shop wherein there are no goods to sell; the farmer does not send his servants into the field without plough, harrow, or spade; the surgeon does not withhold drugs; nor the lawyer parchment and pens from his servant. It is even so with our great Master. He calls us to work, and, if we ask Him, He will qualify us for it. (*T. R. Stevenson.*)    *Self-sufficiency* :—A certain alchemist who waited upon Leo X. declared that he had discovered how to transmute the baser metals into gold. He expected to receive a sum of money for his discovery, but Leo was no such simpleton; he merely gave him a huge purse in which to keep the gold which he would make. There was wisdom as well as sarcasm in the present. That is precisely what God does with proud men, he lets them have the opportunity to do what they boasted of being able to do. I never heard that so much as a solitary gold piece was dropped into Leo's purse, and I am sure you will never be spiritually rich by what you can do in your own strength. Be stripped, brother, and then God may be pleased to clothe you with honour, but not till then. (*C. H. Spurgeon.*)    *Strong in Christ Jesus :*—When Wingfield expressed his pity for Kirby, who was condemned to die for the truth, the undaunted martyr replied, "Fire, water, and sword are in His hands, who will not suffer them to separate me from Him." Here was power from on high perfected in human weakness. Nor was it less manifested in another who exclaimed, "If every hair on my head were a man, they should suffer death in the faith in which I now stand." It was in the exhaustion of age, and after long imprisonment, hardship, and ill-treatment, that Latimer, when brought out to be burnt at Oxford, lifted his wrinkled hands towards heaven, and cried, "O God, I thank Thee that Thou hast reserved me to die this death." (*C. Graham.*)    *Christ's sufficiency never failing :*—In travelling through the West of England, you come ever and anon upon large tracts of country, bleak, barren, and desolate ; no tree, no flower, no blade of grass, no habitation of man. In these wild and dreary wastes you find proofs in abundance that the spots were not always desert. The deep, black, yawning shaft of many a mine ; the broken or decaying timbers which still stand around, or over the mouth of those mines ; the remains of cottages ; all, all tell you that the place was not always a wilderness. But the mines have been opened, the last bucket of precious ore has been drawn up to the surface of the ground ; there is nothing more to be gotten from the once rich earth ; and so the miners have all departed to seek a supply elsewhere. Now, as you stand there, in that solitude and desolation, hearing no more the miner's song, and missing the busy hum of labour, which perhaps years before had greeted you as you walked over those Cornish lands, you can scarcely help contrasting those empty mines with that ever rich and overflowing treasury of blessing which a gracious God has opened to all His people in Jesus Christ. (*A. C. Price, B.A.*)    *Strong through faith :*— On an occasion of great drought, which the rain-makers attributed to the missionaries, a Bechuana chief with twelve spears came to command Robert Moffat to leave the territory on pain of death ; but he said, "You may shed my blood, you may burn my dwelling ; but my decision is made : I do not leave your country." And the cause of all this was his faith. He was a man of wonderful faith ; he believed the Gospel was the power of God unto salvation, through faith in Christ Jesus. He felt that his Master was ever as near to him, and as full of love, as the wife of his bosom ; he felt that Christ must reign until He should put all things beneath His feet ; and just because he was so strong in faith, he was so strong altogether. (*J. C. Harrison.*)    *The conflict and the strength* (vers. 1–7):—In these seven verses I see—I. THE APOSTLE ENUMERATING THE SORT OF LABOURS AND SUFFER-INGS WHICH HIS YOUNG DISCIPLE TIMOTHY WOULD HAVE TO ENDURE. II. THE GRACE WHICH IS SUGGESTED TO TIMOTHY AS SUFFICIENT TO SUPPORT HIM. (*D. Wilson, M.A.*) *The holy calling of the minister of the Lord :*—I. THE EXTENT OF THIS CALLING (vers. 1–7). Presented under figures 1. Of the soldier. 2. Of the athlete. 3. Of the husbandman. II. MOTIVES FOR THE EXERCISE OF THIS CALLING (vers. 8–13). 1. A look backwards (ver. 8). 2. A look around about one (vers. 9, 10). 3. A look orwards (vers. 11–13). (*Van Oosterzee.*)

Ver. 2. **The things that thou hast heard of me among many witnesses commit to faithful men, able to teach others also.**—*How the Church is to be continued :*—I. CARE IS TO BE HAD THAT THE CHURCH MAY BE CONTINUED. Art thou a ruler in Christendom, like Jehosaphat ? Send Levites into the dark corners of the land. Rich ? Found colleges, relieve the sons of the prophets, and repair the decayed walls of Jerusalem. Hast thou children ? Nurse them up in the fear of God, teach them the principles in the holy letters, and, with Hannah, dedicate thy firstborn to the Lord. If thou be poor, yet pray for Jerusalem. II. BY THE WORD PREACHED THE CHURCH IS CONTINUED. III. THE MORE WITNESSES, THE GREATER ENCOURAGEMENT TO WELL-DOING. IV. ALL MINISTERS ARE TO TEACH THE SAME THINGS. As there is but one true God, one Saviour, Redeemer, Faith, Love, &c., so but one law, gospel, doctrine, baptism, which is to be preached for their glory and our salvation. Thrash thy corn out of God's barn, beat it forth of the apostolical rick of the holy letters ; bring thy grain into the market of the Church, which prophetical spirits have in former ages set to sale ; and it shall feed thee and thine to life eternal, for be thou assured that the soundest testimony is this, that the mouth of the Lord hath spoken it. V. MINISTERS MUST

BE FAITHFUL. And this faithfulness is in—1. Doctrine. 2. Life. Thou hast known, saith Paul to Timotheus, my doctrine, manner of living. To be faithful in doctrine, the matter what, and the manner how, to be delivered are both to be regarded. For matter, it must be what we have received from the Lord. For the manner, a double condition is to be observed. First, that the word of truth be divided aright; each person have his portion, according to his spiritual estate and disposition. And secondly, the doctrine must be intelligible, else how should the people be edified? Now, as faithfulness in doctrine, so in life is required of a minister. What they preach they are to practice, for the vulgar sort be more led by examples than rules, patterns than precepts. Should ministers be faithful? Then let such as have in their power ordination, and induction, lay hands rashly on no man; make choice of faithful, able persons. VI. ABILITY TO TEACH IS NECESSARY FOR A MINISTER. 1. Some knowledge of the tongues and arts is necessary. For as the form lieth closely couched in the matter, the kernel in the shell, so doth the truth in the several languages. 2. To be an able man requires a sound memory. For the truth being invented, orderly disposed, is then firmly to be retained. 3. A door of utterance is also necessary. When we have invented, judged, and methodically disposed of Divine truths, then we must clothe them with the garment of apt words. 4. And to omit many; an able minister must have his whole carriage in the delivery of his doctrine, suitable and correspondent to it. His countenance, elevation, pronunciation, gesture, and action, are to vary and be altered as the matter in handling requireth. And let all men make mention of them in their prayers. VII. THE SAME TRUTH SHALL BE CONTINUED UNTO THE END OF THE WORLD. For Christ received it from the Father, the Holy Ghost from Christ, the apostles from Him, faithful men from them; and so by a successive communication it shall continue for ever. As one sun shall enlighten the world, so one gospel the minds of men, until Jesus returns to judge all the posterity of Adam. (*J. Barlow, D.D.*) *Able teachers:*—The apprentice, who has just entered the blacksmith's shop, may wear a leathern apron, and blacken his hands and face, but though he may try to make other boys think he is a blacksmith, everybody knows that it requires years of hard labour to make him an able workman; and even after an apprenticeship, some men are but very poor hands at their trade. So, the having one's name entered as a certified instructor does not certify that a man is an able teacher. Is not goodness higher than arithmetic, and is not virtue nobler than grammar? Is it not a glorious position to be a teacher of little children? A certain philosopher was often talking about the garden in which he studied and recreated, and one day a friend calling to see it, was surprised to find it consisted of only a few square yards. The friend said, "Why this is a very small place; it is only a few strides across!" The philosopher replied, "Small! Ah, you only look at the ground; but if you look up, you will see that it reaches to the sky!" So it is with a little child. It may be small; you have power to break its back across your knee, as well as break its heart; but in this little child there is a pathway to the heart of God, and angels walk therein. Lord Beaconsfield said of Greece, "Let it be patient; it has a great future"; so I say that you must be patient with every child, for it has a great future. Let us be gentle in the teaching of little children. Do you know how barbarous men teach bears to dance? Let me tell you. They play a flute, and put the bear on a hot iron. Do not let us teach children as if they were bears. Children have to be "trained." You know how a crooked plant is trained. It is held in its place by a soft band that will not hurt it, until it grows in the right direction. So children should be trained in mind and body, gently yet firmly, to be good and strong. No two children are alike either in body or mind, and individual peculiarities must be studied and accommodated. We should, one and all, become teachers of children by our example, which is far more powerful than precept; and we should take care that our faults do not turn them against the religion we profess. (*W. Birch.*) *A faithful custodian:*—The grand battlefield of Drumclog is where the hardy, faithful Covenanters routed the cruel Claverhouse. I have stood upon that battlefield and looked upon a schoolhouse erected there by a Scotchman, though there was not a house to be seen near it, because he wanted the faith and the zeal of his forefathers to dwell in those that might come afterwards. I went, after looking at that field, into the house of a poor weaver. I heard he had a relic of the great fight in his possession, and I thought I should like to purchase it. He unfurled a flag that had been held by his forefathers on the great day of the fight, and on that flag were these words, "God and our sworn covenant." I asked him if he would sell the flag. "I will never sell the flag," said he, "except with my own life. I hold it as an heirloom, and, however poor I may be, I will hand it down to my children; and I hope they will hand it down to their children." The incident reminds us that Christians carry a banner, and are pledged by their covenant relationship to Christ to seek the salvation of sinners, and thus be true to the memory of those who preceded them in the holy warfare. (A. McAulay.) *The undying energy of truth :*—Sir Bernard Burke thus touchingly writes in his "Vicissitudes of Families": "In 1850 a pedigree-research caused me to pay a visit to the village of Fyndern, about five miles south-west of Derby. I sought for the ancient hall. Not a stone remained to tell where it had stood! I entered the church. Not a single record of a Finderne was there! I accosted a villager, hoping to glean some stray traditions of the Findernes. 'Findernes!' said he, 'we have no Findernes here, but we have something that once belonged to them: we have Findernes' flowers.' 'Show them me,' I replied, and the old man led me into a field which still retained faint traces of terraces and foundations. 'There,' said he, pointing to a bank of garden flowers grown wild, 'there are the Findernes' flowers, brought by Sir Geoffrey from the Holy Land, and, do what we will, they will never die!'" So be it with each of us. Should our names perish, may the truths we taught, the virtues we cultivated, the good works we initiated, live on and blossom with undying energy. (C. H. Spurgeon.) *Setting others to work :*—Nasmyth says that when he introduced his great steam-hammer, it not only itself produced marvellous results, but "its active rhythmic sound, by some sympathetic agency, quickened the strokes of every hammer, chisel, and file in his workmen's hands, and nearly doubled the output of work." And is not this true of some noble workers whom we could name? More than half Mr. Moody's power consists in his capacity of setting other people to work by his own earnestness. (W. Fullerton.) *The genius of the true teacher :*—Speaking of art training, Mr. Ruskin says: "Until a man has passed through a course of academy studentship, and can draw in an improved manner with French chalk, and knows foreshortening and perspective, and something of anatomy, we do not think he can possibly be an artist. What is worse, we are very apt to think that we can make him an artist by teaching him anatomy, and how to draw with French chalk; whereas the real gift in him is utterly independent of all such accomplishments." So the highest powers of the teacher or preacher, the power of interpreting the Scriptures with spiritual insight, of moving the hearers to earnest worship and decision, may exist with or without the culture of the schools. Learned Pharisees are impotent failures compared with a rough fisherman Peter anointed with the Holy Ghost. Inspiration is more than education. (H. O. Mackey.) *The worth of colleges :*—The great importance of the work done in our educational institutions for young ministers was never more strikingly emphasised than by the 'missionary Judson, who said, as he was approaching Madison University, "If I had a thousand dollars, do you know what I would do with it?" The person asked supposed he would invest it in Foreign Missions. "I would put it into such institutions as that," he said, pointing to the college buildings. "Planting colleges, and filling them with studious young men, is planting seed corn for the world." *An ignorant preacher :*—Of the late Bishop Ames the following anecdote is told. While presiding over a certain conference in the West, a member began a tirade against the universities and education, thanking God that he had never been corrupted by contact with a college. After proceeding thus far for a few minutes, the bishop interrupted with the question, "Do I understand that the brother thanks God for his ignorance?" Well, yes," was the answer; "you can put it that way if you want." "Well, all I have to say," said the bishop, in his sweetest musical tone—"all I have to say is, that the brother has a good deal to thank God for." *College life :*—He whose spiritual life evaporates under processes of ministerial culture could hardly resist the temptations of any other form of life. (H. Allon, D.D.)

Ver. 3. **Endure hardness as a good soldier.**—*The Christian soldier :*—Every Christian, and especially every Christian minister, may be regarded as a soldier, as an athlete (ver. 5), as a husbandman (ver. 6); but of the three similitudes the one which fits him best is that of a soldier. Even if this were not so, St. Paul's fondness for the metaphor would be very intelligible. 1. Military service was **very** familiar to him, especially in his imprisonments. He must frequently have seen soldiers under drill, on parade, on guard, on the march ; must have watched them cleaning, mending, and sharpening their weapons ; putting their armour on, putting it off. Often, during hours of enforced inactivity, he must have compared these details with the details of the Christian life, and noticed how admirably they corresponded with one another. 2. Military service was also quite sufficiently familiar to those whom he addressed. Roman troops were everywhere to be seen throughout the length and breadth of the empire, and nearly every member of society knew something of the kind of life which a soldier of the empire had to lead. 3. The Roman army was the one great organisation of which it was still possible, in that age of boundless social corruption, to think and speak with right-minded admiration and respect. No doubt it was often the instrument of whole-sale cruelties as it pushed forward its conquests, or strengthened its hold, over resisting or rebelling nations. But it promoted discipline and *esprit de corps*. Even during active warfare it checked individual license, and when the conquest was over it was the representative and mainstay of order and justice against high-handed anarchy and wrong. Its officers several times appear in the narrative portions of the New Testament, and they make a favourable impression upon us. If they are fair specimens of the military men in the Roman Empire at that period, then the Roman army must have been indeed a fine service. But the reasons for the apostle's preference for this similitude go deeper than all this. 4. Military service involves self-sacrifice, endurance, discipline, vigilance, obedience, ready co-operation with others, sympathy, enthusiasm, loyalty. 5. Military service implies vigilant, unwearying and organised opposition to a vigilant, unwearying, and organised foe. It is either perpetual warfare or perpetual preparation for it. And just such is the Christian life ; it is either a conflict or a pre-paration for one. (*A. Plummer, D.D.*)    *The minister a good soldier :—* Ministers above all should be leaders and exemplars in this contest. For the apostle's fear of disapproval at last relates to him as a herald or preacher to others, calling them to the spiritual warfare. They should be like the statues of ancient heroes in the Palœstra, which the Roman youth were sent to admire and emulate, while they recounted the history of their achievements. (*J. Leifchild, D.D.*) *The good soldier of Jesus Christ :—*Fight, not as Joash, who smote the ground with the arrows thrice and stayed before he was bidden, for which he was denied a full victory. Fight, not as Israel in Canaan, who, instead of seeking the decreed exter-mination of all the ancient inhabitants, suspended their conquests, and allowed many of them to remain in their immediate neighbourhood and intercourse ; for which they received not the promise of full rest and enjoyment. But fight as Joseph, who said, " How can I do this great wickedness and sin against God ! " Fight as Paul did, when he laboured to bring under his body and keep it in sub-jection. Fight as Christ told His disciples to fight, by cutting off the right hand and plucking out the right eye that causes them to offend. Fight as did your great Lord and Master Himself with the arch-traitor, when he sought to inject into His mind thoughts of discontent, of ambition, and of a debasing servility of soul : repelling him with a holy indignation, and saying, " Get thee hence, Satan, for it is written, Thou shalt worship the Lord thy God, and Him only shalt thou serve." (*Ibid.*)    *Aggressive goodness :—*The Saviour expects true saintliness will always be an aggressive thing. Where it is such, its activities rouse enmity. We have different views from the Saviour on this subject of aggressive goodness. We think saintliness is at liberty to be an unobtrusive, self-saving thing : carefully restricting its service to the quiet influence of its example, content to develop its own life sweetly. But the Saviour calls for something more vigorous than passive piety. Prince of Peace as He was, He proclaims : " I came not to send peace on earth, but a sword "—to set a man at variance with those around him. He defines His object to be to " send fire on the earth," and tarries only until it is kindled. He assumes that evil must be assailed, that falsehood will be contradicted, and sin denounced. He intends a true peace to be reached by the disturbance of the false. He expects sanctity ever to have something of the soldierly quality, and that the life will be a fight of faith. He did not contemplate sanctity adopting a live-and-let-live policy in the presence of falsehood and evil. Silence is the earth in which the talent of truth is buried. He expects us to be His witnesses ; bids us say, " Repent ! " not merely to men in general, but to sinners in particular ; expects us to reprove all evil, as well as to point to Him who is the source and pattern of all good. Wherever love is thus aggressive, truth thus bold, mercy thus active —

hatred of the intensest kind must rise. For who can bear to have his ways denounced as evil ; his views as false ; his destiny—perdition ; his duty—repentance? Moreover, the Christian has to be the reformer in a world of vested interests. And there is no evil under heaven, from idolatry to drunkenness, from gambling to gaiety, from heresy to vice, but some have an interest in maintaining it. You will not achieve any usefulness of any sort without the cry, " This our craft is in danger ! " rising to the lips of those profiting by others ignorance, or servitude, or evil. In these circumstances, however meek and peace-making the saint of God may be, if he is faithful to his Saviour, and to the interests of men, he will suffer from the bitter speech or the deed of hatred of those who resent his whole spirit and activity. (R. Glover.) *Earnestness demanded :*—During the Crimean War a young chaplain, newly arrived in camp, inquired of a Christian sergeant the best method for carrying on his work among the men. The sergeant led him to the top of a hill and pointed out the field of action. "Now, sir," said he, "look around you. See those batteries on the right, and the men at their guns. Hear the roar of the cannon. Look where you will, all are in earnest here. Every man feels that this is a life and death struggle. If we do not conquer the Russians the Russians will conquer us. We are all in earnest here, sir ; we are not playing at soldiers. If you would do good, you must be in earnest ; an earnest man always wins his way." Such was the advice of Queen Victoria's servant to the servant of King Jesus. (A. A. Harmer.) *A recruiting sergeant :*—In writing the life of Uncle John Vassar, Dr. Gordon has so dealt with the materials at command that the successive chapters are made to pourtray the " good soldier of Jesus Christ," and to enforce the injunction—" Fight the good fight of faith." Uncle John not only deserves to be called a " good soldier." He was something more, for, while fighting the Lord's battles himself, he was an active recruiting sergeant, and never seems to have missed a chance of pressing home the question, " Who is on the Lord's side ? " Accosting a gentleman on one occasion with the familiar question, " My dear friend, do you love Jesus ? " he was met with the rejoinder, " I do not know that that concerns you, sir." Uncle John was too shrewd a tactician to be disconcerted, and at once followed up the assault with the remark, " Oh, yes it does. In these days of rebellion does it not concern every citizen as to which side every other citizen may take ? How much more when a world is in rebellion against God, should we be concerned to know who is on the Lord's side ! " In this way he fenced the resentment which the obtrusion seemed likely to provoke, and justified his advance as the anxious inquiry of an interested friend. Resisted or repulsed in his spiritual warfare, Uncle John never appears to have been vanquished. The word defeat was not found in his vocabulary. *Every Christian a soldier :*—Not only ministers, but laymen, should be Christ's ambassadors. Must a soldier be an officer in order to fight well? By no means. Minus gold lace and cocked hat, he may do good service. Hard blows may be given, or a sure aim may be taken, by him who is quite destitute of ribbon and medal. Thus is it spiritually. Eminent talent and honourable position are non-essentials in benevolent effort. The humblest warrior in the Saviour's army can be valiant and victorious. And he ought to be. Excuse here is quite vain. None that are saved have a right to be idle ; all are to evangelise. The work is not to be delegated to one order or class. Each is expected to take his share. What should we think of him who refused to rescue a drowning man because he was not connected with the Royal Humane Society ? " Let him that heareth," as well as him that preacheth, " say Come." (T. R. Stevenson.) *Enemies not to be despised :*—It is said that the Duke of Wellington on one occasion, when asked why it was that he was so generally on the side of victory, replied that he never despised an enemy. *Every convert a recruit :*—As the young Hannibal was brought by his father to the altar of his country, and there sworn to life-long hatred of Rome, so should we be, from the hour of our spiritual birth, the sworn enemies of sin, the enlisted warriors of the Cross ; to fight on for Jesus till life's latest hour, when we shall be " more than conquerors through Him that hath loved us." The Spartan mother, as soon as her child was born, looked upon the babe as having in it the possibilities of a hero ; and the whole training of the Lacedemonians aimed solely at producing good soldiers, who would honour the race from which they sprung. So should we look upon every young convert as a recruit ; not merely as one who has been himself saved, but as having within his new-born nature the possibilities of a good soldier of Jesus Christ. (C. H. Spurgeon.) *" In my shirt sleeves " :*—I am much of the opinion of the soldier who, being brought before the Duke of Wellington and a

committee of the House of Lords, on being asked if he had to fight the battle of
Waterloo over again how he would like to be dressed, said, "Please, your Lordship, I should like to be in my shirt sleeves." And, depend upon it, the freest
dress is the right costume of war. There is nothing like the shirt sleeves for hard
gospel work. Away with that high stock and the stiff coat, in which you find it
difficult to fight when you come to close contact with the enemy. You must dispense with pipeclay and bright buttons when it comes to blood, fire, and vapour of
smoke. (*Ibid.*)    *Christ provides for His soldiers :*—Our filthy garments are to be
taken off; we are to go to the Royal Fountain and wash; we are to go to the Royal
Wardrobe to be clothed; we are to go to the Royal Armoury for our equipment;
we are to go to the Royal Banqueting House to be fed; we are to go to the Royal
Treasury to be paid. Christ's soldiers have no reason to care about the future.
(*C. Garret.*)    *A soldier always :*—You cannot be a saint on Sundays and a sinner
in the week; you cannot be a saint at church and a sinner in the shop; you cannot be a saint in Liverpool and a sinner in London. You cannot serve God and
Mammon. You are a soldier everywhere or nowhere, and woe to you if you dishonour your King. (*Ibid.*)    *The inspiration of a true leader :*—The personal
magnetism of General McLellan over his soldiers in the Civil War was a constant
experience. Once when the tide of success seemed to go against the Union forces,
and dismay was gradually deepening into despair, his arrival in the camp at night
worked a revolution among the troops. The news "General McLellan is here"
was caught up and echoed from man to man. Whoever was awake roused his
neighbour, eyes were rubbed, and the poor tired fellows sent up such a hurrah as
the army of the Potomac never heard before. Shout upon shout went out into the
stillness of the night, was taken up along the road, repeated by regiment, brigade,
division, and corps, until the roar died in the distance. The effect of this man's
coming upon the army—in sunshine or in rain, darkness or day, victory or defeat
—was ever electrical, defying all attempts to account for it. (*H. O. Mackey.*)
*Enduring hardness :*—It behoves thee not to complain if thou endure hardness;
but to complain if thou dost not endure hardness. (*Chrysostom.*)    *The Christian
must be prepared for trial and conflict:*—Some of God's people seem to forget this.
They think they are soldiers on pay days and at reviews: but as soon as the fiery
darts begin to fall around them, and the road gets rough and rugged, they fancy
they are deserters. A strange mistake this. You are never so much a soldier as
when you are marching or fighting. I fear the fault of this mistake lies very much
with some of us who may be called recruiting sergeants. In persuading men to
enlist we speak much more of the ribbons, the bounty money, and the rewards,
than we do of the battle-field and the march. Hence, perhaps, the error. But if
we are to blame in this respect our great King is not. The whole of His teaching
is in the other direction. He puts all the difficulties fairly before us, and we are
exhorted to count the cost, so that we may not be covered with shame at last.
(*C. Garrett.*)    *Christian courage :*—Thomas Garrett, of America, when he was
tried and heavily fined for concealing fugitive slaves, and his judge said he hoped
it would be a warning to him to have nothing to do with runaway slaves for the
future, replied: "Friend, if thou knowest of any poor slave who is coming this
way, and needs a friend, thou canst tell him I shall be ready to help him." (*Ibid.*)
*Enduring hardness :*—The old wrestlers did not decline ten months of laborious
and abstemious training to make their bodies supple and their will indomitable;
so much so, that "a wrestler's health" became a proverb. If Plato challenged
his disciples—"Shall our children not have energy enough to deny themselves for
a much more glorious victory?" ("De Leg.," vii. 840), a greater man than Plato
urged, "Now they do it for a corruptible crown, but we for an incorruptible"; and
our ardour, self-denial, and moral training, or, as St. Paul calls it, our spiritual
gymnastics, should exceed theirs, in some such ratio as our prize exceeds theirs;
and thus, "if ye through the Spirit do mortify the deeds of the body, ye shall
live." (*J. B. Owen, M.A.*)    *No feather-bed soldiers :*—A young Christian officer
said, "Our heavenly Captain wants no feather-bed soldiers. He wants those who
are not afraid of camp bed and marching orders, who don't mind 'roughing it a
little' by the way, because they know that perfect rest awaits them when their
home-call sounds, and their race here is ended." *A sham battle :*—At the
festival of Treviso, to which the neighbouring towns were invited, the chief
feature was the storming of a fortress, defended by the most beautiful ladies
and their servants, by noblemen who made war with fruits, flowers, sweet-
meats, and perfumes. (*H. O. Mackey.*)    *A good soldier :*—I remember a story

of a French grenadier, who, in a war with the Austrians, was in charge of a small fort commanding a narrow gorge, up which only two of the enemy could climb at a time. When the defenders of the fort heard that the enemy were near, being few in number, they deserted, and left the brave grenadier alone. But he felt he could not give up the place without a struggle, so he barred the doors, raised the draw-bridge, and loaded all the muskets left behind by his comrades. Early in the morning, with great labour, the enemy brought up a gun from the valley, and laid it on the fort. But the grenadier made such good use of his loaded muskets that the men in charge of the gun could not hold their position, and were compelled to retire; and he kept them thus at bay all day long. At evening the herald came again to demand the surrender of the fort, or the garrison should be starved out. The grenadier asked for a night for consideration, and in the morning expressed the willingness of the garrison to surrender if they might "go out with all the honours of war." This, after some demur, was agreed to, and presently the Austrian army below saw a single soldier descending the height with a whole sheaf of muskets on his shoulder, with which he marched through their lines and then threw them down. "Where is the garrison?" asked the Austrian commander, astonished. "I am the garrison," replied the brave man, and they were so delighted with his plucky resistance that the whole army saluted him, and he was afterwards entitled the "First Grenadier of France." (*Major Smith.*)     *Luxury unfits for soldiership:*—The Commons of England being very importunate with Edward IV. to make war with France, he consented to satisfy their importunity, though willing rather to enjoy the fruits of his wars and toils, and spend the rest of his days in peace. When he took the field he ordered to accompany him a dozen of fat, capon-eating burgesses, who had been most zealous for that expedition. These he employed in all military services, to lie in the open fields, stand whole nights upon the guard, and caused their quarters to be beaten up with frequent alarms, which was so intolerable to those fat gentry accustomed to lie on soft down, and that could hardly sit on a session's bench without nodding, that a treaty being desired by King Louis, none were so forward to press the acceptance of his offers, or to excuse so little done by the king with so great preparations. (*C. H. Spurgeon.*)     *A war for fireside:*—"Home guards to the front!" was the cry of '65. Look at them, slight lads stooping under their heavy muskets, decrepit men tottering on with cane in one hand and gun in the other; convalescent, furloughed soldiers rising like a wounded war-horse. And has war come to this? Yes, and worse. It has seen the nursing mother, and feeble, aged women, and delicate girls, defending the parapet. The hearth must be protected, and the husband, the little lad, and the white-haired father are gone, dead, dead in their blood! Women are to the front only because there are no men, none at all. But wait; there is a war for home and fireside, a war for rights more dear, and from foes more cruel, in which women face its fury, not because the men have fallen first, but because men shirk. Yes, men shirk the discipline, the hardships, the responsibility of this war. Not all men, thank God! yet many do. Happy in their homes, receiving the blessings of Christianity, they are willing to see the wives and mothers fight the battle. The hosts of hell, with black flag unfurled, surround us, menacing the peace of home, threatening slavery and death. With dreadful malice and cruelty they contend for every inch of ground. It is a battle remorseless, ceaseless, momentous. It appeals to all that is manly in men to take their places in it, to submit to its discipline, to endure its hardships, to shoulder its responsibility. (*R. S. Barrett.*) *A good soldier of Jesus Christ:*—I. A SOLDIER MUST BE ENLISTED. II. THE SOLDIER AFTER HAVING BEEN ENLISTED HAS TO BE DRILLED—that is to say, he has to learn his business. A good soldier is not to be made in a day; there must be time and pains spent upon him; he must be trained and taught, and that very carefully, before he is fit to fight against the enemies of his country. And it is just the same with Christian soldiers. They have to learn to act together, so as to support and help one another in the conflict with evil. And then they have to learn the use of their weapons—of one more especially, which is called the "sword of the Spirit." III. WE HAVE ENEMIES TO FIGHT WITH—real enemies, not imaginary ones: "the world, the flesh, and the devil." In order to enable you to understand what is meant by fighting against the "flesh" and "the devil," I will tell you a story, or rather, two stories, both of them true. Some years ago there lived a good and holy man, who was a most useful minister of the gospel. This good man's Christian name was William. Now when he was a little boy, about four or five years old, he one day was left in the dining-room alone, and on the table was a plate of sweet cakes, of which he was particularly fond, but which he had been forbidden to touch. Somebody coming quietly into the room found the boy looking at the cakes, his little hands tightly clasped together behind his back, and saying to himself over and over again, as if he were saying a lesson, " Willie mustn't take them, 'cause they are not Willie's own." Now this was a victory over the " flesh." The flesh said, " These cakes are very nice, Willie ; just smell them. No one will see you, Willie, if you *do* take one. Mamma will not miss the cakes, Willie, there are so many of them." But little Willie would not do wrong, although he was sorely tempted to it. He fought with the " flesh," and came off conqueror. But there was one sad occasion on which Willie, now grown up to be a tall, handsome lad of seventeen, was beaten by the enemy. There was a servant in the family who was a wicked man ; and wicked men, whether they know it or not, are agents for the devil, and do his work. This servant, annoyed at his young master's goodness, said once, in a sneering sort of way, and in William's hearing, " Oh ! as for Master William, he's not man enough to swear." The taunt—it was just like a fiery arrow shot from Satan's bow—stung the young lad beyond endurance ; and for the only time in his life, I believe, he took God's holy name in vain, and swore a terrible oath. Whenever William spoke of the matter—years, long years, after—it was with expressions of the bitterest regret, though he felt in his heart that God had forgiven him. Well, that was a fight with the devil in which the devil was the victor. The Christian soldier was beaten, for the moment. Satan, through the mouth of one of his servants, triumphed over him. IV. THE APOSTLE TELLS US THAT WE ARE TO BE GOOD SOLDIERS OF JESUS CHRIST. A " good " soldier obeys orders strictly ; does not get tired of his duty, but sticks to it; and never dreams of turning his back and running away when the enemy is coming. V. AND NOW LET ME TELL YOU BY WHAT MEANS WE ARE TO BECOME GOOD SOLDIERS. A good general makes good soldiers. He infuses his own spirit into them, and leads them to victory. And we have a good general, the Lord Jesus Christ. Put yourselves, then, into His hands, and He will make you what you ought to be. I wish you especially to notice that you cannot be a true Christian warrior without possessing that loyal devotion to Christ which springs from love. (*G. Calthrop, M.A.*)　　*A good soldier:*—Much as war is at variance with the spirit of Christianity, there are few things to which the Scriptures more frequently allude when treating of the spiritual life. There is reason for this; for, notwithstanding all that is objectionable in the soldier's occupation, there are many things in the personal qualities of the man which pertain to the very noblest type of character. That which makes him a good soldier would also, if combined with other elements, make him a higher style of man. I. THE FIRST THING REQUIRED OF A GOOD SOLDIER IS HEARTY SERVICE. " One volunteer is worth many pressed men." The adage was singularly verified during the war between Austria and Prussia. The Austrian soldiers fought well, but not with the enthusiasm of men who cordially approve of the object for which they fight. Drawn from various nationalities—believing, some of them, that the war was hostile to the dearest interests of their country—they were not so much free agents as machines forced into the strife ; and this fact, perhaps, more than bad generalship or insufficient equipment, accounted for their signal defeat. Whereas the Prussians, although not enlisted voluntarily in the first instance, nevertheless entered voluntarily into the conflict. With an appreciation of the purposes of the war which few gave them credit, believing that it was to promote the much-coveted unity of the Fatherland, they fought with an enthusiasm which is the surest pledge of victory ; and to this, quite as much as to the superiority of their arms and their leaders, did they owe their splendid triumphs. And so to be good soldiers of Jesus Christ, we must freely and enthusiastically engage in His service. II. The second thing required of a good soldier is IMPLICIT OBEDIENCE TO HIS COMMANDER'S ORDERS. Much has been said of the drill and discipline of the Prussian soldiers as accounting for that marvellous succession of victories which, culminating in Sadowa, changed the map of Europe. The far-seeing men who contemplated and conducted the war, with a keen appreciation of the means by which their end was to be gained, had been drilling most severely for years, until the soldier had become a kind of living machine. And that is really what is required in order to good soldiership. III. A third quality essential to the good soldier is FAITH IN HIS LEADER. In the war to which we have referred, the Austrian soldiers, after two or three defeats attributable to mismanagement, lost all faith in the capacity of their general, and not only ceased to fight with spirit, but were forthwith changed into a panic-stricken rabble. Even the brave Italians, with all their enthusiasm, recovered slowly from their defeat at Custozza, because of the manifest bungling which brought about the disaster. Whereas the Prussians, having in their leaders men whose clearness of vision and capacity for command were equal to their own fighting efficiency and power of endurance, do not seem ever to have faltered in their victorious career. Such confidence is manifestly indispensable. The private soldier knows little or nothing of the plan of the battle in which he is an actor, knows not why he is led into this position or that, or how he is to be led out of it, knows not why he is required to do this or that; but his general knows, and unless he has full confidence in the men who are directing the movements of the troops he will fight with very little courage, and prove himself but a poor soldier. And in our warfare we are equally required to have faith in our King. IV. A fourth quality is CAREFUL TRAINING. In the war referred to, the best trained and most intelligent men proved the best fighters. Intelligence consists with, and is conducive to, the highest state of discipline; and of the human machine, which the soldier must needs become, the thinking is by far the most efficient specimen. So in our warfare the best soldier, other things being equal, is the man whose mind is most thoroughly trained. The servants of Christ should seek to understand the requirements of their time, and prepare to meet them. The conditions of warfare and the works required of the Christian soldier now are not what they were once; and unless men have understanding of the times, they may, though with the best intentions, render very bungling service. The worthier the master, the more efficient should his servants be. V. HEROIC EFFORT AND PATIENT ENDURANCE ARE NECESSARY. We cannot understand in what sense they are soldiers of Christ who enter His service simply with a view to their own comfort. Their notion is that they are to have a nice pleasant time, plenty of sweet experiences, and no trials, with temporal comforts to match the unruffled smoothness of their spiritual course. So much has been said of making the best of both worlds, that the highest conception which many form of Christianity is that it is a system which rewards men in the next world for seeking to be comfortable in this. Young men should understand that a soldier's life is one of warfare and endurance. In order to your being good soldiers of Jesus Christ, there must be—VI. CONCERTED ACTION. Union is strength, insomuch that one small band of men, acting together for one purpose and under one head, will scatter thousands who have neither leader nor organisation. (*W. Landels, D.D.*)    *A good soldier of Jesus Christ:*—Many men, many minds. In reference to what a Christian is there have been very many and diverse opinions. Paul's description of a Christian in the text is that of a soldier, and that means something very far different either from a religious fop, whose best delight is music and millinery, or a theological critic who makes a man an offender for a word, or a spiritual glutton who cares for nothing but a lifelong enjoyment of the fat things full of marrow, or an ecclesiastical slumberer who longs only for peace for himself. The Christian is a self-sacrificing man as the soldier must be. A soldier is a serving man. A soldier is full often a suffering man. Once again, the true soldier is an ambitious being. Paul does not exhort Timothy to be a common, or ordinary soldier, but to be a "*good* soldier of Jesus Christ"; for all soldiers, and all true soldiers, may not be *good* soldiers. David had many soldiers, and good soldiers too, but you remember it was said of many, "These attained not unto the first three." Now Paul, if I read him rightly, would have Timothy try to be of the first three, to be a good soldier. I. We shall endeavour to DESCRIBE A GOOD SOLDIER OF JESUS CHRIST. 1. We must begin with this fundamental—he must be loyal to his King. 2. He is obedient to his Captain's commands. 3. To conquer will be his ruling passion. Wellington sent word to his troops one night, "Ciudad Rodrigo must be taken to-night." And what do you think was the commentary of the British soldiers appointed for the attack? "Then," said they all, "we will do it." So when our great Captain sends round, as he doth to us, the word of command, "Go ye into all the world and preach the gospel to every creature," if we were all good soldiers of the cross, we should say at once, "We will do it." The passion for victory with the soldier often makes him forget everything else. Before the battle of Waterloo, Picton had had two of his ribs smashed in at Quatre Bras, but he concealed this serious injury, and, though suffering intensest agony, he rode at the head of his troop, and led one of the greatest charges which decided the fortunes of the day. He never left his post, but rode on till a ball crushed in his skull and penetrated to the brains. Then in the hot fight the hero fell. In that same battle one of our lieutenants, in the early part of the day, had his left fore-arm broken by a shot; he could not, therefore, hold the reins in his hand, but he seized them with his mouth, and fought on till another shot broke the upper part of the arm to splinters, and it had to be amputated; but within two days there he was, with his arm still bleeding, and the wound all raw, riding at the head of his division. Brave things have been done amongst the soldiers of our country—Oh, that such brave things were common among the armed men of the Church militant! 4. A good soldier is very brave at a charge. 5. A good soldier is like a rock under attack. 6. He derives his strength from on high. This has been true even of some common soldiers, for religious men when they have sought strength from God have been all the braver in the day of conflict. I like the story of Frederick the Great; when he overheard his favourite general engaged in prayer, and was about to utter a sneering remark, the fine old man, who never feared a foe, and did not even fear his majesty's jest, said, "Your Majesty, I have just been asking aid from your Majesty's great ally." He had been waiting upon God. In the battle of Salamanca, when Wellington bade one of his officers advance with his troops, and occupy a gap, which the Duke perceived in the lines of the French, the general rode up to him, and said, "My lord, I will do the work, but first give me a grasp of that conquering right hand of yours." He received a hearty grip, and away he rode to the deadly encounter. Often has my soul said to her Captain, "My Lord, I will do that work if Thou wilt give me a grip of Thy conquering right hand." Oh, what power it puts into a man when he gets a grip of Christ, and Christ gets a grip of him! II. Thus I have described a good soldier of Jesus Christ. Give me a few minutes while I EXHORT YOU TO BE SUCH. 1. I exhort you who are soldiers of Christ to be good soldiers, because many of you have been so. Dishonour not your past, fall not from your high standing. "Forward" be your motto. 2. Be good soldiers, for much depends upon it. 3. Good soldiers we ought to be, for it is a grand old cause that is at stake. 4. I implore you to be good soldiers of Jesus, when you consider the fame that has preceded you. A soldier when he receives his colours finds certain words embroidered on them, to remind him of the former victories of the regiment in which he serves. Look at the eleventh chapter of Hebrews, and see the long list of the triumphs of the faithful. Remember how prophets and apostles served God; recollect how martyrs joyfully laid down their lives; look at the long line of the reformers and the confessors; remember your martyred sires and covenanting fathers, and by the grace of God I beseech you walk not unworthy of your noble lineage. 5. Be good soldiers because of the victory which awaits you. 6. Besides, and lastly, if I want another argument to make you good soldiers, remember your Captain, the Captain whose wounded hands and pierced feet are tokens of his love to you. Redeemed from going down to the pit, what can you do sufficiently to show your gratitude? Assured of eternal glory by-and-by, how can you sufficiently prove that you feel your indebtedness. (*C. H. Spurgeon.*) *Fellow soldiers:*—Let no one say that he has no taste for warfare. Each one of us is pledged to fight. Each one of us bears the sign of the Cross, which binds him to be Christ's soldier till his life's end. Once, in the old wars, an English drummer-boy was taken prisoner by the French. They amused themselves by making the lad play on his instrument, and presently one asked him to sound the retreat. The drummer answered proudly that he had never learnt how to do that! So in our warfare there is no retreating. It was the boast of Napoleon's soldiers—the guard dies, but never yields! We Christians are bidden to be faithful unto death, and Jesus promises us a crown of life. When Maximian became Emperor of the West he did his utmost to destroy Christianity. There was in the Roman army a famous legion of ten thousand men, called the Thebian Legion. It was formed entirely of Christians. Once, just before going into battle with the enemy, the Emperor commanded the Thebian Legion to sacrifice to idols. Their leader, in the name of his ten thousand soldiers, refused. The Emperor then ordered them to be decimated—that is, every tenth man to be killed. Still they were firm, and again, the second time, the cruel order was given for every tenth man to be slain. Fully armed, with their glittering eagles flashing on their helmets, the Christian soldiers stood in the perfect discipline of Rome, ready to die, but not to yield. Again they were ordered to sacrifice, and the brave answer was returned, "No; we were Christ's soldiers before we were Maximian's." Then the furious Emperor gave the order to kill them all! Calmly the remaining soldiers laid down their arms, and knelt whilst the other troops put them to the sword. So died the Thebian Legion, faithful unto death! Each one of us is in one sense a martyr, a witness for the Lord Jesus Christ. Those of us who bear hard words, and cruel judgments, and harsh treatment, patiently, rendering not evil for evil, are martyrs for Jesus. Again, as fellow soldiers, let us remember the NAME under which we serve. To a Roman soldier of old the name of Cæsar was a watchword, which made him ready to do or die. In the wars of the middle ages, when our countrymen went into battle the cry was, " St. George for Merry England," and every soldier was ready to answer with his sword. They tell us that the name of the great Duke of Wellington was alone enough to restore courage and spirit to the flagging troops. Once when a regiment was wavering in the fight, the message was passed along the ranks, " The Duke is coming," and in an instant the men stood firm, whilst one old soldier exclaimed, " The Duke—God bless him ! I had rather see him than a whole battalion." The name of our Leader is one indeed to inspire perfect faith, courage, and hope. In all ages certain regiments have had their distinguishing names. Among the Romans of old time there was one famous band of warriors known as the Thundering Legion. In later times there have been regiments known as the " *Invincibles*," the " *Die-hards*." One famous corps has for its motto a Latin sentence meaning " *By Land and Sea*," and another has one word for its badge, meaning " *Everywhere*." These mottoes remind the soldier that the regiment to which he belongs has fought and conquered, served and suffered, all over the world. The proud badge of the county of Kent is " *Invicta* "—unconquered ; that of Exeter is " *The Ever-faithful City*." All these titles belong of right to our army, the Church of Jesus Christ. It is said that in New Zealand, some years ago, many of our troops were mortally wounded by concealed natives, who hid themselves in holes in the earth, and thence darted their deadly spears upward against the unsuspecting soldier. So our spiritual enemy, Satan, hides himself in a thousand different places, and wounds us with some sudden temptation when we are least aware. (*H. J. Wilmot-Buxton, M.A.*) *The children's crusade :*—I suppose many of you have read of those strange wars called the Crusades ? They were undertaken to deliver the Holy Sepulchre of Jesus at Jerusalem out of the hands of the heathen. Thousands of brave men, besides their friends and followers, went to the Holy Land, at different times, to fight in the Crusades. The warriors wore a blood red cross on their clothing, from which they got their name of Crusaders, and their motto was, " *The Will of God*." It was a very good motto, but not a very true one for them, for I am afraid they did many cruel and wicked things which certainly were not the will of God ; and thousands of people perished miserably abroad, who might have been doing useful work at home. Well, amongst these Crusades there was one called the Children's Crusade. A boy in France went about singing in his own language—

" Jesus, Lord, repair our loss,
　　Restore to us Thy Holy Cross."

Crowds of children followed him, singing the same words. No bolts, no bars, no fear of fathers, or love of mothers, could hold them back, they determined to go to the Holy Land, to work wonders there ! This mad crusade had a very sad ending ; of course young children could do nothing, being without leaders, or experience, or discipline, and they all perished miserably either by land or sea. Now I want you to think about another Children's Crusade, in which you are all engaged. What do you think is required of a good soldier ? I. First of all he must be BRAVE. We all like to hear about acts of bravery, like that of the little midshipman who spiked the Russian guns in the Crimean war ; or of the boy Ensign, Anstruther, who at the battle of the Alma planted the colours of the 23rd Regiment on the wall of the great Redoubt, and then fell, shot dead, with the colours drooping over him like a pall. But the courage which is thought most of in heaven is the courage to do right. I have read a story of a wounded soldier lying on a battlefield, whose mouth had been struck by a shot. When the doctor placed a cup of water to his mouth, the man was eagerly going to drink, when he stopped and said, " My mouth is all bloody, it will make the cup bad for the others." That soldier, in giving up self for the sake of others, was more of a hero than when charging against the foe. Try to remember that story, children, and if you are tempted to do anything selfish or wrong, stop and think, " It will make it bad for the others." II. You MUST EXPECT TO FIND ENEMIES AND DIFFICULTIES IF YOU DO WHAT IS RIGHT. Every one was against Daniel because he prayed to God. Every one was against Shadrach, Meshach, and Abednego, because they would not bow down to an idol. But God was on their side. There was once a famous man of God named Athanasius. He was bold enough to maintain the true faith of Christ against Emperors, and Bishops, and he was driven into banishment over and over again. Some of his friends advised him to give in, for, said they, the world is against you; "Then," answered Athanasius, "I am against the world." Now you must, as Christ's soldiers, "learn to suffer and be strong." To win a victory we must fight, to get to the end of a journey we must bear fatigue. Let me tell you a fable about that. Three animals, an ermine, a beaver, and a wild boar, made up their minds to seek a better country, and a new home. After a long and weary journey, they came in sight of a beautiful land of trees and gardens, and rivers of water. The travellers were delighted at the sight, but they noticed that before they could enter this beautiful land, they must pass through a great mass of water, filled with mud and slime, and all kinds of snakes and other reptiles. The ermine was the first to try the passage. Now the ermine has a very delicate fur coat, and when he found how foul and muddy the water was, he drew back, and said, that the country was very beautiful, but that he would rather lose it than soil his beautiful coat. Then the beaver proposed that as he was a good architect, as you know beavers are, he should build a bridge across the lake, and so in about two months they might get across safely. But the wild boar looked scornfully at his companions, and plunging into the water, he made his way, in spite of mud and snakes, to the other side, saying to his fellow-travellers, "Paradise is not for cowards, but for the brave." Dear children, between you and the Paradise of God there lies a long journey, the enemy's country, where the devil and his angels will fight against you, where there are deep pools of trouble to be gone through, rough, stony roads of temptation to be traversed, high rocks of difficulty to be climbed : but don't be afraid, only be brave, and go forward, and follow Jesus your leader, and you will be able to say, as St. Paul said, "Thanks be to God, who giveth us the victory, through our Lord Jesus Christ." III. Well, we have seen that soldiers must be brave, what else must they be? OBEDIENT. God told Saul to do a certain thing, and he did not, and God would no longer have him as a soldier. Do you remember what was said to him? "Behold, to obey is better than sacrifice." (*Ibid.*) *The good soldiers :*—The question before us is,—How may we become good soldiers of Jesus Christ? I. WE MUST WEAR THE UNIFORM OF CHRIST. This uniform is not made up of different-coloured cloth, such as we see other soldiers wear. No; but it is made up of the tempers, or dispositions, which form their character. To wear the uniform of Jesus, then, is to have the same mind, or spirit, or temper that He had. II. The second thing for us to do, if we would be good soldiers of Jesus Christ, is to—OBEY THE ORDERS OF JESUS. Some time ago, a large ship was going from England to the East Indies. She was carrying a regiment of soldiers. When they were about half-way through their voyage, the vessel sprang a leak, and began to fill with water. The lifeboats were launched and made ready, but there were not enough of them to save all on board the ship. Only the officers of the ship, the cabin passengers, and some of the crew, could be taken in the boats. The soldiers had to be left on board, to go down with the ship. The officers determined to die with their men. The colonel was afraid the men would get unruly if they had nothing to do. That he might prevent this he ordered them to prepare for parade. Soon they all appeared in full dress. He set the regimental band on the quarter-deck, with orders to keep on playing lively airs. Then he formed his men in close ranks on the deck. With his sword drawn in his hand, he took his place at their head. Every officer and man is at his post. The vessel is gradually sinking ; but they stand steady at their post, each man keeping step. And then, just as the vessel is settling for its last plunge, and death is rushing in upon them, the colonel cries,—"Present arms !" and that whole regiment of brave men go down into their watery grave, presenting arms as death approached them. Those were good soldiers. They had learned to obey orders. But this is a hard lesson to learn. Several boys were playing marbles. In the midst of their sport it began to rain. One of the boys, named Freddie, stopped and said, "Boys, I must go home. Mother told me not to stay out in the rain." "Your mother—fudge !" said two or three of the boys. "The rain won't hurt you any more than it will us." Freddie turned on them with a look of pity, and yet with the courage of a hero, while he calmly said, "I'll not disobey my mother for any of you." That was the spirit of a good soldier. After a great battle once, the general was talking to his officers about the events of the day. He asked them who had done the best that day. Some spoke of one man who had fought very bravely, and some of another. "No," said the general, "you are all mistaken. The best man in the field to-day was a soldier who was just lifting up his arms to strike an enemy, but when he heard the trumpet sound a retreat, he checked himself, and dropped his arm without striking the blow. That perfect and ready obedience to the will of his general is the noblest thing that has been done to-day." III. We must FOLLOW THE EXAMPLE OF JESUS. When Alexander the Great was leading his army over some mountains once, they found their way all stopped up with ice and snow. His soldiers were tired out with hard marching, and so disheartened with the difficulties before them, that they halted. It seemed as if they would rather lie down and die than try to go on any farther. When Alexander saw this, he did not begin to scold the men, and storm at them. Instead of this, he got down from his horse, laid aside his cloak, took up a pickaxe, and, without saying a word to any one, went quietly to work, digging away at the ice. As soon as the officers saw this, they did the same. The men looked on in surprise for a few moments, and then, forgetting how tired they were, they went to work with a will, and pretty soon they got through all their difficulties. Those were good soldiers, because they followed the example of their leader. (*Richard Newton, D.D.*) *A good soldier :*—I. WHAT IS IMPLIED IN BEING A SOLDIER ? 1. A soldier is a person who has enlisted in an army. Had looked at the reasons for and against entering the army, and at last he enlisted. 2. He is the property of the king. Gives up his free agency. Gives up his very name. Known and called by the number he bears. 3. He is provided for by the king. Must take off his own clothes, whether of best broadcloth or corduroy. Must be clothed, and fed, and armed by the king. 4. He must always wear his regimentals. A soldier can always be recognised as such. 5. He is prepared for trial and conflict. Soldiers are the result of war, and if there were no war, there would be no soldiers. He enlisted to fight. For this purpose he is armed, and trained, and drilled. II. WHAT IS IMPLIED IN BEING A SOLDIER OF CHRIST ? It is implied that Christ is a King, that He has enemies, that He has an army, and that the person spoken of belongs to this army. I have to glance at the ground we have already passed—You have enlisted, &c. III. WHAT IS IMPLIED IN BEING A GOOD SOLDIER OF CHRIST ? There are soldiers and soldiers. There are some who are idle and dissipated : a disgrace to the profession to which they belong. Others only swell the numbers and fill up the ranks, they look very well at reviews, but don't count for much in the battle-field. Others are so true and faithful that they cover the army to which they belong with glory. 1. A good soldier is thoroughly loyal. Not a mercenary, fighting for pay. Proud of his uniform, his name, his king. 2. Patriotic. Loves his country. Every soldier is his comrade. The defeat of the army is his sorrow ; its success his joy. 3. Obedient. He may be at home in the midst of his family—a telegram comes ; by the next train he leaves to join the army, perhaps to cross the seas and perish in a distant land. 4. Earnest. 5. Brave. 6. Patient. Not enlisted for a day, but for life. Often put where there is nothing to excite or gratify ambition. There will be the long wearisome march, or the still more wearisome halt. While his comrades are assaulting cities and winning victories, he has to stand and watch, or lie and suffer. 7. Self-denying. 8. Modest. His motto, Deeds not words. It is said that the word "glory" is not found in the despatches of the Duke of Wellington. He merely states what the army had done. So with the Christian. What are you ? A rebel ? Your defeat is certain. A deserter ? Return. A penitent, longing to be enlisted in Christ's army ? Come. A soldier ? Be "a good soldier." (*C. Garrett.*) *A good soldier of Jesus Christ :*— The contrast between the saints of the Old Testament and of the New Testament is very great, especially in the relation which they bore to war. No great saint or apostle of the New Testament was a soldier. But in the Old Testament we read of the faith of Abraham, of the wisdom of Moses, of the courage of Joshua, of the nobility of David, of the piety of Josiah, of the zeal of Nehemiah ; and all these had at some parts of their lives to go forth to the battle-field. But it was not so with Peter, James, John, Paul, and the rest of the early disciples. The distinction is to be accounted for partly by the circumstances in which they severally lived. In Old Testament and primitive times men had to obtain a footing for their very life, and to contend for national existence. But in the time of Christ the Roman Government secured the safety of person and property, and within certain limits left the Jew to indulge in his national customs. So, in the history of our own country, we see how greatly circumstances have changed. In the time of Queen Elizabeth Englishmen of every creed were compelled to have the soldierly spirit unless they wished to succumb to the Spaniard. And in the time of the Stuarts men were obliged to keep their armour bright unless they were prepared to put their liberties at the mercy of a tyrant. Thus we have in both periods of English history, and also during the struggles of Jewish history, saints who were also and literally soldiers. But there is a deeper reason for the change which has come about. And that reason is to be seen in the gentle and forgiving spirit which is inculcated by the Christian religion. The religion of Christ banishes war by taking away its occasions and its causes. It bids its adherents still enter on a battle. It utilises those pugnacious principles which exist in us all, by confronting us with the great moral struggle between good and evil, where every man must choose his side. There are certain plain and palpable qualifications of a good soldier of Christ which we will point out. I. A GOOD SOLDIER UNDERSTANDS HIS CAPTAIN. II. UNDERSTANDS HIS WEAPONS. III. UNDERSTANDS HIS PLACE IN THE BATTLE. IV. LOVES THE CAUSE IN WHICH HE FIGHTS. (*S. Pearson, M.A.*)     *Christianity and soldiers:*—The metaphor which the apostle here chooses to describe the work of a primitive Christian bishop cannot but strike us as remarkable. Himself a servant of the Prince of Peace, and writing to another servant of the Prince of Peace, he might, we may think, have gone somewhere else for his metaphor than to the profession of arms. How are we to explain the honour which the apostle puts upon the military profession when he points to a soldier as embodying, at any rate, some of the qualities which he desires to see in a ruler of the Church of God? We cannot say, by way of reply, that the metaphor is so accidental or so singular that stress ought not in fairness to be laid on it, for there is a great deal more religious language with a military colour or flavour about it, not merely in the Old Testament, but in the New. The relation between the military profession and religion thus traceable in Scripture reappears in the history of the Church. If, in her higher moments, the Church has done her best to check or condemn bloodshed, as when St. Ambrose excommunicated the Roman Emperor Theodosius, at the very height of his power, for the slaughter of Thessalonica, she has distinguished between the immediate instruments in such slaughter and the monarchs or the captains who were really responsible for it. If, in the first centuries of the faith, Christians were often unwilling to serve in the Roman ranks, and in some cases preferred martyrdom to doing so, the reason was that such service was then so closely bound up with pagan usages that to be an obedient soldier was to be a renegade from the Christian faith. When this difficulty no longer presented itself, Christians, like other citizens, were ready to wear weapons and to serve in the wars, and so long as warfare is defensive—devoted, not to the aggrandisement of empire, but to maintaining the peace and the police of the world—the Christian Church, while deploring its horrors, cannot but recognise in it at times a terrible necessity. When the great Bishop Leo of Rome or the great soldier Charles Martel set their faces against the destructive inroads of barbarism, they had behind them all that was best and purest in Christendom; and the rise of the military orders, the Knights of the Temple and the Knights of St. John of Jerusalem, marks a yet closer intimacy, the form of which was determined, no doubt, by the ideas of the twelfth century rather than of our own, between a soldier's career and the profession of religion. We cannot pass that noble home of the law, as it is now, the Temple, without remembering that it was once tenanted by an Order of soldiers, bound by religious obligations, devoted to the rescue and the care of those sacred spots which must always be dearest to the heart of Christendom. Here, then, let us ask ourselves the question, What are the qualities which are common to a good soldier and to a good Christian? The answer will explain and will justify the language of the apostle. I. THE FIRST IS, THAT EACH, THE CHRISTIAN AND THE SOLDIER, DOES HIS WORK WELL IN THE EXACT DEGREE OF HIS DEVOTION TO HIS COMMANDER. The greatest generals have been distinguished by the power of inspiring an unbounded confidence in and attachment to their persons. This is true in different senses of Alexander, of Hannibal, of Cæsar, of Napoleon. And what is the deepest secret of the Christian life if it be not an unbounded confidence in the Captain of our salvation, Jesus Christ our Lord, devotion to His person, undoubting belief in His Word, readiness to do and to endure whatever He may order? II. AND THE SECOND VIRTUE IN A SOLDIER IS COURAGE. In the conventional language of the world, a soldier is always gallant, just as a lawyer is learned, just as a clergyman is reverend. Whatever be a man's real character, the title belongs to him by right of his profession. There are virtues in which a soldier may be wanting without damage to his professional character, but courage is not one of these. III. AND A THIRD EXCELLENCE IN A SOLDIER IS THE SENSE OF DISCIPLINE. Without discipline an army becomes an unmanageable horde, one part of which is as likely as not to turn its destructive energies against another, and nothing strikes the eye of a civilian as he watches a regiment making its way through one of our great thoroughfares in London more than the contrast which is presented by the unvarying, I had almost said the majestic, regularity of its onward movement and the bewildering varieties of pace, gesture, direction, costume of the motley crowd of curious civilians who flit spasmodically around it. Discipline in an army is not merely the perfection of form, it is an essential condition of power. Numbers and resources cannot atone for its absence, but it may easily with small resources make numbers and greater resources powerless. IV. AND ONE MORE CHARACTERISTIC OF THE MILITARY SPIRIT IS A SENSE OF COMRADESHIP. All over the world a soldier recognises a brother in another soldier. Not only members of the same regiment, of the same corps, of the same army and country, but even combatants in opposing armies are conscious of a bond which unites them, in spite of their antagonism ; and the officers and men of hostile armies have been known to engage in warm expressions of mutual fellowship as soon as they were free to do so by the proclamation of peace. This generous and chivalrous feeling which survives the clash of arms confers on a soldier's bearing an elevation which we cannot mistake. When, in the later years of his life, Marshal Soult, who had been in command in the Peninsula, visited this country, he came to St. Paul's Cathedral, and the monument which most interested him, and which then had been recently erected in the South Transept, was that of Sir John Moore, the hero of Corunna. " Soult," says one who witnessed it, " stood for some time before the monument ; he could not speak ; he could hardly control himself ; he dissolved in a flood of tears." Certainly it was meant to be so in the Church. " By this shall all men know that ye are My disciples, if ye have love one towards another." But there is an important difference between the services. The one terminates, if not before, yet certainly and altogether at the moment of quitting this earthly scene. The last possible point of contact that even a Wellington can have with the profession of his choice is seen in the device on his coffin, in the epitaph on his grave. The other service —that of Jesus Christ—although under changed conditions lasts on into that world to which death is but an introduction, and which He, our Captain, has opened to us by His death on the cross, by His resurrection from the dead. (*Canon Liddon.*) *Endurance :*—Here the apostle is not thinking of the soldier on the field of battle engaged in conflict with the enemy. His exhortation to Timothy is not to fight well, but to endure, or, as the same word is rendered elsewhere (chap. i. 8), to suffer affliction well. He thinks of the soldier being drilled and disciplined for the fight. As a prisoner at Rome he would be, very probably, a daily eye-witness of the severe training through which the emperor's troops had to pass. These were good soldiers of Cæsar. They were true patriots, laying upon the altar of their country their very lives. Now Timothy was, like the apostle himself, a soldier ; but the soldier of a very different King from Cæsar, and had a very different warfare to wage than such wars as the Roman soldiery were so frequently engaged in. He was the soldier of Jesus Christ. I. Let me remind you THAT THERE IS HARDNESS TO BE ENDURED BY ALL OF US. Christianity means to-day as it always did, continual cross-bearing. The word "duty" has still a rough edge. For example, here is a Christian merchant who has so many shares in a concern which he has for some time back had good reason for thinking is in a rather shaky condition, and an opportunity occurs for his selling out, and that at a good price. Just at present a few hundred pounds in hard cash would be of immense service to him in his business. But no, he won't sell. He means to be the true Christian gentleman, and he feels that that he cannot be and sell as good that what he has his doubts about. Yet it is hard, especially if one can see at his back a wife and so many daughters inclining rather to be extravagant, and who cannot appreciate "father's scruples." This is his cross, and as a good soldier of Jesus Christ he bears it. Come what may, he will be honest—will not finger a shilling that does not come to him lawfully. I think, then, that in the region of commercial morality those of us who belong thereto will find occasion for the exercise of the precept, "Thou, therefore, endure hardness as a good soldier of Jesus Christ." II. Let me see if I can give the true word of direction ; if I can at least indicate to you THE SPIRIT IN WHICH WE ARE TO ENDURE. I think Paul does this himself for us. We are to endure hardness as good soldiers of Jesus Christ. That is, we also, like Timothy and like those good soldiers at Rome which Paul saw—are to take to our task kindly. We are not to despise the cross that is laid upon us. We are not to run out of the way of duty. We are not to rebel when our Master chastens. III. Let me see if I can say anything THAT MAY HELP TO STIMULATE US TO DARE AND DO THE RIGHT, so that we may not repeat the mistakes of the past which have brought to us so much misery and unrest. Observe, then, what Paul says—" As a good soldier of Jesus Christ." That is, as a soldier under Jesus Christ. Think of that name—Jesus Christ. Can we for a moment suppose that He would give an unkind command or put upon us an unnecessary burden? Jesus! Why the name suggests all that is kindest, and noblest, and gentlest, and truest. But there is one other thought here I should like to take up and lay upon your hearts, " As a good soldier of Jesus Christ "— that is, of Jesus Christ as our Leader. He is not the Master to say "Go." His way is always to say " Come." The heaviest cross ever borne was that which He bore. (*Adam Scott*.)  *Moral soldiership* :—I. LET US UNDERSTAND THE MEANING OF THE INJUNCTION, " ENDURE HARDNESS." The reference is to the life of privation and suffering which a soldier, far more in those times than now, had to undergo, and which in all times he is expected to bear without murmuring, to endure willingly, as a part of that profession which he has voluntarily embraced. Endurance is not merely bearing suffering, but bearing it manfully. To bear hardship with the spirit of a hero is to " endure hardness as a good soldier." Samuel Rutherford, when in prison, used to date his letters from " Christ's Palace, Aberdeen," and when Madam Guyon was confined in the castle of Vincennes, she said, " It seems as if I were a little bird whom the Lord has placed in a cage, and that I have nothing now to do but sing." Paul, too, did not tell his son in the faith to do more than he had done himself. II. The Christian's profession, as a soldier, IMPLIES A VOLUNTARY CHANGE OF POSITION IN LIFE. III. It is now nearly universally allowed that AN INTELLIGENT ACQUAINTANCE WITH THE PLANS OF THE GENERAL, AND WITH THE PURPOSES FOR WHICH THE BATTLE IS FOUGHT, OR THE CAMPAIGN UNDERTAKEN, BY BEGETTING CONFIDENCE IN HIS LEADER, ENABLES THE SOLDIER TO RENDER MORE EFFICIENT SERVICE. So in proportion as a Christian grows in the knowledge of God and of His plans for the redemption of our world as revealed in the person of Jesus Christ, in that proportion he throws his whole soul into the fight. Four special conditions in which a soldier is called upon to " endure hardness." 1. In standing his ground. Wellington brought peace to Europe by his stand at Waterloo. To retire would have been disgrace, to advance would have been destruction. Holding his position brought victory. The battle of Inkermann was won by an eight hours' resistance of six thousand men to sixty thousand. So a Christian soldier often finds himself so hotly assaulted by the world, the flesh, and the devil, that he is unable to advance a foot. But a firm, resisting stand is conquest. 2. A soldier must endure hardness in marching. The chief care of one who has a long march before him is to be well shod. If this be not attended to, even things so insignificant as thorns and briars will occasion suffering, and may unfit the soldier for the fight. So the lesser vexations and petty cares and trials of patience in everyday life, if not guarded against, will weary and wound the " feet of the soul," as Bishop Horne calls the affections, and, footsore and wearied, he will be ill-prepared for those special encounters with the enemy to which he is always liable. 3. The soldier must endure hardness in action. 4. Although many an earthly soldier endures who is never crowned, no soldier of Christ is overlooked in the day of victory. The only condition is endurance. (*W. Harris*.)  *Soldiers of Christ*:—It sometimes happens that a verse in our English Bible contains a Scriptural rule of the utmost value, though it represents neither the best reading nor the accurate translation. Such is the case with this text. The true translation in reading it is : " Share, my son, in my suffering as a fair soldier of Jesus Christ " ; and yet the words " endure hardness " convey a most valuable general lesson, and involve the exhortation of the entire context. Perhaps some careless epicurean man of the world, perhaps some envious fashionable woman of the world, perhaps some easy, self-indulgent, godless youth asks me, " Why should I endure hardness? Life has troubles enough in store ; why should I add to them? There is no religion in making myself uncomfortable ; how can God be pleased by self-denials which will only be a burden to me? " 1. My first answer to your question is, Do it for your own sakes because we men cannot live like beasts to be cloyed with honey ; because sickness and satiety are the just nemesis of self-indulgence ; because, by the very constitution of the nature God has given you, it is a bad thing as well as ruinous to all earthly happiness that the body should be pampered, since where the body is pampered the spirit is almost necessarily starved. We have bodies ; but we are spirits. He who would truly live must walk in the Spirit, and he who would walk in the Spirit must keep the body under stern control. 2. But we go further and say, endure hardness also because it is the manifest will of God. See what pains

God takes to teach us that it is His will. The everlasting hills are full of their mineral riches, but to get them men must drive the tunnel and sink the shaft. The soil teems with golden harvests, but to win them man must scatter his seeds into the furrow, and breathe hard breath over the plough. Nature has priceless secrets in her possession ; but she holds them out to us clenched in a granite hand, which sheer labour must unclasp. Everywhere in nature God teaches us the same great lesson. Anything worth having is not to be had for nothing. 3. Endure hardness also because it is the training-school of worth. When God wants a nation to do Him high service, to fight His battles, to wrestle in His arenas, then He gives that nation labours and sorrows too. He takes them out of the sluggish levels of Egypt, and makes them climb His granite mountains and listen to the wild music of His desert winds. A nation of greedy slaves might have been contented to live and die in gluttonous animalism ; but when God wants heroes, then out of His house of bondage He calls His sons. Read God's lessons written on the broad page of history. The type of Egypt's centuries of sluggish placidity is but the cruel, motionless, staring Sphinx ; but the type of immortal Greece and the brave flash of her glory is the Apollo launching at the Python with his arrows. What would Sparta have been had she never had Thermopylæ ? What would Athens have been but for Salamis and Marathon ? 4. Endure hardness, scorn sloth, embrace labour, despise sham, practise self-denial in the path of duty, because Christ did it. It is the will of Christ ; because there is no virtue and there is no holiness possible without it. The word "virtue" occurs but once in the whole of the New Testament ; because the pagan world has made of it too dwarfed an ideal, and Christianity had better words than that ; but even the pagan world saw that broad is the path of evil—broad, and straight, and smooth to ruin by the steps of sin. The type of nobleness, even to the pagan world, was not Sardanapalus, but Hercules ; not Apicius, the glutton, but Leonidas, the king. They knew it was difficult to be a good man—difficult, and not so easy as it seems ; they knew that any fool could be a money-getter, or a drunkard, or a debauchee ; that out of the very meanest, vilest clay that ever was you can make an effeminate corrupter, or selfish schemer, or a slanderer, or a thief ; but that it takes God's own gold to make a man, and that it wants the furnace and the toil to make of that gold and fine gold ; and it is strange how unanimous all nations have been on this point. David Hume has a passage in his writings about virtue, and her affability, and her engaging manners, nay, even, at proper intervals, her frivolity and gaiety, and her parting not willingly with any pleasure, and requiring a just calculation, and her ranking us as enemies to joy and pleasure, as hypocrites, or deceivers, or the less favoured of her votaries ; whereupon one of our men of science, far from being a dogmatist, says that in this pæan of virtue there is more of a dance measure than will sound appropriate in the ears of most of the pilgrims who toil painfully, not without many a stumble, along the rough and steep road that leads to the higher life. But if virtue be difficult of acquirement, far more is holiness. (*F. W. Farrar, D.D.*)          *Enduring hardness as a soldier* :—The apostle Paul, a true and valiant hero, gives counsel in the text to each minister of God who stands up in any age to do battle for the Lord. He must not only understand the art of war as a theory, but put his knowledge into practice, going before the mighty host of God's elect in order that they may triumph gloriously—"Endure hardness as a good soldier of Jesus Christ." The apostles all set this example to the world. The advice of St. Paul in the text had reference in its original application to the clergy, but it is no less a rule which is binding on all Christians. The fact that we are Christian soldiers suggests three corresponding duties. I. THE WILL OF THE SOLDIER SHOULD BE WHOLLY ABSORBED IN THAT OF HIS COMMANDER. "My life consists in being, rather than in doing," said a good Christian woman, when cut off from active work by long-continued sickness. "I cannot fight much, but if I can hold the standard for other eyes, I may inspire tired soldiers with fresh courage, and so, if nothing but a colour-bearer, help in the good cause ! " Yes, brave and devoted woman, many a jaded and disheartened one will take heart and hope, as you thus bear aloft with unflinching hand the standard of faith and patience ! II. A soldier, to deserve the name, must possess TRUE COURAGE. III. A SOLDIER MUST BE READY TO ENDURE HARDNESS. (*J. N. Norton.*)          *The good soldier of Jesus Christ* :—Suppose a young man went of his own will for a soldier, was regularly sworn in to serve the Queen, took his bounty, wore the Queen's uniform, ate her bread, learnt his drill and all that a soldier need learn, as long as peace lasted. But suppose that as soon as war came and his regiment was ordered on active service, he deserted at once and went off and hid himself. What should you call such a man? You would call him a base and ungrateful coward, and you would have no pity on him if he was taken and justly punished. But suppose that he did a worse thing still. Suppose that the enemy, the Russians say, invaded England, and the army was called out to fight them; and suppose this man of whom I speak, be he soldier or sailor, instead of fighting the enemy, deserted over to them, and fought on their side against his own country, and his own comrades, and his own father and brothers, what would you call that man? No name would be bad enough for him. If he was taken he would be hanged without mercy, as not only a deserter but a traitor. And who would pity him or say that he had not got his just deserts? Are not all young people, when they are old enough to choose between right and wrong, if they choose what is wrong and live bad lives instead of good ones, very like this same deserter and traitor? For are you not all Christ's soldiers, every one of you? Did not Christ enlist every one of you into His army, that, as the baptism service says, you might fight manfully under His banner against sin, the world, and the devil—in one word, against all that is wrong and bad? And now when you are old enough to know that you are Christ's soldiers, what will you deserve to be called if, instead of fighting on Christ's side against what is bad, you forget you are in His service. But some may say, "My case is not like that soldier's. I did not enter Christ's service of my own free will. My parents put me into it when I was an infant without asking my leave. I was not christened of my own will." Is it so? Do you know what your words mean? If they mean anything, they mean that you had rather not have been christened, because you are now expected to behave as a christened man should. Now is there any one of you who dare say, "I wish I had not been christened"? Not one! Then if you dare not say that; if you are content to have been christened, why are you not content to do what christened people should? But why were you christened? not merely because your parents chose, but because it was their duty. Every child ought to be christened, because every child belongs to Christ. You have now no right to choose between Christ and the devil, because Christ has chosen you already—no right to choose between good and bad, because God, the good God Himself, has chosen you already, and has been taking care of you, and heaping you with blessings ever since you were born. And why did Christ choose you? As I have told you, that you may fight with Him against all that is bad. But if we go on doing bad and wrong things, are we fighting on Christ's side? No, we are fighting on the devil's side, and helping the devil against God. Do you fancy that I am saying too much? I suspect some do. I suspect some say in their hearts, "He is too hard on us. We are not like that traitorous soldier. If we do wrong, it is ourselves at most that we harm. We do not wish to hurt any one; we do not want to help the devil." (*Chas. Kingsley.*)

*Fortitude:*—Weakness and effeminacy have ever accompanied the latter stages of all human civilisation. Either society actually rottens and falls to pieces by the dissolving influence of its own vices, or, weakened by indulgence, it falls a ready prey in its turn to the sword of some ruder but manlier enemy. In the ancient nations of the world such has been the invariable process. The question has often been asked, Does the law still hold good, and must the nations of modern Europe decay and die, as the great nations of antiquity have done? If we had nothing but human nature to look to the reply would be an unhesitating, Yes. But we have another element in our case, what our Lord calls the leaven, to spread its own healthy influence through the otherwise fermenting mass of humanity; and upon its regenerating force all our hopes of a happier future must rest. If Christianity keeps us from effeminacy, it will keep us from ruin. I cannot for a moment doubt its power, because it is the power of God. But it therefore follows that, if it is to save us, it must be a real Christianity—a Christianity such as God originated and such as God will work by. Now it is, I think, the most serious thing in the present condition of the world that, not only has a luxurious civilisation weakened the domestic virtues, especially among some women, whose extravagances have become almost a satire upon womanhood—I say among women, because the love of athletic sports to a considerable degree checks the tendency among men; but that our Christianity itself has caught the infection and is demoralised by self-indulgence. The effeminacy has reached even our religion. Words and sentiments take the place of deeds. The charm of the eye and the ear are substituted for great inward principles; the grandest truths are welcomed, admitted, admired, but not acted upon in daily life. The Church is enormously below her own standard. A refined self-indulgence spreads everywhere, and if it continues to spread till it touches the very heart of the Church and nation, then indeed there can be no hope for us. I cannot doubt that it is the providential object of the struggles of faith belonging to our day to revive the manliness, the independence, the reality, and power of our religion, just as nations amid sufferings and disaster recover the manly virtues which have rusted in prosperity and ease. There are many obvious reasons for cultivating a more robust and manly earnestness in our religion. I. It IS DUE TO THE CHARACTER OF THE GREAT MASTER WHOM WE SERVE. We look up to the Captain of our salvation, and every imaginable motive which can nerve the human heart combines to inspire us with dauntless courage and unflinching fortitude. II. A ROBUST EARNESTNESS IS DUE TO THE NECESSITIES OF THE WORK. God takes every possible precaution in His Word that we should count the cost, before we enlist under our Captain's banner. We have, indeed, Divine strength to help us; but it is given to help, not to supersede. Our battle requires all our strength, and nothing less will suffice. The very saints hardly press into the kingdom : they take it by violence, and enter like soldiers after a hard-fought fight—wounded, bleeding, and weary, but conquering. And this endurance of hardness is the more necessary because, not only are habits of personal self-denial and self-restraint, watchful devotion and earnest effort, the conditions of victory, but they are actual parts of the victory themselves. III. MANLY VIGOUR IS DUE TO THE ABUNDANCE OF THE REWARD. Salvation itself is not of reward; it is all of grace. But once let the soul find Christ, let it be accepted within the family circle, let it fairly take service beneath the banner of Christ as the faithful soldier and servant of a crucified Master, and then God deals with it by rewards. (*E. Garbett, M.A.*) *The Christian a soldier :*—I. THE SOLDIER GIVING UP THE DIRECTION OF HIS OWN ACTIONS AND EXERTIONS, GIVES HIMSELF UP TO THE SERVICE OF ANOTHER. The Roman soldier, to whose case St. Paul must be supposed particularly to refer, was nothing but a soldier. So it is with the Christian : he may not serve the world and his God together. He must either be all Christ's or none of His. II. THE SERVICE INTO WHICH THE SOLDIER ENTERS IS FOR THE MOST PART A SERVICE ACCOMPANIED BY PERIL AND PRIVATION. III. The third point of similarity observed in the conditions of the soldier and the Christian is, that EACH IS BOUND TO BE FAITHFUL IN THE DISCHARGE OF THE DUTIES OF HIS PROFESSION BY THE OBLIGATION OF A SOLEMN OATH. At the time St. Paul wrote, the Roman soldier, when first enrolled, took an oath to obey the commands of his emperor, and never to forsake his standard : and this oath was yearly renewed. A Christianised imagination found a parallel to this in the solemn engagement entered into at baptism, and renewed in the holy communion of the supper of the Lord, "obediently to keep God's holy will and commandments, and to walk in the same all the days of our life." For this very reason those two awful rites of our religion received from the primitive Church the name which they yet bear, the name of sacraments. Sacrament was the usual term for the soldier's military oath, and it was transferred by the ancients to baptism and the eucharist, because in them the believer, as it were, binds himself by solemn compact faithfully to serve in the spiritual armies under the orders of the King of heaven. (*W. H. Marriott.*)

Ver. 4. **No man that warreth entangleth himself with the affairs of this life.**—*Roman soldiers* were not allowed to marry or to engage in any husbandry or trade ; and they were forbidden to act as tutors to any person, or curators to any man's estate, or proctor in the cause of other men. The general principle was, that they were excluded from those relations, agencies, and engagements, which it was thought would divert their minds from that which was to be the sole object of pursuit. (*A. Barnes.*) *The soldier of Jesus Christ, enduring, and unentangled* (vers. 3, 4) :—Soldiers read and scan attentively the military orders which are put forth from time to time by their commanding officers. Let us see what, in the articles of Christian warfare, are placed here for our instruction to-day. I. THE CHRISTIAN SOLDIER IS TO ENDURE SUFFERING FOR CHRIST. This is the true rendering of the expression, "Endure hardness." It means, suffer or endure for Christ's sake. The faithful soldier never deserts his duty. The hardships on the battle-field are fearful, but never, in his thought, unendurable. Officers in the Crimean war (as they themselves have told me) had for weeks nothing else than the hard rock for their pillow, and the sky (often obscured by deluging rain clouds) for their ceiling. Yet they "endured" it, and the soldiers "endured" it with them, and thus they "suffered" or endured hardness together, as "good soldiers" under a gracious queen! 1. The good soldier of Jesus Christ will often "endure" suffering by reproaches for Christ's name. 2. And you must not wonder, if you have to endure persecution also, by taunts openly spoken in your hearing. II. THAT CHRISTIAN SOLDIERS ARE NOT TO "ENTANGLE THEMSELVES WITH THE AFFAIRS OF THIS LIFE." 1. The Christian is a warrior—is a "man that warreth." There is the daily watch to be kept over yourself, and to bar out Satan, and to keep out the world. Ay, and all is not done even then, for there are those occasional surprises, when the enemy would pounce upon us from an ambush; for the Christian knows that sometimes he is vigorously assaulted at the time, and from the point where he thought injury impossible, and when he deemed himself quite secure. Then, too, there is the well-planned attack, when Satan brings all his legionaries to the fight, and the hosts of temptations are directed against you with unceasing violence. 2. Well, then, be mindful you do not entangle yourself. You need not be entangled—if you become so, you entangle yourself. (1) You may entangle yourself by a worldly spirit. (2) Or, you may become entangled by evil company. (3) Or, you may become entangled by any business or any pleasure. How, then, are these dangers to be avoided? I answer—1. By watchfulness against first dangers. You know in an army, "pickets" are sent to the very outskirts of the camp, who give signal of the earliest beginning of any attack. Be you always on your guard; let conscience have fidelity and watchfulness, ever on the alert to give notice of the least cause of danger. 2. Then, next, daily prayer is as needful to a Christian soldier as daily food is to the winner of the earthly fight. 3. And, lastly, you will do well to make a profession. A man is just as brave in fustian as in full regimentals, but it is a fact long ago established, that the ornament and distinctive dress are extremely useful. (*Geo. Venables.*)    *The military discipline:—*1. I begin with the particular matter suggested by the apostle; viz., the putting off or excision of the world, as an interruptive and disqualifying power. The only way to make great soldiership, as the military commander well understands, is to take his men completely out of the home world and have them circumscribed and shut in by drill, as being mortgaged in body and life for their country. Trained to flinch at nothing, and suffer anything, he makes them first impassive, and so, brave. And under this same law it is that all Christian disciples are required to strip for the war, throwing off all their detentions, all the seductions of business, property, pleasure, and affection. All such matters must now drop into secondary places, for the understanding is, that no one gets the great heart, or becomes in any sense a hero, till his very life is drunk up in his commander, and his supreme care to please him that hath chosen him to be a soldier. 2. Consider next how the military discipline raises spirit and high impulse by a training under authority, exact and absolute. Does it reduce the soldiers and all the subordinate commanders of an army to mere cyphers, when they are required to march, and wheel, and lift every foot, and set every muscle by the word of authority; when even the music is commandment, and to feed, and sleep, and not sleep are by requirement? Why, the service rightly maintained invigorates every manly quality rather; for they are in a great cause, moving with great emphasis, having thus great thoughts ranging in them and, it may be, great inspirations. God's all dominant, supreme authority is our noblest educator. 3. How often is it imagined by outside beholders, or felt by slack-minded, self-indulgent disciples, that the military stringency of the Christian life is a condition of bondage. Liberty is not the being let alone, or allowed to have everything our own way. If it were, the wild beasts would be more advanced in it than all states and peoples. No, there is no proper liberty but under rule, and in the sense of rule. It holds high sisterhood with law, nay, it is twin-born with law itself. 4. Ungenial and repulsive as the law of the camp may be, there is no such thing in it as enduring hardness for hardness' sake, no peremptory commandment for commandment's sake. Such kind of discipline would not be training, but extirpation rather. And yet how many of us Christian disciples fall into notions of Christian self-denial that include exactly this mistake. As if it were a proper Christian thing to be always scoring, and stripping, and mortifying ourselves. The truth is, that our human nature is made to go a great deal more heroically than some of us think; and our soldiers in the field are just now making this discovery. Why, if the fires of patriotic impulse can help our sons and fathers in the field to rejoice in so great sacrifice for their country, what pain can there be to us in our painstakings, what loss in our losses, when the love of God and of His Son is truly kindled in us? 5. The military discipline has as little direct concern to beget happiness, as it has to compel self-abnegation. It is never altogether safe for such as we to be simply happy, and that may be the reason why the best and solidest of us never are. 6. There is yet one other point of this military analogy, where in fact it is scarcely any proper analogy at all, but a kind of universal law, running through all kinds of mortal endeavour, secular, moral, mental, and spiritual ; viz., that whatever we get, we must somehow fight for it. What begins in the conflicts of tribes and empires runs down through all kinds of experience. Fighting a good fight is the only way to finish the course, and the crown of glory comes in nowhere, save at the end. (*H. Bushnell, D.D.*) *The Christian warfare :*—What are the things with which we are in danger of entangling ourselves ? 1. Doubtless we are in the greatest danger from our sins and especially from our besetting sin, *i.e.*, that peculiar sin to which each one is liable either from some natural bias, or from acquired habit arising out of the evil within. We are in danger of entangling ourselves with our sins—(1) From their deceitfulness. (2) From the power and force of habit. (3) Because we cannot be the slaves of sin and be the servants of God. 2. But the Christian's dangers arise not only from his sins, but also from the ordinary affairs of daily life. These are more especially meant in the text. And what snare can be greater ? Actual sin we may generally know to be sin. But in the affairs of this life, our daily occupations and our lawful enjoyments, it is often hard to find where the entanglement begins. If as moralists say and as experience proves, the difference between things lawful and unlawful is frequently one of degree, it must require both an enlightened conscience and much self-examination to ascertain the middle path of safety. Then keep as your safeguard the motive the text supplies : " to please Him who hath chosen you to be a soldier." It is possible, we may think we do God service by acts which a more enlightened judgment would convince us do not ; we cannot mistake a sincere desire to please Him. The old Crusader who, his heart aroused by the preaching of a Bernard or a Peter, laid his hand on his breast and swore to scare away the infidel from the holy sepulchre by his good broadsword, needed more light to learn that " our weapons are not carnal " ; and yet who can doubt his desire to please his Saviour ? Let us, then, see to it that we have this motive—Am I desirous to please Him who hath chosen me to be a soldier ? (*G. Huntingdon, M.A.*) *The affairs of this life may entangle us :*—1. From weakness of judgment. 2. From inordinate affection. 3. From the rebellion of the will. Let us use all helps to avoid the danger ; and (1) We must get a sound judgment, to understand what is the chiefest good, and how we are to dispose of all inferior things, for the procuring of it. (2) Labour to see the vanity of all earthly and sublunary things, what, and wherein their natural worth consisteth. (3) Make the Lord thy portion, and be thou assured that He only can content thy heart. (4) Refrain things indifferent (if in thy choice), and watch over thy outward senses. (5) Strive for a taste of spiritual things. They who tasted of the grapes which came from Canaan, desired to see the land : coveted more. So will it be in better things. (6) Beat Satan with his own weapons, outshoot him in his own bow. Doth he show thee the glory of this world ? Tell him, it is thy Father's ; and in serving of Him He will give thee a better. Tempts he thee to wear two swords ? Say that thou art weak, and one sufficeth. Art thou enticed by Rebecca's beauty ? Consider the king's daughter, who is all glorious within. Saith he, thou art a sinner ? Reply, else what needed I a Saviour ? (*J. Barlow, D.D.*) *Not entangled with the world :* —St. Paul does not suggest that Christians should keep aloof from the affairs of this life, which would be a flat contradiction of what he teaches elsewhere (1 Thess. iv. 11, 12). He has a duty to perform " in the affairs of this life," but in doing it he is not to be entangled in them. They are means, not ends ; and must be made to help him on, not suffered to keep him back. If they become entanglements instead of opportunities, he will soon lose that state of constant preparation and alertness which is the indispensable condition of success. (*A. Plummer, D.D.*) *Carnal ease not becoming a soldier :*—Milton excuses Oliver Cromwell's want of bookish application in his youth thus : " It did not become that hand to wax soft in literary ease which was to be inured to the use of arms and hardened with asperity ; that right arm to be softly wrapped up amongst the birds of Athens, by which thunderbolts were soon afterwards to be hurled among the eagles which emulate the sun." Carnal ease and worldly wisdom are not becoming in the soldier of Jesus Christ. He has to wrestle against principalities and powers, and has need of sterner qualities than those which sparkle in the eyes of fashion or adorn the neck of elegance. (*C. H. Spurgeon.*) *Wholly a soldier :*—Let not the minister of the gospel have one foot in the temple and the other in the *curia*. (*Melancthon.*) *Military service :*—Those who regard relationship are not fit for military service. (*Tamil Proverb.*)    *Devotion to duty:*—The Countess of Aberdeen, speaking at Millseat, said, "If you have noticed Mr. Gladstone as I have done, he considers it a sacred duty never to think any part of his time his own while he is in office. He considers he has no right to have anything to do with his own private affairs. He has told me himself that he never reads a book which he does not think will help in some way to prepare his mind for the work which he has to do for the country. He never takes any relaxation, any recreation, but what he thinks is just necessary to prepare him in doing the work of his country. It is a life of hard and continuous work, and yet we all look upon that as the most honourable place in the country, that of being absolutely the servants of the country." (*British Weekly.*)    **That he may please Him who hath chosen him to be a soldier.**—*That I may please Him:*—As we read his epistles, we feel that we know St. Paul better even than those who saw his face or heard his voice; and more and more the consciousness of his greatness becomes impressed upon us. There are two things in this greatness of his which strike us most forcibly. The first is his success in living the Christian life. What was the secret of this strength and success, making St. Paul's life so different from the lives of other men? Another thing which strikes us, as we read his writings, is his deep spirituality. What was the secret of this spirituality? Perhaps the text will furnish us with an answer. There you have the ringing key-note of St. Paul's whole life, the one thought that was ever uppermost in his mind, "That I may please Him." There are three aims, or motives, under which men act, and these three give birth to three different kinds of lives. Each of these principles of action is exclusive. I. LIVING TO PLEASE SELF. This is the keynote of most lives—the central force into which they resolve themselves when they are analysed and dissected. The principle first manifests itself when the unconscious life of childhood passes into the conscious life of manhood or womanhood. II. The second type of life is THAT IN WHICH THE FIRST AIM IS TO PLEASE OTHERS. The highest good, some say, is to sacrifice all for selfish pleasure. The highest good, say others, is to sacrifice all to gain the approbation and admiration of the world. Some men will give honour and reputation for gold. Others will give gold for honour and reputation. Here you have the distinction between these two motives. III. From the slavery of these two motives—living to please self, and living to please others—let us now turn to the glorious liberty of the third—St. Paul's motive—LIVING TO PLEASE CHRIST. The Christian religion is different from all other religions in this one respect: it is founded, not upon a system, but upon a person. Remember that this is not a dead person who lived eighteen hundred years ago, and then went back to heaven. It is not the memory of a life. It is a present life. It is a living person—"Jesus Christ, the same yesterday, and to-day, and for ever." Here is the fountain of spirituality—the constant contact of heart and soul with the living Christ. We Christians are men of but one principle. We, with that feeling of loyalty in our hearts to Christ, have but one simple rule of action: Will it please Him? (*H. Y. Satterlee, D.D.*)    *One mind rules the army:*—Nowhere else is it so true that the will of one becomes lost in that of another as in the case of the soldier. In an army it is contemplated that there shall be but one mind, one heart, one purpose—that of the commander; and that the whole army shall be as obedient to that as the members of the human body are to the one will that controls all. The application of this is obvious. (*A. Barnes.*)    *Heart devotion to Christ:*—Ofttimes a commander is so beloved and idolised by his soldiers, that they know no higher wish than to please him for his own sake. A French soldier lay sorely wounded on the field of battle. When the surgeons were probing the wound in the breast to find the bullet, the soldier said—"A little deeper, gentlemen, and you will find the emperor." So heart-deep was his devotion to his captain. But there never, never was a captain who so held the heart and charmed the love of His soldiers as Immanuel does. For Him they fight, for Him they live, for Him they suffer, and for Him they die! if only they may "please Him who hath called them to be a soldier." This Commander loves to mention His beloved "braves" in His despatches, and these are kept as a book of remembrance. (*J. J. Wray.*)    *Duty more than safety:*—In evil times it fares best with them that are most careful about duty, and least about safety. (*J. Hammond.*)    *Erratic soldiers:*—Erratic Christians, who dash about like Bashi-Bazouks, working according to no law save the bidding of their own caprice, are sorry specimens of soldiers. (*W. Landels, D.D.*)    *Obey orders and leave results:*—When Stonewall Jackson, who was personally a very tender man, was asked whether he had no compunctions in shelling a certain town, which had been threatened unless it surrendered, he replied, "None whatever. What business had I with results? My duty was to obey orders." (*H. O. Mackey.*)

Ver. 5. **Not crowned, except he strive lawfully.**—*Lawful striving :*—The athlete who competes in the games does not receive a crown, unless he has contended lawfully, *i. e.*, according to rule (νομίμως, νόμος). Even if he seem to be victorious, he nevertheless is not crowned, because he has violated the well-known conditions. And what is the rule, what are the conditions of the Christian's contest? "If any man would come after Me, let him deny himself and take up his cross and follow Me." If we wish to share Christ's victory, we must be ready to share His suffering. No cross, no crown. To try to withdraw oneself from all hardship and annoyance, to attempt to avoid all that is painful or disagreeable, is a violation of the rules of the arena. This, it would appear, Timothy was in some respects tempted to do; and timidity and despondency must not be allowed to get the upper hand. Not that what is painful, or distasteful, or unpopular, is necessarily right; but it is certainly not necessarily wrong; and to try to avoid everything that one dislikes is to ensure being fatally wrong. (*A. Plummer, D.D.*)     *Lawful diet :*— The phrase "lawfully" which is found in precisely the same connection in Galen (Comm. in Hippocrates I. 15) was technical, half-medical, and half belonging to the training schools of athletes, and implied the observance of all rules of life prior to the contest as well as during it. Failure to keep to the appointed diet and discipline, no less than taking an unfair advantage at the time, excluded the competitor from his reward. (*E. H. Plumptre, D.D.*)     *Regulations for athletic contests :*—The following were among the regulations of the athletic contests. Every candidate was required to be of pure Hellenic descent. He was disqualified by certain moral and political offences. He was obliged to take an oath that he had been ten months in training, and that he would violate none of the regulations. Bribery was punished by a fine. The candidate was obliged to practise again in the gymnasium immediately before the games, under the direction of judges or umpires, who were themselves required to be instructed for ten months in the details of the games. (*Conybeare and Howson.*)     *Lawful striving :*—I. A CHRISTIAN IS A STRIVER.  1. In the breast and forefront of this strife thou must contend with ignorance, which adversary, though his eyes be put out, and he be as blind as a mill-horse, yet his strength is like behemoths, his weapons Goliahs, his blows the batterings of a tearing cannon; for if this giant be not quelled, killed, he will lead you into mazes of error.  2. This monster being put to flight, you are to encounter with aged superstition.  3. Close after idolatry follows covetousness.  4. At the heels of every striver you shall have sloth and idleness.  II. ETERNAL LIFE IS CALLED A CROWN. For the worth and excellency of it.  III. THE LAWFUL STRIVER SHALL BE CROWNED.  (*J. Barlow, D.D.*) *The lawful strife :*—Man likes to choose his own way; but the gospel of our Lord Jesus Christ has marked out a way for him: hence one reason at least of his unwillingness to go along it. The text tells us that we must put off this perverseness of the old man, and put on all the obedience of the new man, following the direction which the Lord hath given. Man's will is to have no change of his ways, no sorrow for the past, no amendment (but he will not call it amendment) for the future. All this is too humbling to his pride, too much of a curb upon his self-will. But our Lord's precept is repentance: you must come to Me, and receive that which I give along the road of repentance. The making repentance a step, and not a course, merely a gate of introduction, and not a road also of daily conduct, is one of the short cuts by which men think to arrive at the prize, without going through all the prescribed rules of the struggle. And not only must we bring our minds to submit to the rules which our Lord hath laid down, but also our hearts to understand them: indeed, we must first understand them before we can truly accept them. We cannot in any case effectually bind ourselves to a duty of which we know not the extent; we cannot be sure of accomplishing a thing of which we have not counted the cost. Now our blessed Lord hath set before us our course, both by example and precept. And what remains is to make up our minds to rise and follow. In His trials we have the model of our lawful strife. In His ascension unto glory we see the assurance of our crown. His flesh was crucified: so must we crucify the flesh. He rose again; even so we must rise again unto newness of life. He is seated in heaven: so we must set our affections on things above. The rules are plain; they cannot be confounded with the rules of strife for any worldly mastery. We see, then, what we have to contend against. It is a compliance with the course of a sinful world; a reluctance to change our course into one which is not in conformity with it, but even in a contrary direction. It is putting God's end, indeed, before us, even the prospect of eternal life, but not using His means, but putting our own in their place, because we find them much more agreeable: it is, in short, the indulgence of our nature. (*R. W. Evans, B.D.*) *Lawful strife:—* We gather from this figure that in spiritual things there is a striving lawfully and a striving unlawfully, and that the prize is not necessarily given to him who wins the race, if he has not complied with certain rules laid down. I think, then, we may say that there are three distinct ways of striving. 1. There is an unlawful striving after unlawful objects. 2. An unlawful striving after lawful objects. 3. A lawful striving after lawful objects. I. As what is right is often more clearly shown by holding up what is wrong, I shall attempt to describe WHAT IT IS TO STRIVE UN-LAWFULLY AFTER UNLAWFUL OBJECTS. 1. To strive, then, after pre-eminence, to be a Diotrephes in a church (John iii. 9). 2. All strife about vain and idle questions (ver. 14). 3. To seek after a form of godliness, whilst secretly denying the power thereof, or to have a name to live when dead in sin. 4. To strive after fleshly holiness and creature perfection. 5. To seek to find an easier and smoother path than the strait gate and the narrow way. II. But now I come to another kind of striving, which is UNLAWFUL STRIVING AFTER LAWFUL OBJECTS. Now God has laid down in His word of truth three solemn rules, laws you may call them if you like, which constitute lawful striving. 1. The Holy Ghost must begin, carry on, and finish the inward work of grace. 2. The soul must be brought under His Divine teaching to be thoroughly stripped and emptied of all creature wisdom, strength, help, hope, and righteousness. 3. The glory of a Triune God must be the end and motive of all. Any departure from these three rules of striving makes a man strive unlawfully. III. But we come now to the only striving which the Lord crowns—A LAWFUL STRIVING AFTER LAWFUL OBJECTS. 1. Now we will begin with the first rule, which is this, that the Holy Spirit must work in us all the power, wisdom, grace, faith, strength, and life, that we strive with. 2. The second rule of lawful striving is, that the runners in this race should have no strength. "He giveth power to the faint, and to them that have no might He increaseth strength." 3. And this enables you to comply with the third rule of lawful strife—to give God all the glory. Surely you can take no glory to self, when self has been proved, and found wanting. Now these lawful strivers after lawful objects are crowned, and they only. This crown is twofold—a crown here and a crown hereafter, a crown of grace set on the heart below, and a crown of glory set on the head above. (*J. C. Philpot.*) *Lawful striving* (chap. ii. 5 with 1 Cor. ix. 25):—Let us glance first at—I. THE FACT THAT THE CHRISTIAN LIFE IS A WARFARE, A RUNNING AND A WRESTLING, A COURSE OF SELF-RESTRAINT, and of earnest labour and striving after a great end. Let us consider—II. THE MANNER OF THE STRIFE. There are two words which describe this, both of which are significant. "Lawfully" is the one, and "certainly"—or to put the double negative as the apostle has it, "not uncertainly"—is the other; and the "not as one that beateth the air" is only an expletive, or repetition of that. 1. This "lawfully" requires that all our effort and striving should be in accordance with Divine rule. And this implies at least two things—(1) That it should be preceded by our trust in Christ. Nothing we can do is acceptable or valuable until by faith in Christ we have been reconciled to God. (2) In the efforts we put forth we are not to follow our own impulses or inclination, but to be directed by the will of Christ. 2. "Certainly." The certainty is secured by the lawfulness. Those who are guided by Christ's will are not in any doubt either as to what they ought to do, or as to the result of doing it. Let us notice—III. THE OBJECT OF OUR EFFORT AND STRIVING. The apostle defines this object in the words, "I keep under my body, and bring it into subjection," and in this he but describes the warfare of the spirit against the flesh, or of the new man against the old, which is character-istic of the Christian life. And this leads me to notice in the fourth and last place—IV. THE MOTIVE OF THE APOSTLE'S STRIVING. 1. That he might not be a castaway. "A castaway." Try to realise what that word means, if you would understand the full significance of the text, and the mighty force of the motive by which the apostle was actuated. "A castaway." There was a picture so desig-nated painted some years ago, and engravings of it were frequently met with. One of these you may have seen, and the remembrance of it will help you to a conception of what the apostle dreaded. In that picture a gaunt figure with unshaven head and unkempt hair, badly clad and hunger-stricken, is seen seated on a raft in the midst of a raging rainy sea, sheltering his face with his arm from the blinding drift, straining his hollow eyes to descry a sail in the far distance. He is the very picture of unmitigated, hopeless, unpitied misery. He is not only alone in the universe, but the whole universe, so far as it is visible, seems to be against him. The sky frowns on him; the rain descends on his unsheltered head, the wind smites him; the sea dashes over, and threatens to engulf him; hungry monsters of the deep are waiting to make him their prey. There is no ear to hear his cry, no eye to witness his miserable and forlorn plight, no hand to help him, no haven near, no friendly star gleaming through the darkness to show him where he is. He is left alone of men, cast out by the world, persecuted by the elements. The only thing that befriends him is the raft to which he clings. Now to be a castaway in the spiritual sense is worse even than that—unspeakably worse. The word is fraught with all kinds of imaginable and unimaginable horrors. To be rejected by the universe of being, to be despised and spurned, to be expelled from any circle into which it is desirable to enter, to be disowned by all the good, tormented by all the bad, to see every door of hope closed, to find everything in the universe hostile, every force operating unfavourably, every object wearing a frown, no eye to pity, no hand to help, no ear to hear, no voice to utter one consoling word, no means of mitigating, no friendly raft even to bear up amidst the engulfing misery! What conception can be more horrible than that? 2. Paul was not only actuated by the desire to escape being a castaway, but also by the desire to gain a crown. "They do it," he says, of the competitors in the games, "to obtain a corruptible crown, but we an incorruptible." (*W. Landels, D.D.*)    *Law :*—As the chemist, the navigator, the naturalist attain their ends by means of law, which is beyond their power to alter, which they cannot change, but with which they can work in harmony, and by so doing produce definite results, so may we. (*Shorthouse, " John Inglesant."*)    *Obedience :*—If a boy at school is bidden to cipher, and chooses to write a copy instead, the goodness of the writing will not save him from censure. We must obey, whether we see the reason or not; for God knows best. (*New Cyclopædia of Illustrations.*)    *Conquest the condition of entrance into heaven :*—Many years ago the Turks and the Christians had a great battle, and the Christians were defeated, and with Stephen, their commander, they fled toward a fortress where the mother of the commander was staying. When the mother saw her son and his army flying in disgraceful retreat, she ordered the gates of the fortress to be closed against them, and the gates were closed, and then the mother stood on the battlement and cried to her son, " You cannot enter here except as a conqueror." Then the commander rallied his scattered troops, and resumed battle and won the day—twenty thousand scattering like flying chaff two hundred thousand. Ah! my friends, defeated in this battle with sin and death and hell, there is no joy, no reward, no triumph for you. Only shame and everlasting contempt. But for those who gained the victory through our Lord Jesus Christ the gates of the New Jerusalem are open, and you will have abundant entrance into the everlasting kingdom of our Lord. (*T. De Witt Talmage.*)    *Obedience and freedom :*—The truest freedom is secured by the most implicit obedience. Those who profess themselves free in the sense of being superior to law do but make themselves the slaves of sin. It is in the observance of rule that we find the fullest scope for the development of our individuality and the improvement and elevation of all our natural powers. They soar highest, and act with the greatest vigour, and move with the greatest freedom, who keep themselves most completely subject to the restraints of law. Loyalty elevates. We are ensnared and deteriorated when we follow our own caprice; for the liberty which is lawless is essentially degrading. The worlds describe their brilliant course over the dark brow of night because of the force which binds them to their great centre; let that force be destroyed, and they are free to rush whithersoever the centrifugal force propels. Their movement may be swifter than the lightning, and their track more dazzling than its path, but it will soon end in darkness and destruction. And so it is with the mind and the law of duty which binds it to God. The freedom which comes from the violation of that law is a freedom which, instead of securing its welfare and elevation, only lands it in deeper degradation and death. (*W. Landels, D.D.*)

Ver. 6. **The husbandman that laboureth must be first partaker of the fruits.** —*The labouring husbandman :*—The order of the Greek shows that the emphatic word is " labours." It is the labouring husbandman who must be the first to partake of the fruits. It is the man who works hard and with a will, and not the one who works listlessly or looks despondently on, who, according to all moral fitness and the nature of things, ought to have the first share in the fruits. This interpretation does justice to the Greek as it stands, without resorting to any manipulation of the apostle's language. Moreover, it brings the saying into perfect harmony with the context. It is quite evident that the three metaphors are parallel to one another, and are intended to teach the same lesson. In each of them we have two things placed side by side—a prize, and the method to be observed in obtaining it. Do you, as a Christian soldier on service, wish for the approbation of Him who has enrolled you. Then you must avoid the entanglements which would interfere with your service. Do you, as a Christian athlete, wish for the crown of victory? Then you must not evade the rules of the contest. Do you, as a Christian husbandman, wish to be among the first to enjoy the harvest? Then you must be foremost in toil. (*A. Plummer, D.D.*) *The minister a husbandman:*—1. He must prepare good seed—i.e., sound doctrine. For in this sense we may truly say: what a man soweth, he shall reap; such as thy seed is, such will be thy harvest. 2. Understand the nature of the soil, the spiritual estate of thy people, and let the seed be in degree and measure suitable. Seed that is hot and dry must be sown in a cold and moist ground; if cold and moist, in a land that is hot and dry, else no multiplication. He that preaches mercy to the wicked is like him who soweth wheat on dry sandy mountains; judgment to the righteous, rye in wet and watery valleys—neither of both will, can prosper. 3. Get skill in the manner of sowing. 4. When the seed is sown, weeds will grow up with it. These must be plucked up, kept under, else the corn will not prosper. 5. In any case, go not thou beyond thy bounds, but sow in that soil where God commands thee. That great seedsman, Paul, had ill success among the Jews, being chiefly sent to teach the Gentiles. 6. Cast not off thy calling; wax not weary in this husbandry; and to encourage thee, consider the excellency of thy function. The husbandman waiteth long; be thou also patient, for a time of gathering will come—shall come. (*J. Barlow, D.D.*) *What the Christian teacher can learn from the husbandman:*—1. No fruit without labour. 2. No labour without reward. (*Van Oosterzee.*) *The minister a husbandman:*—1. He must cultivate the people, and sow the good seed. 2. He must not be discouraged if he does not reap fruit at once. 3. As the fruits of the ground sustain the husbandman, so should the people sustain the minister. (*W. Burkitt, M.A.*) *Reward of work:*—A few years since, Motley shot up to the first position as an historian. Many wondered; but it was no wonder. He had wrought patiently for years in the libraries of the Old and New Worlds, unseen of men. The success of the great artist Doré was years of study in the hospitals, and practice in the studio behind it. This path to success is open to all. (*New Cyclopædia of Illustrations.*) *No work, no reward:*—Gilbert Wakefield tells us that he wrote his own memoirs, a large octavo, in six or eight days. It cost him nothing, and, what is very natural, is worth nothing. You might yawn scores of such books into existence; but who would be the wiser or better? We all like gold, but dread the digging. The cat loves the fish, but will not wade to catch them. (*J. Todd, D.D.*) *The pleasure of sloth inconsistent with the reward of toil:*—They are utterly out that think to have the pleasure of sloth and the guerdon of goodness. (*J. Trapp.*) *Work and joy:*—Work is heaven's condition of prosperity and enjoyment in everything. A workless world would be a joyless world. (*Homilist.*) *Partaking of the fruit:*—A young man came to a man of ninety years of age, and said to him, "How have you made out to live so long and be so well?" The old man took the youngster to an orchard, and, pointing to some large trees full of apples, said, "I planted these trees when I was a boy, and do you wonder that now I am permitted to gather the fruit of them?" We gather in old age what we plant in our youth. Sow to the wind, and we reap the whirlwind. Plant in early life the right kind of a Christian character, and you will eat luscious fruit in old age, and gather these harvest apples in eternity. *The present rewards of service:*—Of the husbandman it is said that he first shall eat of the fruit of his labour. Here we have an intimation of the rewards of Christian life that come before the final distribution. The soldier must wait until the war is over; the contestant shall not be crowned until the games are over; but the husbandman has continuous incomings of the fruits of his labours all the time. He first partakes of the fruit of his labour. The loaf on his table, the milk in his dairy, the fruit of his storehouse—these are kept plenished and plentiful all the time. Then comes harvest and autumn, with their laden garners and their orchard spoil. So it is with the rewards of the Christian. Let him be as a soldier brave, as contestant striving, as a husbandman diligent and thrifty, and he shall have the reward of his labours even now—in grace and favour, in strength and peace, in hope and heavenly mindedness, and in the joy of doing good. Plenty to go on with, and a harvest to follow—the fruits immortal, that await the plucking from the bending branches of the trees of life! (*J. J. Wray.*)

Ver. 7. **Consider what I say, and the Lord give thee understanding.**—*Reflection aids discernment :*—The better rendering gives, " For the Lord will give thee." This gives also a better meaning : " Make the effort to reflect ; for if thou do, the Lord will give thee the discernment which thou needest." (*E. H. Plumptre, D.D.*) *Enlightenment aids personal application of truth:*—De Wette and others object to this verse, that it is impossible to suppose that St. Paul would imagine Timotheus so dull of apprehension as not to comprehend such obvious metaphors. But they have missed the sense of the verse, which is not meant to enlighten the understanding of Timotheus as to the meaning of the metaphors, but as to the personal application of them. (*Conybeare and Howson.*)	*Consideration:*—I. CONSIDERATION IS A DUTY TO BE PRACTISED. 1. For hath not God given man a discoursive faculty ? What creature but he hath understanding, the angels only excepted ? Were it not vanity to have an eye, and close it ? an ear, and stop it ? a hand, and not move it ? And is it not wickedness to have a faculty of discourse and not employ it ? And wherein better than in consideration ? 2. The life of man differs little from a beast without consideration ? This soundly lessons those that approve of it but never practise it. Will you hear how they excuse, clear themselves ? (1) It is a difficult duty. Grant it be so, what then ? Is it to be rejected ? But what hard things dost thou use for the love of this world ? Take thou the like pains in this profitable action. (2) But I want time. Wonderful! Did God ever command a duty and allow no time to effect it ? What! None to consider? to confer with thy Father ? Lay thy hand upon thy mouth—say no more ; for, for what end is the Sabbath ? (3) I have no convenient place. Imitate David, commune with thyself in bed. But my children cry. Then with Isaac, to the field; Hannah, to the Temple ; or get thee to some garden, solitary mount, as did thy Master. (4) I cannot bring my mind to it. Is it so with thee as thou sayest ? Be the more humbled for it, and make that matter of consideration. Set thou thyself about this necessary duty; it shall recompense all thy painstaking. And—(*a*) Wouldst thou love God ? Then consider how He hath chosen thee, redeemed thee, given thee a being in these glorious days of the gospel, conferred on thee many earthly favours. Consider the many sins He hath pardoned, prevented ; the evils spiritual, corporal, He hath removed ; the petitions He hath granted ; and of what great things thou art assured. (*b*) Is thy faith feeble ? Consider the depth of God's mercy, the firmness of His promise, the might of His power, the unchangeableness of His nature. Shall not these relieve thee ? (*c*) Art thou impatient ? Do afflictions overlade thee ? Consider the greatness of thy sins, whereby thou hast deserved far worse evils. Think, and think often, that they come from the hand of thy heavenly Father; how He hath an eye to thy weakness, that they shall not exceed thy ability; and at their departure, like an overflowing river's rich mud, leave a blessing behind them. (*d*) And what external action can, without consideration, be well discharged? Did magistrates take up their minds, exercise themselves in this duty, would it not make them resolute for the execution of their function? (*e*) Can ministers preach and neglect this action ? (*f*) Why do men hear much, understand little, and practise nothing? It is want of consideration. The most run to God's house, as travellers to an inn, hear the Word as some well-told tale, not knowing, like that rude company, for what end they came together. (*g*) In a word, consideration will give us matter of prayer, and kindle the little spark of grace within us, put us in mind of our vow in baptism, and provoke us to perform it—yea, all our promises. II. GOD'S WORD IS TO BE CONSIDERED. 1. For the Author's sake. Is it not the Book of God? 2. And is not the matter holy, just, good ? 3. What admirable effects will it work ? David hereby became wiser than his teachers—a man according to God's own heart. III. EXHORTATION IS TO BE SECONDED WITH PRAYER. IV. GOD GIVETH MAN UNDERSTANDING. V. MEN OF MUCH KNOWLEDGE MAY BETTER THEIR UNDERSTANDING. Knowledge in a threefold respect may be increased—1. In the faculty. 2. In the object. 3. In the medium of it. VI. IN ALL DIVINE TRUTHS WE ARE TO HAVE UNDERSTANDING. Had not Moses a pattern of the Tabernacle—to a broom, a snuffer, a curtain-ring ? Shall we, then, be ignorant of any one principle in the whole frame of religion ? (*J. Barlow, D.D.*)	*On hearing the Word :*—I. SHOW IN WHAT MANNER WE ARE TO HEAR THE WORD. 1. Consider well the matter or import of what is spoken.

2. Attend to the truth and propriety of what is delivered. 3. Consider the weight and importance of what is delivered. 4. Consider the personal concern you have in the truths delivered. II. THE MOTIVES WHICH SHOULD INDUCE US WELL TO CONSIDER WHAT WE HEAR. 1. Think in whose Name the ministers of the gospel speak, and whose Person they represent. 2. Consider the great end they aim at in their ministrations. 3. By the Word that we hear we shall be judged at the last day. (*B. Beddome, M.A.*)    *The young invited to consider :*—I. I begin by calling your attention to a thought which you should never have wholly absent from your minds— namely, FOR WHAT PURPOSE HAS LIFE BEEN GIVEN YOU? For what other purpose than to prepare for eternity, by loving and serving your Creator now, that you may serve and enjoy Him for ever? II. From this thought, then, which I beg you seriously to lay to heart, consider WHAT PROVISION GOD HAS MADE FOR YOUR ATTAINING THIS GLORIOUS END OF YOUR BEING. III. And this introduces another thought of vast importance. "Consider," then, "what I say," as to THE FITTING PERIOD FOR MAKING THIS SURRENDER OF YOURSELVES TO GOD. When should it be done? Our answer is, it cannot be done too early. IV. Consider THE HAPPINESS OF A LIFE THUS EARLY GIVEN TO GOD, to be spent in His service, to end in His glory. (*J. Haslegrave, M.A.*) *Consideration :*—Consideration is the bed where the incorruptible seed is sown, and on the ground thus prepared the Sun of Righteousness doth shine, and by His warmth produces in the soul all manner of pleasant fruits. (*Anthony Horneck.*) *Men need instruction :* — A man's understanding is very much like a window. The sun-light is all of one colour; but all the light that goes through the window is not. Sometimes the audience have a scarf of yellow running over them, sometimes one of blue, and sometimes one of red, according as the window is painted. Man's reason being like a painted window, the light that goes through it and falls upon his conscience is bizarre, grotesque, wrinkled, bent, or distorted. I have known men whose understanding had in it hideous saints, crowned monsters, apocalyptic visions, and what not—things that took the colours which were painted on the window of that reason. It is very important, therefore, that men should be instructed. (*H. W. Beecher.*)    *God's teaching :*—When the Prince of Wales landed at Portsmouth, after his tour in India, I was in the crowd with my little boys; and as the Prince and his Princess and children drove past, I lifted my younger boy on my shoulder, and this enabled him to see better and further than the tallest person around us. So those whom God teaches and helps will discern better and further than those who just look out for themselves, or merely get information from others. (*H. R. Burton.*)    *Instruction from God :*—When a sceptic once went to a Christian minister to have his doubts and difficulties solved, the minister asked, "Have you gone and asked God, the fountain of light and the source of all wisdom, for the solution of your difficulties?" On the perplexed man's replying he had not, the minister declined to try and assist him out of his perplexities till he had attended to this necessary and important duty. When we ask wisdom as well as light and instruction from God, He will give us mental and spiritual capacities, to prepare us for rightly apprehending truths; and He will also give us sufficient opportunities for gaining wisdom, and then aid and prosper us in our effort to acquire it. Wisdom is to knowledge like what the engineer is to the locomotive—a director, a controller, and a manager. Religion is the highest wisdom of all. (See Prov. iv. 7; Deut. xxxii. 29; Psa. xc. 12; Prov. ii. 6; James i. 5.) (*Ibid.*)    *Thinking of Christ :*—Dr. Cullis tells, in one of his reports, of an aged Christian who, lying on his death-bed in the Consumptives' Home, was asked the cause of his perfect peace, in a state of such extreme weakness that he was often entirely unconscious of all around him. He replied, "When I am able to think, I think of Jesus; and when I am unable to think of Him, I know He is thinking of me."    *Remembrance of Christ :*—There is no Christianity where there is no loving remembrance of Christ. If your contact with Him has not made Him your friend, whom you can by no possibility forget, you have missed the best result of your introduction to Him. It makes one think meanly of the chief butler that such a personality as Joseph's had not more deeply impressed him—that everything he heard and saw among the courtiers did not make him say to himself: There is a friend of mine in the prison hard by, that for beauty, wisdom, and vivacity would more than match the finest of you all. And it says very little for us if we can have known anything of Christ without seeing that in Him we have what is nowhere else, and without finding that He has become the necessity of our life, to whom we turn at every point. (*Marcus Dods, D.D.*)

**Ver. 8. Remember that Jesus Christ, of the seed of David, was raised from the dead.**
—"Bear in mind," the connection seems to be. But, with all its toils and sufferings, the gospel has also its stores of abounding consolation. The remembrance of the risen and victorious Saviour is the comfort and support of His ministers. (*Speaker's Commentary.*) *Remember Jesus Christ :*—Every Christian who has to endure what seems to him to be hardships will sooner or later fall back upon this remembrance. He is not the first and not the chief sufferer in the world. There is One who has undergone hardships, compared with which those of other men sink into nothingness ; and who has expressly told those who wish to be His disciples that they must follow Him along the path of suffering. But merely to remember Jesus Christ as a Master who has suffered and who has made suffering a condition of service will not be a permanently sustaining or comforting thought if it ends there. Therefore St. Paul says to his perplexed and desponding delegate, "Remember Jesus Christ as one *risen from the dead.*" Jesus Christ has not only endured every kind of suffering, including its extreme form, death, but He has conquered it all by rising again. Everywhere experience seems to teach us that evil of every kind—physical, intellectual, and moral—holds the field and appears likely to hold it. To allow one's self to be mastered by this thought is to be on the road to doubting God's moral government of the world. What is the antidote to it? "Remember Jesus Christ as one risen from the dead." When has evil ever been so completely triumphant over good as when it succeeded in getting the Prophet of Nazareth nailed to the tree, like some vile and noxious animal? That was the hour of success for the malignant Jewish hierarchy and for the spiritual powers of darkness. But it was an hour to which very strict limits were placed. Very soon He who had been dismissed to the grave by a cruel and shameful death, defeated, and disgraced, rose again from it triumphant, not over Jewish priests and Roman soldiers, but over death and the cause of death ; that is, over every kind of evil—pain and ignorance and sin. But to "remember Jesus Christ as one risen from the dead" does more than this. It not only shows us that the evil against which we have such a weary struggle in this life, both in others and in ourselves, is not (in spite of depressing appearances) permanently triumphant; it also assures us that there is another and a better life in which the good cause will be supreme, and supreme without the possibility of disaster, or even of contest. What the Son of Man has done, other sons of men can do and will do. The solidarity between the human race and the Second Adam, between the Church and its Head, is such that the victory of the Leader carries with it the victory of the whole band. Once more, to "remember Jesus Christ as one risen from the dead" is to remember One who claimed to be the promised Saviour of the world and who *proved His claim*. And this leads St. Paul on to the second point which his downcast disciple is to remember in connection with Jesus Christ. He is to remember Him as "of the seed of David." He is not only truly God but truly Man. The Resurrection and the Incarnation—those are the two facts on which a faltering minister of the gospel is to hold fast, in order to comfort his heart and strengthen his steps. This is the meaning of "according to my gospel." These are the truths which St. Paul has habitually preached, and of the value of which he can speak from full experience. He knows what he is talking about, when he affirms that these things are worth remembering when one is in trouble. The Resurrection and the Incarnation are facts on which he has ceaselessly insisted, because in the wear and tear of life he has found out their worth. (*A. Plummer, D.D.*) *Our Lord's resurrection :*—The high value which the apostle attributes to the bodily resurrection of the Lord, here and in other passages, is, in a remarkable way, in contrast with the spiritualistic and indifferentistic evaporisation of this chief article of the gospel, on the side of the modern speculative rationalism of our days. (*Van Oosterzee.*) *Remembrance :*—I. DIVINE TRUTHS ARE TO BE REMEMBERED. II. REMEMBERING IS A REFLECTING OF THE EYE OF OUR MIND ON THAT WHICH BY THE SENSES OR THE UNDERSTANDING HATH BEEN PERCEIVED. In remembrance are four things to be considered. 1. The apprehension of an object by the external or internal senses. 2. A reposing of it in the memory. 3. A retaining of it there. 4. A reflecting of the eye of the understanding on it. This last act is properly called remembrance. Helps follow. 1. Get a true understanding of things. 2. Meditate much on that thou wouldst remember. Roll the thing to and fro in thy mind, look often at it, mark it well; so shall it, like a bird by struggling in the gin or lime bush, stick faster. 3. Labour for love. Will a maid forget her ornament? a bride her attire? the covetous man his coin, hid long ago in some secret corner? Wherefore, love the Word once, and then forget it if thou

canst. 4. Be jealous of thy remembrance. He who carrieth a vessel in his hand may suddenly let it fall; whereas had he feared he would have held it faster. For jealousy, though a bad getter, is an excellent keeper. 5. Use repetition. Have that oft in thy tongue thou wouldst hold in thy mind. For repetition, like a mallet, will cause the piles of Divine truths to stick fast in the soil of man's memory. 6. Study for method. Things in order laid in the head will with the more facility be held. Method (say some) is the mother of memory. III. THE CHOICEST OF DIVINE TRUTHS ARE CHIEFLY TO BE REMEMBERED. Have thy senses exercised, through long custom, to discern betwixt things that differ—good and evil. (*J. Barlow, D.D.*) *An appeal to the pattern* :—In the words preceding this text the apostle Paul has been speaking of the labour and conflict and endurance involved in a true profession of faith in Christ. And now that he has on hand to prove the necessity of enduring hardness in Christian life, he is ready with example as well as argument. "Remember that Jesus Christ, of the seed of David, was raised from the dead, according to my gospel." But there is more in these words than a mere confirmation of what has gone before. They are a fresh battery brought up to the siege, adapted especially for an assault upon that strong citadel, the human will. But we have not yet got to the bottom of the apostle's meaning. If we have yielded to the influence of his words they have carried our hearts beyond the subject they were first intended to illustrate. His theme was the endurance of hardship, and his object to brace up the soul of a fellow disciple to this trial; but, in doing so, by the example of the Master Himself, he has done more; for he has reminded Timothy that Jesus Christ not only suffered, but died; and as elsewhere and often he has taught the necessity of our dying by union with Christ, he surely means no less than to put us face to face with the truth in the present passage. Christianity is the masterpiece of God, the wonderful fabric into which He has woven all Divine and eternal principles; and there is no principle or characteristic of Christianity more plain or more abundantly illustrated than the appointment and use of death for the production of a higher life than that which preceded it. It would be strange, indeed, if man, whose peculiar honour it is to be " called into the fellowship of God's Son," were an exception to this rule of death and life; or if, in his case, it were only to be known by the dissolution of his earthly body. But Scripture teaches otherwise. Christ has not merely given His life a ransom for ours. He has done this, indeed, and this is the great news of the gospel; but He has done more. He has put Himself at the head of an army which must conquer as He conquered when alone—by suffering. And thus only can we understand His words, " If any man serve Me let him follow Me ! " " He that taketh not up his cross and followeth not after Me cannot be My disciple" ; " He that loveth his life shall lose it, but he that loseth his life for My sake the same shall find it." (*J. F. B. Tinling, B.A.*)   *Remember Jesus Christ* :—We know how one recollection, distinct and dominant in the mind, has often been the decisive force at a critical moment; how upon the battlefield, for instance, or under the almost overpowering pressure of temptation, the thought of a man's country, of his home, of his ancestral traditions, has reinforced, as with a fresh tide of strength, his faltering heart, and borne him on to victory, whether by success or death. We may recall the scene in one of our African campaigns, the scene preserved for us by a clever artist, where the thought of a man's old school, and the boyish eagerness anyhow to bring it to the front, was the impulse of a splendid courage. Yes, there are images in most men's minds which, if they rise at the right moment, will do much to make them heroes; a word, a glance, some well-known sight, some old familiar strain of music, may beckon the image out of the recesses of the memory, and if the man has in him the capacity of generous action he will use it then. It is on this characteristic of human nature that St. Paul relies as he writes to Timotheus the words of the text. He would avail himself of this; he would raise it to its highest conceivable employment; he would enlist it as a constant, ready, powerful ally on the side of duty—on the side of God. He may never see Timotheus, never write to him again; well then, he will leave dinted into his mind, by a few incisive words, one commanding and sustaining Image. For it is not, as it appears in our English version, an event of the past, however supreme in its importance, however abiding in its results, that St. Paul here fastens upon the memory of his disciple; it is not the abstract statement of a truth in history or theology, however central to the faith, however vast in its consequences; it is a living Person, whom St. Paul has seen, whose form he would have Timotheus keep ever in his mind, distinct, beloved, unrivalled, sovereign—" Bear in remembrance Jesus Christ, raised from the dead." Let us take two thoughts this Easter morning from the counsel which St. Paul thus gives. First, that he is trying to lodge at the heart of Timotheus's life and work that which has been the deepest and most effective force in his own. St. Paul was convinced that he had seen the risen Lord; and the energy, the effect, of that unfading Image throughout his subsequent life might go some way to prove that the conviction was true. Physical weight is sometimes measured by the power of displacement; and in the moral and spiritual sphere we tend, at least, to think that there must be something solid and real to account for a change so unexpected, so unworldly, so thorough, so sustained through every trial, so vast in its practical outcome, as was the conversion of St. Paul. Let St. Paul's conviction be taken in its context; let justice be done to the character it wrought in him; to the coherence and splendour of the work it animated; to the penetrating, sober insight of his practical teaching; to the consistency, not of expression, but of inmost thought and life, which is disclosed to any careful study of his writings; lastly, to the grasp which his words have laid upon the strongest minds in Christendom through all succeeding centuries, the prophetic and undying power which, amidst vast changes of methods and ideas, men widely different have felt and reverenced in these Epistles—let these distinctive notes of St. Paul's work be realised, together with its incalculable outcome in the course of history, and it will seem hard to think that the central, ruling impulse of it all was the obstinate blunder of a disordered mind. This, at least, I think, may be affirmed, that, if there were against belief in Christ's resurrection any such difficulty as the indisputable facts of St. Paul's life and work present to disbelief, we should find it treated as of crucial importance, and that, I think, not unjustly. "Bear in remembrance Jesus Christ raised from the dead." It is the form which has made him what he is, for life or for death, that St. Paul would with his last words, it may be, leave clenched for ever on the mind and heart of his disciple. The vision of that form may keep him true and steadfast when all is dark, confused, and terrible around him. May not we do well to take the bidding to ourselves? There are signs of trouble and confusion in the air, and some faint hearts begin to fail; and some of us, perhaps, "see not our tokens"—so clearly as we did. But One we may see, as we lift our eyes this Easter Day; it is He who liveth and was dead; and behold He is alive for evermore; He who cannot fail His Church, or leave even the poorest and least worthy of His servants desolate and bewildered when the darkness gathers, and the cry of need goes up. (*F. Paget, D.D.*) *The testimony of St. Paul:*—St. Paul was a man who could have been trusted beyond perhaps any other man of his time to take a calm, clear, and accurate view of any alleged historical fact, and to estimate its practical bearings; and if, after the whole evidence for the Resurrection had been brought to bear upon his mind, he felt himself constrained to believe and proclaim it to the dire extremity of martyrdom—that fact becomes the strongest possible evidence for its truth. The testimony of St. Paul to the truth of the Resurrection has a double value. In the first place there is his personal witness, "Last of all He was seen of me also, as of one born out of due time." It is allowed on all hands that Paul at any rate asserted simply what he believed to be the truth. It is, in the judgment of his hostile critics, a case of hallucination, not of wilful perversion of the truth. Well, men are subject to hallucinations, no doubt, especially men of genius. But the world, the hard rough world, is a great dispeller of hallucinations. No man lives and works through a long and intensely active life as the victim of hallucination: either it vanishes and leaves him in free possession of all his faculties, or it makes him incapable of taking part in any real purpose in the business of his fellow-men. It must be remembered that this statement of Paul does not stand alone. It is in harmony with many appearances of Christ after the Resurrection, which rest on the incontestable evidence of numerous disciples; and it seemed real enough to make a vital change in the character, the beliefs, the aims, the life-work of one of the very ablest, most self-controlled, most masterly men whom we meet with in the records of universal history. But there is a second point of view from which the testimony of St. Paul to the truth of the Resurrection is so deeply important. It is the testimony of one who had mastered the whole argument in its favour, and who believed it to be irresistible. We cannot examine the witnesses, and sift their evidence; all the details are beyond our reach for ever; but we have the proofs sifted for us, weighed and stamped as valid beyond shadow of doubt or question by the regal intellect of St. Paul. His evidence has, however, a value beyond this, to which I must call your attention before I close. St. Paul not only was not a disciple, but he had been the most bitter and uncompromising enemy of the truth. Nor had he been a silent opponent. Though but a youth, by his brilliant powers he had already made for himself a name of renown among his countrymen. He was the coming leader of the people, the rising man, on whom the hopes of the elders were set as the future champion of the oppressed nation in the perilous times which were manifestly coming on the world. I have said that the evidence is the evidence of disciples. I have explained how that is its strength and its glory. But one longs sometimes to know what was actually said in the Sanhedrim and in chief-priestly circles against it. We have no contemporary record of this ; if any was written, no note of it has reached us, but St. Paul stands forth to supply the want. His is a voice out of the hostile camp, confessing that the opposition was in hopeless collapse. The fact that a man of such keen and eager intellect, who left no objection unanswered, no nook of argument unexplored, never condescends in any of his writings to notice the counter statements of opponents, is proof absolute that there was no validity in them. They evidently had left on his mind not a shadow of question, and brought forward nothing which it was worth his while to trouble himself to refute. Then, having borne his witness life-long to the Resurrection, he died with the testimony on his lips. (*J. B. Brown, B.A.*) *The resurrection of our Lord Jesus :*—I. Let us CONSIDER THE BEARINGS OF THE FACT THAT JESUS ROSE FROM THE DEAD. 1. It is clear at the outset that the resurrection of our Lord was a tangible proof that there is another life. Have you not quoted a great many times certain lines about " That undiscovered country from whose bourne no traveller returns " ? It is not so. There was once a Traveller who said, " I go to prepare a place for you, and if I go away I will come again and receive you unto Myself ; that where I am there ye may be also." He said, " A little time, and ye shall see Me, and again a little time and ye shall not see Me, because I go to the Father." His return from among the dead is a pledge to us of existence after death, and we rejoice in it. His resurrection is also a pledge that the body will surely live again and rise to a superior condition ; for the body of our blessed Master was no phantom after death any more than before. 2. Christ's rising from the dead was the seal to all His claims. It was true, then, that He was sent of God, for God raised Him from the dead in confirmation of His mission. The rising of Christ from the dead proved that this man was innocent of every sin. He could not be holden by the bands of death, for there was no sin to make those bands fast. Moreover, Christ's rising from the dead proved His claim to Deity. We are told in another place that He was proved to be the Son of God with power by the resurrection from the dead. 3. The resurrection of our Lord, according to Scripture, was the acceptance of His sacrifice. 4. It was a guarantee of His people's resurrection. 5. Once more, our Lord's rising from the dead is a fair picture of the new life which all believers already enjoy. There is within us already a part of the resurrection accomplished, since it is written, " And you hath He quickened who were dead in trespasses and sins." Now, just as Christ led, after His resurrection, a life very different from that before His death, so you and I are called upon to live a high and noble spiritual and heavenly life, seeing that we have been raised from the dead to die no more. II. LET US CONSIDER THE BEARINGS OF THIS FACT UPON THE GOSPEL ; for Paul says, " Jesus Christ was raised from the dead according to my gospel." 1. The resurrection of Christ is vital, because first it tells us that the gospel is the gospel of a living Saviour. We have not to send poor penitents to the crucifix, the dead image of a dead man. Notice next that we have a powerful Saviour in connection with the gospel that we preach ; for He who had power to raise Himself from the dead has all power now that He is raised. 2. And now notice that we have the gospel of complete justification to preach to you. 3. Once again, the connection of the Resurrection and the gospel is this : it proves the safety of the saints, for if when Christ rose His people rose also, they rose to a life like that of their Lord, and therefore they can never die. I cannot stop to show you how this resurrection touches the gospel at every point, but Paul is always full of it. More than thirty times Paul talks about the resurrection, and occasionally at great length, giving whole chapters to the glorious theme. III. THE BEARING OF THIS RESURRECTION UPON OURSELVES. Paul expressly bids us " remember " it. Now, if you will remember that Jesus Christ of the seed of David rose from the dead, what will follow ? 1. You will find that most of your trials will vanish. Are you tried by your sin ? Jesus Christ rose again from the dead for your justification. Does Satan accuse ? Jesus rose to be your advocate and intercessor. Do infirmities hinder ? The living Christ will show Himself strong on your behalf. You have a living Christ, and in Him you have all things. Do you dread death ? Jesus, in rising again, has vanquished the last enemy. 2. Next remember Jesus, for then you will see how your present sufferings are as nothing compared with His sufferings, and you will learn to expect victory over your sufferings even as He obtained victory. 3. We see here, in being told to remember Jesus, that there is hope even in our hopelessness. When are things most hopeless in a man ? Why, when he is dead. Do you know what it is to come down to that, so far as your inward weakness is concerned ? You that are near despair, let this be the strength that nerves your arm and steels your heart, " Jesus Christ of the seed of David was raised from the dead according to Paul's gospel." 4. Lastly, this proves the futility of all opposition to Christ. (C. H. Spurgeon.) The resurrection of Christ:—I. I would first say a few words on THE FACT OF THE RESURRECTION. It is a main point in our faith. The resurrection of Jesus Christ is a pledge of ours. II. I would next direct your attention to THE POSITION OF THE BELIEVER IN THIS LIFE. As connected with the risen Saviour, the believer is regarded in the Word of God as " risen with Christ." We see, then, that Paul would stir Timothy by our text to remember his privileges. He would, in effect, say to him, " Timothy, remember you have the life of Christ now ; and it is His risen life which is to animate you to work and to suffer, and to ' endure hardness as a good soldier of Jesus Christ.' " III. But there is another point to which I would direct your attention, and that is, UNION. It is most important to observe that this oneness of life between Jesus and the believer is just that which constitutes union. Nothing short of this is union. It is the resurrection life of Jesus that believers are united with ; and this is possible only to the " new creature," only to the " man in Christ." We see, then, a little, I trust, of the force of the text. It is a wonderful text, and we see the power there is in it to comfort the believer and to strengthen him for service ; and just as he understands in his own experience these things will he realise his privileges. In Jesus Christ he will see how the doctrine of the resurrection is calculated to make him " endure hardness." (J. W. Reeve, M.A.) The resurrection of Christ:—I desire to speak to you on the importance of connecting the fact of the Saviour's resurrection with two other facts, namely, first, that Christ was of the seed of David, and secondly, that the resurrection of Christ is so essential a part of the gospel of Christ that the one may be described as according with the other. There can be no dispute that it could not be needful for St. Paul to characterise Jesus as of the seed of David, in order to distinguish Him from any other being whom the name might recall to the mind of Timothy. I deny, therefore, altogether, that there is anything whatsoever of the fanciful or the far-fetched in our ascribing any particular emphasis to this casual introduction of the human lineage of Messiah. I look on the name of Jesus, and its every syllable seems to burn and blaze with divinity. I may explain and interpret it ; I may expound it as promising salvation, as eloquent of deliverance to our fallen race ; but in exact proportion as I magnify the wonder, I remove, as it were, the being unto whom it belongs from all kindred and companionship with the sinful tenantry of a ruined creation. The title of anointed Saviour, full though it be of magnificent mercy, consisting of attributes and principles bearing the impress of a superhuman greatness ; and, however stupendous the truth, that Deity has interposed on behalf of the helpless, still the Saviour of man must be one who could hold communion and fellowship with man ; He must not be separated from him by the appalling attributes which mark a Divine Creator. If there must be a celestial nature to afford the succour, there must also be a terrestrial nature to ensure the sympathy. Hence, I think it just to imagine that when the apostle sent to a beloved disciple this short compendium of Christian consolation, which he desired might be carefully borne in mind, he would not fail to interweave into such compendium a distinct reference to the complex nature of the Redeemer's person ; and, not content himself with referring him to Jesus Christ, he would add some such description as this—" of the seed of David," in order to mark His real humanity. There is, however, a distinct allusion to other truths, as well as to the Redeemer's humanity, in this accurate specification. It is a wonderful thing to cast one's eye over the prophetic pages and behold how years past and years that are to come do alike burn with the deeds and triumphs of David's Son, under the name and title of a descendant from the man after God's own heart. It concerns not my argument to examine into the reasons which might induce the frequent introduction of the name of David whenever the triumphs of Messiah are the subject of discourse. I appeal simply to the fact, and demand of every student of Holy Writ whether there be any title under which prophecy tenders so vast a revenue of honour as it does to the seed, or heir, or antitype of David. Truly, the more the mind ponders over the combination of ideas which are gathered into this apparently brief and superfluous message of Paul to Timothy, the more will it be struck with the beauty and consolation it conveys.  Now, I have dealt at sufficient length on the first head of discourse ; and much that I have advanced in illustration of the importance of the clause, "of the seed of David," applies equally to the other, "according to my gospel," which I would, in the second place, exhibit to you, as giving strength and emphasis to St. Paul's commemoration of the death and resurrection of our Saviour.  You remember the strong terms in which St. Paul, when writing to the Corinthians, states the importance of the resurrection as an article of the Christian faith.  He may be said to resolve the whole of our religion, all its truth, all its value, all its beauty, into the one fact that Christ Jesus had been raised from the dead.  "If Christ be not raised"—thus it is he speaks— "your faith is in vain ; you are yet in your sins : then they also which are fallen asleep in Christ are perished."  By stating the fact that life and immortality have been brought to light by the gospel, to which I suppose St. Paul to allude when he speaks of Christ Jesus as "raised from the dead according to my gospel," I suppose him designing to remind his son Timothy, not so much of the simple truth of the Saviour's resurrection as of the colouring and character which this event gave to the whole system of Christianity.  (*H. Melvill, B.D.*)     *The place of the resurrection of Jesus in the theology of the New Testament :*—The resurrection was far more than any mere sign, though so unique and remarkable.  Like the miracles of Christ, only in a still profounder measure, it was in itself a display of mercy—an instrument of His mighty and beneficent mediation.  When the apostles taught it they not only bore witness, but they preached a "gospel"; they not only announced a wonderful fact, but they presented that fact to men as in itself at the same time a measure of Divine grace.  Apart from the resurrection of Christ you could not construct the faith, impart the solace, urge the appeal, or sway the inspiration of Christianity.  It is not simply that there would be no sign, but there would be no power.  It is, so to speak, the blood "which is the life," the blood that circulates through every vein to every limb and member of the Christian system.  This is the fact I want to impress in my present discourse.  Perhaps it will surprise you to hear my full belief that, but for the resurrection, you would have had in your hands no such exposition as you now possess of who and what Christ was and did for men.  Christ Himself did not write any book about His life ; not a line.  How, then, came we to know what we do about Him ?  Right down to the end of His life, to the end of the Gospels, the disciples remained strangely ignorant of the great work their Master came to achieve.  Dull, ignorant, confused, bewildered, they were the last men in the world to take up a forlorn cause, redeem it, and carry it to triumph.  Contrast with this state of mind the speech and conduct of those self-same men in the stirring scenes with which the Acts acquaint us.  You may search all literature, I believe, and you will not find a greater contrast.  How did this happen ?  The only book that gives the history lets us into the secret.  I claim, then, on the authority of this only history, to say that but for the resurrection of Jesus we had had no portraiture of Christ, no Gospels, no Acts, no Epistles, setting Him forth to the world for its salvation and joy.  No other writers of the age have depicted Him ; and these who have all refer their knowledge and appreciation to the illumination of that Spirit whom He sent on His exaltation to heaven.  Again.  It is the constant representation of the writers of the New Testament that Christ offered Himself in some way as a sacrifice for sin, and that that offering was presented in His death.  But what had that sacrifice been without Christ's revival from death ?  With the greatest force does the letter to the Romans teach us, "He was delivered for our offences, and raised again for our justification."  Paul does not hesitate to declare that apart from it there is no pardon : "If Christ be not raised, your faith is vain ; ye are yet in your sins."  Another point of our "precious faith" at which the resurrection of Christ meets us with infinite power and solace is seen at death, when we bury our dead out of sight, or are ourselves laid in the grave.  "For if we believe that Jesus died and rose again, even so them also which sleep in Jesus will God bring with Him."  None of the apostles had a higher standard of the Christian life than the Apostle Paul ; none more keenly realised its contrast with the former habits of sin, or more acutely felt the struggle, fierce and constant, by which it alone was to be attained and maintained ; none more clearly perceived the organic relation of one part of that life to another ; and Paul strove by a most beautiful and expressive image to urge the believer to all vigilance and mortification of unworthy impulse and passion in its culture.  Christ's death and resurrection furnished the image.  "We are buried with Him by baptism into death ; that like as Christ was raised from the dead by the glory of the Father, even so we also should walk in newness of life," &c. If Christ be not risen from the dead, the day of judgment, as solemnly delineated in the New Testament, is denuded of many of its most sublime and thrilling features. There is no judgment-seat of Christ; for though Christ has died, He has not risen and revived that He might be Lord both of the dead and the living. Neither, for the same reason, can we look for His appearing, or expect Him from heaven, since He is not gone thither. I should have to quote a vast number of passages from all the great sections of the New Testament Scriptures were I to set forth the claims, according to their teaching, of the Lord Jesus on our worship, His power and readiness to hear our prayers and satisfy our trust. But these are obviously of no authority and service to us if He did not rise from the grave. The writer to the Hebrews has repeatedly described Him as seated at the right hand of God, but of course he is mistaken; Christ is in the grave. He has imputed illimitable efficiency to His intercession. But he is mistaken; Christ is not capable of making any intercession at all. Believers are designated by Paul as those who call upon the name of the Lord Jesus Christ; but they were all deluded, for Christ was not risen nor ascended. Nor would the example of Christ as an all-perfect pattern of holiness and love in a world governed by infinite holiness and power occasion us less hopeless embarrassment, if He be not risen, than the facts just dismissed. We should, in that case, have the frightful spectacle of a righteousness, truth, goodness, and mercy that never faltered or failed expending themselves to the very uttermost, and this without Divine acknowledgment and vindication. A greater shock to all virtue could not be conceived. And in this instance it would be aggravated by the very measure with which this Great Exemplar had indulged the hope of reward. The resurrection stands to us a pledge and pattern of our own; and while our dust may await its final recovery, our spirits shall be with Him. Nay, He will even be our convoy through the gates of death, and then receive us into the mansions of His Father's house, that where He is we may be also. (*G. B. Johnson.*) *My gospel :*—The apostle is not contrasting his gospel with that of other preachers, as if he would say, "Others may teach what they please, but this is the substance of *my* gospel"; and Jerome is certainly mistaken if what is quoted as a remark of his is rightly assigned to him by Fabricius, to the effect that whenever St. Paul says "according to my gospel" he means the written gospel of his companion St. Luke, who had caught much of his spirit and something of his language. It would be much nearer the truth to say that St. Paul never refers to a written gospel. In every one of the passages in which the phrase occurs the context is quite against any such interpretation (Rom. ii. 16, xvi. 25; *cf.* 1 Tim. i. 11). In this place the words which follow are conclusive: "Wherein I suffer hardship unto bonds, as a malefactor." How could he be said to suffer hardship unto bonds in the Gospel of St. Luke? (*A. Plummer, D.D.*) *Each man has his own conception of the gospel :*—We may be sure, then, that the phrase "my gospel" is not used by St. Paul in the spirit either of the Pharisee or of the bigot. He is not one who refuses to recognise the excellence in those who may not exactly agree with him, or assumes that to him alone is committed a trustworthy form of the faith. Nevertheless, the phrase has a distinct force of its own. It suggests that St. Paul looked at the gospel from his own standpoint, and that the gospel as he represented it had aspects differing somewhat from the same gospel as represented by others. We need not be afraid to admit this. If you look at any great mountain from several points of view, its parts are at once brought into varying relations to each other. Standing here you see clearly great peaks, which from another position would be hidden. Nay, if you look at the same mountain from the same standpoint at different times, it will present different aspects—now dim and mysterious in the grey morning, and now rosy with the after-glow when the sun has set. Yet it is the same mountain, presenting itself in varying guise to different spectators. So with St. Paul. When he speaks of "my gospel," it is not another gospel in the sense of being contradictory, or even deficient as compared with the gospel proclaimed by other apostles. It is the same gospel, seen, however, from his own standpoint—"the gospel according to Paul." (*T. B. Stephenson, D.D.*) *The unity underlying the various conceptions of the gospel :*—The West Indies are a long chain of islands, seeming to be widely and completely separated from each other, each one a lovely jewel resting on the heaving bosom of the sea. But if you look below the surface of the ocean you discover that each of these islands is bound to all the others; that they are, in fact, the topmost points of one long mountain chain which has been submerged. So that whilst each island seems to be separate, all rest upon and are a part of the vast and substantial unity which lies far below.

"My gospel": each one of the Churches may correctly use the phrase, yet these are not many gospels, but in essence and substance one.

Ver 9. **Wherein I suffer trouble, as an evil doer, even unto bonds; but the Word of God is not bound.**—"*The Word of God is not bound*":—The apostle is imprisoned, but his tongue and his companion's pen are free. He can still teach those who come to him; can still dictate letters for others to Luke and the faithful few who visit him. He has been able to influence those whom, but for his imprisonment, he would never have had an opportunity of reaching—Roman soldiers, and warders, and officials, and all who have to take cognisance of his trial before the imperial tribunal. "The Word of God is not bound." While he is in prison Timothy and Titus and scores of other evangelists and preachers are free. Those who are left at large ought to labour all the more energetically and enthusiastically in order to supply whatever is lost by the apostle's want of freedom, and in order to convince the world that this is no contest with a human organisation, or with human opinion, but with a Divine word and a Divine Person. "The Word of God is not bound," because His Word is the truth, and it is the truth that makes men free. How can that of which the very essence is freedom, and of which the attribute is that it confers freedom, be itself kept in bondage? (*A. Plummer, D.D.*) *God's Word free:*—He perhaps changes the expression from "my gospel" to the "Word of God" in order to indicate why it is that, although the preacher is in prison, yet his gospel is free, because the Word which he preaches is not his own, but God's. (*Ibid.*) *Suffering furthers the gospel:*—The sufferings of the witnesses for Christ was, and is at all times, one of the most powerful agencies for the furtherance of the gospel (comp. Phil. i. 12–14; Col. i. 24; 2 Col. i. 5–7). (*Van Oosterzee*). *Suffering for the gospel:*—I. THE GOSPEL MAY OCCASION TROUBLE. 1. For it bruiseth Satan's head, discovereth his plots, overturneth his kingdoms. 2. Besides, it pulleth down the pride of man, provoketh to repentance, presseth him to deny himself, put confidence in Christ, and its worth is not known in the world. II. THE ENEMIES OF THE CHURCH AFFLICT THE GODLY UNDER A PRETENCE OF LAW. 1. For the conversation of the godly is holy, honest, harmless; that without such pretences they could have no seeming cause to afflict them. 2. The wicked, in their generation, are wise; therefore, to cover and cloak their mischiefs they must have some pretence of law. III. GODLY PREACHERS MAY HAVE GREAT PERSECUTIONS. 1. Because not many wise, mighty, or noble men are called neither to embrace the gospel nor preach it. 2. And godly preachers speak with power, curb men's raging corruptions, wound their rebellious spirits, and never prophesy of peace unto them. IV. THE LIBERTY OF GOD'S WORD IS GREATLY TO BE REGARDED. 1. For it is the instrumental cause of man's conversion. 2. It increaseth grace, supports in trouble, and directeth to heaven. 3. And by the Word are not our adversaries foiled? V. THE PERSECUTION OF PREACHERS DOTH NOT ALWAYS INFRINGE THE LIBERTY OF THE WORD. 1. Because then the Lord hath a special care to His own cause. 2. The example of some will embolden others. (*J. Barlow, D.D.*) *The Word of God not bound:*—1. The first idea suggested by the words in their original connection is, that Paul's incarceration did not hinder his own personal exertions as a preacher of the gospel. The practical lesson taught by Paul's example, in this view of it, is obvious. It is a reproof of our disposition to regard external disadvantages, restraints, and disabilities as either affording an immunity from blame if we neglect to use the power still left us, or discouraging the hope of any good effect from using it. 2. It was still true, however, that Paul's bonds diminished his efficiency. While he avoided the extreme of abandoning all hope, he equally avoided that of foolishly imagining that he could personally do as much for the diffusion of the gospel in his own hired house at Rome, as in the wide sweep of his itinerant apostleship. His work, though not yet at an end, was interrupted, and how should his lack of service be supplied? The answer is a plain one: By the labours of others. This was a large ingredient in the cup of the apostle's consolation. He rejoiced not only in the labours of others during his comparative inaction, but in that inaction as the occasion, the exciting cause, of other men's exertions. Nay, he could even go so far as to consent to be wronged and dishonoured, if by that means his ruling passion might be gratified (see Phil. i. 12–21). What is the principle involved in this sublime profession of heroic devotion to the cause of Christ? Plainly this, that while Paul was ever ready to magnify his office as apostle to the Gentiles, and correctly appreciated both the honour and the difficulty of the work assigned to him, he never dreamed that it was meant to be entirely dependent upon his individual activity. It was not at himself, but at the word that he continually looked. Here, too, the lesson to ourselves is obvious. The apostle's example ought to shame us out of all undue reliance upon certain human agencies and influences. Especially ought this to be the case in relation to our own share of the work to be performed for the honour of God and the salvation of the world. 3. One of the most important lessons, couched in this significant expression or deducible from it, would be lost upon us if we went no further. I refer to the doctrine that the truth of God is independent, not only of particular human agents, but of all human systems of opinion, organisations, and methods of procedure. "The Word of God is not bound" or restricted, in its salutary virtue, to the formal and appreciable power exerted upon Churches and Christian communities, or through the ordinary modes and channels of religious influence, however great this power may be, however indispensable to the completion of the work which God is working in our days. We may even admit that it is relatively almost all, but it is still not quite all; and the residuary power may be greater, vastly greater, than it seems to us before attentively considering the other less direct, less formal, less appreciable ways, in which the Word of God, the truth revealed in Scripture, is at this moment operating on the condition of society, apart from its constant and direct communication through the pulpit, the school, and the religious press. These are the agencies, indeed, by which sound doctrine is maintained in your Churches and impressed upon your youth; and this, in its perfection, is the highest end that can be wrought by the diffusion of the truth. But let us not forget that much may be effected even when this highest end is not attained. In many a heresy, for instance, how much truth may be mingled, saving it from absolute corruption, and perhaps the souls of those who hold it, from perdition. Infidelity, in all its forms, affects to treat religion with contempt, as the offspring of ignorance; but its own discoveries are mere mutilations of the truths which it has stolen from its despised enemy. The attempt of infidelity to do away with the great doctrines of religion is the prowess of a dwarf mounting on a giant's shoulders to put out his eyes. The same thing is true as to those slighter and more trivial, but for that very reason more effective, forms of unbelief, which are propagated, not in philosophical abstractions, but in poetry, romance, and other current literature. The novelist or journalist who, with a scorn of Christianity only to be equalled by his ignorance of what it teaches, undertakes to show his readers "a more excellent way," often brings them at last to some elementary truth, already wrought into the mind and stamped upon the memory of every child who reads the Bible. What a tribute is this to the pervading, penetrating force of truth, that it can find its way even into such dark places, and at least serve to make the darkness visible! Look, too, at the schemes of civil government and social order framed by irreligious men, or unbelievers in the Scriptures, and observe these two facts easily established: that every departure from the lessons of God's Word is a demonstrable evil or defect in relation even to the lower object aimed at; and that everything conducive to a good end in the system is an adaptation of some Christian doctrine to a special purpose. It would be easy to pursue the same inquiry through every field of science and every walk of art, and to show that even there the Word of God has first been followed as a guide, and then expelled as an intruder; that its light has first been used to kindle others, and then vain attempts made to extinguish it for ever; in a word, that its enemies have first resorted to it in their time of need, and then ungratefully forgotten or unblushingly denied the obligation. If this be a correct view of the influence exerted even indirectly by the Word of God; if over and above its certain and complete results, it shines through the interstices of unknown caverns, and mitigates the darkness of unfathomed depths; if in fertilising one spot it sheds even a few scattered but refreshing drops upon a multitude of others; if in doing all for some, it incidentally does some for all, let me ask, in conclusion, What should be the practical effect of this belief? 1. We need not tremble for the truth itself. 2. There is some hope for the world itself, and even for those parts of it, and those things in it, which otherwise might seem to be confined to hopeless, irrecoverable ruin. 3. It may teach us a valuable lesson as to the true spirit of philanthropy, as being not a formal, rigid, mathematical attempt to save men's souls by certain rules, and in the use of certain ceremonial forms; but a generous, impulsive, and expansive zeal for the glory of God in the salvation of the lost.

And as the surest way of gaining this end, let us flood the world with the pure and unadulterated Word of God. (*J. A. Alexander, D.D.*)  *Not bound yet :*—I. IN WHAT SENSE IS IT TRUE, that "the Word of God is not bound"? 1. It is not bound so that it cannot be preached. Paul could preach it even when in bonds, and he did preach it, so that the gospel was made known throughout Cæsar's palace, and there were saints in the imperial household. Nineteen centuries after Paul we have still an open Bible and a free pulpit. When Hamilton was burned in Scotland, there was such an impetus given to the gospel through his burning that the adversaries of the gospel were wont to say, "Let us burn no more martyrs in public, for the smoke of Hamilton's burning has made many eyes to smart until they were opened." So, no doubt, it always was. Persecution is a red hand which scatters the white wheat far and wide. 2. "The Word of God is not bound" so as to be no longer a living, working power among men. Sometimes the enemies of truth have thought that they had silenced the last witness, and then there has been an unexpected outburst, and the old faith has been to the front again. The enemies of the gospel have attempted also to bind it by the burning of books. I have in my possession an early copy of Luther's sermons, and I was told how very rare it was, because at first the circulation was forbidden, and afterwards they were bought up and burned as soon as ever they were met with. And what did they do? They only put fire into Luther when they burned his sermons; they drove him to be more outspoken than he otherwise might have been, and so they helped the cause they thought to destroy. As the sun is not blown out by the tempest, nor the moon quenched by the night-damps, so is not the gospel destroyed by the sophistries of perverse minds. 3. The Word of God is not bound so that it cannot reach the heart. God has ways of reaching the hardest hearts and melting them, and He can do it at moments when such a work is least expected. Sometimes it happens to those whom we love that they are removed from the means of grace, but even then the Word of God is not bound. Had we not, a little while ago, an instance of one whom we were praying for at a prayer-meeting, and that night, while we were praying, it was a moonlight night, and as he was walking the deck of the ship, the Lord met with him? When no tongue was able to reach him, the memory of what he had heard at home came over his soul, and he was humbled before God. I was telling, just a little while ago, at our prayer-meeting, a very singular instance of how, just lately, three or four sermons on Sunday evenings have been made most useful to a young friend. He was going away to Australia unconverted, and without God. He went on board to depart, and when the vessel steamed out of dock, it ran into another ship, and he was obliged to wait and spend almost a month here, whilst the vessel was being repaired. The Lord met with him on those Sunday nights, and he has gone now, leaving in his mother's heart the sweet persuasion that he has found his mother's God. But sometimes we are apt to think a case is more hopeless still, when, in addition to natural depravity, and the absence of the means of grace, there springs up a scepticism, perhaps a downright derision of the Word of God, and of things sacred. I knew a man who had lived a life of carelessness and indifference, with occasional outbursts of drunkenness and other vices. This man happened one day, on Peckham Rye, to hear a preacher say that if any man would ask anything of God, He would give it to him. The assertion was much too broad, and might have done harm; but this man accepted it as a test, and resolved that he would ask, and thus would see if there was a God. On the Saturday morning of that week, when he was going early to his work, the thought came upon him, "Perhaps there is a God after all." He was ready to swoon as the possibility struck him, and there and then he offered the test petition, concerning a matter which concerned himself and his fellow-workmen. His prayer was granted in a remarkable manner, and he came then to be a believer in God. He is more than that now, and has found his way to be a believer in all that God has spoken, and has found peace through believing in Jesus Christ. 4. It is not bound as to its power to comfort the soul. 5. The Word of God is not bound in the sense that it cannot be fulfilled. I now allude principally to the promises and prophecies of God's Word. 6. The Word of God is not bound so that it cannot endure and prevail unto the end. II. WHAT ARE THE REASONS WHY THE WORD OF GOD IS NOT BOUND? 1. It is not bound, because it is the voice of the Almighty. If the gospel be indeed the gospel of God, and these truths be a revelation of God, omnipotence is in them. 2. Moreover, the Holy Ghost puts forth His power in connection with the Word of God, and as He is Divine He is unconquerable. 3. If you wanted another reason less strong than these two, I should say, "How can it be bound while it is so needful to men?" There are certain things which if men want they will have. I have heard say that in the old Bread Riots, when men were actually starving for bread, no word had such a terribly threatening and alarming power about it as the word "Bread!" when shouted by a starving crowd. I have read a description by one who once heard this cry: he said he had been startled at night by a cry of "Fire!" but when he heard the cry of "Bread! Bread!" from those that were hungry, it seemed to cut him like a sword. Whatever bread had been in his possession he must at once have handed it out. So it is with the gospel: when men are once aware of their need of it, there is no monopolising it. None can make "a ring" or "a corner" over the precious commodity of heavenly truth. 4. The Word of God is not bound, because, when once it gets into men's hearts, it works such an enthusiasm in them that you cannot bind it. There is Master Bunyan; they have put him in prison, and his family is nearly starving, and they bring him up, and they say, "You shall go out of prison, John, if you won't preach. Go home, and tag your laces, that is what you have to do, and leave the gospel alone; what have you got to do with that?" But honest John answers, "I cannot help it. If you let me out of prison to-day, I will preach again to-morrow, by the help of God. I will lie here till the moss grows on my eyelids, but I will never promise to cease preaching the gospel." III. ONE OR TWO OTHER FACTS RUN PARALLEL TO THE TEXT. Paul is bound, but the Word of God is not bound. Read it thus: the preacher has had a bad week, he is full of aches and pains, he feels ill: but the Word of God is not ill. "What will become of the congregation when a certain minister dies?" Well, he will be dead, but the Word of God is not dead. "Oh, but the worker is so feeble!" The Word of God is not feeble. "But the worker feels so stupid." But the Word of God is not stupid. "But the worker is so unfit." But the Word of God is not unfit. But you bitterly and truthfully lament that Christian men are nowadays very devoid of zeal. "All hearts are cold in every place"; the old fire burns low. But the Word of God is not cold, nor lukewarm, nor in any way losing its old fire. "Yes," says one, "but I am disgusted with the cases I have lately met with of false brethren." Yes, but the Word of God is not false. "But they walk so inconsistently." I know they do, but the Word of God is not inconsistent. "But they say they have disproved the faith." Yes, they have disproved their own faith, but they have not disproved the Word of God for all that. "Oh, but," says one, "it is an awful thing to think of the spiritual ruin of so many that are round about us, who hear the gospel, and yet after all wilfully refuse it, and die in their sins." Truly this is a grievous fact: they appear to be bound by their sins like beasts for the slaughter, but the Word of God is not bound or injured. It was said of old that it would be a sweet savour unto God in them that are saved, and in them that perish—in the one a savour of life unto life, and in the other a savour of death unto death. (*C. H. Spurgeon.*) *The Word of God not bound:*—Liberal Christianity may be defined, not as any belief, nor as any system of opinions, but as something going deeper. It is a habit of mind; a way of considering all opinions as of secondary importance; all outward statements, methods, operations, administrations, as not belonging to the essence of religion. Liberal Christianity comes from that spiritual insight which penetrates the shell and finds the kernel; sees what is the one thing needful, and discovers it to be not the form, but the substance; not the letter, but the spirit; not the body, but the soul; not the outward action, but the inward motive; not the profession, but the life. Liberal Christianity began when the first struggle began between the spirit and the letter, and that was the great battle which emancipated Christianity from Judaism. It was thought, at first, that the Word of God was bound to Judaism, and that no man could be a Christian unless he were also a Jew. Paul rooted that weed out of Christianity, and won for the whole Ethnic world—Greeks, Romans, Egyptians, Persians, Hindoos, Germans—the right of becoming Christians at once, just as they were, without first having to become Jews. But intolerance is the natural growth of strong soils. Out in the West, when the primeval forest is felled, there comes up in regular order, a whole succession of weeds, which are killed out, one after another, by culture. So it has been in the progress of Christian civilisation. This progress has killed off, one after another, a similar series of weeds which came up in the Christian Church. The Jewish intolerance was the first weed. Paul weeded the Church of that so thoroughly that it never came up again. The next weed was the Church intolerance, which said, "No man can be a Christian who is not a member of the Holy Roman

Catholic Church, and partakes of its sacraments, and submits to its authority."
Martin Luther weeded Christianity of this form of intolerance, and made it possible
for man to be a Christian without being a Roman Catholic. But not being as
liberal a Christian as Paul, he left another weed growing in its place—the weed of
dogmatic intolerance. The dogmatists said, "The Word of God is not bound to
the Roman Catholic Church; but it is bound to certain essential doctrines—the
Trinity, total depravity, the atonement, everlasting punishment." This weed has
also been nearly eradicated in our time. The principle of liberal Christianity has
pervaded all denominations. It has taken the shells and husks and outward
coverings from the Word of God, and these are now seen to be like those envelopes
which God puts around the fruits of the earth, until they are ripe, but which then
are taken off and thrown away. Nothing abides, nothing is permanent in Christianity, says Paul, but faith, hope, and love. The Word of God is not bound to any
Church or to any creed; it goes outside of all Churches and all creeds. The same
cool breeze which fans the hot cheeks of the labourers on the plains of Hindostan,
sweeps on across the Indian Ocean, gathering moisture as it goes, and pours it
down in rain on the parched regions of Central Africa. So God sends His prophets
and teachers of truth to every race, to help them according to their separate needs;
sends some knowledge of Himself, some intuitions of duty, some hopes of immortality, to all the children of men. The Word of God is not bound to the Bible. It
is not the prophecies of the Bible which are essential—"for whether there be prophecies, they shall fail." It is not its verbal inspiration which gives to it its
supreme importance—"for whether there be tongues, they shall cease." Nor is
its vitality even in the doctrinal truth it teaches—"for whether there be knowledge,
it shall vanish away." But it is the faith, the hope, the love which are in the
Bible which will abide, and will cause the Bible to remain always a permanent
blessing to mankind. Nor is the Word of God bound to any belief we may have
about the outward history of Jesus—His miraculous birth, His own miracles, or
any particular outward facts of His life. The essential thing, even in His resurrection, is not the outward part of it, but the inward part; not the particular way
in which He arose, as that He did go up to a higher life; that He is now alive,
and that death has no dominion over Him. Faith in Christ is not believing this
or that fact about Him, but it is faith in Himself, faith in the truth and love,
which are incarnate in Him, and which were breathed forth in all He said and did
and was. Deny His miracles, if you please; you cannot deny the great miracle
of His influence on mankind. Such a vast effect must have its cause. If we have
faith in the spirit of Jesus, in the Divine piety which made Him the well-beloved
Son, dwelling always in the bosom of the Father; in the Divine charity which
made Him the Friend and the Helper of the humblest of God's children; if we
have faith in these as the true life to lead here and as salvation hereafter, then
we have the real Word of God in our hearts, and believe in the real Christ. Finally,
the Word of God is not bound to any particular religious experience. Men come
to God in all sorts of ways—the important thing is to come to Him. Some are
converted suddenly; others grow up, by an insensible process, into the love of
God. God has a great many means of making men good. If a man find that
formal and regular prayers help him, let him pray that way. If he finds that he
comes nearer to God by endeavouring to live a pure and honest life, and leaning
on God's help to do it, let him pray that way. He who loves truly prays well.
Here is a poor woman who is obliged to be away from her children all day, working
hard for their support. When she comes home at night she finds that her oldest
boy has been sawing the wood and bringing the water, and that the oldest girl has
been taking care of the little children all the time she has been gone. That pleases
her more than all the affectionate words they could say to her. That is the best
proof of their love. If we take care of God's poor, and His sick and His sorrowful
children, that will be counted to us, I think, for faith and prayer and conversion
and piety. (*J. Freeman Clarke.*)    *The Word of God not bound:*—I. BY ANY
RESTRICTIONS IMPOSED BY GOD. God may permit certain circumstances, but He
has not imposed any restrictions. The Old Testament and New Testament, the
voice of the prophets, and of Him who is greater than prophets, alike concur
(Psa. lxvii. 5; xcviii. 3; Isa. xlix. 6; Mark xvi. 5). The character of God, the end
of the gospel, the state of man, confirm this. II. BY ANY ARTIFICIAL OR CON-
VENTIONAL RESTRAINTS IMPOSED BY MAN. Look at the history and progress of
Christianity (Acts iv. 18; v. 28; vi. 6; x.; xii. 24; xix. 20); history of early
Church—Reformation—of missionary labours. III. BY ANY DEGREE OF HUMAN

GUILT OR DEPRAVITY. Look again at first days of gospel (Luke xv. 2; xix 1–11; xxiii. 39–44; 1 Cor. vi. 9–12. St. Paul himself a witness (1 Tim. i. 12–17). But if the Word of God is not bound, why do not all men receive it, and live by it? Not because the gospel is bound, but because the natural heart is bound. (*E. A. Eardley-Wilmot, M.A.*) *The invincibility of the Divine Word* :—As a word expresses a thought, and so places one in a definite relation to another, so the Word of God is that by means of which He places Himself in a definite or thinkable relation to us. It is an expression of the purpose of God; that purpose in accordance with which He seeks to place Himself in a relation of abiding concord with the children of men, on the basis of which all men may be brought into the perfect knowledge and love of God. By the declaration that the Word of God is not bound, I understand the apostle to assert that this word, as a revelation of the purpose of God to bless and save men, must infallibly succeed in making that purpose known, and must also, from the very nature of the case, effect in some sense and way the realisation of the purpose itself. In so far as the Word of God is concerned, there is nothing to prevent the salvation and everlasting blessedness of every human being. 1. The Word of God is not bound by either of the two conditions of all created existence: the conditions of time and space. The Word of God is not bound as regards time, because it is the revelation of a purpose that runs through all time, originating in eternity and reaching unto eternity. It is true that the revelation is made in time. It moves in the line, works on the plane, and manifests itself through the sphere of the natural world; still its distinctive feature is this, that it is a revelation of that which exists in the supernatural: and, therefore, while existing in time, it also transcends time, and cannot, in the whole extent of its existence, be limited by time. And yet there are people who practically believe that the Word of God is bound as regards time. What is the error of all traditionalism, if it be not this, that nothing is good for us in the matter of religion, but that which has been handed down to us as a finished result from the past; and that, therefore, a new truth is necessarily not a truth at all, having no right to call itself a truth, except on the explicit understanding of its being the merest echo of an idea uttered long ago. Space, again, is that in which we have the notion of the comprehension of existence. It is that in which all things exist, and are held together, each in its own place. Space itself has no outline, but everything, as existing therein, has a given outline, within which it exists. But the Word of God is not bound as regards space. And yet there are those who would confine the Word of God not merely to this earth, which is but a speck in the boundlessness of space, but would limit it still further to some particular spot of the earth. The people who believe in consecrated places, and make pilgrimages to them, in the hope of getting spiritual benefit thereby, are the unhappy dupes of the delusion that the Word of God is bound—bound as to place. 2. The Word of God is not bound by either of the two highest forms of supernatural existence, viz., Christ and the Church. It is in the person of Jesus Christ that God has placed Himself in a definite relation to us. Hence Christ is spoken of as the living or incarnate Word, God manifest in the flesh. Is not the Word of God, then, it may be said, as thus embodied in the person of Christ, in some sense limited or bound? It exists under the conditions of human nature; appears in a particular country; is spoken in a particular language; submits to the restrictions of a somewhat limited sphere, experience, and term of life; and have we not in all this that which fulfils, in the most complete sense, the notion of the conditioned or bound? In a word, is not the Incarnation at best a mere anthropomorphism, under which we have only a partial view of God? To this objection it may be answered in a general way that the supernatural is not necessarily bound when it moves in the line, works on the plane, and manifests its power through the sphere of the natural world, any more than a father is bound, when he freely stoops to take the hand of his child, and keeps pace, for a time, with the shorter step of the little one, in order that the child may ultimately be brought up, as nearly as possible, to the level of the father; and no more is God, as the self-existent One, bound when He reveals Himself under the forms of nature, or comes as Christ into a more definite relation to us, in order that we may be able thereby to think ourselves up to the ideas of God. At the same time, it must be admitted that if the supernatural came down into any form of permanent subordination to the natural, it would undoubtedly to that extent be bound. Accordingly, up to the time of the first advent, or prior to the ascension of our Saviour, to the right hand of God in heaven, there was a sense in which the supernatural was bound, to some extent, in its relation to the natural. That partial and temporary dispensation has given place to the dispensation of the Spirit, under which those former limitations and restrictions have passed away. If, then, the Word of God is no longer bound, even as it was by the circumstances of our Saviour's life upon the earth, how can it be bound by any other individual, such as an infallible Head of the Church upon the earth, by an historical succession of apostles, or priestly caste of any kind, in whose hands alone that Word is supposed to reside, and by whom alone saving grace can be communicated to their fellow-men? The exaltation of Christ to the right hand of God in heaven and to the absolute supremacy of the whole world, puts an end for ever to all such pretensions. But the objection may still be pursued under the form of the Church. We require to lay hold of some clear idea of the Church in its relation to the Word of God. Undoubtedly it is the Divinely-appointed expounder of that Word; but so long as the Church is broken up into so many little sects, and so long as spiritual matters are disposed of by the merest majority, it may be even of a sect, it is difficult to see how the whole truth of the Divine word ever can be brought out before the world, the only organ through which the Holy Spirit speaks in fullest form being a truly Catholic Church. In the existence, then, of such a body there is no restraint put upon the Word of God, because the creed of that Church would be the ever-growing and ever-brightening expression of the mind of God as contained in the sacred Scriptures. 3. The Word of God is not bound by either of the two essential qualities of personal being; viz., thought and speech. If every idea is the identity of a thinking subject and an object thought, the one absolute law of thought is the law of identification. No doubt thought in its course reveals a number of opposites or contradictories, but its last function is to unite the whole. There cannot be legitimately different schools or types of thought, any more than there can be different laws of thought in different individuals, or different principles of understanding and reason in different parts of the world. Therefore, we deem it a fallacy to say that men cannot attain to unanimity of sentiment in regard to the highest of all subjects; because they have only to be true to the deepest principles of their own intellectual being in order to come to the most perfect harmony in respect of all these important matters. If so, the Word of God is not bound when it comes under the conditions of human thought, seeing that, in its essential principles, it is one with the very laws of thought themselves. But it may still be objected—and this is the last point with which we have to deal—that if the Word is not bound by the limits and laws of thought, it is so by the limits and laws of speech. As regards the Bible there need not be much difficulty. It is simply a record of spiritual facts. It merely notes the different points in the historical development of the Divine purpose. It professes, indeed, to be a veritable history of the supernatural, as a phenomenon working itself out, in, and through the natural. And it is altogether to be tested from the point of what it claims to be. The letter of the Bible is no more a fetter on the living purpose of God than any word or letter is to the thought of which it is the free and adequate expression. It is not so evident, however, that the Word of God is not bound, when we come to the written creed of the Church; and on that account some sections of the Church dispense altogether with a written creed. It becomes, therefore, a question as to what the creed of the Church is, and what the relation of the Church to her creed. And the whole question seems to resolve itself into this—that on a basis of perfectly clear and immovable conviction, about which no one can have any real difficulty, who believes in God at all, and without which the Church, as a whole, can have no existence, every one ought to be free to carry out in detail, to the minutest and remotest ramifications of thought, those subordinate shades of spiritual life and conviction that belong to the experience of one individual as compared with another. In such a case the creed would only be an arrangement, in their simple and natural order, of the leading conceptions of Divine revelation; and thus the whole mind of the Church would be left perfectly free to explore the depths, to bring out the riches, and to reveal the glory of the Divine Word. (*F. Ferguson.*) *God's Word not bound:*—Under the Church of Santa Maria via Lata, on the Corso, in Rome, is an ancient house which is said to have been St. Paul's "hired house," where he dwelt during the two years of his abode in the Imperial City; and where, as tradition says, he converted his keeper, a soldier named Marcellus. In this house is to be seen an antique marble pillar and a rusty chain, hundreds of years old, riveted into it, bearing the inscription: "Sed verbum Dei non est alligatum "—

" The Word of God is not bound." Our Divine Master Himself was bound to the accursed tree, but His gracious words are heard throughout the world. St. Paul's bonds turned out to the furtherance of the gospel; and God's Word is set free by the endurance and sufferings of its preachers. The apostle's manacled hand still pointed to the cross of his Divine Lord. When Admiral Ver Huce, a Protestant of whom Buonaparte entertained the highest opinion, went over to London, a few years after the battle of Waterloo, to represent the Bible Society of France, at the annual meeting of the British and Foreign Bible Society, he and Admiral Gambier met on the platform. The last time they had met was in deadly combat on the ocean; met as enemies, amidst the roar of cannon and all the accompaniments of a bloody conflict. Now they met, not simply as friends, but as brethren in the faith of a common Saviour, to advocate and help forward His glorious reign of righteousness and peace. As the two brave old men rushed into each other's arms, and wept aloud, the immense assembly arose with one accord, profoundly moved by a spectacle so unlooked for and so touching. Although the Bible is the best book in the world, it has always had enemies who have tried to do away with its teachings, if they could not succeed in destroying it. For three hundred years after our Saviour lived upon earth, the emperors of Rome did their utmost to hinder the advance of the gospel, by shutting up its ministers in prison, or by putting them to death. They stirred up dreadful persecutions against Christians, some of which lasted ten years; and during one of these, more than a hundred and fifty thousand followers of Jesus were slain. Diocletian was so confident that he had accomplished his purpose that he caused a medal to be struck, bearing this inscription: " The Christian religion is destroyed; and the worship of the gods restored." After the overthrow of the Roman empire, and the rise of the Papacy, stringent measures were inaugurated against the circulation of the Holy Scriptures. Fulgentio once preached in Venice from the text, " Have ye not read?" "If Christ were now to ask you this question," said the bold friar, " all the answer you could make would be, 'No, Lord, we are not suffered to do so!'" On another occasion, when preaching on Pilate's question, " What is truth?" he told his hearers that he had been long searching for it, and had at last found it. Holding up the New Testament, he said, " Here it is in my hand!" Then, returning it to his pocket, he observed, with an arch look, " The Book is prohibited!" He was a little too venturesome in his zeal for the truth, and was burned alive. In 1553, when Pope Julius III. asked some of his counsellors as to the best mode of strengthening the Church, several bishops gave him this advice— the original document being still in existence—" We advise that as little as possible of the gospel be read in the countries subject to your jurisdiction. The little which is usually read at Mass is sufficient, and beyond that no one whatever must be permitted to read. While men were contented with that little, your interests prospered; but when they read more, they began to decay." A company of bigoted priests once met in Earl Street, Blackfriars, London, to consult together concerning an edition of the Bible which Wyclif had just published in the English tongue. As might be expected, they not only condemned this excellent clergyman as a bad man, but they passed this resolution: " The Bible is a dangerous book. It shall not be circulated." These instances of the efforts made to suppress the Holy Scriptures might be indefinitely multiplied; but, instead of dwelling on so painful a subject, let us rather ask, how have such attempts succeeded? It is certainly a wonderful ordering of Providence, that on the very spot where those misguided priests met to destroy the Bible, the building erected for " The British and Foreign Bible Society " now rears its head. Aye, more than this, millions of copies of the Word of God are scattered abroad, every year, in all the languages of the earth. In Rome herself, where the Bible was so long a sealed book, it is now openly sold and distributed by colporteurs; and within a stone's throw of the place where St. Paul was imprisoned, a large apartment has been fitted up, where multitudes of soldiers gather every night to listen to the reading of the Bible, and to learn to read it for themselves. These men come from every part of Italy, and are generally from the better classes of the peasantry. After staying in Rome for three years, they will be removed to other parts of the kingdom, or go back to their homes, carrying the Bible with them. M. Guizot, the famous French scholar and historian, on taking his seat as president of " The French Bible Society," in Paris, truthfully and forcibly remarked, " The more the Bible is contested, the greater the number of devoted defenders who arise to affirm it and to send it forth. The Bible renews itself through trials, and its battles lead only to new conquests."

"The Word of God is not bound" to any person who preaches it. The weak and the unlearned often confound the wise and the mighty. In 1821, some wretched slaves were crowded into a Portuguese ship, on the coast of Guinea, and among them a boy of eleven, who, when the slaver was captured by a British cruiser, was carried to England. The boy manifested such excellent qualities of mind and heart that he was placed at school, where he occupied a high position in his class, and became a tutor, and then a clergyman. He returned as a missionary to his native land, and one of the first who heard the glad tidings of the gospel from his lips was his widowed mother. Converts multiplied, and a bishop was needed to govern and instruct this new community of Christians. All eyes were turned on Samuel Crowther; and on St. Peter's day, 1864, in the grand old cathedral of Canterbury, the slave-boy was consecrated to the high office which St. Paul himself had filled. 2. "The Word of God is not bound" to any form in which it is preached. 3. "The Word of God is not bound" to any time, place, or circumstance. (*J. N. Norton.*) *The Word of God not bound:*—"When I was cast into prison all knew that I was locked up because I had read the Gospel," said Ratushny, a Russian Christian. "When I was locked up for the second time people wondered again, and began to search after the gospel with greater zeal, and to read it. That is how our doctrines have spread, and not, as some people think, through my having propagated it." (*Sunday at Home.*) *Fame through opposition:*—In 1834, there was a little book published by the Abbé de la Mannais, entitled, "The Words of a Believer," which began to make some noise because of its Republican sentiments. The reigning Pope, however, went out of his way to condemn it in an Encyclical letter, which gave it an additional popularity, caused it to be widely read, and translated into the principal European languages. (*H. O. Mackey.*) *Useful though in prison:*—The Earl of Derby's accusation in the Parliament house against Mr. Bradford was that he did more hurt (so he called good evil) by letters and conferences in prison than ever he did when he was abroad by preaching. (*J. Trapp.*)

**Ver. 10. I endure all things for the elect's sake.**—God's chosen ones, whether already in the Church, or to be called into it afterwards. (*Speaker's Commentary.*) *The visible church for the sake of the elect:*—If we were asked what was the object of Christian preaching and instruction, what the office of the Church, considered as the dispenser of the Word of God, I suppose we should not all return the same answer. Perhaps we might say that the object of Revelation was to enlighten and enlarge the mind, or to make us good members of the community. St. Paul gives us a reason in the text different from any of those which I have mentioned. He laboured more than all the apostles; and why? not to civilise the world, not to smooth the face of society, not to facilitate the movements of civil government, not to spread abroad knowledge, not to cultivate the reason, not for any great worldly object, but "for the elect's sake." And when St. Paul and St. Barnabas preached at Antioch to the Gentiles, "As many as were ordained to eternal life, believed." When St. Paul preached at Athens, "some mocked," others said, "We will hear thee again," but "certain men clave unto him." And when he addressed the Jews at Rome, some believed the things which were spoken, and some believed not. Such was the view which animated, first Christ Himself, then all His apostles, and St. Paul in particular, to preach to all, in order to succeed with some. Our Lord "saw of the travail of His soul, and was satisfied." St. Paul, as His servant and instrument, was satisfied in like manner to endure all things for the elect's sake; or, as he says in another place, "I am made all things to all men, that I might by all means save some." And such is the office of the Church in every nation where she sojourns: she attempts much, she expects and promises little. This is a great Scripture truth, which in this busy and sanguine day needs insisting upon. There are in every age a certain number of souls in the world, known to God, unknown to us, who will obey the truth when offered to them, whatever be the mysterious reason that they do and others do not. These we must contemplate, for these we must labour, these are God's special care, for these are all things; of these and among these we must pray to be, and our friends with us, at the Last Day. In every nation, among many bad, there are some good; and, as nations are before the gospel is offered to them, such they seem to remain on the whole after the offer—"many are called, few are chosen." And to spend and be spent upon the many called for the sake of the chosen few is the office of Christian teachers and witnesses. That their office is such seems to be evident from the existing state of Christian countries from the first. Christianity has raised the tone of morals, has restrained the passions, and enforced external decency and good conduct in the world at large. Still, on the whole, the great multitude of men have to all appearance remained, in a spiritual point of view, no better than before. Trade is still avaricious, not in tendency only, but in fact, though it has heard the gospel; physical science is still sceptical as it was when heathen. Lawyers, soldiers, farmers, politicians, courtiers, nay, shame to say, the priesthood, still savour of the old Adam. Human nature remains what it was, though it has been baptized; the proverbs, the satires, the pictures, of which it was the subject in heathen times, have their point still. The knowledge of the gospel then has not materially changed more than the surface of things. Our Saviour's words, spoken of the apostles in the first instance, relate to the Church at large—" I pray not for the world, but for them which Thou hast given Me, for they are Thine." In like manner St. Paul says that Christ came, not to convert the world, but "to purify unto Himself a peculiar people, zealous of good works"; not to sanctify this evil world, but to " deliver us out of this present evil world according to the will of God and our Father." This has been the real triumph of the gospel, to raise those beyond themselves and beyond human nature, in whatever rank and condition of life, whose wills mysteriously co-operate with God's grace, who, while God visits them, really fear and really obey God, whatever be the unknown reason why one man obeys Him and another not. It has laboured for the elect, and it has succeeded with them. This is, as it were, its token. An ordinary kind of religion, praiseworthy and respectable in its way, may exist under many systems; but saints are creations of the gospel and the Church. Not that such a one need in his lifetime seem to be more than other well-living men, for his graces lie deep, and are not known and understood till after his death, even if then. But in process of time, after death, their excellence perhaps gets abroad; and then they become a witness, a specimen of what the gospel can do. There are many reasons why God's saints cannot be known all at once ;—first, as I have said, their good deeds are done in secret. Next, good men are often slandered; they are mistaken by those, whom they offend by their holiness and strictness. Then, again, their intentions and aims are misunderstood. It is no triumph, then, for unbelievers that the gospel has not done what it never attempted. From the first it announced what was to be the condition of the many who heard and professed it—" Many are called, few are chosen." Though we laboured ever so much, with the hope of satisfying the objector, we could not reverse our Saviour's witness, and make the many religious and the bad few. We can but do what is to be done. We cannot destroy the personal differences which separate man and man ; and to lay it as a fault to baptism, teaching, and other ministrations, that they cannot pass the bounds predicted in God's Word, is as little reasonable as attempting to make one mind the same as another. There is nothing to hinder the poorest man from living the life of an angel, living in all the unearthly contemplative blessedness of a saint in glory, except so far as sin interferes with it. I mean, it is sin, and not poverty which is the hindrance. Such is the case with the poor ; now, again, take the case of those who have a competency. They too are swallowed up in the cares or interests of life as much as the poor are. While want keeps the one from God by unsettling his mind, a competency keeps the other by the seductions of ease and plenty. The poor man says, " I cannot go to Church or to the Sacrament of the Lord's Supper, till I am more at ease in my mind ; I am troubled, and my thoughts are not my own." The rich man does not make any excuses,—he comes; but his " heart goeth after his covetousness." No ; such a one may be far other than a mere man of the world,—he may be a religious man, in the common sense of the word; he may be exemplary in his conduct, as far as the social duties of life go ; he may be really and truly, and not in pretence, kind, benevolent, sincere, and in a manner serious ; but so it is, his mind has never been unchained to soar aloft, he does not look out with longing into the infinite spaces in which, as a Christian, he has free range. A sort of ordinary obedience suffices them as well as the poor. Alas ! and is it so? is the superhuman life enjoined on us in the gospel but a dream? is there no meaning in our own case, of the texts about the strait gate and the narrow way, and Mary's good part, and the rule of perfection, and the saying which " all cannot receive save they to whom it is given ? " God grant to us a simple, reverent, affectionate, temper, that we may truly be the Church's children, and fit subjects of her instructions! (*J. H. Newman, M.A.*) *Sufferings on behalf of the elect:*—The question doubtless arises, does St. Paul here, and also in Colossians i. 24, regard his own afflictions as a part of the redemptive suffering by which the elect should receive the gift of Christ's salvation and inherit their eternal glory? This would, undoubtedly, contradict the whole tenor of his teaching elsewhere. "Was Paul crucified for you?" rings out (in 1 Cor. i. 13) his own indignant disclaimer of any such position. Still he does assert his hope and conviction that direct and positive advantages may accrue to the elect of God from his own sufferings. The "salvation" is "in Christ Jesus"; still there are "things lacking" in the afflictions of the Lord which he and other saints are called upon to supplement, to fill up from another source. They are to be filled up in the persons of the members of Christ's suffering body. Because these bitter sorrows effectuate or tend to produce a closer resemblance to Christ, because they may lead to a more intense consecration on the part of the elect of God, he willingly endures them all. We take it that these θλίψεις of Christ are not His atoning or sacrificial agonies, but all the contumely and repression which He endured for us and with us, and also which He endured for us and with us, and also which He, in sublime sympathy, continues to suffer in His body the Church, and which will not be completed until the last battle has been fought and the last enemy overcome. Thus the Lord dignifies every patiently borne cross, every holy death, as part of His own affliction for the sake of the elect. (*H. R. Reynolds, D.D.*) *The redemptive end of affliction:*—I. AFFLICTIONS ARE THE MORE WILLINGLY SUSTAINED WHEN THEY FURTHER THE LIBERTY OF THE GOSPEL. 1. For when the Word runs the plots of the wicked are prevented. 2. The wandering sheep gathered. 3. The body of Christ perfected. 4. The kingdom of God enlarged. II. A GROWN CHRISTIAN CAN SUFFER ALL KINDS OF AFFLICTIONS. 1. For experience have taught him that afflictions are good for him. 2. Many acts make a habit; whence it falls out that tribulation worketh patience. 3. He believeth that though sorrows be bitter at the entrance, they shall be sweet in the end. 4. The Lord assisteth him, by whose strength he can do and suffer all things. III. THERE BE AN ELECT PEOPLE. Now concerning the elect, two things are not unworthy of our consideration—the one, their number, the other their prerogatives. For their number absolutely taken is great. The prerogatives are many, and all excellent, which are proper to the elect, for they be the objects of God's love. The redeemed of His Son; temples of the Spirit; and co-heirs with Christ of all things. IV. ALL THE GOODNESS OF OUR SUFFERINGS IS IN RESPECT OF THEIR GROUND AND END. V. OF THE TWO, A TRUE CHRISTIAN MAN HAD RATHER SAVE SOULS THAN PROSPER IN THIS WORLD. For such know, that to save a soul is more worth than to win the world; and that they shall shine as the sun for ever and ever. (*J. Barlow, D.D.*) *A noble purpose:*—A man's purpose in life should be like a river which was born of a thousand little rills in the mountains; and when at last it has reached its manhood in the plain, though, if you watch it, you shall see little eddies that seem as if they had changed their minds, and were going back again to the mountains, yet all its mighty current flows, changeless, to the sea. If you build a dam across it, in a few hours it will go over it with a voice of victory. If tides check it at its mouth, it is only that when they ebb it can sweep on again to the ocean. So goes the Amazon or Orinoco across a continent—never losing its way or changing its direction for the thousand streams that fall into it on the right hand and on the left, but only using them to increase its force, and bearing them onward in its resistless channel. (*H. W. Beecher.*) *Supporting others:*—A curious old tree that supports other trees is described in a South American journal. It is stated that in Columbus there is a china tree that grew up very tall. Several years ago the top was taken off, leaving the main trunk of the tree about twenty feet high. On the top it has become somewhat decayed, but is making up for lost life by supporting a young forest. There are several different shrubs growing on its top, among others an evergreen three or four feet in height, a black-berry bush, which has put on leaves and flowers, and a water-oak which is about two inches in circumference. It is said that the spectacle is a very remarkable one, and arboriculturists take great interest in it. The old tree is a type of many lives. When God has withdrawn one of His children from active service, he is frequently able to continue his usefulness in another way, by supporting others, lifting them nearer to Heaven and sustaining them with his own stalwart spiritual growth. *Enduring for the elect's sake:*—An ordinary person may rest in his bed all night, but a surgeon will be called up at all hours; a farming-man may take his ease at his fireside, but if he becomes a shepherd he must be out among the lambs, and bear all weathers for them; even so doth Paul say, "Therefore I endure all things for the elect's sake, that they may also obtain the salvation which is in Christ

Jesus with eternal glory." (*C. H. Spurgeon.*)    *Suffering to help others :*—Suppose that by some painful operation you could have your right arm made a little longer; I do not suppose you would care to go under the operation; but if you foresaw that by undergoing the pain you would be enabled to reach and save drowning men who else would sink before your eyes, I think you would willingly bear the agony, and pay a heavy fee to the surgeon to be thus qualified for the rescue of your fellows. Reckon, then, that to acquire soul-winning power you will have to go through fire and water, through doubt and despair, through mental torment and soul distress. (*Ibid.*)    *The believer's salvation obtained by Christ and connected with glory :*— I. LET US CONSIDER THE NATURE OF THIS SALVATION. 1. It is a salvation from the condemnation of a broken law. 2. It is a salvation from the power and dominion of sin. 3. It is a salvation from the bondage of Satan. 4. It is a salvation from the temporary triumphs of the grave. II. LET US INQUIRE IN WHAT RESPECTS THIS SALVATION IS IN CHRIST JESUS. Because it was with His Son Christ Jesus that God was pleased to enter into covenant, respecting human redemption, before the world was. III. LET US GLANCE AT THE ETERNAL GLORY WITH WHICH THIS SALVATION IS CONNECTED. 1. The persons of the saints will then be glorious. The body will be no longer subject to hunger and thirst, to pain and weariness, or to disease and decay. And then in respect to the soul, it will be formed after the Divine image, in righteousness and true holiness, made to partake, so far as a finite creature is capable, of the image of God. 2. The mansions of which the redeemed shall take possession will be glorious. 3. The society to which they will be admitted will be glorious. 4. The employments of the believer will be glorious. (*Essex Congregational Remembrancer.*)    **That they may also obtain salvation.**—Rather, that they also may; they as well as we. (*Speaker's Commentary.*)    *Salvation in Christ :*— Having Christ we have salvation also, while without receiving Christ Himself we cannot have the salvation. Having the fountain we have its issuing streams. Cut off from the fountain the streams will not flow to us. Christ offers Himself to be the Bridegroom of the soul. The mistake is that of seeking the salvation instead of seeking the Saviour. Just the same mistake that the affianced would make if she should seek to have the possessions of him to whom she was engaged made over to her from him, without their union in wedlock, instead of accepting his offer of himself, and having the hymeneal bond completed by which he and all he has would become hers. (*W. E. Boardman.*)    *Salvation :*—I. THE NATURE OF SALVATION. 1. Salvation is the great and constant theme of the whole Bible. 2. Salvation is a word of pleasing import. 3. Salvation is a full and complete deliverance from all past guilt and condemnation. 4. Salvation is a glorious deliverance from all the miseries of sin and the bondage of Satan. 5. Salvation is a deliverance from the envenomed sting of death. 6. This salvation is a deliverance from the resurrection of damnation, the horrors of the judgment, and the miseries of the lost in hell. Now for the peculiar characteristics of this salvation. (1) It is free. (2) Suitable. (3) Present. (4) Gracious. (5) Eternal. II. THE AUTHOR AND SOURCE OF SALVATION. It is "Christ Jesus." III. LET US POINT OUT ITS METHOD. Some persons try to mystify the plan. But it is simple. The way is easy. Some want to purchase the gift of salvation, but it is not to be bought. It is here—"Look unto Me, and be ye saved, all ye ends of the earth." Turn your eyes from the world and sin, and, by faith, LOOK TO CHRIST ! (*R. Key.*)    *Heaven, or the final happiness of the righteous :*—Let us attend to what notices we can gain from the scriptures of truth of the heavenly state, as coming under the notion of salvation and glory. Each of these sometimes is put alone for the whole of it; but being here joined together, they make the description of it more complete; the former directly signifies the negative part, a deliverance from all evil, and the latter the positive, the possession of the highest and greatest good our nature is capable of. And how significantly and emphatically is this salvation with eternal glory said to be in Christ Jesus ? It is in Him, as possession purchased, in whose right we can only obtain it. It is in Him as an inheritance kept in truth, and to be conveyed by Him to the appointed heirs. It is in Him as the grand Exemplar in His human nature of the complete and final happiness of the saints. It is in Him both as a beatific object, and as a perpetual medium through which the blessed will see and enjoy God. I. The Christian shall obtain instantly on his arrival at heaven, and everlastingly possess, a complete salvation, a perfect freedom from all manner of evil. 1. In heaven there will be a perfect and eternal salvation from all sin. 2. The salvation of heaven will be an absolute and perpetual deliverance from the temptations of Satan. In heaven, too, all wicked men, as well as evil angels, shall cease from troubling or tempting; for there shall be none of them there, no more than any matter of temptation in that blessed world. 3. This salvation will be a deliverance from all natural weaknesses; from slowness of apprehension, errors of judgment, slipperiness of memory, levity of will, a rashness or tardiness in resolving, and a heaviness in acting. 4. It will be a deliverance from all the diseases and pains which attend our mortal frame, together with the great variety of disagreeable accidents our life on earth is continually liable to. 5. It will be a deliverance from all God's wrath and anger. 6. It is a deliverance from all relative and sympathising sufferings and sorrows. 7. It will be a deliverance from death. But it is time now to say somewhat—II. Of the positive felicity of the heavenly world, of which the less will suffice, as several of its ingredients are easily understood from the evils and miseries which they stand in opposition to, and because we can have but a general idea of this part, rather knowing what heaven is not, than what in particular it is. However, what belongs to this state is all great, excellent and glorious. It is glory itself. Now, the glory which continues the heavenly happiness is both objective and subjective, and these reciprocally influencing each other and inseparably concurring to form it. There is a glory without, objects of unspeakable lustre and glory which will be exhibited and presented to the saints in heaven to converse with. And there will be a glory within themselves. All the parts and powers of their nature will be rendered inexpressibly glorious, as by an elevation of them into a fitness to converse with the glorious objects before them, so by an actual exercise on them and the most satisfying gratification by them. Hence the frequent expression in Scripture of their happiness in heaven is their being glorified. And it is the glory of God either way, as it is often called. He makes all the glory of heaven; He is the principal object Himself of the saints' beatific converse, and He forms all the other objects, as well as themselves, glorious. And here we may observe that all these glories will be revealed in a propitious and amiable light. God will manifest Himself to His saints as their own God, and all His perfections and operations are arrayed in love. No room will be left for terror and dismay from the full blaze of His Majesty above, as but a few beams of it breaking in on some of His people here have oppressed their souls with the most dreadful apprehensions. Again, the revelation of heavenly glories will be made to the blessed in a measure exactly suited to their faculties and capacities. There will be no deficiency to cause an uneasy and an unsatisfied craving; no excess to over-power and exhaust the spirits. 1. There will be a perfect knowledge in heaven: a knowledge in the very best manner of the best and noblest things. This know-ledge will in a great measure be intuitive, and so consequently very comprehensive, easy, clear, and satisfying. 2. In heaven there will be a perfect rectitude, and regular harmony in all the powers of the soul. As the understanding clearly and steadily beholds the beauties of holiness, the soul will naturally take and keep a correspondent impress, and be satisfied with this Divine likeness. 3. In consequence of this, the active powers will be fully and most delightfully employed in the incessant praises of God and of the Lamb, and in whatever unknown services may be assigned them, all noble and pleasurable. (*J. Hubbard.*)

Vers. 11, 12. **If we be dead with Him, we shall also live with Him.**—*Union with Christ in death and life :*—I. The first branch of this "faithful saying" is, "If we be dead with Him, we shall also live with Him." There seem to be two ways chiefly in which the soul "is dead with Christ." If we look at the operation of the law as a manifestation of the justice of God, the law was the cause of the death of Christ —that is to say, the law being broken by the Church in whose place Christ stood, He, as a Substitute and a Surety, stood under its curse, and that curse was death. If, then, we are to die with Christ, we must die under the law just as Jesus died under the law, or else there is no union with Christ in His death. But further, Christ died under the weight of sin and transgression. Every living soul then that shall die with Christ spiritually and experimentally, must die too under the weight of sin— that is, he must know what it is so to experience the power and presence of sin in his carnal mind, so to feel the burden of his iniquities upon his guilty head, and to be so overcome and overpowered by inward transgression, as to be utterly helpless, and thoroughly unable to deliver himself from the dominion and rule of it in his heart. But there is another way in which the soul dies with Christ. Christ not only died *under* the law and died *under* sin, but He died *unto* the law, and He died *unto* sin. But in living with Christ, there will be, if I may use the expression, a dying life, or a living death, running parallel with all the experience of a child of God, who is brought to some acquaintance with the Lord Jesus. For instance, the apostle says, " I am crucified with Christ, nevertheless I live; yet not I, but Christ liveth in me." II. But we go on to consider another branch of this vital union with Christ. " If we suffer, we shall also reign with Him." There can be no suffering with Christ, until there is a vital union with Christ; and no realisation of it, until the Holy Ghost manifests this vital union by making Christ known, and raising up faith in our hearts, whereby He is embraced and laid hold of. And there is no " reigning with Christ," except there first be a "suffering with Christ." I believe that reigning not only signifies a reigning with Him in glory hereafter, but also a measure of reigning with Him now, by His enthroning Himself in our hearts. III. " If we deny Him, He also will deny us," that is the next branch. The words have a twofold meaning; they apply to professors, and they apply to possessors. There were those in the Church who would deny Him, for there were those who never knew Him experimentally, and when the trial came, they would act as Judas acted. And then there were those who were real followers of Him, but when put to the test might act as Peter acted. (*J. C. Philpot.*)     *Christ and the Christian:*—In matters of great worth and difficulty prefaces are used : so here. Whence observe we, that—I. AFFLICTIONS ARE NOT EASY TO BE ENDURED. II. GOD'S WORD IS FAITHFUL. III. CHRIST AND A CHRISTIAN ARE FELLOW-SUFFERERS. IV. CHRIST AND A CHRISTIAN SHALL LIVE TOGETHER. (*J. Barlow, D.D.*)     *Dead with Christ:*—In the fourth century a young earnest disciple sought an interview with the great and good Macarius, and asked him what was meant by being dead to sin. He said, " You remember our brother who died and was buried a short time since. Go to his grave, and tell him all the unkind things you ever heard of him. Go, my son, and hear what he will answer." The young man doubted whether he understood; but Macarius only said, " Do as I tell you, my son; and come and tell me what he says." He went, and came back, saying, " I can get no reply; he is dead." " Go again, and try him with flattering words—tell him what a great saint he was, what noble work he did, and how we miss him; and come again and tell me what he says." He did so, but on his return said, " He answers nothing, father; he is dead and buried." " You know now, my son," said the old father, " what it is to be dead to sin, dead and buried with Christ. Praise and blame are nothing to him who is really dead and buried with Christ." (*Christian Herald.*)     *Dead with Christ:*—" Believe, my dear Pris, what I am just beginning to learn, and you knew long ago, that the death of Christ is far, very far, more than a mere peace-making, though that view of it is the root of every other. But it is actually and literally the death of you and me and the whole human race; the absolute death and extinction of all our selfishness and individuality. So St. Paul describes it in Rom. vi. and in every one of his Epistles. Let us believe, then, what is the truth and no lie—that we *are* dead, actually, absolutely dead; and let us believe further that we *are* risen and that we have each a life, our only life, a life not of you nor me, but a universal life—in Him. He will live in us and quicken us with all life and all love; will make us understand the possibility, and, as I am well convinced, experience the reality, of loving God and loving our brethren." (*F. D. Maurice to his sister.*)     *Suffering and reigning with Jesus:*—I. SUFFERING WITH JESUS, AND ITS REWARD. To suffer is the common lot of all men. It is not possible for us to escape from it. We come into this world through the gate of suffering, and over death's door hangs the same escutcheon. If, then, a man hath sorrow, it doth not necessarily follow that he shall be rewarded for it, since it is the common lot brought upon all by sin. You may smart under the lashes of sorrow in this life, but this shall not deliver you from the wrath to come. The text implies most clearly that we must suffer with Christ in order to reign with Him. 1. We must not imagine that we are suffering for Christ, and with Christ, if we are not in Christ. 2. Supposing a man to be in Christ, yet it does not even then follow that all his sufferings are sufferings with Christ, for it is essential that he be called by God to suffer. If a good man were, out of mistaken views of mortification and self-denial, to mutilate his body, or to flog his flesh, as many a sincere enthusiast has done, I might admire the man's fortitude, but I should not allow for an instant that he was suffering with Christ. 3. Again, in troubles which come upon us as the result of sin, we must not think we are suffering with Christ. When Miriam spoke evil of Moses, and the leprosy polluted her, she was not suffering for God. When Uzziah thrust himself into the temple, and became a leper all his days, he could not say that he was afflicted for righteousness' sake. If you speculate and lose your property, do not say that you are losing all for Christ's sake; when you unite with bubble companies and are duped, do not whine about suffering for Christ—call it the fruit of your own folly. If you will put your hand into the fire and it gets burned, why, it is the nature of fire to burn you or anybody else; but be not so silly as to boast as though you were a martyr. 4. Be it observed, moreover, that suffering such as God accepts and rewards for Christ's sake, must have God's glory as its end. 5. I must mind, too, that love to Christ, and love to His elect, is ever the main-spring of all my patience; remembering the apostle's words, " Though I give my body to be burned, and have not charity, it profiteth me nothing." 6. I must not forget also that I must manifest the spirit of Christ, or else I do not suffer with Him. I have heard of a certain minister who, having had a great disagreement with many members in his church, preached from this text, " And Aaron held his peace." The sermon was intended to pourtray himself as an astonishing instance of meekness; but as his previous words and actions had been quite sufficiently violent, a witty hearer observed, that the only likeness he could see between Aaron and the preacher was this, " Aaron held his peace, and the preacher did not." I shall now very briefly show what are the forms of real suffering for Jesus in these days. (1) Some suffer in their estates. I believe that to many Christians it is rather a gain than a loss, so far as pecuniary matters go, to be believers in Christ ; but I meet with many cases—cases which I know to be genuine, where persons have had to suffer severely for conscience' sake. (2) More usually, however, the suffering takes the form of personal contempt. (3) Believers have also to suffer slander and falsehood. (4) Then again, if in your service for Christ you are enabled so to sacrifice yourself, that you bring upon yourself inconvenience and pain, labour and loss, then I think you are suffering with Christ. (5) Let us not forget that contention with inbred lusts, denials of proud self, resistance of sin, and agony against Satan, are all forms of suffering with Christ. (6) There is one more class of suffering which I shall mention, and that is, when friends forsake, or become foes. If you are thus called to suffer for Christ, will you quarrel with me if I say, in adding all up, what a very little it is compared with reigning with Jesus ! " For our light affliction, which is but for a moment, worketh for us a far more exceeding and eternal weight of glory." When I contrast our sufferings of to-day with those of the reign of Mary, or the persecutions of the Albigenses on the mountains, or the sufferings of Christians in Pagan Rome, why, ours are scarcely a pin's prick : and yet what is the reward? We shall reign with Christ. There is no comparison between the service and the reward. Therefore it is all of grace. We are not merely to sit with Christ, but we are to reign with Christ. II. DENYING CHRIST, AND ITS PENALTY. " If we deny Him, He also will deny us," In what way can we deny Christ ? Some deny Him openly as scoffers do, whose tongue walketh through the earth and defieth heaven. Others do this wilfully and wickedly in a doctrinal way, as the Arians and Socinians do, who deny His deity : those who deny His atonement, who rail against the inspiration of His Word, these come under the condemnation of those who deny Christ. There is a way of denying Christ without even speaking a word, and this is the more common. In the day of blasphemy and rebuke, many hide their heads. Are there not here some who have been baptized, and who come to the Lord's table, but what is their character? Follow them home. I would to God they never had made a profession, because in their own houses they deny what in the house of God they avowed. In musing over the very dreadful sentence which closes my text, " He also will deny us," I was led to think of various ways in which Jesus will deny us. He does this sometimes on earth. You have read, I suppose, the death of Francis Spira. If you have ever read it, you never can forget it to your dying day. Francis Spira knew the truth; he was a reformer of no mean standing ; but when brought to death, out of fear, he recanted. In a short time he fell into despair, and suffered hell upon earth. His shrieks and exclamations were so horrible that their record is almost too terrible for print. His doom was a warning to the age in which he lived. Another instance is narrated by my predecessor, Benjamin Keach, of one who, during Puritanic times, was very earnest for Puritanism; but afterwards, when times of persecution arose, forsook his profession. The scenes at his deathbed were thrilling and terrible. He declared that though he sought God, heaven was shut against him ; gates of brass seemed to be in his way, he was given up to overwhelming despair. At intervals he cursed, at other intervals he prayed, and so perished without hope. If we deny Christ, we may be delivered to such a fate. (*C. H. Spurgeon.*)　　*Deniers of Christ :*—I. DIFFICULT DUTIES ARE GREATLY TO BE PRESSED. II. TO CONCEIVE THE ESTATE OF A CHRISTIAN IS TO HAVE AN EYE TO HIS LATTER END. III. GOD'S METHOD AND THE DEVIL'S DIFFER. He begins with death, ends with life : but Satan the contrary. IV. CHRIST IS NOT TO BE DENIED. V. THE DENIERS OF

CHRIST SHALL BE DENIED. Helps against this sin—1. Deny thyself. 2. Never dispute with flesh and blood. 3. Look not on death as death: but on God's power, which is manifest in our weakness. 4. Consider the examples of so many martyrs. (*J. Barlow, D.D.*) *The encouragement to suffer for Christ, and the danger of denying Him:*—"It is a faithful saying." This is a preface used by this apostle to introduce some remarkable sentence of more than ordinary weight and concernment. I shall begin with the first part of this remarkable saying: "If we be dead with Him, we shall also live with Him; if we suffer, we shall also reign with Him." 1. What virtue there is in a firm belief and persuasion of a blessed immortality in another world, to support and bear up men's spirits under the greatest sufferings for righteousness' sake; and even to animate them, if God shall call them to it, to lay down their lives for their religion. 2. How it may be made out to be reasonable to embrace and voluntarily to submit to present and grievous sufferings, in hopes of future happiness and reward; concerning which we have not, nor perhaps are capable of having, the same degree of certainty and assurance which we have of the evils and sufferings of this present life. Now, granting that we have not the same degree of certainty concerning our future happiness that we have of our present sufferings, which we feel, or see just ready to come upon us; yet prudence making it necessary for men to run this hazard does justify the reasonableness of it. This I take to be a known and ruled case in the common affairs of life and in matters of temporal concernment; and men act upon this principle every day. The matter is now brought to this plain issue, that if it be reasonable to believe there is a God, and that His providence considers the actions of men; it is also reasonable to endure present sufferings, in hope of a future reward: and there is certainly enough in this case to govern and determine a prudent man that is in any good measure persuaded of another life after this, and hath any tolerable consideration of, and regard to, his eternal interest. In the virtue of this belief and persuasion, the primitive Christians were fortified against all that the malice and cruelty of the world could do against them; and they thought they made a very wise bargain, if through many tribulations they might at last enter into the kingdom of God; because they believed that the joys of heaven would abundantly recompense all their sorrows and sufferings upon earth. And so confident were they of this, that they looked upon it as a special favour and regard of God to them, to call them to suffer for His name. So St. Paul speaks of it (Phil. i. 29). If we could compare things justly, and attentively regard and consider the invisible glories of another world, as well as the things which are seen, we should easily perceive that he who suffers for God and religion does not renounce happiness; but puts it out to interest upon terms of the greatest advantage. I shall now briefly speak to the second part of this remarkable saying in the text. "If we deny Him, He also will deny us"; to which is subjoined in the words following, "if we believe not; *εἰ ἀπιστοῦμεν*, if we deal unfaithfully with Him; yet He abideth faithful, He cannot deny Himself"; that is, He will be constant to His word, and make good that solemn threatening which He hath denounced against those who, for fear of suffering, shall deny Him and His truth before men (Matt. x. 33). If fear will move us, then, in all reason, that which is most terrible ought to prevail most with us, and the greatest danger should be most dreaded by us, according to our Saviour's most friendly and reasonable advice (Luke xii. 4, 5.) (*J. Tillotson, D.D.*) **If we suffer, we shall also reign with Him.**—*Suffering with Christ:*—In the olden time when the gospel was preached in Persia, one Hamedatha, a courtier of the king, having embraced the faith, was stripped of all his offices, driven from the palace, and compelled to feed camels. This he did with great content. The king passing by one day, saw his former favourite at his ignoble work, cleaning out the camel's stables. Taking pity upon him he took him into his palace, clothed him with sumptuous apparel, restored him to all his former honours, and made him sit at the royal table. In the midst of the dainty feast, he asked Hamedatha to renounce his faith. The courtier, rising from the table, tore off his garments with haste, left all the dainties behind him, and said, "Didst thou think that for such silly things as these I would deny my Lord and Master?" and away he went to the stable to his ignoble work. How honourable is all this! (*C. H. Spurgeon.*) *Christ's martyrs:*—Christ's true martyrs do not die, but live. (*E. Thring.*) *Ennobled in death:*—Henry V. on the evening of Agincourt found the chivalric David Gamm still grasping the banner which through the fight his strength had borne and his right arm defended. Often had the monarch noticed that pennon waving in the foremost van of the men of England who that day pierced, broke, and routed the proud ranks of France. The king knighted him as he lay. The hero died, but dying was ennobled!" (*S. Coley.*) *Cyril, the boy martyr:*—Let me tell you of a young soldier of His, who bore much for his Lord. We must go back to the early days of Christianity, and picture a martyr being led to death in the city of Antioch. At the place of execution is the judge surrounded by a guard of soldiers. The man about to die for his love to his heavenly King says to the judge—"Ask any little child here whether we ought to adore the many false gods whom you serve, or the one living and true God, the only Saviour of men, and that child will tell you." Close by there stood a Christian mother and her boy of ten years old named Cyril. She had brought her son there to see how a true servant of God could die for his Lord. As the martyr spoke, the judge spied the lad, and asked him a question. To the surprise of all, Cyril answered—"There is but one God, and Jesus Christ is one with Him." At these words the judge was very angry. "Wretched Christian," he said, turning to the martyr, "it is thou who hast taught the boy these words." Then more gently, he said to the child—"Tell me, who taught thee this faith?" Little Cyril looked lovingly up to his mother, and answered, "The grace of God taught my mother, and she taught me." "Well, we will see what this grace of God can do for thee," cried the judge. He signed to the guards, who, according to the custom of the Romans, stood with their sheaves of rods. They came near and seized the child. Passionately the mother pleaded that she might give her life for that of her son. But none heeded her entreaties. And all that she could do was to cheer her child, reminding him of the Lord who loved him and died for him. Then cruel strokes fell upon the bare little shoulders of Cyril. In a tone of mocking, the judge said—"What good is the grace of God to him now?" "It can enable him to bear the same punishment which his Saviour bore for him," answered the mother decidedly. One look from the judge to the soldiers, and again the cruel blows fell on the tender flesh of the boy. "What can the grace of God do for him now?" again asked the pitiless judge. Few of the spectators could hear unmoved the mother, who, with heart bleeding at the sight of her boy's sufferings, answered—"The grace of God teaches him to forgive his persecutors." The child's eyes followed the upward glance of his mother, as she raised her pleading for him in earnest prayer. And when his persecutors asked whether he would not now worship the gods they did, that young soldier answered—"No, there is no other God but the Lord, and Jesus is the Redeemer of the world. He loved me, and I love Him, because He is my Saviour." Stroke after stroke fell upon the boy, and at last he fell fainting. Then he was handed to his mother, and the question was once more repeated: "What can the grace of God do for him now?" Pressing her dying child to her heart, she answered—"Now above all, the grace of God will bring him gain and glory, for He will take him from the rage of his persecutors to the peace of His own home in heaven." Once more the dying boy looked up and said, "There is only one God, and one Saviour, Jesus Christ—who—loved—me." And then the Lord Jesus received him in His arms for evermore. The boy martyr went in to be with his King, that Saviour "who hath abolished death, and hath brought life and immortality to light through the gospel." *Suffering for Christ rewarded:*—Agrippa, grandson of Herod the Great, once expressed a desire that his friend Caligula might soon come to the throne. Old Tiberius, the reigning monarch, felt such a wish, however flattering to Caligula, to be so little kindly to himself, that he threw the author of it into a loathsome dungeon. But the very day Caligula reached Imperial power, Agrippa was released. The new emperor gave him purple for his rags, tetrarchies for his narrow cell, and carefully weighing the gyves that fettered him, for every link of iron bestowed on him one of gold. Think you that day Agrippa wished his handcuffs and his leg-locks had been lighter? Will Jesus forget the wellwishers of His kingdom, who, for His sake, have borne the burden and worn the chain? His scales will be forthcoming, and assuredly those faithful in great tribulation shall be beautified with greater glory. (*S. Coley.*) *Happy ending of a suffering life:*—We have sometimes watched a ship entering the harbour with masts sprung, sails torn, seams yawning, bulwarks stove in—bearing all the marks of having battled with the storms, and of having encountered many a peril. On the deck is a crew of worn and weather-beaten men, rejoicing that they have reached the port in safety. Such was the plight in which many believers of old reached the haven of rest. They met with dangers and encountered difficulties. But if their course was toilsome, their end was happy. It was their joy to labour and suffer for their Lord's sake, and they are now sharing His kingdom and His glory. (*Bp. Oxenden.*) **If we deny Him, He also will deny us.**—*Denying*

*Christ :*—There are many ways of denying Christ, both by word and action. We may take the part of His enemies, or ignore His supreme claim to our allegiance ; we may transform Him into a myth, a fairy tale, a subjective principle, or find a substitute in our own life for His grace ; and we may assume that He is not the ground of our reconciliation, nor the giver of salvation, nor the sole Head of His Church. If so, we may reasonably fear, lest He should refuse to acknowledge us when upon His approval our eternal destiny will turn. (*H. R. Reynolds, D.D.*)

Ver. 13. **If we believe not, yet He abideth faithful.**—*Faithless :*—"If we are faithless"—that is, untrue to the vows of our Christian profession—the faithlessness implies more than mere unbelief in any of the fundamental doctrines of the faith, such as the resurrection of the Lord or His divinity. (*H. D. M. Spence, M.A.*) *The unchangeableness and independence of Christ, proofs of His divinity :*— If you open any professed treatise on the divinity of Christ, you will find that one series of proofs is deduced from the ascription to our Lord of attributes or properties which can belong only unto God. And the words which we have just read to you from the writings of St. Paul contain, as it would seem, two instances of this kind of evidence. Amongst the characteristics of the Creator, characteristics which can never be transferred to a creature, we justly reckon unchangeableness and independence. You may learn from the context, it is of Christ, "the one Mediator between God and men," that St. Paul affirms that "He abideth faithful," and that "He cannot deny Himself." And first, then, as to unchangeableness. You know that with the Father of lights "there is no variableness neither shadow of turning." When it is said of God "He cannot change," you should understand the phrase in its largest and most literal acceptation. We are as much borne out by reason as by revelation, in pronouncing it impossible that God should change. To suppose that He could change is to suppose that He could cease to be perfect, and we need not prove to you that an imperfect God would be no God at all. There is no passage in the Bible in which this unchangeableness is more distinctly ascribed to the Father than it is in our text to the Son. "He cannot," He is not able to "deny Himself." Such language could never have been applicable to Christ had He not been God. There is nothing in the nature of a creature, not even though it come nearest in glory and greatness to that unchangeable Being from whom its existence was derived— there is nothing, I say, in the nature of a creature which renders it impossible that it should deny itself. Now, unchangeableness is not the only attribute of Godhead which is here ascribed to Christ ; a little examination will show you that independence is equally ascribed. Sublimely as God is enthroned on His own essential majesty, He depends neither on angel nor on man for one jot of His honour, for one tittle of His happiness. And you are to observe that this independence which is necessarily to be reckoned among the Divine attributes is actually incommunicable ; that is, it can belong only to God, and cannot be imparted to what is finite and created. And yet the mode of expression adopted by the apostle in our text appears to me strictly to imply that the being of whom he speaks is independent. "If we believe not," what then ? will it make any difference to Christ ? must His purposes be altered, as though to meet an emergency ? must the terms of His gospel be lowered, so as to square better with our prejudice or our infidelity ? Nothing of all this. "If we believe not, yet He abideth faithful : He cannot deny Himself." Everything will follow the same course ; we may turn the willing ear, or the deaf ; we may march in the train of the Captain of our salvation, or we may fight under the banner of the apostate. "Yet He abideth faithful"; or, as the verse is paraphrased by an old prelate of our church, "He loseth nothing by it ; the misery and the damage is ours ; but for Him, He is the same that He was, whatever become of us." Now, we are very anxious that whenever a portion of Holy Writ on which we are meditating contains any indirect testimony to the divinity of Christ, such testimony should be carefully worked out and set before you in its strength and in its simplicity. And there is no doctrine to which there is a greater assemblage of these indirect testimonies than there is to the divinity of Christ. Passages occur in almost every leaf of the New Testament, which do not indeed assert the divinity of Christ, which do not even seem to allude to the divinity of Christ, but which, nevertheless, are stripped of all force, yea, of all sense, if doubt be thrown on the divinity of Christ. In reading the Epistles we seem reading the writings of men who never thought of the divinity of Christ as of a questionable or debateable thing. They buckle on the armour of controversy when the sinfulness of the human race is to be demonstrated, and when the method of justification is to be vindicated, and when the errors of Judaising teachers are to be exposed; but, except in one or two instances, there is nothing that looks like controversy in regard to the divinity of Christ. And we attach the greatest possible worth to this indirect kind of evidence, a specimen of which we have found in our text. Certain doctrines there may be, which rest only on certain passages, and which consequently we should find a difficulty in establishing if those passages were removed. But this cannot be affirmed of the main pillar of our faith, the divinity of Christ. The doctrine rests not upon isolated passages; leave us a page of the New Testament, and I think you will have left us proof of Christ being God. And now let us take a different view of the text. It contains much both of what is alarming and what is encouraging. The threatenings and the promises of Christ, each of these, as we may learn from the text, will take equal effect, whether we ourselves believe them or whether we disbelieve them. (*H. Melvill, B.D.*)     *Eternal faithfulness unaffected by human unbelief:*—I. THE SAD POSSIBILITY, AND THE CONSOLING ASSURANCE—" If we believe not, yet He abideth faithful." I must take the sad possibility first—" if we believe not," and I shall read this expression as though, first of all, it concerned the world in general, for I think it may so be fairly read. If mankind believe not, if the various classes of men believe not—yet He abideth faithful. The rulers believed not, and there are some that make this a very great point. They said concerning Jesus, " Have any of the rulers believed on Him ? " Well, if our greatest men, if our senators and magistrates, princes and potentates, believe not—it does not affect the truth of God in the smallest conceivable degree—" yet He abideth faithful." Many, however, think it more important to know on which side the leaders of thought are enlisted, and there are certain persons who are not elected to that particular office by popular vote, who nevertheless take it upon themselves to consider that they are dictators in the republic of opinion. However, we need not care because of these wise men, for if they believe not, but becloud the gospel, yet God abideth faithful. Yes, and I venture to enlarge this thought a little more. If the rulers do not believe, and if the philosophical minds do not believe, and if in addition to this public opinion, so called, rejects it, yet the gospel is still the same eternal truth. 2. Now, having spoken of our text as referring to the world in general, it is, perhaps, a more sorrowful business to look at it as referring to the visible church in particular. The apostle says, " Though we believe not," and surely he must mean the visible church of God. 3. Once more I will read the text in a somewhat narrower circle. " If we believe not "—that is to say, if the choicest teachers and preachers and writers believe not, yet He abideth faithful. Here, then, is the fearful possibility; and side by side with it runs this most blessedly consoling assurance—" He abideth faithful." Jesus Christ abideth: there are no shifts and changes in Him. He is a rock, and not a quicksand. He is the Saviour whether the rulers and the philosophers believe in Him or refuse Him, whether the Church and her ministers are true to Him or desert Him. And as Christ remains the same Saviour, so we have the same gospel. And as the gospel is the same, so does Christ remain faithful to His engagements to His Father. II. A GLORIOUS IMPOSSIBILITY WITH A SWEET INFERENCE THAT MAY BE DRAWN FROM IT. " He cannot deny Himself." Three things God cannot do. He cannot die, He cannot lie, and He cannot be deceived. These three impossibilities do not limit His power, but they magnify His majesty; for these would be infirmities, and infirmity can have no place in the infinite and ever blessed God. Here is one of the things impossible with God—-" He cannot deny Himself." What is meant by that? 1. It is meant that the Lord Jesus Christ cannot change as to His nature and character towards us, the sons of men. 2. His word cannot alter. 3. He cannot withdraw the salvation which He has presented to the sons of men, for that salvation is indeed Himself. 4. And then the atonement is still the same, for that, too, is Himself: He has by Himself purged our sins. 5. And the mercy-seat, the place of prayer, still remains; for if that were altered He would have denied Himself, for what was the mercy-seat, or propitiatory, that golden lid upon the covenant ark ? What was it but Christ Himself, who is our propitiatory, the true mercy-seat? 6. And here is another sweet thought : Christ's love to His Church, and His purpose towards her cannot change, because He cannot deny Himself, and His Church is Himself. 7. Nor will any one of His offices towards His Church and people ever fail. 8. Now, my last word is about an inference. The text says, " If we believe not, yet He abideth faithful ": it runs on that supposition. Take the other supposition : Suppose we do believe. Will He not be faithful in that case ? And will it not be true that He cannot deny Himself? (*C. H. Spurgeon.*)     *The Divine immutability:*—Weak as man is, all powerful as God is, there is one thing which weak man can do, and which Almighty God cannot do. Man can pass his word, and almost in the same breath can call it back again. God, on the other hand, cannot promise or denounce a thing without fulfilling it to the very uttermost. This is a doctrine which there are few of us, I fear, who thoroughly believe. Whilst there are many of us who are making light of the threatenings of God, and flattering ourselves with the profane idea that they will never be fulfilled, there are others again who are equally distrustful of God's promises. If we trust God in spirituals we mistrust Him perhaps in temporals. If we believe Him as the God of grace, we sometimes seem to doubt Him as the God of providence. If we trust Him for eternity, we are half afraid to rely on Him for time. (*A. Roberts, M.A.*) *Faith in God ennobles reason; unbelief degrades reason:*— 1. Faith in God involves, in its very act, a rational appreciation of evidence. Hence it is distinct from credulity, which is belief without evidence; from scepticism, which is unbelief, though evidence is at hand; and from infidelity, which is the rejection of evidence sufficient to convince. In each of these there is either the neglect or the abuse of the reason, and a consequent injury to the intellectual as well as to the moral powers of the soul. But faith in God, distinct from all these, is belief on sufficient evidence. 2. Faith in God promotes the highest exercise of reason, because also it rests upon the most substantial and durable foundation. If, in the investigation of natural truth, it is philosophical to seek for first principles, it is equally or more so to require them in the reception of revealed truth. Now to have faith in God is to rest on first principles, and to build up knowledge and hope on a sure foundation. 3. Faith takes in the sublimest truths, and the widest circle of thought. 4. If this be our philosophy we shall not stumble at miracles. While faith admits the miracles as facts, reason co-operates with faith by showing that they are wise and good. Moreover, the great first miracle displayed in the world's creation, which we receive by faith, prepare the mind for all other miracles, however stupendous they may be (Heb. xi. 1). 5. Guided by the philosophy of faith, we shall not stumble at mysteries. For what are mysteries? Grand truths as yet but partially revealed; the first syllables of some vast volume to be unrolled hereafter. 6. Nor at alleged contradictions between science and revelation. We are free to admit that there are difficulties, real difficulties, between science and revelation; and there may be even greater still. What then? We are but in the position in which patriarchs and prophets were placed for ages. 7. Supported by the philosophy of faith, we shall not faint under the delay of promised good. "One day is with the Lord as a thousand years," &c. (*W. Cooke, D.D.*) *Faith and the gospel:*—I. UNBELIEF IS A SIN. What more in the holy letters checked, condemned? Does not Christ dissuade from it? His apostles forbid it? and God everywhere commands the contrary? May not arguments be produced, if any doubt of it, to confirm, ratify it? II. A MAN MAY NOT HAVE FAITH YET POSSESS THE GOSPEL. To try the truth of thy faith, let these two rules following be well weighed of thee: First, he who hath faith receives Christ, as the wife does her husband. He will have Him and no other from this time forward, for better, for worse; for richer, for poorer; in sickness and in health, according to God's holy ordinance, till (and after that) death shall them part. In the second place, how does thy faith work? Faith, if true and sound, will embrace Christ, purify the heart, lift up the wing of thy soul and cause thee to soar on high. It will do what God enjoins, though it strip him of reputation, promotion, life and all. III. IN PREACHING THE WORD MINISTERS ARE NOT TO EXCLUDE THEMSELVES. IV. THE LORD IS FAITHFUL. V. THE LORD IS WITHOUT CHANGE. (*J. Barlow, D.D.*)

Ver. 14. **Put them in remembrance.**—*Repetition:*—I. REPETITION OF THE SAME THINGS IS WARRANTABLE. 1. For at the first delivery of a thing we may not fully apprehend it; the eye of our mind is but opened by degrees. 2. Our faith by often repetition may be confirmed. 3. It is a help to cause the truth in the soil of our memories to take the deeper impression. 4. We are slow to practise what we conceive, believe, and remember: therefore the reduplication of Divine things is profitable. II. THE DOCTRINE OF CHRIST IS ABOVE ALL THINGS TO BE DESIRED. (*J. Barlow, D.D.*) *Repetition:*—A preacher must often repeat an exhortation, because we dwell in a land of forgetfulness. (*Cramer.*) *A good memory:*—Abraham Lincoln had a marvellous memory; nothing seemed to escape his recollection. A soldier once struck a happy description of him when he said, "He's got a mighty fine memory; but an awful poor forgetery." How many Christians have good "forgeteries." **Charging them before the Lord.**—*Preaching in the sight of God:*—The whole section is applicable to ministers throughout the Church in all ages; and the words under consideration seem to be well worthy of attention at the present time, when so many unworthy topics and so much unworthy language may be heard from the pulpit. One is inclined to think that if ministers always remembered that they were speaking "in the sight of God" they would sometimes find other things to say, and other ways of saying them. We talk glibly enough of another man's words and opinions when he is not present. We may be entirely free from the smallest wish to misrepresent or exaggerate; but at the same time we speak with great freedom and almost without restraint. What a change comes over us if, in the midst of our glib recital of his views and sayings, the man himself enters the room! At once we begin to measure our words and to speak with more caution. Our tone becomes less positive, and we have less confidence that we are justified in making sweeping statements on the subject. Ought not something of this circumspection and diffidence to be felt by those who take the responsibility of telling others about the mind of God? And if they remembered constantly that they speak "in the sight of the Lord," this attitude of solemn circumspection would become habitual. (*A. Plummer, D.D.*) **Strive not about words to no profit.**—*The spirit of controversy :*—The spirit of controversy is a bad thing in itself; but the evil is intensified when the subject of controversy is a question of words. Controversy is necessary, but it is a necessary evil; and that man has need of searchings of heart who finds that he enjoys it, and sometimes even provokes it, when it might easily have been avoided; but a fondness for strife about words is one of the lowest forms which the malady can take. Principles are things worth striving about when opposition to what we know to be right and true is unavoidable. But disputatiousness about words is something like proof that love of self has taken the place of love of truth. The word-splitter wrangles, not for the sake of arriving at the truth, but for the sake of a dialectical victory (see 1 Tim. vi. 4). And here the apostle says that such disputes are worse than worthless, they tend to "no profit"; on the contrary, they tend "to the subverting of those who listen to them." This subversion or overthrow is the exact opposite of what ought to be the result of Christian discipline, viz., edification or building up. The audience, instead of being built up in faith and principle, find themselves bewildered and lowered. They have a less firm grasp of truth and a less loyal affection for it. It is as if some beautiful object, which they were learning to understand and admire, had been scored all over with marks by those who had been disputing as to the meaning and relation of the details. (*Ibid.*) *Controversy :*—It has been a favourite device of the heretics and sceptics of all ages to endeavour to provoke a discussion on points about which they hope to place an opponent in a difficulty. Their object is not to settle, but to unsettle; not to clear up doubts, but to create them; and hence we find Bishop Butler in his Durham charge recommending his clergy to avoid religious discussions in general conversation; because the clever propounder of difficulties will find ready hearers, while the patient answerer of them will not do so. To dispute is to place truth at an unnecessary disadvantage. (*Ibid.*) *Strife of words :*—Christians are not to strive about words. 1. It wasteth time, consumeth good hours, which are to be redeemed. 2. Prevents better matter. 3. Kindles strife and contention. 4. And for idle words we are to give an account. Now, for the avoiding of these fruitless disputes, observe these following directions:—1. Get a sound mind, a good judgment, to discern betwixt things that differ. 2. Root self-love and pride out of thy heart. 3. In matters of less moment reserve thy judgment; publish it not, lest thou trouble others. 4. Take heed of overmuch curiosity: pry not into God's ark; neither presume above that which is written. 5. Consider wherein thou and the party with whom thou hast to deal do agree, and let that consent make a stronger union than the dissent can a separation. 6. Abandon such companions as are always complaining of Church government. (*J. Barlow, D.D.*) *The hydrostatic paradox of controversy :*—If a fellow attacked my opinions in print, would I reply? Not I. Do you think I don't understand what my friend the Professor long ago called the hydrostatic paradox of controversy? Don't know what that means? Well, I will tell you. You know that if you had a bent tube, one arm of which was of the size of a pipe-stem, and the other big enough to hold the ocean, water would stand at the same height in one as in the other. Controversy equalises fools and wise men in the same way—*and the fools know it.* (*O. W. Holmes.*) *Controversy :*—Controversy has kept alive a certain quantity of bitterness, and that, I suspect, is all that it would accomplish if it continued till the day of judgment. I sometimes, in impatient moments, wish the laity in Europe would treat their controversial divines as two gentlemen once treated their seconds, when they found themselves forced into a duel without knowing what they were quarrelling about. As the principals were being led up to their places one of them whispered to the other, " If you will shoot your second, I will shoot mine." (*A. J. Froude.*) *Controversy a sign of moral poverty :*—In the course of more than twenty-seven years, I never knew one exemplary Christian a disputer, whether amongst Dissenters or in our own Church; and it is a rule with me to conclude any person who can be taken up with a desire to make men converts to any notion, and not to Christ, or to be zealous for anything more than the life of faith and holiness from knowledge of Christ crucified, is a sounding empty professor, or, at best, in a very poor low state. (*H. Venn.*) *Cavilling and disputation :*—When Endamides heard old Xenocrates disputing so long about wisdom, he inquired very gravely, but archly, " If the old man be yet disputing and inquiring concerning wisdom, what time will he have left to use it ? " Controversy may be sometimes needful; but the love of disputation is a serious evil. Luther, who contended earnestly for the truth, used to pray, " From a vainglorious doctor, a contentious pastor, and nice questions, the Lord deliver His Church." Philip Melancthon, being at the conferences at Spires, in 1529, made a little journey to Bretton to see his mother. This good woman asked him what she must believe amidst so many disputes, and repeated to him her prayers, which contained nothing superstitious. " Go on, mother," said he, " to believe and pray as you have done, and never trouble yourself about religious controversies." (*Sunday School Teacher.*)

Ver. 15. **Study to show thyself approved unto God.**—*Approved :*—The word which he uses (σπουδάζειν) is one which scarcely occurs in the New Testament, except in the writings of St. Paul. And the corresponding substantive is also much more common in his Epistles than it is elsewhere. It indicates that ceaseless, serious, earnest zeal, which was one of his chief characteristics. And certainly if the proposed standard is to be reached, or even seriously aimed at, abundance of this zeal will be required. For the end proposed is not the admiration or affection of the congregation, or of one's superiors, nor yet success in influencing and winning souls; but that of presenting one's self to God in such a way as to secure His approval, without fear of incurring the reproach of being a workman who has shirked or scamped his work. The apostle's charge is a most wholesome one, and if it is acted upon it secures diligence without fussiness, and enthusiasm without fanaticism. The being " approved " implies being tried and proved as precious metals are proved before they are *accepted* as genuine. (*A. Plummer, D.D.*) *The minister approved of God :*—I. In what way and manner a minister ought to show himself approved of God. It appears to me that something more is required to convince men that a minister has the smile of God than his own belief. Our text evidently implies that by his work a minister must show that God is with him. In his work four things will be found which tend to show this. 1. Its quality. It must be such as God commands. 2. Its quantity ; which shall evince diligence. 3. The difficulties attending its performance; which is the trial of sincerity. 4. The spirit in which it is done. It is a work which requires a spirit of compassion and kindness. II. What are the signs of a minister's approval of God which should be accepted by persons ? 1. I would place conversions as an evidence of Divine approval. They show Divine favour. The moral miracle of a true conversion evinces the Divine presence and power equally with any other miracle. 2. The convictions of truth and duty, which are made by his preaching to the consciences of sinners. 3. The last sign we shall notice of God's approbation of His minister, is the effects of his preaching on the hearts of them that believe. Those that are spiritual can judge whether his preaching is scriptural. (*W. Moore.*) *God's approval :*—Advert continually to His presence with reverence and godly fear; consider Him as always looking on the heart; trust in His almighty protection; believe in Him as a holy sin-hating God and reconciled to sinners of mankind only in Jesus Christ; value His favour above all the world, and make it the settled sole aim of your lives to approve yourselves to His pure eyes. (*T. Adam.*) *Desire for God's approbation :*—" If you were an ambitious man," said a person one day to a minister of talent and education, who was settled in a retired and obscure parish, " you would not stay in such a place as this." " How do you know that I am not an ambitious man ? " said the pastor. " You do not act like one." " I have my plans as well as others—the results may not appear as soon, perhaps."

"Are you engaged in some great work?" "I am; but the work does not relate to literature or science. I am not ambitious, perhaps, in the ordinary sense of the term. I do not desire to occupy the high places of the earth, but I do desire to get near my Master's throne in glory. I care but little for popular applause, but I desire to secure the approbation of God. The salvation of souls is the work He is most interested in, and to the successful prosecution of which He has promised the largest rewards." (*H. L. Hastings.*) " *Vibration in unison* " :—" Something is the matter with your telephone; we can hardly hear you," was the response, that in a faint voice came to us from the Central Office when we had answered their signal ring with the usual " Halloo! " A few minutes afterwards a young man from head-quarters stepped into our study, and taking the telephone in his hand commenced to investigate. " Yes, here it is," he exclaimed, as he began to unscrew the ear-piece. " The diaphragm is bulged, and dust has collected around it to such an extent that it does not vibrate in unison with ours up in the office, and that spoils the sound. You see," he added, while brushing the instrument, " that the telephones at both ends of the wire must act in harmony or there will be no voice. There," he said, "it is all right now." And sure enough the lowest word could be distinctly heard. There was, of course, nothing remarkable in this incident, and yet the words "vibrate in unison," " must act in harmony or there will be no voice," suggested higher thoughts as well. The human heart is God's telephone in man. Through it He purposes to speak to our inner consciousness; and when our conscience, our affections, and our desires " vibrate in unison" with the breath of His lips we can hear His voice within us. **A workman that needeth not to be ashamed.**—The single word which represents "that needeth not to be ashamed" (ἀνεπαίσχυντος) is a rare formation, which occurs nowhere else in the New Testament. Its precise meaning is not quite certain. The more simple and frequent form (ἀναίσχυντος) means " shameless," *i.e.*, one who does not feel shame when he ought to do so. Such a meaning, if taken literally, would be utterly unsuitable here. And we then have choice of two interpretations, either (1) that which is adopted in both A. V. and R. V., who *need* not feel shame, because his work will bear examination, or (2) who *does* not feel shame, although his work is of a kind which the world holds in contempt. The latter is the interpretation which Chrysostom adopts, and there is much to be said in its favour. Three times already in this letter has the apostle spoken of not being ashamed of the gospel (chap. i. 8, 12, 16). Does he not, therefore, mean here also, " Present thyself to God as a workman who is not ashamed of being in His service and of doing whatever work may be assigned to him " ? This brings us very close to what would be the natural meaning of the word, according to the analogy of the simpler form. " If you are to work for God," says Paul, " you must be in a certain sense *shameless.* There are some men who set public opinion at defiance, in order that they may follow their own depraved desires. The Christian minister must be prepared sometimes to set public opinion at defiance, in order that he may follow the commands of God." The *vox populi,* even when taken in its most comprehensive sense, is anything but an infallible guide. Public opinion is nearly always against the worst forms of selfishness, dishonesty, and sensuality ; and to set it at defiance in such matters is to be "shameless " in the worst sense. But sometimes public opinion is very decidedly against some of the noblest types of holiness ; and to be " shameless " under such circumstances is a necessary qualification for one's duty. It is by no means certain that this is not St. Paul's meaning. If we translate " A workman that feeleth no shame," we shall have a phrase that would cover either interpretation. (*A. Plummer, D.D.*) *The gospel workman :*—I. Look, first, at the DESIGNATION the Christian minister must try to earn for himself, to be " a workman approved of God," one whose work will bear trying in the fire; having nothing counterfeit about it, but discovering the fine gold of an unadulterated service—truthful, hearty, honest towards God and man. 1. Such a man will strive to be approved of God for his diligence, his earnestness, the anxious concentration upon the duties of the ministry of all the powers which God has given him. 2. "Approved of God," again, a minister should strive to be for his faithfulness. Now, this faithfulness, in relation to the stewardship of souls, consists in a bold and unfaltering adherence to the terms of our gospel commission ; in a jealousy, before all things, for the honour of the Lord we serve ; in a determination that, neither in public nor in private, will we exercise any timid reservations whether men will hear or whether they will forbear. II. But the text invites us, in the next place, to consider the Christian minister in HIS OFFICE as a public teacher. 1. Where note, first, it is the " word of truth " he has to divide; an expression with which we may compare the language of the same apostle on another occasion, where he says, " When ye received the word of God which ye heard of us, ye received it not as the word of men, but as is in truth the word of God." This mode of speaking of Holy Scripture seems well calculated to meet that irrepressible craving for certainty on moral subjects, which is the first need of the awakened mind. 2. But this word or truth, we are told, is to be " rightly divided "; that is, we may interpret the expression, to have all its parts distributed and disposed after some law of connection and coherence and scientific unity. The general spirit of this injunction goes to reprove all that mutilated or partial teaching in which, through an over-fondness for particular aspects of theological truth, a man is betrayed into negligence, if not into culpable reticence, about all the rest. III. But I proceed to the last point which calls for notice in our text, or that which leads us to contemplate the CHRISTIAN MINISTER IN HIS PERSONAL CHARACTER AND QUALIFICATIONS. 1. "Needeth not to be ashamed," in regard of his mental culture, and attainments, and general fitness to cope with the demands of an intellectual age. 2. " Needeth not be ashamed," once more, in regard of his personal and experimental acquaintance with the truths he is ordained to teach. Every profession in life has its appropriate and distinctive excellence. We look for courage in the soldier; integrity in the merchant; wise consistency in the statesman; unswerving uprightness in the judge. What is that which, before all things, should distinguish the Christian minister, if it be not pre-eminent sanctity of deportment, and the spirit of piety and prayer? (*D. Moore, M.A.*)    **Rightly dividing the word of truth.**—*Cutting straight :*—Literally " cutting straight." The figure has been very variously derived; from a priest dividing the victim, the steward distributing the bread or stores, a stonemason, a carpenter, a ploughman, a road-cutter. The last has been most frequently adopted. Perhaps they are right, who, like Luther and Alford, consider that the figure had become almost lost sight of in common usage, and that the word had come to mean little more than to " manage " or " administer." (*Speaker's Commentary.*)    *Fearless faithfulness :*—The metaphor is taken from cutting roads. The characteristic of the Roman roads would be well known to the apostle, and this idea is given in the margin of the revision " holding a straight course in the word of truth." The expression denotes a fearless faithfulness—a simple straightforward-ness in the proclamation of the truth of God, whatever may be the opinions or the conduct of men. The Word has to be preached whether men will hear or whether they will forbear. (*R. H. S.*)    *Defection dangerous :*—I am disposed to think that we may perhaps class this among the medical words with which these Epistles abound, and see in it a reference to the work of the surgeon, in which any deflection from the true line of incision might be perilous or even fatal. The reference in ver. 17 to the gangrene or cancer seems to carry on the train of thought. (*E. H. Plumptre, D.D.*) *Right handling :*—The idea of rightness seems to be the dominant one ; that of cutting quite secondary ; so that the Revisers are quite justified in following the example of the Vulgate (*recte tractantem*), and translating simply " rightly handling." But this right handling may be understood as consisting in seeing that the word of truth moves in the right direction, and progresses in the congregation by a legiti-mate development. (*A. Plummer, D.D.*)    *Straightforwardness :*—St. Paul sum-mons Timothy to a right straightforward method of dealing with the Divine word. He would have him set out clear lines for the intellect, a plain path for the feet, a just appeal to the emotions, a true stimulant of the conscience. (*H. R. Reynolds, D.D.*)    *Rightly dividing the word of truth :*—I. The Vulgate version translates it—and with a considerable degree of accuracy—" Rightly HANDLING the word of truth." What is the right way, then, to handle the word of truth ? 1. It is like a sword, and it was not meant to be played with. It must be used in earnest and pushed home. 2. He that rightly handles the word of God will never use it to defend men in their sins, but to slay their sins. 3. The gospel ought never to be used for frightening sinners from Christ. 4. Moreover, if we rightly handle the word of God we shall not preach it so as to send Christians into a sleepy state. We may preach the consolations of the gospel till each professor feels " I am safe enough ; there is no need to watch, no need to fight, no need for any exertion whatever. My battle is fought, my victory is won, I have only to fold my arms and go to sleep." 5. And, oh, beloved, there is one thing that I dread above all others—lest I should ever handle the word of God so as to persuade some of you that you are saved when you are not. II. But my text has another meaning. It has an idea in it which I can only express by a figure. "Rightly dividing, or STRAIGHT CUTTING." A ploughman stands here with his plough, and he ploughs right along from this end of the field to the other, making a straight furrow. And so Paul would have Timothy make a straight furrow right through the word of truth. I believe there is no preaching that God will ever accept but that which goes decidedly through the whole line of truth from end to end, and is always thorough, earnest, and downright. As truth is a straight line, so must our handling of the truth be straightforward and honest, without shifts or tricks. III. There is a third meaning to the text. "Rightly dividing the word of truth" is, as some think, an expression taken from the priests dividing the sacrifices. When they had a lamb or a sheep, a ram or a bullock, to offer, after they had killed it, it was cut in pieces, carefully and properly; and it requires no little skill to find out where the joints are, so as to cut up the animal discreetly. Now, the word of truth has to be taken to pieces wisely; it is not to be hacked or torn as by a wild beast, but rightly divided. There has to be DISCRIMINATION AND DISSECTION. 1. Every gospel minister must divide between the covenant of works and the covenant of grace. 2. We need also to keep up a clear distinction between the efforts of nature and the work of grace. It is commendable for men to do all they can to improve themselves, and everything by which people are made more sober, more honest, more frugal, better citizens, better husbands, better wives, is a good thing; but that is nature and not grace. Reformation is not regeneration. 3. It is always well, too, for Christian men to be able to distinguish one truth from another. Let the knife penetrate between the joints of the work of Christ for us, and the work of the Holy Spirit in us. Justification, by which the righteousness of Christ is imputed to us, is one blessing; sanctification, by which we ourselves are made personally righteous, is another blessing. 4. One other point of rightly dividing should never be forgotten, we must always distinguish between the root and the fruit. "I want to feel a great change of heart, and then I will believe." Just so; you wish to make the fruit the root. IV. The next interpretation of the apostle's expression is, practically CUTTING OUT the word for holy uses. This is the sense given by Chrysostom. I will show you what I mean here. Suppose I have a skin of leather before me, and I want to make a saddle. I take a knife, and begin cutting out the shape. I do not want those parts which are dropping off on the right, and round this corner; they are very good leather, but I cannot just now make use of them. I have to cut out my saddle, and I make that my one concern. The preacher, to be successful, must also have his wits about him, and when he has the Bible before him he must use those portions which will have a bearing upon his grand aim. V. One thing the preacher has to do is to ALLOT TO EACH ONE HIS PORTION; and here the figure changes. According to Calvin, the intention of the Spirit here is to represent one who is the steward of the house, and has to apportion food to the different members of the family. He has rightly to divide the loaves so as not to give the little children and the babes all the crust; rightly to supply each one's necessities, not giving the strong men milk, and the babes hard diet; not casting the children's bread to the dogs, nor giving the swine's husks to the children, but placing before each his own portion. VI. Rightly to divide the word of truth means to TELL EACH MAN WHAT HIS LOT AND HERITAGE WILL BE IN ETERNITY. Just as when Canaan was conquered, it was divided by lot among the tribes, so the preacher has to tell of Canaan, that happy land, and he has to tell of the land of darkness and of deathshade, and to let each man know where his last abode will be. (*C. H. Spurgeon.*)

*Appropriate truth*:—Paul no doubt meant by this simile, that as a father at the dinner-table cuts and carves the meat, and divides it in proper shares to his family —a big piece for the grown-up son who works hard, and a small tender bit for the wee bairn who is propped up in a high chair next the mother—so all Christian workmen should divide religious truth, according to the capacity and the wants of the people amongst whom they labour. We are told in a fable that a half-witted man invited a number of creatures to a feast, at which he gave straw to the dog, and a bone to the ass. So, unless we think and reason, we shall be giving the wrong sort of food to the people who look to us for spiritual nourishment. When you are invited to visit the death-bed of a man whose life has been self-indulgent and occasionally vicious, and you see the tears of repentance in his eyes, it is a blunder to read him an account of the last judgment in the 25th of Matthew; but it is rightly dividing the truth to open the 15th chapter of Luke, and tell him the touching story of the father's love to his penitent prodigal son. If you are asked to preach religious truth to a sceptic, do not ask him to believe that the whale swallowed Jonah; or that, one day, the sun stood still while an army fought out its battle. It would be like giving straw to a hungry god.  Tell the sceptic the Divine parable of the humane Samaritan, and say, "If you copy the spirit of that man, you shall find it one of the gateways to God."  Would you influence for good a young man who is leaving home for the great city?  Then, tell him the story of virtue as exhibited in the life of Joseph, who as a son, a brother, a slave, a servant, a overseer, a prisoner, and a prince, benefited man and glorified God.  If you have to speak to children, tell them of the child Samuel, who prayed to God, and was consecrated to His service in one of the most illustrious lives of the Old Testament; and when you wish to impress upon a child that he should trust in God, read and expound to him the psalm which begins with the thrilling words, "The Lord is my shepherd, I shall not want"; and tell him of the sacred Saviour who took the little ones in His arms and blessed them, saying, "Of such little children is the kingdom of heaven."  If you are asked to go to a prison and speak to the convicted wretches, tell them of the poor, naked, dying thief on the cross who saw Jesus, believed in Him, prayed to Him, and the same day was received into paradise.  And are you moved to give a word to the outcasts?  Then, give them their share of suitable spiritual food.  Tell them of Mary Magdalene whose heart was cleansed from its impure demons and filled instead with sacred love.  And when the penitent outcasts weep while you speak of the Divine love, one may reply, "But, sir, no good woman will befriend such as we have been!"  Then, tell them that when Mary Magdalene was converted she became the companion of the mother of Christ; and that if they trust in God and do the right, He will make a sacred path for them through the world and make them perhaps as useful and as honoured as the Magdalene whose service to Christ and His mother is the charm of the world.  Yes; there is in this grand gospel history a share of food for everybody; and it should be for us to find it and bestow it according to the needs of the people. (*W. Birch.*)     *Rightly dividing the word of truth :*—Truth is of various kinds—physical, mathematical, moral, &c.; but here one particular kind of truth is referred to, called the word of truth—that is, the truth of the Word of God—the truth of Divine revelation—theological truth.  The Bible was not given to teach men philosophy, or the arts which have respect to this life; its object is to teach the true knowledge of God, and the true and only method of salvation.  1. The truths of God's Word must be carefully distinguished from error.  2. But it is necessary to divide the truth not only from error, but from philosophy, and mere human opinions and speculations.  3. The skilful workman must be able to distinguish between fundamental truths, and such as are not fundamental.  4. Rightly to divide the word of truth, we must arrange it in such order as that it may be most easily and effectually understood.  In every system some things stand in the place of principles, on which the rest are built.  He who would be a skilful workman in God's building must take much pains with the foundation; but he must not dwell for ever on the first principles of the doctrine of Christ, but should endeavour to lead His people on to perfection in the knowledge of the truth.  5. A good workman will so divide the word of truth, as clearly to distinguish between the law and the gospel; between the covenant of works and the covenant of grace.  6. Another thing very necessary to a correct division of the word of truth is that the promises and threatenings contained in the Scriptures be applied to the characters to which they properly belong.  7. But finally, the word of God should be so handled that it may be adapted to Christians in different states and stages of the Divine life; for while some Christians are like "strong men," others are but "babes in Christ, who must be fed with milk, and not with strong meat." (*A. Alexander. D.D.*)     *The right division of truth :*—We will suppose a workman dealing with the yet unrenewed and unshapen material—with the unconverted of his hearers; and we will study to show you how, if he would "rightly divide the word of truth," and approve himself of his Master, he must use different modes according to the different characters upon which he has to act.  To illustrate this we may refer to a passage in St. Jude, where the apostle thus expresses himself— "Of some have compassion, making a difference; and others save with fear, pulling them out of the fire."  Here you have gentle treatment prescribed; and you have also harsh treatment.  Let us see how both will be employed by "a workman, that needeth not to be ashamed."  Of some, the minister is to "have compassion."  Is he not to have compassion of all?  Indeed he is.  Let him lay aside instantly the ministerial office; let him be pronounced utterly wanting in the very first qualification for its discharge, if there be the sinner whom he does not pity, for whom he is not anxious, or whose danger does not excite in him solicitude.  All are to be regarded with a feeling of pity, but all are not to be treated with the same mildness and forbearance. Behold that young man whose family is irreligious, who, with perhaps a sense of the necessity of providing for the soul, is laughed out of his seriousness by those who ought to be urging him to piety—hurried to amusements which are only fitted to confirm him in enmity to God, and initiated into practices which can issue in nothing but the ruin of the soul. I could not treat that young person sternly. I could not fail, in any intercourse with him, to bear in mind his peculiar disadvantages. And though it would be my duty—else could I be " study-ing to approve myself unto God "?—to remonstrate with him on the madness of allowing others to make him miserable for eternity, the very tone of my voice must show that I spake in sorrow, and not in anger. Or, behold, again, that man in dis-tressed circumstances, on whom press the cares of a large family, and who is tempted perhaps to gain the means of subsistence through practices which his con-science condemns—Sunday trading, for example. Could I go to the man in harsh-ness and with severity? I must not, indeed, spare his fault. I must not allow that his difficulties are any excuse for the offence. I had " need to be ashamed as a workman," if I did this; but, surely, when I think on his peculiar temptations, and hear the cries of his young ones who are asking him for bread, you will expect me to feel great concern for the man, and so to " divide the word of truth," as to show that concern, by the manner in which I reprove his misdoing. Or, once more, a man of no very strong intellect, and no very great reading, is thrown into the society of sceptical men perhaps of brilliant powers, and no inconsiderable acquirements. Why, he will be no match for these apostles of infidelity! His little stock of evi-dence on the side of Christianity will soon be exhausted; and he will not be able to detect the falsehoods, and show the sophistries of the showy reasoners; and pre-sently, by a very natural, though most unfair process, he will be disposed to conclude that what he cannot prove wrong must be right. Towards a man thus seduced our prevailing feeling will be compassion—a feeling which you cannot expect us to extend towards those who have seduced him, except in the broad sense that we are aware of their danger, and would snatch them from ruin. Again, it is melancholy to think how many an inquirer may have been repulsed, how many a backslider confirmed in apostasy, how many a softening heart hardened, how many a timid spirit scared by the mode in which the truth has been pressed on their attention. It requires great delicacy and address to deal successfully with a very sensitive nature; more especially where—to use the language of the world—there is much to excuse the faults which we are bound to rebuke. But if there be a right division of the word of truth, it is evident that whilst some of you may require the gentle treat-ment, others will need the more severe. There are cases of hardened and reckless men, reckless men, of the openly dissolute and profane—men living in habitual sin, and showing unblushing contempt for the truth of God. And we must not so speak as to lead you to suppose us sure that there are none amongst yourselves requiring the harsh treatment. There are men who cannot possibly be in any doubt as to the wrongness of their conduct, who cannot plead ignorance in excuse, or the suddenness of temptation, or the pressure of circumstances; but who have a decided preference for iniquity, and a settled determination to gratify their passions, or aggrandise their families—pursuing a course against which conscience remonstrates, and who would not themselves venture to advance any justification. And if we would " rightly divide the word of truth," what treatment must we try with such men? Oh! these men may yet be saved! The word of truth does not shut them up to inevitable destruction. We are not despairing of any one amongst you, and we will not. We can yet again bring you the message of pardon. And thus whilst directed to make an effort to save you, and, therefore, assured that you are not past recovery, the word of truth enjoins severe and peremptory dealing. These are those of whom St. Jude uses the remarkable expression—" Others save with fear, pulling them out of the fire." (*H. Melvill, B.D.*) *Adaptation in preaching :*—King Oswald, of North-umbria, sent for missionaries from the monastery of Iona. The first one despatched in answer to his call obtained but little success. He declared on his return that among a people so stubborn and barbarous success was impossible. " Was it their stubbornness or your severity?" asked Ardan, a brother sitting by; " did you forget God's word to give them the milk first and then the meat?" (*H. O. Mackey.*) *Adaptation :*—A divine ought to calculate his sermon, as an astronomer does his almanac, to the meridian of the place and people where he lives. (*J. Palmer.*) *Close preaching :*—Do you not know that a man may be preached to liturgically and doctrinally, and never be touched by the truth, or understand that to which he listens? Suppose I were to preach to you in Hebrew, how much would you understand? Now, when I preach so that a banker, who has all along been sitting under the doctrinal preaching, but has never felt its application to his particular business, feels the next day, when counting his coin, a twinge of conscience and says, " I wish I could either practice that sermon or forget it," I have preached the gospel to him in such a way that he has understood it. I have applied it to the sphere of life in which he lives. When the gospel is preached so that a man feels that it is applied to his own life, he has it translated to him. And it needs to be translated to merchants and lawyers, and mechanics, and every other class in society, in order that all may receive their portion in due season. (*H. W. Beecher.*) *Eccentric souls to be saved:*—Success in soul winning is only given to skill, earnestness, sympathy, perseverance. Men are saved, not in masses, but by careful study and well-directed effort. It is said that such is the eccentric flight of the snipe when they rise from the earth, that it completely puzzles the sportsman, and some who are capital shots at other birds are utterly baffled here. Eccentricity seems to be their special quality, and this can only be mastered by incessant practice with the gun. But the eccentricity of souls is beyond this, and he had need be a very spiritual Nimrod, a " mighty hunter before the Lord " who would capture them for Christ. (*H. O. Mackey.*) *False exposition:*—Few sermons are more false or dangerous than those in which the teacher professes to impress his audience by showing " how much there is in a verse." If he examined his own heart closely before beginning, he would find that his real desire was to show how much he, the expounder, could make out of the verse. But entirely honest and earnest men often fall into the same error. They have been taught that they should always look deep, and that Scripture is full of hidden meanings ; and they easily yield to the flattering conviction that every chance idea which comes into their heads in looking at a word is put there by Divine agency. Hence they wander away into what they believe to be an inspired meditation, but which is, in reality, a meaningless jumble of ideas, perhaps very proper ideas, but with which the text in question has nothing whatever to do. (*John Ruskin.*) *" Pray that sermon":*—A young beginner at preaching, after throwing off a highly wrought, and, as he thought, eloquent gospel sermon in the pulpit, in the presence of a venerable pastor, solicited of his experienced friend the benefit of his criticisms upon the performance. " I have but just one remark to make," was his reply, " and that is, to request you to pray that sermon." " What do you mean, sir ? " " I mean, literally, just what I say ; pray it, if you can, and you will find the attempt a better criticism than any I can make upon it." The request still puzzled the young man beyond measure ; the idea of praying a sermon was a thing he never heard or conceived of ; and the singularity of the suggestion wrought powerfully on his imagination and feelings. He resolved to attempt the task. He laid his manuscript before him, and on his knees before God, undertook to make it into a prayer. But it would not pray; the spirit of prayer was not in it, and that, for the very good reason—as he then clearly saw for the first time—that the spirit of prayer and piety did not compose it. For the first time he saw that his heart was not right with God ; and this conviction left him no peace until he had " Christ formed in him the hope of glory." With a renewed heart he applied himself anew to the work of composing sermons for the pulpit; preached again in the presence of the pious pastor who had given such timely advice ; and again solicited the benefit of his critical remarks. " I have no remarks to make," was his complacent reply, " you can pray that sermon." (*Sword and Trowel.*) *In the closet:*—Of Mr. John Shepherd, of the United States, it is recorded that he was greatly distinguished for his success in the pulpit. When on his death-bed he said to some young ministers who were present, " The secret of my success is in these three things: 1. " The studying of my sermons very frequently cost me tears." 2. Before I preached a sermon to others I derived good from it myself. 3. I have always gone into the pulpit as if I were immediately after to render an account to my Master." All who knew that devoted man would have united in expressing his secret in three words, " In the closet." (*Ibid.*) *Nor by the depth either:*—A young minister having preached for Doctor Emmons one day, he was anxious to get a word of applause for his labour of love. The grave doctor, however, did not introduce the subject, and the young brother was obliged to bait the hook for him. " I hope, sir, I did not weary your people by the length of my sermon to-day ? " " No, sir, not at all; nor by the depth either." (*Ibid.*) *A useful preacher:*—I know a clergyman who valued as one of the best testimonies to his pulpit ministry the remark of a servant, overheard by a friend, after a sermon specially addressed to servants : " One would think he had been a servant himself." (*J. C. Miller, D.D.*)		*Advice to preachers :*—On the fly-leaf of a Greek Testament used by Dr. John Gregg, Bishop of York, are carefully written out the following memoranda for his own guidance. They will be found interesting to those who aim at speaking in appropriate language on a subject previously studied and thought over, and they will know that the hints given are the results of much experience: " Much depends on vitality and vigour of body, much depends on the mood and spirit in which you are; therefore pray, and feed your mind with truth, and attend to health. Much depends on subject; therefore select carefully. Much on preparation; therefore be diligent. Much on kind and number of hearers. Much on method; therefore arrange. Much on manner; therefore be simple and solemn, spirit earnest, tender and affectionate. Much on language; therefore be choice. All on the Spirit; therefore invoke His presence, and rely on His power, that you may expect *docere, placere, movere.* Energy depends on the state of mind and body, ease on calmness and self-possession; this on constant intercourse with people and variety of ranks, and much practice. Read aloud various passages and portions. Think much, and read select authors. Converse with refined and well-informed persons. Prepare well for each public occasion. Exercise your powers in public often, and always do your best. Let your public manner be an enlargement of your private, and let that be natural and simple, graceful without awkwardness or affectation."

	Ver. 16. **Shun profane and vain babblings.** —*Shun :*—The word rendered " shun " is a strong one, and signifies, literally, to make a circuit so as to avoid; or as Alford paraphrases it, " the meaning seems to come from a number of persons falling back from an object of fear or loathing, and standing at a distance round it." The word is used in Tit. iii. 9. (*H. D. M. Spence, M.A.*)		**They will increase unto more ungodliness.** *Will increase :*—προκόψουσιν. The metaphor is from pioneers clearing the way before an army, by cutting down all obstacles : hence to make progress, to advance. (*Jas. Bryce, LL.D.*)		*A lax life connected with erroneous doctrine :*—The close connection between grave fundamental errors in doctrine and a lax and purely selfish life is constantly alluded to by St. Paul. (*H. D. M. Spence, M.A.*)		*Error is of an encroaching nature :*—Let the serpent but wind in his head, and he will quickly bring in his whole body. He that saith Yea to the devil in a little, shall not say Nay when he pleases. (*J. Trapp.*)		*The odium theologicum, the worst of social devils :*— On approaching my subject I shall premise four things : 1. I have no disposition to underrate the importance of right beliefs in religion. 2. I hold it to be the right of every man to endeavour to propagate his beliefs. 3. I recognise the value of a rightly-conducted theological controversy. 4. The controversy of which I have to speak is that of a conventional theology. By a conventional theology I mean a theology which a man has received from others, rather than reached by his own research ; a theology which has been put into his memory as a class of propositions, rather than wrought out of his soul as spiritual convictions; a theology which is rather the manufacture of other men than the growth of individual reflection and experience ; a theology which is more concerned about grammar than grace—symbol than sense—sign than substance. Now, such controversies, in the nature of the case, must always be marked by two features. (1) Technicality. (2) Per onality. I. SUCH CONTROVERSIES DEVELOP THE MOST IMPIOUS ARROGANCE. All the arrogancy of mere worldly men pales into dimness in the glare of the arrogancy which that man displays who dares pronounce a brother heretic because he subscribes not to his own views. II. SUCH CONTROVERSIES DEVELOP THE MOST LAMENTABLE DISHONESTY. The polemic of a mere scribe theology has ever been a cheat. 1. He cheats by the representation he makes of himself. He would have his readers or hearers believe that he has reached the conclusions in debate by a thorough study for himself of the holy Book. It is false. It is a law that self-reached convictions expel dogmatism. But the polemic of a mere scribe-theology cheats also by representing himself as being inspired only in the controversy by love for truth. It is not love for truth ; it is love for his own opinions. 2. He is dishonest in his representation of his opponents. He imputes motives not felt— ideas and conclusions not held. III. SUCH CONTROVERSIES DEVELOP A MOST DISASTROUS PERVERSITY. The conventional controversialist perverts the Bible, the powers of the intellect and the zeal of the heart. IV. SUCH CONTROVERSIES DEVELOP THE MOST HEARTLESS INHUMANITY. They blind the polemic to the excellences of others. The technical theologue who looks at a brother through the medium of his own orthodoxy, will fraternise with a modern scoundrel if he is orthodox; but, like Caiaphas of old, will rend his robes with pious horror at incarnate virtue if it conform not to his own views. What inhumanities have not been perpetrated in the name of orthodoxy! What built the inquisition? What kindled the flames of martyrdom? What animated Bonner? What prompted Calvin to murder Servetus? What roused the Jewish rabbis to put the Son of God to death? The remarks made will suffice to justify the proposition that the controversies of a mere conventional theology are the most effective means of developing depravity. (*D. Thomas, D.D.*) *Profane babbling to be avoided :*—I. PROFANE VAIN BABBLINGS ARE TO BE AVOIDED. How often does our apostle condemn them? Why are they to be avoided? 1. Because the branches which bear them are evil; as weakness of judgment, frowardness of will, and disorder in the affections. 2. And do they not blemish our reputation? obscure the gloss of grace? hinder the acts of it? kindle corruption? and turn from the faith? II. THE CAUSES WHICH INCREASE SIN ARE TO BE REMOVED. (*J. Barlow, D.D.*)

Ver. 17. **Their word will eat as doth a canker.**—*Gangrene :*—The substitution of "gangrene" for "cancer" is an improvement, as giving the exact word used in the original, which expresses the meaning more forcibly than "cancer." Cancer is sometimes very slow in its ravages, and may go on for years without causing serious harm. Gangrene poisons the whole frame, and quickly becomes fatal. The apostle foresees that doctrines, which really ate out the very heart of Christianity, were likely to become very popular in Ephesus, and would do incalculable mischief. The nature of these doctrines we gather from what follows. (*A. Plummer, D.D.*) *Unsound opinions :*—I. THE CHURCH IN ALL AGES HATH BEEN PESTERED WITH VAIN BABBLERS. II. UNSOUND OPINIONS ARE OF A SPREADING NATURE. And this is true of all sin, original and actual. 1. For doth not corruption, like a disease, disperse itself, and pollute every power of the soul and member of the body? What part is not infected with that leprous contagion? Hath it not spread also, by natural propagation, to all Adam's posterity? 2. Will not all actual sin spread also? For unbelief, hath it not run into atheism? fear, into despair? anger, into fury? and that, to revenge? Foolish mirth will become madness; temporary faith, high presumption; and speculative lust, actual whoredom. Were not images, in the beginning, for civil use, to put men in mind of deceased friends; and are they not at this day, by the Romanists, religiously adored? 3. Shall we not see one error beget another? 4. Moreover, unsound opinions spread from person to person. III. SIN WILL DESTROY, IF NOT DESTROYED. (*J. Barlow, D.D.*) *Justification by faith :*—This is a most striking and accurate description of the nature of heresy—it never remains inactive—it is sure to spread; an error in any essential point is sure, eventually, to corrupt the whole body of truth, just as a gangrene in the human body appearing, at first, as a small spot, gradually spreads, eating into the sound parts near it, and they, in their turn, infecting the rest, until the whole body is destroyed. The reason for this is very simple. The truths of religion are not a set of independent and unconnected notions bound up together in a creed, as men bind loose sticks into a bundle; they are closely connected parts of a great whole, arising one out of the other, so that you cannot deny one without denying or perverting a great many others; for once you admit a truth, you admit all its consequences; once you deny a truth, you must be prepared to deny, in like manner, all its consequences. God declares that false doctrine eats into the faith of the Church like a canker. Sacramental justification does this—therefore it is false. In order to show the injurious results of this false doctrine, we will take, for our example, that Church which most strongly holds it. The Church of Rome gives us the most awful instance of its effects. The Church of Rome holds that, at his baptism, every one is made perfectly holy; that if he remain in this state of grace, or if, after falling from it, he is restored to it again, so that he be in it at his death, then he is saved. Now let us suppose a church, as yet sound upon all other points, adopting this opinion. We shall see how it eats its way. And firstly, it must lead to the perversion of the doctrine of original sin. But further; every one knows that he is constantly committing little faults. "In many things we offend all." But Rome affirms that some sins are venial, while others are mortal. But the law of God commands as well as forbids, and they must, by their good works, continue to deserve God's favour! Now, in such a system, every work must have its own proper value, it must be just so much merit towards justification: a man who works because he has been justified, does not stop to reckon or to price his good works;

he works from love—he cannot do too much ; but he who works that he may be justified, must keep count of his good deeds, and try to ascertain their value, that he may be sure he has really done enough to secure his justification. But this is not all. In such a system of external observances, it is clear that the man most remarkable for his fastings and his many prayers is the holiest man. But we may trace it further still. These holy men, who dwell apart from the common crowd, have clearly attained a degree of holiness greater than is necessary for their own salvation. May they not, then, bestow some of it on others? So far we have been tracing the effects of this false doctrine on those who believe that they are still in a state of justification because they have retained their baptismal purity. We have now to see its effects upon those who have reason to fear that they have lost their justification. Even when men have raised their own righteousness to the utmost, and lowered God's law to the lowest, still the uneasy doubt will intrude itself— What if, after all, I have not done enough? what if I have fallen into mortal sin? Now, in such a case, of whom would the anxious sinner seek advice and consolation? who shall decide for him each nice case of conscience, and say what is venial and what is mortal sin? what are good works and what are not? Who but his pastor, God's minister, whose province it is to study such matters? He will naturally ask him to decide for him what his state may be ; but if so, he must confess all his sins to him : this spiritual physician must know all the symptoms of his case before he can give his opinion upon it ; and, accordingly, the penitent will soon acquire the habit of auricular confession of all his sins to his priest. But what if this adviser, when consulted, shall decide that he has fallen from grace and is even in mortal sin? The priest cannot re-baptize him ; how shall he regain his justification? This confessor has a right to declare God's forgiveness ; he preaches remission of sins ; what if he have a right to give it? it is but a step from saying " You are forgiven," to " I forgive you." The fears of the penitent, the ambition of the priest, soon take it ; the inquisitor becomes a judge, the ambassador assumes the authority of the king, the minister of Christ attempts to give the sinner the peace he needs, by usurping the office of his Lord and Master, who alone has power on earth to forgive sins. The canker eats its way ! There may, however, be cases where time is too short for the performance of penance—death may be imminent. For such a state another provision must be made—it is ready. There is a scriptural and primitive custom, that the elders of the Church should pray over a sick man, "anointing him with oil in the name of the Lord." All that is necessary is, to make of this rite, a sacrament conveying to the insensible, sick man remission of sins, as baptism was supposed to have given it to the insensible infant; and then his salvation is secured. Mark, now, how the true doctrine of justification preserves from all this error. Being justified by faith " I have peace"; what need have I then to confess to man? I may come boldly into the holy of holies, through the new and living way ; I need no man to tell me how great my sins may be ; I can ask God to " pardon my iniquity, for it is great!" If I address myself to my fellow man, it is for counsel and consolation, not for pardon. I have no need of extreme unction, I have "an unction from the Holy One"; I have no need of purgatorial fire, for " the blood of Christ cleanses from all sin." " Being justified by faith I have peace with God." (*W. G. Magee.*)

Ver. 18. **Saying that the resurrection is past already.**—*Error concerning the resurrection :*—The resurrection of the body, always a difficulty in ancient modes of thought, was especially so to those who, with the Essenes amongst the Jews, the Neo-Platonicians, and most of the early sects which afterwards expanded into Gnosticism, had adopted the dualism of the East, and held matter to be evil—sometimes the Evil Principle or his embodiment. Hence they were ready to avail themselves of the other sense of resurrection, the rising of those who were baptized into Christ to newness of life (Rom. vi. 35; Col. ii. 12) ; and they denied that any further revelation was to be believed. This error had been early taught in the Corinthian Church (1 Cor. xv. 12). (*Speaker's Commentary.*) **And overthrow the faith of some.**—*Overthrowing the faith of others :*—After an infidel had succeeded in sapping the foundation of his mother's faith in the Christian religion, he received a letter from her one day, informing him that she was near death. She said that " she found herself without any support in her distress ; that he had taken away that only resource of comfort upon which in all cases of affliction she used to rely, and that she now found her mind sinking into despair. She did not doubt that her son would afford her some substitute for her religion; and she conjured him to hasten to her, or, at least, to send her a letter containing such consolations as philosophy could afford to a dying mortal." He was overwhelmed with anguish on receiving this letter, and hastened to Scotland, travelling day and night; but before he arrived his mother expired. *Unreliable ministers:*—A misplaced buoy caused the wreck of a steamer worth £25,000, the loss of a valuable cargo and peril to many lives recently. The steamer, which was called the *City of Portland*, left Boston on her voyage to St. Johns, N.B., with seventy passengers on board and considerable freight. The night was clear, and as the steamer passed the Owl's Head just before daybreak, the captain saw a striped buoy indicating the presence of a sunken rock. The course was altered in accordance with the position of the buoy, but in a few minutes the steamer struck a ledge. The pumps were started at once, distress colours set, and the boats cleared. The officers and crew retained their presence of mind, and despatched a boat for help. In a short time a steamer arrived, and took off the terrified passengers, but the steamer and cargo were a total loss. The captain of the ship was in no way blameable. The buoy, which was put there to be a means of safety, was by its displacement the cause of disaster. It had drifted. Similarly some preachers drift from orthodox positions, and their change of position may cause the wreck of the souls of those who flock to hear them. *Ministerial responsibility:*—During a voyage, sailing in a heavy sea near a reef of rocks, a minister on board the vessel made, in a conversation between the man at the helm and the sailors, an inquiry whether they should be able to clear the rocks without making another tack, when the captain gave orders that they should put off to avoid all risk. The minister observed, "I am rejoiced that we have so careful a commander." The captain replied, "It is necessary I should be very careful, because I have souls on board. I think of my responsibility, and remember that, should anything happen through carelessness, souls are very valuable." The minister, turning to some of his congregation who were upon the deck, observed, "The captain has preached me a powerful sermon; I hope I shall never forget, when I am addressing my fellow-creatures on the concerns of eternity, that I have souls on board." (*Archbp. Benson.*)

Ver. 19. **The foundation of God standeth sure.**—*Nevertheless:*—We should give full force to the μέντοι. If the spirit of the apostle was perturbed with vain babblings, or cruel mortification, or the spread of plausible or perilous theories, he required to fall back upon great and deep principles. (*H. R. Reynolds, D.D.*)    *The foundation:*—Rather, "God's firm foundation stands," *i.e.*, the Church, the "great house" of ver. 20, but here designated by its "foundation," because the antithesis is to the baseless fabrics of heresy. Other explanations have been: the doctrine of the resurrection of the body, the promises of God, the fidelity of God, Christ, the Christian faith, the election of God. But the context and the analogy of Eph. ii. 19–22 leave little doubt of the correctness of the first interpretation. (*Speaker's Commentary.*) *The foundation of God:*—The scene here is one of destruction and desolation. On all sides houses are shaken and overturned. The houses are individuals or communities professing to believe the gospel. The faith of some, of many diversely minded and diversely influenced, is overthrown. But, amid the storm and wreck occasioned by false principles issuing in corrupt practice, there is a building which standeth sure. Now it may be the Church collective of which it is said, the Church which has the Lord's promise that the gates of hell shall not prevail against her. But it may also be the individual believer that is intended; for the collective Church and the individual believer are on the same footing. For my present purpose I take the text in this latter view, and hold it to be descriptive of the Christian man, continuing steadfast and firm in his faith amid many surrounding instances of backsliding and apostasy. He is a tower, or temple, or building of some sort standing sure; being the foundation of God. And in token of that security he is sealed. He is doubly sealed; sealed on both sides. I. "THE LORD KNOWETH THEM THAT ARE HIS." 1. The Lord knoweth them that are His by signs or marks or tokens bearing on His interest or right of property in them, His ownership of them. Thus, He knows them as given to Him by the Father from before all worlds, in the everlasting covenant. The Lord knoweth them that are His as redeemed by Him. He knows them by the Spirit's work in them also. 2. The other class of marks or tokens by which the Lord knoweth them that are His, those bearing upon their interest or right of property in Him, do unquestionably come within the range and sphere of your consciousness and experience. They are, in fact, in the main, but an expansion, or unfolding, of the last of the three former ones, the work of the Spirit making you Christ's, and Christ yours, and keeping you evermore in this blessed unity. (1) The Lord knoweth them that are His, by the need they have of Him. (2) By the trust they put in Him. (3) By the love they bear to Him. (4) By the work they do for Him. (5) By their suffering for and with Him. (6) As waiting for Him. Now, put together all these marks by which the Lord knoweth them that are His, and say what must His thus knowing them mean? what must it imply and involve? Nay, rather, what will it not include of watchful care, tender pity, unwearied sympathy, unbounded beneficence and liberality and bountifulness? II. "LET EVERY ONE THAT NAMETH THE NAME OF CHRIST DEPART FROM INIQUITY." 1. Naming the name of Christ comes before departing from iniquity. This is the evangelical arrangement. And it is the only one that can meet the sinner's case. 2. Naming the name of Christ is to be followed by departing from iniquity: and that not only in the form of a natural and necessary consequence to be anticipated, but in that of obedience to a peremptory command. It is not said, He that nameth the name of Christ may be expected, or will be inclined, or must be moved by a Divine impulse, to depart from iniquity. But it is expressly put as an authoritative and urgent precept. "Let him that nameth the name of Christ depart from iniquity." 3. Naming the name of Christ and departing from iniquity thus go together. They are not really twain, but one. There is not first a naming of the name of Christ, as if it were an act or a transaction to be completed at once, and so disposed of and set aside; and then thereafter a departing from iniquity, as its fitting consequence and commanded sequel. The two things cannot be thus separated. For, in truth, naming the name of Christ involves departing from iniquity; and departing from iniquity is possible only by naming the name of Christ. (*R. S. Candlish, D.D.*)  *The palace and its inscription :*—I. THE SAFETY OF THE CHURCH IS FOUNDED ON GOD'S IMMUTABILITY. Whether the truth is regarded as an abstract existence, or as personified in the Church, it takes its stand on this attribute of the Divine Being. All ecclesiastical history is but a commentary upon the fact that "the foundation of the Lord standeth sure." The pledge of Church safety rests on Fact and Promise. Time would fail us to trace out the former. We see it in that dark vessel ploughing the waves of an ocean-sepulchre, and settling on the crest of Ararat. We see it in those weeping tribes by the river of Babylon; for though their harps are silent, the very breeze that stirs the willow echoes the voice of Israel's God! We see it in that pillar of cloud and in that pillar of light. We hear Daniel rejoicing over it in the lion's den, and the faithful Hebrews proving it in the furnace of fire, and all the countless multitudes of Christ's confessors deepen the voice of confirmation! History is our stronghold of proof. We dare the sceptic to unbolt the door of the past, and show us wherein the Divine immutability has failed. Shall we turn to Promise, to show the Church's safety? It is like turning to a sky lighted with constellations of suns, or to a world bespangled with rarest flowers, or to a land flowing with milk and honey. To record the promises were a task almost equal to transcribing the entire Bible. II. THE SEAL WITH WHICH GOD HAS ENSTAMPED THE CHURCH PARTAKES OF HIS IMMUTABILITY. There is no mistaking it. Time does not obliterate it. The "seal" cannot be successfully counterfeited in the eye of God. He knows His own. 1. This "seal" is ornamental. A monarch's star is a mere toy—give it time and it will rot. Young men, you seek after the decorative, here it is! It "shall be an ornament of grace unto thy head, and chains about thy neck." 2. This "seal" is a passport to confidence. Christianity has won many compliments in its practical outworking, from those who effect to despise the evidence on which its claim to divinity is founded! 3. This "seal" is an earnest of future glory. Such is the testimony of Scripture (2 Cor. i. 21, 22; Eph. iv. 30). III. THE SEAL INDICATES DISCRIMINATION AND APPRECIATION OF CHARACTER. "The Lord knoweth them that are His." What mean those strange words? In the wide sense of creation all men are God's—in the sense of Providence all are the pensioners of His bounty; and Jesus Christ is the propitiation for our sins, and not for ours only, but for the sins of the whole world. There are standing places in the universe, from which all humanity may be regarded as the peculiar property of God. But there is an inner circle in which are found hearts differing from the majority—hearts bearing the "seal" of God-property. 1. The thought that God appreciates the Christian character, and will finally glorify it, is to the believer a source of comfort. 2. This thought, moreover, imparts a sense of security. 3. This thought, again, suggests principles of action. Fond as we may be of comfort, and anxious to be assured of security, there is something *positive* expected from our Divine relationship. If God knows me, the world must know me too. The

Christian has a profession to maintain.  IV. DISTINCTIONS IN MORAL CHARACTER
MAY EXIST WITHOUT THE SEAL OF DIVINE APPRECIATION.  If all men were God's in
the peculiar sense of the text, there would be no special meaning in its terms.  A
class is referred to, in contradistinction to all other classes.  There are only two
sections in the domain of moral being—the good and the bad ; these again being
broken up into almost endless sub-divisions, shades and stages of development.  To
make the leading proposition clearer, take a sample of instances :—1. Here is a
man of keen religious sensibility.  A tender heart is a great treasure, indeed, but
let not a few tears be considered proof of penitence.  2. Here is the rigid formalist.
Religion is a life, not a form : it is an actual power and not an elaborate creed.
The Cross, and not the pew, is the true way to heaven.  3. A third hopes in the
mercy of God.  A benevolent God, he argues, will not destroy one of His own
creatures.  He forgets the harmony of the Divine attributes.  Overlooking an outraged justice, he hopes in an insulted love.  Terrible is the portion of those who
bear not God's seal (Rev. ix. 3, 4).  V. THE CHURCH, AS A PALACE, MUST HAVE
UNITY, COMPLETION, AND DESIGN.  The Church is not a broken fragment or a shattered limb.  It is a whole, where individual members have their part to play.  The
large stones and the small ones must be side by side.  The position that
each shall occupy in the temple must be determined by the wise Master-
builder.  If one member is jealous of another's position there is an end
to unity and progress.  We are each dependent on the other.  (*J. Parker, D.D.*)
*The firm foundation :*—The time in which we live, presents two striking, and to
many minds incongruous, features.  1. There is great unrest in the realm of religious thought and life.  On every side are heard voices of dissent from both theological and ecclesiastical dogmas.  Schools and Churches are shaken with strife.
Many are anxiously questioning concerning the stability of the Christian faith, and
not a few are prophesying evil.  There is a strong and increasing revolt against
traditionalism.  But with this commotion in the realm of religious thought there
is (2) a great increase of practical Christianity.  Missions both at home and abroad
are pushed more vigorously than ever, and with larger results.  Education for the
people advances with leaps and bounds.  Philanthropic enterprises multiply in
number and increase in wisdom and efficiency continually.  The Church is stripping off her dainty garments and grappling with social problems in a new spirit.
There is a broadening application of Christianity to life, such as no past age has
witnessed.  In a word, the situation is this : The power of dogma wanes, but the
power of truth waxes ; forms are decadent, life is crescent ; religious authority is
challenged on every side, spiritual influence broadens and deepens.  Here is a
seeming contradiction or anomaly.  Many do not understand the times.  In their
alarm over the upheaval in the realm of religious thought they fail to see or to
appreciate the uplift in the realm of religious life.  Can we not see that

> " God fulfils Himself in many ways,
> Lest one good custom should corrupt the world " ?

There is a " firm foundation of God."  A careful study of the Scriptures, of
history, and of experience makes clear—(1) That the essential basis of Christianity
is not an institution, nor even a book.  Christianity was before the Church.  Christianity was before the New Testament.  It produced the Gospels and Epistles, as in
the olden time the prophetic spirit and experience antedated and produced the
prophetic history and literature.  Men forget this.  They forget that God and the
soul, and God revealing Himself to the soul, precede the institutions and records
of religion.  (2) It is clear also that the essential basis of Christianity is not a
creed.  Faith existed before dogma.  It terminates in a personality and not in a
proposition or any series of propositions.  Dogma is the result of an attempt
to express and justify faith as an intellectual possession.  It is natural and inevitable that men should make this attempt.  But the process which goes on in the
sphere of the understanding, or even its result, must not be identified with Christianity any more than physiology should be identified with the exercise of physio-
logical functions, or dietetics with eating, or optics with seeing.  Creeds change as
life and thoughts change.  They *must* change if there is life.  Thought grows.
Experience deepens.  All creeds save the simplest, the most elemental, are left
behind.  They are not basal, but resultant.  They belong to the sphere of the
understanding.  (3) The essential basis of Christianity is a personal revelation of
God in and through " the man Christ Jesus," and a personal experience of a

Divine communion and a Divine guidance. How do we know God? Not by argument, but by experiencing the touch of God on the soul. There is a Divine impact on the spirit of man. Argument is always subordinate to experience. How do we know God as Father? Through the revelation of the archetypal Divine Sonship in Christ and the *experience* of sonship through fellowship with Him. Spiritual experience underlies Christianity. The great spiritual verities comes to us always as experiences. They authenticate themselves in consciousness. "How do you know that Christ is Divine?" said a Methodist bishop to a frontiersman whom he was examining for admission into the ministry. The brawny-limbed and little-cultivated but big-hearted man looked at the bishop a moment in silence, and then, as his eyes filled with tears, he exclaimed: "Why, bless you, sir, He saved my soul!" It was another way of saying: "I *know* whom I have believed, and I am persuaded that He is able to keep that which I have committed unto Him until that day." This experience of God is inseparable from the perception and the acceptance of an inclusive ethical principle that makes life the progressive realisation of a Divine ideal of righteousness. The experience of a Divine communion and the attraction of a Divine ideal belong to the essence of Christianity. "Let every one that nameth the name of the Lord depart from unrighteousness." Christianity has its essential basis, then, in a personal revelation of God in and through the Christ, and a personal experience of God as life and love, as source and goal, as ideal and law. The Book, or the institution, may be a means to the experience, but the experience is fundamental. Along this line of experience lies the test of all doctrines. Truth is realised in *being*. This foundation stands sure. It is not shaken by changes in Church or creed. History is full of illustrations. The Reformation came shattering the mediæval Church as with throes of earthquake. Many sincere souls cried out in dismay that Christianity was overthrown. But the convulsion passed, and Christianity put on new power to bless the world. Within the present century geology began to tell its marvellous story of creation, and many devout souls saw in it a deadly menace to religion. Genesis became a rallying-ground for the alarmed theological hosts. But truth had its way. Old ideas and interpretations of the Mosaic cosmogony fell away, and Christianity spread more and more widely among the people. Then came Darwin, with his appalling and atheistical ideas of evolution! Then, indeed, the ark of God was in danger! Doughty champions of the faith drew their weapons for battle, while the timid were ready to exclaim that Church and Bible alike were doomed unless the new foe were vanquished. The foe has proved the best of friends. Evolution soon appeared to be a great structural principle of thought in all realms of study. It has entered the domains of sociology, politics, history, philosophy, and even theology. Meanwhile Christianity, better understood by the very principle that seemed to threaten its life, increases in power continually. Nothing is shaken and overturned by human progress but what ought to be shaken and overturned. Nothing true ever perishes. Christianity has proved itself hospitable to every advance in knowledge, and to every social and political change that has been a step forward in the long battle-march of humanity. They are guilty of a great error who base the validity of the gospel of Divine love and eternal life on any *theory* of creation or inspiration, or on any fixed scheme of social and political organisation. They say; If this theory of inspiration or salvation or church order is discredited, Christianity is discredited. But a hundred theories have been discredited, and even disproved, and Christianity is better authenticated and has a wider and stronger hold on the world to-day than ever. "The firm foundation of God standeth." These are marks of abiding Christianity: The personal experience of God and the spiritual attraction of righteousness—God in the soul, a motive and an ideal. Cultivate the passion, not for safety, but for righteousness, the realisation of love in conduct. Strive not for fixedness, but for growth. Spiritual permanence is permanence of growth in knowledge and goodness. Love for God and man walks with sure feet through paths where selfishness stumbles and sinks in bogs of doubt and despair. Keep the mind open to the ever-teaching Spirit of God. There are withheld revelations that wait for the unfolding of capacity in man to receive God's disclosure. Be content with nothing. Let faith in God and love to man be the broad base on which to build the aspiring structure of an eternal life. That foundation standeth sure. Trust God for the future of humanity. The world was not made in jest, nor does the kingdom of God rest on a contingency. Faith, as well as love, casteth out fear. Two boys were talking together of Elijah's ascent in the chariot of fire. Said one: "Wouldn't you be afraid to ride in such a chariot?" "No," said the other, "not if God drove!" God drives the chariot of human progress, and it mounts as it advances. God is in His world, not outside of it. He is redeeming it from sin. He is making men. He is fulfilling His holy and beneficent purpose. Fear not, but believe and hope, for the power as well as the glory is His to whom be glory for ever and ever. (*P. S. Moxom.*) *The foundation and its seal:*—I. First, let us think of THE LAMENTABLE OVERTHROW which the apostle so much deplored. 1. The apostle observed with sorrow a general coldness. It was in some respect coldness towards himself, but in reality it was a turning away from the simplicity of the doctrine of salvation by grace through faith (see the 15th verse of the previous chapter). 2. Furthermore, the apostle saw with much alarm that teachers were erring. He names two especially, Hymenæus and Philetus, and he mentions the doctrine that they taught—not needlessly explaining it, but merely giving a hint at it. They taught, among other things, that the resurrection was past already. I suppose they had fallen into the manner of certain in our day, who spiritualise or rationalise everything. 3. In Paul's day many professors were apostatising from the faith because of the evil leaders. Sheep are such creatures to follow something that, when they do not follow the shepherd, they display great readiness to follow one another. 4. Paul also deplored that ungodliness increased. He says that the profane and vain babblings of his time increased unto more ungodliness. II. Now let us turn to the subject which supplied Paul with consolation. He speaks of the ABIDING FOUNDATION : "Nevertheless the foundation of God standeth sure." What is this foundation which standeth sure ? Those who have interpreted the passage have given many meanings to it, but I believe that all those meanings are really one. For the sake of clearness I would give three answers to the inquiry : the foundation is, secretly, the purpose of God ; doctrinally, the truth of God ; effectively, the Church of God ; in all, the system of God whereby He glorifies His grace. III. Now, we are to look at this foundation and observe THE INSTRUCTIVE INSCRIPTION. I think this figure best expresses the apostle's intent; he represents the foundation-stone, as bearing a writing upon it, like the stone mentioned by the prophet Zechariah of which we read, "I will engrave the graving thereof, saith the Lord of hosts, and I will remove the iniquity of that land in one day." The custom of putting inscriptions upon foundation-stones is ancient and general. In the days of the Pharaohs, the royal cartouche was impressed upon each brick that was placed in buildings raised by royal authority. The structure was thus known to have been erected by a certain Pharaoh. Here we have the royal cartouche, or seal, of the King of kings set upon the foundation of the great palace of the Church. The House of Wisdom bears on its forefront and foundation the seal of the Lord. The Jews were wont to write texts of Scripture upon the door-posts of their houses ; in this also we have an illustration of our text. The Lord has set upon His purpose, His gospel, His truth, the double mark described in the text—the Divine election and the Divine sanctification. This seal is placed to declare that it belongs to the Lord alone, and to set it apart for His personal habitation. If I might use another illustration, I can suppose that when the stones for the temple were quarried in the mountains, each one received a special mark from Solomon's seal, marking it as a temple stone, and perhaps denoting its place in the sacred edifice. This would be like the first inscription, "The Lord knoweth them that are His." But the stone would not long lie in the quarry, it would be taken away from its fellows, after being marked for removal. Here is the transport mark in the second inscription : "Let every one that nameth the name of Christ depart from iniquity." The first mark—1. Is concerning God and us. "The Lord knoweth them that are His." 2. The text teaches us that the Lord discriminates. Some who bear His name are not His, and He knows them not. 3. "The Lord knoweth them that are His" signifies that He is familiar with them, and communes with them. They that are really the Lord's property are also the Lord's company : He has intercourse with them. 4. Further, the words imply God's preservation of His own; for when God knows a man He approves him, and consequently preserves him. The second seal is concerning us and God—"Let every one that nameth the name of Christ depart from iniquity." Observe how the practical always goes with the doctrinal in holy Scripture. Those whom free grace chooses, free grace cleanses. This is a sweeping precept as to the thing to be avoided : let him "depart from iniquity"—not from this or that crime or folly, but from iniquity itself, from everything that is evil, from everything that is unrighteous or unholy. The text is very decisive—it does not say, "Let him put iniquity on one side," but, "Let him depart from it." Get away from evil. All your lives long travel further and further from it. Do you know where my text originally came from? I believe it was taken from the Book of Numbers. Read in the sixteenth chapter the story of Korah, Dathan, and Abiram. In the Septuagint almost the same words occur as those now before us. The Lord Jesus is exercising discipline in His Church every day. It is no trifling matter to be a Church member, and no small business to be a preacher of the gospel. If you name the name of Christ, you will either be settled in Him or driven from Him. There is continually going on an establishment of living stones upon the foundation, and a separating from it of the rubbish which gathers thereon. (*C. H. Spurgeon.*) *The stability of God's purpose :*—It may be asked, how did it happen that under the direct observation of the apostles themselves, standing as they did on such exclusive ground, acting in the name and by the authority of the Lord Jesus Christ, and clothed with all the awful powers of their high office—how happened it that so many and such dangerous errors arose? It might be permitted—1. To ascertain the faith and put to the test the obedience of the sincere. There must be heresies that these may be proved and made manifest. 2. To show that the claims of the religion of Jesus Christ are not guided or influenced by secular authority, and that men's minds are left perfectly free, at liberty to think and determine for themselves. 3. To illustrate the nature of the early discipline of the Christian Church. It was not such as affected men's properties or lives, as has too frequently been the case where ecclesiastical authority has been felt. Paul put down error by virtue of his authority as an apostle ; but we find nothing carnal in any of his proceedings. 4. To furnish occasions for developing more clearly the essentials of Christianity. Three topics of reflection are suggested to us here—I. THE STABILITY OF GOD'S PURPOSE. The idea which we found on this part of the subject is, the certain continuance and continual accomplishment of God's purposes, spite of all difficulties, oppositions, and enemies. But it has respect chiefly—1. To the truth of God ; and 2. To the Church of God. II. THE SPECIAL OBJECTS OF GOD'S PURPOSE. "The foundation of God standeth sure ; having this seal, the Lord knoweth them that are His," &c. 1. In speaking of the special objects of God's love, we shall notice chiefly the character under which they are described—they are "His." This implies knowledge, discrimination, approbation, acknowledgment. They are "His"—His by dedication. 2. His in consequence of a gracious influence on their hearts. 3. His in consequence of an interest in Christ. But this question is naturally suggested : How are we to determine whether we are His ? How are we to know that we belong to the number of the called, and chosen, and faithful ? The answer is ready—"Let every one that nameth the name of Christ, depart from iniquity," and this leads us—III. To consider THE HOLY CHARACTER WHICH OUGHT TO RESULT FROM CHRISTIAN PRINCIPLES. Consider here—1. The profession assumed. They "name the name of Christ." This includes in it an admission of His authority—a reception of His doctrines—a public avowal of their sentiments and convictions. 2. The obligation enjoined. Let him "depart from iniquity." To depart from iniquity is to hate it—to be habitually opposed to the commission of it—to avoid it with the greatest circumspection—to seek and pursue whatever is opposed to it. 3. This is enjoined by the authority of Him whose name we bear. Can we think on that holy name without calling to mind the purity it should inspire ? He gave Himself for us that He might redeem us from all iniquity. Think of His character—it was holy and heavenly : of His doctrines—every word of God is pure : of His institutions—they are all designed to promote our sanctification : of the great ends and designs of His government—these are all connected with our purity. There is not a doctrine, not a testimony, not a precept which Christ has laid down, not a promise which He has caused to be recorded, which does not lead to the inculcation of holiness. On all parts of the Christian system we see inscribed, "Be ye holy, for I am holy." 4. This is enforced by the peculiar discoveries of revelation. Can you mention a doctrine which does not lead to holiness ? 5. This departure from iniquity is an essential and constituent part of the salvation of the gospel. 6. This is provided for by the continual agency of the Holy Spirit. 7. This is the design of all gospel institutions. 8. This is the great end of all providential dispensations. 9. It is that without which all our professions would be nullified and useless. (*J. Fletcher, D.D.*) *What is religion :*—We have come in our day into times precisely like those of the apostle, in which there is a great movement throughout the whole civilised world, and a great change of feeling, either of apprehension or of words, in regard to the stability of the Christian religion. I declare that the essential elements of Christianity were never so apparent as to-day; that they were never so influential; that they were never so likely to produce institutions of power; that they never had such a hold on human reason and human conscience; and that the religious impulse of the human race was never so deep and never so strong in its current. In the first place, then, we must recollect that there may be very great changes around about religion, in its external forms, without any essential interior change, nay, even with the augmentation of its interior power. Some men think that anything which is a revelation from God must be always one and the same thing; but God's revelation is alphabetic; it is a revelation of letters, and they can be combined and recombined in ten thousand different words, varying endlessly. The great facts which are fundamental to consciousness, once being given, are alphabetic; and these facts may be combined; and with the development of the human race in intelligence and moral excellence they go on taking new forms, and larger experiences must have a larger expression. It is said that men do not believe in virtue. Well, when a man tells me that the refinements of the schoolmen are lapsing on questions which relate to eternal regeneration through the Son of God, and that many of the fine distinctions between ability natural and ability spiritual are going out of men's thoughts and out of much use, I admit it; but I say that the great fundamental truths of religion— namely, the nature of man, the wants of man, and Divine love as a sufficient supply for human wants—instead of growing weaker are growing stronger in men's minds. After all the pother that is made about the doctrines of human depravity, and the need of regeneration by the power of the Holy Ghost, are they not true? Men kick them about like so many footballs; but do they not recognise them as true when they are stated in a different way from that in which they have been accustomed to hear them stated, and in a way which is suited to the experience of our times? Men think these truths are passing out of the world; but I say they are simply taking another form of exposition. The truths themselves are inherent, universal, indestructible. Religion is not one thing. It means the moving of the human soul rightly toward God, toward man, and toward duty. He who is using his whole self according to laws of God is religious. Some men think that devotion is religion. Yes, devotion is religion; but it is not all of religion. Here is a tune written in six parts, and men are wrangling and quarrelling about it. One says that the harmony is in the bass, another that it is in the soprano, another that it is in the tenor, and another that it is in the alto; but I say that it is in all the six parts. Each may, in and of itself, be better than nothing; but it requires the whole six parts to make what was meant by the musical composer. Some men say that love is religion. Well, love is certainly the highest element of it: but it is not that alone. Justice is religion; fidelity is religion; hope is religion; faith is religion; obedience is religion. These are all part and parcel of religion. Religion is as much as the total of manhood, and it takes in every element of it. All the elements of manhood, in their right place and action, are constituent parts of religion; but no one of them alone is religion. It takes the whole manhood, imbued and inspired of God, moving right both heavenward and earthward, to constitute religion. I ask you to consider what religion is according to the definition of Paul—" The fruit of the Spirit is love, joy, peace, long-suffering, gentleness, goodness, faith, meekness, temperance." I do not care whether a man whitewashes or blackwashes his fence, or whether he uses guano or barn-yard manure, or what his mode of cultivation may be, the question is, Does he get good fruit? If he does, his method is good. Now, I take it that the apostle is speaking of religion when he speaks of the fruit of the Spirit; and the fruit of the Spirit is what? Orthodoxy? Oh, no. Conscience? Not a bit of it. One of the fruits of the Spirit is love; and is love dead? Another fruit of the Spirit is joy; and is joy gone? Peace, the strangest of fruits—is it not slowly coming to be that which is the unison of all other qualities with blessedness in the soul? Ye, then, who mourn because particular modes are changing, and think that religion is dying out, look deeper, and pluck up hope out of your despair, and confidence out of your fear; and to you that think religion is going away because of science, let me say that science is the handmaid of religion. It is the John Baptist, oftentimes, that clears the way for true religion. By religion I do not mean outward things, but inward states. I mean perfected manhood. I mean the quickening of the soul by the beatific influence of the Divine Spirit in truth, and love, and sympathy, and confidence, and trust. That is not dying out. (*H. W. Beecher.*)    *The sure foundations :*—It is the nature of truth, as it is developed by human intelligence and used for practical purposes, to gather to itself instruments and institutions. The permanence of great fundamental truths, and the infinite variability of the exponents of truth, in the form of law, custom, philosophical statement—these are the two great truths with which we are to expound the past history of religion in the world, and by which also we are to prepare the way for its development in the days that are to come. After a while men lose sight of the truth in the instruments of it. They cease to worship the thing, and worship its exponent; so that, by-and-by, it is not the truth that men follow so much as its institutions. And so, as soon as this takes place, men, following their senses and their lower nature, begin a process of idolatry, of professionalism; and they become worshippers of the sensuous. So it comes to pass that all religions tend on the one side downward, and on the other side upward. The tendency to carry on truth to a higher and nobler form co-exists with another tendency to hold the truth in just the same confined forms with which it has hitherto been served. And so Churches find in themselves the elements of explosion and of controversy. Then comes revolution or reformation. Then comes sectarianism—or the principle, rather, from which sects grow. Now, in the time of St. Paul, vast changes were taking place. Mosaism, or religion as developed through the instrumentality of Mosaic institutions, had ripened and gone to seed, and was passing away; and in so far as the Gentile world was concerned, there was no further attempt on the part of the apostles to teach religion by the old forms and under the old methods. If you turn your eyes toward the Greek nation, which was the thinking nation of the world, they had knowledge, philosophy and art, but they had no moral sense. If you turn to the Roman empire, there was organisation, there was law, and an effete idolatry. Now came Christianity. But Christianity in itself, in its very origin, was vexed with schisms, with disputings; and it was in the midst of these confusions that Paul made the declaration of our text, that "the foundation of God standeth sure." No matter what this man thinks, or that man teaches; no matter what shadows come or go, be sure of one thing—that the immutable foundations of religion stand. They will not be submerged permanently, nor will they rot in the ground; and they have this seal or superscription, written, as it were, on the corner-stone: "The Lord knoweth them that are His." There is the great truth of Divine existence, and intelligence, and active interference in human affairs. God is not blotted out by men's doubts, or reasonings, or philosophies, themselves caused by the interpenetration of Divine thought upon human intelligence. "God knoweth them that are His." "Let every one that nameth the name of Christ depart from iniquity." That is the other seal—aspiration for goodness; departure from all evil; an earnest, thorough and persistent seeking after a godly manhood. There are the two elements. There are fundamental elements in a Christian Church which we ought to speak of, and which we ought to mean when we speak of fundamental doctrines, and there are those which are necessary for the formation of the individual character, and for the transformation of man from an animal to a spiritual being. These are the fundamental truths which stand connected with the existence, government, and power of God in the world; and also with the organised development of human nature, that it may rise toward God. Now, it so happens that there are a great many things fundamental to theology which are not at all fundamental to human nature; and it so happens, on the other side, that there are in human nature a great many things which are fundamental to the organisation of a noble and manly character, but are hardly recognisable in theology at all. We ought, then, to clear our minds of the misuse of the term fundamental doctrines. No doctrines are fundamental except those that teach the Divine existence and government, or that teach the condition and wants of human nature, and its reconstruction, its re-organisation into Christian manhood. Men cannot live without religion. They cannot be men without it. The State calls for it; art calls for it; home and domesticity call for it; the voice of mankind and the voice of the ages have called and are calling for it; and they are either ignorant or cowardly who fear that any great disaster is going to befall religion in consequence of the progress which is taking place in the investigation of truth. Do you believe in a providence? Is this great world floating without a rudder, without a pilot or a captain? is time made up of chance-drifts? or is there a God? If there is a God, has He a future, and is He steering time and the race towards that future? And will He sleep or forget, and allow the race to run to ruin? The Word of God, the foundations of God, stand sure. Now, this general fear will lead us to take into consideration the necessity of a closer union and affiliation of true Christian people. It seems to me what we need is, not to go back to old systems, or to cling to the old

Churches, but simply this : that we should search for the great fundamental facts and truths which stand connected with the development of human nature from animalism to spirituality, and work together on these common grounds. Not that I would abolish ordinances, days, or institutions. I say to every sect, " Act according to your belief in regard to these things. Keep your theory ; ordain as you think best ; organise as you think best ; let your ordinances be such as you think best ; make your philosophical systems such as you think best ; but stand with your brethren. Do not let the veins of your life run just as far as the walls of your church, and then come back again ; let them go forth throughout Christendom." (*Ibid.*)     *The foundations of the Christian faith :*—The scepticism which we have to meet to-day concerns itself not with specific doctrine, but with the very roots and foundation of Christian faith itself. Time was when the foundation of Christian faith was the authority of the Church. The authority of the Church as the foundation of Christian faith has passed away. Nor is the Bible, the printed Book, in any true and profound sense the foundation of our Christian faith. Underneath the Bible there is a foundation on which the Bible itself rests. Now modern thought proposes, in lieu of these two foundations, another, the human reason, and it asks us to bring all our questionings and our faiths to the bar of the intellect, and have them adjudged and determined there. I shall not stop to argue whether reason be a sufficient foundation for our Christian faith ; but I undertake to say that it is not the foundation of our Christian faith, and that we believe not because things are asserted by the Church, not merely because they are printed in the Book, not merely because they commend themselves to our reason. Deep down in the human life there is yet a foundation underneath all these. We do not object to bringing all Christian faiths to the bar of reason. We believe our Christian faith is not unreasonable ; but there are truths which are not arrived at by argumentative processes ; they are not reached by processes of logic ; they are not demonstrated ; they are known. Æsthetic truths, we do not prove them, we see them. All our moral beliefs rest on this foundation ; we do not argue them, we know them. Love, patriotism, honesty, justice, truth, by what chemical processes will you analyse these ? How will you put them into the scales and weigh them ; by what logical demonstration will you prove they exist ? Now that which is true in respect of all the æsthetic elements of life, that which is true in respect of the moral element of life is true in respect of the great spiritual realm. Our articles of Christian faith rest on our vital, personal, living experience in them. Why do I believe in God ? Why do you believe in your mother ? You have seen her. I beg your pardon ; you never saw your mother. You have seen the eyes, the forehead, the cheeks, the face—that is not mother. If that be mother, then why, when the form lies prostrate, and you press the kiss upon the lips, and they give no answering kiss back, and you press the hand, and it gives no answering pressure back, why burst you into tears ? Why wring your hands with grief ? The lips are there, the brow is there, the cheeks are there, all that you ever saw is there. But mother is gone ; and love, patience, fidelity, self-sacrifice, long-suffering—that is what makes the mother that you loved—that you have never seen. And we believe in God because we have known the tenderness of His love, because in times of great weakness He has strengthened us, and in times of great sorrow He has comforted us, and in times of great darkness He has guided us, because we have known in our inmost experience the power that is of God in life's struggle. Why do you believe in immortality ? It is not because of the philosophical arguments that have been addressed to you ; it is not because of the proof texts you can find in the Scriptures ; we know that we are immortal, as the bird knows that it has power to fly while yet it lies in its nest, and waits for the moment when it shall soar off into the invisible air. There is no better argument for immortality than that of the French Christian to his deistical friend. When the deist had finished a long scholastic argument, the Christian Frenchman replied, with a shrug of the shoulders, " Probably you are right ; you are not immortal, but I am." Now, when this view of the foundation of the Christian faith is employed, men sometimes object to it and say, " You are appealing to our feelings, you are not willing to test Christian truth where all truth must be tested, in the clear light of reason ; you are appealing to our feelings, to our prepossessions, to our desires, to our sentiments." Not at all. I am putting our Christian faith on that foundation on which all our knowledge and all our belief rest, albeit our Christian faith stands closer to the foundation than anything else. All that science has taught us, all that travel, all that history, all that observation, either of our own or observations of others, all is based, in the analysis, upon this—the truthfulness either of our own personal consciousness, or of the consciousness of others. Now, we carry in our hearts the consciousness of a Divine presence outside ourselves. We look upon this life of Christ, and it stirs within us a new and a Divine life. We know the power there is in the pardoning and atoning grace of the Lord Jesus Christ. Why do we believe the Bible is an inspired Book? Because it is an inspiring Book, because it has given us comfort that no other book ever did, life that no other book ever gave, strength that no other book ever gave, because in our own personal use and experience of it it has been the life of God in our hearts. Moreover, our Christian faith rests not merely upon our own consciousness, it rests upon the concurrent consciousness of innumerable witnesses. But mark you one thing more. Our Christian faith rests on our consciousness, on the concurrent consciousness of witnesses verified by actual testimony. Christianity is not a theory. It proposes to do something for me. Compare old Rome with England or America of to-day with all our vices, with all our shortcomings, with all our corruptions, and behold what is the answer of history to the claim that Christ has made. Why, when Mr. Morse first proposed the magnetic telegraph it was not strange that men were sceptical. When he said "By touching a little key here I communicate a message to a man a thousand miles yonder," no wonder that wise and conservative people shook their heads and shrugged their shoulders, and said, "Impossible!" But when the wire had been laid from Washington to Baltimore, and the first message was flashed through that wire, "Behold what God hath wrought," how could any man doubt when the work was achieved? Some of you will say, "Ah! this will not give us a well-defined theology." Well, perhaps not. But who can stand and look out into the vast future, and define immortality? Who can look up into the heavens and define God? Who can look into his own soul and define there the sins that have oppressed him, or the Saviour that has redeemed him from them? No, no; our experiences do transcend all our definitions, being beyond them. And some of you will say, "This is well for those of you that have this experience, but I have it not." Is that any reason why you should not believe? Now, let us reason this matter one moment. Because you do not enjoy the music of Beethoven will you therefore conclude that all musical enjoyment is a myth? Because you, standing on the deck of an Atlantic steamer, cannot see the light of the far-distant lighthouse which the ship captain with his better trained eye does see, will you conclude that he is mistaken and you are right? If it be true that there is a testimony coming from innumerable hosts of witnesses to the reality of God's presence, to the certainty of immortality, to the inspiration of God's Book, to the vital saving power of a living Christ, will you reject the light because you are blind? Will you deny the truth because you see it not? A father and his son stand on the shores of the Bay of Fundy. A great tidal wave forty feet in height comes rolling in, when the boy catches the father's hand in terror, and cries, "Run, father, run; the ocean is going to wash us away." The father looks and smiles upon the lad, and says, "Wait, wait." The great wave dashes itself into innumerable atoms of foam upon the great rock, and sweeps back into the ocean. And when this tidal wave of scepticism shall have expended its force it will be found broken into innumerable atoms of foam at the foot of a rock which shall stand through all the future, as in all the past, the Rock of Ages. (*L. Abbott. D.D.*) **The Lord knoweth them that are His.**—*All God's people favourites :*—It is said of Tiberius, the emperor, that he never denied his favourite Sejanus anything, and often prevented his request ; so that he needed only to ask and give thanks. All God's people are His favourites, and may have all that their hearts can wish, or their need require. (*J. Trapp.*) *Affectionate remembrance :*—At Bury St. Edmunds, I went to the infirmary of the workhouse, where, amongst other patients in bed, I conversed with an old man, who, if I remember rightly, was over eighty years of age. As it lay outside the counterpane, I noticed that his arm from the elbow to the wrist was covered, after the manner of sailors' tattooing, with numerous letters. On asking him what they were, he said, "Why, you see, sir, I've had nine children, and all are gone ; some I know be dead, and some I don't know whether they be dead or alive, but they're all the same to me ; I shall never see any of 'em again in this world. But I've got all their initials here on my arm ; and it's a comfort to me as I lie here to look at 'em and think of 'em." It was all that this poor old man could do for his sons ; but he held them in affectionate remembrance, though he needed not the sight of their initials to remember them by. Our heavenly Father knoweth and taketh pleasure in all them that are His. He bears them all on His heart, and His power to help and to bless them is as great as His wealth of love. (*B. Clarke.*)    *Hidden Christians :*—There are stars set in the heavens by the hand of God, whose light has never reached the eye of man ; gems lie covered in the dark abysses of earth that have never yet been discovered by the research of man; flowers which have grown in blushing beauty before the sun, that have never been seen by the florist; so there may be Christians, made such by God, who are hidden from the knowledge of this world. (*John Bate.*) *Unknown, yet well known :*—Many of the greatest saints have lived and died unknown and uncared for by the world. These are God's secret ones, unknown to men, well-known to God. About some of the saints and apostles we hear much; the lives and works of St. Paul and St. Peter are familiar to us all. It is not so with St. Bartholomew, and yet none of the martyrs worked more faithfully, or suffered more severely. He who laboured so successfully for Christ, and suffered so severely, is only mentioned four times in the New Testament, and then very slightly. There is no word to record his hard toil, his burning love, his patient suffering, and his noble death. And so it is with many of the greatest of God's saints. No one knows the name of Naaman's little servant, who brought her master to God. The names of the Holy Innocents appear in no earthly book. That pious widow who gave all she had to the Temple is not named ; and there are thousands of others, who though " unknown, are well known " to God, whose names are not written on earth, but are written in heaven. There are many who are now living for God, and working for Him, and suffering for Him, of whom this world knows nothing. There will not be, perhaps, a paragraph about them in the newspapers, but " the Lord knoweth them that are His." God has hidden saints in every place, dwelling under cottage thatch, as well as in great houses. These are the gems which no earthly eye has ever valued, but they will shine none the less brightly on that day when God makes up His jewels. (*H. J. Wilmot-Buxton, M.A.*)    *The Lord knoweth them that are His :*—The Church at Ephesus, at a very early age, suffered from that stumbling-block—the " falling away " of professors. Oh ! I do not wonder at the pain and the perplexity which the young missionary at Ephesus seemed to feel, at the thought of " the falling away " of many whom he had been wont to teach, and love, and hope, and pray for. But mark the delightful emphasis of that " nevertheless "—" Nevertheless the foundation of God standeth sure." Perhaps, of those who set out with you on the road to heaven, some years ago, it may have been your painful lot to see one after another stop, lie down, and go to sleep, and die. " Nevertheless, nevertheless ! the foundation of God standeth sure." Or, look again at that " nevertheless." One by one the friendships and the happinesses of life have been melting away from you. And now every idol has been pulled down; and now almost the only hope of your earthly support is gone : oh ! with what sweetness at such a moment will that thought come back to you, " Nevertheless the foundation of God standeth sure ! " You have a Friend that never can leave you. Or it may come closer than this. It may please God to bring trial more home to your heart. He may lead you through a long, dark cloud, where it may seem to you as if every trace of comfort was obliterated for ever,—" Nevertheless the foundation of God standeth sure." Beneath the feet the " foundation " stands. The building may fall, but the " corner-stone " is safe. There is pardon ; though there is no sense of it. There is faith ; though there is not " the joy in believing." There is Christ ; though there is not the feeling of Christ. That cloud will roll over, and when the morning breaks, it will light up that " foundation," brighter, clearer, and more saving, for ever. For " Nevertheless the foundation of God standeth sure." You see, then, that the whole of a man's peace and all his security depend upon this,—What is his " foundation " ? It is the plainest of all plain Scriptural truths, that the only " foundation " of any soul's safety is the Lord Jesus Christ. " Other foundation can no man lay than that is laid, which is Christ Jesus." " Other foundation " may have a momentary peace; but this only can support the super-structure for eternity. Now this truth the apostle carries out into a little more detail. In order to do it, his mind borrows an image from a ceremony common at the commencement of the erection of a public building, when a king, as he lays the foundation-stone, sets upon it the impression of the royal seal. In like manner, as if to give the believer's hope a two-fold security, God is said not only to " lay the foundation," but to " seal " it ; and when He " seals " it, He seals it to Himself, by the " oath " with which He " confirms it " ; and to the believer, by the Spirit in which He gives it. Now, that " seal," with which God stamps every converted soul, is two-fold. Or, to speak more accurately, it is a single " seal " which has two faces. Accordingly, on the heart of every child of God, on the ground of it, there will be found two inscriptions, which the hand or " seal " of God has engraven there. In other words, there are two fundamental principles which God has placed there. The one stands out clear, legible, and large—" The Lord knoweth them that are His." And the other is like unto it—" Let every one that nameth the name of Christ depart from iniquity." The " seal " must have been twice stamped—both inscriptions must have been there—before the soul is safe, and stands quite " sure." Now, let us look at the two sides of that " seal "; first, separate ; and then together. I. The first in the relation, as also the first that is laid upon the heart, is the impression of God's love. " The Lord knoweth them that are His." This records that truth of truths on which the whole gospel rests, as upon one base—that salvation is all of God's eternal, sovereign love. This must be held by every man who wishes to enjoy the peace of God: that it was God who " knew " me, loved me, and cared for me, and drew me long before I ever had any thoughts of Him. The whole of a man's safety depends upon this : " The Lord knew " me from all eternity ; " the Lord knew " me when He drew me to Himself ; " the Lord knows " me now—all my little thoughts and works : " the Lord knows " I am trying to serve Him ; " the Lord knows " I wish to love Him. But as the one side of God's " seal " is privilege, the other is duty. II. The one is God's love, the other is your holiness. " Let every one that nameth the name of Christ depart from iniquity." The two sides must never be divided. But as the stamp of God's love is laid, so must the stamp of man's obedience be laid. God's love first, to teach that there can be no real obedience till there is first a sense of God's love. Feelings often have deceived us, and they will deceive again. But the question is, practically, Are you " departing from iniquity "? Observe the expression. It is not one single act; but it is a gradual, progressive retiring back from evil, because, more and more, the good prevails. Now, how is it ? Say you have conquered the acts of sin, have you conquered the desires ? Say you have conquered the desires, have you conquered the thoughts ? Do you think that your temper is being every day more subdued ? Is your pride lessened ? Your worldliness, and your covetousness—are they receding ? Would your own family—would your own dearest friend have cause to say, that you are growing every day in grace ? Is it a " seal," think you, that can be " read of all men " upon you ? Could they see it exemplified ? (*J. Vaughan, M.A.*) *Inscriptions on foundation stones :*—The figure is probably drawn from the practice of engraving inscriptions on one or both sides of the foundation-stone. So, in Rev. xxi. 14, the names of the twelve apostles are found on the twelve foundations of the mystical Jerusalem. " The Lord knoweth them that are His." Not as expressing the knowledge that flows from an inscrutable decree, but, as in 1. Cor. viii. 3, xiii. 12 ; John x. 14, the knowledge, implying love and approval, which Christ has of those who are truly His. This represents one side of the life of the believer, but, lest men interpret the truth wrongly, the other side also needs to be put forward, and that is found in personal holiness. (*E. H. Plumptre, D.D.*) *The chosen known to God :*—" The Lord knoweth them that are His " is a citation from the Septuagint of Num. xvi. 5, and a moment's consideration will show how appositely the apostle quotes this passage. Korah, Dathan, and Abiram had gathered themselves together against Moses on the plea of the holiness of the whole congregation : " all the congregation," they said, " are holy, every one of them, and the Lord is among them : wherefore then lift ye yourselves up above the congregation of the Lord ? " Here then certain bad men had got hold of a true principle, but were applying it wrongly and rebelliously. It was quite true that all the congregation were holy, but it was also true that God had especially sanctified the sons of Levi above the remainder of His people. Korah and his company came forward with specious pretensions to superior spirituality ; they asserted that all the people of Israel were priests of God —a great truth in itself, but not, therefore, to supersede another truth, viz., that God had chosen a certain tribe to be specially His priests. So Hymenæus and Philetus asserted a great truth, viz., the nature and importance of the spiritual resurrection ; but because they so asserted it as to supersede by it another plainly revealed truth, they undermined and overthrew the very faith itself, and proved themselves to be the children of Satan, and not of God. (*M. F. Sadler, M. A.*) *Inconspicuous lives related to heaven :*—In modern times it has been found out that, by a wise adaptation of electricity, an organ can be played many miles away, under certain conditions. If the keyboard is connected with the battery, and the wires run, no matter how far, even hundreds and thousands of miles—if the battery be properly charged and the wires run, say, to New Orleans, the organist sitting here may thunder there the majestic tones of an anthem. And if you consider that the human soul is a battery, and that all its wires run into the heavenly land, there are many inconspicuous persons living in the world of whom we see and hear and know nothing, but from whom to heaven wires go, and around whose souls are angel assemblies gathered together chanting joyful songs ; and there are many men a knowledge of whom the telegraph wires are busy communicating, and about whose fame the newspapers pile telegraph upon telegraph ; there are many noisy men respecting whom there is much ado made on earth, but there is not a single wire that runs between them and the other life. (*H. W. Beecher.*)    *God's knowledge of His children :*—I remember a story of Mr. Mack, who was a Baptist minister in Northamptonshire. In his youth he was a soldier, and calling on Robert Hall, when his regiment marched through Leicester, that great man became interested in him, and procured his release from the ranks. When he went to preach in Glasgow he sought out his aged mother, whom he had not seen for many years. He knew his mother the moment he saw her, but the old lady did not recognise her son. It so happened that, when he was a child, his mother had accidentally wounded his wrist with a knife. To comfort him she cried, " Never mind, my bonnie bairn, your mither will ken you by that when you are a man." When Mack's mother would not believe that a grave, fine-looking minister could be her own child, he turned up his sleeve and cried, "Mither, mither, dinna ye ken that ? " In a moment they were in each other's arms. Ah, the Lord knows the spot of His children! He acknowledges them by the mark of correction. What God is to us in the way of trouble and trial is but His acknowledgment of us as true heirs, and the marks of His rod shall be our proof that we are true sons. He knows the wounds He made when exercising His sacred surgery. (*A. Maclaren, D.D.*)    *Pretended spirituality :*— It is as if Paul said, " Here are false teachers who, under a show of great spirituality, have overthrown the faith of some in the Church. They have come as angels of light. They have said, " The only real resurrection is the resurrection of a dead soul to the knowledge of God. Why trouble yourselves about any other resurrection except this ? " And by these specious words—words which apparently only highly spiritual men could say—they have opened the flood-gates of unbelief ; but God, after all, knows who are sound and who are rotten at heart. The Lord knoweth them that are His. The Lord sees through every pretence of sanctity. The sure foundation of God standeth, for God knows the souls who really and truly belong to Him. He knows them infallibly, and no one knows them but He. You see, St. Paul evidently implies that these falsely spiritual teachers, and those who were led by them, were not in heart God's true people. We learn from this that our faith may be subverted and our souls ruined by pretenders to spirituality in religion. We may extend this to our doctrines of the faith besides the resurrection of the body. The two sacraments, for instance, have each an outward part, which touches the body, or which is received by the body ; and God has made the reception of the inward grace of the sacrament to depend, ordinarily speaking, on the reception of the outward sign. And now I have to put you on your guard against another form of specious yet false spirituality, with which a very large proportion of our modern religious literature is saturated. Beware of books and tracts, and appeals and sermons, full of deep doctrine and evangelical statements, without any duty—any lowly, common-place, homely Christian duty, mixed up with such doctrine or Gospel statements. No book of religion can possibly be more spiritual than St. Paul's Epistle to the Ephesians. And yet, what sort of exhortations have we in the fourth chapter of this most spiritual Epistle ? What I have said respecting the teaching of St. Paul is equally true of that of his brother apostles, SS. Peter, James, and John. Remember, then, that if our standard of Christianity is the teaching of the apostles, then writings, full of high experience or sweet assurance, without any inculcation of lowly duty, are simply unscriptural, and so unspiritual. (*M. F. Sadler, M.A.*)    *The seal of the foundation of God :*—The inscription is twofold ; the first part relating to God, the second to ourselves ; the first confirming our faith, the second directing our practice ; the first permitting us to trust our all on our Redeemer, the second inciting us to " work out our own salvation with fear and trembling." I. In the visible Church the bad are mingled with the good. Many bear the name of Christian who have not even the outward appearance of the reality ; others profess much with their lips, but are strangers to the power of religion in the heart : others, again, are despised by man, who yet bear about with them that pearl of great price—a true and lively faith, without which the rich are poor, and with which the poor are richer than all the world could make them. But all this is surrounded with such a mist of circumstances and forms and conventional habits, that the difference is well nigh imperceptible to human eyes. Certain broad lines of distinction between those who may be the Lord's, and those who certainly are not, may easily be drawn ; but much will still be left where we may hope or fear, but cannot know. But God knows. His eye pierces through the outward covering of professions, and looks directly on the heart. And there is much comfort in the belief that God thus " knoweth them that are His." 1. It is a guarantee of the safety of those who are His, whatever may be their station, or how powerful soever their enemies. 2. Joined to this belief also is the comfortable conviction that, where God " has begun a good work, He will perform it unto the day of Jesus Christ " (Phil. i. 6). 3. And this truth furnishes a key to the mystery, that in the visible Church the bad are ever mingled with the good. To human eye they are, but not to God's. II. But this is but part of the seal or inscription on the foundation of God's temple, and the part with which, however confirmatory of our faith and consolatory to our weakness, we have the less immediate concern. This relates to God's knowledge, THE OTHER TO OUR DUTIES. " Let every one that nameth the name of Christ depart from iniquity." 1. God's foreknowledge does not at all diminish man's responsibility, nor detract from the necessity of our own endeavours. 2. Man's holiness is the end of God's predestination. He has chosen those who are His, not simply to be happy, but to be holy. Would we read God's eternal counsels concerning ourselves ? We may do so with reverence and trembling hope ; but only in our growing freedom from sin, and the increasing holiness of our lives. (*John Jackson, M.A.*) **Let every one that nameth the name of Christ depart from iniquity.** —" Iniquity " here includes the teaching of those false men above alluded to, as their teaching led away from the truth, and resulted in a lax and evil way of life. (*H. D. M. Spence, M.A.*) *Departing from iniquity the duty of all who name the name of Jesus :*—We are—I. To show who they are WHOM THE LORD CHARGES TO DEPART FROM INIQUITY. The text tells you it is every one who names the name of Christ. 1. Baptized persons, capable to discern betwixt good and evil. 2. Who profess faith in Christ, and hope of salvation through Him. 3. Who pray to God through Christ. 4. Who profess faith in Christ, and holiness of life also. 5. Communicants who name the name of Christ in a most solemn manner, by sitting down at His table, before God, angels, and men. II. To show WHAT IS IMPLIED IN THIS DEPARTING FROM INIQUITY which God chargeth us to aim at. Here let us inquire in what this departure, this happy apostasy, lies. There is—1. A giving up with our rest in sin. God chargeth you to awake and bestir yourself, to spring to your feet, and prepare to make progress in the ways of holiness. 2. A going off from sin, and giving up with it : " If I have done iniquity, I will do no more " (Job. xxxiv. 32). 3. A standing off from sin, as the word properly signifies : " Avoid it, pass not by it, turn from it, and pass away " (Prov. iv. 15). 4. A going off to the other side, namely, to Christ and holiness. 5. A going farther and farther from sin. Let us inquire what of iniquity God charges us to depart from. It is the accursed thing, with which we have nothing to do. We must depart from all sin, from the whole of it. We must depart—(1) From under the dominion of sin (Rom. vi. 12). (2) From the practice of sin (Isa. lv. 7). (3) From the devising and contriving of sin. (4) From the love of sin (Ezek. xiv. 6). (5) From the enjoyment of the fruits of sin. (6) From the occasions of sin, and all temptations to it (Ezek. xiv. 6). (7) From the workers of iniquity (2 Cor. vi. 17). We now proceed—III. To EXPLAIN THE NATURE OF THIS CHARGE. You may know the nature of this charge given to them in the text, by these following properties. It is—1. An universal charge, and this in two respects. (1) In respect of the persons naming. " Every one," says the text, " who nameth the name of Christ." (2) In respect of the sins which you are to depart from (Exek. xviii. 31). 2. A peremptory charge (Acts xvii. 30). 3. A charge for the present time (Psa. xcv. 7, 8). 4. A charge with certification, a charge upon your highest peril (Heb. xii. 25). We are now—IV. To show WHY THOSE PARTICULARLY WHO NAME THE NAME OF CHRIST ARE CHARGED TO DEPART FROM INIQUITY. All to whom the gospel comes are so charged, but those who profess Christ are in a special manner thus charged. For—1. The practice of iniquity is a contradiction to their profession ; so that they cannot have this practice, but they give the lie to their profession. 2. Whosoever partakes of Christ's salvation departs from iniquity ; for salvation from sin is the leading and chief part of Christ's salvation. 3. The practice of iniquity is in a peculiar manner offensive to God, and grieving to His Spirit. 4. It reflects a peculiar dishonour upon God ; such sins bring a scandal upon that holy name and religion which they profess (Rom. ii. 24). We are now—V. To MAKE SOME PRACTICAL IMPROVEMENT. This doctrine shows us—1. That all and every one amongst us, by the authority of God who made us, and in whose name we were baptized, are obliged to depart from iniquity. 2. That for men to abstain from the sacrament of the supper, to this end that they may not be abridged of their liberty in sinful courses, is not only impious, but childish and foolish. 3. That they are bold adventurers, and run a dreadful risk, who come in their sins, unrepented of, and not sincerely resolved against, and sit down at the Lord's table. 4. Behold here how the Lord's table is fenced, by a fence of God's own making. Our text debars from this holy table whosoever will indulge themselves in, and will not part with, any known sin whatsoever; particularly—(1) All neglecters of the duties of piety towards God. (2) All who make not conscience of their duty towards men, righteousness, mercy, and charity. (3) All those who are not sober in their lives (Tit. ii. 12). (4) All those who suffer their tongues to go at random, and make no conscience of their words. (5) All those who have no conscience of inward purity, the keeping of the heart. (6) All those who entertain and indulge themselves in any known sin, or in the neglect of any known duty, or are not content to have their sin and duty discovered to them (Psa. lxvi. 18). 5. Behold how the door of access to the Lord's table is opened to all true penitents, whose hearts are loosed from, and set against, all sin. 6. This shows us the necessity of self-searching, examining ourselves on this occasion (1 Cor. xi. 28). We exhort you to depart from iniquity, turn from your sins, since you name the name of Christ. (*T. Boston, D.D.*) *How is gospel grace the best motive to holiness?*— I. DEPARTING FROM INIQUITY IS NO CAUSE OF JUSTIFICATION. II. DEPARTING FROM INIQUITY HATH ITS INFLUENCE UPON, THOUGH NO CAUSE OF, OUR SALVATION (Heb. xii. 14). III. HOLINESS IS INDISPENSABLY NECESSARY UNTO ALL JUSTIFIED PERSONS. As it was necessary that Christ should take upon Him our flesh, so it is as necessary that we should receive from Him His Spirit. As it is storied of one who was very debauched and wicked, and, taking up a Bible, which by his religion he had not been acquainted with (being a Papist), he confessed that whatsoever book that was, it made against him; so unless thou dost sincerely labour after holiness, there is never a word in all the book of God that speaks any comfort unto thee, none of the fruit that grows upon the Tree of Life can be tasted by thee. This might be more evinced if we fix our mind on these following reasons :—1. From the nature of God. I mean the essential holiness of His nature, by which He cannot have communion with any one that is unholy, no more than light can have "fellowship with darkness"; but He indispensably hates and opposes all wickedness, and hath declared His enmity against it. Neither can the gospel change God's nature, or make Him less to abhor sin. It is indeed a declaration of the way and means which God hath ordained to exalt his grace and mercy to the sinner by; but it is in saving of him from his sin, and not with it. 2. From the requisites in the gospel itself. All the privileges of the gospel do include or pre-suppose departing from iniquity. How did the Jews search every hole and corner of their houses to find out leaven, and how earnestly did they cast it away! or else the paschal lamb would not have availed them, and the destroying angel would not have passed from them. And "these things are our examples" (1 Cor. x. 7), and tell us, that unless we industriously search out and cast away the leaven of sin and wickedness, the very death of Christ, the Lamb of God, will profit us nothing. Let us take a view of the privileges of those that are saved by the gospel, and see how they are obliged to holiness by them. (1) Election is the first. And if we are "chosen in Christ Jesus," the apostle tells us, that we are "chosen in Him, that we should be holy and without blame before Him" (Eph. i. 4). (2) Our vocation is unto holiness. (3) Our regeneration, or being born again, which the gospel insists so much upon, is in being made like unto God. "Partakers of the Divine nature" (2 Pet. i. 4). (4) And what is glory, which we seek for, and endeavour after, but only holiness in perfection? (Rom. ii. 7.) Grace is glory in the bud, glory is grace in the flower. Christian is not an empty name; and being called so makes us not to be so. Every one is not a scholar, or an artist in any faculty, who is called so. Besides, Christianity is a practical science; and thou hast no more of it than thou dost practise. What should an unholy heart do in heaven? There are no carnal delights. 3. It is written in our very natures, did we but understand them. Every man that receives a reasoning soul is, by his receiving of it, obliged to give God a reasonable service. IV. FREE PARDON THE BEST MOTIVE TO BECOME HOLY. 1. If it be to expiate for by-past offences, or to merit undeserved favours, it must needs be abominable in the sight of God, being the highest act of pride or presumption that can be imagined. Let our works be what they will, though the best "are as filthy rags" (Isa. lxiv. 6), if they be offered unto God by way of barter or exchange, they become most abominable : as if God stood in need of something that we have, or that we were so sufficient as to be able to benefit God too. 2. To depart from iniquity, or to labour in holiness, in order to express our thankfulness unto God for His mercies in Jesus Christ, is most grateful and most forcible. 3. Love unto God for all His glorious excellencies, especially for His mercy in Christ Jesus, is the best principle of holiness and of our departing from iniquity. God requires His children to give Him their heart (Prov. xxiii. 26). Now love is as a fire which "many waters cannot quench." Difficulties will be overcome, and obedience will be permanent, where true love to God is. And this love in the soul to God is begun by and flows from God's love first unto the soul, as fire kindles fire: "He loved us first" (1 John iv. 19). (*Ibid.*) *The obligation of Christians to a holy life:*—I. WHAT OBLIGATION THE PROFESSION OF CHRISTIANITY LAYS UPON MEN TO LIVE HOLY LIVES. 1. He that professeth himself a Christian professeth to entertain the doctrine of Christ, to believe the whole gospel, to assent to all the articles of the Christian faith, to all the precepts and promises and threatenings of the gospel. Now the great design, the proper intention of this doctrine, is, to take men off from sin, and to direct and encourage them to a holy life. 2. He that professeth himself a Christian professeth to live in the imitation of Christ's example, and to follow His steps, "who did no sin, neither was guile found in His mouth." 3. He that calls himself a Christian hath solemnly engaged himself to renounce all sin and to live a holy life. Thus you see what obligation the profession of Christianity lays upon us to holiness of life. From all which it is evident that the gospel requires something on our part. For the covenant between God and us is a mutual engagement ; and, as there are blessings promised on His part, so there are conditions to be performed on ours. II. I come now to the second thing propounded, and that is, TO PERSUADE THOSE WHO PROFESS CHRISTIANITY TO ANSWER THOSE OBLIGATIONS TO A HOLY LIFE, WHICH THEIR RELIGION LAYS UPON THEM. 1. Consider how unbecoming it is for a man to live unsuitably to his profession. 2. Consider how great a scandal this must needs be to our blessed Saviour and His holy religion. As we would not proclaim to the world that the gospel is an unholy and vicious institution, let us take heed that we bring no scandal upon it by our lives, lest the enemies of our religion say as Salvian tells us they did in his time—" Surely if Christ had taught so holy a doctrine, Christians would have lived holier lives." 3. And, lastly, let us consider the danger we expose ourselves to by not living answerably to our religion. Hypocrites are instanced in Scripture as a sort of sinners that shall have the sharpest torments and the fiercest damnation. (*J. Tillotson, D.D.*) *The obligations of Christians to depart from iniquity :*—I. EVERY PROFESSING CHRISTIAN DOES NAME THE NAME OF CHRIST, and is called by His name, even as the disciples were called Christians first at Antioch ; nay, even before that naming at Antioch, every believer in Christ —every one baptized into His name--was virtually so called. And we may say, as every pupil or disciple of the various schools and sects of philosophy acknowledged the master, and assumed the name of the school to which he belonged ; and as the soldier wore the badge of the commander, and of the corps to which he was attached ; and as idolaters had the name of the idol-god whom they worshipped upon their hands or upon their forehead ; so, in like manner, in a far higher and in the most eminent and religious sense, every Christian showed his school, the company, the corps to which he belonged, to be that of Christ Jesus the Lord, whose name he bears, and into whose service he has been admitted. II. PRESS UPON YOU DEPARTURE FROM ALL SIN. 1. One great end of the religion of Jesus is the destruction of sin and the encouragement of holiness. Can any one doubt of this? Can the most superficial examination of its terms, and language, and ordinances, leave any one to doubt of this? I appeal to the testimony of enemies, of wicked men, and of evil spirits in proof of this. Why has the gospel been so hated and opposed? And, from the whole current of prophecies, types, and positive declaration of the great Author of the Gospel, is it not undeniable that the destruction of the works of the devil was the grand end of the wondrous dispensation? 2. If any spark of gratitude be kindled in your hearts to Him who hath given Himself for you, to deliver you from this present evil world, and to bless you in turning every one of you from your iniquities, and who hath done this at such an expensive rate, redeeming you not with corruptible things, as silver and gold, but with His own precious blood, surely you will depart from all iniquity. 3. Again, the credit of religion, regard to the honour of Christ, should lead you to depart from all iniquity. It is said of the Pythagoreans, an ancient sect of philosophers, that they used to send a coffin to unworthy members who had disgraced the sect, intimating that they were considered as dead and gone. 4. Finally, if you would maintain your peace of mind and your good hope through grace, and have the first part of this text and motto secured—" The Lord knoweth them that are His "—see that the second part of it which we have been illustrating be fulfilled and carried through, even " departing from all iniquity." (*W. H. Burns.*)    *Christians bound to cultivate holiness of heart and life :*—I. CONSIDER TO WHOM THE TEXT IS ADDRESSED. 1. It may be said of all professing Christians that they have named the name of Christ. The text is not addressed to infidels. Those who have merely named the name of Christ have His name, but have nothing of His nature; they have something to do before they can depart from iniquity. It is idle to tell the captive to leave his prison till the fetters are broken which chain him to its floor; before a dead man walks he must live; before the branch bears it must be grafted; before the water wells from the frozen fountain the springs must be thawed; and the breeze and the breath of heaven must blow down the valley before its dry bones are changed into living men; and so before a man can, by one step, leave iniquity, he must be made a new creature in Jesus Christ. 2. Our text is addressed to real Christians. When the apostle said, " Let every one that nameth the name of Christ depart from iniquity," it was a very different thing to do so then and to do it now; it is one thing to swim down the stream and another thing to make head against it; the mere naming the name of Christ is nowadays no evidence at all that a man is a true lover of Jesus. II. CHRIST'S PEOPLE ARE CALLED ON TO DEPART FROM INIQUITY. The text calls on you who are lovers of Jesus not only to abstain from open and barefaced iniquity, not only to maintain before the world the high honour of your Master's cause, but to part with your secret and your sweetest sins. III. THE LOVE OF CHRIST SHOULD LEAD US TO DEPART FROM ALL INIQUITY. Can a lover of Jesus think of the shame, the spitting, scourging, crucifying, and very tempest of evils they rained down on the head of a beloved Saviour, and not hate his sins? IV. SEEK DIVINE GRACE TO ENABLE YOU TO DEPART FROM ALL INIQUITY. Sin is like the negro's colour: it is not an accidental property; he is born with it; the water of the broad sea cannot wash it away; the art of man cannot remove it; in change of climate he remains unchanged; you may carry him to shiver amid the snows of Greenland; he may exchange the shadow of his palm trees for a hut of snow, the burning sands for the frozen sea, he is as dark as ever; nothing but a miracle of nature can change the negro's colour, and nothing but a miracle of grace can change the sinner's heart; " though you wash thee with nitre, and take thee much soap, yet thine iniquity is marked before me, saith the Lord." You have one of two things to choose—you must either depart for Christ from iniquity, or you must depart for iniquity from Christ. (*T. Guthrie, D.D.*)    *The moral tendency of the gospel :*—I. THE GREAT DESIGN OF ALMIGHTY GOD IN THE DISPENSATION OF THE GOSPEL is our improvement in holiness and virtue here, in order to the attainment of eternal life hereafter. The gospel is not a fanciful theory, containing a system of speculative opinions, which have little or no connection with virtue and happiness. Universal obedience is declared to be requisite. Having thus considered the nature of our holy religion, we are now—II. To consider THE CONSEQUENCES OF LIVING UNSUITABLY TO THAT PROFESSION. 1. He who names the name of Christ, without departing from iniquity, exposes himself to reproach and contempt. Men will not be imposed upon by an empty possession. They cannot indeed see into our hearts, and notice the motives by which we are actuated; but they can observe our good or bad actions, and judge whether our lives be answerable to our profession. 2. But the consequences of vice in a professed Christian extend farther than to the sinner himself. A wicked life in a professed Christian is attended with more than ordinary mischief : it not only serves to seduce, like every other evil example, but it has a strong tendency to stagger a weak and honest mind. Perplexities crowd upon his mind. He begins to suspect the truth of religion, and to regard it as an empty profession. His zeal abates; he relaxes in the discharge of his duty; and throws religion away as a mere imposition. His enemies rejoice; his friends weep. Religion has lost an advocate; the world has gained a triumph; but his blood will be required of your hands. 3. But the consequences of iniquity, in a professed Christian, extend farther than individuals; they extend to the cause of Christianity; nay, even to our blessed Saviour Himself. It is an indignity offered to Christ, and an outrage committed upon the gospel, in the disguise of a friend. It seems to declare either that Christianity countenances immorality, or that it wants authority to enforce its laws. On both which suppositions it destroys its authority as coming from God.  4. A wicked life, as it injures the weak and reflects discredit on religion and its author, also exposes the sinner himself to the most imminent danger.  There are many circumstances which aggravate the guilt, and will add to the punishment of a wicked Christian.  The more indulgent the father who commands, the more ungrateful is the son who disobeys; the more plain and reasonable the command, the more inexcusable the breach of it; the more powerful the motives to obedience, the more obstinate the disobedience; the more advantages and means of improvement, the more culpable the neglect, and the more dreadful the condemnation.  (*Andrew Donnan.*)  *Particular in small things :*—Ralph Waldo Emerson was a man of rare integrity, and so particular about small things as to be punctilious.  One day a new cooking-stove had been provided for his house, and although the stove came highly recommended it proved thoroughly refractory and aggravating, and did everything but what it was expected to do.  At length the family was in despair, and some one suggested sending it to auction.  "What!" exclaimed Emerson, "transfer our own perplexity to another pair of shoulders?  No, never! unless the stove be labelled 'imperfect.'"  And "imperfect" it was labelled, and sold at a heavy discount.  (*New Zealand Methodist.*)  *A holy life :*—The following testimony borne to the character of the Rev. John Fletcher by Wesley, in the funeral sermon which he preached for him soon after his death, serves to explain the powerful influence which he exerted on the age in which he lived, an influence which has not yet died out.  "I was intimately acquainted with him for about thirty years.  I conversed with him morning, noon, and night, without the least reserve, during a journey of many hundred miles; and in all that time I never heard him speak an improper word, or saw him do an improper action.  To conclude : many exemplary men have I known, holy in heart and life, within fourscore years; but one equal to him I have not known, one so inwardly and outwardly devoted to God.  So unblamable a character in every respect I have not found either in Europe or America, and I scarce expect to find another such on this side eternity."  *Power of holy lives :*—I was once privileged to lead an aged man across a thoroughfare—that old man of whom you may read in a tract called, "I never Lost but Once."  Some rough men, attracted by his patriarchal appearance, cleared a way for him through the carts and boys, and as he acknowledged their kindness with a low bow of his silver head, I heard one man say, "If ever there was a godly party, that is one; the face don't tell lies."  *A good life enforces teaching :*—A gentleman from England wrote that he went to some one of our cities in the morning prayer-meeting of one of the churches; that during the meeting a man spoke with little or no animation, and the address was wanting in all the elements calculated to produce an impression.  Yet, to his astonishment, the entire meeting appeared to be listening with rapt attention, and it was but a little before he saw many of the people were in tears.  He was so utterly surprised at the result that he was led to inquire about it at the close of the service.  He was told that the man who had spoken was so remarkable for his uniform Christian consistency, and was so gentle and affectionate, that his words were always weighty, for that his life had secured him the affection of the whole church.  This visitor wrote further that he went to the meeting the following morning, and was much interested in the whole service, and specially so in a gentleman's address, who spoke with such fervour and eloquence as to excite his feelings intensely, so that he found himself weeping profusely, and supposed that everybody in the meeting would be as much excited as himself; but on looking around, he found that he was the only weeper to be seen.  Again he was astonished; but the solution was the fact that while his brethren did not question his being a Christian, his life had not compelled their homage.  (*S. B. Halliday.*)  *Running from sin :*—We once heard Dr. W. F. Broadus tell of a little girl who, in the days when the conversion of children was not the subject of as much prayer as now, applied for membership in a Baptist chapel.  "Were you a sinner," asked an old deacon, "before this change of which you now speak?"  "Yes, sir," she replied.  "Well, are you now a sinner?'  "Yes, sir, I feel I am a greater sinner than ever."  "Then," continued the deacon, "what change can there be in you?"  "I don't know how to explain it," she said, "but I used to be a sinner running after sin, but now I hope I am a sinner running from sin."  They received her, and for years she was a bright and shining light; and now she lives where there is no sin to run from.  *Sin ruinous :*—A man must have hell taken out of him if he is to escape hell.  (*Norman Macleod.*)  *The stability of holiness :*—A building which demands holiness, carries within itself no ground of dissolution and overthrow.  (*Van Oosterzee.*)  *Inconsistent Christians false witnesses :*—Dr. E. W. Benson (Archbishop of Canterbury) said that a well-known advanced freethinker had told him that he was more impressed by the inconsistency between the theoretical teaching and the social practice of cultivated and active-minded Christians in respect of wealth, advancement, and luxuriousness than by our doctrinal difference. And what was his inference? That the standard of the gospel was too high—that its morality was impracticable, as tested by the lives of those who accepted it, and that it was, therefore, not divine. *The power of a good life :*—A sceptic towards whom a Christian had shown great kindness, said to him, "I don't believe in Christ, but I do believe in you, and I will try to believe in Christ because you tell me it is He who has made you what you are." (*J. Clifford, D.D.*) *Christ dishonoured by the inconsistencies of His professed people :*—A recently-erected edifice has fallen : how do men treat the fact? They instantly connect it with the architect or the builder. When a chemical experiment has failed, how is it looked upon? Instantly the manipulator is blamed for want of skill, or for want of judgment in the selection of the quality of his materials. So all the practices of the Church are carried back to Christ, and He is magnified or "crucified afresh," according to their nature. (*J. Parker, D.D.*)

Ver. 20, 21. **In a great house there are not only vessels of gold and of silver, but also of wood and of earth; and some to honour and some to dishonour. If a man, therefore, purge himself from these he shall be a vessel unto honour.**—*The house and its vessels :*—The words imply a parable which is not formally interpreted. Rising as it does, however, from the thought of the "foundation" in ver. 19, we shall not be far wrong in assuming that the "great house" is (as in 1 Tim. iii. 15) the Church of God. The sequel of the parable presents questions of greater difficulty. Are we, with the majority of interpreters, to identify the vessels made to honour with silver and gold, those of wood and earth with the vessels made to dishonour? In this case the difference between the two sets of vessels is, in the interpretation of the parable, purely ethical. All true members of Christ are as the gold and silver, all unworthy members as the wood and clay. And, as the material of which the vessel is made does not depend upon itself, it might seem at first as if we had here, as in the parable of the tares and the drag-net, to interpolate the thought that the man whom the vessel represents may, by purifying himself, transmute his nature, and pass from the one class to the other. I venture to think that a different interpretation gives a far truer meaning. The classes of vessels correspond to the gifts which men have received (as in the parable of the talents we have the five, the two, the one), and each has its proper use and honour in the great house of the Church of God. But in each case, of the gold as of the clay, it is true that purity is the one essential condition of honourable use. The man of poorer gifts (to pass from the sign to the thing signified) may, if he keeps himself pure, be a vessel made to honour. If the silver and gold are allowed to be defiled by that which is unclean, if "holiest things find vilest using," then even they are in danger of serving only as vessels for dishonour, of showing (not ceasing even then to fulfil a Divine purpose) that the righteous judgment of God is against them that commit such things. In this case the words, "If a man purge himself" retain their full significance, and we have no need to interpolate the idea of a self-transmuting process, changing the earthen vessel into gold. (*E. H. Plumptre, D.D.*) *The Church a kingly house :*—I. THE TRUE VISIBLE CHURCH IS LIKE A GREAT AND KINGLY HOUSE. For, did not the King of kings contrive its platform? lay its foundation? rear its walls? and perfect its building? Doth He not protect it, dwell in it, and prescribe laws to govern it? For its circle, is not that also great, spacious? Doth it not extend itself to the four corners of the world? Who can number the inhabitants of it? or tell the tenth part of this household? Is not its provision wonderful? Do not its servants eat angels' food, bread from heaven, and drink the choicest wines, the water of life? II. IN THE VISIBLE CHURCH ARE GOOD AND BAD PERSONS. III. ALL GOD'S SERVANTS ARE NOT EQUALLY SANCTIFIED. IV. STRONG CHRISTIANS ARE LIKE VESSELS OF GOLD. First, they are resembled to vessels, both good and bad persons; this is common to all. Secondly, unto vessels of gold and silver; this is proper to the good, not the bad. Why to vessels? Because they are capable to receive the water of grace and corruption, as vessels any liquid or solid matter. Again, they are of use in God's house, like vessels in man's. And grown Christians are like golden vessels; for they are rare, precious, pure, glorious; of honour, profit, and will endure the fire, hammer, and come out of the furnace the more purged from tin, dross, corruption. And, as noblemen engrave their arms on the one, so doth God imprint His image on the other. But you will say, How may I know myself to be such? Well enough; for golden vessels have the most fiery trials, endure much hammering, are strongest set on by the devil, have the hottest skirmishes in their captain's army, scatter the words of grace the farthest, and rejoice in the greatest tribulation. V. WEAKER CHRISTIANS ARE LIKE VESSELS OF SILVER. VI. THE WICKED ARE NOT EQUALLY CORRUPTED. VII. PERSONS LESS PROFANE ARE LIKE WOODEN VESSELS. VIII. THE BASEST SORT OF MEN BE LIKE EARTHEN ONES. IX. THE FINAL ESTATE OF MEN IS BUT TWOFOLD. (*J. Barlow, D.D.*) *The house of God and utensils of it :*—I. WHAT IS THE GREAT HOUSE HERE SPOKEN OF? The Church is sometimes in Scripture called the house of God (1 Tim. iii. 15; Heb. iii. 2), and here a great house. If the greatness of that material house of God, erected by Solomon, was measured by the number of workmen, which were 200,000, and of the years wherein it was a building, which were seven; much more may we conceive this spiritual house great, which hath been from the beginning of the world a setting up, both by God's own hand, and infinite numbers and millions of workmen, patriarchs, prophets, apostles, pastors, teachers, martyrs, confessors, professors, and holy men in all ages. And for the parts, the foundation is of pure gold, even Jesus Christ. The stones not dead, as in other houses, but living stones (1 Pet. ii. 5). And the whole house is, saith St. Peter, a spiritual house; so as great things are spoken, and might more be spoken, of this great house of God. II. WHAT ARE THESE VESSELS OF GOLD AND SILVER, OF WOOD AND EARTH? As in the material house of God, the temple, were vessels for all services, both more honourable, of gold and silver, and others of baser matter; so in this spiritual house (typified by that) are vessels, that is, persons of sundry sorts, distinguished in our text. 1. In themselves, by their matter, gold, silver, wood, earth. 2. In their use and end, honour and dishonour. Now, out of each part observe somewhat. 1. In that the Church is the house of God, and we all profess ourselves to be within this house, we learn two things: (1) To walk careful in God's presence, who dwelleth in it. In other great houses many things pass and are done, which the master knows not, for that he is not always at home, and, if he were, yet his eye could not be in all corners. But the owner of this house is never from home, and His eye pierceth into every part of His house, and is on every person, so that nothing can escape Him. (2) To acquaint ourselves with His will and directions. 2. In that the Church is the house of God, it follows every Christian is a part of this house (Heb. iii. 6). And therefore we must—(1) Give the Lord possession of His house. (2) Having once given Him possession, beware of sacrilege. What was once dedicated to God might never be profaned. 1. Note that there must necessarily be a mixture of good and bad in the visible Church; vessels of divers sorts. 2. Note how the Lord esteems of a godly man, though he be good but in part. He calls him a vessel of gold and a vessel of honour, even where much dross remains to be purged. But how shall I know that I am indeed a vessel of honour? 1. In respect of himself, he purgeth himself from these things. What is this purging or purifying? According to our former resemblance, we may conceive the metaphor to be taken from goldsmiths, who used to try and purify their metals from dross, before they can frame it to a vessel of honourable use and service. Even so doth the Lord with His chosen. Who must cleanse and purify? Every man himself, none excepted, that will be a golden vessel. This purging is all one with our sanctification; the whole work of which is God's, as appears—(1) By His promise (Isa. iv. 4). (2) By Christ's testimony (John xv. 2). (3) By His prayer for the whole Church (John xvii. 17). (4) By the prayers of all saints (Psa. li). And yet we are said to purge ourselves; yea, to convert ourselves, and make ourselves new hearts. When—1. Being renewed by the Spirit, we co-operate with Him in using the means. In not resisting His work. From what must a man purge himself? From these things—that is, lusts and defilements, errors in judgment and practice, in faith and manners, of which he had spoken before; implying sin to be the foulest filthiness in the world, and that it defiles the whole man. But when must he purge himself? The apostle speaks in the present time, for there is no purgatory hereafter. Again, the present time noteth a continued act; so as every man must always while he liveth be purging away these things. 2. The second mark for the trial of such a one is in respect of God. He is meet for the Lord. Before God can use men as vessels of honour, Himself must first fit and prepare them to honourable services. We are His workmanship, created in Christ unto good works (Eph. ii. 10). 3. The third is in respect of godliness. Prepared to every good work. Where—(1) The object, works good in the author, rule and kind, piety and mercy. (2) The extent—every. (3) The readiness to it—Whence? of God. (*T. Taylor, D.D.*) *The great house and the vessels in it :*—"After all," says the apostle in effect, though in fewer words, "it is not such a very great wonder that there should be persons in the Church who are not of the sterling metal of sincerity, nor of the gold and silver of truth, which endures the fire. You must not look at Hymenæus and Philetus as if they were prodigies, there have been many like them and there will be many more; these ill weeds grow apace, in all ages they multiply and increase." Where beneath the skies shall we find absolute purity in any community? The very first family had a Cain in it, and there was a wicked Ham even in the select few within the ark. Isaac, with all his quiet walk with God, must be troubled with an Esau, and ye know how in the house of Jacob there were many sons that walked not as they should. "I have chosen you twelve, and one of you is a devil." In the great field which Christ has sown, tares will spring up among the wheat, for the enemy takes pains to sow them; neither is it possible for us to root them up. In the king's garden briars will grow, thorns also and thistles will the most sacred soil yield to us. Even the lilies of Christ grow among thorns. You cannot keep the best of churches altogether pure. Yea, lift your eyes even to the skies, and though there be myriads of stars, yet ye shall mark wandering stars among them, and meteors which are and are not, and are quenched in the blackness of darkness for ever. Until we shall come to the heaven of the Most High we must expect to find chaff mixed with the wheat. Coming to the text, the apostle suggests the encouragement I have already given, under a certain metaphor. The Church of God being in the world has its common side and its common vessels, but being also a heavenly house has also its nobler furniture, far more precious than gold which perisheth though it be tried with fire. I. First let us consider THE GREAT HOUSE. The apostle compares the Church to a great house. We feel sure he is not speaking of the world; it did not occur to him to speak about the world, and it would have been altogether superfluous to tell us that in the world there are all sorts of people, —everybody knows that. The Church is a great house belonging to a great personage, for the Church is the house of God, according to the promise—"I will dwell in them, and walk in them." 1. It is a great house because planned and designed upon a great scale. 2. Because it has been erected at great cost, and with great labour. 3. Because its household arrangements are conducted on a great scale. Speak of fine flour—behold, He has given us angels' food; speak of royal dainties—behold, the Lord hath given us fat things full of marrow, wines on the lees well refined. What a perpetual feast doth the Lord Jesus keep up for all His followers. 4. For the number of its inhabitants. How many have lived beneath that roof-tree for ages. What a swarm there is of the Lord's children, and yet not one of the family remains unfed. The Church is a great house wherein thousands dwell, yea, a number that no man can number. 5. Because of its importance. The Church is a great house because it is God's hospice, where He distributes bread and wine to refresh the weary, and entertains wayfarers that else had been lost in the storm. It is God's hospital, into which He takes the sick, and there He nourishes them until they renew their youth like the eagle's. It is God's great *pharos* with its lantern flashing forth a directing ray so that wanderers far away may be directed to the haven of peace. It is the seat of God's magistracy, for there are set thrones of judgment, the thrones of the house of David. The great house of the Church is the university for teaching all nations, the library wherein the sacred oracles are preserved, the treasury wherein the truth is deposited, and the registry of new-born heirs of heaven. It is important to heaven as well as to earth, for its topmost towers reach into glory. II. We will now go inside the great house, and we at once observe that it is well furnished. Our text, however, invites us to note that it contains a number of MEANER VESSELS, articles of the coarser kind for ordinary and common uses. Here are trenchers and buckets of wood, and pitchers and pots and divers vessels of coarse pottery. Some have thought that this figure of vessels to dishonour relates to Christians of a lower grade, persons of small grace and of less sanctified conversation. Now, although believers may from some points of view be comparable to earthen vessels, yet I dare not look upon any child of God, however low in grace, as a vessel to dishonour. Moreover, the word "these" refers to the earthen and wooden vessels, and surely they cannot represent saints, or we should never be told to purge ourselves from them. Besides, that is not the run of the chapter at all. The real meaning is, that in the Church of God there are unworthy persons serving inferior and temporary purposes, who are vessels to dishonour. They are in the Church, but they are like vessels of wood and vessels of earth, they are not the treasure of the mansion, they are not brought out on state occasions, and are not set much store by, for they are not " precious in the sight of the Lord." The apostle does not tell us how they came there, for it was not his intent to do so, and no parable or metaphor could teach everything ; neither will I stay to describe how some professors have come into the Church of God, some by distinct falsehood and by making professions which they knew were untrue, others through ignorance, and others again by being self-deceived, and carried away with excitement. The parable does not say how they got there, but there they are, and yet they are only vessels of wood and vessels of earth. The vessels in the great house are, however, of some use, even though they are made of wood and earth ; and so there are persons in the Church of God whom the Lord Jesus will not own as His treasure, but He nevertheless turns them to some temporary purpose. Some are useful as the scaffold to a house, or the dogshores to a ship, or the hedges to a field. I believe that some unworthy members of the Church are useful in the way of watch-dogs to keep others awake, or lancets to let blood, or burdens to try strength. Some quarrelsome members of the Church help to scour the other vessels, lest they should rust through being peaceful. There is one thing noticeable, viz., that the wooden and earthen vessels are not for the Master's use. When He holds high festival His cups are all of precious metal. How sad it is that many Christians are useful to the Church in various ways, but as for personal service rendered to the Lord Jesus Christ Himself, in that they have no share whatever and never can have till grace changes them from wood to silver, or from earth to gold. Note that in these vessels of which the apostle speaks the substance is base. They are wood, or they are earth, nothing more. So are we all by nature of base material, and grace must make us into silver or into golden vessels, or the Master cannot Himself use us, nor can our use in the Church ever be to honour. These vessels unto dishonour, though turned to some account, require a good deal of care on the part of the servants. When our forefathers used to eat from wooden trenchers, the time the good wives used to spend in scalding and cleaning to keep them at all sweet to eat upon was something terrible, and there are members of the Church who take a world of time from pastors and elders to keep them at all decent ; we are continually trying to set them right, or keep them right, in the common relationships of life. III. We are now going into the treasury, or plate room, and will think of THE NOBLER VESSELS. These are, first of all, of solid metal, vessels of silver and vessels of gold. They are not all equally valuable, but they are all precious. Did you ever hear how vessels come to be golden ?—

> " There stood a *golden* chalice wondrous fair,
> And overflowing with deep love for him.
> He raised it to His gracious lips, and quaffed
> ' The wine that maketh glad the heart of God,'
> Then took the cup to heaven."

1. On the vessels to honour you can see the hall mark. What is the hall mark which denotes the purity of the Lord's golden vessels ? Well, He has only one stamp for everything. When He laid the foundation what was the seal He put upon it ? " The Lord knoweth them that are His, and let every one that nameth the name of Christ depart from all iniquity." That was God's seal, the impress of the great King upon the foundation-stone. Do we find it here? Yes, we do. " If a man, therefore, purge himself from these he shall be a vessel unto honour." You see that the man who is the golden or silver vessel departs from all iniquity, and that is the token of his genuine character. 2. Notice, however, that they are purged, for the Lord will not use filthy vessels be they what they may. 3. And then notice that these gold and silver vessels are reserved as well as purged. They are made meet for the Master's use. As Joseph had a cup out of which he alone drank, so the Lord takes His people to be His peculiar treasure, vessels for His personal use. 4. Oh, for a holy character and holy communion with God ; then we shall be golden vessels fit for the Master's use, and so, according to the text, we shall be ready for every good work, ready for the work when it comes, and ready at the work when it has come, because completely consecrated to God and subject to His hand. IV. We must speak about THE MASTER. 1. He is introduced here, you see, as having certain vessels meet for His use, and this shows

that He is in the house. Secondly, the Master knows all about the house, and knows the quality of all the vessels. And then reflect that the Master will use us all as far as we are fit to be used. What comes of this, then, lastly? Why, let us bestir ourselves that we be purged, for the text says, "If a man therefore purge himself." (*C. H. Spurgeon.*) *The Christian vessel :*—1. Vessels of gold and silver. We are reminded here of the vessels used in tabernacle and temple service, golden basins for the blood, golden dishes for the bread, golden flagons for the wine, golden snuffers, snuff dishes, and oil vessels, for the lamps. Then there were the silver sockets for the foundations of the tabernacle, silver fillets and hooks, silver vessels, attached to the brazen altar. To prepare these, the gold and silver needed refining that the dross might be purged away by the fire. In figure we see the refining process through which God passes His people that they may be fit for His use (Mal. iii. 2, 3). He sits and watches until the reflection of Himself is visible in the hearts and lives of those whom He is refining. If we would be honoured in special service in the sanctuary, and be found prepared unto every good work, we must cheerfully and willingly submit to the refiner, and the refiner's fire. Self must be consumed, all impurity of motive must be purged away, all the faith that God esteems so precious must be tried to its utmost power of endurance. 2. Vessels of wood and of earth. These are the vessels for everyday and ordinary use—for the Master's constant use in His house. A wooden vessel is formed out of the rough timber, and must undergo the sharp cutting of saw, plane, and chisel. The Lord finds many knots and gnarls in the rough material, from which He fashions these vessels, and He knows how to use the sharp tools of discipline and trial. He will shape our lives according to His own design, and the pattern after which we are made will be a heavenly one. An earthen vessel is made out of the clay under the hands of the potter. "We are the clay" (Isa. lxiv. 8). Some are inclined to boast of superiority of ancestry, but after all it is only clay. To be made into vessels the clay must needs be soft to receive the impression of the hand of the potter. It must be free from grit and other hard substances, otherwise it will not yield to the hand. God would have us as the clay, able to take the impression, and yield to the pressure of His will. He must remove all the grit of self and pride, and the many hard substances that find their way in, otherwise "the vessel will be marred in the hands of the potter" (Jer. xviii. 5). The wheel was a horizontal disk on which the clay was placed, and made to rotate rapidly. Day by day, the wheel of our life spins round, and God would fashion us by our daily circumstances and surroundings. When the wheel stops how will He find us? Finished or unfinished? Unto honour or dishonour? Complete or marred? Has He not frequently almost stopped the wheel, and, finding the vessel marred, has "made it again another vessel, as it hath pleased Him"? Many can thank God for the change in their lives, produced through sickness sanctified to their souls. 3. All the famous porcelain works have their private marks burned into the vessels they produce, so that they can be easily identified at any time. So the Great Potter has placed His private mark on all who are His handiwork, and the mark has been burned in by the fire of His love, thus becoming indelible, and easy of identification. 4. The vessel made and marked, and prepared in the furnace, is now fit for use, and is to be in constant use, by being filled with treasure. Look for a moment into yonder house. It is breakfast-time, and the little white earthenware mug stands full of milk on the table for little Mary. Afterwards it is washed and put away ready for use, and in the course of the morning her little brother asks for a drink of water. Mary fills her mug and give it to him. Again the vessel is put aside ready for use. A friend calls and leaves a nosegay of flowers. Down runs the child to fill her mug with water to revive the flowers, and the house is filled with their perfume. At the door later on a poor creature falls fainting and exhausted, and the mug, ready again, is quickly brought containing some wine or other restorative, that is poured down the sufferer's throat. It is only an earthen vessel, but it is prepared for every good work by being kept clean. What shall we be? Only vessels, to do *one* thing, only a Sunday-school teacher, only a tract distributor, only a church member. Let us ask the Master to use us in every way He chooses. Let us be for Him the basin wherewith He may wash some soiled ones, or a vessel wherewith He may give of the milk of the Word to His babes, or the bearer of the message of atoning blood, or all these, as He may have need. Let us purge ourselves from all filthiness of flesh and spirit ; be sanctified by the truth, and reserved absolutely for His use and for no other. 5. If not a "vessel of mercy," then a "vessel of wrath." If not in His hand for His use in His household, then to be dashed in pieces, and to be but a potsherd cast away amongst the rubbish. (*G. Soltau.*)  *Holy vessels :*—I. THE VESSELS OF HONOUR ARE ORIGINALLY UNHOLY. Were it not thus, why are we commanded to purge, to cleanse ourselves? II. THE VESSELS OF HONOUR ARE TO BE PURGED. III. THE HOLY ARE HONOURABLE. 1. For, are not such the nearest unto the nature of God? 2. Set apart for the most noble ends? 3. Can any else truly hate evil? detest base courses? 4. And who but they shall be crowned with immortal glory? IV. SANCTIFIED MEN ARE MEET INSTRUMENTS FOR THE USE OF THEIR MASTER. V. THE LORD HATH USE FOR HIS HOLY VESSELS. VI. SANCTIFIED PERSONS FOR EVERY GOOD WORK ARE PREPARED. Not for one, but all. They can fast, pray, hear, read, meditate; deny themselves, afflict their souls, give alms, do and suffer anything. What God affirms they believe, what He commands they obey, what He doth they approve. (*J. Barlow, D.D.*)  *Fitness for the Lord's service :*—I. OUR TEXT DESCRIBES THE SERVICE TO WHICH CHRISTIANS ARE CALLED. It is described in three ways. 1. A Christian in his service should be an honour to himself. Worthy of the nature God has given him, worthy of his capabilities, worthy of his privileges, and worthy of his position and opportunities and means. Now we naturally estimate all service by the heart there is in it. There are differences in true service; some lower and some higher. The supreme aim of Christian men must be spiritual service by spiritual means. 2. A Christian in his service must be useful to his Master. "Meet," &c. It is intimated in this view of our service that we do not work apart and alone as master-workmen, choosing our own work, choosing how to do it, and finishing and round-it off by ourselves. We work under a master, we receive our work at his hands, we do it according to his directions, we do it under his eye, and when it is done we bring it to him that he may put it to its proper use. It is the glory of a master-worker that he can use the services of a thousand workmen, give full scope to their faculties, and then by the use he makes of their work double its value. 3. A Christian in his service should be "prepared unto every good work." Prepared for good *work.* There are stages in goodness. There is good desire, the conception and digestion of the plan for carrying out the desire, the provision of means, and, last of all, the actual work. Prepared unto *every* good work. The world is wide; human needs are great; God calls sinful men to a high destiny. The obstacles in the way are great and many; how great must the design be, and how manifold the work which embraces all. But our Master is prepared unto every good work, and He gives His servants power like His own. II. THE PREPARATION NECESSARY FOR SUCH SERVICE. In every department of God's kingdom fitness is the law of service. It is true that what man deems fit may be foolishness with God; and what God deems fit may be foolishness with man. In this sense the Cross, and the preaching of the Cross are foolishness. Again, it has pleased God to accomplish great results by slender human instruments, that He might teach us rightly to estimate the value of our own work and His. But all this does not alter the fact that so far as man's work is used, it is used according to its fitness. God does not employ ignorant men to teach wisdom, nor worldly men to produce spirituality, nor lovers of ease to conduct great enterprises, nor selfish men to generate enthusiasm of love. Wherein does preparation consist? 1. In purity of life. Personal worth is the foundation of service, and the measure of personal worth is the measure of fitness for service. Two considerations show the need of eminent personal worth as a preparation. (1) We never do anything well till we have caught the spirit of it, till it possess us, till we live in it and find our joy in it. (2) Men are slow to believe in goodness—*i.e.*, in goodness as the proper result of personal principle. They are apt to explain it as the result of circumstances, of a good natural disposition, of what is necessary to maintain with credit a Christian profession. This suspicion is often excessive and unreasonable, but there it is; and he who would win men to righteousness must have personal worth to overcome it. 2. Purity of doctrine is not less necessary than purity of life. Personal excellence enables a man to do good chiefly by enabling him to bear witness of Christ. John the Baptist was as eminent in personal worth as any man that ever lived; yet he spoke of himself as only a voice. It was needful for the work appointed him that he should be a man of sterling worth; but what would his personal worth have done for Judea apart from his witness to Christ? The personal worth of God's people does not enable them to save men; but it does enable them to bear witness to Him who can save. (*John Pillans.*)  *The Master's use :*—I. FIRST COMES MEETNESS. In the renewed spirit, the chastened imagination, the energised conscience, the obedient will, we find the highest meetness for spiritual service. 1. Meetness comes from faculty patiently used. This is true of all faculty. Mr. Ruskin shows us how hard it is to draw a straight line, how none but an accustomed hand can do it. Men shrink from commencement. If you wish to skate, you must not mind a fall, the graceful curve is not a gift, but a growth. The most able musician once had the drill of exercises. The most perfect classic once toiled over unpoetical grammar-books. Christian service is not an easy service; to teach a child is not merely an inspiration, but an education. Of course faculty varies, and there are diverse adaptations. Talents are differentiated—ten, five, one—but all *have* talents. 2. Meetness comes through suffering patiently borne. Many of the Church's best angels are not the ablest or the cleverest, but the humblest. Sorrow often does what no other agency can achieve. Suffering creates sympathy and tenderness to the erring, and consciousness of our own frailty. Moreover, the heavenly world becomes clearer to the eye that is purified by trial. 3. Meetness comes from instrumentalities faithfully employed. These are divine and wonderful. As soldiers, we have the perfect panoply of the heavenly armour. As stewards, we have each a many-acred farm to care for. As vine-dressers, we have the sun and shade and shower, and God has given us our own sweet vineyard of Church or home. If we do not the work nearest to us, we shall do no other. Reynolds, it is said, could sit thirty-six hours before the canvas without a break to bring out in beauty the human face divine. How seldom have we ever lingered enthusiastically at our work to bring out on the living canvas of the human heart the beautiful likeness of Jesus Christ! Let us be diligent. Meetness will come through meditation which is prayer in preparation, and prayer which is meditation spoken; and, above all, from the consciousness of dependence on the spirit of the living God, who will strengthen us with all might in our inner man. II. MINISTRATION. We come here to the word "use." Use characterises all the works of God. The running stream is more than a line of silver beauty in the landscape; it brings fertility and blessing with it. The sea bears the freight of commerce, and brings the healthful ozone on its bosom, as well as spreads its broad expanse of beautiful blue. The tree gives you shade in summer, and breathes out its air of oxygen. We cannot as yet discern all uses; but use there is, delicate and exquisite, in all the works of God. 1. The Christian man is to be a useful man, not a self-indulgent one. We are under a Master. Alas! how many take Christ as a Saviour who do not take Him as a Master, and seldom ponder how much they can obey Him! 2. We are of use to the Master. He has condescended to link His kingdom in its extension with our poor endeavours. Christian work is not merely a kind of spiritual exercise. Your living and your loving heart, your sanctified energies, are useful to the Master. 3. We must give our best to the Master. It is sad, in this England of ours, to think how little faculty is cultured. The Scotch set us a splendid example in this respect, so do the Germans. Dr. Guthrie's autobiography shows what Scotch lads did and do to rise, not merely in position, but in attainment! They have had heroes other than those who fought at Bannockburn—heroes of the parish school and college. It is not lamentable to find faculty so little cultivated amongst us? How few fit themselves for higher posts! (*W. M. Statham.*) *The holiness of use :*—Who are they whom the apostle sees enthroned; his vessels unto honour; the people whom the law of creation praises and places on high? They are the "sanctified," he writes. A favourite epithet with him, which our translators frequently rendering thus, have sometimes rendered, "hallowed" and sometimes "holy," and the fundamental idea of which is "separation." Hence its ancient application to the firstlings of the Hebrew flocks and herds as being animals taken out from the rest, and set apart for God, to be laid upon His altar. St. Paul's sanctified ones, then, are God's sacred ones—God's saints. But that is not telling us much. What is it to be a sacred person, we ask; what is a saint? They, you know, have been designated "sacred" who have withdrawn from common mundane pursuits to occupy themselves mainly with religious exercises, in the performance of religious rites and ceremonies; and "saint," you may hear applied, not seldom, with half a sneer, to those who are interested in and zealous for theological dogmas, or scrupulous in abstaining from practices and amusements to which the generality are addicted, or given to church worship and pious talk. The real sacredness, however, the real sanctity in men, consists according to the implication and suggestion of the term employed here, in personal surrender to the Divine claims upon us; in separation from self-indulgence and self-will, from contrary inclinations and propensities, to be what Heaven would have us be, to cultivate conformity to the Divine ideal. This is glory, teaches the apostle; this is to enjoy rank and commendation; being good and doing nobly. But now, we have not advanced very far after all. Our explanatory words wait to be explained. What is it to be good and do nobly, to be worthy and act well our part, which St. Paul describes theologically as "sanctification," or devotion to the will of God? In whom is it exemplified? and our writer answers shortly: In those who are "meet for the Master's use," or, more correctly, in those who are "useful for the Master." The saint, then, is eminently the *useful* person. Holiness is use. It is not in mere having, nor yet in being and doing, that it is reached; but in being and doing beneficially. But while without some use we are naught, there is a certain special use which it is necessary to yield in order to be a saint, and the yielding of which reveals and marks the saint. "Useful for the Master," says the apostle. He has been comparing society to a house containing divers kinds of vessels—of which house he has implied that Jesus Christ is the Lord and Head; and the hallowed vessels therein are the vessels, he tells us, that are profitable to Him. Now, we may be said to be profitable to another, as we are contributing to the fulfilment of his wishes and ideas, as we are instrumental in forwarding his views, in advancing his purposes. We are useful for Christ, can only be useful for Him in that way—by helping to promote His ends. And what are they? What was His grand passion, the object that burdened and consumed Him? Was it not, speaking broadly, and according to His own constant testimony, that men might be quickened and raised to live more abundantly? But here, probably, many an earnest, well-meaning soul will be moved to say, "I really do not know, I really cannot tell, whether or no I am of any such use in the world, and, what is more, I seem to have so little chance or power; my scope is so narrow, my ability so small." And as if to meet and answer these, and encourage and assure them, St. Paul hastens to add to the words, "Useful for the Master," the qualifying explanatory clause, "being prepared or ready to every good work." We do not know, we cannot tell, whether we are divinely helpful. Not a few are so to a considerable extent without perceiving it. They live sincerely and beautifully, and die wearily, unconscious of how noble or wide their effect has been. But while unable to decide concerning the amount of our helpfulness, we can tell whether we are ready to do every good work that may be done by us in our sphere; whether we carry about within us a spirit and disposition to serve; whether we are alive to each open door of opportunity and quick to enter in and occupy; whether we have a heart sensitively responsive to needs that appeal, to the calls and claims of the hour; whether our desire and aim is to make a good work of whatever is laid upon us to do, to do it according to our light and power in the best and perfectest way, let it be the painting of a picture or the sweeping of a room, preaching a sermon or managing a business. We *can* tell whether it is thus with us. But what then? Why the apostle implies that such alertness to do well at every step, on every occasion, is certain to involve the radiation from us of some helpfulness; that you may conclude you are for some use if only you are eager and anxious to discharge faithfully each duty as it presents itself, to answer duly to the requirements of the time and place, to the facts before you. And now a word in conclusion, concerning what is necessary in order to reach and maintain this hallowed state of use in preparedness for every good work. "If a man purge himself from these," says St. Paul, that is, from the vessels unto dishonour, of which he has been speaking, as mixed with others in the house—"If a man purge himself from these, then shall he be a vessel unto honour." It is intimated, you see, that none are found saints to begin with; that to become such and remain such we must need engage and persevere in effort, in effort to cleanse and emancipate ourselves; that there is that which has to be shaken off and risen out of. And there is, around us, morally adverse, morally opposing atmospheres, unavoidable contacts and intercourses that tend to deaden and depress, popular maxims and sentiments, prevailing ideas and fashions, the spirit of the world seeking other things altogether than the things which are Jesus Christ's, and encountered continually at every turn, insinuating and insidious. All this has to be resisted and surmounted. (*S. A. Tipple.*)   *Sanctified and meet for the Master's use :*—For a moment the apostle drops the figure of the house and the foundation, to take it up again in the remaining portion of the sentence. Purification from vessels would be a very incongruous figure. What St. Paul says is—If therefore any man shall have purged himself from these evil associations or corrupting ideas, from persons whose words are like the deadly poison of contagious gangrene, then he will be a vessel unto honour, whether his faculties cause him to resemble the golden goblet or the silver lamp; the wooden bowl or the porcelain vase; if pure and conscientious, faithful and good, he will be consecrated to noblest uses, serviceable to the Master of the house, and prepared for every good work. (*H. R. Reynolds, D.D.*)　*Fit for use :*—I remember reading of a man who, having a grudge against a railway company, threw a bar of soap into their tank of water. The soap was dissolved, introduced into the boiler, and as soapy water does not generate steam, the engine by and by came to a standstill. The fires were all right but there was no steam; and we must, figuratively speaking, keep the soap out, or God cannot use us. Remember we owe allegiance to Him who needs every thought of the heart. (*G. F. Pentecost.*)　*A clean vessel :*—If in haste we would give a draught of refreshing water to a traveller, we take from our shelf the first vessel which is *clean*. We pass over the elegant and richly-chased cup for the earthenware mug, if the latter has a cleanliness which the former lacks. And our Lord Jesus will gladly use us for His service, though we be but common ware, if only we are clean and ready for use. In our hospitals the instruments used in operations are constantly kept in carbolic acid, that they may not carry the slightest contagion to the open wound; and we cannot touch the open and festering wounds which sin has caused without injury to ourselves and others, unless we are ever in the flow of the blood and water of which St. John speaks. (*F. B. Meyer, B.A.*)　*Holiness and service :*—Through the whole of Scripture we find that whatever God sanctifies is to be used in the service of His holiness. Holiness and selfishness, holiness and inactivity, holiness and sloth, holiness and helplessness, are utterly irreconcilable. Whatever we read of as holy was taken into the service of the holiness of God. Holiness is essential to effectual service. In the Old Testament we see degrees of holiness, not only in the holy places, but as much in the holy persons. In the nation, the Levites, the priests and then the High Priest, advance from step to step; as in each succeeding stage the circle narrows, and the service is more direct and entire, so the holiness required is higher and more distinct. It is even so in this more spiritual dispensation; the more of holiness, the greater the fitness for service; the more there is of true holiness the more there is of God, and the more true and deep is the entrance He has had into the soul. The hold He has on the soul to use it in His service is more complete. (*Andrew Murray.*) *Various vessels :*—All the vessels of Christ's house are not of one size. (*S. Rutherford.*)　*What service might have been done by greater sanctification :*—When Nelson served under Admiral Hotham, and a certain number of the enemy's ships had been captured, the commander said, "We must be contented: we have done very well." But Nelson did not think so, since a number of the enemy's vessels had escaped. "Now," said he, "had we taken ten sail, and allowed the eleventh to escape when it had been possible to have got at her, I could never have called it well done." If we have brought many to Christ we dare not boast, for we are humbled by the reflection that more might have been done had we been fitter instruments for God. (*C. H. Spurgeon.*)　*The stimulus of holiness :*—Holiness is a source of every kind of human excellence. For it sets to work all our powers, and sets them to work in the best possible direction. It gives to intellectual effort its noblest aim, viz., to comprehend and to convey to others the life-giving truth of God; and it guards intellectual success from the perils which surround it. It gives the noblest motive for the care and development of the body; for it shows us that the powers even of our perishing body may work out eternal results. And it gives the only pure motive, and a very strong motive, for effort after material good; for it teaches that this world's wealth may be a means of laying up treasure in heaven. Thus holiness quickens, develops, and elevates all our powers. (*J. A. Beet.*)　*The beauty of service :*—Once upon a time, says the legend, a dispute arose between three young ladies as to which had the most beautiful hand. One sat by a crystal stream and dipped her snowy hand into the water and held it up. Another plucked strawberries till the ends of her tapering fingers were pink. Another gathered violets till her hands were fragrant. Thereupon an aged woman passed by, hungry, emaciated, decrepit. "Who will give me a gift," said she, "for I am poor?" All three young ladies denied her request; but a poor peasant girl, who stood near, unwashed in the stream, unstained by the pink of strawberries, unadorned with flowers, gave her a simple gift and cheered the aged pilgrim. Then, turning back, she asked the three young ladies what they disputed about. They told her, and lifted up their beautiful hands for her to decide. "Beautiful, indeed!" exclaimed she, with radiant countenance. "But which is the most beautiful?" asked they. "It is not the hand that is washed in the purling brook," said she; "it is not the hand that is tipped with delicate pink; it is not the hand garlanded with fragrant flowers, it is the hand which gave a gift to the destitute that is most beautiful." And as she spoke her body was slowly transfigured, her wrinkles gradually vanished, her staff suddenly dropped, and there flew up to heaven, in a blaze of glory, the radiant form of an angel of God. Yes, the sanctification of man means the sanctification of all that the man has to do. It means the sanctification of the hand, the feet, the brain, the heart, the temper, the disposition, the pocket, the whole man, inwardly and outwardly. It is the perfecting of the heart that makes the perfection of every state in life. *The service of love:*—We may be blameless without being faultless. If it be asked what practical difference there is in such a distinction, we may take, as an example, a little child whose loving heart is bent upon pleasing her mother. Her first little task of needlework is put into her hands. But the little fingers are all unskilled, nor has she any thought of the nicety required ; still with intense pleasure she sets stitch after stitch, until at last she brings it to her mother ; she has done her best and does not dream of failure. And the mother taking it, sees two things : one is a work as faulty as it well can be, with stitches long and crooked ; and the other is that smiling, upturned face, with its sweet consciousness of love. Not for anything could she coldly criticise that work. She thinks of the effort to please, and how little she could expect in a first attempt. It is the child's best for the time being. So she commends her and even praises the poor, imperfect work, and then gently and most lovingly shows her how she may do still better. The child is blameless, but her work not faultless. It will be nearer and nearer faultless, as day after day she gathers skill, and even new ideas of care and faithfulness in her tasks ; but still in her mother's eyes she is at first, as well as at last, her blameless child. (*S. F. Smiley.*)   *Reasons why you are not used :*—You are admitted into a great house, along the walls of which are four shelves ; on the lower shelf the gold, on the second the silver, on the third the wood, and on the fourth—high, way up where you would think the dust collected—the earthern vessel. Upon one of these four shelves there is each one of those in this congregation. You say, "I am not gold, I am not silver, I am rather wooden if anything, or earthenware ; my place is on the very top shelf," and when I ask if you can tell which of those four shelves holds the vessels to honour, you say, "Oh, I suppose those golden or silver ones beneath, and my lot will never be there." The Master enters. "Wilt Thou tell us to-day, for our hearts are all aflame to be used by Thee in the foreign mission or home mission field, where we may stand, to be vessels of honour ?" And He says : "I cannot tell by the outside appearance. I must look in." He takes the gold, and says : "That won't do, it is not clean." He takes the silver one and puts it back with a sad look. It is not clean. But it may be He comes to those upper shelves, and takes down one of the very commonest of the vessels, and I see a smile come over His face as He lifts it, and He presses it to His lips, and says : "This will do ; this is a vessel to honour, this is a choice vessel, it is clean. If a man cleanse himself he shall be a vessel to honour." "Ah, but, Master, there is nothing inside of it." "That doesn't matter. I will put inside what has got to be put inside. I only want a clean vessel to put it in." God says, "My child, you have failed, not because you lack the talent or power, but are deficient in the one thing you might accomplish, having the cleansed heart." (*F. B. Meyer.*)

**Ver. 22. Flee youthful lusts : but follow righteousness, faith, charity, peace.—** *Flee the passions of youth :*—Timothy was no longer a young man, but he was still in the strength of his manhood, when he might easily suffer from desires and passions which are comparatively venial in a youth. The *juvenilia desideria*, the immoderate hilarity, the irregular longings of the flesh and mind, the rashness of judgment, the self-indulgence, the love of admiration, which are weakness and failure of youth, not its beauty nor its charm. (*H. R. Reynolds, D.D.*) *The Christian young man :*—To the word "lust" a specific meaning is now popularly attached, which we do not find in the original; the term there used being much more extensive, and, with the addition of the epithet, "youthful," much more expressive. It signifies the inclination of the mind ; and thus it includes what is evil in the spark as well as in the flame, in the blossom as well as in the fruit, in the deep, though still fountain, as well as in the rolling, turbid, and impetuous stream. And with good reason ; for however small and obscure the beginning, the end may be most momentous, most irreparable. Hear it plainly stated : "Lust, when it hath conceived, bringeth forth sin ; and sin, when it is finished, bringeth forth death." Watch over inclination, lest it become desire ; watch over desire, lest it become appetite ; watch over appetite, lest it become passion ; watch over passion, lest it become, in the evil and extreme sense, "lust." And this applies equally to voluptuousness, ambition, covetousness, revenge, and all the characteristic vices of youth. I. And this is to be done BY AVOIDING, AS FAR AS IT BE POSSIBLE, THE COMPANIONSHIP OF THE UNGODLY. On this subject, indeed, the wise man, teaching from experience, is earnest even beyond his wont; counselling with an emphatic iteration : "Enter not into the path of the wicked, and go not in the way of evil men ; avoid it, pass not by it, turn from it, and pass away." It is against the first step that young men should be exhorted especially to guard ; to beware of the first act, against which conscience enters and records its solemn protest. II. While, however, you "flee youthful lusts" by avoiding companionship with the wicked, FLEE THEM ALSO BY CULTIVATING COMPANIONSHIP WITH THE HEART ; AND WEIGH WELL THOSE ASSOCIATIONS, HABITS, AND PURSUITS, WHICH GIVE A DIRECTION TO THE MIND. Beware lest inclination assume the reins of action ; beware lest interest or convenience usurp that supremacy over the purposes and the practices, which ought to be exercised only by conscience and by principle. Test all things by one standard ; try all men by one rule; and let that be the Word of God. Whenever, therefore, in a judgment administered upon such principles, and directed to such an end, the bent of the mind and the will are found to be in any particular instance opposed to the great purpose, for which all who bear, by their own consent, the name of Christian, must for that very reason profess to live, it is clear that the course of life must be altered, the stream of thought and desire must be turned, the current must be made to flow in an opposite direction. And if this only be done as soon as the necessity is discerned, it will be done effectually, and it will be done comparatively without an effort. III. Not only, however, are we exhorted in the text to "flee youthful lusts," BUT TO CULTIVATE THOSE CHRISTIAN GRACES AND DISPOSITIONS, WHICH CAN NEVER APPEAR TO GREATER ADVANTAGE THAN WHEN THEY ARE ASSOCIATED WITH THE NATURAL TRANSPARENCY AND INGENUOUSNESS OF YOUTH. 1. Follow, then, after righteousness. Give God what is His due ; and you will never withhold from man what is his. 2. Follow not only after righteousness, but, as the apostle exhorts his son Timothy, after "faith." Account, that as practical righteousness, the rendering of everything that is due to man, so faith is the expectation of all that is needful from God. 3. Next, you are exhorted to follow "charity" or love. Love is the essence of righteousness, for it is "the fulfilling of the law" ; it is also the evidence of faith, for "faith worketh by love." 4. Lastly, in the words of the apostle, "follow after peace." This, indeed, is the subject of one of the most earnest petitions that ever fell from human lips : " Now the God of peace Himself give you peace always by all means." Nor can the apostles of the Lord and Saviour better express the fervour of their love for the brethren than by the prayer that "grace, mercy, and peace may be multiplied to them through Jesus Christ." Yes, peace is indeed an object worthy to be followed by man, a blessing worthy to be multiplied by God. Follow after peace, then, and ye will find it, in all its varieties of excellency and of loveliness. Peace of conscience ; for your sins, however multiplied and aggravated, shall be made as though they had never been. Peace of mind ; for "great peace have they that love Thy law, and nothing shall offend them." Peace with man in life, for "the work of righteousness is peace" ; and peace—the "peace that passeth understanding"—in death, for "mark the perfect man, and behold the upright, for the end of that man is peace." Now we have looked upon four objects of moral excellency and social usefulness, which the young Christian is to follow—righteousness, faith, charity, peace. Let us contrast these with four "youthful lusts," desires, inclinations, or tendencies, call them which you will, from which he is to flee. The love of self, as opposed to righteousness ; the pride of philosophical unbelief—unbelief that calls itself philosophical—as opposed to faith ; covetousness, or the desire of accumulation, as opposed to charity ; and the turbulence of mirth, revelry, and excess, as opposed to peace. (*T. Dale, M.A.*) *Admonitions to the young :*—I. CONSIDER WHAT YOU OUGHT TO AVOID—"Flee youthful lusts." The objects of abhorrence are distinctly specified in this short but impressive caution. No palliating epithets are employed to divest them of their disgusting qualities. They are not pleaded for by being called, as too many in modern times represent them— "mere juvenile indiscretions,"—"youthful follies," which maturer age will correct ; but they are marked by a term, which at once describes and condemns them. Lust, in the language of Scripture, has an extensive latitude of meaning; it is applied to evil desire in general—the desire of what is in itself unlawful and forbidden, or the intemperate desire of what is in itself lawful and allowed. This explanation accords with the assertion of the apostle John in his first Epistle, in which he gives an accurate classification of evil desires : " All that is in the world, the lust of the flesh, the lust of the eye, and the pride of life, is not of the Father, but of the world." The passions and appetites of our nature are powerful principles of action. Were they always subjected to the government of enlightened reason, they would become sources of innocent gratification ; indulgence would leave no stain, and remembrance would awaken no remorse. But from their fatal predominance over the convictions of the understanding, and the remonstrances of conscience, what streams of sin and misery have inundated the world ! To these, as their immediate sources, may be traced innumerable diseases which ruin the body, by causing its premature debility, and securing its inevitable destruction. But their direst evil is that they "war against the soul," impair the mind, and pollute the heart. In order to render the impression more vivid, let us consider to what evil desires the young are peculiarly exposed ; what are the unhallowed passions that require their utmost vigilance and opposition. 1. I would first exhort you, my young friends, to guard against the seductions of sensuality ; against what are emphatically termed "fleshy lusts." On no subject are the sacred writers more frequent, or more alarming in their denunciations than on this. Aware of the wide-spreading nature of the contagion, they continually remind us of its evil, and direct us to the means of counteracting and expelling it. 2. Beware of intemperance. By intemperance, I mean particularly the excessive indulgence of those appetites of our nature on which our existence depends. It is sometimes said that such indulgence, so basely irrational, places a man on a level with the brutes that perish. But it is insulting to brutes to make the comparison. The laws of animal instinct teach them moderation, and the dictates of universal conscience as well as the "grace of God," should teach men, that "denying ungodliness and worldly lusts, they should live soberly in this present evil world." Intemperance is the baneful source of most destructive evils ; it is the powerful stimulus to the commission of crimes, which men would shudder to perpetrate in the cool moments of sobriety. 3. Amongst the evil principles which the apostle warns us to avoid, may be included also high-mindedness, for immediately after the exhortation in the text, he says, "The servant of the Lord must not strive ; but be gentle unto all, apt to teach, patient, in meekness instructing those that oppose themselves." And to enforce this impressive caution he predicts the approach of "perilous times," when all the symptoms of unhallowed self-exaltation should be manifest in the prevailing characters of men. I have adopted a term of extensive application, because it includes the various modifications of pride, haughtiness, conceit, vanity, and ambition. It is worthy of your attentive regard that the admonition in the text is levelled at the very seat and principle of iniquity. The tyranny of the passions is enthroned on the heart ; and it is from that interior dominion they must be expelled. The axe is therefore laid at the root of the tree, that all its branches and fruit may be destroyed. The apostle does not merely say, Flee evil habits, impure connections, and all the scenes of temptation, but he says what virtually includes all this, by denouncing their pernicious origin : "Flee youthful lusts" ; let not the desire be indulged ; "the thought of foolishness is sin." As the venerable Elisha purified the waters of Jericho, by sprinkling salt on the fountain whence they flowed, so the apostle directs us to cleanse the springs of action ; persuaded that they will send forth wholesome streams when healed from the contamination of sin. II. Our next general inquiry respects the opposite principles and tempers which ought to form the objects of your constant and unremitting pursuit. WHAT SHOULD YOU FOLLOW ? He was persuaded that in order to "abhor that which is evil," we must "cleave to that which is good." Let us attend to his wise and salutary directions. 1. Follow righteousness. This term frequently occurs in the sacred writings, with various, though connected acceptations. In its most important reference it is applied to that perfect "obedience even unto death," by which our exalted Lord "magnified the law and made it honourable." The Scriptures which so clearly reveal this righteousness as the exclusive basis of acceptance with God, announce the method of obtaining its blessings. " Not to him that worketh, but to him that believeth on Him that justifieth the ungodly, his faith is accounted for righteousness." This righteousness, the possession of which justifies a sinner in the sight of God, will infallibly secure as its invariable consequence, an inherent rectitude of principle—that personal righteousness, " without which no man can see the Lord." In conformity with this statement, I would earnestly exhort you, my young friends, to cultivate all the fruits of righteousness. Aim at the entire agreement of your spirit and actions with the unerring rule of righteousness, laid down in the sacred Word. There you behold its nature clearly defined, and its wide extent unfolded. It is not a variable, shifting principle, adapted to the changes of custom, and the fluctuations of caprice. Its nature and obligations are not dependent on views of expediency, which may happen to agree with its dictates to-day, and suggest an opposite rule of conduct to-morrow. Righteousness is the conformity of the heart and life to the immutable laws of equity which God has established; an equity, unbending in its decisions, and unalterable in its claims. 2. If you "follow righteousness," your character will be adorned by fidelity. This I conceive is what the apostle meant by "faith"; and the word has precisely this rendering, in the Epistle to Titus, in which servants are exhorted to "show all good fidelity." Fidelity is an important part of righteousness; it is one of the essential expressions of it, and all pretensions to rectitude without it are but as "tinkling cymbals and as sounding brass." 3. With "righteousness and fidelity," the apostle connects charity and peace. The principles and duties of justice are intimately blended with those of benevolence. The latter derive all their value and stability from the former, and give them in return "an ornament of grace—a crown of glory." Charity, or love, is of essential importance to Christian character. It is often referred to as a decisive test of real religion. It is well described by the apostle Paul as the "bond of perfectness." It unites and combines all the other graces, "fitly framing them together," giving them beauty, proportion, and effect. The apostle Paul has presented a full-length portraiture of Charity. Are you surprised that peace should spring from that charity which "endureth all things"? This is its rational and invariable result. The peace which flows from believing, and which consists in reconciliation with God through Jesus Christ, will be connected with a pacific temper and disposition. These are the objects of pursuit exhibited to your attention, in the exhortation of the text. You are commanded to follow them, wherever they may lead you; to aim at attaining them, whatever they may cost you; and with unremitting diligence to persevere in the path which they have prescribed. With peculiar propriety has the apostle connected this wise direction with the preceding caution. Every disposition marked out as the object of pursuit, immediately tends to the subversion of those unhallowed desires which you are warned to avoid. You cannot indulge in one "youthful lust" but you violate the claims of "righteousness, faith, charity, and peace." Let these holy principles exist, and you will be effectually armed against the enemies of your souls. III. WITH WHOM SHOULD YOU ASSOCIATE? "With them that call on the Lord with a pure heart." Religion does not extirpate the social affections of our nature; but it directs their exercise, and consecrates them supremely to the glory of God. The fellowship of a Christian Church is designed to bring them under the guidance of those laws which Christ has revealed in His Word, and to regulate all our voluntary associations. The influence of pernicious example is peculiarly felt in the circle of intimate friendship. There your opinions and practices receive their strongest confirmation; and your character and habits, if at first opposed to the prevailing complexion of those with whom you associate, will be almost imperceptibly changed. Consider the infinite importance of being now "numbered with the saints," "on the Lord's side," that you may not be "gathered with sinners" at the day of final separation and unalterable decision! (*Jos. Fletcher, M.A.*) *Purity*:—Antony William Boehme, a German divine, once preached from Exodus xx. 14: "Thou shalt not commit adultery." A chevalier, who was one of his hearers, felt himself so much insulted that he challenged Boehme to fight a duel, because he thought his sermon designed entirely to offend him. Boehme accepted the challenge, and appeared in his robes; but instead of a pistol he had the Bible in his hand, and spoke to him in the following manner: "I am sorry you were so much offended when I preached against that destructive vice; at the time I did not even think of you. Here I appear with the sword of the Spirit, and if your conscience condemns you, I beseech you, for your own salvation, to repent of your sins and lead a new life. If you will, then fire at me immediately, for I would willingly lose my life if that might be the means of saving your soul!" The chevalier was so struck with this language that he embraced him and solicited his friendship. A bold man was this preacher, and reminds you of another bold man in English history, Hugh Latimer, Bishop of Worcester, who presented to Henry VIII. for a new year's gift a New Testament, doubled down at the leaf where is written, "Whoremongers and adulterers God will judge" (Heb. xiii. 4). God's truth must be told, and not be kept back. The Seventh Commandment concerns our own and our neighbour's chastity: "Thou shalt not commit adultery." It forbids all acts of uncleanness, with all those fleshly lusts which produce those acts and war against the soul; and all those practices which cherish and excite those fleshly lusts, as looking in order to lust, which Christ tells us is forbidden in this commandment (Matt. v. 28). The eyes, like Jacob's cattle, too firmly fixed on beautiful objects, make the affections bring forth spotted fruit, and it is as easy to quench the fire of Etna as the thought fixed by lust. Lusting is often the result of looking, as in David, who saw Bathsheba bathing, and in Joseph's mistress, who set her eyes upon Joseph. Lust is quicksighted. How much better Job, who would not look, lest he should think upon a maid! He had learned to keep in his eyes from roving to wanton prospects. Samson's eyes were the first offenders that betrayed him to unlawful desire of carnal pleasure; therefore are his eyes first pulled out, and he led a blind captive to Gaza, where before he had with carnal appetite gazed on his Delilah. Among the things which in our baptismal vow we promised to renounce are the sinful lusts of the flesh. The text enforces that promise upon us. Carnal pleasures are the sins of youth; ambition and the love of power the sins of middle age: covetousness and carking cares the crimes of old age. "Flee fornication," &c. (1 Cor. vi. 18, 19). He that commits this sin sinneth against his own body; and inasmuch as his body was created for God's Holy Spirit to dwell in, it is a defilement of the temple of God. This sin of fornication is, therefore, the more hateful, because by committing it a man sins both against himself, against his fellow-creature, and against his God. By indulging in this sin he debases his noblest faculties; he defiles and destroys God's handiwork; he makes vile that which God made holy. By the just judgment of God all these irregular and sinful connections are married to death. Neither prostitutes, whoremongers, nor unclean persons of any description can live out half their days. Parents! beware of the example of Eli! He was a good man himself, but his children were extremely wicked—he restrained them not. Parents! see that your children do not associate with corrupt companions—"Evil communications corrupt good manners." Indulged children, like Dinah (Gen. xxxiv.), often become a grief and shame to their families. Her pretence was to see the daughters of the land, to see how they dressed, and how they danced, and what was fashionable amongst them; she went to see—she went to be seen too; she went to gain an acquaintance with those Canaanites, and to learn their way. See what came from Dinah's roving! The beginning of sin is as the letting forth of water—"Give the water no passage, neither an unprotected daughter liberty to gad abroad" (Ecclus). Carefully avoid all occasions of sin and approaches to it. Parents! let your household arrangements be such as never to endanger your children's purity of character; never let the blush of shame be needlessly raised on their cheeks. Whatever sacrifice it may cost you in other ways, do not put them in jeopardy by crowding your family into too small a space, thus rendering it impossible that a sense of decency and modesty should be preserved. It is a false and fatal economy that would tempt you to do this. Much depends on you, landlords, masters, employers of labour. But whatever may be done by parents or by masters, to you, young men and young women, we must mainly look. The celebrated John Newton, as the commander of a slave-ship, had a number of women under his absolute command, and knowing the danger of his situation on that account, he resolved to abstain from flesh in his food, and to drink nothing stronger than water during the voyage, that by abstemiousness he might subdue every improper emotion. Upon his setting sail, the sight of a certain point of land was the signal for his beginning a rule which he was enabled to keep. (*R. A. Taylor, M.A.*) *Helps against lusts:*—1. Get a sound knowledge of them. 2. Mortify thy carnal members. 3. Labour for a broken heart. 4. Be diligent in thy calling. 5. Abandon lewd companions. 6. And strive to taste deeply of the water of life; favour the best things. (*J. Barlow, D.D.*) *Youthful lusts:*—And thy lusts of youth are principally these: pride, idleness, pleasure, wantonness. To avoid these see thou—1. Set a watch over all thy external senses. In presence, view not, touch not. In absence, talk not, think not on wanton affections. 2. Sleep little, eat little, work much, pray much; for take away the fuel and the fire will be quenched. 3. When wandering cogitations or suggestions reflect on thy fancy, divert them the contrary way. Forget not this. 4. Attend to good counsel, and follow it; and see before thou purpose anything what the best men advise thee. (*Ibid.*) *A choice between the higher and lower life :*—Thou hast a double nature. Choose between the worse and the better that is within thee. Thou hast it in thy power to become the slave of passion, the slave of luxury, the slave of sensual pleasure, the slave of corruption. Thou hast it in thy power to become the free master of thyself, to become the everlasting benefactor of thy country, and the unfailing champion of thy God. (*Dean Stanley.*) *Passions to be early checked :*—There was once an old monk walking through the forest with a little scholar by his side. The old man suddenly stopped and pointed to four plants close at hand. The first was beginning to peep above the ground; the second had rooted itself pretty well into the earth; the third was a small shrub; whilst the fourth and last was a full-sized tree. Then the old monk said to his young companion : "Pull up the first." The youth easily pulled it up with his fingers. "Now pull the second." The youth obeyed, but not so easily. "And the third." But the boy had to put forth all his strength, and to use both arms, before he succeeded in uprooting it. "And now," said the master, "try your hand upon the fourth." But lo! the trunk of the tall tree, grasped in the arms of the youth, scarcely shook its leaves, and the little fellow found it impossible to tear its roots from the earth. Then the wise old monk explained to his scholar the meaning of the four trials. "This, my son, is just what happens with our passions. When they are young and weak, one may, by a little watchfulness over self, and the help of a little self-denial, easily tear them up; but if we let them cast their roots deep down into our souls, then no human power can uproot them, the Almighty hand of the Creator alone can pluck them out. For this reason, watch well over the first movements of your soul, and study by acts of virtue to keep your passions well in check." *The bloom of youthful purity :*—There grows a bloom and beauty over the beauty of the plum and apricot, more exquisite than the fruit itself—a soft, delicate flush that overspreads its blushing cheek. Now, if you strike your hand over that, it is gone for ever, for it never grows but once. The flower that hangs in the morning impearled with dew, arrayed as a queenly woman never was arrayed with jewels; once shake it so that the beads roll off, and you may sprinkle water over it as you please, yet it can never be made again what it was when the dew fell silently on it from heaven. On a frosty morning you may see panes of glass covered with landscapes, mountains, lakes, and trees, blended in a beautiful fantastic picture. Now, lay your hand upon the glass, and by a scratch of your finger, or by the warmth of your palm, all the delicate tracery will be obliterated. So there is in youth a beauty and purity of character, which, when once touched and defiled, can never be restored,—a fringe more delicate than frost-work, and which, when torn and broken, will never be re-embroidered. He who has spotted and soiled his garments in youth, though he may seek to make them white again, can never wholly do it, even were he to wash them with his tears. When a young man leaves his father's house with the blessing of a mother's tears still wet upon his brow, if he once lose that early purity of character, it is a spot that he can never make whole again. Such is the consequence of crime. Its effects cannot be eradicated; it can only be forgiven. *Righteousness :*—Let me exhort you to put on the righteousness of Christ Jesus, as by application, so in imitation. When thou art to deal with God, and to appeal in His court, see thou have this wedding garment: clothe thy nakedness with the mantle of Jesus; cover thy sinful person with no other robe; wear not linsey-woolsey; mix not thy pigeon feathers with this eagle's plumes; blend not thy flash water with this fresh wine, lest thy nakedness appear, and death be found in the pot. But with him, who knew what he did (Phil. iii. 8, 9), cast off thy rags, trample them under foot, and apparel thyself with the pure linen of Christ our Lord; for Solomon in all his royalty was not clothed like him, who hath put on Christ Jesus. (*J. Barlow, D.D.*) *Faith :*—By faith the righteousness of Christ is unfolded, apprehended, put on. Knowledge, like the eye, may direct us unto the wedding garment. But faith, as the hand, must take hold of it, apparel ourselves with it. What if we be said to live by faith? so are we by our hands. Yet doth any man eat his fingers? No; it is by that which faith applieth; and the motion of the hand procureth and receiveth. (*Ibid.*) *Following peace :*—For thy help take these directions:—1. Be at peace with God; for that will keep thy heart and mind in the acknowledgment and love of the truth (Phil. iv. 7, 9). 2. Have peace with thyself. In all things be in subjection to the Spirit (James iii. 14, 15). For if wars be in us, peace will not be without us (Gal. vi. 16). 3. Depart with part of thine own rights; so did Abraham to Lot (Gen.

xiii. 9). Christ paid tribute to preserve peace (Mat. xvii., ult.). And for peace sake we should suffer wrong (1 Cor. vi. 7). 4. Abandon self-love, and pray for peace. When men will have their own actions still go forward, without doubt, it is a work of the flesh (Gal. vi. 20). For motives—1. Are we not the sons of God? and is not He the King of Peace? (1 Cor. xiv. 33). 2. Be we not subjects to Him who is the Prince of Peace? (Isa. ix. 6). 3. Is not a Christian called to live in peace? (1 Cor vii. 15). 4. And if we continue in peace, will not the God of love and peace be with us? (2 Cor. xiii. 11). (*Ibid.*) *Self-control inspired by the thought of God :*—A heathen may herein teach multitudes of unconverted men and many professing Christians a lesson. We read of Cyrus, that when, after one of his victories, a captive of singular beauty, Panthea, the wife of Abradates, king of Susiana, was taken, he refused to see her, and entrusted her to the keeping of Araspes, giving him a very prudent admonition respecting his conduct, and was thus assured by him; "Fear nothing; I am sure of myself, and I will answer with my life that I shall do nothing contrary to my duty." This young nobleman was notwithstanding overcome by her beauty, and in danger of basely violating his promise, had not Panthea given Cyrus intelligence of his baseness. Araspes, when cited to appear before his prince, was overwhelmed with shame and fear, and spoke of the control over his desires which he had when in Cyrus' presence, and his weakness when left to himself (see "Rollin's Ancient History," bk. iv., ch. i., sec. iv.). If the presence of a fellow-creature, however marked by purity and modera- tion, availed to curb the passions of a heathen, how much more should the re- collection of a pure and holy God! And if love constrain not, the fear of His displeasure should lead us to beware of danger, and to guard our eyes and our hearts, lest we fall into temptation. *Avoiding danger :*—Have you never heard the story of a lady who wanted a coachman? Two or three called to see her about the situation, and, in answer to her inquiries, the first applicant said, "Yes, madam, you could not have a better coachman than myself." She replied, "How near do you think you could drive to danger without an accident?" "Madam, I could go within a yard of it, and yet you would be perfectly safe." "Very well," she said, "you will not suit me." The second one had heard the question upon which the other had been rejected, and therefore he was ready with his answer, "Danger! madam, why I could drive within a hair's breadth, and yet be perfectly safe." "Then you will not suit me at all." When number three came in, he was asked, "Are you a good driver?" "Well," he replied, "I am careful and have never met with an accident." "But how near do you think you could drive to danger?" "Madam," he said, "that is a thing I never tried, I always drive as far away from danger as ever I can." The lady at once replied, "You are the kind of coachman I want, and I will engage you at once." Get such a coachman as that yourself, to guide your own heart, and lead your own character. Do not see how near you can go to sin, but see how far you can keep away from it. (*C. H. Spurgeon.*) *Abstinence :*—A friend who, in the opinion of all who knew him, was very unlikely to take stimulants to excess, and who had very little sympathy with teetotalism, told me the other day that he had given up wine. When I asked him his reason he gave me this suggestive reply : "Because I was beginning to like it and count on it." It was the wise repression of incipient rebellion before it had asserted itself by overt act. (*A. Rowland, LL.B.*) *Taken unawares :*—We have read that "a debtor seeing a bailiff in quest of him ran three miles to a boundary, beyond which he was safe." The bailiff, seeming calmly to submit to his failure, stretched out his hand and said, "Well, let us part good friends, at any rate." The debtor, off his guard, accepted the offered hand, whereupon the bailiff, with a desperate effort, pulled him across the line, and clapping him on the shoulder, said, "You are my prisoner." So men may be overcome by the evil one when they least expect an assault from him, and think themselves most safe. (*Sunday School Teacher.*) *Self-control:*—Bishop Ryle, in his "Young Men Exhorted," makes some pungent remarks on this duty of self-control. "Resolve at once," he writes, "by God's help, to shun everything that may prove an occasion of sin. It is an excellent saying of good old Bishop Hall: 'He that would be safe from the acts of evil must wisely avoid the occasions.' Never hold a candle to the devil. He that would be safe must not come near the brink of danger. He must look upon his heart as a magazine of gunpowder, and be cautious not to handle one spark of temptation more than he can help. Where is the use of your praying, 'Lead us not into temptation,' unless you are yourselves careful not to run into it?" "*Flee*" :—Prayer is not enough. Many have prayed, and have not found

15

it sufficient. Therefore the advice in the Bible is rational—Flee. The usual receipt for resisting sin is, Fight; but I venture to say the Bible and common sense recommend flight rather. There are many sins we must not even look at; to turn away and run is the only resource. The Bible says, "Flee youthful lusts," and "Look not on the wine." The brave thing, although it looks the cowardly, is to flee. But it is not into space we are to flee. We are to fly upward, to get into a higher mood, and breathe another atmosphere. (*Prof. H. Drummond.*) *Temptation's deceits :*—In the Fisheries Exhibition the nets were so beautifully hung and draped as to form graceful curtains. How many of Satan's nets are made to appear charmingly attractive. (*H. O. Mackey.*) *The conquest of self :*— The following epitaph was once placed over a soldier's grave :—

> "Here lies a soldier, whom all must applaud,
>  Who fought many battles at home and abroad ;
>  But the hottest engagement he ever was in
>  Was the conquest of self in the battle of sin."

*The danger of success :*—There is danger in success. St. Bernard astonished an immense congregation, intensely interested in his sermon, by suddenly exclaiming, "Get thee behind me, Satan." He felt that the devil was tempting him to be proud of his eloquence, as though he would win souls by his own enticing words. And when Lacordaire had enthralled thousands by one of his Lenten sermons in Notre Dame, the young monk who went to summon him to the refectory, found him kneeling before a crucifix, with the tears on his cheeks, and inquired, "Oh, father, why are you so sad?" This was the answer, "My son, I am afraid of success." Be not high-minded, but fear. (*Dean Hole.*) *Undiscovered character :*—Every man has in himself a continent of undiscovered character. Happy is he who acts the Columbus to his own soul. (*Sir J. Stephen.*) **Peace with them that call on the Lord out of a pure heart.**—This last "peace" must be joined with the words immediately following : "With them that call on the Lord," &c. The "peace" here signifies absence of contention; it is well paraphrased by, "that spiritual concord which unites together all who call upon and who love their Lord." (*H. D. M. Spence, M.A.*) *The Christian young man :*— It will be manifest, at the very first glance, that when the apostle expresses with whom his son Timothy should, he implies with what kind of persons he should not associate; with those who do not "call upon the Lord," and with those who do indeed appear to call upon the Lord, but not "out of a pure heart." First, the unbeliever, whether he be such in appearance, or only in practice ; and next, the hypocrite, the formalist, the inconsistent, and the insincere. 1. Our first character is that of the avowed and unblushing sceptic ; that of the man who contemptuously characterises religion as the business of women, the trade of preachers, and the toy of men ; one who mistakes adroitness in contending against truth in argument, for capability of disproving it, and who is as much delighted with himself, when he has hurled a sarcasm or a sneer against the gospel or the Church, as if he had invented an objection which must tend to the overthrow of them both. This class of persons may be ordinarily identified by one generic feature ; namely, that they assume everything, and demonstrate nothing. Avoid, then, as far as possible, all intercourse, all communion, with persons such as these. If they interrogate you, answer; but when you have answered, do not argue. 2. I shall next describe the character of the man whose infidelity is practical ; who is only not an atheist because he is nothing; who does not avow or advocate false principles simply because he has no principles at all; and who remains just as indifferent to all that concerns his moral responsibility or his religious duty, as if indeed he were the base degraded thing, to which he endeavours to assimilate himself; as if in truth he were "the beast, whose spirit goeth downward to the earth" —not the rational, immortal, intelligible, accountable man, whose spirit, when dismissed from and disencumbered of its earthly tabernacle, must "return to God that gave it." The root of the evil is, that so far as the interests of the soul are concerned, persons of this class do not think at all. From such, then, as we have now described, such as "separate themselves" from the assemblies of Christian worship, being "sensual, having not the Spirit" ; such as do not "call upon the Lord" in the house of prayer, and therefore cannot be presumed to call upon Him in the closet—you ought to separate yourselves as far as possible, on no other ground than the simple knowledge of the fact. They are far more likely to injure you than you are likely to profit them; for they have an ally, an accomplice, in your own sinful nature. 3. There is yet another class of characters, from whom in following out the spirit of the text, we are constrained to counsel separation. It is the inconsistent, the undecided, the manifestly insincere; those who "call on the Lord," but not" out of a pure heart"; those who observe proprieties, but who disregard principles; who conform to the ritual without imbibing the spirit of the Church; who profess with their lips that they know God, but in works do deny Him—disguising their practices by their profession, and masking their private vices by their public prayers. Those who "call on the Lord out of a pure heart." But then understand what this means—the heart of such persons is not innately pure; it is not pure from the first. No, nor is it inherently pure by any natural constitution or organisation peculiar to itself. Nor is it independently pure— without the aids of Divine and spiritual operation, or by influence of its own. Nor is it invariably pure—pure without any apprehension of or capability of change. Its purity is derived and imparted from above; purity in the comparative sense, for all human purity is comparative; and produced by the action of the Spirit of God upon the heart. It is first the purposed, attempted, desired separation from all iniquity—because we "name the name of Christ"; the ceasing to regard it with the heart, as well as admit it knowingly into the life. It is next the fixed, settled, honest purpose, to "seek first the kingdom of God and His righteousness"; and to postpone all considerations of present pleasure, interest, or inclination to the "one thing" which is supremely "needful," even to "win Christ and be found in Him." Purity, indeed, is but another name for what is elsewhere called "single-ness of heart"; that which St. Paul exemplified when he declared, "One thing I do; forgetting those things which are behind, and reaching forth unto those things which are before, I press toward the mark for the prize of the high calling of God in Christ Jesus"; and what the Lord Himself delineated when He said, "If thine eye be single, thy whole body shall be full of light." I have already spoken to you about the prudence of avoiding companionship with the ungodly, but this example leads you one step beyond it—to the cultivation of fellowship with the pious. And for this reason: that every friendship, which is formed upon such principles and with such persons, is an additional barrier and defence against the encroachment or aggressions of the enemy. To form a new Christian connection or intimacy is like placing a new warrior within the citadel of the heart, a new sentinel upon the watch-tower, or, it may be, a new defender in the breach. (*T. Dale, M.A.*)

Ver. 23. **Foolish and unlearned questions avoid.**—The Greek word translated "unlearned," is better rendered *ignorant*. These "questions," which the false teachers, with whom Timothy was so much thrown, loved to put forward for discussion, could hardly be termed "unlearned"—much useless learning being often thrown away in these disputings of the schools—but were rather "pointless," "stupid," as well as foolish. (*H. D. M. Spence, M.A.*) *Ignorant questionings :*—I. UNADVISED AND UNLEARNED QUESTIONS ARE TO BE AVOIDED. 1. For the ground of them is not good : such spring either from curiosity or ignorance. 2. The fruit therefore will be bitter; for nothing profitable. II. SIN IN THE FIRST CAUSES IS TO BE PREVENTED. What of less motion or power than a word—a question? yet such of all men are to be regarded. III. THE CAUSES OF SIN ONCE DISCERNED ARE TO BE RESISTED, SHUNNED. Thou knowest that fond reasonings, unadvised disputings, beget quarrels, stir up strifes: therefore reject them, flee from them. IV. FOOLISH QUESTIONS RAISE CONTENTIONS. It is a wonder to see what abundance of ill fruit one branch of fond reasoning hath produced. Like a bone cast amongst curs, an unlearned question will cause men to snarl, bite, and quarrel. (*J. Barlow, D.D.*) *Foolish question-ings :*—A lady, of whom we heard in our travels, had worried several ministers who sought her good by always telling them that she could not believe till they could explain to her how God could be without a beginning. "For," said she, "if He never began, then He has not begun, and there can be no God at all." Very dexterous are certain persons in blocking up their own road, and yet, perhaps, there is no great dexterity in it, for the proverb says, "A fool may put questions which a wise man cannot answer." In the Vatican at Rome we saw the renowned statue of the boy who has a thorn in his foot, and is busy extracting it. He was doing this when we first saw him, and three years after he was attempting the same operation. We have good reason for believing that he is even now in the same posture, and will be found in like attitude fifty years hence. He is carved in marble, and therefore is excused for making no progress; but what shall be said of living, thoughtful individuals who year after year are trifling with imaginary difficulties, and never set foot on the road to heaven? (*C. H. Spurgeon.*)    *Unwise curiosity :*—The over-curious are not over-wise. (*Massinger.*)    *Metaphysical subtleties :*—

> "Defend me, therefore, common sense, say I,
> From reveries so airy, from the toil
> Of dropping buckets into empty wells,
> And growing old in drawing nothing up."        (*Cowper.*)

*Religious strife :*—Haxley came to Baltimore to attend a general conference in 1820. A discussion arose on a question of order, whether presiding elders should be elected by preachers or not, and the dispute had waxed warm, not to say hot. Brother Haxley had said not a word through it all, but at the close of the session the Bishop called upon him to make the concluding prayer. He knelt and said, "Now, O Lord, Thou knowest what a time we've had here discussing and arguing about this elder question, and Thou knowest what our feelings are. We do not care what becomes of the ark; it's only who drives the oxen." (*Christian Age.*)

Ver. 24. **The servant of the Lord must not strive, but be gentle.**—*Conciliation :* —It is noteworthy how, in these Pastoral Epistles—which contain, so to speak, the last general directions to believers in Jesus as to life, as well as doctrine of, perhaps, the greatest of the inspired teachers—so many careful suggestions are given for the guidance of Christians in all their relations with the great heathen world. Conciliation may be termed the key-note of these directions. St. Paul would press upon Timothy and his successors the great truth that it was the Master's will that the unnumbered people who sit in darkness and in the shadow of death should learn, by slow though sure degrees, how lovely and desirable a thing it was to be a Christian; should come at length to see clearly that Christ was, after all, the only lover and real friend of man. (*H. D. M. Spence, M.A* )    *Gentleness becometh a minister :*—He must not be a fighter, quarreller ; but meek, quiet, easy to be entreated : for such are fathers, nurses, surgeons, physicians. Oh, how much pity, tenderness of affection is required of them! Lambs, sucking babes, bones out of joints, stand in need of a gentle heart and finger to feed, nourish, and rightly to place them. To be fierce, cruel, outrageous, better befits a dog than a shepherd. (*J. Barlow, D.D.*)    *True spirit of reform :*—The temper and deportment recommended by St. Paul in the text to those who undertake to serve God in the instruction of man, or in advancing any reformation, approve themselves to our sober judgment as best suited to the work in view, and alone conformable to the example and precepts of our blessed Saviour. But then we look back upon the history of the Church, which is in great part an history of ignorance and instruction, of corruptions and reformations, and we find that among the most prominent of the servants of the Lord, among the most remarkable leaders in religious progress, were those who, though apt to teach were also very apt to strive, and so far from being patterns of gentleness, patience and meekness, were rather remarkable for qualities of an opposite description, for rudeness, for hastiness, and for intemperance of language and action. We ask, whether, considering the task which these men assumed, the obstacles which they were obliged to contend with, and the success which rewarded their efforts, they were not, after all, the right kind of men for the work and for the time; whether their severe and even martial characteristics were not necessary to the accomplishment of their purpose ; and whether a different kind of men, of more peaceful sentiments, and moderate designs and measures, would have made any head at all against the torrent of sin and error which they might endeavour to stem. We think of Luther, of Calvin, of Knox—fiery, arbitrary, and often abusive men. But were they more so than they ought to have been? Here is the gospel rule on the one side, and here, on the other, are these impressive facts. Now, in few of these facts, must not the gospel rule admit of exception and modification? If this has at any time been my opinion, longer reflection has induced me to renounce it; and I am now convinced that truth never requires the sacrifice of love, that wrath and violence are never necessary to reforms, that the cause of Christianity is never really advanced by the operations of an unchristian spirit. Do I then undertake to say, that what we have been accustomed to call reformations are not reformations, and that the leaders of them do not deserve the name of reformers, which has so long been awarded them? I say no such thing. But I do venture to affirm, that these reformations would have been attended with less suffering and evil, and would have been more extensive than they were, if the reformers had manifested more of the Christian spirit than they did. I would attribute the success of those reformers whom I have already named, such as it was, and it surely was great, not to their failings but to their excellences, not to their vices but to their virtues. They possessed in great perfection the energetic virtues: through the force of these virtues, and the force of truth, they succeeded as they did. Their bitterness, their fierceness, did not promote, but on the contrary impeded, the progress of the truths for which they contended. A Christian reform cannot be caused or aided by a spirit which the law of Christ expressly and utterly condemns. The real causes which bring it about are of another character. 1. There is, in the first place, the obviousness of the corruptions which the reformer would abolish, and which the pure and honest portion of society, when their eyes are opened, will unite in abolishing. 2. There is, in the second place, the equal obviousness of some good, which the reformer distinctly presents as an end, and which the well-disposed will assist him to establish. 3. There is, in the third place, the real virtue which the reformer manifests in the exhibition and accomplishment of his purpose. 4. In the fourth place, there is the vast amount of noble enthusiasm which is excited by the prospect of enormous corruptions on the one hand, and of great improvements and blessings on the other, and which enlists itself on the reformer's side. 5. And, to go no further in the enumeration, there is the help of God, which is always bestowed upon those who, with whatever imperfections, are labouring to accomplish a high and worthy object. I find that my opinion is supported by an authority which, on such a subject, is entitled to more than common weight. "I know," says the reformer John Wesley, speaking of the reformer John Knox, and of that fierce and barbarous spirit of his followers, which demolished the finest architecture of Scotland, "I know it is commonly said, the work to be done needed such a spirit. Not so; the work of God does not, cannot need the work of the devil to forward it. And a calm, even spirit goes through rough work far better than a furious one. Although, therefore, God did use at the time of the Reformation. sour, overbearing, passionate men, yet He did not use them because they were such, but notwithstanding they were so. And there is no doubt He would have used them much more, had they been of a humbler and milder spirit." Instances, in sufficient number, might be mentioned beside that of Wesley, of men who, charged with an important message, and meeting with rude and cruel opposition in delivering it, have still delivered it with a kind and loving, and withal a steady voice, and who have been heard and obeyed at last, when opposers grew ashamed of their own ferocity, and sank into quietness from the want of exasperation. But if there were no such instances, I see not what is to forbid our pointing to the Great Redeemer, and requiring that all who work in His name should work with His spirit; and moreover asserting that whatever contradictions of this spirit are manifested by them are to be counted, not among their excellences, nor among qualities which are necessary to their success, but among their defects, and defects which their cause, if a Christian cause, might easily have spared. (*F. W. P. Greenwood, D.D.*) *Gentleness :*—It is a suggestive fact that the dove, which is regarded as the emblem of gentleness, has no gall-bladder. (*H. O. Mackey.*) *Power of gentleness :*—St. Anselm was a monk in the Abbey of Bec, in Normandy, and upon Lanfranc's removal, became his successor as director. No teacher ever threw a greater spirit of love into his toil. "Force your scholars to improve?" he burst out to another teacher who relied on blows and compulsion. "Did you ever see a craftsman fashion a fair image out of a golden plate by blows alone? Does he not now gently press it and strike it with his tools; now with wise art, yet more gently raise and shape it. What do your scholars turn into under this ceaseless beating?" "They turn only brutal," was the reply. "You have bad luck," was the keen answer, "in a training that only turns men into beasts." The worst natures softened before this tenderness and patience. Even the Conqueror, so harsh and terrible to others, became another man, generous and easy of speech, with Anselm. (*Ibid.*) *The quietness of Christ :*—One feature of Christ's teaching which St. Matthew notices, is the quietness in dealing with those by whom it was misunderstood. There was no fighting, no contention of words, no hot disputing, where it could be avoided, but retirement. So we are told that when the Pharisees held a council against Him, how they might destroy Him, He withdrew Himself fulfilling, St. Matthew tells us, the old words, " He shall not strive nor cry, neither shall any man hear His voice in the streets." I must, however, draw your attention to yet one more feature, His teaching was positive, not negative. There was much in the religion of the day that was so small, contemptible, and even base, that it might have seemed right and wise to pull down first and then build. But He, by His actions and His words, was constantly justifying His express statement that He came not to destroy, but to fulfil. So far from fulminating against the dead formality of the temple worship, He tried to make it better by purging it and infusing fresh life into it. His life and words were a continual filling in with a new spirit all that was good and helpful. Where He could transform He would never discard. Could we catch something of His spirit by retiring from, instead of fighting with, determined enemies, by transforming instead of discarding, how helpful our service of man in this respect would be! (*Prof. G. H. S. Walpole.*) *Christian gentleness :*—I remember to-day two masters I was under at school. One was a huge, burly fellow, with a sharp, unkind word, and a sharper punishment for every boy, big or little, who was guilty of an omission or a fault : and every lad, little or big in the school, hated him, and longed for the time when they would see him no more. The other was by no means a weakling, for he was a splendid fellow in the cricket-field; but he was as gentle as a child. And the roughest and wildest lads, who would have scorned to allow their faces to tell what they suffered under a cruel beating from the first, used to dread a quiet five minutes' talk with the second master, who in a sweet low voice always used to begin with "my dear boy." Few lads left the presence of that second master without having felt unable to repress the rising tears, and without a noble resolve to be better for the sake of the Christian gentleness with which the folly or the fault had been dealt with. (*J. Bowker.*)          *Kind words :*—Kind words never blister the tongue or lips, and we never hear of any mental trouble arising from this quarter. Though they do not cost much, yet they accomplish much. They help one's own good nature and good will. Soft words soften our own soul; angry words are fuel to the flame of wrath, and make it burn more fiercely. Kind words make other people good-natured. Cold words freeze people, and hot words scorch them; and bitter words make them bitter, and wrathful words make them wrathful. There are such a number of other kinds of words, that we ought occasionally to make use of kind words. There are vain words, and idle words, and silly words, and hasty words, and empty words, and profane words, and boisterous words, and war-like words. But kind words soothe and comfort the hearer; they shame him out of his sour, morose, unkind feelings. We have not yet begun to use kind words in such abundance as they ought to be used. (*Pascal.*)          *Scholars to be considered rather than subjects :*—If teachers could be convinced that every lesson in which a child, however it has increased its knowledge, has increased its dislike for knowledge, is a lesson worse than lost, then they would consider not only how subjects ought to be treated, but pupils. There are many who do great justice to their subjects, while they do great injustice to their pupils. The nature of the one is understood, but not the nature of the other. (*Sunday School Teacher.*)          **Patient** (see Wisdom ii. 19.)—Endurance of malicious detraction is one of the victories of grace. (*H. R. Reynolds, D.D.*) *Teaching better than controversy :*—This is what the servant of God should really aim at being : the teacher rather than the controversialist—rather the patient endurer of wrong than the fomenter of dissentions and wordy strifes. (*H. D. M. Spence, M.A.*) *Impatience :*—Antony, the hermit, heard praise of a certain brother; but when he tested him he found that he was impatient under injury. Quoth Antony, "Thou art like a house which has a gay porch, but is broken into by thieves through the back door." (*C. Kingsley.*)          *Provocation wisely used :*—The oyster, when it is feeding, lies with its shell open a little way, so that the water may flow through it; and when any of the very little insects and animals on which it feeds comes floating in with the water, the oyster opens its mouth and swallows them. But it sometimes happens that things float in which the oyster does not want, and which it cannot swallow or eat. When it is lying quietly in the sunshine, and enjoying its meal, a little grain of sand may come inside the shell, so small that you and I could scarcely see it, but so hard and sharp, that if it gets under the oyster's soft, tender body, it would irritate and pain it. What does the oyster do? It has no hands to catch hold of it and throw it out. Well, it does not, as we should say, get into a passion, and knock itself about the shell; no, it lies quite still, and with some of that beautiful, white, smooth, glossy matter, with which it has lined the inside of its shell, it covers the sand all over, and so makes it smooth too. And more than that, when the oyster is caught, and its shell is opened, if one of these small round beads is found, it is taken out and called a pearl, and sometimes makes a very valuable and handsome ornament. So provocation should be the occasion of developing the pearl of patience.

Ver. 25. **In meekness instructing those that oppose themselves; if God peradventure will give them repentance to the acknowledging of the truth.**—The phrase is difficult as it stands. Strictly translated it would be, " lest at any time "; but this would be out of harmony with the whole strain of the passage. Grave doubt is expressed, but hope is not extinguished. God is the giver of repentance. Scharlitz, quoted by Fairbairn, suggests " whether God may not still give repentance." Here is expression of the thought that there is room and necessity for the operation of the Spirit of God, over and above the normal action of the truth upon the understanding. (*H. R. Reynolds, D.D.*)   *Timothy's ministry* (vers. 25, 26):—Consider—I. THE CHARACTERS AMONG WHOM IT WAS TO BE EXERCISED—opposers not only of God, but of themselves. They oppose—1. Their duty.   2. Their conscience. 3. Their peace.   4. Their safety.   II. ITS NATURE. It was a ministry of—1. Instruction.   2. Meekness.   III. ITS DESIGN. 1. That sinners may be led to repentance.   2. Led to an acknowledgment of the truth.   3. Recovered from the snares of the devil. (*Anon.*)   *Meekness in the minister :*—He who cannot bear calmly and reply with dignity to contradiction, is just as little fitted for the ministry of the gospel as the physician would be for his profession who would allow himself to become moved by the abusive speech of a patient in fever delirium either to forsake the sick-bed, or to hurl back the abuse. (*Van Oosterzee.*)   *Thunder rare :*—But you may reply that ministers must be Boanerges, Sons of Thunder, rattle in a congregation. True; notwithstanding, meekness is to be retained, practised. But to return an answer suitable to the objection.   1. Every thin vapour, light exhalation, will not afford matter to cause a thunder-crack; so each text, subject, doth not give warrant to denounce terrors.   2. Before it thunder we apprehend a light, and then the voice striketh the organ of hearing, and the eye of the mind is to be enlightened in order ere that judgment be threatened.   3. Thunder is rare, not at every season; should the minister continually shoot the shafts of God's indignation, would not the vulgar begin to smile, laugh him to scorn?   4. After a great crack of thunder the heavens grow black and refresh the earth with sweet showers of water, and when the bolts of justice are cast among the people a preacher is to assume a doleful look, a sad countenance. These rules observed, cry aloud, Thunder and spare not! What shall I more say? In the cause of thy Master be bold, resolute; in thine own, let meekness have her perfect work. (*J. Barlow, D.D.*)   *The spirit of opposition :*—It was written of Thoreau, the author, that " He was by nature of the opposition; there was a constitutional ' No ' in him that could not be tortured into ' Yes.' " (*H. O. Mackey.*)   *The nature of religious truths :*—I. HERE IS A SUPPOSITION LAID DOWN : THAT TRUTH IS SOMETHING REAL IN ITSELF AND OF IMPORTANCE TO MEN ; something that may be found, and which we ought to seek after. Wherever the Scripture speaks of truth it always means such truth as has relation to religion. All truth, of what kind soever it be, is real. But truth in matters of religion is always of the greatest importance; as being the foundation and the support of right practice. These truths of God are like an immovable rock, the basis and foundation of that true religion which approves itself to every man's understanding by clear reason, and glorifies God by making men like unto Him through virtue and righteousness in their practice. All false religions consist in changing these truths of God into a lie (Rom. i. 25).   II. Such is the corrupt state and disposition of mankind, THAT SOME THERE WILL ALWAYS BE WHO WILL SET THEMSELVES TO OPPOSE THE TRUTH. Notwithstanding the native excellency and beauty of truth considered in itself ; notwithstanding the strength and clearness of reason with which it is generally accompanied ; notwithstanding the apparent benefit and advantage which the knowledge of truth always brings to mankind; yet so little sensible are men of the intrinsic excellency of things, so unattentive to the strength of the clearest reason, so apt to be imposed upon in judging concerning their own true interests ; that nothing is more common than to see the plainest and most useful truths in matters of religion violently and passionately opposed.   The principal causes of this opposition are—1. Ignorance. Meaning here by ignorance not a bare want of knowledge. There is a presumptuous ignorance which despises knowledge, and this makes men oppose the truth before they understand anything of it.   2. Carelessness. They blindly, and without any consideration, follow the customs of the place where they happen to live, and the knowledge of truth seems to them to be of no great importance. They take up their religion at adventures, not from the consideration of the laws of nature or of revelation, but merely from the company they chance to be educated amongst, and thus all religions are put upon an equal foot, varying according to the accidental temper· of the persons among whom they prevail. 3. Prejudice. They have accustomed themselves to found their belief entirely in an implicit reliance upon other men, instead of building it upon the evidence of things themselves which is the foundation of truth. 4. But the last and greatest reason of men's setting themselves in opposition to the truth is the wickedness and corruption of their manners, the love of unrighteousness and debauchery, the desire and power of dominion, the concern they are under for the defence and support of a sect or party without having any knowledge how far they are, or are not, in the right. III. THE DIRECTION GIVEN US CONCERNING OUR OWN DUTY, THAT WE OUGHT IN MEEKNESS TO INSTRUCT THOSE WHO OPPOSE THEMSELVES AGAINST THE TRUTH. We cannot always discern who they are that err through ignorance and through a vicious disposition. But if we would, yet meekness is at all times necessarily a fruit of the spirit, and we are commanded to be patient towards all men, towards them that oppose as well as towards them that are only ignorant of the truth. IV. A PARTI-CULAR REASON WITH REGARD TO THE PERSONS TO BE INSTRUCTED, WHY OUR INSTRUCTION TO THEM OUGHT ALWAYS TO BE ACCOMPANIED WITH MEEKNESS. If God peradventure will give them repentance to the acknowledgment of the truth. In the original it is, "Lest God peradventure should give them repentance to the acknowledgment of the truth." The meaning is, we are to instruct them with meekness, lest per-adventure, by our heat and passion, we raise in them a just prejudice against us, when, by meek instruction, they might possibly have been brought to repentance, and to the acknowledgment of the truth, and so we, by our ill-behaviour become answerable for their miscarriage. For this reason we so frequently find repeated in Scripture the following admonitions, which may serve for a proper applica-tion of this whole discourse : 1 Pet. ii. 12, iii. 15 ; 1 Cor. x. 32 ; Col. iv. 5 ; 1 Tim. iii. 7 ; Phil. ii. 15, iv. 5 ; Matt. v. 16. (*S. Clarke, D.D.*) *Repentance the design of preaching :*—1. One principal end of the ministry is to bring men to repentance. 2. By meek preaching God may work repentance. 3. Repentance is hopeful and yet doubtful. 4. Ministers are to preach and leave the success to the Lord. (*J. Barlow, D.D.*) *Meekness in controversy :*— When Dr. Swift was arguing one day with great coolness with a gentleman who had become exceedingly warm in the dispute, one of the company asked him how he could keep his temper so well. "The reason is," replied the dean, "I have truth on my side." A cobbler at Leyden, who used to attend the public disputations held at the academy, was once asked if he understood Latin. "No," replied the mechanic, "but I know who is wrong in the argument." "How?" replied his friend. "Why, by seeing who is angry first." (*Sunday School Teacher.*) *Many qualities requisite in a minister :*—The medical attendant of my brother has just been expressing his surprise to see how much I am worn within this last half-year ; I am very sensible of it myself, and expect that I shall be much more worn if my people continue in such a grievous state. I would that my eyes were a fountain of tears to run down day and night. Would you believe it? I have been used to read the Scriptures to get from them rich discoveries of the power and grace of Christ: to learn how to minister to a loving and obedient people ; I am now reading them really and literally to know how to minister to a conceited, con-tentious, and rebellious people. Two qualities, I am sure, are requisite, meekness and patience, yet, in some cases, I shall be constrained to rebuke with authority. I have been used to sail in the Pacific. I am now learning to navigate the Red Sea, that is full of shoals and rocks, with a very intricate passage. I trust the Lord will carry me safely through ; but my former trials have been nothing to this. (*C. Simeon.*) *Plain instruction :*—Who expects to find "Bradshaw" full of Latin questions? You get it as a guide, and you want it to be as plain as possible. You have lost your way among some mountains one night, and are overtaken by some classic—who says, "I will tell you the way to get home in sixteen different languages," none of which you comprehend. I think you would reply, "I would rather be told it, sir, in one that I could understand." Or, if some profound professor should inform you that he could explain the geological strata and formation of the soil on which you were standing, I think you would say, "If you could point me to my own abode, I should be more grateful." And I think if some poor ragged girl or shepherd boy could tell you of a way by which you could escape that wood or yonder precipice and reach a hospitable shelter, such information would undoubtedly be more profitable to you.　The sign-post that points the way by the side of the roads never have a quotation of poetry upon them, or sentences from Isocrates or Sophocles.　There is just the word, and that is enough.　(*C. H. Spurgeon.*)

Ver. 26. **And that they may recover themselves out of the snare of the devil, who are taken captive by him at his will.**—And that they may return to sobriety from the benumbing intoxication of false philosophy and bad habits, here represented as a snare of the devil, in which, though held captive, they were not yet killed—" out of the snare of the devil, being made living captives of by him." So far, there is no difficulty, but the last clause, " according to the will of Him," leaves the reader in doubt as to its meaning, since two pronouns are used which generally, if not universally, refer to two different subjects.　De Wette, Huther, and Davidson disregard the difference of the pronouns, and make them both refer to the devil. But the contrast of the two pronouns is remarkable, and the sense of the passage very obscure, the " will of the devil" being an otiose addition, unless it be translated, as by Davidson, " to do his will." If ἐκείνου refers to the more remote antecedent, then " God's will" is suggested as the gracious accompaniment and occasion of this gift of repentance, or as the exposition of the state of new life, into which such penitents may be brought.　The passage will read as follows :— " Whether haply God would grant them repentance, and also whether haply they may return to society, into harmony with His will, out of the snare of the devil, seeing they have been made living captives by him." (*H. R. Reynolds, D.D.*) *Satan's temptations are like snares :*—The devil is a fowler, beholds the world like a great and spacious forest full of all kinds of beasts and birds, and setteth snares and gins in every corner to catch them. 1. In a snare there is subtlety, so in Satan's temptations.　(1) He never propounds a temptation in his own name. No, should he do so, his plot would be discerned prevented.　How cunningly crept he into the serpent and seduced the woman ?　He conveyed himself into such things as we are least suspicious of.　Who would have thought that any snare had been in the words of the apostle, Master pity thyself ?　Yet doth not Christ reply, " Get thee behind Me, Satan " ?　(2) He can lay a snare in the very Scriptures. Though they be milk for babes, strong meat for grown men, he can poison all.　Let Christ answer him by Scripture, straight he replies, tempting him by a place of Scripture. " Cast thyself down ; for it is written, God shall give His angels charge over Thee that thou dash not Thy foot against a stone." (3) He can convey a temptation in the frame of a man's spirit.　He conceives that some are apt to pride, malice, coveteousness, melancholy, mirth, silence, liberalness of speech, and according to our natural inclination he sets his gins for us.　Thus he provides a wanton object in the time of idleness, a beautiful woman washing herself, and so the good king is caught in his net.　What way the tree leans he thrusts it, and where the fence is weakest he seeks to enter.　So subtley will he here lay a snare that we will hardly be brought to believe it is a temptation of Satan, but think rather it proceeds solely from our natural disposition. 2. In a snare there is cruelty ; so here. He is called Abaddon, Apollion, a murderer, a destroyer. 3. In a snare is strength, and is it not to be found in Satan's temptations ? 4. You shall find in Satan's temptations, as in snares, pleasures and suddenness.　Were it not thus they were not snares properly.　Was not the tree, in the eye of Eve, good for meat, pleasant, and to be desired to get knowledge (Gen. iii. 6) ?　Were not the daughters of men fair (Gen. vi. 2) ?　And in these was not a bait to catch the beholders ?　Have not fowlers a lure and call, as if they were birds themselves, to allure and deceive ?　Will they not scatter corn and all to seduce and bring within danger the little-suspicious birds ?　Do they not creep on their hands and knees, stand in close and secret places, and when the fowl is within reach how suddenly is the net pulled ! Per- adventure, when she is singing, playing, suspecting nothing, she is wound in. When Satan assaults, how eagerly, busily, and suddenly will he follow the prey ? He sets a man's affections on fire, kindles such a heat within him that for the present the object of temptation seems wonderful fair, delightful, honourable ; though when he is ensnared he perceives no such thing, but the direct contrary (*J. Barlow, D.D.*)　　*The deluded captives :*—These words are the concluding portion of a solemn address to Timothy, in reference to the instruction of the ungodly, and is the end pointed out as resulting from that instruction—" And that they may recover themselves out of the snare of the devil." They present to the thoughtful mind a sad picture, bringing before us on the one hand the devil, in the character of fowler ; and on the other hand his victims, as deluded, taken alive, under a hard bondage. I. THE CHARACTERS SPOKEN OF. II. THE MEANS BY WHICH THEY ARE HELD IN BONDAGE. III. THE MEANS BY WHICH THEY MAY BE RECOVERED FROM THAT BONDAGE. I. They are spoken of as those who are ensnared by Satan, and "taken captive by him at his will." 1. We must notice who is the captor. It is the devil, the murderer and liar, the destroyer of souls ; represented here under the character of a snarer or fowler. It is very important to notice Satan in his character, because it manifests his subtlety. The fowler must be subtle in hiding his net, or otherwise he would miss his prey. It is plain from Scripture that sin was introduced through Satan's subtlety. 2. In the next place, see the awful force of the language. The expression, " taken captive," is rendered in the margin " taken alive " ; it is an idea derived from fowling, in which the prey is taken alive in snares : so the devil takes men's souls alive by his subtlety : nay, more, unless they be recovered out of his snares, they must be alive for ever under his sway : lost, yet alive ; hopeless, yet alive ; tormented, yet alive ; ever desiring to die, but never able. The other expression, " at his will," may bear a double interpretation. It may mean that they have been ensnared by Satan's arts unto his will ; *i.e.*, they were so influenced by him that they complied with his will. It is most important to notice this, because it at once brings out the humiliating truth, that the ungodly comply with Satan's will. The man who lives in drunkenness, who is a sensualist ; or to pass on to sins which are thought little of in the world, the man who is untruthful, a backbiter, a slanderer or deceitful, is complying with Satan's will. The man who is a neglecter of salvation, who never prays, who is putting off the thought of eternity to a convenient season, is complying with Satan's will. Again, the expression " at his will," may have reference to the devil's will concerning his victims—viz., their destruction. Hence those who are taken alive by Satan at his will are taken alive by him for their destruction, he is leading them on, step by step, with the one end and the one object of dragging them alive into that pit of darkness and agony prepared for himself and his angels. Oh, look upon this other picture—while Satan wills your destruction, God wills your salvation. " He would have all men to be saved, and to come to the knowledge of the truth." 3. In the next place, notice the bondage itself. It is worse than Egyptian bondage. A sinner, taken captive by Satan, has his immortal soul in captivity, bound in fetters which none can break but the Lord of glory. But we may see the fearfulness of this bondage by looking at it in a threefold point of view. (1) The master whom the captive serves. Dread thought ! it is not Jesus, the sinner's great Deliverer, but it is the devil, the sinner's great destroyer. Ah ! and what a master ! one who hates him ; one who watches closely to prevent his victim's escape, binding around him every day tighter and tighter the cords of his destruction. Look again —(2) At the state of the captive. It is one of misery and wretchedness. " The way of transgressors is hard." It is utterly impossible to experience true peace and happiness while walking in the pathway of the devil. Christ's yoke in opposition to Satan's ; the one is perfect liberty while the other is the most galling bondage. Look again—(3) At the end of this bondage. Now, Satan does not make his bondage felt, for fear of alarming the victim, and leading him to seek deliverance from it : but in eternity, when all hope of deliverance is past, he will make his bondage felt in all its overwhelming force. II. THE MEANS BY WHICH SATAN KEEPS SINNERS CAPTIVE. He does so by his snares. We must look at some of those principle snares by which he deludes and holds captive the unwary. 1. The first snare of Satan which I shall mention is, his making sin pleasant, and hiding its awful consequences. He makes the sinner believe the command not to sin, to be a restriction of his liberty, and, therefore, one which he has no right to listen to. It is the present, and the present only, which the devil seeks to force on the captive's mind ; the present and its gain ; but the awfully mysterious future he puts out of sight, veiling from the sinner's mind his dread connection with it. 2. A second snare of Satan's is, his insinuating doubts into the mind as to the truth of God's Word. 3. A third snare of Satan's is, his presenting God to the soul as one made up of all mercy. 4. A fourth snare of Satan's is, by persuading the soul that the work of repentance is an easy work : that it need not be thought of till laid on a bed of sickness or a bed of death : and he will suggest to the sinner's mind examples from God's Word to bear out this delusion. 5. Another snare of Satan, by which he takes souls captive, is by making himself an object of ridicule. This is one of

" the depths of Satan " : he knows that the Bible puts him forward as an object of dread ; he takes care, therefore, to put himself forward as an object of ridicule, so as to blind the ungodly, and keep them captive at his will. Mark the consequence : all the warnings of Scripture concerning him, all the representations of him as an adversary, a murderer, fall on the ear of his captives as unmeaning titles, they cannot comprehend why he is to be dreaded. And why is this ? Just because they are ignorant of the real reason why they cannot comprehend it—viz., Satan has deceived them, deceived them as to his character, deceived them as to his object, deceived them as to their danger, deceived them as to their end, and, will deceive them to that very hour when, as lost and wretched, they shall open their eyes, to learn then, but, alas ! too late, that though the devil appeared to them " an angel of light," yet he was indeed a deceiver, a liar, and a murderer. 6. Another snare by which Satan takes souls captive at his will is, by making them rest in outward forms instead of true conversion. III. The means by which souls may be recovered from his bondage. " And that they may recover themselves out of the snare of the devil." The word which is rendered " recover " is in the margin, " awake." It properly means to become sober again, as from intoxication ; to awake from a deep sleep ; and then to come to one's self, or to a right mind. The idea is, that while men are under the bondage of the devil, they are like men intoxicated, or in a deep slumber, unconscious of their danger. How are they to be roused to a sense of their danger ? The answer is given in the previous verse, we are to set before them the " truth," the simple truth of Christ, "If peradventure God will give them repentance to the acknowledging of it." Acknowledging, implying not merely confession of the truth, but a vital reception of it as it is in Jesus. It is the truth of Christ borne home to the heart by the Holy Ghost, which is the means of conversion. As long as Satan can spread over us the veil of darkness, so long are we his captives, but no sooner does the light of Christ's truth break in on the soul, than the darkness is dispersed, Satan is vanquished, and the sinner delivered out of darkness into light, and from the power of sin and Satan unto God. But mark you, it is God alone who can effect this transformation ; it is God alone who can bear home the word to the heart, and make it a converting word. (*A. W. Snape, M.A.*) *The snare of the devil :*—Forbidden fruit is sweet. It is sweetened by the devil. One forbidden tree in Eden seemed better than a thousand trees allowed. That terrible magician has power to concentrate our gaze upon one object—power to withdraw our eyes from the pure and wholesome fruits of many trees, and rivet them upon that one forbidden thing. He so intensifies our thought upon that one desire that it outgrows all desires, and perhaps life itself for the time seems stale and flat unless that one desire be gratified. That is one of the supernatural powers of the serpent to charm his victims. This dreadful delusion, this deadly fascination, fills common objects with dazzling beauty. The coloured lights of hell are reflected upon earthly things and make them appear heavenly. Thus the gaming-table is made to assume attractions which make money and land and houses insignificant trifles in comparison. Thus a glass of liquor grows in beauty and power that will out-dazzle the love of family, or the joys of home, or even the hopes of heaven. (*R. S. Barrett.*) *Snared through over-confidence :*—Naturalists tell us that amongst birds and butterflies, the swiftest, strongest fliers approach man much nearer than those with weaker wings, feeling confident that they can dart away from any threatened danger, and this misplaced confidence brings them into the net of the collector. (*W. L. Watkinson.*) *Caution necessary :*—In mountain ranges there is often a loose *detritus* especially dangerous to mountaineers ; these loose or crumbling stones being called " the devil's stones," for, owing to their treacherous character, if you step on one incautiously you may be precipitated into the depths. There are many such stones in the path of life. False maxims with sophistical colourings ; license stealing the name of liberty ; harmful speculations, luring as grand chances ; methods of trade outlined square, yet full of betrayal ; sandy doctrines simulating the rock ; friendships which are flowery graves ; occupations, recreations which promise rest and serve only to slip us into mire ; these are the things of peril : life is full of them ; and he only walks surely who walks discreetly. (*Ibid.*)

## CHAPTER III.

VER. 1. **Perilous times shall come.**—*Perilous times:*—I. THE MANNER OF THE WARN-
ING.—" This know also." 1. It is the duty of ministers to foresee and take notice of the
dangers which the churches are falling into. 2. It is the great concern of all professors
and believers to have their hearts very much fixed upon present and approaching
dangers. 3. Not to be sensible of a present perilous season is that security which
the scripture so condemns ; and I will leave it with you under these three things—
(1) It is that frame of heart which of all others God doth most detest and abhor.
Nothing is more hateful to God than a secure frame in perilous days. (2) A secure
person, in perilous seasons, is assuredly under the power of some predominant lust,
whether it appears, or not. (3) This senseless frame is the certain presage of
approaching ruin. II. THE EVIL ITSELF. " Perilous times "—times of great difficulty, like those of public plagues, when death lies at every door. III. THE MANNER
OF INTRODUCTION—" Shall come." Our great wisdom then will be to eye the displeasure of God in perilous seasons, since there is a judicial hand of God in them :
and we see in ourselves reason enough why they should come. IV. THE TIME AND
SEASON OF IT—" In the last days." You may take it in what sense you will : the
last days, the days of the gospel ; the last days towards the consummation of all
things ; the last days following the days of the profession of churches ; and the last
days with many of us, with respect to our lives. 1. The first thing that makes a
season perilous is, when the profession of true religion is outwardly maintained
under a visible predominancy of horrible lusts and wickedness (see vers. 2–5). (1)
Because of the infection. (2) Because of the effects. When predominant lusts have
broken all bounds of Divine light and rule, how long do you think human rules will
keep them in order ? (3) Because of the consequences—the judgments of God
(2 Thess. ii. 10, 11). 2. A second perilous season is, when men are prone to forsake
the truth, and seducers abound to gather them up that are so ; and you will have
always these things go together. If it be asked, how we may know whether there
be a proneness in the minds of men in any season to depart from the truth ? there
are three ways whereby we may judge of it. (1) The first is that mentioned in 2 Tim.
iv. 3. When men grow weary of sound doctrine, when it is too plain, too dull, too
common, too high, too mysterious, one thing or other that displeases them, and they
would hear something new, something that may please. (2) When men have lost
the power of truth in their conversation, and are as prone and ready to part with the
profession of it in their minds. Do you see a man retaining the profession of the
truth under a worldly conversation ? He wants but baits from temptation, or a
seducer to take away his faith from him. (3) The proneness to depart from the truth,
is a perilous season, because it is the greatest evidence of the withdrawing of the
Spirit of God from His Church. 3. A third thing that makes a perilous season is,
professors mixing themselves with the world, and learning their manners. Such a
season is dangerous, because the sins of professors in it lie directly contrary to the
whole design of the mediation of Christ in this world. Christ " gave Himself for us,
that He might purge us from dead works, and purify us unto Himself a peculiar
people " (Tit. ii. 14). " Ye are a royal nation, a peculiar people." 4. Another
perilous season is when there is great attendance on outward duties, but inward,
spiritual decays. 5. Times of persecution are also times of peril. Use 1. Let us
all be exhorted to endeavour to get our hearts affected with the perils of the day
wherein we live. (1) Consider the present things, and bring them to rule, and see
what God's Word says of them. (2) If you would be sensible of present perilous
times, take heed of centring in self. Whether you pursue riches, or honours, while
you centre there, nothing can make you sensible of the perils of the day. (3) Pray
that God would give us grace to be sensible of the perils of the day wherein we live.
Use 2. The next thing is this, that there are two things in a perilous season—the
sin of it, and the misery of it. Labour to be sensible of the former, or you will never
be sensible of the latter. Use 3. Remember there is a special frame of spirit required in us all in such perilous seasons as these are. And what is that? It is a
mourning frame of spirit. Use 4. Keep up church watch with diligence, and by
the rule. When I say rule, I mean the life of it. Use 5. Reckon upon it, that
in such times as these are, all of us will not go free. (*John Owen, D.D.*) *Perilous
times in the last days :*—1. The notification of an event as future—" Perilous times
shall come." (1) Times wherein it will be hard for people to keep their feet, to
know how to carry themselves, to keep out of danger, and keep a good conscience.

(2) "Shall come." They will be on men, in the course of providence, to try what metal they are of ; as darkness comes on after light, and adversity after prosperity, in their turn. 2. The time of that event—"In the last days." The days of the gospel are the concluding period of time. In these last days are several particular periods ; the first of which was the last time of the Jewish state, beginning from the time of our Saviour, to the destruction of Jerusalem ; and more periods followed, and some are yet to come ; but from the time of our Saviour to the end of the world, is " the last days." 3. The notice to be taken of that event—"This know also " ; rather, " Now know this "; consider it duly, and lay it to heart, that being fore-warned, ye may be armed against the " perilous times." I. WE SHALL CONSIDER " THE DAYS OF THE GOSPEL AS THE LAST DAYS." And so we may take them up in a threefold view. 1. As the last days of the world, the latter end of time. With rela-tion to them that oath is made (Rev. x. 6). The morning and forenoon of the world are over ; it is afternoon with it now, and drawing toward the evening. 2. As the days of the last dispensation of grace towards the world, with which God's dealing with sinners for reconciliation shall be closed (Rev. x. 7). There have been three dispensations of grace in the world : the Patriarchal dispensation in the first days; the Mosaical dispensation in the middle days; and now the Christian dispensation in the last days. The first two are now off the stage, and shall never come on again ; the third now is ; and after it there shall never be another. 3. As the best days of the world in respect of the greatest advantages attending them. The last works of God are always the greatest, as ye may see in the account of the Creation (Gen. i.) ; so the circumstances of the world to come are greater than those of this. The gos-pel-dispensation far excels the other two, in clearness, extensiveness, and efficacy, through a larger measure of the Spirit. II. THE DIFFICULT AND PERILOUS TIMES THAT COME ON IN GOSPEL DAYS. We must inquire what makes these perilous times. 1. An old controversy lying over untaken up. They that are in debt are always in danger. The Jews were from generation to generation murderers of their prophets ; there was an old debt on the head of the generation in our Saviour's time (Matt. xxiii. 31) ; and made their time perilous, for it was like a train lying, which at last came to blow them up (ver. 35). So good Josiah's days were perilous times, by reason of an old controversy laid in the days of Manasseh his grandfather (2 Kings xxiii. 26). Our times are so, by reason of the iniquity of the late times, which is like that of Baal-peor, that brought " a plague on the congregation of the Lord " (Josh. xxii. 17). 1. Error or corruption of principles spreading. This was foretold to happen in the latter days (1 Tim. iv. 1). 2. Immoralities abounding. (*T. Bos-ton, D.D.*) *Evil of the last days :*—These (evil characters) will swarm like flies in the decay of the year. (*C. H. Spurgeon.*) *Corruptions within :*—Not so much on the account of persecutions from without as on the account of corruptions within. (*M. Henry.*) *Traitors :*—Two traitors within the garrison may do more hurt to it than two thousand besiegers without. (*Ibid.*) *Fidelity in evil times :*—The worse the times we live in are, the greater will our honour be, if we be faithful. It was Lot's commendation that he was good in Sodom, and Job in an heathenish Uz. The more sin abounds, the more our grace should abound ; and the more sin appears in the world, the more should we appear against it. The Lord hath done more for us of this last age of the world than He ever did for our forefathers, and therefore He expects more from us than He did from them ; where He bestows much He looks for much again ; where we bestow double cost, we look for a double crop. It is a shame for us if we do not do our work better by sunlight, than others that have had but twilight. (*T. Hall, B.D.*) *Sin makes the times bad :*—It is worth our noting that the apostle doth not place the peril and hardness of the last times, in any external calamity or penal evils, as sword, plague, famine, persecution ; but in the prodigious sins and enormities of such as profess religion. Sin is the evil of evils, and brings all other evils with it. Let the times be never so miserable, and the Church lie under sad persecutions ; yet if they be not sinful times, they are not truly perilous times, but rather purging and purifying times. (*Ibid.*) *Sinners swarm even in gospel days :*—Vermin of this kind will then abound everywhere ; weeds grow nowhere so rank as in fat soil. (*Ibid.*) *Prudence in perilous times:*—This spiritual prudence can hurt neither pastor nor people, but will advantage us much. This pre-vision is the best means of prevention; in vain is the snare laid in the sight of a bird. Observe God's singular love unto His people, in that He warns them of perilous times long before they come. The people of God, and specially His ministers, His Timothies, should be so prudent as to know and observe when perilous times are approaching, as the prudent man foresees the evil of punishment

before it comes (Prov. xxii. 35). (*Ibid.*)     *Time aiding proficiency in sin:*—As it is in every art, by length of time, custom, and experience, it is improved to a greater degree of fineness and exactness; so it is in this of sinning; time and experience make men more cunning in ways of sin, and more subtle to defend them. (*Ibid.*) *Making the times better :*—We should all make the times and places we live in the better, and not the worse, for us. (*Ibid.*)

Ver. 2–5. **Men shall be lovers of their own selves.**—*The nature and kinds of self-love :* —I. SELF-LOVE, CONSIDERED IN THE GENERAL, ABSTRACTING FROM PARTICULAR CIRCUM- STANCES, IS NEITHER A VICE NOR A VIRTUE. It is nothing but the inclination of every man to his own happiness. A passionate desire to be always pleased and well-satis- fied, neither to feel nor fear any pain or trouble, either of body or mind. It is an instinct of nature common to all men, and not admitting of any excess or abatement. Self-love directed to, and pursuing, what is, upon the whole, and in the last result of things, absolutely best for us, is innocent and good; and every deviation from this is culpable, more or less so, according to the degrees and the circumstances of it. II. When we blindly follow the instinct of self-love, coveting everything which looks fair, and running greedily upon it without weighing circumstances or considering consequences; or when, to get rid of any present pain or uneasiness, we take any method which first offers, without reflecting how dearly we may pay for it afterwards; I say, when we do thus, THEN IT IS THAT OUR SELF-LOVE BEGUILES US, DEGENERATES INTO A VICIOUS, OR AT LEAST, SILLY APPETITE, and comes under the name of an overweening, excessive, and inordinate self-love. He suffers the natural instinct of self-love to carry him too far after present satisfaction, farther than is consistent with his more real and durable felicity. To understand the nature of this enchantment, and how it comes to pass that those who love themselves so well, can thus consent to ruin themselves, both bodies and souls, for ever; let us trace its progress. 1. To begin with pride. All the happiness of life is summed up in two articles—pleasing thoughts and pleasing sensations. Now, pride is founded in self- flattery, and self-flattery is owing to an immoderate desire of entertaining some kind of pleasing thoughts. 2. Another instance of inordinate, ill-conducted self- love is sensuality. This belongs to the body more than to the mind, is of a gross taste, aiming only at pleasing sensations. It so far agrees with pride that it makes men pursue the present gratification at the expense of the public peace and to their own future misery and ruin. 3. A third instance of blind and inordinate self-love is avarice or self-interestedness. This is of larger and more diffusive influence than either of the former. So great a part of temporal felicity is conceived to depend upon riches, that the men of this world lie under the strongest temptations to this vice of any. If the case be such, that treachery and fraud, guile and hypocrisy, rapine and violence, may be serviceable to the end proposed; the blind self-lover will charge through all rather than be defeated of his covetous designs, or bear the uneasiness of a disappointment. Thus he comes to prefer his own private, present interest, before virtue, honour, conscience, or humanity. He considers not what would be good for him upon the whole and in the last result, but lives extempore, contrives only for a few days, or years at most, looking no farther. The height of his ambition reaches not beyond temporal felicity, and he miscalculates even in that. III. CONSIDERATIONS PROPER TO PREVENT OR CURE IT. It is very evident that the self-lovers are not greater enemies to others in intention than they are in effect to themselves. Yet it is not less evident that they love themselves passionately all the time, and whatever hurt they do to their own selves they certainly mean none. They run upon it as a horse rushes into the battle, as an ox goeth to the slaughter, and as a bird hasteth to the snare, and know not that it is for their life. It is for want of thinking in a right way that men fall into this fatal misconduct, and nothing but serious and sober thought can bring them out of it. I shall just suggest two or three useful considerations, and then conclude. 1. We should endeavour to fix in our minds this great and plain truth, that there can be no such thing as true happiness, separate from the love of God and the love of our neighbour. 2. A second consideration, proper to be hinted, is, that man is made for eternity, and not for this life only. No happiness can be true and solid which is not lasting as ourselves. 3. To conclude, the way to arrive at true happiness is to take into consideration the whole extent and compass of our being; to enlarge our views beyond our little selves to the whole creation round us, whereof we are but a slender part; and to extend our prospect beyond this life to distant glories. Make things future appear as if they were now present, and things distant as if they were near and sensible.

(*D. Waterland, D.D.*)     *Self-love :*—1. Self-love is vicious, when it leads us to judge too favourably of our faults. (1) Sometimes it finds out other names for them, and by miscalling them endeavours to take away their bad qualities. (2) Sometimes it represents our sins as weaknesses, infirmities, the effect of natural constitution, and deserving more pity than blame. (3) Sometimes it excuses them upon account of the intent, pretending that some good or other is promoted by them, and that the motive and the end sanctify the means, or greatly lessen the faultiness of them. (4) It leads us to set our good in opposition to our bad qualities, and to persuade ourselves that what is laudable in us far outweighs what is evil. (4) It teaches us to compare ourselves with others, and thence to draw favourable conclusions, because we are not so bad as several whom we could name; it shows us the general corruption that is in the world, represents it worse than it is, and then tells us that we must not hope, and need not endeavour to be remarkably and singularly good. 2. Our self-love is irregular, when we think too well of our righteousness, and overvalue our good actions, and are pure in our own eyes. 3. Our self-love is blameable when we overvalue our abilities, and entertain too good an opinion of our knowledge and capacity; and this kind of self-love is called self-conceit. One evil which men reap from it is to be disliked and despised. The reason why self-conceit is so much disliked is that it is always attended with a mean opinion of others. From self-conceit arise rash undertakings, hasty determinations, stubbornness, insolence, envy, censoriousness, confidence, vanity, the love of flattery, and sometimes irreligion, and a kind of idolatry, by which a man worships his own abilities, and places his whole trust in them. The unreasonableness of this conceit appears from the imperfections of the human understanding, and the obstacles which lie between us and wisdom. 4. Our self-love is irregular when we are proud and vain of things inferior in nature to those before mentioned, when we value ourselves upon the station and circumstances in which not our own deserts, but favour or birth, hath placed us, upon mere show and outside, upon these and the like advantages in which we surpass others. This conceit is unreasonable and foolish; for these are either things which the possessors can hardly call their own, as having done little or nothing to acquire them, or they are of small value, or they are liable to be irrecoverably lost by many unforeseen accidents. 5. Lastly, our self-love is vicious when we make our worldly interest, convenience, humour, ease, or pleasure, the great end of our actions. This is selfishness, a very disingenuous and sordid kind of self-love. It is a passion that leads a man to any baseness which is joined to lucre, and to any method of growing rich which may be practised with impunity. (*J. Jortin, D.D.*)     *Self-love :*—I. I shall endeavour TO TRACE OUT MORE PARTICULARLY THE WORKINGS OF THIS NOXIOUS PRINCIPLE, AS IT RESPECTS MATTERS OF RELIGION; for it is said of these lovers of themselves, that "they have the form of godliness, but deny the power thereof." 1. Self-love may carry men out in desires after Christ (see Mark i. 37; John vi. 26). Many would partake of Christ's benefits, who reject His government; receive glory from Him, but give no glory to Him. If they can but go to heaven when they die, they care not how little they have of it before; and are unconcerned about the dominion of sin, if they can but obtain the pardon of it; so that their seeking and striving are now over. 2. Self-love may be the sole foundation of men's love to, and delight in, God. And indeed it is so with all hypocrites and formalists in religion. Many mistake a conviction of mind, that God is to be loved, for a motion of the heart towards Him; and because they see it to be reasonable that He should be regarded by them, they imagine that He is so. But the highest regard that a natural man can have to the Divine Being, if traced back to its origin, or followed to its various actings, will be found to be self-love. 3. Self-love may be the principle that first excites, and then puts fervour and ardency into our prayers. How coldly do some put up those requests, "Hallowed be Thy Name, Thy kingdom come"; but are much more earnest when they come to those petitions in which their present comfort and future happiness are so much interested: "Forgive us our trespasses," and "Give us our daily bread," "Let me die the death of the righteous." 4. Self-love insinuates itself into the severer acts of mortification; nay, it often runs through and corrupts the whole course of religious duties. It is like the dead fly which taints the whole box of precious ointment. From this principle some neglect duties as burdensome, and only seek privileges; a reward without labours, victory without fighting. 5. Self-love runs through all their affections, exertions, and actions, with respect to their fellow-creatures. If they rejoice at others' prosperity, it is because they themselves may be benefited by it. If, on the other hand, they grieve at their calamities, it is because they are likely to be sharers in them, or some way or other injured by them. II. From what has been said, you see THAT SELF-LOVE IS AN INSINUATING PRINCIPLE, APPEARING IN VARIOUS FORMS, EVEN IN THE RELIGIOUS WORLD, AND UNDER MANY ARTFUL DISGUISES, HARD TO BE DISCERNED, BUT HARDER STILL TO BE GUARDED AGAINST. To stir you up to this, let me set before you some of the evils resulting from this easily-besetting, and alas, too universally prevailing sin. 1. It is the root of hypocrisy. So far as self-love and self-seeking influence, we are void of sincerity and integrity. 2. It promotes pride, envy, strife, uncharitableness, and an evil temper and conduct towards all with whom we are conversant. A man who loves himself too well, will never love his God or his neighbour as he ought. 3. All evil may, perhaps, be reduced to this one point: All our desires, passions, projects, and endeavours, centred in self. This was the first sin: "Ye shall be as gods"; and it has continued the master-sin ever since. It is the corrupt fountain, sending forth so many impure and filthy streams. (*B. Beddome, M.A.*) *A sermon against self-love, &c.:*—1. What kind of self-love is it which St. Paul does here so severely censure? 2. By what manner of influence self-love makes times and seasons become perilous. 3. What times the apostle means by the Last Days; and whence it is that self-love operates with such successful prevalence in those days as to render them the Evil Days. 4. What reflections are fit to be made by us, upon occasion of this argument in relation to our age, and to ourselves, and our present affairs, in order to that which all ought to fast and pray, and labour for the stability of our times and the peace of Jerusalem? I. To consider WHAT KIND OF SELF-LOVE St. PAUL SPEAKS AGAINST as the fountain of public mischief; for there is a self-love which is a very natural and a very useful principle. No man ever yet hated his own flesh; no man, without the loving of himself, does either preserve or improve himself. If Almighty God would not have suffered men to love themselves, He would not have moved them to their duty by their personal benefit, and especially by so great a recompense as is that of life eternal. It would conduce to the felicity of men, even in this world, if they truly loved themselves; for then they would not waste their fortunes by an unaccountable profuseness, nor destroy their bodies by the extravagances of rage, and luxury, and lust. The self-love here condemned by St. Paul is that narrow wicked affection which either wholly or principally confines a man to his seeming personal good on earth. An affection which either opposeth all public good, or at least all that public good which comes in competition with man's private advantage. Of such lovers of themselves the apostle gives a very ill character in the words that follow the text. He says of them, in ver. 2, that they are covetous; their heart is like the mouth of a devouring gulf, which sucks in all into itself with deep and unsatiable desire. He continues to mark them, in ver. 3, as persons without natural affection, as people who have no bowels for the miserable part of mankind; as such who rejoice at a public wreck, not considering the loss of others, nor the dismal circumstances of it; but minding with their whole intention the profit which they may gather up for their inhuman selves. He adds, in the same verse, that they are despisers of those who are good. They vilify men of a public spirit. II. This straight and uncharitable affection is of SO MALIGNANT AN INFLUENCE, that where it prevails no age can be calm, no government stable, no person secure. And that it is of such perilous consequence may be demonstrated on this manner. God, who is good and does good, designed, that whilst man was here on earth, it should be competently well with him in case of his obedience, though He intended not to give him all his portion in this life. He knew that men could not subsist apart with such conveniences as they might obtain by being knit into regular societies. He, therefore, united them in civil and sacred bodies, that by conjoined strength they might procure those benefits which, in a separate state, and by their single selves, they could not come at. For, consider, how void of comfort a life of entire solitude would have been to man; with what a life of fear would they have been crucified who had stood perpetually by themselves on their own defence; with what a life of labour and meanness would men have been burdened if every one of them must have been his own only servant; if every one had been obliged to build and plant, and till the ground, and provide food and physic and garments for himself by his own solitary power. And how could a man serve himself in any of these necessary offices in times of sickness, lameness, delirium, and decrepit old age? To such a perilous and laborious life as I have been speaking of, indiscreet and vicious self-love tends; for as far as men do mind and seek themselves alone, so far they dissolve society and lessen its benefits, being rather *in* it than *of* it. So that the soul which animates society, whose advantages are so considerable, is the great and generous spirit of charity. That violates no compacts, that raises no commotions, that interrupts no good man's peace, that assaults no innocent man's person, that invades no man's property, that grinds no poor man's face, that envies no man, that supplants no man, that submits its private convenience to the public necessities. Concerning this vile affection, St. Paul taught that it would possess the men of the last days. III. To consider WHAT TIMES HE MEANS BY THOSE DAYS, and in what sense he speaks of self-love as the distemper of the last days, seeing it has been the disease of every age. By the last days he means the last age of the world, the age of the Messiah, not excluding that part of it in which he himself lived. There were several precedent periods : that of the fathers before the flood, that of the patriarchs before the Law, that of Moses and the prophets under the Law. But after the age of the Messiah, time itself shall be no more. To this age all evil self-love cannot be confined, for that dotage had a being in the world from the very beginning of it. The murder of Cain was so early, that he sinned without example; and from his selfishness his murder proceeded. We therefore misunderstand St. Paul, if we interpret him as speaking, not of the increase, but of the being, of self-love ; for it is not its existence, but its abundance, which he foretells. What he wrote has been true in fact, from the times of Demas and Diotrephes, to this very hour. Light is come into the world, a glorious gospel which shines everywhere ; and men love darkness rather than light, and shut up themselves in their own hard and rough and private shells. Selfishness cannot be the direct natural effect of the gospel of Christ, which, of all other dispensations, depresseth the private under the public good. The age of the Messiah is the best of ages in His design, and in the means of virtue which He gives the world ; and if the men of it be worse than those of other generations, the greater is the aggravation of their guilt, whilst, under a gospel of the widest charity, they exercise the narrowest selfishness. But, however, so it is : whether it be that wicked men, by a spirit of contradiction, oppose charity where they are most earnestly pressed to it ; or that the devil, having but a short time, is the more passionately industrious in promoting the interests of his kingdom ; or that the further men are from the age of Divine revelations, the less firmly they believe them. It concerns us then—IV. To MAKE SERIOUS REFLECTIONS UPON THIS ARGUMENT, and to suffer our selves to be touched with such deep remorse for the guilt of our partiality, that God may be appeased, and our sins pardoned, and our lives reformed, and that perilous times may be succeeded by many prosperous days. And—1. Let us give glory to God, and take shame to ourselves, upon the account of that selfish principle which hath long wrought among us, and still worketh. 2. May we not only bewail but amend this great defect in our nature, and in our civil and Christian duty. (1) The regaining of a public spirit is at all times worthy our care. We can do no greater thing than to " follow God, who is concerned for all, as if they were but one man ; and for every single person, as if he were a world." God hath disposed all things in mutual subserviency to one another : the light, the air, the water, are made for common good ; and because they are common, they are the less, but they ought, for that reason, to be the more esteemed. There is not an humble plant that grows to itself, or a mean ox that treads out the corn merely for his own service ; and shall man be the only useless part of the creation ? It is a most unworthy practice, upon the account of self-interest, to multiply the moral perils of the world, whilst there are inconveniences enough in insensible Nature. It is enough that the natural seasons are tempestuous ; men's passions should not raise more storms. It is enough that famine can destroy so many ; uncharitableness should not do it. What is it that is worthy the daily thoughts and the nightly studies of a man of understanding, and of an excellent spirit ? Is it the supplanting of a credulous friend, or the oppressing of an helpless neighbour ? Alas ! these are designs so base and low, that he who calls himself a man should not stoop to them. But that which is worthy of a man is the service of his God, his Church, his country ; the generous exposing of himself when a kingdom is in hazard. (2) A public spirit, as it is worthy our care at all times, so at all times it needs it. For it requires the utmost application of our minds, seeing self-love insinuates with great art and subtlety into all our designs and actions. (*Thomas Tenison, D.D.*)   *Self-love odious :*—Here you see how far self-love is from being proposed to our practice, when you find it standing in the front of a black and dismal catalogue of the most odious and abhorred qualities. That I may contribute, if possible, to the making men less tenacious, and more communicative, I shall make it my present business to set the two characters in an opposite light, and to show—I. THE ODIOUSNESS OF SELF-LOVE.

II. THE AMIABLENESS OF A GENEROUS AND PUBLIC SPIRIT. There is, indeed, a kind or degree of self-love which is not only innocent, but necessary. The laws of nature strongly incline every man to be solicitous for his own welfare, to guard his person by a due precaution from hurts and accidents; to provide food and raiment, and all things needful for his bodily sustenance, by honest industry and labour; to repair as far as he is able, such decays as may attend his bodily constitution, by proper helps and the best means that are afforded him; and much more to make it his grand concern to secure the everlasting happiness of his immortal part. Such a self-love as this goes little farther than self-preservation, without which principle implanted in us the human species would be soon lost and extinguished, and the work of our great Creator be defeated. But that which St. Paul speaks of with abhorrence is a love merely selfish, that both begins and terminates in a man's single person, exclusive of all tender regards for any one else: this is, in the worst and most criminal sense, taking care of one only. If we will but look into our own nature, and reflect on the end and design of our creation, the reach and extent of our faculties, our subordination to one another, and the insufficiency of every man as he stands by himself alone, we shall soon be convinced, that doing good and affording each other reciprocal assistance is that for which we were formed and fashioned, that we are linked together by our common wants, as well as by inclination, and that tenderness of disposition and natural sympathy that is implanted in us. That we are born and educated, that we enjoy either necessaries or comforts, that we are preserved from perils in our greener, or ever arrive at riper years, next under the watchfulness and protection of Almighty God, is owing to the care of others. And can anything be more just and reasonable than that we, too, in our turn, should give that succour we have received, and do, not only as we willingly would, but as we actually have been done unto? There is a certain proportion of trouble and uneasiness, as well as of pleasure and satisfaction, that must of necessity be borne by the race of men; insomuch that he who will not sustain some share of the former, is unworthy to partake of any of the comforts of the latter. But here the selfling will interpose, and say: "It is true I have occasion for the help of others, and the help of others I have. I have occasion for the attendance of servants, and by servants I am attended. I want to be supplied with those conveniences of life which artificers provide in their respective occupations, and I am supplied accordingly. So long as I am furnished with sufficient store to pay them an equivalent, I am in no danger of being left destitute of anything that money can procure. This is the commerce I carry on in the world; thus I approve myself a social member of the commonwealth. But what have I to do in parting with my substance to them who can give nothing to me in return?" And sometimes we see it does please Almighty God to make examples of this sort: to humble such haughty and self-confiding men, by reducing them from their towering height, and all the wantonness of prosperity, to the extremity of want and misery. And whenever this happens to be the case, who are then so pitifully abjected? But the universal hatred which such a person naturally contracts will not always be suppressed, nor his former aversion to doing good offices be covered by a charitable oblivion, nor be lost under the soft relentings and a melting commiseration of his present sufferings. In short, since every man has an equal right to confine all his care and endeavours to the promoting his own separate interest, that any one man has, what must be the consequence if such a narrow way of thinking and acting should become universal? Love and friendship terminate at once if every man were to regard himself alone, and to extend his care no farther! Such a situation would put an end to all intercourse and commerce; men would be destitute of all confidence and security, and afraid to trust each other. And this may suffice to show that odious and malignant quality of selfishness, or mere self-love. Let us now consider—II. THE AMIABLENESS OF A GENEROUS AND PUBLIC SPIRIT. He who has a heart truly open and enlarged, over and above that reasonable thoughtfulness and contrivance with which every prudent man will be possessed, about providing for his own, and how to proportion his expenses to his revenue, as well as how to obtain more ample acquisitions, if fair and honourable methods of advancing his fortunes present themselves in his way; I say, beyond this domestic care, he will have room enough in his thoughts to let them be employed sometimes in the service of his friends, his neighbours, and his country; which have not only his best wishes and hearty desires for the success of their affairs, but he makes it his study to promote their welfare, and puts himself to a voluntary trouble and expense in order to extricate them from difficulties and free them from dangers. He has the pleasure of reflecting that a beneficial act is done, and that although he has not been able to animate others to promote it in the same degree with himself, he has, however, been instrumental in causing some good to be done, and the receivers are heartily welcome both to his pains and his contributions. This may appear but a poor satisfaction to little and grovelling minds, who have no idea of any joy that can arise from the reflection on anything that is not attended with present profit, and look upon everything as a losing bargain where more is expended than received. But large and capacious souls have far nobler sentiments; they know how to value and enjoy a loss, and find a secret pleasure in the diminution of their fortune when honourably and worthily employed. We are sure that God Almighty, who gives everything, and receives nothing, is a most perfectly blest and happy being; and the nearer we resemble Him in any of our actions, by so much we advance our own happiness. Such a friendly promoter of the good of others may survey the objects of his love with some degree of that satisfaction wherewith God beheld His workmanship when He had finished the several parts of the Creation, and pronounced that they were good. And as for a man's name and character, who would not rather choose not to have it mentioned at all, than not mentioned with respect? This seems to be the only end that is sought after by those who delight in show and pomp; and yet this very end might be much better compassed by another way than by that which they affect. For does it not give a sweeter fragrancy to a man's name? And does not every one speak of him with higher expressions of honour and esteem, who has been a common benefactor, and relieved a multitude of necessitous persons? (*Andrew Snape, D.D.*) *Self-love the great cause of bad times:*—1. To inquire what this self-love is which the apostle here speaks of, and wherein the nature and evil of it consists. 2. To show that wherever such self-love spreads and becomes general there must needs be perilous or bad times. 3. To use several arguments to prevent men's being poisoned and over-run with this dangerous and pernicious principle of self-love. I. LET US INQUIRE WHAT THIS SELF-LOVE IS WHICH THE APOSTLE HERE SPEAKS OF, AND WHEREIN THE NATURE AND EVIL OF IT CONSISTS. Now all self-love when taken in an ill sense, as it is plain this is here by the apostle, must come under one or other of these following notions. 1. Self-love may be considered in opposition to a love of God, and a making His glory and the interests of religion the principal and ultimate end of all our designs and actions; to our loving Him with all our hearts, with all our souls, and with all our minds, and our seeking first, or before all other things, His kingdom and righteousness. And then we may be properly said to be self-lovers in this sense, when we are so very intent upon ourselves and our own interests as not to concern ourselves at all, or to be sure not much and chiefly about God and religion. 2. Self-love may be considered in opposition to that honest and commendable self-love which every man oweth to himself, which is a love of our whole beings, soul as well as bodies, and of every part of them in due measure and proportion to the excellence and worth of them; and then it signifieth a love only of one part of ourselves, or at least an immoderate and disproportionate love of one part above any or all the rest. And in this sense it is to be feared most men are guilty of self-love. And, agreeably to this notion, we find the word self used in Scripture to signify the sensual and carnal part of man. 3. Self-love may be considered in opposition to charity or a love of our brethren; and then it signifieth such a stinginess and narrowness of soul as will not suffer us to have any concern, or take any care for anybody but ourselves, such a temper as is the exact reverse of that which the apostle commendeth, which seeketh not its own, but the things of another, and hardly ever thinks, much less acts, but for itself. Nature has implanted in us a most tender and compassionate sense and fellow-feeling of one another's miseries, a most ready and prevailing propension and inclination to assist and relieve them; insomuch that pity and kindness towards our brethren have a long time passed under the name of humanity, as properties essential to, and not without violence to be separated from, human nature. And then as to reason, what can possibly be more reasonable than that we who are of the same mass, of one blood, members of each other, and children of the same Father, should love as brethren? That we, who live in a very fluctuating and uncertain state, and though rich to-day, may be poor to-morrow, should act so now towards others as we shall then wish others may act towards us? 4. And then, lastly, as to religion, especially the Christian, besides that this doth acquaint us with a new and intimate relation to each other in Christ Jesus, and consequently a new ground and obligation to love and assist each other. Nay, so great a value do the Scriptures set upon this duty of mercy or charity to our brethren, that wherever they give us, either in the Old or New Testament, a short summary of religion, this is sure to be mentioned, not only as a part, but a main and principal part of it. Nay, farther yet, it sometimes stands for the whole of religion, as that universal name of righteousness given to it is said to be the fulfilling of the law. 5. Self-love may be considered in opposition to a love of the public and a zeal for the common good, and then it signifieth a preferring of our own particular and private interests to those of the whole body. II. To show that wherever such self-love spreads and becomes general there must needs be perilous or bad times. 1. I say, self-love will make men neglect the public and decline the service of it, especially in times of danger, when their service is most needed. And for this reason we always find it a very difficult task, if not impossible, to engage such men in any public service merely upon a prospect of doing public good. They will use a thousand little shifts and artifices to get themselves excused. Nay, and which is rare in self-lovers, who have always a good stock of self-conceit, rather than fail, they will speak modestly and humbly of themselves, and plead incapacity and want of ability for their excuse. But never is this so plainly to be seen as in times of public danger, when there is most occasion for their assistance. For self-love is constantly attended with a very great degree of self-fear, and this makes mere weather-cocks of such people as are acted by it, continually bandying them about, hither and thither, backwards and forwards, and never suffering them to fix anywhere till the storm is over, the weather begins to clear up, and they can pretty certainly discern the securest side. 2. That though they do pretend to serve the public, yet it is for their own private ends, and consequently their self-love will suffer them to serve it no farther or longer than these shall be advanced by their so doing. And this but a very poor and uncertain service, and even worse than none at all; for their supreme end being their own private interest, all other ends must of course crouch and become subordinate to this. 3. Their self-love will probably turn them against the public, and instead of preserving and securing it, make them undermine and destroy it; and if so, it is still better they should have no concern with it, because the more concern they have with it the greater will be their opportunity of doing mischief to it. Self-love is a very tyrannical and domineering principle, and generally makes perfect slaves of her subjects, and carrieth them on to all such excesses and extravagances as she shall think fit. For, alas! self-love is the blindest, as well as the greediest, and least able to deny itself of all loves, and will very hardly be brought to see any objections against itself; or at least, if it must see them, it will accept of very easy answers to them, and be a wondrous gentle casuist to itself; so, that, if there but come a good lusty temptation in our way, it is too much to be feared that our self-love will close with it, be it attended with never such hard terms, and that, out of eagerness for the bait, hook and all will go down. III. To use all the arguments we can to prevent men's being poisoned and overrun with this dangerous and pernicious principle. And—1. As to ourselves, there cannot certainly be a better argument than the danger which we were brought into by some men's immoderate love of their private interest in the late reign. 2. Let us consider that this principle of self-love is a very foolish principle, and really defeats its own end. For this, I take it for granted, I may lay down as a maxim, that every man's private good is best secured in the public, and, consequently, whatever weakens the public, doth really weaken every private man's security; and, therefore—3. This self-love is a most base, pitiful, and mean principle, and will certainly make us odious and contemptible in the sight both of God and man. (*William Dawes, D.D.*) *Sin multitudinous:*—See here what a concatenation of sins there is, and how they are linked together—self-lovers, covetous, boasters, proud, &c. Sins (especially great sins) seldom go alone. As great men have great attendance, so great sins have many followers; and as he that admits of a great man into the house must look to have all his ragged regiment and blackguard to follow him, so he that admits but one great sin into his heart must look for Gad, a troop of ugly lusts to throng in after. Sin is like a tyrant, the more you yield to it, the worse it tyrannises over you. (*T. Hall, B.D.*) *Self-love foolish:*—This is, with the silly bird, to mind nothing but the building of our own nests when the tree is cutting down; and to take more care of our private cabin than of the ship itself when it is sinking. (*Ibid.*) *Self-love hereditary:*—Hereditary diseases are hardly cured. Self-love is hereditary to us; we are apt to have high conceits of ourselves from the very birth; till grace humble and abase us, all our crows are swans, our ignorance knowledge, our folly wisdom, our darkness light, and all our own ways best though never so bad. (*Ibid.*)     *Self-love a manifold disease :*—This is a disease that hath many other diseases included in it, and so is more hard to cure. Hence spring all those errors and heresies which are so rife in these last days. (*Ibid.*)     *Self-love self-deceptive :*—As a man that is in love doth think the very blemishes in his love to be beautiful, so those that are in love with themselves, and dote on their own opinions, think their heresy to be verity, and their vices virtues. This will bring vexation at last ; it troubles us to be cheated by others in petty matters, but for a man to cheat himself wilfully, and that in a matter of the highest concernment, is the trouble of troubles to an awakened conscience. (*Ibid.*)     *Self-love odious to God :*—The more lovely we are in our own eyes, the more loathsome in God's ; but the more we loathe ourselves, the more God loves us (Jer. xxxi. 18, 20). (*Ibid.*)     *Self-love a primary sin :*—This sinful self-love is set in the front, as the leader of the file, and the cause of all those eighteen enormities which follow : 'tis the root from whence these branches spring, and the very fountain from whence those bitter streams do issue. (*Ibid.*)     *Pious self-love communicative :*—There is a pious and religious self-love, considered in relation to God and the common good ; thus a man may love himself as an instrument of God's glory, and as a servant for the good of others, else our Saviour would never set our love to ourselves before us as a pattern of our love to our neighbours. Now, upon these grounds, and in relation to these ends, we may not only love ourselves, but seek ourselves too. This love spreads and dilates itself for God and the good of others. The more noble and excellent things, the more communicative and diffusive they are of themselves. The sun is herein a more noble thing than a torch, and a fountain than a ditch. Christ emptied Himself of His glory, not for His own, but for our benefit (Phil. xxiii. 6) ; it will make us part with our own right for peace (Gen. xiii. 8, 9 ; 1 Cor. vi. 7) ; it will make us condescend to those of the lower sort (Rom. xii. 16), not seeking our own profit, but the profit of many (1 Cor. x. 33) ; yea, and though they be free, yet love will make them servants to all (1 Cor. ix. 19). On the contrary, self-love contracts the soul, and hath an eye still at self in all its undertakings. 'Tis the very hedgehog of conversation, that rolls and laps itself within its own soft down, and turns out bristles to all the world besides. (*Ibid.*) *On self-conceit :*—Sometimes in our imagination we assume to ourselves perfections not belonging to us, in kind or degree. Sometimes we make vain judgments on the things we possess, prizing them beyond their true worth and merit, and consequently overvaluing ourselves on their account. There is indeed no way wherein we do not thus impose on ourselves, either assuming false, or misrating true advantages, so that our minds become stuffed with fantastic imaginations, instead of wise and sober thoughts, and we misbehave ourselves towards ourselves. 1. We are apt to conceit ourselves on presumption of our intellectual endowments or capacities, whether natural, or acquired, especially of that which is called wisdom, which in a manner comprehends the rest, and manages them : on this we are prone to pride ourselves greatly, and to consider that it is presumption, hardly pardonable to contest our dictates : yet this practice is often prohibited and blamed in Scripture. " Be not wise in thine own eyes," saith the wise man ; and " Be not wise in your own conceits," saith the apostle. If we do reflect either on the common nature of men, or on our own constitution, we cannot but find our conceits of our wisdom very absurd ; for how can we take ourselves for wise, if we observe the great blindness of our mind, and feebleness of human reason, by many palpable arguments discovering itself ? if we mark how painful the search, and how difficult the comprehension is of any truth ; how hardly the most sagacious can descry any thing, how the most learned everlastingly dispute, about matters seeming most familiar and facile ; how often the most wary and steady do shift their opinions ; how dim the sight is of the most perspicacious, and how shallow the conceptions of the most profound ; how narrow is the horizon of our knowledge, and how immensely the origin of our ignorance is distended ; how imperfectly and uncertainly we know those few things to which our knowledge reacheth. If also a man particularly reflected on himself, the same practice must needs appear very foolish ; for that every man thence may discover in himself peculiar impediments of wisdom ; every man in his condition may find things apt to pervert his judgment, and obstruct his acquisition of true knowledge. Such conceitedness therefore is very absurd, and it is no less hurtful ; for many great inconveniences spring from it, such as gave the prophet cause to denounce— " Woe unto them that are wise in their own eyes." It hath many ways bad influence on our souls, and on our lives ; it is often our case, which was the case of

Babylon, when the prophet said of it, "Thy wisdom and thy knowledge hath perverted thee; for thou hast said in thy heart, I am, and none else beside me." It is a great bar to the receiving instruction about things; for he that taketh himself to be incomparably wise, will scorn to be taught. It renders men in difficult cases unwilling to seek, and unapt to take advice; hence he undertaketh and easily is deceived, and incurreth disappointment, damage in his affairs. It renders us very rash in judging; for the first show of things, or the most slender arguments, which offer themselves, being magnified, do sway our judgment. Hence also we persist incorrigible in error; for what reason can be efficacious to reclaim him whose opinion is the greater reason? It renders men peevish; also insolent in imposing their conceits on others. Hence they become censorious of those who do not agree with their notions. 2. Again, we are apt to prize highly and vainly our moral qualities and performances, taking ourselves for persons of extraordinary goodness, without defects or blemishes; which practice is both foolish and mischievous. It is very foolish; for such is the imperfection and impurity of all men, even of the best, that no man who strictly searches his heart can have reason to be satisfied with himself or his doings. Every man is in some degree sinful; conceit therefore of our virtue is very foolish; and it breeds great mischiefs. Hence springs a great carelessness of correcting our faults: a contempt of any means conducive to our amendment, such as good advice and wholesome reproof. It breeds arrogance even in our devotions to God, like that of the conceited Pharisee; also a haughty contempt of others: it disposes men to expect more than ordinary regard from others; and as it causes a man to behave himself untowardly to them, so thence he behaves unseemingly towards himself, of whom he becomes a flatterer, and profane idolater. 3. Self-conceit is also frequently grounded on other inferior advantages: on gifts of nature, or of fortune; but seeing that these things are in themselves of little value, and serving no great purpose; seeing they are not commendable, as proceeding from chance; seeing they are not durable or certain, but easily may be severed from us, the vanity of self-conceit founded on them is so notorious, that it need not be more insisted on. (*Isaac Barrow.*) *On vain-glory:*— When a regard to the opinion or desire of the esteem of men is the main principle from which their actions do proceed, or the chief end which they propound to themselves, instead of conscience of duty, love and reverence of God, hope of the rewards promised, a sober regard to their true good, this is vain-glory. Such was the vain-glory of the Pharisees, who fasted, who prayed, who gave alms, who " did all their works that they might be seen of men," and from them obtain the reward of estimation and applause: this is that which St. Paul forbiddeth: " Let nothing be done out of strife or vain-glory." 1. It is vain, because unprofitable. Is it not a foolish thing for a man to affect that which little concerns him, and by which he is not considerably benefited? Yet such is the opinion of men; for how do we feel the motions of their fancy? 2. It is vain, because uncertain. How easily are the judgments of men altered! how fickle are their conceits! 3. It is vain because unsatisfactory; for how can one be satisfied with the opinion of bad judges, who esteem a man without good grounds, commonly for things which deserve not regard? 4. It is vain, because fond. It is ugly and unseemly to others, who despise nothing more than acting on this principle. 5. It is vain, because unjust. If we seek glory to ourselves, we wrong God thereby, to whom glory is due: if there be in us any considerable endowment of body or mind, it is from God, the author of our being, who worketh in us to will and to do according to His good pleasure. 6. It is vain because mischievous. It corrupts our mind with a false pleasure that chokes the purer pleasures of a good conscience, of spiritual joy and peace, bringing God's displeasure on us, and depriving us of the reward due to good works performed out of a pure conscience, &c. "Verily they have their reward." (*Ibid.*) *Some general remedies of self-love:*—1. To reflect on ourselves seriously and impartially, considering our natural nothingness, infirmity, unworthiness; the meanness and imperfection of our nature, the defects and deformities of our souls, the failings and misdemeanours of our lives. 2. To consider the loveliness of other beings superior to us; comparing them with ourselves, and observing how very far in excellency, worth, and beauty they transcend us. (1) If we view the qualities and examples of other men, who in worth, in wisdom, in virtue, and piety, do far excel us; their noble endowments, what they have done and suffered in obedience to God, their self-denial, their patience, how can we but in comparison despise ourselves? (2) If we consider the blessed angels and saints in glory—their purity, their humility, their obedience—how can we think of ourselves without abhorrence? (3) Especially if we contemplate the perfection, the purity, the majesty of God; how must this infinitely debase us in our opinion concerning ourselves, and consequently diminish our fond affection toward things so vile and unworthy? 3. To study the acquisition and improvement of charity toward God and our neighbour. This will employ and transfer our affections; these drawing our souls outward, and settling them on other objects, will abolish or abate the perverse love toward ourselves. 4. To consider that we do owe all we are and have to the free bounty and grace of God: hence we shall see that nothing of esteem or affection is due to ourselves; but all to Him, who is the fountain and author of all our good. 5. To direct our minds wholly toward those things which rational self-love requireth us to regard and seek: to concern ourselves in getting virtue, in performing our duty, in promoting our salvation, and arriving to happiness; this will divert us from vanity: a sober self-love will stifle the other fond self-love. (*Ibid.*) *Self-centred:*—Original cause of all wickedness, so that they make their own I the centre of their thinking, feeling, willing and doing. (*Van Oosterzee.*) *Self-love:*—Such a love of self as to lead us to secure our salvation is proper. But this interferes with the rights and happiness of no other persons. The selfishness which is condemned is that regard to our own interests which interferes with the rights and comforts of others; which makes self the central and leading object of living; and which tramples on all that would interfere with that. As such, it is a base, and hateful, and narrow passion. (*A. Barnes.*) *Selfishness common:*—How many are there who occupy public places with private spirits? While they pretended to undertake everything for the good of others it has appeared that they undertook nothing but for the good of themselves. Such suckers at the roots have drawn away the sap and nourishment from the tree. They have set kingdoms on fire, that they might roast their own venison at the flames. These drones stealing into the hive have fed upon the honey, while the labouring bees have been famished. Too many resemble ravenous birds, which at first seem to bewail the dying sheep; but, at last, are found picking out their eyes. These people never want fire, so long as any yard affords fuel. They enrich their own sideboard with other men's plate. There is a proverb, but none of Solomon's, "Every man for himself and God for us all." But where every man is for himself, the devil will have all. Whosoever is a seeker of himself is not found of God. Though he may find himself in this life, he will lose himself in death. (*T. Secker.*) *Selfishness condemned by philosophy:*—Plato anticipated one half of a Christian doctrine by saying, "Ye are not your own, but the State's." (*J. F. B. Tinling, B.A.*) *The Divine Nemesis:*—It is a remarkable revelation of the Divine Nemesis, that they who, with the denial of the faith, begin not seldom with the beautiful phrase, that they are zealous for morality, and wish to maintain the morals of the gospel, while they reject dogma, just upon this road advance gradually to the most decided immorality. He who digs out the tree, cannot also enjoy the fruit. Emancipation from all authority theoretically leads practically to the promulgation of the rights of the flesh. (*Van Oosterzee.*) **Covetous.**—*Covetous:*— If selfishness be the prevailing form of sin, covetousness may be regarded as the prevailing form of selfishness. Entering with the first transgression, and violating the spirit of the whole law, it has polluted and threatened the existence of each dispensation of religion; infected all classes and relations of society; and shown itself capable of the foulest acts. (*J. Harris, D.D.*) *Covetousness seen in human life:*—Commerce is covetous; competition is without bounds; rapid fortunes, sudden falls, speculations without end, hazards, excitements for gaining under all forms; such is the new mode of satisfying the old thirst for gold. Industry is covetous: those admirable inventions which are continually succeeding one another aim less at the progress of art than at the making of money; produced by the hope of gain, they hasten toward gain. Ambition is covetous; that solicitude for office which crowds all the avenues to authority aims less than formerly at honour, and more at money. The struggle of parties is covetous. Legislation is covetous: in it money is the chief corner-stone; money chooses the arbiters of our social and political destinies. Marriage is sometimes covetous: the union of man and woman becomes a secondary matter. Literature is covetous; impatient of producing, and more impatient of acquiring, the literature of the present day spends its strength in unfinished, defective, extravagant works, perhaps immoral and impious, which cater for the tastes of the multitude, and pour into the hands of their authors streams of gold unaccompanied by glory. (*A. Monod, D.D.*) *Covetousness barren of grace:*— We may as soon expect a crop of corn on the tops of barren mountains, as a crop of grace in the hearts of covetous cormorants. (*T. Hall, B.D.*) *Covetousness revealed in* *talk :*—" Out of the abundance of the heart doth the mouth speak." (Matt. xii. 34.) What is in the warehouse will appear in the shop, what is in the heart, the tongue tells you. As is the man, such is his language ; as we know what countryman a man is by his language ; a Frenchman speaks French, &c. So we may guess at men by their language; a good man hath good language, he speaks the language of Canaan ; an evil man speaks the language of the world (Isa. xxxii. 6.), discourse with him of that, and he is in his element; he can talk all day of it, and not be weary : but talk to him of spiritual things, and he is *tanquam piscis in arido,* out of his element, he hath nothing to say. It is a sure sign men are of the world, when they speak only of the world (1 John iv. 5). (*Ibid.*) **Boasters.**—*Meanness of boasting :*—Lord Bacon told Sir Edward Cooke when he boasted, " The less you speak of your greatness, the more I shall think of it." Mirrors are the accompaniments of dandies, not heroes. The *men* of history were not perpetually looking in the glass to make sure of their own size. Absorbed in their work they did it, and did it so well that the wondering world saw them to be great and labelled them accordingly. (*S. Coley.*) *Vain boasting :*—A gourd had wound itself around a lofty palm, and in a few week climbed to its very top. " How old mayest thou be ? " asked the new-comer. " About a hundred years." " About a hundred years and no taller ? Only look : I have grown as tall as you in fewer days than you count years ! " " I know that very well," replied the palm; " every summer of my life a gourd has climed up around me, as proud as thou art, and as short-lived as thou wilt be." *Boasters :*—This sin is fitly linked to the former; for when men by covetous practices, have gained riches, then they begin to boast and glory in them (Prov. xviii. 11; 1 Tim. vi. 17), because of the supposed good which they think riches will procure them, as friends, honours, fine clothes, fine buildings. The Greek word is diversely rendered, yet all tend to one and the same thing, and are coincident ; for he that is a boaster is usually a vain-glorious, lofty, insolent, arrogant man : it notes one that is inordinately lifted up with a high esteem and admiration of his own supposed or real excellencies ; and thereupon arrogates and assumes more to himself than is meet; or, one that boasts of the learning, virtues, power, riches, which he hath not, and brags of acts which he never did. The proud man boasts of what he hath, and the boaster brags of what he hath not. This vice is opposed to verity ; and in proper speaking it consists in words, rather than in the heart; for as pride, in exact and proper speaking, hath relation to the heart, rather than the words ; so this sin of boasting hath relation to our words, rather than our hearts : so that this sin is the daughter of pride, for when pride lieth hid in the heart, it shows itself by arrogant boastings, and high-flown words. (*T. Hall, B.D.*) *Boasters discontented :*—Thus when men set a high rate upon their own parts and perfections, they be very impatient and discontented, if others will not come to their price, and because other men will not, they will canonise themselves for saints. (*Ibid.*) *Boasting of vice :*—It is dangerous to excuse and defend sin, but to boast of vices, as if they were virtues, is the height of villany. (*Ibid.*) *Boasting no recommendation :*—When men's mouths are so full of their own praise, it augurs an emptiness of grace within ; full vessels make little noise, when empty ones sound loud. Empty carts make a great rattle, when the loaded ones go quietly by you ; your poor pedlars that have but one pack, do in every market show all they have, when the rich merchant makes but a small show of that whereof he hath great plenty within. The worst mettle rings loudest, and the emptiest ears of corn stand highest. Labour therefore for the contrary grace of modesty. (*Ibid.*) **Proud.**—*Downfall of pride :*—A kite having risen to a very great height, moved in the air as stately as a prince, and looked down with much contempt on all below. " What a superior being I am now ! " said the kite ; " who has ever ascended so high as I have ? What a poor grovelling set of beings are all those beneath me ! I despise them." And then he shook his head in derision, and then he wagged his tail; and again he steered along with so much state as if the air were all his own, and as if everything must make way before him, when suddenly the string broke, and down fell the kite with greater haste than he ascended, and was greatly hurt in the fall. Pride often meets with a downfall. (*Cobbin.*) *Pride abounding :*—And is not this the master-sin of this last and loose age of the world; when did pride ever more abound in city and country, in body and soul, in heart, head, hair, habit ; in gestures, vestures, words, works ? (*T. Hall, B.D.*) *Pride hated by the proud :*— It is so base a sin, that even the proud themselves hate it in others. (*Ibid.*) *The natural heart full of pride :*—Naturally we are all as full of pride as a toad is of poison. The sea is not more full of monsters, the air of flies, the earth of vermin, and the fire of sparks, than our corrupt natures are of proud, rebellious imaginations against God. (*Ibid.*)　*Pride poisons virtuous actions:*—It is the poison of virtuous actions; the meat may be good in itself, but if there be poison in it, it becomes deadly. Praying, preaching, alms, are good in themselves, but if pride get into them, it leavens and sours the best performances. It is a worm that devours the wood that bred it. He that is proud of his graces, hath no grace; his pride hath devoured it all. (*Ibid.*)　**Blasphemers.**—*Gradation in sin:*—He tells us, men shall be self-lovers, silver-lovers, boasters. proud, insulting over their brethren, and, which is worse, they spare not God Himself, but are blasphemers of Him. (*Ibid.*)　*Blasphemy ungrateful:*—It argues the highest ingratitude in the world for a man, like a mad dog, to fly in the face of his master, who keeps and feeds him, and to use that heart and tongue which God made for His praise, to the dispraise and disparagement of his Creator, to load Him with injuries, who every day loads us with mercies, and to curse Him who blesseth us. What greater ingratitude? (*Ibid.*)　**Unthankful.**—*Enormity of ingratitude:*—Philip, King of Macedonia, caused a soldier of his, that had offered unkindness to one that had kindly entertained him to be branded in the forehead with these two words, *Hospes ingratus.* Unthankfulness is a monster in nature, a solecism in manners, a paradox in divinity, a parching wind to dry up the fountain of further favour. (*J. Trapp.*)　*Connection of ingratitude with other evils:*—There be three usual causes of ingratitude upon a benefit received—envy, pride, covetousness; envy, looking more at others' benefits than our own; pride, looking more at ourselves than the benefit; covetousness, looking more at what we would have, than what we have. (*Bp. Hall.*)　*Ingratitude mars friendship:*—It is a lump of soot, which, falling into the dish of friendship, destroys its scent and flavour. (*Basil.*)　**Without natural affection.**—*Want of affection:*—Fontaine's character was such that it seemed incompatible with strong attachments. He married at the persuasion of his family, and left his wife behind him when he went to live at Paris at the invitation of the Duchess of Bouillon. His only son was adopted by Harley, the archbishop, at the age of fourteen. Meeting the youth long afterwards, and being pleased with his conversation, he was told that this was his son. "Ah," said he calmly, "I am very glad of it."　*Cruelty to children:*—Twice in six months one father had to be sent to prison whom it seemed a shame to send at all. When he had gone his second time, there was found on his table "The Floating Matter of the Air," by Tyndall, with his book-mark at page 240, to which he had read. Had you passed him and his wife together in the street, you would have unconsciously felt a certain pride in the British workman; yet was he not ashamed to express openly a desire to be rid of the tasks and limitations his children set to his life, and twice in one night he gave an infant of fifteen months old a caning for crying of teething. His clenched fist could have broken open a door at a blow, and with it, in his anger, he felled a child three years and a half old, making the little fellow giddy for days, and while he was thus giddy felled him again; and because the terrible pain he inflicted made the child cry, he pushed three of his huge fingers down the little weeper's throat—"plugging the little devil's windpipe," as he laughingly described it. He denied none of the charges, and boldly claimed his right—the children were his own, he said. (*Contemporary Review.*)　*Natural affection:*—A team was running away with a small child, when a mother, seeing its danger, cried in agony, "Stop that waggon, and save the child!" as loud as she could. A heartless man said, "Silly woman! don't fret yourself; it isn't your child." The woman replied, "I know that; but it's somebody's child."　**Truce breakers.**—*Covenant proof:*—They will make no more of a covenant than a monkey doth of his collar, which he can slip off and on at his pleasure. In the last days, men will not only be sermon-proof and judgment-proof, but covenant-proof; no bonds so strong, so sacred, but they can as easily break them as Samson did the bonds of the Philistines. It is not personal, sacramental, or national vows that can keep the men of the last times within the circle of obedience. (*T. Hall, B.D.*)　*How rightly to covenant:*—Now that we may covenant rightly, we must do it—1. Judiciously. 2. Sincerely. 3. Unanimously. 4. Affectionately, with—(1) Fear. (2) Love. (3) Joy. (*Ibid.*)　**False Accusers.**—*Faults invented:*—If they can find no faults, they will invent some, as the devil did by Job (Job ii. 9–11, ii. 5), and this properly is slandering. (*Ibid.*)　*The back-biter:*—As those buy at one place and sell at another, so these pedling devils make merchandise of their words, hearing a false tale at one house and selling it at another. The back-biter is a mouse that is always gnawing on the good name of his neighbour. Sometimes he whispers in secret, and anon he openly defames, yet subtlely covering all with a deep sigh, professing his great sorrow for such an one's fall; when they should delight in the virtues of others, they feed upon their vices. (*Ibid.*) *Actions to be kindly interpreted :*—It is a rule in heraldry, and it holds good in divinity, that in blazoning arms and ensigns the animals must be interpreted in the best sense, according to their noble and generous qualities—*e.g.*, if a lion or a fox be the charge, we must conceive his quality represented to be wit and courage, not rapine and pilfering. So, and much more, in blazoning my brother's name, I must find out what is best, and mention that; if I meet with a sin of infirmity and humane frailty, I must conceal it; it is the glory of a man to pass it by (Prov. xix. 11.) (*Ibid.*) *Slander poisonous :*—It is the custom in Africa for hunters, when they have killed a poisonous snake, to cut off its head and carefully bury it deep in the ground. A naked foot stepping on one of these fangs would be fatally wounded; the poison would spread in a very short time all through the system. This venom lasts a long time, and is as deadly after the snake is dead as before. The Red Indians used to dip the points of their arrows in this poison; so, if they made the least wound, their victim would be sure to die. The snake's poison is in its teeth; but there is something quite as dangerous, and much more common, in communities, which has its poison on its tongue. Indeed, your chances of escape from a serpent are greater. The worst snakes usually glide away in fear at the approach of man, unless disturbed or attacked. But this creature, whose poison lurks in its tongue, attacks without provocation, and follows up its victim with untiring perseverance. We will tell you his name, so you will always be able to shun him. He is called " Slanderer." He poisons worse than a serpent. Often his venom strikes to the life of a whole family or neighbourhood, destroying all peace and confidence. (*Dictionary of Illustrations.*) *Slander, overruled :*—After reading a slanderous article in an evening paper, an anonymous friend sent to the Church Missionary Society, as a protest, a cheque for £1,000. Livingstone said, " I got two of my best friends through being ill-spoken of." (*J. F. B. Tinling, B.A.*) **Incontinent.**—*Rules to be observed in our feasting :*—1. It must be done seasonably. 2. Soberly. 3. Discreetly. 4. Religiously. (*T. Hall, B.D.*) *How to know a drunkard :*—Question : But how shall we know a drunkard? Answer : By his affections, words, and actions. (*Ibid.*) *Preservatives against incontinency :*—1. Take heed of intemperance in eating and drinking ; when men are fed to the full, then, like pampered stallions, they neigh after their neighbours' wives (Jer. v. 9 ; Ezek. xvi. 49). Take away the fuel, and the fire goeth out ; take away the provender, and you will tame the beast. Drunkenness and whoring are joined together (Prov. xxiii. 31, 33 ; Hos. iv. 11.) 2. Idleness breeds uncleanliness, as standing pools do mud. 3. Take heed of evil company ; come not near the house of the harlot (Prov. v. 8–11). He that would not be burnt, must not come too near the fire. 4. Set a watch over the eyes. The devil gets into our hearts by these windows of the soul. (*Ibid.*) **Fierce.**—*The fierceness of sin :*—This is the thirteenth sin which helps to make the last days perilous. Men will then more especially be of a fierce, rude, savage, barbarous, inhuman disposition. They will be cruelly and bloodily disposed. There will be in them no meekness nor mildness to regulate the passions ; but, like brute beasts, they will bo ready to slay all such as oppose them. This is a fruit of that self-love and covetousness before mentioned. (*Ibid.*) *Wickedness ferocious :*—This verity is made one special note of the wicked (Prov. xii. 10, xvii. 3 ; Gen. xlix. 7). Hence in Scripture they are compared to lions (Job iv. 10); to wolves (Hab. i. 8) : bears (Prov. xvii. 12) ; horses, which must be restrained from hurting with bit and bridle (Psa. xxxii. 19); serpents (Psa. lxxiv. 13, 14); dogs (Phil. iii. 2 ; Matt. vii. 6) ; boars (Psa. lxxx. 13); threshers, which bruise and oppress the people of God (Amos i. 3) : millers, that grind them with their cruelty (Isa. iii. 75); and to butchers, which do not only fleece, but slay the sheep. (*Ibid.*) *Lessons :*—1. Then let men get grace, that breeds humanity, civility, and candid carriage towards all. Such will not, dare not, hurt their brethren in body, soul, goods, or good name (Psa. xv. 3). We need not fear those that truly fear God. 2. As grace will keep you from being fierce against others actively, so it will be a shield to keep you from the rage of fierce men passively (Isa. xxxiii. 15, 19). It is disobedience which brings fierce men against a people (Deut. xxviii. 50); but when we are obedient, God will restrain their rage, and bound them, as he doth the proud waves of the sea (Job xxxviii. 11). 3. Admire the goodness of the Lord, who preserves His lambs in the midst of so many fierce lions. Did not the great Lord, Keeper of the world, watch His vineyard night and day, the boar out of the wood would soon lay it waste. The thorns would soon over-top this lily, and the birds of prey devour God's turtle. (*Ibid.*)        **Despisers of those that are good.**—*Antipathy between good and evil :*—1. If we consider that strong antipathy and enmity which is between the righteous and the wicked, there is an irreconcileable war and hatred between them (Gen. iii. 15). 2. In respect of the dissimilitude of their manners. They have contrary principles, practices, ends, and aims. 3. To try and exercise the faith, hope, patience, and constancy of His people (Isa. xxvii. 9; 2 Thess. i. 4; Dan. xii. 10). 4. To wean them from the world. It is easy to love a good man for his riches, learning, parts, gifts; this is but a carnal love, and springs from carnal ends and principles (James ii. 1-4). True love is a spiritual love, springing from spiritual considerations; it makes men love the saints for their faith, zeal, &c., and not for any by-respect. (*Ibid.*)        **Traitors.**—Now of these traitors there are three sorts—1. Traitors political. 2. Ecclesiastical. 3. Domestical. (*Ibid.*) *Fidelity :*—Let us be faithful to the truth of God, faithful to the land of our nativity, and faithful in all our relations. Fidelity is the chiefest bond of human society; take away this, and you take away all peace and commerce from amongst men. It is only to the faithful that the promises run (Psa. xxxi. 32). The Lord will preserve the faithful, and make them to abound with blessings (Prov. xxviii. 10). (*Ibid.*) *William Tyndale's betrayal :*—The immediate agent of Tyndale's troubles is known to have been an English ecclesiastic, Phillips by name, who acted the part of a Judas, by artfully ingratiating himself into the translator's confidence, and then conspiring with Pierre Dufief, the procureur at Brussels, to arrest him. The martyr's capture was effected in the street, as Tyndale and Phillips were leaving the house of Poyntz to dine together. Poyntz had expressed to his friend his suspicions of the lurking Englishman; but so adroitly did Phillips act the hypocrite by affecting zeal for the Reformation and love for the Bible, that he found himself courted and trusted, while Tyndale disregarded all warnings. (*Sword and Trowel.*) **Heady.**—In the last days men will be heady, hasty, rash, inconsiderate; they will be carried by the violence of their lusts without wit or reason. They will set upon things too high and too hard for them, like young birds which, flying before they are fledged, fall to the ground, and so break their bones: so much the word implies. They will make desperate adventures; they will be rash in their words and works, precipitate and inconsiderate in all their undertakings; what they do will be raw, rude, indigested, unconcocted. Hence the word is rendered " rash " and unadvised. (*T. Hall, B.D.*)        **Lovers of pleasures more than lovers of God.**—*Lovers of pleasure described and warned :*—I. WHO BELONG TO THIS NUMBER. 1. All whose fondness for pleasure leads them to violate the commands of God—(1) By indulging in forbidden pleasures. (2) By inordinate pursuit of pleasures not in themselves sinful or expressly forbidden. 2. All who are led by a fondness for pleasure to indulge in amusements which they suspect may be wrong, or which they do not feel certain are right. When we love any person supremely, we are careful to avoid not only those things which we know will displease him, but such as we suspect may do it. 3. All who find more satisfaction in the pursuit of worldly pleasures than they do in God's service. 4. All who are deterred from immediately embracing the Saviour, and commencing a religious life, by an unwillingness to renounce the pleasures of the world, are most certainly lovers of pleasures more than lovers of God. II. THEIR SINFUL, GUILTY, AND DANGEROUS CONDITION. 1. That the apostle considered them as sinful, in no common degree, is evident from the company in which he has placed them. It is still farther evident from the description which he gives of them in some of the verses succeeding the text. For instance, he there informs us that such are persons of corrupt minds. What can be a more satisfactory proof of a corrupt state of mind in a rational, immortal being, than a preference of unsatisfying, transitory, sinful pleasures to his Creator. 2. In the second place the apostle informs us that they resist the truth. This they must do, for their deeds are evil. Such persons hate the truth, because the truth condemns their sinful but beloved pleasures. 3. Hence they are represented as despisers of good men. They consider such men, whose conduct reproves them, as the enemies of their happiness, and ridicule them as rigid, morose, superstitious, or hypocritical persons, and who will neither enjoy the world themselves, nor allow others to do it. 4. Lastly, the persons we are describing are represented as being dead in trespasses and sins. She that liveth in pleasure, is dead while she liveth. They are dead as it respects the great end of their existence; dead to everything that is good; dead in the sight of a holy God; loathsome to Him as a corpse is to us, and as unfit for the society of the living Jehovah, as the naturally dead are for the society of the living. (*E. Payson, D.D.*)      *The Christian view of amuse-ments :*—I. AMUSEMENT IS TO BE USED AS RECREATION. The clerk who has been hours at the desk, the mechanic in his shop, the student with his books, will take exercise and bring the unused muscles into play, and so reinvigorate the frame, or the weary brain will be soothed by the excitement and absorption of some game, or the mind, perplexed with life's mysteries and sorrows, will wander away into the world of imagination under the spell of some master spirit, while another will plunge into long-hidden secrets of nature revealed by our modern science, and wonderingly learn the Creator's wisdom, power, and love. But do you observe the assumption underlying this principle? The assumption is, that you are hard at work at your life's task. But now, supposing you have found, and are engaged in, your life's work, apply this principle of amusement as recreation. Nothing is lawful which deteriorates any of your powers or hinders the effectual discharge of duty. What is helpful in moderation becomes harmful in excess; amusement begun as a recreation may end in dissipation. If a man spends his holiday in toil-some excursions by day and revellings at night, and returns to his work unfitted for his daily calling, he loves pleasure rather than God. Had he loved God supremely, he would have always kept in mind that he was having a holiday to fit himself for the due discharge of his God-given work; but he has thought of amuse-ment for its own sake, and has been abusing it. Further, if that is unlawful which dissipates, that which corrupts is still worse. If your recreation brings you neces-sarily into corrupting companionships, it is thereby condemned, and it is to be renounced. II. WE MUST OBSERVE IN OUR RECREATIONS THE GOLDEN RULE OF DOING TO OTHERS AS WE WOULD HAVE THEM DO TO US. We must ask at what cost to them-selves do others produce what amuses and recreates us. If your amusement demands loss of modesty, it demands what must harm you, as well as injure her who loses modesty. In the old slave days our fathers and mothers denied themselves sugar, refusing to eat the forced produce of their outraged brothers and sisters. But this principle applies still more widely, not only to woman, but to man; not only to human beings, but to animals as well; with regard to all these, we shall require that our recreation involves the shame, suffering, and ruin of none. A word should be said with regard to the waste of time involved in many harmless recreations. (*A. N. Johnson, M.A.*)      *The love of pleasure :*—The moral effects of this exorbitant and over-mastering love of pleasure are very awful. In cases of the greatest excess, the very body gives way under it. Gluttony, drunkenness, licentiousness, not only eclipse the mental lights, and scorch the moral sensibilities of the soul, but they hasten the body to dissolution; they dig many a dishonoured grave. But apart from these physical consequences, and even in those cases where they do not follow, the moral effects of the love of pleasure are very sad. Take a tree that needs firm rooting and fresh air, and put it in a hothouse, or in some steamy vaporous place where no winds reach it, and where light is dim, and see how weak and how faded it will become. Such is the man who has blotted out the word " duty" from the plan of his life, and written "pleasure" there in its stead; who feels life no longer to be a moral strife, with God and goodness as its end, but only a low and ignoble endeavour to snatch enjoyment and secure comfort. That man must wither even while he seems to bloom; he must fall, however he may appear to rise; to him there are no stirrings of noble impulse, no victories of the will, no clear light of supreme law. Life is a song, a play, a picture, a feast, a superficial shallow thing —for the man is a lover of pleasure more than a lover of God. And when men sink thus far, it is very hard to raise them. The worm is at the heart of the tree—the corrosive stain is beneath the surface—it is eating the metal through and through. " She that liveth in pleasure is dead while she liveth." Dead in this sin, the love of pleasure. The noblest things have gone now. There is nothing left to which we can appeal. I. FROM SUCH TURN AWAY, not only from the wicked men described in the passage, but from pleasure lovers. Turn away from them, from the frivolous, the butterfly race, who find no seriousness in life, who take no time for thought, who have no spirit of prayer, and no love of God. Such people can do you only harm. If they were willing to bless you, they have no means of doing it. Their life is a scanty rill; and if you find that you cannot influence them, then turn from them, lest you put your own soul in peril. II. We may take this as a guiding rule of invariable and universal application—THAT DUTY IS TO STAND MORALLY SUPREME IN OUR LIFE. It is to be far above enjoyment of every kind. We shall never be safe otherwise. If life is moral, it must be moral all through—from its lowest to its

highest things.   III. THERE MUST BE SELF-DENIAL IN EVERY TRUE HUMAN LIFE.
We are not safe without that.   We shall not keep our life wholesome, green, and
growing, without a good deal of self-denial in it.   Self-denial is like the pulling of
the reins now and again, just to see that we have those fiery coursers, the passions,
well in hand.   It is like the touching of the helm when the sea runs high, or the
tides are treacherous, to make sure that the ship will answer to it if there should be
sudden need to turn her course.   IV. THE LOVE OF GOD, POSSESSED AND CULTURED,
WILL CERTAINLY SAVE US FROM THE DEGRADATION AND THE DOOM OF SUCH A LIFE AS
THAT AGAINST WHICH WE ARE HERE WARNED.   The love of pleasure is not put in
the text against the love of God, as if they were direct opposites.   The sin is to
love pleasure more than God; the cure is to love God more than pleasure, and
pleasure only in a moderated sense in Him.   (*A. Raleigh, D.D.*)	*Amusements :*
—I. THE SPIRIT OF AMUSEMENTS.   Amusements are dangerous things.   Can any
of you explain how it comes to be that in amusements in general there is such a
lack of all reference to God ?   Where is the party that will more brutally resent the
intrusion of religion, or flee more abashed at its mention, than just the party of
pleasure ?   Instinctively there is felt an incongruity between the two.   The
startled response to Mr. Blackwood in a ball-room, I take to be the outspeaking
of the universal feeling—" For goodness' sake, Mr. Blackwood, don't introduce that
here ! "   In the lull of a dance, he had spoken to his partner something about the
Saviour.   This utter absence of God in amusements is an ominous symptom.   As
a rule they are thoroughly secular.   Even when they begin with a mixture of
religion, how soon that drops, and the secular takes its place.   The natural history
of entertainments has been one away from God.   The several stages of their course
have been religious, semi-secular, worldly, the profane, the lewd.   I must ask you
Christians to look that fact straight in the face, and ponder it to its full weight,
because it is full of import.   To me it is a revelation of the spirit of all these
amusements, for it is by this means that we can most certainly discern the spirit.
Generally speaking, the initial beginning between right and wrong has the form of
a narrow fork like the points in a railway line.   With the slightest jolt, you are
shunted from one track to the other.   Can you determine the exact point when
you have left the right line?   But soon as the divergence grows you know to
your pains.   Two seeds are before you.   Each has within it a hidden germ, the
image and ideal of a great tree.   Can you determine their species in the seed?
You may not be able, and argument will be useless.   But plant them, and when
one has grown into an ash and another into a maple, then the difference and the
kind is patent.   Yet these seeds were specifically different.   A different germ, a
different life principle, resided in each; and they could grow only into what they
originally were.   Each had a potency to become what they eventually grew into.
Your pleasures grow from a germ, a spirit.   A life principle pervades the whole.
I refuse to argue the matter at a microscopic stage, the seed difference, the narrow
railway point.   Taking the Master's great principle, we know them by their fruit.
Can that be right which needs the Bible laid aside, prayer neglected, God forgotten,
and to which the name of Jesus is a jar?   II. THE DESIRE FOR PLEASURE A MORBID
SYMPTOM.   The healthiest tone in manhood and society is when people are busy,
when they are bent on some great ideal, and do not need to be amused.   Even a
healthy child needs far less to be amused than mothers and nurses think.   Its great
idea of amusement is to do something.   The honest workman, the colonist, say, in
a new country, busy in felling timber, reclaiming land—his own now—erecting his
homestead, and in other works of homely husbandry, give him the solace of his
wife's society, the prattle of his children, his Bible, a rest in the evening, and the
church on Sabbath, and he will live a life above entertainment—a life of such
solid satisfaction, that entertainments would be a mockery to it.   The kingdom
that is at its best, the society that is at its healthiest, and the Church of God at its
most useful stage, do not need entertainments.   In the old days, when old Rome
was slowly climbing the splendid height of mistress-ship of the world, her citizens
were sober, frugal, and industrious.   Her dictators held the plough, and her matrons
the distaff.   Then the gladiatorial shows had no existence, and adultery was
unknown.   The men were freemen, and the women virtuous.   It was when the
citizens had let themselves be debauched by the games and consented to be amused,
that they sank into the position of public beggars, issuing of a morning from their
squalid cabins for their daily dole of the public bread, to idle away the livelong day
on the benches of the amphitheatre and circus, with an occasional lounge in the
public baths, doing no work, all labour being considered degrading as the lot of

slaves. Then was the time of Rome's decay, till at last they lost to the hardier Goths that semblance of liberty they were too effeminate to defend. Drill your minds, steer your course through life with the grand helm of duty, and not let yourselves roll on the wave of self-indulgence and entertainment. III. WHAT, THEN, SHOULD BE THE CHRISTIAN'S ATTITUDE TOWARDS AMUSEMENTS? In answering this, let me distinguish between Christians in their collective capacity as the Church, and the Christian by himself as an individual. As for the Church of Christ, or Christians collectively, I fail to see that she has got anything to do with amuse. ments whatever. God never instituted the Church to amuse people; so to speak, it is outside her commission. Since Christians cannot go down to the world's pleasures, all the more sedulously should they cultivate that domain which relates to the pleasant in their own religion; for there is distinctly a pleasurable depart- ment in Christianity. The restfulness, the kindness, the sincerity, the readiness to oblige and put one's self about to please, the unfeigned humility and readiness to commend—yea, and relish for all that beauty so copiously strewed in nature without. The cause of conversion often is said to be, "These Christians seemed so much happier than I was." Instinctively, somehow or other, the unsaved feel that if you profess religion you belong to another party from them, and ought to be better; and when they see you indulging in the amusements they indulge in, and which they probably have a shrewd idea are not just the right thing, they are the first to feel the incongruity and to wonder at you. Their idea of religion is taken from you, and you are found false witnesses of God. Perhaps the impression your conduct may produce on their minds is utter scepticism of the reality of all vital religion whatever. The Christian that goes down to worldly pleasures is guilty of bringing a slander on his religion. IV. AMUSEMENTS AND THE UNSAVED. I know that in touching your amusements I am touching the apple of your eye. 1. Let me tell you frankly, then, that your worldly entertainments and amusements are sinful. Sinful, for they are to you the rivals of Christ, and keep you from salvation—yea, even more than ridicule and persecution. 2. They are also unseasonable. There are positions in life in which all acknowledge that anything like jollity or mirth is out of place. If a man has committed a crime, and he is placed in the dock to be tried for his life, frivolity and laughter would be counted exceedingly unbecoming. If you, as the Bible tells you, are a sinner; if you have done things that have angered God that is above, and if His wrath is abiding in your souls, is mirth seemly in your state? Sorrow, repentance, prayer, a turning to Christ, realising that your state is one of sin against the Infinite Jehovah—that is the becoming state for you to be in. (*Alex. Bisset, M.A.*)    *Worldly pleasures:*—Worldliness is often condemned in the New Testament. It is not, as some seem to think, any particular object or pursuit. It is nothing external, but resides in ourselves. It is a condition of soul, not of circumstance—a mind which is more carnal than spiritual, more earthly than heavenly, more self-seeking than God-fearing. Persons who have no relish for society, or music, or public amusements, may yet be intensely worldly in the prosecution of business, in the gaining and spending or hoarding of money, in the management of a household, in the manner of bearing trials, in excessive care, in intellectual pursuits, and even in the affairs of benevolence and religion. It is especially tested in the selection of our pleasures and the degree in which they are indulged. Pleasure-providing is a trade in which, as in others, there is fierce competition. Many places of amusement are not remunerative, and every effort is put forth to increase the revenue. For this end the lowest tastes must be pandered to, and new excitements must be found. Must not such plea- sures tend to corrupt a nation? Christians cannot hesitate as regards their own duty. We do not denounce pleasure as such. Rest as well as labour is from God, laughter as well as tears, recreation as well as toil. Pleasure becomes sin when we are "lovers of pleasure more than lovers of God." This is always the case when our pleasures are opposed to purity and piety. Besides this, we may love inordinately that which is in itself innocent and useful. Excess in what is lawful may become wrong by violating a higher obligation. Whenever we find that our pleasures are interfering with our piety, that they occupy the chief place in our minds, that we are loving them more than we love God, then we may be sure that we are wrong, whatever the nature of those pleasures may be, or whatever the sanction which they claim. (*Newman Hall, LL.B.*)    *Carnal pleasure ruling in man:*—Such were those libertines (James v. 5; 2 Pet. ii. 13; Jude iv. 18, 19). Peradventure they may give God some external worship of cap and knee; but they keep their hearts and best rooms for their carnal lusts and pleasures. (*T. Hall,*

*B.D.)      Godly pleasure :*—Many are so bewitched with their lusts and pleasures, that they do even sacrifice their time, wit, wealth, lives, souls, and all unto them. They are even led by them (2 Pet. ii. 10), as an ox to the slaughter (Prov. vii. 22, 23). They make them their chiefest good, and place their happiness in them. How many spend their precious time in playing, which they should spend in praying and in serving God in some vocation. (*Ibid.*)      *The poison of pleasure :*— 1. That sensual pleasures are the very poison and bane of all grace in the soul; they war against the peace and purity of it (1 Pet. ii. 11); they blind the eye, that it cannot attain to saving knowledge (chap. iii. 6, 7); the love of pleasures eats out the love of God and goodness out of the soul.   2. It is these sensual pleasures which stop the ears against God's call, so that no reason nor religion can work on men. These choke the good seed of the Word, that it cannot grow (Luke viii. 14).   That is the best pleasure which springs from the knowledge and love of God.   We call not upon you to forsake, but to change your pleasures.   Change your sordid, sinful, sensual delights, into sublime, spiritual, and noble delights.   3. The better to wean your hearts from carnal pleasures, consider the vanity and shortness of them.   They are like a fire of straw—a blast, and gone.   Do not, then, for a mite of pleasure, purchase a mountain of misery; for momentary joys, endure eternal sorrows.   4. They do emasculate and weaken the mind.   Whoever was made more learned, wise, courageous, or religious by them?   They rob man of his reason, and besot him (Hos. iv. 11); they take away the man, and leave a swine or beast in his room.   5. This world is a place of weeping, conflicting, labouring, to all the godly, and not of carnal mirth and rejoicing; carnal mirth must be turned into mourning (James iv. 9, 10); the way to heaven lies through many afflictions. 6. Consider, those sensual pleasures end in sorrow.   The end of such mirth (whatever the beginning is) is sorrow.   Men call them by the name of pleasures, pastimes, delights; but in God's dictionary their name is Madness (Eccles. i. 17, ii. 2), Sorrow (Prov. xiv. 13), and is attended with poverty. (*Ibid.*)      *Voluptas :*—Voluptas, the goddess of sensual pleasures, was worshipped at Rome, where she had a temple.   She was represented as a young and beautiful woman, well dressed and elegantly adorned, seated on a throne, and having virtue under her feet.   This representation is just enough; the love of pleasure is too often attended with the sacrifice of virtue. (*C. Buck.*)      *Culling pleasure :*—The world may have many pleasures; but it is culling flowers from the enemy's land, and we Christians must take care that no nightshade and henbane mix unwittingly with our garland.      *Worldly pleasures vain :*—Pleasures, like the rose, are sweet, but prickly; the honey doth not countervail the sting; all the world's delights are vanity, and end in vexation; like Judas, while they kiss they betray.   I would neither be a stoic nor an epicure; allow of no pleasure, nor give way to all; they are good sauce, but nought to make a meal of.   I may use them sometimes for digestion, never for food. (*J. Henshaw.*) *Pleasure-mongers :*—Better be preserved in brine than rot in honey.   These pleasure-mongers are at last as the worst of all.   Such a one was Catullus, who wished all his body was nose, that he might spend all his time in sweet smells.   Such was Philoxenus, who likewise wished that his neck was as long as a crane's, that he might take more delight in meats and drinks.   Such was Boccas, the poet, who said that he was born for the love of women. (*J. Trapp.*)      *Pleasure-loving professors :*—It is always a terrible condemnation of a church member that no one should suspect him of being one.   We have heard of a young lady who engaged for many months in a round of frivolities, utterly forgetful of her covenant with Christ.   One Sunday morning, on being asked by a gay companion to accompany him to a certain place, she declined on the ground that it was the communion Sunday in her own church.   "Are *you* a communicant?" was the cutting reply.   The arrow went to her heart.   She felt that she had denied the Lord who died for her.   That keen rebuke brought her to repentance and a reconversion.   Are there not many other professors of Christ who appear to be "lovers of pleasure more than lovers of God"? (*T. L. Cuyler, D.D.*)      *Emblem of worldly pleasure :*—It was a remarkably hot and sultry day.   We were scrambling up the mountain which rises above the east shore of the Dead Sea, when I saw before me a fine plum-tree loaded with fresh-blooming plums.   I cried to my fellow-traveller, "Now, then, who will arrive first at that plum-tree?"   And as he caught a glimpse of so refreshing an object, we both pressed our horses into a gallop, to see which should get the first plum from the branches.   We both arrived at the same time, and each snatching a fine ripe plum put it at once into our mouths, when, on biting it, instead of the cool, delicious, juicy fruit which we expected, our mouths were filled with a dry, bitter dust, and we sat under the tree upon our horses, sputtering and "hemming," and doing all we could to be relieved of the nauseous taste of this strange fruit. We then perceived, to my great delight, that we had discovered the famous apple of the Dead Sea, the existence of which has been doubted and canvassed since the days of Strabo and Pliny, who first described it. (*R. Curzon.*)    *Death of a lover of pleasure :*—Monsieur de L'Enclos, a man of talent in Paris, educated his daughter Ninon with a view to the gay world. On his death-bed, when she was about fifteen, he addressed her in this language: "Draw near, Ninon; you see, my dear child, that nothing more remains for me than the sad remembrance of those enjoyments which I am about to quit for ever. But, alas! my regrets are useless as vain. You, who will survive me, must make the best of your precious time."

Ver. 5.—**Having a form of godliness, but denying the power** —*Form and power of godliness :*—This form is a profession of religion; the outward appearance of piety; the external performance of holy duties. Its power is the inward experience of its saving efficacy; that is attested by a holy, heavenly walk. This power is denied, not merely by the declaration of the lips, but by all those actions which are inconsistent with it, and which prove that we do not feel its influence. I. A FORM OF GODLINESS IS ABSOLUTELY NECESSARY IF WE WOULD BE SAVED. We are unequivocally commanded to assume the form of godliness; to testify by external acts our allegiance to the Lord; and to attend on those ordinances and sacraments which He surely did not appoint that we might with impunity neglect them. Say not that you secretly and in your hearts worship and love Him. It is impossible that there should be internal piety without some outward manifestation of it. If "with the heart man believeth unto righteousness, with the lips confession will be made to salvation." Besides, what right have you to withhold the acts of external worship from Him who is "the God of all flesh," as well as the "Father of spirits"; who made your body as well as your soul; who confers upon it daily mercies: who purchased it by the sufferings of His Son, who, when He was offered a sacrifice, not only endured agonies of soul, but was also crucified in His body; and who offers at the last great day to raise it up from the grave and crown it with immortality and glory! "Glorify Him therefore in your body and your spirit, which are His." Without the form of godliness, you will probably render yourselves guilty of the blood of souls; be accessory to the eternal perdition of some who are dear to you. There is no one, whose example has not some influence on those with whom he associates. II. BUT THIS FORM IS INSUFFICIENT, UNLESS IT BE UNITED WITH THE POWER OF GODLINESS. 1. This mere outward service is a worship not conformed to the nature of God. 2. It is not conformed to the commands of God (Prov. xxxiii. 26). 3. It is not conformed to the design of the mission of the Saviour, and the gift of the Holy Spirit. 4. It is not conformed to the nature of that covenant which is the foundation of our hopes (Jer. xxxi. 33.) 5. It is not conformed to the examples of the pious; all of whom have used language the same in substance with that of Paul, "The God whom I serve in my spirit" (Rom. i. 9). 6. It is not conformed to the example of the blessed Redeemer; concerning whom none can be so blasphemous, as to doubt whether His whole soul was engaged in doing and in suffering the will of God. 7. It is not conformed to the great ends of religion. These are to deliver the soul from guilt, to renew it, to re-impress upon it the image of God, to make us meet for the inheritance of the saints in light. And how certain is it, that for these great purposes "bodily exercise profiteth little." (1 Tim. iv. 8.) III. YET NOTWITHSTANDING THE CLEAR EVIDENCE OF THIS TRUTH, THERE ARE MANY WHO SATISFY THEMSELVES WITH THE FORM WITHOUT THE POWER OF GODLINESS. 1. At their head must be placed the intentional hypocrite, who knows that he is utterly destitute of love to God and the Redeemer, who has no desire for holiness, but who assumes the mask of religion to cover his sinful purposes. 2. The cold formalist. 3. The vain enthusiast. 4. The worldly-minded professor. 5. The bitter sectarian. 6. The censorious professor. 7. The unfruitful professor. (*H. Kollock, D.D.*) *Form and power.*—I. TRUE RELIGION IS GODLINESS—*i.e.*, moral likeness to God. II. GODLINESS HAS ITS FORM, or way of expressing itself. 1. Towards God— confession, prayer, praise, worship. 2. Towards man—respect for the right, compassion for the miseries, and a loving desire for the happiness of all. III. THE FORMS OF GODLINESS SOMETIMES EXIST WITHOUT ITS POWER. 1. There is often a great deal of external worship where there is no godly devotion. 2. There is

often a great deal of external philanthropy where there is no godly devotion.
IV. HAVING THE FORM WITHOUT THE POWER IS PRACTICAL INFIDELITY. To have
nothing but the mere form is to deny the power. 1. The mere form mis-
represents the power. 2. The mere form counteracts the power. (*Homilist.*)
*Form and power.*—I. EVERY GENUINE EXISTENCE HAS TWO CHARACTERISTICS—
ESSENCE AND FORM. II. THE ESSENCE OF EVERY GENUINE EXISTENCE IS A POWER.
This is true in the highest sense of godliness, which is eminently a "power"; and
the greatest among men, because it is the channel whereby we communicate with
the truth and love of God Almighty. 1. It is a formative power. Originating.
(1) Forms of conception (Rom. ii. 20). (2) Forms of words to express the conceptions (2 Tim. i. 13). (3) Forms of worship, using as handmaids the kindred
fine arts. (4) Forms of society, embodying the grand principles of godliness, and
of its cognate humanity. 2. It is a controlling power, especially over itself. 3.
It is a benificent power over others for their instruction and quickening. III.
THOUGH THERE CANNOT BE POWER WITHOUT FORM, THERE MAY BE FORM WITHOUT
POWER. A man may have the logic and words of godliness, the litany, music,
architecture of godliness; but if he have not godliness itself! IV. THE POSSES-
SION OF THE FORM WITHOUT THE POWER DISPOSES TO THE DENIAL OF THE POWER.
He who has the form alone is apt to be deceived, and satisfied with appearances;
he resents, as an impertinence to himself, the claims of anything further: he
denies it. 1. He strives to ignore it (John ix. 29). 2. When it is forced on his
notice he denies its existence (John ix. 32). 3. When this is impossible, when
the power becomes an evident fact, he clothes it with misrepresentation, obloquy,
ridicule (Matt. xii. 22). 4. When the power becomes too formidable he persecutes
it, and strives to counteract and annihilate it. "Crucify Him!" (*C. Wills, M.A.*)
*Form of godliness:*—I. THERE IS SUCH A THING AS A FORM OF GODLINESS. 1. It
is natural. 2. Beautiful. 3. Advantageous. II. A FORM OF GODLINESS MAY
EXIST WITHOUT ITS VITAL POWER. 1. This is possible. Church at Laodicea. 2.
A lamentable fact. 3. Most alarming consequences. (1) There will be no
searchings of heart. (2) No pungent sorrow for sin. (3) No love to truth. (4)
No conformity to the Divine will. III. THE POSSESSION OF A MERE FORM OF
GODLINESS DOES NOT ENTITLE A PERSON TO CHRISTIAN FELLOWSHIP. 1. The formalist has no sympathy with the sentiments of true Christians. 2. He would detract from their usefulness. 3. He is unfit for any exalted pleasure. (*J. H. Hughes.*)
*The form of godliness:* In these words the apostle tells us—1. What these
men have, viz., a form of godliness. 2. What they want, viz., the power
of it. 3. How we must behave ourselves towards them, viz., we must shun
their society; from such turn away. For the first, they have a vain and
empty show of faith and holiness. They are not men without the pale of
the Church, such as heathens and Jews, which are open enemies to the
gospel; but they have a form of godliness, an external profession of religion
in words, ceremonies, and gestures; they make great shows, and put on
the vizard of piety; like stage players, they act the part of a king, but strip
them of their robes, and they are beggarly rogues. They have not the true
form and essence of godliness, which consists in an inward change, and doth
denominate and give being to things: but they have formality or an outward show
and shadow of holiness. Like pictures and images, which have an external show
and shape of a man, whose lineaments and proportion may be so drawn to the
life, that there wants nothing but life indeed to act them: they will be great professors, and look what a sincere Christian hath in substance, that have these formalists in semblance, they have no life, no power, no principle of operation in
them. (*T. Hall, B.D.*)    *Profession in excess of sanctification:*—The complaint
is general, there is not that mortification, self-denial, and circumspect walking as
formerly. There's more light, but less life; more shadow, but less substance;
more profession, but less sanctification, than formerly. There is more fasting,
praying, preaching; but where's the practice and power of religion? As Isaac
said to Abraham, behold the wood, but where's the lamb? So behold the duties,
but where, oh where's the life, the power, the truth of what is done? The voice
is Jacob's voice, but the hands are the hands of Esau; for they deny the power of
religion not only in their hearts, but also in their works (Titus i. 16; 1 Tim. v. 8).
They so live, as if godliness were but an airy notion, and a matter of fashion,
without all force or efficacy. (*Ibid.*)    *Self-love under a form of holiness:*—The
text may be considered two ways—relatively or absolutely. 1. Relatively. as it
relates to the eighteen sins before mentioned; so this sin is the cloak to hide and

cover them all; men will be lovers of themselves, but under a form of godliness. Hence observe—that a man may have a form of godliness, and yet live in all manner of wickedness. It is true, the power of godliness cannot consist with the power of ungodliness; but the more ,the power of godliness is lifted up in the soul, the more the power of ungodliness will be suppressed; as the house of David grows stronger and stronger, so the house of Saul grows weaker and weaker. But yet the form of godliness may stand with the power of ungodliness. A man may be a glorious professor in the highest form, and yet a puny in the form of grace. He may be a blazing comet for profession, and yet be a devil incarnate in life and conversation. (*Ibid.*)    *The fair covering the foul:*—They put on a fair glove on a foul hand, and get on the vizard of holiness better to deceive.    (*Ibid.*) *Satan covers sin:*—The devil cannot endure that sin should be seen in its proper dress, for then it would be so odious that all men would abhor it; the devil, therefore, puts a garment and cover upon it. (*Ibid.*)    *Profession cannot carry men to heaven:*—This may as soon carry you to heaven as a dead horse can carry a man a journey, a painted ship save a man from drowning, a painted helmet save the head from wounding, or painted food keep a man from starving. (*Ibid.*)    *Formalism:*—1. His knowledge is merely notional, discursive, and speculative, it is in his head, and not in his heart. Hence it is called a *form* of knowledge, *i.e.*, a mere empty shadow and show of knowledge (Rom. ii. 20). But he that hath the power of godliness hath a rooted, affective, saving, sanctifying, experimental, practical knowledge. He knows Christ as the truth is in Him (Eph. iv. 21); he knows and doth Christ's will (John xiii. 17). It is a soul-convincing and converting, a sin-crucifying and conquering light (Ephes. v. 14). It is not a dim, glimmering, vanishing, light; but a thorough, soul-awakening, soul enlivening light. 2. The formalities, obedience and practice, is merely external in words and shows; in their deeds they deny the power of godliness, they live as if godliness were but an empty name and matter of fashion, void of all force and efficacy. Such are like a wicked minister in a white surplice, *extimè lineus, intimè lanius*, fair without, but foul within, or like an inn that hath an angel without and a devil within. Of such we may say as Erasmus said of a friar's cowl—it covers a multitude of sins. He comes short in all ordinances: if he read, pray, hear, or frequent the sacrament, it is all *pro forma*—God is nigh to their mouths, but far from their hearts. (*Ibid.*) *Helps against formality:*—1. Go unto God, who is a quickening Spirit, and beseech Him to quicken thy dead heart   So did David, Psa. cxix. So God can make dry bones to live. 2. Act and use your graces, this is the way to increase and quicken them, bring good motions into resolutions and actions; blow till the spark become a flame. This stirring is painful, but gainful. 3. Delight in quickening company, get acquaintance with humble, holy, active men, and shun the company of dead, formal, earthly-minded men; we must stand up from the dead before Christ will give us life (Eph. iv. 14). There is a quickening virtue in the society of God's people. As one living coal sets his fellow on fire, so God hath ordained the gifts and graces of His people for the benefit of others, that those who dwell under their shadow might return (Hos. xiv. 7). 4. Get sincerity, for therein lies much of the very power of godliness. Let your faith, love, obedience, be unfeigned, and without hypocrisy. Be not only nominal and formal, but be real Christians, be Israelites indeed. Christ says to us as Alexander said to one of his name—either fight like Alexander, or never bear his name; so either act like Christians, or else put off that name. To quicken you, consider that this grace is: commanded, commended, rewarded. 5. It is the grace of our graces, it is not properly a distinct grace, but the perfection of them all. If a man have faith, repentance, obedience, if they be not sincere, they are worth nothing. A pearl if counterfeit is good for little. Gold, if mixed with brass or baser mettle, is debased. It is sincerity that puts a lustre on all our duties. It is the salt that seasons them and makes them savoury. 6. Let the noise of God's judgments awaken thee out of thy sleepy formality; if a man be in a dead sleep, a great noise will awaken him. God's judgments have a voice, and we should mark what it says. (*Ibid*). *The form and the power of godliness:*—Godliness, what is it? It is, as the very word implies, God-likeness. Godliness is the God in the man; godliness is the man being like his God; and seeing that this image has been lost, godliness in man now is a restored godliness—restored through the mediation of Christ Jesus, and by the ministrations of the Holy Ghost. I. In our text we read of THE FORM OF GODLINESS WITHOUT THE POWER—without that power which belongs to the form, and which ought to be inseparable from that form. If you pick up an empty shell, you know that there has been a living creature in that shell: just so there is a power belonging to the external form of godliness; but the two things may exist apart. Many examples might be given of form without power. Take a statue representing some man; it is a form without power. There is the form of the eye, but no power of sight; there is the form of the ear, but no power of hearing; there is the form of the mouth, but no power of speech; there is the form of the arm, and of the hand, but no power of working; there is the form of the legs and of the feet, but no power of walking. There is the form that does embody life, but there is no power of life in that form. And a painting, if it be a portrait, is a form without power. Thus in the form of godliness there is the *appearance* of spiritual knowledge without the knowledge; the appearance of the soul listening to God and hearkening to the voice of His word, without the attentive ear; the appearance of a nature breathed into again by the spirit of life, although still dead in trespasses and sins, and therefore without life. The outward appearance of godliness—what then may it be? 1. It is the appearance of faith in the doctrines which are according to godliness. And where shall we find the appearance of faith without faith? Why here. These doctrines may be held in some articles, or creeds, or theological writings, by the intellect alone. They may be understood as statements, and held by the understanding without being spiritually and religiously appreciated; and they may be held by the tongue. 2. The outward appearance of godliness may be the appearance of sympathy with the ordinances and institutions which are intended alike to express and to cherish godliness. 3. Or the form of godliness may be the appearance of obedience to the laws which are the requirements of godliness. Now these may be fulfilled in the letter and broken in the spirit. For example, I may love my fellow-creature in word and in tongue, and fail to do it in deed and in truth. 4. There may be also the appearance of oneness with the godly through associating with such without communion of spirit. Many things may lead me to associate with the godly—things which are not Christian, considerations which are not Christian motives. I may associate with a man who is a godly man, because he happens to be very intelligent, a well-read man, a man of exquisite taste, and I may fancy that I make him my companion, because of his godliness. The godliness of the man is, however, an accident of my association with him. The probability is that if the man were ungodly, I should associate with him still for his intellectuality; for while he stands on my right hand, and I associate with him, there is a man on my left, not so well educated, not so refined, who is more godly than my well-educated friend, and I pass him by. I might with immense advantage to myself associate with that man, but I do not; his godliness is no attraction to me. Now what does this show? Why it shows that I have the appearance of oneness with the godly, without the affection for the image of God, which would bring me into profitable contact with all who really have and who manifest that image. 5. Further, there may be the appearance of enjoyment of the blessedness of godliness; and this appearance may be made in speech and in tongue, and in a cheerful face on religious occasions. "Having the form, but denying the power." II. Now WHERE IS THE POWER? The power of godliness is true faith in the doctrines which are according to godliness; the power of godliness is worship in spirit and in truth; is doing the will of God from the heart; is love for the godly as godly persons; is joy in God as God; and, I may add, the power of godliness is that external godliness which is the fruit of an internal godliness. . . . III. Now, LISTEN TO THIS EXHORTATION: "From such turn away." You know that this is not fashionable advice. The advice nowadays given is, Turn away from no person, as a protest against the principles and character of that person—especially if that person be much thought of, or be in a high position; or be rich, or from any cause popular. Now, it strikes me that for our soul's health, and especially for our uprightness, we need translate into action some of these directions which demand separation. Let us, therefore, solemnly look at the conduct to be pursued. 1. You see the precept before us requires us to form a judgment of the character of others. You must do so, or you cannot obey this precept. Elsewhere you are forbidden to judge, but you are to bring into harmony that prohibition with this direction. You are to do both. It often strikes me as exceedingly odd, that men who object very much to our forming judgments of the character of others in religious matters, do form judgments of the characters of others in commercial matters. A young man applies for a situation, and the employer, who happens to object to any judgment being formed as to the religious life of another, will thoroughly investigate the character of that young man—not his business habits merely, but everything about him—all his moral habits, and, it may be, even his religious tendencies and dispositions. Well, if the thing be right in one sphere, why is it not right in another? If it have God's sanction in one sphere, why has it not God's sanction in another? 2. By the text, too, we are required to act upon an unfavourable judgment when that judgment is unfavourable. You decide that certain persons have the form of godliness, but are denying the power, and from such you are to turn away. What does this show? This shows that, so far as we can secure it, the communion of Christians must be pure. But let us look again at this precept. "From such" let the confessedly religious man "turn away"—from the men who have the form of godliness without the power. 3. From such let the inquirer turn away, he will learn nothing of these. And from such, let the really religious man, as a matter of stern duty in every sphere, turn away where his association with such would seem to be a sanction. (*S. Martin.*) *Religion more than formality :*—I. THE "POWER" OF GODLINESS IS HERE DISTINGUISHED FROM THE MERE "FORM": and indeed it is easy to show the difference between them. The one is the name—the other is the thing; the one is the appearance—the other is the reality. The one is the body—the other is the soul, that inspires every member, and penetrates every particle of the frame. Behold then the life of the real Christian, and trace the operation of the power of godliness there. 1. It appears with regard to the ordinances of divine worship. Others who have only the form, come without expectation and prayer, and return without reflection and concern; they are satisfied with their attendance—but he is not. He is anxious to derive spiritual advantage from it: he enters the closet before he approaches the temple, and his language is, "O that I knew where I might find Him, that I might come even to His seat!" 2. It appears with regard to the dissipations of the world. He voluntarily resigns those amusements in which he once placed so much of his happiness: and returns no more to them. And why? If he were mindful of the country whence he came, he has opportunity to return: he is surrounded with the same allurements as others—why then does he not engage in these diversions again? Because he has found something infinitely more noble and more satisfying. And a greater good has power to abolish the impressions of a less. When the sun arises, the stars disappear. And the grapes of Eshcol cause us to forget the leeks and onions of Egypt. 3. You may see it in the mortification of sin. He denies himself; he crucifies the flesh with the affections and lusts; he plucks out a right eye, and cuts off a right hand. You may see it in what he is willing to sacrifice and to suffer. Read history: read the book of martyrs; read the eleventh chapter of the Epistle to the Hebrews—and see what the force of this powerful principle can accomplish. 4. The vigour of this principle appears also in other sufferings. How many are there at this moment, enduring a variety of grief in private, whose names will never be published in history, but who, in the eye of God, are greater than the admired heroes of the age! II. INQUIRE WHENCE IT IS THAT SO MANY WHO DENY THE POWER ARE STILL DISPOSED TO MAINTAIN THE FORM. 1. The form of godliness requires no strenuous exertions; demands no costly sacrifices. It is the power of it that renders the Christian life a "striving to enter in at the strait gate"; a "wrestling with principalities and powers"; a "running the race that is set before us"; a "fighting the good fight of faith." And it is this, too, that incurs opposition from the world. It will indeed be acknowledged that sometimes the very form draws forth the rancour of others: and of all people those are most to be pitied who are persecuted for what they have not; who are reproached as Christians without deserving the honour. But upon a nearer inspection of these mere formalists, the world is generally made quite easy. They see that they were mistaken in the characters; they find that they are "of their own," though wearing a religious uniform. 2. Persons are sometimes induced to take up the form of godliness through the influence of their connections. From some of them they feel the influence of authority; from some, the influence of friendship; from some the influence of business. "Hence," says M. Henry, "they assume a form of godliness to take their reproach, but not the power of it to take away their sin." 3. They avail themselves of the form of godliness to preserve peace within. For, without something of religion, conscience would rage and clamour; but by means of this, it is amused and quieted; and this renders it so extremely dangerous. (*W. Jay.*) *Godliness—its form and its power :*—I. BY THE FORM OF GODLINESS MAY BE PROPERLY UNDERSTOOD, NOT ONLY A SPECIOUS PRACTICE OF RELIGIOUS DUTIES, EXHIBITED TO PUBLIC NOTICE, BUT ALL EXTERNAL ACTS OF WORSHIP, ALL RITES AND

CEREMONIES, all stated observances, and all compliance with temporary and local injunctions and regularities. In ages and countries in which ignorance has produced, and nourished, superstition, many artifices have been invented of practising piety without virtue, and repentance without amendment. As almost every man is, by nature or by accident, exposed to danger from particular temptations, and disposed to some vices more than to others ; so all are, either by disposition of mind, or the circumstances of life, inclined or compelled to some laudable practices. Of this happy tendency it is common to take advantage, by pushing the favourite, or the convenient, virtue to its utmost extent, and to lose all sense of deficiency in the perpetual contemplation of some single excellence. II. THE POWER OF GODLINESS IS CONTAINED IN THE LOVE OF GOD AND OF OUR NEIGHBOUR ; in that sum of religion in which, as we are told by the Saviour of the world, the law and the prophets are comprised. 1. The love of God will engage us to trust in His protection, to acquiesce in His dispensations, to keep His laws, to meditate on His perfection, and to declare our confidence and submission, by profound and frequent adoration, to impress His glory on our minds by songs of praise, to inflame our gratitude by acts of thanksgiving, to strengthen our faith, and exalt our hope, by pious meditations, and to implore His protection of our imbecility, and His assistance of our frailty by humble supplication ; and when we love God with the whole heart, the power of godliness will be shown by steadiness in temptation, by patience in affliction, by faith in the Divine promises, by perpetual dread of sin, by continual aspirations after higher degrees of holiness, and contempt of the pains and pleasures of the world, when they obstruct the progress of religious excellence. 2. The power of godliness, as it is exerted in the love of our neighbour, appears in the exact and punctual discharge of all the relative and social duties. He whom this power actuates and directs, will regulate his conduct, so as neither to do injury, nor willingly to give offence. III. How FAR IT IS NECESSARY TO THE CHRISTIAN LIFE, THAT THE FORM AND POWER OF GODLINESS SHOULD SUBSIST TOGETHER. It may be with great reason affirmed that, though there may be the appearance of godliness without the reality, there can hardly be the reality without the appearance. The form of godliness, as it consists in the rites of religion, is the instrument given us by God for the acquisition of the power ; the means as well as the end are prescribed ; nor can he expect the help of grace, or the Divine approbation, who seeks them by any other method than that which infinite wisdom has condescended to appoint. (*John Taylor, LL.D.*)      *Of the form and the power of godliness :*—The word μόρφωσις, which is here translated " form," signifies the show or image of a thing, which is dead and ineffectual : in opposition to the reality and life, which is quick and powerful. And, I think, this word is but once more used in the New Testament, and much in the same sense ; viz., for an empty and ineffectual knowledge of religion without the practice of it (Rom. ii. 17-20, 21). I. To SHOW WHEREIN A FORM OF GODLINESS DOTH CONSIST. In general it consists in an external show and profession of religion, or of any eminent part of it, or of that which is reputed to be so. 1. An external devotion. 2. An orthodox profession of the Christian faith. 3. Enthusiasm and pretence to inspiration. 4. A great external show of mortification. 5. An imperfect repentance and partial reformation. 6. The appearance and ostentation of some particular grace and virtue. 7. A great zeal for some party, or opinions, or circumstances of religion. 8. Silliness and freakishness, and either a pretended or real ignorance in the common affairs and concernments of human life. 9. Much noise and talk about religion. II. WHEREIN THE POWER OF GODLINESS DOTH CONSIST. 1. A due sense of God, and suitable affections towards Him. This is the principle and fountain of all religion, from whence all actions of piety and goodness do spring. 2. A sincere and diligent use of the means and instruments of religion, such as prayer, reading, and hearing the Word of God, and receiving the sacraments. 3. A firm and steady resolution of well-doing. This is the result of a true and sincere repentance, and the great principle of a new life ; and if it be firm and steadfast, it will derive its influence into all our actions ; but if it be wavering and inconsistent, it is only the occasion of a religious mood and fit, but not the principle of a religious state. 4. As the proper and genuine effect of all these, the practice of a good life, in the several parts and instances of it. (1) In the mortifying of our lusts, the lusts of intemperance and uncleanness, covetousness, and ambition. He that is a slave to any of these, his religion is but a form, how glorious a show soever it may make. (2) In the subduing of our passions, wrath, hatred malice, envy, and revenge. (3) In the government of our tongues. (4) In the several virtues of a good life, in opposition to these and all other vices; such as are the truth and justice, humility and meekness, patience and contentedness with our condition, peaceableness and charity to those that are in want and necessity, a readiness to forgive our enemies, and an universal love and kindness to all men. III. SOME MARKS WHEREBY WE MAY KNOW WHEN THESE ARE SEPARATED, WHEN THERE IS A FORM OF RELIGION WITHOUT THE POWER OF IT. 1. He hath only " a form of godliness," who minds merely the external part of religion, without any inward sense of it. 2. He that useth only the means of religion, without regard to the end and effect of it. 3. He that is grossly and knowingly defective in the practice of any part of it. IV. THAT A FORM OF GODLINESS, WITHOUT THE POWER OF IT, IS INSIGNIFICANT TO ALL THE GREAT ENDS AND PURPOSES OF RELIGION. The great ends that men can reasonably propound to themselves in being religious, are these three: 1. The pleasing of God. 2. The peace and tranquillity of our own minds. 3. The saving of our souls. Now a form of godliness, without the power of it, is unavailable to all these purposes. V. THAT HE WHO TAKES UPON HIM A FORM OF RELIGION, WITHOUT THE POWER OF IT, DOTH NOT ONLY LOSE ALL THE CONSIDERABLE ADVANTAGES OF RELIGION, BUT HE HATH TWO GREAT DISADVANTAGES BY IT. 1. He hath the trouble of making a show and appearance of religion, without the real benefit of it. 2. He incurs a heavier sentence upon this account, that he hath a form of religion, and yet is destitute of the power of it. Concluding inferences: 1. To take heed of mistaking the form of religion for the power of it. 2. To take heed of being captivated and seduced by those who have only a form of godliness. 3. To persuade men to mind the life, and power and substance of religion. (*Archbp. Tillotson.*) *The form of godliness without the power:*—I. THE MEN. 1. What they had—"A form of godliness." (1) What is a form of godliness? (*a*) Attention to the ordinances of religion. (*b*) Attendance with the assemblies of God's people. (*c*) A great deal of religious talk Tongue-godliness is an abomination if the heart be destitute of grace. (*d*) More than this, some have a form of godliness upheld and published by religious activity. It is possible to be intensely active in the outside work of the Church, and yet to know nothing of spiritual power. (2) But now, as these people had not the power of godliness, how did they come to hold the form of it? (*a*) Some come by the form of godliness in an hereditary way. Their ancestors were always godly people, and they almost naturally take up with the professions of their fathers. This is common, and where it is honest, it is most commendable. But remember, not generation, but regeneration, makes the Christian. (*b*) Others have accepted the form of godliness by the force of authority and influence. There is danger lest we fail to have personal repentance and personal faith, and are content to lean upon the opinions of others. (*c*) So have I seen the form of godliness taken up on account of friendships. Many a time courtship and marriage have led to a formal religiousness, lacking heart. (*d*) I do not doubt that, in these silken days, many have a form of godliness because of the respect it brings them. (*e*) Certain persons assume the form of godliness from a natural religious disposition. They could not be happy unless they were attending where God is worshipped, nor unless they were reckoned among the believers in Christ. They must play at religion, even if they do not make it their life business. (*f*) From the days of Iscariot until now, some have taken up the form of godliness to gain thereby. To make gain of godliness is to imitate the son of perdition. (*g*) A form of godliness has come to many because it brings them ease of conscience, and they are able, like the Pharisee, to thank God that they are not as other men are. 2. What they did not have—"The power." (1) What is that power? God Himself is the power of godliness. The Holy Spirit is the life and force of it. (2) What is the general history of those who have not this power? Well, their course usually runs thus: they do not begin with denying the power, but they begin by trying to do without it. They try to persuade themselves that they have been changed: they accept emotion as regeneration, and a belief of doctrine for belief in Christ. It is rather hard at first to reckon brass as gold, but it grows easier as it is persisted in. At the first they are a good deal suspicious of themselves, but they industriously kill every question by treating it as a needless doubt. Thus, by degrees, they believe a lie. The next step is easy: they deceive themselves, and come to believe that they are surely saved. At last they take the daring step of denying the power. Being without it themselves, they conceive that others are without it also. *They* get on very well without any supernatural power, and others, no doubt, do the same; only they add a little cant to it to please the very godly folk. They practically deny the power in their lives, so that those who see them and take them for Christians say, "There really is nothing in it; for these people are as we are. They have a touch of paint here, and a little varnish there, but it is all the same wood." Practically, their actions assure the world that there is no power in Christianity; it is only a name. Very soon, privately, in their hearts they think it is so, and they invent doctrines to match. By and by, in some cases, these people profanely deny the Divine power of our only faith, and then they become the greatest enemies of the Cross of Christ. II. THE WICKED FOLLY OF THIS HYPOCRITICAL CONDUCT. 1. They degrade the very name of Christ. If there is no spiritual power in godliness, it is worth nothing. 2. There is no value in such a dead form. I have read that the swan was not allowed to be offered upon the altar of God, because, although its feathers are as white as snow, yet its skin is black. God will not accept that external morality which conceals internal impurity. 3. There is no use in mere formality. In the depth of winter, can you warm yourself before a painted fire? Could you dine off the picture of a feast when you are hungry? 4. There is no comfort in it. The form without the power has nothing in it to warm the heart, raise the spirits, or strengthen the mind against the day of sickness, or in the hour of death. 5. To have the form of godliness without the power of it, is to lack constancy in your religion. You never saw the mirage, but those who have travelled in the East, when they come home are sure to tell you about it. It is a very hot and thirsty day, and you are riding on a camel. Suddenly there rises before you a beautiful scene. Just a little from you are brooks of water, flowing between beds of osiers and banks of reeds and rushes. Yonder are palm trees and orange groves. Yes, and a city rises on a hill, crowned with minarets and towers. You are rejoiced, and ask your guide to lead you nearer to the water which glistens in the sun. He grimly answers, "Take no notice, it is the mirage. There is nothing yonder but the burning sand." You can scarce believe him, it seems so real; but lo, it is all gone, like a dream of night. So unsubstantial is the hope which is built upon the form of godliness without the power. The white ants will eat up all the substance of a box, and yet leave it standing, till a touch causes the whole fabric to fall in dust: beware of a profession of which the substance has been eaten away. Believe in nothing which has not the stamp of eternity upon it. 6. In reality, this kind of religion is in opposition to Christ. It is Jannes and Jambres over again: the magician of hypocrisy is trying to work miracles which belong to God only. Nobody can do so much damage to the Church of God as the man who is within its walls, but not within its life. 7. This nominal godliness, which is devoid of power, is a shameful thing. (*C. H. Spurgeon.*) *The power of godliness:* I. GODLINESS IS POWERFUL BECAUSE IT IS THE EMBODIMENT OF GOD. II. GODLINESS IS POWERFUL BECAUSE IT IS A NEW BIRTH TO RIGHTEOUSNESS, TRUTH, AND LOVE. III. GODLINESS IS POWERFUL BECAUSE IT IS A GROWTH. IV. GODLINESS IS POWERFUL BECAUSE IT IS A PERSONAL PROPERTY. You see upon the desk of that organ a music book; but the book does not sing. The gospel is like a music book. Here are the rules for the harmony of life. Godliness is singing from the book of Christ; it is playing upon the heavenly harp; it is putting the music of God into one's own life. (*W. Birch.*) *Motives and dissuasives from familiarity with wicked men:*—1. Consider that familiarity with wicked men will make us like them, we are very apt to resemble those that we converse with, and as he that walks with wise men shall be wiser (Prov. xiii. 20), so he that walks with wicked men shall be worse. The best mettles, when mixed with baser, are embased thereby; mix gold with brass or silver with copper, and you debase the coin; for saints to familiarly join with the limbs of Satan, not only endangers, but debaseth them. Man is a poor, weak, unconstant creature, and apt to go astray, and therefore we should shun temptations. 2. This familiarity with them may harden them in their sin, God hath ordained our separation, and withdrawing ourselves from them, as a means to humble them, and turn them from sin (1 Thess. v. 22.) 3. There is no comfort to be found in such society; when trouble comes, miserable comforters are they all. When Judas fell into trouble of conscience, he ran to his wicked associates, but see what miserable comforters they are to him in his extremity (Matt. xxvii. 4). 4. It is a dishonour to our Lord and Master to be familiar with known traitors and rebels to Him. Every wicked man rebels against God. 5. It is impossible that ever we should be good so long as we delight in wicked company. 6. By familiarity with such we do not only endanger our spiritual, but our temporal estate also. (*Ibid.*) *Form and power:*—I do not suppose that these words need much explanation. "Godliness," in the New Testament, means not only the disposition which we call piety, but the conduct which flows from it, and which we may call practical religion. The form or outward appearance of that we all understand. But what is the "denying the power thereof"? It does not consist in words, but in deeds. In these latter epistles we find "denying" frequently used as equivalent to "abjuring," renouncing, casting off. For instance, in a passage singularly and antithetically parallel to that of my text, we read "denying ungodliness and worldly lusts," which simply means throwing off their dominion. I. Observe THE SAD FREQUENCY OF SUCH A CONDITION. Wherever any great cause or principle is first launched into the world, it evokes earnest enthusiasm, and brings men to heroisms of consecration and service. And so, when Christianity was first launched, there was less likelihood of its attracting to itself men who were not in earnest, and who were mere formalists. As years go on, the primitive enthusiasms die out, and the cause which was once all freshly radiant and manifestly heaven-born becomes an earthly institution, there is a growing tendency to gather round it all sorts of superficial, half-and-half adherents. And every church has its full share of such people ; loose adherents, clogs upon all movement, who bring down the average of warmth like the great icebergs that float in the Atlantic and lower the temperature of the summer all over Europe. They make consecration "eccentric"; they make consistent, out-and-out Christian living, "odd," "unlike the ordinary thing." And they pull down the spirituality of the Church almost to the level of the world. II. Think, next, of THE UNDERGROUND WORKING OF THIS EVIL. These people about whom Paul is speaking in my text were, I suppose, mostly, though by no means exclusively, conscious pretenders to what they did not possess. But the number of hypocrites, in the full sense of the word, is amazingly small, and the men whom you would brand as most distinctly so, if you came to talk to them, would amaze you to find how entirely ignorant they were of the fact that they were dramatising and pretending to piety, and that there was next to no reality of it in them. A very little bit of gold, beaten out very thin, will cover over, with a semblance of value, an enormous area. And men beat out the little modicum of sincerity that they have so very thin that it covers, and gives a deceptive appearance of brilliancy and solidity to an enormous amount of windy flatulence and mere pretence. The worse a man is, the less he knows it. The more completely a professing Christian has lost his hold of the substance and is clinging only to the form, the less does he suspect that this indictment has any application to him. The more completely a man's limbs are frost-bitten the more comfortable and warm they are, and the less does he know it. I need say little about the reasons for this unconsciousness. We are all accustomed to take very lenient views, when we take any at all, of our own character; and the tendency of all conduct is to pull down conscience to the level of conduct, and to vindicate that conduct by biassed decisions of a partial conscience. The underground enemies of our Christian earnestness are far more dangerous than the apparent and manifest antagonists ; and there are many men amongst us who would repel with indignation a manifest assault against their godliness, who yield without resistance, and almost without consciousness, to the sly seductions of unsuspected evil. The arrow that flies in darkness is more deadly than the pestilence that wasteth at noonday. III. Further, notice THE EVER-OPERATING CAUSES THAT PRODUCE THIS CONDITION. 1. I suppose that one, at any rate, of the main examples of this "form" was participation in the simple worship of the primitive Church. And although the phrase by no means refers merely to acts of worship, still that is one of the main fields in which this evil is manifest. Many of us substitute outward connection with the Church for inward union with Jesus Christ. All external forms have a tendency to assert themselves, and to detain in themselves, instead of helping to rise above themselves, our poor sense-ridden natures. Seeing that the purest and the simplest of forms may become like a dirty window, an obscuring medium which shuts out instead of lets in the light, it seems to me that the Churches are wisest which admit least of the dangerous element into their external worship, and try to have as little of form as may keep the spirit. I know that simple forms may be abused quite as much as elaborate ones. Let us be very sure that we do not substitute Church membership, coming to chapel, going to prayer-meeting, teaching in Sunday schools, reading devout books, and the like, for the inward submission to the power. 2. Another cause always operating in the tendency which all action of every kind has to escape from the dominion of its first motives, and to become merely mechanical and habitual. Habit is a most precious ally of goodness, but habitual goodness tends to become involuntary and mechanical goodness, and so to cease to be goodness at all. And the more that we can, in each given case, make each individual act of godliness, whether it be in worship or in practical life, the result of a fresh approach to the one central and legitimate impulse of the Christian life, the better it will be for ourselves. 3. And then, still further, there is the constant operation of earth and sense and daily duties and pressing cares, which war against the reality and completeness of our submission to the power of godliness. Grains of sand, microscopically minute in the aggregate, bury the temples and the images of the gods in the Nile Valley. The multitude of small cares and duties which are blown upon us by every wind have the effect of withdrawing us, unless we are continually watchful, from that one foundation of all, the love of Jesus Christ felt in our daily lives. IV. So, lastly, let me point you to THE DISCIPLINE WHICH MAY AVERT THIS EVIL. 1. First and foremost, I would say let us cherish a clear and continual recognition of the reality of the danger. Forewarned is forearmed. Rigid, habitual self-inspection, in the light of God's Word, is an all-important help to prevent this sliding into superficiality of our Christian life. In a country which is only preserved by the dykes from being swallowed up by the sea the minutest inspection of the rampart is the condition of security, and if there be a hole big enough for a mouse to creep through the water will come in and make a gap wide enough to drown a province in a little while. And so, seeing that we have such dangers round about us, and that the most formidable of them all are powers that work in the dark, let us be very sure that our eyes have searched, as well as we can, the inmost corners of our lives, and that no lurking vermin lie beneath the unturned-up stones. 2. And then, lastly, and as that without which all else is vain, let us make continual and earnest and contrite efforts day by day to renew and deepen our personal communion with Jesus Christ. He is the source of the power which godliness operates in our lives, and the closer we keep to Him the more it will flood our hearts and make us real, out-and-out Christians, and not shallow and self-deceived pretenders. The tree that had nothing but leaves upon it hid its absence of fruit by its abundance of foliage. The Master came, as He comes to you and to me, seeking fruit, and if He finds it not He will perpetuate the barrenness by His blasting word, "No fruit grow upon thee henceforward for ever." (*A. Maclaren, D.D.*) *Forms of religion necessary:*—1. Forms are necessary to religion as the means of its manifestation. As the invisible God manifests His nature—His power, wisdom, and goodness, in visible material forms, in the bright orbs of heaven, in the everlasting hills, in the broad earth with its fruits and flowers, and in all the living things which He has made,—so the invisible soul of man reveals its convictions and feelings in the outward acts which it performs. A form is the flag, the banner, the symbol of an inward life; it is to a religious belief what the body is to the soul; as the soul would be utterly unknown without the body, so religion would be unknown without its forms, a light hidden under a bushel, and not set up in a candlestick that it may give light to all that are in the house. 2. Forms are necessary not only to the manifestation of religion, but to its nourishment and continued existence. A religion which expressed itself in no outward word or act would soon die out of the soul altogether. The attempt to embody truth and feeling, to express it in words and actions, is necessary to give it the character of living principle in the soul : in this respect forms are like the healthy exercise which at once expresses and increases the vigorous life of the body, or they may be compared to the leaves of a tree, which not only proceed from its inward life, but catch the vitalising influences of the light, the rain, and the atmosphere, and convey them down to the root. 3. What, then, is that formalism which is everywhere in the Scripture, and especially in the discourses of our Lord, described as an offence and an abomination in the sight of God ? It is the substitution of the outward rite in the place of the inner spirit and life of the soul; it is the green leaf which still hangs upon the dead branch which has been lopped off. (*Christian Age.*)  *Form without power :*— Some years ago the captain of a Greenland whaling vessel found himself at night surrounded by icebegs and "lay-to" till the morning, expecting every moment to be ground to pieces. As the morning dawned he sighted a ship at no great distance. Getting into a boat with some of his men he carefully picked his way through the lanes of open ice towards the mysterious looking craft. Coming alongside he hailed the vessel with a loud, " Ship ahoy! " but there was no response. He looked through the porthole and saw a man, evidently the captain, sitting at a table as if writing in a log-book. He again hailed the vessel, but the figure moved not. It was dead and frozen ! On examination the sailors were found, some frozen among the hammocks, others in the cabin. From the last entry in the log-book it appeared this vessel had been drifting about the Arctic seas for thirteen years—a floating sepulchre, manned by a frozen crew. And there are souls to-day who have refused the Divine offer of life, forsaken the centres where they were warmed with hallowed influences, and drifted into the chilling regions of Arctic darkness and frost. Many of these have certain appearances of Christian life, and a name to live. (*Christian Journal.*)   *A deceptive form :*—On the farm of Manorlees, in Fifeshire, and in the house of Mr. Alexander Gibson, a large and very tempting ham hung from one of the rafters running across the ceiling.   In the same house there was a rat, whose taste lay strongly in the direction of ham, and this rat, with rare instinct, gnawed a hole in the woodwork directly over the tempting morsel, and, descending, ate itself into the inside of it.   How long the excavating went on is not known, but one day the housewife found it necessary to commence operations on the ham, when, on lifting it down, out bolted the depredator.   The ham was a perfect shell, skin and bone only remaining to show its form.   The animal, after feeding sumptuously, had commenced to build a nest inside.   This anecdote is not simply amusing; it serves well to illustrate the operation of secret sin, eating away our spiritual life till nothing remains but a deceptive form of godliness—the mere rind and shell of religion.   (*Christian Herald.*)   *Form without power:*—Across your path, and on the ground, lies stretched out in death, a mighty tree, tall and strong—fit mast to carry a cloud of canvas, and bear unbent the strains of tempests. You put your foot lightly on it; and how great your surprise when, breaking through the bark, it sinks deep into the body of the tree—a result much less owing to the pressure of your foot than to the poisonous fungi and foul, crawling insects that have attacked its core.   They have left the outer rind uninjured—but hollowed out its heart.   Take care your heart is not hollowed out, and nothing left you but the crust and shell of an empty profession.   (*T. Guthrie, D.D.*)   *Religion, false and true :*—A painter has undertaken to portray on his canvas flames of fire.   He does it so exactly that you can hardly detect it from real flames.   But look ! you see flies and other insects passing across it ; they could never pass across real flames.   Just so spiritual insects, in the shape of sins, will pass across the mere professor, which they could never do across one who had the power of real religion in his heart; the former has but the " form " of flames " of godliness," the influential power is wanting.   (*Dr. Jenkyn.*)   *Hollow professors :*—Hollow professors are as hollow trees in an old wood—tall, but pithless, sapless, unsound. Their formality is fitly compared to a bulrush, whereof the colour is fresh, the skin smooth : he is very exact that can find a knot in a bulrush (Isa. lviii. 5).   But peel it, and what shall you find within but a kind of spongeous, unsubstantial substance ?   These, as if religion were a comedy, do in voice and gesture act Divine duties, in heart renounce them.   Hypocrites only act religion, play devotion; like they are to the ostrich, saith Hugo, which hath wings, but flies not.   The swan in the Law was rejected for sacrifice because of her black skin under white feathers.   Art may take a man more than nature ; but with God, the more art the less acceptance : He loveth truth in the inwards (Psa. li. 6).   (*J. Trapp.*)   *Formalism not religion :*—A hypocrite is a contemptible person, whether he is in the Church or out of it; whether he is deceiving in the name of respectability or religion.   He is not a Christian any more than a crocodile is a nightingale or a fungus is a lily.   *Formalism in religion :*—A gentleman once entered a hall with his son.   They saw a number of well-dressed people—some of them standing together in groups, others apart; some sitting in various postures.   The son's attention was fixed by a pleasant-looking gentleman, somewhat gaudily dressed.   He said, "Father, who is that gentleman?   He seems a mild, pleasant-looking person; but what a singular dress he wears !   Who is he ? "   " Ask the gentleman who stands near you," said the father.   " If you please, sir, can you inform me who that gentleman opposite is ? "   No answer.   The boy thinks it strange. At last the father tells him, " My son, those are only wax figures : there is no life in them; they are all outside, very fair to look at, but there is no soul, no life : they are outside and nothing else."   So it is with those who have no internal religion.   (*Dictionary of Illustrations.*)   *False profession :*—Pharnaces, the son of Mithridates, the king of Pontus, sending a crown to Cæsar at the time he was in rebellion against him, he refused the present, saying, " Let him first lay down his rebellion, and then I will receive his crown."   There are many who set a crown of glory upon the head of Christ by a good profession, and yet plant a crown of thorns upon His head by an evil conversation.   (*T. Secker.*)   *Danger of the office of preacher :*—There is always danger to those who have to talk much about religion that their religion may become that of the head, rather than the true religion of the heart. I have found it necessary myself to dedicate an hour or two at midnight to serious meditation, self-examination, and prayer. (*Dean Hook.*) *Formalism :*—Some may live upon forms, but there is no dying upon forms. Formalists, like Pharaoh's lean kine, are full-fed, yet lean. To pursue the ways of God with a guilty conscience is Satan's great receipt for perpetual failure.

Ver. 6.—**Lead captive silly women.**—*Creeping into houses :*—The expression "which creep into houses," although perfectly natural, and one which, even in these Western countries, could be used with propriety to express the method in which these deceiving and perverting men make their way into households, yet, when we remember the comparative state of seclusion in which women usually lived, and still live, in Eastern lands, the words used by Paul acquire an increased force. Special fraud and deceit was needful for these false teachers to creep into the women's apartments in Asia. (*H. D. M. Spence, D.D.*) *Sneakiness :*— Cheaters must get some credit before they can cozen; and all falsehood, if not founded in some truth would not be fixed in any belief. (*T. Fuller.*) *Woman and sin :*—There lies in the womanly character the foundation ; as for the highest development of the power of faith, so also for the highest revelation of the power of sin (comp. Rev. xvii.). Josephus also states that the Pharisees especially had found much support amongst women ("Antiq." xvii. 2). Compare the account, moreover, of the rich Fulvia of Rome, who was induced by two Jewish impostors to furnish a considerable sum of gold, under the supposition that it was for the temple at Jerusalem (" Antiq." xviii. 3). (*Van Oosterzee.*) *Impostors :*—1. As they are impudent, so they are of a fraudulent, subtle, sly, insinuating temper ; they vent not their errors openly (especially, not at first) but they secretly and slily creep into private houses, and there they sell their wares (Jude 4), they privily bring in damnable heresies (2 Pet. ii. 1 ; Gal. ii. 4). Truth loveth the light and seeks no corners. 2. These impostors observe a method in seducing silly women, who, being the weaker sex, are sooner won over to their way, as being less able to withstand the shock of a temptation. As warriors go about a city observing where the wall is weakest, lowest, and unguarded, and there they make their greatest assault ; and as thieves set not upon strong, armed men, but upon weak, unarmed ones, so seducers love not to set upon strong, grounded, judicious, discerning Christians, but it is the weak and ignorant which cannot discern their frauds, but like children are tossed to and fro with every wind of doctrine, that become their prey (Prov. xiv. 15 ; Rom. xvi. 18 ; Eph. iv. 14) ; man is, or at leastwise should be, more strong and prudent to resist temptations than women are. They catch not grave and truly pious matrons, but light women which prefer their lusts before Christ. It is the light chaff which is tossed with every wind, when the massy wheat abides in the floor. (*T. Hall, B.D.*)

Ver. 7. **Ever learning, and never able to come to the knowledge of the truth.**— *Ever learning, never attaining :*—This is one of the features of the "perilous times" of the "last days." "Men shall be selfish." This lies at the root of all. Self enthroned where God ought to be—self pampered, to the neglect alike of duty and charity—this will explain anything in the longest and blackest list of vices. The text presents another characteristic of the perilous times. These selfish men, without natural affection, despisers of all that is good, lovers of pleasures more than lovers of God, yet tenacious of the form of that godliness of which they have utterly set at nought the power, shall exercise a strange empire, none the less, over the homes and over the lives and over the consciences of women. Professing themselves religious, calling themselves teachers of truth, they will insinuate themselves into houses, and captivate by their offers of an indulgent and accommodating Christianity, just those who need above all others a discipline of plain speaking—silly women laden with sins, led this way and that way by divers lusts. It is of these captives, these victims, of a debased and degenerate teaching, that the words of the text were written. There are those who, though they are ever learning, are never able to arrive at this sort of knowledge of truth. They are not careless hearers, they are not inattentive readers, they are not uninterested inquirers. If they were this, the wonder of the non-attainment would be at an end. But there is a wonder. The cry and the complaint is, "I am always learning. I never allow a new book, which promises light upon some part of the truth, to escape my notice. I am athirst for knowledge ; I would give all I possess to be quite sure." 1. There is in some minds an impatience of process and progress, fatal of itself to safe and solid attainment. "By little and little" is the motto of the spiritual dealing, whether it be in the "putting out of enemies" or in the discovery of truth. 2. Another cause of disappointment lies in confusion of thought as to the nature of spiritual certainty. If God speaks, certainly He will give me proof of it; but a proof in the same region and in the like material with the thing to be proved; not an evidence of sight, touch, or smell, as to things which, by their very hypothesis, lie outside it, but an evidence appealing to conscience, heart, and soul, as He made each; satisfying the whole (not one part) of me, that the thing of which He gives me the information is beneficial, is wholesome, is good for me—and, because good, therefore also true. 3. A further error contributes, in many, to this defeat of knowing, and it is the want of instant action on the footing of the thing learned. Many men listen to a sermon without the slightest intention of doing any one single thing in consequence. A man has been interested in a treatise upon Prayer, upon Inspiration, upon the Atonement. He closes the book with a feeling of satisfaction—now he can give a reason for the hope that is in him. Yet he feels that he has not "come to the knowledge" of that truth. It is not a part of him. It does not enter into his thought, mind, and life. It does not influence him; it has not flowed into him—for that is influence; it will not flow out from him into any one else. Why is this? Because he has not acted upon the thing learned. He has not carried out the acquisition of the head into the heart, if that is its province; or into the conduct, if its region of operation is there. A man powerfully impressed with the reasonableness of prayer will instantly set himself to pray with a new stimulus and a new intensity. If he does not he may have "learned"—as St. Paul would have us distinguish—but he cannot be said to "know." A man who has received a new instruction on the subject of inspiration, forthwith opens his Bible, kneels on his knees with it, feels the breath of God in it all as he reads, and echoes each sentence of it in earnest prayer. (*Dean Vaughan.*) *Ever learning, and never able to come to the knowledge of the truth*:—The case here represented may perhaps strike us as having something in it rather extraordinary. That they who take no pains to learn should never grow wiser is what we can readily understand, but that there should be those who do labour in the work of religion and yet never succeed is surely not a little remarkable. Strange, however, as it may on the first view appear, the case is by no means uncommon. It will, then, be useful to investigate the causes of this. We may lay it down for a certain truth, that it is not owing to anything unattainable in the object itself. 1. The knowledge which is necessary to salvation is open to the most ordinary capacity. The great leading truths of the Bible are plain and simple, and, where the mind is in a right disposition, are easily understood. 2. The knowledge of the truth is not unattainable, because we have the promise of Christ that it shall be imparted to every one, be his condition what it may, who is sincere in seeking it. Without Divine illumination it is impossible for any human being to become wise unto salvation. But this illumination God is willing to pour upon the minds of all who call upon Him for that purpose. The causes of their failure are to be traced entirely to themselves. (1) One great cause of their coming short of saving knowledge is this—that they do not seek it in the right way. In the Bible God's will is revealed to us, but to understand the Bible, and to derive effectual and saving information from it, we must have recourse to the Author of the Bible. But this method the persons of whom we are speaking do not pursue. Reason, with them, is all-sufficient. Reason, they think, is equal to the investigation of every subject; and the consequence is, that what reason cannot account for, what reason cannot comprehend, they refuse to admit. "The meek will He guide in judgment; and the meek will He teach His way." (2) Another reason why men, though continually learning, come not to the knowledge of the truth, is that they make a wrong use of the means of knowledge; that is, they mistake the means for the end—they mistake the means of religion for religion itself. They have hitherto satisfied themselves with the performance of the outward duties of prayer, reading, and hearing, without ever looking further; without ever asking themselves seriously, "What do we these things for? Have the ordinances of religion produced in us any of the effects for which they were designed?" (3) The secret love of sin is another obstruction to the attainment of saving knowledge. God tells the house of Israel that He will not be inquired of by them because they "set up their idols in their heart, and put the stumbling-block of their iniquity before their face." "If any man will do His will he shall know of the doctrine whether it be of God." "The secret of the Lord is with them only that fear Him." (4) They refuse to obey their convictions. They do not act up to the light they possess. (*J. Boucher, M.A.*) *Caution against enticement from the truth :*—1. I wish this were not the sin of silly men as well as of silly women, to be always learning, yet never come to the knowledge of the truth ; how many are men in years, yet children in understanding (1 Cor. xiv. 20). And when for the time they might have been teachers, they had need to be taught the elements of religion (Heb. v. 12). Though the knowledge of the best in this life be imperfect, and we are always learners here, yet we must strive toward perfection and not always stick in the place of bringing forth (Hos. xiii. 13) ; nor be like a horse in a mill, still going round in the same place ; or like a picture that grows not, but is the same now that it was twenty years ago. Such barren trees are nigh to cursing (Luke xiii. 9), and such unprofitable learners are left by God justly to the power of seducers, as malefactors are to jailers. This is the true cause of all those errors and sins amongst us (Psa. xcv. 10 ; Jer. ix. 3 ; Matt. xxii. 19). As for ourselves, let us inquire for the good way, and when we have found it, sit not still, but be walking from knowledge to knowledge, from grace to grace, and from strength to strength, till at last we come to our celestial Sion. 2. Since seducers are so ready to seduce women, how careful should that sex be to shun conversing or disputing with them. Let every one know his own strength, and, if he be wise, keep within his own bounds. 3. Since women often are Satan's instruments, by which he seduceth many, take heed of women; let not those syrens enchant thee so as to leap into the depths of errors. Consider how many of thy betters have fallen by them. Whosoever they be that seek to draw thee from thy God, let thy heart and thy hand be against them (Deut. xiii. 6, 8, 9). (*T. Hall, B.D.*) *Unsanctified education :*— There is a right and wrong way of looking at everything. As a rule, whatever is most valuable in its use is most harmful in its abuse. The keener the surgeon's knife, the more serviceable it is in skilled hands, but the more dangerous in hands unskilled. Education—learning—is of the utmost value, rightly acquired and rightly used. Misapplied—used as an end, not a means—it is a cogent factor of evil. 1. It is unsatisfactory and embittering. As a man who ascends the mountain-side far enough to enter the blinding mists, but not far enough to overlook them, so is the man of godless learning. 2. It destroys the humility and childlike simplicity so essential to a knowledge of real truth. 3. It is inefficient to cleanse from sin. Science, philosophy, all the learning of all the schools cannot, without Christ's atonement, regenerate sinful man. Give us, then, education; but let it be complete, as far as it goes—moral building up as well as intellectual. Cried Grotius, the eminent historian, on his death-bed : " Ah! I have consumed all my life in a laborious doing of nothing. I would give all my learning and honour for the plain integrity of John Urick "—a poor man of remarkable piety. (*Homiletic Monthly.*) *Resultless study :*—What would be thought of a chemist who should conduct an experiment day after day, making a number of little variations in his method, but always withholding the deciding element from the crucible, or else persistently refusing to look at the result ? Or what would be thought of a merchant always reckoning up his figures, but never writing down the final sums? Or what of a captain who should sail his ship in a circle ? Or of a traveller always on the road, never reaching home or inn? (*A. Raleigh, D.D.*) *Activity without progress :*—Two sailors happened to be on a military parade-ground when the soldiers were at drill, going through the evolution of marking time. One sailor, observing the other watching the movement of the company very attentively, with eyes fixed and arms akimbo, asked him what he thought of it. " Well, Jack," replied his comrade, "I am thinking there must be a pretty strong tide running this morning, for these poor fellows have been pulling away this half-hour, and have not got an inch ahead yet." *No further on the road :*—" How wise I am ! " cried the finger-post to a willow-stump by his side. " Are you ? " said the willow. " Am I ? " indignantly retorted the post. " Do you see my arms ? Are not the name to the great town, and road to it. and distance from it, plainly written there ? " " Ah, yes ! " said the willow. " Then you must acknowledge how superior I am to you. Why ! I am a public teacher." " True, indeed," answered the willow, " and learned you are ; but, as to wisdom, I see little difference between you and me. You know the way to the city, I believe, and are the means of enabling many to find it; but here you have stood these twenty years, and I don't see that you have got a step farther on the road than I have, who don't profess to understand anything about it." (*Original Fables.*)

Vers. 8, 9. **As Jannes and Jambres withstood Moses.**—*Jannes and Jambres :*—I. THE NATURE OF THE OPPOSITION OFFERED BY THESE MEN TO MOSES. You do not find that they tried to make light of the miracles of Moses, or call in question their genuineness, or anything of the sort. No, they simply tried by imitations to depreciate the value of the real. They so surrounded the true diamond with cut glass copies that in the eye of an undiscerning public it was difficult to tell the difference. This is the kind of resistance the Church has to struggle against in the present day. The old, rough, brutal, physical opposition has passed away. It would be folly on the part of Satan to try and use such weapons now. Like a skilful angler he suits the fly on his hook to the season of the year. Variety, if not pleasing, is profitable to him in this respect. Having failed to do away with Christians, he now seeks to make the whole world Christian after his sort. Stamping out the genuine having proved an utter failure, he now seeks to swamp them with imitations of his own manufacture. II. THE INFLUENCE OF JANNES AND JAMBRES. Jannes and Jambres wield an immense power in the present day, and it is no use shutting our eyes to the fact. Jannes is not to be got rid of with a laugh, nor Jambres with a smile of indifference. Their existence is a source of constant danger, and their presence in the professing Church does more to paralyze its testimony than all the outward opposition and persecution it has ever met. This form of Satanic resistance is an awful proof of the deep-sightedness of the great adversary. He knows that nothing can possibly deaden the power of the Church's testimony more than flooding it with a number of cold formalists, who in the eyes of the world can do as much as the genuine Christian. And then when the world detects they are but shams and finds that it has been deceived, so much the better for him, for he knows that the whole Church will be judged by the impostors, and all put down as belonging to the same family. Counterfeits destroy confidence. This is true in everything. It is unprincipled rogues that make it so hard for honest men to get their bread. It is quackery that keeps the true medicine out of the field. It is bubble joint-stock companies that eat out all commercial trust, and make the very name to many a synonym for fraud. Everywhere the true and real are suffering through the influence of the false and base imitations. I have heard an anecdote somewhere that so exactly sets forth the idea I have in my mind I cannot but tell it. One gentleman made a wager with another that if he stood on London Bridge with a tray full of sovereigns and offered them to the public for sixpence each, he would not sell half a dozen of them in the day. All day long the man cried out, "Real sovereigns for sixpence," and declared with all earnestness that he could guarantee their genuineness. Of course no one believed him and he sold none. Why? Because the public had so often seen sham sovereigns for sale that it never doubted they were the same. The gilt having come first had destroyed all faith in the gold. Just so in the spiritual world. The existence of Jannes and Jambres eats out all faith in the reality of any Christian life. III. THE END OF THEIR RESISTANCE. They were put to shame (see Exod. viii. 18). Ah Jannes, it must have been a bitter moment when you stood convicted before all of being an impostor! How complete the collapse of their pretensions. So shall it be with their followers of to-day. This Paul most distinctly states in the verse following our text, "But they shall proceed no further: for their folly shall be manifest unto all men as theirs also was." "Folly"? No other word could better describe their resistance. The hypocrite is of all fools the greatest. He is almost certain to be unmasked in time, and even should he carry on the horrible deception unto the last, what shall it profit him when God calleth for his soul? Now just as Jannes and Jambres failed to do all that Moses did, so there are some things that the mere formalist can never accomplish. I will but mention two. 1. He has no power to bear trouble with joyfulness. His whole life being one of externals, when he is driven by force of circumstances to seek his joy in the life within, he fails, and fails utterly, for there is no life there. A sham Christianity withers up in days of trouble. It has no arms to put beneath a man when the dark waters of sorrow roll and surge around him. No, it can do none of these. It fails like the magicians when needed the most. The "form" may do for bright and sunny days when sorrow and sickness are unknown, but it requires the "power" to triumph in the winter night, and to "take joyfully the spoiling of the goods." Put a Jannes or Jambres amidst a number of anxious souls, and tell him to speak to them and point them the way of peace. See how he fails. 2. If not, I pray you to remember that Jannes and Jambres were included in the doom of the Egyptians. When the angel of death walked through the streets of Egypt, there was no exception made. The form of religion does not save—the appearance of piety is of no avail. (*A. G. Brown.*) *Men must guard against error:*—This must teach us to keep our judgments pure, and our understandings clear, for it is our guide, and if that mislead us, we must needs fall into the ditch. Corruption in judgment (in some respects) is worse than corruption in manners, especially when the mind hath been enlightened with the knowledge of the truth; for this is the root of those corrupt manners that are amongst us. In the time of the Law, the leprosy in the head was of all other leprosies the most dangerous and destructive; the man that had it in his hand or feet was unclean, but if it were in his head then he was to be pronounced utterly unclean (Lev. xiii. 44). Hence the Scripture gives so many caveats against errors and erroneous ones (Deut. xiii. 3; Philip. iii. 2; Col. ii. 8; 2 Pet. iii. 17; Matt. vii. 13). Beware of false prophets; the word implies a diligent study and singular care, lest we be caught by such subtle adversaries. Keep your judgments pure. 1. There have been false teachers in all ages to oppose the truth and the professors of it. As Jannes and Jambres here oppose Moses, a meek, a learned, a faithful servant in all God's house. 2. That as the devil hath his Jannes and Jambres to oppose the truth, so God hath His Moses and Aaron to uphold it. As the devil hath his domestic chaplains, so God hath His armed champions; and as the devil raiseth up oppressors, so God sends saviours. 3. A corrupt head and a corrupt heart usually go together; no sooner are men's minds corrupted, but presently it follows they are reprobate concerning the faith; and if once men make shipwreck of faith, they will soon part with a good conscience too. Corrupt principles breed corrupt practices; and corrupt practices teach men to invent corrupt principles. Be sure, then, to keep your heads free from error, if ever you would have your hearts and hands pure from sin. 4. That false teachers are very dangerous persons—they are not such meek, innocent, harmless persons as some imagine. The apostle here tells us that they are impudent, fraudulent, resisters of the truth, men of corrupt heads, hearts, and hands; and what could he say more unless he should call them devils? and so he doth (ver. 3), in the last days, men, especially seducing men (for all these nineteen sins are applicable also to the false teachers of the last times, as appears by the context (vers. 5, 6). These study to please men, and therefore they are no servants of Christ (Gal. i. 10), all their fine speeches are but like poison given in honey, which destroys more swiftly. They set a gloss upon their false tenets as tradesmen do upon their bad stuffs to make them sell the better. They can cite Scripture to draw you from Scripture, and tempt you to be irreligious by religious arguments misapplied. This is the devil's great masterpiece which he hath now upon the wheel, he carries his deadliest poison in a golden cup (Rev. xvii. 4). 5. They wrest and abuse the Scriptures for their own ends. They do violence to the Law (Zeph. iii. 4), they wrest and wring it, they add, they detract, they change the sense, they set it on the tenters to fit it to their fancies, they turn it this way and that way as may best serve their purposes; they set it on the rack, and so make it speak what it never thought. They compel the Scriptures to go two miles, which of themselves would go but one. They deal with them as chemists do with natural bodies, which they torture to get that out of them which God and nature never put into them (2 Pet. iii. 16). 6. They seek their own glory, not God's. They cry up nature, and decry grace, they cry up a light within them (which is no better than darkness), and cry down God's word without them. Simon Magus sets up himself instead of God (Acts viii. 9, 10), they drive at self in all their actings (Rom. xvi. 18; 2 Pet. ii. 3, 14). Impostors are always great self-seekers. These are contrary to God's faithful ministers. (*T. Hall, B.D.*) *Resistance of the truth:*—1. Its weapons. 2. Its sworn comrades. 3. Its stubbornness. 4. Its final fate. (*Van Oosterzee.*) *Bounds set to spread of error:*—As God set bounds to the sea, saying, Hitherto shall ye come but no further, and here shall thy proud waves be stayed (Job xxxviii. 11), so He limits the malice and madness of men how far they shall prevail; He only can stop these seas of error, and bound these floods of false doctrine which are ready to overflow the face of the world. (*T. Hall, B.D.*) *Deceivers subject to providence of God:*—Our comfort is that both the deceivers and the deceived are ordered by the providence of God (Job xii. 16); He sets down the time when they shall begin, and limits them how long they shall continue, He orders how far men shall deceive, and to what height they shall come and prevail, and when to stop them, that they may proceed no further: for as the maliciousness, so the deceivableness of men would know no bounds if God did not bound it; but because He doth, therefore though they would, yet they shall proceed no further. No man can do good till God assist him, and no man shall do hurt when God will stop him (Rev. xx. 3). (*Ibid.*) *Heresies short-lived:*—Heresies are seldom long-lived—such meteors last not long, such mushrooms soon vanish; witness Becold, Knipperdolling, Phifer, &c. Though for a time they may deceive many, yet in a short time God discovers their hypocrisy to their reproach. (*Ibid.*) *Error vanisheth, truth increaseth :*—Heresy is like a cloud which for a little time darkens the Church, and then vanisheth. But truth, though it meet with opposition at first and hath few followers, yet increaseth and prevails against all opposition. It hath its *plus ultra*, it is perpetual and endures for ever. (*Ibid.*) *Impudent error near its end :*—Pride and impudence, they do not only preach but print their blasphemy: a sign their end is near. Smoke, the higher it riseth the sooner it is scattered (Psa. lxviii. 1, 2). (*Ibid.*) *The fall of error :*—They shall fall—1. Irrecoverably. 2. Easily. 3. Suddenly. 4. Surely. (*Ibid.*) *False teachers exposed :*—Observe, that God will overthrow false teachers, by discovering their coverings and making known their delusions to the world. As a disease discovered is half cured, so an error discovered is half conquered. Usually before God overthrows wicked men He discovers their vileness first, that the glory of His justice may be the more apparent, and His people may come out from amongst them. (*Ibid.*) *A faithful ministry the best safeguard against error :*—When the sun ariseth the clouds scatter, and where the Son of Righteousness is powerfully preached and published, heretics hide themselves, and dare not make that open sale of their wares as they do in dark corners. Let us therefore pull off their masks of liberty, their sleeves of sanctity, and their trappings of hypocrisy: let us expose their error, stripped and naked in their own natural deformity, and they will soon be exploded by all, so that they shall proceed no further. (*Ibid.*) *Error utilised and subjugated at last :*—He is infinitely just, though His ways be secret and full of darkness to us, yet they are always just. When clouds and darkness are round about Him, then righteousness and judgment are the habitation of His throne (Psa. xcvii. 7). He can make a medicine of the poisonous oppositions of wicked men, their malice shall be as horse-leeches to suck out the bad blood, as a file to take off the rust, as rubbish to cleanse the vessel and wash away the filth, and as a touch-stone to try the graces of His children. And though His providences seem to cross His promises, yet wait the conclusion, and you shall see and say He hath done all things well. We see in a clock though the wheels run cross and contrary one to another, yet they all conduce to the going of the clock. Joseph's imprisonment is the way to his preferment, and Jonah's drowning was the means to save him from drowning. We must not judge of God's actions before they be formed and finished. (*Ibid.*) **Their folly shall be manifest unto all.**—*The efficiency of the Divine Government seen in the limitations of wickedness :*—1. This is seen in the manifest folly of sin. Sin is always folly, but this is not always made manifest in the course of human affairs. But God's government is such that, though the folly of sin be not in every case made manifest, it is always made clear that God thwarts the designs of wicked men, no matter how ingenious they may be. Men play the knave, only to show themselves fools. Their deeds ever pass in review before the never-closing eye of Him who holds every destiny in His hand. Under every wise system of government sin is demonstrated to be folly, though it may not always be exposed. 2. One of the declared principles of this effective government is, that crime shall be its own warning. There are earnests of penalties and promises of penalties, no less pronounced, in every-day life, than in the written moral code, the latter to follow us hereafter. The trial and punishment of law-breakers remain unfinished here, though there are generally enough admonitions to associate sin with approaching danger. Owing to the cross-workings of law upon law, here the danger is not so apparent; but the Divine economy marks its criminals before they are arraigned. 3. Sin is often limited by exposure, pain, and special judgments, so that God Himself becomes the greatest restraint. Destruction of Sennacherib's army. 4. Divine grace often limits sin in action. Conversion of Paul. Lessons :—1. If there is a limit to wickedness, and to wicked men, in their course, there must be a limit to individual sins. The believer has to struggle more or less with sin while in this world, but there will be an end of all that conflict. 2. Living under such a government, how unwise to lead wicked lives! 3. The Christian can be faithful and energetic in his work. Sin is sure to fail, and righteousness to succeed. (*W. M. Barbour, D.D.*) *The true nature of scepticism :*—Some time ago I was a little alarmed at the stealthy progress which that accursed system—secularism—was making in Lancashire. But God settled it. God sent us the cotton famine; that settled it: and secularism has never rallied since. When the secularists used to come out to meet us, they said to the people, " Don't listen to these men ; all they want is your money. All their talk is about the next world. They do not care about this. They do not care about your having food, clothes, and healthy homes."

And thus we were taunted everywhere. Then occurred the outbreak of that terrible cotton famine. Where were the secularists then? Like the Arabs of the desert, they folded up their tents and silently stole away. And they who had said it was their special mission to deal with temporalities, forgot all temporalities but their own, and came up to London to lecture upon anything—"admission threepence." (*C. Garrett.*)    *Manifest folly :*—Dr. John Hall, in one of his sermons, compared the attacks of infidelity upon Christianity to a serpent gnawing at a file. As he kept on gnawing, he was greatly encouraged by the sight of the growing pile of chips, till, feeling pain and seeing blood, he found that he had been wearing his own teeth away against the file, but the file was unharmed.    *The folly of opposition to Christ :*—You have heard of the swordfish. It is a very curious creature, with a long and bony beak or sword projecting in front of its head. It is also very fierce, attacking other fishes that come in its way, and trying to pierce them with its sword. The fish has sometimes been known to dart at a ship in full sail with such violence as to pierce the solid timbers. But what has happened? The silly fish has been killed outright by the force of its own blow. The ship sails on just as before, and the angry swordfish falls a victim to its own rage. But how shall we describe the folly of those who oppose the cause of Christ? They cannot succeed ; like the swordfish, they only work their own destruction. (*G. S. Bowes.*)    *Error cannot stand :* —Error is a palace of ice, which at last must melt and tumble down necessarily, when but one ray of the sunlight of truth penetrates it.    (*Van Oosterzee.*)    *The gospel and its enemies :*—Luther heard one day a nightingale singing very sweetly near a pond full of frogs, who, by their croaking, seemed as though they wanted to silence the melodious bird. The Doctor said, "Thus 'tis in the world ; Jesus Christ is the nightingale, making the gospel to be heard ; the heretics and false prophets are the frogs, trying to prevent his being heard." (*Table Talk.*)

Vers. 10, 11. **But thou hast fully known my doctrine, manner of life.**— *Apostolic imitation :*—1. Doctrine. 2. Conversation. 3. Purpose. 4. Faith. 5. Long-suffering. 6. Love. 7. Patience. 8. Persecutions. 9. Afflictions.    (*T. Hall, B.D.*) *Precedents better than precepts :*—Now since we are more easily led by precedents than by precepts, the apostle propounds his own example for our imitation, wherein we have the lively pattern and portraiture of a faithful pastor, whose office it is not only to preach sound doctrine, but also to practise what he preacheth in his own life, that so he may be able to speak from the heart to the hearts of his people, and may not bring his food as birds do to their young ones—in their beaks, not in their breasts. (*Ibid.*)    *The example of superiors powerful :*—In that Paul propounds his own example for Timothy to consider and follow. That the pious example of the godly must be imitated by us. Younger ministers especially must observe the doctrine and conversation, the pious ways and walking of the elder and graver ministers, and must follow them. Aged Paul propounds his virtues to young Timothy for imitation. Many young men praise the gravity, solidity, wisdom, industry, mortification, and self-denial of ancient ministers, but they do not follow them. They deal by them as the world doth by honesty, they praise it, but they never practise it. As Gideon said to his soldiers (Judg. vii. 17), "Look upon me, and do likewise"; so you that are young and unsettled, rash, and conceited, look upon the doctrine, discipline, hair, habit, ways and works of the holy, and the grave; follow them now you are young, and then you will be good long. Great is the power of the example of superiors. (*Ibid.*)    *A copy to write by :*—God hath set them before us as our copy to write by, and our pattern to live by, and we must answer not only for sinning against the light of the word, but against the light of good example also. It will be one day said, "You had such and such to go before you in paths of piety, and yet you would not follow." The faithful are called witnesses (Heb. xii. 1; Rev. xii.). Now if we walk contrary to their light they will witness against us, as Noah and Lot did against the sinners of their age ; but if we walk answerable to their light they will witness for us. Their practice may comfort and confirm us in God's way; they declare the possibility of obtaining such a grace, and make it thereby the more easy, when we have seen it done before us. If a man have a torch to light him in a dark and dangerous path, how glad is he : the godly shine like lights in the midst of a crooked generation (Phil. ii. 15, 16), their life is a commentary on the Scripture. Now since the nature of man is apter to be guided by example then precept, therefore God hath prepared abundance of glorious examples for our imitation, and thus the saints that are now at rest and triumphant in glory, their lives are to be our looking-glasses to dress ouselves by, our compass to sail by, and our pillar of a cloud to walk by. (*Ibid.*) *We must come up to the best patterns :*—We can have no excuse in these days of light if we come not up to the best patterns, because we have more of the spirit, more light, and more clear manifestation of God than they had. (*Ibid.*) *The best patterns defective :*—The saints have had their failings, and the best have a great deal of the old Adam in them. They are pillars of cloud for us to walk by, but this cloud hath its dark part, which if we follow we shall fall as they did. There are four sorts of actions which the Scripture tells us were done by saints. (*Ibid.*) *Both doctrines and graces must be good :*—Our Saviour by the truth of His doctrine proved Himself to be sent of God (John vii. 16, 17, 18, and xii. 49, 50). Paul commands Timothy to keep the pattern of wholesome words (2 Tim. ii. 13), and Titus must be careful in appointing ministers for the Church, to choose such as hold the faithful word (Titus i. 7, 9). Moral virtues may be found with a false faith; let not those apples of Sodom deceive you, for as there may be good doctrine where the life is bad, so there may be false doctrine where the life is seemingly good. Look, therefore, in the first place to the doctrine, and in the second place to the virtues which seem to commend it. So doth Paul here; first he tells you his doctrine was sound, and now he comes to declare his graces, and how he lived. (*Ibid.*) *Patience in ministers :*—A little patience will not do, for we have no little enemies to oppose us—it must be all patience and all strength. This also is a virtue very requisite for a minister, who hath to do with all sorts of men; some are dull, some froward, some weak, some wayward; so that without patience there is no good to be done. It is for pusillanimous spirits to be always murmuring, complaining, and seeking revenge. The weakest creatures are most vindictive. This is an ornament of great worth, not only in the sight of man, but also of God (1 Pet. iii. 4). Without it we are unfit for duty, as the troubled sea unfit for voyage. Without it we double and increase our burthens; like a wild bull in a net, or the untamed heifer, we may gall our necks, but never break the yoke. Without patience no grace is perfect, faith hath but half its strength, and hope is feeble (Jas. i. 4). By our patience we please God, displease the devil, rejoice the angels, and many times melt and convert our enemies. By this means we heap coals of conversion or coals of confusion upon their heads (Rom. xii. 20). This will keep us good in a bad condition, so that a man enjoys himself when he hath nothing else; and though he have nothing, yet is as one that possesseth all things. The consideration of this made Tertullian to cry, " Farewell all, so I may but get patience." (*Ibid.*) *Christian consistency :*—Paul did not pull down by his living what he built up by his preaching. (*M. Henry.*) *Life an eloquent sermon :*—Of Donne's romantic career it has been said that his life is more poetical than his poetry. We might without exaggeration adapt this epigram to his preaching, and say that his life was a sermon more eloquent than all his sermons. If, then, I were asked to describe in few words the secret of his power as a preacher, I should say that it was the contrition and the thanksgiving of the penitent acting upon the sensibility of the poet. (*Bp. Lightfoot.*) *The preaching that tells :*—There is a legend which tells how a saint once in vision saw a band of Franciscan friars standing round Jesus in heaven. He noticed that the lips of each were crimson. He asked the meaning of this, and to him the Lord said, " These are the great preachers of my Cross, for the story of My redeeming love only comes with power over lips that are red with My precious blood." Yes; the preaching that will save preacher and hearers is the preaching that comes from crimson lips. (*British Weekly.*) *The stimulus of example :*—The other evening a gentleman told me that he went into the room where his son was taking lessons in singing, and found the tutor urging the boy to sound a certain note. Every time the lad made the attempt, however, he fell short, and his teacher kept saying to him, " Higher! higher! " but it was all to no purpose until, descending to the tone which the boy was sounding, the musician accompanied him with his own voice, and led him gradually up to that which he desired him to sing; and then he sounded it with ease. (*W. M. Taylor, D.D.*)

> " Example is a living law, whose sway
> Men more than all the written laws obey."
> (*Old Poet.*)

Example is the school of mankind, and they will learn at no other. (*Burke.*) *The power of a godly life :*—" Whenever I read Scripture, a thousand atheistical thoughts were injected in my soul. . . . Being in Mr. T. H.'s house, a godly and prudent man, his company did me much good . . . For the universal carnality of professors, with their discouragements, living so short of their principles, did much help forward my atheism, as it made me think that a saint was but a fancy; but truly I thought mine eyes saw something of a saint and New Testament spirit in him, and was something persuaded, by feeling his holiness, his cheerfulness in God, and his deep reach in spiritual mysteries, that there was a God, and a holiness attainable." (*Life of James Fraser of Brea.*)    *Cassock and character:*—I like that remark of Whitfield's, when some one of a bad character wondered how he could preach without a cassock. "Ah," he said, "I can preach without a cassock, but I cannot preach without a character." (*C. H. Spurgeon.*)   *Paul's path of suffering:*—The path of suffering of the apostle Paul a revelation—1. Of the power of sin which pursued him. 2. Of the greater power of faith which sustained him. 3. Of the omnipotence of the Lord who delivered him out of all. (*Van Oosterzee.*) *Commands should be enforced by example:*—During the siege of Sebastopol Gordon was one day going the round of the trenches when he heard an angry altercation between a corporal and a sapper. On inquiring the cause, he learnt that the men were instructed to place some gabions on the battery, and that the corporal had ordered the sapper to stand on the parapet, where he would be exposed to the enemy's fire, and to place the gabions, while he, perfectly sheltered, handed them up from below. Gordon at once jumped upon the parapet, ordering the corporal to join him, while the sapper handed them the gabions. When the work was done, and done under the fire of the watchful Russian gunners, Gordon turned to the corporal and said, "Never order a man to do anything that you are afraid to do yourself." *Wicked men hate the good:*—All wicked men hate the good, as all wolves do the sheep. (*T. Hall, B.D.*)   *Persecution beneficial:*—Such shakings make way for Christ (Hag. ii. 7). The Church, like a quick-set hedge, grows the thicker for cutting, this vine is the better for bleeding, and this torch burns the better for beating. The more Pharaoh oppressed the Israelites the more they increased (Exod. i. 12). (*Ibid.*)   *Deliverances to be noted:*—Not only our dangers, but also our deliverances must be observed and recorded by us. (*Ibid.*)

Ver. 12. **All that will live godly in Christ Jesus shall suffer persecution.**—*A Christian is not a favourite with the world:*—Who can help admiring the frankness of Scripture ? It shows us the difficulties as well as the enjoyments of religion; the sacrifices it requires, as well as the rewards it insures. This is perfectly just, and in every way profitable. I. THE LIFE DESCRIBED. It may be taken with two distinctions. 1. It is not merely a moral life, but a godly one. We by no means depreciate morality. A man cannot be religious without being moral, but he may be moral without being religious. It is well to be a good master, a good neighbour, a good subject—but how are you disposed towards God ? 2. It is not merely a godly life, but a Christian one. We are not only to live godly, but to live godly " in Christ Jesus ; " *i.e.*, in all our religious concerns—To be governed by the revelation of Jesus Christ—To be conformed to the example of Jesus Christ—To be actuated by the grace of Jesus Christ—And to depend on the mediation of Jesus Christ. II. THE CONDITION ANNOUNCED AS THE CONSEQUENCE OF THE LIFE DESCRIBED. " Shall suffer persecution." 1. That ever since the Fall there has been an irreconcilable enmity between the " seed of the woman and the seed of the serpent "; that " man being alienated from the life of God," loves nothing that reminds him of God ; that the tempers and actions of the righteous necessarily reprove and upbraid the wicked ; that their endeavours to save disturb them in their sins; that the gospel condemns the worldly as well as the vicious, and the formal as well as the negligent ; that, as there is nothing in Christianity that flatters sin, so there is nothing that flatters self; and that every man is naturally as self-righteous as he is depraved. 2. To this we may add another source of the inevitableness of persecution. It is taken from the Christian himself. Suffering is necessary for his trial and his triumph. Without this how could he prove that he loves God better than friendship, reputation, wealth, or life? How could he over-come evil with good ? It is warfare that makes a good soldier. A Christian is like the firmament, and it is the darkness of affliction that makes his starry graces to shine out. He is like those herbs and plants that best effuse their odours when bruised. Concluding reflections:—1. There are some who suffer persecution that do not live godly in Christ Jesus. The people of the world cannot easily distinguish between " the form of godliness and the power," and therefore the pretending and the sincere frequently fare alike. The hypocrite loses heaven for the sake of earth, and earth for the sake of heaven, and is of all creatures the most miserable. 2. With what caution and prayer should we assume a profession of religion! 3. If any man suffer as a Christian, let him not be ashamed, but let him glorify God on this behalf. It gives you an opportunity to prove your thankfulness for His goodness, and your adherence to His gospel. 4. But what shall we say to persecutors? If you feel enmity against the godly, and would injure them were it in your power, it is "a token of perdition." You may now be placed above them in circumstances; and may love to misrepresent and to vilify them. But "their Redeemer is mighty." He is "near that justifieth them." He "will plead their cause." He that "toucheth them, toucheth the apple of His eye." (W. Jay.) Persecution of Christians by the world:—The greater part of our sufferings are not distinguishable from the common afflictions of life; and many of the trials that some foolish professors frequently charge on religion, religion would teach them to avoid, if its admonitions were regarded. But, on the other hand, it must be allowed—1. That human nature is essentially the same in every age; and that a tiger may be chained and not changed. Under every form of government "the heart is deceitful above all things, and desperately wicked." And where there is a strong active propensity against anything (as, in this case, there must be against real godliness), it will show itself as opportunity offers; and such opportunity there must be in a world like this. 2. That persecution admits of various degrees. It includes every kind of injury or vexation, from a fiery stake to a scornful sneer. How often has genuine religion produced the loss of friendship, or chilled the warmth of attachment into cold civility! Where power is possessed, it is frequently exerted as far as safety or a regard to appearances will allow. This is seen in the attempts of husbands, parents, and masters, to restrain from following their religious convictions their wives, their children, and their servants. With regard to relations, a Christian will sometimes find a greater trial in their affections than in their frowns. Here is a mother, in all other respects tender and kind; she takes her daughter aside, and weeps to think she should favour a doctrine "everywhere spoken against." 3. If modern Christians frequently escape persecution, may it not be asked whether, in many instances, it does not arise from their less fully exemplifying the spirit of their religion than the primitive Christians did? (1) The one is concealment. This is dastardly and mean. We should never be drawn out of a corner by the praise of man, nor be driven into a corner by the fear of man. (2) The other is accommodation. And it is awful to think how one doctrine and usage after another has been given up! Christianity, says one, will never be received by Jews and Mahometans, while you "honour the Son as you honour the Father." It will never be acceptable, says another, to men of taste and learning, till you abandon the barbarous notion of the atonement and of original sin. Now, upon this plan, what would be left after all the objectors were satisfied? Christianity allows of no alteration. It needs none. The change required therefore is, where it ought to be—in the world. (W. Jay.) A good man a good mark for the arrow:—The better the man, the sooner persecuted; the devil shoots his arrows at the whitest marks. (T. Hall, B.D.) A good man a miracle of preservation:—It is a miracle of mercy to consider how the lily subsists in the midst of so many briars and thorns, how the Lord's wheat grows in the midst of so many tares, how His doves live in the midst of so many birds of prey, and His lambs in the midst of so many roaring lions. Were not the Almighty her defence, those bands of ungodliness would soon destroy her. (Ibid.) God honoured by His suffering servants:—Hereby we honour God, and so bring honour to ourselves. God hath much honour by His suffering servants, when out of love to Him they can sacrifice their lives and estates for Him. God glories in such; as He suffers in their sufferings so He triumphs in their conquests. (Ibid.) Best when worst:—God is pleased to reserve the sweetest manifestations from the bitterest afflictions. The fountain runs most sweetly when the cistern is broken. When comforts are most needed they will be most prized. The traveller in summer, when the sun shines, casts off his cloak, but in winter, or when the wind blows hard, he wraps it closer to him. So when we bathe ourselves in creature comforts we value not the promises of God, but when we are stripped of all then we look after God. When the salt waters are dried up, then there are fresh springs in God. (Ibid.) The good man happy in adversity, the bad man miserable in prosperity:—See the happiness of a child of God. Take him at worst, and he is better than a wicked man at best. The one in prosperity hath no joy, the other in adversity is full of joy. (Ibid.) Brave martyrdom:—At Perth, in 1554, there were three male prisoners and one woman—Helen Stirk—

put to death for their adherence to the gospel of Jesus. The latter was taken to see her husband suffer before she followed him. They embraced under the gallows. "Husband," she said, " we have lived together many joyful days; but this day in which we must die ought to be most joyful to us both, because we must have joy for ever. Therefore I will not bid you good-night. Certainly we shall meet again in the kingdom of heaven." The executioners seized their prey, and she, too, was then led away to be drowned. When she reached the water's edge she gave the child to a nurse, she was hurled in, and the justice of the Church was satisfied.

Ver. 13. **But evil men and seducers shall wax worse.**—*Graduating in ungodliness:*—1. If we consider wicked men as they are in themselves, they are all strongly bent to apostasy; every day they grow worse and worse. As godly men are graduates in God's school, growing from strength to strength, and from one degree of grace unto another, till they become perfect men in Christ, every sermon makes them better, and every ordinance improves them. So wicked men are graduates also, and take degrees in the devil's school; they stand not at a stay, but they grow from evil to worse. As he that is righteous will go on and be more righteous, so he that is filthy will go on in his filthiness (Rev. xxii. 11). It is the proper character of wicked men that they fall away more and more (Isa. i. 5; Prov. i. 22). 2. But secondly, let us consider them specifically and divisively for such evil men as are deceivers and impostors, and these we see experimentally grow worse and worse. They have no foundation to rest on; they know no stay when once they have passed the bounds of the word, no more than a violent stream doth when it hath broke over those bounds and bonds which before kept it in. Error knows no end; when once men forsake the way of truth they wander *in infinitum*. As it is in logic, grant one absurdity and I will infer a thousand, and as sin begets sin, blood toucheth blood, and one murder begets another (Hos. iv. 2). So error is very fertile and prolific; it speedily brings forth a great increase. One error is a bridge to another; ill weeds spring apace and spread far, when good herbs grow thin and low. A little of this leaven will quickly sour the whole lump (Matt. xvi. 6). When once men begin to tumble down the hill of error they seldom rest till they come to the bottom. (*T. Hall, B.D.*) *Deceiving others and being deceived in turn:*—They cozen others, and the devil cozens them, leading them into far greater errors; and so they shall be punished on a double account. 1. Because they err themselves and resist the truth. 2. Because they have drawn others into error. The participle of the present tense notes their assiduity and constancy; they make it their trade to deceive others: they are still deceiving one or other with their smooth, flattering language. As God loves to employ good men for the conversion of others (not that He needs the help of man, but), for the exercising of the graces of His servants, and for the greater manifestation of His own glory, so the devil, who is God's ape, loves to deceive men by men. He hath his agents and emissaries everywhere. As good men delight in converting others, so wicked men delight in perverting others; as those would not go to heaven alone, so these would not go to hell alone: and therefore they labour to make others twofold more the children of the devil than themselves. (*Ibid.*) *Satan the great deceiver:*—As thieves when they would rob a man draw him aside out of the highway into some wood, and then cut his throat, so this grand deceiver and his agents draw men aside from the right way of God's worship into some bypaths of error to their ruin. The devil he is the cheater of cheaters, and deluder of deluders; it is his constant trade, as the participle implies. And this is the reason why many false teachers may die with boldness and courage for their opinions, viz., because they are blinded and deluded by the devil; they think themselves martyrs, when they are grand deceivers and grossly deceived. We had need, therefore, to pray for the Spirit of grace and illumination that we may see the methods, depths, and devices of Satan and avoid them. (*Ibid.*) *Worse and worse:*—Things alter for the worse spontaneously, if they be not altered for the better designedly. (*Bacon.*) *Being deceived:*—A man may tell a lie till he believes it to be the truth. (*J. C. Gray.*) *Self-deception:*—Mr. Robert Sutcliffe, a member of the Society of Friends, travelling in America early in the present century, had a tough argument with a man engaged in the slave trade, of whom he says: " At length, being hard pressed, he gave up the point in a good deal of warmth, with this remarkable declaration : " Why, sir, you can't suppose that the Almighty looks so narrowly into our actions as you do." (*Leisure Hour.*) *Changed by sin:*—Allowed sin always masters a man in time. The man may loathe his master, yet he obeys him; he may fear his

master, yet still he does his hateful bidding. But there is here an awful warning
as to the sure change of the very being of a man under the once invited presence
and the permitted occupation of the forces of evil. The man himself changes—
imperceptibly at first to himself—others see it. He is often unaware of it himself,
till the last stages are reached. It must be so—there must be a change. If you
think there is no such thing as standing still in life—in spiritual, in natural life.
As the solid tower reels and sways beneath the crashing of the ringing bells, so there
is movement even in the most solid, calm-seeming life. (*Canon Wilberforce.*)
*Development of evil:*—Secular history tells us that when Tiberius (Luke iii. 1)
became emperor of Rome, he was remarkable for his kindness, amiability, and
moderation. But he became one of the most wicked and cruel of tyrants. Nero,
too, was so affable and kind in early life, that he was quite popular at the beginning
of his reign; but he afterwards caused his mother, his wife, his old tutor Seneca,
with multitudes of Christians and others, to be put to death, many of them in
excessively cruel ways; and he was guilty of such other enormities, that his
people at length conspired against him, when, to escape their malice, he killed
himself in the thirty-first year of his age. Robespierre, "the tyrant," and the
leading spirit during "the reign of terror" in Paris, through whom thousands
of both his friends and foes were slaughtered or subjected to the greatest cruelties,
was, in private and early life, amiable and kind. He once, when young, resigned
his situation as a member of a criminal court, because he had such an objection
to the barbarity of capital punishment, which he characterised as "base assassi-
nation." The devil and his angels, Cain, Henry Wainwright, &c., show to what
evil an immortal spirit may fall. Wherefore avoid bad company, give up evil or
doubtful habits, get God's restraining, converting, and preserving grace. (*H. R.
Burton.*)    *Productivity of sin:*—Referring to the terrible productivity of sin,
Mr. Varley once mentioned that when in Tasmania, he had heard of a snake
recently killed there which had given birth to thirty-seven young ones. "But,"
said he, quoting Joseph Cook, "sin is an eternal mother." *Progressiveness of sin:*—
A gentleman was walking with a friend one day through his beautiful grounds,
when they came to a fine large tree which was decayed to the very core. "That
tree," said the proprietor, "was destroyed by a single worm. A short time
since it was as vigorous as any of its companions, when one day a wood-
worm was discovered forcing its way under the outer bark. A naturalist who
was at that time my guest remarked on seeing it that if left alone it would
ultimately kill the tree. It seemed so improbable, that the worm was suffered
to remain. Gradually it bored its way into the fibre of the tree, slowly but
surely doing its work. The following summer the tree shed its leaves much
earlier than usual, and in the second season it was a dead, worthless thing.
The worm which seemed so very insignificant had found its way to the heart
of the once noble tree and destroyed its life." How forcibly do we see this
same thing illustrated in the common walks of every-day life. A young man is
persuaded by his companions to take his first glass of wine. It seems like a
little thing, but it is the beginning of a course of degradation and eternal shame.
The clerk in the bank appropriates a few shillings of the funds entrusted to his
care. One step leads to another, until at last he is arrested and cast into prison
as a defaulter. A boy begins to practise little deceits at school or at home
which, unless discovered and checked, will make him a base and unprincipled
man. Such is the destructive power of little sins when the continued indulgence
in them is practised.

Vers. 14, 15. **Continue thou in the things which thou hast learned.**—*Service must be
constant and faithful:*—God's servants must continue constant in the truth received.
They must not play fast and loose, be off and on; but they must be still the same,
like well-tuned bells, which have the same note in foul weather as they have in
fair (Job. i. 21), we must hold fast the truth (1 Thess. v. 21), abide in it and walk
in it (Rev. iii. 3). 1. This constancy is a note of sincerity, then are we Christ's
disciples indeed, when we abide in the truth (John viii. 32; Job. ii. 3), when no
storms nor tempests can remove us from it, but we stand like Mount Sion, which
never moves, and, like seasoned timber, never warps nor yields. 2. All the promises
of heaven and happiness run only to such as are faithful to the death (Rev. ii. 10),
endure to the end (Matt. xxiv. 13), and continue in faith (Rom. ii. 7; Matt. x. 22;
Col. i. 22, 23; Heb. iii. 6, 14). 3. Lay a good foundation, dig deep; he that will
build high, must lay low. Our learning doth not hinder but further the work of

the Spirit in our souls. Timothy, that had a plentiful measure of the Spirit (for he was an Evangelist), yet must give himself to reading and meditation still. As Moses was faithful, and would not part with a hoof to Pharaoh, so we must not part with a tittle of God's truth to His enemies ; for all truths, even the least, are precious ; truth is like gold, which is glorious in the ray and spangle, as well as in the wedge. As it is in practicals, he that makes no conscience of little sins, will quickly be drawn to greater ; so it is true, and holds in doctrinals, he that admits of a little error, will soon be drawn to a greater. Though every truth be not funda-mental, yet every truth is a guard to the foundation, the outer skin of an apple lies remote from the heart, yet if you pluck that off the heart will soon be rotten. The finger is not a vital part, but a gangrene in the finger will, in a short time, reach to the very vitals and corrupt the blood with the spirits. Not only the garment of truth, but the fringes thereof are useful, and must be preserved (Num. xv. 38–40). We experimentally see that those who forsake truth, in discipline, quickly fall to errors in doctrine. We shall hardly find a man that errs in the one, to be found in the other. As therefore we must count no sin small, so we must esteem no error small ; for the least truth of God's kingdom doth in its place uphold the whole kingdom of His truth. 4. If you preserve the truth it will preserve you in the hour of temptation, as Solomon says of wisdom (Prov. iv. 8). 5. It is a great honour to a person or nation to be the conservators and preservers of the truths of God. It is not only our duty, but our glory. There are many spiritual cheaters abroad ; the greater will our honour be in maintaining God's truth against them all. Say not I am but one, and a weak one too, but remember what great things the Lord did by Athanasius and Luther. (*T. Hall, B.D.*) *The excellency of the teacher makes the doctrine the more taking :*—This we see even in human and moral learning, the Platonic doctrine grew famous because it was professed by Socrates, and the Peripatetic by Aristotle. The scholars of Pythagoras did so confide in the dictates of their master, that when any one asked them a reason of what they held, they would give no other answer but " Our master said so." Young ministers should suspect their own judgments when they vary from a holy, aged Calvin Beza, and all the churches of God. As young lawyers and physicians observe the principles and practices of the serious and grave professors of their way, especially when grounded on maxims and rules of art, so should young divines. It ill becomes a young raw physician to contradict a whole college of physicians, or a puny lawyer a bench of judges, or a young divine a whole assembly of divines. (*Ibid.*) *Continuance in the faith :*—I. The things in which we are to continue. 1. We must learn those things in which we are to continue. 2. The things in which we are commanded to continue are the things of which we have been assured. II. In what respects we are to continue in them. 1. We must continue in the belief of them. 2. We must continue to profess that truth which we believe. 3. We must continue in the practical improvement of the truth. What is the chaff to the wheat ? Such is every other doctrine to the doctrine of the Bible ; and its energy and effects are proportioned to its excellency, when it is received with faith and love. (*G. Lawson, D.D.*) *The necessity of correct belief :*—Comprehensively, we may say that there are two things to be noticed in this passage : first, that the proper use and end of all religious know-ledge is the promotion of good conduct and character ; and, secondly, that there is a definite and important relation between certain truths and certain moral results. The same fruits will not follow as well from one set of principles as from another. Right belief has much to do with right conduct. Believing is the basis of all instruc-tion and education. Every parent, every teacher, every moralist, as well as every preacher of righteousness, holds that human life and conduct will largely depend upon the things that men are taught to believe. There has sprung up a popular notion that it makes no difference what a man believes concerning religion if only he be sincere. There is just enough truth in the phrase, in some of its applications, to make it plausible, and to give it currency. And so it has come to be a proverb. When it is said, " It matters little what a man's creed is if his life be right," if it meant, " It matters little what a man's headknowledge is, so that he is sound in his heart," and by sincerity is intended, not sincerity in belief, but sincerity in life or godliness, a great truth is expressed—a truth that is not enough recog-nised. In education it is of great importance what sort of truth you employ, for some kinds of teaching are a great deal more likely to produce godliness than others. But, whatever the teaching has been, if the man is a good man, however strange it may appear that such a creed should have such a disciple, however far he may be from the average results which ordinarily follow the teaching of such things as he believes, his godliness is to be acknowledged in spite of the beliefs. There are thousands that are not half as good as they ought to be, considering the things that they believe. A man's creed does not necessarily make him good. And there are thousands that are better than their creeds. But generally this maxim does not mean sincerity of life in the form of godliness; it means that it does not matter what a man believes, so that he only believes it sincerely. The first question then, that arises, is this: What are we to understand by a man's belief? Do we understand by it simply those things of which he has an intellectual conception? Do *they* amount to a belief? Truth that touches a man not merely through a cold perception, but through some warm feeling—that is the kind of truth the Scripture teaches to constitute belief. It may be intellectually conceived; but no moral truth and no social truth is ever presented so as to be believed, unless it be presented in such a way as to carry sympathy and feeling with it—and that is not the case with all kinds of truth. Physical truths, scientific truths, do not touch the feelings, and do not need to. Arithmetic deals with truths that have no relation directly, except with the understanding. They never come with desire, sorrow, pity, or emotion of any sort. But all truths that relate to dispositions in men, to moral duties—they never stop with the understanding, but touch the feeling as well. A man cannot be said to believe a moral truth unless he believes it so that he carries some emotion with it. And, in this respect, it makes great difference what a man believes. Let us, then, look at this a little in the light of the experience of men in this world. In regard to the truths of the physical economy of the globe, does it make any difference what a man believes? Would it make any difference to a machinist whether he thought lead was as good for tools as steel? Would it make any difference to a man in respect to the industries of life if he thought that a triangle was as good as a circular wheel in machinery? In respect to the quality of substances, the forms of substances, the combination of substances, and the nature of motive powers, does success depend upon *sincere* believing or on *right* believing? Suppose a man should think that it made no difference what he believed, and should say to himself, "I wish to raise corn, but I have not the seed; so I will take some ashes and plant them; and I believe sincerely that they are as good as corn," would he have a crop of corn? What would his sincerity avail? Take one thing further. There are affectional and social truths. Does it make no difference what a man believes in respect to these? Is there no difference between pride, vanity, and selfishness on the one hand, and tenderness, sympathy, and love on the other? As it is with the lower forms of moral truth, so experience teaches us it is with the higher forms of moral truth. There is a definite and heaven-appointed connection between the things a man holds to be true, and the results that follow in that man's mind. All truths are not alike important, and all truths do not show the effects of being believed or rejected with equal rapidity. There are many truths which bear such a relation to our every-day life, that the fruit of believing or rejecting appears almost at once. These are spring truths, that come up and bear fruit early in the season. There are other truths that require time for working out their results. They are summer truths, and the fruit of belief or disbelief does not ripen till July or August. Other truths, in respect to showing the results of belief or disbelief, are like late autumnal fruits, that require the whole winter to develop their proper juices. Thus it is a matter of great importance whether a man believes in his obligation to God or not; whether he believes that he is sinful or not; whether he believes in the necessity of the influence of the Spirit in regeneration. A man's belief is not the only thing that works upon him. There is a great mistake in saying that as a man believes so is he, if you mean that his character depends upon his belief in any technical theological truth. What a man is depends in a great measure upon his father and mother, and brothers and sisters, and friends; that is, it depends partly on the things that he believes, and partly upon the influences that are working upon him in the family, in the society, and in the party to which he belongs. There are a thousand and one circumstances that have much to do with what a man is; and his character is not formed alone by his technical beliefs. Let us apply the foregoing reasonings and explanations to the more important truths which we are appointed to preach. We preach, then, that this life is a very transient scene; that we are strangers and pilgrims here; that we are started here to be transplanted; that we are undergoing a process of education in this life with reference to a life to come. We are taught in the Word of God that all men are sin-struck, and that every man that lives needs the grace, and forbearance, and forgiveness of God, and moral renovation at the hands of God. If a man believes that he is good enough, of course he becomes listless, and heedless, and inattentive. If another man by his side believes that he is sinful, and needs to be born again, with what a constantly quickened and watchful conscience must he needs live! and how, with all his moral power, must he perpetually strive to live a godly life! Does it make no difference what a man believes in respect to the character of God, the nature of the Divine government in this world, its claims upon us, and our obligations under it? What, then, is the application, finally, of this? It is just this: that, according to the tenour of the passage from which our text is taken, it makes all the difference in the world which you believe in respect to those truths that are connected with godliness—with purity of thought, purity of motive, purity of disposition. You must believe right about them. If there are any truths to be indifferent about, they are those that relate to your worldly good; and if there are any truths that you cannot afford to be indifferent about, they are those that relate to your character, to your immortality, and to the eternity that awaits you. Indeed, your character and destiny depend upon your beliefs in truth. If, then, any of you have hitherto been reading the Word of God as a book of curiosity, I beseech you remember that it is not made known to you for the purpose of curiosity. It is made known to you to be your guide from sin, from sorrow, from earthly trouble, toward immortality, and toward glory. Now when I sit in my house, where there is no gale, and with no ship, and read my chart out of curiosity, I read it as you sometimes read your Bible. You say, " Here is the headland of depravity; and there is a lighthouse—born again; and here is the channel of duty." And yet every one of you has charge of a ship—the human soul. Evil passions are fierce winds that are driving it. This Bible is God's chart for you to steer by, to keep you from the bottom of the sea, and to show you where the harbour is, and how to reach it without running on rocks or bars. It is the book of life; it is the book of everlasting life; so take heed how to read it. In reading it, see that you have the truth, and not the mere semblance of it. You cannot live without it. (*H. W. Beecher.*) *Value of personal conviction :*—Without this subjective conviction of the heart, it would not have been possible for Timothy to hold out in the things he had learned, amid so many persecutions. (*Van Oosterzee.*) *Continue :*—The capital word in this injunction is doubtless " continue." Timothy's teachers had been his grandmother Lois, his mother Eunice, and the apostle Paul himself. From his childhood he had been taught in the Scriptures, and now the apostle urges him to remain steadfast in his early teaching. But was such an exhortation consistent with the greater light that would come to the young learner as he grew older and increased in knowledge? Might he not have occasion to change his beliefs, to revise his creed, as he made intellectual advancement? Let us see if he was right. What relation should subsist between " the things learned " and the increasing light of greater knowledge? It should be kept in mind that, notwithstanding much shifting of positions in human thought, the essence of religion remains unchanged; it is fundamentally the same. There are those who seem to think that greater light will revolutionise all our beliefs, and that therefore it is folly to cling so tenaciously to the old orthodox positions in religion or anything else. Suppose for a moment that this were true. Then there could be no certainty, no assurance. We should not dare to pin our faith to anything in religion or science or common sense. Even those mathematical truths that have been so confidently held as axioms would stand on an insecure foundation, for who knows that further research might not shatter them, and raze to the ground the proud superstructure? Besides, these progressive thinkers themselves, who advocate certain theories with so much gusto, are guilty of folly; for, according to their own hypothesis, new light may change their beliefs, and prove them but the phantoms of a day. Do you see where this theory, that all our knowledge is in a fluctuating state, subject to constant change, will land us? In the harbour of nowhere? Let those who will sail for that port. Many of us prefer a definite destination after the voyage of life is over, and a more reliable guiding star while it lasts. But let us look around us for analogies. Are there not many things that abide amid all changes? The zephyrs still blow softly on the blushing cheek, the storm still howls, the stars still twinkle, the waves still roll and dash upon the shore, men still breathe and eat and sleep and love, as they did in the olden times; that is, the fundamental things continue. And the like is true of the principles of Christianity; amid all fluctuations " the foundation of God standeth sure," and we still have " hope as an anchor of the soul, both sure and steadfast." (*Christian Globe.*) *Things learnt at school :*—

1. First among these special lessons of a public school, I will place the value of time. I know not how to express my sense of what we all owe to what I may call a life of compulsory order. Every little duty of the day has, with us, its place and its time. 2. I will mention as one of the lessons of a place like this, the forming a right estimate of yourselves. It is one of the greatest benefits of this kind of education, that it leaves you in no doubt as to your comparative powers and attainments. Be not presumptuous, be not arrogant, be not self-confident. Take a just, not a fanciful, estimate of yourselves, both ways. 3. A third important lesson learned here is, the necessity and the power of adapting yourselves to a variety of persons and circumstances. 4. A fourth lesson here learned is the meaning of a social as opposed to a selfish life. 5. There is a fifth thing taught here, as it can scarcely be but by a system of public education, and that is the great lesson of the consequences of actions. 6. All these things are true, and capable of much enforcement, but I hasten to that chief lesson of all, without which all else would be poor indeed —I mean, the Divine aspect of life; its relation to God Himself through Christ, as our present help, our one hope and object, the very stay and strength and life of our life. That surely is the meaning of all our meetings for worship. (*Dean Vaughan.*)    *Continue in the things learnt :*—What are the things that you have learnt—what are the lessons that I would write upon your hearts in letters that the fire of experience shall bring to the light? 1. The dignity of work. Try to realise how much you owe to the labours of others who have gone before you, and try to labour for others in your turn. Do not be mere triflers and spendthrifts. Lay one stone, if it be one only, in the temple of human progress. Seek to learn something and to do something that is good. 2. The sovereignty of conscience. The age in which we live is democratic. "Vox populi vox Dei" is its watchword. Let me warn you against that great and fruitful error. There is no Divinity in numbers. God reveals Himself not to the many, but to the few. The greatest crime ever wrought was wrought by one who desired to do the people's pleasure. You may sympathise with the people as much as you like, you may hold it right that the will of the people should be done; but nothing that the people say or do can alter by one hair's breadth the law of right and wrong for you. 3. The duty of philanthropy. Every generation has its own duties and responsibilities. Nobody can tell why certain questions arise at a particular time and come to the fore; it is God's will. And there can be no doubt that the distinguishing duty of your generation will be to soften and hallow the lives of the toiling poor. 4. How shall you do this? What shall be your motive power in this great work? It shall be the fourth—the last—of the principles which I have impressed upon you, and which I leave with you as a legacy of remembrance—the paramount value of religion. "I thank God," said Lord Russell on the scaffold—"I thank God for having given me a religious education; for even when I forgot it most, it still hung about me and gave me checks." May it be so with you! May religion be your guide, controlling, inspiring, leading you ever to a higher and diviner life! (*J. E. C. Welldon, M.A.*) *Paul's charge to Timothy :*—Yield to the influence of authority in doctrine and life. "But continue thou in the things which thou hast heard and hast been assured of, knowing of whom thou hast learned them." This advice is strangely unlike what we are accustomed to hear. Our time is impatient of authority. "The new Timothy" is exhorted to be perfectly unbiassed in the formation of his religious opinions. He must go back to the sources of things, if he can; if he cannot, he must improvise opinions, and thereafter be his own authority. Unverified personal impressions, and conclusions hastily reached, are better than the testimony of the wisest and most faithful witnesses touching the doctrines and duties and experiences of Christ's religion. To Paul it seemed far otherwise. He would have Timothy strongly biassed in favour of the teaching which he received in youth, by the Christian character of those who taught him. Grandmother Lois and mother Eunice gave the testimony of experts. They knew whereof they affirmed. Religion was not to them a matter of opinion merely, it was a life. Their faith was "unfeigned." It had power to rule their lives. Why should not their teachings take on an authoritative quality from their lives? The limits of authority must be carefully set. Discriminations must be made. "Profane and old wives' fables" must be avoided. But the authoritative teaching of a holy life is not to be disregarded because unholy lives assume to be authoritative. Mental freedom is to be coveted; but the freedom which assumes that each age must begin anew the study of the "ways of God" with men is too great. (*Monday Club Sermons.*)    **From a child thou hast known the Holy Scriptures.**—*The Holy Scriptures :*—So here

what a large encomium and high commendation the Holy Ghost gives of the Scriptures, even such as is given to no other book in the world besides. 1. He commends them in respect of one special property and adjunct, viz., their holiness. The holy Scriptures. 2. From their effects: they are able to make us wise unto salvation. 3. From their authority, utility, perfection. Now the Scriptures are called holy in five respects. 1. In respect of their Author and principal cause— viz., the most holy God. 2. In respect of the penmen and instrumental cause: they were holy men of God (2 Pet. i. 21). 3. In respect of their matter: they treat of the holy things of God; they teach nothing that is impure or profane. They teach us holiness in doctrine and practice. 4. In respect of their end and effect— viz., our sanctification (John xvii. 17). By reading, hearing, and meditating on God's Word the Holy Ghost doth sanctify us (Psalm xix. 8,·9). 5. By way of distinction and opposition; they are called holy to distinguish them not only from human and profane, but also from all ecclesiastical writings. 1. This must teach us to bring pure minds to the reading, hearing, and handling of God's holy Word. 2. Take heed of profaning the holy Scriptures by playing with them, or making jests out of them. 3. Love the Scriptures for their purity; as God is to be loved for His purity, so is His Word. Many love it for the history, or for novelty, but a gracious soul loves it for its purity, because it arms him against sin, directs him in God's ways, enables him for duty, discovers to him the snares of sin and Satan, and so makes him wiser than his enemies. The Word of God alone is able to make us wise unto salvation (Psa. xix. 7; Luke xvi. 28, 19; John v. 39, and xx. 31; James i. 22, 25). No other knowledge can bring us to salvation, but only the knowledge of the holy Scripture. The Word of God cannot save nor profit us without faith. Such is our blindness, deadness, dulness, yea, enmity against the Word, that without faith we cannot see, conceive, or receive it (1 Cor. ii. 14; Rom. i. 16; Heb. iv. 2; John iii. 19, 20). If a man offer us never so good an alms, yet unless we have an eye to see it, with a hand and heart to receive it, we are never the better for the tender of it. 1. Observe. Parents ought to instruct their children betimes in the Word of God. It is good seasoning the vessel betimes with goodness. It is a singular mercy to have good parents, and specially a good mother, for she being much about her children hath many opportunities of dropping good things into her little Lemuels, as Bathsheba did into Solomon (Proverbs xxxi. 1). The mothers of the kings of Israel are constantly mentioned, and as they were good or evil, so were their children. But at what age would you have parents begin to teach their children? So soon as ever they begin to learn wickedness, we should teach them goodness; so soon as ever they begin to curse and swear, we should teach them to bless and pray. There are many reasons why youth should be seasoned betimes with good principles. 1. In respect of that natural rudeness and ignorance which cleaves so close unto them (Eccles. iii. 18; Job. xi. 12; Jeremiah iv. 22, and x. 14). We are all by nature like wild ass colts, unteachable, untractable. 2. The Lord oft blesses this seasoning in ˉyouth with good success. 3. It is usually blessed with continuance and perseverance; such as are good young are oft good long; what the vessel is first seasoned withal it will have a taste of it a long time after. 4. This is an excellent means to propagate goodness to posterity. As we see here, Timothy's grandmother teacheth his mother, and his mother teacheth him, and he teacheth the Church of God, &c. So if you teach your children, they will teach their children, and thou mayest be a means to propagate God's truth and honour from one generation to another. So that you may comfort yourselves when you come to die that yet your piety shall not die, but shall survive in your posterity, who shall stand up in your stead to profess God's name and truth before a sinful world. 5. Such well-bred and timely-taught children are usually great comforts and ornaments to their parents (Proverbs xxiii. 15, 16, 24, 25), as we see in Abel, Joseph, Samuel, Josiah (2 Chron. xxxiv. 3), Obadiah (1 Kings xviii. 18, 12), David, Daniel, Jeremy. 6. Children are the seminary and nursery of the Church and commonwealth; now, as our seminaries and seed-plots are, such is the nation; as the parents, house, and school are, such are towns and cities. 7. Youth is most teachable and tractable, like soft wax or clay fit to be formed and framed to anything, ready to take any impression. Like a tender twig you may bend it which way you please, but let it grow to be a tree, and you may sooner break it than bend it. We should therefore take this fit season of seasoning youth betimes with saving truths, and killing the weeds of sin which begin to appear in their lives. No creature so wild but it may be tamed if taken whilst young. We see those that would teach or tame horses, lions, hawks, dogs, bears, they begin with them betimes; the horse is broken whilst a colt, and the lion tamed whilst it is a whelp, &c. As in the Ark there was the rod and manna, so in every well-ordered family there must be the manna of instruction and the rod of correction. It must stir up young persons to devote the flower and best of their days unto God, who is the best of beings. Show me any that can show better title to thy youth than God can do, and let him take it. He gives the best wages, and so deserves the best work; godliness hath the promise (Prov. xxii. 4; Matt. vi. 33; 1 Tim. iv. 8). And if we serve Him in our good days, He will help us in our evil ones; if we spend our youth in His service, He will support us and supply us in our old age (Isa. xlvi. 3, 4). If it were in our power, yet we may in no wise deal so disingenuously with our God as to give the devil the marrow of our youth, and reserve the dry bones of our old age for God. It is no wisdom to lay the greatest load on the weakest horse. Old age (though in itself it be a blessing) yet is accompanied with many troubles, sicknesses, and diseases; they are the dregs, the lees, the winter of our days. As all rivers meet in the sea, so all diseases meet in old age—hence it is called the evil day (Eccles. xii. 3–5), &c. Then the eyes grow dim, the ears deaf, the hands tremble, and the legs are feeble, and the memory fails. (*T. Hall, B.D.*) *Religion in youth :*—1. It is more easy; anything taken when it is young is more easily wrought upon. A twig is easily bent; a disease taken in the beginning is easily cured, when everything by delay grows worse. When the fingers are grown stiff, it is ill learning to play on the lute. An old disease is hardly cured. The longer a tree grows, the harder it is to pull up. The further a nail is driven, the harder it is to pull it out again. The acting of sin strengthens the habit, and when sin is become habitual, connatural, and customary, it is hardly cured (Jer. xiii. 23; Isa. xxvi. 10). 2. It is more fruitful; we shall do more good, and receive more good; to him that hath shall be given. We shall bring forth much penitential fruit, which will bring much glory to God, and in glorifying Him lieth our glory (Job xv. 8). Suppose a man should never repent till he were old and ready to die; though such a man may be saved, yet his graces are not so conspicuous, nor can he do that good, nor bring that glory to God as a young man that begins betimes to serve Him. It is a thrifty course to be an early convert; the sooner we submit to the Spirit's conduct the better, the more peace and liberty we shall attain. 3. It is more beautiful and lovely. Everything is beautiful in its season (Eccles. iii. 11); now God's usual season for repentance is when we are young. 4. We shall resemble the servants of God; all their obedience hath been prompt and speedy. They are endued with the wisdom which is from above, which is easily entreated to any goodness. 5. Consider the shortness and uncertainty of our days. It is a notable spur to speedy repentance; for as presumption of long life doth harden men, so realising of death, and looking on it as present, doth quicken and awaken men. Now our life in Scripture is compared to a span that is soon measured (Psa. xxxix. 5); to a tale that is soon told (Psa. xc. 9); to a vapour that quickly vanisheth (James iv. 14); like a flower that soon fades (Isa. xl. 6–8; Job. xiv. 2; Psa. cii. 11, and ciii. 15; James i. 10; 1 Pet. i. 24); like a post or a weaver's shuttle that fly speedily (Job. vii. 6, and ix. 25). 6. The seasons of grace are short; time itself is short; but opportunity is much shorter. Every day in the year is not a fair day, and every day in the week is not a market day. Grace is not every day's offer, and therefore we should walk in the light whilst we have the light. 7. In this we may learn wisdom from the men of the world. The smith strikes whilst his iron is hot; the husbandman makes hay whilst the sun shines. The mariner observes his wind and tide, the lawyer his terms, the chapman his fairs and markets, and the gardener his seasons. Yea, shall the stork, the crane, and the swallow know the time of their coming, and shall we not know the day of our visitation? (Jer. viii. 7). Doth the bee lose no fair day, and doth the ant in summer provide for winter? (Prov. vi. 8). And shall not we in the summer of youth provide for the winter of old age? 8. Neglecting the day of our visitation increaseth wrath, and provokes the Lord to cut off young persons in the flower of their days. If a man should every day be adding sticks to the fire, and oil to the flame, it must needs make the fire very terrible at last. (*Ibid.*) *The Christian education of the young :*—1. "FROM A CHILD THOU HAST KNOWN THE HOLY SCRIPTURES." That must have been a privilege of no slight importance in the estimation of Paul, which he considered worthy of peculiar mention, at such a time, and in his dying charge to his most beloved friend and companion. And when Timothy himself traced back the course of his life to his earlier years—when the memory of those youthful days rose upon his melting mind, as he perused the apostle's touching allusion, he too would most readily acknowledge the gracious hand of providence in having thus blessed him with the inestimable advantages of an early religious education. Men, who deem themselves philosophers, may sneer at the knowledge of a child, and the piety of a child, thinking it impossible that childhood can intelligently either know or love God. How soon can it comprehend the meaning of a father's authoritative and commanding frown, or the checking and controlling, yet affectionate smile of a mother! And, by the very simple process of combining these perceptions, and comparing in order to elevate them, how soon it may be taught to form some idea of a Being whose authoritative laws are similar, though vastly superior, to those of a father, and yet whose surpassing love, infinitely transcending that of a mother, shall endure when hers may have waxed cold, or waned utterly away, or been hid behind the darkness of the tomb! II. CONSIDER WHAT IS THE ADVANTAGE OF BEING TRAINED TO KNOW THE HOLY SCRIPTURES. This Paul declares to be, that they are able to make us wise unto salvation. It might be shown, had we at present scope for the investigation, that the wisdom of the world is wholly ineffectual for accomplishing the moral regeneration of man; nay, effectual only, or at least chiefly, in cultivating and enlarging his capacity of evil. It is the knowledge of the holy Scriptures, and that alone, which can make men wise unto salvation. Results so strikingly different must proceed from originating principles not less diametrically opposed. Let us, therefore, briefly examine some of the leading principles of the wisdom of the world, marking the contrast between them and those of the Scriptures. Now, the main intention of the world's wisdom is, to fit men for living on this earth; that of the Scriptures, to prepare them for heaven. Plans constructed upon such very different principles, and for such very different ends, begin to diverge at their very commencement. The world trains children to a similarity with itself—with its pride, its luxury, its self-indulgence, its vanity, and its self-approbation; the Scripture principle is, " the nurture and admonition of the Lord," self-denial, humility, acknowledgment of sin, and dependence upon God alone for help. The world inculcates the love of gain, as a ruling object; the Bible declares that " the love of money is the root of all evil." The world is loud in its praises of those who acquire advancement and distinction in life; Christianity teaches us to be content with such things as we have, threatens the fall of the mighty and the proud, and pronounces a blessing upon the meek, the lowly, and the humble. The world allows, nay, inculcates, selfishness; Christianity bids us seek not our own welfare only, but also that of others. The world approves a bold, contentious spirit, as one likely to force its jostling way through all opposition; Scripture says, " The servant of the Lord must not strive." The world allows dissimulation, selfish delusion, petty fraud, and all the thousand knaveries of common life and business; Christianity requires that the whole life and conduct should be characterised by the very transparency of truth, as ever in the presence of the God of truth and holiness. III. We come now TO OFFER SOME REMARKS ON THE PRINCIPLE OF THIS SAVING WISDOM—that by which it is accomplished, viz., "Through faith which is in Christ Jesus." (*W. M. Hetherington, M.A.*) *Knowledge of Bible in youth:*—David Livingstone gained a New Testament in the Sabbath school when nine years old by repeating the 119th Psalm on two successive evenings with only five errors. (*W. G. Blaikie.*)　　*John Wesley's estimate of the Bible:*—I am a creature of a day, passing through life as an arrow through the air. I am a spirit, coming from God, and returning to God: just hovering over the great gulf; a few moments hence, I am no more seen; I drop into an unchangeable eternity! I want to know one thing; the way to heaven; how to land safe on that happy shore. God Himself has condescended to teach the way. He hath written it down in a book. Oh, give me that book! At any price, give me the book of God! I have it: here is knowledge enough for me. Let me be a man of one book. Here, then, I am, far from the busy ways of men. I sit down alone; only God is here. In His presence I open, I read His book; for this end—to find the way to heaven. *The Bible and the family:*—One evening a man, who resided in Southwark, attended a missionary's meeting for the special purpose of lauding Paine and Voltaire as writers whose moral sentiments surpassed in beauty anything of the kind found in the Bible. What this objector to the gospel had to say was listened to with deference, and then he was asked if ever he had read the volume he contemned. Yes, he had read the Bible in common with other books. "Have you a family?" asked the missionary who was presiding over the little assembly. Yes, the speaker possessed a wife and little ones. Which, then, would he recommend to them—the life-companion who was dear to him and the children whom he loved—

Infidelity or Christianity? The company may have looked curiously to see what shape the infidel's answer would assume, but they could little have suspected what its import would be. What was their astonishment when the champion of unbelief of a few minutes before burst into tears, and then cried, " I never heard that kind of argument before. I would rather give them the Bible than any infidel book." (*G. H. Pike.*)   *The Bible and the light of God :*—Lord Byron and Mr. Hobhouse explored together a cavern in Greece. They lost themselves in its abysses, and the guide confessed in alarm that he knew not how to recover the outlet. They roved in a state of despair from cave to cell. They climbed up narrow apertures, but found no way of escape. Their last torch was consuming ; they were totally ignorant of their whereabouts, and all around was darkness. By chance they discerned through the gloom what proved to be a ray of light gleaming towards them. They hastened to follow it and arrived at the mouth of the cave. Would that all the torches which are blinding men to the light of God would burn out, and that speedily ! Blessed be darkness and despair if through them men discern the beams which shine from heaven and reveal salvation. (*H. Batchelor.*)   *Education of the young :*—A lady was once talking with an archbishop upon the subject of juvenile education, and, after some time, the lady said, " Well, my lord archbishop, as for myself, I have made up my mind never to put my child under religious instruction until he has arrived at years of discretion." He replied, " If you neglect your child all that time, the devil will not." *Early and lasting impressions :*—In our great museums you see stone slabs with the marks of rain that fell hundreds of years before Adam lived, and the footprint of some wild bird that passed across the beach in those olden times. The passing shower and the light foot left their prints on the soft sediment ; then ages went on, and it has hardened into stone ; and there they remain, and will remain for evermore. That is like a man's spirit ; in the childish days so soft, so susceptible to all impressions, so joyous to receive new ideas, treasuring them all up, gathering them all into itself, retaining them all for ever. (*A. Maclaren, D.D.*)   **Which are able to make thee wise unto salvation.**—*The Scriptures and Christ :*—Christ is the central theme of the Bible's prophecies. The hope of Christ echoes through its Psalms. Every page gains new meaning when brought into relation with Christ. In the great lighthouses along our coast reflectors of immense power are placed around the lamps. They are composed sometimes of as many as a thousand pieces of highly polished crystal. Each of these sends out its own image of the central light. All combine to form the refulgent beam that shines a score of miles across the sea. So from each separate part of the Bible Christ is in some way reflected, and when we recognise Him throughout, it is all bright with interest and truth. *The saving use of the Bible :*—There are many people to whom the Bible does not amount to much. If they merely look at the outside beauty, why, it will no more lead them to Christ than the Koran of Mahomet, or Washington's farewell address, or the Shaster of the Hindoos. It is the inward light of God's Word you must get or die. I came up to the Church of the Madeleine, in Paris, and looked at the doors, which were the most wonderfully constructed I ever saw, and I could have stayed there for a whole week ; but I had only a little time, so having glanced at the wonderful carving on the doors, I passed in, and looked at the radiant altars and the sculptured dome. Alas, that so many stop at the outside door of God's holy Word, looking at the rhetorical beauties, instead of going in and looking at the altars of sacrifice, and the dome of God's mercy and salvation that hovers over every penitent and believing soul. Oh, my friends, if you merely want to study the laws of language, do not go to the Bible. It was not made for that. Take " Howe's Elements of Criticism "—it will be better than the Bible for that. If you want to study metaphysics, better than the Bible will be the writings of William Hamilton. But if you want to know how to have sin pardoned, and at last to gain the blessedness of heaven, search the Scriptures, " for in them ye have eternal life." (*T. De Witt Talmage, D.D.*)   *Wise unto salvation through faith :*—The addition is remarkable. St. Paul's experience had taught him that without that faith the study of the sacred writings might lead only to endless questionings and logomachies. Targums and the Talmud remain as if to show how profitless such a study might become. (*E. H. Plumptre, D.D.*)   *The faith-torch :*—Faith in Christ is, as it were, a torch, by the light of which we can first read aright and understand the dim colonnades and mysterious inscriptions in the ancient venerable temple of the Old Covenant. (*Van Oosterzee.*)   *Wise unto salvation :*—I. THAT THE SCRIPTURES ARE ABLE TO MAKE WISE UNTO SALVATION. The Scriptures do, indeed, contain the truth that makes wise to salvation, but it is "by faith that is in Christ Jesus." It is when the Scriptures are believed, when they are received in the love of them, that man becomes a partaker of a blessing. Here it may be said, what strange language!—believe the Scriptures!—why, we always believed them! Those who utter such observations may imagine they believe, but they never believed "faith worketh by love"—"faith purifies the heart"—"faith overcomes the world"—faith is not a fancy—faith is not something floating through the mind of man, but it is of the operation of God. If, then, a man is careless about his soul, he does not believe; if he thinks more highly of the testimony of the world than he does of the testimony of his God, he does not believe; if he depends on his own poor doings, and makes them the ground of his hope, he does not believe; "for other foundation can no man lay than that which is laid, Christ Jesus." If a man neglects the various relative duties of life, and spends his time and money in satisfying in any way the lusts and desires of his flesh, that man, whatever he may be, or whatever he may say, does not believe. II. THAT TIMOTHY WAS INSTRUCTED IN THESE SCRIPTURES FROM HIS YOUTH. Here we have a direct answer given to those who would withhold from the young the book of God. No man of sense, or common understanding, or ordinary feeling, would withhold a medicine from his sick child, in consequence of that child being unable to ascertain the nature of the medicine, or calculate the effect of its operation. (*P. Roe, M.A.*) *The blessedness of children Scripturally taught:*—I. WHAT THE HOLY SCRIPTURES CAN DO. "Make thee wise unto salvation." Exceedingly high praise: can be affirmed of no other book. Were the Bible a book to teach men the art of becoming rich, many would read it who now refuse; all "that will be rich" would then study their Bibles as diligently as their ledgers. If it taught men to be philosophers, another class would read it more than they commonly do. If it were a mere road book, many would consult it who now do not as they pursue the road of life. But the Bible proposes to make men rich towards God, wise unto salvation, pilgrims on the way to heaven. It teaches the best means of attaining the best end; and that is true wisdom. II. HOW THE HOLY SCRIPTURES PRODUCE SUCH GREAT EFFECTS. "Through faith which is in Christ Jesus." The Scriptures do not work as a kind of charm. It is not by having the Bible in the house, nor in the school, nor in the church; but it is by having the Bible in the heart, its contents heard, read, marked, learned, and inwardly digested—that they make us "wise unto salvation through faith which is in Christ Jesus." The infidel can read them and scoff; the poet can read them and only admire their sublimity; the historical student can consult them only as ancient records; the formalist can read them just to get through a certain stated portion; yea, wicked persons have read them for bad purposes—to copy the sins which the Scriptures hold up to abhorrence. Of all such it may be said that the Word preached or read "did not profit them, not being mixed with faith in them that heard it." The Word profits when we hear as Lydia heard, "whose heart the Lord opened, that she attended unto the things which were spoken of Paul." Therefore the study of the Scripture should always be connected with prayer for Divine grace. III. THE ADVANTAGE OF KNOWING THE HOLY SCRIPTURES, IF POSSIBLE, EVEN FROM EARLY YOUTH. "From a child"; there is the time when Scriptural instruction should begin. The word here rendered "child," denotes childhood in its infantile stage. To early education, blessed of God in His own time and way, the Church has owed some of her greatest ornaments. Augustin, who made a noble stand for the gospel in the fifth century, always attributed his conversion to the prayers, the tears, and the instructions of his mother, Monica. God, in fact, appears to have remarkably honoured Christian mothers, whether they stood singly, or were supported in their endeavours to imbue their children's minds with Holy Scripture. Dr. Doddridge, one of the most eminently pious men among the Nonconformists in this country, used to relate that his mother taught him the histories of the Old and New Testament before he could read, by the aid of some Dutch tiles in the chimney of the room where they usually sat; and her religious instructions were the means of making good impressions upon his mind that were never obliterated. (*J. Hambleton, M.A.*) *First duty of parents:*—1. Paul found Timothy, in their earliest acquaintance, a person who, though young in years, was fitted to enter the world in situations of great trust and confidence. 2. Paul had to think of Timothy, whilst employed in the onerous duties of his vocation, as one whose bodily constitution was sickly, and hence as one who was liable to severe illness or early death. 3. Paul had to experience the contemplation of being shortly separated from Timothy, having before his own eyes the certain prospect of martyrdom. Yet, in all his reflections, arising from the various circumstances attending his connection with this beloved disciple, one sufficient consolation filled St. Paul's affectionate heart. He knew that Timothy, even from his childhood, had known the Holy Scriptures; and this knowledge relieved him from all apprehension and anxious pain about his beloved friend. He could confidently trust him in the world; he could bear to lose him out of it; and he could with comfort leave him in it, when his own expected death arrived. And you who have children of your own, or are in any way entrusted with the guardianship of the young, will find that those three cases which I have cited concerning Paul and Timothy, may minutely represent your connection with the rising members of the human family. 1. In the first place, many a parent's heart is often anxiously burdened with a conviction that soon the world must be opened to a son or a daughter; that the veil of domestic virtue and innocence, which has hitherto screened these children's eyes from a sight of the vanity and wickedness which exist in the highway of life, must be rent asunder; and that the allurements of pleasure, the fascinations of sin, the temptations of gain, the suggestions of ambition, will all assail their inexperienced feelings, with a force to which their own natural inclinations will only lend congenial aid; and this will be so, even with those who have been most carefully and religiously trained. How, then, are parents to defend their offspring, and how are the young to be secured from the corrupting influence of the ordeal through which, in entering the world, these inexperienced ones must necessarily pass? Shall they be supplied with money, to save them from the thirst of gain, when it will give them the means also of indulging in sinful pleasure? Shall they be highly educated, and taught all that the accumulated learning of the philosopher has discovered, when this may fill the head without cleansing one affection of a naturally depraved heart? Shall they be shut out from the world, when the devil has already taken possession of them in those bosom lusts and appetites which human flesh and spirit universally inherit along with breath? All these resources, and all which are like unto them, are useless, vain, and idle; and the only effectual fortification against the seductions of this world, which it is the duty of all men to enter and purify by a good example, is that Divine knowledge acquired in childhood, which Timothy, when a child, had been taught by a holy mother. Armed with this instruction, the parent may trust his child to the duties of life; and youth may boldly go into the world, to bless and be blessed by contact with its evil influences, to which he will neither conform nor yield. 2. It is the sad lot of many parents to see, in the early life of those for whom a mother's pangs have been borne, the blighting shadow of infirmity, or the ravages of violent disease, appear, with ominous warning that sickness and death are no respecters of age. Even in the contemplation of a sickly or a dying child, there is a consolatory reaction from the grief which the spectacle presents, if father and mother can then conscientiously feel that, even from a child, their dear one had known the Holy Scriptures, whatever else they might have omitted in their instructions; and that whether renewed health come, or death carry off their treasure, they have thus made their young one wise unto salvation, through faith which is in Christ Jesus. 3. Parents constantly have the prospect before them of separation, by their own deaths, from those who, naturally, owe their lives to them. It were well, therefore, that they should make provision for this day of consternation and account. To leave riches without righteousness is the poorest of all inheritances; and poverty, though accompanied by patience and decency, will be no excuse for the want of that holiness which springeth only of faith. Happy only, therefore, can be the death of that parent, be he rich or poor, high or low, who can say, with his last breath, to each of his offspring, "From a child thou hast known the Holy Scriptures." (*A. Gatty, M.A.*)    *Wisdom unto salvation :*—(To children.) I am going to say something to you to-day about Timothy, and something about the knowledge which, St. Paul says, Timothy had from childhood. "That the soul be without knowledge, it is not good." All knowledge is good, but the knowledge of the Holy Scriptures is the best; for the Holy Scriptures are able to do for us what all other things are not able to do—to make us "wise unto salvation." How is it that man manages the wind, the water, the steam, the lightning, though once he was a little babe, knowing nothing and able to do nothing? Just because he gets knowledge and wisdom; by knowledge and by wisdom he can do all these things. If you get knowledge, and by knowledge wisdom, you may become like angels; but if you get knowledge and do not use it rightly, if you do not fear God and serve Him, if you lie, and steal, do you think you will be like angels? Oh! there are a great many children brought up to be wise in this world, but the greater number are allowed to be foolish. God says, "Wisdom is the principal thing, therefore get wisdom," get it at any price, and do not part with it for anything. Remember, wisdom is of two kinds—wisdom for this world, and wisdom for the world to come. We have a short life here, but we will have a long eternity there. We have a very nice world here, but there is a beautiful world there. Timothy had wisdom for this world, and wisdom for the other world, too. Children, the way to be wise with the wisdom that is from God is to know the Scripture ; the other wisdom will teach you about this world : how to get food for the body, which comes out of the ground ; clothes for the body, they come out of the ground ; a house for the body, and that comes out of the ground ; how to get money, and it comes out of the ground. Look up ; your treasure is above, not in the ground. The wisdom for this world we get out of the works of God ; the wisdom for the next world we get out of the Word of God. The wisdom from the Word of God teaches us how to get bread for the soul—that is Jesus—raiment for the soul, shelter for the soul. All these we have in Jesus Christ ; and this we know, and Jesus we know, by the Scriptures. So, then, the way to be wise unto salvation is to know the Scriptures. In order to understand the Scriptures we must have a new heart, and when we have a new heart we become wise unto salvation. The Scriptures make us " wise unto salvation," because they tell us what salvation is, and where salvation is. And where is it, children ? I know where the light is—it is in the sun ; I know where the water is—it is in the ocean ; I know where nourishment is—it is in food. But salvation, which is the best thing, and the sweetest thing, is not in the sun nor in the ocean, is not in the moon nor in the stars. Where—where is it ?—in what place can we find it ? There is nothing so good, nothing so great, nothing so lasting, nothing so enriching as salvation. Those who get it will never suffer, never sin, never sorrow, never die. This salvation is a grand thing ! with it, you will be rich ; without it, you will be poor. It will make you like God in holiness and happiness. Oh ! salvation!—where is it ? It is in Jesus. I remember reading about a little boy who went to sea. One night a great storm arose, and the storm lifted up the waves very high, and the wind raged, so that the sails were torn ; the masts were carried away, and the ship was tossed about like a cork on the waters ; and then a great wave came and dashed the ship upon the rocks, and every one on board, big and little—all, all—went like a stone to the bottom ! Two or three days after the body of a boy was found lying on the shore. He was in a sailor's dress ; and when they searched his clothes they felt something hard in his bosom. It was a Bible ! with the name of the Sunday-school where he got it, and the name of the teacher who gave it to him written in it ; and the book had marks of being much read. Children, if that boy loved that book, and read it ; if he knew Jesus and loved Him, though the night was dark and the sea was stormy, he had light in his mind and peace in his heart ; and he has now a life that will never end, and a treasure that will never be spent. Though his body was dashed on the wild shore, his spirit will be with God in heaven for ever. Millions of such children are waiting in heaven for the morning of the resurrection, when they will get their bodies out of their little graves, and Jesus will change them, and make them like His own glorious body, and they shall live and reign with Him for ever and ever. Would it not be a sad thing if any of you who are now hearing about Jesus should be lost ! His blood can wash you; His Spirit can sanctify you. Go to Him—trust in Him—or you will perish. (*J. Gregg, D.D.*) *The sufficiency of Holy Scripture :*—I. The glorious purpose which God intended Holy Scripture to accomplish. To " make them wise." The very statement of such an object is fitted to commend the book that is to accomplish it to our appreciation and our love. What is there, that can be compared with wisdom ? It is the greatest acquisition that immortal man can make. But to be made wise " unto salvation " must be the supreme end and aim of all wisdom, worthy of the name. For if man be pregnant with immortality, to have meetness for heaven must be the chief end of man during the days of his pilgrimage here below. Salvation " through Christ Jesus." The end so glorious, how sure and simple the way ! " Faith which is in Christ Jesus." II. The sufficiency of Holy Scripture to accomplish this glorious object. " Inspiration of God " : have you weighed the expression ? What thanks we owe to our gracious Father, that He has not left us an imperfect, mutilated, shifting, and uncertain standard, but has given us a standard that in itself remains complete and unchangeable as His own eternal throne ! III. The fitness of Holy Scripture to accomplish that purpose even in one of the little lambs of the flock of Christ. The Word of God is of all the books that the world contains the most suited to a child's mind and a child's heart. " I thank Thee, O Father, Lord of heaven and earth, that Thou hast hid these things from the wise and prudent, and hast revealed them unto babes; even so Father, for so it seemed good in Thy sight." (*H. Stowell, M.A.*)     *The gift of the Scriptures, and how it should be improved :—* I. WHAT YOU OWE TO THE SCRIPTURES IN A WAY OF PRIVILEGE. Is truth valuable?—they are called "the Word of truth." Is righteousness valuable?—they are called "the Word of righteousness." Is grace valuable?—they are called "the Word of His grace." Is life valuable?—they are called "the Word of life." Is salvation valuable?—they are called "the Word of this salvation." 1. Let us view these Scriptures as inspired. They claim no less a pre-eminence for themselves. And how delightful is it, in a world of uncertainties, conjectures, and errors, to find something concerning which we may say, Well, this is truth, upon which we may rely secure. "Heaven and earth shall pass away, but My words shall not pass away." 2. Let us view these Scriptures as preserved. 3. Let us view these Scriptures as translated. The first translation of the Scriptures was the Septuagint, executed by a number of learned men at Alexandria, who translated the Scriptures of the Old Testament into Greek. This was peculiarly overruled by the providence of God. Alexander, by his victories and dominion, was the means of spreading the knowledge of the Greek language, and thus the Scriptures could be easily read; and thus an expectation was commonly entertained of a future Messiah and Benefactor. The New Testament was, also, soon translated into several languages; but it was a long time before the Bible was translated into our own language. When Elizabeth came to the throne, by an act of grace she opened the prisons, and a number of the citizens addressed her, thanking her for her generosity; but ventured piously and ingeniously to say, "May it please your Majesty, there are four very excellent and worthy men who have been denied to walk abroad in the English tongue—Matthew, Mark, Luke, and John"; and from that time they have been allowed to walk at liberty, and to speak to you in your own tongue, in public and private, of the wonderful works of God. 4. Let us view these Scriptures as printed. A certain writer says, when London Bridge was first built, a copy of the Scriptures would cost nearly as much as one of the arches; and the whole of a labourer's work through life would not have been sufficient to have furnished him with a copy! How is it now? Now, you see, by means of this invention, they may be multiplied to any degree; and every family, yea, every individual, may be in possession of a Bible, either by donation or by easy purchase. 5. Let us view the Scriptures as expounded. Now we owe much to many of those who have thus written. 6. Let us view the Scriptures as preached. Nothing in the communication of knowledge has ever yet been found like a living address from man to man. Nothing can produce so much impression and effect. 7. Let us view the Scriptures as experienced. There are many who have the Scriptures without them, but not in them. There are many who have the Scriptures in their own country, in their churches, in their houses, in their hands, and some of them even in their mouths, but not in their hearts. But there are others to whom they are as a "well of water, springing up into everlasting life." II. WHAT YOU OWE TO THE SCRIPTURES IN A WAY OF DUTY. 1. Surely you owe nothing less than to peruse them, and to value them, as David did. He said, "I rejoice at Thy Word as those who find great spoil." "I esteem the words of Thy mouth," says Job, "more than my necessary food." And, says David, "The law of Thy mouth is better unto me than thousands of gold and silver." And what said the celebrated Robert Boyle?—"I would prefer a single twig of the tree of life to all the riches of the world." But let it be remembered that the Scriptures will not profit unless they are "mixed with faith in them that hear them." 2. What less can this duty be than to understand them. 3. Surely this duty cannot be less than the practising of what the Scriptures teach. "If ye know these things, happy are ye if ye do them": and even "faith, without works, is dead, being alone." We read of "obeying the truth," and of "walking in the truth." 4. Surely this duty cannot include less than your distributing them. The Scriptures were designed for all. The Scriptures are not given you as a blessing only to enjoy, but as a talent, also, to employ. (*W. Jay.*)     *The Sunday-school and the Scriptures :—*I. The work of God's grace in Timothy COMMENCED WITH EARLY INSTRUCTION—"From a child thou hast known the Holy Scriptures." 1. Note the time for instruction. The expression, "from a child," might be better understood if we read it, "from a very child"; or, as the Revised Version has it, "from a babe." Babes receive impressions long before we are aware of the fact. A special vantage-ground is lost when even babyhood is left uncultured. The Holy Scripture may be learned by children as soon as they are capable of understanding anything. It is a very remarkable fact, which I have heard asserted by many teachers, that children will learn to read out of the Bible better than from any other book. I scarcely know why : it may, perhaps, be on account of the simplicity of the language ; but I believe it is so. A Biblical fact will often be grasped when an incident of common history is forgotten. There is an adaptation in the Bible for human beings of all ages, and therefore it has a fitness for children. Give us the first seven years of a child, with God's grace, and we may defy the world, the flesh, and the devil to ruin that immortal soul. 2. It is well to note the admirable selection of instructors. We are not at a loss to tell who instructed youthful Timothy. "When I call to remembrance the unfeigned faith that is in thee, which dwelt first in thy grandmother Lois, and thy mother Eunice ; and I am persuaded that in thee also." Nowadays, since the world has in it, alas ! so few of Christian mothers and grandmothers, the Church has thought it wise to supplement the instruction of home by teaching held under her fostering wing. I regard this as a very blessed institution. 3. Note the subject of the instruction. "From a child thou hast known the Holy Scriptures " : he was lead to treat the book of God with great reverence. I lay stress upon that word " *Holy* Scriptures." One of the first objects of the Sabbath-school should be to teach the children great reverence for these holy writings, these inspired Scriptures. The Jews esteemed the Old Testament beyond all price ; and though unfortunately many of them fell into a superstitious reverence for the letter and lost the spirit of it, yet were they much to be commended for their profound regard to the holy oracles. Especially is this feeling of reverence needed nowadays. Observe that Timothy was taught, not only to reverence holy things in general, but especially to know the Scriptures. Suppose we get the children together on Sabbath days, and then amuse them and make the hours to pass away pleasantly ; or instruct them, as we do in the week-days, in the elements of a moral education, what have we done? We have done nothing worthy of the day, or of the Church of God. 4. Once more upon this point : it appears that young Timothy was so taught as a child that the teaching was effectual. "Thou hast known the Holy Scriptures," says Paul. II. That this work was QUICKENED BY A SAVING FAITH. The Scriptures do not save, but they are able to make a man wise unto salvation. Children may know the Scriptures, and yet not be children of God. 1. Faith in Jesus Christ is that grace which brings immediate salvation. Many children are called of God so early that they cannot precisely tell when they were converted. You could not have told this morning, by observation, the moment when the sun rose, but it did rise ; and there was a time when it was below the horizon, and another time when it had risen above it. The moment, whether we see it or not, in which a child is really saved, is when he believes in the Lord Jesus Christ. 2. Notice, that by this faith in Christ Jesus we continue and advance in salvation. The moment we believe in Christ we are saved ; but we are not at once as wise as we may be, and hope to be. 3. Observe, that the text gives us a plain intimation that by faith knowledge is turned into wisdom. Exceedingly practical is the difference between knowledge and wisdom. See it in the text. " Knowledge is power," but wisdom is the application of that power to practical ends. Knowledge may be bullion, but wisdom is the minted gold, fit for circulation among men. 4. Learn yet again, that faith finds her wisdom in the use of knowledge conferred by the Scriptures. Faith never finds her wisdom in the thoughts of men, nor in pretended revelations ; but she resorts to the inspired writings for her guidance. This is the well from which she drinks, the manna on which she feeds. Faith takes the Lord Jesus to be her wisdom. The knowledge of Christ is to her the most excellent of the sciences. III. That sound instruction in Holy Scripture, when quickened by a living faith, CREATES A SOLID CHARACTER. The man who from a child has known the Holy Scriptures, when he obtains faith in Christ will be grounded and settled upon the abiding principles of the unchanging Word of God. IV. As this early teaching creates a fine solid character, so will it PRODUCE GREAT USEFULNESS. (*C. H. Spurgeon.*) *True Wisdom :*—The apostle here refers to the Old Testament Scriptures ; showing that there was no want of conformity, but the reverse, between those Scriptures and the doctrines he had preached. What advantage had the Jew? Chiefly that to him belonged the oracles of God. It was a great privilege which Timothy in his childhood had—that he could read, and did read, the holy writings : a great privilege, in like manner, it is, that the entire Bible, the canon in its complete state, with the superaddition of the New Testament, is given " to us and to our children, and to all that are afar off, and to as many as the Lord our God shall call." I. THE HOLY WRITINGS. Will you mark the force and emphasis of the word ? It is not the print ; it is the " writings." The Scriptures then were not produced by types and blocks, by the modern mode of producing copies; each copy was written by the hand of man. But it is very delightful to reflect that the exact transcript, the pure and spotless copy of the things written down by the hand of Moses and David, and Isaiah, and John, and St. Paul have come down in their clearness and certainty to us. We know what the writings are to which St. Paul specifically and in this chapter exclusively refers. The Book of Genesis—the details of the fall, and the deluge, and the call of Abraham; Exodus—the emancipation from Egypt and the Decalogue; Leviticus—the laws and ordinances of the Levitical Church; Numbers—their movements and acts; Deuteronomy—a reiteration, or going over again; Joshua—the pictures of the conquest; Judges—the early difficulties and confusions; Samuel—the development of the regal character, the examples and achievements of Saul and David; and so on, through the historical books, to the Psalms and the prophets. In relation to all these we are certain that we have the exact copies, because the Jews preserved them with an unsurpassed care and vigilance, with an interest and a concern which amounted even to superstition. In addition to these, as I have said, we have as the holy writings the four Gospels, the facts of our Lord's life and death and resurrection—the Acts of the Apostles, the early triumph of the faith—the Epistles, opening doctrine, enforcing precepts, explaining ordinances—and to put the crown and diadem upon the head, as it were, of the entire person, the whole body of revelation, that great and marvellous book called the Revelation. Wonderful writings! An amazing richness and extent and vastness and variety and plenitude of truth and fact, of history and prophecy, of doctrine, of knowledge and of wisdom, opened and poured forth from these gushing fountains. But "*holy* writings." Mark that word: "holy," as emanating directly from God, as being the fruit and product of immediate and miraculous inspiration. And we have the strong affirmation, "All Scripture is given by inspiration of God, and is profitable for doctrine, for reproof, for correction, for instruction in righteousness, that the man of God may be perfect, throughly furnished unto all good works." And in this sense, of an immediate dictation from Heaven, a Divine breathing from above, the afflatus of the Holy Ghost, the writers being full of the Holy Ghost—in this sense, as a communication from the infinite and uncreated Mind, as a product of the wisdom and intelligence of Heaven, I take the book to be "the holy writings," to have a style of its own, an authorship of its own, a permanence of its own. A holy book, as the product and emanation of the thrice holy God, and as having in all the parts and branches of it a holy tendency. It is a revelation of God; and God here makes Himself manifest as holy, in connection with the exhortation, "Be ye holy, for I am holy." In every part of it we see sin punished—virtue, obedience fostered; above all, in the great manifestation of Christ—in His sacrifice, sufferings, and death, that God "might be just and the justifier of him that believeth in Jesus," we behold ineffable justice; and in the example of the Lord Jesus, which we are required to follow, putting our foot into His footprints, there is the same demand. It is a book marvellously adapted to the wants of a fallen and guilty world—preserving from presumption, on the one hand, and from despondency, on the other—that we sin not; but if we are overtaken by transgression, there is the sacrifice and the propitiation. And as actually producing holiness—as being the cause of this beautiful product, the root (if I may so say) of this sweet and lovely and Divine flower; for the "law of the Lord is perfect, converting the soul; the commandment of the Lord is pure, enlightening the eyes." Men are good in proportion as they direct themselves to the study of the Scripture, and as they walk according to its rules. "I cannot tell," Jonathan Edwards says, "how it comes to pass, but so it is, that the more I read the Scriptures, and the more I familiarise myself with the Divine contents of the heavenly book, the more pure, the more peaceful, the more benevolent, and the more happy I find myself." Why, it is cause and effect. If you put yourself in contact with the cause, the effect will be sure to follow; and you may know that the men who are wise in the Scriptures, and who love the Scriptures, are in the same proportion and degree holy men. The Scriptures help them in their walk with God, in the maintenance and preservation of their piety, in its noblest, sweetest, most elevated and pure aspirations and desires. The Bible, the Holy Bible, is the source and fountain of the light and life and power of the Church. II. The Holy Scriptures are "ABLE TO MAKE US WISE UNTO SALVATION." "Are able." There is a power, then, affirmed respecting them. They are true, genuine. If put to the proof they will demonstrate their capacity. They are "able," as supplying the information by the light of which we may be saved. It is said in the Old Testament—"As the rain cometh down, and the snow from heaven, and returneth not thither, but watereth the earth, and maketh it bring forth and bud, that it may give seed to the sower, and bread to the eater : so shall My Word be." It is said in the New Testament, "My Word is quick and powerful, sharper than a two-edged sword." It is "able," as it brings the likeness of Christ into me, and is accompanied by the enlightenment, influence, and grace of the Spirit; for the Spirit who dictated and indited these heavenly communications abides in the Church, and diffuses His unction and grace upon the understandings and hearts of men, whereby, in His light seeing light, they discern the meaning of the expressions and the principles, and are able to appropriate, apply, and bring them home. "Wise." Be upon your guard if any man is going to make you wise. The first thing the devil did was to persuade Eve that he could make her wise. Somebody arises with a new doctrine and a new interpretation—something which is to enlighten the eyes : be upon your guard, to say the least. Yet be "wise" in respect to the truth which is in Jesus ; "wise" in respect to what is good—simple in respect to what is evil ; in malice children—in understanding men. The Bible will make men "wise." Even the uneducated, what is called by Isaiah "the wayfaring man, though a fool," shall not err in the rudiments and elements, in the great salutary, refreshing, and saving principles. But if you want to be wise up to the full measure—to know the exact meaning of every book, the time of its being written, the purpose for which it was written, the literature associated with every book of the whole Bible, why, it is a vast range of knowledge, and it is marvellous how every kind and variety of knowledge can be made to bear upon the elucidation of the inspired books, so that they come out manifested and revealed in their own light and lustre, amid the unbounded and universal intelligence of men. But "wise unto salvation." If you know the holy writings, and are acquainted with the book, you can answer for yourselves the marvellous questions—"How am I to be saved? How is sin to be forgiven, transgression blotted out? How am I to regain the ancient position, and to be dealt with as though I had never sinned?" The holy writings furnish you with the answer. By being sprinkled from an evil conscience by the blood of the Immanuel, cleansed from all sin by the blood of the Son of God. Faith in Him brings home the light upon this subject. I can know nothing of all this, except by the holy writings. And this is the chief wisdom. You may be wise in the world to get money ; you may be wise in philosophy and science, and deep in literature ; you may be wise in frivolities and gaieties and fashions and adornments. What will your wisdom amount to? What is it in comparison with wisdom unto salvation? III. It is "BY FAITH IN CHRIST JESUS." We are not directed by the apostle to exalt the holy writings against Christ, or Christ against the holy writings, as if there were any competition between the two. It is Christ as revealed in the holy writings. Yet it is not that we are "wise unto salvation" by faith in the holy writings, but by faith in Christ Jesus, the living Christ. The holy writings tell me that the anointed Saviour, the Son of God, has done the work, completed the great and wonderful achievement which the Bible ascribes to Him ; and my soul by faith cordially accepts the testimony and reposes upon the truth. IV. TIMOTHY WHEN A CHILD KNEW THIS. Ah! his mother taught him, and his grandmother—his mother Eunice and his grandmother Lois. Oh, sweet child! oh, beautiful teachers! How they taught him! and how he listened! For when Paul says, "From a child thou hast known the Holy Scriptures," he means not merely the speculative and theoretical doctrines, but the experimental and practical had taken possession of his heart and enlightened his mind. Mothers! hear this. Early education, which is the most permanent in its effects, and the most influential upon character, depends mainly and chiefly upon the mother. Search into the Scriptures, then, and let it be said of you that you know them ; that you have a measure of understanding, and that you take means perpetually for its improvement and advance. And those who teach the children of others voluntarily are greatly to be commended. It is a service acceptable and well-pleasing to God. (*James Stratten.*) *Upon reading the Scriptures :*—I. THE OBLIGATIONS WE ARE UNDER TO APPLY OURSELVES TO THE KNOWLEDGE OF THE HOLY SCRIPTURES. II. THE GREAT ADVANTAGE THAT WILL ATTEND THIS STUDY. III. THE PARTICULAR HAPPINESS OF AN EARLY EDUCATION IN THIS KNOWLEDGE. IV. SOME RULES FOR DIRECTION IN THIS DUTY. 1. We must read the Scriptures frequently, because from hence we shall receive the greatest assistances in understanding them. 2. We must read them with attention. Without this, indeed, barely to run over the words of Scripture in a negligent, cursory manner, is a profane disregard to the Almighty Author, whose name they bear. 3. We must read them with reverence. (1) By reverence I understand that humility of mind which is due from us to our great Creator, that submission and subjection of our hearts and understandings to His Divine will, which disposes us readily to comply with whatsoever He proposes to us, whether it concerns our faith or practice. (2) But besides this reverence to God the author, there is a farther instance of our humility to be shown, in not being too hasty or peremptory of ourselves to determine the meaning and sense of the Holy Scriptures. 4. We must read them without prejudice. A fault we shall never avoid unless we observe the former rule, and approach those sacred oracles with reverence and humility, with an open heart, and a teachable disposition. (*J. Rogers, D.D.*) **Through faith which is in Christ Jesus.**—*Faith in Christ the key to the Bible:*—Faith in Christ is the key which will unlock and give access to the treasures of saving wisdom which are laid up in the Old Testament. The Bible is an organised whole, and Christ and the Cross of Christ are wrought into the structure of it, although they do not always meet the eye. He who by faith sees " Christ and Him crucified " in the Scriptures is in immediate possession of the ground-plan of the holy volume. He will observe how the original promise respecting " the seed of the woman " was a germ of hope planted in the earth, which, by constant accretions from new prophecies and new types, had expanded itself into full blossom when the Virgin-born appeared to fulfil it. He will observe how, as the ages rolled away, the light of revelation grew brighter, and how the prophets, in the greater spirituality of their religious precepts, and the greater explicitness of their predictions, were many steps in advance of the law. He will observe how, from the sacrifice of Abel downwards, every victim which fell at the altar of Jehovah prefigured the great sacrifice of the death of Christ. And in reciting the Psalms he will feel that the Spirit of Christ, which was in those sweet psalmists of Israel, testified darkly beforehand of the sufferings of Christ and the glory which should follow. Thus the whole of Scripture is welded together in the counsel and design of God ; and we know that, as regards man, that counsel and design is all bound up in one word—" Christ." He was " the Lamb slain " in the counsels of eternity " from the foundation of the world "; and accordingly in every chant of God's holy prophets, which have been since the world began, there has always been an undersong of Him, an undersong which may be caught by every spiritual ear. (*Dean Goulburn.*) *The Bible in early youth:*—From the time that, at my mother's feet, or on my father's knee, I first learned to lisp verses from the sacred writings, they have been my daily study and vigilant contemplation. If there be anything in my style or thoughts to be commended, the credit is due to my kind parents in instilling into my mind an early love of the Scriptures. (*Daniel Webster.*)

Vers. 16, 17. **All Scripture is given by inspiration of God.**—*Inspiration of Scripture :*—The word Inspiration itself is evidently a figure. It may be illustrated by another word. " Inspiration " is a *breathing into :* " influence " is a *flowing into :* neither word is self-explanatory ; the former, like the latter, may clearly admit of degrees and modifications. The word Inspiration occurs twice in the English Version of the Bible. " But there is a spirit [πνεῦμα] in man : and the inspiration (πνοή) of the Almighty giveth them understanding " (Job xxxii. 8). " All Scripture is given by inspiration of God [θεόπνευστος], and is profitable for doctrine," &c. (ver. 16). In the one passage instruction is the chief thought, in the other edification. The word occurs twice also in the Prayer-book. " Grant to us Thy humble servants that by Thy holy inspiration we may think those things that be good," &c. (Collect for the fifth Sunday after Easter). " Cleanse the thoughts of our hearts by the inspiration of Thy Holy Spirit, that we may perfectly love Thee," &c. (Collect in the Communion service). In both these sanctification is the end in view. Definition is still wanting. In several passages of the Epistles (as, for example, Rom. xv. 4, and 2 Peter i. 20, 21) strong terms are employed to describe the objects and uses of Old Testament Scripture as a whole, and its source in the agency of the Holy Spirit. Nothing can be more inclusive than St. Paul's ὅσα προεγράφη, nothing more emphatic than St. Peter's ἐλάλησαν ἀπὸ Θεοῦ ἄνθρωποι. Yet definition is still wanting alike of the word and of the thing. Theories of Inspiration have been many, but it is not in conjecture or in reasoning that our idea of it should be sought. The only true view of Inspiration will be that which is the net result of a lifelong study of Scripture itself, with all freedom in registering its phenomena, and all candour in pondering the question, " What saith it concerning itself ? " It is easy to see (and the Church of the present day is honest in avowing it) that the real truth must lie somewhere between two extremes—the extreme of verbal inspiration on the one side, and the extreme of a merely human composition on the other. I. AGAINST THE IDEA OF A VERBAL INSPIRATION OF SCRIPTURE WE ARE WARNED BY MANY CONSIDERATIONS. Amongst these we may place—1. Its utter unlikeness to all God's dealings in nature and grace. " Where the Spirit of the Lord is there is freedom "—freedom, not bondage ; freedom, not rigidity. 2. The language of the New Testament as to the difference between "letter" and "spirit," between γράμμα and πνεῦμα—the deadness of the one, the power of the other. As soon as Inspiration itself is tied to the clause and the sentence, to the precise shape and form of the utterance, and the black and white page of the written or printed book, it too is turned from the πνοὴ into the χειρόγραφον, and has lost the very φορὰ of the Spirit which made it a προφητεία (2 Pet. i. 21). 3. Such passages, for example, as the opening verses of St. Luke's Gospel, which speak only of diligent research and a thoughtful judgment as his guides in composing ; or St. Paul's expressions in the seventh chapter of his First Epistle to the Corinthians, as to his speaking not always with authority, but sometimes in the tone of suggestion and advice ; or again, St. Peter's remarks upon the Epistles of St. Paul, which in the same breath he describes, by clear implication, as " scriptures," and yet characterises with a freedom which would be irreverent and almost impertinent if each line of those " scriptures " had been verbally inspired. 4. The observation of differences of style and method between one Scripture writer and another ; the employment, for example, by one of irony and sarcasm, by another of no weapons but those of simple persuasion. 5. The fearful importance attached to each reading and each rendering of each verse and clause of Scripture, if one was, and another was not ; the very word dictated or the very thought breathed from heaven. 6. Also the utter grotesqueness of such an idea as the revelation of science, whether astronomy, geology, or ethnology—which yet there would have been if, where such objects are involved, the phrases and the sentences had been literally and verbally inspired of God ; implying an anticipation, perhaps by many centuries, of discoveries for which God had made provision in His other gift of reason, and which it would have been contrary to all His dealings thus to forestall. " Man's extremity is God's opportunity " ; that which He had given faculties for finding out in time, He would not interpose, before the time came, to precipitate. 7. The terrible risk to mankind of pinning down the faith to statements utterly indifferent to spiritual profiting, which yet, if philosophically accurate, must for whole ages bear the appearance of error. And who shall guarantee the Bible, even if accurately written up to the science of the nineteenth century, from being condemned by the science of the twentieth? II. If such are the confusions and contradictions of the one extreme, THE OTHER EXTREME IS YET MORE PERILOUS. The practical elimination (now so common) of the Divine element in Scripture is fatal in every sense to its inspiration. 1. It reduces Scripture to the level (at best) of works of human genius ; and, when this is done, makes the question, for each book, a comparative one, in which some books would be exposed to a disparaging judgment. 2. It sends us back to human reasoning, which is on many topics (such, for example, as immortality, forgiveness, and spiritual grace) human guessing, for all our information on things of gravest concern. 3. It contradicts (1) express declarations of the New Testament Scriptures as to the Divine authority of the Old, as well as (2) express assertion of Divine illumination, promised and experienced, in the New Testament writers themselves. 4. It does violence to the continuous doctrine of the Church of all ages, which has from the very first been express and peremptory in its view of the Divinity of the Scripture. 5. It leaves us practically destitute, even of a revelation. Because, though there might be a revelation without an inspiration (that is, a gospel of Christ, brought into the world by Him, and by Him communicated to His apostles, and by them to after ages, without a separate inspiration of the writers of its records), yet, as a matter of fact, it is by Scripture that we test our revelation, and that which shakes the authority of Scripture shakes the certainty of the revelation which Scripture enshrines. III. BETWEEN THESE TWO EXTREMES LIES SOMEWHERE THE VERY TRUTH ITSELF ABOUT INSPIRATION. It would be arbitrary to define it so precisely as to unchristianise those who cannot see with us. That there is both a human and also a Divine element in the Bible is quite certain. Some things we may say with confidence. 1. Inspiration left the writer free to use his own phraseology, even his mode of illustrating and arguing. 2. It did not level the characteristic features of different minds. No one could imagine the Epistle to the Galatians written by St.

John, or the Epistle of St. James written by St. Paul. 3. It did not supersede the necessity of diligence in investigating facts, nor the possibility of discrepancies in recording them; though it is more than probable that most or all of these would be reconciled if we knew all. 4. While it left the man free in the exercise of all that was distinctive in his nature, education, and habits of thought, it communicated nevertheless an elevation of tone, an earnestness of purpose, a force and fire of holy influence, quite apart and different from that observable in common men. 5. It communicated knowledge to the man of things otherwise indiscoverable, and also to the writer of things which it was the will of God to say by him to the hearer or reader. IV. While we refrain from definition, IT IS OUR DUTY AS CHRISTIANS TO FORM A HIGH CONCEPTION OF THE THING ITSELF FOR WHICH INSPIRATION IS THE NAME. 1. Let us think what would have become of the $\pi\alpha\rho\alpha\phi\acute{\eta}\kappa\eta$ itself, under whichever or whatever dispensation, if it had been left to depend upon oral transmission. 2. Let us give weight to the passages (some of them quoted above) which assert Inspiration in the strongest possible terms. 3. Most of all, let us live so much in the study of Scripture, as to acquire that reverent and devout conception of it which is ever deepest and strongest in those who best know it. A Christian man able to treat the Bible slightingly would be a contradiction in terms. (*Dean Vaughan.*) *Inspiration :*—The word which is here rendered "inspired of God" is common enough in heathen writers, but this is the only place in which it occurs in Holy Scripture. As the word was common in heathen writers, so is the idea. "Best," says an ancient Greek poet, "is the word of inspired wisdom." Another Greek writer speaks of "dreams inspired of God." The Roman orator Cicero says, "No man was ever great without a certain Divine inspiration." This last example reminds us that in the Bible also inspiration is in the first instance the attribute of men, not of books. The prophet in the Old Testament is also called the man of the Spirit. Men from God, the Second Epistle of Peter tells us, spake as they were moved of the Holy Ghost. There is a spirit in man, we read in Job, and the inspiration of the Almighty giveth them understanding. The Divine breath, for that is the idea contained in the words "inspired of God," is first in a human soul; it is only through the soul that it can be communicated to any word or work. Scripture can only be a body of inspired writings because it is the work of a body of inspired men. Now let us approach the subject from this side, and I think it will lead us to some serviceable truths. All men are not equally capable of inspiration—some have a much greater fitness than others for receiving the Spirit of God. If we wish to see the perfect type of inspiration—inspiration not limited or hampered by any unfitness in its instrument—we must find one in whom there is no sin, but an entire and perfect sympathy with the mind and will of God. One such there is in Scripture, and one only—the man Christ Jesus. No one ever had the Spirit without measure except Him; in other words, no one ever walked the earth besides who was in the true and full sense inspired of God. The Divine breath was in Him, and Him only, the life of every thought and word. Hence the words of Christ have a solitary and supreme value. He says so Himself: "The words that I speak unto you, they are spirit and they are life." The difficulties which are felt at the present time in connection with inspiration should all be brought under review in this light. Every scripture, the text tells us, at least by implication, has a Divine breath in it; there is a Divine purpose which it has once served, and which, at a certain stage of human progress, it may profitably serve still; but not every scripture is equally inspired; not every scripture has the final and permanent validity of the words of Christ; and as long as these last find their way to our hearts and work the will of Christ in us, we need not disquiet ourselves because we cannot define the inspiration of Esther, for instance, or of Second Chronicles. When we take the words of Christ as the perfect type of inspired words, and the record of them as the perfect type of inspired Scripture, we see what the essential contents and purpose of inspiration must be. Christ's words are not monotonous; they are inexhaustible in their fulness; but in them all there is the undertone: One thing is needful. Christ is always saying the same things, and about the same things. The nature of God, the will of God, the true life and destiny of man—these and all that gathers round these are His theme. He aims at making men wise, but it is wise unto salvation. He never taught a school of history or of science, or even of speculative theology. It was His meat to do the will of Him that sent Him, to declare that will, to win others to do it likewise. We cannot come nearer than the study of His words brings us to a true idea of inspiration; and if what I have said is true at all, it follows that inspiration has to do only with the will of God. The man of the Spirit is not necessarily an infallible observer, an infallible scientist, an infallible historian; in matters unconnected with his inspiration he may share the ignorance or the prejudices of his uninspired contemporaries; but he is, in the measure of his inspiration, an infallible interpreter of the will of God. Could anything be more true than that the words of Christ are profitable for doctrine, or to put it in commoner words, useful for teaching? The truth about God and man and all spiritual realities is revealed in them, and brought home to the mind and heart. They have filled and fertilised the intellect of Christendom for centuries. Are they not useful also for reproof, or more exactly, for conviction? Are there any words in the world that can quicken a dead conscience and make it sting, like His? How many of us have been revealed to ourselves as we listened to Him, and been compelled to cry like the woman of Samaria —"Come, see a man that told me all things that ever I did"? Are they not profitable also for correction, for the putting right of what is wrong, and for discipline in righteousness? But, some one may say, though all this is plain enough in regard to Christ's words, it is very difficult to apply it to everything in the Bible— for instance, to the historical books; yet the text speaks of every scripture. That is true, and no doubt by every scripture the apostle has the Old Testament in view; there was no other scripture to speak of when he wrote. But I think a little patience and attention will show that this general and practical definition of inspiration is applicable to the whole of the Bible; and if the Bible, from first to last, has this inspiring and educative power for practical spiritual purposes, we must not deny its inspiration on other and alien grounds. Let us take examples from the historical books to make clear what I mean. There are parts of the Old Testament that belong to the clear daylight of history—for example, the story of the last years of David. That story is told in 2 Sam., from chap. xi. onward. I hardly need to recall it even by mentioning the names of Bathsheba, Uriah, Amnon, Tamar, Absalom, Ahithophel, Joab, Shimei. No one knows who wrote it, but it is not possible to doubt that it rests on the authority of some one in immediate contact with the facts. Now consider how it might have been written. A newspaper reporter often has to deal with the same materials, and the chances are a thousand to one that in his hands they minister to the defilement and degradation of the community. A secular historian would probably handle them lightly, as the inevitable disorders of an oriental despotism—the natural result of such a situation as David occupied. In neither case would there be room to speak of inspiration. But as it stands in the Bible, that terrible record of crime and its consequences, is in the full sense of the word inspired. It is not written by a sensational reporter, or a pragmatical historian, but by a man of the Spirit. We see lust and blood in it, not with the sensual eye which feels the fascination of moral horrors, but with the holy eye of God. No man ever read it but was awed, shocked, disciplined in righteousness by pity and fear. It is in that sense that the story is inspired. The facts were not inspired; they were the common property of men with and without the Spirit. There could not be a more signal illustration of the power of inspiration than that a narrative like this—all of foulest crime compact—should have virtue in it, when told by an inspired man, to quicken the conscience, and educate the man of God. Take one example more, in some ways the most difficult of all, the first eleven chapters of Genesis. According to the usual chronology these cover a space of something like two thousand years. They do not contain many incidents—Creation, the Fall, the Flood, the origin and dispersion of the nations, are the chief. Now nobody lived through all that period, and at the very earliest these narratives were not written as we have them for centuries after it expired. To what extent they embody traditions; how nearly or how remotely, in any given case, tradition may be related to things as they actually happened; whether a primitive revelation survives in them here or there—all these are questions on which men have been very positive, but on which simple regard for truth precludes positiveness. And what I want to insist upon here, is that the inspiration of these chapters, like that of the rest of the Bible, is not affected by any decision to which we may come on these points. Inspiration has to do with the spirit of the writer, not with his materials. The inspiration of Luke did not provide him with facts about the life of Jesus; he had to learn them from eyewitnesses and catechists; he had to scrutinise and compare documents like another historian. Neither did inspiration, as I believe, supply the writer of Genesis with his materials. What is inspired in his story is what speaks to the spirit, what serves to convict, to correct, to discipline in righteousness; and judged by this standard, there is nothing in the Bible better entitled to claim inspiration than the story, *e.g.,* of the Fall. Compare such a narrative with the use made of similar materials by a pagan writer—a comparison that can fortunately be made—and we see how wonderfully the author must have been filled and uplifted by a Spirit above his own. It is because his writing has this spiritual quality, this permanent power to reveal to us both God and our own heart, that it answers to the description given by Paul of every inspired Scripture. There is only one proof, in the long run, that the Spirit of God is in the Bible ; and that is, that it exerts its power through the Bible. The perfection of Scripture is perfection for its purpose, and that purpose is the transformation of character. (*Jas. Denney, B.D.*) *The inspiration and utility of the Scriptures* :—I. THE INSPIRATION OF THE SCRIPTURES. 1. What is inspiration? It is not revelation, but the infallible record of an infallible revelation. 2. The extent of inspiration. How far were these men guided by the Holy Ghost in the composition of the Scriptures ? To every line and word. Yet was not the self-control or intelligent consciousness of the writer destroyed. Each writer retains his own style (see 1 Cor. ii. 13 ; xii. 6). 3. The object of inspiration. To give certainty to that written under its guidance. 4. The proofs of inspiration. Internal evidence. Arguments drawn from the history of these books, from their contents. Christ's appeal to the Old Testament as of Divine origin. The claim of both writers of Old and New Testaments. II. THE UTILITY OF THE SCRIPTURES. "PROFITABLE FOR," &c. 1. As an unvarying standard of doctrine. Not a theological statement, but the germ of all true doctrine. From it all doctrine must be derived, and to it all doctrine must be referred. 2. Useful in the confutation of all religious error. "Profitable for reproof." 3. Useful as an infallible standard of right and wrong. We cannot trust a pope, a church. 4. Useful for instruction in righteousness. By following its teachings we are brought into fuller measures of perfection. Our sanctification is by the Word. "Sanctify them through Thy truth ; Thy Word is truth." (*James Hunter.*) *Inspired Scriptures, and their Divine purpose* :—I. THE NATURE OF THE WRITINGS HERE SPOKEN OF. II. THE OBJECT FOR WHICH THE SCRIPTURES WERE WRITTEN. This object is twofold ; first, what the Bible would make man ; and next, how it would accomplish its purpose. 1. What the Scriptures would make man. "That the man of God may be perfect, thoroughly furnished unto all good works." It does this by first making him a "man of God." Religion is not an abstraction—it is a Divine life, and a life which in man makes him a man of God. 2. The standard after which he ever aims is perfection! 3. But we have not only the standard announced, we have also the style of the spiritual education determined—"that the man of God may be perfect, thoroughly furnished." III. HOW THE SCRIPTURES PROPOSE MAKING "MEN OF GOD, THROUGHLY FURNISHED, UNTO ALL GOOD WORKS." "All Scripture is given by inspiration of God, and is profitable." 1. "For doctrine"; that is, for conveying those truths and that learning needful to salvation. 2. Becoming "profitable for reproof." This word "reproof," means "conviction." 3. It becomes "profitable for correction." This is equally necessary in a volume suitable to save men. 4. Lastly—by "instruction of righteousness." The unlearning of man's love to sin, the undoing of his evil habits—this is correction. But after all this is but the negative part of Christian character. It is the abnegation of evil. Christianity inculcates positive good. IV. THE WORK WHICH HOLY SCRIPTURE IS YET DESTINED TO DO. 1. By the Bible the Church of God must be purified. 2. By the Bible, as an instrument, the Jews must be converted. 3. By the Bible the great apostasy must be destroyed. 4. By the Bible, instrumentally, the heathen must be converted. (*A. M. Brown, LL.D.*) *The Bible superhuman* :—I shall content myself with stating some plain facts about the Bible, which can neither be denied nor explained away. And the ground I shall take up is this—I. THAT THESE FACTS OUGHT TO SATISFY EVERY REASONABLE INQUIRER THAT THE BIBLE IS OF GOD, AND NOT OF MAN. 1. It is a fact that there is a superhuman fulness and richness in the contents of the Bible. It throws more light on a vast number of most important subjects than all the other books in the world put together. It boldly handles matters which are beyond the reach of man when left to himself. 2. It is another fact that there is a superhuman wisdom, sublimity, and majesty in the style of the Bible. Strange and unlikely as it was, the writers of Scripture have produced a book which even at this day is utterly unrivalled. With all our boasted attainments in science and art and learning we can produce nothing that can be compared with the Bible. To talk of comparing the Bible with other "sacred books" so called, such as the Koran, the Shasters, or the book of Mormon, is positively absurd. You might as well compare the sun with a rushlight—or Skiddaw with a mole-hill—or Saint Paul's with an Irish hovel—or the Portland vase with a garden pot—or the Koh-i-noor diamond with a bit of glass. God seems to have allowed the existence of these pretended revelations in order to prove the immeasurable superiority of His own Word. 3. It is another fact, that there is a superhuman accuracy in the facts and statements of the Bible, which is above man. Here is a book which has been finished and before the world for nearly 1800 years. These 1800 years have been the busiest and most changeful period the world has ever seen. During this period the greatest discoveries have been made in science, the greatest alterations in the ways and customs of society, the greatest improvements in the habits and usages of life. But all this time men have never discovered a really weak point or a defect in the Bible. Over and over again the enemies of the Bible have fancied they have detected defects. Again and again they have proved to be mistaken. The march of intellect never overtakes it. The wisdom of wise men never gets beyond it. The science of philosophers never proves it wrong. The discoveries of travellers never convict it of mistakes. Are the ruins of Nineveh and Egypt ransacked and explored? Nothing is found that overturns one jot or tittle of the Bible's historical statements. 4. It is another fact that there is in the Bible a superhuman suitableness to the spiritual wants of all mankind. It feeds the mind of the labourer in his cottage, and it satisfies the gigantic intellects of Newton, Chalmers, Brewster, and Faraday. It is the only book, moreover, which seems always fresh and evergreen and new. I place these four facts about the Bible before you, and I ask you to consider them well. Take them all four together, treat them fairly, and look at them honestly. Upon any other principle than that of Divine inspiration, those four facts appear to me inexplicable and unaccountable. Not only were its writers isolated and cut off in a peculiar manner from other nations, but they belonged to a people who have never produced any other book of note except the Bible! There is not the slightest proof that, unassisted and left to themselves, they were capable of writing anything remarkable, like the Greeks and Romans. Yet these men have given the world a volume which for depth, sublimity, accuracy, and suitableness to the wants of man, is perfectly unrivalled. How can this be explained? To my mind there is only one answer. The writers of the Bible were Divinely helped and qualified for the work which they did. II. Let us now consider THE PRIVILEGES WHICH THE POSSESSION OF AN INSPIRED BOOK CONFERS UPON US. 1. It is a privilege to possess the only book which gives a reasonable account of the beginning and end of the globe on which we live. 2. It is a privilege to possess the only book which gives a true and faithful account of man. 3. It is a privilege to possess the only book which gives us true views of God. 4. It is a privilege to possess the only book which gives a clear account of the full, perfect, and complete provision which God has made for the salvation of fallen man. 5. Finally, it is a privilege to possess the only book which explains the state of things that we see in the world around us. III. Let us now consider THE DUTIES WHICH THE POSSESSION OF GOD'S ORACLES ENTAILS UPON US. 1. First and foremost, let us honour the Bible by making it the supreme rule of faith, the standard measure of truth and error, of right and wrong in our churches. 2. In the next place, if we believe the Bible to be "the oracles of God," let us show the reality of our belief by endeavouring to spread it throughout the world. (*Bp. Ryle.*) *Inspiration of the Holy Scriptures :*—I. IN CONFIRMATION OF THIS DOCTRINE, WE WOULD ASK ATTENTION TO THE FOLLOWING CONSIDERATIONS AND ARGUMENTS. 1. We would offer a short, clear, and strong argument, from Mr. Wesley. "The Bible," says he, "must be the invention either of good men or angels, bad men or devils, or of God." (1) It could not be the invention of good men or angels; for they neither could nor would make a book, and tell lies all the time they were writing it, saying, "Thus saith the Lord," when it was their own invention. (2) It could not be the invention of bad men or devils; for they would not make a book which commands all duty, forbids all sin, and condemns their souls to hell to all eternity. (3) Therefore we must draw this conclusion, that the Bible must have been given by Divine inspiration—that it is the work of God. 2. Our second argument is derived from prophecy. The ability to foretell future events, especially hundreds of years beforehand, belongs to God alone. 3. The declarations of the Scriptures themselves plainly prove this doctrine. But will not this be proving inspiration by inspiration? It would be so, indeed, did we assume the Bible in this argument to be inspired. But now we take it only as a book of truth, declaring true doctrines and true history; as such we receive it, and by itself prove its inspiration. II. WE PASS TO CONSIDER SOME OBJECTIONS. 1. The first, and one which is frequently in the mouths of infidels, is that there are contradictions in the Scriptures, and therefore they cannot be inspired. 2. Another class of objections against the plenary inspiration of the Scriptures is founded on the imperfect state of the text, its variations in the reading and punctuations. 3. Another objection which has been urged against plenary or verbal inspiration is founded on the individuality of the sacred writers. The following is our answer:—God speaks to man after the manner of men; and hence He uses human language, and, of course, human language with its imperfections. Inferences: 1. If the Holy Scriptures are Divinely inspired, human reason ought to be held in abeyance to their teachings. 2. If Divinely inspired, they must teach us truth without any admixture of error. 3. We also infer that, if Divinely inspired, they contain a sufficiency of truth for our salvation. (*Stephen M. Vail, M.A.*)    *The Word of God commended to the man of God in the perilous times of the last days:*—1. The subject of this text is our own precious Bible. 2. And, assuredly, of the very deepest interest must such a subject be to the sort of person to whom in the text the Spirit, by Paul, addresses Himself, on the Divine inspiration, and authority, and profitableness of the Bible. For it is to "the man of God" the apostle here speaks in commendation of the Word of God. It is to one he writes who (vers. 14, 15) had "learned" and "been assured" of "the things" revealed in "the Holy Scriptures," which "from a child he had known"—who had experimentally proved them to be "able to make him wise unto salvation, through faith which is in Christ Jesus." To that sort of person no theme could be more attractive of the deepest interest, than the incalculable preciousness of the Holy Bible (Psa. xix. 7–11). One thing only could enhance such a man's estimate of their infinite value, and that one thing was the character of "the times" in which, as peculiarly threatening of dangerous assaults on the Christian faith, the apostle commended the profitableness of the Scriptures and exhorted the man of God to continue to confide in the profitableness of "all Scripture" as "given by inspiration of God." 3. And yet, though thus employed as the means of enforcing his exhortation to Timothy to "continue in the things which he had learned," the "perilous" controversies of "the times" are not suffered by any insinuation on the part of the apostle to disturb the certainty in which his young disciple had "been assured" of "the things which he had learned." 4. Are we "men of God," "taught of God" to know Him, and with profoundest reverence to acknowledge His authority speaking in His own Word? Then we are of those who spiritually see. To our renewed hearts, as to open healthy eyes, the light of Holy Scripture has come and entered in, carrying with it its own evidence of its Divine authority, and with a power that is irresistible. I. WHENCE HAVE WE THE BIBLE? It is "of God"—its authority is Divine. When God speaks the highest exercise of man's reason surely is, in silent submission, to believe and obey, simply because it is the Word of God that is spoken. It is the exercise of a prerogative the noblest birthright of man, to believe God's truth. In that submission of human reason to the authority of Divine truth, man escapes into freedom! The truth as nothing else can do, emancipates the mind from the debasing slavery to the opinions of men. It puts man as to unseen things in immediate and direct communication alone with God. No creature is allowed to intervene as the Lord of the conscience, when, for the authority of God speaking in it, the word in Holy Scripture is believed. God is then by His Word and Spirit in actual contact with your soul, for your enjoying the most ennobling fellowship with Himself, in the light of truth, and in the perfect freedom of a willing obedience of the truth. II. IN WHAT MANNER IS IT GIVEN US BY GOD?—"It is given by INSPIRATION OF GOD!" The text here, you observe, does not point to such a mode of communication with man as was used in the Garden of Eden, when, in the cool of the day, the voice of God was heard by Adam talking with him. Nor yet does the text here refer to such a mode of writing down what the voice of God had uttered in man's hearing, as was once and again practised, when, on two tables of stone, the ten words of the Holy Moral Law were engraven by the immediate finger of God. The text does plainly testify to the Word of God being written, but observe, to that result being attained by what is called "inspiration." It is God-breathed. That, what is written in the Bible is the Word of God, results from the inspiration by God of men employed by Him to write it. The Word in Holy Scripture results from that miraculous operation of the Spirit of God, whereby He did so communicate Himself to the writers of these Scriptures for the revelation of His will to man, as to secure the infallible truth and Divine authority of what is written in the Bible. Of the manner of that miraculous operation of the Spirit of God we know nothing. III.

To WHAT EXTENT IS THE BIBLE INSPIRED?—" All Scripture is given by inspiration of God." It is thus that the Divine Author of the book Himself declares to what extent it is inspired. In whatever manner the Divine influence that " gave the Word " worked—by whatever means, by means of however many varied manuscripts, as by many different compilers—the result we have in this Bible is throughout Divinely inspired. IV. WITH WHAT DESIGN HAS IT BEEN GIVEN BY INSPIRATION OF GOD? It was given to be profitable, in order " that the man of God may be thoroughly furnished unto all good works," and for that end profitable in a way manifold and many-sided. 1. The Bible is " profitable for doctrine." By its revelation of truth as an objective reality, it really gives man truth to love. It thus stands in the boldest contrast to the utterly unsatisfying vanity of modern rationalism, which gives you nothing but the question whether there be revealed truth at all. 2. The Bible is " profitable, too, for reproof." By its deep and searching spirituality the Bible deals with man's state as a sinner before God. It reveals the truth as to man lost. It reaches the deepest needs of his condition. It thus utterly dispels all the delusive fancies of modern rationalism, whereby man is tempted to think well of himself; and so to count that a gain to him which, if ever he be saved, he must be content to count as loss for Christ. 3. The Bible is profitable, besides, " for correction " of every such groundless hope in man. By the revelation of grace to us as fallen, and of deliverance from the guilt and power of our sin by the death and resurrection of the Lord Jesus, the Bible gives a Divine contradiction to every rationalistic theory of human progress, by which redemption is attempted to be explained without the cross and the sacrifice of the Redeemer. 4. The Bible is profitable, finally, for instruction (or discipline) in the life and walk of righteousness. In direct opposition to the wild ravings of modern rationalism about " emancipation from the external law of revealed truth "—for the solemn rebuke of that delusive licence which is sought in following the light within us, rather than the Word of God without us—the Bible plainly asserts that, " under the law to Christ," this is the love of the new life in Christ, that we keep His commandments—a life of obedience of " the law of liberty "—even as Christ Himself "kept His Father's commandments and abide in His love." (*R. H. Muir.*) *On the Scriptures :*—I. HUMAN ABILITY HAS BEEN INADEQUATE TO THE PRODUCTION OF ANYTHING WHICH WOULD JUSTIFY US IN ATTRIBUTING TO IT THE PRODUCTION OF THE SCRIPTURES. II. God having graciously resolved to recover the human race from the state into which they had fallen, and to this end having spoke in times long past to the fathers by the prophets, and in the latter days to the world, by His Son, IT IS REASONABLE TO SUPPOSE THAT, FOR THE BENEFIT OF THE GENERATIONS TO COME FOR EVER, HE WOULD CAUSE A RECORD TO BE MADE OF THE COMMUNICATIONS OF HIS WILL. III. THE CONNECTION AND AGREEMENT OF THE SEVERAL PARTS OF THE SACRED VOLUME, INTIMATE STRONGLY ITS DIVINE INSPIRATION. IV. TRADITION HAS ACCOMPANIED THE HOLY VOLUME IN ALL AGES AND PLACES OF ITS BEING, TESTIFYING ITS CLAIM TO BE CONSIDERED AS THE WORD OF GOD. V. THE PROVIDENTIAL CARE OF GOD OVER THE HOLY SCRIPTURES MAY WELL LEAD US TO BELIEVE THAT THEY ARE HIS OFFSPRING. VI. The completeness of the sacred writings, whereby I mean THEIR SUFFICIENCY AND PERFECTION AS A RULE OF FAITH AND CONDUCT ; THEIR ADEQUATENESS TO OUR NECESSITIES IN THIS PRESENT STATE. 1. This we may clearly deduce from what has already been established. Being " given by inspiration of God," the Scriptures must be perfect for the purpose whereunto He sends them ; and if they are finished, so that no further addition to them is to be expected, they must be perfect in all generations for ever, for the use of the children of men. 2. And this, if we now advert to the sacred writings, will be found to be really the case. Upon every subject of a religious or moral nature, concerning which mankind have been inquisitive, we may here find ample information. And concerning the conduct which is proper, in every situation in which mankind may be placed, we may here find explicit instruction. 3. But, it may be objected, if the Scriptures are thus complete, whence is it that so many to whom they are sent, are brought by them neither to right faith nor to right practice ? 4. And this brings me to observe in illustration of the completeness of the sacred volume, that if any who have access to it are deficient in knowledge or virtue, the cause of the deficiency is altogether in themselves. The Law of the Lord is perfect ; and His Spirit is ready to render His Word efficacious to every attentive and humble mind. But we must approach it with docility. It is owing to men's lusts and passions, to the pride of their minds, to the perverseness of their hearts, to the carnality and viciousness of their lives, that they do not all perceive the excellence and perfection of the

Word of God, and find it a savour of life unto life to their souls.    VII.
WE FIND OURSELVES IN POSSESSION OF A VOLUME, WONDERFULLY ADAPTED TO
THE NECESSITIES OF OUR NATURE, and "given by inspiration of God." It becomes
us to inquire, what is the object for which it is given? 1. And let me observe
that it is for no purpose of benefit to the Almighty that the volume of His Word is
given to our world.   Neither our faith nor our obedience can profit the Most High.
2. I must also premise that whether any other beings than ourselves are interested
in them, and whether their contents will be of utility to us in the other world, are
questions which need not be discussed as essential to the inquiry we are about to
consider.   It is enough, in order to raise our estimation of them, to be assured
that into the mysteries revealed to us the angels desire to look, and that by the
dispensations of God to the Church on earth His manifold wisdom is made known
to higher orders of beings.   From the nature of things we may also be certain that
those general principles of duty and virtue which have not respect to mutable stations
and relations are the principles by which the conduct of perfect beings is regulated
in all worlds.   3. But what I am now principally concerned to consider is the end
or uses of the sacred volume to men, to whom it is given, in the present world.
And this is nothing less than our recovery from the state of ignorance, sinfulness,
and misery into which we are fallen, and our exaltation to the hope of eternal
life.   That I may more distinctly set before you the gracious design of the Almighty
in giving us the volume of His Word, allow me more particularly to observe that it
is the efficacious means of all those changes and graces by which the Christian
character is formed and perfected.   We are told, you know, that we must be born
again in order to the knowledge and enjoyment of the kingdom of God.   It is
through the instrumentality of the Scriptures that this regeneration is accomplished.
They are the seed of this new birth.   Again : it is necessary that we should be
sanctified and made holy in heart and life before we can enter into the kingdom of
heaven.   And the Holy Scriptures are the means by which the Spirit of God
accomplishes this important part of our salvation.   Further : it is required of us
to grow in grace ; and we have need to be constantly nourished in all goodness, if
we would not relapse into our vile state, but advance to perfection in knowledge
and virtue.   The sacred writings are the granary from which this daily sustenance
of our souls is to be obtained.   They reveal the truths, they contain the virtues,
they give efficacy to the ordinances, by which we are nourished into eternal life.
Finally : it is necessary to our comfort, and to the full accomplishment of our
deliverance from the miseries of our natural state, that we should have joy and
peace in believing.   And the reservoir of all spiritual joy is the Word of God—the
gospel of our salvation.   VIII. From these truths THERE ARE SEVERAL INFERENCES
of a very serious nature and great practical importance to which I must now ask
your attentive consideration.   1. And from the views we have taken of the sacred
volume we may perceive its claim to our highest estimation.   2. But if we value
the Scriptures we shall also study them.   The consequences of not reading the
Holy Scriptures are of a more serious nature and greater in extent than you may
suppose.   It is to this, I apprehend, that we are to attribute, in a great measure,
the total ignorance of religion in some and the decay of it in others.   It is in this
that we are to look for the cause of the instability of Christians.   Here we may
find the reason why error prevails.   Here we may discover the source of fanaticism
and of superstition.   To this it is owing that the best seem unconscious of the
degree of holiness to which they are called ; and that all rest easy under imperfections of knowledge and deficiencies of virtue which a thorough acquaintance with
the Scriptures would both reprove and correct.   3. In the course of our observations upon the Holy Scriptures, we have shown that God hath a merciful purpose
in conferring them upon us, even to recover us from our ignorance, sinfulness, and
misery, and exalt us to the hope of everlasting life.   It behoves us, therefore, to
inquire how far His desire and gracious intention have been accomplished in us?
And this inquiry you will most safely answer, not by adverting to your occasional
feelings and transient fervours, but by looking to your principles and your lives.
Are you brought to a clear knowledge of the only true God, and of Jesus Christ
whom He hath sent ?  Are those traits of excellence which are distinctly exemplified
in the lives of the Scripture worthies, and which are all combined and perfected in
the example of our blessed Lord, imitated by you in the several conditions and
relations in which the Most High hath placed you ?  If, at the day of judgment, we
shall be found, notwithstanding our advantages, to have remained unchanged and
unrenewed, the very heathens will rise up in judgment and condemn us. 4. On

this solemn account I cannot forbear adding what is powerfully enforced by our subject, the importance of bringing to the oracles of truth, whenever we recur to them, becoming dispositions and conduct. Endeavour, if possible, to make it the standard by which you would regulate all your thoughts and actions. 5. The character of the sacred writings, and your privilege in possessing them, impose on you an obligation to extend the knowledge of them as far as you are able, and especially to make them the source from which you furnish your children with the principles and rules of life. (*Bp. Dehon.*)     *The true teachings of the Bible :—* " Every Scripture inspired of God," is the declaration, " is profitable." Profitable for what? Well, " for teaching, for reproof, for correction." It is a good teaching-book. It is a good book out of which to get instruction, provided you seek the right sort of instruction—instruction in righteousness. What is righteousness? Right living. In the Old Testament and the New the ideal pattern is that of a man living right in himself, in his social and civic relations, in his whole orb of self. A man must have some ideal pattern before him, and he must live according to it. The Bible is said to be inspired—that part of it which *is* inspired. " Every Scripture inspired of God is also profitable for teaching, for reproof, for correction, for instruction in righteousness." For what purpose? Why, " that the man of God may be complete, furnished completely unto every good work." There are two radical views of the function of sacred Scripture. First, it is held that it is a book proceeding directly from the mind of God, in the same sense in which Milton's poems proceeded from his mind, or in which Newton's discoveries proceeded from his mind, or in which any legislation proceeds from the minds of the legislators, and that it contains a substantial revelation of God's moral government, both in this life and in the other world. In part, it is such a book ; but that is not the genius of the Bible. Such is not the grand end of this book. The second view is the Scriptural theory. It is contained in the text. The Bible is a book that under-takes to teach men how to live so that they shall live hereafter ; and in regard to that aim and design of the Bible there is no divergence of opinion. All Scripture, then, is not inspired. Why should we suppose that the genealogies, and the land laws, or the laws of property, among the Jews, needed to be either inspired or revealed? Was it to supersede the natural operation of human reason that the Bible was given? If the division of property sprang up in the Hebrew common-wealth, and if there were many minute economies, all of which were of a nature such as that they could be born out of the human mind, and it was perfectly within the power of the human mind to write them down, what inspiration was needed for that purpose? No inspiration is necessary to record things that common human intelligence cannot miss, and cannot very well fail of recording. Proverbs and national songs, manners and customs, of the Hebrew commonwealth—all lay within the natural function of human reason ; and when it is said, " All Scripture that is inspired," doubtless it was with the conception that many of these things were natural and not supernatural. The existence of God ; a belief in the moral order of the universe, or supervising Divine Providence ; conscience, or the know-ledge of what is right and what is wrong, and sensibility to that which is right as well as reaction from that which is wrong ; the nature of things that are right and the nature of things that are wrong ; sanctions for virtue, and sanctions also, penal, for vice, selfishness, wickedness, cruelty—all these things are constitutional, if I may say so, in the Bible. Here, then, is the life that you must *not* live, and here is the life that you *must* live. Was there ever a man that wanted to take anything away from that? The whole Bible is an attempt to correct a man, and take him away from this under-passionate life of which we have been hearing the registra-tion, and to persuade him to come out of it into the higher and spiritual life. The genius of the Bible is to lift men to righteousness, and to show the things to be avoided, and the things to be taken on. It is a book of instruction in righteous-ness, that the man of God may be thoroughly furnished to every good work ; and here are the work and the qualities. Now, I should like to know if there is any infidel in this world on that subject, or can be. A great many do not believe that God can exist in three persons ; but is there anybody that ever doubted that love was beautiful, was true, was desirable? A great many men have had theories of the Atonement of Jesus Christ ; there are some fifteen or twenty different theories or modifications on that subject ; but did men ever have any difference of opinion as to love, joy, peace, long-suffering, kindness, goodness, faithfulness, meekness, or any of these other qualities? About them there is absolute unity. (*H. W. Beecher.*) *The Divine authority and perfection of the Scriptures :*—I. THAT THE SCRIPTURES

ARE GIVEN BY INSPIRATION OF GOD. 1. In order to judge whether persons are inspired, we must carefully inquire into their moral character; into their doctrine or message; and into the credentials or proofs of their mission. 2. The other external proof of an inspired person is the fulfilment of prophecy. II. THE PER-FECTION OR SUFFICIENCY OF THE SCRIPTURES. 1. They are profitable for doctrine to acquaint us with our lost and miserable condition by the entrance of sin into the world, and the train of fatal consequences that attended it; with our recovery by Christ; the covenants of redemption and grace; the offices of Father, Son, and Spirit in the work of our redemption, and with all those other mysteries which were kept secret since the world began, but are now made manifest by the Holy Scriptures for the obedience of faith (Rom. xvi. 26). 2. For reproof, or the discovery of our pernicious errors in doctrine and practice. 3. The Scriptures are profitable for correction of vice and wickedness. "Wherewithal," says the Psalmist, "should a young man cleanse his way but by taking heed thereto according to the Word of God?" There we have a collection of all Christian graces and duties, with their opposite vices. The fruits of the spirit and of the flesh are distinguished with the greatest propriety; and the most engaging motives to the practice of the one, and awful threatenings against the other, are represented with the greatest strength and advantage. 4. For instruction in righteousness. That is, either in the righteousness of God, which is by faith of Jesus Christ unto all and upon all that believe, or in the practice of moral righteousness, the nature and excellency of which is better explained and illustrated in the sermons of our blessed Saviour than in all the writings of the ancient philosophers. III. THE CLEARNESS AND PERSPICUITY OF THE SCRIPTURES. 1. They were written in the vulgar language, and therefore designed for the use of the common people. 2. Our Saviour, in His sermons to the people, appeals to the Scriptures, and exhorts His countrymen, the Jews, to search them. The Bereans are commended for this practice (Acts xvii. 11), and Timothy appears to have been acquainted with them from his childhood. If, then, it be proper to teach our children the Scriptures, and if it be the duty of grown persons to search them, it must follow that they are sufficiently clear in all points necessary to salvation. Lessons: 1. Hence we may learn that the religion of a Christian should be his Bible, because it contains the whole revealed will of God, and is a perfect rule of faith and practice. 2. Let us be thankful that we have the Scriptures in the vulgar language. 3. Let Christians of all ranks and capacities revive this neglected duty of reading the Scriptures in their families and closets: it is both a delightful and useful employment. 4. When we read the Scriptures, let us consider them, not as the words of men, but as in deed and truth the Word of God. 5. In judging of controversies among Christians, let us not be carried away by the authority of great names or the numbers of them that are on one side, but keep close to the Scriptures. 6. When we read the Scriptures, let us pray for the instructions and teachings of the Holy Spirit, whose office it is to remove the prejudices and enlighten the understandings of those who are truly sincere. (*Daniel Neal.*) *The inspiration of the Scriptures:*—I. THE NATURE OF THE INSPIRATION. Inspiration means that which is breathed into the human mind of God. In the same way as Christ breathed upon the apostles, and said, "Receive ye the Holy Ghost," so inspired men receive that influence and power which enlightens, and purifies, and sustains their judgment and their capacity whilst they are writing it. Exactly in the same way as a musician, out of an instrument, by the touch of his fingers, will evoke such sounds, such harmonies, as his own skill, his own will, or his own pleasure may design, the writers of the Holy Scriptures are the instruments out of which the Holy Ghost evokes the melodies of truth—the harmonies of heavenly and Divine doctrine—that which makes us happy in time, and prepares us for the happiness of eternity. There is a slight distinction to be made between inspiration and dictation. Dictation addresses itself to the ear, and goes through the ear into the understanding and the heart; inspiration is more that which is within a man—it is a power dwelling in the interior of his soul, and influencing his thoughts and expressions accordingly. 1. There is inspiration in matters historical —that which relates to the histories and biographies contained in the Bible. 2. We come to the inspiration which is doctrinal, or which has to do with abstract truth, such truth as the human faculties could never elicit, invent, or evolve; such truth as, if known at all by man, must be made known by God. 3. I advert to that inspiration which I denominate legislative—that which is associated with the giving of law and the enunciation of commandments. 4. There is the inspiration which is devotional. 5. I shall mention but one other form: that is, the form of prophecy—the inspiration which relates to the prophetic Word. I take this to be the fullest, most perfect, and unmingled of all the inspirations, because to man in no case is there vouchsafed any foresight. II. SOME OF THE LEADING EVIDENCES, THE MORE STRIKING PROOFS, THAT THE BIBLE DOES COME FROM THAT SACRED AND CELESTIAL SOURCE TO WHICH WE ASCRIBE IT. 1. First it claims to be so; i isays of itself that it is so. Moses did as the Lord commanded him. Again and again we read, "the Lord spake unto Moses"; and every prophet came with this annunciation, "Thus saith the Lord." We find Paul saying, "I command; yet not I, but the Lord"; "The Spirit speaketh expressly"; "Ye have received the Word of God." 2. There is another evidence which arises from the nature of its contents—from the original, exalted, enlightened, amazing principles, which it contains. I hold it as an axiom that God only can reveal God—that God is never known but by His own teaching and by His own inspiration. Here is God revealed. 3. There is also an argument arising from the self-evidencing power of truth. Light is self-evidencing. When a child sees light, it does not want any logical argument to say that it is light. When intellect flashes, when genius sparkles, when genius coruscates, you say, this is mind; you want no other evidence—the thing demonstrates itself. So does the truth in the book of God. Read out the doctrine, make known the precept, let us see the history; why, it is of God; it carries its own evidence. 4. Then there is the harmony of all its parts. 5. I must add the evidence of its holiness. The Bible, received in the heart and mind, makes a man pure, gentle, and Christlike; received into a family, it makes a scene of peace and unity; received into a nation, it purifies and elevates; and the world, did it receive the Bible and act upon its principles, would be paradisaical; almost all the miseries of it would be gone at a stroke; whatever is peaceful and felicitous for the glory of God and for the happiness of man would multiply, prosper, and abound. 6. There is one other argument, that arising from prophecy, in connection with the total want of human foresight, and the vastness and extent of this proof: "We have a more sure word of prophecy, whereunto we do well to take heed, as to a light shining in a dark place." III. THE USE AND PURPOSE: "That the man of God may be perfect, throughly furnished unto all good works." You note the expression, "man of God." I take it to be a very noble and magnificent thing to be a man; I glorify God every day of my life that I am a man; I mean, that I have the capacities, the mind, the thinking powers, the will of a man. Then it is said, "man of God." There are the faculties consecrated, the grace and light, the emanation and power of Deity beaming upon the man, making him a "man of God." (*James Stratten.*) *The inspiration of Scripture*:—We can form no more distinct conception of what inspiration is in itself than that implied in the word—the breathing of God upon, or into, the minds of His servants. He imparted to them an extraordinary degree of influence, whereby they were instructed what and how to speak and write. This special Divine influence distinguishes them from all other teachers, and their writings from all other books. The manner of inspiration is beyond our knowledge; indeed, the working and influence of the Divine Being anywhere are to us a profound mystery. Motion, life, and growth, the fruitfulness of the earth, and the order and harmony of all things must be traced to Him; but how they are produced we know not. In Him we live and move and have our being; He besets us behind and before, and lays His hand upon us; but His manner of doing this is too wonderful for us to understand. We are bound to recognise His influence in the mental power, wisdom, and goodness of men; but how He comes into contact with the mind it is impossible to explain. So also of the prophets and apostles. They were inspired of God; He breathed into their minds, and endued them with a supernatural power of seeing and teaching spiritual truth—this we know; but beyond this point we cannot pass. Observe a threefold effect of inspiration—the revelation of truth, intensity of feeling, and abiding power in the words. I. FIRST, THE INSPIRED MAN WAS A "SEER"; THE VEIL WAS TURNED ASIDE, AND HE WAS PERMITTED TO LOOK INTO THE SANCTUARY OF TRUTH. Think of the Hebrew prophets to whose writings the text refers. The unity, personality, and spirituality of God were revealed to them. They beheld His glory as others did not, and therefore spoke of it in sublime and incomparable language. The teaching of the Bible should be judged of by this: Do the prophets and apostles reveal spiritual truths in a clearer light than the ancient philosophers did? To this a thoughtful man can only return one answer—they do. Read, for instance, the Meditations of Marcus Aurelius, and then turn to the Epistles of St. Paul, and I think you will be obliged to acknowledge that moral and spiritual truth shines in the verses of the apostle with a brilliancy and strength not to be found in the words, wise and beautiful though they are, of the imperial Stoic. Seeing, then, that the prophets and apostles speak with such deep spiritual insight, the question is, How this came to pass? They were not philosophers, scholars, and orators, as the great and learned men of Greece and Rome were. The true explanation is, "holy men of God spoke as they were moved by the Holy Ghost." II. THEIR MENTAL ILLUMINATION WAS ACCOMPANIED BY DEEP AND INTENSE FEELING. Their spirits were "moved"—they felt the burden of "the word of the Lord"—the truth was in their heart "as a burning fire." Therefore speech became a necessity, for by speaking they lightened the burden that oppressed them and gave out the fire that burned in their bosoms. When they had messages of peace and good tidings to deliver, their "doctrine dropped as the rain, their speech distilled as the dew, and as the small rain upon the tender herb." But when the sins of the nation and the judgments of heaven were their themes, they cried aloud, and their language was as terrible as a midnight alarm. To speak as the prophets spoke we also must be enlightened and "moved" by the Holy Ghost. III. THE ABIDING POWER IN THE WORDS. They are instinct with the love, the pity, the sympathy, and the power of the Divine mind. "They are spirit, and they are life." The ancient sacred fire that descended from heaven continues to burn on the altar of the Bible. (*T.*'*Jones.*)　　　*The Bible :*—I speak of THE BIBLE FIRST AS THE GREAT TEACHER OF MANKIND, because it must ever continue to be of the supremest importance to the race of mankind. It contains the record of God's special revelations to one chosen people, and of that final all-inclusive revelation, wherein He has spoken and is speaking to us by His Son. The Bible is not by any means God's only revelation. It always has been an evil when it has been so considered. It contains, however, some of the clearest and directest lessons which God has ever spoken to man through the mind and utterance of his brother man. Take but one illustration of its unique supremacy. After all these thousands of years of the world's existence, after all splendours of literature in all the nations and in all ages, there is no book in the whole world which can supersede the Bible as an instrument for the education of the young. After all these millenniums it remains the most uniquely glorious book which the world has ever known. "Its light," says Cardinal Newman, "is like the beauty of heaven in all its clearness, its vastness like the bosom of the sea, its variety like the scenes of nature." Perhaps testimony from a religious teacher might be regarded as purely official. Let me, then, quote the testimony of an eminent living man of science; the testimony of a man like Professor Huxley on this subject will, at least, not be suspected. "I have been seriously perplexed to know," he says, "how the religious feeling which is the essential basis of conduct can be kept up without the use of the Bible. The pagan moralists lacked fire, and life, and colour, and even the noble Stoic, Marcus Aurelius, is too high and refined for an ordinary child. For three centuries this book has been woven into the life of all that is best and noblest in English history. It forbids the veriest hind who never left his village to be ignorant of the existence of other countries and other civilisations, and of the great past stretching back to the furthest limit of the oldest nations of the world. By the study of what other book could children be so much humanised or made to feel that each figure in that vast historical procession fills, like themselves, but a momentary inter-space between two eternities, and earns the blessings or the curses of this and of all time, according to his efforts to do good and to hate evil, even as they also are earning their payment for their daily work?" Unhappily, however, the Bible in age after age has been liable to such boundless misinterpretation, that it is not possible or honourable to speak of it as the most blessed among the teachers of mankind, without admitting, as St. Peter did eighteen hundred years ago, that it may very easily be wrested to our own destruction. Century after century men, misled by their religious teachers, have failed altogether to see what the Bible is; they have made a fetish of it, and under the plea of its sacredness have taken advantage of its many-sidedness to get rid of its most central and essential teaching; they have made it like the *fainéant* monarchs who have been surrounded with splendid state and almost Divine reverence, while care was taken that their real voice should never be heard, and their real wishes never known. Men have used the Bible to find an excuse for hating and cursing and burning one another, they have torn it into shreds and turned each shred of it into a fluttering ignoble ray of some party pennon; they have dislocated its phrases and built false theologies on the perversions of its texts. . . . But having eliminated these errors, we may dwell without stint on the priceless value of Scripture as a whole—of Scripture in its best and final teaching to the heart of man. The Talmud and the Koran, and even the writings of the Indian and the Buddhist, have stolen its precious gems. It has exercised the toil of men like Origen and Jerome, and fired the eloquence of Chrysostom and Augustine. It dictates the supreme and immortal songs of Dante and of Milton. It has inspired the pictures of Fra Angelico and Raphael, the music of Handel and Mozart. There is scarcely any noble part of knowledge worthy of the mind of man, but from Scripture it may have some direction and light. The hundred best books, the hundred best pictures, the hundred best pieces of music, are ten times over involved in it. The sun never sets upon its gleaming page. " What a book," exclaimed the sceptical poet Heine, after a day spent in the unwonted task of reading it. " Vast and wide as the world, rooted in the abysses of creation and towering up beyond the blue secrets of heaven; sunrise and sunset, promise and fulfilment, birth and death, the whole drama of humanity, are all in this book." " In this book," said Ewald, the foremost of modern critics, when Dean Stanley visited him, and the New Testament, which was lying on the table, fell accidentally to the ground—" in this book," he said, as he stooped to pick it up, " is all the wisdom of the world." II. TEST IT ONCE MORE BY THE IMMEASURABLE COMFORT AND BLESSING WHICH IT, AND WHICH IT ALONE, HAS BROUGHT AND EVER CAN BRING TO DYING MEN. Millions have loved it passionately who have cared nothing for any other literature, and it alone has been sufficient to lead them through life as with an archangel's hand. " Into Thy hands I commend my spirit "; in age after age Polycarp, Augustine, John Huss, Jerome of Prague, St. Bernard, Luther, Melanc-thon, Columbus, Francis Xavier, and I know not how many thousands more, have died with these words upon their lips. " That book, sir," said Andrew Jackson, President of the United States, pointing to the family Bible upon the table, as he lay upon his death-bed, " that book, sir, is the rock on which our Republic rests." " I have only one book now," said the poet Collins, " but that is the best." " Bring me the book, sir," said Sir Walter Scott to Lockhart on his death-bed. " What book ? " asked Lockhart. " *The* book, the Bible," said Sir Walter, " there is only one." Every shallow and ignorant freethinker thinks he can demolish the Bible; he might as well try to demolish the Himalayas. The greatest men have esteemed it most. Infidels babble about the contradictions between Scripture and science. I have quoted the testimony of one of the most eminent living men of science ; let me quote one of the most illustrious dead. Once, when the famous Faraday was lying ill, his physician, Dr. Latham, found him in tears with his arm resting upon a table on which lay the open book. " I fear you are worse," said Dr. Latham. " It is not that," said Faraday, with a sob ; " but why will people go astray when they have this blessed book to guide them ? " Its words speak to the ear and to the heart as no other music will, even after wild and sinful lives. " Though I walk through the valley of the shadow of death I will fear no evil, for Thou art with me, Thy rod and Thy staff comfort me." Those words were written by his physician to Daniel Webster on his death-bed, and the great man, the despised, broken idol of a great nation, who had cast the destiny of all his life on one throw of ambition and had lost the cast—the great man faltered out, " That is what I want—Thy rod, Thy rod, Thy staff, Thy staff," and they were the last words he said. III. I WOULD THEN URGE YOU ALL TO A CONSTANT AND REVERENT, BUT AT THE SAME TIME A WISE AND SPIRITUAL, STUDY OF THIS BOOK. " If we be ignorant," said the translators of 1611, " the Scriptures will instruct us ; if out of the way, they will bring us home ; if out of order, they will reform us ; if in heaviness, comfort us ; if dull, quicken us ; if cold, inflame us." *Tolle lege, Tolle lege;* take them and read, take them and read. Only beware how you read. Read as a scoffer read as a pharisee, and it will be useless. Read rightly, and then the Bible will be a light unto your feet, and a lamp unto your path. Read teachably, read devotionably. The saving knowledge of Scripture is a science, not of the intellect, but of the heart. Read, above all, as Christ taught us to read, not to entangle yourselves in the controversial or the dubious, but go to the very heart of the central significance. (*Archdeacon Farrar.*) *The Holy Scriptures :*—I. THE BIBLE IS THE MOST ANCIENT BOOK IN THE WORLD, AND YET IT IS NOT ANTIQUATED, but always fresh and fragrant, as the beauty of the morning, and the breath of spring. Like the angel of the resurrection, the spirit of the Bible is clothed and crowned with immortal youth, and rejoices in the possession of undecaying strength. II. THE BIBLE IS THE MOST EXPANSIVE BOOK IN THE WORLD. It was the saying of Malebranche, the great philosopher, that if he had all truth, he would let forth only a ray at a time, lest it should blind the world. And this seems to be the principle which underlies the whole revelation in the Word of God. The truth is unveiled to men according as they are able to bear it. III. THE BIBLE IS THE MOST INSPIRING BOOK IN THE WORLD. We may hold certain mechanical views of inspiration, but the question for each one of us is to ask, Does the Bible really inspire us? The Bible is inspired because it is inspiring, and if it fails of this effect, then the mere theoretical knowledge of the inspiration will be of little value. And yet if we derive no inspiration from Scripture, we must not therefore lay the blame upon the Bible, and conclude that it has failed to stand the test. There are certain qualities of mind and heart which we must bring to the interpretation of all things. Nature herself will not inspire us if we have no eye to see her beauty, or heart to understand her charm. It is the poet who sees in nature a glow and glory which may be hidden from others, because he is possessed with a certain sympathy. So it is in regard to the Bible. We must bring to its study an innocent eye and a pure heart, a longing desire for truth, and a purpose to obey it; and then we shall feel inspired by the revelations which it makes known to us. IV. THE BIBLE IS THE ONLY PERFECT BOOK IN THE WORLD. Perfection is the sign and signature of all God's works. If you put under the microscope a bee's sting and an ordinary sewing needle, you will at once see the difference between man's handiwork and God's. They are both very like each other when examined by the naked eye; but when brought beneath the lens we perceive the mighty difference. The needle is rough and rugged, full of bulges and bends, like the undressed bough of a tree, whereas the sting of the bee retains its arrowy point and perfection under the closest scrutiny. And so it is with all God's works in contrast with man's. The Bible is the only perfect book, because it is the work of God. The law of the Lord is perfect, says the Psalmist, the sun rules in the heavens, and divides the day from the night. And so with the Word of God. The light which shines through it rules the mind and will and heart of man, and divides the darkness from the light. But the Word of God is not only perfect, but it is designed to make man perfect—that the man of God may be perfect—fully furnished unto every good work. (*J. Coats Shanks.*) *The incidental advantages of study of the Bible :*— It is common to urge upon men a study of the Bible as a matter of duty—a part of the "thou shalt" of God; and also as a matter of worship—the other part of prayer and praise. While it is fortunate that we have a book which can lay the claim of duty upon us, and still more fortunate that we have a book worthy to be incorporated into our worship, there are other aspects in which the Bible offers itself, which might be called its advantages. Set aside now the fact that it is a religious book, and all religious considerations, and regard it simply as a book to be studied, and there is no book the study of which brings so many advantages as the Bible, because there is no other one book that embraces so many departments of truth and knowledge or treats them in so wise a way. I. Look at it as A BOOK OF HISTORY. The Bible begins with the creation out of chaos, and ends with humanity lifted into the heavens, and the whole mighty sweep is history. But the great advantage of studying history through the Bible is that we thus follow the main current of human progress in all the ages; we are tracing an idea, a principle, a force, and that the greatest the world has ever felt. II. LOOK AT IT AS A BOOK OF POLITICAL SCIENCE. A study of the Hebrew Commonwealth is valuable because it shows how close and real is the relation of the nation to God, and how vital is righteousness and fidelity to God. We have in the Bible the finest illustration of patriotism to be found in all history. There was no individualism, there was no communism, but a happy balance between man as an individual and as a member of the race, such as we find in nature. We are individuals; we are also members of the race, and both exist in God. A true nation is a true expression of this threefold fact. Nowhere is it so clearly set forth as in the Hebrew Commonwealth. Its institutions, also, are well worth studying. The details of life are treated sacredly. A Divine emphasis is laid upon trivial matters of well-being. Filth and contagious diseases are an abomination in the sight of God. Health is well pleasing to God. Family, property, personal rights, sex are guarded by Divine sanctions. III. LOOK AT IT AS A BOOK OF BIOGRAPHY. "The proper study of mankind is man." The Bible is permanently a book of biographies. It is a book of religious history, but the history is always turning on a man. It is a book of religion, but the religion is that of real life, and of separate men. When men of great natures move through great scenes, and do great deeds, or when they unfold qualities and traits that are fine and rare and strong, then we have the materials for biography. By such a standard the Bible is most rich in this material for study. IV. LOOK AT IT AS A BOOK OF LITERA-

TURE. Dr. Johnson once read the Book of Ruth to a company of literary infidels. "What a charming idyl!" they said. "Where did you find it?" There are four fields of literature in which the Bible rises higher than all other books—ethics, religious poetry, religious vision, and the drama in its high sense as a discussion of human life. The Proverbs and Book of Ecclesiastes are the wisest, aptest, most varied, and best expressed maxims of practical life ever made, and outweigh in value all others taken together. The Psalms, considered simply as expressions of religious feeling, find no rival. They touch every mood, sink to all depths, rise to all heights; they are as free and natural as the winds, and cover human nature as it weeps and struggles and hopes and rejoices. The prophetic utterances are not only unique, but are fuller of passion, sublimer in expression, bolder in imagery, loftier in conception, than anything to be found in profane literature. And they have this unique quality: they are the products of an actual experience, and not mere creations of the imagination. They have also this transcendent value—one that should make them dear to every thoughtful man: they are expressions of patriotism, and contain the philosophy of national life as existing in God. V. Look at it as a book FULL OF UNDEVELOPED FORCES AND TRUTHS. I mean the opposite of the common assertion that it is an exhausted book. I mean it in a sense that excludes it from being classed with other books called sacred. I admit that there are a few books which seem to hold within themselves truths capable of infinite expansion, and to touch truths not yet realised. Such are some of the great philosophies and poems and essays; but, after studying them awhile, the sense of finiteness begins to gather about them; we come to limitations, to boundaries; there is a solid firmament above, and the truths run round the world and not into endless heavens; we detect faults; we feel the weakness of a human personality; we say, "Thou hast seen far, but not the end, nor the whole." It is not so when we read the Bible. One reason why some men reject it or pass it by is that it so quickly carries them beyond their depth and outruns their conception. And one reason why other men delight in it, and write books upon books about it, is that it brings the infinite and the mysterious within reach, enkindling their imaginations and stirring their spirits by the outlooks thus gained. I spoke of the Bible as a book of undeveloped spiritual forces. I mean that we find in it those facts and laws and truths which are working out the destiny of man. They are spread out in a life; they are uttered in words. The parables of Christ—if we but knew it—contain the history of the world and of mankind for all eternity. The Sermon on the Mount states the laws by which human society progresses, and will reach its goal of perfection. The acts of Christ's life illustrate or reveal how this material world is immersed in the real world of the spirit, where the miraculous becomes natural. The whole life of Christ is simply a true life—perfectly obedient to God, wholly sacrificed for man, duty itself, love itself, lost and so found, Divine and human, and claiming a oneness for humanity with itself in God. I anticipate the day when the Bible will stand higher in the estimate of men than ever before. It will not be blindly worshipped as in the past, but it will be more intelligently read. It is not a book of the past, but of the future. As we move up toward it we shall find that it reflects the world on its pages, and that it contains the true order of human life. Meanwhile, it is not amiss for us to study the Decalogue for social guidance; the Beatitudes for guides in daily life; and Christ, in all the light and mystery of His being and character, as the Way, the Truth, and the Life—the way through this tangled world, the truth in this world of perplexity, the life in this world where all things else perish and pass away. (*T. T. Munger, D.D.*) *What is the Bible?*— The first thing I want to say to you is this: You are not to look in the Bible for a complete and comprehensive presentation of Divine truth. You are not to look in it for a revelation or disclosure of science of any kind, physical or metaphysical, natural or supernatural. It is not at all a scientific treatise. It does not aim or purport so to be. Nor are you to regard the Bible as an infallible book of equal value and equal authority in all its utterances and all its parts; as a book "without any intermixture of error." An infallible book would require, first of all, that the writers should be infallibly informed as to the truth; in the second place, that they should be able to utter it infallibly; in the third place, that they should have a language for the communication of their ideas which was an infallible vehicle of thought; in the fourth place, that, if they died, the manuscripts in which their thoughts were contained should be infallibly preserved, without any intermixture of error, through the ages after their death; fifthly, that, if the language in which they wrote were changed, the translators should be themselves capable of giving an infallible translation; sixthly, that, if the book were to be infallibly applied to the actual conditions of life, men who interpreted and applied these principles should be infallible interpreters. And, finally, it would require that the men who received should be able infallibly to apprehend what was given. The treasure of truth in the Bible is not a minted treasure with the stamp of the Divine image upon it. It is like the gold hid in the bosom of the mountain. It must be mined, dug out with the alloy with which it is intermixed, washed, burned in the furnace, and the stamp must be put upon it before it is ready for currency. But as soon as this is done, the process begins over again. The Bible yields its treasure only to him who digs for it as for a hid treasure; the promise of the Bible is only to him who seeks and knocks. No age can do this seeking, this knocking, for another. The structure and the history of the Bible alike demonstrate that what God has given us here is not a substitute for thought, but an incentive to thinking. Lessing said, " If God were to offer me in one hand Truth and in the other Search for Truth, I would accept Search for Truth." What God gives us in the Bible is Search for Truth. What, then, is the Bible? It is a selection of literature evolved out of eighteen centuries of human life, comprising all various literary forms, written by men of all various types and temperaments, without concord, without mutual understanding, without knowing that they were making a book that was to last for all time. It is a collection of the most spiritual utterances, of the most spiritual men, of the most spiritual race, of past time. You are to come to it as such a collection. It is as such that you are to study and take advantage of it—as such a record of spiritual experiences. I. In the first place, then, in view of this generic statement, I urge on you to have your Bible—not merely *a* Bible, but YOUR BIBLE. Mr. Shearman has a copy of the Bible which Mr. Beecher carried for something like forty years— perhaps more—with his marking scattered through it. It is more than a Bible—it is Mr. Beecher's Bible; and the pencil-marks in it tell the story of his own spiritual experience, while they emphasize the spiritual experiences of the ages that are past. So, have your own Bible, into which your life shall be woven, around which your spiritual associations shall cluster, and which shall become sacred to you, not so much for the voice that spake to Abraham, to Moses, to David, to Isaiah, or Paul, so many centuries ago, but for the voice that has spoken to you—through Abraham, Moses, David, Isaiah, or Paul—in your own life-experience. II. USE YOUR BIBLE. The Bible that is to lay hold on you is a Bible that you must lay hold upon. Familiarise yourself with the Bible. It is a coy acquaintance. It does not let every one into its heart, or disclose to the chance acquaintance the secret of its power. You must love it. If you are to love it you must acquaint yourself with it. You must take it with you into your experience. You must make it the man of your counsel in your perplexity; you must go to it for comfort in your sorrow; you must find in it inspiration when the deadening process of life has brought you earthward; you must seek in it those experiences for which your own heart and soul hunger. III. You must, in your use of the Bible LOOK BEHIND THE BOOK TO THE TRUTH WHICH IS IN THE BOOK, and which really constitutes the book. Studying Biblical criticism is not studying the Bible. Behind all form and structure is the truth which makes the Bible. What is the Bible? This thing that I hold in my hand? Not at all. Were it in Greek, it would still be the Bible. Not the book—the truths that lie behind the book, they make the Bible. Such truths as these: the man is immortal—not that he is going to live a thousand or a hundred thousand years after death, but that he has in him a spirit that death cannot and does not touch; that he is under other laws than those that are physical, that he is under the great moral laws of right and wrong; that there is a God who knows, thinks, feels, loves; and that there is a helping hand reached down out of heaven to lay hold of and to give help to every struggling man seeking, working, praying, wrestling toward a nobler manhood; an immortal spirit, a personal God, a forgiveness of sins—that is the Bible. Go to the Bible, not for an infallible philosophy of human life, but for unveilings and disclosures of infinite, helpful, inspiring truth. IV. But behind this truth there is something further to be sought. FOR LIFE IS MORE THAN TRUTH, AND EXPERIENCE IS MORE THAN PHILOSOPHY. The Bible is the most human of books. It is the record of human life, and of the noblest and divinest experiences in human life. It is because it is a human book that it appeals to humanity. It is because it is a human book that humanity finds light and life and power in it. Writers of the Bible are not like lead pipes that take water from a distance and bring it a long way and deposit it for you, without the trouble of your drawing. Writers of the Bible are like the mountain-side, saturated with water which pours from its side in springs when we ask to drink. The Bible writers were saturated with Divine truth; then out of that saturation the truth sprang forth into utterance. In the Bible you come into association and fellowship with men who are living in the spiritual realm; you come in contact with men who are struggling, not for art, not for wealth, not for culture, not for refinement, but for walking with God. They blunder; they do not know; they have dim visions, oftentimes, of God—they see Him as that blind man saw the trees as men walking. Their notion is intermingled with the notion of their time; but in it all, throughout it all, inspiring it all, is that hunger and thirst after righteousness that shall be filled. To come into the Bible is to come, not into words graven on stone, however true, but into living experiences of love, of faith, or hope, wrought in imperfect lives, but glorifying them by the glory of an indwelling God. V. And behind the truth and behind the experience you are to look for something still more than either—YOU ARE TO LOOK FOR GOD HIMSELF. Back of all Bible truth is the human experience of the Divine. Back of all human experience of the Divine is the God that inspires, irradiates, and creates it. Do I value the locket less because I know it is a human handiwork? It is not the locket I care for. It is the picture of the beloved that is in the locket. It is not the frame and form and structure of the book, but it is the God who dwells in the book that makes it dear to me. Kaulbach's famous cartoon of the Reformation presents Luther holding aloft an open Bible, while grouped around and before him are the inventors, the discoverers, the thinkers, the writers of genius, that were nurtured in the cradle of the Reformation. It is a true picture. Where that open Bible has not gone, there to-day is darkness illimitable. Where that Bible has gone, partly opened and partly closed, there is a dawning of the day. And where it is an open Bible with a free page and a well-read one, there is the illumination of civilisation. (*Lyman Abbott, D.D.*) *What use do we make of the Scriptures?*—All our practical knowledge of God is comprised in the Bible. The Bible then ought to be to us that which the chart and the compass are to the mariner on a stormy ocean; we have absolutely no other guide, no other directory to our course. In what light, then, do we practically regard the Bible? Is it enough to possess the Scriptures, to have been instructed out of the Scriptures in infancy, to hear them read in public worship, to have a general approbation of their contents? Would it be satisfactory to the mariner merely to possess a compass on board his vessel; to have received information as to its use in infancy, to admire its utility, or to discourse sometimes publicly of its merits; meanwhile he is driving on, it may be, to rocks, to shoals, to sands, or quite away from his course? But how many an individual lives in this precise manner, as to his use of the Scriptures! Day passes after day, week after week, month after month, year after year, and God marks not his anxious eye pondering over this chart of life. Politics, science, poetry, history, it may be lighter productions—these can arrest his attention and interest his mind; but the Bible which notifies the waymarks to eternity—this excites no interest. And yet such a person perhaps expects God's favour—expects to reach the harbour of endless peace, and never even dreams of the probability of intervening shipwreck! Mournful and inconsistent expectations! Many, however, are to be found who are by no means chargeable with this entire neglect of the Scriptures. Some have, from infancy, acquired regular habits of reading the Bible, and peruse, as a daily or at least as a weekly task, their allotted chapters. But they do this oftentimes without anxiety, and without progress in religious knowledge. The *fact* of reading is to them more important than the *contents* which they read. They manifest no submission of the heart to God's teaching—no godly diligence to lay up in the soul His statutes and promises. Eternity fastens not upon their thoughts—the wonders of redeeming love attract not their affections. They read with coldness, and languor, and unconcern. There is no scrutiny as to the effect of their knowledge—as to the conformity of their views, and sentiments, and habits, with the decisions and intentions of God! The heart makes no progress in its voyage—it is no nearer to God—no nearer to the dispositions of Heaven than it was many years ago. Think again of the mariner—his eye glances daily upon his compass—or once a week he fixes his look upon the needle; but he uses not the helm—he brings not the vessel into the prescribed course! As well then might the compass be cast into the depths of the sea! Now, it is evident that this is not the use of the Scriptures which God demands—this is not to possess any anxiety as to the knowledge of God's will. Those who thus neglect, or thus imperfectly respect the Scriptures, are not among those who "work out their salvation with fear and trembling." (*Christian World Pulpit.*) *Scrip-*

*ture manifold yet one :*—The Bible is, to use the language of Prof. Westcott, " a book *manifold* by the variety of times and circumstances in which its several parts had their rise, *one* by the inspiring presence of the same spiritual life." It may be compared to a cathedral whose parts have been built at different successive ages : the traces of these ages are easily seen in the architectural style, but all are knit together in one holy temple of God. Closer investigation of this cathedral shows that the historical range of its growth is greater and wider than was at first supposed. The stones which have been built in, it seems, were drawn from widely-scattered quarries ; here are marbles which must have been imported from distant lands ; here are great blocks of stone which must have been conveyed from unthought-of hills ; here are richly-carved capitals which show some foreign skill : but all these have found their fitting place. Each stone, each ornament, drops into the spot prepared for it ; arch, pillar, buttress, mullion and pinnacle, whatever their greater or their lesser antiquity, are lending support or beauty, and fulfilling their functions as parts of one vast sanctuary, whose purpose is not lost or altered because antiquarians have made its stories doubly interesting and doubly dear by enlarging the bounds of its history and adding new elements to the story of its growth. (*Bp. W. B. Carpenter.*) **Profitable for doctrine, &c.**—*The uses of the Scriptures:*—The Scriptures give Divine, and therefore infallible, direction " for doctrine "—the didactic teaching of the truth concerning God ; " for reproof "—the refutation by proof of error concerning God ; " for correction "—the setting right or rectifying the wrong principles of practical ethics ; " for instruction in righteousness "—the positive nurture of the soul in experimental knowledge of the way in which a sinner may be accounted righteous before God. And this, it will be perceived on a little reflection, is a marvellously logical classification of their uses ; and it is exhaustive, as covering all the possible wants that man can desire to have met by a revelation. As a being endowed with reason, and capable of believing only what he conceives to be truth, his religion must embrace a " doctrine " of God and his relations to God. As a creature liable to be deceived, by error and unbelief concerning God and his relations to God, his religion must have a guide to warn against and expose the wiles of error, that are ever tampering with his " evil heart of unbelief." As a being whose passions are ever blinding his conscience in reference to duty toward God and man, his religion must supply him with a rule of right, by which to correct his crooked judgments and amend his crooked ways. As a being capable of a birth to a new and everlasting life, his religion must supply him with a nurture under the new law of righteousness which the faith that is unto salvation teaches him. So that it may be affirmed with truth, that no want of the human soul can be conceived, which is not provided for under one or other of these four heads. (*S. Robinson, D.D.*) *The profitableness of Scripture :*—The Scriptures are " profitable for reproof." The word here means *conviction*. The teaching has reference to the ignorance of men. the conviction refers to their errors and prejudices. The mental state presupposed here may be thus expressed : First, there is ignorance ; secondly, error, wrong thoughts and beliefs ; thirdly, prejudice in favour of the errors that are present, and against the truth that is absent. The declaration of the apostle is that the Word of God has power to convince those who are in this state ; that it will destroy their errors and remove their prejudice. One great reason why there is so much prejudice in many minds with regard to religion is, that they do not study the sacred Scriptures. They read all sorts of books concerning the Bible, but the Divine book itself is neglected. They prefer the water that is brought to them through pipes and curious contrivances of men to the fountain of living water, pure, clear as crystal, which springs up from the primeval rocks close to their own door. They gaze upon the cold and spiritless engraving rather than examine the grand original picture. The honest and earnest study of the Bible would produce a mighty revolution in the minds and hearts of thousands, both Christians and others. Akin to this there is another thought that follows. The Scriptures are profitable for correction. Some read to criticise. They cannot admire the great opening poem of the Book of Genesis, in which the inspired muse sings the creative power of the Almighty in notes " harmonious with the morning stars," because it does not speak with scientific precision. It is quite right to point out whatever inaccuracies may be discovered in the history of the deliverance from Egypt and the sojourn in the Wilderness, but one cannot help remarking that that is a peculiar state of mind in which a man can read through the wonderful story without being once struck with its spirit, its grandeur, and its awfulness. Others turn the sacred pages to find supports for the systems they have formed. This is the same as if a man constructed a theory of nature, and afterwards went in search of the facts whereby its truth must be proved. Others, again, read for comfort. They have been disappointed by the world in which they placed too much trust; or death has broken in upon their charmed circle and filled their hearts with sorrow; or their health is failing, and there are indications that the end is not distant; or their sin has been a burden from which they seek rest. Well, let them read for comfort, for the Bible is the book for sorrowful people. Its deep expressions of Divine love, sympathy, and tenderness have in them a power to heal the broken heart. But we should also know that the Scriptures are given for our " correction." He is the wise reader of God's Word who tries his opinions, beliefs, principles, life, and character by the Divine standard, and is willing to have them corrected. This brings us to the high purpose for which the Scriptures were given to us, namely, to impart "instruction in righteousness, that the man of God may be perfect"—right in every respect, in thought, feeling, character, and therefore right in state and condition—right in himself, right in his relations to his fellows, and right before God. The aim of the husbandman in the plants he cultivates is to have fruit; but Nature is as careful of the blossoms and the foliage as of the fruit, for her purpose is a perfect tree. Men cultivate parts of their nature. Some educate and develop their physical nature, and not much else. Others pay attention to the sensuous soul—they love music, art, eloquence, and light literature. There are persons who are mere thinkers; the cultivation of the intellectual powers is the one important thing in their estimation. Some spend their lives in small activities—things that are good in themselves, but which become harmful when done to the neglect of more important duties. There is good in all of these; but none of them aim high enough. The Divine purpose is not physical perfection, nor intellectual strength, nor refinement of taste, not even morality and devotion, but the full development of the whole nature, " that the man of God may be perfect." (*T. Jones.*)    *The proper way to test the Bible:*—You see a recipe for making bread. What is the way to test that recipe, but to put the materials together according to its direction? If the bread is good, the recipe is good, is it not? If it is good, I do not care where it came from—I do not care if King Pharaoh wrote it; and if it is not good, I would not care any more for it if it came from the angel Gabriel. It is the *thing* that proves the thing, The effect proves what is the nature of the cause. And if there are prescriptions in God's Word to heal pride, and selfishness, and all forms of sin and diseases, and on trial the prescriptions are found to do what they profess to be able to do, the effect justifies the cause. Now, the Bible does not profess to be a book of theories or philosophies. It professes to be "profitable for doctrine, for reproof"—it is the best book in this world for all sorts of reproof addressed to the weaknesses and wants of human life—" for instruction in righteousness: that the man of God may be perfect, throughly furnished unto all good works." Where a man wants to be a good man, where a man wants to be thoroughly furnished, and he goes to the Bible, he will have the best evidence that any man can have that it is a Divine book; for it will furnish him with those things which his experience shows him he needs. Here is a roll of charts of a difficult harbour. They were drawn, it may be, by Robert Small. They are handed by him to Admiral Dupont. The Admiral, the moment he sees them, laughs right out, and says, " Do you call this a chart?" It was made with a burnt stick. Robert Small, you know, was a slave; and he had to get his knowledge as other slaves get theirs. He was a pilot in Charleston harbour, however, and he knows where the shallow places are, where the deep places are, where the obstructions are, and where it is clear sailing; and he makes a rough sketch of the whole vicinity, and puts it into Admiral Dupont's hand; and the Admiral says, " Do you suppose I am going to steer my ships by a chart that a nigger made?" Or he says, " When did you make this? On what kind of a table did you make it? What did you use to make it with?" Does he say this? Under such circumstances what would Admiral Dupont do, who is a sensible man, and who has so much sense that he knows how to employ negroes, and take the advantage of their aid? He would say to those under him, " Take a cutter, man it, and go out, and sound, and see if the chart is correct"; and they would find the shoals and channels to be just as they were represented to be; and after they had put the chart to proof, and found it to correspond to the fact, they would report to him, and he would say, " That is a good chart, if a black man did make it. It is true, and that is the reason why it is good." Now, the Bible is a chart. It teaches men how to steer where that sandbank of temptation is; where that rock of danger is; where that whirling vortex of passion is. The Bible is a chart of salvation; and if a man only knows his course by this, he will go through life, with all its storms, and come safely into the port of heaven. The way to test the Bible is not to criticise it, and compare its rude marking with the more modern ways of making charts : the way to test the Bible is to put your sounding lines into the channel, and try it, and see if it is not true. But that is the test men do not employ. (*H. W. Beecher.*) *Scripture teaches a religion of grandeur and joy :*—I do not wonder that the men nowadays who do not believe the Bible are so very sad, when they are in earnest. A writer in one of our Reviews tells that he was studying the poems of Matthew Arnold, who believes not in a living God, but in a something or other, which somehow or other, at some time or other makes for righteousness. The sad and hopeless spirit of the poet passed for the time into the reviewer, and he felt most miserable. He went out for a walk. It was a bleak wintry day, and he was then at Brodick in Arran. The hills were in a winding-sheet of snow, above which arose a ghastly array of clouds. The sky was of a leaden hue, and the sea was making its melancholy moan amid the jagged, dripping rocks. The gloom without joined the gloom within, and made him very wretched. He came upon some boys shouting merrily at play. "Are you at the school?" he asked. "Yes," was the reply. "And what are you learning?" "I learn," said one, "what is the chief end of man." "And what is it?" the reviewer asked. The boy replied, "Man's chief end is to glorify God and to enjoy Him for ever." He at once felt that the boy was taught a religion of grandeur and joy, while the poet's was a religion of darkness and despair. (*J. Wells, M.A.*) *All Scripture profitable :*—In the plainest text there is a world of holiness and spirituality : and if we, in prayer and dependence upon God, sit down and study it, we shall behold much more than appears to us. It may be, at once reading or looking, we see little or nothing ; as Elijah's servant went once and saw nothing, therefore he was commanded to look seven times. "What now?" says the prophet. "I see a cloud rising like a man's hand," and by and by the whole surface of heaven was covered with clouds (1 Kings xviii. 44). (*J. Caryl.*) *Scripture to be used in daily life :*—A good husband having received a bag of money, locketh it up safe, that none may rob him of it, and as occasion is he fetcheth it down and layeth it out, some of it for food, some for clothes, some for rent, some for servants' wages, some for this thing, and some for that, as his necessities require ; so, friend, do thou lay up the precious treasure of the Word safe in the cabinet of thine heart, and bring it out as occasion calls for it, in thy daily life. (*G. Swinnock.*) *Adaptation of the Bible :*—The eyes of a good portrait follow the spectator wherever he stands, to look him exactly in the face ; and so, whoever a man may be, and whatever his case, the Bible confronts him with its warning if he be doing ill, its warranty if he be doing well, and its wisdom under any, and for all, circumstances. *Apology for the Bible :*—King George III. on first hearing of Bishop Watson's "Apology for the Bible," said, "Apology for the Bible ! I did not know that the Bible wanted any apology." *The pulpit and the reading-desk :*—John Wesley said to one of his followers, who urged upon him the deficiencies of some of the clergy, as a cause of separation, "If you have nothing but chaff from the pulpit, you are abundantly fed with the finest of the wheat from the desk." *Scripture its own evidence :*—It has been for thirty years the deep conviction of my soul that no book can be written on behalf of the Bible like the Bible itself. Man's defences are man's word . . . the Bible is God's Word, and by it the Holy Ghost, who first spoke it, still speaks to the soul that closeth itself not against it. (*E. B. Pusey, D.D.*) *Revelation and conscience :*—If we admit the agreement of revelation with conscience to be an evidence of Divinity in the Bible, do we thereby make conscience the criterion of what is Divine in it ? Some say so and make this the door to Rationalism. But it is surely possible to make conscience a *witness*, without exalting it into a *judge*. (*J. Ker, D.D.*) *The Bible penetrative :*—In the Bible there is more that finds me than I have experienced in all other books put together ; the words of the Bible find me at greater depths of my being; and whatever finds me brings with it an irresistible evidence of its having proceeded from the Holy Spirit. (*S. T. Coleridge.*) *Scripture profitable :*—A threefold account. 1. For their dignity and authority. 2. For their utility. 3. For their perfection. (1) They are profitable for doctrine and instruction : they teach men what to know and believe, they instruct us in all truth necessary to salvation, viz., concerning God, man, Christ, law, gospel, heaven, hell. He first begins with doctrine, which in order must go before all the rest ; for it is in vain to reprove or exhort unless we first teach a man and inform him of his duty. (2) For reproof of error and confutation of false doctrine. We need not run to general councils or send for ancient fathers to determine controversies or confute errors; we have the Holy Scriptures that enable the man of God, and furnish him richly for that purpose.   (3) For correction of sin and evil manners, which is done by admonition and reproof denouncing God's judgments against them, that those which go astray may be brought into the way by repentance.   (4) The Scripture teacheth us how to lead a holy and righteous life according to the will of God, and so is profitable for instruction in righteousness and good works, it being the most perfect rule of righteousness.   (5) The Scripture allures us to piety by the sweet promises of the gospel, and so is profitable for consolation (Rom. xv. 4).   This God hath ordained as a lamp for our feet, that we miscarry not amidst those many by-paths that are in the world.   Let us, then, make use of it in the course of our lives.   If a carpenter have a rule or line, if he tie it to his back and never use it, his work must needs be crooked; so if we have Bibles and never read them, nor meditate on them to practise them, our lives must needs be irregular.   They are, then, to be reproved who set up false rules to walk by, as—1. Antiquity.  2. Custom. 3. Fathers.   4. The Church.   5. Reason.   6. Universality.   7. Enthusiams.  (*T. Hall, B.D.*)     *Profiting in Scripture to appear :*—Let us imitate the sheep, which boast not how much they have eaten, but show it actually by their fat, fleece, and young.  (*Ibid.*)     *How to profit by Scripture :*—Observe, such as meddle with God's Word must profit by it.   We abuse the Word when we read or hear it only for speculation, novelty, and curiosity, but not for practice, that we may know, love, and fear God, and so be happy for ever.   God gave them for this end, that we might profit by them.   Those ministers, then, are to be blamed that play with Scripture and feed their people with the chaff of airy notions, frivolous questions, idle distinctions, and foolish controversies, seeking their own ends and praise, and not the benefit of God's people.   Let such remember that the Scripture was given to profit us, but not play withal.   (*Ibid.*)     *Perfection of Scripture should win regard :*—This perfection of the Scripture should stir up our love to it.   As imperfect things are slighted by us, so complete and perfect things are highly esteemed by all the sons of wisdom.   No book to be compared to this for perfection, and therefore no book should be so loved, read, studied, and prized by us.   Here's nothing vain or superfluous, but all things full of life and spirit; whatever good the soul can desire, 'tis here to be had.   Here is food for the hungry, water for the thirsty, wine for the wearied, bread for the weak, raiment for the naked, gold for the poor, eye-salve for the blind, and physic for the sick.   If thy heart be dead, this will quicken thee; if hard, this will soften it; if dull, revive it.   In all our temptations, this is a David's harp that helpeth to still them (Acts xv. 31).   We should therefore with joy draw water out of these wells of salvation (Isa. xii. 3).   We see how worldlings delight to view their bills and bonds, their leases and indentures, by which they hold their lands and livings; and shall not we delight to study the Scripture, which assureth us of never-fading riches ?  (*Ibid.*)     *Plainness of Scripture :*—A lady of suspected chastity, and who was tinctured with infidel principles, conversing with a minister of the gospel, objected to the Scriptures on account of their obscurity and the great difficulty of understanding them.   The minister wisely and smartly replied, " Why, madam, what can be easier to understand than the Seventh Commandment—' Thou shalt not commit adultery' ? "  (*C. Buck.*)     *The Bible a guide :*—The Bible is not a puzzle to wise heads, but a lamp for the wayfaring man.  (*Daniel Moore.*)     *The Bible a guide :*—No ; I say, destroy the Bible, and still everything remains the same— except that you have lost your guide.   If a party of voyagers who are passing through a dangerous channel were to say, " Away with the chart ! it is such a worry to be always looking at it ; and it expects one to be so very careful, too ; away with it ; it's a nuisance ! " you might easily get rid of your chart, but the rocks and shoals and sunken reefs and all the perils of the channel would remain there just the same.   Suppose a community were to say, " Banish your doctors. Let's have no medical books here, no treatises on disease.   ' Throw physic to the dogs.   We'll none of it ! ' "   They could do that, of course, if they liked.   But the laws and conditions of health and disease, of life and death, would remain precisely where they were before.   And it is conceivable that men might get rid of the Bible. Practically, many do get rid of the Bible ; but what do they gain ?   Only the loss of a guide.   The facts of the universe, the facts about man and about God, the facts about the mutual relation of the one to the other, remain precisely the same.  (*G. Calthrop, M.A.*)     *Restraining power of the Bible :*—The Rev. Charles Vince, of Birmingham, told the following incident at a meeting of the Bible Society in 1863 :—

" The Hill-top Auxiliary in the 'Black Country' determined to send round two or three Christian men every Saturday evening, with packages of Bibles, to visit the public-houses and persuade the miners and puddlers of the district, while they had their money, to spend some part of it in buying the Word of God. While they were carrying out this plan a miner said, 'Wouldn't it be a good thing for us to have a copy to read down in the pit at dinner-time?' The proposition met with general approval, and they agreed to buy a copy for this purpose. Of the first copy handed to them the landlord said the print was too small to read down in the pit, and offered to give a shilling towards the cost of a better type. This was bought, and one of the men said with great simplicity, 'If we have the Bible at dinner-time, we mustn't have any swearing.' This, too, was carried, and a fine imposed upon the man that should break the rule. Is there any other book in the world that you could carry into the company of men and make them say, 'If we open this, and begin to look at it, we must begin to put away some of our sins'?" (*Family Treasury.*) *The Bible instructive* :—A Hindoo paper, published in Bengal, speaks as follows of the excellence of the Bible:—" It is the best and most excellent of all English books, and there is not its like in the English language. As every joint of the sugar-cane, from the root to the top, is full of sweetness, so every page of the Bible is fraught with the most precious instruction. A portion of this book would yield to you more of sound morality than a thousand other treatises on the same subject. In short, if anybody studies the English language with a view to gaining wisdom, there is not another book which is more worthy of being read than the Bible." (*Sword and Trowel.*) *Faraday's testimony to the value of Scripture* :— One of the best and greatest Fellows of the Royal Society in the present century was ill, and sitting in his room, when one of the best of my profession that ever lived in this country, Dr. Latham, went in to him and found this great man in tears, sitting by his fireside. Latham told me this story himself. He said, " My good friend, I fear you feel more ill to-day; what is it?" " No," he said, " not that; I was thinking what a sorrow it is that the world will go astray when it has this blessed book to guide it." This man was Faraday, and I need not say that the book on his table was the Bible. (*Sir H. W. Acland, M.D.*) *The poor widow's treasure* :—" Did ye ask me if I had a Bible?" said a poor old widow in London; " Did ye ask me if I had a Bible? Thank God I have a Bible. What should I do without my Bible? It was the guide of my youth, and it is the staff of my age; it wounded me, and it healed me; it condemned me, and it acquitted me; it showed me I was a sinner, and it led me to the Saviour; it has given me comfort through life, and I trust it will give me hope in death." *The principles of Scripture to be applied* :—Professor Newman complained, some years ago, against our Bible, because it does not tell every father to what business or profession he should put his sons. For such infinite particulars and detailed advices we should require, not a portable manual, but a British Museum. Far wiser and truer is the principle enunciated by the orator Burke, when he says, " Reading, and much reading, is good. But the power of diversifying the matter infinitely in your own mind, and of applying it to every occasion that arises, is far better; so don't suppress the living force." (*J. Clifford, D.D.*) *The Bible a lighthouse* :—A lighthouse looks like a tall pillar rising out of the sea, or built upon some high bluff. The top is a large lantern, where a bright light is kept burning all night, which is seen far out at sea; and it says to all ships and sailors sailing by, " Take care! take care!" One is built on a ledge of rocks; its warning light says, " Give wide berth to these sunken rocks." Another says, " Steer clear of this dangerous reef." Another, " Keep clear of this dangerous headland. If you come here, you are lost." There are a great many lighthouses on the coast: how does a sailor know which is which? He sees a light gleaming through the darkness and the storm; but where is it? He has a chart in the ship, and that tells. A chart is a map of the coast, with all its rocks and sandbanks and lighthouses put down, and everything that a sailor ought to know in order to steer his ship safely across the ocean. If he faithfully consults it, and keeps a good look out, he is likely to ride out the storm and come safely into port. **That the man of God may be perfect.**—*Character* :— The superiority of man is everywhere manifested on earth. True greatness is measured by character. I. To PERFECT THE CHARACTER OF MAN IS THE AIM OF CHRISTIAN TRUTH. II. IN DEVELOPED CHARACTER IS TO BE FOUND THE GREAT MORAL RICHES OF THE WORLD. III. IN IT WE HAVE A STRIKING PROOF OF MAN'S IMMORTALITY. IV. IT SUPPLIES A TEST BY WHICH TO MEASURE THE VALUE OF THE SERVICES OF THE SANCTUARY, THE VALUE OF THE BIBLE, OF ALL THINGS—ITS ABILITY TO DEVELOP TRUE MANHOOD. Have we grown in Christian character? Have the Church services proven barren or fruitful to us ? (*R. S. Storrs, D.D.*)　　*The Bible the book for the man of God :*—Jerome was versed in the polite literature of his day and in the works of classic writers. He tells us that in a dream he once thought himself arraigned before the judgment seat of Christ, where he was asked the nature of his profession. He answered, " I am a Christian." " Thou art not ! " said the Judge ; " thou art a Ciceronian, for the works of that author possess thy heart." The Judge then gave order that he should be scourged by angels. Although it was only a dream, his chastisement never was forgotten ; it changed the direction of his thoughts. " From that time," he says, " I gave myself to the reading of Divine things with greater diligence and attention than I had ever read the other authors." To give undue attention to secular reading, to the neglect of sacred literature, is a temptation peculiar to the cultivated believer, and it is a real temptation ; for one may be as sordid in the acquisition of knowledge as in the pursuit of wealth. *The man of God's equipment :*—I. THE MAN OF GOD IS INSTRUCTED—1. Concerning God. 2. Concerning man. 3. Concerning duty. 4. Concerning responsibility. II. THE MAN OF GOD IS DISCIPLINED. 1. Joy in prosperity. 2. Hope in adversity. 3. A cheerful submission to the will of God at all times. III. THE MAN OF GOD IS INSPIRED. 1. The mind is illumined. 2. The affections are sanctified. 3. The whole life is made the reflex of revelation. (*Weekly Pulpit.*)　　*Development of character :*—An English barrister who was accustomed to train students for the practice of law, and who was not himself a religious man, was once asked why he put students, from the very first, to the study and analysis of the most difficult parts of the Sacred Scriptures ? " Because," said he, " there is nothing else like it, in any language, for the development of mind and character."　　*The Bible the text-book of character :*—Professor Matthew Arnold represents modern literature, and is often regarded as one of the severest critics of the current Christianity ; yet he says, " As well imagine a man with a sense for sculpture not cultivating it by the help of the remains of Greek art, or a man with a sense for poetry not cultivating it by the help of Homer and Shakespeare, as a man with a sense for conduct not cultivating it by the help of the Bible." Professor Huxley represents modern science, and is the *bête noire* of controversial theologians ; yet he says, " I have been perplexed to know by what practical measures the religious feeling, which is the essential basis of conduct, was to be kept up . . . without the use of the Bible."

---

## CHAPTER IV.

VERS. 1, 2. **I charge thee.**—*An earnest charge :*—Cold preaching makes bold sinners, when powerful preaching awes the conscience. Matters of greatest importance must be pressed with greatest vehemence. God putteth not forth great power but for great purpose (Eph. i. 18, 19). (*T. Hall, B.D.*)　　*Charged before God :*—The master's and the commander's eye make the servant and the soldier active (Matt. vi. 6 ; Acts x. 4). (*Ibid.*)　　*Earnestness in preaching :*—It is weakness to be hot in a cold matter, but worse to be cold in a hot matter. (*J. Trapp.*) *The judgment :*—Dr. John Brown, speaking of a minister's leaving his people for another pastorate, says that he mentally exclaims, " There they go ! When next they meet it will be at the judgment ! " (*H. O. Mackey.*)　　*Ministers at the judgment :*—Adalbert, who lived in the tenth century, was appointed Archbishop of Prague. This preferment seemed to give him so little satisfaction that he was never seen to smile afterwards ; and on being asked the reason, he replied : " It is an easy thing to wear a mitre and a cross, but an awful thing to give an account of a bishopric before the Judge of quick and dead." (*W. H. Baxendale.*)　　*An ordination charge :*—I. WHERE FAITHFUL MINISTERS STAND—" Before God and the Lord Jesus Christ." 1. Before God. (1) As a sinner saved by grace. Once far off, but brought nigh by the blood of Christ. (2) As a servant. In prayer, how sweet to kneel at His footstool, no veil, no cloud between the soul and God. In preaching, how sweet to say, like Elijah, when he stood before Ahab, " I stand before the Lord God of Israel." 2. Before Jesus Christ. (1) The faithful minister has a present sight of Christ as his righteousness. He, like Isaiah, saw " His glory and spake of

Him." (2) The faithful minister should feel the presence of a living Saviour (Jer. i. 8; Acts xviii. 10). (3) Within sight of judgment. II. THE GRAND BUSINESS OF THE FAITHFUL MINISTER. 1. Preach the Word. (1) Not other matters. (2) The most essential parts especially. (3) More in the manner of God's Word. 2. Reprove, rebuke, exhort. Most ministers are accustomed to set Christ before the people. They lay down the gospel clearly and beautifully, but they do not urge men to enter in. Now God says, exhort; not only point to the open door, but compel them to come in. III. THE MANNER. 1. With long-suffering. There is no grace more needed in the Christian ministry than this. This is the heart of God the Father towards sinners—"He is long-suffering to usward, not willing that any should perish." 2. With doctrine—the clear and simple statement of the truth preceding the warm and pathetic exhortation. 3. With urgency. If a neighbour's house were on fire, would we not cry aloud and use every exertion? If a friend were drowning, would we be ashamed to strain every nerve to save him? 4. At all times. Satan is busy at all times—he does not stand upon ceremony—he does not keep himself to Sabbath-days or canonical hours. Death is busy. Men are dying while we are sleeping. The Spirit of God is busy. Blessed be God, He hath cast our lot in times when there is the moving of the Great Spirit among the dry bones. Shall ministers then be idle, or stand upon ceremony? (*R. M. McCheyne.*) *Urgency of the ministerial office :*—In a visit which I once made, when a young clergyman, to the churches of Belgium, so remarkable for the grandeur and elaborate carving of their pulpits, my attention was especially attracted by one well suited to enforce a solemn lesson on every one who might occupy it. There arose from the back of it a gigantic figure of death, stretching its gaunt skeleton form over the head of the preacher, and holding in one hand a scythe, and with the other presenting a scroll on which was inscribed "Hasten thou to gather in thy harvest, for I must soon reap mine." Yes! it is the brevity of the opportunity and the inestimable interests at stake which render the ministerial office of such urgency that no season may be missed, no effort spared, in order that it may accomplish its work. (*Bp. Baring.*) *Preaching in the sight of God :*—Bishop Latimer having one day preached before King Henry VIII. a sermon which displeased his majesty, he was ordered to preach again on the next Sabbath, and to make an apology for the offence he had given. After reading his text, the bishop thus begun his sermon: "Hugh Latimer, dost thou know before whom thou art this day to speak? To the high and mighty monarch, the king's most excellent majesty, who can take away thy life if thou offendest; therefore, take heed that thou speakest not a word that may displease. But then consider well, Hugh, dost thou not know from whence thou comest—upon whose message thou art sent? Even by the great and mighty God! who is all-present! and who beholdeth all thy ways! and who is able to cast thy soul into hell! Therefore, take care that thou deliverest thy message faithfully." He then proceeded with the same sermon he had preached the preceding Sabbath, but with considerably more energy. The sermon ended, the Court were full of expectation to know what would be the fate of this honest and plain-dealing bishop. After dinner the king called for Latimer, and, with a stern countenance, asked him how he dared to be so bold as to preach in such a manner. He, falling on his knees, replied, his duty to his God and his prince had enforced him thereto, and that he had merely discharged his duty and his conscience in what he had spoken. Upon which the king, rising from his seat, and taking the good man by the hand, embraced him, saying, "Blessed be God I have so honest a servant!" **At His appearing.**—*The second advent :*—I. THE MANNER. 1. In mystery. 2. In glory. 3. With universality. II. THE PURPOSE. 1. To reveal the true judgment of righteousness. 2. To proclaim open verdict on probationers. 3. To ensure an effectual separation of character. III. THE RESULTS. 1. The vindication of righteousness. 2. The triumph of love. (*U. R. Thomas.*) **Preach the Word.**—*The ministry of the Word :*—Preaching is God's great ordinance now, as it has been in the past. Its source and substance is the Word. The truth you are to preach is a Divine revelation, a written system of truth. Your teaching is not the tradition of men on the one hand, or their mysterious speculations on the other, but the revealed Word of the living God. You are not the inspirer or discoverer of truth, you are only its interpreter. It is no light matter to represent with freshness and force the truth when reached. Much work goes to that, not to elaborate but to simplify. The test of clear thinking is clear expression. Let the teaching of Christ be your pattern—words clear and simple as the light of heaven—thoughts deep as eternity. Have faith therefore in hard work. But labour is not enough. The mere interpreter can see but a little way into religious truth. The heart sees best. The rays of truth, that shine down into the closet, are the brightest and the best. Have faith in prayer as well as in toil. But while preaching the Word in its fulness, preach it also in its unity—that is, preach Christ. A Bible without Christ, a pulpit without Christ, would be a world without God. Give Christ the place in preaching that He holds in the Word : Christ's death —the sinner's only hope ; Christ's life—the believer's only pattern ; the righteous- ness of Christ—the ground of pardon ; the grace of Christ—the riches of believers ; the love of Christ—the power of new obedience. It is only from the height of the Cross that we can get a full view of the Word. Not that you are always to be preaching on the central doctrine of the Cross, just as you are not always looking right up to the sun ; but as you view all things on earth in the light that streams from the sun, so should you see all truth in the light that streams from the Cross. That is no narrow theme, or soon exhausted. Christ can enter into everything, into all doctrine, all duties, all experience. Christian doctrine is just Christ's portrait, drawn at full length. Christian morality is just Christ's portrait, embodied in the life. Christian experience is Christ realised in the heart. Christian usefulness is Christ's glory, carried out into all the details of life. And, last of all, preach the Word, for it is the "power of God unto salvation to every one that believeth." Preach it for salvation ; not only for instruction, that you may save yourself and them that hear you. All its truths are revealed for this end. (*J. Riddell.*) *Preach the Word :*—I. We must preach the Word with reference to the Divinity of its Author. II. We must preach the Word with reference to the wonders of His love! III. We must preach the Word with reference to the efficacy of His atoning sacri- fice. IV. We must preach the Word with reference to the sanctifying influences of His Spirit. V. We must preach the Word faithfully and fully, in its precepts, as well as its doctrines. VI. We must preach the Word in its catholic and evangelical spirit. VII. We must preach the Word as the grand means of promoting the Saviour's glory ; and of accelerating the approach of the millennial day. (*J. Parsons.*) *Conditions of success in working for Christ :*—1. A sound conversion is essential to successful effort. 2. An intimate association with Christ is an element of great success. Let a minister go out into the fields with Jesus to glean, and he shall come back at even, "bearing his sheaves with him." Let him go out helped by genius, by culture, by learning, by wealth, by position, leaving Christ behind, and his words are as sounding brass and a tinkling cymbal. 3. Christians must orga- nise for victory. A sleepless vigilance and a tireless activity are as essential to success in the Church as in business. A progressive man holds fast to what has been attained, and reaches forth to possibilities laid bare to his eye. 4. A high ideal of a Christian's position and work must be kept in view. 5. The great fight is the preaching of the Word. The men of power and weight are men of the Book ; such represent God. 6. Practise the Word. (*J. D. Fulton, D.D.*) *Preaching the Word :*—To rightly "preach the Word" there is demanded a far-reaching pre- paration. Not for a work like that of the old alchemists and astrologers whose locks and beards grew grey as they bent over their crucibles or gazed at the stars, in the vain hope of solving mysteries. We have little to do with mysteries. It is for the simplicity of the gospel we search, and that leads us to heights and depths. We are to so think and pray and live that we may show to men plain paths for their feet. This makes the minister a student, but none the less a man. It is manly to follow the lead of heavenly lights over rough ways and into clouds. The richest ores and gems of Nature are guarded by her fortresses ; so is it with truth, and no man but the sluggard complains that a full soul, like a full purse, comes through toil and trial. Newton was once asked, "How do you make your great discoveries ?" His reply was : "I keep the subject constantly before me, and wait till the first dawnings open slowly, by little and little, into a full, clear light." This is the key to God's storehouse. The minister, who would be an approved workman, must mingle with those for whom he labours. Surrounding circumstances, bent of mind, temperament, culture, experiences of life, have given to each one of his people a standpoint for discerning truth. Now, the minister of Christ is sent to be the sug- gester of truth. How shall he be able to so hold it up that every one may get a grasp upon it, unless he understands the principles and something of the methods upon which the various activities of life are carried forward ? To gain such a power as this and have it all sanctified, so that he shall neither materialise nor idealise, but rather stamp everything with God's own seal and illumine everything with God's own light, is a work before which the stoutest may tremble. "Who is sufficient unto these things ?" (*E. R. Ingersoll, D.D.*) *Preach the Word, not sceptical objections :*—The habit of perpetually mentioning the theories of unbelievers when preaching the gospel, gives a man the appearance of great learning, but it also proves his want of common sense. In order to show the value of wholesome food it is not needful to proffer your guest a dose of poison, nor would he think the better of your hospitality if you did so. Certain sermons are more calculated to weaken faith than to render men believers ; they resemble the process through which a poor unhappy dog is frequently passed at the Grotto del Cane at Naples. He is thrown into the gas which reaches up to the spectators' knees, not with the view of killing him, but merely as an exhibition. Lifted out of his vapoury bath, he is thrown into a pool of water, and revives in time for another operation. Such a dog is not likely to be a very efficient watch-dog or pursuer of game ; and when hearers Sunday after Sunday are plunged into a bath of sceptical thought, they may survive the experiment, but they will never become spiritually strong or practically useful. It is never worth while to make rents in a garment for the sake of mending them, nor to create doubts in order to show how cleverly we can quiet them. Should a man set fire to his house because he has a patent *extincteur* which would put it out in no time he would stand a chance of one day creating a conflagration which all the patents under heaven could not easily extinguish. Thousands of unbelievers have been born into the family of scepticism by professed preachers of the gospel, who supposed that they were helping them to faith : the fire fed upon the heaps of leaves which the foolish well-intentioned speaker cast upon it in the hope of smothering it. Young men in many instances have obtained their first notions of infidelity from their ministers ; they have sucked in the poison, but refused the antidote. (*C. H. Spurgeon.*) **Be instant in season, out of season.**—*Never out of season :*—Not that the Word is ever out of season in itself, for it is the bread of life ; all other meats have their times and seasons, but bread is the staff of nature, and is never out of season. There is no season unseasonable for so necessary a duty in the opinion of a natural man, and in the eye of carnal reason it seems sometimes to be out of season, as when it is preached on the week-day, when pastor and people have profits and pleasures and worldly employments to draw them off. Now a sermon seems like snow in harvest to such earthly souls, it is out of season with them, yet even these seasons which the world judgeth unseasonable must a minister redeem for preaching. (*Ibid.*) *Not strawberry-preachers :*—We must not be strawberry-preachers (as Bishop Latimer calleth them), which come but once a year and are quickly gone again. (*Ibid.*) *Constant preaching :*—You cannot give God's children too much of their Father's bread. (*Old Puritan.*) *In season, out of season :*—Who has not reproached himself for suffering opportunities of usefulness to pass unimproved— seasons when " a word fitly spoken " might have turned a sinner from the error of his way to the wisdom of the just? Why are we so reluctant to fill this department of usefulness? Who can tell the power of a word? Is it not often more effectual than a sermon? I once spent an afternoon in a family where a young woman had been employed for the day. I ought to have learned her spiritual state, but did not. At the tea-table she remarked that she had done her work. I replied, " If your work is done for time, you must work for eternity." She sat a moment speechless ; then, bursting into tears, she hastened from the room. Surprised and startled at such an effect from a word, I sought to learn from her the cause of this sudden distress. Her heart was overladen with the burden of sin. She had struggled to conceal her sorrow from the family. The cup was full. One drop made it run over, and led to a discovery of her deep conviction. This season of usefulness would have been lost by a few moments' delay, and that anguish of spirit have been to me unknown. (*American Messenger.*) *The seasonable word not to be delayed :*—Dr. Chalmers once lodged in the house of a nobleman near Peebles. He was the life and soul of the discourse in the circle of friends at the nobleman's fireside. The subject was pauperism—its causes and cure. Among the gentlemen present there was a venerable old Highland chieftain, who kept his eyes fastened on Dr. C., and listened with intense interest to his communications. The conversation was kept up to a late hour. When the company broke up they were shown upstairs to their apartments. There was a lobby of a considerable length, and the doors of the bed-chambers opened on the right and left. The apartment of Dr. C. was directly opposite to that of the old chieftain, who had already retired. As the doctor was undressing himself, he heard an unusual noise in the chieftain's room. The noise was succeeded by a heavy groan ! He hastened into the apartment, which was in a few minutes filled with the company, who all rushed in to the relief of the old man.

It was a melancholy sight which met their eyes. The venerable white-headed chief had fallen in the arms of his attendant. It was evidently an apoplexy. He breathed for a few moments and expired! Dr. C. stood in silence, with both hands stretched out, and bending over the deceased. He was the very picture of distress. He was the first to break silence. "Never in my life," said he in a tremulous voice, " did I see, or did I feel, before this moment, the meaning of that text, 'Preach the Word; be instant in season, out of season,' &c. Had I known that my venerable old friend was within a few minutes' reach of eternity, I would not have dwelt on that subject which formed the topic of this evening's conversation. I would have addressed myself earnestly to him. I would have preached unto him and unto you Christ Jesus, and Him crucified. I would have urged him and you, with all the earnestness befitting the subject, to prepare for eternity. You would have thought it, you would have pronounced it, out of season. But ah! it would have been in season—both as it respected him, and as it respects you." *A word in season:*—A poor blacksmith, bending with age and weakness, was passing through a country village; he stopped at a good woman's cottage, and rested himself on the railing before the door. The pious dame came out, and the weary traveller remarked that his time here would be short; he was often ailing; he added, " Ah, Nanny! I sha'n't be long for this world, I reckon!" She thought of his words, and replied, "Well, John, then I hope you'll prepare for your journey!" The blacksmith passed on, and his call was soon forgotten by Nanny; but that simple sentence was impressed on his memory by the Spirit of God, never to be erased. He pondered it while walking home, and soon consumption laid him on a bed of pain. Again and again did he think about " the journey," and about being " prepared " for it. He began to pray, and all around him were continually hearing the old woman's advice. No pious friends were near to converse with him, but it is confidently believed that the aged sinner was led to look to the Saviour through the simple incident related above. Almost his last breath was spent in thanking God that the good old woman ever warned him " Be instant in season, out of season": sow beside all waters, that thou mayest reap a glorious harvest at the coming of the Son of Man. (*Christian Miscellany.*) *Using an opportunity:*—My good and kind friend, Dr. Sale, the late vicar of Sheffield, once gave me an affecting account of a conversation he had in a railway carriage with one of his parishioners, a manufacturer, who was returning from Epsom the day after the Derby, with considerable winnings. The faithful vicar struck home, and soon discovered that the man, with all his seeming elation, was consciously guilty; and showed it, not only by the changes of his countenance, but by his desperate attempts to " change the subject." It was in vain, however, that he strove to get out of the Christian preacher's power. The vicar pressed the charge of guilt, till the sweat started to the gambler's brow, and he cried, " For God's sake, say no more! I know it is wrong. I dare not reflect upon it!" Yet the vicar did not shrink from his duty; but still urged his reproof, till he thought he had reason to believe that the man would give up his sin. (*Thos. Cooper.*) *Making an opportunity:*—The Mogul is a dirty little beer-shop, entirely supported by low and depraved persons. The tap-room was built in the yard beside a skittle ground, and was approached through a long passage. Upon entering it one evening the city missionary, John M. Weylland, found a crowd of at least forty juvenile thieves, vagrants, and bullies. As the noise was great, the only hope of doing good was an effort to enter into conversation with one or two individuals. This, however, was prevented, as many of them knew the visitor, and hit upon a device to get rid of him. A song was started by one of the men, and the chorus was taken up by the full company, who repeated with deafening effect the words, " He's a jolly good fellow." As the song proceeded the repetition became so boisterous that the visitor divined their intention to sing him out. He at once saw the difficulty of his position, as, if they had succeeded, the same practice would have been adopted in other tap-rooms to the hindrance of his usefulness. He, therefore, instead of leaving, took a seat in their midst in a most unconcerned manner. The chorus was kept up until many of the vocalists had bawled themselves hoarse; and as the yelling became feeble the visitor sprang to his feet, and said vehemently, " And they were good fellows, but the magistrates commanded to beat them. And when they had laid many stripes upon them, they cast them into prison, charging the jailer to keep them safely; who, having received such a charge, thrust them into the inner prison, and made their feet fast in the stocks." These words changed the current of feeling. Nearly all in the room had been in prison, and those who had not had a deep sympathy with such. " Who were they ? " " Where was it ? " and " What a shame ! " were the general exclamations. After a pause, which produced absolute silence, the speaker continued: " And at midnight they sang praises unto God." And then, opening his Bible, he, in a solemn, earnest tone, read the narrative of the imprisonment of Paul and Silas. When he came to the words, " He set meat before them, and rejoiced, believing in God with all his house," the reader closed the Book, and in a few telling sentences explained the nature of saving faith in Christ, and the result of that faith—being made " new creatures." After this visit the work was easy in that tap-room, and in the family of the landlord.    *Seasonable fishing :*—The minister is a fisherman, and the fisherman must fit himself to his employment. If some fish will bite only by day, he must fish by day; if others will bite only by moonlight, he must fish for them by moonlight. (*R. Cecil.*)    *Unlikely opportunity used :*—A gentleman one day observed a man in the dress of a clown surrounded by a crowd of some two hundred persons, who were amused at his foolish antics and pitiful jokes. After looking on for some moments with feelings of compassion towards the poor creature who befooled himself to make a living, he drew a tract from a parcel which he carried, and, pressing through the crowd, offered it to the clown. The latter took it, and at once began to read it aloud in mockery, for the further entertainment of the bystanders. It was short, and he read it through to the last words, which were : " Thou fool, this night thy soul shall be required of thee." Overcome with sudden and evident emotion, he left the crowd and hastened away. The giver of the tract followed him, and tried to converse with him ; but all the response he could get for some time was, " I'm lost ! I'm lost ! " However, the gospel was lovingly explained to him, and it entered into his heart. He became an earnest believer, and was soon among the regular labourers for Christ in the East End of London, in 1874. (*J. F. B. Tinling. B.A.*)    **Reprove.**—*Need of reproof :*—He that minds his patient's health will not toy or trifle or play with his mortal diseases ; the flesh must feel the plaster, or it will never eat up the corruption in it. Shouldest thou apply a healing plaster to skin the wound aloft, when there is need of a corrosive to take away the dead flesh, thou wouldest be false and unfaithful to thy friend. Reproof, like salt, must have in it both sharpness and savouriness. Admonition without serious application is like an arrow with too many feathers, which, though we level at the mark, is taken by the wind and carried quite away from it. Some men shoot their reprehensions, like pellets through a trunk, with no more strength than will kill a sparrow. Those make sinners believe that sin is no such dreadful evil, and the wrath of God no such frightful end. He that would hit the mark and recover the sinner, must draw his arrow of reproof home. Reproof must be powerful ; the hammer of the Word breaks not the heart, if it be lightly laid on. It must also be so particular, that the offender may think himself concerned. Some in reproof will seem to aim at the sinner, but so order it that their arrows shall be sure to miss him ; as Domitian, when a boy held for a mark afar off his hand spread, with the fingers severed he shot his arrows so that all hit the empty spaces between his fingers. Be the reproof never so gracious, the plaster so good, it will be ineffectual if not applied to the patient. (*G. Swinnock.*)    *Ministers must be faithful :*—God never made ministers as false glasses to make bad faces look fair ; such make themselves guilty of other men's sins. (*T. Watson.*)    *No harpoons on board :*—A sailor just off a whaling expedition asked where he would hear good preaching. On his return from church his friend said to him, " You do not seem to have liked the sermon ? " " Not much ; it was like a ship leaving for the whale fishing—everything ship-shape, anchors, cordage, sails all right—but there were no harpoons on board."    *Effectual reproof :*—The Rev. Dr. John H. Vincent once reproved a swearer so powerfully and yet so tenderly that he not only subdued him, but melted him in tears. It was in a railway station ; the room was full of passengers waiting for a late train. A man in the room was shocking everybody with his impiety, especially in profaning the name of the Lord Jesus. Suddenly Dr. Vincent began to sing—

> " Jesus, lover of my soul,
> Let me to Thy bosom fly."

—The song ceased ; perfect silence followed. The swearer was reproved. After a time he came to Dr. Vincent and said, " Could I see you for a moment outside ? " They went out together. " How came you," said he, " to sing that hymn just now ? " The Doctor replied : " I heard you swearing and profaning the name of the Lord Jesus, and I thought I would let you know there was somebody there who loved that name." "That's very strange," said the man. "My sister, when she was dying, sang that very hymn, and she made me promise to meet her in heaven. Could you pray for me?" Down they knelt together, and the Doctor prayed for the penitent man, and asked that he might have grace and strength to keep the vow he had made to his dying sister. The train came; they were separated, to meet no more, in all probability, till they meet in eternity. Disciple of Jesus, witness for your Master. Bear His reproach. Confess His name before men. *Personal rebuke best:*—Men need to be reminded of their own sins much more than they do of Adam's sin. The soldier has a deeper sense of danger when the rifle ball rings close by his ears, than by the general roar of the battle; and so a sinner will have a much deeper sense of God's displeasure, when his own sin is brought home to him, than by listening to general remarks on the sinfulness of the race. (*M. Miller.*) *Silent reproof:*—One day, as Dr. Cutler was returning home, a poor woman, whose husband had been very intemperate, called after him, and holding up a pair of chickens, begged him to accept them. "I told her," said he, "she could not afford to give away such a fine pair of chickens." "Mr. Cutler," said she, with a sad expression, "you will hurt my feelings if you do not take them. I have fatted and picked them on purpose for you. It is the only return I am able to offer for the very great service you have lately done me and my little children." "I am not aware," said Mr. Cutler, "of having done you any service of late." "Sir," said the poor woman, "you have reformed my husband." "There must be some mistake," said Mr. Cutler. "I knew your husband was intemperate; but I have never said a word to him on the subject." "I know you never have," said she; "if you had, his pride is such that it might have made matters worse. It has happened, oddly enough, that often, when you have stepped in to say a few kind words to us, he has been taking his dram, or taking down his jug or putting it back again. About two months ago, just after you went out, he went to the door, and to my astonishment poured nearly a pint of rum out of his jug on to the ground, and said, 'Debby, rinse out that jug with hot water. I've done. I can't stand that man's looks any longer! If Mr. Cutler would look savage, I shouldn't mind it; but he looks so sad, and so benevolent all the while, when he sees me taking a dram, that I know what he means just as well as if he preached it in a sermon; and I take it very kindly of him that he didn't give me a long talk.'" (*Memoir of Dr. Cutler.*) *Fruitful rebukes:*—The Rev. John Spurgeon was going to preach at his chapel in Tollesbury, Essex. It was the Sabbath morning, and as he passed a cottage garden he saw a man digging potatoes. He stopped and said, "Am I mistaken, or are you? I have come nine miles to preach to-day, thinking it was the Sabbath-day. As I see you are at work, I suppose I must be wrong, and had better go home." The man coloured, and driving his spade into the ground, he said, "No, sir, you are not wrong, but I am: and I will have no more of it. I will be round this afternoon to hear you preach. Nobody has ever spoken to me before, and you've only done your duty." He was at the chapel, and his wife with him. His wife became a member of the church, and he remained a regular attendant upon the means of grace. (*C. H. Spurgeon.*) *Benefit of reproof:*—There was one particular instance, in which a degree of severity on my part was attended with the happiest effects. Two young men, now blessed servants of the Most High God, came into my church in a most disorderly way; and as usual I fixed my eyes upon them with sternness, indicative of my displeasure. One of them was abashed; but the other, the only one that ever was daring enough to withstand my eye, looked at me again with undaunted, not to say with impious confidence, refusing to be ashamed. I sent for him the next morning, and represented to him the extreme impiety of his conduct, contrasting it with that of those less hardened; and warning him who it was that he thus daringly defied; "He that despiseth you despiseth Me; and he that despiseth Me, despiseth Him that sent Me"; and I enjoined him never to come into that church again, unless he came in a very different spirit. To my surprise, I saw him there again the following Sunday, but with a more modest countenance; and from that time he continued to come, till it pleased God to open his eyes, and to lead him into the full knowledge of the gospel of Christ; and in a year or two afterwards he became a preacher of that faith which he once had despised. (*P. B. Power.*) **Exhort.** *Zealous exhortation:*—The following incident is known only to a few, but is deserving of a wider publicity. "I shall always remember Mr. Moody," said a gentleman, "for he was the means of leading me to Christ. I was in a railway train one day, when a stout, cheery-looking stranger came in, and sat down in the seat beside me. We were passing through a beautiful country, to which he called my attention, saying, " Did you ever think what a good Heavenly Father we have, to give us such a pleasant world to live in ? " I made some indifferent answer, upon which he earnestly inquired, " Are you a Christian ? " I answered, " No." " Then," said he, " you ought to be one at once. I am to get off at the next station, but if you will kneel down, right here, I will pray to the Lord to make you a Christian." Scarcely knowing what I did, I knelt down beside him there, in the car, filled with passengers, and he prayed for me with all his heart. Just then the train drew up at the station, and he had only time to get off before it started again. Suddenly coming to myself out of what seemed more like a dream than a reality, I rushed out on to the car platform, and shouted after him, " Tell me who you are." He replied, " My name is Moody." I never could shake off the conviction which then took hold upon me, until the prayer of that strange man was answered, and I had become a Christian. (*A Faithful Pastor.*)

Vers. 3, 4. **They will not endure sound doctrine.**—*Inclination the enemy of truth :*—The reason is here assigned for this faithful ministry : one that has always been in force, since human nature has always been the same. Men's own inclinations will become the guide of their conduct concerning truth and duty. Because sound or salutary teaching about their own errors and sins is abasing to their pride and crucifying to their selfish passions, it will not be endured. Yet their minds crave stimulus, and even their moral natures demand some opiate. Hence they will resort to various so-called teachers, in order to obtain fancies that please and rules of life that suit their native tastes. And the effect of this will be that they turn themselves away from truth to falsehood, and are at last given up of God to the fixed delusion of believing a lie, to their own perdition. The picture is sad indeed, and common as sad, in this as in every century and land. None believe so wildly, and none are so hopelessly hardened, as those who finally reject the saving truth of God. (*J. G. Butler, D.D.*) *Smooth things preferred :*—Edward Irving found no favour as a preacher in the commencement of his ministry. After various disappointments, Dr. Chalmers heard and appreciated him, and invited him to be his assistant in Glasgow. Irving, in astonishment and doubt, replied : " I will preach to them if you think fit, but if they bear with my preaching they will be the first people who have borne with it." *Dislike to the truth :*—Aristotle writeth that vultures are killed with oil of roses. Sweet smells enrage tigers. Swine cannot live in some parts of Arabia, saith Pliny, by reason of the pleasant scent of aromatical trees there growing in every wood. (*J. Trapp.*) *Sound doctrine forsaken :*—1. The grounds of their apostasy—viz., their hatred of the truth ; they will not endure sound doctrine; they will reject it and cast it behind their backs ; they hate and abhor it. They look upon it as a grievous burden, as Israel did upon the doctrine and visions of the prophets (Jer. xiii. 34, 36). It is not so much they cannot, but they will not endure sound doctrine ; they love their lusts above the law, and therefore they hate him that reproves in the gates. Errors they can tolerate, and superstition they can tolerate, but the truth they cannot bear. 2. A second ground of their apostasy is their delight in false teachers; they so dote on them, that one or two will not content them, they must have heaps of them. They love their lusts, and therefore they seek out for such teachers as may not disquiet them. They wittingly and willingly suffer themselves to be deluded by them. The word signifies—(1) An earnest desire of getting such teachers. (2) It notes an indiscreet and confused gathering together of such a multitude of teachers without wit or reason, without any respect either to their life or learning, head nor tail. The disciples create their doctors, the lusts of their followers are their call. 3. A third cause of their apostasy is that innate malice and inbred concupiscence which is in the hearts of men. But the word in the original is "lusts," which implies, not a simple desire or sudden motion, but a vehement, ardent, earnest desire and pursuit of a thing. 4. They have itching ears; this is another reason why they seek out for false teachers ; they love not such as deal plainly and faithfully with them, they must have such as please their humours, tickle their fancies with novelties and curiosities, but they must in no wise touch their vices. 5. Here is the issue and consequences of their contempt of the truth—viz., the loss of truth, and following fables. This is the devil's method. First he stops the ear against sound doctrine, and then he opens it to error. Like a cruel thief, he draws the soul out of the right road into some wood, by-lane or corner, and there binds, robs, and rifles it.

1. God not only knoweth what men do at present, and what they have done, but what they will do in time to come. He tells Timothy here what will be done many years after he is dead and gone. 2. The more perfidious the world is, and the more false teachers abound, the more careful must Christ's ministers be to oppose them by preaching sound doctrine. The badness of the times approaching must make us to redeem the present season. The sun will not always shine; tempests will arise, and the night will come when no man can work. Those that reverence Moses to-day, to-morrow are murmuring against him (Exod. xiv. *ult.*, and xv. 14). 3. Saving doctrine is sound doctrine. 4. Unsound persons cannot endure sound doctrine. It is salt which searcheth men's sores and puts them to pain. It is light which these sore eyes cannot endure, nor these thieves abide. They do evil, and therefore they hate the light (John iii. 20). They do not only fear, but hate the light. They cannot endure to have the law preached, their consciences searched, nor their sins discovered. But as for sound men, they love sound doctrine; they desire it (Psa. xliii. 3). They come to it (John iii. 21), and bless God for it (1 Sam. xxv. 32, 33). 5. In the last days there will be many false teachers. There will not be one or two, but there will be heaps of them, the world will swarm with them. Men will have variety of lusts, and those call for variety of teachers to uphold them. Good men, and especially good ministers, are rare, they are one of a thousand (Job xxxiii. 23), but wicked ones abound; there is much dross, but little gold; much chaff, but little wheat; many weeds, few good flowers. If the devil have any work to do, he wants no agents to effect it. If men once set open their doors, they shall not want deceivers. When men slight truth they shall have teachers which shall be God's executioners to bind them and blind them, and lead them into error. 6. Observe, as all other parts of man, so amongst the rest the ear hath its diseases. Salt is fitter for such than oil: though it be more searching, yet it is more sovereign. This itching disease was never so common as in our days. There is a sinful spiritual itch upon the soul which is sevenfold—viz., an itch of—(1) Novelty. (2) Curiosity. (3) Singularity. (4) Popularity. (5) Flattery. (6) Disputing. (7) Quarrelling. (*T. Hall, B.D.*)　　*Application in preaching objected to :*—A farmer went to hear John Wesley preach. The farmer was not a converted man; he cared little about religion; on the other hand, he was not what we call a bad man. His attention was soon excited and riveted. John said he should take up three topics of thought—he was speaking greatly about money. His first head was, " Get all you can." The farmer nudged a neighbour and said, " This is strange preaching. I never heard the like of this before. This is very good. Yon man has got things in him; it is admirable preaching." John discoursed of " Industry," " Activity," " Living to purpose," and reached his second division, which was, " Save all you can." The farmer became more excited. " Was there ever anything like this ? " he said. Wesley denounced thriftlessness and waste, and he satirised the wilful wickedness which lavishes in luxury; and the farmer rubbed his hands, and he thought, " All this have I been from my youth up "; and what with getting, and what with hoarding, it seemed to him that " salvation had come to his house." But Wesley advanced to his third head, which was, " Give all you can." " Ay dear, ay dear," said the farmer; " he has gone and spoilt it all." There was now no further point of contact, no interest in the farmer's mind. (*Preacher's Lantern.*)　　**Itching ears.—** *Curious hearers :*—Some come to the Word preached, not so much to get grace, as to enrich themselves with notions—" Itching ears " (ver. 3). Austin confesseth that before his conversion he went to hear St. Ambrose, rather for his eloquence than for the spirituality of the matter. " Thou art unto them as a very lovely song of one that hath a pleasant voice, and can play well on an instrument." Many come to the Word only to feast their ears; they like the melody of the voice, the mellifluous sweetness of the expression, the newness of the notion (Acts xvii. 21). This is to love the garnishing of the dish more than the food; this is to desire to be pleased rather than edified. Like a woman that paints her face, but neglects her health, so they paint and adorn themselves with curious speculations, but neglect their souls' health. This hearing doth neither sanctify the heart, nor the Sabbath. (*T. Watson.*)　　**Shall be turned unto fables.—** *Truth hidden when neglected :* —From these words we learn that there is such a thing as religious truth, and therefore such a thing as religious error. We learn that religious truth is *one*, and therefore that all views of religion *but* one are wrong. And we learn, moreover, that so it was to be that professed Christians, forgetting this, should turn away their ears from the one truth, and be turned, not to one, but to many fables. This is a most solemn thought, and a perplexing one. However, there is another which,

though it ought not to be perplexing, is perplexing still, and perhaps has greater need to be considered and explained—I mean that men of learning and ability are so often wrong in religious matters also. Now, if we consult St. Paul's Epistles to the Corinthians, we shall find the same state of things existing even in the first age of Christianity. Even the apostle speaks of those who were blind, or to whom his Gospel was hid; and he elsewhere describes them, not as the uneducated and dull of understanding, but as the wise of this world, the scribe and the disputer. Does not our Saviour Himself say the same thing, when He thanks His Father, Lord of heaven and earth, that He hath hid these things from the wise and prudent, and revealed them unto babes? Now it should not surprise us when men of acute and powerful understandings more or less reject the gospel, for this reason: that the Christian revelation addresses itself to our hearts, to our love of truth and goodness, our fear of sinning, and our desire to gain God's favour; and quickness, sagacity, depth of thought, strength of mind, power of comprehension, perception of the beautiful, power of language, and the like, though they are excellent gifts, are clearly quite of a different kind from these spiritual excellences —a man may have the one without having the other. This should be kept in mind when Christians are alarmed, as they sometimes are, on hearing instances of infidelity or heresy among those who read, reflect, and inquire; whereas, however we may mourn over such instances, we have no reason to be surprised at them. It is quite enough for Christians to be able to show, as they well can, that belief in revealed religion is not inconsistent with the highest gifts and acquirements of mind, that men even of the strongest and highest intellect have been Christians; but they have as little reason to be perplexed at finding other men of ability not true believers, as at finding that certain rich men are not true believers, or certain poor men, or some in every rank and circumstance of life. A belief in Christianity has hardly more connection with what is called talent, than it has with riches, station, power, or bodily strength. Now let me explain what I mean by a further remark. Is it not plain that earnestness is necessary for gaining religious truth? On the other hand, is it not a natural effect of ability to save us trouble, and even to tempt us to dispense with it, and to lead us to be indolent? Do not we see this even in the case of children—the more clever are the more idle, because they rely on their own quickness and power of apprehension? Is indolence the way to gain knowledge from God? Though there is no art or business of this world which is learned without time and exertion, yet it is commonly conceived that the knowledge of God and our duty will come as if by accident or by a natural process. Men go by their feelings and likings; they take up what is popular, or what comes first to hand. They think it much if they now and then have serious thoughts, if they now and then open the Bible; and their minds recur with satisfaction to such seasons, as if they had done some very great thing, never remembering that to seek and gain religious truth is a long and systematic work. And others think that education will do everything for them, and that if they learn to read, and use religious words, they understand religion itself. And others, again, go so far as to maintain that exertion is not necessary for discovering the truth. They say that religious truth is simple and easily acquired; that Scripture, being intended for all, is at once open to all, and that if it had difficulties, that very circumstance would be an objection to it. And others, again, maintain that there are difficulties in religion, and that this shows that it is an indifferent matter whether they seek or not as to those matters which are difficult. In these and other ways do men deceive themselves into a carelessness about religious truth. And is not all this varied negligence sufficient to account for the varieties of religious opinion which we see all around us? How are the sheep of Christ's flock scattered abroad in the waste world! What religious opinion can be named which some men or other have not at some time held? All are equally confident in the truth of their own doctrines, though the many must be mistaken. In this confusion let us look to ourselves, each to himself. There must be a right and a wrong, and no matter whether others agree with us or not, it is to us a solemn practical concern not to turn away our ears from the truth. Let not the diversity of opinion in the world dismay you, or deter you from seeking all your life long true wisdom. It is not a search for this day or that, but as you should ever grow in grace, so should you ever grow also in the knowledge of our Lord and Saviour Jesus Christ. ("*Plain Sermons by Contributors to 'Tracts for the Times.'*")

Ver. 5. But watch thou in all things.—1. But watch thou. The apostasy and looseness of the times we live in must make us the more watchful. Their falls must be our fears; their levity must quicken us to constancy, and their negligence must quicken our diligence in keeping the watch of the Lord. 2. Good men desire the Church's good after their departure. Paul is dying, yet he commands Timothy to improve his talents for the Church's good when himself was dead. Moses, before he dies, prays the Lord to set up a fit ruler instead (Num. xxviii. 16, 17). Wicked men care not what becomes of the world, when they are dead and gone let heaven and earth come together, and all be in confusion, they care not. But good men have public spirits. 3. As all persons, so ministers especially must watch. The devil hath a special spite at them; he commands his agents, as the king of Aram did his followers, to fight neither with small nor great, but against the king of Israel; so he bends all his strength against the ministers of Israel. (1) The better the man, the more watchful must he be. The pirate sets on the laden ship, and the thief upon the wealthiest traveller. But we must watch as pastors too, and discover wolves that would destroy the flock. (2) We must watch at all times. (a) In prosperity, as pigeons when they fare best fear most. (b) Watch in adversity, the devil is busy then in laying snares, as the fowler doth for birds in frosty weather. (3) In all places, in public and private, at home and abroad; the world is full of snares. (4) Watch in all things, so runs the text. (5) Watch against all sins. We carry about us a proneness to all sin. (6) Watch over all thy senses; stop thine ears; make a covenant with thine eyes (Job. xxxi. 1). Set a watch before thy mouth. The whole soul is out of order, and therefore we must set a guard upon all its faculties. 4. Ministers especially must be hardy men. We are called soldiers, shepherds, watchmen, husbandmen, all which must endure summer's heat and winter's frost. (1) We must endure hardship in our preparatory studies; we must give up ourselves to reading, study and prayer. (2) He must endure hardship in the actual performance of his duty. (3) Most properly and genuinely this hardship in the text consists in a patient undergoing of those injuries and oppositions which we must expect from an ungrateful world. (4) The Lord Himself sometimes is pleased to exercise us, and to inure us to hardship, that we may be the fitter for His service. But let us, like good soldiers of Christ, endure hardship—(a) Patiently. (b) Courageously. (c) Constantly. 5. The ministry is a work. The sweat of the brow is nothing to that of the brain; besides the dangers we are liable to for our work's sake. 6. Do the work or service of an evangelist. Observe, ministers are servants, and their office is service. 7. Of an evangelist. Observe, ministers must preach the gospel. We must publish the glad tidings of a Saviour (what in us lieth to all the world); this is to do the work of an evangelist, viz., soundly and sincerely to publish the gospel. 8. Make full proof of thy ministry. Ministers must fully and faithfully discharge all the duties of their calling. (*T. Hall, B.D.*) *Christian watchfulness :*— None are so likely to maintain watchful guard over their hearts and lives as those who know the comfort of living in near communion with God. They feel their privilege and will fear losing it. They will dread falling from their high estate, and marring their own comfort by bringing clouds between themselves and Christ. He that goes on a journey with a little money about him takes little thought of danger, and cares little how late he travels. He, on the contrary, that carries gold and jewels, will be a cautious traveller: he will look well to his roads, his horses, and his company, and run no risks. The fixed stars are those that tremble most. The man that most fully enjoys the light of God's countenance, will be a man tremblingly afraid of losing its blessed consolations, and jealously fearful of doing anything to grieve the Holy Ghost. (*Bishop Ryle.*) **Endure afflictions.**—*Endurance of hardship :*—Some dyes cannot bear the weather, but alter colour presently; but there are others that, having something that gives a deeper tincture, will hold. The graces of a true Christian hold out in all sorts of weathers, in winter and summer, prosperity and adversity, when superficial counterfeit holiness will give out. (*R. Sibbes.*) *Ministerial hardship :*—I board with a poor Scotsman; his wife can talk scarcely any English. My diet consists mostly of hasty-pudding, boiled corn, and bread baked in ashes, and sometimes a little meat and butter. My lodging is a little heap of straw, laid upon some boards, a little way from the ground; for it is a long room, without any floor, that I lodge in. My work is exceedingly hard and difficult. I travel on foot a mile and a half in the worst of roads almost daily and back again; for I live so far from my Indians. I have not seen an English person this month. These and many other uncomfortable circumstances attend me; and yet my spiritual conflicts and distresses so far exceed all these that I scarce think of them, but feel as if I were entertained in the most sumptuous manner. The Lord grant that I may learn to *endure hardness* as a good soldier of Jesus Christ! (*David Brainerd.*) **Do the work of an evangelist.**— *The work of an evangelist:*—We fancy we still see Dr. Wardlaw standing in the pulpit and beseeching the newly-ordained pastor to approve himself in all things as the faithful servant of God. Some of his sentences still linger in our recollection—"Oh, my brother!" he said, "never forget that the greatest triumph which can be accomplished on earth is the conversion of a soul; and a minister's labours are never so highly honoured as when men are born of God through his instrumentality. It may be of importance to polish the jewel after it has been found, but the chief thing is to dig it out of the mine. It may be, and it is, important to dress up the stone for the front of the building, but he does the greatest work who excavates it from the quarry in which it lay imbedded." (*Evangelical Repository.*)　　*An earnest evangelist:*—While waiting on one occasion in a gentleman's parlour, Vassar opened conversation with his wife, a very fashionable and proud-looking lady, who was sitting in the room. With great concern he began at once to urge the necessity of the new birth and immediate acceptance of Christ upon her. She was thunderstruck, and protested that she did not believe in any of those things. Then followed a most fervent appeal, texts of Scripture, warning against rejecting Christ, the certainty of a wrath to come for any found in impenitence, till my friend said he was fairly alarmed at the boldness of the assault. Suddenly the gentleman came in for whom he was waiting, and called him out. When the gentleman returned to his wife, she said, "There has been an old man here talking with me about religion." "Why did you not shut him up?" he asked gruffly. "He is one of those persons that you cannot shut up," was her reply. "If I had been here," he said, "I would have told him very quickly to go about his business." "If you had seen him, you would have thought he was about his business," was her answer. (*Memoir of Uncle John Vassar.*)　　**Make full proof of thy ministry.**—*Fulfil thy ministry:*—This word "ministry" does not refer exclusively to what we are accustomed to call the Christian ministry, meaning the teaching and pastoral office in the Church. That is but one of ten thousand forms of ministration or service, which may be rendered to our fellows at the call of God. To minister to any one, is to help or serve him; and so every course of action by which we can help and serve others is a ministry, and every such service is truly a Christian work. And as we cannot all render the same service, but can each render particular kinds of service to particular people—relatives, friends or neighbours— that particular description of service which each of us can render is our "ministry." It is a ministry, the object of whose functions lies without us, in contrast to activities which centre in self as their object. And it is "thy ministry," because it is that particular form of helpful activity which it is open to each, separately, to prosecute. Paul's was different from Timothy's, and neither has belonged to anybody since; nor will your ministry, or mine, ever be allotted to anybody else; for no one will be situated as we are, or have exactly our opportunities. But, in some respects, our ministry is like Timothy's and Paul's. It is directed to the same objects: the spread of Christ's truth and Christ's Church. And we are summoned to it by the same Divine Lord, to whom also we shall render an account of its discharge. All the high, sublime elements, then, which belonged to their ministry or service in life, belong to ours, though ours may take less striking outward forms, and be rendered with no eye but God's to watch our performance of it. The sublime considerations, moving to fidelity in it, which Paul urged on Timothy, bear, then, on us. "I charge thee before God, make full proof of"—thoroughly fulfil—"thy ministry." (*T. M. Herbert, M.A.*)　　*The appeal of the elder to the younger generation:*—In the charge of the aged Paul to the young disciple Timothy, there seems to be an appeal which, though unexpressed, is perpetually addressed from the elder generation to the younger. What the one old man said to the single young one, all Christ's servants, whose work is nearly done, seem to say to all those whose work is just beginning. "Fulfil thy ministry, for I am now ready to be offered." Choose what time in the world's history you like, you will always find those two classes well represented; for it is always true that "one generation passeth away, and another cometh." And while the old are always passing to their rest, and the young rising to do their parts, the great aims for which Christian men strive and pray, and the great institution of the Church, through which they further them, lives on; and it is, or should be, the concern of each generation to hand it down invigorated and enlarged, to their successors. But if that is to be done, these successors must be ready to take up these toils and aims; to adapt them to the needs of the coming time, and engage in them with a spirit at least as devoted as that which their fathers showed. So they seem to hear from their father, "Fulfil thy ministry, for I am now ready to be offered." Now if we take our own time, and apply to it these considerations, which hold good of every time, what shall we say? Now, as ever, there is a passing and a rising generation. And the great Church and kingdom of Christ, which has been in the hands of the fathers, will soon be in the hands of the children. That glorious institution will live, though the hands which now sustain it decay. But young hands must receive it from the failing hold of the elders, and by their efforts it must be upheld. Are they ready to take it? Are they prepared to "fulfil their ministry," because their predecessors will soon leave the task in their hands? (*Ibid.*) *Fulfilling one's ministry :*—Several ancient rulers did not find management of their dominions sufficiently burdensome, and so one of them became a fiddler, another a poet, and another an orator. The world never had a worse fiddler than Nero, nor a more wearisome poet than Dionysius, nor a more blundering orator than Caligula; and we might fearlessly assert also that the world never had worse princes than these three. Such instances are exceedingly instructive, and remind us of the sculptor's advice to the cobbler to stick to his last. Each tub had better stand on its own bottom; for when tubs take to rolling about they spill all that they contain, be it either wine or water. (*C. H. Spurgeon.*)

Vers. 6–8. **I am now ready to be offered.**—*The law of sacrifice :*—The interest of the Second Epistle to Timothy is altogether exceptional. It is the interest of a heart-moving tragedy; and yet the tragic gloom which rolls above its heavens is relieved, is almost illumined with golden glory by a strain and temper of pathetic tenderness. It is, as far as we are concerned, the last earthly utterance of an altogether remarkable man; the last will and testament, so to speak, of one in whose character commanding ability, simple and unswerving purpose, unflagging energy, unselfish enthusiasm, and warm and wide and sunny sympathy were combined in a degree unrivalled in the history of our race. And then, too, St. Paul, as he writes, may indeed be "the aged," but age can scarcely slacken power in such a soul, and here, consequently, he wins the unforbidden homage we pay spontaneously to one who, in the fullest vigour and energy of life, looks straight and calmly into the eyes of death. The text is, I suppose, one of the best-known verses in the Bible, an utterance of profound humility and lofty courage and unvarying truth; it is to us altogether interesting—interesting, doubtless, because it reveals the character of such a one as Paul; but more, a word of world-wide import, for at such moments great men are themselves revelations. Paul was alone in a sense in which he had never been before. The dear Churches—that is, the dear souls, loved with such strength and joy as was in him to love with—were far away; their faces he would never gaze upon again; the old places were gone; no more would he see the Holy City so rich in memories, no more the long blue line of the Abarim bounding the land of the chosen race, no more the jagged hills of his native Tarsus, no more the dancing waters of the blue Ægean, no more the Acroceraunian crests, only lately marking the path of his pilgrimage from Corinth to Rome. Nature had closed her doors to the wanderer; from his prison on the Esquiline, or from the cave near the Capitol, or wherever it was that, in their last days, his eyes closed and opened to the light of the Roman summer, those eyes were straining beyond even objects of human affection to the unimagined wonders of another world; he was looking forward. At such a time it is that great natures fall back upon the principles which have governed life; and to us their utterances then, are supremely interesting, for such principles are the exhibition, in fact, of universal law. St. Paul, in his words illustrated by his life, is indeed proclaiming a fundamental law of the Church of his Master. "The Reign of Law!" Need I remind you that of that realm we are all the subjects? It is fundamental, it explains, as it has guided, the Church's influence; it teaches, as it has trained, souls to tread the only way of lasting usefulness. It applies to all. It is not the heritage of the peerless apostle, but also the rule of the quiet Christian; obedience to it decides indeed the value of our choice in crises of destiny, but it also ennobles the "trivial round" of daily life. Here, indeed, it is thrown out in vivid colour from a dark background of death; here, indeed, in full force, it is borne in upon the mind, because it comes as no abstract statement, but the life-rule written in the

heart's blood of a living and a dying man. In him it found a wonderful completeness: it is the fundamental law of the Church of Jesus—the Law of Sacrifice.
And now, I ask, "How for Paul was the grave transfigured?" and the answer is,
"By the same power by which life was governed, by the law of sacrifice." What,
then, is sacrifice? By sacrifice, speaking morally and spiritually, as now, I mean
this : The willing surrender of legitimate desire in submission to a sovereign, an
authoritative claim; and the interest of the text lies in this, not only that it
expresses the rich result of that law operating in its completeness in a human soul,
but also, it limits the stages of trial by which such completeness was achieved.
What, let us ask, were some at least of those stages? 1. First, then, he had
wakened up to the reality and requirements of the spiritual life. Man is a creature
of two worlds, but of one sphere of being; standing he is within the boundary of
time, but one foot is planted across the frontier of eternity. Little we see of man's
real working, just here and there a hint is given by the definite act which meets
the senses, excites our blame or sets the chorus of praise re-echoing through the
halls of history, but day by day and hour by hour man's spirit, shrouded, veiled
from his fellow man, is at work in the spirit sphere. Now to waken up to this,
and to the consequent requirements of duty in this interior life, is to be brought
under the law of sacrifice, because it is at once to be under the necessity of war.
"The Prince of the power of the air, the spirit that now worketh in the children
of disobedience," is no mere tendency to wrong, but a personal spirit, with a
personal power. And surely it has been the experience not only of the saints—the
giant explorers in the regions of spiritual life—but the experience of earnest,
commonplace children of God, that besides their struggle with their own corruption,
they have been conscious of sudden assaults, of well-timed suggestions of sin,
alarming, astounding, distinctly to them distinguishable from any picture of
imagination ; painfully, evidently separated from themselves, and clearly coming
with the force and horror of the agency of a personal tempter. The action of
the hierarchy of evil was indeed perhaps more evident to the Christians when
St. Paul taught and lived than to ourselves. The entire imperial system of Rome
might well appear to him an organisation of evil ; and indeed, so awfully had the
creature forsaken his Creator—read the first chapter of the Roman Epistle and
say was it not so?—that that splendid fabric sprung from the genius of Pagan
civilisation had become little else than a series of well-worked agencies of sin. It
is true that the life of the second Adam permeating the race of the Redeemed
has made of modern civilisation a very different story. But tell me, is there
not enough in modern life to witness to the presence of the same tremendous
power? Can you open your newspaper any morning without being impressed by
the fact that the world is trying to get rid of the incubus of the thought of God?
without being conscious of tones of thought and views of life nowise condemned by
society at large, which would, to say the least, have shocked apostles? Is there not
an air of unruffled indifference, or a tone of quiet patronage assumed towards moral
evil which give the lie to the brave, the necessary hostility taught us in the
Catechism when we were children? Does not this subtle tolerance of sin flow
through society, invade the Church, deprave the mind? Hence men lose all
sense of the severe requirements of a righteous God, because they have first lost
all sense of His character of severe essential holiness ; hence, young men, you
are the victims (are you not?) in business life of habits of language, alliance
with, almost toleration of, which you feel to be inconsistent with any nobility
of mind, not to say any sincerity of Christian character. Ah! how are you to
escape? Certainly not without struggle. Roused to the facts, roused to the requirements of spiritual life, you find yourself in battle ; self must be denied, duty
must be done, strength must be sought (faithfulness is needed in sacraments and
prayer—faithfulness, too, in using strength when given). You must submit, and
heartily, to the law of sacrifice. Spiritual activity on the side of right and truth
and purity and duty—this is a stage towards a complete achievement. Paul had
learned it ; whether his description is drawn from the racecourse or the battle it
matters not ; he had learned at any rate the necessity of struggle. "I have fought
a good fight." 2. It is well, is it not, to awaken to the mystery, to recognise
the reality, of the spiritual world? But there is surely a farther stage for the way-
farer in this path of sacrifice. What shall be the standard to measure and direct
the struggle of life? To an earnest Christian what God forbids is bad—unutterably,
inexcusably bad. Right is right and wrong wrong, without palliation or possibility
of compromise. To do good is not merely wiser than to do ill ; it is the place,

calling, need of the creature; wilful sin, self-chosen evil, is the damnable, ruinous, and sorrowful thing, which may call for a tribute of sadness and pity, but admits of no defence. Need I say it? this necessary revelation of God's will is furnished by the moral law. Conscience speaks first. I do not now pause to define its office or assign its place, or dwell upon the limits of its dominion; only let me remark in parenthesis—Obey your conscience, respect its warnings, listen for its whispers, submit unhesitatingly to its commands; you will be all the wiser, better men. Here Paul had first read and obeyed the will of God, and because he had long been trained in that sincere and accurate submission, he was ready, when the face of Jesus was flashed upon him from the flaming heaven, above the peaks of the Hauran, at once to recognise, and unconditionally to obey. The prophets, the psalmists, the teachers of Israel had for him enlarged upon and enforced the lessons of that primal instruction, as revelation of the Christ, and the New as well as Old Testament Scriptures have ever since done for us all; but for him and for each since his time, the larger laws of Divine guidance have been particularised and pointed by special providence and special trials. The requirements of that Will are often—at least to human frailty—severe. The heart's most fierce desires are not most easily assuaged, the world's most prized successes are not most surely secured, by obedience to the will of God. No. Splendid indeed the results, moral, spiritual, of such adherence and such submission, but the process is pain. Honestly and earnestly to choose that standard is to be subject to the law of sacrifice. Paul chose it, and, like him, each one who does, fulfils, though it be in pain, an allotted mission. "I have finished," says the apostle, "the course marked out for me." 3. But there is one further stage of conquest dependent upon the most stern self-discipline. If there be anything that a man would seem entitled to call his own, it is his thought. Surely in thought, at least, man is free; surely "I can think what I like," as it is the expression of a natural craving, so it is the statement of a truth. Scarcely; for thought, if untrained, undisciplined, and unrepressed, becomes a tyrant, not a slave; and thought, which shares the heritage of our nature's blight, can only fulfil its intended function when purified by submission to the law of sacrifice. My brothers, to plant the footstep of your thoughts on the track of Divine Revelation, to refuse to them the by-paths of ungoverned fancy, to restrain them in their wild impulsive leaps, is to start them, nay, far to advance them, on the journey which ends in God. Be sure that to "learn obedience" to the truths of the Christian Faith, to bathe the mental habits in the cleansing waters of the Spirit, who gives light, humility, courage, and truth, is the one way possible for emancipating the mind from the thraldom of corruption; but to do this, how hard, how full of sorrow, how severe at times the trial and the strain; ah me! as in other things, in this also, "obedience is learned by the things" we "suffer." To leave men's criticism, and desire the Revelation of God; to quit our own miserable inquiries, and choose the path of the Pathless One; to watch against the wilfulness that slights, the sin that weakens our power of believing; this, as it is an evidence of strength, and even of stern decision, is not lacking in an element of trial, requires submission to the law of sacrifice. "Kept the Faith," mark you; for as to reach the path needed some self-conquest, so to keep the track required unflagging earnestness and persevering power. To submit to the Faith, in such an one as Paul, meant moral earnestness; to keep it implied moral force; for him, as for all men, to govern thought by God's revelation implies obedience to the law of sacrifice. Paul, I say, did it, did it utterly, did it also in the face of extremest external difficulty, did it when to be faithful to conviction implied fierce persecution and inevitable death; it is a triumphant climax that last stage of struggle—"I have kept the Faith." So the saintly soul advanced to that completeness of surrender which is completeness of power, and finds expression in the text. In fact, spiritual activity, a creaturely temper, and a humble mind, were the stages of his self-sacrifice. One question remains—Whence came its impulse? whence its sustaining strength? The answer is easy. It came whence only it can come, from super-natural, but personal affection. My friends, we are not all St. Pauls: very much the reverse usually, almost infinitely short of him in spiritual vigour, most of us. But being all professed disciples of Jesus Christ, God demands of each of us in our degree, submission to the law of sacrifice. 1. We are under special trial when the soul is subject to the illumination of some new truth. A light comes—such a course long lived is wrong, or is not the best. We must obey, but to us—for man is very frail and only human—this is sharp. 2. Or we lose something very dear. It may be an old friendship, it may be an old friend; it may be old, long-cherished, long-loved dreams; it may be that the mystery of the freshness of early life, once making all things fresh, has fled. There is, remember, nothing lost without a something gained, if the soul walk by this law, mind this rule. 3. Or, as you may be this week, as you and I have often been, there may be a time of temptation. How sorely some of you are tried I know. How not seldom England's commercial greatness means that young souls must often choose between the loss of place, which means loss of maintenance—sometimes too for wife and children dearer than self—and the loss of peace with God. This I am not forgetting. Oh brother, tempted, you or I, to wrong, in the interests of self-advancement, are we not after all only victims submitted to the law of sacrifice? Do not shrink. It is severe and painful, but it is the law of life. 4. And there is death. True, here we have no choice; but still, when that comes, how we shall comport ourselves may depend in very large, in very serious measure, on our habit of sacrifice now. Every life, believe it, to be trained for God, for goodness, must be trained by sacrifice. Every work, believe it, that you do will be of lasting value in proportion to the amount of sacrifice entailed in doing. In fact, it is by submission to this law that the Church teaches you how to use the world. This world may be viewed in many lights, so many-sided it is, so strange! For instance, it is a burying-earth, a world of death, a huge and sombre grave. "The world is full of death!" We tread on the dust of a thousand generations, and other pilgrims, children of our children, shall tread on ours when we lie low! Stop! A powerful principle can transfigure everything, even the horror of death. The world is an altar of sacrifice: lives have been lived, and therefore deaths have been died of abundant fruitfulness and unending power. Why? Because these souls, which live each an endless life, have expressed themselves in sacrifice, have lost, have strangled the only death-giving principle, the principle of self, in undying devotion to truth and holiness. Further, then: the world is the vestibule of a palace of complete achievement. However, all here seems stamped with imperfection, branded with the trade-mark of unfinished labour, yet death, on such terms, is in truth the entrance to essential life; sacrifice, the birth-throe of a spirit satisfied. (*Canon Knox Little.*) *Ready to be offered:*—I. THINGS WHICH MAKE IT DIFFICULT TO SAY THIS. 1. The enjoyment of life. 2. Attachment to friends. 3. The anticipated pain of dissolution. 4. Uncertainty about the future. II. THINGS WHICH MAKE IT EASY, AT LEAST COMPARATIVELY, TO SAY THIS. 1. The sad experience of life's ills. 2. The consciousness of having finished one's life-work. 3. The pre-decease of Christian friends. 4. An ever-nearing and enlarging prospect of heaven's glory. (*T. Whitelaw, D.D.*) *Death anticipated:*—1. The godly, by a spiritual instinct and sagacity, foresee their ends; so did Jacob (Gen. xlviii. 21), and Joshua (xxiii. 14), and Christ (John xvii. 2), and Peter (ii. 14). They always watch and wait for their Master's coming. Their acts, diseases, and disquietments which they meet withal from the world are as so many petty deaths unto them. A man that dwells in an old crazy house where the walls fall down, the foundation sinks, the pillars bend, and the whole building cracks, concludes such a house cannot long stand. As for the wicked they are insensible and secure, and though grey hairs, which are signs of old age and death approaching, be here and there upon them yet they know it not (Hosea vii. 9). 2. Death is not dreadful to good men. The apostle speaks of it here not by way of lamentation, but of exultation. Death to him was but a departing from one room to another, from a lower room to a higher, from earth to heaven, from troubles to rest, from mortality to immortality. They are long since dead to the world, and so can part with it more easily. The wicked look on death as a dreadful, dismal thing; but God's people looking on it through the spectacles of the gospel, see it to be a conquered enemy, having its sting taken out (Hosea xiii. 15), so that what Agag said vainly and vauntingly, a Christian may speak truly and seriously: "The bitterness of death is past" (1 Sam. xv. 32). 3. The soul of man is immortal. Death is not an annihilation, but a migration of the soul from the body for a time. 4. The death of the martyrs is a most pleasing sacrifice to God. 5. The death of the martyrs doth confirm the truth. The Church is God's garden, and it is watered and enriched by the blood of martyrs. (*T. Hall, B.D.*) *Paul the martyr, Christian, conqueror:*—I. THE INFORMATION HERE GIVEN OF PAUL'S DEATH AS A MARTYR. 1. He looked on his death as an offering on behalf of the gospel. 2. He looked on his death as a departure from every temporal bondage. II. THE DECLARATION HERE GIVEN OF PAUL'S LABOUR AS A CHRISTIAN. 1. As a soldier in the army. 2. As a runner in a race. 3. As a faithful servant to his Master. III. THE DECLARATION HERE GIVEN OF PAUL'S REWARD AS A CONQUEROR.

1. The preciousness of this reward. 2. The excellent Giver of this reward. 3. The solemn time of obtaining this reward. 4. The liberality of the Giver. "Not to me only," &c. (*M. Jones.*)    *Looking out toward heaven :*—1. He looks downward into the grave (ver. 6) whither he was going, and there he sees comfort. 2. He looks backward and views his well-spent life with joy and comfort, and in a holy gloriation breaks forth, "I have fought the good fight," &c. 3. He looks upward, and there he sees heaven prepared for him. But doth not this savour of vain-glory and spiritual pride? 1. Answer: Not at all, for the apostle speaks not this proudly, as if he had merited anything at the hand of God. 2. He speaks this partly to comfort Timothy, and to encourage him to walk in his steps, keeping faith and a good conscience. 3. To encourage himself against the reproach of his reproaching violent death, he eyes that heavenly reward and that crown of life prepared for such as have fought the good fight as he had done. (*T. Hall, B.D.*)    *The Christian's course, conflict, and crown :*—I. THE VIEW IN WHICH THE APOSTLE REPRESENTS HIS DECEASE. 1. He expresses neither terror nor reluctance, on account of the violent nature of the death which awaited him, but speaks of it calmly as a sacrifice and offering to God. His last and most solemn testimony would thus be given to the truths of God, which he had everywhere proclaimed ; and his blood, when poured out, would simply resemble, as his words imply, the mixture of blood and wine which was poured upon the altar in the ancient sacrifices. His death would merely form the concluding part of that offering, which he had made of himself to the service of his Lord ; and he seemed rather to welcome than to withhold the termination of the sacrifice. The decease of every Christian may be likewise called an offering. We are all required to "yield ourselves to God" ; to present ourselves to him as living sacrifices ; and in our dying hour, or in our devout preparations for it, we may bear our testimony to His perfections, by manifesting our firm faith in His promises and our full submission to his will. 2. But the apostle here speaks farther of his decease, in a sense still more applicable to that of all men ; "the time of my departure" (or as his words directly signify, "the time of my loosing anchor") "is at hand." Thus he teaches us to take a much more enlarged view of our existence than to regard our death as, strictly speaking, the last of its acts ; and rather to consider the dissolution of our mortal frames as the transferring of that existence from the service of God on earth to the presence of God in heaven. II. THE REFLECTIONS WITH WHICH THE APOSTLE HERE LOOKS BACK UPON HIS LIFE ON EARTH. 1. Justly does he speak of his life as a fight, in which he had been engaged, and which he had maintained with the most unshaken resolution to that very hour. 2. This service he farther likens to a race, to one of those contests of bodily strength, or speed, or skill, in which it was common in those days for men to seek the prize of victory, and in which it was accounted the highest earthly honour to gain the corruptible crown. "I have finished my course." In this course of the Christian he had long and perseveringly run, and was now approaching the goal with the prize full in his view. He was the more encouraged in his anticipation of the recompense placed before him by the consideration that he had "kept the faith" ; that he had not only run the Christian race, but had duly observed the rules of the contest. "If a man strive for mastery, yet is he not crowned except he strive lawfully" ; and the first law of the race here spoken of is to "walk by faith," "to run with patience, looking unto Jesus," to be animated in every step and turn of your course by a devout love to His name, a humble trust in His grace, a fervent desire of His glory. In this manner had the apostle kept his fidelity to his Lord, both in fulfilling with diligence the portion of service assigned to him and in his course of labour "living by the faith of the Son of God." By His grace and to his glory he has done the work given him to do ; and, through his promised mediation, he now looked for the end of his faith, the salvation of his soul. III. THE HOPES BY WHICH THE DYING APOSTLE IS CHEERED IN VIEW OF AN ETERNAL WORLD. You are thus called to exercise a rational regard to your own true happiness, looking forward to an eternal blessedness, which can be compared to nothing less than crowns and kingdoms ; a settled approbation of perfect righteousness, desiring to receive, as the sources of your felicity, the approbation and favour and future presence of the righteous Judge of all the earth ; a benevolent sympathy in the best interests of others, delighting in the thought that so many of your fellow-creatures may participate in your company, in the same blessed inheritance ; and finally, a devout sentiment of love to the Son of God, anticipating with joy His own appearing, as the consummation of all this felicity

to your own souls and to multitudes of His redeemed of every age and people. (*James Brewster.*) A prisoner's dying thoughts :—I. THE QUIET COURAGE WHICH LOOKS DEATH FULL IN THE FACE WITHOUT A TREMOR. The language implies that Paul knows his death hour is all but here. As the revised version more accurately gives it, "I am already being offered"—the process is begun, his sufferings at the moment are, as it were, the initial steps of his sacrifice—"and the time of my departure is come." The tone in which he tells Timothy this is very noticeable. There is no sign of excitement, no tremor of emotion, no affectation of stoicism in the simple sentences. 1. We may all make our deaths a sacrifice, an offering to God, for we may yield up our will to God's, and so turn that last struggle into an act of worship and self-surrender. 2. To those who have learned the meaning of Christ's resurrection, and feed their souls on the hopes that it warrants, death is merely a change of place or state, an accident affecting locality, and little more. We have had plenty of changes before. Life has been one long series of departures. This is different from the others mainly in that it is the last, and that to go away from this visible and fleeting show, where we wander aliens among things which have no true kindred with us, is to go home, where there will be no more pulling up the tent-pegs, and toiling across the deserts in monotonous change. How strong is the conviction, spoken in that name for death, that the essential life lasts on quite unaltered through it all! How slight the else formidable thing is made. We may change climates, and for the stormy bleakness of life may have the long still days of heaven, but we do not change ourselves. II. THE PEACEFUL LOOK BACKWARDS. We may feel like a captain who has brought his ship safe across the Atlantic, through foul weather and past many an iceberg, and gives a great sigh of relief as he hands over the charge to the pilot, who will take her across the harbour bar and bring her to her anchorage in the landlocked bay where no tempests rave any more for ever. Such an estimate has nothing in common with self-complacency. It coexists with a profound consciousness of many a sin, many a defeat, and much unfaithfulness. It belongs only to a man who, conscious of these, is "looking for the mercy of the Lord Jesus Christ unto eternal life," and is the direct result, not the antagonist, of lowly self-abasement, and contrite faith in Him by whom alone our stained selves and poor broken services can ever be acceptable. Let us learn too that the only life that bears being looked back upon is a life of Christian devotion and effort. It shows fairer when seen in the strange cross lights that come when we stand on the boundary of two worlds, with the white radiance of eternity beginning to master the vulgar oil lamps of earth, than when seen by these alone. All others have their shabbiness and their selfishness disclosed then. III. THE TRIUMPHANT LOOK FORWARD. That crown, according to other words of Scripture, consists of "life" or "glory"—that is to say, the issue and outcome of believing service and faithful stewardship here is the possession of the true life, which stands in union with God, in measure so great, and in quality so wondrous that it lies on the pure locks of the victors like a flashing diadem, all ablaze with light in a hundred jewels. The completion and exaltation of our nature and characters by the illapse of "life" so sovereign and transcendent that it is "glory" is the consequence of all Christian effort here in the lower levels, where the natural life is always weakness and sometimes shame, and the spiritual life is at the best but a hidden glory and a struggling spark. There is no profit in seeking to gaze into that light of glory so as to discern the shapes of those who walk in it, or the elements of its lambent flames. Enough that in its gracious beauty transfigured souls move as in their native atmosphere! Enough that even our dim vision can see that they have for their companion "One like unto the Son of Man." It is Christ's own life which they share; it is Christ's own glory which irradiates them. (*A. Maclaren, D.D.*) A Christian's death :—I. We begin with making some observations on THE SOURCES OF THAT CONSOLATION WHICH SUPPORTED THIS EMINENT SERVANT OF GOD AT THE TIME WHEN HIS DEPARTURE WAS AT HAND. It was the reflection upon a well-spent life; it was the consciousness of a strenuous and immovable fidelity in the religious warfare which formed his habitual preparation for death, and laid the foundation of his joyful hopes. The only sovereign and efficacious remedy against the fears of dissolution is to mortify the power of sin within the soul, and to make all our vicious appetites to die before us, for the sting of death is sin. He that hath risen above the influence of sin can live beyond all possibility of any great annoyance from the terrors of the last enemy. How animating a scene is the deathbed of the righteous man! What can disturb his last and peaceful moments? The recollection of his trials and patience, the many acts of piety and benevolence which his memory can then suggest, all rise to view, to refresh his retiring soul, to smile upon his departing spirit, and render it superior to the frowns of death, which he is thus enabled to consider, not as a stern and inexorable tyrant sent to execute the vengeance of heaven, but as the messenger of love and peace commissioned to close a troublesome and mortal life, and to put him in possession of one glorious and eternal. II. From the manner in which the apostle expresses the foundation of his tranquillity and hopes, we may observe, in the second place, WHAT IS THE NATURE OF THAT SERVICE IN WHICH THE CHRISTIAN IS ENGAGED, and of that strenuous and immovable fidelity which is indispensably requisite to complete his character : " I have fought a good fight, I have finished my course, I have kept the faith." It is the uniform declaration of the Almighty to all the sons of men, that it is no easy thing to be a Christian, but that through much tribulation we must enter into the kingdom of God. We wrestle not with flesh and blood, but with principalities and powers, with the rulers of the darkness of this world, with spiritual wickedness in high places. Our combat does not endure only for a little, nor is our security the reward of a few hours of steady opposition, but almost every step we take through the wilderness of life exposes us to some new attack ; we are often assaulted by all the deceivableness of unrighteousness, and through the whole of life we maintain an unceasing struggle. Nor are all our enemies open and declared. Equally dangerous are our secret foes, these insidious passions which lodge within us, ever ready to catch at the bribes of an alluring world, and to open for it a secret passage to the heart. Thus surrounded with dangers on every hand, how absolutely necessary is it to be strong, to quit ourselves like men, to brace the mind with firmness and vigour, to keep the attention constantly directed to every quarter from which we may be assaulted? Thanks be to God, however, we are not left to struggle alone: there is an omnipotent grace which gives strength to the feeble. The law of the Christian dispensation is this: We are commanded to labour with as vigorous efforts as if the whole success of that work depended on ourselves alone, and, at the same time, with the humility and diffidence of a mind conscious of its own imbecility, and sensible of the necessity of Divine grace to render all its endeavours effectual. The man who is thus disposed has no reason to dread the greatest dangers : " He who is with thee is greater than he who is against thee : the Lord is thy life and thy salvation, whom shalt thou fear ? The Lord is the strength of thy life, of whom shalt thou be afraid ? " The sacred influence of His grace shall continually descend to guide thy doubtful steps, to invigorate every languid effort, to teach thy hands to war and thy fingers to fight, and to crown thee with final success and triumph. III. Which leads us naturally to turn our thoughts, in the third place, TO THAT BLESSED AND GLORIOUS REWARD, SPECIFIED IN THE TEXT, by the expression of a crown of righteousness. This expression has an evident allusion to those crowns bestowed by the ancients on brave and intrepid warriors ; to those marks of honour and respect by which they were wont to distinguish particular feats of valour. It intimates to us that high and splendid triumph which shall be at last conferred on the faithful and undaunted servants of the Most High God ; that ineffable dignity which shall be bestowed on them in the day of Christ's appearance ; and recalls to our thoughts that most interesting period when the Judge of all the earth shall descend with ineffable pomp and majesty, with the voice of the archangel, and with the trump of God. How great, O God, is that goodness which Thou hast laid up for them that serve Thee, and wrought for them that fear Thy name before the sons of men. Thou shalt hide them for ever in the secret of Thy pavilion ; Thou shalt defend them from the strife of tongues, and from the pride of men. Such honour shall all the saints of God possess ; such shall be the reward of the steady friends of Jesus. Thus blessed shall they be who are found holy and undefiled in the world ; they shall have a right to the tree of life ; they shall enter through the gate into the city, and reign with Jesus for ever and ever. IV. Our last observation is founded on the declaration in the text, THAT THIS HONOUR SHALL BE CONFERRED ON THOSE, AND THOSE ALONE, WHO LOVE THE APPEARANCE OF JESUS. Shall the treasures of Divine grace ever be prostituted to enrich the unworthy ? or, shall the impious man ever be raised to that happiness which he hath always despised ? No, the decree hath passed, a decree which shall never be reversed, that unless we are renewed in the spirit of our minds we cannot enter into the kingdom of heaven. This decree is no arbitrary law ; it is founded in nature; it is implied in the very reason of things, that none but the pure in heart are qualified for relishing the pleasures of that immortal inheritacne. For, what is heaven? Not a total alteration of state, but reason, and every pious and virtuous disposition dilated and expanded to its highest pitch. What are the immortal joys which it contains but the security, the increase, and the perfection of virtue? (*J. Main, D.D.*) *Sayings of Christians at the end of life :*—Rev. J. Newton, who lived to a good old age, used to tell his friends in his latter days, " I am like a parcel packed up and directed, only waiting for the carrier to take me to my destination." When Dr. Wardlaw was visited by Norman McLeod in his dying hour, and was asked by him if he could not wish, like Enoch, to escape the pains of death, "No," he said, most touchingly, " I would enter heaven by the way that Jesus went." " I die no more," were the exultant words of old Dr. Redford, as he fell down in death. The Rev. Dr. Punshon, working and suffering, fulfilled a sort of double life until his Divine Master called him home. Then, in deeply reverent tones, looking upward, he said, with a firm voice, "Christ is to me a bright reality. Jesus! Jesus!" What a moment for his beloved wife when she saw a smile of rapture on his face, then marked him bow his weary head, and enter into the rest eternal! *Readiness for death :*—Sir John Burgh, a brave soldier, who received a mortal wound in the Isle of Rees, and being advised not to fear death, but to prepare himself for another world, answered, " I thank God I fear not death; these thirty years together I never rose out of my bed in the morning, that ever I made account to live till night." *Contrasted deaths :*—There is one more point of tremendous reminiscence, and that is the last hour of life, when we have to look over all our past existence. What a moment that will be! I place Napoleon's dying reminiscence on St. Helena beside Mrs. Judson's dying reminiscence in the harbour of St. Helena, the same island, twenty years afterwards. Napoleon's dying reminiscence was one of delirium — *Tête d'armée*—"Head of the Army." Mrs. Judson's dying reminiscence, as she came home from her missionary toil and her life of self-sacrifice for God, dying in the cabin of the ship in the harbour of St. Helena, was, " I always did love the Lord Jesus Christ." And then she fell into a sound sleep for an hour, and woke amid the songs of angels. I place the dying reminiscence of Augustus Cæsar against the dying reminiscence of the Apostle Paul. The dying reminiscence of Augustus Cæsar was, addressing his attendants, " Have I played my part well on the stage of life?" and they answered in the affirmative, and he said, " Why, then, don't you applaud me?" The dying reminiscence of Paul the apostle was, " I have fought a good fight, I have kept the faith; henceforth there is laid up for me a crown of righteousness, which the Lord the righteous Judge will give me in that day, and not to me only, but to all them that love His appearing." Augustus Cæsar died amid pomp and great surroundings. Paul uttered his dying reminiscence looking up through the wall of a dungeon. God grant that our dying pillow may be the closing of a useful life, and the opening of a glorious eternity. (*T. De Witt Talmage.*) *Death a departure :*—It is the most melancholy circumstance in the funerals of our Christian friends, when we have laid their bodies in the dark and silent grave, to go home and leave them behind; but, alas! it is not we that go home and leave them behind; no, it is they that are gone to the better home, and have left us behind. (*Matthew Henry.*) *Bishop Ken in life and death :*—Nothing could be more beautiful than Ken's life. His days at Longleat are amongst the treasured memories of one of England's fairest spots; and his last journeys derive a tender pathos from the singular fact of his carrying his shroud in his portmanteau—he remarking that it " might be as soon wanted as any other of his habiliments." He put it on himself some days before the last; and in holy quietness and peace, his death was as beautiful as his life. (*J. Stoughton, D.D.*) *Passing on the torch :*—Bengel says that Paul was about to deliver up to Timothy before his decease the lamp or torch-light of the evangelical office. Bengel alludes, remarks Dr. James Bryer, to the ancient torch-races of the λαμπαδηφόροι, in which the torch was handed by the runners from hand to hand. *Carrying on the battle :*—A brave soldier in the day of battle, if he hears that a regiment has been exterminated by the enemy's shot and shell, says, "Then those of us that survive must fight like tigers. There is no room for us to play at fighting. If they have slain so many, we must be more desperately valiant." (*C. H. Spurgeon.*) **The time of my departure is at hand.**—*A last look-out :*—I. OUR DEPARTURE. We loose our cable, and bid farewell to earth, it shall not be with bitterness in the retrospect. There is sin in it, and we are called to leave it; there has been trial in it, and we are called to be delivered from it; there has been sorrow in it, and we are glad that we shall go where we shall sorrow no more. There have been weakness, and pain, and suffering in it, and we are glad that we shall be raised in power; there has been death in it, and we are glad to bid farewell to shrouds and to knells; but for all that there has been such mercy in it, such lovingkindness of God in it, that the wilderness and the solitary place have been made glad, and the desert has rejoiced and blossomed as a rose. We will not bid farewell to the world, execrating it, or leaving behind us a cold shudder and a sad remembrance, but we will depart, bidding adieu to the scenes that remain, and to the people of God that tarry therein yet a little longer, blessing Him whose goodness and mercy have followed us all the days of our life, and who is now bringing us to dwell in the house of the Lord for ever. But if I have had to speak in a somewhat apologetic manner of the land from which we depart, I shall need to use many apologies for my own poor talk about the land to which we are bound. Ah, whither goest thou, spirit loosened from thy clay—dost know? Whither goest thou? The answer must be, partly, that we know not. None of us have seen the streets of gold of which we sang just now; those harpings of the harpers, harping with their harps, have never fallen on these ears; eye hath not seen it, ear hath not heard it; it is all unrevealed to the senses; flesh and blood cannot inherit it, and, therefore, flesh and blood cannot imagine it. Yet it is not unknown, for God hath revealed it unto us by His Spirit. Spiritual men know what it is to feel the spirit, their own new-born spirit, living, glowing, burning, triumphing within them. They know, therefore, that if the body should drop off they would not die. They feel there is a life within them superior to blood and bone, and nerve and sinew. They feel the life of God within them, and none can gainsay it. Their own experience has proven to them that there is an inner life. Well, then, when that inner life is strong and vigorous, the spirit often reveals to it what the world of spirits will be. We know what holiness is. Are we not seeking it? That is heaven—perfect holiness is heaven. We know what peace means; Christ is our peace. Rest—He gives us rest; we find that when we take His yoke. Rest is heaven. And rest in Jesus tells us what heaven is. II. THE TIME OF OUR DEPARTURE, though unknown to us, is fixed by God—unalterably fixed; so rightly, wisely, lovingly settled, and prepared for, that no chance or haphazard can break the spell of destiny. III. THE TIME IS AT HAND. In a certain sense, every Christian may say this; for whatever interval may interpose between us and death, how very short it is! Have you not all a sense that time flows faster than it did? In our childish days we thought a year was quite a period of time, a very epoch in our career; now as for weeks—one can hardly reckon them! We seem to be travelling by an express train, flying along at such a rate that we can hardly count the months. Why, the past year only seemed to come in at one door and go out at the other; it was over so soon. We shall soon be at the terminus of life, even if we live for several years; but in the case of some of us, God knows of whom, this year, perhaps this month, will be our last. 1. Is not this a reason for surveying our condition again? If our vessel is just launching, let us see that she is seaworthy. It would be a sad thing for us to be near departing, and yet to be just as near discovering that we are lost. I charge every man and woman within this place, since the time of his departure may be far nearer than he thinks, to take stock, and reckon up, and see whether he be Christ's or no. 2. But if the time of my departure be at hand, and I am satisfied that it is all right with me, is there not a call for me to do all I can for my household? 3. Let me try to finish all my work, not only as regards my duty to my family, but in respect to all the world so far as my influence or ability can reach. 4. If the time of our departure is at hand, let it cheer us amid our troubles. Sometimes, when our friends go to Liverpool to sail for Canada, or any other distant region, on the night before they sail they get into a very poor lodging. I think I hear one of them grumbling, "What a hard bed! What a small room! What a bad look-out!" "Oh," says the other, "never mind, brother; we are not going to live here; we are off to-morrow." Bethink you in like manner, ye children of poverty, this is not your rest. Put up with it, you are away to-morrow. 5. And if the time of my departure is at hand, I should like to be on good terms with all my friends on earth. 6. If the time of my departure is at hand, then let me guard against being elated by any temporal prosperity. Possessions, estates, creature comforts dwindle into insignificance before this outlook. 7. Lastly, if the time of our departure is at hand, let us be prepared to bear our testimony. We are witnesses for Christ. Let us bear our testimony before we are taken up and mingle with the cloud of witnesses who have finished their course and rested from their labours. Let us work for Jesus while we can work for Him. (*C. H. Spurgeon.*)

*The dying Christian* :—It is recorded of one of our most distinguished British essayists, that he addressed to an irreligious nobleman these solemn words, " I have sent for you that you may see how a Christian can die." Many critics have thought that the apostle's request to Timothy, " Do thy diligence to come shortly unto me," was prompted by a desire not only to have his companionship in the time of tribulation, but to impart religious counsel, and above all, that he might be a witness of the last moments of his aged father in Christ, the apostle. Whatever difference of opinion may be entertained of Addison's saying to the nobleman, who can doubt the wisdom and piety of Paul's wish? I. LIFE PRESENT, OR THE APOSTLE'S REFLECTIONS ON DYING. How calm his mind! Whilst our views and feelings may be altered by the nearness of the last enemy, to Paul it seemed the same whether death was dimly seen in the distance, or the interval be measured by a single step. The words, " I am now ready to be offered " probably contain an allusion to the heathen custom of pouring wine and oil on the head of the victim when about to be offered in sacrifice. The apostle felt himself to be as near to death as that very victim ; every preparation having been made, he only had to await the fatal blow. How could such a man fear death when for years he had been a " living sacrifice " in the service of his Master, and was now awaiting death as the consummation of the sacrifice? The other figure is not less beautiful. The apostle had hitherto felt himself bound to the present world as a ship to its moorings, but now anchor was to be weighed, fastenings to be loosened, and sails to be unfurled. But though the vast, the boundless ocean stretched out before him, he felt himself to be no mere adventurer—a Columbus going in search of an undiscovered land. Though known only by report, he knew that the report of this new world was not the speculation or idle conjecture of man. Thus, elsewhere, he is found saying, " having a desire to depart [to loose cable] and to be with Christ, which is far better." How does the repetition of these figures show that his feelings were not transient impulses, but the settled habits of his mind. How intelligent was this confidence! His was not the peace of ignorance, or of a perverted view of the mercy of God. Here was his assurance of a triumph over the last foe, " I know whom I have believed, and am persuaded that He is able to keep that which I have committed unto Him against that day." And is there not something sublime in this state of mind? What a contrast does it present even to some of those cases of supposed religious triumph over death which men of the world have quoted from classic antiquity. For what was it that made the apostle so resigned, so willing, so longing to meet death? Was it a feeling of misanthropy from the base treatment he had received from his fellow creatures, including even his professed friends? Was it disappointed ambition, the world refusing him its laurels? Was it anxious suspense from being in prisons and deaths oft? Was it the infirmity of old age, drying up all the sources of the enjoyment of life? Whilst these may be the secret motives which have urged many men of the world to desire departure, no such selfishness was enthroned in the apostle's breast, as you may learn from his reflections : " For I am in a strait betwixt two, having a desire to depart, and to be with Christ, which is far better." " We are confident, I say, and willing rather to be absent from the body and to be present with the Lord." II. LET US LOOK AT LIFE PAST ; OR, THE APOSTLE'S RETROSPECT. 1. Here is life reviewed in reference to its conflicts. Life is not only a race, but a conflict—not only a stretching forward for the prize, but one continuous struggle with besetting foes: it calls not only for activities, but resistance. Say you this is a repulsive view of religion? We reply, is not self-denial necessary for success in all the departments of life? Is it not, moreover, as salutary as indispensable? Instead of complaining of this battle of life, ask yourselves if the self-knowledge thereby obtained, the opportunity afforded for the development of graces, the vigour given by exercise to every virtue, be not more than a compensation? 2. Life is here reviewed in reference to the individual sphere of active duties. We might here propose several questions. Is a man sent into the world by his Creator only to follow out his own inclinations, or is he in any sense born to the fulfilment of some great end in the kingdom of God's providence? We might ask again if the individual believer sooner or later may not find out his particular vocation, and arrive at some satisfactory conclusion as to what end he was born, or for what cause he came into the world. Do not wants, gifts, counsels of friends, oft unmistakably point to the work assigned by the Disposer of all things? Will not the prayer, "Lord, what wilt Thou have me to do?" be answered, so that the suppliant shall be able to say, " This is my course." If, then, there is a course prescribed by Divine providence for each of us, is it not our interest as well as our obligation to pursue it? 3. Life is here reviewed in reference to religious beliefs, or our fidelity to truth. By the word faith here is meant the Christian religion, so called because it is a revelation made to man's faith; "the righteousness of God is revealed from faith to faith." But all cannot say, "I have kept the faith." Could Phygellus, or Hermogenes, or Hymenæus, utter such words? The patience and the faith of the saints are often severely tried, and blessed are they of whom it was said, "Here are they that keep the faith of Jesus." If any think lightly of adherence to the faith, let them ponder over the death-bed confession of one who had swerved from the truth. "It seemed," says a writer in the *Quarterly Review*, "that Hume received a religious education from his mother, and early in life was the subject of strong and hopeful religious impressions; but as he approached to manhood they were effaced, and confirmed infidelity succeeded. Maternal partiality, however alarmed at first, came to look with less pain upon this declaration, and filial love and reverence seem to have been absorbed in the pride of philosophical scepticism: for Hume now applied himself with unwearied, and, unhappily, with successful efforts, to sap the foundation of the mother's faith. Having succeeded in this dreadful work, he went abroad into foreign countries, and, as he was returning, an express met him in London with a letter from his mother, informing him that she was in a deep decline, and would not long survive. She said she found herself without any support in her distress; that he had taken away that source of comfort upon which in all cases of affliction she used to rely, and that now she found her mind sinking into despair: she did not doubt that her son would afford her some substitute for her religion; and conjured him to hasten home, or at least send her a letter containing such consolations as philosophy can afford a dying mortal. Hume was overwhelmed with anguish, hastened to Scotland, travelling night and day, but before he arrived his mother had expired." Is it nothing, then, to "hold fast the form of sound words," and, on a dying bed, to exclaim, "I have kept the faith"? III. LET US NOTICE LIFE TO COME, OR THE APOSTLE'S SUBLIME ANTICIPATIONS. The race was nearly run, the conflict was well-nigh ended; it now only remained that the crown should be bestowed. The crown was to be one of righteousness. Not that the apostle felt he could claim it, for he who styled himself less than the least of all saints would be the first to cast his crown at the feet of the Royal Redeemer, exclaiming, "Thou alone art worthy"; but it was called "a crown of righteousness" because won in the cause of righteousness, and conferred upon him by One who is "not unrighteous to forget your work and labour of love, which ye have showed towards His name." In every age the attainment of a crown has been the summit of human ambition. For it, usurpers have dethroned monarchs—warriors have stood in the breach—navigators have defied the fury of the deep—philosophers have strained intellect night as well as day; for it the foot-racer, and the boxer, and the charioteer have endured severest bodily discipline—all—all reaching after the goal of worldly honour, all trying to distance their competitors—all dissatisfied with the present, and reaching to that which is before. Now Christianity addresses such aspirants, and points them to something better, to crowns purer, brighter, and more enduring. But what may be the crowns which the Lord the righteous Judge shall bestow, we shall not venture to describe. Sure we are, they are not merely symbols of sovereignty, or ensigns of victory, or tokens of national gratitude to earthly benefactors. The conqueror there will not be crowned with olives, or parsley, or any other such fading leaves. It will not consist in the praises of men, or worldly elevation above the millions of our fellow-creatures. It will not be awarded for human merit, nor will the wearer be conscious of any feeling of claim: the weight of his glory will rather weigh him down. It will not be of such a character as shall endanger his holiness, or that shall afterwards require a thorn in the flesh lest the victor should be exalted above measure. It will not be the joy and rapture of an hour, awakened by the excitement of the novelty, to be followed by *ennui* and disappointment. It will not awaken envy among the millions of the glorified, but rather raise higher joy as they see one wearing a more brilliant diadem than the rest. The crown will consist in nothing that will divert the mind from the Eternal All, and cause it to seek satisfaction in self. The real joy will be that it has been awarded by God's own Son, placed on the brow by His own hand—that it will reflect higher glory on the Giver—that it will be prostrated at His feet. In a word, the honour will consist in the presence and favour and likeness of God. But we pause and tremble, lest we should darken counsel by words without knowledge. We must wait until we wear it, before we shall fully understand the words—" a crown of life "—" a crown of glory "—" a crown that fadeth not away "—" a crown of righteousness." (*J. S. Pearsall.*)    *Ready for home :*—I. As a DEPARTURE TO ANOTHER COUNTRY. As when the ship puts to sea, it is for the purpose of sailing to another port, so Paul looked forward to death as a " departure " for another country. The sailor does not leave the port with the prospect of an eternal cruise in unknown seas, or for the purpose of ultimately losing himself somewhere in some mysterious, undefined nothing. II. As a DEPARTURE TO A BETTER COUNTRY. He was willing to sail. Now Paul was no misanthrope, who had become so sick of human society that he longed to be rid of it. He was not weary of life. Then why did he wish to go ? Was he amongst those eternal grumblers who themselves do all the " howling," and then complain that the world is a "howling wilderness"? By no means! His desire to depart was not because this was bad, but because that was "better"; not because he had had enough of Christian society and Christian service—that was good—but because he wished to be with Christ, which was infinitely preferable. III. As a DEPARTURE TO A BETTER COUNTRY, WHICH WAS HIS HOME. Paul compared himself to a sailor who, lying in a foreign port, was awaiting orders to sail for home. Such a man, though in a land of pleasure and plenty, would sit and long to be away. As he thought of friends beloved across the sea, he would count the weeks and days when he hoped to see them once again. Not unlike this are the Christian's dreams of heaven. IV. As a DEPARTURE FOR HOME, THE TIME OF WHICH WAS FIXED. "The time of my departure is at hand." The Psalmist says, "My times are in Thy hand." "My times ! "—that is, all my future is with God. He knows—1. When I shall depart. 2. Whence I shall depart. 3. How I shall depart. Two Cistercian monks in the reign of Henry VIII. were threatened, before their martyrdom, by the Lord Mayor of that time, that they should be tied in a sack, and thrown into the Thames. " My lord," answered one, " we are going to the kingdom of heaven ; and whether we go by land or water is of very little consequence to us." So our thoughts should be fixed on the goal rather than on the path by which it is reached ; on the rest that remains rather than on the toil through which it is obtained. V. As a DEPARTURE FOR HOME, THE TIME OF WHICH WAS NEAR. "The time of my departure is at hand." The sailor, lying in a foreign port, with his cargo complete, his sails " bent," and the wind fair for home, contemplates with joy the fact that the day is near when the order will come to bid him sail. Thus Paul waited for death. To him the disease, or the accident, or the martyrdom, would be but as the postman who brought the letter—the letter for which he longed with unutterable desire. VI. As a DEPARTURE FOR HOME, FOR WHICH HE WAS PERFECTLY READY. "I am now ready," said he. And so he was. As one by one he saw the cords being unloosened which bound him to this world—as loved ones were taken away—as sickness, disease, or age told him that the time was at hand when he was to depart, he viewed the whole with the complacent satisfaction of the sailor who sees his vessel being unmoored to sail for home. (*W. H. Burton.*)    *Joy of a faithful minister in view of eternity :*—I. THE CHARACTER OF A FAITHFUL MINISTER. 1. He loves the gospel which he preaches. 2. He does not shun to declare all the counsel of God, but endeavours to preach the gospel as fully and as plainly as possible. 3. He will uniformly and perseveringly perform the self-denying duties of his office, which are of a less public nature, but of no less importance, than his ministrations on the Sabbath. In visiting the sick and the dying, he will deal plainly as well as tenderly with them. Whenever he is called to converse with persons about the state of their minds, whether they are in stupidity, distress, or doubt, he will not daub with untempered mortar, nor endeavour to comfort those who ought not to be comforted. He will contend earnestly for the faith which was once delivered unto the saints. II. WHAT REASONS HE MAY HAVE TO REJOICE IN THE NEAR PROSPECT OF ETERNITY. 1. He has good reason to rejoice that he chose the work of the ministry in preference to any other employment in life. The most useful employment must be allowed to be the most important and desirable. 2. He has good reason to rejoice in the close of life and in the view of eternity, that God has enabled him to be faithful. 3. He has good reason to rejoice in the close of his ministry, because God has given him assurance that all his faithful labours shall produce some valuable and important effects, either sooner or later. 4. He has good ground to rejoice when the time of his departure is at hand, because God has promised him an ample reward for all his sincere services. (*N. Emmons, D.D.*)    *A Christian's death :*—I. THE IMPORTANCE OF PREPARATION FOR OUR DEPARTURE. 1. This is the last and closing scene of human life. 2. How serious a thing it is to die. 3. Because disease and the period introductory to our dissolution are special seasons given to us in which to glorify God and bring credit to religion. 4. This is the last opportunity we have of doing anything for God, for the Church, for our families, and for the world. II. THE MANNER IN WHICH A CHRISTIAN SHOULD DIE. 1. Amidst the darkness, languor, and pain of a sick bed, a Christian man ought to engage in commending the ways of God and religion to those about him. The words of dying saints have been called "living oracles"; and so they should be. 2. We should then attend to the duty of exhorting others who are walking in the ways of the Lord. 3. We ought to commend ourselves and others to God in the devout exercise of prayer. 4. In the exercise of strong faith. (*A. Waugh, D.D.*)　*Calmness in death—its philosophy :*—I. A SOUL-ABSORBING INTEREST IN THE GREAT CAUSE OF UNIVERSAL TRUTH AND BENEVOLENCE. II. AN ACCURATE CONCEPTION OF WHAT DEATH REALLY IS TO THE GOOD. III. DELIGHTFUL MEMORIES OF THE MANNER IN WHICH HE HAD SPENT HIS LIFE. IV. A SOUL-ENRAPTURING VISION OF THE FUTURE INTO WHICH HE WAS ABOUT ENTERING. (*Homilist.*)　*Good-bye to the world :*—The way out of this world is so blocked up with coffin, and hearse, and undertaker's spade, and screwdriver, that the Christian can hardly think as he ought of the most cheerful passage in all his history. We hang black instead of white over the place where the good man gets his last victory. We stand weeping over a heap of chains which the freed soul has shaken off, and we say, "Poor man! What a pity it was he had to come to this." Come to what? By the time people have assembled at the obsequies, that man has been three days so happy that all the joy of earth accumulated would be wretchedness beside it; and he might better weep over you because you have to stay, than you weep over him because he has to go. Paul, in my text, takes that great clod of a word, "death," and throws it away, and speaks of his "departure," a beautiful, bright, suggestive word, descriptive of every Christian's release. Now, departure implies a starting-place, and a place of destination. When Paul left this world, what was the starting-point? It was a scene of great physical distress. It was the Tullianum, the lower dungeon of the Mamertine prison. The top dungeon was bad enough—it having no means of ingress or egress but through an opening in the top. Through that the prisoner was lowered, and through that came all the food, and air, and light received. It was a terrible place, that upper dungeon; but the Tullianum was the lower dungeon, and that was still more wretched, the only light and the only air coming through the roof, and that roof the floor of the upper dungeon. It was there that Paul spent his last days on earth, and it is there that I see him to-day, in the fearful dungeon, shivering, blue with cold, waiting for that old overcoat which he had sent for up to Troas, and which they had not yet sent down, notwithstanding he had written for it. Oh, worn-out, emaciated old man, surely you must be melancholy. No constitution could endure this and be cheerful; but I press my way through the prison until I come up close to where he is, and by the faint light that streams through the opening I see on his face a supernatural joy, and I bow before him and I say, "Aged man, how can you keep cheerful amid all this gloom?" His voice startles the darkness of the place as he cries out, "I am now ready to be offered, and the time of my departure is at hand." Hark! what is that shuffling of feet in the upper dungeon? Why, Paul has an invitation to a banquet, and he is going to dine to-day with the King. Those shuffling feet are the feet of the executioners. They come, and they cry down through the hole of the dungeon, "Hurry up, old man. Come, now, get yourself ready." Why, Paul was ready. He had nothing to pack up. He had no baggage to take. He had been ready a good while. I see him rising up, and straightening out his stiffened limbs, and pushing back his white hair from his creviced forehead, and see him looking up through the hole in the roof of the dungeon into the face of his executioner, and hear him say, "I am now ready to be offered, and the time of my departure is at hand." Then they lift him out of the dungeon, and they start with him to the place of execution. They say, "Hurry along, old man, or you will feel the weight of our spear. Hurry along." "How far is it," says Paul, "we have to travel?" "Three miles." Oh, three miles is a good way for an old man to travel after he has been whipped and crippled with maltreatment. But they soon get to the place of execution—Acquæ Salvia—and he is fastened to the pillar of martyrdom. I see him looking up in the face of his executioner, and as the grim official draws the sword, Paul calmly says, "I am now ready to be offered, and the time of my departure is at hand." One sharp, keen stroke, and Paul does go to the banquet, and Paul does dine with the King. What a transition it was! From the malaria of Rome to the finest climate in all the universe—the zone of eternal beauty and health. From shipwreck, from dungeon, from the biting pain of the elm-wood rods, from the sharp sword of the headsman, he goes into the most brilliant assemblage of heaven, a king among kings, multitudes of the sainthood rushing out and stretching forth hands of welcome; for I do really think that, as on the right hand of God is Christ, so on the right hand of Christ is Paul, the second great in heaven. He changed kings likewise. Before the hour of death, and up to the last moment, he was under Nero, the thick-necked, the cruel-eyed, the filthy lipped. But the next moment he goes into the realm of Him whose reign is love, and whose courts are paved with love, and whose throne is set on pillars of love, and whose sceptre is adorned with jewels of love, and whose palace is lighted with love, and whose lifetime is an eternity of love. When Paul was leaving so much on this side the pillar of martyrdom to gain so much on the other side, do you wonder at the cheerful valedictory of the text, "The time of my departure is at hand"? Now, why cannot all the old people of my congregation have the same holy glee as that aged man had? You say you most fear the struggle at the moment the soul and body part. But millions have endured that moment, and why may not we as well? They got through with it, and so can we. Besides this, all medical men agree in saying that there is probably no struggle at all at the last moment—not so much pain as the prick of a pin, the seeming signs of distress being altogether involuntary. But you say, "It is the uncertainty of the future." Now, child of God, do not play the infidel. After God has filled the Bible till it can hold no more with stories of the good things ahead, better not talk about uncertainties. But you say, "I cannot bear to think of parting from friends here." If you are old, you have more friends in heaven than here. Besides that, it is more healthy there for you than here, aged man; better climate there than these hot summers, and cold winters, and late springs; better hearing; better eyesight; more tonic in the air; more perfume in the bloom; more sweetness in the song. I remark again: all those ought to feel this joy of the text who have a holy curiosity to know what is beyond this earthly terminus. And who has not any curiosity about it? A man, doomed to die, stepped on the scaffold, and said, in joy, "Now in ten minutes I will know the great secret." One minute after the vital functions ceased, the little child that died last night knew more than Jonathan Edwards, or St. Paul himself before they died. Friends, the exit from this world, or death, if you please to call it, to the Christian is glorious explanation. It is demonstration. It is illumination. It is sunburst. It is the opening of all the windows. It is shutting up the catechism of doubt and the unrolling of all the scrolls of positive and accurate information. I remark again: we ought to have the joy of the text, because leaving this world we move into the best society of the universe. You see a great crowd of people in some street, and you say, "Who is passing there? What general, what prince, is going up there?" Well, I see a great throng in heaven. I say, "Who is the focus of all that admiration? Who is the centre of that glittering company?" It is Jesus, the champion of all worlds, the favourite of all ages. (*T. De Witt Talmage, D.D.*) *Presentiment of death:*— In one of his last letters Livingstone wrote, "During a large part of this journey I had a strong presentiment that I should never live to finish it. It is weakened now as I seem to see the end towards which I have been striving looming in the distance. This presentiment did not interfere with the performance of any duty: it only made me think a great deal more of the future state of being." *Unconscious sense of the end of life:*—Churchill, in the unfinished "Journey," the last fragment found among his papers, showed a strange unconscious kind of sense of being near his end. He calls it the plain unlaboured Journey of a Day, and closes with the line—"I on my journey all alone proceed!" The poem was not meant to close here, but a greater Hand interposed. That line of mournful significance is the last that was written by Churchill! (*Timbs.*) *Welcoming death:*—Of Bradford it is said, that when the keeper's wife said to him, "Oh, sir, I am come with heavy tidings—you are to be burnt to-morrow"; taking off his hat and laying it upon the ground, and kneeling and raising his hands, he said, "Lord, I thank Thee for this honour. This is what I have been waiting for, and longing for." (*W. Jay.*) *Byron and St. Paul—a contrast:*—For a contrast of worldly despair with Christian confidence at the end of life, compare with the words of Paul in 2 Tim. iv. 6-8 the following, which are reckoned the last verses of Byron's pen:—

> "My days are in the yellow leaf,
> The flowers, the fruits of love are gone;
> The worm, the canker, and the grief,
> Are mine alone.

The fire that on my bosom preys
Is lone as some volcanic isle,
No torch is lifted at its blaze
A funeral pile ! "    (*J. F. B. Tinling, B.A.*)

**I have fought a good fight.**—*The holy war:*—I. THE TWO ARMIES. 1. The army of the saints. (1) Their Captain-General is the Lord Jesus Christ. (2) The officers are the ministers of Christ, and all who are active and useful in His service. (3) The soldiers are the saints. (4) The enlisting—conversion. (5) The uniform—the graces of the Spirit, and the robe of righteousness. (6) The armour—helmet of salvation, &c. (7) The instruction of the young soldiers—Bible. (8) The allies —angels. 2. The army of the enemy. (1) Generals—sin, Satan, and world. (2) Soldiers—the wicked. (3) Allies—evil spirits. II. THE BATTLE. 1. What kind of a battle ? (1) A good battle. (2) A hot battle. (3) A very profitable battle. (4) A battle that must be constant. 2. Where fought? Whole world. 3. When shall it be finished? At death for each individual soldier; at the day of judgment for the whole army. III. THE VICTORY. 1. Is certain. 2. Shall be held in everlasting remembrance. (*A. Fletcher, D.D.*)    *Moral warfare :*—1. It is lawful sometimes to speak of those gifts and graces which God hath given us, that we may comfort and quicken others by our example. 2. The sweetest songs of the saints have been towards their last ends. The sun shines sweetliest when it is setting, the wine of the spirit is strongest in the saints when they are drawing to an end. His motions are quickest when natural motions are slowest ; as we see in Moses his swan-like song (Deut. xxxi.–xxxiii.), and David how sweetly doth he sing a little before he dies of God's mercies to himself, of the covenant of free grace which God had made with him, and His judgments on the sons of Belial (2 Samuel xxii; 1–8). Joshua dying, how sweetly doth he exhort the people to obedience by setting before them the mercies of God (Joshua xxiv.). All Christ's sayings are excellent, but none so sweet and comfortable as those which He delivered a little before His death. Wicked men when they die they set in a cloud, and like the going out of a candle they leave a stench behind them : as their bodies, so their names rot and stink when they are dead and gone. As wicked men grow worse and worse and their last days are their worst, so good men grow better and better, and their last days are their best ; having but a little time to live in the world, they are willing to leave it with a good savour. 3. The sweet resent which a good conscience hath of a well-spent life is matter of singular comfort and rejoicing in death. 4. Every faithful Christian is a spiritual soldier. (1) In war there is watching, soldiers must stand on their guard continually for fear of a surprisal to the loss of all. (2) In warring there must be arming, another man may go unarmed, but he that is a soldier must be armed. (3) He must have skill and knowledge how to manage his weapons, his hands must be taught to war and his fingers to fight. (4) Courage and valour. Even Rabshakeh could say counsel and strength are for war (2 Kings xviii. 20). Policy and power are very requisite for a soldier. (5) In respect of hardship a soldier must be a hardy man. (6) In respect of obedience. A soldier is under the most absolute command of any man. He must obey and not dispute the commands of his commander to whom by oath he is bound to be faithful. (7) In respect of order. In war there is much order. Soldiers must keep rank and file, they must abide in that place and keep on that ground on which their commander sets them. (8) In respect of their unsettled abode. A soldier whilst he is in actual service hath no settled abode, but he is always either marching, charging, watching, fighting, lying in his tent for a night or two and is gone. (9) A soldier must attend the wars, he must forsake house, land, wife, children and other lawful delights (for a time at least), and give up himself to his martial affairs ; he cannot work and war, follow a trade and fight too ; but he must wholly devote himself to his military employment that he may please his commander. (10) In respect of unity, soldiers must be unanimous. United forces prevail much, but if soldiers be divided and mutiny they ruin themselves. (11) Lastly, In respect of activity a soldier's life is a laborious life, they are cut out for action, they must never be idle. Now, the Lord will have us all to fight for these reasons : 1. For the greater manifestations of His own glory. He could deliver His people without fighting, but then the glory of His wisdom, power and goodness in their preservation and deliverance would not be so perspicuous to the world ; nor His justice in downfall of His enemies be so apparent to all. 2. For the good of His people, hereby He exerciseth their graces and keeps them from rusting. Virtue decays if it have not some opposite to quicken it, and draw it out; hereby also He proves their valour and makes it more apparent to others. The skill of a pilot is not known till a storm, nor the valour of a soldier till the day of battle. 3. To make us long for our rest in heaven. 4. This spiritual fight is a good fight. It is not warring after the flesh, but a spiritual, holy, honourable war (2 Cor. x. 3, 4). It is a good fight in nine respects. 1. Of the author. 2. The man. 3. The matter. 4. The manner. 5. The end. 6. The armour. 7. The issue. 8. The fellow-soldiers. 9. The reward. It is a great comfort to be an old soldier of Christ. Men cashier old decrepit men out of their camps; but the older soldiers we are in Christ's Church the better and the more acceptable to Him. (*T. Hall, B.D.*) *The good fight:*—A general retrospect of Christian life may fill the soul with rejoicing at the end of life. It is the life that men live that is the evidence that they are fit to die. As against a selfish, sordid life the gleams of a lately-inspired hope are but doubtful evidences. A consciousness of imperfection and of sins need not dim the hope that men have, nor the triumph that they express in their last hours—nay, it may increase as the sufferings of a campaign lend added lustre to the victory. So, as one glances back and sees how the grace of God sustained him in all the imperfections of a long life, so one may at last be bold to affirm his fidelity and safety and become prophetic of that which is before him. For every man that is born and lives is building; and the builder invariably must hew. For the material of which character is built, as of houses, is either wood or clay, unfitted; and the clay must be moulded, and the brick must be burned, and the carpenter must hew the log, and there will be heaps of chips wherever there has been skilful work. But when at last the mansion stands out in all its fair proportions, and its scaffolding is removed, and the chips and uncleanliness are all taken away, that is what men look at; and he would be a woeful workman that should go, after he has completed his building, to count his chips and all the fragments of stone, lime, and litter. That is indispensable to this process of unbuilding in this life of character, as it is in external dwellings. It is said of Michael Angelo by one of his biographers that when the sacred enthusiasm seized him he went at a statue with such vengeance and vigour, that in one hour he cast off more stones that a workman could carry away in several hours; and Paul was sometimes like that in the vigour with which he was emancipating the true spirit within himself. He had made a good life. He had lived it. He stood therefore in the consciousness: "I am a completed man. No matter how long I was in building; no matter what the dealing was by which I was brought where I am now, I have fought a good fight, I have kept the faith, and I know that there is laid up for me the crown." This was a glorious confidence; the rational certainty that our purposes and fulfilments are not inconsistent with the true humility nor with the realisation that we are saved by grace. Paul looked forward. "I have fought a good fight; I have finished my course; I have kept the faith; henceforth"—manacled, abandoned, as he elsewhere shows himself to have been; the poorest man in creation, the most unfortunate, stripped and barren—"henceforth," he cries, from out of his weary prison, "there is for me"—not captivity—"there is for me a throne, a crown, and a sceptre. I am a monarch." Some men have said this when bereft of reason; but here is a man in the use of his highest reason that is able to say, "A crown is laid up for me"; and as he looked up he could well say, in his thought: "O, crown, wait! I am coming for thee; it is mine; no one shall take it from me; wait for me." "I have a crown laid up for me—a crown of righteousness which the Lord, the righteous Judge, shall give to me that day." What is a crown but a sign of eminence, of glory, and of power? What is a crown of righteousness but a crown that is made up of all the elements that constitute righteousness? It was the sum total of all the highest conditions and fruits of his very nature, and the nature was of Divine origin and likelihood. He had the vision of pre-eminent manhood; a glorified love; a glorified conscience; a glorified sympathy, with all that ordains one to the nobler condition of being laid before Him, and all was expressed in that crown of righteousness. "A monarch, and my monarchy lies in the glorification of my whole nature, for I shall be as the Lord." Here was no anticipation of hoping that he should "get to heaven somehow." There was certainly no intimation that he expected to escape into heaven so as by fire. He had no idea of sleeping a thousand years, or ten thousand years, and then appearing in glory. The vision was before him, near at hand, and the step off the platform of this earth was to be a step on to the pavement of heaven. How the elements of grandeur exist in this life! You are the crown-builders, you that are living for Christ and for heaven. No one that was ever disengaging gold from the quartz would ever see in it those miracles of art that at last shall be made out of it. We are creating, in this life, the material for our crown, for all the things in the soul that are of their nature and tendency Divine—every thorough impulse to the right, every impulse that is willing to sacrifice a present pleasure for the sake of higher joy of purity and nobility— all would seem to us to be the scattering of grace in our lives; they are, all of them, flakes of gold; they are, all of them, the material of which crowns are made, and men, in this life, are caged eagles, that, looking out on the sun and heavens, know that they would fly, but they have not room to spread their wings. Ten thousand intimations, ten thousand aspirations, struggling desires, and longings are breaking in the hearts of men, and, because they cannot execute them and bring them forth to real action in this life, they are not dead. In the early spring the root and the bud are checked and held back. They are not annihilated; they wait. The rose is sealed up and cannot deliver itself, but it is the rose; and the root that dimly throws the evidence of itself above the ground is itself, though it cannot yet develop itself. But by and by, when soft southern rains and sweet suns begin to beam, week after week, the little garden breaks out into blossom. And in this life, where we are checked and hindered and tempted over much, where we find that we cannot carry out our best purposes, and are failing on the right and on the left, the attempts to do it are so many attempts to bud and blossom, but the sun is not warm enough yet. But when, by and by, the Sun of Righteousness shall arise with healing on its beams upon our liberated selves, we shall break forth into the full glory of the kingdom of God. (*H. W. Beecher.*)

*A noble career:*—I. SPLENDID ACHIEVEMENTS IN REGARD TO THE DUTIES OF LIFE. 1. Victorious soldiership. (1) His behaviour was good. (2) His cause was good. (3) His Leader was good. (4) His armour was good. (5) His victory was good. 2. The successful athlete. (1) Ambition. (2) Self-denial. (3) Concentration. (4) Perseverance. 3. The faithful steward. He had—(1) embraced, (2) lived, (3) spread, (4) defended the truth. II. GREAT TRANQUILLITY IN REGARD TO THE TRIALS OF LIFE. 1. His knowledge of them. (1) Of their honours—"To be offered." Martyrdom. (2) Of their nearness—"Is at hand." 2. His preparedness for them—"Ready." 3. His benefit by them—"Departure." III. GLORIOUS EXPECTATION IN REGARD TO THE REWARD OF LIFE. 1. In value it will be the highest possible. "Crowns." 2. In principle it will be the most indisputable. "Crown of righteousness." 3. In bestowal it will be the most honourable. (1) Given by the Highest Being. (2) On the most august occasion. (3) In association with the most distinguished company. (*B. D. Johns.*) *Paul's review of his life:*—I. THE PAST FILLED HIM WITH SATISFACTION. 1. He had been a warrior. And his contest was with no phantom or abstraction; not with a mere principle of evil, employed without will or intelligence, but with a real enemy. Paul evidently acted continually under the impression that he was in an enemy's country,—that he was watched by an invisible foe, resisted by a being mightier than priest or prince. He recognised a terrible unity in sin—an energy and ubiquity which are angelic. He considered himself an officer in an army which has regiments contending in battlefields far away from this earth. Paul's enemy was God's enemy. He had no quarrels of ambition, or revenge, or covetousness, or pride, to settle. His eye was fixed on the prince who led the revolt in heaven, and had brought it down to earth. Against him Paul proclaimed an open and uncompromising war—a war of extermination; and he extended it to everything that enlisted under Satan. Hence it began in his own heart, against the traitors long entertained there; and with them he proclaimed an unrelenting war. 2. He had been a racer, also. What was the goal? It was, to attain and accomplish the highest ends man can seek; the highest personal perfection consistent with being on earth; attaining, as he styles it, "to the resurrection of the dead"; the exalting Christ among men; the leading men to him; the confirmation of the Churches in their faith; the leaving behind him writings which should be the means of glorifying God, edifying His people, and converting men, to the end of time. He had aimed at these achievements; and, by the grace of God, he had accomplished them. 3. He had been a steward. His life presented in this aspect a trust discharged. "I have kept the faith." II. A FUTURE FILLED WITH BLESSEDNESS. He had honoured his Redeemer, and he knew that Christ would honour him. He looked for "a crown." It has been a common thing in the world's history to contend for a crown. The Christian hero here stands on the level of the earthly hero. But, when we come to compare the nature of these respective crowns, the character of their conflicts, and the umpires to whom the warriors look, the Christian rises to an elevation infinitely above the earthly hero. There is nothing selfish in the war, the victory, or the coronation. (*E. N. Kirk, D.D.*)    *Paul the hero:*—I. Here is a man whose entire being is under THE SUPREMACY OF CONSCIENCE. With other men conscience often has theoretical supremacy; with St. Paul its reign was actual. Other men may waver and fluctuate in their obedience to its behests; St. Paul is held to this central power as steadily as the planets to the sun. There was no sham about this man. What he seemed to be, that he was. What he declared to another, that his inmost soul commended as truth and attested to its own secret tribunal. II. His life was also under the dominion of another regnant power—THE SUPREMACY OF AN OVERMASTERING PURPOSE. Every man needs the inspiration of a great purpose and a great mission to lift him above the pettiness and cheapness which are the bane of ordinary lives. Some great undertaking, with an element of heroism and moral sublimity in it, the very contemplation of which quickens the blood and fires the soul and awakens an ever-present sense of the dignity and significance of life—this is an essential condition of all great achievement. Such an inspiring purpose and ennobling work stirred the heart and stimulated the powers of St. Paul. Though nothing low had previously ruled or influenced him, it happened to him—as it has to many another man at his conversion—that the supreme purpose of life was formed in that supreme hour when the transforming touch of the Divine hand was felt upon the soul, and life's sublime work opened before the clarified vision. III. But the supremacy of conscience and of a great purpose are not sufficient in themselves alone to produce such a character and such a life as St. Paul presents for our study. To these two ruling forces must be added another—greater than either, and co-ordinate with both—THE SUPREMACY OF AN ALL-CONQUERING FAITH. Christ to him was not a myth, not merely the incomparable Teacher of Galilee, not the theoretic and historic Saviour of men; He was infinitely more than that, the ever-present Partner of his life, the unfailing Source of his strength. His faith perpetually saw this personal Jesus, felt the warm beating of His loving heart, heard His sacred voice in solemn command or inspiring promise, and walked with Him as with an earthly friend. As well separate the spirit from the body, the beating heart from the respiring lungs, as separate this inspired apostle from this inspiring Christ. Anything is possible to such a man. Indeed, it is no longer a question of human ability at all, but of human co-operation with the Divine Christ—the natural man giving the supernatural agency full play and power. (*C. H. Payne, D.D.*) **I have finished my course.**—*The Christian's course:*—I. We are to consider THE WAY OR PATH IN WHICH THE CHRISTIAN IS TO RUN. 1. The way in which the Christian is to run is a way of faith in our Lord Jesus Christ. 2. The way the Christian is to run is a way of holiness (Psa. cxix. 32; 1 Thess. iv. 7). Christians, in proceeding on this course, do it not with the same life and vigour; some appear cold and indifferent, whilst others are quick and lively; some make great advances, whilst others go on by slow degrees. Some begin the heavenly race soon, in the bloom of life, whilst others loiter till towards the evening of their days. II. We now come to consider HOW WE ARE TO RUN, THAT WE MAY FINISH OUR COURSE WITH ADVANTAGE. 1. That we may run the Christian race well, it is necessary that we cast off every weight. 2. We must begin and continue in a dependence upon Christ. 3. We must run with patience, courage, and resolution. 4. We must be watchful and diligent. Be upon your guard, Christian, the way you run is difficult, and it is attended with many snares and temptations. 5. We must keep pressing forward and persevere to the end of our course. You may meet with many discouragements, but still keep on, the further you go, the less ground remains to be trod, therefore let not your hearts be troubled. III. THE ENCOURAGEMENT CHRISTIANS HAVE TO RUN THIS RACE. 1. There is a glorious crown before us. 2. He that begins aright shall at length certainly finish his course. 3. Every one that finishes his course shall as surely receive the prize. To conclude, with some improvement of the point. (1) The further we proceed in our text, the more we see the difficulty of the Christian life, and the vanity of their hopes who content themselves with a mere form. (2) How foolish are all those that run after perishing enjoyments, and neglect the prize of immortality. (3) What arguments are there for running this race. (4) How should every one that has begun this race rejoice in the encouragements that have been offered. (*S. Hayward.*) *The finished race:*—To this end we must run—1. Rightly. 2. Speedily. 3. Patiently. 4. Cheerfully. 5. Circumspectly. 6. Resolutely. 7. Perseveringly. (*T. Hall, B.D.*)    *Best at last:*—In our Christian course it is but too generally and too truly observed, that as we grow older we grow colder; we become more slack, remiss, and weary in well doing. The reverse ought to be the case, for the reason assigned by the apostle when stirring up his converts to vigour and zeal and alacrity: he says, "For now is our salvation nearer than when we believed." In a race the push is made at last. (*Bishop Horne.*)    **I have kept the faith.—** *Keeping the faith* :—What does St. Paul mean by the faith which he has kept? Is he rejoicing that he has been true to a certain scheme of doctrine, or that he has preserved a certain temper of soul and spiritual relationship to God? For the term "faith" is a very large one. There can be no doubt, I think, that he means both, and that the latter meaning is a very deep and important one, as we shall see. But this term, "the faith," did signify for him, beyond all doubt, a certain group of truths, all bound together by their common unity of source and unity of purpose. Paul was too wise and profound not to keep this always in sight. That there must be intellectual conceptions as the base of strong, consistent, and effective feeling is a necessity which he continually recognises; and the faith which he is thankful to have kept is, first of all, that truth which had been made known to him and to the Church by God. The first thing, then, that strikes us is that, when Paul said that he had kept the faith, he evidently believed that there was a faith to keep. The faith was a body of truth given to him, which he had to hold and to use and to apply, but which he had not made and was not to improve. We want, then, to consider the condition of one who, having thus learned and held a positive faith, continues to hold it—holds it to the end. He keeps the faith. We need not confine our thought to St. Paul. An old man is dying, and as he lets go the things which are trivial and accidental to lay hold of what is essential and important to him, this is what comes to his mind with special satisfaction: "I have kept the faith." The true faith which a man has kept up to the end of his life must be one that has opened with his growth and constantly won new reality and colour from his changing experience. The old man does believe what the child believed; but how different it is, though still the same. It is the field that once held the seed, now waving and rustling under the autumn wind with the harvest that it holds, yet all the time it has kept the corn. The joy of his life has richened his belief. His sorrow has deepened it. His doubts have sobered it. His enthusiasms have fired it. His labour has purified it. This is the work that life does upon faith. This is the beauty of an old man's religion. His doctrines are like the house that he has lived in, rich with associations which make it certain that he will never move out of it. His doctrines have been illustrated and strengthened and endeared by the good help they have given to his life. And no doctrine that has not done this can be really held up to the end with any such vital grasp as will enable us to carry it with us through the river, and enter with it into the new life beyond. And again, is it not true that any belief which we really keep up to the end of life must at some time have become for us a personal conviction, resting upon evidence of its own? I know, indeed, how much a merely traditional religion will inspire men to do. I know that for a faith which is not really theirs, but only what they call it, "their fathers' faith," men will dispute and argue, make friendships and break them, contribute money, undertake great labours, change the whole outward tenor of their life. I know that men will suffer for it. I am not sure but they will die to uphold a creed to which they were born, and with which their own character for firmness and consistency has become involved. All this a traditional faith can do. It can do everything except one, and that it can never do. It can never feed a spiritual life, and build a man up in holiness and grace. Before it can do that our fathers' faith must first by strong personal conviction become ours. And here I think that, rightly seen, the culture of our Church asserts its wisdom. The Church has in herself the very doctrine of tradition. She teaches the child a faith that has the warrant of the ages, full of devotion and of love. She calls on him to believe doctrines of which he cannot be convinced as yet. The tradition, the hereditation of belief, the unity of the human history, are ideas very familiar to her, of which she constantly and beautifully makes use. And yet she does not disown her work of teaching and arguing and convincing. She cannot, and yet be true to her mission. She teaches the young with the voice of authority; she addresses the mature with the voice of reason. And now have we not reached some idea of the kind of faith which it is possible for a man to keep? What sort of a creed may one hold and expect to hold it always, live in it, die in it, and carry it even to the life beyond? 1. In the first place, it must be a creed broad enough to allow the man to grow within it, to contain and to supply his ever-developing mind and character. It will not be a creed burdened with many details. It will consist of large truths and principles, capable of ever-varying applications to ever-varying life. So only can it be clear, strong, positive, and yet leave the soul free to grow within it, nay, feed the soul richly and minister to its growth. 2. And the second characteristic of the faith that can be kept will be its evidence, its proved truth. It will not be a mere aggregation of chance opinions. The reason why a great many people seem to be always changing their faith is that they never really have any faith. They have indeed what they call a faith, and are often very positive about it. They have gathered together a number of opinions and fancies, often very ill-considered, which they say that they believe, using the deep and sacred word for a very superficial and frivolous action of their wills. They no more have a faith than the city vagrant has a home who sleeps upon a different door-step every night. And yet he does sleep somewhere every night; and so these wanderers among the creeds at each given moment are believing something, although that something is for ever altering. We do not properly believe what we only think. A thousand speculations come into our heads, and our minds dwell upon them, which are not to be therefore put into our creed, however plausible they seem. Our creed, our *credo*, anything which we call by such a sacred name, is not what we have thought, but what our Lord has told us. The true creed must come down from above, and not out from within. (*Bp. Phillips Brooks.*) *On keeping the faith:*—I. WHAT IS MEANT BY KEEPING THE FAITH. 1. It may signify that we firmly believe the doctrines God has revealed, and steadfastly maintain them. We read of a " faith once delivered to the saints " (Jude 3). These, therefore, coming from God are certainly worthy of our credit, deserve our notice, and ought to be steadfastly maintained by us. 2. The expression signifies that we faithfully observe the vows and engagements we have brought ourselves under, to our glorious Master, and hold on with integrity and constancy in His service. II. THE NECESSITY AND IMPORTANCE OF KEEPING THE FAITH. 1. It is the distinguishing characteristic of a real Christian. That profession that is not set upon good principles will never hold. 2. In keeping the faith, the Christian's comfort is greatly promoted. The glorious doctrines of faith are of the most excellent nature; they abundantly recompense the Christian in his steady belief of and attachment to them, by the unspeakable supports they yield in every circumstance and station of life. 3. Keeping the faith is necessary to promote the honour of Christ, and to secure the Christian from those errors and snares to which he stands exposed. 4. Without a steadfast perseverance in the faith our hopes of heaven are vain and deceitful. Perseverence in the faith does not entitle us to eternal life, but there is no eternal life without it. A word or two of improvement. (1) Is keeping the faith the distinguishing character of a Christian? Then how few are there in the present age. The honours of the world lead away some, the sensualities of life ensnare others. (2) Is perseverance in the faith the character of a real Christian? How melancholy must their state be who never yet set forward in the ways of God. (3) Is it so important to keep the faith? Then let us seriously examine our own hearts concerning it. (*S. Hayward.*) *Guarding the faith:*—I. THE PRECIOUSNESS OF THAT WHICH HE HAD KEPT. He was the emissary of the great Physician, who had but one remedy, one panacea for the one radical disease of man. In Rome he said, " I am not ashamed of the gospel of Christ, for it is the power of God unto salvation unto every one that believeth, to the Jew first, and also to the Greek." In Corinth he would say, " The Jews require a sign, and the Greeks seek after wisdom; but we preach Christ crucified, to the Jews a stumbling-block, and to the Greeks foolishness; but to them that are called, both Jews and Greeks, Christ the power of God, and the wisdom of God." In Galatia he would say, " God forbid that I should glory save in the Cross of our Lord Jesus Christ, whereby the world is crucified unto me, and I unto the world." II. THE STRENUOUSNESS WITH WHICH HE HAD GUARDED IT. Think you that he had no difficulties with which to cope? Was there to him no maze in Providence, no labyrinth which he found it impossible to track and thread? Providence in many of its movements was to him, as to us, an impenetrable mystery; but still he " kept the faith." Think you that he found no difficulties in comprehending the dispensations through which God had manifested Himself to man; and that the wonder never rose up in his mind how it was that thousands of years had to pass away before the incarnation of the Son of God and the redemption of the Cross? He must have been less than man, or greatly more than man, if he could have sounded this depth; but still he " kept the faith."    III. HIS SUCCESS IN GUARDING THE FAITH. How he kept it he does not tell us here; but we catch glimpses, here and there, of the secret of his power. He kept it on his knees, kept it when he prayed night and day with tears. And be sure there is no faith, no true faith, no faith that will hold a man firm, which can be kept apart from fellowship with God. We can keep a creed without Divine help—we can keep a creed through the force of prejudice— through the force of obstinacy—through the force of ignorance—through the force of custom and social sanction—through the force of policy. To keep a creed is the easiest thing in the world, for it can lie, made up and dead, in some undisturbed chamber of the brain. But oh! to keep a faith is far from easy; for a faith to be a faith at all must be living, and if it be living, it must meet the onset of a thousand circumstances by which it will be tested. It will be tested by the influence of our obstinate corruption—it will be tested by the temptations of the world, by its maxims and customs—it will be tested by promises of advantage if only we will be faithless to our profession—it will be tested by changes in our circumstances, whether they be from poverty to wealth, or from wealth to poverty—it will be tested by those strange aspects of providence which bewilder at times the strongest minds, and make their feet almost to slip—it will be tested by the indifference or lukewarm- ness of those around us. Happy the man who brings his faith through all these things. He is like a fire-safe, which guards its treasure unhurt, amid the flames which have raged around it in vain. (*E. Mellor, D.D.*)     *Martyrdom :*—To die for truth is not to die for one's country, but for the world. (*J. P. Richter.*)     *Keeping the faith :*—When Bernard Palissy, the inventor of a kind of pottery called Palissy ware, was an old man, he was sent to the French prison known as the Bastille because he was a Protestant. The king went to see him, and told him he should be set free if he would deny his faith. The king said, "I am sorry to see you here, but the people will compel me to keep you here unless you recant." Palissy was ninety years old, but he was ashamed to hear a king speak of being compelled, so he said, " Sire, they who can compel you cannot compel me! I can die!" And he remained in prison until he died.     *St. Paul keeping the faith :*—Paul kept the faith at Antioch, even when the infatuated crowd attempted to drown his voice with their clamour, and interrupted him, contradicting and blaspheming. He kept the faith at Iconium, when the envious Jews stirred up the people to stone him. He kept the faith at Lystra, when the fate of Stephen became almost his, and he was dragged, wounded and bleeding, outside the ramparts of the town, and left there to languish, and, for aught they cared, to die. He kept the faith against his erring brother Peter, and withstood him to the face, because he was to be blamed. He kept the faith when shamefully treated at Philippi, and made the dungeon echo back the praises of his God. He kept the faith at Thessalonica, when lewd fellows of the baser sort accused him falsely of sedition. He kept the faith at Athens, when, to the world's sages, he preached of Him whom they ignorantly worshipped as the unknown God. He kept the faith at Corinth, when compelled to abandon that hardened and obdurate city, and to shake off the dust from his garment as a testimony against it. He kept the faith at Ephesus, when he pointed his hearers not to Diana, but to Jesus Christ as their only Saviour. He kept the faith at Jerusalem, when stoned by the enraged and agitated mob—when stretched upon the torturing rack, and bound with iron fetters. He kept the faith at Cæsarea, before the trembling, conscience-stricken Felix, when he reasoned of righteousness, temperance, and judgment to come. He kept the faith before Agrippa, and, by his earnestness, compelled the king to say, "Almost thou persuadest me to be a Christian"; and even in the closing hours of life, when the last storm was gathering over his head, when lying in the dark and dismal Roman cell, he wrote these triumphant words, "I am now ready to be offered, and the time of my departure is at hand. I have fought a good fight, I have finished my course, I have kept the faith. Henceforth there is laid up for me a crown of righteousness, which the Lord, the righteous Judge, shall given me at that day." (*J. R. Macduff.*)     *Keeping the faith :*—The apostle kept the faith. But does not the faith keep the man? It does; yet only as he keeps it. The battery keeps the gunners only as they stand to the guns. The fort keeps the garrison, yet only as they guard its walls. Never was a time when fidelity on guard was more needed than now, when the sappers are approaching the citadel of the faith, and there is treason in the camp of heaven— men in Christ's uniform, having been so deceived by successful crime, and so blinded by dalliance with mammon as to give utterance and organisation to the shameless sentiment that the prosperity of a community can be built upon sin. It is a true soldier's business to guard the faith. The Roman sentinel that was exhumed at Pompeii, grasping his spear, perished rather than desert his post. He wears the immortality of earth. But he that guards the faith, when dug out of the forces that overwhelm him while he stands his ground, shall inherit the immortality of God, and walk with warrior feet the streets of gold, a living king over a lofty realm. (*J. Lewis.*)     **A crown of righteousness.**—*The crown of righteousness:*—I. Let us consider THE PRIZE THE APOSTLE HAD IN VIEW, " a crown of righteousness." Royalty is the highest pitch of human grandeur. Those that wear earthly crowns have got to the very summit of earthly honour, and are in that station in which centres all worldly glory and happiness. What an idea is this similitude designed to give us then of that glorious world, where every saint wears an unfading, incorruptible and immortal crown? 1. This crown consists of perfect and everlasting righteousness. The sparks of this crown are perfect holiness and a conformity to God. 2. This crown was purchased by the righteousness of Jesus Christ. It cost a valuable price, and therefore is of inestimable worth. 3. We come to the possession of this crown in a way of righteousness. Its being purchased for us does not lay a foundation for our slothfulness, sin and security. II. Consider THE PERSON BY WHOM THIS CROWN IS BESTOWED, AND HIS CHARACTER AS A RIGHTEOUS JUDGE. This illustrious person is everywhere represented to be our Lord Jesus Christ. Thus, Acts. xvii. 31. Christ is the appointed person, and He is every way fitted for the great and important work, He being God as well as man : He is absolutely incapable of committing the least mistake or error. And He is a righteous judge. He will display His righteousness in the last sentence that He will pass upon every creature. III. Consider WHEN THIS CROWN SHALL BE COMPLETELY POSSESSED AND BE FULLY GIVEN. It is here said to be given " at that day," viz. : The day of Christ's appearance to judge the world. IV. Consider THE PERSONS TO WHOM THIS CROWN SHALL BE GIVEN. " To all those who love His appearing." The apostle was one of that happy number. They love His appearing, for then every enemy will be vanquished. (*S. Hayward.*)     *The heavenly crown assured :*—This assurance is—1. Attainable. 2. Tenable. 3. Desirable. (*T. Hall, B.D.*)     *The crown of righteousness :*—I. THE REWARD. It is described as a " crown of righteousness "; and, without question, such a phrase conveys the idea of something exquisitely pure, brilliant, and honourable. The crown is the reward of a conqueror; the righteousness is the diadem of deity Himself. And yet we cannot deny that it would be difficult to follow the idea into detail, and keep unimpaired its interest and its beauty. There is something indefinite in the phraseology, if we wish to ascertain from it the precise character of the recompense. When, however, we turn to the Being, by whom the recompense will be bestowed, and find Him described as " the Lord, the righteous Judge," we may gain that precision of idea which is not elsewhere to be procured. For we should never forget that, by our thoughts and actions, we lie exposed to God's righteous indignation. And from this we may proceed to another fact. We require you to observe that a surprising change must have been effected ere a sinner can dwell with anything of delight on the title now under review. We press on you the truth, that if the crown is to be bestowed by the hands of the Lord, the righteous Judge, the recipient must have been the subject of a great moral revolution; for he is not only to be acquitted, he is actually to be recompensed. The bliss of an angel may be great, the splendour of an angel may be glorious; but it was not for angels that Jesus died, it was not for angels that Jesus rose. There will be for ever this broad distinction between the angels and the saints. The angels are blessed by the single right of creation; the saints by the double right of creation and redemption. Who, then, can question that the portion possessed by saints will be more brilliant than that possessed by the angels? II. THE TIME AT WHICH THE CROWN SHALL BE BESTOWED. It must be that day when, with the cloud for His chariot, the archangel's trump for His heraldry, and ten thousand times ten thousand spirits for His retinue, the Man of Sorrows shall approach the earth, and wake the children of the first resurrection. And from this we conclude that St. Paul did not expect the consummation of his happiness at the very instant of his departure from the flesh. He knew, indeed, that to be " absent from the body " is to be " present with the Lord " ; he knew that in the transition of a moment the prison dungeon would be exchanged for the palace, the turmoil of earth for the deep rapture of peace which never ends; but he knew also that the crowning time of the saints shall not precede the second coming of their Lord. The crown, indeed, was prepared, but then it was " laid up." It should never be forgotten, that the resurrection of the body is indispensable to the completeness of happiness. If it be not, the whole scheme of Christianity is darkened, for the Redeemer undertook to redeem matter, as well as spirit. III. THE PERSONS ON WHOM THE CROWN SHALL BE BESTOWED. There is nothing more natural to man, but nothing more opposed to religion, than selfishness. He who has earthly riches, may desire to keep them to himself; he who has heavenly, must long to impart them to others. It is an exquisitely beautiful transition, which St. Paul here makes, from the contemplation of his own portion, to the mention of that which is reserved for the whole company of the faithful: "not to me only, but unto all them also that love His appearing." He could not gaze on his own crown, and not glow with the thought, that myriads should share the coronation. Ye wish to ascertain whether ye be of those who love His appearing. Take these simple questions, and propose them to your hearts, and pray of God to strengthen you to give faithful answers. Do ye so hate what is carnal that it would be delightful to you to be at once and for ever set free from the cravings of earthly desires? Do ye so long to be pure in thought, in word, and in deed, that you feel that perfection in holiness would be to you the perfection of happiness? But, finally, if we would win the "crown of righteousness" which is spoken of by St. Paul, we must use the means. (*H. Melvill, B.D.*) *The crown of righteousness:*—The crown of righteousness is a crown whereof righteousness is the material. This crown is of the same fabric and texture as that which it should decorate; it is a crown whose beauty is moral beauty, the beauty not of gold or precious stones, but of those more precious, nay, priceless things which gold and gems can but suggest to us, the beauty of justice, truthfulness, purity, charity, humility, carried to a point of refinement and of high excellence, of which here and now we have no experience. Once and once only was such a crown as this worn upon earth, and when it was worn to human eyes it was a crown of thorns. It may seem to be a difficulty in the way of this statement that the happiness is said elsewhere to consist in the beatific visions—that is to say, in the complete and uninterrupted sight of God, whom the blessed praise and worship to all eternity. "We know we shall be like Him, for we shall see Him as He is." But what is it that makes this vision of God the source of its promised happiness? What is it in God that will chiefly minister to the expected joy? Is it His boundless power? Is it His unsearchable wisdom? Will they cry for ever, "Almighty, Almighty, Almighty," or "All-knowing, All-knowing, All-knowing"? Will they, do they not say, without fatigue, without desire for change, "Holy, holy, holy"? And why is this? Because essentially God is a moral being, and it is by His moral attributes that He perfectly corresponds to, and satisfies the deepest wants in our human nature. The "crown of righteousness" means a share, such as it is possible for a creature to have in God's essential nature, in His justice, His purity, and His love; since while we can conceive of Him, had He so willed it, as never having created the heavens and the earth, we cannot, we dare not, think of Him, in any relation with other beings as other than just, true, loving, merciful—in other words, as other than holy. He is, indeed, Himself, the "crown of righteousness," the crown with which He rewards the blessed, and there is no opposition between the idea of such a crown and the beatific vision. They are only two different accounts of that which is in its essence the same. "The crown of righteousness!" Some crown or other, I apprehend, most men are looking for, if not always, yet at some time in their lives; if not very confidently, yet with those modified hopes which regard it as possibly attainable. Human nature views itself almost habitually as the heir apparent—of some circumstances which are an improvement on the present. An expectation of this kind is the very condition of effort in whatever direction, and no amount or degree of proved delusion would appear permanently to extinguish it. But the crowns which so many of us hope may be laid up for us somewhere, and by some one—what are they? There is the crown of a good income in a great mercantile community like our own. This is the supreme distinction for which many a man labours without thought of anything beyond. And closely allied to this is another crown—the crown of a good social position. "I have made great efforts, tempered with due discretion; I have finished the course which has appeared to bring me unbounded pleasure, but which has really meant incessant weariness. I have observed those laws of social propriety, which are never to be disregarded with impunity; and so henceforth there awaits me an assured position, in which I indeed may be reviled, but from which I cannot be dislodged—a position which society cannot but award, sooner or later, to those who struggle upward in obedience to her rules." And, then, there is the crown of political power. "I have fought against the foes of my party or my country; I have finished a course of political activity which has borne me onwards to the end. I have kept to my principles, or I have shown that I had reason to modify or to abandon them; henceforth there is laid up for me a crown of political influence which is almost from the nature of the case independent of office, and which a great country will never refuse to those who served it long and have served it well." And once more there is the crown of a literary reputation. "I have had a hard time of it; I have finished what I proposed to it; I have been true to the requirements of a great and exacting subject; henceforth there is reserved for me the rare pleasure of a reputation which wealth and station cannot command, and which envy cannot take away; henceforth I have a place in the great communion of the learned, those elect minds in whom genius is wedded to industry, and whose works are among the treasures of the human race." Here are the crowns, or some of them, for which men toil and with which are they not seldom rewarded. But do they last? . . . . As we get nearer death, the exaggerations of self-love cease to assert themselves; we see things more clearly as they really are; we distinguish that which lasts from that which passes; we understand the immense distinction between all the perishable crowns and the "crown of righteousness." That crown does not pass. It is laid up, it is set aside for its destined wearer by the most Merciful Redeemer, who is also the Eternal Judge, and who watches with an unspeakable, tender interest each conqueror as he draws nearer and nearer to the end of his earthly course, and as, in the name of the great redemption, he dares to claim it. (*Canon Liddon.*)     *A crown of righteousness:*—If I had three things to wish, I should wish for Paul's threefold crown. 1. The crown of grace, a great measure of grace to do Christ much service. 2. His crown of joy, a great measure of joy to go through with that service. 3. The crown of glory which he was here assured of. In the words we have first the concluding particle, henceforth, lastly, as for that which remains. 1. A crown is not given till the victory be gained (chap. ii. 5). 2. It notes the perpetuity of the glory, incorruptible, never fading crown (2 Pet. i. 4; 1 Cor. ix. 24). 3. It notes the perfection of it, as the crown compasseth the head on every side; so there is nothing wanting in this crown of life. So the saints in glory shall be crowned with goodness when all the faculties of the soul and members of the body shall be perfect and filled with glory. 4. It represents to us the dignity of the saints and the glory of their reward. They are all kings and shall be crowned. The day of judgment is their coronation day. Of righteousness—1. Because it is purchased for us by the righteousness of Christ. By His perfect righteousness and obedience He hath merited this for us. 2. In respect of His promise, His fidelity bindeth Him to perform it. God hath promised a crown of life to such as serve Him sincerely (James i. 12; 1 John ii. 25; Rev. ii. 10; iii. 21). 3. It may be called a crown of righteousness, because it is given only to righteous men, and so it showeth who shall be crowned, and what is the way to it; but not for what merits or desert of ours it is given. (*T. Hall, B.D.*)     *The crown of righteousness:*—It is not the diadem of noble, prince, or king, but the wreath of victory for those who have contended (See Matt. xi. 12). This crown can never fit the brows of the indolent, the lover of ease, the self-indulgent man of the world who acquiesces in Christian doctrines and Christian customs, whether of worship or social life, because he shuns the trouble of inquiry and of choice. To contend, to strive, to fight is the first condition of conquering, even as the conqueror alone can win the crown. Who, in that day, will deem the contest too hard when he has received the crown? Then, again, it is the crown of righteousness; and righteousness is the square and the perfection of all moral character and virtue, moulded and shaped by Christ's Spirit after Christ's example. Therefore, only that stage of character in which feeling, desire, choice and motive are genuine and pure, can be expressed by this word. This fabric of righteousness thus inwrought into the man himself will receive its topstone from Christ. No byeways, no short cuts lead to heaven, only the narrow way of righteousness. (*D. Trinder, M.A.*)     *A crown without cares:*—The royal life which Paul anticipated in heaven will not only be a life of dignity, and power, and grandeur, but it will be all that, without any of the disagreeable concomitants which earthly royalty has to experience. In this world greatness and care are twins. Crowns more commonly prove curses than blessings to those who wear them. Isaac, the son of Comnenus, one of the most virtuous of eastern rulers, was crowned at Constantinople in 1057. Basil, the patriarch, brought the crown to him surmounted with a diamond cross. Taking hold of the cross, the Emperor said, "I, who have been acquainted with crosses from my cradle, welcome thee; thou art my sword and shield, for hitherto I have conquered with suffering." Then taking the crown in his hand he added: "This is but a beautiful burden, which loads more than it adorns." The crown of the triumphant Christian is a crown of righteousness, which will neither oppress the head, afflict the heart, nor imperil the life of any that receive it. ((*J. Underhill.*) *Historic crowns :*—Napoleon had a magnificent crown made for himself in 1804. It was this crown that he so proudly placed upon his head with his own hands in the cathedral of Notre Dame. It is a jewelled circle, from which springs several arches surmounted by the globe and cross, and where the arches join the circle there are alternately flowers and miniature eagles of gold. After his downfall, it remained in the French Treasury until it was assumed by another Bonaparte, when Napoleon III. made himself Emperor in 1852. It is now in the regalia of France, which have only just been brought back to Paris from the western seaport to which they were sent for security during the Prussian invasion, just as the Scottish regalia were sent to Dunnottar. If we may judge from some of the German photographs of the Emperor William, the crown of the new German Empire is of a very peculiar shape, apparently copied from the old Carlovingian diadem. It is not a circle, but a polygon, being formed of flat jewelled plates of gold united by the edges, and having above them two arches supporting the usual globe and cross. Of the modern crowns of continental Europe, perhaps the most remarkable is the well-known triple crown or Papal tiara, or perhaps we should say tiaras, for there are four of them. The tiara is seldom worn by the Pope; it is carried before him in procession, but, except on rare occasions, he wears a mitre like an ordinary bishop. Of the existing tiaras, the most beautiful is that which was given by Napoleon I. to Pius VII. in 1805. It is said to be worth upwards of £9,000. Its three circlets are almost incrusted with sapphires, emeralds, rubies, pearls and diamonds; and the great emerald at its apex is said to be the most beautiful in the world. *A lost crown :*—A lady in a dream wandered around heaven, beholding its glories, and came at last to the crown-room. Among the crowns she saw one exceedingly beautiful. "Who is this for?" "It was intended for you," said the angel, "but you did not labour for it, and now another will wear it." *Seeking to obtain a crown :*—A French officer, who was a prisoner upon his parole at Reading, met with a Bible. He read it, and was so impressed with the contents that he was convinced of the folly of sceptical principles and of the truth of Christianity, and resolved to become a Protestant. When his gay associates rallied him for taking so serious a turn, he said, in his vindication, "I have done no more than my old schoolfellow, Bernadotte, who has become a Lutheran." "Yes, but he became so," said his associates, "to obtain a crown." "My motive," said the Christian officer, "is the same; we only differ as to the place. The object of Bernadotte is to obtain a crown in Sweden; mine is to obtain a crown in heaven." *More crowns left :*—On one occasion, preaching from the text of St. Paul, "I have fought a good fight, I have finished my course," he suddenly stopped, and looking up to heaven, cried with a loud voice, "Paul! are there any more crowns there?" He paused again. Then, casting his eyes upon the congregation, he continued, "Yes, my brethren, there are more crowns left. They are not all taken up yet. Blessed be God! there is one for me, and one for all of you who love the appearing of the Lord Jesus Christ." (*Life of Father Taylor.*) *A congruous crown :*—There is such a congruity between righteousness and the crown of life, that it can be laid on none other head but that of a righteous man, and if it could, all its amaranthine flowers would shrivel and fall when they touched an impure brow. (*A. Maclaren, D.D.*) *Preaching for a crown :*—The Rev. H. Davies, sometimes called "the Welsh apostle," was walking early one Sabbath morning to a place where he was to preach. He was overtaken by a clergyman on horseback, who complained that he could not get above half a guinea for a discourse. "Oh, sir," said Mr. Davies, "I preach for a crown!" "Do you?" replied the stranger, "then you are a disgrace to the cloth." To this rude observation he returned this meek answer, "Perhaps I shall be held in still greater disgrace in your estimation, when I inform you that I am now going nine miles to preach, and have but sevenpence in my pocket to bear my expenses out and in; but I look forward to that crown of glory which my Lord and Saviour will freely bestow upon me when He makes His appearance before an assembled world." **Shall give me at that day.**— *St. Paul a witness for immortality :*—As example is better than precept, so is the man more valuable than his doctrine, when he lives it. And when we study the apostle as he appears to us in his last written letter, we come face to face with the exemplification in living reality of a sublime doctrine, which proves itself stronger than adversity, animating and supporting a great soul amid circumstances which threaten to afflict and even crush its hopes. The chains hung round his hands and feet. Death menaced him with every approaching footstep. Only a tyrant's breath stood between him and the executioner's sword. In such a moment a man is likely to be true to himself. False reckonings are corrected, self-flatteries cease; then, if ever, he faces his real position. I. St. Paul bequeaths the example of a finished career. Labour and suffering, threatenings and persecution, have failed to wrest from him the prize which, above all others, is most worth keeping—the faith of God as revealed in Christ. II. What had he in the present? A certain conviction that a treasure was, at the very moment when he wrote, laid up in safe keeping for his future benefit. Though the Roman sword shall soon sever the apostle's wearied head from his weakened, tired body, the crown shall survive, and he, too, who shall wear it. Death will not extinguish his being, nor bear him off into the great stream of existences that have passed away. The followers of Auguste Comte, the so-called Positivist, profess to hope for an immortality in the mass of human beings that follow in our wake, as if the fact that others are living were a compensation for our dying, or as if we could live again in those who carry on the race and profit by our example. Not so the great apostle. There is laid up for *me*, for that being who has wrestled, who has fought, who has kept the faith, the crown of righteousness, even as I am being kept to wear it. III How grandly does the prospect of the future burst upon the keen eye of the faithful warrior! The hope of this crown is not a privilege of a few, still less a monopoly for himself. Not only does he know that it is kept safe for him, but he tells the day and the manner of its bestowal. The day of labour gives place to one of rest, strife is followed by peace, suffering is forgotten in undying vigour of mind and body. This certainty of future recompense at the hand of Christ, the Righteous Judge, blends with what has gone before, and adds to this legacy all that was wanting to its completeness. The benefits of past experience, the certainty of present conviction, and the assured hope of a righteous award in the great day of account, from One who lives and has made His life felt in the holy strivings and faithful efforts of His redeemed servants on earth; these form a triple cord which cannot easily be broken. (*D. Trinder, M.A.*) *An assured hope:*—I. An assured hope is a true and Scriptural thing. It cannot be wrong to feel confidently in a matter where God speaks unconditionally—to believe decidedly when God promises decidedly—to have a sure persuasion of pardon and peace when we rest on the word and oath of Him that never changes. It is an utter mistake to suppose that the believer who feels assurance is resting on anything he sees in himself. II. A believer may never arrive at this assured hope, which Paul expresses, and yet be saved. "A letter," says an old writer, "may be written, which is not sealed; so grace may be written in the heart, yet the Spirit may not set the seal of assurance to it." A child may be born heir to a great fortune, and yet never be aware of his riches; may live childish, die childish, and never know the greatness of his possessions. III. Why an assured hope is exceedingly to be desired. 1. Because of the present comfort and peace it affords. 2. Because it tends to make a Christian an active working Christian. 3. Because it tends to make a Christian a decided Christian. 4. Because it tends to make the holiest Christians. IV. Some probable causes why an assured hope is so seldom attained. 1. A defective view of the doctrine of justification. 2. Slothfulness about growth in grace. 3. An inconsistent walk in life. (*Bp. Ryle.*) **All them also that love His appearing:**—I. Who they are that love the Lord's appearing:—I might answer such a question very shortly by saying, those who are prepared for it. "But who," you may ask, "is the prepared servant?" I answer—he who has received that Lord as his Redeemer, who, he expects, will be his Judge. II. Why they love it. If you had received a multitude of obligations from an unseen friend, you would surely long to set your eyes upon him. If you heard that you were soon to meet him, you would be pleased exceedingly; you would exclaim, "Oh, come the day!" And here then is a reason why the saved sinner loves to think of the appearing of his Saviour. The very sight of his Redeemer will be rapture to his soul. But look at the words immediately before our text, and there you will see a further reason of the fact we are considering. There are we told of a prize which the believer has to look for in the day of his Lord's coming. It will be a day when the present evil course of things will be for ever over. Again, the Lord's people love the day of His appearing, because then He will be All in All. (*A. Roberts, M.A.*) *The love of Christ's appearance the character of a sincere Christian:*—I. I shall open the character of a sincere Christian. 1. There must be a firm persuasion, or assent of mind, upon just grounds, to the truth of this proposition, That Christ will appear; for it is a wise and reasonable love, not a rash and unaccountable thing. They don't love they don't know what, or without a sufficient reason. "They look for these things according to His promise" (2 Pet. iii. 13). 2. It imports earnest desire of it. This is essential to the love of anything. Love always works by desire towards an absent good, and so it is constantly represented. Looking for the blessed hope and glorious appearance. And to them who look for Him shall He appear the second time. The word signifies earnest desire, looking with great expectation. The Church is represented making this return to Christ, "Behold I come quickly: Even so come Lord Jesus" (Rev. xxii. 22). They often think it long, and are ready to say, in the warmth of their desire, and under the sense of present burdens, Oh, when will He come! why are His chariots so long a coming? But then it is not a rash and impatient desire, or an impetuous, unruly passion. Though they earnestly desire it, they are content to stay the proper season, and wait with patience notwithstanding the longest delay, and the greatest exercise in the mean time. 3. There is pleasure and satisfaction in the expectation and hope of it. This is the nature of love too. It is desire towards an absent object, but delight in it when present. Besides that there is a pleasure in the desire. Now, though the appearance of Christ is a future thing, yet the thoughts of it, and the hopes of it, are present things. 4. It is powerful and influential. The expectation of His appearance will not only give a pleasure, but form the mind suitable to it, and direct the conduct of the life. For example, it will engage to answerable diligence, excite to faithfulness, and promote a constant readiness and preparation for it. II. I shall consider THE REASONS of it, and show why sincere Christians have such a love to His appearance. 1. With respect to Christ, who is to appear. This will be evident if you consider either His person or His appearance itself. He is the great object of their love now. Whom having not seen, they love, from the representations of Him in the gospel, and the benefits they receive from Him. And how can they but love His appearance whom they so greatly love? And His appearance will be most highly honourable to Him; for He will appear in the state of a judge and the majesty of a king. He will then appear as He really is, and not in disguise, or under a disadvantage. And how reasonable is the love of His appearance in this view, as every way most honourable to Him, and the greatest display of His glory before the world? 2. With respect to themselves. It will be every way to their advantage. Our Lord says, "Thou shalt be recompensed at the resurrection of the just: When He shall appear, they will be like Him, and receive a crown of life." III. THE PRIVILEGE AND BLESSING annexed to this character, and which belongs to it; the righteous Judge will give them a crown of righteousness. Conclusion. 1. Let us often contemplate the appearance of Christ. This is the noblest subject of thought, and of the greatest concern to us. The consideration of this is proper to raise our love to Him, and reconcile our minds to His dispensations towards us. 2. The great difference between sincere Christians and other men. They love to think of His appearance, but others dread it; they wish and long for it, but others are afraid of it, and wish He would never come at all, or say in scorn, Where is the promise of His coming? 3. Can we make out this character? Are we lovers of His appearance? Is it the powerful motive to proper duty, and all suitable regard to Him? 4. How great is the Divine mercy in bestowing such a blessing upon sincere Christians. (*W. Harris, D.D.*) *Loving the Second Advent:*—See where St. Paul places a "love" of the Second Advent. He was writing as "Paul, the aged," with his own "crown of righteousness" now full in view. But who shall share it? The rest of the college of the apostles? Those who had "fought," his "good fight"—run his "course"—and "kept" his "faith" to the end? He stretches the bond of fellowship far higher. He makes the condition of the attainment very simple; but perfectly definite. All that is required to get the "crown," is to "love" very dearly Him that brings it. There are four attitudes of mind in which we may stand respecting the "appearing" of Christ. By far the worst is "indifference"; and that indifference may be either the dullness of ignorance, or the apathy of the deadness of the moral feelings. The next state is "fear." There is always something very good when there is "fear." It requires faith to "fear." But above "fear" is "hope." "Hope" is expectation with desire; knowledge enough to be able to anticipate, and grace enough to be able to wish it. And here the ladder is generally cut off; but God carries it one step higher—

"love." "Love" is as much above "hope" as "hope" is above "fear"—for "hope" may be selfish, "love" cannot be; "hope" may be for what a person gives, "love" must be for the person himself. Therefore a man might deceive himself, by thinking all was right in his soul, because he "hoped" for the Second Advent; but he might, after all, be set upon the pageant; and the rest; and the reward. But to the individual that "loves" it, there must be something infinitely dear in it; and that one dear thing is the Lord Jesus Christ. All Rome "hoped", for the return and the triumph of Cæsar—but Cæsar's own child "loved" him' Remember no motive concerning anything ever satisfies God, until it is the reflex of His own motive; and God's motive is always "love." Christ will come "lovingly" —therefore He must be met "lovingly." But the "love of Christ's appearing" is, evidently, not a simple idea; but one composed of many parts. I would separate four. which four at least go to make it. The moment of the manifestation—the original word is the epiphany—"epiphany," you know, is the same as "manifestation"— the moment of the manifestation of Christ will be the moment of the manifestation of all His followers. Then, perhaps, for the first time in their united strength and beauty—declared, and exhibited, and vindicated, and admired, in the presence of the universe. And, oh! what a subject of "love" is there. Some we shall see selecting and individualising us, as they come, with the well-remembered glances of their loving smiles. But all sunny in their sacred sweetness and their joyous comeliness. Never be afraid to "love" the saints too much. Some speak as if to "love" Christ were one thing—but to "love" the saints were another thing; and they almost place them in rivalry! But the saints are Christ. They are His mystical body, without which Christ Himself is not perfect. Another part of "the appearing"—very pleasant and very loveable to every Christian—will be the exhibition that will then be made of the kingdom and the glory of Jesus. If you are a child of God, every day it is a very happy thought to you, that Christ gains some honour. Only think what it will be to look all around as far as the eye can stretch, and all is His! "On His head are many crowns!" His sceptre supreme over a willing world! Every creature at His feet! His own, all-perfect! His name sounded upon every lip! His love perfect in every soul! But there is another thing after which you are always panting—you are very jealous over it with an exceeding jealousy. You are in the habit of tracing the ebb and flow of it every night, with the intensest interest. I mean, the image of Christ upon your soul. "Why am I not more like Him? Does His likeness increase at all in me? When shall I be entirely conformed—no separate will—no darkening spot upon the little mirror of this poor heart of mine, to prevent His seeing His own perfect mind there?" But now you stand before Him—in His unveiled perfections—and you are like Him—for you "see Him as He is!" And if "His appearing" is to appear in you, is not that cause to love Him? Therefore all His Church love Him—because then they shall be as that "sea of glass" before the throne, wherein God can look and see Himself again in their clear truth, and their holy stillness, and their unsullied brightness! But why speak of the shadows when you will have the substance? We shall look on Him and there will not be a feeling which ever throbbed in a bosom which will not be gratified! There will not be a desire, which ever played before the eye, which will not be surpassed! Another mark of the believer is that he loves the person of Christ. Others may love His work—he loves Him—for His own sake—because He is what He is. He loves Him to be with him—to see him—to know him—to converse with him. This fills his heart. All that is "love," and it is satisfied. But, will not all other "love," that ever was "loved," be as no "love," to the "love" that will then fill the soul? (*J. Vaughan, M.A.*) *A crown for all the saints :*—A king rejoices in his crown, not only because it is rich in gems and a symbol of power, but because he is the only man in the kingdom who has one or who is permitted to wear one. Suppose that some peer of the realm or some rich commoner should have a crown royal made for himself, and should wear it in public, what would the king do? Would he be glad that there was somebody else who possessed and was worthy of that symbol of royalty? Would he say: "I would that all my people were kings?" No, indeed! That presumptuous, self-crowned subject would either be put in an asylum as a lunatic or in prison as a traitor. Such is the Christian spirit in contrast with that of selfishness. Such is the joy of heaven in contrast with that of earth. Let us see how much purer and nobler it is. The Christian spirit, so beautifully illustrated by the great apostle when he could not think of his own without thinking also of the crowning of his brethren, is the spirit that will fill heaven with the joy that springs from love. Would that we had more of it here and now.

**Vers. 9–11. Come shortly unto me.**—*Companionship :*—I. HUMAN COMPANIONSHIPS ARE VERY NECESSARY. The ear thirsts for a friend's voice; the heart hungers for a friend's love. II. HUMAN COMPANIONSHIPS ARE VERY CHANGING. Changes are caused by distance, death, depravity. III. HUMAN COMPANIONSHIPS ARE OFTEN GREAT BLESS-INGS. Luke was with Paul. Mark was to be brought to him. Timothy was coming to him. IV. HUMAN COMPANIONSHIPS SOMETIMES PROVE GREAT AFFLICTIONS. Demas, Alexander. Men suffer most when "wounded in the house of their friends." V. HUMAN COMPANIONSHIPS MUST SOMETIMES FAIL US. Friends are sometimes scared by poverty, failure, shame. Besides, companionship can do little in our intense bodily pain, mental anguish, spiritual conflict, throes of death. (*U. R. Thomas.*) *The society of good men desirable :*—1. Personal presence is to be preferred before writing. 2. The society and help of good men is much to be desired. There is much comfort and good to be gained thereby. 3. The strongest Christians sometimes may be helped by weaker. A Paul may stand in need of a Timothy. 4. A minister upon weighty and just occasions may lawfully be absent from his flock for a time. 5. We may love one friend more than another. Timothy was Paul's beloved son in the faith (1 Tim. i. 2). (*T. Hall, B.D.*) *Best men—lessons from their life :*—I. THE BEST MEN, IN THE PRESENCE OF DEATH, ARE NOT DISREGARDFUL OF HUMAN SYMPATHY. Even Christ took three disciples with Him to Gethsemane. II. THE BEST MEN ARE SOMETIMES EXPOSED TO GREAT SOCIAL TRIALS. All of us are constantly losing friends, from one cause or another. III. THE BEST MEN ARE SUBJECT TO COMMON NEEDS. Men, if they are to be clothed, must procure their own garments ; if they are to be educated and informed, must use their own faculties. IV. THE BEST MEN ARE SOMETIMES TROUBLED BY THEIR INFERIORS. "Alexander the coppersmith." It requires no greatness to do mischief. The most contemptible characters are always the most successful in this work. Lessons—1. Value true friends. 2. Anticipate social desertions. 3. Do not look for miraculous interpositions to supply your needs. Do not be painfully surprised if you have enemies. (*Homilist.*) *Friends in adversity :*—To-day Colonel C. came to dine with us, and in the midst of our meal we were entertained with a most agreeable sight. It was a shark, about the length of a man, which followed our ship, attended with five smaller fishes, called pilot-fish, much like our mackerel, but larger. These, I am told, always keep the shark company, and, what is more sur-prising, though the shark is so ravenous a creature, yet, let it be never so hungry, it will not touch one of them. Nor are they less faithful to him ; for, as I am in-formed, if the shark is hooked, very often these little creatures will cleave close to his fins, and are often taken up with him.—Go to the pilot-fish, thou that forsakest a friend in adversity, consider his ways, and be ashamed. (*G. Whitefield.*) *Man's craving for society :*—Man is a social being. He is made to feel for, and with, his fellow-men. Sociality is a joy, a strength, a light to him. He is revealed, regaled, renewed, by fellowship. When there is community of views, sympathy of feel-ings, it causes a wonderful development of his nature, and gives it wonderful power. It is a lamp, a feast, a buttress of his being. It is everything whereby he can be ministered unto, or help to minister. God is social : "The God of the spirits of all flesh." Christ is social : "The Head of the body, the Church." Christianity is social : "The fellowship of the gospel." Man is social : "Come shortly unto Me." (*A. J. Morris.*) *Isolation undesirable :*—"One man is no man." True, there are some cold, misanthropic souls that shun their fellows, like some plants that shrink and shrivel at a touch, and that even take an awful pride in solitude and isolation ; but this is disease, or sin, or both. The finest natures are furthest removed from it. (*Ibid.*) **Demas hath forsaken me.**—*Demas :*—I. HIS PREVIOUS HISTORY. (See Philemon 24 ; Col. iv. 14). You see from this noted instance of unfaithfulness how far a man may go in the profession of Christianity, how richly he may seem to be partaking of its privileges, and how highly he may be honoured by its most de-voted friends, and yet have no part or lot in it at last. Trust not in mere professions, however loud—in mere external privileges, however distinguishing—in mere intel-lectual gifts, however excellent—in mere occasional impressions, however lively—in mere outward services to the cause of Christ, however zealous. You may be a fellow-labourer with Paul, and yet a castaway. II. HIS SUBSEQUENT FAITHLESSNESS. He refused to stand by the apostle in his hour of trial, withheld from him his former sympathy, withdrew from those Christian labours in which he had once been noted as a sharer with him, and shunned to be any longer seen in his society. He was not prepared to " endure hardness as a good soldier of Jesus Christ." That want or weakness of faith which he had hitherto concealed from others, and, probably, from himself also, could not be any longer disguised. That world which he had long loved secretly, without perhaps being aware of the strength of his attachment to it, he now openly clung to and embraced. III. The cause. Preferring his temporal interests to his Christian duties, he went back and walked no more with the apostle. To love the world, and the things that are in the world, is one of the chief sources of danger to our soul's welfare—of which we are taught in Scripture to beware. It is true there is no reason why a Christian should not engage as industriously as other men in the necessary business of life, and avail himself as thankfully of its varied blessings. It is one thing, however, to use this world in due subordination to religion, and it is quite another thing to serve if as our master, or to rest in it as our chosen portion. Even with those who do not thus love the world, its influence is hostile in many things to their spiritual welfare. Countless are the hindrances it places in their way—wily and ensnaring the allurements which it spreads for them. By its fair looks, and winning smiles, and flattering and crosses, entices them to sin; while, on the other hand, its frowns, and threats, promises, it and hardships, deter them from duty. Now, if such be the influence of the world even over those who do not set their hearts upon it, how much more powerful must its influence be on such as have yielded up to it their full affection! In them, alas! the wicked world without is fatally seconded by the wicked heart within. The world no sooner knocks, than the kindred spirit is ready to open a wide and effectual door for its admission. Temptations to vanity meeting with a vain heart find it not only a sure but an easy conquest. So was it in the case of Demas. His worldliness of spirit led him to forsake the Christian cause, when he saw that he could not longer adhere to it without endangering or prejudicing his temporal interests. How many a fair promise has it blighted! how many a hopeful beginning has it checked! how often, when the good seed was ready to spring up, have " the cares of the world, and the deceitfulness of riches," checked the rising plant, and rendered it unfruitful! (*T. J. Crawford, D.D.*)      *Demas :*—I. Many of you are young men who have been religiously educated in some distant home, and have been sent here, or have come here, for the pursuits of business. II. Consider, dear friends, whose consciences declare you to belong to this class, what it is you have forsaken, or are forsaking. 1. You are forsaking honour and conscience. 2. You are forsaking the company of those you most respect. 3. And not only so, but you are forsaking the pursuits which will most ennoble your natures. 4. But worst of all, in forsaking religion, you are forsaking you God and Saviour. III. To complete this subject, let us ask for what, considered at its very best, you leave all that is best and noblest and highest ? Demas had forsaken Paul, because he loved the then present world. I suppose that, in some shape or other, is the reason why you have forsaken religion to the extent to which you have forsaken it. It is really Satan's trap into which you have gone; but the bait has been this present world. You do not love penury, disease, privation, remorse, anguish, death. Oh, not at all! you love pleasure, success, money-getting, if you can get it easily. All the other things, the dark sides of this present world, drunkenness, debauchery, covetousness, immorality, over-reaching, you are not in love with these. No! You are lovers of pleasure, according to your idea of pleasure. Suppose you could gain the world, the whole world (and at best it will be an utterly unnoticeable and infinitesimal portion of it you will ever get), and in the chase should lose your own soul! (*R. T. Verrall, B.A.*)      *The apostasy of Demas :*—Now, whatever may have been the circumstances under which Demas first made profession of Christianity, it is very clear that that profession must have exposed him to hardship and danger, for he became a companion of St. Paul at the very time when that apostle was hunted down by persecution. It is not, therefore, to be supposed that, in embracing Christianity, Demas was conscious of acting with any insincerity. He must have considered himself a firm believer in Christ, and must have been so considered by those who had the best power of judging. Ah! it is in this that the case of Demas is full of melancholy warning. We do not find that he was scared by the perils which encompassed the profession of Christianity. It was love of the world which caused this promising disciple to make shipwreck of faith, and of a good conscience. He who could scorn danger or endure hardship could not withstand the blandishments of the world, which plied him with its pleasures. We have no security but in constant prayer, in constant war; and it should make you more diligent than ever in supplication, more vehement than ever in resistance, to hear St. Paul say of Demas—Demas who ministered to him in prison, Demas whom he called his fellow-labourer—that Demas had forsaken him, "having loved this present world." And now we would turn your thoughts from the progress which Demas must have made in Christianity to the advantages which he enjoyed. We wish you to observe him, not merely as forsaking St. Paul, but as forsaking him when that apostle was on the very eve of martyrdom. Who can question that there came to him, in the solitude of his prison, glorious visitations from the invisible world, that the consolations of God abounded towards him, and that, whilst the fetters were on the body, the spirit soared as with an eagle's wing, and gazed upon the inheritance that fadeth not away. Oh! to have been with him as he had to tell of the comforts and satisfactions thus vouchsafed, to have stood by him as the soul came back from its sublime expatiations, laden as it were with the riches of Paradise! Who could have doubted the truth of Christianity—who could have refused to adhere to its profession—who could have hesitated between its promises and any present advantage—with the prisoner Paul for his preacher, with the prisoner Paul for his evidence? Ah, be not too confident! It was the prisoner Paul whom Demas forsook. Forsook? Why, one would have thought the common feelings of humanity would have kept him constant! To desert the old man in his hour of trial—to leave him without a friend as the day of his martyrdom approached—who could be so ungenerous? Ah! pronounce not a hasty judgment. Demas did this—Demas who had for a long time been assiduous in ministering to the apostle—and Demas did this only because, like many—too many—amongst ourselves, he loved this present world. Learn ye, then, how weak are those extraordinary advantages when the heart is inclined to yield to the fascinations of the world—how these fascinations may be said to steal away the heart, so that he who is enslaved by them loses, to all appearance, the best sensibilities of his nature. And let no hearer henceforward think, that because he may have delight in hearkening to the pathetic or powerful speech of a favourite minister, he must be rooted in attachment to Christ and His religion. Let no minister henceforward think, that because he has gained an influence over men's minds, he must have gained a hold on their hearts. And in what mode may Christians hope to deliver themselves from love of the world? This is an important question. It is useless to show how fatal is the love, if we cannot show also how it may be subdued. There is no denying that the world addresses itself very strongly to our affections, and that the correspondence which subsists between its objects and our natural desires, gives to its temptations a force which can hardly be exaggerated; and we are sure that these temptations are not to be withstood, unless love of the world is dispossessed by love of something better than the world. You will not cease to love the world, you will not grow weaker in attachment to the world, through the influence of any proof, however elaborate, that the world is not worth loving. It is only by fixing the affections on things above, that they can be drawn from things below. There may be weariness, there may be dissatisfaction, there may be even disgust with the vanities of earth, but nevertheless these vanities will occupy the heart, unless displaced by the realities of heaven. You see, then, what you have to do. You have to meditate upon God and upon heaven, striving to acquire higher and higher thoughts of Divine majesty. There is not one of you who will become a Demas, if you keep this in mind. This is what you may call a recipe against apostasy. It is not a recipe composed upon abstract and speculative opinions, but drawn from the known workings and pleadings of the heart. The heart will attach itself to what it feels to be a greater good in preference to a lesser. (*H. Melvill, B.D.*)

*The apostasy of Demas :*—In the long line of the Doges, in the grand old palace in Venice, one space is empty, and the black curtain which covers it attracts more attention than any one of the fine portraits of the merchant kings. From that panel, now so unsightly, once smiled the sallow face of Marino Falieri, afterwards found guilty of treason against the state, and blotted out, so far as might be, from remembrance. The text reveals the fate of one who had filled a much more honoured place, and who, yielding to temptation, sank to still lower depths. Poor, foolish Demas has gained for himself a most unenviable notoriety. Once he was not only a Church-member, but he was accounted as no ordinary man among his brethren. Twice in the friendly salutations with which St. Paul usually closes his epistles he mentions Demas with honour (Philemon 24; Col. iv. 14). Two years later he wrote in sorrow of heart, "Demas hath forsaken me," &c. It was neither cowardice nor self-indulgence which had caused his ruin, but simply the love of the world; the very danger to which so many are exposed in our own day, when the beguiling blandishments of sin, rather than the terrors of persecution, are the devil's most successful devices.   There is no shadow of a reason to suppose that Demas had not devoted himself at the outset in downright sincerity and earnestness to God's service; but his weakness was such as might prove the ruin of any one who does not keep every avenue to his heart diligently guarded, lest an inordinate love of temporal things force an entrance there.   It is recorded of the King of Navarre, then claiming to be a good Protestant, that being urged by Beza to behave himself in a more manly way for the cause of God, he made answer, that he was "really the friend of the reformers, but that he was resolved to put out no further to sea than he might get safely back to shore in case a storm should unexpectedly arise."  In other words, he would not hazard his hopes of the crown of France for the sake of his religion.   You know the sequel of his story.   Like Demas, he loved "this present world" better than he loved God. He proved a traitor to his religion, and bartered his heavenly crown for a fading one of earth.   Some years ago, a young woman was hanged in England for murder, who had been tempted to commit the awful deed for the sake of a five pound note, and this note proved to be a counterfeit!   To run such a risk, and to receive such bitter wages!   Do those people fare better than this wretched woman who desert God's service for the world's poor bribes?   Can the possession of hoards of wealth, or the fading memories of past enjoyments, bring peace in a dying hour?   An Arab lost his way in a desert, and was in danger of perishing from hunger, when he was fortunate enough to reach a brackish well, and close by he discovered a little leather bag.   "Ah! here's just what I need," he cried, with joy; "dates, or nuts, to appease my gnawing hunger!"   He hastily opened the bag, but only to cast it away with contempt.   It was filled with pearls!   What value did they possess for one who was about to die?   Just as much as the world will be to those who have sold everything else to gain it.   (*J. N. Norton, D.D.*)    *Demas the deserter:*—I was very much affected—as probably you have been affected—by reading the accounts of the punishment of deserters in the army.   Nothing in battle is so blood-chilling and horrible.   It is so cool, so individual, so premeditated a life-taking.   The leading forth of the offender before his whole regiment; the rehearsal of his disgrace to all his comrades; the pinioning of his arms; the bandaging of his eyes that he may not see what comrade takes his life; the open coffin beneath him hungry for its prey; the file of soldiers all aiming at one poor fluttering heart (as if sportsmen should shoot a bird already caged); the ringing volley; the lightning-like death under a dozen wounds—all this is enough to drive the kindred of the deserter to the verge of madness.   The mother whose son lies in the sacred mould of Gettysburg or Chattanooga is happy in comparison with her whose hapless boy was blown into eternity from the coffin of a deserter!   And why is the deserter's doom made so awful?   Simply because the crime is so great and the consequences of the crime so fatal to the interests of an army and of the cause for which an army fights.   If desertion will destroy an army, then the army must destroy desertion.   His crime is punished so fearfully that other men will be deterred from imitating his bad example.   Now history has marked to infamy more than one deserter of his country, or of a sacred cause.   Benedict Arnold stands already in American history, bandaged, pinioned, shot through with the volleys of a nation's abhorrence!   In Scripture history hangs Judas the arch-deserter.   In our text we read of another.   Paul has pilloried the unhappy man.   Every man who has ever brought disgrace on his Christian profession, or has fallen out of his church-standing had some secret reason for his fall.   He deserted under the seduction of some besetting sin.   If we could come at the sad roll of all the backsliders or open apostates we might read over the specifications like these: "Deserted from moral cowardice," or "Deserted through neglect of prayer," or "Deserted from love of the wine-bottle," or "Deserted through the enticements of irreligious associates," or "Deserted through unbelief."  Demas's name has the Holy Spirit's specification beside his name.   He deserted for "love of the world!"   "Whoso loveth the world, the love of God is not in him!"   This is the last we read of poor Demas.   Tradition says that he sank so low as to become a priest in an heathen temple!   But if this were so or not we need not discuss.   We do know that he forsook his Master's cause in its hour of peril, and preferred the "world" to Christ.   Paul encountered the world; went into its thickest, saw its brightest allurements; met its fiercest assaults, and its most attractive lures to his ambition.   He never deserted.   Why?   He never loved it; he so loved Jesus that he could not love the world.   Demas loved the world.   It would have done him no harm if he had not. It will do you none as long as you keep it out of your heart. But when it works into the soul it eats out the loyalty to Christ and consumes the spirituality of the soul. Do you remember reading in your childhood, in that favourite volume of Oriental stories, about Sinbad's voyage into the Indian Ocean? Do you remember that magnetic rock that rose from the surface, surrounded by a placid and a glassy sea? Silently the ship was attracted towards it; silently the bolts were drawn out of the vessel's sides one by one, by the magnetic rock! And when the fated vessel drew so near that every bolt and clamp was unloosed, the whole structure of bulwarks and masts and spars tumbled into helpless rubbish on the sea, and the sleeping sailors awoke to their drowning agonies! So stands the magnetic rock of worldly enchantments! Its attraction is silent, slow, but powerful to the soul that floats within its range! Under its spell, bolt after bolt of resolution, clamp after clamp of Christian obligation is drawn out. One neglect of duty paves the way for another. One desertion accustoms the man to the path of evil, until he is used to what a Christian never should "get used to"—sinning! A backslider gets so accustomed to neglect of secret devotion that he passes by the bolted closet-door with as little concern as he passes by the doors of his neighbours in the street. He becomes habituated to a deserted Bible, a deserted sanctuary, a deserted Sabbath-school, to a neglected heart, to a deserted Saviour. At length he finds that the Friend he has deserted, deserts him. The God whom he has offended withdraws His presence. This is the penalty of sin! No deserter from Jesus escapes unpunished. And a most invariable penalty which the forsaker of God suffers is —a sense of God's frowns, which sometimes drives the transgressor to recklessness, sometimes to despair. Then does the unfaithful Christian find that "it is an evil thing and a bitter to depart from the living God." His by-path meadow leads to "Doubting Castle" and the dungeons of "Giant Despair." (*T. L. Cuyler, D.D.*) *Demas:*—I. LET US SEE WHAT IS TOLD US CONCERNING THIS DEMAS. 1. This man was no hypocrite. He had not turned Christian for some selfish hope of worldly good or gain. There never are many of these. In those days probably there were none. 2. Nor was he a timid follower of Jesus. It was rather bleak and stormy for Mr. Facingbothways to show himself, who is usually a very dainty and delicate fellow and cannot stand much exposure. Like the cuckoos and the swallows his season is the summer, and the first touch of frost is enough to send him away. 3. Nor was he moved only by a passing glow of enthusiasm. It is not unlikely that some were—the devotion of an impulsive nature to the noble and the good, especially to the noble and the good in persecution. They receive the seed of the Word with joy, but anon the sun is up and it is withered, for it has no root. 4. And further, it was not that Demas had no religious opportunities and fellowship. That little company, knit together as it was by such bonds of sympathy and fellowship constantly met in Paul's house. Think how the soul of Demas was stirred by the great utterances of St. Paul. II. WHAT WAS IT THAT RUINED HIM? Having loved this present world. 1. Was it avarice?—the cursed love of gold? That vice that grows with the years and fattens on its gains: that creeps from prudence to saving, from saving to scraping, from scraping to grubbing, from grubbing to gripping the gold more than life. So clutching his money-bags does Demas go forth, leaving Paul the aged forsaken. The love of money makes many a Demas still. If that was it, pity him. Of all pitiable, ill-tempered, miserable people in the world, this is the worst. Of all fools hell laughs most loudly at the miser, who could not use it when he had it and then left it behind. But how can we warn him? Alas, Demas is the first to sigh and shake his head, and say how dreadful it is, and never suspect that you mean him. The miser never thinks himself rich. 2. Was it love of pleasure, of the world's ways and the world's approbation? The world kills more men with its smiles than with its frowns. Samson can kill the young lion that roars against him, but is himself coaxed to death by Delilah. 3. And yet again, it may have been neither avarice nor worldliness that killed him, but a gradual process of spiritual neglect. So away on the coast I have seen some projecting crag, bold and mighty, joined, as it seemed, and rooted with all the solid continent: one with the ground that stretched down through the round world and away under the seas to the shores of the far west, and inland bound to the hills that were topped and crested with the granite crags—there it stood facing the blasts of the Atlantic, defying them and looking proudly forth on the wild seas that stormed and tossed below it. Yes, winds and waves would never have fetched it down. But within were hollow places, tiny streams that washed the deepening water-courses: then came the silent frosts that gnawed at it, crumbling underneath it; so hollowed out within; then came some day the crash and din of thunder and clouds of dust that darkened heaven and the proud headland was hurled far down below, dashed by the tumbling seas and swept triumphantly by the wild waves. Oh, are you the man, whose prayers were once fervent pleadings with God, and now they are an empty round of phrases? Thy danger is great. A little longer—only that, a little longer, and of thee too it must be spoken—he hath forsaken me. 4. Here is the record of the basest ingratitude. A black ingratitude that rouses our indignation. St. Paul had most likely been the means of bringing him to the knowledge of the truth. He could not have failed to lead him to the richer enjoyment of the truth. Now when his company would have cheered the apostle in his dungeon loneliness we find the record—"Demas hath forsaken me, having loved this present world." Ah, thou Demas of to-day, think how the Lord Jesus Christ hath come down from His glory in very love to thee. He sighs—He saith, Thou hast forsaken Me. Oh, Demas, thou hast made a bad bargain. Thirsty ambition in place of quietness and rest. The devil as thy master in place of the loving Lord. The bondage instead of the life of goodness. And for wages at the last heaven given up for hell. Thou hast a thorn in thy pillow. Thy religion is dead, buried; but its ghost haunts thee still and will haunt thee. It meets thee in still and lonely places and whispers of what used to be. Thy religion gone and thyself spoiled for this world, and undone for the world which is to come. (*M. G. Pearse.*) *The danger of backsliding :*—I. IT IS THE LOT OF GOD'S DEAREST CHILDREN TO BE OFTENTIMES FORSAKEN OF THOSE THAT HAVE BEEN MOST NEAR UNTO THEM (Matt. xxvi. 56; Psa. cxix. 87; xxvii. 10; 1 Kings xix. 10). 1. That they may be made conformable to their head, Christ Jesus, who was left alone of His beloved disciples, and had none to comfort Him. 2. That they may fly to Christ, in whom all true comfort lies. II. THOSE THAT HAVE GONE FAR IN RELIGION MAY YET, NOTWITHSTANDING, FALL AWAY, AND BECOME APOSTATES. 1. Because they rest on their own strength, and there is no support in man to uphold himself. 2. Because Satan, that grand apostate, is fallen from the truth himself, and he labours to draw others to fall back with him. III. How SHALL WE PERSEVERE IN GOODNESS? 1. Labour for a true grace. 2. Get a strong resolution against all oppositions. 3. Labour to know the truth, and to practise what thou knowest. 4. Get the love of God in thy heart. 5. Strive to grow daily in a denial of thyself. 6. Labour to have Divine truths engrafted in thee, that so they may spring forth in thy life. 7. Grow deeper and deeper in humiliation. IV. THE LOVE OF CHRIST AND THE WORLD CANNOT LODGE TOGETHER IN ONE HEART. They are two masters, ruling by contrary laws. (*R. Sibbes.*) *The falling away of Demas :*—1. The expression, "Demas hath forsaken me," &c., probably means, in the first instance, that he loved his life too well to risk it by farther companionship with one, all but condemned, and whose martyrdom might be the signal for his own. 2. But the expression involves something more. That "love of this present world," which assaulted Demas under the lone roof of the apostle, is what we can all understand, and a snare which is more or less laid for us all. It was the result of not having counted the cost of what might be required of him; a perilous "looking back," after "having put his hand to the plough," and therefore being "unfit for the kingdom of God." In his former home at Thessalonica there might be a comparative security to be obtained. There he might find a comparative easement from a confessor's labour; a retirement from the responsibility of a more marked and active disciple. There, at all events, he might not be called upon to defend his faith; to sustain it against the onset of impiety and false doctrine; but might indulge the illusion of adhering to it in what the world calls "peace." There, in short, freed from the severer claims of an appointed trial, he might live as seemed best in his own eyes; and cling to the vain hope of reconciling the duty of a Christian with the divers conflicting habits and temptations, which beset the man of "this present world." (*Canon Puckle.*) *Demas :*—Observations: 1. It is lawful (in some cases) to name men. The apostle, to make others fear apostasy, names this backslider. Our application must be as a garment fitted for the body it is made for: a garment that is fit for everybody, is fit for nobody. What is spoken in general to all, few will apply to themselves. The only way to benefit our people is to apply the plaster to their particular sores. This made Ahab to put on sackcloth (1 Kings xxi. 20), and brought in so many thousand converts (Acts ii. 37). One preacher that thus faithfully applieth the Word to his people, shall do more good in one year than another that preacheth in a general way, and never cometh home to the consciences of the people, shall do in many. 2. The godly must look sometimes to be forsaken by their bosom friend. Demas was Paul's intimate acquaintance and coadjutor, yet "Demas hath forsaken me." True friendship is like a well-built arch which standeth at first at a greater distance, and thence leisurely groweth up into a greater closure at the top, and so it will stand the better for weight. 3. Eminent professors may become grand apostates. Demas is a preacher of the gospel, Paul's coadjutor, and is joined with Luke the evangelist (Col. iv. 14), yet for all this " Demas hath forsaken me." Nothing but sincerity can preserve us from apostasy. Let us therefore, especially at our first setting forth, dig deep, lay a good foundation, consider what the truth may cost us, and ask ourselves whether we can deny ourselves universally for Christ. If we cannot, or will not, we are not fit to be Christ's disciples, we shall shrink in the wetting, and start aside like a broken bow when a temptation comes (2 Thess. ii. 10, 11). 4. The inordinate love of this present world is the highway to apostasy. It is not the world or the creatures which are good in themselves, but the excessive and inordinate love of them, which ruins men. 5. This world shall have an end and all things in it, it is not an everlasting world, it is but this present world, whose pomp and pleasures soon vanish away (1 Cor. vii. 29, 30, 31). 6. Sin blotteth a man's name, and blemisheth his reputation. Demas, for his worldliness, had a brand set on his name to the end of the world. 7. It is an aggravation of a man's sin to sin deliberately against light and conviction. Demas doth not sin here through passion or fear, but deliberately. (1) He sinned against great light, he being a professor, yea, a preacher of the gospel, could not offend (in this kind especially) through ignorance. (2) Demas sinned against great love. God had enlightened him, and made him a preacher of the gospel, gave him a room in the affections of his chosen vessel Paul, who made him his coadjutor. (3) He sinned against the light of good example. Paul went before him in doing and suffering, and glories in all as comfortable and honourable, yet Demas deserts him, and is not this our sin ? (4) To sin upon a light temptation aggravateth a sin. Now Demas had no just ground for flinching. If he feared suffering for Christ, he knew the promise, That he who forsaketh father, or mother, or lands, or life, for Christ,·shall have a hundredfold in this present world, and could he have brought his life and estate to a better market ? If he loved the world and found sweetness in that, is there not more sweetness in Him that made the world ? (5) To draw others into sin, aggravateth sin. Demas, by his evil example, brought an evil report on the gospel, and did tacitly and interpretatively say there is much more sweetness in the world than in Christ, and so drew others from the truth. (6) The greater the person that sins the greater is his sin. Theft in a judge is worse than in an inferior person ; for Demas, a teacher of others, to teach apostasy, draws men into sin. Such cedars fall not alone, but crush the shrubs that be under them. (*T. Hall, B.D.*) *Demas :—* I. THE CHRISTIAN LIFE ACCORDING TO DEMAS. Chrysostom, assuming that Demas left Paul in order to go back to his friends, expressively describes his purpose by saying, "He chose to luxuriate at home." If that was so, he did only what most Christian people are doing now. He still believed in Jesus as the Saviour of sinners, and hoped to be accepted for His sake ; he purposed to abstain from the things forbidden by the law ; and, this done, he thought himself at liberty to seek and enjoy the full measure of worldly good which he was able to obtain. In other words, he wished to lead a Christian life, but with the least possible quantity of self-denial. He wished, in the selfish acceptation of the phrase, to make the best of both worlds. His Christian ideal was a negative one, and consisted in not breaking the gospel commandments, rather than in laboriously doing, or being, anything great or good. It may often happen—in our case it will generally happen—that the best service we can render to others and to Christ is to be done at home ; yet it is possible, it is common, to remain at home, and not to render it, but simply to luxuriate there, our lives regulated by that love of this present world which Demas showed. Indeed, whatever the sphere may be in which we are best able to serve others and Christ— whether the home circle, or the wider arena of social life, or the haunts of business, or the Sabbath-school, or the sick, or the poor—are we not tempted to occupy it after the manner of Demas? II. THE CHRISTIAN LIFE ACCORDING TO PAUL. Not, how little can I do, but, how much, was the ruling principle with Paul. Not, what would be easiest for me, but, what most acceptable to Christ. Not a cold calculation in the interest of self, but a warm devotion to the welfare of all. Loyalty, gratitude, generous enthusiasm, are its features ; and, surely, they are among the noblest qualities of human character. Cold and grudging selfishness marks the other conception. They hardly deserve to be called two forms of the Christian life, for only one has the Spirit of Christ at all. Yes, let us remember even the nobleness of Paul was but a reflection of the nobleness of Christ. It was at that source the flame of his soul was kindled: "The love of Christ constrained him." III THE CHRISTIAN LIFE BEGUN WITH PAUL AND ENDED WITH DEMAS. The Spirit which founded the Christian Church was the spirit of Paul; but, as soon as the days of its freshness and persecution were over, the spirit of Demas prevailed. And the history of individuals is apt to be similar. (*T. M. Herbert, M.A.*) *Demas:*—In old times your London Bridge and our Netherbrow Port in Edinburgh were garnished with human heads; and in days when tyrants and persecutors were on the throne, alongside those of many notorious criminals, many a good and patriotic head hung there to bake and wither in the sun. That may appear to you a barbarous custom; in a sense it was; notwithstanding, it came down, in a way, almost to our own times. Years ago, yet in our time, in sailing down your Thames, you saw certain strange and fearful objects standing up within tide-mark on the shore, between you and the sky; they were gibbets, with dead men hung in chains. Contrary as such a custom is to the feelings and sentiments of the present day, the object of those who observed that custom was a good one. They had a better end in view than merely the frightening of those who, happening to pass that way by night, heard the wind whistle though the holes in the empty skull, or the rusty chains creak as the body swept round and round. Piracy, with all its awful atrocities on men and women, was a much more common crime in those days than it is now; and the sailors who dropped down the river and passed these frightful objects, carried away with them a salutary lesson. They were pirates who were hung in chains, and they who looked saw in them the abhorrence with which society regarded, and the vengeance with which justice would pursue the perpetrators of so great a crime. "Rebuke before all," said the apostle, "that others may fear"; and these men were thus hung in chains that others might see and be afraid. Nevertheless, these monuments of sin and of justice, however offensive they may be to our taste, or however suitable they might be to the ruder customs of ruder times, were not perpetual. The work of decay went on, and bone dropping away from bone left empty the chains; mother earth received into her bosom the last relic of her guilty child, and the crime and the criminal were soon forgotten. More enduring monuments of sin and its punishment than these have perished in the wreck of all things. For long ages the stony figure of a woman stood, with her cold, grey eyes turned on the sea that had buried the sinners, but not the saints, of Sodom. Lonely and awful form—the travellers that skirted the shores of the Dead Sea, and the shepherds that tended their flocks on the neighbouring mountains, regarded her with all horror and terror; and never did living creature deliver such a sermon on the words, "Whoso putteth his hand to the plough and looketh back, is not worthy of the kingdom of God," as did that dumb statue! But time that destroys all things destroyed that, and now travellers have sought in vain for even the vestige of a relic that, were it found, would be far more interesting and far more impressive than all your Greek and Roman marbles, anything dug out of quarry or carved by sculptor's chisel. She who, loving the world too well, looked back on Sodom, has ceased to exist in stone: she lives, however, in story, and we would do well, in and amid the temptations of this world, often to "remember Lot's wife." The purpose our forefathers had in hanging pirates in chains, and the purpose God Himself had in turning that woman into a pillar of salt, the Apostle Paul had in his treatment of this man whom he holds up here as a beacon to all future ages. He did not write this of Demas to revenge himself on Demas; he was above that. He did not write, "Demas hath forsaken me, having loved the present world," out of spleen or anger against this poor and pitiable apostate. Nothing of the kind. Nor was Demas the only man that at one time forsook Paul. There were others stricken with such panic, as will sometimes seize the bravest troops. All his friends deserted him. Ah! but even then there was an essential, and now there is an eternal difference between them. I do not deny that others fled, but then they returned, they rallied; they washed out with martyr's blood the stains of their disgrace. They fled, I grant; they fled the field, but only for a time—Demas for ever; they abandoned the fight—Demas the faith. Theirs was the failing of the disciples for whom our Lord pled the kind apology, "The spirit is willing, but the flesh is weak." Demas's was the sin and crime of Judas. He abandoned for aye and for ever the cause of Jesus. I. DEMAS'S HISTORY AND DEMAS'S FALL. Men live after they are dead. I do not mean merely that they live in another world after they are dead, but that, in a sense, after they are dead they live here—some in their good works, and others in their bad. Many a man would never have been heard of in this world at all but for his crimes. His crimes are the salt, wherewith his memory is salted; he lives in them. But for them he had passed a happy life, obscure, no doubt, but happy; and when he died had gone down to his grave unnoticed and unknown. Now that is not the case of Demas. The truth is, if this Second Epistle to Timothy had never been written, or if it had pleased God to have let this Second Epistle to Timothy perish, like some other writings of the apostles, perhaps you might have called this church after Demas; Demas might have had his name in the calendar of saints. This man fell from a height which few of us have reached or ever will reach, and all the more impressive, therefore, is the story of his fall. He was indeed a fallen star! The reverse of Paul, who fell a persecutor and rose an apostle, this man was an apostle, but is an apostate now; he was a professor, but he is a renegade now; he was a brave soldier of the cross, but he is a base deserter and traitor now, having deserted and abandoned all for which a man should live. What a fall was there! Scripture drops the curtain on Demas just where we see him here, like a dishonoured knight from whose heels the spurs he has won have been hacked—just where we see him as a soldier who, his facings plucked from his breast, is dismissed as a deserter. No other word in Scripture about Demas after that; the curtain drops, and he vanishes. But let tradition lift her curtain, and if she speaks the truth—and there is no reason to doubt her story—it happened that Demas, as I could have prophesied, or you or any one else—went from bad to worse, down and down, and lower still, from one depth of infamy to another, till in the last sight we get of Demas, there he is yonder, a priest in a heathen temple, offering sacrifices to dead stocks and stones! Unhappy, miserable man, whether he died, as he might have died, with a recollection of better days, stung with remorse, howling in despair, or whether he died defiant of Christ, like Julian the royal apostate, who, when vanquished by the Christian hosts, caught the sword from his mortal wound, and tossed it up to heaven, and cried, expiring in the effort, "The Nazarene has conquered!" Unhappy man, whether he died one way or the other! II. WHAT MADE DEMAS FALL? what brought him down from his high position? Sailing once on a Highland loch where the crags went sheer down into the water, the boatman called my attention to a very remarkable fragment of rock. There it stood, tilted up on its narrow edge, threatening destruction to every one below it, and to all appearance ready, at the touch of an infant's finger, to leap with a sudden plunge into the depths below. What had tilted that enormous table into that upright position? No arms of brawny shepherds had set it there; no earthquake, rolling along the mountains and turning it upward, as earthquakes sometimes do, had turned it, nor had lightning, leaping from a cleft on the mountain's summit, struck it, split it, shivered it, or raised it on its narrow edge. The task belonged to a much quieter and less obtrusive agent than these. Borne on the wings of the tempest, or dropped by some passing bird, a seed fell into a crevice of the rock; sleeping the winter through, but finding there a shelter and a congenial soil, it sprang with the spring, fed by rains and by dews it grew, and put up its head and spread out its branches, and struck deep its roots, worming them deep into the crannies of the rock, and wrapping it round and round. That table, as they grew, and thickened, and strengthened, was slowly and silently raised and separated from its bed, and then one day there came a storm roaring down the glen, and seizing the tree, whose leafy branches caught the wind like sails, turned that tree into a lever, and working upon the rock, raised it and set it where I saw it just on the edge of the dizzy crag, and there it stood, waiting till another storm should come to hurl it over into the mossy waters of that wild mountain lake. Whether that stone has fallen yet I do not know, but it will fall; and just as that shall fall, so fell Demas; so many have fallen, and so you and I, but for preserving grace, would fall too. Do not mistake the Bible. The Bible does not say a word against the world. It is not the world, it is not riches, it is not fame, it is not honour, it is not the innocent enjoyment of the world that the Bible condemns; it is the love of the world. Beware of that! Let it once enter, let it get lodgment in your heart, though it is simply a tiny seed, let it grow there, let it be fed by indulgence, let it strike its roots, let it worm them into the crevices and crannies of your heart, and it will do this so silently that you will never suspect it, and you will never know it, and others will never know it, till one day the storm shall come. What was it that brought on Demas's fall? Why was it that persecution destroyed Demas? Why, because persecution acted on Demas just as the storm did on the tree that got its seed into the rock. But that that tree had its seed and its roots round about that rock, the rock had defied all tempests, though they blew their worst; and Demas—persecution might have made him a beggar, persecution might have cast him into the deepest dungeon Rome had, persecution might have brought him to the scaffold, but if Demas had never loved the world, all that persecution had done would have been to destroy his wealth, to destroy his health, and to destroy his life, but it had never destroyed him ; and on that day when Paul stood with his grey head before a mighty crowd coming to see him die, Demas had stood at his side ; they had stood together in the battle-field, they had stood together in the pulpit, they had stood together before Jews and heathens, and that day had they stood together again ; one chain of love, as of iron, binding them still, they had fought together and they had fallen together, their heads had rolled on the same scaffold, one chariot had borne these brothers to the grave, and over their mangled remains, carried by devout men to burial, a weeping church had raised one monument, and I will tell you what she would have put on it; copying the words of David she might have said, " They were lovely and pleasant in their lives, and in their death they were not divided." Alas ! I have an epitaph for Demas, taken from the same touching lament, but consisting of other words—" How are the mighty fallen, and the weapons of war perished !" Such is the epitaph of Demas ! He was laid in an apostate's grave, and, not excepting a drunkard's, there is no grave the grass grows on so hopeless as the apostate's. Lessons : 1. " Put not your trust in princes," says David. " Put not your trust in preachers," says Demas. A blazing star quenched in darkness, oh ! how does Demas teach them that stand high to walk humbly, and them that are high-placed not to be high-minded. It is well to carry a low sail, even when the wind blows strong. 2. Have you a pious father or mother, a pious wife or children, pious brothers or sisters—are you a servant in a pious family, or are your friends pious and your associations good ? Ah ! how does this teach you not to count too much on man ! Why, there is Demas ; what is your society to his ? Demas lived in the holiest society out of heaven ; Demas was the bosom friend and associate of one of the holiest, and I will say of one, in point of soul, of the noblest and loftiest men that ever lived—the Apostle Paul. There is no man in this house so little likely to be engrossed with the business, to be entangled with the cares, to be fascinated with the pleasures of this world, as was that man Demas ; and yet he fell; he fell, and if he fell, who of us is to stand? Oh ! how does his history sound in my ear like that old prophet's voice, " Howl, fir-tree, for the cedar is fallen !" 3. Ah, what a lesson is this for you and me, and all those who live under the best religious influences, for us to take care that we do not reckon upon them, but that we watch and pray lest we enter into temptation. The world's smiles are more to be dreaded than its frowns ; its sordid sophistry, than its sharpest sword. Let the love of the world get into a man's heart, and there is no pleader, no counsel, no man that ever made the worse appear the better, so successful as that is ; for the world has a tongue to convince the man who has the love of it, that virtue is vice, and vice is virtue. (*T. Guthrie, D.D.*) *The relapsed Christian :*—He reminds us of the piteous spectacle of a man emerging from the watery element in which he has been plunged, and for a moment gaining a footing upon the shore, but caught by the retiring wave, or losing his hold, he is once more carried into deep water with the danger of being finally engulfed in the waves, unless by another strenuous effort he should regain the shore and reach a standing above the power of the surge. (*J. Leifchild, D.D.*) **Having loved this present world**—*The connection between love of the world and apostasy :*—Love of the world —love of the world's opinions, and the world's habits, and the world's tastes, and the world's privileges, and the world's dispositions, for their own sakes, diminish faith, by bringing us more into contact with visible things. It is the privilege of faith to gaze upon the invisible, to behold and to lay hold of those things which the natural eye sees not, which the natural intellect comprehends not, and which the natural powers cannot grasp. But if the love of the world constrains me to grovel in the dust, to be busied and exercised and made careful overmuch with the things that are seen, soon may the far-scanning sight of faith be impaired and enfeebled, till at length it scarcely deserves the name, and brings not the comfort and imparts not the joy. Do we not know that the natural eye, when engaged upon minute visible objects which have to be brought near to it, accommodates itself to the distance ; and the strong and healthful eye at length becomes short-sighted, and cannot gaze upon the distant prospect in its brightness, and looks confusedly on the landscape that woos admiration ? And so it is with the spiritual perception. Let me be employed in the minute things of this world—the poor trifles after which the men of this world toil—and I may look upwards in vain ; the spiritual sun may be shining upon me, in its meridian splendour, but my sight may be so dimmed, that with my purblind spirituality I shall be forced to look up and say—Where is it? The love of the world also diminishes our hope; because it induces us to seek, and in a certain sense enables us to find, satisfaction in present enjoyment. The young heart gazes upon the world and upon its enticements, and is it not constrained to say—"How delightful—how attractive"? And the grey-headed worldling, who has luxuriated in worldly enjoyments, has no range of hope beyond that which the little limited circle of his present existence gives him. Let me be content with present enjoyment—let me be content with worldly success—let me be satisfied with all I can perceive while passing as a traveller rapidly through this world, and I apprehend I should not be over-much anxious to build up a "hope" that is "full of immortality"; I should be inclined to say—"I want no better heaven, I do not wish for anything beyond this, I do not desire to hope for more." How it becomes us to entreat you, with all earnestness and affection, to beware of a Christian profession which does not separate you from the world! Nothing is more delusive than to become acquainted with the letter of God's Word, to feel desires after the experience of its comfort, to make a Christian profession, to join Christian assemblies, to mingle in Christian ordinances, and yet to be still numbered with those who say to the world by their conduct—"Thou art my God!" But if you find your profession has been genuine—if you have "tasted that the Lord is gracious"—beware of the first symptoms of decline. (*G. Fisk, LL.B.*)      *The foolish love of the world :—*

> Judge in thyself, O Christian! is it meet
> To set thine heart on what beasts set their feet?
> 'Tis no hyperbole, if you be told,
> You delve for dross with mattocks made of gold.
> Affections are too costly to bestow
> Upon the fair-faced nothings here below:
> The eagle scorns to fall down from on high,
> The proverb saith, to pounce a silly fly;
> And can a Christian leave the face of God
> T' embrace the earth, and doat upon a clod! (*John Flavel.*)

*Worldliness fatal to religion :—*In Brazil there grows a common plant, which forest-dwellers call the matador, or "murderer." Its slender stem creeps at first along the ground; but no sooner does it meet a vigorous tree than, with clinging grasp, it cleaves to it, and climbs it, and, as it climbs, keeps at short intervals sending out arm-like tendrils that embrace the tree. As the murderer ascends, these ligatures grow larger and clasp tighter. Up, up, it climbs a hundred feet, nay, two hundred if need be, until the last loftiest spire is gained and fettered. Then, as if in triumph, the parasite shoots a huge, flowery head above the strangled summit, and thence, from the dead tree's crown, scatters its seed to do again the work of death. Even thus worldliness has strangled more Churches than ever persecution broke. (*S. Coley.*) *Danger of the world :—*As you love your souls, beware of the world; it has slain its thousands and ten thousands. What ruined Lot's wife?—the world. What ruined Achan?—the world. What ruined Haman?—the world. What ruined Judas?—the world. What ruined Simon Magnus?—the world. What ruined Demas?—the world. And "what shall it profit a man, if he shall gain the whole world and lose his own soul?" *The world pictured by fancy :—*In the mirage of the desert, objects are said to become strangely distorted—a mud-bank exhibiting the appearance of a magnificent city with domes and towers, a few stunted bushes are transformed into a forest of stately trees. Is not the world with its hollow, fading distinctions thus transformed in our idle, foolish fancy? We attach an importance to its treasures, praise, ambitions, pleasures, utterly false and exaggerated. (*W. L. Watkinson.*) *The border-land between Christ and the world :—*Centuries ago it was dangerous for any one to live on the border-land between England and Scotland. Let us take care not to dwell on the border-land between Christ and the world. *Counteractives to worldliness :—*Let the declining Christian strive against the deteriorating and retrograding tendency to worldliness. Let him exercise his faith in strong realisations of celestial things, which alone are able to counteract the debasing impressions of terrestrial ones. Let him accustom himself to look upon all things here in the light of eternity. The fascinations of the world will then appear to him as a brilliant bubble, which will soon burst, and its troubles but as a dark vapour that appeareth but for a little while and then vanisheth away. For his warning, let him contemplate the fearful catastrophe threatened to those who draw back from God to the world. He has only to open his eyes to see in what numerous instances this passage of Scripture has been verified: "They that will be rich fall into temptation and a snare," &c., resembling covetous merchants, who overload their vessel with a freight which impedes its course and endangers its safety. What a fatal shipwreck of faith and a good conscience have many suffered from this cause: and who can tell whither it may carry him who surrenders himself to its influence? Upon the principle of a relapse being more difficult to cure than the original disease, let him be doubly on his guard against this tendency. (*J. Leifchild, D.D.*)    **Crescens to Galatia.**—*Crescens is gone to Galatia, Titus to Dalmatia :*—1. Good men will be doing good wherever they are. Paul was now a prisoner, yet he preached constantly in prison, and there converted Onesimus (Philemon 9). 2. Though some may forsake us and the truth, yet God hath others that are faithful. What if Demas be gone, yet Crescens, Titus, Timothy, Mark, and Luke abide constant; no storms nor tempests can beat them off; if Saul oppose David, yet Jonathan will stick to him. (*T. Hall, B.D.*)    **Only Luke is with me.**—*The beloved physician :*—I. THE INDUCEMENTS TO REMAIN WITH ST. PAUL. 1. There was the power of friendship. From the earlier references to Demas, we may conclude that he had been associated with the apostle in companionship in trial and labour. Intimacy and affection were motives to stay with him. 2. There was the sense of chivalry. However Demas might be tempted to go, a noble spirit would have said, Not now, when it is a time of comparative loneliness, need, and danger. 3. Interest in the faith. From his former relationship with St. Paul we must assume knowledge and admiration for the faith. He had seen Christianity, accepted it, and had been privileged to witness its power in the personal piety and devotedness of St. Paul. II. THE TEMPTATIONS TO GO. 1. The world's temptation of Demas was probably not through her seductive glitter of pleasure and pomp, but through her frowns. The apostle was under a cloud. Few seem willing to take him by the hand. Notice how joyously he recognises the courageous kindness of Onesiphorus (chap. i. 16, 17). 2. Perhaps we may hazard a conjecture respecting the character of Demas. May he not have been one of those whose religious life is just strong enough, or rather weak enough, to live in a religious atmosphere, but utterly unable to live when unsupported by Christian society? 3. The way in which such a character would desert. Not openly, but by degrees. Excuses to omit dangerous duties, and even at the last perhaps only leave St. Paul on some plausible pretext to go to Thessalonica. The old apostle saw through it: "Having loved this present world." III. THE CONTRASTED CONDUCT OF ST. LUKE. 1. While Demas at Thessalonica, St. Luke at Rome. His helpfulness to St. Paul. The knowledge of the physician, with its frequently induced sympathetic power and insight. The spiritual refreshment of a brotherly heart. Demas lives the life of him who seeks to save life, but loses it in all its nobility and opportunities of doing kindness. Luke is ready to lose life, but saves its true vitality. 2. For the retrospect of Christendom tells us that St. Luke in his devotedness has saved his life, while Demas has lost it. The latter is a beacon-warning; the former a guiding light, a name in the Church—loved where Christ is loved, honoured where the apostle is honoured, for constancy, kindliness, and intrepid faith. Learn therefore that—1. Chivalry is not strong enough against the world-spirit. 2. A religion which is only dependent on the personal influence of others will prove faulty in the time of trial. 3. Thus only the inner strength supplied by Christ can keep us strong; not Paul, not Apollos, not the wisdom of men, but Christ. For the difference between St. Luke and Demas was not in outward circumstances. They were equally tried. It is Christ in us which is the hope of glory, a glory the earnest of which is seen in the scorn of earth and the triumph of faith over her frown or her smile. (*W. B. Carpenter, M.A.*)    *St. Luke the Evangelist :*—We know but very little, historically, of St. Luke. His birthplace appears to have been Antioch, the metropolis of Syria, and, from his profession as a physician, we conclude him to have been, as indeed his writings prove him, a man of liberal education. Antioch was distinguished as the seat of literature; and St. Luke had probably availed himself of the advantages presented by his native place. We have no information in regard to the calling and conversion of St. Luke, and of his becoming a physician of the soul as well as the body. Many suppose him to have been converted by St. Paul at Antioch, and so to have had no acquaintance with Christianity until after the death of its Founder. Others again maintain that Luke was one of the seventy disciples whom Jesus sent forth to publish the gospel. However this may have been, it is in connection with St. Paul that St. Luke is first mentioned in the New Testament. From

Acts xvi. to xxviii. we learn that he accompanied St. Paul in many of his labours and journeyings, and was with him at Rome during his two years' imprisonment. We are wholly without authentic information as to the after life of St. Luke. Various spheres of labour are assigned to him by various writers, and much obscurity rests on the time, place, and manner of his death. The most ancient authors, however, say nothing of his martyrdom; and this would seem to show that he died a natural death; though others, indeed, allege that he went out of life stretched on an olive tree. But whilst so little material is furnished by the biographers of St. Luke, we are in possession of his writings, and by these " he, being dead, yet speaketh." There has never been debate in the Church that the Gospel which bears his name, and the Acts of the Apostles, were written by St. Luke. These were his legacies to all after ages, and for these must he be held in honour so long as there is any love for the gospel. And with these writings in our hands, who that has any sense of the worth of revelation will hesitate to describe St. Luke as " a brother whose praise is in the gospel throughout all the churches "? Or who, like St. Paul, if he had no other companion, would not feel that, in having this evangelist, he had books on which to draw that he could never exhaust, and which would continually furnish him with spiritual information, so that he could never be in loneliness, never at a loss for guidance and instruction, even though he should have to say with the apostle in our text—" Only Luke is with me." And what we venture to assert is, that the history which he has produced outweighs, in value to ourselves, either of the other three which the New Testament contains. We venture to affirm that, if only one Gospel is to be preserved, that that Gospel should be the Gospel according to St. Luke. The debate must lie between the Gospels of St. Luke and St. Matthew; for neither in the Gospel of St. Mark, nor in that of St. John is any account given of the parentage and birth of Jesus Christ; so that, with no other document in our hands, we should be uninformed upon facts which lay at the very root and foundation of Christianity. We should have no proof of the fulfilment of prophecies declaratory that Christ should be born of a virgin, without taint of original sin; and we could therefore make no way in building up the fabric of our most holy faith. You will admit, then, that if only one Gospel be retained, it must be that of St. Matthew or St. Luke, inasmuch as these contain what is wanting in the others, the account of Christ's miraculous nativity, and this account is indispensable to our knowledge of redemption; but if we are to choose between the Gospels of St. Matthew and St. Luke, the far fuller manner in which St. Luke gives the circumstances of the birth of our Saviour might of itself determine upon which to decide for the history. And when you add to this that St. Luke is the evangelist who has preserved for us the parables and incidents most adapted to our case, and most comforting to our feelings, and that from his writings we draw a prayer which is the very epitome of petitions, " God be merciful to me, a sinner "; that it is he who draws for us that most affecting of pictures, the picture of the father's rushing to meet the prodigal son whilst yet a great way off, folding him in his arms, and giving him his embrace; that in the pages, moreover, of this evangelist it is that we behold the good Samaritan pouring oil and wine into the wounds of the sufferers; that we are warned by the sudden summons to the rich fool, who, within a hair's breadth of death, talked of building larger barns; by the torments of Dives, who exchanged the luxuries of a palace for the plagues of hell; that we are comforted by Christ's gracious words to the thief on the cross;—ay, if it be thus true that we turn to the Gospel of St. Luke for whatever is most exquisitely tender, most persuasive, most encouraging, most startling in the registered actions and sayings of the Saviour, then it is not to be doubted that our chief debt of gratitude is due to this evangelist; that if we had lost all the others—Crescens unto Galatia, Titus unto Dalmatia, Matthew, Mark, and John having departed from this present world—it might still be with the tone of those who felt they had kept the one from whom most might be learned, that we took up the language of our text and exclaimed with St. Paul, " Only Luke is with me." We now turn to look at the Acts of the Apostles, a work which stands quite by itself, and whose worth, therefore, cannot be measured by comparing it with others. If we had not this book we should have no inspired record whatever of the actions and sayings of the first preachers of Christianity, and consequently its value must be estimated by the injury which would be occasioned by the total want of such a record. The removal of the Acts from the New Testament would be altogether a different thing from the removal of one of the Gospels; in the latter case the deficiency would be at least partially supplied by the remaining writings, whereas in the former there would be left no document to which we could refer. The book of the Acts is to the Holy Spirit what the Gospels are to the Saviour—a record of His entering on His office, and fulfilling His great work in the scheme of human redemption. And can we dispense with one record any more than with the other? Is it not indispensable to the completeness of the evidences of Christianity—the showing how each Person in the ever-blessed Trinity has interposed on our behalf—that we should be able to point to apostles and to apostolic men, receiving supernatural gifts, and going forth with a more than human strength to a warfare with principalities and powers? It is one thing to prove a work valuable, and another to show that its loss would be fatal. It is this that we endeavour to do, by exhibiting the Acts as the Gospel of the Holy Ghost, and as the record of transactions which involve the interest and the permanence of the whole Gentile Church. And when we have shown you that without this book you would be left ignorant of the coming of the Comforter; that you would know nothing of the manifestations by which the seal of Divinity was finally set on Christianity—yea, be unacquainted with redemption as the joint work of the three Persons in the Godhead; and when we have further shown you that, take away this book, and you take away all the register of God's ordering the removal of the middle wall of partition, so that the Gentiles might be received without submitting themselves to the institutions of Moses, and we think we have shown enough to convince you that you owe St. Luke, at least, as much for his Acts of the Apostles as for his Gospel; and, therefore, we again say—Crescens might have departed to Galatia, Titus to Dalmatia, and you might be left alone in a prison, almost without associates, almost without books; but could you be lonely? could you be forced to speak as if deprived of high companionship and intercourse with those in whom a Christian has the deepest interest, and access to the best stores of comfort and of knowledge, if you could say of yourself, as St. Paul says in our text—"Only Luke is with me"? (*H. Melvill, B.D.*)          *St. Luke an example of true friendship :*—Most of that which goes by the name of friendship is as rootless as an aquatic plant that turns its broad leaves and flowers to the summer's sun. Men desecrate the holy name of friendship by applying it to alliances, conferences, and leagues. But true friendship is one of the sweetest and best of earthly things, if, indeed, it can be called earthly. Friendship is the best developed fruit of love. It is the escape for the pent-up soul. Friends can do for each other what modesty forbids them to do for themselves. They can keep down each other's vanity, and keep up each other's courage. Friendship has the physician's skill, the nurse's vigilance, the mother's devotion. How may we procure this blessed boon? Friendship cannot be created by the jugglery of oaths and grasped hands. True friendship ought to be grounded in the love of God; it ought to be well chosen, cemented by nature and religion, developed by time, tested by adversity, consecrated by associations. Let such friendship be held at high value. Let no trivial thing imperil it. Let it be cherished by confidence unstinted, by demonstrations of affection, by sincerity and truth, by faith and trust, by mutual forbearance and sacrifice. Such friendship will be an oasis in the arid waste of selfishness, and it will be an anticipation for the life to come. (*R. S. Barrett.*)          *The friendship of St. Luke and St. Paul :*—That St. Paul should be drawn to St. Luke is no wonder, for there must have been great similarity in their tastes, both being men of highly cultivated minds; but that St. Luke should throw in his lot with St. Paul, the homeless, persecuted man, who was an outcast from his own people, and who went in constant danger of his life—this betokens a strength of mind such as is met with but rarely, and a friendship of no ordinary kind. And we can hardly guess at the value to St. Paul of the friendship of such a man as St. Luke, even if we take it on the low standard of the value of services which he would be able to render to the Apostle. Being an educated man, he would be able to assist in many ways; for instance, as his amanuensis, and as being more competent than others to deal with the more cultivated heathen with whom they were brought in contact. But all this would be as nothing compared with the common bond which would knit their souls together, their love for their risen Lord. The world can show us friendship, and that, too, of a high order; it has done so in past history; it can do so, no doubt. even now. Similarity of tastes, the pursuit of a common object, the necessities of daily life, may draw men very closely together, and make them friends in the sense in which the world uses the term. But there is a deeper sense than that; for Christianity has done the same for friendship as it has for whatever else it has touched—it has raised and it has sanctified it. St. Paul and St. Luke were not only friends, but each had a common friend in the Lord Jesus. In Christ Jesus they were knit together by a bond stronger than any which the world could forge, and the secret of St. Luke's devotion to St. Paul was not only community of taste and feeling, but the love of God which was shed abroad in their hearts through Jesus Christ their common Lord and Master. We often hear people speak of others as their friends, or of themselves as being the friends of others; but it would be well if we thought a little more about what a friend might, or what a friend ought to be, before we allowed ourselves to use the word. How can there be true friendship between the Christian and the man of the world? How can there be true friendship between those whose deepest and purest feelings are not in accord? (*W. G. Abbott, M.A.*)　　*Luke, the beloved physician:*—To account for his being alone with Paul at that solemn and trying time we do not need to charge unfaithfulness upon all who had been Paul's companions during his confinement in Rome. Did Paul keep Luke there, perhaps, because he needed his professional care in his old age, after so many toils and hardships and exposures by land and by sea? Did Luke refuse to leave him because his watchful eye saw that Paul needed his professional care more than Paul knew or would willingly acknowledge? Had he the tact to conceal this professional solicitude under the equally true desire to enjoy Paul's company and instruction, and to fill his own mind and memorandum-book with those memories which the Holy Spirit was moving him to write to "most excellent Theophilus" and to us? If I might not be a minister of the gospel, a pastor taking care of souls, I know not what else I would rather be than a physician, skilled to minister at bedsides and in chambers of the sick, worthy to be looked to by anxious households when the chill shadow of death makes them shudder, worthy to be trusted as a sentry by a community when the "pestilence walketh in darkness." The highest skill in medicine is not all that such a trusted and beloved physician must have; or, rather, skill in a physician includes much more than knowledge of anatomy and physiology and the materia medica. It includes high acquaintance with the human soul in its peculiar powers and in their relations to the body. It involves not merely knowledge of the body, as a thing which it has dissected, a machine whose parts it has taken asunder and handled. It involves reverence for that body as the supreme handiwork of Jehovah, whose infinite skill and care are illustrated in all its joints and members, all its parts and organs, all its processes and powers. It involves tender appreciation of all the liabilities and capabilities of such a soul in such a body. It involves genuine sympathy with sufferers, suffusing and beautifying, not enfeebling nor hindering the business of relieving, making it not less effective and successful business because clothed upon with graces which present it ever as intercourse, conversation, fellowship. (*H. A. Nelson, D.D.*)　　*A faithful friend:*—A faithful friend will not forsake us in our deepest distress. A faithful friend—and such a one was Luke—loves at all times (Prov. xvii. 17). Though Paul be a prisoner and ready to be martyred, yet Luke keeps with him still; though all forsake him, yet he will stick to him. Pot-friendship will vanish, especially in adversity. Job (vi. 15) complains of his friends that they had deceived him like a brook; they were not like a river which is fed by a spring and hath a perennity of flowing, but like a brook which runs in moist times when there is least need of it, but in a drought it fails; like swallows which fly about us in summer, but in winter they leave us and hide themselves in hollow trees or the like. Such vermin abound which run to full barns, but outrun them when empty. Most worship the rising, few the setting sun. (*T. Hall, B.D.*) **Take Mark, and bring him with thee.**—*The quarrel about John Mark* (see Acts xv. 36-39):—I. THE SHARP QUARREL BETWEEN PAUL AND BARNABAS. They were both good men, both men of cultivated spirit and of fine Christian character, and yet they got into a violent passion about a matter that one would think might have been easily arranged if discussed forbearingly and wisely. The only wise thing about the whole matter was the separation. It is far better for Christian people who cannot work comfortably together to separate than to keep up an endless bickering, or a dull, sulky anger which only reveals the smouldering fire that sooner or later is sure to burst forth. 1. The most godly men are still liable to sharp and sudden falls. 2. Those who are engaged in the same work may have antagonistic views on matters of prudence. II. THE TWO DIFFERENT STAGES OF MARK'S LIFE. Sometimes a poor-looking material works out better than we expected. The unpromising youth often surprises us by very superior development in after years. Soldiers who have quailed before the first fire of their first battle have distinguished themselves as brave men in after years. There is really nothing more common than this contradiction of all early promises, both for good and bad, which daily life brings to us. Life and character have so many sharp turnings that you can never calculate what direction they shall ultimately take. This was the case with John Mark. In the former of these passages he is brought before us as a young man. The opinion Paul had of him then was a very contemptible one. He had set his hand to the plough, and looked back. Seventeen years after Paul is in prison at Rome, and writes thence this letter to Timothy. And in it comes this honourable and affectionate mention of the very man who seventeen years before he had held at so cheap a rate, "Take Mark, and bring him with thee, for he is profitable to me for the ministry." A bright midday to a very unpromising morning! We are constrained to suspect, after all, that, though Paul had prudence and justice on his side, on that former occasion, yet Barnabas had the finer intuition when he kept his faith in his nephew, notwithstanding his disgraceful delinquency. After-events certainly proved that the unpromising youth had in him the making of a strong man. How much of Mark's after strength was due, on the one hand, to the paternal faith and protection of Barnabas, and, on the other hand, to the tonic administered to him by Paul's contemptuous refusal, we cannot say. Probably both had a good effect. The scornful glance with which a brave man looks on a delinquent, by inflaming his self-respect, may, while it mortifies his soul, impel him to bolder things. And, on the other hand, to feel that though we have miserably failed, there is one heart that still believes in our capacity, and one hand that never loses its grasp of ours, is heaven's good angel to our life. Many a coward life has been made brave by that ministering angel. Many a one-time sinner has been made a saint by the faithfulness with which one hand has continued to hold his in confident love, and not seldom that hand has been the soft hand of a brave and trusting woman. Stick to the coward a little longer, and you may, by God's grace, make a brave man of him yet! Stick to the sinner a little longer, and you may yet write his name in the roll of the saints! (*E. H. Higgins.*) *Good men easily reconciled to good men :*—There was formerly a sharp contention between Paul and Barnabas about this Mark, who for fear forsook Paul and left him in Pamphilia (Acts xiii. 13, xv. 37–39), which made Paul that he would not suffer him to visit the brethren. Superiors in gifts and grace may sometimes have need of the help of inferiors. A Paul may send for a Mark to help him. (*T. Hall, B.D.*)

Ver 13. **The cloke . . . the books . . . the parchments.**—*Paul—his cloak and his books:*—I. Let us LOOK AT THIS MEMORABLE CLOAK which Paul left with Carpus at Troas. Troas was a principal seaport-town of Asia Minor. Very likely the apostle Paul was seized at Troas on the second occasion of his being taken before the Roman emperor. The soldiers usually appropriated to themselves any extra garment in the possession of an arrested person, such things being considered as the perquisites of those who made the arrest. The apostle may have been forewarned of his seizure, and therefore prudently committed his few books and his outer garment, which made up all his household stuff, to the care of a certain honest man named Carpus. Although Troas was full six hundred miles' journey from Rome, yet the apostle Paul is too poor to purchase a garment, and so directs Timothy, as he is coming that way, to bring his cloak. He needs it much, for the sharp winter is coming on, and the dungeon is very, very chilly. 1. Let us perceive here with admiration, the complete self-sacrifice of the apostle Paul for the Lord's sake. Remember what the apostle once was. He was great, famous, and wealthy. Ah! how he emptied himself, and to what extremity of destitution was he willing to bring himself for Christ's name sake. The Saviour must die in absolute nakedness, and the apostle is made something like Him as he sits shivering in the cold. 2. We learn how utterly forsaken the apostle was by his friends. If he had not a cloak of his own, could not some of them lend him one? No ; he is so utterly left, that although he is ready to die of ague in the dungeon, not a soul will lend or give him a cloak. What patience does this teach to those similarly situated! In your greatest trials do you find your fewest friends? Have those who once loved and respected you fallen asleep in Jesus? And have others turned out to be hypocritical and untrue? "Notwithstanding the Lord stood with me, and strengthened me." So now, when man deserts you, God will be your Friend. 3. Our text shows the apostle's independence of mind. Why did not he borrow a cloak? Why did not he beg one? That is not the apostle's taste at all. He has a cloak, and though it is six hundred miles away, he will wait until it comes. A Christian man would do well to remember that it is never to his honour, though it is not always to his dishonour, to beg. 4. We see here, how very little the apostles thought of how they were dressed. Paul wants enough to keep him warm; he asks no more. When good Bishop Hooper was led out to be burnt, he had been long in prison, and his clothes were so gone from him, that he borrowed an old scholar's gown, full of rags and holes, that he might put it on, and went limping with pains of sciatica and rheumatism to the stake. We read of Jerome of Prague, that he lay in a damp, cold dungeon, and was refused anything to cover him in his nakedness and cold. Every saint is an image of Christ, but a poor saint is His express image, for Christ was poor. So, if you are brought to such a pitch with regard to poverty, that you scarcely know how to provide things decent by way of raiment, do not be dispirited; but say, "My Master suffered the same, and so did the apostle Paul"; and so take heart, and be of good cheer. 5. Paul's cloak at Troas shows me how mighty the apostle was to resist temptation. "I do not see that," you say. The apostle had the gift of miracles. Our Saviour, though able to work miracles, never wrought anything like a miracle on His own account; nor did His apostles. Miraculous gifts were entrusted to them with gospel ends and purposes, for the good of others, and for the promotion of the truth; but never for themselves. II. We will LOOK AT HIS BOOKS. We do not know what the books were about, and we can only form some guess as to what the parchments were. Paul had a few books which were left, perhaps wrapped up in the cloak, and Timothy was to be careful to bring them. 1. Even an apostle must read. He is inspired, and yet he wants books! He has been preaching at least for thirty years, and yet he wants books! He had seen the Lord, and yet he wants books! He had had a wider experience than most men, and yet he wants books! He had been caught up into the third heaven, and had heard things which it was unlawful for a man to utter, yet he wants books! He had written the major part of the New Testament, and yet he wants books! The apostle says to Timothy, and so he says to every preacher, "Give thyself unto reading." The man who never reads will never be read; he who never quotes will never be quoted. He who will not use the thoughts of other men's brains proves that he has no brains of his own. 2. Paul herein is a picture of industry. He is in prison; he cannot preach: what will he do? As he cannot preach, he will read. As we read of the fishermen of old and their boats. The fishermen were gone out of them. What were they doing? Mending their nets. So if Providence has laid you upon a sick bed, and you cannot teach your class—if you cannot be working for God in public, mend your nets by reading. If one occupation is taken from you, take another, and let the books of the apostle read you a lesson of industry. III. We now want to have AN INTERVIEW WITH THE APOSTLE PAUL HIMSELF, for we may learn much from him. The poor old man, without his cloak, wraps his ragged garment about him. Sometimes you see him kneeling down to pray, and then he dips his pen into the ink, and writes to his dear son Timothy. No companion, except Luke, who occasionally comes in for a short time. Now, how shall we find the old man? What sort of temper will he be in? 1. We find him full of confidence in the religion which has cost him so much. 2. But he is not only confident. You will notice that this grand old man is having communion with Jesus Christ in his sufferings. 3. Triumphant. 4. In expectation of a crown. (*C. H. Spurgeon.*) *The cloak at Troas:*—Doubtless the cloak was an old companion; it may have been wetted many a time with the water torrents of Pamphylia, and whitened with the dust of the long Roman roads, and stained with the brine of shipwreck, when, on the rocky cliffs of Malta, the Euroclydon was driving the waters into foam; he may have slept in its warm shelter on the uplands under the canopy of the stars; it may have covered his trembling limbs, bruised with the brutal rods of the lictors, as he lay that night in the dungeon of Philippi; and now the old man thinks, as he calls himself, with a passing touch of self-pity, an ambassador in chains, and as he sits shivering in some gloomy cell under the walls, or, it may be, on the rocky floor of the Palladio, in the wintry nights that are coming on, he bethinks him of the old cloak, and asks Timothy to bring it with him. "The cloke that I left at Troas with Carpus, when thou comest bring with thee, and the books, but especially the parchments"—the Biblia and the papyrus books, few we may be sure and yet old friends. Perhaps he had bought some of those very books in the school of Gamaliel at Jerusalem, or had received some of them as presents from his wealthier converts. Perhaps among them may have been some of those books in which, as we can trace from his Epistles, he had read the poems of his native poet, Aratus. or some of the pamphlets of Plato, or the wisdom of Solomon. The papyrus books, then, "but especially the parchments," that is, especially the works inscribed on vellum—what were these? Was there any document amongst them which would have been useful to prove his rights as a Roman citizen? Were there any precious rolls of Isaiah and the Psalms, or the lesser prophets, which father or mother may have given him as a life-long treasure (for in those days parchments were valuable things)in the far-off days when, little dreaming of all that awaited him, he played as a happy boy in the dear old Tarsian home? Dreary and long are the days; longer and drearier still are the evenings in that Roman dungeon, and often the rude legionary soldier, who detests to be chained to a sick and suffering Jew, is coarse and cruel to him. And he cannot always be engaged in the sweet session of silent thought, even in the sweet hopes of the future or the remembrance of the past. He knows Scripture well, but it will be a deep joy to read once more how David and Isaiah, in all their troubles, learned, like his own poor self, to suffer and be strong. Who, as he reads this last message, can help remembering the touching letter written from the damp cells of his prison by our own noble martyr, William Tyndale, one of the greatest of our translators of the English Bible: "I entreat your lordship," he writes, "and that by the Lord Jesus, that, if I was to remain here for the winter, you would beg the Commissary to be so kind as to send me, from the things of mine which he has, a warmer cap; I feel the cold painfully in my head; also a warmer cloke, for the one I have is very thin; also some cloth to patch my leggings. My overcoat is worn out, my shirts even are threadbare. The Commissary has a woollen shirt of mine if he will be so kind as to send it. But most of all I entreat your kindness to do your best with the Commissary to be so good as to send me my Hebrew Bible, grammar, and vocabulary, that I may spend my time in that pursuit.—William Tyndale." The noble martyr was not thinking of St. Paul; but history repeats itself, and what is this fragment from the letter which he, too, wrote so soon before his death, but the same thing as "the cloke which I left at Troas with Carpus, bring with thee, and the books, but especially the parchments"? I. Does it not show us that this great and holy apostle was first a man like ourselves; a tried and suffering man with human wants and human sympathies; aye, and human limitations, and with transcendentally severer trials, yet with no greater privileges than we enjoy? Does he not call to us with more clear encouragement, "Faint not, dear brother, dear sister in the Lord; I, too, was weak; I, too, was tempted; but thou, no less than I, canst do all things through Christ which strengtheneth us"? II. Then, in what a lovely light of manliness, good sense, and contentment does this place the apostle's character! The sword, he well knows, is hanging over his head whose flash shall slay him, but life is life. Until the Lord calls him, there is no reason at all why life should not go on, not only in its quiet duties, but also with such small blessings as it yet may bring. There is no flaring fanaticism, no exaggerated self-denial, here. The wintry nights will be cold and dull; there is no sort of merit in making them colder and duller. That is why he writes for the cloak and the dear old books. God, for our good, sends us all trials enough to bear, but it is only for our good. There is not the least reason—it is not even right—to create tortures and miseries for ourselves which God has not sent us. We are allowed to take and we ought to take every harmless and every innocent gift which God permits to us, and to thank Him for it. III. Then, look at the matter in one more light. What is it that a life of ceaseless ungrudging labour has left to St. Paul? What earthly possessions has the apostle gained as the sum total of services to the world, unparalleled in intensity and unparalleled in self-denial? Perhaps he wants to leave some small memento behind him, some trifling legacy by which some true heart may remember him "ere the rippled sea of life flows smooth once more over his nameless grave." Just as the hermit St. Antony left the great bishop St. Athanasius his one sole possession, which was his sheep-skin cloak, so St. Paul, perhaps, might have liked to leave to the kind and faithful Luke, or to the true and gentle Timothy, the cloak, the books, the parchments. But, oh, how small a result of earth's labours, if earth were everything, worth far less than a dancer gets for a single figure in a theatre, or an acrobat for a fling on the trapeze; not worth one-millionth part of what a patent brings in for some infinitesimal invention! Oh, the work and the reward are not the same for eternity. It is not for such rewards that the great high service of the world is done. Earth's rewards, observe, have marvellously small relations to intrinsic values. The singer who has a fine note in her voice may blaze in diamonds worth a king's ransom. But the thinker who has raised the aim and nature of nations may die unnoticed; and the poet, who has enriched the blood of the earth, may be left to starve. Paul pours out his whole life as a libation on God's altar, in agonies for his fellow-men; he cleanses the customs, he brightens the hope, he purifies the life of men; he adds, for centuries, to the untold ennoblement of generations; what is the sum total of his earthly reward? What is the inventory of all his earthly possessions as he sits upon his prison floor? Just "the cloke that I left at Troas, and the books, but especially the parchments." Would that content you? Do you think that he sighed or was envious of evildoers, when he contrasted his sole possessions—that cloak and those few books, which were all that he had—with the jewels of the adventurer.Agrippa, or the purple of the execrable Nero? Not one whit. They were not what he had aimed at. He sat loose to those earthly interests on which men's minds are sometimes to the last so deplorably and so hideously fixed. No; better as it is. He will thank God for such warmth as he may find in the cloak and such consolation as the books may bring him, and, for the rest, he will trust death, and he will throw himself on God. (*Archdeacon Farrar.*) *Note-books* of his own making or collecting: these are highly prized by students. Julius Cæsar, being forced to swim for his life, held his commentaries in one hand above water, and swam to land with the other. (*J. Trapp.*) *A great love of books :*—An incident of my own experience has often interested me, and may not be without interest to you. I learnt one evening in London—it was at an evening party at which many persons were assembled—from a friend of mine that a friend of his and mine was lying dangerously, and, as it turned out, fatally ill in his chambers in the Temple. That friend of mine was the late Sir David Dundas, who was for many years in Parliament, and with whose friendship for many years I was favoured. I went down the next morning to ask after him, and, if it were proper, to see him. He invited me, through his servant, into his room, and I found him upon his bed of sickness, feeble, not able to talk much, and scarcely able to turn himself in his bed. We had some little conversation, and in the course of it he offered to me something like a benediction. He said—I remember his words very well—"I have never pretended to be a learned man or a scholar, but God has given me a great love for books." He then referred to the writings of the celebrated Lord Bacon, and taking a quotation from a letter which that eminent person had written to a friend, he turned to me and said, "May God lead you by the hand." That was one of the passages fixed in his mind from his reading of the words of Lord Bacon. Now, that was a solemn hour with my friend—if I may quote a very expressive and beautiful line from one of Scotland's real, but one of her minor poets, Michael Bruce—"When dim in his breast life's dying taper burns." At that solemn hour, reviewing his past life, reviewing the enjoyment he had partaken of, he thanked God for having given him "a great love of books." Two days after that—I think the second or third after that interview—that "dying taper" was extinguished, and my friend passed into the unseen world. (*John Bright.*) *A good book a lasting companion :*—Truths which it has taken years to glean are therein at once freely but carefully communicated. We enjoy communion with the mind, though not with the person of the writer. Thus the humblest man may surround himself by the wisest and best spirits of past and present ages. No one can be solitary who possesses a book; he owns a friend that will instruct him in moments of leisure or of necessity. It is only necessary to turn over the leaves, and the fountain at once gives forth its streams. You may seek costly furniture for your homes, fanciful ornaments for your mantelpieces, and rich carpets for your floors; but, after the absolute necessaries for a home. give me books as at once the cheapest, and certainly the most useful and abiding embellishments. (*Family Friend.*) *Choice of books :*—What books you will choose as your intimate friends will depend upon your humour and taste. Dr. Guthrie's choice seemed to me charming. He told me that he read through four books every year—the Bible, "The Pilgrim's Progress," four of Sir Walter Scott's novels, which he reckoned as one book, and a fourth book, which I have forgotten, but I think it was "Robinson Crusoe." You will choose some books because they soothe and quiet you; some because they are as invigorating as mountain air; some because they amuse you by the shrewdness of their humour; some because they give wings to your fancy; some because they kindle your imagination. (*R. W. Dale.*) *Mental occupation in prison :*—Exile and imprisonment are among the darkest tragedies of existence. But Ovid, banished from the luxurious and learned capital to the barbarians of Tomis, in the inhospitable waste along the Euxine, stripped of property, wife, and children, saved himself from despair by labour, and, surrounded by hopeless savagery, produced some of the finest of his works. Boethius, the last and noblest of the ancients, before the darkness of the Middle Ages fell on Europe, lying under unjust sentence of death in the tower of Pavia, forbidden books, intercourse with fellow-scholars, preserved his sanity and fortitude to face a cruel death by writing " The Consolation of Philosophy." " Don Quixote," which convulsed a nation with merriment, was the solace of an undeserved imprisonment, which bodily suffering made more unendurable. The dungeon of Walter Raleigh was his calm study. In the condemned cell Madame Roland, less moved by the certainty of her own fate than by apprehension for her beloved husband, fortified her mind against possible madness by the composition of her memoirs. Lady Jane Grey and Mary Queen of Scots beguiled imprisonment of half its terrors with hard study and careful writing. (*Harper's Bazaar.*)	*An affection for a cloak :*—Newman tells us (in 1840) how he kept an old blue cloak which he got in 1823, and "had an affection for it," because it had " nursed me through all my illness. I have it still. I have brought it up here to Littlemore, and on some cold nights I have had it on my bed. I have so few things to sympathise with me that I take to cloaks."	*An endeared garment :*—A shawl with a strange history was buried with the late Professor Cocker, of Michigan University. Shortly before his death, Dr. Cocker called the attention of his pastor to a worn and faded shawl spread on his bed, and requested to have it wrapped around his body and buried with him. He had made it himself when a young man in England; had worn it in all his journeyings to and from over the Atlantic and Pacific Oceans, when residing in Australia, when he escaped from the Fiji Islanders as they were preparing to kill and roast him, and when he was shipwrecked. It accompanied him when he landed in the United States, and even clad the remains of his dead child when, penniless and disheartened, he first arrived in Adrian. It is not surprising that a garment with such associations had, though worn and faded, become precious to him, and his desire that his body should be enshrouded in it is easily understood.	*Use of a cloak :*—John Welch, the old Scotch minister, used to put a plaid across his bed on cold nights, and some one asked him why he put that there. He said : "Oh, sometimes in the night I want to sing the praises of Jesus, and I get down and pray. Then I just take that plaid and wrap it around me to keep myself from the cold."	*Cloak, books, and parchments :*—Winter was coming on, and his somewhat emaciated frame was less able than formerly to withstand the cold. He remembers that when he was last at Troas, he left his heavy overcoat there, in charge of his friend Carpus, probably because he preferred to take a portion of his journey on foot. He will be sure to need it as the weather becomes more severe, so he requests Timothy, who is now at Ephesus, to bring it with him when he comes west to Italy.	I. TAKE CARE OF YOUR BODILY HEALTH. Young men are often particularly neglectful on this matter. Many is the man whose constitution has been undermined for life by his own carelessness as a youth in respect of food, rest, and clothing.	II. MAINTAIN THE CULTURE OF YOUR MIND. Do not be so engrossed with business, that you rarely open an instructive book. Do not forget that your intellect wants to be stimulated and fed, as it cannot be if you think of nothing but bills, and accounts, and orders, and invoices, and what is vulgarly and expressively called " shop." A sailor, who had circumnavigated the globe with Captain Cook, was pressed by his friends to give them some account of the wonders he had seen, and at last consented to do so on a certain evening. A large and eager company assembled, in expectation of a great intellectual treat ; when the rough mariner thus began and ended his description of his travels : " I have been round the world with Captain Cook, and all that I saw was the sky above me and the water beneath me." And, truth to tell, there are young men who show little more discernment than that blunt sailor. They have no intellectual ambition, no thirst for knowledge, no passionate desire for self-improvement. If business is going on well, and their salary is regularly paid, and they have enough to eat and drink, they are content. There is no systematic study; no training of the mind, no whetting or sharpening of the intellectual faculties. I warn you, young men, against so ignoble a use of what is, in some respects, the best part of life. Lord Bacon's opinion upon books he thus expressed: " That histories make men wise ; poets, witty ; mathematics, subtle ; natural science, deep ; moral philosophy, grave ; logic and rhetoric, able to debate." As you would possess such qualities, then, your reading must be catholic and extensive.	III. ESPECIALLY SEE TO THE WELFARE OF THE SOUL. However limited be your reading, see that the Bible has its rightful place. It is said that in the British Museum alone there are so many books that the mere mechanical reading of them would demand a thousand years. So you cannot read everything—you must make your selection; but oh! let this peerless volume reign supreme in your library.   Let it be the monarch of your bookshelves.   There is an old Latin proverb, which is good enough so long as the Bible is out of account, *" Cave ab homine unius libri "*—i.e., " Beware of a man of one book."   But when that one book is the Book of God, the counsel may be inverted; for there is no man more to be sought after than the man who daily feeds from this table, and drinks from this well.   " Especially the parchments."   Let no general reading, however excellent and instructive, elbow this to one side.   Be diligent students of God's Word, "and," as Dr. Doddridge said, " you shall be excellent scholars ten thousand years hence "; whereas, however proficient in secular knowledge, if the Bible be neglected, you shall be unfitted for the occupations of the redeemed in heaven.   You have a richer Bible than ever Paul possessed.   Those clumsy, greasy " parchments," written by laborious scribes, would form a strange contrast to such triumphs of modern skill as are now sent out in millions from the great repository in Queen Victoria Street; and you can place in your waistcoat-pocket treasures of inspiration, which in the apostle's time would have taxed the strength of a man to carry.   The greater, then, your responsibility.   Oh, make good use of your Bibles!   Above all, accept without delay the Divine salvation revealed.   (*J. T. Davidson, D.D.*)   *The cloak and the parchments; or, man's needs :*—We have here—1. A striking illustration of the manner of Divine inspiration.   The divinest communications of truth appear in connection with things of personal and secular concern.   2. A beautiful display of spiritual self-possession.   3. An affecting utterance of human needs.   With all his present principles, past achievements, and future destiny, he has yet necessities as well as resources.   Spirituality did not destroy his physical sensibilities; heroic courage and independence did not deaden his social affections; supernatural illumination did not make him depreciate the ordinary means of information and excitement.   I. PHYSICAL.   " The cloak."   Paul needed a garment, and wished for one.   To slight the body is a mark of heretics; to destroy it is to be a murderer.   What a world of need is caused by its possession!   What urgent demands does it make on care and effort, skill and labour!   But the thought here is, that the body is a source of trouble, inconvenience, dependence;—that small things may lead to its discomfort and injury.   Let but the ordinary laws of nature be broken; let but the ordinary operations of life be suspended; let there be but a little accident, a slight mistake, a temporary forgetfulness; and how bitterly are we made to feel the pressure and responsibility of our material charge!   We cannot afford to trifle with or ignore it.   The most spiritual and independent must remember the mislaid or forgotten dress.   II. THE SOCIAL.   " When thou comest."   " Do thy diligence to come shortly unto me."   Man is a social being—made to feel for and with his fellow-men.   He is revealed, regaled, renewed by fellowship.   It is a lamp, a feast, a buttress of his being.   It is everything whereby he can be ministered unto, or help to minister.   Fellowship in woe, in joy, in work, in thought, is a rich delight, and in most cases a great necessity.   III. THE SPIRITUAL.   " The books, especially the parchments."   We know not what these were, but are sure they were books tending to cultivation of mind and heart.   What a field of thought is opened up by these words!   See the ministry of minds; see their working and results preserved and propagated by the use of letters; see the labours and rewards of some made the inheritance of others; and all this beyond the sphere of personal presence and immediate influence see it done for men and ages unborn.   What a debt we owe to books!   What information and stimulus! what means of growth! what instruments of knowledge, joy, and power!   " Especially the parchments."   Some think these were a kind of commonplace book, in which the apostle put his own reflections and precious passages met with in his reading.   If so, we have an important thought.   That is most a man's own which he has originated, or thoroughly appropriated by meditation.   Books are nothing but as they are "read, marked, learned, and inwardly digested."   Lessons : 1. The subject teaches humility.   2. Gratitude.   3. Benevolence.   4. Self-interest.   (*A. J. Morris.*)   *The cloak at Troas :*—It appears to us that Paul's request for his cloak left at Troas affords an undesigned proof of a striking feature in his character—viz., that sobriety of mind which, on the one hand, never separates the things of earth from the things of heaven; nor, on the other hand, ever esteems spiritual-mindedness, and the ardent contemplation of unseen things, to be inconsistent with attention to the ordinary ongoings, the common duties, and little details of every-day life.   Paul was not further removed from the worldliness which never seeks to ascend in heart to heaven, than from the fanaticism and morbid pietism we sometimes witness, which only condescends to visit earth. The "light of life" which he enjoyed filled and blended into one common glory the things of earth and heaven, of time and of eternity! At one moment, for instance, we hear him exclaim (vers. 6–8). Yet, when his course was being finished, his death near, his reward sure, and while he sees the glories of heaven opening before his enraptured eye, it is even then that he expresses his anxiety to obtain his cloak from Troas. What evidence does this coincidence afford of calmness, peace, and sobriety of mind! Such we have some-times witnessed, too, in aged Christians of long experience, who, on their death-beds, could gaze upon the unseen world of everlasting rest, on which they were entering with perfect peace and full assured hope, while, at the same time, they attended with cheerful spirit to those common household duties and family arrangements from which, in person, they were soon to be for ever severed. (*Edinburgh Christian Magazine.*)

Ver. 14. **Alexander the coppersmith did me much evil.**—*Indignation an important quality in a true man:*—At a party at Dalkeith Palace, where Mr. —— in his mawkish way was finding palliations for some villainous transaction, Adam Smith waited in patient silence until he was gone, then exclaimed, "Now I can breathe more freely. I cannot bear that man; he has no indignation in him." (*W. H. Baxendale.*) *Of whom be thou ware:*—1. We must shun the society of incurable sinners. Whilst men are hopeful and curable we must try all means to win them. 2. Opposing of the truth is very grievous to a gracious soul. "For he hath greatly withstood our words." God's people are baptized with fire as well as with water, and must be hot and not lukewarm or indifferent in the things of God. 3. Wicked men do not so much oppose our persons as our preaching. They hate us not as men, but as ministers, because we publish the truth that condemns their wicked practices. (*T. Hall, B.D.*)

Vers. 16–18. **All men forsook me.**—*Paul, a Christian's example:*—I. PAUL FOR-SAKEN, AND YET FORGIVING THOSE WHO HAD WITHDRAWN FROM HIM. 1. The apostle was forsaken by his friends when most he needed them. 2. Paul's friends leaving him, made him the more helpless. 3. Paul's friends leaving him, discovered their frailty. 4. The apostle's forgiving spirit is particularly worthy of our notice. II. PAUL UPHELD, AND THEREFORE PREACHING. 1. Paul was upheld by Divine grace. 2. The Lord was present with His servant. 3. The Lord stood by the apostle that his kind of preaching might be fully known. 4. We who are Gentiles have heard the apostle's kind of preaching. III. PAUL DELIVERED, AND SO ACKNOWLEDGING. 1. This was a seasonable deliverance. 2. This was a great deliverance. 3. The Lord was the accomplisher of this deliverance. 4. Paul gratefully acknowledges his deliverance. IV. PAUL ENCOURAGED, AND THEREFORE GLORIFYING. 1. The apostle was encouraged to look for a glorious destination—heavenly kingdom—the kingdom of glory. 2. The apostle was encouraged to look for Divine preservation—shall deliver still. 3. The apostle was encouraged in his expectations by former deliverances (2 Cor. xi. 24–27; 31–33). 4. In the whole, Paul glorified the Lord. Conclusion: 1. To those who question us with regard to our hope, we should be able to give an answer. 2. We should exercise a forgiving spirit towards our brethren. 3. When we feel our own weakness, this should lead us to look to the Lord for assistance. 4. We should glorify God for all our deliverances. 5. We should remember that the Lord alone can save and preserve us. What will those do who forget this? (*John Miller.*) *The adversity of the good:*—I. THAT GREAT ADVERSITY FREQUENTLY BEFALLS THE BEST OF MEN. This shows—1. That neither adversity nor prosperity is any test of character. 2. That there must come a period of retribution. II. THAT GREAT ADVERSITY EXPOSES THE WEAKNESS OF OUR BEST FRIENDSHIPS. III. THAT GREAT ADVERSITY DEVELOPES THE MAGNANIMOUS IN THE HEART OF THE GOOD. "I pray God," &c. Like Stephen under shower of stones, and Christ on cross. IV. THAT GREAT ADVERSITY DEMONSTRATES EVER MORE THE FAITHFULNESS OF GOD. "Notwithstanding the Lord stood by me" (Job v. 19). (*Homilist.*) *Man's extremity is God's opportunity:*—1. All men forsook me, but the Lord stood by me. Hence, observe: that man's extremity is God's opportunity, or when man's help faileth then God appeareth, He then cometh in as an Auxiliary. The Lord only is immutable, He never faileth His at their need. God's people are never less alone than when they are most alone; never less forsaken than when they are forsaken of all. 2. Strengthening grace is the gift of God. "And strengthened me." He doth not only give us renewing grace and then leave us to our own free-will, but

He giveth us persevering grace also. As He is the Author of our grace by vocation, so He is the finisher of it by preservation. 3. Whilst God hath any work for His servants to do, He will assist and uphold them in spite of all oppositions. "That by me the preaching might be fully known." Though Nero rage against Paul, and all men forsake him, yet God will assist him that He may preach the gospel to the world. Our comfort is, that our times are not in our enemies' hands but in the hands of a gracious God. 4. God would have His truth revealed to the sons of men. "And that all the Gentiles might hear." He would have the gospel known —fully known—to the Gentiles. Truth is good, and the more common it is the better. Where it getteth ground, Satan's kingdom falleth like lightning from heaven suddenly and irresistibly (Luke x. 18). Let none then hide their talents, but as the sun freely communicateth its light and heat to us, so let us freely impart our gifts unto others. 5. The Church's enemies ofttimes are lions. "And I was delivered out of the mouth of the lion." Lions for potency, lions for policy (Psa. xvii. 12), lions for cruelty, lions for terror. Be serpents for policy, and not for poison, lions for prowess, and not for rapine. Be not familiar with these lions, come not near their dens lest they make a prey of you, have no fellowship with such unfruitful works of darkness but reprove them rather. 6. God many times suffers His dearest children to fall into the mouths of these lions, so that to a carnal eye they seem hopeless and helpless. 7. That God will deliver His from this great danger. He that brought thee into the mouth of the lion will bring thee out again (Dan. vi. 22). (T. Hall, B.D.) God's goodness in the greatest distresses:—I. PAUL'S EXPERIENCE of God's loving care for him in his past deliverances. 1. The enemies of the truth are oft for power, always for malice—lions. 2. God suffers His dearest children to fall into the mouths of lions. 3. In their extremities God delivers them—(1) By suspending the malice of their foes. (2) By raising up one lion against another. (3) By diverting them from their intended prey. (4) By changing their nature to lambs. (5) By showing Himself a lion. (6) By making them lions to themselves. (7) By making them friends, putting some conceit or fancy into their heart. (8) By making His own people lions to their adversaries. II. PAUL'S ASSURED HOPE, built upon his experience. 1. "The Lord shall deliver me from every evil work." God preserves from evil works by planting the graces of faith and fear in us. 2. "And will preserve me unto His heavenly kingdom." By Himself, and by inferior agencies. III. THE ISSUE OF BOTH HIS EXPERIENCE AND HIS HOPES. As they flow from God's grace, so he ascribes to Him the glory. We honour ourselves when we honour God; our praising God causes others to do so. (R. Sibbes, D.D.) Deliverance and salvation through death:—"Deliver us from evil, for thine is the Kingdom, the power and the glory, for ever. Amen." So our Lord taught us to pray. Is there not an echo of the prayer in these words of the prisoner? Surely it is not accident that so many of the keywords of the closing petitions of the Lord's Prayer recur here. And this burst of triumph is his very last word to his friend Timothy, with the exception of one or two closing personal salutations. That bird could sing in a darkened cage, and had the firmest and brightest hopes when all seemed darkest. I. Consider then, first, THE PRISONER'S CONFIDENCE. It is quite clear that he expected nothing but death. Only a few verses before he has said, "I am now in the very act of being offered, and the time of my departure is at hand." And yet, with death staring him in the face, and with nothing more clear to his anticipation than that his work was done, and that there only remained for him to wait for the crown, he breaks into this rapture of triumph, and says, "The Lord will deliver me from every evil work, and will preserve me," or, to take the pregnant expression of the text, "save me into His heavenly kingdom." May we not learn from this what the true meaning of deliverance from evil is; and what therefore is meant by the petition when it occurs in the pattern prayer? It is not exemption from trial, not escape from even the uttermost severity of it. Whosoever is able in the midst of all, to keep firm hold of his faith and, by his faith, of his Saviour, has received deliverance from the evil which pours all its vials of plagues upon his head. For the only thing that really does us harm is that which drags us away from God. "He shall deliver me from every evil work"; not because the sword will not fall upon my neck, but because, when it does, it will not part me from my Christ. "He shall deliver me from every evil work"; not because I shall not taste the full bitterness of the cup that is commended to my lips, but because in the very act of drinking the most nauseous potion I shall take it as a cup of salvation, and call upon the name of the Lord. That is deliverance. The same line of thought may be suggested in reference to the other clause of this expression of confidence, which teaches us to look at the last of the so-called evils. Paul expects to be " delivered *from* " and to be " saved *into*." The former phrase contemplates removal from the sphere of evil, the latter, the bringing safely into another sphere where evil is unknown, even that kingdom in the heavens over which Christ serenely held sovereign sway, while Nero afflicted the earth with a delirium of blood and lust. And what was the prose fact which presented itself to Paul's faith, thus radiantly clad in robes of triumph? Nothing else than that grim form of Death, feared and hated of men as the worst of all calamities, seems to him a deliverer and angel-messenger of salvation, who came " not to destroy men's lives, but to save them," not to drive them into the gloomy dominions of the grave, but to lead them safe into the heavenly kingdom of his Lord and theirs. For Christ's servants Death is the lackey who opens the doors of the presence-chamber of the King. The apostle employs in my text a different preposition to describe this ultimate deliverance from that which he does when he says, " I was delivered *out of* the mouth of the lion." In one case he represents the peril as though he was, as it were, dragged from between the teeth that threatened to devour him. In the other case the deliverance is more complete, and implies complete removal away from the sphere in which evil works. Taken together, the two prepositions in the two clauses, *from* and *into*, present the idea of change of place, or, as we may say, a migration from one realm and order of things to another. Thus the final saving is here regarded as a deliverance which lifts us out of the lower levels of the atmosphere, where evil, like some wild cyclone sweeps howling and destroying, and carries us into the quiet regions above, where loud winds never call, but " all the air a solemn stillness holds," though stagnation is as far away as tumult. II. A second consideration is suggested by these words— namely, THE GROUND OF THE PRISONER'S CONFIDENCE. The " and " at the beginning of the text is very probably spurious, but none the less is the confidence expressed in the text based upon the experience narrated in the preceding sentence. There Paul thankfully tells Timothy, " I was delivered out of the mouth of the lion." Therefore he is sure that the future will be like the past—" I was delivered " —" the Lord shall deliver." That experience, then, is the first ground of his confidence. God's " hitherto " has always wrapped up in it a " henceforth." All that He has been He will be. There are no tenses in His verbs. The past and the future are smelted down into one eternal and unchangeable present. But there is another ground of confidence on which I may touch for a moment. If I am at all correct in tracing any kind of connection between the words of my text and the Lord's Prayer, that very prayer is the basis of the confidence which is here expressed, and Paul is sure that God will deliver, and that he will come to Christ's heavenly kingdom because Jesus Christ taught him to pray, " Deliver me from evil." So he makes his prayer into a promise, and out of all these Christ-taught petitions he wins the assurance of Christ-given hopes. Happy they who so pray as that out of their prayers they can construct confidences! III. Lastly, note THE PRAISE THAT SPRINGS FROM THE CONFIDENCE. " Unto Him be glory for ever and ever. Amen." Paul's thankfulness arises from his anticipation, and not from the realisation, of deliverance. So completely did this man's faith make real to him at the moment the future deliverance that irrepressibly there bursts from his lips this great thanksgiving and doxology. If the anticipation led to such sweet music of praise, what would the reality do? Ought we not to entertain our yet unreceived blessings with as full a welcome and credence, and with as lively a gratitude, as speaks here? Should we not draw them to ourselves before they come, in the exercise of a hope based upon God's faithful promises which will open our lips to show forth His praise? We should note still further in this doxology the unconditional attribution of Divine honour to Jesus Christ. It is Jesus who is here called " the Lord," and while the word does not necessarily imply Christ's divinity, the ascriptions of praise here unhesitatingly laid at His feet can neither be explained nor justified, unless the speaker owned Him as Divine. Paul's Christ was not a Christ who had once done sweet and great things, and could do such no more, but a Christ working to-day for His servant. Note, too, that the ascription to Jesus of glory that shall shine through ages of ages is here connected with Paul's salvation. He did not think himself as of such exceptional importance that his salvation would bring more glory to Jesus Christ than that of others would do. Lowly self-oblivion and wondering gratitude, not arrogance, speak here. Precisely because he is so unworthy and weak does the apostle think that the power and love which would and could save him call for endless praise. The poorer the material the more the artist's glory. For ever and ever the praise of the glory of God's grace in

Christ will ring through the universe. (*A. Maclaren, D.D.*)  *Conserving grace :*—1. The experience of God's former deliverances must make us rest upon Him for future. 2. " From every evil work." Though God doth not save His people from suffering, yet He will save them from sin ; and though He leave in them infirmities, yet He will free them from enormities, and from total apostasy. 3. God is the preserver of His people. " And He will preserve me to His heavenly kingdom." But especially He keeps their souls in an holy frame till He bring them to glory. It is not sufficient that we light a lamp, but there must be a continual supply of oil, else the light will go out. So it is not sufficient that we have preventing, preparing, renewing grace, but we must also have subsequent, conserving, perfecting, persevering grace daily given in to preserve us from apostasy. We have always need of a Divine maintenancy till we have finished our course (Psa. lxxiii. 23). And this He will do in despite of all our enemies ; if anything destroy us it is sin, and for that we have God's hand here that He will deliver us from every evil work that might any way ruin us, and so preserve us till He have brought us to heaven. He keeps heaven for the saints, and the saints for heaven. 4. God's goodness to His people is wholly free. All His dispensations to His are free grace and pure mercy. 5. God is a good and bountiful Master to His people. 6. In our deepest distress we should have an eye to this heavenly kingdom. So doth Paul here. Whatever thy sorrows or sufferings be here, yet remember there is a heavenly kingdom will pay for all. 7. God will bring His people to a kingdom, to an heavenly kingdom. (*T. Hall, B.D.*)  *Never a friend :*—Paul might have said, as Socrates did, My friends, I have never a friend. And as Plato, A friend is a very mutable creature. (*J. Trapp.*)  *Why earthly props are removed :*—" See, father ! " said a lad who was walking with his father, " they are knocking away the props from under the bridge ; what are they doing that for ? Won't the bridge fall ? " " They are knocking them away," said the father, " that the timbers may rest more firmly upon the stone piers which are now finished." God only takes away our earthly props that we may rest more firmly upon Him. (*Elon Foster.*)  *Folly of persecution :*—In the Indian legend a mighty, wicked sorcerer seeks, with very poor success, to keep the sun, moon, and stars in three separate chests ; and those who have sought to suppress God's servants have succeeded no better. John was banished to Patmos, but, far from sinking out of view in the solitary sea, he stands before the world amid sublimest illuminations, like his own " angel standing in the sun." They drove Luther into the Wartzburg ; but there, in translating the Scriptures into German, he became the cynosure of all eyes. Bunyan's enemies consigned him to Bedford Gaol, and so he became known to the race, one of the foremost of the immortals of Christendom. (*W. L. Watkinson.*)  *Divine protection :*—Mr. J. G. Oncken was the Baptist pioneer in Germany, and in his younger days suffered for the truth's sake, both fine and imprisonment. We remember his pointing out to us the spot upon the Alster where he baptized his converts at dead of night, and we shall never forget his story of the burgomaster of Hamburg, who held up his finger and said, " You see that finger ! As long as that can move I will put you down." " Sir," said Oncken, " I see your finger, but I also see an arm, which you do not see, and so long as that is stretched out you cannot put me down." (*C. H. Spurgeon.*)  *Confidence in God :*—John Wesley once stood out very nobly in disregarding the eyes of men so long as he stood acquitted in the sight of God. Among his many persecutions are to be numbered the falling back of former friends, including his wife. These turned against him, and published many spiteful things, even defaming his character in a shocking manner. Brother Charles hastened off in alarm and indignation to inquire what defence Brother John would set up. There was no time to lose ! The eyes of the world were upon him, and God's enemies and his own would be glad to make capital out of so contemptible a business ! What was Charles's surprise to find that John was resolved on doing simply nothing ! The great preacher was calm and comfortable in mind, being entirely free from any concern for the future. Why should he be perplexed when he had entrusted God with his all—even with his reputation ? None are so safe as those whose characters are in God's keeping. Such often consider that they dishonour God by setting up puny defences of their own against the cavils of the wicked. They think more of that one eye of God which is ever looking on them than of the eyes of men. (*C. H. Spurgeon.*)  *The faithfulness of Jesus :*—It is recorded of a good man that his last day, with the exception of a few intervals, was passed in unconsciousness. Seeing a look of returning intelligence, one asked, " Are you thinking of Jesus to-day ? " His reply of loving trust was never to be forgotten :

"When I am conscious I am thinking of Jesus; when I am unconscious Jesus is thinking of me." *Looking up for help:*—One morning, not long after my arrival at Llandrindod, the artist was showing me a "printed proof" of a likeness of myself recently taken, when, in reply to a remark, he said, ▌You see, sir, you have such a habit of looking up." The words came to me with a meaning he did not intend them to convey. I quite rejoiced to hear them. (*J. T. Wrenford, M.A.*) *Prayer and trust:*—This is the true inmost essence of prayer—not that we should prescribe to Him how to answer our desires, but that we should leave all that in His hands. The apostle Paul said, in his last letter, with triumphant confidence, that he knew that God would "deliver him and save him into His everlasting kingdom." And he knew, at the same time, that his course was ended, and that there was nothing for him now but the crown. How was he "saved into the kingdom" and "delivered from the mouth of the lion"? The sword that struck off the wearied head that had thought so long for God's Church was the instrument of the deliverance and the means of the salvation. For us it may be that a sharper sorrow may be the answer to the prayer, "Preserve Thy servant." It may be that God's "bowing down His ear" and answering us when we cry shall be to pass us through a mill that has finer rollers, to crush still more the bruised corn. But the end and the meaning of it all will be to "rejoice the soul of the servant" with a deeper joy at last. (*A. Maclaren, D.D.*)

Ver. 19. **The household of Onesiphorus.**—*An extensive blessing:*—As the dew that falleth on the mountains runs down to the valleys, and the precious ointment that was poured upon the head of Aaron ran down to the skirts of his clothing (Psa. cxxxiii.), so the blessing which God pours on governors extendeth itself to such as are under them. (*T. Hall, B.D.*)

Ver. 20. **Trophimus sick.**—*Unaccomplished aims:*—How many broken-down servants of God are there to-day, Christian men and women, who have proved their sincerity, who do prove their sincerity, but whose thin hand can do little or nothing in raising the stones of the shrine they so passionately desire to build? As in the busiest thoroughfares of great cities we behold wistful faces looking down from hospital windows, longing to share in the strong life of the streets; so are there frail, broken-down watchers of the work of God who long to share the toil and sacrifice of God's workmen. (*W. L. Watkinson.*) *Use of sickness:*—Hannah More made the following entry in her journal (Jan. 21, 1798): "Many temptations this week to vanity. My picture asked for two publications. Dedications—flattery without end. God be praised, I was not flattered, but tired—twenty-four hours' headache makes me see the vanity of all this." (*J. F. B. Tinling, B.A.*)

Ver. 21. **Come before winter.**—*Winter voyages:*—I. THE VOYAGE TO THE ETERNAL CITY. 1. The departure. 2. The voyage. 3. The guidance of the helmsman. 4. The propulsion of all progress must come from the winds of heaven. 5. Industry on board the ship. 6. The shipping of the anchor. 7. The end of the journey. II. THE AVOIDANCE OF WINTER RISKS. Put not off to old age, &c. III. THE ADVENTURE OF DILIGENCE. Make haste. There is no time to lose. (*S. H. Tyng, Jun., D.D.*) *Friendships:*—Of such friendships biography happily furnishes us with many examples:—Gray, the poet, and Mason; Cowper and Mrs. Unwin; Tennyson and Arthur Henry Hallam; Keats and Severn; Elizabeth Carter and Bishop Secker; Mrs. Tait and Miss Marsh. This collocation of names reminds us of the old fallacy that true friendship can subsist only between individuals of similar character and disposition. Never was there a greater delusion! A man's friend is never his counterpart, but his complement; supplies that which is wanting in himself. And this is the use and value of friendship, it is like an offensive and defensive alliance between two equal powers, in which the one undertakes to furnish a military and the other a naval force, it provides for each party to the bond that which he or she most needs. (*The Fireside.*) **Eubulus and Pudens, and Linus, and Claudia.** Eubulus is mentioned here only. It has been thought possible that Pudens may be the friend of the poet Martial, whose marriage with Claudia, a foreign lady, he celebrates in Epigram viii. lib. iv., supposing that other epigrams which are not favourable to the moral character of Pudens were written before his conversion. An inscription found at Colchester mentions a site given by one Pudens for a temple, built under the sanction of a British king, Claudius Cogidubrius; and it has been conjectured that this was the same Pudens who was a centurion in the army, and who may have married the daughter of Cogidubrius, whose name would consequently have been Claudia. The Claudia Rufina of Martial was a Briton, and may have received the name of Rufina from Pomponia, the wife of Aulus Plantius, commander in Britain, who was connected with the Rufi family, and was accused of holding foreign superstitions. All this, however, is very uncertain. Linus is probably the same Roman Christian who became the first bishop of the Church there, according to Ignatius and Eusebius. (*Bp. Jackson.*)

Ver. 22. **The Lord Jesus Christ be with thy spirit.**—*The highest wish of true friendship :*—I. MAN HAS A SPIRITUAL NATURE. "pirit is something that is unlike matter—indivisible, self-active, self-conscious, religious. That man has a spirit is— 1. A fact most demonstrable. 2. A fact most practically ignored. 3. A fact the most distinguishing—marking us off from all mundane existences. II. MAN'S SPIRITUAL NATURE NEEDS THE COMPANIONSHIP OF CHRIST. 1. Christ alone can centralise its affections. 2. Christ alone can enlist unbounded reliance. III. COMPANIONSHIP WITH CHRIST IS AN ATTAINABLE BLESSING. (*Homilist.*) *Christ with us :*—I. LET US INQUIRE IN WHAT SENSE THE LORD JESUS CHRIST IS WITH HIS PEOPLE. We cannot hope to enjoy His bodily presence. It was expedient that He should go away ; and still it is expedient that He should remain away. Yet in His spiritual presence He can be with us. II. He is with us WHEN, AS THE UNIVERSAL RULER, HE GOVERNS ALL THINGS FOR OUR GOOD. But the prayer of Paul for Timothy is, "The Lord Jesus Christ be with thy spirit." What we need is a consciousness of Christ's presence—the enjoyment of fellowship with Him. As the eagle soars towards the sun, so he soars towards God. The spirit of man needs God ; especially God manifest in the flesh. It is only as He is with us—filling us with all the fulness of God, that our spirits find rest. Then we are assured of reconciliation, forgiveness, and eternal blessedness. III. THE REQUIREMENTS OF OUR EARTHLY STATE cause us to need the presence of Christ. We are exposed to temptation ; how shall we resist it unless He help us? IV. Have you ever thought of THE GREAT AND MANIFOLD BLESSINGS which the presence of Christ brings to us ? No visitor brings such gifts. 1. How largely He increases our store of knowledge ! What glorious revelations He makes of His own beauty and worth, shining before us, like the sun, in the brightness of His own light ! 2. Then, among the blessed results of Christ's presence, and not the least, is assimilation to His image. (*W. Walters.*) *The presence of Christ with His people desirable :*—All who desire the ministry, which Christ has established amongst them, to be useful, and wise, and successful, ought frequently to pray, "The Lord Jesus Christ be with thy spirit." Nor is it less important in respect to their own individual piety, their growth in grace, and their preparation to go into eternity, that the Lord Jesus Christ be with their own spirits. This will appear : I. FROM A CONSIDERATION OF THE INQUIRY. In no other way, except by the presence of Jesus, can we arrive at a purifying and sanctifying knowledge of the Word of God. II. The importance of praying, the Lord Jesus be with our spirits, will be manifest FROM THE NECESSITY OF HIS PRESENCE IN OUR DEVOTIONS. This alone can cause our prayers to go up before God as a sweet savour. III. The importance of praying for the presence of Christ is manifest FROM ITS INFLUENCE ON OUR INTERCOURSE WITH THE IMPENITENT. Do we desire to set an example such as Christ set, and to have such an influence as He shed around Him, and to cause the mite of our moral power to fall into the current of that which our God, and the Lamb, and all the saints, have poured forth on an ungodly world? And shall we not desire that the Lord Jesus Christ would be with our spirits ? IV. WHAT CAN WE DO IN OUR INTERCOURSE WITH THE CHURCH WITHOUT THE PRESENCE OF CHRIST ? V. WHAT CAN WE DO IN SICKNESS WITHOUT THE PRESENCE OF CHRIST ? Conclusion : 1. From the subject we learn the reason why so many are fluctuating in their religious characters. It is because the Lord Jesus Christ is not with their spirits. 2. The subject shows why there is so little effort for the salvation of the impenitent amongst us. It is because the Lord Jesus Christ is not enough with our spirits. 3. The subject explains some facts, which we have long witnessed but have not understood. (1) It explains why so many, who have named the name of Christ, do not appear to be Christians. (2) It explains why so many, who occasionally appear to be Christians, are generally without any evidence of piety—The Lord Jesus Christ is not with their spirit. (3) It explains why so many are changing their religious views and feelings, while they do not appear to wish to abandon religion itself—The Lord Jesus Christ is not with them. (4) It shows why the impenitent have so little respect for the Christian character amongst us—The Lord Jesus is not with us, as a Church. (5) It shows why, when so many persons in the Church and around it profess to be full of faith and love, there are few or none converted. (6) It shows what is necessary to a genuine revival of religion—That the Lord Jesus be with us. (7) It shows that all who are not labouring for one, seeking for one, and praying for one, are without Christ—He is not with them. (*J. Foot, D.D.*) **Grace be with you.**—*Continual grace :*—The acts of breathing which I performed yesterday will not keep me alive to-day; I must continue to breathe afresh every moment, or animal life ceases. In like manner yesterday's grace and spiritual strength must be renewed, and the Holy Spirit must continue to breathe on my soul, from moment to moment, in order to my enjoying the consolations, and to my working the works of God. (*Toplady.*)

# THE BIBLICAL ILLUSTRATOR

## TITUS

THE

# BIBLICAL ILLUSTRATOR

BY

JOSEPH S. EXELL

TITUS

BAKER BOOK HOUSE
GRAND RAPIDS, MICHIGAN 49506

# INTRODUCTION TO THE EPISTLE TO TITUS.

TITUS.—Extremely little is known of Titus, either as a man or as an evangelist. His name never occurs in the history of the Acts, which is somewhat strange, as we know, from the Epistle to the Galatians, that he was with Paul and Barnabas at Antioch, and accompanied them to Jerusalem when they went to have the dispute settled about circumcision (Gal. ii. 1–3). We learn, from the brief notice given us of what took place on that occasion, that Paul sternly refused to have him circumcised, as some of the Jewish Christians wished, because he saw that in *his* case the principle of gospel liberty was at stake, and must, at whatever hazard, be vindicated. It therefore appears not only that Titus was a Gentile, but that he must also have been employed chiefly in ministering to the Gentiles, or to churches in which these formed the predominating element. He appears, at a later period, to have been with Paul and Timothy at Ephesus, doubtless sharing with these in the manifold labours attendant on the planting of the Church in that centre of idolatry and corruption. From Ephesus he was sent forth by Paul to Corinth, for the purpose of stimulating the brethren to get forward their contributions for the poor saints at Jerusalem (2 Cor. viii. 6; xii. 18). He rejoined the apostle in Macedonia, and cheered him with the report he brought, not only of the progress of the contributions, but also of the salutary effect produced by the First Epistle of Paul to the Church at Corinth (chap. vii. 6–15). (*P. Fairbairn, D.D.*)

TITUS A STRONG MAN.—The love of apology, stimulating suggestion, and fatherly counsel manifested towards Timothy differs greatly from the manner of every reference to Titus, who evidently could take care of himself and be safely entrusted with intricate, difficult, and delicate negociations. St. Paul appears to have been more dependent upon Titus than Titus was upon Paul. He is described as the apostle's "brother and companion and fellow-labourer" (2 Cor. viii. 23); and if he were the bearer of the First Epistle to the Corinthians, and enforced the advice of the apostle upon the Church which had for the moment been thrown into violent confusion by "that wicked person," he must have been a man of strong nerve and fine tact. . . . Titus not only discharged his task with admirable patience and success, but was ready, even eager, to go back to Corinth with the second letter, and to complete the delicate service which he had commenced a year before (*cf.* 2 Cor. viii. 6 with xii. 18). Since he had begun, Paul desired him also to finish among the Corinthians the same grace or gift. The eager interest with which he responded to the appeal seemed like a Divine inspiration. "God," says Paul, "put it into his heart." A private letter addressed to Titus in the midst of these negociations would have possessed great interest; but we know nothing of his proceedings until many years have elapsed. (*H. R. Reynolds, D.D.*)

BIOGRAPHICAL DETAILS.—St. Paul's first imprisonment is concluded, and his last trial impending. In the interval between the two, he and Titus were together in Crete (chap. i. 5). We see Titus remaining in the island when St. Paul left it, and receiving there a letter written to him by the apostle. From this letter we gather the following biographical details :—First we learn that he was originally converted through St. Paul's instrumentality (chap. i. 4). Next we learn the various particulars of the responsible duties which he had to discharge in Crete. He is to complete what St. Paul had been obliged to leave unfinished (chap. i. 5), and he is to organise the Church throughout the island by appointing presbyters in every city. Instructions are given as to the suitable character of such presbyters (chap. i. 6-9); and we learn, further, that we have here the repetition of instructions furnished by word of mouth (chap. i. 5). Next, he is to control and bridle (chap. i. 11) the restless and mischievous Judaisers, and he is to be peremptory in so doing (chap. i. 13). Injunctions in the same spirit are reiterated (chap. ii. 1, 15; iii. 8). He is to urge the duties of a decorous and Christian life upon the women (chap. ii. 3-5), some of whom (chap. ii. 3) possibly had something of an official character. He is to be watchful over his own conduct (chap. ii. 7); he is to impress upon the slaves the peculiar duties of their position (chap. ii. 9, 10); he is to check all social and political turbulence (chap. iii. 1), also all wild theological speculations (chap. iii. 9), and to exercise discipline on the heretical (chap. iii. 10). When we consider all these particulars of his duties, we see not only the confidence reposed in him by the apostle, but the need there was of determination and strength of purpose, and therefore the probability that this was his character; and all this is enhanced if we bear in mind his isolated and unsupported position in Crete, and the lawless and immoral character of the Cretans themselves, as testified by their own writers (chap. i. 12, 13). The notices which remain are more strictly personal. Titus is to look for the arrival in Crete of Artemas and Tychicus (chap. iii. 12), and then he is to hasten to join St. Paul at Nicopolis, where the apostle is proposing to pass the winter. Zenas and Apollos are in Crete, or expected there; for Titus is to send them on their journey, and supply them with whatever they need for it (chap. iii. 13). (*Dean Howson.*)    From his lonely cell on the eve of his martyrdom, St. Paul penned his second letter to Timothy, and in that touching epistle we find the final reference to Titus, who is said to have gone into Dalmatia. There is no reason whatever for believing that Titus had deserted his father in the faith, or that in this journey he had done other than fulfil the wishes of the dying apostle. . . . Titus left behind him in Crete a name and a sacred memory. The modern Candia claims the honour of his tomb. Two considerable churches were dedicated to him in the island, and he was regarded as its patron saint. After the conquest of Crete by Venice, the Venetians also claimed Titus, by the side of St. Mark, as their patron too. Pashley discovered a fountain, said to have been used by St. Paul for the baptism of his converts, and, amid other superstitious tributes to his memory, found that the apostle was credited with having driven the wild beasts from the island. (*H. R. Reynolds, D.D.*)    Titus shares with Timothy the glory of having given up everything in order to throw in his lot with St. Paul, and of being one of his most trusted and efficient helpers. What that meant the Epistles of St. Paul tell us—ceaseless toil and anxiety, much shame and reproach, and not a little peril to life itself. He also shares with Timothy the glory of being willing, when the cause required such sacrifice, to separate from the master to whom he had surrendered himself, and to work on by himself in isolation and difficulty. The latter was possibly the more trying sacrifice of the two. To give up all his earthly prospects and all the sweetness of home life, in order to work for the spread of the gospel side by side with St. Paul, was no doubt a sacrifice that must have cost those who made it a great deal. But it had its attractive side. Quite independently of the beauty and majesty of the cause itself, there was the delight of being associated with a leader so able, so sagacious, so invigorating, and so affectionate as the apostle who " became all things to all men that he might by all means save some." Hard work became light, and difficulties became smooth, under the inspiriting sympathy of such a colleague. But it was quite another thing to have given up everything for the sake of such companionship and support, or at least in the full expectation of enjoying it, and then to have to undergo the hard work and confront the difficulties without it. The new dispensation in this respect repeats the old. Elisha leaves his home and his inheritance to follow Elijah, and then Elijah is taken from him. Timothy and Titus leave their homes and possessions to follow St. Paul, and then St. Paul sends them away from him. And to this arrangement they consented, Timothy (as we know) with tears, Titus (we may be sure) with much regret. And what it cost the loving apostle thus to part with them and to pain them we see from the tone of affectionate longing which pervades these letters. (*A. Plummer, D.D.*)

GENUINENESS.—With regard to modern objections, it may be freely admitted that there is no room in St. Paul's life, as given in the Acts, for the journey to Crete, and the winter at Nicopolis, required by the Epistle to Titus. But there is plenty of room for both of these *outside* the Acts—viz., between the first and second Roman imprisonments of the apostle. And, as we have already seen good reason for believing in the case of 1 Timothy, the condition of the Church indicated in this letter is such as was already in existence in St. Paul's time; and the language used in treating of it resembles that of the apostle in a way which helps us to believe that we are reading his own words, and not those of a skilful imitator. For this imitator must have been a strange person; very skilful in some things, very eccentric in others. Why does he give St. Paul and Titus a work in Crete in which there is no mention in the Acts? Why does he make the apostle ask Titus to meet him in Nicopolis, a place never named in connection with St. Paul? Why bracket a well-known person, like Apollos, with an utterly unknown person, such as Zenas? It is not easy to believe in this imitator. Yet another point of resemblance should be noted. Here, as in 1 Timothy, there is no careful arrangement of the material. The subjects are not put together in a studied order, as in a treatise with a distinct theological or controversial purpose. They follow one another in a natural manner, just as they occur to the writer. Persons with their hearts and heads full of things which they wish to say to a friend, do not sit down with an analysis before them to secure an orderly arrangement of what they wish to write. They start with one of the main topics, and then the treatment of this suggests something else; and they are not distressed if they repeat themselves, or if they have to return to a subject which has been touched upon before and then dropped. This is just the kind of writing which meets us once more in the letter to Titus. It is thoroughly natural. It is difficult to believe that a forger in the second century could have thrown himself with such simplicity into the attitude which the letter pre-supposes. (*A. Plummer, D.D.*)

TIME AND PLACE OF COMPOSITION.—It is not possible to determine whether this letter was written before or after the First to Timothy. But it was certainly written before the Second to Timothy. Therefore, while one has no sufficient reason for taking it before the one, one has excellent reason for taking it before the other. The precise year and the precise place in which it was written, we must be content to leave unsettled. It may be doubted whether either one or the other would throw much light on the contents of the letter. These are determined by what the apostle remembers and expects concerning affairs in Crete, and not by his own surroundings. (*A. Plummer, D.D.*) The striking resemblance of this Epistle to 1 Tim. justifies us in assigning it to the same year (say 67 A.D.). It may have been written in Asia Minor when the apostle was on his way to Nicopolis. (*J. A. McClymont, B.D.*)

CRETE AND THE CRETAN CHURCH.—Crete is a large island in the Greek seas, with a range of high hills running through its entire length from east to west, from which fertile valleys open upon a continuous strip of flat shore round the coast line. On the north it possesses good natural harbours. In its palmly days these served as outlets for the abundant crops of wheat, wine, and oil which it then yielded to the industry of a dense population. Descended from an ancient Greek stock, its early inhabitants were employed partly as cultivators in the interior, partly as seamen on the coast. They were a somewhat rude, turbulent, and independent race, among whom the usual defects of the Greek character in its less cultured condition were very strongly marked. Of these defects, falsehood, both in the form of over-reaching and in that of treachery, has always been the foremost. To this vice there were joined, in St. Paul's time, gross forms of licentiousness and a readiness to swift, insolent brawling such as has never been quite cured among the maritime Greeks of the Archipelago. (*J. Oswald Dykes, D.D.*)    There is no *record* of any visit of St. Paul to Crete, except in Acts xxvii. 7. He *may* have gone there from Ephesus or Corinth during the period of his life embraced in the Acts ; but it is far more probable that the visit referred to here took place after his first imprisonment at Rome. This island, although famous in the mythology of early Greece, had played no important part in its subsequent history. It had been added to the Roman Empire by Metellus (B.C. 67), and was united in one province with Cyrenaica, on the African coast. There are indications of considerable Jewish settlements on this island. Tacitus, indeed, mentions, among several traditions of the origin of the Jews, that they came from Crete ; perhaps from a confusion between them and the Cherethites, or Cherethim, who are supposed to have been Philistine mercénaries. The Septuagint translates these names by Cretans in Ezek. xxv. 15 ; Zeph. ii. 15, where, too, in ver. 6, for " sea-coast " it reads " Crete." Jews in Gortyna, a city of Crete, are alluded to in 1 Mac. xv. 23. Josephus mentions the Jews in Crete, in connection with Alexander, the pretended son of Herod ; and Philo, in the reign of Caligula, speaks of Crete as being, like other islands of the Mediterranean, full of Jews. Cretes were among the devout Jews who were sojourning at Jerusalem at the day of Pentecost (Acts ii. 11). When, or by whom, Christianity was planted on this island, is quite uncertain. It could hardly have been by St. Paul, unless we suppose some visit previous to his first imprisonment to which no allusion is made in the Acts. But in that case we shall rather expect to find some mention of " brethren " there, when the apostle touched at the Fair Havens on his way to Rome (Acts xxvii. 8). The directions in this Epistle indicate an imperfectly organised Church, but one which had been in existence long enough to admit irregularities, and to be endangered by false teachers. (*Bp. Jackson.*)

THE FALSE TEACHERS.—The heretics (chap. i. 9) belong especially to Judaism (chap. i. 10). While boasting of their special knowledge of God, they lead a godless life (chap. i. 16), condemned by their own conscience (chap. iii. 11). What they bring forward are Jewish myths (chap. i. 14), genealogies, points of controversy about the law (chap. iii. 9), and mere commands of men (chap. i. 14). They are idle babblers (chap. i. 10), who, with their shameful doctrine (chap. i. 11), seduce hearts (chap. i. 10), cause divisions in the Church (chap. iii. 10), and draw whole families into destruction (chap. i. 11) ; and all this—for the sake of shameful gain (chap. i. 11). (*J. E. Huther, Th.D.*)    They made much of the law of Moses. Not of its moral elements, however ; nor even of its religious ritual ; nor of its observance as a means of attaining to righteousness. What they appear to have chiefly insisted upon was the distinction it drew between what was ceremonially " clean " and " unclean" in food, and the like external matters—portions of Mosaic legislation which many, even among the Hebrews, had come to regard as its least important or permanent features. On such points, they added new Rabbinical prohibitions to those of the original law. They had even introduced doctrines foreign to the whole spirit of Hebrew thought and history. For example, they discouraged marriage and extolled celibacy, as well as denied a literal resurrection of the body. It is clear, therefore, that the root idea which underlay their speculations and practical rules was the same belief in the essential evil of matter which for some years had been operating injuriously (as we see from the letter to Colosse) upon the churches of Asia Minor, and which, after St. Paul's decease, was destined to blossom into the vast and many-headed heresy of Gnosticism. The legitimate offspring of all speculations of this complexion, which assign moral evil as a property to matter, not to the spirit, is, first, a false asceticism, and, at the next remove, immoral indulgence. To this last, even, it had already come with certain of the Jewish teachers at Crete. They were worming their way into Christian families, undermining authority in the household, and seeking by all means to win proselytes to their views, for the purpose of enriching themselves ; and, under a garb of self-denial, they indemnified themselves for ascetic restraint by flagitious laxity. Such are the charges brought against them by St. Paul. It was, therefore, no abstract error which had to be combated. A " gangrene " of immorality, as the natural product of fanciful speculations which were dangerous as well as false, was laying waste the Church, demoralising the behaviour of professed believers, and endangering the very existence of a healthy Christianity in the island. The evil was by no means peculiar to Crete, although it had there acquired unusual development. It was destined to overrun all churches. It was the same evil the foresight of which, in its finished form, darkened the last days of Paul, and which is dealt with by the pens of St. Peter and St. Jude. All the more interesting does it become to note how the great missionary dealt with it in the present case. No sooner was he on the spot, than he felt the need for a prompt and drastic remedy. The mischief had gained too firm a footing to be readily expelled. It found support in the low morals of the Cretan population. Before it could be counteracted, it would therefore require courage, plain speaking, a vigorous enforcement of discipline, and, above all, a faithful exhibition of gospel truth in its essential connection with sound morality. (*J. Oswald Dykes, D.D.*)

CONTENTS.—After a somewhat elaborate preface, Paul reminds Titus that he had left him behind in Crete for the purpose of ordaining presbyters in the churches there. The qualities are named which the presbyter ought to possess, and Paul points out the upholding of the pure gospel as the most important requisite of all, that the presbyter may be able to withstand the continually growing influence of the heretics. The mention of the heretics in Crete gives the apostle an opportunity of quoting a saying of Epimenides, which describes the character of the Cretans, while at the same time he sketches the heretics, with their arbitrary commands and their hypocritical life, and vindicates against them the principle of life in the gospel (chap. i. 5–16). Then follow rules of conduct for the various members of the Church, for old and young, men and women, together with an exhortation to Titus to show a good example in work and doctrine, and especially to call upon the slaves to be faithful to their masters. These exhortations are supported by pointing to the moral character of God's grace (chap. ii. 1–15). Then follows the injunction that Titus is to urge the Christians to obedience towards the higher powers, and to a peaceful behaviour towards all men. The latter point is enforced by pointing to the undeserved grace of God which has been bestowed on Christians (chap. iii. 1–7). To this are added warnings against heresy, and directions how Titus is to deal with a heretic (chap. iii. 8–11). The Epistle closes with an injunction to come to the apostle at Nicopolis, some commissions, greetings, and the benediction. (*J. E. Huther, Th.D.*)

# THE BIBLICAL ILLUSTRATOR.

## TITUS.

## CHAPTER I.

VER. 1. **Paul, a servant of God.**—*A servant of God.*—"Servant of God," "servant of Jesus Christ"—this is the title by which each one of the writers of the Epistles of the New Testament describes himself in one place or another. The title indicates their work in life, the place they hold in the world, and the definite object to which all their powers are devoted. For them God had tasks as much above the tasks and trials of Christians generally as the tasks of a great servant of State are above the responsibilities of those whom the State protects. St. Paul had parted company with what men care for and work for here, as the enthusiast for distant travel parts company with his home. I. THIS CHARACTER IS EXCLUSIVE IN ITS OBJECT AND COMPLETE IN ITS SELF-DEDICATION. St. Paul knew no other interest here but the immense one of his Master's purpose in the world; this scene of experience, of pain and pleasure, of life and death, was as if it had ceased to be, except as the field on which he was to "spend and be spent" in persuading men of what his Master meant for them. II. IT CONTEMPLATES as the centre of all interest and hope, the highest object of human thought and devotion, a presence beyond the facts of experience, THE PRESENCE OF THE INVISIBLE GOD. What St. Paul lived for, so whole-hearted, so single-minded, was to be one with the will and purpose of Him who had chosen him from the millions of mankind to bear His name before the world. III. IT ACCEPTS, AS THE MEASURE OF ITS LABOUR AND ITS ENDURANCE, THE CROSS OF JESUS CHRIST. For such a life a price had to be paid, and St. Paul's price was the acceptance of the fellowship of the cross of Christ. The likeness of the cross pervades every life of duty and earnestness—in lifelong trouble, in bereavement, in misunderstanding, in unjust suffering, in weary labour, in failure and defeat—God's proof and test of strength is laid upon us all. But we must not confound with this that partnership in their Master's sufferings which was the portion of servants like St. Paul, and for which he sought expression in the awful language recalling the Passion—"I am crucified with Christ"; "I fill up that which is behind of the afflictions of Christ," &c. There is no reason why, without extravagance, without foolish or overstrained enthusiasm, we should not still believe that a life like St. Paul's is a natural one for a Christian to choose. We still reverence his words; and his words have all along the history of the Church found echoes in many hearts. There is a great past behind us—a past which is not dead, but lives—lives in every thought we think and every word we speak, lives in our hopes, in our confidences and joy in life, lives in those high feelings which thrill and soothe us at the grave. May we not be unworthy of such a past! (*Dean Church.*) *The honour of being a servant of God :*—This being the first title whereby the apostle would get himself authority, teacheth that the very name of a servant of God is full of honour and authority. The apostle, comparing the glory of Christ with the glory of the angels (Heb. i. 14), advanceth them as far as possibly he can, that Christ's glory, being so much more excellent than theirs there described, might be most highly exalted; and yet the highest ascent of their honour which he can rise unto is to title them "ministering spirits" standing about God, from which service they are honoured with glorious names, of thrones, dominations, powers, rulers, principalities; and although the Scriptures most usually under this title express the low and humble condition of Christ, "who took on Him the form of a servant," yet also thereby the Lord would sometimes signify His great glory, as Isa. xlii. 1.   1. This serves to teach ministers their duty, that seeing the Lord hath so highly honoured them as to draw them so near unto Himself, as it were admitting them into His presence-chamber—yea, and unto His council-table—they are in a way of thankfulness more straightly bound to two main duties—(1) Diligence ; (2) thankfulness.   2. This doctrine ministereth comfort unto those that are faithful in their ministry, whom, howsoever the world esteemeth of them, their Lord highly respecteth, admitteth them into His privy councils, and employeth in a service which the angels themselves desire to pry into.   3. Teacheth people how to esteem of their ministers, namely, as the servants of God, and consequently of their ministry as the message of God, which if it be, Moses must not be murmured at when he speaks freely and roughly ; and if Micaiah resolve of faithfulness, saying, " As the Lord liveth, whatsoever the Lord saith, be it good or evil, that will I speak," why should he be hated and fed with "bread and water of affliction " ? Is it not a reasonable plea, and full of pacification in civil messages—" I pray you be not angry with me ; I am but a servant "?   4. Let every private Christian account it also his honour that the Lord vouchsafeth him to become His servant ; and hereby harden thyself against the scorns and derisions of mocking Michals, who seek to disgrace thy sincerity.   If the ungodly of the world would turn thy glory into shame, even as thou wouldest have the Son of man not to be ashamed of thee in His kingdom, be not thou ashamed to profess thyself His servant, which is thy glory.   (*T. Taylor, D.D.*)      *Willing service :*—Before the time when Abraham Lincoln emancipated three millions of coloured people in the Southern States of America, there was one day a slave auction in New Orleans.   Amongst the number was a beautiful Mulatto girl, who was put upon the " block " to be sold to the highest bidder, like a cow or a horse.   The auctioneer, dilating on the graces of the girl, her skill in working, and the beauty of her form, asked for a bid.   The first offer was five hundred dollars, and the bids quickly rose to seven hundred dollars. Then a voice called from the outside of the crowd, " Seven hundred and fifty dollars ! "   The slave-owners thereupon advanced their bids to eight hundred, eight hundred and fifty, and nine hundred dollars.   The bids continued to rise, but whenever there was a pause the unseen bidder offered fifty dollars more, and at last the girl was knocked down to him for 1,450 dollars.   He then came forward, and, paying the money, arranged to receive delivery of the lot in the morning.   The slave girl saw that her purchaser was a Northerner, one of the hated " Yankees," and was much disgusted to become his slave.   The next morning her new owner called at the house, when the poor girl said with tears, " Sir, I am ready to go with you."   He gently replied, " But I do not want you to go with me ; please look over this paper ! "   She opened the paper, and found that it was the gift of her freedom. The Northerner said, " I bought you that you might be free ! "   She exclaimed, " You bought me that I might be free !   Am I free ?   Free !   Can I do as I like with myself ? "   He answered, " Yes, you are free ! "   Then she fell down and kissed his feet, and almost choking with sobs of joy, she cried, " Oh, sir, I will go with you, and be your servant for evermore ! "      **And an apostle of Jesus Christ.**—*High office means chief service in the Church :*—The apostle, by joining these two together, a servant and apostle, teacheth us that the chiefest offices in the Church are for the service of it.   Was there any office above the apostles in the Church ?   And yet they preached the Lord Jesus, and themselves servants for His sake.   Nay, our Lord Jesus Himself, although He was the Head of His Church, yet He came not into the world to be served, but to minister and serve.   1. Ministers must never conceive of their calling, but also of this service, which is not accomplished but by service ; thus shall they be answerable to Peter's exhortation (1 Pet. iii. 3) to feed the flock of God depending upon them, not by constraint, but willingly ; " not as lords over God's heritage, but as examples to the flock."   2. Would'st thou know what ambition Christ hath permitted unto His ministers ?   It is even this, that he that would be chief of all should become servant of all.   (*T. Taylor, D.D.*)      **According to the faith of God's elect.**—*God's elect :*—I.  GOD HATH SOME WHO ARE ELECT AND CHOSEN, AND OTHERS ARE NOT.   Men may be called the elect of God three ways.   1. In respect of some temporal function or ministry to which the Lord hath designed them (John vi. 70).   2. In regard of that actual election and choice of some people and nations above others, unto the true means of life and salvation, so to become the people of God's election.   3. In respect of that eternal election of God, which is according to grace, whereby of His good pleasure He chooseth from all eternity, out of all sorts of men, some to the certain fruition and fellowship of life eternal and

salvation by Christ.  These elect of God are here meant, the number of which is comparatively small; "for many are called, but few chosen"—a little flock, and a few that have found the narrow way.  II. THESE ELECT HAVE A SPECIAL FAITH, DISTINCT BY THEMSELVES.  1. For there is an historical faith, standing in an assent and acknowledgment of the truth of things written and taught.  2. There is also an hypocritical faith, which passeth the former in two degrees.  First, in that with knowledge and assent is joined such a profession of the truth as shall carry a great show and form of godliness.  Secondly, a kind of gladness and glorying in that knowledge; for it is ascribed to some, who in temptation shall fall away, "to receive the Word with joy."  To both which may be joined sometimes a gift of prophecy, sometimes of working miracles, as some in the last day shall say, "Lord, have we not prophesied and cast out devils in Thy name?" and yet they shall be unknown of Christ.  Neither of these is the faith of the elect here mentioned, but a third kind, called saving faith, the inheritance of which is the property of the elect; for the just man only liveth by this faith, which in excellency passeth both the former in three worthy properties.  (1) In that here, with the act of under-standing and assent unto the truth, there goeth such a disposition and affection of the heart as apprehendeth and applieth unto it the promise of grace unto salvation, causing a man to rejoice in God, framing him unto the fear of God and to the waiting through hope for the accomplishment of the promise of life.  (2) In that whereas both the former are dead, and not raising unto a new life in Christ, what shows soever be made for the time, the sun of persecution riseth, and such moisture is dried up.  This is a lively and quickening grace, reaching into the heart Christ and His merits, who is the life of the soul and the mover of it to all godly actions, not suffering the believer to be either idle or unfruitful in the work of the Lord.  (3) Whereas both the former are but temporary, this is perpetual and lasting.  The other, rising upon temporary causes and reasons, can last only for a time, as when men, for the pleasure of knowledge or the name of it, by industry attain a great measure of understanding in Divine things, or when, for note and glory or com-modity, true or apparent, men profess the gospel.  Let but these grounds fail a little, or persecution approach, they lay the key under the door, give up the house, and bid farewell to all profession.  Thus many of Christ's disciples, who thought they had truly believed in Him, and that many months, when they heard Him speak of the eating of His flesh and drinking His blood, went back, and walked with Him no more.  But the matter is here far otherwise, seeing this faith of the elect hath the promise made good to it that the gates of hell shall never prevail against it.  III. THIS PECULIAR FAITH IS WROUGHT IN THE ELECT BY THE MINISTRY OF THE WORD.  1. If this be the principal end of the ministry, let ministers herein employ their first and principal pains to bring men unto the faith.  2. The minister ought to propound before him God's end in performance of every ministerial duty, and that is by enlightening, converting, confirming, comforting, to bring and stablish men in the faith.  3. The Lord having set out the ministry for this use, let every hearer acknowledge herein God's ordinance, and yield themselves with all submis-sion unto the ministry and the Word there preached, that thereby they may have faith wrought in their hearts.  4. Every man may hence examine himself, whether in the use of the ministry he finds saving faith begotten and wrought in his heart; and by examination some may find their understandings more enlightened, their judgments more settled, their practice in some things reformed; but a very few shall find Christ apprehended and rested in unto salvation, seeing so few there are that live by faith in the Son of God, for of all the sins that the Spirit may and shall rebuke the world of, this is the chief, because they believe not in Christ.  (*Ibid.*)
**And the acknowledging of the truth which is after godliness.**—*On the gospel being the truth after godliness :*—Here we have a full though compendious account of the nature of the gospel, ennobled by two excellent qualities.  One, the end of all philosophical inquiries, which is truth; the other, the design of all religious institutions, which is godliness; both united, and as it were blended together in the constitution of Christianity.  Those who discourse metaphysically of the nature of truth, as to the reality of the thing, affirm a perfect coincidence between truth and goodness; and I believe it might be easily made out that there is nothing in nature perfectly true but what is also really good.  It would be endless to strike forth into the eulogies of truth; for, as we know, it was the adored prize for which the sublimest wits in the world have always run, and sacrificed their time, their health, their lives, to the acquist of; so let it suffice us to say here that as reason is the great rule of man's nature, so truth is the great regulator of reason.  I. Now in

this expression of the gospel's being " THE TRUTH WHICH IS AFTER GODLINESS," these three things are couched. 1. It is a truth, and upon that account dares look its most inquisitive adversaries in the face. The most intricate and mysterious passages in it are vouched by an infinite veracity : and truth is truth, though clothed in riddles and surrounded with darkness and obscurity ; as the sun has still the same native inherent brightness, though wrapped up in a cloud. Now, the gospel being a truth, it follows yet further that if we run through the whole catalogue of its principles, nothing can be drawn from thence, by legitimate and certain consequence, but what is also true. It is impossible for truth to afford anything but truth. Every such principle begets a consequence after its own likeness. 2. The next advance of the gospel's excellency is that it is such a truth as is operative. It does not dwell in the mind like furniture, only for ornament, but for use, and the great concernments of life. The knowledge of astronomy, geometry, arithmetic, music, and the like, they may fill the mind, and yet never step forth into one experiment ; but the knowledge of the Divine truths of Christianity is quick and restless, like an imprisoned flame, which will be sure to force its passage and to display its brightness. 3. The third and highest degree of its perfection is that it is not only operative, but also operative to the best of purposes, which is to godliness : it carries on a design for heaven and eternity. It serves the two greatest interests in the world, which are, the glory of the Creator and the salvation of the creature; and this the gospel does by being " the truth which is after godliness." Which words may admit of a double sense—(1) That the gospel is so called because it actually produces the effects of godliness in those that embrace and profess it. (2) That it is directly improvable into such consequences and deductions as have in them a natural fitness, if complied with, to engage the practice of mankind in such a course. II. There are three things that I shall DEDUCE FROM THIS DESCRIPTION OF THE GOSPEL. 1. That the nature and prime essential design of religion is to be an instrument of good life, by administering arguments and motives inducing to it. (1) Religion designs the service of God, by gaining over to His obedience that which is most excellent in man, and that is the actions of his life and continual converse. That these are the most considerable is clear from hence, because all other actions naturally proceed in a subserviency to these. (2) The design of religion is man's salvation; but men are not saved as they are more knowing or assent to more propositions, but as they are more pious than others. Practice is the thing that sanctifies knowledge ; and faith without works expires, and becomes a dead thing, a carcase, and consequently noisome to God, who, even to those who know the best things, pronounces no blessing till they do them. (3) The discriminating excellency of Christianity consists not so much in this, that it discovers more sublime truths, or indeed more excellent precepts, than philosophy (though it does this also), as that it suggests more efficacious arguments to enforce the performance of those precepts than any other religion or institution whatsoever. (4) Notwithstanding the diversity of religions in the world, yet men hereafter will generally be con‑ demned for the same things; that is, for their breaches of morality. 2. That so much knowledge of truth as is sufficient to engage men's lives in the practice of godliness serves the necessary ends of religion; for if godliness be the design,it ought also, by consequence, to be the measure of men's knowledge in this particular. 3. That whatsoever does in itself or its direct consequences undermine the motives of a good life is contrary to, and destructive of Christian religion. (*R. South, D.D.*) *The doctrine of the gospel :*—I. THE DOCTRINE OF THE GOSPEL IS THE TRUTH ITSELF.—1. Because the Author of it is truth itself, and cannot lie, it being a part of His Word, who can neither deceive nor be deceived. 2. Because the penmen of it were inspired by the Holy Ghost, and spake and wrote as they were moved by Him, who is called " the Spirit of Truth " (John xiv. 17). 3. Because it is a doctrine of Christ, and aimeth at Him who is the Truth principally, as well as the Way of our salvation. II. THE KNOWLEDGE OF THIS TRUTH IS THE GROUND OF FAITH. 1. Then slight is the faith of most, whatsoever men profess. 2. Waverers in religion and unsettled persons in their profession may hence be informed to judge of themselves and their present estate. We hear more than a few uttering such voices as these : " There is such difference of opinion among teachers that I know not what to hold or whom to believe ; but is not this openly to proclaim the want of faith, which is not only assuredly persuaded of, but certainly knoweth the truth of that it apprehendeth ? 3. If the elect are brought to the faith by the acknowledging of the truth, then, after long teaching and much means, to be still blind and not to see the things of our peace is a most heavy judgment of God ; for here is a forfeit of faith and salvation.

III. Whosoever in truth entertain the doctrine of the gospel, the hearts of such are framed unto godliness. 1. If this be the pre-eminence of the Word, to frame the soul to true godliness, then it is a matter above the reach of all human learning; and therefore the folly of those men is hence discovered who devote and bury themselves in profane studies, of what kind soever they be, thinking therein to obtain more wisdom than in the study of the Scriptures. 2. Every hearer of the truth must examine whether by it his heart be thus framed unto godliness, for else it is not rightly learned; for as this grace "hath appeared to this purpose, to teach men to deny ungodliness and worldly lusts, and to live soberly and justly and godly in this present world," so it is not then learned when men can only discourse of the death of Christ, of His resurrection, of His ascension, except withal there be some experience of the virtue of His death in themselves. (*T. Taylor, D.D.*) *Redemptive truth :*—I. A grand enterprise. 1. An enterprise devoted to the highest purpose. (1) The promotion of the faith of God's elect; (2) the promotion of the knowledge "of the truth which is according to godliness." 2. An enterprise employing the highest human agency. II. A transcendent promise. 1. Transcendent in value. 2. In certitude. 3. In age. III. A gradual revelation. 1. It was manifested at a proper time. 2. By apostolic preaching. 3. By the Divine command. IV. A love-begetting power. "Mine own son." The gospel converter becomes the father in the highest and divinest sense of the converted. (*D. Thomas, D.D.*) *Lessons :*—I. An honourable designation. 1. "Servant of God." 2. Apostle of Christ." II. A glorious purpose—"According to," or rather, perhaps, "with reference to," the faith of God's people. Sent by Jesus Christ in order to promote the faith of "God's elect." III. The reasonableness of religion—"The acknowledging of the truth." Faith is the central doctrine of Christianity, but is to be distinguished from blind credulity. The faith of the Christian is based on knowledge, on fact, on truth (2 Pet. i. 16; 1 John i. 1–3). IV. The practical character of religion—"The truth which is after godliness"; that is, piety. Original word probably derived from one signifying "good, brave, noble." Paul was himself emphatically a model of manliness and devout courage. (*F. Wagstaff.*) *The grandest end and means of life :*—In this verse the apostle speaks of himself as—1. Possessing a character common to the good of all worlds—"Servant of God." All creatures are servants of God—some without their will, some according to their will. Paul served God freely, cordially, devotedly. 2. Sustaining an office peculiar to a few—"Apostle." Peculiar in appointment, number, and authority. 3. Engaged in a work binding on all Christians. To promote "the faith of God's elect"—that is, of His people—and "the knowledge of the truth which leads to godliness." I. Godliness is the grandest end of being. In the Old Testament the good are called "godly" (Psa. iv. 3; xii. 1; xxxii. 6; Mal. ii. 15). In the New Testament goodness is called "godliness" (1 Tim. ii. 2; iv. 7, 8; vi. 3, 5, 6; 2 Tim. iii. 5; 2 Pet. i. 3, 6, 7; iii. 11). Godliness is moral likeness to God. II. Truth is the grandest means of being. All truth is of God, natural and spiritual. The truth here referred to is the gospel truth—"the truth as it is in Jesus"—which, while it illustrates, vivifies and emphasises all other truth, goes beyond it, opens up new chapters of Divine revelation. It is not only moral truth, but redemptive truth, and redemptive truth not in mere propositions, but in a Divine life. This truth is the power of God unto salvation; it delivers from depravity, prejudice, guilt; it raises to purity, truth, peace. (*Homilist.*) *Truth as a medium of godliness :*— Suppose that a person wishing to send a message from London to Edinburgh by lightning knows how to construct an electric battery; but, when he comes to consider how he will transmit the impulse through hundreds of miles, he looks at an iron wire and says, "This is dull, senseless, cold; has no sympathy with light: it is unnatural, in fact irrational, to imagine that this dark thing can convey a lightning-message in a moment." From this he turns and looks at a prism. It glows with the many-coloured sunbeam. He might say, "This is sympathetic with light," and in its flashing imagine that he saw proof that his message would speed through it; but when he puts it to the experiment, it proves that the shining-prism will convey no touch of his silent fire, but that the dull iron will transmit it to the farthest end of the land. And so with God's holy truth. It alone is adapted to carry into the soul of man the secret fire, which writes before the inner eye of the soul a message from the Unseen One in the skies. (*T. W. Jenkyn, D.D.*)

Ver. 2. In hope of eternal life.—*Christianity a hope-inspiring promise :*—I. It is an absolutely certain promise. It is God's promise, and God cannot lie. II. It

IS AN INFINITELY RICH PROMISE. "Eternal life," *i.e.*, eternal well-being. III. IT IS A VERY OLD PROMISE. "Before the world began." (*Homilist.*)    *Hope reaching beyond the revolutions of time :*—I. IT IS GLORIOUS IN ITS OBJECT. "Eternal life"— a life of eternal goodness. II. IT IS DIVINE IN ITS FOUNDATION. 1. Inviolable. 2. Eternal. 3. Conditional. (*Ibid.*)    *Lessons :*—I. A GLORIOUS PROSPECT—"Eternal life." II. A TRUTH-SPEAKING GOD—"That cannot lie" (Num. xxiii. 19 ; Heb. vi. 18). III. AN OLD-STANDING PROMISE—"Before the world began." (*F. Wagstaff.*)    *The covenant—its deathless life and hope :*—I. THE GENERAL DOCTRINE. 1. God, he tells us, who cannot lie, made a certain promise before the world began. Not, observe, formed a purpose merely. We know well, indeed, from many a scripture, that He formed a purpose. But the apostle says that He did more,—that He made a pro- mise — and to this belongs the special character under which he presents the adorable God here, "God that cannot lie." But to whom was the promise made? It could only be to the Son of God, our Lord Jesus Christ. 2. It was "eternal life" of which God, before the world began, made promise. The Son of God could not receive such a promise for Himself. He could receive it only as the predestined Mediator—the Head and Surety of a people "given to Him by the Father," to be in time redeemed by Him, and eternally saved. 3. And thus does there arise a third momentous truth, namely, that this promise could be made to Christ only on a certain condition—only on supposition, and in respect of His whole future obedience unto death in behalf of His people. II. A HOPE unspeakably glorious and stable in its character. 1. Its glory. "Hope of eternal life." I cannot tell what this is. "It doth not yet appear," &c. This, at least, we know, that the "eternal life" shall have in it the expansion to the full of all the faculties and affections of the renewed nature ; the perfect harmony of those faculties and affections both among themselves and with the will of the adorable God ; the end of the last remnants of sin ; all tears for ever dried up ; body and soul reunited in a holy, deathless com- panionship, and made perfectly blessed in the full enjoying of God to all eternity ! 2. Its immovable stability. (1) First, the apostle says that it is built on the "pro- mise of God who cannot lie." Ah, if that is not security enough, then farewell, at least, to all possible security in the universe ! (2) Nor is this *a* promise of God merely—one among many ; it is, in a sort, *the* promise, the promise pre-eminently, of Jehovah, as the words intimate, "eternal life which God, that cannot lie, pro- mised before the world began." So we read, "This is the promise that He hath promised us, even eternal life." And again and again we read of "eternal life," as of the grand central blessing—"I give unto My sheep eternal life." "Thou hast given Him power over all flesh, that He should give eternal life to as many as Thou hast given Him." "Whoso eateth My flesh, &c., hath eternal life." (3) Again, the promise which this hope is built on was made by God "before the world began." See the immovable stability which lies here. For this world is one of ceaseless fluctuations, vicissitudes. Had the promise arisen amidst the changes and emergencies of time, then, one of them having begotten it, another might perad- venture have made a final end of it. But it was anterior to them all—made in full foresight of them all—made an eternity before them all. And thus none of them can in any wise affect its stability. (4) The promise this hope is built on is, as we have seen, the promise of a covenant—a promise made only on express and deter- minate conditions. And own that these have been to the uttermost fulfilled, it has become matter of justice no less than truth—of rectitude, as well as faithfulness. Concluding inferences :—1. See the absolute security of the ransomed Church of God, and each living member of it. 2. Remember those words in Romans, "There- fore it is of faith, that it might be by grace ; to the end the promise might be sure to all the seed." That is to say, there is an open entrance for all of us, sinners, into the whole inviolable security of this covenant of promise, by faith alone, with- out the deeds of the law—"it is of faith, that it might be by grace." 3. I end with the "hope" (daughter of the faith)—the undying hope—the "hope of eternal life, which God, that cannot lie, promised before the world began." What a hope this for storms and tempests—"anchor of the soul" indeed, "sure and steadfast"! What a hope for afflictions, to sustain under them ; for duties, to carry through them; for death and the grave, to give the victory over them ! (*C. J. Brown, D.D.*)    *The grace of hope :*—I. Every faithful teacher must conceive it to be his duty TO DRAW MEN'S HEARTS FROM THINGS BELOW TO THE CONTEMPLATION OF THINGS OF AN HIGHER STRAIN, and from seeking the things tending to a temporal, unto such as belong to life eternal. 1. This was the aim of all the men of God, whose faithfulness the Scriptures hath re- commended unto our imitation. All that pedagogy during the law was only to train men unto Christ, and to salvation by Him. 2. All other professions further men in their earthly estates, some employed about the health of the body, some about the maintaining of men's outward rights, some about the framing of tender minds in human disciplines and sciences; all which further our fellowship and society among men; only this, of all other professions, furthereth men in their heavenly estate, and fitteth them, yea maketh up for them their fellowship with God (Eph. iv. 11, 12). 3. Hereby men lay a sure groundwork of profiting men in godliness, for this expectation and desire of life eternal once wrought in the heart, it easily bringeth men to the denial of themselves, both in bearing the cross for Christ, as Moses esteemed highly of the rebuke of Christ—for he had respect unto the recompense of reward—as also in stripping themselves of profits, pleasures, advancements, friends, father, wife, children, liberty, yea, of life itself. II. TRUE FAITH NEVER GOES ALONE, BUT, as a queen, IS ATTENDED WITH MANY OTHER GRACES, as knowledge, love, fear of God; among which hope here mentioned not only adorneth and beautifieth, but strengtheneth and fortifieth the believer, and as a helmet of salvation, causeth the Christian soldier to hold out in repentance and obedience. 1. The original of it. It is a gift of God and obtained by prayer as faith also is, whence the apostle prayeth that the God of our Lord Jesus Christ would give the Ephesians to know what the hope is of his calling. 2. The subjects in whom it is. The saints, for as the practise of believers before Christ to wait for His first coming in humility, as we read of Simeon, Hannah, and many others, so now believers as constantly wait for his second coming and the comforts of it (Rev. xxii. 17). 3. The object of this hope. Things to come, and, namely, after the resurrection, life eternal. In which regard the apostle calleth it a hope laid up in heaven, which is all one with that in the text, hope of life eternal, unto which it lifteth up the heart and affections. Where the excellency of the grace may be conceived from the excellency of the object; it is not conversant about momentary and fleeting matters, nor insisteth in things below, but about durable and eternal things to come; and not only comforteth the soul here below on earth, but crowneth it hereafter in heaven. 4. It is added in the description that this grace of hope doth firmly and not waveringly expect this eminent object, and this it doth, both because it is grounded not upon man's merit, power, or promises, but upon the most firm promise of God, as also in that the Holy Ghost, who first worketh it, doth also nourish it, yea, and so sealeth it up unto the heart as it can never make ashamed; it may, indeed, be tossed and shaken with many kinds of temptations, yet in the patient attending upon the Lord it holdeth out and faileth not. (*T. Taylor, D.D.*) *Eternal life:*—I. WHAT IS THAT ETERNAL LIFE which is the object of faith and expectation. Complete deliverance from all evil, and the positive and perfect enjoyment of all good for ever. II. WHY DO WE BELIEVE IN IT? 1. God has promised it. 2. Christ has actually taken possession of it. 3. The Holy Spirit, given to them that believe, is expressly said to be the earnest and first-fruits of eternal life. 4. The real Christian has an undoubted and undeceiving foretaste of this blessedness. III. THE INFLUENCE WHICH OUR BELIEF OF THIS GREAT TRUTH SHOULD HAVE UPON OUR SPIRIT AND CONDUCT. 1. It should influence us to a due consideration of, and a diligent preparation for, the eternity to which we are destined. 2. It should influence us to a decided consecration of ourselves to that blessed Master whose service on earth is connected with so great and so substantial a reward in heaven. 3. It should induce us to a cheerful renunciation of the world as our portion. 4. It should influence us to cheerful and patient suffering under all the ills which can possibly crowd upon us in the present state of existence. 5. It should influence us to indefatigable diligence in seeking the salvation of the human soul. 6. Lastly, what comfort may not this subject inspire in the prospect of our departure hence, our descent into the cold grave, and our introduction into that state, of which we have feebly enunciated the reality. (*G. Clayton, M.A.*) *The inspiration of hope:* —"Look up!" thundered the captain of a vessel, as his boy grew giddy while gazing from the topmast,—"look up!" The boy looked up, and returned in safety. Young man, look up, and you will succeed. Never look down and despair. Leave dangers uncared for, and push on. If you falter, you lose. Do right, and trust in God. **God, that cannot lie.**—*What God cannot do:*—Truth once reigned supreme upon our globe, and then earth was Paradise. Man knew no sorrow while he was ignorant of falsehood. Falsehood is everywhere; it is entertained both by the lowest and the highest; it permeates all society. In the so-called religious world, which should be as the Holy of Holies, here too, the lie has insinuated itself. We have everywhere to battle with falsehood, and if we are to bless the world, we must confront it with sturdy face and zealous spirit. God's purpose is to drive the lie out of the world, and be this your purpose and mine. After wandering over the sandy desert of deceit, how pleasant is it to reach our text, and feel that one spot at least is verdant with eternal truth. Blessed be Thou, O God, for Thou canst not lie. I. THE TRUTH OF THE TEXT. 1. God is not subject to those infirmities which lead us into falsehood. You and I are such that we can know in the heart, and yet with the tongue deny; but God is one and indivisible; God is light, and in Him is no darkness at all; with Him is no variableness, neither shadow of turning. 2. The scriptural idea of God forbids that He should lie. The very word "God" comprehendeth everything which is good and great. Admit the lie, and to us at once there would be nothing but the black darkness of atheism for ever. I could neither love, worship, nor obey a lying God. 3. God is too wise to lie. Falsehood is the expedient of a fool. 4. And the lie is the method of the little and the mean. You know that a great man does not lie; a good man can never be false. Put goodness and greatness together, and a lie is altogether incongruous to the character. Now God is too great to need the lie, and too good to wish to do such a thing; both His greatness and His goodness repel the thought. 5. What motive could God have for lying? When a man lies it is that he may gain something, but "the cattle on a thousand hills" are God's, and all the beasts of the forest, and all the flocks of the meadows. Mines of inexhaustible riches are His, and treasures of infinite power and wisdom. He cannot gain aught by untruth, for "the earth is the Lord's, and the fulness thereof"; wherefore, then, should He lie? 6. Moreover, we may add to all this the experience of men with regard to God. It has been evident enough in all ages that God cannot lie. II. THE BREADTH OF MEANING IN THE TEXT. When we are told in Scripture that God cannot lie, there is usually associated with the idea the thought of immutability. As for instance—"He is not a man that He should lie, nor the son of man that He should repent." We understand by it, not only that He cannot say what is untrue, but that having said something which is true He never changes from it, and does not by any possibility alter His purpose or retract His word. This is very consolatory to the Christian, that whatever God has said in the Divine purpose is never changed. The decrees of God were not written upon sand, but upon the eternal brass of His unchangeable nature. There is no shadow of a lie upon anything which God thinks, or speaks, or does. He cannot lie in His prophecies. How solemnly true have they been! Ask the wastes of Nineveh; turn to the mounds of Babylon; let the traveller speak concerning Idumea and Petra. Has God's curse been an idle word? No, not in one single case. As God is true in His prophecies, so is He faithful to His promises. His threatenings are true also. Ah! sinner, thou mayst go on in thy ways for many a day, but thy sin shall find thee out at the last. III. HOW WE OUGHT TO ACT TOWARDS GOD IF IT BE TRUE THAT HE IS A "GOD THAT CANNOT LIE." 1. If it be so that God cannot lie, then it must be the natural duty of all His creatures to believe Him. If I doubt God, as far as I am able I rob Him of His honour; I am, in fact, living an open traitor and a sworn rebel against God, upon whom I heap the daily insult of daring to doubt Him. 2. If we were absolutely sure that there lived on earth a person who could not lie, how would you treat him? Well, I think you would cultivate his acquaintance. 3. If we knew a man who could not lie, we should believe him, methinks, without an oath. To say "He has promised and will perform; He has said that whosoever believeth in Christ is not condemned; I do believe in Christ, and therefore I am not condemned," this is genuine faith. 4. Again, if we knew a man who could not lie, we should believe him in the teeth of fifty witnesses the other way. Why, we should say, "they may say what they will, but they can lie." This shows us that we ought to believe God in the teeth of every contradiction. Even if outward providence should come to you, and say that God has forsaken you, that is only one; and even if fifty trials should all say that God has forsaken you, yet, as God says, "I will never leave thee, nor forsake thee," which will you take—the one promise of God who cannot lie, or the fifty outward providences which you cannot interpret? 5. If a man were introduced to us, and we were certain that he could not lie, we should believe everything he said, however incredible it might appear to us at first sight to be. It does seem very incredible at first sight that God should take a sinner, full of sin, and forgive all his iniquities in one moment, simply and only upon the ground of the sinner believing in Christ. But supposing it should seem too good to be true, yet, since you have it upon the testimony of One who "cannot lie," I pray you believe it. (*C. H. Spurgeon.*) *Lessons :*—1. If God cannot lie, then whatsoever His ministers promise or threaten from Him, and out of His Word, is above all exception; seeing He hath spoken it, who cannot lie, deceive, or be deceived; which should stir up every man to give glory unto God (as Abraham did) by sealing to His truth—that is, by believing and applying unto his own soul every word that proceedeth out of the mouth of God, for whosoever thus receiveth His testimony hath sealed that God is true, than which no greater glory can be given unto Him. Whereas not to believe Him on His Word is as high a dishonour as any man can cast upon Him, for it is to give God the lie; he that believeth not hath made Him a liar, which in manners and civility we could not offer to our equal, and which even a mean man would scorn to put up at our hands. 2. Seeing God cannot lie let every one of us labour to express this virtue of God—first, and especially the minister in his place, seeing he speaketh from God; nay, God speaketh by him, he must therefore deliver true sayings worthy of all men to be received, that he may say in his own heart that which Paul spake of himself, "I speak the truth in Christ, I lie not," and justify that of His doctrine which Paul did of his writings, "the things which now I write unto you, behold I witness before God that I lie not." (*T. Taylor, D.D.*)    *God cannot lie :*—I. AN ARGUMENT FOR TRUST. God, in all views of His character, may be safely trusted. He is wise, mighty, good, and faithful.   II. AN ARGUMENT FOR TRUTH. God, who cannot lie Himself, hates lying in others. Be truthful, for God cannot be deceived. (*J. Edmond, D.D.*)    **Promised before the world began.**—*All the promises, promises to Christ :*—St. Paul speaks only of the promise of "eternal life," but you will admit at once that such a promise must be regarded as including every other.  In promising "eternal life," God is to be considered as promising whatsoever is required for the attaining eternal life.  The promise of eternal life is a sort of summary of all the promises; for every other promise has to do with something which is helpful to us in our course; with those assistances in duty, or those supports under trial, without which eternal life can never be reached.   To whom, then, did He make the promise?  If He promised before the world began, He must have promised before there were any human beings, with whom to enter into covenant.  If the promise were then made, the two contracting parties must have been then in existence or intercourse; whereas there was then certainly no Church, no man, to form a covenant with the Almighty.  There can be little debate that it must have been to Christ, the second Person in the ever-blessed Trinity, that God made the "promise of eternal life before the world began." "Before the world began" the apostasy of our race was contemplated and provided for in the councils of heaven.   A solemn covenant was entered into between the Persons of the Trinity, each undertaking an amazing part in the plan for our redemption; and though the Mediator had not then assumed human form, He already acted as the Head or Representative of the Church, engaging to offer Himself as a sacrifice for sin, and receiving in return the promise that the sacrifice should be accepted, and should prevail to the full salvation of all such as believe on His name. Eternal life was promised to Christ, on behalf of the Church; it was promised to the Church for the sake of Christ; or, rather, it was promised to Christ, as that result of His obedience and endurance in the flesh, which He might bestow on all those who should have faith in the propitiation.   But whilst this seems sufficient to explain the strangeness of our text, you can hardly fail to observe that the explanation involves a great general doctrine or truth; even the same doctrine or truth which is elsewhere announced by St. Paul when, speaking of Christ, he says that "all the promises of God are in Him yea and amen"; in other words, that God has promised nothing to man, but in Christ or on account of Christ, and that all that He hath thus promised hath on His account been fulfilled.  In order to the clearing and understanding of this, you are to observe that Adam, as the father of all men, stood federally in their place. And when the whole race had thus fallen, in the person of their representative, there were no blessings and no mercies for which man could look.  Human nature had become so necessarily and entirely exposed to Divine vengeance that there was no room whatsoever for promise. Therefore, if He promised at all, it could only have been in virtue of His having covenanted with another Head; with One who had put the race which He represented into such a moral position, that it would no longer be at variance with the Divine character, to extend to them the offices of friendship. Because it was His own Son who had undertaken to be this Head of humanity, and because it was therefore certain that the required ransom would be paid to the last farthing, God could immediately open to man the fountain of His benevolence, and deal with man as a being who stood within the possibilities of forgiveness and immortality.  But if this be the true account why, after his transgression, man could still be the object of the promises of God, it follows distinctly that, according to the doctrine of our text, these promises, however announced to the sinner at or after the time of his sin, were promises originally made to another; and that, too, "before the world began." There could have been no promises, it appears, had not "the Word which was in the beginning with God, and which was God," previously engaged to become the Surety for the beings who had just woven death and woe and shame into their inheritance. Assuredly it follows from this that whatsoever is now promised to man is not promised to man in himself but to man in his representative. It must have been promised to Christ before it was promised to man; or rather, the promise must have been made unto Christ though the thing promised should be given to man. Fix not, then, as the origin of a promise, the occasion when the promise was clothed in human speech; associate not the making of that promise with the human being to whom it was first uttered. The promise was made before man was created; the promise was given to a higher than man, to a higher than any finite being. And when you have taken, as you justly may, all the promises of God, and gathered them into the one emphatic summary, the "promise of eternal life," you are not to say, "This clause of the promise was made to Adam, this to Moses, this to David, this to Paul"; you are to say, generally, of the whole, with the apostle in our text, that "God, which cannot lie, promised it"—and to whom could He then promise but to Christ?—"promised it before the world began." Now we have been so occupied with the great doctrine of our text, with the fact of all God's promises being promised to Christ, and to us only for the sake of Christ, and in virtue of His merits, that we have made no reference to what St. Paul here says of God's truthfulness—"God, that cannot lie." He uses a similar expression in his Epistle to the Hebrews: "That by two immutable things, in which it was impossible for God to lie, we might have a strong consolation." It is one of Satan's most frequent and dangerous devices, to put before you your unworthiness, and to strive to make this hide the rich provisions of grace. It looks so like genuine humility, to think oneself unworthy to have a promise made good, that the Christian will almost fancy it a duty to encourage the suspicion which the devil has injected. But you are to remember that your own unworthiness has nothing whatsoever to do either with the making or the performing the promise. God did not originally make the promise to you; He made it to His own dear Son, even to Christ, "before the world began"; and the performing the promise, the making good His own Word, is this to be contingent on anything excellent in yourselves? Nay, it is for His own sake, for the glory of His own great name, that He accomplishes His gracious declaration. He is faithful, He "cannot lie"; heaven and earth may pass away, but not one jot nor one tittle can fail of all which He hath covenanted with Christ, and, through Christ, with the meanest of His followers. (*H. Melvill, B.D.*)

Ver. 3. **But hath in due times manifested His Word through preaching.**— *A timely revelation :*—I. A TIMELY REVELATION—the purpose of salvation through Christ Jesus. II. A SACRED TRUST—to preach the unsearchable riches of Christ. III. A DIVINE COMMISSION—to preach "according to the commandment of God." (*F. Wagstaff.*) *Salvation revealed :*—I. That salvation is more clearly revealed than in former ages appeareth in that all the time of the law was but the infancy and nonage of the Church, which then was as a child under tutors and governors; and as a child was initiated in rudiments and elements of Christian religion, and endued with a small measure of knowledge and faith, because the time was not come wherein the mysteries of Christ were unfolded. II. The Lord (who doth not only by His wisdom order His greatest works, but every circumstance of them) effecteth all His promises and purposes in the due season of them. III. The manifestation of salvation is to be sought for in the preaching of the Word. Which point is plain, in that the preaching of the Word is an ordinance of God. 1. To make Christ known, in whose name alone salvation is to be had. 2. To beget and confirm faith in the heart, by which alone, as by an hand, we apprehend and apply Him with His merits to our salvation. (*T. Taylor, D.D.*) *God's Word manifested through preaching :*—I. THE MANIFESTATION OF GOD'S WORD. This was gradually made to men—to all nations, both Jews and Gentiles—in general, and to particular places. II. THE INSTRUMENTALITY EMPLOYED FOR THAT MANIFESTATION. We should imitate the simplicity, zeal and affection displayed in the apostle's preaching. (*W. Lucy.*) *Preaching in God's name :*—An American gentleman once went to hear Whitefield for the first time, in consequence of the report he heard of his preaching powers. The day was rainy, the congregation comparatively thin, and the beginning of the sermon rather heavy. Our American friend began to say to himself, "This man is no great wonder, after all." He looked round, and saw the congregation as little interested as himself. One old man in front of the pulpit had fallen asleep. But all at once Whitefield stopped short. His countenance changed. And then he suddenly broke forth in an altered tone: "If I had come to speak to you in my own name, you might well rest your elbows on your knees, and your heads on your hands, and sleep; and once in a while look up, and say, What is this babbler talking of? But I have not come to you in my own name. No! I have come to you in the name of the Lord of Hosts" (here he brought down his hand and foot with a force that made the building ring), "and I must, and will be heard." The congregation started. The old man woke up at once. "Ay, ay!" cried Whitefield, fixing his eyes on him, "I have waked you up, have I? I meant to do it. I am not come here to preach to stocks and stones. I have come to you in the name of the Lord God of Hosts, and I must, and will, have an audience." The hearers were stripped of their apathy at once. Every word of the sermon was attended to. And the American gentleman never forgot it. (*J. C. Ryle.*) *The best ally in Christian work:*—Frederick the Great was once in company with a number of French wits, and there was a brave Scotchman also at the table, who was the ambassador of England. Frederick the Great was then contemplating a war, in which he would be dependent upon English subsidies, and by and by the ambassador, as he listened to the king and these French wits making fun of religion, and speaking of its certain and sudden decay, said, "By the help of God England will stand by Prussia in the war." Frederick turned round and said, rather sneeringly, "By the help of God! I did not know that you had an ally of that name." But the Scotchman turned round to the king, and said, "May it please your majesty, that is the only ally England has to whom England does not send subsidies." Now, let me say, that we as a Christian Church and as a missionary society have an ally of that name. Our ally is the Lord of Hosts, and it is because His name has been upon our banners that we have succeeded in the past. (*T. H. Hunt.*)      **Which is committed unto me, according to the commandment of God our Saviour.**—*The Christian ministry:*—I. Every minister called by God IS ONE OF CHRIST'S COMMITTEES, unto whom He betrusteth now after His departure the care and oversight of His spouse, who is dearer unto Him than His own life, appeareth in that they are called stewards of this great house, having received the keys to open the kingdom of heaven, and to distribute to the necessity of their fellow servants; chosen vessels, as Paul, not to contain, but to carry the pearl and the treasure of the kingdom; feeders, as Peter, husbandmen, to whom the vineyard is let out till His return.  1. The honour of a minister is faithfulness in the diligent and careful discharging himself of that trust committed unto him; the principal part of which repose standeth in the faithful dispensing of Christ's legacies to His Church, according to His own testament; which as it is his duty enjoined (1 Cor. iv. 2), so is it his crown, his joy, his glory, that by his faithful pains he hath procured the welfare of his people, and bringeth with it a great recompense of reward; for if he that showeth himself a good and faithful servant in little things, shall be ruler over much; what may he expect that is faithful in the greatest?  2. The ministry is no calling of ease, but a matter of great charge; nor contemptible, as many contemptuous persons think it too base a calling for their children; but honourable, near unto God, a calling committing unto men great matters, which not only the angels themselves have dispensed sundry times, but even the Lord of the angels, Jesus Christ Himself, all the while He ministered upon earth; the honour of which calling is such, as those who are employed in the duties of it, are called not only angels, but co-workers with Christ in the salvation of men.  II. Whosoever would find comfort in themselves, or clear and justify their callings to others, or do good in that place of the body wherein they are set, MUST BE ABLE TO PROVE THAT THEY ARE NOT INTRUDERS, BUT PRESSED BY THIS CALLING AND COMMANDMENT OF GOD: that as Paul performed every duty in the Church by virtue of his extraordinary calling, so they by virtue of their ordinary. For can any man think that a small advantage to himself, which our apostle doth so dwell upon in his own person, and that in every epistle, making his calling known to be committed unto him, not of men, nor by men, but by Jesus Christ? (See Gal. i. 1, ii. 7; Eph. iii. 2; 1 Thess. ii. 4.)  1. Let no man presume to take upon him any office in the Church uncalled; no man taketh this honour to himself. Christ Himself must be appointed of His Father.  2. Let none content himself with the calling of man separated from God's calling; for this was the guise of the false apostles against whom our apostle opposeth himself and calling almost everywhere, who were called of men, but not of God. 3. In all other callings let men be assured they have God's warrant, both in the lawfulness of the callings themselves, and in their holy exercise of them; passing through them daily in the exercise of faith and repentance, not forgetting daily to sanctify them by the Word and prayer. III. MINISTERS MAY AND OUGHT TO BE MORE OR LESS IN THE COMMENDATION OF THEIR CALLING, as the nature and necessity of the people to whom they write or speak do require. 1. As the apostle here magnifieth his authority in that he is a servant of God. 2. An apostle of Jesus Christ. 3. That he received his apostleship by commission and commandment of Christ Himself; and 4. All this while hath by sundry other arguments amplified the excellency of his calling: the reason of all which is not so much to persuade Titus, who was before sufficiently persuaded of it; but partly for the Cretians' sake, that they might the rather entertain this doctrine so commended in the person of the bringer; and partly because many in this isle lifted up themselves against him and Titus, as men thrusting in their sickles into other men's fields too busily; or else if they had a calling, yet taking too much upon them, both in correcting disorders and establishing such novelties among them as best liked them; so as here being to deal against false apostles, perverse people, and erroneous doctrines he is more prolix and lofty in his title; otherwise, where he met not with such strong opposition, he is more sparing in his titles, as in the Epistles to the Colossians, Thessalonians, &c. (*T. Taylor, D.D.*)

Ver. 4. **To Titus, mine own son after the common faith.**—*Lessons:*—I. A SPIRITUAL RELATIONSHIP (*Cf.* Acts xv.; Gal. ii. 2; 2 Cor. ii. 13, vii. 6, &c.) II. A THREEFOLD BLESSING. 1. "Grace," the source of our redemption. 2. "Mercy," displayed in our redemption. 3. "Peace," the result of our redemption. III. THE SOURCE AND MEDIUM OF THE BLESSING. God the Father from whom it comes, and Christ the Son through whom it comes. (*F. Wagstaff.*) *Spiritual parentage:*—I. THAT MINISTERS ARE SPIRITUAL FATHERS TO BEGET CHILDREN TO GOD, appeareth in that the Hebrew phrase not only styleth them by the name of fathers. 1. Who indeed are so properly by the way of blood and natural generation? 2. Neither, only those who are in a right descending line, though never so far off. 3. Neither, only those who adopt others into the room and place of children. 4. But those also that are in the room of fathers, either generally, as all superiors, in age, place, or gifts; or more specially such as by whose counsel, wisdom, tenderness and care, we are directed as by fathers; who in these offices and not in themselves (for sometimes they be inferiors otherwise) become fathers unto us. Thus was Joseph an inferior, called a father of Pharaoh; that is, a counsellor. Job, for his tenderness and care, called a father of the poor. Scholars of the prophets, called sons of the prophets. Elisha, saith of Elijah, my father, my father; and Jubal was the father of all that play on harps. But much more properly is the minister called the father of such as he converts unto the faith, because they beget men unto God, as Paul did Onesimus in his bonds, in which regeneration the seed is that heavenly grace whereby a Divine nature is framed, the instrument by which it is conveyed, is the Word of God in the ministry of it. Now if any be desirous to carry themselves towards their ministers, as children towards their parents, they must perform unto them these duties. 1. They must give them double honour (1 Tim. v. 17), reverencing their persons, their places. 2. They must partake in all their goods, as the Levites in the law did; yea, if need be, lay down their necks for their sakes (Rom. xvi. 4) in way of thankfulness. 3. No accusations must be received against them under two or three witnesses; a dutiful child will not hear, much less believe, evil reports of his father. 4. In doubtful cases of conscience resort unto them for counsel, as children to their father. 5. Obey them in all godly precepts, endure their severity, be guided by their godly directions, as those who have the oversight of souls committed unto them, even as the child ingeniously imitateth and obeyeth his father. II. FAITH IS ONE AND THE SAME IN ALL THE ELECT, AND IS THEREFORE CALLED THE COMMON FAITH (Eph. iv. 5), there is one faith which is true. Which grace is but one, and common to all the elect, notwithstanding there be diverse measures and degrees of it peculiar to some. Hence the apostle Peter calleth it the like precious faith. 1. In respect of the kind of it being a justifying faith, by which all that believe have power to be the sons of God (John i. 12; Gal. iii. 26). 2. Of the object of it, which is one Christ, the same yesterday, and to-day, and for ever; who dwelleth in the hearts of every believer (Eph. iii. 17), whom, although the fathers of former ages beheld Him to come, and the latter ages already come ; yet both rejoice in seeing His day with the same eye of faith : the difference is, that one seeth it somewhat more clearly than the other. 3. Of the same end of it, which is salvation, common to all believers; called therefore by Jude the common salvation. (*T. Taylor, D.D.*) *Spiritual children :*—Calvin's three children all died in infancy. Of the last he wrote to a friend : " The Lord gave me another son, and the Lord hath taken him away; but have I not thousands of children in the faith of Christ ? " **Grace, mercy, and peace.**—*Grace bringing peace :*—I. THE GRACE OF GOD IS THE WHOLE SUFFICIENCY OF HIS PEOPLE. The first, middle, and last cause of every good thing conveyed unto them, or issuing from them : not once did the Lord enforce this point upon His own people, teaching them by things temporal, their spiritual estate and condition (Deut. vii. 7). II. ONLY THEY THAT ARE BY GRACE AND MERCY ACCEPTED OF GOD HAVE THEIR PORTION IN THIS PEACE HERE MENTIONED. 1. Peace, that is all kind of prosperity, is promised only to the godly. They shall prosper in everything ; and the apostle pronounceth it, only upon the Israel of God. 2. It is accordingly bestowed upon those only that are justified by faith ; seeing they only have peace with God, which is the principal part of it. 3. To show it to be a fruit of God's grace, sundry phrases in Scripture might be alleged ; as that it is called the "peace of God," and that God is called the "God of peace"; as also that difference which is worthy to be observed between the salutations of the Old and New Testament. In the Old Testament, grace and peace are never joined. The ordinary form of salutation was, " peace be with thee," " peace be to this house," " go in peace " ; but the apostles, after the mystery of redemption was revealed and perfected before the ordinary salutation, prefix this word—grace, or mercy, or both ; that as they are never joined in the Old Testament, so are they never separated in the New, to show that we cannot look to have one of them alone, or separate them, no more than we can safely sunder the branch from the root, or the stream from the fountain. (*T. Taylor, D.D.*) *Peace through Christ :*—A minister was asked to visit a poor dying woman. The messenger being ignorant could give no account of her state, except that she was a very good woman and very happy, and was now at the end of a well-spent life, therefore sure of going to heaven. The minister went, saw that she was very ill, and after a few kindly inquiries about her bodily condition, said : " Well, I understand you are in a very peaceful state of mind, depending upon a well-spent life." The dying woman looked hard at him, and said : " Yes, I am in the enjoyment of peace. You are quite right ; sweet peace, and that from a well-spent life. But it is the well-spent life of Jesus ; not my doing, but His ; not my merits, but His blood." Yes ; only one man has spent a life that has met all the requirements of God's holy law, and on which we rest before God. (*Preacher's Lantern.*)

Ver. 5. **Set in order the things that are wanting.**—*Church order :*—I. IN EVERY CHRISTIAN COMMUNITY THERE SHOULD BE THE MAINTENANCE OF ORDER. Confusion in a Church is a calumny of Christ, and obstructive at once to its peace, power, prosperity, and usefulness. II. THE MAINTENANCE OF CHURCH ORDER MAY REQUIRE THE MINISTRY OF SPECIAL SUPERINTENDENTS. The words elder, bishop, pastor, &c., all refer to the same office—that of overseer. Such a one is to maintain order, not by legislating but by loving ; not by the assumption of authority, but by a humble devotion to the spiritual interests of all. III. THE SUPERINTENDENTS SHOULD BE MEN OF DISTINGUISHED EXCELLENCE. (*D. Thomas, D.D.*) *Perfecting the order of the Church :*— 1. It noteth what was the special work of an evangelist; namely, that being the companions of the apostles, they were to bring on the work of the Lord to perfection, both by establishing that foundation they had laid, and building on further by their direction where they left off. The office was middle between the apostle and the pastor ; the calling was immediate from the apostles, as the apostle was immediate from Christ. 2. Notwithstanding many defects and wants in this Church and those great ones, and that in constitution, for we see their cities were destitute of elders and Church governors ; yet was it neither neglected by Paul, nor separated from by Titus as a cage of unclean birds ; teaching us not presently to condemn a number and society of men (much less of Churches) for want of some laws or government (for no Church is not wanting in some), if they join together in the profession of truth of doctrine and worship ; for so many of the Churches, planted by the apostles themselves, might have been refused for wanting some offices for a time, although they were after supplied. 3. We learn hence, that no Church is hastily brought to any perfection. The apostles themselves, the master builders, with much wisdom and labour, and often in long time, made not such proceedings ; but that, had they not provided labourers to follow them with a diligent hand, all had been lost. Much ado had they to lay the foundation, and prepare matter for the building; and yet this they did, by converting men to the faith and baptizing them; but after this to join them into a public profession of the faith, and constitute visible faces of Churches among them, required more help and labour, and for most part was left to the evangelists. So as the building of God's house is not unlike to the finishing of other great buildings, with what labour are stones digged out of the earth? with what difficulty depart they from their natural roughness? what sweat and strength is spent ere the mason can smooth them? As it is also with the timber; and yet, after all this, they lie a long time here and there scattered asunder and make no house, till, by the skill of some cunning builder, they be aptly laid, and fastened together in their frame. So every man's heart, in the natural roughness of it, is as hard as a stone; his will and affections, like the crabbed and knotty oaks, invincibly resisting all the pains of God's masons and carpenters, till the finger of God in the ministry come and make plain, and smooth way, working in their conversion. (*T. Taylor, D.D.*)    *Titus left in Crete:*—I. THE POWER LEFT TO TITUS. "*I left thee*"—I, Paul, an apostle of Christ. II. THE USE AND EXERCISE OF THIS POWER. 1. To set in order things that are wanting. 2. To ordain elders in every city. III. THE LIMITATION OF THESE ACTS. "As I had appointed thee." Titus must do nothing but according to commission, and by special direction. (*W. Burkitt, M.A.*)    *Ministers as moral leaders:*—I. THAT MINISTERS HAVE SPECIAL WORK AS WELL AS GENERAL. II. THAT THE WORK OF THE BEST OF US NEEDS REVISION BY OTHERS. "Set in order," lit., "revise, make straight." III. THAT EVERY COMPANY OF CHRISTIANS SHOULD HAVE A LEADER OR OVERSEER. "Elders in every city," is suggestive of the widespread influence of the gospel in Crete, which was famous for its cities. Homer, in one place mentions, that the island had a hundred cities, and in another ninety. (*F. Wagstaff.*)    **Ordain elders in every city.**—*An embertide sermon:*—Our Lord Himself is the sole source and origin of all ministerial power. He is the Head of the Church—none can take office in the Church except with His authorisation; He is our great High Priest—none can serve under Him, unless by His appointment; He is our King—none can bear rule in His kingdom, except they hold His commission. This ministerial power our Lord conferred upon His apostles. In the Acts of the Apostles and other parts of the New Testament, we learn how the apostles carried out this commission. Their first act after the Ascension was to admit another to their own ranks. St. Matthias was co-opted into the room of the traitor Judas. After a time the needs of the growing Church required them to appoint subordinate officers, they themselves still retaining the supreme control. These officers were, in the first place, deacons, whose special duty it was to attend to the due distribution of the Church's alms, but who also, as we learn from the subsequent history of two of them, SS. Stephen and Philip, received authority to preach and to baptize; and in the second place, elders who were appointed to still higher functions, to be pastors of congregations, to feed the flock of God and have the oversight thereof. We read of the elders first in Acts xi. 30. The word "elder," wherever it occur in the New Testament, is a translation of the Greek word "*presbuteros*," from which our words "presbyter" and "priest" have come, the latter by contraction. If the word had been left untranslated, as the words "bishop," "deacon," and "apostle" were, and appeared as "presbyter" or "priest," the English reader would have been saved from much perplexity, and much danger of erroneous inferences. Thus the apostles, in order to keep pace with the requirements of the Church, shared, by degrees, their functions with others, admitted others by prayer and the laying on of hands into the sacred ministry. But one prerogative they still retained in their own keeping, that was, the power of ordaining others. Yet if the Church was to be continued, if the promise of Christ was to be fulfilled, "Lo, I am with you alway, even unto the end of the world," this power also must be transmitted. And so we find that the college of apostles was gradually enlarged. One there was, St. Paul, who had received the apostolate, with all its prerogatives, directly from heaven. Others, such as St. Barnabas, were also admitted to the apostolic ranks and placed on an equal footing with the original Twelve. And, finally, in the Pastoral Epistles we come to the last link of the chain which connects the apostolic rule of the Church with the episcopal superintendence which followed. As the apostles travelled through the whole known world, and established Churches and ordained clergy in every city to which they came, they found at last that the oversight of all these Christians of whom they were the spiritual fathers had become too much for them. It was felt to be a necessity to place over each Church a local superintendent, who, within a fixed district, should be armed with full apostolical authority—with power to rule the Church, to administer discipline, to ordain clergy. When we open the Pastoral Epistles we find that it was to just such an office that SS. Timothy and Titus were appointed. And history informs us that immediately after the apostles' times the Christian Church in all parts of the world was governed by bishops, who claimed to be successors of the apostles, and who alone had the power to ordain, with priests and deacons under them. Why the bishops did not retain for themselves the name of apostles we know not; but probably they thought themselves unworthy to share that title with such eminent saints as those who had been called by Christ to be His original apostles, and therefore they adopted a designation which had less august associations attached to it, having formerly been borne by clergy of the second order. For more than 1,500 years no other form of Church government was known in any part of Christendom. Turn where we will, north or south, east or west, or take any period of history previous to the Reformation, and we can discover no portion of the Church which was not governed by bishops, or where there were not these three orders of ministers. By the good providence of God, in the great crisis of the sixteenth century, we were permitted to retain the ancient organisation of the Christian Church. The Reformation in these islands was the act of the Church itself, which, while it rejected the usurped supremacy of the Bishop of Rome, and returned in other respects to the purer faith of primitive times, carefully maintained unimpaired the three Orders of the Ministry. There was no severing of the link which bound us to the men to whom the Great Head of the Church said, "As My Father hath sent Me, even so send I you." What abundant reason have we, clergy and people alike, to be thankful to God for this! We clergy can go about our work with no misgivings as to whether we are indeed ambassadors for Christ or no. We know that in all our ministerial acts He is with us, that He indeed is acting through us, and that our feeble, unworthy efforts to advance His kingdom and glory are backed and supported by an infinite Power which can turn our weakness into strength. And the people, too, should bless and thank God that, through His great goodness towards them, the sixteenth century proved in these islands a true Reformation in religion—not a Revolution, as it did elsewhere; that you belong to the very Church founded by the apostles, and that Church, too, released from mediæval corruption, and saved from those debasing modern superstitions into which Roman Christianity has fallen; that you have free access to the means of grace which Christ appointed for His people; that the Sacraments which are generally necessary to salvation are here duly ministered according to God's ordinance in all those things that of necessity are requisite for the same; that you have a ministry which can speak to you in Christ's name, and bear to you His message of reconciliation; for they have been set apart to their office by Himself—by Him to whom alone all power has been committed in heaven and in earth; that you are "fellow-citizens with the saints and of the household of God, and are built upon the foundation of the apostles and prophets, Jesus Christ Himself being the chief corner stone." On a valid ministry depends the very existence of a Church. On a faithful ministry depends the well-being of a Church. And how largely does the character of the ministry depends upon the people? How largely is it in the power of the people to assist the bishop in making a choice of fit persons for Holy Orders? I am not now alluding to the direct power the people possess to prevent the ordination of an unworthy man. It is for this express purpose that the *Si quis*, as it is called, of the candidate is appointed to be read in the parish church previous to the ordination. The name of the candidate is published, and the people are invited to object if they can allege any impediment. And another opportunity of the same kind is given at the ordination itself. I am now alluding specially to your prayers. "Brethren, pray for us," was the earnest request of St. Paul to the Christians of his day, and surely the successors of the apostles now need no less the prayers and sympathy of their people. (*J. G. Carleton, B.D.*) *Directions regarding the appointment of elders:*—1. It is Titus himself who is to appoint these elders throughout the cities in which congregations exist. It is not the congregations that are to elect the overseers, subject to the approval of the apostle's delegate; still less that he is to ordain any one whom they may elect. The full responsibility of each appointment rests with him. Anything like popular election of the ministers is not only not suggested, it is by implication entirely excluded. 2. In making each appointment Titus is to consider the congregation. He is to look carefully to the reputation which the man of his choice bears among his fellow Christians. A man in whom the congregation have no confidence, because of the bad repute which attaches to himself or his family, is not to be appointed. In this way the congregation have an indirect veto; for the man to whom they cannot give a good character may not be taken to be set over them. 3. The appointment of Church officers is regarded as imperative: it is on no account to be omitted. And it is not merely an arrangement that is as a rule desirable: it is to be universal. Titus is to go through the congregations " city by city," and take care that each has its elders or body of elders. 4. As the name itself indicates, these elders are to be taken from the older men among the believers. As a rule they are to be heads of families, who have had experience of life in its manifold relations, and especially who have had experience of ruling a Christian household. That will be some guarantee for their capacity for ruling a Christian congregation. 5. It must be remembered that they are not merely delegates, either of Titus, or of the congregation. The essence of their authority is not that they are the representatives of the body of Christian men and women over whom they are placed. It has a far higher origin. They are " God's stewards." It is His household that they direct and administer, and it is from Him that their powers are derived. As God's agents they have a work to do among their fellowmen, through themselves, for Him. As God's ambassadors they have a message to deliver, good tidings to proclaim, ever the same, and yet ever new. As " God's stewards " they have treasures to guard with reverent care, treasures to augment by diligent cultivation, treasures to distribute with prudent liberality. (*A. Plummer, D.D.*)

Ver. 6. **If any be blameless.**—*Lessons :*—I. CHARACTER, THE PRIMARY QUALIFICATION FOR OFFICE IN THE CHURCH. II. DOMESTIC AND SOCIAL RELATIONSHIPS, CONDUCIVE, RATHER THAN HINDRANCES, TO CHRISTIAN SERVICE. III. GOOD FAMILY GOVERNMENT, A GUARANTEE FOR CHURCH GOVERNMENT. (*F. Wagstaff.*)   *A man of scandalous life is unfit to be a minister :*—1. Our apostle here first insisteth upon the life of him that is to be chosen, and afterwards requireth his fitness for doctrine : and so in his charge to Timothy that he should lay hand on no man rashly, addeth, that some men's sins go beforehand, and some men's sins follow after judgment : as though he had said more largely, Use all the circumspection thou canst, yet some hypocrites will creep into the ministry. Some are inwardly profane, and such close sinners thou canst not discern, till afterward they manifest themselves. Others are open sinners, of which thou mayest judge aright ; these latter thou art to hinder, the former reclaim, or seasonably remove, and so salve up the sore again : for how requisite is it that such a sweet and favourite doctrine should be matched with a sweet and savoury Christian conversation ! 2. That such an high calling is to be graced with an unreprovable life was typified in the law sundry ways, as after we shall more clearly see in the positive virtues required, especially in that prohibition that none of Aaron's sons, or seed, that had any blemish in him, might once press to offer before the Lord, neither come near the vail, nor stand by the altar. 3. A scandalous and obnoxious person shall never do good in his calling. For although the things of Christ, as the Word, sacraments, and doctrine, depend not upon the person of the minister, but on the ordinance of Christ, neither in themselves are the worse in bad men's hands, no more than a true man's piece of gold in the hands of a thief ; yet by our weakness, in such a man's hand, they are weaker to us : and although no man can answer or warrant the refusing of pure doctrine (which is not to be had in respect of persons) for the spotted life of the minister, who, while he sitteth in Moses's chair (be he Pharisee, be he hypocrite) must be heard, yet can it not be but that the wickedness of Eli's sons will make the people abhor the offerings of the Lord, which what a grievous sin it was before the Lord (see 1 Sam. ii. 17). Again, how can he benefit his people whose hands are bound, whose mouth is shut, and cannot utter the truth without continual galling and sentencing of himself? and when every scoffer shall be ready to say to him, " Art thou become weak like one of us ? " and the word shall be still returned upon himself, how can it be expected that he should do good amongst them? 4. It is a most dangerous condition to himself to be a good teacher of a bad life, for such a one is in the snare of the devil, that is, when he seeth his life still more and more exprobrated, and himself more despised every day than other (for it is just with God that with the wicked should be reproach), then he begins to grow so bold and impudent, as that he casts off all shame and care, and as one desperate and hardened in sin, prostituteth himself remorselessly unto all lewdness and ungodly conversation. (*T. Taylor, D.D.*) *Rules to keep a man unreprovable:*—1. Labour with thy heart to see itself still in the presence of God, and this will be a means to keep it in order ; whereas otherwise an unruly heart will break out one time or other. 2. Have a care of a good name, as well as a good conscience ; not so much for thy own as for God's glory : neither because thyself, but others stand much upon it. 3. Avoid occasions of sins, appearances of evil, seeing thy motes become beams. 4. Study to do thy own duty diligently, meddle not with other men's matters. 5. Curb and cover thine own infirmities, buffet thy body, and bring it in subjection (1 Cor. ix.). 6. Daily pray for thyself, with a desire of the prayer and admonition of others. (*Ibid.*) *Importance of good ministerial character :*—Personal character is of the utmost moment in the work of admonition. We must not try to remove motes from the eyes of others while we have beams in our own. Quarles reminds us that " He who cleanses a blot with blurred fingers, makes a greater blot. Even the candle-snuffers of the sanctuary were of pure gold " (Exod. xxxvii. 23). We may not urge others to activity, and lie still like logs ourselves. A quaint old preacher of the sixteenth century has put this truth into homely, pungent words : " Beloved in our Lord and Saviour Jesus Christ, it is a very monstrous thing that any man should have more tongues than hands. For God hath given us two hands and but one tongue, that we might do much and say but little. Yet many say so much and do so little, as though they had two tongues and but one hand ; nay, three tongues and never a hand. Such as these (which do either worse than they teach, or else less than they teach, teaching others to do well and to do much, but doing no whit themselves) may be resembled to divers things. To a whetstone, which being blunt itself, makes a knife sharp. To a painter, which being deformed himself, makes a fair picture. To a sign, which being weather-beaten, and hanging without itself, directs passengers into the inn. To a bell, which being deaf and hearing not itself, calls the people into the church to hear. To a goldsmith, which being beggarly, and having not one piece of plate to use himself, hath stores for others which he shows and sells in his shop. Lastly, to a ridiculous actor in the city of Smyrna, who pronouncing ' O cœlum,' O heaven, pointed with his finger toward the ground. Such are all they which talk one thing and do another ; which teach well and do ill." (*C. H. Spurgeon.*) *The secret of a blameless life :*—Archbishop Benson, speaking after Earl Granville had unveiled the memorial to his predecessor, adorned the occasion by a reference to the secret of the beautiful life of the late Archbishop Tate. " I have heard," he said, " and I believe it is true, that on the first day of his wedded life he and his bride pledged themselves to each other that they would never quarrel with any one, and I believe that, with God's blessing and help, that pledge was kept to the end." *Husband of one wife :*—In the corrupt facility of divorce allowed both by Greek and Roman law, it was very common for man and wife to separate, and marry other parties during the life of each other. Thus, a man might have three or four living wives, or women who had successively been his wives. An example of this may be found in the English colony of Mauritius, where the French revolutionary law of divorce had been left unrepealed by the English Government ; and it is not uncommon to meet in society three or four women who have all been wives of one man, and three or four men who have all been husbands of one woman. Thus, successive rather than simultaneous polygamy is perhaps forbidden here. (*Conybeare and Howson.*) *The husband of one wife :*—The family arrangements in the Isle of Crete were the result of heathenism, and, of course, polygamy had prevailed. Many believers had several wives, as is often the case in heathenism at the present time, and one of the most difficult questions of modern missions is how to treat such cases. When a man and his two wives, for example, all at the same time become Christians, and demand baptism and the Lord's supper, what am I to do ? There is no passage that I know of in the Word of God to guide me in the matter ; and I am left to the general rules of Scripture, to the dictates of wisdom and prudence, and to the leadings of Divine Providence. If, however, such a man wished to become an elder, I would say, No, for a bishop must be blameless, the husband of one wife, and not of two wives, according to the decision of the apostle Paul. (*W. Graham, D.D.*)

Vers. 7–9. **For a bishop must be blameless.**—*An ideal bishop :*—I will try in five words to set before you the ideal of a bishop : humility, self-sacrifice, simplicity of heart, undaunted courage, moral faithfulness. Of holiness and of diligence I need hardly speak—no bishop could ever imagine himself to be a true bishop without these ; but glance for a moment at the others, for they go to the very root of the matter. 1. First, utter humility—" not lording it over God's heritage," &c. Pride is a sin foolish and hateful enough in any man, but it seems doubly so in a bishop. How instructive is that story of Augustine, the first Archbishop of Canterbury. When he summoned the other bishops to meet him, they asked a holy hermit of Bangor how they might know whether Augustine was or was not a man of God, and he answered that they might follow him if they found him to be of a meek and humble heart, for that was the yoke of Christ; but if he bore himself haughtily they should not regard him, for then he was certainly not of God. They took his advice, and hastened to the place of meeting, and when Augustine neither rose to meet them nor received them in any brotherly sort, but sat all the while pontifical in the chair, they would not acknowledge him or denote that they owed him any obedience but that of love. One of the noblest men the Church has ever seen—St. Thomas Aquinas—was also one of the most truly humble. Once a celebrated cardinal was seen passing to the high altar of his cathedral in scarlet robes and jewelled pectoral, in the midst of magnificent ecclesiastics; but one who knelt behind him, seeing a little stream of blood trickling where he knelt, observed that under the sweeping silken robes the great cardinal had been walking with bare feet over the flinty path, that his heart might be mortified amid the splendour of his state. Deep humility within—a violet which scarcely ever grows except at the foot of the cross—should be the mark of a true bishop. 2. Nor is utter self-sacrifice less necessary. If pride is detestable in a bishop, greed is no less so. The bishop who uses the revenues of his church to enrich his family, is false to one of the first duties of his post. The brother of the Bishop of Lincoln, in the twelfth century, complained that he was still left a ploughman. "Brother," said the great bishop, "if your cow dies, I will give you another, and if your plough wants mending I will have it mended; but a ploughman I found you, and a ploughman I mean to leave you." The income of the see should be spent upon the see. Poverty is never so honourable as in men who might be rich. When Archbishop Warren, Cranmer's predecessor, was told on his deathbed that he had only thirty pounds in the world, he answered with a smile, "Enough to pay my journey to heaven." 3. Simplicity of heart. None but small and unworthy men would lose by it. Neither pomp, nor wealth, nor office—prizes of accident as oft as merit—ever made any small man great. Once I was staying as a boy in a bishop's house, and there was dug up the brass plate from the tomb of one of his predecessors, and I have never forgotten the inscription on it: "Stay, passer by! See and smile at the palace of a bishop. The grave is the palace they must all dwell in soon!" 4. Unbounded courage. Scorn of mere passing popu- larity should be among his first qualities. When that persecuting emperor, Valens, sent his prefect to threaten St. Basil, and was met by a flat refusal of his demands, the prefect started from his seat and exclaimed, "Do you not fear my power?" "Why should I?" answered Basil. "What can happen to me?" "Confiscation," replied the prefect, "punishment, torture, death." "Is that all?" said Basil. "He who has nothing beyond my few books and these threadbare robes is not liable to confiscation. Punishment! How can I be punished when God is everywhere? Torture!—torture can only harm me for a moment; and death—death is a bene- factor, for it will send me the sooner to Him whom I love and serve." "No one has ever addressed me so," said the prefect. "Perhaps," answered Basil, "you never met a true bishop before." You may think that bishops in these days have no need for such courage. They will not have to face kings and rulers, I dare say; but I wish all had the bolder and rarer courage to face the false world; to tell the truth to lying partisans, religious and other; to confront the wild and brutal ignorance of public opinion; to despise the soft flatteries of an easy popularity; to know by experience that Christ meant something when He said, "Blessed are ye when all men revile you for My name's sake." 5. Again, I ask, are bishops never called upon by their duty to exceptional moral faithfulness—to be, as it were, the embodied con- science of the Christian Church before the world? That was the splendid example set by St. Ambrose. Theodosius was a great, and in many respects a good, emperor; but in a fierce outburst of passion he had led his soldiers into the amphi- theatre of Thessalonica, and had slain some five or six thousand human beings, the innocent no less than the guilty, in indiscriminate massacre. Courtiers said nothing; the world said nothing; civil rulers said nothing; then it was that St. Ambrose stood forth like the incarnate conscience of mankind. For eight months he excluded the emperor from the cathedral, and when he came at Christmastide to the Communion, he met him at the door, and, in spite of purple and diadem and prætorian guards, forbad him to enter till he had laid aside the insignia of a guilty royalty, and, pros- trate with tears, upon the pavement, had performed a penance as public as his crime.

(*Archdeacon Farrar.*)    *Qualifications for the eldership :*—St. Paul had never shown himself indifferent to the local organisation of each little community which he founded.  On his very earliest missionary tour, he and Barnabas had ordained presbyters over the Gentile Churches at Derbe, at Lystra, at Iconium, and at Pisidian Antioch.  It seems likely that, as he grew older and realised how soon both he and the other temporary chiefs of the new society must be withdrawn, he only came to feel more strongly than at first the importance of providing for its permanent administration through stationary office-bearers who could be continually replaced.  Such a case as this which had come to his knowledge in Crete must have sharpened that conviction.  As error spread, and especially such error as led to lax morals, the office of ruler in the young community grew to be of the higher consequence, and it became more important to secure that those who were admitted to office possessed the requisite qualifications.  It throws a good deal of light on this point to observe where the stress is laid in Paul's catalogue of these qualifications. Ability on the elder's part to argue with Jew and heathen, or even to edify disciples, is not put in the foreground.  On the contrary, the qualification insisted upon with most detail is one of character.  Among the little companies to be found in the towns of Crete few men would probably be found competent to discuss points of theology, or to hold their own on subtle questions of Mosaic law with glib talkers of "the circumcision."  Certainly there could not as yet exist a class of professional divines, expert in controversy or specially educated to instruct their brethren.  What was to be had was just a few men of some years' Christian standing and of grave and approved Christian character, who, knowing from experience that the true faith of the Lord Jesus was a faith " according to godliness," could bring new-fangled doctrines to this plain test : Did they contribute to promote wholesome manners, or did they betray an evil origin by their noxious influence upon practice ?  In effect, it was by their pure example, by the weight of their character, by the sober and balanced judgment which Christian experience forms, and, above all, by that instinct with which a mature Christian mind, however untrained in theology, recoils from morbid views of duty, dangerous errors of mischievous speculation : it was by the possession of gifts like these that the elders were fitted to form a salutary force within the Church ; and the best service they could render it at that conjuncture would be to keep the flock in old safe paths, guarding its faith from poisonous admixture, that, amid the restlessness of a fermenting period, men's minds might be settled in quietness upon the simple teaching of the gospel. It cannot surprise us therefore to find, when we come to look at the qualifications Paul desires in the Cretan elder, that the condition first insisted on is, not simply character, but reputed character.  He must be a man against whom public rumour lays no scandalous charge, either within or without the Christian society.  There may have been something in the condition of the Cretan Church which rendered it specially desirable that its representatives should stand well in the esteem of their neighbours.  But it is plain that upon this qualification must always depend in every Church the real value and influence of the eldership.  It matters comparatively little how active or zealous or even devout a church-ruler be, if men cannot respect him because they either see, or imagine that they see, such flaws as seriously detract from the total impression his character ought to make upon them.  However useful in other ways a man of blemished estimation may prove, he is not likely to lend dignity to sacred office or attract to it the confidence and reverence of the people.  The general conception of "blamelessness" St. Paul breaks up into eleven particulars ; of which five describe what the elder must not be, and six what he ought to be.  Of the negative requirements, the first and the last need not surprise us.  Many a good man exhibits an unconciliatory and unpliant temper ; but such a disposition is a peculiarly unfortunate one in the official who has to act along with others in the management of a large body of brethren, and to preserve that peace which is the bond or girdle of perfection.  The stubborn man who insists on having his own way at too heavy a cost makes a bad elder.  So of the fifth negative.  The instance of the false teachers at Crete showed how readily in that age a greedy man might take unworthy advantage of the confidence of the Church, not to say by downright peculation, but at all events by making a good thing out of his position.  Such a temptation lay near to a trader in one of the Greek seaports, as many among these new-made presbyters would be.  But the spirit of covetousness is hard to exorcise from the ministry at all times ; the harder now, because

the ministry has come to be a "profession." Let us hope that the modern ecclesiastic stands in less danger of the group of things forbidden which lies between
these two : "not soon angry ; not given to wine" (or in the R.V., "no brawler");
literally it means one who is not rude over his cups), "no striker." All three
expressions picture for us a type of character with which Paul and the Church at
Crete were possibly too familiar ; a hot-tempered man, apt to get excited, if not a
little tipsy, on jovial occasions ; and, when heated with wine, only too loud in his
talk and too prompt with his fists. The seaboard of these Greek islands must
have offered plenty of specimens of this sort of fellow ; but we should scarcely
have supposed it needful to warn a Christian congregation against making an
"elder" of him. Although the temptation to drink drags too often even presbyters
from their seats, we should not elevate to that position a quarrelsome tippler if
we knew it. I suspect that the surprise we feel when we meet such items in a
list of disqualifications for office, serves in some degree to measure the progress
in social manners which, thanks to the gospel, we have made since these words
were written. Our holy religion itself has so raised the standard of reputable
behaviour, at least among professors of the faith, that we revolt from indulgences
as unworthy even of a Christian which Cretan converts needed to be told were
unworthy of a presbyter. When we turn to the positive virtues which Paul desired
to see in candidates for sacred office, we are again reminded of our altered circumstances. No modern writer would think of placing hospitality at the top of the
list. But in times when travelling was difficult, and the inns few or bad, those
Christians, whom either private business or the interests of the gospel compelled
to visit foreign cities, were exceedingly dependent on the kindly offices of the few
who in each chief centre owned and loved the same Lord. At heathen hands
they could count on little friendship ; the public usages of society were saturated
with the associations of idolatry. The scattered members of the Christian body
were therefore compelled to form a little secret guild all over the Mediterranean
lands, of which the branches maintained communication with each other, furnishing their members with letters of introduction whenever they had occasion to pass
from one port to another. To receive such stranger disciples into one's house,
furnish them with travelling requisites, further their private affairs, and bid them
God speed on their journey, came to be everywhere esteemed as duties of primary
obligation, especially on the official leaders and wealthier members in each little
band of brethren. Hospitality like this would be a part of the elder's public duty;
it was to be wished that it should spring out of a liberal and friendly disposition. Hence to the word "hospitable" the apostle adds, "a lover of good men,"
or of all noble and generous acts. The main emphasis, however, in Paul's sketch
of the good "bishop" rests on the word our Authorised Version renders, not very
happily, "sober." This favourite word of the apostle throughout the Pastoral
Epistles describes, according to Bishop Ellicott, "the well-balanced state of mind
resulting from habitual self-restraint." As he grew older St. Paul appears to have
got very tired of intemperate extravagance both in thought and action, even
among people who called themselves Christians. He saw that mischief was
threatened to the Christian cause by wild fantastic speculation in theology, by
the restless love of novelty in matters of opinion, by morbid one-sided tendencies
in ethics, and generally by a high-flying style of religiousness which could minister
neither to rational instruction nor to growth in holiness. Sick of all this, he
never wearies in these later letters of insisting that a man should above all things
be sane—morally and intellectually ; preserving, amid the bewilderment and
"sensationalism" of his time, a sober mind and a healthy moral sense. If the
new elders to be ordained in Crete did not possess this quality, they were likely to
effect extremely little good. The unruly Jewish deceivers, with their "endless
genealogies," legal casuistry, and "old wives' fables," would go on "subverting
entire households" just as before. It certainly pertains to this balanced or sober
condition of the Christian mind that it rests firmly and squarely on the essential
truths of the gospel, holding for true the primitive faith of Christ, and not lending
a ready ear to every new-fangled doctrine. This is the requirement in the presbyter
which at the close of his instructions St. Paul insists on with some fulness (ver. 9).
The mature and judicious believer who is fit for office must adhere to that
faithful (or credible?) doctrine which conforms to the original teaching of the
apostles and first witnesses of our holy religion. Otherwise, how can he discharge
his twofold function of "exhorting" the members of the Church in sound
Christian instruction, and of "confuting" the opponents? (*J. O. Dykes, D.D.*)

**As the steward of God.**—*Ministerial stewardship :*—I. First, the word implieth thus much, that God is a great Householder (Matt. xxi. 33) ; THAT HIS HOUSE IS HIS CHURCH, where He as a great personage keepeth His residence, more stately and honourable than the court or standing house of any earthly king in the world, in that herein He pleaseth to manifest His presence by His Spirit working in the Word and ministry ; and as it is with other great houses, so the Spirit of God speaketh of this as committed not to one but many stewards, who take the charge of it to order and govern it according to the mind of the Master and unto His greatest honour and advantage. And these stewards are the ministers, so called —1. Because as the steward in a house is to dispense all necessaries unto the whole family according to the allowance and liking of his lord, even so the minister receiveth from God power to administer according to the necessities of the Church all the things of God, as Word, sacraments, prayer, admonition, &c. 2. As the steward receiveth the keys of the house to open and shut, to lock and unlock, to admit or exclude out of the house, for so is it said of Eliakim (Isa. xxii. 22), even so every minister receiveth the keys of the kingdom of heaven to open and shut heaven, to bind and loose, to remit and retain sins, as Matt. xvi. 19. 3. As the steward sitteth not in his own as an owner or freeholder, but is to be countable and to give up his bills monthly or quarterly when the master shall call for them, so every minister is to be countable of his talents received, and of his expenses, and how he hath dispensed his Master's goods (Heb. xiii. 17). " They watch for their souls as they which must give account." II. The second thing in this similitude to be considered is the force of the argument, which is this : THAT BECAUSE EVERY MINISTER IS CALLED TO A PLACE SO NEAR THE LORD AS TO BE HIS STEWARD, THEREFORE HE MUST BE UNBLAMEABLE. Where we have the ground of another instruction. Every man as he is nearer unto God in place must be so much the more careful of his carriage : that he may both resemble Him in his virtues, dignify his place, and walk more worthy of Him that hath drawn him so near Himself. Besides that, every master looketh to be graced by his servant ; and much more will the Lord be glorified either of or in all those that come near Him (Lev. x.). For as the master quickly turneth out of his doors such disgraceful persons as become reproachful to the family, even so the Lord, knowing that the infamous courses of the servant reacheth itself even to the master, turneth such out of His service which are the just subjects of reproach. (*T. Taylor, D.D.*) *Stewards of God :*—It is worthy of remembrance that Archbishop Tillotson and Burnet, Bishop of Salisbury, considered their large revenues as trusts committed to their care. Accordingly they set aside what remained after their maintenance in a plain way for bettering the condition of the poor clergy and repairs in churches, besides using hospitality to the poor. It is said of Burnet that when his secretary informed him he had in hand about £500, he remarked, " What a shame for a Christian to have so much money unemployed ! " and ordered its immediate distribution for useful purposes. *A faithful steward :*—The other day I received a communication from a lawyer, who says that a very large owner has discovered that a very small piece of property belongs to him and not to the small proprietor in whose possession it has for a very long time remained. The matter seemed a trifling one. We had a conference, and there came the steward with the lawyers, and he was furnished with maps, and, putting on his spectacles, examined them with great care. Why? It was a small matter to him, but because he was a steward he was expected to be faithful. And when he found that this small piece of ground belonged to his lord he was determined to have it. So let me say—as stewards of the gospel of God—never give up one verse, one doctrine, one word of the truth of God. Let us be faithful to that committed to us, it is not ours to alter. We have but to declare that which we have received. (*S. Cook, D.D.*)      **Not self-willed.**—*Frowardness most dangerous in a minister :*—1. It is the mother of error in life and doctrine, yea, of strange opinions, schisms, and heresies themselves ; and it cannot be otherwise, seeing the ear of a self-conceited person is shut against all counsel, without which "thoughts come to nought, as where many counsellors are is steadfastness." And as everywhere almost the wicked man is termed a froward man, and a wicked and ungodly heart a froward heart, so is it generally true which the wise man observed, that such a froward heart can never find good, but evil and woe cleaveth unto it : and therefore David, when he would shut the door of his soul against much evil, said, " A froward heart shall depart from me : I will not know," that is, affect and act, " evil." 2. Whereas men think it a note of learning and wisdom not to yield an inch in any opinion they take up, the Spirit of God brandeth it with a note of folly: and it is no other than the way of the fool which seemeth good in his own eyes. Indeed, neither minister nor ordinary Christian may be as shaking reeds, tossed hither and thither with every blast of wind; but yet is it a wise man's part to hear and try and not stick to his own counsel as a man wiser in his own conceit than seven men that can give a reason: for there is greater hope of a fool than of such a one. 3. There are many necessitudes and occasions between the minister and people: he must admonish the inordinate, raise with comforts the afflicted, restore those that are fallen, and set their bones again tenderly by the spirit of meekness, and privately encourage those that do well. Again, they must consult with him, ask him sometimes of his doctrine, lay open unto him their grief as to their physician under Christ, and seek for particular direction in special cases from him: in all which and many more mutual duties they may not by this inordinate humour be deterred and hindered, but rather with all meekness and lenity be allured, lovingly entertained, and contentedly dismissed from him. Use—1. The minister must learn to be docile and affable: the former fitteth him to learn of others, the latter to teach others; for none can be apt to teach others who is not apt to learn of others; and in the minister especially a tractable and teachable disposition is a singular inviting of others by his example more easily to admit his teaching, whether by reprehension, admonition, or howsoever. 2. So hearers (seeing frowardness is such an impediment to instruction) must learn to cast it from them, which in many (otherwise well affected) is a disposition hard to please: in some making them seldom contented with the pains, matter, or manner of their ministry; but having a bed in their brain of their own size, whatsoever is longer they cut off, whatsoever is shorter they stretch and rack it: for their own opinions may not yield, not knowing to give place to better. Others are secure, and therein grown froward against the Word. (*T. Taylor, D.D.*)

**Not soon angry.**—*Hastiness to anger a great blot in a minister:*—For—1. Whereas a minister ought to be a man of judgment, knowledge, and understanding (for these are most essential unto his calling), yea, a man of such wisdom as whereby all his actions, ministerial and common, should be ordered; this flashing anger overturneth for the present, yea, and drowneth all his judgment, for what other is it than a little fury and a short madness? 2. The pestilent effects and fruits of anger, and the natural daughters resembling the mother are such, as in a minister of all men are intolerable: as, swelling of the mind so high, and so full as there is no room for good motions and meditations (which should wholly take up the minister's heart) to dwell by it: the often arising of God's enemies, and harming and wounding of His friends, for anger is cruel and wrath is raging: it cares not for any, nor spares any that come in the way of it; for who can stand before envy? And from this indignation of heart proceed usually impiety against God, for all prayers and parts of His worship are interrupted; contumely against men, for the bond of love is broken; clamour of speech, violence of hands, temerity of actions, late repentance, and many more such symptoms of this desperate disease: for he hath lost all the bridle and moderation of himself. Now what government is he worthy of, especially in the Church of God, that ordinarily loseth all the government of himself? 3. The minister standing in the room and stead of God ought to be a mortified man, for till he have put off this filthy fruit of the flesh can he never lively express the virtues of God, who is a God of patience, meekness, much in compassion, slow to wrath; and much less can he fitly stamp and imprint that part of His image on others, yea, or teach them to withstand such hot and hasty affections which so suddenly surprise and inflame himself. 4. As the minister is to be a means of reconciling God unto man, so likewise of man unto man; which commendable duty a hasty man can never to purpose perform: nay, rather he stirreth up strife and marreth all: whereas Solomon observeth that only he "that is slow to wrath appeaseth strife," for this unruly passion will disable a man to hear the truth of both parties indifferently, nor abideth to hear the debate, but it will be thundering threats before time serve to take knowledge of the matter. 5. This vice prejudiceth all his ministerial actions. (1) In his own heart. For the minister shall often meet in his calling with those, both at home and abroad, who in many things are far different from him both in judgment and practice; yea, some of weakness, and others of obstinacy, loathing even his wholesome doctrine. Now his calling is, and consequently his care should be, to gain these to the love and liking of the truth : to which end he is not presently to break out into anger : for thus he sets them further off, and scandaliseth such as otherwise he might have won, no more than the physician is or may be angry though the weak stomach of his patient loathe and cast up his wholesome physic, for that would set the patient into further distemper ; but such must be restored by the spirit of meekness. (2) In his people's hearts, by alienating their love and affection, which are easily worn away with the distasteful fruits of this hasty anger : let him instruct, admonish, reprove, every one findeth this evasion, one he doth in anger, another not in love, and so his whole work is lost and become fruitless : whereas by loving usage he might have pierced his people with a permanent and lasting affection, and won better entertainment to all his proceedings. (*Ibid.*)   *Means to repress rash anger* :—The means to bridle and stay this rash and unadvised anger stand partly in meditations, partly in practices.   1. For the former—(1) Meditate on the providence of God, without which not the least grief or injury could befall us, for even the least is a portion of that cup which God's hand reacheth unto us to drink of. (2) On the patience and lenity of God, who with much mercy suffereth vessels ordained unto destruction. How long did He suffer the old world? how loath was He to strike if in a hundred and twenty years He could have reclaimed them! And add hereunto the meekness of our Lord Jesus Christ, who hath commanded us to learn it of Him : His voice was not heard in the streets; a bruised reed He would not break : how long bare He with Judas, being no better than a devil within His family! (3) On the unbounded measure of God's mercy, whose virtue His child must endeavour to express.   God forgiveth to that man which injureth thee much more than thou canst; He forgiveth him infinite sins, and canst not thou pass by one offence? and thou hast more reason, for thou knowest not his heart nor his intention ; it may be he meant better unto thee : neither art thou acquainted with the strength of his temptation, which perhaps was such as would have overthrown thyself, nor the reason why the Lord suffereth him to be overcome and fall by it.   And yet if all this cannot bridle the headiness of this vile lust, apply this mercy of God to thyself : thou standest in need of a sea of God's mercy for the washing of so many soul offences; and wilt not thou let one drop fall upon thy brother to forbear and forgive in trifling wrongs. (4) Upon the danger of retaining wrath, which is an high degree of murder, thou prayest to be forgiven as thou forgivest : the promise is, forgive and it shall be forgiven you : the threatening is, "that judgment merciless shall be to him that showeth not mercy" : and be sure that what measure thou metest unto others shall be measured to thee again and returned into thine own bosom.   2. And for the practices—(1) In thine anger make some delay before thou speakest or doest anything, which point of wisdom nature hath taught her clients to observe.   That of Socrates to his servant is better known than practised, "I had smitten thee but that I was angry" : and memorable is that answer of Athenodorus to Augustus, desiring him to leave him some memorable document and precept, advised him that when he was angry he should repeat over the Greek alphabet before he attempted any speech or action. But although this be a good means, yet will it be to no purpose without the heart be purged of disorder : therefore (2) Apply to thy heart by faith the death of Christ, to the crucifying of this lust of the flesh : nothing else can cleanse the heart but the blood of Jesus Christ, who, as He was crucified, so they that are His have also crucified the flesh and the lusts of it. (3) After the inward disposition use outward helps, as—(*a*) Avoid occasions, as chiding, contentions, multiplying of words, which, though they be wind, yet do they mightily blow up this fire.   (*b*) Depart from the company of the contentious, as Jacob from Esau, and Jonathan avoided the fury of his father by rising up and going his way. (*c*) Drive away with an angry countenance whisperers, tale-bearers, flatterers, who are Satan's seedsmen, by whom he soweth his tares everywhere, and his bellows by whom he bloweth up these hellish sparkles, desirous to bring all things into combustion and confusion. (4) Pray for strength and grace against it, especially for the contrary virtues of humility, meekness, love, and a quiet spirit which is of God much set by : and having obtained strength and victory against the assaults of it, forget not to be thankful, but break out into the praises of God as David (1 Sam. xxv. 32, 33). (*Ibid.*)     **Not given to wine.**—*Drunkenness* has been the ruin of multitudes of the most learned and gifted ministers of the Church of God.   It has slain its thousands and tens of thousands in all ages, to the scandal and ruin of the Church of God.   If there was a danger in the wine country of Crete, what must be the danger in the spirit countries of the north? But a man may be πάροινος (ver. 7; 1 Tim. iii. 3)—viz., by wine, sitting long by his wine—without being a drunkard; and this, also, is condemned by the apostle. A man once said to me, "I drink wine regularly; I like it, and require a bottle or two daily, but I never drink to excess; I am no drunkard, and in all my life I have never been rendered incapable of doing my duties by wine." Very likely, but yet you are πάροινος. You like your wine, and sit long by it, and therefore you are condemned by the apostle. Generally speaking, the more simply and abstemiously we live the better; and bishops especially should in this, as in all others, be examples to the flock. (*W. Graham, D.D.*) *Why a minister should not be addicted to wine:*— 1. To be addicted to the wine or strong drink "taketh away the heart" (Hos. iv. 11), that is, troubleth the understanding, confoundeth the senses, and equalleth a man to the brute beast without understanding: and thus disableth the man of God in all the practice of his calling. As the wise man therefore saith (Prov. xxxi. 4), so much less is it for the minister and pastor set over God's people, lest he forget God's decrees and change His judgments as Aaron's sons did. 2. This sitting at wine calleth him from the duties and means of his fitness unto his calling; he cannot attend to reading, exhortation, doctrine, which is straightly enjoined (1 Tim. iv. 13). 3. Such a man is so far from performance of any faithful duty, that he cannot but become rather an enemy to those that do. Thus the love of wine makes them fail in vision: and the sitting at wine lulleth them asleep, "even on the top of the mast" (as Solomon speaketh of the drunkard), that in times and places of most present and desperate dangers, they see none nor fear any. 4. It disableth all the duties that such a one in his most sobriety can perform (suppose them never so commendable), seeing he hath made himself and calling so contemptible: for what authority can an oracle have out of a drunken man's mouth, which is so accustomed to speak lewd things? and one who hath shaken hands with the most base and wicked companions in a country, which is another inseparable companion of this sin (Hos. vii. 5). (*T. Taylor, D.D.*) **No striker.**—"*No striker*":—It is said of Bishop Bonner, of infamous memory, that, when examining the poor Protestants whom he termed heretics, when worsted by them in argument he was used to *smite them with his fists*, and sometimes scourge and whip them. But though he was a most ignorant and consummate savage, yet from such a Scripture as this he might have seen the necessity of surrendering his mitre. (*Adam Clarke.*) **Not given to filthy lucre.**—*Rules for the subduing of covetous desires:*—1. Meditate—(1) On God's commandment (Prov. xxiii. 4; Matt. vi. 25). And reason there is, that seeing distracting and solicitous thoughts are the ground of covetous practices, the care of a Christian must be to walk diligently in his calling, but leave all the success and blessing of it unto God. (2) On God's promises (Psa. lv. 24; 1 Pet. v. 7). Make these promises thy purchase and possess them by belief, and they shall be instead of a bridle unto all covetous and greedy desires of gain. And thus the apostle dissuadeth it (Heb. xiii. 5). Let your conversation be without covetousness, and be content with things present. They might ask, but how shall we attain hereunto: have we not cares and charges upon us? True; but you have where to lay them: for He hath said, "I will not leave thee nor forsake thee." (3) On thy own deserts: whereby Jacob in want stayed his mind, "I am less than the least of Thy mercies." (4) On the inordinancy of thy desire: for how little is nature contented with! and a very little above a little choketh it: and yet grace is contented with much less: it careth not how little it see about it, for it believeth the more, hopeth the more, trusteth the more, prayeth the more, and loveth the more. All the labour of a man (saith Solomon) "is for his mouth"; the mouth is but little and strait, soon filled, "yet the desire is not filled": noting it to be an unnatural desire in many men, who labour not as men who were to feed a mouth but a great gulf fit to swallow whole Jordan at a draught, or such a mouth as the Leviathan which receiveth the cart and drawers of it. 2. Practise these rules following— (1) Carry an equal mind to poverty and riches, and aim at Paul's resolution, "I can want and abound," I can be full and hungry, in every condition I can be content. If the world come in upon thee, use it as not using it; if it do not, yet account the present condition the best for thee, because the Lord doth so account it: and the way to get wealth is to give it up into God's disposition, as Abraham by offering up Isaac to the Lord kept him still. (2) Turn the stream of thy desires from earthly to heavenly things, making, with David, God thy portion; then shalt thou be better without these than ever thou wert or canst be with

them. (3) Thou must go one step further, daily to cross the affection directly—
(*a*) By daily seeking the assurance of the pardon of sin. (*b*) By daily prayer
against this sin especially. (*c*) By daily reading the Scriptures, which are the
sword of the Spirit to cut off such lusts, wisely observing and applying such
places as most cross it. (*d*) By being ready to do good, and distribute, and
exercising liberality upon all good motions and occasions. (*T. Taylor, D.D.*)
**A lover of hospitality.**—*The true hospitality* :—By this is not meant what is
called keeping a good open table, of which we have, and have ever had, many
examples in England, and much money, time, and health have been spent at
these luxurious and hospitable banquets. The apostle does not mean the great
dinners of friendship, such as we have now, when luxuries are drawn together
from the ends of the earth, to renew the sated appetite, and anticipate not only the
real but the imaginary wants of the guests ; he refers not to the sparkling of the
wine, or the brilliancy of wit when the spirit is high, or those postprandial exhibitions which have been called the feast of reason and the flow of soul. No ; this
is not his meaning : but the bishop must be a lover of hospitality in a higher and
far nobler sense of the word ; his house and his heart ever open to the poor and
needy (Luke xiv. 13) ; if he has two coats, the first naked man whom he meets
gets one of them ; if the Lord has given him wealth, he actually realises the 25th
of Matthew, by feeding the hungry, clothing the naked, and visiting those that
are in prison. He loves to see the learned and the good, the advanced Christian
and the weak believer, assembled round his table, in free and full and unrestrained
conversation ; it is his noble privilege to meet with all classes, mix with all
classes, and still be a blessing to them all ; he can fare with a peasant or feast
with a prince, and be equally satisfied with either. (*W. Graham, D.D.*)
*Hospitality in ministers* :—I. THE OCCASION OF THIS PRECEPT WAS THE DISTRESSED
ESTATE AND CONDITION OF THE CHURCH, which by reason of many tyrants and
persecutors was driven into many straits, partly perceived in present and partly
foreseen by the prophetical spirit of the apostle, not only in the ten persecutions
then imminent, but also in the several afflictions of the world, in which they were
to find tribulation even to the end of it. For as it is in this aspectable world,
which is subject to so many changes and mutations, because it standeth in the
vicissitudes of years, months, days, and nights, so much more is it in the spiritual
world of the Church, which in the earth is acquainted with her winter as well as
summer, her nights as well as days : sometimes the Sun of Righteousness most
comfortably shining and imparting His heat and light by His near approach unto
her ; yea, and sometimes there be two suns in this firmament, for together with
the sun of the Church, the sun of the world affordeth warm and comfortable days
for the full beauty, liberty, and glory of the Church. But sometimes, again, this
sun departeth in displeasure and carrieth the sun of the world with him, then is a
black winter of the Church, nothing but storms and tempests, persecutions and
trials, one in the neck of another, and scarce one fair gleam between. Now in
such times the poor Church is driven to travel for rest, and the innocent dove of
Christ cannot find in her own land any rest for the sole of her foot ; well may she
fly abroad to seek her security. In all which times every Christian is bound by this
and such like precepts to give her harbour and safe conduct till the dash and storm
be over. Besides, suppose the Church in general at her best estate, yet the particular members of the Church are for most part poor and needy, and even then
subject to many troubles for keeping the faith and good consciences, by means
whereof they are often driven from house and home, and sometimes are in banishment and exile, sometimes in prison and bonds ; all whom the Lord commendeth
to the charitable and Christian devotion of Christian men, and bindeth them to the
cheerful receiving and relieving of them in such necessity ; let them be strangers
yet, if they be of the household of faith, they have right to harbour and relieve, and
in the practice of this duty the apostle requireth that the minister be the foreman.
II. It will be inquired WHETHER EVERY MINISTER MUST BE HARBOUROUS AND HOSPITABLE,
and if he must, what shall become of them whose livings are scarce able to harbour
themselves ; and much more of the swarms of our ten-pound men, and very many scarce
half that to maintain their family ? it seemeth that every minister ought to be a rich
man. I answer, that the poorest minister may not exempt himself from this duty,
neither is altogether disabled from it ; a poor man may be merciful and comfortable to
the distressed some way or other, as if with Peter and John he have not money or meat
to give, yet such as he hath he can give—counsel, prayers, and his best affections.
III. THE REASONS ENFORCING THIS PRECEPT UPON THE MINISTER ESPECIALLY. 1. In

regard of strangers he must take up this duty whether they be strangers from the faith, that hereby he might win them to the love of true religion which they see to be so merciful and liberal, or else if they be converted much more that he may comfort and confirm such as are banished, or otherwise evil entreated for the confession and profession of the truth, for if every Christian, much more must the minister be affected to those that are in bonds, as though himself were bound with them, and consequently look what kindness he would receive if he were in their condition, the same to his power he is to bestow upon them. 2. In regard of his own people, upon whom by this means he sealeth his doctrine sundry ways; but especially if he keep open house for the poor Christians in want he bindeth the souls of such receivers to obey the Word, and encourageth them by his entertainment in their entertainment of the gospel. IV. THE USE. 1. It teacheth that it were to be wished that the maintenance of every minister were competent, certain, and proper unto himself, that he might have wherewith to perform this so necessary a duty. 2. In regard of poor strangers, to stir up ministers and people to a liberal heart towards them all, but especially if they be such as, the land of whose own possessions being unclean, come over unto the land of the possession of the Lord, wherein the Lord's tabernacle dwelleth. How few children hath Abraham, the father of our faith, among us, who sit in the door of their tent to watch for and enforce strangers to receive their best entertainment! Few be our Lots, who will undergo any loss, any indignity, before strangers shall sustain any harm at all; he will offer his own daughters to their violence, he will use reasons, they had known no man, and that which would have persuaded any but the Sodomites he used last, that they were strangers and were come under his roof. Few Jobs, who will not suffer the stranger to lodge in the street, but open their doors to him that passeth by the way. (*T. Taylor, D.D.*) **A lover of good men.**—*The lover of the good:*—1. A good man is always deeply sensible of the opposite of goodness—of moral evil—in himself and in the world around him. The inner cry of his heart often is, "O wretched man that I am," "When I would do good, evil is present with me!" It is present, but not allowed; hated rather, mourned over, repented of, put away in purpose. The goodness of the man is shown in this internal preference—a preference of which, in the first instance, only the man himself is conscious, but which is certain to become apparent to others. For, be sure of this, that what we most deeply regard in our own hearts cannot be permanently hidden from others. Exactly so it is with regard to evil in the world around him, that is, the evil that is in other men. A good man cannot look upon evil with favour or allowance; the instinct that is within him will put him in a moment in moral opposition to the evil that is in the world. Conscience says, with Luther, "Here I stand. I can do no other. So help me, God!" The world's way is a way of universal conciliation and compliance and apology. 2. A good man, while standing in direct moral opposition to evil will, at the same time, be pitiful and compassionate towards the subjects of it. He will be like God in this. God hates evil. God pities those who are caught in its toils, and who suffer its penalties and are loaded with its curse. He pities them and comes to save them. 3. A good man is humble, modest, moderate in his own esteem. He has the sense of his frailty, of his sin, and all the limitations of his nature, and the sorrows and troubles of this earthly life to keep him humble. A proud man is foolish, in the deepest sense, and ignorant. 4. A good man is one who does good. As the righteous man is one who doeth righteousness; as the merciful man is one who "sheweth mercy," and the generous man one who gives at some self-sacrifice; so in a larger sense the good man is one who does good, as he has opportunity, at his own cost, with some intelligent purpose for the benefit of his fellow-men; who does good from a grateful sense of the great goodness of God to him; does good from a real love of the action, and a love of the people to whom he does it;—who, in one word, is like God Himself, who giveth to all men liberally, and upbraideth not—"who sends His rain on the just and on the unjust." A good man is one, in short, who has the active and passive virtues more or less in exercise. They are not in perfect exercise: some of them may be scarcely in sight at all, but he is inclined to all the virtue and set, in the temper of his mind, against all evil. 5. There is on the whole not much difficulty in distinguishing such a man from a man who is not good—who is not true, who is not faithful; who is not generous, nor humble, nor helpful; who has no likeness to Christ, who is not morally a child of God. The difficulty is greater when we come to compare this real Christian goodness with some of the more promising types of natural amiability. Some men are made to be loved. They are so kind, so bright, so helpful, so full of sympathy, and they carry all this somehow so much in their temper, and in the whole habit of their life, and even often on their very countenances, that they make their way at once wherever they wish to be. After all some of them may be good and true in the deepest and most essential sense; many of them may be good up to the point of their knowledge—"He that doeth righteousness is righteous." He that doeth good is good; and without any fear we may be "lovers of" such good men. 6. If we love good men, we shall observe them thoughtfully, we shall look at their spirit and character, their aims and their purposes in life. Love will soon die, love of any kind, unless it be fed by thought and kindled anew by remembrance. "Therefore will I remember Thee from the land of Jordan." "When I remember these things"—the privileges and joys of bygone days—"I pour out my soul in me"; in distress and apprehension lest they should never be renewed, and yet in fervent hope that they may; that I shall again ascend the hill of Zion, and sing at her feasts among the bands of the faithful and the good. 7. If we love good men we shall associate with them. They will be our hearts' aristocracy, the very uppermost circle of life to us, "our joy and crown." By such association we shall get social and spiritual advantages that could not otherwise come to us. (*A. Raleigh, D.D.*) *Good companionship:*—This is no doubt intended to rebuke the tendency in many most hospitable men to surround their tables not with the good but the bad; not with the sober, the wise, and the saintly, but the vilest, because they may be brilliant, and the most immoral, because they may be attractive and refined. The Christian bishop should be a lover of good men : his house should be a magnet to attract the just, the generous, and the holy from all quarters; not a scene of luxurious revelry to attract the riotous and the profane. Except in the pulpit the apostolical bishop has nowhere so great an influence as in his own house and at his own table; and his example in privacy being noble and Christian is even more attractive and influential than in his public ministrations. His guests have generally an open ear, and the faithful bishop has a word in season for them all. A godly bishop (if he had the means), in the neighbourhood of a university might influence in this way the minds of hundreds of young men who are to be the future lights and guides of the nation. (*W. Graham, D.D.*) **Just, holy, temperate.**—*Good ministerial qualities :*—1. Just refers to the principles of equity in our conduct with one another. In the entire management and government of his Church, but especially in discipline, the bishop or elder requires this qualification. He must look upon the poor and the rich, the ignorant and the learned, in this respect with an equal eye. 2. Holy, on the other hand, expresses more especially our relations towards God, who is so often called in Scripture "the Holy One of Israel." He is a saint, and rejoices to be numbered with the company of those that are sanctified. His external conduct, which is altogether just, is not superficial but real, and flows from holiness of heart; and all his noble actions in the sight of man are based on the new heart, the new nature, and the new hope within him. He is holy : his presence rebukes the ungodly, and the tongue of the wicked is silent before him; the atmosphere around him is pure, salubrious, and serene; his words when he speaks are like ointment poured forth ; his holy exhortations and heavenly prayers are full of the blessing of the Lord; and his whole walk in the midst of the people is like the sun, brighter and brighter unto the perfect day. This twofold relation of man to his neighbour and to God was known to the heathen, for Polybius says (xxiii. 10, 8), "Just in respect to our fellow-man, and holy in things pertaining to God." Both of these meet in the Christian bishop and form the greatest perfection of his character. He is distinguished by justice among his fellow-creatures on earth, and his holiness connects him with his Lord and Head in heaven. 3. He is also temperate, ἐγκρατῆς, (*cf.* 1 Cor. vii. 9; ix. 25)—powerful, master of himself, having self-control, and hence continent, which is undoubtedly the meaning of it here. He has renounced the world, the devil, and the flesh, and he will not be drawn away from his high calling by sensual pleasure. (*Ibid.*) **Holding fast the faithful Word.**—*The characteristics of a successful preacher :*—I. Personal conviction of the truth. II. Aptness to teach others. III. Power of persuasion and conviction. (*F. Wagstaff.*) *The faithful Word :*—I. The Word of God is a faithful Word, and infallible. 1. The author is holy and true (Rev. iii. 7, 14). 2. The instruments were led by the immediate direction of the Holy Ghost (2 Pet. i. 21). 3. The matter of this Word is an everlasting truth ; the law an eternal rule of righteousness as ancient as God Himself; the gospel an everlasting gospel, containing promises of eternal truth, &c. 4. The form of it, which is the conformity of it with God Himself, maketh it appear that if God be faithful this His Word must needs also be so ; in that it resembleth Him in His omnipotency, for this power and arm of God never returneth in vain but doth all the work of it. In His wisdom giving most perfect and sure directions, resolving all doubtful cases, and making wise unto salvation. In His purity and perfection being an undefiled and perfect law. In His omniscience it searcheth the heart, discovereth the thoughts, divideth between the marrow and bone (Heb. iv. 12). In His judgment acquitting believers, to whom it is a sweet savour of life to life; condemning infidels both here and much more at the last day (John xii. 48). In His truth and verity as here, and Col. i. 5, it is called the word of truth. 5. The ends show the certainty and faithfulness of it, it being the only means of regeneration (1 Pet. i. 21), of begetting faith, (Rom. x.), and, consequently, both of freeing men from hell and of assuring them of that freedom; the only word that can supply sound and firm consolation, yea settled and assured comfort unto distressed consciences, none of which ends could it ever attain if itself were unsound and uncertain. II. Now AS IT CARRIETH WITH IT ALL THESE GROUNDS, SO ARE THERE A NUMBER WITHOUT IT MORE whereby we may confirm the same truth, as—1. It is the foundation of the Church (Eph. ii. 20), against which if hell gates could ever prevail the Church were utterly sunk. 2. Hereunto hath the Lord tied His Church, as to an infallible direction, to the law, and to the testimony, without which there is nothing but error and wandering; ye err not knowing the Scriptures. 3. This truth hath been above all other oppugned by Satan, heretics, tyrants, yet never a whit of it was ever diminished; Solomon's books may be lost, but not these of the true Solomon, Jesus Christ. 4. This Word hath been so certainly sealed in the hearts of the elect of all ages that where it once was harboured in truth it could never be shaken out by any kind of most exquisite torture and torment. (*T. Taylor, D.D.*) *The faithful Word to be improved:—* Unto hearers this doctrine affordeth special use of instruction. 1. If it be so faithful a Word every man must attend unto it (2 Pet. i. 19); we have a surer word, to which ye do well that ye attend. 2. To lay up this Word surely, as being the sure evidence of thy salvation, and of thy heavenly inheritance among the saints. Men lock up their evidences or conveyances of land in sure and safe places, delight often to read them, suffer no man to cousen them of them, whatsoever casualty come these are by all means possible safeguarded, and shall any man carelessly neglect such an evidence as this is, without which he hath no assurance of salvation, nor the tenure (out of his idle conceit) of one foot in heaven; a lame man, if he hold not his staff, falleth; and whosoever loseth his part in the Word loseth his part in heaven. 3. Here is a ground of thankfulness, in that the Lord hath not only vouchsafed us life and glory and immortality when we were dead, and when nothing could be added to our misery; but hath also given us such a constant guide and direction thereunto. Now what can we do less than in way of thankfulness (1) Yield up ourselves to be directed by this faithful Word. (2) Believe it in whatsoever it commandeth, threateneth, or promiseth, in that it is such a faithful Word; and hereby we set also our seal unto it. (3) Constantly cleave unto it in life and in death, and not to be so foolish as to be soon removed to another gospel, nor so fickle as children, to be carried about with every wind of doctrine, but hold fast such a stable truth, so full of direction in all the life, and so full of comfort at the time of death; for it is as a fast and faithful friend, tried in time of adversity, standing closest to a man in his greatest necessity. (*Ibid.*) *The Bible inflexible in its requirements:—*When I was a boy I was engaged in the building trade. I didn't know much about it, and I was set to do any odd jobs, any work in a dark corner that could not be much seen. I worked by the side of a man who on one occasion made a sarcastic remark that I shall never forget. It made me so angry, nearly as angry as you are when you are hit hard from the pulpit. He said, "Tom, when I go home I will call at the saddler's and order a leather plumb-rod for you." He meant that my work was so crooked that I wanted a bending and not a straight plumb-rod. Builders use a wooden plumb that will not bend at all. The Bible is not a leather plumb-rod to be accommodated to us, but is like a wooden one, inflexible in its requirements, and to which we must accommodate ourselves. (*T. Champness.*) **That he may be able by sound doctrine both to exhort and convince.**—*Sound doctrine and faithful exhortation:—*1. In that the Word is called doctrine, and no doctrine is without a teacher; it behoveth every man to repair to the teachers of it. 2. As this doctrine implieth teachers, so doth it also learners and scholars. Teaching us that we must all of us become learners of this Word and doctrine, for so long as there is doctrine and teaching on God's part so must there be an hearkening and learning on ours, and the rather, both because that which is said of all knowledge, that it is infinite, is much more true of this, for God's commandments are exceeding large, as also seeing in this school we are to become not only more learned but better men. 3. In that the apostle calleth that here wholesome doctrine, which in the words before he called a faithful Word, and fitted for doctrine. Note that the men of God, when they fell into speech of the Word of God, they spoke not slightly of it and away, but were hardly drawn from it without leaving behind them some notable eulogy or other upon it (Rom. i. 16) : the gospel the power of God to salvation (John vi. 68). Peter saith not, Master, Thou hast the word of God, but Thou hast the words of eternal life ; and what a number of glorious things are ascribed unto it (Heb. iv. 12). Hence according to their several occasions are all those excellent epithets ascribed unto it through the Scriptures, some of the penmen looking at the author, some at the matter, some to the qualities, some to the effects, and accordingly invest it with titles well beseeming it. 4. Whereas the apostle is not contented that the minister should teach but exhort also ; it teacheth ministers to labour for this gift whereby an edge is set upon their doctrine, and wherewith as with a goad they prick on the affections of those that are under the yoke of Christ. A difficult thing it is, for teaching is an easy task in comparison of it, and yet so necessary as that all the ministerial work is called by this name (Acts xiii. 15). 5. Whereas the apostle addeth that exhortation must go with wholesome doctrine, we note that then is exhortation powerful and profitable, when it is firmly grounded upon sound and wholesome doctrine. (*T. Taylor, D.D.*)     *Victory through preaching sound doctrine :*—Seldom has a better answer been rendered to the enemies of Christ than that given by Pastor Rolland in a Catholic canton, where the gospel has but recently gained a footing. The incident is thus described : Absolutely discarding controversy he preached the simple, clear gospel. The Capucine monks came to preach a mission against the " heretical invasion," the " Vaudois venom " permeating the canton ; and, in no measured language, thundered their calumnies and anathemas. People came to the pastor : " You surely will not let this drop, but roundly answer them ? "   " Only you come next Sunday," replied he, " and you will hear how I will serve them out ! " The church was filled, and the pastor preached on the love of God through Christ Jesus, and on the love He sheds abroad in our hearts towards all men—not an allusion throughout to the bitter words which had been spoken. The contrast was immensely felt. The writer goes on to say that the people who had crowded the church were profoundly touched, and a grander victory was won than by any amount of hard words. The simple story of the love of God in Christ moved and melted the hardest hearts. The incident is worth noticing as an example which might well find followers.

Vers. 10, 11. **For there are many unruly and vain talkers and deceivers.**—The conjunction " for " showeth that the words following contain a reason of the matter preceding, viz., why the minister should be a man so qualified with able parts, both to maintain the truth and censure the falsehood. The reason is drawn from the description—1. Of teachers, in these two verses ; and 2. Of hearers, in the twelfth. The teachers are described by three arguments. 1. From their indefinite number, there are many, not two or three, who are easily set down, but many. 2. By their adjuncts, which are two. 1. They are disobedient or refractory, such as will not submit themselves to the true doctrine and discipline of the Church. 2. They are vain talkers ; that is, such as being given to ostentation and vanity, contemn the study and delivery of sound and profitable doctrine, and search out words and matters of wit and applause, both of them of more sweetness unto the flesh than soundness unto the soul and spirit. 3. By their most dangerous effects, and these also are two. 1. Their deceiving of minds ; for which ungodly practice he especially brandeth them of the circumcision ; that is, either by metonymy, the Jews themselves circumcised, or else Gentiles Judaising, embracing Jewish opinions, mixing the law and gospel, Moses and Christ, circumcision and baptism together, making indeed an hotchpotch of religion by confounding things that can never stand together. The second effect of them is their subversion of whole houses ; that is, they poison and infect whole houses, yea, and where the grounds and foundation of religion hath been laid they overturn and overthrow all. This last effect is declared by two arguments. 1. From the instrumental cause of it, and that is by their false doctrine, teaching things which they ought not. 2. From the final cause of it, that is, covetousness, for filthy lucre sake. Now these teachers being so many, so dangerous and hurtful, their mouths must needs be stopped. Which is a common conclusion set between the two verses, as having reference unto them both, as a common remedy against all the mischief which anyway may be let in by them, and therefore those that are to be admitted into the ministry must be of ability to stop their mouths. (*T. Taylor, D.D.*) *Hindrances to religion :*—I. THE CHIEF HINDRANCES TO RELIGION ARE OFTEN IN THE CHURCH ITSELF. The persons alluded to were members and professed teachers. 1. Words without sincerity are "vain." 2. Great attention may be paid to the letter of the law, while its spirit is violated—"they of the circumcision." 3. The distinction between good and bad preachers—the former live to preach, while the latter preach to live. II. HINDRANCES IN THE CHURCH MUST BE REMOVED. "Whose mouths must be stopped." 1. Discipline must be exercised in love. 2. The prosperity of the Church of God must be considered before that of individuals. 3. Every age has its own obstructions to the truth — intemperance, covetousness, selfishness, the chief hindrances of the present. III. COMMUNITIES ARE AFFECTED BY THE CONDUCT OF INDIVIDUALS. The characters of men are transferred to their country; here the Cretians became a bye-word. So, drunken Englishmen abroad, compromise the character of their fellow-countrymen. Four vices—1. Untruthfulness. 2. Passion—"evil beasts." 3. Sensuality. 4. Slothfulness. (*F. Wagstaff.*) *The characteristics of false teachers :*—1. In that the first thing taxed in these false teachers by the apostle is disobedience, we learn THAT DISOBEDIENCE COMMONLY IS THE GROUND OF FALSE DOCTRINE. For—1. It is just with God to give up those to errors and delusion that receive not the truth in the love of it, for wheresoever it is received in love obedience cannot but be yielded unto it. 2. The nature of sin is ever to be excusing itself, and is loath to be crossed, although never so justly, but studieth how to defend itself as long as it can, even by wresting the Scriptures, and by taking up one error for the maintenance of another. 3. The tenor of Scripture joineth these two together (2 Pet. ii. 1, 10, 12 ; Acts xiii. 8, 10; 3 John 9). II. PREACHERS WHO THEMSELVES ARE DISOBEDIENT UNTO THE WORD, FOR MOST PART BECOME IN THEIR MINISTRY NO BETTER THAN VAIN TALKERS. 1. In regard of themselves, being vain-glorious persons, affect applause rather than godly edifying, which is a most vain thing. 2. In respect of their labour, which is all in vain, never attaining the end and right scope of the preaching of the gospel unto salvation ; for he that soweth vanity what else can he look to reap ? 3. In regard of the hearers, who also spend their pains in vain : they hear a great noise and pomp of words, and a glorious show of human wisdom, which may wrap the simple into admiration, but they are left without reformation; their ear is perhaps a little tickled, but their hearts remain untouched ; neither are their souls soundly instructed nor fed with knowledge, but they go away as wise as they came. These Paul calleth vain talkers and vain janglers (1 Tim. i. 6), and again, profane and vain babblers, and that justly. 1. Because their puffed discourses proceed from the profanity of their hearts. 2. They are as strange fire from the Lord's altar, opposed to that which the Lord hath sanctified to the salvation of His people. 3. They are so far from the edifying of the Church that they cause men to increase unto more ungodliness and profaneness. III. HOW DID THESE FALSE TEACHERS DECEIVE MEN'S MINDS ? 1. By suppressing the truth; for by their vain jangling and speaking, liker poets, philosophers, historians, than prophets, apostles, or any successors of theirs, they made a cleanly conveyance of the light from the people, and, withholding the truth and light, they led them from Christ, from the right knowledge of the Scriptures, from sound godliness and religion in judgment and practice, and so they remained as dark in their understanding, as erroneous in their judgments, as froward in their affections, and as wicked in their lives as ever before. 2. By flattery; for they would not deal directly against the sins of the age, as godly ministers do, but deceitfully, that they might not displease ; herein imitating Satan himself, who was wont of old to answer in riddles, as he answered Cresus, that if he would transport himself over the river Halys he should overthrow a most mighty kingdom, namely, his own. But Micaiah will not deceive nor flatter with Ahab, although it stand upon his life. 3. By letting men see their estate in false glasses, so as they never see the truth of it, for people taught by fables and novelties think, and are borne in hand, that they are in heaven's highway ; their souls are brought on sleep, and coming from such frothy discourses, they sit down and please themselves in that they have done their task required, especially if they can bring home a jest or some witty sentence, when perhaps they scarce heard a word of Christ, of their justification, of their mortification, or of their glory. 4. By placing religion in bodily exercises, not in matters of spirit and truth (Col. ii. 20) ; thus did the Pharisees in their times, the Papists in these, and whosoever urge the decrees of men more than the commandments of God. IV. But whose minds are deceived ? 1. First their own and then others, for they are blind leaders of the blind, deceiving, and being deceived, and although our apostle expresseth not here who they be that are deceived, yet elsewhere he doth, as Rom. xvi. 18, " they deceive the hearts of the simple," and 2 Tim. iii 6, " they lead captive simple women," and 2 Pet. ii. 14, " they beguile unstable souls," whence we see that ignorant, inconstant, and unsettled souls, which hand over head receive any doctrine without examination or trial, whose simplicity disableth them to judge between truth and falsehood, and whose levity makes them like shaken reeds, these are the carcases on which such vultures do seize. (*T. Taylor, D.D.*) *Danger from false teachers :*—Herodotus tells of a Scythian river having marvellous sweetness till a little bitter mingles with it, and gives it ever after an uncommon bitterness. So evil counsel, in some emergencies of the soul, will poison the whole current of its existence. You may poison a well from which a neighbourhood drinks, and yet be less guilty than to contaminate the flow of eternal thought. There are times when the greatest trust which one human being can repose in another is the confidence of wise direction. Confiding in the integrity of others, men sometimes commit their credit, their wives and children, to their keeping, and are guided by them through fiery coursers over the land, or by steam-vessels over the seas ; but when a man goes with his soul, and trusts that to what a fellow-being may direct, the trust is as momentous as eternity itself. Yet this is done, for as by man came death, so by man comes life. Oh, ye who watch for souls, as every Christian should, see to it that you ask of God that which is profitable to direct, before you point out the way for a deathless mind to travel in. Example is said to speak louder than words. **Whose mouths must be stopped.**— *Faithful teachers must oppose seducers :*—The duty of every faithful minister is, when occasion is offered, timely to oppose himself against seducers, and stop the mouths of false teachers, wherein also the Church ought to back and strengthen him. For—1. The example of Christ must be our precedent, who most bodily and freely vindicated the law from the corrupt glosses and expositions of the Pharisees, and that in His first sermon. 2. In regard of the particular members of the Church, that they may be preserved in soundness from starting away and forsaking of the truth. And this is made one end of the precept ; the madness of the false apostles must be made manifest, that they may prevail no longer. 3. In regard of the false teachers themselves ; fools, saith Solomon, must be answered, lest they be wise in their own conceit ; neither shall the labour be wholly lost upon them, for it shall be a means either to convert them and bring them to the knowledge of the truth, or else so to convince them as they shall be made excuseless. And further, the Church must strengthen every minister's hands in this contending for the faith, and so manifest herself to be the ground and pillar of truth, which is committed to her trust and safe-keeping, against all gainsayers. This ministerial duty requireth a great measure of knowledge, and a man furnished with gifts of variety of reading and soundness of judgment. (1) He must be well read and skilful in the Scriptures, that by them in the first place he may be able to shut the mouth of the adversary. (2) To all this knowledge is required a sound judgment, that he may be able to infer good and necessary consequence upon the granting of the truth he standeth for, and on the contrary, the absurdities and inconveniences which necessarily follow his adversaries' false positions. (*Ibid.*) *The silencing of evil talkers :*— Whose mouths must be stopped, does not mean that you are to throw them into an inquisition and gag their mouths, as was, and is, the practice of the Papacy. The heathen persecutors adopted the same method of dealing with the faithful martyrs of the Lord ; for, in order to prevent them speaking of His grace, they cut out their tongues. The Moslems have the same bloody principle from their Koran ; so that the Pope, the heathen, the grand Turk, are, on principle, persecutors. This is neither taught in our text, nor in any other part of the New Testament. On the contrary, the saints are persecuted, but they never persecute ; they are to follow their Lord and Master to the cross, not the example of those who crucified Him. But their mouths must be stopped in a quite different manner from gagging ; they must be opposed by reason, faithfulness, and love ; their influence must be destroyed by the faithful preaching of the gospel ; and if they be members of the Church, they must be silenced by discipline, and if still refractory, cast out of the communion of the faithful. (*W. Graham, D.D.*) *Stopping foolish speech :*—The heights and recesses of Mount Taurus are said to be much infested with eagles, who are never better pleased than when they pick the bones of a crane. Cranes are prone to cackle and make a noise (Isa, xxxviii. 14), and particularly so while they are flying. The sound of their voices arouses the eagles, who spring up at the signal and often make the talkative travellers pay dearly for their impudent chattering. The older and more experienced cranes, sensible of their besetting foible and the peril to which it exposes them, take care before venturing on the wing to pick up a stone large enough to fill the cavity of their mouths, and consequently to impose unavoidable silence on their tongues, and thus they escape the danger. Persons troubled with unruly tongues may learn a lesson from the elder cranes. All Christians ought to bridle their tongues by watchfulness and prayer. The Psalmist formed a noble resolution : " I said, I will take heed to my way, that I sin not with my tongue."

Vers. 12, 13. **The Cretians are always liars.**—*A classical quotation :*—It is not often that St. Paul quoted from the treasuries of classic literature, and when he did so he did not draw upon the most celebrated of the Greek poets. The Hymn of Cleanthes gave him a text in his speech on Mars' Hill ; the treatise of Epimenides " concerning oracles " furnished him with another. Epimenides was a Cretian poet of religious character and prophetic claims, who visited Athens 599 B.C., and who shortly afterwards died, at the advanced age of a hundred and fifty. He appears to have uttered a terse drastic proverb, a bitter epigrammatic characterisation of his fellow-countrymen, a portion of which, " The Cretians are always liars," was quoted by Callimachus in his hymn to Zeus. Theodoret attributes the whole quotation to Callimachus. Jerome, Chrysostom, and Epiphanius, agree to refer this severe indictment against the Cretians to Epimenides, the semi-mythical and prophetic minstrel and priest. The severity of the condemnation did not interfere with the tradition preserved by Diogenes Laertius, that the Cretians did sacrificial honour to him as a god. According to Diogenes, stories manifestly fabulous are told of Epimenides, and he is credited with having written numerous treatises and poems. (*H. R. Reynolds, D.D.*) *The character of the Cretians :*—The charge of falsehood is repeated undoubtedly by Callimachus, and this characteristic must have been deserved, if we are to trust the host of testimonies to the same effect from other sources. The very word " Cretize " was invented, meaning, " to play the part of a Cretian," and was identical with " to deceive, or to utter and circulate a lie." " Evil beasts " is a phrase expressive of untamed ferocity, truculent selfishness, and greed; while " idle bellies," or " do nothing gluttons," completes a picture of most revolting national character. (*Ibid.*) *Falsehood :*—I. Falsehood and deceit in word and deed is condemned, not only by the light of the Scriptures, BUT BY THE LIGHT OF NATURE ITSELF. Which appeareth expressly not only by the testimony of this Pagan poet, but by other lights in nature ; for the natural conscience of man accuseth and checketh for it ; yea, in children themselves, it maketh them blush at the report of a lie. Besides, the most graceless of men account it the highest disgrace to have the lie given them, the infamy of which vice is such as none will take to it, none will confess it. And on the contrary, the heathen so extolled truth, in word, in practice, as of all other virtues it was said to be the only daughter of Jupiter, as whom most nearly it resembled. II. How SHOULD WE WHO WOULD BE REPUTED GOD'S CHILDREN ABHOR THAT PRACTICE, which even the sons of men are ashamed of ? Shall the sparkles of natural light make the natural conscience of a heathen, and graceless man accuse him of this sin ; and shall not the clear light of grace force the conscience of professed Christians to reprove them ? Is it justly reputed a disgrace to common men, to be taken with a lie, how disgraceful should it be to Christian men ? Shall the heathen profess truth to resemble God so expressly, as that it is His dear and only daughter, and shall Christians who find in the Scriptures the whole image of God, styled by the title, and comprehended under the name of truth, in their practice scarce express it as a part of that image ? 1. Every lie is hurtful whether in jest or earnest, for evil or for good, because it is an enemy to truth, and against the ninth commandment. 2. For jesting or sporting lies, the threatening is general (Psa. v. 6), untruths may not be spoken although they be not thought. And many of the heathen themselves saw the silliness and folly of this shift ; we read of the Lacedemonians, that they would not suffer their laws to be gainsaid in jest, and yet the law of the Lord may be controlled, and gainsaid in jest of Christians. When Thespis, the first stage-player, was asked if he were not ashamed to utter so many lies in such a worthy audience, he answered, he did it in sport. But wise Solon replied, If we approve and commend this sport we shall find it in earnest in our contracts and affairs ; and even so by God's just judgment it befalls Christians, who, using to lie in sport, got an habit of lying in earnest, and by his jesting lies, raiseth a suspicion of his words, that he cannot be believed, be he never in such earnest. 3. For officious lies, so called, there can be no such, because in every lie some office or duty is violated. But they hurt no man; yes, if they hurt not another, they hurt a man's self many ways; again, if they hurt not the parties for whom, yet they hurt the parties to whom they are told, who are abused, and urged to believe a lie, and were not this, yet they hurt and prejudice the truth which ought to prevail. But the end of them is good, Yea, but that which is evil in the nature and constitution may never be admitted, let the end be never so good which is pretended. The least evil may not be committed for the greatest good; to help man we may not hurt God. Nay, we may not tell the least lie for God's greatest glory, and much less for man's good (Job xiii. 9, 10). But they be not against charity. Yes, for charity rejoiceth in truth, and if they were not, yet are they directly against piety, which two loving friends may admit no divorce. III. AND TO HELP OURSELVES IN THIS DUTY MEDITATE ON THESE REASONS. 1. All falsehood and lies are directly against God Himself, who is truth itself; so as by them a man becometh most unlike unto God, and most like to the devil, who is the father and first founder of them. 2. That therefore the liar casteth himself into the gulf of God's displeasure, seeing as He hateth all the works of the devil, so hath He testified special hatred against this. A lying tongue is one of the six things which the Lord hateth, and is abomination unto Him (Prov. xii. 22), and therefore doth with them as we do with the things we abhor; either removeth them out of sight by barring them out of heaven, or destroyeth them (Psa. v. 6). 3. That although that be the greatest plague to have the face of God set against them here, and to be cast from out of His face and blessed presence of joy hereafter, yet there are other inferior evils not to be contemned which wait at the heels of this sin. (1) That it maketh the sinners of this suit justly hateful even unto men, as those who are the main enemies unto human society, which is upheld by truth and faithfulness. (2) Such deceitful and fraudulent persons are occasions of the multiplication of oaths and perjuries among men, for which the land mourneth. (3) In themselves it argueth the want of God's Spirit in their hearts, who, being the Spirit of truth and light, cannot abide to dwell in a heart that is pleased and delighted with nothing more than darkness and falsehood. (4) They lose justly their own voice and credit, and are worthy not to be believed when they speak truth; and men must deal with them as with their father the devil, whose works they accustom themselves unto, suspect even the truth from them, and not receive any as from them. (*T. Taylor, D.D.*) *The punishment of liars :*—When Aristotle, a Grecian philosopher and tutor of Alexander the Great, was asked what a man could gain by uttering falsehoods, he replied, "Not to be credited when he shall tell the truth." On the contrary, it is related that when Petrarch, an Italian poet, a man of strict integrity, was summoned as a witness, and offered in the usual manner to take an oath before a court of justice, the judge closed the book, saying, "As to you, Petrarch, your word is sufficient." From the story of Petrarch we may learn how great respect is paid to those whose character for truth is established; and from the reply of Aristotle the folly as well as the wickedness of lying. In the country of Siam, a kingdom of Asia, he who tells a lie is punished, according to law, by having his mouth sewed up. This may appear dreadful; but no severity is too great against one who commits so great a sin. We read likewise that God Almighty struck Ananias and Sapphira dead for not speaking the truth. *The gospel offered to the worst :*—This is indeed a fearful character, which the apostle says is perfectly true. The island must have been in a fearful condition, for the apostle is always in the habit of speaking mildly even of those who are blameworthy. If their guilt had not been enormous, he would never have rebuked them so severely, nor given such stringent commands to Titus to rebuke them sharply, that they might be sound in the faith. And here we should remark how wonderful the love of God is, which reaches down to the lowest of the species, and elevates such brutish natures into the likeness of the Son of God, and lifts them up to the throne of His glory! In the midst of that pandemonian isle is the Church of God planted, like an oasis in the desert waste, like a lighthouse in the raging seas, to give rest and direction to all who will listen to the calls of Divine mercy. Oh, how admirable, how glorious, is that God, who, like the father of the lost son, opens His house and His bosom to a vile, wretched, prodigal world! Art thou a Cretian? art thou a liar, a glutton, and a brute? then the message of the love of God is to you—even to you; and if you receive it you shall shine among the saints in light for ever! The world says perhaps of you, as the proverb did of old, "The three worst C's in the world are Cappadocia, Crete, and Cilicia "; yet unto these habitations of iniquity and dens of devils the grace of God penetrated, and multitudes were drawn to the Lord. The gospel is for thee, brother, in all thy vileness and guilt; and Jesus, who loved thee, is the same yesterday, to-day, and for ever. Come to Him, and be saved. (*W. Graham, D.D.*) **Evil beasts.**—*Bestiality in men:*—1. In becoming without understanding, and in all the things of God by nature as ignorant as the brute beasts (Psa. lxxiii. 22 ; Jer. x. 14; Prov. xx. 24). 2. By giving up themselves to be led with sensuality as brute beasts (2 Pet. ii. 12). This naturally arises out of the former ; for when men are deprived of understanding, judgment, reason, as every natural man is in the things of God, they must needs be led by other guides, of lusts, appetite, sense, and sight, even as the beasts are. 3. By the practice of many beastly and brutish properties. For what properties have unregenerate men, which are not more beseeming evil and hurtful beasts than men? (1) If we consider the respect between God and him his heart knoweth no subjection; but as was said once of Israel, he is as an unruly heifer, he knoweth no yoke, acknowledgeth no master, lifteth up his heel against his feeder, and careth not for the owner of his fat pasture. (2) If we consider natural men in themselves, no beast is so unclean and foul as they whose filthy hearts are fit for nothing, but to be stinking cages and dens for filthy birds and beasts, wholly bespotted as the leopards (Jer. xiii. 23), swinish men, wallowing in the dirt and mire of sinful pleasures, and revolting from every good way as dogs to their vomits ; for so the apostle termed such Jews as revolted from Christianity to circumcision, beware of dogs. (3) Consider them in respect of their neighbour, no evil beast is so cruel and venomous as they ; in regard of the former the Scriptures ascribe the property of the devil himself unto them, calling them ramping and roaring lions, such as David and Christ Himself had to do withal (Psa. xxii. 13) such a one was Nero whom Paul had to do withal (2 Tim, iv. 17). And for their savageness and greediness they are called dogs and wolves (Zeph. iii. 3). And for subtlety and craft to hurt they are termed foxes (Luke xiii. 32). In regard of the latter, namely, their poison and venom, Christ calleth them serpents and generation of vipers ; their tongues are like stings, sharpened against good men, and the poison of adders and asps is under their lips (Psa. cxl. 3), hence doth the Lord threaten most cruel and inevitable enemies under such speeches (Jer. viii. 17). Whereby he would describe and signify the implacable and virulent malice and rage of the Chaldeans. Now man being above all other born a sociable creature, and to live in society with God and men in the family, Church, and commonwealth, hath by his hostility against God, and enmity against man, after a sort put off the nature of man, and by such degenerating of good right hath lost even the name of man also. (*T. Taylor, D.D.*) *Like a beast :*—We have a common saying when we see ourselves overseen or overtaken in any temporal and outward thing, Oh, what a beast was I ! but well were it if we would seriously thus accuse ourselves when we have failed in our godly course, and to say, Oh, what a beast was I to leave the direction of the Word, and suffer myself to be led by my appetite, or by the lust of my heart, or the sight of mine eyes to this or that sin? Alas, that I to whom God hath given reason, judgment, election, deliberation, yea, His Word and Spirit, should live all this while as one destitute of all these. I understand not what the good and acceptable will of God is, but am yet like the horse and mule without understanding. I have stopped my ears like the deaf adder, and have refused the things of my peace ; I have barked against God and godliness ; I have wallowed in my uncleanness like a swine in his own filth ; I have been unmerciful and cruel as any lion or wolf ; I have spared no prey, and as subtle as any fox to deceive my brethren. I have spit out my venom both to the face and behind the backs of my neighbours, and especially against the household of faith, the professors of religion. Oh, what a beast was I in all this ! But now seeing my understanding is restored unto me again, I will never hereafter carry myself but like a man, not making my lusts my law any longer, but reason shall be my guide ; nay, nor that only, but, like a Christian man, I will by God's grace suffer myself to be guided henceforth by renewed reason, yea, by the Word and Spirit of God. If I must needs in anything resemble the beasts it shall be the ox and ass, in knowing my Lord and Master; the stork, and crane, and swallow, in acknowledging the seasonable time of my repentance, the serpent in Christian wisdom, the lamb and dove in Christian meekness and innocence, and thus resembling them, I neither shall be nor accounted a beast, nor yet be condemned by any of them. But if any, loath to leave his brutish properties, will be a beast still and follow his lust, it is fit he should see the end of his way in one of his predecessors (Prov. vii. 22). (*Ibid.*) **This testimony is true.**—*Ministers must not be discouraged from their duty, though they have to deal with a brutish and wretched people:*—This testimony being true, Titus might have been discouraged, and occasioned hereby to meditate his departure from them as a hopeless people, or to repine that the apostle should place him among such a company of beasts rather than men. But yet Titus must and does with courage go on in his work among them, and plough up to the Lord even this stiff ground. It is the lot of many gracious ministers to be called and planted among rude, barbarous, and beastly people, such as these Cretians were, yea, among viperous broods who will reward their faithful pains and travail in begetting them to God with extremity of wrong and violence (Jer. xxvi. 8). And little comfort find they, unless the Lord give them a breathing time by the means of some Ahikam or other (v. 24.) Now what must the minister do in this case? Surely, as he came not of his own head, so now is he not at his own hand to remove himself at his pleasure. And if he should depart upon this ground, he should perhaps meet with less comfort in leaving an uncomfortable people than in staying amongst them. If God bid Jonah arise and go to Nineveh, but he will betake himself to a ministry of more credit and less labour, the Lord will teach him, before he get to Tarshish, that he is not his own man, and that no creature shall shelter him from trouble whilst he flieth it as fast as he can. If Moses be called to speak to Pharaoh, he must not excuse the matter, saying, "But they will not believe me." The Lord is said to hold the ministers in His hand, and Christ the "seven stars in His right hand" (Rev. i.). First, in regard of His disposition of them here and there at His pleasure. Secondly, of His protection of them in their labours. And some He sendeth, and all the heartening they have of Him beforehand is, "But they will not receive thee," as Moses and some of the prophets; and that is not all, but they must prepare brows of brass, their shoulders to bear reproaches and wrongs, their backs for stripes, their feet for fetters and stocks, yea, their necks for the very block itself. In like manner Christ, sending out His disciples, forbids them to possess gold and silver, and wisheth them to possess patience, for they should stand more in need of that than the other; and telleth them, that if Himself, the green tree, could not be spared, much less should they the dry branches; and that if the master be called Beelzebub, the servant must not look to escape scot free. And therefore ministers called to such an uncomfortable condition must imitate Paul who, although he knew that bonds and imprisonment did abide him in every city, yet forward he must, and provoketh his own readiness and cheerfulness not only to be bound, but to suffer also the pains of death, for the testimony he beareth: considering well—1. That the disciples themselves, sent from the side of Christ, must make account to be hated of all men for His name's sake. 2. That although they see no great comfort or fruit of their works with men, yet their work is with the Lord. 3. That the Lord Jesus, foretelling His death at Jerusalem, yet went forward, and would not pity Himself for all Peter's friendly counsel, but pitied His flock, His body, His Church, more than Himself: a worthy example for the practice of all His ministers. (*Ibid.*) **Rebuke them sharply.**— *Sharply:*—Here we have another adoption of the phraseology of health or "soundness" in relation to the faith. Probably it was suggested to the apostle by the previous adoption of phrases indicative of disease, and of severe remedies. A sharp knife, instruments of cautery, firm handling, free incisions, are needed for some poisonous and putrefying sores; and as in former days Titus had to show the Corinthians how to purge out the old leaven, to deliver wicked persons to Satan, to rebuke pretentious sciolism and proclaim "no quarter" to certain kinds of vice, so once more he had to lift up his voice like a trumpet, and out of sheer kindness was commanded not to spare them. (*H. R. Reynolds, D.D.*) *Different modes of dealing with different sins:*—According to the nature of sins and sinners we must set an edge upon our reproofs and sharpen them; for all sins are not of one size, nor all sinners of one strain; but some sins are more enormous than others, and some sinners are more obstinate than others. Some sins are of ignorance, some of malice; some secret, some open; some sinners are as wax to work on; some are stony and stiff-necked; some have here and there their freckles and frailties on them: others are spotted all over like leopards, or, like the Ethiopian, they never change their hue; no washing doeth them good. Now, we must wisely put a difference between both. Compassion must be showed upon some; and others, whom love cannot allure, fear must force. Some must be saved by love, and some be pulled out of the fire. Some sores need but a gentle lenitive, some a sharper drawer; some require but the prick of a needle to open them, others a more painful lancing and cutting; and some a cutting off. (*T. Taylor, D.D.*) *Christian reproof :*—I. CHRISTIAN REPROOF SHOULD ALWAYS BE BASED ON A CERTAIN CONVICTION. Mere hearsay insufficient; general rumour unreliable. Inquisitorial curiosity different from faithful watchfulness. II. CHRISTIAN REPROOF SHOULD BE THOROUGH AND EFFECTIVE. A cutting rebuke need not be unkind. Sarcasm, satire, scorn—these are unbecoming a Christian teacher. Soft words break hard hearts; warmth melts, while coldness freezes. III. CHRISTIAN REPROOF SHOULD BE FOR THE SINNER'S GOOD.—"That they may be sound in the faith." Wrong motives:—1. To save appearances. 2. To maintain dignity. 3. To gratify revenge. Right motives:—1. To save the purity of the Church. 2. To prevent the spread of contagion. 3. To restore to spiritual life and privilege. (*F. Wagstaff.*) *The object of rebukes :*—The sharpest rebukes in the Church ought to aim at this end, the recovery of diseased Christians to soundness in religion both in judgment and practice; which appeareth in that the greatest ordinary censure in the Church is not mortal but medicinal. For as a surgeon cuts off arms and legs that the body and heart may be saved, so in this body, parts and members are cut off that themselves may be saved as well as their whole body. Paul excommunicateth the incestuous person that his spirit might be saved. Hymineus and Philetus were cast out to Satan that they might learn not to blaspheme. Those whom Jude wisheth to be pulled out of the fire by violence, must be saved thereby. If any object against this that in 1 Cor. xvi. 21, "If any man love not the Lord Jesus, let him be had in execration to the death." And therefore edification and salvation is not the end of this censure. I answer, "It is one thing for the Church to excommunicate, another to curse and execrate; the one is an ordinary censure, the other very extraordinary and rare; the one against those who may be friends of the Church, the other only against desperate enemies, and open and obstinate apostates, even such as Julian, whom the Church judgeth to have sinned the sin against the Holy Ghost, and therefore execrateth and accurseth. (*T. Taylor, D.D.*)    *Sharp rebukes sometimes needed :*—The words is a metaphor taken from surgeons, who cut out dead flesh to the quick, but it is in order to healing. Cutting words have done great cures : many a diseased, festered soul has been made sound, both in faith and manners, by severe reprehension. Learn hence, that although, generally speaking, we ought to temper our reproofs with much gentleness and meekness, yet there is a time when we must reprove sharply, that men may be "sound in the faith." We may, we must speak cutting words when kind words will not do. (*W. R. Burkitt, M.A.*)    *A sharp rebuke :*—A young clergyman came to the house of his sister, and found quite a company round the table—among them a talkative military gentleman, who rather freely flavoured his wit with perverted Bible quotations and anti-Christian inuendos. A bantering remark about God that amounted to no less than a parade of his atheism aroused the hostess at last. "You seem to forget that my brother here is a minister of the gospel," she said. " Oh ! " quoth the unabashed officer, " my clerical friend and I understand each other"; and turning to the young man, with patronising impudence he asked, " Is it not so, sir? Your office requires you to tell the old story, which for the ignorant may do very well to believe, but as a man of culture you yourself cannot put faith in these worn-out doctrines." The clergyman eyed his questioner a minute, and then said, " Sir, before answering your question, I must ask you three. You are an atheist. Such people have always been in the world. One class of these are thinkers who have speculated and groped till they have fallen into despair, and said, ' There is no God.' Do you belong to that class ? " " No," laughed the officer; " thinking is not to my taste. I am no philosopher." " Another class are those who speak frivolously of God merely because they learned to do it where such talk was the fashion. Are you one of them ? " " No, sir," said the officer, slightly reddening; " I am not a blind follower of others." " There is but one more class of atheists," quietly continued the minister—" those who have wallowed in sin till they must either expect the horrors of remorse or kill their conscience; and, as the shortest way to get rid of it, they declare that there is no God." This time the clergyman did not utter his question; but the eyes of the whole company, turned on the confused scoffer, made both question and answer needless.    *Fidelity in administering reproof :*—The Rev. Joseph Alleine was very faithful and impartial in administering reproof. Once, when employed in a work of this kind, he said to a Christian friend, "I am now going about that which is likely to make a very dear and obliging friend become an enemy. But, however, it cannot be omitted; it is better to lose man's favour than God's." But, so far from becoming his enemy for his conscientious faithfulness to him, he rather loved him the more after, as long as he lived. *The reproof of a good man:*—The reproof of a good man resembles fuller's earth; it not only removes the spots from our character, but it rubs off when it is dry.

Ver. 14. **Not giving heed to Jewish fables.**—*The perverting power of trivialities:* —Trivialities, and mere human conceptions, exert a perverting power—(1) by distracting attention from the essentials of religion; (2) by dissipating the strength of the mind; (3) by attributing to the human an authority belonging only to the Divine. Truth, in its essence, always of more importance than the form in which it is clothed. The "spirit" is greater than the "letter." (*F. Wagstaff.*) *Jewish fables to be rejected:*—I. ALTHOUGH ALL FABLES IN MATTER OF RELIGION ARE TO BE REJECTED, YET ESPECIALLY HE MENTIONETH THESE OF THE JEWS, BECAUSE THEY WERE MOST DANGEROUS OF ALL. 1. Because they directly opposed themselves as the over-throwers of the whole doctrine of the gospel and the merit of Christ. 2. They were persuaded under most strong pretences, for they came as from God's own mouth, and from His own people, from such as were born under the law, so as they were urged as things of surest ground and strongest authority from God Himself and His greatest prophet Moses. II. BUT WHAT WERE THESE FABLES? 1. Under this head may be comprehended all the false glosses and false interpretations of the law of Moses, urging the external and literal, but not the internal and spiritual meaning of the law; for which corruption Christ challengeth the Jewish teachers (Matt. v., vi., vii.). 2. All their fabulous invention in their Talmud, such as that concerning the coming of the Messiah, and the great feast at His coming; and of the fruitfulness of the earth, which at that time shall bring forth instead of ears of corn, loaves of bread; and a number such, of which St. Paul saith, they are for number infinite, and for use unprofitable. 3. But the context in the verse following pointeth us to expound them of some other than these, namely, of all those doctrines of the Jews which conceived the legal and ceremonial observation of days, meats, drinks, garments, washings, persons and peoples: for the Jews taught that the same difference remained to be obtained still, as Moses from the Lord commanded it; so as yet some meats were common and some clean; some days were more holy than others; so garments and persons much more lay open to legal pollution by issues, touchings, &c., whereas the appearing of Christ procured final freedom from all such impurity, so as, according to Peter's vision (Acts x.), no man, no thing is to be called polluted or unclean. III. BUT WHY DOTH THE APOSTLE CALL SUCH DOCTRINES FABLES seeing—1. They were from God. 2. Necessarily imposed upon God's own people in pain of death and cutting off from His people in case of contempt, yea or omission. 3. They included in them that evangelical truth whereby both they and we are saved. Yet for all this he termeth them so. 1. Because even these legal constitutions of God Himself, when they were at the best, were but actual apologies, or shadows of things to come, carrying a show or figure of truth, but not the body, nor the truth itself: to the same effect, saith Paul (Gal. iv. 24), that they were allegories; that is, being the things that they were, signified the things that they were not. 2. Because those constitutions, although they had their times and seasons, yet now were they dated: and now to teach or urge them was as vain, as void of ground out of Scripture, as void of profit, as void of truth, as if they had taught the most vain, fictious, and unprofitable falsehoods that men could possibly devise. (*T. Taylor, D.D.*) **That turn from the truth.**—*Rules to preserve us from being turned from the truth:*—1. Entertain it not for outward respects; neither for the laws of the land, nor the encouragement it hath, &c., as very many do, but for the love of itself: for that we affect, we easily turn not from it, no, nor are driven from it; and if we love it for outward respects, as those outward respects change, so will our affections. For example, if we love it for the prosperity of it, times of persecution will make us fall off, with Demas. If we hold it because we would hold our temporalities, the loss of it will be light in comparison of loss of goods, dignities, country, world, liberty and life, the least of these will the heart fasten upon, although with the loss of the truth, and with it of salvation also. 2. Practise so much of it as thou knowest, and the more thou practise, the more thou knowest, and the more thou knowest thus, the more thou lovest, and the surer dost thou bind it upon thyself; and this is the surest hold (John vii. 17), when as in religion, faith and good conscience are joined together, for such as thy conscience is, such shalt thou be found in religion ; without which, hear every hour a sermon, read over the Bible as often as he did, who gloried that he had read the text and gloss also fourteen times over, all this knowledge will not lift thee up to heaven. 3. Call no ground of this Divine truth into question, suspect not that which thou canst not reach, but accuse thine own weakness and ignorance : our first parents yielding at the first onset of Satan to call into question the truth of God, were turned away from all that image of God which stood in truth and holiness. 4. Beware of indifference in God's matters ; many think it good wisdom and policy to be on the yielding hand, and as wax fit to take all forms and the print of any religion ; but the truth is, that such persons as are not rooted and stablished in the truth, when winds and storms arise, or the evil day approach, they shall not be able to stand ; but as they have been long tottering, so their fall shall be great. (*Ibid.*)

Ver. 15. **Unto the pure all things are pure.**—*The supreme importance of moral character :*—1. There is an essential difference in the moral characters of men. 2. The outward world is to men according to this difference. I. The morally PURE in relation to all things. 1. In relation to appearance. A good man is neither given to suspicion nor censoriousness ; he sees some good in all men. 2. In relation to influence. A good man, like the bee, can extract honey from the bitterest plant ; or, like the Æolian harp, can turn the shrieking wind into music. 3. In relation to appropriation. A corrupt soul appropriates, even from the most strengthening and refreshing means of spiritual improvement, that which weakens and destroys. II. The morally DEFILED in relation to all things. 1. The sphere of the defilement. 2. The cause of the defilement. 3. The hideousness of the defilement. (*D. Thomas, D.D.*) *Purity :*—For the evils of this world there are two classes of remedies—one is the world's, the other is God's. The world proposes to remedy evil by adjusting the circumstances of this life to man's desires. The world says, give us a perfect set of circumstances, and then we shall have a set of perfect men. This principle lies at the root of the system called socialism. Socialism proceeds on the principle that all moral and even physical evil arises from unjust laws. If the cause be remedied, the effect will be good. But Christianity throws aside all that as merely chimerical. It proves that the fault is not in outward circumstances, but in ourselves. Like the wise physician, who, instead of busying himself with transcendental theories to improve the climate, and the outward circumstances of man, endeavours to relieve and get rid of the tendencies of disease which are from within, Christianity, leaving all outward circumstances to ameliorate themselves, fastens its attention on the spirit which has to deal with them. I. The principle that St. Paul has here laid down is, THAT EACH MAN IS THE CREATOR OF HIS OWN WORLD ; he walks in a universe of his own creation. As the free air is to one out of health the cause of cold and diseased lungs, so to the healthy man it is a source of greater vigour. The rotten fruit is sweet to the worm, but nauseous to the palate of man. It is the same air and the same fruit acting differently upon different beings. To different men a different world—to one all pollution—to another all purity. To the noble all things are noble, to the mean all things are contemptible. In its strictest sense, the creation of a new man is the creation of a new universe. Conceive an eye so constructed as that the planets and all within them should be minutely seen, and all that is near should be dim and invisible like things seen through a telescope, or as we see through a magnifying glass the plumage of the butterfly, and the bloom upon the peach ; then it is manifestly clear that we have called into existence actually a new creation, and not new objects. The mind's eye creates a world for itself. Again, the visible world presents a different aspect to each individual man. One man sees in that noble river an emblem of eternity ; he closes his lips and feels that God is there. Another sees nothing in it but a very convenient road for transporting his spices, silks, and merchandise. To one this world appears useful, to another beautiful. Whence comes the difference ? From the soul within us. It can make of this world a vast chaos—" a mighty maze without a plan " ; or a mere machine—a collection of lifeless forces ; or it can make it the living vesture of God, the tissue through which He can become visible to us. In the spirit in which we look on it the world is an arena for mere self-advancement, or a place for noble deeds, in which self is forgotten, and God is all. Observe, this effect is traceable even in that produced by our different and changeful moods. We make and unmake a world more than once in the space of a single day. In trifling moods all seems trivial. In serious moods all seems solemn. II. THERE ARE TWO WAYS IN WHICH THIS PRINCIPLE IS TRUE.

1. To the pure, all things and all persons are pure, because their purity makes all seem pure. There are some who go through life complaining of this world; they say they have found nothing but treachery and deceit; the poor are ungrateful, and the rich are selfish, yet we do not find such the best men. Experience tells us that each man most keenly and unerringly detects in others the vice with which he is most familiar himself. Persons seem to each man what he is himself. One who suspects hypocrisy in the world is rarely transparent; the man constantly on the watch for cheating is generally dishonest; he who suspects impurity is prurient. This is the principle to which Christ alludes when He says, "Give alms of such things as ye have; and behold all things are clean unto you." Once more, to the pure all things are pure, as well as all persons. That which is natural lies not in things, but in the minds of men. There is a difference between prudery and modesty. Prudery detects wrong where no wrong is; the wrong lies in the thoughts, and not in the objects. There is something of over-sensitiveness and over-delicacy which shows not innocence, but an inflammable imagination. And men of the world cannot understand that those subjects and thoughts which to them are full of torture, can be harmless, suggesting nothing evil to the pure in heart. Here, however, beware! No sentence of Scripture is more frequently in the lips of persons who permit themselves much license, than the text, "To the pure, all things are pure." Yes, all things natural, but not artificial—scenes which pamper the tastes, which excite the senses. Innocence feels healthily. To it all nature is pure. But, just as the dove trembles at the approach of the hawk, and the young calf shudders at the lion never seen before, so innocence shrinks instinctively from what is wrong by the same Divine instinct. If that which is wrong seems pure, then the heart is not pure but vitiated. To the right minded all that is right in the course of this world seems pure. 2. Again, to the pure, all things not only seem pure, but are really so because they are made such. (1) As regards persons. It is a marvellous thing to see how a pure and innocent heart purifies all that it approaches. The most ferocious natures are soothed and tamed by innocence. And so with human beings, there is a delicacy so pure, that vicious men in its presence become almost pure; all of purity which is in them is brought out; like attaches itself to like. The pure heart becomes a centre of attraction, round which similar atoms gather, and from which dissimilar ones are repelled. A corrupt heart elicits in an hour all that is bad in us; a spiritual one brings out and draws to itself all that is best and purest. Such was Christ. (2) Lastly, all situations are pure to the pure. According to the world, some professions are reckoned honourable, and some dishonourable. Men judge according to a standard merely conventional, and not by that of moral rectitude. Yet it was in truth, the men who were in these situations which made them such. In the days of the Redeemer, the publican's occupation was a degraded one, merely because low base men filled that place. But since He was born into the world a poor, labouring man, poverty is noble and dignified, and toil is honourable. To the man who feels that "the king's daughter is all glorious within," no outward situation can seem inglorious or impure. (*F. W. Robertson, M.A.*) *Purity:*—I. Who are meant by pure persons. The persons here called pure are such as by faith are set into Christ, by whose blood they are justified, and by whose Spirit, through the means of the Word, that immortal seed of regeneration, they are sanctified and reserved unto life everlasting. And hence to both these is the purifying and cleansing of sinners ascribed in the Scriptures. 1. Because by faith every member of the Church layeth hold upon Christ's most absolute purity. 2. The spirit of regeneration hath washed every part, although in part only, nor so clean as it shall be, yet so as that perfect purity is sealed and assured to the soul by it. 3. The Lord doth account every such believer pure even for the present, and imputeth never a spot unto them, but reputeth in His Christ all fair. 4. Hath promised them that for time to come they shall become so absolutely clean as though they had never been defiled. II. How all things are pure or impure. 1. Seeing all things were pure in their creation, we may herein, as in a glass, behold the purity of God in all His creatures, admiring that goodness of His which bewrayed itself even in the meanest of them; yea, provoking ourselves to love, reverence and fear before Him, the image of whose goodness shineth out not only in angels and men, but even in the silly worm and fly, yea in the lifeless creatures themselves. And further, hence we may gather our own duty towards the creatures, namely—(1) Reverently meditate and speak of them. (2) Purely to use them. (3) Mercifully to deal with them. All which we shall the easier do if we can spy out some part of God's image in them. 2. Consider our misery, and the

woeful fruit of our sin, which hath debarred us from all comfort in heaven and earth, from God or any of His creatures. The sweetest sins would carry a bitter taste, if we would but remember what sweet comfort of the creatures we have forfeited for them. 3. The restitution of us to our former right is only from our Lord Jesus Christ, and our first right is recovered to us in this manner. First, as we were at odds with the Creator, and consequently with the creature, even so first we are reconciled unto God through Christ, and then to the creatures; for when Christ (who is our peace) hath wrought our peace with God, He bringeth back our peace, both the inward peace of our own consciences, which before could do nothing but accuse and terrify, as also peace with others, friends and enemies, yea even with the beast of the field, and stone in the wall, and everything striketh a covenant of peace with him who hath entered into league with the Creator of it. If any man, then, would have any right in any creature he useth, he must not hold it by the broken title in the first Adam, but by a recovered and new purchase in the second Adam, who is the Lord of glory, blessed for ever. III. How ALL THINGS ARE PURE TO THE PURE. That we may rightly and properly conceive the apostle's meaning, we must know—1. That the universal particle "all things" admitteth restraint, and may not be extended beyond the apostle's intendment, who speaketh only of such things as are not forbidden by the law of God, or nature; or rather only of things of an indifferent nature, which in themselves are neither commanded nor forbidden, and neither good nor evil in their substance and nature, but are to be used or not used according to the circumstances and occasions of them; such things as these are meat, drink, apparel, recreation, sleep, marriage, single life, riches, poverty, bondage, freedom, &c. And it may not seem strange thus to restrain this general proposition, seeing we have it thus limited in sundry other places (1 Cor. vi. 4). "All things are lawful, but not profitable" (1 Cor. x. 23). "All things are lawful for me, but not expedient" (Rom. xiv. 20). "All things indeed are pure, but destroy not for meats," &c. 2. By pure is meant nothing else but that all such things are free now to be used in good conscience, without scruple, by means of our Christian liberty. 3. In that he addeth "to the pure," he showeth how we come to have title in this liberty, even by becoming believers and getting our hearts purified by faith. In one word, all indifferent things are pure, and free to be used of the pure and believing person, with this one condition; so they be purely and rightly used. (*T. Taylor, D.D.*) *Purity of mind indispensable:*—I. THE IMPORT of the terms. By "the pure" is not meant sinless. Evangelical purity is connected with faith (1 Pet. i. 22; Acts xv. 9). The mind and conscience are governing powers; if they be polluted, all the man is so. II. ILLUSTRATE THE SENTIMENT. 1. On a believing mind the doctrines of Christ will have a sanctifying effect, and the contrary on an unbelieving mind. 2. On a believing mind precepts and even threatenings produce a salutary effect. 3. Mercies and judgments humble, melt, and soften some, but harden others. 4. The evils which occur amongst men, differently influence different characters. 5. The treatment received from men brings out the state of the heart. (*A. Fuller.*) *Purity:*—A pure lake is beautiful as it reflects the loveliness of the heavens, but a pure heart is more beautiful as it reflects the loveliness of God. (*W. M. Statham, M.A.*) **Even their mind and conscience is defiled.**—*The faithlessness of conscience:*—That the conscience is so perverted in our present condition, that no confidence can be placed in its decision, is evident. I. From the fact that these decisions can be correct in no other cases but those in which Divine truth is fully understood. II. That the decisions of conscience are not always in accordance with the truth is evident from the fact that sinners are not always convinced of sin. III. This position is also sustained by the fact that the agency of the Holy Spirit is requisite to convince the world of sin. IV. The faithlessness of conscience is apparent in the fact that hypocrites have not always an appalling sense of their hypocrisy. V. This view of the subject is strengthened by the fact that even Christians do not always detect their own sins. VI. This doctrine is evident from the fact that there is no command in the Scriptures to follow the dictates of conscience. VII. And while there is no direction to follow the dictates of conscience, it is true that the Scriptures designate different consciences, and perhaps different states of the same conscience, by different and directly opposite terms. VIII. This view of the subject is confirmed by the fact that the way to ruin seems to be the way of peace and eternal life. This is a very common and perhaps a general trait of the human family. The light that is in them by nature is darkness. They discern not the way in which they should go. Lessons:—From this subject I infer—I. That God has placed no rule of duty within ourselves. Our reason was never designed to be our guide in spiritual things. Its only office is to understand the things which God has revealed in His Word, and in all cases reverently to bow to His authority. So long as its eyes are not opened by the power of the Holy Spirit, the understanding is in deplorable darkness. And even if it were capable of discerning all the principles of duty, its office is to gather them from the Word of God. II. The subject teaches us that to live conscientiously is not in all cases to live godly. Conscience in its decisions has respect to some principles of life. These principles may be the fruit of our own reason. In this case, the decision will approach no nearer to truth than the principles are according to which the decision is made. Or it may decide according to the maxims of duty which it has learned from others. In this instance, as in the former, its decisions can claim no higher authority or greater correctness than the maxims according to which they are made. Or, if even the Scriptures be the rule according to which the decisions are made, then it will follow that the decisions themselves must be affected by the blindness of the understanding and by the weakness of conscience itself. And hence, to live conscientiously may vary widely from living accordingly to the commands of God. III. The subject teaches what estimate to set on professions of acting conscientiously. IV. The subject suggests the importance of praying for the purification of our conscience. V. The subject suggests that our condition is very deplorable. We are exceedingly inclined to rely on our understandings to discover the way of life, and on the testimony of our consciences that we are walking in it. But not only are our natural understandings too blind to discover it, but our consciences are exceedingly apt falsely to decide that we are walking in it, even while we are wandering in darkness. Thus we are liable to think we are something when we are nothing. The way which we take may seem right unto us, but the end thereof are the ways of death. (*J. Foot, D.D.*)

*Pollution of mind and conscience :*—By the mind is meant the whole understanding part of the soul, which, being the eye of the soul, carrieth with it reason, judgment, and election. The pollution of which is, to be taken up with darkness and blindness (1 Cor. ii. 14); to be filled with vanity (Eph. iv. 17); with fleshliness (Col. ii. 18); in so much as all the natural wisdom of man is fleshly and devilish. By conscience is meant that faculty of the soul which, by applying particular things judged of and done, doth determine them either with or against them ; which, depending upon the former, must necessarily be led into the errors of it, no otherwise than one blind man is led by another into a ditch. The pollution of it is when it is either idle or ill occupied ; the former, when it is sleepy, senseless, or seared, doing nothing at all, neither accusing, nor excusing ; the latter, when it doth both these, but neither of them as it ought, but accuseth where it should excuse, and excuse where it ought to accuse. I. We have here a GOOD ARGUMENT OF THE DIVINITY OF SCRIPTURE, in that it can, and doth (as God Himself) enter upon, and judge the thoughts of men ; and of men themselves (not as men) from things without, but from things within, even according to their cleanness or uncleanness before God. From this argument the apostle proveth the same thing (Heb. iv. 12). II. We learn further, WHAT IS THE ESTATE OF A MAN UNREGENERATE, whom the apostle setteth out thus. 1. He is one that is unclean. 2. An unbeliever. 3. One to whom nothing is pure. 4. His mind. 5. His conscience is polluted. In all which respects he is a most odious person, in whom is nothing but filthiness of flesh and spirit, the which the pure eyes of the Lord cannot abide. III. BEFORE THIS NATURAL UNCLEANNESS BE PURGED EVERYTHING IS UNCLEAN UNTO A MAN ; the unbeliever tainteth everything that he toucheth ; nothing within him, nothing without him, which is not polluted, although not in his own nature, yet unto him and in his use. Let a natural man turn him to any action, word, or thought, all of them, not excepting the best, are against God, because they proceed from unclean minds and consciences. 1. His actions spiritual, even his best services, as praying, hearing, reading, receiving the sacraments, alms, all these being the sacrifices of the wicked, are abomination unto the Lord, who first looketh to the person, and then to the gift, who if he turn his ear from hearing the law, even his prayer is abominable ; if he choose his own ways, let him kill a bullock for sacrifice, it is all one as if he slew a man ; if he be a polluted person that toucheth any of these holy things, shall they not be unclean ? Yes, surely, the most Divine ordinances are turned to him to sin ; for the Lord first requireth pure parts, and then pure actions (Ezek. xxxvi. 26). 2. His civil actions, his honest dealing in the world, his buying, selling, giving, lending, his labour, care, yea, all the duties of his calling, are in and to him no better than sins. 3. His natural actions, as eating, drinking, sleeping, recreation, physic, all are unclean unto him. 4. All God's creatures and human ordinances, as meat, drink, clothes, goods, lands, buildings, marriage, single estate; in a word, "the whole way of the wicked is abomination to the Lord" (Prov. xv. 9). All these are witnesses of his sin and filthiness, all of them are enlargers of his woe and damnation, because he wanteth faith to lay hold on the Lord Jesus, whereby the just do live, have their heart purified, and so are made lords over the creatures. (*T. Taylor, D.D.*) *Defilement of mind and conscience :—* The "mind" is more than the mere intellective faculty, and includes the activity of the will; and "conscience" is the moral self-consciousness which brings self, and the fact, and the entire behaviour of the soul and spirit, into judgment. This conscience may be "good" in the sense of being approving, or in the sense of being active; it may be "evil" in that it is torpid, seared or dead, and also in respect of its being accusing or condemnatory. Defilement of "mind" must mean that thoughts, ideas, desires, purposes, activities, are all corrupted and debased. Defilement of "conscience" would mean that the sentinel sent to watch was bribed to hold his peace, or that the guide to loftier standard was eagerly applying some base-born man-made perilous rule as all-sufficient. (*H. R. Reynolds, D.D.*) *A pure conscience cast aside :—*In the majority of cases conscience is an elastic and very flexible article, which will bear a deal of stretching, and adapt itself to a great variety of circumstances. Some people by prudent management, and leaving it off piece by piece, like a flannel waistcoat in warm weather, even contrive in time to dispense with it altogether; but there be others who can assume the garment and throw it off at pleasure; and this, being the greatest and most convenient improvement, is the one most in vogue. (*Old Curiosity Shop.*)

Ver. 16. **They profess that they know God.**—*Conventional Christians :—*I. Conventional Christians are PROFESSIONAL ATHEISTS. II. Conventional Christians are PRACTICAL ATHEISTS. 1. They deny God's authority in every-day life; ignore the claims He has upon their existence, powers, possessions. 2. They deny His teaching. He teaches that spiritual interests are supreme. They declare in their daily life that temporal interest are paramount. He teaches that no man should live to himself, but should be inspired by that benevolence that will promote the common weal. But they practically declare that self-interests are supreme, that every man should work for himself, regardless of the common good. He teaches to honour all men on account of what they are. They declare that those only are to be honoured who are endowed with wealth, and move in the pageantry of worldly pomp and power. (*Homilist.*) *The judgment of hypocrisy :—*I. HYPOCRISY THE OCCASION OF ATHEISM. False and inconsistent professors cause more scepticism than the active propagandism of infidels. II. HYPOCRISY IS OFFENSIVE EVEN TO THE UNGODLY. III. HYPOCRISY IS PRACTICAL DISOBEDIENCE. The law is first for the spirit, then the letter: for the life through the heart. IV. HYPOCRISY UNIVERSALLY CONDEMNED. Though in appearance full of "good works," the hypocrite is condemned as destitute of any. (*F. Wagstaff.*) *Hypocrites in the Church :—* I. THERE WILL ALWAYS BE HYPOCRITES IN THE CHURCH. Although the Lord could easily and at once purge His floor of them, yet in great wisdom He suffereth them. 1. In regard of His own glory, that His holiness might appear in the daily discovering of them and purging His Church; for he cannot abide that hypocrites should go in the tale and account of His children. But one time or other, one way or other, will be sanctified in all them that come near Him; at which time His glory also shineth out unto others in their just judgment. 2. In regard of the wicked, that they should the more stumble at the truth by reason of some hypocrites among professors. 3. In regard of the godly, that they should partly be exercised by this means, and partly driven to examine what truth is in them. 4. In respect of the truth itself, which getteth some testimony hence, as Christ on the cross by the very title of His enemies, affirming that He was the King of the Jews. II. THE CHARACTER OF THE HYPOCRITE. 1. The hypocrite is a great professor of religion, and hence cometh to be answerable to his name, in seeming to be, and sustaining the person that he is not. As a clown or knave on a stage playeth the part of a noble, or king, but is well known to be the next remove from a rogue, so these fellows whom the apostle noteth have often in their mouths the name of God and of Christ, the title of the Church, and pretend great knowledge of God and cunning in the Scriptures, and other ecclesiastical writings; yea further, make a great show of faith and pity, and if bare profession would lead to heaven, these could not be the least or last there. And to make this a little more plain, an hypocrite can carry himself so level and even in his course, as no man shall be able outwardly to accuse him, or impute anything unto him, no more than the disciples could accuse Judas, when every man said, "Master, is it I?" but none of them said, Master, is it Judas? 2. The second note is in these words, But indeed they deny him. That is, all the religion of an hypocrite is only in outward profession, separated from the inward sincerity of the heart. All that we have spoken of him is but a lifeless form of godliness, in which the power of it is denied (2 Tim. iii. 5). Men may be said to deny a thing three ways. 1. With the tongue. 2. With the heart; thus the atheist denieth God (Psa. xxiv. 1). 3. With the life or actions, which is here properly meant. For ask the tongues and words of these men concerning their courses, all will appear to be fish whole, but ask their lives, and you shall hear their works (which are far more evident witnesses with or against a man, than his words) speak otherwise. Or, grant they do many glorious works to the eye, yet even herein after a sort God is denied, in that they are lame, and, indeed, carcases of good actions, without any soul to quicken them; all is external, and in such works they may be very busy, but spiritually they perform nothing. 3. The third note or character, is in a further degree of the sin, in that they are said, rebellious to God's commandment, and disobedient to the doctrine of God. The Word giveth us to discover two vices in these titular Christians. (1) Infidelity. (2) Rebellion, or in one word, the want of the obedience of faith. True it is they make a great show of faith, but the apostle distinguisheth of faith; one kind is feigned, another is unfeigned: the former may be joined with much knowledge, much talk of piety, but never with a pure heart and good conscience, as the latter. Now this unfeigned faith, being the mother and mistress of unfained obedience, and the only root whence this fruit can bud and blossom, whosoever are destitute of the former cannot but be barren of the latter. What are the fruits of unbelief, see Acts xvii. 5; 2 Thess. iii. 2; Heb. iii. 12. 4. The fourth note is yet in a further degree of the sin, and goeth near the detection of him; when after long custom in sin, and cracking his conscience checking him, he becomes as a crazy pitcher which is unfit to hold water; so is he reprobate to every good duty; now can he do nothing but rush into sin thick and threefold, and dowse himself over head and ears in impiety. III. THE MISERABLE CONDITION OF THE HYPOCRITE. They are abominable to God, which appeareth both—1. In their persons. 2. Their actions. 3. Their punishment. For their persons, they are but half Christians, neither hot nor cold, and therefore the Lord cannot digest them, compared to cakes but half baked (Hos. vii. 10), and not turned on the other side. Seeing, therefore, they are such as withdraw their best part from God, the soul of God can take no pleasure in them. Their actions, although never so good in themselves, never so specious unto others, yet are abominable unto God. Yea, in their most devout services, they do nothing but (as Ephraim) compass the Lord with lies, and deceit (Hos. xi. 12). Their punishment showeth them to be every way abhorred of God; for as men deal with things they hate, so the Lord—1. Casteth them out of His sight (Job. xiii. 16). The hypocrite shall not come before Him; the workers of lies shall not enter within the walls of that holy city. Yea, sometimes they are cast out of His presence, as Cain was, even out of the visible Church, as they are ever out of the invisible, to show that they shall never be endured hereafter. 2. Destroyeth them; for their destruction from the Lord sleepeth not, but shall surprise them; perhaps while they are in the body, as Ananias and Sapphira, but certainly hereafter. (*T. Taylor, D.D.*) *Professing God, but denying Him:*—Here learn—1. That hypocrites are generally great professors: they profess great knowledge of God, and great zeal for Him. 2. That to deny God is a very heinous sin, and an abominable wickedness: there is a twofold denial of God; first in words, expressly and openly; secondly, in practice, closely and consequentially; "They profess that they know God; but in words they deny Him." There may be at once a professing of God, and a denial of Him; many a man's practice speaks loud, that there is no God, when he makes a fair confession and profession of Him with his mouth and tongue. 3. That no sorts of persons are so odious to God, and abominable in His sight as those who make a profession of His holy name and truth, but walk contrary in their lives to that profession. (*W. Burkitt, M.A.*) *A tarnished Christian:*—"I laid aside a coin one day but did not remember just where I had put it, till one day I found it in a corner, encrusted with rust. At first, I thought it was copper, but careful examination proved it to be silver. It had lain there so long that it was tarnished and unrecognisable. Just as many Christians, alas! are so covered with the grime and filth of this world that it is no wonder that the unconverted and Christians look upon them as copper instead of being good silver." *Inconsistencies of Christians :—* In true kindness of heart, sweetness of temper, open-handed generosity, the common charities of life, many mere men of the world lose nothing by comparison with such professors; and how are you to keep the world from saying, "Ah! your man of religion is no better than others; nay, he is sometimes worse!" With what frightful prominence does this stand out in the answer—never-to-be-forgotten answer—of an Indian chief to the missionary who urged him to become a Christian. The plumed and painted savage drew himself up in the consciousness of superior rectitude; and with indignation quivering on his lip and flashing in his eagle eye, he replied, "Christian lie! Christian cheat! Christian steal!—drink!—murder! Christian has robbed me of my lands, and slain my tribe!" adding, as he turned haughtily away, "The devil, Christian! I will be no Christian." Many such reflections teach us to be careful how we make a religious profession! And having made the profession, cost what it may, by the grace of God let us live up to it; and act it out. It is better not to vow, than, having vowed, not to pay. (*T. Guthrie, D.D.*) *Religion not to be rejected because of hypocrites :—*Many people are offended with the profession of religion, because all are not religious who make a profession. A little consideration will correct this error. Does the sheep despise its fleece because the wolf has worn it? Who blames a crystal river because some melancholy men have drowned themselves in its streams? The best drugs have their adulterants. And will you refuse an opiate, because some have wantonly poisoned themselves with it? Though you have been cozened with false colours, yet you should not dis-esteem that which is dyed in grain. He is a bad economist who, having a spot in his garment, cuts off the cloth, instead of rubbing off the dirt. God rejects all religion but His own. (*T. Secker.*)

---

# CHAPTER II.

Ver. 1. **But speak thou the things which become sound doctrine.**—*Connexion with previous chapter: on the true pastor in contrast with the false :—*Titus' duty is laid down by way of opposition, and knit to the former matter and chapter by the conjunction, But teach thou. As if he had said, Although the false teachers whom I have described dote upon dreams, and feed their hearers with fancies and doctrines of men, to the corrupting and poisoning of souls, and turning men away from the truth, thou must be utterly unlike them in thy preaching; they speak pleasing things, but thou must speak profitable; they, by despising the simplicity of the gospel, fall not only into dangerous errors which they broach, but into loose and idle discourses which bring diseases upon the soul; but thou, on the contrary, must plainly and familiarly discover unto all estates of men and women their estates and duties, that thereby they may be brought to soundness; they cannot but speak and teach as they are; but let them trifle as they will, and live as they list, thou hast betaken thee to another service than that of man, and must carry thy ministry as becometh a sound teacher of the truth, which is according to godliness. (*T. Taylor, D.D.*) *Lessons for ministers :—*I. No Christian minister nor man must be so shaken at the ungodly courses of others in their rank as that they either give over or give back from their uprightness in their duties, for Titus, although he might seem to be cried down by the general voice of false and pompous teachers, yet must he not be silent; and though he might be troubled and opposed, yet must he not be timorous or sluggish; and though his doctrine was not received nor obeyed, yet he must not be weary of tendering and teaching it; yea, be it that the world would rather applaud mockers and time servers, yet must not he discontentedly with Jonas turn another way, but look unto his own duty in serving God, his Church, and men's salvations. Let others stand or fall to their own masters, it is safe for every man so to lay his counters as that his Master may find him doing, yea, well-doing. II. The scope of every minister in his teaching must be to feed the people of God with wholesome doctrine, such as may bring the souls of men to health and soundness. For—1. If the common talk of Christians must be edifying, ministering grace, bring sweetness to the soul, and health to the bones; if it be required of every righteous man that his lips should feed many, nay, more, if the law of grace must sit under the lips of every virtuous woman, much more must the minister's, whose office in peculiar bindeth him to be a pastor or feeder, and that according to God's own heart, he having for this purpose received his calling, gifts, and approbation of God. 2. Otherwise he perverteth the whole course of his life and calling, and is no better than those false apostles who, turning themselves from sound teaching to unfruitful discourses, called vain jangling, are said to rove and err from the right aim, like unskilful darters or shooters. (*Ibid.*) *Sound doctrine :*—I. We have only to look at the remaining part of this chapter to learn WHAT PAUL MEANS BY " SOUND DOCTRINE." In this first verse he states the subject generally, and then branches it out into its various parts. Through the subsequent verses he directs Titus to explain to his flock the duties of their several stations, and to enforce these duties from motives suggested by the gospel. He was to exhort the aged and the young, masters and servants, male and female, to acquit themselves of every obligation which their situations imposed, and thus adorn the doctrines of God their Saviour. The performance of all their duties as Christians forms the perfection of holiness. 1. The apostle Paul says (chap. iii. 8), " This is a faithful saying, and these things I will that thou affirm constantly, that they which have believed in God might be careful to maintain good works." The same apostle in another place, distinguishing between true and false professors, says, " For many walk of whom I have told you often, and now tell you even weeping, that they are the enemies of the cross of Christ, whose end is destruction, whose God is their belly, and whose glory is in their shame, who mind earthly things ; but our conversation is in heaven, from whence, also, we look for the Saviour, the Lord Jesus Christ." " We are His workmanship, created in Christ unto good works, which God hath before ordained, that we should walk in them." The whole of the sixth chapter of the Epistle to the Romans is written to show that the true end of the doctrine of grace is to sanctify men. But to mention particularly all the passages which oblige us to holiness would be to recapitulate almost all the Bible ; the whole book enforces obedience to the precepts of our Divine Master. It is sufficient to recollect His own words, " Let your light so shine before men, that they may see your good works, and glorify your Father which is in heaven." " Herein is My Father glorified, that ye bear much fruit." The religion of Christ, which is intended to bring us into communion with God, brings us first to holiness, without which this communion is not to be attained. Believers are temples of the Holy Ghost ; but, while we live in sin, can the Spirit of God dwell in us ? Can He dwell in a man without producing the effects of His power and of His grace ? Can He possess the heart, and yet leave the affections enslaved to sin ? 2. From the tendency of its doctrines, considered as motives to action, the same thing is evident. There is no discrepancy betwixt the various parts of the gospel. While it inculcates purity and holiness of life, it affords us the most powerful motives to live soberly, righteously, and godly. Do we examine its precepts and rules of conduct ? These give us an idea of holiness in a manner at once lively and impressive. Do we consider the manner in which the nature of vice is represented ? Its miseries are described so fully and so well that we cannot but hold it in abhorrence ; everywhere the Bible abounds with reasons most powerfully enforcing the necessary practice of a good life ; all its mysteries point to this ; all its doctrines are as strong bonds to bind our hearts to the obedience of faith—they are so many weapons of war, mighty through God to cast down imaginations and every high thing—to bring into captivity every thought to the obedience of Christ. The gospel consecrates to holy uses even what the light of nature teaches us, as, that God is our Creator, who, at the beginning, called us into existence ; that He is our Preserver, who, by a perpetual influence, supports us—that it is His providence that watches over the whole universe—particularly guards us, and furnishes us with whatever His goodness and wisdom judge needful for us. What can more forcibly incline us to the practice of obedience than these important truths, if well considered? Since God is our Creator, who gave us life, ought we not to devote that life to Him? Be it ours to view the mercies of God aright, and acknowledge that they all demand holiness unto the Lord. But these motives to holiness, however great and powerful, are as nothing compared with those which the gospel does not take from the light of reason, but from revelation. These latter motives, comprehended in Christ and His economy, are such as must affect every soul which is not dead in sin and insensible to every right impression. That the Almighty, after all our crimes, should be reconciled to us ; that He should give His Son—give Him to be made man—to be our brother—our example ; that He should give Him to die for us the most ignominious and cruel death; is not this love and mercy worthy of eternal praise? Are not these the strongest inducements to be holy in all manner of conversation? Who shall be found so ungrateful as to be capable of sinning against a God so merciful—of counting the blood of such a covenant an unholy thing? II. Let us next consider THE MANNER IN WHICH SOUND DOCTRINE IS TO BE SPOKEN. The view of the Christian revelation already given is a sufficient reply to allegations against the two common modes of preaching. Some complain that the explanation and enforcement of precepts is not preaching Jesus Christ, while others complain that doctrines are stated and enlarged upon which have no relation to practice. While we preach Christ crucified, or exhort to virtuous conduct, let none say that we overlook the end of revelation, for each part, properly stated, does, in the most explicit manner, promote the end of the gospel—the sanctification of believers. Let it be remembered, then, that whether a minister enforces a precept or explains a doctrine, he is bringing that precept or that doctrine to take its share in the grand design of the whole—the salvation of mankind; and that, in choosing either as the subject of discourse, he does not lose sight of what the gospel constantly keeps in view—that men who would inherit the kingdom which cannot be moved must " serve God acceptably with reverence and godly fear." III. We next consider WITH WHAT MIND AND IN WHAT MANNER THIS " SOUND DOCTRINE IS TO BE HEARD." Though the preacher speak " never so wisely," if the hearers neglect the means of instruction, his labour must be vain. Give attendance to reading, to exhortation, to doctrine, to prayer. You ought to hear with serious attention, having repaired to the house of God with holy awe, having composed your spirits by prayer, lay aside each low and earthly thought, and earnestly devote your minds to learn the things that are profitable unto salvation. You must hear with meekness. Come to the house of God with modest and tractable dispositions, bring along with you the persuasion that you need frequently to be reminded of your duty. They only, who in good and honest hearts receive the Word, keep it, and bring forth fruit. You must hear with particular application. When you hear a vice reproved of which your conscience accuses you, apply the reproof to yourselves, " O my soul, thou art the man." Let the instructions which you hear be carefully laid up in your hearts, and reduced to practice in your lives. You must be " doers of the Word and not hearers only." Religion is not an empty amusement or an airy speculation; it is the science of holiness, a practical art, a guide and director of human life. Make your prayer before the Lord your God, that you may understand His truth; God alone can seal the instructions you may receive. Whoever may plant, it is God that giveth the increase. Ask, in faith, wisdom from above, and " God, who giveth to all men liberally and upbraideth not, will give it you." (L. Adamson, D.D.) The minister's directory :—I. HE SHOULD BE A PREACHER. "Speak." II. HE SHOULD BE HIMSELF. "Thou." III. HE SHOULD BE A STUDENT. " Sound doctrine." IV. HE SHOULD BE PRACTICAL. "The things which become." (F. Wagstaff.) Lessons for hearers :—Hearers are hence taught sundry duties. As—1. To desire only this wholesome food that their souls may be well liking, laying aside their itching ears, which hunt after novelties, for the ministry is not appointed to beat the ear as music, but to sink into the soul as the food and medicine of it, by becoming the means and rule of life. Athenian hearing is the cause of Athenian preaching, and the diseases running upon such hearers showeth the curse of God on them, who with contempt of the manna from heaven, with the onions, garlic, and flesh of Egypt; these things they have upon their desire, and with them more than they desire, for they rot even between their teeth. 2. To receive the wholesome doctrine, as for the body we receive wholesome food whatsoever it be, or from whomsoever; let it be bitter sometimes, or seem too salt, yet if it be wholesome hunger findeth it savoury; no man but will strive to receive a bitter potion to restore his body out of any weakness to soundness; and yet who is it that will suffer a wholesome reproof to the recovery of soundness to the soul? and others stand so much upon toothsomeness of their meat, and must know their cooks so well, that before they can be resolved in these two, the plausibleness of the doctrine and the friendliness of the person, their souls are well nigh starved to death. Hence is it that we hear so many complaints. Oh, saith one, he seeketh not the goodwill of his hearers, nor casteth to please them; he is of a tart and bitter spirit; he seeketh to wound and gall, but he healeth nor suppleth not. But what preacheth he, whether any errors or the pure doctrine of God? No, say they, we cannot except against his doctrine. True, for they never trouble themselves so far as to examine it by the Word or themselves by it. But then, say

I, is it the Word of God thou hearest, and the truth by thine own confession? Why dost thou then not tremble at that Word? 3. Hearers must hold wholesome doctrine when they have received it (2 Tim. iii. 14). Continue in the things thou hast received; buy the truth, but sell it not, and bind it fast upon their hearts. And good reason, for if the meat be never so wholesome, if the stomach of the soul keep it not, but it slip the memory, and is not by meditation digested, the soul is as surely diseased as is the body when no sustenance will stay to strengthen it. 4. Hearers must so desire, receive, and hold this wholesome food, as they may grow by it, showing by their thriving in grace that they have wholesome meat (Psa. cix. 4), for as in the body, if meat, when it is digested, send not virtue whereby the operation of it appeareth in all the parts, the body is diseased, some obstruction or opilation hindereth the work of it, so is the soul obstructed with the itching ear, covetous thoughts, hardness of heart, formal worship, all which keep the soul barren and empty of grace, yea, lean and ill-looking in the eyes of God. Seeing, therefore, the Lord hath spread His table for us, and liberally furnished it with store of this wholesome food, let it appear in our souls, by our strength to labour in Christian duties to which we are called, to overcome the temptations unto sin, to carry our victory in our strife against our own lusts. (*T. Taylor, D.D.*) *Genuine morality* :—I. Genuine morality LEGISLATES ALIKE FOR ALL MANKIND. 1. Age. 2. Sex. 3. Relationship. II. Genuine morality REACHES TO THE SPRINGS OF THE HEART. III. GENUINE MORALITY IS THE GRAND PURPOSE OF GOSPEL TEACHING. (*D. Thomas, D.D.*) *Healthy teaching:*—Sound teaching, according to Paul, is not teaching that has the conventional ring, not teaching that is divested of all freshness, originality, and stimulating force, but whatever goes to make moral fibre, whatever tends to build up strong men and women, whatever brings a healthy colour to the cheek, and gives life a true zest. I. IT IS THE HEALTHY MIND ALONE THAT CAN IMPART HEALTHY TEACHING. A healthy mind is a free and untrammeled mind; a mind that plays freely around all questions, and forms its own unbiassed conclusions. A mind that has the clear vision of health, a mind that has the keen appetite of health, a mind that has the unvitiated palate of health, a mind that has the hardy courage of health, a mind that takes the world as it finds it. An independent mind, a mind that makes its own observations, draws its own inferences, is not a mere servile echo of other minds. II. HEALTHY TEACHING IS THAT WHICH IS HEALTHFUL IN ITS EFFECTS. Bad food cannot build up a robust frame. I will imagine that a mother has a puling, pining infant to rear. There is a question between divers kinds of diet. One authority says: "You ought to use mine, because it has the correct label on it, and is done up in the proper regulation tins." But the mother says: "I have tried it, and the child starved upon it." "But it has all the requisite chemical constituents in their due proportions. It must have been the native perversity of the child which prevented its thriving. It is the recognised thing, endorsed and recommended by the entire faculty." "I cannot help that," says the mother; "labels or no labels, tins or no tins, faculty or no faculty, all I know is that I have tried that food, and that if I had gone on with it, my child would have been dead by this time." And then she is induced, by some old wife, perhaps, to try another preparation, natural and simple, nobody's patent, with no label or endorsement whatever. But, lo, and behold! the child grows fat and plump, the hue of health comes gradually to its cheeks, and it weighs heavier every day! "But this is not an accredited compound. The great authorities on diet have not prescribed it. It cannot be wholesome." Once more the mother retorts: "No matter. My child is alive and well." Now, that is the true test to apply to religious teaching. What sort of men and women does it make? "Sound doctrine" is that which produces a healthy, spiritual life, which builds up character. (*J. Halsey.*) *Wholesome doctrine must be applied to the several ages and conditions of men :*—Every faithful minister must fit and apply his doctrine to the several ages, conditions, and occasions of his people, that every man and woman, young and old, superior and inferior, may know not only what is lawful, but what is most expedient and beseeming our age, place, and condition of life. It is true that all virtues in general are commanded, as all vices in general are forbidden, to all persons, of what sex or estate soever; yet there be some special virtues which are more shining ornaments in some age and condition than others, as in young men staidness and discretion are special beauties, but are not (if wanting) such blemishes in their years, as in old men, because of their observation and experience. So there be some special vices (though all are to strive against all) which are fouler spots and stains to some ages than to others, and some to which men and women are more subject by reason of their age or sex, as youth to headiness and rashness; old age to testiness, frowardness, covetousness, &c.; women to curiosity, loquacity, &c., against all which the man of God must in special furnish and arm his people, instantly striving to root out such noisome weeds as of their own accord appear out of the earthy hearts of men, as also to plant the contrary graces in their stead. Examples of this practice we meet withal everywhere in the Epistles. Paul, in divers of his Epistles, as to the Colossians, but especially to the Ephesians, describeth in particular the duties of wives, husbands, children, fathers, servants, masters (see chap. v. 6). Peter, in the second and third chapters, is as large in the distinct offices of subjects, wives, husbands, servants. And from this practice the apostle John dissenteth not (1 John ii. 12), where he giveth his reasons why he writeth to fathers, to babes, to old men, and to young men. Besides these examples are sundry weighty reasons to enforce the doctrine. 1. As first, the faithfulness of a wise steward herein appeareth, namely, in distributing to every one of his master's family their own portion of meat in due season (Luke xii. 42). 2. To this purpose is the Word fitted, to make every man ready and absolute to every good work; and thus the wisdom of God is made to shine to all eyes, who can behold such a perfect rule of direction in faith and manners. 3. Well knew our apostle, with the other men of God, that general doctrines (though never so wholesome) little prevail, are but cold, and touch not men to the quick, without particular application to their several necessities; till Peter come to say, "You have crucified the Lord of glory," we read of no pricking of their hearts. (*T. Taylor, D.D.*) *Dealing with individuals :*—Richard Baxter adopted the method of individual dealing with the parishioners of Kidderminster, bringing them to his house and taking them apart one by one. He tells us that, because of it, he had reason to believe that more than a third of the grown-up inhabitants of the place were converted to God. The late Mr. Grant of Arndilly was so intent upon this habit of individual intercourse that in three months he had dealt with fifteen hundred souls, while the refrain of all his letters, as Mrs. Gordon says, was always this, "Speak a word for Jesus."

Ver. 2. **That the aged men be sober.**—*The temptations and duties of old men :*— I. SINS TO BE AVOIDED. 1. Indulgence in wine. 2. Irreverence. 3. Folly. "Temperate" here is really prudent, sound-minded. II. VIRTUES TO BE CHERISHED. 1. Stability. 2. Love. 3. Patience. (*F. Wagstaff.*) *The duty of old men :*— Our apostle exempteth not old men from being subject to the doctrine of God because of their age, but rather sendeth them first to school, notwithstanding all that knowledge and experience which they might pretend (1 John ii. 13). For God's school is as well for old as for young, in which men are not only to be initiated in the principles of religion, but also to be led forward unto perfection of wisdom; and seeing no man can attain in this life unto perfection, therefore every man is still to press forward, and to wax old daily learning something. And there is great reason that as old men must first be instructed by Titus, so they should be the first in learning their duty. 1. First, in regard of example, for their presidence prevaileth much, and would be a great inducement to the younger, who need all encouragements in the ways of God, which example not being generally given by our elder men, besides that they entangle themselves in the sins of the younger, we cannot marvel at the licentiousness of our youth. 2. The honour of their age, yea, the ornament and crown of their years, is to be sound in the ways of righteousness, that is, in a life led holily and justly, which two can never be found but in a heart submitted to the Word of God, the rule of both. 3. Whereas old men are delighted with relations of idle antiquities, and things formerly passed as long as they can recall, the Holy Ghost recalleth them from such unfruitful spending of their time, and showeth them that Christ and His doctrine, both of them being from the beginning, are most ancient, and consequently the knowledge and remembrance of Him is a matter best beseeming them; to have their senses and tongues exercised herein should be the delight of their age; to be conversant in the holy exercises which witness of Him should be their chief business, as old Hannah went not out of the Temple, and old Simeon waited there to see his salvation. 4. Their time by the course of nature cannot be long to fit themselves to heaven, and therefore they had not need slack any opportunity which might hasten them thither. (*T. Taylor, D.D.*) *Suitable characteristics for the aged :*—Sobriety in all things is the peculiar character befitting age. Hasty, impulsive, intemperate speech, frivolous gaiety, thoughtless indulgence, are hateful in the old. The Christian elders should at least aim to possess the virtue without which hoary hair would be a disgrace rather than a crown of glory. They are not only to be "sober," but "grave and discreet," terms which nobly pourtray and illustrate the highest characteristics and the truest consecration of age.

> Age should fly concourse, cover in retreat
> Defects of judgment, and the will subdue;
> Walk thoughtful on the silent, solemn shore
> Of the vast ocean it must sail so soon.

"Healthy," or sound, must they be "in respect to their faith, love, and patient endurance." The apostle, in his earliest Epistle (1 Thess. i. 3), congratulated that Church on "work" of theirs which originated in "faith," on "labour unto weariness" which was dictated by "love," and on "patient endurance" which was born of Christian "hope." In writing to the Corinthians (1 Cor. xiii. 13), he says, "Now abideth faith, hope, love." The Lord, from His throne of glory, addressed the Ephesian Church (Rev. ii. 2) thus: "I know thy works, thy labour unto weariness, and thy patient endurance." The passages throw light upon each other. Occasionally "hope," the child of faith, the source of patience, the secret of peace, and the well-spring of joy, is substituted by the apostle for one or other of the emotions with which it is so closely associated, either as antecedent or consequent. But, making allowance for this characteristic touch, it is profoundly interesting to trace in this—one of the latest of the Pauline Epistles—the vibration of a note struck by him in his earliest; an argument of no small weight in determining the authenticity of the Pastoral Epistles. Paul would have Titus cultivate among the aged men of Crete the root-principles out of which all holy living proceeds. The peculiarity of the Pastoral Epistles—reference, *i.e.*, to the being "sound" or "healthy" in these respects—suggests the possibility that "faith" may be undermined or perverted; that "love" may become irregular, sentimental, partisan, or hysterical; and that "patience" may degenerate into listlessness, obstinacy, or stoicism, if it be not fed at the fountains of Christian "hope." Does not the reference here to the causes and sources of holy living, rather than to those effects of them on which he had enlarged when writing to the Thessalonians (1 Thess. i. 3), suggest to us that the longer St. Paul lived, he more and more acquired the habit of putting confidence in Christian principles and "sound" motives? (*H. R. Reynolds, D.D.*)    *Behaviour suitable for the aged:*—He that hath received much must bring forth much fruit, as the servant that had five talents committed unto him gained five other talents. So old men must be grave and sober, and carry a majesty in their countenance, that they may after a sort resemble the majesty of God. As gravity and sobriety agreeth to every age, so most especially to the elder age, contrary to which is lightness, lasciviousness, and waywardness, which make them not honourable, but odious, not to be reverenced, but to be despised in the eyes of the younger sort. Let them adorn their years with those virtues which the apostle nameth. If they be careful to express these things which become wholesome doctrine, they shall manifestly show that their living so in the world hath not been in vain; but honour is not seemly for a fool. The wise man saith, "The beauty of the young men is their strength, and the glory of the aged is the grey-headed," that is, wisdom, counsel, experience, whereby they are more adorned than the young man is beautified by his bodily strength. For the ornaments of the mind are to be preferred before the properties of the body. Again, they must be examples of a godly life and holy conversation, that youth may stand in fear to commit any indecent and unseemly thing in their presence. Thus Job saith of himself (chap xxix.), "When I went out of the gate, the young men saw me, and hid themselves." But when the elder sort are ringleaders and examples of an evil and corrupt life, there is more gravity on their heads than piety in their hearts; in their white hairs than in their behaviour; and so the crown of honour is taken from them, and they are justly condemned, despised, and reproached of those of whom they should be honoured. For we may see old men so hardened in wickedness, that if a man would find whole heaps of wickedness, he need seek no farther but to them. We are all to honour the grey head and to magnify old age, for (as Solomon saith) "Age is a crown of glory when it is found in the way of righteousness," whereby he meaneth that old age, seasoned with a godly life and upright, bringeth with it as great glory as a crown on the head and a sceptre in the hand doth unto a king, and therefore such old men are greatly to be reverenced and highly to be esteemed. But many, except they should be honoured for their ignorance, superstition, frowardness, maliciousness, waywardness, covetousness, drunkenness, licentiousness, and self-will, there is nothing else to be found in them, to be learned of them, to be gathered from them. By these foul enormities they bring themselves into contempt, and bring shame and reproach upon their own heads, so that no man defameth and dishonoureth them so much as themselves. Surely, if young men misbehave and misgovern themselves, they are not to be excused, but to be reproved, because they ought to order their lives aright, and remember their Creator in the days of their youth, and not deserve to be evil spoken or reported of ; but old folks are doubly worthy of the shame that men do them, if they be not honoured for their virtues. They should learn by their long life and old age to grow in the knowledge of God and His Son Jesus Christ, to hate sin, to delight in righteousness, and daily to die unto the world. (*W. Attersoll.*) *The theological use of old age :*—One of the uses of the aged is to keep our theology sweet. I should be very much afraid for evangelical doctrine if there were none but young men in the Church. Youth loves to speculate. Old age loves to rest in ascertained realities. Youth is destructive. You have seen a boy when he has got a gun. He goes popping at everything—sparrows, cats, barn-doors. He can hardly resist levelling even at his own father. So, when a young man becomes conscious of the possession of reason, he is for exercising it upon everything. Nothing is so sacred as to be beyond the reach of this destructive weapon, and truths are often in danger of being swept away along with the falsities. But, on the other hand, old age is proverbially conservative, and so the needful counteractive is supplied. A man may have gone very wide in his young days, but, as a rule, he comes round again to the old starting-point—comes home to the old centre when he is verging upon threescore years and ten. A soul that is consciously on the brink of eternity cannot do with the shallow fallacies that once passed muster as excellent substitutes for the old faith. It finds that, after all, the old gospel is the thing it wants. The late learned Dr. Duncan said to a student, "I do not forbid you to speculate. I like speculation. I have speculated a great deal during my life, but now that I am turning an old man, I am in love with the facts." Then he added in a quasi-humorous tone, "Now that I'm an auld man, I have just come back to the theology of the old wives and the bairns. I like that." This is a useful element in the Church. Thank God for the aged and for their tenacious grasp of the essential verities of the gospel. (*J. Halsey.*)     *If age be blended with naughtiness, the older the worse:*—An old river without water quencheth not our thirst. An old friend that hath lost his honesty is worse than an old picture that hath lost its colour. Old wine no man commends ; when it is turned to vinegar, let them take it that like it. An old house is no safe harbour when it is ready to fall on the inhabiter's head. An old man that hath lost his experience is like a boulter ; much good flour hath gone through it, but there is nothing left in it but bran. (*T. Adams.*)     **Temperate.**—*The limit of law and reason :*—Notice the frequent occurrence of a single epithet which may almost be said to characterise Christian behaviour, as St. Paul, in his later days, came to conceive of it. The repetition of the word I mean is veiled from readers of the Authorised Version by variations in the rendering of it. In one form or another it really occurs in these verses four times. First, old men are to be "temperate" : that is its first occurrence. Then, elderly females are to teach the young wives to be " sober," another use of the same word. Next, the younger women are to be " discreet," the same word. Finally, it is the solitary require- ment for young men that they be " sober-minded," where once more the same word is retained. What is this moral quality which Paul felt it to be so necessary to enforce upon every age and on both sexes ? It denotes that moral health which results from a complete mastery over the passions and desires, "so that," in Archbishop Trench's words, " they receive no further allowance than that which the law and the right reason admit and approve." Self-control would probably come as near the idea as any single word we can employ. But it includes such moral sanity or wisdom of character as is only to be attained through the habitual control of the reason over loose, illicit, or excessive desires of every kind. It is by no means to be wondered at that St. Paul should have laid much emphasis on this virtue. Heathen society in its later periods was remarkable for the weakening of self-control. Self-indulgence became at once its danger and its disgrace. When religion came to be thoroughly divorced from ethics, no curb remained strong enough to restrain the bulk of men either from angry passion or from sensual gratification. Against this tendency of the later classical period philosophers and moralists were never weary of inveighing. The very word which St. Paul here uses was with them the technical name for a cardinal virtue, the praises of which, as "the fairest of the gifts of the gods," they were always sounding. But the foolish excess which heathen religion had failed to check defied heathen philosophy too. The time had come for Christianity to try its hand. The task was a hard one. I have no doubt Paul beheld with anxiety the growing inroads which, before his death, the loose and reckless habits of his age had begun to make even upon those little sheltered companies that had sought a new refuge beneath the Cross. In these latest writings he reiterates the warning to be sober-minded with no less urgency than Plato or Aristotle. We may well thank God that he based the admonition on more prevailing pleas. It took a long time for Christianity to lay the foundations of a manlier and purer society; but it did so in the end. The old civilisation was past remedy and perished. Into the new, which should take its place, the gospel inspired a nobler temper. The restored authority of Divine law and the awful sense of the evil of sin, which were the Church's inheritance from Judaism, the value of personal purity which it learned at the Cross, the new conception of sanctity which Christ created, the hopes and dreads of the hereafter: these things trained our modern nations in their youth to a reverential sobriety of character, an awe for what is holy, and a temperate enjoyment of sensual delights, such as had utterly disappeared from the Greco-Roman world. It is for us to take heed, lest, amid the growth of wealth, the cheapening of luxuries, and the revolt against restraining authority which distinguish our own age, we should forfeit, before we are aware of it, some of that chastened decorous simplicity and manly self-control which lies so near the base of a noble Christian character, and which has been one of the gospel's choicest gifts to human society. (*J. O. Dykes, D.D.*)

Vers. 3–5. **The aged women.**—*The dangers and duties of women:*—I. WOMEN HAVE PECULIAR DANGERS ACCORDING TO THEIR AGE. The older ones are tempted to seek the excitement of stimulants, or of slander; the younger ones to instability of affection, to impurity of life, or other inconsistency of conduct. II. WOMEN HAVE DUTIES PECULIAR TO THEIR AGE. The younger have duties of obedience; the middle-aged have the cares of home life; the aged have the instruction of the younger. (*F. Wagstaff.*) *Religious home life:*—I. TRUE RELIGION IS THE FOUNDATION OF HOME HAPPINESS. II. TRUE RELIGION IS THE SECRET OF DOMESTIC PROSPERITY. III. TRUE RELIGION AT HOME CAN ALONE INSURE THE ESTEEM AND RESPECT OF THOSE ABROAD. (*Ibid.*) *Apostolic advice to the aged women:*—The gospel revealed the lofty destiny of woman, and it is not surprising that St. Paul should continue his advice to Titus thus: " Enjoin that the aged women in like manner, should preserve in their demeanour holy propriety." As Jerome has it, " Their gait and motion, their countenance, their speech, and their silence, should exhibit a certain dignity of sacred decorum." The very word seems to convey the fine thought that there is a consecration, a sacerdotal eminence and sanctity, possible and even normal, in the life of woman. The aged woman should have in her looks and ways something better than the garment of the priest or the aureole of the saint. It is fitting and seemly that she should. The apostle adds a grim touch after this hint of saintly sacerdotal beauty. He knew the temptation of " old women " of both sexes to be censorious, blundering, and self-indulgent, and so he adds, " Let them not be slanderous, nor enslaved by much wine." They are, moreover, to be " mistresses of honour," capable of " beautifully instructing " by their word and example those who look up to them for counsel. (*H. R. Reynolds, D.D.*) *Holiness consists of little duties:*—Did a holy life consist of one or two noble deeds—some signal specimens of doing, or enduring, or suffering—we might account for the failure, or reckon it small dishonour to turn back in such a conflict, But a holy life is made up of small things of the hour, and not the great things of the age, that fill up a life like that of Paul or John, like that of Rutherford, or Brainerd, or Martyn. The avoidance of little evils, little sins, little inconsistencies, little weaknesses, little follies, little indiscretions and imprudences, little foibles, little indulgences of self, little bits of covetousness and penuriousness, little exhibitions of worldliness and gaiety, little indifferences to the feelings or wishes of others: the avoidance of such little things as these goes far to make up at least the negative beauty of holy life. And then attention to little duties of the day and hour in public transactions, or private dealings, or family arrangements; to little words, and looks, and tones; little self-denials and self-restraints and self-forgetfulness: these are the active developments of holy life, the rich and Divine mosaics of which it is composed. What makes yon green hill so beautiful? Not the outstanding peak or stately elm, but the bright sward which clothes its slopes, composed of innumerable blades of slender grass. It is of small things that a great life is made up; and he who will acknowledge no life as great, save that which is built up of great things, will find little in Bible character to admire or copy. *The bloom of the aged:*—A good woman never grows old. Years may pass over her head, but if benevolence and virtue dwell in her heart, she is as cheerful as when the spring of life first opened to her view. When we look upon a good woman we never think of her age; she looks as charming as when the rose of youth first bloomed on her cheek. That rose has not faded yet; it will never fade. In her neighbourhood she is the friend and benefactor. Who does not respect and love the woman who has passed her days in acts of kindness and mercy—who has been the friend of man and God—whose whole life has been a scene of kindness and love and devotion to truth? We repeat, such a woman cannot grow old. She will always be fresh and buoyant in spirit and active in humble deeds of mercy and benevolence. If the young lady desires to retain the bloom and beauty of youth, let her not yield to the sway of fashion and folly; let her love truth and virtue, and to the close of life she will retain those feelings which now make life appear a garden of sweets, ever fresh and ever new. (*Great Thoughts.*)    **Not false accusers.**—*Rules to avoid false accusing*: —1. Look to thine own calling and the necessary duties of it, that so following thine own plough, thou mayest have no leisure to intermeddle in other men's affairs: busy-bodies and prattlers are joined by the apostle. 2. Beware of envy, which is still hatching and inventing evil: the saying is true, "Malice never spake well," but is suspicious, and depraving the best persons and practices, and is one of the greatest enemies of truth, in which God's image chiefly consisteth. 3. Learn to esteem the good name of thy brother, the next thing to his life, considering the truth of that homely speech, that he that wanteth a good name is half hanged; and there is great reason that those who would have their names tendered by others should tender the good name of others, doing as they would be done unto, which is the golden rule of all equity. 4. In receiving reports excuse parties absent as far as well we can, as also facts done, so far as they may be well interpreted; and where we cannot do so to advise the reporter to look well unto and consider himself. (*T. Taylor, D.D.*)    *False accusation:*—Often are the most painful wrongs inflicted through the medium of covert inuendoes and malignant insinuations. Half of a fact is a whole falsehood. He who gives the truth a false colouring by a false manner of telling it is the worst of liars. Such was Doeg in his testimony against the priests. He stated the facts in the case, but gave them such an artful inter-pretation as to impart to them the aspect and influence of the most flagrant falsehoods. It was through the same mode of procedure that our Lord was condemned. A perverse misconstruction was given to His words, so that what was spoken in loyalty to the highest truth, was transformed into treason worthy of death. (*E. L. Magoon.*)    **That they may teach the young women.**—*The education of young women:*—The young women are mentioned here as under the teaching and authority of the aged. What now are some of the first elements which Paul insists on in the education of a Christian family? He omits many things which one would have supposed to stand high in the list of young ladies' accomplishments; for example, music, dancing, and the art of binding themselves into the shape of sand-glasses. Perhaps the apostle thought them sufficiently advanced in such acquirements, and that therefore he might pass them over in silence. He insists, however, that these aged governesses shall teach the following great elementary principles. 1. That the young woman be sober, wise, of a sound mind, prudent and discreet members of the Church of Christ. The first element, then, in the education of your daughters is wisdom or prudence; and if you begin anywhere else with them, you begin at the wrong end. This wisdom or prudence is not easily defined, but it will appear in the entire character and conduct of their future life; it will enable them to avoid the snares which the ungodly lay for them, and conduct themselves in a manner worthy of the name and the religion of their Redeemer. This prudence is opposed to rashness, enthusiasm, and impulsive resolutions, to which the young mind, and especially the young female mind, is naturally inclined. 2. Then secondly, they are to love their husbands, for without this the house will become a pandemonium, and profligacy and impurity fill the land. Their love to their husbands should be ardent and unchangeable, yielding neither to the seduction of strangers nor to the husband's coldness and neglect at home. 3. To love their children. It may be asked, Is not this love natural? and if so, where is the necessity for teaching it? I answer, bad habits in society can eradicate many of the principles of our nature, and make us more degraded and unfeeling than the brutes. Edmund Burke relates that J. J. Rousseau would not keep his children in his house, but sent them to be brought up in an hospital; and then remarks, " that bears love their young, and lick them into shape, but bears are not philosophers." In India the natural love of our offspring was conquered by the tyranny of a terrible custom, and millions of female infants were destroyed in infancy by the mother's hands! Is the murder of infants altogether unheard of in among us? Are there no Foundling hospitals within the bounds of Christendom? Then remember that the Isle of Crete was one of the wickedest places in the world, and the inhabitants mere heathen, and you shall see the force of the exhortation to " love their children." It is an awful fact, which I first heard of in Hamburgh, that in the continental cities there is a class of old wives, real old devils, who are called " child-murderesses," and whose office it is to save the mother and destroy the child! In this way myriads of innocent infants are sacrificed, and no eye but the eye of God, the mother, and the murderess, ever knows anything about it! 4. They are to be discreet, which is the same as sober, mentioned in the fourth verse; chaste, viz., placing all their happiness in their husbands and families alone; keepers at home, that they may attend to the affairs of the household, and be an example to their children. It is not the duty of a married woman with a family to engage much in public business, even though it should be of the most important kind. Her place is the family circle, and her duty is to stay at home. We may say the same of much visiting. It is impossible to gad about and take care of the family at the same time; and as to the mother handing over her children to the care of servants, and then giving herself little or no concern about them, I say with Edmund Burke that such conduct would be a slander on the instinct of the brutes! 5. Good; they are to be good wives, faithful and diligent in their household duties. Good is a very expressive word, and is used to denote the highest excellence (Acts xi. 24). Good (from which our word God comes, the Good One) I take in its most general acceptation to signify the disposition to bless; it is the fountain of kindness within, from which love, mercy, and all gentle and kind actions flow; " obedient to their own husbands, that the Word of God be not blasphemed." The great duty of the wife is obedience, and in this she is a type of the Church's obedience and submission to Christ. Love is common to both, though the natural order is that his should go before and hers follow after, as in the case of Christ and the Church; then obedience is her special duty, even as protection and defence are his. The command, probably, has a special reference to wives who were united to unbelieving or heathen husbands, and teaches that grace never delivers us from the obligations of nature—they are, though believing, to be obedient to their husbands though unbelieving, and the husband, though unbelieving, is bound to love, support, and protect his wife, though she is a believer in the gospel. (*W. Graham, D.D.*) *Pastoral dealings with young women:*—A delicate tact may be observed in St. Paul's management of the younger women. To them he does not bid Titus address himself at all. Although he thinks of them as already married, yet the admonitions of the pastor are to pass, as it were, through the lips of the senior matrons. Some of these may have been official " deaconesses " (like Phœbe at Cenchræa), but this is by no means essential to the spirit of his instructions. Whether officially set apart to minister among her own sex, as was the salutary habit of the early Church, or not, it is in the privacy of the home, or the retired gathering for prayer and female industry, that the wholesome influence of a Christian matron of experience and weight of character may most advantageously be exerted. And it is through the familiar intercourse of such " mothers in Israel " with their younger sisters that a Christian minister can most suitably and safely reach the maidens and young housewives of his flock. So at least St. Paul judged. The homely housewifely virtues which are here specified do seem to be best taught by female lips. In seven particulars has this unmarried old man succeeded in covering the circle of a young wife's duties. Her devotion to husband and babes, her discipline of herself into suitable decorum, her womanly purity, her household industry, her benign sweetness of temper, her due deference to her husband: such are the graces by which within her gracious realm of home the youthful matron is to glorify her Saviour and her God. What a surprising elevation did the gospel confer on woman at its first promulgation! The sudden discovery that " in Christ Jesus there is neither male nor female " might have a tendency at the first to relax somewhat those restraints which sex and marriage impose on woman ; but, if the wholesome influence Paul desired could be exerted by matrons of maturer character, it is plain that so far from the Christian wife giving her husband (heathen though he might still be) any cause to speak ill of her new faith—her chastity, her meekness, her dilligence, her obedience, would be certain to recommend the gospel in which her soul had found the secret of a behaviour so gracious and so beautiful. (*J. O. Dykes, D.D.*)    *A husband endeared :*—"I am thankful to the Nihilists for one thing," says the Czarina.  "They have made me love my husband dearly.  Our home-life has become so different since I began to look on him as though he were under sentence of death.  You can't think how deeply his menaced state attaches me to him."   *A heartless mother reproved by a sparrow :*—Down in a London slum there lived a working man, his wife, and four children, all wretched and miserable through drink.  The drunken wife one evening, wandering about in misery, saw a sparrow pick up a crumb and carry it to her young in her nest.  The poor woman turned pale, trembled for a moment, and burst into tears.  The day of repentance had come to her.  "Oh!" she exclaimed, "that sparrow feeds her young birds, and I neglect my young children.  And what for?  Drink.  Nothing but drink!" And she wrung her hands and wept.  Then she arose and went home to pray.  She cried unto God in her distress and He sent His message of forgiveness to her soul. Then her face wore a new beauty, and her husband and family looked wonderingly upon her.  She kissed them all, one by one, and told them how she had become changed.  The husband, under his wife's teaching, became a Christian, and a happy home, with comfort, peace, and plenty, soon followed. (*G. W. McCree.*) *A faithful wife :*—There is nothing upon this earth that can compare with the faithful attachment of a wife ; no creature who for the object of her love is so indomitable, so persevering, so ready to suffer and to die.   Under the most depressing circumstances, a woman's weakness becomes mighty power ; her timidity becomes fearless courage ; all her shrinking and sinking passes away ; and her spirit acquires the firmness of marble—adamantine firmness—when circumstances drive her to put forth all her energies under the inspiration of her affections. (*D. Webster.*)    *Influence of a good wife :*—Oftentimes I have seen a tall ship glide by against the tide as if drawn by some invisible bow-line, with a hundred strong arms pulling it.  Her sails unfilled, her streamers were drooping, she had neither side-wheel nor stern-wheel ; still she moved on, stately, in serene triumph, as with her own life.  But I knew that on the other side of the ship, hidden beneath the great bulk that swam so majestically, there was a little toilsome steam-tug, with a heart of fire and arms of iron, that was tugging it bravely on ; and I knew that if the little steam-tug untwined her arms, and left the ship, it would wallow, and roll about, and drift hither and thither, and go off with the refluent tide, no man knows whither.  And so I have known more than one genius, high-decked, full-freighted, idle-sailed, gay-pennoned, who, but for the bare, toiling arms and brave, warm-beating heart of the faithful little wife that nestles close to him, so that no wind or wave could part them, would have gone down with the stream, and have been heard of no more.   *Early Christian women :*—"What women these Christians have!" exclaimed the heathen rhetorician Libanius, on hearing about Anthusa, the mother of John Chrysostom, the famous "golden-mouthed" preacher of the gospel at Constantinople in the fourth century.  Anthusa, at the early age of twenty, lost her husband, and thenceforward devoted herself wholly to the education of her son, refusing all offers of further marriage.  Her intelligence and piety moulded the boy's character and shaped the destiny of the man, who, in his subsequent position of eminence, never forgot what he owed to maternal influence.  Hence, it would be no overstrained assertion to say that we owe those rich homilies of Chrysostom, of which interpreters of Scriptures still make great use, to the mind and heart of Anthusa.   *A mother's love :*—The intensity of maternal affection was illustrated in the observation of a little boy, who, after reading Bunyan's "Pilgrim's Progress," asked his mother which of the characters she liked best.  She replied, "Christian, of course : he is the hero of the story."  The dear child responded, "Mother, I like Christiana best, because, when Christian set out on his pilgrimage, he went alone ; but, when Christiana started, she took the children with her."   *Christianity at home :*—I have no faith in that woman who talks of grace and glory abroad, and uses no soap at home.  Let the buttons be on the shirts, let the children's socks be mended, let the roast mutton be done to a turn, let the house be as neat as a new pin, and the home be as happy as home can be ; and then, when the cannon-balls, and the marbles, and the shots, and even the grains of sand, are all in the box, even then there will be room for those little deeds of love and faith which, in my Master's name, I seek of you who love His appearing. Serve God by doing common actions in a heavenly spirit, and then, if your daily calling only leaves you cracks and crevices of time, fill them up with holy service. (*C. H. Spurgeon.*)    *True marriage:*—Husband, in our old Saxon speech meant *houseband*—the stay of the house; and a wife should be a "help-meet" for the husband.    She should be a "keeper at home." Phidias, when he depicted a woman, made her to sit under a snail shell, this signifying, that like the snail she should never be far away from her home. (*J. G. Pilkington.*)    **Discreet.**—*Discretion:*—A virtue before required both in the minister (chap. i. 8.), and in elder men (chap. ii. 2.), and now in younger women, being a grace requisite for all estates, ages, sexes, and conditions of life; requiring that the reins of affections be subjected unto reason, and moderated by judgment, not suffering a thought to be entertained and settled in the mind which is not first warranted in the Word, without which, if the reins be slacked but a little, the mind is suddenly vanquished, taken, and lead captive of manifold lusts. This grace, then, is the watchman and moderator of the mind, keeping and guarding it from pleasures altogether unlawful, and in lawful curbing and cutting off excess and abuse.    It watcheth also over the affections of the heart and actions of the life, resisting all light behaviour, all childish carriage, all unquiet and troublesome passions, such as are suspicions, jealousies, which are the fuels and firebrands of much mischief; and the distempers of flashing anger, rage, and unjust vexation. It suffereth not undutifulness to the husband, unnaturalness towards the children, unmercifulness towards servants, untowardness in her own duties, unthankful meddling with other folks' affairs. It is a procurer and preservative of many graces, a bond of her own and others' peace, a settler of the comfort of her life, an ornament of her head, and of her house; which once let her to be disrobed of, she may bid farewell to her family's welfare; for let any vile affection bear sway but for a little while, as of anger, impatience, excessive grief, intemperance, or any such, how is the whole house in a kind of tumult! which as a commonwealth in the commotion and rising of some one rebel, cannot be composed and settled till the rebel be subdued; which they find too true who in their match were left unto themselves, to make choice of such as wanted then, and yet have not attained with the fear of God the practice of this virtue. (*T. Taylor, D.D.*)    **Keepers at home.**—*Home the place for women:*—Not that a woman is never to be found without her house over her head, for many necessary and just occasions call her often abroad, namely—1. As a Christian, the public duties of piety and God's worship; as also more private duties of love, and works of mercy in visiting and helping the sick and poor.    2. As a wife, both with her husband when he shall require her, and without him for the necessary provision of the household—and such like.    But the thing here condemned is the affection of gadding at any or all hours, with disposition of hearing or telling news, or affecting merriments, company, expense or excess, accounting the house rather a prison than a home, and so easily forsaking it without all just occasion. And justly is this course condemned, for—1. This is a forsaking and flying for the time out of the calling wherein they ought to abide, for their calling is commonly within doors to keep the household in good order, and therefore for them to wander from their own place, is as if a bird should wander from her own nest.    2. This were the highway to become busybodies, for what other more weighty matters call them out of their calling, but to prattle of persons and actions which concern them not?    Whence the apostle (1 Tim. v. 13) coupleth these two together, they are idle, and busybodies; which if any wonder how they can be reconciled, thus they are easily: those that are idle in their own duties are busy bodies in other men's; and these busybodies have two special marks to be known by to themselves and others, namely, their open ears, and their loose tongues. 3. The Holy Ghost maketh this a note of an whorish woman, she is everywhere but where she should be, sometimes gadding in the streets with Thamar, sometimes in the fields with Dinah, sometimes without at her door, sometimes at her stall, but her feet cannot abide in her house: and if against her will her body be within doors, her heart and senses will be without. Jezebel must be gazing out of the window: whereas if the angel ask where Sarah is, answer will be made, she is in her tent; and the daughters of Sarah will be in their tents, not in the taverns, nor straggling so far abroad but that their husbands can readily answer where they be. 4. What desperate and unavoidable evils do they (and justly) lay themselves open unto, who make no bones of violating the commandment of God? how doth Satan watch all advantages to take them when they are out of their ways? and how easily doth he prevail against them when they have plucked themselves from under God's protection? Dinah was no sooner assaulted than overcome in her wandering; and Eve no sooner absent from Adam than set upon, and no sooner set upon, than vanquished. (*Ibid.*) *A worker at home :*—Here is a note written by Mrs. Garfield to her husband some years ago, and originally designed for no eye but his. It may be helpful to many others whose lot is hard work :—"I am glad to tell that, out of all the toil and disappointments of the summer just ended, I have risen up to a victory; that silence of thought since you have been away has won for my spirit a triumph. I read something like this the other day : 'There is no healthy thought without labour, and thought makes the labour happy.' Perhaps this is the way I have been able to climb up higher. It came to me one morning when I was making bread. I said to myself, 'Here I am, compelled by inevitable necessity to make our bread this summer. Why not consider it a pleasant occupation, and make it so by trying to see what perfect bread I can make?' It seemed like an inspiration—and the whole of life grew brighter. The very sunshine seemed flowing down through my spirit into the white loaves; and now I believe my table is furnished with better bread than ever before; and this truth—old as creation—seems just now to have become fully mine, that I need not to be the shirking slave of toil, but its regal master, making whatever I do yield its best fruits." (*Christian Age.*) *Christian home life :*—Home is specially Teutonic, word and thing. Teutonic sentiment, we know, from very early times, was proud, elevated, even austere, in regard to the family and the relations of the sexes. This nobleness of heathenism Christianity consecrated and transformed into all the beautiful shapes of household piety, household affection, household purity. The life of home has become the great possession, the great delight, the great social achievement of our race. The absence of this taste for the quiet and unexcited life of home is a formidable symptom in portions of our race across the Atlantic. And when home life with its sanctities, its simplicity, its calm and deep joys and sorrows, ceases to have its charm for us in England, the greatest break-up and catastrophe in English history will not be far off. (*Dean Church.*) **Obedient to their own husbands.**—*A sermon to young wives :*—I. TAKE AN INTEREST IN ALL THAT CONCERNS YOUR HUSBAND. When he speaks, listen. When he is depressed try to cheer him. When he is exultant share in his rejoicing. When he is overwhelmed with work see if you can assist him; and certainly never, at such troubled and anxious times, increase his burden by any domestic disorder. Luther had such a wife. She entered into his enthusiasm. She read and prized his books. She surrounded him with the invigorating atmosphere of true love. She helped him in his labours. Lord William Russell had such a wife. She shared with him in all his efforts. Stood by his side in the time of his misfortune. Acted as his secretary when on his trial. Visited him in the Tower of London, and did her best to console him before he was beheaded. Then went back home to train her family to be worthy of the name of so courageous a father. Flaxman, the eminent sculptor, had such a wife. When he ventured on matrimony Sir Joshua Reynolds declared him to be a ruined man. But the future proved the opposite. For thirty-eight years his wife did her utmost to aid him in his calling. Her admiration of his work, and her devotion to his comfort, assisted to make him what Byron pronounced, "the best translator of Dante." Hood had such a wife. Though a woman of unusual cultivation and literary taste, yet she yielded gracefully to the whims and fancies of her husband. She good humouredly accepted his practical jokes, and became indispensable to his happiness. So much so that Hood could not endure her absence from home. Without her he was restless and impatient. Bishop Wilberforce had such a wife. She entered into his clerical duties and responsibilities. When, after thirteen years of unalloyed comfort, she died, the life of the bishop became tinged with sadness. Hence, referring to his wife, he once wrote, "It is most sad going home. If I went home to *her* it were beyond all words." The late Earl of Beaconsfield had such a wife. When, as Benjamin Disraeli, he published "Sybil," and dedicated it "to the most severe of critics—but a perfect wife," he let in a flood of light upon the character of the future countess. And nothing could be a stronger proof of her thorough devotion to her husband's interests, than that afforded by her conduct on one occasion when driving with him to the House of Commons. By accident her finger was crushed in closing the carriage door. Thinking that any cry of pain would disturb the mind of Benjamin, who was deep in the great speech he was that night to deliver, the faithful, sympathetic wife nobly endured the agony without a single word, till her husband was in his place in the House. II. LET IT BE MANIFEST THAT HOME HAS THE PRECEDENCE IN YOUR THOUGHTS AND AFFECTIONS. Hume tells us, in his history, that in the reign of Henry VIII. a proclamation was issued forbidding women to meet together for babble and talk, and directing husbands to keep their wives in their houses. Such a proclamation gives us a sorry insight into the domestic life of our ancestors. Society has improved since then. Still, there are now not wanting very strong temptations to gadding about. Never were there more numerous or more attractive exhibitions on view, never were there more frequent or more important public meetings for benevolent and religious purposes, and never were there greater facilities for transition from spot to spot. And, alas! there are some young wives who seem to feel it incumbent on them to be present and assist at every gathering designed to promote some useful enterprise. The result is that home is often neglected, the children run riot, the domestics grow careless, and the husband returns, after a day's activities and annoyances, to find, what should be a quiet refuge from the world's turmoil, a deserted, disorderly, cheerless spot. I ask you to remember, young woman, that a wife's true orbit is home. In ancient Rome a high compliment was paid a queen by the epitaph, " She staid at home and spun." The ancient Greeks suggested the same feminine duty by carving Venus on a tortoise. In ancient Bœotia, when a bride was conveyed to her husband's house the wheels of the vehicle in which she travelled thither were burned at the doors, as an intimation that they would not be needed again. So to-day in Turkey, in India, in Spanish America, and elsewhere seclusion is the true sign of respect-ability. To be high-bred is to be invisible. Whilst, in our own land, though women enjoy freedom to think, and act, and speak, and are denied no rights of real and enduring value, yet they are most trusted and loved by their husbands and families who are good keepers of home, who make their first and foremost study the temporal and spiritual welfare of those nearest at hand and dearest at heart. There is something quaint, however questionable, in the observation of a clergyman who ventured to preach upon the subject of women's sphere. He chose for his text " Where is thy wife? Behold, she is in the tent." He started his discourse by the remark: " There she ought to be, and the less she is heard outside the better." I would qualify that preacher's words and say: " By all means let her be heard and seen outside the tent if she have fully and faithfully discharged her duty inside the tent. But if to be seen and heard outside she must neglect her own household, then let her keep at home." III. DO YOUR UTMOST TO RETAIN THE CONFIDENCE AND AFFECTION OF YOUR HUSBAND. As you examine the magnificent monument in Hyde Park, erected in memory of the late Prince Consort, you observe that the only figure that is represented twice is that of the celebrated Michael Angelo. Among the painters he leans upon the chair of Raphael. Among architects and sculptors, he is the middle of a far-famed group. And justly is he thus honoured, for his genius was exceptionally great. But far above his fresco in the Sistine Chapel, far above his " Last Judgment," far above his cupola of St. Peter's, far above his " Sleeping Cupid," which Raphael pronounced worthy of Phidias or Praxiteles, stands the sonnet to his wife. Angelo profoundly loved and adored Vittoria Colonna. When she died he lingered by her corpse, and kissed affectionately the clay-cold hand; his only regret afterwards being that he had not kissed her cheeks. And why such deep and enduring affection? Because the wife elicited it, and by constant care retained it. She impressed him with the preciousness of virtue. She elevated his thought and inspired him to write:—

" For oh! how good, how beautiful, must be
The God that made so good a thing as thee."

Macaulay describes the painful scene at the death of Mary, wife of William of Orange. The king's agony was intense. Amid scalding tears he testified to the excellency of the departed Queen, saying to Bishop Burnet, " I *was* the happiest man on earth, and I *am* the most miserable. She had no fault—none; you knew her well but you could not know, nobody but myself could know, her goodness." Not unworthy of notice is the homely advice given by an old lady to her newly-married daughter, " Never worry your husband. A man is like an egg, kept in hot water a little while he may boil soft, but keep him there too long and he hardens." IV. BE GOVERNED IN ALL YOUR RELATIONSHIPS BY TRUE RELIGION. Let the sound, safe, significant principles of godliness guide you. Let the love of Christ constrain you in all your household and family engagements. Do what you are called to do heartily as unto the Lord. Remember that there is One greater, better, wiser, and more loving and loveable than your earthly husband—One who claims and deserves all the affection of your heart, all the homage of your mind, all the service of your life. "Thy Maker is thy husband." The Lord Jesus is the bridegroom of your soul. As a wife renounces old familiar scenes, customary engagements, and long-known associates for her husband, so you are asked to be ready to renounce all for Jesus. As a wife surrenders all her time, influence, and possessions to her husband, so you are asked to make a voluntary and joyful surrender of yourself and all your belongings to Christ. As a wife consents to share with her husband in all vicissitudes, in adversity as well as prosperity, so you are asked to follow the Lord whithersoever He may lead, through evil and through good report, counting it an honour to be partaker of His sufferings. As a good wife cultivates love for her husband so that every day augments the volume of her affection, so you are asked to foster and evince love for Christ. We have read in history how, when Edward I. was wounded by a poisoned dagger, his wife Eleanor, from the deep love she bare her husband, sucked the poisoned wound, and so ventured her own life to save his. Such love you are asked to cultivate for Christ. If He be wounded by the poisonous tongues of the ungodly, by reproaches, blasphemies, and persecutions, do you learn to say, "Let the reproach of Christ fall upon me"—"Let me suffer rather than Jesus and His truth!" (*J. H. Hitchens, D.D.*) **That the Word of God be not blasphemed.**— *The highest motive to duty :*—Here the great law of the family is put on the highest Christian ground. If those who profess the gospel of Christ fail in any of these respects, it is more than possible that the blame will be thrown upon God's Word (*cf.* 1. Tim. vi. 1). If Christians profess to be influenced by a supernaturally strong and sacred motive, and then fail to do what lower and ordinary motives often succeed in effecting, the world charges the failure on the lofty motive itself, and Christ bears once again the sins of His people: He is crucified afresh and put to open shame. (*H. R. Reynolds, D.D.*)

Ver. 6. **Young men likewise exhort to be sober-minded.**—*Sober-mindedness :*—I. WHAT IT IS. 1. You must be considerate and thoughtful, not rash and heedless. Take time to think ; learn to think freely—to think for yourselves, of yourselves. 2. You must be cautious and prudent, not wilful and heady. Fix rules of wisdom. Use reason and conscience. Be diffident of your own judgment. Study Scripture. 3. You must be humble and modest, not proud and conceited. Be not above your business, above reproof, above religion. 4. You must be temperate and self-denying, not indulgent of your appetites. 5. You must be mild and gentle, not indulgent of your passions. 6. You must be chaste and reserved, not wanton or impure. 7. You must be staid and composed, not giddy and unsettled. 8. You must be content and easy, not ambitious and aspiring. 9. You must be grave and serious, not vain and frothy. II. CONSIDERATIONS TO ENFORCE THIS EXHORTATION. 1. You are reasonable creatures. 2. You are sinners before God. 3. You are setting out in a world of sorrows and snares. 4. Multitudes of the young are ruined for want of this sobriety of mind. 5. You are here upon trial for heaven. 6. You must shortly go to judgment. III. APPLICATION : 1. Examine yourselves. 2. Exhort one another. 3. Contemplate the advantages of sober-mindedness. You will—(1) Escape vanity of childhood and youth ; (2) Recommend yourselves to the favour of God and all wise men ; (3) Prepare for a useful and comfortable life, and a happy death. 4. Directions to make you sober-minded. (1) Espouse sober principles. (2) Meditate on serious things. (3) Choose sober companions. (4) Read sober books. (5) Abound in sober work. (*Matthew Henry, D.D.*) *Sober-mindedness :*—I. THE SPIRIT AND CONDUCT TO WHICH THIS EXHORTATION IS OPPOSED. Sober-mindedness, if we are to take the primary meaning of the word, is to be "safe" or "sound-minded." But perhaps the best English equivalent for the word would be "discreet" or "self-restrained." We have to restrain and keep ourselves in check as much as needful ; and yet, at the same time, to cultivate such habits of thought that much check will not be required. 1. This exhortation is opposed to undue self-esteem (see Rom. xi. 20, xii. 3–6 ; Phil. ii. 3). There ought to be a certain amount of self-esteem or self-respect. Where that is wholly wanting, there will be little or no force of character. Where there is no self-respect, one of the strongest arguments against evil will be lost. If we do not respect ourselves, we shall not act so as to gain the respect of others. But the excess of this self-respect is as injurious as its want ; and it is to this excess that youth is naturally prone. When we enter upon life it is with an exalted idea of our own attainments and importance. We are soon led to smart in consequence of this; we soon find our own level. But O! how much pain, how much humiliation should we be spared, if we did but learn at the onset to esteem others better than ourselves! And O! young men, when we look into our own hearts, how much there is there to humble us. 2. This exhortation is opposed to all rash speculations upon spiritual things. The forms of pride are very various; but in whatever form pride presents itself, it is still an evil against which we should be on our guard. There are some forms of pride which are simply despicable and ridiculous. For instance, the pride of dress, the pride of personal appearance, the pride of life, or the pride of birth. But there is another form of pride which does not appear so offensive as these—I mean, the pride of intellect— of those faculties which God has given us, by which we are distinguished above the lower orders of creation, and by which when cultivated we are raised in the social scale. But still, this form of pride, like every other form is inexcusable. Why should we boast of those faculties which have been given us by God, and of which at any moment He could deprive us? And if under no circumstances it is excusable, it is more especially offensive if it lead us to cavil at the statements of this holy book, respecting the character, and the will, and the dealings of the Most High. 3. This exhortation is opposed to all ambitious efforts to amass wealth, and to rise unduly in the social scale. Do not suppose that I would object to any amount of progress, either intellectually or socially. To the young I would say, Do all the good you can, get all the good you can, and enjoy to the utmost all those good things which God has placed within your reach. But, at the same time, remember this, that anything, however good it may be in itself, ceases to be good as soon as it is used in excess, or when it interferes with your highest interests. Now, keeping that statement in view, just consider the result of the ceaseless striving of men in the present day, not only to accumulate wealth, but to imitate the habits, the customs, and the dress of the station above them. Shun—shun as a plague all those books which would render you dissatisfied with the position in which God has placed you. Rest assured that that position is the best possible position for you. Remember that this is but the first stage of your existence. Learn to look upon this as a training school—as a state of discipline in which you must bear much that you do not like, in which you must do much that you would rather not do, but in daring to do which you will be enabled to conform to God's will and to rise to a higher state of being. 4. This exhortation is opposed to all impatience and unwillingness to listen to the counsels and cautions of those who are older than ourselves. You know that one of our poets has observed :—

> " At thirty man suspects himself a fool—
> Knows it at forty—and reforms his plan."

And oh! how much misery would be saved, if when we were young we were content to receive the experience of others, rather than gain that experience for ourselves by a very painful process. II. SOME CONSIDERATIONS BY WHICH THIS EXHORTATION CAN BE ENFORCED. Be sober-minded, and this will elevate your character. "He that humbleth himself shall be exalted." Be sober-minded, and this will greatly increase your influence for good here below. Be sober-minded, and you will escape many a snare in which others have fallen, and been destroyed. There is a passage which I would commend to the attention of young men; describing the death-bed of an ungodly youth—" Lest thou mourn at the last, when thy flesh and thy body are consumed "—the flesh of thy body consumed by indulgence in evil practices— " and thou say, How have I hated instruction, and my heart despiseth reproof; and have not obeyed the voice of my teachers, nor inclined mine ear to them that instructed me. I was almost in all evil in the midst of the congregation and assembly." That is the result of the spirit and conduct opposed to sobriety of mind. Cultivate this in the last place, because it will prove that your religion is a reality, and not a name, (*R. C. Pritchett.*)    *Sober-mindedness as opposed to excitement :*—The word sober-minded has many meanings, or at least many applications; but I think that we should approach most nearly to a comprehension of them all, if we explained it as the opposite of excitement, and regarded the charge in the text, to exhort young men to be sober-minded, as practically equivalent to a charge to exhort them to avoid excitement. 1. There is the excitement of intemperance and of all approaches to it, of sensuality in all its forms; an excitement so strong, and for the moment so pleasurable, that he who has once yielded to it soon forms the habit of such indulgence, and he who has once formed the habit, almost always persists in it till his sin is his ruin ; no persuasions and no convictions, no experience of misery and no resolutions of amendment, are of any avail; the man who has allowed the body to become his master is in this sense, as in all others, indeed a slave, that he cannot escape from his bondage, he must live on in it, and die in it too. The word intemperance may be too strong to express anything which you are at present in danger of, or anything indeed which the present fashions of society make perilous (speaking generally) for any one in your rank of life : but none the less would I caution you with the most anxious earnestness, against bodily excitement of a sinful kind : no change in national customs will ever make the body cease to be the chief enemy of the soul : other enemies come and go, temptations from companions, from occupations, from circumstances of life : this one alone is always with us, an enemy in the very camp, and able too to mask his assaults under the show of friendliness and good will. 2. As sinful excitement, so excessive excitement, even in forms not sinful, is here plainly forbidden. God has established a certain order and gradation amongst the parts of our nature. He bids us think of this intricate framework of human life as composed of three parts, which to our present comprehension we may best explain under the names of body, mind, and soul. Every one of these is most important : in each one a great work has to be done within a limited time : each one is destined to immortality, and has to be prepared for it by us. But, though each of these three parts is valuable, each immortal, each worthy of thought and care and culture, each the object (for our sakes) of God's special regard ; yet they are not equally valuable : the soul stands first, far first, in this respect : that part of us which is capable of knowing and loving God, of resembling Him, of being His own dwelling-place, ought always to be the first also in our own regard : we ought to think far more seriously of its hunger, or its disease, than we all do of that of the body : we ought to be far more vexed when our soul loses one of its meals, which are opportunities of prayer, public and private, opportunities of reading or hearing God's Word, or of joining in the Holy Communion, than when we are debarred by accident or want of appetite from a bodily meal : all these things are necessary consequences of the most elementary faith in God, and Christ, and eternity. Next to it comes the mind; that part of man which understands and judges, thinks and knows ; that part which has to be stored and practised in youth, for the service of God and our generation in mature life. Young men likewise exhort to be sober-minded. Bid them, if you be a faithful minister of Christ, bid them, whether they will hear or whether they will forbear, but with all earnestness of entreaty that they will listen, to think first of their souls, and next of their minds, and last of that which is bodily : tell them that, though God wills that their bodies should be active, hardy, and skilful, He does not will that every other part of them should be backward, awkward and stunted ; that, because He loves them, because He desires their happiness, because He desires to bless them and to do them good, because He would have them with Him hereafter, and in order to do this must first fit them for His presence, therefore He exhorts them to be not excited but sober-minded in things which are transitory and temporal; bids them set Him before them even in their amusements ; bids them ask His blessing every day, as before they work, so also before they play; bids them accept their bodily pleasures, like all other, from Him, remember Him in them, moderate them for His sake, and above all use for His glory alone, in self-control, in temperance, in purity, those bodies upon which they bestow so much labour. 3. To be sober-minded is, in other words, to have a sound mind ; a mind neither trifling, nor giddy, nor inconstant, nor morbid ; a mind just in its views, wise in its aims, moderate in its expectations, inflexible in its principles, authoritative in its self-control, right with God. It implies that we have a just view of life ; that we not only profess but feel its true object, as a preparation for eternity, as an opportunity of doing the will of God and promoting His purposes towards us and towards all men. It implies that we neither expect to be able, nor feel it to be desirable, in all things to please ourselves, or to have our own way. It implies that we are thankful for whatever God gives, and patient under His withholding, controlling and even chastening hand. That we are willing to be what He would have us to be, even when our own inclination might point to a very different lot. All this it is, but more also. A sound mind, in the highest sense of the word, cannot be where the Holy Spirit is not ; where God Himself is not present in the soul, through Jesus Christ, by His Spirit, as the Guide and Lord and Comforter, wisdom and quietness and strength, the life of our life and the hope of glory. Little can they who have not this be depended upon : natural cleverness and good sense may do much for us ; it may cover up many faults, it may enable us to originate many good counsels ; but it breaks down in the time of trial, when it is most of all important to be right, most of all fatal to be wrong. A sound mind, a sober mind, in the true sense, can only be where the soul of man has been changed (to use the Scriptural figure) into the spirit of man by the indwelling of the holy and blessed Spirit of God. (*Dean Vaughan.*) *Sober-mindedness :*—I. To BE SOBER-MINDED IS TO BE—1. Thoughtful and considerate, in opposition to giddiness and levity of disposition. 2. Humble and diffident in opposition to an assuming and self-sufficient spirit. 3. Temperate and self-denied, in opposition to the unrestrained indulgence of the passions. 4. To give an habitual preference to eternal over temporal things. 5. That we never put off to a future period that which ought to be done now. II. REASONS FOR URGING TO SOBER-MINDEDNESS. 1. You are reasonable creatures, and it is the office of reason to govern the passions, &c. 2. You are guilty creatures, but the means of salvation are placed within your reach. 3. You are dying and accountable creatures, but the means of eternal happiness are enjoyed only in this world. (*W. Peddie.*) *Exhortation to young persons :*—I. As for THE REASONS WHY SOBRIETY OF MIND SHOULD IN PARTICULAR BE RECOMMENDED TO YOUTH, among others, we may assign these which follow. 1. It will be acknowledged that it is impossible for a person, with any constant tenor, to act well that does not think wisely, or to think wisely that does not think soberly. But what is of constant necessity in every stage of life must be of special importance in that upon which the rest depend ; and, by consequence, he that sets out with this advantage, is in the most probable method to go on and prosper. 2. The morning of our life, our early and flourishing years, ought especially to be armed with this precaution, because it is then we are exposed to the greatest dangers ; when the passions are the strongest, and so the most apt to transport us with their violence ; when the pleasures and entertainments of sense have their full taste and relish, and are therefore the more capable of betraying us into excess ; when we are the most easy, credulous, and complying, and so the most open to the attempts of others, the likeliest to be insulted and overborne by the confident, or ensnared by the designing, or perverted by those that go astray. Wherefore, experience coming so late should, if possible, be supplied by more early consideration, and reason should invite us before affliction constrains us to be serious. 3. As most ornaments, whether of mind or body, sit best upon the young, flourish in the spring of life, and look with peculiar gracefulness in the bloom and beauty of Nature, so this excellent temper of which we speak, which is the chief attire of the soul, and to which most other good qualities that it can put on are but appendages, is then in the exactest manner fit and becoming; and if it be real and not counterfeit, natural and not affected, easy and not precise, it has indeed the finest lustre, and renders those who wear it the most amiable and charming. 4. As youth has many natural gifts and endowments that speak in its behalf, and entitle it to favour, so it has one natural disadvantage, in respect of time, which it would be glad, if possible, to balance or compensate. In this regard it has been excellently well observed of birth or quality, that it gives a person at eighteen or twenty the same esteem and deference which another of inferior rank acquires at fifty ; so that the former has thirty years gained at once. Now, the privilege which custom and civility allow to the noble, reason and justice demand, and generally obtain, for the sober and discreet ; and they are the happiest who possess it by a double title. II. This may the better suffice as to the offering some reasons why sobriety of mind should particularly be recommended to youth ; since, by representing THE BENEFITS AND ADVANTAGES it then specially affords, we are to show the effect of those reasons, and of that particular application. 1. Sobriety of mind confirms and settles the principles of religion. Great has been the happiness of your birth, and the advantage of your education, but that either of these should be lasting and effectual depends upon yourselves. What admonitions and advices you have heard, what cautions you have received from parents or friends, books or conversation, are a ready stock committed to your management and improvement : a treasure in which you cannot make too much haste to be rich, an inheritance which indeed renders them the happiest to whom it comes the soonest. You are left to make your first steps in the world, which being so rough and uneven ground, and so plentiful in occasions of falling, it imports you the more to have regard to Solomon's rule (Prov. iv. 15, 16). To which you will give me leave to add that great and excellent lesson which he received from his father, and which some of you, I presume, have received from yours (1 Chron. xxiii. 9). 2. As sobriety of mind has such a power in keeping the principles of religion firm and stable, it has no less in rendering the practice of religion easy. We say all things are easy to a willing mind; but a sober mind is as willing as it is wise. For that which brings in most of the difficulties of a good life is our too late consideration, when having gone so far without thought, we cannot retire without pain. 3. It is a strong defence against temptations. "I have written to you young men because ye are strong," says St. John; "Or what imports the same," says an eloquent divine, "because you are vigorous; that is, you are now in such a state of body and soul and affections as is most subservient to piety—most quick and governable, and most successfully applied to the offices of duty. Govern, therefore, your appetites before the evil days come. Now you may gird them, and carry them whither you will, but if you neglect the season, they will hereafter gird you, and carry you whither you would not." 4. It affords the greater opportunities of eminent piety and virtue. For he that is thus armed is, we see, the fittest and most expedite not for defence only but for action; so that when occasions present themselves, he is ready to meet them with delight, and improve them to advantage. (*B. Kennet, D.D.*) *Sobriety of mind urged on young men :*—The word in our text, strictly translated, means "sound-minded," or healthy-minded, and implies the conviction that there is a certain standard of character, or condition of the mind which bears an analogy to health of body, a condition in which all the functions of the mind are in their right state, in which sound or healthy views of things are taken, in which no part of human nature is either inoperative or unduly developed. In this large sense, soundness of mind may serve as a description of the harmony or regular action implied in virtue; but inasmuch as the passions and desires, excited by objects which have strong influence over us in our present state of being, more than anything else destroy sanity of mind, the term is usually confined to the control over worldly desires, and to views of life which commend themselves to right reason. Thus, soundness of mind includes self-restraint and temperance, the former of which is the power of governing the passions, and the other the habit of using all pleasures without going to excess. But soundness or sobriety of mind is more radical than either of these, for it includes those just views of life, that appreciation of the value of enjoyment and of the world compared with duty and the higher life of the soul, without the sway of which in the soul it can neither exercise continence, nor self-control, nor temperance. Soundness or sobriety of mind, also, is far from stopping at the boundaries of the passions, especially the sensual; all the desires, even those which have little to do with the body, as the desire of fame, of power, of superiority, and the desire of wealth—the means of gratifying all other desires—are placed under its control. I. As THUS UNDERSTOOD, SOBRIETY OF MIND IS TO BE DISTINGUISHED FROM A NATIVE SLUGGISHNESS OR CAUTIOUSNESS WHICH MAY CONSPIRE WITH IT TO PREVENT EXCESS. If a man, for instance, can never become angry, he may be saved from many foolish and sinful acts, but it is many times better to have a power of subduing anger, which you have acquired by exertions which have cost you something, than to be a stone. Moreover, if such native sobriety of mind exists, it is rare. There is generally some weak spot, where passion can with success approach men who seem like icicles. What class of persons is more thoroughly worldly than many who are proof against the allurements of vice, but speculate with the gambler's intense excitement, or burn with a devouring lust for power. Perhaps the greatest insobriety of mind belongs to those who, in most respects, have an entire mastery over themselves—who view the world on many of its sides as it is, but concentrate all their forces on one object, with an untiring restless fever of soul which the votary of pleasure seldom knows. II. THE APOSTLE'S SOBER-MINDEDNESS IS NOT TO BE CONFOUNDED WITH THAT SELF-CONTROL WHICH SPRINGS FROM WORLDLY PRUDENCE AND SHREWD CALCULATIONS OF SUCCESS IN LIFE. There are men who live exclusively for earthly enjoyment, who yet have attained to a mastery over their own lusts. They know what the laws of health will allow, what the body will bear, how far they may go in pleasure consistently with prudence and economy, what degree of restraint is demanded to preserve their reputation. They will, therefore, keep themselves sober while their less discreet, and perhaps less corrupt, companions are intoxicated at their side; they live a long healthy life, while others die of the effects of vicious indulgence, and retain their good name while others ruin themselves in the opinion of society. Verily, they have their reward; but their sober-mindedness is certainly no such virtue that even a philosopher could commend it. III. SOBRIETY OF MIND, BEING SOMETHING MORE THAN A TEMPERAMENT AVERSE TO EXCESS, SOMETHING MORE THAN SELF-CONTROL ON SELFISH PRINCIPLES MAY BE LOOKED AT AS A PHILOSOPHICAL, OR AS A CHRISTIAN VIRTUE.

In both cases, it is a subordination of the desires and passions to the higher principles of the soul; in both, it is a spontaneous self-government according to the rules of right living, not according to calculations of temporal advancement. When we speak of Christian sobriety of mind, we mean nothing generically different from the notion which philosophy had already formed. But we mean sobriety of mind sustained by Christian principles, enforced by Christian motives, and dwelling amid other manifestations of a Christian or purified character. Let us consider it when thus broadly understood, in some of its most prominent characteristics. 1. It involves an estimate of earthly pleasure and good formed under the power of faith. With Christ's advent into the world, a new idea of life began, and the victory of the spirit over the flesh is rendered possible. 2. But it is not enough to have a standard of character; the young man, if he would be sober-minded, must have rules of living calculated beforehand to resist the allurements of the world when they arise. It is the part of Christian ethics to make known what rules are needed for our moral guidance, and to enforce them by the appropriate motives. In this place, no such thing can be attempted, and yet I cannot pass on without calling your attention to one or two parts of conduct, where it is peculiarly important to have well settled principles of action. (1) In regard to the bodily appetites, Christian sobriety begins to be lost as soon as they are made ends in themselves, without regard to something higher. (2) In regard to amusements and diversions, sobriety consists in keeping them in their place, as recreations after bodily and mental toil. They must not then usurp the rights of labour, unless we are resolved to destroy the earnestness and seriousness of character, which grows out of a conviction that life is full of meaning. 3. Need I add that rules must be followed by a settled purpose, by a resolution formed in the view of spiritual and divine truth to adopt such a course of life as sobriety of mind requires. (*T. D. Woolsey.*) *Exhortation to sober-mindedness :*—I. The necessity of this exhortation. This arises from—1. The ignorance and inexperience of youth. 2. Those constitutional inclinations which predominate in some more than in others. 3. The temptations by which youth is surrounded. 4. The vast importance of commencing well a course of life. II. The character of that sober-mindedness which the text recommends. 1. Its basis. Reverence for God, contrition for sin, &c. 2. Its contrasts. Pride, rashness, obstinacy, petulance, sullenness, presumption, &c. 3. Its objects. It should make you moderate in all things, &c. III. The advantages which result from the possession and display of this sober-mindedness. 1. It will qualify you for your relations to society. 2. It will greatly contribute to your usefulness wherever you are placed. 3. It will greatly increase your comfort. (*J. Clayton.*) *Discretion the safeguard of youth :*—This concise statement as to the exhortation to be addressed to young men may be regarded as a summary of all youthful virtues. The sins and follies of youth largely arise from want of thought. This fact, while it is no excuse for the sins committed, is an indication of the remedy to be sought. Let youths be trained to cultivate discretion, and, humanly speaking, they will be kept safe from the follies so common to their age. In a sermon to young men, discretion may be commended thus :—I. As the cultivation of the mental and moral powers with which God has endowed them. II. As the fulfilment of the destiny which they are to fulfil in life. III. As the fitting preparation for a higher life hereafter. (*F. Wagstaff.*) *Sober-minded youth :*—I. Some characteristics of this sober mind. 1. A habit of moral thoughtfulness. 2. Practical prudence and circumspection. 3. A modest and humble deportment. II. Some particulars in which this grace of character should be displayed. 1. In all your plans and schemes for worldly happiness. 2. In all parts of your social intercourse—dress, discourse, choice of recreations, &c. III. A valuable agency by which this sober-mindedness may be promoted. (*D. Moore, M.A.*) *On sober-mindedness :*— What is it that may properly be called "sober-mindedness"? This is to ask, in other words, What is it that we are all charging the want of upon our fellow-mortals, while we are all, on all hands, censuring, reproaching, or ridiculing them, for folly, absurdity, extravagance, for running into all extremes, for being the sport of fancies, tempers, and passions? Plainly, the effectual predominance of sound reason. That then is the general description of sober-mindedness—that there be in habitual exercise a just judgment of things, and that this judgment be in real effective authority. But a little more particularly. There cannot be the required state of mind, unless there be some great master principles, decidedly fixed in the very habit of thinking and feeling—principles applicable to almost all things in our interests and practice —principles so general that many special ones will grow out of them for particular application.  One is—that in all things and at all events, God is to be obeyed. Another—that there is the essential distinction of holiness and sin in all conduct, both within the mind, and in external action, and that sin is absolutely a dreadful evil.  Another—that that cannot be right long in which there is no self-denial. Another—that must not be done which must be repented of.  Another—the future should predominate over the present.  Such things, we said, must be established firmly and operatively in the mind.  But then how can this be without much and frequent exercise of serious thought?  Do such principles grow and establish themselves spontaneously?  Alas! let any young person look into his own mind and see ! Without much of serious thought, therefore, there cannot be " sober-mindedness." And therefore, again, there cannot be this required state of mind, if principles are admitted, or practical determinations adopted, from mere impressions of fancy and feeling, perhaps from some casual situation into which a person is thrown ; perhaps from the pleasing impression made by some new acquaintance, or a friend, while no account is taken of the whole comprehensive view of the matter ; nay, perhaps, the judgment actually withheld from attempting this.  Again, no principles can suffice for the true " sober-mindedness " in young persons or any others, unless as consciously held as under the sanction and as having the authority of the Supreme Power.  For the term must imply a steady tenor of feeling and proceeding, not fluctuating, confused, alternating.  And it implies a calm independence of spirit and conduct, not at the mercy of the winds and circumstances—the opinions and wills—of the surrounding world ; which holds one certain plan and aim, right onward through all the causes of interference and perversion.  But how can this be but by the vital connection of our governing principles with the unchangeable Spirit?  Again, there cannot be a high degree of that well-ordered state, " sober-mindedness," without the person's forming a sound judgment of his own mind.  If there be an insensibility to the general corruption of the soul, throughout its very nature, how little to the purpose will any scheme of self-government be !  And then there are the special and peculiar circumstances and tendencies ; the particular weaknesses or wrong propensities ; the liability to some one evil in a strong and dangerous degree.  Without an attentive and deep cognizance of things so important, the person enjoined to maintain sober-mindedness will not at all know what he has to do ; not know against what he has to maintain it.  We may add a most self-evident thing ; that it is of the essence of sober-mindedness to maintain a systematic strong restraint on the passions, fancy, temper, appetites.  And this was probably the most direct object of the apostle's exhortation to young men.  In these respects, it is the very first point of sober-mindedness for youth to be aware how perilous their condition is.  Let young persons observe what is actually becoming of those who surrender themselves to their passions and wild propensities.  What numbers!  Then, in themselves, observe seriously whither these inward traitors and tempters really tend ; and then think whether soberness of mind be not a pearl of great price, and whether there can be any such thing without a systematic self-government.  Young persons of any hopefulness will often have serious thoughts about what is to be the main grand purpose of their life.  Immense interests are exhibited before them, as immortal natures.  It is for them to consider, whether they will be consigned down just merely to this, to be gay and joyous creatures for a few years, and busy ones the rest?  Or, whether they shall early in life have a greater purpose and concern, rising above the world, and extending beyond time. Now here is to be the application of those principles we were endeavouring to illustrate ; and without them we have ample and deplorable manifestation what the notion and purpose of life in young persons will be.  But again, this sober-mindedness is quite necessary for the subordinate schemes and pursuits of life.  In the want of it, a young person may form schemes ill adapted to his character, his qualifications, and abilities—or his circumstances.  For want of it, many have rushed into wild ill-concerted projects, which have ended disastrously, or frustrated the most laudable designs.  Companionship and friendly connections are among the most favourite interests of young persons.  Sober-mindedness is eminently important here.  This would keep them clearly aware that the mere pleasure of friendly association is a trifle as compared with the influence and effect.  Soberness of mind, again, would be of high value to young people, as to the terms on which they shall stand with what is called the world.  This is the denomination for a sort of system of maxims, customs, modes, and fashions.  And it takes upon itself a high and tyrannic authority, if we may judge from the number of submissive slaves.  The firmly sober-minded young person would, in numerous instances and considerable degrees, set at nought the prescriptions of the despot; would act just as he thought proper; and would have his reason to assign; "I really have something else to do with my time and thoughts, than to study and follow your caprices, modes, and vanities." So much for the situation of young persons in the world; it is almost too obvious to be added that for what concerns their preparation to go out of it, there is the utmost necessity for everything implied in sober-mindedness. We conclude with a consideration or two for the enforcement of the exhortation. And let it not be forgotten that youth will soon be passed away. In the case of not a few young persons, their youth is appointed to be the whole of their life. Now supposing that in any particular instance this were certain and known: in that instance, all opinions would agree as to the propriety and necessity of sober-mindedness: yes, the vainest, the giddiest, unless totally ignorant or unbelieving of the hereafter, say, "Yes, certainly he or she should be sober-minded." But now judge soberly whether the propriety is reversed by the circumstance of uncertainty; that a young person may only have his youth for the whole of his life. When this may be the case, were it not infatuation to live as if it most certainly would not? But assuming that life will be prolonged into the more advanced stages, consider that then a great change of feeling from that of youth will certainly take place. Experience, disappointment, difficulty, will have begun their process. Now consider; is it not a most ungracious thing that the altered state of feeling in more advanced life should come just wholly as disappointment, as mortifying experience, as sober sense forced upon reluctant folly? Whereas, sober-mindedness in youth might have anticipated a great deal; might, through wisdom, have made the change much more smooth; might have caused it to be much less, and less mortifying, and made it less reproachful in reflection on the sanguine delusion of early life. We would enforce one more consideration; namely, that things will have their consequences. If there be a vain, giddy, thoughtless, ill-improved youth, the effects of it will infallibly come in after life. If there be a neglected understanding, a conscience feebly and rudely constituted, good principles but slightly fixed or even apprehended, a habitual levity of spirit, a chase of frivolities, a surrender to the passions; the natural consequences of these will follow. And what will they be when a man is advanced into the field of important and difficult duties? when he shall himself be required to be a counsellor of youth? when he shall be put upon strong trials of both his judgment and conscience; when he shall have to sustain afflictions; when advancing age shall force him to see that he shall ere long have to leave life itself behind? We add but one consideration more, which we could wish to press on young minds with peculiar force. They love cheerfulness, spiritedness, vivacity; and they are right. But then! on the supposition of life being prolonged, would they be content to expend away the greatest portion of this animation in the beginning of life? Would they drink out the precious wine of life in the morning, and leave but the dregs for the evening of life's day? If there be any possible way of throwing a large portion of this vital element, this animation, into the latter, the latest part of life, were not that the highest wisdom? (*J. Foster.*) *Hints to young men:*—1. Young men must take notice of that great bundle of folly which is naturally bound up in their hearts, the corruption of that age being such as needeth not any occasion without itself to cast it down. 2. That the means to redress it is the study of the Scriptures, unto the rules whereof they must have regard, and not to the example of men. 3. That if they will needs be given to imitation, then must they imitate not the most, but the best of that age; such as was young Daniel, who in tender years was able to utter knowledge (Dan. i. 4); young Samuel, who so soon as he is weaned, must stand before the Lord (1 Sam. i.); young Josiah, who at eight years old walked uprightly (2 Kings ii.); young Timothy, who knew the Scriptures of a child; yea, of Christ Himself, who increased in wisdom as in stature, so as at twelve years old He was able to confound the doctors and great rabbis of the Jews. 4. That against all the discouragements they shall meet withal from men, as that they are too forward, soon ripe, and young saints, &c., they must oppose the Lord's good pleasure, who requireth firstlings, first fruits, first-born of man and beast; the first month, yea, the first day of that month, for the celebrating of the passover; and delighteth in whole and fat offerings, not in the lame, lean, and blind sacrifices which His soul abhorreth: for of all the sons of men, the Lord never took such pleasure as in such who were sanctified even from the womb. Some of the learned call men to the timely service of God, from the allusion of Moses's rod (Exod. iii.), and Isaiah's vision (chap. ix.), both of the almond tree, because of all trees that soonest putteth forth her blossoms. How sound that collection is, I will not stand to inquire; only this is true, that such as would be trees of righteousness, and known to be of the Lord's planting, laden (especially in their age) with the fruits of the Spirit, must with the almond-tree timely bud, and blossom, and bear, that their whole lives may be a fruitful course, whereby God may be glorified, and themselves receive in the end a more full consolation. (*T. Taylor, D.D.*)	*Our young men :*—" Tell me," said Edmund Burke, " what are the prevailing sentiments that occupy the minds of your young men, and I will tell you what is to be the character of the next generation." This is but an echo of the epigrams of the ancients. The modern statesman but repeats the wisdom of the past. The dominant power of the young men of a nation has been recognised in all ages. It was because he taught her young men, that Socrates was feared at Athens. Standing in the market place, visiting the gymnasia, or speaking from the porticoes, he wielded a power that senators viewed alike with envy and with dread. When Wesley was desired to leave Oxford to take a local parish, he refused, because, he said, the schools of the prophets were there, and he felt that in forming the sentiments of young men he was doing a greater work for the next generation than he could possibly do in any other locality.	*Rules for young men :*—The Hon. Stephen Allen, who had been Mayor of New York, was drowned from on board the *Henry Clay*. In the pocket-book was found a printed slip, apparently cut from a newspaper, a copy of which we give below. It is worthy to be engraven on the heart of every young man :—" Keep good company, or none. Never be idle. If your hands can't be usefully employed, attend to the cultivation of your mind. Always speak the truth. Make few promises. Live up to your engagements. Keep your own secrets if you have any. When you speak to a person look him in the face. Good company and good conversation are the very sinews of virtue. Good character is above all things else. Your character cannot be essentially injured except by your own acts. If any one speaks evil of you let your life be so that none will believe him. Drink no kind of intoxicating liquors. Ever live (misfortune excepted) within your income. When you retire to bed, think over what you have been doing during the day. Make no haste to be rich if you would prosper. Small and steady gains give competency with a tranquil mind. Never play at any game of chance. Avoid temptation, through fear you may not withstand it. Earn money before you spend it. Never run into debt unless you see a way to get out again. Never borrow if you can possibly avoid it. Do not marry until you are able to support a wife. Never speak evil of any one. Be just before you are generous. Keep yourself innocent if you would be happy. Save when you are young, to spend when you are old. Read over the above maxims at least once a week."	*Self-control :*—" In the supremacy of self-control," says Herbert Spencer, " consists one of the perfections of the ideal man. Not to be impulsive, not to be spurred hither and thither by each desire that in turn comes uppermost; but to be self-restrained, self-balanced, governed by the joint decision of all the feelings in council assembled, before whom every action shall have been fully debated and calmly determined—that it is which education, moral education at least, strives to produce." This is the one determining quality on which success or failure in after life most depends. Failing here, your failure is absolute and irremediable. Success here is success assured henceforward. Here are two youths—the one college-bred, but without self-government; the other was never in a college, but knows and possesses the power of self-control. For all worthy work in life the latter is immeasurably superior; he will make a better banker, manufacturer, legislator, general. Knowledge of Greek and mathematics and Latin is valuable, but placed in the balance against self-control, it has not the weight of a feather or the worth of a farthing. But true education embraces self-control, and, with other acquisitions, gives the scholar great advantage. Mr. Pitt was once asked what quality was most essential for a Prime Minister. One of the party said, " Eloquence "; another, " Knowledge "; another, " Toil." " No," said Pitt, " it is Patience," and patience with him had its real meaning of self-control. In this quality he himself excelled. There is an instructive monument to this great statesman in Westminster Abbey. Pitt stands erect with extended hand; another figure represents Anarchy writhing in chains at his feet, while a calm-browed figure representing History is writing down the record of his victorious achievements for posterity to read. There is pressing need for other Pitts to conquer self, and then conquer their fellows in this disordered world. Anarchy and wrong yet ravage the land. They need strong, self-conquered men to put them in chains. And be assured, impartial history waits to immortalise the name of the great moral heroes of to-day.

Vers. 7, 8. **In all things shewing thyself a pattern.**—*A good example :*—Having propounded the several precepts fitted to all ages of men and women, the last whereof was unto young men, our apostle here inserteth a precept unto Titus himself, whence it is probably gathered that Titus was now a young man, as Timothy also was, in the same office of an evangelist ; and being a minister, in him he closely again instituteth every minister, notwithstanding he hath been most ample in that argument, as though ministers could never sufficiently be instructed.    In these two verses we will consider two things. 1. A precept. 2. An enforcement of it. I. The precept is, That Titus show himself an example to others.  For as all the persons formerly taught, so more especially the last sort, namely, young men, for the slipperiness of their age need the benefit of good example as well as good doctrines and counsel. And this exhortation is enlarged by setting down wherein Titus must become an example, which is done, first, more generally, " in all things," we read it, " above all things " ; others, " above all men," which readings may be true, and grounds of good instruction, but I take the first aptest to the place.  Secondly, by a more particular enumeration of shining virtues, as—1. Uncorrupt doctrine.    2. Good life fruitful in good works ; and these not one or two, or now and then in good moods, but there must be a constant trading in them throughout a grave and pure conversation.    3. There must be joined gracious speeches and words, for I take it fitliest interpreted of private communication, described by two necessary adjuncts. 1. It must be wholesome.   2. Unblameable, or not liable to reproof.  II. The enforcement of the precept is taken from the end or fruit of it, which is twofold.  1. Shame. 2. Silence to the withstanders and opposers.   And thus the general scope of the verses is, as if he had more largely said, " That this thy doctrine, O Titus, thus aptly applied to all sorts of men, may carry more weight and authority with it, see thou that (considering thou art set in a more eminent place, and clearer sun, and hast all eyes beholding and prying into thee) thou show thyself a pattern and express type wherein men may behold all these graces shining in thy own life : let them look in thy glass, and see the lively image of a grave and pure conversation, which may allure them to the love of the doctrine which thou teachest : let them hear from thy mouth in thy private conferences and speech nothing but what may work them to soundness ; at the least, keep thou such a watch over thy tongue, as that nothing pass thee which may be reprehended, and hence will it come to pass that although thou hast many maliciously minded men, seeking by all means to oppose thy doctrine and life, and to destroy the one by the other, these shall either be put to silence and have nothing to say, or if they take boldness to speak anything, it being unjust, the shame shall be removed from thee and fall justly upon themselves ; and all the reproach shall return home to their own doors.  (*T. Taylor, D.D.*)      **That he that is of the contrary part may be ashamed.**—*Lessons :*—I. It is the lot of faithful ministers to have opposites and adversaries : yea, such as are just contrary and directly opposite, for so the word is used (Mark xv. 39).   The case is clearer than needeth proof.  How the prophets were entertained our Saviour showeth by that speech to the Jews, " Which of the prophets have not your fathers persecuted and slain ? "   Moses was often resisted by the people, and before he shall go scot free, his own brother and sister shall withstand him ; and as he was resisted by Jannes and Jambres, so in all ages to the end men of corrupt minds shall start up to resist the truth.   That the disciples and apostles, notwithstanding their apostolical rod and power, were resisted, appeareth by Alexander the coppersmith, who was a sore enemy to Paul's preaching ; and Elimas, who was full of subtlety to pervert the truth, and strongly withstood the apostles.  How was Christ Himself, the chief Doctor, withstood by the Scribes, Pharisees, Sadducees, rulers, and people, that He had never come into the world if He had not made His reckoning to give His back to the smiters, His face to shame and spitting, yea, Himself to the shameful and accursed death of the cross.  If it was thus to the green tree, we shall need seek no further what was done to the dry, but rather to inquire into the reason hereof, and that is this : So long as there is a devil, darkness, and death in men's souls, so long will there be resistance unto God, His light, and life, in whomsoever it is ; the devil not only suggesting, but working effectually in the hearts of reprobates, and natural men, to withstand God's work, as Sanballat and Tobiah used all means to hinder the building of Jerusalem.  And so do his instruments, the spirits of devils, go about the world to provoke men unto war against Christ and His little flock. Those spirits of devils are graceless and wicked men, carried by devilish motion and violence against Christ and His kingdom, and the battle between Michael and his angels, and the devil and his angels, shall not cease till time be no more. II. These that

OPPOSE THEMSELVES TO GOOD MINISTERS AND MEN ARE EVER SPEAKING EVIL, AND OPENING THEIR MOUTHS WITH REPROACHES AGAINST THEM AND THEIR GODLY COURSES. Moses was charged, and that not in corners, but to his face, that he took too much upon him, whereas he was unwilling to undertake all that the Lord laid upon him. It went current in court and country that Elias troubled all Israel. Amaziah accuseth Amos to the king, that the land is not able to bear all his words. Diotrephes not only withstood the apostle John, but prattled against him. But what is the reason of all this, have they any cause given them? The reason is partly positive in themselves, and partly negative in the other. 1. In themselves. (1) The malice of their heart is such as cannot but continually out of the abundance thereof set their tongues at work: the fire within sendeth out such smoke abroad. (2) With this malice is joined exceeding pride and swelling, which moveth them to seek the raising of themselves, although with the fall of others, and make the reproach of others as a ladder for themselves to climb by. (3) With this malice and pride is joined exceeding subtlety and policy in their generation. Well know they that they have gotten ever more conquests by the strokes of their tongues than of their hands, and seldom have they failed of their purposes. 2. Now the negative reason in good men themselves, why their withstanders speak evil of them, is set down (1 Pet. iv. 4). III. EVERY GODLY MAN'S ENDEAVOUR MUST BE TO STOP THE MOUTHS OF SUCH ADVERSARIES, AND SO MAKE THEM ASHAMED. But it is an impossible thing they will have always something to say. Yet so live thou as thou mayst boldly appeal unto God. Let thine own conscience be able to answer for thy uprightness, and so thou openest not their mouths; if now they open them against thee, it is their sin and not thine, and thus this precept is expounded (1 Tim. v. 14). Give no occasion to the adversaries to speak evil. And is enforced with special reason (1 Pet. ii. 12, 15). This is the will of God, by well doing to silence the ignorance of foolish men. If any shall say, "Why I care not what they say on me, they are dogs and wicked men," and what are we to regard them? The apostle telleth us that yet for God's commandment sake we must not open their mouths, but perform all duties of piety and humanity unto them. 2. Because they watch occasions to traduce, we must watch to cut off such occasions (Luke vi. 7). The Scribes and Pharisees watched Christ whether He would heal on the Sabbath, to find an accusation against Him. Christ did the good work, but by His question to them cut off so far as He could the matter of their malice, by clearing the lawfulness of it. So out of their malice we shall draw our own good, and thus it shall be true which the heathen said, that the enemy often hurteth less and profiteth more than many friends. 3. What a glory is it for a Christian thus to slaughter envy itself? To keep shut that mouth that would fain open itself against him? To make him be clothed with his own shame, who sought to bring shame upon him and his profession? When a wretch cannot so put off his forehead as to accuse him whom he abhorreth, no more than he can the sun of darkness when it shineth; yea, when the Prince of the world cometh to sift such a member of Christ, yet He findeth nothing justly to upbraid him withal? (*Ibid.*) *A scoffer silenced :*—I remember a story connected with my native place. One of the most saintly of men lived there, Dr. Andrew Symington, a Cameronian minister, Professor of Theology to the Reformed Presbyterian body who represented the old Scottish Covenanters. He was one day walking down the streets of Paisley, and when he came to the Cross there was a knot of men lounging there, among whom was a sort of ruling spirit, a man who liked to scoff at spiritual matters, and at people who lived a spiritual life. Dr. Symington was passing through the group, with his grave, tender look, and as he passed by the crowd, with the scoffing man in their midst, an awe and silence came upon them. He went on; and the man who scoffed just looked after him and whispered, "Enoch walked with God!" What a sermon to preach! and yet the good man never knew it! (*Prof. Graham.*) *A consistent Christian :*—A friend told me of a young man who was a true soldier of the Cross, and suffered much in consequence, not only from his companions, but from his own father, who was overseer in the same works. That young man showed forth Christ in all his actions, even when his companions who worked with him were unusually provoking in tormenting him about his religion, and, I am ashamed to say, were often encouraged in their wickedness by his own father. One morning, after enduring their cruel and insulting words for some time, he turned to them with a calm look and said : "Friends, tell me, is there anything in my life that is not consistent in a Christian? If there is, tell it to me, and I will kneel in your presence and ask God to forgive me." Complete silence fell on the men, not one dared to open his mouth as that young man stood there and challenged them to find anything against him. (*Major Mathers.*)

Vers. 9, 10. **Exhort servants to be obedient.**—*The duties of servants :*—I. Those duties enumerated. 1. Obedience. 2. Acceptableness of service. The idea is really, approbation based upon virtuous actions. 3. Respectfulness of manner. 4. Honesty. 5. Fidelity. II. Motives of duty. That the religion of Christ might be honoured in the consistency of its professors. (*F. Wagstaff.*) *Duties of servants :*—I. The first and proper duty of every servant is subjection, or a stooping under the authority of his master. This consists—1. In an inward reverencing in heart the image of God in His superiority. This reverent subjection of the heart the Lord in His own example requireth in all His servants, " If I be a master, where is My fear? " (Mal. i. 6), and is the first duty of that commandment, "Honour thy father and mother." The apostle (Eph. vi. 5) calleth for fear and trembling from servants toward their masters. 2. In the outward testimony of this inward reverence, both in speech and gesture before his master, and behind his back ; but especially in the free obedience of all his lawful, yea, and unequal commandments, so as they be not unlawful (Col. iii. 22). 3. In patient enduring without resistance, rebukes and corrections, although bitter, yea, and unjust (1 Pet. ii. 18, 19). II. The second virtue required of servants towards their masters is, that they please them in all things. How will this precept stand with that in Eph. vi. 6, where servants are forbidden to be men-pleasers? To serve only as men-pleasers, as having the eye cast only on man is hypocrisy, and the sin of many servants, pleasing man for man's sake, and that is condemned by our apostle ; but to please men in God and for God is a duty in servants next unto the first ; who, to show themselves well-pleasing to their masters, must carry in their hearts and endeavour a care to be accepted of them, even in the things which, for the indignity and burdensomeness of them, are much against their own minds. For this is the privilege of a master to have his servant devoted unto his pleasure and will, for the attempting of any business, the continuance in it, and the unbending of him from it ; and when the servant hath done all he can, it was but debt and duty, and no thanks are due to him from his master (Matt. viii. 9). But wherein must I please my master or mistress? In all things, that is, in all outward things which are indifferent and lawful. I say in outward things, so Eph. vi. 5, servants obey your masters according to the flesh ; wherein the apostle implieth two things. 1. That the masters are according and over the flesh and outward man ; not over the spirit and inward man, over which we have all one Master in heaven. 2. That accordingly they are to obey in outward things, for if the dominion of the one be bounded so also must needs be the subjection of the other. Again, these outward things must be lawful or indifferent ; for they must not obey against the Lord, but in the Lord. III. Servants are in the third place prohibited crossly and stubbornly to reason, and dispute matters with their masters ; but in silence and subjection to sit down with the worse, even when they suffer wrong ; for as they are to carry a reverent esteem of them in their hearts so must they bewray reverence, love, and lowliness in all their words and gestures ; neither are they here coped from all manner of speech, for when just occasion of speech is offered, as by questions asked, they must make respective answers and not in sullenness say nothing, for Solomon condemneth it as a vice and great sin in servants, when they understand, not to answer (Prov. xxix. 19). IV. " Not purloining." By the former, servants were taught to bridle their tongues ; by this precept, their hands. The word properly noteth the setting somewhat apart to one's private use, which is not his, and is used (Acts v. 6). Ananias kept away and craftily conveyed to his private use that which should have gone another way. So that servants are forbidden to pilfer the least part of their master's goods to dispose to their own or other's use without the acquaintance of their masters. And herein, under this principle, all manner of unfaithfulness is inclusively condemned, as the opposition in the next words showeth. V. " But showing all good fidelity." 1. In his master's commands, readily and diligently to perform them of conscience, and not for eye service, but whether his master's eye be upon him or no. Wherein Abraham's servant giveth a notable precedent. 2. In his counsels and secrets, never disclosing any of his infirmities or weaknesses, but by all lawful and good means covering and hiding them. Contrary hereunto is that wickedness of many servants, who may, indeed, rather be accounted so many spies in the house, whose common practice is, where they may be heard, to blaze abroad whatsoever may tend to their master or mistress's reproach, having at once cast off both the religious fear of God, as also the reverent respect of God's image in the persons of their superiors. 3. In his messages abroad, both in the speedy execution and dispatch of them, as also in his expenses about them ; husbanding his master's money, cutting off idle charges, and bringing home a just account; hereby acknowledging that the eye of his own conscience watcheth him when his master's eye cannot. 4. Unto his master's wife, children, servants, wisely with Joseph distinguishing the things which are committed unto him from them that are excepted. 5. Lastly, in all his actions and carriage, so also in every word, shunning all lying, dissembling, untruths, whether for his master's, his own, or other men's advantage; in the practice of which duties he becometh faithful in all his master's house. (*T. Taylor, D.D.*) "*Not answering again*":— A lady once, when she was a little girl, learned a good lesson, which she tells for the benefit of whom it may concern:—" One frosty morning I was looking out of the window into my father's farmyard, where stood many cows, oxen, and horses, waiting to drink. It was a cold morning. The cattle all stood very still and meek, till one of the cows attempted to turn round. In making the attempt she happened to hit her next neighbour, whereupon the neighbour kicked and hit another. In five minutes the whole herd were kicking each other with fury. My mother laughed and said : ' See what comes of kicking when you are hit. Just so, I have seen one cross word set a whole family by the ears on some frosty morning.' Afterward, if my brothers or myself were a little irritable, she would say, ' Take care, my children. Remember how the fight in the farmyard began. Never give back a kick for a hit, and you will save yourselves and others a great deal of trouble.' " **Not purloining.**--*Honesty in little things:*—I. The NATURE OF THE SIN AGAINST WHICH THE TEXT WARNS US. Stealing is a term applicable to the conduct of a man who goes to the house, or the farm, or the shop of another, and takes away his goods or other property. We turn an act of theft into one of purloining when a servant helps himself, without an understood allowance from his master or mistress, to that which is under his care, or to which he has access ; or when a workman pockets, for his own use, what he thinks he may bear away without detection ; or when a labourer carries away from his master's farm something to add to his own little stock, or to maintain his own family. To steal is to take what is not our own. To purloin is to take what is not our own too ; but it is something we had in trust, or to which we had access. If purloining be practised on a large scale, it changes its name and becomes embezzlement. II. The EXCEEDING SINFULNESS OF THIS SIN. There are many excuses which are brought forward in extenuation of this offence. 1. The change of its name. There is a wonderful imposition in words ; and many purloiners quiet their consciences by changing the name. Because it is not commonly called stealing, they think it does not involve the guilt of stealing. 2. Another plea is, that however great the amount may be in the course of months or years, you are pleased to make the depredations small in detail. It is a petty affair of every day, and so very little as not to be worth thinking about. It does not say, " Thou shalt not steal much ! " but, " Thou shalt not steal ! " 3. The next plea is, that the master is rich and will not miss it, and so it will do no harm. This law does not merely forbid them to steal from the poor, leaving them at liberty to steal from the rich. III. The MOTIVES WHICH ENFORCE THE OPPOSITE CONDUCT. The servants whom Titus was to exhort were those of his own congregation. They formed a Christian community ; and however the title may be applied now, it was then given to those who had renounced Paganism. The admonition was to men who had embraced not only the profession of faith, but the faith itself. It is right that, for every kind of unrighteousness, men should be reproved ; for " the wrath of God is revealed," &c. The more they are burdened with a sense of sin, the more will they feel the importance of repentance. (*T. Chalmers, D.D.*) *Fidelity in a servant :*—Selim, a poor Turk, had been brought up from his youth with care and kindness by his master, Mustapha. When the latter lay at the point of death, Selim was tempted by his fellow-servants to join them in stealing a part of Mustapha's treasures. " No," said he, " Selim is no robber. I fear not to offend my master for the evil he can do me now, but for the good he has done me all my life long." **That they may adorn the doctrine of God our Saviour.**— *Servants adorning the gospel :*—I. The DOCTRINE OF THE GOSPEL : THE DOCTRINE OF THE GOSPEL IS CALLED THE DOCTRINE OF CHRIST. 1. Because He is the argument and subject of it. 2. Because He is the first and chief messenger and publisher of it. 3. Whosoever have been the teachers and publishers of this doctrine from the beginning, either by word or writing (not excepting prophets or apostles themselves) or shall be unto the end. They all do it by commandment from Him, yea, Himself preacheth in them and in us. 4. As it proceedeth from Him so it tendeth wholly unto Him, and leadeth believers to see and partake both of His grace and glory shining in the same. II. Christ is called GOD OUR SAVIOUR. 1. To prove His own deity, not only in express terms being called God, but also by the epithet agreeing only to a Divine nature, our Saviour. 2. To imply our own misery, whose infinite wretchedness only God could remove, and whose infinite good none but God could restore. 3. And especially in regard of this doctrine. (1) To confirm the divinity of the same, it being a doctrine of God and a doctrine of salvation proceeding from our Saviour. (2) To enforce the duty towards it, namely, that seeing the author of it is God, the matter Divine, the effect salvation, meet it is that such a saving doctrine a doctrine of such tidings, should be beautified and adorned. III. THIS DOCTRINE IS ADORNED WHEN IT IS MADE BEAUTIFUL AND LOVELY UNTO MEN, and this by two things in the professors of it. 1. By an honest and unblamable conversation, for carnal men commonly esteem of the doctrine by the life, and the profession by the practice of the professor. 2. By God's blessing which is promised and is attending such walking, whereby even strangers to the Church are forced to begin to like of the profession: for God's blessing upon His people is not only profitable to themselves, but turneth to the salvation of many others. So we read that when Licinius was overcome by Constantine, and the persecutions ceased, which had almost for three hundred years together wasted the Church, how innumerable of them, who before had worshipped their idols, were contented to be received into the Church. On the contrary, the gospel is dishonoured when the Lord is forced to judge and correct the abuse of His name in the professors of it (Ezek. xxxvi. 20). IV. Servants adorn the gospel, when professing it, they, by performing all faithful service to their masters in and for God, SEEK AND OBTAIN THE BLESSING OF GOD IN THE CONDITION OF LIFE WHEREIN HE HATH PLACED THEM. (*T. Taylor, D.D.*) *The duty of advancing the Christian religion :*—I. THE EXPLANATION OF THE TERMS USED. 1. By " the doctrine of God our Saviour " the apostle means the Christian religion, or that institution of faith and manners which Jesus taught and published when here on earth. 2. To " adorn the doctrine of God our Saviour " is to advance the credit and reputation of Christian religion in the world. It is so to govern and demean ourselves that we may reconcile its enemies to a good opinion of it ; that we may procure and even force regard and veneration towards it. 3. By the " they " in the text, the persons upon whom this duty is incumbent, we may fairly understand the whole body of Christians. II. THE NATURE, ACTS, AND EXERCISES OF DUTY. How a man may adorn the doctrine of God our Saviour—1. As it is a rule of faith, or an institution of religion, which we believe and own as of Divine authority. By manifesting, beyond any reasonable exception, that we unfeignedly assent unto it, that we firmly believe it to be, what we pretend, of Divine original. And this will be evident to all—(1) If our faith be perfect and entire. If we receive our religion as it is in itself, in all its parts, in every article, and in their plainest sense. (2) If we are steady, firm, and constant in the profession of it. (3) If we express an affection, a prudent zeal in the profession of it. 2. As it is a rule of life and manners. To this purpose it is absolutely necessary—(1) That our obedience be entire and universal. (2) That our obedience be free and cheerful. (3) If in cases doubtful we determine our practice on the side of the law, and of our duty. (4) By an eminent practice of some particular virtues, as of mercy and charity. Wherever these are expressed to the life—habitually, bountifully, freely—all that observe it will esteem the religion from whence such a spirit flows. III. THE REASONS WHICH OBLIGE US, AND THE ENCOURAGEMENTS WHICH MAY PERSUADE US, TO THE PRACTICE OF IT. 1. To adorn the doctrine of God our Saviour by such a faith and practice as I have now described is the most infallible assurance, both to ourselves and others, that our principle is sincere and perfect. 2. To live such a life as shall cause our religion to be esteemed and honoured in the world, is the greatest blessing, as well to ourselves as to others, that we can either imagine or desire. 3. Another encouragement to such a profession and practice of our religion as shall adorn it are the particular promises which are made to those who shall attain unto it. 4. The particular peace and satisfaction which will arise from such a faith and life. (*J. Lambe.*) *Slaves adorning the doctrine of God :*—As the number of slaves in the first century was so enormous it was only in accordance with human probability that many of the first converts to Christianity belonged to this class; all the more so, as Christianity belonged to this class; all the more so, as Christianity, like most great movements, began with the lower orders and thence spread upwards. Among the better class of slaves, that is those who were not so degraded as to be insensible of their own degradation, the gospel spread freely. It offered them just what they needed, and the lack of which had turned their life into one great despair. It gave them something to hope for and live for. Their condition in the world was both socially and morally deplorable. Socially they had no rights beyond what their lord chose to allow them. And St. Chrysostom in commenting on this passage points out how inevitable it was that the moral character of slaves should as a rule be bad. They have no motive for trying to be good, and very little opportunity of learning what is right. Every one, slaves included, admits that as a race they are passionate, intractable, and indisposed to virtue, not because God has made them so, but from bad education and the neglect of their masters. And yet this is the class which St. Paul singles out as being able in a peculiar way to adorn the doctrine of God our Saviour in all things." " To adorn the doctrine of God." How is the doctrine of God to be adorned ? And how are slaves capable of adorning it? " The doctrine of God " is that which He teaches, which He has revealed for our instruction. It is His revelation of Himself. He is the author of it, the giver of it, and the subject of it. He is also its end or purpose. It is granted in order that men may know Him, and love Him, and be brought home to Him. All these facts are a guarantee to us of its importance and its security. It comes from One who is infinitely great and infinitely true. And yet it is capable of being adorned by those to whom it is given. There is nothing paradoxical in this. It is precisely those things which in themselves are good and beautiful that we consider capable of adornment and worthy of it. Thus adornment is a form of homage : it is the tribute which the discerning pay to beauty. But adornment has its relations not only to those who bestow, but to those also who receive it. It is a reflection of the mind of the giver ; but it has also an influence on the recipient. And, first, it makes that which is adorned more conspicuous and better known. A picture in a frame is more likely to be looked at than one that is unframed. Adornment is an advertisement of merit : it makes the adorned object more readily perceived and more widely appreciated. And, secondly, if it is well chosen and well bestowed, it augments the merit of that which it adorns. That which was fair before is made still fairer by suitable ornament. The beautiful painting is still more beautiful in a worthy frame. Noble ornament increases the dignity of a noble structure. And a person of royal presence becomes still more regal when royally arrayed. Adornment, therefore, is not only an advertisement of beauty, it is also a real enhancement of it. All these particulars hold good with regard to the adornment of the doctrine of God. By trying to adorn it and make it more beautiful and more attractive, we show our respect for it ; we pay our tribute of homage and admiration. We show to all the world that we think it estimable, and worthy of attention and honour. And by so doing we make the doctrine of God better known : we bring it under the notice of others who might otherwise have overlooked it : we force it upon their attention. Moreover, the doctrine which we thus adorn becomes really more beautiful in consequence. Our acceptance of the doctrine of God, and our efforts to adorn it, bring out its inherent life and develop its natural value, and every additional person who joins us in doing this is an augmentation of its powers. It is within our power not only to honour and make better known, but also to enhance, the beauty of the doctrine of God. But slaves—and such slaves as were found throughout the Roman empire in St. Paul's day—what have they to do with the adornment of the doctrine of God ? Why is this duty of making the gospel more beautiful specially mentioned in connection with them ? That the aristocracy of the empire, its magistrates, its senators, its commanders—supposing that any of them could be induced to embrace the faith of Jesus Christ—should be charged to adorn the doctrines which they had accepted, would be intelligible. Their acceptance of it would be a tribute to its dignity. Their loyalty to it would be a proclamation of its merits. Their accession to its ranks would be a real augmentation of its powers of attraction. But almost the reverse of all this would seem to be the truth in the case of slaves. Their tastes were so low, their moral judgment so debased, that for a religion to have found a welcome among slaves would hardly be a recommendation of it to respectable people. And what opportunities had slaves, regarded as they were as the very outcasts of society, of making the gospel better known or more attractive ? Yet St. Paul knew what he was about when he urged Titus to commit the " adorning of the doctrine of God " in a special manner to slaves: and experience has proved the soundness of his judgment. If the mere fact that many slaves accepted the faith could not do a great deal to recommend the power and beauty of the gospel, the Christian lives, which they thenceforward led, could. It was a strong argument *à fortiori.* The worse the unconverted sinner, the more marvellous his thorough conversion. As Chrysostom puts it, when it was seen that

Christianity, by giving a settled principle of sufficient power to counterbalance the pleasures of sin, was able to impose a restraint upon a class so self-willed, and render them singularly well-behaved, then their masters, however unreasonable they might be, were likely to form a high opinion of the doctrines which accomplished this. And Chrysostom goes on to point out that the way in which slaves are to endeavour to adorn the doctrine of God is by cultivating precisely those virtues which contribute most to their masters' comfort and interest—submissiveness, gentleness, meekness, honesty, truthfulness, and a faithful discharge of all duties. What a testimony conduct of this kind would be to the power and beauty of the gospel; and a testimony all the more powerful in the eyes of those masters who became conscious that these despised Christian slaves were living better lives than their owners! The passionate man, who found his slave always gentle and submissive; the inhuman and ferocious man, who found his slave always meek and respectful; the fraudulent man of business, who noticed that his slave never pilfered or told lies; the sensualist, who observed that his slave was never intemperate and always shocked at immodesty—all these, even if they were not induced to become converts to the new faith, or even to take much trouble to understand it, would at least at times feel something of respect, if not of awe and reverence, for a creed which produced such results. Where did their slaves learn these lofty principles? Whence did they derive the power to live up to them? Nor were these the only ways in which the most degraded and despised class in the society of that age were able to "adorn the doctrine of God." Slaves were not only an ornament to the faith by their lives; they adorned it also by their deaths. Not a few slaves won the martyr's crown. What slaves could do then we all of us can do now. We can prove to all for whom and with whom we work that we really do believe and endeavour to live up to the faith that we profess. By the lives we lead we can show to all who know anything of us that we are loyal to Christ. By avoiding offence in word or in deed, and by welcoming opportunities of doing good to others, we can make His principles better known. And by doing all this brightly and cheerfully, without ostentation or affectation or moroseness, we can make His principles attractive. Thus we also can "adorn the doctrine of God in all things." "In all things." That all-embracing addition to the apostolic injunction must not be lost sight of. There is no duty so humble, no occupation so trifling, that it cannot be made into an opportunity for adorning our religion (1 Cor. x. 31). (*A. Plummer, D.D.*)     *Christians making the gospel beautiful:*—I. THE WONDERFUL POSSIBILITY that is opened out here before every Christian that he may add beauty to the gospel. He may paint the lily and gild the refined gold. For men do quite rightly and legitimately judge of systems by their followers. The astronomer does not look directly up into the sky when he wants to watch the heavenly bodies, but down into the mirror, on which their reflection is cast. And so our little low lives down here upon earth should so give back the starry bodies and infinitudes above us that some dim eyes, which peradventure could not gaze into the violet abysses with their lustrous points, may behold them reflected in the beauty of your life. Our lives should be like the old missals, where you find the loving care of the monastic scribe has illuminated and illustrated the holy text, or has rubricated and gilded some of the letters. The best Illustrated Bible is the conduct of the people that profess to take it for their guide and law. II. THE SOLEMN ALTERNATIVE. If you look at the context you will see that a set of exhortations preceding these to the slaves, which are addressed to the wives, end with urging as the great motive to the conduct enjoined, "that the Word of God be not blasphemed." That is the other side of the same thought as is in my text. The issues of the conduct of professing Christians are the one or other of these two, either to add beauty to the gospel or to cause the Word of God to be blasphemed. If you do not the one you will be doing the other. There are no worse enemies of the gospel than its inconsistent friends. Who is it that thwarts missionary work in India? Englishmen! Who is it that, wherever they go with their ships, put a taunt into the lips of the enemy which the Christian workers find it hard to meet? English sailors! The notorious dissipation and immorality amongst the representatives of English commerce in the various Eastern centres of trade puts a taunt into the mouth of the abstemious Hindu and of the Chinaman. "These are your Christians, are they?" England, that sends out missionaries in the cabin, and Bibles and men side by side amongst the cargo, has to listen, and her people have to take to themselves the awful words with which the ancient Jewish inconsistencies were rebuked: "Through you the name of God is blasphemed amongst the Gentiles." And in less solemn

manner perhaps, but just as truly, here, in a so-called Christian land, the inconsistencies, the selfishness, the worldliness of professing Christian people, the absolute absence of all apparent difference between them and the most godless man
that is in the same circumstances, are the things which perhaps more than anything else counteract the evangelistic efforts of the Christian Church. III. THE
SORT OF LIFE THAT WILL COMMEND AND ADORN THE GOSPEL. 1. It must be a life conspicuously and uniformly under the influence of Christian principles. I put
emphasis upon these two words "conspicuously" and "uniformly." It will be of
very little use if your Christian principle is so buried in your life, embedded
beneath a mass of selfishness and worldliness and indifference as that it takes a
microscope and a week's looking for to find it. And it will be of very little use,
either, if your life is by fits and starts under the influence of Christian principle;
a minute guided by that and ten minutes guided by the other thing—if here and
there, sprinkled thinly over the rotting mass, there be a handful of the saving salt.
2. Remember, too, as the context teaches us, that the lives which commend and
adorn the doctrine must be such as manifest Christian principle in the smallest
details. What is it Paul tells these Cretan slaves to do that they may "adorn the
doctrine"? Obedience, keeping a civil tongue in their heads in the midst of provocation, not indulging in petty pilfering, being true to the trust that was given to
them. "That is no great thing," you may say, but in these little things they were
to adorn the great doctrine of God their Saviour. Ay! The smallest duties are in
some sense the largest sphere for the operation of great principles. For it is the
little duties which by their minuteness tempt men to think that they can do them
without calling in the great principles of conduct, that give the colour to every life
after all. The little banks of mud in the wheel-tracks in the road are shaped upon
the same slopes, and moulded by the same law that carves the mountains and lifts
the precipices of the Himalayas. And a handful of snow in the hedge in the
winter time will fall into the same curves, and be obedient to the same great
physical laws which shape the glaciers that lie on the sides of the Alps. You do
not want big things in order, largely and nobly, to manifest big principles. The
smallest duties, distinctly done for Christ's sake, will adorn the doctrine. 3. And
then again, I may say that the manner of life which commends the gospel will be
one conspicuously above the level of the morality of the class to which you belong.
These slaves were warned not to fall into the vices that were proper to their class,
in order that by not falling into them, and so being unlike their fellows, they might
glorify the gospel. For the things that Paul warns them not to do are the faults
which all history and experience tell us are exactly the vices of the slave—petty
pilfering, a rank tongue blossoming into insolent speech, a disregard of the master's
interests, sulky disobedience or sly evasion of the command. These are the kind
of things that the devilish institution of slavery makes almost necessary on the
part of the slave, unless some higher motive and loftier principle come in to
counteract the effects. And in like manner all of us have, in the class to which we
belong, and the sort of life which we have to live, certain evils natural to our position; and unless you are unlike the non-Christian men of your own profession and
the people that are under the same worldly influence as you are—unless you are
unlike them in that your righteousness exceeds their righteousness, "Ye shall in
no wise enter the kingdom of heaven." (*A. Maclaren, D.D.*) *Religion adorned:*—
I. THE PURITY OF TRUTH. The other day we read in the newspapers that in Berlin
there is a wonderful gem, a sapphire weighing ten ounces, and said to be worth—if
it were pure—a million pounds. But there is a flaw in it; it is not "one entire and
perfect chrysolite." Ah, *if* it were only pure! We damage our cause and prevent
people from joining us sometimes because we are not true to the principles we
profess. Deceit is always ugly; truth is ever beautiful. To be pure and truthful
in all we say or do cannot be accomplished by merely wishing; it will probably
take an entire life for a man to become genuine as Jesus Christ was. Still, let us
try; and though we fall, we should not despair. The finest trait of beauty in a
man's character is when he is so true that his word may be trusted as much as his
bond, and people remark of him, "Well, if he says so, it must be true." II. THE
RHYTHM OF LIFE. Not only wear a flower in your breast, but let there be the beauty
of truth and the perfume of kindliness in your looks, words, and actions. Let me
tell you of a famous soldier who went to the palace one day to have an audience of
the king of England. Having to wait a little, he paced up and down the ante-
chamber impatiently, and as he walked, his sword dragged and rattled behind him.
The king opening the door, said to a courtier loud enough for all the others to hear,

"Dear me, what a nuisance that man's sword is!" The veteran exclaimed, "So your Majesty's enemies think." That was the "retort courteous," wasn't it? Of course the sword was powerful, and while the hand that wielded it was strong and the heart of the soldier true and brave, still I think he might have carried his sword quietly; though it was terrible in the battle, need he to make it a nuisance in the palace? Therefore, be thoughtful of the feelings of others. More unpleasantness is caused by want of thought than by want of feeling. Make your life as musical and poetical as possible, agreeable in passing and pleasant in remembrance. III. THE GLORY OF USEFULNESS. In being useful you are adorning the religion of Christ; pluck up your heart, and seek out opportunities to do good. Be a true Christian minister; and remember that though you are a slave to circumstances, you may adorn religion more than a cathedral can do. When you thus live, prompted by love to God and love to man, life shall be a blessing, and your heaven shall be begun below. (*W. Birch.*)   *The grammar of ornament:*—I. THE GRANDEUR OF CHRISTIAN DOCTRINE. "The doctrine of God." If the gospel of Christ be the doctrine of God it ought to reflect the attributes of God. We venture to say it does thus reflect its Author; the New Testament bears conspicuously the grand characteristics of divinity. 1. Think of the vastness of the gospel. We feel in it the infinitude of God. We are redeemed before the foundation of the world; the redemption disclosed is that of a race; it is worked out through the ages; its issues are in the great eternity beyond. 2. Think of the purity of the gospel. There is a strange purity in revelation. The Old Testament stretches like a stainless sky above the wild, sensual, corrupt nations of antiquity; the New Testament bears the same relation to the life of modern nations. As we look into the pure blue of the firmament far beyond our smoky atmosphere, so do we look up to the righteousness revealed in Christ as the body of heaven for clearness. 3. Think of the love of the gospel—comprehending men of all nations, languages, tribes, and tongues. 4. Think of the power of the gospel. We feel in revelation the energy of suns, the force of winds, the sound of many seas. There is a majestic moral power in the gospel that we do not find in the sublimest philosophies of men, that is also painfully missing in the noblest sacred literature of the heathen (Rom. i. 16). 5. Think of the permanence of revelation. Science says, "Persistence is the sign of reality." How divinely real, then, is the gospel of God in Jesus Christ! It is the only thing on the face of the earth that does persist. Every now and then when a new heresy starts up there is a panic, as if the authority of revelation had come to an end; but if you wait awhile it is the heresy and the panic which come to an end. A gentleman told me that he was walking in his garden one day when his little child was by; suddenly the little one burst into tears and cried out in terror, "Oh! father, the house is falling." The child saw the clouds drifting over the house, and mistook the movement of the clouds for the movement of the house—the house was right enough, it is standing now. So sometimes we think that revelation is falling and coming to nought, but it is soon clear that the movement is elsewhere. Nations, dynasties, philosophies, fashions, pass like fleeting vapours and shadows, but the gospel stands like a rock. Ah! and will stand when rolling years shall cease to move. II. THE SUPREME DEMONSTRATION OF CHRISTIAN DOCTRINE IS FOUND IN CHRISTIAN CHARACTER. "That they may adorn the doctrine of God our Saviour in all things." The gospel is not a mere speculation, a superb philosophy, a grand ideal; it is intensely practical; it is to prove itself the doctrine of God by making all who believe in it like God. 1. "Adorn the doctrine." That is, reveal, display, make conspicuous and impressive the splendid contents of your faith. The doctrine of God is in the Testaments in suppressed magnificence, and the saints are to give it expression, embodiment: they are to flash out the unrevealed glory in their spirit and language and conduct. The vastness, the depth, the tenderness, the beauty of their creed is to be made tangible. Our creed must transfigure our life; our life must demonstrate the divinity of our creed. As the stars adorn astronomy, as the roses of June adorn botany, as the rainbow adorns optics, so our conduct must flash out the hidden virtue and glory of the doctrine of God. 2. Adorn the doctrine "in all things." The saints are to illustrate the doctrine of God in all its fulness—to do it justice at all points. And so we have much to do. Every system of morality outside the Christian Church: Platonic, Aristotelian, Stoic, Epicurean, Utilitarian, Positivist; every system concerns itself with some pet virtue, or with some special class of virtues; but Christianity is most comprehensive—it concerns itself with whatever is just, true, lovely, or of good report; everything virtuous and praiseworthy is made an object of aspiration. We must do justice to the doctrine of God throughout our whole personality. At one end of our complex nature are the grand faculties of intelligence, conscience, will, imagination, linking us with the upper universe; at the other end of our being are basal instincts and affinities establishing a kinship between us and the world below our feet. We must see to it that our faith hallows our whole personality, that our splendid faculties are sacred to their lofty uses, that our inferior instincts are duly chastened, that we live sanctified in body, soul, and spirit. The ethics of Christianity comprehend the whole grammar of ornament. The faith of Christ is a salvation from all sin, a salvation into all holiness. As everybody knows, Shakespeare was a great lover of the old English flowers, frequently making them to spring forth in his poems with the freshness of nature itself, and so some years ago, when his admirers restored the cottage in which the dramatist was born, they resolved to plant in its grounds all the sweet things of summer found on the bard's immortal page: rosemary, ox-lip, wild thyme, pansies, peony, lily, love-in-idleness, cuckoo-buds, lady-smocks, freckled cowslip, daisies pied, eglantine, woodbine, nodding violets, musk-roses, red roses—all were carefully planted out in the sun. What a catalogue of virtues could we compile from revelation! What a multitude of graces are here, and fine differentiations of sublime qualities and principles of moral life! Now all these we are to realise in actual life as season and opportunity may permit, until the whole range of our character and action is filled with beauty and fragrance as the garden of the Lord. In adorning the doctrine of God in all things we render that doctrine the most valuable service any may render it. The world is not persuaded by logic, by learning, by literature, but by life; the multitude believes in what it can see—in the eloquence of conduct, the logic of facts, the feeling and power of deeds. We may see this very clearly illustrated in another direction. Why do we all believe in astronomy? Why have we such a positive faith in a science which professes to give the true account of the distant mysterious firmament; which assumes to weigh suns, to analyse stars, to calculate the movements of endless orbs and comets? Do we believe in all this because we have read Sir Isaac Newton, mastered his reasonings, verified his calculations and conclusions? Not for a moment. The faith of the million rests on what it can see. Our common faith in astronomy is derived not immediately from Newton's *Principia*, but indirectly through the penny almanac. At the beginning of the year we learn that an eclipse of the sun or moon is predicted, and on the palpable fulfilment of that prediction rests the firmest faith of modern times—faith in astronomy. On the day or night of an eclipse myriads of people look into the sky who never look into it at any other time, and the exact fulfilment of the prediction brings conviction to their mind touching all the large assumptions of celestial science. People believe in what they see; the popular faith is based entirely on the darkened orb. So the faith of men generally in Christianity does not rest on theology, criticism, logic, but on Christianity as it finds expression in the spirit and life of its disciples. Once more men believe in what they see, only this time they are not called to look upon a darkened orb, but on a Church bright as the sun shedding on men and nations moral splendours like the light of seven days. (*W. L. Watkinson.*) *The duty of adorning our Christian profession:*—I. TAKE A GENERAL VIEW OF THE DOCTRINE OF GOD OUR SAVIOUR. It is not the doctrine of God, as our Creator, Preserver, Benefactor, Governor, &c., which is here meant, but the doctrine that concerns our salvation — our fall in Adam, and its consequences (Rom. v. 12), ignorance, insensibility, sinfulness, guilt, condemnation, &c; our redemption by Christ (1 Cor. xv. 1–3; Rom. v. 6–10; 1 Pet. i. 18) the means whereby we partake of this redemption, viz., repentance and faith (Mark i. 15; Acts xx. 21); the effects produced, as justification, whereby we pass from condemnation and wrath to acquaintance and favour with God, and are entitled to eternal life (Acts xiii. 38; Tit. iii. 7); as renovation of nature, whereby we are qualified to bring forth fruit to the glory of God; the necessity of continuing in this state of salvation, and increasing in holiness (John xv. 1; Rom. xi. 19–22); our enemies and hindrances— Satan, the world, the flesh (Eph. vi. 10–19; 1 John ii. 14, 15; Rom. viii. 12, 13); our friends and helps—God (Rom. viii. 31), Christ (Heb. iv. 14–16; 2 Cor. xii. 9), the Spirit (Rom. viii. 26), angels (Heb. i. 14), the people of God: that we are upon our trial for eternity, and many eyes upon us (Heb. xii. 1): the issue of all, the death of the body, the immortality of the soul, the resurrection, judgment, eternal life. II. SHOW WHAT IS MEANT BY ADORNING IT. Here is an allusion to the ornaments of dress. Dress may be fit or unfit for us, suitable or unsuitable: our temper and conduct must be suitable to the gospel.

Instance, in the doctrine of our fall and its consequences. Does the gospel teach that we are fallen, depraved, &c. ? then all high thoughts of ourselves, all self-confidence, and impenitence are unsuitable to this doctrine; humility, self-abasement, and godly sorrow, are suitable thereto. In the doctrine of our redemption; unbelief, diffidence, despondency, are unsuitable; faith, confidence in God, and peace of mind, are suitable thereto. 2. Another end for which dress is used is to represent and exhibit the persons who wear it in their true character and proper loveliness. Just so, our temper and conduct should be calculated to set forth the doctrine of the gospel in the most correct and clear point of view. 3. A third end, which some have in view in adopting various kinds of dress, is to add to their comeliness and beauty, and make themselves appear more agreeable than they really are. We cannot possibly give greater beauty to the gospel than it has, but there are certain graces and virtues which are more calculated to set forth its beauty and amiableness, and to show it to advantage. Such are the graces and virtues recommended (Rom xii. 9–18; 1 Cor. xiii. 4–7; Col. iii. 12–17); and in the verses preceding the text, as truth, uprightness, justice, mercy, charity, meekness, gentleness, benevolence, sobriety, industry, frugality, liberality, cheerfulness, gratitude. III. How THIS MUST BE DONE " IN ALL THINGS." In all persons, old and young, rich and poor, high and low. In all conditions and states, as married or single, parents or children, masters or servants. In all places: at home, abroad, alone, in company, in the church or market, with our friends or enemies, the righteous or wicked. In all employments: in religious, civil, and natural actions. At all times: on the Lord's days; on other days; at morning, noon and night; in childhood, youth, manhood, middle age, old age. (*J. Benson.*)    *Adorning:*—Raphael, the prince of modern painters, made ten pictures of Bible scenes. Three of them were lost, and somehow the rest lay neglected and forgotten for more than a hundred years in a garret at Arras. There Rubens found them, and persuaded Charles I. of England to buy them for his palace. They were put into good order, and by and by a room in Hampton Court Palace was built to receive them. They are now admired by thousands in the South Kensington Museum, and, by means of engravings, are better known, it is said, than any other work of art in the world. The gospel in Crete was like Raphael's pictures in the Arras garret. It was a despised thing, overlaid with frightful prejudices, under which its beauty was buried. But Paul feels that if the poor Christian slaves lived Christian lives, they would do for it what Rubens did for the defaced and dusty paintings of Raphael; they would rescue it from neglect, and discover its heavenly grandeur to admiring thousands who would multiply and spread it throughout the world. Every adorner of the doctrine walks along a highway which has these stages. I. SAVING FAITH, A HEARTY FAITH. A doctrine in logic or metaphysics appeals only to my head: it has little or nothing to do with the heart; but " the doctrine " must win the assent of the mind and the consent of the heart. The gospel plants all its artillery before the heart till the everlasting gates are lifted up that the King of glory may enter and reign without a rival. And you must obey Him; for, being God as well as Saviour, when He commands you must obey. You are like the wounded soldier on the battlefield, to whom healing is offered by the doctor, who has all the authority of the kingdom at his back. The sick man has no right to refuse, he must accept healing that he may be fitted for the Queen's service. The offers of mercy, so gentle, have behind them all the authority of heaven. Christ as Saviour wins the heart, and as God He claims obedience. II. TRUE CONFESSION. Christ comes from heaven, and gives His testimony about God and yourself, about sin and salvation. You in your turn take up and repeat His testimony. You receive His record, and set to your seal that He is true. Your confession is to be as a true trademark, declaring the maker and quality of what is within. The foot, or the hand, or the eye must not contradict the lip. And you are to put away all mean shame; for no one ever adorned a doctrine of which he was ashamed before men. III. DAILY DUTY, A HEAVENLY MORALITY. Some make much of duty, but think that they can get on well enough without doctrine. Were the captain of a steamer to say, " I want steam, but don't bother me with coals—dirty, dull, heavy lumps; steam, but no coal for me," you should think him a very foolish man. Now he is as foolish whose motto is, " Not doctrine, but life. The apostle, you see, unites the two. He makes one thing of doctrine and piety, and one thing of piety and morality. To him duty is the adorning of the doctrine. (*James Wells.*)    *Adorning the truth:*—The word " doctrine," as used here, means instruction—any or all of the great truths set forth in the Divine word. The word " adorn " means to decorate or beautify, as with gems or garlands or goodly apparel.  I. This exhortation applies first TO ALL WHO, IN ANY SENSE OR SPHERE, ARE TEACHING CHRISTIAN TRUTHS.  1. It is largely violated in two opposite directions.  (1) On the one hand, we find the doctrines of grace set forth as bold, ugly, and repulsive *dogmata*.  (2) On the other hand, we find men attempting to render the gospel attractive to the carnal heart by simply leaving all its strong doctrines out of it.  2. Between these extremes, and equally opposed to both, lies the true method of teaching.  It is not the work of a costumer, arranging either a harlequin for farce or a gibbering ghost for tragedy; but it is a blessed imitation of Christ, beautifying the whole heavenly body of truth by " adorning its doctrines."  II. This exhortation APPLIES EQUALLY TO ALL CHRISTIANS, bidding them make all these doctrines beautiful by the power of their daily lives.  Let us only live as if the gospel we profess, instead of making us gloomy fanatics or self-righteous pharisees, made us rather kind and gentle, and lovely and joyous; never taking from us a single truly good thing on earth, but only adding to each a new charm and power.  Thereby we shall wonderfully adorn that gospel.  The humblest man in our midst, if he live imitating his Master, his life pervaded with the principles of his faith, truly glorifies the gospel.  Behold these humble children of suffering and toil—that faithful-hearted woman, plying her needle into the waning night that she may earn scanty bread for her fatherless children, amid all temptations and trials keeping Christian faith and love unstained; and as she fashions that coarse garment she is working as well a lustrous robe for God's glorious gospel!  See that weary toiler in shop or field, amid all antagonisms to good and solicitations to evil making exhibition of all that is honest and lovely and of good report; and while he plies the hammer, or holds the plough, he is making Divine truth beautiful, as with gems and fine gold fashioning a diadem for the gospel of Christ.  Oh, what a beauty and glory it casts over this low world and this common life, just to feel that amid all weary labour and perplexing cares we are at work not merely for ourselves and our beloved ones, or for the higher good of our day and generation, but verily and directly as well for the infinite God and His glory; that there is not one of us so ignorant or obscure that he may not, in his own sphere and lot, be reflecting splendour on every Divine attribute, bringing forth nobler regalia for the coronation of Christ!  (*C. Wadsworth, D.D.*)     *Gospel adornment:*— I. A NAME OF ADORNMENT FOR THE GOSPEL.  "The doctrine of God our Saviour."  1. It sets forth its greatness: "doctrine of God."  (1) Our fall, ruin, sin, and punishment were great.  (2) Our salvation and redemption are great.  (3) Our safety, happiness, and hopes are great.  2. It sets forth its certainty.  It is "of God."  (1) It comes by revelation of God.  (2) It is guaranteed by the fidelity of God.  (3) It is as immutable as God Himself.  3. It sets forth its relation to Christ Jesus: "of God our Saviour."  (1) He is the author of it.  (2) He is the substance of it.  (3) He is the proclaimer of it.  (4) He is the object of it.  The gospel glorifies Jesus.  4. It sets forth its authority.  (1) The whole system of revealed truth is of God.  (2) The Saviour Himself is God, and hence He must be accepted.  (3) The gospel itself is Divine.  God's mind is embodied in the doctrine of the Lord Jesus, and to reject it is to reject God.  II. A METHOD OF ADORNMENT FOR THE GOSPEL.  1. The persons who are to adorn the gospel.  In Paul's day, bond-servants or slaves; in our day, poor servants of the humblest order.  Strange that these should be set to such a task!  Yet the women slaves adorned their mistresses, and both men and women of the poorest class were quite ready to adorn themselves.  From none does the gospel receive more honour than from the poor.  2. The way in which these persons could specially adorn the gospel.  (1) By obedience to their masters (ver. 9).  (2) By endeavours to please them: "please them well."  (3) By restraining their tongues: "not answering again."  (4) By scrupulous honesty: "not purloining" (ver. 10).  (5) By trustworthy character: "showing all good fidelity."  3. The way of adornment of the doctrine in general.  (1) Adornment, if really so, is suitable to beauty.  Holiness, mercifulness, cheerfulness, &c., are congruous with the gospel.  (2) Adornment is often a tribute to beauty.  Such is a godly conversation: it honours the gospel.  (3) Adornment is an advertisement of beauty.  Holiness calls attention to the natural beauty of the gospel.  (4) Adornment is an enhancement of beauty.  Godliness gives emphasis to the excellence of doctrine.  (*C. H. Spurgeon.*) *Living ornaments:*—1. I sometimes think that the doctrine of God our Saviour, may be likened to a guide book, which tells us how to attain a holy character.  When buying a book, I always give preference to one that is illustrated.  I prize my Bunyan's "Pilgrim's Progress" as much for its charming pictures as for its letterpress.  As pictures adorn a book, so let our kindly words and loving deeds be pleasant illustrations of the Christ who dwells within. Paul said, " I live, yet not I, but Christ liveth within me"; but people cannot see the Christ within you. They are like children, who cannot read the words of a book, but can understand it from the pictures. Therefore, let your life be an adorning picture of the doctrine that the gentle and loving Christ dwells within His disciples. 2. It may also be likened to a letter from a loved one. A month or two ago, I received a loving letter from Southport, from one of our orphan children who is now dangerously ill; and in her letter, she enclosed two or three beautiful flowers which she had begged from somebody's garden. The letter was not elegantly expressed or beautifully written, but those flowers spoke to my heart; they made the letter beautiful. Let us adorn the epistles of our lives with the beautiful flowers of peace and gentleness. Your life may be but humble and poor—some people may even call you vulgar ; but still you may adorn yourself with the perfume of love, and your life shall lead men to God. 3. I think, too, that Christianity may be likened to a shelter in the wilderness of a prodigal's life. See him yonder, afar off, half naked, hungry, brokenhearted, looking for home, and while he looks and longs for home, his father runs, and falls on his neck, and kisses him, and orders a feast to welcome him. But soon after, his elder brother drew nigh to the house, and hearing music and dancing, he cried, " What means this ? " When he was told that it was done to welcome his younger brother, he was angry and would not go in. The elder brother did not adorn, but blurred the doctrine of God our Saviour. The father adorned the doctrine that God loves the penitent sinner ; and you should copy his spirit into your life. When you forgive men, do it kindly and thoroughly. A man or a woman—it may be your workmate, or your brother, or child—having been sorely tempted, the weak one has fallen, and comes to your door hungry, naked, friendless, and penniless. Take her in, of course, with a kindly welcome ; and thus, adorn the doctrine that God freely and cheerfully pardons His human children. 4. The Christ-life may be further likened to seed—it is a thing of growth, and generally of slow growth, as is the case with things that are to be lasting. While character cannot be wholly transferred, the seeds of love and purity can be planted in us. The seeds of truth are planted in the receptive soil of our heart, which has to be prepared for it, and kept watered by prayer and faith, and continually weeded of those wild inclinations which always choke the plant. Like a divine graft, the Christ-life of purity and self-sacrifice is joined to us, and becomes our life, our love, our delight. When His Spirit dwells within us, we grow like Him in our character, and our fruit is after His kind. 5. When we receive the truths of Jesus and practise them from day to day, our lives shall exhibit and adorn His doctrine of sacred charity. We need more charity ; the charity which covereth a multitude of sins, and holds on to the erring ones to the very end, copying from Christ, who never forsook His wayward disciples. Let us show our charity when men need it most. If a man have plenty of friends fawning upon him, you need not bestow your friendship ; but when he is hungry, naked, or sick, or in grief, then be to him the adornment of the doctrine of charity. Show men that you believe in Christ by carrying out His teaching in the friendship and charity of your life. It is said that Francis the Second, of Prussia, took as his motto these words : " The king of Prussia shall be the first servant of his people." If you would be great in God's sight ; if you would be a power not only in this world but in the next, be a servant to your fellow-men, especially in their sore distress. One day, when Napoleon was walking in the streets of Paris, a man came along bearing a heavy burden on his shoulder. Napoleon at once stepped from the footpath into the carriage road, and allowed the man to pass. Some of his officers were very much surprised, saying, " Sire, why did you give way to that wretched man ? " Napoleon replied, " Should I not respect his burden ? " So, let us respect the misfortunes of our fellow-men. Let the men, women, and children in your street, through your noble life, be led to praise God ; and let your light so shine that all men may see the goodness of the Lord through you and be drawn unto Him. (*W. Birch.*) *Adorning the doctrine of God :—* We have been so educated that we are apt to think of beauty as simply an attribute of matter. We are apt to think that it can be transferred to moral conduct only by a figure of speech. Now, while we do not deny that in the constitution of the human mind there is such a condition of faculty as that the perception of outline, or colour, or harmony in matter, or materialness, produces a certain enjoyment, or, as we call it, a certain sense of the beautiful, we affirm that that right conduct— moral excellence as well as intellectual excellence—produces upon the mind just as clearly a sense of beauty. I might appeal to every man's own experience in his home-life—if his home-life is fortunate—whether the qualities that he discerned in father and mother were not admirable to him in his childhood; and whether they were not admirable to him all the way up. And to many of you, I speak with confidence when I say that, when you have wandered far from technical faith, yea, when you have largely fallen under the chill of doubt and unbelief, there still remains to you a silver cord not yet loosed, and a golden bowl not yet broken, and that that cord which holds you to faith is the mother's heart, and that that bowl is the father's heart, and that you believe against reason and in spite of unbelief, because of the faith yet lingering in your soul in the moral qualities that you have witnessed in the household. Is not courage beautiful? Is not disinterested benevolence beautiful? There is the case of the engineer who would not abandon his engine, but stood steadfast because he knew he had a hundred lives behind him. He stood upon the board, obviously knowing that he was rushing into the darkness of death. Then there was that other engineer who, on the burning ship upon Lake Erie, stood by the wheel, and steered for the shore, amidst the gathering and gaining flames, refusing to escape, and perished in the wheelhouse, in the vain effort to save those who were committed to his charge. Are not such deeds grand? Are not the qualities that inspire them beautiful? Is there any temple, is there any sculptured statue, is there any picture, that thrills the soul with such enthusiastic admiration as acts like these? And what are they but moral acts? How do all men say of them—"They are grand, they are beautiful, they are sublime." Look at the disinterestedness of woman's love. She was won from the father's house and household with all that was hopeful before her, to begin a life of love. He was full of generosity, full of manliness, and full of promise. The buds of young developing life hung on the bough, and were blossoming, until the fatal snare was set for him: until the growing habit of intoxication fastened upon him, and degradation settled down upon him, and little by little her life, with anguish of foresight, and with anguish of love, is overclouded. And yet, though her father's door stands open to call her back, she will not abandon him. She thinks of her children, she thinks of their future, and she will not abandon him. He grows morose. More and more he becomes like the animals. The beauty which she first saw in him lives now only in memory. The recollection of the past, or some dimly-painted dream of the future, is all the source of joy that is left her; for the present to her is full of woe, and sorrow, and humiliation. Gradually his friends forsake him. He is abandoned by one and by another. He is cast out of work and out of position. More and more is he degraded and bestialized; and well might she cry, "Who shall deliver me from the body of this death?" But she cries no such thing. No angel in heaven ever ministered more patiently, more tenderly, or more indefatigably for a soul than does she for him. And when at last he dies, and every person in the whole neighbourhood breathes freer, and says, "Thank God, he is gone, and she is free at last!" she is the only mourner; she is the only one that remembers the good that was in him; and she stands at his grave bowed down with real grief. She stood by him through good report and through evil report, as she promised; and love triumphed. Tell me, unbrutified men, is there no beauty in self-denial or in self-sacrifice? Take every single moral quality. Take those fruits of the Spirit recorded in the word of God which you will find in the fifth chapter of Galatians. Love—is not that beautiful? Is there anything that makes the face so seraphic as the full expression of a noble and high-minded love? Joy—even a curmudgeon of avarice will look with admiration upon the cheery face of outbursting joy in children. Peace, such as we often see when the passions are burned out, when the day and its heat are gone, and the soul in its old age sits waiting for the final revelation—this is beautiful. The beauty of the house is in the cradle or in the arm-chair. Long-suffering, gentleness, goodness, faith, meekness, self-control—are not these, when they exist in plenary power, esteemed by mankind honourable and beautiful? and do they not excite the involuntary exclamation of surprise? Now, it is on account of the intrinsic beauty of moral quality that piety and religious life, in their higher forms, are spoken of in the word of God as beautiful; and the consummation of piety in the social estate, in the Church, whether in the present or in the future, is celebrated all the way through the Bible as beautiful. When the beauty that is in moral quality shall be developed and made conspicuous; when not merely here and there a person, or a handful, or a household, are harmonious, all the others being relatively at discords; when not only single families in a neighbourhood, or single members in a Church are at peace; but when, in serried ranks, men shall shine with the beauty of holiness, and be lifted into a higher state in which they are able to give positiveness to the fruits of the spirit; when neighbour does it to neighbour, and it becomes the public sentiment, and the air is full of it—then will come the millennial day; then will be realized that enchanting vision which danced in the air before the prophet's eye; then shall men live together in righteousness; then shall that state be known which is symbolized by the lying down of the lion with the lamb; then all brute natures, all that live by vice, and cruelty, and wickedness, shall be cleansed out of the earth; and all men shall rejoice in the light, and in the glory, and in the supremacy of those spiritual experiences which belong to a religious life. It is often the case, when persons are brought into the Christian life—especially when in great numbers, and under great excitement—that the first thought of every one is, "Now, what shall I do?" And some begin to think of tracts, and wonder if it would not be well for them to have a district. Others inquire if they had not better go out and see their young friends, and preach to them. They are taught explicitly that they must go to work. It is said to them, "You are converted; now go to work. Start prayer-meetings. Bring in the neighbourhood." I do not say that these things are to be deprecated: on the contrary, in due degree, and with proper discretion, they all may be duties; but to represent a Christian life as having its first exhibition and its peculiar testimony in setting itself to work on and about somebody else is a grave mistake. My advice to every one of you that has found the Lord Jesus Christ, and that is living in a joyful faith, is, make yourselves more comely. Look to your thoughts and dispositions. Begin with yourself in your relations to brother and sister, or to father and mother. Let every duty that is incumbent upon you as child, or husband, or wife, rise instantly to an exalted place, and become more luminous, more beautiful, better. And if, having made home more heavenly, if—your disposition being ripened and beautified—there be opportunity for enterprise with others, do not by any indolence or misconception neglect that opportunity. Wherever you are, make those who are next to you in the relation of life see that you are a better man since you became a Christian than you were before, as a door-keeper, or as a doer of errands, as a book-keeper, as a salesman, as a schoolboy or a schoolgirl. In whatever station God has placed you, in the performance of your special duty, let the testimony of the Lord Jesus Christ be so borne that men, seeing the things which you do, may be attracted to Him by the exhibition of your personal character in your relations. Remember that the essential power of the gospel of Christ, in so far as you are concerned, will lie in how much of Christ you have in you. It is not profession, nor is it doctrine, though it were preached by never so eloquent lips, that has power with the world; it is Christlikeness in men. It is living as Christ lived, not in outward condition, but in inward disposition. He came down that we might go up. Though He was rich, for our sakes He became poor, that we through His poverty might become rich. He wept that we need not weep. He was a man of sorrows and acquainted with grief, that He might lift others out of the lower sphere. He accepted poverty as a means of enriching us. You are to follow Christ's example; and you can preach no more of Him than you practise. (*H. W. Beecher.*)  *All-round Christianity:*—In this Titus is counselled to place plainly before the several classes of people who claim to belong to the Church of Christ the virtues they are expected to cultivate and the vices they must carefully shun. Each class and each rank has its own special duties to perform, its own special temptations to resist, its own testimony for Christ to bear. There is no class, and there is no individual exempt from this. Titus must make no respect of persons, and neglect no class. He must not influence class against class, but address himself to each, and tell each how to act towards the others. Each class is under obligation to fulfil its duties towards others so faithfully that it may be seen at once that they are the disciples of Christ. Now, if every class of professing Christians were to act in this way, were to strive so to act—were to think less of the failure of others in the fulfilment of duty and more of their own, were to look at home first and set about correcting what is wrong there—what a wonderful transformation would be effected in the face of society. Masters would ask, not, "Are my workmen as diligent as they ought to be?" but "Do I deal as fairly with them as I should?" Servants would ask, not "Is my master as just towards me as the law of Christ commands?" but "Am I doing what in me lies to fulfil my duty towards him, as Christ would have me?" Landlords would ask, not "Are my tenants as industrious and thrifty as they might be?" but "Am I dealing with them in as fair and brotherly a spirit as I should?" Tenants would ask, not "Is my landlord not exacting from me more than he ought?" but "Am I as careful over his property as I should be—as I might be?" And so on throughout all the relationships of life. But, alas! few think of adopting this method of adorning their Christian profession. They think it enough to adorn that profession if they point out to one class the faults of the others, or bemoan the wrongs done to themselves, forgetful of, or heedless to, the wrongs they themselves do to others. It was not thus that our Lord desired His people, His followers, to act. No; each man was to begin with himself, pull the beam out of his own eye before he set himself to extract the mote out of his neighbour's. But not only are we apt to overlook the applicability of the law of Christian duty to ourselves; we are apt also to overlook its thoroughness and comprehensiveness. There are not a few whose adornment of the Christian doctrine goes little, if any, further than the acceptance of the Church creed, and attendance with more or less regularity on certain church services. It is not an uncommon thing to meet men and women who boast of, who are sincerely proud of, their orthodoxy and Church attendance, and who do not think it wrong to practise in business what are called, say, the "tricks of trade," or in private life to indulge in some one or more vices. I have myself heard a person in a maudlin state of intoxication lamenting the sad condition of a friend who had expressed himself doubtful of the expediency of infant baptism. Then, again, we have instances of people who magnify one particular virtue, which they happen to practise, and who become so proud of it that they quite forget the other virtues which our Christian faith inculcates quite as much on them. The virtue may, after all, however, not be in their case a virtue at all, or be very little of a virtue. Christ would not have the temperate man less temperate than he is, but He would ask him, though he has no inclination towards strong drink, to examine himself and see if he has no inclination towards something else which is bad, and set himself against that. Christ would ask him, not to think himself perfect because he did not indulge in a sin that has not the least attraction for him, but to try and find out the sins that do "beset him," and show his perfection—the strength of his character and the power of his faith—by overcoming them. It may be a temper that is not yet under his control—a querulous disposition that destroys the peace of his home—a spirit of fault-finding and uncharitableness that mars the blessedness of all intercourse with him, and transforms even his very truths into falsehoods. Christ would have us adorn the doctrine of God our Saviour in not one thing but in all things— have us show that it raises us above the vice of drunkenness, certainly, but also above that of malice, covetousness, selfishness, and all uncharitableness. But this, I repeat, is what too many professing Christians forget or overlook. Men are everywhere prone to make compromises in the matter of Christian duty—to hold, it may be, by the creed and forget the commandments, to think of the sins of others and forget their own, or cling to one virtue and make it to do duty for all the others. Let us be warned against this folly. Let us remember that our Christian faith, if it brings us light, lays on us also obligation; if it reveals the love of God towards us it reveals also what He requires of us. Let us remember how comprehensive is its scope, and how personal is its appeal to us. It is the spirit of a new life—a new life that must pervade our whole being and manifest its sanctifying presence in every act we do and every word we say. (*W. Ewen, B.D.*)

Vers. 11–14. **The grace of God that bringeth salvation.**—*The gospel :*—I. WHAT IS HERE SAID OF ITS NATURE. 1. The name. "The grace of God." 2. The subject. "Bringing salvation." 3. The manifestation. "Hath appeared." (1) None are excluded from its benefits. (2) None are exempt from its appointments. II. ITS INFLUENCE. 1. How the gospel teaches. (1) Precept. (2) Example. (3) Motive. (4) Real and spiritual operation and efficiency. 2. What the gospel teaches. (1) What it teaches us to deny? "Ungodliness and worldly lusts." (2) What it teaches us to do? "To live soberly, righteously, and godly in the present world." (3) What it teaches us to expect? "Looking for that blessed hope and the glorious appearing of the great God and our Saviour Jesus Christ." (4) What it teaches us to acknowledge? "Who gave Himself," &c. (*W. Jay.*)    *The gospel of the grace of God :*— I. ITS DISTINGUISHING CHARACTERISTICS. "The grace of God." 1. The gift. 2. Its objects. 3. Its purpose. II. THE UNIVERSALITY OF ITS APPEARANCE. 1. Adapted for all. 2. Revealed for all. 3. To be proclaimed to all. III. THE INESTIMABLE BOON WHICH IT BESTOWS. "Salvation." 1. From the condemning power of sin. 2. From the defilement of sin. 3. From the love of sin. 4. From the power of sin. 5. From the punishment of sin. IV. ITS PRACTICAL INFLUENCE. "Teaching us," &c. The way of salvation is the highway of holiness and of purity; the unclean may not pass over it; and within the gates of the celestial city "there shall enter nothing that defileth, that worketh abomination, or that maketh a lie." Wherever this gospel hath come, "in demonstration of the Spirit and with power," it hath swept away the obscure and execrable rites, the foul abominations, the detestable practices of paganism. Wherever this gospel hath come "in demonstration of the Spirit and with power," it hath purified the polluted, it hath made the dishonest honest, the intemperate sober, the licentious chaste. It has converted the monster of depravity into the humble, correct, consistent, temperate disciple of Christ. The abandoned woman it has purified and refined; and he who was at once the disgrace, the dishonour, of his family, of society, and of his country, renewed, reformed, sanctified, made holy, it has placed at the feet of the Redeemer, like the recovered maniac, "clothed and in his right mind." (*T. Raffles, D.D.*) *The extensiveness of the gospel offers:*—That the message which Jesus was anointed to deliver emanated from the sovereign goodness and everlasting mercy of Jehovah, whereby before all worlds He had devised a plan for the restoration of ruined man, and contains a revelation of His will, is a truth at once most animating and important. It is a firm conviction of this momentous truth which induces the believer to set a proper value on the gospel as the message of glad tidings of great joy. I. Our thoughts are directed, first, to THE SOURCE OF THE GOSPEL, and that source is the grace of God. The proper signification of the word "grace" is favour—unmerited goodness and mercy in a superior conferring benefit upon others. The grace spoken of in the text is the revelation of the Divine will set forth in the gospel, which, in the strictest sense, may be termed "the grace of God"; it being a revelation to which man had no title, setting forth promises of which man was utterly unworthy, unfolding a plan of redemption which man had no reason to expect. This grace "bringeth salvation." Herein consists its importance. "What shall I do to be saved?" "What good thing shall I do to inherit eternal life?" "Wherewith shall I come before the Lord, and bow myself before the high God?" These are vitally important questions—questions which will frequently present themselves even to the most careless, and they can be satisfactorily answered in the gospel alone. The gospel bringeth salvation, for it points out to man the means of his recovery from guilt and degradation. This salvation is complete and infinite, including all the blessings of the everlasting covenant—that covenant which displays to us the mercy and love of God the Father; the benefits of the incarnation, life, crucifixion, ascension, and intercession of God the Son; and all the enlightening, enlivening, and sanctifying influences of God the Holy Ghost. In the possession of these consists our salvation. The gospel directs man to a Saviour who has promised, and is able and willing, to bestow any blessing upon those who believe in Him: it promises pardon, reconciliation, peace; it unfolds the glories of the eternal world; and it invites and stimulates the sinner to strive, through grace, to become meet for the heavenly inheritance. II. Now consider THE PERSONS for whose benefit this grace of God hath appeared. The apostle says, "The grace of God, that bringeth salvation hath appeared unto all men"; or, according to the translation in the margin of our Bibles, "The grace of God, which bringeth salvation to all men, hath appeared"; and this rendering I conceive to be the more correct. The gospel, then, is described as bringing salvation to all men; that is, as offering to all who accept it free and full remission of sin, through the blood of the Lord Jesus; as opening to all believers the gate of the kingdom of heaven. The gospel is precisely suited for all the wants of a fallen sinner; it meets him in the hour of difficulty; and, consequently, its offers of mercy are addressed to every sinner. In the manifestation of Jesus to the wise men, who came from the east to worship Him; in the prophetic declaration of the aged Simeon, that the Child whom he took up in his arms should be a light to lighten the Gentiles; in the rending of the veil of the temple, when Jesus had given up the ghost; in the unlimited commission— "Go ye into all the world, and preach the gospel to every creature"; and in their qualification for this important work, by the miraculous gift of tongues, we discover that the new dispensation was designed for the spiritual and eternal benefit of the whole human race. The rich dispensation of mercy revealed in the gospel beautifully illustrates the gracious character of our heavenly Father. It is calculated to remove all erroneous views of His attributes, His mercy, His compassion, His tenderness towards the works of His hands. Why that gospel should not have been clearly manifested for so many ages after the fall of man—why eighteen centuries should have elapsed, and millions of our fellow-creatures should still be immersed in the gross darkness of heathen superstition—is one of those secret things which belong to the Lord our God. It is not our province to sit in judgment on the wisdom of Jehovah's plans—to weigh the wisdom of Jehovah's counsels; neither are we to seek to pry into the mysterious dealings of His providence. We are, rather, thankfully to acknowledge the blessings bestowed upon ourselves, and earnestly seek to improve them to the uttermost; recollecting that responsibility is commensurate with privilege. (*T. Bissland, M.A.*) *The grace of God :*—I. THE ORIGINAL FIRST MOVING CAUSE OF ALL THE BLESSINGS WE HAVE FROM GOD IS GRACE. 1. Survey all the blessings of the covenant, and from first to last you will see grace doth all. Election, vocation, justification, sanctification, glorification, all is from grace. 2. To limit the point. Though it is of grace, yet not to exclude Christ, not to exclude the means of salvation. 3. My next work shall be to give you some reasons why it must be so that grace is the original cause of all the blessings we receive from God; because it is most for the glory of God, and most for the comfort of the creature. (1) It is most convenient for the glory of God to keep up the respects of the creature to Him in a way suitable to His majesty. (2) It is most for the comfort of the creature. Grace is the original cause of all the good we expect and receive from God, that we may seek the favour of God with hope and retain it with certainty. II. GRACE IN THE DISCOVERIES OF THE GOSPEL HATH SHINED OUT IN A GREATER BRIGHTNESS THAN EVER IT DID BEFORE. 1. What a darkness there was before the eternal gospel was brought out of the bosom of God. There was a darkness both among Jews and Gentiles. In the greatest part of the world there was utter darkness as to the knowledge of grace, and in the Church nothing but shadows and figures. 2. What and how much of grace is now discovered? I answer—(1) The wisdom of grace. The gospel is a mere riddle to carnal reason, a great mystery (1 Tim. iii. 16). (2) The freeness of grace both in giving and accepting. (3) The efficacy and power of grace. (4) The largeness and bounty of grace. (5) The sureness of grace. III. THE GRACE OF GOD REVEALED IN THE GOSPEL IS THE GREAT MEANS OF SALVATION, OR A GRACE THAT TENDS TO SALVATION. 1. It hath a moral tendency that way; for there is the history of salvation what God hath done on His part; there are the counsels of salvation what we must do on our part; and there are excellent enforcements to encourage us to embrace this salvation. 2. Because it hath the promise of the Spirit's assistance (Rom. i. 16). The gospel is said to be "the power of God unto salvation," not only because it is a powerful instrument which God hath appropriated to this work, but this is the honour God puts upon the gospel that He will join and associate the operation of His Spirit with no other doctrine but this. IV. THIS SALVATION WHICH THE GRACE OF GOD BRINGETH IS FREE FOR ALL THAT WILL ACCEPT IT. God excludes none but those that exclude themselves. It is said to appear to all men—1. Because it is published to all sorts of men; they all have a like favour in the general offer (John vi. 37). 2. All that accept have a like privilege; therefore this grace is said to appear to all men. There is no difference of nations, nor of conditions of life, nor of lesser opinions in religion, nor of degrees of grace. See all summed up by the apostle (Col. iii. 11). (*T. Manton, D.D.*) *The Epiphany and mission of grace :*—To this important statement the apostle is led up by the consideration of certain very homely and practical duties which fall to the lot of Christians in various walks of life, and these matters he refers to as "the things pertaining to sound doctrine." He has a word of practical counsel for several distinct classes of persons; for he knows the wisdom of being definite. In the connection indicated by that little word "for" we have both an introduction to, and a striking illustration of, the great truth that the passage is designed to set forth. It is the gospel with its wondrous revelation of grace that is to provide us with new and high incentives to a life of practical virtue and holiness. It is because we are not under the law, but under grace, that the righteousness of the law is to be fulfilled in us. To destroy the works of the devil, and to restore and perfect the grandest work of God on earth, was indeed an undertaking worthy of such conditions as the Incarnation and the atonement. The apostle speaks of grace itself before he proceeds to indicate the effects of grace, and of the first grand object and work of grace before he proceeds to enlarge upon its ulterior effects. He begins with the assertion that "the grace of God which bringeth salvation to all men hath appeared." In these opening words, first our attention is invited to this central object, the grace of God, then to the fact of its epiphany or manifestation, and then to its first most necessary purpose and mission—the bringing of salvation within the reach of all men. I. ALL TRUE AND EVANGELICAL RELIGION MUST HAVE ITS COMMENCEMENT IN THE APPREHENSION OF DIVINE GRACE, AND THEREFORE IT IS OF NO SMALL IMPORTANCE THAT WE SHOULD ENDEAVOUR CLEARLY TO UNDERSTAND WHAT IS DENOTED BY

THE WORD. Divine grace, we may say, is the child of love and the parent of mercy. The essential love of the great Father's heart takes definite form, and accommodates itself to our need; reveals itself in facts, and presents itself for our acceptance; and then we call it grace. That grace received rescues from the disastrous effects of sin; heals our inward diseases, and comforts our sorrows; and then we call it mercy. But grace does not exhaust itself in the production of mercy any more than love exhausts itself in the production of grace. The child leads us back to the parent; the experience of mercy leads us back to that "grace wherein we stand"; and the enjoyment of grace prepares us for the life of love, and for that wondrous reciprocity of affection in which the heavenly Bridegroom and His Bride are to be bound together for ever. Thus of the three mercy ever reaches the heart first; and it is through accepted mercy that we apprehend revealed grace; similarly it is through the revelations of grace that we learn the secret of eternal love. And as with the individual so with mankind at large. Mercy, swift-winged mercy, was the first celestial messenger that reached a sin-stricken world; and in former dispensations it was with mercy that men had most to do. But if former dispensations were dispensations of mercy, the present is pre-eminently the dispensation of grace, in which it is our privilege not only to receive mercy, but to apprehend the attitude of God towards us from which the mercy flows. But let us remember that though specially revealed to us now, the grace of God towards humanity has existed from the very first. The Lamb was slain in the Divine foreknowledge before the foundation of the world. But the grace of God has in it a further and higher object than the mere provision of a remedy for human sin—than what is merely remedial. God has purposed in His own free favour towards mankind to raise man to a position of moral exaltation and glory, the very highest, so far as we know, that can be occupied or aspired to by a created intelligence. Such is the destiny of humanity. This is the singular favour which God designs for the sons of men. God's favour flows forth to other intelligences also, but not to the same degree, and it is not manifested after the same fashion. This eternal purpose of God, however, which has run through the long ages, was not fully revealed to the sons of men until the fulness of time arrived. It was revealed only in parts and in fragments, so to speak. From Adam to John the Baptist every man that ever went to heaven went there by the grace of God. The grace of God has constantly been in operation, but it was operating in a concealed fashion. Even those who were the subjects of Divine grace seem scarcely to have known how it reached them, or in what manner they were to be affected by any provision that it might make to meet their human sins. Before the full favour of God could be revealed to mankind it would seem to have been necessary first of all that man should be put under a disciplinary training, which should induce within him a conviction of the necessity for the intervention of that favour, and dispose him to value it when it came. Grace, we have already said, is the child of love and the parent of mercy. We discover now that the love of God is not a passive, inert possibility, but a living power that takes to itself definite form, and hastens to meet and overcome the forces of evil to which we owe our ruin. II. But further, the apostle not only calls our attention to Divine grace, but he proceeds to state with great emphasis THAT IT HAS APPEARED OR BEEN MADE MANIFEST. We are no longer left in doubt as to its existence, or permitted to enjoy its benefits without knowing whence they flow. In order to be manifested, the grace of God needed not only to be affirmed, but to be illustrated, I may say demonstrated, and then only was man called upon to believe in it. It might have been written large enough for all the world to see, that God was love. It might have been blazoned upon the starry heavens so that every eye might have read the wondrous sentence, and yet I apprehend we should have been slow to grasp the truth which the words contain, had they not been brought within reach of our finite apprehension in concrete form in the personal history, in the life, in the action, in the sorrow, in the death of God's own Son. When I turn my gaze towards the person of Christ I am at liberty to doubt God's favour towards me no longer. I read it in every action, I discover it in every word. Here is the first thought that brings rest to the heart of man. It has been demonstrated by the Incarnation and by the Atonement, that God's attitude on His side towards us is already one of free favour—favour toward all, however far we may have fallen, and however undeserving we may be in ourselves. You often hear people talking about making their peace with God. Well, the phrase may be used to indicate what is perfectly correct, but the expression in itself is most incorrect, for peace with God is already made. God's attitude towards us is already an assured thing. We have no occasion to go about to ask ourselves, "How shall we win God's favour?" It is possible for a person to be full of friendly intentions to me, and yet for me to retain an attitude of animosity and enmity towards him. That does not alter his character towards me, or his attitude towards me; but it does prevent me from reaping any benefit from that attitude. And so, I repeat, the only point of uncertainty lies in our attitude towards God, not in His attitude towards us. III. Thus the apostle affirms that THIS GRACE OF GOD "BRINGETH SALVATION TO EVERY MAN." Yes, God's free favour, manifested in the person of His own blessed Son, is designed to produce saving effects upon all. God makes no exception, excludes none. All are not saved. But why not? Not because the grace of God does not bring salvation to every man, but because all men do not receive the gift which the grace of God has brought to them. There are necessarily two parties to such a transaction. Before any benefit can accrue from a gift there must be a willingness on the one side to give, and a willingness on the other side to receive, and unless there be both of these conditions realised no satisfactory result can ensue. Here then is a question for us all: What has the grace of God, which is designed to have a saving effect upon all men, done for us? Has it saved us, or only enhanced our condemnation? Now we maintain that the enjoyment of the knowledge of salvation by the remission of sins is needed before our experience can assume a definitely Christian form. The first thing that grace does is to bring salvation to me; and until I accept this I am not in a position to accept her other gifts. Grace cannot teach until I am in a position to learn, and I am not in a position to learn until I am relieved from anxiety and fear as to my spiritual condition. Go into yonder prison, and set that wretched felon in the condemned cell to undertake some literary work, if he is a literary man. Put the pen into his hand, place the ink and the paper before him. He flings down the pen in disgust. How can he set to work to write a history or to compose a romance, however talented or gifted he may be by nature, so long as the hangman's rope is over his head and the prospect of a coming execution staring him in the face? Obviously the man's thoughts are all in another direction—the question of his own personal safety preoccupies his mind. Give him that pen and paper to write letters which he thinks may influence persons in high quarters with a view to obtaining a reprieve, and his pen will move quickly enough. I can understand his filling up reams of paper on that subject, but not on any other. Is it likely that a God who has shown His favour towards us by the gift of His own Son should desire to keep us in uncertainty as to the effects of that grace upon our own case? Does not the very fact, that it is grace that has brought salvation to us, render it certain that it must be in the mind of God that we should have the full enjoyment of it? Let us rather ask, how can we obtain this knowledge of salvation, this inward conviction that all is well? The answer is a very simple one. Grace brings salvation within our reach as something designed for us. Not to tantalize us by exciting desires destined never to be realised, but in order that we may have the full benefit of it—the free favour of God has brought salvation within our reach to the very doors of our hearts. Surely we dishonour God when we for a moment suppose that He does not intend us to enjoy the blessing which His grace brings to us. All the deep and precious lessons that grace has to teach are, we may say, simply so many deductions from the first great object lesson—Calvary. It is through the Cross of Christ that the grace of God hath reached a sinful world; it is on the Cross that grace is revealed and by that Cross that its reality is demonstrated. But we may also add that it is in the Cross that grace lies hidden. Yes, it is all there; but faith has to search the store-house and examine the hidden treasure, and find out more and more of the completeness of that great salvation which the grace of God has brought within our reach; nor shall we ever know fully all that has thus been brought within our reach until we find ourselves saved at last with an everlasting salvation—saved from all approach of evil or danger into that kingdom of glory which grace has opened to all believers. (*W. H. M. H. Aitken, M.A.*) *The grace of God in bringing salvation to all men :*—I. THE ORIGIN OF SALVATION. 1. Man did not deserve it. 2. It was unsolicited. 3. It was entirely the result of Divine grace. The grace of God—(1) Made all the arrangements necessary for salvation. Devised the astounding plan. Fixed upon the means, time, &c. The grace of God—(2) Brought the author of salvation. "Ye know the grace of our Lord Jesus Christ," &c. (2 Cor. viii. 9). (3) It brought the message of salvation. Gospel is emphatically the gospel of the grace of God (Acts xx. 24). (4) It brings the application of salvation to the soul. We are called by His grace—justified freely by His grace—sanctified by His grace—kept and preserved by His grace—and the topstone is brought on amid ascriptions of "Grace,

grace unto it." II. THE EXTENT OF SALVATION. The grace of God bringeth salvation—1. To all classes and degrees of men.   To the rich and the poor ; noble and ignoble ; monarch and the peasant; the ruler and the slave.   2.   To men of all grades of moral guilt.   It includes the moralist, and excludes not the profane.   3. To men of all ages.   III. THE INFLUENCE OF SALVATION ON THE MORAL CHARACTER OF MAN.   It teaches and enforces the necessity of—1. The abandonment of ungodliness and worldly lusts.   2. Sobriety of conduct.   3. Righteousness of life.   4. Godliness of heart.   Application : 1. How we should rejoice in the riches and fulness of Divine grace.   2. How necessary that we cordially receive the invaluable boon it presents.   3. And how important that we practically exemplify the moral lessons it communicates.   (*J. Burns, D.D.*)       *The gospel described :*—1. A choice and excellent description of the gospel ; it is the grace of God, that is the doctrine of God's free grace and gratuitous favour declared in Christ to poor sinners.   2. The joyful message which the gospel brings, and that is salvation ; the gospel makes a gracious tender of salvation, and that universally to lost and undone sinners.   3. The clear light and evidence that it does hold forth this message in and by ; it has appeared or shined forth like the day-star or the rising sun.   4. The extent of its glorious beams, how far they reach. It is tendered to all without restriction or limitation. (1) As to nations, Jew or Gentile.   (2) As to persons, rich or poor, bond or free.   (3) Without restriction in reference to the degree of their graces.   5. The great lesson which the gospel teaches, negative and positive.   (*a*) Negative, to deny ungodliness and worldly lusts ; where, by ungodliness, understand all sins committed against the first table ; by worldly lusts, all sins committed against the second table ; called worldly lusts because the object of them is worldly things, and because they are the lusts of worldly men.   (*b*) Positive, to live : (1) Soberly : he begins with our duty to ourselves, then to our neighbour, and last of all to God, and so proceeds from the easier to the harder duties : and observe the connection, soberly and righteously and godly, not disjunctively ; as if to live soberly, righteously, or in pretence godly, were sufficient.   A sobriety in speech, in behaviour, in apparel, in eating and drinking, in recreations, and in the enjoyment of lawful satisfactions.   (2) Righteously, exercising justice and charity towards our neighbour ; he that is uncharitable is unjust and unrighteous, and the unrighteous shall no more enter into the kingdom of God than the unholy ; and all a person's pretences to godliness are but hypocrisy without righteousness toward our neighbour.   (3) Godly, godliness has an internal and external part ; the internal and inward part of godliness consists in a right knowledge of Him, in a fervent love unto Him, in an entire trust and confidence in Him, in an holy fear to offend Him, in subjecting our wills entirely to Him, in holy longings for the fruition and enjoyment of Him.   The external and outward part of godliness consists in adoration and bodily worship ; this is due to God from us ; He was the Creator of the body as well as of the soul, and will glorify the body as well as the soul ; therefore we are to glorify God with our bodies, and with our spirits, which are the Lord's.   6. The time when and the place where this lesson is to be learned, in this present world.   Here is the place, and now is the time when this duty of living soberly, righteously, and godly in this present world is to be performed by us.   Learn, that a sober, righteous, and godly life in this present world is absolutely necessary in order to our obtaining the happiness and glory of the world to come. (*W. Burkitt, M.A.*)       *The grace of God :*—Although the doctrine of the Churches of the Old and New Testament be the very selfsame in regard—1. Of the author, who is God ; 2. Substance and matter, which is perfect righteousness required in both ; 3. Scope and end to the justification of a sinner before God ; yet are there diverse accidental differences between them which, that we may the better understand both the offices and the benefits by Christ, are meet to be known.   Some of them we shall note out of these words as we shall come unto them. (1) The first difference is in that the gospel is called grace, which word the law acknowledgeth not ; nay, these two are opposed, to be under the law and to be under grace.   To be under the law is not to be under it as a rule of life, for so all believers on earth, yea the saints and angels in heaven, are under it ; but to be under the yoke of it, which neither we nor our fathers were able to bear.   For to omit the least part of the yoke, standing in the observation of—1. Many, 2. Costly, 3. La︰or-ious, 4. Burdensome ceremonies, what a killing letter is the law which commandeth inward and perfect righteousness, for nature and actions, and that in our own persons ? which promiseth life upon no other condition but of works, " Do this, and live " ; and these must be such as must be framed according to that perfect light and holiness of nature in which we are created, which wrappeth us under the curse of sin. Now to be under grace is to be freed from all this bondage; not only from those elements and rudiments of the world, but especially—1. When the yoke of personal obedience to justification is by grace translated from believers to the person of Christ our surety, so that He doing the law we might live by it. 2. When duties are not urged according to our perfect estate of creation, but according to the present measure of grace received; not according to full and perfect righteousness, but according to the sincerity and truth of the heart, although from weak and imperfect faith and love: not as meriting anything, but only as testifying the truth of our conversion, in all which the Lord of His grace accepteth the will for the deed done. 3. When the most heavy curse of the law is removed from our weak shoulders and laid upon the back of Jesus Christ, even as His obedience is translated unto us, and thus there is no condemnation to those that are in Him. 4. When the strength of the law is abated so as believers may send it to Christ for performance, for it cannot vex us as before the ministry of grace it could; which is another law, namely of faith, to which we are bound, the which not only can command us as the former, but also give grace and power to obey and perform in some acceptable sort the commandment. And this is the doctrine of grace which we are made partakers of. (*T. Taylor, D.D.*) *Genuine Christianity*:—I. A TRUE AND GRAPHIC OUTLINE OF DOCTRINE ESSENTIAL TO SALVATION. 1. How ancient the purpose of this grace. 2. How great and glorious its nature. 3. How benignant its design. 4. How unrestricted its manifestation. II. A VIEW OF THOSE WORKS WHICH ACCOMPANY SALVATION. 1. Vigilant self-denial. 2. The right governance of the moral relations of life. III. MOTIVES BY WHICH COMBINED FAITH AND OBEDIENCE MAY BE SUSTAINED AND ENFORCED. 1. The temporary nature of the discipline. 2. The self-sacrifice of Christ. 3. The future manifestation of Christ. (*Jas. Foster, B.A.*) *The soul-culture of the world*:—I. THE INSTRUMENT OF TRUE SOUL-CULTURE. "The grace of God," *i.e.*, the gospel. 1. It is the love of God. 2. The love of God to save. 3. The love of God revealed to all. II. THE PROCESS OF TRUE SOUL-CULTURE. 1. The renunciation of a wrong course. 2. The adoption of a right course. 3. The fixing of the heart upon a glorious future. III. THE END OF TRUE SOUL-CULTURE. 1. Moral redemption. 2. Spiritual restoration to Christ. 3. Complete devotedness to holy labour. 4. The self-sacrifice of Christ. His gift teaches the enormity of moral evil. (*D. Thomas, D.D.*) *The soul's rest*:—When the illustrious, learned, and wealthy John Selden was dying, he said to Archbishop Usher, "I have surveyed most of the learning that is among the sons of men, and my study is filled with books and manuscripts (he had 8,000 volumes in his library) on various subjects; but at present I cannot recollect any passage out of all my books and papers whereon I can rest my soul, save this from the sacred Scriptures: 'The grace of God that bringeth salvation,'" &c. **Hath appeared to all men.**—*Love made visible*:—I. The apostle sets forth, as the foundation of all, THE APPEARANCE OF THE GRACE OF GOD. Grace, the theological term which, to many of us, sounds so cold and unreal and remote, is all throbbing with tenderness and warm with life if we understand what it means. It means the pulsation of the heart of God pouring a tide of gracious love on sinful men, who do not deserve one drop of it to fall upon them, and who dwell so far beneath His loftiness that the love is made still more wonderful by the condescension which makes it possible. The lofty loves the low, and the love is grace. The righteous loves the sinful, and the love is grace. Then, says my text, there is something which has made this Divine love of God, so wonderful in its loftiness, and equally wonderful in its passing by men's sinfulness, visible to men. The grace has "appeared." Scientists can make sounds visible by the symmetrical lines into which heaps of sand upon a bit of paper are cast by the vibration of a string. God has made invisible love plain to the sight of all men, because He has sent us His Son. II. NOTICE THE UNIVERSAL SWEEP OF THIS GRACE. The words should be read, "The grace of God, that bringeth salvation to all men, hath appeared." It brings salvation to all men. It does not follow from that, that all men take the salvation which it brings. Notice the underlying theory of a universal need that lies in these words. The grace brings salvation to all men, because all men need that more than anything else. In the notion of salvation there lies the two ideas of danger and of disease. It is healing and it is safety; therefore, if it be offered to all, it is because all men are sick of a sore disease, and stand in imminent and deadly peril. That is the only theory of men's deepest need which is true to the facts of human existence. III. NOTICE THE GREAT WORK OF THIS GRACE MADE VISIBLE. It seems to be a wonderful descent from "the grace of God which bringeth salvation to all hath appeared" to "teaching us." Is that all? Is that worth much? If by "teaching " we mean merely a reiteration in words, addressed to the understanding or the heart, of the great principles of morality and conduct, it is a very poor thing, and a tremendous come-down from the apostle's previous words. Such an office is not what the world wants. To try to cure the world's evils by teaching, in that narrow sense of the expression, is something like trying to put a fire out by reading the Riot Act to the flames. You want fire engines, and not paper proclamations, in order to stay their devouring course. But it is to be noticed that the expression here, in the original, means a great deal more than that kind of teaching. It means correcting, or chastening. Our Physician has in His great medicine-chest balm and bandages for all wounds. But He has also a terrible array of gleaming blades with sharp edges, and of materials for cauterising and burning away proud flesh. And if ever we are to be made good and pure, as God wants to make us, it must be through a discipline that will often be agony, and will often be pain, and against the grain. For the one thing that God wants to do with men is to bring their wills into entire harmony with His. And we cannot have that done without much treatment which will inflict in love beneficent pain. No man can live beside that Lord without being rebuked moment by moment, and put to wholesome shame day by day, when he contrasts himself with that serene and radiant pattern and embodiment of all perfection. And no man can receive into his heart the powers of the world to come, the might of an indwelling Spirit, without that Spirit exercising as its first function that which Christ Himself told us it would perform (John xvi. 8). (*A. Maclaren, D.D.*) *The universal offer of salvation:*—Salvation is offered to all men—I. IRRESPECTIVE OF THEIR VARYING MORAL CONDITIONS. Though "all have sinned," yet all are not sinners in the same degree, or after the same fashion. Sinners are of many kinds—young, old, beginners in offences, hardened in crime, sinners through ignorance, against light, &c. II. BECAUSE ALL MEN NEED IT. God recognises degrees of guilt and punishes "according to transgression." There are "few stripes" and "many stripes"; yet all need salvation, and all men may have it. III. BECAUSE GOD LOVES ALL. He is no respecter of persons, and has no delight in the death of him that dieth. "God so loved the world," &c. IV. BECAUSE CHRIST DIED FOR ALL. (*F. Wagstaff.*) *The gospel for all sorts of men:*—It bringeth salvation to all men, that is, all kinds and conditions of men, not to every particular or singular of the kinds, but to all the sorts and kinds of men, to servants as well as masters, to Gentile as well as Jew, to poor as well as rich. Thus is it said that God would have all men saved, that is, of all sorts of men some. So Christ healed all diseases, that is, all kinds of diseases; and the Pharisees tithed all herbs, that is, all kinds; for they took not every particular herb for tithe, but took the tenth of every kind, and not the tenth of every herb. (*T. Taylor, D.D.*) *The grace of salvation appearing to all men:*—The grace of God is the prime mover in the work of salvation. It "bringeth salvation." Man had nothing to pay for it, and man could not merit it. I. BUT IN WHAT RESPECTS DOES THE GRACE OF GOD BRING SALVATION? Here we remark generally, that it brought it forward in the decree from everlasting. Again, the grace of God brought salvation forward another stage, by publishing the promise of it to man after his ruinous fall. This promise was to be the ground of man's faith and hope in God; and these graces were necessary for giving sinners an interest in the Divine salvation. The grace of God advanced salvation work still further when it brought the First-begotten into the world. It was on this occasion that it was purchased. To gain it, Christ had to sustain the rejections of men, the malice and wrath of evil spirits, and the wrath of His heavenly Father. No less conspicuous is the grace of God in applying to the soul the benefits of purchased redemption. It is not when persons have ceased from the love and commission of sin, that the Holy Spirit comes with power to call them effectually, and to unite them to the Lord Jesus Christ. No; He addresses Himself to His work when sinners are dead in trespasses and in sins—alienated from the life of God—without God and without hope in the world. But there is still another stage of the grace of God that bringeth salvation, and it is the time when Christ will raise His people from the dead, and make them sit visibly as they now sit representatively in heavenly places with Himself. II. We shall now turn your attention to THE NATURE OF THE SALVATION WHICH THE GRACE OF GOD THUS BRINGS TO SINNERS. And here you will notice in general that the term salvation implies a state of danger, or of actual immersion in suffering; and denotes the averting of the danger, or the deliverance from the suffering. We say of a man who has been delivered from a house on fire, that he has been saved. We also assert of him who has been drawn from a shipwreck and brought in life to land, that he has been saved. And in like manner, we affirm in regard to the man who has been set free from transgression and its train of consequences, that he has obtained salvation. More particularly, you will observe—1. That it is a salvation from the guilt of sin. 2. It includes deliverance from the defilement of sin. 3. Deliverance from the power of sin. 4. Deliverance from the very being of sin. 5. Liberation from the curse of God. 6. Freedom from the wrath of God. III. We have thus given you an outline of the salvation spoken of in the text, WE SHALL NOW INQUIRE IN WHAT RESPECTS IT APPEARS TO ALL MEN. There is one class of persons to whom salvation does more than appear; for they shall enjoy it in all its length and breadth. The chosen of God shall be set free from the guilt, the power, and being of sin, and redeemed from the wrath and curse of God. But there are some respects in which the salvation which they enjoy, presents itself to the view of others, who never come to the actual enjoyment of its precious blessings. 1. The grace that bringeth salvation appears to all, because time and space are given them for seeking and obtaining it. 2. The grace of salvation appears to all in the inspired Word and appointed ordinances. 3. The grace of salvation appears to all, inasmuch as mercy is offered to them without distinction. 4. The grace that bringeth salvation appears to all, in the common operations of the Holy Spirit. From our subject see—(1) Ground for accepting the salvation of the gospel. (2) Learn reason to fear lest we should not enter the heavenly rest through unbelief. (3) Ground of gratitude on the part of the people of God. They are distinguished above the rest of mankind. While salvation appears to others, it is possessed and enjoyed by them. We now propose—IV. To INQUIRE INTO WHAT IS MEANT BY THE TERMS ALL MEN. As to the import of the terms "all men," you will observe—1. That they cannot mean every individual of our race. It is matter of fact that many, both in the days of the apostles were, and in our own time are, wholly unenlightened by the good news of salvation. 2. The grace of God appears to men of all countries. This is no contradiction of what we formerly said; for although salvation has not yet been shown to all the individuals of our race, yet some of almost every kingdom under heaven have been made acquainted with the gospel of God's Son; and it is matter of promise that all the ends of the earth shall yet see the salvation of our God. 3. The grace of God appears to all kinds of men. None are excluded from it who do not exclude themselves. It is presented to persons of all ages and all ranks, to men of every kind of culture and attainment. Nor does the gospel inquire into a man's character, in order to discover whether he is entitled to salvation. Grace is offered to the moral and immoral—to the virtuous and the vicious. V. WE ARE NOW TO INVESTIGATE THE RESPECTS IN WHICH THE GRACE OF GOD APPEARS TO MEN IN GENERAL. Our text does not assert that the grace of God is enjoyed by all, but only that it appears to them. They behold in somewhat the same manner as Balaam said he would see the star that was to arise out of Judah: "I shall see Him, but not now; I shall behold Him, but not nigh." It is but a distant sight that the unregenerate obtain of the grace of salvation. It appears to them as a beauteous and glowing star in the remote horizon, which they may admire, but do not reach. 1. Time and space are given them for accepting salvation. 2. The grace of God appears to men in general in their enjoyment of Divine ordinances. Ordinances are the appointed means of salvation. They are not effectual of themselves to the communication of saving benefit; but they are the medium through which spiritual blessings are imparted. 3. The grace of God appears to all in the offer of salvation to every individual. 4. The grace of God appears to men in general in the common operations of the Spirit. 5. The grace of God appears to men in general in the impressions of Divine truth upon the heart. (1) What a great privilege is possessed by the hearers of the gospel. (2) Reason for great anxiety. Look after the evidences of your real Christianity. (*A. Ross, M.A.*)    *All men must come to the grace of salvation:—* The American officer who was appointed to measure the boundaries of Mexico and the United States tells us touchingly that the springs which occur at intervals of sixty or a hundred miles apart in the desert are perforce the meeting-places of life. All living creatures must gather there or die in an agony of thirst. There comes the American panther, and laps luxuriously the stream beside the timid hare—the one tamed by thirst, the other made brave by thirst; and there come the traveller and the trader and light the camp-fire beside the wigwam of the scalp-clothed warrior of the prairie, civilised by thirst; they quaff the waters together. So the waters of life should be resorted to by all mankind. **Teaching us that denying ungodliness.**—*Grace our teacher:*—The apostle proceeds to state that grace not only saves but undertakes our training; and this, of course, is a life-long work, a work that will only be concluded when grace ends in glory. Now, obviously, if this work is to be done as it should be done, the soul must, first of all, be in a position to receive teaching. If grace is really to undertake our training, and to teach us such lessons as only grace can teach, surely she must first of all calm the tumultuous misgivings which fill our hearts ; and until grace has done this for us, how can she instruct us ? If I am learning my lesson with a view to obtain grace, it cannot be grace that is acting the part of the teacher, for she can only teach where she has been already obtained. Grace cannot at one and the same moment be my teacher, and also that to obtain which I am being taught, for this, of course, involves a contradiction in terms. Hence, as we have said, unless this first point be settled, and we know that we are in the enjoyment of God's salvation, we are not in a position to learn from grace, whoever else it be that we may learn from. And thus it comes to pass, as a matter of simple fact, that a large number of nominal Christians are taught, indeed, after a certain fashion, but they are not taught by grace. They seek to learn of Christ in order that they may obtain the grace of Christ ; they endeavour to become conformed to Christ in order that their resemblance to Christ may dispose the heart of God to regard them with the same favourable consideration which He bestowed on Him whom they seek to resemble. Such persons are under the law. Grace, then, is to be our instructress, and she has plenty of work before her in the training and preparation of the human subject for the glorious destiny which lies before him. Then only is it possible, after the adoption has taken place, for the education to begin. With these thoughts in our mind we will proceed to consider grace as our teacher, and first we will point out the contrast between the training of grace and the operation of law. Before the grace of God appeared men were under another teacher, and his name was "Law." Grace is our teacher, and she teaches us far more power-fully, far more efficiently, and far more perfectly than law can ever teach us. But observe, she will not share her office of teacher with law. The Christian is not to be a kind of spiritual mongrel, nor is his experience to be of a mongrel type—part legal, part spiritual, part savouring of bondage, part savouring of liberty : but the design of God is that we should stand fast in the liberty where-with Christ has made us free, and never allow ourselves, even for a moment, to be entangled in a yoke of bondage. How many Christians are there who never seem to have perceived that we are no more to be saved by grace and then trained by law, than we are to be saved by law and then trained by grace ? How many who need to learn that as we are to be saved by grace at first, so we are to be trained by grace afterwards, until at last the corner-stone is raised upon the wondrous structure which only grace has reared, amidst shouts of "Grace, grace unto it ! " All is of grace from first to last. Now in order that we may very clearly apprehend what the teaching of God's word is on this subject, let us just put side by side the teach-ing of law and the teaching of grace, contrasting them one with the other, and then we shall see how much to the advantage of grace the contrast is. Grace teaches better than law. 1. She teaches better than law, first, because she delivers to us a fuller and more distinct exhibition of the mind and will of God as regards human conduct, based upon a more complete manifestation of the Divine character. Grace, as she takes possession of our heart, makes us acquainted with the mind and will of God in a manner in which we should never have become acquainted with these by the mere influence and teaching of law. If you reflect for a moment, you will see that the object of law is not to reveal the mind and the will of the Lawgiver, but to lay down certain positive precepts for the direction of those to whom the legislation is given, or for whom the legislation is designed. If an Act of Parliament is passed by the British Legislature, by both Houses of Parliament, and a person were to ask, " What is the object of this Act? " nobody would reply, " To reveal to the British public what is the mind and will of the members of our Legislature." Nothing of the kind. The object of the Act is to meet some specific political need, or to give some specific political direction to those who are subject to its authority. Even so the law delivered from Sinai was not primarily designed to reveal the mind and will of God. The law contained only a very partial revela-tion of the mind and will of God. The law consisted of certain positive precepts, which were given in the infancy of the human race for the direction and guidance of mankind. The rules and precepts which are laid down in the nursery are not designed to exhibit the mind and will of the parent, although they are in accord-ance with that mind and will. They are laid down for the convenience and for the benefit of those for whom the rules were made. A child knows somethin of the mind and will of the parent from personal contact with that parent, but not from the rules, or only to a very slender degree from the rules, which are laid down for its guidance. But when we turn from law to grace, then we see at once that we now are dealing with a revelation of the mind and the will of Him from whom the grace proceeds. Each act of favour which a parent bestows upon his child, or which a sovereign bestows upon his subject, is a revelation, so far as it goes, of the mind and will of the parent towards that particular child, or of the sovereign towards that particular subject, as the case may be. And even so every act of grace which we receive from God is a revelation, as far as it goes, of the mind and will of God towards us who are affected by the act. 2. Not only is the teaching of grace in itself fuller and more complete, but we are still more impressed by the superiority of the mode in which the teaching is given—the form in which this new doctrine is communicated. In the decalogue you are met with, " Thou shalt," or, " Thou shalt not "—and you observe at once that the command addresses itself directly to your will. Children are not appealed to so far as their understandings are concerned. They are told to act in a certain particular way, or not to act in a certain particular way ; and if a child stops to reason with its parents, an appeal is at once made to parental authority. " Your duty, my child, is to obey, not to understand." Or, once again, the decalogue makes no appeal to the affections of those to whom it was delivered ; it deals not with our moral states, or with the motives from which actions proceed ; it simply concerns itself with those actions, and speaks to the will which is responsible for them. But when we turn from the decalogue to the sermon on the mount we find that all is changed. It does not begin with a direct appeal to the will, and yet the will is touched by a stronger influence, and moved to action by a more mighty force, than ever operated upon the will of the Israelites at Sinai. Grace is our teacher ; and we observe that the first word that she utters in this lesson is a blessing. The law had summed up its all of teaching with a curse— " Cursed is he that continueth not in all things that are written in this book to do them." 1. She does not say, " Ye shall be blessed if ye will become poor in spirit." Grace drives no bargains ; but she explains to us that a state of experience from which most of us would naturally shrink is a state of actual blessedness. Here you will observe that she appeals to our enlightened understanding, indicating to us a new and a higher view of self-interest, showing that God's will, so far from being opposed to our truest well-being, is in complete and full harmony with it ; for He is our Father, and He loves us, and therefore desires to see us supremely happy like Himself. Does she not teach better than law? Once again. Not only does she teach by giving us a fuller and a deeper revelation of the mind and will of God, and exhibiting these to us in such a way as that she appeals not merely to our own will, demanding action, but to our understanding, and, through our understanding, to our feelings, kindling holy desires, and so setting the will at work almost before it is aware that it is working ; but she does more than all this. 3. Grace teaches us by setting before our eyes the noblest and the most striking of all exemplars. Grace speaks to us through human lips ; grace reveals herself to us in a human life. Now we all know how much more we learn from a personal teacher than from mere abstract directions. To watch a painter, and to see how he uses his brush, and carefully and minutely notice the little touches that give so much character and power to the product of his genius, does far more for us in the way of making us painters than any amount of mere abstract study of the art itself. This in itself may suffice to show the superiority of grace as a teacher. While the thunder sounded from Sinai and the fiery law was given, God still remained concealed. When the veil was taken away, and God was made flesh in the person of Christ, human eyes were allowed to look at Him, and human ears heard the sound of His voice. Perfection stood before us at last in concrete form. When grace teaches us, she always teaches us by leading up to Christ—by exhibiting fresh views of His perfection, drawing out our heart in admiration towards Him. Happy they who thus set themselves to learn Christ as their life-lesson, not as a mere duty—that is legality—but because they have fallen in love with Christ ! Happy they who learn Christ just as the astronomer learns astronomy ! Why does he study astronomy ? Would a Newton tell you that he has spent all those hours in the careful examination of the phenomena of nature, or absorbed in profound mathematical calculations, because he thought it his duty to do it ? And even so those who are under the teaching of grace learn Christ, not because they are under a legal obligation to learn Him, but because they are mastered by an enthusiastic admiration for the Divine object. There is a beauty in Christ which wins the heart. But grace does more than even this. 4. She not only sets before us the highest of all exemplars, but she establishes the closest possible relationship between that Exemplar and ourselves. Grace is not content with merely setting an example before us ; she takes us by the hand and introduces us to the Exemplar, tells us not only that this Exemplar is content to be our friend, but, more wonderful still, that He is content to be one with us, uniting Himself to us, that His strength may be made perfect in our weakness. " Know ye not," says grace, " that Christ is in you ? " In you ; not merely outside you as a source of power, not merely beside you as a faithful companion on life's journey, but in you. " Christ is your life," says grace. Do you prefer to be under the law ? Do you really elect to be bondslaves ? You say your prayers in the morning ; it is your duty to do it. You do not feel comfortable if you do not say them. You go to church ; but it is not because you love to go and cannot stay away, or because you want to know more and more of God, or delight in His worship. " I was glad when they said unto me, Let us go into the house of the Lord." You go because it is your habit. May God save us from such bondage as this ! Let us remember that all the while that we are thus trifling there is within our reach, if we would but have it, the glorious liberty of the children of God. (*W. H. M. H. Aitken, M.A.*) *Our teacher's mode of teaching :*—You will observe that inasmuch as grace proposes to form Christ in our nature, she proceeds upon an altogether different method from that which is followed by law. Grace purposes to make the tree good, and then concludes, reasonably enough, that the fruit will be good ; whereas law aims, so to speak, rather at improving the fruit than at regenerating the tree. Grace deals with the springs of action, and not primarily with action itself. She deals with actions, but deals with them only indirectly. She begins her beneficent operations by setting right that part of our nature from which actions proceed, and so, from first to last, grace is chiefly concerned with our motives, checking the sordid and the unworthy, and developing the noble and the godlike. Now, the contrast here lies between an outward objective law exhibited to the human understanding, claiming the homage of the will, and an inward and subjective law which became part and parcel, so to speak, of the nature of him who receives it. Now it is by the teaching of grace that this new state of things is introduced ; it is by the operation of grace that the Father's Law is to be written upon the hearts of His once rebellious children. She effects this blessed result, first by opening up to us through His Son a revelation of the Father's heart, and by showing us how deep and strong is His love towards us ; in the second place, by sweeping away all obstacles between the Father's love and our experience of it ; and thus in the third place, by bringing our humanity under the mighty operation of the Holy Spirit of God, whose work it is to form within us the nature of Christ ; and once again, in the fourth place, grace indelibly inscribes God's law upon our hearts in the very terms of her own manifestation. For it is from the Cross that Grace is manifested and it is involved in the terms of its acceptance, that to the cross the eye of him who accepts it should be turned. We have just said that the first effect of grace is to reveal the Father's love to us, and to sweep away all the barriers which interfere with our enjoyment of that love ; by this first act of grace we are introduced into what may be described as the life of love—a life in which we are no longer influenced by mere considerations of moral or legal obligation. The love of God shed abroad in the heart, like the genial rays of the sun, produces a responsive love within us which is simply the refraction, so to speak, of those rays ; and this love, the gospel teaches us, is the fulfilling of the law. 1. But love fulfils the law, not by a conscious effort to fulfil it, but because it is the voluntary response of the soul to the Person from whom the law has emanated. Love fulfils the law, not by commanding me to conform my conduct to a certain outward and objective standard, but by awakening within me a spiritual passion of devotion for the Person of Him whose will is law to those who love Him. Love knows nothing about mere restriction and repression —love seeks to please, not to abstain from displeasing ; and so love fulfils, not merely abstains from breaking, the law. Thus we see that love takes us up to an altogether higher level than law. I cannot illustrate this point better than by referring for a moment to our earthly relationships to each other. There are certain laws which are applicable to these relationships. For instance, there are certain laws of our land, and there are certain laws contained in the Bible, which apply to the natural relationships of the father and of the husband. It is obviously the duty of the father and the husband to care for his wife and his children, to protect them, to provide for them, to endeavour to secure their well-being so far as in him lies.

A man who occupies that relationship is bound to do not less than this. But does a really affectionate husband and father perform those various offices because the law constrains him to do so, because it is his legal duty to do them? Does he perform acts of tenderness towards his wife and towards his child because the law demands them of him? Even so the man whom grace has taught finds a new law within his nature, the law of love, in surrendering himself to which he fulfils indeed the outward and objective law, not because he makes an effort to fulfil it, but because he is true to his new nature. So that I may say, to put the thing concisely, grace is not opposed to law, but is superior to law; and the man who lives in grace lives not " under the law," because he is above the law. We imprison the wife-beater. Why? Because he has fallen from the level of love altogether, and thus he has come down to the level of the law, and is within the reach of the law. Even so here the only persons who are not under law are the persons who are above law. Is the law written within our hearts, or is it only revealed from without? In our attempt to do what is right, do we simply do, or endeavour to do, what is right because we have recognised a certain external standard of duty, and are endeavouring to conform our conduct to it? Or do we do what is right because we are living in happy, holy intercourse with an indwelling God in whose love we find our law, and in surrendering ourselves to the influence of whose love, our highest enjoyment? Herein lies the test of the difference between legal experience and evangelical experience. 2. But here let me point out that grace, whilst she teaches us gently and tenderly, and in a very different way from law, has nevertheless sanctions of her own. They are the rewards and punishments which are congruous to the life of love, whereas the rewards and punishments of legal experience are such as are congruous to the life of legal servitude. We shall detect in a moment what these sanctions are if we reflect upon the nature of our relation to Him who has now become to us our law of life. It is the glory of the life of love that we have something to love. Our love is not merely an empty abstraction, nor is it merely a wasted energy that wanders in infinity; it is attracted towards a living Person. In the enjoyment of His society, which to the real Christian is not a matter of sentiment, but a matter of practical experience, the soul finds its highest privilege. Ah! grace disciplines as well as teaches. She does not spoil her children. She is not like some fond and indulgent mother, who fancies that she is benefiting her children when she is really injuring them more cruelly than in any other way she possibly could, by always giving them their own way. Grace does not teach us to be negligent, thoughtless, heedless, careless. Grace does not whisper in our ears, "Now that you are saved once you are saved for ever. Go on, and never mind what happens to you." But grace teaches us very delicately. " I will guide thee," says grace, " with my eye." Grace teaches us. She brings out the scales of the sanctuary, and into the one she puts our worldly idol—our love of popularity, our self-seeking, our slothfulness, our self-indulgence, our pride of heart, all those little and great things which we are so apt to set against the society of Jesus, or rather which we are so apt to allow to come in between us and the society of Jesus. Yes, grace has her sanctions. And I am afraid that there are only too many Christians who have often to feel the force of those dread sanctions. Their whole life has come to be a clouded, unsatisfactory, melancholy, woe-begone life. How many Christians are there of whom it cannot be said that the joy of the Lord is their strength! And why? They are under the discipline of grace. Yes, God does not forsake them altogether. He has not left them to their own waywardness, but He has visited their offences with the rod and their sin with scourges. They cannot be happy in the world since they have tasted something better in Christ. Nor can they be happy in Christ while they cast longing looks towards the world. But grace has also her rewards, and I love to think of them. What are they? The eye, perhaps, wanders on towards the future, and we think of the glories that are to be revealed. In this present world, amidst all the trials to which the Christian may be exposed, the school of grace has its prizes. Grace has her prizes. " The fruits of the Spirit are love, joy, peace." Grace teaches indeed, but she teaches by first of all correcting, nay, by regenerating, the secret springs of our actions. Unless these are set right, how can our actions be right? How can you love God unless the love of God has conquered your heart? (*Ibid.*) *The negative teaching of grace; the denial of ungodliness :*—Two things, it will be observed, exist in every physical organism—a mysterious inward energy or life-power, and an inherent law of being, or condition of existence. Between these there can be no kind of contrariety or antagonism. We do not see life exerting its energies in defiance of the subjective laws of the organisms that it inhabits, nor do we see those laws fulfilled save by the inward energies of life. Even so the new creature in Christ Jesus has a certain law of being or condition of existence which properly belongs to him, and it is this that the Holy Spirit proceeds to fulfil, working out and forming in us a new nature in the image of Jesus Christ Himself. On the Cross our new life is purchased; but not the less on the Cross our old man is crucified. In the very act of extending mercy grace teaches her first great lesson. We are saved because we have died and risen again with Christ; but if so, we have already denied ungodliness and worldly lust. Let us observe, then, that this first lesson taught by grace is a negative lesson. Before teaching us what to do, she teaches us what we are to have done with; before introducing us into the positive blessedness of the new life, she first of all separates our connection with the old. This negation of the old must always come before the possession of the new; and unless our experience follow this order, we shall find that what we mistake for the new is not God's new at all, but simply Satan's travesty of God's new creation. Let us not fail to observe that the apostle here speaks of our " denying ungodliness." He does not speak of our combating ungodliness, or of our gradually progressing from a state of ungodliness into a state of godliness. " If any man be in Christ Jesus, he is a new creature: old things are passed away, and all things are become new. And all things are of God." It is a strong word, this word denial. Now it is upon this primary fact that grace bases her teaching. She may save, but does not undertake to train, the graceless. The only improvement of the old man that grace recognises is his legal execution; but this she teaches us has already taken place in the case of those who are in Christ Jesus. Let us ask ourselves, Are we in the habit of denying, or only of opposing? But before pursuing our consideration of the mode of denial, let us pause to contemplate the objects here spoken of as being denied, and we shall then be in a position to return to this point of denial and treat of it more fully. The first thing we are represented as denying is ungodliness. This sounds a very' strong word, and I dare say at first most people would be disposed to affirm that they cannot be charged with this, whatever else they may be guilty of. They may not have been as good as they might, but ungodly they certainly have not been. We must endeavour to find out what ungodliness is. This is certainly important, because unless we understand what it is, it is impossible to deny it. Let me then begin by saying that ungodliness is the cardinal and root-sin of the world. It was the first sin committed in the history of the world; and it was the parent of all other sins, and it is usually the first sin in the life of each individual, and equally the parent of all the sins that follow. In the happy early days of human history when man, created in God's own image, was living in fellowship with his Creator, the characteristic of that pristine experience was doubtless godliness. But there came a change, a blight, a cloud, a darkness, a horror. What was it? The entrance of ungodliness. Here was man's first temptation; and here came man's first sin. It consisted in ungodliness or impiety, exhibited in a determination to put self in the place of God. So was it with the first sin, and so it has been with all its successors. Ungodliness, in one form or another, has been at the root of them all, and the deadly growth from this evil root has cast its baleful shadow over universal history. Now we are in a position to form some idea of what ungodliness really means. 1. Ungodliness consists, first of all, in the repudiation of God as the final cause of our being; that is to say, the end for which we live. A man is ungodly when he lives not for God. I do not care what outward complexion it wears. It may be the life of a zealous ritualist devoted to his party, or of an earnest churchman, or of a staunch protestant, or of a decided evangelical, or of a stout nonconformist; it makes no difference. Whatever complexion our outward life may wear, the man that is not consciously living for the glory of God is leading an ungodly life. He has fallen from the original position which belongs to man in relation to God. 2. The second characteristic of ungodliness will be exhibited in an indisposition on man's part to take God as the efficient cause of all that he is or wishes to be. Ungodliness begins when we decline to live for God; ungodliness is developed in an incapacity or an indisposition to live by God. The apostle was describing a godly experience when he said, "I live; yet not I, but Christ liveth in me: and the life which I now live in the flesh I live by the faith of the Son of God, who loved me, and gave Himself for me." "Man shall not live by bread alone." He needs that. "As the eyes of servants look unto the hand of their masters, and as the eyes of a maiden unto the hand of her mistress; so our eyes wait upon the Lord our God, until that He have mercy upon us." Is that the kind of life of dependence that we are leading, drawing all our strength for action from Him, receiving all our guidance in action through Him? Happy they who live thus. 3. The next characteristic of the life of ungodliness is that as, in the first place, man does not live for God; and as, in the second place, he does not live by God, so, in the third place, he does not live with God. He knows not what it is to enjoy the Divine society. The man that knows what it is to be godly—to "live godly in Christ Jesus"—finds that he cannot do without God at home any more than he can do without God at church; he cannot do without God in the place of business any more than he can do withot God in his closet. He needs God. God has become a kind of necessity to him. Jesus always near, always dear, is more than life to those of us who really know Him. The godly live with God. 4. Once more, the ungodly life will not only be a life which is not lived for God, and not only a life which is not lived with God; but it will also be a life which is not lived in God, and a life in which God lives not in us. There is something more blessed even than living in the company of Jesus; and that is to know by faith that we live in Him, and to realise in our inmost experience the still more wonderful fact that He lives in us. But how does grace provide for this complete separation between us and this root-sin, which seems to have become hereditary in the family of man? how does the denial of ungodliness take place? We seek an answer by referring to two remarkable expressions which fell from our blessed Master's lips, shortly before His own passion. On that memorable occasion on which a supernatural voice responded to His prayer, "Father, glorify Thy name," He proceeds to state, "Now is the judgment of this world; now is the prince of this world cast out." Elsewhere He supplements these words by another similar statement. "When the Holy Ghost is come," He says, "He will convict the world concerning judgment, because the prince of this world is judged." Most mysterious though these utterances may seem they will be found to throw a good deal of light upon this particular subject. How is ungodliness to be denied? It is to be denied by recognising God's judgment against it. The prince of this world is the very representative, as he is the author, of the world's ungodliness. Satan succeeds in obtaining the worship of humanity in a thousand different forms. But, however we may serve him, he is judged. If we ask how and when, only one reply seems possible. Strange and paradoxical though it may seem, he is judged and condemned on Calvary, in the Person of Him who exhibited more than any other filial piety and true godliness. The ungodliness of the world, the revolt of human independence against Divine authority, is represented by the world-victim upon the cross of Calvary, and meets in Christ with its proper doom. Against that world-sin, against that ungodliness which is the root and source of every kind of iniquity, all the wrath of God has been already revealed. I discover it as I witness the dying agonies of Emmanuel. A godless world will not have God; by and by it shall not have Him. It turns its back upon God; God must needs turn His back upon it. "My God, My God, why hast Thou forsaken Me?" Surely this is the true explanation of that bitter cry that was wrung from the breaking heart of Emmanuel. There we see the judgment of the world passed upon the representative of the world's sin, and it is because that judgment has expended itself on Him that there is therefore now no condemnation for those that are in Him. But, observe, it is only as our faith sees our ungodliness crucified there that we are in a position to enjoy this immunity from condemnation. We thus judge that He died for all, that we who live should not henceforth live to ourselves, but to Him who died for us and rose again. (*Ibid.*) *Grace and its lessons:*—The " saving grace of God which has appeared to all men " is described by the apostle as "teaching us," or rather educating, training us in such a way as to secure the precious fruits that follow. It is a characteristic feature of the gospel that it does men good by putting them to school, by making them disciples, not simply for the purpose of communicating knowledge, but for that of forming and maturing character; for education in the highest, largest, and most emphatic sense. This pedagogical design of true religion is stamped upon all its institutions, and legible even in its phraseology. It is not by an unmeaning figure of speech that Christians are continually called disciples, that is, learners, pupils, and that the ministers of Christ are spoken of as teachers. The church is Christ's school; he who enters it must enter as a learner, a disciple, with as real and sincere a deference to his great teacher as the little child feels, when it trembles for the first time in the presence of a master. Such submission is the more imperative in this case, because more truly than in any other case the process of instruction is moral as well as intellectual; it is not mere teaching, it is training, education; not the mere acquisition of knowledge, although that does lie at the foundation, but the cultivation of the powers and affections, as a preparation for the joys and services of heaven, as well as for the duties and the trials of this present state. The design and the legitimate effect of this disciplinary process are distinctly stated in the text, with reference both to the present and the future; both in a negative and positive form. The negative design of all this training is that we deny, repudiate, or abjure allegiance to the sinful dispositions and affections which are paramount in fallen nature, but the objects of which perish in the using, being limited to this world, so that they may be described as "worldly lusts" or desires, and may be said, so far as they predominate, to put man on a level with the brutes, whose highest good is present enjoyment of the lowest kind. By all who would be saved, these worldly, temporal, and short-lived lusts must be denied, renounced; and this is never done without a simultaneous or previous denial of ungodliness, of all indifference and enmity to God, which is indeed the source of the other, for when human hearts are right towards God, the paramount control of worldly lusts becomes impossible. This, however, is only the negative part of the effect produced by the spiritual discipline to which we are subjected in the school of Christ. It has a positive side also. It teaches us how we are to live. In reference to himself, the true disciple in this school is educated to be sober or sound-minded; the original expression denotes sanity as opposed to madness, not in its extreme forms merely, but in all its more familiar and less violent gradations—all those numberless and nameless aberrations of the judgment which give character to human conduct, even in the absence of gross crime or absolute insanity. In opposition to this "madness," the saving grace of God trains its subjects to be rational or sober, and thus in the highest sense and measure to be faithful to themselves. But at the same time it trains them to be faithful to others, to be just, in the wide sense of the term; including all that one can owe another—including, therefore, charity and mercy, no less than honesty and rigorous exactness in the discharge of legal obligations. Justice or rectitude, in this enlarged and noble sense, as opposed to every form of selfishness, is no less really a dictate and a consequence of spiritual training, than sanity or soundness of mind, as opposed to the chimeras and hallucinations of our state by nature. But "soberness" and "justice," in the wide sense which has just been put upon the terms, have never yet been found divorced from "godliness." As we have seen already, in considering the negative effects of training by Divine grace, it is man's relations to his God, that must adjust and determine his relations to his fellow-creatures. The symmetrical position of the points in the circumference arises from their common relation to a common centre. Such are the objects and effects of Christian training, that is, of the method by which Christ trains His disciples, with respect to the present state or stage of man's existence, as distinguished from those future states or stages to which he cannot but look forward. For although the sobriety of mind produced by the discipline of God's grace, causes men of a morbid, penurious disposition to lose sight of present duties and enjoyments in a vague anticipation of the future, it is so far from excluding expectation altogether, that our very salvation is prospective. "We are saved in hope," and that hope is a blessed one; a hope of blessedness to be revealed and realised hereafter; a hope, that is, an object of hope, not yet fully enjoyed, but only "looked for," and to look for which is one of the effects and marks of thorough training in the school of Christ. This hope is neither selfish nor indefinite. It does not terminate upon ourselves, our own deliverance from suffering, and our own reception into heaven; nor does it lose itself in vague anticipations of a nameless good to be experienced hereafter. The Christian's hope is in the highest degree generous and well-defined. It is generous, because it rises beyond personal interests, even the highest, even personal salvation, to the glory of the Saviour as the ultimate end to be desired and accomplished. It is well-defined, because, instead of looking at this glory in the abstract, it gives it a concrete and personal embodiment; it is glory, not in the sense of the metaphysician or of the poet, but in that of the prophets, saints, and angels; it is manifested and apparent excellence, a glorious epiphany, analogous to that which marked Jehovah's presence in the Holy of holies, but unspeakably transcending it in permanence and brightness; the glorious appearance, not of any mere creature, even the most noble, but of God Himself, and yet not of God in His essence, which is inaccessible to sense, nor even in some special and distinct manifestation of the Father, or the Godhead, under an assumed or borrowed form of which the senses may take cognisance, but in the well-known person of His Son, who is the brightness of His glory, and the express image of His person, in whom dwelleth all the fulness of the

Godhead bodily; and therefore it is not the untempered brightness of the Divine majesty, and holiness, and justice, which to us is, and must be, a consuming fire; and yet it is the manifested glory of God, of the great God—great in all conceivable perfections, but, as the object of this hope, emphatically great in mercy—great in the power, not to punish and destroy, but to forgive and save, to save the sinner, to save us;—the glorious appearing of our great God and Saviour Jesus Christ. Let it not be overlooked, however, that the gospel, while it sets Christ before us as an object of believing expectation, sets Him also before us as an object of believing recollection, and thus brings into a delightful harmony the hope of favours yet to be experienced with gratitude for those experienced already. It is not simply as a glorious person, human or Divine, that we look for His appearing; it is not simply as a Saviour or Deliverer from evil in the general; it is not simply as a potential Saviour or Deliverer, one who can save us if He will, and will if we should need it at some future time; not merely a Saviour whose ability and willingness to save are yet to be displayed and proved, but as an actual deliverer, as one who has already done His saving work, by giving Himself for us, the highest gift, it may in a certain sense be said, of which even He was capable, for us, His creatures, His rebellious subjects, His despisers, and His enemies! What, then, was His object? To redeem us, to buy us back from bondage, to save us by the payment of a ransom price, not only from the punishment of sin, but from its power, from its love, from its pollution, from its foul and hideous embrace, no less than from its sword and from its chains. It was to set us free from sin itself that Christ redeemed us; not from some sin, but from all sin; not that we should still remain, or afterwards fall back under the dominion of the very tyrant from whose power He redeemed us; not that we should merely exchange one hard master for another, or for many;—no, He " gave Himself for us," He laid down His life for us, He died upon the cross for us, " that He might redeem us from all iniquity." Nor was this deliverance from sin as well as punishment intended merely for our advantage, but for His. He had an end to accomplish for Himself. He died to purify us, not merely that we might be pure and therefore happy, but also to purify a people for Himself; a *peculium*, a possession of His own, a Church, a body of which He should be the Head, a kingdom of which he should be the Sovereign. (*J. A. Alexander, D.D.*) *The lessons that grace teaches:*—Observe—1. Grace teacheth us holiness. (1) It teaches by way of direction what duties we ought to perform, and so it makes use of the moral law as a rule of life. Obedience respects the command, as love doth the kindness and merit of the lawgiver. (2) It teacheth by way of argument; it argueth and reasoneth from the love of God (Gal. ii. 20). The law and the prophets do not beseech, but only command and threaten; but the grace of God useth a different method in the New Testament. (3) It teacheth by way of encouragement, as manifesting both help and reward. Uses. 1. Of information. It showeth us—(1) What is true holiness, such as cometh from the teachings of grace, obliging conscience to the duty of the law, inclining the heart to obey out of the sense of God's love, and encouraging us by faith, drawing strength from Christ, and looking to God for an acceptance from Him. (2) That grace and corruption draw several inferences and conclusions from the same premises. A bee gathereth honey from whence a spider sucketh poison. (3) That it is the greatest wrong one can do to grace to slacken any part of our duty for grace's sake (Jude 14). 2. Of trial. Whether we are made partakers of the grace of God in the gospel? Have we these teachings and arguings? Many can endure to hear that grace bringeth salvation, but that it teacheth us to deny ungodliness, there they flinch. Men would have us offer salvation and preach promises; but when we press duty, they cry out, " This is a hard saying." The cities of refuge under the law were all cities of the Levites and schools of instruction, to note that whoever taketh sanctuary at grace meeteth instruction; it is no benefit to thee else. In the general, doth it persuade you to make a willing resignation of yourselves to God? (Rom. xii. 1.) (1) Doth it press you to deny lusts? (Ezra ix. 13, 14.) (2) Doth it press you to good? (1 John v. 3.) 2. Grace teacheth us both to depart from evil and also to do good (Psa. xxxiv. 15), 'Depart from evil, and do good "; Isa. i. 16, 17, " Cease to do evil, learn to do well." We must do both, because God hates evil and delights in good; we must hate what God hates, and love what God loves. That is true friendship—*eadem velle et nolle*—to will and nill the same thing. I durst not sin, God hates it; I durst not omit this duty, God loves it. Let it press us not to rest in abstaining from sin merely. Many are not vicious, but they are not sanctified; they have no feeling of the power of the new life. 3. We must first begin with renouncing evil; that is the first thing grace teacheth. Since the fall, the method is analytical, to unravel and undo that which hath been done in the soul. So it is said of Christ (1 John iii. 8). Dagon must down, ere the ark be set up. It cannot be otherwise, it must not be otherwise; there must be mortifying and subduing of sin by acts of humiliation and godly sorrow before there will be experience of grace. 4. It is not enough to renounce one sin, but we must renounce all; for when the apostle speaks of denying ungodliness, he intends all ungodliness. Compare this with 1 Peter ii. 1; James i. 21. I might give you several reasons. One sin is contrary to God as well as another. There is the same aversion from an eternal good in all things, though the manner of conversion to the creature be different. Again, one sin is contrary to the law of God as well as another; there is a contempt of the same authority in all sins. God's command binds, and it is of force in lesser sins as well as greater; and therefore they that bear any respect to the law of God must hate all sin—"I hate vain thoughts, but Thy law do I love" (Psa. cxix. 113). God hath given a law to the thoughts, to the sudden workings of the spirit, as well as to actions that are more deliberate; and therefore, if we love the law, we should hate every lesser contrariety to it, even a vain thought. And all sin proceedeth from the same corruption; therefore, if we would subdue and mortify it, we must renounce all sin. Use 1. Direction what to do in the business of mortification. We must deny all ungodliness; not a hoof must be left in Egypt. Grace will not stand with any allowed sin; and in demolishing the old building, not one stone must be left upon another. (1) In your purpose and resolution you must make Satan no allowance; he standeth hucking, as Pharaoh did with Moses and Aaron; first he would let them go three days into the wilderness; then he permitted them to take their little ones with them; but they would not go without their cattle, their flocks, and their herds also; they would not leave anything—no, not a hoof—behind them. So the devil would have a part left as a pledge, that in time the whole man may fall to his share (2 Kings v. 18). (2) We should often examine our hearts, lest there lurk some vice whereof we think ourselves free (Lam. iii. 40). (3) Desire God to show you if there be anything left that is grievous to His Spirit (Job xxxiv. 32). (4) When any sins break out, set upon the mortification of them. Do not neglect the least sins; they are of dangerous consequence; but renew thy peace with God, judging thyself for them, and mourning for them, avoiding temptations, cutting off the provision for the flesh (1 Cor. ix. 27). Use 2. Of trial. Do we renounce all sin? But you will say, "Who can say I have made my heart clean, I am pure from sin?" (Prov. xx. 9.) I answer—(1) It must be done in purpose and resolution. In conversion there is an entire surrender of the soul to God. (2) There must be a serious inclination of the will against it. Carnal men will profess a purpose and faint resolution, but there is no principle of grace to bear it, no bent of the will against it—"I hate every false way" (Psa. cxix. 104). A child of God doth not escape every false way; but he hateth it, the inclination of the new nature is against it, and therefore sin is not committed without resistance. 3. There must be endeavours against it. The case of obedience must be universal, though the success be not answerable—"Then shall I not be ashamed when I have respect unto all Thy commandments" (Psa. cxix. 6); not when I have kept them, but when I have a respect to them all. We should never be able to look God in the face if our acceptance lay upon keeping all His commandments; but we must respect them all, and endeavour to keep them all, and dispense with ourselves in no known failing, and still the work of denying all sin must be carried on by degrees. (*T. Manton, D.D.*) *The effects of the grace of God :*—1. What does this grace teach us to deny? and the answer is "Ungodliness and worldly lusts." (1) Ungodliness means impiety, blasphemy, and all forms of public infidelity; and most certainly all such evils are condemned in the passage: but surely the mere negative form is intended to include far more than these. Ungodly means not godly, and points to the condition of the soul in which God is simply shut out. A godly man is a man in whom God dwells—a man who thinks, speaks, and acts for God. Even so an ungodly man is a man who simply thinks, speaks, and acts without any reference to God— he seeks his own pleasure or interest, and guides his conduct according to the maxims of sagacity and worldly prudence. He thus becomes rich, or learned, or eloquent, or victorious in battle; but seeing God was neither consulted nor cared for in the whole of it, he remains an ungodly man. (2) But what are these worldly lusts, these cosmical desires? All that relates merely to the kosmos, or great material visible world—all that the men of the world hunt so eagerly after, and long to possess. Your quiet retreat in the bosom of green fields and enchanting

scenery delights and satisfies you, and that is worldly lust; you make your calculation in the counting-house, and look forward with contentment to the success of
your mercantile speculations, and that is worldly lust; you set your heart upon
excelling your fellow-men, be it in science, or in wisdom, or in warfare, and that
too is worldly lust. Everything whose end is in this fallen state of things is worldly
lust; everything, however honest and noble and praiseworthy among men, which
has not God for its motive and its end, is worldly lust. 2. But how are we to live?
(1) Soberly. This refers to our own character, and implies many of the duties that
we owe to ourselves. It denotes soundness of mind, as well as temperance regarding the indulgence of the appetites. (2) Righteously. This means justly, and sums
up the duties which we owe to our fellow-men. Justice is one of the exact virtues,
which can be easily recognised and definitely measured; and hence it is the great
palladium of the nations, the very basis of social intercourse and mercantile prosperity. Justice is a noble, but not one of the highest virtues, and therefore it is
well fitted to be the common medium or life of a community. An act of injustice
is recognisable and punishable; not so avarice, ambition, or forbidden pleasure;
and here, too, we see its fitness for moulding and strengthening the natural character.
(3) This is the idea of natural justice, and forms the staple commodity with
publicists and jurists; but righteousness, as defined in the person of Christ and in
the Scriptures, is a much higher and nobler principle. Justice is based upon rights;
and the Christian, as such, has none, save to love all men, and be put to death for
this love, as his Master was. Right says, Smite the smiter till he gets his due; but
the gospel says, Turn the other cheek. (4) Lastly, we should live godly—viz.,
with God, in God, and for God. This is the glorious end, so far as this world is
concerned, which the saving grace of God is intended and calculated to accomplish
in the believing Church of Christ. Like their Divine Master, they are not of the
world, though in it; and though in the midst of defilement, they remain undefiled.
This is the victory that overcometh the world, even our faith. 3. But what does
this grace teach us to look for? I answer, in the first place, the apostle directs the
believer's eye here, as elsewhere, to the glorious Person of the Lord Jesus Christ, as
the centre and home of the longing heart. (1) What is our position? It is that
of waiting for, and looking for, the coming of the Lord—not waiting upon the Lord
merely, which is also a duty, but waiting for the Lord from heaven, who shall
change our vile bodies, and make them like unto His glorious body. He is the
centre in which the ages, ceremonies, and dispensations all meet and have their
stability—the unity which harmonises time and eternity, creation and Creator—the
living fountain which sends forth the benediction of God over the ages, dispensations, and nations in a thousand streams. As the Jews hoped and waited, so we
hope and wait. Our position is the same, and the Person whom we wait for is the
same; they waited for His coming in the flesh, and we for His coming in glory.
(2) Is this hope an important doctrine of the New Testament? I answer, Very
important; for our text calls it the blessed hope, so that it is full of real blessing
to the believer. What can be more blessed to the soul than the person of the adorable Redeemer, whom even unseen we love so ardently? All our hopes are about
to be realised in His glorious appearing, when we shall be with Him and like Him
for ever. (*W. Graham, D.D.*) *The practical effects of the grace of God:*—I. The
FOUNDATION OF ALL TRUE RELIGION. Not our own reason or wisdom, which cannot
give us light and knowledge; not our own righteousness, which can never merit
salvation or recommend us to God; not our own strength or ability, which is
insufficient to help us to do or suffer the will of God, to be pious or virtuous
(John xv. 4, 5; 2 Cor. iii. 5); but the grace of God in these different senses—viz.,
Divine Light from the Word and Spirit of God; this instructs (παιδευουσα),
" teaching us," as a master his pupils, as we are able to receive it, the free favour
and unmerited love of God; this, by justifying and adopting, encourages and
inclines, adds correction and discipline to instruction, and gives us the will to be
the Lord's: the influence of the Spirit; this gives resolution, fortitude, and power.
We may infer from this that they who are not acquainted with, nor possessed of,
the grace of God, can have no true religion; or their religion is a superstructure
without a foundation; that is, it is only imaginary, illusive, unreal. II. The
SUPERSTRUCTURE TO BE RAISED ON THIS FOUNDATION. Religion itself is the superstructure that must be raised on this foundation, the stream that must flow from
this fountain. It consists of two parts. 1. It is negative; " denying ungodliness
and worldly lusts." In this way true religion first appears, and manifests its
reality: it makes us " cease to do evil" before we can " learn to do well;" it strips

us of "the old man" before it clothes us with "the new." Without this there can be no religion; there is not even repentance if there be not its fruits (Matt. iii. 8; Luke. iii. 8). 2. But it has a positive part, which is to "live soberly, righteously, and godly." Man is here considered as an individual on earth, as a member of society connected with his fellow-creatures, and as a creature—a redeemed creature —a subject and servant and child of his Creator, Preserver, King, and Lord. III. THE HAPPINESS THAT AWAITS ALL THAT DO THIS, AND THE BLESSED PROSPECT OPENED BEFORE THEM. "Looking for that blessed hope," &c. Hope here is put for the object of hope, a state of future and eternal blessedness, perfection, and felicity, both in soul and body. The grace of God begets us again to a well-grounded and "lively hope" of it; the gospel enlightens us as to this hope, and reveals it; the free, unmerited mercy and love of God justifies, adopts, and entitles us to it; the Spirit of Grace renews and fits us for it. In the way of godliness, righteousness, and sobriety, we wait for it, and are brought to it. "The glorious appearing of the great God," or, of our great "God and Saviour," shall raise our bodies, and after the process of the final judgment, shall put us in the possession of it. (*J. Benson.*) *The purpose of the discipline of grace :—*I. THE FAIR PICTURE OF WHAT OUR LIVES SHOULD BE. 1. Because we are to a large extent made up of blind desires which take no account of anything except their appropriate food, the commandment comes from the deepest recesses of each nature, as well as from the great throne in the heavens—"Live soberly." The engines will work on all the same, though the bows of the ship be turned to the rocks, and driving straight on the reef. It is the engineers' business to start them and keep them going; it is their business to turn the screw; it is somebody else's business to look after the navigation. We have our "humours under lock and key," in order that we may control them. And if we do not, we shall go all to rack and ruin. So "live soberly" says Paul. 2. The next requirement is "righteously." We stand in certain relations to a whole universe of things and of people, and there does rise before every man, however it may be accounted for, or explained away, or tampered with, or neglected, a standard of right and wrong. And what Paul here means by "live righteously" is, "Do as you know you ought to do," and, in shaping your character, have reference not merely to its constitution, but to its relations to all this universe of outside facts. So far as the word may include our duty to others, I may just remind you that "righteousness" in reference to our fellows demands mercy. The common anti- thesis which is drawn between a just man, who will give everybody what they deserve, and not one scrap more nor less if he can help it, and a kindly man is erroneous, because every man has a claim upon every other man for lenient judg- ment and undeserved help. He may not deserve it, being such a man as he is; but he has a right to it, being a man at all. 3. The last of the phases under which the perfect life is represented here takes us up at once into another region. If there were nobody but myself in the world, it must be my duty to live controlling myself, since I stand in relations manifold to creatures manifold, and to the whole order of things, it is my duty to conform to the standard, and to do what is right. And just as plainly as the obligations to sobriety and righteousness press on every man, so plainly is godliness necessary to his perfection. For I am not only bound by ties which knit me to my fellows, or to this visible order, but the closest of all bonds, the most real of all relations, is that which binds us each to God. And if "man's chief end be to glorify God," and then, and thus, "to enjoy Him for ever," then that end, in its very nature, must be all-pervasive, and diffuse its sweetness into the other two. For you cannot sliver up the unity of a life into little sections and say, "this deed has to be done soberly, and that one righteously, and this one godly"; but godliness must cover the whole life, and be the power of self-control and of righteousness. "All in all or not at all." Godliness must be uniform and universal. II. NOTICE WHAT A HARD TASK THE MAN HAS WHO WILL LIVE SO. The apostle, very remarkably, puts first, in my text, a negative clause. The things that he says we are to deny are the exact opposites of the characteristics that he says we are to aim after. Now, says Paul, there is no good to be done in the matter of acquiring these positive graces, without which a life is contemptible and poor unless, side by side with the continual effort at the acquisition of the one, there be the continual and resolute effort at the excision and casting out of the other. Why? Because they are in possession. A man cannot be godly unless he casts out the ungodliness that cleaves to his nature; nor can he rule himself and seek after righteousness unless he ejects the desires that are in possession of his heart. You have to get rid of the bad tenant if you would bring in the good one. You have to turn the current, which is running in the wrong direction. And so it comes to be a very hard, painful thing for a man to acquire these graces of which my text speaks. If it were only advancing in practice, or knowledge, or sentiment, or feeling, that would not be so difficult to do; but you have to reverse the action of the machine; and that is hard. Can it be done? Who is to keep the keepers? It is difficult for the same self to be sacrifice and priest. It is a hard matter for a man to crucify himself, and we may well say, if there can be no progress in goodness without this violent and thorough mutilation and massacre of the evil that is in us, alas! for us all. III. WHAT GOD GIVES US TO MAKE SUCH LIFE POSSIBLE. Christ and His love; Christ and His life; Christ and His death; Christ and His spirit; in these are new hopes, motives, powers, which avail to do the thing which no man can do. An infant's fingers cannot reverse the motion of some great engine. But the hand that made it can touch some little tap or lever, and the mighty masses of polished iron begin to move the other way. Jesus, who comes to us to mould our hearts into hitherto unfelt love, by reason of His own great love, and who gives to us His own Spirit to be the life of our lives, gives us by these gifts new motives, new powers, new tastes, new affections. He puts the reins into our hands, and enables us to control and master our unruly tempers and inclinations. If you want to clear out a tube of any sort, the way to do it is to insert some solid substance, and push, and that drives out the clogging matter. Christ's love coming into the heart expels the evil, just as the sap rising in the trees pushes off the old leaves that have hung there withered all the winter. As Luther used to say, "You cannot clean out the stable with barrows and shovels. Turn the Elbe into it." Let that great flood of life pour into our hearts, and it will not be hard to "live soberly." He comes to help us to live "righteously." He gives us His own life to dwell in our hearts, in no mere metaphor, but in simple fact. And they that trust in Jesus Christ are righteous by no mere fiction of a righteousness reckoned, but by the blessed reality of a righteousness imparted. He comes to make it possible for us to live "godly." For He, and He alone, has the secret of drawing hearts to God; because He, and He alone, has opened the secret of God's heart to us. (*A. Maclaren, D.D.*) **And worldly lusts.**—*The denial of worldly lust :*—All things in outward nature have their element, and our moral nature must have its element, in which to live, and move, and have its being. Beasts live on earth, birds fly in air, fishes swim in water; but each of these animal organisms requires its own element, and no amount of education will make a fish enjoy fresh air. Even so the ungodly man has this world for his element, even as the true believer has God for his element. The ungodly is of the earth earthy; he receives the world's spirit; he enters into its mind; he forms his character in accordance with its genius; he submits to its dictates; he measures everything by its standard. He lives in the world, and is of the world, just as the true believer lives in God, and is of God. He is one with the world, and the world with him. He is represented by the world; for he is in the world, just as the Christian is in Christ, and the world lives in him, just as Christ lives in the heart of His own people, forming its own nature within him, and conforming him to its character. Yes, the child of the world will always be like the world that he makes his god. You remember what the Psalmist says about the gods of the heathen. "Their idols are silver and gold, the works of men's hands." Then he goes on to add the startling assertion, "They who make them are like unto them; so are all they that put their trust in them." And "they that make them are like unto them"—not only do we become the slaves of that which we have created, but we also become assimilated to the creation of our own perversity. I mean to say that those who live in the world and for the world become worldly; and if that sounds but a little thing to some ears, let me say that, if my observation have not failed me, "worldly" means hollow-hearted, empty-headed, frivolous, selfish, sordid, incapable of realising the true dignity of our own nature, insensible to higher motives, heedless of grave responsibilities, unreal, conventional, hypocritical, false, deceiving and deceived. Shall I give an example of what I mean? There are scores of mothers in our land who are at this moment quite prepared to sell their daughters to the highest bidder. The question with them is not "What is the moral character?"—far less "What is the religious character of the man that shall marry my daughter?"—but "How many thousands a year has he? What will be his position in society?" I only mention that as one of the many instances that could be given of the hollowness and heartlessness of the worldly life; because we see it here conquering and paralysing one of the very strongest and purest instincts of nature—a mother's love. So the world goes on, getting hollower and hollower. The very conversation of the worldling is suggestive of the havoc which the spirit and genius of worldliness have made in the man's true character. What is worldly conversation for the most part but an exhibition of littleness and frivolity? It never seems to get below the surface. Men of the world know nothing of the fellowship of heart with heart. Just think how impossible it would be for two such persons to discuss with each other their inner life and heart experiences. Oh, empty, hollow, world, is this man s best substitute for God! Now the apostle affirms that we have denied worldly lust as well as ungodliness. We have renounced and repudiated it for ever. But here rises the question, How have the world and worldly lust been thus denied? or how are we to deny it? and how are we to be freed from it? Various answers to this inquiry meet us from different quarters. "Turn your back upon the world," says the ascetic. "Wander into the depths of the desert. Shut yourself up in an eremite's cave, or hide yourself within a monastic enclosure." But even so, how shall I be sure that I may not carry a little world of my own along with me? How shall we get rid of the world's bondage? or how shall we deny this worldly lust, and rise above it? "Despise it," says the cynic. "Be indifferent to all considerations of pain and pleasure. Never mind what the world thinks of you. Rejoice in being peculiar." May not our Diogenes be creating for himself a greater conqueror, or a greater tyrant, in his own inflated self-consciousness, than ever was an Alexander or a Xerxes? No; we want a better answer than this. Again I ask, "How am I to deny worldly lust?" It is all round me. "God forbid that I should glory, save in the Cross of our Lord Jesus Christ, whereby the world hath been crucified to me, and I unto the world." That is the answer. Grace had taught St. Paul that lesson. He did not learn it on Sinai, but at Calvary. "There was a time when thou didst think well of the world, wast elated by her blandishments, wast alarmed at the thought of her frown. Thou didst value her good opinion, and didst shrink above everything else from forfeiting it; thou wast attracted by her glitter, and blinded by her display. But now, behold the world is revealed as a traitress and a usurper, a rebel against Infinite Benevolence, and a deceiver of all her deluded votaries; for in her judgment theirs is revealed. Child of God, the world is crucified to thee. There she hangs, represented in the great Victim of her malice under the ban of God's wrath, blighted with a curse, blasted by the dread thunderbolt from the hand of Omnipotent Justice. Thou seest her now exposed to shame and everlasting contempt. Nor canst thou make a cunning compromise between thy God and her whom thou seest crucified yonder; for there can be no compromise between a condemned culprit and his judge. No: 'If any man love the world, the love of the Father is not in him'; for the friendship of the world is enmity towards God. And even that is not all," Grace goes on to say. "By that same Cross thou, too, art crucified unto the world. To the world He is a despised, rejected outcast, crucified outside the camp; and as He is, so art thou in this present world. Surely thou canst not refuse to bear His reproach, to whom thou owest thy all of dignity and honour. But even this is not all. Thou art crucified unto the world; 'for thou art dead, and thy life is hid with Christ in God.' Thy old worldly life has been forfeited; but through death and resurrection thou hast been born again as a citizen of the New Jerusalem. Thou art raised up into the heavenly places in Christ Jesus; and now thou art not of the world, as He is not of the world. Art thou content to accept the privileges of the Atonement? Thou rejoicest to accept them. Then understand that one of the privileges of the Atonement is, that thou shouldst be separated, by the very terms of the Atonement, from thy old relationship to a God-resisting world—a world which has presented itself to the hearts of its children as a substitute for the Being to whom it owed its origin." Can we conceive it possible for a true believer to address his Saviour thus: "O Lord, I desire to escape hell, and I understand that Thy Atonement has been made in order that I may escape it; but I understand also that Thy Atonement had in view several other objects, about which I have no concern. I gather that it was also designed to save me from sin; but about that I am indifferent, so long as I escape sin's consequences. I will accept the immunity from condemnation. I will be very glad to know that the doors of hell are shut in my face, and that the doors of heaven are opened. But further than this I have no desire; indeed, were I to accept more, the consequences to myself might not be pleasant." It is, perhaps, impossible to conceive of such language in the lips of any true child of God; yet I fear that such words describe only too accurately the attitude assumed by too many who think themselves Christians indeed. They seek to retain sufficient religion to enable them to entertain the hope of heaven; but they cover this over so skilfully with a cloak of worldly conformity, that they are hardly suspected by their acquaintance and friends of possessing any religion at all. Such Christians attempt to lead a double life in religious society; they can talk as well as any one on religious subjects, and may pass with strangers for earnest and decided Christians; but amongst the citizens of the world they assume quite a different manner, and can be as flippant and frivolous and insincere as any with whom they associate. Yes; it must be one thing or the other—the world or God; we cannot choose both. If we decide to choose the world and seek a substitute for God, then let us get the very best substitute we possibly can find. Do you select money for your substitute? If it be pleasure you select, then live for pleasure. Our choice lies between the two; but ere we decide for the world, let us remember the solemn sentence uttered by inspired lips, but amply confirmed by daily observation, " The world passeth away, and the lust thereof." If we make choice of it, we cannot keep it; if we decline to deny it, it will soon deny us. (*W. H. M. H. Aitken.*) **Live soberly, righteously, and godly, in this present world.**—*Present day Christian life:*—Is this a good time for a sober, righteous, and godly life? " Business standards," it is said, " are relaxing; home habits, loose; self-seeking, the common rule; plain living and high thinking, not the custom of the time." in such a state of mind two things seem possible. One is to yield to the pressure of the age. Accepting its inconsistency with the Christian life, one may adapt himself to standards which his conscience never can approve. That is the common worldliness of the present age, surrendering character to the social pressure of the time. The other thing to do is to run away from the age. That is what thousands of the choicest souls have done throughout Christian history. They have thought it impossible to live a sober life in the full current of their own time; and so they have fled from its influence, hiding themselves in monasteries and peopling the desert with their caves. No one can survey the story of these ascetics and hermits without a glow of admiration. It is a great thing that the enticements of each age which have overpowered so many souls have been powerless over a few. But none the less this whole story is not the story of a battle, but of a flight. And it was a fruitless flight. Fleeing from the world, they fled from all the chance they had to make it better. If, then, the sober, righteous, and godly man is not to yield himself to the present age, nor yet to flee from it, what is he to do? Why, he is to use it—to take it just as it is, as the God-given material out of which the Christian character fit for the present time is to be wrought. The saints of the past have been, for the most part, those who have fled from the world; but the Christian saint of to-day is the person who can use the world. Such a person may be all unconscious that he is doing anything heroic. He is simply the man in the business world who, amid looseness and dishonour, keeps himself true and clean; simply the woman who, amid luxury and affectation, keeps her simplicity and sympathy; simply the youth who, without the least retreat from the influences which beset him in a place like this, makes them contribute to his growth of character. That is a harder thing than to be a hermit, and quite as noble as to be a saint. It is the sober, righteous, and godly life lived in the midst of this present age. The man who hides himself behind the spirit of the age, and makes it the apology of his own folly or sin, is simply deceived. He is like many a man in that western country, who has thought himself standing in a hopeless desert when he really stood in what might be a garden of the world. He simply abandons it to barrenness, instead of turning upon it the stream of service which is at his command, and for which the desert longs. The man, who throws a sober and a godly life into the main movement of the present age, is but contributing the fertilising power to a receptive and responsive world; and the hills and valleys about him will shout for joy at their redemption by that pure and abundant stream. (*F. G. Peabody, D.D.*) *Every-day life:*—I. THE INGREDIENTS OF EVERY-DAY LIFE. **1.** Conversation is a large element of every-day life. The power of speech is one of the grand distinctions of man and of his life upon the earth. It is thus he clothes invisible thought with form, and confers upon the subtle intangible reality an immortality of earthly recognition. Our daily conversation determines all the tone of our mind; it stamps and it stereotypes our temper. It reveals whether charity and virtue, manly or womanly grace, dignify our character; or whether we are frivolous, vain, heartless, and worldly. **2.** Wish is an equally extended department of every-day life. It is in our nature to be conscious of desires after a great many things, and these desires are not in themselves sinful; they are even neces-

sary to the maintenance of life, to the onward progress of mankind, to the subduing and replenishing of the earth which God has lent to us, and in which He has
given us a life-interest. These desires of all kinds are the spring of nearly all that
we do in this life. Let us bring them up now, and see what is the revelation they
will give us of ourselves. Perhaps we shall find a legion of devils, which must be
cast out; a storm of passions, which must be hushed; a brood of revenges, vexations, bad resolves, unbrotherly triumphs, impure hankerings, which must be
trampled out of us. Perhaps they are humble, virtuous, charitable, reasonable,
modest, chaste, holy desires, fit for a brother or sister of Jesus. A moment's
thought will prove that these desires of ours, these genuine intentions, these self-
born, or heaven-inspired, wishes, are our very self; and if we are to be religious
men, religion must have sway over these. 3. Work is another main element in
life. The business of life, the daily toil and drudgery of a man, these help to constitute his every-day life. It must be possible to bring all this under the empire of
religion—to supply a set of motives that can dignify the commonest occupation,
consecrate the humblest toil, and make " daily drudgery divine "—motives which
can explode and deflagrate those wretched purposes and evil desires that have so
often issued in violated laws and broken hearts; and motives which will hallow
and purify all our service and every talent. 4. But there is another large department of every-day life to which it is necessary to refer—I mean Recreation. That
which is recreation to one man would be a complete penance to another; that which
some of you think a most enjoyable relaxation is to others an intolerable weariness.
Some mode of spending the leisure hour is necessary to every man; and perhaps
nothing more surely indicates his temper and spirit than the method in which he
finds it most agreeable to while away his spare time and gather strength for
further duty. As religion penetrates every-day life, the whole tone of recreation rises in character, until it becomes harmless, pleasant, virtuous, holy,
religious, and useful. To promote this end is one great enterprise of the Church.
II. THE REQUIREMENTS OF THE GOSPEL AS TO EVERY-DAY LIFE. 1. Sobriety means the
chastisement of all our passions, the resolute endeavour to gain and keep the control of all our desires, the determination to repress angry feelings as well as impure
fancies, to subdue inordinate affection quite as much as depraved taste. Sobriety
means resistance to every form of temptation. It has its realm in work quite as
much as in recreation—in recreation quite as much as in work. 2. Righteousness
is clearly something more than a refusal to commit an act of cruelty or dishonesty.
Righteous living includes this; but it means very much more than this. We
must respect every just claim upon us, not merely upon our money, but upon our
affection, our reverence, and our good offices—and we must recognise and yield the
right to every man who has one, to our good words, to our time, to our service, to
our best efforts—or we are not acting justly. 3. The life here spoken of is to be a
life of godliness; we must date and draw our motives from the highest source. The
government of all our passions, the recognition of every just claim upon us, must
spring from no mere vague notion that it is right to do this, but from the discovery
of the ground of our nature, our relation to the living God, our obligation to the
suffering Saviour, and our responsibility to the Spirit of grace. (*H. R. Reynolds,
D.D.*) *The true value of morality :*—This passage is an admirable example of the
manner of the apostle in mingling exhortation to present duties with the recognition and enforcement of that Divine power from which true obedience springs.
In other words, we find blended here morality and spirituality. Both
the one and the other are made to cohere, and to be in consistency with each
other; and both of them spring from considerations of manhood in ourselves, and
of gratitude and allegiance to God. It is difficult to give—nor is it necessary that
we should give—a definition of morality. It is a phrase in every man's mouth. It
does not mean the same with all, however. Men take their ideas of morality, not
only from the communities in which they live, but from the circles in which they
associate in any one community; and what would be considered as morality in a
certain sort of neighbourhood in this city, would not be considered as continental
morality. Morality in a neighbourhood may not be morality in a family of refinement and culture. There is something higher than morality in a cultured household. But yet men are regarded as moral who act in accordance with the laws of
the land and with the customs of the community, and who avoid any outbreaking
sins which shock the average conscience. It may be said, in the first place, that
morality possesses the benefit of the most important negatives. A truly moral man,
in the judgment of all, should be a man who does not get drunk, and does not steal,

and does not commit burglary, and does not bear false witness. In other words, he is one who is rid of outbreaking vices and outrageous crimes. Well, that is creditable. You ought not to be guilty of such things. And if you have had a strong bias in your nature in any of these directions, and have arrested it, and that under circumstances where influences from without threatened to carry you away, it is no small thing. It is a great thing that you have avoided those pitfalls in which so many have been destroyed. Still, that is not the sum of all excellence. It is not enough for you to congratulate yourself upon, as I think we shall see. I not only recognise the import and excellence of morality in such sterling virtues as these, but I exhort men to them; and I say: "If you cannot go any further, go as far as that. It is a great deal better to go so far than not to reach that point. It may be only a beginning, but it is a beginning." Secondly: Morality includes those simple virtues which are indispensable to a wholesome life in society. A man can scarcely be called moral who is destitute of worldly honour. Honour is a sort of secular and partial conscience. It is functional; but within its limits it serves a most important end, and keeps alive those fragmentary elements of a higher life, of a higher moral sense, to which all men should be brought. Truth is one of those elements which is regarded as indispensable to morality—that is to say, such ordinary truth as passes current in life. Therefore morality includes honour, and truth, and fidelity, as well as honesty and fairness. And men say, "I am a moral man," meaning by that that they are possessed of these social and business-like virtues. The experiences of civil life and commercial life have found out many things which are very necessary for the easy conduct of affairs. For the regulation of society, for the living together of great masses of men, various things are inculcated, as essential to morality. Public sentiment demands certain things which are necessary to morality. The law prescribes certain things which are indispensable to morality. The customs prescribe certain negatives which enter into the popular idea of morality. And all of these are designed to take away the friction from the machinery of life, and to raise men above animal violence and above deceit, and put them upon a certain plane of moral sentiment. All that I complain of in reference to them is, that they are so low, that they are such uneducated and undeveloped forms of excellence, that they tend to dampen men's ambition, and to render them satisfied with the germs of things, instead of leading them to aspire after higher excellences of which these are but the basilar leaves. For—first; Morality in this grand sense founded upon external convenience, and not upon the requirements of things relating to man's whole nature. So it is a mere fragmentary thing; and it is a fragmentary thing in its lowest stages of development. Secondly: It restrains the outplay of evil; but it does not attempt to purify and to cure the sources of evil. Thirdly: It permits heinous faults which impoverish character, and waste the heart of man. Thus, a man may be a moral man who is peevish, morose, fretful. Fourthly: Morality aims to build up a man outwardly in his condition, but not inwardly in his character. It does not seek to develop one single spiritual grace. Lastly: It leaves out, wholly, the world to come, and all the obligations which we owe to God, and all the relations which are established between the soul and the Saviour Jesus Christ. It leaves out religion. That is to say, it leaves out the highest forms of aspiration and of duty, and all that which faith brings within the circuit of our knowledge and makes imperative. Here, then, are the deficiencies of morality. I have said that in conduct, in its lowest form, it has its value; but I think you will now perceive that it cannot be a substitute for religion. And yet, men who have only morality, say, "What lack I yet?" Now, if an Indian, with a fragmentary dress, should present himself as a full-dressed man before you, would you deride the idea that he was properly clad? Would you have him throw away the little he had before he got more? Complete dress is what one wants; but is nothing short of that of any value? I do not say to the young, "These moralities are of no value to you." They are of great value to you. Truth-speaking, fidelity, industry, cleanliness, punctuality, frugality, enterprise—these are real excellencies. Have these at least. Have these anyhow. But will you be content with these? Is there not something in every human soul which has the touch of inspiration in it, and which leads it to aspire to something more than these qualities, which belong to the undeveloped mass of mankind? Morality is not in any sense, then, a substitute for spiritual religion, any more than industry and frugality are substitutes for patriotism. Every man ought to be frugal and industrious; but many are frugal and industrious who have no patriotism. "Well, then," you will say, "what about those qualities when a man dies? A man has been industrious, and frugal, and honest, and moderately truth-speaking all his life long; and when he dies, and goes to judgment, what is to be done with these qualities which you say are good?" Well, they are of benefit to you now; they are of benefit to you in a thousand ways in this world; but they do not constitute that character which is to fit you for the world to come. They do not go to make the golden key which unlocks those mysteries of love which you. have need of. These minor qualities are not a substitute for it. You go forth an ungrown spirit; you go forth with lower leaves without the bloom and the fruit; and the lower is no substitute for the higher. Moreover, out of every one of these lower states, if we did but know it, may be developed, by the Divine grace, that which shall bring forth the true spiritual life. If you know enough to take one step, take a second. If you know enough to recognise law and obligation, and that low sense of character which is required by society, you have that foundation on which moral government itself rests, and you know enough to go on from step to step, and from strength to strength, and develop out of your lower knowledges higher attainments. Spirituality is only the normal and legitimate development of men in their higher forms, Divinely inspired, Divinely led, and Divinely blessed. It is God that works in those who work out their own salvation. It is the Divine co-operation and guiding influence that works upon your mind; and out of this joint working come all the grace, all the hope, all the faith, all the sweet fruition of love, the sense of immortality, and the longing for it, which we experience. And whatever is just, and true, and pure, and sweet, and of good report, upon earth, and in the heavenly circle—all this comes, to be sure, by the grace of God; but it comes by the grace of God through the development of your own faculties, and through your own striving. (*H. W. Beecher.*)　　*Good works :*—This passage has deen described as "a concise epitome of the Christian system in its practical bearing on human experience and conduct." St. Paul's great theme was faith, but no one acquainted with his writings can charge him with indifference respecting works. I. The WORKERS. A careful study of the passage will show that these are—1. Redeemed ones, "Might redeem us" (ver. 14). The bond slaves of Satan cannot work for God. David said, "O Lord, truly I am Thy servant; Thou hast loosed my bonds." 2. Saved ones, "Bringeth salvation" (ver. 11). The believer does not work for salvation, but from it. Like the new-born child, he does not move to get life, but because he has it. 3. Instructed ones, "Teaching us" (ver. 12). The Christian needs to be taught what to do (Acts ix. 6), and how to do it, "His way," (Psa. xxv. 9). 4. Hopeful ones, "Looking for that blessed hope" (ver. 13). The hope of the Lord's coming is a great stimulus to holiness and activity (Heb. x. 25). II. The WORKSHOP. "This present world" (ver. 12). The believer's first sphere of action is in the world. This is—1. A good sphere for the believer. It must be, for our Lord prayed not that His people should be taken out of the world (John xvii. 15). Conflict with evil is bracing (1 John ii. 14). 2. A sphere of much danger. This present world is an evil world, "This present evil world" (Gal. i. 4). Demas was damaged by it (2 Tim. iv. 10), and our Lord, remembering the presence of the evil, prayed that His disciples might be kept from it (John xvii. 15). A sphere of usefulness. Here Christ achieved His gracious and beneficent purposes, "He was in the world" (John i. 10). Here is the material which may be shaped into crowns to adorn the Redeemer's brow. We may say, as Dr. Macleod said to Dr. Guthrie, in reference to the Cowgate in Edinburgh, "A fine field of labour, sir." III. The WORKS. What have God's workmen to do? Many things. Note—1. The rejection of bad models, "Denying" (ver. 12). A bad model will result in bad work. See this in the case of Nadab, "Way of his father" (1 Kings xv. 26). To deny (ἀρνέομαι) is to disown. The believer disowns "ungodliness," that which is not in the likeness of God or after the mind of God. (See 2 Pet. ii. 5, 6.) "Worldly lusts" are those things which are the staple of the desires of worldly men (John viii. 44; 1 John ii. 16). 2. The maintenance of a healthy moral sense, "Live soberly." "Sobriety," says Mr. Aitken, "according to the Greek moralist, Aristotle, is that which preserves or protects and maintains in due activity our moral sense." Temptation often produces moral intoxication. It destroys the balance of mind, and reason is in a measure dethroned. Against this evil we must be constantly watching, or there will be discord and disorder in our lives. 3. The production of what is right, "Righteously" (ver. 12). The believer must do right in his relation to his family, his friends, society, and the whole world. 4. The imitation of the best model, "Godly" (ver. 12). The believer is to be God-like. He must aim at no lower standard. (Matt. v. 48; 1 Pet. ii. 21.) IV. The WORKMANSHIP.

" Zealous of good works " (ver. 14). The best work can only be accomplished by
the enthusiastic worker. This is true of works of art. Think of the enthusiasm
of Michael Angelo, of Rubens, of Mozart, of Palissy. The best work is
work for God, and for this the highest enthusiasm is required. What a stimulus
to zeal we have in the example of our Lord, " Who gave Himself " (ver. 14).
Well might Brainerd say, " Oh that I were a flaming fire in the service of my
God ! " (*H. Thorne.*)    *The Christian's business :*—I. THE CHRISTIAN'S BUSINESS,
while an inhabitant of this present world. 1. What he must renounce. (1) Ungodliness. (2) Worldly lusts. 2. What he must cultivate. (1) With regard to
his personal character he is to " live soberly." While *in* the world, he is not *of* the
world. His heart is weaned from its honours, riches, and pleasures. He uses this
world without abusing it. (2) We now pass on to view the Christian in his social
capacity. He is to live " righteously " as well as " soberly." This term includes
all his relative obligations. (*a*) With regard to the relation in which he stands to his
fellow creatures in general, he looks upon himself as a member of one great family,
all of whom have suffered a common shipwreck. He sees himself rescued from the
wreck by an act of infinite grace, and, therefore, he cannot exult over the rest of the
crew as though by his own right hand, or by his own arm he had gotten himself
the victory. Tender compassion towards the whole race fills his breast. He longs
to tell the whole world of " the grace of God which bringeth salvation " ; and he
uses every means in his power to diffuse the knowledge of this unsearchable grace.
(*b*) In his relation also to the Church of Christ the Christian would live
" righteously." He must here, also, be influenced by the law of love. Consider
the many ties which bind Christians to each other. Having a common Father,
redeemed by the same precious blood, pervaded by the same Spirit, possessing one
hope of their calling—what more can they need to cement the bond that unites
them ? (3) In his religious duties he is to cultivate godliness. (*a*) He seeks to
please God. (*b*) He loves to hold communion with God. (*c*) He delights to think
of God. (*d*) He glorifies God in his body and in his spirit. II. THE CHRISTIAN'S
HOPE IN PROSECUTING HIS BUSINESS. What is it that urges on the worldling to labour
and toil? What is it that keeps him in one unbroken course of regular and well-
sustained exertion? Or, again, what is it that excites the shipwrecked mariner to
stem the foaming surge ? What is it that keeps him clinging with invincible firmness to the friendly plank? Is it not hope? Now if the expectation of worldly
gain, and of a temporal salvation can yield such support, oh ! say, what should
be the sustaining power of your hope—the hope of your Saviour's second coming.
Whether we consider the blessedness of your hope, a complete salvation ; or whether
we consider the time of its consummation, the glorious appearing of the Redeemer ;
or, whether, again, we look to the character of your expected Saviour—in whatever
point of view we behold your blessed object of hope—we cannot but feel how
mighty should be its influence in stirring you up to " live soberly, righteously, and
godly in this present world." (*H. Cadell, M.A.*)    *Right living :*—I. SOBERLY. 1.
We must have control over all the base passions of our nature. The monarch of
himself is king of men. 2. There is to be a proper restraint over the more refined,
the æsthetic elements of our nature. If you can build a fine house and pay for it
with your own money—not your neighbour's, nor God's—build it, adorn it with
statuary, beautify it with paintings : but make art the handmaid of religion. See
to it that the more you spend on yourself, the more you give to God. 3. There
must also be a wise control over our professional pursuits. Remember, this world
is not all. Let eternal verities dwarf earthly vanities. II. RIGHTEOUSLY, or
rather " justly "—the word points to moral rectitude. 1. We are not needlessly to injure our neighbour. His property, person, and good name are
sacred. 2. We are to render to every one his due. We must be just in
all our dealings. 3. We are to strive to lead all to salvation through
Christ. Our duty to man is not negative. Duty is " due-ty." The Christian is to
be Christlike : thus he will draw men to God. III. GODLY. Regard to God runs
through all our other duties ; personal and relative duties must be done with an eye
to His glory. But some duties refer at once to Him. 1. Repentance towards God
—a heart broken for and from sin. 2. Faith in Jesus Christ. You cannot please
God if you refuse to trust Him. 3. Obedience. This includes all duties. (*R. S.
MacArthur, D.D.*)    *The sober life :*—Hitherto we have been occupied in considering the negative teaching of Grace, by which her pupils are trained to deny
ungodliness and worldly lust. Grace begins by separating us from connection with
the old, that she may hasten to introduce us into connection with the new. She

does not rest satisfied with inducing merely the denial of ungodliness and worldly lusts. Grace begins by communicating life, and along with it a new life-power, which is to manifest its presence in the character and conduct of those who receive it. We must possess the new life before we can live it. It must be received before it can be manifested. You might just as well expect a piece of dead wood to grow into a tree the moment you planted it in the ground, and attached to it by some artificial process a few bunches of leaves, or clusters of fruit. Your own common sense tells you that you may plant your walking-stick in your garden, and, with the utmost possible care, you may prune it, and water it, and perform all other possible horticultural operations upon it, but it remains a dead stick at the end of the process, and nothing but a dead stick; and you cannot make it grow into life. Let us desist from conceiving that we can ever grow into a state of spiritual vitality by our efforts to improve ourselves. Not only are we taught that Grace saves us from and separates us from the old, but that it introduces us into the new. Not only is the ransomed soul dead unto sin, but alive unto God. We rise into a state of vitality when first we begin to trust ourselves to Christ for life; then only can we receive the gift of life in Jesus Christ from the hand of God, and begin to be, in the full sense of the word, living souls. Are we trying to live soberly, righteously, and godly, because law claims it of us? or are we living thus because we claim it by faith of God, as the law of our new nature that we should do so? Let us proceed to consider the positive characteristics of our new life, to which the apostle here calls attention. We notice that of the three words that he employs—the first brings before us primarily that which we owe to ourselves; the second, chiefly that which we owe to our fellow-man; and the third, exclusively that which we owe to God. The first suggests to our minds the thought of the relations of the various parts of our complex nature to each other; the second, of our relations to society; and the third, of our relations to God. Let us begin by considering the first of these three words as suggesting an important, we may say an essential, lesson of Grace. It is the privilege of the true child of God to lead a sober life. The ancient Greek moralist, Aristotle, in speaking of this word, suggests an etymological derivation of the term, which, though not perhaps philologically correct, may yet serve to indicate the true character of the idea conveyed by the expression to his own mind and the minds of his contemporaries. He speaks of the word here used as formed of two words, signifying the preservation of the moral sense, and accordingly defines temperance or sobriety to be that which preserves or protects, and maintains in due activity our moral sense. This, at all events, gives us a good idea of what an intelligent Greek-speaking man would understand by the word "sobriety." Let us reflect for a moment upon the idea thus suggested to our minds. It implies, we observe, the possibility of our moral sense being lost, or so interfered with as for the time being to be rendered inoperative. How different things appear when we contemplate them in the abstract and in cold blood, so to speak, from what they do when once they have become causes of actual temptation to us. How readily did the moral sense of David reprobate the pitiless injustice and rapacity of the wealthy despoiler! How often is this blinding influence exercised by passion! Or, again, with respect to worldly lust, which is a common form of moral insobriety, how easy is it for us, in our calmer moments, to deride the world, to look down contemptuously upon it.—" Well, after all, what an idle show it is—what a poor painted pageant!" And then we come down from the mount of contemplation, we find ourselves sucked into the stream before we know what is happening; and there we are, just as worldly as other people. What has happened? We have lost our moral sense. We are blinded by the force of the temptations to which we have been exposed, and the influences by which we are surrounded. Now, let us endeavour to get an idea into our minds of some of the various forms which this insobriety may assume (Rom. xii. 3). A man who thinks more highly of himself than he ought to think, might not at first sight appear to us to be one who is leading a life wanting in sobriety; and yet that is just the description that St. Paul gives of such a person. In 1 Peter iv. 7, we have a solemn warning given to us upon this subject: " The end of all things is at hand: be ye therefore sober." Keep your heads clear, the apostle seems to say. You are only down here for a few short days. The end of all things is at hand. Now observe, that where this intoxicating influence prevails, man becomes a prey to inward discords and disorders. The higher elements in his nature are no longer able to master the lower and keep them in their proper place. Now Grace proposes to introduce and maintain moral harmony within our nature; so that, instead of element being arrayed against element, and part against part, the whole may live, and continue to live, under the perfect law of liberty. Grace undertakes so to train us that passion shall not be able to tyrannise over the understanding, or desire ride rough-shod over conscience ; but that those elements in our nature which are necessarily highest shall occupy their own proper position, and those elements which are necessarily lower shall be subordinated to the superior and commanding faculties which God has set over them. Such in general terms is the character of the sober life. But how are we to establish this inward harmony ? How is this most anarchical world one day to be set in perfect order ? When and how will the true *cosmos* be realised ? We, basing our hope upon a most sure word of prophecy, look forward to that glorious period of the future, of which I read, " Behold, a king shall reign in righteousness, and princes shall execute judgment in the earth." There is a time coming when Messiah's sceptre shall sway the hearts of men, and "the kingdoms of this world shall become the kingdoms of our Lord and of His Christ." Meanwhile, until that glorious day come, it is possible for us, each one of us, in our own souls to realise a millennium, where "the wolf and the lamb shall lie down together, and the lion shall eat straw like the ox." The millennium begins within each human heart when Jesus Christ is King. We have all read of the horrors of the first French Revolution. We recall with a shudder the ghastly tale of that reign of terror, when the guillotine was the prominent object in Parisian history, and the noblest and the best blood of France was flowing in the gutters. Yes, it was a terrible time ; but in what occurred then you have a picture of what occurs in every human heart where insobriety is rampant. What is to be done to remedy this terrible moral disorder ? How is sobriety to be established ? Thus we see that this virtue of sobriety is something more than a mere negation. It consists not merely in escaping from the tyranny of lust, but in possessing such a sound judgment, such a calm recollectedness, such an administrative capacity, so to speak, as shall enable us to hold the reins of government under Divine authority in the commonwealth of our being, as " a king against whom there is no rising up " (Prov. xxx. 31)—our renewed will becoming God's own vicegerent within our redeemed and consecrated nature. Sobriety regulates, but does not exterminate— modifies, but does not ignore—our natural propensities, which in themselves become only good or bad as they are kept in their proper place, or allowed to depart from it. Nor, again, is sobriety to be confused with phlegmatic dulness and insensibility ; on the contrary, it is perfectly compatible with the loftiest enthu- siasm, and is often the guide and supporter of burning zeal. Nor, once more, must we fail to distinguish between sobriety and moroseness. There is nothing gloomy, nothing misanthropic, nothing affected or unnatural, though much that is super- natural, in the sober life. The sober Christian sees things, not so much by the " dry light " of the ancient philosopher as in the warm light of Divine love that pervades everything. Are we living a sober life ? Do we know what it is thus in God's name and by God's power to possess our souls ? How common a thing, for example, is it to meet with Christian people who are the victims, not the masters, of an evil and irritable temper, which is ready to be excited on even the slenderest provocation, and to suggest the stormy word, the bitter thought, the hasty and unjustifiable action ! Such a habit of soul is simply one form of that moral insobriety, that incapacity of self-control, which erases from our minds, so to speak, for the moment, the sober conclusions of reason, silences our moral sentiment, or so bewilders and confuses it, that it is no longer able to form a just estimate of conduct, to condemn the wrong and maintain the right. But are you living by Grace ? Can Christ in you exhibit a bad temper ? The truth is, we come down from the level of Grace and " walk as men," and then we need scarcely wonder that the old tree brings forth the old evil fruit. Or, to take another illustration, how many professing Christians are hampered and marred by some form of worldli- ness, by vanity, love of money, or by the ambitious dreams of youth ? This is but another form of insobriety ; our spiritual apprehension has been confused by the insurrection of lower desires unworthy of our Christian character. How many Christians have to complain of their bondage to their own sensual propensities ? Let me point out that as Grace provides us with the power, so in the very first great lesson that she gives us she teaches how the power is to be applied. It is through faith that we receive the first great blessing that Divine Grace communicates ; it is through faith that we receive all others. Our will has indeed to be exercised, but it has to be exercised rather in admitting its own inability, and in surrendering to Another the task for which it feels incompetent, than in endeavouring to perform the task itself. (*W. H. M. H. Aitken.*) *The righteous life :*—The word "righteous-

ness " sometimes signifies, or at any rate includes, what is here spoken of as
temperance or sobriety, and sometimes what is here spoken of as "godliness."
But inasmuch as it here stands side by side with these two other terms, we believe
it to be used in a narrower sense, and to have special reference to our relations
with our fellow-man. The true meaning of the word "righteousness" is suggested
to us by a reference to the root word "right," from which it is derived, just as
analogously in the Greek language the word δικαιοσύνη draws its essential import
from its connection with its root word δίκη. The idea of righteousness springs from
the recognition of right. There are certain rights which have their origin in the
nature of our relations with others, which they are justified in claiming that we
should respect, and from which we cannot escape, and the recognition of these
rights and the fulfilment of these claims is that which we understand by "righteousness." We are under certain obligations in the first instance to God, and God
has certain rights in us which He cannot for a moment ignore or decline to assert
and enforce. In recognising these rights, and in responding to these claims, we
fulfil the law of righteousness, so far as God is concerned. Further, there are
certain rights which our fellow-men have in us, which we are not less bound to
respect; and inasmuch as we are at present using the term righteousness in the
somewhat restricted sense that I have indicated, it will be desirable to give this
second class of rights our special consideration. Yes, our fellow-men have certain
rights in us from which we cannot free ourselves. We owe to society a great debt.
Perhaps we do not sufficiently let our minds dwell upon the thought of our debt to
society, yet everything around might well remind us of it. The very food that we
eat is the product of social labour. We are dependent upon society, and hence are
constantly indebted to it. The very money which we offer in return for these
benefits is but the symbol of the accumulated labour of mankind; and those who
are born in the possession of most of it are therefore the greatest debtors of all. It
is true that some of us endeavour to contribute to the wealth of society by our
labour, thus making some return for what we have received; but if we reflect how
very different our condition is from what it would have been had we been cut off
from society from our early years we shall be able to see how much our debt
exceeds our capacities of repayment. The Christian feels that he owes an even
heavier debt than this to his fellow-man. He cannot forget that it was through the
devotion of human messengers, who jeoparded their lives in the task, that the glad
tidings of the gospel ever became so widely known as to reach his ear. He cannot
forget his debt to the Church of Christ all through the ages, nor his obligations to
those who have represented her beneficent influences towards him. Who shall
say how much we may have been influenced for God and for good, by comparatively
trivial circumstances, which have not even left their impress upon our memory, or
perhaps of which we have never known at all? "All souls are Mine," says the
great Father of spirits; and because they are His, therefore they possess a certain
definite claim upon our consideration, indifference to which must needs argue
indifference to Him. There are certain things which society has a right to claim
that we should not do, and there are others which society has a right to claim that
we should do. Now, as a rule, human laws only recognise the negative claims of
right. They provide means for checking men from performing unlawful deeds.
When we turn from laws, Divine and human, to conventional morality, here also we
find ourselves mainly dealing with the negative side of moral obligation. The idea
of righteousness most generally entertained by society is negative rather than
positive. Men flatter themselves that if they have done no very definite harm to
any one they have pretty well fulfilled the law of righteousness. How often are we
told by those whom we seek to convict of sin, and of their need of a Saviour, that
they have always endeavoured to do their duty by God and man; and when we
come to examine what their idea of duty is, we discover that they simply mean that
they are not criminals or open offenders against public decency! But let us observe,
in spite of the common sentiment, that the positive claims of the law of righteousness are just as strong and just as incapable of being defeated as are its negative
claims. In plain language, we are just as much bound to live for the good of our
fellow-men as to abstain from injuring them; and even if we can satisfy ourselves
that we have abstained from injuring our fellow-men, unless we can also show that,
according to the measure of our opportunity, we have actually benefited them, we
are not in a position to claim that we have even made an attempt to fulfil the law of
righteousness. But have men as a rule as much right as they think they have, to
conclude that they have fulfilled even the negative claims of the Divine law? We

may wrong our neighbour without any overt action, and perhaps more grievously than if we had injured his body with our hand. The scandalous story, even the uncharitable thought, which may be the parent of so many cruel actions, who shall say how much of base injustice there may be in these, and yet the world thinks lightly of them. How much of selfish grasping and pushing may strain the relations of man with man, and yet no such act of dishonesty or violence be committed as could be taken cognisance of by law. All this may pass for justice amongst men, but does it appear so in the eyes of God? So what does it matter how little we pay our commercial clerks, or our half-starved sempstresses; or what does it matter if we deny a Sabbath to our cab and omnibus drivers, and keep them slaving, some fourteen hours a day, all the year round. Justice, after all, is not such a very common virtue amongst mankind. But it is possible for us to injure our neighbour in other ways than these, and thus equally to offend against the negative demands of the law of righteousness. How many are ready enough to affirm "that they have never done any harm to anybody," who have never even reflected upon the injury that may have been caused even to their nearest friends by the unholy effect of their influence or example. How many a once pure-minded and innocent girl is wrecked and ruined for life, by learning only too well the lessons of vanity and levity taught by companions and acquaintances, who never seemed to themselves to be vicious. But even when it can be shown that we are blameless in this respect, we have yet to face its positive claims. The same authority that claims that we should do justly tells us also that God requires that we should love mercy. This is as much a matter of obligation, arising out of our relations with our fellow-man, as is the other; and the man that does not love mercy, although he may flatter himself that he does justly, has not fulfilled the law of righteousness. But while under the Old Dispensation the legal obligation was distinctly recognised, we shall see here also how much better and more effectually grace teaches than law. Grace is not content with laying down the positive precept; she presses this lesson upon our mind more forcibly than any commandment could, by setting before us this as the most prominent and striking characteristic of the life of Him whom she has already taught us to trust and love. His was no cold negative morality, no mere abstinence from sin in every form; His morality was the fulfilment of the law, because it was the continuous exhibition of love to the sons of men. His career is thus epitomised by one who was an eyewitness of it. "He went about doing good, and healing all that were oppressed of the devil; for God was with Him." More than this; Grace not only exhibits to us this perfect ideal, and sets before us a personal example of pure unselfish benevolence in His life and history, but she offers to us all her best benefits as the result of His having possessed and exercised towards us those qualities which she desires us to imitate. "The love of Christ constraineth us," exclaims the apostle; that is to say, not our love for Christ, but the consciousness of His love to us—"because we thus judge, that if one died for all, then all died: and that He died for all, that they who live should not henceforth live unto themselves, but unto Him who died for them, and rose again." Who that has been a recipient of Divine favour can be insensible to such an argument as that? How can we avail ourselves of the self-sacrificing love of Christ for our own salvation, and yet be unmindful of the obligation under which this lays us? We owe our salvation, our immunity from condemnation, and our justification before God, to the fact that, as representing our unrighteousness, Christ died, while, representing the righteousness that God expects of us, He lived. But if this be so, how can we claim the benefits of His life and death without repudiating that which in Him was crucified, and accepting that which in Him won the smile of the Divine Father's approval? To sum up then, Grace teaches us to live righteously, first by showing in a human life what righteousness, both negative and positive, is, next by loading us with all the spiritual benefits that we enjoy in virtue of the righteousness of this our Great Exemplar; so that gratitude to Him binds us to a life of righteousness, and further by the illustration of God's judgment against all unrighteousness and sin, and by the fulfilment of that judgment upon the person of the sinner's Representative on the Cross of Calvary, and as the necessary sequel to this legal condemnation by the introduction of the Divine Spirit as a power of righteousness into our hearts. Surely there is no lack of means towards the end in the school of grace. She is well supplied, not only with lessons, but with all that is needed to bring the lessons home. But further, our idea of righteousness must ever be relative to our subjective condition. That which does not offend my sense of righteousness to-day, I may distinctly condemn and repudiate a twelvemonth hence. We can speak with assurance of extreme forms, either of evil on the one hand, or of good on the other; but our judgment begins to waver and assurance to forsake us as we approach the border line, and it is only as we become through Grace possessed more and more of God, and more and more taken possession of by God, that our vision becomes clear enough to enable us to discern the dividing line, or even anything that closely approaches to it. But the learners in the school of Grace have one great advantage. They are not students of ethics, but children of God ; and therefore it is less their habit to inquire whether a thing is right or wrong, than to endeavour to discover whether or not it be in accordance with the mind of God concerning them. They have no desire to discover the minimum of obligation, but a great ambition to reach the maximum of devotion. As the knowledge of the Divine will opens more and more clearly upon their apprehension, they yield their members more and more fully servants of righteousness unto holiness ; for this is how Grace teaches us to live righteously. The just or righteous man lives by his faith. He is not only quickened by it at first, but lives by it when he is quickened, and herein lies his power for righteousness. But such an one cannot be satisfied with mere negative morality ; for love glows within his heart, kindled by the breath of God; and love is the fulfilling of the law. He owes it to his God, he owes it to his new life, he owes it to society, to live not for himself. (*Ibid.*) *The godly life :*—We proceed now to consider the crowning characteristic of the new life and grandest lesson that Grace essays to teach. All her other lessons, however important in themselves, are designed to lead up to godliness ; and unless this lesson is learnt, all others must remain incomplete ; for this word brings before us the true end of man. The true end of man is to be attained in his own personality ; it is in the proper development and education of the highest and most spiritual faculties of his nature, and in the concentration of these upon their proper object, that man rises to his true destiny and fulfils the great purpose of his being. That object is God; and in the development of those faculties which have God for their proper object, and in their concentration upon Him, consists the state or habit of godliness, while the education and training of these faculties is the work of grace, as she teaches us to lead a godly life. Christianity is a religion, not a mere ethical system, and designed to produce spirituality rather than morality—to teach man to realise and take advantage of his proper relations with God, not to show him how he can improve himself independently of any such relations. God is the centre around which all the moral teaching of the New Testament revolves, or from which it radiates. In the Christian system the revelation of the attributes of God in the person of His Son is the standard of moral truth, and relation of our conduct to God's will thus revealed the criterion of its moral character. The word "conversion," with which modern evangelising preaching has made us all familiar, and more particularly the word in the original Greek which we thus translate, is very well chosen as being suggestive of the only possible commencement of the life of godliness. It signifies not only a turning, but a turning towards God. When first His Divine influences begin to move us, He finds us with our hearts averted from Him, and our lives setting in an opposite direction. Then comes the first great change : the godless heart is brought by the influences of the Holy Spirit to feel its need of God, and in yielding to this sense of need, and in the endeavour to satisfy it, the godly life finds its commencement. "Jesus Christ died for our sins, the just for the unjust, to bring us to God." When that great change has taken place, which we usually call conversion, its most salient feature is always the complete alteration and, we may say, reversal of all our previous relations with God. Instead of flying from Him, we have now boldness to approach Him ; instead of looking upon His service as a yoke of bondage, we find it the only freedom. It is doubtless with a view to this end that faith has been Divinely appointed as the subjective condition of justification. He has appointed simple faith in Himself; for this reason, amongst others, that faith brings us into the closest and most personal relations with God Himself. No man who accepts the Christian revelation at all can fail to recognise the justice of the Divine claims. Created at God's pleasure, and for His glory; redeemed by the life of His Son, and consecrated by the gift of the Divine Spirit ; the believer must, as a matter of theory at any rate, admit that he is under an obligation to his God, from the force of which it is impossible to escape. Two thoughts, however, about these rights of God in His creature we may call attention to in passing. The first is, that these claims of God upon us are not arbitrary in their character, or despotic in their operation ; they are perfectly consistent with, and indeed they are the expression of, Divine love towards man, and therefore they are most strictly in accordance with our true interests. The apparent opposition that sometimes seems to exist between man's interest and God's will arises from the fact that man does not clearly apprehend his own interests, and confuses between his real good and his temporary gratification; while, on the other hand, he misunderstands the nature of the Divine will. If we could only obtain a firm and practical grasp of this great truth, that our interests and God's will must coincide, what different lives we should lead! The second thought to which I desire to refer flows from this, an ever-necessary sequel. Since God's claims cannot be opposed to our truest well-being, therefore they can never be withdrawn or even modified. Were God to ask less than He does He would be doing us an injury, not a benefit; for He would be teaching us to be satisfied with something less than our highest good. These claims of God upon us are like the claims of the law of righteousness, both negative and positive. From certain forms of conduct the law of godliness demands that we should abstain; while, on the other hand, there are certain things which it enjoins. " Ye cannot serve God and mammon." This first negative claim of God upon His creature man is represented in the Decalogue as being attributable to a certain attribute of the Divine character, which is denoted by the word "jealousy." Such being the nature of the first claim of the law of godliness, and such the attribute to which it is due, let us proceed to consider the second, and then to observe how Grace teaches us to comply with these claims. "Thou shalt love the Lord thy God with all thine heart, and with all thy soul, and with all thy might " (Deut. vi. 5). This claim includes all others; for here also " Love is the fulfilling of the law." But how shall we respond to these claims? The Law might say to the Israelites, "Thou shalt have none other gods but Jehovah." But none the less Israel proceeded to copy the idolatries of Egypt and Canaan. And the law may repeat its solemn prohibition to men in our own day, but will that keep them from worshipping at the shrine of Mammon, or Pleasure, or Fashion? The Law might tell the Israelites to love the Lord their God with all their heart; but that did not prevent them from turning their backs upon Him altogether. "My people have forgotten Me days without number." Grace presents to us the claims of God in the light of privileges, ever pointing to the Cross for an argument to move our wills, and appealing to the true character of the Divine purpose for a justification of her claims. Here is a specimen of the way in which she urges God's claims, " I beseech you therefore, brethren, by the mercies of God, that ye present your bodies a living sacrifice, holy, acceptable unto God, which is your reasonable service. And be not conformed to this world: but be ye transformed by the renewing of your mind, that ye may prove what is that good, and perfect, and acceptable, will of God." So long as our hearts resent or even demur to the claims of God upon us we cannot enjoy the fellowship of God. We are not agreed. But as soon as we have joyfully accepted these claims, even though we may have only begun very inadequately to fulfil them, the cause of disagreement is removed, and there is nothing to prevent the soul from enjoying the life of fellowship with God. It is not difficult to see the connection between this habit of fellowship with God and the next feature of the life of godliness to which we will refer, and the development of which constitutes frequently the next forward step in Christian experience. Reconciliation is necessary to fellowship, fellowship is necessary to personal love. This affection is the result of personal knowledge, and increases with it. They must perforce love Him most who know Him best, and they must know Him best who are most in His society, who live in the secret of His presence. Nor is this love of the soul for God a mere enthusiasm of admiration, though admiration must ever be one of its most prominent elements. Nor is this love of the soul for God a mere sentiment, a sickly enthusiasm. Men have been prompt to turn their backs upon the dearest earthly affection, the tenderest ties, because the love of God led them on. But the love of God must needs produce very definite subjective effects upon him who knows its blessedness. Even amongst us men, where persons are bound together by close and mutual affection, it has often been observed that a certain assimilation takes place between them, even though they may have originally been very unlike each other—an assimilation that affects not only character, but outward manners and habits, sometimes even extending to the expression of the countenances and the tones of the voice. It is not surprising, then, that they who walk with God, and thus come completely under the influence of the love of God, should be conformed unto the Divine image. "Beholding His glory, we are changed into the same image from glory to glory, as by the Spirit of the Lord," The characteristics of the godly life are of the most practical kind, for true godliness influences everything, elevating and purifying all, and he who lives it will offer such a contrast in his life and conversation to those who live it not, that men shall still be constrained to marvel at such, and to take knowledge of them that they have been and still are with Jesus. Are we living godly in Christ Jesus? It often happens that present salvation, in virtue of the atoning work of Christ, has been accepted without any very definite apprehension of what I may describe as the moral and actual benefits ensured to us by that work, and of the claims that God makes upon us in consequence of it. Where this has been the case, a change so marked and definite that it is sometimes described as a second conversion often takes place, when first the eyes are fully opened to see what the fulness of God's provision actually is. My next word of counsel would be, that the soul that wishes to grow in godliness should cultivate a habit of delicate sensibility to the Divine influences. This is chiefly to be done by making prompt and unquestioning response to the Divine motions. Yield to those heavenly desires, those Godward aspirations, which suddenly interrupt the ordinary occupations of the mind. Next I would say, Be very jealous of idols. The object may be in itself an innocent one; it becomes most guilty when it takes in any degree the place of God. And lastly, do not be satisfied with anything that seems to be beneficial until you find God in it. The Bible will be a " well of salvation," just in so far as God speaks to us from its pages through the Incarnate Word, and by the Divine Spirit. (*Ibid.*) *Sobriety and righteousness:*—1. The doctrine of grace teacheth not only to abstain from evil, but also to do good, and is the mistress of true sanctification in both parts of it, both the mortification of sin, as also quickening in righteousness. For as it is in the lighting of a dark house, first darkness must give place, and light must succeed, so is it in the shining of this light of grace, the night must pass, and then the day must come; the old man must be cast off with his lusts, and then the new man put on. 2. Note that where the gospel bringeth to any person salvation, there it looketh for return of some recompense; and namely this, that it be entertained with sobriety, righteousness, and godliness, which are the three graces which go hand in hand, and every one looking at another. Sobriety keepeth the house, and moderateth the mind at home; righteousness looketh forth, and giveth every man his due abroad; piety looketh up unto God, and giveth Him His right. Sobriety preserveth, and is content with its own estate and portion; righteousness preserveth, and is content that other men enjoy their estate and portion; piety preserveth, and is willing that God's part be reserved unto Him. Again, sobriety must go before as a nurse of the other two, for he that dealeth not soberly, cannot deal justly, but depriveth the Church, the commonwealth, and family of their due. Righteousness without godliness is but atheism, and a beautiful abomination; and piety without righteousness is but hypocrisy; for how absurd it is to be precise with man and careless how wickedly we deal with God? Now as sobriety, the first, is the nurse of the two latter, so piety, the last, is the mother of the two former, which, where it is wanting, neither of the former, nor both of them, can commend a man unto God. Therefore, none of these three adverbs of Paul (as a learned writer speaketh) must be forgotten, which jointly contain all the rules of Christian life. (*T. Taylor, D.D.*) *In this present world:*—1. Note that godliness must not so lie hid in the heart, but it must appear in the eyes of the world, neither must it be neglected till death, but exercised in this present world: a point the more needful to be propounded, in that every man naturally wisheth with Balaam to die well and godly; but forgetting the practice of piety in their life time, we see the most men would be put in mind of God at their death, and send for the minister when the physician hath left them hopeless of life, yea, albeit they have forgotten the Almighty, and neglected acquaintance with Him all their days, yet at the finishing of them they would seem to seek unto Him. But it is most righteous with God that an ungodly life be finished with a proportional death, whatsoever it seemeth to be: and, therefore, it is a safe rule worthy our remembrance, that whatsoever we would be found doing on our dying day, to be doing it every day while we live. 2. Note hence that it is a most deceitful and desperate argument thus to conclude—If I be ordained to salvation let me never pray, never serve God, and do what I will I shall be saved, and on the contrary; and hence to cast off all the care of godliness; for this openly proclaimeth want of grace, which directeth men to the means, and leadeth them the way of salvation in this present world. God in wisdom hath combined to every end His means in all His ordinary courses; as to natural life, bread, sleep, physic; so to the spiritual, the word, sacraments, prayer, sobriety, righteousness, piety; and therefore the argument will be found in the contrary thus: If God have appointed me to die the death of the righteous, He hath ordained me to the means, namely, to live the life of the righteous; if to glory, then to grace; if to the full revelation of glory hereafter, then to the firstfruits of it here in grace; if to the city of the great King hereafter, then to the suburbs here; there is no jumping to heaven, no more than a man can leap from one city to another upon earth. 3. Note hence what is the proper end of every man's life in this present world, namely, that in the way of a sober, righteous and religious life, he may attain everlasting happiness hereafter. Alas, how do many pervert the end of their lives, some to get wealth, honour, and great estates; others to sit down to eat and drink, and rise up to play; others to trade in some one or other special sin and lust, but let us that will be wise to salvation, seeing it is called to-day, and our acceptable time and day of salvation is come upon us, beware of hardening our hearts. Let us not dare to strive against the Holy Ghost in the ministry, for contemners of grace in this present world shall never partake of the glory of the just hereafter. (*Ibid.*) *Godliness must calculate the resisting element*:—Power is calculable by the results it yields, but if we are attempting to estimate the force of a projectile, we shall take account not only of the velocity at which it moves, but also of the quality and tenacity of the resisting material which it shows itself competent to penetrate. One evidence of the vital energy of Christianity is shown in this, that in all its movements and demands and prohibitions, it runs steadily counter to the whole grain of natural desire. Whatever Christianity has done or may yet be doing in the world, it is doing it all in the teeth of spontaneous impulse. It is a system that requires us to love our neighbour as we do ourselves. It enjoins upon us to crucify our affections and lusts. It is a religion that is contented with nothing less than sacrifice. It meets the soul at the level of its higher needs, to be sure; but that is not the level at which we find it our first impulse to live. Christianity prohibits our doing a host of things that we would like to do, and requires us to do another host of things that we have no disposition to do. Every inch that Christianity has gained, or may still be gaining, it has gained by a square fight. All advance that it has made has been so much conquest on the one side, over against so much reluctant and contested surrender on the other. In estimating the draught-power of a locomotive, we must consider not only the rate at which it moves and the tons of freight it drags, but the grade at which it is pulling. If I can row eight miles an hour, it is important to know whether I can do it with the wind, or in the teeth of it. There is nothing evangelical in a man's first impulses. So in estimating the inherent vigour of Christianity, it must be studiously considered that in all its advances it has steadily trained upon it the charged and primed artillery of man's natural lust and congenital ambition. All the way from the last man that became a Christian, back to Peter who forsook his fishing-tackle at the Lord's call, the process of becoming a Christian has been a process of surrender. Count that carefully in calculating the spiritual dynamics of the doctrine of the Nazarene. (*C. H. Parkhurst, D.D.*) *Duty to our Father in heaven must be united with duty to our brother on earth*:—You have a son, I will suppose, in a distant land. He has been prosperous, he has become honoured, influential, and beloved. He has won golden opinions from all for his abilities, his charities, his devotion to the interests of the community. He is known as a tender father; he is reputed a munificent benefactor and large-hearted philanthropist. The colony rings with his praises. Does not your paternal heart throb with a pardonable pride as you hear of the goodness and the greatness to which he has attained? "Alas!" you say, "what might be my pride is my pain. My boy has been absent for twenty years, and took a father's fond blessing with him, but during that long period he has sent no tidings to his parents. His commercial correspondence has been carried on with most commendable regularity, but never a solitary line has he written home. All the news we get of him comes at second hand. We hear of his bounties to others, but we are getting poor in our old age and no token has come to us. He has not shown in any way that he is even aware of our existence." Now what are your ideas of such sonship as that? Are not the benefactions of such a man an abomination, and his fascinations an offence? Here, then, is a picture of the behaviour of the man who, just in all earthly dealings, and tender in all human relations, yet lives, with regard to his highest obligations, simply as though God were not. (*J. Halsey.*) **Looking for that blessed hope.**— *The hope of the resurrection*:—"I believe in the resurrection of the body." And what does this imply? Does it merely mean that we assent to there being such a thing, as a bare truth in the abstract? Does it mean, "I believe that men's bodies shall rise?" And when we continue, "And in the life everlasting," do we merely intend by this, "I believe that some shall live for ever?" Oh, surely not: we cannot have such a cold unworthy idea of the articles of the Christian faith as this. When I utter these words in church, when I profess them as my belief, I must surely mean that I regard them as facts in my own life and course. I take the words as they stand in the Nicene Creed, where the very same expression is used as in our text: "I look for the resurrection of the dead, and the life of the world to come." That is, I expect in my own case, I look forward to witnessing, and sharing in, the things thus spoken of. If you ask me what reason have I in my own case to look for such blessed participation in the resurrection to life eternal, my answer is plain and decisive. "I look for the resurrection of the body, and the life everlasting," because God has assured these blessings to me in my covenant relation with Him in Christ as a member of Christ's body. Now, many of you are aware that in saying this I am touching on a question much debated among religious writers of a certain stamp: I mean the question as to what is called personal assurance: the question as to whether it is, or is not, an essential portion of the Christian's faith to be assured of his own part in Christ, and his own ultimate share in Christ's salvation. Now, this is a question which no Christian Churchman can be at any loss how to answer. He will answer it as we have done above; and tell the inquirer that his own personal part in God's covenant and God's promises is not a matter which can be left to uncertain and easily mistaken feelings and experiences of his own, but is, as we said before, at the foundation of his whole spiritual life, which is built up upon it, as it is built on the fact of God's mercies to him in Christ. And this being so, important effects are produced, or ought to be produced, on our views of several things, either present or in prospect. 1. The first of which I shall speak is our view of death. If a blessed resurrection in an incorruptible body is to be ours, any one can easily see that the act and state of death, so terrible where this hope is not, at once loses its formidable character, and shrinks up into utter insignificance. Doubtless it will and must be a conflict when it comes, that solemn moment of parting from the body: but what is a conflict where victory is assured to us? What soldier ever dwells long and gloomily on the fearful incidents of battle, by way of bracing his courage to meet it? Is it not ever the rule, and should it not ever be our rule, to dwell on the triumph beyond, and so to forget the struggle by which it is to be reached? 2. And as this confidence of hope will alter our view of death, so will it also of life. What is life to the man of this world—to the poor creature who does not know whether it is not to be cut short for ever at the day of death? Life to him is simply a snatching-time: to get as much as he can out of it, to eat and drink, and amass gain, and earn repute, and win importance, and fill as large a space as he can with what credit he may: and there is an end of it. Thousands on thousands are leading just this life and nothing more: often varnished over with pure and bright colours—decent charities, expected attendance on religion, and the like: but none can deny that, judging by the practice of most men, such is the general view of life; that as to eternity and so on, it is an uncertainty after all, and it is better to take the present good in hand, than to lay up for such an uncertainty. Now then, does a man, in his heart, in his deepest thoughts and views of the future, look for the resurrection of the body and the life everlasting? And can he any longer think thus of life? Why, to the other man, this life is all: he knows of nothing beyond it; but to this man, what is beyond it is almost all, and this life is as compared to it almost as nothing. But how? Even as the seed-time, which though in a certain field it may be but one morning in a year, yet on that one morning depends all the use and produce of that field for that year—so is it with the Christian believer's estimate of this life. It is, as compared with that beyond the grave, but as a moment—but as a point hardly to be appreciated: yet in the use of this moment, in the conplexion of this little point, is involved the whole character and degree of blessedness of that immeasurable eternity. Life is now not a snatching-time, but a laying-up time: a time of treasuring up things which may be of account there. 3. There is another thing concerning which, if we look in our own persons for the resurrection of the dead and the life everlasting, our views will necessarily undergo a change, and that is, the body. It may not be very easy to say what the mere worldly man thinks of the body in which he finds himself dwelling. But I am afraid we should not be far wrong in believing that the very last thing which he expects is, that it will rise from the grave, and be his dwelling for ever. This doctrine, at which the wise Athenians scoffed, is still despised by those who think themselves wise after this world's measure.  They have some vague notion of a probability of the immortality of the soul and a future judgment, without ever reflecting that we shall be judged in the body for the deeds done in the body.  And the consequence is that in their view the man is not one, but two persons, soul and body : the soul is meant to be saved by religion, but the body has little or nothing to do with religion.  And then those who are not only worldly, but irreligious, go further than this ; and pretend to tell us, from the speculations of misused science, that the life which is so mysteriously placed in the body is necessarily and inseparably united to it, and therefore perishes when the body decays.  How different an aspect do the things of the body present to him who regards it as his companion through a blessed eternity—to him who reads and feels what the apostle tells us, that Christ is the Saviour of the body ;— that we are now waiting for the adoption, that is, the redemption of the body.  How careful will he be to train this his future servant for its blessed ministrations there ; —to put it entirely under the power of God's purifying Spirit of grace :—to subdue in it all impure and unholy desires, all inordinate indulgences of lawful appetite, and render it a habitation if it may be worthy of Him whose temple it ought to be. 4. Yet another change will be wrought by looking for the resurrection of the body, and the life everlasting : and that will be in our views of and affections towards others around us.  If the painter who painted for posterity needed more care in every touch than the other, who painted merely for the day, will not he who loves for eternity love more wisely, more tenderly, more cautiously and self-denyingly than he who merely gratifies a present predilection?  A fellow-member of the body of Christ—one with whom I hope to hold converse which shall never know parting nor end in the presence of Him who is Love—if I remember this, and act on this, can I wantonly wound the feelings of such an one?  Can I hinder such an one in the path to glory?  Can I to such an one act a part, and put on guile, to serve any worldly purpose?  " They take the sun out of heaven, who take away friendship out of life " : thus wrote the heathen philosopher ; but we may say a worthier thing—they take away the sun out of heaven, who take the hope of the resurrection out of friendship. 5. Once more, he who looks for the resurrection of the dead and the life everlasting, will, in proportion as this blessed hope is present to him, find his thoughts of Christ evermore changed and exalted, and made more precious to him.  From a distant historical character to a present Saviour—this is the first great change in a man's thoughts of Christ.  From a present Saviour to be the desire of his soul—one whose likeness, and nothing else, will satisfy him ; this is the next change, and it is no less an one than the former : it is, after all, that which constrains a man, that which leads him on, that which will transform him into Christ's image from glory to glory.  And I see not how this latter change can take place, without a man's looking for this blessed hope of the resurrection. (*Dean Alford.*)     *The happy hope :*—There are two appearances spoken of in this context—the appearance of " the grace of God that bringeth salvation "; and parallel with that, though at the same time contrasted with it, as being in very important senses, one in nature and principle, though diverse in purpose and diverse in manner, is what the apostle here calls " the glorious appearing of the great God."  I. THE APPEARANCE OF THE GRACE LEADS TO THE APPEARANCE OF THE GLORY. The identity of the form of expression in the two clauses is intended to suggest the likeness of and the connection between the two appearances.  In both there is a visible manifestation of God, and the latter rests upon the former, and completes and crowns it.  But the difference between the two is as strongly marked as the analogy ; and it is not difficult to grasp distinctly the difference which the apostle intends. While both are manifestations of the Divine character in exercise, the specific phase (so to speak) of that character which appears is in one case "grace," and in the other "glory."  If one might venture on any illustration in regard to such a subject, it is as when the pure white light is sent through glass of different colours, and at one moment beams mild through refreshing green, and at the next flames in fiery red that warns of danger.  The grace has appeared when Divine love is incarnate among us.  The long-suffering gentleness we have seen.  And in it we have seen, in a very real sense, the glory, for " we beheld His glory—full of grace."  But beyond that lies ready to be revealed in the last time the glory, the lustrous light, the majestic splendour, the flaming fire of manifest Divinity.  Again, the two verses thus bracketed together, and brought into sharp contrast, also suggest how like, as well as how unlike, these manifestations are to be.  In both cases there is an appearance, in the strictest sense of the word, that is to say, a thing visible to men's senses.  Can we see the grace of God?  We can see the love in exercise, cannot we?

How? "He that hath seen Me hath seen the Father; and how sayest thou then, Show us the Father?" The appearance of Christ was the making visible in human form of the love of God. My brother! The appearance of the glory will be the same—the making visible in human form of the light of throned and sovereign Deity. What we look for is an actual bodily manifestation in a human form, on the solid earth, of the glory of God! And then I would notice how emphatically this idea of the glory being all sphered and embodied in the living person of Jesus Christ proclaims His Divine nature. It is "the appearance of the glory"—then mark the next words—"of the great God, and our Saviour." The human possesses the Divine glory in such reality and fulness as it would be insanity if it were not blasphemy, and blasphemy if it were not absurdity, to predicate of any simple man. The words coincide with His own saying, "The Son of Man shall come in His glory and of the Father," and point us necessarily and inevitably to the wonderful thought that the glory of God is capable of being fully imparted to, possessed by, and revealed through Jesus Christ; that the glory of God is Christ's glory, and the glory of Christ is God's. And then I must touch very briefly another remarkable and plain contrast indicated in our text between these two "appearings." They are not only unlike in the subject (so to speak) or substance of the manifestation, but also in the purpose. The grace comes, patient, gentle, sedulous, labouring for our training and discipline. The glory comes—there is no word of training there! What does the glory come for? The one rises upon a benighted world—lambent and lustrous and gentle, like the slow, silent, climbing of the silvery moon through the darkling sky. But the other blazes out with a leap upon a stormy heaven, "as the lightning cometh out of the east, and shineth even unto the west," writing its fierce message across all the black page of the sky in one instant, "so shall also the coming of the Son of Man be." II. THE APPEARING OF THE GLORY IS A BLESSED HOPE. The hope is blessed; or the word "happy" may, perhaps, be substituted with advantage. Because it will be full of blessedness when it is a reality, therefore it is full of joy while it is but a hope. The characteristics of that future manifestation of glory are not such that its coming is wholly and universally a joy. There is something terrible in the beauty, something menacing in the brightness. But it is worth noticing that, notwithstanding all that gathers about it of terror, all that gathers about it of awful splendour, all that is solemn and heart-shaking in the thought of judgment and retribution for the past, the irreversible and irrevocable past, yet to Paul it was the very crown of all his expectations of, and the very shining summit of all his desires for, the future—that Christ should appear. The hope is a happy one. If we know "the grace" we shall not be afraid of "the glory." If the grace has disciplined in any measure we may be sure that we shall partake in its perfection. They that have seen the face of Christ looking down, as it were, upon them from the midst of the great darkness of the cross, and beneath the crown of thorns, need not be afraid to see the same face looking down upon them from amidst all the blaze of the light, and from beneath the many crowns of the kingdoms of the world, and the royalties of the heavens. Whosoever hath learnt to love and believe in the manifestation of the grace, he, and he only, can believe and hope for the manifestation of the glory. III. THE GRACE DISCIPLINES US TO HOPE FOR THE GLORY. The very idea of discipline involves the notion that it is a preparatory stage, a transient process for a permanent result. It carries with it the idea of immaturity, of apprenticeship, so to speak. If it is discipline, it is discipline for some condition which is not yet reached. And so, if the grace of God comes "disciplining," then there must be something beyond the epoch and era within which the disciple is confined. Here is a perfect instrument for making men perfect, and what does it do? It makes men so good and leaves them so bad that unless they are to be made still better and perfected, God's work on the soul is at once an unparalleled success and a confounding failure—a puzzle, in that having done so much it does not do more; in that having done so little it has done so much. The achievements of Christianity upon single souls, and its failures upon those for whom it has done most, when measured against, and compared with, its manifest adaptation to a loftier issue than it has ever reached here on earth, all coincide to say—the grace—because its purpose is discipline, and because its purpose is but partially achieved here on earth—demands a glory, when they whose darkness has been partially made "light in the Lord," by the discipline of grace, shall "blaze forth as the sun" in the Heavenly Father's kingdom of glory. Yield to the discipline, and the hope will be strengthened. You will never entertain in any vigour and operative power upon your lives the expectation of that coming of the glory unless you live soberly, righteously, and godly in this present world. That discipline submitted to is, if I may so say, like that great apparatus which you find by the side of an astronomer's biggest telescope, to wheel it upon its centre and to point its tube to the star on which he would look. So our anticipation and desire, the faculty of expectation which we have, is wont to be directed along the low level of earth, and it needs the pinions and levers of that gracious discipline, making us sober, righteous, godly, in order to heave it upwards, full-front against the sky, that the stars may shine into it. The speculum, the object-glass, must be polished and cut by many a stroke and much friction ere it will reflect "the image of the heavenly"; so, grace disciplines us, patiently, slowly, by repeated strokes, by much rubbing, by much pain—disciplines us to live in self-restraint, in righteousness and godliness, and then the cleared eye beholds the heavens, and the purged heart grows towards "the coming" as its hope and its life. (*A. Maclaren, D.D.*) *The blessed hope :*—I. THE GREAT OBJECT OF THE CHRISTIAN HOPE. The true rendering is not "the glorious appearing," but "the appearing of the glory." There are two appearings—that of "the grace of God," and that of "the glory." These two manifestations are paralleled in many respects, as is shown by the very fact that the same word is employed in reference to both, but they differ substantially in this, the aspect of the Divine character manifested by each. The one is like the silver moon flooding all things with silvery and gentle light; the other is like the flash of the lightning from one side of the heavens to the other. Both the manifestation of the grace and that of the glory are given through the same medium. Jesus Christ is the means of making the grace visible; and Jesus Christ will be the means of making the glory visible. And these two appearances are connected in such a manner that the former is evidently incomplete without the latter. As certainly as the cradle at Bethlehem required the open grave and the ascension from Olivet, so certainly does the ascension from Olivet require the return to judgment. The past has in it one great fact, to which the world must turn for light, for leading, for life. And that past fact, like an eastern sky that flings its colouring into the furthest west, irradiates the future and points onwards to His return again. So that past fact and its companion yet to be are like two great towers on opposite sides of some fathomless abyss, from which stretch the slender rods which are sufficient to bear the firm structure on which we may tread across the gulf, defiant of the darkness, and find our way into the presence of God. II. THE CHRISTIAN ANTICIPATION OF THE APPEARING. "Looking," says the apostle, "for that blessed hope." How comes he to call it blessed? If it be a flashing forth of the Divine glory, and if it be, as it distinctly is, a coming to judge the earth, there must be much about it which will touch into activity not unreasonable fears, and may make the boldest and the truest shrink and ask themselves the old question, "Who shall stand when He appeareth?" But Paul here stretches out the hands of his faith, and the yearnings of his desire to it. Whence comes this confidence? It comes from the power of love. How beautiful it is, how merciful, and how strange that the very same yearning after bodily presence, the same restlessness in separation, and the same fulness of satisfaction in companionship, which mark the lower loves of earth, can be transferred wholly to that higher love! This hope is blessed because of the power of the assurance which we all may have that that coming can bring no harm to us. "Herein is our love made perfect, that we may have boldness before Him at the day of judgment." It is blessed because the manhood which is thus lifted to participate in and to be the medium of manifesting to a world the Divine glory, is our manhood; and we shall share in the glory that we behold, if here we have trusted in the grace that He revealed. "He shall change the body of our humiliation that it may be fashioned after the likeness of the body of His glory." And the hope is blessed because, in contradistinction to all earthly objects of hope, it is certain—certain as history, certain as memory. It is as secure as treasures that we keep in the cedar-presses of our remembrances. It is also blessed because, being thus certain, it is far enough in advance never to be outgrown, never to be fulfilled and done with here. So it outlasts all others, and may be laid in a dying hand, like a rosebud clasped in cold palms, crossed on each other, in the coffin; for not until we have passed the veil shall we receive the hope. He will come to the world; you and I will go to Him; either way, we shall be for ever with the Lord. And that is a hope that will outlast life and death. III. THE TEACHING OR CORRECTION WHICH STRENGTHENS THE HOPE. The fact that the first manifestation is of an educational and corrective kind is in itself an evidence that there is another one to follow. For the very idea of training implies that there is something for which we are being trained; and the very word "correction" or "discipline" involves the thought of an end towards which the process is directed. That end can be no less than the future perfecting of its subjects in that better world. God does not take the rough bar of iron and turn it into steel and polish it and shape it and sharpen it to so fine an edge, in order that He may then break it and cast it "as rubbish to the void." You will find in prehistoric tombs broken swords and blunted spears which were laid there with the corpses; but God does not so break His weapons, nor is death the end of our activity. If there be discipline there is something for which the discipline is meant. If there be an apprenticeship there is somewhere work for the journeyman to do when he has served his articles and is out of his time. There will be a field in which we shall use the powers we have acquired here; and nothing can bereave us of the force we made our own, being here. Grace disciplines, therefore there is glory. Again, our yielding to the grace is the best way of strengthening our hope of the glory. The more we keep ourselves under the influences of that mighty salvation that is in Jesus Christ, and let them chasten and correct us, and submit our inflamed eyes to their healing pains, the more clearly will they be able to see the land that is afar off. Telescope glasses are polished in order that they may enable the astronomer to pierce the depths of the heavens. Diamonds depend for their brightness on the way in which they are cut, and it is poor economy to leave some of the precious stones on the mass, if thereby its reflecting power and its radiance be diminished. God cuts deep and rubs hard, in order that He may brighten the surface and the depth of our souls, that they may receive in all its purity the celestial ray, and flash it back in varied colours. So, if we would live in the buoyant hope of the manifestation of the glory, let us docilely, prayerfully, penitently, patiently, submit ourselves to the discipline of the grace. (*Ibid.*) *The Christian's blessed hope :*—I. THE FORCE AND FITNESS OF THE ARGUMENT DRAWN FROM THE HOPE OF A CHRISTIAN. The ground of our hope lies not in our merit, but in God's mercy; the reward for which we are encouraged to look is not of debt, but of grace. And supposing it a very small and inconsiderable thing, yet, upon all the principles of reason, it is encouragement to do what otherwise we are indifferently bound and obliged to do. But the abundant grace of our God in Christ Jesus hath invited us to expect an abundant reward; and whatever force there is in hope to move men to action, is all bent to push them on to well-doing, by a just view of that reward which God hath promised. If hope can stimulate men to vigour and vigilence in any case, it wants not something to look for in the course of well-doing and on a better foundation than can be attained respecting any comfort in life. II. THE TIME WHEN THIS BLESSED REWARD SHALL BE CONFERRED. That is the great day when our great God and Saviour Jesus Christ shall appear. And if we consider the design and manner of this appearance we shall see abundant reason to live soberly, righteously, and godly in expectation of it. 1. The design of it is to judge the world in righteousness, to call every man to account for his conduct in life, and render to every one according to his works. Then the godly shall receive the glorious reward of eternal life with glorious advantages, as we shall see more particularly if we consider—2. The manner of that appearance which is here expressed by a peculiar epithet, serving to distinguish it from all other appearances, particularly from His first appearance in our nature. III. THE TEMPER AND TURN OF MIND FIT AND NECESSARY TO GIVE THESE ARGUMENTS THEIR PROPER INFLUENCE UPON US. Looking is in Scripture common style to express the principles and disposition of the mind with respect to things Divine and heavenly. And with regard to the blessed hope and glorious appearing here mentioned, it means—1. A firm persuasion of the truth and reality of those things. No wonder if they are ungodly and slaves to worldly lusts who look not for a future reckoning. 2. Looking for the blessed reward signifies a lively hope of obtaining it, which, on that very account, is called the blessed hope. 3. Looking here denotes an earnest longing, an ardency of desire to obtain the blessed hope, and see the blessed day when Christ shall appear. 4. Looking for the blessed hope means a constant and habitual attention to this as the chief end and object we ought to have in view. (*Wm. Best.*) *The glorious expectation :*—I. THE LIFE OF THE BELIEVER NOW IS ONE OF EXPECTATION. We are "looking for." 1. Our condition is one of continual expansion—growth in grace. The child is never satisfied. Clothes become too small, toys loose their charm, sympathies are enlarging, and he is constantly looking for something else. The child of God is in that position—the heart is enlarging, and expectation is the natural result. 2. The resources of the gospel are unfolding. The love of God swells, the Cross of Jesus is higher, and communion with the Saviour is closer. Travellers continued their search until they found the great lakes in Central Africa which form the water-shed of the Nile. So the streams of grace lead us on to the fountain. Our course is God-ward. II. THE LIFE OF THE BELIEVER HEREAFTER WILL BE ONE OF REALISATION. So we interpret the words of the apostle—looking for the object or fulfilment of our blessed hope. 1. Jesus is to come to take the government of the Church, and assert His sway over mankind. This is a glorious thought, especially when we remember how little we are able to do in extending His kingdom. 2. Jesus will appear in the last day as the judge of all. He will be accompanied by myriads of saints and angels, not as a root out of the dry ground, without form or comeliness, but in the glory of His Father. 3. Jesus will appear to take home His disciples as they pass through physical death. (*Weekly Pulpit.*)    *The hope of the Church under the gospel dispensation :*—I. WHAT THIS HOPE IS. II. WHO ARE ENTITLED TO LOOK FOR THE GLORIOUS APPEARING AS A BLESSED HOPE TO THEM. III. THE INFLUENCE WHICH THIS BLESSED HOPE MUST HAVE ON ALL WHO ARE REALLY POSSESSED OF IT. (*F. Hewson, M.A.*)    *The blessed hope of grace :*—Grace teaches us, not only by referring us to the great facts of the past, but also by setting before our awakened hope the sublime and crowning event of the future, and in this respect also she exhibits the superiority of her teaching to that which law could offer. Under the law the future could hardly be contemplated without terror ; for who could feel so secure of his legal righteousness as to be able to look forward to that day without a misgiving ? We cannot entertain such happy anticipations with respect to the future unless we are quite sure of our own relations to God in the present. Let us put a case. If our Queen were about to make a progress through this realm, and if it was understood that, as soon as she reached the city of York, of one dozen felons confined in the prison yonder, six were to be taken out and promptly executed at the moment of her arrival, while six should be liberated ; and if of those twelve felons no single one knew for certain whether he were one of the six that were to be set free, or of the six that were to be executed, is it conceivable under such circumstances that any of those felons would long for and entreat Her Majesty's speedy advent? Would it not be far more conceivable that they would all, if they were permitted, petition her to defer her visit, and, if possible, to abandon it? Not otherwise must it be with us, as we look forward to this dread event of the future, unless we know that by the saving grace of God we are prepared for it. But while our attitude towards this great event of the future may serve as a test of the reality or unreality of our religion, it may also be employed by the true Christian as a gauge of his spiritual condition. Do we really love His appearing ? Is it a subject much in our thoughts ? Does it cheer us, or does it make us uncomfortable to think of it ? How apt are even those who have known something of the grace of God to take root, as it were, here upon earth, instead of living as strangers and pilgrims ! But the love of Christ's appearing is not only a test of our spiritual health and progress, it may also largely contribute to the promotion of these. The truth is the life and the hope act and react upon each other. Personal godliness must ever strengthen and intensify our hope ; but then again our rejoicing in hope will ever stimulate our desires after growth in grace. What the effect of Advent light upon our daily lives must needs be is indicated by numerous passages of Scripture. " We know that when He shall appear, we shall be like Him ; for we shall see Him as He is. And every man that hath this hope in Him purifieth himself, even as He is pure." It is not difficult to understand in how many ways we may be favourably affected in our present personal experience by the thought of this blessed hope. Surely much of the gloomy despondency or depression that frequently paralyses our spiritual activities might be more easily mastered if we only lived more in the Advent light, cheering our hearts with the anticipations of coming glory. But the thought of this blessed hope does more than cheer us amidst the vicissitudes of life ; it also tends to strengthen our faith, and thus to invigorate our whole spiritual experience ; for while we dwell upon the thought of the complete victory that Christ is one day to win, the thought will naturally suggest itself to our minds, as we return to the consciousness of the present from the hopes of the future, Cannot He who will one day conquer the world conquer even now our old nature? Thus the very contemplation of these glorious prospects in the future proves a source of strength as well as of cheer in the present. But most of all, the thought of this blessed hope is specially designed to induce watchfulness. " Therefore be ye also ready," cries our blessed Lord ; " for in such an hour as ye think not the Son of Man cometh." One other benefit likely to arise from the thought of the glorious appearance of our

Saviour, and affecting our conduct and character, suggests itself here.   Surely we cannot fail to find in this prospect a mighty stimulus to our zeal.   The time is short.   Soon the Master will come to take account of His servants.   Fain would we be able to say when He appears, as He was able to say to His Father, " I have finished the work that Thou gavest Me to do."   But if this habit of looking for that blessed hope is likely to be productive of so many advantages in our present experience, it may be asked, How is such a habit to be formed ?   Strangers passing through a hostile land cannot but look forward to a change in their position.   Grace teaches us then to love the Lord's appearing, by reminding us that we are already citizens of the heavenly kingdom, in the revelation of which we are to find a full satisfaction, which cannot be ours amidst the hostile influences of the house of our pilgrimage.   We long for the moment when the power of the usurper shall be overthrown, and our King receive the homage which is His due from all, just as a Hushai or Ittai must have longed for the restoration of David, and the downfall of the odious traitor Absalom.   Nor does the expectation of the true Christian end even here.   He cannot forget that human history is to be crowned by "the marriage of the Lamb."   In that mysterious event of the future the destiny of the creature is to be attained, and the pleasure of the Creator in His own work is to be fulfilled.   But it is Grace, and Grace alone, that bids us cherish such hopes as this.   Law might train a servant, but could not prepare a bride.   To sum up, we may say that Grace teaches us to love Christ's appearing by revealing to us the mystery of our spiritual union with Him, from which there arises a certain identity of interests, and consequently of desires.   As He is, so are we in this present world, " despised and rejected of men " ; where He is, there in Him we are in the world of glory—seated in heavenly places with Christ Jesus, accepted of the Father in the Beloved.   As He shall be, such shall we be by and by, when He appears in His kingdom.   " We know that when He shall appear we shall be like Him ; for we shall see Him as He is."   Surely it is indeed " a blessed hope," and every one that hath it must needs " purify himself, even as He is pure."   We see then that while our hope becomes bright and real just in so far as we walk soberly, righteously, and godly in this present world, so the cultivation of this blessed hope helps us and stimulates us thus to live.   (*W. H. M. H. Aitken.*)        *The tonic of hopeful life :*— These words of Goethe, repeated by Carlyle in the happiest and most auspicious moment of his life, ought to be in the heart and on the lips of every earnest man and woman.   Half the energy of the world is wasted in vain regrets or in paralysing despair.   The world needs, more than anything else, a continual reinforcement of its faith in the noblest things and in its own future.   Its mistakes are of small account so long as it is true to high aims and firm in the conviction that they can be realised.   The moment of waning faith and fading hope is also, and pre-eminently, the moment of despair.   A glance beneath the surface of any decaying civilisation in the past always discovers an expiring belief in progress ; a glance beneath the surface of any advancing and triumphant civilisation always discerns a high, aspiring hope which believes that all things are possible to those that strive.   Pessimism, the religion of despair, once generally accepted would paralyse the race.   Half the world is weary, faint-hearted, overborne by calamity and sorrow ; it needs, most of all, courage, cheer, and the contagious hope that goes from strong men like an atmosphere.   There is a surplusage of truth in the world ; men know what they ought to do well enough, but they lack the power to do it. What they need above all things is impulse ; instruction is to be found on all sides, but power is not so common.   Christ started with the conception of a sick and weary world, and He lived and taught that men might be comforted and healed. Strong, buoyant natures forget too often the hourly need of a world that is still sick and weary ; the cry of the children does not shadow often enough the sunshine in which they live.   The first, the most imperative, duty of every earnest man and women is to be strong, in order that strength may go from them through every channel of expression and activity.   Make yourselves rich in hope, in order that you may have the supreme happiness of giving to the poor.   There are men and women in every community who have a tonic quality in them, whose very presence inspires hope and reinforces faith.   They carry in their faces a revelation of the strength which comes with a strong healthy grasp upon life, and a clear, far-sighted outlook upon its experiences and vicissitudes.   They say, with the force of personal example and influence, " We bid you hope."   Is this your message to the men about you ?   *Waiting the coming of Christ :*—When I was a boy, just after the marriage of the Prince and Princess of Wales, it was announced that they were to visit the town in which I lived. On the appointed day a rumour spread amongst the expectant crowd that their route was changed for some reason, so that it was probable they would not come. I shall never forget the appearance of the streets and houses. The streets were thronged with working men, shop-keepers, merchants along with their wives and daughters; the windows and the roofs of the houses were filled with anxious people. They wondered whether the royal pair would come or not, but very few went away. Many had stood there for six hours when the word came, "They are coming in two hours." Did the crowd disperse? No; they waited long and patiently to see a face bowing from a carriage window. The Prince never did anything for them, nor did they expect him to do anything for them, but still they waited, and when he passed, rent the air with cheer after cheer to show their loyalty. How many Christians are waiting longingly for the coming of their Prince and King? (*D. McEwan.*) **The glorious appearing of the great God.**—*The two appearings, and the discipline of grace:*—I. OUR POSITION. 1. The people of God stand between two appearances (vers. 11, 13). We live in an age which is an interval between two appearings of the Lord from heaven. Believers in Jesus are shut off from the old economy by the first coming of our Lord. The times of man's ignorance God winked at, but now commandeth all men everywhere to repent. We are divided from the past by a wall of light, upon whose forefront we read the words Bethlehem, Gethsemane, Calvary. We date from the birth of the Virgin's son: we begin with *Anno Domini.* All the rest of time is before Christ, and is marked off from the Christian era. The dense darkness of the heathen ages begins to be broken when we reach the first appearing, and the dawn of a glorious day begins. We look forward to a second appearing. Our outlook for the close of this present era is another appearing—an appearing of glory rather than of grace. This is the terminus of the present age. We look from Anno Domini, in which He came the first time, to that greater Anno Domini, or year of our Lord, in which He shall come a second time, in all the splendour of His power, to reign in righteousness, and break the evil powers as with a rod of iron. See, then, where we are: we are compassed about, behind and before, with the appearings of our Lord. Behind us is our trust; before us is our hope. 2. Our position is further described as being in this present world, or age. We are living in the age which lies between the two blazing beacons of the Divine appear-ings; and we are called to hasten from one to the other. It is but a little time, and He that will come shall come, and will not tarry. Now it is this "present world": oh, how present it is! How sadly it surrounds us! Yet by faith we count these present things to be unsubstantial as a dream; and we look to the things which are not seen, and not present, as being real and eternal. We hurry through this Vanity Fair: before us lies the Celestial City and the coming of the Lord who is the King thereof. II. I have to call your attention to THE INSTRUCTION which is given to us by the grace of God which has appeared unto all men. A better trans-lation would be, "The grace of God that bringeth salvation hath appeared to all men, disciplining us in order that we may deny ungodliness and worldly lusts." 1. Grace has a discipline. We generally think of law when we talk about school-masters and discipline; but grace itself has a discipline and a wonderful training power too. The manifestation of grace is preparing us for the manifestation of glory. What the law could not do, grace is doing. As soon as we come under the conscious enjoyment of the free grace of God, we find it to be a holy rule, a fatherly government, a heavenly training. We find, not self-indulgence, much less licen-tiousness; but on the contrary, the grace of God both restrains and constrains us; it makes us free to holiness, and delivers us from the law of sin and death by "the law of the spirit of life in Christ Jesus." 2. Grace has its chosen disciples, for you cannot help noticing that while the eleventh verse says that "the grace of God that bringeth salvation hath appeared to all men," yet it is clear that this grace of God has not exercised its holy discipline upon all men, and therefore the text changes its "all men" into "us." 3. The discipline of grace, according to the apostle, has three results—denying, living, looking. (1) When a young man comes to college he usually has much to unlearn. If his education has been neglected, a sort of instinc-tive ignorance covers his mind with briars and brambles. If he has gone to some faulty school where the teaching is flimsy, his tutor has first of all to fetch out of him what he has been badly taught. The most difficult part of the training of young men is not to put the right thing into them, but to get the wrong thing out of them. We have learned lessons of worldly wisdom and carnal policy, and these we need to unlearn and deny. The Holy Spirit works this denying in us by the discipline of grace.    (2) But then you cannot be complete with a merely negative religion ; you must have something positive ; and so the next word is living—that " we should live soberly, righteously, and godly, in this present world." Observe, that the Holy Ghost expects us to live in this present world, and therefore we are not to exclude ourselves from it.    This age is the battle-field in which the soldier of Christ is to fight.    Society is the place in which Christianity is to exhibit the graces of Christ.    You are to shine in the darkness like a light.    This life is described in a threefold way—(a) You are, first, to live " soberly "—that is, for yourself.    " Soberly " in all your eating and your drinking, and in the indulgence of all bodily appetites—that goes without saying.    You are to live soberly in all your thinking, all your speaking, all your acting.    There is to be sobriety in all your worldly pursuits.    You are to have yourself well in hand : you are to be self-restrained.    (b) As to his fellow-men the believer lives " righteously."    I cannot understand that Christian who can do a dirty thing in business.    Craft, cunning, over-reaching, misrepresentation, and deceit are no instruments for the hand of godly men.    Dishonesty and falsehood are the opposites of godliness.    A Christian man may be poor, but he must live righteously : he may lack sharpness, but he must not lack integrity.    A Christian profession without uprightness is a lie.    Grace must discipline us to righteous living.    (c) Towards God we are told in the text we are to be godly.    Every man who has the grace of God in him indeed and of a truth, will think much of God.    God will enter into all his calculations, God's presence will be his joy, God's strength will be his confidence, God's providence will be his inheritance, God's glory will be the chief end of his being, God's law the guide of his conversation.    Now, if the grace of God, which has appeared so plainly to all men, has really come with its sacred discipline upon us, it is teaching us to live in this threefold manner.    (3) Once more, there is looking as well as living.    One work of the grace of God is to cause us to be " looking for that blessed hope of the glorious appearing of the great God and our Saviour Jesus Christ."    What is that " blessed hope "?    Why, first, that when He comes we shall rise from the dead, if we have fallen asleep ; and that, if we are alive and remain, we shall be changed at His appearing.    Our hope is that we shall be approved of Him, and shall hear Him say, " Well done, good and faithful servant."    This hope is not of debt, but of grace : though our Lord will give us a reward, it will not be according to the law of works. We expect to be like Jesus when we shall see Him as He is.    III. The text sets forth certain of OUR ENCOURAGEMENTS.    1. In this great battle for right, and truth, and holiness, what could we do if we were left alone ?    But our first encouragement is that grace has come to our rescue; for in the day when the Lord Jesus Christ appeared among men, He brought for us the grace of God to help us to overcome all iniquity.    He that struggleth now against inbred sin has the Holy Spirit within him to help him.    He that goes forth to fight against evil in other men by preaching the gospel has the same Holy Ghost going with the truth to make it like a fire and like a hammer.    2. A second encouragement is that another appearing is coming.    He who bowed His head in weakness, and died in the moment of victory, is coming in all the glory of His endless life.    When the hour shall strike He shall appear in the majesty of God to put an end to the dominion of sin, and bring in endless peace.    Satan shall be bruised under our feet shortly; wherefore comfort one another with these words, and then prepare for further battle.    Grind your swords, and be ready for close fighting !    Trust in God, and keep your powder dry. 3. Another encouragement is that we are serving a glorious Master.    The Christ whom we follow is not a dead prophet like Mahomet.    Truly we preach Christ crucified ; but we also believe in Christ risen from the dead, in Christ gone up on high, in Christ soon to come a second time.    He lives, and He lives as the great God and our Saviour.    4. Then come the tender thoughts with which I finish, the memories of what the Lord has done for us to make us holy : " Who gave Himself for us."    Special redemption, redemption with a wondrous price—" who gave Himself for us."    He died—forget not that—died that your sins might die, died that every lust might be dragged into captivity at His chariot wheels.    He gave Himself for you that you might give yourselves for Him.    Again, He died that He might purify us—purify us unto Himself.    How clean we must be if we are to be clean unto Him !    The apostle finishes up by saying that we are to be a people " zealous of good works."    Would to God that all Christian men and women were disciplined by Divine grace till they became zealous for good works!    In holiness zeal is sobriety.    We are not only to approve of good works, and speak for good works, but we are to be red-hot for them.    We are to be on fire for everything that is right and true. (*C. H. Spurgeon.*) *Expectation of Christ's coming :*—I. True believers in Jesus Christ look and wish that He may come, AS HE WILL BE THEN GLORIFIED IN A WORLD WHERE HE HAS BEEN SET AT NOUGHT AND DESPISED. If the sun, after a whole day's dark and uninterrupted gloom of clouds, sets in an evening of thick mists and impenetrable darkness, who is there that rejoices not when the next morning opens in a clear and radiant sky, and a full and unclouded effulgence of his splendour ? And if Jesus, the Sun of Righteousness, thus leaves our world in darkness and reproach, all those who have a sincere and cordial value for Him will hail Him when He returns the second time in His own and His Father's glories, and will often wish, during the night of His absence, that the hour was come when He shall appear in that might and majesty, in that honour and glory which belong to Him, and by which He will dissipate all the misconstructions concerning Him, as the bright beams of the rising sun scatter the shades of thickest darkness, and pour glory and heat, peace and pleasure, over the face of gladdened nations. II. True believers look and wish for the coming of Jesus Christ, in order TO PUT AN END TO THEIR PAIN AND SORROW. The wound that was inflicted upon our nature at the first grand apostasy has been kept open and bleeding on through all generations ; and when we take a view of mankind, what misery and wretchedness from all quarters meet our eyes, and affect our hearts ! Not to mention those great capital calamities which with an enormous scythe lay waste whole cities and kingdoms at once, *i.e.*, earthquakes, famines, pestilence, and war. There are many smaller mischiefs that harass and afflict us ; I mean the dreadful train of common diseases, from which no city or town, it may be, is ever entirely free, and which often bring us to an untimely grave, even in the very bloom and strength of our constitutions. Add to all this, that pain and sorrow have still a wider spread in our world, from the ten thousand vexations and disappointments of the present state. Such and so various are the pains and sorrows of the present state, but they shall all be ended at the second coming of our Lord Jesus Christ. When this wished-for period shall arrive, " God shall wipe away all tears from our eyes," from what causes soever they have flowed, and " there shall be no sorrow nor crying, neither shall there be any more pain, for the former things are passed away." III. Another reason why true believers look and wish for the second coming of Christ is, BECAUSE HE WILL AT HIS SECOND COMING FINISH THE REIGN OF DEATH. How dismal and distressing is the reign of death at present ! What havoc does he make, in a few years, in our world ! How many of our dear relatives, the brethren of our flesh, and of our friends, the brethren of our souls, have fallen victims to the power of this great and general destroyer ? And we ourselves must soon expect to feel the stroke of this king of terrors. We may literally say that we are dying daily. In the midst of life we are in death. Death has sent us the heralds of his approach, and we hear the sound of his feet and the sharpening of his dart in every disease and pain, in every infirmity and decay that we feel. But when Christ comes, death shall be no more. His prison, the grave, shall be broken up, and his chains, powerful as they may be, shall all be burst asunder. " Because Christ lives, His people shall live also." IV. Another reason why true believers look and wish for Christ's second coming, is taken from THE GREAT GLORY AND THE CONSUMMATION OF THEIR FELICITY WHICH THEY SHALL THEN OBTAIN. They are then acknowledged, approved, and welcomed as the children of God, and the brethren and joint-heirs with Jesus Christ. And as their positive felicity, their joy without measure and without end, in the presence and fruition of God and the Lamb, lies before them, and ages appear rolling on after ages in the immense eternity, all bright in glory and rich in blessing, so neither is there any possible fear that their bliss shall ever fail, or that the possessors shall ever be removed away from their enjoyments. Lessons : 1. Let our thoughts dwell upon this great and glorious subject. Even the very make of our bodies themselves, though our inferior part, shows us that we are not to grovel upon earth, but to view and contemplate our kindred skies ; and shall not our souls mount up from this low world, and its vain scenes, and look forward " to the things which are not seen ? As risen with Christ seek those things which are above, where Christ sitteth on the right hand of God ; set your affection on things above, not on things on the earth " (Col. iii. 1–4). Oh for the telescope of faith to be often lifted up to explore not only the land that is afar off, but the coming of the Prince of it in all His glory ! Let us see the heavens opening to give Him a passage unto our earth, the solemn state of His majestic Person, the bright armies of the skies in attendance upon Him, to augment the glory of His coming, and to perform His will. 2. What a miserable portion have those souls who have no interest in the blessedness and glories of this day! To be excluded from a lot and portion in the honours and happiness conferred on the children of God and the redeemed of the Lamb at His second coming, and to be consigned over to the miseries of endless perdition with the devil and his angels; to dwell with devouring flames and everlasting burnings; what a fearful end is here! And if this be the end of sinners, then what avail all their present worldly possessions, pleasures, and honours? 3. Let us give all diligence that we may be prepared for the second coming of our Lord Jesus Christ. Let us keep this solemn day in our continual view, and let none of the vanities of this life be ever suffered to intercept its prospect, or darken its glories. And whilst we contemplate it, let us be getting ready for it. Let us be concerned that our corruptions may be more and more subdued, and that our graces may be more and more exercised and strengthened. (*J. King, B.A.*) *Our state of expectation and the reasons for it:*—I. It is clear THAT THE NATURE OF OUR EXPECTATION DEPENDS UPON THE NATURE OF THE PROMISES WHICH EXCITE IT; it will be more or less strong and definite as they are more or less so. Now when we examine these promises, we find in them a remarkable mixture of certainty and of uncertainty; certainty as to the event—uncertainty as to the time of its occurrence. History, as well as prophecy, viewed as a whole, gives the Christian student the same result—certainty, and yet uncertainty; assuring us of His coming, and yet leaving the time of that coming a mystery. And the nature of our expectation must, as we have said, correspond to the nature of the revelation which excites it: it, too, must be thus certain, and yet uncertain. We are fully persuaded as to the event; doubtful, and in anxious suspense, as to the time of it;—now "lifting up our heads because our redemption draweth nigh," now saying, "Why tarry the wheels of His chariot?" Now full of joy at some sign accomplished—now filled with sadness at finding that it is yet to be fulfilled: fear mingling with our hope, and yet hope brightening our despondency; but, through all, sustained by the assured certainty of the event which so perplexes us by the uncertainty of its arrival. II. BUT WE HAVE NOW TO INQUIRE WHY WE ARE THUS KEPT IN THIS STATE OF UNCERTAINTY. The answer to this question is to be found in that fact which explains so much that is difficult in Scripture, namely, that this present dispensation is merely preparatory to another. The whole life of each Christian, and, therefore, the whole life of the Church, is the time given for the acquisition of that character which we shall need in heaven. To this, every event in our life, every arrangement in our dispensation, was designed to be conducive; and, if you bear this in mind, you will see how it was necessary that there should be this mixture of assured certainty and anxious suspense in our expectation of the Lord's second coming. In the first place, the fact that Christ shall come must be clear and indubitable, in order to fix, steadily, the hope of the Church, in all ages, upon Christ, her future King. Beyond time, and the things of time—above its mists and its storms, we must see, and see clearly, Jesus Christ our King. It is for this reason that the coming of Christ is assured to us by every possible assurance that can be given, so that doubt concerning it is, to him who believes the Bible, impossible. This much, then, of our present state is clearly intelligible: we can see why the fact of the second advent should be certain; but why should the time be uncertain?—why are we in this state of anxious suspense as to when our Lord is to appear? We understand this when we remember that besides the general purpose of giving us a love for, and a dependence upon, Christ, by setting His coming before us as the one thing to be looked for, the promise of His coming is to have certain special effects upon us; it is to produce in us certain particular tempers and feelings—two especially: it was designed to comfort us under trial, and also to be a strong motive to watchfulness. Had the time of our Lord's second coming been known from the first it would have utterly frustrated the design of making this life a state of probation and of gradual sanctification. The early Church would have been languidly indifferent; the later Church intensely and absorbingly expectant: the one would have been tried above measure, the other have had no trials at all. The one would have been patient, but not watchful; the other would be watchful, but not patient; neither, in the true sense of the word, could have been said to wait for the coming of Christ. But if, on the contrary, the date of this event is concealed, and the prophecies and signs of it so contrived that at any given moment there may be reason for thinking it to be near at hand, and reasons, also, for pronouncing it to be far off; if now it needs the straining gaze of ardent faith to catch a glimpse of it, and now it seems advancing full upon our view; if now it seems to approach, and now to recede, so that the earlier Church might sometimes deem it nigh, and the latest generation sometimes think it far off, then at all times, and in all ages, would this event have its full practical effect upon the Church. III. BUT THIS IS NOT THE ONLY REASON WHY THE TIME OF HIS COMING SHOULD BE THUS UNCERTAIN. So far we have been viewing it with reference only to the saints ; it may, and should, be viewed with reference to the ungodly. To those who love Him not, as well as to those who do, it is said, " Behold, I come quickly." And what is the promise of the second advent meant to be to such ? A solemn warning ; and a fearful snare if they neglect that warning. (*Abp. Magee.*) *The second advent of Christ :*—I. AN IMPORTANT CHARACTER. 1. His Divine character—" the great God." " Great " in majesty, wisdom, knowledge, power, love. Crowned with all perfections peculiar to Deity. 2. His relative character—" our Saviour." 3. In this combined and glorious character He will make His second appearance. II. AN IMPORTANT EVENT. 1. Sudden. 2. Glorious. 3. A contrast to His first appearance in humiliation. III. AN IMPORTANT EXERCISE. " Looking for," &c. (*Homilist.*) *The coming of Christ :*—I. CHRIST COMES TO THE PENITENT SOUL IN CONVERSION. II. CHRIST COMES TO THE TRIED AND AFFLICTED CHRISTIAN TO HELP AND COMFORT. III. CHRIST COMES TO THE DILIGENT SERVANT TO ENCOURAGE AND AID HIM. IV. CHRIST COMES TO THE DYING CHRISTIAN TO RECEIVE HIS SPIRIT. (*F. Wagstaff.*) *The appearing of Christ :*—I. AN EXALTED CHARACTER. 1. God. 2. Saviour. II. AN INTEREST- ING EVENT. 1. His own appearing will be glorious. " His countenance will be as the sun shineth in his strength." 2. The manner of His appearing will be glorious. He will take the clouds for His chariot; He will come in the clouds with power and great glory. 3. The attendants at His appearing will be glorious. An innumerable multitude of celestial spirits will grace His train and perform His will. 4. The circumstances of His appearing will be glorious. The heavens will pass away with a great noise ; the dead shall be raised; the Son of Man shall ascend His great tribunal, and before Him shall be gathered all nations ; the final sentence will be pronounced and executed. III. A JOYFUL EXPECTATION. 1. The hope of a blessed resurrection. 2. The hope of a blessed mansion. 3. The hope of a blessed society. 4. The hope of obtaining the most blessed enjoyments. 5. The hope of being employed in the most blessed services. IV. THE BELIEVER'S CONDUCT in the prospect of this blessedness. " Looking for that blessed hope," &c. What is meant by this expression ? 1. It includes a full conviction of the certainty of Christ's appearing. The ground of our persuasion is the Word of God. Our faith is built on the Divine testimony. 2. To look for the glorious appearing of the great God and our Saviour Jesus Christ is to love and desire His appearing. 3. To look for the appearing of Jesus Christ is to wait patiently for it. 4. In looking for the appearing of Christ the believer makes it His constant study to be always ready for His appearing, so to have his lamps trimmed that he may be prepared, at a moment's warning, to meet the bridegroom. (*The Pulpit.*) *The future state :*—The present state is not permanent, neither do its circumstances render it desirable that it should be so. Its perishing hopes, groundless fears, profitless pur- suits, faithless friendships, its toils, stripes, afflictions, make it far from happy. The Christian, then, looks for something better. The future state—1. Is necessary to solve the mysteries of Providence. 2. Is requisite to complete human happiness. 3. Is the end of the Christian faith. 4. Is the declared purpose of God. 5. Is advisable as a development. (*Homilist.*) *The glorious appearing of Christ :*— I. In view of such an experience, made sure to us in the near future, our religion should be a source of perpetual comfort and joyous expectation. II. Present ills and seeming losses and self-denials should be borne with resig- nation and composure, in view of the imminence of the glorious appearing of the great God and our Saviour Jesus Christ, to finish His appointed work and reward His faithful ones. III. There is no influence so potent on the faith, heart, and life of the Christian, as the near and daily contemplation of this revelation of Jesus Christ in the power and glory of heaven to consummate His work of grace and His reign of love. (*J. M. Sherwood, D.D.*) *The revisers' rendering of this passage :*—" The appearing of the glory of our great God and Saviour Jesus Christ." Among the foolish charges which have been brought against the revisers is that of favouring Arian tendencies by blurring those texts which teach the Divinity of Jesus Christ. The present passage would be a sufficient answer to such a charge. In the A.V. we have "the glorious appearing of the great God, and our Saviour Jesus Christ," where both the wording and the comma make it clear that " the great God " means the Father and not our Saviour. The revisers, by omitting the comma, for which there is no authority in the original, and by placing the " our " before both substantives, have given their authority to the view that St. Paul means both "great God" and "Saviour" to apply to Jesus Christ. It is not any Epiphany of the Father which is in his mind, but the "Epiphany of the glory of our great God and Saviour Jesus Christ." The wording of the Greek is such that absolute certainty is not attainable; but the context, the collocation of the words, the use of the word "Epiphany," and the omission of the article before "Saviour," all seem to favour the revisers' rendering. And, if it be adopted, we have here one of the plainest and most direct statements of the Divinity of Christ to be found in Scripture. As such it was employed in the Arian controversy, although Ambrose seems to have understood the passage as referring to the Father and Christ, and not to Christ alone. The force of what follows is enhanced if the revisers' rendering, which is the strictly grammatical rendering, is maintained. It is as being "our great God" that He gave Himself for us, that He might "redeem us from all iniquity"; and it was because He was God as well as man, that what was uttered as a bitter taunt was really a glorious truth; —" He saved others; Himself He cannot save." (*A. Plummer, D.D.*) **Who gave Himself for us.**—*Christ's gift to us, and ours to Him:*—I. THE UNSPEAKABLE AND ALL-POWERFUL GIFT. Christ began to give Himself when from the depths of eternity He passed within the limitations of men, and, drawn by our need, and impelled by filial obedience and fraternal love, entered within the conditions of our existence, "and, forasmuch as the children were partakers of flesh and blood, Himself likewise took part of the same." It was much that Christ should stretch out His hand to bless, should "give His back to the smiter and His cheeks to them that plucked off the hair," and bear His cross on His own shoulders, and should be fastened to it on Calvary. Did you ever think that it was perhaps more that He should have a hand with which to bless, and a back to be bared to the scourge, a cheek that did not flush with one angry spot when rude spittings were shot upon it and traitorous kisses touched it; shoulders to bear His cross, and a body to be nailed upon it. Why had He these but because, ere He had them, He gave Himself for us? And so, having its roots in eternity, that gift included all His wonderful self-oblivious and world-blessing life and culminated in the death upon the cross. But then, mark still further, that the apostle here gives us another thought which deepens the wonderfulness and the preciousness of this gift; for, speaking to a man who had never come near Jesus Christ in the flesh, and including in his words the whole race of mankind to the last syllable of recorded time, he declares that "He gave Himself for us." How did He give Himself for us unless in the giving He had the knowledge of us and His heart turned to us; unless when He yielded Himself to life and to death, the thoughts of all the men in the world, and that should thereafter be in it, were the motives that impelled Him? And how did "He give Himself for us" unless He gave Himself for me and for thee? II. THE REDEEMING POWER OF THE GIFT. It is noteworthy that here, in the apostle's summing up of the great purpose of the life and death of Jesus Christ, he isolates from all other consequences of that mighty fact, blessed as those are, and selects as the sole object to be considered this power to deliver men from the bondage of evil. Jesus Christ died for—not only that He might redeem you from the penalties of sin, nor from its guilt, but that He might redeem you from doing it. You want more than culture, more than the morality of prudence, more than education of conscience, in order to weaken passion and to strengthen will, so that a man may shake off the bondage of the evil which he has done, and may begin to walk in newness of life. I know of no power that enables a poor man, beset and burdened by torturing tyrants of his own passions, and feeble against the strong seductions of outward temptation, to stand fast and overcome them all, shaking their fetters from his emancipated limbs, but the realisation of that infinite sacrifice, that changeless Divine human love, that mighty pure Brother's life, from which there flow into men's hearts motives and powers and impulses which, and which alone, are strong enough to make them free. III. THE ANSWERING GIFT THAT CORRESPONDS TO, AND IS EVOKED BY, CHRIST'S GIFT OF HIMSELF. The only way by which we can win another for ourselves is by giving ourselves to that other. Hearts are only bought by hearts; love's flame can only be kindled by love's flame. The only way by which one spiritual being can possess another is when the possessed loves and yields to the love of the possessor. And thus Jesus Christ makes us His own by giving Himself to us for our own. There is no power known in humanity that can, I was going to say, decentralise a human life and lift it clean off its pivot of self except the power of the unspeakable love of Jesus Christ on the cross. We revolve round our own centres, self is our centre; but that great

Sun of Righteousness has mass enough to draw hearts and lives from their little orbit, and to turn them into satellites of its own. And then they move in music and in light around the Sun of their souls. IV. THE ENTHUSIASM FOR GOOD WHICH THAT GREAT GIFT WILL KINDLE. " Zealous of good works." The apostle means substantially the same thing as he and the others mean by "righteousness"—the deeds of all kinds which correspond to men's place and power—"whatsoever things are lovely and of good report." He thinks that if a man has rightly pondered and yielded himself to the influence of that serene and supreme example of a beautiful work, Christ's giving of Himself for us, he will not only do such works, but be passionately desirous of opportunities for doing them. It is a deal easier to be zealous for the Church, for a society, for a political or religious party or school, for a movement or a cause, than to be " zealous for good works." And all that zeal is froth unless the other be with it. All Christ's flock are earmarked thus. They are zealous for good. They like and they seek for good works. (*A. Mac-laren, D.D.*) *The great redemption :*—How great a theme—how glorious a work is this! To redeem a few bodies from slavery, what has it cost! To effect but a partial alleviation of their suffering, a prospective and future freedom, what efforts, what sacrifices, what a hard and protracted struggle have been necessary! But we " are not redeemed with silver and gold from our vain conversation (that is, our life of iniquity), but with the precious blood of Christ." I. WE NOTICE WHAT WAS THE IMPLIED CONDITION OF MANKIND THAT INDUCED JESUS CHRIST TO UNDERTAKE THIS ARDUOUS WORK ON THEIR BEHALF. We were under the influence of moral evil. 1. We were held under the sentence of the supreme law—a law undeniably just and pure, calculated to maintain the prerogatives of the sovereign Lord, and worthy of being feared as the expression of His righteous will. 2. The human soul, created at first in God's image, was polluted and degraded. As a temple now in ruins, desecrated, and perverted from its original purpose, no longer fit for him to inhabit. 3. The condemnation and pollution of the soul involved its ultimate, if not its present misery—the loss of all pure felicity and pure immortality. " Sin, when it is finished, bringeth forth death "—a privation of all happiness, a subjection to all suffering. II. WE OBSERVE WHAT IT IS HERE SAID CHRIST DID FOR US—He gave Himself for us.—This, under any view, was an act of stupendous goodness and compassion. But its peculiar features must be distinctly traced. 1. The Person who gave Himself. The Father's co-equal and co-eternal Son, whom angels worship and devils dread, whom the universe acknowledges as its author. He gave Himself for us, a ransom-price of ineffable excellence and worth! 2. What was the deed? The most entire self-sacrifice. He gave Himself, not only to teach us, comfort us, labour for us, but to die for us. 3. The unparalleled magnanimity of the act. Who so great as He? who so mean as we? What being so glorious as He? who so worthless as we? III. LET US DISTINCTLY APPRECIATE HIS PURPOSE, OR THE END OF HIS WONDROUS SELF-DEVOTEMENT. To redeem us from all iniquity. 1. To rescue us from the sentence pronounced upon all iniquity by the Divine law; and this by being made a curse for us. The law has no more power over you. 2. To redeem us from the dominion of sin in our hearts and minds. He designed that we should not continue slaves of iniquity, vassals of Satan, and victims of guilt. What a noble purpose, to regenerate that which was so degenerate, and restore that which was in ruins, and purify that which was so polluted! 3. His design included the recovery of our immortal life; for to redeem from all iniquity must signify to redeem from all the effects, all the consequences, all the privations and inflictions which iniquity in all its possible relations can incur. IV. WE NOTICE HOW THIS DEED OF HIS EFFECTS THE PURPOSE HE PROPOSED. 1. His death is the moral substitute for ours; or that great moral consideration on account of which God is pleased to pardon sin, to accept the repenting sinner, and justify the ungodly who believes in Jesus. Here we can perceive that there is a reasonable foundation for the practical display of the Divine love to lost souls. It is a conception of the Divine and infinite mind, and evidently worthy of that mind, since it is " glory to God in the highest, on earth peace, good-will towards men." 2. We may perceive, also, that the sacrifice of Christ becomes the basis on which Divine influences are granted to renovate fallen man. The Holy Spirit becomes our sanctifier, because Christ has restored us to Divine favour, satisfied the law, and removed every barrier to our adoption. 3. The discovery of this grand fact of Christ's sacrifice is found the most efficient, indeed the only successful, means of recovering us to a sincere obedience and a lively hope of glory. This works the great moral miracle of transforming a heart of stone to one of flesh, a heart of sin to one of virtue, a heart of enmity to one of love. Application : 1. Can we say, "He hath loved me, and given Himself for me"? Then let us prove our vital union by all the fruits of godliness. 2. Can we find no evidence that we are redeemed from our iniquity? then let us fear the impending issue, and flee for refuge to lay hold on the hope set before us. (*The Evangelist.*)  *Christ's gift of Himself for our redemption :*—I. THE PERSON HERE SPOKEN OF. "The great God," &c. II. THE GIFT. 1. The dignity of the person bestowing it. 2. The sacrifice at which it is made. 3. Its value. 4. The motive which impelled the donor to bestow it—love. 5. The benefit which accompanies it. (*A. Alexander, D.D.*)  *Christ's gift of Himself:*—In that Christ gave Himself—1. We learn that there can be neither other priest nor other sacrifice than Christ Himself : both which our apostle accurately noteth in a diverse phrase, which at the first seem to sound the self-same ; neither doth our English so distinguish them as the Greek doth. The former is in our text, which more properly betokeneth that Christ offered no other oblation or sacrifice than Himself : hence is it said that for this end God gave Christ a body, that in the same He might perform this part of His Father's will. The latter is in 1 Tim. ii. 6, which implieth more directly that Christ Himself gave Himself, and that there can be no other priest in this oblation than He that is the sacrifice : neither, indeed, can He be offered of any other save Himself, who for this purpose "sanctified Himself," as the altar sanctifieth the gift and the temple the gold. 2. In that it is said that Christ gave Himself we may note that He gave Himself wholly, both His body and soul, in sacrifice, and spared neither: for we had deserved a double death which it was meet that Christ by a double death should destroy; by His bodily death pull out the sting of the death of our bodies, and utterly abolish the death of our souls by the death of His soul; and to this purpose, that our consolation might be full, the Scripture showeth how that His soul was heavy unto the death, and that a little before His suffering His soul was sore troubled. And Isaiah expressly affirmeth that His soul travailed in His death, and that He made His soul an offering for sin and poured out His soul unto death, and that He made His grave with the rich in His death: where note, that he speaketh in the plural number to note this double death of Christ; and what other thing did Himself proclaim with such a loud voice upon the cross when He cried, "My God, My God, why hast Thou forsaken Me?" For what other is the death of the soul but to be separated from God, the fountain of life? which point helpeth us to understand such places of the Scripture as affirm that Christ suffered and died according to the flesh (John vi. 51), and that Christ offered His body (Heb. x. 10), and all those which ascribe all our salvation to the blood of Christ. All which must be synecdochically understood, under one kind comprehending all His suffering and never excluding any part of it, every one of them being equivalent to this speech of the apostle, "who gave Himself" : that is, both His body and soul, or wholly unto the death ; neither can the death of the cross be other, which is joined with the malediction of God from which we by it were wholly delivered. 3. Where it is said that Christ gave Himself it may be further noted that His whole passion and death was voluntary ; for what is more free than gift? and this appeareth in that He was wont to say beforehand that He must go away unto His Father, that He must leave the world and His disciples, that He had power to lay down His life and take it up again and that no man could take it from Him ; for who could take that life from Him, whose sinless nature of itself was not obnoxious to death, it being the stipend of sin? (*T. Taylor, D.D.*)  *Christ must be received :*—1. If Christ gave Himself for us, then suffered He not for His own sins, for He knew no sin, being most holy in His conception, without original sin; according to the word of the angel "That holy thing that shall be born of thee" (Luke i. 35); as also most innocent in all His life, for no guile was found in His mouth; and who could accuse Him of sin, of which innocency, not only His friends, the prophets and apostles, but His greatest foes also, by God's providence, became witnesses? Pilate's wife wished her husband to have nothing to do with that just man. Pilate himself confessed he found no fault in Him. The centurion said, surely this man was the Son of God. Caiaphas said, that one man must die, not for Himself, but for the people ; the thief on the cross, "this man hath done nothing amiss." Nay, Judas himself cried out that he had betrayed innocent blood; not to speak anything of the many confessions of the devils themselves, that He was the Son of the Most High. 2. If Christ have given Himself for us, we must receive this gift and the benefit of it, seeing a gift not received is to no purpose or profit. And the means to receive Christ and apply Him with all His benefits is—(1) To know Him, for darkness comprehendeth Him not; and He came to His own, but they not knowing Him received Him not, but crucified Him, whom had they known, they would never have crucified the Lord of Glory. (2) By prizing the gift above gold, silver, pearls; esteeming the precious blood of the immaculate Lamb above every corruptible thing under the sun, all which cannot redeem our soul. (3) By opening the door of the heart, purified by faith, to entertain Him, while He offereth Himself with all His merits in the Word and sacraments, and this not as a stranger, by giving a night's lodging, but as our husband and head, never to be departed. 3. If Christ has given Himself so willingly to such a cursed death for us, we must also in way of thankfulness give ourselves unto Him. He gave His body, His soul, His glory, and all for us; we must not think much to part with body, goods, name, liberty, or life itself, for His sake, when He calleth us unto Him. The law of thankfulness requireth that we should part with such things as in comparison are but trifles for Him, who thinketh not His dearest things too good for us; and the rather, because when we have done all we can, we can never be sufficiently thankful for this greatest gift that ever was given to the sons of men; we can never speak sufficiently of it, nor ever wade deep enough into the ocean of that love that presenteth us with such a gift as this is. (*Ibid.*) *Christ's gift of Himself for us:*—I. THE PERSON REFERRED TO. Show—1. His Divinity. 2. His humanity. 3. Union of both. 4. Superiority to angels and all other existences. II. WHAT THIS PERSON DID. "Gave Himself for us." 1. Voluntarily. 2. Personally. 3. Sacrificially. III. THE PURPOSE FOR WHICH HE GAVE HIMSELF FOR US. 1. To "redeem" or deliver us; not from poverty, or affliction, or death, but from "iniquity"—all iniquity—its guilt, condemnation, power, inbeing, consequences. 2. To "purify" us; to separate us unto Himself from the world and sin; "a peculiar people"—in nature, names, possessions. 3. "Zealous of good works"—not passive, but active. Lessons: Our redemption is—1. Wrought out by love and blood. 2. Entire and perfect. 3. Into blessed experience and useful living. (*Local Preacher's Treasury.*) *The duty of using one's life for others:*—"Who gave Himself for us." We are familiar with the expression that Jesus Christ gave His life for man. I would not take anything away from the meaning and magnitude of the act of dying; but I should be glad to give more emphasis and power to the fact that Christ gave His life as much while He was living as while He was dying, and that to give life may mean either to use it or to lay it down. All Christ's was a giving. Although comprehensively viewed, it was a single gift, yet it was a continuous gift, developing in every direction. It was a multiple force, ever varying. It was one prolonged giving of Himself away to others. For He lived not for Himself. He sought not His own. He did not employ His reason, nor His moral sentiments, nor His active forces, nor His time, nor His power, for Himself. He honoured His Father, and sought the welfare of men. And the three years, or nearly three, that preceded His death, were in some respects a far more remarkable gift than was the death itself. And in the case of our Divine Lord, He gave Himself both while living and while dying. So the lesson to be derived, it seems to me, from many of the descriptions of Christ's gift of Himself, is a lesson to be pondered in regard to the use of our lives, rather than in regard to their termination. We give our life best, not when we die, but while yet we are living. It is true that men often give their lives in some sense as Christ did; but the more obvious and the more common and attainable imitation of the Lord Jesus Christ is that which seeks to imitate His life, rather than His death. No man can give his life for the world as Christ did. Though a man may give his life for the world, no man can stand sinless; but He did. No man is related to God as was the Saviour. From no man reaches out those threads which connect him with the spiritual and invisible realm as Christ was connected with it. What the other-side influence was I have said we do not know; but that there was one we are told. And this we cannot have. Here is a grand official difference. There is a universal character belonging to the influence of the death of Christ which does not and cannot belong to that of any man. Yet, in so far as moral influence is exerted by one's death on his fellow-men, it is possible, though in a far lower sphere, and in a far less degree, that we should follow and imitate our Lord by giving our life for one another. Every patriot who is sacrificed, on account of the heroic fidelity of his life, to the public weal; every martyr whose blood is shed as a seal and witness of that holy faith by which he would illumine and bless the world; every prisoner lingering in dungeons, and, with long dying, suffering unseen and forgotten by the multitude for whose welfare his life is spent; every man who goes forth to lands of fever and malaria, and to early death, knowing that he carries religion, civilisation, and liberty to the ignorant at the price of his own life, and cheerfully dies in the harness there, where men, being most degraded and thankless, are on that very account more needful of this very sacrifice of some one—all these, and all others whose death is brought about by persistent adhesion to the welfare of men, follow their Lord not less really because the sphere is lower and narrower. They follow their Lord in death and, through death. While, then, it is possible, literally, to give our life for others, and while we may sometimes be called in the performance of our duty to do it, so that we shall not say that dying for others is antiquated; yet, in the main, if we are to follow our Lord, and to give our lives for others, it must be by the use which we make of those lives. Now, he who devotes the active hours of his life to those spheres to which Providence calls men, is really giving himself for others. When a man stands upon the deck, and at the bench, and by the forge, and in the furrow, and in the colliery—then, if ever, if he has a life to live of true piety, is the time; and there, at the post of duty, is the place. For all the humblest avocations and employments are so arranged that, while they serve to support the actor, they do a hundred times as much for the community as they do for him that follows them. Why, that old smith, rugged himself, almost, as the storms he prepares to combat, hammers morning and night upon the links that form the chain which clasps the cable. It may be, as in the olden time, yet more ponderously, that he in the smithy works on the huge shank of the anchor, and when his summer's work or winter's toil is done, and it is sold for the ship, men ask him, " What got you for your labour ? " Nobody ever thinks of saying to him, " You have worked a whole winter to make a gift; what have you given to the community? What has he given? It may not be known for a long time. On voyage after voyage the ship goes, and there lies his gift useless and unsuspected. Some day the ship bears back a thousand precious souls, among them mothers whose flowers lie at home waiting for them to return; fathers, who cannot be spared from the neighbourhood; public men of signal service—the very salt of the times in which they live; heroes and patriots many. Then it is that the storm beats down and seeks to whelm them all in the sea, and to whelm the community in mourning. Then it is that, when every other effort has been made in vain, the anchor is thrown out. And now the storm rages with increased violence, as if it were yet more angry because it is thwarted. But the good blacksmith's work holds. Sinking far out of sight, and grappling the foundations of the earth, it will not let go. And we, for the first time, see the value of his gift. Every link has been properly welded; and, though the wind howls, and the sea wages a fierce and desperate battle, and the strain is tremendous, the storm passes by, and there rides the gallant ship safe ! There is what he gave. He gave a chain, an anchor, to the community, and salvation to the hundreds on board the ship, and joy and peace where the tidings came of souls saved from the remorseless deep. And yet, how many men think simply that he made an anchor, and got so many hundred dollars for it ! He made an anchor and saved a hundred lives. So men that fill our houses with conveniences, with comforts, with various instruments by which our time is redeemed to higher and nobler uses; men that make implements—they give my brain a gift. He that makes a machine emancipates me. For if matter cannot be made to toil upon matter, then men must toil upon it. And just in proportion as you make slaves—the only slaves that are fit for this world—machine slaves— just in that proportion you redeem the mind to greater leisure, and to a larger sphere for the moral functions of manhood. And all men that labour thus productively and skilfully are real benefactors of the community. Let every man, then, follow the occupation that God has given him, and understand that in following it he is rendering a service to his fellow-men; and let him feel, " I am honoured in these appointed channels of God's providence, that I am permitted to give my life for my fellow-men—that is, to live it for them." Now, in proportion as you are noble, in proportion as God has made you wise and stronger than anybody else, in proportion as study and opportunity have refined you and cultured you—in that proportion God requires that you should give the benefit of your gifts and attainments to the whole community. You cannot follow Christ except you do it. Lastly, consider the wickedness of what seldom passes for a wicked life. I am not speaking of a life of vice and of crime, which is the diseased form of all wickedness —wickedness carried to its most morbid condition. But see how, all through life, men of repute, men of standing, men of influence, men that are praised while they live and are eulogised when they die, are men that are given to the lust of pride and vanity. They live inordinately for themselves. They do not actually do harm, it may be; but they are men who are full of ambition all for themselves. They are like the oak which stands in the night to gather dew for itself, and then, if the wind in the morning shakes it, is willing to part with the few drops that it really cannot hold on to; and they call themselves benevolent! There are men that spread abroad gigantic arms, and gather the wealth of heaven—whatever God's bounty can give them—meaning it all for themselves; and a few accidental drops of kindness here and there give them some claim to generosity and benevolence. But where are the channels into which their life flows? Where are the uses that these great forces, concentrating in them, subserve? They live for pride, for vanity—the meanest of all feelings when it is in excess—and for self. They live for everything but others. You need not be a criminal, you need not be a very wicked man, you may neither riot or debauch, you may neither steal nor gamble; and yet, you may live stained, leprous, spotted, and hideous before God, before all holy angels, and before right-thinking men. Your life may be a vast activity; and yet may be a huge vortex where everything tends to that centre—-self. And that is to be wicked enough. You do not need to be any wickeder. And yet, you may be as wicked as that, and still be very respectable in the eyes of men. This question comes home very nearly to us. What we are doing for others is to measure our following the Lord Jesus Christ; and not what we are doing of necessity, but what we are doing on purpose, what we are doing consciously, what we are striving to do, what we put our heart and soul into. If there be any of you, then, that desire to follow the Lord Jesus Christ, and to give yourselves for others, as He gave Himself for our comfort, living or dying ye are the Lord's—living or dying, and the one as much as the other. (*H. W. Beecher.*)        **That He might redeem us from all iniquity.**—*The redemption from lawlessness :*—When we hear that we are not under the law, there is a danger of our allowing ourselves to feel a vague impression that the requirements of the gospel cannot be quite so strict, and that we are now a good deal more free to take our own way than if we were under the old bond of legal restraint. A general laxity of moral tone has too often been disguised under a title of Christian liberty; and a reference to the consolations of the gospel and the provisions of grace has too frequently prevented any serious distress and contrition at the consciousness of the inconsistencies and shortcomings of an unholy, self-indulgent life. In making the Christian revelation, God has been careful to guard against such an abuse of gospel truth by exhibiting side by side, as correlative and mutually dependent truths, the proclamation of pardon, and the provision for holiness. If we fall into the Antinomian snare, it will be not only in spite of the plain teaching of Christ, but also in defiance of the great moral lesson exhibited in the Atonement. "Who gave Himself for us, that He might redeem us from all iniquity," that is the negative object of the teaching of grace; and purify "unto Himself a peculiar people, zealous of good works," that is the eternal and positive purpose of God towards the elect bride of His Divine Son. The word translated in our version of this passage—iniquity—might literally be rendered lawlessness, and suggests the moral attitude and condition of him who is altogether ignorant of, or indifferent to, the claims of the Divine law, or who wantonly sets them at defiance. From such a state of soul and habit of life Christ is here represented by St. Paul as dying to redeem us, and we may add, from all that in any way savours of or leads up to these; for it is from all lawlessness that we are redeemed, whatever specific form it may assume. Let us consider a little more closely how our natural disposition towards lawlessness is affected by the influences of true Christian experience; in other words, how grace guards against or triumphs over lawlessness. This life of lawlessness is quite compatible with knowledge of the law; indeed it only assumes its worst moral type when the sinner is familiar with the law's claims and sanctions, just as the worst criminals are those who know that the State has enacted laws against the crimes they are committing, and who yet continue to commit them; but, whether ignorant of it or familiar with it, the lawless will resent or endeavour to evade legal restraint, and to a greater or less extent act as though no law existed. The great attraction of the life of lawlessness is the liberty which it seems to promise. The lawless soul recognises no superior authority, and is ready to ask defiantly, "Who is Lord over us?" For while the life of lawlessness appears to be a life of liberty, when we come to examine it a little more closely, we make the startling discovery that it is really a life of skilfully concealed bondage. The truth is, that lawlessness itself becomes a law, and operates with inexorable force upon those who have sought their liberty in it—the apostle calls it "the law of sin and death." We may illustrate this by referring to the analogies of social life. We know well that in human society lawlessness must mean tyranny. Any one member of society who acts out of law will be sure to infringe the rights of some other which the law was designed to protect. The thief leads a life of lawlessness, but it is at the expense of others on whom he preys. Lawlessness must ever mean the subjection of the weaker to the stronger, and from this we may judge what must inevitably be the condition of the lawless man. If in such an one the higher elements were really the stronger, no worse consequences perhaps might happen than the production of a morbid asceticism or a stoical insensibility ; but unhappily with such this is not the case. The lawless man, by his very lawlessness, is cut off from God, and therefore from all those holier influences which might have stimulated these higher elements of his nature, and enabled them to hold their own, while by the same lawlessness he is exposed to the influence of the great author of lawlessness, with whose spirit in this respect he is in perfect sympathy. Hence the lower elements in the man's nature, in one form or another, are sure to carry all before them, and to exercise a certain tyrannous supremacy by virtue of the right of the stronger. Thus we see that there comes into existence a certain law of lawlessness, which is the most execrable of all forms of slavery, and which binds, as with an iron yoke of bondage, those who, to realise their foolish dream of independence, have turned their back on the law of God. Lawlessness becomes law, and when, wearied with the tyranny of lawless forces, the lawless heart would fain return to a state of allegiance to law, it finds itself precluded from doing so by that anarchical force, that other law in the members, which will not submit to the dictates of the will, any more than to the commands of God. Herein lies the most startling illustration perhaps that can be found of that dread law of Nemesis in which the ancients believed so firmly, and not without good cause. By and by voluntary yielding becomes compulsory submission, and he is the slave to a greater or less extent of that habit of lawlessness to which he has surrendered himself. But there is more than this to be said. When we consider the position of God as the moral Governor of the universe, it is easy to see that it is a just and righteous thing that they who reject His authority should be allowed to find their punishment in their own miserable experiences, that He should ordain the self-imposed tyranny of lawlessness to be the scourge of lawlessness. But if this be so, this cursed bondage comes upon the lawless not merely as a natural sequel attributable to the force of habit, but as a part of the effect of that Divine law of retribution which backs with terrible sanctions the revealed law of God, the complete effects of which will be exhibited in the doom of the lost. Now if a man turn his back upon his allegiance to the law, it will follow as a matter of right as well as of necessity that he shall fall under the supremacy of the great lawbreaker, and become the slave of that spirit that now worketh in the children of disobedience. Hence, although Satan's authority over us is a usurpation, yet there is a certain sense in which his sway is backed by right. We have given him a claim over our desecrated nature by our wilful apostasy from God. Sin and death form as much the subjective law of the sinner's experience as life and holiness constitute the law of the experience of the saint. Just as this outward world itself has laws of its own laid down by infinite wisdom, which regulate its motion and form its character; as every flower of the field is possessed of a law of its own, in obedience to which it assumes a certain form, and passes through a definite process of development; even so the experience of the lawless has a certain subjective character, and is governed by laws which belong to it. As nature has fixed laws of its own, so fallen nature has fixed laws of its own ; and this law of fallen nature, the law of sin and death, springs into existence, as I have been endeavouring to show, as the direct Nemesis of sin. With these thoughts present to our mind, clearly discerning that lawlessness works out its own Nemesis and prepares its own retribution, we proceed to ask how can man be saved from penalties so justly incurred, and delivered from those legal provisions which render him the victim of his own lawlessness? St. Paul's words in the passage supply us with the only satisfactory answer, revealing to us an undertaking that was indeed worthy of a God. In one way only could a means be provided to enable those who had become the lawful captives of the anarchical powers of darkness to pass from that condition into lawful liberty. Whatever God does must be in accordance with law. God's dealings with humanity must be consistent with His dealings with other intelligences. God cannot, and will not, arbitrarily exercise towards man, however favoured man may be, an unjust and unholy partiality. So we read in this passage that "Christ gave Himself for us, that He might redeem us from all lawlessness." It was only by redemption that alike the claims of law and the force of lawlessness, as against the sinner, could be met; and the only redemption price that the great Judge of all could either propose or accept is that which is indicated in our text—"Christ gave Himself for us." Now it is evident that if the redemption of humanity is to be effected by the sufferings of Christ as the voluntary victim of the broken law, His sufferings should bear some close resemblance to those which sin has incurred; otherwise the great lesson suggested by His sufferings must be lost, and one supreme object of them be defeated. The passion of man for self leads man to submit to the tyranny of sin, even though he hates and despises it while he yields to it. The passion of Christ for human souls led Him to submit to be made sin for us, though He knew no sin, and intensely loathed it, even while He represented it. But the similarity extends even further. We have seen that it is part of the Nemesis of lawlessness that the lawless sinner comes under the power of him who is emphatically the lawless one, and that, having renounced all allegiance to Divine law, he should experience the results of the negation of law amidst the representatives of lawlessness beneath. Even so our blessed Lord was content to be given over, not only into the hands of wicked men, but in some mysterious sense to the cruel animosity of the lawless spirits of evil. "This," He exclaims, "is your hour, and the power of darkness." Perhaps, without intruding into mysteries that are too profound for our limited knowledge, we may even go a step further, and suggest that as it is doubtless part of the just retribution on lawlessness that the lawless should be left to himself, and cut off from all connection with Him who is the eternal source of law, even so Christ, representing our lawlessness, was cut off from all conscious connection with His Divine Father in those terrible moments spent upon the Cross, when the confession of inward and agonising desolation was wrung from His breaking heart. I picture to myself the dying Son of Man as in some sense outlawed, denied all recognition and protection from above, and victimised by violence and cruelty below. In this voluntary submission of the Son of God to penalties such as are due to the lawlessness of man, we have presented to our minds the most solemn and striking tribute that ever was paid to the majesty of Law. And now that the ransom has been paid, it is our blessed privilege to claim the full benefits of this redemption from all lawlessness, and to return in our own actual experience to the happy liberty of the law. From henceforth ours is to be a life of law, but not such a life of law as we vainly tried to lead before we accepted His redemption. Christ has not redeemed us from one form of bondage only to place us under another. He has redeemed us from lawlessness not to place us under law, but to place us in law, and law in us. Thus St. Paul speaks of himself as being, not without law, or lawless towards God, but lawbound to Christ. It suggests the thought that devotion to Christ had become a law of life to St. Paul, in the fulfilment of which he found his "perfect law of liberty." We are redeemed from lawlessness that we may enjoy the liberty and not feel the constraint of law, and this end is attained when law coincides with inclination, which it will when its seat is within the heart. Law is liberty when we live from law, not by law. The Christian carries the law of his being within him, just in the same way as the objects of the natural world carry the law of their own motion or development in themselves. He has but to be true to his new nature, to recognise its instincts, to yield to its impulses, to respond to its claims, to gratify its desires, and he will find himself fulfilling the law without any thought of fulfilling it, indeed without a thought of its being law. Christ has redeemed us from lawlessness that He may Himself become our life-law, because He is our new nature. Two things surely are manifest in New Testament Scripture; first, that in redemption all has been done for us that is necessary to render it possible for us to "attain the prize of our high calling"; second, that we shall only attain the prize of our calling as we by faith appropriate to ourselves what has thus been made ours. It is most instructive, with these two thoughts in our minds, to notice how throughout the New Testament the work is represented as done, and yet to be done; the blessing as bestowed, and yet to be appropriated. A few instances out of many must suffice; but they might be multiplied almost indefinitely. We are spoken of as already saved, and as being saved, and yet are directed to work out our own salvation (Acts ii. 47; Phil. ii. 12). We are dead with Christ, and our old man is crucified with Him, and yet we are to mortify our members that are on the earth (Rom. vi. 6, 8; Col. iii. 5). We have put off the old man, and yet we are taught to put him off (Col. iii. 9, 10; Eph. iv. 22). Do you believe really that Christ has redeemed you from all lawlessness, whether in little things or in great? and do you claim the practical effect of the deliverance in the same way in which you once claimed the practical effect of His expiation for your justification? How many of us can believe readily enough that His redeeming grace may raise us above flagrant forms of iniquity, and yet doubt His ability to save us from the more common, and therefore less startling, forms of infirmity and sin. From all He has already redeemed us. For sin shall not have dominion over you; for Christ gave Himself for us, that He might redeem us from all lawlessness; and He gives Himself to us, that He may become Himself our law. Yes, let us believe it, from all lawlessness. That embraces the little things as well as the great things. It embraces the little tempers, which are so lawless, the rattle of the tongue, which is a very lawless member. Be no longer satisfied with hoping and longing, and desiring, and wishing for better things; but bring your strong faith to bear upon God's fact. Christ died to ransom you from all lawlessness, and He has not died in vain. Believe that you are redeemed, and claim it of the Redeemer that He shall apply His own redemption. (*W. H. M. H. Aitken.*) *Redemption and its obligations:*—I. CHRIST'S WORK OF REDEMPTION. 1. This redemption is presented to us in the Word of God in a threefold aspect. In one place—" Christ hath redeemed us from the curse of the law, being made a curse for us." In our text—" Christ hath redeemed us from all iniquity "—that is, from the power of indwelling sin. And in other passages the day of Christ's second advent is spoken of as the day of redemption, because it is at His return that the glorification of His redeemed people will be consummated by the "redemption of our bodies." The price at which this redemption was effected is declared by St. Peter not to have been a corruptible price, as silver and gold, but the precious blood of Christ, as of a lamb without blemish and without spot. Thus, then, you will perceive that the basis of Christ's redemption is this—His self-surrender is a sacrifice for the sins of man, His death in its design was an expiatory sacrifice for the sins of the world. 2. The fountain has its source from the throne of Deity, and the rise of the stream of mercy is lost amid the depth of the eternal counsels. The work of Christ was not the cause but the fruit of the Father's love. Christ Himself, the provision of Christ, the surrender of Christ, is the manifestation of the love of God. II. THE DESIGN OF REDEMPTION, AND THE CONSEQUENT OBLIGATION OF THE REDEEMED. The redemption which is in Christ Jesus involves this great and mighty principle—that if I have been bought by the precious blood of Christ I am not my own; that henceforth the love of Christ is to constrain me, that henceforth I am not to live to myself, but to Him that died for me and rose again, and that I am to glorify God in my body and in my spirit, which are God's. (*J. C. Miller, M.A.*) *A perfect redemption:*— 1. If Christ hath freed and redeemed us from all iniquity, then hath He made no partial redemption; He satisfieth not for the fault, and leaveth us to satisfy for the punishment; neither redeemeth us from the eternal punishment, but giveth us leave to satisfy for the temporal. But if Christ have redeemed us from all iniquity, if He said on the Cross, It is finished, that is, the whole work of man's redemption is consummate and perfect; if at one time He made one perfect expiation, and thereby brought in an everlasting redemption, here is artillery and gunshot against all popery; down go all other satisfactions for sin in this life, down go all satisfactions after this life in purgatory, down goeth their doctrine of all other merits save this of Christ. 2. This consideration must stir us up to a love of our Lord Jesus, who hath discharged us of such a debt, and ransomed us from such an unutterable thraldom. 3. It must work in us a detestation and watchfulness against all sin, which bringeth such vassalage upon us; for shall Christ take upon Him our debts, that we, like desperate prodigals, should do nothing but augment them? Shall He ransom us, and give us perfect freedom that we, with the unthankful Israelites, should run back again to our former bondage? Shall we, with Solomon's fools, make but a mock of sin, which cost Christ so dear to expiate? 3. Hence also is ministered no small consolation to the faithful; for if Christ have redeemed us from all iniquity, who can lay anything to our charge? Seeing that Christ hath justified, who can condemn? (*T. Taylor, D.D.*) *A threefold description of Christians:*—I. "REDEEMED FROM ALL INIQUITY." We have been brought out of the dominion and thraldom of sin with the heart's blood of the Son of God. What have we, then, to do any more with the works of darkness? What has the emancipated slave to do any longer with his old bondage and his old toil? He is a free man now. The owner's lash is no longer for his shoulders to bear. He and slavery have parted company for ever, and he never experiences a single moment's desire to return to it. II. "A PECULIAR PEOPLE." We are God's own purchased possession; we are His sole property, and belong to Him alone. The remembrance of this truth cannot fail to produce in us a life that will appear eccentric to the world, but there is no warrant in it for practising eccentricities. III. "ZEALOUS OF GOOD WORKS." Not merely practising good works, but boiling in their desire to do them. (*G. A. Sowter, M.A.*) *Christ the promoter of the right:*—The supreme mission of Christ to this earth was not so much to give correct creeds as correct conduct. Iniquity is the want of equity, the negation of rectitude. I. HE REVEALS THE STANDARD OF RECTITUDE. The will of God. II. HE SUPPLIES THE MOTIVE TO RECTITUDE. Supreme love to God. III. HE PRESENTS THE MODEL OF RECTITUDE. He Himself is a perfect example of what all men should be. (*Homilist.*) *The consecrating Saviour and the consecrated people:*—I. THE CONSECRATING SAVIOUR. 1. He gave Himself (John x. 18). 2. He gave Himself a ransom. 3. The object of this was to purify men; to save from sin. Note the distinction between being saved from the penalties of sin, and from sin itself. II. THE CONSECRATED PEOPLE. 1. Freed from the power of sin. 2. Brought under the Divine rule. "From all iniquity; literally, "from all lawlessness." 3. Specially devoted to good; "peculiar," 4. Ardent; "zealous." 5. Diligent, devoted to "good works." (*F. Wagstaff.*) **Purify unto Himself a peculiar people.**—*Cleansing through Christ's death:*—1. In that the death of Christ serveth for our continual cleansing while we live in this world; we are to take notice and acknowledgment of much filthiness and uncleanness even in the best, it is no slight soil or stain that hath fouled our natures, which will easily be blown or brushed off, for it sticketh nearer us than our skins, that the very power of Christ's death itself doth not wholly destroy it while we live; but we have cause to cry out with the leper in the law, I am unclean, I am unclean: nay, the godly see what blackamoors they are, and how hardly they change their skins and what leopards they are, hardly parting with their spots. And this made the apostle take such pains that he might attain this fruit of Christ's death and resurrection after he had been long able to maintain his justification against all challenges, and say who shall lay anything to the charge of God's elect, and what shall separate us from the love of God? Well knew he how fast this uncleanness cleaveth unto our natures (Heb. xii. 1). 2. Hence may be noted that wheresoever sin is pardoned it is also purged (Rom. viii. 2). That is not only from the curse of the law, but even that law and the power of sin itself which would still hold us in the service of it. He shall die in his sin that dieth not unto his sin, not that sin can be so dead as not remain; but if it lie not bleeding by virtue of that stroke which Christ in His death hath given it if the force of it be not abated, and thou escaped from the rule of it Christ's blood doth thee no good. 3. Let both these considerations move us to be ever washing and cleansing ourselves from our uncleanness, and never to be at rest till we find ourselves, although not free from blackness, yet comely, as the Church confesseth of herself. (*T. Taylor, D.D.*) *Why believers are called a peculiar people:*—1. Because they are the most precious of men, even the most noble persons of the earth, descended of the blood of Christ. 2. In regard of God they are a peculiar people, distinct from others by His grace of election by which they are chosen out of the world and set high in His favour above all others. For they lie before Him in the righteousness of Christ in whom the Father is well pleased; they are bought from the earth and stand before Him in the work of His own fingers, namely, their new birth and second creation in which He also delighteth to behold. Hence are they called a holy nation, the spouse of Christ, the daughter of God, the choice of God, and God's delight. 3. They are a peculiar people in regard of their whole manner and condition of life, which made Balaam say of Israel that it was a people dwelling alone and numbered not himself among other nations, that is, altogether different in laws, customs, manner, and condition of life. But let us see this truth in some instances. (1) Their original are not some few families coming out of some corner of the earth; but they sprung of Christ, of whom all the families in heaven and earth are called. (2) Their country is no part of earth, for they are here but strangers and pilgrims, but heaven, to which they tend and from whence they look for a Saviour. (3) Their King is neither born nor created, but the everlasting King of glory who ruleth not some one country but from sea to sea, yea, to the world's end, and not for an age, but as He is a King for ever and His kingdom an everlasting kingdom, so He ruleth for ever and ever, and of His king-

dom there is no end.  (4) Their laws are spiritual, to govern the conscience as well
as the outward man, most perfect, never changed, never abrogated as men's be.  (5)
Their war and weapons are not carnal, but spiritual, as their chiefest enemies; their
Captain was never foiled nor can be, and therefore before they strike a blow they are
sure of victory, and for their external enemies they conquer them, not by smiting
(as others), but by suffering.  (6) Their language is the language of Canaan, their
speech bewrayeth them to be citizens of heaven, hence are they called people of a
pure language, no filthy, unsavoury, or corrupt communication cometh out of their
mouths, but such as is holy, tending to edification, and ministering grace to the
hearers.  (7) Their apparel is devised and put on by God Himself, even garments
of innocency, long white robes died red in the blood of the Lamb.  (8) Their diet
not rising out of the earth, but descending from heaven ; Jesus Christ is the Bread of
Life, and that manna that came down from heaven, and that water which gusheth
out of the rock, of whom whosoever feedeth and drinketh he hath tasted of the tree
of life and of the water of life, he cannot but live everlastingly.  (*Ibid.*)     *Peculiar
but not eccentric :*—The phrase employed in our version, " peculiar people," has no
doubt tended to suggest and foster exceedingly erroneous ideas of what God expects
His people to be.   It certainly does not mean a people who affect all kinds of peculiarities.   Not only is this phrase associated with some of the most extraordinary
exhibitions of fanaticism that have been witnessed in modern times, but I apprehend
that there are not a few earnest and even devoted Christians whose minds have
been more or less warped and their lives distorted by a misapprehension of the true
significance of the phrase here used.   There are some good people whose religion,
to the casual observer at any rate, seems mainly to consist in making themselves
very extraordinary, and they are disposed to claim that others should copy their
peculiarities if they desire to follow the Lord fully.    Such persons need to be
reminded that God does not seek for an eccentric people, but for a people whose
essential singularity lies in the fact that they are His.  Be true to your calling as
espoused to Christ, and this will save you from having to attempt the solution of
many otherwise perplexing questions.  You will not then have to ask, as too many
Christians do, " How far may I go in the direction of worldly conformity without
actually forfeiting my religion ? "   Can you conceive a loyal and devoted bride
making any such inquiry, " How far may I go in the way of associating with those
who are the enemies and detractors of my affianced husband, who have done all that
they could to wrong him, and rob him, and injure him ?   How far shall I be justified
in choosing such persons for my friends and companions, and in sharing in their
pursuits and pleasures where his name is never mentioned except in scorn?   What
length may I go in this direction without altogether forfeiting his affections, and
bringing my relations with him to an abrupt termination ? "   Pity the bridegroom
who has such a bride in prospect !  But such a bride the Lord's will never be.  We
need not court peculiarity ; without going out of our way to make ourselves ridiculous
or absurd, those of us who live right out for Christ will make themselves peculiar
enough in a world that does not live for Christ at all.  The man who counts all
things dung and dross that he may win Christ, will be a very peculiar person in a
world that counts Christ dung and dross so that it may win its own pleasures and
gratifications. (*W. H. M. H. Aitken.*)     **Zealous of good works.**—*The practical result
of the teaching of grace :*—" Zealous of good works."  Such is the practical fruit of
the training of Grace ; such its effect upon the outward lives of those who learn in
her school.  Herein Grace as a teacher returns a triumphant answer to her traducers,
who would fain represent her as robbing man of his energies and paralysing his
activities by withdrawing the legal motives for action.  Who are at this moment
foremost in every good work of charity and benevolence throughout our land, but
the very persons to whom the doctrines of Grace are dear as their own lives, and who
have learnt most assiduously at her school?  Nor is it difficult to see how, even on
psychical grounds, apart from any reference to the introduction of supernatural
power, such results should follow from the acceptance of the gospel revelation.  For,
first, he who receives the salvation that Grace brings finds himself a new creature,
dead to his old life, and cut off from all connection with its baleful associations.  He
is therefore in a position to make a really new start in life without being paralysed
in the future by the fatal influence of the past.  Next, he is under the influence of
feelings of the liveliest gratitude to Him to whom he owes his present happiness
and his hopes for the future ; to Him he feels under the deepest obligation ; and his
appreciation of the heroism that has purchased his redemption awakens within him
a genuine and ardent enthusiasm for the person of his Benefactor ; his feeling is

that it is impossible to do too much for One who has done so much for him. Once again, he is at ease in his mind as to his own personal salvation, and therefore has a mind sufficiently " at leisure from itself " to feel for the miseries of those around him. And further, he has vividly before his mind the contrast between his own byegone misery and his present happiness; and the contrast speaks to all of humanity that there is in his nature, urging him to lay himself out for the salvation of those whose condition is as wretched as his own once was, and may become as blessed as his is now. Undoubtedly the enthusiastic benevolence of the true believer may thus to a great extent be accounted for by the character of the belief he entertains; but whence came that creed that reaches and moves so wondrously the subtle mechanism of our nature? Would any profound philosopher, whether ancient or modern, have thought of framing a scheme that seems at first sight so little likely to produce the desired results? But when we have spoken of these natural effects of the acceptance of Christian truth, we have by no means exhausted our list of the real forces which generate this lofty enthusiasm. The believer feels the mighty energies of a new life throbbing within his soul. He is now in a position to draw from the Divine Store-house all that he needs to equip him for his life's work. So it is that, in spite of the cavil of unbelief and the à priori conclusions of unfriendly criticism, Grace proves herself the most practical of all teachers; and the greatest benefactors of mankind are to be found amongst her most faithful scholars. She does not allow those who learn of her to think only of their own spiritual advantage, or to be indifferent to everything except their own personal growth in holiness. Our life's work is twofold; it lies without us and within us; and we cannot neglect either branch of our work without injuring both. We cannot hope to grow in grace while we are leading lives of selfish indolence and uselessness; nor can we expect to be really and extensively useful unless we are fully consecrated to the Lord. Grace trains us then to be enthusiasts or, to use St. Paul's word in this passage, to be zealots, and this is evidently quite in accordance with her genius and customary mode of procedure. Such enthusiasm, if we surrender ourselves to it, will almost always lead to self-denial and even self-sacrifice; but these will rather increase than damp its ardour. There are some expansive forces in the natural world that seem to acquire their intensity by opposition; steam, for example, is only a power when it is compressed. Even so the mighty moral force which eighteen centuries ago shook the heathen world becomes all the mightier when obstacles have to be faced, opposition encountered, sacrifices endured. Some this holy enthusiasm will lead to turn their backs on home and country and expose themselves to the hardships and risks of a missionary life. Others the same enthusiasm will lead to find their work at home amidst our perishing thousands. Nor do we need less but rather more enthusiasm if the same inward call summon us to find our field of toil amidst scenes of fashion and luxury, rather than amidst the hovels of the poor. Self-denial to preach Christ crucified in a drawing-room than in a cellar; where sin is glossed over with a varnish of respectability and refinement, than where it flaunts its naked hideousness before the eyes of all beholders. But for this most difficult of all tasks, which only Christian religion would think of as a possible task at all, and only Christians would dream of undertaking, Grace can supply her disciples with a sufficient motive-power in the enthusiasm which she inspires. But while Grace provides us with a sufficient motive-power in the form of a holy enthusiasm, she is also careful to train us to spend that zeal in the production of really good works. There seems to be a prevalent notion in our day that so long as a man is in earnest it matters little what form his earnestness takes; but Grace teaches us to be particular about the quality as well as the quantity of our work. Our object is not to do much work, but to do good work—so good that it will not need to be done over again. We fear that this is hardly the character of much of the work that is being done in our own busy day. " I am painting for eternity," exclaimed the illustrious Italian, when asked why he spent such pains over his canvas. How many Christian labourers work with a similar feeling? Are we working for eternity, or only for the passing hour? A work, to be a good work, should certainly be, according to the apostle's phrase, " for necessary uses." We are to work for some definite good purpose, and not merely for the sake of keeping ourselves employed. It is needful, therefore, as far as possible, to avoid unnecessary labour, to use the best, and not necessarily the most laborious, means towards the attainment of the end in view, in order that we may have the more time and strength for that which needs to be done. Again, a work to be good needs to be done thoroughly, not in a superficial perfunctory manner. This will naturally be the besetting sin of all mere legal service.

Once again, a work to be good needs to be done in the power of the Holy Ghost. "Apart from Me," our blessed Lord has taught us "ye can do nothing." Once again, a work to be really good needs to be done in the spirit of faith, with the full assurance that the Lord who sends us will use us and work out His own blessed purposes through us. He who does not expect God to use him need express no surprise at not being used; but rather the marvel would be if he were used at all. Yet once again, if our work is to be as good as it should be, it must needs be "a labour of love." This point is amply illustrated by the career of Him whom grace sets before us as our Exemplar. His career was one long exhibition of that hidden love of God which the world was so slow to believe in. If our work is to be really good it must be characterised by the patience of hope. Much work that once promised fairly is marred and spoilt for lack of perseverance. Christians are not steadfast, immovable, and therefore always abounding in the work of the Lord. Good work is not to be produced by a series of extraordinary and spasmodic efforts. We need that patient continuance in well-doing which shows that we seek honour, glory, and immortality. But here again the teaching of Grace comes to our aid. Not only does she set before us an example in One who was no stranger to apparent failure in His own ministry, but she also reminds us of His great forbearance towards us. Such are some of the characteristics of good work in which we are to be zealots, and in which we are to find our outward occupation while God leaves us here. Our day cannot at most be very long; its twelve hours, how rapidly they slip away! and the night cometh when no man can work. Yes, the worker's life is after all the only happy life, even though it may entail toil, hardship, and privation. The true labourer has Christ Himself for his companion in toil, and the smile of His approval for his dearest reward. (*Ibid.*)

*God's family, a school of good works*:—A Christian, by God's ordinance, is no longer allowed to consider himself as standing alone in the world, but as one among many in a holy family. And this puts all his duties in a peculiar point of view, not always regarded as it ought to be, even by serious and well-meaning men. This piece of instruction is conveyed in the text by the words "peculiar people." The title was at first applied to the holy seed, the Children of Israel, when God had redeemed them to Himself by bringing them out of the land of Egypt. The natural condition of all mankind is no better, you see, than a slavery, out of which we needed to be bought and redeemed, before we could be capable of the mighty blessings which God in His mercy had prepared for us: just as the Jews needed deliverance from Egypt, before they could be brought into Canaan. This slavery the whole world, both Jew and Gentile, were continually making worse, by the bad habits in which they indulged, and the power which they allowed evil spirits to gain over them. Christ died to redeem the sinner from those chains of evil custom, which have wound themselves so round him by length of time, that he feels as if shaking them off would be losing a part of himself. Christ died to redeem the drunkard from his drunkenness, the impure from his debauchery, the unkind from his malice, the godless and careless man from his love of this present world. Observe now to what purpose the Son thus made us free. Not to leave us in such a condition as many seem to delight in imagining, the moment they hear of freedom and liberty—not to turn us out into the world, loose and independent of all restraint—but to make us more dependent on Him, more closely confined within His laws, for every day and hour that we live as Christians. In a word, the peculiar, chosen people, whom Christ vouchsafed to redeem to Himself, were meant, above all things in the world, to be always "zealous of good works"; not only rather good than evil, such as might pass well enough in the world, but "zealous," eager, earnest in good; every man striving and trying to be every day better than he was yesterday. And in order that each particular Christian might answer the better this intention of our gracious Redeemer, He has not left us to stand, as it were, separate and apart from one another, but has appointed that all who believe in Him should make up one people, one household, one body; should feel a deep interest one in another, as if their welfare were bound up together: so that "whether one member suffer, all the members should suffer with it; or whether one member be honoured, all the members should rejoice with it." The whole plan of the Christian Church is, in short, as entirely opposite to the natural pride and self-sufficiency of man as anything can well be imagined. It will not let you for a moment dream that you can stand alone and be independent. If any be tempted to the irreligious fancy of saying, "they never made the promise; others made it in their name, and they cannot be bound by it"; certainly it is in their power, if they will, to disavow and break their word given to God : but let them remember that at the same time they cast away all the privileges of their Christian calling. By the very act of coming to the Holy Communion, you renounce, before God and man, that proud unchristian notion of standing alone, being independent. You yourself profess to stand in continual need of all the means and instruments of grace; the prayers, the intercession, the good example, of your brethren; all the helps which the Son of God has so graciously provided in His Church and household. And surely, as to zeal in good works, every one who thinks at all on the subject knows that one chief purpose of the Holy Communion was to encourage and strengthen men in *that*. (*Plain Sermons by Contributors to " Tracts for the Times.")       The zeal of God's people for good works :*—They are zealous because—1. The spirit of the work is in them. A disposition, a bias, a zeal, consonant with the nature of the work, whose relation to God makes it a good work, is implanted in them, and they have naturally a pleasure in its performance. 2. Christ's command is that they should so act that they should bring forth fruit unto His glory. His commands are precious to them because they love Him. 3. In the performance of good works the Christian finds his daily support. The way of good works is the way of salvation, and there abound its consolations. 4. In the way of good works the people of God obtain fellowship with God. Here are the shinings of His face. It is here that darkness turns into light before them. It is here the Lord speaks to His people, and where He strengthens their hearts against folly. It is in the ways of holy exercise that " the God of peace " is with them. These are the " galleries " in which the King is held. Truly here " our fellowship is with the Father and with His Son Jesus Christ." (*D. Charles.*)       *Zeal in works and worship :*—1. Zeal is an intense earnestness for the accomplishment of an object—not a great excitement of feeling, not mere demonstrative warmth of expression, but something far more deep and enduring. It is a working, practical energy; it is a power which may be directed to things indifferent, things good, or things bad ; and accordingly the word is sometimes used in the New Testament in a good sense, and sometimes in a bad one. Thus in a good sense, " Your zeal hath provoked very many "; " I am jealous over you with a godly jealousy." And in a bad sense where the apostle enumerates among the works of the flesh "envyings and emulations." What zeal is we know by experience. For instance, what zeal is shown by men of science when they explore the remotest bounds of the earth, from torrid zones to the everlasting snows of the far North, or when they leave their bones to whiten in Australian wildernesses, to settle a question of geography. What zeal is shown by them in a nobler cause when they sacrifice their own lives—in some cases consciously—in the study of disease and the result of the battle with death. So in things bad, what zeal is shown by infidels in the propagation of their opinions on all occasions and in every place. What in the sacrifices of violent revolutionists, &c. When I turn from such illustrations I blush for the apathetic condition of our Church. 2. Now, such a zeal can only spring out of a great motive, just as the rush of the limpid stream at the mountain side shows the abundance of the water that feeds it. Zeal is force ; it is the great working force of our world ; and force can only arise from an adequate motive, just as the great river is not fed by the scanty summer shower, but gathers its strength from rains that fall upon a thousand hills. Now, the motives furnished in this passage are common to all Christian men, just as the grace they must produce must be common to Christian men likewise. The ultimate spring is love—love, purest, holiest, sweetest, most abiding of all motives—the very essence of true religion, the Alpha and the Omega of its strength, the one thing which of all earthly things approaches most to Omnipotence, because it is the reflection of God and His peculiar prerogative. It is love for Christ awakened by His love for us—the deep echo of a converted human soul to the suffering cries and agonising tears of a dying Saviour ; love quickened by the grateful experience of the peace which fills the heart when leaning its weary guilt upon the Sin Bearer, and which feels itself redeemed from all iniquity ; love deepened by profound obligation as it remembers that the very purpose of that love was to purify us unto Himself ; love strengthened by adoring admiration, which has called us to be His peculiar people and filled our breasts with a world of wealth, of which the unconverted man has no knowledge. 3. There is one thing more by which a habitual zeal must necessarily be characterised. If it be the common grace of all Christians ; if it springs from motives which are abiding as the life of a redeemed soul ; if it is taught by the power of the Almighty Spirit of God then it must be a steady, permanent force—not transient, not occasional, not flickering up into a vehement flame now and then and dying away again, but like the sun in the midst of the heavens, or like the laws of nature which hold sun and moon and stars revolving ever in their courses round their central orb. (*E. Garbett, M.A.*)     *Good works :—* I. WHAT ARE GOOD WORKS? 1. No work can be good unless it is commanded of God.   2. Nothing is a good work unless it is done with a good motive ; and there is no motive which can be said to be good but the glory of God.   3. Furthermore, when we have faith in God and perform all our works with the best of motives, even then we have not so much as a solitary good work come from until the blood of Christ is sprinkled thereon.   II. WHERE DO GOOD WORKS COME FROM? 1. From a real conversion brought about by the Spirit of God.   2. From union with Christ.   III. WHAT is THE USE OF GOOD WORKS? 1. They are useful as evidences of grace.   The Antinomian says—But I do not require evidences ; I can live without them.   This is unreasonable.   Do you see yonder clock?   That is the evidence of the time of day. The hour would be precisely the same if we had not that evidence.   Still we find the clock of great use.   So we say good works are the best evidence of spiritual life in the soul.   Is it not written, " We know that we have passed from death unto life, because we love the brethren "?   Loving the brethren is a good work.   Again, " If any man abide in Me, he shall bring forth fruit."   Fruits of righteousness are good works, and they are evidences that we abide in Christ.   If I am living in sin day by day what right have I to conclude I am a child of God?   2. They are the witnesses or testimony to other people of the truth of what we believe.   A sermon is not what a man says, but what he does.   You who practise are preaching ; it is not preaching and practising, but practising is preaching.   The sermon that is preached by the mouth is soon forgotten, but what we preach by our lives is never forgotten. 3. They are of use to a Christian as an ornament.   The adornment of good works, the adornment in which we hope to enter heaven, is the blood and righteousness of Jesus Christ ; but the adornment of a Christian here below is his holiness, his piety, his consistency.   If some people had a little more piety, they would not require such a showy dress ; if they had a little more godliness, to set them off, they would have no need whatever to be always decorating themselves.   The best earrings that a woman can wear are the earrings of hearing the Word with attention. The very best ring that we can have upon our finger is the ring which the father puts upon the finger of the prodigal son when he is brought back ; and the very best dress we can ever wear is a garment wrought by the Holy Spirit—the garment of a consistent conduct. (*C. H. Spurgeon.*)     *An acquaintance with Christ the foundation of experimental and practical religion :—*I. IT LAYS THE FOUNDATION OF CHRISTIANITY IN A PROPER ACQUAINTANCE WITH AND FAITH IN THE KINDNESS AND BOUNTY OF OUR GREAT REDEEMER.   II. THE EXPERIMENTAL RELIGION TO BE BUILT ON THIS FOUNDATION. III. THIS DOCTRINE INCULCATES THE IMPORTANCE OF CHRISTIAN PRACTICE. (*J. Benson.*) *Zeal in good works :—*I. Note that before the apostle speaks of good works we hear of redemption, and purging, and washing, and of a peculiar people that must do them, for, indeed, the best works are so far from justifying and purging that none can be good before the party be justified and purged.   II. Note that whosoever are justified and sanctified they must needs bring forth good works, for else Christ should be frustrate of His end in those for whom He gave Himself. (Eph. ii. 10). III. Note that the thing that God requireth in a professor is zeal, forwardness, and earnestness in well-doing, and that his whole course should be a studious prosecuting of good works.   The effects of zeal for good are, 1. It preserveth in the heart a fitness and preparedness to every good work required of every believer (2 Tim. iii. 17).   2. It exciteth to diligence and haste in the things we do ; it abandoneth idleness, slothfulness, and delays, by which occasions of well-doing are often cut off : the zeal of David made him prepare diligently for the temple ; zeal in the magistrate causeth in him diligence throughout his government; zeal in the minister maketh him like Apollo, of whom we read that being fervent in spirit he taught diligently the way of God ; zeal and fervency in private men causeth them to shake off slothfulness in their duties, and removeth in all conditions the curse which is denounced against the man that doeth the work of the Lord negligently : most fitly, therefore, doth the apostle combine those precepts : " Not slothful to do service, fervent in the spirit, serving the Lord " (Rom. xii. 11).   3. Zeal causeth continuance in well-doing, which is also required in every good action as well as in prayer ; it contenteth not itself with one or two good actions, but is plentiful in them, and bringeth the party professing it to be rich in good works and to shine lightsomely therein ; yea, it maketh a man hold out, and keep a constant tenor in good courses, and that as well in adversity as prosperity, so as he is neither choked by preferments, as very many, nor discouraged by distresses, as not a few.   4.

Zeal setteth such a high price unto the glory of God and performance of conscionable duties, that it causeth the party to attempt and go through, though with never so much difficulty, whatsoever he seemeth himself bound unto; it hardeneth the face like brass against dangers and losses, the loss of the world in his judgment gain, yea, all things are loss and dung so as he may win Christ; this alone yieldeth joy in the spoiling of goods, by this can a man hate father and mother in comparison of his obedience, and be contented to be hated of all men for well-doing, in which case the loss of friends is but light. This zeal for God maketh a man's liberty small in his eye; nay, in standing out in a good cause his life will not be so dear unto him as the finishing of his course with joy; yea, he can rejoice to be offered up upon the sacrifice and service of the Church's faith, as Paul. And which is yet much more, the zeal of God's glory will so burn in the heart as it can carry a man so far beyond himself as that he shall neglect his own salvation and wish to be accursed, yea, and blotted out of the book of life, if God may be more honoured by the one than by the other. (*T. Taylor, D.D.*) *The necessity of positive duty or actual goodness:*—I. Positive duty, or the actual exercise of goodness, is indispensably required at our hands. 1. This will appear in a general way, if we do but turn a thought to the state and order of created beings and the designs of their Creator. For though no virtue or vice can be ascribed to those beings which have no understanding, yet remiss and negligent man may form a just and useful reproof to himself upon this observation, that whilst he, who is the glory of visible creatures, fails of exercising his powers and abilities, and of answering the ends of his creations, all the other parts, even of the natural world, do exert themselves to their utmost capacity in promoting and fulfilling the great ends and purposes of nature. 2. This will further appear from that more particular consideration of this point, which is now to be added to the general one already offered. Where I shall represent an obligation to good works, or, to the actual exercise of goodness, as such good works may be considered—(1) In respect of God, as we are created and redeemed by Him, and subject to Him, and therefore, obliged to contribute our utmost to His honour. (See 1 Cor. vi. 20; Matt. v. 16; John xv. 8.) (2) In respect of our neighbour. It is not our keeping to the letter of the Sixth Commandment that fills up the measure of duty to our neighbour in regard to his life; for, as we must not destroy it, we stand further obliged to protect it and to crown it with comforts, by proper acts of our own, to the utmost of our power. (3) Necessary to prove our fidelity in the service of God. (4) An engaging recommendation and endearment of religion to others. (5) Necessary to that perfection which the gospel requires. II. Zeal is the necessary qualification of positive duty, or acts of goodness. When good works are done with a negligence and unconcern, as if it were perfectly indifferent to the man, whether they be undertaken or let alone, whether they succeed or miscarry, they then sit upon him with a very ill grace, and he may easily expect that what is performed with so much coldness will meet with a cold reception. It is the life and spirit, the sprightliness and fervour of religious enterprises, that must recommend them to God, the discerner of spirits. (*W. Lupton, D.D.*)

Ver. 15. **These things speak, and exhort, and rebuke.**—*The duties of the episcopal function:*—In all this Epistle it is evident that St. Paul looks upon Titus as advanced to the dignity of a prime ruler of the Church, and intrusted with a large diocese. I. The duties of his place. In a word, it is every bishop's duty to teach and to govern; and his way to do it is, "not to be despised." 1. The first branch of the great work incumbent upon a church ruler is to teach. It is a work of charity, and charity is the work of heaven, which is always laying itself out upon the needy and the impotent: nay, and it is a work of the highest and the noblest charity; for he that teacheth another gives an alms to his soul: he clothes the nakedness of his understanding, and relieves the wants of his impoverished reason. Now this teaching may be effected two ways: (1) Immediately by himself. Change of condition changes not the abilities of nature, but makes them more illustrious in their exercise; and the episcopal dignity, added to a good preaching faculty, is like the erecting of a stately fountain upon a spring, which still, for all that, remains as much a spring as it was before, and flows as plentifully, only it flows with the circumstance of greater state and magnificence. But then, on the other hand, let me add also, that this is not so absolutely necessary as to be of the vital constitution of this function. He may teach his diocese, who ceases to be able to preach to it; for he may do it by appointing teachers, and by a vigilant exacting from them the care and the instruction of their respective flocks. He is the spiritual father of his diocese; and a father may see his children taught, though he himself does not turn schoolmaster. (2) Mediately, by the subordinate ministration of others; in which, since the action of the instrumental agent is, upon all grounds of reason, to be ascribed to the principal, he who ordains and furnishes all his churches with able preachers is a universal teacher; he instructs where he cannot be present; he speaks in every mouth of his diocese, and every congregation of it every Sunday feels his influence, though it hears not his voice. That master deprives not his family of their food who orders a faithful steward to dispense it. 2. The second branch of his work is to rule. "Rebuke with all authority." (1) It implies exaction of duty from the persons placed under it: for it is both to be confessed and lamented that men are not so ready to offer it where it is not exacted. (2) Government imports a protection and encouragement of the persons under it, in the discharge of their duty. (3) Coercion and animadversion upon such as neglect their duty; without which all government is but toothless and precarious, and does not so much command as beg obedience. II. THE MEANS ASSIGNED for the discharge of the duties mentioned. "Let no man despise thee." 1. We will discourse of contempt, and the malign hostile influence it has upon government. As for the thing itself, every man's experience will inform him that there is no action in the behaviour of one man towards another, of which human nature is more impatient than of contempt, it being a thing made up of those two ingredients, an undervaluing of a man upon a belief of his utter uselessness and inability, and a spiteful endeavour to engage the rest of the world in the same belief and slight esteem of him. He that thinks a man to the ground will quickly endeavour to lay him there; for while he despises him, he arraigns and condemns him in his heart; and the after bitterness and cruelties of his practices are but the executioners of the sentence passed before upon him by his judgment. Contempt, like the planet Saturn, has first an ill aspect, and then a destroying influence. By all which, I suppose, it is sufficiently proved how noxious it must needs be to every governor; for, can a man respect the person whom he despises? And can there be obedience where there is not so much as respect? 2. Those just causes, that would render them, or indeed any other rulers, worthy to be despised. (1) Ignorance. A blind man sitting in the chimney corner is pardonable enough, but sitting at the helm he is intolerable. If men will be ignorant and illiterate, let them be so in private, and to themselves, and not set their defects in a high place, to make them visible and conspicuous. If owls will not be hooted at, let them keep close within the tree, and not perch upon the upper boughs. (2) Viciousness and ill morals. Virtue is that which must tip the preacher's tongue and the ruler's sceptre with authority: and therefore with what a controlling overpowering force did our Saviour tax the sins of the Jews, when He ushered in His rebukes of them with that high assertion of Himself, "Who is there amongst you that convinces Me of sin?" (3) Fearfulness of, and mean compliances with, bold, popular offenders. (4) A proneness to despise others. (*R. South, D.D.*) *Hints to ministers:* —The Christian teacher should always act with mildness, yet with firmness. There are gradations to be observed. 1. Instruction: "these things speak." 2. Expostulation: "exhort." 3. Reproof: "Rebuke with authority." (*F. Wagstaff.*) *Teaching out of the Scriptures:*—These things, saith our apostle: for this purpose hath the Lord in great wisdom furnished the Scriptures to make the man of God able both to teach, instruct, and improve, so as he need go no further to seek for profitable things. Which teacheth such as will stand in God's counsel, to fetch from hence all their doctrines, all their proofs, all their exhortations, and all their reproofs; for so shall they be just, so shall they be powerful to work a work of edification, and so shall they be unresistible in the consciences of men. These things if men would tie themselves unto, they should increase men with the increasings of God in spiritual wisdom, watchfulness, and the fear of God. Then should we not meet with so many pretors for sin and liberty to the flesh, straining their wits to legitimate bastardly broods of opinions, which the Scriptures never acknowledged here. Nor so many who in their reproofs glad the hearts of the impenitent, and make heavy the hearts of those to whom the Lord hath spoken peace; who strike at the best things and men; and so as soon as ever they have delivered a truth in these, lest they should leave it while it is true, misapply it in the hypothesis; girding at godliness as too much scrupulosity and preciseness; accounting conscience a hypocrite, and the fear of God dissembling before men. Hence are discovered as sinful all reproofs of sin by jesting, interluding, and stage representations, in which fools make a mock of sin, and open a public school of all lewdness and iniquity; and if any devil or sin be cast out there, it is by Belzebub, the prince of the devils. Further, all reproofs by satirising, and by slanderous libels, and secret calumniations (all which commonly wreck themselves rather upon the persons than sins of men) are here reproved; which, although they be indeed sharp and biting means, yet hath the Lord appointed fitter and sharper arrows to smite His enemies withal, even sound and sufficient convictions out of the Word, which is able to wound and daunt kings themselves; and prescribed them also to be publicly drawn, and shot in such grave, reverent, and seemly sort, as is befitting. 1. Both the person and calling of the reprover. 2. The things themselves, which are weighty and serious: as also 3. The presence of God and His congregation, whose matters are debated, and whose sentence against sin is in denouncing and executing. Small wisdom, therefore, it is, for men in these cases of the salvation and damnation of men to suffer their wits to play upon sin so lightly and jestingly as becometh rather some vain spectacle, or professed jester; then either the errand of the Lord, or a messenger from the Lord of hosts. (*T. Taylor, D.D.*)     *A summary of the "things" Titus was to "speak" :*—1. The central idea of the passage appears to be a life of sobriety, righteousness, and godliness, issuing in and sustaining the practical advice previously offered to old men and maidens, to matrons, aged and young, to youths, and slaves of all degrees. 2. The subjective condition of this heavenly life on earth is explicitly stated—a denial of all godliness and worldly passions. 3. This "life" and its "conditions" are originated and promoted by a process of Divine discipline. Here are processes, mental and disciplinary, which augment and stimulate this life of godliness. 4. This entire subjective process rests upon two groups of sublime objective realities: (1) The historic epiphany of the grace of God in the Incarnation; (2) the anticipated and prophetic epiphany of the glory of our great God and Saviour Jesus Christ. Thus it calls for the exercise of the twofold energy of "faith" and "hope." 5. The "grace" and the "glory of God," received and appropriated in Christian faith and hope, attain their highest expression in the redemptive self-sacrifice of the God-man. 6. By way of closing the circle of the thought, it is expressly stated that the end of the redemptive work is the creation of "a holy people," who are not only His "peculiar treasure" and inheritance, but who have, as the law and charter of their incorporation, this grand distinction, that they are charged with the genius of goodness—the passion for godliness. They are the very "zealots of goodness," passionately eager for all that will help and move them to realise the ideal of the Divine life. (*H. R. Reynolds, D.D.*)     *Care in presentment of Divine truth :*—Philopoemen, a Grecian general, was so enamoured of military tactics, that when he travelled he used to be pointing out to his friend the difficulties of steep or broken ground, and how the ranks of an army must be extended or closed, according to the difference made by rivers, ditches, and defiles. By such observations, and acting upon them in real warfare, he became one of the most skilful and successful generals in his time. Were Christian ministers to attend with as much care to the arrangement of Divine truth in their public instructions; were they to consider with as much attention what plans, all things considered, are most proper to be adopted in order to extend their usefulness, it might be expected their lives would be more useful than they often are. **Let no man despise thee.**—*The causes of disrespect in the character of a clergyman :*—The esteem of mankind, especially that of the wise and good, who are competent judges of moral excellence, is certainly a valuable blessing. It confirms the testimony of conscience, gives a lively satisfaction to the mind, procures the respect and services of mankind, extends the sphere of our own utility, and increases the opportunities of doing good. If a respectable character, in the opinion of the best judges, was thought so necessary to an orator to conciliate the favour of his audience, and give weight to his speech, must it not, for the same reasons, be infinitely more requisite in a preacher of the everlasting gospel of Jesus Christ? Esteem is the natural ground of confidence and respect; and in proportion as we sink in the opinion of mankind, they will suspect our integrity, contemn our authority, and disregard our instructions. In pointing out the causes of disrespect in the character of a clergyman, I do not allude to those grosser vices which are an outrage against religion, and would expel men from the sacred office. I would point to those inconsistencies of conduct, or defects of accomplishment, which fall not under the lash of discipline, but tarnish the reputation, and lessen the utility of a minister of the gospel. 1. In the character of a minister of the gospel, ignorance is both a derogatory and a hurtful quality.  2. Another, and a still juster, cause of contempt is negligence in discharging the duties of his office.  Ignorance, although always a humiliating circumstance, may sometimes proceed from defect of understanding; and whenever it arises from that cause, however deserving it may be of pity, it is neither the ground of censure, nor the proper object of contempt.  But wilful negligence, as it proceeds entirely from ourselves, and always implies a defect of principle, justly lays us open to reproach, and must bring us down in the estimation of mankind.  3. Another ground of disrespect is bigotry and imprudence.  As by neglecting the duties of our office we may suffer piety to decline and immorality to increase, so by an ignorant and furious zeal we may sow the seeds of superstition and folly, or promote a spirit of rancour, to the great prejudice of holiness and virtue.  From the same rash and precipitate temper, by reproving vice at an unseasonable time, or in an imprudent manner, we may exasperate rather than reclaim offenders; or, by an unnecessary severity of discipline, we may drive men on to obstinacy, and confirm them in impenitence and opposition.  4. Another cause of contempt in a minister is servility.  From false modesty, or from interested policy, from a desire of vain glory or a fear of reproach, we may be tempted to descend beneath the dignity of our character, and to be drawn into servile compliances.  From an undue attachment on the one hand, or from a secret resentment on the other, we may be led into unbecoming partialities of conduct, treating the same offence with lenity in some, and with severity in others.  From a vain desire to ingratiate ourselves with the great, or a servile dread of incurring their displeasure, we may comply with their follies, assent to their opinions, enter into their licentious conversations, and even connive at their vices.  Such abject servility must be universally detested.  Even those to whom we hope to recommend ourselves by our unworthy complaisance, though they may behave with civility to us, will despise us in their hearts as unworthy of our sacred office, and a disgrace to our profession.  For however men may practise vice themselves, or be pleased with it in others, yet they universally detest it in a teacher of religion on account of its gross inconsistency.  (*A. Donnan.*)  *Despising the preacher :*—1. Men will despise a preacher when his life and his doctrine do not agree.  2. When he delivers his message with half-heartedness, as one who does not really believe it himself.  3. When it is evident he has bestowed no pains or labour on preparation for his work.  4. When by his manner he makes it plain that he desires to give prominence to himself, and excite admiration.  5. When he is evidently influenced by other motives than God's glory and man's good.  (*F. Wagstaff.*)  *Lessons :*—1. Let no man despising thee prevent the full discharge of certain duty.  " He that despiseth you, despiseth Me, and he that despiseth Me, despiseth Him that sent Me."  2. If men will despise God and Christ, the human messenger may well consent to be despised along with them.  Let them despise thee, but let not the effect be caused by cowardly suppression, or disingenuous corruption of the truth on your part.  As a faithful messenger of God and an ambassador of Christ, let men despise you if they will, or if they must—let them despise you at their peril.  But as a traitor to the truth and to its Author, let no man despise thee.  (*J. A. Alexander, D.D.*)  *Ministers to be preserved from contempt :*—1. First, how people and hearers should entertain the ministers sent them of God, seeing they cannot without great sin despise them; for seeing the Lord, who could by Himself work the salvation of men, yet is pleased to use as His helpers herein weak and base men, whom He assumeth into fellowship with Himself, to become co-workers with Him, although not in the act of conversion, yet in the ministry of it.  Who dare despise such whom the Lord so far honoureth?  And therefore calleth them His white horses—horses, in that He useth them in His battles against sin, the world, and wicked ones; and white, for the purity of their doctrine and integrity of their lives.  Yea, His angels, namely, such as by whom He revealeth His good pleasure unto us; and His own voice, by whom He beseecheth men to be reconciled.  2. Secondly, how careful is the Lord to preserve His ministers from contempt, when He affirmeth that such as despise them, despise Himself that sent them.  In which sense we read that the posterity of Cain, contemning the preaching of Noah, despised and contended against God's spirit; so Israel, murmuring against Moses and Aaron, Moses saith, " He hath heard your murmurings against the Lord, for what are we that ye have murmured against us? "  3. Thirdly, how unnatural a part were it for children to despise their fathers : and what severity hath the Lord showed against it in His law.  But godly ministers are the fathers of their people.  "I am your father," saith Paul; and Onesimus, yea, and Titus here begotten by him unto the faith, he calleth his sons. Let no cursed Cham presume to scorn them, which is not so hurtful to them as dangerous to themselves, being the next way to bring themselves under the curse. On the contrary, let the natural children of the Church—1. "Know them" (1 Thess. v. 12), that is, both in heart acknowledge them the ministers of Christ, and in affection, love them as His ministers, accounting their feet beautiful, 2. Render then double honour (1 Tim. v. 17), in which precept the Holy Ghost hath made—(1) reverence, (2) obedience, (3) thankfulness, (4) comfortable maintenance, their due from their people. Ministers are hence taught so to order their lives and doctrine, as they lay not their persons open to reproach, nor prostitute their authorities unto contempt, and so lose it both from themselves and others. For this is the way for ministers to win authority and reverence in the hearts of men by their lives and doctrine, to become examples unto the flock. And thus shining in the purity of doctrine and conversation, they show themselves stars in the right hand of Christ. (*T. Taylor, D.D.*) *A sermon to ministers of the gospel :*—It is impossible for any man to keep himself from being hated. Hatred may exist without cause. There is another strange trait in human nature. Whenever injury has been done it is usually the injurer who hates. In general the ignorant hate the wise and the intelligent. This superior knowledge in others is like the sun's light to bats and owls and moles, painfully blinding—and they hate at once the knowledge and the man who knows. In general the bad hate the good, because goodness is always a most impressive and powerful rebuke of badness, even when good men are silent. But a man can keep himself from being despised. The rule is that only the despicable are despised. The exception is when a man, not in himself despicable, is despised by some one who does not know him. In that case it is not the real individual who is despised, but some ideal person. It is a greater misfortune to be despised than to be hated. A man may hate you now who, when his own character is changed, may come to love you with a passion strong and ardent as his former hatred. But if one despise you, even when he comes to know you better he will find it difficult to discriminate between you and the idea he has had of you. "Let no man despise thee." The plain meaning is—live in the ministry so that no man can despise you, however much he may hate and oppose your person and your ministry. A minister of the gospel makes himself despicable whenever he does anything which is proof that he himself does not believe the message he proclaims to others. No lie is noble. I. In the first place IT MAY APPEAR IN A MINISTER'S ASSUMING WHAT DOES NOT OF RIGHT BELONG TO HIM. To hold a position for which one is evidently not capacitated by nature or grace or education, is to make one appear badly in the eyes of one's fellows. A man who undertakes small things and does them well, appears much better than a larger and stronger man who undertakes what he is obviously not able to accomplish, and what he should have done was beyond his depth. A minister of the gospel ought to know just what it is his position demands of him, and assume nothing beyond. He is a servant of the souls of men, to wait on those souls, bringing all spiritual help from the gospel to those souls. He is no more. II. Another cause of contempt for some ministers may be found IN THEIR CLAIMING CERTAIN IMMUNITIES WHICH DO NOT IN RIGHT REASON BELONG TO THEM SO FAR AS OTHER MEN CAN SEE. Age, position, attainments, usefulness, are claims to respect, but the minister should share them with men of other professions. He should expect to be honoured simply in proportion to his abilities and his usefulness. A man who really is not respectable in his character cannot be rendered honourable by any office or position. III. Again: a minister may render himself despicable BY RELYING UPON WORLDLY MEANS ALONE IN ORDER TO SECURE SPIRITUAL ENDS. When men detect that in a minister, it seems at once to convince them that the man never had a true faith in the existence of a spiritual world, and in the existence and offices of that Holy Ghost of whom the Bible speaks and of whom he must sometimes preach. When a minister makes his Church a mere secular establishment, which shall gratify and even in some sense educate the people in architecture, ecclesiastical decoration, classic music, oratory, liberal views, and polite manners—when he shall work as if the aim were simply to crowd the house with a large select audience, who should generate the necessary animal and mental magnetism to make all things pleasant, and whose pew-rents should produce a large financial exhibit—when he shall have even succeeded in all that, as a lyceum manager he is splendid, but as a minister of Jesus he is despicable. The obverse fault is the use of one's position as a spiritual teacher to gain worldly ends, whether personal or partisan. A fair use of secular instrumentalities for the accumulation of money or fame perhaps no reasonable mind would censure. But when a man who professes to have devoted himself to the spiritual improvement of mankind clearly employs his place to enrich himself, he is despicable. IV. Again : a minister may make himself disreputable BY NEGLECT-ING TO PREPARE HIMSELF FOR THE PROPER DISCHARGE OF THE FUNCTIONS OF HIS OFFICE. He has to deal with the most complex and profound questions of life and destiny ; and he has to conduct these discussions not so as to merely entertain or even satisfy the intellects of his hearers. He is an utter failure if he do not make all those discussions profitable to their souls. A lawyer is a failure if he never carries a case, however much he may entertain the court and the jury. The world makes rapid progress in all science. No chemist expects a minister to be up in chemistry as he is ; no political economist expects him to be "posted" on all the minutiæ which go to solve the great problems of civil and social advancement. But they do expect him to know something beyond a few dry theological propositions and a few dry jokes. They do expect him to be a worker. They work. V. Again : there is much to be learned from what Paul teaches Timothy in connection with the precept, "Let no man despise thy youth," when he adds, "BE THOU AN EXAMPLE OF THE BELIEVERS, IN WORD, IN CONVERSATION, IN CHARITY, IN SPIRIT, IN FAITH, IN PURITY." What will save a minister from loss of respect in his youth will keep him in honour through all his ministry. 1. If other men spoil their reputation by loose tongues and careless and corrupt speech, how very careful of his speech must be a minister of the gospel, who is supposed to be always holding close to his own heart and conscience and to his fellow-men the realities of a world which fleshly eyes do not behold. Nor do sensible men like canting parsons. Words are things. To him who uses them they may be empty things, and he is despicable who employs the divine gift of speech to scatter empti-ness over the world. 2. Then the apostle holds that a minister's intercourse with society may make him despicable. A grasping, stingy, mean minister is con-temptible. And so is a minister who allows others to cheat him just because he is "a parson." He ought to know his rights and dare maintain them. He who is not aiming to be a gentleman is not fit to be a minister. 3. The apostle instances charity also. He who preaches the gospel of love cannot be respected if men per-ceive that he is not animated by a real and deep love for God, and an earnest brotherly affection for all the race for which Christ died. And this temper must pervade his intercourse with society. 4. The apostle next instances spiritual-mindedness ; which does not mean a neglect of the things which are seen and a contempt for them, a voluntary humiliation and castigation of one's self. 5. The apostle enjoins fidelity, entire faithfulness to every trust, faithfulness toward God and man, faithfulness in allowing no evil to spread in the Church because it is the besetment of his special friends. He must deal honestly in the preaching of the Word and in the administration of the discipline of his Church. He must not be drawn from the discharge of any duty by fear, favour, affection, reward, or the hope of reward. 6. The last thing mentioned by the apostle is purity ; and no one can confine this to mere chastity, a perfectly apparent indispensable to the ministerial position ; it must cover his whole life. (*C. F. Deems, D.D.*)

---

## CHAPTER III.

VERS. 1, 2. **Put them in mind to be subject.**—*Obedience to civil magistrates :*—I. WHO ARE TO BE UNDERSTOOD BY CIVIL RULERS. All those who are in the peaceable possession of civil power. II. IT IS THE DUTY OF SUBJECTS TO OBEY THEIR CIVIL RULERS. 1. The Scripture expressly enjoins this duty upon subjects. 2. The duty of submission naturally results from the relation which subjects bear to their rulers. There would be no propriety in calling the body of the people subjects, unless they were under obligation to obey those in the administration of government. 3. All subjects ought to obey their rulers for the sake of the public good. III. MINISTERS OUGHT TO INCULCATE SUCH SUBMISSION TO CIVIL MAGISTRATES. 1. Preachers are expressly required to press this plain and important duty upon the people of their charge. 2. It becomes the preachers of the gospel, in this case, to follow the example of the inspired teachers—John the Baptist, Christ, &c. 3. It no less belongs to the office of gospel ministers to teach men their duty towards civil rulers than to teach them any other moral or religious duty. 4. There are some peculiar reasons why the duty of submission to civil authority should be more especially inculcated upon the minds of subjects. (1) Men are extremely apt to forget that they are under any moral obligation to obey the rulers of the land. (2) There is scarcely any duty more disagreeable to the human heart than submission to civil government. (3) The safety and happiness of the whole body politic more essentially depend upon each member's performing this, than any other duty. Where there is no subordination, there can be no government; and where there is no government, there can be no public peace nor safety. Concluding reflections: 1. There is no ground to complain of the ministers of the gospel for inculcating political duties. 2. There appears to be no more difficulty in determining the measure of submission to civil government than the measure of submission to any other human authority. 3. It is extremely criminal to disobey civil rulers, and oppose the regular administration of government. 4. It is criminal not only to disobey and resist civil authority, but also to countenance, cherish, and inflame a spirit of disobedience and rebellion. 5. Those in executive authority are under indispensable obligation to give rebels and traitors a just recompense of reward. They are God's ministers to execute wrath upon them that do evil; and they ought not to hold the sword of justice in vain. (*N. Emmons, D.D.*)   *The Christian's loyalty to secular government:*—I. Its NATURE. 1. Subjection to the general government. 2. Obedience to the local authorities. 3. Readiness to help the government in times of emergency. 4. Carefulness in respect to the reputation of their fellow-citizens. 5. Peaceful and order-loving. II. Its REASONS. 1. The spiritual change wrought upon believers. 2. Some blessed features of the source of this change. (1) Its graciousness. (2) Its method. (3) Its abundance. (4) Its justifying power. (5) Its benefits and tendency. Lessons: 1. The superiority of Christianity. (1) The best thing for the State. (2) The best thing for individuals. (3) The best thing for the family. 2. The unmistakable evidences of the Divine origin of Christianity. (1) In its love of man. (2) In its legitimate effects on man and on society. (*D. C. Hughes, M.A.*)   *The subject's duty:*—I. THE MANNER OF PROPOUNDING THE COUNSEL. Titus is here enjoined two things: 1. To call back into their minds an old doctrine—not what they had newly learned since their becoming Christians, but what nature and reason had taught them long before. 2. To inculcate, or beat often upon this point. (1) Because men generally are ambitious of liberty, unwilling, if lust or pride of heart be listened to, to be subject to any yoke, whether of God or man; ever ready to think one man as good as another, and with Korah to suggest that every Moses and Aaron takes too much upon him. (2) Because the dispersed Jews (of whom there was no small number at that time in Crete) stood very much upon temporal privileges; as upon Abraham, the temple, the law, &c. And ever loath they were to stoop to the authority of the Gentiles. (3) Because the Christians at that time, both of Jews and Gentiles, stood as much upon spiritual privileges, not thinking it sufficient to be set free from the thraldom of Satan, and bondage of sin, and so to be made spiritual kings unto God and the Lamb; unless by a boundless (Christian) liberty, as they supposed, they might be at their own hands to do as they listed. II. THE SUBSTANCE OF THE PRECEPT ITSELF. 1. The duties required. (1) By subjection is meant honour, reverence, and respect to the persons whom God has set in authority over us. (2) By obedience is meant a free voluntary readiness of mind to yield to, and to execute whatsoever lawful command of a superior. Where there is conscience of subjection, there will be cheerfulness in obedience. 2. The second considerable in the substance of the precept is—(1) The persons to whom these duties belong, namely, to all magistrates, which are here distributed into two ranks, principalities, powers. By the former we understand such who have primary and plenary power under God, and by this their proper power and authority have an absolute command within their several dominions; such are Cæsars, kings, and chief governors in free states. The latter signifieth such as exercise delegated authority, that is, hold from those higher powers; and such are all inferior officers, whether in Church or State, who have no authority to act in any public business, but what they receive from the supreme magistrate. 2. The persons from whom these dues are to be paid. This is soon decided. The persons solvent, are all Christians in general, without any exception, but of the supreme magistrate himself, clergy as well as laity—all who are under authority. The apostle includes all in the word αὐτούς, put them in mind, that is, all inferiors.

Every soul must be subject to the higher powers. Having thus far explained the subject matter of the apostle's command, I proceed to the observations arising out of it. 1. Christian religion destroys not government or civil authority but ratifieth and confirmeth it. 2. The kingdom of Christ is not of this world, His authority divideth not civil inheritances, His sceptre swalloweth not up (as did Aaron's rod the others) the sceptre of worldly monarchs. His weapons are not carnal; the keys of His kingdom are no temporal jurisdiction. 3. One ordinance of God doth not abolish another. The laws of Christ in His Church bring not in lawlessness into the Commonwealth; nor is God the God of order in the first, and the Author of confusion in the latter. For one ordinance of God to destroy another would argue want of wisdom in God, the Ordainer. The very thought thereof is blasphemous. Nay, on the contrary, for the Church's sake (which He loveth) He keepeth order, and maintains government in commonwealths, that His Church, whilst it is a-gathering in the world, might find safe harbour therein; that this dove of Christ might have a place where to set without danger the sole of her foot. (*John Cleaver, M.A.*) *Ministers remembrancers :*—1. The scope of the ministry is to put men in mind, and keep in them the remembrance of every Christian duty. Thus, ministers may be called the Lord's remembrancers, not only for putting the Lord in mind of His covenant towards His people, and of the people's wants, but also that they must not be silent, but restless in whetting the doctrine of God, legal and evangelical upon the people, and so be ever putting them in mind of their covenant and duty unto God. Paul acknowledged himself such a remembrancer (Rom. xv. 15). 2. None is so far instructed, but is wanting much in knowledge, and much more in the cheerful practice of that which he knoweth; and therefore every one hath need of quickening and stirring up. 3. None are so strong but they stand in need of this confirmation, as well as the former quickening, neither can any caution or any admonition be too much in things of such moment. 4. No man's memory is so sound, but as out of a leaking vessel good things are ever running out; and when such things are slipt away, they had need be renewed and recalled again. (1) Ministers must not desist from teaching and exhorting, as many that think a little enough; nor discouraged when people forget their wholesome doctrine; but encourage themselves in their duty, which is to keep in men's memories the mindfulness of their duties. (2) When they come to teach, they may not seek out vain and strange speculations, which were never heard of before, but teach plain things, yea, and deep mysteries in plain manner, as such who respect the weakness both of the apprehension and memory of their hearers. (3) An wholesome thing it is to teach the same things often, whereby things delivered are recalled into the memory. Curious men cannot abide repetitions, nor hear common things, notwithstanding these be excellent helps of memory, which is the cause of such gross and everywhere palpable ignorance in the most familiar principles of religion. But the wisdom of godly teachers will be not too much to yield unto the niceness of their hearers; nor to fear to do that which is the safest for them, as Paul speaketh; which if it be, let it be to us what it will or can, it will be our part that by our practice they may find the profit. We learn hence, also, what it is that should profess and take up the memories of Christians, namely, those lessons of Christianity which they hear in the ministry. For—1. The commandment must be bound up upon our hearts, and we ought to make our memories the statute book of our souls, and by diligent meditation, chain this book unto ourselves (Prov. iv. 21). 2. Herein standeth the sanctity of the memory, partly by retaining the rules of life, and partly in presenting and offering them unto the mind upon occasion of practice, both to direct and urge the conscience to obedience. Thus David hid the Word in his heart, the blessed fruit of which was that he did not sin against God; and indeed holy memory preserveth the holiness of the whole man. 3. Forgetfulness of the Word is everywhere in the Scriptures taxed as a grievous and hateful sin: "Be not forgetful hearers, deceiving your own selves," saith James; "Have you forgotten how I fed so many thousand," &c., saith Christ to the disciples; and the author to the Hebrews, "Have ye forgotten the exhortation?" (*T. Taylor, D.D.*) *Subjection to civil rulers :*—I. PUBLIC AUTHORITY PRESUPPOSED. II. SUBJECTION AND OBEDIENCE ENJOINED. Put them in mind to obey magistrates, to be ready to every good work—intimating to us that we must show our obedience by our ready compliance in good works; for if the magistrate command what is evil, there is no obligation to perform it, because nothing can oblige us to do evil. But what if the thing commanded be neither good nor evil, but of an indifferent nature; what must we do in that case? Why then we must undoubtedly obey it; for otherwise there will be nothing left wherein the magistrate may use his power. What is good or evil in itself must be done or avoided for God's sake. What is not so in itself, but only in regard of the end for which it is enacted, being judged so by the magistrate for the good of the community, this must be observed, both for God's sake and his too, because God requires our obedience to Him in these things, But what then becomes of our liberty, if another must judge for us? It is where it was before; we must obey, and yet we are as free as Christ hath made us; nay, I doubt not to add, we are most Christ's freemen when we duly obey our governors' just laws; for seeing Christ hath commanded us to be subject not only for wrath, but for conscience sake, that so we may avoid the guilt of sin, that obedience which keeps us from sin (which is the only vassalage of a Christian) can by no means infringe, but does rather advance our Christian liberty. III. THE DUTY OF PASTORS AND TEACHERS INCULCATED. Put them in mind, admonish them often of it, and bring it to their remembrance, as St. Peter does twice together in another case (2 Pet. i. 12, 13). 1. Let us consider that obedience to magistrates is a prime duty of piety and religion, wherein the honour and authority of God are particularly concerned; not only because He requires it by manifold precepts, but because magistrates are His officers and ministers, by whom He governs the world and administers His providence towards men, and to whom He has given part of His own power for that purpose. 2. The exigence of our civil affairs, and the preservation of the public does exact this duty from us. For the execution of justice between man and man, the safe and quiet enjoyment of God's blessings, and the welfare and peace of the whole community, are extremely concerned and advanced by it. 3. Obedience to our governors is founded on the highest equity and reason; for day by day we receive invaluable benefits by the influence of their government and conduct; protection of our lives and estates, of our privileges, properties, and religion; secure possession of the gifts of God, and liberty to increase our substance by trade and traffic, and to eat the fruit of our labour, &c. 4. Obedience to our governors is a duty incumbent on us in point of ingenuity and gratitude. For in preserving the peace and prosperity of the nation, they do not only preserve ours, but for our advantage also they undergo many cares and troubles, great toil and labour, attending continually for this very thing (Rom. xiii. 6). 5. No man can disobey his governors without breaking the most sacred laws of justice and honesty; without downright perjury towards God, and perfidiousness towards man. (*Henry Dove, D.D.*) *Duty:*—I. In relation to CIVIL GOVERNMENT. 1. Man's social tendencies indicate it. 2. Man's social exigencies indicate it. II. In relation to GENERAL SOCIETY. 1. Usefulness. 2. Charitableness. 3. Courteousness III. In relation to our MORAL SELF. It is a duty which every man owes to himself, to remember all the wrong of his past life—1. That he may be charitable towards others. 2. That he may be stimulated to efforts of self-improvement. 3. That he may adore the forbearance of God in His past dealings. 4. That he may devoutly appreciate the morally redemptive agency of Christ. 5. That he may realise the necessity of seeking the moral restoration of others. Lessons: 1. The possibility of the moral improvement of souls. 2. The obligation to the moral improvement of souls. (*D. Thomas, D.D.*) *The authority of law:*—I. LAW IS OF GOD. Therefore godly men are obedient to human laws, when not inconsistent with the dictates of conscience, as being ordinances of God. II. AUTHORITY IS DERIVED FROM GOD. Therefore righteous lawgivers and just judges are to be esteemed as God's gifts to a nation. III. OBEDIENCE TO LAW AN ESSENTIAL PREPARATION FOR GOOD WORKS. No amount of religious profession, and no degree of activity in the performance of Christian duties, can compensate for the neglect of social duties or disregard of the claims of citizenship. (*F. Wagstaff.*) *The Christian citizen:*—1. Individual excellence is what makes national strength. St. Paul tells Titus that he must preach personal purity, obedience, and peace to all the citizens around him. 2. Charity to others is best promoted by an honest consideration of what we are ourselves. No man, who is conscientious, can fail to remember many a mean act he has during his life committed. 3. The apostle tells Titus that he will make the better citizen the oftener he recalls to mind how much he owes, and must for ever owe, to sovereign grace, as a child of God and an heir of heaven. People nowadays are excessively diffident in attributing their successes or their virtues to their piety. Yet now and then the world will find it out for itself. "Havelock's men" in campaigns wrote their record by their prayers as well as by their prowess. 4. The apostle adds a lesson for Titus about his preaching, which every Christian, trying to instruct others, might lay well to heart; namely, that the best of all teaching in truth is the teaching of a true life. He tries to lead him away from mere formulas, and force him to deal with real things in a real way for greatest good. "After the first phase of Christian life," remarks Merle d'Aubigné, " in which a man thinks only of Christ, there usually ensues a second, when the Christian will not voluntarily worship with assemblies opposed to his personal convictions." That is a gentle way of saying that, after a new convert cools a little in piety, he takes a time of becoming denominational and belligerent. Perhaps the Apostle Paul imagined Titus was going to do that, and so told him he had better not. If there be any truth in the line, " The child is father of the man," it is manifest most plainly in religious life. The young believer perpetuates himself in the old. Maurice, son of William the Silent, at the age of seventeen, took for his device a fallen oak, with a young sapling springing from its root ; to this he gave the motto, *Tandem fit surculus arbor*, " The sapling will by and by become a tree." It seems very trite to write all that out soberly ; but really it is a thing most unfortunately forgotten. (*C. S. Robinson, D.D.*) *Civil duties :*—The rule of Rome, which then lay upon all those lands in which the gospel was being preached, was a rule which rested on the sword. Everywhere ancient nations had been subjugated, venerable thrones had been overturned, the freedom of commonwealths, jealous of their independence, had been ruthlessly suppressed ; and, although it was the policy of Rome to leave the old forms of administration untouched wherever possible, it was of course as impossible to conceal from the conquered peoples the degrading tokens of their subjection, as it is for us to do so in our Indian Empire. Roman troops sentinelled the palaces where Roman proconsuls sat in the seats of dèthroned kings ; Roman judges administered the law ; writs ran in the Roman tongue ; oaths were sworn to the Roman Cæsar ; taxes were paid in Roman coin. The military power which imposed such subjection upon haughty and once mighty nations was at the best a heavy yoke. The imperial laws were on the whole just, but they were stern and could be mercilessly enforced. Nor were the imperial courts above the imputation of corruption. The imposts were very heavy. Provincial governors were usually rapacious. The provincial revenues were drained off to feed the monstrous dissipation of the capital. For the most part, therefore, the provinces groaned beneath a burden which the strongest of them was unable to shake off, but which was enough to goad the most passive into turbulence. It was into a society thus honeycombed with political disaffection, and ready at every point to burst into revolt, that Christianity entered with its new conceptions of human dignity and spiritual freedom. Its entrance could not fail to add to the ferment. It quickened in men's minds that sense of injustice which oppression breeds. It deepened their irritation at the insolence and wrong-doing of the dominant race. It produced a longing for the happier era when the kingdom of God, which they had received into their hearts, should be also a kingdom of social equity and brotherhood. Hence it became an urgent duty with the leaders of the young society to warn their converts against political restlessness. Do as they might, the Christians could hardly hope, under a government like Nero's, to escape suspicion. They were pretty certain to be reckoned among the dangerous forces in a community which heaved with discontent. But to do anything to encourage such suspicion, or afford the authorities a pretext for repression, would have been foolish as well as wrong ; for it would have compromised the gospel at its outset by mixing it up in matters with which the gospel has nothing directly to do. Indirectly, no doubt, the new faith was sure to affect in the long run political affairs, as it affects every province of human life. No community of brave men who are animated by the lessons of Christianity will always sit still, contented in a condition of vassalage. The gospel has proved herself the mother of freedom. The most resolute and successful resistance that has ever been offered to arbitrary power has been offered by men whom the truth had made free, and who carried their Bible beneath the same belt to which they buckled their sword. But personal and political liberty is a secondary effect of the gospel, after it has penetrated the structure of society and has had time to reform nations on its own lines. For the individual convert in the age of Paul to revolt against the emperor or to run away from his master, would have been to misrepresent his faith to his contemporaries. The question at what time or in what way a Christian state is justified in deposing its tyrant, in order to organise itself as a free commonwealth, is a question which, as it concerns the Christian community and not the individual merely, so it can only arise under a different condition of things altogether. What the gospel enjoins upon private citizens, so long as governments stand and a successful resistance by the people at large is out of the question, is—submission. They are to discern underlying all authority, so long as it is legitimate, a Divine ordinance, and to render such obedience as is due to the magistrate within his proper sphere, not merely through dread of consequences, but still more for the sake of a good conscience towards God. (*J. O. Dykes, D.D.*) *Christians should be taught good citizenship :*—The schools should teach the children that their first duty and highest privilege is to become good citizens; and a good citizen, be he cobbler or manufacturer, tailor or senator, upholsterer or cabinet officer, will never condescend to become an incompetent or unworthy member of the community. Were all the boys and girls to leave school fully imbued with this knowledge, the country would be safe; the political firmament would be sustained upon shoulders firmer than those of Atlas, and its stars would shine with ever-increasing number and brilliancy. The third and highest form of spiritual power is moral and religious. Give me leave simply to state my belief that the only solid basis for an enduring nation is the Rock of Ages. Any other foundation is unstable and insecure as the sands of the seashore. Let the tower be built in obedience to God's laws, and it will reach unto heaven, the children of men will re-unite in permanent harmony, science and religion will coincide, and the one universal speech will be of God's Word written on the sun, moon, and stars, on the solid earth itself, and in the gospel. (*Professor B. Peirce.*) *Honouring authority :*—It was held in the olden time, but is not now, that authority came from God to the king, and then descended, in the form of law, from the king to the people. We have turned that theory bottom-side up, although there are texts of Scripture which run that way. Now we find no difficulty in this land, since we are republicans, in jumping those texts. "Honour the king," meant honour the king; but we say, "Yes, honour authority; and the king represents authority." So we bridge the difficulties without much trouble. When the people have committed their interests to the hands of individuals, they are justly jealous, because they have seen that human nature is fragile timber, like the slender supports of a bridge over which too much must not go, or it will break down under the pressure; properly, there is a wise watchfulness of those who are empowered to execute the law, and to represent, in the various spheres of magistracy, from the lowest to the highest, the will and interests of a great people; but the untaught and unbalanced way in which men exercise this proper watchfulness leads—somewhat in connection with the other things of which I have spoken—to what amounts to almost a universal suspicion. If there is one corrupt judge on the bench, ten judges suffer. If there is one bad senator, the whole senate suffers. If there are a score of purchaseable legislators, then the whole legislature suffers. There is no discrimination made in that matter. Our people have come to look upon those who are entrusted with power as being suspicious persons. The way men get that power rather tempts to this injustice. The rude and mischievous ways of partisans tend to inimical feeling in this same sphere. Men and brethren, do you ever reflect that he that hauls down a magistrate, except where there is absolute and assignable evidence of corruption; that he that deteriorates the authority of a judge; that he that takes from the responsibility and respectability of the representatives of the people, or of the members of the general government, or of governors; that he that makes an assault upon them which shall lower the respect and confidence of the community for them, is striking at the whole system of law and government? Worse than that, it is a blow aimed at the faith of whole classes of men in virtue, in patriotism, and in integrity. A class of men has grown up—and is growing up continually, with the spectacle before them, on every side, of rude and unjust criticisms and depreciations—who say that everybody is selfish, and that nobody but illusionists suppose that there is any such thing as a disinterested service of one's country. I am ashamed to see so many young men growing up with the feeling that heroism of patriotism is unknown except as a poetic adornment, or a mere spangle on the dress of pretentious patriots. (*H. W. Beecher.*) *The Christian citizen :*—The civic virtues planted and fostered by Christianity are a theme interesting and profitable for study. One of the credentials of its Divine origin is its usefulness for this world. Finding mankind individually and socially disordered, and full of painful suffering in consequence, it is an antiseptic, arresting deadly processes, a balm, full of gentle healing, and a tonic which strengthens every manly purpose, and enters integrally into all true life of the state. It first purifies and exalts, then it directs, though using only moral forces. I. CHRISTIANS MUST BE LOYAL SUBJECTS TO GOVERNMENT, READY FOR EVERY GOOD WORK. They must be often reminded of the obedience due to principalities, powers, and magistrates. The essential excellence and authority of human law can best be understood and appreciated by those who know the worth and heed the claims of the Divine. They know that the fabric of society is in some true sense a Divine institution. But, you say, government is corrupt, and God cannot be the author of political corruption. Very true, but the whole idea and framework of government is not corrupt. There is a sum of truth underlying the simple fact of government which is entitled to respect. Abuses should be keenly recognised, but remedies should be sought for them not by angry assault or disgusted contempt or sullen neglect. In healing the body politic, the laws of life must be respected, and employed as patiently and intelligently as when the physical body is to be healed. The practical side of Christianity in such teaching is specially timely and important to-day. Monetary values, domestic peace and security, time-honoured institutions, received ideas and principles, are assailed by influences and methods before which the wise, the good, and the strong well may stand somewhat in dread, if not in awe. What shall save the fairest portions of earth from such refluent waves of barbarism? The gospel is the only complete remedy. Bayonets and grape-shot may quell a temporary demonstration; but the only effectual cure is in that respect for government which Paul learned of Jesus Christ, and which Christian experience alone can fully understand. Then faithful reconstruction is possible by methods constructive, not destructive, in a spirit reverent to the essential dignity and claims of government. The Christian is not unmindful of the ills of the world, nor is he careless about their remedy. He is a man of affairs. He neither ignores nor scorns nor idly dreams about the ravages of sin wherever manifest. He deliberately and boldly grapples with them, but he uses methods which respect the laws of life and healing, laws written in the nature of things and the will of God. He knows meekness is compatible with manliness. The meek man thrusts no one aside, frowns not upon the humblest, but lives in abiding consciousness of the wants, powers, and claims of others. When this is the spirit of the world, there will be no more riots, forcible levies, assassinations; and it is only by cultivating this and kindred virtue, in the spirit of the gospel, that the world's peace will be secured. II. WHAT ARE THE MOTIVES AND CONSIDERATIONS UPON WHICH THE APOSTLE RESTS THESE URGENT INSTRUCTIONS? Not, as we might have expected, because such walk and conversation were useful and becoming, but he points (vers. 3–7) to the sad degradation of their own past lives, full of the opposites of all Christian virtues—foolishness, disobedience, lustful pleasures, malice, envy, and hatreds. From these they have just escaped; they must pity the moral ruin which stains and disables those yet blinded. He adduces a yet stronger consideration—their difference is all a pure gift, through " the kindness and love of God our Saviour." Out of such experience, all the more because it is exalted and refined, Paul admonishes to the most practical and assiduous performance of Christian duty under the general name of " good works." In these instructions to Titus, Paul was in full sympathy with the gospel in our Lord's time, in all time. Let us note the practical workings of Christianity for the individual and the state. 1. Christianity is the only source and safeguard of lasting patriotism. Patriotism is more than aroused sensibility, or quickened emotions, however worthy. There must be loyalty to principles, and those principles take root in the teachings of Him who valued humanity not by its degradation, but by its possibilities, who revealed the law of self-sacrifice, and who enforced all his precepts by a corresponding life of voluntary humiliation and unfailing service. 2. Organised and efficient philanthropy is unknown apart from Christianity. Man is not by nature wholly regardless of the sufferings and wants of his fellow men; but sinful practices soon blunt and disable humane promptings. 3. Christianity promotes harmony, and the best conditions of growth in society and the state. Intelligence is also an incident to the prevalence of the gospel; and before it, the dark vagaries of demagogues and fanatics appear in their repulsive deformity. Patience and forbearance with those who oppose themselves are essential conditions of prosperous life in all circles from the neighbourhood to the republic. These virtues are permanently active only when inspired by Christian benevolence. " Charity suffereth long and is kind." In short, Christian doctrines and institutions are the foundation of all public utilities and perpetuity. (*Monday Club Sermons.*)　　**Ready to every good work.**—*Christian duty:*—I. EVERY CHRISTIAN MUST MAKE ACCOUNT WITH HIMSELF THAT EVERY CHRISTIAN DUTY BELONGS TO HIM. 1. This doctrine first teacheth us to learn the rule of every good work, legal or evangelical. Content not thyself that thou canst say the commandments, nor if thou canst say that thou hast kept the whole letter of the law from thy youth; but study the whole Scripture, which is an exposition and large commentary of those ten words ; hear it, read it diligently, meditate upon it, apply it to thy heart and life, else knowest thou not how to begin any good work. 2. If every good work belong to every Christian then may not men post over the matter to the minister. The common conceit is, that the clergy should be holy, hospitable, and so qualified as we have heard in the first chapter ; but for common men and unlearned it will be acceptable enough if they be almost Christians, that is, as good as never a whit ; whereas the Lord bindeth upon every Christian, of what condition soever, the practice of every good work which is offered him within the compass of his calling. 3. If a Christian must employ himself in every good work, then must men so cast and contrive their courses, and neither duties of piety hinder the duties of their calling, nor these stand in the way of the other. And he that hath the heart of the wise to know time and judgment, forecasteth both wisely, and knoweth one of these to be subordinate, but not opposite unto the other. Hence must Christians forecast, and remember the Sabbath beforehand, and so order and husband their times and seasons, that there may be place and time and opportunity for every good work in the week-day, and especially for the best works, whether public exercises of religion or private prayers and exercises in the family. II. That every Christian ought to keep in himself a fitness and readiness to every good work is plain in the Scriptures. For—1. In duties of piety, we are enjoined not only to come to the house of God, but to take heed to our feet, and to wash our hands in innocency before we compass the altar, and first to sanctify ourselves before God and reconcile ourselves to men, and then bring our gift. If we preach, we must do it readily, and of a ready mind, and then we have reward. If you hear, you must be wise to hear, and ready to hear, rather than to offer a sacrifice of fools. 2. In performance of duties of love and mercy unto men, we are called to readiness in distributing (1 Tim. vi. 18), and mindfulness to distribute (Heb. xiii. 16). 3. In private duties, when God giveth us peace and opportunity, we must serve Him with cheerfulness and good hearts (Deut. xxviii. 47). 4. In private injuries, we must be ready to receive, yea, to offer reconciliation, and to forgive, which is another good work, and so in the rest. Reasons—1. We herein become like unto God, whose nature is to accommodate Himself to our good ; whose readiness to give bountifully and forgive freely is hereby shadowed. 2. Hereby we also beautify, and as it were gild our duties, when they come off without delays, without grudging, murmuring, or heaviness, but as from men inured to well-doing. 3. Hereby we may lay hold of Christian consolation, in that this ready and willing mind is accepted, where often power of doing good is wanting, and indeed the regenerate often want power and ability unto good, but to want will and desire is dangerous. III. Some rules of practice for the better setting us forward in this duty. 1. Get into thy soul the conscience of this commandment, accounting it worthy of all thine obedience, being so often urged in the Scriptures, and made in the end of the former chapter, the end of Christ's purchasing of us. This reason drawn from the fear of God prevailed so far with Job, that thence he was moved to use mercifulness to all sorts of men ; for God's " punishment was fearful unto me, and I could not escape His highness." 2. Take every opportunity of well-doing while it is offered, for else the opportunity may be cut off from thee, or thou from it. This is the apostle's rule, " While we have time do good unto all " (Gal. vi. 10), that is, take the present occasion of doing all the good thou canst. (1) In regard of thyself, perform the principal and main duty, know the day of thy visitation ; slack not this thy term-time, but get the oil of faith, knowledge of God, and obedience to His Word, that thy lamp may ever be shining to the glorifying of the Father which is in heaven ; in one word, forget not while thou hast time to give all diligence to make thine election sure. (2) In regard of others, if now thou canst do them good in soul or body, delay it not. " Say not unto thy neighbour, go, and come again to-morrow, and I will give thee, if now thou hast it " (Prov. iii. 28) ; and what knoweth any man, whether this may be the last day wherein he can do good to himself or others ? 3. Go yet one step further, to seek and watch occasions of doing good, and be glad when thou hast obtained them, that so thou mayest ever be furthering thy reckoning. We read of the patriarchs, Abraham and Lot, how they sat at their doors watching to entertain strangers, that they espied them afar off, ran out to meet them, and most earnestly entreated them to abide and refresh themselves ; show thyself herein the son of Abraham. (*T. Taylor, D.D.*)　　*Christian usefulness :—* I. The course specified. " Every good work." Every department of religion may be so denominated, repentance, faith, restitution, obedience, prayer, praise.

1. There is the work of mercy to the bodies of our fellow-men. Our fires will burn brighter, our clothes be warmer, our food sweeter, our slumbers more refreshing, if we tread in the steps of the blessed Jesus, who went about doing good. 2. There is the good work of compassion to the souls of our fellow-men. How many are ignorant and out of the way. What can we do to win souls to Christ? 3. There is the good work of affection and kindness to the household of faith. II. THE DIRECTION GIVEN. 1. The qualification. "Be ready." (1) That we have the disposition. Naturally, we have not the disposition. But the grace of God always imparts it. If the heart be good, then we shall have dispositions of goodness. (2) That we do good cheerfully. That it is not our burden. Not a sacrifice. Not a painful, but easy yoke. (3) It is to do good promptly. "To be ready." To be at the call. Everything nearly depends upon being in season. (4) Includes perseverance. Never to wish to cease, till the Saviour says it is enough. 2. The extent of the direction. "Be ready to every good work." As you have ability and opportunity. 3. The motives which should influence us. (1) Our religion is emphatically one of goodness. It allows of nothing malignant, or malevolent, even to enemies. (2) Our spiritual improvement is connected with it. It is by acting that we are conformed to Christ. (3) Our happiness is inseparably connected with it. It is heaven on earth. The joy of angels, felt and realised by man. (4) Our future amount of glory is connected with it. We are to be judged by our work, not by our faith, gifts, &c. Application.—1. Urge on the unregenerate the work of repentance. 2. Urge believers to be ready, &c. (*J. Burns, D.D.*)     *To the active Christian :*—I. THE COURSE OF ACTION ENJOINED. 1. Good works to the bodies of others. 2. Good works to the souls of others. 3. Good works to the Christian Church. II. THE QUALIFICATIONS SUPPOSED. 1. Cheerfulness. 2. Promptitude. 3. Perseverance. 4. Catholicity. III. THE MOTIVES. 1. The genius of our religion. 2. The example of Christ. 3. Personal improvement. 4. Future reward of grace. (*G. Brooks.*) *Readiness to good works explained and recommended :*—I. WHAT THIS ADVICE IMPLIES. To "be ready" is to be prepared, by laying a proper foundation in ourselves for doing good works. And this must be by the attainment of Divine knowledge and grace. 1. Knowledge is first necessary. Ignorance unfits and hinders many from doing good works. They know not the nature of good works, their necessity, that without them "faith is dead," their utility, amiable character, the will of God on this subject, nor how they may perform their duty in this respect. 2. By the attainment of grace (2 Cor. ix. 8), pardoning grace ; a consciousness of guilt burdening and discouraging the mind, and hindering good works; renewing grace; only a good tree bringeth forth good fruit ; strengthening grace ; enabling us to break, or shake off, the fetters of sin, which incapacitate us to do the will of God. II. THE IMPORTANCE OF BEING THUS READY. The glory of God is herein greatly concerned (Matt. v. 16 ; John xv. 8 ; Phil. i. 11). God is glorified by our holy tempers and heavenly affections, but especially by our substantial, good, and useful works. Great credit and honour is thus brought to the gospel. "These things are profitable to men," by lessening their miseries, or preventing or enabling them to obtain happiness. Our own good is involved herein. It is an evidence of our sincerity, and of the genuineness of our religion, to ourselves and others ; an evidence of our repentance, faith, hope, love, our justification, regeneration, and growth in grace. Our own peace of mind, as well as our religious character, is involved in this point. It is the means of exercising our grace and gifts, and thereby retaining them (Matt. xiii. 12 ; John xv. 2). III. THE MEANS TO BE USED IN ORDER THAT THIS ADVICE MAY BE COMPLIED WITH. The Word of God is the chief means of knowledge and of grace, whereby we may have the preparation, inclination, and ability mentioned above for every good work (2 Tim. iii. 15–17). This must be heard, read, searched, and diligently studied. It must also be received in faith and love, be obeyed in an humble and submissive spirit, through the influence and succour of the Holy Spirit (2 Cor. ix. 8). This Spirit must be sought in sincere, fervent, and importunate prayer, without which we shall not possess either the right disposition, or sufficient ability to do good works. Christian fellowship is a further means. We must "exhort one another" daily (Heb. x. 25), and take example from such as appear, or have appeared, eminent in usefulness. (*J. Benson.*)    **To speak evil of no man.**—*On evil-speaking :*—I. THERE ARE SEVERAL REASONS FOR WHICH CHRISTIANS OUGHT TO BE EXHORTED TO REFRAIN FROM EVIL-SPEAKING. 1. It is not only a mean and shameful, but a pernicious fault ; it produces much harm in society, and is a cause why many live hateful and hating one another, and die in the same unfriendly disposition. 2. It is a common and widespread fault, and few, very

few, are entirely free from it. It is not confined to wicked and profane persons; it is to be found in some measure even in those who have their virtues, their good and useful, and amiable qualities and accomplishments, who live soberly and honestly, who love their friends and are active to serve and oblige them, who are not uncharitable to the poor, who have a sense of religion, and worship God both in public and in private. 3. They who are addicted to it, either seldom reflect upon its odious nature, or are not sensible when and how often they thus offend, or have several plausible though vain excuses to justify themselves. II. EVIL-SPEAKING CONSISTS IN SPREADING REPORTS TO THE DISADVANTAGE OF OUR NEIGHBOUR; and of this fault there are three distinct kinds or degrees. 1. The worst kind of it is to spread lies of our own invention concerning others. 2. The next is to report things to their disadvantage, of the truth of which we are not sufficiently assured. 3. The lowest degree is to say of them that evil which we know to be true. III. There is no occasion to prove and expose the folly and dishonesty of the two former kinds. It would be losing time and words. I shall, therefore, chiefly discourse of the latter, and SHOW HOW BLAMABLE EVEN THIS IS FOR THE MOST PART. 1. We should not be too forward to publish the faults of others, because it is no sufficient excuse for us, that what we say is true, and that they against whom we speak deserve such usage. 2. Another argument against censoriousness is contained in this plain precept of the gospel—" Whatsoever ye would that men should do unto you, do ye so unto them." 3. We should not accustom ourselves to discourse about the faults of our neighbour, because it may betray us by degrees into a worse kind of evil-speaking. 4. We should not be forward to expose the faults of others, because by so doing we may bring upon them a punishment too heavy for the offence. 5. We should be cautious how we censure others, because we may misrepresent them, and yet say nothing of them that is not true. 6. To disclose the faults and indiscretions of others is often very pernicious to society, raises infinite variances amongst men, and tends to destroy the slender remains of love and charity which subsist in the Christian world. 7. Since for the most part we cannot discern the exact nature and degree of other men's faults, we may easily think too hardly and judge too severely of them. Their faults, when we know not the circumstances attending them, are like objects seen by us at a great distance, or at twilight : we see them neither in shape, nor in size or colour, such as they really are. 8. That we may restrain ourselves from talking of the faults of others, we should also consider that such discourse is produced by bad causes, and proceeds from a corrupted heart; and that all good and wise persons who hear us will judge of us accordingly. Speech is the child of thought; and a child it is which greatly resembles its parent. When the discourse is censorious and malicious, the mind which conceives it is no better. 9. Besides, this is an offence which seldom escapes correction. If human laws cannot chastise it, except in some few cases, the persons who are ridiculed or censured will fully supply that defect. 10. Lastly, we should be cautious not to give way to this inclination, because if we be once accustomed to it there is no probability that we shall ever leave it off. Of all bad habits, those of the tongue are, perhaps, the hardest to be cured. The reason is this : We deceive ourselves in thinking that words can do little or no hurt, and that the guilt of them is inconsiderably small, and consequently we speak at random what comes uppermost. (*J. Jortin, D.D.*)    *Evil-speaking* :—I. THE NATURE OF THIS VICE. It consists in saying things of others which tend to their disparagement and reproach, to the taking away or lessening of their reputation and good name; and this whether the things said be true or not. If they be false, and we know it, then it is downright calumny; and if we do not know it, but take it upon the report of others, it is, however, a slander; and so much the more injurious because really groundless and undeserved. If the thing be true, and we know it to be so, yet it is a defamation, and tends to the prejudice of our neighbour's reputation; and it is a fault to say the evil of others which is true, unless there be some good reason for it; besides, it is contrary to that charity and goodness which Christianity requires, to divulge the faults of others, though they be really guilty of them, without necessity or some other very good reason for it. Again, it is evil-speaking, and the vice condemned in the text, whether we be the first authors of an ill-report or relate it from others ; because the man that is evil spoken of is equally defamed either way. Again, whether we speak evil of a man to his face, or behind his back: the former way indeed seems to be the more generous, but yet is a great fault, and that which we call reviling : the latter is more mean and base, and that which we properly call slander, or backbiting. And lastly, whether it be done directly and in express terms, or more obscurely and by way of oblique insinuation; whether by way of downright reproach, or with some crafty preface of condemnation; for so it have the effect to defame, the manner of address does not much alter the case: the one may be more dexterous, but is not one jot less faulty. II. THE EXTENT OF THIS PROHIBITION. In what cases, by the general rules of Scripture and right reason, are we warranted to say the evil of others that is true? 1. It is not only lawful, but very commendable, and often our duty, to do this in order to the probable amendment of the person of whom evil is spoken. But then we must take care that this be done out of kindness, and that nothing of our own passion be mingled with it; and that under pretence of reproving and reforming men we do not reproach and revile them, and tell them of their faults in such a manner as if we did it to show our authority rather than our charity. 2. This likewise is not only lawful, but our duty, when we are legally called to bear witness concerning the fault and crime of another. 3. It is lawful to publish the faults of others in our own necessary defence and vindication. 4. This also is lawful for caution and warning to a third person that is in danger to be infected by the company, or ill example of another; or may be greatly prejudiced by reposing too much confidence in him, having no knowledge or suspicion of his bad qualities: but even in this case we ought to take great care that the ill character we give of any man be spread no farther than is necessary to the good end we designed in it. III. THE EVIL OF THIS PRACTICE, both in the causes and the consequences of it. 1. We will consider the causes of it. And it commonly springs from one or more of these evil roots. (1) One of the deepest and most common causes of evil-speaking is ill nature and cruelty of disposition: and by a general mistake ill nature passeth for wit, as cunning doth for wisdom; though in truth they are nothing akin to one another, but as far distant as vice and virtue. And there is no greater evidence of the bad temper of mankind than the general proneness of men to this vice. (2) Another cause of the commonness of this vice is, that many are so bad themselves in one kind or other. For to think and speak ill of others is not only a bad thing, but a sign of a bad man. (3) Another source of this vice is malice and revenge. When men are in heat and passion they do not consider what is true, but what is spiteful and mischievous, and speak evil of others in revenge of some injury which they have received from them; and when they are blinded by their passions, they lay about them madly and at a venture, not much caring whether the evil they speak be true or not. (4) Another cause of evil-speaking is envy. Men look with an evil eye upon the good that is in others, and think that their reputation obscures them, and that their commendable qualities do stand in their light; and therefore they do what they can to cast a cloud over them, that the bright shining of their virtues may not scorch them. (5) Another cause of evil-speaking is impertinence and curiosity; an itch of talking and meddling in the affairs of other men, or any bad thing that is talked of in good company. (6) Men often do this out of wantonness and for diversion. But what can be more barbarous, next to sporting with a man's life, than to play with his honour and reputation? 2. The ordinary, but very pernicious consequences and effects of it, both to others and to ourselves. (1) To others; the parties I mean that are slandered. To them it is certainly a great injury, and commonly a high provocation, but always matter of no small grief and trouble to them. (2) The consequences of this vice are as bad or worse to ourselves. Whoever is wont to speak evil of others gives a bad character of himself, even to those whom he desires to please, who, if they be wise enough, will conclude that he speaks of them to others, as he does of others to them. But there is an infinitely greater danger hanging over us from God. If we allow ourselves in this evil practice, all our religion is good for nothing. IV. SOME FURTHER ARGUMENTS AND CONSIDERATIONS to take men off from this vice. 1. That the use of speech is a peculiar prerogative of man above other creatures, and bestowed upon him for some excellent end and purpose; that by this faculty we might communicate our thoughts more easily to one another, and consult together for our mutual comfort and benefit, not to enable us to be hurtful and injurious, but helpful and beneficial to one another. 2. Consider how cheap a kindness it is to speak well, at least not to speak ill of anybody. A good word is an easy obligation, but not to speak ill requires only our silence, which costs us nothing. 3. Consider that no quality doth ordinarily recommend one more to the favour and goodwill of men, than to be free from this vice. 4. Let every man lay his hand upon his heart, and consider how himself is apt to be affected with this usage. 5. When you are going to speak reproachfully of others, consider whether you do not lie open to just reproach in the same, or some other kind. Therefore give no occasion, no example of this barbarous usage of one another. 6. Consider that it is in many cases as great a charity to conceal the evil you hear and know of others, as if you relieved them in a great necessity. And we think him a hard-hearted man that will not bestow a small alms upon one in great want. V. SOME RULES AND DIRECTIONS FOR THE PREVENTION AND CURE OF THIS GREAT EVIL. 1. Never say any evil of any man, but what you certainly know. 2. Before you speak evil of any man consider whether he hath not obliged you by some real kindness, and then it is a bad return to speak ill of him who hath done us good. 3. Let us accustom ourselves to pity the faults of men, and to be truly sorry for them, and then we shall take no pleasure in publishing them. 4. Whenever we hear any man evil spoken of, if we know any good of him let us say that. 5. That you may speak evil of any, do not delight to hear ill of them. 6. Let every man mind himself, and his own duty and concernment. Do but endeavour in good earnest to mend thyself, and it will be work enough for one man, and leave thee but little time to talk of others. 7. Lastly, let us set a watch before the door of our lips, and not speak but upon consideration ; I do not mean to speak finely, but fitly. Especially when thou speakest of others, consider of whom and what thou art going to speak : use great caution and circumspection in this matter: look well about thee ; on every side of the thing, and on every person in the company, before thy words slip from thee, which when they are once out of thy lips are for ever out of thy power. (*Archbishop Tillotson.*)    *Detraction :*—I. Consider THAT RASH AND INCONSIDERATE CENSURES ARE INCONSISTENT WITH THE JUSTICE WHICH YOU OWE TO YOUR BRETHREN. The Author of our nature hath wisely ordained that approbation should follow virtue as its natural reward. This the virtuous are allowed to propose to themselves as an inferior motive of conduct; and this they expect as what belongs to them of right. The esteem which a man hath merited by his integrity and usefulness may be considered as a property of which he cannot innocently be deprived ; and the extent of the injury done by detraction, is proportioned to the value of the possession which it invades. Now, what interest is dearer to the ingenuous than the preservation of their good name ? You detest the villain who robs the industrious of their well-earned store ; you abhor the oppressor who plunders the innocent and the deserving of the means of their support; yet how light and trivial are such injuries as these in comparison of the ruin of their virtuous name, which, even in the midst of poverty, would ensure them respect. Would men weigh duly the mischiefs which detraction occasions, that pernicious humour would be less frequently indulged ; for it is not always from malice and cruelty of nature that detraction proceeds : it arises, often, from an inconsiderate gaiety of mind, and means not to ruin the character which it delights to expose. The effects of such conduct are not, perhaps, obvious, because they are not immediate ; but they are not, on this account, the less certain, or the less direful. With a man's reputation his usefulness and success are closely connected ; and one unguarded expression may involve a deserving family in want and wretchedness. The only compensation which you can possibly make is to vindicate the violated character at the expense of your own ; and this is an atonement most humiliating to yourselves, yet to the unhappy sufferer often of little avail; for many listen with avidity to the tale of slander, who will lend to your exculpation an indifferent ear ; nor will your influence be sufficient to repair the reputation which your levity or your baseness hath ruined. II. THAT A CENSORIOUS TURN OF MIND IS DESTRUCTIVE ALSO OF YOUR OWN FELICITY. The man who is addicted to this odious vice, acquires, by degrees, an unhappy acuteness in marking the imperfections of his brethren. To him, therefore, the society of men can have no charms ; for he beholds in every human being an object of dislike. Is not that man's mind ill-formed for happiness, who, amidst the various appearances which nature exhibits, dwells always on such as are dismal and destructive ; who observes only the inhospitable desert, the blasting lightning, and the wintry storm; but marks not the beauties which adorn the spring, the riches which descend in the shower, or the stores with which autumn gladdens the earth? Nor does his happiness suffer merely from the effect of detraction on his own disposition. His conduct renders him an object of general aversion. Even his gay companions, whom his destructive pleasantry may entertain for a season, despise and dread the promoter of their mirth. They know that the edge of his satire will soon be turned against themselves ; and that their own characters are destined to bleed by the very same weapons by which others have been assailed. Those who have suffered by his calumny, are entitled to vindicate, at his expense, their injured reputation ; and every friend of innocence will aid them in the attempt. Merely to refute his slander, implies a reproach to which no prudent man would choose to expose himself. But how rarely doth human resentment confine itself within such moderate bounds. The rage of the injured will probably prompt them to retaliate. The security of others will seemed to be concerned in the cause. It will not appear sufficient that the aspersion be removed. The character of the detractor is devoted to ruin. In the snare which he hath laid for others, his own feet are entangled, and he falls by the sword which he hath whetted against his brethren. (*W. Moodie, D.D.*). *Evil-speaking :*—I. All evil speaking MAY BE REFERRED TO TWO HEADS, FOR IT IS (1) EITHER THE UTTERING OF FALSE AND EVIL THINGS, OR (2) OF TRUE THINGS FALSELY AND EVILLY. 1. The former. (1) When men speak upon no ground, as when men, present or absent, are accused of the evils which they never did (2 Sam. xvi. 3). (2) When men speak some evil of others upon weak and insufficient grounds, as when any either publicly or privately chargeth some other man before his face or behind his back with evil upon suspicions (2 Sam. x. 3). (3) When men cast railing, cursing, or reviling speeches upon another, present or absent, openly or secretly, and covertly by insinuation (2 Sam. xv. 3) 2. The latter kind of evil-speaking is in true things, as—(1) When a man speaketh of something done or spoken, but destroyeth the sense (Matt. xxvi. 61 ; John ii. 19). (2) In uttering nothing but truth, but with wicked insinuations and collections of evil (1 Sam. xxii. 9, 10). (3) In speaking of good things, but either lessening them or depraving them, as done of bad intent for bad ends in hypocrisy. (4) In speaking of things evil and not so well done. (*a*) By uncovering infirmities, which is the guise of cursed Chams, who are ever revealing to their brethren other men's nakedness, which an ingenious disposition, yea, humanity itself (if there were no religion), would cover and hide (Prov. xi. 13). (*b*) Whereas we can excuse our own faults twenty ways, by amplifying the faults and offences of others, be they never so apparent, we become evil speakers in a high degree, as sycophants who make the scapes of men far greater than they are, affirming often that to be done of deliberation which was done rashly and in hot blood, or presumptuously when it was perhaps done but weakly, and imputing that to want of conscience which perhaps was want of heedfulness and foresight ; and thus the sin is heightened when men so wickedly speak of that which they ought altogether to be silent in and not to speak at all. II. Now, because of all sins, there is not a more manifest and general mischief in all the life of man, WHEREIN EVEN CHRISTIANS THEMSELVES ARE NOT EXEMPTED, who carry a very world of wickedness about with them, and yet wipe their mouths as though all were well with them ; therefore will it not be amiss to take a little pains with this sin, scarce so accounted of, and to show—1. How unseemly it is for a Christian. 2. How dangerous in itself. 3. The means to repress and avoid it. 1. For the first—(1) To utter slander, saith Solomon, is a note of a fool ; and the slander itself is a fool's bolt, which is soon shot. And the apostle in so many places affirming it to be the practice of the old man, which must be cast off, maketh it hence an unbeseeming thing for Christians that profess new life to walk in such heathenish courses. (2) This cursed speaking, whereby our brethren are hurt in their names, is the devil's language, who thence hath his name, and argueth a venomous and hateful disposition not becoming the children of God. (3) True religion will not stand with such a tattling course as many Christians take up, who, like the Athenians, delight in nothing more than hearing and telling news ; and once getting a tale by the end, they are in travail till they have delivered it to others, and with these all opportunity of good and edifiable speech perisheth. (4) Were it not most disgraceful for a Christian to be counted a thief, or a continual robber in the highway, or a continual breaker of the peace? and yet this sin is a greater breach of love than theft or spoiling of the goods, for a good name is more precious than gold, more sweet than the sweetest ointment. 2. The second point is the danger of this sin, which cannot but attend it, unless we conceive no danger in breaking such express commandments as we have (Lev. xix. 16 ; James iv. 11). The defence of many a man is, I speak nothing but the truth, and so long I may speak it. But if that thou speakest be a tale true or false (as it is if without a calling thou playest the pedlar, and settest to sale the name of thy brother), these commandments cast and condemn thee. Others think it is a fault indeed, but not so great a fault to speak the thing we know by another ; but look upon it, not as it may seem in thine eye, but in the penalty the Scripture hath set upon it; (Psa. xv. 3) it hindereth the entrance into the holy mountain of God, and (1 Cor. vi. 10) railers and revilers shall not enter into the kingdom of heaven; and therefore it is no such small matter as many take it for. Others reply, What are words but wind? and God is not so strait-laced; if a man should go to hell for every word, who shall come to heaven? This, indeed, is an ancient natural conceit that outward profession and ceremony will carry a man to heaven, although in the particulars of the life the power of godliness be never expressed. But mark how the Lord answereth such vain conceits (Psa. l. 19, 20). God hath His time then to call upon old reckonings, and then thou shalt not think words wind, but know to thy cost that life and death was in the power of thy tongue. Others yet see no such danger, or, if any be, it is far off. But this sin, beside the just hire of it hereafter, carrieth a secret plague with it for the present, for look, as thou dealest with another man's name, so shall thine be dealt with, and with what measure thou metest to others shall men measure to thee again. 3. The third thing to be considered is the means to avoid this sin of evil-speaking, which may be reduced to five rules. (1) Look to thine heart, for if it, being the fountain, be corrupted, the issues and streams cannot but be bitter; and if thou giveth thyself leave to think evil of any man, as accounting the thought free, thou canst not but one time or other utter it. Purge well thine heart, therefore—(*a*) Of pride, which maketh a man speak disdainfully of those who want the things which themselves seem to have, and liberally take up any language if he can make the detraction of another a ladder for himself to climb upon. (*b*) Of envy, which, grieving at the graces and good things in another, seeketh to darken them, as Satan, envying Job's prosperity, said, "He serveth not God for nought." (*c*) Of flattery, which for favour or reward will tune the tongue to any ear. (2) Be careful to contain thyself within thine own calling; follow thine own plough; beware of the sin of busybodies, who love to play the bishops in other men's dioceses, who, if they had not with the witch in the fable, put off their own eyes at home, they might find foul corners enough well worthy of reformation in themselves; but therefore load they others, because they spare themselves; they throw no stones at their own faults first, and therefore they are at good leisure to pry into other men's, and so become the devil's gunpowder for want of better employment. (3) Beware in all thy speeches with men of strife of words, for from hence evil speeches arise, and many words want not iniquity. (4) In all companies pray to the Lord to set a watch before thy mouth, and to keep the door of thy lips, for the tongue can no man of himself tame, being such an unruly evil. (5) Beware of consenting to this sin in another, for as thou art bound not to relate, so not to receive, any evil speeches of thy brother. Solomon counselleth not to meddle with the slanderer and flatterer; wise chapmen must beware of such base pedlars. (*T. Taylor, D.D.*) *Evil-speaking:*—I. THE PRECEPT. 1. We should never in severe terms inveigh against any man without reasonable warrant, or presuming on a good call and commission for the purpose. 2. We should never speak so of any man without apparent just cause: we must not reproach men for things innocent or indifferent, for not complying with our humour or interests. 3. We should not cast reproach on any man without some necessary reason: in that charity which covereth a multitude of sins, we are bound to extenuate and excuse the faults of our brethren, so far as truth and equity permit. 4. We should never speak ill of our neighbour beyond measure, be the cause never so just, the occasion never so necessary. 5. We should never speak ill of any man out of bad principles or for bad ends; from no sudden anger, inveterate hatred, revengeful disposition, contempt, or envy; to compass any design of our own, to cherish any malignity or ill-humour; neither out of wantonness nor out of negligence and inadvertency; in fine from no other principle but that of charity, and to no other intent but what is charitable. II. INDUCEMENTS TO ITS OBSERVANCE. 1. Let us consider that nothing more than railing and reviling is opposite to the nature, and inconsistent with the tenor of our religion. 2. It is therefore often expressly condemned and prohibited as evil. 3. Against no practice are severer punishments denounced. St. Paul adjudges the railer to be banished from good society (1 Cor. v. 11), and from heaven (1 Cor. vi. 10). 4. Such language is in its nature the symptom of a weak and distempered mind: a stream that cannot issue from a sweet spring. 5. This practice plainly signifies low spirit, ill-breeding, and bad manners, and is thence unbecoming to any wise, honest, or honourable person: all such have an aversion to it, and cannot entertain it with complacency. 6. He that uses this kind of speech, as he harms and troubles others, so does he create thereby great inconveniences and mischiefs to himself. 7. Hence with evidently good reason is he that uses such language called a fool; and he that abstaineth from it is commended as wise (Prov. xviii. 6, 7). 8. Lastly, we may consider that it is a grievous perversion of the design of speech, which so much distinguishes us above other creatures, to use it in defaming and disquieting our neighbour: far better were it that we could say nothing than that we should speak ill. (*Isaac Barrow, D.D.*) *Avoiding evil-speaking:*—Philip Henry used to remind those who spoke evil of people behind their backs of that law, "Thou shalt not curse the deaf." Those that are absent are deaf; they cannot right themselves; therefore say no ill of them. A friend of his, inquiring of him concerning a matter which tended to reflect upon some people, he began to give him an account of the story, but immediately broke off, and checked himself with these words, "But our rule is to speak evil of no man," and would proceed no further in the story. The week before he died a person requested the loan of a particular book from him. "Truly," said he, "I would lend it to you, but that it takes in the faults of some which should rather be covered with a mantle of love." (*W. Baxendale.*) *Sin of evil-speaking:*—Remember, this contradicts your nature and your destiny; to speak ill of others makes you a monster in God's world. Get the habit of slander, and then there is not a stream which bubbles fresh from the heart of nature—there is not a tree that silently brings forth its genial fruit in its appointed seasons, which does not rebuke and proclaim you a monstrous anomaly in God's world. (*F. W. Robertson, M.A.*) *Cure for evil-speaking:*—When will talkers refrain from evil-speaking? When listeners refrain from evil-hearing? At present there are many so credulous of evil, they will receive suspicions and impressions against persons whom they don't know, from a person whom they do know—an authority to be good for nothing. (*A. W. Hare, M.A.*) **No brawlers.**—*Contention to be avoided:*—I. NOT THAT EVERY STRIKING AND FIGHTING IS HEREBY FORBIDDEN. For—1. Every man is bound to contend in his place for the truth—for religion, truth, and sound doctrine against falsehood, error, heresy, and superstition. 2. The ruler and people may by lawful war repel openly either idolatry or injury from Church or commonwealth, for if it had been altogether unlawful, John Baptist would have advised the soldiers rather to have given over their calling and taken no wages at all than to have been content with their wages. 3. Private men may seek the face of the ruler to prevent or redress an injury, and thus contend in judgment, which is no sin unless it be for trifles or of revenge: so Paul appealed to Cæsar, and helped himself by the benefit of law. 4. It is lawful for every Christian, in defect of the magistrates' aid, in the lawful defence of themselves, lives, and goods, to become magistrates unto themselves, in which case they may without sin both strike and slay, so as desire of revenge and intent of bloodshedding be absent. 5. Neither is domestical discipline excluded by this precept, whereby fathers and masters may, if the fault require, put on severity in their just corrections of their servants and children. II. But the sin here condemned is when men suffer their lusts so far to sway, as they not only follow the things which make to Christian peace, BUT ARE ENEMIES UNTO CONCORD AND BROTHERLY LOVE—men of such violent affections as are ready, not only to return injury with injury, but with seventy-fold revenge; right Lamechs and rough Ismaels, whose hand is against every man; men of a word and a blow, fitter for the camp than the congregation of Christian men. Now, what an hateful thing is it that a Christian should be indited at the Lord's bar for a common barrator and quarreller? How unlike should he be to God, who is a God of peace, and loveth peace and the sons of peace? How far from having any part in the merit of Christ, who hath dearly by His precious blood bought the reconcilement of all things? How unanswerable were it unto this profession of Christianity, which cannot become a kingdom divided against itself? How prejudicial to Christian duties, both interrupting prayers and withstanding the acceptation of them, when the gift is brought without a reconcilable mind? How doth this course in Cain's way violate all bonds both of nature and grace? signing a man to be out of the commission, out of the natural fraternity in the first Adam, and much more out of the spiritual in the second, yea, arguing such fierce men to be rather of the serpents' and crocodiles' seed, between which and man God hath put an enmity, than of men, seeing they have put off all respect of creation, of adoption, of flesh, and of faith. III. If any ask, But BY WHAT MEANS SHALL I AVOID THIS SIN OF CONTENTION AND QUARRELLING? 1. Bridle the tongue, for this is an immediate follower of evil-speaking, and it runneth from the tongue into the hand. 2. Let the consideration of our common brotherhood be a means to cut off contention (Gen. xiii. 8). 3.

Consider what a scandal it is to profane scorners of religion that such as profess themselves scholars of Christ should live together like dogs and cats (as we say), and by ungodly quarrels and heartburns be still building up the works of the devil which Christ hath destroyed; why should such a thing be heard in Gath and Askelon? why should Priamus and his son laugh us to scorn? 4. Get a low conceit of thyself and be small in thine own eyes, for whence riseth contention and strife but from the lust in the members, namely, the inordinate bearing of a man's self above that which is meet? Only by pride (saith Solomon) man maketh contention, and, indeed, experience showeth that the most suits at this day are not so much for right and equity as for victory. 5. Because some in their own temper are of more mild and quiet spirits, and rather lie open to this sin by others' instigation than their own propensity and disposition. That rule of Solomon is worth noting, to take heed of part-taking, of meddling, and mingling oneself in other men's strifes and contentions, for this were to take a dog by the ears or a bear by the tooth. (*T. Taylor, D.D.*)        **Gentle.**—*Christian gentleness :*—We are called to the practice of that property of wisdom which is from above, which is peaceable and gentle, and to buckle unto us, as the elect of God, tender mercy, kindness, humbleness of mind, meekness, longsuffering, forbearing one another, and forgiving one another. The benefit will be exceeding great. For—1. This wisdom teacheth us to be soft in our speeches, as they that know how a soft answer breaketh wrath, a rare example whereof we have in Judg. viii. 2. 2. It teacheth us softness in our whole conversation and exercise of our personal and general callings. It suffereth not the magistrate to be so stern that an inferior should come to him as a man that were to bring a bottle to an elephant, which he is afraid of, which timidity Augustus reproved in a petitioner. It suffereth not the minister to be lordly in his doctrine or discipline, but compassionate and tender in both. It suffereth not the father or master to be a lion in his house, but causeth them to govern sweetly and to dispense severity, and weigh out correction as physic to the children and servants. 3. It teacheth even the superior to yield some part of his right to his inferior, as Abraham to Lot, "If thou take the right hand, I will turn to the left," nay, as Christ Himself being God and Lord of all, yet for peace' sake, and to avoid offence, did pay tribute unto Cæsar. 4. Further, how necessary a virtue this is cannot but appear to him that considereth how frail our flesh and blood is, how full of infirmities, how lying open to offences, how needful of much forgiveness at God's hand and man's; and yet no forgiveness at God's hand, but on condition of our forgiveness of men, for so is the petition in the Lord's Prayer; nor at man's, for what measure ye mete out to men shall men measure to you again. 5. How sweet a grace it is appeareth also in that it preserveth the outward peace of a man, and especially the peace of a good conscience. (*Ibid.*)        *Gentleman defined :*—A Christian is God Almighty's gentleman. The real gentleman should be gentle in everything; at least in everything that depends on himself—in carriage, temper, constructions, aims, desires. He ought, therefore, to be mild, calm, quiet, even, temperate: not hasty in judgment, not exorbitant in ambition, not overbearing, not proud, not rapacious, not oppressive: for these things are contrary to gentleness. (*J. C. Hare.*)        **Showing all meekness unto all men.**—*Christian meekness :*—I. THE NATURE OF THIS GRACE will appear in the description of it. Meekness is a grace of God, whereby the heart and affections are inclined unto a mild and loving, a kind and courteous carriage towards our neighbour, even then when they might be provoked to anger. Where three things are laid down to be further opened to the better knowledge of this virtue—1. That it is a grace of God, for the next verse will teach us that we are born as rough as Esau in our corrupted nature; and therefore this strippeth and goeth beyond the best nature, being a fruit of the Spirit, and is called the spirit of meekness, because it is such a peculiar work of the Spirit, and proceedeth not of the flesh. 2. The work of it is properly to preserve Christian affection, in moderating all revengeful passions, not suffering the heart to be easily overcome with bitterness, but is as a wall or fence of the soul, receiving all the shot of injurious and hostile actions and speeches, and yet keeping all safe within, not permitting the possessor hastily or violently either to offer to another or remove from himself such injuries. The mother of it is humility, the daughter is long-suffering, and therefore we read it set between these two in diverse places. It preserveth peace within when it is provoked to war, to anger, and return of wrongs, for then is the chief use of this grace, which is therefore added, because many men seem to have attained this virtue, when it is never a whit so. Let them alone, offend them not, you shall have them gentle, courteous, affable, and tractable enough; but cross them a little, and stir their blood, oh, now you must pardon them; they have their affections, and you shall know they can be passionate and angry as well as others; here shall you see the best nature betraying her meekness. But Christian meekness must step in to overcome evil with good when it is provoked to return evil, or else what great thing doest thou? It is no hard thing for the very Infidel and Turk to be kind to the kind, nay, the wild beast, if thou goest no further, will be as meek as thou, who the most of them hurt not unprovoked. II. THIS MEEKNESS MUST BE SHOWED FORTH, not hid with ourselves, but it must be brought into the light, that others may have the benefit of it, for as this grace is a sign and pawn of our election, which, as the elect of God, we must put on and array ourselves withal (Col. iii. 12), so also must it be the ornament of our vocation, whereby we glorify God, adorn our profession, and win others unto the liking of it. Hence the apostle, praying the Ephesians to walk worthy of their high calling, teacheth them that this they shall do if they put on humbleness of mind, meekness, longsuffering, &c. (Eph. iv. 2), for otherwise, if men partake not in these graces, the unity of the spirit in the bond of peace cannot long last undissolved. III. THIS MEEKNESS MUST BE SHOWED TO ALL MEN—believers, unbelievers, friends, enemies, the better and the worse, which is a special point not to be neglected, because it is the ground of the verses following. (*T. Taylor, D.D.*) *The might of meekness:*—Conversing the other day with a friend on some point of domestic difficulty, it was replied by the latter, " Should I give up in that way, and be as meek as a lamb, I should be good for just nothing at all." " No," I answered, " there is nothing mightier than meekness." This sentiment, which, at the time, flashed upon my mind like a gleam of new truth, I have found, by subsequent reflection, to rest on a broad basis. I. In the first place, meekness INVOLVES THE LARGEST SELF-CONTROL. 1. Meekness is not mental indolence. A person may be too lazy to resent a wrong, too intellectually lazy—like some big house-dog in the farmer's kitchen, submitting with marvellous resignation to be kicked or pulled by the ears, if only he may be left in his snug, warm corner, and meeting it all with a most humble and beseeching whine. If this were meekness, we would not hesitate to pronounce it the weakest thing on earth. 2. It is not impassibility. Some are natural stoics. In some respects they are fortunate beings; utter strangers to that red-hot sense of injustice which sometimes bursts forth in words of heaven-lit prophecy—sometimes in words set on fire of hell. They escape that terrible knowledge—the soul's capacity to suffer. And yet, doubtless, they are not to be envied; for the words of the poet are equally true when reversed:—

" Chords that vibrate sweetest pleasure
Thrill the deepest notes of woe."

3. Nor is it dulness of perception. Some seem not to know when they are ill-treated. They are ignorant of the proprieties of life, of what is due to position; there is an entire lack of native dignity of character. True meekness, on the contrary, achieves its highest triumphs where the perceptions are most quick-sighted, the sensibilities keenest, and the mind most active and vigorous in all its operations. It is just here that we can best discern its true nature, its inherent might, the hiding of its power. So far from being a mere passivity, it is activity in its highest form. It is self-control in its broadest sway when girding itself in its full strength. It is victory over all that is mightiest in pride and passion, attained by the full and conjoint action of all the nobler powers of the soul. It is man in his sovereignty, ruling within the realm of his spirit, as the prince-subject of Jehovah. Its highest embodiment was Jesus of Nazareth. II. Again, MEEKNESS IS MIGHTY IN GOD'S MIGHT. He loves the meek. They are the most like His Son—resembling Him in just that quality which was His most prominent characteristic. Still again, the might of meekness is seen in its power to secure happiness. Life is a perpetual wild chase after happiness. Who are winners? Pride? Passion? Ambition? Wealth? " Nay, nay, not yet," they each exclaim as they rush by, dripping with sweat; and catching breath, they add, " but the goal is just ahead, and then the prize is ours." The result is " even as when a hungry man dreameth, and behold he eateth; but he awaketh, and his soul is empty." Yet, far off, away from the bustling and anxious crowd, I behold the meek man already inheriting the earth, in sweet fruition of the world that now is, and in joyous expectancy of that which is to come. The reign of passion is over. He has learned to recognise, in all events that affect him, not accidents, but Providence; not a stern and blind fate,

but a kind and wise Father; not the present means and instruments merely, but the aim of final result. The peace of God that passeth understanding keeps his heart. The whole world has become a Beulah; and while meekly performing its duties, its eye catches sweet glimpses of the far-off land; his heart leaps betimes at snatches of the distant music, and his temples are fanned, ever and anon, by the refreshing breezes that are wafted thitherward. He has an antepast of heaven; a joyous earnest of his inheritance. Here, then, I say, is might. He gains what worldlings of every class toil and tug for, but always lose; or, as Cicero says, respecting another point, "They desire it, he has it." Once more: there is nothing like meekness to overcome the resistance of passion and pride in others. And yet it is just here that the worldly-wise despise it most. I am assailed. I erect myself in proud might. I bid defiance to wrath. I mock at the deadliest threats of my enemy. I dare him to do his worst. Like Achilles before Agamemnon, I fling at his feet the oath-pledge of battle. By all that is most fearful I swear to stand him foot to foot to the death. And what is the result of all this? Why, Greek meets Greek. Words fly back to words, wrath flashes to wrath, threats are hurled to threats, and pride towers aloft to pride. But what boots it all? You turn from the encounter, leaving your enemy never stouter in his resistance, while the tiger passions tear your own bosom, or react in paroxysms of futile tears. Now, what has meekness accomplished in just such cases? Silenced the proud words of the enemy; extinguished his raging wrath; roused up the elements of his better nature, and turned them against himself. It has completely subdued him; and the proud Greek has sat at the feet of his foe a weeping child. I say, then, let passion exhaust all its resources—let it tower to very sublimity, let it be a fit subject for an epic, let a Homer immortalise its deeds. Meekness is mightier; it will accomplish what passion shall labour for in vain. *Meekness:*—Meekness is the quality which heathenism everywhere has scouted as meanspiritedness, but which the gospel of Christ has canonised. It is that one condition of soul which, springing out of genuine penitence for sin, a profound sense of personal unworthiness, and a profound appreciation of the Divine mercy, predisposes a man to forbearance under provocation and forgiveness for injury. It has nothing in common with pusillanimity, but it has its origin in the religious experience which we call conversion; for it is when the sap root of human pride is broken by a thorough crushing down of the soul under the discovery of its sinfulness before God; it is when the strong man, reduced to cry for mercy at the hands of Infinite Justice, is fain to receive forgiveness, and hope, and peace with God as unmerited gifts from the very grace of his Redeemer; it is then, and through that religious change, that the heart grows susceptible of true meekness. Then humbleness enters—humbleness, the child of penitence, and mild charity too, for all men, and a tender feeling—a feeling that one who has himself done so much evil in his day ought to bear with the evil-doing of other men, that one who owes everything to mercy should be, above all things, merciful. (*J. O. Dykes, D.D.*) *Meekness:*—A little lad on being asked, "What is meekness?" replied, "Mary is meekness." "Mary?" "Yes, my sister Mary, for she always gives smooth answers to rough questions."

Ver. 3. **We ourselves also were sometimes foolish.**—*The transforming power of the gospel:*—I. WHAT EVEN CHRISTIANS WERE. Their lives and characters were distinguished by—1. Folly; 2. Disobedience; 3. Liability to deception; 4. Sensuality; 5. Passion; 6. Unloveliness; 7. Unbrotherliness. II. WHAT CHRISTIANS BECOME. Their lives display—1. Humility of spirit; 2. Gentleness in action; 3. Truthfulness in word. (*F. Wagstaff.*) *Before conversion and after:*— This verse layeth down a weighty reason whereby our apostle would bow and bend the minds of Christian men to the practice of the former virtues, namely, of equity, lenity, long-suffering, and meekness towards all men, foes as well as friends, yea, the worst as well as the best. The reason is drawn from the consideration of the present condition of converted Christians, compared with that estate they were in before their conversion and calling to the faith, to which purpose he is very large in describing. 1. Our estate of corruption (ver. 3). 2. Our estate after conversion (vers. 4–6), from both which the apostle thus concluded the same thing thus: First, the former; if we ourselves were in times past in the self-same condition, which other men are not called out of, then ought we to be meek and merciful even to those who are not yet converted. But we ourselves were in times past as they are; we lay in the same puddle of corruption, were hewn out of the same pit, and though we may think we were never so graceless, as we see some others, yet we cannot charge them so deeply for time present, but they may come over us with the same in times past, as this third verse will teach us, and therefore we ought to show all lenity and meekness to all men. Secondly, from our latter condition of conversion, thus our apostle frameth his reason. If God have been so bountiful a benefactor unto us, when we were so unworthy, as the former verse describeth, that His mere and alone mercy saved us; then must we in imitation of our heavenly Father do the like to our brethren. But God hath done thus (vers. 4, 5) so as from both we may well reason that a new condition requireth a new conversation; new men must have new manners; we being Christians may not carry ourselves so crookedly as in times past, nor so roughly towards those who now do the same things which then we did, considering our own selves. (*T. Taylor, D.D.*) *The difference between the present and the past of life*:—1. The consideration of the common condition is a notable ground of meekness and moderation towards those who are yet uncalled to the faith. For—(1) Whereas pride maketh the heart to swell against the brother, and is a root whence these bitter fruits arise, this consideration pulleth those peacock feathers, and humbleth the heart, so as when it can find no other reason of forbearance, here it never wanteth a most effectual one. 2. This consideration not only subdueth that violent affection of pride, but worketh the heart to such affections as not only beseem ourselves but befit the offender, and these are two—(1) For time present pity and compassion. (2) Hope for time to come. 3. Whosoever are called unto the faith have experience of a double estate in themselves, one in time past, another for the present, the one of nature, the other of grace. Our apostle affirmeth it of all believers, of which there is none but he had his once, his time past, in regard of which he may now be said to be changed into another man (Rom. vii. 5, 6). The time was when the Romans were in the flesh, when sinful motions had force in them unto death; and there was an aftertime when they were delivered from the law, and served God not in the old-ness of the letter, but in the newness of spirit (Eph. ii. 3). Among whom the Gentiles we believers had our conversation in time past. "Wherein ye walked also once, but now," &c. (1 Cor. vi. 11). "And such were some of you, but ye are washed." And good reason there is that he that is now beloved should see that once he was not beloved, and that he who now is in the state of grace should see that he was once in the state of wrath as well as others, which will cause him to love much; and indeed the elect could not be elect, nor justified, nor washed, if they were always the children of God, and were it not for this once, and time past, wherein there was no difference between them and the reprobate, but only in God's counsel and possibility of calling. I add, further, that the converted may and must have experience of this change, for the conversion of a sinner is a miracle above all natural wonders; and therefore, except in some Jeremiah, John Baptist, and some few sanctified from the womb, is no such insensible thing as cannot be perceived. It is no such natural change as is effected by insensible degrees, as when he that was a child is now become a man; but a supernatural change by the Spirit of grace, such as when a man is born into the world, or when a blind man is restored to his sight, or rather a dead man unto life, which are things of much note and manifest alteration, and that of the whole man. Again, faith it is which as an internal instrument purgeth the Augean Stable, and purifieth the foul cage of the heart. Now this we may know, and must examine whether we be in the faith or no; know ye not that Christ is in you, unless ye be reprobates. "Know ye not that ye are the temple of God, and that the Spirit of God dwelleth in you?" (1 Cor. iii. 16). "Know ye that ye are dead to sin, but are alive to God in Jesus Christ our Lord" (Rom. vi. 11). Labour to find this change in thyself and examine whether thou canst put difference between time past and time present, for otherwise I see not but thou must set thyself down without comfort, as one that hath no sound proof of thy conversion. Hence may many a one learn what to think of himself. Some profess they love God with all their hearts and have ever so done since they can remember; they always believed in Christ and never doubted but they were ever dear unto God. But all this is nothing but a deceitful skinning over the sores of their souls with peace, peace, whereas the case that was ever so good was never good at all; no, if thou canst not remember the time past, when thy state was worse than nought, I can never be persuaded that it is good for the present. Every Christian learn hence—1. If we see a change in ourselves or others to bless God that hath made this separation (Rom. vi. 17). God be thanked that ye were such, but now ye obey the form, and blessed be God for this unspeakable gift. 2. Not to deem of men as they were once in time past, when once this change is come, the Lord esteemeth of men according to the present grace received, and never casteth them in the teeth with that they were in time past; and why should we upbraid men with sins or infirmities past, which the Lord hath covered? Paul accounted not James, John, Peter, fishermen, as they had been in times past, but highly esteemed of them as apostles of Christ, being called thereunto. (*Ibid.*)    *Foolish :* —1. The main property of fools and silly bodies is that they know not the end of their lives, why God made them and put them into this world; even to ask many men why God did inspire the breath of life on their faces, how few would give this direct answer, that by glorifying God in my calling I might be led to a better life hereafter. Ask many a man concerning heaven, and earth, and sea, and other sensible things, and they will give some sensible answers, as that the earth was made for man and beast to live upon; the sea for fish and navigation; the air for man and beast to breathe in; the sun, moon, and stars for light, heat, and comfort; the beasts, fishes, fowls, &c., for man; but why thyself? Fewest would say for God; but if they speak true, some for themselves, some for their family, some for their pleasures, some for wealth, or some baser end, to which such a noble creature as man is should be destinated.    2. As fools live for the present time if they can get meat, drink, clothes, and necessaries for the present, they forecast nothing to come; even so ungodly men, if they can get wealth, and lay up things present for many years to come, they dream of no other heaven, they forecast no day of death, nor judgment; but oh, fool, what if thy soul be taken away this night? This was that which that fool thought not of; and as of their own, so they judge of all other men's felicity by things present, into which folly David himself was sliding when he confesseth himself as ignorant as a beast in this point, until he went into the sanctuary.    3. Fools are indocible and incorrigible; so the natural man put him to school, he learneth nothing by the book of the creatures, nor of the Creator in the Scriptures. Let God the great schoolmaster whip him, and bray him in the mortar of His judgments. He is a fool still, he leaveth not his old wonts.    4. Fools are so wise in their own conceits as they will abide no counsel; the natural man is wiser in his own eyes than seven men that can give a reason. (*Ibid.*)    *A significant contrast :*—The whole sentence is in form a contrast. It reminds the Cretans of what they had been in their unconverted condition. Against that it sets their present position as Christians. It grandly magnifies the Divine grace which had made them to differ. Out of this little biographical sketch there sprang two arguments for a meek behaviour. In the first place, these heathen neighbours, whose abusive attitude is so irritating, are not at all different from what you used to be. Recall what you were before God's grace changed you : precisely such as they are to-day. You did not then see your own foulness—not then, before the light came; neither do they see theirs now. Yet contemplate the hateful picture! What is pagan life?    1. So dark on religious matters as to possess no true acquaintance with God nor any just apprehension of spiritual truth at all.    2. As a result in part of this ignorance, disobedient in practice to all the requirements of Divine law.    3. Deluded indeed and misled to false conceptions of duty and false superstitions in worship.    4. Worse than that, enslaved to the desire for enjoyment, given over to indulgence in what seems most pleasant, no matter how immoral.    5. Socially leading a life too selfish to be either just or generous to others, cherishing rancour against one another for imagined slights and jealousy on account of superior fortune. Is this a just picture of the natural life as it mirrors itself in the enlightened Christian conscience? Sum it up in a single word : Are not such men repulsive as well as repellant—hateful as well as hating? Yet such were you. By the recollection of your former state, remembering the old darkness out of which you indeed have been rescued but not they, bear with them tenderly, think of them kindly! To this argument, a second joins itself : Out of that universal degradation of unregenerate nature, how is it that you have been rescued? By an effort of your own, or by Another's favour? Nay; not through any righteous actions or meritorious struggles to grow better, as you very well know; but through the mere mercy and cleansing and renewing power of "God our Saviour"; by a salvation which came to you unsought, found you helpless, surprised you with its benefits, and by its own virtue made new men of you in that day when you turned from your idols to become through Jesus Christ the heirs of life eternal! Saved thus by the sheer philanthropy of Heaven, have you none for your unsaved brothers? Changed by Divine mercy from a state like theirs, where is your mercy to them? They are as you were : treat them, then, as God treated you! How if

He had been as resentful against us, as quick to take offence and ready to strike? Ah, how ill it becomes a Christian to speak evil of others, to brawl, to give back word for word and blow for blow! By the kindness your Saviour has returned for your wrong, show to your still wrongful fellows what is that love of God to man which has been manifested unto you; that they too may be won to taste that God is good! (*J. O. Dykes, D.D.*)    *Transforming power of the Holy Spirit :*—Many years ago the people of Paris used to throw out the offal of fish and other garbage into the streets to be carted away as useless, but a clever man found out a way to extract from this filth a sweet scent, so pleasant and good that the Queen on her throne has it in her boudoir.    This is an example of what men can do with vile materials ; but God can do greater and mightier things with man than this, He can and will take the vilest person out of the mire and slime of sin's foul gutter, and make him glorious like His own Son by the transforming power of the Holy Spirit. (*J. Lawson.*)    **Disobedient.**—*Frowardness :*—This second degree of corruption of mind showeth that we are not only ignorant but froward in the things of God, and such as will not be persuaded, as the word in the original sounded ; and this is nothing else but a perverse disposition which fighteth against the truth.    Which a little better to understand, we must know that before our fall the mind of man had two faculties about the truth of God.    1. The knowledge of it so far as was meet.    2. An assent approving that knowledge.    Instead of which are succeeded two contrary corruptions since the fall.    1. Darkness instead of that light of knowledge.    2. Frowardness or reasoning against it.    For example : when the understanding of man, unconverted, conceiveth something of that we deliver out of the Word, whereas it should assent unto the law that it is good, and the gospel that it is the arm of God unto salvation, the wisdom of the flesh on the contrary, it becometh enmity to all this ; it can find evasions to shift off the curse ; it can covenant with hell and death.    And for the gospel, it is to one foolishness, to another offence.    Paul's preaching shall be counted madness, or malice, or something else which shall be reason and warrant enough to contemn it. (*T. Taylor, D.D.*)    **Deceived.**— *Various kinds of deceived persons :*—I. First, what a fearful deceit is that of many who strengthen themselves in their sins, sometimes PUTTING OFF ALL THE FEAR OF GOD'S JUSTICE, AND GROWING INTO CONTEMPT OF HIS JUDGMENTS ; sometimes absolving themselves from the guilt and curse of sin in hope of impunity, as though the Lord were become an idle essence, who hath put off the power of judging the world and revenging the wickedness of it.    Zephaniah noted in his time such a knot of ungodly men that were frozen in their dregs ; but how came they to this settledness in sin? "They said in their hearts, Tush ! the Lord will do neither good nor evil." And did this sin die with that age ?    II. A second and as fearful deceit as the former is that proud CONCEIT OF A KIND OF INBRED AND INHERENT RIGHTEOUSNESS of many reputed Christians, but indeed of such as wanting Christ's righteousness, seek to sew their own fig-leaves together.    The Pharisees in their time thanked God that they were not as other men ; they were whole and needed no physician.    The Laodiceans took themselves to be rich and increased and stood in need of nothing, but were deceived, and saw not themselves in a true glass, which would have showed their blindness and nakedness and poverty.    So how many civil, just-dealing, and harmless men everywhere are there at this day who overthrow themselves with this deceit, which ariseth sometimes by measuring themselves with themselves, as the proud preachers of Corinth seemed somewhat comparing themselves with themselves, and otherwhiles comparing themselves with others, whom they take greater sinners than themselves as the Pharisees did ; but especially through ignorance, or a dead knowledge of the righteousness of the law, they see not what strict righteousness God requireth, not their own corruption boiling within them, and so neglect all the sense of their secret lusts rising up against the love of God or man and that incessantly in them ? III. A third sort of men as far deceived as the former are SECURE PERSONS, who being baptized into the name of Christ as yet never came unto Him, but plod on in all dirty and sinful ways with many pretences underpropping themselves, but never examining duly whether they be right or no.    1. Superstitious persons who take up a voluntary religion which hath some show of wisdom and humbleness of mind ; worship God they think they do, but it is uncommanded ; devout they are, but resist the truth as those devout women which resisteth Paul.    2. General or Catholic Protestants of all, any, or no religion, these content themselves with the Jews to say, " the temple, the temple, the covenant, Abraham's seed," &c., so these find a religion established, and they love it because it is crowned and bringeth in abundance of property with it.    3. A rabble of idle Protestants whose carnal hearts turn the grace of God into wantonness.  4. The fourth sort may well carry the title of crafty Christians, as also of free-will Protestants, who for the present walk in a secure path and will not yet be acquainted with repentance for their sin they think. 5. The fifth sort of secure persons may be called sensible Protestants, who by outward things judge themselves high in God's books ; and many, both rich and poor, tread in this path.   Thus David observed of wicked rich men ; their houses were peaceable without fear, and because they are not in affliction like other men, pride compasseth them as a chain ; they seek not after God, nor sound and settled peace in Him, but little know they the end of that fat pasture.   He learned at the sanctuary that they were lifted up above other, as felons on the ladder, to come down with a greater mischief and breakneck.   But more marvellous it is that corrections and afflictions should become a pillow for security in many, which are God's spurs in the flank of the godly to prick them up, and rouse them from their drowsiness ; and yet many determine hence, and conclude without further ground, the Lord's love towards them, because of long and durable afflictions, of which they could never come to make good use, nor take any profit by them, whom God loveth, say they, He chasteneth.   And we are judged of the Lord, that we should not be condemned of the world, and when they are exceeding crossed in the world, and indeed cursed in their counsel and attempts, they thank God they have their punishment here in this life and so secure themselves from all future pains.   But this is but a guile and stratagem of Satan to cast his poison into the Lord's cup, and bane and destroy men with that which might be a special mean of their good, even a special provocation to make them seek reconciliation with God in Jesus Christ. IV.   The fourth and last sort of men who are deceived and wander out of the good way are SOME THAT SEEM TO THEMSELVES AND OTHERS TO BE VERY GOOD CHRISTIANS, AT LEAST NONE OF THE WORST, and yet many of them little better than some of the former. And these are of two sorts ; some are deceived in regard of their sins, others in regard of their graces or virtues.  1. Of the former sort.   There be some who, because they are not carried to such sins as they see others, they conclude presently that they are in the right way to heaven, whereas there may be a work of the Word and Spirit forcible against many sins, where there is no saving grace in the soul. 2. The latter sort are they that deceive themselves in turning their eyes from their sins to some virtues or graces which they find in their souls.   Hence have we men that can be diligent in hearing the Word, and that gladly with Herod, and think that enough to dispense with their holding of their Herodias, some sweet sin or other.   Others can rejoice and be affected as we have known soft-hearted Protestants, that could melt at sermons into tears with great affection, and yet have made little conscience of their ways, but not mortifying the deeds of the flesh, have yielded to their lusts the reins in all liberty.   Others can receive the Word, talk of it, yield a seemly obedience unto it ; any man would say they were surely good Christians, yet as bad ground they give it not depth enough ; they give it the understanding and some affection, but the will and the whole joy is not carried unto it. If they talk of it, it is but as such as only have tasted it with their tongues, as cooks do their services, but they have not filled their belly with it, as they for whom it is prepared.   Their sightly obedience is like Herod's, who did many things because John was a good man.   In a word, they can be reverent and liberal to ministers, kind to professors, forward in good motions, can lend their hands or purses to help the godly out of trouble, and yet in all these commendable duties are like a deceitful bow, which being cast and crooked, let the eye aim never so right at the mark, it casteth it quite besides all the way ; even all these, proceeding from deep hypocrisy, and done not purely, but sinister respects furthering them, deceive the soul and keep it far from the happiness of it.   (*Ibid.*)        **Serving divers lusts and pleasures.—** *Lusts and pleasures :*—Sins are called lusts because they be indeed so many inordinate desires against the commandment.   And pleasures, because of the imagination of them that commit sin, being carried away with the present pleasure and sweetness of them.   And diverse pleasures—1. Because they are many in themselves, and though every man yield not service to every one, yet some serve this, and some that, and every wicked man some.   Samson will be slave to his Delilah, in the lust of the flesh and uncleanness ; Nabal to his wealth, in the lust of the eye ; Herod to his vainglory, in the lust of pride of life.  2. Because they diversely carry men, even as a man in the sea is carried backward and forward and hurried with divers waves, for there is no stability nor settledness but in the fear of God.   The wicked are like the raging sea, and there is no peace to them, saith the Lord ; but as slaves having served one lust, they must presently be at the call and command of another, and if it command they must obey, although it call to the clean contrary course. (*Ibid.*)    *The slavery of sin:*—What slavery is like the slavery of sin? In every other case there is hope; there are lulls, at least, and intervals of anguish; there are alleviations, though perhaps they may be few and rare; there is patience, there is prayer; there may be the comfort of the cherished Spirit of God in the inner heart; there is death, in which the consummation of earthly tyranny works its own cure, and the slave is free for ever; but in the slavery of sin there is no hope, no lull, no check, no flight, no patience, no prayer, no inward peace of a religious spirit counterbalancing the outward misery of the fettered limbs; and death, the limit of the one slavery, is but the terrible " beginning of the end " of the other; when sin, which has been allowed to rule in the heart and members during life, declares itself visibly and unmistakably to be the very tyrant of souls himself, the Prince of Darkness, to whose sway his slave is consigned to all eternity. (*Bp. Moberly.*)    **Living in malice and envy, hateful, and hating one another.**—I. First, TO DISTINGUISH THE WORDS. The first of them, malice, is an evil affection of the heart, which properly desireth the hurt of our neighbour and rejoiceth in his fall. Envy is a contrary affection, but as wicked, for it grieveth at the neighbour's good, and fretteth itself at his prosperous and fortunate success in anything. Hateful may to good purpose be taken either actively, as it is read, namely for such as are in such extremity of wickedness, as they in every way are abominable creatures in themselves; or else passively, and so may be read hated, that is, justly execrable and odious unto others, both God and men. And hating one another, as full of poison and venomous hatred towards others as they could be unto us, requiting like for like, all which, although they show a most godless and comfortless condition, yet we lived in this graceless course, that is, passed our days, or at least a great part of them in time past, before we came to know the grace of God. II. Now this being the estate of every natural man, that his whole conversation is monstrously depraved, so as he spendeth his days and consumeth his time in malice, envy, hatred, and such hateful courses, IT MAY LET MANY A MAN SEE HOW LITTLE THEY ARE ESCAPED FROM THE FILTHINESS OF NATURE. For—1. How do the lives of most men show that the spirit which lusteth after envy ruleth them? and how doth that bitter root of malice and hatred shoot forth buds and blossoms at all seasons? (1) In affection, when as men grieve at the good and greatness of another, and cannot look upon the prosperity of a man whom they wish not so well unto, but with an evil eye, and the more they look upon it, the sorer still groweth their eye, accounting themselves after a sort wronged by him, if they cannot attain to his estate. (2) In men's speeches, how doth Satan tip many men's tongues and set them on fire with all manner of malicious and murdering speeches? What is more common speech than detraction and impairing from the just praise of men? (3) In the actions of life, what a cloud of frivolous suits, and yet fiery enough, witness the malice and envy of men's hearts. If a man's beast look but over another man's hedge, and so make but offer of a trespass, or any other such trivial colour is sufficient to fire the gunpowder within, and to carry the controversy with such violence, as one must yield or both be blown up. But the most fearful and wretched work of this inbred corruption is most apparent in the pursuit of good men, because they are good; for who, be he never so good, can stand before envy, which feedeth even upon virtue and goodness itself? 2. This must teach us that profess ourselves to be the Lord's, to abhor all the sins of this suit, and to banish such filthy fruits of the flesh, which God giveth them up unto who are of a reprobate mind; and have nothing to do with such wicked inmates, which are ever plotting to set the whole tenement on fire, and which bring rottenness into their own bones and bowels. As well said a godly man of Cain, he had half killed and consumed himself with malice before he killed his brother. And not to urge the multitude of reasons which to this purpose offer themselves, I will only name those two which are couched in the verse. (1) Because that we profess that we were such in times past, but now are begotten unto God, which were it not a forcible reason, the apostle would not so often beat upon it (Col. iii. 8; 1 Cor. v. 8; James i. 18). (2) These hateful sins make us justly odious—(*a*) To God (Prov. xiv. 32). The wicked is cast away for his malice both root and fruit. (*b*) To man, in that they wage battle against Christian love, which is the preservative of all society. 3. Lastly, let every one learn timely to take in hand this crooked nature before he be accustomed to evil; for else as hardly as a blackamoor changeth his skin shalt thou become changed when wicked nature and worse custom have both barred thy repentance and bound thy sins faster upon thee. And because much of this folly is bound up in the hearts of children and servants, let masters and fathers seek seasonably to drive it out; fathers especially, because they helped their children into it, must by Christian instruction, godly example, and the rod of correction, labour to help them out, and thus do their best to make their children a part of amends. Zuinglius calleth this corruption the disease of nature. And herein it fitly resembleth the diseases of the body, the which the longer they continue the more incurable they are; and if they be let go too long they bring certain death; and therefore let parents and masters, many of whom are careful enough to prevent and seek out for help against the diseases which threaten the bodily death of their children and servants, take up some care to remove that everlasting death which this evil threateneth, and will certainly bring if in due season it be not repressed. Teach thy child and train him in the Scriptures from a child; teach thy servant the trade of Christianity and godliness, for thou art no less bound to deliver him the principles of this calling, as the particular to which he is bound. Use good means to get them the light of knowledge, opposed against this blindness of mind; work upon their wills to break them from the follies and vanities of youth, opposed to this rebellion of will; bring them at least to outward conformity in their conversation, opposed to this general depravation of manners. These things they will not forget in their age, or if they do, the peril is their own; thou hast done thy duty. One thing remember: thy servants, thy children are all poisoned, and have need of some present antidote. (*T. Taylor, D.D.*) *Malice:*—Malice is the devil's picture. Lust makes men brutish, and malice makes them devilish. Malice is mental murder; you may kill a man and never touch him. "Whosoever hateth his brother is a murderer." (*T. Watson.*) *Malice self-destructive:*—A bee, in inflicting a sting, it is said, leaves it barbed weapon in the wound, and, being thus mutilated, inevitably dies. The bee stings itself to death in trying to sting some one else. Your stinging may hurt others and kill yourself. *Malice and rancour:* —Malice, in Latin, *malitia*, from *malus*, bad, signifies the very essence of badness lying in the heart. Rancour is only continued hatred; the former requires no external cause to provoke it, it is inherent in the mind; the latter must be caused by some personal offence. Malice is properly the love of evil for evil's sake, and is, therefore, confined to no number or quality of objects, and limited to no circumstances; rancour, as it depends upon external objects for its existence, so it is confined to such objects only as are liable to cause displeasure or anger. Malice will impel a man to do mischief to those who have not injured him; rancour can subsist only between those who have had sufficient connection to be at variance. (*G. Crabb.*)

Vers. 4–7. **But after that the kindness and love of God.**—*The power of God's kindness:*—In the incarnation of Christ, His life and miracles and mercies and divinest teaching; in His sacrificial death upon the cross, His resurrection and ascension, we have that manifestation of the kindness of God which is intended and calculated to lift us up out of our sins, and to bring us into His own most holy fellowship. And see how broad and far-reaching this kindness is; it is not for the elect nor for the Church, though these of course are included, but for man as such —for the whole human family, without exception. Wide as the world is Thy command, vast as eternity Thy love! We know something of this power of kindness to subdue the evil and develop the good even between man and man. It has many a time succeeded where everything else has failed, and where it fails we know of nothing else likely to succeed. Pinel, the celebrated Frenchman, was the first to introduce into Europe a more humane treatment of the insane. In the madhouse at Paris there had been confined for some twenty years a sea-captain, furious in his madness, ferocious and untameable. Two of the keepers had been struck dead by him with a blow from his manacled hands. He was chained to his seat when Pinel approached him, and with cheerful face and kindly manner, said, "Captain, I am going to release you and take you into the open air." The mariner laughed out right and said, "You dare not do it." It was done, the poor wretch staggered to the door accompanied by Pinel, and lifting up his eyes to the blue heavens above, a sight he had not seen for twenty years, said, as the tears coursed down his face, "Oh, how beautiful!" and from that hour became perfectly docile. If human kindness meets such returns, shall God's love go unrequited, no echo answering to the Divine from the human? (*J. W. Lance.*) *St. Paul's gospel:*—Note at the outset two points. First, the central words, on which as on a peg the whole structure both of thought and of expression hangs, is the proposition—"He saved us." In what sense is man lost? In what must his salvation consist? What is necessary in order to it ? In proportion as these questions are answered in a profound or in a shallow way will be our appreciation of those redemptive actions of God—the mission of His Son and the outpouring of His Spirit. Next, let it be noted that in this saving of man by God three leading points have to be attended to : The source or origin of it ; the method of it ; the issues and effects of it. What we have to ask from St. Paul is a distinct reply to these three great queries—1. FROM WHAT SOURCE DID GOD'S SAVING ACTIVITY ON OUR BEHALF TAKE ITS RISE ? 2. Through what methods does it operate upon us ? 3. To what ultimate issues does it conduct those who are its objects ? I. The answer to the first of these need not detain us long. True, it is a point of primary importance for the immediate purpose of the writer in the present connection. What he is engaged in enforcing upon Cretan Christians is a meek and gentle deportment toward their heathen neighbours. With this design, it is most pertinent to observe that they have not themselves to thank for being in a better state than others—saved Christians instead of lost heathen ; not themselves, but God's gratuitous kindness. It is worth remarking too in this connection, how singularly human are the terms selected to express the saving love of God. Two terms are used. The one is God's "kindliness" or sweet benignity, like that gentle friendliness which one helpful neighbour may show to another in distress. The other is God's "love for man," literally, His philanthropy, or such special benevolence to all who wear the human form as might be looked for indeed among the members of our race themselves, but which it startles one to find is shared in by Him who made us. These curiously human phrases are chosen, it is to be presumed, because St. Paul would have us imitate in our dealings with one another God's behaviour towards us. In substance, however, they describe just the same merciful and compassionate love in God our Saviour, to which the whole New Testament traces back man's salvation as to its prime or fontal source. It is quite in harmony with this ascription of our salvation to God's love as its fountain-head, that, throughout his account of the process, Paul continues to make God the subject of his sentence, and man its object. All along the line God appears as active and we as receptive ; He is the doer or giver, man the field of His operations and the recipient of His benefits. II. We pass next from the epiphany of God's unmerited kindness in the advent of the Saviour, TO THAT PROCESS BY WHICH INDIVIDUALS, at Crete or elsewhere, BECOME PARTAKERS IN HIS SALVATION. The conversion of one born a heathen wears a conspicuous character, which is usually awanting to cases of conversion among ourselves. The day of their baptism, on which they sealed their conversion to the Christian faith, had marked a complete revolution in every department of their life. It had in many cases severed family ties. It had in all cases made them marked men in society. It had brought them into the circle of a strange community, and affiliated them to new comrades under the badges of a foreign religion. Outwardly, no less than inwardly, they were become new creatures; the old had passed away and all things were become new. The font at which they sealed their vows of discipleship had proved to be a second birth—the starting-point for a changed life. Of course it is still the same among the converts who are won at our mission stations abroad ; and we require to keep the condition of an infant missionary church well in mind if we would do justice to such language as St. Paul has here employed to describe the conversion of his readers. He speaks of the change in phrases borrowed both from its outer and inner side, its ritual and its spiritual elements. Inwardly, the convert was saved by the power of the Holy Spirit regenerating and renewing him. Outwardly, this spiritual second birth found its expressive seal in the bath or laver of holy baptism. Paul's language could not mislead his Cretan readers. But it was admirably adapted to revive their most touching recollections. As they read his words, each one of them seemed to himself to stand once more, as on the most memorable and solemn day of his life, beside the sacred font. Once more he saw himself descend into the laver to symbolise the cleansing of his conscience from idol worship, from unbridled indulgence, from a vain conversation, by the precious death and burial of his Lord. By that act how utterly had he broken once for all with his earlier life and its polluted associations, leaving them behind like a buried past ! Coming up afresh to commence the new pure career of a Christian disciple, he had received the symbolic white robe amid the congratulations of the brotherhood, who thronged around to welcome the new-born with a kiss of love—to welcome him among that little band who, beneath the cross, had sworn to fight the devil in Jesus' strength, and, if need arose, to shed their blood for Jesus' name ! How keenly, as all this rushed back upon the Christian's recollection, must he have felt that a change so wonderful and blessed was the Lord's doing. What power, save God's, could have turned backward the currents of his being, reversing the influences of education with the traditions of his ancestry and the usages of his fatherland? What hand but the Almighty's could have snatched him out of the doomed nations over which Satan reigned, to translate him into that kingdom of light—the kingdom of God's dear Son? Where was the spiritual force that could have opened his eyes, cleansed his conscience, quickened his heart, and made a new man out of the old one, save that Divine Spirit whose advent at Pentecost had been the birthday of a new era for the human family? The grateful praise which could not fail to mount to the lips at such a recollection, was a doxology to the Triune God, into whose name he had been baptized: to the Father unseen, eternal fountain-head of mercy; to the Incarnate Son, sole channel for its manifestation to guilty men; to the Holy Ghost, who, like a stream of life, had been plentifully poured forth from the Father, through the Son, to be the effectual giver of life in sinful souls! III. Consider, in the last place, WHITHER THIS SAVING ACTIVITY ON THE PART OF THE GODHEAD IS CARRYING SUCH AS SURRENDER THEMSELVES TO IT. What is to be the outcome of His redemptive undertaking? In this alone, that the sinner is justified freely by His grace? Is the release of the guilty from condemnation and penalty the issue of all that God has done in His kindness? No; but that, "having been justified, we should be made heirs." Birth of the Divine Spirit involves sonship to God Himself. The privilege of sons is to inherit; "heirs," therefore, of "life eternal." The word is one which opens, as it were, a door into heaven. It is true that it is not yet apparent what the children of God shall hereafter be, for purity, for freedom, for wisdom, for felicity. But forth from that opened door, how there streams to meet us a radiance of the unseen glory, which in the twilight of this lifetime dazzles our earthly eyes! For that undiscovered heritage of the saints in light we can only hope. To this point, therefore, and no further, does the Christian gospel conduct its disciple. Here for the present it leaves him, sitting patient and expectant by the gate of Paradise, to await, with steadfast heart, the moment that shall disclose to him his patrimony of bliss. While he sits and waits, shall he not behave himself as a child of God, and strive to grow more meet for the heritage of the holy? (*J. O. Dykes, D.D.*) *God's kindness :*—The sun that shines on you shall set, summer streams shall freeze, and deepest wells go dry; but God's love is a stream that never freezes, a fountain that never fails, a sun that never sets in night, a shield that never breaks in fight. *God's kindness only partially seen by the soul :*—The sun appears red through a fog, and generally red at rising and setting, the red rays having a great momentum which gives them power to traverse so dense an atmosphere, which the other rays have not. The increased quantity of atmosphere which oblique rays must traverse, loaded with the mists and vapours which are usually formed at those times, prevents the other rays from reaching us. It is thus that but a few of the rays of God's love—like the red rays—reach the soul. Sin, passion, and unbelief surround it as with a dense atmosphere of mists and vapours; and, though the beams of God's love are poured out innumerable as the sun's rays, they are lost and scattered, and few of them shine upon the soul. (*H. G. Salter.*) *God's love incomparable :* —If an angel were to fly swiftly over the earth on a summer morning, and go into every garden—the king's, the rich man's, the peasant's, the child's—and were to bring from each one the choicest, loveliest, sweetest flower that blooms in each, and gather them all in one cluster in his radiant hands, what a beautiful bouquet it would be! And if an angel were to fly swiftly over the earth into every sweet and holy home, into every spot where one heart yearns over another, and were to take out of every father's heart, and every mother's heart, and out of every heart that loves, its holiest flower of affection, and gather all into one cluster, what a blessed love-garland would his eyes behold! What a holy love would this aggregation of all earth's loves be! Yet infinitely sweeter and holier than this grouping of all earth's holiest affections is the love that fills the heart of our Father in heaven. (*John R. Miller.*) *God's love to men :*—I was leaving a gentleman's house where I had been paying a visit, said a minister [of the gospel, when I put this question to the servant-maid who was about to open the door: "My friend, do you love God?" "I am afraid not," she answered, "and I fear I never shall." "Well," I said, "you may at least depend on this—it is certain that God loves you." "How can you possibly tell that?" asked the master of the house, who was going downstairs with me. "This is the first time you have ever seen this woman; you know nothing about her character. You cannot tell whether she attends to her duties properly or not." "Never mind about that," I said. "It is certain that God loves her, and you too. I am quite sure of this, because God has told us that His love to us does not depend on what we are, or what we deserve. The Bible tells us, ' God so loved the world that He gave His only begotten Son' to die for it; and again it tells us, ' Herein is love ; not that we loved God ; but that God loved us, and sent His Son to die for our sins ' " (1 John iv. 10). " If that is so," said the gentleman, " and your words seem to prove it, what a shame it is that I don't love Him. May I say to myself, without any fear of making a mistake, ' It is certain that God loves me ' ? " " Indeed you may," I said ; " and I pray to God you may soon be able to say, ' It is certain that I love Him.' " And Jesus may well be called a loving messenger, because He came into the world, not only to tell us this great truth, but also to be Himself the proof of it. (*Richard Newton.*) *The disposition of God :*—God's forgiveness is unspeakably generous, and, if I may so say, unspeakably more fine, delicate, and full of strange gentleness than ours. I believe the more we come to know the disposition of Almighty God, the more we shall find in it, in magnitude and power, those traits which we call, among men, rare in their excellence. And when God undertakes for us, if we have thrown ourselves upon His mercy, and we have really meant to be His, and are really striving to be His, I believe that His feeling toward us transcends that of the tenderest love, of the most generous parentage, and of the most romantic friendship in men ; that He is not less than men in these emotions of friendship and of generosity in it, but transcendently more ; that in Him they spread over a broader ground, and take on a more wondrous experience. And instead of being likely to over-estimate the volume of the Divine goodness and mercy towards those who fear Him, we are always under the mark. We always think less of God, and more meanly of the Divine nature than we ought to do. (*H. W. Beecher.*) **Not by works of righteousness.**— *Salvation, not of works, but of grace :*—I. WORKS OF RIGHTEOUSNESS WE CANNOT PERFORM, AND THEREFORE THEY CANNOT SAVE US. 1. Could we render such works, they would save us. 2. Without rendering such works, we cannot be saved. II. REDEMPTIVE MERCY HAS BEEN VOUCHSAFED TO US, AND THEREFORE WE MAY BE SAVED. 1. The special work of this redemptive mercy. (1) Cleansing. (2) Renewal. 2. The Divine Administrator of this redemptive mercy—the Holy Ghost. 3. The glorious medium of this redemptive mercy—Jesus Christ. 4. The sublime result—" That being justified," &c. (1) This rectitude inspires with the highest hope. (2) Inaugurates the highest relationship —" Him." (*Homilist.*) *The source of salvation :*— I. SALVATION BASED UPON DIVINE MERCY. " Kindness" or goodness, "Love." Margin, " pity." Literally, " philanthropy " ; that is " the love of man" (John iii. 16). II. SALVATION INDEPENDENT OF HUMAN MERIT. 1. There is in the best of us an absence of good (*i.e.*, meritorious) works. 2. Redemption can only be attained by a new creation. " Regeneration," or " new birth." III. SALVATION PROVIDED ABUNDANTLY. 1. Abundantly—as an exhibition of abundant mercy. 2. Abundantly—as a remedy for great sin. 3. Abundantly as a provision for all who will repent. IV. SALVATION EVERLASTING. 1. Justification a ground of hope. 2. Hope of eternal life. (*F. Wagstaff.*) *The way of salvation :*—I. SALVATION IS NOT EFFECTED BY HUMAN AGENCY. 1. Where there is no salvation, there are no works of righteousness (Gen. vi. 5 ; Gal. v. 19-21). 2. Works of righteousness, even where they exist, possess no saving effect. They are the evidences, not the causes, of salvation. 3. The Bible disclaims the merit of human agency in salvation (Isa. lxiv. 6 ; Dan. ix. 7 ; Rom. iii. 20-28, xi. 5, 6 ; Gal. ii. 21 ; Eph. ii. 8, 9). II. SALVATION ORIGINATES IN THE DIVINE COMPASSION. " According to His mercy He saved us," &c. 1. Our salvation accords with the tender sympathies attributed to that mercy (Psa. xxv. 6, li. 6 ; Isa. lxiii. 15 ; Luke i. 78 ; James v. 11). 2. It accords with the readiness ascribed to that mercy (Neh. ix. 17 ; Isa. xxx. 18 ; Mic. vii. 18). 3. It accords with the description given of the greatness, fulness, and extent of that mercy (Num. xiv. 19 : Psa. v. 7 ; Neh. ix. 19 ; Psa. cxix. 64, cxlv. 9). 4. It accords with the perpetuity of that mercy (Psa. cxviii. 1). III. SALVATION IS ATTENDED BY AN IMPORTANT CHANGE. We are saved " by the washing of regeneration," that is, delivered from sin and all its tremendous consequences in the other world. 1. Delivered from the love of sinful pleasures and carnal delights, by having the " love of God shed abroad in our hearts." 2. From the guilt of sinful practices, by having a knowledge of salvation by the remission of our sins. 3. From the prevalence of sinful habits, by the principles of holiness, and the power of the Divine Spirit. 4. From the commission of sinful acts, by the total regeneration of our natures (1 John v. 18). IV. SALVATION IS ACCOMPLISHED BY A DIVINE INFLUENCE. " By the renewing of the Holy Ghost." All the influences of God upon the human soul are effected by the agency of the Holy Ghost. 1. The light and information which we receive on Divine subjects are communicated by the Holy Ghost (John xiv. 26; 1 Cor. ii. 11, 12 ; 1 John ii. 20). 2. The conviction we have of our personal danger is derived from the same source (John xvi. 8). 3. The change which is produced in the minds of Christian believers is attributed to the Holy Ghost (John iii. 5–8 ; 1 Cor. vi. 11 ; 2 Cor. iii. 18). 4. The assurance of salvation is by the witness of the Holy Ghost —the Comforter (John xiv. 16; Rom. viii. 16). Inferences : 1. How awful the delusion of those who depend on themselves or their works for salvation! 2. How deeply we are indebted to the Divine mercy for salvation! Let us sing of the mercies of the Lord for ever. 3. How indispensable is. regeneration! Salvation without it is impossible. 4. How deeply anxious should we be to secure the influences and agency of the Holy Ghost (Luke xi. 13). (*Sketches of Sermons.*) *Salvation :*—I. SALVATION IS NOT BY WORKS. 1. Because of our relation to God. We are His creatures; we owe Him everything always; and therefore never can acquire any surplus merit to place to the account of past shortcomings and offences. 2. Because of our moral inability to perform works of righteousness, on account of the depravity and corruption of our nature. 3. Because every attempt to procure salvation by works implies the principle of " value for value," and our works would be no equivalent for the salvation required. II. THE TRUE SOURCE AND CHARACTER OF SALVATION. 1. It has its origin in God's kindness and love toward man (ver. 4). 2. His kindness and love were manifested through Jesus Christ our Saviour (ver. 6). 3. This salvation includes justification by His grace, adoption into His family by His love, regeneration by the power of the Holy Ghost, the blessed hope of eternal life while here, and the blessed reality of eternal life hereafter (vers. 5, 7). (*O. McCutcheon.*) *Salvation by grace :*—I. PREVIOUS CHARACTER. Two great lessons— 1. Adoring gratitude. 2. Deep humility. II. PRESENT STATE. Sinners saved by grace. 1. The originating cause of salvation. 2. The efficient means of salvation. III. FUTURE EXPECTATIONS. 1. This hope is supporting. 2. Sanctifying. (*Expository Outlines.*) *Salvation viewed from God's side :*—In this passage, which is a brief but pregnant epitome of the gospel, the scheme of man's salvation is regarded only from the side on which it is wholly God's work, without taking note of the conditions and qualifications which, however much they too are God's work, are required from the co-operation of man. The apostle was dwelling on the truth that the change referred to in ver. 3 is not due to ourselves or our own merit, but to God's grace. He therefore had no occasion to allude here to the qualifications or stipulations required at baptism, nor to the faith by which man is justified, nor to " the working out his own salvation," which is one of the instruments by which the Holy Ghost renews us day by day, nor to the holiness which is the character and badge of the heirs of eternal life. All this is needed ; but, viewed from God's side, it is not by anything which man has done or could do, but by His own free mercy that God has saved him. (*Bp. Jackson.*) *Working hard for salvation :*—A Christian lady was visiting a poor, sickly woman, and after conversing with her for a little she asked her if she had found salvation yet. " No," she replied, " but I am working hard for it." " Ah, you will never get it that way," the lady said. " Christ did all the working when He suffered and died for us, and made complete atonement for our sins. You must take salvation solely as a gift of free, unmerited grace, else you can never have it at all." The poor woman was at first amazed beyond measure, and felt for the moment as if all hope had been taken from her ; but very soon the enlightenment came, and she was enabled to rest joyously on Jesus alone. When speaking afterwards of the friend who had been so helpful, she said, " Oh, how I will welcome her into heaven, for she guided me to the Saviour." *Good works no ground of acceptance with God :*—A man whom I knew in Chicago failed in business, and got into difficulties. He had paid his creditors what proved to be worthless notes, for he had no assets. He coolly proposed to put matters right by handing to his creditors more worthless notes. Now, many of you are trying to act like that. You have no spiritual assets, you have nothing with which to pay, and yet you are proposing to pay God with what is worthless to save you. Suppose you owe a grocer £20, and you go and tell him that you are not going in debt in future, what answer would you expect? He would say : " All very well so far as it goes; I'm glad to hear it. But your keeping out of debt in the future won't pay what you owe me now. What about that £20 already due ? " A hundred years ago, when Prince Charles the Pretender headed a rebellion, many risked their lives and property for his sake, feeling sure that if he succeeded he would reward them handsomely. But he did not succeed. He lost, and so they lost. What could they get from him, when he had nothing to pay? At the close of our late American Civil War, between the Federals and rebel Confederates, a man in Georgia wanted to pay, as his tax, money issued by the Confederate Government. But of course the officer representing the revenue of the Federal Government said, "That won't do. Your money is worthless. It was issued by rebels, and we cannot accept it." The man who expects God to accept him on the ground of his good works, or of anything that he can do, is acting like that. In America no man lost his life or his estate through engaging in that great rebellion, because mercy was shown. But for all that the government could not recognise the currency of rebels. Mercy is offered to all men, but everything with which they hope to purchase pardon and peace is simply worthless. (*Major Whittle.*) *Good works not to be relied on:*—Though good works may be our Jacob's staff to walk with on earth, yet they cannot be our Jacob's ladder to climb to heaven with. To lay the salve of our services upon the wound of our sins, is as if a man who is stung by a wasp should wipe his face with a nettle; or as if a person should busy himself in supporting a tottering fabric with a burning fire-brand. (*T. Secker.*) **The washing of regeneration.**—*Regeneration:*—The main thoughts which run through these verses are the cause and method of redemption. These are set against the old state of sin, in which we were "foolish, disobedient, deceived, serving divers lusts and pleasures, living in malice and envy, hateful, and hating one another." I. SALVATION AS TO ITS PRIMARY CAUSE. The cause is Divine, lodged within the Divine heart, and is twofold. 1. Love. The love of God for a "world of sinners lost," is the first cause of man's redemption. That love is like Himself—free, boundless, inexplicable, and eternal. "For God so loved the world," &c. "God is love." 2. Mercy. The object of love can only be touched by the hand of mercy. This speaks of the sinfulness of our nature, and that compassion which has found a way for love to operate on the human heart. The original of the gospel is not a human device, or the work of righteousness, but the gift of God to fallen man. II. SALVATION AS TO ITS METHOD. There are here also two observations made by the apostle. 1. The removal of guilt. The washing of regeneration means the removal of the guilt of the soul, and the acceptance of the peace of the Father. It was the custom to sprinkle the proselytes with water, in token of their renouncing their idolatry, and be made clean to enter the service of the true God. 2. The renewal of Divine influences. The Spirit rests on believers to light them, and to guide them; also to comfort them. Regeneration must be followed by the indwelling Spirit. This is a comparison taken from nature, where all living things are renewed in the spring of the year. Thus we are reminded of the necessity for the constant power of the Holy Ghost in our daily life. (*Weekly Pulpit.*) *Regeneration:*—I. THE RENEWING. 1. It creates a new thing in man (2 Cor. v. 17). Like a vessel with a new commander, steering a new course, by a new compass, to a new haven. The old nature remains, though the new nature has come, and there are now in the one man the carnal and the spiritual mind—the human and the Divine life—that which is born of the flesh, and that which is born of the Spirit—the old man of sin that is to be crucified, and the new man that is to be renewed daily in the image of Him that created him, until he shall come to the full stature of a man in Christ Jesus. 2. It is a restoration of a former state. That which was lost by sin is restored by regeneration. 3. It is a renovation of the whole man. Though every part be not thoroughly sanctified, yet the regenerate are sanctified in every part. They have a perfection of parts, though not of degrees. The renewing is going on in every part, though every part is not perfectly renewed. The seat and centre of this renewing work is the heart. The might of the Spirit is exerted in the inner man. And from thence He works outwardly to the utmost extremity. Just as the vital fluid is driven by the propelling power of the animal heart to every extremity of the body, so is the renewing energy sent forth from the centre of moral and spiritual life—the inner man by the power of the indwelling spirit. And so will He continue to work until the day of perfection shall come, when we 'shall be presented faultless before the throne of glory, without spot or wrinkle, or any such thing. II. THE RENEWER. "The Holy Ghost." 1. Not an influence, but a Person, having ascribed to Him in Holy Scripture the attributes and actions of a person, and that a Divine and omnipotent person. To Him is confided the work of carrying out the purposes of the Father by applying the truth and work of the Son. It is by the Spirit's overshadowing of the soul that the new creature is conceived and brought forth. The babe of grace can call no man on earth father. And while a man's regeneration is not of his fellow-man, neither is it of himself. They which are born of the flesh contribute nothing to their own being, neither do they that are born of the Spirit; they are begotten of God. 2. But the Holy Ghost, in His renewing, uses—Instrumentality. The one grand instrument is the Word (James i. 18; 1 Peter i. 23). (1) It may be by the Word read. Augustine and Luther tell us they were converted by the reading of the Word; so have many thousands of others. In Madagascar we have a striking illustration of this, in the conversion of many thousands by reading only fragments of .the Word of God, left in their country by the banished missionaries. (2) It may be by the Word remembered. I read once of an aged man, who had lived an ungodly life, and had wandered thousands of miles away from his native home, who one day, while he was sitting under a tree, had suddenly brought to his remembrance truths he had read and heard when a child and youth, but which had been long forgotten. They came with such irresistible power that his conversion was the result. (3) It may be by the Word lived and acted out. There are those who will not read the written Word, neither will they go to hear the Word preached, but who are willing readers—unconscious readers of the lives of Christians among whom they dwell. God expects His people, whom He has regenerated, to be " living epistles of Christ, known and read of all men." Was it not in this sense that Paul exhorted believing wives to win their unbelieving husbands " without the Word," by their " chaste conversation, coupled with fear." (4) It may be by the Word spoken—as a man would speak to his friend. The kind and faithful teachings of friendship have often proved the instrument, in the hands of the Holy Ghost, for the accomplishment of this great object. " I owe much to the public ministry of the Word," said a recent convert to his minister; " but it was the Word spoken by a friend that was made by God the immediate instrument of my conversion." (5) But it is principally by the preached Word that God works. The public ministry of the Word is God's appointed institution for the accomplishment of this glorious end. The preacher is the spiritual husbandman, sowing broadcast the incorruptible seed of the Word, which shall spring up and bring forth fruit, some thirty, some sixty, and some a hundred-fold. This is all the minister can do; sow the seed in prayer, and faith, and hope—God must give the increase. (*H. Quick.*)     *The laver of regeneration :—* I. We must conceive that IN EVERY SACRAMENT THERE BE THREE ESSENTIAL PARTS, the absence of any of which destroys the whole. 1. The sign. 2. The thing signified. 3. The analogy between them, which is the union of them both. The first is some outward and sensible thing; the second, inward and spiritual; the third, mixed of them both. As in baptism the sign is water, the thing signified the blood of Christ. The analogy or union standeth in this resemblance, that as the former outwardly washeth the filthiness of the body, so the latter inwardly purgeth the soul from all sin. By reason of which relation and near affection between the sign and the thing signified, it is usual in the Scriptures by an improper, but sacramental speech. 1. To call the sign by the name of the thing signified, and contrarily. And thus baptism is called the washing of the new birth, because it is a sign, seal and instrument of it. 2. To ascribe that to the sign which is proper to the thing signified, and so baptism is here said to save, as also 1 Pet. iii. 21, which is indeed the property of the blood of Christ (1 John i. 7), but by the near affinity of these two in the sacrament it is said so to do, to note unto us—(1) Not to conceive of the sacramental elements as bare and naked signs, so to grow into the contempt of them. (2) As we may not conceive them idle sins, so neither idle signs by insisting in them as though they were the whole sacrament, for they are but outward, whereas the principal matter of a sacrament is spiritual and inward. (3) That then we truliest conceive of a sacrament, when by looking at the one of these we see both, neither making the sign a vain symbol, nor yet ascribing anything to it transcending the nature of it, such as are the peculiars and the prerogatives of God, but in the sign and action, which is outward, be led to those which are spiritual and inward. II. HOW IS BAPTISM THEN THE LAVER OF REGENERATION ? 1. As it is an institution of God signifying the good pleasure of God for the pardoning of sin, and accepting to grace in Christ; for as the word signifieth this, so doth also the sacrament which is a visible word. And thus is it truly said of the Word and sacraments too that they save and sanctify, because they signify the good pleasure of God in saving and sanctifying us, even as we say a man is saved by the king's pardon, not that the pardon properly doth it, for that is the mere merciful disposition of the king, but because the pardon (written and sealed perhaps by another), signed by the king, is the ordinary instrument to manifest the merciful mind of the king in pardoning such a malefactor, 2. As it is a seal or pledge of our sanctification and salvation, as certainly assuring these to the soul of the believer, as he is or can be assured of the other, that as a man having a bond of a thousand pounds sealed him may truly say of it, here is my thousand pound, that is, a security, as surely confirming it unto me as if I had it in my hands, or as I have this even so may the believing party baptized say of his baptism, Here is my regeneration, here is my salvation. 3. As it is a means to excite and provoke the faith of the receiver to lay hold upon the grace of the sacrament, and apply it to these purposes, in which regard it be as truly said to renew as faith is said to justify, and that is only as it may be a means or hand to lay hold on Christ our righteousness; so baptism is a means helping forward our renewing by the true understanding and conscionable and serious meditation of it. 4. In that in the right use of it, it giveth and exhibiteth Christ and all His merits to the fit receiver, for then God's grace putteth forth itself, and after a sort conveyeth itself in and by this instrument into the heart of the worthy receiver. And thus principally it is the laver of regeneration, because in it and by it as a means and organ the Holy Ghost freely worketh His grace in such as in whom He delighteth. (*T. Taylor, D.D.*) *The laver of regeneration :*—On man's side there is the washing with water ; and on God's side there is the washing away of sin and pouring out of the Spirit. The body is purified, the soul is purified, and the soul is hallowed. The man is washed, is justified, is sanctified. He is regenerated : he is " a new creature." " The old things," his old principles, motives, and aims, then and there " passed away": " behold, they are become new " (2 Cor. v. 17). Can any one reasonably doubt that, when the apostle speaks of " the washing of regeneration," he means the Christian rite of baptism, in which, and by means of which, the regeneration takes place ? We are fully justified by his language here in asserting that it is by means of the baptismal washing that the regeneration takes place ; for he asserts that God " saved us through the washing of regeneration." The laver or bath of regeneration is the instrument or means by which God saved us. Such is the natural, and almost the necessary meaning of the Greek construction. And there are numerous analogies which throw light upon the question, proving to us that there is nothing exceptional in God (who of course does not need any means or instruments) being willing to use them, doubtless because it is better for us that He should use them. In what way is the employment of perceptible means a help to us ? In two at least. It serves the double purpose of being both a test to faith and an aid to faith. 1. The acceptance of divinely appointed means is necessarily a test of faith. Human intellect is apt to assume that Omnipotence is above using instruments. "Is it likely," we ask, " that the Almighty would employ these means ? Are they not altogether beneath the dignity of the Divine nature ? Man needs tools and materials ; but God needs neither. It is not credible that He has ordained these things as conditions of His own operation." All which is the old cry of the captain of the host of Syria. Therefore humbly to accept the means which God has revealed as the appointed channels of His spiritual blessings is a real test of the recipient's faith. He is thus enabled to perceive for himself whether he does sincerely believe or not; whether he has the indispensable qualification for receiving the promised blessing. 2. The employment of visible means is a real aid to faith. It is easier to believe that an effect will be produced, when one can perceive something which might contribute to produce the effect. It is easier to believe when one sees means than when none are visible ; and it is still easier to believe when the means seem to be appropriate. The man who was born blind would more readily believe that Christ would give him sight when he perceived that Christ was using spittle and clay for the purpose; for at that time these things were supposed to be good for the eyes. And what element in nature is more frequently the instrument both of life and of death than water? What could more aptly signify purification from defilement ? What act could more simply express death to sin and a rising again to righteousness than a plunge beneath the surface of the water and a re-issuing from it ? Faith in the inward gift, promised by God to those who believe and are baptized, becomes more easy when the outward means of conferring the gift, not only are readily perceived, but are recognised as suitable. In this way our faith is aided by God's employment of means. Is the " renewing of the Holy Ghost " the same thing as the " washing of regeneration " ? In this passage the two expressions refer to the same fact, but in their respective meanings they are not co-extensive. The Greek construction is ambiguous like the English; and we cannot be sure whether St. Paul means that God saved us by means of the washing and by means of the renewing, or that God saved us by means of a laver, which is both a laver of regeneration and a laver of renewal. The latter is more probable : but in either case the reference is to one and the same event in the Christian's life. The laver and the renewing refer to baptism; and the regeneration and the renewing refer to baptism; viz., to the new birth which is then effected. But, nevertheless, the two expressions are not co-extensive in meaning. The laver and the regeneration refer to one fact, and to one fact only : a fact which takes place once for all and can never be repeated. A man cannot have the new birth a second time, any more than he can be born a second time : and hence no one may be baptized twice. But the renewing of the Holy Spirit may take place daily. (*A. Plummer, D.D.*) *Spiritual washing :—* The following is related in the life of the late Dr. Guthrie. James Dundee, a weaver, lived on a lone moor, where, beyond his wife's, he had no society but that of God and nature. James might have been a poet, though I don't know that he ever cultivated the muse; a man he was of such an impassioned nature, lofty thoughts, and singularly vivid imagination. On the morning of a communion Sabbath he rose, bowed down by a sense of sin, in great distress of mind. He would go to church that day, but, being a man of a very tender conscience, he hesitated about going to the Lord's table. He was in a state of great spiritual depression. In this state of mind he proceeded to put himself in order for church, and while washing his hands, no one being by, he heard a voice say, " Cannot I, in My blood, as easily wash your soul, as that water does your hands? " " Now, minister," he said, in telling me this, " I do not say there was a real voice, yet I heard it as distinctly, word for word, as you now hear me. I felt a load taken off my mind, and went to the table and sat under Christ's shadow with great delight." *The renewing of the Holy Spirit :*—The word " renewing " is used in the Scriptures in reference to the starting-point of the Christian life—regeneration, and to the progressive development of it, day by day. Consider it now in the latter sense, that is in connection with the Holy Spirit's work in those who have " life eternal." I. ESTABLISHING. 1. Bringing back the wanderer (Hos. xiv. 1, 2 ; Job. xxii. 23). 2. Settling the unstable (Psa. li. 10, lvii. 7 ; Eph. iii. 17). 3. Comforting the fearful (Psa. xxiii. 3, li. 12). II. STRENGTHENING. 1. Separating us from the things that hinder our growth (2 Cor. vi. 16–18). 2. Bringing us into closer contact with the Fountain of Supply (Isa. xl. 31 ; Eph. iii. 17). 3. Enlarging our capacity and powers of reception (2 Cor. iv. 16). III. TRANSFORMING. 1. Illuminating the mind (Rom. xii. 2; Col. iii. 10). 2. Gladdening the heart (Rom. xv. 13, xiv. 17). 3. Energising the will (Eph. iii. 16, iv. 23). 4. Transfiguring the character (2 Cor. iii. 18). (*E. H. Hopkins.*) **Renewing of the Holy Ghost.**—*The renewing of the Holy Ghost :*—I. BRING TOGETHER SOME OF THE MORE STRIKING SCRIPTURE TESTI- MONIES TO THE NECESSITY OF THIS AGENCY. 1. As embodied in the devotional sentiments of holy men. Hear David. " Create in me a clean heart," &c. " Cast me not away from Thy presence," &c. " Teach me to do Thy will," &c. " Thy Spirit is good ; lead me," &c. And so Paul. " Now the God of peace fill you with all joy," &c. 2. As a fulfilment of ancient promise. " I will pour water on him that is thirsty, and floods upon the dry ground." " I will pour My Spirit upon thy seed, and My blessing upon thine offspring." " A new heart also will I give you, and a new spirit will I put within you." " And I will put My Spirit within you, and cause you to walk in My statutes." If from these examples we pass to the New Testament, to consider how far the supposition of this great spiritual change enters into the pleas and arguments by which the sacred writers exhort their con- verts to the duties of practical godliness, we find the great promise of Whitsuntide sharing equally with our Lord's proper oblation a claim to be received as among the very necessities of our salvation. " If any man have not the Spirit of Christ he is none of His." " Now we have received not the spirit of the world, but the Spirit which is of God." " Know ye not that ye are the temple of God, and that the Spirit of God dwelleth in you? " " Hereby we know that we dwell in Him, and He in us, because He hath given us of His Spirit." These passages, with number- less others which might be quoted, show to us how completely the work of Christ for man, and the work of the Spirit in man, are looked upon by the inspired pen- man as joint and co-equal parts of a common salvation, the constituent elements of one great truth, successive and inseparable links in that chain of mercy by which sinners are to be lifted up from earth's lowest pit, and set down with Christ on heaven's highest throne. 3. As practically attested by the great facts of gospel history. The great miracle of Pentecost is one standing witness that without the agency of the Divine Spirit there never was, and never can be, such a thing as true conversion. It was not Peter's preaching that turned the hearts of those three thousand. He might have exhibited truth to the understanding of that great audience; he might have addressed powerful appeals to their consciences; he might even have lodged a deep conviction of the truth of all he said in their very souls; but so to convince them as to make them yield, so to prick their hearts that into its open pores there should be received and welcomed " the truth as it is in Jesus," this was a work to be done, " not by might, nor by power, but by My Spirit, saith the Lord of Hosts." The manner in which the notorious Earl of Rochester describes his conversion is strikingly illustrative of some great influence from without, acting upon, though still concurrently with his own natural faculties. He was reading, he tells us, the 53rd chapter of Isaiah, and his language is that there was some inward force upon him which convinced him that he could resist no longer, for the words had an authority which did shoot like rays or beams in his mind; and this power did so effectually constrain him that he did, ever after, as firmly believe in his Saviour as if he had seen Him in the clouds. II. How THIS RENEWING OF THE HOLY GHOST IN THE SOUL OF MAN IS ACCOMPLISHED. 1. First, we attribute to Him a true and proper indwelling in our souls (John xiv. 17). 2. Again, by the influences of this Spirit alone, are both produced and maintained within us all those affections and dispositions which constitute the renewed man. 3. Further, it is helpful to that renewing process which the Spirit of God carries on within us, that He testifies to the reality of His own work. Without raising the question of how much or how little of assurance must be inseparable from true conversion, the various expressions, witness of the Spirit, earnest of the Spirit, seal of the Spirit, must imply that one office of this Divine Agent is to supply some form of corroborative testimony to our own minds that we are the children of God. " He that believeth on the Son of God hath the witness in himself." 4. Once more, the renewing power of the Holy Ghost is to be looked for in the daily sanctification of our souls, and the preparing them for a condition of endless life. (*D. Moore, M.A.*) *The difficulty of removing the pollution of sin :*—At Portland navy-yard one of the United States ships came in for repair and fumigation, as yellow-fever had broken out amongst her crew during her previous voyage. She was thoroughly scraped and repainted, and then put into commission again, but she was less than a month at sea when the fever once more appeared. It was decided to open her up and expose the fever-spores to a thorough freezing during the winter, as medical men said that the spores could not live in cold weather. In the spring she was again painted and re-furnished, but the fever appeared again. Then it was found that, though a noble-looking vessel, death was in her, and she was towed to sea and sunk. So is it with all who have not been born again; they carry within their hearts the seeds of a fatal fever, and unless they are completely cleansed from it by Christ they will one day go down in the sea of the Divine wrath. **Which He shed on us abundantly, through Jesus Christ.**— *Abundant supply of grace :*—I. THE GRACES OF THE SPIRIT ARE PLENTIFULLY POURED OUT UPON US AS OUT OF A FULL AND RICH MERCY. For—1. We have the accomplishment of many prophecies and promises, as Isa. xi. 9; Dan. xii. 4. Many prophecies were then sealed, and the book shut until the term of time; but then many should run to and fro, and knowledge should be increased. 2. We have the truth of many types and resemblances, as of the waters running from under the threshold of the sanctuary, still rising to increase; and of the proceedings of the New Testament, typified in the cloud which at the first appearance was no bigger than a man's hand, but after rose to that greatness as to cover the whole heavens. 3. If we compare our Church with that of the Jews' we shall observe that the Lord did but drop and sprinkle these graces here and there upon a few persons where He pleased, but now hath poured out His Spirit and opened a fountain of grace to the house of Judah and Jerusalem, even for all true believers. (1) If such plenty of grace be poured out upon us, our care must be to be found answerable thereunto, that according to our proportion our increase may be; for we may not think the return of one talent sufficient if we have received five or ten, seeing where much is given much will be required. Hath the Lord so richly shed out His Spirit that whereas the most excellent patriarchs saw Christ only afar off, the most simple of our age may see Him in the Word and sacraments even crucified before his eyes, and will it not be expected that in all things we should be made rich in Him? And thus have we ministered unto us a ground of examination whether we find the fruits and work of these waters upon us. (2) If upon this examination we feel not this plenty of grace, we must beware of accusing God, but condemn ourselves in whom all the fault is, as who refuse and despise so great grace. If any ask how it can come to pass that such excellent grace should be refused, I answer there are three main causes of it—1. Ignorance and blindness of mind. 2. Hardness of heart. 3. Security, which three destitute us of so abundant grace as is offered. II. All the grace that is bestowed on us IS BY MEANS OF JESUS CHRIST, FOR WITH HIM IS THE FOUNTAIN AND HEADSPRING; yea, He is the head which sendeth life, sense, motion, and direction into all the members, resembled in that holy ointment which ran down from Aaron's head and beard even to the skirts of his garment. The evangelist, after he had affirmed that Christ was full of grace and truth, addeth that of His fulness we receive grace for grace, so the apostle (Col. ii. 9, 10). (1) Want we any grace? call upon God in the name of Christ. "Whatsoever ye ask the Father in My name, He will give it unto you." Get Christ to be thine own, become a true believer, that thou mayest in Him begin thy prayer with Our Father; this is the way to be rich in grace. (2) Hast thou received any spiritual grace? sacrifice not unto thine own net, but be thankful unto God in Christ. (3) Take heed of quenching that grace, neither grieve that good Spirit of God by thy sin, for thou camest hardly by it, for Christ must come down from heaven, humble Himself to the death, rise again, ascend, and now make continual intercession before He could procure thee the least grace. A thing very little thought of. (*T. Taylor, D.D.*) *Eminent holiness:*—Our text combines doctrine and practice, faith and morals, and makes the one the proper foundation of the other. That, being justified by His grace, we should be made heirs. This is a faithful saying—that they which have believed be careful to maintain good works. It is worthy of remark that there are four passages of Scripture in which the expression "a faithful saying" is employed, and each faithful saying is worthy of all acceptation (1 T.m. i. 15, iv. 8, 9; 2 Tim. xi. 11–13; Titus iii. 8). And they all mark out the connection between faith and obedience—between holiness and happiness—between principle and practice. I. THAT THE DOCTRINE OF OUR ACCEPTANCE IN CHRIST, WHILE IT FORMS THE ONLY FOUNDATION OF A SINNER'S HOPE, HAS A DIRECT TENDENCY TO PROMOTE EMINENT HOLINESS. 1. The doctrine of justification by faith, through the merits and advocacy of Christ, constitutes the alone basis of our acceptance with God. We are said to be justified by His grace. This doctrine forms the only answer to the question which in every age has baffled the wisdom of the wise, and brought to nought the understanding of the prudent. How shall man be just with God? A cordial reception of Jesus Christ as the end of the law for righteousness to every one that believeth, entitles the returning offender to life by a merciful appointment, and brings him into a state of personal acceptance with God. This doctrine may well be considered as the cardinal doctrine of Christianity, and as lying at the very foundation of all our hopes for eternity. So deep and aggravated is our guilt, that it is quite evident that if we be not accepted by the merits and righteousness of another we cannot be accepted at all; for it is clear we have no righteousness of our own. This therefore forms, as the text states, a singular exhibition of Divine benignity and grace. Grace provided the Saviour revealed in the gospel—grace accepted His substitution in the sinner's place—grace communicated the principle of piety implanted in the human heart—grace preserves that principle from extinction, amidst all the storms and tumults of this opposing world—and grace crowns the subjects of its influences with glory at last. 2. The doctrine of justification, so far from lessening the obligations to obedience, furnishes the most powerful of all inducements to eminent holiness. The pardoned offender is not rendered lawless; a justified state is not exempted from obligation. We are not without law to God, but under the law to Christ. It is no part of the Divine design to raise up one light in order to extinguish another. What was once truth is always truth; what was once duty is always duty. All the original grounds of moral obligation remain. If God was our Creator before our conversion, He is our Creator still—a faithful Creator. If God was our Judge before, He is our Judge still. Neither does Divine grace destroy or change any of the relations in which we previously stood to each other, nor cancel any of the duties arising out of those relations. Neither does Divine grace alter the nature of sin, nor render it one whit less than before the abominable thing which God hateth. The plague does not cease to be the plague because a remedy has been mercifully provided for it. The gospel has produced no change in our moral relation to God, nor in our relation to our fellow-man; and, therefore, all the antecedent obligation to obedience remains unchanged; and they that have believed in God are enjoined carefully to maintain good works. The gospel superadds motives and inducements unknown before to induce conformity to the Divine will. The grace of God, that bringeth salvation, teacheth us that, denying ungodliness and worldly lusts, we should live soberly, righteously, and godly. All false religions attempt to lower the standard of morals, in order to fall in with the weakness or wickedness of mankind. But Christianity presents us with raised views of the spirituality of the Divine law. It presents us with the most powerful motives to holiness—derived from the love of God—the Cross of Christ—the glories of the coming world, and especially from the great work of redemption. II. That these principles, in their connection with each other, are to be explicitly asserted and maintained. "These things I will that thou affirm constantly." They are to be affirmed in their connection with each other—that is, the doctrine of justification is to be affirmed—and the doctrine of sanctification is to be affirmed too: the one as the cause, the other as the effect; the one as the root, the other as the fruitful branch. And observe to what class of characters the exhortations and commands of the gospel are to be specifically addressed—That they which have believed in God might be careful to maintain good works; plainly proving that the most advanced Christians require to be frequently admonished. Our text says these truths are to be constantly affirmed. These good works are to be expressly enjoined upon those who believe. We are not to leave them to implication and inference, as though we presumed that they would follow as a necessary result from the mere belief of the doctrine of justification, but they are to be plainly stated and enforced. This is to be done in defiance of opposition and contradiction, which supposes objection and denial on the part of some. The reasons why we should thus constantly urge these truths will be perceived at a glance. 1. Because we are always liable to overlook and forget them amidst the active engagements and snares of life. The gospel ministry was instituted for this purpose. 2. Because the personal sanctity of Christians is the final object of the dispensation of mercy. To this everything in the Divine economy tends; in this everything terminates. It is no inferior degree of excellence to which we are taught to aspire; we are not to begin only, but to advance and persevere—we are to maintain good works, and to be careful to maintain them. The marginal rendering is more emphatic still—the force of the Greek word being to go before in good works—to excel, to emulate—to attain eminence in holiness and devotion. Plutarch tells us that it was the aim of Tully, that it was his ambition, to be eminent in all that he undertook. How much more should Christians desire to attain the highest measures of moral and religious excellence. 3. Because advancement in holiness is essential to the enjoyment of all genuine consolation. The state of grace is only evidenced by the sanctities of the Christian character. 4. Because the absence of these good works proves the destitution of Christian principle, and leaves the individual exposed to a fearful disappointment and a final doom. III. That from the faithful exhibition of these truths the happiest results are to be anticipated to the church and the world. These things are good and profitable to men. They are good in themselves, and good in their influence upon the mind. Many things may be good that are not profitable, and some may be thought profitable that are not good; but these are both good and profitable. They are good in the Divine esteem—good as the transcript of His own infinite excellence—good as perfectly accordant with all His revelations to man—good in their origin—good in their progress—good in their end. They come from heaven and lead to it. They are good and profitable, as opposed to those "foolish questions, and genealogies, and contentions, and strivings about the law," which we are told in the next verse to avoid as unprofitable and vain. (*The Evangelist.*) **That being justified by His grace.**—*Justification; faith; works:*—I. The moral rectification of the soul. 1. All souls in their unrenewed state are unrighteous. 2. Restoration to righteousness is the merciful work of God. 3. In this moral rectification of soul there is the heirship of eternal good. II. The essential foundation of all true faith. To believe in God implies—1. To believe in what He is in Himself—the only absolute existence, without beginning, without succession, without end, who is in all and through all, the All-Mighty, the All-Wise, the All-Good Creator and Sustainer of the universe. 2. To believe in what He is to us—the Father, the Proprietor, and the Life. III. The supreme purpose of moral existence is to maintain good works. 1. Good works are—(1) Works that have right motives. (2) Works that have a right standard. 2. The maintenance of these works requires strenuous and constant effort. 3. The great work of the Christian ministry is to stimulate this effort. (*D. Thomas, D.D.*) *God's method of justification:*—1. The originating cause is the grace, the free, sovereign, undeserved, and spontaneous love of God towards fallen man (Titus iii. 4, 5; ii. 11; Rom. iii.

24). 2. Our Lord Jesus Christ is the sole meritorious cause. All He did, and all He suffered, in His mediatorial character, may be said to have contributed to this great purpose. 3. The instrumental cause of justification. The merit of the blood of Jesus does not operate necessarily so as to produce our pardon as an immediate and unavoidable effect, but through the instrumentality of faith. Hence—1. We are not justified, in whole or part, by the merit of our own works, whether past, present, or future. 2. Our repentance is neither the meritorious course, nor the immediate instrument of justification. 3. The Holy Spirit's work of regeneration and sanctification is not the previous condition of our free justification or the pre-requisite qualification of it. 4. Our justification is not by the merit of faith itself; but only by faith, as that which embraces and appropriates the merit of Christ. (*J. Bunting.*) *Relation of justification to regeneration :*—Justification is a qualification of title; regeneration of nature. Justification alters the relative character; regeneration the personal. Justification reconciles us to the Divine favour; regeneration to the Divine service. Justification removes every obstacle of law; regeneration every obstacle of disposition. Justification destroys the incapacity of guilt; regeneration the resistance of depravity. Justification makes us one with God in acceptance; regeneration makes us one with Him in will. Justification opens heaven; regeneration causes us to walk in its white. Justification furnishes the song of deliverance; regeneration teaches us to modulate it. (*R. W. Hamilton, D.D.*) *The finished work of Christ :*—A poor man was very anxious about his soul. Though he knew the Bible well, yet he could not get over one difficulty, which was that he wanted to do something to save himself; it was too easy a way to be saved by Christ without doing anything to merit salvation himself; at least so he thought. One day an evangelist called at his workshop, and saw a gate all painted and varnished, ready to be hung in its place. "John," he said, "is this gate complete?" "Yes, sir; it is quite finished; it has got the last coat of varnish." "You are perfectly certain?" "Yes, quite." The evangelist took up a plane, and in a moment had taken a shaving off the top bar. "Stop, stop, sir!" cried John, "you are spoiling the gate." "Ah, John, that is what you want to do with Christ's work; He has completed the work of your salvation, yet you want to spoil it by doing something—you don't know what—to improve upon it!" This practical hint was just what John needed, and there and then he gave up trying to improve upon the work of Christ, and gave himself up to be saved at once, just as he was, in the workshop. **We should be made heirs.**—*Heirs of eternal life :*—In these words is laid down the second end of that new condition into which believers are brought. In which for the meaning two parts must be considered—1. The right and privilege of believers who, being once justified by faith, are made heirs of life eternal. 2. Their present tenure of this their inheritance by hope. I. For the former, THE WORD HEIR IN THE FIRST AND PROPER SIGNIFICATION BETOKENETH A LOT, and is used sometimes in the New Testament with allusion unto the twelve tribes, whose portions were divided and distributed unto them by lot, as Eph. i. 11, whence that people were more peculiarly called the lines and heritage of the Lord, as whom Himself made partakers of all the good things of that land; and by proportion those also who by faith laid, or shall lay, hold upon His covenant, for all those spiritual and eternal good things shadowed out thereby. But commonly it signifieth those who after a man's death succeed him in his goods and possessions, especially children, whose right it is to inherit their father's lands and possessions; and thus must we become heirs by becoming the sons and children of God. Now, whereas children are either natural or adopted, our title to this inheritance cometh in by the grace of adoption, seeing Christ is the only natural Son, as we confess in our creed; and the phrase of the text is observable, which faith we are made heirs, but not so born; so as this inheritance belongeth properly unto Christ the natural son, the heir, and firstborn of many brethren, and consequently through Him communicated unto us, who are sons by adoption (John i. 12). II. THE PRESENT TENURE OF THIS INHERITANCE IS BY HOPE, for our inheritance is not so much set before our bodily eyes as the eyes of our faith, which is not of things present, but of things to come. And yet although it be an estate to come, the Lord would not leave us without such graces as being conversant about it might serve us in this life to retain our hold and comfort therein, such as are faith, hope, and patience. Now hope signifieth two things —1. The thing hoped for. "Hope which is seen is not hope" (Rom. viii. 24). "What is the hope of the calling" (Eph. i. 18). 2. For the gift whereby we hope and expect good things promised, and this must of necessity here be meant, because life eternal of which we have spoken is the thing hoped for. This grace hath the Lord for our encouragement and comfort, in and for the state of this life only, put into the hearts of His elect, that they might hereby have a certain hold and expectation of all that good which God of His mercy through the merit of His Christ hath promised; the which shall cease when they come once to see that which they now hope for, seeing hereafter can be no hope, not in heaven, for the godly shall enjoy all blessedness their hearts can wish; not in hell, for the damned can never hope for any good. 1. That which the apostle specially aimeth at is that heaven is not merited, but a free gift; here it is called eternal life, which is the gift of God (Rom. vi. 23). It is called here an inheritance, in that the elect are called heirs; it is against the nature of an inheritance to come any way but by free gift, legacies we know are most free without desert, without procurement, and what an absurd thing were it for a child to go to his father to offer to buy his inheritance? It is said here further that we are made heirs, that is adopted, not born to the inheritance, and therefore it is so much the more free. And lastly, it is here called an eternal inheritance, which, if it be so, how can it be merited, being so far disproportionable to anything we can do. 2. It teacheth us if we would have right to eternal life to become the sons of God, and consequently heirs; seek to be resolved that thou hast a child's part in heaven. How shall I come to know this? A man may know himself an heir of grace by two things—(1) By the presence of faith, for this intitleth into the covenant. Noah by faith was made heir of the righteousness which is by faith (Heb. xi. 7). Faith in the Son of God it is which maketh thee the King's son and free born; this is the means of thy freedom, here cometh in thy title, if thou reliest only upon the mercy of God in Christ for thy salutation. (2) By the presence of sanctification of heart, sanctimony of life (1 Cor. vi. 10, 11). 3. This doctrine teacheth us to set our hearts upon this inheritance; a man that hath any possibility to befal him cannot keep his mind, but it will be running after it, insomuch as many wicked children in regard of their patrimony will inquire into their fathers' years, and grow sick of their mothers, and it is ordinary that such as look for windfalls by decease will be feeding their hearts with their hopes; so should it be with us, who may, without injury to our Father, long after our inheritance in heaven; and as we see men take no content in any part of the earth, no nor in the whole, comparable to that peace or portion which is their own, even so should not we suffer our hearts so to wander after earth or earthly things, as that we settle our contentment anywhere but where our inheritance and our treasure is. The which desire if it filled our hearts, three worthy fruits of it would manifest themselves through our lives. (1) It would moderate the eager cares of this life, and would not suffer men to become drudges, or sell themselves as slaves unto the earth, for he that taketh himself to be an heir of heaven is well enough provided and cared for already, his Father hath left him so well as he need not basely shift for himself. (2) It would content the mind with any present condition. 4. Set thyself well to keep this inheritance and the deeds of it, lay up the covenant safe in the closet of the soul, hide the Word, which is the indenture of God passing it unto thee, in the midst of thy heart, let not Satan nor any cheater defraud thee of it. 5. This doctrine affordeth sundry grounds of most sweet consolation. (1) The meanest believer is a great heir, and that to all God's best blessings, a truth which few see as they might and ought, and therefore fail of that comfort which God hath put into their hands. (2) God's children being such heirs, they cannot but in the meantime be well provided for till their patrimony fall. We know that great heirs in their minority are well and honestly maintained, their fathers being rich and kind will not suffer them to want things fit for them, and what they want in the purse they have in their education, and if they be any way scanted for the present they shall afterward find it with much advantage. (3) In any want thou, being thy Father's heir, mayest boldly repair to thy Father, with good hope to speed in any request which He seeth fit for thee and making for thy good. (*T. Taylor, D.D.*) *Looking for the hope of eternal life:*—One bright morning last summer, while travelling in Switzerland, I took my seat on the top of a diligence as we passed along the magnificent country from Geneva to Chamounix. I was full of expectation to see Mont Blanc. Our driver said, as we drew nearer the object of our journey, "Unless a cloud sails up and covers its forehead you will see it leaning up against the clear blue sky." I need not tell you I kept looking up, feeling that every moment brought me nearer to the sight I so much wanted to see. (*Mrs. Bottome.*)

Ver. 8. **Maintain good works.**—*The maintenance of good works:*—I. WHAT WE

ONCE WERE. A threefold set of evils is here described. 1. The first set consists of the evils of the mind : " We were sometimes foolish, disobedient, deceived." We were foolish. We thought we knew, and therefore we did not learn. Every lover of vice is a fool writ large. In addition to being foolish, we are said to have been disobedient; and so we were, for we forsook the commands of God. We wanted our own will and way. We were unwilling to yield God His due place either in providence, law, or gospel. Paul adds that we were deceived, or led astray. We were the dupes of custom and of company. We were here, there, and everywhere in our actions : no more to be relied upon than lost sheep. 2. The next bundle of mischief is found in the evils of our pursuits. The apostle says we were " serving divers lusts and pleasures." The word for "serving" means being under servitude. We were once the slaves of divers lusts and pleasures. By lusts we understand desires, longings, ambitions, passions. Many are these masters, and they are all tyrants. Some are ruled by greed for money ; others crave for fame ; some are enslaved by lust for power ; others by the lust of the eye ; and many by the lusts of the flesh. 3. We were also the bond-slaves of pleasure. Alas! alas! that we were so far infatuated as to call it pleasure! Looking back at our former lives, we may well be amazed that we could once take pleasure in things whereof we are now ashamed. The Lord has taken the very name of our former idols out of our mouths. A holy man was wont to carry with him a book which had three leaves in it, but never a word. The first leaf was black, and this showed his sin ; the second was red, and this reminded him of the way of cleansing by blood ; while the third was white, to show how clean the Lord can make us. I beg you just now to study that first black page. It is all black; and as you look at it it shows blacker and blacker. What seemed at one time to be a little white darkens down as it is gazed upon, till it wears the deepest shade of all. Ye were sometimes erring in your minds and in your pursuits. Is not this enough to bring the water into your eyes, O ye that now follow the Lamb whithersoever He goeth? 4. The apostle then mentions the evils of our hearts. Here you must discriminate and judge, each one for himself, how far the accusation lies. He speaks of "living in malice and envy, hateful and hating one another." That is to say, first, we harboured anger against those who had done us evil; and, secondly, we lived in envy of those who appeared to have more good than we had ourselves. II. WHAT HAS BEEN DONE FOR US? 1. First, there was a Divine interposition. The love and kindness of God our Saviour, which had always existed, at length "appeared" when God, in the person of His Son, came hither, met our iniquities hand to hand, and overcame their terrible power, that we also might overcome. 2. Note well that there was a Divine salvation. In consequence of the interposition of Jesus, believers are described as being saved : "not by works of righteousness which we have done, but according to His mercy He saved us." Hearken to this. There are men in the world who are saved : they are spoken of, not as " to be saved," not as to be saved when they come to die, but saved even now—saved from the dominion of the evils which we described under our first head : saved from folly, disobedience, delusion, and the like. Whosoever believeth in the Lord Jesus Christ, whom God has set forth to be the propitiation for sin, is saved from the guilt and power of sin. He shall no longer be the slave of his lusts and pleasures; he is saved from that dread bondage. He is saved from hate, for he has tasted love, and learned to love. He shall not be condemned for all that he has hitherto done, for his great Substitute and Saviour has borne away the guilt, the curse, the punishment of sin ; yea, and sin itself. 3. There was a motive for this salvation. Positively, "According to His mercy He saved us"; and, negatively, "Not by works of righteousness which we have done." We could not have been saved at the first by our works of righteousness ; for we had not done any. "No," says the apostle, "we were foolish, disobedient, deceived," and therefore we had no works of righteousness, and yet the Lord interposed and saved us. Behold and admire the splendour of His love, that "He loved us even when we were dead in sins." He loved us, and therefore quickened us. 4. There was a power by which we were saved. The way in which we are delivered from the dominion of sin is by the work of the Holy Ghost. This adorable Person is very God of very God. This Divine Being comes to us and causes us to be born again. By His eternal power and Godhead He gives us a totally new nature, a life which could not grow out of our former life, nor be developed from our nature—a life which is a new creation of God. We are saved, not by evolution, but by creation. The Spirit of God creates us anew in Christ Jesus unto good works. We experience regeneration, which means—being generated over again, or born again. 5. There is also mentioned a blessed privilege which comes to us by Jesus Christ. The Spirit is shed on us abundantly by Jesus Christ, and we are "justified by His grace." Both justification and sanctification come to us through the medium of our Lord Jesus Christ. 6. Once more, there comes out of this a Divine result. We become to-day joint-heirs with Christ Jesus, and so heirs of a heavenly estate ; and then out of this heirship there grows a hope which reaches forward to the eternal future with exceeding joy. III. WHAT WE WISH TO DO. "Be careful to maintain good works." 1. This precept is full in its meaning. What are good works? The term is greatly inclusive. Of course we number in the list works of charity, works of kindness and benevolence, works of piety, reverence, and holiness. Such works as comply with the two tables of command are good works. Works of obedience are good works. What you do because God bids you do it, is a good work. Works of love to Jesus, done out of a desire for His glory, these are good works. The common actions of every-day life, when they are well done, with a view not to merit, but one of gratitude—these are good works. "Be careful to maintain good works" of every sort and kind. 2. This precept is special in its direction. To the sinner, that he may be saved, we say not a word concerning good works, except to remind him that he has none of them. To the believer who is saved, we say ten thousand words concerning good works, beseeching him to bring forth much fruit, that so he may be Christ's disciple. For living works you must have a living faith, and for loving works you must have a loving faith. When we know and trust God, then with holy intelligence and sacred confidence we work His pleasure. 3. This precept is weighty in importance, for it is prefaced thus: "This is a faithful saying." This is one among four great matters thus described. It is not trivial, it is not a temporary precept which belongs to an extinct race and a past age. "This is a faithful saying"—a true Christian proverb, "that they which have believed in God might be careful to maintain good works." Let the ungodly never say that we who believe in free grace think lightly of a holy life. 4. I am afraid that this precept of being careful to maintain good works is neglected in practice, or else the apostle would not have said to Titus, "These things I will that thou affirm constantly." There are still persons in our Churches who need to have the ten commandments read to them every Sabbath-day. It is not a bad plan to put up the ten commandments near the communion table where they can be clearly seen. Some people need to see them; though I am afraid, when they come in their way, they wink hard at some of the commands, and go away and forget that they have seen them. Common morality is neglected by some who call themselves Christians. 5. This, mark you, is supported by argument. The apostle presses home his precept by saying: "These things are good and profitable unto men." Men are won to Christ when they see Christianity embodied in the good and the true. (*C. H. Spurgeon.*)    *The connection of faith and good works :—* Truth is many-sided. And though like a pure gem, it is on all sides equally bright, it cannot all be seen at once. No merely human mind can so take it all up as to give to every part the same sharp and well-defined outline. Truth in the mind of Christ was like light in the sun, pure and undivided, and ever came out in its glorious integrity. In the minds of his followers it was like light in the prism, in which the rays are separated, or like light in the bow, in which, according to certain laws, the rays are first refracted, and then reflected in the drops of rain, and in which we see the conquering splendour of the light in its struggle with darkness. Faith and works were never separated—not even in idea—in the teaching of Christ. In His own mind they were indissoluble, and so in His instructions. If faith did not express itself in corresponding action, He denied the existence of the principle, or rather He treated men as still on the side of the world and of self. His apostles, on the contrary, gave to all truth their own mental cast and colouring, and unless these various colours are allowed to meet and mingle, we shall lack the pure light. Though Paul and James are treating of one and the same subject, each has his own mode of statement; and the light in which he places it depends on his own individual state of mind. Both apostles are teaching and enforcing the same doctrine, but the parties whom they have in view are not the same. The teachers occupy exactly the same position; but those to whom they address themselves have assumed entirely opposite and conflicting points. The contrariety is not in the statements of the inspired men, but in the minds of Christian professors. Each is a firm believer in the article of justification by faith, but it has different phases, and according as it appears to the one or the other, is his representation. The aim of St. Paul is to set forth God's method of forgiveness and acceptance through the mediation of His Son ;—that this is revealed for faith, and that through faith alone do we come to participate in all the provision of redeeming love. Faith, and not. justification, is his theme. There is but one ground of dependence—but one foundation on which the soul can rest her hope of eternal life, and from which all works are necessarily and for ever excluded. But having been once brought to repose our faith in the Divine method of salvation, it remains that we give evidence of the fact. We cannot be in communion with the Redeemer of our souls without partaking His higher life ; and we cannot be in communion with the Spirit of life without producing the fruits of the Spirit. Hence the challenge of St. James addressed in words of sharp-pointed irony to those who were boasting of their faith as something separate and separable from a life of practical holiness — " Show Me thy faith without thy works." If it have no outward expression, how is it to be known or discovered ? " As the body without the spirit is dead, so faith without works is dead also." As the spirit is the inward animating and informing principle, and manifests itself in the outward acts and movements of the body, so faith has in it an element of life, which cannot but develop itself in practical godliness and holy activity. It follows that there is not one faith to justify a sinner and another faith to justify a believer. The same faith justifies both ; or rather, the faith which brings a man to simple dependence on the propitiation set forth by God for the remission of sins, has in it such a force and vitality as ever afterwards to come out in those buds and blossoms which have their fruit unto holiness and the end everlasting life. If this simple fact had been but kept in view, no discrepancy would have been found in the statement of these two inspired men. The one wholly excludes the human element from the Divine method of reconciliation and life, and demands the most childlike faith in Heaven's revealed and published plan of mercy—the other sets it in the clearest light that wherever this pure unsophisticated faith has existence in the soul, it will ever manifest itself in a course of lofty and persevering righteousness. While faith, and not justification, is the subject treated of by both apostles, it may not be amiss just to glance at the doctrine commonly denominated justification by faith. There are two errors common on this subject. First, justification is confounded with acquittal ; and, secondly, man is said to be treated as righteous for the sake of the righteousness of another. Now if he be acquitted, he needs not to be treated as righteous. He is righteous ; and is entitled to be dealt with according to his rectitude. And if he be righteous, it is absurd and contradictory to speak of his acquittal. Man has sinned ; and the proof of his guilt is overwhelming. With the sentence of condemnation lying heavy upon his heart, he may be pardoned, but he can never be declared to be innocent. But is not the righteousness of Christ said to be imputed to us, and that we become righteous on the ground of His righteousness ? In creeds, and catechisms, and commentaries, it certainly is so, but nowhere in the Book of God. The righteousness of Christ is a phrase which never occurs but once in the whole of the Christian Testament. When the great apostle of the nations would heighten our idea of the grace of God, by setting the blessings of redeeming love over against the evils entailed upon our race by the introduction of sin, he says, " As by the offence of one, judgment came upon all men unto condemnation ; even so by the righteousness of one, the free gift came upon all men unto justification of life." He does not represent the righteousness of the One, as something imputed or transferred from Christ to man, but simply as the procuring cause of our forgiveness and life. The righteousness is put for the whole work of the Saviour's mediation, and this is declared to be the sole ground on which the blessings of Divine mercy are extended to our fallen world. Nor is more than this to be extracted from the deep saying of this same apostle, when in words that breathe, he thus expresses the inmost feeling of his soul : " I have suffered the loss of all things, that I may win Christ and be found in Him, not having mine own righteousness which is of the law, but that which is through the faith of Christ—the righteousness which is of God by faith." The idea here is, that he was supremely anxious to be kept from even the attempt of laying a foundation in his own strivings and doings for his acceptance with God, and that he might ever be led to repose by a simple faith in the one Divine method of forgiveness and salvation. The righteousness of God is God's revealed plan of saving man through the propitiatory offering of His Son. Faith in this propitiation involves an act of perfect self-renunciation, an acknowledgment of conscious sin and weakness, and a resting upon another for help and succour. Our justification introduces us into a new and loftier relation. Our Father in heaven may not treat us as righteous, but He will most surely bless us as His adopted ones. If we can prefer no claim we may yet possess all good. If salvation can never be of works it can ever be of grace. If life is not a right it is yet our high privilege and our mightier joy. This life is progressive. As the first ray of light that gilds the mountain's height predicts a meridian sun, and as the first blush of the opening flower promises a full and perfect bloom, so the faintest indications of the life of God in the soul assure us of continued growth and progress, till, from its fulness and exuberance, it burst into all the beauty and perfection of heaven. The power that quickens is the power that purifies. There are spots on the disc of the sun, only they are invisible through the effulgence and the fulness of his light, and there are but few spirits so highly sanctified and refined as to render indiscernible, through the glory which surrounds them, those sin-spots which daily alight upon their renewed nature. Nor can the work of inward holiness be perfected so long as we are in this body of death. It is in the act of shaking mortality off that the Spirit puts forth his last and latest effort in the soul; and it is only when the soul has burst her prison-wall, let fall the last link of the chain which bound her to earth, and is on her way to the great world of light, that she is conscious of her final and everlasting separation from sin. Up to that mysterious point we may become day by day more closely assimilated to God our Saviour. Our sanctification is inseparable from our justification. It is not enough that we live. It is the will of God that we should enjoy the fulness of life. Life can have fellowship only with life. We must, therefore, detach ourselves from every opposing element and influence. We must give up the material and the visible for the spiritual and the unseen. Enjoyment without activity would not be an unmixed good. It follows that as life is quickened and our nature is purified, we are freed from sloth and sluggishness. The soul moves with a freedom and a swiftness corresponding to the unconfined liberty of heaven. That is a world of never-ending activity, and, in proportion as we rise into conformity with the pure spirits that surround the throne of God, shall we, like them, employ all our renovated powers in holy and active service? Christianity is love—universal, unbounded love—and embraces within itself the present and the everlasting interests of man. And the more we partake its spirit, the more entire will be our consecration—the more unreserved our activity and our service. Let no one be startled and offended with the doctrine of good works. They necessarily flow from faith. They are faith in action. They are " the living effluence of the tide of Divine love," which refuses to be confined within any prescribed limits, and flows out in deeds of unwearied benevolence and piety. He who repudiates a life of well-doing in the dreamy belief that in the same proportion he is exalting the grace of God, is not the man whose character exhibits the closest correspondence to the pure and sublime requirements of the Book. It is a grand mistake to suppose that the law is repealed by the gospel. In Christianity the law reappears; only it is transfigured and glorified. Every utterance which was given in the thunder-tones of Sinai, is re-echoed with heightened emphasis in the Sermon on the Mount, only it comes silent as the light and gentle as the dew from the lips of Incarnate Love. We hold that salvation is by grace and not by works; but where the works are wanting the grace cannot be present. Our activity and our service will be the everlasting recognition and expression of the fact that we have been redeemed by blood and saved by grace. We should be unfaithful to our ministry and to your souls did we dare to say that sin committed by a professed believer is less criminal or less damnable than what we discover in the unregenerate and the unholy. Sin is sin by whomsoever committed, and involves the same tremendous consequences. It is of infinite moment that they who believe in God should be careful to maintain good works—that their life should be pure, their character transparent, and their conduct patent. Their principles should be above suspicion, and their whole course of action such as may challenge the higher light of the world to come. (*R. Ferguson, LL.D.*) *The practice of good works :*—I. IT IS NOT ENOUGH TO BELIEVE WHAT GOD HATH SAID TO BE TRUE, AND TO GIVE OUR ASSENT TO THE CERTAINTY OF DIVINE REVELATION, UNLESS OUR BELIEF INFLUENCES OUR HEART AND LIFE. Christ's laws, as well as any other, run in this disjunction—either do or suffer; either live holily, or perish everlastingly : nothing is therein promised, but upon condition of our obedience. The main thing our Saviour aimed at all His life was to restore human nature to its primitive purity and perfection, and to advance true piety and holiness in the world; to bring men to a good opinion of and a ready compliance with God's laws, so that it influences all their actions, faith not being enough to denominate a man a true Christian, unless he goes on to add to his faith virtue, &c. II. THE PRACTICE OF GOOD WORKS, TAKEN EITHER FOR PIETY TOWARDS GOD OR CHARITY TOWARDS MAN, IS ABSOLUTELY NECESSARY FOR ALL UNTO SALVATION. 1. They render our services more acceptible unto God. Purity and holiness in the heart, before these be or when there is no opportunity to work, are in themselves good ; but when they are demonstrated by godly and charitable actions, then smell they sweet, and are sacrifices well-pleasing. 2. By them God's name is more glorified (Matt. v. 16). 3. By them we shall be the greatest gainers or losers, in that by them we make our calling and election sure (2 Pet. i. 10). III. WHY THOSE ARE MORE INDISPENSABLY OBLIGED TO BE EXEMPLARY IN ALL GOOD WORKS, WHO HAVE BEEN MORE PARTICULARLY ACQUAINTED WITH GOD'S WILL, AND EARLY INSTRUCTED IN IT. As we may be supposed to have been, whose parents were our spiritual guides, as well as fathers of our flesh, and under whose roof we were early seasoned with their daily instructions and good example. We shall, therefore, reflect upon their memory and care, we shall cause others to uncover their ashes with dishonour, unless we adorn that faith our fathers believed, which they taught us, and which we saw them practise. (*Thos. Whincop, D.D.*)   *On the necessity of good works :* —I. THE CERTAIN TRUTH AND CREDIBILITY OF THIS SAYING OR PROPOSITION, that they which have believed in God ought to be careful to maintain good works. 1. If we consider the great end and design of religion in general, which is to make us happy, by possessing our minds ·with the belief of a God, and those other principles which have a necessary connection with that belief, and by obliging us to the obedience and practice of His laws. 2. If we consider the great end and design of the Christian religion in particular, which was to reform the world, to purify the hearts and lives of men from corrupt affections and wicked practices, to teach men to excel in all kinds of virtue and goodness. II. THE GREAT FITNESS AND NECESSITY OF INCULCATING FREQUENTLY UPON ALL THAT PROFESS THEMSELVES CHRISTIANS, the indispensable necessity of the practice of the virtues of a good life. (*Abp. Tillotson.*) *Good works :*—I. THAT BELIEVERS ARE UNDER OBLIGATIONS TO MAINTAIN GOOD WORKS is so evident, not only from the text, but from the whole tenor of the Scripture, that I know of no sect of Christians that pretend to deny it. But, with regard to their place and importance as connected with our salvation, great mistakes have been made. It will certainly then be worth our pains to inquire from the oracles of God, " How far and in what respect are our good works necessary to be maintained with regard to salvation." 1. In my negative answer to this question, I must first observe that we are not to do good works in order to change God's purposes and designs towards us ; or to excite His benevolence and compassion to us. Our business is to come to Christ and learn of Him, to bow our necks to His yoke, to do good works from faith in Christ, and out of love and obedience to Him ; and in that way to hope in God for mercy, for Christ's sake, and for His own sake, and not for ours. 2. We are not to do good works with a view to qualify us for our reception of Christ by faith, or for obtaining an interest in Him. The gospel brings glorious tidings of salvation to perishing sinners. It exempts and excludes none who will come to Christ for life, who will come to Him as lost sinners under a sense of their guilt and unworthiness, who will "buy of Him wine and milk without money and without price, and who will take the water of Life freely." 3. I must further add that we are not to do good works in expectation that we shall by them obtain a title to the future inheritance. Heaven is a purchased possession ; our title to it, our qualification for it, our perseverance in the way that leads thither, and our eternal enjoyment of the glorious inheritance, are all purchased by the blood of Christ. In all these respects Christ Jesus is our Hope ; and when we "rejoice in hope of the glory of God," we must "rejoice in Christ Jesus, having no confidence in the flesh." 4. I shall only add that we must not depend upon our good works for re-newing supplies of grace, and for continual progress in holiness, and comfort unto God's heavenly kingdom. We are not only justified by faith, but we must be sanctified by faith too, and of Christ's " fulness must receive even grace for grace." II. I proceed now to show you IN WHAT RESPECTS GOOD WORKS ARE OF NECESSITY ; and to that purposes they must be done by all those who would approve themselves Christians indeed. 1. Good works are necessary as being one design of our redemp-tion and effectual calling. Though not the fountain and foundation of a renewed nature, they are always the streams that flow from that fountain, and the super-structure upon that foundation. Though they do not sanctify us they are the natural and necessary actings and operations of a sanctified heart. 2. Good works are necessary, as they belong to the way leading to heaven. "Without holiness no man shall see the Lord." We must not only " enter in at the strait gate, but walk in the narrow way which leadeth unto life." They who would hope for heaven hereafter must have it begun in their souls here. Their hearts must be in some measure conformed to the Divine nature and will, that they may be qualified for the enjoyments and employments of the heavenly world. 3. Good works are necessary as acts of obedience to God's commands, and a just acknowledgment of His dominion over us. Our freedom from the curses and demands of the moral law as a covenant of life is so far from freeing us from our duty towards it as a rule of practice, or excusing us from a careful observation of its precepts, that the glorious liberty we are made partakers of is given us for this very end that we may serve " God without fear, in holiness and righteousness before Him all the days of our life." 4. Good works are necessary as expressions of our gratitude to God for all His goodness to us, more especially for gospel-grace, and the influences of His blessed Spirit. They who have ever tasted that the Lord is gracious, and have any suitable sense of their obligations to Him, will study what they shall render to the Lord for all His benefits ; they will delight in endeavours to glorify Him, they will be solicitously careful of a constant conformity to His will, and a peculiar delight in following after holiness. 5. Good works are necessary to honour our profession, to adorn the doctrine of God our Saviour, and to bring glory to His name. 6. Good works are likewise necessary to our inward peace and comfort. A truly tender conscience will always remonstrate against the indulgence of any sin, either of omission or commission. And how unhappy and miserable must that man be to have his heart condemning him ; to have a worm gnawing in his breast, to have conscience applying the terrors of the Lord, and representing to Him his guilt and danger ! And yet this cannot be avoided without a life of good works. We cannot have grounds of rejoicing, but from " the testimony of our conscience, that in simplicity and godly sincerity, not with fleshly wisdom, but by the grace of God we have our conversation in the world." (*J. King, B.A.*) *Morality the proper subject of preaching :*—Among the many causes which have concurred to render our holy religion thus unsuccessful, the indifference and neglect with which many sects of Christians have been accustomed to treat the moral precepts of the gospel deserves, I think, to be considered as none of the least. By giving an imaginary importance to subjects of speculation, concerning which wise and good men have always thought, and will probably continue to think, differently, they have turned aside the attention and zeal of mankind from those things in which their present and future happiness are really and principally concerned. My design is to counteract the influence of these prejudices, as far as I am able, by showing that the principal end of public preaching is to recommend the practice of virtue ; and that those who attend upon it should be best satisfied with such discourses as clearly explain and strongly inculcate the several branches of morality as it comprehends our duty to our Maker, our fellow-creatures and ourselves, without entering further into subjects of speculation and controversy than is of evident importance to the moral improvement and happiness of mankind. 1. I observe, in the first place, that if the duties of morality and religion were made the principal subjects of public preaching, it would remove or prevent many evils which have arisen from the contrary practice. The divisions and contentions, the persecutions and cruelties, which have disgraced the Christian Church, from its first establishment to the present day, are so well known that I may be excused the painful talk of entering into a particular enumeration of them. The time, however, seems to be at length arrived, in which men are beginning to see the folly of hating and persecuting one another for a difference in opinion on subjects concerning which it is impossible that they should be agreed. And shameful indeed must be the weakness, and fatal the delusion of mankind if the experience of so many ages hath not been sufficient to teach them this one plain but important lesson, that all zealous contentions about particular modes of faith or worship are unfriendly to the interests of religion, and the happiness of the world. From these circumstances one may hope that the present time is the dawning of a happy day, in which all distinctions of sects shall be abolished and all dissentions and animosities will be forgotten ; in which we shall all love one another with pure hearts fervently, and shall cordially unite in the worship of one God, the Father of us all. And what can be more likely to hasten the approach of this delightful period than for the ministers of religion to overlook and as much as possible discourage every party distinction and useless speculation, and constantly to direct the attention of their hearers to those subjects concerning which we are all agreed, and in which we are all immediately interested ; I mean the great duties of morality and religion? 2. Another reason why these duties should be the constant subjects of public preaching is because we may speak concerning them with the greatest perspicuity and certainty. That we ought to venerate the most excellent and perfect of all beings; that we should devoutly and thankfully acknowledge the hand which feeds and clothes us, and gives us richly all things to enjoy; that we should cheerfully submit ourselves to the direction of that Being who ordereth all things well; that we should observe the great laws of equity in all our transactions with mankind; that we should pity, and, if possible, relieve a brother in distress; that we should love our friends, be grateful to our benefactors, and forgive our enemies; that we should behave with honour and generosity, kindness, and charity towards all men; that we should govern ourselves with prudence and discretion, and diligently cultivate the powers which God hath given us; these are truths as obvious as they are important; truths concerning which all mankind in every country, and of every sect, are agreed. They are, therefore, of all others, the most proper subjects of public discourse. 3. I add this strain of preaching is best adapted to the understanding and taste of the generality of mankind. If a preacher endeavours to establish received opinions, or if he takes pains to overturn them; if he recites the comments of the most learned and celebrated fathers of the Church on difficult texts of Scripture, and supports them; or, if on the other hand, he attempts to explain them in a different manner, and, on this explanation, to ground a more rational scheme of faith; he may perhaps amuse and please a few; but he will, most probably, offend some, soar above the understandings of many, and reach the hearts of none. But if he exhorts his hearers to maintain good works; if he appeals to their consciences for the reasonableness and importance of the duties which he recommends; if he gives them just and lively representations of the influence which the observance or neglect of these duties will have upon their peace and happiness; if he touches the springs of gratitude, benevolence and humanity, of self-love, of hope and fear in their hearts, and calls forth every power and passion within them to assist him in pleading the cause of virtue; he will generally find his audience attentive and serious, and may hope to send them away not only pleased but improved. 4. Further, we may remark, that to exhort Christians to maintain good works is the proper business of the Christian ministry. Jesus Christ was eminently a Preacher of righteousness. This character He supported during the whole course of His public ministry. All the doctrines which He taught; all the wonderful works which He performed; all the pains and sufferings to which He submitted, were with this immediate view, that He might take away sin and bring in everlasting righteousness. Now, by what means can the teachers of religion so properly merit the character of Christian ministers as by pursuing the same important plan with Him whom they acknowledge as their Lord and Master? 5. The last consideration which I shall mention to evince the reasonableness of making the duties of morality and religion the constant subjects of public preaching is, that they are of the highest importance to the happiness of mankind, and that, in comparison with them, all other subjects are unprofitable and vain. 6. I will conclude by earnestly recommending it to you to take heed that you hear with the same design with which your ministers do or ought to preach, that you may be confirmed in all goodness. Attend upon public preaching, not with a view to have your favourite opinions established, your curiosity gratified, or your imaginations amused; but to have your evil habits corrected, your good dispositions strengthened, and your characters continually improved. "Be ye doers of the Word, and not hearers only." (*W. Enfield.*)  *The maintenance of good works the fruit of faith:*— This text places Christian morals upon a basis sufficiently firm and extended to support the fabric. Well aware of the absolute necessity of preaching sound principles in order to attain to a holy practice, and of the mighty influence which evangelical doctrine, if rightly understood and fairly stated, hath upon holiness in the life, St. Paul heaps privilege upon privilege, and within the compass of three short verses, enumerates the leading articles of our holy religion—giving such a view of them in their connection and influence upon practice, as must delight, constrain and ravish the heart of every believer. From hence I would humbly suggest this general remark, which, by the favour of our God, I intend to prosecute in the sequel of this discourse—whoever in the ministry would really advance the interests of holiness must be constant assertors and unwearied defenders of the doctrines of free grace. I. Glance at THOSE THINGS IN THE FAITHFUL SAYING WHICH OUR APOSTLE WOULD HAVE THE MINISTERS OF CHRIST TO AFFIRM CONSTANTLY, FOR THE EXPRESS PURPOSE OF PROMOTING HOLINESS. The very humbling doctrine of universal depravity (ver. 3).    We have little reason to be proud or vainglorious, severe or censorious of others, or to despise those who have not obtained mercy with ourselves—a vice which frequently deforms the character even of a child of a God.    But by frequently insisting upon the doctrines of universal depravity, the graces of humility, meekness, mildness, tenderness, and benevolence are perceived to be of the highest request for adorning the Christian character, and promoting the happiness of men; and hence the necessity as well as the advantage of affirming it constantly.    2. The Divine benevolence to man (ver. 4).    According to this statement, the gospel of our salvation is a system of love—of Divine love—of the love of God towards foolish, disobedient, and enslaved men.    3. Our salvation is all of grace (ver. 5).    Men cannot be too diligently cautioned against seeking salvation by the works of the law, nor too distinctly taught to ascribe the glory of the whole to "the Lord our righteousness."    4. Grace displayed in regeneration (ver. 5).    The reality and necessity of regeneration, the Divine Agent by whom the gracious change is accomplished, the manner in which this happy change is effected, with the unbounded mercy and love displayed, both by the Father and the Son, in giving the Holy Ghost for such a purpose.    These things cannot be too constantly affirmed: for, till this change be wrought on the nature and the heart, no true reformation will ever adorn the life.    5. Justification only by grace (ver. 7).    This is a cardinal article in the scheme of salvation, according to the Scriptures.    Well may the preservation or loss of it be designed the mark of a standing or falling Church.    It is the glory of the gospel, the melody of the joyful sound, the admiration and the joy of redeemed men, the most powerful motive to holiness which can be presented.    6. The title secured by justification to the enjoyment of eternal life (ver. 7).    It is both pleasant and very encouraging to mark, in this statement preceding my text, how regeneration, justification, adoption, and eternal glory, are so linked together in the same chain, that by holding one of the links, the happy possessor is infallibly secured of all the rest.    A most glorious and eternal truth—an assurance eminently calculated to enliven the believer's hope of eternal life in Christ.    And "whosoever hath this hope in Him purifieth himself," as Jesus Christ, his hope "is pure."    II. Show THAT THE CONSTANT AFFIRMATION OF THE DOCTRINES OF THE GOSPEL IS THE ONLY SCRIPTURE METHOD OF PREACHING GOOD WORKS.    Good works is a general expression for the practice of holiness, or the performance of every part of new obedience, whether it respect moral, civil, or religious duty.    To maintain good works, according to the signification of the original word, is to take the lead in the practice of them.    The term is of a military illusion.    As the officers of an army stand before, or a little in advance of the line, both to display heroism and preserve the order of the troops, so the believer in God is expected and commanded to stand forth, in the view of the world, in the sight of the Church, and particularly in the presence of younger disciples of Christ, as examples of regularity, sobriety, tenderness, and devotion.    To be emulous to excel, so as to provoke one another to faith, "to love and to good works."    An emulation this eminently worthy of being cherished!    To be "careful to maintain good works," is to be wholly intent upon the study and the practice of new obedience; for, except the mind feel a deep interest in holiness, from a love to God and a desire to be like Him, the external performance of good works will be cold, formal, and remiss. Hence it follows that the constant affirmation of these doctrines, so happily calculated to cherish the exercise of faith, must be peculiarly friendly to the interests of holiness; nay, more, that the constant affirmation of these things is the only Scriptural and consistent plan of engaging the believer in God to be careful to maintain good works.    This I hope to make manifest to your satisfaction from these four considerations.    1. These doctrines contain the principles, powers, and privileges, by which alone any of the human race become qualified for maintaining good works. 2. In these doctrines the believer is presented with the most powerful and proper motives and inducements to maintain good works.    3. These doctrines, when firmly believed, excite an inveterate antipathy at everything contrary to the nature and holy will of God.    4. The constant affirmation of these things affords the Christian moralist every advantage to state his subject in all its force.    (*W. Taylor.*) *On the necessity of Christian morality:*—I. THE NECESSITY OF GOOD WORKS IN REGARD TO OURSELVES.    1. The practice of good works is necessary to prove the reality and sincerity of our faith.    Faith or belief is a hidden principle which no man can see, and there is no other way of testifying that we possess this principle, but by the benevolent sentiments which it breathes, and the good actions which it prompts us to perform.    2. Good works are necessary to promote our moral improvement.

We know very well that there is such an indissoluble connection between a true faith and eternal salvation, that the man who is a sincere believer will be justified and sanctified and glorified ; but his sanctification is entirely distinct from, and is only a consequence of, his faith and justification. It is therefore necessary that the principle of a Divine life should operate in transforming him from glory to glory, and from one degree of religious and moral improvement unto another, until he be conformed to the image of the Son of God, and attain to the measure of the stature of a perfect man in Christ Jesus. It is not merely necessary that he should cease to do evil ; but he must learn to do well. In short, by a diligent and unremitting attention to the duties of religion and morality, he must cultivate the principle of universal righteousness and perfect holiness in the fear of the Lord. 3. Good works are necessary to qualify us for heaven. They are necessary to form us to the temper and disposition of Christ, who went about continually doing good ; in order that the same mind may be also in us that was in Him ; for we may depend upon it, that if we have not the spirit of the Lord Jesus, we are assuredly none of His. II. How THESE THINGS ARE GOOD AND PROFITABLE UNTO MEN. 1. These works are good, because they flow from a faith or belief in the command of God, and are done from a principle of conformity to His will. 2. But the apostle not only characterises these things as good, he also affirms that they are profitable unto men. We shall, therefore, conclude, by briefly pointing out how these good works are especially profitable to those to whom they are performed ; and we are espressly enjoined in Scripture to do good to all men as far as we have opportunity. Now, all who believe in God have it in their power, more or less, to do good to the bodies and the souls of men. This is one substantial reason why we are required to prove our faith by our works. He has ordained many to be rich, and more to be poor, that those to whom He has been bountiful might glorify Him with His own. He has bestowed wisdom and knowledge upon many, that they should instruct the ignorant, reclaim the wandering, and those who are out of the way. He commands us to defend the fatherless and plead for the widow ; to be the stranger's shield and the orphan's stay ; to relieve the oppressed ; to pour the balm of consolation into the wounded spirit ; to feed the hungry and clothe the naked, that the blessing of those who are ready to perish may come upon us. (*D. Stevenson.*) *Good works :*— I. DEFINE GOOD WORKS. 1. That our works may be good, they must be—(1) Performed by good persons ; (2) Required by God's Word ; (3) Done from a sound principle ; (4) Done to a right end. 2. How these good works must be maintained—(1) Attention to God's Word ; (2) Solicitude to know God's mind ; (3) Watchfulness against temptations ; (4) Embracing every opportunity of doing good ; (5) Pressing forward in knowledge ; (6) Exciting others to do the same. II. THE FAITH WHICH PRODUCES GOOD WORKS. 1. Knowledge of God. 2. And of the Word of God. 3. Faith is a composing grace. 4. A receptive grace. 5. An operative grace. 6. A rooting grace. 7. A humbling grace. 8. An elevating grace. 9. A strengthening grace. 10. A uniting grace. 11. A working grace. 12. A saving grace. III. How GOOD WORKS ARE PROFITABLE TO MEN. 1. As evidences of true faith. 2. Testimonies of gratitude to God. 3. Strengthening to assurance. 4. Edifying to others. 5. Condemning the world. (*T. B. Baker, M.A.*) *Practical Christianity :* —I. Practical Christianity is GOOD IN ITSELF. 1. It accords with the will of God. 2. It is an object of moral approbation to all minds. II. GOOD IN ITS INFLUENCE. Nothing is so useful to men as a Christly life. (*Homilist.*) *Some hints to preachers :*—I. FUNDAMENTAL TRUTHS ARE TO BE CONTINUALLY ENFORCED. II. PRACTICAL PREACHING IS NEVER OUT OF SEASON. III. CHRISTIAN DUTIES ARE OF UNIVERSAL APPLICATION. IV. TRIVIAL QUESTIONS OUT OF PLACE IN THE PULPIT. Inferences—1. It is possible to have repetition without sameness: " affirm constantly." 2. Belief that does not change the life is useless (James ii. 17). 3. The law is to be obeyed in spirit, rather than letter. (*F. Wagstaff.*) *Creed and conduct :*—The things that Titus is to " affirm constantly," as we shall see presently, are the doctrines of Christianity. What for ? " In order that they which have believed in God " might be orthodox ? Guarded against heresies ? Certainly ! But something more than that. In order that they might " give their minds to being foremost," as the word might be rendered, " in good works." That is what you are to preach your theology for, says Paul ; and the only way to make sure that your converts shall live sober and righteous lives is to see that they be thoroughly saturated in the great and recondite truths which I have taught you. I. THE GOSPEL IS DEGRADED UNLESS IT IS ASSERTED STRONGLY. " These things I will that thou affirm constantly " ; or, as the word might be rendered, " asseverate pertinaciously," persistently, positively, affirm and assert constantly and confidently. That is the way in which Paul thinks it ought to be spoken. "These things." What things? Well, here they are (vers. 4–7). There are all the fundamentals of evangelical Christianity packed into three verses. They are all there —man's sin, man's need, the Divinity of Jesus Christ, His sacrificial death, the gift of the Holy Spirit, the act of faith, the inheritance of eternal life. And these are the things which are to be asserted with all the energy and persistency and decisiveness of the speaker's nature. Paul did not believe in fining them down because people did not like them. He did not believe in consulting the "spirit of the age," except thus far, that the more the spirit of the age was contrary to the truth, the more need for the men that believed it to speak out. II. THIS POSITIVE ASSERTION OF THE TRUTHS OF REVELATION IS THE BEST FOUNDATION TO LAY FOR PRACTICAL GODLINESS. "I will that these things thou affirm constantly, in order that they which have believed might be careful to maintain good works." Rightly understood and presented, the great body of truth which we call the gospel, and which is summarised in the preceding context, grips daily life very tightly, while, on the other hand, of all the impotent things in this world, none are more impotent than exhortations to be good, which are cut away from the great truths of Christ's mission and work. The world has been listening to these ever since it was a world, and it is not a bit better for them all. There is only one thing that supplies the requisite motive power for practical godliness, and that is the great sacrifice of Jesus Christ and His indwelling in our hearts. The motives that the gospel gives for goodness, for holiness, for purity, for self-sacrifice, for consecration, for enthusiasm, for widespread sympathy and benevolence, for contempt of the material and the perishable—the motives that Christianity gives for all things that are lovely and of good report—are the strongest that can ever be brought to bear upon men, as regards their fulness, their depth, their sweetness, and their transforming energy. Then, if it be true that the best foundation for all practical goodness is in the proclamation and the possession of the great message of Christ's love, two things follow. One is that Christian people ought to familiarise themselves with the practical side of their faith, just as Christian ministers ought to be in the habit of insisting, not merely upon the great revelation of God's love in Jesus Christ, but upon that revelation considered as the motive and the pattern for holy living. And another consequence is that here is a rough but a pretty effective test of so-called religious truth. Does it help to make a man better? It is worth something if it does; if it does not, then it may be ruled out as of small consequence. III. THE TRUE TEST AND OUTCOME OF PROFESSING FAITH IS CONDUCT. In the text the fact that these Cretan Christians "believed in," or rather, perhaps, we should translate simply, "believed God," is given as a reason why they ought to maintain good works. That is to say, those who profess to have Him for their Lord and Father, those who avow that they are Christians, are by that profession bound to a conduct corresponding to the truth which they say they have received; and to conformity to the will of the God in whom they say that they have believed. Religious knowledge is all very necessary, but what is it for? It is to make us like God. Religious emotion is very necessary, too, and very delightful. It is right that Christian men should feel the glow of love and gratitude, the joy of forgiveness, the lofty and often unspeakable delights of calm communion with Him. All these are essential parts of a deep and true Christian character, but all these are for a purpose. If we are Christians we know God and we feel the emotions of the religious life, in order that we may be and that we may do. IV. NO ONE WILL KEEP UP THESE GOOD WORKS WHO DOES NOT GIVE HIS MIND TO IT. "That they . . . might be careful to maintain." The word that the apostle employs is a very remarkable one, only used in this one place in the New Testament; and the force of it might be given by that colloquialism which I have ventured to employ—"Giving their minds to maintaining good works." You have to make a business of it if you would succeed in it. You have to make a definite effort to bring before you the virtues and the excellencies which you ought to possess, and then to try your best to have them. And my text suggests one chief means of securing that result, and that is, the habit—which I am afraid is not a habit with a great many professing Christians—the habit of meditation upon the facts of the gospel revelation looked at in their practical bearing on our daily life and character. We should bring ourselves into that atmosphere, and saturate our minds and hearts with the thoughts of God's great love to us in Jesus Christ's death for us, of the pattern in His life, of the gift of His Spirit, of the hope of inheritance of eternal life. We should, by frequent meditation, submit ourselves to the power of these sacred thoughts, and we shall find that in them, one by one, are motives which, twisted together, will make a cord of love that shall draw us up out of the pit of selfishness and the mire of sense, and shall attract us joyfully along the path of obedience, else too hard for our reluctant and unaccustomed feet. (*A. Maclaren, D.D.*) *Good works :*—By flowers, understand faith ; by fruit, good works. As the flower is before the fruit, so is faith before good works ; so neither is the fruit without the flower, nor good works without faith. Faith and works.— 'Twas an unhappy division that has been made between faith and works. Though in my intellect I may divide them, just as in the candle I know there is both light and heat ; but yet, put out the candle, and they are both gone ; one remains not without the other. So 'tis betwixt faith and works ; nay, in a right conception, *fides est opus* (faith is work) ; if I believe a thing because I am commanded, that is *opus* (work). (*T. Selden.*)

Ver. 9. **Avoid foolish questions.**—*Foolish questions reproved :*—I. Amongst the QUESTIONS TO BE AVOIDED, such as the following may be included. 1. Those which savour of scepticism and unbelief, or which imply a doubtfulness of the truth of Divine revelation, or of any of its fundamental doctrines. Religion is not intended to gratify our curiosity, or to answer our speculative inquiries ; its object is to renew and sanctify the heart, and to meeten us for heaven. 2. Intricate and controversial questions are in general to be avoided, as engendering strife rather than ministering to godly edifying. 3. Prying questions relative to futurity, and which tend only to gratify a vain curiosity, ought to be avoided. 4. Questions arising from impatience and discontent are generally in a high degree improper, and unworthy of a Christian. When the mind is disquieted and full of trouble, we are commonly dissatisfied with everything about us, and wish if it were possible to have it otherwise. But this is a spirit which the Scriptures condemn, as utterly inconsistent with submission to the will of God, and as savouring of presumption and unbelief. 5. Perplexing and disquieting questions, which have no tendency to promote the great objects of practical religion, but only to excite unnecessary doubts and fears, are also prohibited in the text. Instead of asking the anxious question, for example, Are we elected ? our great concern should be to know whether we be effectually called ? Not, are our names written in heaven, but is God's law written in our hearts ? 6. Trifling and uninteresting questions which serve only to amuse and not to impart any useful information, ought by all means to be avoided. There is too great a disposition, even in serious people, to indulge in frivolous disputes, or in a strife about words rather than things, to the neglect of the weightier matters of the law, judgment, charity, and the love of God. II. Notice some things that are NECESSARY TO A PROFITABLE CONVERSATION. 1. Beware of loquacity, or too much speaking. Let not your words go before your thoughts ; think twice before you speak once. 2. Accustom yourselves to a sober way of thinking and talking, using at all times sound speech which cannot be condemned. 3. It may be proper to lay in a stock of interesting questions as matter for after conversation. Inquiries relative to our state, tending to promote experimental religion, both in ourselves and others, would at all times be useful and edifying. We cannot too frequently ask ourselves, Are we in a state of acceptance with God ; do we grow in grace ; do we hate sin and love holiness ; are we more weaned from the world, and fit for heaven ? An awakened sinner would naturally inquire, What must I do to be saved ? and those who have believed through grace should be anxious to inquire, What shall we do that we may work the works of God ? 4. Living as in the sight of God, and under a conviction that for every idle word we must give an account in the day of judgment, will exclude a great deal of light and trifling conversation, and give a savouriness to our speech, which will minister grace to the hearer. (*B. Beddome, M.A.*) *Religious disputes :*—Never was there a time wherein there was more talk or bustle and ado made about religion, and yet so little of the power of it seen in the world, whilst every one is most eager and busy in defending and propagating those doubtful doctrines which distinguish their several sects and factions, and so few mind those great and certain truths wherein they all are, or at least pretend to be, agreed. I. THAT OUR SAVIOUR AND HIS GOSPEL GAVE NO REAL JUST OCCASION FOR THOSE CONTROVERSIES, which since have been so hotly moved, will appear if we consider a little His doctrine and way of teaching whilst He was here on earth, for we shall find all along that He delivered His message not in any studied, artificial, spruce, and affected method, but with the greatest perspicuity and plainness imaginable. He accommodated not His discourses to the learned or wiser part of mankind only, but to the ignorant and simple. Thus also, if we consult the Acts of the Apostles, we shall find it was in the first and early times of the gospel. Much pains it cost them to convince Gentiles and Jews of the truth of our Saviour's religion, and to take off their prejudices against it and His person, and to resist and gainsay apostate Christians who would set up new religions of their own in opposition to Christ's, but little or none, in comparison, to make them understand the doctrine of it when once they were ready to follow and embrace it. They did not perplex their hearers with any quirks and intricacies, but avoiding all needless disputations, which engender strife and are not unto edification, told them plainly that Jesus commanded them everywhere to repent of their sins, and to forsake them, and to believe His gospel, and become His disciples, and obey what He enjoined in being temperate, humble, just, and charitable, and they should be for ever happy in the other world; and that for the effecting of this the Son of God came down from heaven, and lived here amongst men, and died, and rose again, of which they were witnesses. II. IT IS TRUE SOME DISPUTES SOON AROSE IN THE CHURCH, AND WHAT GAVE OCCASION TO THEM I AM NEXT TO INQUIRE. Some did arise even in the apostles' days, occasioned either by that great respect and veneration the Jews had for Moses' laws and institutions, or that fond presumption they had of God's particular inconditionate favour to them, and His absolute election of the seed of Abraham only; or else by the wickedness of those who for some private ends would pretend to Christianity, but, being unwilling to undergo the severities of it, invented such doctrines as might best serve to patronise their lusts or impieties. Thus though there were disputes, then, yet they were chiefly between Christians and their open and professed enemies, or such as had apostatised from them, or were but in part converted; but for some considerable time (whilst the persecutions lasted) the Christians amongst themselves lived in all love and peace, professing the same faith, joining in the same worship, and agreeing in the same principles and practices. But when once our religion had triumphed over all others and brought the greatest part of the world to its subjection, and the princes of the earth and the great and wise men became Christians, and there was no public enemy, either Jew or Gentile, to oppose, and find work for busy wits, then they began to fall out about their own religion; and this still increased more as the Christians grew more learned and idle, and less honest, and found time and leisure to study philosophy, the greatest part of which about that time was nothing else but sophistry, or the art of wrangling, and making plain things obscure. III. But yet by anything I have now said I WOULD NOT BE THOUGHT TO PERSUADE YOU THAT THERE WAS NOTHING IN OUR RELIGION THAT WAS DIFFICULT OR MYSTERIOUS. There are, without all doubt, some things contained in Scripture which are past our understandings, the particular modes and circumstances of which we cannot perfectly comprehend, but only that it would have been much more for the honour of God, the interest of Christianity, and the good of souls, if men would have suffered those things which were mysterious to have remained so, and also left those things that were plain in the same condition they found them. IV. Had I time in particular to show HOW SUCH IDLE DISPUTES IN MATTERS OF RELIGION ARE STILL CONTINUED IN THE WORLD, I MIGHT TELL YOU—1. Some men there are of a voluble tongue and of a talking, prating humour, who debate and dispute about everything, and therefore religion shall not escape if it ever comes in their way; you can say nothing but they presently contradict and oppose it. 2. Others there are that are pretty cool, tame, and calm, and can discourse freely and civilly about any ordinary common affair; but let the smallest and most inconsiderable point of religion be started, and they shall be presently all on fire, and as quarrelsome as if they had been born disputing, and as fierce as if at the pronouncing of every article of their belief their swords were to be drawn, and it was to be fought out. 3. Others there are who furnish themselves for dispute by reading a great deal of Scripture and getting it by heart, and so pouring it forth upon all occasions, interpreting it as peremptorily, and explaining it as confidently, as if they were guided by the same infallible spirit that the writers of it were endued withal. 4. Others there are who are very eager in maintaining a great many opinions, which are not to be found in Scripture, but in some authors they have great esteem of, or first chanced to read, or were directed to by those whose judgments they most valued; and these men's books such make their Bible, and from them fetch all their divinity. V. But whatever be, and many more there are, occasions of these quarrels and debates in religion, THE INCONVENIENCE OF THEM IS GREAT AND NOTORIOUS. 1. This foolish contending consumes so much time of our lives, which ought to be spent in our honest employments, in serious devotions, and doing the offices of justice, friendship, and charity one towards another; and I doubt not but much of our religious brawling and disputing shall be accounted for at the last day as idle words, for which neither ourselves, nor neighbours, nor anybody else was anything the better. 2. That which is a greater mischief than this, from hence men's lusts learn to dispute, and from these controversies in and about religion men have found out how to quiet their consciences in a way of sin, and to go on securely and undisturbedly, hoping by the help of a distinction or two they shall for all that get to heaven at last. 3. These disputes have been the occasion of those great breaches that have been made amongst Christians, whose care it ought to be to be of one mind, of one faith, and of one Church, and to adorn the doctrine of our Saviour by their mutual good will and serviceableness to one another; but instead of this, Christians, by their several little models of faith and their passions, have made it their business to divide the Church, excluding as many from salvation and their communion as are not just of their own way and fancy. (*B. Calamy.*)    *Unanswerable questions to be avoided:*—The writer remembers calling, late one Saturday evening, on a friend, an able theologian, whom he found seated at his writing table, evidently almost in a state of despair, and with tears in his eyes. "Why are you so sorrowful?" he said to him. In reply, the theologian only smiled sadly, and pointed to his waste-paper basket, which was full of torn-up manuscript. "See," he said, "the remains of eighteen quires of paper, which I have written all over since Monday morning, endeavouring to get my thoughts into order for my sermon to-morrow. But now I am more stupid and perplexed than when I began. I wanted to show how the two truths can be harmonised, that God knows everything and is the cause of everything, and yet that man is a free agent." It was no wonder that, notwithstanding all the intense thought and all the expenditure of paper, pens, and ink, that sermon did not get itself finished; for the more earnestly a man ponders on such problems the deeper and darker does the Divine mystery become. He who does not wish to lose his senses will postpone the consideration of such unanswerable questions to eternity, and then there will be no fear of his wanting occupation there. (*Otto Funcke.*)    *Profitless questions:*—A story is told of a man who spent most of his time interpreting the mysteries of Revelation. He said to a friend one day, "I can't quite understand about those seven trumpets, can you?" "No," was the answer; "but if you would pay more attention to your seven children and less to the seven trumpets, more of your real problems would be solved." The teacher must rule out unprofitable speculations and discussions. "Let us call up a great logician to help us out," said a pastor on one occasion, breaking in on such a debate in his class. "'Without controversy, great is the mystery of godliness.' Now, when I eat fish, I don't wear myself out grinding on the bones. I just leave them and go for the meat. Now for some meat from this lesson. Brother," turning to the combatant, "what have you found in this Scripture to help you this week?"    *Avoiding unprofitable questions:*—I once heard him tell an amusing story about a scientific man and popular author, who left a very celebrated minister for a seat in Bloomsbury Chapel. He brought a letter from Dr. H—— to Dr. Brock. "Before you open it, sir," said the author, "allow me to state that I am a man of science, and that I have much to do with beetles, butterflies, and spiders. Well, I get tired of them in six days, and on the seventh, the Sabbath, I don't want to hear anything about them. But our good, genial minister is also a man of science, and he will talk about scientific topics in the pulpit to illustrate the Word. Well, last night, the Sabbath, you know, he gave us a sermon full of spiders! I could not stand it any longer, so I went into the vestry, and said, 'Doctor, that sermon on spiders has finished me; give me a letter to Dr. Brock.'" "So," said the pastor, laughing, "he came to us because he knew I didn't preach about spiders." (*Memoir of Dr. Brock.*)    *The polemical and the practical Christian:*—Two learned physicians and a plain honest countryman, happening to meet at an inn, sat down to dinner together. A dispute presently arose between the two doctors on the nature of aliment, which proceeded to such a height, and was carried on with so much fury, that it spoiled their meals, and they parted extremely indisposed. The countryman, in the meantime, who understood not the cause, though he heard the quarrel, fell heartily to his meat, gave God thanks, digested it well, returned in the strength of it to his honest labour, and in the evening received his wages. Is there not sometimes as much difference between the polemical and practical Christian?    *Controversy foolish and unprofitable:*— As in the burning of some wet fuel we cannot see the fire for smoke, so the light of the Scriptures is dusked by the vapours of controversies. (*T. Adams.*)    *It is better not to try to understand too much:*—He that would comprehend all things, apprehends nothing. As he that comes to a corn heap, the more he opens his hand to take, the less he graspeth, the less he holdeth. Where the Scripture hath no tongue, we should have no ear. (*Ibid.*) **Genealogies.**—*The right and wrong use of genealogies:*—I. The second thing which Titus must resist are genealogies, which also must be rightly taken, because there always was, and yet is, an excellent use of them in Scripture. Before Christ they were so necessary, as the Jews were commanded to keep public and private records of their tribes and families—yea, and if there were any that could not tell or find his genealogy, he was not to be admitted, or, if inconsiderately he were, was to be deposed from public office (Numb. i. 18; Neh. vii. 62); and to this purpose some holy writers of Scripture have set down for the use of the Church to the end whole books of genealogies, but especially that the Jews might be able to bring their descent from the patriarchs, as we read of Paul, who no doubt could bring his line down from Benjamin (Phil. iii. 5). The use of these genealogies was to manifest the truth of God in the Scriptures. I. In the accomplishment of many special prophecies to particular persons. II. What is it, then, the apostle condemneth? Not any such as serve to the edification of the faith of the Church, whereof this of Christ a public person and Saviour of the world is the chief of all; neither the keeping of the descent so far as serveth to the preservation of right justice and civil peace. In which respect kings and nobles, yea, and other inferior persons, may inquire into that right which their ancestors have made their due, and must so hold their genealogy as they may hold their right against all claims. But here is condemned all that recounting of kindred and pedigree in all sorts of men, which proceedeth from a vain mind, and tendeth to worldly pomp and vainglory. For this was the sin of the Jewish teachers, that whereas now by Christ's appearance all distinction of families was in religious respect abrogated, and now was no such need of genealogy as before, unless it were before infidels and such as were not persuaded of the right descent of Christ, yet they out of their pride would be much and often in extolling of their tribes and kindred, and so not only for these accessories let go the substance of religion, but, as if they would build up that polity again which was now abolished, to the great hurt of their hearers, would much busy themselves in fruitless discourses. (*T. Taylor, D.D.*)

Vers. 10, 11. **An heretic . . . reject.**—*The treatment of heresy:*—I. HERESY IS NOT AN UNSOUND OPINION, BUT AN UNSOUND LIFE. A man may hold an erroneous opinion, and hold it sincerely; but the word used here denotes one who seeks to promote discord in the Church (See Rom. xvi. 17). II. HERESY IS TO BE DEALT WITH FIRMLY, BUT GENTLY. 1. Firmly—by admonition. 2. Gently—by repeated admonitions. III. HARDENED HERETICS ARE TO BE REJECTED. 1. But this only applies to exclusion from Church fellowship. 2. It is no warrant for persecution. 3. Excluded heretics are to be deemed objects of pity. (*F. Wagstaff.*) *Treatment of heretics:*—Paul having exhorted Titus both to teach the truth according to godliness, as also to resist all such foolish and vain doctrine as might do hurt in the Church of God. Titus might object: This indeed is my duty wherein I extend to exercise myself with diligence; but when I have laboured and done all I can, many there are who will not yield to the truth, nor submit themselves to this ordinance of God; how am I to carry myself towards such? Answer: The apostle, careful to prevent all such things as he foresaw might be hurtful to the Church, giveth direction in these two verses how to proceed in this business also. The former, giving direction and laying down the duty; and the latter, enforcing the same by moment of reason. In the former are three things to be considered: 1. The persons against whom Titus is to deal—here called heretics. 2. The direction how he is to behave himself towards them—reject them. 3. The orderly manner of proceeding, after once or twice admonition. The latter verse containeth the reason of this severity, because such persons are incurable and incorrigible; which is proved by two arguments. 1. Such a one is subverted, that is, turned or cast off the foundation. 2. He sinneth against his own conscience, being damned of his own self, that is, he wittingly and willingly spurneth against that truth of which his conscience is by the former admonition convinced. (*T. Taylor, D.D.*) *Heresy not to be trifled with:*—I am asked sometimes to read an heretical book. Well, if I believed my reading it would help its refutation, and might be an assistance to others in keeping them out of error, I might do it as a hard matter of duty, but I shall not do it unless I see some good will come from it. I am not going to drag my spirit through a ditch for the sake of having it washed afterwards, for it is not my own. It may be that good medicine would restore me if I poisoned myself with putrid meat, but I am not going to try it : I dare not experiment on a mind which no longer belongs to me. There is a mother and a child, and the child has a book to play with, and a blacklead pencil. It is making drawings and marks upon the book, and the mother takes no notice. It lays down one book and snatches another from the table, and at once the mother rises from her seat, and hurriedly takes the book away, saying : "No, my dear, you must not mark that, for it is not ours." So with my mind, intellect, and spirit; if it belonged to me I might or might not play tomfool with it, and go to hear Socinians, Universalists, and suchlike preach ; but as it is not my own, I will preserve it from such fooleries, and the pure word shall not be mingled with the errors of men. (*C. H. Spurgeon.*)    *Contagion of false doctrine :*—Sin is like the bale of goods which came from the East to this city in the olden time, which brought the pest in it. Probably it was but a small bale, but yet it contained in it the deaths of hundreds of the inhabitants of London. In those days one piece of rag carried the infection into a whole town. So, if you permit one sin or false doctrine in a church knowingly and wittingly, none can tell the extent to which that evil may ultimately go. The Church, therefore, is to be purged of practical and doctrinal evil as diligently as possible    That sour and corrupting thing which God abhors must be purged out, and it is to be the business of the Christian minister, and of all his fellow-helpers, to keep the church free from it. (*Ibid.*)    *Dilution of the truth :*—I have likened the career of certain divines to the journey of a Roman wine cask from the vineyard to the city. It starts from the wine-press as the pure juice of the grape, but at the first halting-place the drivers of the cart must needs quench their thirst, and when they come to a fountain they substitute water for what they had drunk. In the next village there are numbers of lovers of wine who beg or buy a little, and the discreet carrier dilutes again. The watering is repeated, till, on its entrance into Rome, the fluid is remarkably different from that which originally started from the vineyard. There is a way of doctoring the gospel in much the same manner. A little truth is given up, and then a little more, and men fill up the vacuum with opinions, inferences, speculations, and dreams, till their wine is mixed with water, and the water none of the best. (*Ibid.*)    *Wilful heresy :*—Heresy, in the New Testament, is most commonly used in an indifferent sense, and but seldom in a bad one. It generally signifies no more than a sect or party in religion. Thus we read of the sect, or heresy, of the Sadducees; of the sect, or heresy, of the Pharisees; St. Paul is styled a ring-leader of the sect, or heresy, of the Nazarenes; and he says of himself that, after the strictest sect (where the same Greek word is used) of the Jewish religion, he lived a Pharisee. In this last passage particularly nothing can be more plain than that the word has an innocent meaning, since the apostle rather commends than charges himself with anything criminal for having been a Pharisee before his conversion to the Christian faith. And we find it applied in the same manner in Acts xxviii. 22. I shall mention but one text more, and that is, "For there must also be heresies among you," &c. (1 Cor. xi. 19). The evident design of which is, that considering the various tempers of men, their different views, passions, prejudices, their selfishness, ambition, vanity, and the like, it was natural to expect that they would divide into parties about religion, as well as about politics, and the civil affairs of life ; and that the providence of God wisely permitted this for the trial of their integrity, and to distinguish the indolent, careless, and insincere from the real friends of truth, persons of an honest, inquisitive, and ingenuous temper. Now, according to this account, the general notion of a heretic is no more than this, viz., one that sets up to be the head, or chooses to join himself to a particular religious sect. I say who makes this the matter of his choice because it is implied in the original signification of the word; and, besides, nothing can be supposed to have any concern with religion but what is a voluntary action. A heretic, therefore, in a bad sense, must be one who knowingly espouses a false doctrine, is insincere in his profession, and asserts and defends what he is convinced is contrary to Christianity, and, consequently, one who maintains and supports the interest of a faction, to serve some base designs. According to St. Paul's account in the text, a heretic is not only subverted or turned aside from the true faith, he not only entertains wrong sentiments of Christianity, but sinneth, *i.e.*, doth this wilfully, and with an ill attention. He is one that makes religion a cloak for his immoralities, and espouses and propagates what he knows to be false, to promote the ends of his ambition, covetousness, or sensual pleasure; who, indeed, thinks it his interest to retain the name of a Christian, and in that circumstance only differs from a thorough and wilful apostate from Christianity, but which incurs the greater guilt may perhaps be hard to determine; for as the one rejects the Christian religion altogether, the other out of choice corrupts it, and opposes its true doctrines, even while he pretends to believe and reverence its authority. Such as these, I say, persons of such vile and dishonest principles, and of so flagitious a character, are the heretics condemned by St. Paul; and therefore to fix it as a term of reproach on any in whom there does not appear hatred of the truth, a sensual mind, and a profligate conscience, must be unchristian and scandalous. And if we examine other passages of the New Testament we shall find that they all concur in giving us the same idea of heresy. It is represented as a work of the flesh, because it has its foundation in the corrupt inclinations of human nature. It is reckoned among the most heinous and execrable vices—such as adultery, idolatry, hatred, variance, seditions, murders. And heretics are constantly described as men of no probity or honour, strangers to all the principles of virtue, and embracing such opinions only as were calculated for the gratification of irregular appetites, and advancing selfish and worldly views (1 Tim. i. 19; 2 Pet. ii. 1.) 1. It appears from what has been said that no mere error of the judgment can be heresy. For heresy is a high degree of wickedness; and necessarily supposes irregularity of the affections and a depraved and vicious choice; whereas erroneous conceptions and apprehensions of things are no crime at all, but natural to mankind in the present weak and imperfect state of the faculties. 2. We may infer that no honest man can possibly be a heretic. He may, indeed, have errors (and who is there among us that has not?)—nay, he may err in points of importance too, but his mistakes cannot be dangerous while he takes care to maintain a good conscience. 3. If heresy be an error of the will, and such only can be guilty of it who are condemned of themselves, how can we certainly know, in most cases at least, whether a man be a heretic or not? Let each of us put this question to himself impartially, and if we cannot answer it to our satisfaction, let us, however, learn thus much from our ignorance, to be modest in the censures we pass upon others. If it be said that such wicked deceivers are generally known by their fruits, and that their vicious lives will show us by what views they are acted, and the vile design of their imposture, I answer that, even upon this supposition, I should think it better that they be rejected for their immorality, which is notorious and palpable, than for heresy, of which we cannot so certainly judge. 4. Though it be a point of great nicety to judge of heresy in particular instances, the persons who come nearest the character of the old heretics are violent party men, who confine Christianity to their own faction, and excommunicate all that take the liberty to differ from them; the rigid imposers of human schemes of doctrine and modes of worship, as essential branches of religion, and laws binding conscience, these, I say, are most like the heretics condemned in Scripture, notwithstanding their insolence and presumption. (*James Foster.*) I. WHAT PATIENCE THE LORD USETH IN HIS JUST PROCEEDINGS, EVEN AGAINST THE WORST MEN, WHOM HE WILL NOT HAVE CONDEMNED NOR CAST OUT OF THE CHURCH UPON SUSPICIONS, OR SURMISES; no, nor presently after an open sin is committed; but there must be a time between wherein the Church must rightly inform herself, that she may know the nature and degree of the sin before she turn her to any censure or sentence. Yea, and further, the sin being apparent, she must not reject any, till all good means of reclaiming have been in vain used. Which may teach us, that to hasten excommunications *ipso facto;* or (as it is often) before the party can come to the knowledge or suspicion of any such proceeding, is to swerve from the rules of the Word, and those weighty reasons also upon which they are grounded. As namely: 1. Some offenders are curable; and what man in his wits will cut off his arm or leg so soon as it beginneth to ache and pain him, and not rather use means of surgery and cure? is any member in the body so despised? 2. Ourselves must not be so uncharitable as presently to despair of any man's conversion. God may in time raise the most desperate sinner unto repentance. 3. The means used are not lost; for if it attain no other end, yet shall it make them more inexcusable, the censure more just, and the Church's proceeding more equal and moderate. 4. Add here unto the Lord's example, who never striketh before He have sufficiently warned; He never precipitateth either sentence or execution, but first cometh down to see (Gen. xviii. 21), and hearkeneth and heareth (Mal. iii. 16), and accordingly passeth sentence. II. Note THAT WHEN A SINNER IS KNOWN TO SIN OF OBSTINACY, THE BEST WAY IS TO AVOID HIM AND CAST HIM OUT. 1 For labour is but lost on such a one. 2. He doth but tread holy things under his feet; of which holy things the Church is the keeper, and must be faithful. 3. He sins not only of judgment and reason, but of affection; and this is the reason why very few heretics are converted, when many unregenerate men and outrageously wicked in other kinds are, who sin not of affection and wilfulness, but of corrupt judgment only. 4. The Lord's example (Hos. iv. 17). III. Note hence, also, WHAT USE THE LORD MAKETH OF A WICKED CONSCIENCE, EVEN IN DESPERATE SINNERS. It shall be the accuser, witness, and judge to pronounce the sentence of death against his own soul; and so shall make way unto the Lord's most righteous judgment. Use. 1. It letteth us see what an intolerable torment a wicked conscience is. Use. 2. This further teaches us not to neglect the checks of conscience, nor our own hearts reproving us of our ways; as those men who are resolved to hold on their lewd courses, let the word and spirit, yea, their own spirits, suggest what they will or can against it. For the time cometh when thou canst not set the voice of thy conscience so light, and then that conscience which hath checked thee shall judge thee, and that heart which hath reproved thee shall torment thee, and thou shalt never be able to turn off the charge of it, but shalt by it be accused and convicted to have been a wilful chooser of thine own destruction. Use. 3. This consideration also teacheth us to look that in everything we keep good consciences before God and all men, the use of which will be manifold. (1) To keep us from errors and heresies, and contain us in the profession of the true faith; for let good conscience be put away, there must needs follow a shipwreck of faith; as is to be seen in all heretics. Hence are we counselled to make pure conscience as the coffer to keep faith in (1 Tim. iii. 9). (2) In doing any action lawful in itself, a good conscience only maketh it good to the doer; for to do even the will of God against my conscience is sin to me, be the same in itself never so materially good. (3) In suffering or enduring anything for well doing (as not the pain, but the cause maketh a martyr so), not the cause so much as the conscience of the sufferer worketh out his boldness and peace in the midst of the combat, and giveth him security in his conflict; whereas a bad conscience will betray the best cause. (4) In enjoying any condition of this present life, a good conscience is a sweet companion; even a dry morsel with peace of heart is better than a house full of sacrifices with strife and war within. In outward afflictions there is inward rejoicing, for let the heart be pacified in God, it can rejoice in tribulation. The disciples can go away rejoicing from the council that they were counted worthy to be beaten and suffer rebuke for Christ (Acts v. 41). The martyrs can kiss the stake, embrace the fire, and sing in the midst of the flames. (5) Yea, it doth not only through the whole life minister joy and comfort even in the remembrance of death, as in 2 Tim. iv. 7, 8, but it followeth a man after death, when all things else forsake him; and as a most faithful friend it goeth with him before God's judgment seat, and pleadeth for him at the bar of Jesus Christ; yea, testifieth with him, and cleareth, and quite acquitteth him from the judgment of the great day. All which being so, what pains and labour can be thought too much in the getting and keeping of such a jewel, which bringeth in so rich a recompense for so little labour, and how worthily doth he forfeit all these sweet fruits of it, who will be at no costs nor pains for it. (*T. Taylor, D.D.*)          *Heresy-hunters:*—You can imagine a husbandman who would neglect to care for his soil, and go out after squirrels and all manner of vermin that were eating his grain—if he had any that they could eat—who would go out to shoot weasels in the wall, foxes in the field, wolves in the wood, and bears everywhere; and who, when he could find nothing to shoot, would lie out at night, watching for racoons, and range up and down through the day, searching for some stray dog, where there should be sheep, but where there are none. There are in the Church what may be called heresy-hunters. They always carry a rifle—a spiritual rifle—under their arm. You will find them for ever outlying, watching for heresy—not so much in their own hearts, not so much in their own Church, not so much in their own minister, but in other people's hearts, in other people's Churches, in other people's ministers. If any man happens to hold an opinion respecting any doctrine which does not accord with their own peculiar views, they all spread abroad to run him down. They are taking care of and defending the faith! They are searching for foxes, and wolves, and bears, that they suppose are laying waste God's husbandry! They never do anything except fire at other folks. I have no doubt that Nimrod was a very good fellow in his own poor, miserable way, but a Nimrod minister is the meanest of all sorts of hunters. (*H. W. Beecher.*)          *Treatment of heretics:*—In what way are the directions here given to Titus to be used for our own guidance at the present time? They do not apply to persons who have always been, or who have ended in placing themselves outside the Christian Church. They refer to persons who contend that their self-chosen views are part and parcel of the gospel, and who claim to hold and teach such views as members or even ministers of the Church. Secondly, they refer to grave and fundamental errors with regard to first principles; not to eccentric views respecting matters of detail. And in determining this second point much caution will be needed; especially when inferences are drawn from a man's teaching. We should be on our guard with regard to assertions that a particular teacher virtually denies the Divinity of Christ, or the Trinity, or the personality of God. But when both these points are quite clear, that the person contradicts some of the primary truths of the gospel, and that he claims to do so as a Christian, what is a minister to do to such a member of his flock? He is to make one or two effects to reclaim him, and then to have as little to do with him as possible. In all such cases there are three sets of persons to be considered: the heretic himself, those who have to deal with him, and the Church at large. What conduct on the part of those who have to deal with him will be least prejudicial to themselves and to the Church, and most beneficial to the man himself? The supreme law of charity must be the guiding principle. But that is no true charity which shows tenderness to one person in such a way as to do grievous harm to others, or to do more harm than good to the person who receives it. Love of what is good is not only consistent with hatred of what is evil; it cannot exist without such hatred. What we have to consider, therefore, is this. Will friendliness confirm him in his error? Would he be more impressed by severity? Is intercourse with him likely to lead to our being led astray? Will it increase his influence and his opportunities of doing harm? Is severity likely to excite sympathy in other people, first for him, and then for his teaching? It is impossible to lay down a hard and fast rule that would cover all cases; and while we remember the stern instructions which St. Paul gives to Titus, and St. John to the " elect lady," let us not forget the way in which Jesus Christ treated publicans and sinners. (*A. Plummer, D.D.*)      *Condemning of himself:*—Ferdinand, Emperor of Germany, possessed a great number of watches, in collecting of which he had a fancy. " It pleased him once," says our quaint author, " to put this, his variety of speaking gold, upon a table, as if he would expose it to sale: he then stepped aside. A stander-by, driven by a desire of stealing, filched one of them (a repeater), which the emperor espying aslant, called him, and without accusation, kept him in various discourse till the watch striking disclosed the hour and his theft. (*Saturday Magazine.*)

Ver. 13. **Bring Zenas the lawyer.**—*Sermon to the legal profession:*—This man of my text belonged to a profession which has often had ardent supporters of Christ and the gospel. Among them, Blackstone, the great commentator on English law; and Wilberforce, the emancipator; and Chief Justices Marshall, and Tenterden, and Campbell, and Sir Thomas More, who died for the truth on the scaffold, saying to his aghast executioner: "Pluck up courage, man, and do your duty: my neck is very short; be careful, therefore, and do not strike awry." Among the mightiest pleas that ever have been made by tongue of barrister, have been pleas in behalf of the Bible and Christianity—as when Daniel Webster stood in the Supreme Court at Washington, pleading in the famous Girard will case, denouncing any attempt to educate the people without giving them at the same time moral sentiment, as "low, ribald, and vulgar deism and infidelity"; as when Samuel L. Southard, of New Jersey, the leader of the forum in his day, stood on the platform at Princeton College commencement, advocating the literary excellency of the Scriptures; as when Edmund Burke, in the famous trial of Warren Hastings, not only in behalf of the English government, but in behalf of elevated morals, closed his speech in the midst of the most august assemblage ever gathered in Westminster Hall, by saying: " I impeach Warren Hastings in the name of the House of Commons, whose national character he has dishonoured; I impeach him in the name of the people of India, whose rights and liberties he has subverted; I impeach him in the name of human nature, which he has disgraced; in the name of both sexes, and of every rank, and of every station, and of every situation in the world, I impeach Warren Hastings." Yet, notwithstanding all the pleas which that profession has made in behalf of God, and the Church, and the gospel, and the rights of man, there has come down through the generations a style of prejudice against it. So long ago as in the time of Oliver Cromwell, it was decided that lawyers might not enter the parliament house as members, and they were called "sons of Zeruiah." The learned Doctor Johnson wrote an epitaph for one of them in these words:

> "God works wonders now and then,
> Here lies a lawyer, an honest man!"

There is no man who has more temptations, more trials, or graver responsibilities than the barrister, and he who attempts to discharge the duties of his position with only earthly resources, is making a very great mistake. Witness Lord Thurlow, announcing his loyalty to earthly government in the sentence: "If I forget my earthly sovereign, may God forget me," and yet stooping to unaccountable meanness. Witness Lord Coke, the learned and the reckless. No other profession more needs the grace of God to deliver them in their temptations, to comfort them in their trials, to sustain them in the discharge of their duty. While I would have you bring the merchant to Christ, and while I would have you bring the farmer to Christ, and while I would have you bring the mechanic to Christ, I address you to-day in the words of Paul to Titus, "Bring Zenas the lawyer." By so much as his duties are delicate and great, by so much does he need Christian stimulus and safeguard. God alone can direct him. To that chancery he must be appellant, and he will get an answer in an hour. Blessed is that attorney between whose office and the throne of God there is perpetual, reverential, and prayerful communication. That attorney will never make an irreparable mistake. True to the habits of your profession, you say, "Cite us some authority on the subject." Well, I quote to you the decision of the Supreme Court of Heaven: "If any lack wisdom, let him ask of God, who giveth to all men liberally, and upbraideth not, and it shall be given him." There are two or three forms of temptation to which the legal profession is especially subjected. 1. The first of all is scepticism. You get so used to pushing the sharp question "why" and making unaided reason superior to the emotions, that the religion of Jesus Christ, which is a simple matter of faith, and above human reason, has but little chance with some of you. Scepticism is the mightiest temptation of the legal profession, and that man who can stand in that profession, resisting all solicitations to infidelity, and can be as brave as George Briggs of Massachusetts, who stepped from the gubernatorial chair to the missionary convention, to plead the cause of a dying race: then on his way home from the convention, on a cold day, took off his warm cloak and threw it over the shoulders of a thinly-clad missionary, saying: "Take that and wear it, it will do you more good than it will me"; or, like John McLean, who can step from the Supreme Court room of the United States on to the anniversary platform of the American Sunday School Union—its most brilliant orator—deserves congratulation and encomium. O men of the legal profession, let me beg of you to quit asking questions in regard to religion, and begin believing. If you do not become a Christian, O man of the legal profession, until you can reason this whole thing out in regard to God, and Christ, and the immortality of the soul, you will never become a Christian at all. Only believe. "Bring Zenas the lawyer." 2. Another mighty temptation for the legal profession is to Sabbath breaking. What you cannot do before twelve o'clock Saturday night, or after twelve o'clock Sunday night, God does not want you to do at all. Beside that, you want the twenty-four hours of Sabbath rest to give you that electrical and magnetic force which will be worth more to you before the jury than all the elaboration of your case on the sacred day. Every lawyer is entitled to one day's rest out of seven. If he surrender that, he robs three—God, his own soul, and his client. Lord Castlereagh and Sir Thomas Romilly were the leaders of the bar in their day. They both died suicides. Wilberforce accounts for their aberration of intellect on the ground that they were unintermittent in their work, and they never rested on Sunday. "Poor fellow!" said Wilberforce, in regard to Castlereagh—"Poor fellow! it was non-observance of the Sabbath." Chief Justice Hale says, "When I do not properly keep the Lord's day, all the rest of the week is unhappy and unsuccessful in my worldly employment." 3. Another powerful temptation of the legal profession is to artificial stimulus. The flower of the American bar, ruined in reputation and ruined in estate, said in his last moments: "This is the end. I am dying on a borrowed bed, covered with a borrowed sheet, in a house built by public charity. Bury me under that tree in the middle of the field, that I may not be crowded; I always have been crowded." 4. Another powerful temptation of the legal profession is to allow the absorbing duties of the profession to shut out thoughts of the great future. You know very well that you who have so often tried others, will after awhile be put on trial yourselves. Death will serve on you a writ of ejectment, and you will be put off these earthly premises. On that day all the affairs of your life will be presented in a "bill of particulars." No *certiorari* from a higher court, for this is the highest court. The day when Lord Exeter was tried for high treason; the day when the House of Commons moved for the impeachment of Lord Lovatt; the day when Charles I. and Queen Caroline were put upon trial; the day when Robert Emmet was arraigned as an insurgent; the day when Blennerhasset was brought into the court-room because he had tried to overthrow the United States government, and all the other great trials of the world are nothing compared with the great trial in which you and I shall appear, summoned before the Judge of quick and dead. There will be no pleading there "the statute of limitation"; no "turning State's evidence," trying to get off ourselves, while others suffer; no "moving for a non-suit." The case will come on inexorably, and we shall be tried. You, who have so often been advocate for others, will then need an advocate for yourself. Have you selected Him? The Lord Chancellor of the Universe. Lord Ashburton and Mr. Wallace were leading barristers in their day. They died about the same time. A few months before their decease they happened to be at the same hotel in a village, the one counsel going to Devonshire, the other going to London. They had both been seized upon by a disease which they knew would be fatal, and they requested that they be carried into the same room and laid down on sofas, side by side, that they might talk over old times and talk over the future. So they were carried in, and lying there on opposite sofas, they talked over their old contests at the bar, and then they talked of the future world upon which they must soon enter. It was said to have been a very affecting and solemn interview between Mr. Wallace and Lord Ashburton. My friends, my subject to-day puts you side by side with those men in your profession who have departed this life, some of them sceptical and rebellious, some of them penitent, childlike, and Christian. These were wandering stars for whom is reserved the blackness of darkness for ever, while these others went up from the court-room of earth to the throne of eternal dominion. Through Christ, the advocate, these got glorious acquittal. In the other case, it was a hopeless lawsuit. An unpardoned sinner *versus* the Lord God Almighty. O what disastrous litigation! (*T. De Witt Talmage, D.D.*) **That nothing be wanting unto them.**—*Titus' duty to his fellow-ministers :*— Ministers ought to abound in the fruits of kindness to one another, and most to those whose circumstances render the expressions of brotherly kindness needful. Probably Titus could not, from his own purse, furnish everything that was needful to his brethren who were travelling in the service of the Churches. But he might, through his influence, do by the hands of others what was not in his own power. The apostle had already said that the doctrine of salvation by grace teaches and constrains men who believe it to maintain good works. And here he calls on the believers under the care of Titus to embrace the occasion that was presented to them, of testifying their faith by their works, and learning to practise the duties by which they were to approve themselves unto God as faithful Christians. There are too many who form good resolves, but when opportunities offer of putting them into practice, suffer them to pass unimproved. They intend to do what they know to be right, but are in no haste to perform it. But let ours, those who belong to our holy society, learn not only to do, but to stand foremost in doing, good works, on all necessary occasions. An opportunity for doing good ought to be as much valued by us as an opportunity for receiving it, for we are sure that "it is more blessed to give than to receive." We know not what opportunities we may afterwards have to do good; but the present opportunity will not return; and we may feel the same disposition to neglect a second and a third as a first opportunity of usefulness. How then shall we approve ourselves fruit-bearing branches in the true vine, and not to be found among the barren branches against whom the terrible sentence is pronounced, that the great Husbandman will take them away, and they shall be gathered, and cast into the fire and burned? "Bring Zenas the lawyer, and Apollos, diligently on their way," and in supplying their necessities let our people learn to excel, or go before others, in good works, that they be not unfruitful. Zenas had probably been a Jewish lawyer. And against that class of men awful things had been spoken by our Lord. Amongst others, it is said that they took away the key of knowledge from men. But the grace of God can make a most effectual change in those from whom least good and most evil is to be expected. He was now travelling with the key of knowledge to open the mysteries of the kingdom of heaven to Gentiles as well as Jews. Apollos was a well known and an eminent labourer in the gospel. And those who were not ready to afford encouragement and facilities to such labourers for Christ, and for the souls of men, gave too much reason to suspect that they were themselves barren and unfruitful in the knowledge of our Lord and Saviour. Let us be fellow-helpers to the truth, that we may not incur the punishment of those who are lukewarm in the cause of Christ (Rev. iii.). (*G. Lawson, D.D.*)     *Christianity enjoins courtesy :*—Christianity hindereth not, but commendeth and enjoineth civil courtesy and all kind of humanity. For—1. Whatsoever pertaineth to love and good report, that must believers think on and do (Phil. iv.). 2. The wisdom which is from above is gentle, peaceable, full of mercy and good fruits (James iii. 17). 3. Those many commandments, that Christians should salute and greet one another, and that with a holy kiss (1 Thess. v. 26), called by Peter the kiss of love; usual in those East countries, by which outward testimony they declared mutual love and kindness. 4. Outward courtesy is a necessary virtue even for the maintaining of the bond of Christian peace; yea, availeth much for the nourishing and increasing the communion of saints, and society with God's people. 5. How disgraceful a thing were it for the profession of Christ, that such as profess faith in the Lord Jesus should show themselves inhuman or hoggish, who should be as lambs and little children, for such are they who have entered into the kingdom of Christ, as the prophet witnesseth. Let this point, therefore, be well thought of, that as faith and love cannot be separate, so must good conscience and good manners go together. (*T. Taylor, D.D.*)

Ver. 14. **Let our's also learn.**—*The mutual property and purpose of good men :*—
I. THE MUTUAL PROPERTY OF GOOD MEN. "Ours." 1. A mutual appreciation.
2. A mutual accumulation. II. THE MUTUAL PURPOSE OF GOOD MEN. "To maintain good works." 1. What are good works? Works that grow out of supreme love to God, and tender and disinterested sympathy with man. 2. Why is the maintenance of good works so transcendently important? (1) Because they are essential to the building up of a true moral character. (2) Because they are necessary to the spiritual reformation of mankind. (*Homilist.*)     **That they be not unfruitful.**—*Christianity fruitful :*—The metaphor implieth that as the Church is God's orchard or garden, and His ministers are His planters and waterers, so the faithful are the trees, even trees of righteousness, the planting of the Lord, and planted by the rivers of waters, that they might bring forth their fruit in due season ; and teacheth that true Christianity is not a barren but a fruitful profession, unto which Christians are everywhere called. In Ezek. xlvii. 12 we have a notable resemblance of those manifold fruits, which by the power of the gospel should be by believers produced in the Church of the New Testament. The vision was of waters which ran from the Temple, and from under the threshold of the sanctuary. And wheresoever these waters should run, they should cause admirable fruitfulness, in so much as on both sides of the river shall grow all kind of fruitful trees, whose leaves shall not fade, and their fruit shall not fail. These waters are the gospel which issue from under the threshold : that is, from Christ the door, typified by that beautiful gate of the Temple; from the Temple at Jerusalem these waters were with swift current to run not only over Judæa, but all the world in a short space : hence was the Church mightily increased, for though these waters run into the dead sea, wherein (if we believe histories) abideth no living thing, yet such a quickening power they carry with them, as even there everything shall live ; such as were dead in trespasses and sins are hereby quickened, and become trees of righteousness green and flourishing, yea, and constantly fruitful in all godly conversation. And this the same which our Saviour noteth (John xv. 1), that His Father is the husbandman, Himself is the Vine, Christians are the branches of that vine, who if they be found, His Father purgeth that they may bring forth more fruit ; teaching us hereby that it is the Lord's scope and aim that Christians should be abundant in fruits beseeming their profession. The Apostle Paul accordingly exhorteth the Philippians to be much in goodness, to abound in love, in knowledge, and in all judgment; yea, to be filled with fruits of righteousness which are by Jesus Christ unto the glory and praise of God. And the same apostle calleth rich men to be rich in good works. I. THE CONDITIONS OF THIS FRUITFULNESS. 1. Every Christian must be fruitful ; for every fruitless branch is cut down and made fuel for the fire. 2. Every Christian must bring forth good fruit. 3. This fruitfulness must proceed from good causes. (1) The tree must be good, for men gather not grapes of thistles. (2) He must have a good root (John xv. 4). (3) He must draw thence good sap and juice through the fellowship and

communion of Christ's death and resurrection. (4) He must have the Spirit of the Son to be a principal agent in the setting and ripening of these fruits. (5) He must have the love of God within him, constraining him, which will be as the sun helping on these fruits to their perfection. (6) He must have good ends in his eye, viz., God's glory and man's good (Phil. i. 2). 4. Every Christian must bring forth much fruit, and not for clusters scarce berries, trees of righteousness are laden with the fruits of the Spirit; and herein is the Father glorified, that ye bring forth much fruit (John xv. 8). 5. Christians must continue fruitful, and grow daily more fruitful (John xv. 2). II. REASONS TO MOVE CHRISTIANS TO THIS FRUITFULNESS. 1. God's pains and costs with us. 2. It is more than time to yield up our fruits. Let us consider how much we have already lost, and how little remaineth behind, and this cannot but be as a loud voice in our ears unto fruitfulness. 3. Heavenly wisdom which is from above is full of good fruits; which, if it have taken up our hearts, will bewray itself in love, in joy, peace, long-suffering, gentleness, goodness, faith, meekness, temperance, and such like; and as naturally we rejoice to see everything about us fruitful—our fields, our cattle, our orchards—even so this supernatural wisdom would make it the delight of our souls to see our hearts and lives laden with the best fruits. 4. The barren condition hath little comfort in it, and the danger of unfruitfulness is very great; for God's fearful displeasure disburdeneth itself, and seizeth on such persons by sundry degrees. (1) The Lord rejecteth them. (2) Degree of God's curse on such fruitless branches is the withering which presently followeth their casting forth, and this the Lord bringeth on them two ways: sometimes by removing means of fruitfulness, and so having laid His vineyard waste, He threateneth, in the next place, that the clouds should not rain upon it (Isa. v. 6): and sometimes by blowing upon the gifts He had given, he shall lose his sap and greenness he once had; the unprofitable servant after conviction must have his talent taken from him; and this curse is so eminent upon many men that, comparing them with themselves not long since, a man may say, as the disciples of the fig tree, against which the curse was passed from the mouth of Christ, "How soon is the fig tree withered!" (3) Another degree is, that no means shall be able henceforth to do such a person any good; but the curse being passed against him, this is one branch of it, that he shall be like the heath in the wilderness, which shall not see when any good cometh. Now the heath it hath good coming upon it, the rain falleth, the sun shineth, the spring and summer season returneth upon it, but it seeth none of this good, but remaineth a dry and parched heath still; even so it is with a barren soul which God hath begun to curse—the rain, the sun, the season, the Word, sacraments, days of grace, Jesus Christ Himself do him no good; he sees no good towards him in all these; nay, the Word judgeth him, the sacraments are poison unto him, and Christ Himself is a rock of offence to him, on whom he breaketh the neck of his soul. (4) After all these cometh the heavy sentence, unto which by all these this sinner hath been prepared. Cut him down, bring now the axe, for the pruning-knife hath done him no good; hew him down by death from the ministry under which he hath been so long fruitless, bind him hand and foot, make a faggot of him, and cast him into hell fire—cast, I say, that unprofitable servant into utter darkness, there shall be wailing and gnashing of teeth: and this is the woeful hire of unfruitfulness. III. THE HINDRANCES OF THIS FRUITFULNESS. 1. Superfluity of lusts and inordinate desires, which are as dead branches, and therefore must be lopped off before fruit can be expected; the denial of a man's self so far as corrupt is the first lesson in Christianity. 2. The unfitness of the soil, as if it be stony, or near unto a rock where it cannot take deep roots; the hard and stony heart suffereth not any good seed to take root, and much less rise up to fruit. Or if the soil be a dry ground on which the rain falls not, or on a high and hilly ground on which the rain stayeth not; so the haughty and proud heart shutteth off the rain as fast as it cometh; it moisteneth the crust and outside a little, but it stayeth not to get within it to prepare it to fruitfulness. Or if the ground be shaded that the sun cannot, or seldom, look upon it; if the mind and affections are otherwise distracted, that seldom men set themselves under the means of instruction; the Sun of Righteousness shining in His Church not enlightening, not warming nor cherishing them, not bringing back a new spring upon them, how can we expect fruit from such, unless we can look that a tree which hath been fruitless all the summer should be laden with fruit in the midst of winter. 3. Sundry vain conceits suggested by the devil, and assented unto by men to keep them in unfruitful courses. (1) As many will not stick to object, I hope notwithstanding I have not been hitherto so fruitful as you speak of, yet I have done well enough all this while, and why may I not do so still? and thus resolve because God hath used patience and spared them, He will therefore spare them still in their unfruitfulness. But this is the devil's logic, the clean contrary whereof is the conclusion of the Scripture. Hath God spared thee the second and third year, and art thou still fruitless? He must now needs call for the axe, and this is that which thou must expect. (2) Another saith, "Oh, but I am a member of the Church, and what talk you to me. I hear the Word, receive the sacraments, and though I be not so forward and strict, I hope I shall do well enough." Which is all one as if a fruitless tree should reply to the master and say, "I hope, master, thou wilt not cut me down, I am in thy orchard, and stand near thy house; if I were in the waste I should think thou should care less for me." But will not the master reply, that "Thou must rather go down, because thou standest unprofitable in my orchard." (3) Others say, "Oh, but we are not so fruitless as you take us, and what desire you more?" Whereunto I say, that such have great need to desire better evidences to allege for themselves than this. Thou must not be a privative, but a positive Christian, laden with the fruits of the Spirit, else thou hast lost all thy labour. (*T. Taylor, D.D.*) *Fruifulness the true test :*—It is with professions of religion, especially such as become so in a time of outpouring of the Spirit of God, as it is with blossoms in the spring; there are vast numbers of them upon the trees which all look fair and promising, but yet many of them never come to any-thing, and many of those that in a little while wither up, drop off, and rot under the trees, yet for a while look as beautiful and gay as others; and not only so, but smell sweet and send forth a pleasant odour, so that we cannot, by any of our senses, cer-tainly distinguish those blossoms which have in them that secret virtue which will afterward appear in the fruit, and that inward solidity and strength which shall enable them to bear, and cause them to be perfected by the hot summer sun that will dry up the others. It is the mature fruit which comes afterward, and not the beautiful colour and smell of the blossoms, that we must judge by. (*Jonathan Edwards.*)

Ver. 15. **Greet them that love us in the faith.**—*Christian love :*—Hence note that religion bindeth man to man in the straightest bond; for—1. The Spirit is the tier of it; and hence is it called the unity of the Spirit in the bond of peace; and indeed it must be a wonderful bond that can reconcile such deadly enemies as men are before they come into the kingdom of Christ (Isa. xi. 6). 2. God's image, wheresoever it is, is exceeding beautiful, and a great binder, especially where renewed and repaired; which being once espied, let the outward condition be what it can be, a religious heart seeth sufficient matter of love, and will knit the soul unto the soul of such a one. 3. It addeth strength and firmness to all other bonds of nature, affinity, desert, &c., and maketh them more natural. What a true friend was Jonathan to David! Because he saw that God was with him his soul clave unto him; though the kingdom was to be rent from him for it, yet could he not rend his heart from David. If Joseph had not had more than nature, he could not but have revenged such infinite wrongs upon his brethren; whereas the grace of his heart made him say, "It was not you, my brethren, but God sent me before you." Consider also of the example beyond all imitation of our Lord Jesus Christ, who gave Himself to the death for us when we were yet His enemies. 4. This love must needs be most lasting; for being love in the truth for the truth's sake, it shall continue so long as the truth doth; but the truth abideth with us, and shall abide with us for ever; and this is the cause, that whereas the love of nature dieth with it, and the love of wicked men dieth with their persons, this love liveth in death, yea, when it goeth to heaven with a man, and getteth strength and perfection then faith ceaseth, and hope vanisheth away. Use 1. Whence we are taught most familiarly to embrace them that love us in the faith, and to make most account of their love. Many love in the face, many in the flesh, many in nature, only the love of Christians is a fruit of faith, a work of the Spirit, and therefore a surer bond than they all. Well knew the apostle that none was in comparison worth having but this; he calleth for no other, he careth for no other, he mentioneth no other. 2. Such as set into any society with others, if he would have it comfortable unto him, let him strengthen all other natural or civil bonds by this bond of religion; let him labour to begin his love in the faith, or, if he have begun elsewhere already, let him reform the same hereby if he look for any sound comfort in his estate; for this is the cause that men often have so little return of love from their wives, so little obedience from their children, so little duty from their servants, so slender respect from their equals, because they begin their love and duties at a wrong end, and have for other respects affected those with whom they live, but the least, if at all, for grace and religion, which of all is the soundest, most profitable, and most comfortable. (*T. Taylor, D.D.*) *Shake hands :*—Shake hands with somebody as you go out of church. The more of it the better, if it is expressive of real interest and feeling. There may be a great deal of the spirit of the gospel put into a hearty shake of the hand. Think of St. Paul's four times repeated request—" Greet one another "—after the custom then in common use, and one which is expressive of even warmer feeling than our common one of hand-shaking. Why not give your neighbours the benefit of the warm Christian feeling that fills you to your finger tips, and receive the like from them in return? You will both be benefited by it; and the stranger will go away feeling that the Church is not, after all, so cold as he had thought it to be. *Christian love :*—A lady and her little daughter, passing out of church, the child bade good-bye to a poorly dressed little girl. " How did you know her? " inquired the mother. " Why, you see, mamma, she came into our Sabbath School alone, and I made a place for her on my seat, and I smiled and she smiled, and then we were acquainted."

# THE BIBLICAL ILLUSTRATOR

## PHILEMON

THE

# BIBLICAL ILLUSTRATOR

BY
JOSEPH S. EXELL

PHILEMON

BAKER BOOK HOUSE
GRAND RAPIDS, MICHIGAN 49506

# INTRODUCTION TO THE EPISTLE TO PHILEMON.

AUTHORSHIP.—The testimonies to the Pauline authorship of this Epistle are abundant. 1. External. It is not quoted so often by the earlier Christian fathers as some of the other letters; its brevity and the fact that its contents are not didactic or polemic, account for that omission. We need not urge the expressions in Ignatius, cited as evidence of that apostolic father's knowledge and use of the Epistle, though it is difficult to regard the similarity between them and the language in ver. 20 as altogether accidental. The Canon of Muratori, which comes to us from the second century, enumerates this as one of Paul's Epistles. Tertullian mentions it, and says that Marcion admitted it into his collection. Sinope, in Pontus, the birthplace of Marcion, was not far from Colosse where Philemon lived, and the letter would find its way to the neighbouring churches at an early period. Origen and Eusebius include it among the universally acknowledged writings of the early Christian times. It is so well attested historically, that De Wette says its genuineness on that ground is beyond doubt. 2. Internal. It is impossible to conceive of a composition more strongly marked within the same limits by those unstudied assonances of thought, sentiment, and expression, which indicate an author's hand, than this short Epistle as compared with Paul's other productions. It will be found also that all the historical allusions which the apostle makes to events in his own life, or to other persons with whom he was connected, harmonise perfectly with the statements or incidental intimations contained in the Acts of the Apostles or in the other Epistles of Paul. (*H. B. Hackett, D.D.*) The *authenticity* of this Epistle was probably never very seriously denied; its *inspiration* was unpopular in certain quarters, external to the Church. It is very necessary to remember that the objections to the inspiration of the letter came from anti-dogmatic, not from dogmatic Christians; that "in the battle of the creeds" the defenders of the Catholic doctrine are the champions of the Epistle; that "the fierce current of prejudice," stemmed by Jerome, Chrysostom, and Theodore of Mopsuestia, set in from a quarter external to the Church. Jerome states that the arguments used against the Epistle were, either that it was not St. Paul's, or that, if it came from his hand, he was not always inspired. Its subject, they argued, proved that it was a commendatory note, not a dogmatic document. Jerome argues that its universal reception by all churches in the whole world is unaccountable, except on the hypothesis of a Pauline origin. As to apparent triviality and everyday style, he points to such passages as 2 Tim. iv. 13, Gal. v. 12, 1 Cor. vii. 12, with their apparently petty details, outbursts of human feeling, admissions of uncertainty. For the brevity of the letter he refers to the Minor Prophets, and concludes by a quaint quotation of Rom. ix. 28, as if the very shortness of Philemon were in consonance with the spirit of the gospel. (*Bp. Wm. Alexander.*) The beautiful Epistle to Philemon contains nothing inconsistent with its genuineness, and bears everywhere marks of the hand and character of Paul. Among these last must be reckoned the absence of any request for the manumission of Onesimus. Tact so delicate belongs not to a forger. The names sending greeting to Philemon are a valuable coincidence with the same names in the Epistle to the Colossians. (*Prof. J. A. Beet.*)

PLACE, TIME, OCCASION, AND OBJECT OF WRITING.—We have to bring before our thoughts the picture of St. Paul's life at Rome during the two years' sojourn in his hired house, in custody, a prisoner so far though not in prison (Acts xxviii. 30). Friends and visitors were allowed free access to him.  When the churches which he had founded heard of his being at Rome, it was natural that they should send messengers with their gifts, their offers of personal help, their affectionate remembrances.  Such as these were Epaphroditus from Philippi, Epaphras from Colosse, Onesiphorus and Tychicus from Ephesus.  It was a time when, apart from the danger which might attach to their position as Christians, a visit to the imperial city was not without its special dangers.  There was a serious epidemic which affected all classes of the community.  The emperor himself was so ill that sacrifices were offered in all the temples for his recovery (Philostratus, "Life of Apollonius of Tyana," b. iv., c. 44).  It may be inferred from Phil. ii. 25–27, that Epaphroditus nearly fell a victim to the disease.  It was under such circumstances that an unlooked-for visitor would seem to have made his way to the apostle's quarters.  We may picture him as in early manhood.  He looks outwardly in evil case.  His face is that of one weary and alarmed, oppressed alike by the consciousness of guilt and by the fear of punishment.  It was a common story enough.  He had yielded to the temptations of his calling and had robbed his master, either by direct purloining or by indirect fraud or culpable negligence.  He had been afraid of punishment— perhaps all the more afraid because he thought that Philemon's higher standard of duty as a Christian would make him more rigorous than other masters—and had run away.  The punishment of such a crime might have been scourging or imprisonment.  He might have been branded with the three letters (F U R = thief) which would stamp him with an indelible ignominy.  When flight had been added to his guilt, Roman law would hardly have interfered had the scourging or the torture ended in death.  It is not difficult to picture to ourselves how the apostle received that confession; how he would clasp the hands of the penitent, and lay his hands in blessing on his head, and tell him of the love of Christ and the death upon the Cross, and tell him that his sin was forgiven.  Was this followed by a night of prayer and a morning baptism?  Was it a time to which St. Paul looked back as one in which he, the prisoner, shut out from most opportunities of evangelistic work, had yet been able, in the might of intercession, to save a soul from death, to win a new spiritual son for God and for himself?  That new life was, at any rate, implanted, and it showed itself, as was natural, in love and reverence to the teacher to whose influence it was due.  To wait upon the apostle, ministering to his infirmities, to mitigate the inevitable discomforts of his imprisonment, to watch over him with a devotion which was at once filial and fraternal—this was the return which Onesimus strove to make for the great blessing of his new birth to a higher and Diviner life.  With a gentle playfulness St. Paul loved to dwell on the thought that the slave was now "profitable" to him, and would be profitable when he re-entered his former master's service also.  That re-entry was the subject of the Epistle to Philemon. . . .  Of the after-history of those whom the Epistle has brought before us, we are left to guess.  We can picture to ourselves the arrival of Onesimus and the presentation of the letter.  We can scarcely doubt that his reception, both by his master, and by the company of believers at Colosse, was such as St. Paul desired.  We can think of him telling the story of his conversion, and of all that he owed to the tender, fatherly kindness of the apostle, or reporting what he had seen of the growth and work of the Church at Rome.  If, with most recent writers on St. Paul's life, we believe that he was released from his first imprisonment, and carried into effect his intention of revisiting the Macedonian and Asiatic churches, we may believe that the "lodging" for which he asked was not prepared in vain, and that the three—the apostle, the master, and the slave—met once more, to give thanks for all the great things God had done for them, to pray together for each other's welfare, to partake together in the breaking of bread, of that which was the pledge and symbol of their brotherhood in Christ. (*Dean Plumptre.*) What a picture rises in the mind as one tries to conceive the scene! There, in his wooden cabin, often "crowded" by anxious hearers of the Word, sits a scholar and a gentleman, exhausted by the labours of the day. The lamp shines down on his bald forehead, lights up the keen aquiline features of his oval face, shaded with grey hair, and glitters from the armour of the brawny Prætorian who lounges beside him, and from the links of the chain which binds them wrist to wrist. Paul dictates sentence after sentence to Luke, the learned physician, who carries his pen and ink-horn at his waist. He is inditing a letter to his friend Philemon in far-away Phrygian Colosse, about a runaway slave, pleading for the outcast, promising that if in anything the slave has wronged his master, he (Paul) will be answerable for it. The thought strikes him that the promise will carry more weight with it if written by his own hand. He interrupts the flow of speech; cries, "Here, Luke, give me the reed!" and with benumbed, labouring fingers inscribes these words, "I, Paul, write this *with my own hand*—I will repay it." It is touching, is it not, to think of so great a man in such miserable conditions. A man so like the Master whom he serves that, while he carries whole races and churches on his heart, he yet has a special love for every wretched outcast who will accept his love; and is not only bent on serving him, but will take thought how he may best serve him, and spare no pains to make his service effectual. (*S. Cox, D.D.*)

CHARACTER AND STYLE.—This Epistle has one peculiar feature—its æsthetical character—which distinguishes it from all the other Epistles. It has been admired deservedly as a model of delicacy and skill in the department of composition to which it belongs. The writer had peculiar difficulties to overcome. He was the common friend of the parties at variance. He must conciliate a man who supposed that he had good reason to be offended. He must commend the offender, and yet neither deny nor aggravate the imputed fault. He must assert the new ideas of Christian equality in the face of a system which hardly recognised the humanity of the enslaved. He could have placed the question on the ground of his own personal rights, and yet must waive them in order to secure an act of spontaneous kindness. His success must be a triumph of love, and nothing be demanded for the sake of the justice which could have claimed everything. He limits his request to a forgiveness of the alleged wrong, and a restoration to favour and the enjoyment of future sympathy and affection, and yet would so guard his words as to leave scope for all the generosity which benevolence might prompt towards one whose condition admitted of so much alleviation. These are contrarieties not easy to harmonise; but Paul, it is confessed, has shown a degree of self-denial and a tact in dealing with them, which in being equal to the occasion could hardly be greater. (*H. B. Hackett, D.D.*) Dignity, generosity, prudence, friendship, affection, politeness, skilful address, purity, are apparent. Hence it has been termed with great propriety, "the polite Epistle." The delicacy, fine address, consummate courtesy, nice strokes of rhetoric, render the letter an unique specimen of the epistolary style. (*S. Davidson, D.D.*) This Epistle showeth a right noble, lovely example of Christian love. Here we see how St. Paul layeth himself out for the poor Onesimus, and with all his means pleadeth his cause with his master; and so setteth himself, as if he were Onesimus, and had himself done wrong to Philemon. Yet this doeth he not with power or force, as if he had right thereto; but he strippeth himself of his right, and thus enforceth Philemon to forego his right also.

Even as Christ did for us with God the Father, thus also doth St. Paul for Onesimus with Philemon: for Christ also stripped Himself of His right, and by love and humility enforced the Father to lay aside His wrath and power, and to take us to His grace for the sake of Christ, who lovingly pleadeth our cause, and with all His heart layeth Himself out for us. For we are all His Onesimi, to my thinking. (*Luther.*)    The Epistle to Philemon holds an unique place among the apostle's writings. It is the only strictly private letter which has been preserved. It is addressed apparently to a layman. It is wholly occupied with an incident of domestic life. The occasion which called it forth was altogether commonplace. It is only one sample of numberless letters which must have been written to his many friends and disciples by one of St. Paul's eager temperament and warm affections, in the course of a long and chequered life. Yet to ourselves this fragment, which has been rescued, we know not how, from the wreck of a large and varied corre-spondence, is infinitely precious. Nowhere is the social influence of the gospel more strikingly exerted; nowhere does the nobility of the apostle's character receive a more vivid illustration than in this accidental pleading on behalf of a runaway slave. (*Bp. Lightfoot.*)    " Though he handleth a subject," says Calvin, " which other-wise were low and mean, yet after his manner he is borne up aloft unto God. With such modest entreaty doth he humble himself on behalf of the lowest of men, that scarce anywhere else is the gentleness of his spirit portrayed more truly to the life." " A true little *chef d'œuvre* of the art of letter-writing," exclaims M. Renan, characteristically. " We have here," writes Sabatier, " only a few familiar lines, but so full of grace, of salt, of serious and trustful affection, that this short Epistle gleams like a pearl of the most exquisite purity in the rich treasure of the New Testament." Even Baur, while laying violent hands upon it, is constrained to speak of this " little letter " as " making such an agreeable impression by its attractive form," and has penetrated " with the noblest Christian spirit."

THE ATTITUDE OF CHRISTIANITY TOWARDS SLAVERY.—It is worthy of note that in this Epistle Paul does not require or ask Philemon to liberate Onesimus. Moreover, while Onesimus was still a slave in the house of Philemon, the latter was apparently a recognised Christian and a beloved friend of Paul. This, together with the silence of the rest of the New Testament, implies that the apostles did not forbid their converts to hold slaves. Yet, not only has the gospel put an end to slavery where throughout the world it has gained power, but it is the only religious system which has done anything effective in this direction. The reason of this apparent tolerance of slavery is not far to seek. By asserting the Fatherhood of God, the gospel pro-claims the brotherhood of man ; and thus asserts a principle utterly inconsistent with one man treating another as his property. On the other hand, had Christ and His apostles forbidden the holding of slaves, they would have arrayed against the gospel all those interested in maintaining the existing order of society, and thus have needlessly placed in its way most serious obstacles. And, worse still, by raising a standard of revolt against a social injustice, they would have rallied around them-selves multitudes anxious only for relief from a social grievance. An appeal to such classes would have utterly misrepresented Christianity, and their help would have ruined it. Christ therefore offered to men only a spiritual liberation. But this carried with it the living germ of every kind of freedom. For these reasons the apostles tolerated slavery. We have no trace of fault found for holding Onesimus as a slave. It does not even lessen Paul's warm recognition of Philemon's excellence. And, even if Onesimus resume his former position, Paul will gladly be Philemon's guest. Yet, while refusing to claim for the slaves a liberty for which they were not yet prepared, and which would have loosened the very framework of society, Paul taught that in Christ the distinction of bond and free no longer exists, and that a believing slave is already virtually free (Gal. iii. 28 ; 1 Cor. vii. 21). And in Col. iv. 1 he teaches that slaves have just claims upon their masters, claims recognised by a Master in heaven. Such teaching at once improved the lot of the slave and prepared gradually a way for the emancipation which our day has seen. From the example of the apostles in the matter of slavery we may learn an important lesson. There are many things contrary to the spirit of the gospel, which it is inexpedient at once to forbid by civil or ecclesiastical law. In some few cases such prohibition would appeal to unworthy motives. And verbal prohibition can be effective only when supported by the public conscience. The gospel works always from within, shedding light upon broad principles of right and wrong, light which ultimately reaches and illumines all the details of practical life. But, for this inner illumination, time is often needful. Legislation is effective only when it registers an inward growth of the moral sentiment. (*Prof. J. A. Beet.*)

# THE BIBLICAL ILLUSTRATOR.

## PHILEMON.

VER. 1. **Paul a prisoner of Jesus Christ.**—*A pathetic commencement :*—St. Paul does not give himself the title of "apostle" in this place. The very first word in which he speaks of himself is pathetic. He refers to his chains no less than five times in this short letter (vers. 1, 9, 10, 13, 23). He feels it glorious to suffer shame for his Lord's sake, and blessed to inherit the beatitude of those who are persecuted for righteousness' sake (Matt. v. 10). He literally fulfils the exhortation of St. Peter (1 Pet. iv. 14–16). (*Bp. Wm. Alexander.*) *A lofty title :*—To me it seems a loftier thing that he should style himself "prisoner of Jesus Christ" than "apostle." The apostles gloried because they were counted worthy to suffer shame for the Name (Acts v. 41); but the authority of bonds is irresistible. He who is about to plead for Onesimus feels that he should plead in such a form that he could not be refused. (*Jerome.*) *The bondman seen to advantage :*—We dwell on the circumstances of his imprisonment—we fondly recall his vexatious position—because the whole "surroundings" of this letter lend additional effect to its inherent grace. It is when the fragrant herb is pressed that it gives forth the richest odour; and it is when Paul's heart is being tried that it breathes out the tenderest sympathy. Himself a bondman, "with gyves upon his wrist," he pleads the cause of that other bondman, whose story is the burden of the letter. It is when he is a much-wronged captive that he begs forgiveness for a wrongdoer, and when society is making war upon himself he plays the part of peacemaker with others. As dewdrops are seen to best advantage on the blades of grass from which they hang, or gems sparkle brightest in their appropriate settings, so may we regard Paul's imprisonment as the best foil to the design of this letter. Wrongs and oppressive suffering may drive even wise men mad; but here it only seems to evoke Paul's tenderest feelings, and open wide the sluices of his affectionate sympathies. (*A. H. Drysdale, M.A.*) *Christ the Christian's supreme motive :*—"Paul, a prisoner of Jesus Christ." The one point in this clause that we have to do with now is that wherever Paul was and whatever he was doing, the place he was in and the work he was about were always coloured by reminiscences and considerations of the relation in which he stood to his Divine Lord, Jesus Christ. If it was any kind of service he was rendering, why, he writes himself "the servant of Jesus Christ." If he viewed himself in the character of a message-bearer, why, then, always it was from Christ he received the message; and he writes himself "the apostle of Jesus Christ." That relation of his to his Lord underlay every other relation: it was the fundamental fact in his experience, and determined everything that pertained to him, inwardly and outwardly. And now in this letter to Philemon it is "Paul, a prisoner of Jesus Christ." This means not simply that it was Christ that had imprisoned him, or that his imprisonment came about in consequence of his having preached Christ's gospel; he means all of this, perhaps, but he means, besides, that in whatever place he is, in whatever relation he stands, he is Christ's in that place and relation; Christ was the Greenwich from which he counted longitude, the Equator from which he reckoned latitude. If he was out of doors and at liberty, why then he was the Lord's freeman; if he was in prison and fettered, then he was the Lord's prisoner. This same determining influence comes out in the fourteenth chapter of his Roman letter, when he says, "Whether we live, we live unto the Lord; and whether we die, we

11

die unto the Lord: whether we live, therefore, or die, we are the Lord's." This explains the compactness of Paul's life—the gathering in of all the loose ends—the unity of it. Wherever you touch him, after his conversion, you find him the same man all through. At the same time, nobody finds in the devotedness to Christ of this man Paul anything unwholesome. That is one of the startling and instructive features of his case. We are constantly encountering people who have a great deal of piety, but who take piety in a hard way. They are what we are going to call cranks—holy cranks. Not impostors, but holiness that has passed the line that divides between health and fever. Paul's letters make good reading for any one who suspects that there is any inherent antagonism between ordinary sense and a mind all alive unto the Lord. The more reason a man has, the more opportunity there is for faith ; and the greater his faith, the more need of reason to foster, sustain, and guarantee it. If what are known as very holy people are sometimes intellectually out of joint with the good sense of the people about them, it is due to some other cause than the whole-heartedness of their devotion to the Lord Jesus Christ. Abnormal specimens of piety ought not to be taken as indices of the true quality and import of piety, any more than deranged minds should be accepted as fair exponents of what intelligence is and can do, or than a man with an excess of fingers, or two heads, or a club foot, should be counted a just exponent of human anatomy. It is rather surprising, and betrays lack of honesty, that in matters of religion objectors pick for the most unlucky examples, and insist on estimating religion by them, but in other matters grade their judgments by the best obtainable exponents. Because buildings sometimes fall beneath their own weight, we do not give up our faith in architecture ; and when we go into a new town to live, the first thing we seek for is a house to live in. Do not, then, be repelled from this matter of whole-hearted commitment to Jesus Christ because you know of some people who have made very hard and awkward and morbid work of being holy. Select the most winning specimens, not the most repellent, you know of, and take from the best the law of your estimate. In that way only can you be just to yourselves and just to the truth. Besides this, in insisting upon the unifying of our nature —this bending of it all to one end, in order to the largest attainments in Christian character and living—we are only commending that same policy of whole-hearted-ness which prevails in secular matters, and which, unfortunately, asserts itself there with a good deal more constancy and strenuousness than it does in affairs distinctively personal and Christian. Other things being equal, the amount that we attain in any department will be according to the intensity with which we concentrate ourselves upon the one object that we are in pursuit of. No one understands this better than the business men and the money-makers that are here this morning. Concentration pays. Incompatible motives weaken results. I only want it should be realised what a practical thing this whole-heartedness is, and how full of effect it is. All of this points one way. It means that you must gather yourself in upon a purpose if you are going to succeed in it. It is just as true in art, law, medicine, literature, as in money-making. Attainments are according to the degree in which we make ourselves solid in their pursuit. There is, then, nothing absurd or impracticable in the matter of concentration. When, therefore, we ask a man to become solid for Christ, we are only asking him to bend himself beneath the sweep of one imperial motive, and to aim at Christian results along the only way by which in any field of acquisition the largest results are attainable. This matter goes by supreme motive. And it is not hard to find out the supreme motive. We have occasional warm days in winter, but there is no difficulty deciding whether it is January or July. If you fall in with a man who has devoted himself in any generous, cordial way to art, you never have difficulty in saying whether he is an artist or an engineer. His conversation will carry the flavour of art ; his library or studio will exhibit the literature and tokens of art. His whole style, taste, choices, phrases, haunts, will be redolent with his æsthetic engrossments. These matters are not brought in review by way of criticism. A man can do nothing well while working counter to the grain of his impulses. A man's hands will not do good work, his thoughts will not do good work, unless heart goes with them. If a man who is engrossedly an artist brings everything to the arbitrament of beauty, then a man who is engrossedly a Christian brings everything to the arbitrament of Christ ; and wherever he is, the conscious or unconscious sense of what Christ is to him will shape his thoughts, mould his affections, determine his purposes, and engender his activities. I hope it is not necessary to say that this does not stand in the way of men's having other aims and ends. Christianity has never embarrassed wholesome art, or science, or literature, or trade, or commerce ; rather has she been the foster-mother of all these. Because the moon goes around the sun does not hinder its going around the earth every day on its way round. Christ is the Christian's sun. Whatever other orbits he describes—and there will be a good many of them, according to the various relations in life in which he is naturally and properly and necessarily placed—whatever other orbits he describes, they will only be fluctuations this side and that of the one continuous circuit about the solar centre. To any one, then, who asks what it is to be a Christian, and who wants a definite answer, here is a definite answer. Take that man whose character and life are delineated in the evangelists ; familiarise yourself with that delineation ; walk by faith with the unique person it depicts—call it, to begin with, what you please, but walk with it ; let it show itself to you and tell its best story to you, and let it, so fast as it becomes revealed to you, decide for you what you shall be and what you shall do. You perceive we are saying nothing about doctrines ; we are talking about a life. We are not urging you to accept something that you find yourself mentally incapacitated from believing. Let the unique figure delineated in the gospels grow upon you, if it will, and it probably will, if you lend yourself to it ; and then so fast as it does become a personal fact and a real presence to you, let it settle for you the questions of daily living in the order in which they come up to be settled, making it the final court of appeal, and saying in each perplexity, What does the light of such a life as that show that I ought to do in this exigency ? I am distressed by the dilettanteism that is in our Christian communities, by which I mean the numbers, even inside of the Church, who have taken up Christianity simply as polite pastime ; men and women who are not supremely motived by Christ, and who gain a little smattering in the matter because it is rather a nice thing to do, or take it up on occasion when there is nothing else pressing ; men and women who are worldly in all their heart-experiences and ambitions, and to whom Christianity—what they have of it—is only a wash or a veneer. The initial act in becoming a Christian is to subordinate everything to Jesus Christ, and then the question as to field and occupation comes in for adjustment afterwards. (*C. H. Parkhurst.*) *The blot wiped out :*—The title of a prisoner, in the eyes of the world, is full of reproach ; but when it is for Christ's sake the blot is wiped out. (*W. Attersoll.*) *A prisoner for Christ :*—The apostle testifieth he was a prisoner for Christ and the gospel, not for his own sins and offences. It is not our suffering barely considered can honour us with the reward of glory and the crown of martyrdom, but the cause in which we die and the quarrel in which we suffer. True it is, afflictions are common to the godly and ungodly, they are imprisoned alike ; but albeit the afflictions be one and the same, yet the cause is not one and the same for which they are afflicted. The ungodly are punished for their sins ; the godly are afflicted for a good conscience. Abel is murdered of his brother ; Cain is cursed and condemned to be a fugitive upon the earth. Both of them are afflicted, but the cause is diverse. Abel is killed for his godliness ; Cain is punished for his wickedness. Christ had His feet and His hands nailed on the Cross, so had the two thieves ; they suffered all one punishment, but how contrary were the causes of Him and them, seeing He suffered without cause, but they justly had the sentence of death executed upon them, as one of them confessed (Luke xxxiii. 5). Let us not, therefore, only fasten our eyes and look upon the bare punishment, but consider what the cause is, and, according to the cause, esteem both of the person and of the punishment. Some are prisoners of men, others are prisoners of the devil, of whom they are holden captive, and both of them for their wickedness ; but if we will be martyrs of Christ we must be the prisoners of Christ. (*Ibid.*) *Lessons :*—I. This Epistle came out of the prison. The Spirit, therefore, was Paul's companion in the prison, and so is He to all God's children that are prisoners of Jesus Christ, and in more special sort communicating Himself unto them, whereby it cometh to pass that at such times, and in such estates, they are more fit for holy duties than in any other. Then pray they more feelingly and fervently (Rom. viii.), then also as here we see writ, they exhort more powerfully and passionately, as me thinketh, in those Epistles which Paul wrote in the prison, there seemeth a greater measure of holy zeal and fervent affections than in any other. II. But now Paul, writing this Epistle in the prison, as many others also, herein further appeareth the good providence of God. 1. In that even in the time of this his restraint, he had yet liberty of pen, will, and paper, yea, and of a scribe too, sometimes, and those which did minister unto him. 2. God's providence also herein did show itself that would not suffer Paul, so skilful a workman, to be idle and do nothing in the business of the Lord, but would have a supply of his apostolical preaching made by his writing. III. Again, it is to be observed that St. Paul doth not simply call himself prisoner, BUT WITH THIS CONDITION, OF JESUS CHRIST. The title of a prisoner in itself is ignominious; but when he addeth "of Jesus Christ" all stain of ignominy is clean wiped away. IV. But here is not all that we must look to in our sufferings, that our cause be good, BUT ALSO THAT WE SUFFER FOR A GOOD CAUSE, IN A GOOD MANNER. The which point is further commended unto us in Paul's example, who was not only a prisoner of Jesus Christ, but also a cheerful and courageous prisoner of Jesus Christ; for so far was he from being ashamed of his chain, wherewithal for the hope of Israel's sake he was bound, that he even glorieth in it, accounting it far more honourable than a chain of gold about his neck. V. Lastly, we are to observe in Paul's example the duty of all the ministers, namely, TO MAKE GOOD THEIR PREACHING BY THE PRISON, IF NEED BE, THEIR SAYINGS BY THEIR SUFFERINGS. Oh, base is that liberty, yea, baser than the basest bondage, which is got by flinching from that truth, which we have preached and professed. (*D. Dyke, B.D.*) *A prisoner of Christ:*—Samuel Rutherford, in prison, used to date his letters, "Christ's Palace, Aberdeen." He wrote to a friend: "The Lord is with me; I care not what man can do. I burden no man. I want nothing. No king is better provided than I am. Sweet, sweet, and easy is the cross of my Lord. All men I look in the face, of whatsoever rank, nobles and poor. Acquaintance and strangers are friendly to me. My Well-beloved is kinder and more warm than ordinary, and cometh and visiteth my soul. My chains are over-gilded with gold. No pen, no words, no engine, can express to you the loveliness of my only Lord Jesus. Thus in haste I make for my palace at Aberdeen." *The Lord's prisoner:*—When Madame Guyon was imprisoned in the Castle of Vincennes, in 1695, she not only sang but wrote songs of praise to her God. "It sometimes seemed to me," she said, "as if I were a little bird whom the Lord had placed in a cage, and that I had nothing now to do but sing. The joy of my heart gave a brightness to the objects around me. The stones of my prison looked in my eyes like rubies. I esteemed them more than all the gaudy brilliancies of a vain world. My heart was full of that joy which Thou givest to them that love Thee in the midst of their greatest crosses." **And Timothy our brother.**—*Paul and Timothy—the old and the young:*—I. In the text we see AGE AND YOUTH TOGETHER. Not separate, not looking ashamed at each other, not divided by incompatibilities or jealousies, but in union. The young often flee from the old. The old are often impatient with the young. Here is an instance of union. The advantages are obvious. 1. The old will contribute the wisdom of experience. 2. The young will quicken the animation of hope. No doubt temporary difficulties will arise. II. Though age and youth are together, yet AGE TAKES PRECEDENCE OF YOUTH. It is Paul and Timothy, not Timothy and Paul. A principle of right settles all questions of priority. It is not beautiful, because it is not right, that youth should take precedence of age. There are many ways of taking virtual precedence. 1. Contradiction. 2. Impatience. 3. Neglect. III. Though age takes precedence of youth, yet both age and youth are ENGAGED IN COMMON SERVICE. Paul and Timothy are both servants, it is not Paul the master and Timothy the servant, they are both included under one name. See how one great relationship determines all minor conditions and attitudes; as between themselves, Paul was father, and Timothy was son; Paul was renowned, and Timothy was obscure; Paul was senior, and Timothy was junior; but looked at as before Christ the one Lord, they were both servants. Many reflections arise out of this regulating power of one absorbing relationship or union. The Alps and Apennines are great mountains in themselves; yet they are less than pimples when looked at in their relation to the whole world. The earth itself is a "great globe" to its own inhabitants; it is a mere speck of light to the nearest star. A man who is a very important tradesman in a small town, may not have been so much as heard of in the great city. Through and through life we see how relationships supremely important as between themselves, are modified by one great bond. The right way to take our proper measure, and to chasten our ambition, is to look at the highest relationships of all. The great citizen dwindles into his right proportions when he looks at the Creator; the mighty potentate, when he looks at the King of kings; the philanthropist, when he looks at the Saviour. The noisy, rushing, furious train seems to be going fast; let it look at the flying stars, and be humble! Compared with them it is a lame insect toiling in the dust. Life should never **be** looked at as merely between one man and another. Look at it as between the finite and the infinite—between the momentary and the eternal—between the ignorant and the omniscient. It will thus be elevated. No man will then think of himself more highly than he ought to think. The Alps will not scorn the molehills. (*J. Parker, D.D.*) *Brotherhood in Christ:*—In the Church of Christ all are brethren. They have " one heavenly Father ; one first-born brother, Christ ; one seed of regeneration, the Divine Word ; one inheritance of eternal life.' Mutual love is the basis of true Church fellowship. " As natural relationship produces natural affection, so spiritual relationship produces spiritual affection." It will be —1. An unfeigned love (1 Pet. i. 32). Not the profession of the lip, which may fail if put to a practical test. 2. A pure love. In sympathy with whatever is god-like in fellow-believers. Grace in the heart seeking and fostering its kindred grace in others. There is need of clearer evidence that the love which is of God has place in hearts on earth. 3. A fervent love. A fire burning up natural selfishness. An habitual consideration of the things of others rather than our own. 4. A lasting love. It has come from God, the eternal source of light, and it bears us on to Him again. (*A. W. Johnson.*) *Lessons:*—I. THE HUMILITY OF PAUL, who, though an apostle in the highest degree of the ministry (Eph. iv. 11 ; 1 Cor. xii. 28), yet disdaineth not to yoke himself, not only with the Evangelist Timothy, an inferior degree, but even with an ordinary pastor, Philemon, who was yet of a lower place than Timothy. Art thou a pastor ? Speak and do as a pastor to thy fellow-pastors, and not as though thou wert an apostle or evangelist. II. I observe THE CAUSE OF PAUL'S LOVE TO PHILEMON by the conjunction of these two things together, BELOVED AND FELLOW-WORKER. The latter is the cause of the former, therefore was Philemon beloved of Paul, because his fellow-worker in the ministry. Those that are joined together in the same calling ought in this regard more dearly to love one another. True it is that the general calling of a Christian should be a sufficient bond to knit together in true love the hearts of all Christians. But when to this bond there cometh a second of our special callings, our hearts should be more firmly knit together, that so it might appear that when our hearts shall be linked together by the bond of nature, or Christian and special calling, that a three-fold cord is not easily broken. But where shall we find this sweet conjunction of beloved and fellow-worker ? In the most men the proverb is verified. One potter envies another. But far be this envy from all Christians of what calling soever, specially of the ministry. The ministers must love together as brethren, and with one heart and hand give themselves to the Lord's business. Far be from them the mind of the monopolists, that they should go about to engross the Word of God to themselves ; nay, rather with Moses let them wish that all God's people were prophets. (*D. Dyke, B.D.*) *Two better than one:*—Paul joineth Timothy with him in this suit, because howsoever he were in great credit with Philemon, and able to obtain a great matter at his hands, yet he knew he should prevail better by the help of another than he could do himself alone, seeing two may prevail more than one. He honoureth him also with the name of a dear brother, whom oftentimes, because he had converted him, he calleth a natural son, that his gifts and graces may be considered with his person, and carry the greater weight in his suit, and so Philemon sooner yield his consent and grant this request, being requested, and as it were set upon by so many. From this practice of the apostle we learn that what good thing soever we take in hand we shall better effect it with others than alone by ourselves. The joining unto us the hand and help of others is profitable and necessary to all things belonging unto us for the better performing and accomplishing of them. Two are better than one. Abimelech, being directed by God to stir up Abraham, obtaineth by his means, who prayed for him, that which he could not compass and accomplish alone by himself. Absalom not being able to purchase and procure of himself the goodwill of his father, moved Joab to deal for him, Joab useth the help of the subtle woman of Tekoah, whereby he is reconciled to his father. Hereby it cometh to pass that Paul so often requesteth the prayers of the Church that utterance may be given unto him, that he may open his mouth boldly to publish the secrets of the gospel. All those places of Scripture prove plainly and directly unto us, that what matter of weight and importance soever we enterprise and go about, it is good for us to take to ourselves the help of others to further us therein. (*W. Attersoll.*) **Unto Philemon our dearly beloved, and fellow-labourer.**—*A Christian household:*—The names of the receivers of the letter bring before us a picture seen, as by one glimmering light across the centuries, of a Christian household in that Phrygian valley. The head of it, Philemon, appears to have been a native of, or at all events a resident in, Colosse, for Onesimus, his slave, is spoken of in the Epistle to the Church there as " one of *you*." He was a person of some standing and wealth, for he had a house large enough to admit of a " church " assembling in it, and to accommodate the apostle and his travelling companions if he should visit Colosse. He had apparently the means for large pecuniary help to poor brethren, and willingness to use them, for we read of the refreshment which his kindly deeds had imparted. He had been one of Paul's converts, and owed his own self to him. He is called " our fellow-labourer." The designation may imply some actual co-operation at a former time. But more probably the phrase is but Paul's gracefully affectionate way of lifting his humbler work out of its narrowness, by associating it with his own. All who toil for furtherance of Christ's kingdom, however widely they may be parted by time or distance, are fellow-workers. The first man who dug a shovelful of earth for the foundation of Cologne Cathedral, and he who fixed the last stone on the topmost spire a thousand years after, are fellow-workers. However small may be our capacity or sphere, or however solitary we may feel, we may summon up before the eyes of our faith a mighty multitude of apostles, martyrs, toilers in every land and age as *our*—even our—work-fellows. The field stretches far beyond our vision, and many are toiling in it for Him whose work never comes near ours. There are differences of service, but the same Lord, and all who have the same master are companions in labour. (*A. Maclaren, D.D.*) *Fellow-labourers :*—They that put to their helping hand any kind of way, for the furtherance of the gospel, are the minister's fellow-labourers, that edify their brethren in the most holy faith, that exhort one another while it is called to-day, that comfort one another, that are as bells to toll others to Christ, are the preacher's fellow-labourers. So was the woman of Samaria that called the whole city to Christ, those women that ministered to Christ of their own substance, also Priscilla and Aquila, who expounded to Apollos the way of God more perfectly. Let us all thus be fellow-labourers, and our labour shall not be in vain in the Lord. (*W. Jones, D.D.*) *Philemon :*—He addresses himself unto Philemon as his dearly beloved and fellow-labourer. Now if he was so dearly beloved by Paul he could not but love one by whom he was so much beloved; and if he had that love for Paul, which Paul's love for him challenged as a suitable return of gratitude, he would give him a testimony of his affection by gratifying him in his request. It was a great honour to Philemon to be beloved by so eminent an apostle as St. Paul. It was still a greater honour to be numbered amongst his dearest friends. He could not doubt of the sincerity of St. Paul, when he made these large professions of love and kindness to him. It was not agreeable with the character of the apostle to use these expressions, as empty forms, words of course, and idle compliments ; but they came from his heart as well as from his pen. Philemon had found real and undoubted proofs of St. Paul's love to him in the pains he had taken in his conversion to Christ. He had received from him the greatest instances of kindness that one man could receive from another. He had been turned by him from darkness unto light, and from the power of Satan unto God, and owed to him the means of grace and the hopes of glory. If, therefore, he had any sense of gratitude, any sparks of generosity in him, he must be very desirous to find out some opportunity of making his acknowledgments to one to whom he was so deeply indebted. He could not but with great greediness embrace an opportunity which was put into his hands of obliging one to whom he was so highly obliged. He could now no longer be at a loss how he might in some measure requite St. Paul for the great and inestimable benefits he had received from him, since he could not doubt but what was so earnestly asked by the apostle would be in a peculiar manner acceptable to him. And as the apostle thus strongly enforces his request, by applying to Philemon as his dearly beloved, so doth he give it yet farther advantage by addressing to him under the notice of his fellow-labourer. For if Philemon was an assistant of St. Paul in ministering unto him in the execution of his apostolical office, he would not complain of the absence of Onesimus, who did in his place and stead minister to the apostle. He would be pleased that he tarried with St. Paul to supply his absence and to do his work. He would not think himself deprived of the service of Onesimus whilst he was employed in that work in which he himself was a labourer. This his servant would be even then looked upon as doing his master's business, whilst he was subservient to the apostle, whose minister his master was. (*Bp. Smalridge.*) *St. Paul's relations with Philemon :*—During his three years' stay at Ephesus he had come across a trader from Colosse, who carried on in that city the business of a cloth-weaver and a dyer, for which the three cities of the valley of the Lycus—Laodicea, Hierapolis, and Colosse itself—were all alike famous, and who had come to the city of Artemis probably during the month of May, which was sacred to the goddess, to seek a market for his goods. The work of making up the bales of cloth into curtains, hangings, and the like, was one which fell in with St. Paul's calling as a tent-maker, and as Aquila and Priscilla had left Ephesus to return to Rome (Rom. xvi. 3), he was glad to be able to carry out his rule of maintaining himself by the labour of his own hands, by entering into partnership with one in whose character there was so much to esteem and love (ver. 17). When they first became acquainted with each other, Philemon was as one of those not far from the kingdom of God, a Gentile who, like the centurion at Capernaum and Cornelius at Cæsarea, had come to be a worshipper of the God of Israel, and to share the hope of the children of Abraham in the manifestation of His kingdom. To him the apostle had pointed out the more excellent way of faith in Christ crucified, risen, ascended, as the Head of that kingdom; and he was accordingly baptised with his wife Apphia, and his son Archippus. The master of a warehouse, well-to-do and benevolent, with many slaves and hired labourers working under him, was naturally an important personage. His employés themselves were a congregation. His house became the meeting-place of an " ecclesia," which included friends and neighbours as well. St. Paul was a frequent guest there, spoke as a teacher, and took part in the Eucharistic meal on the first day of the week. As elsewhere (Gal. iv. 14, 15), he gained the affection and goodwill even of those who were as yet outside the faith. The very slaves learnt to love one who never lost his temper, never gave a harsh command, who found in all men, as such, that which was a ground of brotherhood. They would run errands for him, wait upon his wants, nurse him when he was ill. The partnership was, however, interrupted by St. Paul's plans for his work as an apostle. He left Ephesus, and if he contemplated any return to it at all, it was not likely, to be till after the lapse of some years. Then came the journeys to Macedonia, and Achaia, and Jerusalem, the two years' imprisonment at Cæsarea, the voyage to Italy, the shipwreck at Melita, the two years' residence at Rome. And now the apostle had at last heard some tidings of his former friends. (*Dean Plumptre.*) *Inferences from the subject-matter of this Epistle:*—1. We should not despise any persons by reason of the meanness of their outward condition; we should love and esteem men, not so much by the rank and place they bear in the world as by the inward qualities and graces of their souls; we should not treat even servants with an air of haughtiness and insolence, as if they were creatures of another kind from us, and of a species below us, but should show them all that humanity, which is due to them as men, who are partakers of the same nature, and with all that love and affection which are due to them as Christians, partakers of the same grace with ourselves. 2. We should use that interest we have with men of power and authority for the advantage of those who stand in need of our patronage and help. 3. We should not despair of the reclaiming of any sinners, be they at present never so wicked. 4. When sinners are reclaimed from their vicious courses, we should not upbraid them with their past faults. 5. Those who have ministered to others in spiritual things should not from thence assume over them a right of commanding and influencing them in temporal affairs. 6. We should not look upon the first preachers of the gospel as men of no skill, no learning, no address. We have a convincing proof to the contrary in this Epistle. 7. If this part of Scripture, which hath been generally looked upon as the most dry, and barren, and un-edifying, is thus fruitful of wholesome, and practical, and useful truths, we should have an high esteem and reverence of these Divine oracles, which are so well fraught with wisdom and knowledge. (*Bp. Smalridge*) *Lessons:*—1. It is not without its use to observe the persons to whom the Epistle is ad-dressed—the father, the mother, the son, and the Church at the house. How widely contrasted were they, but all were Christians, sending a voice of en-couragement to persons of all classes and through all time! 2. While we contemplate with admiration the separate individuals of this group of early believers, our attention is turned to the fact that they were assembled with others of like spirit, and along with them formed, according to the apostle's language, an *ecclesia* or Church. Happy those who possess the faith that gives admission to this Church; the truth that commends its spirit directs its worship and secures its permanence and promotes its peace; and the holiness that prepares for its full approaching glory! 3. The Church, or the company of the out-called and separated, who received the apostle's greetings, and who were "at the house" of Philemon, consist, in the first instance, of the various members of his household. When converted himself, he would naturally strengthen his brethren. A man who has learned that faith in the Son of God is essential to his own happiness, and "deliverance from the wrath to come," is no more able to keep the discovery to himself than he would withhold the knowledge of a medicine of sovereign value from the sufferers he saw dying around him in the wards of a fever hospital. Religion, accordingly, begins at home. (*R. Nisbet, D.D.*)

Ver. 2. **Our beloved Apphia.**—*Apphia :*—It seems in the highest degree probable that Apphia was Philemon's wife ; probable, but in a lower degree, that Archippus was their son. The mention of a woman between two such men, one the apostle's "fellow-labourer," the other his "fellow-soldier," is a noble example of the spirit of the gospel (Gal. iii. 28). It is an unobtrusive yet real hint of the elevation of woman, as the whole letter is of the release of the other victim of classical civilisation, the slave. "Thus, supported on both sides, she seems to have the place not of her own sex, but of her worth." (*Bp. Wm. Alexander.*) *A new reading :*—The reading "the sister" seems preferable to "the beloved." It is superior in uncial authority. It is of course conceivable that "beloved" might have been exchanged for "sister" from motives of false delicacy. (*Bp. Lightfoot.*) *Sister :*—On the other hand, the adjective applied to Philemon might readily have suggested the same prefix to Apphia. The reading "beloved" seems scarcely grave enough for the dignified reserve which St. Paul never forgets in his tenderest moments. Above all, the word "sister" distinctly adds to the meaning. For it shows that Apphia had embraced the gospel, and was a baptised member of the Church, and thus preserves the line of thought in the sentiments balancing the epithets "fellow-worker," "fellow-soldier," applied to Philemon and Archippus. (*Ibid.*) *Addressed to both :*—Her friendly reception of the runaway would be quite as important as Philemon's, and it is therefore most natural that the letter bespeaking it should be addressed to both. (*A. Maclaren, D.D.*) **Archippus our fellow-soldier.**—*Archippus :*—He was perhaps Philemon's son ; or a family friend ; or the minister of the family ; the former hypothesis being perhaps the most probable, as the letter concerns a family matter. (*Dean Alford.*) *Archippus* was a Christian pastor at Colosse (Col. iv. 7), and a fellow-soldier of St. Paul, in fighting the good fight of faith against the enemies of the gospel. (*Bp. Chris. Wordsworth.*) *Fellow-soldier :*—The notion of the spiritual life—more especially as connected with definite ministerial functions—being a warfare, a campaign, a soldier's life, passed into New Testament from Old Testament (*cf.* Num. iv. 23 ; viii. 24 ; 1 Sam. ii. 22 ; 1 Cor. ix. 7 ; 2 Cor. x. 4 ; 1 Tim. i. 18 ; 2 Tim. ii. 4). The "gospel campaigns" in which Archippus was St. Paul's comrade in arms may have been those during the apostle's sojourn at Ephesus (A.D. 54–57). Those who hold that St. Paul had a personal connection with Colosse will also point to Acts xviii. 23. (*Bp. Wm. Alexander.*) *Soldier instead of worker :*—The variation of "soldier" for "worker" probably is due to the fact of Archippus being the bishop of the Laodicean church. In any case, it is very beautiful that the grizzled veteran officer should thus, as it were, clasp the hand of this young recruit, and call him his comrade. How it would go to the heart of Archippus! (*A. Maclaren, D.D.*) *A stern message :*—A somewhat stern message is sent to Archippus in the Colossian letter. Why did not Paul send it quietly in this, instead of letting a whole church know of it? It seems at first sight as if he had chosen the harshest way ; but perhaps further consideration may suggest that the reason was an instinctive unwillingness to introduce a jarring note into the joyous friendship and confidence which sounds through this Epistle, nor would he bring public matters into this private letter. The warning would come with more effect from the church, and this cordial message of goodwill and confidence would prepare Archippus to receive the other, as rain-showers make the ground soft for the good seed. The private affection would mitigate the public exhortation, with whatever rebuke may have been in it. (*Ibid.*) *Fellow-soldier :*—He calleth him a fellow-soldier because they of the ministry (if they be faithful) are in continual warfare, not only against the continual engines and assaults of Satan, who withstandeth their ministry, but against false teachers, and against many other unreasonable men, as also against the sins and corruptions that reign or arise in their several charges. We see how men destitute of faith make continual war against

them one way or other. (*W. Attersoll.*)　*Ministers are soldiers :*—I. IN THE FIELD.
1. Conflict. (1) With Satan's temptations. (2) With persecutions (Tim. ii. 3). (3)
With the perverse understanding, will, and affections of sinful man (2 Cor. x. 4).
2. In victory. (1) Over the elect, who are taken captive and made willingly to
submit themselves to Jesus Christ, against whom formerly they fought under Satan's
banner. (2) Over the reprobate, who are quite killed with the spiritual sword, and
because they will not bend, are broken to pieces. II. IN THE GARRISON. Though
returned home glorious in victory, yet he must not sit down and rest, as though all
were now despatched, but on with his defensive weapons, that he may be able to
maintain his own. And herein first of all consisteth the second part of the minister's
soldiership at home, namely, in having a wakeful eye to discern even the clouds of
danger even arising afar off, and thereupon to give warning. Secondly, having so
done, which is the half-arming of his people, according to the proverb, "Fore-warned,
fore-armed," he must fortify and make them strong against the power of the adversaries. First, by instructing them how to carry themselves, how both to wear and
how to use that complete harness of the Christian soldier. Thus like a good
captain doth he train his soldiers, teaching their hands to fight and fitting their
fingers for the battle. Secondly, by praying for them ; wherein he playeth the
valiant soldier indeed, combating and conflicting with the Lord God Himself. This
is called standing in the gap, and making up of the hedge (Ezek. xxii. 30). Look as
the wife and provident martiallist will see where the city is weakest when the walls
are anything decayed, and will bend his forces most of all to fortify that place,
knowing the enemy will be sure to take advantage of that place for his more easy
entering upon them, so likewise doth the faithful minister consider with himself
where the sins of the people have most weakened them, and made any breaches in
their walls, any gaps in their fence for God's judgments to run in upon them,
and there doth he make up the breach and stand up in the gap by earnest praying
and calling upon the name of the Lord, as Aaron (Num. xvi. 47). (*D. Dyke, B.D.*)
*The warfare of work :*—Paul, indeed, loves to think of himself as a soldier ; for in
all earnest work there is verily something of war. Real labour itself is but a war
against sloth and self-indulgent idleness. Agricultural labour is war on the weeds
and the stubbornness of the soil. And so shall all work that kindles into the white
heat of earnestness burst often into a war-flame. (*A. H. Drysdale, M.A.*)　*Fulfilling the true soldiership :*—We look past the lounging mercenary at his wrist.
Not he, but Paul, is fulfilling the true soldiership of the world. We see the apostle's
work, by its intensity, rising into warfare ; and as we hear him in his prayers, the
warfare rises into worship before the Lord. (*Ibid.*)　*Christians are fellow-
soldiers :*—Those who speak of the Christian warfare, as I have observed,
almost always limit it to the narrow path in which one treads alone. That
was the idea so grandly wrought out by Bunyan in his "Pilgrim's Progress."
But that sort of warfare belonged to the days of knight-errantry. The modern
soldiers of the Cross, like other soldiers, are massed in armies. No doubt each
Christian has many a fight single-handed with the adversary. But those thrilling
appeals in the Epistle to the Ephesians, concerning taking the whole armour of
God, were addressed to the Church collectively. Individualism has its perils.
Christians are fellow-soldiers. We need to build a common barrier against the
common foe. Side by side we need to charge on the enemy's works. And then, in
the final day of triumph, we shall join with "thousands of thousands, and ten
times ten thousand," in shouting the glad chorus of victory. (*J. Hovey.*)　**The
church in thy house.**—*Early Christian churches :*—As vast buildings, publicly
consecrated and set apart, were impossible from the nature of the case in the
earliest years of Christianity, houses of considerable size were employed for
worship—like those of Aquila at Rome, of Nymphas or Philemon at Colosse—and
the name of "church" seems to have been transferred at an early period from the
collection of living souls to the building in which they met. (*Bp. Wm. Alexander.*)
*An act of zeal :*—This was one way in which Philemon might be said to have
"refreshed the bowels of the saints" (ver. 7), and to have shown his Christian
faith and love to his poorer brethren. Here probably it was that St. Paul preached
when at Colosse. This concession of some apartment in their own houses for the
purposes of the public worship of the Christian Church, "a sect everywhere spoken
against" in those days, was an act of zeal and courage on the part of the wealthier
members of the Christian community, and seems to have elicited special expressions
of notice, approval, and affection from St. Paul and the other apostles (Rom. xvi.
5, 23 ; Col. iv. 15 ; *cf.* 2 Tim. i. 16, iv. 19 ; 3 John 6, 7). (*Bp. Chris. Wordsworth.*)

*A comprehensive salutation :*—He did not omit the *slaves* here ; for he knew that the words of slaves can often change a master's purpose, and especially when they plead for a fellow-servant. Some of them perhaps had stirred up Philemon against Onesimus. He does not permit them there to have any feeling of grudge, as he addresses them with the family. Nor does he give the master just reason for anger. If he had addressed the slaves by name, Philemon probably would have been displeased. See, then, how prudently he deals. For the word " Church " does not permit masters to be angry, if they are numbered with slaves. For the Church knows not the distinction of master and slave (Gal. iii. 28). (*Chrysostom.*) *Tact :*— Meyer remarks the tact of the apostle in associating with Philemon those connected with his *house,* but not going *beyond* the limits of the house. (*Dean Alford.*) *The domestic church :*—1. A Christian's household a church of Christ. 2. Means and influences suited to make it such. 3. Pleasures and secular habits which tend to prevent it ; (1) by quenching the religious spirit ; (2) by interfering with domestic worship and training ; (3) by placing godliness in a secondary position. 4. Motives which should urge the Christian to utmost effort to secure it. (1) Salvation of children and servants greatly dependent on him ; (2) God holds him responsible ; (3) world needs well-trained workers. (*A. W. Johnson.*) *A Church in a house :*—1. In this pious household there had been one graceless member. Onesimus must often have witnessed the holy engagements of this " Church ! " listened to reproofs and appeals of God's Word ; seen the joyfulness of Christian faith and life. This aggravated the wrong he had done, and his sin against God and conscience. 2. Yet the holy influence was not lost. It prepared his heart for the apostle's doctrine. 3. Apphia's share in this influence may be safely reckoned upon. There is no power in a home like that of a mother or mistress. Women's work may seem the slowest, but it is the surest. (*Ibid.*) *The family church :*—Christians families should be little churches. How may a family come to deserve this title ? For this purpose many things are required, whereof some are common to all in the family, others proper to some. Common to all are these two points—1. If we would have our families churches then we that are members in families must labour to become true members of the Church. For a company of profane men is not the house of God, but a den and dungeon of thieves, adulterers, atheists, conspiring together against God. The which yet is not so to be understood, as if the name of a church could not be attributed to a family in which there are some not members of the Church, for even in the Church itself there are some in it that are not of it. Let therefore every one of a family be desirous the house he dwells in should be Bethel— God's house—bring one stone to the making of this spiritual house that so he may be able to say, This house is a holy edifice and I am one of the living stones that help to the making of it so. 2. That a family may obtain the commendation of being a Church, this is another thing that we require generally of all in the family, namely, that look what kind of men they are, or at least would seem to be, in the Church and public congregation, the same they would show themselves to be in the family and private conversement one with another. These be things common to all ; now follow those peculiar to some—first to the chief, secondly the inferior. Those things which respect the chief are specially these—first, as much as in them lies, let them entertain none into their family whom God hath not first entertained into His. The Church doth not indifferently receive all and admit into her society by the sacrament of baptism the children of Turks and cannibals, strangers from the covenant, but only such ordinarily as are of a holy seed, the offspring of religious parents. So likewise must our families, if we would have them like churches, be something dainty who they receive. David's example is to be imitated (Psa. ci.), whose " eyes were unto the faithful of the land," that he might pick even the choicest of them for his service, and that so much the rather because far more easily may we keep out than cast such guests out of our houses. Secondly, the chief in the family must resemble the chief in the Church, namely, the pastors, &c., thereof ; and that not only in those things which concern God's service, but outward discipline also. For the first. There are two special duties of the pastor respecting God's service, preaching and praying. In both these, in some measure, should the governors of the family be like to the pastors of the Church. First, therefore, they must instruct the whole family in that doctrine which is according to godliness. This they must do, first, in words ; which Paul commandeth (Eph. vi.), and which God Himself commendeth in Abraham (Gen. xviii.). Here, then, is censured that government of the family which is only civil, not religious. Assuredly, if the Word of God found not in thy house as in the Church it is unworthy the name of a church? Secondly, they must teach likewise by example. With David, walking in the uprightness of their hearts in the midst of their house; for the eye of the whole family is upon the governors thereof, as is the eye of the Church upon their pastors. Secondly, as in preaching, so likewise in praying, must they imitate the pastors; for the house of God is called the house of prayer. If, therefore, this principal part of God's service be wanting in any house, how can it be called God's house? Thus must they be like the pastors in things concerning God's service. Secondly, they must resemble them in their discipline, causing their household discipline to be answerable to the Church discipline. First, that which is the ground of all good discipline, they must have a very watchful and attentive eye over every soul in the family, so that they may know the several natures, conditions, and dispositions of all, and so proportion their government accordingly. This is rightly to play the bishop, who hath that name from his careful overseeing of the flock (Acts xx. 20). Secondly, after that the eye hath laid these foundations the hand must build thereon. First, as soon as it hath received warning from the eye of some evil that is in brewing, in stretching forth itself and arming itself to hinder it, and keep the authors thereof within their bounds. For this purpose both admonitions and threatenings must be used, but especially wholesome laws must be enacted for the prohibiting and preventing of things unlawful. Secondly, the same hand which made the sword of good laws for the prevention of evil to come must draw it out for the punishment of evil past, and not suffer it to lie rusting in the sheath. If, then, any shall break those good laws which the governors of the families have made, let the punishments threatened be inflicted, that so those who would not obey the precepts of the law may perforce be constrained to obey the threatenings thereof. Now herein must there be an imitation of Church discipline. Look, then, as in the Church the offender is first admonished divers times, and at length, not profiting by those admonitions, is excommunicated and dis-synagogued, so likewise in thy family, finding wicked and ungodly ones, first must thou deal with them by admonition, reprehension, castigation; and if, for all these means, they still remain incorrigible, then cast them out of thy house, and think their room better than their company. If the king were to come to thy house, and there were some in it he could not abide, wouldest thou not discharge them thine house, if so be thou wert desirous of the king's presence? And entertaining traitors in thy house, traitors against God, thinkest thou that He will come and pitch His tent and take up His lodging with thee? These be the things proper to the chief. Now follow those which belong to the inferiors, in the which, as in the former, their governors resembled the pastors of the Church, they must resembled the rest of the body of the Church. First, in matter of doctrine. As the Church acknowledgeth those that are over her, in the Lord, and obeyeth them (1 Thess. v; Heb. xiii.), so must those that are under government carry themselves reverently and respectively towards their governors, cheerfully and consciorably obeying, as all other of their lawful commands, so especially those which concern God's worship. And as by the example of the pastors, the rest of the Church are stirred up to godliness (Phil. iv. 9), so must the inferiors in the family be encouraged and inflamed to virtue, when they shall see their superiors going before them. Secondly, they must resemble the Church in matters of discipline. First, enduring those chastisements, either verbal or real, which for their deserts are inflicted, and freely acknowledging the equity of them. Secondly, if at any time they see any of their fellows misbehaving himself, first let them try what they can do themselves by admonition; but if that way they prevail not, then according to the example of the ecclesiastical discipline (Matt. xviii.), let them acquaint their governors therewithal. (*D. Dyke, B.D.*) *A Christian household:*—We have here shown to us, by one stray beam of twinkling light, for a moment, a very sweet picture of the domestic life of that Christian household in their remote valley. It shines still to us across the centuries which have swallowed up so much that seemed more permanent, and silenced so much that made far more noise in its day. The picture may well set us asking ourselves the question whether we, with all our boasted advancement, have been able to realise the true ideal of Christian family life as these three did. The husband and wife dwelling as heirs together of the grace of life, their child beside them, sharing their faith and service, their household ordered in the ways of the Lord, their friends Christ's friends, and their social joys hallowed and serene—what nobler form of family life can be conceived than that? What a rebuke and satire on many a so-called Christian household! (*A. Maclaren, D.D.*) *Family worship:*—Robert Hall's words on this subject are as beautiful as they are true. "Family worship," he says, "serves as edge or border to prevent the web of life from unravelling." *Influence of personal contact:*—Said General Havelock, in reply to a remark of a friend as to his influence over the men of his regiment, "I keep close to them—have personal contact with each man, and know each man's name." (*Preacher's Lantern.*)    *Refreshment in the Church:*—The bee cannot gather honey on the wing. No more can Christ's disciples gain refreshment and sustenance in the midst of the world's bustle, save by habitually alighting and drawing on the resources of Christ's presence and grace afforded in the assemblies of the saints.    Not as though the " Church " were only a convalescent home for recruiting spiritual energies—it is no less a field for their exercise and development.    It is the seat and centre of witnessing for Christ and of working for Him.    His disciples need not think to carry dark lanterns.    Loyalty to Him will not be ashamed to confess His name before men. (*A. H. Drysdale, M.A.*)    *The mission of the Church:*—For as the lowly bush receives the dew of heaven, not to absorb it on itself, but to distil a portion on the yet lowlier plant that may grow at its root, so must " the Church in the house " learn " to do good and distribute," as a steward for Christ of that gospel which is committed to it in trust for others.    Even the lordly mountain catches the first outpourings of the skies, not to treasure them up in its own bosom, but to send them down in limpid and refreshing streams along the valleys and meadows below.    And so it is the mission of the Church of Christ at large to fulfil such offices of gospel mercy as shall make " the wilderness and solitary place be glad for them, and the desert rejoice and blossom as the rose," and to be the instrument of Christian enterprise and effort to the ends of the earth. (*Ibid.*)

Ver. 3. **Grace to you, and peace.**—*A touching prayer:*—The word " grace " would be peculiarly touching to Philemon in connection with the plea for Onesimus.    The speech to us of " grace " is to remind us of our sins and of their forgiveness by an infinite compassion.    "Think," he seems to say, " how much God hath forgiven *thee*, how *thou* art saved by grace.    Imitate thy God." (*Bp. Wm. Alexander.*)    *A loving wish:*—The two main points to be observed are the comprehensiveness of the apostle's loving wish, and the source to which he looks for its fulfilment.    It is perhaps accidental that we have here the union of the Greek and of the Eastern forms of salutation.    Just as the regal title of the King, whose throne was the Cross, was written in the languages of culture, of law, and of religion, as an unconscious prophecy of His universal reign; so, with like unintentional felicity, we have blended here the ideals of good which the East and the West have framed for those to whom they wish good, in token that Christ is able to slake all the thirsts of the soul, and that whatsoever things any races of men have dreamed as the chiefest blessing, these are all to be reached through Him, and Him only.    But the deeper lesson here is to be found by observing that " grace " refers to the action of the Divine heart, and " peace " to the result thereof in man's experience.    " Grace " is free, undeserved, unmotived, self-springing love.    It is love which stoops, forgives, communicates.    Hence it comes to mean, not only the deep fountain in the Divine nature, and that property in His love by which, like some strong spring, it leaps up and gushes forth by an inward impulse, in neglect of all motives drawn from the lovableness of its objects, such as determine our poor human loves, but also the results of that bestowing love in men's characters, or, as we say, the " graces " of the Christian soul.    " Whatsoever things are lovely and of good report," all nobilities, tendernesses, exquisite beauties, and steadfast strengths of mind and heart, of will and disposition—all are the gifts of God's undeserved and open-handed love.    The fruit of such grace received is peace.    That old Eastern salutation " peace " recalls a state of society when every stranger might be a foe; but it touches a chord which vibrates in all hearts.    We have little fear of war, but we are all weighed upon with sore unrest, and repose sometimes seems to us the one thing needful.    All the discords of nature and circumstances can be harmonised by that grace which is ready to flow into our hearts.    Peace with God, with ourselves, with our fellows, repose in the midst of change, calm in conflict, may be ours. (*A. Maclaren, D.D.*) *The apostle's prayer:*—1. The matter of his prayer, what it is.    He asketh not the favour of men, but of God; he craveth not earthly and worldly peace, but spiritual and heavenly.    True it is, the favour of God and goodwill of men, the outward peace and tranquillity one with another, are excellent gifts, but the free and fatherly favour of God, together with peace with God the Father, being reconciled unto us in His dear Son, are much to be preferred in our desires.    2. As we learn chiefly to ask spiritual blessings, so we see what blessings among such as are spiritual are the principal and predominant—to wit, the favour of God and peace of conscience. He that is possessed of these two, hath a hidden mine of treasures, with which all the riches of the world are not to be compared. For these blessings are heavenly, spiritual, eternal; whereas all the substance of this world is temporal, transitory, corruptible. 3. The apostle in some of his Epistles useth three words—grace, mercy, and peace. Here he contenteth himself with naming two—grace and peace, wherein there is no contrariety, forasmuch as mercy is included under peace. For by mercy is understood our justification, which consisteth partly in the forgiveness of our sins, and partly in the imputation of Christ's righteousness, which do bring true peace with them. 4. We see from whom he asketh all these—first from God the Father, to teach that he is the author of every good and perfect gift. If then we stand in need of them we can receive none but of Him. 5. We see that to God the Father he joineth Jesus Christ; for all blessings are bestowed through Christ, the Mediator of the New Testament. God the Father is the fountain, Christ is the pipe or conduit, by whom they are conveyed unto us. He that hath not Him hath not the Father. He that is not in Him, remaineth in death. He that believeth in the Son, hath everlasting life, and he that obeyeth not the Son, shall not see life, but the wrath of God abideth on him. 6. The title given unto Him: He is called the Lord of His Church; it is a kingdom, whereof He is the Prince; it is a city, whereof He is the governor; it is a house, whereof He is the master or owner; it is a body, whereof He is the head. So then, all obedience is due to Him, and all men must acknowledge His worship over them. Lastly, in that he craveth grace and peace from Christ our Lord, as well as from God the Father, it confirmeth our faith in a fundamental point of Christian religion, touching the Deity of Christ, Who is God equal with the Father. (*W. Attersoll.*)

*Grace:*—I. From hence let us observe the CHIEFEST CAUSE OF GOD'S FAVOUR TO US, NAMELY, HIS OWN FREE WILL AND GRACIOUS DISPOSITION TO FAVOUR US. The use of this doctrine is to humble us in ourselves, as having not the least spark of goodness in ourselves, and to make us ascribe all glory in everything to God, whose grace is the fountain and foundation of all good things whatsoever. II. In the example of Paul, in all his salutations wishing first of all grace, that is, the favour of God, we learn WHAT IT IS THAT WE SHOULD CHIEFLY DESIRE, EITHER FOR OURSELVES OR FOR OTHERS, our children, wives, kindred, fathers and mothers, acquaintance, &c., viz., the grace of St. Paul. 1. God's favour is the ground of all other mercies whatsoever; it is the main and mother-blessing, the very seed of all other mercies whatsoever—so that in desiring it, we desire all other, and getting it, we get other. 2. God's grace is instead of all other blessings, in case they be wanting. III. Since whatsoever we desire, we are likewise TO SEEK IT, IN THE USE OF THE MEANS. Paul in his example commending unto us the desire of God's favour withal further showeth us that we must use means for the attainment of it. 1. Taking thorough notice of that disgrace and displeasure thou art in with God, and that most deservedly for thy sins, thou must first of all come as Benhadad's servants came to Ahab, even with a halter about thy neck, creeping and crouching before the throne of grace, abasing and abjecting thyself at His footstool, in the humble and penitent confession of thy sins. 2. Thou must shroud thyself under Christ's wings. Clothe thyself with His righteousness, that so thou mayest appear lovely in the eyes of the Lord, for in Christ only is the Father well pleased; and so if thou wouldst have Him well pleased with thee, thou must become a member of Him, bone of His bone, and flesh of His flesh. This thou doest when by faith thou layest hold upon Christ's righteousness, and gripest the promises of the gospel. 3. By faith having clad thyself with the robes of Christ's imputed righteousness, thou must be clothed upon with the garment of thy own righteousness and obedience, which howsoever being in itself a menstruous cloth as it comes from us yet being of the Spirit's own weaving, in that regard is acceptable to God, and causeth Him to take a further delight in us. (Prov. iii. 3.) (*D. Dyke, B.D.*)

*Grace to be used:*—Grace is always a gift, and not to be enjoyed only but to be used. For it is use that makes all things bright in creation, that keeps the diamond from accretions, and the fine gold from being tarnished. The great lesson of the universe is the blessedness of use. The purest atmosphere obeys the law of circulation, and the most crystal river is always sending up clouds of blessing from its living waters. (*W. M. Statham, M.A.*) *Varieties of grace:*—Ever in each individual Christian life there is seen a manifold grace—grace of forgiveness, grace of new life and peace, grace of birth at the Cross, grace of growth by the Holy Spirit, growth in power and purity and in likeness to God. How many varieties of life Nature has! We are struck with her grace and beauty in her myriad forms. She never seems to exhaust the variety of her wardrobe, as in garments of light, now of subdued colour, now of effulgent beauty, she proclaims the majesty and glory of God. (*Ibid.*) *Peace :*—I do willingly assent to those who by peace understand all prosperity and felicity, both earthly and heavenly, in this life, and that to come. 1. First, the inward peace of conscience with God, which springeth out of the grace and favour of God (Rom. v. 1). A man's conscience will never be at quiet within him till it feels this grace. 2. The peace of charity among ourselves. This also is an effect of God's grace, which as it maketh a man at peace with himself and God, so with his brethren. The love of God shed into our hearts will make us love our brethren also. 3. The peace of amity, and a holy kind of league with all God's creatures. This also is an effect of grace ; for when we have His favour, who is the Lord, we have the good will also of His servants the creatures. 4. Outward prosperity and good success in our ways ; so it is commonly taken in all their salutations (1 Chron. xii. 18). Now, the reason why outward prosperity is signified by this name of peace is—first, because to the godly they are pledges of that sweet peace they have with God. Secondly, they are notable maintainers of the peace and quietness of our affections ; for in the want of outward things how are we disquieted. But peace, in this fourth signification, is so taken for outward prosperity, that which all this outward prosperity hath security annexed unto it, and is a forerunner of that eternal prosperity and felicity in God's kingdom ; for both these things are understood by the name of peace. I. From hence observe, that as we may lawfully desire for ourselves and others outward prosperity and the blessing of this life, so HOW AND IN WHAT MANNER WE MUST DESIRE THEM. 1. Having desired grace in the first place " First seek the kingdom of God " (Matt.vi.) ; and then in the second place we may seek temporal things ; but now men are all for peace, " Who will shew us any good ? " few or none for grace ; peaceable men, as I may call them, enough, very few gracious men that do first of all seek God's grace, and then in the second place peace. 2. In desiring of outward things we must moderate our desires, that they go not beyond their bounds, to desire abundance and superfluity of them ; for we desire them by the name of peace : therefore no more must we desire, but that which will serve us, to attend the works of our calling with free and quiet minds, without disturbance or distraction. II. Paul first desiring grace and then peace, showeth us THAT PEACE, NAMELY, OUTWARD PROSPERITY, IS A FRUIT OF GRACE, and so, that the nearest and most compendious way to get peace, is first to get grace and favour with God. Joseph and David had wonderful success in all their ways, and the reason the Holy Ghost yieldeth thereof is this, " The Lord was with them " (Gen. xxxix. ; 1 Sam. xviii.). Grace is the only means to draw on peace. When we have got Christ's righteousness, it is that grace which makes us graceful to God (Matt. vi.). Then outward things come voluntarily, as it were, without our seeking or desiring ; no marvel then if oftentimes things go cross with us, we by our sins having drawn down the curse of God upon all our enterprises. This is the reason why God's children live better, even with greater credit and reputation in the world with a little, than many times the wicked do, which have far more. God's blessing sets forward the one, and his curse blows upon the other. But we oftentimes see those that are not in greatest favour with God abounding with these earthly blessings. And on the contrary, those that have greatest store of grace, to have a very small pittance of peace. 1. For the godly, who, having their part in grace, have always in some measure their portion in peace also ; for—(1) The end of all his afflictions, whereto they are disposed, is peace. (2) He hath the peace of security in his greatest distresses (Psa. iii. 6 ; iv. 9). (3) He hath the peace of contentation, grace supplying and sweetening the want of peace, and turning very war itself into peace, darkness into light to the godly, his heart is at rest and at peace within itself. There is no warring of the affections against God, whatsoever his outward estate is. 2. For the wicked. It is far otherwise with them in their peace, which being a graceless peace, is in truth a peaceless peace, for in the midst of their peace they want the peace of security, their hearts tremble like an aspen leaf, in fear of change ; or if they have security, it is a presumptuous and false security ; for when they cry, " Peace, peace," then is their destruction at hand (1 Thess. v. 3). And let their peace be never so flourishing, yet still want they the peace of contentation. They think all too little ; if they had the whole world, with Alexander, they would grieve there were no more for them to get. Again, as the end of the godly man's warfare is peace, so the end of the wicked man's peace is warfare, even an eternal warfare, and wrestling with the anger of God in hell. Therefore a sound and safe peace ariseth only from the grace of God. (*D. Dyke, B.D.*) **From God our Father, and the Lord Jesus Christ.**—*The unity of the Divine Father and Son:*—The placing of both names under the government of one preposition implies the mysterious unity of the Father with the Son; while conversely St. John, in a parallel passage (2 John 3), by employing two prepositions, brings out the distinction between the Father, who is the fontal source, and the Son, who is the flowing stream. But both forms of the expression demand for their honest explanation, the recognition of the divinity of Jesus Christ. How dare a man, who thought of Him as other than Divine, put His name thus by the side of God's, as associated with the Father in the bestowal of grace? . . . The double source is one source, for in the Son is the whole fulness of the Godhead: and the grace of God, bringing with it the peace of God, is poured into that spirit which bows humbly before Jesus Christ, and trusts Him when He says, with love in His eyes and comfort in His tones, " My grace is sufficient for thee; My peace give I unto you." (*A. Maclaren, D.D.*) *God our Father :*—Dr. Pentecost said that he once gave some Bible readings at Wellesley College, in America, where about three hundred young ladies were being educated. The principal of the College asked him to give them to two of the students who were confined to their room by sickness. On being introduced to them, he inquired if they were Christians. One replied, " I hope so "; the other answered, " Sometimes I think I am, and sometimes I think I am not." Mr. Pentecost said : " If I met your father in Boston and told him that I had met a young lady at Wellesley who said that she thought that you were her father, what would he think? " The tears streamed over her cheeks as she replied, " Do you mean to say that it is our privilege to call God our Father in the same way as our earthly father ? " This circumstance was the means of leading her to Christ. *Grace from God :*—We may conceive of " grace and peace " being connected with " God our Father and the Lord Jesus Christ," as we conceive of the water with which a town is supplied in relation to the reservoir of storage on the one hand, and the channel of communication and distribution on the other. We may think of God our Father as the exhaustless fount of these perennial blessings—He is " the God of all grace," and the " very God of peace." Yet all this grace and peace are not gathered up in Him like water in some lake from which there is no outlet, but, like reservoir supplies, these unspeakable mercies are meant to be communicated and enjoyed through the channel and conduit of the Lord Jesus Christ. And while the whole appliances are regulated and managed by the continual operation of the Holy Ghost, there is nothing derogatory to that Divine Spirit, although in this salutation no specific mention is made, in so many words, of His work and offices, because the greater function includes all the separate distributions for individual use and benefit. Grace, therefore, is peace prepared for us, and peace is grace enjoyed by us. For grace is simply that free favour that spontaneously emanates from love—the grace of God our Father and the Lord Jesus Christ being the self-moved and self-moving operations of Divine love to sinful men. Such kindness is called " grace," because the inherent goodness of the Divine disposition alone can account for it—" grace " being the word that brings into special prominence the Divine motive in redemption as unbought, unsought, and unconstrained by principles from without, just as " mercy " has reference particularly to the unworthy character of its objects. A many-sided word like grace is best explained by analogies suggested by some similar many-sided word, such as "life," "vegetation," and the like. Grace, like life, may be regarded as a great and blessed gift from without, or a Divine power working mercifully towards us, and ultimately working in us ; bringing salvation for us, and securing its mightiest triumph when it secures a lodgment of itself within us. And just as life receives various names from the various blessings it includes—feeling, moving, seeing, hearing, which are but varieties of the one great privilege of living—so grace is the comprehensive term including the supply of all favours and privileges needful for our fallen and undeserving condition as sinners to be saved. It is enlightenment for darkness, pardon for transgression, comfort for trial, hope for despondency, strength for weakness, and all help for all need. And just as life brought into play as a power within us will be sight if it operate through the eye, speech if through the tongue, hearing if through the ear; so with grace—if it work upon our convictions of sin, it will be the grace of repentance ; if on God's testimony, it is the grace of faith; if on God's commandments, it is the grace of obedience—and so on through the whole range of Christian excellence. We thus use " grace " with the varied applications attachable to any kindred word, like " vegetation "; as when we say " Vegetation is at work," we mean the hidden power or influence which produces the buds, leaves, fruits, and all the riches and beauty of the face of nature ; or when, on the other hand, we say, " Vegetation is looking lovely," we refer to the effects themselves of the hidden power as they strike and delight the eye. So grace is the Divine agency or quicken- ing power which, when it takes hold of us, produces all good thoughts, all holy desires, and all heavenly life, while it is no less the name for those thoughts, desires, and graces themselves, considered as its fruits. If, further, it be viewed as dealing with Divine truth and promise, with God's gospel-message of mercy, with Christ and His work, with the Holy Spirit's aid, with the heavenly inheritance, and the like, under the aspect of blessings appropriated and enjoyed, then grace becomes peace. When, in short, we think of spiritual and saving benefits as connected with the Divine nature, and as communicated through our Lord Jesus Christ, we call them all grace; and, on the other hand, we call them all peace when we think of them with special relation to our own good—when we think of their precious value for us, and their tranquillising and enjoyable effects upon us. Oh ! if our peace were not of grace, we should be doomed to perish for want of it, like a population whose whole water supply depended on two or three trickling streams, that might dry up and fail when most needed. If we are to live beyond the fear of our peace getting exhausted, it must be by drawing on the perennial resources of heavenly grace, ever full and ever flowing among the everlasting hills—the free, the sovereign, self- moving and redeeming love of God in Christ Jesus our Lord. What an appeal there is to Philemon in such a salutation ! As if the apostle would say, " This is sufficient to enable you to do all I am to ask at your hands. And as you would find grace and favour with the Lord yourself, or enjoy peace in your own soul, you may not be inexorable or ungracious towards Onesimus, but must seek peace and pursue it, by sealing its comforts on the penitent's heart." (*A. H. Drysdale, M.A.*)

Ver. 4. **I thank my God.**—*A thankful commendation :*—Paul has the habit of begin- ning all his letters with thankful commendations, and assurances of a place in his prayers. The exceptions are 2 Corinthians, where he writes under strong and painful emotion, and Galatians, where a vehement accusation of fickleness takes the place of the usual greeting. But these exceptions make the habit more conspicuous. But though this is a habit, it is not a form, but is the perfectly simple and natural expression of the moment's feelings. He begins his letters so, not in order to please and to say smooth things, but because he feels lovingly, and his heart fills with a pure joy which speaks most fitly in prayer. To recognise good is the way to make good better. Teachers must love if their teaching is to help. The best way to secure the doing of any signal act of Christian generosity, such as Paul wished of Philemon, is to show absolute confidence that it will be done, because it is in accor- dance with what we know of the doer's character. " It's a shame to tell Arnold a lie ; he always trusts us," the Rugby boys used to say. (*A. Maclaren, D.D.*) *A thankful interest in God :*—God cannot be possessed except as a personal good ; and yet cannot be possessed and enjoyed as a personal good only, any more than sunshine can be held as mere private property. The more of such blessings a neighbour enjoys, there is the more for any one else to use and enjoy. So there is that in vital personal interest in God which at once guarantees a thankful spirit in the possessor, and acts as a safeguard against the spirit of self-worship. The law of the solar system is that " the more quickly a planet revolves round the sun, the more slowly it turns round its own axis"; and the very principle which regulates its speed makes it sway to and fro from its own centre towards neighbouring orbs, while keeping it balanced in its course round the central one of all. No wonder there exhales from Paul's heart the incense of pure thanks to God for all the evidences of Philemon's goodness and grace, as inwrought by saving mercy, and as working outwardly in acts of love and kindness unto others ! Far from the expres- sion of his self-interest, " My God " being self-confined, his very thanks are absorbed with the good in another. The more a fire shoots its flame and heat towards heaven, the farther out from itself will it shoot its warmth. So the more vehemently the soul can possess itself of God and be possessed by Him, the more ardently will it be carried upward with its thanks and outward with its intense desires for the good of others. Thoughts of God's mercies will ever be found lying very close to thoughts of others' needs. To be able to thank God sincerely for the good we see in others, is the best security for our feeling intensely solicitous for their further good. (*A. H. Drysdale, M.A.*) *Prayerful thanksgiving :*—I. HIS PRAYERFUL THANKSGIVING. 1. The mingling of thanks with intercession is true prayer—the discovery of a reason in blessings bestowed for craving and expecting more (Psa. cxv. 12). 2. Thanksgiving insures further grace by fostering a spirit of dependence. 3. Gratitude for the good in others is a spiritual grace. Disinterested love—the prime feature of heavenliness—Christlikeness. II. THE OCCASION OF HIS GRATITUDE. Two leading characteristics of Christianity are specified as being possessed by Philemon. 1. Faith fixed on Christ. This is—(1) The absolute source of salvation. (2) The principle of the saved life. (3) The spring of beneficent activity. 2. Love of the brethren proving the faith. Such affection—(1) Impartial. (2) Discriminating. (3) Active. A grace of the heart first, the force of life afterward. III. THE OBJECT OF HIS PETITION. Twofold: Increase—1. In practical godliness. "Be ye enlarged" is the Divine mandate in the natural and spiritual realm. Paul "prays for that very thing for which he 'gives thanks.' The most perfect need prayers for their perseverance and progress." 2. In the number of believers. The eloquence of good deeds cannot be resisted. "Everything in us that is good makes known our faith" and impels us to make "acknowledgment" of our relation to Christ. His reflected light in us will attract men to seek Him for themselves. IV. THE GREATNESS OF HIS JOY. Greatheart he who could be glad for others' sakes under such conditions! 1. His triumph in adversity. Thinks little of his own troubles. Mentions them only to appeal to his friend's heart in the interests of another. 2. His unselfishness. "The hearts of the saints are refreshed." This was the fountain of his pleasure. "Singular love to feel so much joy on account of the benefit received by others." Learn: 1. To cultivate sympathy. 2. To master circumstances. 3. To commend the gospel. 4. To advance in every good. (*A. W. Johnson.*) *Praises and prayers :*—I. THE OBJECT. "I thank my God," &c. 1. God is the Author of all good (Hos. xiv. 8). 2. To him, therefore, is all praise due (1 Chron. xxix. 13, 14). 3. It is the privilege of good men to approach Him as their God. 4. Our prayers and praises should be for others as well as for ourselves. II. THE CIRCUMSTANCE. "Always," &c. III. THE MATTER. 1. Of his praises, on account of Philemon—(1) Love for Christ. (2) Faith in Christ. (3) Love to saints. 2. Of his prayers. (1) That fruits may abound. (2) That others may be won. (3) That God may be glorified. IV. THE REASON. (*M. Henry, D.D.*) *The growth of graces :*—We learn from hence that all Christians (especially teachers) are greatly to rejoice and praise God when they see that professors grow forward in heavenly graces. It is a matter of great joy and comfort to see men grow in graces as they do in years, and to increase in heavenly things as they multiply their days. 1. It serveth exceedingly to advance the glory of God that men grow in godliness, which ought to be an effectual reason to move us to rejoice; for what is there that should more cheer us, than when God's name is magnified, and His truth extolled among the sons of men. 2. The forwardness of one is a notable means to draw forward another. For as one wicked man maketh another, and he that is seduced is an instrument to seduce another; so he that is truly converted will not rest in the quiet fruit and inward comfort of his own conversion, but labour to convert others, and so make them partakers of that comfort which they have found. 3. It is a great comfort to the pastors and teachers of the Church, when such as are taught do grow in grace and prosper by those means that are brought and offered unto them. The apostle calleth the Philippians his brethren, beloved and longed for, his joy and his crown; wherein he accounteth their growth, his honour; their increasing, his rejoicing; their faith, his hope; their flourishing, his felicity. It is a great comfort to the husbandman after his toiling and tilling, after his planting and ploughing, to see the fruits of his labours, and to behold the increase of the earth. So it fareth with the spiritual husbandman, whose labour is greater and oftener, enduring all the year long, whose patience is greater in waiting for the early and latter rain, whose gain and profit is less in tilling a dry and barren soil, that yieldeth little or no increase, but a crop of cares, a bundle of briars and bushes, and an harvest of thorns and thistles, that are reserved for the fire. 4. The graces of God, and the growing in these graces, are fruits of their election, and seals of their salvation, so that the angels in heaven rejoice at the conversion of a sinner. (*W. Attersoll.*) *Christian congratulation :*—I. FOR HIS GRATULATION, OR REJOICING WITH PHILEMON IN HIS GRACES, IT IS SET DOWN IN THE FORM OF THANKSGIVING, "I thank." 1. Where observe, the manner of true Christian congratulating and rejoicing with our friends, for any good thing they have; namely, to rejoice in the Lord; giving Him first of all His due, the praise of all that good they have. The rejoicing of the world is carnal and profane. God is never so much as thought upon. The parties whom we congratulate, they are dignified and almost deified. "Oh, I admire your wisdom, eloquence, learning," &c., will the flatterer, or the inordinate lover of his friend, say. But Paul would say, "I admire the goodness and mercy of God towards you, in enriching you with these gifts, I thank God for your wisdom," &c.; so all the praise is given wholly to God, whereas before it was wholly derived from God to man, and so God was defrauded and defeated of His right. Not that it is unlawful to praise men endued with the graces and gifts of God's Spirit; nay, it is a duty we owe unto them; but it must be performed in that wise sort, that God in the first place be praised; for by this means we shall both in ourselves take away suspicion of flattery, and in our brother commended, suspicion of pride. 2. The title that Paul giveth God in this his thanksgiving, "My God." (1) The privilege of every true Christian. He hath a peculiarity and special propriety in God, that look as a man may say of his inheritance, his house and lands, "These be mine," so he may as truly say of God, "God is mine;" I am righted and interested in Him. This privilege is conferred upon us in the covenant of grace which runs in this tenor, "I will be thy God, and thou shalt be one of My people." (2) The nature of true justifying faith, which is, to apply God in special to the believer. True faith doth not only believe that God is the God of His elect in general, but that He is his God in special, as Paul here saith, "My God." II. The second effect WHEREBY PAUL DECLARETH HIS LOVE TOWARDS THEM, IS HIS DAILY PRAYING FOR THEM. "Making mention of you always in my prayers." 1. Even in our private and solitary prayers, we must be mindful of our brethren. 2. Observe, that Paul did pray even for those for whom he gave thanks; from whence it followeth, that there is no man so perfect that he hath need only to give thanks for that good he hath received, and not to ask some good thing he wanteth. Unto thanksgiving, there-fore, for ourselves or others, petition must be annexed both for the continuance and increase of that good we give thanks for. III. We may observe, THAT PHILEMON WAS SUCH AN ONE AS MINISTERED TO PAUL JUST OCCASION, AS OF PRAYER, SO LIKEWISE OF THANKSGIVING. We must labour herein to be like him, that others, specially God's ministers, who either see us, or hear of us, may have cause not only to pray for us, but also to praise God for us. (D. Dyke, B.D.) **Making mention of thee always in my prayers.**—*Good men need our prayers :*—The best men, cumulated with the greatest graces of the Spirit, had need be prayed for. St. Paul was rapt up into the third heaven, where he saw secrets not to be uttered, yet he desires the Ephesians' prayers. St. Peter was a stout champion; yet Christ prays that his faith should not fail. Philemon abounded in all good gifts, of knowledge, faith and love, yet St. Paul ceased not to pray for him. 1. The best of all know but in part, love in part; therefore we had need to pray for them, that their defects may be supplied, that they may increase daily more and more. 2. Here we are wayfaring men, we are not come to our journey's end; therefore we had need to be prayed for, that we may persevere to the end, and have the crown of life. (W. Jones, D.D.) *Happy in being prayed for :*—Alexander counted Achilles happy, that he had such a trumpeter of his praises as Homer was. Philemon might count himself happy, that he had such a worthy man to pray for him as St. Paul. (*Ibid.*) *A large prayer-list :*—What a list of persons for whom he daily entreated God must St. Paul have had! If he thus prayed especially for this convert in the comparatively small city of Colosse, what numbers must he have mentioned in Corinth, in Ephesus, in Philippi, in Thessalonica? And notice how in these supplications for private persons he mentions thanksgivings. He remembers not only their wants, but the blessings already bestowed upon them. (M. F. Sadler, M.A.) *The benefit we may confer on others by praying for them :*—When we are poor and can do our brethren no other good, yet may we benefit them by our prayers. When we see our brethren in necessity, in danger, in affliction, in persecution, in sickness, and in great misery; when we have no hand to help them, no power to deliver them, no means to succour them, no favour to speak for them; yet, we have hearts to lift up for them to God, the Father of all mercies, and the God of all consolation, and by praying unto Him for them, we shall do them much good, give them much comfort, minister unto them much help, and procure unto them speedy deliverance. This shall be more available and profitable unto them than all other means of help and succour used for their safety without this. Let such as are of the greatest gifts earnestly crave and call for the prayers of those that have lesser and smaller gifts. This reproveth such as never regard them, nor require them, that think they have no need of them, nor know the necessity of them. It is all one to these men, whether they be prayed for or not; whom God no doubt doth oftentimes cross in the works of their hands, that they do not prosper, because they make no account of the Church's prayers. It reproveth such also as regard not the public assemblies of the faithful, and the meeting of the congregation of Christ in one place, where prayers are made for the Church, where praises are sung, and thanks are rendered for the blessings of God ; yea, heaven and earth are made to ring and rebound with sounding out His glory, as it were with the voice of one man. All our churches, for the most part on the Lord's day, assemble at one hour, we come together at one time, a blessed hour, a blessed time ; the best hour, the best time in the whole week. Oh, how should we love it, how should we desire it, how should we delight in it? Then do we pray for the Church, then the Church prayeth for us ; then are we mindful of our brethren, then are our brethren likewise mindful of us ; then is God mindful of us all. (*W. Attersoll.*) *Intercessory prayer a means for diffusing good :*—It is matter of thankfulness that the privilege of intercession is the property of all Christians. While perishable good—such as friends, health, riches—are denied to thousands, there is not one so poor or so powerless as may not be a benefactor, not to individuals merely, but to the Church and to mankind, through the common privilege of prayer. It enables the weakest and most lonely to direct the arm of Omnipotence, and to help the objects of their affection from afar. It gives power to bless those who are separated from our presence by half the globe, and secures to the absent child the comfort of a parent's presence, whom he shall never meet except in heaven. " Surely some good Christian is praying for us to-night," has been heard from the lips of a pious seaman, when the tempest that was driving them in resistless fury towards destruction suddenly veered round, and saved them from the rocks on which they expected to be dashed the next moment ; and God only, and the good angels whom He sends to minister to His children, can tell what good thoughts have been inspired, what temptations have been averted, what peace has been communicated, through the power of some absent believer's prayers. Let it be our care to make use of this practicable and powerful instrument of diffusing good. The poorest can obtain it ; the humblest believer is already in possession of it. Say not thou canst do nothing for men if thou canst give them thy love, thy Christian example, and thy prayers. (*R. Nisbet, D.D.*) *Prayer and attainment :*—Prayer is based on a supreme contentedness with Divine gifts and blessings but also on a sublime uncontentedness with human attainments in them. It therefore catches up thankfulness and petition into a happy unity, as the railway train holds its passengers at rest and yet in motion at the same moment. True prayer is free alike from querulous discontent and from cloddish self-content. The very satisfaction of the traveller at the well with the water it affords, bids him draw more largely on its supply for himself and others. And so Paul is thankful for all that God is and does, for all He has and offers, as manifested in the evangelic faith and love of Philemon ; but he cannot think of either Philemon or himself resting satisfied where so much more remains to be possessed. To have nothing further to ask and yearn after were to have the mainspring of activity and improvement utterly broken. To pray is therefore a privilege and a relief. To pray for others is especially so to a loving and benevolent heart. We might have been permitted to pray only for ourselves; but amid the separations and scatterings of earth, God has been pleased to put intercession for one another as an instrument of mutual interest and blessing into the hands of all who would promote each other's good. (*A. H. Drysdale, M.A.*)

Ver. 5. **Hearing of thy love and faith.**—*A true human love :*—Some translators in ancient times, and many in later days, would at once accept M. Renan's version, as an equivalent, and, indeed, as a judicious correction—" De ta foi au Seigneur, de ta charité pour tous les saints." Yet those who reverence Scripture may justly maintain that St. Paul's own arrangement of the words has a higher rhetoric, under the guidance of a better wisdom. Let us suppose a writer to have before him two propositions, one of which is of special importance for his immediate purpose. He might be able to bring out that purpose most effectively by beginning and ending his sentence with the motive to which he wished to give prominence. From this point of view, it is instructive to compare the two contemporary letters to the Ephesians and Colossians. In those more elaborate and dogmatic pieces the idea of *faith* is of principal significance, and in one or other of its aspects is the leading subject of consideration. But in the Epistle to Philemon the writer's great object is to appeal to the principle of Christian humanity, to that true human love which flows from the constraining power of Divine love, believed in and accepted. "Love toward the saints," and therefore to the brother for whom he pleaded, is consequently placed in the forefront. It is the first note of the whole strain. Let us conceive the epistle presented to Philemon, when the delegates first arrive, and the returned fugitive anxiously awaits his master's decision. The letter is received with reverential joy. Philemon listens, or reads, in breathless expectation, and the very first word which falls upon his ear, or meets his eye, after the salutation, is— *love.* It has a force in this place which no other word could supply. St. Paul, therefore, places *love* first; but as he never can forget *faith,* and Christ as the central object of faith, he puts *love* first, the object of the love last, faith towards Christ in the middle between the extremes. (*Bp. Wm. Alexander.*) *Love first :—* Love is put before faith. The significance of this sequence comes out by contrast with similar expressions in Eph. i. 15 ; Col. i. 4. The reason for the change here is probably that Onesimus and Epaphras, from whom Paul would be likely to hear of Philemon, would enlarge upon his practical benevolence, and would naturally say less about the root than about the sweet and visible fruit. The arrangement then is an echo of the talks which had gladdened the apostle. Possibly, too, love is put first because the object of the whole letter is to secure its exercise towards the fugitive slave ; and seeing that the apostle would listen with that purpose in view, each story which was told of Philemon's kindness to others made the deeper impression on Paul. The order here is the order of analysis, digging down from manifestation to cause ; the order in the parallel passages quoted is the order of production, ascending from root to flower. (*A. Maclaren, D.D.*) *Love and faith, the principal points of salvation :—*1. He reduceth the principal points of salvation to two heads—faith and love. In these standeth the happiness of the godly. By these, a Christian man perfected, for they are the chief graces of the Holy Ghost. 2. He beginneth with love, and placeth it before faith ; deed is more precious, but it is inward and hidden in the heart, and in name and order goeth before love. But he first nameth love because it is better known to us, better seen of us, and is as the touch-stone to try our faith. For though the cause be more worthy than the effect, yet the effect is more conspicuous and manifest. So faith, being the cause of works, is more excellent, and love as an effect is more evident. 3. We see, that albeit faith be set in the last place, for the reason rendered before, yet faith is first defined, and so the order somewhat inverted. Now, it is described and declared by his object, that it respecteth Christ Jesus. (*W. Attersoll.*) *Faith and love in the Christian life :—*This faith embodies the theoretic principles of Christian life, while this love for saints embodies these principles on their practical side. Like heart and lungs in the body, each has its own functions ; and, though separate, the one never acts apart from the other—life being the combined play of both. Faith binds to all Christian verities, translating them into personal convictions ; while love binds to all Christian motives, translating these into personal activities—love being well called the daughter of faith and the mother of virtue and good works. (*A. H. Drysdale, M.A.*) *Faith and love acceptable to God :—* I. THE REASONS FOLLOW TO CONFIRM THIS DOCTRINE. 1. They give us good acceptance with God and man, because they are evident marks and notable testimonies of our election and perseverance. They are as two ear-marks, to know and discern whose sheep we are. 2. God hath given praise and glory as an inseparable companion of godliness and goodness; and on the other side, He hath allotted shame to follow sin. He hath joined these together, to wit, glory with piety, and shame with iniquity. These draw together, as it were, in one yoke, so that one cannot be without the other. The apostle speaking of the ungodly, faith, their glory shall be to their shame. Seeing, therefore, the graces of God's spirit are testimonies of election, and companions of praise and glory, we must from hence conclude that the good gifts of God that are found in us make us accepted of God and man. II. THE USES FOLLOW TO BE CONSIDERED AND LEARNED OF US. 1. Seeing faith in Christ, and love toward the saints give us a good report in the Church, and lay up a good foundation for us in heaven, we see that only godly men have a good name, and evil men shall leave the blots of an evil name behind them. The memorial of the just shall be blessed, but the name of the wicked shall rot. This overthroweth three sorts of men that offend, and esteem not of men according to their faith and profession. (1) Such as slander the godly, and bring up an evil report of the faithful people of God, and seek to take away their good name from them, which is a jewel more precious than silver and gold. But we shall less esteem what they speak, if we consider who they are that speak. For the witness of an enemy is by no law to be taken, but always to be suspected. (2) Such as magnify and advance the ungodly, give them the praise of the world, speak well of them, as of the only honest men that deserve to be commended. But so long as they live in sin, their own wickedness doth testify to their faces, and their ungodly hearts proclaim their own shame, and shall bring upon them utter confusion. Let this be written and engraven in our minds, that ungodliness will leave a reproach behind it. (3) It convinceth such as are civil men, and can say they are not drunkards, they are not adulterers, they are not thieves, they lead an honest life, they pay all men their own. These men have a good liking of themselves, and are accounted the only men among others. But a man may do all this, and be a Pharisee, yea, no better in the sight of God than a Turk and Infidel. He may carry the countenance and have the report of such a liver, and yet smell strongly, and savour rankly in the nostrils of God, of ignorance, of unbelief, of pride, and of self-love. If we would deserve true praise indeed, we must not rest in these outward practices and in this moral civility, we must plant religion in our hearts, we must have a sound faith in Christ, we must know the doctrine of the gospel, we must worship God aright. 2. Seeing faith and love give us a good commendation and report, let us by these and such like graces of God's Spirit, seek after a good name, let us not hunt after the praise of men, but that which is of God. The other is a blast of wind; this is certain and never fadeth. (*Ibid.*) *Love and faith not separated :*—1. Seeing these two gifts are coupled together one with another, it followeth that they must never be separated in a Christian man. He that is joined with the head, must also be joined with the members ; and he that hath his part in the communion of saints, hath his fellowship with Christ. 2. Seeing faith and love go together, and dwell together, we are put in mind of a notable duty, and are thereby directed to prove our faith by our love, and our love by our faith, and to make one of them serve to assure the other. The cause will prove the effect, and the effect will manifest the cause. We may prove fire by the heat, and the heat by the fire ; a good tree by his fruit, and the fruit by his tree. (*Ibid.*) *Thankful for the graces of others :*—I. See in Paul's example, WHAT IS THE EFFECT THAT THE GOOD REPORT WHICH THE GODLY HEAR OF THEIR BRETHREN, USETH TO WORK IN THEIR MINDS. Commonly men suck in their own praises with very greedy ears, but they cannot with patience endure the praises of others, thinking that the praises of others is a close kind of dispraising themselves, and that so much is taken from them as is given unto another. Hence it is that the speech of those that are much in the commendations of others is so troublesome to us, in that thereby we feel ourselves stirred up to wrath, fretting, envy, and such like distemper of corrupt affections. But it is far otherwise with the children of God, who have the circumcised ears of Paul, that not only with patience, but with great joy, can hear the commendations of their brethren, and upon the hearing of them break forth not into fretting and fuming, but into a holy lauding of the Name of the Lord. II. Observe, THAT THANKS ARE DUE TO GOD, NOT ONLY FOR THOSE BENEFITS WHICH HE BESTOWETH ON US OURSELVES, BUT ON OUR BRETHREN ALSO. And therefore if we pay him not this debt, he may justly charge us with ingratitude. For shall we confess it our duty to pray for our brethren, that they may be enriched with these graces ; and shall we not think ourselves equally bound to give thanks to God, when He hath heard our prayers ? III. If in Paul's example others are bound to give thanks for our graces, then it is our part, who through God's mercies are possessed of any of His graces SO TO USE THEM THAT WE MAY MINISTER JUST CAUSE TO OUR BRETHREN TO GIVE THANKS FOR THEM. IV. Paul saying that he heard of the faith and love of Philemon, PLAINLY SHOWETH, THAT THERE WERE SOME THAT RELATED AND REPORTED THEM TO HIM. By whose example we must learn to have a special respect of the good name of our brother, being always ready, as occasion shall serve, to speak of those good things that are in others. V. Observe GOD'S PROVIDENCE, RECOMPENSING FAITH WITH FAME AND GOOD NAME. When faith shall open our hearts and mouths to extol God's name, God will open our brethren's, yea, sometimes our enemies' mouths, to extol ours (Heb. xi. 13). "By this" (namely faith) "our elders obtained a good report." This was the means whereby they became so famous. What marvel, then, if thou hast an ill name, when thou hast an ill conscience ? Naughty faith and fame, cracked credit and conscience, commonly go together. (*D. Dyke, B.D.*) *Faith and love :*— By faith understand justifying faith, which only is able to bring forth true love, either to God or man. And by love, as the apostle showeth, not only love to God, but also to man. Here observe—I. THE DISTINCTION OF THESE GRACES of faith and

love. They are named distinctly as two virtues (1 Cor. xiii. 13). II. THE CON-
JUNCTION OF THESE TWO GRACES, for howsoever they are to be distinguished, yet not
to be divided. Wheresoever true faith is, there necessarily love, both to God and
our brethren, will follow. For though faith be alone in justification, yet not in the
justified. As the eye, though alone in seeing, yet not in him that seeth, but joined
with the ears, nose, and many other members of the body. Faith therefore is a
fruitful mother of many daughters, and love is the firstborn of them. Faith,
though it be in regard of God a beggar, always holding out the hand to receive, and
crying, "Give, give," yet in regard of those in whom it dwelleth, it is like a sovereign
lord and king, and hath as a king his officers under him, and among the rest, love, his
almoner, to distribute and disperse those treasures which itself hath received from
the Lord. 1. Our love towards God proceedeth from faith, which, apprehending
God's love to us, enflameth our affections again with the love of God. The beams
of God's love lightning upon our hearts reflect back upon God Himself by the virtue
of our faith. " The love of Christ," saith the apostle—namely, being apprehended
by our faith—"constraineth us." An example whereof we have in Mary Magdalen,
whose faith, believing that much was forgiven her, caused and constrained her to
love much. (1) This plainly convinceth the faith of many to be nothing but
vain presumption, because their love to God is so lukewarm. (2) But as this
doctrine is terrible to the hypocrite, whom it unmasketh of his vain vizard of faith,
so it is no less comfortable to the true Christian. For what dost thou feel thy soul
panting in the earnestness of desire after God ? Dost thou find thyself grieved
when thou missest of thy desire ? Doth thou find thy heart to arise when thou
seest God's Name dishonoured, &c. ? Surely, these things as they are arguments
of sincere love, so likewise of faith not feigned. If thou canst with David (Psa.
xviii. 1) say " I love the Lord," thou mayest as truly use the words following, and
say, " The Lord is my Rock." (3) This doctrine of love flowing from faith,
confuteth those that teach, our election dependeth upon our foreseen obedience.
By that which hath been delivered it appeareth that our love of God is caused and
stirred up in us by His love, to us apprehended by our faith. 2. Our love of our
brethren springeth likewise from faith, for the apostle speaketh here of both loves.
This will appear, if either we consider those duties of love, which we owe generally
to all, or in special to some. (1) For the first this is a duty which we owe to all
indifferently, to be ready to forgive one another, being offended. Now what is that
which will make a revengeful nature yield to this, but faith, which, when once it
hath apprehended God's love, forthwith reasoneth, as the Master in the parable
with His servant (Matt. xix.). The Lord hath freely forgiven me my whole debt,
ought not I then to show the like compassion to my fellow-servant? Therefore the
Lord enjoining the duty of forgiveness ; the apostles pray, Lord, increase our faith
(Luke xvii. 4, 5). (2) Other duties there are which we owe specially to some.
(*a*) As first, to those that are yet unconverted, the desiring of, and by all means
possible labouring after their conversion. Now, it is faith only which will make a
man do this. For, when by faith we have felt the sweetness of God's love ourselves,
we cannot but call upon others, and with the prophet David invite them to the
eating of the same dainties with ourselves (Psa. xxxiv.). "Come, and see, and taste
how good," &c. (*b*) But yet a more special love, which therefore hath a special
name of brotherly love, is due unto those which are already effectually called, and
so made members of Christ. This love also cometh from faith, which, causing us
to love God, must needs also force us to love all those in whom we shall see the
very face and lively image of God Himself so clearly shining. 1. Uses : by this
then once again we may try our faith. A working faith hath laborious love even to
our brethren annexed (1 Thess. i. 3). If then thou art of a hard nature, of a memory
fastly retaining injuries of affections vindicative, which the Scripture calls feet
swift to shed blood, this shows thou hast no part in the blood of Christ by faith.
The like is to be thought of those which are moved with no compassion towards the
soul of their brethren sitting in darkness and the shadow of death, but can suffer
them to pine and perish away in their sins, and never reach forth the hand to pull
them out of the ditch. 2. This doctrine serveth not only for the trial of our faith,
but also of our love to our brethren. For as that faith, which is without this love,
is an idle, and imaginary faith, so that love of our neighbour, which cometh not
from faith, is blind and foolish, and in the end will prove a deceitful and unfaithful love. Natural men, that seem to love very dearly to-day, to-morrow are at
deadly feud. The reason hereof is because their love comes not from faith. 3. It
may be asked, How could others declare to Paul the love and faith of Philemon,

which are secret and hidden virtues, that be in the innermost corners of the heart, far from the sight of the eye? They saw not Philemon's faith, but his outward works, and by them they judged, and so did Paul too of his faith, discerning the tree by the fruit. (*D. Dyke, B.D.*) **Toward the Lord Jesus.**—*Faith toward Christ:*—Sometimes faith is spoken of as " in " Christ, sometimes as " unto " or " upon " Him; here it is " toward " Him. The idea is that of aspiration and movement of yearning after an unattained good. And that is one part of the true office of faith. There is fruition and contact in it. We rest " in " Christ by faith. It incorporates us into His mystical body, and brings about a mutual indwelling. We lean " on " Christ by faith, and by it build the fabric of our loves, and repose the weight of our confidence upon Him, as on the sure foundation. We reach " unto," and, in deepest truth, pass " into " Christ by faith. But there is also in faith an element of aspiration, as of the soaring eagle to the sun, or the climbing tendrils to the summit of the supporting stem. In Christ there is always something beyond, which discloses itself the more clearly, the fuller is our present possession of Him. Faith builds upon and rests in the Christ possessed and experienced, and just therefore will it, if it be true, yearn towards the Christ unpossessed. (*A. Maclaren, D.D.*) *Faith towards Christ:*—For faith is just like the coupling-chain of a railway-carriage—everything depends on where its fastenings are ultimately attached. The carriage moves only if its coupling-chain communicate with the moving power. And faith saves only as it takes hold of the Saviour for itself, and terminates in Him as its object. This precious faith is a bond of attachment. It cannot be a single isolated act, but an abiding attitude of confidence towards the Lord Jesus. (*A. H. Drysdale, M.A.*) *Love to Christ:*—A gentleman when visiting in a hospital in London sat beside the cot of a little girl. Wishing to win her confidence, he said, " My child, do you love your mother?" With a very serious look she replied, " Yes, I do indeed." " But why do you answer so gravely; what is that you are thinking about, my dear?" Then she replied with great earnestness, " Because I can never love my mother anything as she loves me." Can any of you say of Jesus as the little girl said of her mother, " Yes, I love Him indeed, but I can never love Him in any way as He loves me?" **Toward all saints.**—Clearly their relation to Jesus Christ puts all Christians into relation with one another. This was an astounding thought in Philemon's days, when such high walls separated race from race, the slave from the free, woman from man; but the new faith leaped all barriers, and put a sense of brotherhood into every heart that learned God's fatherhood in Jesus. . . . The love which is here commended is not a mere feeling, nor does it go off in gushes, however fervid, of eloquent emotion. Clearly Philemon was a benefactor of the brotherhood, and his love did not spend only the paper-money of words and promises to pay, but the solid coin of kindly deeds. Practical charity is plainly included in that love of which it had cheered Paul in his imprisonment to hear. Its mention, then, is one step nearer to the object of the letter. Paul conducts his siege of Philemon's heart skilfully, and opens here a fresh parellel, and creeps a yard or two closer up. " Surely you are not going to shut out one of your own household from that wide-reaching kindness." So much is most delicately hinted, or rather left to Philemon to infer, by this recognition of his brotherly love. A hint lies in it that there may be a danger of cherishing a cheap and easy charity that reverses the law of gravity, and *in*creases as the square of the distance, having tenderness and smiles for people and churches which are well out of our road, and frowns for some nearer home. (*A. Maclaren, D.D.*) *Love extending to the saints:*—Philemon's love extended itself to the saints, as is here avouched of him; yet it was not cooped up within the pen of the saints: the saints must have the prime place in our love, but not the whole. " Do good to all men, chiefly to them of the household of faith ": chiefly, but not wholly. Aristotle gave an alms to an unworthy man: one reproved him for it. Says he, I gave it to the nature of the man, not to the man; the nature is God's, and must be sustained: the vice is his own and the devil's, and must be reformed. (*W. Jones, D.D.*) *The saintly household:*—1. This teacheth that there ought to be among all the faithful a communion of saints; they are as a family or household among themselves. They have a near fellowship, they are near brethren, they are fellow-members of one body, they are knit together by one spirit, they are called under one hope, they are made Christ's by one faith, they are made one by one baptism, they have one bread to feed upon, they have one cup to drink of, they have one table to meet at, they have one God that they worship, they have one salvation that they aim at (Eph. iv. 2, 3). We are charged to have a care of all mankind, but as it is fit and convenient that they which are of the same family should be helpful one to another rather than to such as are of another family, which are not so nearly joined unto them (Phil. ii. 1, 2). The gifts of God to be imparted to our brethren are of two sorts. For as we consist of two parts, the soul and the body, so the gifts are of two kinds—spiritual graces, and temporal blessings. We must bestow upon them spiritual gifts, procuring their good by example, exhortation, comfort, prayer, reproof. Touching temporal blessings, we must be ready and content to bestow such goods as God hath bestowed upon us, for the good of our fellow-members. If we have this world's goods we must not hide our compassion from them, for then we cannot assure ourselves that the love of God dwelleth in us. 2. Seeing we are charged to provide for the godly poor, and not to see them want, it teacheth that we are all the Lord's stewards, to dispense and dispose His blessings to others. For properly we are not lords, but tenants ; not owners, but stewards ; not possessors, but borrowers ; and whatsoever we enjoy, it is not ours only, but ours and the poor's—they have their share and portion with us. A Christian man, though he be the freest man upon the earth, yet he is a servant to all, especially to the Church of God. This condemneth— (1) Such as seek for nothing but to settle themselves and maintain their own estates, to enrich themselves that they may live in ease and wealth, like the rich man mentioned in the gospel : these make no conscience of swearing, forswearing, lying, dissembling, oppressing, and such like unfruitful works of the flesh. These men may allege and plead for themselves what they will, but in truth they never yet knew what the communion of saints meaneth. (2) It reproveth such as waste and consume the good creatures of God in riotousness, in drunkenness, and in all excess, and when they are in brotherly love and Christian compassion admonished, do answer, "What have you to do with my spending ? I spend nothing but mine own, I spend none of yours." Yes, thou spendest that which is thy wife's, thy children's, thy family's, the poor's, the Church's, yea even that which is God's, for which thou shalt give an account at the great and dreadful day of judgment. (3) Seeing we are debtors to all men, but specially to the faithful, it reproveth such as show the chiefest fruit of their love and charity upon the ungodly and profane, whom it were many times more charity to see punished than relieved : and corrected than maintained. (*W. Attersoll.*) *Why believers are called saints :*—1. Because they are thereunto called and chosen in Christ, they are thereunto justified and redeemed by Christ. For we are chosen before the founda- tions of the world to be holy (Eph. i. 4 ; 1 Thess. iv. 3, 7 ; Luke i. 68, 74, 75). 2. The servants of God must be saints, to the end there may be a conformity and likeness unto Him that hath had mercy upon us. It is requisite that there should be a resemblance between God and His people. God is holy, it is one of His names, He is called the Holy One ; Christ is Holy, and He is called the Holy One of God ; the Spirit is holy, and therefore is called the Holy Spirit. The Son beareth the image of His Father, and thereby is easily known whose Son He is. If we be the sons of God we must express His image in holiness and true righteousness (Lev. xi. 45 ; 1 Pet. i. 14, 15). 3. The faithful are called by the name of saints, that there might be a difference between that which we have of ourselves, and that which we receive from God : between the old man and the new man ; between our first birth and our second birth ; between nature and grace. No man is a saint by nature, we have no holiness from ourselves, but we are strangers to it, and that is a stranger to us ; nay, we are enemies to holiness who love nothing else but profaneness, and desire to be anything else than to be saints and holy. (*Ibid.*) *Love of Christ a bond of brotherhood :*—An unknown man one day dropped dead in New York. He seemed to have been very poor, for in the pockets of his shabby clothes there was not a cent. His description was published in the news- papers, and among other details, mention was made of a tattoo mark on his right arm. It represents a tomb overhung by the branches of a weeping willow. Below was the inscription, " In memory of my mother." Nothing was known of him ; but one thing was clear—he had once had a mother whom he loved. The body was sent to a station-house, and the next day would have been buried in Potter's Field at the expense of the city, if a merchant had not interposed. He asked permission to pay the cost of a decent funeral in a cemetery for the man. He did not know him, but he, too, had lost his mother, and the memory of her had been enshrined in his heart for many years. He felt a brotherhood with the man whose love of his dead mother was displayed in the tattoo marks, and desired to do a brother's part to him. If every Christian felt that the love of Christ, common to him with other Christians, constituted a bond of brotherhood with its claims upon him, how much hardship and pain would be relieved! *Love to saints:*—The magnetised needle turns to the invisible North Pole whenever it turns to any visible object that lies due north of itself; and so, love to saints, as saints, is love to Christ Himself personally, because it is love to whatever of Christ is manifest in them. (*A. H. Drysdale, M.A.*)

**Ver. 6. The communication of thy faith.**—*Communication:*—There is some doubt respecting the allusion in the word "communication." It is translated "fellowship" in Acts ii. 42, 2 Cor. xiii. 14, and "communion" in 1 Cor. x. 16. It may mean that the imparting to others of their faith (when they see the fruits of it) may be effectual, &c.; or "communication" may be taken as meaning distribution. If Philemon loved the saints he would distribute liberally to their needs. Both senses are true: faith "may become effectual by the acknowledging of every good thing." In the eyes of St. Paul it was needful, not only that there should be secret good in a man, but that it should be acknowledged on all hands as good springing from the grace of God and Christ, somewhat analogous to "Let your light so shine," &c. (*M. F. Sadler, M.A.*) *Christian beneficence a means of spiritual growth:*—Philemon's "communication of faith" will help him to the knowledge of the fulness of Christ. The reaction of conduct on character and growth in holiness is a familiar idea with Paul, especially in the prison epistles (see Col. i. 10). The faithful carrying out in life of what we already know is not the least important condition of increasing knowledge. If a man does not live up to his religion, his religion shrinks to the level of his life. Unoccupied territory lapses. We hold our spiritual gifts on the term of using them. The practice of convictions deepens convictions; not that the exercise of Christian graces will make theologians, but it will put in larger possession of the knowledge which is life. While this general principle is abundantly enforced in Scripture and confirmed by experience, the specific form of it here is that the right administration of wealth is a direct means of increasing a Christian's possession of the large store treasured in Christ. Every loving thought towards the sorrowful and needy, every touch of sympathy yielded to, and every kindly Christlike deed flowing from these, thins away some film of the barriers between the believing soul and a full possession of God, makes it more capable of beholding Him and of rising to communion with Him. (*A. Maclaren, D.D.*) *A communion of gifts:*—As there is a communion of saints, so there must be a communion of gifts. A good thing, the more common it is, the better it is. The sun communicates his light to the world, and shines the brighter for that; the springs and fountains communicate their water, and are the fuller for that; a nurse or mother communicates her milk to the infant, and her breasts are replenished still: the communication of faith, of knowledge, and other gifts, is not a diminution, but an augmentation of them. Let us joyfully communicate that which we have, one to another. (*W. Jones, D.D.*) *The gifts and blessings of God:*—I. IT IS THE DUTY OF ALL MEN EARNESTLY TO DESIRE AND PROCURE THE GOOD OF OTHERS, AND TO STIR UP OURSELVES AND OTHERS TO INCREASE IN THE GRACES OF GOD'S SPIRIT. The growing and proceeding of our brethren in the best things should be sought for of us. Reasons: 1. Christian profession is a way in which men must not stand still; they must not stay in one estate, but be always stirring forward. 2. Christians are compared to children. Children are always growing in age, increasing in stature, going forward in knowledge. So must we grow in grace, until we come to a perfect aged man in Christ. 3. We must so walk in our way and hasten to our journey's end, that we may obtain the prize. He that overcometh and holdeth out to the latter end only shall be saved. He that giveth over is a faint soldier, a weak workman, a slow runner, a feeble wrestler. (1) We learn that God hath a just action and suit to commence against all idle and unprofitable drones, that be truants and no proficients in the school of Christ. (2) We are bound to use the means that may further these gifts in us, that is, the ministry of the Word, which being reverently used hath a promise of blessings. (3) Seeing we should desire our own profit and others, it condemneth three sorts of men: first, such as stand at a stay; secondly, such as go backward; thirdly, such as envy the good and growth of others in the best things. (4) Seeing we should all seek to profit ourselves and others in godliness, we must know that it is our duty to stir up the gifts of God in us, that we do not bury them as in a grave; we must exercise the gifts that we have by continual practice. Use maketh men prompt and ready, want of use maketh men untoward. II. The gifts and blessings of God, whether temporal or eternal, bestowed upon any, must not lie hid or dead, but be used and employed to the good of others, and so yield a fellowship and communion to others. Reasons: 1. We are servants unto all, to do them good and to further their salvation. 2. We are members of the same body, and therefore in this respect should profit one another. We see it is so in every part of our body: the eye seeth not for itself, the head inventeth not for itself, the hand worketh not for itself, the foot walketh not for itself, but they do these duties for the whole body. Thus it ought to be among all the faithful; if Christ Jesus be our head, we must be affected as mutual members one to another. 3. We are all of us stewards and disposers of the manifold graces of God. God committed His goods to us, and made us stewards of His family, to minister in season to all in the household, and He will take an account how we use them. Uses: (1) This teaches us to remember the benefit and good of others, and not only to desire, but to effect the same as much as we can, especially their eternal good. It is a good thing to do good unto the bodies of our brethren, but the chiefest good is to do good to their souls. (2) Such are reproved as have gifts and yet use them not but hide them, and so diminish them by idleness and want of conscience. (3) Seeing we must employ that which we have received to the benefit of others, it serveth greatly to comfort such as have been careful to communicate to others those things that they have received, and to make them partakers of the same comfort that they have reaped by them. III. It is the duty of every one to manifest and show forth, yea, to spread abroad and to speak of the gifts of God bestowed upon themselves and others. When God is good towards us, and distributes His graces among us, we must be ready to acknowledge them, when we feel them in ourselves, or see them in others. Reasons: 1. To the end that God's graces being seen and known He may be glorified and blessed for them, who is the author and giver of them. It ought to be our chiefest desire and study that God may have His praise and glory among us. 2. Because the more they be known and farther they are spread, the larger praise and more abundant thanksgiving may be given unto God and yielded to His name by many. 3. In respect of others, because the more the goodness and graces of God are spoken of, and the more largely they are dispersed, the more by that means may be stirred up to an imitation of their example. Uses: (1) We see there may be sometimes a foolish modesty in concealing those good things which should be uttered and published, if they may further the cause of religion, or provoke others to godliness, or bring glory to God. God is not ashamed of us to be called our God, and to do us good; let us not, therefore, be ashamed to acknowledge Him to be good unto us, and confess His goodness to the sons of men. (2) Seeing it is our duty, when God hath been good unto us or others, to make known His goodness. We learn hereby how the saints of God may be rightly and religiously honoured of us, and remembered to their everlasting praise. It is our duty to give thanks to God who hath blessed them with His graces and governed them by His Holy Spirit, and to pray unto Him so to direct us and dispose of our ways that we may follow their godliness and walk in their steps wherein they have gone before us. (3) We must beware that vainglory be not the end which we seek for. We are to give the glory to the author, not to the instrument; to God, not to man; to the Creator, not to the creature. (*W. Attersoll.*) *The efficacy of faith:*—I. That efficacy of faith which here Paul desireth for Philemon was two. First, in regard to Philemon himself, that it might work effectually in him; secondly, in regard of others, that it might be exemplary to them, and so might be effectual in provoking them to the like. And that the apostle had some reference, even to this latter kind of efficacy, the words following seem to import— that whatsoever good thing is in you may be known: for when the light of our faith shineth to others, it very effectually stirreth them up to the glorifying of God's name. Hence observe—1. That true faith may sometimes faint, and be, as it were, raked up under the ashes. A kind of sleepiness may sometimes seize upon it, and disable it for spiritual exercises. As we see in the disciples, who being oppressed with carnal grief for the departure of Christ now at hand, were not able to attend the exercise of prayer, no, not one hour, with our Saviour. So likewise in Phil. iv. 10. Of whom, when the apostle says, that they were revived, or, as the word signifies, waxen green or fresh again, in their love and liberality towards Him; thereby he declareth that for a time they were like trees, that in the winter are in their widowhood, having lost their leaves, and appearing outwardly as dead, all their sap being in the root within. 2. Observe how faith, being by Satan's craft cast into this deep sleep, may be awakened, and how it may shake off this spiritual laziness, viz., by this spiritual exercise of prayer. 3. Paul here plainly teaches us that true faith in his own nature is effectual, lively, full of vigour and spirits (1 Thess. i. 3). I discern the picture of a man, though never so lively, to be no true man, because it stands still and stirs not. Therefore, though it have show of eyes, mouth, feet, &c., yet when I see it neither goes, sees, nor speaks, I know it is no man. So, when I look upon thy faith, and find, for all the colours of outward profession, that it is idle, I conclude forthwith that it is an idol, a shadow, void of truth and substance. II. WHEREIN THIS EFFICACY OF FAITH HERE PRAYED FOR CONSISTS; FIRST, in communication; secondly, in the knowledge of every good thing. 1. For the first, observe, that faith is no sparing niggard, but of a very bountiful and liberal disposition. It hoardeth not, it hideth not those treasures which she receiveth of God, but communicateth them to others. 2. The second thing, wherein this efficacy of faith consisteth, is the knowledge of all that good. That faith then is effectual which hath all other graces at command; so that when it says to one, Go, it goeth; to another, Come, it comes; to all of them I would have you known of others, they forthwith come forth into the open light, and by practice make themselves known to all. If a king command and be not obeyed, it shows his power is not great—that he is not as yet thoroughly confirmed in his authority. So it is an argument that faith as yet is but weak and of small force when it commands not with a kingly and imperial majesty and authority, so that without further delay his commands are obeyed. " That thy faith may be effectual." But how? In the knowledge of every good thing that is in you. (*D. Dyke, B.D.*) **By the acknowledging of every good thing.**—*The acknowledgment of good in others:*—We must acknowledge the good things that are in others. The Queen of Sheba extolled the good things that were in Solomon, and blessed God for them. The elders of the Jews acknowledged the good things that were in the centurion. God set the good things that were in Job, as on a stage, and the devil himself could not but acknowledge them, though maliciously he depraved them. Christ, though He was the giver of them, acknowledged the good things that were in Nathaniel. St. Peter acknowledges the good things that were in St. Paul. Augustin acknowledged the good things that were in Jerome, and Jerome also the good things that were in Augustin, as appears by their epistles one to another. We are injurious to God if we do not acknowledge them. No painter but would have his picture acknowledged: every good man is the beautiful picture of God Almighty; they be envious persons that will not acknowledge them. (*W. Jones, D.D.*)

Ver. 7. **We have great joy and consolation in thy love.**—*The far-reaching consequences of good deeds:*—No man can ever tell how far the blessing of his small acts of kindness, or other pieces of Christian conduct, may travel. They may benefit one in material fashion, but the fragrance may reach far beyond. Philemon little dreamed that his small charity to some suffering brother in Colosse would find its way across the sea and bring a waft of coolness and refreshing in the hot prison house. Neither Paul nor Philemon dreamed that, made immortal by the word of the former, the same transient act would find its way across the centuries, and would " smell sweet and blossom in the dust " to-day. Men know not who are their audiences or who may be spectators of their works; for they are all bound so mystically and closely together, that none can tell how far the vibrations which he sets in motion will thrill. (*A. Maclaren, D.D.*) *Refreshing ministries:*—The Moors, five hundred years ago, occupied Granada in Spain, and if you go there to-day you may find traces of that occupation. But where will you find them? Their empire has fallen. Their creed has passed away. Their palaces have crumbled into dust. But you will find traces of them in the irrigating rivulets which they were the means of calling into existence. The traveller who may pass under the heights of Granada to-day hears the murmuring music of those beautiful streams. The men who dug them have gone; but there are these streams telling their own story and doing their own work. So let us cut channels through which God's blessing may flow. It is hard work. We have to remove the rock and the soil, but by and by others will come, and as they stoop down and drink of these beneficent streams, they will look up and say, " Thank God for the workers who have gone before! " *Spiritual blessings bestowed on others give occasion of joy to the saints:*— It is our duty greatly to rejoice, when we see spiritual blessings in heavenly things given to the children of God (see Luke xv. 5, 6, 9, 10, 32). David rejoiced with great joy when he saw that the people offered willingly unto the Lord with a perfect heart, and he blessed the Lord God of Israel. When the Jews heard of the con-

version of the Gentiles, and that the Holy Ghost fell upon them, as upon themselves at the beginning, they held their peace and glorified God, saying, "Then hath God also to the Gentiles granted repentance unto life." When the apostle perceived the notable zeal of the Thessalonians, in receiving and entertaining the gospel, not as the word of man but as it is indeed the Word of God, he witnesseth that they were his hope and his joy, his crown and his glory in the presence of our Lord Jesus Christ at His coming. Likewise the apostle John rejoiced greatly when the brethren testified of the truth that was in Gaius, and how he walked therein. He had no greater joy than this, to hear that his sons walked in the verity. Reasons: 1. The glory and praise of God is much increased, which should comfort the hearts and rejoice the spirits of the saints. The more we abound with spiritual blessings the more God is honoured and His name glorified. 2. The general good of the Church must lead us to this duty and cause us to rejoice, which next unto God should be dearest to us. Who can have such hearts of flint or of iron as not to be moved with joy, beholding the enlarging of the kingdom of Christ? 3. The ordinances and laws of God are observed, and so His blessings procured and obtained. Now, when God is obeyed, men should rejoice and be glad; and when His laws are broken, they should be much grieved and troubled. Uses: 1. First of all, seeing God's graces upon others must work joy in ourselves, we learn the truth of that article of our faith, which all profess to believe, but many do not understand, to wit, the communion of saints. There is a double communion, one which we have with Christ; the other, which the Church hath among themselves, and the former is the cause of the latter. Our communion among ourselves consisteth in three things—(1) In the affection of the heart. (2) In the gifts of the Spirit. (3) In the use of temporal riches. 2. We learn to desire the best gifts, that we may rejoice and comfort the godly. For when we profit in good things, we cheer the hearts and minds of the faithful. Every living thing hath his prospering and proceeding, and is known to have life in it by increasing from one degree of perfection to another. The grass springeth, the plant shouteth, the corn flourisheth, the tree groweth. If we have any life in us of God's Spirit, and be not as grass that is withered, as plants that are dead, as corn that is blasted, and as trees that are plucked up by the roots, we must go forward from one measure of grace to another, from a lesser to a greater. 3. It is our duty to seek the good and prosperity of the Church by all good means, and to draw them and move them, to embrace the ways of salvation. This duty hath many branches growing from it. For, seeing God's graces bestowed give occasion of great joy, it ought to teach us to exhort one another, to comfort them that are comfortless, to reprove them that go astray, to pray for our brethren, to seek to gain and win them to the faith; and when they are gained and won, to rejoice unfeignedly at their conversion, and if we see any hope of their repentance and turning to God, to converse with them, and not to be ashamed of their company. (*W. Attersoll.*)    *Thankfulness for love:*—
I. THE REASON OR CAUSE THAT MOVED PAUL TO GIVE THANKS FOR PHILEMON'S LOVE. 1. His joy, which Philemon's love ministered to him, and that no small or slender joy, but great joy. 2. His comfort, which he received by the same love, and this latter is an amplification of the former: for Paul hereby signifieth that the joy he took in Philemon's love was not a simple joy but a comfortable joy, such a joy as did countervail and swallow up all the grief of his present afflictions. Here observe—1. That whatsoever breeds joy is a just matter of thanksgiving; for this is the reason of Paul's thanksgiving for Philemon—"For we have great joy in thy love." 2. That joy is a singular and wonderful blessing of God, for which special thanks are due unto him. 3. Observe what that is which must stir us up to thanksgiving, and cause us to perform it in due manner, namely, the feeling of joy in the benefit bestowed upon us. 4. Mark that Paul did not only take joy but comfort in Philemon's love; comfort pre-supposeth grief as a medicine, a disease. Therefore Paul gives us to understand that Philemon's love was a kind of counter-poison to the grief which his imprisonment and other afflictions wrought him. Whereby we may learn what is that which will bring ease and comfort to the minds of God's children in their troubles, namely, the virtue and good carriage of those whom they love and respect. As this will be the comfort of good ministers in their afflictions, if their flocks stand fast in that truth which they have preached. 5. Observe what that is, wherefore we are to take joy in another, viz., his grace. "We have great joy in thy love." This is that which may justly cause parents to rejoice in their children, one friend and kinsman in another. II. THE CONFIRMATION OF THIS REASON. 1. Here observe that Paul doth not say he hath joy in his love because

his own bowels were refreshed by him, but because the saints' bowels were refreshed. Many will rejoice in that love which is profitable to themselves; but where is he that will as well rejoice in that love which is profitable only to others? 2. Mark that then as a most seasonable time of rejoicing when we see the bowels of God's saints refreshed—the Church and people of God relieved in their distresses. 3. In Philemon's example we are all, according to our power, taught to refresh the bowels of God's poor distressed saints, if we will show ourselves to have that love which we profess. 1. In speeches of comfort (Psa. xli. 1). 2. In commending and remembering their afflicted estate to God in prayer. 3. In the works of liberality, as the need of the afflicted shall require, and our own ability give us leave. Let us imitate Philemon in refreshing the bowels of the saints, knowing—1. That God Himself hath pronounced such blessed (Psa. xli.; Matt. v.). 2. That herein we imitate the Spirit of God (Rom. viii. 26), whose office it is to comfort the hearts of the afflicted saints. 3. That by the same means we refresh the bowels, not only of the afflicted but also of others, who long to bear the afflictions of their brethren. 4. Yea, not only so, but we shall refresh the bowels of Christ Himself. 5. That hereby we shall enlarge the spirit, not only of the afflicted but of all other good men besides, to whom our love is known, in praying to God for us. 6. That if we reap not this benefit of our love from men, who may prove ungrateful and unmindful, yet God is not unjust, that He should forget the labour of our love which we have showed towards His name, ministering to the saints (Heb. vi.). Nay, He will cause it to be as seed, that shall bring us a plentiful harvest of many temporal blessings in this life, and of eternal life itself at the resurrection of the just. (*D. Dyke, B.D.*) *Delight in love manifested by others:*—He will never want for supplies of joy and consolation who finds a great delight in love manifested by others or enjoyed by them; who, free from envy, takes an exalted pleasure in the gifts and graces of others, and who, ever on the outlook for occasions to be thankful, is willing to regard as mercies to himself what are blessings to others. The vulgar joy of earth would snatch at everything for itself; but the divinely beautiful disposition of being happy in the diffusion of happiness, grows radiant with a sunshine akin to the Divine blessedness itself. If any one go after his own personal joy and comfort with an all-consuming and self-seeking eagerness, he may as well think to get the rainbow by chasing it. To be absorbed in our own private comfort, and pursue it for itself, is to fare like the man who in his foolish over-anxiety to catch a delicate creature alive, suddenly puts his foot on it, and finds it just dying when he gets it in his hands. "I had much joy in thy love, because the hearts of the saints have been refreshed by thee, brother," as the apostle very touchingly adds, in token of his kindly and fraternal feeling to Philemon, in recalling his acts of benevolence. (*A. H. Drysdale, M.A.*) **The bowels of the saints are refreshed by thee.**—*Almsgiving—alms, or a work of mercy, is a singular work above others:*—1. It makes men like God. A bountiful man is the image of God. 2. It is a fair broom that makes all clean (Luke xi. 41). As the first-fruits in the time of the law did sanctify the rest of the fruit, so alms in the time of the gospel sanctify all unto us; all that we possess are unclean without them. 3. It is an usury approved by God, more gainful than any other usury. "He that hath mercy on the poor lendeth to the Lord," &c. 4. It is an harbinger that goes before to provide thee a place in heaven (Acts x. 4; 1 Tim. vi. 18). Therefore let us refresh the bowels of the saints here, that we may enter into the place of eternal refreshing hereafter. We are too straitlaced; we make this mammon of unrighteousness our enemy, whereas we should make him our friend. Nazianzen's mother carried such a bountiful mind to the poor, that a sea of wealth could scarce have sufficed her. She was contrary to Solomon's horse-leech, that cried, "Give, give," namely, to me; she cried, "Give, give, to the poor." He heard her often say that she and her children should want before the poor should want: we are all for ourselves, our wives and children; nothing for the poor. Amadeus, Duke of Sabandia, being asked whether he kept hounds or not? Yes, says he; come to-morrow, and you shall see them. They being come, he opens a window into his hall, where a great multitude of poor people were dining: these are my dogs, said he, and with them I hope to get eternal life. (*W. Jones, D.D.*) *Benevolence encouraged:*—I. THE PROPER OFFICE OF LOVE. Should be exercised towards all, even enemies; but is due in especial manner to "the saints" (Gal. vi. 10). Not on any party principle. Due to them—1. Because dearer to God than others. (Chosen, Eph. i. 4–6; called, Rom. viii. 30; begotten, 1 Pet. i. 3; heirs, Rom. viii. 16, 17. Hence, 1 John v. 1). 2. Because Christ is more deeply interested in them. Have sought Him, hope in Him, one with Him (Eph. v. 30; 1 Cor. vi. 17).

3. Because more nearly related to ourselves. Naturally alike, spiritually different (Eph. ii. 19; 1 Cor. xii. 12, 20, 27). 4. Because they are themselves of superior worth (Prov. xii. 26; 2 Pet. i. 4; John xiv. 23). The Lord's property. If. ITS EXCELLENCE, WHEN SO EMPLOYED. Paul had a high idea of its excellency, because he felt—1. How pre-eminently God was honoured by it. He commands it; it displays His care for saints, and His character; it excites praise to Him (2 Cor. ix. 12, 13). 2. How greatly the gospel also was recommended and adorned. Love, in all practical forms, the spirit of the gospel. 3. What extensive benefits accrued from it to the Church. 4. What an evidence it gave of substantial piety in him who possessed it. An evidence to himself (1 John iii. 14, 18, 19); to others (John xiii. 35). (*C. Simeon, M.A.*) *The duty of looking after and relieving the poor* :—I. IT IS NOT ENOUGH FOR US TO GIVE GOOD WORDS, OR TO UTTER FROM OUR MOUTHS GOOD WISHES, BUT WE MUST, IN OUR SEVERAL PLACES AND PARTICULAR CALLINGS, DO OUR UTMOST ENDEAVOUR THAT RELIEF MAY EVEN BE SEALED TO OUR POOR. It is not enough to give to those that ask and crave the fruit of our liberality, but we must learn to inquire of the wants of the saints, and to search what is their condition. It belongeth unto us, not only to have ears prepared to hear but to have mouths opened, to ask of the welfare of those that are in necessity. We would desire to be so dealt withal ourselves; and therefore let us be so minded toward our brethren. This we see in Abraham: he stayed not till those strangers came into his house, till they desired to be received and have lodging; but he went out of his tent of his own accord, to see whom he could espy, that he might bring them to his house. So did Lot, so dealt all the fathers. Thus did Nehemiah, when he saw some of his brethren that were come from Jerusalem; he asked then concerning the state of the Church, and of the residue of the captivity. We must not always wait till we be entreated and urged to show mercy, but offer it to ourselves to testify the willingness of our hearts. As Christ hath loved us, so let us love one another. There have ever been poor that make not their wants openly known, and are so dejected and rejected of many, that they are ashamed to show their necessity. II. IT REPROVETH THOSE THAT DO NOT RIGHTLY CONSIDER WHAT POOR THE APOSTLE MEANETH, AND SETTETH BEFORE US AS OBJECTS OF OUR COMPASSION. He doth not understand the idle beggar, or sturdy rogue, or vagrant companion, who, not applying himself in any lawful calling, maketh a profession of beggary, and liveth altogether upon the spoil of other men's goods. Neither doth he mean such manner of persons as are continual haunters of ale-houses, spend-alls, carders, dicers. These are excluded and wiped out of the register of the poor saints spoken of in this place, being worse than infidels, and denying the faith. But the apostle pointeth out such unto us, to be holpen and comforted, as it hath pleased God not to bestow so great a portion of worldly blessings upon them, as upon others, as the artificer, the handicraftsman, and day-labourer, yet labour diligently. III. IT REPROVETH SUCH AS NEVER OPEN THEIR MOUTHS TO KNOW THE ESTATE OF THE POOR SAINTS, OR TO INQUIRE HOW THEY FARE. Alas! how should they offer their help of their own accord, and open the bowels of pity before they be entreated, that will depart from nothing, but urged and constrained by force of law, or taxation of others? Or how should they extend their compassion to the poor that are absent? It is noted to the great commendation of David, that after the death of Saul, his enemy, he sought not revenge upon his issue and posterity, but did good to his children's children, and said—"Is there any left of the house of Saul, that I may shew mercy for Jonathan's sake?" So ought we to seek out the servants of God, and to find out the poor, and to inquire after the distressed saints, and say, Is there any of the poor yet left, to whom we may show mercy for the Lord's sake? (*W. Attersoll.*) *Commendation of Philemon's liberality* :—How high a commendation is this of Philemon's bounty, that it afforded joy, not only to those who were relieved by it but also to the apostle who heard of it; that not only the indigent were supported by it in their necessities, but St. Paul also comforted by it in his imprisonment; that the tidings of it were so welcome to the apostle, that they made his chains fit easier upon him, and gave him consolation in his distress; that as the bowels of the saints were refreshed, so also the spirits of the apostle were revived, by the diffusive charity of this his proselyte, whom he might style his son, as having begotten him in Christ Jesus through the gospel, but whom he here styles his brother, that he might not seem to affect a superiority over him, but might place himself on the same level with him. How apt an introduction is this applause, given by St. Paul to Philemon, to that request, which he was now to usher in? Had he been so universally kind to all the faithful, and would not the same good disposition incline him to be kind to St.

Paul? Had he by his charity towards the saints gained so great a reputation, and would he forfeit his character by an unkind repulse of the apostle's request? Had the apostle found so much joy and consolation from the report of his charity towards those who were strangers to St. Paul, and would he not contribute to his pleasure and comfort, by being merciful and kind to Onesimus, for whom the apostle was so nearly and affectionately concerned. (*Bp. Smalridge.*)

Ver. 8. **Though I might be much bold in Christ to enjoin thee.**—*Mingled command and entreaty :*—The balance and propriety of St. Paul's language in this place is not always understood. He does not say "I have no right at all to command you," but "authority I have to command your obedience—not, indeed, of earthly rank, but in the sphere of Christ." This mingled tone of command and entreaty is the exact reflex of the mingled respect and affection which, in his earliest Epistle, he claims for the ministerial office (1 Thess. v. 12, 13). There are two spirits which have prevailed in the Christian ministry at different times and in different circumstances—the spirit of the heirarch and the spirit of the religious demagogue. St. Paul's tone here shows that he was too humble for the first, too full of gentle dignity for the second. (*Bp. Wm. Alexander.*)     *Authoritative in Christ :*—He has no authority in himself, but he has in Christ. His own personality gives him none, but his relation to his Master does. It is a distinct assertion of right to command, and an equally distinct repudiation of any such right, except as derived from his union with Jesus. (*A. Maclaren, D.D.*)     *Ministerial boldness :*—Ministers may be bold in the execution of their office. 1. God commands it (Jer. i. 17). 2. It is that which they themselves beg by earnest prayers at the hand of God (Acts iv. 29, 30; Eph. vi. 18, 19). 3. The dignity of their office requires it (2 Cor. v. 20). 4. God's protection may encourage unto it (Jer. i. 18). 5. It procures admiration even with the very enemies (Acts iv. 13). (*W. Jones, D.D.*)     *The ministerial office is one of power and authority :*—1. If we consider the names that are given unto them, and the honourable titles whereby they are called, we shall be moved to confess their calling to be accompanied with power under Christ. If, then, the true ministers of Christ be fathers, shepherds, ambassadors, and captains under Christ, the great Shepherd of the sheep, their office cannot be without jurisdiction and authority over the people of God committed to their charge. 2. If we consider the fruits and effects that are ascribed in the Word to the ministers of the Word, we shall see that their ministry is joined with authority. They are the means to bring us to the knowledge of Christ, to the bosom of the Church, and to the kingdom of heaven. Their office is to convert sinners and to save souls. 3. There is a co-operation of God and the minister's office together, and an admirable sympathy between them. If, then, God and the minister do work together, he may lawfully enjoin men to do their duties. Uses—1. (1) It condemneth those that think the ministers proud and presumptuous, and accuse them as saucy and malapert when they command us from the Lord as His ambassadors, and arrest us for our sins as His sergeants. It is their duty not only to teach and admonish, to exhort, and to comfort, but to convince and reprove, to threaten, and to denounce judgments from God against the obstinate and impenitent. (2) It reproveth those that account the ministers their vassals and slaves, whereas the case of a pastor is not to be made an underling or a block for every one to insult and tread. (3) The high excellency of this calling reproveth those that account the office too base and low for them and for their children. Many there are that live by the gospel that are ashamed to preach the gospel. (4) If it be a calling of such dignity, it reproveth those that run before they be sent, and wait not a lawful calling from God, that they may discharge it afterward with peace of heart and comfort of conscience. (5) It reproveth such as regard not the censures of the Church inflicted upon evil doers. 2. Seeing boldness to command under Christ belongeth to the office of minister, it teacheth us and putteth us in mind of many good duties; as—(1) To ask this gift of God, and crave of Him to endue us with the zeal of His glory and other graces of His spirit, that we may speak the Word boldly, as we ought to speak. (2) It teacheth the ministers not to lose their authority, and so to shame their calling, and their Master that hath put them in their calling, bringing themselves and their ministry under the subjection and slavery of others. (3) It teacheth the ministers to take heed they abuse not their authority and turn it into tyranny, but employ it unto edification, not to the destruction of the Church, or any member thereof. (4) It serveth for instruction of the people, that they despise not the ministry of the Word, but alway be ready to hear it with reverence. For wheresoever there is authority in the speaker there should be fear and reverence in the hearer. (*W. Attersoll.*)　　*Wise ministerial exhortation:*—I. Observe, first, in the example of the apostle, THAT MINISTERS MUST DEAL IN THE MILDEST ATD GENTLEST MANNER THAT MAY BE WITH THEIR HEARERS, entreating, persuading, exhorting, beseeching, even then when they may lawfully command. II. Observe, further, in Paul's example, THAT SOMETIMES WE ARE TO YIELD OF OUR RIGHT, neither always may we do those things which of themselves are lawful and indifferent. Here, then, is condemned the tenacity and temerity of some in the use of that liberty which the Word hath granted them in things indifferent. Their tenacity, that they hold their own stiffly, and will not let go the least part of their right, though the glory of God and good of their brethren do earnestly crave it at their hands. Their temerity, not only that they themselves rush venturously upon all things that in themselves are lawful, not considering whether in regard of some circumstances it may not be unlawful for them, what inconvenience may ensue, what hurt may also arise to the gospel, but also censure and condemn others, who, kept back by Christian wisdom and charity, dare not run with them to the same excessive use of their liberty. Let them remember that Paul, in this place, having much liberty of commanding, yet chose rather to entreat. III. Observe, thirdly, WHAT IT IS THAT WILL MAKE A CHRISTIAN ABRIDGE HIMSELF SOMETIMES OF THE USE OF HIS LIBERTY; NAMELY, THE LOVE OF GOD AND OUR BRETHREN. For love's sake I rather beseech thee. For this is reckoned among the properties of love by the apostle; that it seeketh not her own, but His, whom it loveth. If God's glory and the Church's good be dear unto us, we will not use our liberty to the full in those things which may hinder and hurt both. (*D. Dyke, B.D.*)

Ver. 9. **Yet for love's sake I rather beseech thee.**—*A beautiful specimen of Christian humility and genuine pathos:*—I might be bold to *command* thee in Christ's name, by which I am *strong;* but thou dost not *need* any argument derived from my *strength:* and for *love's* sake I rather *beseech* thee by my own *weakness*, by my years, and by my chains. Such language—the language of entreaty—best befits me now in my prison and in my old age. (*Bp. Chris. Wordsworth.*)　　*The entreaty of love:*—Love naturally beseeches, and does not command. The harsh voice of command is simply the imposition of another's will, and it belongs to relationships in which the heart has no share. But wherever love is the bond, grace is poured into the lips, and "I order" becomes "I pray." So that even where the outward form of authority is still kept, as in a parent to young children, there will ever be some endearing word to swathe the harsh imperative in tenderness, like a sword blade wrapped about with wool, lest it should wound. Love tends to obliterate the hard distinction of superior and inferior, which finds its expression in laconic orders and silent obedience. It seeks not for mere compliance with commands, but for oneness of will. Its entreaties are more powerful than imperatives. The lightest wish breathed by loved lips is stronger than all stern injunctions—often, alas! than all laws of duty. The heart is so tuned as only to vibrate to that one tone. The rocking stones, which all the storms of winter may howl round and not move, can be set swinging by a light touch. Una leads the lion in a silken leash. Love controls the wildest nature. Authority is the weapon of a weak man, who is afraid of his own power to get himself obeyed; or of a selfish one, who seeks for mechanical submission rather than for the fealty of willing hearts. Love is the weapon of a strong man, who can cast aside the trappings of superiority, and is never loftier than when he descends, nor more absolute than when he abjures authority and appeals with love to love. (*A. Maclaren, D.D.*)　　*Gentle means of persuading men to be used rather than severe:*—I. REASONS. 1. We are bound to use those means and to take that course which is most forcible and effectual. But to deal with love, and to handle our brethren kindly and meekly, is most likely to prevail with most men. Therefore the apostle requireth that the servant of God must not strive, but must be gentle toward all men, apt to teach, suffering the evil, instructing them with meekness that are contrary minded. There is no way so available to bring evil men out of the dangers wherein they stand, who are, as it were, made bondslaves to do the devil's will, than to allure them by gentleness, to draw them by long-suffering, and to overcome them by patience. 2. This course, well and duly observed, serveth to persuade them with whom we deal of our love and tender affection towards them. For loving and friendly dealing argueth loving and affectionate minds, and the ready way to bend and incline him unto that which is good, and to turn him from that which is evil, when his persuasions are perceived to tend to the profit and benefit of him whom we would persuade. 3. We are to imitate our Head and Master, Christ Jesus; He used not His authority and power that was in Him; He dealt not roughly and severely with His enemies, but meekly and mercifully, and most compassionately; He was meek, and as a lamb before the shearer. II. Uses. 1. We learn that mercy and compassion—yea, all tokens and testimonies of love—are to be showed toward malefactors, even when justice is to be executed and punishment inflicted. 2. Seeing we are to win men rather by gentleness and love, we must acknowledge that great wisdom and discretion is required in the ministry, to divide the Word of God aright, and to be able to apply himself to every degree and calling of men. When the people of God went out to war, the Lord commanded them to offer conditions of peace to that city; if it refuse to make peace, they should besiege it, smite it, and destroy it. So should we, when we execute our office, first offer peace before we proclaim war; first allure by gentleness before we thunder out judgments; first exhort before we threaten. In the material building, all the stones that are to be fitted to the building are not of one nature; some are soft and easy to be fitted and hammered; others more hard and of a flintier marble disposition—they require sharp tools, strong blows, before they can be brought into form, or be squared for that place which they are to hold. So it is with the lively stones of the spiritual temple of God: some have soft hearts of flesh, and are of humble and contrite spirits, like the bruised reed or the smoking flax; others have hearts hard as the adamant, and cannot easily be brought to feel the strokes of the Word of God. These are not to be dealt withal and handled alike, but after a divers manner. This is the counsel of the apostle Jude, "Have compassion of some in putting difference, and others save with fear, pulling them out of the fire, and hate even that garment which is spotted by the flesh." This serveth to reprove, first, such as use unseasonable lenity when godly severity is required. Some diseases require sharp medicines. Secondly, it reproveth such as are too sharp and vigorous against offenders, and forget all rules of charity toward them. True it is, the pastors and ministers are to rebuke such as are fallen; but when they see sorrow for sin, and repentance from dead works wrought in them, they should begin to raise them up again and comfort them with the precious promises of the gospel, lest they should be overwhelmed with despair and be swallowed up with over-much heaviness. 3. And, last of all, we learn for our obedience, that whensoever entreating, gentle, or loving dealing is used to call men home to God and to themselves, it is their duty to yield themselves and to embrace earnestly the mercies of God offered unto them. The sin of contempt and contumacy is fearful, when the bountifulness of God is despised, His mercies loathed, His patience and long-suffering abused. If we will not hear when He crieth to us, we shall cry also in the days of our misery, and He will not hear us in our trouble, but mock at our affliction. (*W. Attersoll.*) *Love more effective than severity :—* One winter morning, as the Wind set out on his day's work, he found the trees loaded with ice. Every tiny twig was bending under an armour many times its weight. The little white lady birches had drooped until their heads touched the ground. A great groan to be delivered went up from all the trees. "This will never do!" cried the Wind; and straightway he went to work with all his might. The branches of the giant elms swung and creaked. The brown, curled leaves still clinging to the oaks were snatched away and went whirling through the air. There was a great rustling in all the wood. But the ice did not move. Still harder the wind blew. And now whole branches came crashing down, until they lay thick on the ground in their glittering winding-sheets. But still the ice did not move. At last the Spirit of the Woods came forth, frowning. "Do you call this helping?" cried she. "You are ruining my trees. To get rid of the ice, forsooth, you are breaking off the boughs. Get you gone!" The Wind retired to his cave, and was melancholy all day. He had had a sincere desire to do good, but now he saw that he had only done harm. He shuddered as he thought of the wrecks he had made in his untempered zeal. "What is the use of my trying to do anything?" he sighed. Many an eager soul has known such hours, when it had thought to add its note of praise to the great chorus, and has only succeeded in making a discord. The next morning the Sun knocked at the door of the cave, and cried, in genial tones, "Come on, friend! I want your help. The trees must be rid of their load. I will shine on them, and then do you gently wave their branches and shake off the loosened ice." They went forth together, and the Sun shone on the forest. An hour passed. The only visible result was here and there a drop of water from the icy boughs. "We shall never get through at this rate!" panted the Wind.

" Gently, friend, gently ! All in good time ! " replied the Sun. " The ice was a day and a night in forming. Could you hope to get rid of it by one fierce gust ? When I get higher in the sky, I can strike the trees more directly with my beams." After another hour of silent shining, the Sun whispered, " Now, friend, with your wings ! But not too violently. See, now, some pieces are falling. Two or three hours of work like this, and our task is done. There is another piece loose." So the Sun shone on, and the wind from time to time shook down the loosened pieces of ice, and what did not rattle down dissolved in fast-flowing tears under the gentle yet burning eye of the Sun. The birches gradually lifted their pliant forms. The Spirit of the Woods came out with her blessing for the two workers. And that night the Wind returned to his cave humbled but joyous, because he had found the " more excellent way." **Paul the aged.**—*The aged Christian :*—We have —I. In Paul's CIRCUMSTANCES the OCCUPATIONS OF THE AGED CHRISTIAN. 1. He preaches and teaches. 2. He is full of care for distant Churches. 3. He is tenderly interested in individuals near him. II. In Paul's RECOLLECTIONS the MEMORIES OF THE AGED CHRISTIAN. 1. Trials. 2. Labours. 3. Graces. III. In Paul's ANTICIPATIONS THE HOPES OF THE AGED CHRISTIAN. 1. Hope of renewed service on earth. 2. Hope of the victory of the truth on earth. 3. Hope of blessedness in heaven. (*U. R. Thomas.*) *Paul the aged :*—We are accustomed to think of Paul the persecutor, the Christian, the missionary, the apostle, the inspired scribe, the sufferer for Christ. Here another and unexpected epithet pictures him to us as " Paul the aged." The word is from his own pen. Perhaps now he is learning for the first time that his days of mature vigour are past. Manifold labours, perils, trials, have broken him in premature age. I. PAUL WEARS OLD AGE AS A CROWN (see Prov. xvi. 31). There is a pleasant story told of Frederick the Great. At a parade of the guard in the King's apartments at Berlin, Frederick's quick eye picked out among the splendid crowd the brave old Ziethen, who, though turned eighty-five years, had come to pay his duty to his monarch. Greeting the veteran with a cry of joy, the King called for a chair. Objections were in vain. " Sit down, good father," said the King. " I will have it so, or I must instantly leave the room." The old soldier yielded, and Frederick the Great continued standing before him, the centre of the illustrious circle that had gathered around, and so " honoured the face of the old man." The aged Christian has his peculiar infirmities, but he also has his peculiar joys. To the aged saint come the fullest revelations of God, the most comfortable words of Christ, the sweetest visitations of the Spirit. II. PAUL'S OLD AGE HAD ITS DUTIES AND LABOURS. He does not excuse himself from duty on the ground of age. He will do what he can for Onesimus. He writes for him with a delicacy, a tact, a tenderness, an urgency, such as he himself never surpassed. The aged Christian is still a unit in the host of society, still kindred to some and neighbour and friend to others. And still, however much he may be lost, duty remains—duty to himself, to others, and in all to God. Life is lengthened that it may labour for Christ. And is not the old the best workman ? The young may attract more attention, but it is the experienced hand that does the most and best. III. PAUL USED HIS AGE AS A PLEA OF LOVE. Where we may command, it is wise to request. Love wins love. Gentleness calls out gentleness. IV. PAUL IS " PAUL THE AGED " NO MORE. He has escaped, through death, from all earthly prisons, and is oppressed by old age no longer. He is " with Christ, which is far better." (*G. T. Coster.*) *Reverence due to old age :*—Old men are to be reverenced—1. For their very age, because they draw nearest to the Ancient of Days (Lev. xix. 32). 2. For their wisdom. 3. For their experience. 4. For their piety (Prov. xvi. 31). (*W. Jones, D.D.*) *The aged minister :*—I. REVIEW HIS PAST HISTORY. 1. His character ; and how, during this long period, he has conducted himself : what reputation he has spent so many years in building up, and in what estimate he is now held when grey hairs are upon him. 2. His labours. True, his toils are chiefly mental ; but who knows not that, on this account, they are the more exhausting and wearing ? 3. His usefulness. How many have been impressed by his example, enriched by his beneficence, blessed by his prayers, and instructed by his principles. 4. His trials. Ah, you know a minister's joys far better than you know his sorrows. You see his sails, but not his ballast. You follow him in his public walks of labour, but not in his Gethsemane retreat, where he goes to pray and agonise alone. He calls you to share his felicities, but he carries his perplexities and his griefs to his closet and his God. Look, then, at the hoary man over whom the clouds of fifty years have rolled. How many storms have burst upon that aged tree, tearing off its branches, stripping off its leaves, and dismantling it in some cases, till little else but the mere trunk and a few boughs remain of all that once umbrageous top. Still, however, the venerable trunk does remain, and there is life in it to the last. How much of Divine power and faithfulness and grace we associate with that sacred antique. 5. His temptations. A minister is the chief mark for Satan's arrows. II. ESTIMATE HIS PRESENT CLAIMS. 1. He is entitled, if a holy and faithful man, and in proportion to his sanctity and fidelity, to respect and veneration. 2. He is entitled to affection. It is not claimed for what he is in himself, but what he is to his people as their friend and counsellor; in fact, the instrument of their salvation and the promoter of their progressive sanctification. 3. He has a right to expect gratitude. 4. I next mention candour and forbearance as virtues which an aged minister is entitled to expect, and of which, in some cases, by the gathering infirmities of declining years, he will stand in need. 5. And has he not a claim upon your attendance upon his ministry? To desert him when he is old is a poor reward for the more effective services of younger and stronger days. III. ANTICIPATE HIS FUTURE DESTINY. Growth, decline, and death, are the law of all life on earth, from which there is no exemption on behalf of the minister of the gospel. The weary, worn-out labourer goes to his rest and to his reward; goes to be associated with those who were his hope and joy on earth, and now are to be his crown of rejoicing in the presence of Christ; goes to meet his Maker, and hear Him say, "Well done, good and faithful servant; enter thou into the joy of the Lord." (*J. A. James.*) *A review of life and a glimpse of glory :*—This language—1. Supposes childhood and the scenes of life already past. 2. Suggests a review of the events of individual life. 3. Reminds us of the infirmities which years witness. 4. Shows Paul to us as an old disciple—not only a man, but a "new man," a man in Christ. 5. Contains a touching plea. 6. Suggests that the aged Christian has nearly finished his course. (*J. S. Pearsall.*) *The standard of age :*—He was, perhaps, sixty, perhaps a few years more. Labour, sorrow, the storms of ocean and the fires of thought, possible sickliness—the sad and solemn maturity which is the portion upon earth of men who believe intensely —had done their work. Roger Bacon wrote " *me senem* " at fifty-two or fifty-three, and Sir Walter Scott at fifty-five calls himself sadly " an old grey man and aged." In truth, the standard by which old age is measured is pretty much subjective. At an age about fifteen years earlier than that of St. Paul at this time, Chateaubriand writes, " Déjà je n'appartenais plus à ces matins qui se consolent eux-mêmes—je touchais à ces heures du soir qui ont besoin d'être consolées." At different periods of life we adopt a different standard. It was said by Victor Hugo that forty is the old age of youth, and fifty the youth of old age. (*Bp. Wm. Alexander.*) *Anxieties tell on age :*—Such a multitude of anxieties and endurances as are recounted in 2 Cor. xi. 23–30 must have told upon him and exhausted his manly vigour. (*M. F. Sadler, M.A.*) *Christian old age :*—No more beautiful picture of the bright energy and freshness still possible to the old was ever painted than may be gathered from the apostle's unconscious sketch of himself. He delighted in having fresh young life about him—Timothy, Titus, Mark, and others—boys in comparison with himself, whom yet he admitted to close intimacy, as some old general might the youths of his staff, warming his old age at the genial flame of their growing energies and unworn hopes. His was a joyful old age, too, notwithstanding many burdens of anxiety and sorrow. We hear the clear song of his gladness ringing through the epistle of joy—that to the Philippians—which, like this, dates from his Roman captivity. A Christian old age should be joyful, and it only will be; for the joys of the natural life burn low when the fuel that fed them is nearly exhausted, and withered hands are held in vain over the dying embers. But Christ's joy "remains," and a Christian old age may be like the polar midsummer days, when the sun shines till midnight, and dips but for an imperceptible interval ere it rises for the unending day of heaven. Paul the aged was full of interest in the things of the day—no mere " praiser of time gone by," but a strenuous worker, cherishing a quick sympathy and an eager interest, which kept him young to the end. And over his cheery, sympathetic, busy old age there is thrown the light of a great hope, which kindles desire and onward looks in his dim eyes, and parts "such a one as Paul the aged " by a whole universe from the old whose future is dark and their past dreary, whose hope is a phantom and their memory a pang. (*A. Maclaren, D.D.*) **Now also a prisoner of Jesus Christ.**—*Duty enforced by personal consideration :*—He holds up his fettered wrist, and in effect says, " Surely you will not refuse anything that you can do to wrap a silken softness round the cold, hard iron, especially when you remember for whose sake and by whose will I am bound with this chain." He thus brings personal motives to reinforce duty which is binding from other and higher considerations. Christ does thus with His servants. He does not simply hold up before us a cold law of duty, but warms it by introducing our personal relation to Him as the main motive for keeping it. Apart from Him, morality can only point to the tables of stone and say, " There! that is what you ought to do. Do it, or face the consequences." But Christ says, " I have given Myself for you. My will is your law. Will you do it for My sake ? " Instead of the chilling, statuesque ideal, as pure as marble and as cold, a Brother stands before us with a heart that beats, a smile on His face, a hand outstretched to help ; and His word is, " If ye love Me, keep My commandments." (*Ibid.*)

Ver. 10. **I beseech thee for my son Onesimus.**—*Softened by the entreaty of a friend :*—This and the previous verse taken together seem to contain two references to the Roman law. "For the love's sake I rather *beseech*—being such an one as Paul, an old man, and, as it is, a prisoner of Jesus Christ, I *beseech* thee for my son, Onesimus." We have here a twofold reference—a plea for legal pardon, a hint at emancipation. 1. I beseech—I beseech thee—puts Paul in the position of a formal *precator.* The law gave the Roman slave one real right. It relented with humane inconsistency upon one point, and one only. For the slave in the Roman Empire the right of asylum did not exist. His only conceivable resource was that he might, in his despair, fly to a friend of his master, not for the purpose of concealment, but of intercession. The owner, who was absolute as far as any formal tribunal was concerned, might be softened by the entreaties of the friend who took upon himself the office of intercessor. The Roman jurisprudence formally declared that the slave in flying to a friend of his proprietor with this intention did not incur the enormous guilt of becoming *fugitivus.* St. Paul, indeed, was unable to appear with Onesimus. But in the emphatic and repeated "beseech," he seems to declare himself the legal *precator.* 2. The hint at the emancipation is contained in the recognition of Onesimus by St. Paul as a son. Of the various forms of *manumissio justa,* the adoptive stands in the first rank. With the title of son, the rights of domestic and civil life flow in upon the slave, new born into the common family of humanity. May there be a yet further allusion ? St. Paul, indeed, hopes to see Philemon again (ver. 22). Yet he may die. In these literally *precativa verba* ("I beseech," "I beseech thee," vers. 9, 10), in what may be his last will and testament, he lays upon Philemon, as if his heir, the duty, not only of pardoning, but of giving manumission to the penitent slave. (*Bp. Wm. Alexander.*) *The compassion of the gospel :*—I. How COMPASSIONATE THE GOSPEL MAKES A MAN TOWARD HIS SUFFERING FELLOW-MEN. Though the greatest man then alive—far greater than the Emperor of Rome himself—Paul, illustrious in the estimation of all the angels, is trying to do good to a poor runaway slave, whom the pagan Romans looked upon as a mere dog, the like of whom many a Roman master had flogged to death, and then flung into the pond to feed the fish. He acts towards Onesimus as a father ; calls him his " son converted in his bonds." Then notice the prudence and tact with which Paul writes. When a prudent person wishes to convey a piece of painful news to another, he tries to prepare the mind of the hearer for the tidings. For example, when the messenger conveyed to Achilles the news of the death of his beloved friend Patroclus, he used a word which means both to be dead and to be asleep. So if we wanted successfully to plead the cause of a son who had grievously offended his father, we should keep out of sight as long as we could the faults of the son, and mention all we could in his favour. So Paul acts in pleading the cause of Onesimus. In order to induce Philemon to take back Onesimus, he first calls him " his child " ; and of course Philemon would respect any one Paul called by so tender a name. He then calls him " his convert " ; and of course Philemon would treat with affection any convert of Paul. He then speaks of his conversion during his imprisonment ; and then—ast—comes his name, " Onesimus." II. How MYSTERIOUSLY GOD OFTEN WORKS IN THE CONVERSION OF SINFUL MEN. Onesimus was probably born at Colosse, in Asia Minor. There he was in the service of Philemon, and, having robbed his master, he travelled hundreds of miles to Rome, to hide himself from pursuit. Yet there the Lord met him. Perhaps it was the result of the merest accident that he was induced to enter Paul's humble abode. Perhaps he was in the deepest poverty, and meditated drowning himself in the Tiber, when some Christian person saw him, pitied him, and induced him to listen to that gospel he had often heard and slighted at Colosse. We lately heard of a young man who robbed his master of £10, and from fear of detection escaped to India. The preaching of a missionary was the means of his conversion, and, as soon as possible, he sent to his master threefold the amount stolen, with a full and contrite confession of his guilt. III. THE AFFLICTIONS OF GOD'S SERVANTS NEED BE NO BARRIER TO THEIR SPIRITUAL USEFULNESS. Paul was a prisoner in Rome when the conversion of Onesimus took place. Martin Luther was called to endure a long and dreary confinement, but during it he produced his marvellous translation of the Bible. Richard Baxter wrote some of his most beautiful works in prison, or at seasons of bodily affliction; and if John Bunyan had not been in Bedford jail, most likely the "Pilgrim's Progress" would never have been written. Persecutors have tried to trample under foot the piety of the people of God, but, like the aromatic herb, the more it was pressed, the more sweet odours it sent forth. If we have the will we have the power to serve God and benefit our fellow-creatures. In health, in sickness, in death, we can alike glorify God and honour Christ. IV. A FAINT EMBLEM OF THE COMPASSION OF CHRIST FOR HUMAN SOULS. Says Martin Luther, "To my way of thinking, we are all like poor Onesimus, and Christ has come down from heaven to restore us to our Divine Friend and Father." (*Homilist.*)      *Brotherly regard in the Church:*—I. We learn from this love appearing in the apostle THAT THE BASEST PERSON IN THE CHURCH, TRULY CONVERTED AND BROUGHT UNTO CHRIST, SHOULD NOT BE CONDEMNED, BUT MOST LOVINGLY, TENDERLY, AND BROTHERLY REGARDED. The least and lowest member that belongeth to God ought not to be rejected and debased, but highly for Christ's sake to be honoured and respected. Reasons: 1. Those that are least esteemed, and are of lowest condition, were bought with as great and high a price as any others. 2. There is no respect of persons with God. 3. They shall receive with others the same recompense of reward. Uses: 1. Seeing we are bound to love the lowest in the Church that belong to Christ, we learn that our affections must be carried most earnestly, and in the greatest measure to those that have the greatest measure of heavenly graces, not regarding riches, or kindred, or outward respects before the other. 2. Seeing every member of Christ must be much esteemed, be he never so mean, it teacheth us not to have the religion of God and the faith of Christ in acceptation of persons. 3. This giveth comfort and contentment to the meanest and smallest of God's saints, and putteth them in remembrance not to be discomforted and out of heart for their mean calling or for their low estate, for they are nothing the less regarded of God, or to be esteemed of His Church. II. We learn from this name given unto Onesimus converted to the faith THAT THERE OUGHT TO BE THE SAME AFFECTION BETWEEN THE PASTOR AND THE PEOPLE, WHICH IS BETWEEN THE FATHER AND THE SON. Uses:—1. Seeing the minister and people ought to love as father and son, it teacheth both of them to cut off all occasions of discord and division and to nourish love and mutual concord one with another. It may be many occasions may arise, which if by wisdom they be not smothered and suppressed in the beginning, they are as little sparks that quickly break out into a flame, and the flame suffered to continue consumeth all things that are near unto it. We must show ourselves ready to bring water to quench this fire. It is a deceitful snare, and wonderful subtilty of Satan to cast matters of dissension between the minister and people that so though the Word be among them, yet that it may by that means be with less fruit and profit with them. 2. These most loving titles applied to the minister and people show the duties required of pastors toward their charge, and teach them to love them as their children, to tender their good, to exhort them to lay up for themselves spiritual riches. Great is the love of parents towards their children. If the child be sick or wayward, they do not cast him out of doors or withdraw their affection from him. Hence it is that Christ when He saw the people scattered abroad, and dispersed here and there as sheep without a Shepherd, "He had compassion upon them, and showed great love toward them." We see how Christ applieth this to the conscience of Peter, and willeth him to try his love toward Him by feeding His sheep and lambs, thereby assuring him that if he persuaded himself to love Christ Jesus, and yet was not careful to teach His people, he deceived himself and lied to the Holy Ghost, who would find him out in his sin. Seeing the minister and people ought to be as father and son, this showeth the duty of the people that are under their ministry that they regard their ministers as their parents, honouring them, yielding them due recompense, esteeming them as workers together with God, to beget them to Christ, to turn them to salvation. Of our parents we have received only to be, of our ministers we have received to be well. Of our parents we have taken our first birth, of our ministers we have obtained our second birth. Of our parents we have been brought into the world by generation, of our ministers we have been brought into the Church by regeneration.

Our first begetting was to death, our second or new life is to life and salvation. By the first birth we are heirs of wrath, by the second we are made the sons of God. (*W. Attersoll.*)    *Onesimus :*—1. The love which St. Paul felt towards his convert, the yearning desire with which he longed for his good.    He overlooked all distinctions of rank; all that was swallowed up by a deeper bond of sympathy, namely, that St. Paul had been the means of bringing him out of darkness, and of teaching him the gospel of Christ Jesus.    I believe there is no union more lasting and true than the spiritual union which exists between those who have done and those who have received good.    It is what every clergyman longs for, that he may know that his ministrations have been a blessing to those among whom he ministers.    No encouragement, no praise, will compare for a moment with the joy of feeling that he has souls for his hire.    No grief is so heavy as the fear of an unblessed ministry, of souls not drawn towards himself, because not drawn by him to Christ Jesus.    2. St. Paul quite foresaw that it might be hard for Philemon to receive back his slave in a forgiving spirit, and to look on him as a brother through faith in Christ, and as an equal in the sight of God.    And is not that same difficulty of daily occurrence among us ?    People always like to keep up the notion of their own superiority over others that they are above, and others below them.    And we stand on our rights, and we resent an injury, and we remember a wrong that has been done us, and we should be as likely as Philemon was to speak in disparagement of the change which is said to be wrought in any one who once has done us harm.    And here comes up the evidence of a truly Christian spirit.    To forgive those who have injured us ; to care not for our own, but for another's wealth ; to do to others as we would be done by ; to think no evil, to bear no malice, to rejoice in any one's conversion to Christ ; here are the signs of a heart renewed and sanctified by the grace of the Holy Ghost. 3. The words of St. Paul may remind us how careful we ought to be, how much of pains and thought we ought to take about those who are closely connected with us in the affairs of our daily life.    Just think of the relations which should exist between masters and servants, between employers and employed.    As a matter of fact, how little there is for the most part of mutual interest in each other's welfare beyond the mere giving and receiving of wages, and the good-natured liking which may exist between the one and the other.    How seldom the matter is looked on from a Christian point of view.    How seldom the master cares for more than to prevent dishonesty and vice, and to avoid scandal in his house.    Is he really anxious about the spiritual welfare of his dependents ?    Or take the opposite side.    For those who go out to service, how little thought is given to any part of the engagement beyond the amount of wages, or the lightness of the work, or the pleasantness of the place.    Whether the household be one where God is really served is a less common question.    Everything seems to be remembered but the one chief thing of all, the care of the soul.    And the same thought may be applied to other relations of life, to parents and children, to acquaintances and neighbours and friends.    God allows us to have such relations one to another, but God requires that He should stand first in everything.    We cannot be serving God in sincerity and truth ; we cannot be fulfilling the charge which God has committed to us, unless we be anxious for others as well as for ourselves, unless we would depart with them from evil, and increase with them in good.    And when we heartily desire and pray that others, as well as ourselves, may have God's highest blessing, we shall find how wonderfully the Lord answers that wish.    How strange that the running away of Onesimus from his master should have led to his conversion, and so to his return.    But not one whit more strange than are the great results which have come to us all from what seemed the smallest and most unimportant events.    A word will change the current of a man's life, will lead to the awakening of conscience, to the searching for and finding salvation.    (*H. R. Nevill.*)    *The courtesy of the gospel :*--I. THE GENTLE COURTESY OF THE APOSTLE.    No Christian ought to be rude or harsh.    This letter is a model of true politeness—" a charming and masterly example of Christian love." II. THE ELECTING LOVE OF GOD.    Philemon was a Christian ; a Christian minister too ; yet the heart of Onesimus, his servant, remains hardened.    No doubt his master had given him up.    But the Lord had not.    The Lord willed not that he should perish.    III. THE POWER OF THE GOSPEL.    The Holy Ghost brought it home with power to the heart of Onesimus.    He saw the evil of sin, the love of Jesus, the worth of his soul.    IV. THE VALUE OF A CHRISTIAN SERVANT (ver. 11).    Now Onesimus is really a changed man, he will be " profitable " to Philemon.    A truly Christian servant will serve his earthly master well, because he serves a Master in heaven. He will work with a good conscience, and prove himself faithful and true.    V. THE

GROUND ON WHICH ST. PAUL URGES HIS REQUEST (ver. 19). Those who are God's instruments in bringing others to Jesus ought to get gratitude from their spiritual children. Strange to say, this is almost rare. We warmly thank friends who help us in regard to this world, while spiritual blessings are too often forgotten. (*F. Harper, M.A.*) *Spiritual children:*—Calvin's three children all died in infancy. Of the last he wrote to a friend: "The Lord gave me another son, and the Lord hath taken him away; but have I not thousands of children in the faith of Christ?" (*J. F. B. Tinling, B.A.*) *The after-life of Onesimus:*—Ignatius mentions an Onesimus as Bishop of Ephesus at the time of his journey to his martyrdom at Rome, and though we must allow an interval of forty-four years between that time and the date of this Epistle, it is at least possible that the converted slave may have risen to that high position. It is suggestive that Ignatius speaks of him in the highest terms as a man of "inexpressible love," and exhorts all the members of the church to love and honour him, and that he reproduces St. Paul's allusion to the meaning of his name. "May I," he says, after naming Onesimus, "have joy or profit of you, if indeed I be worthy of it." Another Onesimus appears half a century later, as writing to Melito, bishop of Sardis, to urge on him the compilation of a volume of extracts from the Scriptures; and it may, perhaps, be inferred from its occurrence there and elsewhere, in the regions of Asia Minor, that the memory of the Colossian slave had invested the name with a special popularity. (*Dean Plumptre.*) **Whom I have begotten in my bonds.**—*Spiritual parentage better than natural:*—St. Paul, then, was Onesimus's father—not natural but spiritual; and we are more beholden to our spiritual than to our natural fathers. 1. They beget us of a woman; these of the Church which is the spouse of Christ. 2. They beget us of mortal seed, therefore we die; these of the immortal seed of the Word of God, whereby we live for ever. 3. They beget us to a temporal life; these to an eternal. 4. They to the miseries of the world; these to the joys of the world to come. Therefore let us love them, let us have them in singular love for their works' sake. As Alexander professed he was more beholden to Aristotle than Philip; the one gave him *esse*, being, the other *bene esse*, his well-being. Yet this is little considered of. (*W. Jones, D.D.*) *Eager for usefulness:*—I. THAT MINISTERS MAY LOVE THEIR SONS WITH AN UNEQUAL LOVE, THEY MAY LOVE SOME MORE THAN OTHERS, as Christ did John above the rest of the disciples; namely, those in whom they behold a more lively image of Christ, and in the begetting of whom they had greater experience of God's power and mercy than in others. II. THAT THE SPIRIT OF GOD AND THE WORD OF GOD IS NOT BOUND TOGETHER WITH THE BODIES OF THE MINISTERS, for both these, namely, the Spirit and Word of God, were now effectual in the prison for Onesimus's conversion. The adversaries then must not think that the restraining of the ministers and of the gospel will prove one work. The Earl of Derby's accusation in the Parliament House against M. Bradford was that he did more hurt (so he spake, calling good evil) by letters and conferences in prison than ever he did when he was abroad by preaching. III. PAUL SAYING THAT HE BEGOT HIM IN HIS BONDS, hence it is easy to gather that after, by speech had to and fro with him in the prison, he understood in what case he was, he presently wrought upon him, to bring him to a sight of his sin, and so to a godly sorrow for it. By which example ministers must learn that it is their duty, not only in their public meetings to seek men's conversion by their general preaching to all, but if at any time, by God's providence, they shall light upon any whom they see miserably to stray out of the ways of God, though it be in private places and companies, as Philip and the Eunuch in journeying, they are by all means possible, no just cause detaining them, to endeavour the conversion even of such, and to do the part of a good Samaritan towards them, whom they find so dangerously wounded by Satan. IV. But as all ministers are greedily to catch those occasions which God offers for furthering the salvation of their brethren, so ESPECIALLY THOSE WHO, BEING IMPRISONED, ARE RESTRAINED FROM THEIR PUBLIC PREACHING, that so by this means the want of their public sermons may in some measure be supplied. Now, how goodly a thing it is for ministers, even then when they are poorest, to make others rich (2 Cor. vi. 10), and when they are bound and captive, to make others free! (*D. Dyke, B.D.*) *Preaching in chains:*—The following incident is related by one of the leading Christians of Russia:—" One of our converts was wrongfully accused of blasphemy for breaking his images. He was sentenced to transportation to Siberia. This involved trudging on foot one thousand miles in chains through the snow. A fellow convert went to see him depart, and to cheer him up as he left his friends and home behind. To his astonishment he found the prisoner full of peace and joy. 'Thank God,' said the exiled one, 'for the privilege of preaching Christ in chains to my fellow prisoners.' A nobler example of Christian fortitude than this it would be difficult to find in any religious movement." The effect of persecution generally has been to spread the gospel, and it appears that Russia will be no exception.

Ver. 11. **Now profitable to thee and to me.**—*A new leaf turned over :*—The apostle has had but short experience of his convert, but he is quite sure that he is a Christian ; and, that being the case, he is as sure that all the bad, black past is buried, and that the new leaf now turned over will be covered with fair writing, not in the least like the blots that were on the former page, and have now been dissolved from off it by the touch of Christ's blood. It is a typical instance of the miracles which the gospel wrought as every-day events in its transforming career. Christianity knows nothing of hopeless cases. It professes its ability to take the most crooked stick and bring it straight, to flash a new power into the blackest carbon, which will turn it into a diamond. Every duty will be done better by a man if he have the love and grace of Jesus Christ in his heart. New motives are brought into play, new powers are given, new standards of duty are set up. The small tasks become great, and the unwelcome sweet, and the difficult easy, when done for and by Christ. (*A. Maclaren, D.D.*)    *Self-profitableness :*—St. Paul does not commend Onesimus for being profitable to himself, but to him and Philemon. He that is not good for himself is good for nobody : there our goodness must begin, but it must not stay there ; do good to all, so be profitable to all. (*W. Jones, D.D.*)    *The hurtful made profitable by conversion :*—Philemon might object, " I have found him hurtful; why, then, should I receive into my house as a member of my family that servant which will cause more harm than bring profit ?  I have had experience of the damage that he hath done me ; what homage he will do me I know not."  To this the apostle maketh a double answer—first, by granting, then by correcting that which he hath granted, and both ways by comparing the time past with the time present—the time before he embraced religion with the time of his conversion ; as if he should say : " True it is, and I grant he was once unprofitable to thee, for while he was unfaithful to God he could do no faithful service unto thee ; but why dost thou urge the time of his ignorance?  And why dost thou consider so much what he hath been ?  For now he has become a new man ; he has tasted of the true religion ; he hath learned to know God, to know himself, to know thee, and to know me—to know God, his merciful Creator ; to know himself, a wretched sinner ; to know thee, his loving master ; to know me, his spiritual father ; whereas in former times he was ignorant of all these.  As he regarded not to know God, so he could not regard thy good, but now thou shalt receive a new Onesimus, a new servant, a new man, the same in substance, but renewed in quality, and altered from the crown of the head to the sole of the foot.  He was not before so profitable, but now thou shalt find him as profitable unto thee as I have found him both diligent and dutiful unto me in my bonds and imprisonment." (*W. Attersoll.*)    *Altered by conversion :*— Before he was Onesimus in name, now he is so indeed ; before he held the title, now he hath the truth; before thou sawest the shadow, now thou shalt see the substance; thou hast had experience of his unprofitableness, now shalt thou have the benefit of the profit that he bringeth with him; being made a new creature in Christ Jesus. We learn from hence that Christian faith or religion of a man unprofitable maketh him profitable, and of one unfit maketh him fit to every good work. The conversion of men to the true faith worketh the greatest change and alteration that can be, and maketh them good, profitable, and helpful unto others that have been before unjust, injurious, cruel, and hurtful. (*Ibid.*)    *Conversion of heart produces alteration in the life :*—Where is a right conversion of the heart there is also a true alteration of the life, and where there is an embracing of the true Christian religion there is a change of our conversation.  I. THE REASONS OF THIS DOCTRINE ARE EVIDENT, and shine as clearly as the sun at noonday.  1. If we consider our natural estate and condition, what we were before our conversion, we shall easily be brought to acknowledge both where and what and whence the change is ; for naturally we hate the truth and the professors of the truth.  2. When men are truly converted they will make conscience of hurting ; they will abstain from wrongs and injuries ; they will be ready to do good to others, to profit others, to walk in all the duties of their callings, and to keep a good conscience toward God and man.  3. True conversion worketh in us the love of God and men, and so maketh us fruitful in all good works ; it suffereth us not to be barren and unfruitful, and it subdueth the rage and corruption of our sinful nature.  II. Now let us come to the consideration of THE

USES, AND TO THE APPLICATION OF THE DOCTRINE TO OURSELVES. 1. We see hereby that they are greatly deceived that think true godliness to be unprofitable, and no gain at all to return to the practiser of it. Great is the benefit of true religion, and much is the profit of our conversion. When once we are truly converted we have gotten Christ; He has become ours; we have Him dwelling in us—Him, I say, in whom dwelleth the fulness of the Godhead bodily, who is the Head of the Church, whom to know is eternal life. By Him our bondage is turned into freedom, our beggary into riches, our thraldom into liberty, our death into life. Who is it, then, can be so simple or ignorant to affirm that profession to be without gain and profit that bringeth Christ Jesus with it, in whom all treasures are hid and had? 2. Seeing Christian religion, planted in the heart of a man, maketh him good and helpful to others, who before was unjust and unprofitable, let every one prove his effectual calling and true conversion by earnest seeking after the good of others, and by a careful abstaining from hurting, troubling, and wronging of others. It is to be chosen as a better thing to suffer than to offer wrong, to receive than to require, to take than to give. 3. Seeing it is the turning of us to God that turneth us to the good of men, it serveth as a notable direction unto us, to teach us that whosoever desireth that such as belong unto him should be profitable and faithful unto him, let him labour to plant godliness in their hearts and to sow the seeds of eternal life in their minds. (*Ibid.*) *Religion makes us profitable :*—To render us profitable is the design of religion, and it is easy to see that it must be the effect of it. Religion is social and diffusive. According to our Saviour's language the possessors of Divine grace are the salt of the earth to keep it from corruption. They are the lights of the world to keep it from darkness; and this light is not to be concealed " under a bushel," but to be fixed " on a candlestick, that it may give light to all that are in the house." The blessings they enjoy they are to communicate. Divine grace never leaves us as it finds us. It produces a change the most wonderful and glorious and beneficial. Divine grace destroys those vices by which we are injurious to others. For the best charity I can exercise towards my fellow-creatures, says a good man, is to leave off sinning myself. Every company and neighbourhood is the better for us: we are as "a dew from the Lord." And thus the promise is fulfilled in every child of Abraham by faith : " I will bless thee, and thou shalt be blessing." Finally, we remark that our being useful does not depend upon our abilities and station. See Onesimus, a slave, profitable even to such men as Philemon and Paul—profitable to "thee and me." It is with the community as it is with the body (1 Cor. xii. 14–21). Thus we behold, in the world and in the Church, difference of rank, of office, of talents; but there is a connection between the whole, and a dependence arising from it. And from this none are exempted; even " the king is served by the labour of the field." Every man, whatever be his condition and circumstances, is of some importance in society, and we should labour to impress our minds with this reflection, especially in three cases. Let us remember it when we are in danger of pride and disdain with regard to any of our fellow-creatures. Perhaps he is more necessary to you than you are to him. Let us remember it when discouraged from exertion. He that is "not faithful in little" has no reason to believe that he would be "faithful in much." We should also remember it when we are tempted to do good in unlawful ways. What I mean is this : some suppose that they can only be useful in such a particular station or office, and hence they are ready to leave their present condition to rush into it. But, says the apostle, "Let every man abide in the calling in which he is called of God." Things are so constituted that if any man wishes to do good he may do it in the circumstances in which he is placed; he has some influence. Let us conclude with two reflections. First, if religion renders people, in all situations, valuable and useful, how deserving is it of encouragement! Let, therefore, all unite to promote it. Secondly, if religion be profitable to others, it is much more so to ourselves. It sanctifies all our mercies. It sweetens all our trials. It teaches us " in whatever state we are therewith to be content." (*W. Jay.*)  *Manhood raised :*—Being supplied with religious principle and animated with ennobling motives, his life will be pervaded by a new and improved spirit. The man was raised. His service will rise with him. Paul had found it so. (*A. H. Drysdale, M.A.*)

Ver. 12. **Whom I have sent again.**—*Christianity and slavery :*—Not many years ago the conscience of England was stirred because the Government of the day sent out a circular instructing captains of men-of-war, on the decks of which fugitive slaves sought asylum, to restore them to their " owners." Here an apostle does the same thing—seems to side with the oppressor, and to drive the oppressed from the sole refuge left him, the horns of the very altars. More extraordinary still, here is the fugitive voluntarily going back, travelling all the weary way from Rome to Colosse in order to put his neck once more beneath the yoke. Both men were acting from Christian motives, and thought they were doing a piece of plain Christian duty. Then does Christianity sanction slavery? Certainly not; its principles cut it up by the roots. Historically it is true that as Christianity has grown slavery has withered. But the New Testament never directly condemns it, and by regulating the conduct of Christian masters, and recognising the obligations of Christian slaves, seems to contemplate its continuance, and to be deaf to the sighing of the captives. This attitude was probably not a piece of policy or a matter of calculated wisdom on the part of the apostle. He no doubt saw that the gospel brought a great unity in which all distinctions were merged, and rejoiced in thinking that " in Christ Jesus there is neither bond nor free "; but whether he expected the distinction ever to disappear from actual life is less certain. The attitude of the New Testament to slavery is the same as to other unchristian institutions. It brings the leaven and lets it work. That attitude is determined by three great principles. First, the message of Christianity is primarily to individuals, and only secondarily to society. It leaves the units whom it has influenced to influence the mass. Second, it acts on spiritual and moral sentiment, and only afterwards, and consequently on deeds or institutions. Third, it hates violence, and trusts wholly to enlightened conscience. So it meddles directly with no political or social arrangements, but lays down principles which will profoundly affect these, and leaves them to soak into the general mind. If an evil needs force for its removal, it is not ready for removal. If it has to be pulled up by violence, a bit of the root will certainly be left, and will grow again. The only true way is by slow degrees to create a state of feeling which shall instinctively abhor and cast off the evil. There will be no hubbub and no waste, and the thing once done will be done for ever. So has it been with slavery; so will it be with war, and intemperance, and impurity, and the miserable anomalies of our present civilisation. Coming centuries will look back on the obtuseness of the moral perceptions of nineteenth-century Christians in regard to matters of Christian duty which, hidden from us, are sun-clear to them, with the same half-amused, half-tragic wonder with which we look back to Jamaica planters or South Carolina rice-growers who defended slavery as a missionary institution, and saw no contradiction between their religion and their practice. (*A. Maclaren, D.D.*) **Thou therefore receive him.**—*Forgiveness:*—I. The duty of forgiveness. 1. An imperative gospel demand (Matt. vi. 15, xviii. 21, 22; Mark xi. 25; Luke vi. 36, xvii. 4; Eph. iv. 32; Col. iii. 13; James ii. 13). To fail in this is to seek judgment for ourselves. 2. Culture essential to its discharge. This virtue results from experience, trial, exercise. More natural for men to consider themselves ingenious as they are able to detect an injury, and manly as they promptly and energetically resent it. The vengeful spirit among the earliest revelations of childhood. A child hurts himself in his efforts to walk; incipient revenge on table or chair. Parents often show how little they apprehend the virtue of forgiveness. The spirit of retaliation lives long within us. " Revenge is sweet" has become a hideous proverb. Louis XII. said: " Nothing smells so sweet as the dead body of an enemy." We are supposed to have got beyond that. Yet what is the measure of grace within us? 3. Christian faith is equal to the demand. Intimate fellowship with Christ will " transform by the renewing of the mind." " Learn of Me," says Jesus; and " He that doeth His will shall know " (Col. iii. 12–16). II. The prayer for forgiveness. A model for imitation, whether God or man be approached. Contains—1. Humble confession. Apostle, for Onesimus, assumes becoming attitude of an offender. But deals more tenderly with the offence than the guilty one himself could do. Apostle shows the part of the wrong-doer as well as of the wronged. On the one hand acknowledgment, which is a manly because a severe duty, as first steps towards moral elevation; on the other pardon, complete and absolute, as proof of sympathy with Christ, and in imitation of His example. Intention of Epistle missed if both obligations be not recognised. Only by confession can it be known that pardon is desired or deserved. Honest avowal to one who knows the Lord will—(1) Insure success of suit. The spirit that would reprove will be disarmed. (2) Restrain from future error. Memory of struggle to tell of sin and shame will strengthen in seasons of weakness and peril. 2. Implicit expectation (ver. 21). The whole spirit of the gospel warrants the expectation that wrong frankly confessed will, by him who is subject to the gospel, be freely forgiven. Vindictiveness alien to kingdom of Christ, as darkness to light. Christianity God's own protest against revenge. III. THE LAW OF FORGIVENESS. The special instance of generous love solicited by apostle was claimed—1. On the ground of friendship. A true fellowship gives right of mediation. 2. On the stronger ground of Christian relationship. Friendship had sprung from highest and holiest source, and was thereby intensified and glorified. Still more, Paul was the agent in Philemon's salvation. 3. On the strongest ground of Christ's will. "In the Lord," "In Christ Jesus," appear throughout. IV. THE POLICY OF FORGIVENESS. 1. Each needs it himself. "Who is he that doeth good, and sinneth not ?" Our necessity of Divine forbearance prohibits resentment. 2. Our wrong is against God. Customary to measure guilt by the rank of the person injured. Consequences of insolence and wrong not so serious when offered to a private person as when committed against a magistrate. Penalty greater still when the sin is against a king. Act may be the same, but punishment gauged by dignity of offended person. How great the grace we claim when we pray "forgive"! 3. Aggravations of sin increase our need. Careful in reference to men, while unrestrained before God, whom we cannot see. These we fear, Him despise! His love despised, His Word, Son, Spirit. As, therefore, forgiveness is desired, forgive. (*A. W. Johnson.*) *The sinner's Substitute :*—I. GENEROUS CONDUCT OF THE APOSTLE—HE PLEADS FOR A FUGITIVE. II. INTERESTING PARALLEL TO THIS EXAMPLE—OUR SALVATION BY CHRIST. III. PRACTICAL REMARKS. 1. How abundant is the comfort against sin provided for believers in Christ. 2. How much it concerns every soul to be a partaker of Christ's mercy. 3. How binding is the example of Paul, and the greater example of Christ, upon the Church, to welcome penitents of every class. (*Biblical Museum.*) *Forgiveness—connection between forgiveness and readiness to forgive :*—1. Forgiveness makes us ready to forgive. 2. Readiness to forgive inspires us with courage to seek forgiveness. 3. The spirit of forgiveness ever joins the two more closely together. (*J. P. Lange.*) *He who cannot forgive man cannot find forgiveness with God :*— 1. Because he will not believe in forgiving love. 2. Because he will not act upon its directions. (*Ibid.*) *In what sense is it true that he who forgives shall be forgiven ?*—1. His forgiving is not the ground, but the evidence of his forgiveness. 2. His forgiving is an evidence that the forgiveness of God preserves him. 3. His forgiving shows the truth of his testimony, that there is forgiveness. (*Ibid.*) *The duty of reconciliation :*—There must be a reconciliation between Christians : all offences must be buried (Col. iii. 12). 1. God offers reconciliation to us ; and shall we be so hard-hearted as not to be reconciled one to another ? 2. All we do is abominable in the sight of God without it (Matt. v. 23, 24). God should be first served, yet He will have His own service to stay till thou be reconciled to thy brother. 3. We can have no assurance of our reconciliation to God without it (Matt. xviii. 35). 4. We have no certainty of our lives. This night may our souls be taken from us. Jovinian the emperor supped plentifully, and went to bed merrily, yet was taken up dead in the morning ; and if death take us before we take another by the hand, as a token of hearty reconciliation, what shall become of us? (Eph. iv. 26). Johannes Eleemosynarius, Archbishop of Alexandria, being angry in the day with Nicetus, a senator, towards night sends this message to him : "My honourable brother, the sun is setting ; let there be a setting of our anger, too." If we do it not within the compass of a day and night, yet let us do it within the compass of our lives ; let not our anger be like the fire of the temple, that went not out day nor night. Let our anger be the sting of a bee, that is soon gone ; not the sting of a serpent, that tarries long, and sometimes proves fatal. (*W. Jones, D.D.*) *Forgiveness :*—Count Enzenberg, who was formerly Resident Minister of Hesse in Paris, has in his album of autographs three entries on the subject of forgiveness. M. Guizot has written : "In the course of my long life I have learnt two wise rules : the first to forgive much, the second never to forget." M. Thiers follows this with : "A little of forgetfulness would not injure the sincerity of the forgiveness." Below these Prince Bismarck penned the striking words : "I have learnt in my life to forget much, and to make myself much forgiven." *Forgiveness of others :*—He that cannot forgive others breaks the bridge over which he must pass himself ; for every man has need to be forgiven. (*Lord Herbert.*) *Reconciliation of brothers :*— The reconciliation of two brothers, gentlemen of position in Liverpool, was effected by the late Rev. Dr. McNeile as follows :—Although, on account of an unhappy feud which was publicly known, they scarcely recognised each other, yet they both attended Dr. McNeile's church. He therefore preached on one Communion Sunday on the duty of brotherly reconciliation, taking his text from Matt. v. 23, 24.

The blessed effect upon the alienated brothers was simultaneous. They remained as if by consent to communicate, and as they advanced from their respective pews towards the Communion-table the pastor motioned them into juxtaposition at the rails, and as they knelt side by side he, in silent but expressive action, joined their hands together in the mutual grasp of restored fraternal affection, continuing till they sealed their reconciliation over the memorials of their Lord's dying love. Their widowed mother rejoiced as only a fond Christian mother could over the reunion of her children. **Mine own bowels.**—*Paul's affection for Onesimus :*—Of course " mine own bowels " is simply the Hebrew way of saying " mine own heart." We think the one phrase graceful and sentimental, and the other coarse. A Jew did not think so, and it might be difficult to say why he should. It is a mere question of difference in localising certain emotions. Onesimus was a piece of Paul's very heart, part of himself ; the unprofitable slave had wound himself round his affections, and become so dear that to part with him was like cutting his heart out of his bosom. Perhaps some of the virtues, which the servile condition helps to develop in undue proportion, such as docility, light-heartedness, serviceableness, had made him a soothing and helpful companion. What a plea that would be with one who loved Paul as well as Philemon did ! (*A. Maclaren, D.D.*) *Christian love for converts :*—We learn from hence that the love which Christians ought to bear to all the saints, especially to those whom they have been the means to convert, ought to be entire, hearty, earnest, most faithful, and most fervent. It is our duty to love all men, more especially the saints, but most especially such as have been gained to the faith by us. The reasons that may be rendered to uphold this doctrine are many and infallible. 1. For, first, there is great labour employed, long time spent, many means used, and continual care bestowed to convert a soul to God. It is no idle work ; it is not brought to pass without much ado. 2. Secondly, by testifying of our love and showing forth the fruits thereof we gather great assurance that we are of the company of the faithful, of the communion of saints, and of the society of them that belong to the truth, when we love unfeignedly those that are of the truth. 3. Lastly, it is the sum of the whole law, and a token and testimony that we make conscience to walk in the ways and commandments of God. Uses : 1. This, then, being a virtue so necessary that every one which belongeth to the Lord Jesus Christ must yield their obedience, even to love the brethren, and show himself a true Christian by showing charity to his neighbour, let us consider the nature and properties of this love, that we may have right and true use of this doctrine. (1) First, therefore, let us know what brotherly love is. It is a work of God's Spirit, whereby a man is moved to affect his brother for God's sake, and to show forth the fruits of this affection. (2) Secondly, we are to consider the property of this love, how it is to be performed ; for, as we have seen the parties who are to be loved, even all, so we must mark the manner how they are to be loved—that is, fervently and earnestly. (3) Thirdly, we must know the form and manner how we are to love our brethren ; to wit, even as ourselves. 2. Seeing this is the love that must be found in us towards the saints, it serveth to meet with many enormities, and to reprove many sins that reign in the world, and are as the forerunners of the full and final ruin thereof. (1) Our love to others is a cold love ; frozen, without heat ; dead, without life ; barren, without fruit ; such as our Saviour speaketh of in the gospel : " Because iniquity shall be increased, the love of many shall be cold." But our love is hot toward ourselves ; we have abundance of self-love, which overfloweth in us, and overcometh true love. This is almost, or for the most part the only love that remaineth in the world in these days, which is the corruption, nay, the bane and poison of true love. (2) As we see self-love checked and controlled, so they are condemned that place brotherly love in fair words and gentle speeches (and yet many fail in these, and cannot afford them, as if every word of the mouth were worth gold), whereas in such is no sound religion, but a vizor only of holiness. True love must be shown in the fruits, in sustaining, helping, pitying, and relieving those that crave our release and are in necessity. (3) It reproveth such as give themselves to fraud and deceit, to cruelty and oppression, to subtlety and circumventing their brethren, to lying and using false weights and measures ; for if this should be the rule of our love, that it ought to be fervent, we should examine our own hearts whether we would have another man to deceive and oppress us by forgery and falsehood. 3. Seeing all are to be loved, but especially such as have been converted by us, it teacheth us to further their salvation that have been brought into the way by us, and never to forsake them until we have brought them to their journey's end ; for what a vain thing were it to find a man wandering out of his way and going astray from the right path, and when we have brought him back to leave him without further direction? or what an unnatural part were it for a mother to bring forth her child into the world and then to take no more care of it, neither to wash it in water nor to wrap it in swaddling clothes, nor to have any compassion upon it, but to cast it out into the open field. (*W. Attersoll.*)

Ver. 13. **In thy stead he might have ministered unto me.**—*What is this ministering?*—No doubt it is aiding Paul in his ministerial work, or he would not have said, "In thy stead." It is scarcely to be supposed that Philemon would have ministered to St. Paul in the capacity of a domestic servant; and if Onesimus was to have ministered to the apostle, it was to supply the absence of Philemon in being St. Paul's deacon. There must have been something peculiarly thorough in the conversion of Onesimus, that the apostle should so desire him to be near him. (*M. F. Sadler, M.A.*) *A ministering friend:*—There is no need to enlarge on the winning courtesy of these words, so full of happy confidence in the friend's disposition, that they could not but evoke the love to which they trusted so completely. Nor need I do more than point their force for the purpose of the whole letter, the procuring a cordial reception for the returning fugitive. So dear had he become, that Paul would like to have kept him. He goes back with a kind of halo round him, now that he is not only a good-for-nothing runaway, but Paul's friend, and so much prized by him. It would be impossible to do anything but welcome him, bringing such credentials; and yet all this is done with scarcely a word of direct praise, which might have provoked contradiction. One does not know whether the confidence in Onesimus or in Philemon is the dominant note in the harmony. In the preceding clause, he was spoken of as, in some sense, part of the apostle's very self. In this he is regarded as, in some sense, part of Philemon. So he is a link between them. Paul would have taken his service as if it had been his master's. Can the master fail to take him as if he were Paul? (*A. Maclaren, D.D.*) *Christian ministration:*—The gospel is the common cause, that concerns us all: if any suffer for it, we are bound from the highest to the lowest to assist them with our purses, prayers, and personal presence too if conveniently it may be; yea, though we be never so great personages. Our Saviour Himself washed His disciples' feet. St. Cyprian writes to the priests and deacons, to provide all things necessary for them that were in prison, wishing that he himself were present with them, readily and willingly he would perform all obsequious duties of love unto them. Helena, the mother of Constantine, when at Jerusalem herself served meat to the virgins there. Placilla, the wife of Theodosius the Emperor, ministered to the poor in her own person; and Philemon himself should have ministered unto St. Paul. The angels minister to us, yea, when we be in prison, as to St. Peter; and shall we scorn, be we never so wealthy, worshipful, honourable, to minister to them that are in bonds for the gospel? Let us count it an honour to us. In ministering to them we minister to Christ, and He will reward it. (*W. Jones, D.D.*) *A welcome service:*—I. The apostle intimateth his desire to have retained Onesimus with him, and that he was loath to suffer him to depart from him: which declareth THAT THE PRESENCE OF THOSE THAT ARE DEAR UNTO US IN CHRIST IS WELCOME, PLEASANT, COMFORTABLE, AND MUCH SET BY, AND WE GREATLY DESIRE TO KEEP THEM CONTINUALLY WITH US. For as love is the knot of conjunction that bindeth us together, though we be absent and far severed one from another, so it craveth and requireth the bodily presence of those whom we entirely love, which howsoever we cannot obtain in this life, forasmuch as our earthly affairs will not suffer it, yet we shall be sure to enjoy it perpetually and without end in the life to come, when we shall have the greatest joy and comfort one in another that can be wished or desired; such as the eye hath not seen, nor the ear heard, neither hath it entered into the heart of man to conceive. II. Note with me the end why he desired to retain Onesimus with him, THAT THE SERVANT MIGHT DO SERVICE TO HIM IN THE MASTER'S STEAD. The end, then, is the ministry and attendance which Paul might of duty require of Philemon himself. If then the master be bound to do his service, and wait upon the apostle, much more the servant! Whereby we may note how great right and jurisdiction he that hath gained a man to Christ hath over him whom he hath gained, so that he may challenge not only one of his servants, but himself to minister unto him, and to help him in temporal and transitory things. For he that hath received spiritual blessings cannot without great unthankfulness deny corporal benefits, so that it cannot be expressed how well he hath deserved of that person whom he hath won by the Word of God. "And delivered him by his ministry from the power of darkness, and translated him into the kingdom of His dear Son." III. We may observe in the apostle's correcting of his former grant, that as he is commended that doth his duty that is required of him, freely and willingly, so he is worthy to be praised and commended, that DOTH NOT GO ABOUT TO WRING AND WREST A BENEFIT AGAINST A MAN'S WILL, though it be due debt and a bounden duty, but laboureth by all means, that it may be voluntary, and not upon necessity; for hereby it cometh to pass oftentimes, that he not only getteth a benefit, but winneth his heart and good will that giveth it, and many times it falleth out that the mind of the giver is more to be respected than the gift itself, as we see in the poor widow mentioned in the gospel, who casting into the treasury two mites, is said to have given of her penury more than all the rich men that bestowed of their superfluity. (*W. Attersoll.*) *Ministering to the saints:*—I. WHATEVER GIFTS ARE BESTOWED UPON US, TO THIS END THEY ARE BESTOWED TO PROFIT WITHAL, TO HELP ONE ANOTHER, and to edify that body whereof we are members. II. It is our duty TO FOLLOW THE EXAMPLE OF OUR LORD AND MASTER CHRIST JESUS, He came to serve, not to be served: to minister, not to be ministered unto: to redeem, not to rule. III. TRUE RELIGION CONSISTETH IN MINISTERING TO THE SAINTS, IN HELPING AND SUCCOURING OF THE POOR, in employing himself to the good of others, as a candle that spendeth and wasteth itself to give light to them that are in the house. It consisteth not in bare knowledge, but in practice; not in an idle faith, but in the fruits of love. Uses: 1. This serveth to reprove those that have forgotten all true service to the faithful. Many there are that have no feeling of the troubles that fall upon the servants of God. Their eyes are closed, and their hearts are hardened; they have no bowels of compassion to minister unto them, they have no hands open to relieve them. The rich of our Churches, who have this world's goods given unto them, are either in their unsatiable desires poor, wrongfully getting, miserably keeping, unconscionably scraping, and unjustly pulling from others without mean or measure; or else they spend their wealth and consume their substance, some in sumptuous apparel, others in excessive feastings, others in worse uses, all being unnecessary and fruitless things, unprofitable for the Church or commonwealth, so that little can be spared for the poor saints, and that which is spared is as hardly drawn from them as a piece of flesh out of their sides. These men never think of doing service to others, but of serving their own turns and commodities, which ought not so to be among them that profess Christ Jesus, who served not Himself. 2. Seeing we are servants to all, to help them by all the means we can, by comfort or counsel, by word or deed, by our wealth or authority, or whatsoever God shall enable us; from hence ariseth a great comfort unto a man's conscience, and an assurance of his peace and acceptation with God, to pray unto Him with comfort for His graces, not doubting to obtain them, if we have been serviceable and comfortable unto others, especially to the servants of God, that are as dear to Him as the apple of His eye. It is a means of excellent joy and peace to a man, to consider that he hath employed all the good things he hath to the use of God's house and His household servants, for when any common danger shall fall, or he find anguish and affliction of conscience for sin, he may be assured of comfort, seeing God hath wrought this sincerity, and set it as a seal of His mercy in his heart. 3. Seeing God requireth of all true Christians, of what condition soever they be, according to the means afforded unto them, to use their gifts, their power, their possessions, and whatsoever benefits they have received, to use them to the comfort and service of God's saints, it kindleth the affections of God's people to bless and praise God for them, to speak well of them, to pray unto God for them, and to obtain greater blessings for them than they have bestowed. Thus they that do good to the Church do good to themselves; they that give much unto them do receive more themselves, and such as have been helpful and serviceable to God's people, shall find them as their remembrancers to God, who will not forget the labour of their love, and the duty of their service. 4. Seeing God requireth service to His Church at our hands to do all good to them by all good means, it is our duty to inquire and learn the estate of the distressed Church, that we may know and be informed where and when and how it is afflicted. This is one misery of the faithful, that men do not regard them when they are in misery. The Lord hath determined that there shall be always some objects offered unto us and set before us to exercise the fruits of our faith and love. (*Ibid.*)

Ver. 14. **Without thy mind would I do nothing.**—This final resolution was, no doubt, the result of several motives. 1. To harbour and detain a slave, who applied to him to become a *precator*, beyond a limited period, would have been distinctly to violate the Roman law. 2. The apostle might have seemed to inflict a pecuniary loss upon Philemon by depriving him of a "chattel personal," and morally constraining him to put up with the loss by imposing a severe strain upon the bonds of friendship. 3. Onesimus, in the depth and reality of his repentance, saw the duty of returning. What truer piece of restitution was ever made? 4. St. Paul was peculiarly "sensitive" as to the scandal which the Church might occasion, if slaves received encouragement to become fugitives. See Col. iii. 22; 1 Tim. vi. 1. (*Bp. Wm. Alexander.*) *Servants not to be detained from their masters :*—Servants must not be detained without their masters' liking. Eustathius, Bishop of Armenia, was deposed from his see because under a colour of piety he had taken servants from their masters. (*W. Jones, D.D.*) **Willingly.**—*Voluntary virtue :*—Jerome from this passage justly deduces as a conclusion that St. Paul held the principle that nothing in moral action is good which is not voluntary. He applies it to the solution of the question which has been so often asked—"Why God did not make men absolutely good?" God might have made man good without man's will. But, had He done so, the good would not have been voluntary, but necessary. But what is necessarily good is not good in the highest sense, and is even relatively and in another point of view evil. Therefore, in leaving us to our own free will, He made us more truly after His image and likeness. *Freedom essential to virtue :*—Freedom is essential to virtue. If a man "could not help it" there is neither praise nor blame due. That freedom Christianity honours and respects. So in reference to the offer of the gospel blessings, men are not forced to accept them, but appealed to, and can turn deaf ears to the pleading voice, "Why will ye die?" Sorrows and sins and miseries without end continue, and the gospel is rejected, and lives of wretched godlessness lived, and a dark future pulled down on the rejecters' heads, and all because God knows that these things are better than that men should be forced into goodness, which indeed would cease to be goodness if they were. For nothing is good but the free turning of the will to goodness, and nothing bad but its aversion therefrom. The same solemn regard for the freedom of the individual and low estimate of the worth of constrained service influence the whole aspect of Christian ethics. Christ wants no pressed men in His army. "Must" is not in the Christian vocabulary, except as expressing the sweet constraint which bows the will of him who loves to harmony, which is joy, with the will of Him who is loved. Christ takes no offerings which the giver is not glad to render. (*A. Maclaren, D.D.*) *Voluntary goodness :*—It is a received axiom—That which is good of necessity, is not good, yet this is to be understood of a coacted necessity, not of a voluntary. God is necessarily, yet willingly, good. Death comes necessarily upon all; yet some die willingly. But the good which is done upon a constrained necessity, loses the name of good : patience perforce is no patience. A willing mind in a good action is all in all. If Solomon had not willingly built the temple, it had not been pleasing to God; if the centurion had not willingly set up the synagogue, God would not have respected it; if the woman of Shunem had not willingly entertained the prophet, it had been no good work in the sight of God; if Dorcas had not made the coats willingly, they had not been acceptable to God. (*W. Jones, D.D.*) *Spontaneity in goodness :*—I. A PREFERENCE WITH RESPECT TO GOODNESS. Paul was anxious not simply about the pardon of Onesimus, but as to—1. The moral quality of the action of Philemon. Spontaneousness is an element of the highest goodness. The necessity which dictates to the Christian should be from within rather than from without. 2. The principle it was to illustrate. That Christianity is not a mere adjustment of external relations, but a spirit which interpenetrates and transfigures all. 3. Its spiritual effect upon the age. It has a greater effect upon the receiver, and upon onlookers, when a good deed is perceived to be spontaneous and not due to the influence of another. II. A SPIRIT OF CONSIDERATION FOR THE FREEDOM AND INDIVIDUAL RESPONSIBILITY OF A FELLOW CHRISTIAN. St. Paul's behaviour throughout this episode is an example to us all of the courtesies that ought to soften and dignify the general relations of life; but of greater value is its suggestiveness in the spiritual sphere. It teaches us—1. To do justice to the spiritual life of others. 2. To respect the diverse operation of the One Spirit. 3. To maintain a confident faith in the promptings of Christian principle. (*A. F. Muir, M.A.*) *Willinghood in service :*—1. Seeing no man must perform any holy duty to God or man upon compulsion, or against his will, but with all his mind and might, we learn that every action or duty is accounted of by God, not according to the greatness of the worker, or outward show of the work, but according to the will and affection of the doer; it is the manner of doing that God more accepteth than the action or deed itself. A child in his obedience to his father is esteemed for his reverent, loving, obedient, and dutiful heart, and not for the greatness or worthiness of his work. For what can he do when he hath endeavoured to the utmost to pleasure his father? So it is with us, when we have done all that we can, we must confess we have been unprofitable servants, and therefore God more respecteth the intention than the action, the workman than the work, the affection than the effect. 2. Seeing only that duty which is done freely and not by compulsion deserveth due commendation, this reproveth all those things that are done upon wrong grounds and evil foundations. It is not enough to do a good thing, but we must do it well; it is not sufficient to do those things that are godly, but we must do them in a godly manner. 3. This confuteth those who ascribe all to the work done, and regard nothing at all either the mind of the doer or the manner of doing. Outward observations of religion will deceive us if we rest upon them and put our trust in them. If we perform a worship to God without the heart, we dishonour God, we deceive our own souls, and we increase our condemnation. We must make the house of God a paradise, or place of pleasure; we must make His word our meat and drink, and our continual hearing must be a daily refreshing unto our souls. 4. Seeing all Christian duties must be performed of us willingly, we are hereby guided and directed in our obedience, that we are not to hinder the necessary duties of Christianity belonging unto us by objecting fleshly reasons, as it were laying stumbling blocks in our own ways, to keep us back from a willing, free, and cheerful going forward in the works of our calling, and in the parts of God's worship. (*W. Attersoll.*)

Ver. 15. **Perhaps.**—*Contingency :*—The word is used to express every degree of contingency from the faintest possibility to the highest probability. Two reasons may underlie the peculiar timidity and hesitation implied. 1. This "departure" might have been allowed with a view to a higher good. This case might have been like Joseph's (Gen. xlv. 5). Certainly a beginning which appeared so unpromising looked like the very path that had led to happiness. Had not Onesimus fled from Philemon, he would not have arrived in Rome, nor have found St. Paul. Had not Paul been imprisoned, Onesimus would never have believed, or been baptized, or become a minister of Christ—perhaps a bishop and martyr. Taking the two extreme points of the story, and connecting them together, it might be said, Onesimus became a minister of the gospel, *because* he fled from his master. St. Paul softens the sentence by the words, "it may be," because the judgments of God are hidden, and it is culpably rash to pronounce *certainly* on that which must be *doubtful* for creatures like ourselves. 2. If he had not so qualified his statement, slaves might have appealed with too much readiness to the example of Onesimus. (*Bp. Wm. Alexander.*) *Perhaps :*—Paul will not be too sure of what God means by such and such a thing, as some of us are wont to be, as if we had been sworn of God's privy council. "Perhaps," is one of the hardest words for minds of a certain class to say; but in regard to all such subjects, and to many more, it is the motto of the wise man, and the shibboleth which sifts out the patient, modest lovers of truth from rash theorists and precipitate dogmatisers. Impatience of uncertainty is a moral fault which mars many an intellectual process; and its evil effects are nowhere more visible than in the field of theology. (*A. Maclaren, D.D.*) "*Perhaps,*"—"*therefore*" :—I. UNCERTAINTIES. God often allows us no more than a "perhaps"; and for a time does not give us the slightest indication in any direction of what good turn our trial is to take. And it is wonderful of what use this "perhaps," with its uncertainty, is to the believer. While he is saying "perhaps this," or "perhaps that," his mind wanders away far afield, seeing how a blessing may come from this unlikely quarter or from that, and how his trouble may link in with one thing and another, until he gets up from his thoughts full of wonder at what God's resources are, and full of happiness at the thought that he is within such reach of blessing, and that it can travel to him by such hundreds of hitherto unknown ways. The very uncertainty which is so harassing to the natural man is educational to the believer; he is taught to look out for God in all possible directions; the very uncertainty prevents his trying to fix God to this mode of action, or to that. The "perhaps" of the believer never dies; when it sees one door plainly closed, it immediately opens another; that is its very nature. II. SEPARATIONS. 1. Separations are to be traced farther back than what we call the accidental circumstances which apparently have caused them. It is soul teaching, and soul strengthening, when we discern that things are " of the Lord." 2. We have God deep in the background of trial for good, if we by our waywardness hinder Him not. The loss for a season to Philemon of the services of Onesimus was great; but it was to be met by a greater gain. The bringing of good out of evil is the prerogative of God. He permits the evil, to produce the good. 6. Here there seems to meet us, also, a working of what might almost be said to be a law of God's dealing with us in our present fallen state, viz., that loss must precede gain; that seed corn must die, before harvest corn can be reaped. III. RESTORATIONS. If we could but introduce those words " for ever " in their deep meaning into our trials—into the decision as to the course of action we would pursue—into the results which naturally belong to them, how differently would things be often done from the way in which they are now. Let us apply the " for ever " to earth's great things to make them small, and to Christ's small things to make them great. The tears which at the most we can shed are but few —the watercourse of a cheek is short; but who can tell the depth of the pure river of the water of life, clear as crystal; or, whither flows that stream, concerning which all that we are told is this—" that it proceedeth out of the throne of the Lamb." It is through temporary losses that we, if we yield ourselves to their teaching and power, pass to eternal gains. (*P. B. Power, M.A.*) *The runaway slave sent back :*—I. " PERHAPS HE THEREFORE DEPARTED," &c. Wonderful dealings of God in providence—ordering all, overruling even faults. Onesimus had done wrong; yet God, instead of giving him up to the consequences, in mercy overruled all for good; led him to Rome; brought under Paul's teaching, where converted. Doubtless he had suffered hardships and want. Humbled thus perhaps. Thus often. Chastisement, suffering; yet good at last. Even faults often overruled. Some in prison for crime have there learnt the way of salvation. Wild young man enlists, sent abroad, there learns " the way." Boy goes to sea, endures hardship, brought to repentance. The " therefore " runs through all. II. OBSERVE HOW CONFIDENTLY PAUL ASKS PHILEMON TO FORGIVE. Could he have done so, unless Philemon had been a Christian? No. Little hope of mercy otherwise. Nothing would have been thought too heavy punishment for dishonest runaway slave. What change the gospel makes! Thankful for it even in this view. Thankful to be born and live under it. Paul, we may be sure, appealed not in vain. Onesimus forgiven and restored. All past forgotten. Of all the fruits of the gospel, none more striking or peculiar than forgiveness of injuries. III. BUT MORE THAN FORGIVENESS WAS EXPECTED OF HIM, and doubtless not in vain. He and Onesimus now, not merely master and servant, but fellow-Christians, brethren. Surely he would be a slave no more! 1. This is such forgiveness as we receive, returning and confessing. Not bare pardon, but rich and full blessing too. Made free; made happy. Servants, yet children too. All in Christ 2. Such also the forgiveness we should practise. Not grudging, but bountiful, generous. And every Christian we should treat as a brother. (*F. Bourdillon, M.A.*) **Departed for a season.**—*Sin not to be exaggerated :*—He does not say, " Perhaps he therefore ran away "; he uses a word of better report : he " departed," was separated from thee, by the permissive hand of God's providence. After men have repented of their sins, we must not aggravate, but in some measure extenuate them. Not "Noah's drunkenness," but "Noah's unadvised drinking"; not " David's adultery," but "the matter of Uriah "; not " Peter's apostasy," but " Peter's denial "; not " Onesimus' running away," but " departing." Before they be humbled, we must be as trumpeters to waken them out of their sins; after that, we must be as nurses to cherish them : before corazives, after lenitives : before, we must come with the law as a schoolmaster to whip them; after, with the gospel to comfort them; before, we must be Boanerges, sons of thunder; after, Barnabases, sons of consolation. (*W. Jones, D.D.*) *Philemon and Onesimus :*—I. WHAT SORT OF RESULTS ST. PAUL EXPECTED TO FLOW FROM THE RECONCILING AND COMBINING POWER OF THE CHRISTIAN FAITH. Certainly slavery was repugnant to the spirit of Christianity, to the spirit of Him who had vindicated the rights of our human nature, and who had indefinitely enhanced its dignity by taking that nature upon Him at His incarnation. But the business of the apostles was of a higher and of a Diviner sort then that of inaugurating a violent social revolution. The revolt of Sparticus with all that had followed was still fresh in the memory of the world, and the apostles addressed themselves to the practical task of lodging the Christian faith and life in the minds and hearts of masters and slaves alike, confident that in time that faith would act as a powerful solvent upon the institution, by eating out its very spirit. The Christian master would feel that the slave was certainly as a man his equal, and possibly in the kingdom of the Redeemer his superior, and that he too, the while, had a Master in heaven. And the Christian slave would feel that the circumstances of this life mattered little if, through the Divine redemption, he were secure for the next ; and he would see in his master's will, wherever he could, nothing less than the will of God. The apostles, then, would not anticipate the slow but certain action of the Christian principles upon society, the infiltration of the Christian spirit into the Imperial codes ; the gradual legislation of the great Catholic councils; the work which, too long delayed, is associated in our latter days with the honoured names of Wilberforce and Clarkson. When Philemon received Onesimus, a great Christian enterprise of reconciling classes had indeed begun. What are we doing to further it? II. How ENTIRELY, FOR THE TIME BEING, ST. PAUL'S INTEREST IS CONCEN-TRATED ON A SINGLE SOUL. He writes just as though there was no person in the world to think about except Onesimus, and relatively to Onesimus his master Philemon. Now, here is a lesson which is much needed, it seems, in our day. Our fashion is to think and speak of religion as an abstract influence, to forget that to be worth anything it must be a power reigning in the individual life. We talk grandly and vaguely about the tendencies of the age, about the dangers of the age, about the modern spirit, about a number of fine abstract phrases and conceptions, which just slightly, each one of them, stimulate the imagination, and which exact no sacrifice whatever from the will. We utter or we listen to these imposing abstractions at a public meeting, and we forget that they mean nothing—nothing whatever—apart from the life and experience of each separate soul. They are creations of our own thought ; but souls, they are independent realities. The soul is there, whether we think about it or not. All the real good that is to be done in the Church or in the world must begin with individual characters, with single souls. Phrases die away upon the breeze—souls remain. They remain in their ignorance, in their per-plexity, in their sorrows. They remain awaiting death, awaiting eternity. Many a teacher of two or three children, of a few pupils, who seem dull and irresponsive, and little likely to do their instructor credit—many a teacher is often tempted to wish that he had what is called a larger sphere of action, where he might control great issues, and become a leader or a fashioner of the thought of the time. If any such one hears me, let him think of Paul, the aged apostle of the nations, working away as the dreary hours passed, working away on the dull brain and on the sluggish affections of the slave Onesimus. The world, it has been well said, is not saved by abstract ideas, however brilliant. The world is saved by the courageous individualising efforts of Christian love. III. How A CHRISTIAN SHOULD LOOK AT THE EVENTS OF LIFE, at the commonplace and trivial events, as well as those which appear to be striking and important. Every such event has a purpose, whether we can trace it or not. It is a purpose which will be made plain in the eternal world, in the mysterious state of existence which awaits every one of us when we have passed the gate of death. To St. Paul, the future life was just as certain as the shining of the sun in the heavens, and therefore he writes quite naturally to Philemon : "Perhaps Onesimus was therefore parted from thee for a season, that thou mightest receive him for ever." And yet observe the "perhaps"|! St. Paul will not encourage us in a rash and presumptuous confidence when we endeavour to interpret in detail God's providences in this life by the light of the next. We may conjecture that such and such an event is permitted for such and such an end, which will be agreeable to the known will and attributes of God ; we cannot know that it is so. Some well-meaning, but unthinking people, undertake to interpret a human life, just as they undertake the Revelation of St. John, with an easy reliance on their own insight, which nothing but ignorance of the real difficulties of the subject can possibly explain. St. Paul saw as far as most men into the purposes of God, and yet, when he would interpret God's purpose in respect of a given human life, he reverently adds "Perhaps"—"Perhaps he therefore was parted from thee for a season, that thou mightest receive him for ever." St. Paul describes what took place, but in his own religious language. Onesimus had robbed Philemon and had fled from justice : St. Paul says, "He was parted from thee for a time." St. Paul sees a higher hand in what seemed to be only the act of Onesimus. If Onesimus robbed and fled from his master, God permitted him to do so, and this permission we are told was probably given in order to bring about the conversion of Onesimus to the Christian faith and his reunion with his master Philemon, first in this life at Colosse, and then for ever in the life everlasting. Now, what is here remarkable is that even the misconduct of Onesimus seems to have been, according to St. Paul, permitted for a purpose which would be made plain in the future life. God knew what he was doing in permitting the misconduct of Onesimus. It was for Philemon to forget the petty and personal aspects of the case, to recognise God's hand and mind in it ; to throw his thought upward and forward from the present to the future ; upward from the lower world of sense and time, to the mighty world, with its immense proportions, of eternity. Observe this is a rule of thought. It is not for us men a rule of action. Never are we authorised to do evil that good may come, though we are bound to extract all the good we can out of the evil that may be done by others ; and to trace God's hand in bringing good out of evil which He permits His creatures to work. (*Canon Liddon.*) *The story of a runaway slave :*—I. Look at Onesimus as AN INSTANCE OF DIVINE GRACE. 1. In his election. Were there no free men, that God must elect a slave ? Were there no faithful servants, that He must choose one who had embezzled his master's money ? Were there none of the educated and polite, that He must needs look upon a barbarian ? Were there none among the moral and the excellent, that infinite love should fix itself upon this degraded being, who was now mixed up with the very scum of society ? " I will have mercy on whom I will have mercy, and I will have compassion on whom I will have compassion," rolls like thunder alike from the cross of Calvary and from the mount of Sinai. The Lord is a Sovereign, and doeth as He pleases. Let us admire that marvellous electing love which selected such a one as Onesimus ! 2. In his conversion. Look at him ! How unlikely he appears to become a convert. He is an Asiatic slave of about the same grade as an ordinary Lascar, or heathen Chinee. He was, however, worse than the ordinary Lascar, who is certainly free, and probably an honest man, if he is nothing else. This man had been dishonest, and he was daring withal, for after taking his master's property he was bold enough to make a long journey, from Colosse to Rome. Some of us, I have no doubt, are quite as wonderful instances of Divine election and effectual calling as Onesimus was. Let us, therefore, record the lovingkindness of the Lord, and let us say to ourselves, " Christ shall have the glory of it. The Lord hath done it ; and unto the Lord be honour, world without end." 3. The grace of God was conspicuous in the character which it wrought in Onesimus upon his conversion, for he appears to have been helpful, useful, and profitable. So Paul says. What wonders the grace of God can do ! Many plans are employed in the world for the reformation of the wicked and the reclaiming of the fallen, and to every one of these, as far as they are rightly bottomed, we wish good success; for whatever things are lovely and pure, and of good report, we wish them God speed. But mark this word—the true reforming of the drunkard lies in giving him a new heart; the true reclaiming of the harlot is to be found in a renewed nature. The lowest strata of society will never be brought into the light of virtue, sobriety, and purity, except by Jesus Christ and His gospel; and we must stick to that. Let all others do what they like, but God forbid that I should glory save in the cross of our Lord Jesus Christ. II. A very interesting INSTANCE OF SIN OVERRULED. The Lord must have Onesimus in Rome to hear Paul, and the sin of Onesimus, though perfectly voluntary on his part, so that God had no hand in it, is yet overruled by a mysterious providence to bring him where the gospel shall be blest to his soul. Now, I want to speak to some of you Christian people about this matter. Have you a son who has left home ? Is he a wilful, wayward young man, who has gone away because he could not bear the restraints of a Christian family ? It is a sad thing it should be so, but do not despond. You do not know where he is, but God does ; and you cannot follow him, but the Spirit of God can. Many a sailor boy has been wild, reckless, God-less, Christless, and at last has got into a foreign hospital. Ah, if his mother knew that he was down with the yellow fever, how sad her mind would be, for she would conclude that her dear son will die away at Havannah or somewhere, and never come home again. But it is just in that hospital that God means to meet with him. A sailor writes to me something like that. He says, " My mother asked me to read a chapter every day, but I never did. I got into the hospital at Havannah, and, when I lay there, there was a man near to me who was dying, and he died one night ; but before he died he said to me, ' Mate, could you come here ? I want to speak to you. I have got something that is very precious to me here. I was a wild fellow, but reading this packet of sermons has brought me to the Saviour, and I am dying with a good hope through grace. Now, when I am dead and gone, will you take these sermons and read them, and may God bless them to you. And will you write a letter to the man that preached and printed those sermons, to tell him that God blessed them to my conversion, and that I hope He will bless them to yourself?'" It was a packet of my sermons, and God did bless them to that young man who, I have no doubt whatever, went to that hospital because there a man who had been brought to Christ would hand to him the words which God had blessed to himself and would bless to his friend. You do not know, dear mother, you do not know. The worst thing that can happen to a young man is sometimes the best thing that can happen to him. III. Our text may be viewed as AN EXAMPLE OF RELATIONS IMPROVED. "He therefore departed for a season, that thou shouldest receive him for ever; not now as a servant, but a brother beloved, specially to me, but how much more unto thee?" You know we are a long while learning great truths. Perhaps Philemon had not quite found out that it was wrong for him to have a slave. Some men who were very good in their time did not know it. John Newton did not know that he was doing wrong in the slave trade, and George Whitfield, when he left slaves to the orphanage at Savannah, which had been willed to him, did not think for a moment that he was doing anything more than if he had been dealing with horses, or gold and silver. Public sentiment was not enlightened, although the gospel has always struck at the very root of slavery. The essence of the gospel is that we are to do to others as we would that others should do to us, and nobody would wish to be another man's slave, and therefore he has no right to have another man as his slave. Perhaps, when Onesimus ran away and came back again, this letter of Paul may have opened Philemon's eyes a little as to his own position. No doubt he may have been an excellent master, and have trusted his servant, and not treated him as a slave at all, but perhaps he had not regarded him as a brother; and now Onesimus has come back he will be a better servant, but Philemon will be a better master, and a slave-holder no longer. He will regard his former servant as a brother in Christ. Now, this is what the grace of God does when it comes into a family. It does not alter the relations; it does not give the child a right to be pert, and forget that he is to be obedient to his parents; it does not give the father a right to lord it over his children without wisdom and love, for it tells him that he is not to provoke his children to anger, lest they be discouraged; it does not give the servant the right to be a master, neither does it take away from the master his position, or allow him to exaggerate his authority, but all round it softens and sweetens. Rowland Hill used to say that he would not give a halfpenny for a man's piety if his dog and his cat were not better off after he was converted. There was much weight in that remark. Everything in the house goes better when grace oils the wheels. The mistress is, perhaps, rather sharp, quick, tart; well, she gets a little sugar into her constitution when she receives the grace of God. The servant may be apt to loiter, be late up of a morning, very slovenly, fond of a gossip at the door; but, if she is truly converted, all that kind of thing ends. She is conscientious, and attends to her duty as she ought. The master, perhaps—well, he is the master, and you know it. But when he is a truly Christian man—he has a gentleness, a suavity, a considerateness about him. The husband is the head of the wife, but when renewed by grace he is not at all the head of the wife as some husbands are. The wife also keeps her place, and seeks, by all gentleness and wisdom to make the house as happy as she can. (*C. H. Spurgeon.*) *A runaway converted:*— Some years ago I was talking with an aged minister, and he began fumbling about in his waistcoat pocket, but he was a long while before he found what he wanted. At last he brought out a letter that was well nigh worn to pieces, and he said, "God Almighty bless you! God Almighty bless you!" And I said, "Friend, what is it?" He said, "I had a son. I thought he would be the stay of my old age, but he disgraced himself, and he went away from me, and I could not tell where he went, only he said he was going to America. He took a ticket to sail for America from the London docks, but he did not go on the particular day that he expected." This aged minister bade me read the letter, and I read it, and it was like this:— "Father, I am here in America. I have found a situation, and God has prospered me. I write to ask your forgiveness for the thousand wrongs that I have done you, and the grief I have caused you, for, blessed be God, I have found the Saviour. I have joined the Church of God here, and hope to spend my life in God's service. It happened thus: I did not sail for America the day I expected. I went down to the Tabernacle to see what it was like, and God met with me. Mr. Spurgeon said, 'Perhaps there is a runaway son here. The Lord call him by His grace.' And he did." "Now," said he, as he folded up the letter and put it into his pocket, "that son of mine is dead, and he is in heaven, and I love you, and I shall do so as long as I live, because you were the means of bringing him to Christ." (*Ibid.*) *The providence of God in human life :*—The great idea underlying the present turn of thought is, that in every event of life, good or bad, God has not only an interest, but a meaning or purpose through it, all His own. There is not merely a general superintendence of Providence over the affairs of men, but a Providential agency at work in the very midst of them. Very different, no doubt, is the Divine agency from the human, with which it mysteriously mingles. Not more distinct is the Lord of all from the works of His own hands, than is His providential government distinct from what it regulates ; yet moving freely in the midst of His creation, He no less freely interlaces human agencies with His own. Man's history, in short, is not the mere sum of his own thoughts and doings, any more than the well-compacted web is the mere sum of the weft-threads shot across its range—there are the slowly unrolling warp-threads as well ; and not less surely is there the unfolding of a providential agency to bind into one the crossing and recrossing lines of human activity. Hence we continually see results issuing from trivial matters which the actors in them never contemplated. But the special feature in Divine Providence on which the apostle's argument proceeds is the fact that God brings good out of man's evil. (*A. H. Drysdale, M.A.*) *The providence of God in the life of man :*—I. An encouraging view of the providence of God. 1. The minuteness of its operation. 2. The beneficence of its operation. "Why did God permit evil in the world?" (1) To bind man more closely, lastingly, lovingly to Himself. (2) To awaken nobler developments of human character. (3) To manifest more conspicuously His own character and glory. (4) To increase human joy. The joy of gratitude for redemption, of deliverance from direst perils, of victory over subtlest, strongest foes, &c. II. A view of the pre-eminence of spiritual relationships. 1. Christianity does not weaken any of the bonds of our civil or other earthly relationships. 2. Personal Christianity exalts and ennobles all other relationships. 3. Spiritual relationships are pre-eminently over all others. (1) They are independent of differences of rank and condition. (2) They are perpetual in their duration. (3) They centre and subsist in Jesus Christ. (*W. Jones.*) *More than a servant :*—1. Mark that the apostle entitleth the shameful running away of Onesimus, the servant of Philemon, by the name of a departure. If we will speak properly, a departing is one thing, a running away is another thing. For albeit every one that runneth away departeth ; yet every one that departeth runneth not away from his master, because he may depart by consent either having leave and licence, or that the time of his service is expired. So a little before (ver. 11), he called him "unprofitable," whereas he might lawfully have given him a harder title. This was not done in regard of the offence because it was small, but in regard of his repentance because it was great. 2. In the apostle's answer to Philemon's objection we may mark that we are bound to forgive and forget injuries and offences done unto us, when once God hath forgiven and covered the sins committed against Him and received the sinner that repenteth to mercy ; when God maketh all things turn to our good that love Him and thereby recompenseth by a double benefit the loss and damage that we have sustained. 3. We may observe that Christian religion doth more strongly bind all persons to their particular callings and ᵔaketh the knot greater than it was. For that which he speaketh here of a Christian servant, even a brother, is true of all callings in the family and commonwealth. For as a faithful servant is more than a bare servant, so a Christian king is more than a king ; a Christian master is more than a master ; a Christian father is more than a father ; a Christian husband is more than a husband ; so on the other side a Christian wife is more than a wife ; a Christian subject is more than a subject ; and so of all the rest. 4. The apostle notwithstanding the great account he maketh of this servant doth not deny subjection to his master nor exempt him from the condition of a servant, but he addeth "More than a servant." He saith not, he is no more a servant, but he is more than a servant ; so that our Christian calling doth not abolish policy and politic constitutions and domestic government ; but rather doth strengthen and sanctify them. He that is called to the truth being a servant, must not be discouraged and discontented, but rejoice in this that he is the Lord's freeman. 5. When he styleth him "A brother" he doth after a sort signify he is equal unto him. For albeit in the commonwealth and private family it be necessary that some should be superiors and other inferiors; and that this disparity and inequality among men be the ordinance of God; yet in the kingdom of God and in Christ Jesus there is no distinction. 6. We may observe that he joineth love with Christian brotherhood, and calleth Onesimus " A beloved brother," not only a servant, not only a brother, but a brother dear and beloved; signifying thereby that where a Christian calling is found, there charity and love is as a due debt required. (*W. Attersoll.*) **For ever.**—*A brother for ever :*—There may probably be here an allusion to that which is written in the Hebrew law about the slavery of " the children of the strangers that sojourned among the Israelites " (Lev. xxv. 46). Onesimus was to be his master's property—his to have and hold, to enjoy as his possession—" for ever," as the old law said of the slave in permanent servitude. But in how much a deeper and truer sense! To be with him not only for time, but in eternity, in the eternal communion of saints. The time of the absence of Onesimus, during which he was " parted " from Philemon, might have entailed some little discomfort upon his master. What of that? Why count up the weeks and months? They were but as the slave's " little hour " of holiday compared with the gain of a brother " for ever." (*Bp. Wm. Alexander.*) *Eternal friendship :*—Since he left Onesimus had obtained eternal life, and eternal life involves eternal interchange of friendship. His services to his old master were no longer barred by the gates of death. (*Bp. Lightfoot.*) *All things, even sin itself, are turned by God's providence to the good of the elect :*—I. THE REASONS OF THIS DOCTRINE ARE APPARENT, TO SETTLE OUR HEARTS AND CONSCIENCES THEREIN. 1. The infinite wisdom and unsearchable power of God, who, as the apostle teacheth, bringeth light out of darkness, and worketh by contrary means, such as men count foolishness, as to save men by the foolish preaching of the gospel, that is, which is esteemed among the wise men of the world no better than foolishness. 2. It is the pleasure of God to confound the wisdom of man that cannot attain to great matters but by great means (1 Cor. i. 27). God disposeth of all things as pleaseth Him, and often-times crosseth the devices of men. They intend one thing, but God bringeth to pass another; they purpose one end, but He will have another come forth to teach man's wisdom to be but foolishness. 3. He expresseth His wonderful love, making all things that fall out in the world to serve His Church. II. THIS DOCTRINE SERVETH FOR REPROOF, FOR COMFORT AND FOR OBEDIENCE. 1. For it serveth to reprove and convince sundry persons, that either know not or knowing do abuse this providence of God whereby He taketh care of all things that are in the world and directeth them to a right end. (1) And first of all, we set against it and oppose unto it the dreams of atheists, epicures, libertines, who either deny wholly there is a God, or make Him sit as idle in heaven as themselves are upon the earth: so that albeit He know and see all things yet He worketh or ordereth not the special actions of men that fall out. These are they that pull God out of His kingdom and set up chance and fortune as an idol and make it their God. We must all learn and confess that the Lord, that is the Creator of heaven and earth, is also the Ruler and Governor of all creatures. The whole world, from the highest heaven to the centre of the earth, is subject to His providence. (2) It reproveth such as from hence take encourage-ment to commit sin, to break out into sundry outrages, or to live securely because God can turn it to our good and maketh it serve to set forth His mercy. This is that presumption and sin of rebellion touched by the apostle, " Why do we not evil that good may come thereof, whose damnation is just." So in another place. " What shall we say then? Shall we continue still in sin that grace may abound? How shall we that are dead in sin live yet therein? " We confess, indeed, that God is the sovereign cause of all events that are brought to pass, and whatsoever the enemies of the Church intend and enterprise, whether the sons of men, or the devil and his angels, He stayeth and hindreth or represseth and disappointeth, and always dis-poseth it to the good and salvation of His children. Nevertheless, this doth not excuse or free the instruments that He useth from fault. They do the will of God blindly and ignorantly, but they do cross His will openly and purposely, so that His providence doth not exempt the wicked from their evil doing. 2. This doctrine serveth greatly to comfort us both in prosperity and adversity, and that for the time to come we should repose our whole hope in God. For seeing all things come to pass by the providence of God so that not so much as sin itself is committed with-out His will, it is a great comfort many ways to God's Church and chosen children. We know that He can moderate and will moderate the rage of the devil and the malice of wicked men that they shall not hurt or hinder their salvation. For the devil is the Lord's servant or slave to work His will, albeit he do it unwillingly and by compulsion. 3. This providence of God in everything teacheth contentment of mind in every estate; yea, in adversity when we lie under the cross, so that all things go against us; forasmuch as God's providence hath appointed us our lot and portion. 4. This should be a very strong reason unto us not to be unmeasurably dismayed when offences and great evils break out among us as oftentimes it falleth out, whereby many are ready to shrink back, and others are much disquieted to see the Church of God so troubled. We are not to think it strange or to forsake the faith through these scandals, for God would not suffer any evil to come to pass unless out of that evil He were able to bring good, and out of that sin to bring forth righteousness to the glory of His great name, and for the salvation of His dear Church. 5. Seeing God's providence extendeth to everything that is, and disposeth it according to His own pleasure, it directeth us in our obedience and putteth us in mind of a Christian duty, namely, to be patient in all adversity. This will keep us that we do not rage against second causes, that we do not mutter and murmur against God, that we seek not revenge against our enemies. We are ready in sickness to complain, in poverty to repine, in injuries and oppressions to retail and return like for like, and in all troubles to be impatient and to use unlawful means to deliver ourselves, not attending the Lord's leisure; and the reason is because the providence of God is not learned of us we cannot depend upon Him, we know not that He hath all things in His power to employ them to His glory and to use them to our good. (*W. Attersoll.*) *God's power to bring good out of evil:*—This must not make us do evil that good may come of it, which we are forbidden (Rom. iii.), for God only hath this skill, by reason of His infinite wisdom and power, to work good out of evil, to draw light out of darkness. He only hath the philosopher's stone to turn dross into gold. In vain, therefore, is it for us to assay any such thing. The right use of this doctrine is for us to comfort ourselves when we see wicked men plotting and practising mischief against God's poor Church. Their heads and hands work not so fast but God works as fast. When they go and strive one way He sets them awork another way; as the sun going in his own proper motion one way is every day, by the violent circumvolution of the heavens, turned another way: nay, He makes their striving against His glory and His Church's good to be the means of furthering both. As in a boat, when the rowers go with their faces striving towards the east, they set the boat going apace towards the west. Onesimus in running away from his master's house, the Church of God, did as much as in him lay, strive against his own conversion, and yet it is made a means of conversion. Joseph's brethren in selling him thought to have frustrated his dreams and to have made him sure for ever having dominion over them; and yet their selling of him was the special means of accomplishing his dreams. Satan, in Christ's death, thought to have wounded the Church to the death; and yet thereby we were healed of his deadly wounds. This is the work of the Lord, who knoweth how to catch the wise in their own wiles, and it must be marvellous in our eyes. Let not, then, the power and policy of all the Achitophels and Machiavels in the world, combining themselves against the gospel, dismay us; for God hath His oar in their boat, He hath a special stroke in all actions whatsoever, and can easily overreach and make stark fools of the wisest by making their own counsels and endeavours like Chushais, to overthrow those intentions which they seem to support. (*D. Dyke, B.D.*)

Ver. 16. **A brother beloved.**—*Christian brotherhood:*—As has been well said, " In the flesh, Philemon has the brother for his slave; in the Lord, Philemon has the slave for his brother." He is to treat him as his brother, therefore, both in the common relationships of everyday life and in the acts of religious worship. That is a pregnant word! True, there is no gulf between Christian people nowadays, like that which in the old times parted owner and slave; but, as society becomes more and more differentiated, as the diversities of wealth become more extreme in our commercial communities, as education comes to make the educated man's whole way of looking at life differ more and more from that of the less cultured classes, the injunction implied in our text encounters enemies quite as formidable as slavery ever was. The highly-educated man is apt to be very oblivious of the brotherhood of the ignorant Christian, and he, on his part, finds the recognition just as bad. The rich mill owner has not much sympathy with the poor brother who works at his spinning jennies. It is often difficult for the Christian mistress to remember that her cook is her sister in Christ. There is quite as much sin against fraternity on the side of the poor Christians who are servants and illiterate, as on the side of the rich who are masters or cultured. But the principle that

Christian brotherhood is to reach across the wall of class distinctions is as binding to-day as it was on Philemon and Onesimus. That brotherhood is not to be confined to acts and times of Christian communion, but is to be shown and to shape conduct in common life. "Both in the flesh and in the Lord" may be put into plain English thus—a rich man and a poor one belong to the same Church; they unite in the same worship; they are "partakers of the one bread," and therefore, Paul thinks, "are one bread." They go outside the church door. Do they ever dream of speaking to one another outside? "A brother beloved in the Lord"— on Sundays, and during worship, and in Church matters—is often a stranger "in the flesh" on Mondays in the street, and in common life. Some good people seem to keep their brotherly love in the same wardrobe with their Sunday clothes. Philemon was bid, and all are bid, to wear it all the week, at market as well as church. (*A. Maclaren, D.D.*) *Regard for those in whom grace is found:*— Here we see the apostle reasoneth for Onesimus; to have him received and respected above an ordinary servant because he was truly converted, and had in him a good measure of grace, and was become a true and sound Christian. We learn from hence that the more grace appeareth in any, the more should they be tended and regarded of us, whether they be servants, children, neighbours, pastors, people, wife, kinsfolk, or acquaintance. In whomsoever the greatest store of heavenly things is to be found, such are most of all to be loved and regarded, tendered, and respected. I. THE REASONS HEREOF ARE PLAIN TO INFORM US. 1. Where grace is, it bringeth blessedness to that society, kingdom, congregation, family, and person, as appeareth by the confession of Joseph's master (Gen. xxxix. 2, 3), whom he served. Now, who are more to be regarded, or better to be thought of, than such as are blessed, and cause blessedness to others? 2. We see that God is most gracious to such as have most grace in their hearts; He tendereth them as the apple of His eye, and loveth them as His own sons. Indeed, We loveth all the works of His hands as they are His creatures: He maketh His sun to shine, His rain to fall, His fruitful seasons to refresh them: He had not left Himself without witness among the infidels, that He might make them without excuse. He giveth to beasts and to beastly men their food; their corners and garners are full, and abounding with divers sorts; but God is specially known in Judah; His name is great in Israel. He showeth His Word and His statutes among them; He hath not dealt so with every nation, neither have they known His judgments. 3. The more grace appeareth in any, the nearer he doth resemble God, the more evidently doth the image of God show itself in him. The image of God standeth and consisteth, especially in holiness and true righteousness. II. LET US GATHER THE USES THAT ARISE FROM THIS DOCTRINE. 1. This ought to stir us all up to labour to grow in grace and in the gifts of the Spirit, that thereby we may procure and deserve the love of men. They that grow in grace are truly to be reputed and accounted gracious. 2. Seeing it is our duty to respect every one of the faithful, according to the grace of God measured out unto him, it is required of all men to look always to the best things in the choice of the companions of their life. 3. Seeing it belongeth as a special duty unto us, to show our greatest affection to such as have in their hearts most religion; it serveth as a comfort and encouragement to all callings, even the lowest that are amongst men, to labour after good things, and to seek to serve and fear the Lord, seeing such as are the meanest, and of basest reckoning with many, are respected and recompensed of Him. (*W. Attersoll.*) *Brethren in Christ:*—1. Seeing that in Christ, who is the Elder Brother of the house, we are all made brethren and sisters together, having one Father, which is God; one mother, which is the Church; one inheritance, which is heaven. It is our duty, being nearly joined by so strong bands, and in so fast and firm a society, to love one another, to seek the good one of another, and to cut off all occasions of discord and division that may arise among us. For, shall such as are members of one body be divided one against another? 2. Seeing the gospel of Christ teacheth us to account ourselves as brethren, albeit, it take not away the degrees of persons and the differences of callings; it serveth as a good instruction to all superiors, to use all mildness and moderation, patience and meekness towards those that are their inferiors, and placed under them, and to teach them not to contemn and abhor them, not to despise and disdain them. For howsoever there be one way a great inequality between them in matters of this world, and in the things of this life, inasmuch as God set superiors above us in an higher place, and requireth subjection, reverence, and obedience of those that are beneath, yet in another respect they are matches and equals, having a like portion in Christ, and a like interest in the means of salvation. 3. This title of brethren communicated to all the faithful, serveth as a comfort and consolation to all inferiors, and to teach them this duty, that they ought not to grudge, or to be grieved that they are placed in a low estate, as though they were therefore less esteemed and regarded of God. 4. Seeing God respecteth all alike, and hath made all as one, and as brethren that are in Christ, it serveth as a reproof, and threatening, and terror, to all drowsy and secure persons that think they shall escape the judgments of God for their high places. There is no difference with God, there is no inequality with Christ, to them that are in Christ; high and low are all alike with Him. None are saved for their highness; none are condemned for their lowness. Christ Jesus accepteth no man for his glory; He rejecteth no man for his ignominy. Let us, therefore, not bear ourselves bold and confident upon our outward excellency, but stand in fear of His judgments, and prepare ourselves with all reverence and diligence, that we may be found worthy to stand before the great God in that great day of account. (*Ibid.*)

*Christian brotherhood :*—I. Here note the spiritual kindred that is betwixt true Christians. They are all brethren—brethren by the Father's side, having one Father, God the Father of spirits; brethren by the mother's side, lying in the same womb of the Church, having one and the self-same elder brother, Christ Jesus, begotten with the same spiritual seed; fed at the same table with the same nourishment. This brotherhood must far exceed the natural, even as God's fatherhood towards us far exceedeth the natural fatherhood among men. Look, then, what nature tieth natural brethren to, that doth grace much more tie spiritual unto, as— 1. Amity and unity (Psa. cxxxiii. 10). How, then, do they show themselves brethren that do bite, yea, and devour those that are of the same holy profession with themselves? Even as in the sea, the greater fishes swallow up the lesser. 2. It is the part of brethren to take one another's part, to cleave one to another, taking that which is done to their brother as done to themselves. 3. It is the property of a brother, though at other times he have been something more unkind to his brother; yet in his affliction and extremity, then to feel nature working in him, and to show and express his affection by doing his best (Prov. xvii. 17). If we then will show ourselves true and natural sons of God, and so brethren to His children, when we see His honour ready to be trod under foot, when we see His children evil intreated, then is it high time for us to manifest our affection. II. Observe that this spiritual brotherhood is betwixt all Christians indifferently, whatsoever difference there be amongst them in outward civil respects, yet they are nothing prejudicial to this spiritual fraternity in Christ: for here Philemon and Onesimus, the master and the servant, are made these kind of brethren. This doctrine is of special use, both for comfort to inferiors and for humiliation and moderation of mind to superiors, inasmuch as the servant is Christ's free man, and the master is Christ's servant. (*D. Dyke, B.D.*)

*Christianity and slavery :*—Christianity entered on no superficial and obvious contest with this ancient, consolidated, and haughty iniquity, so general in the world and so intricately involved with the customs of the rude, the laws of the advanced, with barbarian ferocities, Grecian philosophies, Roman power. It sent no formal challenge to the system, to which it was as fatally hostile as it was to idolatry. But it smote it with blows more destroying than of arms, and caused it to vanish as summer skies and melting currents consume the glacier, which we call an iceberg, which has drifted down from Arctic coasts. The Sermon on the Mount, God's affectionate and watchful Fatherhood of all, the brotherhood of disciples, the mutual duty and the common immortality of poor and rich—these were the forces before which slavery inevitably fell. Where philosophies had utterly failed and eloquence had been wanting, and the progress of arts, cities or states, had only clenched tighter the manacles of the bondman, He who taught on the narrow Galilee beach overwhelmed, by the mystic energy of His words, the consummate oppression. It fell before Him as the warrior falls, more surely than by bullets, by famine and thirst; as the giant's strength fades in fatal atmospheres. "Not now a slave, but above a slave, as a brother beloved, so receive him"; it was the voice not of one apostle only, though he were the chiefest, but of the whole Church, to the master who was himself in Christ. "The grace of God that bringeth salvation hath appeared to all men," before that announcement slavery could not stand, any more than flax before shrivelling fires. (*R. S. Storrs, D.D.*)

*Care for servants :*—The celebrated Earl of Chesterfield left, by his will, legacies to all his menial servants, equal to two years' wages each, considering them "as his unfortunate friends, equal by birth, and only inferior by fortune." John Claude when on his dying bed, thus addressed his son, who, with an old servant, was kneeling before him—" Be mindful of this domestic; as you value my blessing, take care that she wants nothing as long as she lives." *Mutual obligations of Christian masters and servants:*—Onesimus might remain a slave; there might be no change in their relative positions; but then as the slave went about his ordinary duties; duties in which there was nothing degrading—for duty cannot be degrading; if it is actually God to whom it is rendered; and, I might, therefore, dare to say that it must be honourable—as the slave then went about his ordinary duties, the master was to regard him as the free man of Jehovah, the heir, with himself, of an incorruptible inheritance. The slave was to regard his master as possessing authority from God, to whom he was bound to yield a devoted obedience; but at the same time, as a fellow traveller with himself to a city where each should be judged according to his works. And what but a holy and close brotherhood could subsist between the master and the slave when each thought of the other as he appeared in God's sight, and each being himself accountable to that God for every word and every work? Would that rich and poor would both keep more in mind these which are the only levelling principles of the Christian religion. It would do more towards cementing together the several classes of society, now, alas, so much disjoined! than all the well meant endeavours of statesmen and economists. It is a grievous thing for a country, more grievous than foreign invasion, when there is little or nothing of kindly feeling between the several ranks, but jealousy and envy separate them even more than titles and property. The rich and the poor filling their respective places in a well-ordered community, each class dependent on the other, and neither able to subsist by itself, ought to present the same spectacle as the members of the body; their offices different, but their concord so great, that the whole framework is sensitive to the least injury done to the least part. And we know of nothing but the diffused influence of Christianity which can either produce this state, or restore it when impaired. This, however, can, and that, too, on the simple principle that while it puts a sort of sacredness around civil institutions, and thus is a better upholder of the rights of the rich than despotism with its armies, or legislation with its statutes; it puts also a dignity round poverty, and lifts it to at least equality with wealth, by merging all human distinction in the being sons of God, and heirs of God. Let the rich feel this, and where is pride? Let the poor feel this, and where is discontent? Oh, the beauty of the spectacle which might be presented if the brotherhood which Christianity recognises and enforces were practically instituted throughout a community! There is little else needed for the making that millennium on which prophecy has poured its most gorgeous colouring. (*H. Melvill, B.D.*) **Specially to me, but how much more unto thee, both in the flesh, and in the Lord.**—*Reasons for the increase of mutual love:*—Hereby there is offered to our considerations this lesson to be learned, that the more bands and reasons are given unto us of God to care for any, the more we are bound to care for Him, and to respect Him. A professor of the gospel is more to be regarded than he that is without. One of the same nation, more than a stranger; one of our own kindred, more than another farther from us; a neighbour, more than one that dwelleth many miles from us; one of a man's house, more than him that is out of his house; a kinsman converted to the faith, and become a true and perfect Christian, more than a kinsman not converted; a child that hath the sparks of grace in him, more than a child void of them; a servant fearing God, more than a servant in the same family that doth not fear God, nor regard His Word, nor make conscience of the means of his salvation. The reasons being wisely considered will make this plainly to appear unto us. 1. It is a general sentence delivered by Solomon in the book of Ecclesiastes, " Two are better than one, and a threefold cord is not easily broken." Wheresoever there are stronger cords to tie us, and no bands to join us together, our love ought to be the greater one towards another. Many sticks make the greater fire, and many strings the better music. 2. It is a thing very well pleasing in the sight of God, to consider what means He hath afforded to increase mutual love and society one with another. This is the reason urged by the apostle to persuade the children and nephews of poor widows to take care for their parents according to their ability, because that is an honest thing, and acceptable before God. Now we are bound unto them by many effectual reasons, as it were with bars of iron, and bands of brass, to nourish those that have nourished us, that have fed us, that have clothed us, that have begotten us, and brought us into the world, so that we must acknowledge it both right and reasonable. 3. Such as break these bands and cast away these cords from them, do set themselves against the doctrine of Christ, and may be sent to school to the infidels; nay, to the brute beasts, which are not void of a certain natural affection. This the apostle teacheth, "If there be any that provideth not for his own, and specially for them of his household, he denieth the faith, and is worse than an infidel." For howsoever they profess the faith in words, yet in deed and in truth they deny it. But God is delighted with our works, not with our words, and looketh upon the substance, not the show of our religion. (*W. Attersoll.*)    *Love for ever:*—Very dear was Onesimus to the apostle; dear as being a spiritual son, whom, as he expresses it, he had "begotten in his bonds." But dearer still must he be to Philemon who had not succeeded in the endeavour to turn him from the error of his ways. It may be, and it should be, a deep gladness to the minister of Christ if God employ him in inducing the prodigal to return to his home. But even this gladness is nothing to that of a parent or guardian who receives back the wanderer, and views in his conversion the fruit and the recompense of his prayers and his tears. The parent seems to have laboured in vain when another is employed where all his efforts have failed. But oh, think not on this account that the joy is transferred from the parent to the minister—"A brother beloved, specially to me, but how much more unto thee." I have not robbed thee of thy rapture through taking from thee the office wherein thou didst so devotedly toil. I have gained indeed a rich delight for myself; but there is a richer—richer as succeeding to fear, and watching, and anxiety—richer as thou now dost receive back a beloved one, of whom thou thoughtest that thou hadst lost him for ever. Surely, the apostle seems here to imply that ties of earthly relationship and family, though they will not subsist hereafter in anything of their present selfishness and contraction, shall nevertheless not wholly disappear from our future and everlasting condition. He speaks, you observe, of Philemon as having received Onesimus for ever; and of Onesimus as dearer to Philemon than even to himself who had turned him to the Lord. If it was for ever that Onesimus was received; and if he have reason to be dearer to his master than to any one beside, we can hardly avoid the inference, that in a higher and better state of being there will be something corresponding to human friendships and associations—that parents and children, husbands and wives, brothers and sisters, will be more to each other than parties, who have been wholly strangers on earth; that although in that lofty and ethereal condition, "they neither marry, nor are given in marriage," still it will be in the purifying and refining rather than in the actual destruction of earthly relationships that the future shall be distinguished from the present. All of you, we believe, admit that those who have known each other on earth shall know each other in heaven. This seems to follow on our preserving our identity; on our remaining, and on our feeling ourselves the same persons hereafter as here. You all, moreover, admit that the saints in heaven shall constitute but one vast family, every member of which shall be bound to every other by intimate as well as indissoluble ties. But it seems necessary in order to there being any worth in the first part—that of our knowing each other in heaven, that this should not interfere with the second part—that all the redeemed shall constitute one family above, that we suppose human associations so far to remain that Philemon should single out Onesimus and regard him as with a special affection. There is perhaps but very little that is cheering in the prospect of a reunion with friends whom we have long lost, if they are to be nothing to us through eternity but what others will be whom we never saw. It will hardly help to dry the tears of the mother as she weeps over her child, to tell her that she shall see that child again, but see it only where it shall be to her nothing more than what a thousand others are. There must be some place, some play for human affections, else shall we so spiritualise the future as to strip it of all influence on such beings as ourselves. And there is place, and there is play for human affections. (*H. Melvill, B.D.*)

Ver. 17. **If thou count me therefore a partner.**—*A partner, not a prelate:*—He does not say, If thou count me a prelate, a ruler of the Church, but a partner; he is content to be one of them, not above them. The angels count us partners (Rev. xix. 10); Christ counts us partners (Heb. ii. 14); and shall we disdain to call one another partners? There are partners in nature, so are we all; partners of the same air, water, fruits of earth, misery, death; there are partners in office, as churchwardens, and constables; there are also partners in grace—partakers of the Divine nature, of one Christ, of one heaven. Such a partner did St. Paul desire to be accounted; and happy are they that are in this partnership. (*W. Jones, D D.*)

*A partner :*—Philemon and the apostle had been at one time associated as partners in their secular calling. The latter accordingly now falls back upon the language which business men who are so connected use in writing to each other. "If thou count me a partner, receive him as myself. Let the runaway slave stand on the footing of my agent, and be treated as the agent of a partner ought to be." But then there came the fact which, both for the sake of justice and of the penitent himself, St. Paul had no wish to gloss over, that there had been a wrong committed. Onesimus had stolen or embezzled. How was that to be dealt with? Here also he falls into the business language of partners. "If he hath wronged thee," &c. He was ready to debit himself with that responsibility. (*Dean Plumptre.*)    *New arguments :*—The words in this verse are not many, but the observations are not few that might be concluded and collected out of the same. 1. First of all, many may marvel that the apostle is so earnest, importunate for a servant, and especially for such a servant. Surely, fear of hard and severe dealing might have moved Onesimus to distrust and despair, and therefore he useth all means to hold him up, to cherish his faith, and to further the good work begun in him, being as yet a young plant, a new convert, as a joint newly restored, and having yet, as may be thought, a tender conscience; whereby he provoketh us and all others, to seek tenderly the upholding, maintaining, confirming, and comforting, such as have given witness of their true repentance, not to quench the smoking flax, nor to break the bruised reed. For seeing we are with all mildness to receive unto us such as are weak in the faith; woe unto them that stay them that are coming forward, and lay stumbling-blocks in their way to bring them back, and to cause them to return to their vomit with the dog, and to the wallowing in the mire like the sow that was washed. And seeing the sinner is thus to be helped, which hath approved his conversion unto us, that we are to make intercession unto others, to obtain pardon for the penitent: we are admonished, that they are much more favourably to be handled, and carefully to be received, and gently to be remitted by ourselves. 2. We see that to the old request he added a new reason; for we shall never find in this epistle his petition barely and nakedly propounded. He hath used diverse arguments before to persuade Philemon, yet here we have another annexed, to move him to grant it without denial or resistance. This giveth instruction to the ministers of the gospel, to teach the truth soundly and substantially, as that the consciences of the people may be well grounded and thoroughly settled therein. When matters of weight and importance are in question they must not deal rawly, they must not use weak proofs and unsufficient reasons, whereby men may be rather hardened in their errors than helped out of their errors. 3. The apostle doth not simply say : If our things be common (as he might have done), but if thou account them common, and us to have a communion between ourselves, declaring thereby that it is not enough to know a truth, unless we also yield unto it as unto a truth. It is one thing to know what is good in our judgments, and another thing to embrace it in our practices. It is one thing to know what is evil in our minds, and another to refuse it in our actions. We must labour not only to have our thoughts cleared, our understanding and our judgments rectified, to see the truth, but to have our hearts and affections sanctified to follow it. It behoveth therefore not to rest ourselves satisfied with general notions, but so to ensue after them, as that we make special application of them. David in general knew that adultery was evil; Noah knew that drunkenness was beastly; Peter knew that denying of his Master was fearful, yet in the brunt of temptation, though the mind had knowledge of it, the affections would not refuse it, but yielded as a city besieged by an enemy. 4. The apostle putteth Philemon in mind, that seeing there was so near a conjunction between them twain, that they were become as it were one man, and had one mind in two bodies ; it followeth that whosoever was joined to one of them ought of necessity to be joined to the other. Whereby we see that such as are our friends ought to be also the friends of our friends, that is, of those that are joined unto us. Philemon was the friend of Paul, and therefore if Onesimus were the friend of one he must needs be the friend of the other. Paul and Philemon were as two brethren ; if then Onesimus were the brother of Paul he ought also to be accounted the brother of Philemon, and therefore he would have him received as himself. It is no true friendship when one maketh profession to love another man, and yet hateth him which is his chiefest and dearest friend ; for if indeed we loved him we would for his sake love the other that loveth him. This we see in the covenant made with Abraham, who is called the friend of God, whereby it appeareth that the Lord promised to be a friend to his friends, and an enemy to his enemies. 5. In the amplification of the conclusion he addeth (as myself), thereby showing that he would have him regarded no otherwise than himself. Whereby we learn that our love to the brethren ought not to be in word, or in tongue, or in show, but in deed, in truth, and in heart. This is Christian love, this was in Christ towards us, and this should be in all of us one toward another (1 John iii. 18 ; Rom. xii. 9; 1 Pet. iv. 8). (*W. Attersoll.*)

Ver. 18. **If he hath wronged thee, or oweth thee ought.**—*Theft:*—The form only is hypothetical. The case is put as one which is absolutely unquestionable. No doubt Onesimus robbed his master when he ran away. The consequence of this is a debt at present unpaid. He wronged Philemon once for all, and consequently is in debt. Flight and theft were instinctively associated in the minds of Romans as the kindred offences of slaves. It will be observed that St. Paul's teaching was not socialistic. Not private property, but the abstraction of it, was theft in his estimation. (*Bp. W. Alexander.*) *Ownership of goods:*—We learn from hence that the communion which is among the faithful saints doth not take away the private possession, dominion, distinction, and interest, in the things of this life. Albeit the things belonging to this temporal life be in some respect common, yet in another respect they are private. They are common touching use, they are private touching possession. I. This truth will yet further and better appear unto us, if we enter into the CONSIDERATIONS OF THE REASONS THAT SERVE TO STRENGTHEN IT. 1. It is confirmed by the Commandments of God, and by the fourth petition of the Lord's Prayer. The Eighth Commandment forbiddeth us to steal away our neighbour's goods, and to do him the least hurt therein. The Tenth Commandment restraineth the inward lusts and motions that arise in our minds, and condemneth the coveting of his house, of his wife, of his servant, of his ox, and his ass, or of anything that belongeth unto him. If then God commandeth the preservation of every man's goods, and forbiddeth all injuries to be offered unto them, it standeth us upon to acknowledge a right and interest that every one hath in earthly things given unto him. Likewise our Saviour Christ teacheth us daily to ask our daily bread, so that no man ought to desire that which is another's bread, but every one to know his own, what God hath given him, and what he hath given to others. If then there be bread that is ours, then also there is bread that is not ours. And if somewhat be ours and somewhat not ours it followeth that every one hath an interest in his own goods, and cannot lay hold of another man's. 2. The invading of other men's inheritances, and the encroaching upon their private possessions, is the fruit either of a confused anarchy, or of a loose government; and both of them are contrary to that ordinance which God establisheth, and the order that He requireth. 3. Every one hath a proper and peculiar possession, his own servants to order, his own ground to till, his own fields to husband, his own family to govern, and his own domestical affairs to manage, that he may provide things honest in the sight of God, that he may rejoice in the labour of his own hands, and be thankful to the Father and giver of all good things. It is a rule taught by nature, approved by experience, strengthened by customs, and established by the founders of cities and kingdoms, that whatsoever is cared for of all is cared for of none as it ought to be, but is neglected of all. II. As we have seen the reasons that confirm this doctrine, so let us see the USES THAT INSTRUCT US IN MANY PROFITABLE POINTS TENDING TO EDIFICATION. 1. This confuteth and convinceth the detestable sect who deny to men any property in anything, but would have all things common. 2. Seeing every man hath a state in his own goods, it teacheth us this duty, that we ought to be content with the portion which we have, be it more or less, be it a simple or a worthy portion, and to be by all means thankful for it ; considering with ourselves that the difference of places, lands, possessions, with the properties thereof, be of God, and are to be acknowledged as His gift. 3. We learn from this doctrine to take good heed that we do not abuse our property and dominion of those gifts that God hath given us, bestowing them only to our private use, and withholding the comfort of them from others, to whom they ought of right to be imparted and employed. For albeit the possession of them be ours, yet there is a use of them belonging to the saints; the property of goods and the communion of saints standing together. Whensoever we have these outward things we must not withhold them, when they may profit the Church and refresh the saints. (*W. Attersoll.*)
**Put that on mine account.**—*Taking the slave's debt:*—The verb used here for " put to the account of " is a very rare word ; and perhaps the singular phrase may be chosen to let another great Christian truth shine through. Was Paul's love the

only one that we know of which took the slave's debts on itself? Did anybody else ever say, " Put that on mine account"? We have been taught to ask for the forgiveness of our sins as " debts," and we have been taught that there is One on whom God has made to meet the iniquities of us all. Christ takes on Himself all Paul's debt, all Philemon's, all ours. He has paid the ransom for all, and He so identifies men with Himself that they are " received as Himself." It is His great example that Paul is trying to copy here. Forgiven all that great debt, he dare not rise from his knees to take his brother by the throat, but goes forth to show to his fellow the mercy he has found, and to model his life after the pattern of that miracle of love in which is his trust. It is Christ's own voice which echoes in " put that on mine account." (*A. Maclaren, D.D.*) *Suretyship:*—From this offer that Paul maketh, which is, to satisfy another man's debt, we learn that it is a lawful thing for one man to become surety for another, and to engage himself for his sure and faithful friend, of whom he is well persuaded. Howsoever suretyship be to some very hurtful, and to all dangerous, yet it is to none in itself, and of its own nature, unlawful or sinful, when the merciless creditor shall take his debtor by the throat and say, " pay me that thou owest." I. And if we require better grounds to satisfy us in this truth, LET US ENTER INTO THE STRENGTH OF REASON TO ASSURE US, WITHOUT ANY WAVERING HEREIN. 1. Weigh with me the example of Christ, an excellent pattern and president of the practice of this, an example far beyond all exception, an example that overshadoweth, and dazzleth, and darkeneth, all that cloud of witnesses produced by the apostle in the Epistle to the Hebrews ; He became surety for His Church unto His Father, to pay the debt of our sins, and to satisfy His justice. 2. It is a fruit of love and brotherly kindness, even this way to relieve and help such as are like to suffer damage and detriment by want of outward things. There is no man so rich but may become poor ; no man so high but may be brought low ; as there is no full sea but hath his ebbing. Now humane society and Christian piety requireth that one should sustain and succour another in their necessity. We are commanded to help up our enemy's ox that is fallen, or his ass that is sunk down under his burden ; how much more ought we to show pity and compassion to our brother himself, vexed with the creditor, terrified with the prison, oppressed with the debt, and dismayed and discouraged with the payment at hand that is to be made ? So then, whether we do consider that Christ Jesus is made our surety, and that suretyship is a fruit of Christian love one toward another, in both respects we see that in itself it is not to be disallowed or condemned. II. THE USES OF THIS DOCTRINE ARE DILIGENTLY TO BE CONSIDERED OF US. 1. If it be lawful to become surety one for another, it convinceth and confuteth those that hold it to be evil and unlawful, to give their word, or offer their hand, or tender their promise, for their brethren. Love is a debt that we owe to all men, as the apostle testifieth (Rom. xiii. 8), and therefore we ought not to fail in the performance thereof. 2. Seeing we have showed it to be lawful to enter into suretyship (for if it had been simply and altogether forbidden Paul would never have proffered himself to be surety unto Philemon for Onesimus), this serveth divers ways for our instruction. For hereby we are directed to be careful to use it lawfully. It is good and lawful if a man use it well and lawfully. But if we use it and enter into it rashly, not rightly, ordinarily, not warily, foolishly, not wisely, desperately, not discreetly ; if we entangle ourselves with it without much deliberation, without good circumspection, and without due consideration, it becometh unlawful unto us. Wherefore that this giving of assurance to others, and for others, either by our word or hand, may be performed lawfully to the good of others, and not the hurt of ourselves, we must mark and practise two points :—(1) Consider the persons of others for whom it is done. (2) Our own persons that do it ; and these two are caveats for all sureties. Touching those persons for whom we become sureties, we must know that we are not to engage ourselves and our credit, for every one that will crave it at our hands, and enter into bands for them, and promise us fair to see us discharged ; but in such men, who oftentimes have a greater feeling of their own wants and necessities than of freeing them out of woe that have pledged themselves for them, we are to observe three things. (*a*) That they be well known. (*b*) That they be honest and godly. (*c*) That they be sufficient to pay that which they would have us bound unto another, to assure him that they will pay. 3. Touching our own persons, before we are to enter into band or suretyship for others we must mark and meditate upon two things. (1) What is the sum for which we shall be obliged. (2) The means how we may be discharged. It standeth us greatly upon to bethink ourselves both what is the quantity, and what is our ability to answer it. It is a moral precept and wise saying, worthy to be written in our hearts, "be not surety above thy power; for if thou be surety, think to pay it." Let every man therefore well weigh his own strength. It were foolish pity for the saving of another man's life to lose our own. It were a merciless kind of mercy to leap into the water and drown ourselves while we seek to deliver another. We are commanded to bear the burden one of another, but it were more than foolish pity to break our own shoulders, by sustaining the weight and bearing the burden of another man. Again, as we are to mark our own strength, so we are to consider our own discharge, how we may be secured and set at liberty. For, before we pass our word, or give our band and hand for the payment of other men's debts and duties, we must know how we shall be assured to be delivered from that burthen and bondage that we have undertaken. We ought indeed to bear good will to all men, but our good will should not be a loser. It is no charity to receive a blow upon our own heads to keep the stroke from another. Know what kind of man he is for whom thou becomest a surety. If he be a stranger to thee meddle not with him; if he have broken his credit with any before, suspect him; if he be a shifting companion, discard him; if he be unsufficient to pay his own debt, deny him; if the sum be great and thy ability little so that it may hinder thee and thy calling, if thou be driven to pay it, enter not into it; and if thou cannot see which way thou mayest be freed from the peril and danger that hangeth over thy head, fly away from it as from a serpent that will sting thee, as from a canker that will consume thee, as from a gulf that is ready to swallow thee. 4. Seeing it is not unlawful or forbidden to bind a man's self by band or otherwise to another, it ought to teach all creditors and lenders not to be rough and rigorous over a surety. No cruelty toward any is lawful. (*W. Attersoll.*) *The atonement—an illustration :*—Suppose, then, that Philemon had demanded the repayment of what he had lost to the uttermost farthing; suppose that for many months St. Paul had had to work very hard, and to live very sparely, in order to earn the required sum, and that at last he had actually paid it to the rich Philemon, in order that Onesimus might be got out of his debt: would *that* have been wrong and base? wrong of St. Paul, I mean. Would you, would any man, have blamed him for it? Would you not, rather, have been moved to an enthusiastic admiration of the man who was capable of so singular and so signal an act of self-forgetting generosity and compassion? And what would you have thought of Philemon if he had taken the money? Surely you would have been as quick to condemn him as to admire Paul. "Which things may be allegorised." Let us, then, for our instruction in righteousness, turn this story into an allegory or parable. Let Philemon, the just and kind master, stand for God, our Father and Lord. Let St. Paul, the generous debt-assuming apostle, stand for Christ, our Saviour. Let Onesimus, the fraudulent and runaway slave, stand for man, the sinner. And then, sinful man, fleeing from the God he has wronged, falls into the hands of Christ, and comes to know and hate his sins. Christ goes to the Father saying, "If he [*i.e.*, man] hath wronged Thee, or oweth Thee ought, put that to My account; I will repay it." And, according to one theory of the Atonement at least, God takes the money; He demands that Christ should exhaust Himself with toil and suffering in order that man's debt may be paid, and then blots out the debt from his account. Assuming for a moment this theory of the Atonement to be a true theory, what are we to think of Christ? Was it wrong, was it blameworthy of Him, to take the sinner's place, to pay the sinner's debt, to atone the sinner's offence? If we hold to our parallel, so far from thinking it wrong, we can only pronounce it an unparalleled act of generous and self-forgetting love: so far from blaming Him for it, we can but honour and admire Him for it with all our hearts. But if God took the money —if He would not release man from his debt till some one, no matter who, had paid the debt—what are we to think of Him? Had Philemon taken St. Paul's money, we agreed that in him it would have been an action almost incredibly mean and base; we agreed that we should have felt nothing for him but contempt. Are we to lower our standard, and alter our verdict, because it is God, and not man, who is called in question—God, from whom we expect, and have a right to expect, so much more than from man? No, we cannot, we dare not, either lower our standard or alter our verdict. What would have been wrong in man would have been at least equally wrong in God. And as God can do no wrong, either our parallel does not hold good, or this theory of the Atonement must be radically misleading and incomplete. Is the parallel at fault, then? Look at it again. Philemon was a just and kind master. And does not God Himself claim to hold a similar relation to us? Onesimus was an "unprofitable" servant—running away from a master he had robbed. And have not we again and again robbed God of His due, and left His service to walk after our own lusts? St. Paul loved Onesimus "as his own heart," " as himself " (vers. 12, 17) ; and, in his love, he even put himself in the place of Onesimus, assumed his debt, interceded for him with his justly offended master, and raised him from the status of a slave to that of a " brother beloved." Are there any words, even in the Bible itself, which more accurately and happily describe Christ's relation to us? The parallel holds good then. We may take Philemon as setting forth God's relation to us, Onesimus as setting forth our relation to God, and St. Paul as setting forth Christ's relation both to God and man. But as the parallel does hold good, must not that theory of the Atonement to which I have referred be radically misleading and incomplete? No doubt any theory of the Atonement must be incomplete, for the Atonement is the reconciliation of man to God ; and which of us fully comprehends either God or man? How, then, can we comprehend and express that Divine act or process, " that miracle of time," by which the relations of God with man and of man with God were or are being drawn into an eternal concord? No theory of the Atonement conceived by the human mind, and expressed in human words, can possibly be perfect and entire, lacking nothing. The great " mystery of godliness " must ever remain a deep " in which all our thoughts are drowned." And any man who assumes that he can comprehend it, and crush it into some narrow and portable formula, does but prove that he pertains to that well-known category or class which presumes to " rush in where angels fear to tread." Still we may refuse to hold any theory of the Atonement which is obviously untenable. We may know, we may learn from Scripture at least enough of the Atonement for faith to grasp, and for the salvation that comes by faith. And, surely, it is impossible to deny that in sundry places Scripture does teach what is known as the vicarious or substitutionary theory of the Atonement ; that it speaks of Christ as taking our place, paying our debt, suffering in our stead. Whether we like it or not, there it is : the writings of St. Paul are full of it. Whatever the moral effect of it were, candour would compel us to confess that this aspect of Christ's work and ministry of reconciliation is set forth in the Scriptures of the apostles—not as the *only* aspect, only, indeed, as one of three or four, but still as a true aspect, as demanding our acceptance. Nevertheless, I confess that I for one should hesitate to accept it, were I unable to see and to show that the proper moral effect of it is not evil, but good ; that it does not tend to weaken our hatred of sin, or to relax our struggle against it, but tends rather to strengthen our hatred of it, and to brace us for new endeavours to overcome it. And I value this story of Onesimus very highly because it suggests a reasonable and a complete answer to this common difficulty and objection. For, consider : Was St. Paul's offer to pay the debt of Onesimus in the very least degree likely to confirm Onesimus in his knavery? Suppose the offer accepted ; suppose he had seen the busy and weary apostle toiling night and day, suffering many additional hardships, in order to clear him of his debt—would Onesimus, after having thus seen what his crime had cost, have been the more likely to rob Philemon again? Would that have been the natural and proper effect on his mind of the apostle's generous and self-sacrificing love for him? We know very well that it would not. We know very well that Onesimus, touched and melted by the love St. Paul had shown him, would rather have starved than show himself wholly unworthy of it. Why, then, if we believe that Christ Jesus, in the greatness of His love, took our place, paid our debt, toiled and suffered for our sins, and so reconciled us to the God we had wronged—why should *that* have a bad moral effect upon us? If Christ so loved us as to give Himself for us, the just for the unjust ; if we clearly and honestly believe that, surely its proper moral effect on us will be that we shall love Him who so loved us : and how can we love Him, and yet not hate the evil that caused Him so much pain? But here we come back to a still graver difficulty. As St. Paul, to Philemon, for Onesimus, so Christ says, to God, for us, " If they have wronged Thee, or owe Thee ought, put that to My account ; I will repay it." Let it be granted, as I have tried to show, that this assumption of our place and debt by Christ Jesus was an act most noble and generous and Divine. Let it be granted, as I have also tried to show, that by our faith in His great love we are incited to more strenuous efforts after moral purity and righteousness, instead of being degraded and demoralised by it. Grant both these points : and, then, what are we to think of God if He took from Christ the money which paid our debt? All that series of Scriptural figures which represents our sins as debts, and the Father Almighty as keeping a book in which they are entered, and as blotting them from that book when they are paid, may be necessary, and may once have been still more necessary than it is now, to set forth certain aspects of spiritual truth. But we need not conceive of God's book as though it were a ledger, nor of God Himself as a keen, hard-eyed merchant, still less as a peddling huckster, indifferent where his money comes from so that he gets it, and gets enough of it. All this is not in the Bible, though it may be in certain creeds and systems of divinity which, although they "have had their day," have not even yet altogether "ceased to be." And even the mercantile and forensic metaphors which are in the Bible are but metaphors after all; *i.e.*, they are but human forms of Divine truth adapted to the weakness and grossness of our perceptions. Nor do they stand alone. Lest we should misinterpret them, they stand side by side with figures and words which set forth other aspects of the self-same truth in forms we cannot easily mistake. Recall and consider, for example, such sayings as these:—"God so loved the world that He gave His only begotten Son, that whosoever believeth in Him might have eternal life"; and again, "God was in Christ reconciling the world unto Himself"; and again, "Herein is love, not that we loved God, but that He loved us, and sent His Son to be the propitiation for our sins." Are not these words sufficiently simple and clear and direct? Are they not instinct—charged and surcharged— with a Divine tenderness? But if these sacred and tender words be true; if God was in Christ, if He against whom we had sinned Himself took our debt upon Him that He might frankly forgive us all, is there any lack of love and kindness in Him then? "It was noble in St. Paul," you admit, "to take the debt of Onesimus upon him; but it would have been ignoble of Philemon to let the apostle pay it." Granted. But suppose—for even impossibilities are supposable—that St. Paul had been both himself and Philemon. Suppose that when, in the form of Philemon, he had been robbed at Colosse, he forthwith posted to Rome in order that, in the form of St. Paul, he might bring Onesimus to repentance, in order that, at any cost of toil and suffering to himself, he might wipe out his debt and atone his wrong. Would not that have been nobler still? And if God, the very God whom we had defrauded, from whom we have fled, Himself came down into our low and miserable estate, to toil and suffer with us and for us, in order that He might bring us back to our better selves and to Him, in order that He might wipe out the debt we had contracted, convince us that He had remitted it, and raise us to a new life of service and favour and peace—what was that but a love so pure, so generous, so Divine, that the mere thought of it should melt and purify our hearts? We are to think of God, then, not simply as taking the money offered Him by Christ on our behalf, but also as paying it; not as exacting His due to the uttermost farthing, but rather as Himself discharging a debt we could never have paid. In the terms of our parable, He is Paul as well as Philemon—not only the Master we have wronged, but also the Friend who takes the wrong upon Himself. And we owe to Him both whatever service and duty the forgiven Onesimus owed to Philemon, and whatever gratitude and love he felt for St. Paul. (*S. Cox, D.D.*) *Reparation to God:*—And what a light is shed on the gospel idea of making reparation to God by means of a substitute, according to this earthly analogy! How finely the apostle here follows in the footsteps of Him who, on a higher plane, offered Himself as pledge or pawn for us who had failed to render the service that was due! Sin is no doubt much more than debt, but it is debt in so far as human defalcations stand in the account with God. Through melancholy faithlessness and dereliction and apostasy toward Him, what debts have been accumulating beyond all human power to liquidate! Neither regrets nor promises can here avail. Debts must be paid, if they would creditably be written off. The grace of the Lord Jesus admits of Him being debited. To the trusting soul He says: "I am your written and covenant surety"; and so far as sin is a load of debt to God, it is His alone to say: "Put this down to My account. I will repay." Not as if there were any transference of moral qualities, or confusion of merit. Human guilt or blameworthiness can never be transferred to Christ, only imputed or reckoned to His account. What is actually transferred is the liability. And so must Christ's merit be ever His own—its benefits only can be transferred, when it itself is imputed or put to any human account. In this sense Christ is ever holding Himself forth as able and ready to bear away the burden of human debt, and cancel sin, in the account of any soul with God. (*A. H. Drysdale, M.A.*)

**Ver. 19. Written it with mine own hand.**—St. Paul may have written the whole of this letter with his own hand, contrary to his usual practice. (*Jerome.*) *A precious* *relic :*—What a precious relic, in that case, for Philemon and his family! (*Bp. Wm Alexander.*) *A signed bond :*—It does not follow from this sentence that the *whole* Epistle was written with the apostle's own hand; rather it would seem that he made this engagement of repayment to be more emphatic and significant by distinguishing it from the rest of the Epistle, and by taking the pen from the hand of his secretary, and by inditing that particular clause with his own autograph, well known to Philemon. (*Bp. Chris. Wordsworth.*) *A Christian's word should be enough :*—If we did live as becometh Christians, there should need no greater bond than the word of a Christian. The saying is, " By the word of a king "; who would not take a king's word, so royal are they in their performances? Christ has made us all kings, to God His Father; therefore we should have a singular care of any of our bare words; though the witnesses die, yet God who heard our word lives for ever. But we are fallen into such an age that many men's bonds are of no validity. Samson broke the cords; and some break the seals of green wax at their pleasure; they make no account of paper or parchment bonds till they be cast into iron bonds. Some put their hands and seals to a writing, that make no conscience of the accomplishment of that which they have written. They are content to go so far with Pilate as to acknowledge their handwriting—" What I have written, I have written "; but they will not say, " What I have written I will perform." St. Paul was of another mind; as he gave him his hand for the payment, so he gives him his heart and faithful promise to pay it. (*W. Jones, D.D.*) *Written covenants :*— We learn from hence, that civil instruments and covenants in writing, together with other assurances that may be asked and granted, are good and lawful, even amongst the best and greatest friends. I say, when debts are owing, when bargains are made, when money is lent, when lands are sold, and when there are mutual contracts between man and man, between friend and friend, between kinsman and kinsman, assurance in writing with hand and seal may be interchangeably given and received. And if we would enter into a further consideration of this truth we shall see a plain confirmation of it by sundry reasons. 1. It is a common proverb among us, fast bind, fast find. That which is loosely bound is lightly lost; but a three-fold cord, weil tied and twisted by word, by writing, by seal, is not easily broken. A word affirmeth, a writing confirmeth, a seal assureth, and every one of them bindeth to confirm our promise. We see by daily experience that men are both mortal and mutable, and words prove oftentimes but wind, albeit ratified with the greatest solemnity. True it is, our word ought to be as good as a thousand obligations, but deceit is bred naturally in our hearts, so that we cannot ground upon the bare word of men to find good dealing. Otherwise, the Lord would never have given so many laws to restrain wrong and injustice, fraud, and oppression. All these, or at least a great part of them, are prevented by setting down our covenants and agreements in writing under our hands and seals. 2. It is needful to have this manner of dealing among us, to the end that equity and upright dealing might be observed among us, and that all occasions of wrangling and wresting of words and bargains might be cut off as with the sword of justice. 3. That all occasion of controversy and cousenage might be taken away. For if there were no writing to show (the memories of men being frail, and their practices being unfaithful) the world would be full of all loose dealings, and concord would be banished from among men. 4. Good assurance is to be allowed and received, to the end we may safely dispose of such things that are in our power and possession, either to our posterity or otherwise. Hence hath been in all ages, the laudable and commendable use of making wills and testaments, which the word of God approveth by delivering divers rules belonging to that profession. The law of God and of nature hath taught: that the will and testament of the dead ought not to be abrogated or altered; and that no will is of force until the testator be dead. Now we know not whether the gifts that we give, and the legacies that we bequeath, be of our own proper goods or the goods of other men, except we have beforehand a sufficient assurance of them made unto us. Seeing, therefore, where there is a fast knot, there is a sure keeping; seeing upright dealings is to be observed; seeing occasions of quarrels and contentions are to be stopped; and seeing the goods that God hath given unto us are rightly to be bestowed: it followeth that every one is to provide for the security and quietness of his estate by all lawful means, not only by word of mouth, but by assurance in writing, that thereby he may foresee the danger that may come upon him and be wary and circumspect in all his doings, according to the saying of Christ, the Teacher and Author of true wisdom, " Be ye wise as serpents and innocent as doves. For if wisdom do season all our affairs, then also our contracts that are common in this life. (*W. Attersoll.*)    *Man's debt remitted by Christ :*—Of what has not man robbed God? He has assailed His government, His laws, His honour, He has stolen and prostituted His gifts, time, health, mind, influence, to the service of sin, and striven to dethrone Him in the very world which He made, and in the heart whose every pulsation is at His will. Who shall atone for the great wrong? Only a surety, and He a Divine one, who is willing to draw upon His own head the punishment, and submit to "be wounded for our transgressions, and bruised for our iniquities," and to do and suffer whatever the claims and honour of Divine love required, till He could say, " It is finished," and depart in peace, the Author of an eternal salvation to all that believe on His name. Graciously has God made earthly relations between man and man the representatives and explainers of higher things, and Paul's generously undertaking the debt of the guilty Onesimus sets vividly before us that Saviour whom it was his whole life to preach and his brightest hope to enjoy. (*R. Nisbet, D.D.*)    **Thou owest unto me even thine own self besides.**—*Man restored to himself :*—Very pregnant words indeed. He that accepts the gospel of Christ is made the true possessor of himself. Before this his soul was enslaved to evil, so that, humanly speaking, it would have been better for him if he had not been born. Now his true being is restored to him, so that by God's grace he can fulfil that purpose for which he was created and redeemed—the glorifying of God in his whole self—in his body and in his spirit, which are God's. (*M. F. Sadler, M.A.*)    *We owe ourselves to Christ :*— Does not Christ speak to us in the same language? We owe ourselves to Him, as Lazarus did, for He raises us from the death of sin to a share in His own new, undying life. As a sick man owes his life to the doctor who has cured him, as a drowning man owes his to his rescuer who dragged him from the water and breathed into his lungs till they began to work of themselves, as a child owes its life to its parents, so we owe ourselves to Christ. But He does not insist upon the debt; He gently reminds us of it, as making His commandment sweeter and easier to obey. Every heart that is really touched with gratitude will feel that the less the giver insists upon his gifts, the more do they impel to affectionate services. (*A. Maclaren, D.D.*)    *What do you owe ?*—Have not all of us received benefits? Have we paid our gratitude? I do not mean how much you owe to the grocer, baker, and landlord; but how much do you owe to yourself, to humanity, to God. I. God is our Father who cares for us, and we therefore owe SUBMISSION TO HIS WILL when crosses and tribulation come. Tribulations borne with resignation shall mellow our nature, and be as a mould to fashion our character like unto Christ. II. Do you not owe to yourself and to your fellow-men the DOING OF DUTY ? As the men who built Jerusalem, each repaired the wall before his door, so let us each do the duty that lies next us. We are not like the spectators in a theatre. We are the tragedians; we are the actors; daily life is our stage ; Christ, and the angels, and our fellow-men, are the spectators. Let us do our duty manfully, as Christ did. Do it because it is right ; and remember that duty well done will honour us at the judgment day. III. PAY YOUR DEBT OF RELIGION TO THE WORLD. When passing Westminster Abbey or St. Paul's Cathedral, if I have a quarter of an hour to spare, I always enter the sacred building and walk reverently over the graves of the good men of the past, and while looking on their partly obliterated names, I am inspired by their example to pray that my life may also be beneficial to my fellow-men. What can be grander than a life which exhibits true Christian religion ! Cannot you make yours such a life ? Is it not a debt you owe to your neighbour? Pay the debt by embodying in your life the eternal truth which Christ has given to the world. (*W. Birch.*) *Reverence and love due to ministers :*—From hence we learn that such as have gained us to God, or preserved us in the state of salvation by the preaching of the gospel, ought to be most dear unto us, we owing unto them even ourselves, and whatsoever we have besides to do them good. The benefits bestowed upon us by the ministry of the Word can never be sufficiently esteemed, nor worthily enough prized, nor abundantly enough be recompensed and rewarded with our love and the fruits of our love. Neither should this seem strange unto us. 1. They are most of all to be loved and highly esteemed of us that do us most good ; we are most deeply indebted unto them that labour most for our benefit. 2. Again, they are unto us instead of Christ. They are His officers that He hath appointed in His Church, who, when He ascended into heaven, gave gifts unto men and ordained those that should teach His people unto the end of the world. 3. They are the ministers by whom we believe, and consequently by whom we are saved. They are our fathers in Christ, by whom we are begotten to eternal life. The uses arising from hence are of divers sorts. (1) It directeth us to other necessary truths to be learned of us. It is noted by the apostle to be one general use of the Scripture, that it serveth and sufficeth to teach all truth needful to salvation, so the former point being received will help us to find out and conclude other truths. First we learn that, wheresoever there is a true profession, a sound feeling, a true taste of religion, or joy of salvation, there will be a reverent account and joyful entertainment of the teachers and publishers of the gospel. On the other side, a light and slender account of the ministers argueth a light account of the word of Christ, of the doctrine of salvation, and of the trueness of religion. Thus then we see how we may prove ourselves whether we be in the faith or not, even by the good estimation that we have of such as are the bringers of it. Secondly, we may gather from hence that the greatest part of the world lieth deeply and dangerously in condemnation, because such hath been the unthankfulness thereof toward the ministers and messengers of salvation, that it never respected them or gave them any reverence. (2) As this doctrine serveth to teach, so it is profitable to reprove divers sorts of men; but I will only touch these three. First, it maketh against such as make a bad and base account of the ministers of God, and think they owe no duty to their pastors, but reckon them as their vassals and servants; suppose that they are bound to please them and follow their humours, and account their teachers beholden unto them for vouchsafing to hear them as crediting their ministry by their presence. If a man abuse an ambassador of a prince and set him at nought, it is reputed and revenged as a disgrace and dishonour done to the prince himself; so, if we shall abase and disgrace the ministers of the gospel, which are the messengers of God, we shall never escape without punishment, but bring upon ourselves swift damnation. Is not he a godless and ungracious child that mocketh and despiseth his father, after the example of cursed Shem, who tasted of God's wrath for his contempt? Lastly, it reproveth such as refuse to give them sufficient maintenance, and do bar them of that competent and convenient portion that God hath allotted unto them in His word. For, if such as have spent their strength to bring us unto God, ought above all others to be regarded of us and have a worthy recompense of their labours; surely they deserve to be checked and controlled that deal niggardly toward them, who have kept back nothing from them, but revealed unto them the whole counsel of God. Thirdly, seeing the benefits brought unto us, both upon our bodies and souls, by the means of the ministry, can never be worthily esteemed and sufficiently expressed; it serveth to instruct us in the necessary duties of our obedience, even to testify our love to the truth by reverencing and respecting them that are the Lord's messengers to bring the truth unto our doors. Lastly, seeing they by whose ministry we are gained to God and preserved in the state of salvation being gained, ought to be most dear unto us, we owing unto them our own selves; this must teach the ministers of God a necessary duty and lesson to be marked of them, to wit, to endeavour by their daily diligence and continual preaching of the gospel, to make the people indebted unto them. For how do the people come so much in their debt but that they receive heavenly doctrine by their ministry as from the mouth of God? All men are not to be handled after one manner, but one after one manner, and another after another. He were a bad and mad physician that would use all his patients to one receipt. Some have gross humours in them, and stand in need to be purged; some more strongly, others more gently, according to their condition and constitution. Others have more need to have nature restored than purged, such must have cordials and restoratives ministered unto them. So it is with such as need physic for the soul. (*W. Attersoll.*) *Ourselves received from and given to Christ:*—I venture to take these words as spoken to each Christian soul by a higher and greater voice than Paul's. "I will repay it; albeit I do not say to thee how thou owest unto Me even thine own self besdies." I. OUR TRANSCENDENT DEBT. The Christian teacher may say to the soul which by his ministrations has been brought back to God and to peace in a very real sense: "Thou owest thyself to me." But I pass from that altogether to the consideration of the loftier thought that is here. It is a literal fact that all of you Christian people, if you are Christians in any real sense, do owe your whole selves to Jesus Christ. Does a child owe itself to its parent? And has not Jesus Christ, if you are His, breathed into you, by supernatural and real communication, a better life and a better self, so that you have to say, "I live, yet not I, but Jesus Christ liveth in me." And if that be so, is not your spiritual being, your Christian self, purely and distinctly a gift from Him? Does a man that is lying wrestling with mortal disease, and who is raised up by the skill and tenderness of his physician, owe his life to the doctor ? Does a man that is drowning, and is dragged out of the river by some strong hand, owe himself to his rescuer ? And is it not true that you and I were struggling with a disease which in its present form was mortal, and would very quickly end in death ? Is it not true that all souls separated from God, howsoever they may seem to be living, are dead ; and have not you been dragged from that living death by this dear Lord, so as that, if you have not perished, you owe yourselves to Him ? Does a mad man who has been restored to self-control and sanity owe himself to the sedulous care of him that has healed him ? And is it not true, paradox as it sounds, that the more a man lives to himself the less he possesses himself ; and that you have been delivered, if you are Christian men and women, from the tyranny of lust and passions, and from the abject servitude to the lower parts of your nature, and to all the shabby tyrants, in time and circumstance, that rob a man of himself ; and have been set free and made sane and sober, and your own masters and your own owners, by Jesus Christ ? To live to self is to lose self, and when we come to ourselves we depart from ourselves ; and He that has enabled us to rule our own mutinous and anarchic nature, and to put will above passions, and tastes, and flesh, and conscience above will, and Christ above conscience, has given us the gift which we never had before of an assured possession of our own selves. II. THE ALL-COMPREHENDING OBLIGATION BASED UPON THIS. If it be true that by the sacrifice of Himself Christ has given us ourselves, what then ? Why, then, the only adequate response to that gift, made ours at such cost to the giver, is to give ourselves back wholly to Him who gave Himself wholly to us. Christ can only buy me at the cost of Himself. Christ only wants myself when He gives Himself. In the sweet commerce of that reciprocal love which is the foundation of all blessedness, the only equivalent for a heart is a heart. As in our daily life, and in our sweet human affections, husband and wife, and parent and children, have nothing that they can barter the one with the other except mutual interchange of self ; so Jesus Christ's great gift to me can only be acknowledged, adequately responded to, when I give myself to Him. And if I might for a moment dwell upon the definite particulars into which such an answer will expand itself, I might say this entire surrender of self will be manifested by the occupation of all our nature with Jesus Christ. He is meant to be the food of my mind as truth ; He is meant to be the food of my heart as love ; He is meant to be the Lord of my will as supreme Commander. Tastes, inclinations, faculties, hopes, memories, desires, aspirations, they are all meant as so many tendrils by which my many-fingered spirit can twine itself round Him, and draw from Him nourishment and peace. Again, this entire surrender will manifest itself in the devotion of our whole being to His name and glory. Words easily spoken ! words which, if they were truly transmuted into life by any of us, would revolutionise our whole nature and conduct ! And further, this entire surrender of self will manifest itself in regard not only of our being and our acting, but of our having. I do not want to dwell upon this point at any length, but let me remind you, that a slave has no possessions of his own. And you and I, if we are our own owners, are so only because we are Christ's slaves. Therefore we have nothing. In the old bad days the slave's cottage, his little bits of chattels, the patch of garden ground with its vegetables, and the few coins that he might have saved by selling these, they all belonged to his master because he belonged to his master. And that is true about you and me, and our balance at our bankers', and our houses and our possessions of all sorts. We say we believe that ; do we administer these possessions as if we did believe it ? III. THE REPAYMENT. Jesus Christ stops in no man's debt. There is an old story in one of the historical books of the Old Testament about people who, in the middle of a doubtful negotiation, were smitten by conscience and drew back from it. But one of them, with commercial shrewdness, remembered that a portion of their capital was already invested, and he says, " What shall we do for the thousand talents that we have given, and are now sacrificing at the bidding of conscience ? " And the answer was : " The Lord is able to give thee much more than these." That is true of all sacrifices for Him. He has given us abundant wages beforehand. What we give is His before it was ours. It remains His when it is called ours. We but give Him back His own. There is really nothing to repay, yet He repays in a hundred ways. He does so by giving us a keen joy in the act of surrender. " It is more blessed to give than to receive." Christ bestows ourselves upon ourselves that we may have some portion of that joy. And with it come other gladnesses. There is not only the joy of surrender and the enhanced possession of all which is surrendered, but there is the

larger possession of Himself which comes always as the issue of a surrender of ourselves to Him.  When we thus yield He comes into our souls.  (*A. Maclaren, D.D.*)

Ver. 20. **Let me have joy of thee in the Lord.**—In that thou doest what thou
doest through the grace of Christ, through His dwelling in thee, and particularly
thou imitatest Him in the breaking of bonds and freeing the captive.  (*M. F. Sadler, M.A.*)    *Christ the true sphere of action :*—If Philemon receives his slave for
Christ's sake and in the strength of that communion with Christ which fits for all
virtue, and so for this good deed—a deed which is of too high and rare a strain of
goodness for his unaided nature—then " in Christ " he will be helpful to the
apostle.  In that case, the phrase expresses the element or sphere in which the act
is done.  But it may apply rather, or even also, to Paul, and then it expresses the
element or sphere in which he is helped and refreshed.  In communion with Jesus,
taught and inspired by Him, the apostle is brought to such true and tender sympathy with the runaway that his heart is refreshed, as by a cup of cold water, by
kindness shown to him.  Such keen sympathy is as much beyond the reach of
nature as Philemon's kindness would be.  Both are " in Christ."  (*A. Maclaren,
D.D.*)    *Provoked to virtue by a good example :*—Let me have profit of thee.
There is here a play on the slave's name, and the words are equivalent to, " Be
thou to me an Onesimus."  He would extinguish the rising feeling of conscious
merit and of boasting Philemon might entertain in compliance, and reminds him
that by such compliance he would still be less helpful to him than had been Onesimus.  He had Paul's messenger, servant, fellow-worshipper, and friend, and all
he would have Philemon do was so to act as not to allow one of so despised a class
to surpass him in generosity.  It is good for men that are provoked to emulation
by the Christian virtues of those around them.  Their presence slays pride and
inflames zeal, and invites to effort and to prayer, and makes it matter for shame
even should slender abilities and advantages cast superior endowments into shade,
should a Philemon be surpassed in Christian feeling and usefulness by an Onesimus.
(*R. Nisbet, D.D.*)

Ver. 21. **Having confidence in thy obedience.**—*A good opinion of others :*— In
these words the apostle excuseth that he hath hitherto been so earnest with Philemon, declaring, that notwithstanding his exact and effectual manner of handling
the matter, he doubted not of his receiving of him into his favour again.  So then
his drift is to show his good opinion of him, that he would not stick to forgive him
but yield readily to every honest and reasonable request.  He knew not certainly
what Philemon would do, he knew what wrongs he had received and what losses he
had sustained at his servant's hands ; yet we see how, grounding himself upon the
former trial of his faith and obedience, he hopeth the best, he doubteth not the
worst ; he trusteth in his obedience, he feareth not his denial.  I. From hence we
learn THAT IT IS OUR DUTY ALWAYS TO HOPE WELL and to think the best, not to
suspect the worst, of our brethren.  1. It is a property of love to be charitably
affected, as the apostle testifieth in his description of it, " Love thinketh not evil "
(1 Cor. xiii. 5–7).  Again, he saith, " It suffereth all things, it believeth all things,
it hopeth all things, it endureth all things."  The wise man also teacheth "that
love covereth a multitude of sins."  So then, where Christian love and brotherly
kindness is, there is the best opinion and judgment one of another.  2. It is a fruit
of a righteous man to hope the best and to judge charitably of his brother.  The
best man doth hardly suspect others to be bad.  It is a common proverb, " A man
doth muse as he doth use " ; as himself useth to do so he imagineth of another.
He that judgeth lewdly of another by mere suspicion or supposition is commonly
lewd himself.  For such as are wicked do think others as wicked as themselves ;
and such as are hypocrites themselves are most forward to tax others of hypocrisy.
Seeing therefore to be charitably minded is both a property of love and a fruit of
righteousness, it followeth that we ought to hope the best of all our brethren.  II.
THE USES REMAIN TO BE CONSIDERED.  1. This serveth to reprove sundry abuses
that are crept in among us and are too common in our practice, and are directly
condemned in the Ninth Commandment, which tend to the hurt of our brother's
good name, as all hard conceits and evil surmises, all uncharitable opinions and
suspicions against them.  The good name of a man is very precious, better than
silver ; yet it hath many enemies.  If then we be charged to conceive the best in
doubtful cases one of another, the capital sin of calumniation or slander is hereby
condemned as the chief opposite to a man's estimation and credit.  This hath

many branches that are breaches of the law : all of one kind and kindred, and all enemies unto the good names of our brethren. In this number are arranged these three as companions one of another : the tale-breeder, the tale-bearer, the tale-believer. 2. It is our duty to expound and interpret all doubtful things in the best part before the truth do plainly and clearly appear unto us, and labour what we may to cover their infirmities. We must not be suspicious without great cause or good ground, but to give all uncertain and wandering reports of our brethren the best interpretation, according to the rule before remembered, " Love believeth all things, it hopeth all things." 3. Albeit we are to hope the best of others and to judge charitably of them, yet we must know that it is our duty to admonish one another and seek to convert one another from going astray. Hereby we shall save a soul, clear their good name, and cover a multitude of sins. For it is most certain, we can never conceive a good opinion of them, nor have them in any estimation, nor entertain a charitable judgment of their doings, unless we show ourselves forward to exhort and admonish them when we see they walk not with a right foot nor tread in the steps that lead unto eternal life. 4. Lastly, seeing it is our duty to hope and esteem the best of one another, let this be acknowledged and confessed of us, that we must judge of no man before the time ; we must take heed of rash judgment. We must despair of no man's salvation but hope the best of them, that God will give them repentance to come out of the snares and subtleties of the devil whereby they are holden captives to do his will. III. This offereth unto us these meditations. 1. It is a comfort to those that at the last are brought to repentance. No man is excluded from grace in this life, and from glory in the world to come, that turneth unto God with all his heart. Let none despair through the greatness, heinousness, and multitude of his sins, but rather make haste and delay not the time to put off from day to day, considering how ready the Lord is to embrace him, to receive him, to forgive him. 2. Albeit the gate of mercy be set wide open for all penitent persons, yet this ought not to harden men's hearts in carelessness and security. For the ungodly that continue in their sins have no defence for themselves and their presumption in God's mercy, by the example of those that were called at the last hour of the day. Mark, that so soon as the thief and labourers were called, by and by they repented : the reason why they turned from their sins no sooner was because grace was no sooner offered unto them : but when God spake, they heard His voice with joy ; when God called, they answered without delay : whereas these impenitent persons have had the means oftentimes offered unto them, and yet refuse the calling of the Lord. 3. We are to hope the best of our brethren, to commend them unto God, to pray for their conversion. There cannot be a greater injury done unto them than to pass the sentence of condemnation upon them, and as much as lieth in us to blot them out of the book of life. Hence it is that the apostle saith (1 Cor. iv. 5). (*W. Attersoll.*) *Earnest confidence in others :*—I. Paul's confidence abates not his earnestness. Even where there is greatest hope of speed, it is no error to put to our best strength. Even the most forward may be quickened. Assurance of speed should not cool our fervour in our suits for God. God loves not only obedience but a cheerful spirit therein. Though we be assured of men's obedience, yet who knows what oppositions, reluctations, and discouragements may come from Satan, and a man's own corrupt heart ? How seasonable then in such cases may some motives be ! and how may our warmth heat another ! It is no absurdity in this case to put spurs to a running horse. II. Mark what hath all this while made Paul so earnest with Philemon, "having confidence of thine obedience." Never hath a man a better heart to speak than where he hath an hope to speed. Surely people's zeal kindles ministers', the forwarder they are to hear the forwarder are they to speak. Philemon's obedience puts heat and life into Paul and makes him earnest. A man hath but little heart to speak where he hath but little hope to speed. When a man fears he shall have but a cold suit of it, it chills his affections and makes him a cold suitor. Examine therefore thine own heart, and try if thou find not the cause of thy minister's defects in thyself. Many a minister would be better if he had a better people, and a good people makes a good minister as well as a good minister makes a good people. III. See the credit, yea the honour, that conscience and obedience puts upon a man. Paul makes no question but to prevail with Philemon, because he knew him even before to make a conscience of yielding obedience. IV. The property of a gracious and an enlarged heart. It is not so illiberally and niggardly disposed as to give God no more than His just dues in extremity, but enlarges itself so as to go further than it is tied by express command-

ment. (*D. Dyke, B.D.*)      **Thou wilt also do more than I say.**—*Something more :*—
What was the something which lay outside of, beyond, and over, the wide range of all
that St. Paul had claimed—forgiveness of two great offences on the part of Onesimus
—deletion of his debt, his exaltation and ennoblement into a brother? There were
overwhelming reasons why St. Paul should not demand the manumission of Onesimus. The slave would thus have been forced by St. Paul's action into a position
in which he would have derived an enormous gain from gross wrong-doing.
Philemon, besides, would have been a pecuniary loser without a free and hearty
consent. Yet there has been a very general feeling that the word "liberty" fills
St. Paul's heart, hangs upon his lips though unuttered, and hovers over his pen
though unwritten. (*Bp. Wm. Alexander.*)      *Obedience :*—If St. Paul had thought
Philemon a churlish, hard man, he would not have written such a letter, but he
knew him to be a kind, considerate man, and so he would be ready, not only to
comply, but to go beyond the expressed desire of the apostle. Notice the word
"obedience." It is the only one in the letter which implies apostolic authority,
but it *is* in the letter, and justly reminds Philemon that it was no ordinary servant
of Christ who was making the request. (*M. F. Sadler, M.A.*)      *More hinted than
stated :*—Was he hinting at emancipation, which he would rather have to come from
Philemon's own sense of what was due to the slave who was now a brother, than
be granted, perhaps hesitatingly, in deference to his request? Possibly, but more
probably, he had no definite thing in his mind, but only desired to express his
loving confidence in his friend's willingness to please him. Commands given in
such a tone, where authority audibly trusts the subordinate, are far more likely to
be obeyed than if they were shouted with the hoarse voice of a drill-sergeant. Men
will do much to fulfil generous expectations. Christ's commands follow, or rather
set, this pattern. He trusts His servants, and speaks to them in a voice softened
and confiding. He tells them His wish, and commits Himself and His cause to
His disciples' love. Obedience beyond the strict limits of command will always be
given by love. It is a poor, grudging service which weighs obedience as a chemist
does some precious medicine, and is careful that not the hundredth part of a grain
more than the prescribed amount shall be doled out. A hired workman will fling
down his lifted trowel full of mortar at the first stroke of the clock, though it would
be easier to lay it on the bricks ; but where affection moves the hand, it is delight
to add something over and above to bare duty. The artist who loves his work will
put many a touch on it beyond the minimum which will fulfil his contract. Those
who adequately feel the power of Christian motives will not be anxious to find the
least that they durst, but the most that they can do. (*A. Maclaren, D.D.*)      *Superabounding obedience :*—The doctrine arising from hence is this, that righteous men
being moved to honest, charitable, just, and necessary duties, will yield more than
men can well request and require them to do. 1. The obedience of the faithful will
super-abound because they set before them the example of God and delight to come
near unto Him. They have experience of His bountiful dealing toward them, He
is ready to grant not only what they ask but more than they ask. 2. The children
of God have a free and willing mind, and seek to walk before Him with a perfect
heart. And what will not a willing heart do? Will it not strive to attain to perfection? 3. Their joyfulness in the works of righteousness and godliness do exceed
the trial of necessity. Though the Lord try His people with manifold afflictions,
yet they are so far from quailing and cooling their willing readiness and ready
willingness to do according to that they are required, nay, above that they are
required, that they make the same much more excellent and famous. 4. They acknowledge all things to be from God and to be His ; and therefore they will yield
freely where He requireth and what He requireth and as far as He enableth them
to their uttermost strength. The uses remain to be handled. 1. From hence we
learn this point, that forwardness and zeal in good things is greatly to be commended.
We cannot yield more than is looked for at our hands, unless we be earnest and
fervent in the Spirit as men that are led by the Spirit. True it is there is no warrant
to walk without our warrant or to run too fast without any guide. Hence it is that
Solomon saith (Eccles. vii. 18, 19). Meaning thereby that as we should not suffer
sin to reign in our mortal bodies (though we cannot wholly drive it away), so we
should not seek a righteousness beyond the law. So then we must understand that
albeit we are to be ready to yield more than can be required of us, yet we must not
think to do more than God requires of us. If we speak of the duties that God commandeth, we come far short when we have done what we can, and we must confess
we are unprofitable servants ; but when we speak of good and Christian duties which

our ministers or brethren crave of us and desire us to practise, we should willingly perform more than they ask at our hands. Let us therefore be fervent and zealous in all lawful and honest things. It is good always to be earnest in a good thing. 2. This doctrine is a comfort to ourselves and to other the servants of God, and an occasion of great joy when as we ourselves or others are forward and cheerful beyond expectation in good things. A notable example of both is offered to our consideration in the provision that was made and the furniture that was provided for the building of the Temple (1 Chron. xxix. 9). Where we see that when David himself having a great zeal and delight in the house of his God gave of his own gold and silver, and the people and princes following his example spared no cost and expenses, it is said, " The people rejoiced when they offered willingly, for they offered willingly to the Lord, with a perfect heart : and David the king also rejoiced with great joy." Again, there is great occasion offered unto us to glorify God and to praise His Name, whensoever He worketh this willingness in the hearts of His children, and when we see their zeal to abound and their readiness to go beyond any request that we can make unto them. Lastly, it is the duty of every man to labour to be answerable at the least to the expectation that the Church hath had of him, and to endeavour to be as good as he hath made show of, performing therein the practice of his profession, not deceiving any of the servants of God therein. This requireth of us a careful observation and marking of the manners of men, both of their beginnings and proceedings, and not to stand, as idle beholders, gazing in the air ; that we may understand the time, the means, the forwardness, the knowledge, the show that hath been in many ; all which have promised much and caused us to expect good things at their hands, and yet oftentimes in vain. (*W. Attersoll.*)

*Philemon's willing-heartedness :*—There are labourers whose hammers or spades move more or less briskly according as the foreman is near at hand or away. They need both an overseer and a stint of work. There are also those whose work is turned off changeably as to quantity, according to the terms of agreement signifying " by the day " or " by the job." Selfishness is not easily laid aside always when, hired to perform work for another, one lays off the coat to set about it. That under garment still remains, fitting more closely than tailor ever cut ; Nessus-like, cleaving to the very skin. But an unselfish workman, even though but hired, is more like a partner in the firm. What interest he manifests in the successful issue ! With hearty love for the end to be accomplished, making the work his own apparently, see how the better motive keeps every muscle up to its full tension ! Not easily does he tire. Stint him, and, if possible, he will over-do the stint. No danger but that in a full day he will accomplish a full day's work—without any overseer. There are such Christian workmen. Paul regarded Philemon as one of this sort. Some one has suggested that that accounts for Philemon's Epistle having but one chapter. Writing to him, Paul needed not to spin out directions and exhortations page after page. Twenty-five verses were sufficient. No more than that to Philemon—whose heart was in the work ! Possibly certain congregations, clamorous for short sermons, in these days might take a hint from the brevity of Philemon's Epistle. At least shorter sermons might find more appropriate place if Philemon's spirit was more generally diffused throughout the Churches. As it is, may they not already be disproportionately brief, especially as we consider the half-heartedness for the Christian task with which so many of us go to our work ? We deserve watching. We deserve stinting. We deserve long epistles, like overseer's lash, laid over us. It is the boy who hates work to whom his father must address himself with ever-wearying particulars of direction each morning. " Before you go off to play to-day, you must saw twenty-five sticks at the wood-pile, or help mother about the house two hours and a half. That's your stint." Such a boy one must be particular with, or, likely as not, he'll do nothing. You know very well he will do no more than he has been directed to do. But the boy Philemon—when his father is leaving home, and must give directions to the hired servant for the management of affairs about the place during his absence, will he need directing also ? Is his father anxious about him ? " What will he be about while I am away so long ? " Oh, no ! Philemon has a son's interest in the work to be carried forward. " I've told him a few things to be remembered ; but he is as much interested in affairs as I am, and he will do much more than I have said. I can trust Philemon ! " Philemon-Christians, too, require but short sermons. To the Corinthians, however, chapter after chapter ! Specific information how to conduct themselves : Not to vex their brethren, going to law with them ; not to defile themselves shamelessly ;

not to eat meats offered to idols, nor cover their heads in prayer, nor profane the
Lord's Supper by over-drinking. Finally, Paul had even to add that, notwithstanding all his instructions, he feared, when he should come again to them,
lest there should be " debates, envyings, wraths, strifes, swellings, and tumults "—
enough to require some more very long sermons, just such as Paul could preach
on occasions, as at Troas, where one poor man got asleep under it and fell out of
the window. But Philemon—a whole church full of such Corinthians as he
would have required very simple directions by epistles or sermons—in fact, would
have constituted a model Church, no less than one easy to preach to in these hot
days of summer. Somehow, a minister rather longs for Philemons in the pews,
with hearts so much in the work they need little but leading ; never pushing, never
stinting, never overseeing, never long sermons. (*G. G. Phipps.*)

Ver. 22. **Prepare me also a lodging.**—*A lodging :*—1. If St. Paul's direction
here arose from a real anxiety upon the subject of the "lodging" itself, we shall
not be likely to suppose that he required much comfort or preparation for an ample
retinue. The lodgings, as Jerome happily says, " were for the apostles rather than
for Paul. He anticipated a large concourse of hearers. This would involve a
situation convenient of access ; large enough to hold a number of people ; in a
locality of good report, and undisturbed by a troublesome neighbourhood." 2.
St. Paul had evidently changed his plans since writing Rom. xv. 24–28. With
this verse *cf.* Phil. ii. 24. 3. Rhetorically, this request would tell doubly—(1)
"Prepare me a lodging, or arrange for me at an inn." Nay, surely he will be the
honoured and beloved guest of Philemon and Apphia. Will not Onesimus be
there ? And in what position ? (2) St. Paul wrote to a true and devoted friend.
This simple direction would excite hope and joy, the passions which beyond all
others make the human heart unable to refuse anything to those whom it loves.
(*Bp. Wm. Alexander.*)      *A hope of liberty :*—A thought concerning himself, introduced here not for the sake of himself, but because, as he adds, they prayed to God
that his presence might be vouchsafed to them, not only for their personal gratification, but that he might impart to them some spiritual gift as an apostle (Rom.
i. 11; *cf.* Phil. i. 25 ; ii. 24), where a similar hope of liberation is expressed. (*Bp.
Chris. Wordsworth.*)      *St. Paul coming to Philemon :*—Whereas, therefore,
Philemon might have thought with himself, and thus reasoned touching Paul's
suit. " It skilleth not whether I grant it or not, he hath been a most lewd servant
unto me, and Paul liveth far off from me, he is held in prison at Rome ; either he
will not hear what becometh of Onesimus, or if he does hear, peradventure he
shall never be delivered out of prison, but remain a prisoner all the days of his
life; and therefore I will deal with Onesimus as seemeth good to myself." These
and such like imaginations the apostle putteth out of his head, and telleth him he
should shortly look for his coming unto him, whereby he should know what account
he made of his words, and what obedience he would yield to his request. Hence
it is that for this cause Paul craveth to have lodging prepared for him rather by
Philemon than any other citizen at Colosse ; not that he required much provision
and preparation to be made for his entertainment, who had taught others, and
learned himself to be content with a little, but because by this commandment, as
by a sharp sword, he would pierce the bowels of Philemon, and as by a strong
engine, batter the fort and bulwark of his heart, and thoroughly persuade him and
prevail with him to receive Onesimus, both into his house and into his favour.
(*W. Attersoll.*)      *Christian friendship :*—I. ITS DEPENDENCE (ver. 22). 1. On God.
His restoration would be an act of Divine grace. 2. On each other. Mutual dependence a privilege as well as necessity. Includes—(1) Intercession. (2)
Hospitality. II. ITS RECIPROCATION (vers. 23, 24). 1. Of faith and feeling. As a
thousand particles of iron are held together by invisible magnetic current, so the
hearts of men by unseen force of faith in Jesus and love for Him. 2. Of labour
and endurance. The first named in the salutation is more than a fellow-worker.
He had joined the apostle in combat with the powers of darkness, and now shared
his captivity. III. ITS BENEDICTION (ver. 25). 1. Testimony concerning Christ.
Main teachings of the gospel concerning Him concentrated here. (1) That He is
alive and a Divine Benefactor. (2) Anointed "Lord." Appellative of Jehovah in
Old Testament. So in Col. i. 16 ; John i. 1–3 ; Heb. i. 2. Equal with God, whose
grace alone can sustain the spirit of men. (3) Faith in Him the origin and power
of all worthy life (ver. 5, 6). No good done without His grace. All and in all. 2.
Teaching for followers of Christ. Grace of Christ the supreme fount of goodness

and blessing. The Alpha and Omega of joyfulness and power. Thence comes—
(1) Forgiveness (Matt. i. 21; Eph. i. 7; 1 John i. 7, 9). (2) Renovation. Onesimus a "new creation" (2 Cor. v. 17). (3) Sanctification (2 Cor. v. 21). (4)
Wisdom (1 Cor. i. 24, 30; Col. ii. 3; Eph. i. 8). (5) Hope (Rom. v. 2; 1 Pet. i.
3–8). (6) Consolation (2 Cor. i. 5, xii. 9; Heb. iv. 15). All we need and can
wish. (*A. W. Johnson.*) *Christian hospitality :*—I. THIS DUTY IS URGED UPON
US BY DIVERS EXAMPLES IN THE HOLY SCRIPTURES. 1. It is to be practised of us
because it is the commandment of God that we should love and lodge strangers,
and show all pity and compassion toward them, to succour them in their necessity.
This it is which Moses saith, "Love ye the stranger, for ye were strangers in the
land of Egypt" (Deut. x.). Hereunto cometh the rule of the apostle, "Distribute
to the necessities of the saints, give yourselves to hospitality" (Rom. xii.). This is
the precept of the apostle Peter, "Be ye harbourers one towards another without
grudging" (1 Pet. iv. 9). Seeing, therefore, God commandeth, it is our part to obey,
and submit ourselves to His will and pleasure. 2. As God requireth this duty of
us, so we have His own example to teach it unto us. It is a property of God to
love strangers, and therefore to be imitated and followed of all that belong unto
Him. This reason is expressed in Deut. x. 18. 3. God doth greatly honour such
as honour strangers. They have been so far honoured by God as that angels have
entered into their houses, been entertained by them, and have blessed them. II.
THE DOCTRINE BEING THUS CLEARED, THE USES REMAIN TO BE SHOWED. 1. This
declareth that hospitality is a commendable virtue, and a worthy fruit of love;
yea, an excellent ornament in the children of God, whereby they receive good
report of the Church. 2. Secondly, this doctrine serveth for reproof. Of all,
of such as think that hospitality consisteth in feasting and keepeth great cheer,
and bidding the rich to their tables; whereas the Scripture understandeth by it a
courteous entertainment of such poor Christians as are banished out of their
countries. 2. This meeteth with the corruption of our times, we cannot abide
those that are strangers, but are enemies to the very name when we hear of it.
But all neglect of them and injurious dealing towards them is a great sin, and
such as are haters of strangers are grievous sinners. 3. It is our duty to take the
opportunity offered unto us of God; nay, it is required of us to seek the opportunity
to express our obedience to God, and our love to our people, in doing all good to
such as stand in need. 4. Lastly, it is a great comfort and peace to a man's conscience that God will in His Son Christ regard him, when with a single heart he
hath been careful to testify his love toward distressed strangers for the truth's
sake. Let us rejoice in this consolation, that we shall be assured that God will
pity us when we have thus pitied others. (*W. Attersoll.*) *Letters do not blush :*—
It is a known observation that letters do not blush. What men would be ashamed
to ask in person, that they are bold enough to ask by letter; and it is as true that
the readers of letters do not blush; they are hardy enough to deny that to their
absent friends, which they could not refuse them if present. The apostle therefore
intimates to Philemon his intention to visit him shortly, who must for that reason
be the more inclined to gratify him as not being able to look him in the face and
to bear his presence, if he should deny him this small, this reasonable, this importunate request. (*Bp. Smalridge.*) **I trust that through your prayers.**—
*Prayer for temporal blessings :*—The limits of Paul's expectation as to the power of
his brethren's prayers for temporal blessings are worth noting. He does believe
that these good people in Colosse could help him by prayer for his liberation, but
he does not believe that their prayer will certainly be heard. In some circles
much is said now about "the prayer of faith"—a phrase which, singularly enough,
is in such cases almost confined to prayers for external blessings—and about its
power to bring money for work, which the person praying believes to be desirable, or to send away diseases. But surely there can be no "faith" without a
definite Divine *word* to lay hold of. Faith and God's promise are correlative; and
unless a man has God's plain promise that A. B. will be cured by his prayer,
the belief that he will is not faith but something deserving a much less noble
name. The prayer of faith is not forcing our wills on God, but bending our
will to God's. The prayer which Christ has taught in regard to all outward things
is, "Not my will, but Thine be done," and "May Thy will become mine" That
is the prayer of faith, which is always answered. The Church prayed for
Peter, and he was delivered. The Church, no doubt, prayed for Stephen, and
he was stoned. Was, then, the prayer for him refused? Not so, but if it were
prayer at all, the inmost meaning of it was, "Be it as Thou wilt"; and that was

accepted and answered. Petitions for outward blessings, whether for the petitioner or for others, are to be presented with submission ; and the highest confidence which can be entertained concerning them is that which Paul here expresses : " I *hope* that through your prayers I shall be set free." (*A. Maclaren, D.D.*) *The duty of praying for ministers :*—1. In regard of the love, which is due from people to minister. People are bound to love their pastors. Now love seeks not her own things. He that prays not for his minister, loves him not. 2. In regard of their great charge wherewithal they are betrusted. A charge of greater worth than all the world—the soul of their people. The greater the charge the greater the gifts required to discharge it. The more graces they need the more earnest should our prayers be to procure the same. 3. In regard of their danger as in the former point. They are in danger of Satan's malice, he knows if he can but with his tail cause these stars to fall from heaven, that he shall cause the greater darkness and the greater scandal; their corruption in life or doctrine will be exemplary and infectious. They are also in danger of unreasonable men (2 Thess. iii. 2). The greater reason that they should be holpen with our prayers. 4. Pray for your ministers, because in praying for them you pray for yourselves, and procuring their good you procure your own. The better ministers are, the better is it for people. Many people complain of the insufficiency of their teachers, and as many ministers may complain of the negligence of their people. For if they were more diligent in prayer their ministers would be more able to preach if they would pray more for them, then should they be able to preach better unto them. What be the things we should beg for them ? Paul specifies some particulars, wherein he would be remembered. As—(1) Free and bold utterance of the gospel (Eph. vi. 19 ; Col. iv. 3, 4). (2) Free passage of his ministry (2 Thess. iii. 1). (3) Deliverance from wicked men (Rom. xv. 30 ; 2 Thess. ii. 3). (4) Other particulars are mentioned (Rom. xv. 31). (*D. Dyke, B.D.*)   **I shall be given unto you.**—*Answered prayer unmerited :*—The meaning of the apostle is thus much in effect. The prayers of the saints shall prevail with God, and being offered up for my deliverance, shall not return to them without comfort, nor ascend to Him without effect, nor concern me without profit. Notwithstanding, albeit, they shall not go empty away, but have their full force and power, yet it is to be acknowledged and learned that they so obtain, as that my deliverance is to be wrought out by the free gift of His grace, not by the merit and desert of your prayers. If we would know the causes and reasons why the graces of God are freely bestowed upon us, and nothing given for our deserts. 1. Let us consider that all matter of boasting is taken from us, and God will have the glory of His own work, and the praise of His mercy. 2. There are no such properties in any man's works as that they can merit, or proceed from any other fountain than grace. Let us therefore see what properties are necessarily required in works to make them meritorious. (1) They must be done of a man of himself, and by himself ; but we have nothing of our own to give Him, but are most poor men and mere beggars, and can but pay God with His own. Without Him, therefore, we can do nothing ; it is He that must work in us the will and the deed. (2) They must be such works as are not due unto Him, they must not be due debt, they must come from our own free will, they must be such as God cannot justly challenge at our hands. We are miserable bankrupts, we have nothing, we have less than nothing to pay. (3) The work must be done to the benefit and profit of Him, from whom we look to be repayed. But our goodness and well-doing reacheth not to the Lord (Psa. xvi.). We may benefit men, but we cannot benefit our Maker, from whom we have received soul and body. Now they that cannot give anything to God can deserve nothing from Him. (4) Whatsoever is imperfect cannot stand in the presence of the most just and perfect God. We must bring nothing before Him but that which is absolute and able to bear and sustain His wrath. But all that we do offer, or can offer, unto God is maimed and imperfect. Lastly, the work and the reward must be in proportion equal, for if the reward be more than the work it is not a reward of desert, but a gift of good will. For grace and glory are unmatchable, no price can purchase them, no merits can match them. This doctrine being thoroughly strengthened, let us see what uses may be grounded from thence. (1) We learn from thence that seeing God giveth not by desert, but of His mercy; that whatsoever we have obtained and received by any prayer, or other means from the hand of God, we must ascribe all to the glory and praise of His name, and acknowledge Him to be the Author and Giver. (2) As by the free bestowing of the graces of God we are taught to give Him all possible praise, so it taketh away all opinion of the merits of works wherein proud flesh is ready to trust. Lastly, seeing all God's gifts come from Him to us of grace and mercy, it is our duty, above all things, to desire mercy, and to crave the free gifts of God. (*W. Attersoll.*)

Ver. 23, 24. **There salute thee.**—*Apostolic salutations:*—The salutations which the apostle delivered in such numbers and so earnestly—1. Rest on faith and a confession of the one true Church of the Lord. 2. Are an expression of the feeling of our communion, of our higher, heavenly relationship in the family of God. 3. Furnish significant proofs of Christian love. (*Nitzsch.*) *Observations:*—I. We see the apostle setteth down A SALUTATION PROCEEDING FROM OTHERS which teacheth that salutations are an ordinary means ordained of God to nourish and cherish mutual love, and that union and conjunction which the members of Christ's body have one with another. II. Albeit the apostle were a prisoner for the faith's sake, yet GOD DOTH NOT LEAVE HIM ALONE. Thus we see the endless mercy of God towards His afflicted and distressed servants, He raiseth them up some comfort, verifying the promise made to His Church, "If I depart, I will send the Comforter unto you." He knoweth our infirmities, He seeth how ready we are to yield and slide back, and therefore as He strengtheneth us by others, so He maketh us means to strengthen others. III. He calleth Epaphras A PRISONER OF CHRIST, as he also had called himself before in the beginning of this Epistle. The reason is, because he had preached Christ. There might haply be others in the same prison who might suffer as malefactors, and justly deserve the restraint of the prison, but such were none of Paul's fellow-prisoners. Hereby we learn that persecutions often follow the sincere preaching of the gospel, not that it is the property of the gospel, but the cause is the malice of such as will not receive the gospel, and therefore they hate and persecute those that believe in Christ and give entertainment to the gospel. This is it our Saviour teacheth (Mat. x. 34, 35). So, then, let us not think it a strange thing when we see such tumults arise, but arm ourselves with patience. Learn to be wise as serpents and innocent as doves, and condemn those that are the authors and beginners of those broils and contentions. IV. Observe the titles that he giveth unto our Lord and Saviour—HE DESCRIBETH HIM BY TWO NAMES. First he calleth Him Christ, then he calleth Him Jesus. Christ signifieth as much as anointed. Under the Law the priests were anointed (Exod. xxx. 30); so were the kings (1 Sam. x. 1; xvi. 13); and the prophets (1 Kings xix. 16). Christ is the true anointed Priest, King, and Prophet of His Church (Acts iv. 27; x. 38), and the only person that had all these offices, and therefore is said to be anointed with the oil of gladness above all His fellows (Psa. xlv. 7; Heb. i. 9; John iii. 34). From this title it is that we are called Christians (Acts xi. 26; Psa. cv. 15). Jesus importeth as much as a Saviour, who was so called because He saveth His people from their sins (Mat. i. 21). From whence observe that Christ is the King, the Prophet, and the Priest of His Church, to govern us, to teach us, to redeem us, to save us. This is His office, for these ends and uses He was anointed of the Father with the Spirit of God itself. This serveth to our great good, and the benefit of it is communicated unto us; He maketh us kings and priests to God His Father (Rev. i. 6). He armeth us with power and strength against sin, the flesh, the world, the devil, and maketh us able to overcome them. Through Him we have access to the Father, and may boldly appear in His sight, and offer up our prayers with assurance. Yea, He enableth us to offer up ourselves, our souls, and bodies, an holy, lively, and acceptable sacrifice unto Him, which is our reasonable serving of Him. He doth instruct us in the will of His Father, enlighten us in the knowledge of the truth, and maketh us, as it were, His household disciples and scholars to reveal unto us all things needful for our salvation. Let us therefore confess Him to be the only Son of God, perfect God and perfect Man, the sole Mediator between God and man. V. Observe that speaking of Marcus, Aristarchus, Demas, and Luke, HE CALLETH THEM HIS FELLOW-HELPERS; whereby he putteth the ministers of the gospel and all the children of God in mind to be helpers to the truth, and to further the preaching and propagation of the gospel by all possible means that God hath enabled them. This reproveth those that employ their wits and bestow their strength to hinder the truth and the professors thereof. These have no part nor fellowship in the ministration, nor in the sound profession of the gospel, but are professed enemies to the faith of Christ. Moreover, this shall minister unspeakable comfort unto us to consider that we have been helpers to the truth and furtherers of the faith which is in Christ Jesus, we shall leave a good name behind us, and receive an incorruptible crown of eternal glory. (*W. Attersoll.*) *Courteous*

*speeches are becoming to Christians :*—I. Our well wishing one to another is a fruit of our love, and a means to maintain and continue love among us. If we would maintain love, we must wisely and carefully entertain such helps as may further us in the performance of that duty, whereof this that now we speak of is one, so that we are to express our inward love by outward tokens, to the end that it may be seen and appear unto others. II. Our salutations are remembrances of our care and good affections toward those whom we greet well. It is a sign that we are not forgetful of them, but do greatly regard and respect them. III. To desire the good of others from the heart is both a fruit of the Spirit and a good sign and testimony to our own selves that we are chosen of God to eternal life. 1. We learn that courtesy with civil, gentle, friendly, and soft speeches are to be entertained of the servants of God. A fire is soonest quenched by water, and anger is soonest appeased by gentleness. Let us plant this in the garden of our hearts, and learn to give good speeches one to another, and show a friendly countenance, even to them that wrong us and abuse us, without any purpose or desire to revenge. This is a virtue hard to be found in these days among the sons of men, they cannot speak well one of another. This gentleness that teacheth us to deal courteously toward each other is thinly sown in the furrows of our hearts. Wherefore, we must know that humanity and courteous dealing are not, as some imagine, excluded from Christians, as if nothing should be in them but rigour and austerity. Indeed they are to deal roughly and rigorously with wilful and wicked men that are offensive and unruly, but we must be gentle, meek, and lowly toward such as are willing to be instructed. Let us therefore accustom our tongues to civility, to blessing, and wishing all good one to another. This becometh our profession, and witnesseth to all the world that we are of pure conversation. 2. This doctrine serveth for reproof of divers and sundry abuses that are too rife and common among us. It seemeth a light and ridiculous thing to many to salute and to be saluted, but it is of great force, and availeth much to the obtaining and getting of good will. It is a point of courtesy and humanity to salute others and to pray for them. Let no man say these are very small matters to be spoken of and stood upon. We must acknowledge that our obedience is to be showed even in the least, and not in the greatest matters only. And a true Christian is to be seen and known when he will yield in the practise of lesser points and such as are not of greatest importance. 3. Seeing we are taught to use all gentle and courteous communication, and all loving salutations and well-wishing one toward another, this teacheth us that we must all diligently study and practise the government of the tongue, to order it aright and in due manner. This is a worthy study, it is a hard study, it is a profitable study (Psa. xxxiv. 12, 13 ; xxxix. 1). To this purpose the apostle teacheth us to be slow to speak and swift to hear. This virtue appeared notably in Elihu (Job xxxii.), who waited till Job had spoken, for they were more ancient in years than he. In our speaking we must be careful that our words be gracious, and seasoned with wisdom, truth, reverence, modesty, meekness, and sobriety, as it were with salt, which are contrary to the foolish, rotten, and graceless talk that aboundeth in our days, wherein men are grown to be very beasts (Rom. iii. 13, 14). (*Ibid.*)
*Courtesy :*—Courtesy is not confined to rank, or wealth, or station. Nature's noblemen, without lineage, or heraldry, or fame, may be found sitting in the cottage, working in the fields, toiling with their hands. Though unlettered and untrained, their instincts are the instincts of gentlemen. They speak restrainedly, they would not wrong another for any gain ; they would put themselves to any trouble for another's sake. Courtesy is not mere manners ; neither does it spring from mere amiable meekness. True courtesy is wedded to true pride and a fearless self-respect. The strong man is courteous because he is strong. The vacillating man is uncivil because he is weak. True courtesy shines most brightly in the sphere of home. The stripling, who is all grace to outside young ladies, and neglects his mother ; the girl who is radiant as a butterfly at a ball, and surly as a wasp at home ; the apprentice who addresses his employer as " Sir," and talks of his father as " the old boy," may possess the polish, but have not the principle, of courtesy. Courtesy shows itself not only upon great occasions, but also in little things. In a drawing-room it will listen to playing or singing which may not be very brilliant, for the performer's sake. True courtesy is kind to inferiors and servants. It knocks at the cottage door just as it rings at the mansion's hall. It is chivalrous to woman, not because she is rich, or young, or handsome, or gifted, but because she is woman. It is kind to old age : the grey head is venerable in the eyes of courtesy. The same fine feeling which is called courtesy in secular conduct

leads to reverence in sacred things. Irreverence is a coarse form of rudeness. Courtesy makes us bow to our fellows: reverence makes us kneel before God. What would be bad conduct in a drawing-room is worse than bad conduct in church. Courtesy of heart overflows in courtesy of action. By imitating the gentleness of Christ, Christians become Christ's gentlemen. (*J. W. Diggle.*)

Ver. 25. **The grace of our Lord Jesus Christ.**—*Grace the gift of Christ :*—1. At the beginning of the Epistle Paul invoked grace upon the household "from God our Father and the Lord Jesus Christ." Now he conceives of it as Christ's gift. In Him all the stooping, bestowing love of God is gathered, that from Him it may be poured on the world. That grace is not diffused like stellar light through some nebulous heaven, but concentrated in the Sun of righteousness, who is the light of men. That fire is piled on a hearth that, from it, warmth may ray out to all that are in the house. 2. That grace has man's spirit for the field of its highest operation. Thither it can enter, and there it can abide, in union more close and communion more real and blessed than aught else can attain. The spirit which has the grace of Christ with it can never be utterly solitary or desolate. 3. The grace of Christ is the best bond of family life. Here it is prayed for on behalf of all the group, the husband, wife, child, and the friends in their home—church. Like grains of sweet incense cast on an altar flame, and making fragrant what was already holy, that grace sprinkled on the household fire will give it an odour of a sweet smell, grateful to men and acceptable to God. 4. That wish is the purest expression of Christian friendship, of which the whole letter is so exquisite an example. Written as it is about a common, every-day matter, which could have been settled without a single religious reference, it is saturated with Christian thought and feeling. So it becomes an example of how to blend Christian sentiment with ordinary affairs, and to carry a Christian atmosphere everywhere. Every Christian ought by his life to be, as it were, floating the grace of God to others sinking for want of it to lay hold of, and all his speech should be of a piece with this benediction. (*A. Maclaren, D.D.*)   *Grace to be most desired :*—I. First of all, we see here, that as in the entrance of the Epistle, and, as it were, at their first meeting, he wished unto him the grace of Christ, so he doth in the farewell and departing, hereby teaching that nothing is better or more to be desired than His grace; that all our salutations and farewells should be grounded in His grace; this must be the beginning and the ending of all our talk and communication; and as he began with prayer, so he endeth with prayer. Thus ought our actions to be, that whatsoever we do in word or in deed, we should do all in the name of the Lord Jesus (Col. iii. 17). This bringeth good success to our works, and maketh that which we do to prosper. II. When the Son of God is called Jesus, we observe again that He is a perfect and absolute Saviour ; the alone Saviour, inasmuch as the work of our salvation and redemption is wholly and only wrought out by Him, and no part left unfinished and reserved for any creature in heaven or in earth. III. The Son of God is called Christ, which signifieth as much as anointed. IV. Let us consider the third title given to the Son of God. He is called our Lord ; which teacheth us to acknowledge Him to be the Ruler and Governor of His Church, and of every particular member thereof. And if He be the Governor and Guide, woe unto them that will not be ruled and governed by Him. V. Observe that the grace here asked for Philemon and others to whom the apostle wrote, is called the grace of Jesus Christ, to teach us that God's graces and benefits come upon us through Him, and as nothing was made without Him that was made, so nothing is given without Him that is given. If, then, we would have right and interest in any of the blessings of God, we must labour to be in Christ and to have assurance that we are in Christ. (*W. Attersoll.*)   *The apostolic benediction :*—1. Some explanation of the words of the text, " The grace of our Lord Jesus Christ." 2. What we may learn from it. (1) The grand foundation of a sinner's hope. (2) How to make a practical use of Christian doctrines. (3) The simplicity of the faith and the fervency of the love of the primitive Church—the Church of the apostle's time. (*R. Cecil, M.A.*) *The Christian's prayer for his brethren in Christ :*—1. Breathes family affection— affection to all who love Christ—affection to them as brethren, for—(1) They are born of the same Father. (2) They are taught by the same preceptor. (3) They are severed from the world and dedicated to God, body, soul, and spirit. 2. Invokes a family blessing—grace—the grace of Christ. 3. Describes family experience. If we have realised the text in our experience, then we have attained the climax of Christian attainments. (*J. Dillon, D.D.*)   *Grace :*—1. The sum of all other blessings. 2. Obtained through Christ. 3. The greatest happiness we can desire for others. (*J. Lyth, D.D.*) *Grace :*—1. Its source. 2. Its fulness. 3. Its flow. 4. Its power. (*Ibid.*) *Grace :*—1. Is needed by all. 2. Is provided for all. 3. Is offered to all. 4. Is supplicated for all. 5. May be enjoyed by all. (*Ibid.*) *The grace of the Lord Jesus Christ :*—Very powerful was the impression which Lady Fanny Shirley on her sick bed made upon the surrounding attendants. Once, as a reigning beauty at Court, Chesterfield had addressed to her some of his most famous epigrams; since then she chose that better part which could never be taken from her. " I am quite at a loss to explain how Lady Fanny is enabled to bear such a severity of suffering with so much tranquillity and so few symptoms of restlessness and murmuring," said her physician to Mr. Venn. " Can you account for it, sir ? " " Sir," answered Venn, " that lady happily possesses what you and I ought daily to pray for, the grace of her Lord Jesus Christ, the love of God, and the fellowship of the Holy Ghost." *Grace :*—With a prayer for this grace Paul had opened the Epistle, and with a prayer for this grace he now will close. It is the most all-inclusive wish for good he can indite in so few words— the free and saving favour of the Lord, with all its holy and happy influences for soul and body, for time and for eternity. This grace sanctifies earth's fellowships, and protects them from degeneracy and social corruption. It raises life above the entanglements of *ennui* and chagrin, of cynicism and despair. It weans the heart from the world, without permitting it to be soured. It lends dignity to suffering, and gilds the gloom of sorrow with radiant hope. To the apostle had been often verified the soul-sustaining words, " My grace is sufficient for thee." As the day grows, the warmth increases and the shadows flee away; so, as grace is realised, the heart basks and suns itself in the glow of heaven's love, and everything gets bathed in heaven's own light. (*A. H. Drysdale, M.A.*) Amen.—This is set down in a word, and yet it containeth more than the prayer itself. For in prayer we testify our desire, by this we witness our faith. By this we observe that unto our requests and petitions in prayer must be joined faith and belief that God will grant the things craved. To pray without faith is not to pray at all. And to say amen in the end of our prayers, and yet to pray with doubting, and without believing, is to make a lie and to teach our tongues to deceive our hearts. For this is a great jar and discord when infidelity is in the heart and faith in the tongue ; when inwardly we waver, and outwardly the mouth uttereth amen. Moreover, so often as we use public prayers they must be pronounced and delivered with that plainness, feeling, and zeal, as that the people, being thereby moved, and their faith and affections going with that which is delivered and prayed for, may answer amen unto that which is desired. This is it which the apostle teacheth (1 Cor. xiv.).